THE HARPERCOLLINS DICTIONARY OF RELIGION

THE
HARPERCOLLINS
DICTIONARY
OF
RELIGION

GENERAL EDITOR

Jonathan Z. Smith

ASSOCIATE EDITOR

William Scott Green

AREA EDITORS

Jorunn Jacobsen Buckley	Alf Hiltebeitel
Lawrence S. Cunningham	Richard C. Martin
Gary L. Ebersole	Carole A. Myscofski
Malcolm David Eckel	Jacob Neusner
Sam D. Gill	Hans H. Penner

with the American Academy of Religion

HarperSanFrancisco
An Imprint of HarperCollinsPublishers

PUBLICATION STAFF

SENIOR EDITOR John B. Shopp

ASSISTANT EDITOR Judith Kleppe

PRODUCTION EDITORS Lisa Zuniga Carlsen, Terri Goff

COPYEDITORS Ann Moru, Pam Suwinsky, Nancy Haught, Virginia Rich

PRODUCTION ASSISTANTS Mark A. Nigara, Cullen Curtiss, Adrienne Armstrong

PROOFREADERS Steven Anderson, Dahlia Armon, Jennifer Boynton, Carol
Lastrucci, Laurie McGee, Antonia Moore, Karin Mullen, Kimberley Spears,
Annelise Zamula

EDITORIAL ASSISTANT Matthew Harray

PHOTOGRAPHIC CONSULTANT Professor Richard M. Carp, Northern Illinois
University

DESIGN Design Office, San Francisco

DESIGN MANAGER Martha Blegen

TYPESETTER TBH/Typecast, Inc.

TEXT PRINTER AND BINDER R. R. Donnelley & Co.

Photograph credits begin on page 1153.

FIRST EDITION

Library of Congress Cataloging-in-Publication Data:

The HarperCollins dictionary of religion / general editor, Jonathan Z. Smith ; associate editor William Scott Green ; area editors, Jorunn Jacobsen Buckley... [et al.] ; with
the American Academy of Religion.

ISBN 0–06–067515–2 (cloth)

1. Religion—Dictionaries. 2. Religions—Dictionaries. I. Smith, Jonathan Z. II. Green,
William Scott. III. Buckley, Jorunn Jacobsen. IV. American Academy of Religion.

BL31.H37   1995

200'.3—dc20   95–37024

95 96 97 98 99 RRD(C) 10 9 8 7 6 5 4 3 2 1

CONTENTS

Section of Illustrations Follows Page 770

EDITORIAL BOARD

CONTRIBUTORS

JONATHAN Z. SMITH
  University of Chicago
  Chicago, Illinois

Religions of Antiquity

JORUNN JACOBSEN BUCKLEY
  Area Editor
  Boston University
  Boston, Massachusetts

LAWRENCE J. ALDERINK
  Concordia College
  Moorhead, Minnesota

PERTTI ANTTONEN
  Nordic Institute of Folklore
  Turku, Finland

LARISSA BONFANTE
  New York University
  New York, New York

JOHN BUSSANICH
  University of New Mexico
  Albuquerque, New Mexico

RON D. CAMERON
  Wesleyan University
  Middletown, Connecticut

ALAN COOPER
  Hebrew Union College
  Jewish Institute of Religion
  Cincinnati, Ohio

WILLIAM R. DARROW
  Williams College
  Williamstown,
  Massachusetts

ULF DROBIN
  University of Stockholm
  Stockholm, Sweden

JARL FOSSUM
  University of Michigan
  Ann Arbor, Michigan

MARIJA GIMBUTAS (D. 1994)
  University of California
  Los Angeles, California

DEIDRE GOOD
  General Theological
  Seminary
  New York, New York

FRANCES V. HAHN
  University of California
  Santa Barbara, California

JOHN HELGELAND
  North Dakota State
  University
  Fargo, North Dakota

KENNETH G. HOGLUND
  Wake Forest University
  Winston-Salem, North
  Carolina

SUSAN TOWER HOLLIS
  Sierra Nevada College
  Lake Tahoe, Nevada

M. H. JAMESON
  Stanford University
  Stanford, California

HANS J. KIPPENBERG
  Institute of Advanced
  Studies
  Princeton, New Jersey

LEONARD H. LESKO
  Brown University
  Providence, Rhode Island

DEBORAH LYONS
  University of Rochester
  Rochester, New York

MARK MCPHERRAN
  University of Maine
  Farmington, Maine

NANNO MARINATOS
  Swedish Institute of Athens
  Athens, Greece

LUTHER H. MARTIN
  University of Vermont
  Burlington, Vermont

RICHARD P. MARTIN
  Princeton University
  Princeton, New Jersey

RUTH I. MESERVE
  Indiana University
  Bloomington, Indiana

MARVIN W. MEYER
  Chapman University
  Orange, California

PIOTR MICHALOWSKI
  University of Michigan
  Ann Arbor, Michigan

WILLIAM L. MORAN
  Harvard University
  Cambridge, Massachusetts

DENNIS PARDEE
  University of Chicago
  Chicago, Illinois

PETER A. PICCIONE
  University of Chicago
  Chicago, Illinois

EDGAR C. POLOME
  University of Texas
  Austin, Texas

FRANCESCA ROCHBERG
  University of California
  Riverside, California

BENSON SALER
  Brandeis University
  Waltham, Massachusetts

JENS PETER SCHJODT
  Aarhus University
  Aarhus, Denmark

ALAN F. SEGAL
  Barnard College
  Columbia University
  New York, New York

SUSAN C. SHELMERDINE
  University of North
  Carolina
  Greensboro, North
  Carolina

NICOLAS D. SMITH
  Virginia Polytechnic
  Institute and State
  University
  Blacksburg, Virginia

GRO STEINSLAND
  University of Oslo
  Oslo, Norway

JAMES D. TABOR
  University of North
  Carolina
  Charlotte, North Carolina

JAVIER TEIXIDOR
  Institut d'Etudes
  Semitiques
  Paris, France

GARTH TISSOL
  Emory University
  Atlanta, Georgia

DAVID ULANSEY
  Institute of Integral Studies
  San Francisco, California

JOANNE PUNZO WAGHORNE
University of North
Carolina
Chapel Hill, North Carolina

GERNOT WINDFUHR
University of Michigan
Ann Arbor, Michigan

PAUL ZIMANSKY
Boston University
Boston, Massachusetts

Buddhism

MALCOLM DAVID ECKEL
Area Editor
Boston University
Boston, Massachusetts

EDWIN BERNBAUM
University of California
Berkeley, California

STEVEN COLLINS
University of Chicago
Chicago, Illinois

COLLETT COX
University of Washington
Seattle, Washington

LUIS O. GOMEZ
University of Michigan
Ann Arbor, Michigan

PAUL GRIFFITHS
University of Chicago
Chicago, Illinois

CHARLES HALLISEY
Harvard University
Cambridge, Massachusetts

ANNE KLEIN
Rice University
Houston, Texas

JAN NATTIER
Indiana University
Bloomington, Indiana

REGINALD A. RAY
Naropa Institute
and the University of
Colorado
Boulder, Colorado

FRANK REYNOLDS
University of Chicago
Chicago, Illinois

JOHN STRONG
Bates College
Lewiston, Maine

DONALD SWEARER
Swarthmore College
Swarthmore, Pennsylvania

Religions of China, Japan, and Korea

GARY L. EBERSOLE
Area Editor
University of Chicago
Chicago, Illinois

NORMAN J. GIRARDOT
Special Editor, Chinese
religions
Lehigh University
Bethlehem, Pennsylvania

JOHN I. GOULDE
Special Contributor,
Korean religions
Sweet Briar College
Sweet Briar, Virginia

JOHN MAJOR
Special Contributor,
Chinese religions
New York, New York

FRANCISCA CHO BANTLY
George Washington
University
Washington, D.C.

DAVID L. BARNHILL
Guilford College
Greensboro, North
Carolina

CATHERINE M. BELL
Santa Clara University
Santa Clara, California

COLLEEN BERRY
Indiana University
Bloomington, Indiana

JOHN BERTHRONG
Boston University
Boston, Massachusetts

STEPHEN BOKENKAMP
Indiana University
Bloomington, Indiana

JAMES BUCHANAN
Rochester Institute of
Technology
Rochester, New York

ROBERT CAMPANY
Indiana University
Bloomington, Indiana

CONSTANCE A. COOK
Lehigh University
Nazareth, Pennsylvania

ROGER J. CORLESS
Duke University
Durham, North Carolina

MICHAEL DEMARCO
Via Media Publishing
Company
Erie, Pennsylvania

H. BYRON EARHART
Western Michigan
University
Kalamazoo, Michigan

JAMES HARLAN FOARD
Arizona State University
Tempe, Arizona

RICHARD A. GARDNER
Sophia University
Tokyo, Japan

PAUL GRONER
University of Virginia
Charlottesville, Virginia

CHARLES B. JONES
Carleton College
Northfield, Minnesota

RUSSELL KIRKLAND
University of Georgia
Athens, Georgia

THEODORE M. LUDWIG
Valparaiso University
Valparaiso, Indiana

CHIA-LI LUO
Indiana University
Bloomington, Indiana

MARK WHEELER MACWILLIAMS
Bucknell University
Lewisburg, Pennsylvania

JEFFREY F. MEYER
University of North
Carolina
Charlotte, North Carolina

ALAN L. MILLER
Miami University
Oxford, Ohio

DAVID W. PANKENIER
Lehigh University
Bethlehem, Pennsylvania

JULIEN PAS
University of
Saskatchewan
Saskatoon, Saskatchewan,
Canada

RICHARD K. PAYNE
San Jose State University
San Jose, California

THOMAS V. PETERSON
Alfred University
Alfred, New York

LAUREN F. PFISTER
Hong Kong Baptist
University
Kowloon, Hong Kong,
China

RICHARD PILGRIM
Syracuse University
Syracuse, New York

DON A. PITTMAN
Tainan Theological College
and Seminary
Tainan, Taiwan

MURRAY RUBINSTEIN
Baruch College
City University of New
York
New York, New York

MARY EVELYN TUCKER
Bucknell University
Lewisburg, Pennsylvania

SHOUCHENG YAN
Indiana University
Bloomington, Indiana

Christianity

LAWRENCE S. CUNNINGHAM
Area Editor
University of Notre Dame
Notre Dame, Indiana

DOUGLAS ADAMS
Pacific School of Religion
Berkeley, California

DIANE APOSTOLOS-
CAPPADONA
Georgetown University
Washington, D.C.

ROLLIN S. ARMOUR
Mercer University
Macon, Georgia

JOHN BALDOVIN
Jesuit School of Theology
Berkeley, California

DAVID BARR
Wright State University
Dayton, Ohio

PAUL F. BRADSHAW
University of Notre Dame
Notre Dame, Indiana

JOHN J. CAREY
Agnes Scott College
Atlanta, Georgia

DENISE LARDNER CARMODY
Santa Clara University
Santa Clara, California

JOHN CARMODY
Santa Clara University
Santa Clara, California

CONRAD CHERRY
Indiana University-Purdue
University
Indianapolis, Indiana

KEITH J. EGAN
St. Mary's College
Notre Dame, Indiana

RONALD B. FLOWERS
Texas Christian University
Fort Worth, Texas

BRADLEY HANSON
Luther College
Decorah, Iowa

DANIEL J. HARRINGTON
Weston Jesuit School of
Theology
Cambridge, Massachusetts

SAMUEL S. HILL
University of Florida
Gainesville, Florida

ELIZABETH A. JOHNSON
Fordham University
New York, New York

PHYLLIS H. KAMINSKI
Saint Mary's College
Notre Dame, Indiana

JOHN KELSAY
Florida State University
Tallahassee, Florida

ELIZABETH STRUTHERS
MALBON
Virginia Polytechnic
Institute and State
University
Blacksburg, Virginia

TERENCE J. MARTIN
Saint Mary's College
Notre Dame, Indiana

WATSON E. MILLS
Mercer University
Macon, Georgia

WALTER L. MOORE
Florida State University
Tallahassee, Florida

RANDALL C. MORRIS
William Jewell College
Liberty, Missouri

M. E. O'KEEFFE
Mercy Hurst College
Erie, Pennsylvania

WILLIAM L. PORTIER
Mt. St. Mary's College
Emmitsburg, Maryland

STEPHEN G. POST
Case Western Reserve
University
Cleveland, Ohio

JOHN F. PRIEST
Florida State University
Tallahassee, Florida

CARL RASCHKE
University of Denver
Denver, Colorado

DON E. SALIERS
Candler School of
Theology
Emory University
Atlanta, Georgia

MARY LEA SCHNEIDER
Cardinal Stritch College
Milwaukee, Wisconsin

MILTON SERNETT
Syracuse University
Syracuse, New York

GRANT S. SPERRY-WHITE
St. Paul School of Theology
Kansas City, Missouri

MARK KLINE TAYLOR
Princeton Theological
Seminary
Princeton, New Jersey

SUSAN THISTLETHWAITE
Chicago Theological
Seminary
Chicago, Illinois

JOSEPH WAWRYKOW
University of Notre Dame
Notre Dame, Indiana

RICHARD WENTZ
Arizona State University
Tempe, Arizona

JAMES WIGGINS
Syracuse University
Syracuse, New York

ROBERT WILKEN
University of Virginia
Charlottesville, Virginia

PETER W. WILLIAMS
Miami University
Oxford, Ohio

Religions of India

ALF HILTEBEITEL
Area Editor
George Washington
University
Washington, D.C.

LAWRENCE A. BABB
Amherst College
Amherst, Massachusetts

ROBERT D. BAIRD
University of Iowa
Iowa City, Iowa

AGEHANANDA BHARATI (D.)
Syracuse University
Syracuse, New York

MADELEINE BIARDEAU (RET.)
Ecole Pratique des Hautes
Etudes
Sorbonne
Paris, France

DOUGLAS R. BROOKS
  University of Rochester
  Rochester, New York

WILLIAM CENKNER
  Catholic University of
  America
  Washington, D.C.

FRANCIS X. CLOONEY
  Boston College
  Chestnut Hill,
  Massachusetts

FRED W. CLOTHEY
  University of Pittsburgh
  Pittsburgh, Pennsylvania

THOMAS B. COBURN
  St. Lawrence University
  Canton, New York

GEORGE CORDONA
  University of Pennsylvania
  Philadelphia, Pennsylvania

PAUL COURTRIGHT
  Emory University
  Atlanta, Georgia

WENDY DONIGER
  University of Chicago
  Chicago, Illinois

ANNE FELDHAUS
  Arizona State University
  Tempe, Arizona

JAMES FITZGERALD
  University of Tennessee
  Knoxville, Tennessee

ANDREW O. FORT
  Texas Christian University
  Fort Worth, Texas

ANNE GRODZINS GOLD
  Syracuse University
  Syracuse, New York

LINDSEY HARLAN
  Connecticut College
  New London, Connecticut

WILIAM HARMAN
  DePauw University
  Greencastle, Indiana

JOHN STRATTON HAWLEY
  Barnard College
  Columbia University
  New York, New York

GLEN A. HAYES
  Bloomfield College
  Bloomfield, New Jersey

BALAJI NARAYANA HEBBAR
  Silver Spring, Maryland

THOMAS J. HOPKINS
  Franklin and Marshall
  College
  Lancaster, Pennsylvania

D. DENNIS HUDSON
  Smith College
  Northampton,
  Massachusetts

STEPHANIE W. JAMISON
  Harvard University
  Cambridge, Massachusetts

MARK JUERGENSMEYER
  University of California
  Santa Barbara, California

GURUDHAM SINGH KHALSA
  Fairfield, Pennsylvania

DAVID R. KINSLEY
  Mcmaster University
  Hamilton, Ontario, Canada

W. RANDOLPH KLEOTZLI
  Washington, D.C.

DAVID M. KNIPE
  University of Wisconsin
  Madison, Wisconsin

DAVID N. LORENZEN
  El Colegio de Mexico
  Mexico City, Mexico

PHILIP LUTGENDORF
  University of Iowa
  Iowa City, Iowa

MARY MCGEE
  Vassar College
  Poughkeepsie, New York

W. H. MCLEOD
  University of Otago
  Dunedin, New Zealand

WILLIAM K. MAHONY
  Davidson College
  Davidson, North Carolina

GURINDER SINGH MANN
  New York, New York

FREDERIQUE APFFEL MARGLIN
  Smith College
  Northampton,
  Massachusetts

EVELINE MASILAMANI-MEYER
  University of Zurich
  Zurich, Switzerland

RANDALL BLAKE MICHAEL
  Ohio Wesleyan University
  Delaware, Ohio

ROBERT N. MINOR
  University of Kansas
  Lawrence, Kansas

PAUL E. MULLER-ORTEGA
  Michigan State University
  East Lansing, Michigan

VASUDHA NARAYANAN
  University of Florida
  Gainesville, Florida

HARJOT SINGH OBEROI
  University of British
  Columbia
  Vancouver, British
  Columbia, Canada

PATRICK OLIVELLE
  University of Texas
  Austin, Texas

S. S. RAMA RAO PAPPU
  Miami University
  Oxford, Ohio

INDIRA PETERSON
  Mount Holyoke College
  South Hadley,
  Massachusetts

MICHAEL RABE
  Saint Xavier College
  Chicago, Illinois

JAMES D. REDINGTON
  Zimbabwe, Africa

HOLLY BAKER REYNOLDS
  Washington, D.C.

ARSHIA SATTAR
  Bangalore, India

WILIAM SAX
  University of Canterbury
  Christchurch, New Zealand

DAVID DEAN SHULMAN
  University of Jerusalem
  Jerusalem, Israel

BRIAN K. SMITH
  University of California
  Riverside, California

H. DANIEL SMITH
  Syracuse University
  Syracuse, New York

DEBORAH A. SOIFER
  Bowdoin College
  Brunswick, Maine

DORIS METH SRINIVASAN
  George Washington
  University
  Washington, D.C.

TONY K. STEWART
  North Carolina State
  University
  Raleigh, North Carolina

BRUCE M. SULLIVAN
  Northern Arizona
  University
  Flagstaff, Arizona

GUY R. WELBON
  University of Pennsylvania
  Philadelphia, Pennsylvania

CHARLES S. J. WHITE
  American University
  Washington, D.C.

DAVID GORDON WHITE
University of Virginia
Charlottesville, Virginia

RAYMOND B. WILLIAMS
Wabash College
Crawfordsville, Indiana

GLENN YOCUM
Whittier College
Whittier, California

PHILLIP B. ZARRILLI
University of Wisconsin
Madison, Wisconsin

ABBIE ZIFFREN
George Washington
University
Washington, D.C.

Islam

RICHARD C. MARTIN
Area Editor
Iowa State University
Ames, Iowa

MAHMOUD AYOUB
Temple University
Philadelphia, Pennsylvania

JUAN EDUARDO CAMPO
University of California
Santa Barbara, California

MICHAEL G. CARTER
New York University
New York, New York

FREDERICK M. DENNY
University of Colorado
Boulder, Colorado

DALE F. EICKELMAN
Dartmouth College
Hanover, New Hampshire

CARL W. ERNST
University of North
Carolina
Chapel Hill, North Carolina

JOHN L. ESPOSITO
Georgetown University
Washington, D.C.

PATRICK D. GAFFNEY
University of Notre Dame
Notre Dame, Indiana

ALAN GODLAS
University of Georgia
Athens, Georgia

SIDNEY GRIFFITH
Catholic University of
America
Washington, D.C.

WADI Z. HADDAD
Hartford Seminary
Hartford, Connecticut

PETER HEATH
Washington University
St. Louis, Missouri

MARCIA HERMANSEN
San Diego State University
San Diego, California

VALERIE J. HOFFMAN-LADD
University of Illinois
Urbana, Illinois

TH. EMIL HOMERIN
University of Rochester
Rochester, New York

TAZIM R. KASSAM
Middlebury College
Middlebury, Vermont

JOHN KELSAY
Florida State University
Tallahassee, Florida

KATE KOLSTAD
University of California
Santa Barbara, California

BRUCE B. LAWRENCE
Duke University
Durham, North Carolina

JANE DAMMEN MCAULIFFE
University of Toronto
Toronto, Ontario, Canada

BARBARA D. METCALF
University of California
Davis, California

MUSTANSIR MIR
University of Michigan
Ann Arbor, Michigan

AZIM A. NANJI
University of Florida
Gainesville, Florida

GORDON D. NEWBY
Emory University
Atlanta, Georgia

ERIC ORMSBY
McGill University
Montreal, Quebec, Canada

FRANCIS E. PETERS
New York University
New York, New York

A. KEVIN REINHART
Dartmouth College
Hanover, New Hampshire

ABDULAZIZ A. SACHEDINA
University of Virginia
Charlottesville, Virginia

ANNEMARIE SCHIMMEL
Harvard University,
emeritus
Cambridge, Massachusetts

MICHAEL A. SELLS
Haverford College
Haverford, Pennsylvania

DANIEL G. SHAW
University of Colorado
Colorado Springs,
Colorado

JANE I. SMITH
Iliff School of Theology
Denver, Colorado

TAMARA SONN
University of South Florida
Tampa, Florida

JOSEF VAN ESS
University of Tubingen
Tubingen, Germany

JOHN VOLL
Georgetown University
Washington, D.C.

STEVEN WASSERSTROM
Reed College
Portland, Oregon

EARLE H. WAUGH
University of Alberta
Edmonton, Alberta,
Canada

BERNARD WEISS
University of Utah
Salt Lake City, Utah

CAROLINE WILLIAMS
William and Mary College
Williamsburg, Virginia

MARK R. WOODWARD
Arizona State University
Tempe, Arizona

Judaism

JACOB NEUSNER
Area Editor
University of South Florida
Tampa, Florida

SAMUEL ADLER
Eastman School of Music
Rochester, New York

ALAN J. AVERY-PECK
College of the Holy Cross
Worcester, Massachusetts

DAVID ELLENSON
Hebrew Union College
Jewish Institute of Religion
Los Angeles, California

DARRELL J. FASCHING
University of South Florida
Tampa, Florida

PAUL V. M. FLESHER
University of Wyoming
Laramie, Wyoming

MARVIN FOX
  Brandeis University
  Waltham, Massachusetts

LESTER L. GRABBE
  University of Hull
  Hull, England

WILLIAMS S. GREEN
  University of Rochester
  Rochester, New York

EDWARD L. GREENSTEIN
  Jewish Theological
  Seminary
  New York, New York

JOSEPH GUTMANN
  Hebrew Union College
  Cincinnati, Ohio

JUDITH HAUPTMAN
  Jewish Theological
  Seminary
  New York, New York

LAWRENCE HOFFMAN
  Hebrew Union College
  Jewish Institute of Religion
  New York, New York

ABRAHAM J. KARP
  Jewish Theological
  Seminary
  New York, New York

RONALD C. KIENER
  Trinity College
  Hartford, Connecticut

GARY G. PORTON
  University of Illinois
  Urbana, Illinois

SAMUEL ROSENBAUM
  Temple Beth El
  Rochester, New York

ANTHONY J. SALDARINI
  Boston College
  Boston, Massachusetts

JONATHAN D. SARNA
  Brandeis University
  Waltham, Massachusetts

MANFRED VOGEL
  Northwestern University
  Evanston, Illinois

ELLIOT WOLFSON
  New York University
  New York, New York

ALAN ZUCKERMAN
  Brown University
  Providence, Rhode Island

New Religions

CAROLE A. MYSCOFSKI
  Area Editor
  Illinois Wesleyan
  University
  Bloomington, Illinois

MARGOT ADLER
  Washington, D.C.

EILEEN BARKER
  London School of
  Economics and Political
  Science
  London, England

ROBERT M. BAUM
  Wesleyan College
  Macon, Georgia

HORACE CAMPBELL
  Syracuse University
  Syracuse, New York

ROBERT S. ELLWOOD
  University of Southern
  California
  Los Angeles, California

STEPHEN D. GLAZIER
  University of Nebraska
  Kearney, Nebraska

JULIA DAY HOWELL
  Australian National
  University
  Canberra, Australia

DAVID K. JORDAN
  University of California,
  San Diego
  La Jolla, California

JEFFREY KAPLAN
  Arctic Sivunmun Ilisagvia
  Coll
  Barrow, Alaska

VIRGINIA KERNS
  College of William and
  Mary
  Wiliamsburg, Virginia

MARY MACDONALD
  Lemoyne College
  Syracuse, New York

JOSEPH M. MURPHY
  Georgetown University
  Washington, D.C.

VICTOR L. OLIVER
  Atlanta, Georgia

IAN READER
  University of Stirling
  Stirling, Scotland

THOMAS ROBBINS
  Rochester, Minnesota

DEBORAH BIRD ROSE
  Australian National
  University
  Canberra, Australia

KAREN SINCLAIR
  Eastern Michigan
  University
  Ypsilanti, Michigan

OMER STEWART (D. 1991)
  University of Colorado
  Boulder, Colorado

JILL WATTS
  California State University
  San Marcos, California

The Study of Religion

HANS H. PENNER
  Area Editor
  Dartmouth College
  Hanover, New Hampshire

LARRY D. BOUCHARD
  University of Virginia
  Charlottesville, Virginia

JOHN W. DIXON
  University of North
  Carolina
  Chapel Hill, North Carolina

H. MICHAEL ERMARTH
  Dartmouth College
  Hanover, New Hampshire

NANCY K. FRANKENBERRY
  Dartmouth College
  Hanover, New Hampshire

TERRY F. GODLOVE, JR.
  Hofstra University
  Hempstead, New York

RONALD M. GREEN
  Dartmouth College
  Hanover, New Hampshire

GILES GUNN
  University of California
  Santa Barbara, California

THOMAS F. HEAD
  Yale University
  New Haven, Connecticut

MARLENE ELIZABETH HECK
  Dartmouth College
  Hanover, New Hampshire

ROGER A. JOHNSON
  Wellseley College
  Wellseley, Massachusetts

STEVEN T. KATZ
  Cornell University
  Ithaca, New York

E. THOMAS LAWSON
  Western University
  Kalamazoo, Michigan

E. ANN MATTER
University of Pennsylvania
Philadelphia, Pennsylvania

CHRISTOPHER MOONEY
Fairfield University
Fairfield, Connecticut

WILLIAM PADEN
University of Vermont
Burlington, Vermont

KAREN PECHILIS PRENTISS
Drew University
Madison, New Jersey

WAYNE L. PROUDFOOT
Columbia University
New York, New York

ROBERT A. SEGAL
Lancaster University
Lancaster, England

CHARLES STINSON
Dartmouth College
Hanover, New Hampshire

LAWRENCE E. SULLIVAN
Harvard University
Cambridge, Massachusetts

JOHN M. WATANABE
Dartmouth College
Hanover, New Hampshire

JOHN WILSON
Duke University
Durham, North Carolina

Religions of Traditional Peoples

SAM D. GILL
Area Editor
University of Colorado
Boulder, Colorado

NEWELL S. BOOTH, JR.
Miami University
Oxford, Ohio

THOMAS BUCKLEY
University of
Massachusetts
Boston, Massachusetts

DAVID CARRASCO
Princeton University
Princeton, New Jersey

ANGELIQUE ESPINOZA
Boulder, Colorado

JOHN GRIM
Bucknell University
Lewisburg, Pennsylvania

RONALD GRIMES
Wilfrid Laurier University
Waterloo, Ontario, Canada

THOMAS HARDING
University of California
Santa Barbara, California

HOWARD L. HARROD
Vanderbilt University
Divinity School
Nashville, Tennessee

ELAINE A. JAHNER
Dartmouth College
Hanover, New Hampshire

JOANN W. KEALIINOHOMOKU
Northern Arizona
University
Flagstaff, Arizona

ROXIE MCLEOD
Boulder, Colorado

KENNETH MADDOCK
MacQuarie University
Sydney, New South Wales,
Australia

KENNETH MORRISON
Arizona State University
Tempe, Arizona

THOMAS OVERHOLT
University of Wisconsin
Stevens Point, Wisconsin

THOMAS PARKHILL
St. Thomas University
Fredericton, New
Brunswick, Canada

JAMES L. PEACOCK
University of North
Carolina
Chapel Hill, North Carolina

KAY A. READ
DePaul University
Chicago, Illinois

IRENE SULLIVAN
Golden, Colorado

TOD D. SWANSON
Arizona State University
Tempe, Arizona

CHRISTOPHER VECSEY
Colgate University
Hamilton, New York

JAMES WEST-HILL
Boulder, Colorado

INTRODUCTION

BY JONATHAN Z. SMITH

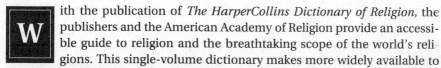ith the publication of *The HarperCollins Dictionary of Religion*, the publishers and the American Academy of Religion provide an accessible guide to religion and the breathtaking scope of the world's religions. This single-volume dictionary makes more widely available to the general public both the results of the best of contemporary scholarship on the world's religions and an account of the most significant issues and categories that inform present-day practices within the academic study of religion.

The HarperCollins Dictionary of Religion is the result of an unusual collaborative effort between a major learned society, the American Academy of Religion (AAR), and a major publishing house, HarperCollins, to ensure that the work will be authoritative, attractive, and usable for the general reader.

Under the corporate leadership of a general editor, an associate editor, and ten area editors, each appointed by the AAR, an international team of 327 scholars was commissioned to prepare more than thirty-two hundred articles on the major and lesser-known religious traditions as well as articles on interpretative categories employed in the study of religion. Each author is an acknowledged expert, bringing to his or her individual contributions years of study and publication as well as a balanced sense of judgment regarding the most current scholarship of other specialists. Each was chosen not only for learning but also for abilities in communicating knowledge to scholars and nonscholars alike. The result is a dictionary remarkable for its authority, as well as for its scope and format.

SCOPE

This dictionary treats representative and significant religious formations of humankind from every geographical area and from the Paleolithic era to the present day. Given this range, it cannot be complete; it is necessarily selective. The choice of items for inclusion, a process that extended over several years, engaged every scholarly resource available to the editors. Each item included was chosen because (1) it represents a significant religious tradition or is essential for the understanding of a significant religious tradition; (2) it is representative of a wider set of religious phenomena or of issues recurrent in the study of religion; or (3) it is a term that occurs in public discourse about religion and might, therefore, be encountered by our readers.

Within these necessary limitations, *The HarperCollins Dictionary of Religion* seeks to expand public understanding of religion by going beyond the usual concentration on major world religions. In addition to this, significant attention has been devoted to religions of traditional peoples, to extinct religions of antiquity, and to new religious movements (the last-named being the second largest set of entries). Because this work is in dictionary format, the diversity of the religious expressions and experiences of humankind is largely represented through defining native religious terms, that is, a particular group's words for itself and for central elements in its traditions.

The *Dictionary* seeks to expand public understanding of religion in a second way: by presenting, in addition to native vocabulary, terms in common use by scholars for describing and understanding religions, often from outside the tradition under discussion. This relatively new field, the academic study of religion, constitutes one of the most exciting endeavors within the human sciences over the last one hundred years.

On occasion, the reader will be invited to join the scholars in critical reflections on their enterprise. One issue will be persistent: the degree to which "our" language, whether our native Western religious language or our generic academic terminology, distorts "their" language.

To some degree, distortion is inevitable. Our language is, at best, a translation of theirs, and translations can never be complete or exact. The larger problem, however, is not at the level of a word itself, the particular translation term, but rather with all the associations our word evokes or fails to evoke. For example, when a term such as *scripture* is used by one of our authors, it carries for many of our readers the connotation of (1) a fixed collection of (2) revealed or inspired books, two senses rarely appropriate when speaking of the sacred literature of the majority of literate religions of humankind. (For this reason, the *Dictionary* largely employs the term *authoritative books* in place of *scripture*.) On the other hand, when authors use the translation term *priest* to describe a professional ritualist, they are also usually describing a hereditary office. This connotation is largely lacking in the English use of the term.

Sometimes the degree to which we have imposed alien understandings on others is so massive, so unrelenting, that it appears to us to be quite natural. Perhaps the most ubiquitous example of this in the *Dictionary* is the chronological designation B.C., which the editors have quite self-consciously decided to retain to remind the reader that we in American and European culture routinely organize the dating of all religions' histories by a Christian schema. The difficulty with B.C. is not at the level of nomenclature and is, therefore, not solved by changing B.C. ("before Christ") to B.C.E. ("before the common era"—a commonality that only includes Christians and Jews). The problem is in the numeration. Here, all other traditions are being required to abandon their native decisions concerning important events: Judaism, which begins the year one with creation; Islam, with the Hijra in 622; Buddhism, with the Buddha attaining *nirvana* in 544 B.C.; or Japan, which begins the year one with the accession of each new emperor.

Concealed within this previous example is another instance of an imposed understanding that seems quite natural to us, the names by which we designate the various religions. For example, when we name a religion "Hinduism," we are employing an Arabic geographical term, first used by India's Muslim Mughal conquerors, denoting people who live near the Indus River. When we hear this tradition name itself in Sanskrit, *sanatana dharma* ("imperishable truth"), we are hearing what it most values about itself—in this case, that it has no temporal founder. While many of the older names of religions (Judaism, Christianity) were not initially self-designations but were imposed by colonial authorities, they have become the native terms. The majority of names, however, are inventions of nineteenth-century European scholars who replaced, with proper nouns, more general terms such as *pagans* or *idolaters* by which religions other than Judaism, Christianity, and Islam were previously designated in Western literature. Taking as their model the name *Christ*, embedded in Christianity, they christened a whole host of religions after the names of their founders, such as Confucianism (which calls itself *ju chia*, "the School of the Scholars"), Zoroastrianism (which names itself after its God, *Daena Mazdayasni*, "the Good Religion of the Worshipers of Mazdah [the Wise Lord]"), as well as the improper and insulting designation of Muhammadism for Islam, or the soon abandoned name, Mosaism, for the religion of Israel.

FORMAT

Within any dictionary, alphabetization, the very device that makes possible quick and easy reference on a particular topic, works to disassemble the organic relations that characterize the components of any religious tradition. Terms that belong or regularly occur together may be separated by hundreds of pages owing to the sheer chance of their initial letter. (Think of the common Christian formula "Jesus Christ Son of God": the three titles will be separated and distributed at the middle, beginning, and end parts of any dictionary.) The major tool available to overcome this fragmentation is the cross-reference, a device we have included at the end of many articles, which sends the reader who wants more information to other, related articles in the *Dictionary*.

The editors and contributors have worked particularly hard at overcoming fragmentation in the *Dictionary* and have introduced a system of cross-referencing that seeks to multiply the number of relationships the reader is invited to consider for any particular term.

For example, the reader may have heard the native term *bris* and been unable from context to guess at its meaning. In this dictionary, the alphabetical entry will give its approximate English pronunciation, provide its etymological derivation, and define the word as "Jewish ritual circumcision." The reader may, quite appropriately, choose to halt his or her inquiry at this point. The word is no longer a foreign one; its verbal meaning has become clear.

The cross-reference at "bris" will invite the reader to look up the generic term *circumcision*. This entry will note as examples not only circumcision as practiced by Jews, but also Muslim circumcision and circumcision as a common ritual within the religions of traditional peoples. With this, the reader will begin to have the possibility of comparison, of considering similarities and differences across religious traditions. The cross-references appended to the "circumcision" article are more numerous, suggesting several parallels for possible exploration. Some cross-references are to academic terms (*initiation rituals, puberty rituals*) that are used to describe not only some practices of circumcision but also other ritual acts that share a similar function or structure. Other academic terms focus on the specific mode of ritual activity, leading the reader to other rituals involving operations performed on either the male or female genitals (*clitoridectomy, subincision*). Either set of articles concerned with academic terminology will guide the reader through an ever-widening range of practices, including a lengthy, comprehensive entry on "ritual," which introduces the variety of theories, debates, and understandings of ritual itself.

Other cross-references included with the "circumcision" entry will take the reader in another direction, deeper into those particular religions in which the ritual of circumcision appears. By looking up the "Judaism (life cycle)" and "Islam (life cycle)" entries, the reader will be able to place circumcision within a set of rituals undergone by the typical male Jew or Muslim beginning with birth and extending through death. These entries, in their turn, will invite consideration of other central aspects of these two religious traditions.

Another reader may come to the *Dictionary* with a quite different set of expectations, not to gain particular information, but with a desire to obtain a general education about one of the major religious traditions, about broad categories of religion, or about what present-day scholars are thinking and arguing about religion. With this sort of reader in mind, the alphabetical arrangement has been supplemented by another mode of organization: the *Dictionary* may be read as a set of *eleven* books within the larger book.

Each of the area editors has written a major article designed to introduce the reader to both the subjects and interpretative issues that characterize their fields of expertise:

Religions of Antiquity
Buddhism
Chinese Religion
Christianity
Hinduism
Islam
Japanese Religion
Judaism
New Religions
The Study of Religion
Religions of Traditional Peoples

Of these featured articles, those corresponding to historical religious communities and traditions are accompanied by maps, timelines, and other appropriate illustrative devices enabling the reader to gain an overview of the tradition under discussion. In addition, each major article is accompanied by a set of comprehensive entries treating an appropriate set of central topics. These most frequently include:

art and architecture
authoritative texts and their interpretation
festal cycle
life cycle
thought and ethics

The "Study of Religion" article is also closely accompanied by a set of comprehensive entries:

religion, anthropology of
religion, definition of
religion, explanation of
religion, phenomenology of
religion, philosophy of
religion, psychology of
religion, sociology of

To enhance the *Dictionary*'s usefulness to the general reader, whenever persons or places are mentioned they are identified, and their location or dates given with as much precision as possible. Pronunciation guides are provided when necessary, and all foreign-language terms have been defined. Special maps, timelines, charts, bar graphs, family-tree diagrams, and drawings have been commissioned in order to clarify verbal descriptions or to present large amounts of information in an attractive, easily readable form. Photographs have been chosen with care, not only to illustrate particular traditions but also to invite comparisons among them. In each case the captions clarify their significance.

The result of these efforts in both ensuring a broad scope and providing an innovative format is a highly readable, authoritative, and reliable summary of the best of contemporary knowledge about the religious traditions of humankind and the achievements and issues attendant on their study.

ACKNOWLEDGMENTS

This undertaking could not have been brought to completion without the cooperation of many individuals, including editors and contributors, without whose labors neither the contents nor the authority of this volume would have been possible. The various members of HarperCollins, each of whom has become a colleague in the six years it has taken to prepare the work, are owed a debt of gratitude: John B. Shopp, senior editor, who has guided this work from its inception to its conclusion; Judith Kleppe, assistant editor, who has supervised the final editing of the manuscript and procurement of the illustrations; Lisa Zuniga Carlsen, production editor; Terri Goff, editorial production manager; Martha Blegen, design manager; and Professor Richard M. Carp of Northern Illinois University, photographic consultant. The American Academy of Religion, under whose scholarly oversight this dictionary was produced, has been unfailingly cooperative, most especially its Executive Director from 1983 to 1991, Professor James Wiggins, and its current Executive Director, Professor Barbara di Concini, as well as Professor Robert Detweiler, who chaired the Academy's Research and Publications Committee, which first proposed this undertaking. The University of Rochester made possible the filing processes by which the thousands of pages of manuscript were first assembled, especially through the heroic efforts of Jeanine Korman, assistant in the Department of Religion and Classics.

A special thanks goes to the Image Bank for Teaching World Religions for its contribution of photographs to this project. Many of the images reproduced in this book and other annotated images concerning the world's religions can be obtained by contacting the Center for the Study of World Religions at Harvard University, 42 Francis Avenue, Cambridge, MA 02138.

Each of these individuals, and many more, contributed to this extraordinary, cooperative venture in scholarship and publication, one that is faithful to the maxim of one of the giants of the field: "He who knows but one religion knows none." The study of religion constantly plays on the relationships between the near and the far, hoping through its interpretative labors to make familiar those traditions that at first sight seem strange or alien, and hoping, at the same time, to defamiliarize, to reveal unexpected aspects of those traditions that are thought to be close to home. The scholars of the AAR invite the readers of this dictionary to join with them in undertaking this exciting process of discovery.

ABBREVIATIONS

Arab.	Arabic	abbr.	abbreviated
Aram.	Aramaic	b.	born
Chin.	Chinese	ca.	about
Egypt.	Egyptian	cf.	confer, compare
Eng.	English	ch.	chapter
Fr.	French	d.	died
Ger.	German	ed.	edition
Gk.	Greek	esp.	especially
Heb.	Hebrew	fem.	feminine
Ital.	Italian	fl.	flourished
Jap.	Japanese	lit.	literally
Kor.	Korean	masc.	masculine
Lat.	Latin	neut.	neutral
Russ.	Russian	pl.	plural
Skt.	Sanskrit	pron.	pronounced
Span.	Spanish	r.	ruled
		sing.	singular
		trans.	translated
		vs.	versus
		*	reconstructed proto-Indo-European root
		?	uncertain

PRONUNCIATION KEY

SYMBOL	SOUND	SYMBOL	SOUND
a	cat	ng	sing
ah	father	o	hot
ahr	lard	oh	go
air	care	oi	boy
aw	jaw	oo	foot
ay	pay	*oo*	boot
b	bug	oor	poor
ch	chew	or	for
d	do	ou	how
e, eh	pet	p	pat
ee	seem	r	run
f	fun	s	so
g	good	sh	sure
h	hot	t	toe
hw	whether	th	thin
i	it	*th*	then
i	sky	ts	tsetse
ihr	ear	tw	twin
j	joke	uh	ago
k	king	uhr	her
kh	ch as in German *Buch*	v	vow
ks	vex	w	weather
kw	quill	y	young
l	love	z	zone
m	mat	zh	vision
n	not		

NOTE ON TRANSLITERATION

The HarperCollins Dictionary of Religion has undertaken the unusual and difficult task of providing pronunciation guides and transliterations for words in
more than one hundred languages. These should be taken as each scholar's
best approximation and judgment.

When there is a difference between common English pronunciation and a
more correct form, this will be indicated (for example, "Baha'i, bah-hi', or, more
properly, bah-hah'ee"). There are languages that are no longer spoken (such as
Sumerian, Akkadian, and classical Greek) whose pronunciation remains controversial or uncertain. There are living languages (for example, Turkish with
twenty-seven vowels) that strain the capacity of English sounds or the Latin
alphabet to represent them. In some cases, the editors have had to choose
between rival accepted theories of transliteration, for example, Chinese, where
the same name may be represented as either Ching ho or Jing he, or Tibetan,
where the same name may be transliterated as either Gzis-ka-rtse or Shingatse.
In other cases, native language speakers are themselves divided, such as in the
differences between Israeli (Sephardic) and Euro-American (Ashkenazic) pro-
nunciations of Hebrew. Words in other languages are not pronounced the way
they are spelled, either because of rules of euphony (for example, the Greek
word from which "angel" is derived is spelled aggelos but pronounced angelos)
or because, as in Korean, grammatical indicators are pronounced but not
written. Other languages, such as Japanese, do not stress syllables. Many of the
languages of traditional peoples have not yet been reduced to writing (an enterprise largely undertaken by foreigners), or, when they have, there is no standardized form. Finally, in the interest of general readability, the editors have
deliberately omitted many of the phonetic refinements introduced to improve
accuracy of transliteration in specialist publications, ranging from the use of
diacritical marks in Sanskrit and other Indic languages to the representation of
the hamza in Arabic.

It is important to call these matters to readers' attention to remind them that
even when they are confronting a term in the dictionary in a foreign language
they are, in effect, already encountering a translation and an act of scholarly
judgment.

LIST OF ILLUSTRATIONS

Maps and Charts

Graphs

Timelines

Family-Tree Diagrams

Floor Plans and Other Drawings

THE HARPERCOLLINS DICTIONARY OF RELIGION

A B C D E F

G H I J K L

M N O P Q

R S T U V

W X Y & Z

Aaron (air'uhn), in the Hebrew Bible, the brother of Moses and the first Israelite priest.

Abbas Effendi. *See* Baha'i.

Abbasid Empire (uh-ba'sid; Arab.), Islamic rulers from 750 to 1258. The Abbasids came to power when they overthrew the Umayyads. This victory shifted the center of the Muslim caliphate, or leadership, from Syria to Iraq and a more cosmopolitan ruling elite replaced the Arab-oriented Umayyad rulers. The Abbasid caliphate was the political framework for the great cultural synthesis of medieval Islamic civilization. Centralized control weakened in the ninth century, and effective control of Abbasid lands passed to military commanders who ruled as sultans. The Abbasid caliphs remained as political symbols controlled by others. Formal Abbasid rule ended with the Mongol conquest of the Abbasid capital, Baghdad. *See also* caliph; Umayyad.

abbess/abbot (Aram. *abba*, "father"), title for the superior of a Christian monastery of women (abbess) or men (abbot). *See also* monasticism.

abbot. *See* abbess/abbot.

Abelard, Peter (a'bay-lahrd; 1079–1142), French Roman Catholic theologian and philosopher. One of the strong representatives of Christian Aristotelianism, in his major work *Sic et non* (Yes and No) he juxtaposes quotations from authoritative scriptural and theological writings that appeared contradictory and suggests how they might be reconciled. Several of his works were condemned as heretical and burned.

Within Christian lore, Abelard is best known for his autobiographical volume, *Historia calamitatum* (History of My Troubles), which, among other incidents, recounts his ill-fated love for Heloise, with whom he had a child. Heloise, the daughter of the canon of Notre Dame in Paris, was sent to a convent; Abelard was forcibly castrated and became a monk.

Abhidharma (uh-bee-dahr'muh; Skt., "about the doctrine," "higher doctrine"), the exegesis of Buddhist doctrine. The term designates either the study of Buddhist doctrine or the genre of texts that systematically elaborate the doctrine expounded in the *sutra* (scriptural discourse) portion of the canon. A complete set of canonical Abhidharma texts, including later commentaries, treatises, and digests, survives for only the Theravadin and Sarvastivadin Buddhist sects. Abhidharma is characterized in style and method by the systematic analysis of Buddhist teaching, beginning with simple catechetical lists and matrices, proceeding to more comprehensive taxonomies and dialogue, and culminating in an exhaustive account of reality providing a doctrine of salvation buttressed by philosophical arguments. *See also* Buddhism (authoritative texts and their interpretation); exegesis.

Abhinavagupta. *See* Kashmir Shaivism.

ablution, ritual washing, most frequently with water, in order to remove pollution. *See also* baptism; conversion; Elchasai, Elchasaites; foot washing; Hinduism (worship); Ganga, Ganges; holy water; Kumbha Mela; Mandaeans; mikveh; prayer; purity and impurity; ritual; sweat, sweat lodge.

Hindus performing ablutions in the Ganges and thereby gaining access to the purificatory powers of the holiest river in India as it flows through the sacred city of Banaras (Varanasi).

abortion, premature termination of pregnancy. All societies possess techniques for abortion. Many religions recognize the legitimacy of abortion to protect the mother's health (i.e., therapeutic abortion). Voluntary abortion is more controversial, especially among Christian groups in the United States. *See also* birth control; infanticide.

Christianity: The New Testament makes no reference to abortion. By the second century, Christian social thought condemns abortion, as it does infanticide and contraception. Some writers consider abortion worse than murder because it condemns the soul of the unbaptized to hell. Augustine (d. 430) condemns abortion as "lustful cruelty," indicating the extent to which Christians were concerned with the unrestrained sexual indulgence that lay at the roots of abortion. Augustine thought that the body is infused with a soul slightly more than forty days after conception; before that point abortion, while still condemned, is not homicide.

In medieval Catholicism, Aristotle's (d. 322 B.C.) view of animation combined with Augustine's theory of ensoulment led most theologians not to consider abortion a homicide if induced within forty days after conception for male fetuses and eighty days for females. Thomas Aquinas (ca. 1225–74) agrees with this view, although he frowns on abortion for any reason but threat to the mother's life. A more conservative position is found in one canon of the medieval *Decretales,* holding that abortion at any time is homicide and should be punished as such. This, however, is a minority view.

Through the Protestant Reformation, the ensoulment theory remains dominant. Martin Luther (1483–1546) accepts the Catholic position and condemns abortion.

In Roman Catholicism, by the nineteenth century, the ensoulment theory gives way to the view that abortion is homicide from the moment of conception. Even acts to save a mother's life, as in cases of ectopic pregnancy and uterine cancer, are limited to the indirect killing of the fetus.

Modern Protestants such as Helmut Thielicke and Paul Ramsey oppose abortion in part by emphasizing the commitment and steadfast love with which Christians should conceive life. In 1952, the American Lutheran Conference declared against abortion except as a measure to save the life of the mother.

In the United States, many liberal Christians in the 1990s support a woman's right to elective abortion, although they resist being designated as pro-abortion. After the 1973 *Roe v. Wade* decision by the United States Supreme Court legalizing elective abortions, some conservative Christians joined forces in opposition to the pro-choice position. While most Christian feminists are pro-choice, some are defining a pro-life feminist position that opposes elective abortion. They argue that few women would opt for elective abortions if poverty and serious consequences could be avoided. European nations provide the public support for adoption and child care that makes elective abortions much rarer than in the United States. Abortion divides Christianity, and the debate is acrimonious. The common ground is that most view abortion as tragic, however justifiable. *See also* soul.

Abraham (ay'bruh-ham; Heb.,"father of a multitude"), ancestor of the Hebrews. In Jewish, Christian, and Islamic traditions Abraham is seen as a model of faith. *See also* akedah.

Islam: Ibrahim (Arab.) is the "friend of God" and major prophet in the indivisible Islamic chain of prophecy culminating in Muhammad. The Qur'an relates how Abraham, questioning his father's religious beliefs, came to advocate monotheism and denounce idolatry. The Qur'an states explicitly that Abraham was neither Jew, Christian, nor pagan, but, rather, a believing monotheist (*hanif*) who was prepared to sacrifice his son, either Isaac or Ismail (Heb. *Ishmael*), in submission to God's will. Further, Abraham, together with Ismail, built the Kaaba in Mecca and established the pilgrimage (*Hajj*) there. *See also* Hajar (Islam); Islam (festal cycle); Ismail; Kaaba; Messenger of Allah.

Abrahamic religions, popular designation for Judaism, Christianity, and Islam, emphasizing their common heritage.

Abrasax. *See* Abraxas.

Abraxas (ah-braks'uhs), or Abrasax, the world creator in Basilides's Gnostic system. Depicted as rooster- or ass-headed, Abraxas marks the typically Gnostic, devalued Jewish God. *See also* Basilides; Gnosticism.

abrogation (Arab. *nashk*), Islamic doctrine, explicit in the Qur'an (2:106; 13:39; 16:101; 17:86; 87:6–7), that Allah ("God"), in his progressive self-revelation to Muhammad, rescinded or caused the Prophet to forget previous revelations, those revelations having been only temporary. A notorious instance of this is the annulment of the so-called "satanic verses" advocating Meccan polytheism (53:19–20: "Have you thought upon al-Lat and al-Uzza and Manat, the third, the other?" followed by the now abrogated passage: "These are the intermediaries exalted, whose intercession is to be hoped for"). A later revelation (22:52) abrogated this endorsement of Meccan polytheism and suggested that Satan had whispered that message to Muhammad.

In later Islamic jurisprudence (*fiqh*), jurists used the doctrine in two ways. First, they argued that the revelation of the final and perfect scripture, the Qur'an, annulled the authority of all earlier revelations (i.e., the Judeo-Christian scriptures). Second, many, citing the passages listed above, used the doctrine to argue that some of the existing injunctions of the Qur'an, though still in the scripture, have been abrogated by passages revealed later. Though the text remains, the commandment is not binding. This helped early jurists reconcile apparently contradictory passages in the scripture as well as advance legal opinions contrary to certain injunctions of the Qur'an. *See also* exegesis; Islamic law.

absolute, unconditioned, concept found in Western metaphysics and philosophy of religion from the early nineteenth century to the 1990s. It was developed fully in German and in some strands of Anglo-American thought. The absolute functions as a semisecular philosophical equivalent of the Hellenistic Christian concept of God. As such, it is conceived of as unconditioned by any reality outside of or other than itself. It is independent, unrelated, beyond any limiting conditions, outer or inner, and without finite attributes. It is thus contrasted sharply with the finite, related, limited realm of creatures as that which transcends them. Often, though not always, it is part of a general idealistic metaphysics in the style of nineteenth-century German philosopher Georg Friedrich Wilhelm. Hegel, for whom the absolute is mind (or spirit), which dialectically includes and transcends relative realities.

absolution, the declaratory statement that sins are forgiven, uttered by the priest in the administration of the Christian sacrament of penance. *See also* confession; penance.

abstinence. 1 A general term for asceticism, particularly celibacy. 2 In American Protestant usage, especially the avoidance of alcoholic beverages. *See also* asceticism; celibacy.

academies (Korea), private and public. Education in Korea before the modern period was directed toward the training of civil servants in the traditions of Confucian letters, rituals, and statecraft. The institutions for this training were of two types: the public academies, which were established and maintained by successive Korean governments in the capital and in key provincial cities, and the private library-academies, established by bureaucrat-scholars in the countryside.

Private Academies: The first private academies (Kor. *sojae*) were established in the tenth century by retired bureaucrat-scholars. Unlike their public counterparts, these private schools were better off financially, were not subject to the vagaries of government support and court politics, and, because they were usually located in remote areas, suffered little from the depredations of the Khitad, Jurched, and Mongol invasions. Though both the private and public academies prepared students for the literary and classics civil service examinations and for fur-

ther studies at the National Academy in the capital, the private academies tended to foster a greater appreciation for the ethical, ritual, and metaphysical side of Confucian learning and were responsible for the growing Confucianization of Korean society and government in the centuries that followed. So successful were these private schools in training students for government service that their students came to dominate the civil service examination and bureaucracy from the mid-eleventh through the end of the thirteenth century, a period marked by strong bureaucratic and weak monarchical control of the government. In that same period twelve great teacher-student lineages evolved and when the military usurped the government (1170–1258), it was these private schools and lineages that kept education in Confucian classical texts, poetry, and composition alive.

Shrine-schools: While the Koryo-period (918–1392) private academies focused on education for the sake of government service, the Choson-period (1392–1910) private academies (*sowon*), under the banner of Neo-Confucian ritual orthodoxy, were established as shrines honoring one or more great Korean Confucian scholars. These shrine-schools served as hermitages for scholars who refused to serve in the central government or had retired from it. It was in such shrine-schools that the ideal of the righteous scholar-recluse (*sarim*), the Confucian equivalent of the Taoist and Buddhist recluse, was to flourish.

At the Choson-period shrine-schools scholars and their students led austere lives marked by absolute loyalty to the monarch under all circumstances and engaged in studies that went far beyond the requirements of employment in the central government, such as the study of metaphysical and ethical theory, the practice of meditation, local and national geography and history, medicine, and geomancy. Scholars at the private academies in time built a base of power in the provinces by creating and enforcing Confucianized village codes and serving as village schoolmasters. The result was a deeper and broader penetration of Confucian values and rituals at all levels of society.

These shrine-schools also preserved and developed particular lines of Neo-Confucian thinking and trained men to implement that thinking in local and national politics. By the seventeenth century there were hundreds of such academies and, as their students rose in the ranks of the bureaucracy, there was increasing competition for royal charters and gifts. These charters included large tracts of cropland, slaves, books, and, like the Buddhist temples of the Koryo dynasty, special exemptions from taxation and corvee labor. By the eighteenth century the power of the private academies, the factions they spawned, the regionalism they fostered, and the wealth they controlled constituted a major political and economic threat to the central government and the monarchy. While the private academies had done much to stabilize and Confucianize Korean society during the Choson kingdom, their inherent conservatism and moral absolutism eventually became obstacles to the reform and renewal needed to bring Korea into the modern era. By the end of the nineteenth century, all but forty-seven of the private academies were ordered closed and all government subsidies withdrawn.

Christian Missionary Schools: Late-nineteenth-century Confucian private academies were succeeded by Western Protestant missionary schools at the primary, secondary, and postsecondary level. These missionary schools, established and maintained by churches in the United States, Canada, and Australia, specialized in the education of women as well as men and, unlike the Confucian academies, focused their attention on the middle and lower economic classes. These Protestant schools followed the curricula of their American and European counterparts and, in addition to classes on the Bible and, Christian dogma, taught English, reading and writing in the Hangul script, science and mathematics, and social and domestic sciences. Graduates of these schools went on to higher studies abroad or began careers at home in the religious, medical, and educational fields.

In the twentieth century the Protestant schools have been followed by Catholic, Buddhist, and other religious and independent schools, but apart from mandatory and voluntary classes in religion and institutional specialties, the organization, finances, staffing, and curriculum of the private schools follows that set by the Korean Ministry of Education.

Public Academies: The public academies established and maintained by successive Korean governments for the training of civil servants were of two types, the National Academy (Kor. *Taehak, Kukjagam*) in the capital, and the lower provincial academies (*hyanggyo*) established in key provincial cities throughout the peninsula.

Three Kingdoms Period: The first National Academy was founded in the Koguryo kingdom in 372 for the training of royal and aristocratic family members in the civil and military arts. Students at the National Academy were also responsible for the worship of Confucius and his learned disciples at the academy. This was followed by similar establishments in the kingdoms of Paekche and Silla. These early establishments played an important role in the transformation from tribalist and clan-shared monarchies to centralized, single-family hereditary monarchies working through an established aristocratic bureaucracy. They were also important in the spread of continental Chinese culture and the establishment of foreign relations with China and Japan.

Silla Period: With the unification of the peninsula by Silla in the seventh century, a single National Academy was established in the capital at Kyongju and, like its predecessors, housed a shrine where the portraits and statues of Confucius and his worthy disciples were worshiped. The Silla government established the first examination system in literary and historical studies at the National Academy, but restricted admission to lower-ranking Sillan and subjugated Kaya, Paekche, and Koguryo aristocrats. Students successful in the examinations could be appointed to provincial posts and low-ranking capital posts, or they could go to China and seek to raise their status at home through success in the Chinese examination system.

Koryo Period: In the succeeding Koryo kingdom (918–1392) a full-fledged examination system in civil and military subjects was established in 958, and the sons of collateral branches of the royal family and aristocrats were educated at the academy in the capital at Kaesong. Entrance to the academy and qualifications for the examinations now included a mastery of poetic and prose composition and a record of Confucian ethical behavior. Once admitted, students and faculty were supported by the government through the allocation of national lands and landbound peasants. Provincial schools and libraries were also established and maintained by the government as a means of bringing candidates to the capital from all over the country.

The national academy in Kaesong, though, was never able to achieve the kind of success that the private academies did, and several times throughout the Koryo period was left empty of students and faculty. During the military government of the twelfth century, government public education was neglected as the military governors had little need for trained scholars, except as scribes and archivists. After the restoration of monarchical control and the establishment of peace with the Mongols, the national and provincial academies were only gradually reestablished. It was during this period that Korean scholar-bureaucrats often went to China to complete their education and do apprenticeship service in the Mongol government.

Upon their return, they would introduce new policies, reform education, and work to improve the civil service examination. One such student, Yi Saek (1328–96), was able to reestablish the National Academy in 1367 with the new title of Songgyu'gwan, or Hall for the Establishment of Balance. Yi Saek also succeeded in changing the largely literary curriculum to one that emphasized the study of the Four Books and Five Classics, texts that formed the core of Neo-Confucian learning and civil service examination in the Mongol, Ming, and Ch'ing periods. A contemporary of Yi Saek, Chong Mongju (1337–92) helped create the Five Confucian Academies (*obu haktang*) in the capital and helped promote the creation of Confucian academies and shrines in major provincial towns and cities (hyanggyo). In 1398 when the capital was moved to Hanyang (modern-day Seoul) the Songgyu'gwan was moved to its present location.

Choson Period: In the Choson period (1392–1910) the National Academy grew both in size and importance. At its height the Songgyu'gwan could accommodate more than two hundred students and their attendants. It was endowed with lands and slaves and its status, rules, and properties were recognized in the Yi dynastic code. Like its predecessors, the Songgyu'gwan also housed the Shrine to Culture (Munmyo), which was expanded over the years to accommodate the enshrined spirit tablets of Korean scholars. Many of the founding merit subjects of the Choson kingdom had either studied at or taught in the National Academy. As bureaucrats they ensured the academy's independence from the throne and kept royal relatives from attending. The result was that faculty and students became a counterbalance to both the power of the throne and the aristocratic bureaucracy. Heavily politicized graduates and undergraduates of the academy would, under the aegis of Confucian orthodoxy, freely remonstrate with the throne on political, military, and bureaucratic issues. The success of such political involvement eventually spawned its own factionalism, and many of the brightest and most capable students left and returned to the private academies.

Modern Period: Nineteenth- and twentieth-century reforms in government and education led to the disestablishment of the National Academy and the provincial academies. Private Confucian associations reorganized the National Academy as the School for the Study of Classics (Kyonghak won) and maintained at their own expense the spring and autumn rituals (*sokchon*) to Confucius and his disciples. The

Kyonghak won was later reorganized as Songgyu'gwan University, a private university in Seoul. Though Confucian education has, in the modern day, become a matter of private choice and one aspect of Korean heritage, the status, expectations, even reverence once accorded to students and faculty at the National Academy have been transferred to Seoul National University. *See also* Confucianism; Korea, Confucian virtues in; Shrine to Culture; Yi Saek.

accretions, a charge, often made by religious reformers, that the original, pure faith has been overlaid with subsequent corruptions.

acculturation, cultural change within one tradition by virtue of contact with another. *See also* diaspora; diffusion; nativistic movements; syncretism (Japan).

Achaemenid (ah-kee'men-id), Persian imperial dynasty that ruled Iran, the Near East, and Anatolia from 550 to 331 B.C. Cyrus II founded the empire; Alexander the Great conquered it.

Achamoth (ak-uh-moth'; a corruption from the Heb. *hokma,* "wisdom," and *moth,* "death"), another form of the Valentinian Gnostic Sophia. *See also* Gnosticism; Sophia; Valentinianism.

acharya (ah-chahr'yuh; Skt., "teacher"), an instructor in Indic traditional knowledge, a spiritual guide learned in religious texts.

Two *acharyas,* brought from India, ensure the proper performance of the ritual consecrating a new Hindu temple in Ashland, Massachusetts, May 1990. The temple, dedicated to Shri-Lakshmi, a goddess associated with wealth and good fortune, is one of a number of recent constructions serving the more than seven hundred thousand practicing Hindus in North America.

acolyte (Gk., "attendant"), layperson who assists the

priest during the celebration of the Christian liturgy.

A.D. *See* B.C./A.D.

adab (ah'dab; Arab.), in Islam, one of many terms that at base denotes a custom or norm of conduct. In the early centuries the term came to convey an ethical connotation of proper personal qualities or an implication of either proper knowledge or the cultivation of a range of sensibilities and skills. In its plural form, *adab* acquired the meaning of rules of conduct, often specified for a particular social group. In addition, adab specified all that made one polished and urbane, master of the arts not subsumed under the category of religious learning. Often in recent times, adab has meant simply literature in the narrow sense.

Underlying the concept of adab is a notion of discipline and training, denoting as well the good breeding and refinement that results from training. In all its uses, adab reflects a high valuation of the employment of the will in proper discrimination of correct order, behavior, and taste. The term implicitly or explicitly distinguishes cultivated behavior from that deemed vulgar, for example, from pre-Islamic custom. The term's root sense of proper conduct and discrimination, of discipline and moral formation, especially fostered in the Sufi tradition, has been brought to the fore in many recent reform movements. In that sense, adab is often coupled with *akhlaq* ("manners," "ethics"). *See also* Islam (ethics).

Adam and Eve (Heb., "human being" and Heb., derivation uncertain), in the Hebrew Bible, the first human couple. Their creation is narrated twice: in the first account (Genesis 1:26–27) Adam is the generic name for humankind; in the second account (Genesis 2–3) Adam is the proper name of an individual, the first man, and Eve is the first woman. The story of their creation, disobedience, and expulsion from Eden is rarely alluded to in the Hebrew Bible but became the subject of much later elaboration in the Jewish pseudepigrapha, rabbinic traditions, the New Testament, and Christian theologies. *See also* Fall.

Islam: Adam (Arab. *Adam*) is the father of humankind and God's first prophet. God formed Adam from clay, breathed his spirit into it, and taught Adam the names of all things. Adam is God's vice-regent (*caliph*) on earth. A group of angels, led by Iblis, refuse God's command to bow down to Adam, resulting in their expulsion from heaven. Iblis takes revenge by tempting Adam and Eve (Hawwa) to eat the fruit of the forbidden tree. *See also* Iblis.

Adi-buddha (ah-dee-bood'dah; Skt., "Original Buddha"), the primordial Buddha from which all other Buddhas issue. This concept, associated with the esoteric Buddhist traditions, is found with considerable variations in Nepal, Tibet, and Japan. *See also* Buddhas.

Adi Granth (ah'dee gruhnth; Punjabi, "Original Book"), the sacred scripture of the Sikhs. The *Adi Granth* was compiled by the fifth Guru, Arjan, in 1603 and 1604, using two earlier volumes that had been recorded at the command of Amar Das, the third Guru. The earlier collection (the *Mohan Pothis* or *Goindval Pothis*) contained the works of the first three Gurus and of other Sant poets whose views corresponded with those of the Gurus. To them Guru Arjan attached his own works and those of the fourth Guru; and at a later date the works of the ninth Guru were also added. In 1705, shortly before he died, the tenth Guru, Gobind Singh, declared that the functions of the Guru would pass to the scripture and the community at his death. The *Adi Granth* thereafter became the *Guru Granth Sahib* ("the revered Book which is Guru").

History: The history of the *Adi Granth* manuscript is obscure until the annexing British discovered it in the Lahore treasury in 1849. Following the death of Guru Arjan it evidently came into the possession of Dhir Mal, grandson of the sixth Guru, who wanted it in order to buttress his claims to be Guru. Since that time it apparently remained in the village of Kartarpur, except when the orthodox Sikhs briefly recaptured it and later when it was held in Lahore by Maharaja Ranjit Singh and his successors. The British restored the manuscript to the descendants of Dhir Mal and apart from a brief period when it was under litigation it has remained in that family ever since.

Content: The *Adi Granth* consists almost entirely of religious songs praising God for his greatness and holding out to humankind liberation of the soul through meditation on the divine Name (by which is meant all aspects of God). Although the script is Gurmukhi (as in modern Punjabi), the language is generally Sant Bhasha ("Sant language"), based on the same foundation as the Punjabi and Hindi of today.

The contents are divided into an introductory section, main text, and epilogue. The introductory section includes works that had acquired a liturgical function for Sikhs; and the epilogue largely consists of works that could not be accommodated elsewhere. The main text takes each *raga* (or meter) in turn, dividing it up into the various songs, mainly according to length; and then it divides each variety according to author, beginning with those of Guru Nanak (1469–1539).

Treatment of the Adi Granth: Because it is the Guru, extreme deference is shown by Sikhs to the *Adi Granth*. In its presence the head must be covered and no shoes worn. The mere presence of a copy makes a room a *gurdwara* (Sikh house of worship); upon entry each person is required to bow the forehead to the floor. When carried it must be borne on the head and when put down it must be placed at a higher level than any people in the same room. *See also* Sikhism; Sikhism (authoritative texts).

Aditi (uh′di-tee), a goddess of Vedic India, mother of the Adityas, a group of gods guarding the moral order, including Varuna, Mitra, and Aryaman. Aditi's name signifies boundlessness, freedom, and innocence. *See also* Veda, Vedism.

adolescence. *See* life-cycle rituals; puberty rituals.

Adonai (ad′oh-ni; Heb.,"lord"), divine title in the Hebrew Bible, used in Jewish liturgy as a substitute for the divine name, YHWH. *See also* Judaism, God in; Tetragrammaton; YHWH.

Adonis (uh-don′is; Gk., may derive from *Adon,* Semitic for "Lord"), a Greco-Oriental deity. In Assyrian myth, Aphrodite and Persephone, quarreling over the infant Adonis, appealed their cases to the Olympian deities, who decreed that Adonis should spend part of each year in the upper world with Aphrodite and the remainder in the underworld with Persephone. In the more familiar Ovidian version of the myth, Adonis is killed by a wild boar while hunting and the event is commemorated by Aphrodite with a flower. In a later combination of the two stories Persephone restored Adonis to life on the condition that he spend part of the year with her and the remainder with Aphrodite. This has been adduced by scholars as an example of the "dying and rising god" motif, which narrates and annually represents a young son/lover of the Mediterranean "Great Mother Goddess," who dies and comes to life again, as does vegetation. The early version of the myth, however, contains no mention of Adonis's death and resurrection, while the Ovidian version tells only of his death, and the combined versions establish his alternative periods of habitation in the upper and lower worlds prior to his death. References to a joyful celebra-

tion of new life following upon the well-attested summer rituals mourning Adonis's disappearance are ambiguous and come from the Christian era. Recent scholarship suggests that Adonis represents immature sexuality in contrast to the ideal of marriage and family in Greek social life. *See also* Magna Mater; mother goddess.

Adoptionism, a Christian Christological position arguing that Jesus Christ was by nature human, becoming adopted Son of God at some point in his earthly career. *See also* Christology.

adultery, extramarital sexual relations. Most cultures prohibit adultery; some do not consider relations with a member of another social group to be adulterous.

Advaita-Vedanta. *See* nondualism, Hindu.

Advent, in the Christian liturgical year, the month of penitential preparation before the celebration of the feast of Christmas. *See also* calendar (Christian).

Adventists, Christian groups that share an expectation of the imminent Second Coming, or Advent, of Jesus Christ.

Adventism arose in early-nineteenth-century America as a perspective within Protestant churches regarding Christ's thousand-year reign on earth (the millennium). After the Civil War, Adventism splintered into several independent bodies. Originally, Adventism was one of several movements born of the widespread outbursts of revivalism and religious experimentation in an emergent American culture. Its largest current manifestation, the Seventh-Day Adventist Church, is an international movement that draws most of its members from outside the United States.

Millerites: Adventism sprang from the conversion, vision, and biblicism of a charismatic leader stirred by revivalism. William Miller (1782–1849), a Baptist in Low Hampton, New York, who was delivered from his religious skepticism by a local revival in 1816, set out to study the Bible. He was especially attracted to biblical prophecy and by 1818 became convinced that the book of Daniel, with its "days" interpreted as "years," forecast the Advent—a date when Christ would return, divide the righteous from the unrighteous, destroy the earth, and inaugurate a new heaven and a new earth—in March 1843. At first Miller was reluctant to spread his notions of the end-time, but through the encouragement of neighbors and ministers and the prompting of a dream in which God commissioned him to warn the world, he was ordained a Baptist minister in 1833 and published his predictions in 1835. Assisted by the organizational and publicity talents of Boston pastor Joshua Himes, Miller addressed revivalist camp meetings, winning audiences across the country.

Miller and his followers suffered the "Great Disappointment" when the Advent failed to materialize in 1843 or, after recalculations, in March or October 1844. Many Adventists were not only disappointed but, ridiculed and disciplined by the Protestant churches of which they were members, abandoned the cause. Others, including Miller himself, withdrew from their churches to form separate congregations and sought to coordinate their churches through the Evangelical Adventist Association. By the 1920s, the Association had dissolved, and by the 1980s only about ten thousand members were claimed by small, distinct Adventist churches such as the Advent Christian Church, the Church of God (Adventist), and the Church of God (Seventh-Day). Much of the failure of the Adventist churches to attain organizational unity owed to their disagreement over the meaning of the imminent Second Coming. Some held that Christ on the predicted day had fulfilled prophecy by "cleansing a heavenly temple" rather than an earthly one, others that Christ had returned to earth but had not been recognized by mortal eyes, still others that the Advent was being delayed by the popish (Roman Catholic) observance of the Sabbath on Sunday.

Seventh-Day Adventists: One branch of Adventism found in the person of Ellen Gould (Harmon) White (1827–1915) a force for unification and immense growth. This Adventist prophetess from Maine, converted to Miller's views in 1842, experienced thousands of visions and ecstatic transports before her death in 1915. She poured her ideas into a stream of publications that filled eighty volumes, and she inspired a worldwide religious organization that would include hospitals, universities, and missionary programs.

White and her followers taught that the Advent was delayed by the failure of Christians to follow the Ten Commandments, especially the keeping of the Sabbath on the seventh day of the week. They also came to believe, by virtue of revelations to White, that a holy life pursued in preparation for Christ's return entailed the cultivation of health through vegetarianism, abstention from alcohol and tobacco, and the avoidance of drugs in the treatment of illness. Dr. John Harvey Kellogg, a disciple of White,

conceived of his cornflakes as a vegetarian health food. Both Sabbatarianism (observing Saturday as the Sabbath) and concern for bodily health remain central convictions of Seventh-Day Adventists. Other distinctive beliefs deriving from White are that death is a form of sleep from which the righteous and the unrighteous are awakened by the Advent; the righteous will remain in heaven during the millennium; and at the end of the millennium Satan will be defeated, the unrighteous will be destroyed, and the righteous will be allowed to return to earth for eternity.

The Seventh-Day Adventists have developed into an imposing Christian denomination that is missionary-minded, active in lay leadership, and effective in utilizing the communications media. By the 1980s, the denomination had grown to over a half-million members in the United States, an increase of 35 percent in a ten-year period. Of its 3.5 million members worldwide, 76 percent reside in the Third World. *See also* Jehovah's Witnesses; Miller, William; Protestantism; White, Ellen Gould.

Aeneid (i-ne′eed), epic by Vergil (70–19 B.C.), who came to be regarded by Romans as their national poet. The *Aeneid* can be divided into two general parts—travel and war. In it Vergil connects the Roman culture to the Greek, for after wandering the world over Aeneas, the hero, goes from the destroyed Troy to Rome and there, with numerous portents, founds the Roman capital. In the second part of the epic one can sense the Roman weariness at a succession of civil wars. Octavian (Augustus) brings stability to the world in the form of the new Roman Empire. *See also* Vergil.

aeon. 1 Word of Greek origin signifying an enormous period of time, a stage in a cosmic cycle. 2 In Neoplatonic and Gnostic theologies, in plural form denotes successive emanations from the realm of pure Being, connecting the upper to the lower worlds. *See also* Aion/Aeon.

Aesir (ay′seer), a group of Scandinavian gods including Odinn, Frigg, Thor, Baldr, Heimdall, and Loki. *See also* Nordic religion.

Aetherius Society (ee-ther′ee-us), a group founded in London in 1956 by George King and centered on belief that its founder is the Primary Terrestrial Channel for the advanced spiritual beings who dwell on various planets of the solar system. Its headquarters are in Los Angeles and branches may be found in England and New Zealand. *See also* Europe, new religions in.

affliction, involuntary possession, either by demonic initiative or by sorcery, interpreted as negative. *See also* possession.

Africa, new religions in. Since the European conquest and colonial occupation in the latter half of the nineteenth century, well over seven thousand religious movements have been created and have attracted significant followings in sub-Saharan Africa. These new religious movements, structurally autonomous religious communities developed in the colonial or postcolonial eras, are normally associated with Christian churches that have developed in Africa. There are also important new movements that have developed within African Islam and African traditional religions, as well as new religious movements that have spread within Africa but whose origins are external to the continent. Most of these movements stress the importance of African control of African religious institutions and seek to address the spiritual concerns of African populations in a colonial or postcolonial state. While they vary widely in the size of their memberships, approximately one-tenth of the population of sub-Saharan Africa are members of these groups.

Most theories of the development of new religious movements in Africa stress the disruptive effects of the colonial conquest and subsequent occupation, which generated a crisis of confidence in the viability of indigenous political, social, and religious institutions. As the trauma of foreign domination deprives African societies of their abilities to explain and control their world, new religious movements, often led by charismatic leaders claiming privileged communication from spiritual beings, seek to restore the ability of the society to understand its changing world by introducing new or revitalizing older teachings and practices. Other theories stress the role of culture contact as a catalyst for new religious movements or suggest that the leaders of successful religious movements point out or even create the disjunctures of the colonial situation before they provide ways to restore a society's ability to explain its world.

By far most of the new religious movements in Africa are Christian. While most of these have developed in areas where Protestant missionaries were active, several new religious movements have emerged from Roman Catholic churches. Explanations for the frequency of new Christian movements focus on a combination of church-specific and historical factors. Since the Reformation, several hundred Protestant churches from Europe and the Americas have sent missionaries to Africa. This profusion of churches, divided by cultural as well as theological differences, has encouraged a similar diversity among African Christians. The development of African churches also has been encouraged by the spread of literacy and the translation of the Bible into African languages.

The slowness of many missionary societies to establish self-propagating churches with indigenous clergies also fueled the desire for African-controlled religious institutions. Missionary indifference to the more instrumental spiritual concerns of African Christians—specifically in relation to disease, infertility, exorcism, and witchcraft accusations—and the missionaries' determination to inculcate European social norms along with Christian teachings also contributed to the rise of Christian movements with African leaders. The greatest number of new Christian movements have developed in southern Africa, where massive land alienation, segregation in church and state, labor migration, and the use of Christian teachings to legitimate apartheid have created the greatest need for indigenously controlled religious institutions and a greater receptivity to new prophets speaking to an African Zion.

Ethiopian Churches: The oldest of the African Christian movements, usually classified as Ethiopian churches, broke away from mission-controlled churches. Ethiopian churches appear to stress African control over their own religious institutions more than innovations in doctrine or in ritual practice. These churches first developed in the late nineteenth century and are particularly common in southern Africa and Nigeria—areas heavily proselytized by Protestant churches and where missionaries quickly translated the Bible into African languages. One of the first African churches, founded by Mangena Mokone, a South African Wesleyan minister, was called the Ethiopian Church. Established in 1892, it took its name from Psalm 68:31, "Ethiopia shall soon stretch out her hands unto God." Mokone's church inspired others who also utilized the name Ethiopia in their church names as they generated autonomous Christian institutions. In Nigeria, the earliest Ethiopian churches were established after the Church Missionary Society arbitrarily removed Bishop Samuel Ajayi Crowther, the first Anglican African bishop, in 1890. Ethiopian churches in Nigeria included the African Church Movement, made up of disaffected Anglicans, and the pan-Africanist West African Church, inspired by E. W. Blyden.

Separatist Churches: Separatist churches, like Ethiopian churches, broke away from established mission churches—both Catholic and Protestant—and stress indigenous control over religious institutions, but they also tend to indigenize church teachings and ritual.

Churches separated from the Catholic church include the Jamaa movement and the Legio Maria ("Legion of Mary"). The Jamaa movement began as a fellowship within the Catholic Church of Katanga, Belgian Congo (Zaire), in the late 1940s. It was influenced by Father Placide Tempels, whose years of mission work in the region resulted in his study of the Lunda tribe's system of thought, *Bantu Philosophy*, and led him to emphasize the idea of community-based spirituality and a conceptualization of the Trinity as the Holy Family. Initially tolerated by the Catholic hierarchy, by 1953 the Jamaa movement was forced to develop as an independent church. The Legio Maria grew out of an Irish lay organization and became an important independent church movement among the Luo of Kenya. In 1963, an ex-catechist, Simeon Ondeto, and Guadencia Aoko, the mother of several children who had died, decided to create a separate church organization. Within a year, they had gathered more than one hundred thousand members, many of whom wished to retain the Latinate Mass, as well as a Catholic sense of church hierarchy. Members of the legion saw themselves as Catholics in Africa rather than in Rome. Their focus on protection against disease and witchcraft, as well as spirit possession, which were major issues in western Kenya, while using familiar Catholic church structures, attracted a considerable following among the Luo.

Separatist churches were also important among Protestants. One of the most important was the Balokole ("Saved Ones") or East African Revival. This movement, which began as a breakaway movement from the Rwanda Mission of the Church Missionary Society in the 1930s, spread rapidly into Uganda and western Kenya. Stressing a personal experience of salvation, it lessened the dependence of new Christians on missionary expertise. Its critique of levirate marriage and polygyny also helped to empower women to reject certain aspects of gender roles in East African societies.

Independent Churches: A third type of Christian religious movement developed during the colonial era is the indigenous or independent church, created as a result of a religious leader's claim to direct revelation from the Trinity or a saint, who appointed this leader to bring Christianity to Africa. Sociologists of religion have grouped these churches according to the nature of the claims that the religious leaders made about their authority. Prophetic indigenous churches are new African churches whose founders claim to be prophets based on divine or saintly revelations. A second group of churches are called messianic indigenous churches because their founders claimed to be messiahs who had come to usher in a new world for the believers who joined their church. The distinctions between these two types of churches are not always clear. In many cases followers of particular religious leaders attributed greater powers to them than they claimed for themselves. Nevertheless, these indigenous churches have a common stress on revelation to an African religious leader, who offered hope of deliverance from suffering in this new world order and was often concerned about religious problems of daily life, from the problem of disease to infertility and drought. Such emphases largely were absent from the mission churches.

Among the many indigenous churches, the two most important clusters in West Africa were the Harrist churches in Ivory Coast and Ghana and the Aladura churches, primarily in southwestern Nigeria and Dahomey. The Harrists were inspired by the teachings of William Wade Harris (ca. 1860–1928), a Grebo from Liberia. Having worked as a seaman and a schoolteacher before involving himself briefly in Grebo resistance to Liberian rule, he found himself in prison, where he began having visions of the angel Gabriel. In 1913, after accepting Gabriel's call, Harris entered the French Ivory Coast and initiated the most dramatic campaign of religious proselytization ever experienced in West Africa. Dressed in white robes, he traveled from village to village preaching the rejection of traditional religions and strict adherence to Christian teachings. He did not start his own church. However, in less than two years he had generated such enthusiasm for Christianity that 120,000 people were baptized. Converts flooded the few Catholic and Protestant missions. Fearful of any mass movement in the recently pacified Ivory Coast, the French deported Harris, despite his lack of a political agenda. French officials also destroyed many churches built by his followers while they awaited the establishment of mission stations.

While many Harrists joined mission churches, others kept alive oral traditions concerning the mission of the Prophet Harris. In 1923, Methodists visited Ivory Coast and were stunned to find thousands of Harrist Christians seeking ministers. One of these missionaries visited Harris in Liberia and returned with a letter from the prophet urging people to join the Methodist Church and to avoid both Catholicism and African religions. Concerned by the authoritarian structure of the Methodist mission, its insistence on tithing, and its condemnation of polygyny, John Ahui led a Harrist delegation to Liberia in 1926 and returned with Harris's last will and testament. This document delegated Harris's prophetic role to Ahui, tolerated polygyny, and supported independent churches. Several Harrist churches developed during this period, most notably the Deima church, founded by Marie Lalou, and Grace Thannie's Church of the Twelve Apostles. Freed from persecution after 1945, Harrist churches became a major religious force in Ivory Coast and Ghana.

The Aladura (lit., "praying people") movement started as praying bands within established mission and independent churches under the leadership of charismatic individuals who had visionary experiences of angels or the Holy Spirit, in which the individuals were commanded to preach and to heal. The devastation wrought by the influenza epidemic of 1918 to 1919, which killed thousands of people in southwestern Nigeria, gave added impetus to this concern for spiritual healing. The most important prophetic figures were Moses Orimolade and Christianah Abiodun, who founded the Cherubim and Seraphim Society, and Joseph Babalola, who founded the Diamond Society of the Faith Tabernacle Church. The Diamond Society changed its name and its overseas affiliations several times before becoming fully independent in 1939 as the Christ Apostolic Church. All of these churches share the belief that God answers all prayers and stress the importance of divine healing. Direct revelation through dreams and visions provides authority for most Aladura teachings and practices. These churches began in the urban areas of southwestern Nigeria and were especially popular among clerks and artisans who had left rural areas for greater economic opportunities in the cities. Aladura churches remain a major force among the Christian Yoruba and have spread to other areas of southern Nigeria, Benin, and Ghana.

Zionist Churches: In southern Africa, indigenous churches are usually called Zionist churches. This term was applied to South African indigenous churches influenced by the teachings of John Dowie and his Evangelical Christian Catholic Church, founded in 1896 and based in Zion City, Illinois. There are more than two thousand churches in southern Africa, and central to their teaching are a strict rejection of all forms of African traditional religious practices and a strong focus on spiritual healing and divine revelation. Many Zionist churches have millennial expectations that only those believers who have deep convictions and follow the strict rules of the church community will be able to enter into this new Zion. Both church rules and ritual structures are said to be based on direct revelations to the prophetic founder, but the former often include the dietary regulations found in the biblical book Leviticus.

The most important South African Zionist church is the amaNazaretha Baptist Church, founded by Isaiah Shembe (d. 1935) in 1911. After a series of visionary experiences in which he was ordered to bring Christianity to the Zulu, Shembe had a dream in which he saw his own corpse. In the dream, God warned Shembe against his sinful ways and urged him to begin his prophetic mission. In later visions he was tempted by supernatural powers, but vowed to remain true to his mission to Jehovah. Shembe believed that God had granted him the powers to heal the sick and to exorcise demons. He quickly attracted a large following. As prophet of the amaNazaretha, he surrounded himself with much of the pomp of the recently humbled Zulu kings and incorporated both Zulu oral poetry and songs and Zulu age-grade organizations into the ritual life of his church. He established two major pilgrimage sites for his followers within Zulu-controlled areas of Natal province. His followers saw him as God's emissary to the Zulu, occupying much the same position as Jesus and Moses in their missions to the Jews. After his death, his son, Johannes Galilee Shembe, took over the leadership of the church.

In central Africa, indigenous churches tended to focus on inspired leaders who saw themselves as associated with the New Testament apostles. Most notable of these churches are the Apostles of John Maranke (1912–63) or Bapostolo and the Apostolic Church of John Masowe, both founded in 1932. These churches were started among the Shona of Southern Rhodesia, though the former quickly became a multiethnic church of more than 150,000 members in six countries. John Maranke began to have visions as a six-year-old boy and sought the advice of his Methodist minister about the significance of his visions. As a young man he had such an overpowering vision that he felt compelled to found his own church. A voice told him that he was John the Baptist and that he must go out and preach to all nations to live moral lives and to keep the seventh-day Sabbath. Apostles carefully separate themselves from the world, avoiding excessive social interaction with nonmembers and avoiding such worldly goods as money or luxury items. Their wearing of white robes, not only in ritual but in the activities of daily life, is another way of marking their detachment from the mundane world. Before Maranke died, he assembled a book of his visions called *The New Witness of the Apostles*, which continues to be an authoritative text for the church that he founded.

Until his prophetic calling John Masowe had been known as Shoniwa, but as a result of the visions he received during a near-death experience, he took on the name of John of the Wilderness (Masowe) and began to preach. His teaching stressed to his followers the necessity of abandoning European goods and ceasing all labor in order to usher in the kingdom of God. To support themselves, his followers formed artisan cooperatives, primarily in the basketmaking and tinsmithing trades, and pooled their profits in order to establish church communities. Masowe rejected all Christian sacraments other than baptism, which he personally administered to his converts.

The most important of the indigenous church movements in Equatorial Africa is a series of churches associated with the BaKongo prophet Simon Kimbangu (1889–1951). L'Eglise de Jesus-Christ sur la terre par le prophete Simon Kimbangu (Church of Jesus-Christ on Earth by the prophet Simon Kimbangu) is the

largest of these churches. Kimbangu was educated in Baptist Missionary Society schools and worked as a catechist. Beginning in 1918, he had visions commanding him to teach and to heal. He resisted this prophetic calling until April 1921, when he began to heal the sick. His spiritual healing and his critique of mission Christianity and BaKongo *nkisi* ("powerful medicines," "charms") attracted a massive following. His claim of revelation from Jesus brought Christianity directly into the lives of the BaKongo in a way that missionaries could not. Despite the absence of an overtly political message in Kimbangu's teachings, Belgian authorities viewed his mass following with alarm and ordered his arrest. In September 1921, he was sentenced to death, though this was eventually commuted to life imprisonment.

Despite Kimbangu's arrest, his teachings continued to be followed in rural communities and among his imprisoned followers. Other prophetic figures emerged, claiming inspiration from Kimbangu and developing distinct interpretations of the Kimbanguist message. One of the most influential was Mpadi Simon, who created his own church, the Mission des Noirs ("Mission of the Blacks"), which was openly anti-European and stressed the need for African self-determination in the political and religious spheres.

Firewalking by members of the Apostles of John Maranke (or Bapostolo), a Christian African independent church founded in 1932 and concentrated in southern and central Africa. Walking through fire, placing hot coals in one's mouth, healing, and prophecy are considered both spiritual gifts and confirmation of being in a state of purity.

In the 1950s, Belgian authorities allowed Kimbangu's sons to establish the Eglise de Jesus-Christ sur la terre par le prophete Simon Kimbangu. In the postcolonial era, they managed to become the official Kimbanguist church, preventing government recognition of other Kimbanguist churches in Zaire. A variety of churches tracing themselves back to Kimbangu are found throughout the region, although the church established by Kimbangu's sons has become not only the largest of the Kimbanguist churches but the largest independent church in Africa.

Islamic Movements: While not usually studied as new religious movements, there have been several new Islamic movements that developed in sub-Saharan Africa during the colonial era. The most important have been the creation of new Sufi Islamic brotherhoods (Arab. *tariqas*) in the late nineteenth and twentieth centuries. The most influential of these new Islamic movements was the Mouride brotherhood, founded by Amadou Bamba (1850–1927), who had his first visionary experiences near the central Senegalese village of Touba in 1890. In the wake of the French conquest of the Wolof kingdoms of northern Senegal, Amadou Bamba attracted a large following, both among Muslims and followers of Wolof traditional religion. His stress on the intercessory role of the Muslim cleric (*marabout*), who could transmit the blessings (*baraka*) of God to disciples who served the cleric, provided both an alternative social structure and series of religious institutions during the chaotic situation following the French conquest. Followers came to Bamba to serve him rather than to study. He set them to work growing peanuts in order both to support themselves and to serve God's work. The French worried about Bamba's large following and exiled him for seven years, initially to Gabon and then to Mauritania. While he was in exile a miracle tradition developed about him, giving added impetus to his teachings once he was allowed to return. Numbering close to a million adherents, this is the largest Islamic brotherhood in the Senegambia region. A smaller Muslim brotherhood, the Layenne, has become an important influence among the Lebou of the Cap Vert region of Senegal. Muslim brotherhoods have had an increasing influence in other parts of sub-Saharan Africa, but they have tended to be older more established Sufi organizations, most notably the Qadiriyya and Tijaniyya.

African Traditional Religions: There have also been important new religious movements within what are often called African traditional religions. In the wake of the colonial conquest a series of new religious movements emerged, focused on prophetic figures who sought to restore the autonomy of African peoples. Often seeing the European conquerors as a divine chastisement, such prophetic figures as Kinjeketile in Tanganyika and Rembe in northern Uganda sought to purify their communities of the pollution caused by witchcraft and to introduce new ritual forms that would revitalize their traditional religions, often on a multiethnic basis. These early-twentieth-century religious movements offered spiritual protection to the faithful who struggled to expel the European conquerors through military means and who eschewed the particularistic aims of witchcraft and traditional medicines. Protection focused on a water medicine that had been blessed by a water deity who was revered among several of the region's religious communities.

Other traditional religious leaders, like the woman visionary Alinesitoue among the Diola of Senegambia, introduced a series of new cults that stressed public access to spiritual knowledge and power and the direct involvement of the supreme being in daily life in an effort to curb the divisive influences of Christians and Muslims, who were actively proselytizing in Diola communities. Alinesitoue worked to preserve traditional forms of agriculture, including more drought-resistant forms of rice than the Asiatic rice introduced by the French, and rejected the cash crop of peanuts, which diverted men from collective family work in the rice paddies, leaving the staple crop entirely to the labor of women. She began teaching during a period of severe drought, political instability caused by Vichy rule over the French colony, and renewed competition with missionaries. In January 1943, after only a year of teaching, she was arrested by the French and convicted of embarrassing the colonial administrators. Her whereabouts remain unknown, but her series of new cults continue to be practiced. A series of new prophets have arisen among the Diola and have continued to offer new teachings to address the problems of the Diola in postcolonial Senegambia.

Other new African traditional religious movements have resembled more closely the structural organization of Christian churches. Most notable perhaps are the Bwiti Church among the Fang of Gabon and the Eglise de Dieu de Nos Ancetres ("Church of the God of Our Ancestors"), both of which sought to revitalize traditional religious forms with the type of organization and ritual forms that were better suited to the culturally pluralistic, Western-dominated societies of twentieth-century Africa.

Finally, some new religious movements have originated outside of Africa. Groups such as

Transcendental Meditation, the Unification Church, the Ahmadiyya Movement, and American televangelism have become active in many parts of sub-Saharan Africa. While their influence is relatively small, they have worked in the region for a comparatively short time. **See also** African apostolic churches; Aladura; Apostles of John Maranke; Apostolic Sabbath Church of God; Balokole movement; Ethiopian churches; Haile Selassie; Harrist movement; Jamaa movement; Kimbanguist Church; new religions; Zionist churches.

Africa, traditional religions in. Some 70 million Africans are classified in a 1994 survey as follow-

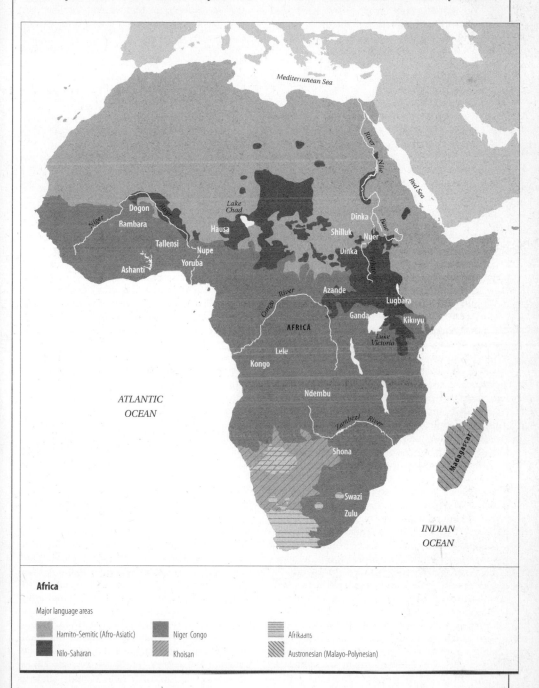

Africa

Major language areas

- Hamito-Semitic (Afro-Asiatic)
- Nilo-Saharan
- Niger Congo
- Khoisan
- Afrikaans
- Austronesian (Malayo-Polynesian)

A group of male Yoruba (southwest Nigeria) on their way to attend an Engungun ritual, where the collective spirits of the patrilineal ancestors are personified by dancers wearing elaborate cloth constructions (1983).

ers of traditional religions in contrast to Africa's 341 million Christians and 285 million Muslims. The same survey reports that in Benin, Botswana, Burkina Faso, Cameroon, Cote d'Ivoire (Ivory Coast), Ghana, Guinea-Bissau, Liberia, Mozambique, Sierra Leone, Togo, Zimbabwe, as well as Madagascar, the bulk of the population practices traditional, indigenous religions.

Diversities: Africa is the second largest continent. Its landmass, some 11,700,000 square miles, is bounded on the north by the Mediterranean, on the west by the Atlantic, on the east by the Indian Ocean and the Red Sea, and on the south by the waters of the Indian Ocean and the Atlantic. This geographical description signals the issues that recur with respect to African religions. On the one hand, there is a sense of a continental boundary, an entity that might properly be called "Africa." On the other hand, a vastness coupled with a sense of fuzzy boundaries—the mingled oceanic waters of the south, let alone the vexing question of whether the islands frequently associated with the continent, from Madagascar to the southeast to Tristan da Cunha to the southwest, are properly part of Africa—call into question any simple notion of Africa.

If anything, a cultural map of Africa is even more complex and questions more rigorously any sense of unity that might overcome the overwhelming impression of diversity. Africa's 703,090,000 people have been divided into some three thousand tribes speaking almost as many languages and dialects. (Since fewer than thirty African languages have more than a million native speakers, a large number of languages of convenience have been developed—such as varieties of colloquial Arabic; Swahili and Lingala, Bantu languages heavily influenced by Arabic; Fanagalo, or "kitchen Kaffir," a pidgin Zulu with English and Afrikaans loanwords; and Sango, a pidgin Ngbandi with French loanwords.) There is no agreed-upon classification of tribes. There is a controversial division of the languages of Africa into four major families: Hamito-Semitic, Nilo-Saharan, Niger-Congo, and Khoisan, with two groups classed separately: the languages of South Africa influenced by the Indo-European Afrikaans and the Austronesian languages of Madagascar. Here, again, these simple and well-known facts point to difficulties: the lack of any one-to-one correlation between tribal units, linguistic families, and present-day nations in Africa and the heavy presence of colonial influence, whether Islam in the north or European Christian in central and southern Africa.

Generalities: Attempts to describe the traditional cultures and religions of Africa in terms of geographical region (northern, western, west-

Divination, at the beginning of a Ndembu (northwest Zambia) healing ritual, Ihamba. The healer is determining, from patterns of clay and medicinal substances in the mortar he's pointing to, the nature of the "shadow-soul" of a dead hunter whose tooth is biting the patient, causing illness.

Ngo-ouka, a water-spirit-carrying woman (*oro-kuro*) of the Ijo people of the Niger Delta, in trance (1978) embodying an old man, one of the forms of her water-spirit husband, Damen. Marked off by various forms of illness, a potential oro-kuro is cured by marrying the afflicting water spirit, thereby gaining powers of divination and healing.

central, eastern, central, and southern) conceal the theory that environment determines cultural and religious phenomena. Nothing of a general nature can be presumed concerning African traditional religions other than that they are not Eurasian imports (though they may be heavily influenced by and practiced simultaneously with such imports, chiefly Islam and Christianity) and that they occur somewhere on the continent. Conventionally, several elements have been pointed to as common but by no means universal features of African traditional religions.

High Gods: Most traditional African cosmogonies feature a high god and a mythology of rupture. Once, the creator deity lived close to the earth and the ancestors of humans. Something strained that relationship and the deity removed itself to the sky, the ancestors being transformed by that same rupture into their present form as humans. The mythology of rupture is often linked to one of death, in which what marks off the ancestors from humans is a fateful choice by the ancestors that resulted in death for their human descendants.

Superhuman Beings: Alongside the high god and the ancestors, most African religions recognize a plurality of superhuman beings who often manifest themselves through "natural" phenomena and are translated in the scholarly literature by a range of terms from *gods* to *spirits*. Some of these may take the form of trickster figures; others appear to represent deep oppositions between male and female, twin brothers, etc. There are also a variety of culture heroes who have led the people to the land in which they dwell today and are bearers of the gifts of technologies such as agriculture and metalworking, as well as major social and religious institutions such as marriage, initiatory societies, and priesthood. The patrilineal ancestors (in the genealogical rather than the mythical sense), the dead, kings, and priests may also be viewed as superhuman in some traditions.

Ritual: A full range of life-cycle and annual rituals are practiced. While the most elaborate rites usually focus on the initiation of young men and women into adulthood, age-grade initiations are often followed by initiation into one or another secret society.

Sacrifices, offerings, meals, and dance are the predominant ritual forms. Sacrifices and offerings establish relations and communications between the divine and human worlds. Meals and dance are not only modes of social celebration but also function to evoke the presence of divine beings.

Hereditary office and ritual specialization are not common, though a variety of ritual functionaries—priests, elders, rainmakers, diviners, prophets, and healers—are found in most tribal units.

Healing and divination appear most characteristic of African traditional religions. Both are concerned, to some degree, with the detection of witchcraft and sorcery and with the ritual means of their control.

African American Catholic Congregation. *See* African Americans (North America), new religions among.

African Americans (North America), new religions among. Many religious alternatives have appeared in the African-American community in the United States since the end of the Civil War in 1865.

New religious movements among African Americans developed out of a complex cultural heritage and a quest for equality. Kidnapped into slavery, cut off from family, friends, and communities, African-American slaves forged a new religion composed of a variety of traditional African faiths and Christianity. A synthesis of several theologies, slave religion not only addressed existential questions but also served as a vehicle for self-protection and social protest, producing a foundation for future black religions.

After emancipation (1863), African-American religion continued to function as a social force. With freedom, the opportunity to establish independent black churches increased. Additionally, the rising tide of segregation in the late nineteenth century and a desire for self-determination drove African Americans to organize separate congregations. Most of these groups maintained ties with mainstream black or white denominations, like the Methodists or Baptists.

The socioeconomic status of African Americans continued to deteriorate, and by 1900 alienation from mainstream religious orders set in. White denominations became increasingly exclusionary and patronizing. Many black churches had lost touch with the needs of their constituencies. These black denominations offered an ephemeral theology, promising salvation in heaven, and seemed more preoccupied with internal politics than with fighting Jim Crow segregation. Furthermore, black churches in urban areas, surviving on limited budgets, could not meet the demands for social assistance from the massive numbers of blacks migrating to the cities.

Out of black urban frustration, storefront churches, independent sects located in rented rooms or buildings, appeared and quickly multiplied in American cities. Despite their limited resources, storefront churches attempted to fulfill the functions neglected by institutionalized black churches. Many storefront churches developed out of migrants' desire to recreate old religious affiliations. Often spurned by familiar denominations because they were from rural areas or of a different socioeconomic class, newcomers organized their own congregations, hoping to simulate familiar religious practices.

Storefronts also evolved out of a quest for a new identity. Black migrants left rural areas searching for a new life and, in turn, developed religious alternatives that reflected and reinforced their new identities. Coming into contact in American cities with people from all over the nation and the world, black migrants exchanged thoughts and opinions, broadening their awareness. This flow of information and ideologies led to an explosion of black religious alternatives in the United States after 1900.

Many new African-American religions drew from the teachings of Marcus Garvey (1887–1940). A black Jamaican who migrated to New York in 1916, Garvey founded the Universal Negro Improvement Association (UNIA), a political and economic organization dedicated to elevating the status of African Americans. Garvey encouraged black pride and formulated a Back-to-Africa program, envisioning people of African heritage establishing an independent nation on the African continent. Garvey declared that God and Jesus Christ were black and anticipated global redemption of people of African heritage. He appointed George Alexander McGuire in 1921 to organize the African Orthodox Church, which mingled the UNIA's philosophy with Episcopalian practices. Garvey's teachings impacted many new black religions, some directly tracing their lineage to him, others indirectly exhibiting his influence.

Some patterns appeared among new African-American religions. All groups pursued a theological plan for liberation and most offered some type of social welfare. New black sects grew in number and membership during times of increased racism and economic hardship. They boosted confidence and imparted pride and self-respect. Most emphasized temperance and health, combating the alcoholism and high disease rate prevalent in black communities. Many black sectarian leaders viewed themselves as the deliverers of African-American people, rescuing them from destruction, striking down false doctrine, and restoring true faith. These leaders considered their congregations to be God's chosen and forecast imminent redemption of black Americans. Despite these similarities, black sects differed widely and are commonly grouped under three categories: black Jewish movements, African-American Islamic sects, and African-American Christian sects.

Black Jewish Movements: Black Jewish movements developed, in part, from African-American identification with the persecution of the Jews and their status as God's chosen people. Slave sermons were replete with comparisons between African-American bondage in the United States and the enslavement of the Jews in Egypt. After emancipation, interest in Judaism may have led many black Americans to investigate the faith. By the early twentieth century black Jewish itinerants traveled the United States, an organized congregation of African-American Jews appearing shortly afterward.

Much of the attraction to black Judaism rested in the opportunity to cast off Christianity, perceived by many as the religion of white Americans, and the chance to establish a faith independent of white ties. Black Jews believed they were members of one of the lost tribes of Israel, stripped of their true heritage by hundreds of years of white oppression. Many black sects, and some white Jewish scholars, contended that African Americans were descendants of Ethiopian Jews known as "Falashas." Black nationalism, the belief that African Americans should maintain a separate identity, appears in many black Jewish sects. But black Jews disagree on theology and practice. All accept the Talmud or Old Testament as primary scripture but have adopted and adapted Judaism in varying degrees and forms.

The first identifiable congregation of black Jews was the Church of God and Saints in Christ, founded by Prophet William S. Crowdy. In 1905 he established a black Jewish congregation in Belleville, Virginia. He contended that the original Jews were black, and his congregation observed Passover and a Saturday Sabbath. But the church relied heavily on the New Testament, practiced baptism, celebrated communion, and required members to make a public confession of faith in Jesus Christ.

Another early sect that fused Judaism with Christianity was the Church of God established by Prophet F. S. Cherry in Philadelphia in 1915. Cherry also taught that blacks were the original and only authentic Jews. He asserted that white skin was a curse from God, charging that white Jews were impostors. According to Cherry, God was black, and Jesus Christ came to fulfill the prophecies of the Old Testament. Cherry's followers practiced baptism and performed gospel music, but they also subscribed to Judaic customs and rituals. They celebrated only Jewish holidays and refused to eat pork; men wore skullcaps to worship services.

Other groups followed more orthodox Judaic practices. The Commandment Keepers of the Living God, founded in 1924 by a former Garveyite, Arnold Josiah Ford, and led by Rabbi Wentworth A. Matthew, repudiated Christianity and strictly observed Jewish tradition. Members followed kosher dietary laws and men covered their heads at all times, wearing skullcaps and phylacteries to synagogue. Matthew organized a Hebrew school and trained future leaders at the Ethiopian Hebrew Rabbinical College in Harlem.

The group maintained friendly relations with white Jews, considering them to be members of another tribe of Israel. But they distinguished themselves from mainstream Judaism through the practice of cabalistic science, more popularly known as Voodoo and derived from African religion. Followers believed that practitioners like Matthew healed the sick, assured financial security, and protected them from harm.

These older Jewish sects persisted into the late twentieth century, joined by several newer groups. The Original Hebrew Israelite Nation (Black Israelites), founded in Chicago in the 1960s, also strove to follow orthodox Judaism. The Black Israelites advocated a separatist philosophy, Black Zionism, and have attempted, first in Liberia and later in Israel, to establish an independent black colony.

One of the most controversial of the later sects was the Nation of Yahweh (Hebrew Israelites), founded by Yahweh ben Yahweh (Heb., "God, son of God") in the 1970s. Considered a savior by his followers, Yahweh ben Yahweh taught that God was black and that black people would return to Israel. Followers kept kosher and wore white, symbolizing their faith. The group also worked toward racial cooperation, believing that anyone, regardless of race, could be saved by Yahweh ben Yahweh.

The Nation of Yahweh also promoted economic advancement and invested in business and real estate. The group provided community relief and supported voter registration and education. In the late 1980s, the federal government investigated Yahweh ben Yahweh, resulting in his arrest in 1990. Followers equated his situation with that of Jesus Christ and insisted that Yahweh ben Yahweh was suffering for the benefit of humanity.

Finally, the Rastafarians, a transplanted Jamaican religion, was another black Jewish movement that attracted many followers in the United States. Influenced by Marcus Garvey, Rastafarians adhere to Ethiopianism, which predicted that God will redeem people of African heritage and return them to their true ancestral homeland, Ethiopia. They derived their name from Ethiopian ruler Haile Selassie (born Ras Tafari Makonnon, 1892–1975) whom they believed was a messiah sent to black people. Rastafarians adopted many black Judaic concepts, contending that God was black and Africans were his chosen people. Rastafarians were pacifists, devoting much time to prayer and studying the scriptures. They considered *ganja* ("marijuana") to be a sacred herb, aiding in religious meditation. Many regarded white culture as evil and denounced Western materialism.

Black Islamic Sects: Like black Judaism, African-American Islam rejected Christianity, viewed as the religion of the oppressor, in favor of a religion that adherents contended was the original faith of people of African descent. Black Muslims urged African Americans to find racial self-awareness through Islam. While most pursued advancement through black enterprise, they differed dramatically over theology and ritual.

African-American Islamic sects began appearing in the early twentieth century. Among the first was the Moorish Science Temple founded in Newark, New Jersey, in 1915 by Prophet Noble Drew Ali (Timothy Drew, d. 1929). Ali maintained that blacks were not Africans, but Asiatic Moors whose true homeland was Morocco and original religion was Islam. The cursed descendants of Noah's son Ham, the white race, had conquered Moorish Americans by enslaving them and deceiving them into believing they were Africans. Liberation consisted of a rejection of white religion, Christianity, and separation from Euramericans. By embracing Islam, Moorish Americans would return to power. Male followers wore red fezzes emblazoned with a crescent and star, a configuration they believed would appear in the sky signifying the beginning of black redemption. An advocate of capitalism, Ali marketed a line of toiletries. The movement also provided philanthropic assistance to the surrounding community. After Ali's murder in 1929, membership in the movement declined.

In 1930 Wallace Fard (Master Wali Fard Muhammad), a yard-goods peddler, revived African-American Islam and founded the Lost-Found Nation of Islam in Detroit. Of unknown origins, Fard claimed to be a prophet from Mecca bearing Allah's message to black Americans. Fard taught that Islam was the true religion of African Americans, who in reality were descendants of "Asiatic black men," the original human race designated by God to bring civilization to the world.

Fard predicted that blacks would soon reclaim their power, ending white rule and white Christianity. He encouraged the celebration of Islamic holidays, observation of Muslim dietary codes, and practice of Islamic prayer. He also established the University of Islam to promote his teachings and organized the Fruit of Islam, a paramilitary group of young men trained in the use of weapons and charged with the protection of the Nation of Islam and its members.

In 1934, Fard disappeared and a former Garveyite, Elijah Muhammad (born Elijah Poole, 1897–1975), assumed leadership. Muhammad focused on economic advancement, encouraging followers to open and patronize black businesses. Muhammad also proposed complete separation of blacks and whites and the formation of a black state in the southern United States. In his view, whites were an inferior race, devils created by experiments in genetic mutation conducted by an evil scientist Mr. Yacub. God had permitted whites to dominate African Americans as a test of the black race. Initially the movement grew slowly, impeded by Muhammad's imprisonment for antiwar activities during World War II. But his experience in prison inspired him to focus on recruiting incarcerated blacks. His prison ministry netted many converts, one of the most important of these was a former burglar, Malcolm Little, who became known as Malcolm X (1925–65).

By the late 1950s, Malcolm X emerged as the Nation of Islam's foremost spokesperson. He urged black Americans to be proud of their heritage and to insist on immediate equal rights. He rejected the passive resistance philosophy of Martin Luther King, Jr., and advocated using self-defense against white violence. Malcolm X's work succeeded in attracting much publicity and many converts.

Before long, friction developed between Malcolm X and Elijah Muhammad. In 1964, Malcolm X broke from the Nation of Islam. He had returned from a journey to Mecca maintaining, like many others, that the Nation of Islam had distorted Muslim teachings. After worshiping in Mecca with Muslims of all races he became convinced that interracial harmony was possible through orthodox Islam. He continued his fight against white racism and founded the Organization of Afro-American Unity, but he was assassinated by a follower of Elijah Muhammad.

The Nation of Islam persisted and survived into the 1970s. Upon the death of Elijah Muhammad, the group split into several factions. One, led by Muhammad's son Wallace (Warith Deen Muhammad, b. 1933) and known as the American Muslim Mission, admitted whites to its ranks. Affiliated with Sunni Islam, the sect promoted cooperative capitalism and has secured contracts from the United States government.

Another faction retained Nation of Islam as its name and grew steadily under the leadership of Louis Farrakhan (b. 1933), who sought to preserve the orthodox teachings of Wallace Fard and Elijah Muhammad. A separatist, Farrakhan was an outspoken critic of the United States government, demanding reparations to African Americans and calling for people of African heritage to return to Africa to organize an independent state. He advocated black self-help and enterprise, arguing that economic power was the most effective tool against white domination. His militant comments induced many to charge that he was anti-Semitic and antiwhite. By the mid-1980s he was the most influential Black Muslim leader in America, but many African-American politicians and public officials distanced themselves from him, fearing negative publicity. Regardless, under Farrakhan the Nation of Islam experienced a revival in the late 1980s and early 1990s, attracting members from the inner cities to college campuses.

African-American Christian Sects: While many black Judaic and Islamic alternatives derive their appeal by rejecting Christianity, African-American Christian sects attracted followers by claiming to furnish a revitalized and more relevant Christianity. They viewed Christianity as a positive spiritual force perverted by manipulating and self-serving church leaders. Racism had further robbed the faith of its true meaning. Leaders of black Christian sects maintained they were restoring the original church and pure gospel. Based on the Old and New Testaments, African-American Christian sects proclaimed faith in Jesus Christ as a savior. These groups also fought for equality, some through separatism and others through integration. Widely ranging in form and belief, they vastly outnumbered their Jewish and Muslim counterparts.

Black Holiness churches arose as one of the earliest alternatives to mainstream Christianity. The Holiness movement first developed among whites dissatisfied with institutional churches, but it quickly spread into the black community. Many independent African-American denominations and storefront churches adopted the Holiness doctrine of sanctification, believing that conversion experiences freed congregants of sin and assured them of salvation. Worship was energetic, filled with spontaneous song and testimony. The number of black Holiness sects grew rapidly, and it persisted into the late twentieth century as a major faith in black communities.

Another popular religious option was the Pentecostal movement, originating out of the Azusa Street Revival of 1906 led by African-American minister William Seymour. The practice of glossolalia, or speaking in tongues, drew pilgrims of all races and from around the world to the revival held in an abandoned warehouse in downtown Los Angeles. Considered by many to be the father of American Pentecostalism, Seymour insisted that glossolalia was a direct gift from God, the final step in sanctification. Seymour's ministry stimulated the growth of both black and white Pentecostal churches.

But Seymour's influence stretched beyond Pentecostal circles and influenced the formation of one of the most highly visible of the new African-American religions, the Peace Mission movement. Its founder, Reverend M. J. "Father" Divine (formerly George Baker, d. 1965), attended the Azusa Street Revival, which inspired his ministry dedicated to saving humankind and reforming society. He developed a unique theology composed of various elements of Pentecostalism, African-American Christianity, Methodism, Catholicism, and the power of positive thinking ideology, New Thought. Urging followers to believe he was God, Father Divine encouraged them to channel his spirit through positive thoughts to achieve health, prosperity, and salvation. His worship services consisted of banquets with endless courses, designed to demonstrate his ability to generate abundance.

His mind-power message was especially appealing during the Great Depression of the 1930s, giving Americans suffering from poverty and racism hope for change and a sense of control over their destiny. An integrationist, he attracted both black and white followers, actively campaigning for civil rights. He also instituted a strict moral code, demanding that followers abstain from sexual intercourse, alcohol, drugs, and tobacco.

Pooling the earnings of followers, the Peace Mission built a network of successful businesses and nationally popular relief shelters during the 1930s. Father Divine's seemingly endless financial resources and his activist leadership drew much attention, his ministry constantly scrutinized by the media and the authorities. With economic recovery in the 1940s, his mind-power message became less appealing and the movement began to dwindle. Reduced significantly in size by the time of his death, the Peace Mission continued under the guidance of his second wife, Mother Divine.

African-American Christian sects flourished during the economic chaos of the 1930s. The Church of the Living God, The Pillar and Ground of Truth; Refuge Church of Christ of the Apostolic Faith; George Becton's, World Gospel Feast; Fire Baptized Holiness Church of God of the Americas; Elder Solomon Michaux's, Church of God; National David Spiritual Temple of Christ Church Union; Prophet Jones's, Universal Triumph/The Dominion of God Incorporated; and the Anthony Spiritual Temple were a few of the movements active during the Depression. But only Bishop Charles Emmanuel "Daddy" Grace (d. 1960), leader of the United House of Prayer for All People, came close to rivaling Father Divine.

Patterned after Holiness churches and espousing sanctification, the United House of Prayer grew in membership throughout the 1930s. But in a departure from Holiness doctrine, followers worshiped Daddy Grace in place of God or Jesus Christ. Disciples kneeled before Daddy Grace's portrait and prayed for his blessings and protection. From their donations to his ministry, he built a million-dollar financial empire, acquiring real estate and establishing a line of beauty and health care products. Although Daddy Grace's integrity was widely questioned, his United House of Prayer remained firmly entrenched long after his death.

During the Depression, several African-American women emerged with religious alternatives. Elder Lucy Smith's All Nations Pentecostal Church, Mother Rosa Horne's Mt. Calvary Assembly Hall of the Pentecostal Faith of All Nations, and Bishop Ida Robinson's Mt. Sinai Holy Church had branches in the major northeastern cities. These denominations drew from Holiness and Pentecostal doctrine, stressing sanctification and glossolalia. These women professed to have holy gifts, such as the ability to heal the sick, and conducted community outreach, combating poverty and destitution. They also challenged gender roles. Historically, black women have provided most of the support for African-American churches, but in sects founded by female ministers, women participated even more actively and occupied many leadership positions traditionally reserved for men.

African-American Christian movements continued to appear in the 1980s. In Crescent City, Florida, Prophetess Mother Essie Mae MacDonald organized the Mt. Zion the Overcoming Body of Christ Church, which sponsored a communal home known as the Ark. In Trenton, New Jersey, Charles Berry Brinson, the Pope Bishop of the Brinson Memorial Showers of Blessings Churches Worldwide Incorporated, conducted a financially booming ministry focused on a theology of prosperity.

The African American Catholic Congregation, organized by Bishop George A. Stallings, was the most notable black religious alternative to surface in the 1980s. A black priest, Stallings broke from the Roman Catholic Church in 1989 to establish a denomination dedicated to addressing African-American needs. By blending Catholicism with African-American religious traditions, Stallings incorporated gospel music, shouting, clapping, and testimony into the traditional Catholic worship service. Charging that the Catholic Church neglected African Americans, Stallings also attacked the Church's position on women, in 1991 ordaining Rose Vernall into the priesthood of his breakaway sect.

As the twentieth century neared an end, increased racial tensions and national economic decay ushered in yet another decline in African-American communities. Gang warfare, drug abuse, poverty, and the HIV virus were only a few of the complex problems facing black Americans. In the 1990s, many in the African-American community looked to the church for answers, some prophesying an impending revival of black religion. New African-American religions were born out of a struggle against oppression and adversity, and these sects continued to function as a foundation of faith and hope. *See also* African Methodist Episcopal Church; American Muslim Mission; Black Israelites; Black Jewish movements; black theology; Drew, Timothy; Fard, Wallace D.; Farrakhan, Louis; Father Divine; Garvey, Marcus M.; Haile Selassie; Holiness churches; Malcolm X; Moorish Science Temple; Muhammad, Elijah; Muhammad, Wallace D.; Nation of Islam; new religions; Rastafarians; Yahweh ben Yahweh.

African apostolic churches, a collective term for a group of independent African churches founded by prophetic figures who modeled themselves on the role of John the Baptist in the Christian tradition. The two most important such figures were John Masowe and John Maranke, from the Shona areas of Southern Rhodesia. In 1932, Masowe founded the Apostolic Sabbath Church of God and Maranke established the African Apostolic Church of John Maranke (the Bapostolo).

Both churches stressed the role of the prophet as a healer and teacher, the purification of the congregation through adult baptism by immersion and rites of confession, and strict adherence to church rules in order to separate them from the world.

John of the Wilderness (Masowe), previously known as Shoniwa, began to preach after seeing visions received during a near-death experience. Masowe believed that the economic independence of his followers from Europeans would help usher in the kingdom of God. As a result, his followers boycotted European goods and refused to work for Europeans, instead forming artisan cooperatives to support themselves. With the profits from their crafts, primarily basketry and tinsmithing, they established church communities. Masowe rejected all Christian sacraments other than baptism, which he personally administered to his converts. Because of the anti-European dimension of his work, Masowe went into hiding. In 1943, some of his followers settled in the South African township of Korsten, near Port Elizabeth, but they were forced to return to Rhodesia in 1960.

John Maranke, who was raised as a Methodist, claimed to have had his first vision at the age of six. In 1932, he had such an overpowering vision that he felt compelled to found his own church. He heard a voice tell him that he was John the Baptist and that he must go out and preach to all nations to live moral lives and to keep the seventh-day Sabbath. Bapostolo services are held outside, on holy ground, rather than in the confines of buildings like other religious groups. The most important holiday of the year is Passover, a time for confession of one's sins and for those who have received charismatic gifts to be confirmed in their use. Apostles carefully separate themselves from the world, avoid excessive social interaction with non-members, forgo such worldly items as money or luxury goods, and wear white robes both in ritual and in the activities of daily life. Before Maranke died, he assembled a book of his visions called *The New Witness of the Apostles*, which continues to be an authoritative text for the church that he founded. By 1970, the Bapostolo had grown into a multiethnic church with more than 150,000 followers in Zaire, Malawi, Zambia, Rhodesia, South Africa, and Botswana. *See also* Africa, new religions in; Apostles of John Maranke; Apostolic Sabbath Church of God.

African Church movement. *See* Africa, new religions in.

African Methodist Episcopal Church, a Christian African-American denomination founded in 1816. The AME Church originated out of the protest, in the post–Revolutionary War period, of African-American Christians against racial discrimination. The AME Church grew to about fifty thousand members by the Civil War, then expanded to nearly a half-million by the end of the century, largely due to aggressive mission work among ex-slaves in the South. The largest black Methodist denomination in the 1990s, it conducts a wide variety of activities in the United States and elsewhere, notably in Africa. *See also* Methodism.

African Orthodox Church. *See* African Americans (North America), new religions among.

Afro-Americans (Caribbean and South America), new religions among, recent Afro-Caribbean religious movements related to the regional processes of indigenization and outreach. Because almost everyone in the Caribbean is from someplace else, Caribbean religious movements have been greatly affected by the presence of Africans, Europeans, Americans, and—to a lesser extent—Asians.

The majority of new religions in the Caribbean have an African or Christian base. There is also a significant Asian presence going back to the nineteenth century, and Asian religions—along with localized variants of Islam—have been among the fastest growing religions. The Kali cult has become increasingly important in Trinidad, and syncretisms of Hinduism and Christianity—such as the cult of Maldevidan in Martinique—occur with greater frequency among Asians and Afro-Americans.

It is not fruitful to look at new religions in the Caribbean as "religions of protest" or as "religions of the oppressed." Such interpretations are based on data collected more than thirty years ago and ignore changes in Caribbean religions and societies over the past three decades.

Indigenous Visions—Ras Tafari and the Earth People: Ras Tafari (Rastafarianism) is perhaps the best known of the new religions, largely due to the widespread influence of *reggae* music. It is difficult to estimate the number of Rastafarians because they refuse to be counted, although scholars estimate their numbers in the hundreds of thousands. This may be an exaggeration, but their influence far exceeds their numbers in Jamaica, elsewhere in the Caribbean, in Europe, and in the United States.

The movement traces its history to a number of early-twentieth-century indigenous preacher-leaders, most notably Leonard Howell, Joseph Hibbert, Archibald Dunkley, Paul Earlington,

Vernal Davis, Ferdinand Richetts, and Robert Hinds. Each of these, working in isolation from the others, came to the conclusion that Ras ("Prince") Tafari, then enthroned as Ethiopian emperor Haile Selassie, was "the Lion of Judah," who would lead blacks in the promised land of Africa.

Rasta is not an organized, hierarchical, or uniform movement. As in other new religions, there are no formal creeds, few written texts, and no seminaries to enforce orthodoxy. Because adherents share so few beliefs and values, it is not possible for Rastafarians to present a uniform front or to form an organized, cohesive group. Nevertheless, there are shared values and beliefs.

Initially, Rastafarians belonged to small autonomous groups that were augmented by persons who attended the meetings or sympathized with the aims of the movement. In these early years, *ganja* ("marijuana") was not smoked and dreadlocks were a less prominent feature of the movement than later. Rastafarians were bitter about racialism and about class differences in Jamaican society. They railed against the white man and the black traitors—politicians, the police, clergy, landholders, teachers, and business and professional people—who were said to have mistreated and misled the people.

Originally, there were seven basic Rastafarian beliefs: black people were exiled to the West Indies because of their moral transgressions; the wicked white man is inferior to black people; the Jamaican situation is hopeless; Ethiopia is heaven; Haile Selassie is the living God; the emperor of Ethiopia will arrange for all expatriated persons of African descent to return to their homeland; and black people will get revenge by compelling whites to serve them.

Today, Ras Tafari is much more heterogeneous than it was in the 1950s. Different subgroups stress different elements of the original creed, and some modifications are discernible. For example, the death of Haile Selassie (1975) has raised significant questions about his role in the movement. For many Rastafarians, there is less emphasis on Ethiopia and more on pan-Africanism.

Doctrines concerning the whites have also undergone some changes. For some adherents, the essence of Rastafarian teaching is that all races are basically equal. Moreover, Rastafarian claims that they are the chosen people of God do not signify superiority as much as dictate a prophetic role putting them in the service of all nations.

Repatriation to Africa has received less attention in some groups, and there has been greater stress on themes of black power and black cultural ascendancy.

At the same time, Ras Tafari has played an important role in the development of Jamaican popular music. Although frequently portrayed as a music of the oppressed, reggae also celebrates Jamaican heroes, freedom, and ganja.

By the mid-1970s, Ras Tafari had become the culture and/or counterculture of a sizable percentage of the Jamaican population. Although the movement earlier had been considered subversive and a force to be eliminated, today Jamaicans of all social classes accept some aspects of the Ras Tafarian vision. This has resulted in tactical accommodation. For example, while some Rastas see themselves as fighters against oppression, others believe that peaceful living will bring about a victory against evil.

Another indigenous vision—the Earth People—has its origins in Trinidad in the 1970s. Each year, members of the group come to the capital city, Port of Spain, to repeat their messages and to recruit new members. They attract attention because members are nudists and deliberately use obscenities. The group's founder, Mother Earth, boldly announces that there is no God and that she is the Biblical Devil, the Mother of Africa and India, and Nature Herself.

Prior to founding the Earth People, Mother Earth had been a Spiritual Baptist. After the birth of her twins, she began to experience a series of revelations giving rise to an awareness that the Christian doctrine of God the Father was untrue. The universe, she discovered, is actually the work of a primordial mother, who had created a race of black people. But a rebellious son reentered his mother's womb to create a race of white people who are the race of death. Whites, acting as the son's agents, enslaved blacks and continue to exploit them through technology, cities, clothes, factories, and wage labor. The way of the mother is the way of nature: nakedness, cultivation of the land, and nonexploitation in human relationships. Mother Earth sees her role as facilitating a return to nature by organizing her coastal community called Hell Valley, the Valley of Decision, to prepare for a return to the beginning. It is her mission to combat the distortions of the Bible, which put the son over the mother. At any given time, the movement claims between fifty and a hundred sympathizers, but there is a high rate of turnover. Some neighboring Rastafarians are sympathetic to Mother Earth's teachings but are sometimes put off by the nudity and Mother Earth's repudiation of Haile Selassie.

Afro-Catholic Outreach—Vodun, Santeria, and Maria Lionza: Vodun (also Voodoo, or Vodou), the Afro-Catholic folk religion of Haiti, combines an impressive continuity with ancestral African elements with a remarkable openness to change. Like many Afro-Caribbean religions, Vodun appears to be both heterodox and orthodox at the same time.

A Haitian Voodoo (or Vodou) priest prepares a meal welcoming the various spirits of the dead (*gede*) who will appear during All Souls' and All Saints' days (October 31, November 1). The bowls contain pieces of cassava bread, cooked plantain, wedges of avocado with salted herring cooked with onions and peppers, and pieces of spicy fried meat, the favorite foods of Baron Samdi ("Saturday"), head of the gede.

The period from 1730 to 1790 is usually seen as Vodun's formative stage. It was at this time that the religious beliefs of the Dahomeans, Senegalese, Congolese, Yoruba, and other Africans were combined with selected ideas concerning Catholic saints to form the complex religious system we now call Vodun.

The central focus of Vodun, in all its manifestations, is devotion to the *loa* ("deities"). The African origin of many loa, including all important members of the Vodun pantheon, is re-

flected in their names: Damballah, Ezurlie, Obatala, Legba, Ogun, Shango, etc. Confusion in beliefs surrounding these deities is due partly to contradictions in the Dahomean religious system as it was adopted by the Haitians, as well as to the addition of the Yoruba pantheon to the Dahomean religious system.

The relationship between devotees and the loa is thought to be a contractual one, and relations with the loa are an individual responsibility. It is widely believed that neglect of one's loa will result in sickness, the death of relatives, crop failure, or other misfortunes.

There is evidence that Vodun is moving in an accommodative direction, becoming more international in scope. One can find variants of Vodun throughout the United States, Europe, and especially in the Dominican Republic, where the religion has become a major new movement.

Vodun has no well-defined body of doctrine

The heavily powdered face of this member of a Haitian Voodoo (or Vodou) temple indicates that he represents one of the *gede* (spirits of the dead).

and no formal mythology on which to base a theological system. Traditions vary from family to family and cult house to cult house, where contact with spirits is direct and intimate. It is primarily through dreams and possession-trance that spirits reveal themselves to humans.

Cuban Santeria also combines European and African beliefs and practices. Unlike Vodun, however, Santeria derives mainly from one African tradition—the Yoruba. During ceremonies, blood—the food of the deities—flows onto sacred stones belonging to the cult leader. These stones are the objects through which the gods are fed and in which their power resides. Although the regime of Fidel Castro has attempted to curb the expansion of Santeria, the religion continues to flourish in Cuba.

A significant religious development during the past twenty years has been the large-scale transfer of Haitian Vodun and Cuban Santeria to urban centers in the United States and Canada. It is estimated, for example, that there are currently more than one hundred thousand Vodunists and Santeros in New York City, making these among the largest and fastest growing religious movements in the city. Similar assessments could be made for the cities of Miami, Toronto, and Los Angeles. Santeria has also spread to Venezuela, where it has influenced the indigenous Maria Lionza movement.

Maria Lionza is a popular religion that resembles Brazilian Umbanda with its emphases on spiritualism and ritual healing. Over the past twenty years, Maria Lionza has diffused throughout the Venezuelan countryside and has been especially influential among the urban poor. The majority of cult leaders are Venezuelans, but a number of leaders are of Colombian or Antillean origin.

According to legend, Maria Lionza is an Indian princess who governs water, wild animals, and plant life. She is surrounded by lesser spirits, including Indian leaders who fought against the Spanish. In recent years, African spirits (Ogun, Shango, Ezurlie) have been joined by Buddhist spirits. From Europe have come spirits as diverse as Adolf Hitler, Simon Bolivar, and Pope John XXIII. Dr. Jose Hernandez (a deceased healer from Caracas) has become such an important member of the pantheon that in some areas he has inspired cult houses of his own.

Beliefs and rituals in Maria Lionza centers are not uniform. The majority of adherents consider themselves Catholic, but there is little formal doctrine and tremendous competition among leaders. Devotees attend rituals for the purpose of obtaining spiritual and material help by entering into agreements with the spirits. Over the past ten years, both Trinidadian and Cuban leaders have introduced the practice of blood sacrifice into Maria Lionza ceremonies.

Afro-Protestant Outreach and Indigenization— Cumina, Convince, Revivalism, Pocomania, the Spiritual Baptists, and Shango: On a continuum from pure African-based to pure Christian-based religious movements in Jamaica, Cumina would be at the African end. The earliest published reference to a Cumina ceremony is in 1943, but ceremonies clearly predate this century. The religion is centered primarily in the parish of St. Thomas among descendants of Maroons of the Blue Mountains. It is possible that the religion emerged in this location because of the presence of a large number of Bantu-speaking people from the Congo-Angola area. A pivotal element in Cumina religion is the invocation of ancestral spirits that take possession of the living.

Cumina, like other Afro-Caribbean religious movements, is organized into nations or sects served by special deities. Each Cumina has its chief who is responsible for every aspect of ceremonies, assisted by a queen or mother of the Cumina. Rituals begin with the greeting of the spirits and by beating the rims of drums with a specific rhythm. The spirits are welcomed and fed before ceremonial dancing begins. Rituals may extend for a night and a day, but rarely longer.

Aspects of Cumina ceremonies have gained considerable publicity as an art form, and Cumina is seen as a vivid, active, and creative form of cultural expression.

Convince, practiced in Jamaica, includes many more Christian elements. While recognizing God, Christ, and other Christian ideas, members of Convince consider Christian forms too remote and otherworldly to be of practical value. Instead, they focus attention on lesser beings who are thought to be more accessible and more directly involved in the world of humans. Many of these lesser beings are believed to be departed ancestors and/or individuals who were once members of the Convince religious group. Spirits are said to "mount" their devotees who, in turn, honor them with refreshments and sacrifices.

At the Christian end of the continuum stand the religious movements of Pocomania ("a little madness") and Revival. These movements have been mostly urban, have developed stable organizational structures, and have a well-defined priesthood. A major difference between Pocomania and Revival in West Kingston is that Pocomania puts less emphasis on preaching and Bible explanation and greater emphasis on singing and spiritual dancing. Revival leaders, it is claimed, use neither rum nor marijuana, while Pocomania leaders use both.

Pocomania began in the 1920s, but its roots may go back to the Great Revival of 1860 to 1862. Adherents consider the term *Pocomania* derisive and prefer to have their religion designated Baptist or Zionist. Members are organized into bands under a leader. Among important rituals are baptisms, communion services, and various healing functions (mostly entailing ritual baths and use of balms and herbal medicine). The Bible is used as a means of revelation through dreams and visions.

Although Pocomania is sometimes called "Revival" or "Revival Zion," not all sects that carry the name *Zion* in their title are necessarily connected with the Revival Zion movement. Within nearly all Revival groups, there is an elaborate hierarchy. Leaders and subleaders are referred to as Shepherds or Captains; in some instances—as among the Spiritual Baptists—the highest-ranking members are referred to as Father and Mother. Women have important functions within Revival groups, sometimes equivalent to those of the men. Jamaican Revivalism lost considerable membership during the 1960s and 1970s, but the religion is now on the rebound.

The Spiritual Baptists are an international religious movement with congregations in St. Vincent (where, some Baptists claim, the faith originated), Trinidad and Tobago, and Grenada, Guyana (where they are known as Jordanites), Venezuela, Toronto (Canada), Los Angeles, and New York City. A number of new religious movements on other islands have rituals similar to those of the Spiritual Baptists (e.g., the Tieheads of Barbados and the Spirit Baptists of Jamaica), but Spiritual Baptists do not consider these others part of their religion and do not participate in joint worship, pilgrimages, missions, and other services. Spiritual Baptists do, however, maintain active ties with their coreligionists in other nations.

Baptist membership is predominantly black, and, like many other Afro-Caribbean religions, the early appeal was as a religion of the oppressed. In recent years, however, congregations in Trinidad have attracted membership among middle-class blacks, as well as sizable numbers of wealthy East Indians, Chinese, and Creoles. Over the past ten years, membership has remained stable at about ten thousand.

Many Trinidadians confuse Spiritual Baptists with an African-derived cult known as Shango

and assume that Spiritual Baptist and Shango rituals are identical. Members of these faiths, however, do not share this confusion, and a large number of Spiritual Baptists condemn Shango rituals as heathen worship. Shangoists, for their part, claim that Spiritual Baptists copy their ideas and try to steal their power.

Both the Spiritual Baptists and Shango combine rituals and beliefs from many religions. A major difference in Shango and Baptist belief systems is that Baptist rituals are directed toward their version of the Christian Trinity, while Shango rituals are directed toward African or African-derived deities. Spiritual Baptists are ostensibly Christians, but this is not to say that Baptists do not believe in the existence of African deities. A majority of Spiritual Baptists do believe in Shango powers but do not feel that they should be venerated.

Although the Spiritual Baptists and Shango are clearly separate ritual traditions, they are interrelated on a number of levels. Their memberships overlap. About 80 percent of all Shangoists in Trinidad also participate in Baptist services, and about 40 percent of all Baptists also participate to varying degrees in Shango.

A central ritual in the Spiritual Baptist faith is called the mourning ceremony, which does not relate directly to death and bereavement but is an elaborate ritual involving fasting, lying on a dirt floor, and other deprivations. A major purpose of the rite, according to Baptists, is to discover one's true rank within the church hierarchy.

Mourning rites are believed to have curative powers, and because so many participants enter the rite in an unhealthy state, occasionally someone dies during the ordeal, resulting in a government inquiry. While government prosecutors assert that poor diet and damp conditions in the mourning rooms contribute to mourners' deaths, leaders claim that they take every possible precaution to ensure the mourner's survival.

Conclusions: The growth of new religious movements in the Caribbean is not easily explained in terms of protest or deprivation. Many changes have taken place in Caribbean societies over the past thirty years, and a large number of Jamaicans, Trinidadians, and—to a lesser extent—residents of the smaller islands have experienced some degree of upward mobility. The consequences of affluence for new religious movements, whose primary appeal had previously been among the poor, remain uncertain.

A critical issue in the study of new religious movements in the Caribbean is the difficulty in separating indigenous and foreign elements. Because there is so much outreach, it may prove impossible to discover the origin of any one faith. Because all of these religions lack denominational chains of command, the most accurate statements refer to individual groups and their leaders—not denominations or denominational organizations. To examine movements such as Ras Tafari, Maria Lionza, the Earth People, or the Spiritual Baptists as if they were unified denominations on the European model is to present an overly coherent picture of an incredibly fragmented situation. *See also* Cumina religion; loa; new religions; Rastafarians; Santeria; Shango; Voodoo.

Afro-Americans (North America), new religions among. *See* African Americans (North America), new religions among; Kwanzaa; new religions; North America, new religions in; World Community of Islam.

Afro-Brazilian religions. A variety of new groups developed from contact between religions of the African diaspora and native Brazilindian, Roman Catholic, and spiritist traditions. Rooted in the covert practices of enslaved Africans and their freed and mixed-race descendants, Afro-Brazilian groups continue to recognize the ancestral divinities of Africa in rituals centered on trance possession and individual spiritual enhancement. The religions exhibit considerable regional variations and are a strong, though underrecognized, presence in modern Brazilian society.

History: The history of the Afro-Brazilian religions is intertwined with the history of the enslavement and transportation of Africans to Brazil, a process that began in the late 1500s, grew only gradually in the following century, but accelerated in the eighteenth and nineteenth centuries. The preservation of significant portions of African religious life was a remarkable achievement under such repressive conditions, and slaves apparently availed themselves of the opportunities allowed by the inconsistencies in the actions of the ruling classes. Efforts to perpetuate Portuguese society in Brazil and to eliminate African culture and thwart solidarity among the slaves included the splitting of tribal groups and families, as well as forced conversion to Roman Catholicism. Seen not only as an introduction to religious "truth" but also as the path to civilization, proselytization of slaves was, however, often superficial and, after a hurried baptism, consisted of little more than required presence at and acknowledgment of the

external rituals of the late medieval church. While colonial historians reported that rural plantation owners permitted the slaves to hold nighttime dances (such as the *calundus* or *batuques*), considering them to be merely simple customs, the descriptions of the dances, as well as Afro-Brazilian folk history, suggest that these festivities founded the new religious tradition. Worship of African deities apparently continued under the guise of or in assimilation with the widespread Catholic cult of the saints. Additionally, the popular *congadas* (processions) in honor of Sao Benedito, patron saint of Africans in Brazil, commemorated moments of African history and fostered independent pride in the black community.

In the nineteenth-century Portuguese empire, pressures to conform to the Luso-Brazilian society changed as avenues for slight social and religious advancement opened. Freed African men and men of mixed descent were particularly encouraged to "whiten" their prospects through participation in lay Catholic brotherhoods or in the lower ranks of religious orders. Nevertheless, the neo-African traditions, cloaked under or adapted to Roman Catholicism, emerged in the early 1800s in distinct sects.

Overview: Although the earliest manifestations of the African beliefs and practices fundamental to Afro-Brazilian religions are not recorded, it is most likely that priests and mediums from the different African tribes, especially Yoruba, Fon, Ashanti, Congo, and eastern Bantu groups, covertly continued their distinctive religions and that communities formed on plantations or in towns with substantial numbers of tribal members. Initially, ethnic solidarity may have built strong divisions between groups, but the shift of ancestral family and locative cults to the New World elicited the reinterpretation and, eventually, fusion of formerly separate religious elements.

Because of the relatively late arrival of Yoruba tribal members in Brazil and the vigorous preservation of their cultural identity, Yoruban theology, cultic structure, and language have predominated in Afro-Brazilian religions, perpetuating the worship of the deities of West Africa, modified with the Christian concepts of mediation and salvation. Bantu cosmology and native Brazilian ritual elements were also influential in some regions. Communities combined the separate divine cults, as well as the several priestly and mediumistic roles, such that each group, led by a ritual priest or priestess and guided by a divination expert, honored a pantheon of deities linked with natural phenomena and made present in celebratory rituals through possession of mediums.

Contemporary centers typically feature a room divided into two spaces, the sacred area separated from the congregants' seating area. Statues and other symbolic representations of divine presence are placed on a front altar decorated with candles and flowers. Each deity, called *orixa* (Yoruba, "divinity") or *santa/santo* (Portuguese, lit., "saint," but used as the translation for orixa), is identified with a Catholic divine aspect (creator, Jesus) or saint and linked with other deities in a cosmic network of powers. The more well-known are the gods Olorun, Obatala, Oxala, Shango or Xango, Ogun, Oshossi or Oxossi, and Exu, and the goddesses Yemanja, Oxum, and Yansan. Other powers venerated or invoked in an Afro-Brazilian center (*centro*) are Brazilian Indian spirits, souls of the dead, and, more recently, Asian spirits.

Membership usually begins with individual identification of and dedication to a patron divine spirit. The mediums for divine possession, *filhas* ("daughters") or *filhos de santo* ("sons of the saint/deity"), form the core of the religious community and enter religious service through complicated initiations traceable to African rituals. From their ranks rise the leaders for the independent centers, the priestesses and priests or *maes* and *pais de santo* ("mothers" and "fathers" of the saint/deity"). Until the 1950s, the majority of the members, mediums, and leaders of Afro-Brazilian religions were women of African descent from Brazil's working classes; recent decades have seen tremendous diversification across gender and racial and class lines, particularly through the phenomenal growth of Umbanda.

Regional Differences: Early accounts of Afro-Brazilian religious groups are replete with speculation on the historical tribal connections, not only of each regional type but also of each doctrinal, practical, or linguistic element in the religion. The divergent regional communities certainly maintain the heritage of African, Brazilian, Christian, and spiritist traditions, but Afro-Brazilian religions are characterized by their supersession of ethnic ties and deliberate universalism.

Candomble is regarded as the oldest and the most traditionally African of the Afro-Brazilian groups. It is centered at the sacred sites of Engenho Velho, Gantois, and Axe de Opo Afonja in Salvador (Bahia), which trace their founding lineages to the early nineteenth century. Candomble has emphasized Yoruban priestly roles,

initiatory and cleansing rituals, symbolism, and orixas. The framework of its theology parallels late medieval Christianity, for the followers acknowledge a high creator deity, Olorun, but invoke the intermediary patron deities for intercession in human affairs. Other aspects of African mythology have diminished to lists of divine attributes—linking each divine spirit to one type of natural phenomenon, color, day of the week, and temperament—while the central Christian concepts of sin and salvation are present in the acceptance of human imperfections and ultimate dependence on superhuman aid.

Candomble priestesses, women of unambiguous African descent, have been significant spiritual leaders in Salvador; in their religious roles, they perform animal sacrifices and divination rituals for individual devotees, as well as oversee all training and calendrical ceremonies. The central rituals are spectacular dramas of possession: during dances accompanied by traditional drum rhythms and chants, the mediums—mostly women—enter trance states and, as "horses" for the divine, are "mounted" by the orixas and assume elaborate costumes representing their patrons. Each medium undergoes extensive training—lasting as long as seven years—and initiation before first experiencing full trance and possession by a guiding deity. During the ceremonies, followers may consult with or offer worship to the deity, temporarily in material form and responsive to the worshiper. Male priests, musicians, and council members served chiefly in auxiliary roles until the 1970s, when the proportion of male priests and mediums increased significantly.

Catimbo flourishes in the coastal states near the Amazon and is heir not only to Christian and African traditions but also to the *caboclo* (backlander or Indian-European) traditions based in the native religions. Its centers are simple buildings housing an altar, a few statues, and seating. Rituals are performed by the *page* or *curandeiro* ("healer") who leads the community in petitioning the spirits for health and a good life and drinking the intoxicant *jurema* to induce visions. Among most Catimbo groups, the possession experience is limited to the leader, who may, however, receive any type of spirit during a ritual. The invoked powers include the traditional Brazilindian gods Tupa and Ituapa, stereotypical Indian spirits Iracema and Master Healer, Christian saints Antonio and Josaphat, and some of the African deities worshiped elsewhere; these spirits or *encantados* (lit., "enchanted ones") inhabit nonmaterial villages, states, and kingdoms aligned with similar

A *Candomble* procession in Ponta de Areia, Brazil, as part of a two-day festival (February 1–2, 1983) honoring the Yoruba-Brazilian water goddesses Yemanja and Oxum. The women are carrying decorated water jars, symbolic of the full breasts of the goddess. The decorations include mirrors, combs, cosmetics, and flowers, all associated with beauty, which appeals to the goddesses.

powers. The native Brazilian influence on Catimbo, excepting the continuing use of jurema, has been muted by centuries of contact with Christianity, but Catimbo structure reflects Bantu cosmology in the organized cosmic geography and the central healing rituals and possession trances.

Other regional sects echo the differences noted above: *Xango* in Pernambuco and other northeastern states is analogous to Candomble, and *Tambor de Mina* in Maranhao and *Pagelanca* in Amazonas parallel Catimbo.

Macumba represents the more recent trend in Afro-Christian spirituality, blending Bantu (divine names, leadership roles, rituals), Christian (divine titles, theology), and Brazilindian (spirit names) traditions with spiritist metaphysics. Macumba centers are led by *embandas* ("priests") and their mediums embody the divinities and spirits known to other groups, as well as souls of the enlightened dead. Spread nationwide from its beginnings in Rio de Janeiro and Sao Paulo, Macumba rituals and teachings are quite similar to those of Bahian Candomble but are often reduced to simpler core elements by the fractioning of larger communities. In some interpretations of the phenomenon in Rio, there has also been division by intent: positive rituals remain under Macumba while negative

or evil-manipulating magical rites are called *Quimbanda*. Recent scholarship suggests that the name Macumba has been indiscriminately applied to nascent Umbanda groups, as well as to older communities.

Umbanda is considered the most Brazilian of the Afro-Brazilian groups and represents a break from the traditionalist religions such as Candomble. The origins of Umbanda are linked with a small group that sought in the 1920s to integrate neo-African religion with spiritist cosmology by abandoning African-centered doctrines and ritual practices—especially animal sacrifices—and emphasizing the charitable spiritual healing rendered by exalted souls in a cosmic hierarchy.

Umbanda communities, now found throughout Brazil after explosive growth in the 1970s and 1980s, continue aspects of all of Brazil's religious past. Brazilian Indian spirits are prominent, as are use of tobacco and herbal potions, and stereotypic native symbolism. Roman Catholic theological concepts of salvation, immortality, and hierarchical but benevolent divine-human relationships are central tenets, while saints are identified with Indian and African divine powers. The divinities, community structure, and possession rituals were developed from other neo-African religions and the cosmology from Kardecism, a European Spiritist movement.

Umbandists maintain that their religion's universalist teachings emerged with the human race, were influenced by ancient Hindu laws, continued by the Mayans and by Greek, Egyptian, and Jewish priests, and preserved in Africa until revival through the reuniting of three branches of humanity—Indians, Europeans, and Africans—in Brazil. At the pinnacle of Umbanda's cosmic hierarchy is God the creator, the transcendent source and destination of all spirits. His son, Jesus Christ, is the highest communicating power; entities below him are other nonincarnate spirits who make up the celestial court and four categories of formerly incarnate spirits who communicate through possessed mediums: spirits of dead Brazilindians; souls of dead African slaves; the spirits of dead children; and spirits of malicious women and men, especially dead Europeans. According to Umbanda, human beings, composed of body and evolving soul, undergo reincarnation according to the laws of *karma* and are subject to spiritual illnesses resultant from social evils and personal problems. Each person may, however, improve fate through study, prayer, ritual cleansings, and practice of the highest virtue, charity.

The most important rituals in Umbanda are the *giras* ("dances"), during which the ritually purified and specially attired mediums dance to achieve a trance state and the spirits descend. Bearing positive messages from the higher celestial ranks, the possessing spirits consult with members of the congregation, offer advice on personal problems, and cleanse the members of evil influences.

A substantial portion of Afro-Brazilian doctrine and practice was kept secret during the long years of suppression and persecution by local and federal governments of a religion whose members were potential opponents of the Roman Catholic and white dominant class. The growing national community, which holds infrequent congresses, faces new challenges in the 1990s, such as reconsideration of its assimilation with Roman Catholicism, conflicting pressures for universalism, and recent aggressive proselytization by Protestant evangelical missions from North America. *See also* Candomble; filha de santo; Macumba; new religions; orixa; Umbanda.

Afro-Surinamese new religions. Major variants of new religions in Suriname include Winti and various Maroon groups. Winti, the name given to the popular polytheistic religion of the majority of coastal Creoles, means wind; members believe that their deities are as invisible as the wind. The religion's worldview orients life for its adherents; its rites include elements that are common to both Europe and Africa.

Among the major powers within the stratified pantheon of Winti are a variety of *kromanti* ("spirits of the sky"), *apuku* ("spirits of the forest"), and *aisa* ("water spirits"). The most prominent water spirits are associated with snakes, for example, *vodu* (boa) and *aboma* (anaconda). A major focus of the religion is to cure illness and remedy misfortune with the help of spirits speaking through mediums. Winti ceremonies are supervised by a *bonuman*, who may be male or female.

There are currently six Maroon groups living along rivers in the interior of Suriname. The Djuka and Saramaka are the largest groups, with more than twenty thousand members; the Matawai, Aluku, Paramaka, and Kwinti number far fewer. All are descended from slaves who escaped from coastal plantations in the seventeenth century.

A majority of Maroons participates in a religion that is mostly African in orientation, with ritual life and social organization well-integrated. The principal deities (*gadu*) are Gaan Gadu, Agedeonsu (the goddess of fecundity), Tebu, and Na Ogu ("the danger"). Each has been the focus of popular cults. There are also four independent pantheons of minor deities: spirits of the deceased ancestors (*jorkas*), reptile spirits (Papa Gudu or *Vodu*), bush spirits (*ampuku*), and sky spirits (*kumanti*). No lines of authority connect one pantheon with the others. The spectacular feats of kumanti mediums are legendary, including touching red-hot blades and climbing trees covered with thorns without injury. Also notable are the extensive rituals surrounding birth, life crises, and death. Funerals constitute the single most important ritual event, spanning a period of many months and often involving many hundreds of people. *See also* new religions.

afterlife, the fate of humans after death. *See also* afterworld; ancestral rites; ancestors; apotheosis; ascension; burial; Celtic religion; cremation; damnation; dead, rituals with respect to the; death; deification; descent to the underworld; Egyptian religion; eschatology; ghost; grave, graveyard; heaven and hell; hell (Christianity); immortality; islands of the blessed; Judgment Day; life-cycle rituals; limbo; metempsychosis; paradise; purgatory, the Roman Catholic; rebirth; reincarnation; resurrection; revenant; sky; soul; spirits.

afterworld, the abode of the dead. *See also* afterlife; Chinvat; death; Hades; happy hunting ground; heaven (Christianity); heaven and hell; Hel; hell (Christianity); Huang-ch'uan; islands of the blessed; limbo; paradise; purgatory, the Roman Catholic; shaman; sky; Tartaros; Tibetan Book of the Dead; Valhall.

agape (ah-gah′pay). 1 In Christian writings, the Greek word for selfless love as distinguished from *eros* (sexual love) and *philia* (the love of friendship). 2 An early Christian ritual meal.

Age of Aquarius, forthcoming era of peace and spiritual advancement under the astrological sign of Aquarius the Water-bearer; a major eschatological theme in esoteric thought and a centerpiece of the 1960s counterculture. Though datings differ, the year 2000 is often cited for its advent. *See also* New Age movements.

age-sets, categories into which traditional cultures often divide the human life cycle for ritual and social purposes. Usually an age-set spans several years, and refers to a set of people who were initiated together. For girls it often means a group who came of marriageable age together. Because age-sets orient people in relation to different age-sets and other social categories, the entrance or exit of one set affects all the others. The formation of an age-set is not always on a biological basis; for example, in some cultures, the death of a chief opens a new age-set, and not until then can people of that age marry. In other cultures, both men and women shift age-sets when they have their first child.

Age-sets integrate the human life cycle into the larger temporal and spatial patterns of the cosmos. Relations between the age-sets can be described as relations between cardinal directions, seasons, celestial bodies, or animal species. The Inca, for example, coordinated the male life cycle with the solar journey by dividing the male life into twelve age-sets, each with different social tasks and status.

During festivals, the age-sets frequently engage in ritual battles that enact the creative tension between opposing parts of the cosmos. The Brazilian Sherente, for example, divide the four athletically active age-sets into east/west pairs for log races. Such contests become beginnings of lifelong ritual friendships between sparring partners, sponsors and initiates, or initiates and designated helpers of the opposite gender. Each of these newly forged friendships serves as a metaphor for the interplay between parts of the cosmos separated in ancient times. *See also* gender roles; initiation rituals; life-cycle rituals; men's houses; ritual.

ages of the world, stages of development of the cosmos from creation to destruction to re-creation. *See also* Age of Aquarius; antediluvian/postdiluvian; apocalypticism; chaos; cosmology; cyclical time; Degenerate Age of the Dharma; dispensationalism; Edda; Etruscan religion; golden age; Hesiod; Joachim of Fiore; macrocosm, microcosm; mappo; Mesoamerican religion; myth; yuga; Zoroastrianism.

aggadah (ah-gah-dah′; Heb., "narrative"), a native category of rabbinic Judaism, defined in contrast to *halakah* (Heb., "law," "practice"). *Aggadah*, narrative lore, retells Hebrew Bible stories and fabricates parables and tales of rabbis to make exemplary points about right thinking and virtuous behavior. *See also* halakah; Judaism (authoritative texts and their interpretation).

aggregates (Skt. *skandha,* "mass," "heap"), the basic categories constituting all psychophysical phenomena in the Buddhist analysis of existence. Denying any substantial or permanent essence, Buddhists instead see all existents as the result of the varying combination of five basic components: corporality, including the four fundamental elements of earth, water, fire, and wind and their derivatives; sensation, whether agreeable, disagreeable, or neutral; conception; motivation, or proclivities to action; and perceptual consciousness. The last four originate in the contact between the six sense organs, including the mind, and their respective objects. *See also* Buddhism (thought and ethics); impermanence.

Agni (uhg′nee; Skt., "fire"), deified "Fire," a god of Vedic and later India. He is associated with ritual fire, as receiver and conveyor of oblations to heaven, and with the domestic hearth. *See also* Hinduism; sacrifice; Veda, Vedism.

agnosticism (Gk. *agnos,* "unknowable"), the view that there is insufficient evidence to posit either the existence or nonexistence of God, and by extension, of the immortal soul. Agnosticism functions as an intellectual mid-position between theism and atheism. The term was coined in 1869 during the Victorian debate over Western biblical faith and the new Darwinian outlook in science and cosmology. There are, as well, forms of religious agnosticism, which avow ignorance about the mystery of the divine nature. *See also* atheism; theism.

Agnus Dei (ahg'noos day'ee; Lat., "Lamb of God"). 1 Christian title applied to Jesus (see John 1:29). 2 A common part of the Catholic Mass sung before taking communion. 3 A small Christian devotional medallion, often in wax, and blessed by the pope, with an impression of a lamb upon it.

Agonshu (ah-gon-shoo), a Japanese new religion founded by Kiriyama Seiyu (Tsutsumi Masao) in 1978. Based on the veneration of the Buddhist Agama Sutras and the use of esoteric Buddhist fire rituals, Agonshu teaches that the cause of all problems stems from the spirits of the dead.

Its membership is estimated to be about 250,000, although its annual Hoshi Matsuri (Star Festival), a dramatic fire ceremony held each year near Kyoto, attracts upwards of half a million people. Adherents recently built a large headquarters outside Kyoto. *See also* fire ritual (Japan); Japan, new religions in.

agriculture, religious aspects of. Scholars distinguish between the grain agriculture characteristic of Eurasia and Mesoamerica and the tuber cultivation characteristic of Oceania and the Amazon region. Grain cultivators perceive the cosmos in sexual and periodic terms. The seed is planted, it grows, it is harvested and replanted; birth, death, and rebirth are but moments in one life-sustaining process.

Tuber cultivation is an asexual process. The tubers are stored, cut in pieces, and the pieces grow into mature plants. The myths and rituals emphasize the creative power of killing, dismembering, and violence. Rather than the central deities being a divine couple, as in grain agriculture, the central figure for tuber cultivators is often a male or female who is killed and dismembered resulting in natural and cultural products. Violent initiations, headhunting, and cannibalism are characteristic ritual activities.

Both types of agriculturalists practice what are termed *seasonal rituals*, which seek relationships among the rhythms of the divine realm, the human world, and the world of vegetation. *See also* hunting, religious aspects of; myth; ritual.

Agrippa of Nettesheim, Heinrich Cornelius (a-grip'-pah; 1486–1535), German Christian hermetist and scholar who argued both for a magical occult in-

terpretation of the world (*De occulta philosophia*, On Occult Philosophy) and for a skeptical view toward both the sciences and the occult (*De incertitudine et vanitate scientiarum et artium*, On the Uncertainty and Vanity of the Arts and Sciences) as compared to scripture.

Agudah Party, political branch of Agudat Yisrael (Heb., "union of Israel"), Orthodox movement to unite all Jews. Founded in 1912, it organized as an Israeli political party in 1948.

A.H. (Lat. *anno Hegirae,* "in the year of the Hijra"), Islamic dating system with the year one equivalent in the Christian system to A.D. 622, the date of Muhammad's flight from Mecca to Medina.

ahimsa (ah-him'suh; Skt., "noninjury," "not desiring to harm"), a fundamental moral quality valued in many Indian religions, including Hinduism, Buddhism, and Jainism. *Ahimsa* is often translated as "nonviolence," but is also a compassionate feeling toward others. Literally it is the state of not desiring harm toward others. This requires a high degree of self-control, and ahimsa has often been associated with religious renunciation in India. It is a central and enduring theme in the Jain tradition, a value commended to both ascetics and laity. Mahatma Gandhi (d. 1948) made it a key part of his religious and political program. *See also* Buddhism (thought and ethics); cow (Hinduism), veneration of; Gandhi, Mohandas Karamchand; Jainism; King, Martin Luther, Jr.; pacifism, Christian; satyagraha; vegetarianism; violence and religion.

Ahl al-Kitab. *See* People of the Book.

Ahl al-Sunna wal-Jamaa (ah'-l oos-soon'nuh wal-ja-ma'uh; Arab., "people of the [Islamic] practice and community"), a reference in traditional Sunni Islam to those who constituted the orthodox community of Islamic belief and practice. The term *jamaa* has more recently been used in compounds such as al-Jamaat al-Islamiyya to refer to Muslim reform groups. *See also* Sunni.

Ahmadiyya (ah-ma-dee'yuh; Arab.), a heterodox Islamic sect that emerged in the Indian Punjab at the end of the nineteenth century. Members are sometimes also called Qadiyanis after the place of the sect's origin in India, Qadiyan. Ahmadiyya beliefs and practices are based on the teachings of Mirza Ghulam Ahmad (ca. 1835–1908), who is believed by some of his followers to have been a prophet, and by the Lahore branch to have been a saint. Prophethood after the Prophet Muhammad is regarded as heresy by orthodox Muslims. Consequently, the Ahmadiyya became the object of many agitations in Pakistan, where most of them migrated after the partition of India in 1947. They were ultimately declared non-Muslims by the government of Pakistan in 1974 and more explicitly restricted in practicing and promulgating their beliefs in 1984. Since then, the Ahmadiyya in Pakistan have had to keep a low profile in worship and other religious activities, although they continue extensive missionary work in Africa, Asia, and the West.

Ahriman (ah'ree-mahn; Pahlavi, "Hostile Spirit"), in Zoroastrianism, the source of evil and leader of the demonic *daivas;* he will be defeated at end of time. *See also* daivas; Zoroastrianism.

Ahura Mazda (ah'hoo-reh maz'dah; Avestan title of unnamed Iranian high god, "Wise Lord" or "Lord Wisdom"), a proper name and object of worship by the sixth century B.C. both in the earliest stratum of Zoroastrian scriptures and in Achaemenid inscriptions. Ahura Mazda is celebrated as maintainer of cosmic law, creator of the world, and leader of forces of good. *See also* Zoroastrianism.

Ainu religion (i'noo, more properly ah-ee-noo; Ainu, "human"). The Ainu, traditionally hunter-gatherers, lived in Hokkaido, Sakhalin, the Kurile Islands, and, previously, the northern part of the main island of Japan. Ainu religion is centered around the notion of *kamui,* or gods, a term applied to a wide range of benevolent and malevolent beings. Religious lore is orally transmitted in a variety of epics (*yukar*). The Ainu cosmos is composed of a number of worlds paralleling the human world populated by different types of kamui. Men usually take a priestly and women a shamanic role in negotiating the relation of these worlds. The beings of the human world (including animals, birds, fish, plants, rivers, etc.) are held to be kamui visiting the human world in their respective disguises. The notion of the "visitor" is thus central to Ainu religion. In the Ainu bear festival (also found in other arctic and subarctic cultures), the bear (the kamui of the mountain and chief of the animals) is treated as an honored visitor and then killed to enable the bear to return to its own country, whence it will eventually return to be hunted and treated as an honored guest again. *See also*

bear ceremonialism; circumpolar religions; hunting, religious aspects of; kamui; shamanism.

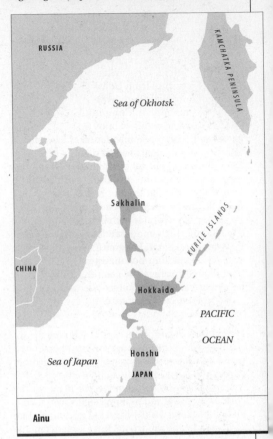

Ainu

Aion/Aeon (ay'on/ee'on), the personification of time in Greek mythology. Associated with Orphism, it is problematically identified with the lion-headed figure of Mithraism and designated in Gnosticism as obstructive ages separating the unredeemed soul from the "unknown God." *See also* aeon; Gnosticism; Mithraism.

Aisha (a'ee-shuh), the beloved younger wife of Muhammad in Medina. Aisha (d. ca. 678) was the daughter of Muhammad's close companion Abu Bakr, the first caliph. She survived the Prophet and became an advocate of keeping religious leadership in the family of the Prophet. She also was an important transmitter of traditions (*hadith*), about family life in particular.

Akali (uh-kahl'ee; Punjabi, "immortals"), a term in Sikhism that generally applies to anyone who is a devotee of God (*akal,* "the timeless one"). In particular, it refers to Sikh warriors in the eighteenth and nineteenth centuries noted for their bravery and to followers of a twentieth-century political party, the Akali Dal ("army of the followers of God").

The Akali movement took shape early in this century in the Punjab region of India as a militant group intent on seizing Sikh *gurdwaras* (houses of worship) from Udasis and other Hindus who controlled them. After the Shiromani Gurdwara Prabandhak Committee (SGPC) was created as a representative body over gurdwaras, the Akalis became a political faction within the SGPC. From the 1930s to the present the Akali Dal has been a political party in the state legislature, the only one proclaiming itself the guardian of Sikh interests. In the 1980s and 1990s, however, the Akalis became seriously divided over the degree to which they supported Sikh militancy. The moderate faction was led by Sant Harchand Singh Longowal, who was assassinated in 1985 after negotiating a compromise with Prime Minister Rajiv Gandhi. The radicals, fragmented among several factions, were briefly united in the late 1980s under the leadership of Simranjit Singh Mann. *See also* Sikhism.

Akal Purukh (uh-kahl' poo-rook'; Punjabi, "the Timeless Being"), the major Sikh designation for the divine, which emphasizes his unity and uniqueness. He is the transcendent creator who is also immanent in the creation, directing the world by his command, which expresses his justice and grace. *See also* Akali; Sikhism.

Akbar (the Great) (ak'bahr), Moghul Muslim emperor who ruled India from 1542 to 1605. He ascended to the throne at age fourteen. Akbar developed a strong interest in comparative religions, and he sponsored debates among scholars from India's many religious communities. He is portrayed as tolerant toward Hinduism; his chief consort was a Hindu Rajput princess, and he forbade the slaughter of cows, abated the poll tax (*jizya*) on non-Muslims, and gave high positions at court to Hindus. More controversial were Akbar's efforts to found a small and elite cult known as the *Din-i-Ilahi* ("divine religion") around his own person and his attempts to use his authority as ruler to change elements of Muslim belief and practice. *See also* Moghul Empire.

akedah (ah'kay-dah; Heb., "binding"), in the Hebrew Bible, the episode in Genesis 22 in which Abraham, in obedience to a divine command, prepares to sacrifice his son, Isaac. *See also* Abraham.

Akhenaton (ahk'en-ah'tuhn; Egypt., "he who acts effectively for the sun disk"), pharaoh of Egypt ca. 1350 to 1334 B.C., often called (erroneously) the first monotheist of recorded history. He first came to the throne as Amenhotep IV and worshiped traditional gods. However, after his fourth year, he elevated a minor deity, the Aton, i.e., the "disk of the sun" (a form of the sun god, Re), to the position of state god of Egypt and changed his name to Akhenaton to reflect his devotion to that deity. His pantheon consisted of a trinity that included the Aton, Akhenaton, and Nefertiti (also the name of his wife), which was the focus of popular worship. While Akhenaton was worshiped as the unique son of the Aton, Nefertiti was celebrated for her fertility. Common people were excluded from worshiping the Aton itself. Egyptians could worship only the royal couple; the couple in turn worshiped the sun disk. The new religion was maintained by Akhenaton's popular appeal as king, but it quickly passed away after his death. Akhenaton's motives in promulgating his beliefs were political and religious, since he elevated himself to the status of a god higher than customary for an Egyptian king. Akhenaton's religion recognized both Egyptians and foreigners as equal beneficiaries of the same god, and it overturned established conventions in Egyptian language and art. *See also* Egyptian religion; kingship, sacred.

akhlaq. *See* adab; Islam (ethics).

Akitu (ah-kee'too), the greatest festival in the religious calendar of Mesopotamia in the first millennium B.C., celebrated in association with the New Year in many major cities of Babylonia and Assyria. In the most influential of the Akitu festivals, in Babylon, the city and national god, Marduk, was carried in procession and enthroned in his temple, and the "creation epic" *Enuma elish* was recited. *See also* Enuma elish; Marduk; Mesopotamian religion; new year festivals.

Aksobhya (ahk-shoh-byah; Skt., "Imperturbable One"), a Buddha whose paradise is to the east. His name alludes to his vow as a Buddha-to-be (*bodhisattva*) never to become angry with any sentient being. Although sometimes the object of his own cult within the Mahayana, he generally is honored as part of a pantheon of five celestial Buddhas. *See also* Bodhisattvas; Buddhas.

Aladura, a mass religious movement that began among the Yoruba of Nigeria in the wake of the influenza epidemic of 1918 and 1919. Aladura (lit., "praying people") began within established churches under the leadership of charismatic individuals who had visionary experiences of angels or the Holy Spirit. Leaders prohibited all participation in traditional Yoruba rituals. The most important prophetic figures were Moses Orimolade and Christianah Abiodun, who founded the Cherubim and Seraphim Society, and Joseph Babalola, who founded the Diamond Society of the Faith Tabernacle Church. The Diamond Society eventually broke its affiliation with the Faith Tabernacle Church in the United States and established an affiliation with the British Apostolic Church, before becoming fully independent in 1939 as the Christ Apostolic Church. All of these churches share the belief that God answers all prayers and stress the importance of divine healing. Through dreams and visions direct revelations provide authority for most Aladura teachings and practices. Especially popular among clerks and artisans who had left rural areas for greater economic opportunities in the cities, Aladura churches remain a major force among the Christian Yoruba and have spread to other areas of southern Nigeria, Benin, and Ghana. *See also* Africa, new religions in.

Albertus Magnus (ca. 1193–1280), Christian Dominican theologian and saint, teacher of Thomas Aquinas (ca. 1225–74). He substituted Aristotle for Plato as the foundation of medieval science.

Albigensians, a twelfth- and thirteenth-century Christian movement in southern France that held the dualistic belief that a second god is the source of all evil in the world. Supported by leading noble families, Albigensians prevailed over Catholic Cistercian and Dominican preaching missions, which were eventually supplanted by the Albigensian Crusade (1208–18) conducted by northern French nobles, and, beginning in the 1230s, by the papal Inquisition. *See also* Catharism.

alchemy, a premodern science that employed chemical operations to convert base metals into gold and to greatly prolong life or even attain physical immortality. Alchemy has flourished in several traditional societies and has long been considered to have a spiritual component if not foundation.

Hinduism: Alchemy is considered a branch of Hindu Tantrism by which the human body becomes endowed with superhuman powers and longevity through the internal use of mercurial preparations combined with the practice of *hatha yoga* (a discipline of physical techniques to control the body). The golden age of Indian alchemy spanned the tenth to fourteenth centuries, after which certain of its techniques became incorporated into traditional Indian medicine.

According to alchemical theory, mercury, identified with the semen of the god Shiva, is compounded with sulphur, representing the uterine blood of the goddess Shakti, his consort, to produce an all-transmuting elixir. This chemical manifestation of the combined sexual essences of god and goddess is first applied to base metals, to transmute them into gold, as a sort of litmus test. It is thereafter applied to the alchemist's body, which through the power of these combined essences (manifested in chemical mercury and sulphur, and divine and yogic semen and blood) is itself transmuted into a body possessed of divine powers and longevity. *See also* Shiva; Tantrism (Buddhism); yoga.

Chinese Religion: Chinese alchemy represents the pursuit of personal spiritual perfection through a transformative process expressed in chemical terms. Though often considered "Taoist," Chinese alchemy originated independently of any form of Taoism and was seldom practiced by Taoists of any description before the late fourth century. Second-century texts like the *Chou i ts'an-t'ung ch'i* (Concordance of the Three According to the Book of Changes) were considered divine revelations that, when supplemented by proper oral instruction, permitted the manipulation of cosmic forces to achieve immortality. This manipulative process, symbolized as simple chemical interactions controlled by the adept, could be interpreted either as an inner process of spiritual refinement (through meditative visualization) or as an external, material process of compounding a potent "elixir" (*tan,* referring to cinnabar, not gold). Historical figures (including several emperors) who died after consuming such elixirs have often been viewed as victims of insidious superstitions. Doubtless, some failed to realize that it was the process, not the product, that was central and sought only to prolong their lives through magic potions. It is also true that many alchemists worked with medicines that had great healing properties. For those who pursued alchemy as self-cultivation, alchemy had a wholly different end. Rather than an effort to preserve one's physical life, alchemy was actually a method of transcending mortality and ascending to a higher plane of existence. *See also* fang-shih; hsien; tan.

Taoism: In Shang-ch'ing Taoism, the ultimate goal was ascent to perfection, defined as the transcendent state enjoyed by the perfected ones (Chin. *chen-jen*) who dwell in heavenly spheres. Alchemy was one practice employed to elevate an aspirant's spiritual state in hopes of such ascent. The manufacture of an elixir was perilous, for ingesting a formula prepared without adequate spiritual and ritual safeguards could result in death without the intended spiritual ascent. Hence few persons were admitted to the study of alchemy, and all alchemical undertakings were rigorously controlled by knowledgeable masters. However, anyone desiring to ascend to the heavens necessarily had to forgo life on the earthly plane, so the alchemical enterprise inherently involved physical death in the expectation that a perfected self, no longer subject to aging, would be reborn from the corpse. From around the eleventh century, Taoists generally abandoned all operative practices (*wai-tan*, "external alchemy") in favor of "inner alchemy" (*nei-tan*), the purely meditative pursuit of reunion with the Tao as expressed in chemical metaphors. *See also* Shang-ch'ing Taoism.

Western Religion: In the West, alchemy—a precursor of modern chemistry—can be traced back at least to Hellenistic times. Linked to other cognate disciples such as astrology and the Neoplatonic theory of correspondences, alchemy was part of the Hellenistic era's endeavor to make the cosmic humanly significant through correlations between the processes of nature and the spiritual quest. Alchemy in the Middle Ages and, for some modern scholars, especially in its Renaissance and early modern heyday, made the chemical quest for gold or longevity an allegory of the search for spiritual transformation. As scientific alchemy developed into chemistry, its spiritual wing became part of the background of Rosicrucianism and, eventually, of recent analytic psychology.

Alcoholics Anonymous, American group founded by recovering alcoholics in 1934 to help themselves through a Twelve Step fellowship program. Although it does not understand itself to be a religious organization, its spiritual practices borrow from religious traditions.

Alcuin (al'kwin; ca. 735–804), English Catholic scholar largely responsible for the Christian revival under Charlemagne (the Carolingian Renaissance).

Alexander the Great (356–323 B.C.), King of Macedonia from 336 B.C., Alexander the Great embarked on military campaigns conquering Persia and parts of Asia. *See also* Hellenism.

Alids (ah'lids), descendants of Ali ibn Abi Talib and Fatima, daughter of Muhammad (d. 632). The Prophet's two grandsons, Hasan and Husayn, and their descendants have played a unique role in the devotional and political life of Muslim society; they are addressed by the titles *Sayyid* ("master") and *Sharif* ("noble"). According to Shiite belief, the descendants of Ali and Fatima are the Prophet's viceregents (*caliphs*) and *imams* of the Muslim community. Their noble descent notwithstanding, Alids have had a mixed career, oscillating between high spiritual and political status and violent persecution. Some Alids were able to establish short-lived states.

Ali ibn Abi Talib (ah'lee ib'in ah-bee tah-leeb'; 600–661), the cousin and son-in-law of the Prophet Muhammad. Ali is regarded as the fourth caliph by Sunni Muslims but esteemed by Shiites as the first *imam*. He was ten to eleven years old when he embraced Islam, the first after Muhammad's wife Khadija to do so. During the night of Muhammad's emigration (Hijra) from Mecca to Medina in 622, Ali occupied the Prophet's bed, a ruse that allowed Muhammad to escape. Following this event, Ali joined the Prophet in Medina. Some months later, Ali married Muhammad's daughter Fatima; their two sons, Hasan, and especially Husayn, played important roles in the formative period of Islamic history. During the Prophet's lifetime, Ali participated in almost all expeditions that resulted from the conflict between the Prophet's community in Medina and his opponents in Mecca. Ali's bravery is legendary.

After Muhammad's death in 632, a dispute arose between Ali and other associates of the Prophet on the matter of succession. It was this dispute that divided the Muslims into two major factions. Those sympathetic to Ali's claim were known as the Shia or Shiites (partisans) of Ali and regard him as the first imam of Muslims; the Sunni, who accepted Abu Bakr, Umar, and Uthman as the first three caliphs placed Ali as fourth after Uthman's assassination in 656. At that moment, then, Ali inherited the consequences of events he could not avert, especially regarding the political and ethical implications of Uthman's murder. In the year 660, a member of the Kharijite sect, which had seceded from Ali's partisans, struck Ali down with a sword in the mosque of Kufa, Iraq. He died two days later and was buried at al-Najaf, some miles from Kufa. Ali's mausoleum at al-Najaf is an important site for Shiite pilgrimage and a center of Shiite scholarship.

Ali's stature as a distinguished judge, pious believer, and ardent warrior for Islam is virtually unanimous among Muslim biographers, historians, and jurists. Other estimations of him, such as the belief that, along with God and the Prophet, Ali is a pivot around which religious belief revolves, are rejected by Sunni Muslims. In the Shiite and Sufi hagiographic literature, where Ali's profoundly religious spirit is emphasized, he is raised to the status of *wali* ("friend") of God and is regarded as the saint in whom the divine light resided. The most moderate Shiite views about him are held by the sect known as the Twelvers (*Imamiyya*). *See also* Alids; imam; Ithna Ashari Shia; Shia.

Alinesitoue. *See* Africa, new religions in.

Allah (ahl'lah; Arab.,"God"). **1** The foremost name for the supreme being according to Islamic belief. **2** A term applied to God generally by Arabic-speaking peoples, be they Muslims, Jews, or Christians.

Allah in the Qur'an: Since its promulgation in seventh-century Arabia, Muslims have first looked to the Qur'an, the self-proclaiming word of Allah, for knowledge about him. Therein he is portrayed (in masculine gender) as the only true god, eternal sovereign lord of the universe, creator of heaven and earth who neither rests nor sleeps, source of life and death for creatures, merciful bringer of fortune and misfortune to all humans, the judge who will revive the dead on the day of resurrection to consign the righteous to paradise and wrongdoers to hell. He reveals himself to humans through occurrences in nature and through prophets who have conveyed his word through the ages. In opposition to orthodox Christian dogma and some forms of polytheism, Allah cannot be engendered, nor does he procreate; he creates by commanding things to be. Humans are called to worship and devote their faith only to him; hence he is the object of *islam* ("submission"). (See e.g., *suras* 1:2–4; 2:117, 164, 255; 13:16; 15:23; 24:34–46; 37:4–5; 40:62; 59:22–24; 64:1–4; 112:1–4.)

Allah in Islamic Speculative Theology and Mysticism: The establishment of an Arab Muslim state during the mid-seventh century in lands formerly under Byzantine and Persian rule presented an array of new challenges and opportunities for all Muslims. Discourse about God was not immune to these developments. Conflict over the leadership of the community led to debates about divine destiny and human free will, as well as the nature of good and evil. Conversion from and interaction with long-standing Christian, Jewish, and Persian communities obliged Muslims to systematically defend Allah's unity and the anthropomorphic representations of Allah in the Qur'an, as well as articulate the relation of the Qur'an as the word of Allah to Allah himself. During the ninth century, Muslim appropriation of Hellenistic learning entailed the penetration of Islamic theological disputation by Greek science and philosophy.

In the absence of a church organization and episcopal councils, Muslims advanced diverse theological formulations through the centuries. Among Sunni theologians, the median position on Allah (best defined by al-Ashari [d. 935] and his followers) maintains that Allah alone commands both good and evil; everything, including human acts, occurs by his will; his attributes (knowing, speaking, hearing, seeing, hands, face, etc.) are absolutely real and distinct from those of creatures; the Qur'an is his speech, which is an uncreated divine attribute. For Twelver Shia thinkers, however, Allah in his justice can only be the source of good; his attributes metaphorical; the Qur'an is his created speech. Both of these branches of Islam forbid depicting Allah in figural art.

Often using metaphors of purity and love, Sufis affirmed the spiritual bonds between Allah and creatures. These bonds were discovered through detachment from mundane concerns, followed by self-annihilation in Allah's presence. Alternate Sufi, Shii, and theosophic movements posited that the cosmos had emanated from Allah, which made divine incarnation among humans plausible.

Most Muslims acknowledge their belief in Allah, for example, by practicing the Five Pillars of Islam, daily recitation of the Qur'an, and inscribing his names in their homes and buildings. Many carry one of his ninety-nine "beautiful names" as their own by affixing it to the Arabic word for "servant of" (e.g., Abd Allah, Abd al-Nasir, Abd al-Jabbar).

Allah Akbar (ahl'lah ahk'bahr; Arab.,"God is most great"), Islamic exclamation. Called the *takbir*, this phrase is uttered frequently in formal prayer and on many other occasions, including calls to defense of the Muslims, as an expression of approval at gatherings, and as a potent funeral litany.

allegory (Gk.,"to speak other"), a way of reading texts in which the surface ("literal" or "plain") sense is seen as a code concealing a deeper meaning. *See also* exegesis.

All-Father, a supernatural being, formerly the subject of widespread belief in southeast Australia, who acts as father to all persons. Human in form, he is credited with a leading role in shaping the world and in originating aboriginal laws, initiation ceremonies, and arts of life. From his home in the sky, where he lived with a wife or wives and children, he would visit the Aborigines when young men were initiated. He taught remarkable powers to magicians. Christian influences on this figure have been suggested, but there seems no reason to deny the native authenticity of the All-Father belief and cult. *See also* myth.

All-Mother, type of earth goddess celebrated in the cults and myths of northern Australia, who acts as mother to all persons. An important creator figure, she is associated with major ceremonies, especially those of the Kunapipi type, in which she is said to swallow and regurgitate novices, a process suggestive of symbolic death and rebirth. The All-Mother is commonly represented as having the form of a giant snake within whom almost all life was once contained. When so depicted she is often identified with rainbows and rainbow snakes, and hence with both the destructive and the rejuvenative forces of nature. *See also* myth; rainbow snake.

All Saints' Day, a Christian feast now celebrated in the West on November 1, commemorating all those who reside in heaven. The feast seems to have started in Rome in the eighth century. *See also* calendar (Christian); dead, rituals with respect to the.

All Souls' Day, in Roman Catholicism the day to pray for the deceased. Since the tenth century it has been observed on November 2. In some countries it is also called the Day of the Dead. *See also* calendar (Christian); dead, rituals with respect to the.

almanac (China), a state calendar, issued by the imperial government since ancient times, containing important information concerning political, social, economic, and ritual matters. Many unofficial almanacs were also circulated among the people and are still published today, appearing four to six weeks before the lunar New Year. Modern almanacs contain day-by-day descriptions of recommended actions, moral stories for edification, advice concerning diet and health,

A Zapotec-speaking woman in Oaxaca, Mexico, wearing a mesh mask representing the returning spirits of the dead at the Feast of the Dead (October 31–November 2). Originally a pre-Conquest November festival for the remembrance of the dead, the native Day of the Dead has been assimilated to the Catholic All Souls' Day as a time for the joyous reunion with dead members of one's family, who are attracted to the occasion by the smell of food and flowers. The local Catholic authorities have rejected the festival, closing the churches and refusing to participate in the rituals.

lists of talismans, prognostications by means of hand and face analysis, and predictions for the coming year according to the cycle of twelve animals. *See also* calendar (China); state cult, Chinese.

almsgiving, the gift of money or other donations to the poor. Almsgiving is an obligatory feature of many religious traditions, in some serving also as a means of support for religious orders whose members have undertaken vows of voluntary poverty. *See also* tithing.

Islam: A major goal of the Qur'an is the establishment of an ethical social order in this world, a viable and just society in which individuals meet their obligations for the good of the larger community. Greed and economic exploitation are to be opposed and distributive justice must be sought for the public welfare. This aim underlies the quranic injunction for every economically self-sufficient adult Muslim to pay obligatory alms (Arab. *Zakat*), which are assessed annually on all personal wealth above a set minimum. In addition, the Qur'an urges believers to donate voluntary alms to the community, and this charity, known as *sadaqa* ("to tell the truth"), is believed to confirm the truthfulness of the giver's religious conviction. Though Muslims have debated whether it is better to give these alms openly or in secret, all agree that proper motives and good intent are requisite if alms are to be useful for the expiation of a donor's previous transgressions.

By far the most valuable institution for Muslim charity has been the *waqf* ("pious endowment"). Waqf literally means the "prevention" of a thing from becoming another's property, and the term came to designate real estate, agricultural lands, and occasionally agricultural produce and livestock whose revenues are to be applied in perpetuity to religious and public works including the building and maintenance of mosques, shrines, schools, hospitals, and water projects. The waqf is legally exempt from taxation and state seizure, although both have occurred in fact. The founder of the waqf may appoint a paid administrator for the endowment or administer it himself but, over time, substantial endowments are usually acquired and administered by important religious or state officials who use the waqf and its revenues to enhance their personal power and prestige. Yet, despite such abuses, the waqf system remained for centuries the major contributor to Muslim religious and public welfare.

Beginning in the nineteenth century, Muslim charitable institutions witnessed two major changes. First, most Islamic states annulled many previous pious endowments or confiscated their lands, centralizing their administration under state control and curtailing the economic power and independence of the religious establishment. Secondly, a number of private charitable societies have been formed to collect and distribute contributions for religious and social causes, such as missionary activities, teaching the Qur'an, providing vocational training, and supporting neighborhood health clinics. *See also* Five Pillars; mendicancy (Islam); Zakat.

Buddhism: Although Buddhism has always affirmed support of the destitute as a commendable thing, the alms it emphasizes are the donations made to members of the Buddhist

Young novice monks in the Theravada Buddhist tradition collecting alms, chiefly food, in Mandalay, Myanmar (Burma) (1980).

monastic community. Indeed, the Sanskrit words for Buddhist "monk" and "nun" (*bhiksu, bhiksuni*) simply mean "beggar" and reflect material dependence upon the laity.

Traditionally in India, and still today in such places as Thailand and Myanmar (Burma), Buddhist monks go out on their begging rounds every morning. With serious demeanor, they silently stop at the homes of laypersons who fill their bowls with food, which is then consumed upon their return to the monastery. On occasion, other needed items (robes, supplies, money) are donated to the monks.

Though monks may be "beggars," they are held in very high esteem, and the custom of giving alms to them is one of the fundamental expressions of the Buddhist practice of giving. This not only provides material support and sustenance to the community, it also gives laity an opportunity to make merit. As a result of their almsgiving, Buddhist laypersons can hope to better their situation in this or a future lifetime. At the same time, their offerings are more than gestures of generosity; they are also cultic acts of reverence, expressing devotion and respect.

The almsfood given by Buddhists to monks is called *pinda*, a word that, in India, traditionally referred to the lumps of rice that were offered to the spirits of one's dead ancestors. To a certain extent, then, the giving of alms to monks (who have abandoned their families) may be seen as a Buddhist reformulation of the practice of making offerings to the dead. Certainly later, in both Indian and Chinese Buddhism, the feeding of monks was recognized as one way of transferring food to the neglected spirits of hungry ghosts.

On the other hand, the giving of alms may be more broadly symbolic of the giving up of oneself. As an act of selflessness it has the spiritual aim of lessening one's attachment to the world, something that is often emphasized in Buddhist legends about great almsgivers whose generosity toward the monastic orders is presented as paradigmatic. These model laymen include such figures as the Buddha in many of his past lives (especially in his life as Prince Vessantara); Anathapindada (an early lay follower of the Buddha whose very name reflects his munificence); and the emperor Ashoka (who is said on several occasions to have made offerings to the monas-tic community of his entire kingdom, his wives, his son, and his own person). On a more mundane level, other stories magnify the importance of seemingly insignificant gifts made by poor people who give all they have. *See also* Ashoka; devotion (Buddhism); merit; Vessantara.

alpha and omega, the first and last letters of the Greek alphabet, used in Christianity to signify that Christ is the beginning and end of all things (Revelation 1:8).

alphabet mysticism, assignment of secret qualities to the shape of letters or to their numerical equivalents. The latter, known in Greek and Hebrew as *gematria*, maintains that words with the same numerological value are, therefore, equivalent. *See also* exegesis; gematria.

altar (Lat., "a high place"). 1 A place, especially a raised platform, where sacrifices or offerings are made to an ancestor or a god. 2 A table or stand used for sacred purposes in a place of worship. *See also* sacrifice.

Christianity: In early Christianity, the altar was a movable wooden table on which the Eucharist was celebrated; it became, after the fourth century, a stone encasement for relics. Medieval

Korean shaman's altar displaying offerings of fruit and a side of beef, in Seoul. In Korea, the shaman (*mudang*) is usually a woman, skilled in relations with the ancestral dead.

Christians distinguished the "high altar" of the liturgy from the "lesser altars" dedicated to individual saints. Protestants, favoring wood construction, relocated the eucharistic altar closer to the congregation. *See also* Christianity (art and architecture); Eucharist, Christian.

altered states of consciousness, mental states different from ordinary consciousness. Such states are generally perceived as the result of some intervention, either self-induced or attributed to divine agency. *See also* dreams; hallucinogens; meditation; mysticism; possession; psychedelic substances; psychoactive plants; religious experience; trance.

Alvar (ahl'vahr; Tamil, "one who is deeply immersed"), name given to twelve South Indian Hindu poet-saints who lived between the seventh and ninth centuries and composed devotional hymns in Tamil expressing their devotion to the lord Vishnu. The eleven men and one woman are considered to be paradigmatic devotees by the Shrivaishnava community, although some of them were from low castes. The Alvars sing about the many incarnations of Vishnu but focus on his manifestations in the many temples of South India. The songs of the Alvars were organized in the eleventh century in a text called the *Nalayira Divya Prabandham* (The Sacred Collect of Four Thousand Verses). Selections are recited daily in Shrivaishnava temples and homes and the entire collection is recited in annual cycles. The Alvars, especially the woman saint Antal, are enshrined in Shrivaishnava temples and venerated by the community. *See also* Bhagavata Purana; path of devotion; Shrivaishnavism; Vaishnavism.

A.M. (Lat. *anno mundi,* "in the year of the world"), Jewish dating system with the year one equivalent to the traditional date for creation, 3760 B.C. in the Christian system.

Amagahara. *See* Takamagahara.

Amana Society, American Christian communitarian society, founded in Germany in 1714 and incorporated in the United States in 1859. Also known as the Community of True Inspiration, it became a private enterprise corporation in 1932 and is best known for the manufacture of electrical appliances.

amaNazaretha Baptist Church. *See* Africa, new religions in.

Amaterasu (ah-mah-teh-rah-*soo;* Jap., "heaven-illuminator"; also Amaterasu Omikami, oh-mee-kah-mee; "heaven-illuminating great deity"), the central deity in Shinto, associated with the sun and considered the progenitrix of the imperial line. *See also* cosmogony; cosmology; Ise Shrine; Japanese myth; Ryobu Shinto; Shingon shu; Shinto; Susano-o.

Ambedkar, Bhimrao Ramji (uhm-bayd'kahr, bim-rah'oh rahm'jee; 1891–1956), writer and politician who founded a major Buddhist reform movement, the Buddhist Society of India. Born an untouchable in the Indian state of Maharashtra and educated in India and abroad, Ambedkar campaigned aggressively for laws that would ban the practice of untouchability during the years that led to the independence of India in 1947. Attracted to the ideal of Buddhism as a rational, humane, and egalitarian tradition, near the end of his life he and many of his followers converted to Buddhism. *See also* caste; Reform Hinduism.

Ambrose (am'brohz; ca. 339–397), bishop of Milan, Italy, one of the four Doctors (along with Jerome, Augustine, and Gregory the Great) of Roman Catholic theological tradition.

A famous preacher, liturgist, and defender of orthodoxy, Ambrose played a key role in relating Greek to Latin Christian thought. He is best known for his role in the conversion of Augustine (386).

AME Church. *See* African Methodist Episcopal Church.

amen (Heb., "so be it"), an emphatic statement of religious affirmation in the Bible. In Jewish and Christian traditions, it is a frequent ending to formulaic prayers.

America, Hinduism in. More than 95 percent of approximately 650,000 Hindus in the United States are Asian Indians admitted after revision of immigration law in 1965. Immigrant lay leaders are quickly forming an American Hinduism, just as earlier immigrants created American Catholicism, Judaism, and Protestantism.

Home Shrines and Temples: Home shrines containing images of deities and saints provide focus for daily rituals, as important to Hinduism as temple worship. Independent Brahmans (members of the priestly class) in most metropolitan areas go to homes for family life-cycle rituals (Skt. *samskaras*)—"baby showers," marriages, thread ceremonies, funerals, and death anniversary ceremonies—and auspicious bless-

A sacrificial fire at the Hindu temple in Ashland, Massachusetts, dedicated to the goddess Shri-Lakshmi, who is associated with wealth and good fortune. Clarified butter (ghee) is being offered.

ing rituals (*satya narayan pujas*) for special occasions. Priests from some larger temples also provide these rituals for set fees.

Almost fifty major Hindu temples have been constructed since 1975 and many others installed in smaller buildings and houses. Most contain several families of deities generally not found in the same temple in India. South Indian temples, with elaborately sculpted towers and Brahman priests recruited from South India, provide a full range of daily, seasonal, and life-cycle rituals. The Tirumala Tirupati Devasthanam and the Andhra Pradesh State Government provide financial and architectural assistance. The Venkateshvara Temple in Penn Hills near Pittsburgh (dedicated in 1976) is the oldest, most active, and wealthiest. North Indian temples have different constellations of images and are often founded and maintained by *gurus* (spiritual leaders) or *sadhus* (ascetics) who have proprietary interest. Temple representatives have failed in attempts to establish a national Hindu temple board.

Sectarian Groups: Groups affiliated with specific institutions (*sampradaya*) in India have national organizations and local affiliates in many metropolitan areas. Swaminarayan Hinduism of Gujarat is the most successful regional/linguistic group. Beginning in 1972 with twenty-nine individuals, it now has over forty thousand followers in two branches, seven temples, sites for three more, and over fifty centers for weekly meetings. Other groups, such as Swadhya Samaj and Manu Seva Mandal, actively serve Gujaratis, who form approximately 40 percent of Asian Indians in America. The constituency of the Arya Samaj is primarily North Indian Hindi and Punjabi and meets in several temples. Bengalis gather for the annual Durga Puja. The Chinmaya West Mission has many centers, regular publications, annual tours by its leaders, and Hindu heritage summer camps for children. Satya Sai Baba is a small but active group. The Vishwa Hindu Parishad promotes Hindu unity and cooperation among these sects and temples.

Small, intimate, primary groups meet in homes, rented halls, or Indian cultural centers to study sacred texts such as the *Bhagavad Gita* or to sing sacred songs (*bhajans*) in regional languages. Sunday schools for children meet under several auspices in most metropolitan areas, teaching Hindu religion, Sanskrit chanting, Indian culture, and regional languages.

Hinduism in America is created and administered by people who are not religious specialists. Indeed, it is difficult to recruit and gain permanent resident status for appropriately trained specialists for Hindu institutions. Few religious specialists are permanent residents, but many gurus, lecturers, and musicians tour

America every summer, encouraging Asian Indians to remain faithful to their Hindu heritage, gathering support for programs in the United States and India and advising individuals and institutions.

Small bell-metal statues of the deities being washed with water from India prior to the installation of their larger stone images (in background), carved in India, at the dedication ritual of the Shri-Lakshmi temple in Ashland, Massachusetts, May 1990.

Missionary Hinduism: Missionary Hinduism refers to attempts as diverse as those by the Vedanta Society and by the International Society of Krishna Consciousness (ISKCON) to attract followers who have no ethnic ties to India.

Swami Vivekananda (1863–1902) presented Vedanta philosophy to the Parliament of World Religions at the Chicago World's Fair in 1893, attracting a following. After World War II, some prominent immigrants from Britain—Aldous Huxley, Gerald Heard, and Christopher Isherwood—reinvigorated the Vedanta Society. Centers in several metropolitan areas and a rural ashram in Michigan propagate Vedanta philosophy.

Abhay Charan De (1896–1977) arrived in New York in 1965 to teach devotion to Krishna and founded ISKCON, popularly known as the Hare Krishna movement. He attracted young Americans to Krishna devotion, established urban temples, vegetarian restaurants, and several rural communes. The most prominent is New Vrindaban in West Virginia (recently expelled from the movement). After his death, a group of gurus from among his American followers assumed leadership, each with responsi-

bility for a geographical area. Division, litigation, expulsions, and scandal have reduced the core membership to below two thousand and stifled new initiations. ISKCON attracts some Asian-Indian Hindus to their temples and festivals, with the result that American converts of the late 1960s and 1970s now serve as religious specialists for a predominantly Asian-Indian clientele. *See also* North America, new religions in; Vedanta Society; Vivekananda.

American Indian, outdated name for the indigenous peoples of North America. *Native American* is the preferred term.

Americanism, an American Catholic reform movement begun in 1887 by progressive clerics to adapt Catholicism to the political freedoms of American culture. Influenced by the nationalist expansionism of the 1890s and hoping to reform European Catholicism on an American model, the Americanists internationalized through contacts in France, Germany, and Italy. Conservative opposition in France led to Pope Leo XIII's censure, in the apostolic letter *Testem Benevolentiae* (1899), of a set of theological opinions under the general rubric of Americanism. Scholars still debate whether Americanist reformers held the censured opinions.

American Muslim Mission, an outgrowth of the Nation of Islam led by Wallace D. Muhammad (b. 1933). Interracial and affiliated with Sunni Islam, it promotes cooperative enterprise. *See also* African Americans (North America), new religions among; Muhammad, Wallace D.; World Community of Islam.

Amesha Spentas (ah-may'shah spen'taz; Avestan, "Holy/Bounteous Immortals"), instrumental divinities of the Zoroastrian god Ahura Mazda. There are usually thought to be six, each represented by a physical element. *See also* Ahura Mazda; Zoroastrianism.

am haaretz (ahm hah-ah'rets; Heb., "people of the land," "inhabitants"). 1 In the Bible, various Israelite and non-Israelite groups, especially the Judeans not exiled to Babylonia, who opposed the religious reforms of the returnees Ezra and Nehemiah. 2 In rabbinic texts, Jews ignorant of rabbinic rules and traditions. 3 In later Jewish usage, an ignoramus or commoner.

amidah (ah-mee-dah'; Heb., "[the prayer said while] standing"), one of two central rubrics to statutory daily worship in Judaism, known properly as *haTefillah* ("*the* prayer [par excellence]"); it is a series of blessings, primarily petitionary and largely messianic. *See also* Judaism, prayer and liturgy of.

amir (a-meer'; Arab.,"prince"), local ruler over an Islamic territory; often in compound titles, such as the designation "Prince of Believers" for the caliph.

Amish, collective name for a number of Christian Anabaptist groups that originated in the 1590s in a split led by Jacob Amman from Swiss Mennonites over disciplinary issues, while continuing to adhere to pacifism, adult baptism, and other Anabaptist tenets. A century later, Amish began to emigrate to southeastern Pennsylvania and then spread westward to Ohio, Indiana, and other Midwestern states. Of the several extant Amish groups, the best known are the Old Order Amish, who dress in Reformation-era fashion and eschew modern technology and secondary education.

The Amish in America have generated a number of significant court cases, involving the right to separate education and the distinctive Amish practice of shunning delinquents, that have helped define First Amendment protections of religion. *See also* Anabaptists.

Amitabha (ah-mee-tah'bah; Skt.,"Immeasurable Light"), a Buddha who is represented in Mahayana Buddhism as presiding over a paradise in the western part of the universe.

As the Buddha-to-be (*bodhisattva*) Dharmakara, Amitabha made a series of vows to create a paradise of unmatched magnificence for those who depended on him completely for salvation and expressed their trust by the invocation of his name (*Namo Amitabha Buddhaya,* "Homage to the Buddha Amitabha"). Amitabha appears to those who trust in him in a beatific vision at the moment of death. Those who are reborn in Amitabha's "Pure Land" are able to listen to his teachings until they themselves attain enlightenment.

Although Amitabha was acknowledged as a Buddha in India and Central Asia, a distinct movement devoted to him was established in China only around the sixth century. "Pure Land" Buddhism, as this movement is known, is one of the most popular forms of Buddhism in East Asia. *See also* Bodhisattvas; Buddhas; Mahayana; Pure Land.

Amitayus (ah-mee-tah'yuhs; Skt.,"Immeasurable Life"), an alternate name for the Buddha Amitabha. *See also* Amitabha; Buddhas.

Amoghasiddhi (ah-moh-gah-sid'dee; Skt.,"Unfailingly Successful"), one of the five celestial Buddhas; his paradise is represented in Mahayana Buddhism as being to the north. He apparently did not have an independent cult. *See also* Bodhisattvas; Buddhas; Mahayana.

Amoghavajra (ah-mohg-ah-vahj'rah; Chin. *Pu-k'ung*), Indian Tantric master who arrived in China in the eighth century to lead the Buddhist esoteric school. *See also* China, Buddhism in; Esoteric Buddhism in China.

Amritsar (uhm-rit'sahr), the sacred city of the Sikhs in the Indian state of Punjab, founded in 1577 by Guru Ram Das. The "Golden Temple" and the headquarters of the Akali Dal are located there. *See also* Akali; Golden Temple; Sikhism.

amulet, or talisman, an object, either natural or of human manufacture, believed to possess power when worn or carried by a person, attached to an individual's possessions, or placed in an area where its influence is desired. Some scholars distinguish an amulet as conferring protective power from a talisman as conferring beneficial power, but the terms are usually employed interchangeably. Both *amulet* and *talisman* refer to the object and should be distinguished from *charm*, which refers to a verbal formula, often employed to empower an amulet, although popular usage has extended the term charm to include the object. A further complication is introduced by the fact that a large class of amulets consists of written texts, and it is the wearing or display of these texts that confers power rather than their recitation. *See also* charm; phylactery.

Chinese Religion: Amulets and talismans (Chin. *fu, fulu*) are used in Taoism and folk practices primarily for healing and protection, especially the protection of young children. They may be stamped with a seal or written out by hand on paper with the appropriate color ink by a Taoist priest or other professional. Most talismans display divinatory diagrams and a highly stylized script understood to be heavenly writing. Talismans are usually burned and the ashes ingested or scattered, but they may also be worn on one's person or mounted on a wall. *See also* Chinese popular religion.

Japanese Religion: Amulets and talismans are obtained at most Shinto shrines and Buddhist temples (also at centers for new religions) for blessing or protection. *Ofuda* (Jap., "talismans," "amulets"); *omamori* ("protectors," "amulets"), and *ema* ("picture horses," "votive tablets") are made of wood, paper, cloth, metal, or plastic and feature the name (and/or picture) of a *kami* (divinity, divine presence) or Buddha and often a written formula or Buddhist scriptural passage. They are deposited at a shrine or temple, kept on or about the person, or placed in the home or in a vehicle (or a ship). A large variety of amulets play a major role in the practice of Japanese religion; the most popular amulets today are for traffic safety, academic success, and protection of the family. *See also* Japanese folk religion.

Anabaptists (Gk., "to baptize again"), the generic name for a variety of radical sixteenth-century Protestant groups who insisted on adult baptism and on the strict separation of church and state. Many Anabaptist groups were pacifist as well. They were often condemned by both Catholic and Protestant authorities, and although they began in Europe, many Anabaptist sects fled and formed communities in the United States. *See also* Amish; Hutterites; Mennonites; Protestantism.

Anahita (ah-nah-hee'tah; Avestan, "immaculate"), title that became name of Iranian goddess of water and royalty; her cult is attested among later Achaemenids (fifth–fourth centuries B.C.). *See also* Iranian religions.

Analects. *See* Lun Yu.

ananda (ah'nuhn-duh; Skt., "bliss"), in monistic, contemplative, and devotional Hinduism, the state of unconditioned union of the self with the Godhead. *See also* Hinduism (mysticism); path of devotion; satchidananda.

Ananda (ah'nuhn-duh; fl. sixth century B.C.), cousin, disciple, and personal attendant of the Buddha. Known for his devotion, his exceptional memory, and his support of women disciples, Ananda was called upon to recite all the Buddha's sermons and played a leading role in the formation of the Buddhist community after the Buddha's death. *See also* Gautama.

Ananda Marga (ah'nan-dah mar-ga; Skt., "Path of Bliss"), a yoga society founded in India by Prabhat Ranjan Sarkar in 1955, which teaches a path to *ananda* ("bliss") through initiation, yoga, and meditation. The close-knit organization also has promoted social and economic reform. Controversial in India, it has nonetheless established numerous centers around the world.

Anandamayi Ma (ah'nuhn-dah-mah'yee mah; Bengali, "the mother filled with bliss"), a title applied to the Bengali Hindu holy woman Nirmala Sundari Devi (1896–1982). Attracting a wide following to her religious centers at Dakka and Dehradun, she demonstrated the presence of the divine in feminine form through mystical experiences granted her disciples. *See also* Hinduism (mysticism).

anaphora (ah-naf'oh-rah; Gk., "a lifting up," "an offering"), the solemn eucharistic prayer of the Christian Orthodox and Catholic liturgies. The prayer begins with an opening dialogue between priest and congregation and ends with words of praise (a doxology) and a solemn "Amen." The general shape of the anaphora took form in the mid-third century. *See also* Eucharist, Christian.

Anat (an'at), one of three principal goddesses of ancient Ugaritic mythology. Sister and consort of Baal, she was renowned for pugnacity and sexuality. *See also* Baal; Canaanite religion; Ugarit.

anathema (ah-nath'ey-mah). 1 In the New Testament, a Greek term referring to a curse. 2 In Catholicism, a declaratory condemnation directed by Church authority against those who are deemed immoral, heretical, or blasphemous. *See also* blasphemy.

ancestors. 1 The spirits of the deceased to whom one can pray for help, and whom one is obligated to honor or to appease. Their favor is powerfully beneficent and their disfavor equally maleficent. In many African, Asian, and Native American religions as well as in the traditional religion of China there is a cult of ancestors, a Chinese form of which survives in the Confucian concept of honoring one's ancestors. In Celtic religion in the autumn, on *Samhain*—the pre-Christian Halloween—the spirits of the dead were honored and set at peace lest they cause trouble for the living. In ancient Mesopotamia, Egypt, and Israel as well as in Greece and Rome, the ancestors were revered but not invoked as causative powers. *See also* afterlife; ancestral rites. 2 In some traditions (for example, Australian Aborigines), term for powerful divine beings whose activities shaped the present world. *See also* Australian and Pacific traditional religions; Changing Woman; Dreaming, the.

ancestor worship, an inappropriate term for ancestral rites. *See also* ancestors; ancestral rites.

ancestral rites, rituals that unite the living and

the deceased members of a family into a single community by means of attention to the prestigious dead, the ancestors. *See also* ancestors; Cumina religion; dead, rituals with respect to the; domestic ritual; Garifuna religion; ritual.

Hinduism: Despite widespread regional and textual variations, there is general uniformity in funeral traditions throughout Hindu India and Nepal. Textual bases for ancestor rituals (Skt. *shraddhas*) derive from the Vedic period, particularly the *Shrauta Sutras* and *Grihya Sutras* compiled in the last half of the first millennium B.C. The later Dharmashastras, Puranas, and medieval manuals expanded upon Vedic ritual patterns, accommodating late Vedic doctrines of *karma* (meritorious and demeritorious actions) and rebirth. Rites are concerned with disposal of the body, creation of an ancestor (*pitar*, lit., "Father") from the disembodied spirit (*preta*), and nurturance of that ancestor toward eventual promotion from otherworldly realms into another rebirth. Funerary specialists appointed guardians of *mantras* (sacred utterances) and rituals have traditionally been Brahmans, members of the highest social class, the priestly class, although non-Brahman ritualists practicing variations on the ancient models are known throughout the subcontinent. The oldest living son of the deceased is usually chief mourner and performer of the funeral. As such, he then becomes a performer of ancestral rites in general.

Funerals—Disposal of the Body: The funeral is a sacrifice, literally the "final offering" (*antyeshti*) of the body abandoned by the remainder spirit. Cremation on a pyre of logs a few hours after death is considered standard for adult corpses. Soon afterward bone fragments are collected for later deposition in a sacred river. Earth burial or deposition in a river is generally practiced for those who do not become normal ancestors—children, some ascetics, those who commit suicide, and certain others who die untimely deaths. For a few large communities, particularly among non-Brahmans in South India, burial is the preferred ritual for all.

Creation of an Ancestor: A ten-day period following cremation, symbolic of the ten lunar months of human gestation, is devoted to ritual construction of a temporary intermediate body for the disembodied spirit. On the tenth day—the only day of rituals in some abbreviated versions—a ball of cooked rice (*pinda*) signifies full assembly of this subtle body. Such creation eliminates both the preta's vulnerability and its potential danger to the survivors. In this period of impurity (*ashaucha*) for the family, household rituals and hospitality are suspended. Regional practices include hanging a water pot that drips slowly either onto a basket of earth sprouting nine different food grains or onto ground at the base of a pipal tree inhabited by the preta; wrapping a triangular stone in a piece of the funeral shroud; tying a piece of the shroud or its substitute around the chief mourner's neck. On the eleventh day a set of sixteen shraddhas serves in modern times to satisfy a requirement of one year of rituals up to the death anniversary. The twelfth day includes the dramatic *sapindikarana* ritual of joining the newly created ancestor with those of preceding generations, accomplished by blending a cooked-rice ball for the deceased with three that represent his father, grandfather, and great-grandfather.

Nurturing the Ancestors: Once ritually promoted to ancestorhood, the deceased is a temporary deity resident in the lowest of three cosmic levels (earth, midspace, heaven), with the two preceding generations located hierarchically above. This set of three pitars requires routine offerings of food, water, and mantras, for which they are invited in a variety of rituals. In turn, pitars provide wealth, prosperity, and long life for their descendants. Beyond are the remote ancestors, already in progress toward rebirth and no longer directly attached to the living. In the past, stricter rituals required a daily offering to the pitars (one of the five *mahayajnas*), a monthly shraddha on new-moon day, a death-anniversary shraddha (*samvatsarika*), shraddhas known as *mahalaya* during the dark half of the lunar month of Bhadrapada (September-October), and shraddhas during the mid-January solstice, Sankranti. In modern times only the most dedicated Brahmans perform all monthly shraddhas, but the three annual events are still widely observed by all four *varnas* (classes in the caste system). As well as the standard paternal triad of pitars, a maternal lineage may also be recognized, either in the three wives of the paternal line or through a mother's paternal ancestors. As in ancient times, it is believed that ancestors come to the place of shraddha to eat food prepared for them by entering into Brahmans invited by the sacrificer. Cooked rice, sesame seeds, ghee, barley, and water are the basic substances offered with mantras; uncooked grains are offered by Shudras (the lowest class) without mantras. Invited Brahmans representing the gods, Soma and Agni in particular, are also fed. Fear of impurity prevented most Brahmans from accepting food for the dead, resulting in categories of degraded Brahmans employed for corpse bearing, shraddha feasts, and other ill-omened tasks such as removal of the influence of malevolent planets. *See also* caste; devayana/pitriyana; Hindu domestic ritual; Hinduism (worship); sacrifice.

Chinese Religion: Identity formation in Chinese society has traditionally involved learning to recognize the fabric of familial relationships that bind one both to the living and the dead. Deceased members of a family or clan have been understood as meaningful participants in the drama of the living and therefore as worthy of remembrance and veneration. Filial piety (Chin. *hsiao*) has required the living to provide for the needs of the ancestors according to principles of reciprocity and ritually to commune with them. Property inheritance creates a special obligation. While one's own ancestral spirits have been viewed as primarily beneficent, if neglected or offended they may act punitively.

Early Evidence: Inscriptions on oracle bones and bronze sacrificial vessels from the earliest historical period, that of the Shang kingdom (ca. 1766–1122 B.C.), show that ancestral spirits were petitioned for blessings, guidance, and intercession with more powerful deities and Shang-ti, the supreme "Ruler on High," who may have been the first Shang ancestor. In the following Chou period (ca. 1122–221 B.C.), ancestral temples were established by the royal family and the nobility. Ritual feasts for important ancestors were held at times determined by divination. A complex theory of the human soul was developed in relation to the dichotomy between *yin* and *yang,* the two primordial forces of the universe. The human being came to be viewed as composed of a gross material, or yin, energy called *p'o* and a subtle spiritual, or yang, energy called *hun.* At death, the material aspect was believed to return to the earth while the ethereal aspect ascended to the celestial realm as a deified spirit, or *shen.* If not properly interred and provided for through sacrificial offerings, a person's yin soul might be encountered as a malevolent ghost, or *kuei.* Restless and malevolent spirits must be appropriately placated, repelled, or exorcised.

Domestic and Lineage Rites: Elaborate funeral rites, which involve family mourning garments, ritual wailing, and a ceremonial procession to an auspiciously situated gravesite selected by geomancy (*feng-shui*), have been prescribed by ancient tradition. Six or seven years later, the corpse is often disinterred and the cleaned bones reburied in a ceramic pot. Tombs must be well maintained by family members and are the locus of periodic sacrifices offered throughout the year, especially during the important Ch'ing ming (Clear and Bright) festival. The hun, or

yang, soul is provided a wooden spirit tablet (*shen-chu*) as a seat of residence. It is inscribed with the deceased's name and enshrined on a home altar or that of a clan's ancestral temple. In the home, normally for several generations after an ancestor's death, daily food offerings and incense are presented on the altar and occasional reports made concerning significant family developments. If a family is a member of a clan sufficiently prosperous to maintain an ancestral temple, the spirit tablets of the lineage are displayed together where, periodically, solemn rituals in veneration of the ancestors are performed, reinforcing clan solidarity. *See also* Chinese popular religion; Chinese religions (festal cycle); Chinese rites controversy; Ch'ing ming; Chou religion; geomancy; hsiao; kuei; Shang religion; Shang-ti; shen-chu; yin and yang.

Japanese Religion: Ancestor veneration is the principal religious activity of the family, performed to some degree by nearly every Japanese. Regarded as the foundation of morality, it is central to the teachings of many religious groups. The rites are largely Buddhist, but involve Confucian and folk motifs. Two patterns exist: rites for recently deceased individuals and those for the collective, more remote dead. The former are performed before the Buddhist altar in the home (Jap. *butsudan*) or in a Buddhist temple on certain anniversaries of the death, ideally extending for thirty-three or forty-nine years. The latter include Obon, the summer visit by the dead to the village and home, and grave visiting during the two equinoxes, all three of which are national holidays. In addition, daily rites are often performed before the home altar and major family events are announced to the ancestors there. *See also* Japanese folk religion; Japanese religion; Japanese religions (festal cycle).

Korean Religion: A common religious practice throughout East Asia, the veneration of clan and family ancestral spirits has permeated Korean society at all levels and is ritually manipulated by Confucianism, Buddhism, shamanism, and more recently, Christianity. In all its forms it is the ritual basis for Korean clan and family solidarity and the minimum standard of ethical behavior. At the local and national level Korean ancestral veneration has broadly included the semiannual rites to Confucius and his Chinese and Korean disciples (Kor. *sokchon*) offered at the Shrine to Culture on the grounds of the National Academy in Seoul, South Korea; the worship of Tan'gun, the mythical founder of Korea's first kingdom and guardian spirit of the Korean people, the worship of Kija, founder of another ancient kingdom and teacher of Chinese civilization; the devotion offered to royal ancestors by each ruling house on the peninsula; and the memorial and feasting rites offered to the teachers and founders of Buddhist, Confucian, and other religious lineages. In modern times it includes government-sponsored memorial rites for military victims of the Korean War and worship at the government shrine to General Yi Sun-sin (1545–1611), a defender of the peninsula during the period of Japanese invasions and a model of absolute loyalty to civil authority.

In its most common form, Korean ancestral veneration was and still is carried out through use of the Confucianized ritual feasting with the souls of the dead (*chesa*) either at the graveside or at a shrine set up for this purpose. This ritual feasting is normally performed on the death anniversary successively for three years. Thereafter, a smaller version or memory rite (*kije*) is performed twice a year at the time of the New Year (Sindan) and the Harvest Festival (Ch'usok). At such times family members gather at the gravesite or clan shrine, clean the site, and then make a food offering before a spirit tablet or, in more recent times, a photograph of the departed. Before the table of offerings a small incense burner is placed and incense and cups of wine are offered by the male members of the worshiping group. The order of the rite, whether large or small, usually involves an invocation and welcoming of the spirits of the dead, a series of prostrations and wine libations, an acknowledgment that the spirits have feasted well and that all merits and blessings of the worshiping group are due to their graciousness, and the consumption of food by those present.

In Korean Buddhist variants of ancestral rites Buddhist clerics read prayers and scriptural passages for the final liberation of the dead in other realms. Water, candles, incense, and strips of paper on which are written prayers may be placed on a temple altar before a photograph or spirit tablet, behind which is the urn or box containing the ashes of the deceased. Buddhist memorial rites for the dead may be commissioned as needed (on anniversaries of birth and death) or commissioned yearly at the time of the Festival of All Souls. Buddhist memorial rites for lineage personalities (teachers, patriarchs, former abbots and abbesses) are usually held daily or yearly at a shrine within the monastery compound or at a reliquary site.

Korean shamanistic rituals for the dead (*ogugut, nokkut,* and *paridegigut*) manipulate and send forth the spirits of the recent dead, helping them turn into ancestors and establishing them in a paradisiacal afterlife.

Finally, Korean Christian rituals for ancestral spirits, reinterpreted as a memorial rite, tend either to follow the traditional Confucian feasting rituals or Western forms of memorial masses and prayer services conducted at a church.

anchorite. *See* hermit.

ancient Near Eastern religions. *See* Mesopotamian religion.

androcentrism, a persistent pattern in religion and other cultural formations of focusing on the male to the deliberate exclusion or subordination of the female. *See also* feminism; patriarchal.

androgyny, having both male and female characteristics in either mythic or ritual contexts. 1 The mythic tradition that originally both sexes were found in the same being and subsequently separated. 2 Androgynous deities found in religious representations and mythic texts, usually as part of a symbolism of totality. 3 Bisexuality or asexuality often held as an ideal in ritual activities, as expressive of a state of transcendence over mundane categories. *See also* Ardhanarishvara; Caitanya; gender and religion; Indo-European religion; myth; sexuality and religion.

angel (Gk. *angelos,* "messenger"), a superhuman being who serves as an intermediary between the divine and human realm. The term is appropriately applied in those Western religious traditions that place great emphasis on divine transcendence (Christianity, Gnosticism, Islam, Judaism), but potentially misleading when used to translate classes of intermediaries in other traditions.

Christianity: In the Bible angels are mentioned frequently either as messengers or as those in heaven who praise God. In the Christian tradition Dionysius the Areopagite's *Celestial Hierarchy* (sixth century) categorizes angels into three triads based on a harmonization of selected biblical texts: Seraphim, Cherubim, and Thrones; Dominations, Virtues, and Powers; Principalities, archangels, and angels. Only the latter triad acts as intermediaries on earth. Medieval and postmedieval theologians speculate at length about the nature of angels, their powers, and their duties, but the most immediate impact of the Dionysian categories is on popular religion, religious iconography, symbolism (e.g., Dante's heaven is divided into nine angelic spheres), and devotionalism.

The Christian tradition views the rebellious

Anglicanism

angels as damned and servants of Lucifer (Lat., "Light bearer"), the Lord of the damned. *See also* archangels (Judaism and Christianity); cherub/cherubim; demon; Fallen Angels; Gabriel; Lucifer.

Islam: The Qur'an refers frequently to angels, beings described as perfect in their obedience to God. Among their functions is constant and unceasing praise of the Lord. Several of the angels are acknowledged as having special responsibilities. Chief among them is Gabriel, who mediated the message of God to the Prophet Muhammad in the Arabic language (some Muslims say the angel Michael shared in this) and accompanied him on his night journey (Arab. *miraj*) to the celestial realms.

In this tradition death itself is portrayed as the angel Israil who takes the souls from the dying bodies, and the fearsome angels Munkar and Nakir are believed to question the dead in the grave concerning matters of faith. Another angelic figure, Israfil will sound the trumpet at the Last Judgment (Yawn al-Akhina).

Every individual is said to have a personal angel who witnesses and records what has been said and done each day. The results of this recording will determine one's future state in the hereafter, revealed on the judgment day. The quranic suggestions that angels are winged creatures has inspired fantastic descriptions in terms of size and number of wings in some of the traditional writings.

Several issues in relation to the nature and being of angels are left unclarified in the Qur'an. Some traditions suggest that they are created of light, while others classify them with lower extrahuman creatures (*jinn*) that the Qur'an identifies as created from fire. Muslim scholars differ as to whether the angels are capable of sin. *See also* Gabriel; Iblis; jinn.

Anglicanism, a form of Christianity that has been shaped in the British Isles, particularly England. Anglicans are those Christians throughout the world who gather liturgically according to some authorized edition of *The Book of Common Prayer*, whose religious ideas and practices owe a deference and loyalty to the Church of England and the leadership of the archbishop of Canterbury. Although influenced by the sixteenth-century Reformation on the European continent, Anglicanism is a distinctive tradition of Christianity.

Anglican Beginnings: The roots of Anglicanism lie in the Romano-British Christianity of ancient Britain as well as in the Catholic Christianity of Ireland, Scotland, and Brittany. Certain influences from the Orthodox East intermingled with these existent traditions after the Council of Whitby (644), which struggled with the question of whether the allegiance of English Christianity should be Roman or remain under the direction of the monasteries of Celtic Christianity. Pope Gregory had sent Augustine of Canterbury to England in 597 to establish the Roman presence and coordinate Christian practice. Whitby decided in favor of Rome.

However, the history of the Church of England offers constant testimony to the devotional style and intellectual freedom of Celtic Christianity. For almost a century after Whitby the English Church developed its native leadership, held regular councils of clergy, and generated innovative scholarly and cultural ideals. The work of Alcuin of York (ca. 735–804) and the Venerable Bede (ca. 673–735) is representative of this early period. To it must be added the missionary endeavors of such figures as Boniface (680–754) and Willibrord (658–739) to Germany and Frisia.

The coming of the Normans in the eleventh century brought extensive building of new stone churches and the establishment of Benedictine abbeys. During the later Middle Ages, the bishop became a feudal baron and ecclesiastical courts acquired separate status. Thus were sown the seeds of potential conflict between church and state that ultimately led to the murder in 1170 of Thomas a Becket, archbishop of Canterbury, whose struggle with Henry II centered on the question of where the power of the Church court ended and that of the royal court began. Throughout the thirteenth and fourteenth centuries, the papacy asserted its control over English church life, arousing the anger of people whose spiritual values had been shaped by a history of independence, a sense of national pride, and a devotional life ill at ease with restrictive systems.

The Church of England: Out of this larger context of the Catholic Church in England, the Church of England emerges in the sixteenth century during the reign of Henry VIII. The English Reformation begins with a declaration of independence from papal control, the first step of a struggle to determine whether Catholic Christianity could survive in a national setting without papal allegiance. The story of that struggle is the distinctive history of Anglicanism.

The first phase of the struggle is characterized by the conflict of the English Catholic spirit with the forces of continental Reformation. These protestantizing influences existed in counterpoint to the repeated resurgence of the loyalist efforts of those hoping to reassert papal authority. This phase ends with what is called the Elizabethan Settlement. Queen Elizabeth I

(1533–1603) opposed the protestantizing forces of the Puritans and sought to manage a national Christianity that could permit diversity of doctrinal interpretation while maintaining a common liturgical life through the use of *The Book of Common Prayer.*

Although the Puritan revolution sought to put an end to Anglican claims to continuity with the undivided Church of the first six centuries, the restoration of Charles II in 1660 revealed that Anglicanism had survived. Richard Hooker's *Laws of Ecclesiastical Polity* (1594) had established an Anglican basis of authority that sought to steer a course between the *sola scriptura* (Lat., "scripture alone") of Protestantism and the magisterial authority of the papal Church.

In the seventeenth century the so-called Caroline Divines developed Anglicanism into a tradition of great spiritual and poetic power, with the emergence of what has been called the High Church movement. The poets John Donne (1572–1631) and George Herbert (1593–1633) are important figures in this tradition.

In the eighteenth century, an evangelical movement emerged, emphasizing divine judgment and the vocation of preaching in order to encourage conversion experience. During the early nineteenth century the Oxford or Tractarian Movement restored the earlier High Church emphasis upon apostolic succession.

The Principles of Anglicanism: Anglicanism is a Christian tradition that emphasizes the importance of common liturgical life as the context for prayer and for theological activity. The Catholic substance of Christianity is preserved in the liturgy, which permits freedom of theological interpretation. Anglicanism emphasizes the implications of the Christian doctrine of the Incarnation. The fact of God's embodiment in Jesus Christ invests the entire created order with the sacramental power to show forth the glory of God. Anglicanism has fostered a positive attitude toward the power of human reason. Reason is the mind of God at work among humans. Therefore in the human sciences as well as in theology, there is no absolute discontinuity between the divine and the human. Anglicanism has always been distinguished by a love of learning and a concern for bridging the apparent gaps between theology and other intellectual enterprises. *See also* Alcuin; Augustine of Canterbury; Becket, Thomas a; Bede, Venerable; Boniface; Book of Common Prayer; Celtic church; High Church, Low Church; Hooker, Richard; Oxford Movement; Protestantism; Separatist; Thirty-nine Articles; Westminster Abbey.

An Hyang. *See* An Yu.

aniconic, lacking images. *See also* iconoclasm; images, veneration of.

animals and birds in Japanese religions. Traditional Japanese religion, particularly its folk stratum, tends to see virtually all natural objects as having life and all life as having human faculties of consciousness, will, and reason. Thus communication is possible with trees, mountains, birds, and animals. All (especially white birds and animals) are at least potentially sacred and thus have powers that can be important to the well-being of humans. Approached with reverence, they may be benevolent; if not, they may cause harm; in either case, they may be enshrined and accorded formal cultic treatment. The bird form is a favorite of celestial *kami* (divinities, divine presences) and souls of the dead. There are many folktales in which swans or cranes become divine wives of men. The crow and pheasant are important in myth as messengers of the kami. The phoenix, of Chinese origin, is an auspicious sign of long life and good fortune. Among animals, the fox and badger are often seen as malevolent creatures who entice humans to their doom or as tricksters, while the monkey, although often comical, is usually depicted as being wise in relation to foolish and greedy humans. The dragon, who lives beneath the sea or in pools, is generally associated with good fortune, while its close relative the snake is more often malevolent, associated with unbridled sexual energy. The horse is often honored at Shinto shrines, perhaps as the steed or messenger of the kami. Among fish, the carp is associated with strength and valor desirable in boys, and the catfish is thought to cause earthquakes from its underground home. *See also* Inari shrine; Japanese folk religion; kami; tanuki.

animal worship, an obsolete term for the belief, rooted in an evolutionary theory of religion, that people reverenced animals as deities. Animal worship according to this theory is a very early (primitive) stage in the development of religion and is often associated with totemism. We now know that animal worship and totemism are products of the scholars' imagination. Animals play a significant part in many religions. Their significance in a religion is dependent upon the relationship the animal has with other parts of the religious system, and is not due to some inherent quality. *See also* origin of religion; totem.

animism (Lat. *anima,* "soul"), an obsolete term employed to describe belief systems of traditional peoples that appear to hold that natural phenomena have spirits or souls. Introduced in

1871 by the British anthropologist E. B. Tylor (1832–1917), it should be used with caution as a cross-cultural term of comparison or as designating a stage in the evolution of religion. *See also* origin of religion; religion, anthropology of; soul.

ankh (angk), a cross with a looped top (also known as *crux ansata*). **1** In Egyptian iconography, a symbol of life-giving power in representations of deities or kings. **2** An occult amulet believed to confer protective power when worn by an individual.

Annen (ah-nin; ca. 841–889), a Japanese Tendai Buddhist monk who systematized the Tendai position on Tantric Buddhism. He wrote major works on the Tendai position on various exoteric themes including the Buddhist precepts, the realization of Buddhahood with this very body (*sokushin jobutsu*), and the realization of Buddhahood by grasses and trees. *See also* sokushin jobutsu; Tantrism (Buddhism); Tendai school.

annulments (Christianity), marital, judicial declarations of the nonvalidity of the marriage contract. Such declarations are distinguished from decrees of divorce. A marital annulment says, in effect, that a true marriage did not take place. A divorce, by contrast, dissolves the bond of a legitimate marriage.

In the Christian tradition such annulments are granted after church weddings by the Catholic, Orthodox, and Anglican churches through legal procedures specific to each tradition. Roman Catholic polity recognizes Church annulments but not divorce. Annulments may be granted for a spectrum of reasons: for example, if one party was forced into the marriage (lack of consent); prior impotence; some form of fraud (bigamy); or lack of informed consent due to mental illness or youth or psychological immaturity. *See also* marriage.

annunciation. **1** In the New Testament (Luke 1:26–38), the visit of the angel Gabriel to Mary announcing that she would become the mother of Jesus. **2** A feast day celebrated on March 25, commemorating the annunciation.

anointed in the Spirit, a Christian notion based on 2 Corinthians 1:21–22, "[God] has put his seal upon us and given us his Spirit in our hearts as a guarantee." This passage has been interpreted as referring to the believer's being "anointed in the Spirit," i.e., the condition whereby God confirms the believer and his or her relationship

to Christ and "seals" it with his own guarantee. By extension this anointing is understood as equipping the believer to understand the faith and to live the Christian life. *See also* confirmation.

anointing, ritual consecration through the application of vegetable or animal oil. *See also* chrism; Messiah; ritual.

anointing of the sick, Christian rite marking a sick person with blessed oil combined with prayers for the restoration of health. This rite is considered a sacrament in both the Roman Catholic Church, which no longer uses the term *extreme unction*, and the Orthodox Church, where it is called *euchelaion*. *See also* anointing; Christianity (life cycle); healing.

Anselm (1033–1109), British Christian Benedictine monk and saint. One of the earliest Scholastic thinkers, Anselm is best known for his version of the ontological proof and for developing a satisfaction theory of Christ's atonement, where recompense is owed God, as the injured party, by humans, as the offenders due to sin, and Christ serves as the payment, through his death. *See also* ontological argument.

antediluvian/postdiluvian, pertaining to the widespread mythic motif dividing history into two stages, preflood and postflood. *See also* flood stories.

Anthony (ca. 250–355), Egyptian Christian saint traditionally understood as the first monk.

anthropogony, a myth of the origin of human beings, as different from cosmogony, a myth of the origin of the world. *See also* myth.

anthropomorphism (an'throh-poh-mor'fiz-uhm; Gk. *anthropos,* "mankind" and *morphe,* "form"), the ascription of human characteristics to referents of religious language, especially those culturally postulated superhuman agents that are represented (in different forms and with varying degrees of centrality) in the conceptual schemes of various religions. Theologians frequently employed the term pejoratively, the idea being that a proper description of the characteristics of a deity would be more metaphysical and less metaphorical. This bias against anthropomorphic language and imagery has influenced scientific and philosophical discourse about religious referents. As a consequence, all three of these traditions of inquiry (the theological, scientific, and philosophical) regard anthropomorphic language and imagery as an inferior form of concrete conceptualization that fails to achieve an appropriate level of abstraction.

Such pejorative views occur not only in scientific, theological, and philosophical descriptions of religious imagery but also in everyday religious views about other, different religious conceptual schemes. One religion's anthropomorphism is another religion's abstraction.

Anthropomorphic language and imagery is sometimes regarded by both critics and apologists of religious thought as an important symbolic rather than literal interpretation of religious referents.

Terms such as *anthropomorphism* are not theoretical terms at all and are, therefore, incapable of either interpreting or explaining religious thought and action. Such pseudotheoretical concepts presuppose the very language and imagery for which they are supposedly accounting. For example, one can't argue that God has a human (or animal or mineral or vegetable) form until some theoretical semantic sense has been given both to the term *God* and to the acquisition of such forms.

Religious systems come as wholes. They are systems capable of being interpreted and explained by coherent and testable theories. If, for example, one argues that terms such as God refer to culturally postulated superhuman agents that are only one aspect of a complex and well-ordered conceptual scheme, then terms such as anthropomorphism are neither necessary nor sufficient to either describe or explicate the symbolic-cultural systems in which such agents play a role. The syntactic and semantic roles, whether anthropomorphic or not, that the term plays in a religious system are what is important, not what properties, such as humanlike characteristics, the agent is believed to have. *See also* Greek religion; Judaism, God in; religious language; Shekhina; symbol.

Anthroposophical Society, a group founded in 1912 and centered on the teachings of Rudolf Steiner (1861–1925), a former head of the German section of the Theosophical Society. Departing from what he saw as increasingly Eastern and speculative tendencies, Steiner retained such fundamental features of Theosophy as emphasis on the inner spiritual components of reality and the importance of cosmic spiritual evolution. He also stressed close coordination with scientific thought and the need to express spiritual vision through such media as agriculture, education, and the arts.

Although the Anthroposophical Society usu-ally presents only lectures and discussions, it is closely linked to a religious group, the Christian Community, which offers eucharistic and other worship aligned with anthroposophical concepts. Society members also are involved in a variety of activities based on Steiner's teachings, such as organic farming, herbal and homeopathic medicine, eurhythmic dance and exercise, and the well-regarded Steiner or Waldorf schools. Though not numerically large, the movement has had influence and is found throughout the world, especially in Europe and English-speaking nations. *See also* Steiner, Rudolf; Theosophy.

Antichrist, the final opponent of Christ in the end-time. Occurring throughout Christian literature, the Antichrist, who performed evil under the cloak of sanctity, is an impersonator of Christ. He is frequently identified with wicked popes, or rulers who persecuted the Church. *See also* eschatology

antinomianism. 1 The belief that a particular religious allegiance frees one from obedience to any secular law. 2 The belief that secular laws are evil and ought to be deliberately broken as a sign of one's religious stature. *See also* Frankists; Gnosticism.

anti-Semitism, antagonism to Jews and to Judaism, which can range from a set of attitudes to a formal doctrine and from mild antipathy to active efforts to kill Jews. The term itself was first used in 1880 by the German writer Wilhelm Marr to distinguish modern European secular antipathy to Jews from hostility to the Jewish religion. In recent usage, the term has come to denote hatred of Jews and Judaism in all forms.

Religious Anti-Semitism: Anti-Semitism as a phenomenon and an ideology presupposes the theological and historical enmity between Judaism and Christianity. Christianity emerged from Judaism, and early Christian writers needed to distinguish the new religion from its predecessor. For example, in the New Testament, the apostle Paul, one of the earliest Christian writers, draws a sharp contrast between the two religions, "If righteousness comes through Torah, then Christ died for nothing" (Galatians 2:21). Early Christian literature, from the New Testament through the writings of the church fathers, continued to develop the theme of Christianity's separation from, and superiority over, Judaism. Some Christian writers, particularly Melito of Sardis (d. 180) and John Chrysostom (347–407), extended arguments against Judaism to condemnations of the Jews themselves, including the charges of rejecting the Messiah and of deicide. When, with the conversion of the emperor Constantine in 321, Christianity became the official religion of the Roman Empire, the anti-Judaic myth of early Christian writing took on long-term political consequences for the Jews, who became a politically disenfranchised and socially stigmatized group.

The position of the Jews in European polity and in cultural imagination worsened almost steadily after Constantine's conversion to Christianity. Decrees of Theodosius (439), Justinian (531), two Lateran Councils (1179, 1215), and of the Council of Montpelier (1195) gradually deprived Jews of their rights and compelled them to wear special badges and clothing. From the thirteenth to the sixteenth centuries Jewish life in central and western Europe was largely ghettoized, and Jews were regarded as the quintessential aliens in Christian society. In a range of locations, they were unjustly accused of a variety of heinous crimes.

In the nineteenth century, the Enlightenment and its quest for a neutral and secular society allowed the Jews to enter European society and polity, but even secular preceptions of the Jews reflected long-standing Christian attitudes. Many Enlightenment thinkers, for example, Diderot and Voltaire, published attacks on Jews, and other intellectuals hoped and expected that Jews emancipated from the ghettos would assimilate to the mainstream culture. Jews' emergence in general society made them more visible and led to an increased awareness of them. The emergence of so-called scientific racism in the nineteenth century led to a different, non-Christian and nonreligious kind of hatred of the Jews, one grounded in ethnic and racial theories. This racial anti-Semitism became a foundation of the Nazi state and led directly to the murder of millions of Jews in the Holocaust.

Political Anti-Semitism: In the years before World War I, political anti-Semitism entered the campaign appeals of right-wing political parties; it appeared in the demonstrations and pronouncements of students seeking to limit the number of Jews in universities and in the actions of governments, most notably those of the Tsarist empire, to curtail access to jobs, housing, and education. The Dreyfus Affair is the most dramatic example. In 1894, the false accusation of treason against Alfred Dreyfus, an army officer, led to a split that colored French politics for more than a generation. Political anti-Semitism opposed the Jews as one element in a strategy defending the various social and political groups. Declining rural economies raised the vulnerability of those in direct economic competition with Jews, especially the traders and merchants in small towns and cities. Others, particularly peasants in western and central Europe, contrasted their increasing poverty with the mobility and prosperity of the Jews. In Wilhelmine Germany and Austria, competition among the newly formed political parties increased the number, intensity, and visibility of political claims against the Jews. In the years before World War I, political anti-Semitism was an important theme in the development of modern European states.

In the interwar years, the severity of political attacks on Jews increased. Governments in Poland and Hungary passed legislation sharply curtailing the ability of Jews to obtain jobs, access to markets, and entry into the universities. The Soviet governments destroyed the institutions of the Jewish communities under its rule, while providing economic and educational opportunities for Jews. In Germany, Hitler led the National Socialist German Workers Party to power in 1933. During the first six years of rule, the Nazis destroyed the bases of Jewish life in Germany, and a majority of the German Jews fled. In 1939, the Nazis began World War II, which culminated in the destruction of European Jewry.

Anti-Semitism and Anti-Zionism: The defeat of the Nazis and the creation of the State of Israel transformed manifestations of anti-Semitism. The social sciences reject all racial theories. The pluralist societies and democracies of the United States and Canada have been particularly hospitable to Jews and their communities. In the former Soviet Union and eastern Europe, however, anti-Semitic policies remain in place, leading to a large migration of Jews to the United States and Israel. Soon after the creation of Israel, Arab governments adopted anti-Semitic policies, occasioning a mass emigration of Jews. Most fled to Israel. A significant portion of the Jews of North Africa went to France. Political anti-Semitism has surfaced at the United Nations, particularly in the effort to equate Zionism and racism, and in other attempts to delegitimate Israel. Anti-Semitism now appears in the form of attacks on Israel and Zionism. *See also* Holocaust, religious responses to the.

An Yu (ahn yoo; 1243–1306), also An Hyang, a Korean Confucian scholar of the late Koryo period (918–1392) who rose to prominence for his attempts to revivify public Confucian education on a national level after the period of the Ch'oe military rule (1170–1258). An was the disciple of Yu Kyong, a civil official who assassinated the last of the military governors. He devoted much of his early career to reestablishing the National Academy and creating a treasury for public education from contributions from the throne and court officials. In 1287 An Yu accompanied King Ch'ungnyol (r. 1274–1308) to the Yuan capital at Tatu (Peking), where he became acquainted with the works of the Neo-Confucian scholar Chu Hsi (1130–1200). After his return to Korea he studied and taught these Neo-Confucian texts privately. In 1298 he again traveled to China and purchased books with funds from the treasury he had helped to establish. He spent the rest of his life promoting the cause of Confucian education. He was put in charge of the Koryo Shrine to Culture (Kor. *Munmyo*), Korea's national shrine to Confucius, housed at the National Academy, and six years after his death his spirit tablet was placed in that same shrine.

Later Choson-period Neo-Confucian sources portray An Yu as an opponent of Korean Ch'an Buddhism (Son Pulgyo), a Buddhist development that had been fostered by the military rulers of the time and a movement that the Neo-Confucianism of the orthodox Ch'eng-Chu school had singled out for attack. With the growth of Neo-Confucian orthodoxy in the Choson period, reverence for the work of An Yu as an early Neo-Confucian educator grew and a royal charter was bestowed on the Soso Sowon, a private academy that had been established specifically for the worship of An Yu's spirit. *See also* Ch'eng-Chu school; Shrine to Culture.

Aphrahat (af'rah-hat; early fourth century), Syrian Christian monk whose writings are the earliest preserved from the Iranian Syriac church. He is best known for his twenty-three *Homilies* on biblical texts. *See also* Syria, Christianity in.

Apocalypse of John. *See* Revelation, Book of.

apocalypticism (Gk. *apokalypsis*, "uncovering" or "revelation"). **1** Social movements emphasizing the evilness of the present age and the imminent coming of a new age of righteousness. *See also* ages of the world; eschatology; millenarianism. **2** In Judaism, when Antiochus IV (175–164 B.C.) launched his persecution of Jews faithful to the Law, a new apocalyptic theology argued that people suffer because the present age is under the control of evil powers. This explanation built on older elements of Israel's prophetic movement, which looked forward to a coming new age, and ancient mythologies, which portrayed a cosmic struggle between God and the powers of Chaos. There may also be influence from Persian religion, which posited an ultimate dualism

as twin gods, one good, one evil, struggle for control. *See also* dualism; Zoroastrianism.

Apocrypha (uh-pahk'ref-uh; Gk., "hidden"), a collection of books or chapters of books not included in the canonical Hebrew Bible as transmitted in Judaism, but part of various Christian versions of the Old Testament. The majority of these books are of Jewish composition (third century B.C.–A.D. first century). Roman Catholic Bibles print twelve apocryphal books as part of their Old Testament and add three more as an appendix; Greek Orthodox Bibles contain fifteen apocryphal books, with one additional book as an appendix; Russian Orthodox Bibles contain seventeen apocryphal books. Each of these Christian traditions accepts the authority of the apocryphal books, at times distinguishing between the protocanon ("first canon") of the Hebrew Bible and the deuterocanon ("second canon") of the Apocrypha. Protestantism rejects their authority; hence Protestant Bibles either omit the Apocrypha or print it as a separate section, most commonly between the canonical Old and New Testaments.

In addition to the set of books designated the Apocrypha, there are a large number of Jewish and Christian works (third century B.C.–A.D. sixth century) that rewrite portions of the Hebrew Bible, resemble biblical texts, or are attributed to figures in the Hebrew Bible. These are designated pseudepigrapha ("writings with false attributions") While rarely forming a part of any canon (a few are found in the Ethiopian Christian Old Testament), they have been important in both Jewish and Christian traditions. *See also* canon; Hebrew Bible; pseudepigrapha.

Christianity: The term *Christian Apocrypha* is used by biblical scholars to designate non-canonical Christian writings that, for the most part, purport to contain information about Jesus and other prominent first-century Christian leaders. All of the major New Testament genres, Gospels, Acts, Letters, and Apocalypses are represented. Although fragments of early tradition may be found in texts such as the Coptic *Gospel of Thomas* or the Greek *Gospel of Peter*, the primary value of these writings lies in providing information about the beliefs and practices of movements in early Christianity. They also contribute insight into the history of the formation of the biblical canon. *See also* canon; New Testament.

Buddhism: The Chinese Buddhist Apocrypha consist of indigenous texts self-consciously modeled on Indian canonical works in order to be accepted as authentic scripture. *See also* Awakening of Faith; China, Buddhism in.

RELIGIONS OF ANTIQUITY

"A ntiquity" in this article denotes those religions that either preceded Christianity in the areas of its major expansion or were supplanted by it. It does not designate a simple chronological division. Neither Paleolithic religions nor the early religions of Asia (for example, Indus Valley culture) find a place within antiquity's domain. What is understood as "the ancient world" or "the classics" is hedged about with strictly patrolled borders, and those who understand themselves as carriers and caretakers of the Western tradition look back to "antiquity" with a sense of ownership. This is so because the tradition functions as a venerable ancestor whose memory and continued presence need to be awesomely secured, above all with respect to religious, aesthetic, and moral values. But "ownership" of the ancient world is hardly possible anymore, and that world's hallowed status is no longer taken for granted.

Even less certain are the borders of that world: in this volume religions of antiquity include many religions that are dead and that do not belong in clearly defined categories. Thus we find here the expected Greeks and Romans, but also peoples of the ancient Near East; then we turn northeast, making a swing to Inner Asia, then westward to the ancient Finns and Vikings. To be sure, inclusivity creates its own problems, but at least these problems are different from the old, exclusivist ideals. "Whose" antiquity is invoked now? It is no longer that of the educated gentleman mourned earlier, but antiquity may not "belong" to anyone else, either. The question of ownership simply ought to be dropped, and we should rather ask why the religions of antiquity are worth studying.

The answer is (and this holds, of course, for all religions): because such study is an exercise in the confrontation of the alien with the familiar. One's own religion always seems "familiar," its stranger features often willfully hidden, consciously or not. When traditional Western scholars and gentlemen felt they "owned" antiquity (in its exclusivist sense), their claim rested on the consoling, though facile, conviction that the "classical age" was somehow familiar, understandable, desirable, and highly worthy of emulation. When they cared to examine features of antiquity less amenable to essentially nineteenth-century European values, they were repelled and declared these features to be intrusive, decadent, and uncivilized. It would be in bad taste to dismiss them as "pagan," for the classical authors *were* pagan, but pagans of the right kind, loftier, equivalent to the "noble savage."

Some present-day scholars often note how the old, unquestioned habit of making the proponents of the classical age "like us" has swung to its opposite extreme; now, hands thrown up in bewilderment, specialists revel in the strangeness of the ancients. But this too can mark an abdication. What is strange needs examination, not openmouthed awe or tight-lipped repulsion, and the familiar ought to be put under disciplined scrutiny in order to be made odd. Constructing two columns listing items "strange" and "not strange" in religions of antiquity would not take us very far, for the real life of such items, their contexts, would be lost. Instead, a variety of examples from the religions of antiquity (as understood in this dictionary) and a few selected, loosely contextualized topics simultaneously odd and familiar will be presented. Humor, death, and magic are sometimes connected, sometimes not, but the attempt will be made to place them within frameworks of power. "Power" here means forces manipulated for good or for evil, depending on who is wielding force, when, and under what conditions.

ESCAPES

In the medieval English poem *Sir Gawain and the Green Knight* laughter is presented in ways both expected and unsettling. Sir Gawain, nephew of King Arthur and a knight at his table, volunteers to cut off the head of the gigantic, mysterious Green Knight, who suddenly shows up at the King's party and laughingly demands to be beheaded. As the still living Green Knight rides off, his own head in hand, Sir Gawain and King Arthur both laugh at the spectacle. Beneath their merriment, however, they are anything but amused, for in accordance with the code of chivalry, Sir Gawain has promised to do battle with the Green Knight at a future date, and the beheading in the King's palace has been a grisly sight. But King Arthur's own peculiar rule is to blame: he will not eat at his own party before some joke, story, or spectacle has been performed. Now he has obtained more than he asked for. The two laughing men are covering up their own fear, publicly feigning amusement, but in reality they are humiliated (especially the King) and frightened at the battle awaiting Sir Gawain.

When the Green Knight, at the beginning, laughs in derision and challenge, he has the power. The two others laugh in order to hide that they have lost theirs: they have been upstaged but cannot show it. For them, to laugh is an attempt to level the situation, to minimize the reality of competition and imbalance of power. Before Sir Gawain goes off to his confrontation, King Arthur laughs when Sir Gawain comes for the Christmas party (he feigns cheerfulness in order to quell his knowledge of what is in store for the young knight), and the King's court pretends merriment, "joylessly joking for that gentle knight's sake."

Later, at the estate of the Green Knight, he and Sir Gawain laugh together as they seal their bargain: each will give to the other what he has gained hunting during the day. Sir Gawain is at a disadvantage; he hunts nothing but is himself hunted daily by the Green Knight's wife, who tries to seduce him. Against heavy odds, he keeps his virtue and dutifully gives to the Green Knight the kisses he,

Sir Gawain, has obtained from the other's wife. The Green Knight, in turn, displays his catch, animals symbolizing worldly and fleshly entrapment. As long as Sir Gawain does not give in sexually to his host's wife, the two men continue the game and simultaneously defuse it as competition.

Sir Gawain finally allows the Green Knight's wife to tie on him her magical belt, a charm against evil and also a proof of his weakness toward her. Many events later, when Sir Gawain is safely back at King Arthur's palace and blushingly displays the belt to the assembled lords and ladies, they laugh, not so much to mock him as to offer relief, to support the young man's need for a protective charm. Their laughter marks that danger has now passed, virtue has vanquished evil, and royal power as well as knightly virtue are firmly established.

In the Greek epic the *Iliad*, an ugly, common soldier, Thersites, insults the Greek leaders on the eve of a battle. Mutiny and treachery threaten to erupt, for the rest of the soldiers are clearly frightened, trying to avoid their duty, running toward their ships in hope of escape. Odysseus crushes Thersites, and the troops, just a moment ago siding with Thersites, now laugh in relief that he, not they, are punished. By laughing, the troops show that they are again on their leaders' side; order is restored, and if the soldiers are going to die, they will die in battle and not as punishment for treachery.

Death or the prospect of death is no laughing matter, and yet death vanquished can become a source of ridicule. Safe in his conviction of resurrection, the Christian apostle Paul mockingly wags his finger at death, asking, "Where is your sting?" Humor is not usually associated with Christianity, nor, more precisely, with the idea of resurrection. But it is possible to see this religious notion as a joke. Death redescribed becomes life: bodily death leads to eternal life in heaven. Turning things upside down in this manner runs the risk of paradox, a term usually treated with reverence. But if paradox goes unappreciated, it turns into blasphemy or absurdity.

Scholars of early Christianity do not usually suggest that the ideology of martyrdom is the ultimate joke on death, that martyrs savored their practical joke. Yet, the idea of resurrection, pushed to a logical extreme, might justify a new view. The utterly serious act of dying for the faith in order to attain eternal life may become utterly ridiculous. If pagan spectators were impressed at the strength of the faith of early Christian martyrs, they might just as easily ask themselves whether the martyrs' action is any way to build an organization. The possibility was not lost on the budding church, which soon suppressed the practice. If you preach that life is death and vice versa, the mystery of faith can soon become an absurdity.

HERESY

Sometimes it falls to the so-called heretics, those who choose to see things differently, to focus the lens in such a way that the most sublime mystery turns out to be a joke on the believer. In the *Book Baruch,* a Christian Gnostic text transmitted by the third-century church father Hippolytos, the followers of the (unidentified) religion are to be imbued with a mystery enabling them to ascend to a heavenly abode, the residence of "the Good." The mystery requires silence and secrecy, and Elohim himself (modeled on the God of the Old Testament) ascended to "the Good" after having promised to keep a secret oath. Precisely what the secret is, is never revealed, of course; all one needs is the assurance of its effectiveness.

Once one has reached the heavens, the residence of "the Good," it is revealed that this entity, supposedly entirely otherworldly and living up to its name in terms of virtue, is none other than the admittedly obscene Greek fertility principle Priapus, symbolized by fruits and an erect penis. This means that earthly voluptuousness and bodily entanglements, which the devotee thought were now safely far behind, are gleefully present in the figure Priapus as supreme ruler in the heavens. So, the joke on the believer is that what he thought he had escaped from equates the goal; life on earth and in the upper realms is ruled by the same earthly divinity. One can now appreciate the text's emphasis on the need for secrecy, for if word gets out that the ascent is illusory—that one ends up where one began, that upward is merely sideways—the religion may lose adherents. Or perhaps the religion is a haven for those who enjoy this type of humor; others may be embarrassed. Not a few scholars dealing with the *Book Baruch* have exhibited the latter emotion, trying to explain away Priapus as an illicit intrusion into the text.

Willful reinterpretations of "canonical" traditions are the delicious privilege of heretics like the Gnostics, a bee in the bonnet of the Christian tradition as it struggled to achieve hegemony and a sheen of orthodoxy. Heresy gains force by publicly expressing views counter to those taken for granted, by exposing the arbitrariness of dogma. It says, "Why not look at things from a different angle?" So we find, in the Gnostic text from the Nag Hammadi the *Apocryphon of John*, a smiling Jesus revealing to the perplexed John (one of the Zebedee sons) that Moses was wrong when he wrote that the Spirit moved to and fro (Genesis 1:2). It was not the Spirit, says Jesus, but the aeon (heavenly figure) Sophia who moved about in a confused manner after having strayed from her origin. Likewise, Jesus criticizes "Moses'" statement that God put Adam to sleep (Genesis 2:21), for the sleep was really forgetfulness (this makes sense from a Gnostic viewpoint because God is a "wrong" god). Even worse, the smiling Jesus reveals that he, Jesus, taught Adam and Eve to eat of the fruit. The astounded John has, of course, always thought that the serpent was the agent. But Jesus says that the serpent taught the first human couple lust, but he, savior that he is, instructed them in wisdom by means of fruit.

Even the crucifixion does not escape parody; in the *Apocalypse of Peter* (also a Nag Hammadi text), Jesus reveals to Peter one of his "selves," a laughing man hanging on the cross. This is the living, spiritual Jesus who escapes death, while the ignorant tormentors strike and hammer nails into a mere phantom, a fleshly figure without spiritual life. This docetic idea (i.e., the view that Jesus merely appeared to suffer) exemplifies opposition to the dogma of Jesus' double citizenship—earthly and divine. As noted above regarding resurrection as a redescription of death, the paradoxical mystery of faith may turn into a joking matter. The paradox is held up to ridicule: by splitting apart the entities allegedly held together in the mystery of coexistence, the proponents of the *Apocalypse of Peter* refuse a suffering savior and accept only the victor.

MAGIC

Rewriting and reinterpreting texts or traditions constitutes a form of magic exerted on those texts. Such operations move the power of the text onto new exegetes, wrest it away from its reputedly "original" owners, and may redirect the forces invoked or conjured. If the powers handled in magic are malignant, care is taken to steer them away from the user or his patient. The medieval Icelandic saga about Eigill Skallagrimsson has an instructive story in this regard. Visiting his friend Thorfinn, Eigill notices that his host's daughter, Helga, is sick, wasting away, and unable to sleep. The father tells Eigill that he has had a neighboring man carve runes for Helga, but she has only become worse. Eigill goes to work: he removes the woman from her bed, searches the bedclothes, and finds a rune-carved whalebone. Having read the runes, he scrapes them off the bone, burns scrapings and bone, throws out the bedclothes, and derides Thorfinn with the verse "None should write runes who can't read what he carves; a mystery mistaken can bring men to misery. I saw cut on the curved bone ten secret characters; these gave the young girl her grinding pain."

Then Eigill carves other runes and places them under the girl's pillow. She immediately shows signs of recovery, and Eigill leaves. When he later comes back to the farm, the girl is well. The saga now tells that the man who carved the original runes was in love with Helga, but his love was unrequited. Undeterred, he tried to carve love runes for her, but he had not sufficient skill, so the runes instead made her ill. Carved words carry power on their own; the carver himself may only be the tool. But a bad tool—the lovesick, inept, probably also hostile man—makes matters worse, for his creation is beyond his ken and control. Because the carver did not know what the secret characters meant, they took on a life of their own.

A more confident magician may threaten his tools if they do not perform properly. A Greek magical papyrus gives a spell, to be said before sunrise, for picking a plant,

> "I am picking you, such and such a plant, with my five-fingered hand, I, NN, and I am bringing you home so that you may work for me for a certain purpose. I adjure you by the undefiled name of the god: if you pay no heed to me, the earth which produced you will no longer be watered as far as you are concerned—ever in life again, if I fail in this operation (magical formulas follow); fulfill for me the perfect charm."

The plant, which seems to be held personally responsible if no rain ever falls again, will, one assumes, be scared into performing correctly. The menacing tenor of this text places the magician in the position of power. Still, the plant is endowed with a will of its own, which must be controlled.

One solution is to merge with one's magical tools, as in the example of the Jewish aficionado of magic who was apprehended on the Egyptian border at a time when export of Egyptian magic (the most powerful in the then-known world) was forbidden because his body was tattooed with magical formulas.

(The Greek author Kelsos accuses Jesus of smuggling magic in this manner.) Such mergings of messenger and message are known from "classical" Greek texts, as when rulers would send secret messages written onto the shaved heads of slaves who had to let their hair grow a bit before embarking on their mission. Drawings on a body, penetrated words, ingested food, beheld objects, inhaled aromas can all confer power, drain the recipient of it, or protect the recipient from malignant powers. It is all a matter of intent and know-how.

CRITICISM

An obedient slave and a submissive plant are, at times, merely wishful thinking, for resistant individuals or groups often shake off, say, their state's attempts to exert power over the citizens. Ridiculing and protesting society's rules for decent behavior and productive citizenship, "heretics" like the Greek Cynics (lit. "dogs"), claim a higher moral vision, devotion to loftier principles than state custom and religion. As noted earlier, heretics have the task of exposing the arbitrariness of "the system." The Cynic traditions ascribe to Diogenes acts such as insulting royalty, masturbating in public, and provocative shows of poverty. And the Cynics' revered ancestor, the pre-Socratic philosopher Herakleitos, denounced the frivolous habits, pride, and complacency of his countrymen. According to legend, he ended his life by crawling into a dung heap and dying there—perhaps demonstrating how he esteemed his fellow Ephesians.

Protest figures like these Greek philosophers work within their societies, providing for themselves mental, but not physical, separation from their cultures. The time of Hellenism is especially rife with all sorts of splinter groups breaking away from their established contexts. Such conditions foster polemics and intellectual warfare because the "new" religious organizations need to articulate distance from their origin and forge identities of their own. As religious traditions collide, redistribution of power takes place, and the proponents may engage in diatribes and name-calling. Such fights are worthy of attention. Mandaeism, a still-extant, non-Christian, Gnostic religion with sectarian Jewish roots eager to poke fun at the religions surrounding it, in this case Judaism and Christianity, provides an example.

In the Mandaean *Book of John*, John the Baptist is busy with his work in the River Jordan. Jesus comes to him and requests baptism. He tries to entice John, saying, "If I prove myself as your disciple, I will mention you in my book; if I do not prove myself, then erase *my* name from *your* book!" John will not stand for this kind of bribery or flattery; he refuses, and accuses Jesus of having violated Jewish customs by forcing his own followers to become celibate. Jesus denies John's allegations, and the two men engage in an argument. After Jesus has twice repeated his request to be baptized, a letter comes from the (Mandaean) heavenly world to John, commanding John to "baptize the betrayer." He complies, but the female devil figure Ruha ("Spirit") makes the sign of the cross over the Jordan and the waters turn into various colors, which deeply satisfies Ruha.

This looks like a defeat for Mandaeism, a bad result of dangerous toying with opposing religious forces. But the letter from the heavens was only joking, for the text immediately assures the reader that the ritual did not work on Jesus. Instead of the Mandaean baptism (which Jesus wanted as guarantee for his soul's salvation despite his planned deceitful mission, according to a modern Mandaean view), Jesus has received a counterfeit baptism, sacred meal, headgear, and sacred staff. What looked like regular Mandaean features in the baptism ritual magically turned into those of Christianity. Even the normally exuberantly flowing Jordan transmuted itself into a mere trickle. This is a jab at the Christian custom of using "cut-off," that is, stagnant baptismal water. Jesus is now barred from Mandaeism's protective power and launched into his own, new religion.

Only a religion with a modicum of self-assurance or protection can afford this type of complex polemics, engaging its two archenemies. At times, a religion may explicitly confront its own, more homegrown dilemmas. An example

A Mandaean baptism, Iraq (ca. 1954). Mandaeism, along with Judaism, Christianity, and Samaritanism, is one of the few religions of late antiquity to continue into the twentieth century.

of this in Mandaeism is that believers are not to resist death or to mourn dead relatives, for death means entry into real life in the heavenly world. In one of the *Left Ginza* texts, the angel of death comes to call Adam home to the upper world, for he is now a thousand years old and it is time to go. Offended, Adam protests, saying that he is indispensable on earth. The angel has to return empty-handed. He is sent down again, repeats the message, and Adam, annoyed as before, suggests that the angel take Adam's son Seth instead. Seth is only eighty years old and afraid to die, but he is even more afraid of offending the heavenly powers. So he departs. Later, Adam sees a vision of Seth in the upper worlds, and now Adam wishes to die. But Seth sternly addresses his father, calling him a foolish old man, saying that nobody may request death: Adam will have to wait.

As noted earlier with respect to Christianity, death redescribed becomes life. The Mandaean story deals with life turning to death turning to life. It also reverses hierarchical structures (the son berates the father), exhibits the folly of substitutes (the victim is victor), and shows that human control is illusory. It is no excuse that Adam, being the first man, did not know better, for the heavenly powers mock Adam's inflated self-importance.

Whether one deals with mythologies or rituals, social or individualistic forms of religion, magic or lofty metaphysics, religions of antiquity display tapestries of the familiar and the alien. Varying cultural fashions or political ideologies tend to judge certain religious forms as better or more advanced than others. But it is necessary to cultivate an awareness of how any given culture will try to dictate (even "religiously") the study of religions. One might take a lesson from the studied avoidance of the word *magic* when the first seminar on ancient magical papyri was announced at the University of Heidelberg in 1905. The word could not be used in the announcement, clearly because the word itself was offensive, dangerous, and through sheer print might conjure up its own existence. Such faith in the power of words demonstrates an understanding deeply at home in antiquity.

See also Aramaean religion; Baltic religion; Canaanite religion; Celtic religion; Cycladic religion; Egyptian religion; Etruscan religion; Finnish religion; Gnosticism; Greek and Roman philosophy; Greek religion; Harranians; Hellenism; Hermetism; Hittites; Hurrians; Indo-European religion; Inner Asian religions; Iranian religion; Israelite religion; Mandaeans; Manichaeism; Mesopotamian religion; Minoan religion; Mithraism; Mycenaean religion; Mystery religions; Nabataean religion; Nordic religion; Old European religion; Orphism; Phoenicians; Roman religion; Samaritans; Zoroastrianism.

Apollo (uh-pol'oh), a major ancient Greek god, patron of young men entering the communal assembly, of purification, and of music and poetry. He was associated with oracle shrines, especially Delphi. *See also* Delphi; Greek religion.

Apollonius of Tyana (d. ca. A.D. 98), Greek Neo-Pythagorean philosopher, reformer, and miracle worker. His biography, by Philostratus (ca. 220), has often been compared to the Gospel accounts of Jesus. *See also* aretalogy; divine man.

apologetics (Gk. *apologia,* "defense"), that branch of theology in which a body of doctrine is defended against criticism. Some scholars distinguish between outer apologetics, which are directed toward those who are not members of the tradition, and inner apologetics, which serve to strengthen the beliefs of members of the tradition.

Christianity: Apologetics, or defense of faith on intellectual grounds, is usually considered a branch of theology, but the term may be more generally applied to any other-directed communication of religious belief that makes certain assertions about knowing and serving God and claims the truth of this knowledge. Whereas apologies for faith in Christ have existed as long as there have been Christians, formal apologetics began in the second century with writers like Justin (d. ca. 165) and Tertullian (d. ca. 220) who used the classical apology as a genre of testimony of the superiority of Christianity to nonbelievers or a defense of Christianity in the period of persecution. Soon apologetics took on the task of defending orthodox teaching against errors and dissent from within. In the Middle Ages apologetics was directed against Judaism and Islam, but Thomas Aquinas (ca. 1225–74) developed a positive defense of belief in God based on Aristotelian theories of a first cause of the universe. Post-Reformation apologetics often focused on polemics and controversial issues within Christianity. Modern apologetics became more comprehensive as theologians defended revealed religion, Christianity, or perhaps a particular form such as Roman Catholicism, as true. Friedrich Schleiermacher (1768–1834), Rudolf Bultmann (1884–1976), and Paul Tillich (1886–1965) have made significant contributions to modern Protestant apologetics; in Catholicism major contributions have come from Maurice Blondel (1861–1949), Pierre Rousselot (1878–1915), and Karl Rahner (1904–84). As twentieth-century theologians deal with evolution, Marxism, psychoanalysis, postmodern philosophy, and global concerns, the nature and function of apologetics becomes problematic. Current hermeneutical theory offers important insights for the reformulation of apologetics.

apostasy, the public act of leaving one religious tradition and joining another. *See also* conversion.

apostle (Gk., "one sent out"), a member of one of the earliest groups of followers of Jesus sent out to preach the gospel. The term is used for the twelve disciples, for Paul, for witnesses to Jesus' resurrection, and for early Christian missionaries generally. The biblical books of Matthew, Mark, and Luke narrate Jesus' selection of (Matthew 10:1–4; Mark 3:13–19; Luke 6:12–16), "sending out" to preach and heal (Matthew 10:5–14; Mark 6:7–13; Luke 9:1–6), and commissioning to baptize and teach (Matthew 28:16–20) twelve disciples, or apostles. ("Twelve" is probably symbolic of the twelve tribes of Israel.) In the biblical book of Acts of the Apostles, the apostles—as witnesses to Jesus' life, death, and resurrection (1:21–22)—serve as leaders of the Jerusalem church. Paul, missionary founder of the first Christian churches outside of Palestine and writer of many New Testament books, claims and defends in his Letters the title "apostle," arguing that, although he did not know Jesus when alive, he had a vision of the resurrected Christ. When early Christian writers refer to "the Apostle," they usually mean Paul. *See also* disciple.

Apostles' Creed, a short formulary of Christian belief. Known only in the West, this creed (Lat., "belief") was popularly thought to have been composed by the apostles. It took its present form in eighth-century Gaul but was derived from earlier baptismal professions of faith in the Father, Son, and Holy Spirit.

There is a long tradition of commentary on the parts of this creed that extends in Christian literature to the twentieth century. Widely used in Christian devotional and liturgical life, the Apostles' Creed has been suggested as a starting place for ecumenical discussion. *See also* creed.

Apostles of John Maranke, or Bapostolo, an African independent church founded in 1932 by John Maranke (Muchabaya Momberume), now a multiethnic church in Southern and Northern Rhodesia and the Belgian Congo. From his youth, Maranke felt called by the Holy Spirit to teach, prophesy, heal, and to establish a new church. *See also* Africa, new religions in; African apostolic churches.

Apostolic Sabbath Church of God, a separatist group, also known as the Apostolic Church of John Masowe, founded in 1932 by a man who preached to the Shona of Southern Rhodesia about his millennial visions. He demanded that his followers minimize contact with Europeans and with European goods, supporting themselves only from self-employment as farmers or artisans. Some of Masowe's followers settled near Port Elizabeth, South Africa, though they were forced to return to Rhodesia in 1960. *See also* Africa, new religions in.

apostolic succession, the Christian principle of continuous succession of ministry from the time of the apostles.

As early as the end of the first century there is evidence of concern that the authenticity of Christian ministry be guaranteed on the basis of a continuous community directed by bishops as heirs of the original apostles. Generally speaking, this is the Catholic understanding of apostolic succession shared by Roman Catholicism, Eastern Orthodoxy, and Anglicanism. In 1876 the Vatican denied the legitimacy of the Anglican orders of succession.

Many Protestant churches have understood apostolic succession to conform to their notions of authentic ministry. When the gospel is rightly preached and the Lord's Supper rightly administered, the ministry is assumed to be in harmony with the faith of the apostles.

apotheosis, the Greco-Roman ritual act by which a human being is raised to the status of a deity. *See also* afterlife; deification; kingship, sacred; ritual.

apotropaic ritual, rites or verbal formulas intended to prevent evil. *See also* ritual.

apple, popularly understood to be the unidentified forbidden fruit eaten by Adam and Eve in the Garden of Eden based on a Latin pun on *malum,* which can mean both "apple" and "evil." *See also* Fall.

Apsaras (ahp'suh-rahs; Skt.,"going in the waters or between the clouds'waters"), in Hindu mythology, a seductive nymph, mistress to the celestial musicians, and dancer for the gods who can assume any form at will.

Apuleius (a-puh-lay'uhs; ca. 124–170), Roman rhetorician, poet, and philosopher, born in Madaurus, Africa. His novel, *Metamorphoses,* or *The Golden Ass,* is related to the Mysteries of Isis. *See also* Isis; mystery religions.

Aquarian Gospel of Jesus Christ, a modern gospel, first published 1911, describing the travels and teaching of Jesus in India. It was received through Levi Dowling, an American, by spiritualistic mediumship.

Aquinas, Thomas (ca. 1225–74), leading medieval Catholic Dominican theologian and saint. Aquinas is best known for his adaptation of Aristotelian philosophy to distinguish between matters of faith and matters of reason. His *Summa Theologiae* became the central text of Scholasticism. *See also* Scholasticism; Summa Theologiae; Thomism.

Arab, originally, the Semitic tribal peoples indigenous to the Arabian peninsula; currently, all who speak Arabic as a mother tongue and who share the associated cultural heritage. Broadly, the term incorporates a number of distinct ethnic groups occupying more than twenty states extending from Morocco to Oman (although the term may exclude some peoples, such as the Druze or Arabic-speaking Jews). Today, Arabs number about 120 million, of whom approximately 4 percent are Christian and virtually all of the rest are Muslim.

Arabic, the mother tongue of about 120 million Arabs in North Africa and the Middle East. Arabic is related to Hebrew, Ethiopian Geez, and some dialects of the Yemen as survivors of the 4,500-year-old Semitic language group. Arabic first appears in third-century inscriptions. It evolved a complex and expressive tribal poetry long before Muhammad elevated it to a vehicle of revelation in the early seventh century. Since then, Arabic has become the instrument of a universal Islamic culture. Inspired by Islam, an enormous religious and secular literature was produced in the Middle Ages, and in modern times Arabic has adapted to an ever-changing world with energy and inventiveness. It is an official language of the United Nations.

Arabic displays the classic features of the Semitic languages, with its large number of guttural consonants, relatively few grammatical categories, and general syntactic simplicity. It dramatically exploits the Semitic system of word formation, which generates words by combining three root consonants with formative vowels and auxiliary consonants. The Semitic method of forming the plural by changing the internal

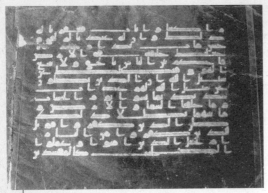

Arabic page of the Islamic holy book, the Qur'an, copied in the ninth or tenth century in Kairouan, Tunisia.

structure has been developed far beyond its limited use in the earlier languages, and contemporary borrowings are still easily accommodated to this system.

There is probably no other religion that relies so profoundly as Islam upon the single linguistic event of its revelation. It is an article of faith that every Arabic letter, word, and verse of the Qur'an is a direct utterance of God transmitted by his prophet Muhammad. For the orthodox Muslim, a personal experience of God is attainable only through recitation of the Qur'an, which is thus comparable to the Christian experience of Christ's body through the Eucharist, the difference being that in Islam the Word never became flesh. Instead the Word and all its doctrinal implications remained a purely linguistic entity, with the result that the Arabic language itself soon became and has never ceased to be identified with divine perfection. Arabic has been preserved and protected ever since from all change and is still, in theory at least, the sole authentic medium for Islamic religion.

Even today the literature of high culture and public oratory are composed in essentially the same classical Arabic as they were fourteen centuries ago. But at the same time, a lively and varied family of dialects has evolved, languages as yet without an established literature but in the process of becoming a second cultural mode. It has been observed that literate Arabs are virtually bilingual, functioning both in the archaic, but still vigorous, classical language and in the colloquial.

All the Muslim languages are heavily influenced by Arabic. Many, such as Persian (Farsi) and Urdu, have adopted the Arabic script, and everywhere Islam has enriched their vocabulary with Arabic loan words. Spanish to this day bears the traces of seven centuries of Arab rule, and even Turkish, which abandoned the script in 1928, is still recognizably indebted to Arabic. It is a profound question whether Arabic will go the way of Turkish and have to translate its own past into a new medium, but the receptivity of modern Arabic to technological and cultural innovation, and its unique religious status as the language of the Qur'an, make this seem unlikely. *See also* Islam (authoritative texts and their interpretation).

Arai Hakuseki (ah-rah-ee hah-*koo*-say-kee; 1657–1725), a leading Japanese Confucian statesman and historian who became an adviser on domestic affairs, economic reforms, and foreign policy for several Tokugawa shoguns. *See also* Japan, Confucianism in.

Aramaean religion (ahr-uh-mee'uhn). The Aramaeans were a Northwest Semitic people known through personal and tribal names in Akkadian texts of the second millennium B.C. By the eleventh century B.C. the Aramaeans appear settled in confederacies in north Syria from where they gained control of the Syrian desert and its caravan routes. Their inscriptions were written in alphabetic characters borrowed from the Phoenician script. Later the Assyrians subdued them, but the Aramaeans preserved their language. Their gods, called on in treaties and religious texts, became the deities of all of Syria up to Roman times. A weather god praised as "the irrigator of heaven and earth," Hadad, was their supreme god. His temples at Aleppo and Damascus constituted centers of an intense religious life. In Greco-Roman times Hadad's identity was concealed under the Greek epithets of Zeus, "the Thunderer," "the Bringer of Fruits," "the Lord." His consort was Atargatis, and the cult of this couple prevailed at Hierapolis (Manbij in north Syria). According to the Greek writer Lucian of Samosata (b. ca. A.D. 120), the statues of Hadad and Atargatis were carried in procession to the sea twice a year by pilgrims who had arrived from all over the Middle East.

In the first millennium B.C., there was an important Aramaean cult at Harran, in northwestern Mesopotamia, dedicated to the moon god under his Mesopotamian name, Sin. The cult had traveled from southern Babylonia to Harran with the Aramaean nomads. The few known inscriptions of the first part of the first millennium B.C. record only the religious views of the ruling class. From the middle of the millennium down to the first centuries A.D., however, the Aramaic inscriptions reveal popular forms of piety. Moreover, Aramaean religion became influenced by the Babylonian cults of Bel-Marduk and Nabu and by the Phoenician cult of Baal. The pantheons of Dura-Europos on the Euphrates, of Palmyra in the Syrian steppe, and of Edessa in southern Turkey disclose a new religious syncretism. *See also* Harranians.

Aranyakas (uh-ruhn'yuk-kuhz; Skt.,"of the forest or wilderness"), a type of Vedic text (ca. 800 B.C.) featuring esoteric meditations about the meaning of the sacrifice and the structure of the cosmos. *See also* Brahmanas; Upanishads; Veda, Vedism.

archaic, a widely used euphemism for the derogatory term *primitive* in the study of religion. *See also* primitive religion.

archangels (Judaism and Christianity), one of the powerful ranks of angels who stand before God and are concerned with human affairs. Archangels are commonly four in number (Michael, Gabriel, Uriel, Raphael), but sometimes seven (adding Chamael, Jophiel, Zadkiel). *See also* angel.

archbishop, a Christian ecclesiastical title designating a bishop who presides over a church distinguished either for its antiquity or importance as an urban center.

archdiocese, in Roman Catholicism, the geographical area presided over by an archbishop.

archetype (Gk. *arche,* "beginning" or "first," and *typos,* "figure" or "form"), in Greek philosophy, the mental blueprint for the universe and its parts preexisting in the mind of the creator god. It remained an important concept in medieval and Renaissance cosmologies and is found as late as Immanuel Kant's *Critique of Pure Reason* (1781–87). The twentieth-century depth psychologist Carl Jung has given archetype a new and widely used meaning: a visualizable master symbol generated by unconscious processes in all human minds. Surfacing in dreams and waking consciousness, it is then expressed in external images. These universal archetypes form for Jung the "collective unconscious" of humanity. *See also* myth; religion, psychology of; symbol.

archimandrite (ahr-ki-man'drit), in Orthodox Christianity, the title given to a distinguished monk as an honorific or the title of the head of a monastery.

architecture and religion. Architecture, the most complex of the fine arts, is both the art of designing and constructing buildings, and the buildings themselves. Religious architecture denotes those structures designed and built specifically in the service of religious traditions.

Not all religions require an architectural setting. Some traditions did not build as much as transform the natural landscape, as in the fifteenth-century B.C. Egyptian mortuary tombs, first-century B.C. Buddhist assembly halls, and the Byzantine cave churches of Cappadocia, all of which were carved out of rocky cliffs. Yet most of the world's religions have erected specialized structures dedicated to religious use.

Sacred buildings are the most visible sign of a religion's authority and resources. Typically they are the most extraordinary architectural achievements of their culture, as they are crafted of the finest and most permanent materials, their scale exceeds that of most or all other buildings, and their decorative schemes are executed by the most gifted artists. Religious architecture characteristically is more conservative than secular constructions, since the architect and builder often are constrained by traditions that govern the design of sacred structures.

Religious buildings are symbolically powerful because each religious tradition embodies cosmologies, rituals, and the social relations of its creed in its use of architectural features. Cosmic beliefs are architecturally expressed through verticality, enclosure, axiality, orientation, and geometry. Hindu gateways permit entry only at the cardinal directional points, mosques are oriented toward Mecca, while Jewish and Christian altars and sanctuaries are placed at the eastern end of synagogues and churches. Specific traditions dictate ornamental schemes, and decorative elements instruct as well as embellish, as in the sculptural programs of Hindu and Egyptian temples, the carved portals of Gothic cathedrals, and the tiled calligraphic inscriptions of mosques.

It is most relevant to discuss the relationship between architecture and religion in terms of typologies of use, with the temple, congregational structure, and shrine being the most common religious building types.

Temples: The temple is a building that enshrines and protects images and tokens of the gods to whom it is dedicated. Archaeological and extant evidence suggests that temples are among the oldest type of religious structures. The greatest Egyptian temple complex, at Karnak in Upper Egypt, dates from the fourteenth and thirteenth centuries B.C. Temple prototypes were often wood structures whose simple post-and-beam construction was later easily rendered in more permanent materials, a process best illustrated by the development of Greek temples. Builders initially erected simple wooden structures whose design may have closely resembled that of domestic buildings. But as markers of Greek civic pride, a more permanent and grander architectural statement developed. Finely crafted marble and limestone classical temples that retained the form of early structures replaced frame predecessors and became the model for centuries of temple building.

Temple siting is a deliberate act, corresponding with both cosmological themes and an architectural concern for prominence, whether at the center of urban activity or at remote, isolated locations. Hindu temple grounds are carefully selected and ritually purified to prepare them for the habitation of a divine image. As part of Hellenic urbanization, each Greek city came to be associated with a particular god, and temples were constructed as the principal buildings of each city. Greek priests chose building sites that embodied attributes of the deity. The selection of elevated temple sites on an acropolis visually distinguishes the structure while confirming its importance. Roman builders brought their temples into the city, but increased their scale and elevated them on podiums, architectural devices that were copied by subsequent designers.

Local circumstances and specific religious practices account for the variety of architectural forms. Ornamental schemes beautify while supplying rich visual instruction. The formal, spare forms of the Egyptian and Greek temples contrast sharply with the ornate masses and elaboration of the Hindu and Buddhist temples. Most Egyptian temples exhibit similar overall forms and nearly identical interior organization. A massive, heavily carved and decorated facade marks the division between the outside, earthly world and the inner, inviolable domain. Because of their dependence on mathematical order and a shared architectural vocabulary, a coherence of form exists among Greek temple designs. The faded hues of temple ruins belies their original polychromed features. Temple forms may correspond to cosmologies, as in Hindu temples, which are built in the shape of a square, a configuration thought to be holy and perfect in form. A Hindu temple is conceived as a microcosm of the universe, and its dimensions are subject to strict mathematical calculation. Usually massive and blocklike in form, the structure is likened to the mountain where the gods reside. Ornamental carvings and sculpture densely cover the Hindu temple, animating its exterior walls with narratives enacted by deities, worshipers, and animals.

A typical South Indian outer gate building (*gopuram*) giving access to the Hindu Shri Rangam Temple in Tamil Nadu.

While temples range in scale from small single chambers to elaborate complexes, the processional path through them typically is arranged along an axis. Temple interiors are hierarchically organized, with fences, doors, and secured chambers keeping all but the elite from the inner precincts. Various chambers may be used for devotions, praise, sacrifice, or other ritual directed to the god whose image or essence is enshrined within. The Egyptian temple interior is an axially organized succession of columned halls and broad courtyards. The small darkened sanctuary that holds the image or substance of the divine is preceded by a narrowed path and dimmed light. As in the Egyptian temple, lay worshipers are barred from the Greek temple interior, which is divided into two rooms. Rows of columns create aisles within these windowless ceremonial spaces. The smaller first room gives way to the principal chamber that houses the effigy of the god, where offerings were made. The vitality of the exterior of a

Hindu temple contrasts sharply with its calm, cavelike interior. Scale and light diminish as one moves toward the sanctum, a small, usually windowless chamber at the very center of the temple where the consecrated images reside. On the exterior the temple's highest tower marks the location of this inner sanctum. A powerful axis of cosmic power is thought to extend vertically from the sacred chamber up and out through the tower. Greek and Hindu temples provide examples of a transformation in architectural and cosmological principles, from the building as the repository of a shrine or tabernacle to the entire structure as tabernacle.

Congregational Structures: Congregational structures are religious buildings specifically meant to house worshipers beneath a single roof in a common ritual practice. They often evolved from the practice of gathering in a domestic or natural setting. The first congregational structures served also as a communal or social center for a community, where the faithful gathered to affirm ethnic and religious identities. Construction of shrines or holy places associated with the earthly ministry and death of Jesus precedes the construction of churches. Early Christians (first–fourth centuries) initially gathered in houses. These houses were not altered from their domestic uses, and proved to be too small to accommodate the growing number of believers. Congregations erected buildings specifically for religious use, but continued to pattern them after domestic models. For Jews the synagogue is the principal religious setting. Sparse, early evidence points toward the probable adaption of houses as synagogues. These renovated spaces served as both social centers and places of ritual assembly for Jewish communities. While mosques are the Muslim place of worship, they frequently are associated with schools, legal gatherings, hospitals, kitchens, and other charitable institutions. The Prophet's Mosque in Medina is the architectural prototype for a religion that eventually would stretch from North Africa around the Mediterranean to Spain, and east to Indonesia. In the first century of Islam, the faithful gathered in courtyardlike spaces, or appropriated churches or shrines in conquered cities. Later mosques developed as rectangular or square buildings.

The exterior organization and ornamental programs of congregational structures changes continually in reaction to changing fortunes, theological shifts, and stylistic preferences, as demonstrated by the stylistic evolution of the Christian church. Early synagogues follow no set model of design, but instead reflect local building practices. By the third century appear new buildings constructed specifically as synagogues. Jewish communities modified the indigenous designs of their surroundings, adapting the styles and formal characteristics of Byzantine, Gothic, and Renaissance religious structures to conform to Jewish ritual requirements. Because liturgical practices remain constant, the individual design of Islam's principal religious structure is largely conditioned by local circumstances and construction traditions. Regional mosque types developed in Syria under the Umayyad caliphates, in Iraq under the Abbasid rule, in Persia during the Seljuk dynasty, in India during the Moghul period, and in Turkey under Ottoman rule.

The interiors of congregational structures typically are composed of a single, open chamber, as they are organized principally for prayer and preaching. For Christians the "house church" building type prevailed, continuously enlarged and adjusted, until the early fourth century, when during the rule of Constantine the basilica emerged as the dominant building type. Adapted from a Roman public building, basilicas are organized into three or five long columned aisles. The central aisle, or nave, accommodates the procession of clergy that

Interior of the Sephardic Synagogue in Amsterdam, The Netherlands, constructed between 1671 and 1675.

moves toward the altar and their seats at the structure's eastern end, while the faithful stand in the side aisles. Decorative screens, stained-glass windows, icons, and inscribed tablets provide both interior elaboration and religious instruction. Basilican churches, such as Old St. Peter's (fourth century) in Rome, are often constructed over the burial place of the saint to whom the structure was dedicated, and thus function as both shrine and place of assembly. Once selected as a suitable building type, basilicas were constantly rebuilt and enlarged to enclose ever larger congregations and in response to changing aesthetic ideals and liturgical practices; the building type endures to the twentieth century with only minor alteration or adjustment as the dominant Christian church type. The open interiors of synagogues are designed for the recitation of prayer and the Torah readings, practices that have essentially remained unchanged. Assembled faithful of Jewish communities are directed toward the east, toward the Holy Ark, which holds the Torah scrolls, and the pulpit from which the scolls are read. From the Middle Ages onward, much of the interior ornament was dropped from synagogues. Islamic ritual practice requires only a wall, or *qibla*, that often is broken by a recess, called a *mihrab*, to indicate the direction of worship toward Mecca. Typically the finest and most detailed ornament is reserved for the qibla wall. Carvings or calligraphic quranic inscriptions enrich the mihrab, and a partial dome may surmount it. Early mosques are characterized by their many columned aisles, but engineering advances by Ottoman architects in the sixteenth century permitted the construction of the most familiar mosque design, that of a large centralized structure capped by a dome buttressed by smaller semidomes.

Shrines: Shrines, including those objects or structures that commemorate the site of a mysterious or miraculous event and those that mark the burial place of important religious figures or the repository of revered relics, constitute a third significant type of religious architecture. These memorial structures range in scale from small,

individual tombs or mortuary chapels to great architectural monuments. Shrines often are strikingly designed and are found free-standing or isolated in the landscape. Many shrine interiors are circular or square to facilitate circumambulation of the tomb, sacred site, or the ritual practice of pilgrims. The most pervasive Buddhist architectural form, the *stupa*, exemplifies the salient characteristics of a shrine. The stupa is not a building, but a memorial mound. Early examples tend to be hemispherically shaped, while later versions are conical, pyramidial, or pillar forms. Evocative of the burial mound that houses the relics of Gautama Buddha, a stupa may be small and enclosed within a temple, or monastic assembly hall, or of grand scale and free-standing, as at the stupas at Sanchi, India (third century B.C.). As a cosmological symbol, the stupa is fixed to the earth by an axial post that emerges through the top of the sphere. A circular balustrade or gateway open at each of the cardinal points encircles the stupa and guides ritual worship. Relics are housed in an enclosure that rests on the dome and above them floats one or more parasols, the insignia of the royalty.

Students of religion increasingly recognize the importance of architecture as religious expression. Careful documentation of the construction histories of religious buildings informs the study of cosmologies and liturgical practices and provides a detailed picture of social and theological transformations. *See also* altar; art and religion; basilica; cathedral; Chinese religions (art and architecture); Christianity (art and architec-

stupa

pagoda

Buddhist *stupas* characteristically have a dome, whether hemispherical or bell-shaped. In China, Japan, and Korea, the multiterraced stupa, originally developed in India, evolved into the equally characteristic many-storied *pagoda* tower. Both the domed stupa and the pagoda are not only associated with relics but also with architectural models of the cosmos.

ture); circumambulation; directional orientations; foundation rites; Hinduism (temple art and architecture); mandala; mosque; pilgrimage; pyramid (Egyptian); relics; shrine; stupa; synagogue; temple; ziggurat.

Ardhanarishvara (ahr-dah-nahr-eesh-vahr'ah), a Hindu half-female god. Like the Vishnu-Shiva composite, Harihara, this iconographic representation of Shiva with female attributes on his left side reflects a concern for unity behind apparent diversity. *See also* androgyny; Shiva; Vishnu.

aretalogy (air-uh-tahl'uh-gee; from Gk. *aretai,* "miracles, wonders"), a collection of miracle stories intended as praise of and propaganda for a deity or an extraordinary (divine) human. Between the first century B.C. and the fifth century A.D., such works were routinely written in biographical form in praise of such figures as Alexander, Augustus, Apollonius of Tyana, and Jesus. *See also* divine man; gospel; hagiography.

arhat (ahr'huht; Skt., "worthy"), one who has attained the final stage of enlightenment in Theravada Buddhism. The Buddhist tradition knows four types of enlightened beings: stream-enterers (subject to seven more rebirths), once-returners (subject to one), non-returners (subject to none), and *arhats* who have achieved full enlightenment here and now, rid themselves of all defilements, and escaped from the cycle of death and rebirth.

Buddhists have held varying opinions on whether laypersons or only monks and nuns can become arhats and on whether arhatship is still attainable today. Clearly, the Buddha was an arhat; so too were most of his disciples, who differed from him in that they did not discover but depended on his teaching.

Early on, arhatship may have been a necessary qualification for participating in certain elite assemblies of elders. Later, distinctions arose between arhats and *bodhisattvas* (Buddhas-to-be) who were thought to postpone their own personal escape from rebirth and remain in this world for the sake of others. From this perspective, some Mahayanists came to malign arhatship as an inferior and selfish enterprise lacking in the compassion of the bodhisattva.

There also evolved, in China and Southeast Asia, a tradition of arhats who did not abandon the world completely but extended their life spans and remained guardians of Buddhist teaching. This coincided with the rise of a popular cult of saints—arhats invoked for specific boons. *See also* bodhisattva; enlightenment; Theravada.

Arianism, a heretical Christian movement named after Arius (d. 336), an Alexandrian priest and proponent of subordinationist views of Christ's divinity. Arius's strict monotheism and uncompromising view of divine transcendence made it unthinkable to regard the divine Logos in Christ as equal to God. Drawing on Proverbs 8:22–31, Arius maintained that the Logos was created before the times, unique, divine, and unchangeable, an "angel" of God. Though superior to the rest of creation, it was subordinate to God, a mediating being with salvific powers. Arius was condemned at the Council of Nicaea (325), which defined the Logos as "one in being" with God the Father (Gk. *homoousios*), "begotten not made." Later Arians divided between the Anomoeans (the Son is unlike the Father in essence) and the majority of Arian Greek bishops who spoke of the Son's essence as being like the Father's (*homoiousios*). *See also* Christology.

Arica (ah-ree'kah; Span.), a system of immersion in emotional, bodily, and intellectual transformation, inspired by the ideas of Georgei Ivanovich Gurdjieff, and by Asian, Sufi, and modern psychological concepts. Originated in the late 1960s in Arica, Chile, by Oscar Ichazo, the program organizes workshops to redress personality imbalances through a holistic approach to reawakening complete perception of reality in the individual self. *See also* North America, new religions in.

Aristophanes (air-i-stah'fuh-neez; ca. 450–388 B.C.), the leading Athenian comic poet, whose eleven surviving plays mix fantasy, political satire, frank sexuality, and exuberant poetry with an incisive critique of society. Aristophanes often parodies myth and cult (as in *Frogs,* featuring a comic god Dionysos), although this was not taken as impious. His clever plots and diction associated him in the view of some with the sophisticated and intellectual tragedian Euripides, despite the latter's being a target of Aristophanes's abuse.

Aristotle (air'is-tot-uhl), enormously influential Greek philosopher (384–322 B.C.). He attended Plato's academy (ca. 367–347), taught Alexander the Great (342–339), and founded his own school (335). His early works are lost, but his extensive scientific and philosophical treatises survive.

Aristotle's interests ranged from biology to

political theory to metaphysics. His views are often a reaction to Plato's; e.g., in place of separated Forms he postulates the primacy of individual substance (e.g., a statue) composed of matter (bronze) and form (its shape). Human beings are thus perishable composites of body and soul (form), and so there is no individual immortality. Aristotle's theology includes arguments for the existence of an eternal, immaterial "Unmoved Mover," a divine Intelligence responsible for movement in the universe. *See also* Plato.

Arius (256–336), Alexandrian Christian thinker, associated with Arianism. *See also* Arianism.

Arjuna (ahr'juh-nah; Skt., "white"), the third of the five Pandava brothers and hero of the Hindu epic *Mahabharata;* he is a warrior with royal and ascetic aspects, whose spiritual instruction by the avatar Krishna is related in the *Bhagavad Gita.* *See also* Bhagavad Gita; Krishna; Mahabharata.

ark in Judaism (ah-rohn' ha-koh-desh'; Heb., "holy ark"), the receptacle in which the Torah scrolls are kept, located on the wall of the synagogue facing Jerusalem. The ark is the holiest part of the synagogue, after the scrolls themselves. The earliest arks were movable chests, often placed in a niche in the synagogue wall. Later the ark became a permanent fixture in which the scrolls stand upright, wrapped in cloth and topped with finials. *See also* synagogue; Torah scroll.

ark in the Hebrew Bible. 1 Boat constructed by Noah to escape the Flood (Genesis 6:5–9:17); 2 Basket in which the infant Moses was hidden (Exodus 3:12). *See also* ark in Judaism.

Armageddon (ahr-muh-ged'uhn), in Christian tradition, the place where the rulers of the world will assemble for battle on the last day of the world's existence (Revelation 16:16); in common parlance, the fiery end of the world. *See also* eschatology; millennialism.

Armenia, Christianity in. Armenia's Christian civilization began with the late-third-century evangelization of Armenia by the Cappadocian bishop and missionary Gregory the Illuminator. Missionaries from both Asia Minor (Cappadocia) and Edessa (home of Syriac-speaking Christianity) were early influences upon the emergent Armenian church.

Mesrop is credited with inventing an alphabet for the Armenian language in the late fourth or early fifth century. Translation of the Bible and writings of Greek and Syriac authors followed. The result is a rich collection of ancient Christian literature, which in some cases contains the only available text of works otherwise lost in the original, including many apocryphal Christian writings.

The Armenian liturgical tradition blends Cappadocian, Syrian, and Byzantine elements, although the Byzantine influence is greatest. There are traces in Armenian baptismal rites of the old Syrian practice of anointing the candidate only once, before baptism. The East Syrian influence on the Armenian liturgical tradition also appears in the Armenian calendar, while the Armenian eucharistic rite is based to a large extent upon Cappadocian rites. The eucharistic rite underwent Byzantinization from the seventh century, and from the time of the Crusades (twelfth through the fourteenth centuries) some Latin Christian features entered the Armenian Eucharist.

A distinctive office in the Armenian church is the *vardapet,* a celibate cleric who is chosen for the work of preaching and teaching.

In 506 the bishops of the Armenian church rejected the christological definition of the Council of Chalcedon (451). However, many believe that the Armenian stance toward the Chalcedonian Christology was determined more by faulty translation of the decrees of the council into Armenian than any specific theological orientation. A reaction against Byzantine authority may also have played a role in the rejection of Chalcedon, whose decisions were backed by imperial authority.

In the 1990s there are both Orthodox Armenian Christians (also known as Gregorian Armenians), and Eastern-rite Catholic Armenians, not only in Armenia but in communities in the Near East, Europe, North and South America.

Arminius , Jakob (ahr'min-ee-yuhs; 1560–1609), also known as Hermandszoon, Dutch Protestant theologian within the Calvinist tradition. Arminianism took exception to aspects of Calvin's doctrine of predestination, emphasizing the compatibility of human free will and divine sovereignty and the role of God's unceasing love. While condemned for a period in Holland, the theological positions of the Arminians, as expressed in the *Remonstrance* (1610), both established a liberal position within the Dutch Reformed Church and were influential on later movements such as Methodism. *See also* Calvinism; predestination; Wesley, John.

arms, uplifted. *See* orant.

art and religion. The relationship between art and religion, two major forms of cultural creativity, has long been a topic of speculation and controversy, both within religious traditions and in modern scholarship on religion.

Functions of Religious Art: Traditionally, works of religious art are not "art," objects made for detached observation and pleasure. They perform a particular function. These functions can be defined by type, although each work of art can serve more than one function.

Since the idol contains the god, makes the god present (either temporarily or permanently), the worshiper prays to the idol, and offers sacrifice to the god in the idol. The worshiper does not pray to the icon but through

Exiled Tibetan Buddhist at the Happy Valley community, Mussoorie, South India, painting a cloth scroll (*tanka*) to be used as an aid in meditation after it is consecrated by a *lama*.

and by means of it. The divinity or the sacred person is on the other side of the icon, which is considered (for example, in Eastern Orthodoxy) to be transparent. The icon is the instrument, not the object, of worship.

Images are made in a particular way; the specific way (the form) is determined by the conception of divinity and the sacred held by those who make the image. The forms also express the feelings of the maker and affect the feelings of the worshiper. Perceiving the form shapes the imagination and, therefore, the consciousness, the personality, of the worshiper who approaches the work devoutly. This is the devotional function of the image.

Images and representations also have a teaching function. One does not worship the image, said Pope Gregory the Great, but one learns from the image who it is one should worship.

The basic themes of art are the basic human themes: the achievement of order by some reconciliation of the primal elements of energy and structure. The work of art is traditionally considered a representation of what is there. The primal concerns of art are space (actual in architecture, represented in painting, implied in sculpture), time (implied by the dominance of geometry or energy, represented in action and particularly in narrative), rhythm (established by spacing between units, represented in the forms of bodies), cause and generation (implied by the relation of dominance or subordination to the material, represented in human forms and in narratives) and, finally, appearances.

The instrumental functions of art and its more fundamental functions can appear in the same work. The icon and the idol can teach through the representation of the gods and by

Tibetan Buddhist *stupa* hung with prayer flags at the Rongbuk Monastery, Mt. Everest, Tibet (1988). The stupa is a characteristic Buddhist form of architecture associated with relics.

the telling of the sacred stories. Both the representation and the telling require all the elements and the themes so the functions are not isolated. The great stupa at Borobudur, Java, tells the Buddhist story in great detail. It represents the

Buddhist cosmos from bottom to top. Its traversal around and up is the pilgrimage from the prison of this earth to the ultimate enlightenment.

A basic function of religious art is participation. The form defines both the object and the nature of the participation. Nature is the primary context of human life. Much religious art is a participation in the essential energies of the natural order. It is probable that the splendid representations of animals deep in prehistoric caves had a ritual purpose: participation in the primal energies of the animals. The same might be said of the small images of obese, pregnant, faceless women who are probably not goddesses but who relate to participation in the energies of generation.

Dominant Elements in Religious Art: Egyptian sculpture subdues all organic energies to the unchanging, eternal stillness of geometry, the reflection of the essence of the pitiless, life-giving sun above the symmetrical, fertile earth. The purposes of the soul are achieved by participation in the rigorous order of geometry. The crystalline form of the pyramid is the symbol of the eternal order to which the gods themselves are subject. In Mesopotamia, subject to the energies of a capricious climate and land, the gods are willful and all-powerful; their sculpture is an uneasy tension between heavy mass and powerful energies. Human representations show the arrogance of the divine king (Sargon) or the humble submission before divine power (Gudea). The ziggurat is the stairway to heaven.

Architecture is by its nature geometric and is the prime embodiment of spatial symbolism. The central importance of geometry is made explicit in the Renaissance church: the initial act of divine creativity is geometric; participating in the forms of the church is participating in the divine order.

Geometry can be affirmed, as in the intricate linear harmonies of the Gothic church or subdued in the impassioned sculpturesque movement of a Baroque church. The first suspends time in the exaltation of the timeless, the second is an exultant manifestation of time. The Romanesque church is a heavy, geometric mass, all weight and power, a shelter against the dangers and evils of the world. The delicate geometry of the Gothic church is a framework for the windows whose richly colored light transfigures space into ecstasy; light and space are both icon and sacrament.

Geometry governs much of Chinese architecture; the forms of the buildings and their rhythmic relations are a reflection of the heavenly order above. Participation establishes that

harmony in the disorder of human life. A similar principle recurs in modern times, without relation to a specified religion. The paintings of Mondrian and the transparent glass buildings of some modern architecture are intended to implant pure order in the sensibility of the spectator.

Organic energy is equally a preoccupation in some religions. India contains both desert and jungle, its seasons an alternation between absolute dessication and absolute fecundity. Its religions include an aniconic, world-denying asceticism and the extreme affirmation of fertile energies.

Some Indian temples are dug into the earth, absorbing the worshiper into the generative origins, the echoing ritual chant dissolving the sense of individual personality. Indian temples constructed on the earth reproduce the hiddenness of the cave in the small, dark, encompassing interior whose shrine is the "womb cell" centered on the generative symbols of the *lingam* (phallus) and the *yoni* (female genitals). The exterior obscures the geometry in encrusted ornament and some are explicitly phallic (*Lingarajah*, "Royal Phallus"). The ornament includes erotic figures and acts. The figures are like ripe fruit, growing from the inside out. Sex is a primal energy; in the context of religion, participation in it is participation in the sacred energies, a dissolving of separate individualities. Shiva, Lord of the Dance, is a prime symbol in Indian religion, the ceaseless rhythm of the dance returning on itself, the figure both male and female, the eternal return of circular time, generation and dissolution.

Sex is a presence in much art but central in few. Another serious treatment is in Baroque Christianity. Sexuality may be employed as an aspect of depicting a complete personality (Michelangelo, Tiepolo, Rubens). In the works of Giovanni Bernini it is a true symbol of the divine-human encounter, in the paintings of Peter Paul Rubens, the luminous exuberance of divine creativity.

Chinese landscape paintings show little interest in the energies of generation and fertility. The calm, quiet landscape is infinite in extension, subdued in action, human beings and human works a harmonious part of the infinite harmony of nature. Its function is the training of the spirit through contemplation. It is a statement of that primary devotional motif, silence and emptiness, equally present in a delicate combination of representation and abstraction in the Japanese sand garden.

A more muted emphasis on fertility and a similar emphasis on quiet harmony returns in the nineteenth-century landscape painting of Germany and the United States. These paintings are not part of any religion, except an undefined pantheism. This vague pantheism recurs in the twentieth-century "organic architecture" of Frank Lloyd Wright, distinctively harmonizing the natural and the geometric. Wassily Kandinsky introduces a new principle: the harmonic relations of undefined forms do not signify anything and are spiritual in themselves, with no reference beyond themselves except in their effect on the sensibility of the spectator.

There are also arts that seek a reconciliation between geometry and energy. Navaho dry painting combines on the earth various natural materials in complex geometric patterns, some of which represent the figures of the sacred myth. By the painting and the accompanying chanted ritual, the disordered harmony of body

Native American Navajo sandpainter creating the sacred design "Many Tongues, Many Nations" (ca. 1960s).

or mind is restored to communion with the sacred order. Art is more sacrament of sacred order than icon. Some African sculpture presents the parts of the body as discontinuous geometrical forms juxtaposed in the vital rhythms of the sacred dance.

Classical Greece, heir to Bronze Age Greece, the Semitic Near East, and Egypt, sought a harmony of geometry and physical energy. Classical human forms manifest a singular balance and restraint, organic energies disciplined by a framework of geometric order. The ordinariness of life and the individuality of forms that make up human experience are transcended in the presentation of a timeless essence. A Greek temple is a harmonious balance between order and energy, a setting for the representation and the stories of the gods in their majesty and beauty.

Gods are seen as the perfection of the human; humans have a part in the dignity and the grace of the gods. Roman gods are specific, present in every object and action. Roman art, immediate and earthy, is insistently representational of the appearance of things and persons.

The temple is the habitation of the god or the place where the god comes. It defines the sacred places and is the object of pilgrimage. The temple is placed on the earth, often on a high place, in the light and the sun. Worship is outside; the interior space is intended for the presence of the god in the cult statue. The interior shrine is often hidden, remote, and dark. A pilgrimage may end at the entrance of the shrine or extend to various points on the interior; the final shrine belongs to the priests.

The synagogue, the mosque, and the church are places for worshiping congregations. Judaism is rigorously iconoclastic. Islam is both iconoclastic and aniconic. Apart from some secular painting in the East, its great art form is calligraphy, the embodiment of the Word of the Qur'an. The mosque is an open courtyard or a domed interior. The canonical type of the Ottoman mosque is adapted from the Byzantine church. The church is the image of heaven, all interior, mass dissolved in light by the gleaming mosaic. It maintains the processional way from entrance to altar, the pilgrimage from this world to the next. The mosques are wholly nondirectional, full of an even light, a pure icon of the indivisible God.

Christian art stands at the intersection of Hebraism, Hellenism in its Olympian religion and its mystery religions, and the interaction of the two in the Hellenistic period and in republican and imperial Rome. Christian artists added their own emphasis: the man-god.

The early Christians contributed the principle of an image as visual prayer, which modulated into the Byzantine icon, weightless, luminous, and transparent to the ultimate reality beyond.

The forms of northern Christianity are rooted in the art of the pre-Christian Celts that reject substantial form and representation, and therefore image, nature, and the body. Art is reduced to its least palpable elements, color and the endless, infinitely moving line. The Celtic interlace is a true symbol of the infinite, beyond the sensuous and the organic. Irish monks incorporated images that later fused with the powerful weight of the Romanesque. This line was a central element of Gothic art. Later, fusing it with the organic forms of Mediterranean art, the

Germans made it into a prime symbol of power and energy.

Gothic figures are highly individual in appearance, but each has the same radiant serenity of the central figure of Christ. Renaissance artists transform these individuals to full personality. Personalities have individual wills and interact with others in dramatic situations. Thus sacred narrative presents the moral significance of the story in forms that require the full empathetic participation of the worshiper.

Protestantism was largely aniconic or iconoclastic. Where religious art appears, the direction is reversed: the divine comes to the human, the humbling of the Word in the ordinary. *See also* aniconic; anthropomorphism; architecture and religion; Chinese religions (art and architecture); Christianity (art and architecture); Hinduism (temple art and architecture); icon; iconoclasm; idol; idolatry; Islam (art); Japanese religions (art and architecture); Judaism (art and architecture).

Artemis (ahr'te-mis), the ancient Greek goddess of hunting, virginity, and childbirth. Daughter of Zeus and Leto and sister of Apollo, she is identified with Hekate and other goddesses. *See also* Greek religion; Hekate.

Arthashastra (ahr-tah-shah'struh; Skt., "teachings regarding material welfare"), a fourth-century B.C. court manual written in India delineating a king's responsibilities and opportunities and, more generally, the political ideology based on those lessons. *See also* kingship, sacred.

Aryan Nations (air'ee-an), a contemporary manifestation of the Christian Identity movement pastored by Richard G. Butler, a former student of California Identity, and Ku Klux Klan leader Wesley Swift. From its closed compound located at Hayden Lake, Idaho, Butler has sought since the 1970s to unite the disparate elements of the far right wing of American politics under the Aryan Nations banner, most notably through the annual International Congress of Aryan Nations held at Hayden Lake. In this ecumenical endeavor, Butler's extreme formulations of Identity doctrine have lost much of their original focus over the years, concentrating now on themes of racial separation, a neo-Nazi blueprint for government, and the conspiratorial belief that the United States has succumbed to Zionist control. In recent years, the appeal of the Aryan Nations' vision appears to have declined considerably, based on the diminishing crowds attending the congress (only about one hundred in 1991). The Aryan Nations, however, retains an influential prison ministry through its publication, *The Way*. *See also* Identity Christianity.

Aryans (from Skt. *arya*, "noble"), a term of social distinction used in the Vedic period to distinguish members of the Indian privileged class of society from others. There are three classes of Aryans: Brahmans (priests), Kshatriyas (warriors and rulers), and Vaishyas (commoners). These classes are known as "twice-born" because only they may be initiated into Veda study and participation in the sacrificial cult. *See also* caste.

Arya Samaj (ahr'yuh sah-mahj; Skt., "Society of Aryans"), a nineteenth-century Hindu reform movement founded in 1875 by Dayananda Sarasvati (1824–83). The Arya Samaj considered authoritative only the original Vedic texts, rejecting later scriptures as sectarian and erroneous. It held that the Vedas taught monotheism and that the various hymns were addressed to one god under a variety of designations. The Arya Samaj supported caste based on character rather than birth and permitted divorce and remarriage under certain circumstances. Polygamy, dowry practice, and widows' self-immolation were opposed. Through its purification movement (*shuddhi*) it sought to reclaim for Hinduism converts to Islam and Christianity. *See also* Reform Hinduism.

asana (ah'suh-nuh; Skt., "sitting position"). 1 Any one of eighty-four physical postures practiced in yoga, a Hindu discipline. 2 In Hinduism the seat offered the image of a deity in worship. *See also* Hinduism (worship); yoga.

Asatru (ah-sat'ru; Icelandic, *asa*, "gods," *tru*, "faith"), popularly known as *Odinism*, preferred term of modern adherents working to reconstruct pre-Christian Germanic and Norse religion. The primary thrusts of the current reawakening of the tradition are concentrated in the areas of theology (rites and myths), magic, runes, and ethics. The sources for these endeavors are the poetic and prose *Eddas*, saga literature and runic inscriptions dating primarily from the era of the Christianization of the Germanic and Norse peoples (twelfth century).

The earliest attempt to reconstruct Odinism in its modern form may be credited to the eccentric and virtually forgotten Australian A. Rud Mills, whose *The Odinist Religion: Overcoming Jewish Christianity* appeared in 1933. The current Asatru revival is generally credited to Texan Steve McNallen, who formed the Asatru Free Assembly ca. 1972. Asatru groupings also developed, largely independently, at the same time in Scandinavia, Germany, and England.

Asatru is currently organized according to an idealized pre-Christian "golden age" model, where individual adherents will form "kindreds" and kindreds may choose to associate with larger alliance groupings, meeting at periodic *althings* (gatherings) to vote on policy matters, i.e., a pseudoclan structure forming a proto-tribal group. An incipient priesthood is emerging as well. The Asatru Free Assembly disbanded in 1987. Its successors are the Asatru Alliance and the Ring of Troth. Specialized guilds have formed as well around such facets of Asatru as rune study and mead brewing.

Asatru adherents today are deeply divided over the issue of race. From its inception, the Asatru revival attracted a significant minority of neo-Nazis and other racialists, who argue that the attempt by most primary Asatru theorists, notably Steve McNallen and Edred Thorsson, to delineate a boundary between racial pride and racial mysticism is artificial, and that the modern "berserker" (warrior) should be a soldier for the white race. Thus, a growing segment of Asatru followers come from prison ministries, motorcycle clubs, and the like. The complexity of the racial question can be seen in the debate over metagenetics, a theory championed by Thorsson, which holds that the Asatru tradition is a matter of biological inheritance for all descendants of the Germanic and Norse peoples. The difficulty of reawakening this religious inheritance in a pluralistic society without, as a consequence, demonizing outsiders to the community is the essence of the current division within Asatru. *See also* Odinn.

ascension, human journey to the upper realms of the gods. There is a widespread belief in ascension and various traditions emphasize differing conditions: the journey is made while alive or just after death; in a dream or in a state of ecstasy. The result is almost always a boon: the individual becomes divine, brings supernatural gifts or knowledge, or changes status. *See also* afterlife; apotheosis; soul.

Christianity: In the New Testament, Jesus returns to heaven after his resurrection, as depicted in Luke 24:51 (in many manuscripts) and Acts 1:9. The Christian feast day is observed forty days after Easter. In the Hebrew Bible, both Enoch (Genesis 5:24) and Elijah (2 Kings 2:1–14) ascend to heaven prior to death.

Islam: The Qur'an relates several visions experienced during Muhammad's lifetime (d. 632) that form the basis for later accounts of his *miraj*

(Arab., "ladder," "ascent") or heavenly ascension. "Glory be to him who caused his servant to travel by night from the Sacred Mosque to the Further Mosque, whose environs we have blessed, that we might show him some of our signs . . . (17:1). According to Muslim tradition, this cryptic verse refers to a nocturnal journey (*isra*) made by Muhammad and the archangel Gabriel from the Meccan Kaaba to the temple precinct in Jerusalem, from which they ascended to heaven.

In standard accounts of these events, Gabriel wakes Muhammad at the Kaaba, purifies the Prophet's heart, and then mounts him on Buraq, a winged steed often described as having a woman's face and a peacock's tail. Together they fly to Jerusalem, where Muhammad leads an assembly of all previous prophets in prayer. Then Muhammad either climbs a ladder or rides on Buraq through the seven heavens, where he meets with their respective prophets while Gabriel testifies that Muhammad has received God's revelation. At last, Muhammad approaches God's throne in the seventh heaven, and he asks God to reduce Muslim daily prayers from fifty to five. This granted, Muhammad returns to Mecca the same night. While tradition claims that Muhammad ascended bodily into heaven, some Muslims have viewed the ascent as a spiritual, not literal, event, symbolizing the soul's return to an angelic condition or the mystic's journey from ignorance to gnosis.

ascension rituals, practices designed to enable the participant to journey to the heavens or experience flight. Though characteristic of many traditions, such rituals are central to shamanism. *See also* ritual; shaman.

asceticism (Gk. *askesis*, "exercise," "training"), the renunciation of physical pleasures or other forms of bodily self-denial as a means of spiritual development. The underlying assumption of asceticism is that the training of the body will aid in the training of the will or the soul and hence aid in the attainment of greater virtue or spiritual perfection. Asceticism is often practiced in conjunction with spiritual exercises such as meditation and contemplative prayer.

While *asceticism* is a word of Western origin, the term is used to refer to practices common to many religious traditions. No single definition, however, can be universally applied; each tradition uses its own terms for these practices. The Buddha, for example, preached the utility of *dhuta* (Skt.), those actions that one vows to undertake for a period of time and that literally aid in "shaking off" bodily passions. Indeed, Buddhism is a tradition, like Catholic Christianity and classical Hinduism, in which asceticism is central to the practice of the religion. There are, however, some traditions in which it remains relatively undeveloped, such as Shinto, Zoroastrianism, Confucianism, classical Judaism, and most Protestant denominations.

Ascetic Practices: The most common forms of ascetic renunciation focus on food and sexual relations. The practices range widely in rigor: from simple abstinence from certain forms of food (most typically meat) to long-term fasts in which the ascetic survives on meager foods (such as bread and water); from the chaste avoidance of sexual passion to a vow of lifelong virginity. Other important practices include the rejection of money or personal property in favor of a life of voluntary poverty, and the withdrawal from normal modes of social interaction to live in seclusion or in an isolated community of like-minded ascetics. In extreme instances asceticism can go beyond self-denial to self-inflicted mortification, although the propriety of such action has been vigorously debated.

Ascetic practices are distinguished from the ordinary pious actions required of all adherents of a given religion. In general such a distinction is a matter of extent, intensity, or duration. All Muslims, for example, are required to fast during the month of Ramadan, but members of some Sufi orders practice rigorous fasting for their entire lives. Similarly, in certain historical periods, ordinary Christians were required to abstain from meat on certain days of the year in imitation of the total abstinence of monks.

While the practices that constitute asceticism bear many similarities across cultures, the meanings these actions carry may differ radically from one religious tradition to another, and even from period to period or from school to school within individual traditions. Monks follow ascetic life-styles in both Theravada Buddhism and Christianity. The former tradition, however, denies the ultimate existence of the personal self, while the latter preaches the centrality of a personal salvation. Thus the Theravada monk practices fasting and chastity in an attempt to extinguish the self in the attainment of nirvana, while the Christian monk who acts in a similar fashion is striving to gain posthumous entrance into heaven. Similarly, the ascetics of many traditions, including Christianity and Hinduism, modify their normal diet in extreme and nearly continuous fashion, while in other traditions, such as Judaism, moderate fasting is prescribed as a periodic and routine means of attaining ritual purity.

The Development of the Western Ascetic Ideal: In its ancient origins, the Greek word *askesis* referred to exercises performed by soldiers and athletes. By the fifth century B.C. philosophers had adopted the word to refer to their own physical regimen, which was intended to train the body in search of spiritual benefit. The varied schools of Greek philosophy employed different forms of bodily training: Stoics, for example, ate a very spare diet, while Cynics could be recognized by their simple clothing and aversion to money. All shared a vision of the human individual as divided into a (superior) spiritual soul and a (inferior) material body. The Greek philosopher Plato (fourth century B.C.) wrote eloquently of the need for withdrawing the soul from the body. The goal was to purify the soul by controlling the body's appetites and thus achieve a state devoid of passion.

Christianity developed in a Hellenistic environment and inherited this ideal of physical training in search of spiritual perfection, as well as the misogynistic assumption that women were more material than men and hence less capable of spiritual development. (While ancient Israel had largely eschewed asceticism as defined here, rabbinic Judaism came to adopt it from the same Hellenistic environment in which Christianity developed.) Christians, however, set the practice of asceticism within the context of the search for salvation. Early Christian saints were frequently referred to as "soldiers of Christ" or "athletes of God."

This context added a moral dimension to asceticism, because it was practiced for the purpose of penance as well as purification. The body was seen as sinful and in need of punishment in order to attain spiritual perfection. It was not sufficient to withdraw the soul from the body; rather the ascetic had to withdraw from human society, which was sinful in its fallen state. The differences between classical and Christian asceticism can be illustrated with regard to sexual relations. While Greek philosophers valued continence and self-control, they also preached the necessity of the philosopher (presumed to be male) performing his social duty and fathering children. Christians, on the other hand, came to regard virginity as the surest means of making the soul holy. Through virginity Christian ascetics sought not only to purify their bodies, but to remove their bodies from the bonds of society. Virginity also allowed a woman to negate the perceived incapacities of her gender.

The most enduring expression of ascetic ideals within Christianity is the monastic movement. By the fourth century, Christian ascetics had begun to create an alternative society by forming communities in desolate places such as the Egyptian desert, which became, as one author remarked, "a city." The monastic life then and later was marked by a spare diet, frequent fasts, a vow of lifelong chastity, lack of personal property, and silence broken for prayer but not personal conversation. Monastic communities were restricted to a single sex and fewer developed for women than for men.

The sixth-century monk Benedict of Nursia described the monastery as "a school for God's service." One purpose of asceticism for the Christian monks was to share in the sufferings of Christ and thus to gain salvation. As Benedict explained, "Never departing from God's guidelines, remaining in the monastery until death, we patiently share in Christ's passion, so we may enter into the kingdom of God." This ideal for salvation was rejected by the Protestant Reformers, but monasticism has continued to be important in Orthodox and Catholic Christianity.

The World Renouncer in Asian Religions: An analogous set of ascetic institutions developed from a concept of ancient importance in Indian thought, that of world renunciation. The *sannyasin* relinquishes all property and social relations in order to take up life as a wandering beggar who possesses only a begging bowl, a staff, and a simple robe. This poverty assures a certain level of asceticism, but many renouncers undertake further feats of self-mortification, such as extended fasts that leave them emaciated or lead to their deaths. Asceticism serves to eliminate all attachments: the robe of the renouncer resembles a burial shroud and thus serves as a symbol of death to the world. The purpose of renunciation is to seek liberation of the self from the world and thus from the cycle of reincarnation. Traditionally this life is considered to be a possible final stage in the life cycle of a Brahman. While in theory available to women, it is in practice usually undertaken by men and only after their sons have male offspring.

Gautama Buddha was a world renouncer, as was Mahavira, the founder of Jainism. Their new religions incorporated the concept of renunciation as a fundamental organizing principle. Both are divided between a laity, composed of those who live in society and thus accept the near inevitability of reincarnation, and a monastic order, which includes those who renounce such a life in search of the extinction of the self. The use of asceticism, however, distinguishes the Buddhist monk from the Hindu sannyasin. One of the discoveries the Buddha made on his path to enlightenment was that the feats of self-denial

he had performed as an ascetic had focused his attention on his body and thus actually hindered his quest. The Buddha therefore preached the need for moderation in monastic asceticism. Nonetheless, Buddhist monks have no personal property and practice chastity; they eat only what they beg, then moderately, and nothing after the noon hour. Historically there was a monastic order for women: in Buddhism it became extinct only to be refounded recently, while it has survived in Jainism.

Other Forms of Asceticism: These brief sketches by no means exhaust the variety of ways in which asceticism is practiced or of goals for which it is used. The monk and the world renouncer both use asceticism as a means of separating themselves from ordinary human society. Other ascetics, however, choose to remain within it. Many followers of schools of ascetic meditation, such as yoga and Zen, have ordinary vocations and lead lives otherwise typical of their society. The Greek philosopher and the Confucian sage traditionally played important social roles as teachers. Figures as different as the Christian preacher Francis of Assisi (thirteenth century) and the Indian nationalist Mohandas K. Gandhi (twentieth century) have used voluntary poverty as a means of undertaking social reform.

While the institutional forms of monasticism and world renunciation seek the attainment of spiritual purity through the renunciation of physical pleasure, other forms of asceticism stress the acquisition of spiritual powers through bodily exercise. Schools of yoga, for example, counsel long periods of physical exercise that are designed to allow the human body to assume those postures best suited to meditation. Shamans commonly utilize long fasts and vigils to enter the trance states in which they converse with the spirits or visit sacred locales, such as the land of the dead. In Tantrism the adept turns traditional asceticism around through the sacramental enjoyment of forbidden foods and activities as a means of improving meditation. Sexual intercourse, for example, is not only allowed, but prolonged, although not permitted to reach the point of male orgasm.

Asceticism and Dualism: The practice of asceticism implies the belief in an intimate relationship between body and spirit. The relationship asceticism most commonly implies is a dualist one: the body and spirit are separate, but linked, entities, and the spiritual aspect is superior. Dualism, however, does not necessitate asceticism; Zoroastrianism is an example of a dualist religion that shuns asceticism in favor of notions of ritual purity. Moreover, ascetic renunciation of physical pleasure does not imply rejection of the corporeal as useless or evil. The Christian ascetic who fasts in search of union with the divine, for example, may shun pleasure and actively seek suffering in imitation of Christ, but in the process that ascetic also recognizes the body as necessary to the pursuit of salvation.

The focus on the body has meant that the ideals and practice of asceticism have often been shaped by attitudes about gender. The tendency of ascetics to shun sexual relations has led many ascetics to avoid contact with the opposite sex. Conversely, asceticism has in some traditions provided a means for women to compensate for their perceived inferiority to men. But fewer opportunities have traditionally been provided to women for entrance into ascetic communities, such as Christian or Buddhist monasteries.

Ascetic training is never an end unto itself, but is undertaken for a purpose. As the athlete trains to improve the body for better performance, so the ascetic trains to achieve spiritual perfection. Most often asceticism is linked to some form of meditation or contemplation. In traditions that allow for a union between the individual and the divine, asceticism is almost always a necessary part of the mystical path. Asceticism is deemed useful for salvation by its practitioners in various forms of Islam, Christianity, and Judaism. Similarly in traditions that preach the extinction of the personal self, some form of asceticism is usually invoked as useful. For those who practice it, asceticism is a means toward their ultimate spiritual goal. *See also* abstinence; body; celibacy; fasting; hermit; monasticism.

Hinduism: Asceticism within the Hindu traditions neither represents a single institution nor advocates a uniform ideology. It has, therefore, no single origin or common meaning.

On the basis of indigenous legal and theological texts, scholars commonly distinguish two types of asceticism represented by the institutions of the forest hermit and the religious mendicant. In all likelihood, however, these two institutions were themselves the products of Brahmanical theology that sought to reduce the variety of concrete life-styles to two classes.

Ascetic Origins: The view, once common, that asceticism originated among the non-Brahmanical or even the non-Aryan peoples of ancient India is without historical foundation. But to argue that asceticism is purely an internal development of the Vedic religion is to ignore historical complexities. The rise of asceticism was probably influenced by a variety of social, economic, and religious factors, including non-Brahmanical religious practices, anti-Brahmanical protests, and theological developments internal to the Brahmanical tradition.

Solitary Hindu ascetic meditating along the trail to Kedarnath, Uttar Pradesh, India.

We know very little about the origins of the ascetic forms subsumed under the institution of hermits. The institution itself became obsolete in classical Hinduism when the religious mendicant came to represent the typical holy person.

Ascetic forms associated with religious mendicancy can be traced back to the sixth century B.C., which saw the rise of kingdoms, cities, and a merchant class along the upper Ganges Valley. Mendicancy, in all likelihood, was originally an urban phenomenon and arose partly as a response to the spiritual malaise resulting from urbanization. This form of asceticism is closely associated with the worldview centered around the concepts of rebirth (Skt. *samsara*) and liberation (*moksha*) and becomes a central institution also in Buddhism and Jainism.

Ascetic Life-styles: Hermits withdrew physically from civilization, living a settled life in huts constructed in the woods. Their asceticism was characterized by a return to nature and the refusal to use any culturally mediated products, including cultivated food, and by extreme bodily torture, including subjecting the body to extremes of heat and cold, standing motionless for long periods, and fasting.

Mendicants severed all social ties, leaving home and family, abandoning all possessions, begging their food, and living a life of constant wandering. Their act of renunciation was considered so total that it was defined as a social and ritual death that dissolved all social contracts, including marriage, debts, and property rights. Yet their practice of begging brought them into daily contact with society.

Ascetic Ideology: Celibacy and the absence of fire were considered the two central features of religious mendicancy. Beyond the obvious control of sexual passion, celibacy denied religious value to procreation. Maintaining sacred fires and offering sacrifices in them were major components of the Vedic religion. The abandonment of fire symbolized the nonritual state of a mendicant, a necessary condition for aspiring to liberation.

The worldview of samsara, however, considered action (*karma*) as a cause of the rebirth cycle, and ritual was karma par excellence. Ascetic ideology, therefore, regarded celibacy and the absence of fire as symbols of the mendicant's rejection of the two central obligations associated with societal religion: offering sacrifices and begetting children. The ideology and value system on which the mendicant life was based thus represented a total reversal of the socioreligious world of ancient India.

Domestication of Asceticism: The ascetic's withdrawal from society, however, was neither as total nor as completely successful as demanded by ascetic ideology. Inscriptions show the ascetics' continuing concern for their parents; and literature often paints an unflattering picture of ascetics as spies and go-betweens for lovers.

From the earliest times there was also a strong antiascetic tendency within the Brahmanical tradition. Beside defending domesticity, it created structures that sought to domesticate asceticism. One such structure was the system of four "life stages" (*ashramas*), which incorporated asceticism into the individual life cycle in such a way that the early and productive years of a person's life were spent within society, while ascetic pursuits were confined to old age.

Asceticism itself required society; mendicants depended on society for sustenance. Not all ascetics, moreover, lived isolated lives. Most became ascetics within the context of sects with a recognized leadership and a lay following. In medieval India, many Hindu sects were founded or led by ascetics. They lived in monasteries and controlled temples and property. Within the context of these sects, ascetics represented a significant element of society.

Over time, therefore, asceticism became incorporated into the institutional, ideological, and even ritual dimensions of Hinduism to such a degree that historical Hinduism embraces both society and its negation, both domesticity and its renunciation. *See also* ashrama/ashram; Brahmanism; liberation; sadhu; tapas.

Christianity: The paradigm for Christian asceticism is the Gospels' portrait of Jesus, who fasted, preached renunciation, and practiced other ascetic acts and who suffered and sacrificed his life for others. John the Baptist is taken as another model of the Christian ascetic. Paul's Letters reveal not only his own asceticism but also his recommendation that Christians also practice it. Through self-control and discipline Christians participate, according to Paul, in the passion and death of Jesus.

Early Christianity saw widowhood, virginity, and especially martyrdom as ways to demonstrate Christian commitment. A formalization of ascetical doctrine and practice grew with desert monasticism. The archetype of the ascetical life was Anthony (d. 356) as he became known through the influential *Life* composed by Athanasius (d. 373). This *Life* reflected a drawing back from an earlier mystical orientation and emphasized asceticism as a restoration of human spiritual capacities. An ideal of the desert was *apatheia* (Gk.), the purification of passion and desire attained through renunciation. Later, mortifications became a way of recapturing the glory of martyrdom. The writings of Jerome (d. ca. 419) and of John Cassian (d. ca. 432) popularized in the West the asceticism of the monastic East. Resistance to Pelagian attitudes by Augustine (d. 430) put an emphasis on grace, not external actions. Yet, Augustine's Platonism fostered some dualism in the tradition. The sixth-century Benedictine Rule set a tone of moderation for physical asceticism that lasted until the beginning of the twelfth century. Bernard of Clairvaux in the twelfth century and the Franciscans in the thirteenth century developed an intense devotion to the humanity of Jesus, his sufferings and death. Asceticism thus became associated with the cross of Christ. In the later Middle Ages the *Devotio moderna* movement brought monastic asceticism to the laity in writings that systematized the life of prayer and ascetical disciplines.

With its doctrine of justification through faith, Protestantism rejected much of the ascetical practice of the Middle Ages including clerical celibacy and the whole of monasticism. In the seventeenth century, Protestant Pietism reacted against this wholesale rejection of the ascetical tradition by restoring a more positive assessment of human effort and discipline. Among Catholics, Ignatius of Loyola (d. 1556), reacting against the externalism and severity of late medieval asceticism, recommended an asceticism at the service of pastoral ministry. John of the Cross (d. 1591) emphasized an asceticism of the heart as a way of freeing one from inordinate attachments. Moderation in physical practices was also taught by Francis de Sales (d. 1622).

Over the centuries various ascetical practices have been common among Christians, especially in monastic circles: fasting, abstinence from certain foods, silence, voluntary poverty, abstinence from sex, vigils, the limitation of sleep, withdrawal from society, the wearing of uncomfortable clothing such as the hair shirt, and self-flagellation. Celtic spirituality espoused self-exile and perpetual pilgrimage for the sake of Christ. As exiles and missionaries, the Irish monks spread a desertlike asceticism throughout Europe.

Asceticism always runs the danger of distortion. The ascetic can put exclusive emphasis on the external, become self-absorbed or proud, denigrate the body, or forget the needs of others. However, the Christian tradition at its best has consistently cautioned moderation in physical asceticism and has always affirmed asceticism's positive orientation as a liberation from whatever prevents love of God and neighbor.

The formalism and externalism of asceticism bred a suspicion of traditional practices of self-denial. Fasting and abstinence from meat, practices that once marked Catholic life especially during Lent are now only minimally required but still common in the Orthodox tradition. Despite modern suspicions of asceticism, there is an intense and growing interest in movements that confront addictions. A dialogue with this secular asceticism is a task of contemporary Christian spirituality.

Since Vatican II (1962–65) there has been a concerted search for a more positive orientation to asceticism in Catholicism. The theologian Karl Rahner (1904–84) sees asceticism in the context of a life of faith. For him a new asceticism could be developed through the joyful fulfillment of one's responsibilities. For Rahner asceticism is necessary to leading a mature spiritual life directed to the love of God. In the 1980s Protestant theologian Margaret Miles discovered that there has been in the tradition an asceticism whose purpose was the search for a fullness of life. Miles has shown that the early tradition had a more positive view of the body than has been presumed by some. The recovery of a positive theology of the body is a key to a wholesome asceticism. The contemporary Catholic theologian Elizabeth Dreyer has taken Rahner's suggestion for an asceticism of everyday responsibilities and has recommended a graceful response to the demanding challenges of a consumer and addictive culture. For Dreyer there may be no more demanding forms of self-denial than letting go of illusion and acceptance of reality, courageous confrontation of the diminishments of aging and death, and responsible parenting. *See also* monasticism.

Islam: Asceticism has had only limited appeal to most Muslims. A variety of disciplines, including fasting and seclusion, aimed to confine temptation, though permanent celibacy was viewed as a violation of quranic and prophetic proscription. However, among the mystics it became a periodic regimen for purification, harnessing self-denial for self-control and spiritual illumination. *See also* Sufism.

Japanese Religion: From ancient times forms of abstinence, such as refraining from foods and sexual contact, and forms of purification, such as use of water, were practiced and these have continued within Shinto. Taoist practices like abstaining from grain were rarely followed (in the case of self-mummified Buddhas, *miira*), but popular Taoist customs such as all-night vigils and avoidance of sex were widespread. The most pervasive ascetic influence in Japanese practice is Buddhism; the most characteristic term is *shugyo* (Jap., "ascetic practice"), which is used for formal Buddhist austerities and also for extraordinary exertions (such as pilgrimage) by laypeople. Ascetic practices vary widely, from deprivation of sleep and food to intense and extended forms of meditation and recitation and even to physical pain, but the intention of all forms is intensified religious experience and/or extraordinary power. Examples of such asceticism include confinement (on a mountain, in a cave, in a temple), repeated water ablutions (or standing under a waterfall), or—especially for laypeople—walking barefoot back and forth a hundred times between specially designated stones within shrine or temple grounds while reciting formulas of repentance. *See also* Shugendo.

Asclepios (a-skle'pee-ohs), an ancient Greek healing divinity, symbolized by a snake. Devotees sought cures in his temples by incubation (diagnosis through dreams). *See also* Greek religion; healing.

Asgardr (os-gahr'thr; Norse, "the home of the gods"), dwelling place of the Scandinavian gods, at the center of the world, reached by a rainbow bridge. *See also* Nordic religion.

Asharite, an adherent to the basic theological methodology and doctrine of Abu al-Hasan al-Ashari (d. 935). Al-Ashari employed reason in the defense of the traditionalist Muslim creed, especially the creed of Ahmad ibn Hanbal (d. 855), which was based on the Qur'an and the *hadith* (traditions). But, while the latter renounced the use of reason or speculative theology (i.e., *kalam*), al-Ashari justified its use in defending the true faith against external attacks and internal deviators. Al-Ashari and his followers nonetheless were critical of the extreme rationalism of the rival Mutazilite School. The Asharites also rejected the blind emulation of other scholars, be they pious ancestors or contemporary scholars, and advocated the obligation of individual believers to use reason (and as a minimum, the simplest kind of reasoning) in proving doctrines to their own satisfaction before they adhered to them. Asharites thought it necessary to demonstrate rationally the existence of a creator (God), and that he is one, unique, and eternal; and to establish the veracity of the claimant to prophecy. They affirmed seven essential eternal attributes of God: life, will, omnipotence, omniscience, speech, vision, and hearing (some, like al-Baqillani, added permanence [*baqa*]). As to the relation of these attributes to the essence of God, Asharites offered the perplexing formula: "they are not He [God's essence] nor other than He." Affirming God's various attributes, the later Asharites interpreted anthropomorphic expressions allegorically. They also introduced discussions of epistemology. Asharites affirmed the Qur'an to be the speech of God, uncreated, thus taking a stand on one of the most disputed issues in medieval Islam. Many Asharite theologians distinguished between God's "self speech," which is eternal, and the speech of God in the Qur'an, which is written on paper with ink, recited by the tongue, and memorized in the heart—all created things. Yet, what is conveyed thereby is the uncreated speech of God.

Another debated issue was human physical and moral control over action. The Asharites said that human capacity over action is acquired (*kasb* or *muktasab*) from God for the action and at the very moment of action. But they maintained that while God creates the power for the action, a human being is responsible and held accountable for the action. Their detractors, the Mutazilites, accused the Asharites of holding to predestination, and although the later Asharites added the affirmation that humans have choices over their actions, the claim was too qualified to be convincing.

The Asharites claimed to be the defenders of the true doctrine. For a time they dominated the core land of the Muslim caliphate and some of the western provinces, but in the course of time they could not reach the populace, which was mainly traditionalist and anti-kalam. For a while, the Asharites were cursed, in some mosques from the pulpit, as in Khurasan during the rule of the Saljuq Turk, Tughril Beg, a Sunni Hanafite warlord in the eleventh century. The Asharites recovered under another Saljuq, Nizam al-Mulk, who established colleges— called the Nizamiyya after himself—and utilized the Asharites as professors. Some of the famous Asharite theologians are: al-Baqillani (d. 1013), al-Juwayni (d. 1085), al-Ghazali (d. 1111), al-Shahrastani (d. 1153), and Fakhr al-Din al-Razi (d. 1210). *See also* Hanbalite; Islamic philosophy; Mutazila.

Ashkenazi (ahsh-ke-nah'zee; Heb.), a Jew originating in central or eastern Europe. Ashkenazi Jews adopted Yiddish, based on medieval German, and have their own culinary traditions, which derive in part from their Polish, Romanian, Russian, and German neighbors. The name *Ashkenaz* comes from the name of the eldest son of Gomer son of Japheth (Genesis 10:3), which became identified with Germany. Ashkenazi Jewry originated in Speyer, Worms, and Mainz in the tenth century and gradually moved eastward into Germany and Bohemia, then Poland, Lithuania, Belorussia, the Ukraine, and elsewhere. The majority of American Jews are Ashkenazim. *See also* Sephardi; Yiddish.

Ashoka (uh-shoh'kuh), emperor of India from 272 to 236 B.C. Ashoka is best known for his royal edicts in which he propounded his polity of Dharma, a program advocating religious tolerance, common ethical observances, an end to violence, and active social concern. In Buddhist legends, he is presented as a convert to Buddhism who becomes a model of kingship and a patron of the monastic community. Pali sources portray him as upholding orthodoxy, convening a great council of elders at Pataliputra, and sending out missionaries to various lands. Sanskrit legends feature his construction of eighty-four thousand *stupas* (reliquary mounds). *See also* kingship, sacred; stupa; universal monarch.

ashrama/ashram (ahsh'ruh-muh/ash'ruhm; Skt./Eng.). **1** Hindu term for each of the four stages of life: student, householder, forest dweller, and homeless wanderer. **2** A place for spiritual retreat. *See also* asceticism; four goals of life (Hinduism).

Ashtoret. *See* Astarte.

Ashura (ah-shoo-ra'; Arab.), tenth day of Muharram, first month of the Muslim calendar, originally the Jewish fast of the tenth day of Tishri. Muslims fasted the day until the institution of Ramadan in 624. Ashura attained special significance in Muslim piety as a day commemorating the martyrdom of Husayn ibn Ali. *See also* fasting; Husayn ibn Ali; Islam (festal cycle).

Ashvattha tree (uhsh-vuht'tuh; Skt., "under which horses stand") in Hinduism the holy fig tree (*ficus religiosa*), also called *peepul*. In Indus Valley seals a buffalo-horned goddess stands in its branches. In Vedic ritual it is used for one or both of the firesticks, conceived as the womb of fire, and for the *soma* vessel. Passages in the Vedas, Upanishads, and *Bhagavad Gita* identify it as the inverted cosmic tree: roots above in the transcendent realms, branches below in the earthly realms. It is the Buddhist Bodhi Tree, and in Jainism the symbolic tree of the fourteenth Tirthankara Anantanatha. *See also* Bodhi Tree; Veda, Vedism.

Ashvins (uhsh'vinz; Skt., "possessing horses"), twin gods of Vedic and later India. Handsome young men, they are physicians of the gods who also perform miraculous rescues, protect humans, and guide them to enlightenment. *See also* Veda, Vedism.

Ash Wednesday, the first day of the Christian penitential season of Lent signaled by the rite of having ashes marked on the forehead by a priest as a sign of penitence or mortality. Before the tenth century it was the day in the Roman church when sinners began their period of public penance. *See also* calendar (Christian).

Assemblies of God, largest mainly Caucasian Pentecostal denomination in the United States. The Assemblies of God was organized in Hot Springs, Arkansas, in 1914 as the Pentecostal movement was spreading rapidly throughout the nation, and several diverse regional constituencies of Reformed (rather than Holiness) background (especially groups based in Alabama, Illinois, Ohio, and Texas) were seeking to combine coordinated action with local autonomy. Although the founders resisted creedal statements other than an appeal to scripture, doctrinal controversies soon led to the enunciation of a trinitarian position in the Assemblies' "Statement of Fundamental Truths" (1916) against the "Oneness" doctrine that had gained adherence among some Pentecostals. Other doctrinal controversies would later periodically trouble the denomination, but did not prevent its rapid growth and pursuit of such activities as the publication of the periodical *The Pentecostal Evangel*, foreign missions, and, gradually, Bible schools. In 1918, its headquarters were moved to Springfield, Missouri, where they remain; polity is basically presbyterian, with a General Council meeting biennially. The Assemblies of God benefited greatly from the surge of interest in conservative Protestantism during the 1970s and 1980s, and by the mid-1980s had over ten thousand local churches and two million members. *See also* Pentecostalism.

assumption, a traditional Roman Catholic and Orthodox belief that the Virgin Mary, upon her death, was taken up body and soul to heaven, promulgated as a divinely revealed dogma by Pope Pius XII in 1950. It is usually celebrated by a feast day on August 15. *See also* Mary.

Assyro-Babylonian religions. *See* Mesopotamian religion.

Astarte (ast'ahr-teh), the Phoenician name of the ancient Near Eastern goddess also known as Babylonian Ishtar, Canaanite Athtart, and Syrian Atargatis—bestower of fertility and consort of the high god. She is anathematized in the Bible as Ashtoret, although she was undoubtedly venerated in both local and official Israelite cults. *See also* Aramaean religion; Atargatis; Canaanite religion; Ishtar; Mesopotamian religion; Phoenicians.

astral body, in occult systems, the form of the soul or inner self outside the physical body or in the astral plane. Thus disembodied, the conscious self is thought to be capable of travel around and beyond the world, into other realms of existence to gain esoteric knowledge or to communicate with other like souls. *See also* occult, the.

astral projection, in occult systems, the sensation that the soul or inner self exists outside the body. Advanced by Spiritualists since the 1800s and supported by New Age movements since the 1970s, belief in astral projection postulates that the disembodied conscious self may travel to otherwise unknowable realms of the universe for otherwise unachievable wisdom. *See also* occult, the.

astral spirits (Korea). The public and private worship of the spirits of stars and constellations in Korea draws upon native traditions and the imported traditions of Confucianism and Taoism. The most prominent star spirits are the Seven Stars or Big Dipper (Kor. *Ch'ilsong*), the Two Hidden Stars of the Nine Polar Stars (*Misong*), the Pole Star (*Paeksong*), the Star of Peace or Canopus (*Noinsong*), the Star of Horse Spirits

(*Majo*, located in Scorpio), and the Star of Grain Cultivation (*Yongsong*, also located in Scorpio). Each of these stars or constellations represents a celestial palace in which a spirit or several spirits reside and from which the spirit or spirits can be called to intervene in human affairs. There is no organized hierarchy among the star spirits and depending upon the rites performed different spirits with different functions may be worshiped within the same celestial palace, as is the case of the worship of the Queen Mother of the West, Tan'gun, the Lord on High, the Bodhisattvas Three and Seven Star, and the local village mountain god—all of which reside in the Big Dipper.

The iconographic representation of these astral spirits in paintings and statues portrays them as human figures dressed in the costumes of royal, military, or civil authority and accompanied by auspicious, protecting animals. The most widespread representation is that of a bearded ancient sitting or resting on top of a tiger beneath a pine tree, which, some have argued, may represent the remnant of a very ancient Korean belief in the Lord of the Animals or Lord of the Hunt, a belief also found among Siberian and Tungusic tribes.

Worship of these star spirits on a national level is most in evidence during the Koryo (918–1392) and Choson periods (1392–1910), when designated shrines and altars were established and yearly rituals ordered by the government. In the modern period, the worship of astral spirits is private and increasingly confined to rural village areas where the local mountain tutelary is astrally placed and worshiped as part of the New Year community renewal rites. In urban areas the worship of astral spirits is in decline but may be still found in some Buddhist temples, where an altar to the Bodhisattva Lord of the Seven Primal Stars is maintained, among urban shamans and their clients who invoke the power of the star spirits during the performance of *kut* (shamanistic rites), and among women who make tribute offerings (*kosa*) to the household gods, one of which is called Seven Stars. *See also* kosa; kut.

astrological animals (China). Within the sixty-year time cycle of the Chinese calendar there are five subcycles of twelve years, each dominated in turn by the five agents (*wu-hsing*) or, more popularly, by the astrological animals. The sequence of the twelve animals is fixed: rat, ox, tiger, rabbit, dragon, snake, horse, goat, monkey, chicken, dog, pig. The legend is that the Buddha summoned all the animals to a lecture, but only twelve appeared; each of them was then rewarded with one year, in the order of their arrival. *See also* calendar (China).

astrology, belief in and practice of determining the influence of the stars. The origin myths of stars recount the adventures of the *zodiac* (a term deriving from the Greek word *zodiakon*, meaning a collection of animals). An alternate etymology, from *zoidion* (a figure carved out of some larger mass), is equally revealing. In many cultural mythologies around the globe, the stellar animals (or figures with animal emblems) took up their heavenly posts after being hunted down, slain, partially dismembered, carved up, or consumed. At the very least, they were hounded from their primordial habitat. Such is the case for the lizards and serpents of Polynesian astronomical myths; the llamas, alpacas, and tinamous of Andean astronomies; the anacondas and tapirs of Amazonian peoples' zodiacs; the rheas of communities in the Gran Chaco of South America; and so on.

Astrological Mind-set—A World of Correspondences: The displacement of mythical star beings plays a principle role in systems of correspondences that include the animals; their associated symbolism; the cardinal points and intercardinal axes; the zenith and nadir of the universe; and a host of colors, shapes, sounds, weather patterns, plants, and relations mentioned in their myths and legends. The myths and legends of star origins often appear to generate arbitrary strings of associations, but they disclose key relations that exist in the cosmos.

Astrology bases itself on these relations and correspondences: since diverse symbolic orders arise in the same mythic episodes, those events that generate the life of the stars can orient the universe into a coherent system. Astral order and the governing structures of space and time appear as constructs of the religious imagination, which establishes imaginal links between the placement and displacement of mythical heavenly beings, between the regular appearance and disappearance of the resultant stars, and between the moving forces of heaven and the effects of those movements on earth. Astrology builds upon the knowledge of those irreversible events that originated the passage and reckoning of time and set the constellations in motion. The fates of cosmic and human existence are but ripples and resonances of these larger, primordial movements.

The bodily parts of slain mythical beings serve as metronomes of human fate. The movements of limbs or wings in flight through the night sky create temporal and spatial markers. The light, time, and space of the stars still reveal something of the reality they first inhabited. Each celestial animal has its own species of time, manifest in the breeding, gestation, growth, and molting cycles of its emblem animal, but also in the unique movements of their limbs, amputated or interrupted while moving in full stride. Now those dancelike steps mete out incessantly the varied rhythms of time to which the cosmos moves and by which the time of human festival and fate is measured.

Based on their appearances and reappearances and their shifting relations to one another, the constellations differentiate synodical rhythms, lunar phases, Venusian cycles, and annual circuits of distinct measure. Together they form one cosmos and the mythology of stars show why these separate rhythms may be coordinated into a megacycle, or calendar, and how calendars suggest that the connective forces of the universe transcend the parts in favor of the whole that was lost. That wholeness must now be imagined. It may only be glimpsed in the ceaseless recycling of the broken parts. Astrology professes to provide that glimpse of the whole, much like a composite afterimage spread throughout periodic time. The mind-set of astrology seems not unrelated to the convictions among atomic scientists today that much about the determinative structure and direction of cosmic matter can be known clearly if a supercollider can mime the movement of particles that occurred once and for all in the first fraction of a nanosecond of the universe's first big bang. The reappearance of primordial movements can provide the measure of their effects, effects that constitute the universe.

In a world of correspondences, the interdependence of all forms of periodic existence is a measure of reality. Changes in the sky, in animal or human form, in weather or season mutually affect one another. Through the generally regular changes of the stars, astrology seeks to divine the effects of change on the human condition.

Astrological Practice: To glimpse how astrology operates in practice, we may briefly outline structures that have passed from Greek and Roman systems through Renaissance astrology. The astrology of Hellenism as it is known from the third century B.C. is ascribed to a synthesis of Greek, Egyptian, and Chaldean sources. Its variant forms were concerned with correspondences among figures of the zodiac, other planets and stars, marked features of the landscape, and the parts and disposition of the human body. Also factored into some systems

(such as that of Hipparchus of Alexandria in 150 B.C.) were plants, metals, gemstones, the ages of the world, the fate of planets, and the heavenly signs that ascended into the sky in the first instant that the earth was made. For example, the days of the week were set in correspondence with metals and planets: Sunday, gold (sun); Monday, silver (moon); Tuesday, iron (Mars), and so on.

In the second century, the Greek astronomer Ptolemy gathered together many of the extant variable systems and attempted to standardize them. By the middle of the eighth century, there was a lively Arabic interest in astrology, driven partly by the translation of Greek works that had survived in Pahlavi translations. The Arabic works were to have a considerable influence on astrological systems of the Renaissance and their derivatives, beginning in 1202, when Leonardo of Pisa (Fibonacci) introduced the Arabic system of numerals. Shortly thereafter the Norman kingdom of Sicily sponsored the translation of Greek texts from Arabic into Latin, with the aid of Arab and Jewish scholars. Michael Scotus, the astrologer of Frederick II, was knowledgeable and influential in the development and diffusion of the astrological tradition. In Toledo in 1252 King Alfonso X of Castile sponsored an assembly of fifty Jewish and Christian scholars to translate the works of Ptolemy, among other scientists, from Arabic into Castilian.

In general, this tradition of astrological systems functioned by overlaying one complex system on another: the system of the stars of heaven on the system of apportioned human conditions and fates. But it must be noted that in the most powerful and perduring astrological systems, the relation of heavenly macrocosm to human microcosm was not simple, not a closed, one-to-one correspondence. Given the variables involved and exploited in the complexities of each system, what results is a generative, open-ended metasystem capable of mapping an infinite number of variables. Astrology served as an immense information storage and retrieval system.

Key elements in the system include the constellations, the houses, and the seven planets. The twelve major constellations of the zodiac lie in the path of the planets, each sign with its distinctive gender, ethos, location, and form. Each is assigned a section of the circle of the sky (divided into three sections, or "decans," of ten degrees each). They are frequently grouped and regrouped in recombinant triads, in which one or another sign is regnant. Each of the four triads becomes associated with primal elements, seasons of the year, cardinal directions, and so on. The houses are the prescriptive divisions into twelve parts of the path taken by the zodiacal signs. Usually there are twelve such houses (e.g., health, wealth, marriage, death, travel, honor, life) through which rotate the twelve signs of the zodiac (divided into at least thirty-six decans). And the seven planets have their own sundry aspects, qualities, and subordinate signs.

Into each configuration and conjunction of moving parts is read a significance. Various astrological methods of reading focus on one or another set of variables: between stars and body, or signs, decans, and planets, or planets, stars, and animals, and so on. The concerns of a specific individual can be inserted into the permutation program by reckoning with the position of key variables at the very moment of the individual's birth, especially the position of the planet or sign rising on the eastern horizon. The astrologer then reads all the combinatorial permutations that emerge when these positions are set in relation to three fixed points in the system. This principle still serves as the basis of most contemporary horoscopes (from *hora* and *skopein*, that "seen" at the "time [of one's birth]").

As astrological systems of many cultures around the world come to be examined with more care, the astrological traditions descending from the Mediterranean are likely to be recovered, renewed, and reshaped. Indeed, through contact with Islam and Christianity in particular, many astrological systems have arrived at transmutations whose history and function are little known. *See also* starlore and ethnoastronomy.

Hinduism: As terrestrial events are believed by many Hindus to correspond to celestial phenomena, astrology is popularly used in Indian culture to explain past as well as future events. Related to Hindu astrology is *jyotihshastra* (Skt.), the science of astronomy, one of the subsidiary fields of the Vedas (Vedanga), which was used to determine the appropriate times for Vedic sacrifices. In the medieval period, having been influenced by Western astronomy and adopting the zodiacal system, Indian astronomy became a tool of astrology, the art of prognostication. Natal astrology (*jatakashastra*) in particular is widespread among Hindus. Astrologers are consulted on the proper time for marriages, paying debts, life-cycle ceremonies, occupying a new house, investments, travel, etc. Astrology is used especially in arranging marriages and in selecting children's ritual names. In natal astrology, a

horoscope is cast based on the exact moment and place of birth and is used to predict one's character, temperament, longevity, health, and prosperity. Despite similarities, Hindu and Western astrologies also differ. The Hindu system does not correct for the precession of the equinoxes and considers the moon rather than the sun to be of fundamental importance. It recognizes the twelve signs of the zodiac (*rashi*), twenty-seven lunar mansions (*nakshatra*), and nine planets (*graha*), namely, the five visible planets, the moon, the sun, and the ascending and descending points at which the orbit of the moon intersects the earth's orbital plane, respectively known as Rahu and Ketu. *See also* auspicious/inauspicious (Hinduism).

Chinese Religion: Intimately linked with cosmology, Chinese astrology uses astronomical data as well as various philosophical-religious concepts: the five agents theory (Chin. *wu-hsing*), *yin-yang* speculation, the eight trigrams (*pa-kua*), and the Ten Heavenly Stems and Twelve Earthly Branches. The Chinese traditional worldview stresses the unity of heaven and earth so that heavenly bodies and earthly powers all affect human fate. Particularly popular is fate calculation based on the time of birth recorded in relation to year, month, day, and hour. These "four pillars" indicate the precise influences of the heavenly bodies on a person's future life. *See also* cosmology; pa-kua; wu-hsing; yin and yang.

New Religions: Contemporary Western astrology relies on the Greek calendar, which divided the skies into twelve sections or houses of the zodiac; astrologers chart the dominant section or sign at the moment of one's birth, along with the placement of other planets and notable celestial objects, in order to ascertain which cosmic forces might affect each individual life. Astrologers similarly predict the influence of planetary conjunctions or of extraordinary phenomena such as eclipses or novas on earthly history.

astronomy (China). Since the late Neolithic the Chinese have been acute observers of the heavens, attaching signal importance to the signs or "images" (*hsiang*) suspended overhead. According to tradition it was contemplation of celestial patterns that prompted Fu-Hsi, first of the legendary sovereigns, to devise the multivalent diagrams of the *I-ching* (Book of Changes). Throughout Chinese history celestial omens— eclipses, planetary conjunctions, comets, and unusual meteorological phenomena—have invariably been interpreted as portentous events.

To the early Chou kings they communicated Heaven's decrees regarding the fate of the dynasty; to the later imperial courts they were an unpredictable facet of political reality that could sometimes be manipulated, but never ignored; for hundreds of generations of ordinary Chinese they foretold the passing of the great and the advent of unsettling change. Confucius himself considered the seasonal revolution of the "heavenly offices" (the constellations) about the immovable pole the perfect symbol of the sage-king who accomplishes all in timely fashion without having to bestir himself. Judging from the imperial nomenclature applied to the circumpolar stars, especially T'ai-i ("Great Unique") and T'ien-ti-hsing ("Celestial Emperor"), both ancient pole stars in the constellation Draco, it is likely that in high antiquity this singular location was considered the abode of the high god Ti. Since the ancient Chinese acquired the habit early on of harmonizing their activity with the regular motions of the sun, moon, and stars, it was entirely in character for them to respond with alarm to unforeseen revelations from above. *See also* I-ching.

Asuka period (ah-soo-kah; ca. 550–710), the age when Chinese culture, including Buddhism, writing, and a complex bureaucracy, was first assimilated in Japan. *See also* Japanese religion.

asura (uh'soor-uh; Skt., "lord"). 1 In Vedic and later India, a supernatural being portrayed as an implacable enemy of the gods (*devas*). Stories of hostile competition between the *asuras* and the devas, their older brothers, abound. 2 In the earliest Vedic literature, a title used of gods (devas). *See also* demons; Veda, Vedism.

Atargatis (a-tahr-ga'tees), also known as "the Syrian goddess," whose cult spread to Greece and Egypt by the third century B.C. and then to Italy. *See also* Aramaean religion; Astarte; Lucian of Samosata.

Aten. *See* Aton.

Atharva Veda (uh-thahr'vuh vay'duh; ca. 1000 B.C.), one of the four Vedas that form the classical Hindu canon; it contains spells and unusual rites and hymns. *See also* Ayurveda; Veda, Vedism.

atheism (Gk. *a-theos*, "no god"), a critical stance toward divinity. Ancient forms of atheism, for example, the Greek atomist school of philosophy, did not deny the possible existence of gods but did deny their permanence and immortality. The atomists viewed the gods—if they existed—as merely higher forms of life within nature. Buddhism does not exempt the gods from the cycle of karmic reincarnation. Modern naturalistic atheism descends from atomism but goes further and denies the existence of any superhuman beings, of any form of transcendent order or meaning in the universe. These notions, it insists, are merely temporary human projections onto a reality alien to human thinking. In practice, atheism denotes a way of life conducted in disregard of any alleged superhuman reality. Existential atheism is a positive form of the teaching: it argues that if humans are to be authentically free in the universe, then it is necessary that God not exist since that would limit human liberty. *See also* agnosticism; theism.

Athena (ah-thee'nah), ancient Greek goddess. Born from her father's head, she was the warlike, virginal daughter of Metis and Zeus; she appears in armor as preserver of Athens. *See also* Greek religion.

Athos, Mt., a marble promontory on the Chalcidice peninsula in northern Greece, also known as "the holy mountain." Since the tenth century, it has been the home of numerous Christian Greek Orthodox monastic settlements. The monasteries are noted for their rigorous discipline and for the conservation of Orthodox ideals. Since 1060, women and female animals have been barred from the mountain. The monasteries form a self-governing community recognized by the current Greek constitution (1927). *See also* monasticism; Orthodox Church; pilgrimage.

Atlantis, mythical prehistoric island submerged in the Atlantic Ocean, first described in Plato's fable of an ideal civilization whose inhabitants vanished when the island sank. In recent retellings, the island's inhabitants survive to found other great civilizations (Egyptian or Mayan); form an occult coterie of supremely powerful mystics; or ascend to earthly or unearthly heights as the Ascended Masters, whose channeled revelations inspire several divergent New Age groups. *See also* Cayce, Edgar; Lemuria; occult, the; paradise.

atman (aht'muhn; Skt., "breath"), in Hinduism, the individual soul or life-force, eternal, indestructible, identical to the Godhead and of the nature of pure being, consciousness, and bliss. *See also*

Hinduism; Hinduism (thought and ethics); six systems of Indian philosophy.

Aton (ah'ten), or Aten, the Egyptian sun disk, the object of veneration under King Amenhotep IV (Akhenaton, fourteenth century B.C.). *See also* Akhenaton; Egyptian religion.

atonement. 1 Reestablishment of a proper relationship between the divine and human realms by means of some positive action, most commonly sacrifice. 2 In Christian thought, the application of the sacrificial model to Jesus' death. *See also* ritual; sacrifice.

Atonement, Day of. *See* Yom Kippur.

Attis (at'ees), in Phrygian mythology, a mortal youth, whether shepherd or prince, beloved by the goddess Cybele, to whom he pledged his fidelity and who drove him mad after he fell under the spell of a nymph. In a frenzy, he castrated himself, thus rendering himself immune to human desires. This ritual act of permanent purification in service to Cybele was characterized in Greek texts as "becoming feminine" and was considered prototypical by her eunuch priests, the *Galli*. Attis is often identified as an example of the "dying and rising" type of deity, who disappears with the harvest only to be resurrected in the spring with the vegetation. However, Attis is a mortal and not a divine figure, and there is no mention in myth of his returning to life. The cult of Attis was rare in Greece but arrived in Rome in 204 B.C. with the cult of Cybele. Attis achieved equal status with her in the cult by the mid-second century. An Attis festival was celebrated in Rome on March 22 with a procession bearing a pine tree, the emblem of Attis, to the temple of Cybele. This was followed on March 24 by the Day of Blood, a day of mourning in commemoration of the castration. A Day of Joy celebrated on March 25, the third day, is not for the resurrection of Attis, for which no evidence exists, but for purifying Cybele. In the later Roman Empire, Attis took on celestial attributes as a solar deity. *See also* Roman religion.

Auditors (aw'dee-torz; Lat., "listeners"), in Manichaeism the lower class of Manichaeans, as opposed to the Elect, the upper class, the monklike leaders. *See also* Manichaeism.

Augsburg Confession, the basic confession of faith of the Lutheran churches. Written principally by Philipp Melanchthon and first pre-

sented to Emperor Charles V at the Diet of Augsburg (1530), its theological platform, in twenty-one articles, sought to show that in essential matters it did not differ from the Catholic Church's and listed abuses that had been corrected. The "unaltered" version, as published in 1580, has always been authoritative for Lutherans; a subsequent version prepared by Melanchthon in 1540 is accepted by many Reformed (Calvinist) churches in Germany. *See also* creed; Lutheranism.

augurs, professional class of diviners. *See also* divination.

Augustine of Canterbury (aw'guhs-teen; d. ca. 604), first Christian evangelizer of southern England and first archbishop of Canterbury.

Augustine of Hippo (aw'guhs-teen; 354–430), a major Christian theologist. Born in Tagaste in North Africa, Augustine devoted his youth to experimentation with a variety of religions and philosophies in North Africa and Italy. In Milan, under the influence of friends and teachers, Augustine converted to Catholic Christianity in 386. In the following years, he lived the contemplative life first in Italy and then in North Africa. On a visit in 391 to Hippo Regius, the townspeople drafted him as a priest. In 396 he became the bishop of Hippo, thereafter playing an influential role in the life of the North African Church.

Augustine used his skills as a writer to attack three principal challenges. In his writings against the Manichees, he rejected their notion that an evil god is responsible for evil in the world, arguing that the source of evil lies in the misuse of the human will. Against the Donatists (North Africans who insisted on complete moral purity), Augustine stated that the expulsion of sinners from the community of the saved must, except in egregious cases, be left to God. In the writings against the Pelagians, Augustine insisted on divine prevenience, grace that precedes the choice of free will, and on the utter gratuity of the salvific process.

Augustine's *Confessions* (ca. 400) provides a moving account of his progress to Christianity in which he praises God for bringing him to the truth. *On Christian Doctrine* (396–427) describes the correct way to read scripture. The *City of God* (413–426), written to defend Christians against the charge that they were responsible for the collapse of the Roman Empire, offers a theology of history. The *Trinity* (399–419) presents a series of meditations on the triune God and notes the traces of the Trinity in the world that make it possible to attain a deeper knowledge of God.

Aum. *See* Om/Aum.

Aum Shinrikyo (oh-m*oo* shin-ree-kyoh), a Japanese new religion. The term *Aum* is a borrowing of the Sanskrit sacred syllable *om; Shinrikyo* is usually translated "Supreme Truth." Founded by Chizuo Matsumoto (b. 1955), who changed his name to Shoko Asahara, it became a legally recognized religion in 1989. Based on his experience of enlightenment in the Himalayas in 1986, Asahara established a teaching combining meditative and ascetic practices from Hinduism and Buddhism together with Japanese and some Western elements; he encouraged followers to intensify their spiritual energy to counteract evil energy and avert a catastrophe at the end of the 1990s. *See also* Japan, new religions in; Om/Aum.

aura (or'ah), in esoteric lore, a pattern of physical or supraphysical radiation said to surround a human being and other living organisms and to be visible to clairvoyants. The shape and color of the aura is often said to indicate the health and spiritual condition of the subject. *See also* occult, the.

auspicious, inauspicious (Hinduism), gloss for a variety of Sanskrit and vernacular terms, most frequently *mangala* and *shubha* and their opposites, *amangala* and *ashubha*. When positive, the terms refer to whatever furthers well-being and the enhancement and continuity of life. No time, object, or person is inherently auspicious or inauspicious; it is made so by a conjunction of objects, persons, astral bodies, or events in a particular relationship to each other. Whether someone or something is auspicious or not thus varies contextually. To see a married woman carrying a pot is auspicious, but not if the pot is empty.

The concern with auspiciousness/inauspiciousness is central for householders and kings, a kingdom being modeled on the household. It is this-worldly and pervades ritual life. In certain Hindu traditions such as Shrivaishnavism, auspiciousness can also be the spiritual path to liberation.

Married women whose husbands are alive and consort goddesses, especially Shri-Lakshmi, are particularly associated with auspiciousness. A king's ability to perform his role as guarantor of prosperity, well-being, and fertility in his kingdom depends on his being wedded to Shri-Lakshmi. Shri's human incarnations are wives and *devadasis* ("women temple servants"). When Shri leaves a king, prosperity and well-being depart from his realm. *See also* astrology; devadasi; Shri-Lakshmi; Shrivaishnavism.

Australia, new religions in, millennial, accommodative, and revivalistic movements begun in Australia over the past century. Related to the disruptions of native cultures in contact with European colonial powers, new religions in Australia are grounded in the most ancient beliefs and practices of the continent.

The first human inhabitants arrived in Australia about fifty thousand years ago. Their occupancy appears to have been undisturbed by foreign incursions, and over that long period these aboriginal (indigenous, usually referred to as aboriginal) hunting and gathering people developed a complex religious life, which, despite much cultural and social diversity, centered on shared themes. Celebrations of the beings who create the world, maintenance of the laws that accommodate difference to produce continuity through time, and regeneration of creation and of humanity's place in the great scheme are common to all aboriginal cultures.

The first major disruptive incursion is dated to the arrival of Captain James Cook in 1788, when the English explorer claimed much of the continent for Great Britain and opened the way for colonization. In many parts of Australia, aboriginal population loss through massacres, introduced diseases, starvation, enforced settlement and subsequent dependence on addictive substances was about 95 percent. Many social problems that resulted from this history continue to affect aboriginal peoples adversely.

For nearly a century, scholars assumed that aboriginal life—intellectual, social, and spiritual—was rigidly incapable of change. The idea that aboriginal people could and would seek creative responses to the devastating impact of outsiders was virtually unthinkable. Across the continent, however, there is evidence of the aboriginal genius for accommodation: footprints of Jesus, remnants of Noah's ark, and places where God visited are to be found. Aboriginal Australia simmers with religious creativity: new religious movements, Christian revivals, Captain Cook(s), crystals, and healing techniques. The specific content varies both in time and in space.

Millennial Movements: One type of response to the coming of outsiders is the millennial movement, which prophesies the overthrow of the existing order. The Mulunga cult, which spread rapidly from Queensland and New South Wales to South Australia around the turn of the century, is the first of this type to be documented. The Mulunga cult consisted of rituals and myths that portrayed Europeans as shooting Aborigines, after which the Europeans themselves were destroyed by a spiritual power called the "Grandmother," who came from the sea.

A similar religious movement, better documented, emerged in northeast Western Australia in the early 1960s. It focused on a reported vision of a personage called Jinimin, or Jesus, who had appeared in the east and told aboriginal people that they would regain control of their land only if they adhered rigorously to their own laws and religious practices. Jinimin-Jesus promised that after the successful fight with Europeans, Aborigines would receive white skins. In the same area there is a set of beliefs about Noah's Ark, which is said to have come to rest nearby and to be loaded with mineral wealth that belongs to aboriginal people. One story asserts that a future flood will destroy the unrighteous, while Aborigines will go back into the ark and be saved. Other movements continue to emerge from this spiritually fertile area.

Christian Movements: In the late 1950s the aboriginal people of Elcho Island (Northern Territory) built a memorial on the Methodist missionary grounds. They displayed publicly the sacred objects that had previously been shown only to initiated men. The Aborigines expected that once they had shown their sacred objects to the missionaries, the Aborigines would receive educational and employment opportunities and be granted greater control over their lives. Reciprocity was not forthcoming, and the Elcho Islanders languished for several decades. Recently a new Christian revival movement has come from Elcho and spread through Arnhem Land and into Western Australia. Called the "Black Crusade," it combines indigenous ritual practices with Christian teachings.

Rituals and Beliefs of Accommodation: One prominent figure in efforts to accommodate invasion within traditional cosmologies is Captain Cook. For residents of the northwest part of the Northern Territory and Western Australia, Captain Cook personifies the whole process of conquest. As the ultimate figure of immoral activity, he is contrasted with other Europeans who are defined as moral, the most significant of whom is the Australian culture hero Ned Kelly. Believers have adopted a millennial perspective, speaking of a time when justice will be restored. In Arnhem Land, by contrast, Captain Cook is a culture hero who wrestles with and defeats Satan. In this tradition, Captain Cook returns home only to be killed by his relations. After his death, Australia is invaded by a new group of false Captain Cooks, who kill, steal, cheat, and lie.

Spiritual Healing: Along the south coast of New South Wales many aboriginal people have adopted the discourse of New Age spirituality in order to communicate their own spiritual concepts and practices among themselves and to non-Aborigines. This emergent movement of spiritual revitalization is closely linked to environmental and social concerns. South coast people have the longest history of dealing with Europeans. Fluent in English, educated, disillusioned with what they see as the sterility of traditional European Christianity, and proud of their aboriginal heritage, many of these people reach out to non-Aborigines both at home and abroad. They seek to offer to all people an aboriginal understanding and experience of the spiritual dimension of human existence. Working with traditional media, such as crystals and herbal medicines, and maintaining close contact with sacred sites, they offer healing that goes beyond bodily ills and seeks to ease the spiritual pain brought about by the savage conquest of the continent. *See also* new religions.

Australian and Pacific traditional religions, the religions of Australian Aborigines and the Pacific islanders of Papua-New Guinea, Melanesia, Micronesia, and Polynesia, which have provided a fertile field for speculative theorizing about religion. Emile Durkheim's *The Elementary Forms of the Religious Life* (1912) was stimulated by the intricacies of totemism among the Aranda tribe of Australia, and the Polynesian/Melanesian concept of *mana* (misleadingly translated as nonpersonalized supernatural power) to argue that humankind's earliest form of religion lacked a concept of spirit beings or gods. A better understanding of Pacific religions led to rejection of this theory, since no religion of record is based exclusively on the mana concept. Similarly, totemism, whether in its most elaborate expression among aboriginal Australians or in the reduced forms found among some other Pacific peoples, is not accurately described as a religion.

For over a century, anthropologists and missionaries have been the principal students of traditional religious life in the Pacific. Their earliest tasks were to describe beliefs and practices in a manner that was intelligible to Westerners. The proper study of religion in the context of community life began only in the 1920s, with the application of the method of intensive fieldwork pioneered in New Guinea by the Polish-English anthropologist Bronislaw Malinowski (1884–1942).

Owing to the early successes of Christian missionaries, native religious institutions were among the first casualties of Western intrusion, with the result that our knowledge of the traditional religions is regionally biased, being most complete for those areas in which the traditional ways of life endured the longest. These areas are northern and central Australia and Melanesia, New Guinea, and the Solomon Islands in particular. Virtually everywhere, however, indigenous religious elements have persisted, apart from or embedded in forms of native Christianity, or as part of active nativist revivals.

The nature and diversity of Pacific religions and their place in the lives of traditional societies challenge such familiar distinctions as sacred versus profane, nature versus the supernatural, empirical versus nonempirical knowledge, and religion versus magic. The nature of Pacific religions makes little provision for the spiritual concerns of Western or Eastern world religions. Neither morality nor divinely mediated salvation are central concerns of the religious beliefs and conduct that are pervasively influential in traditional peoples' daily lives.

The Pacific peoples do not distinguish a cultural domain equivalent to that of religion in Western societies.

Cosmology: Oceanic cosmologies do not consist of explicit formulations of cosmic order. Rather, the conceived order is deduced from myth, rituals, and the things people say and do in a variety of everyday and special contexts. One New Guinea people describe the universe as "the big place." The cosmological ideas of Oceanic peoples can be summarized as follows:

1. The universe includes the human realm of people, social relations, and culture, which is separate from the physical realm of plants, animals, and the earth's natural features, and from the suprahuman realm of spirit beings and invisible forces.

2. The universe, or at least significant parts of it, has definite beginnings. This is invariably true of the human realm, including human beings themselves and the use of fire, agriculture (with the exception of the Australian hunter-gatherers), war, marriage, clans, etc., and by implication the entire sociocultural order. Some peoples think that the physical world has always existed, and they possess no accounts of creation, but for most, the world, or parts of it, was created. Some Polynesians believe the world has evolved from a primordial void with the help of self-created

In the Amanamki village, Papua New Guinea, a native carver, Bapmes, displays his traditional ceremonial dress outside the Men's House.

deities and their progeny. For aboriginal Australians, the physical world existed as a featureless plain in which the spirit beings slumbered. Creation of humans, culture, animals, plants, and natural features followed the awakening of the spirit beings and occurred in the course of their wanderings. Much Australian mythology consists of tales of the spirit beings' travels and exploits, and as they were prodigious travelers as well as creators, tribes came to possess localized fragments of vast intertribal myths that provided a basis for amicable intergroup contacts serving both religious and practical ends.

The beginnings of the suprahuman realm are diverse, in accordance with the differentiated character of extrahuman entities. Deities begat or produced other deities in various ways, chiefs were deified upon death, souls of the dead became ghosts, and so on. As in the human realm and the physical world, elements of the suprahuman realm were created or activated in the mythic creative era while other elements were reproduced or continually renewed. Invisible forces, such as *mana* ("efficacy"), dependent as they were on deities or ancestral ghosts, likewise had a beginning.

3. The universe has definite process characteristics that are dependent upon the close conjunction of the human, physical, and suprahuman realms. The three realms are linked in a compact set of relations; they exist in close proximity. Just beyond the village clearing are forests inhabited by bush spirits; the living and the dead might interact on a daily basis; spirits frequently assume the form of or are manifested in a great variety of natural objects; deified chiefs are a part of Polynesian societies; in Hawaii the highest-ranking female chiefs are considered to be earthly goddesses; in dreams a person's soul departs the body and traffics with spirits; deities speak through human mediums; illness, injury, and minor mishap are spirit-caused; mana or "efficacy" is necessary for the success of most human endeavors, and so on. The cosmic order is directed by the suprahuman realm, initially and on a continuing basis, and the human and physical realms operate according to the cyclical patterns of seasonal and generational succession. Major disturbances or deviations are expected since, in particular, volcanic eruptions and devastating typhoons are experienced recurrently by many Pacific peoples. But apart from such dramatic and catastrophic events, which could hardly help to evoke a cosmological response, there is inherent unpredictability owing to the belief that spirit beings combined humanlike emotions with extraordinary capabilities. Who could say, for example, whether a Melanesian culture hero who, according to myth, had vanished after performing his creative feats, might not suddenly reappear and take up an active role affecting human affairs? The possibility existed, and when myths even included a vague prophecy of return, it is easy to understand the disposition to identify newly arrived Europeans themselves as well as their deities with beings of the traditional pantheons. Over a wide area of northern New Guinea, people not only identified a prominent myth culture hero with Jesus, but also amended their myths in order to account for his return and what this portended.

4. The universe has no end, either of an apocalyptic kind or a long-term entropic death. If it had any expansionary or evolutionary phase, this terminated with the completion of creation. The usual view of the cosmos is utopian: the world as constituted is the best of all possible worlds. The past may be considered superior to the present because the past displayed wondrous beings and archetypical events, but it is not considered a golden age. In a significant sense the past is not over, since the life-promoting forces or principles of the mythic era—the Dreamtime of the uncreated and eternal, as the Australians term it—are still operative. There is no universal hope of achieving a future world that is different from and superior to the present. Traditional Pacific societies have creative thinkers and innovators, but they do not appear to have been troubled by dystopian critics and zealous reformers.

To speak of three realms—the human, physical, and suprahuman—and their interrelations as comprising the cosmos is a succinct way of grasping the essentials of traditional thought while avoiding the connotations of terms such as *supernatural* and *sacred*, which owe too much to the Western cultural tradition. But this three-way distinction and the propositions that followed would not be offered by the traditional practitioner, whether a specialist or ordinary person.

The suprahuman realms of many Polynesians, with their panoplies of gods and elaborate genealogies that embrace gods, ancestors, and the living, are well integrated, and reflect the hierarchical ordering of their societies. In the suprahuman realms of the tribal, egalitarian Australians and Melanesians, the various beings and forces act independently of one another. Each influence they exert makes itself felt in isolation from the others; no principle functions so as to bind or subordinate one to another. They simply coexist.

It is not so much the problem of looking for system where apparently none exists, but rather of searching in the right places. Some have looked at words, the texts of orally recited myths that Westerners wrote down. But anthropologists have also examined the nonverbal performances of ritual. For example, one of the foremost students of Australian religion, William Stanner, proposed that postures, gestures, facial expressions, laughter, cries, wailing, mimes, dances, plastic and graphic arts, and stylized acts are arranged in patterned ways in ritual so as to symbolize ideas. Words are not the only or necessarily the most evocative elements of languages of the mind. Similarly, the New Guinea cosmologists studied by Fredrik Barth, and whose society is notably poor in myths and even spells and verbal explanations of ritual, employ modes of association that are characteristic of gifted artists in Western culture rather than the abstract conceptualization of philosophers and scientists.

The loose integration of Pacific cosmologies means also that they should not be regarded, as they sometimes have been, as closed systems of thought. To be sure, there are basic assumptions about how the world is constructed. But there are also problematic ideas, recognized as such, alternative interpretations, and matters open to doubt and possible reformulation. For example, that the recitation of myths or sacrifices of pigs to ancestral ghosts help taro to grow may be beyond dispute. At the same time, people may have different ideas about how this occurs, and they may also confess that they do not now know how the process works.

Religion in Practice: To understand the peoples' cosmic views is to comprehend that it was within such conceived systems and upon certain aspects of them that religions were designed to operate. Though this is to put the matter in rather mechanistic terms, it is nonetheless consonant with the pragmatic rationality that so obviously informed traditional religious activity, from the bountiful Polynesian high islands to the arid Australian center. Religion, or more properly, the magico-religious system, is a principal means by which people deal with the problems of existence, both the opportunities and dangers of life, and is the preeminent means of understanding and explaining the world. It is not only concerned with evoking and maintaining special ritual or spiritual states of individuals and groups, or with the conditions of one's soul in the afterworld (for the most part a matter of low priority). Religion is also concerned, fundamentally, with helping people to maintain the cosmic order, and however variable the scope of the human role, it is deemed to be of critical or vital proportions. By means of magico-religious knowledge and ritual, people are equipped to succeed in life, to secure food, mates, offspring, material prosperity, health, and social standing; and while premature death, illness, accident, defeat in war, etc., could not always be averted, they could be satisfactorily explained. Physical and spiritual survival, fertility, human reproduction, the natural world, and the sociocultural order, and exemption or protection from misfortune—these are the great ends of religion. Herein lies the explanation for the substantial amount of energy and resources that

Pacific peoples devote to magico-religious activity, the high value placed on esoteric knowledge and the favored social status of people who possess it, and the wide incidence of religion such that there seems to be a religious rite associated with virtually every action in life.

The ability to generalize effectively about Pacific religions is roughly proportional to the general cultural and linguistic diversity of the conventional groupings of societies. Diversity is least in Polynesia, greater in Australia and Micronesia, and the greatest by far in Melanesia, particularly in New Guinea with its seven hundred or more languages. There are pan-Pacific features (either universal, featured widely, or found in societies of all four cultural-geographic regions) such as belief in the existence of spirit beings and souls, in afterworlds and sorcery, that occur in other parts of the world as well. Generalizing about religious practices demands caution, because of the diversity of cultures and the fact that, particularly in Melanesia, the variation has not been fully charted.

Interacting with the Suprahuman Realm: The suprahuman realm is populated by more than one kind of being: spirits that may be termed deities if they are named and have some creative or regulatory role; ancestral ghosts; spirits of the dead; and demons or forest spirits. Ghosts and deified chiefs, of course, are of human origin; other spirit beings are autonomous, or their origins are obscure. In general, spirit beings greatly outnumber human beings. Though they share human attitudes and motives, spirit beings have extraordinary powers of mobility and can change their forms or manifest themselves in diverse objects. Whether they are generally malevolent or punitive, neutral or indifferent, or beneficent in their actions toward people, as well as whether they intervene in human affairs or in natural processes affecting humans, varies with the category of being and from society to society.

Spirit beings make their intentions and influence known by means of their effects on natural and human events, such as crop failure or the outbreak of disease; in omens; in dreams; in the actions of physical objects or beings in which they are manifested—Polynesian gods were regularly incarnated in birds, for example—and they might speak through human oracles. People take the initiative in communicating with spirits by means of prayers and offerings, including human sacrifice in a number of Polynesian societies, and spells and chants, which frequently make use of special or liturgical languages.

The anthropologist's attention, however, has often focused on periodic rituals, public or semipublic in character (since women and the uninitiated were often excluded). Posing a difficulty in the present context is that ritual is such a large and diverse category of behavior. Given the rule-bound, patterned character of "ordinary" social life, which includes the observation of taboos sanctioned by the suprahuman realm, where does ritual begin and end? Moreover, in view of the fact that the more elaborate and protracted rituals were often multipurposed, how is one to determine their religious salience?

There are rituals in which the cosmic order is acted out; others, such as the ritual cycle of the Polynesian Tikopia known as "the work of the gods," which is said to have been instituted by Tikopia's most powerful deity, display the order of society. In Melanesia one finds mortuary rituals that seem to have little to do with the ongoing relations of the living and the dead, a basic theme of Pacific religions. Rather, these rituals are the means by which new political leaders rise to prominence, taking the place of deceased big men, though at the same time a successful ceremony demonstrates that leaders have come to terms with dangerous and powerful spirits. The Australian *corroborees*, or intertribal ceremonies, seem to make ritual temporally and spatially separate from mundane social life. But the Australians believe in ritual as the necessary means of maintaining the cosmos in good working order. In the reigning totemic philosophy, totems (plants and animals, but also a variety of other objects), people, their social groups, natural features created by the spirit beings or into which they transform themselves, and the Dreamtime spirit beings themselves are eternally bound together by relations of mutual influence. Rituals are performed to promote human procreation, to enable the social and spiritual development of the individual, to ensure the fertility of the totemic species, and to provide for the renewal and maintenance of society. Not only the performances of ritual, but also social life carried on in prescribed fashion—observing totemic food taboos or marrying according to totemic social categories—work to maintain the cosmos. The practice of religion may be wider than ritual, or social practice may be informed by religious considerations. All of this is not to say, however, that there are not many rituals that, in a straightforward manner, are designed to enlist the cooperation of extrahuman powers. Failing such support, human projects generally could not hope to succeed.

Magico-religious Knowledge: Knowledge of the suprahuman realm and of the techniques by which spirits and invisible forces can be induced or forced to assist people in achieving their goals is supremely valued. Mere technical knowledge, acquired informally as a part of growing up, is freely available to all. Esoteric knowledge, by contrast, is restricted, its acquisition, application, and transmission hedged by secrecy. As a whole it is monopolized by senior men, which is a critical reason why the religious role of women is secondary or even insignificant.

Among aboriginal Australians, songs, which contain a large part of mythology, are the most treasured form of wealth; young men give meat to their elders to "loosen" them, to encourage them to teach the songs. Melanesian leaders achieve prominence by excelling in a number of activities such as feasting, war, and oratory, but mastery of esoteric knowledge is usually a requirement. In smaller and poorer societies of the New Guinea hinterland, leaders are primarily distinguished by their magico-religious expertise. Leaders in a number of Melanesian societies practice sorcery (magic that inflicts death or disease) or hire sorcerers in order to secure political advantage or domination. In Polynesia, high-ranking chiefs are descendants of gods and they possess mana that is transmitted by descent. In addition to having priestly roles themselves, chiefs are served by professional priests who acquire their positions by both heredity and intensive training.

In every Pacific society, the possession and exercise of magico-religious knowledge, or superior access to the suprahuman realm via intermediary experts, is a major pathway to social prominence. Esoteric knowledge is a gift of the gods—the Australian songs, for example, are the work of the totemic ancestral spirits—and any additions to the stock of knowledge are by revelation alone.

Morality and Religion: It has been said that Pacific religions have little ethical content; deities are not lawgivers, or if they are, they are lawbreakers as well; spirit beings are liable to punish people for lapses or failures in relations with them, but they are not concerned with violations of rules governing relations among humans. It is true that many societies rely on their own devices to deal with immoral and disruptive behavior. Nevertheless, the exceptions to these generalizations are sufficiently numerous as to make the entire issue of the moral content and incidence of religion problematic. There is the oft-cited example of the Manus of the Admiralty Islands, whose conduct is subject to constant ghostly surveillance and the threat of punishment with illness for a variety of infractions. The Huli of highland New Guinea have a deity who punishes violations of the code governing the behavior of kin, though he is unconcerned with how strangers treat one another. For incest or fratricide, the ancestral ghosts of the Yap Islanders visit death on members of the kin group. As part of the Tikopia ritual cycle, the highest-ranking chief, speaking for the gods as a medium, delivers a sermon admonishing the islanders to refrain from theft and brawling, to exercise forethought in the use of resources, and to use restraint in procreation in the interest of the general welfare. The people themselves emphasize the moral message of the chief's annual address. People initiate and maintain relations of moral obligation with spirit beings on the basis of the principle of reciprocity, though necessarily by different means, as they do with fellow humans. People can do many things to please spirit beings and possibly secure their favor, from reciting myths or chanting songs recounting their exploits to dancing the hula and walking on beds of fiery coals. *See also* All-Father; All-Mother; mana; rainbow snake; taboo; tjuringa.

Authorized Version. *See* King James Version.

Avalokiteshvara (ah-wah-loh-ki-tesh'wah-rah; Skt., etymology obscure but traditional explanations suggest a compassionate gaze on the suffering of the world), the Buddhist Bodhisattva of compassion, who assumes the appearance of every human or nonhuman living being that calls upon his name. Avalokiteshvara (Chin. *Kuan-yin;* Jap. *Kannon*) sometimes takes female forms, especially in East Asia where she appears as the matron of children and childbirth. Under the name of Chenrezig, he is the patron of Tibet, where it is believed, reborn in the form of a monkey, he gave birth to the Tibetan people and taught them how to cultivate the "six staple grains." He later came to the aid of the Tibetan people by repeatedly reincarnating in various human forms. Each one of the Dalai Lamas of Tibet is believed to be one such incarnation of Chenrezig. *See also* Black Hat; Bodhisattvas; compassion; Dalai Lama; Kannon; Kuan-yin.

avatar (Skt. *avatara,* "descent"), the descent of a deity to earth. Although in Hinduism the concept of an avatar as a manifestation of a deity or its literal descent from the heavens to earth is not confined to one particular deity, it has been most popularly associated in mythology and worship with Vishnu. This mythology is mainly found in the eighteen Puranas, composed in the period ca. 400 to 1200. During this time and later, the avatars became associated with sacred places and festivals throughout much of India and continue to be venerated through pilgrimage, festival worship, and iconographic representation, as well as in popular literature.

Although for many centuries the number and character of Vishnu's avatars was fluid, the concept of ten became the most prevalent. In his first avatar, Vishnu descends to earth in the form of a fish (Matsya), which is caught by Manu ("man"). In return for letting the fish go, Manu is warned by Vishnu of the imminent coming of a great flood that will destroy the earth. Manu prepares by building a boat and survives the flood, his vessel safely moored to Vishnu, the fish.

As Kurma, the tortoise, Vishnu provides a stable base for the churning stick of the gods and demons as they churn the ocean of milk in an effort to produce an elixir of immortality. Vishnu, in his third avatar, the boar (Varaha), dives into the cosmic ocean to rescue the submerged earth. As Narasimha, the terrifying manlion, Vishnu outwits and brutally slays the demon Hiranyakashipu, who has stolen heaven from the gods and is wreaking havoc on earth.

Vishnu as Vamana, the dwarf priest, also outwits a demon, Bali. As the demon is about to perform a sacrifice that will guarantee him sovereignty over the three worlds, Vishnu arrives disguised as a dwarf but expands to cosmic proportions, regaining the three worlds for the gods.

In martial guise, Vishnu descends next as Parashurama ("Rama with the ax") to avenge Brahmans (priests) persecuted by Kshatriyas (warriors). As Prince Rama, famed hero of the epic poem *Ramayana,* Vishnu saves his wife Sita from the clutches of Ravana, demon king of Lanka, and regains his own throne.

The mythology of Krishna, the eighth avatar of Vishnu, spans his lifetime from his eventful birth and childhood escapades in Vrindavana, his youthful idylls with the lovestruck cowgirls (*gopis*), to his integral role as friend and adviser to the Pandava brothers in the epic *Mahabharata.*

Disguised as Buddha, Vishnu in his ninth avatar leads immoral people astray with a "false doctrine." Vishnu's tenth avatar, Kalkin, will appear in a future age riding a white horse and heralding in the cataclysm that will end this cosmic age.

The idea of an avatar as an appearance or partial incarnation of a deity or divinity itself has persisted beyond this mythology into the modern age. For example, the modern Hindu saint

Satya Sai Baba (b. 1926) is believed to be the appearance of the deities Shiva and Shakti incarnate in one body. *See also* Krishna; Mahabharata; Puranas; Ramayana; Vaishnavism; Vishnu.

Ave Maria (Lat.,"Hail Mary"), Roman Catholic prayer based on Luke 1:28. *See also* rosary.

Avesta (a-ves'tuh; Middle Persian, "the instruction"), the primary collection of Zoroastrian sacred texts. While probably dependent on a period of oral transmission, the texts were written and codified during the third to seventh centuries. About a quarter of this original collection has been lost. The central text is the liturgical Yasna. Within this collection is a smaller group of seventeen metrical hymns, the Gathas, and a prose text, "the Yasna of Seven Chapters." These two documents are often attributed to Zoroaster. Other materials have been added to Yasna at a later date. Other important books within the collection, likewise of later date, include the Vendidad, concerned mainly with purity laws, and the Yashts, a collection of hymns that illustrate Zoroastrian adaptations of earlier Iranian religious traditions. *See also* Gathas; Yashts; Yasna.

avidya (uh-vid-yah'; Skt., "ignorance," lit., "absence of wisdom"), Hindu term for the inability to discriminate the truth about reality, thus causing suffering and rebirth. *See also* Hinduism (thought and ethics); maya; samsara.

Awakening of Faith (Chin. *Ta-shen chi-hsin lun*), fifth-century apocryphal text attributed to Ashvaghosha, an Indian poet and Mahayana philosopher, that was influential in the development of Chinese Buddhist doctrine. *See also* Apocrypha; China, Buddhism in.

aya (a'ya; Arab.,"sign,""verse [of the Qur'an]"), signs or tokens provided by God, in Islamic belief, of his lordship in nature and especially in the revelation of the Qur'an.

ayatollah (a'yat-*ool*-lah'; Arab., Persian,"sign of God"), an Islamic title of highest rank among religious leaders of the Ithna Ashari Shia. *See also* Ithna Ashari Shia.

Ayurveda (ah-yoor-vay'duh; Skt., "knowledge of [long] life"), traditional medicine in India. In this system, the body, like the cosmos, is composed of five elements—earth, water, fire, air, space—that produce three humors—wind, bile, phlegm. Health is proper balance and separation of humors, disease is imbalance and mixing that must be treated by a physician (*vaidya*) with herbal, mineral, dietetic, and other therapies. This system is sometimes considered an Upaveda, as well as a supplement to the Atharva Veda. Classical Sanskrit Ayurvedic texts claim their teachings were revealed through a lineage of deities and sages. Ayurveda departments in Indian universities train physicians who treat large segments of India's population alongside practitioners of other medical systems today. *See also* medicine and religion.

Azalis. *See* Babism.

Azhar, al- (el-az'hahr; Arab., "luminous," "radiant"), mosque and religious college established in Cairo in the late tenth century and the oldest medieval university in Europe and the Middle East. It was a grand *madrasa*, a law college, mosque, and library complex, patronized by successive governments for training religious jurists. In the late twelfth century, the Sunni Ayyubid ruler Salah al-Din (Saladin) ousted the Fatimid (Ismaili Shiite) rulers and converted al-Azhar to a Sunni university. Al-Azhar remains Islam's preeminent Sunni university.

A

B

CDEF

GH

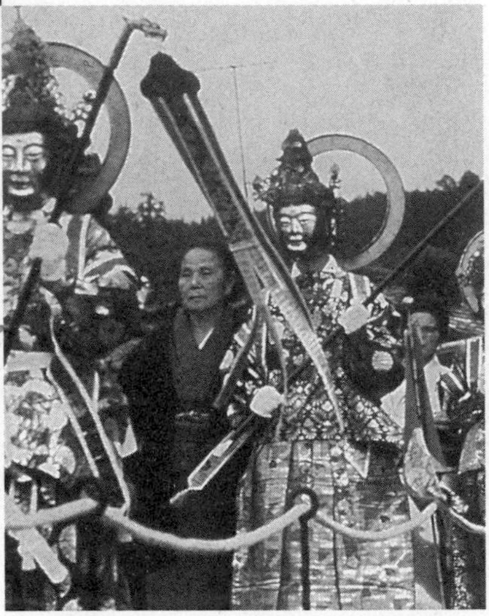

L

MN Q

RSTUV

WXY&Z

Ba (bah), in ancient Egyptian religion, the soul of a god or living person depicted as a human-headed bird. *See also* Egyptian religion; soul.

Baal (ba'al; a common Semitic noun meaning "lord, husband"), the epithet or proper name of the high god of Northwest Semitic pantheons in the second and first millennia B.C. Baal typically controlled the weather and bestowed fertility. *See also* Aramaean religion; Canaanite religion.

Baal Shem Tov (ca. 1700–1760), called by the acronym Besht and also known as Israel ben Eliezer, Baal Shem Tov founded eastern European Hasidism. Baal Shem Tov means "master of a good name" and was a professional title for one who performed healings and other miracles by means of divine names. The Besht was an itinerant exorcist and wonder-worker and employed similar techniques to induce mystical experiences. The principal element of his teaching was the emphasis on constant worship of God through both physical and spiritual means culminating in the ecstatic state of cleaving to the divine light present in every aspect of existence. *See also* Hasidism.

babalawo (bah'bah'lah'woh; Yoruba, "father of the mystery"), priestly office originating among the Yoruba people of Nigeria and Benin and carried to the Americas by slaves. The priests' mastery is expressed in a large, memorized corpus of ritual, divinatory, and herbal knowledge known as *Ifa*. *See also* orisha.

Baba Ram Dass, formerly Richard Alpert, contemporary American New Age spiritual leader who abandoned experimentation with hallucinogens and began the Hanuman Foundation in 1974 for loving service to humanity. *See also* New Age movements.

Baba Yaga (bah'bah yah'gah; Slavic, "disease grandmother"), a witch of Russian tales, originally a pre-Indo-European goddess of death and regeneration. *See also* Old European religion.

Babel, Tower of (ba'bul; Heb., "Babylon"), in the Hebrew Bible, a tower built to reach the heavens, the punishment for which was the imposition of many languages and the dispersal of peoples (Genesis 11:1–9). The biblical text plays on the linguistic similarity of the name Babylon and the Hebrew word for "confusion" (*balal*) in describing what appears to be a characteristic Near Eastern religious building (ziggurat). Despite the apparent similarity, there is no relation to the English "babble." *See also* ziggurat.

Babism (bab'iz-uhm), an Iranian religion centered on Mirza ali Muhammad's (d. 1850) claim to be the *Bab* (Arab., "gateway"), the means of access to the Hidden *Imam* of Twelver Shiite Islam. From May 23, 1844, the date of the Bab's claim, through 1852, Babism inspired a number of religious rebellions resulting in the death of many of its followers.

In the *Banyan* (Persian, "revelation") of the Bab, mediating between the unknowable, transcendent world of God and the human material world are a series of "manifestations," including Abraham, Moses, David, Jesus, and Muhammad. Each manifestation teaches a historically conditioned form of revelation that supercedes its predecessor. The eternal substance of the revelation, however, is unchanging.

Babism continues in its late twentieth century in something like its late twentieth century in something like its original form among the Azalis of Iran. A schismatic group developed after 1863, when one of the Bab's disciples, Baha Allah (1817–92), declared himself to be the "one whom God shall make manifest" (Arab. *man yuzhiruhu Allah*), founding the religion known as Baha'i. The Azalis hold that the "one" is still to come. *See also* Baha'i; prophet.

Babylon, Whore of, polemic phrase based on biblical prophecy. In Revelation 17:1–6, the whore symbolizes Rome; in later Protestant polemics, the Roman Catholic Church.

Babylonian Captivity. 1 The exile and deportation of groups of Israelites to Babylonia in 597 and 586 B.C. 2 In Catholic literature, the exile of the popes to Avignon (1309–77). 3 In Protestant polemics, applied to Roman Catholicism.

Bacchae (bak'kee), frenzied female worshipers, also called Maenads, of the ancient Greek god Dionysos (Bacchus). *See also* Dionysos; Euripides; Greek religion; Maenad.

Bacchus (bak'uhs), the Latin name for the Greek god Dionysos, also known as Bacchos. Adopted by the Romans, he played a more important role in private than in public cult. *See also* Dionysos; Roman religion.

Baha'i (bah-hi', or, more properly, bah-hah'ee; Persian *bahai*, from Arab. *baha*, "splendor"), an Iranian religion founded in 1863 by Mirza Husayn ali Nuri

(1817–92), known as Bahaullah (Persian, "splendor of God") or Baha Allah (Arab., "splendor of God"). Originally a part of Babism, the Baha'i tradition split with the Azali tradition over Baha Allah's claim, first announced privately in 1863, to be the "one whom God shall make manifest," the promised "manifestation" of Babist tradition.

From 1852 to 1877, Baha Allah was either imprisoned or exiled, a period during which he began the *Kitab al-aqdas* (Arab., The Most Holy Book), completed in 1884. After his death, his son, Abbas Effendi (1844–1921), known as Abd al-Baha ("the servant of the glory [of God]"), was designated by Baha Allah's will as the leader of the community and the authoritative interpreter of his father's writings. Abbas Effendi elevated Baha'i from a local sect centered in Iran and Acre, Palestine, to a world religion by undertaking missionary journeys to Egypt (1910) and America and Europe (1911–13). Following Abbas Effendi's death, Baha'i was first led by the eldest son of his eldest daughter, Shoghi Effendi Rabbani (1899–1957), and then by a Council of the Hands of the Cause (1957–62), residing in Israel. Since 1962, Baha'i has been administered by the International House of Justice, elected every five years, located at the Baha'i administrative center in Haifa, Israel. In 1985, it was estimated that there were between one and a half to two million Baha'is, with the greatest areas of recent growth in Africa, India, and Vietnam. Until the 1979 Iranian revolution, Baha'i was that country's largest religious minority.

Baha'i has no public or private rituals. Its members are to assemble every nineteen days, to keep the equivalent of the Islamic fast of Ramadan, to abstain from alcoholic beverages, and to pray in private daily. Although there is no ritual, the Baha'i scripture recommends the erection of a nine-sided building, a *mashrig al-Adhkar* (Arab., "a place where the mention of God rises at dawn"), open to all religions.

Perhaps the most distinctive religious concept of Baha'i is that of continuous prophecy. Each age requires a new message. While the work of each "manifestation" of the revelation of God has been successful and complete, the ongoing task of revelation will never achieve its final "seal"; even Baha Allah is not the Last. According to the *Kitab al-aqdas,* Baha'i itself will be superceded, though not for "a thousand years." *See also* Babism; prophet.

Bailey, Alice (1880–1949), a British citizen and former Theosophist, who in 1923 established the Arcane School on the basis of revelations concerning a coming new age. *See also* esoteric movements; Theosophy.

Balarama (buh-luh-rahm'uh), in Indic tradition, elder brother of Krishna, son of Rohini, also known as Balabhadra, elder brother of Jagannatha. *See also* Jagannatha; Krishna; Vishnu.

Baldr (bahl'duhr), Scandinavian god, son of Odinn. Baldr's death from mistletoe is associated with Ragnarok. *See also* Nordic religion; Ragnarok.

Balokole movement (bah-loh-koy'lay; "saved ones"), a Christian mass movement, also known as the East African Revival, begun in the 1920s. Leaders stressed personal experience of the Holy Spirit, resulting in their becoming *balokole*, public confession of sins, and proselytization. The revival also attracted women who sought religious justifications for opposition to polygyny, or a man having more than one wife. *See also* Africa, new religions in.

Baltic religion. The pre-Christian religion of the Baltic peoples of Latvia, Lithuania, and Old Prussia. Below the Indo-European stratum, brought from the east, is a pre-Indo-European indigenous layer called the Old European (ca. 4500–2500 B.C.). The religion of the Balts must be reconstructed from archaeological remains and from linguistic evidence embedded in folklore and etymologies in Latvian, Lithuanian, and Old Prussian.

The Old European (Matriarchal) Layer: In the Old European ideology, a female deity created the world. Central to this worldview is a pantheon of goddesses who bring life and health, and death and misfortune, as well as rebirth. Their creative energy is of the earth, waters, moon, stones, plants, and all of nature. They are grouped in clans or large families headed by a queen, reflecting the pre-Indo-European matrilineal social structure. Male gods existed secondarily as either seasonal gods of vegetation or protectors of herds, wild animals, and forests.

The main goddesses controlling cosmic life energy, the powers of creation, and destruction and regeneration are Laima and Ragana. Laima is responsible for the birth of humans and animals and appears as a zoomorphic pregnant bear. Until the early twentieth century, she was worshiped by a ritual in the sauna (*pirtis*) presided over by the grandmother of the family. The ritual included the sacrifice of a hen and offerings of linens to the goddess. As a prophesier of spring, she is a cuckoo. She is also a menhir, standing stone, and is the owner of life-giving waters, wells, and streams. Deities closely linked to Laima are the hearth fire goddess Gabija (whose name derives from the verb *gaubti*, "to cover," "to protect") and the benevolent snake (Gyvate, Zaltys), both of whom protect the family, stimulating fertility and vitality. Austeja, the bee goddess, is the protectress of marriageable women and a benefactress of families. Laima's sister image is Death, Giltine, who appears as a white woman, a bird of prey, or a poisonous snake.

Ragana is the fearsome and powerful goddess of destruction and regeneration, goddess of night, the dark moon, and winter. She is extremely dangerous when nights are short. It is she who ties rye ears into knots at harvesttime, shears sheep, stops the milk in cows, and controls the sexuality of men and women. On a cosmic scale, she can cut the full moon in half or even cause an eclipse of the sun. Ragana is the overseer of the cycles of nature, killing the power of life to secure cyclical renewal, balancing the forces of life and death. She also knows the magic of herbs and can heal the sick and regenerate the dead. Her epiphanies are the toad, fish, hedgehog, and the moth or butterfly.

The second group of Old European goddesses and gods is associated with the birth and death of vegetation and with the fertility of crops, animals, and humans. The main divinity is Zemyna, moist, fertile, black Mother Earth, who creates life out of herself. Her functions concern fertility and multiplication, and the interdependence of humans, animals, and plants within the cycles of seasonal awakening, growing, fattening, and dying. Zemyna's veneration continued into this century. Late-seventeenth-century sources describe a black suckling pig being offered to Zemyna during the harvest feast, presided over by a priestess.

Zemyna has a brother, Zemininkas or Zemepatis, protector of animals in pastures. Another male god is Vaizgantas, protector of flax and hemp. He is a year god, related to the Greek Linos and Dionysos, born from the earth and tortured as flax (Lithuanian *linai*), who dies and is resurrected each spring.

The Indo-European (Patriarchal) Layer: The Old European pantheon was superimposed by pastoral, patriarchal warrior gods from the third millennium B.C. In this contrasting ideology, sovereign male gods create the world, and almost all are associated with heavenly bodies, sky phenomena, horses, or cattle. A binary division is typical: light/dark, white/black, shining sky/dark underworld.

There were three main gods, whose names are constructed from old Indo-European roots. The first was Dievas, God of Heavenly Light, who was a year god, manifesting himself in four aspects of the seasons. To the dominion of this god belong his twin sons, Dievo suneliai, Dieva deli; the Sun Maiden, Saulyte; the Dawn, Ausrine; the Moon, Menulis; and the Heavenly Smith, Kalvelis, who forges heavenly bodies. Second was Perkunas, the Thunder God, Overseer of Right and Order, Purifier and Fructifier; and third, Velinas, God of Death and the Underworld.

Temples were built for Perkunas, Dievas, and Velinas. Excavations and place-names suggest the existence of sacred tribal centers on hill forts. There was undoubtedly a hierarchical order of priests. *See also* Indo-European religion; Old European religion.

bamboo (Chin. *chu*), aesthetic, moral, and religious symbol in China. With the orchid, plum, and chrysanthemum, it is one of the "four gentlemen" of Chinese painting. It symbolizes Confucian filial piety, learning, and the superior person (*chun-tzu*); lack of prejudice (hollow stem) and modesty (drooping leaves); and the life force, the breath (*ch'i*) of Tao. *See also* ch'i; chun-tzu.

Bamboo Annals, record of Chinese history from the legendary Huang-ti down to 296 B.C., recovered in A.D. 281 from a royal Wei tomb. *See also* Huang-ti.

Banaras (buh-nahr'uhs), India's most famous sacred city, and central Hindu pilgrimage site. The ancient and now official form of the name is Varanasi. For Hindus, its fame derives from its location on the holy Ganges River, a manifestation of the goddess Ganga; at Banaras the Ganges flows north rather than in its usual southeastern direction. Pilgrims flock to Banaras, also known as Kashi ("City of Light"), for a bath in the holy waters; many come to await death here, for, according to popular tradition, one who dies in this sacred city will immediately achieve liberation (Skt. *moksha*).

Lord Shiva, or Vishvanatha ("Lord of All"), as he is popularly called, is the patron deity of Banaras. Shiva promised that he would never forsake Banaras, and that any meritorious activity performed within its perimeters would be greatly rewarded. *See also* pilgrimage; Shiva.

Bankei Yotaku (bahn-kay-ee yoh-tah-koo; 1622–93), a Japanese Rinzai Buddhist monk who developed a form of Zen that appealed to vast numbers of lay believers as well as monks by focusing on the "Unborn" (Jap. *musho*), a synonym for "suchness" and emptiness. His disciples compiled a collection of his sermons and sayings demonstrating his straightforward manner of preaching. *See also* emptiness; Rinzai.

Bapostolo. *See* Apostles of John Maranke.

baptism (Gk. *baptizein,* "to dip in water"), Christian initiatory ritual centering around the immersion of converts in water, or the pouring or sprinkling of water over them.

Origins: The almost universal adoption of this ceremony as the essential rite of admission to Christianity derives from its institution in New Testament times, though whether its observance began with Jesus himself or later with his disciples is unclear. Equally uncertain is the source from which the practice arose: it appears to have been derived from John the Baptist, but scholars disagree as to whether he was influenced by the ritual ablutions of the Jewish Essenes, by a possibly contemporary custom of baptizing converts to Judaism, by the Old Testament tradition of prophetic symbolism regarding water, or by a combination of all three.

New Testament writers interpret the symbolic meaning of baptism in a variety of ways, including being cleansed from sin and being anointed in the Holy Spirit, being united with Christ in his death and resurrection, being born again, and being enlightened. What else the ritual might have included at that time besides the use of water is not made explicit. Accounts of baptismal practice from the centuries that follow show considerable development. There was probably a preliminary time of instruction, culminating in a profession of belief in the lordship of Christ made at the baptism itself. By the third century in the West this had evolved into a lengthy and more structured period of preparation known as the catechumenate, culminating in a solemn renunciation of evil and a series of three questions concerning faith in the Trinity. There were other ritual acts performed in different locales in conjunction with baptism, especially anointing with oil. By the fourth century, the rites became highly dramatic.

Infant Baptism: Whether young children were at first included with adults in the initiatory process is disputed. The earliest certain evidence for their participation dates from the beginning of the third century, but infant baptism did not become universal until several centuries later, when the high mortality rate coupled with Augustine's (d. 430) teaching on original sin led to a desire to ensure that babies should not risk failing to obtain salvation by dying unbaptized.

A contemporary Protestant minister performs the ritual of infant baptism at St. David's United Church (United Church of Canada), Calgary, Alberta, Canada.

The eventual disappearance of adult baptisms, however, brought significant changes to the rite. Since the catechumenate no longer served any useful purpose, it gradually withered away. Sponsors or godparents who had originally vouched for the genuineness of the conversion of adult candidates now made the profession of faith on behalf of the uncomprehending infants. The necessity of performing such baptisms without delay made them private affairs concerned principally with the washing away of sin instead of part of the religious life of the whole local Christian community. The consequent need for bishops to delegate the act to priests gave rise in the West to a separate rite of confirmation, administered at a later age, which was thought to bestow the Holy Spirit on the candidates. At first, infants continued to be admitted to communion immediately after baptism, just as adults had been, but by the late Middle Ages this too was generally deferred in the West until the child was older. Thus, while Christian initiation remained as a single rite in the Eastern Orthodox tradition and in other oriental churches, it became in the West a series of separate stages associated with particular points of biological development.

The Reformation: Some of the sixteenth-century Reformers rejected infant baptism as unscriptural, and regarded as legitimate only the baptism of those old enough to profess their own faith. These Reformers were known as Anabaptists, and their later successors as Baptists. The majority of the Reformation churches, however, continued to baptize infants and to allow them to take the Eucharist when they were older. The

Reformers tried to strip the baptismal rite of many of its medieval accretions and to restore it as a public ceremony performed during the regular Sunday worship of the congregation. Some abolished the rite of confirmation altogether, while others transformed it into a public affirmation of faith before admission to communion.

The Twentieth Century: Many of the churches that practice infant baptism have reconsidered their policy since the 1960s. They make provision for appropriate rites for both infants and adults, the latter including a restored catechumenate. They stress the need for the rites to be performed within the worship of the local congregation and for those baptized as infants to be brought up within a context of genuine Christian faith, if the rite is to have its true initiatory meaning. Some have begun to admit young children to participation in the Eucharist on the basis of their baptism alone, and to regard confirmation as an opportunity for a mature affirmation of faith at a much later age. Roman Catholicism, while continuing to view confirmation as a sacramental rite in which the Holy Spirit is bestowed, has reunited it to baptism in the case of adult converts and included within it a public profession of baptismal faith in the case of those already baptized in infancy. *See also* ablution; Christianity (life cycle); Christianity (worship); Elchasai, Elchasaites; initiation rituals; Mandaeans; ritual.

Baptists, members of a Protestant church movement characterized by adult or believers' baptism, congregational independence, and an advocacy of religious freedom and separation of church and state. The movement originated in seventeenth-century English Separatism. The name *Baptist* was adopted in the eighteenth century to replace names such as *Church of Christ* and the *Baptized Church of Christ.*

Beginnings: The Baptist movement began in England in a congregation of Puritan Separatists led by John Smyth, an ordained Anglican, that met in Gainsborough, near Lincoln. To escape the religious restrictions of James I, the congregation moved to Amsterdam, Holland, in 1607 (a sister congregation migrated to Leiden, Holland, and in 1620 to Plymouth, Massachusetts).

In Holland, Smyth's group debated the topics of church membership and baptism and in 1609 moved to believers' baptism, thereby forming the first Baptist congregation. When Smyth appeared interested in joining the Mennonites, Thomas Helwys, a British merchant, led part of the Baptist group back to England around 1612

to found the first Baptist congregation on British soil. Helwys's *A Short Declaration of the Mistery of Iniquity* (ca. 1612) presented the first argument for religious liberty in the English language. Because of their Arminian view of the atonement, that Jesus died for everyone and not merely the elect, this group came to be called General Baptists.

A second group of Baptists was formed in the 1630s from an Independent church founded earlier by Henry Jacob. Their Calvinistic view of the atonement brought them the name *Particular Baptists.* In 1641, after a study of the practice of baptism and a contact with Waterlander Mennonites in Holland, the Particular Baptists changed their mode of baptism from pouring to immersion. Soon both Baptist groups used immersion.

Growth in England: The Baptist movement grew rapidly in seventeenth-century England as populist movements mushroomed in the Commonwealth period, and they thrived even under the repressive measures of Charles II.

In the eighteenth century General Baptists moved toward Unitarianism, while the Particular Baptists adopted a hyper-Calvinism. In 1710, General Baptists organized the New Connection of General Baptists, which emphasized spiritual experience. Particular Baptists, with their strict predestinarian theology, opposed the cobbler William Carey when he proposed in 1792 that Baptists undertake foreign missions. Self-taught in seven languages, the industrious and scholarly Carey overcame his critics and went to India as a Baptist missionary. His work was a major contribution to the development of the Protestant missionary movement.

The American Colonies: Baptist life in the American colonies began in Rhode Island with the 1639 formation of a Baptist congregation in Providence. Roger Williams, the founder of the Rhode Island colony, was a member for a brief time. Massachusetts, Maine, Pennsylvania, Virginia, and the Carolinas were other colonies of major Baptist settlement, though Baptists often struggled against restrictive religious policies, particularly in Virginia.

By the time of the American Revolution, Baptists composed 10 percent of the colonial population. Baptists lobbied the Continental Congress unsuccessfully for a guarantee of religious freedom.

Growth in the United States: The number of Baptist churches grew with the westward migration of the settlers and became a major factor in frontier religious life, particularly in the South. Influenced by the first Great Awakening of New

England in the 1740s, Baptists were active participants in the second Great Awakening on the frontier in the early 1800s. The revivalism that developed out of the two Awakenings has remained a common pattern among Baptist churches, particularly the evangelical ones.

The nineteenth-century debate over slavery divided Baptists in America. The resultant divisions of North and South became official in the formation of the Southern Baptist Convention in Augusta, Georgia, in 1845, an action that split the older (since 1814) Triennial Baptist Convention and the American Baptist Home Mission Society, the locus of much of the debate.

By the time of the Civil War a substantial number of African Americans were Baptists. In the South and to some degree elsewhere, their status as slaves relegated them, at best, to a second-class status in the white-led churches. By the end of the nineteenth century African Americans had developed their own organizations, which became part of the structure and life of American denominationalism.

Baptist churches in the United States have frequently been divided by the debates between fundamentalism and liberalism, in the North earlier in the twentieth century, and in the South today. Major groups in the United States are the American Baptist Churches in the U.S.A., the National Baptist Convention of America, the National Baptist Convention of the U.S.A., Inc., the Progressive National Baptist Convention, Inc., and the Southern Baptist Convention.

Baptists Worldwide: The Baptist movement has been largely Anglo-American: some 90 percent of the approximately thirty-four million Baptists in the world today are British or American. The remaining 10 percent are scattered among Europe, Asia, Central and South America, and Canada. These various groups are linked through the Baptist World Alliance, founded in London in 1905. *See also* Great Awakening; Helwys, Thomas; Protestantism; revival; Smyth, John; Williams, Roger.

baraka (bah'ruh-kuh; Arab., "blessing"), a sacred force that adheres to the holy man (*wali*) in popular Islam. It can be passed on through contact, by touching, breathing, or ritual spitting. *Baraka* also adheres to the tomb of the wali, making it the object of visitations from those seeking cures, empowerment, or insight. *See also* holy person; pilgrimage; shrine; wali.

Barbelo (bahr'be-loh), in Gnosticism, the First Thought of the Perfect Spirit, capable of appearing in many forms. *See also* Gnosticism.

Barclay, Robert (bahr'klee; 1648–90), Scottish Quaker theologian, best known for his *Apology for the True Christian Divinity, being an Explanation and Vindication of the People Called Quakers* (1678), which contains an authoritative exposition of the notion of "Inner Light." He was instrumental in the establishment of Quakerism in America and also served as governor of East New Jersey (1683). *See also* Friends, Society of.

Bardesan (bahr'de-sahn), a Syrian philosopher at the court of Abgar IX (179–216) in Edessa who combined Gnostic Christianity, astronomy, and Greek wisdom. Bardesan wrote dialogues against the Marcionites and around 150 hymns and propounded a tempered dualism, advocating free will over and against planetary and zodiacal powers. *See also* Gnosticism; Marcion.

bardo (bahr'doh; Tibetan, "intermediate state"), period between death and rebirth advocated by some Indian Buddhist schools in Tibet; it is forty-nine days in length. During the *bardo*, consciousness is believed to dwell in a bodiless condition and to undergo experiences determined by former meritorious and demeritorious actions. *See also* afterlife; karma; Tibetan Book of the Dead.

bar mitzvah/bat mitzvah (bahr meets-vah'/baht meets-vah'; Heb., "one who is commanded"), a full-fledged member of the Jewish community. When boys reach thirteen and girls twelve, ages roughly corresponding to physical maturity, they become bar or bat mitzvah and are expected to meet all requirements of ritual and civil law, such as

Bat mitzvah of the Wisberg triplets at the Keneseth Israel synagogue, Pittsfield, Massachusetts. The first American bat mitzvah was celebrated in 1922.

praying daily, observing Sabbaths and holidays, honoring parents, and giving charity. At this age, as determined by the Jewish calendar, the youngster may also receive synagogue honors. It is standard practice to mark this change in status publicly by inviting the young man or woman who reaches the proper age to read from and comment upon the weekly Torah and Haftarah portion. The occasion is also celebrated with a festive meal for family and friends. *See also* Judaism (life cycle); puberty rituals.

Barth, Karl (bahrt; 1886–1968), Swiss Reformed theologian, one of the most influential Christian thinkers of the twentieth century.

Associated with a type of theology called Neo-Orthodoxy or dialectical theology, Barth insisted on the "wholly other" nature of God, and on the insufficiency of (human) religion over against the mysterious "Word of God." Barth's earlier thinking is best expressed in *The Word of God and the Word of Man* (1924) and his commentary on Paul's Epistle to the Romans (1918). His later thought is represented by the unfinished *Church Dogmatics* (begun in 1936). Barth is also well known for his leadership role within the Christian resistance to Hitler (the Confessing Church). *See also* Confessing Church; Neo-Orthodoxy.

base community, a grassroots Christian group, led by laity, whose members come together to share their faith and promote sociopolitical change. Latin America has been the great spawning ground of base communities (Span. *communidades de base*), though other regions have followed suit. Roman Catholic groups have predominated, but Protestants have also formed many groups. Usually, a base community focuses on listening to scriptural readings and discussion, leading the members to try to make sense of their current circumstances. Both the personal and the social aspects of faith come under consideration. As a result, the base communities have often been wellsprings of resistance to unjust regimes.

Basho (b. Matsuo Basho; mah-ts*oo*-oh bah-shoh; 1644–94), one of Japan's most famous poets. Basho perfected the short (three lines of five, seven, and five syllables, respectively) poetic form called *haiku* and used it to give expression to his own Buddhist-influenced religio-aesthetic beliefs and sensibilities. *See also* Japanese religions (art and architecture).

basilica. 1 A Christian church characterized by three aisles, walls with high window openings, a wide nave, and a simple altar area. Derived from Roman civic building, it is a characteristic form of early Christian architecture. 2 In Roman Catholicism, an honorific title designating certain privileged churches. *See also* Christianity (art and architecture).

Basilica of Our Lady of Vailankanni in Tamil Nadu, India. Completed in its present form in 1933, this typical cruciform Roman Catholic church is a pilgrimage and healing site for both Indian Christians of all denominations and non-Christians.

Basilides (ba-see'li-deez), one of the great second-century Christian Gnostic theologians, active in Alexandria, Egypt. His teachings include the ineffable, nonbeing God and 365 intermediary worlds, the last of which, ours, is presided over by Abraxas. The unknown God ultimately covers everything in ignorance—not knowledge. *See also* Abraxas; Gnosticism.

Basil of Caesarea (ba'zuhl; d. ca. 379), one of the four Fathers (along with John Chrysostom, Gregory Nazianzus, and Athanasius) of the Greek Orthodox Church. Also referred to as Basil the Great, he is best known for his attacks on Arianism. *See also* Arius.

basmala (buhs-muh-luh'), an Islamic Arabic acronym standing for "In the name of God, the Merciful, the Beneficent." The basmala formula introduces almost all chapters of the Qur'an and is pronounced at the beginning of Muslim sermons, speeches, lectures, and on virtually all occasions when it is appropriate to invoke God's name and presence. *See also* blessing.

bathing. *See* ablution.

baul (bah'ool; Bengali, "mad"), a wandering performer of Hindu religious songs in Bengali, especially in the villages of northeastern India and Bangladesh. *See also* Vaishnava Sahajiya.

bazaar (ba-zahr'; from Persian, Arab. *suq*), places where goods are sold or exchanged. The term refers principally to traditional Middle Eastern markets, which are dominated by small-scale enterprises. Although transformed since the nineteenth century by Western practices, bazaar commerce remains characterized by strong linkages to Islamic institutions and practices. Religious endowments own many shops and stalls. Trades and crafts are often clustered together, with activities regulated by prayer times and religious occasions. In many areas, occupations are also associated with specific Sufi orders.

B.C./A.D. ("before Christ"; Lat. *anno Domini*, "in the year of our Lord"), Christian dating system, the year one being fixed at a sixth-century calculation of the date of the Incarnation (1 January, 754 years after the foundation of Rome).

The use of A.D. for the Christian era became common by the eleventh century; B.C. became popular only at the end of the seventeenth century.

B.C.E./C.E. (abbr., "before the common era"/"common era"), recent circumlocution for the Christian dating system, B.C./A.D., that retains the Christian numeration but avoids the explicit Christology. *See also* Judeo-Christian tradition.

beadle, an usher who keeps order in English Christian churches, maintains the church building, and oversees the prayer books and hymnals.

bear ceremonialism, set of circumpolar rituals and traditions honoring bears.

Respect and honor for the bear—largely because it can stand upright and sustain itself through long winter hibernation—is found among cultures in Finland, Eurasia, eastern Canada to the southwest of Hudson Bay, the Pacific Northwest, northern Siberia, and Japan (the Ainu of Hokkaido). Some Algonquian tribes and the Plains tribes of Blackfeet and Cree honor the bear, and some Pueblo cultures (American Southwest) associate it with medicine and war.

In most hunting rituals, the bear is addressed apologetically before it is killed. The apology often requests that the bear not allow the spirits of other bears to be angry with the hunter.

After its death, the bear is methodically skinned, leaving the fur on the head and paws intact. All meat is consumed or burned in a fire. Certain parts of the bear may be distributed to members of the community based on rank and sex. Dogs are kept away. The bones of the bear are respectfully buried. The leader or shaman sometimes wears the skin. The bear's head is honored by being hung on a pole and decorated with ribbons or other ornamentation.

In some northern Siberian cultures and among the Ainu of Japan, bear cubs were raised as members of the family. The young bear, when about two years old, was ceremonially killed. Preparation for the ceremony included feeding the bear its favorite dishes and taking it to visit all the village dwellings where it had been nursed. *See also* Ainu religion; circumpolar religion; hunting, religious aspects of; ritual; traditional peoples, religions of.

beatific vision, in Roman Catholic theology, the term describing the state of those in heaven who see God directly through knowing and loving.

Beatitudes (Lat., "blessed"), in Christianity the name given to the nine sayings of Jesus in Matthew 5:3–12 and the four in Luke 6:20–23 that begin with "Blessed are." Matthew's Beatitudes open the Sermon on the Mount, while Luke's begin the Sermon on the Plain.

Masin tribal members of the Anglican Church of (coastal) Papua New Guinea celebrate the feast day of St. Thomas a Becket (December 29) by dancing (1981).

Becket, Thomas a (ca. 1118–70), English Catholic official, archbishop of Canterbury, who was assassinated by order of Henry II. Becket's grave is an important pilgrimage site. *See also* Anglicanism.

Bede, Venerable (beed; 672–735), British Catholic monk, best known for his *Ecclesiastical History of the English People* (731). *See also* Anglicanism.

bedouin (bad'oo-win; Arab., "tent dweller"), nomadic pastoralists who occupy desert regions of the Middle East. While most profess to be Muslims, many retain non-Islamic practices.

Beelzebub (bee-el'zay-buhb), in the Hebrew Bible, a Philistine deity, "lord of the lofty abode," polemically punned in Hebrew as "lord of the flies." In the New Testament, Beelzebub is identified as "the prince of demons" (Mark 3:22–26), and the name later used as a title for Satan. *See also* Satan.

begging bowl, a sign of a Buddhist monk's renunciation of the world. Originally, monks were expected to eat only the food collected in their bowls as alms on daily rounds to laypeople's houses. Such expectations have relaxed, and the bowl is now a symbolic vestige, although reformers often advocate a strict interpretation of its use. *See also* almsgiving; bhiksu/bhiksuni; merit; Sangha; Vinaya.

Behemoth (be-hay'muth), a mythical large land animal in the Hebrew Bible (Job 40:15–16), the terrestrial counterpart of the sea monster Leviathan.

Beijing. *See* Peking.

Bel. *See* Marduk.

belief, a disposition to act, based on the attitude of holding true a paired assertion. Thus, someone who holds it true that the room needs cleaning and who, under appropriate circumstances, will clean the room, believes that the room needs cleaning. Beliefs serve crucial explanatory purposes, as in the case of a parishioner who seeks a priest's blessing because the parishioner believes that the priest's authority derives from God. Along with the meaning of one's utterances and the content of one's desires, belief makes it possible to understand human action, including religious action. It has been debated whether belief or ritual takes priority in religious life. In fact, there is no belief without the propensity to act, and one who acts intentionally must believe that one is so acting.

Belief and Communication: Much of the point of

the concept of belief lies with its role in communication. One may be interested in what a person believes for its own sake, as when one is seeking advice. In such cases, easiest access to belief comes via honest assertions in a language already understood. Other times, the real interest is in understanding what a person has said, and an appeal is made to a person's beliefs only as a means to that end. For example, one hears someone say, "There is the evening star," while looking at what we know to be Jupiter. The range of possible interpretations includes failing eyesight and irony. But if one knows that the speaker has no astronomical learning (no relevant beliefs) and tends toward self-importance (wrongly believes himself or herself master of many subjects), then one interprets the speaker as having said something false.

There is another way to make clear belief's contribution to meaning. Someone asks for ice, and another person goes to the freezer. The confidence that when the speaker says "ice" the speaker means ice is based on an assumption that the speaker and the actor believe much the same things about ice: that it is a solid, is cold, melts when warmed, is a form of water, is naturally clear, and so on. If one knew that the speaker did not believe these things, one would not go to the freezer, for one would not know what had been requested. These examples illustrate the fundamental importance of the interdependence of belief and meaning: access to a person's beliefs often comes most naturally through a speaker's words, whereas another's understanding of the speaker's words often depends on an assessment of the speaker's beliefs.

Belief is also connected to behavior. As with linguistic meaning, this connection is double-edged. One may be puzzled by the purchase of an umbrella on a cloudless day—until one learns of the buyer's history of skin cancer. Here the behavior wants explaining, but often the transparency of a person's behavior allows one to fill in the associated beliefs. (Notice, however, that one would not take someone to be washing his or her hands unless one thought he or she believed them unclean.)

Beliefs are most naturally encountered in communicative contexts, where they help people understand one another's words, behavior, choices, and preferences. We may drop the first two items in this list, for to understand a person's words is merely to understand why that person chose or preferred just those words in just that place and time; and to fathom a person's behavior is to see why, then and there, that person chose to do this rather than that. We arrive, then, at the view that beliefs are best understood as they rationalize choices or preferences. This view has been given sophisticated, quantitative expression in twentieth-century economic decision theory.

Degrees of Belief: Our definition of belief appeals to a disposition to act, based on the attitude of holding true a paired assertion. Each clause contains a term that admits of degree. A person can be more or less disposed to act, and can hold something true with more or less intensity. Clearly, the former is dictated by the latter. The person who strongly holds that a given horse will win the derby will, for that reason, be strongly disposed to bet on that horse—indeed, the odds accepted are a natural measure of the strength of the belief.

This simple connection between a wager and strength of belief can be applied to the circularity problem outlined earlier. There it was argued that access to beliefs can often come only through interpreted utterances, and that those very interpretations can often be made only with their associated beliefs in hand. In response to this perceived circularity, many philosophers and decision theorists are now proposing that the evidential base for an adequate theory of belief should record preferences between propositions or sentences holding true. One could then talk of degrees of belief in the truth of propositions or sentences, and of the relative strength of desires that propositions be true. A person's preferences could then be explained by assigning beliefs and interpreting words. Thus, a wager of $400.00 rather than $450.00 balances the preference that the money not be lost against the belief that the horse will win. When generalized across a person's behavior—or, better, across the behavior of a community of persons—it shows how it is possible to attribute belief and meaning in ignorance of both.

The strength of beliefs, then, grades off, and this will be of crucial importance in our discussion of religious belief. This grading assumes that the content of the belief is clear. That is, of course, often not so, and this leads to a second sort of grading. Besides grades of strength, a belief may have grades of clarity. Persons who hold true (believe) sentences containing such words as *love, modernity, liberal, electron,* and *large* will probably not believe precisely the same things. Yet they may be close enough, if the sentence held true can be faced with evidence admitted by both parties. However, in those cases where one does not know how to test for clarity, one may suspect the person of having no belief after all.

The concept of belief requires the concept of

objective truth. In all of the above examples, the interpreter measures the believer's actions (interprets the believer's beliefs, preferences) against the public world, invoking publicly available standards. With the notion of belief one marks the difference between what is held true by someone from what is true.

The Nature of Religious Belief—Concrete: Since religious belief is a species of belief, in general, we should expect it to accept the same general treatment. In fact, it does, at least where the object of the religious belief is natural or fairly concrete. For example, in some Indian Hindu traditions, certain fires become personified into the god Agni. Under appropriate circumstances, Agni is believed to perform certain actions, such as changing ordinary rice cakes into special rice cakes. The human participants perform many actions in this ritual that can only be understood by ascribing to the participants beliefs of the sort described earlier—that is, by seeing the ritual participants as holding true (or as preferring that) certain sentences (be true).

The belief that the fire is a god may well be equivalent to, for interpretive purposes, the ordinary nonreligious belief that the cat is on the mat (when it is). The same might be said of the belief that our ancestors require our prayers, that the rock fell on someone's head because the rock spirit had been slighted, and that sacrifice to the moon god can increase one's sexual potency. If they are equivalent, then they will be religious beliefs by virtue of their object (superhuman, supernatural, sacred, etc.), and not by any special logical or mental or linguistic peculiarity. This was essentially the view of the early-twentieth-century philosopher William James. Whether they are equivalent or not is, of course, an empirical question. If the Hindu really believes that the fire is Agni then he will go through elaborate procedures to extinguish it; he will perhaps prefer that "I am undergoing financial hardship" be true rather than that "I have failed to extinguish the fire correctly" be true. One can explain these preferences by assigning such content to his beliefs and words.

While these beliefs are unusual and interesting because they draw on superhuman or supernatural agents, they need not be for that reason either weak or unclear. It may be obvious that the belief that a certain rock is animated by a capricious spirit can be held firmly; it is equally important that the belief may be clear. That is, one knows what it would be for a rock to act; one can imagine it, and one can imagine evidence that would be convincing. None of these or similar beliefs need grade off into obscurity.

The situation becomes more complex with abstract monotheisms such as Judaism, Christianity, and Islam. There are enormous variations among and within each of these. But all officially appeal to an invisible, intelligent power. The question, then, is whether belief in such a deity can be analyzed in the same way as the belief that the cat is on the mat, or that the fire is Agni.

The Nature of Religious Belief—Abstract: Consider someone who believes in a God who transcends space and time, has no body, and yet performs actions that affect things in space and time; in a God who has no sensory receptors yet hears prayers and sees acts of sacrilege and piety. What does this belief amount to? If one applies the earlier test, one must ask what disposition to action is associated with this putative belief. One such action will presumably be to assent to the question, Do you believe in an invisible, intelligent power? But by itself this is insufficient. A belief must be held on the basis of some evidence, real or imagined. But with very abstract conceptions of God one cannot easily entertain the concept, much less ask after its evidence. Such a putative belief may be held with great intensity, even to martyrdom, and yet its clarity may have graded off to a vanishing point.

This point is perhaps best appreciated by placing this sort of belief in its native communicative context. One wants to know what content to give to someone's apparent belief in an invisible, intelligent power. One examines the behavior. One sees and hears the person pray to something (one knows not what) that accepts a name; one sees the believer accept ritual blessings from something. If anything, these and like actions (these and like prepossessions) bespeak an embodied deity, one having some location in space and time. One then turns to the second evidential source, the meanings of the believer's words. One finds that the believer uses words to describe God that people use to describe each other, only greatly elevated: *loving, just, wise, powerful, creative,* and so on. The trouble is that the words, like the actions, require an entity—something in space and time—to accept them. Thus, the nature of interpretation makes it difficult to ascribe to anyone belief in an invisible, intelligent power.

There are philosophers and theologians who argue that some beliefs are by their nature theoretical and abstract. They draw examples from particle physics, or from theories of prehistory, or physical cosmology; these, they argue, are objects of belief that, like the abstract God of Judaism, Christianity, and Islam, cannot be directly observed. In response, most philosophers point out that, while these cases perhaps cannot be settled by observation, the contending parties can marshall evidence on one side or the other of the issue, evidence that will influence research programs and that will lead to corollary hypotheses, etc. The moral is that, between such unambiguous cases of belief as "the cat is on the mat" and such tenuous ones as "God is love," there is a limitless spectrum of strength and clarity. It is probably not possible to draw a firm line on this spectrum marking off legitimate from illegitimate belief.

Two further points can be made. First, belief in an abstract monotheistic god is, in fact, often not so abstract. For example, many Jews, Christians, and Muslims will say that God has no body, but, as many anthropologists have pointed out, their actual working conception of God may be very different. Indeed, the tendency toward giving God humanlike form has proved ineradicable over the ages. Here the requirements of theology and interpretation clash outright: belief, striving for legitimacy, demands substance, while orthodox doctrine rules it out. Second, even where the believer maintains a pure, abstract conception of the deity, the believer may hold corollary religious beliefs that are quite concrete. Thus, a belief in life after death is often invoked to explain acts of martyrdom.

Questions about the nature of religious belief (concrete or abstract) as belief should be separated from questions about its wider significance. Into the latter category fall, for example, theories about the origin and function of religious belief and its relation, for example, to social structure, to morals, or to aesthetic feeling.

Variations in Belief: One of the most striking features of religious belief is its variability. Besides the basic distinction between concrete and abstract, there are monotheistic and polytheistic religious traditions, and some that appear to worship no deity whatsoever. Some religions require, whereas others outlaw, ritual suicide; some emphasize elaborate cosmological schemes, while others urge concentration on the here and now. Some differ only over the status of infant baptism, while others diverge over the deity's (or deities') gender(s).

While what tends to strike the eye is this variation of belief, the earlier discussion of interpretation allows one to discern a more fundamental level of agreement and commonality. A single belief about, for example, ice depends on many related beliefs about water, cold, melting, solidity, etc.—related beliefs that the interpreter shares with the believer. Philosophers have recently termed this the *holism* of the mental; roughly, the claim is that any particular belief can be identified or selected only on the basis of surrounding, shared belief. When applied to religious belief, holism yields important results. Those traditions that can be meaningfully said to differ over ritual suicide must first agree in many respects about what a person is; identification of cosmological issues depends on prior agreement about the visible world; disagreement over infant baptism makes sense only between persons who share many beliefs about what infants are; contention over notions of male and female presupposes a common ability to identify each one.

Belief is by its nature holistic. Reflection on this can bring into focus the vast extent of belief necessarily shared by all believers, religious or not, a background of commonality that enables divergences of belief to stand out with renewed clarity. *See also* religion, philosophy of; religious language.

Bellarmine, Robert (bel'ahr-meen; 1542–1621), Italian Jesuit theologian, best known as a controversialist against Protestantism during the Roman Catholic Counter-Reformation. *See also* Counter-Reformation.

bells, ringing devices used by many Christian churches for calling worshipers to services, for tolling the dead, and for celebrating occasions. In Orthodox churches, long wooden planks, struck with a mallet, substitute for bells. In Catholicism, bells are used to signal important parts of the liturgy.

Bema (bee'mah; Gk., "throne," "platform"), in Manichaeism an annual feast commemorating Mani's death and a category of hymns. *See also* Manichaeism.

Benedictines, Christian monks who subscribe to the Rule of St. Benedict of Nursia (ca. 480–547). Benedictine monasticism has played a significant role in Western civilization, and the centuries from the eighth to the fourteenth have with considerable justification been called the "Benedictine centuries." Benedictine missionaries in the eighth century brought the Christian message from England to Germany and raised the level of Christianity practiced in the Frankish lands west of the Rhine. As they grew wealthier through the generous donations of lay patrons, Benedictine monasteries became important landowners and thus came to play an essential role in the feudal economy. Benedictine scholars also contributed greatly to intellectual life. Benedictine scriptoria were largely responsible for preserving the classical and early Christian inheritance through the Middle Ages. *See also* monasticism.

benediction. 1 In Christian worship, the blessing called down upon the congregation at the conclusion of the service. 2 In Roman Catholicism, a brief service in which the congregation is blessed with the consecrated eucharistic elements. 3 Any formula of blessing. 4 The act of blessing. *See also* blessing; ritual.

Benedict of Nursia (ca. 480–547), Italian Catholic monk, often termed "the father of Western monasticism." While little is known of his life, he founded the monastery on Monte Cassino (ca. 529), the original site of the Benedictine order. The order comprises those monastic associations governed by Benedict's Rule: a year's probation, a lifelong vow, strict poverty, regular liturgical practice, physical labor, and spiritual studies. *See also* Benedictines; monasticism.

berakah (buh-rah-khah'; Heb., "blessing, benediction"), the rabbis' favored prose genre for Jewish prayers. In short form, the opening "Blessed art Thou, Lord our God, Ruler of the universe who . . ." is followed by a conclusion related to the occasion at hand, introducing the performance of commandments or mediating the Jew's interaction with nature (e.g., eating, drinking, observing a rainbow), which is taken to belong to God and so requires a blessing to transform it for human enjoyment. Longer blessings constitute basic building blocks of statutory prayer service and present theological statements around religious themes, such as revelation or redemption. *See also* blessing; Judaism, prayer and liturgy of.

berdache. *See* gender crossing.

Bernadette of Lourdes (b. Marie Bernarde Soubirous, 1844–79), French Catholic saint. The daughter of a miller in Lourdes, her visions of the Virgin Mary (February 11–July 16, 1858) established Lourdes as a major European pilgrimage site. She was canonized in 1933. *See also* Lourdes.

Bernard of Clairvaux (1090–1163), French Catholic monk, Cistercian abbot, best known for his mystical writings and for his championing of the Second Crusade.

Berossus (buhr-aw'soos; ca. 350–280 B.C.), a Babylonian priest who was the author of *Babyloniaka*, a work in Greek on Babylonian history and intel-

lectual achievements. *See also* Mesopotamian religion; Oannes.

berserk, ecstatic, invulnerable warrior in old Scandinavian tradition. *See also* Indo-European religion; Nordic religion.

Besht. *See* Baal Shem Tov.

Bethel (beth'uhl; Heb., "house of God"). 1 In the Hebrew Bible, the site of Jacob's dream of a ladder stretching from earth to heaven (Genesis 28:10–22). 2 A name used by Christian denominations for their house of worship.

Bethlehem, a city five miles south of Jerusalem celebrated as the birthplace of Jesus.

Beza, Theodore (bee'zuh; 1519–1605), French Protestant theologian and historian. The successor to Calvin as Reformed leader in Geneva, Switzerland, Beza is best known for having produced the first critical edition of the Greek New Testament (1565) and for discovering the late-fifth-century New Testament manuscript that now bears his name (Codex Bezae). *See also* Calvinism.

Bhagavad Gita (buh'guh-vuhd gee'tah; Skt., "Song of the Blessed One"), Sanskrit poetic text written around 200 B.C. to A.D. 200 exalting the Hindu god Krishna and proposing a synthetic religious path. Throughout history Indian thinkers wrote commentaries on the text, each understanding it to teach the writer's own tradition. It became most popular in the modern period due to its compact size (seven hundred verses) and promotion of active involvement in this world, which was seen to counter criticisms of Hinduism as otherworldly and nonethical. Hundreds of translations in Indian and Western languages exist today. It was popular among American transcendentalists and among recent Western movements that trace their inspiration to India.

The text was apparently inserted in the *Mahabharata* by an unknown author who sought to provide another alternative to the religious paths of the day. It portrays itself as a correct understanding of the early Upanishads. As found in the *Mahabharata*, it begins immediately before two branches of the Bharata clan fight a great battle for the dominion of the world. Arjuna, the hero, surveys both armies and refuses to fight. His charioteer, Krishna, whom the text eventually reveals is Vishnu, Lord of All, attempts successfully to convince him to fight in order to protect his family name and the caste system. Thus, Krishna upholds the threatened social order, while teaching that liberation from *karma* (the consequences of meritorious and demeritorious actions) and rebirth is attained through a path combining *karma yoga* (acting without concern for the results, nonattachment), *jnana yoga* (realization of the true self, which is uninvolved in the actions of the world, through thought and meditation), and *bhakti yoga* (devotion of all actions to Krishna, realizing he is the ultimate doer in all that transpires). Chapter 11 describes a vision in which this is vividly revealed. *See also* karma; Krishna; liberation; Mahabharata; path of devotion; path of knowledge; path of (ritual) action; yoga.

Bhagavan (bah'guh-vuhn; Skt., "Beloved One"), in sectarian Hinduism, a title describing Vishnu, and often Krishna, as the supreme and loving deity. *See also* Bhagavata Purana; Krishna; Shrivaishnavism; Vaishnavism; Vishnu.

Bhagavata Purana (bah'guh-vuh-tuh poo-rah'nuh), a Hindu sectarian text emphasizing devotion to Vishnu, especially in his incarnation as Krishna. Also known as the *Bhagavatam*, it is one of the so-called Mahapuranas that laid the foundation for theistic Hinduism during the latter half of the first millennium.

Written most likely in the Tamil region of South India between the mid-ninth and early tenth centuries, the *Bhagavata* is one of the latest, the most unified and artistic, the most philosophical, and the most consistently devotional of the major Puranas. Many of its themes and stories are based on the earlier *Vishnu Purana*, but the *Bhagavata*'s expanded portrayal of Krishna's childhood relations with the cowherd maidens (*gopis*) in Vrindavana also reflects characteristic features of the emotional devotion developed by the Tamil Vaishnava poet-saints known as the Alvars during the intervening three centuries.

The *Bhagavata* had great authority and influence in later Vaishnava movements and was an important factor in the spread of popular devotion to Krishna. Apart from the treatment of Krishna's story, the *Bhagavata*'s major contribution was its detailed accounts of Vishnu's numerous other incarnations and exemplary devotees within a theological framework that combined Vedanta and Samkhya philosophies to explain the world and provide a rationale for devotion. *See also* Alvar; Samkhya; Shrivaishnavism; six systems of Indian philosophy; Vaishnavism; Vedanta; Vishnu.

Bhaisajyaguru (bi-shahj'yah-goo'roo; Skt., "Master of Healing"), a Buddha who is an important member of the Mahayana pantheon. As a Buddha-to-be (*bodhisattva*), Bhaisajyaguru vowed to alleviate the sickness of those who called upon him. He is able not only to ease the physical symptoms of illness, but to transform the ultimate causes of an individual's illness. Historically his cult was found mainly among Buddhists in Central and East Asia. *See also* Bodhisattvas; Buddhas; Mahayana.

bhakti. *See* path of devotion.

bhiksu/bhiksuni (bik'shoo/bik'shoonee; Skt., masc./fem., "beggar"), two of many terms for Buddhist monks and nuns. As etymology suggests, the terms express the expectation that Buddhist monastics should obtain their food by begging. This is no longer an expectation, and the terms refer simply to members of the Buddhist monastic order.

An essential part of the Buddha's career as a religious teacher was the establishment of a monastic order (Sangha), which preserved his teaching and provided a social context for its practice. The monastic order is divided into independent male and female branches. In South and Southeast Asia, the ordination of nuns ceased at some point in the medieval period, and consequently the female branch is no longer found in those areas. A further distinction is made in the monastic order between novices and those who have undergone a higher ordination. The terms *bhiksu/bhiksuni* are often reserved for the latter. A monk who has received higher ordination is expected to observe over two hundred rules, a nun more than three hundred, the precise number varying between schools.

The regulations for monastic behavior (*Vinaya*) are especially concerned with external practice covering the kinds of habitation suitable for monks and nuns, obtaining and wearing monastic robes, permitted nourishment, the use of money, and abstinence from sexual relations. Another concern of the regulations is maintenance of an appropriate communal life, and they provide for the expulsion of members unable to conform to these external practices.

Buddhist monastic history is a record of disputes over the interpretation of Vinaya regulations. These disputes may appear to be over quite minor issues, such as whether a monk may carry salt to flavor his food, but the Buddhist tradition has consistently interpreted external practices as necessary instruments for the cultivation of a desired inner life.

The *Dhammapada*, an anthology of the Buddha's sayings, makes clear that external practices alone are not the whole of a monk's or nun's life. The envisioned inner life that should accompany external practice was often expressed in "folk etymologies" such as "Bhiksu because he sees the fear in rebirth" or "because he has broken that which leads to rebirth." The portrayal of the inner life of the ideal bhiksu or bhiksuni varies more than do specific monastic regulations. The Theravada often employs a scheme consisting of morality, mental cultivation, and wisdom, while the Mahayana adopts ideas from the *bodhisattva*'s (Buddha-to-be's) career, emphasizing compassion and wisdom. *See also* almsgiving; merit; monk; nun; Sangha; Vinaya.

bhiksuni. *See* bhiksu/bhiksuni.

Bhu/Bhudevi (*boo/boo-day'vee*). **1** The earth as Hindu goddess; she is the second and dark wife of Vishnu, repeatedly rescued by his avatars (assumed forms). **2** In Hindu Samkhya, the final evolute of primal matter, completing creation. *See also* cosmology; Earthmother; Goddess (Hinduism); Samkhya; Vishnu.

Bible, ancient Judaic interpretation of. *See* Judaism (authoritative texts and their interpretation).

Bible, Christian (Gk. *ta biblia,* "the books"), the collection of writings considered canonical by the Christian churches. The Bible is divided into two parts, the Old Testament (Hebrew scriptures, or Tanakh) and the New Testament.

Hebrew scriptures consist of twenty-four books divided into three sections: the Law, the Prophets, and the Writings. Protestant versions of these scriptures (the Old Testament) reproduce exactly their content but by dividing some books into two or more separate units that results in a total of thirty-nine. Roman Catholic and Eastern Orthodox churches include seven more books plus additions to the books of Esther and Daniel, known as the Apocrypha in some Protestant Bibles. There are some minor differences between the Roman Catholic and Orthodox canons.

The New Testament contains twenty-seven books—the four Gospels, the Acts of the Apostles, twenty-one Letters, and the book of Revelation. (Some Syrian churches omit the Letters of 2 Peter, 2, 3 John, Jude, and Revelation, while some Ethiopic churches include I Enoch and Jubilees as canonical.)

The process by which the material in the Hebrew scriptures gained canonical status is a complicated and disputed issue. It is generally agreed, however, that by the end of the first century the present collection was accepted by major segments of Judaism. Early Christianity largely considered the Hebrew scriptures as its Bible; however, by the middle of the second century some Christian writings, the Letters of Paul, and various Gospels were considered authoritative in some traditions and were regularly used in Christian worship.

The boundaries of the New Testament remained somewhat flexible during the first four centuries. Certain books were considered canonical by some churches and rejected by others. A consensus was gradually achieved and, with minor exceptions, the present twenty-seven books were accepted. It is commonly asserted that the first official list is to be found in the Easter Letter of Athanasius in 367, but this represents the culmination of a process rather than an official ecclesiastical decree.

All branches of Christendom, in one way or another, consider the Bible the basic source of belief and practice. There remains, however, dispute as to the relationship between the Bible and tradition and the function of contemporary interpretation of the Bible.

The Bible, in addition to its function within religious communities, has had profound influence on Western secular social structures and legal systems. It has also been a primary resource for much of Western high culture, especially the visual arts, literature, and music. *See also* Bible, interpretation of the Christian; Bible, translations of the Christian; canon.

Bible, interpretation of the Christian, the process and procedures for explaining what the writings sacred to Christians meant for the writers and original audience (exegesis), as well as what they mean for the church today (hermeneutics).

The Bible also requires interpretation because most Christians regard it as important and authoritative: the Bible presents the revelation of God and God's dealings with humankind. The Bible also needs explanation or interpretation because its books were written in ancient Near Eastern and Mediterranean cultures. Modern readers need information about ancient history and geography, social customs, literary genres by which people expressed themselves, assumptions about the human condition and nature, and so forth.

In the Gospels Jesus sometimes quotes or alludes to texts from the Hebrew Bible to argue a point or to encourage a way of acting. Although Jesus accords authority to these biblical texts, he is also portrayed as their authoritative interpreter. The earliest Christians interpret their Bible (the Jewish scriptures in their Greek version) in the light of Jesus' life, death, and resurrection. Thus, the details of his death on the cross are explained with reference to Psalm 22 and Isaiah 53. Matthew, Paul, and other New Testament writers understood the Old Testament as "fulfilled" in Jesus Christ.

From the Patristics to the Enlightenment: In the patristic period (second century to the beginning of the Middle Ages) the Bible consists of two Testaments (Old and New). The tension between what the Bible meant and what it means is reflected in the division between the literal (Antiochene) and allegorical (Alexandrian) approaches. Without denying the spiritual truths in scripture, Antiochene interpreters such as John Chrysostom (d. 407) and Theodore of Mopsuestia (d. 427) emphasize the historical realities in scripture, insisting that any spiritual sense be based on the literal sense of the text. Alexandrians such as Clement of Alexandria (d. ca. 211) and Origen (d. ca. 254) use the methods of allegorical interpretation developed by Greek pre-Christian interpreters of Homer and by the Jewish philosopher Philo (d. ca. 50) to uncover the spiritual truths beneath the surface of the biblical texts.

Medieval interpreters discern four biblical senses: literal (what happened), allegorical (the hidden theological truth), anagogical (the heavenly sense), and moral or tropological (the meaning for one's behavior). While not rejecting the several senses of scripture, Thomas Aquinas (ca. 1225–74) insists that the spiritual sense be based on the literal and presuppose it. In his biblical commentaries Aquinas uses human reason to explain the scriptures and seeks to integrate biblical and philosophical truth.

Renaissance humanism inspires an interest in studying the scriptures in Hebrew and Greek in their historical settings. Erasmus (ca. 1466–1536) produced a new edition of the Greek New Testament and called on Greek and Latin classical writings to supplement the biblical interpretations of the church fathers. The Protestant Reformers appeal to the Bible as the best means of restoring the purity of Christian life, and emphasize the Bible's clarity and authoritative sufficiency. Enlightenment thinkers champion human reason over the claims of divine revelation and church tradition. So Benedict de Spinoza (1632–77) and other philosophers argue that in a conflict between the Bible and human reason (as in the case of miracles) the Bible is to be rejected as the final authority and the matter explained in the light of reason.

Types of Criticism: Historical criticism refers to the complex of methods used in establishing the text of the biblical writings, understanding their content and style, and determining their origin and authenticity. Its techniques were generally developed outside of biblical research and can be applied to any literature. The goal is to help one to know as much as possible about the text in its original historical setting.

Textual criticism seeks to reconstruct a text close to the one written by the original author. The most important Greek manuscripts of the New Testament come from the fourth and fifth centuries. The earliest complete manuscripts of the Hebrew Bible are dated to the tenth and eleventh centuries. Using the best manuscripts along with earlier fragmentary evidence (Dead Sea Scrolls, Greek papyri), the textual critic determines the original reading on the basis of external (the number and genealogy of manuscripts) and internal (language, style) considerations, and then explains how the variant readings arose.

In its broad sense literary criticism refers to the systematic analysis of a text's words and images, characters, structure, form, and meaning. These procedures are useful in studying all kinds of literature. Source criticism establishes where previously existing materials have been incorporated into a biblical writing. In addition to classifying literary forms and genres, form criticism seeks to determine the historical settings in which the forms functioned before they became part of the larger text. Redaction criticism examines the ways in which the biblical writer used and adapted sources to address concerns and problems facing the original readers.

Historical critics also study biblical writings in their historical settings, as these are known from textual discoveries and archaeological excavations. Parallels to biblical books enable historical critics to know which ideas and ways of expression were current, and to appreciate where biblical authors adhere to or deviate from cultural patterns. Using all of these approaches, introductions to the Bible describe individual books in terms of author, date, audience, language, purpose, content, structure, and theology.

The term *historical criticism* is often used in a narrow sense to refer to the task of determining the events behind the text, e.g., what really happened at Israel's exodus from Egypt or on the first Easter. A major obstacle facing such historical critics is that biblical writers usually did not distinguish between events and their interpretation. Historical criticism took shape especially in the German universities during the nineteenth and twentieth centuries. Its opponents claim that it reflects the concerns of the Enlightenment and tells us at best what the text meant but not what it means. Its modern practitioners either accept these limitations, or argue that historical criticism can be practiced in an ideologically neutral way and is the necessary basis for trying to convey what a biblical text means today.

Historical criticism of the Bible can tell Christian preachers and teachers what a text meant in its original setting, warn them against fanciful interpretations, and generate ideas and themes. But the hermeneutical task also involves getting from "there" (the world of the Bible) to "here" (the world of the twentieth century). The task of the preacher (or any Christian interpreter) is to bring the biblical text to bear on the life of a specific community, while remaining faithful to the biblical tradition. Fundamentalists make a direct transfer, on the assumption that there is no real gap, or that God's Word leaps over whatever gap there may be. Other Christians look more cautiously for the symmetries or parallelisms between biblical and modern situations. They draw universal principles out of specific texts, identify themselves with characters in the texts, discover spiritual truths in the texts, and adapt the texts to modern situations.

In the 1990s, as always, biblical interpretation is influenced by currents in the intellectual and religious community. It has become common to use terms, methods, and models developed in the social sciences (especially anthropology) along with methods from contemporary literary criticism (structuralism, narrative criticism, deconstructionism). Other approaches are more closely tied to contemporary Christian theological movements (liberation theology, feminism, canonical criticism). *See also* Bible, Christian; Bible, translations of the Christian; exegesis.

Bible, Jewish. *See* Hebrew Bible; Judaism (authoritative texts and their interpretation); Torah.

Bible, translations of the Christian, the rendering of the original Hebrew/Aramaic and Greek books of the Bible into other ancient and modern languages. The oldest extant translation is that by Jews of the Hebrew Bible into Greek (Septuagint) in the third to first centuries B.C.

Several versions of the Septuagint are extant, and at least three other Greek translations appeared in the first and second centuries. The rapid spread of Christianity brought about, as early as the second century, translations into Syriac and Latin, and by the fifth century there were versions in Coptic (Egyptian), Ethiopic, Georgian, Armenian, and Gothic. Slavonic and Arabic translations were produced not later than the tenth century. The most influential translation for Western Christianity was Jerome's Latin Vulgate, prepared in the last decades of the fourth century, which held sway for at least a millennium.

As Latin came to be known less and less by the populace, translations into the various European vernaculars were necessary. By the middle of the sixteenth century translations into virtually every modern European language were available. Missionary activity led to translations into the languages of Asia, Africa, the Pacific Islands, and many vernacular languages of the Americas. As of 1988, the entire Bible has appeared in at least three hundred languages and portions in approximately nineteen hundred others. Twenty-five new languages were added in 1988 alone. *See also* Bible, Christian; Bible, interpretation of the Christian; Jerome; King James Version; Lollards; Origen; Septuagint; Tyndale, William; Vulgate; Wycliff, John.

bida (bid'uh; Arab., "innovation"), an Islamic term for changing or adding to religious belief and practice. The aversion to *bida* is based on the conviction that God's Word (Qur'an) and the *Sunna* (practice) of the Prophet Muhammad contain all that is necessary for a valid life in the path of God. *See also* tradition.

Big House movement, a twelve-night ceremony of the Native American Delaware tribe to secure well-being for the coming year, which emphasized fidelity to ancient ritual patterns and recital of visions. *See also* new year festivals; North America, traditional religions in.

bilocation, the capacity to be in two places at the same time. In some traditions, bilocation is one of the marks of a holy person. In late-nineteenth-century theories of religion, the experience of bilocation by a dreamer was held to be one of the causes of animism. *See also* animism; holy person.

binary opposition. *See* myth; religion, the study of.

birth control, prevention of conception. All societies possess techniques for birth control. For some religious traditions, it is a forbidden or controversial practice.

Christianity: The early church father Augustine (d. 430) condemned birth control along with abortion and infanticide. Primitive understanding of procreation made contraception difficult to distinguish from abortion. Also, Christian marriage was justified for the sake of procreation rather than the pleasure of physical intimacy, so that contraception was discouraged. The Hebrew Bible's narrative of Onan, who was struck dead by God for spilling his seed on the ground (Genesis 38:8–10), coupled with the Roman jurist Ulpian's (d. 228) theory of natural law were also determinative in the association of birth control with sin. Coitus was viewed according to natural law as ordained for procreation. It was Thomas Aquinas (ca. 1225–74), following Aristotle (d. 322 B.C.), who first justified pleasure in association with procreative acts.

In modern Christian ethics, most Protestant churches have voiced no opposition to birth control, although some individual ethicists such as Helmut Thielicke have expressed some general reservations. Roman Catholicism officially opposed birth control in Pius XI's *Casti Connubii* (1930); in *Humanae Vitae* (1967), issued by Paul VI; and in John Paul II's *Evangelium Vitae* (1995). Roman Catholics have been deeply divided on this issue. Some historians suggest that the Roman Catholic rejection of birth control was in part a reaction to the Anglican Church, which condoned the practice in 1929. *See also* sexuality and religion.

Birth Grandmother (Kor. *Samsin Halmoni*), Korean tutelary household spirit entrusted with the protection of conception, childbirth, and the nurturing of young children. Faith in the power of the Birth Grandmother is largely held by women and may be contrasted to the Confucianized belief in heaven, fate, or simple agnosticism held by men. Women recognize that it is through the grace of the Birth Grandmother who resides in each household that the generations of a family continue. The Birth Grandmother is said to reside in an earthenware jar of rice grain, which is kept in the inner room (*anbang*) of the house, where conception, birth, and lactation occur. Women worship the Birth Grandmother through the tribute offering (*kosa*) of rice cakes, wine, and sometimes other delicacies. The Birth Grandmother, if slighted, may prevent conception or cause newborn and young children to sicken and die. The Birth Grandmother also functions as a tutelary spirit of many shamans who are protected by her when they induce possession by their familiar spirit in order to communicate with the dead. *See also* kosa; life-cycle rituals; shamanism.

birth rituals. *See* life-cycle rituals.

bisexuality. *See* androgyny; gender and religion; gender crossing.

bishop, the overseer or chief cleric of a geographical area of the Christian church. In Roman Catholicism the bishop is chief priest and authoritative pastor of a designated region of the Church.

New Episcopal bishop receives his crook-shaped staff (crozier) as an insignia of office at his ordination ceremony, San Juan Bautista, California (1990).

biwa hoshi (bee-wah hooh-shee; Jap.,"lute priest"), blind itinerant lay Buddhist priests who sang ballads with lute accompaniment, most notably the thirteenth-century *Heike monogatari* (Tale of the Heike).

Black Elk (1863–1950), Oglala (Sioux) religious figure. In the life of Black Elk, two religious visions—the symbolic universes of Lakota spirituality and Roman Catholic Christianity—interact. Also revealed through the prism of his life is a tragic clash of worlds, culminating in the bloodletting at Wounded Knee in 1890. In John G. Niehardt's *Black Elk Speaks* (1932), Black Elk's inner life and powerful vision experiences are poetically set forth.

Black Hat (Tibetan *zhva-nag*), also known as "black crown," hat worn by the Tibetan Buddhist "incarnate lama" (Karma-pa) symbolizing spiritual power and institutional authority. In tradition, it was presented by *dakinis* (female spiritual beings) to the first Karma-pa upon his enlightenment. It was woven of the hair of a hundred thousand dakinis and symbolized the compassion of Avalokiteshvara, whose incarnation the Karma-pa is, and was visible to those of pure vision above the heads of all subsequent Karmapas. The emperor of China, having seen the crown above the fifth Karma-pa (fourteenth-fifteenth century), had a physical replica made and presented to him. This became the treasure of the Karma-pa line; it is displayed in a ritual in which the Karma-pa, wearing the crown, reveals his identity with Avalokiteshvara. *See also* Avalokiteshvara; Karma-pa; Tibetan religions

Black Head Taoist, a Taoist priest (Chin. *tao-shih*) who can perform funerals and ceremonies dealing with the underworld, which a Red Head Taoist cannot. This manner of distinguishing between Taoist priests is prevalent in the southern traditions, particularly in Taiwan and Fukien province in mainland China. *See also* tao-shih.

Black Israelites, also Original Hebrew Israelite Nation, a black Jewish sect originating in Chicago in the 1960s, advocating migration to Israel. *See also* African Americans (North America), new religions among; Black Jewish movements.

Black Jewish movements, organized congregations of African-American Jews appearing in the United States beginning about 1905. Black Jewish sects probably sprang, in part, from the identification of African Americans with the persecution of the Jewish people, who were enslaved in Egypt. There is evidence of the existence of black Jewish itinerants, who traveled about preaching during the early years of the twentieth century.

Black Jewish movements vary widely in theology, but most agree that African Americans are members of one of the lost tribes of Israel and most consult the Talmud or Old Testament. Some sects maintain friendly ties with white Jews, considering themselves descendants of the Falashas (Ethiopian Jews). Others contend that the only true Jews are people of African heritage and view white Jews as impostors. Black Zionism, the concept of redemption and return to Ethiopia, prevails among some of these factions.

Black Jews differ over the applicability of Christianity. Many groups rely heavily on the New Testament, maintain the centrality of Jesus Christ, and celebrate select Christian holidays. These Black Jews wear skullcaps and phylacteries, reject pork, and celebrate Passover, but also practice baptism, receive communion, and sing gospel hymns. Other sects reject Christianity completely, viewing it as the religion of white oppressors and striving toward orthodox Judaism. These Black Jews consider Hebrew a sacred language, and many also learn Yiddish. Some sects maintain black Hebrew and rabbinical schools to educate their youth and promote their teachings in African-American communities. *See also* African Americans (North America), new religions among.

black magic, the common designation of occult or spiritual powers used for evil ends, such as selfish gain or to harm rivals and enemies, often contrasted with white or beneficent magic. It constitutes a native category in the West and many traditional religious cultures.

black mass, a parody, often obscene, of the Roman Catholic Mass, performed by Satanists as a means of evoking and worshiping the devil. While often only an allegation in the past, it has now become an element of practice in some groups. *See also* Satanism.

Black Muslims, followers of the Nation of Islam; a term occasionally applied to other African-American Islamic sects. *See also* African Americans (North America), new religions among; Nation of Islam.

black theology, a mode of Christian theological reflection that emerged in the late 1960s in the United States emphasizing blacks' liberation from white racism and cultural dominance. On June 13, 1969, the National Committee of Black Churchmen issued a statement on "Black Theology," which included the following: "Black Theology is a theology of 'blackness.' It is the affirmation of black humanity that emancipates black people from white racism, thus providing authentic freedom for both white and black people."

James Cone, of Union Theological Seminary, New York City, became known as one of the most important voices of the black theology movement with the publication of *Black Theology and Black Power* (1969). The publication of

J. Deotis Robert's *Liberation and Reconciliation: A Black Theology* (1971) sparked additional debate concerning the relationship of theology to politics, of black theology to more traditional Christian theology, and, more specifically, of Cone's interpretation of black theology. In subsequent years, proponents of black theology have sought to establish dialogue with leaders in the established black denominations, white theologians in the United States and Europe, and theologians in Africa, Asia, and Latin and South America who have been struggling to define theological modes of reflection that are indigenous to their cultures and instrumental in promoting political and economic liberation.

black/white gods, iconograph indicating the fusion of the dual nature of divinity as destructive/creative. Gods may change color according to their role in a pair. In Hinduism, Shiva assumes the white half when paired with the destructive goddess Kali but is black when paired with Parvati, his gentle consort. *See also* dualism.

Bladder Festival, communal feast of the western Bering Sea coast of Alaska and the Aleutian Islands, held annually in late fall or during the December full moon, to honor the life forms (souls) of seals and other marine mammals. The souls of these animals, it is believed, are held in the bladders. Properly treated bladders will reincarnate, bringing abundant game to the village.

During the year the bladders of seals, whales, walruses, and polar bears are kept inflated. At the beginning of the Bladder Festival the bladders are brought to the newly cleaned *kashim* or *qasgiq* (the central men's house in a village), painted, and hung on stakes. They are treated with quiet respect and offered food and water. The weeklong festival includes games and dances with masks, drumming, and marionettes, as well as carvings of wood and ivory.

Midweek in the ceremony holes are cut in the ice. Men dance and sing, welcoming the rest of the village to the festival. On the last day of the ceremony the men spear the bladders and push them under the ice as rapidly as they can. A fire is lit on the ice, and the entire village gathers to sing and dance. The men then retire to the kashim for a sweat bath. *See also* circumpolar religions; fishing rites/whaling rites.

blasphemy (Gk., "speaking evil"), a public act of verbal religious offense through mocking or reviling beliefs, sacred persons, or objects.

Judaism: In the Hebrew Bible, blasphemy (Heb. *hillul hashem,* "profaning the name"), consists of cursing God, desecrating the Temple precincts or its service, or behaving immorally. The latter is expanded in later Judaism to include any behavior by a Jew that reflects adversely on the Jewish religion or the Jewish people.

Christianity: In its narrowest sense, blasphemy is the violation of the biblical prohibition against cursing God (Exodus 22:28); in its broadest, it is any view considered heretical. Extended to include both verbal utterances and sacrilegious actions, blasphemy is any word or deed intended to revile or desecrate that which is sacred or to manifest gross disrespect toward sacred beings, places, or persons. In Christian countries, blasphemy was once punished under civil law; the penalties today are ecclesiastical (e.g., excommunication).

Islam: Giving insult (Arab. *saab*) to Allah, Muhammad, or any element in the quranic revelation or tradition is a crime under Islamic law punishable by a loss of all legal and religious rights or, in extreme cases, by the death penalty. An act of public repentance sets aside the penalty. When blasphemy is perceived as a sign of apostasy (*riddah*) or infidelity (*kufr*), the deliberate rejection of Islam by a Muslim, the death penalty is most frequently invoked and repentance is not possible. In theological usage, blasphemy is often extended as a general name for heresy.

Blavatsky, Helena Petrovna (1831–91), a Russian immigrant to the United States and cofounder of the Theosophical Society in New York in 1875 and its chief intellectual catalyst. Her major books, *Isis Unveiled* (1877) and *The Secret Doctrine* (1888), feature such teachings as reincarnation, cosmic evolution, and hidden masters of wisdom. *See also* Theosophical Society; Theosophy.

blessing. 1 The human possession of supernatural powers. *See also* baraka. 2 A type of prayer. *See also* basmala; berakah; blessings, Christian; ritual.

blessings, Christian. 1 In Christianity, a formula or extemporaneous prayer asking God's aid or protection over places, persons, or things. 2 A formula used to consecrate something for sacred use. 3 A prayer of thanksgiving and praise to God for something received. *See also* benediction.

blood, a powerful ritual substance and religious symbol, it is always perceived as highly ambivalent: dangerous and salutary, death dealing and life sustaining, polluting and cleansing. The three most important blood contexts are sacrifice, menstruation, and ritual wounding. *See also* menstrual blood; mutilation; ordeal; sacrifice.

Blue Cliff Record (Chin. *Pi-yen lu*), Chinese collection of one hundred Buddhist *kung-an* (paradoxical teachings that transcend logical or conceptual thought) compiled by Hsueh-tou (980–1052), to which explanatory commentary was later added. *See also* Ch'an school; kung-an.

B'nai Noah (buh-nay; Heb., "children of Noah"), a contemporary movement composed of approximately five hundred former Christians who have adopted the Seven Laws of Noah as the basis of a strongly philo-Semitic belief system that rejects Christianity but discourages full conversion to Judaism. Consciously evoking the ideal of the God-fearers, a controversial sect of Gentiles who may have been associated with diaspora Jewish communities in the first two centuries of the Christian era, the modern B'nai Noah seek teaching and guidance from the Jewish rabbinate on the *halachic* ("legal") and moral aspects of the Noahide Code, as well as on other aspects of Judaism.

The Noahide Code itself is based on the juxtaposition of the Adamic (Genesis 2:16–17) and Noahide covenants (Genesis 9:3–13). The seven Noahide laws may be traced to the third-century Tosefta, from which they were further elucidated by the rabbinical sources in tractate Sanhedrin of the Babylonian Talmud. The most prominent medieval exponent of the laws was Maimonides (1135–1204), who serves as a primary source for the B'nai Noah today. The Noahide laws mandate the appointment of judges over the Children of Noah and prohibit blasphemy, idolatry, sexual sins, murder, theft, and the eating of the limb of a living creature. A Noahide (Gentile), who obeys these laws in the belief that his or her action is commanded by God, is judged as righteous and is accorded a place in the messianic life to come. Beyond the minimal requirement of obedience to the seven laws, the Noahide may, on a discretionary basis, follow other of the 613 halachic requirements incumbent upon the observant Jew.

The French former Catholic Aime Palliere was the first public follower of Noahism in the interwar years, but the genesis of the modern movement may be reliably traced only to the 1970s, when several Christian ministers and laymen, on the basis of intensive Bible study, concluded that divinity had been posthumously and falsely accorded to Jesus. The de-divinization of Jesus is thus the crucial element of B'nai Noah theodicy, and the doctrinal base upon which the study of Jewish religious texts is built. While a number of seekers from throughout the world claim to have come to the Noahide concept independently and virtually simultaneously, founding important centers of Noahide thought in the Netherlands, Belgium, the former Soviet Union, and Nigeria, it is the Noahide movement in the United States that has been the most active.

The core leaders of the American Noahide movement are former Protestant fundamentalist ministers. These include J. David Davis in Tennessee, Jack Saunders in Georgia, and Vendyl Jones in Texas. Through their efforts, the B'nai Noah have initiated a large media outreach to publicize their beliefs to potential adherents and Jewish supporters. Jones was the key figure in instituting annual conferences, bringing the B'nai Noah together with rabbinical supporters from the United States and Israel. Davis is the driving force behind the expanding web of alliances that link the American B'nai Noah with influential sectors of the Israeli religious establishment, including the Chief Rabbinate, and with other sectors of Israeli Jewish activism, including the Temple Institute, whose primary activities center on reclaiming the Temple Mount in Jerusalem as the site of the reconstituted Third Temple. Crowning this close association with the Israeli rabbinate is the current construction of a B'nai Noah Study Center in Jerusalem. *See also* Judaizers; Temple Mountain movement.

Bodh Gaya (bohd gi'yuh), the town in the North Indian state of Bihar where Gautama Buddha experienced enlightenment, a major center of Buddhist pilgrimage. *See also* Gautama; pilgrimage.

Bodhidharma (boh-dee-dahr'muh; late fifth century), Indian meditation master credited with transmitting Ch'an Buddhism into China. A legendary tale recounts his initial banishment from South China by Emperor Liang of Wu. The emperor inquired whether Bodhidharma had attained merit from his lifelong activities of temple building and worship offerings. Bodhidharma answered, "No merit at all," emphasizing the importance of meditation over external works. Bodhidharma served as a focal point for lineage claims of later Ch'an sects, whose doctrine of mind-to-mind transmission claimed a direct inheritance of Buddhist enlightenment through Bodhidharma all the way back to the original

Buddha. *See also* Ch'an school; patriarchal succession.

bodhisattva (boh-dee-saht'vah; Skt., traditionally interpreted to mean "a living being committed to awakening" or "one who [pursues] awakening with courage and vigor"), in Buddhism, a living being who has made a commitment to follow the Path leading to the full awakening, or "enlightenment," of a Buddha. *See also* holy person.

General and Early Meanings: In a general sense, a bodhisattva is one whose life is committed to the attainment of the condition of a Buddha. The process of reaching that goal requires an unimaginably large number of lives (reincarnations). A *bodhisattva's* spiritual and moral qualities vary from the human virtues of a beginner to the marvelous, superhuman powers of a bodhisattva at the end of the Path. The common theme of this spiritual career is the determination to follow the arduous task to the end, expressed in a vow marking the beginning of the Path for all bodhisattvas, the solemn promise to attain perfect awakening for the sake of all living beings.

In non-Mahayana Buddhism the term bodhisattva is an epithet primarily used retrospectively to refer to the previous lives of a person—historical or mythical—presumed to have become a Buddha. In this context, the term refers to a person from the moment the resolution (vow) to attain awakening is made to the moment immediately preceding the attainment of full awakening. Before the advent of Mahayana, the term was applied primarily to the historical Buddha, Sakyamuni, who was seen as a rare—and in this age, unique—individual. During his long spiritual career, the many previous lives on the Path to Buddhahood, he is called "the Bodhisattva." Once he attains enlightenment, he becomes "the Buddha."

As archetype or paradigm, Sakyamuni's early lives reveal the milestones in the career of every bodhisattva. First, in a former life, Sakyamuni, then called Sumedha, declared himself bodhisattva by pronouncing a vow (*pranidhana*) to seek and attain enlightenment before a full Buddha. Sakyamuni took his vow under the former Buddha Dipamkara, who then confirmed the validity of this vow by pronouncing a prophecy (*vyakarana*) stating the place and time when Sakyamuni would attain full enlightenment. Sakyamuni then embarked on a long and arduous career that took him through all the virtues of a Buddha, especially the virtue of compassion and the perfection of generosity.

General Mahayana Usage: In Mahayana belief, where several Buddhas may appear in a single era and cosmic system, a plurality of bodhisattvas becomes possible. The term bodhisattva is used more inclusively and can be applied to anyone who has taken the formal vow of the bodhisattva, as well as to a vast array of mythical Bodhisattvas who appear in response to the invocation of believers. Sakyamuni remains the paradigm of the bodhisattva Path, but as one among many—paradigmatic but not unique. Other bodhisattvas become the focus of myth and ritual and the embodiments of Mahayana ideals, while Sakyamuni plays the role of historical mouthpiece and authoritative voice for the new bodhisattva ideal.

In Mahayana Buddhism and some of the early schools, the title of bodhisattva was usually reserved for those aspirants to enlightenment who, although capable of following the Buddhist Path to its culmination in the freedom of *nirvana*, are motivated by "great compassion" to remain in the world of suffering in order to rescue other living beings from "the ocean of sorrow." This ethical ideal is often combined with a fantastic mythology that depicts the bodhisattva as a superhuman being capable of miraculously intervening to assist living beings in distress and following a spiritual career in distant, supernal worlds in the presence of myriad Buddhas from other worlds. Thus, bodhisattvas are also called "Great Beings" or "Possessed of Great Courage" (*mahasattva*), because their vow has committed them to the energetic pursuit of goals that transcend normal human aspirations: bodhisattvas aspire to know the thoughts, spiritual disposition, and aspirations of all beings; to train in the Path and purify all living beings; to know thoroughly and purify all the Buddha-fields everywhere; and to serve, honor, and understand all the teachings of all Buddhas in all world systems in the universe. The Mahayana bodhisattva is defined primarily in terms of a renunciation of the peace of nirvana, the affirmation of "awakening for the sake of living beings," and the altruistic ideal of remaining in or returning to the world of rebirth to labor for the welfare of others.

The Bodhisattva Path: The Path of the Mahayana bodhisattva is defined by several milestones and stages, sometimes echoing pre-Mahayana conceptions. Technically only a human being can set out on the Path, although bodhisattvas can later choose to be reborn in animal form or as heavenly beings. Most schools also adhere to the pre-Mahayana exclusion of women from the ranks of the bodhisattvas, but a number of important texts allow for female bodhisattvas. Bodhisattvas first awaken to their sacred mission in a moment of intuition called "the arising of the aspiration for enlightenment" (*bodhi-*

citta). This aspiration is then expressed in the presence of a Buddha in the form of a resolution or solemn pronouncement called the bodhisattva vow. In its general form, this is a solemn promise to follow, for the sake of all living beings, the Path to full and perfect enlightenment without interruption and without regard for one's own suffering. The vow's altruistic ideals imply renouncing all moral and religious merit; but merit is renounced by giving it (through merit transference) to other living beings and dedicating it to enlightenment. The vow also implies renouncing the bliss of nirvana in order to be able to remain in the cycle of rebirth until all living beings in the universe have been "ferried across to the safe shore" of nirvana. The Buddha acting as witness to this vow then pronounces the "prophecy," guaranteeing the success of the bodhisattva's endeavors.

Extending for a period of many cosmic ages, the bodhisattva's progress toward enlightenment involves several stages, each dedicated to the cultivation of an essential virtue of the enlightened being. The most common list is that of the ten "terraces" (*bhumi*) found in the *Dasabhumika Sutra* and other Mahayana texts. In the first stage, called "Joyful," the bodhisattva practices the perfection of generosity. According to late scholastic analyses, at the end of this stage bodhisattvas have a deep insight into the nature of all *dharmas* (basic constituents of existence), and this insight establishes them on the "Path of Vision" whereby they become saints (*arya*). In the second stage, "the Pure," the perfection of morality is cultivated; in the third stage, "the Light Giver," the perfection of patient understanding; in the fourth stage, "the Radiant," the perfection of courage and energy and the thirty-seven auxiliaries to enlightenment (*bodhipaksiya-dharmas*); and in the fifth stage, "the Difficult to Conquer," primarily the perfection of meditation. Meditation prepares the mind for the perfection of insight or wisdom (*prajna*), which forms the focus of the sixth stage, called "Face to Face," because in it the bodhisattva stands at the portal of nirvana. In the seventh stage, however, the bodhisattva renounces nirvana and develops the perfection of skillful means (*upaya*), which characterizes the bodhisattva as a person free from the world but engaged in it. This stage is called "Far Going." In the next stage, the eighth, called "Immovable," the bodhisattva becomes "irreversible." Progress in the Path is guaranteed, and the bodhisattva focuses on the perfection of the vow, developing the capacity to visit other worlds in order to worship the Buddhas of the universe, rescue living beings, and purify a Buddha-field. In the ninth

stage, "the Successful," the bodhisattva cultivates the perfection of the powers (*bala*). In the tenth stage, "the Cloud of Dharma," the Bodhisattva cultivates the perfection of liberating knowledge (*jnana*)—the special knowledge that gives access to the liberating powers of Buddhas. Although a certain degree of enlightenment is achieved at the end of the first and seventh stages, perfect enlightenment comes only at the end of this last stage, when a bodhisattva attains the special knowledge of a Buddha. The bodhisattva thereupon enters the eleventh stage, the stage of a Buddha.

Celestial Bodhisattvas: The ten-stage plan attributes to the bodhisattva knowledge and powers similar to those of a Buddha. As perfect saints (*arya-pudgala*) and saviors of living beings, bodhisattvas are extraordinary spiritual beings who epitomize spiritual growth and stand at the center of Mahayana faith. They are believed to inhabit distant celestial Buddha-fields, where they act as attendants to the Body of Bliss (Sambhogakaya) of many Buddhas and by the power of their vows and the transfer of their merit purify their own future Buddha-field. On the portal of full Buddhahood and nirvana they can be distinguished from Buddhas only by their refusal to enter nirvana and by their readiness to respond to the cries of living beings in distress by intervening miraculously or by assuming apparitional bodies that take the form and speech of the suppliant. Some inhabit the Akanistha Heaven (the highest sphere of the form realm), while others inhabit the Tusita Heaven (the fourth heaven of the realm of desire), Maitreya, the future Buddha of our world, already awaits the time of his rebirth as a Buddha in the human realm.

Human Bodhisattvas: The lofty ethical and spiritual ideals of perfect bodhisattvahood play an important role in the daily life of a Mahayana believer. The ideal spiritual life of a common human follower of the Mahayana Path centers on devotion to Bodhisattvas, daily ritual, and the concept of transference of merit. The daily ritual includes among its most important elements the taking of refuge in the Three Jewels (sometimes redefined as Buddhas, Dharma Body, and the Community of the Bodhisattvas), confession of one's transgressions, taking the vows of the bodhisattva, and dedication of merit. Like the mythical Bodhisattvas, common human aspirants to bodhisattvahood take the vow before the Buddhas of the universe and surrender all their merit, transferring it to the quest for enlightenment and to all living beings.

In the daily life of the believer, the bodhisattva ideal also represents an ethical model of compassion and service. For bodhisattvas the happiness and pain of others are their own. Bodhisattvas remain indifferent to their own suffering while giving of themselves for others. Mahayana believers regard the ethics of the bodhisattva as superior to those of other Buddhists, because concern for the well-being of others is its central principle. The bodhisattva's ethical goals are threefold: restraint, which has its equivalent in the ethics of non-Mahayana Buddhists; the cultivation of positive qualities; and the carrying out of what is beneficial to all living beings. Both lay believer and monastic pursue all three goals, reinforcing the last through the bodhisattva vows. In a Mahayana ordination ceremony, the aspiring monastic also adopts the traditional Vinaya rules, which are then followed by special bodhisattva precepts. In some of the Japanese schools, the traditional Vinaya rules have been replaced by the bodhisattva rules of the *Brahmajala Sutra.*

The possibility and symbolic importance of human bodhisattvas places the ideal in a social context. Not only are living persons transformed into bodhisattvas through the ritual of the vows, but particular human beings, legendary or living, may receive the honorary title of bodhisattva. The great Indian philosophers Nagarjuna (fl. second century) and Vasubandhu (fl. fourth–fifth centuries) are called bodhisattvas. In China and Japan, leading religious figures who led exemplary lives could receive the official title of bodhisattva. For instance, the Japanese monk Gyogi (668–749), who was active in social welfare and the foundation of religious establishments, was granted the title Bosatsu (Jap., "bodhisattva"). He was also considered a manifestation of the Bodhisattva Manjushri. *See also* Bodhisattvas; Buddhas; enlightenment; Mahayana; merit; nirvana; Pure Land.

bodhisattva precepts (boh-dee-saht'vah), ten major and forty-eight minor Chinese Buddhist vows articulated by the *Fan-wang ching. See also* bodhisattva; Fan-wang ching.

Bodhisattvas (boh-dee-saht'vahz; Skt., pl., "living beings committed to awakening"), the myriad mythical Bodhisattvas of Mahayana belief, sometimes called "celestial" Bodhisattvas, that represent the active dimensions of enlightenment and often appear as attendants to mythical Buddhas believed to inhabit distant Buddha-fields.

The Myriad Bodhisattvas: Less specific representations of Bodhisattvas focus either on the marvelous saving powers of Buddhas and Bodhisattvas or on the worship of celestial Buddhas by fantastically large numbers of devoted Bod-

hisattvas. The image of huge numbers of Bodhisattvas conveys a sense of spiritual presence and protection. The preferred representation of Bodhisattvas in popular belief, however, is as individual mythical saviors whose assistance can be invoked in times of need.

Celestial Bodhisattvas: Although all bodhisattvas are technically living beings on their way to Buddhahood, the spiritual career of many "celestial" Bodhisattvas is virtually frozen in mythical time to allow them to function as embodiments of the eternal ideal of compassion and as agents of salvation with individual personalities. A number of these Bodhisattvas are taken to epitomize specific dimensions of the Mahayana Buddhist ideal of spirituality. As symbols of Buddhist virtues and practices, they are often grouped in constellations representing fundamental polarities or complementarities in the Mahayana Path. For instance, Avalokiteshvara, the Bodhisattva of compassion, is paired with Mahastamaprapta, a Bodhisattva of wisdom, and both are seen as attendants to the Buddha Amitabha. Representing the practice of the vows and virtues of the Bodhisattvas, Samantabhadra is often depicted next to Manjushri, the Bodhisattva of wisdom par excellence. It is not uncommon for these Bodhisattvas to occupy a position rivaling, or even surpassing, that of Buddhas in Mahayana and Tantric myth and ritual.

Mahayana literature groups some of these Bodhisattvas into formulaic lists. For example, a list of eight Bodhisattvas usually includes Avalokiteshvara, Manjushri, Samantabhadra, Mahastamaprapta, Akasagarbha, Vajrapani, Ksitigarbha, and Maitreya (the next Buddha of the present cosmic age). In Tantric Buddhism, specific Bodhisattvas are associated with specific dimensions of awakening and compassion. Their physical (iconographic) and spiritual attributes form an integral part of the graphic and mental representation of *mandalas* and Tantric visualization techniques.

Bodhisattvas in Buddhist Piety: In Buddhist practice Bodhisattvas often become the main object of devotion as the central figure in pilgrimage cycles (e.g., Chin. *Kuan-yin;* Jap. *Kannon*); as the patron or protector of a special group or location (e.g., the Japanese Jizo as protector of children and crossroads and Chenrezig as patron of Tibet); as the focus of lay devotional societies (e.g., the cult of Kuan-yin); and, in the case of Maitreya, as the center of a religion of hope (e.g., in Chinese messianic movements). *See also* Avalokiteshvara; bodhisattva; Jizo; Kannon; Kshitigarbha; Kuan-yin; Mahayana; Maitreya; Manjushri; merit; Pure Land.

Bodhi Tree (boh'dee), the fig (*ficus religiosa*) under which Gautama Buddha was enlightened. The particular tree was considered a Buddha relic and cuttings from it were highly prized. The species of tree collectively serves to commemorate the Buddha's enlightenment and thus is considered worthy of honor and worship. *See also* Ashvattha tree; devotion (Buddhism); Gautama.

bodily secretions, polluting substances. The body is understood to be a container; any fluid that leaks out is dangerous, transgressing the boundary between self and world. *See also* blood; menstrual blood; purity and impurity; ritual; taboo.

body, the human physical form. Most recently the body has been seen by structuralists as a blank site or foundation on which multiple social constructions are erected, and by poststructuralists as a variable boundary that is itself discursively produced and hence never found in a state of nature but inherent in culture. Most modern theorists have assumed that the body is to nature as gender is to culture, but many postmodern thinkers contest this assumption and view the body primarily as the effect, not the cause, of the apparatus of cultural construction designated by gender. Occupying the shifting border between nature and culture, the body historically has been positioned first on one side and then on the other of the dualities that have constrained the interpretation of bodies for some two thousand years.

From the ancient Greeks to the nineteenth-century neurologist Sigmund Freud, pairs of opposites have played off a single flesh in which they did not inhere, so that fatherhood/motherhood, man/woman, culture/nature, masculine/feminine, honorable/dishonorable, legitimate/illegitimate, hot/cold, right/left were read into a body that did not itself mark these distinctions but instead had order and hierarchy imposed upon it. Historically, differentiations of gender preceded differentiations of sex.

Differentiation itself is bound up with bodies and bodies with boundaries. According to the twentieth-century anthropologist Mary Douglas, the body is a model that can stand for any bounded system. The very contours of the body are established through markings that seek to establish specific codes of cultural coherence. Any discourse that establishes the boundaries of the body serves to naturalize certain taboos regarding the appropriate limits, postures, and modes of exchange that define bodies. Bodily margins are thought to be invested with power and danger, because all social systems are vulnerable at their margins, and all margins are accordingly considered dangerous. Thus, the body, as a part, is taken for the whole, the social system itself, and any unregulated permeability can invite pollution and endangerment.

Religions offer a variety of different techniques to suppress, purify, or modify the body in order to attain a state of perfection, happiness, purity, or supernatural power. They also produce "docile bodies" that may be used, subjected, transformed, and improved. In the Christian ritual of the Eucharist this is accomplished by infusing something pure into the body, in Buddhist disciplines by defusing the grip of ego identifications.

As an attribute of humans and a feature of gods and goddesses, the body is open to a wide array of astral and earthly influences, as well as to startling transgressions of gender. In the history of religions, its cosmological and cosmogonic roles are multiple. Genesis according to the Veda is the process by which Purusha (primordial Man) is dismembered so that each part of his body may become one of the elements of the natural, social, and ritual world. In Taoism, the body, characterized by colors and defined by numerical relations, is perceived as a microcosmic replica of the cosmos whose laws govern its own space. In Soto Zen, the body's breathing is the very prototype of *wu-wei* (Chin., "nonaction"). In Judaism, embodiment is explicitly forbidden as an attribute of the creator, who is devoid of any representable content or form. In Hinduism, where differences in embodiedness do not define the relation between gods and humans, incarnations abound. In Christianity, the Body of Christ incorporates three major sites of religious significance: the human body of Jesus transformed at the resurrection; the consecrated bread whose eucharistic reception ritualizes a form of symbolic cannibalism; and the church as the People of God, the community that is the vehicle of God's redemptive activity on earth. "Because there is one loaf, we who are many are one body, for we all partake of the one loaf" (1 Corinthians 10:17).

In the Christian West the bold affirmation of the body implicit in the idea that "the Word became flesh," supported also by the doctrines of creation and the resurrection of the body, was undercut by its association with certain Greek philosophical assumptions.

The ontological disjunction between mind and body, like the related binary oppositions dividing reason from passion, culture from nature, and self from other, has deep roots in Western philosophy. In the intellectual tradition beginning in the fourth century B.C. with Plato and continuing into the seventeenth century with Rene Descartes and into the twentieth century with Edmund Husserl and Jean-Paul Sartre, the conceptual distinction between body (inert matter, nothing) and soul (consciousness, mind) produces and rationalizes an implicit gender hierarchy in which mind is associated with the male and body with the female. Thus, the capacity to conceive is distributed to women as reproductive bodies and to men as productive minds.

Proliferation of discourse involving various bodily organs, such as the head, serves to naturalize relations and institutions of inequality and produces, as in Augustine (354–430), a fullblown conception of the phallic response to the female body politically coded as a rebellion against the head. In late classical antiquity learned debate flourished on the question of woman as incomplete, a misbegotten and deformed male. As mortification came into practice during medieval times and ascetic bodies were starved for attention, pious souls aimed not so much to debase the body as to elevate it into a means of access to the sacred.

In religious literature and iconography in general, the female body is most often seen from the point of view of males, framed as spectacle, receptacle, or source of pollution and symbolizing sex, sin, and the fall of the human race. The male body, in its conflation with the universal, is in all cases and in all periods considered the standard of the human body and its representations. Both male and female bodies in religion have been open to the interpretative demands of culture. *See also* asceticism; chakras; dualism; gender and religion; gender roles; kundalini; purity and impurity; ritual; sexuality and religion; Tantrism (Buddhism).

Taoism: In Taoist thought and practice the body is a central symbol and ritual focus rooted in older traditions of spirit possession, alchemy, and the search for longevity and immortality. The Taoist body is a microcosm of the geographical country (the five main organs correspond to the five sacred mountains of China), of the social and administrative state, and, ultimately, of the whole cosmos. Taoist practice has used two interdependent approaches to the body. The first cultivates the body for longevity or immortality through practices that include visualization techniques, meditation, respiratory or gymnastic exercises, dietary practices, sexual techniques, and ingestion of alchemical drugs. In a related set of images and practices the

Taoist body is that of a woman with child: visualization techniques "cultivate life" (Chin. *yang-sheng*), uniting *yin* and *yang* (the complementary principles) within the body to create an immortal embryo that is liberated after death. Communal Taoist ritual constitutes a second approach to the body. Cosmic deities are internalized in the body in the course of participation in ritual practices, particularly in the ordination and career of a Taoist priest (*tao-shih*), who internalizes the same pantheon of cosmic deities that is summoned forth at the opening of important rites to assemble in the temple. At that critical moment, revitalizing energy (*ch'i*), personified as a trio of gods, simultaneously descends into the community, temple, and body of the priest. *See also* alchemy; physiological techniques (Taoism); tao-shih; yin and yang.

Boehme, Jakob (buh'mah; 1575–1624), German Protestant mystic whose theosophical writings have deeply influenced a succession of Christian movements and thinkers from Quakerism and Romanticism to twentieth-century theologian Paul Tillich and philosopher Martin Heidegger. His works, based on revelatory experiences and published posthumously, are couched in a difficult vocabulary, in part deriving from alchemy and astrology.

Boghazkoy (boh-ahz'koi), in modern Turkey, site of Hattusha, the ancient capital of the Hittite Empire. Destroyed ca. 1200 B.C., the site provides cuneiform texts and archaeological information relating to the Hittites. *See also* Hittites; Yazilikaya.

Bogomils, a Bulgarian neo-Manichaean movement beginning in the ninth century. *See also* Catharism; Manichaeism.

Bon (bohn), a Tibetan religious tradition that, according to its adherents, represents the authentic, pre-Buddhist religion of Tibet. Modern scholars view the Bon religion as a complex combination of indigenous and foreign practices influenced profoundly by Tibetan Buddhism but justified in maintaining its status as a distinct religion.

The Tibetan word *bon* functions for Bon-pos (the practitioners of Bon) as the word *chos* (which translates the Indian word *dharma*) does for Buddhists. It is used to refer to truth, reality, a teaching about reality, and also the religious tradition through which that teaching is expressed.

The earliest known references to the practitioners of Bon in Tibetan literature depict them as a group of priests who presided over rites for the dead during the period of the ancient Tibetan monarchy (seventh–ninth centuries). These early Bon-pos performed elaborate funeral rituals in which the soul of the dead person was conveyed into the next world by an animal such as a yak, a horse, or a sheep sacrificed during the course of the rite. Modern Bon-pos claim an unbroken connection with these early priests.

The Bon tradition as we now know it took shape during and shortly after the period Tibetan Buddhists call "the later diffusion of the Dharma" (tenth–twelfth centuries). In this period, when Tibetan Buddhism was being cast in the form in which it has endured to the present day, the Bon-pos acquired a canon of scripture, the story of founder, and a body of monastic practices to match their Buddhist rivals.

The Bon Canon of Scripture: The Bon scriptures are divided into two sections: the *Kanjur,* containing the teaching of the founder, and the *Tenjur,* containing commentaries and independent treatises by later scholars. A common summary of Bon teaching divides it into "nine ways," including practices as diverse as divination, astrology, exorcism, monastic discipline, and the higher forms of Tantric meditation. The Bon view of the nature of the world, suffering, and the path to enlightenment shows important similarities with the teaching found in comparable schools of Tibetan Buddhism. Classic Bon texts insist that even practices such as divination and exorcism are infused with "the aspiration to enlightenment" (*byang-chub-sems,* corresponding to the Skt. *bodhicitta*), the attitude of mind in which the practitioner vows to bring benefit to all living beings.

Many of the texts in the Bon canon, like texts in the Nyingma sect of Tibetan Buddhism, are considered "treasures" (*gter-ma*). They are thought to have been concealed in caves, underground, in temples, or in the minds of disciples and then discovered centuries later by "treasure revealers" (*gter-ston*).

The Founder of the Bon Tradition: The texts of the Bon canon trace the origin of the tradition through the region of Shang-shung in western Tibet to a land called Tazik (sTag-gzigs). The name Tazik is reminiscent of the land of the Tajiks in Central Asia and has been identified by a number of modern scholars as Persia. In Tazik, according to Bon sources, lived Shenrap, the founder of the Bon tradition. Shenrap is described as a fully enlightened being (using the Tibetan word for "Buddha"). As a prince, Shenrap traveled the countryside with his family to propagate Bon. Late in his life he was ordained a monk and retired to the forest to live as a hermit.

Bon Monasticism: The foundation of the Bon-po monastery Menri (sMan-ri) at the beginning of the fifteenth century heralded a full-scale adoption of the Buddhist model of monastic organization. Since the fifteenth century, Bon monasteries have been deeply influenced by the traditions of study and debate that dominate the great Buddhist monasteries of the Geluk-pa (Geluk school). There also, however, has been a strong Bon tradition of independent, solitary asceticism.

The Bon Tradition in Modern Tibet: In the early part of the twentieth century, the largest centers of Bon-po population were in eastern Tibet. There also seem to have been important Bon-po communities in central Tibet as well as among nomads and in the border areas of southern Tibet and northern Nepal. Bon-po monasteries suffered the same intense persecution as their Buddhist counterparts during the Chinese Cultural Revolution in the 1960s, but the experience has not destroyed the vitality of the tradition. Since the relaxation of Chinese control over religious practices in Tibet in the 1980s, Bon institutions have been revived, and there is a lively Bon presence in Tibetan refugee communities in India. *See also* Tibetan religions.

Bonaventura (bon'ah-ven'toor-ah; b. Giovanni di Fidanza, 1221–74), Italian Catholic theologian and mystic, known as the "Seraphic Doctor." Minister General of the Franciscan order, his description of the soul's mystical journey (*Itinerarium*) to God was deeply influential on subsequent ascent literature, while his commentary on the *Sentences* of Peter Lombard remains a monument of Scholastic theology.

Bonhoeffer, Dietrich (bon-huhf'uhr; 1906–45), German Protestant theologian, imprisoned and executed by the Nazis for his leadership in the Christian resistance (the Confessing Church).

His posthumously published *Letters and Papers from Prison* (1951), one of the first positive religious treatments of secularism, were of particular importance in Christian theological discussions of the 1960s. *See also* Confessing Church.

Boniface (bon'e-fis; 680–754), English Catholic monk who was, by tradition, leader of the first Christian mission to Germany.

Book of Common Prayer, the authoritative liturgical book for Anglican churches. First printed and authorized by an act of the British Parliament in 1549, it was radically revised in 1552, with more minor revisions in 1559, 1604, and 1662. Further revisions were not attempted until the twentieth century. The revised version of 1927 to 1928 was rejected by Parliament; since 1965, there has been extensive experimentation with the Anglican liturgy through the serial publication of *Alternative Services.*

When *The Book of Common Prayer* is referred to, the 1662 edition is most often meant. However, local versions abound, for example, the Scottish (1764; revised 1912, 1929, 1966), the American Episcopalian (1789; revised 1892, 1928, 1973), the Irish (1878; experimental revision 1967–72), and the Canadian (1918; revised 1959, 1963). Perhaps the most influential of these has been the *Liturgy* of the Church of South India (1950; revised 1954, 1962, 1972). *See also* Anglicanism.

Book of Documents. *See* Shu-ching.

Book of History. *See* Shu-ching.

Book of Poetry/Book of Songs. *See* Shih-ching.

born-again Christian, a person who has had the confirmatory experience of knowing Jesus, sensing the Spirit, and putting off the old self. The experience is an intra-Christian conversion. *See also* confirmation; conversion; testimony.

bow/catalpa (Jap. *azusayumi*), a Japanese instrument used since ancient times for summoning spirits; it is associated with shamanic figures. *See also* Japanese folk religion; shamanism.

Boxer Rebellion (1899–1901), a Chinese anti-Western and, at first, antidynastic revolt spearheaded by heterodox sectarian groups whose members combined martial arts with ecstatic religious behavior. The growth of the Boxers was caused by harsh economic times in Shantung province and by resentment of missionaries and their Chinese converts. The Boxers countered these influences and challenges by making use of spells, amulets, and rites, including the martial arts, especially ritual boxing, that they believed endowed them with supernatural powers and invulnerability to bullets. These ritual practices gave them their Chinese name, "Righteous and Harmonious Fists" (*I-ho ch'uan*), rendered by Europeans as "Boxers."

Initially the movement was antidynastic as well as antiforeign, but officials in the Ch'ing central government expressed their support of Boxer objectives and encouraged the Boxer attacks. The court declared war on the foreign powers and, soon after, groups of Boxers entered Peking and attacked the legation quarter. A dramatic two-month siege followed that led to the defeat of the Ch'ing court by the Western allies. *See also* Chinese sectarian religions; martial arts; nativistic movements.

Brahma (brah-mah'; Skt.), the creator deity of classical Hinduism. Brahma is the personification and embodiment of the sacred power (*brahman*) of Vedic texts and rituals. Brahma is the symbolic representation of the Brahman (priestly) class among the gods and represents the this-worldly values of ritual and social actions rather than the otherworldly values of asceticism and liberation from rebirth. He is often called Pitamaha (Grandfather) and is regarded as the ancestor and teacher of the gods and demons. Between 500 B.C. and A.D. 500 Brahma was worshiped extensively, but his cult diminished thereafter. *See also* cosmogony; Hinduism; trimurti; Veda, Vedism.

Brahma Kumari (brah'mah koo-mah'ree; Hindi, "daughter of the creator"), a modern Hindu sect. Founded in 1937 and supported by a mostly female membership, the sect asserts that those who follow its prescribed celibate life-style and special system of meditation will enjoy a paradise following the imminent destruction of the world.

brahman (brah'muhn; Skt., "expansive"), in Hindu philosophy, the absolute and unified ground of all being. Tradition regards this unchanging reality as either the subtle yet immanent essence of everything, in which case it is known as "brahman-with-qualities" (*saguna brahman*), or transcendent of all categories, thus the ineffable "brahman-without-qualities" (*nirguna brahman*). Some schools understand brahman to be of the nature of subtle sound, thus the source of sacred verbal revelation. The intuitive realization of brahman within the individual soul is said to bring freedom from the limitations of time, space, and causation and, thereby, from death. *See also* Hinduism (thought and ethics); liberation; nirguna/saguna; six systems of Indian philosophy.

Brahman, a member of the highest of the four classes according to Hindu social theory. Supposedly created in the beginning of time from the head or mouth of the creator god, Brahmans are (ideally) priests, intellectuals, religious teachers, and guardians of spiritual values. Historically, this class has provided the authors, preservers, and interpreters of the Veda and most of the other literature of India and those who have usually taken leadership roles in religious life. Their ancient claim to be "human gods" underlines the Brahmans' function in Indian society as yardsticks of caste purity. *See also* ancestors; caste; holy person; priest/priestess; Purusha; sacrifice; Veda, Vedism.

A Brahman priest in Karimpur, Uttar Pradesh, India (1975), seated before a sacred square awaiting the arrival of an infant from a Brahman family, who, at eleven days old, will be formally accepted into the family. At the conclusion of the ceremony, the priest will whisper the ritual name into the infant's ear.

Brahmanas (brah'muhn-uhz; ca. 1000–700 B.C.), a class of Hindu texts within the Veda that explicate, through homologies, the mythological, philosophical, anthropological, and cosmological meanings of the Vedic sacrifice. *See also* sacrifice; Veda, Vedism.

Brahmanism, the name sometimes given to the "classical" Hinduism first systematized in the post-Vedic texts (ca. 400 B.C.–A.D. 600) that center around the concept of *dharma* (Skt., "duty" or "principle"), particularized according to class and stage of life. Brahmanism provides the pan-Indian superstructure for most Hindu sects. *See also* Dharmashastras, Dharmasutras; Hinduism; Veda, Vedism.

Brahmashiras (brah-muh-shihr'uhz; Skt., "Head of Brahma"), name for the Hindu doomsday weapon obtained by Shiva, the destroyer, after severing the fifth head of the creator god, Brahma. *See also* Brahma; Shiva.

Brahmin. *See* Brahman.

brahmodya (brah-maha'yah; Skt., "speech about *brahman*"), in Vedic religion, a patterned verbal exchange or contest, generally in an antagonistic mode, between two or more trained contestants, often at prescribed moments in the sacrificial ritual. The *brahmodya* treats the mysterious correlations between levels of existence in the cosmos in enigmatic terms; usually four obliquely stated questions receive four hermetic answers. The formalized brahmodya of the classical ritual emerged from more open-ended contests of the early Vedic period; this early type recurs in the speculative riddling of the Upanishads, whole sections of which are, in effect, extended brahmodyas. *See also* Upanishads; Veda, Vedism.

Brahmo Samaj (brah'moh sah-mahj'; Skt., "The Society of Brahman"), a religious and social reform movement involving an elite Bengali Hindu group founded in 1828 by Ram Mohun Roy (1772–1833). It rejected polytheism, use of images, sacrifice of animals, self-immolation of widows, child marriage, and polygamy. Roy's first book was a defense of monotheism, which he believed was taught in the Upanishads. Contact with Christian missionaries led him to accept the ethics of Jesus while rejecting trinitarian and Christological formulations. *See also* Reform Hinduism.

Branch Davidians, a Christian Adventist group whose settlement, "Mt. Carmel" in Waco, Texas, was the object of a U.S. government siege in 1993. The Branch Davidians were formed as the result of a schism within the Davidian Seventh-Day Adventist Association descending from an initial split within the Adventists begun between 1930 and 1935 by Victor T. Houteff. Following Houteff's death in 1955, his wife gained control of the group and predicted that on April 22, 1959, the period of waiting (Revelation 11:3) would be concluded and God would intervene directly in Palestine to restore the Davidic monarchy. Following the failure of this prophesy, the Davidian Association was disbanded in March 1962.

The Branch Davidians were one of several splinter groups who did not accept Mrs. Houteff's authority and continued as a separate entity, coming eventually under the leadership of Vernon Howell (1958–93), who split the group, assuming the messianic name of David (the king of Israel is to be a son of David) Koresh (the Hebrew name of Cyrus, king of Persia, the only non-Israelite to bear the title *Messiah* in the Hebrew Bible).

Following Koresh's interpretation of the New Testament book of Revelation, the group stockpiled weapons for the imminent final conflict, attracting the attention of government officials, which led to the siege that resulted in the burning of the complex and the death or arrest of many members. Since 1993, the group has continued with few members and no clear leadership. Its conflict with the government and its fiery end has been taken up as a symbol of resistance by various Identity Christian and paramilitary Aryan groups. *See also* Adventists; Seventh-Day Adventists.

bread and wine, the basic elements of Christian eucharistic services. In some denominations unfermented grape juice is used in lieu of wine. *See also* Eucharist, Christian.

breath, air inhaled or exhaled. In many languages there is a connection between breath, wind, self, and soul. Each is seen as a divine medium of relationship and/or communication. Hence many cultures feature breathing rituals ranging from the control of breath to the inhaling of smoke. The notion of being taken over by divine breath gives rise to theories of possession and inspiration. Loss of breath (death) was seen by religious scholars as one of the sources of animism. *See also* animism; ch'i; ch'i-kung; hatha yoga; inspiration; possession; soul; tobacco and hallucinogens; yoga.

Brethren of Purity (Arab. *Ikhwan al-Safa*), the name of a circle of tenth-century Muslim thinkers in Basra belonging to the Ismaili Shiite sect. Known primarily from a collection of fifty-two epistles written anonymously in Arabic, the Brethren of Purity synthesized Greek science and philosophy with their own religious perspective, which was focused on the Ismaili Imam (religious leader) as the source of salvation. Although the identification of the authors has been controversial, the composition of the epistles probably began as early as 900 and concluded by 965. This period coincides with the establishment of the Ismaili movement of the Fatimids in North Africa and their conquest of Egypt. The subjects treated in the epistles include mathematics, physics, psychology, cosmology, and metaphysics. The epistles are designed to lead the inquiring reader through a curriculum of learning that naturally culminates in the search for the Ismaili Imam. The authors did not overtly reveal their Ismaili doctrines, but they placed suggestive allusions throughout the work to draw the reader in this direction. Neoplatonic, Hermetic, and Pythagorean overtones dominate the scientific and philosophic portions of the text. The *Epistles of the Brethren of Purity* were aimed at philosophers, mystics, and political leaders.

While the epistles did not bring about the triumph of Ismaili Islam that their authors seem to have envisioned, they have held a perennial interest for Muslim intellectuals because of their attractive synthesis of the Greek tradition with Islamic spirituality. *See also* Ismaili Shia.

Brethren of the Common Life. *See* Ruusbruec, Jan van.

bricolage. *See* myth; religion, the study of.

Bridget of Sweden (ca. 1303–73), also Birgitta, Catholic mystic, patron saint of Sweden, and foundress of the Brigittine Order. Her widely read account of her mystical experiences, *Revelations*, was first published in 1492.

Brigittine Order. *See* Bridget of Sweden.

bris (bris; Yiddish, from Heb., "covenant"), Jewish ritual circumcision. *See also* circumcision.

British Israelism. *See* Identity Christianity.

British Israelites. 1 Nineteenth-century belief held by certain Christian fundamentalists that the British people descend from ten lost tribes of Israel who were deported from their homeland by the Assyrians in 722 B.C. The theory was advanced at times to support British expansion into the Middle East following World War I. 2 Movement founded by Richard Brothers in 1794; continues to have influence on contemporary Identity Christian groups. *See also* Identity Christianity.

bronze vessels (China), the crowning achievement of Chinese Bronze Age (ca. second–first millennia B.C.) artistry and metalworking technology, often bearing commemorative inscriptions; the vessels were used for offerings of food and drink in the royal ancestral cult and in state sacrifices to the forces of nature, their durability a symbol of dynastic continuity. *See also* Chou religion; Shang religion; state cult, Chinese.

brotherhood, a characteristic term for voluntary association among males where social language replaces that of biological kinship.

Browne, Robert (ca. 1550–1633), English Puritan writer and radical separatist who so influenced early Congregationalism that its members were often called Brownists. *See also* Congregationalism.

Brownists. *See* Browne, Robert.

Bruno, Giordano (broon'oh; 1548–1600), Italian Christian Renaissance philosopher active in integrating Neoplatonic and Hermetic thought with Christian theology. Often censured for unorthodoxy, he was an early champion of Copernicus' theories that he combined with natural and mathematical magic. He is claimed as a founder of both occult Christianity and modern science. *See also* Hermetism.

Buber, Martin (1878–1965), Jewish philosopher, theologian, and educator, best known for his book *Ich und Du* (I and Thou, 1923) and his philosophy of dialogue and relation. Buber argued that open, direct, nonmanipulative, and mutually affirming human relationships, which he called "I–Thou" relationships, actualize and reveal God ("the Eternal Thou"). "I–It" relationships, which treat others as objects, create alienation and block knowledge of God. His thought is influenced by his extensive studies of Hasidism and by existentialism. With Franz Rosenzweig, he translated the Hebrew Bible into German. A Zionist, Buber left Germany for Palestine in 1938, where he advocated Jewish-Arab rapprochement.

Bucer, Martin (boos'uhr; 1491–1551), Protestant Reformer and liturgical scholar. Originally a German Dominican monk, Bucer was excommunicated and became an influential figure in the continental Reformation. Emigrating to England, he was a supporter of the reforms of Thomas Cranmer and a major author of the Second Prayer Book of Edward VI.

Buchman, Frank (buhck'muhn; 1878–1960), an American Lutheran minister, founder of the Oxford Group (1929), which became known after 1938 as Moral Rearmament. *See also* Moral Rearmament.

Buddhaghosa (boo-duh-goh'suh; fifth century), Buddhist commentator who gave definitive shape to the Theravada tradition of Southeast Asia. Sources written many years after Buddhaghosa's death suggest that he came from India. Buddhaghosa's productive career was spent at the Mahavihara (Great Monastery) at Anuradhapura in Sri Lanka. He organized, codified, and translated (into Pali) a large body of Sinhalese commentaries on the Pali canon. His greatest work, *The Path of Purification*, functions as the authoritative outline of the Buddhist path in the Theravada tradition. *See also* Buddhism (authoritative texts and their interpretation); Theravada.

Buddha image (boo'duh), a representation of the form of the Buddha in stone, wood, metal, or other material. Buddha images are frequently used as focuses of meditation and objects of devotion. Buddhist legends trace the origin of the Buddha image to events in the life of the Buddha, but the practice of representing the Buddha's physical form appears to have arisen in the Buddhist community in India in the first centuries B.C. The earliest images of the Buddha were strongly influenced by representations of the human figure in Hellenistic art as well as by indigenous Indian artistic traditions. *See also* Buddhas; devotion (Buddhism).

Meditating Buddha, a twentieth-century bronze statue from Sri Lanka depicting the Buddha in characteristic meditation posture, Los Angeles County Museum of Art.

Buddha-nature (Chin. *fo-hsing*), in Chinese Buddhism the inborn essence of all sentient beings that endows them with potential for Buddhahood. *See also* Buddhas; Ch'an school; China, Buddhism in.

Buddhas (bood'duhz; Skt., Pali, "Awakened Ones," "Enlightened Ones"), an epithet given to those who have attained the goal of the Buddhist religious life. An idea central to all of Buddhist thought and practice, the notion of a Buddha has been the subject of much discussion in the various Buddhist traditions for more than two thousand years. The diversity of Buddhist opinion about the meaning of the word and its proper referents makes it difficult to move comfortably from the very simple statement that a Buddha is one who is awake to a more elaborate account of the nature and attributes of a Buddha.

Special note should be taken that this article employs the term *a Buddha*. This is in contrast to the tendency of many modern scholars to focus in the first instance on the notion of the Buddha in connection with life and teaching of Gautama, the historical founder of Buddhism. Although it is certainly the case that Gautama stands at the head of the Buddhist movement, it is impossible to trace a single developmental sequence from the life of this singular and charismatic teacher to notions of the Buddha with connotations of supremacy and greatness, then to a more general classification of Buddhas in which numerous Buddhas in addition to Gautama are included, and finally to a doctrinal conceptualization of Buddhahood in which the nature and qualities of a Buddha are abstractly and systematically defined. Although such a sequence has a logical appeal, largely because it draws on assumptions about a natural development of a religion, it can draw no inspiration from historical evidence. The information about the Buddha available to us from the Buddhist traditions always includes each of these levels of understanding in complex interrelations with each other. Even the earliest biographical fragments about Gautama employ abstract notions about Buddhahood and presuppose that he is only one in a line of successive Buddhas.

The Historical Buddha: There is little doubt among scholars that Gautama was a historical figure. Thus a scholarly interest in retrieving the biography of Gautama remains legitimate, but the limitations on what can be known must constantly be kept in mind. Although the evidence preserved in the Buddhist traditions is rich and detailed, its complex character makes it difficult to extract—except by the most arbitrary criteria—information to be used in a reconstruction of his life that would meet the standards of a critical history. For example, a well-known climax in the traditional biographies of Gautama is his encounter with an aged man, a sick man, a corpse, and an ascetic; this encounter sets the stage for Gautama's aspiration to renounce household life and become a Buddha. In traditional biographies, this encounter does not simply occur but is manufactured by the gods. This latter fact is frequently omitted in scholarly summaries of Gautama's life, giving the impression that his decision to renounce the world was motivated only by his acute sensitivity to human suffering.

Given the impossibility of separating fact from fiction in a story like this, some scholars have attempted to construct an alternative contextual biography of Gautama, creating a portrait of the Buddha based on what we can gather from Hindu, Jain, and Buddhist sources about the cultural and social world in which he lived. Gautama appears then as a participant in a trend toward asceticism that emerged in India beginning in the sixth century B.C. This movement was a product of broad social and political changes taking place in India at that time: more developed and cosmopolitan urban communities emerged, state formation became more elaborate, and challenges to established religious orthodoxies became more common. In this context of change, in which many people were alienated from the older patterns of religious order and meaning, religious experimentation seems to have been appreciated. Like other experimenters in this context, the historical Buddha was apparently attracted to and later advocated the renunciation of the religious practices and morality prevalent in society. Like others, he taught a program of self-cultivation that was to culminate in a state of peace and freedom from the sufferings of life. We might also infer that Gautama had certain organizational skills because, unlike most of his contemporaries, he was successful in establishing a community of followers that was able to survive his death.

Of course, such a portrait is painted in broad strokes. Just how broad becomes apparent when it is remembered that there is no certainty about the century in which the historical Gautama lived. Different Buddhist traditions accept various dates for his birth and death, although there is agreement that he lived for eighty years. Buddhists in Sri Lanka and Southeast Asia date the life of the Buddha from 624 to 544 B.C. East Asian Buddhists generally give a later date, 448 to 368 B.C. Modern scholars offered a correction to the earlier dating and argued that Gautama's life was between 566 and 486 B.C., and although these dates are still commonly used, many scholars today argue for a later date closer to the East Asian chronology.

This contextual biography, although inadequate as a picture of Gautama as an individual, is helpful for shedding light on those teachings attributed to the Buddha and on the early Buddhist movement more generally. But the creation of a biography by context is less helpful for understanding what Gautama, as a Buddha, has meant for subsequent Buddhists. This too is a legitimate aim and, if taken, it can neither afford to ignore traditional testimonies about Gautama nor to limit inquiries to what Buddhists say about him in particular. The goal will be to know not only Gautama as the Buddha, but also how he is one among other Buddhas as well as an instance of Buddhahood itself.

Over the centuries, all Buddhists have apparently assumed that there is more than one Buddha. They have also had various conceptions of these multiple Buddhas, the interrelations between them, and the ways in which humans might interact with them. In one view, attested in the earliest literature, there were Buddhas in previous eras who taught exactly what Gautama did in careers almost identical to his. Knowledge of these previous Buddhas enhances the understanding of the nature of "our Buddha," Gautama, the teacher for this era. Awareness of them encourages one to see "our Buddha" not as a unique figure, but one in a sequence that will continue into the future; a future Buddha, Maitreya, is now waiting in heaven for the appropriate time for his birth. Although this sequence of past and future Buddhas has an obvious heuristic value for understanding the significance of Gautama, humans have little other involvement with these previous Buddhas, but it is common for Buddhists to aspire to be reborn near Maitreya in the future.

In another schema developed in Mahayana Buddhism, other Buddhas are seen as existing simultaneously in different areas of the cosmos: just as our Buddha taught in this world, so they teach and save in their own worlds. More significantly, however, these Buddhas are of differing capabilities, and some with extraordinary power and compassion are greater in comparison to Gautama. Although these Buddhas are distant from humankind in space, they are not completely inaccessible. People have access to them, because of their compassion and power, through worship and meditation. Such Buddhas, including Vairochana, Amitabha, Aksobhya, and Amoghasiddhi, are sometimes spoken of as celestial Buddhas and they frequently displace Gautama as the focus of Buddhist worship and devotion. Finally, some Buddhists have insisted that the state of Buddhahood is only one, and that the various Buddhas are only manifestations of this state.

Obviously when one begins with the notion of Buddhas in the plural, the interpretive challenges become of a completely different order than when one begins with the life of the historical Gautama: rather than discerning a simple sequential development of concepts, there is a fluid and shifting complex of interrelated ideas.

Key to understanding this complex are the connections between different ideas of a Buddha. These connections are themselves varied, and they seem to be highlighted in particular modes of talking about a Buddha. The rest of this article will discuss three of these modes: biographies, doctrines, and rituals. In Buddha biographies, polarities and tensions come to the fore; in doctrines, these polarities are often removed in a search for systematic consistency and connections tending toward identity are stressed; while in ritual, connections between a Buddha and those who approach him are the most visible, but the ramifications of these connections are perhaps the most radical.

Buddha Biographies: Two features, however, typically stand out in traditional biographies of a Buddha. First, the biographical particularities of a specific figure and the more generic features of a Buddha seem to mutually constitute each other, and second, the biographies seem to show more interest in the activities leading up to the attaining of enlightenment than in the career of a Buddha properly speaking.

The surprising coincidence of the specific and the general is apparent in even a brief and simplified summary of the life of Gautama. According to various biographies, he was born the son of a king after a period of time waiting in heaven. His future career as a Buddha was foretold at his birth, but his father, Suddhodana, tried to forestall this eventuality because he wanted his son to succeed him as king. He raised Gautama in luxury to keep him ignorant of the sorrows and troubles endemic to human life. But the staged encounter with an aged man, a sick man, a corpse, and an ascetic prompted Gautama to reexamine the value of life. He then left home in search of "the Deathless," and after a period of trial and error with other teachers, he became enlightened. He began his teaching career after some hesitation shortly thereafter.

Early in the history of the Buddhist movement a pattern for a Buddha biography developed that followed this sequence exactly. In one canonical text, the *Mahapadanasuttanta*, the parts of this biography are introduced as being of the order of things: "It is the rule that when a future Buddha descends into a mother's womb, no illness whatsoever befalls his mother" (*Digha Nikaya* 2.14). Thus, all Buddhas wait in heaven for the appropriate time for their birth, all Buddhas have their future foretold in their childhood, all Buddhas are raised in luxury but renounce the world after an encounter with the four sights, and all Buddhas attain enlightenment and teach after a period of hesitation. This standard biographical structure may derive from the biography of Gautama himself, but Buddhists may also have read the details of the biography of Gautama in light of each other, which would have served to connect his life as an individual to a more generic, ahistorical pattern.

The biography of Gautama also illustrates the primary interest of Buddhist authors in the process leading up to the beginning of his career as a Buddha and a comparative lack of interest in his subsequent career. The simple summary above presents in a sequential fashion the events leading up to the Buddha's enlightenment and his first sermon. In this, at least, the summary is typical of traditional biographies of the Buddha. Few—and those that do are relatively late in Buddhist history—venture much further into his teaching career. Of course, quite a lot is known about the Buddha's teaching career from the many texts that preserve his sermons and dialogues, but it is impossible to put this vast body of teaching into any coherent temporal order. It is equally impossible to provide a narrative account of the Buddha's travels during his forty-five years of teaching. This lack of a biography of the Buddha as Buddha highlights the polarity between his life in the world and his fundamental identity beyond the world; the lack of a narrative about his teaching career seems to emphasize that as a Buddha, he cannot be contained within the structures of time.

There are, however, some biographical accounts of the miracles the Buddha performed during his forty-five-year career. These include his creation of a magical double of his body and his gentle taming of a dangerous wild elephant. Such fragments were sometimes associated with each other through a kind of loose "miraculous biography" organized around a theme of eight great miracles; this miraculous biography was very important in medieval Indian Buddhism and was commonly portrayed in art. It includes Gautama's birth, the defeat of the personification of evil, Mara, just before Gautama's enlightenment, the first sermon, the creation of a double of his body, his descent from heaven after teaching his deceased mother there, the taming of the wild elephant, a gift of honey by a monkey, and Gautama's death; this is perhaps as close as we come to a complete birth-to-death biography of Gautama, although it is not given in a connected narrative.

More commonly, traditional biographies of the Buddha either end shortly after the first sermon or they skip decades of teaching and pick up the narrative again only in his last days, giving an account of his final days and his funeral.

These two features—a polarity between the universal and the particular and an emphasis on the preparation for becoming a Buddha—are also found in the biographies of other Buddhas, such as those of the celestial Buddhas. Texts that contain biographical narratives of celestial Buddhas like Aksobhya, Amitabha, and Bhaisajyaguru tend to focus on their careers as Buddhas-to-be (*bodhisattvas*) and especially the vows they took that resulted in the character that they now have as a Buddha. Bhaisajyaguru, for example, took a vow to alleviate the sickness and suffering of all beings, while Amitabha took a vow to bring all beings who put their faith in him to his Pure Land. Here again, however, the specific vows are connected to the more generic pattern of a bodhisattva found in the Mahayana: every bodhisattva utters a vow that has a determining influence on his subsequent career.

Doctrinal Definitions of a Buddha: Is there any possible explanation for traditional biographies of Gautama tending to end at the beginning of his career as a Buddha either with his enlightenment, his first sermon, or the ordination of his first disciples and the establishment of a monastic order? Perhaps the choice of an ending may reflect in each case a particular understanding of what it means to be a Buddha. An author who ends with Gautama's enlightenment may accept or wish to emphasize a conception of a Buddha that gives priority to his knowledge or wisdom realized in his experiences on the night of enlightenment, while an author who ends with his first sermon or the establishment of the monastic order gives due recognition to the Buddha's compassion and his activity for the sake of others. Both of these attributes—wisdom and compassion—are basic to the definition of every Buddha. Buddha biographies would appear then not to give an account of the life of a Buddha for its own sake, but as an aid to understanding the nature and attributes of a Buddha.

Buddhists have also thought about the nature and attributes of a Buddha systematically, constructing generic and abstract definitions of what constitutes a Buddha. In contrast to the Buddha biographies, where the particularity of a specific Buddha is held in tension with more generic patterns of a Buddha's life, doctrinally the interest is in discovering what all Buddhas have in common at the expense of the particularities of individual Buddhas. Identities and commonalities typically replace polarities. According to the *Questions of King Milinda*, a text from the first centuries A.D., there is no distinction in form, morality, concentration, wisdom, or freedom among all the Buddhas, because all the Buddhas are the same with respect to their nature.

Doctrinally, Buddhas are defined as possessing a fairly standard list of properties to the highest degree. These properties are too numerous to list here, even by general categories, but they refer to a Buddha's appearance, action, awareness, attitude, and control. Thus a Buddha's physical appearance is always supremely attractive and pleasing to those who see it. With respect to his action, he always does the right thing at the right time. A Buddha is omniscient, compassionate, always in control of all of his thoughts, words, and deeds. In short, a Buddha is perfect and unsurpassed in everything necessary to make him a Buddha. For some Buddhists this meant that Gautama could not have been a real human being, for the imperfections and impurities of all human bodies would have been incompatible with the nature of a Buddha. Instead such Buddhists took a docetic view, arguing that Gautama only appeared to be human, but his appearance was not an accurate guide to his true nature.

Such arguments were part of larger efforts on the part of some Mahayana Buddhists to order various conceptions of multiple Buddhas into a single coherent schema. Some Mahayana Buddhists, especially in East Asia, spoke of the multiple Buddhas as emanations or manifestations of a transcendent and ineffable Buddha, such as Adibuddha or Vairochana. Multiple buddhas were also connected in a single identity through a conception of the three bodies of a Buddha. This theory distinguished between a *dharmakaya*, or absolute body, that is the ground of the other two and is often considered to be coextensive with reality itself; a glorious body seen in the visions of devotees, such as the appearance of Amitabha to his disciples as they await rebirth in his Pure Land; and a magical and unreal body of appearance, such as the physical body Gautama displayed to his disciples.

Doctrinal thinking about Buddhas was generally embedded in the more general systematic thought of the different Buddhist communities. As with all systematic thinkers, Buddhist scholastics valued consistency in their philosophical views, and they attempted not only to articulate connections between different concepts of a Buddha but also connections with other basic metaphysical positions they held. This sometimes resulted in some apparently odd conclusions. For example, some medieval Indian philosophers questioned whether it is even possible for a Buddha to speak, because in order to speak he would have to have a desire to speak, and since Buddhas by definition are free of such negative qualities as desire, they thus could not speak.

Later Buddhist scholastics increasingly identified Buddhahood, that which gave a single identity to all Buddhas, with ultimate reality itself; whatever properties reality has could be attributed to Buddha. But in this conception, then, there are not multiple Buddhas, only Buddha in the singular, just as there is only one reality. Thus Buddha is permanent, without beginning or end, not captured by the structures of time, a theme we have already seen in the biographies of the Buddha.

A Buddha Known in Ritual: Buddhist systematic philosophers lived in communities that were ritually involved with Buddhas and this may help show why they focused their intellectual attention on the nature and attributes of a Buddha: they were seeking to understand better what they already knew in their ritual lives.

But what is known about a Buddha in ritual? First a distinction should be made between a Buddha known in worship and a Buddha known in some forms of Buddhist meditation. In worship, a Buddhist approaches a Buddha as an Other, separate and distinct from the worshiper. What is critical in this approach is the encounter between a Buddha and a person and the connection, usually one of honor, gratitude, and devotion, made between the worshiper and the worshiped. Buddhas thus are not only represented as supremely great, but they are addressed as "My Lord," "Mother," "Father," "Physician." As in the Buddha biographies, a polarity is implicit in a Buddha known in ritual, but the polarity is not only between the universal and the particular but also between the supremacy and accessibility of a Buddha. The wonder of a Buddha's accessibility is accentuated in worship; it is a conventional part of Mahayana liturgy, for example, for worshipers to confess their faults before a Buddha, increasing the gulf between their own capabilities and his attainment, and put their trust in the compassion and grace of a Buddha to assist them in this life or after death.

Buddhist worship seeks to focus attention on a Buddha, to make him present in a significant way by directing the worshiper to images and reminders of him. But worship of images and reminders also makes one aware of absence, and thus a significant contribution of ritual to knowledge about a Buddha may come from its ability to generate simultaneously feelings of a Buddha's absence and presence in a worshiper.

Buddhas known through meditation are known quite differently. Meditation is to approach a Buddha or Buddhahood more abstractly, not as an Other but as oneself. In meditation, one comes to realize one's already existing identity as a Buddha and one becomes self-conscious of what one already is. Thus, in some schools of Buddhism, such as Yogachara and Zen, it is affirmed that all beings have this original Buddha-nature, which can only be discovered in the practice of meditation. A Buddha known in contemplation is nothing other than what the contemplator already is. *See also* Aksobhya; Amitabha; Amoghasiddhi; Avalokiteshvara; Bhaisajyaguru; Buddhism; devotion (Buddhism); Maitreya; Vairochana.

Buddhas and Bodhisattvas (Korea). The practice of Buddhism in Korea began in the late fourth century as part of the diplomatic relations between Koguryo and the state of Ch'in. It is not known what type of Buddhism was practiced in Koguryo, but accounts of the activities of Chinese and Central Asian monks in Koguryo indicate a high degree of interest in thaumaturgical ritual and miraculous curing. This was followed a century later by the worship of the Bodhisattva Maitreya (Kor. *Miruk Posal*) and the Amitabha Buddha (*Amitabul*), savior-lords of future and present Pure Lands, whose worship helped in the consolidation of centralized monarchies in Koguryo and Paekche by providing those monarchies with heightened status as incarnations of these two Buddhas and their national and cultural systems as representations of Pure Land conditions. In the sixth and seventh centuries Buddhism permeated the Silla kingdom, again in the forms of the worship of Maitreya and Amitabha, followed by the worship of the Bodhisattva Manjushri (Munsu Posal) as the sword-bearing destroyer of ignorance and evil and the worship of the Bodhisattva Kshitigarbha (Chijang Posal) as the destroyer of military hosts. Both Manjushri and Kshitigarbha are important Bodhisattvas within the tradition of esoteric Tantric Buddhism, and Silla's predilection for the worship of Manjushri and Kshitigarbha was tied to its own warrior culture and was most supported and promoted during Silla's century-long conquest of the peninsula.

With the unification of the peninsula under Silla, and thereafter by Koryo (918–1392), Buddhist scholastic and cultic sectarianism expanded and with it the worship of more Buddhas and Bodhisattvas, including Vairo-

chana (Pirochanabul), the Primordial Buddha of Light and the central figure in Hua-yen and *Lotus Sutra* scholasticism; Avalokiteshvara (Kwanum Posal) as the compassionate savior, healer, and protector of travelers; and Samantabhadra (Pohyon Posal) as the protector of clerics and preachers of religious texts. As part of the Ch'an (Son) reformations in the middle and late Koryo period, an emphasis on the worship of the historical Sakyamuni (Sokabul) appeared, though he had already been recognized as a transformation body of the Buddha Reality (Popsin) in Hua-yen and *Lotus Sutra* scholasticism.

Choson Period: With the various disestablishments of Buddhism in the strongly Confucianized Choson period, worship of Buddhas and Bodhisattvas continued among a declining number of Buddhist adherents. Although the Ch'an, or Son, school came to dominate what was left of the Buddhist clergy, Buddha worship continued to focus on the figures of Samantabhadra, Avalokiteshvara, and Amitabha Buddha, and their statues were and are today usually worshiped together at a single altar as part of Korean devotion to the *Lotus Sutra*. The Choson period also saw the popularization of the worship of Taoist and shamanistic mountain gods (*sansin*), astral divinities (Ch'ilsong, Paeksong), and the god of longevity (Toksong) within temple compounds. Two further developments in the Choson period were the increased worship of *arhats* (Skt.; Kor. *nahan*), enlightenment-seeking Buddhist recluses who mirrored the fate of Choson Buddhist clergy and appealed to clergy and layfolk alike as the Buddhist equivalent of Taoist immortals, and the worship and invocation of the Ten Judges of Hell, royal figures responsible for the judgment of souls during the forty-nine-day mourning period.

In the modern day, worship of Buddhas and Bodhisattvas continues as it did in the Choson period. Though the worship of Sakyamuni is known and practiced and his birthday (Ch'opa'il) is celebrated as a national holiday on the eighth day of the fourth lunar month, it is the nonhistorical, cosmic Buddhas and Bodhisattvas that have been and are more readily recognized and worshiped. Koreans have, as have Buddhists in other Asian countries, also conferred the title of bodhisattva on eminent patrons, protectors, teachers, and scholars of Buddhism who have died and established memorial shrines and reliquaries in their honor. *See also* Bodhisattvas; Buddhas; Korea, Maitreyism in; Pure Land school (Korea).

BUDDHISM

O ne of the world's major religious traditions, Buddhism traces its origin to the figure of Siddhartha Gautama (ca. 566–486 B.C.), the man who is revered in Buddhist tradition as the Buddha (Skt., Pali, "the Awakened One"). From its origin in northern India, the Buddhist tradition gradually expanded throughout the Indian subcontinent and much of the rest of Asia. Under the patronage of the Indian emperor Ashoka, Buddhist teaching was introduced to Sri Lanka in the third century B.C. and from there to other regions of Southeast Asia. Buddhist monks carried the tradition to China in the second century, to Korea in the fourth century, and to Japan and Tibet in the seventh century. In the last two centuries the Buddhist tradition has made its way to Europe and North America, making it one of the most widespread and influential of the world's religions.

As the Buddhist tradition developed in India and expanded throughout Asia, it adapted to so many different cultural settings and assumed so many different forms that it is difficult to point to a single doctrine or practice that constitutes the essence of Buddhism. Buddhists also have a profound aversion to language that suggests an essence, particularly in a movement as varied as the one we call "Buddhism." To define this complex tradition it is better not to look for a single, essential feature but for a point of orientation around which Buddhist people have organized their societies, their cultures, and their individual lives. One of the most basic points of orientation is the story of the founder, the man who became the Buddha.

THE STORY OF THE BUDDHA

As is common in other Indian religious traditions that assume a doctrine of reincarnation, the story of the Buddha begins not with the birth of Siddhartha Gautama, but with the previous lives of the *bodhisattva* (Skt., "future Buddha"), who prepared for his final birth as Siddhartha Gautama by performing acts of generosity and self-sacrifice in a succession of lives. The stories of these lives are told in a body of literature known as Jataka (Pali, "Birth") tales. Many of these read like Aesop's fables, in which the stories of animals or human beings are used to illustrate simple moral lessons. In the Jataka tales, there is a story of the future Buddha as the leader of a herd of deer who sacrifices himself to save the herd from destruction, as a monkey who makes a bridge of his body to help other monkeys to safety, and as a partridge who teaches a lesson about respect

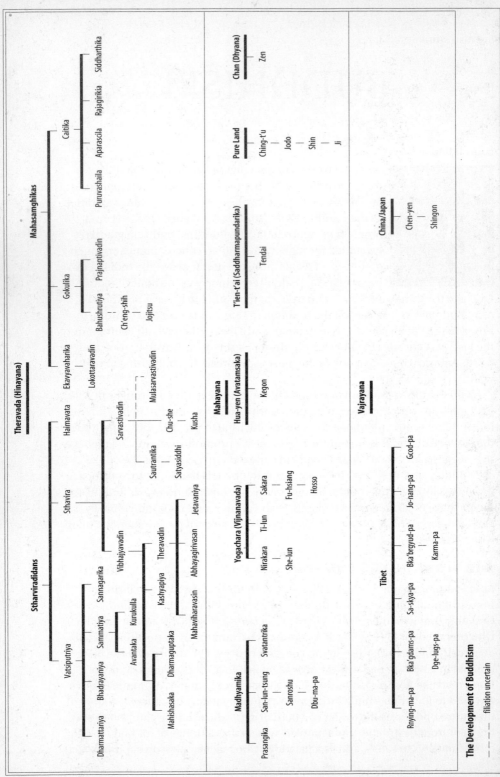

The Development of Buddhism

----- filiation uncertain

for elders by demonstrating his seniority to an elephant and a monkey. There are also stories of human beings who embody basic moral virtues, such as a prince who became a paragon of generosity by giving up all of his possessions, including his kingdom and his family. The Jataka tales continue to function in many Buddhist societies as important models of behavior and sources of moral instruction.

The career of the bodhisattva culminated in the birth of Siddhartha Gautama in a royal family in a region of northern India that is now southern Nepal. Prince Siddhartha was raised in a palace, married, had a child, and then, in his early thirties, saw "four sights" that provoked a major change in the course of his life. He saw a sick person, an old person, a corpse, and finally an ascetic (*samana*)

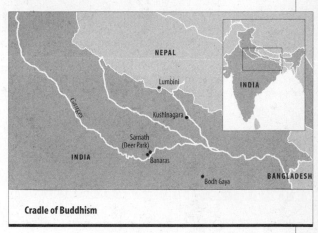

Cradle of Buddhism

who was attempting to escape the problems of suffering and death by renouncing the responsibilities and pleasures of ordinary existence. In an event that is described in Buddhist tradition as the great "Going Forth," Prince Siddhartha left his life in the palace and became a wandering monk. At first he engaged in a strict discipline of asceticism designed to deny the pleasures of the senses, but when this radical self-denial failed to bring the success he sought, he took up a balanced form of discipline, called the Middle Path, in which he avoided the extremes of self-denial and self-indulgence. He then sat down under a tree known as the Bodhi Tree and resolved not to get up until he had found a solution to the problems of suffering and death. After a series of temptations and a complex process of meditation, he broke through to the realization he had been seeking. In this moment of realization, he became a Buddha—someone who has "awakened" from the sleep of ignorance that binds living beings to the suffering of this world.

After the event of his awakening, the Buddha got up from his seat under the Bodhi Tree, walked to Deer Park (the same park that was associated with his earlier life as the leader of the herd of deer) near Varanasi (Banaras), and preached his first sermon to a small group of friends. This sermon is known in Buddhist tradition as the first "turning of the wheel of the Dharma." The Dharma, or the Buddha's teaching, is symbolized by a wheel, and the wheel of the Dharma often functions as a symbol of the Buddhist tradition as a whole. The content of the Buddha's first sermon is summarized in the Four Noble Truths: the truth of Suffering, the truth of the Origin of Suffering, the truth of the Cessation of Suffering, and the truth of the Path to the Cessation of Suffering. After the Buddha had preached his first sermon, he continued to elaborate his teaching and gather a group of followers that are known as the Buddhist Sangha, or community. The Sangha has traditionally been composed of four

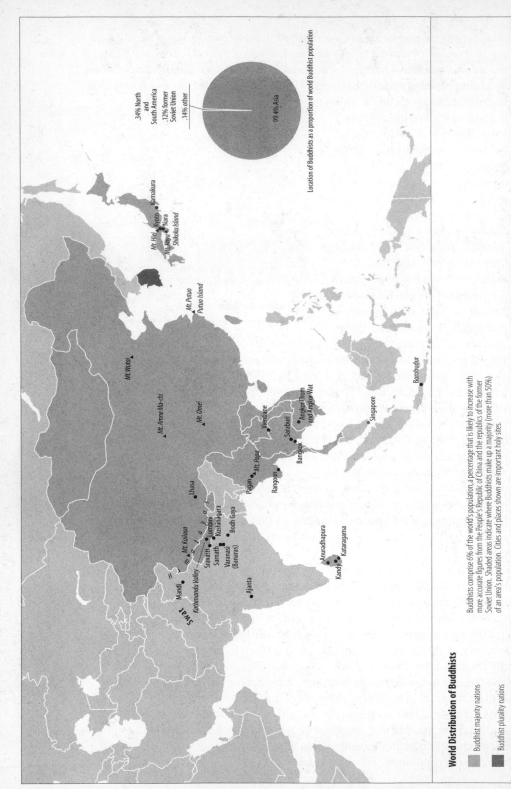

Location of Buddhists as a proportion of world Buddhist population

99.4% Asia

.34% North and South America
.12% former Soviet Union
.14% other

Kamakura
Mt. Hiei Kyoto Nara
Mt. Koya Shikoku Island

Mt. Putuo
Putuo Island

Mt. Wutai

Mt. Amne Ma-chi
Mt. Omei

Vientiane
Angkor Thom and Angkor Wat
Saraburi
Bangkok
Singapore
Borobudur

Lhasa

H i m a l a y a s
Lumbini
Mt. Kailasa Kushinagara
Sravasti Bodh Gaya
Mandi Samath Mt. Popa
Kathmandu Valley Varanasi (Banaras) Pagan
Swat Rangoon
Ajanta

Anuradhapura
Kataragama
Kandy

World Distribution of Buddhists

Buddhist majority nations

Buddhist plurality nations

Buddhists comprise 6% of the world's population, a percentage that is likely to increase with more accurate figures from the People's Republic of China and the republics of the former Soviet Union. Shaded areas indicate where Buddhists make up a majority (more than 50%) of an area's population. Cities and places shown are important holy sites.

Buddhism*

600–500 B.C.	500–400 B.C.	400–300 B.C.
Siddhartha Gautama, the Buddha (566–486 or 448–368)	Buddha enters nirvana, beginning of Buddhist era (486) First Buddhist Council (Rajagriha), possibly legendary (483)	Second Buddhist Council (Vaishali) (383) A Buddhist council at Pataliputra (367 or 346) Moggalliputta Tissa (342–322) First schism in archaic Buddhist community: the Sthaviras/Mahasamghikas, leading to the "18 Schools" (ca. 340)

300–200 B.C.	200–100 B.C.	100–1 B.C.
Mahinda (ca. 282–222) Reign of Ashoka (ca. 268–239) First Buddhist missionary activity outside India (ca. 251) Third Buddhist Council (Pataliputra) (247) Devanampiyatissa (ca. 247–209)	Dutthagamani (fl. 2nd century)	Fourth Buddhist Council (Anuradhapura) (25)

* See also the timelines that accompany the feature articles "Chinese Religion" and "Japanese Religion."

parts—laymen, laywomen, monks, and nuns—although the practice of ordaining Buddhist nuns has now fallen into disuse in many Buddhist countries.

After a period of about forty years, during which the Buddha wandered the roads of northern India elaborating his teaching and providing, by rule and example, a code of conduct for his followers, the Buddha reached the definitive conclusion of his long career as a bodhisattva. He gave a final discourse, lay down between two trees, and passed away, never to be reborn. This event is known in Buddhist tradition as the Buddha's *parinirvana*, the complete cessation of the process of rebirth. Accounts of the Buddha's parinirvana tell us that a group of laypeople was assigned the responsibility of arranging for the Buddha's cremation. After the cremation, the relics of the Buddha's body were divided and enshrined in a series of reliquary mounds, or *stupas*, where they served as the focus of worship. The Buddha's monastic followers arranged for a council of elders to recite the Buddha's teaching and thus began a process that led gradually to the formation of a canon of Buddhist scripture.

The events of the Buddha's life are now known to us from traditions and legends that are very difficult to confirm, but there is little doubt among modern scholars of Buddhism about the basic elements of the Buddha legend. There seems genuinely to have been a man who was born in a princely family, left it behind, and established a tradition of monastic practice that became the basis of a major world religion. The story of the Buddha, however, is more than a dim

Buddhism

1–100	100–200	200–300
Kaniska (late 1st to early 2nd century)	Ashvaghosha (2nd century)	Reign of Siri Sanga Bo (251–253)
Entry of Buddhism into China (65, traditional date)	Nagarjuna (2nd century)	Aryadeva (3rd or 4th century)
	Rise of Mahayana Buddhism (100–150)	
	Lotus Sutra (end of 2nd century)	

reflection of the life of an ancient sage. Even in its barest outline, it shows the hand of the Buddhist community shaping its common tradition, and it suggests many of the key elements that have defined Buddhism as a religious tradition throughout much of its history.

BUDDHISM AS A MIDDLE PATH

According to traditional accounts of the Buddha's first sermon, the Buddha began his presentation of the Dharma with a description of the Middle Path: "Avoiding the two extremes (of self-denial and self-indulgence) the Tathagata (Skt., Pali, lit., "one who has gone beyond," referring to the Buddha) has realized the Middle Path: it gives vision, it gives knowledge, and it leads to calm, to insight, to awakening, to nirvana." In spite of the complex evolution of the Buddhist tradition after the life of the Buddha, Buddhists have retained the practical focus of this first sermon. Buddhist teaching presents a path for living—a path that is balanced and oriented toward the cessation of suffering. The Path often is divided into eight categories: right views, right thoughts, right speech, right action, right livelihood, right effort, right mindfulness, and right concentration. It is possible, however, to group the eight parts of the Path in three categories: moral precepts, concentration, and wisdom. The five "moral precepts" (*sila*) are not to kill, not to steal, not to lie, not to abuse sex, and not to take intoxicants. "Concentration" (*samadhi*) has to do with the practice of mental discipline that is commonly called "meditation." Practices of concentration differ considerably from one variety of Buddhism to another, but many share a traditional form of discipline of mindfulness of breathing. To practice

300–400	400–500	500–600
Asanga (4th–5th centuries)	T'an Yao (mid-5th century)	Bhavaviveka (ca. 490–570)
Buddhaghosa (4th–5th centuries)	Buddhapalita (ca. 470–540)	Paramartha (499–569)
Vasubandhu (4th–5th centuries)	T'an-luan (ca. 476–542)	Vintaruci (5th century)
Tao-an (312–385)	Dignaga (ca. 480–540)	Reign of Emperor Wu (Liang dynasty) (502–549)
Hui-yuan (334–416)		Sthiramati (510–570)
Kumarajiva (344–413)		Shilabhadra (529–645)
Tao-sheng (ca. 360–434)		Dharmapala (ca. 530–560)
Seng-chao (374–414)		Bodhidharma (d. 532?)
Journeys of Fa-hsien (399–418)		Korean Buddhism enters Japan (538 or 552)
		Chih-i (538–597)
		Hsin-hsing (540–594)
		Tao-ch'o (Jap. Doshaku) (562–645)
		Prince Shotoku (574–622)
		"Golden Age" of Chinese Buddhism (589–906)

this form of discipline, one sits down in a stable posture and concentrates on the movement of the breath. As thoughts arise in the mind, one observes them and lets them flow away, returning to concentration on the movement of the breath. Wisdom (*prajna*) constitutes the insight that finally frees a person from suffering and from the cycle of death and rebirth. While defined differently in different parts of the Buddhist world and in different phases of Buddhist history, wisdom involves an awareness of the Four Noble Truths, particularly the truth of Suffering, and the doctrine of no-self.

BUDDHISM AS A QUEST FOR NIRVANA

If one were to define Buddhism not by the principle that governs a Buddhist way of life but by the ultimate goal to which that life is directed, the key would be the concept of *nirvana:* the definitive cessation of the suffering that plagues human existence. The concept of nirvana gains its meaning and much of its importance in classical Buddhist thought from the assumption of reincarnation or transmigration (*samsara*), an assumption that Indian Buddhists shared with their Hindu and Jain counterparts. Classical Buddhist sources pictured human life as a continuous cycle of death and rebirth. A person, or "sentient being," could rise on the scale of transmigration as far as the gods in heaven or fall down through the realm of animals to one of the lowest hells. The realm of a person's birth in a future life was determined by the actions (*karma*) performed in this life. Good, or meritorious (*punya*), actions could bring a good rebirth, bad actions a bad rebirth. In either case, however, the results were impermanent. Even the actions that brought rebirth in the highest heaven eventually

Buddhism

600–700	700–800	800–900
Beginning of Chan (Zen) Buddhism; Vajrayana Buddhism in Tibet (7th century)	Shen-hui (684–758)	Ennin (794–864)
Shantideva (7th–8th centuries)	Chien-chen (Jap. Ganjin) (688–763)	Construction of Borobodur (Java) (9th century)
Candrakirti (ca. 600–650)	Reign of Empress Wu Chao (690–705)	Lin-chi (9th century)
Dharmakirti (600–660)	Aryadeva (8th century)	Vo Ngon Thong (9th century)
Hsuan-tsang (ca. 600–664)	Jnanagarbha (8th century)	Angkorean period (Cambodia), major construction of temple complexes (802–1432)
Shen-hsiu (ca. 606–706)	Padmasambhava (8th century)	
Shan-tao (613–681)	Shantiraksita (8th century)	Tendai Buddhism (Japan) founded by Saicho (805)
Wonhyo (617–686)	Amoghavajra (705–774)	Shingon Buddhism (Japan) founded by Kukai (806)
Uisang (625–702)	Pai-chang Huai-hai (720–814)	
I-ching (635–713)	Kamalashila (ca. 740–795)	Enchin (814–891)
K'uei-chi (636–682)	Saicho (Dengyo Daishi) (767–822)	Tai-mitsu Tendai founded by Ennin (847)
Shubhakarasimha (637–735)	Kukai (Kobo Daishi) (774–835)	Miidera Tendai founded by Enchin (858)
Hui-neng (638–712)	Tsung-mi (780–841)	
Fa-tsang (643–712)	Shantaraksita (d. 788)	
Chinese Buddhism enters Japan (658–666)	A Buddhist council at Lhasa (792–794)	
Gyogi (668–749)		
Classical period of Korean Buddhism (668–935)		

would decay and condemn a person to wander again through the realms of rebirth. The only way to escape the cycle altogether was to extinguish the ignorance and desire that drive a person again and again into the realms of re-birth. In classical Buddhist thought this extinction was called nirvana, the "blowing out" of the fire of ignorance and desire.

BUDDHISM AS A SYSTEM OF SOCIAL RELATIONSHIPS

The different responses to the problem of reincarnation have been institution-alized in a distinction between monks and nuns, on the one hand, and laymen and laywomen, on the other. Laypeople focus on the process of accumulating the merit that will bring them good fortune in this life and the next, while monks and nuns follow the example of the Buddha by renouncing family re-sponsibilities and material possessions and living lives of deliberate simplicity. Monastic life began in India with small groups of wandering monks but quickly settled into established monasteries. In many Buddhist countries the monaster-ies became complex and sophisticated centers of ritual life and learning and had profound influence on the conduct of politics and public life. In Tibet the monasteries functioned for many centuries not merely as the center of Tibetan

900–1000	1000–1100	1100–1200
Koya (903–972)	Atisha (982–1054)	Parakramabahu I (12th century)
Yen-shou (904–975)	Tilopa (988–1069)	Shariputta (12th century)
Genshin (942–1017)	Abhayakaragupta (ca. 11th century)	Dug-gsum-mkhyen-pa (Karma-pa I) (1110–93)
Rin-chen bzang-po (958–1055)	Khyung-po Rnal-'byor Tshul-khrims (11th century)	Saigyo (1118–90)
	Mgon-po (11th century)	Honen (1133–1212)
	Ratnakirti (11th century)	Eisai (1141–1215)
	Shin Arahan (11th century)	Jien (1155–1225)
	Beginning of influence of Buddhism in Central Asia, continuing to present (11th century)	Chinul (1158–1210)
	Construction of Pagan (Ceylon); revival ("new tradition") of Buddhism in Tibet (11th–12th centuries)	Bencho (1162–1238)
		Koben (1173–1232)
	Classical period of Southeast Asian Buddhism (11th–15th centuries)	Shinran (1173–1262)
	Maitripa (1007–85)	Japanese Pure Land (Jodo) Buddhism founded by Honen (1175)
	'Bron ston-pa (1008–64)	Shoku (1177–1247)
	Marpa (1012–96)	Chia'gak Hyesim (1178–1234)
	Naropa (1016–1100)	Sa-skya Pandita (1182–1251)
	Milarepa (Mi-la-ras-pa) (1040–1123)	Rinzai Zen transmitted from China to Japan by Eisai (1191)
	Ma-gcig Lab-sgnon (ca. 1055–1149)	
	Uich'on (1055–1101)	
	Sgam-po-pa (1079–1153)	

religious life but as the dominant force in the Tibetan state. Alongside the complex and public institution of the monastery, the Buddhist tradition also has nurtured and venerated the ideal of the recluse or forest saint who lives on the fringes of Buddhist society and maintains a strict regimen of meditation and self-discipline. Many of the great saints of the Buddhist tradition, like the Tibetan yogi Milarepa, had very little contact with settled monasteries and yet were forceful examples of the detachment and renunciation that characterize the Buddhist monastic ideal.

Relations between monks and laypeople are best typified by the morning begging round that is such a familiar part of Buddhist life in Southeast Asia. In the morning the monks, who are prohibited from keeping food from one day to the next, take their begging bowls and walk to the homes of their lay supporters to receive their alms. The act ties the monks and the laypeople together in a network of mutual support. While the monks receive the food that will sustain them in their life of renunciation, the laypeople develop the attitude of generosity and gain the merit that will help advance them in a future life. The same relationship is mirrored in other, more dramatic acts of generosity by laypeople toward monks. In some Southeast Asian Buddhist societies the yearly rain re-

Buddhism

1200–1300	1300–1400	1400–1500
Dogen (1200–1253)	Bu-ston Rin-poche (1290–1364)	Dge-'dum-grb-pa (Dalai Lama I) (1391–1475)
Nichiren (1222–82)	Klong-chen Rab-'byams-pa (1308–63)	Ikkyu Sojun (1394–1481)
Jodo Sin (True Pure Land) founded in Japan by Shinran (1224)	Tsong-kha-pa (1357–1419)	Dhammaceti (1412–92)
'Phags-pa (ca. 1235–80)		Rennyo (1415–99)
Parakkamabahu II (1236–71)		Lo Ch'ing (1443–1527)
Ippen (1239–89)		Chos-graga-rgya-mtsho (Karma-pa VII) (1454–1506)
Gyonen (1240–1321)		
Nikko (1246–1333)		
Hokke (Lotus), later known as the Nichiren school, founded in Japan (1253)		
Kumararaja (1266–1343)		
Keizan (1268–1325)		
Ji Buddhism founded in Japan by Ippen (1275)		
Muso Soseki (1275–1351)		

1800–1900		
Mongkut (Rama IV) (1804–68)	Kyongho (1857–1912)	Daisetsu Teitaro Suzuki (1870–1966)
Kong-sprul Blo-gros mtha'yas (1813–99)	W. W. Vajirananavorasa (1860–1921)	Fifth Buddhist Council (Mandalay) (1871)
Mindon Min (1814–78)	Anagarika Dharmapala (1864–1933)	Makiguchi Tsunesaburo (1871–1944)
'Jam-dbyangs Mkhyen-brtse'i dbang-po (1820–92)	Peak period Japanese immigration into U.S., 2nd wave of American Buddhist "churches" (1868–1907)	Chulalongkorn (1873–1910)
Shwegyin Sayadaw (1822–93)		Edwin Arnold, *Light of Asia* (1879)
Peak period Chinese immigration into U.S., beginning of American Buddhist "churches" (1854–83)	Nishida Kitaro (1870–1945)	Mahi Bodi Society (Sri Lanka) (1891)
	Acharn Mun (1870–1949)	

treat, when monks gather in monasteries for the monsoon rains, concludes with a great festival. Laypeople gather at the monasteries to cook food for the monks and offer the possessions the monks will need to sustain themselves for another year. The monasteries themselves are often the result of great acts of generosity in which wealthy donors provide the facilities for the monks to carry out their monastic practice.

The relationship of mutual support between monks and their lay followers has been mirrored in Buddhist societies by the relationship between monks and kings. From the time of Ashoka in the third century B.C., Buddhist history is replete with examples of rulers who assumed the role of "righteous king" (*dharmaraja*) and became protectors of the monasteries. The association lent the king a sense of moral and religious legitimacy and gave the monasteries the support they needed not only to sustain their own practice but, in many cases, to send out the missionaries that spread the Buddhist tradition to other parts of

1500–1600	1600–1700	1700–1800
New wave of Buddhism in Mongolia (16th century)	Ou-i Chi-hsu (1599–1655)	Hakuin Ekaku (1686–1769)
Sosan Hyujong (1520–1604)	Blo-bzang rgya-mtsho (1617–82)	V. Saranamkara (ca. 1698–1779)
Chu-hung (1534–1615)	Bankei Yotaku (Dalai Lama V) (1622–93)	Ryokan (1758–1831)
Tz'u-po Chen-k'o (1543–1603)	Shogu Rojin (1643–1721)	
Han-shan Te-ch'ing (1546–1623)		
Dbang-phyug-rdo-rje (1556–1603)		
Neyici Toyin (1557–1653)		
Takuan Soho (1573–1645)		
Suzuki Shosan (1579–1655)		

1900–		
T'ai hsu (1889–1947)	Bdud'joms Rinpoche (1904–87)	Sixth Buddhist Council (Rangoon) (1954–56)
Naganuma Myoko (1889–1957)	Buddhadasa (1906–)	2,500-year anniversary of founding of Buddhism (Buddha Jayati) (1956)
Pak Chung-bin (1891–1943)	U Nu (1907–)	
Bhimrao Ramji Ambedkar (1891–1956)	Norodom Sihanouk (1922–)	Dalai Lama XIV receives Nobel Peace Prize (1989)
T'ang Y'ung-t'ung (1893–1964)	Tenzin Gyatso (Dalai Lama XIV) (1935–)	
G. P. Malalasekera (1899–1973)	Chogyam Trungpa (1939–87)	
Toda Josei (1900–1958)	World Fellowship of Buddhists founded (1950)	
Kotani Kimi (1901–71)		

Asia. The spread of Buddhism in China, Tibet, and Japan was greatly aided by the patronage of Buddhist kings, and the practice of Buddhism in Southeast Asia was closely allied throughout its history with the institution of the monarchy. The story of King Mongkut (1804–68) of Thailand, who began his adult life as a monk and then undertook a major reformation of the Thai monastic order, shows how deeply Buddhist kings can become involved not only in the passive support of monasteries but in their active guidance. And the connection between Buddhist values and the centers of political power is not limited to the relationship between monks and kings. In a number of contemporary Buddhist countries, Buddhist values have been brought to bear in situations of political conflict to represent not only the dominant community but also the powerless and the oppressed. Two recipients of the Nobel Peace Prize, the Dalai Lama of Tibet and Aung San Suu Kyi of Burma, are eloquent, modern representatives of a political Buddhism.

BUDDHISM AS A SYSTEM OF CULTIC ACTION

The basic patterns of Buddhist worship and cultic life can be traced to some of the early accounts of the Buddha's parinirvana, the cremation of the Buddha's body, and the distribution of the Buddha's relics. Simply to place garlands, perfumes, or paint at a shrine of the Buddha's relics or to use them as a place to calm the mind will bring a person "profit and joy." The earliest texts refer to only a few reliquary mounds, or stupas, constructed at major sites of Buddhist pilgrimage. With subsequent division and distribution of relics and with the proliferation of other types of Buddhist shrines, including images of the Buddha and the relics and images of other Buddhist saints, Buddhist worship can now be focused at an enormous variety of shrines and sacred objects. The major centers of pilgrimage, particularly Bodh Gaya, where the Buddha became awakened, and Sarnath, where he preached his first sermon, are still treated with great reverence and respect. There are other shrines that command national or international respect, such as the Jokhang in Tibet, the Temple of the Tooth in Sri Lanka, and the Temple of the Emerald Buddha in Thailand. But Buddhist worship can be offered at simple shrines in a home or an office as well as in the great temples at Buddhist holy sites. The worship at these shrines is similar to the process in the earliest accounts of the worship of the Buddha's relics: a person makes offerings of flowers, incense, candles, or prayers and seeks, in the presence of the shrine, a certain calmness of mind. The goals of such worship can be as different as the accumulation of merit, gaining good luck or success in some worldly undertaking, or attempting to experience the detachment that characterized the Buddha's nirvana.

THE GREAT VEHICLE

Most of the features that have just been described are present in one form or another throughout the Buddhist world, particularly in the Buddhist communities of Southeast Asia, but the Buddhist tradition also has undergone major changes, and new varieties of Buddhism have developed that depart substantially from the traditional model of Indian and Southeast Asian Buddhism. The most important and widespread changes are associated with a movement known as the Mahayana, or "Great Vehicle." The Mahayana emerged as a reform movement within the Buddhist community in India during the first century or two B.C. It is unclear how or in what social or cultic context the Mahayana first appeared, but it is clear that the Mahayana brought with it a new story about the transmission of the Buddha's teaching and a new vision of what it meant to follow the example of the Buddha.

The early texts of the Mahayana trace their origin to a "second turning of the wheel of the Dharma," in which the Buddha presented a new and challenging teaching to a select group of disciples. According to Mahayana tradition, this teaching was then passed on in secret for several centuries before it was widely promulgated in the Buddhist communities of India. The new teaching shifted attention away from the solitary quest for nirvana (associated with the story of the Buddha's final rebirth) toward the ideal of the bodhisattva (associated with the stories of the Buddha's previous lives), and it advised its adherents to become bodhisattvas themselves. They were not to seek a solitary nirvana as the fulfillment of the Buddhist path, but to delay their nirvana and return to this world to engage in the acts of self-sacrifice and compassion that characterized a bodhisattva's gradual progress toward the awakening of the Buddha. The ideal of the bodhisattva was not simply a quest for the wisdom that would release one from suffering, but a combination of wisdom and compassion that made the bodhisattva path a quest for the welfare of others.

Along with the bodhisattva ideal came a remarkable expansion in the possibilities for Buddhist worship and cultic action. The Mahayana tradition conceived of bodhisattvas not merely as human beings who followed the example of the Buddha's bodhisattva career, but as celestial beings who could serve as the focus of devotion and come to one's aid in extraordinary ways.

One of the most important of these celestial bodhisattvas is Avalokiteshvara ("The Lord Who Looks Down"), the great bodhisattva of compassion. Avalokiteshvara's compassion is said to focus particularly on beings who have fallen into danger, but Avalokiteshvara is also invoked to grant children to barren women and to serve as a guide through the realms of the afterlife. For many devotees of Avalokiteshvara, the Bodhisattva's compassion is crystallized in the sacred formula or mantra *om mani padme hum*. The words of the mantra are often translated, "O, the jewel in the lotus," but the meaning of the mantra lies more in its function than in the reference of its individual words. In Tibet the devotees of Avalokiteshvara inscribe the mantra on rocks, flags, and prayer wheels to ward away danger and fill the land of Tibet with the power of Avalokiteshvara's compassion. According to Tibetan tradition, Avalokiteshvara has been manifested in the figure of Srong-btsan-sgam-po, a seventh-century king who played a prominent role in the introduction of Buddhism to Tibet, and more recently in the lineage of the Dalai Lamas. In China Avalokiteshvara is frequently visualized in female form as Kuan-yin, the mother of compassion.

The veneration and worship of celestial Bodhisattvas is closely related in Mahayana tradition to the worship of celestial Buddhas. These are Buddhas who have completed the bodhisattva path and passed beyond the level even of great bodhisattvas such as Avalokiteshvara and attained the stage of perfect Buddhahood. One of the best known of the many celestial Buddhas in the Mahayana is Amitabha ("Infinite Light"), known in Japan as Amida. According to the story of Amitabha's career, Amitabha (or, more properly, the bodhisattva whose career led to the awakening of the Buddha Amitabha) made a vow to create a paradise, known as the Pure Land, and to transport devotees to that paradise if they invoked his name with faith. The invocation is expressed in the phrase *Namo 'mitabhaya buddhaya* ("Homage to Amitabha Buddha"). Devotion to Amitabha played a significant role in the Indian Mahayana, had great popularity in medieval China, was elaborated even further in Japan, and is a major constituent in the complex of modern Japanese Buddhism and in the Buddhism of North America.

The emphasis on compassion in the Mahayana was associated with a new understanding of wisdom and a new vision of reality. In many of the sources of the earlier tradition, to know reality was to understand that nothing had an enduring self, that reality constituted nothing but a stream of momentary phenomena. The basic texts of the Mahayana insisted that nothing was ultimately real, including the "moments" that seemed to make up this stream of reality. The result was the Mahayana doctrine of emptiness—the doctrine that everything is illusory or "empty" of any real identity. The doctrine of emptiness was elaborated quite differently by philosophers in the two major schools of Mahayana philosophy, the Yogachara and the Madhyamaka, and it was expressed in many different ways in Mahayana meditation, ritual, and art. But the core of the doctrine is perhaps best expressed by two interlocking assertions: the nature of all things is their emptiness, and there is ultimately no difference between any two things. This means that all things share a common nature (sometimes referred to as their "Buddha-nature") and are connected in a network of being. From this last claim grows the Mahayana conviction that compassion, or the living sense of connectedness with all beings, is an essential part of any practice that attempts to embody the Mahayana vision of reality.

The doctrine of emptiness is clearly reflected in the tradition of meditation that in its Japanese form is called Zen. The Zen tradition took shape in China (under the Chinese name of Ch'an) as a combination of Indian monastic meditation and a form of Chinese contemplation associated with Taoism. Zen practice often involves long periods of study, with meditation sessions extending from early morning long into the night. It also involves intense struggle with the cryptic questions, called *koans,* that are intended to push students through to moments of awakening. But the most accessible expressions of Zen ideals to an outsider often appear in the arts, such as painting or poetry, where an artist or poet attempts to capture the feeling of stillness in the midst of great activity that lies at the heart of the Mahayana understanding of emptiness.

BUDDHIST TANTRISM

The nondualistic aspect of the Mahayana is given vivid, practical expression in the movement known as Buddhist Tantrism, also referred to as Vajrayana ("the Diamond Vehicle") or Mantrayana ("the Vehicle of Sacred Phrases"). Tantrism emerged as an active force in the Indian Buddhist community in the seventh century and, like the Mahayana, traces itself through a hidden transmission to the figure of the historical Buddha. Many early Tantric texts present the tradition as a powerful form of practice meant to bring a practitioner to awakening in a much shorter time than would be required by the standard practice of the bodhisattva path. Tantric discipline stresses the importance of dependence on a *guru* (teacher), makes heavy use of ritual and symbol (including geometric symbols, such as the mandala), and often visualizes the experience of nonduality in a radical reversal of conventional dualities, such as purity and impurity or good and evil. This understanding of nonduality is expressed in the image of a "wrathful Buddha" as well as in the image of a Buddha as the union of male and female. One indicates that the Buddha's awakening is beyond the distinction between anger and serenity, the other that it is beyond the distinction between male and female. Buddhist Tantrism flourished in India from the

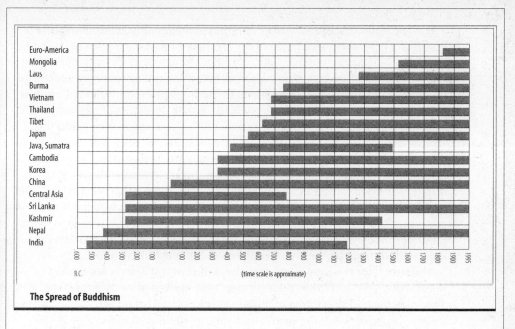

The Spread of Buddhism

seventh to the twelfth centuries, had a brief period of efflorescence in China, contributed to Japanese Buddhism through the influence of the Shingon school, and has had a long and rich history in the Buddhism of Tibet.

CONCEPTUAL PROBLEMS IN THE DEFINITION OF "BUDDHISM"

The Buddhist tradition has undergone so many changes and given rise to so many alternate varieties over the course of its twenty-five-hundred-year history that it seems difficult to recognize any longer the story of the solitary prince who set out from the palace to solve the problem of transmigration. It is important to recognize that, while the story of Siddhartha Gautama may serve as a point of orientation for the Buddhist tradition and may set the stage for important developments in Buddhist life and thought, it does not exhaust the meaning of the word *Buddhism*. There are at least as many conceptual difficulties in the definition of "Buddhism" as there are in the definition of "religion."

One type of difficulty has to do with boundaries. What criterion or type of analysis should one use to decide whether an aspect of a particular culture is Buddhist or not? Should the decision be based on the conceptual coherence of the tradition itself? Should it be based on a sense of historical continuity? Should it be based on phenomenological observation—the judgment that something shows the form or appearance of a Buddhist practice or teaching? Or should it be based on association—the observation that a practice is found in close social or cultural proximity with practices that are identifiably Buddhist? And whose judgment should be taken as authoritative? Should it be the judgment of Buddhists themselves? If so, who counts as a Buddhist? Or should it be the judgment of scholars who observe the tradition in some fashion from the outside?

It is generally recognized that a definition of religion involving veneration or worship of gods or supernatural beings is misleading when applied to the Buddhist tradition. Many Buddhists acknowledge the existence of "gods" or supernatural beings, but gods and supernatural beings are not integrally connected to the pursuit of nirvana. It is more useful in the conceptual study of the Buddhist tradition to follow the impulse behind Paul Tillich's definition of religion as "the state of being grasped by an ultimate concern" and to look not for a Buddhist equivalent of "God" but for an ultimate goal or principle, such as nirvana or Dharma, that gives to Buddhist lives a sense of ultimate meaning. The concept of an ultimate concern tempts one to identify a single element of the Buddhist tradition as essential and interpret all other elements from that perspective. This approach to Buddhism has obvious strengths, not the least of which is a sense of conceptual unity. But it is easily influenced by the interpreter's own ideological program, and it runs the risk of relegating to the periphery aspects of the Buddhist tradition that are far from peripheral to Buddhists themselves.

The search for essential features in the Buddhist tradition is not limited to outside observers. Buddhist philosophers have spoken of the "essence" or "heart" of the tradition (often identified as the doctrine of no-self or emptiness) for many centuries. But the search took on new significance in the late nineteenth and early twentieth centuries as Buddhist leaders attempted to respond to the challenge of religious ideas from the West. Under the influence of Colonel Henry Steele Olcott, cofounder of the Theosophical Society, a series of Buddhist leaders in Sri Lanka, including Anagarika Dharmapala and Walpola Rahula, have attempted to define a purified and reformed Buddhism. This reformed Buddhism (sometimes referred to as "Protestant Buddhism") returns to the scriptures of the Pali canon to discover the basic teachings of the Buddha and presents these teachings as pragmatic, down-to-earth, and compatible with the insights of modern psychology and philosophy. Writers in this tradition are even wary of referring to Buddhism as a religion at all, lest it be associated with the "superstitions" of theistic worship. The movement represented by Dharmapala and Rahula has played an important role in Buddhist modernism comparable to the role played by Ram Mohan Roy and Vivekananda in the modernization of the Hindu tradition. But their account of Buddhism is more of an ideal construct than an account of what Buddhist people actually do.

There has been a strong tendency in the recent academic study of Buddhism to shed the constraints involved in a search for essential or purified Buddhism and to look at the Buddhist tradition, in the words of the anthropologist Stanley Tambiah, as "a total social phenomenon." This approach questions the easy identification of Buddhism with the religious dimension of culture, as the approach of Dharmapala did, but it questions it from a completely different direction. While Dharmapala distills Buddhism into its rational and scientific essence, Tambiah expands his vision of Buddhism to include not merely religion, but society, politics, and economics as well. Is Buddhism a religion? Is Buddhism more than a religion? Or is Buddhism not religious at all? The diversity of modern answers to these questions is a reflection of the richness and complexity not only of the movement we call "Buddhism," but of religion itself.

Buddhism (authoritative texts and their interpretation).

The various collections of texts considered authoritative sources of religious truth or vehicles of ritual power by Buddhist communities were composed in India over a period of approximately one millennium (ca. 500 B.C.– A.D. 600), but later texts or texts composed in other Buddhist countries may also be included.

Buddhist Concepts of "Scripture": Buddhists do not share a common notion of textual authority or authenticity: there is no "Buddhist Bible," no single textual source of religious truth, no single corpus accepted by all Buddhists. In the first place, the sheer volume and diversity of Buddhist scriptural texts makes it virtually impossible for any collections of texts to be both inclusive and authoritative. Second, differences between authoritative scriptural collections are significant, and even within traditions that share the same canon, critical differences exist in the selection of particular sections as privileged or key proof-texts. Last, Buddhist scriptures diverge significantly in their language, genres, sectarian affiliation, and geographic origins.

Buddhists in most of Southeast Asia adhere to the Pali language canon (*Tipitaka*) of the Theravada school. Tibetan Buddhists use a corpus of scriptures composed for the most part of texts translated into Tibetan from Indian languages. Buddhists in China, Korea, Japan, and Vietnam refer to one of several versions of a collection of Chinese language texts that includes native Chinese works as well as translations from Indian languages. Some Buddhists also use derivative canons, such as the Mongolian canon, translated from the Tibetan, and the Manchu, translated from the Chinese.

All Buddhist canonical or quasi-canonical collections are comprehensive repositories of centuries of tradition and include numerous texts from different periods, which add up to collections of formidable size. One edition of the Chinese Buddhist canon, for instance, in English translation amounts to over five hundred thousand pages. The Pali canon includes early materials, possibly from a stage prior to the systematization of classical Buddhist doctrine, side by side with commentaries that may be as late as the second century B.C. The Chinese canon contains equally early materials beside Indian exegetical and philosophical works from as late as the eighth century. Japanese versions of the Chinese canon add works written as recently as the nineteenth century; the most recent Japanese edition (1912–25) also adds texts from the caves of Tun-huang that date to the

eighth century but were only discovered at the beginning of the twentieth century.

Tradition asserts that the Buddhist scriptures form a tripartite collection called the *Tripitaka* (Skt., "three baskets," "three collections"; Pali, *Tipitaka*), divided into three genres: *Sutra*, *Vinaya*, and *Abhidharma*. The *Sutra* section is supposed to contain discourses attributed to the Buddha and his immediate disciples; the *Vinaya* purportedly contains the monastic rules promulgated by the Buddha, and the *Abhidharma* is reserved for treatises expounding Buddhist doctrine in abstract and theoretical terms. In practice, however, only one surviving canon, the Pali *Tipitaka*, is divided in this fashion; some early canons, now lost, may have had five divisions or more. The distribution of genres and topics is not always clear-cut or obvious. The Pali *Tipitaka*, for instance, includes under the *Sutra* (Pali *Sutta*) section works that are clearly exegetical or systematic treatises. The Pali *Vinaya* includes the legendary early history of the Buddhist monastic order.

During the five hundred years following the death of the Buddha (ca. 486 B.C.), Indian Buddhist texts were transmitted orally by reciters who specialized in different groups of texts. Around the first century some of these texts were organized to form larger collections that eventually became, in written form, the authoritative scriptural collections of the present. Some of these collections became explicitly closed collections or canons proper; others remained open collections. The Pali *Tipitaka* of the Theravada school is the only surviving closed canon. This collection was first committed to writing in 29 B.C. under King Vattagamani of Sri Lanka; but it was still undergoing changes in the fifth century, when it took a form very close to its present state. Still, not all Theravada Buddhists use exactly the same canon: the Burmese *Tipitaka*, for instance, includes works considered noncanonical by Buddhists in Sri Lanka. Some collections have remained substantially unchanged for a relatively long time, but not by any explicit decision of a synod or monarch. Thus, the Tibetan canon, although never officially declared closed, has not undergone any major change since the tenth century. The Chinese corpus, on the other hand, remains open, although throughout the ages different recensions and printings of this "canon" have acquired quasi-canonical currency, if not authority.

Content of the Canons: Among all extant collections, the Pali *Tipitaka*—used by the Theravada school—is the most conservative. It is composed of three *Pitakas*: *Sutta* (Skt. *Sutra*), *Vinaya*, and

Abhidhamma (Skt. *Abhidharma*). The *Sutta Pitaka* is divided into five collections called *Nikayas: Digha, Majjhima, Samyutta, Anguttara,* and *Khuddaka.* The criteria for grouping texts in these collections are inconsistent. Works included in the *Digha, Majjhima,* and *Khuddaka Nikaya* represent works of extended, medium, and reduced length, respectively. But the *Khuddaka Nikaya* eventually became a category for miscellaneous, rather than short, texts—it includes today a variety of genres ranging from ascetic verses (*Thera-* and *Theri-gatha*) to the stories of the Buddha's former lives (*Cariyapitaka*), from rich poetry (*Dhammapada*) to textbook prose (*Khuddakapatha*). It includes also Abhidharmic material in the *Patisambhidamagga,* and one of the earliest Buddhist texts, the *Suttanipata.*

Only a small fraction of the *Sutra Pitaka* of the Sarvastivada is extant today. Originally written in Sanskrit, it parallels the Theravada in its main divisions and some of its texts. The Sarvastivada *Nikayas* were called *Agamas,* and numbered only four: *Dirgha, Madhyama, Samyukta,* and *Ekottara.* Many of the works in the Pali *Khuddaka* have no parallel in the Sarvastivada canon. The canons of schools like the Mahisasaka, Dharmaguptaka, and Mahasanghika, which are now lost, included a *Ksudraka-agama* or *Ksudraka-pitaka* that corresponded only roughly to the Pali *Khuddaka.* Some of the *Agamas,* or parts thereof, from the Sarvastivada and other schools are preserved in Sanskrit or in Tibetan and Chinese translations.

The *Vinaya Pitakas* of several ancient canons are also preserved in various forms: a complete Theravada *Vinaya* in Pali; a partial Sanskrit version and complete Tibetan and Chinese translations of the Mulasarvastivada *Vinaya;* and more or less complete Chinese translations of the *Vinayas* of the Dharmaguptaka, Sarvastivada, Mahasamghika, and Mahisasaka. The Pali *Vinaya* is composed of three main parts: a commentary on the *Pratimoksa,* or monastic precepts (227 precepts for monks and 311 for nuns), called *Suttavibhanga;* a discussion of the general rules and the history of the order, called *Khandhaka* and divided into *Mahavagga* and *Cullavagga;* and a late commentary on the Vinaya, called *Parivara.* Only the first two parts of this *Vinaya* have substantial parallels in the *Vinaya* of other schools.

Only two *Abhidharma Pitakas* survive: the Theravada *Abhidhamma,* preserved in Pali, and the Sarvastivada *Abhidhamma,* originally written in Sanskrit, but now preserved for the most part only in Chinese translation. Although both collections contain seven books, the works of the two *Abhidharmas* are not parallel in content or title. The seven books of the Theravada *Abhidhamma* are *Dhammasangani, Vibhanga, Dhatukatha, Puggalapannati, Kathavatthu, Yamaka,* and *Patthana. Dhammasangani* and *Vibhanga* are probably the oldest and provide the model for the "matrix-list" analysis of Abhidharma doctrine. The *Kathavatthu,* the latest of all seven, describes the doctrines and controversies of the early "Eighteen Schools" of Buddhism. The seven books of the Sarvastivada *Abhidharma* are *Jnanaprasthana, Prakaranapada, Vijnanakaya, Dharmaskandha, Prajnaptisastra, Dhatukaya,* and *Samgitiparyaya. Jnanaprasthana* was considered "the body" of the *Abhidharma* and the other six, "the limbs." The most influential work of Sarvastivada *Abhidharma,* however, is a voluminous extra-canonical commentary to the *Jnanaprasthana,* the *Mahavibhasa,* preserved only in Chinese.

Mahayana and Tantrism: No complete Indian Mahayana collection survives; it seems likely that there never was anything like a Mahayana canon in India. The Tibetan canon is supposed to follow the model of Indian Mahayana and Tantric Buddhist libraries in the ancient universities of Nalanda and Vikramasila, but very little is known about these collections, except that they were probably as fluid as the later Tibetan and Chinese canons and remained always open to the addition of new texts. Although there is no clear explanation of why some canons should remain open, it seems less than a coincidence that the scriptural collections that have remained open are those of Mahayana and Tantric Buddhists. Ambivalence regarding what is authoritative may have been due to sociopolitical circumstances as well, but the acceptance of ahistorical or suprahistorical revelation in Mahayana Buddhism played an important role in this development.

Taking the extant Chinese canon as the prototypical Mahayana collection, one notes that it includes non-Mahayana texts such as the *Agamas, Avadanas* and *Jatakas,* and Abhidharmic texts. The authority of these texts is not rejected outright, but is seen as secondary to the authority of Mahayana texts. Mahayana works claiming to be *Sutras* (teachings of Buddhas or Bodhisattvas) are classified into subcategories accepted in both the Tibetan and Chinese collections. Works on the "Perfection of Wisdom" form the *Prajnaparamita* section of the canon. The *Buddhavatamsaka* section is formed of forty-five works held by a loose frame story—it includes the *Gandavyuha Sutra* (the story of the pilgrim Sudhana) and the *Dasabhumika Sutra* (on the ten stages of the bodhisattva Path), both of which are also extant in Sanskrit. The *Maharatnakuta* collection includes several works still extant in Sanskrit, such as the *Kasyapaparivarta*, a Sutra that was very influential in India. The Sutras inspiring the Pure Land tradition are also included in the *Maharatnakuta*, as are some of the key sources for the doctrine of Tathagatagarbha. The *Mahasannipata* collection, used as a class of texts by the Chinese, but not by the Tibetan canon, includes several texts that were well known in India, such as the *Aksayamatinirdesa* and the *Questions of Gaganaganja*, as well as texts that had more currency in China, like the *Vows of Kshitigarbha* and the *Vows of Akasagarbha*. The Chinese collection also reserves a special section for the various Chinese versions of the Mahayana *Mahaparinirvana Sutra*, and another section for the *Lotus Sutra* and its various recensions and translations. Tibetan translation equivalents to these works appear under the heading of *Miscellaneous Sutras* in the Tibetan canon. Some works classified as *Miscellaneous Sutras* in the Chinese canon, such as the *Suvarnaprabhasa* and the *Bhaisajyaguru*, are considered *Tantras* in the Tibetan collection. Among the texts classified as miscellaneous in both the Chinese and the Tibetan collections are the two Sutras favored by the Yogachara school of philosophy, the *Sandhinirmochana* and the *Lankavatara* Sutras.

The Mahayana *Vinaya* also includes non-Mahayana texts, but adds its own so-called *Bodhisattva Vinaya* texts. The most famous among these are the *Bodhisattva Pitaka*, the *Bodhisattva Pratimoksa*, and the *Questions of Upali*. The Chinese canon also includes the influential *Brahmajala Sutra*, a text that is most probably a Chinese creation.

Although Mahayana collections include works of non-Mahayana *Abhidharma*, particularly of the Sarvastivada school, the true Mahayana equivalent of the *Abhidharma* are the scholastic and philosophical treatises called *Sastras*. The two major schools represented in the *Sastras*, according to canonical classification, are the Madhyamaka and the Yogachara. Many of these works are preserved in Sanskrit, Chinese, and Tibetan, but some major works are only preserved in Chinese or in Tibetan.

Tantric scriptures are best described from the perspective of the most representative collection, the Tibetan canon (although some texts have Chinese counterparts). Tantric literature ranges from the poetry of the Indian Siddhas or Mahasiddhas, called *Caryagiti*, to highly techni-

cal texts on Tantric thought, iconography, and ritual and from incantations (*mantra, dharani*) to meditation rituals (*sadhanas*). Tantric scriptures are usually classified following a schema attributed to the Tibetan polymath Bu-ston (1290–1364), although neither the Tibetan *Kanjur* (where *Tantra* is the first subdivision) nor the Chinese *Ta-tsang* follow his order of classification. The first class in Bu-ston's list is that of the "Ritual" (*Kriya*) *Tantra*. This group includes works that would otherwise appear to be ordinary, albeit ritually significant, Mahayana *Sutras*—such as the *Suvarnaprabhasa* and the *Bhaisajyaguru* (both still extant in Sanskrit). The second class, that of the "Practice" (*Carya*) *Tantra*, includes, among other texts, the *Mahavairochana Tantra* (or *Sutra*), part of a pair of texts forming almost a canon unto themselves for Chinese and Japanese Tantric Buddhists. The second member of this pair, the *Sarvatathagatatattvasamgraha*, forms part of the third class, the *Yoga Tantra*. The last group, the *Tantra of the Highest Yoga* (*Anuttarayoga*), is subdivided into "Father" and "Mother" *Tantras*, the first focusing on the presence of the absolute in the here and now, the second on the transcendent nature of the absolute. An example of a *Father Tantra* is the *Guhyasamaja*, and of *Mother Tantras*, the *Hevajra* and *Samvarodaya Tantras* (all three are still extant in Sanskrit). The *Kriya Tantras* represent an earlier stage, the others date from approximately the seventh or eighth centuries. Subsequent centuries saw the production of numerous commentaries, and eventually the appearance of a new type of Tantric text, *Kalacakra Tantras* of the eleventh century. This last type of literature, and the *Anuttarayoga Tantras*, are not extant in Chinese.

Scriptures and Sectarian Apologetics: In spite of the fluidity of its conception of canonicity, Buddhism is not immune to polemics regarding the authority or authenticity of scripture. Legend and history are used to bolster the validity of texts. The Theravada tradition, for instance, claims to trace its *Sutra* and *Vinaya* back to a complete recitation of this part of the canon at the Council of Rajagriha, held one year after the death of the Buddha (485 B.C.). Mahayana Buddhists concede that the scriptures of the pre-Mahayana schools were in circulation earlier than their own, but assert that the Mahayana *Sutras* were preached by the Buddha secretly, or only to gods or divine serpents, or to celestial Bodhisattvas. Thus, although more recently made public, Mahayana texts were seen as more sacred and subtle. Another important issue, that of the original language of the Buddha, is closely connected to the question of what is accurately the word of the Buddha. Most Buddhists, especially Mahayanists, have favored the view that the word of the Buddha can be expressed in any language and that the crucial issue is to preserve the spirit through the technical accuracy of the transmission. Accordingly, some Buddhist traditions have devoted much energy to the proper and thorough translation of Buddhist scriptures —such were the systematic efforts mounted in Tibet from the early ninth to the late fourteenth centuries, and the less organized series of translation projects that created, from the third to the ninth centuries, the Chinese canon. In all of these projects technical terminology and its accurate rendition were considered a vehicle for canonicity and homogeneity.

The key issue in Buddhist exegesis, however, is that of the proof-text. Most Buddhists even today do not read texts as whole texts, but as sources for the decisive passages, or "proof-texts," that define Buddhist orthodoxy. Thus, different schools favor particular texts or passages, so that one can speak of the *Sutras* favored by the Madhyamaka (e.g., *Samadhiraja*) or by the Yogachara (e.g., *Lankavatara*). Cults, sects, and secret societies also tend to cluster around specific texts, e.g., Chinese lay societies and secret societies using the *Lotus Sutra* as authority and modern Japanese "new religions" also based on the *Lotus*. The quest for *the* single, final, authority takes many forms. For instance, the Nyingma sect of Tibet claims to have found, under rocks and in caves, new scriptures (Tibetan *gterma*, "treasures") with new revelations. Even if such claims are not made, Buddhists often give the status of scripture to new creations such as the poetry of inspired mystics, e.g., Milarepa (1040–1123), and the collected works of great polymaths, e.g., Tsong-kha-pa (1357–1419).

East Asian traditions tend to focus on a small number of *Sutras* of real or purported Indian origin or on select native religious writings as the source of their scriptural authority. The Hua-yen school claims to derive its doctrines and practices from the *Buddhavatamsaka Sutra* (Chin. *Hua-yen ching*), but falls back primarily on its own commentaries and speculative tracts. The T'ien-tai school (Jap. *Tendai*) claims to derive all of its teachings from the *Lotus Sutra*, but also uses its own Chinese commentaries and treatises as authoritative texts. The same *Sutra* became the key and single most authoritative text for the Nichiren sect as well. The Pure Land traditions of Japan trace their teachings back to three Mahayana *Sutras:* the *Larger Sukhavativyuha*, the *Smaller Sukhavativyuha*, and the

Sutra on Contemplating the Buddha of Infinite Life. These are collectively known, at least since Honen (1133–1212), as *Jodo-sanbukyo* (The Tripartite Pure Land Sutra). As already noted, however, the Jodo Shinshu branch of Pure Land also refers to some of the works of its Japanese founder, Shinran, with the honorific name "*Holy Sutra*" (*o-kyo*). The denominations of Ch'an or Zen Buddhism, while paying lip service to one *Sutra*, the *Lankavatara*, use the "recorded sayings" (Chin. *yu-lu*) of ancient masters as their most sacred and authoritative texts. Thus, the Chinese term for *Sutra*, *ching* (Jap. *o-kyo*), is used for a text that the sect itself recognizes as non-Indian, the authoritative *Platform Sutra*, attributed to the sixth Chinese "Patriarch" of the school, Hui-neng (638–713). The Soto branch of Japanese Zen appeals to the writings of its founder, Dogen (1200–1253), as the ultimate source of authority. The Rinzai branch, on the other hand, still appeals to classical "recorded sayings," especially those written in the form of short anecdotal question-and-answer exchanges between disciple and Zen master. *See also* Abhidharma; Buddhism; Tripitaka Koreana; Vinaya.

Buddhism (festal cycle). The Buddhist festal cycle defines the life of the Buddhist community primarily in relationship to the paradigmatic events in the life of the Buddha and the early Buddhist community (Sangha). Other referents for annual Buddhist festivals include the seasonal and agricultural cycles calibrated to planting and harvest and the religious and political histories of particular Buddhist countries, e.g., Sri Lanka, Thailand, Tibet, and Japan. Because of these diverse underpinnings, the Buddhist festal cycle provides a particular illustration of the complex nature of popular Buddhism within various Buddhist cultures.

In any given Buddhist country the Buddhist festal cycle can be studied chronologically from the beginning to the end of the calendar year. From this perspective the Buddhist festal cycle is defined in terms of the annual calendric festivals in Tibet, Thailand, Sri Lanka, etc. However, a general study of annually celebrated Buddhist festivals should be concerned with three separate areas: festivals celebrating the person of the Buddha, his teaching (Dharma), and the founding of the monastic order (Sangha); the relationship between the Buddhist tradition and its sociopolitical contexts; and the articulation of the Buddhist festal cycle in relationship to the agricultural/natural seasons.

Festivals Honoring the Buddha: Festivals celebrat-

Chanting ceremony in the nearly completed Buddha hall of the Chinese Buddhist Pao Wah Temple, San Jose, California, January, 1990. While the Chinese New Year is not part of an explicitly Buddhist festal cycle, it is customary to visit Buddhist temples immediately after the New Year.

tinues through the seminal events of the Buddha's life as recounted in such popular commentaries as the *Nidana Katha*. In Sri Lanka the day might also be honored by acts of social service such as feeding the poor and visiting the sick in hospitals.

The life of the Buddha also assumes a place of importance in the Buddhist festal cycle in Mahayana Buddhist traditions. In Tibet the seminal events of the Buddha's life are celebrated independently. The traditional religious year includes honoring the Buddha's conception or incarnation on the fifteenth day of the first lunar month, the attainment of Buddhahood on the eighth day and his death on the fifteenth day of the fourth month, and the Buddha's birth on the fourth day of the sixth month of the Tibetan year. Since the first of these events occurs around the time of the celebration of the Tibetan New Year, it occupied a more prominent place in the Tibetan festal cycle. In particular, it was a day for special *pujas* (Skt , "devotions") to the Buddha's mother.

The procession and bathing of Buddha images is a special characteristic of Buddha's Day celebrations in China, Korea, and Japan. The *Mahasattva Sutra* designates the eighth day of the fourth lunar month as the most propitious time to lustrate Buddha images in order to achieve rewards and good luck. The Buddha's enlightenment signals victory over suffering and rebirth (*samsara*). On the popular level the power of the Buddha's enlightenment has less to do with the attainment of *nirvana* (liberation), than with achieving material blessings. Buddha's Day celebrations embody this paradox.

Buddha images may be honored as a physical representation of the enlightened one (*Tathagata*) or of celestial Buddhas, e.g., Amitabha, or they may be treated as powerful objects worthy of veneration and respect in their own right. Thus, it is not unusual for the Buddhist festal cycle to include celebrations honoring particular Buddha images. For example, Bangkok's famed Emerald Buddha has been revered as a royal palladium by both the Lao and Thai. Ceremonies honoring the image regularly occurred around the New Year and irregularly at times of crisis, e.g., the 1820 cholera epidemic in Thailand.

The Buddhist festal cycle not only honors the seminal events in the life of the Buddha and, by extension Buddha images, it also celebrates Buddha relics. The cult of relics has an ancient history in the Buddhist tradition. According to the *Mahaparinibbana Sutta*, after the Buddha's death his relics were divided among the eight

ing the life of the founder of a religious tradition are at the heart of that tradition's festal calendar. Buddhism is no exception. Among Theravadins, Buddha's Day, or Visakha Puja, is considered to be the most holy day of the Buddhist year. It commemorates the birth, enlightenment, and death of the Buddha, believed to have happened miraculously on the same day of the week. It occurs on the full-moon day of the lunar month of Visakha (April–May).

Given the specifically religious nature of the occasion, Visakha Puja celebrations in the Theravada cultures of Sri Lanka and Southeast Asia focus on the monastery. Devotees flock to the monasteries to observe the Five Precepts, listen to a traditional sermon on the life of the Buddha, circumambulate the reliquary, water the Bodhi Tree, and lustrate sacred Buddha images. In Thailand, the traditional Visakha sermon continues throughout the entire night. It begins with the wedding of Suddhodana and Mahamaya, Prince Siddhartha's parents, and con-

pious rulers (Pali *cakkavatti*) of India. They enshrined them in reliquary mounds at eight locations throughout the country. This legendary account reflects a historical tradition of enshrining relics at Buddhist pilgrimage sites going back at least to the time of the Mauryan king Ashoka in the third century B.C.

Various Buddhist chronicles provide evidence that Buddha relics have been commemorated at various times and places throughout Buddhist history. The ninth-century Chinese Buddhist pilgrim Fa-hsien provides an account of the annual festival in Kandy, Sri Lanka, celebrating the Buddha's tooth relic. The relic was brought to the island kingdom in the latter part of the fourth century. Fa-hsien records that the festival was held on the full-moon day of the third lunar month and that it included a procession of five hundred costumed people representing the five hundred *bodhisattva* (Buddha-to-be) incarnations of the Buddha as recorded in the Pali Jataka stories. Today the festival of the tooth relic is held in Kandy during the lunar month of Asalha, which usually falls in late July.

Chinese chronicles from the T'ang dynasty (618–907) describe festivals held during the second or third lunar month honoring the Buddha's fingerbone relic from the Fa-men temple in the ancient capital of Ch'ang-an. Han Yu records that the display of the Buddha's fingerbone relic from the Fa-men temple created frenzied, extreme forms of devotion.

Festivals in Honor of the Buddha's Teaching: In the Buddhist tradition the person of the Buddha cannot be separated from his teaching, the Dharma. It is natural, therefore, that particular Buddhist texts, especially those considered most sacred and powerful by particular schools and sects, would also be the occasion of annual celebrations.

In Tibet each monastery annually honored the particular *tantra* (text) to which its school ascribed special importance, and a national festival on the fifteenth day of the third lunar month commemorated the preaching of the *Kalachakra Tantra*. In Japan the *Ninnokyo* (Sutra of the Benevolent Kings) became an object of a public cult from the seventh to the thirteenth centuries. Annual ceremonies at the Japanese court honoring the text were held in order to ensure the continuation of the dynasty and its welfare. The *Lotus Sutra* (*Saddharmapundarika Sutra*), the basic text of the T'ien-t'ai and

The July to August procession (Asalha Perahera) of the Buddha's tooth relic in Kandy, Sri Lanka, 1970. The piece of the Buddha's tooth, said to have been brought to Sri Lanka ten days after the Buddha attained *nirvana* and housed in the Temple of the Tooth (Dalada Maligawa), is a sacred object both for Buddhism and the state. The annual circumambulation of the tooth relic around the capital is part of a twelve-day ceremony.

Nichiren schools and of widespread significance in China, Korea, and Japan, was also the object of major annual rites.

In Theravada countries the Buddha's First Discourse (*Dhammacakkappavattana Sutta*, "Setting the Wheel of the Law in Motion") is honored on the full moon of Asalha, the eighth lunar month. This ceremony is held at the auspicious occasion of the beginning of the monsoon rain retreat. Furthermore, this event commemorates the Buddha's preaching of the *Abhidharma* to his mother in heaven and the *Patimokkha*, the core of the monastic discipline. In short, Asalha Puja celebrates all three divisions of the Pali canon of Theravada Buddhism—the *Vinaya*, *Sutta*, and *Abhidharma*.

The *Vessantara Jataka* ranks as the most popular story in the Buddhist cultures of Sri Lanka, Myanmar (Burma), Laos, and Cambodia. It is the story of the selfless generosity (*dana*) of a young prince, Vessantara, who gives away all that he has, including his wife and two children. In the end all that he has given away and more is returned as a reward for his charity. The tale epitomizes the Buddhist doctrine of merit (*punna*) that good deeds, especially meritorious giving, will be rewarded. Its popularity also stems from the fact that in the Jataka tradition the bodhisattva's subsequent rebirth was as Prince Siddhartha.

In Laos the legend of Prince Vessantara is commemorated in an all-night preaching ceremony of the thirteen chapters of the Lao version of the story. Noted monks are invited to deliver the most popular episodes from the story. After each chapter has been preached, elaborate offerings are presented to the monks by lay sponsors of the event. The ceremony often begins with a reenactment of part of the story.

Festivals Honoring the Monastic Order (Sangha): The Buddhist festal cycle celebrates the founding of the monastic order and its spread throughout various parts of Asia. It also marks the rhythm of the monastic year, especially the beginning and end of the monsoon rain retreat (*vassa*) and the lives of founders, reformers, and saints.

According to legend the Buddhist Sangha was founded in Rajagriha in northern India at a time when 1,250 *arhats* ("worthy ones") converged on the Veluvana monastery without prior arrangement. According to legend the Buddha used this occasion to teach the core of the monastic disciplinary rules (the *pratimoksa*) to his assembled followers. In Theravada countries such as Myanmar and Thailand this event is honored on the full-moon sabbath of the third lunar month (Magha) and is, therefore, known

as Magha Puja. The celebration lacks the significance and elaborateness of Visakha Puja. Two main ritual acts characterize the event: reliquary circumambulation and the preaching of sermons. In Thailand the traditional text used for the occasion focuses on the monastic order as a field of merit achieved through constant attention and heedfulness. This theme reflects the Buddha's instructions to the monks at Veluvana to do no evil of any kind, be established in the good, and to maintain a clear mind. In a more general sense these three admonitions function as the catechetical core of Buddhist ethics for both monk and laity. Annual popular Buddhist celebrations such as Magha Puja illustrate the interdependence of these two formal dimensions of the Buddhist community.

Particular countries honor the arrival of the Buddhist Sangha in their own cultures. In Sri Lanka Mahinda's missionary journey to the island and his warm reception by King Devanampiyatissa are honored about a month after Visakha Puja with the Poson festival. The major celebrations take place at Anuradhapura and Mahintale, where the meeting between Ashoka's son and the Sinhalese king was reputed to have taken place.

All major Buddhist monasteries and temples also celebrate their founding with annual festivals often lasting for several days. In many instances events honoring the founding of religious centers also celebrate monarchs and dynasties. For example, in Japan the Shomusai festival of the Todaiji in Nara held in May commemorates the death of the eighth-century emperor Shomu and his patronage of Buddhism. In the case of Wat Haripunjaya in Lamphun, Thailand, the anniversary of the founding of the monastery is virtually inseparable from the founding of the ancient Mon Buddhist kingdom of Haripunjaya.

Annual temple festivals have the atmosphere of a fair. Monks can be seen rubbing elbows with the laity as all enjoy an evening's entertainment of traditional plays and dances, local comedians, and modern movies and videos. Loudspeakers blare out local popular music as well as announce the names of charitable donors for whom the annual temple fair is an opportunity to earn spiritual merit as well as enhance social prestige.

The monastic core of the Buddhist tradition is honored by ceremonies marking the beginning and end of the monsoon rain retreat, which occur in Theravada countries in July and October, respectively. The Indian Buddhist monastic tradition gradually evolved from a mendicant form to a settled, cenobitic style of monastic life. According to Buddhist historical legends this change emerged from the tradition of monks using the three-month rainy season for a time of collective study and meditation. Hence, the time of monastic rain retreat, as it came to be known, was considered by the entire Buddhist community as one of particular sanctity and power. Since young men or adolescent boys are often ordained for only one rain retreat period, ordinations mark the inception of the rain retreat period. Collective ceremonies mark its end. These include elaborate gift-giving processions including the presentation of new monastic robes (*kathina*).

In Theravada countries the highlight of the kathina festivals is the presentation of "wishing trees" (*padesa*) to the Sangha. These elaborately constructed structures, to whose limbs are affixed monetary and material gifts, symbolize the trees of the southern island of the Buddhist cosmology that supply the people with all their needs simply for the asking. In terms of the ideology of merit, giving gifts to the Sangha at the conclusion of this period of unusually rigorous training provides the occasion to tap into the meritorious power generated by the monks' ascetical practice. Paradoxically, then, one of the most sacred periods in the monastic year becomes the occasion for an annual, popular Buddhist festival with more consequences for material benefit of the laity than nirvanic attainment of the monks.

Other annual festivals honoring the Buddhist Sangha pay respects to particularly important monks, reformers, and saints, many of whom take on mythic or divine status. For example, Padmasambhava, who brought Buddhism to Tibet, is honored in a sequence of monthly ceremonies: the tenth day of the first month celebrates his flight from the world; the tenth day of the second month, his taking religious vows; the tenth day of the third month, his changing fire into water after having been consigned to the flames by a certain king, and so on. In Japan Bodhidharma, the founder of the Ch'an (Zen) school of Buddhism in China, is honored in a celebration of his death anniversary on the fifth day of the tenth lunar month. Annual ceremonies commemorate other Zen founders, for example Pai-chang's Day on the nineteenth of the first month.

Celestial Bodhisattvas such as Tara, one of the patron deities of Tibet, and Kuan-yin, the compassionate helper and savior in China, are also honored with annual celebrations. The Chinese traditionally celebrated Kuan-yin's birthday on the nineteenth day of the second lunar month, her enlightenment on the nineteenth day of the sixth month, and her entry into nirvana the same day of the ninth month.

In short, events that define the history and meaning of the Buddhist tradition from the life of the Buddha and his teachings to the lives of culturally constituted Buddhist saints provide the primary referent for the Buddhist festal calendar. Other referents are the seasonal cycles and the regnal-political histories of particular Buddhist countries.

Seasonal Cycles and Regnal-Political Histories: The Buddhist festal year also celebrates the regular transition periods in the life of a community and of individuals. In Japan, for example, seasonal celebrations include New Year's Eve Day (Joya-e) and New Year's Day (Oshogatsu), December 31 and January 1; the heralding of spring (Setsubun-e), February 3; spring and fall equinox (Higan-e), March 21 and September 21; Festival of the Dean (O-bon), July 15; and Buddhist Thanksgiving Day (Segaki-e), sometime in the summer.

Of the seasonally based Buddhist festivals none surpasses New Year's in extent and significance. The Buddhist element in various of the culturally defined New Year celebrations takes second place to non-Buddhist, indigenous, animistic elements. Thus, although the Tibetan New Year, Losar, incorporates the great miracle at Sravasti, its primary meaning is to exorcise the evil influences from the old year and call up good fortune for the year to come. The Thai New Year (*songkran*) celebration at the end of the dry season in April includes various ceremonies at monasteries and temples, but its overriding meaning points to the transition from an old temporal order to a new one and, in particular, to magical acts intended to bring about the onset of the monsoon rains.

A combination of religious and seasonal referents marks several of the junctures in the Buddhist festal calendar. For example, in Sri Lanka the seed-sowing festival (Vap Magula), traditionally held for the prosperity of the nation, is coupled with the legend of Prince Siddhartha's presence at the plowing ceremony held under the leadership of the Minister of Agriculture and Development and is ostensibly a firstfruits offering to the Buddha and the guardian deities of the country.

In all Buddhist countries specifically religious events such as Visakha Puja or Sangha-based rain retreat ceremonies are often a part of or closely related to seasonal events such as New Year, planting, and harvest. Through this kind of combination the specifically Buddhist level of meaning is expanded to include the natural cycle of individual and community life. Similarly, the natural seasons of life take on an explicitly Buddhist signification.

Individual life-cycle transitions do not ordinarily occupy a place of national annual cultural significance except in the case of rites for the dead. In China, Korea, and Japan annual festivals for the deceased are tied to the propitiation of the ancestral spirits, which continue to have a totemic significance for both family and state. In China offerings made to ancestral spirits during the All Souls' Feast held in the seventh lunar month were believed to rescue ancestors for seven preceding generations. In Japan the O-bon festival in mid-July includes home and temple rites as well as special vegetarian feasts. Although indigenous animistic beliefs may undergird the primary meaning of annual death anniversary celebrations, a specific Buddhist legitimation exists. According to legend, the Buddha told one of his favorite disciples, Maudgalyayana, that offerings on behalf of his deceased mother would save her from the torments of hell.

The dialectic between specific events in the Buddhist calendar and seasonal transitions in the life of a community has its parallel in the regnal-political histories of Buddhist countries. Thus, the founding of dynasties in countries like Tibet, China, Japan, and Thailand was celebrated annually not only or even primarily as a "secular" event; it was as much a part of the religious history of these countries as the festivals honoring religious founders.

In Thailand, April 6, Chakri Day, honors the founding of the current dynastic reign. The king, who is the ninth in succession in this royal line, plays a role in the ceremonies. Accompanied by the queen, members of the royal family, and various government officials, he first pays homage to the Emerald Buddha, the palladium of the Chakri dynasty, in the chapel of the royal palace. They then pay respects to the statues of the former Chakri kings enshrined in a special building in the compound of the Temple of the Emerald Buddha. Finally the king and his retinue lay wreaths at a statue of Rama I, the founder of the dynasty, and light candles and incense at a Buddha altar erected for the occasion to pay reverence to the Buddha as well as his royal ancestors.

The Buddhist festal cycle calibrates the Buddhist religious year. In doing so it celebrates the person of the Buddha, his teachings, the founding of the Buddhist community and its historical development in various Buddhist countries. The festal cycle's specifically Buddhist referent, however, incorporates other dimensions of meaning not specifically Buddhist in conception. The two most important are the natural transitions in the life of the community and the individuals composing it, and the community's regnal-political history. *See also* Buddhism; Buddhism (life cycle); devotion (Buddhism); Losar; periodic rites; Vessantara; Visakha Puja.

Buddhism (life cycle). All religions mark the major and various minor junctures in the life cycle with rites of passage. These rituals integrate individual life crises into the social fabric of the community. They also relate them to the sacred, eternal patterns of the cosmos, assuring everyone that life's turning points, especially those fraught with threatening ambiguity, will not destroy the fabric and meaning of existence.

Buddhist life-cycle rites are calibrated to these various transition points in the life cycle of individuals and communities. They also express fundamental Buddhist beliefs about the causal nature of all human action (Skt. *karma*), rebirth (*samsara*) and the cosmology of heavens and hells, the nonphysical or spiritual dimensions of bodily life, the intercessary power of Buddhas and holy saints (e.g., *bodhisattvas, arhats*), the meritorious potency of ritual acts and words (*mantra*), and, ultimately, the possibility of a state of being beyond the suffering and uncertainty of ordinary, mundane existence.

Buddhist life-cycle rituals have much in common, but they also reflect the diversity of cultural backgrounds and belief systems that make up various Buddhist traditions. Buddhism at the popular or mass level is inherently complex. As an important aspect of popular Buddhist belief and practice throughout Asia, life-passage celebrations have integrated non-Buddhist elements distinctive to the cultural traditions of South, Southeast, Central, and East Asia. This process continues as European and American Buddhism develops its own distinctive forms.

Birth, Childhood, and Adolescence: In doctrinal terms Buddhism links birth to death or, in more general terms, to suffering. Nothing symbolizes this linkage more pervasively and powerfully than the Wheel of Becoming (*kalachakra*) and the philosophical principle of dependent co-arising (*pratitya-samutpada*). The life process, the constant cycle of birth/death/rebirth (samsara) begins with ignorance (*avidya*), moves through various stages of sense formation and sense attachment to birth (*jati*), decay, and death (*jaramarana*). Birth and death coexist as the last two steps in the classic cycle of becoming or suffering.

From a doctrinal point of view one of the most distinctive and debated Buddhist beliefs has been the doctrine of no-self (*anatman*). Philosophically the concept of no-self has been at the heart of much sectarian debate. Popular Buddhist belief and practice, however, especially life-passage rites, have unfailingly incorporated belief in a soul or spiritual dimensions to the visible, physical world, including the human body. Thus, while the concepts of karma, merit, rebirth, heaven, and hell figure prominently in Buddhist conceptions of birth, life-crisis transitions, and death, various culturally defined notions of soul or spirit (e.g., Thai *khwan*; Chin. *shen/kuei*; Tibetan *bla/srog*) are even more fundamental to life-passage rituals. Furthermore, officiants at these rituals may be practitioners of a Buddhicized folk religion rather than Buddhist monks, or there might be an appropriate division of labor between Buddhist monks and folk religion specialists.

A look at the eleven traditional Burmese rituals of birth, childhood, and adolescence will serve to illustrate the eclectic nature of life-transition ceremonies within a Buddhist culture. These are a pregnancy ceremony, a birth ceremony performed during labor, a head-washing ceremony a few days after the birth of the child, a hair-shaving ceremony, a cradle ceremony when the infant is placed into a new cradle, a naming ceremony, a cloth-wearing or first-dressing ceremony, a rice-feeding ceremony, an ear-boring ceremony for girls, a hair-tying ceremony for boys, and initiation as a novice monk for boys. These rituals will be performed between birth and the age of twelve or thirteen.

Buddhist elements within these rites vary. In some, such as the pregnancy and hair-shaving ceremonies, there are none. Buddhist monks may be asked to recite protective chants during the birth ceremony; monks may also be invited to the home for the cradle ceremony, where they will be fed. A food offering to monks is one of the most pervasive forms of merit making (*punya*). The monks will also chant auspicious texts and may preach a sermon. Symbolic as well as explicit Buddhist elements may appear in life-passage rites. For example, during the rice-feeding ceremony the baby will be fed three mouthfuls of cooked rice representing the Three Jewels—the Buddha, his teaching (Dharma), and the monastic order (Sangha). Note that the Buddhist dimension is not at the center of any of these rituals, however. The same may be said for similar life-cycle rites in other Buddhist countries. In the case of Japan and China, for example, respective Shinto and Confucian elements dominate early life-passage ceremonies. Since temporary ordination into the monastic order has functioned as an adolescent life-passage rite in many Buddhist cultures, and is the most explicitly Buddhist ceremony of the life cycle, it will be discussed at some length.

Ordination as an Adolescent Life-cycle Rite: Ordination into the Buddhist Sangha may take place at virtually any age from seven to seventy. Some men and women are ordained for a lifetime, others for varying lengths of time depending on personal motivations and social ethos. In various Buddhist cultures at different historical times it was customary for parents to have one or more of their sons ordained a monk for one rain retreat (*vassa*) or for one or more years. Indeed, in Tibet it was virtually expected that the oldest son would enter the order. Often entry into the monastic order occurred about the time of puberty. For political and historical reasons this custom has died out in many Buddhist cultures, although it continues where there are strong, continuous, and relatively intact monastic traditions, e.g., Burma and Thailand.

There are several reasons for entering the monastic order. First, having a son join the order is karmically a source of merit; that is, it brings spiritual if not material benefit to the parents. Second, spending a period of time in the monastery is a socially sanctioned passage into adult social membership. In this sense, ordination functions as a life-cycle rite of passage. Third, monastic life is conducive to appropriating highly esteemed Buddhist social values, e.g., discipline and equanimity. Fourth, education is an important component of the monastic life, even more so in those places and times when it was virtually the only educational institution.

As the above indicates, temporary ordination in the early teens functioned as a male rite of passage in various ways. It instructed adolescent boys in the social values of discipline and respect for authority; it taught them reading and writing, acquaintance with Buddhist texts, and the ritual knowledge expected of adult males in a Buddhist society; and, perhaps above all, it symbolized the transformation of a youth into an adult with the responsibilities of marriage and family life. Common lore in Thailand, for example, held that only after spending time as a monk was a young man sufficiently "ripe" to marry. Ripeness in this case implies physical, moral, and mental maturity.

The ordination ceremony expresses the

theme of transformation in several ways. One seems to alter the meaning of the legend of Prince Siddhartha's quest for a higher truth that led to his renunciation of the householder life. In the case of temporary novitiate ordination in which a youth may actually reenact Prince Siddhartha's going forth, "renouncing" the world, i.e., joining the monastic order, has less to do with supermundane attainment than the mundane goal of social maturation and development. In Southeast Asia, furthermore, the ceremony of novitiate ordination is referred to as "ordaining the serpent." The serpent (*naga*) is a Buddhist symbol of both potency and transformation. As the serpent or snake transforms itself by shedding its skin, so the youth is transformed not only into a monk, but later into a qualified adult member of the larger society.

The ordination rite also serves as a community celebration involving family, friends, and in villages virtually the entire social unity. In Myanmar (Burma) adolescent girls also have a part in the ceremony. They, as well as their male counterparts, are dressed in elaborate, royal costume. While the boys have their heads shaved and don monastic robes, the girls have their ears bored. On the surface, gender greatly differentiates the meaning of the Burmese ordination rite—the boys acquire the sign of a renunciant and the girls the sign of a marriageable female. Such an interpretation, however, ignores the fact that for both male and female the ceremony marks passage into adult society.

Was the monastic life exclusively a male pursuit? Although historically Buddhist nuns have been subordinate to their male counterparts, a female monastic order was established in India. The female order did die out in Theravada countries, but it has had a continuous history in Central and East Asia. Furthermore, today Buddhist nuns and female lay practitioners throughout the world have found the spiritual ideals of Gautama Buddha to be an empowering resource for their self-identity in an increasingly violent and aggressive world.

Adulthood, Old Age, and Death: The principal life-passage rite of young adulthood is marriage. Although Buddhist monks do not actually perform the wedding ceremony, in Sri Lanka and Myanmar monks are often invited to the home of the bride to recite protective chants for the well-being of the bride and groom. In Sri Lanka the monks may chant in an elaborate pavilion or recitation hall made from wood and paper and decorated with betel leaves and areca nut flowers. In northern Thailand and Laos monks invited to the bride's home will be present throughout the ceremony. The bride and groom as well as assembled guests will take the Three Refuges (Buddha, Dharma, Sangha) and the Five Precepts (to abstain from taking life, stealing, sexual misconduct, false speech, intoxicants). After the monks chant auspicious scriptural verses a lay officiant "calls the spirits" of the bride and groom, the heart of the ritual. In content it is often a Buddhist homily on the virtues of married life. After the spirits have been called, they are symbolically tied into the bodies of the bride and groom. A sacred cord connects a Buddha image altar with a bowl of food offerings to the spirits. The ceremony concludes in the late morning when the bride and groom present food offerings to the assembled monks, who in turn chant a final blessing on behalf of the couple, their parents, and the guests.

Throughout Buddhist Asia horoscopes are traditionally consulted regarding the appropriateness of marriage partners as well as the auspicious time for the wedding ceremony. Although Buddhist monks might play a peripheral role in the ceremony, for example, chanting auspicious scriptural texts to bless a marriage, in other Asian cultures a Buddhist element may be entirely absent. For example, in China, the Confucian idiom of filial piety dominates the marriage ceremony, and in Japan a traditional wedding may take place in a Shinto shrine. In short, as with other life-cycle rituals Buddhism is one of several cultural variables. In some cases it is virtually absent; in others, it competes with native concepts of the meaning of the life process.

In traditional Asian societies old age is a respected and honored stage of life marked by deferential behavior on the part of children, grandchildren, other family members, and friends. Old age, however, also entails the uncertainty of physical and mental decline as well as a growing inability to function as a responsible member of the social group. The completion of the fifth astrological cycle or the sixtieth birthday represents a particularly crucial juncture in the life cycle. It may, as a consequence, be marked by a religious ceremony. In northern Thailand, for example, a special "life extension" ritual may be held in the home. Buddhist monks are invited to chant scriptural texts to ensure the health and long life of the individual who has completed the fifth cycle. The spirits are called while the subject of the ritual sits under a symbolically potent triangular structure made of bamboo and sugarcane stalks, coconuts, and bananas. At the conclusion of the ceremony the monks are given food offerings. The final chant

At a funeral among the Yi people of Szechuan province, China, 1988, a Taoist priest reads Buddhist scriptures for the soul of the deceased. The priest's cymbals accompany the chanting, which begins the night before the funeral and ends the next day when the coffin is carried to the gravesite.

transfers a meritorious blessing to all sentient beings.

Funerals or death rituals mark the last of the life-cycle passages. Without exaggeration it can be said that throughout Asia this life-transition rite is the one most associated with Buddhism. In China, Korea, and Japan, for example, Buddhism is more associated with death rites than with the other life-cycle rituals. This may be a consequence of the close association between the life process and death in the Buddhist world-view of the Buddhist emphasis on overcoming suffering; or, perhaps Buddhism has been more preoccupied with questions of rebirth and life after death than other religious traditions.

Elaborate funeral rites characterize all Asian Buddhist cultures. In Tibet complex rituals take place for extracting the soul from the corpse and directing it to the Buddha Amitabha's paradise or to a more fully liberated state. A lama may whisper the syllables of the *Bar do thos grol* (Tibetan Book of the Dead) into the ear of the dead person to lead him or her in the afterlife journey, to reverse the planes of existence from the time-bound realm of samsara to the liberating freedom of nirvana. Elaborate rituals for expelling the death demon from the house reflect indigenous Tibetan animism. Necromatic chanting

rites may be held once a week for forty-nine weeks.

Buddhist funerals in Southeast Asia include a variety of activities. Foremost are extensive *sutra* recitations that in the case of distinguished monks and community leaders last over several days. The recitations focus on the theme of the impermanence of life. Other activities include merit-transference rites, including ordinations, feasting, and funeral processions.

The elaborate nature of funeral rites reflects the uncertainty, ambiguity, and threat death opens up for the living. Disembodied spirits are potentially more dangerous than embodied ones. Thus, it behooves the living to do everything possible to propitiate them and to harness their extraordinary power.

Death, furthermore, points to states of higher existence and even liberation not only for the deceased, but for the living. All die; all will be reborn; all eventually attain liberation from suffering and rebirth. The final life-cycle rite integrates and refocuses virtually all levels of Buddhist belief and practice. *See also* Buddhism; Buddhism (festal cycle); life-cycle rituals; merit.

Buddhism (thought and ethics). The Buddhist tradition has generated a large and sophisticated body of analytical reflection that is widely referred to as Buddhist "philosophy." This critical analysis of the categories of reality and the means of knowledge plays a central role in Buddhist practice and the pursuit of enlightenment.

Philosophy as Vision: The Indian words translated "philosophy" often suggest a form of vision. Philosophy can be referred to as *vipashyana* (Skt., "discriminating vision") or *darshana* ("seeing"). Vipashyana is paired with *shamatha* ("calming") in a two-part system of meditation: a person first calms the mind, then learns to discriminate reality from illusion. In other systems of discipline, "seeing" is understood as following the act of "hearing": a student first hears teaching from an informed and knowledgeable teacher, then investigates it directly. In both cases, "vision" is intended to bring the practitioner a clear, direct, and unmediated understanding of reality.

Philosophy as a Middle Path: Buddhist philosophy also can be pictured as a path. To understand reality is to proceed along a path (*pratipad*) or to reach (*adhigama*) a goal. To tread the correct path, a student has to find the Middle Path between extremes. Sometimes the extremes have to do with practical discipline, as in the Buddha's first sermon, in which a person is advised to avoid excessive self-indulgence and excessive self-denial. Sometimes the extremes have to do with thought, as in the systems that attempt to avoid an excessive affirmation of reality and an excessive denial.

Philosophy as Knowledge: Behind the image of philosophy as vision and a path lies the pursuit of knowledge. Early Buddhist sources speak of wisdom (*prajna*) as a key virtue and one that is coterminous with the Buddha's enlightenment (*bodhi*). Philosophy develops both wisdom (prajna) and knowledge (*jnana*) and often focuses not only on questions about reality (ontology) but on questions about the means of knowledge (epistemology).

Philosophy as a Practical Discipline: Buddhist philosophers insist that their tradition is not concerned with speculation for its own sake, but with achieving the practical goal of freedom (*nirvana*) from suffering. The practical dimension of Buddhist philosophy is illustrated by a story about an encounter between the Buddha and a disciple named Malunkyaputta. According to the story, Malunkyaputta confronts the Buddha and says that he will not take up the religious life until the Buddha gives him the answers to a series of questions: "Is the universe eternal? Is the universe finite? Is the soul identical to the body? Does the Buddha exist after

death?" The Buddha responds to Malunkyaputta by telling a parable: "Suppose that a man is shot by a poisoned arrow. When his friends bring him to a surgeon, he refuses to let the surgeon pull out the arrow until he knows who shot the arrow, what kind of bow was used to shoot it, and what the arrow was made of. That man would die before he could know any of those things. The same is true of someone who refuses to live the religious life until he knows the answers to your questions."

This story of Malunkyaputta and the arrow is taken to mean that philosophy should be pursued with a practical intent: to remove the illusions that generate suffering. The greatest of these illusions is the conviction that there is a permanent self (*atman*). The philosophical process can be used to show that there is no self, to remove attachment, and to bring the peace of nirvana.

The Central Themes of Buddhist Philosophy: Accounts of the Buddha's first sermon divide the basic teaching into the Four Noble Truths: the truth of Suffering, the truth of the Origin of Suffering, the truth of the Cessation of Suffering, and the truth of the Path that leads to the Cessation of Suffering.

The first Noble Truth is expressed by the saying that "everything is suffering," a claim that has given the Buddhist tradition an unjustified reputation for being pessimistic. It is more appropriate, from a Buddhist perspective, to say that Buddhist tradition is attempting to be realistic by looking the painful aspects of life in the face, understanding how they arise, and understanding how they can be overcome.

The truth of Suffering is closely related to two other important doctrines: the doctrine of impermanence (*anitya*) and the doctrine of no-self (*anatman*). Buddhist commentators argue that, while some things are painful in an obvious sense (when a person experiences them, they hurt), other things only become painful as they change and pass away. Anyone who tries to hold on to the unstable and impermanent things of this world and not allow them to change will eventually experience them as suffering. Buddhist commentators carry the point further and argue that because things are subject to change, they lack the identity or the "self" that we conventionally attribute to them. The doctrine of "no-self" became one of the most fundamental claims in Buddhist philosophy and the subject of intense debate.

According to the second Noble Truth, suffering comes from desire, and desire comes, through a complicated process called the twelvefold chain of dependent origination (*pratitya-samutpada*), from ignorance. Like suffering, the concept of ignorance has more than a single meaning. To see the world without ignorance, a person has to be able to recognize things that are palpably painful, but also to realize that everything changes and is devoid of any permanent identity. The most fundamental form of ignorance is the misconception that there is a "self," and knowledge that there is no self unravels the chain of dependent origination and leads to the Cessation of Suffering.

The Cessation of Suffering, also known as nirvana, constitutes the third Noble Truth. The word nirvana refers literally to a "blowing out," as if the flame of desire and the fire of the personality were allowed to flicker out like the flame of a candle. The concept of nirvana in its traditional form has a negative flavor that sometimes puzzles Western interpreters, but it is not difficult to understand if it is read against the background of Indian views of reincarnation. Buddhists, like their Hindu and Jain counterparts, assume that the life of an individual follows a cycle of death and rebirth with no beginning and potentially no end. The goal of the Buddhist path is to bring this cycle to an end. Nirvana is not merely the cessation of desire and ignorance: it is liberation from the cycle of reincarnation.

The Path to nirvana constitutes the fourth Noble Truth. Traditional outlines of the Path speak of it as having eight parts (the Noble Eightfold Path), beginning with "right understanding" and proceeding through "right action" and "right livelihood" to "right mindfulness" and "right concentration." The eight parts can be grouped into three: moral precepts, concentration, and wisdom. The moral precepts for laypeople include no killing, no stealing, no lying, no abusing sex, and no taking of intoxicants. The practice of concentration includes a variety of disciplines that are generally referred to as "meditation." Of these the most common and, in many ways, the most basic is the practice of sitting in a stable posture and concentrating on the movement of the breath. The purpose of this concentration is similar to the purpose of the moral precepts, although it has a mental rather than a physical focus: to allow the negative tendencies that afflict the mind to pass gently away so that the mind can begin to see clearly the flow of phenomena that make up ordinary experience. Finally, the practice of the Path calls for a person to infuse this clear mind with the wisdom, or the awareness of no-self, that unravels the chain of suffering.

The Schools of Buddhist Philosophy in India: Given the importance of wisdom in the practice of the Buddhist Path, it would be wrong to argue that Buddhist philosophy belongs to a late stage in the development of the Buddhist tradition. The pursuit of wisdom was an integral part of the quest for nirvana from the very beginning of the Buddhist tradition. As the organization and the curriculum of Buddhist monastic communities became more sophisticated in the centuries after the death of the Buddha, however, the practice of Buddhist philosophy became more specialized, more self-critical, and more diverse. It also generated internal controversies and became divided into rival schools.

One of the most important of the early doctrinal controversies had to do with the existence of a "person" (*pudgala*). In the third century B.C., about two hundred years after the death of the Buddha, a school known as the Vatsiputriyas claimed that, while there is no "self" (atman), there is something called the "person" that continues from one life to the next. Other schools felt that the distinction between the "self" and the "person" was merely superficial and that the Vatsiputriyas were attempting to smuggle the doctrine of the "self" back into Buddhist teaching by another name. The doctrine of the "person" was eventually rejected by the vast majority of Buddhist schools, but not without considerable controversy.

Among the early schools, two stand out as worthy of particular notice: the Sautrantikas and the Sarvastivadins (or Vaibhashikas). The Sautrantikas emerged out of the Sarvastivadin school in the second century B.C. As their name indicates, the Sautrantikas relied for authority only on scriptural discourses (*sutranta*) and not on the doctrinal summaries of the Buddha's teaching found in the third basket of the canon, known as the *Abhidharma*. They viewed reality as a stream of momentary causal elements in which only present elements could be considered real. The Sarvastivadins claimed, in contrast, that "everything exists." They argued that even the causal factors of the past and the future were real and capable of affecting the present. By the first century, the Sarvastivadins possessed a full canon of scripture in Sanskrit, including an *Abhidharma*. They also produced a large body of commentary on the scriptures, known as the *Vibhasha*, from which they get the name Vaibhashikas ("the commentators"). The Sarvastivadins were particularly influential in northwestern India (the region that is now Kashmir), and significant Sarvastivadin works have been preserved in Chinese.

With the spread of the Mahayana ("Great Vehicle") in the first and second centuries, Buddhist doctrinal controversies took on a new dimension. Mahayana texts referred to the teachings of earlier schools as a Hinayana ("Lesser Vehicle") and argued that the Mahayana represented a more complete and more profound version of the Buddha's teaching. When the controversy between the Mahayana and the Hinayana appears in the works of Mahayana philosophers, it often takes the form of an argument about the nature of scriptural authority and the contents of the canon.

In the second and third centuries, with the appearance of the Indian philosopher Nagarjuna, the Mahayana began to develop schools of its own. Nagarjuna's works, including the *Mulamadhyamaka-karikas* (Fundamental Verses on the Middle Way), extend the doctrine of emptiness from the Mahayana scriptures to the categories then used by philosophers to describe reality. The first verse of the text gives a good indication of the direction of Nagarjuna's argument. The text opens by saying, "Nothing arises from itself, from something else, from both, or from no cause." To say that things do not arise is to say that they are empty (*sunya*) of identity (*svabhava*): they not only are impermanent in the sense that they change over time, but they also have no identity even in the present. They are, in other words, completely illusory (*maya*). Nagarjuna insisted that the negation involved in the doctrine of emptiness was the "ultimate truth" about the nature of things, but he also insisted that this ultimate truth had to be balanced by a "conventional truth" in which one accepted, in a practical or provisional sense, the reality of the ordinary world. The balance of these two perspectives constitutes the Middle Path from which Nagarjuna's Madhyamaka ("Middle") school gets its name.

Nagarjuna's works became the focus of detailed analysis by a series of commentators, and disputes arose about his logical method. Bhavaviveka (sixth century) argued that Madhyamaka philosophers were required to maintain "independent" (*svatantra*) arguments. Bhavaviveka is thus considered the founder of the Svatantrika branch of the Madhyamaka tradition. Candrakirti (seventh century) argued that Madhyamaka philosophers should merely reduce their opponents' positions to "logical absurdity" (*prasanga*). Candrakirti is thus considered the chief representative of the Prasangika branch of the Madhyamaka tradition. Both branches were influential in the introduction of Buddhism to Tibet. The Svatantrika philosophers Shantarak-sita and Kamalashila (eighth century) played important roles in the founding of the first Tibetan monastery, and the Prasangika philosopher Atisha had important impact on the reestablishment of Buddhism in Tibet in the eleventh century.

Nagarjuna's Madhyamaka school was joined in the fourth or fifth centuries by another school of Mahayana philosophy known as the Yogachara ("the practice of yoga"). The Yogachara school was presented in a series of commentaries and independent treatises by Asanga and Vasubandhu. These two brothers argued that the Madhyamaka interpretation of Emptiness was one-sided and needed to be brought back into balance. They represented reality as consisting of "three natures" (*trisvabhava*)—an imagined (*parikalpita*) nature, a dependent nature (*paratantra*), and a perfected (*parinishpanna*) nature. They argued that the category of dependent nature maintained the balance that was intended in the Buddhist view of reality as a Middle Path: it did not exist insofar as it was identified with imagined nature, but it did exist insofar as it could be identified with perfected nature.

The adherents of the Yogachara school also maintained a doctrine of "mind-only" (*cittamatra*) and, for this reason, are often referred to as Vijnanavadins ("those who hold the doctrine of consciousness"). The doctrine of mind-only has been interpreted as a form of Buddhist idealism in which one denies the reality of the external world but affirms the reality of the mind.

With its emphasis on the analysis of consciousness, the Yogachara school helped reinforce an important shift in the priorities of Mahayana philosophy. Buddhist philosophers had always been interested in the workings of the mind, but the fifth and sixth centuries saw Buddhist philosophy turn even more explicitly toward an analysis of the means of knowledge. Within the Yogachara tradition, the philosophers Dignaga (fifth century) and Dharmakirti (sixth century) developed a system of epistemology known as Buddhist logic (*bauddha nyaya*) that had wide influence across the spectrum of Indian philosophy.

Madhyamaka philosophers such as Bhavaviveka and Candrakirti liberally borrowed the techniques of Buddhist logic, and a string of brilliant Buddhist logicians carried on lively debates with their Hindu opponents for many centuries until the decline of Buddhism in India at the end of the twelfth century. A measure of the impact of these debates on the Buddhists' opponents can be found in a verse attributed to the

Hindu logician Udayana (eleventh century). Udayana is said to have visited a temple one day and found the door locked. Furious that he could not get in to perform his devotions, Udayana addressed the following verse to God: "Drunk with the wine of your own Godliness, you ignore me, but, when the Buddhists are here, your existence depends on me."

The Schools of Buddhist Philosophy in China and Japan: When Buddhist philosophy was carried to China, the earliest schools reflected the preoccupations of their counterparts in India. There were important Chinese versions of both Madhyamaka and Yogachara. Sometimes these were expounded with great learning and sophistication, as in the works of the Chinese scholar Hsuan-tsang (seventh century), who traveled to India, studied Yogachara philosophy, and returned to spread the tradition in China.

The most innovative developments in Chinese Buddhist philosophy, however, took place in the schools that developed on Chinese soil and produced their own distinctive syntheses of Indian and Chinese values. The T'ien-t'ai school of Chih-i (sixth century) produced a distinctive scheme of interpretation called "Five Periods and Eight Teachings" that attempted to bring order to the diversity of the Mahayana scriptures. The Hua-yen school, associated particularly with Fa-tsang (seventh–eighth centuries), used the *Jewel Garland Sutra*, an Indian Mahayana text, to develop a picture of the world as the interpenetration of principle (Chin. *li*) and phenomena (*shih*). Every point in space and moment in time was viewed as a jewel in a net, reflecting the light of every other point and moment.

Some of the most influential developments in Chinese Buddhist thought occurred in schools that were oriented less toward theory than toward practice. The devotional practices that eventually flowered in Japanese Pure Land Buddhism took shape originally in China, and the powerful, contemplative vision of Emptiness that has characterized Zen Buddhism in Japan was anticipated by the great masters of Ch'an Buddhism in China during the T'ang dynasty (618–907). One of the most powerful thinkers in the history of Buddhist philosophy was the eminently practical Dogen (thirteenth century), whose account of Zen meditation and the Zen vision of the world has had wide impact on Japanese Buddhism.

In the twentieth century, there have been a number of important attempts by Buddhist thinkers to respond to the intellectual challenge of the West. The Kyoto School in Japan, represented by Nishida Kitaro and Nishitani Keiji, gives a contemporary account of the doctrine of emptiness. Nishitani's *Religion and Nothingness*, published in Japanese shortly after World War II and published in English in 1982, argues that the movement toward nihilism that is reflected in Western thought by philosophers such as Nietzsche and Heidegger needs to be completed in the Buddhist doctrine of absolute nothingness, or emptiness.

Another contemporary Buddhist philosopher with important influence is Tenzin Gyatso, the fourteenth Dalai Lama. As a winner of the Nobel Peace Prize and a tireless campaigner for the cause of Tibetan self-determination, the Dalai Lama has become one of the most visible, modern representatives of Buddhist causes. His philosophy is an updated version of the ancient tradition of Nagarjuna with emphasis on the virtues of wisdom and compassion.

Buddhist Ethics: The Buddhist Path includes firm guidelines for behavior. The Five Precepts, which include no killing and no stealing, apply to all Buddhists, including laypeople, and additional precepts apply to monks. The practice of meditation also includes an attitude of "friendliness" (*maitri*) in which monks attempt to serve the welfare of all beings. This "friendliness" can be focused particularly in the role of "spiritual friend" (*kalyana-mitra*), in which monks serve as teachers and guides for the laity and for one another. The traditional emphasis on "friendliness" was further augmented in the Mahayana by the elevation of "compassion" (*karuna*) to a central place in the practice of the Path. The ideal Mahayana practitioner is a *bodhisattva*, a "future Buddha," who cultivates the virtues of wisdom and compassion simultaneously to help lead all beings to Buddhahood. The virtues of friendliness and compassion give a picture of a Buddhist society in which interdependence is prized and everyone functions, in some sense, by supporting and being supported by everyone else.

The virtue of compassion and the vision of society as a network of interdependent relationships have implications for the "just" distribution of society's benefits and for the protection of the ecosystem that have made Buddhist teaching a popular resource for contemporary thinking about the structure of society and the environment. But a more traditional Buddhist image of a just society is associated with the image of the Dharmaraja, or "righteous king."

Buddhist societies throughout Asia have looked back, at one time or another, to the image of King Ashoka (third century B.C.) as a righteous protector and defender of the Buddhist community. The institution of the monarchy in Thailand is modeled explicitly on Ashoka's example. In times of conflict, it is possible for the Buddhist king and the army that represents him to take up arms to defend the community. Many of the Buddhist countries of South and East Asia have been as susceptible to violent ethnic conflicts and political insurgencies as countries in other parts of the world.

When the Buddhist tradition is viewed not simply as the solitary pursuit of nirvana but as a total social phenomenon, with a role for police and kings as well as for ordinary laypeople and monks, Buddhist ethics present a complex picture in which the values of compassion and nonviolence exist side by side with the values of power and force. To focus on one element and disregard the others ignores the complexity and vitality that has allowed Buddhism to thrive as a religious tradition in Asia for over two millennia. *See also* Buddhism; cosmology; emptiness; Four Noble Truths; impermanence; Madhyamaka; Mahayana; meditation; Path (Buddhism); Precepts (Five, Eight, and Ten); Pure Land; Theravada; T'ient'ai school; Yogachara.

Buddhism in China. *See* China, Buddhism in.

Buddhism in Japan. *See* chingo-kokka; danka system; engi; hongaku; Hosso school; Japanese religion; Jishu; Jodo Shinshu; Jodoshu; Kamakura schools; Kegon school; mujo; Nara schools; nembutsu; Nichiren; Obaku Zen; ordination; relics; Rinzai; Risshu; Sanron school; Shingon-shu; Soga clan; Soniryo; Soto school; temple; Tendai school; ujidera; warrior monks; Yuzu-nembutsu school; Zen.

Buddhism in Korea. *See* Buddhas and Bodhisattvas (Korea); Chogye Buddhism; comprehensive Buddhism; Korea, Maitreyism in; National Protection Buddhism; Nine Mountain schools; Pure Land school (Korea); scripture rites, Korean Buddhist rituals including; Tripitaka Koreana; Uich'on; Uisang; Vinaya (Korean Buddhism); Won Buddhism; Wonhyo.

Buddhist Society of India. *See* Ambedkar, Bhimrao Ramji.

bullroarer (term derived from a British children's toy), a flat stick, pointed at one end with a leather thong or strings attached to the other, that is whirled to produce a loud whirring sound; used in religious performances of native peoples of North and South America, Australia, and New Guinea. In Navajo (American Southwest) practice, bullroarers are used by singers or healers to imitate the sound of thunder and ward off negative influences. In the Hopi (American Southwest) Flute Ceremony, the bullroarer serves as a warning to those who might threaten the ceremony's successful performance. Among the Wiradthuri (Australia), the bullroarer is used in initiation practices to represent the voice of the spirit Dhuramoolan. *See also* traditional peoples, religions of.

Bultmann, Rudolf (1884–1976), German theologian, arguably the most influential twentieth-century New Testament scholar. A student of Martin Heidegger, Bultmann spent most of his academic career teaching at the University of Marburg. He is best known both for his investigations of the preliterary stages of early Christian gospel traditions and for his procedure of demythologization, which seeks to replace the archaic Christian mythical language of the New Testament with its contemporary existential equivalent. *See also* demythologization.

Bundahishn (buhn'dah-heshn; Pahlavi, "primal creation"), a tenth-century Pahlavi Zoroastrian text. Two versions exist of this encyclopedia on cosmogony and Iranian epic history. *See also* Zoroastrianism.

bundle, in Native American tradition, a collection of materials and objects wrapped in skin or cloth. For Plains tribes, bundles are symbolic objects connected with elaborate ritual processes; they play an important religious role in both individual and tribal life. In many oral traditions, the origin of tribal bundles is traced to the vision experience of an important predecessor. An example of this type is the Arrow Bundle of the Cheyennes, which arose as a consequence of the experience of the culture hero, Sweet Medicine. As compared with tribal bundles, individual bundles are more closely tied to personal visions. While individual bundles are owned, and are sometimes buried or scaffolded with the individual's body at death, tribal bundles are handed down through generations. The transfer of tribal bundles might be relatively open, as in the case of the Blackfeet, or may be more socially controlled, as in the case of the Cheyennes. In addition, the transfer process may follow kinship lines, whether matrilineal or patrilineal. Among the Mandans, for example, tribal bundles are passed along the matrilineal line and, at least in theory, are held within a particular clan. Bundles typically include items such as pipes, skulls (whether animal or human), skins of animals and birds, body paints, sage or sweet grass, and tobacco. The objects in a tribal bundle are often associated with narratives of origin. These origin narratives sometimes form the basis for ritual processes that often feature a tribal member playing the role of the culture hero, a supernatural being from the beginning of time. The enactment of tribal bundle rituals has significance for the welfare and continuity of the entire group. For example, the Natoas bundle is the central ritual object in the Blackfoot Sun Dance and the Arrow Bundle is central to an elaborate renewal ritual among the Cheyennes. *See also* medicine bundle; North America, traditional religions in.

burial, ritual act of interring a corpse. Cremation and burial are the two most common methods for disposing of the dead. *See also* afterlife; cremation; Egyptian religion; grave, graveyard; haniwa; life-cycle rituals.

Burial Society (Aram. *hevra kadisha,* "holy society"), a Jewish group that cares for the deceased from the time of death to the time of burial. The society originated in medieval Europe. Among its duties are keeping a continuous watch over the body, washing it, dressing it in shrouds, and preparing the coffin and grave. Men tend male corpses; women, female. *See also* Judaism (life cycle).

bushido (boo-shee-doh; Jap., "the way of the warrior"), the ethical code of the warrior (*samurai*) class in Japan. *Bushido* refers specifically to the martial-ethical system stemming from the earlier warrior society that had a lord-retainer system and was fully articulated in the Tokugawa period (1600–1867). Warrior training in medieval Japan drew inspiration from Zen Buddhism; besides warrior spirit and skill, bushido included devotion to duty, strong personal honor, absolute loyalty to one's lord, and willingness to sacrifice one's life in battle or ritual. In the Tokugawa period bushido took on the Confucian ethical idea that samurai should devote themselves to moral virtue and political leadership, and as such it played a role in the Meiji Restoration. *See also* giri; Meiji Restoration.

busk (buhsk; Creek *posketa,* "fast"), a ritual preparation for the four- to eight-day festival of green corn ceremonies of eastern and southeastern Native American tribes. The ceremonies are celebrated at the ripening of corn from green to yellow, which marks the end of an old year and the beginning of a new year.

Old clothes, worn-out utensils, and corn and grains from the previous year are gathered and burned in a communal fire. Homes and hearths are cleaned out and fires extinguished. Friendships are renewed, wrongs forgiven.

A square-shaped ceremonial ground is cleared with low log sheds built on each side of the square. The openings of the sheds face the middle, where men stay while they fast and purge themselves with emetics. Groups of men and women dance during the first few days of the fast. Food taboos are observed by the entire village. No new corn can be eaten until the end of the three-day fasting period, when a new fire, known as "breath master," is started with a fire drill performed at the center of a square formed by four logs that point to the four directions.

Medicine men blow medicines onto the new fire, and offerings of green corn are made to the fire. The women take fresh coals from the fire to start new fires in their homes. The green corn ceremonies end with feasting on new corn and other foods. There are mock battles among the men and singing and costumed dancing to celebrate the beginning of the new year. *See also* agriculture, religious aspects of; corn ceremonies, green; new year festivals; North America, traditional religions in.

butsudan (boo-tsoo-dahn; Jap., "Buddha altar"), an altar in the Japanese home containing memorial tablets, used in the family's ancestral rites. Larger versions may be found in temples or monasteries. *See also* ancestral rites; domestic ritual; Japanese religion.

Bwiti. *See* Africa, new religions in.

Byzantine liturgy, eucharistic liturgy of the Eastern Christian churches. On Sundays and weekdays the Liturgy of St. John Chrysostom is usually celebrated in three parts: Office of Preparation, Liturgy of the Catechumens (Synaxis), and Liturgy of the Faithful (Eucharist). The preparation is performed privately by the priest and deacon at the side altar (prothesis). The public portion of the service is a service of hymns, prayers, and scripture readings. Following a procession in which the Gospel is carried to the altar (Little Entrance), the Synaxis climaxes with the reading of the Gospel and ends with the dismissal of the catechumens. In the Liturgy of the Faithful, the priest carries the elements to the altar in another solemn procession (Great Entrance). The Eucharist climaxes with the prayer asking the Holy Spirit to transform the elements (epiclesis). After communion of bread and wine, the liturgy concludes with a blessing and the distribution of a blessed but not consecrated bread (the antidoron).

In addition to the Liturgy of St. John Chrysostom there are three other services. The Liturgy of St. Basil, celebrated ten times a year, adheres to the same structure as that of John. The Liturgy of St. James is used once a year on Saint James's Day. The Liturgy of the Presanctified is used during Lent and on the first three days of the Holy Week. *See also* Mass; Orthodox Church.

Byzantium, ancient Greek colony founded in the seventh century B.C.; also a term for the Byzantine Empire.

Early History: The city of Byzantium was refounded as the "new Rome" by Emperor Constantine I the Great in 324 and was given the name Constantinople (City of Constantine). Byzantium was selected as the site for the capital of the newly unified Roman Empire because Rome was too remote to be an effective administrative center. Byzantium was strategically located along the east-west land route where Europe and Asia meet, and at the southern end of the Bosphorus connecting the Black Sea and Mediterranean. Its location along the trade routes and its superb natural harbor, the Golden Horn, provided Constantinople with great economic vitality. Constantine built new city walls, effectively tripling the size of Byzantium, and encouraged new settlers with offers of free bread and citizenship. Constantinople's population swiftly exceeded 250,000, and to accommodate this growth and protect vital water supplies the existing city walls were built in 413 by Emperor Theodosius II. In addition to these walls the major monuments from the first two centuries include the Porphyry Column erected by Constantine I, the Aqueduct of Valens, two triumphal arches (the Golden Gate and the Arch of Theodosius I), and the Church of St. John the Baptist.

Religious Significance: Constantinople was inaugurated with Roman and Christian dedication rites in 330. Non-Christian religions were tolerated until 391, when the temples were closed by Emperor Theodosius I. The importance of Constantinople as an ecclesiastical center, meanwhile, rapidly increased, owing to its position as the seat of imperial government. At the Council of Constantinople (381) the bishop was given "precedence of honor" after the Bishop of Rome because Constantinople was the new Rome. This elevation of Constantinople provoked struggles with the ancient Sees of Antioch and Alexandria for supremacy in the East. Canon 28 of the Council of Chalcedon (451) bestowed, over papal opposition, patriarchal powers on the Bishop of Constantinople. Tensions with Rome increased because of the Orthodox designation of the Bishop of Constantinople as the Ecumenical Patriarch and the development in the West of the rival claim for papal primacy over all bishops.

As well as being the symbolic center of the Eastern Church and See of the Ecumenical Patriarch, Constantinople was a center of monasticism and spiritual life. Over three hundred monastic foundations of men and women between 330 and 1453 have been identified. The most famous of these is the Stoudios, whose rule was adopted by other monastic communities and whose monks contributed to the religious life of Orthodoxy through their manuscripts and liturgical hymns. Monks were also a political force frequently opposed to the civil and church authorities over such issues as icon veneration and politically motivated compromises aimed at unification with Rome.

Reign of Justinian I (527–565): Constantinople underwent extensive reconstruction following the Nika riots in 532, which destroyed large sections of the city. In addition to a new senate building, underground cisterns, and public baths, Justinian erected numerous churches, including St. Irene, the Church of the Holy Apostles, the Church of Sts. Sergius and Bacchus, and Hagia Sophia, or the Church of Divine Wisdom. Hagia Sophia, with its large central brick dome (thirty-two meters in diameter), was built in only five years, yet it remains one of the great achievements of architectural history. For over nine hundred years Hagia Sophia served as the center of Eastern Orthodox religious life. The ninth-century Byzantine rite in use at Hagia Sophia eventually became the standard liturgy of the Orthodox church.

Constantinople was devastated between 541 and 543 by bubonic plague, which had spread from Egypt to the capital. The population of Constantinople at the beginning of Justinian's reign is estimated to have been approximately five hundred thousand; perhaps half perished from the plague. The city and the empire never fully recovered from this initial devastation and subsequent periodic outbreaks.

Decline and Fall: The Byzantine Empire, under constant economic and military pressure, entered a period of steady decline after the reign of Basil II (d. 1025). The Latin maritime states, especially the Venetians, secured trading privileges in Constantinople and a monopoly over the city's foreign trade. Resentment among Greeks led initially to the arrest of all Venetians and confiscation of their property in 1171, and then to a massacre of Latins in 1182. In return the armies of the Fourth Crusade, at the instigation of the Venetians and under pretext of restoring the deposed Byzantine emperor Isaac II, captured Constantinople, and for three days massacred its citizens and pillaged the city. Baldwin I (a crusader from Flanders) was made emperor and Thomas Morosini, a Venetian, was confirmed by Pope Innocent III as patriarch. An Orthodox patriarch in exile continued to lead the church until Constantinople was retaken in 1261 by Michael VIII Palaeologus.

The Byzantine Empire came to an end with the conquest of Constantinople by the Ottoman Turks. The siege of the walls began in April 1453. A chain across the mouth of the Golden Horn protected the harbor from attack, but the sultan dragged his ships overland and into the harbor. The ancient walls were finally breached and the city fell, defended by the Genoese and Greeks, on May 29, 1453. This marked the end of Constantinople as the capital of the Byzantine Empire, yet the Patriarch of Constantinople continued to oversee the Church during Ottoman rule and still remains the honorary head of Eastern Orthodoxy. Byzantium's name was officially changed to Istanbul by the Turkish government in 1926. *See also* Orthodox Church.

A B C D E F
G H I
M N O
R S T U V
W X Y & Z

Cabrini, Frances Xavier (1850–1917), a naturalized American-Italian nun who labored among poor immigrants in the United States from 1899 until her death. She is the first U.S. citizen to be canonized a saint in the Roman Catholic Church.

Cain, mark of, in the Hebrew Bible, a mark placed on Cain's forehead by Yahweh after the murder of Abel to prevent Cain from being killed (Genesis 4:15). In popular understanding, its meaning has been reversed, and the mark is interpreted as branding Cain a murderer.

Cainites, ancient Gnostics who attributed creation to Hystera (Womb) and venerated Judas Iscariot, described by Christian opponents as licentious. *See also* Gnosticism.

Caitanya (ch*i*-tuhn'yuh; Skt.; 1486–1533), a charismatic Bengali god-man worshiped by Hindu devotees as Lord Krishna or his avatar and as the Radha-Krishna androgyne. Born Vishvambhara Mishra, a Brahman householder-pandit in Navadvipa, Bengal, he converted to Krishna devotion and received the name Krishna Caitanya. After extensive pilgrimage, he resided in Puri, Orissa, where he suffered the emotional ecstasy of Radha's love, thereby providing the model devotional religious experience. He promoted congregational singing in praise of Krishna and inspired followers in Bengal, Orissa, and Braj to form a movement called Gaudiya or Bengal Vaishnavism (devotional worship of Vishnu-Krishna). *See also* avatar; Krishna; liberation; path of devotion; Vaishnavism.

calendar. *See* festal cycle.

calendar (China). The origins of the traditional Chinese calendar may be traced back to the oracle-bone inscriptions of the Shang dynasty (ca. 1766–1122 B.C.). Most distinctive about the earliest calendar is the conventional practice of naming the days using a sexagenary cycle made up of sixty unique combinations of twenty-two individual signs, the Ten Heavenly Stems and Twelve Earthly Branches. Numerals were used to name the months, alternately twenty-nine or thirty days long, with occasional intercalation of thirteenth and even fourteenth months. Evidently, this lunar calendar was only infrequently calibrated with the tropical seasons (the Shang recognized just two), and then in ad hoc fashion at year's end. Intermediate between days and months is the continuous weekly cycle of ten

days. It appears that the Ten Heavenly Stems originally may have named the ten days of the weekly cycle. These fundamental features of the calendar have persisted; indeed, the cyclical count of the days has continued uninterrupted to the present.

By the third century B.C. the calendar had become luni-solar, incorporating a regular scheme of intercalation based on the metonic cycle, solstices and equinoxes at the midpoints of the four seasons, and the twelve months of the tropical year (designated by the Twelve Earthly Branches) subdivided into twenty-four fortnightly periods whose ancient names recall their agricultural and meteorological origins. Subsequently, the familiar cycle of twelve animals was introduced to name the years. *See also* almanac (China); astrological animals (China); astrology; cosmology.

calendar (Christian). Festival days in the church's yearly cycle commemorate various aspects of the person and work of Christ, the saints, or days of special fasting and prayer. Particular readings, prayers, antiphons, and hymns are provided for the liturgical celebration of these days. Christian worship understood, from its beginnings, that the ordering of time carries theological significance. Having inherited from Judaism a pattern of feasts that were ritual occasions of remembering what God had done in history, Christian worship developed yearly, weekly, and daily cycles for remembering and enacting what God had done in and through Jesus Christ, and for the sanctification of daily life. Feasts and holy days thus give the liturgical calendar of public liturgy and personal devotion its distinctive theological character.

Two primary cycles of time constitute the classical church year: the temporal and the sanctoral. The temporal cycle of feasts and their attendant seasons is christological; that is, these occasions celebrate the birth, life, ministry, suffering, death, and resurrection of Christ. The sanctoral cycle of holy days focuses upon the witness of martyrs, confessors, the apostles and those most closely associated with Christ, and other saintly women and men whose lives exemplified faithfulness in a notable manner. Roman, Anglican, and Orthodox traditions have placed special emphasis on feasts devoted to Mary, known as "Marian feasts," and have retained the sanctoral cycle, while most Protestant traditions have reduced or done away with the sanctoral cycle. Preceeding the principal feast days of the temporal cycle are periods of preparation, involving disciplines such as fasting and special devotions. The temporal cycle consists of movable days (Easter and Pentecost) and fixed dates that may fall on various days of the week (Christmas and Epiphany); while the sanctoral cycle consists entirely of fixed dates on the anniversaries of saints' deaths and assigned days for apostles.

Feasts and Seasons in the Early Church: In one sense, Sunday may be seen as the defining feast day for Christians. By the end of the first century the term *Lord's Day* had become the Christian designation of the first day of the week, now associated with both creation and the "eighth day" of resurrection. By the mid-second century Sunday was well established across the churches as the weekly feast of the Eucharist. The New Testament witness, especially in Pauline Letters and in Luke and Acts, links Sunday with the resurrection. Easter became known as "the day of all days" because it so fully manifested the mystery of Christ's death and resurrection. Some even came to refer to every Sunday as a "little Easter."

The yearly pattern of feasts and holy days developed more gradually over the course of the first four centuries, though Passover and Pentecost figure prominently in Paul's writings and the practices of first-generation Christian communities. These two principal festivals were inherited from Judaism, but were transformed in meaning by the events surrounding the cross and resurrection. Christianity claimed that the Pascha (Passover) now celebrated the actual saving work of the Messiah, and that Pentecost celebrated the bestowal of the Holy Spirit upon the church and "all flesh" as a consequence of messianic fulfillment in Christ.

A third major festival, Epiphany (Gk., "revealing" or "manifestation") was not Jewish, though its actual origins remain obscure. Epiphany focuses upon the mystery of the incarnation: God's Word made human in Jesus of Nazareth. Three dimensions of the coming of Christ were associated with Epiphany from earliest time—Jesus' birth, his baptism, and the first miracle at Cana. Later in the Western (Latin) Church, the feast of the Nativity (Christmas) came to overshadow Epiphany, thus becoming associated primarily with the birth story, leaving Epiphany associated more with the coming of the Magi.

These three great feasts each began as single, unitive liturgical occasions. But during the fourth century they became subdivided and extended into several distinct commemorations. In Jerusalem, at historical sites narrated in the account of Jesus' passion and death, the liturgy of Pascha was extended over a whole week,

Roman Catholic nuns in a Palm Sunday procession while on a pilgrimage to the Holy Land, Jerusalem (1970s).

known ever since as "Holy Week." Each day centered on one of the events of the week, from Palm Sunday's entry procession, through the betrayal and trial on Wednesday, the Lord's Supper and Gethsemane of Thursday (later known as Maundy Thursday), Friday's crucifixion, culminating in the great Easter Vigil celebration. The last three days of Holy Week, from sundown Thursday through nightfall on Sunday, are referred to in the West as the sacred *triduum,* the three holiest days of the Christian year. In some early traditions, especially in the East, the week of Easter from Sunday to Sunday (the "octave of Easter") kept a clear sense of the original unitive Pascha.

Pentecost and Ascension Day became separate feasts as well, reckoned by counting fifty days to Pentecost from Easter, and forty days to the ascension event as recorded in the book of Acts. But of greater significance was the period between Easter and the fiftieth day, regarded by many early traditions as a continuous sacred feast. Many references are made to the "Great Fifty Days" in which fasting and kneeling were prohibited and the joy of Easter extended. Some called this whole period "Pentecost," though it is now referred to as the Easter or Easter-Pentecost season.

The festivals of the incarnation and the birth also became separated. Christmas as a distinct day arose in the West in the early fourth century. This eventually became fixed on December 25, thus generating related feasts on other days: the Annunciation on March 25 (nine months earlier), Circumcision on January 1 (eight days after the birth), Presentation in the Temple on February 2, Mary's visitation to Elizabeth, and the like.

Each of the three feasts developed periods of preparation as well as extensions such as the fifty days. Thus, Lent, which may have begun as forty days of fasting following Epiphany (baptism of the Lord), eventually became a baptismal preparation period for Easter in which catechumens underwent the final intensities of conversion. Advent as preparation for Christmas was most likely in its beginning a three-week period leading to Epiphany.

Thus the three principal feasts of the Christian year anchor two sequences of the temporal cycle: birth and manifestation (Advent-Christmas-Epiphany), and Pascha (Lent-Easter-Pentecost). All other feasts first developed in relation to the mysteries of faith inherent in these feasts and seasons. These basic structures have remained despite many obscuring developments and attempts at reform throughout the subsequent millennium and a half.

The Sanctoral Cycle—Origins and Development: Early in the second century, the remembrance of men and women of heroic virtue began to be observed by numerous local churches. The mar-

Ethiopian Christian priest, on the left, carrying a copy of the Ark of the Covenant (*tabot*) wrapped in cloth on his head as part of the celebration of the Feast of St. John the Baptist, commemorating Jesus' baptism and the life of John. One of the oldest forms of Christianity, the Ethiopian church holds the ark especially sacred. It is usually kept within the inner sanctuary, which cannot be entered by laity or visitors unless the ark is removed.

tyrdom of Polycarp, bishop of Smyrna, in 155 is traditionally regarded as the most evident starting point for saints' days. Specific prayers and readings of particular persons' lives were assigned to these days. Such anniversaries focused not on death so much as on the holy person's birth into the realm of God, now sharing in the triumph of Christ. Gradually these martyrs' holy days became, with the confessors (who witnessed in prison and in exile), established feasts in many churches. Alongside such days were feasts devoted to persons most intimately related to the whole work of salvation: Mary, especially following the Council of Ephesus in 431, Joseph, John the Baptist, and events surrounding their lives. These commemorations, along with the apostles' days, became part of the Eucharist itself, often celebrated at the tombs of martyrs or in churches erected to honor Mary, John the Baptist, or the apostles and martyrs. This may be seen as the origin of eucharistic celebrations for specific intentions known later as votive masses. By the fifth century, lists of saints were incorporated into the liturgical prayers at every celebration, especially on Sundays. Patronal feasts arose to remember the particular saints for whom local churches were named.

In a matter of a few centuries, however, the sanctoral cycle expanded to include increasing numbers of commemorations of saints. Originally the significance of saints' days was directly

A street carpet of flowers, wet sawdust, and dye, constructed as part of the Roman Catholic celebration of Easter Week in Antigua, Guatemala. On Holy Thursday, a figure of Jesus will be carried over the carpet on the way to the Cross; on Good Friday, his body will be returned from the Cross.

related to the saving work of Christ and to the primary themes of death and resurrection. But with the development of the cult of saints' relics and the invocation of saints, the primary feasts of the temporal cycle were obscured by attention given to the burgeoning number of both local and universal saints' days. The theological significance of remembering the apostles and martyrs was overshadowed by devotion to relics, now transported from place to place. Since these holy days occurred on many weekdays, the centrality of the Sunday Eucharist was also displaced. These developments led eventually to the necessity of revision and even radical reform. The Reformation churches all attacked the sanctoral cycle on biblical and theological grounds. Martin Luther (1483–1546) wished to purify the whole liturgical calendar of the saints' days, celebrating "only on Lord's Days and on Festivals of all the saints." Yet he included the feast of the Annunciation and the Presentation in the Temple as christological, like Epiphany. The more radical reformers, such as the Mennonites or the Church of Scotland following John Calvin (1509–64), rejected saints' days, all Marian feasts, as well as much of the temporal cycle. *The Westminster Directory* (1645) declared: "Festival days, vulgarly called Holy Days, having no warrant in the Word of God, are not to be continued," although public fasting or public thanksgiving were retained so far as these reflected actual needs of the church and the society.

The Anglican tradition retained both the temporal cycle and a modified set of commemorations of Mary and the saints mentioned in scripture, along with the November 1 celebration of All Saints' Day, a ninth-century Western development. Ember Days, four sets of three days each for fasting and intercessions in Lent, Pentecost, September 14 (Holy Cross Day), and December 13 (St. Lucy's Day) were eventually restored.

American Free Church and evangelical churches of frontier influence tended to be pragmatic in their approaches to feasts of the traditional church year while rejecting saints' days. In practice, Christmas and Easter, devoid of preparation and extensions in seasons, were heavily influenced by local customs and eventually by commercialism.

Twentieth-century Reforms: The liturgical reforms of the Council of Trent (1545–63), responding to the Reformation's theological and liturgical changes, modified and cut back the luxurious profusion of the sanctoral cycle. Yet by the mid-twentieth century, as a result of popular piety and growth of regional saints' days, the need for more thoroughgoing reform of holy days emerged. Vatican II (1962–65) undertook the restoration of the primacy of the temporal cycle, with special emphasis on Sunday and the christological character of the Christmas and Easter periods. The basic feast days were now called "solemnities" and given primacy; subsidiary days of lesser importance were designated "feasts," and saints' days "memorials." Thus, the oldest pattern of liturgical time, dating from the fourth century, was restored, and the sanctoral cycle reoriented to the temporal. Among the days from the sanctoral cycle, seven were named solemnities, including the Marian festivals, while twenty-five were named "feasts," and 150 named "memorials," more than half of which are now optional, and which involve only the use of a special collect (prayer).

The new Roman Catholic calendar became official on the first Sunday of Advent in November 1969. Nearly all of those reforms, except for the number of "memorials," have been taken up and adapted by the major Protestant traditions around the world that retain a more liturgical form of worship. *The Book of Common Prayer* provides for some twenty biblical saints' days, with lesser feasts provided. The most dramatic development across a wide ecumenical spectrum has been the attempt to reorient the church's celebrations around the pattern and theological meaning inherent in the origins of the main feasts of Easter-Pentecost, with its Lenten Baptism preparation, and of Christmas-Epiphany with its Advent preparation. The central importance of Sunday and of the "economy of salvation" over time, focused especially in the Pascha and the feasts of the birth and incarnation, now provide the practices that are the framework for recent sacramental theology.

Among Reformed, Free Church, and more evangelical traditions, recent interest has been growing in some uses of the church year and the spiritual and theological integration of Christmas and Easter celebrations. Ecumenical cooperation has thus combined with continuing liturgical reform to provide fresh theological and pastoral/liturgical thinking about feasts and holy days. The ritual keeping of time is necessary for memory and identity. The restoration of feasts, seasons, and holy days in the Christian liturgical year, as participation in the gift of salvation and the hope of the world in God's future (eschatological hope) is itself a remarkable achievement. *See also* Advent; All Saints' Day; All Souls' Day; Ash Wednesday; assumption; carnival; Christianity (festal cycle); Christmas; Easter; Epiphany; Good Friday; Holy Thursday; Holy Week; Lent; Mardi Gras; Palm Sunday; Pentecost; Sabbath; saint; Sunday.

caliph (kay'lif; from Arab. *khaleefa*, "successor" to the Prophet Muhammad; or God's "vice-regent"), supreme Arab religious and temporal leader of the unified Muslim community from 632 to 1258 according to Sunni doctrine. Actually, after the ninth century, the caliph's powers were assumed by competing kings, sultans, and, in religious affairs, the religious notables (*ulama*). Shia factions contested his legitimacy on behalf of their *imams*. *See also* Islamic political theory.

calligraphy (China), the art of brush writing reflecting cultivated inner power and literary accomplishment. It is the ability to map black Chinese characters onto white paper creating microcosms of harmoniously channeled *ch'i* (vital energy) often in imitation of ancient epigraphic forms. Since antiquity, when scribes were also diviners and astrologers, the calligraphy of a political leader has been viewed as a sign of spiritual legitimation or control. In prerevolutionary China, people still performed sacrifices at the altars of the legendary founder of writing, Tsang-chieh, and the god of literature, Wen Ch'ang, and folded bits of ancient texts into charms designed to ward off evil. *See also* ch'i; Chinese religions (art and architecture).

calling. 1 In Reformed Christian theology, the grace of God that causes a person to respond to a predestined salvation. 2 God's impulse that attracts certain persons to a life of ministry in the church (also called a vocation). 3 Any grace or impulse from God that prompts a person to a more devoted life of faith. 4 In evangelical churches, the plea that asks people to come forward to publicly proclaim their faith in Jesus Christ.

Calvary, Mt. Latin name for the traditional site of Jesus' crucifixion. Both Calvary and its Aramaic name, Golgotha, mean "place of the skull." In medieval interpretations, the skull is identified as that of Adam.

Calvin, John (1509–64), a leading figure in the Protestant Reformation. Centered in Geneva, author of *Institutes of the Christian Religion* (1536), he is best known for his teachings on church organization and predestination. *See also* Calvinism; Reformation, Protestant.

Calvinism. 1 The teachings of John Calvin (1509–64), leader of the Protestant reform in Geneva, Switzerland. 2 The theological tradition developed in the late sixteenth and seventeenth centuries by some of Calvin's followers, among them Theodore Beza (1519–1605), Calvin's successor in Geneva. In this sense, Calvinism is often contrasted with the doctrines of Lutherans and Catholics, especially with respect to the doctrine of predestination and the organization of the church. The attempt to define theological Calvinism produced a series of important confessions and catechisms, among them the *Heidelberg Catechism* (1563), the *Second Helvetic Confession* (1566), the *Canons of the Synod of Dort* (1618–19), and the *Consensus Helveticus* (1675). 3 An international religious movement of Protestants who sought to reshape society into a holy commonwealth and who stood in the tradition of Geneva but in a broader sense than that expressed in the theological confessions.

In its second and third meanings, Calvinism is found mainly in Switzerland, France, Holland, and the British Isles. *See also* Beza, Theodore; Bucer, Martin; Calvin, John; Heidelberg Catechism; Presbyterianism; Protestantism; Reformed churches; Zwingli, Huldrych.

Campbell, Alexander (1788–1866), Irish founder of the American denomination, the Disciples of Christ (Churches of Christ), in 1832 as an outgrowth of Scottish Presbyterianism. The Disciples rest everything on scripture. Congregationally organized, the Disciples feature a persistent emphasis on Christian unity in their attempt to return to "primitive Christianity" (in their terms, the "Restoration").

In 1840, Campbell established Bethany College in West Virginia and served as its first president until his death. His best-known writings include a version of the New Testament, *The Living Oracles* (1926), and many articles published in *Christian Baptist* (later, *Millennial Harbinger*), which he founded and edited.

Campus Crusade for Christ, a Christian evangelical collegiate fellowship founded by California businessman William R. "Bill" Bright at the University of California, Los Angeles, in 1951. It is one of the largest such groups in the United States and maintains military and athletic ministries as well as domestic and foreign campus ministries.

Canaanite religion. The religion of the Canaanites, inhabitants of the southwestern Levant during the Late Bronze Age (sixteenth–thirteenth centuries B.C.), was the precursor of Iron Age Phoenician and Israelite religions. Canaanite beliefs and practices are attested in two distinct manifestations: local cults centered around small temples in agrarian communities and royal cults situated in cosmopolitan urban centers.

Local Cults: Local temples featured raised central altars and benches along the front and side walls. They contained small stands and vessels for offerings. These offerings were of two types: recurrent offerings of flock animals and produce made at critical times of the two-season agricultural year, spring "reaping time" and fall "gathering time," the latter of which marked the new year; and occasional offerings of animals, food and drink, jewelry, pottery, seals, figurines, etc.—presumably gifts of devotion and thanks, payment of vows, and entreaties of divine favor. Individual acts of dedication predominated; the temples were too small to accommodate large public ceremonies.

The deities propitiated at local shrines, tombs, and private homes were represented on stelae, in bronze figurines, in clay and stone reliefs, and in molded terra-cotta plaques. A voluptuous goddess, a composite of the three major goddesses known from Ugaritic mythology—the mother goddess Athirat (Asherah) and the warrior-goddesses Athtart (Astarte) and Anat—was ubiquitous. She bestowed fertility and protection and served as an intermediary between the people and her consort, the more remote high god. A composite of the father god El and the young warrior Baal, the high god was represented sometimes as enthroned, but more often as the storm god brandishing lightning bolts in his upraised arm.

Royal Cults: The urban cult of ancient Ugarit (modern Ras Shamra on the north coast of Syria) was a highly organized sacrificial cult under the king's patronage. The mythology of the Middle Bronze Age fertility cults was co-opted by the royal cult. The sacred Baal Cycle, originally a seasonal myth, was reinterpreted as an allegory of Ugaritic kingship, including the etiology of the great Baal temple on the acropolis of Ugarit. This reworking probably took place under the aegis of King Niqmad II (ca. 1360–1330 B.C.), who ordered the sacred cultic texts to be committed to writing. Beside the Baal Cycle, other important texts were the epics of Aqhat and Kirta, edifying tales about deified dead kings.

The official pantheon of Ugarit comprised about thirty gods. The head of the pantheon was El, a general Semitic title meaning "god." El was a transcendent deity, creator of the world and "father" of gods and humans. His spirit was thought to abide in sacred places and in the tangible presence of the deified dead. His special affection was reserved for the king of Ugarit (perhaps the earthly embodiment of Baal), who was known as the "fair lad of El." El's consort was Athirat; styled "creatrix of the gods," she was nursemaid to gods and kings.

Baal, whose name is the general Semitic title meaning "lord" or "master," was, in contrast to El, an immanent deity, bringing fertility and fecundity to the land; but he was also subject to nature's flux. The Baal Cycle relates how Baal's defeat at the hands of Death brought about infertility and the collapse of political order. His return, effected by the zealous intervention of his sister and consort, Anat, restored order to the world in the form of Baal's kingship over the gods.

Most of the known Ugaritic rituals were performed by or on behalf of the king, with the aid of many cultic functionaries (all male, except for the queen). These rituals were intended to secure the gods' aid and protection. The best-attested rite entailed a lustration, sacrificial offerings to one or more deities, recitation of prayers (probably to musical accompaniment), and a rite of desacralization.

Popular Religion: No fixed festivals can be positively identified, but there was one religious assembly in which the entire population of Ugarit took part. It appears to have been a mass purgation of sin, intended to protect Ugarit from its enemies.

The people of Ugarit took a lively interest in the mantic arts. Both Babylonian-style omen interpretation (especially liver omens) and the West Semitic type of oracular divination were practiced. Little is known of the practitioners of these arts, who apparently operated on the fringes of the royal cult.

Ugaritic religion (and probably the local cults as well) was much concerned with propitiating the spirits of the dead (Ugaritic, lit., "healers"). The most important of these, Ugarit's dead kings, were summoned by prayers and offerings to participate in a banquet that was an occasion for drunken revelry. This all-souls' feast was intended to invoke the great power of the dead ("the gods of the earth") on behalf of the living. *See also* Anat; Astarte; Baal; Ebla; Israelite religion; kingship, sacred; Phoenicians; Semites; Ugarit.

candles. *See* lights.

Candomble (kahn-dohm-blay′), Brazilian new religion found principally in northeastern coastal cities, led by ritual priestesses and priests under whose supervision mediums accept possession by divine spirits.

Regarded as the oldest sect drawing on both African and Christian traditions, and the most traditionally African of the Afro-Brazilian groups, Candomble is centered at the sacred sites of Engenho Velho, Gantois, and Axe (de) Opo Afonja in Salvador (Bahia), which trace their founding lineages to the early nineteenth century. Although the origin of the word *candomble* cannot be precisely established, its etymology is presumed to be African and given as related to *candombe* from *ka* ("custom," "dance") and *ndombe* ("black"). The history of Candomble is also uncertain, but colonial period accounts of nighttime dances (*calundus*, *batuques*) among enslaved Africans may have been reporting nascent forms of Afro-Brazilian religions such as Candomble.

Descended from African, Christian, and (to a lesser extent) native Brazilian religions, Candomble has primarily continued Yoruban priestly roles and symbolism. It has named its patron deities (*orixas* or *santos*) with Yoruban names of gods (Obatala, Oxala, Shango, Ogun, Oshossi or Oxossi, and Exu) and goddesses (Yemanja, Oxum, and Yansan). Evidence of Candomble's heritage from other Sudanese and from Bantu tribal traditions is less conspicuous. The framework of Candomble theology parallels late medieval Christianity, for the followers acknowledge a high creator deity, Olorun, but invoke the intermediary patron deities for intercession in human affairs. It is only the intermediaries—identified individually with Christian saints or divine powers—who descend to "mount" followers during possession rituals. Other aspects of African mythology have diminished to lists of divine attributes, while central Christian concepts of sin and salvation and Brazilian Indian influences are present, if less important, than in other Afro-Brazilian groups.

Candomble priestesses, or *maes de santo* ("mothers of the saint/deity/holy one"), women of unambiguous African descent, have been significant spiritual leaders in their communities. In their religious roles, these women perform animal sacrifices and divination rituals for individual devotees, as well as oversee all training and calendrical ceremonies. In the central possession rituals, the mediums, or *filhas de santo* ("daughters of the deity/saint"), assume elaborate costumes after entering trance states. Each medium undergoes extensive initiation—lasting as long as seven years until recent decades—before first experiencing full trance and possession by a single patron deity. During the ceremonies, followers may consult with or worship the deity, temporarily in material form and responsive to the worshiper. Male priests, musicians, and council members served in auxiliary roles until the 1970s, when the proportion of male priests and mediums increased substantially.

Each Candomble center functions independently and may evince slight variations in symbolic interpretations. A substantial portion of doctrine and practice has been kept secret because of long years of suppression and persecution by local and federal governments. This branch of Afro-Brazilian religion has been in decline since the 1960s, owing to the explosive popularity of other Afro-Brazilian religions, such as *Umbanda*, and aggressive proselytization by Protestant evangelical missions from North America. *See also* Afro-Brazilian religions; filha de santo; orixa; Umbanda.

Canisius, Peter (kan-is'ee-yuhs; 1521–97), Jesuit scholar and one of the strongest German opponents of the Reformation. His *Great Catechism* (1554), containing 211 theological questions and answers, was one of the defining documents of the Catholic Counter-Reformation. *See also* catechism; Counter-Reformation.

cannibalism, the eating of human flesh. Regular ritual cannibalism (as opposed to occasional survival cannibalism) is a rare religious phenomenon more often present in stereotyped portrayals of another culture's practices than in fact. *See also* Hamatsa; ritual.

Aztec Religion: Although cannibalism was a widespread and ancient practice throughout Mesoamerica, it finds its most famous expression in the Aztec ceremonial cycles recorded in sixteenth-century reports. The ritual eating of selected parts of the bodies of enemy warriors was related to yearly warfare and large-scale human sacrifices carried out throughout the Aztec world.

The Festival of Tlacaxipeualiztli, the Feast of the Flaying of Men, held for twenty days during the month when "all the captives died" by ritual combat, is a typical example. In these sacrifices, the warrior's heart was torn out and offered to the sun, which was believed to be fed by the blood and substance of the human body.

This theme of incorporation of the dead human into the cosmos was reiterated when each captor took a "green bowl with a feathered rim," to "every place" in the ceremonial complex and placed the blood of the captive on the "lips of the stone images" of gods. The pattern of feeding the deities was concretized in the human community when the body of the dead captive was cut to pieces in the home of the captor and distributed. After the body was flayed and the skin worn in public displays, one of the thighs was sent to the ruler of the city. All the blood relatives of the captor were brought to his house and each was fed a bowl of stew of dried maize upon which "went a piece of the flesh of the captive."

This pattern of sacrifice and ritual cannibalism shows the importance of cosmological parallelism in which both gods and humans incorporate the bodies of humans into their being. The recent argument by scholars that Aztec cannibalism was directly related to the acquisition of protein has been shown to be entirely false. *See also* Mesoamerican religion.

canon, general term for an authoritative set of sacred writings. *See also* Apocrypha; Buddhism (authoritative texts and their interpretation); ching; pseudepigrapha; Tao-tsang; Tripitaka Koreana.

canon law, the body of church regulations that govern the life and practice of the Roman Catholic, Orthodox, and Anglican churches.

Cantimbo. *See* Afro-Brazilian religions.

cantor, European designation of traditional Jewish liturgical leader (Heb. *hazzan*). In medieval Judaism, the cantor rather than the rabbi led the worship service. In many forms of contemporary Judaism, where the rabbi directs the service, the cantor's role is limited to leading chants and hymns. *See also* Judaism, music in; Judaism, prayer and liturgy of.

Cao Dai (kou-di'; Vietnamese, "high tower," "palace"), a new religious movement indigenous to Vietnam. Its name refers to the creator god who, together with the mother goddess Duc Phat Mau, represent the male and female principles that give harmony and balance to the universe.

The Cao Dai movement includes political, social, as well as religious aspects. Officially inaugurated in South Vietnam in 1926 with its center at Tay Ninh, it has attracted more than two million adherents in its seventy-year history.

Cao Dai doctrine is drawn from Mahayana Buddhism, Taoism, Confucianism, and some aspects of Western philosophy and religion reformulated in the Vietnamese cultural context. This synthesis is evident in such common Cao Dai practices as priestly celibacy, vegetarianism, seance inquiry and spirit communication, reverence for ancestors and prayers for the dead, fervent proselytism, and sessions of meditative self-cultivation.

The underlying goal of a disciple is to escape the continuing cycle of reincarnation through devotion to the practice of good and the avoidance of evil. One must observe the five interdictions against killing, lying, luxurious living, sensuality, and stealing; show kindness to animals and plant life; and, finally, one must serve society. Devotees view Cao Dai teaching as the most complete and final revelation of the divine plan for humanity.

Until the Buddhist-sponsored revolution of the 1960s the Cao Dai movement was one of the two major politico-religious forces in South Vietnam. Little is known of the current status of the movement and its adherents.

Cappadocian Fathers (kap-ah-doh'shuhn), three Christian theologians central to the defeat of Arianism at the Council of Constantinople (381): Basil of Caesarea (ca. 330–379), Gregory Nazianzus (330–389), and Gregory of Nyssa (ca. 330–395). *See also* Arianism.

cardinal, a Christian designation for the suburban bishops, parish priests, and deacons of the church at Rome. In the early Middle Ages they were formed into a college, which governed the Roman church after the death of a pope. Today there are both residential cardinals in Rome and nonresidential cardinals; their main task is the election of a pope, who is ordinarily but not necessarily chosen from among their numbers.

cardinal virtues, or natural virtues, in Christian tradition, are prudence, justice, temperance, and courage. Roman Catholicism places great emphasis on the cardinal virtues, while Protestantism stresses the theological virtues of faith, hope, and charity. *See also* theological virtues.

cargo cults, religious movements in Melanesia whose participants await the arrival of an abundance of goods and a social utopia.

The Term: Cargo cults were so named because of an emphasis on the acquisition of the kind of goods introduced by traders, planters, colonial administrators, and missionaries. In Tok Pisin, the pidgin English common language of Papua New Guinea, *cargo* (from Eng. *cargo*, written *kago*) is the word for trade goods or supplies. However, the word has come to suggest all the good things for which people long, including a world in which they will live together coopera-

tively. The term *cargo cult* refers then, in popular parlance, to movements that seek to attain a lifestyle characterized by wealth and good relationships. Although Melanesia is particularly noted for its cargo cults, parallel movements are found in Africa and the Americas.

Response to Colonialism: Cargo cults probably have some continuity with wealth rituals and exchange activities that were part of the precolonial Melanesian world. Precontact economic activities such as gardening, hunting, and fishing had corresponding rituals, while reciprocal exchanges of valuable items such as pigs, shells, and pottery were means of negotiating human relationships. Notions of reciprocity informed relationships with human beings and with the various kinds of spirits. In retrospect, it seems that Melanesians participated in the rituals introduced by missionaries to find the "road of the cargo," the way to acquire the goods and prestige enjoyed by white-skinned people. Because colonial administrators and missionaries expressed little interest in the material goods possessed by Melanesians, the way of exchange employed in traditional society would not work. Cargo similar to that of the white people was, it seemed, needed in order to negotiate relationships with them.

Cargo cults proliferated in Melanesia following first colonial contact. In about 1860 missionaries in Irian Jaya wrote a report on a cult that foretold a golden age. In 1877 the Tuka Cult emerged in Fiji with a prophet announcing that the present order would be reversed, with Fijians becoming the masters and the British the servants, and the roles of chiefs and commoners also being reversed. In the following century, more than two hundred cults were reported throughout Melanesia, and many more mentioned in government and missionary reports. Cults have declined since the attainment of independence by most Melanesian countries in the 1970s and 1980s. There is, however, some overlap between the classic cargo cults and both current Christian revival movements and socioeconomic/political movements. Several of the political movements, such as the Pomio Kivung movement in East New Britain, developed from cargo cults. Some cults have also developed into independent churches, such as the Paliau Church in Manus and the Hehela Church on Buka Island.

In Irian Jaya, where the Free Papua movement has been trying since the mid-1960s to establish a Melanesian state independent of Indonesia, there have been recent reports of anti-Indonesian cargo cults. These cults place their hope in the help of the ancestors to drive out the Indonesians. Some of their members also belong to rebel groups of the Free Papua movement.

Characteristics: Cargo cults look forward to a time when the ancestors will return and the colonial masters depart, or to a time in which whites will share their wealth, and the knowledge of how to acquire it, with Melanesians. Under colonial rule, people experienced a sense of deprivation leading to anticolonial sentiment and a nostalgia for the way of the ancestors. A prophet or messiah figure who claims to bear a message from the ancestors or from God is usually the stimulus to cult development.

The cults, like indigenous religions, and like Christianity, which was introduced during the colonial period, are sustained by myths and rituals. There are many Melanesian myths that describe the relationship of two brothers, and such myths are frequently retold to emphasize the ideal relationship that should prevail between black and white people. Cargo cults often have attracted the attention of government officers because of their ecstatic or threatening elements. In order to end the unsatisfactory colonial age and to usher in a new era, existing gardens, livestock, and dwellings may be destroyed. In order to enlist the aid of ancestors and indigenous spirits, adherents may enter trance states in which to receive messages. In order to signal the new age, former proprieties may be reversed and sexual promiscuity encouraged. Such excesses tend to alarm authorities, but in the logic of the cults they are part of the preparation for the new dispensation.

Occurring in situations of rapid socioeconomic and religious change, cargo cults tend to draw elements from indigenous tradition, from Christianity, and from experiences of modern technology. Hence, cult leaders and members may, for example, reinstate indigenous rituals, insist on an absolute observance of the Ten Commandments, and erect telephone lines to communicate with the ancestors. Because wealth and the exchange of wealth are important aspects of precolonial Melanesian societies, it is not surprising that wealth (cargo) should become a focal symbol in the vision of a golden age. The image of ships or airplanes arriving laden with abundant wealth for all point, like images of abundant pigs and shells in traditional mythology, to the possibility of a rich and peaceful life.

Change in Cargo Cults: Some cargo cults are short-lived, while others go through many phases. One cult dating from the late nineteenth century in the southern Madang area of Papua New Guinea began with the attempts of Melane-sians to learn the myth and the ritual that, they assumed, went along with the way of life of the German missionaries and colonial officers prior to World War I and with that of the Australians and Americans afterward. The participants alternately rejected Christianity and placed their reliance on indigenous myth and ritual and combined Christianity with indigenous traditions. Associated with the move toward self-government and independence in the early 1970s, the movement continues today in independent Papua New Guinea, taking the form of a Christian congregation. *See also* Jon Frum; Melanesia, new religions in; millenarianism; new religions.

Carmelites, Members of a Catholic religious order that originated as an organization of lay hermits near Haifa on Mt. Carmel ca. 1200. Around 1238 conditions in the Latin Kingdom of Jerusalem forced the Carmelites to emigrate to Europe. There, Innocent IV (1247) approved changes in their life-style that included permission to settle not only in desert sites but in the towns of Europe. At that time the Carmelite hermits became friars. Hermitical origins and a mendicant status created the basic Carmelite tension between solitude and (ministerial) community.

While laypeople were affiliated with the order from the thirteenth century, there were no Carmelite nuns until 1452. The best-known Carmelites are Teresa of Avila (1515–82), John of the Cross (1542–91), and Therese of Lisieux (1873–97). The reforms of Teresa of Avila and Teresa of Touraine (seventeenth century) resulting in the Discalced (Lat., "barefoot") Carmelites were a return to solitude and a development of the contemplative orientation of the Carmelites.

There are two branches of the order: Carmelites of the Ancient Observance and Discalced Carmelites, with women and men and lay affiliates in both. *See also* John of the Cross; monasticism; Teresa of Avila; Therese of Lisieux.

carnival (Lat., "put away meat"), the three-day period of revelry preceding the Christian Lenten season of penance. The last day of carnival is Mardi Gras (Fr., "Fat Tuesday"). *See also* Lent; Mardi Gras; ritual.

Carpocrates (kahr-pok'ruh-teez), a second-century Christian Gnostic who taught libertine ethics and had male and female disciples; his son was Epiphanes. *See also* Gnosticism.

Cassandra, a legendary Greek heroine, the daughter of Priam. Her rejection of Apollo dooms her to prophesy Troy's fall and other events in vain.

Cassian, John (kas'ee-yehn; ca. 360–435), Rumanian Christian monk influential in bringing Eastern Christian monastic practices to the West. The *Institutes*, a set of rules for monastic conduct (ca. 415) for the monasteries he founded in Marseilles, France, were an important source for later monastic codes, especially the Rule of St. Benedict. *See also* Benedict of Nursia.

cassock, also called a soutane; a long straight black gown, either buttoned down the front or held with a sash, which is the traditional garb of Roman Catholic priests. The cassock can be worn under liturgical vestments. *See also* Geneva gown.

Castaneda, Carlos (b. 1931), author of a series of popular books that purportedly recount his initiation into Yaqui Indian shamanism through hallucinogenic and visionary experiences. Through the invention of a Yaqui sorcerer named Don Juan, Castaneda has created an imaginative metaphysics rooted in sources as diverse as Greek Neoplatonism and Asian meditative traditions with terminology taken from Mesoamerican religion. Distinguishing between ordinary reality called *tonal* (a term usually meaning "guardian spirit") and the realm of pure potentiality and ultimate meaning called *nagual* (a term usually identifying a sorcerer's animal form or alter-ego), Castaneda proposes that true reality is only perceptible through intense spiritual experience and the unflinching effort to "see." Discrepancies in the descriptions of the region, borrowings from other explorations of the occult, and internal contradictions indicate that his work, once treated by some as an authentic and eloquent rendering of indigenous philosophy, may be fiction. Discounted by many ethnologists, his work is often viewed as spiritual allegory, fantastic speculation or, by a few, as a broad parody of American anthropology. *See also* Don Juan.

caste. The caste system, a complex network of interdependent yet separated, hereditary, endogamous, occupationally specialized, and hierarchically ordered social groups, is the distinctive social institution of India. Based on and guided by religious principles, the caste system has sometimes been regarded as one of the only defining features of Hinduism. On the other hand, caste as an institution transcends the Hindu religion from which it derives its legitimating ideology. Muslims, Jains, Buddhists, Parsis, Sikhs, Christians, Jews, secular humanists, and others in India are all subject to the overarching dictates of caste. The basic structure of the caste system can be traced back thousands of years and, although the system is breaking down to some extent in modern urban areas, it persists as a dominant feature of everyday life in the villages where the vast majority of Indians still dwell.

Varna and Jati: The term *caste* comes from the Portuguese word *casta*, meaning "breed," "tribe," "race," "kind," or "color." "Caste" imperfectly translates the ancient Sanskrit word for the social groups of Indian society, *varna*, or "class." There are hundreds, perhaps thousands, of distinct castes (properly termed *jatis*) in India, each with its own local subdivisions and differing position in a geographically specific social hierarchy. Anthropologists and historians of religion are divided about the exact nature of the relation between the jatis, the actual social groups of the caste system as it is practiced "on the ground," and the varnas, the more generalized, pan-Indian categories. But in indigenous discourse, every caste can in theory be reduced to one or another of the four classes (or some combination thereof): Brahman priests, Kshatriya rulers and warriors, Vaishya commoners (composed of agriculturalists, merchants, and traders), and Shudra servants. The varna system is the theoretical and philosophical backdrop for the caste system, and perhaps also provides the historical origin of the latter.

The varna system is the Indian variant of what has been identified as an Indo-European "tripartite ideology," the social manifestation of which divides society into three "functions": religion and rule, defense, and productivity. In ancient India, however, this "ideology" was modified in two ways. First, rulership dropped from the "first function" and was repositioned into the "second function," i.e., it became the exclusive province of the Kshatriya warrior class, while Brahmans monopolized religion and the priesthood. As a result, some scholars claim that in India there occurred a rift between status and power, spiritual authority and temporal authority; others maintain that the Kshatriya king nevertheless maintained considerable "spiritual" prerogatives.

Second, the tripartite scheme of the Indo-Europeans was enlarged into a quadripartite one in ancient India, apparently in response to the expansion of Vedic society to include within it the non-Aryan indigenous inhabitants of

South Asia. The Indo-European "third function" eventually subdivides into the Vaishyas (agriculturalists, traders, merchants) and the Shudras, who are charged with serving the rest of the social body. As the system further developed over time, a fifth large class, the "untouchables" (later renamed by Gandhi the "Harijans" or "children of God") was added to the bottom of the social hierarchy.

The varna system, which has been called "the caste system in embryo," is already described in some detail in the Vedas, the earliest texts of the Aryans in India dating back to the second and first millennia B.C. In those texts, the social classes are presented as part of creation itself, originating, together with all other parts of the universe, at the beginning of time. The "Cosmic Man," or Purusha, was dismembered in a primordial sacrifice and from his body parts came, among other things, the four classes: "When they divided the Cosmic Man, into how many parts did they apportion him? What do they call his mouth, his two arms and thighs and feet? His mouth became the Brahman; his arms were made into the Kshatriya; his thighs the Vaishya; and from his feet the Shudras were born" (*Rig Veda* 10.90.11–12). Social functions are here correlated with anatomical parts: the Brahman priests are linked to the creator's mouth (and thus make their living through the power of speech, through the recitation of sacred texts and *mantras*, or sacred utterances); the Kshatriya warriors are, naturally enough, said to spring from the strong arms of the creator; the Vaishyas come from the thighs (elsewhere the stomach and/or genitals) to associate them with their function as producers; and the Shudras are connected to the feet, the lowest (and most "impure") part of the cosmic anatomy but also the foundation for the rest of the physical and social body.

The classical sources for the theoretical underpinnings of the caste system are in the Dharmasutras and Dharmashastras (beginning ca. 400 B.C.). These texts had as their chief aim to expand the ritualistic universe of the Vedas to every corner of everyday life, to bring within their purview all aspects of what was called *dharma*, "duty" or "law." In the course of such a hegemonic project, the Dharmasutras and Dharmashastras focused on the four social classes, each with its own set of distinctive traits (innate, but also to be realized through behavior) and specific duties. The cosmogony of the *Rig Veda* becomes the starting point for the elaboration of the duties, or dharmas, the creator allocated to each of the social classes:

But to protect this whole creation, the lustrous one made separate innate activities for those born of his mouth, arms, thighs, and feet. For Brahmans, he ordained teaching and learning [the Veda], sacrificing for themselves and sacrificing for others, giving and receiving. Protecting his subjects, giving [to the Brahmans], having sacrifices performed [by the Brahmans], studying [the Veda], and remaining unaddicted to the sensory objects are, in summary, for a Kshatriya. Protecting his livestock, giving, having sacrifices performed, studying, trading, lending money, and farming the land are for a Vaishya. The Lord assigned only one activity to a Shudra: serving these [other] classes without resentment (*Manu Smriti* 1.87–91).

Intercaste Oppositions: This quadripartite social hierarchy is really formed out of a series of binary oppositions that create divisions of several sorts between the three or four classes. First, the Brahman class is separated from and placed above everyone else. Brahmans are enjoined not only to learn the Veda, offer sacrifices, and give gifts, but also to teach others, act as sacrificial officiants for patrons of other classes, and be recipients of the gifts of others. The Brahmans thus monopolized the functions of priesthood and transmission of the sacred Veda, and as the repositories of sanctity, or what has been called "purity," they are the proper recipients of gifts (*danas*) by which donors obtain religious merit. The Brahmans' claims to superiority in these texts (which, by the way, were composed by members of this class) often are quite unrestrained: Brahmans, it is said, are "human gods" to whom all creation owes respect and obedience.

As a second kind of binary opposition within the quadripartite varna structure, Brahmans and Kshatriyas united are together regarded as the ruling classes, with all others becoming the ruled in relation to them. The Kshatriya king, charged with the protection of all others, was to govern only in cooperation with the Brahman court priest (*purohita*), who was said to be half of the very self of the Kshatriya he serves. Although the king is depicted as divine, the human consolidation of the deities themselves, it is only when impelled and inspired by a Brahman priest that his actions conform with dharma. When united, the Brahmans and Kshatriyas are mutually benefited and righteously rule over the great majority of society, the Vaishyas and Shudras.

Third, Brahmans, Kshatriyas, and Vaishyas are separated from the Shudras. It is the first three classes who are regarded as "twice-born" or full members of Aryan society, for it is they who are allowed to pass through the initiation ritual (*upanayana*) and receive a "second birth" through learning the Veda and offering sacrifices. Conversely, the "once-born" and lowly Shudra servants are not allowed the initiation, are excluded from the sacrifice, and are prohibited from learning—or even hearing—the Veda.

This relational organization of the social classes may also be understood in terms of overlapping and hierarchically ordered domains of "mastery" or "lordship." The Brahman, as the superior social entity, is the "lord" of the cosmos as a whole by virtue of, among other things, his control of the sacrifice and other rituals that supposedly have universal effects: "For when a Brahman is born he is born at the top of the earth, as the lord of all living beings, to guard the treasure of dharma. All of this belongs to the Brahman, whatever there is in the universe; the Brahman deserves all of this because of his excellence and his high birth" (*Manu Smriti* 1.99–100). The Brahman encircles within his domain what the texts call "this all" (*idam sarvam*) and is himself "this all"; he is thus the most complete manifestation of the human being and encompasses within his lordship all the domains of the other social classes.

The Kshatriya, as ruler, is master over the "earth," i.e., society and all its parts, save for the Brahmans, who exempt themselves from the Kshatriya's overlordship and demand protection and gratuities from him. The Kshatriya's lordship, then, is primarily over the subjects of the body politic and also over "immoveable wealth," i.e., the land or kingdom. The Vaishyas control the more limited domain of "moveable wealth" of various sorts, most particularly cash, agricultural produce, and livestock. This class is therefore "encompassed" within the lordship of the Kshatriya, for it is the latter that controls the land that was the source for such "moveable wealth." Similarly, while the Vaishya's lordship was over the animals, the Kshatriya exercised mastery over both animals and people; while the Vaishya was lord over his own household, the Kshatriya ruled all households in the kingdom: "The Kshatriya says whenever he wants to, 'Hey Vaishya, bring me whatever you have laid away!'" (*Shatapatha Brahmana* 1.3.2.15). Elsewhere, the Vaishya is described as a "tributary to another, to be eaten by another, and one who may be dispossessed at will" (*Aitareya Brahmana* 7.29). The Shudras are assigned mastery over nothing other than their own bodies, and sometimes not even that: a member of this class is but "a servant of another, to be dismissed at will, and to be murdered at will" (ibid.).

The social classes, then, are each assigned a particular set of affinities correlated to the series of overlapping, hierarchically ordered domains over which each varna exerts mastery. Each domain, and each social class, is encompassed within the realm of the higher, and each domain is assigned to a particular social class because of the inherent traits that class reputedly possesses. Thus, Brahmans are given lordship over the religious sphere because the Brahman class has innate qualities and powers (including intellectual ability, spiritual predisposition, etc.) that are supposed to "naturally" incline it toward mastery of that realm; and the same is true with the other social classes and their domains. These inherent traits are, however, to be actualized through practice or conduct; if they are not, the individual sinks (if not in this life then in the next) and in some cases is stripped of his or her caste and becomes, one might say, an "outcast." Correlatively, if a member of a particular class enacts his or her "own duty," or *svadharma*, he or she will progress up the ladder in future rebirths.

Interpreting Caste: Both the class (varna) and caste (jati) systems are grounded in and propelled by religious principles. The French anthropologist Louis Dumont in 1966 identified the ruling ideology of caste as the opposition between the "pure" and the "impure." The Brahman is the "yardstick of purity" against which other castes measure their own status. Insofar as a particular caste approximates the habits, lifestyles, and dharma of the Brahmans (e.g., the practice of nonviolence and vegetarianism), it may claim a higher place in the social hierarchy. Conversely, insofar as a caste resembles the untouchables and their "impure" or "polluted" ways, it is located lower in the pecking order. The place of the Kshatriyas, however, is anomalous in such a vision of the social hierarchy, for that group's practices (including eating meat and an occupational bent toward violence) would seem to belie its high place in the hierarchy, second only to the Brahmans. Dumont explains this inconsistency by claiming that "power" (exemplified by the Kshatriyas) has surreptitiously entered the system as a "secondary" principle complementing "purity."

Others, however, have argued that Dumont's radical separation of "power" and "purity" is wrong and prefer terms such as *dominance, auspiciousness* (vs. *inauspiciousness*), or *the sacred* (divided into *good sacred* and *bad sacred*) to describe the socioreligious undergirdings of caste.

Others contend that it is not the Brahman who is the "yardstick of purity" but the world-renouncer or ascetic (the *sannyasin*), who lies outside the social world of caste altogether. Among the principal alternatives to Dumont's theory is that of the contemporary American anthropologist McKim Marriott and his followers, who argue that the caste system is far more dynamic and interactional than Dumont allows. Castes are seen in terms of both the shared "bodily substance" (*dhatu*) of their members and the particular "code for conduct" (*dharma*) ascribed to them. These two are conceived of nondualistically as "coded substance," which defines a particular caste in relation to others with whom it transacts. Indeed, in such transactions the individual's identity is blurred and transformed and caste boundaries become fluid and shifting.

The Dharmasutras and Dharmashastras claim that the hundreds of jatis or castes per se, each with its own occupational specialty, arose out of the intermixture of the four original varnas, or classes, (*varnasamkara*). Thus, for example, the "hunter" caste is said have originated from the union of a Brahman man and Shudra woman, the "charioteer" caste is the product of a Kshatriya man and a Brahman woman, and so forth. Furthermore, these "half-breed" castes were also supposed to have intermingled, thereby creating the welter of possibilities that characterize the caste system (see *Manu Smriti*, 10.8ff.).

By offering such an explanation, however, the indigenous theorists are in fact obliged to admit that there are two different, even opposed, social principles at work in India: an ideal separation of the complementary but exclusivistic classes and the actual interrelation between those classes that results in castes. And the paradox does not end there. For the caste or jati system itself adheres to the principle of separation characteristic of the varna scheme: it is a strictly endogamous social system. While the origin of castes is explained as a corruption of varna integrity, members of the castes thus created out of interclass unions are prohibited from marrying outside their own group. The caste system thus attempts to retrieve the apartheid ideology of the ancient Indian class scheme that caste has contravened in its origins. By doing so, the jatis also come to reclaim the ideological premise of varna: the social groups should be separate.

Whether or not the theory has historical validity, varnasamkara does point to the fact that the principle of separation that guides both the class and caste systems is complemented by the necessary reality of interdependence. Although both the class and caste system of India are premised on the ideals of occupational specialization, endogamy within one's caste, strict rules guiding commensality, and the dichotomy between "purity" and "impurity," in fact the caste system (like all other social systems) necessitates a great deal of interaction between members of its parts. Some of these are highly ritualized, like the exchange of specialized labor guided by what is called the *jajmani* system or the exchange of food. For some theorists, it is these interactions among, rather than the essences of, the various castes (manifested in various sorts of transactions) that is determinative of rank. Other sorts of interactions entail complex calculations of the relationship between various aspects of the person (including, but not exclusively, one's caste affiliation) and other parts of the world and society. The "South Asian person" is an entity both more complicated and less self-contained than the identification by caste would allow.

Some scholars have recently questioned the emphasis anthropologists and historians of religion have placed on "the caste system" as definitive of Indian society (and often also of Indian religion and culture), claiming that envisioning India as governed by caste and hierarchy is a caricature produced by Western orientalism. Others have suggested that the caste system as we know it today may be a rather recent invention, the result of either the fall of Hindu kings in medieval times or the bureaucratic impositions of British colonial administrators. From another perspective, certain scholars wish to expand the use of the term *caste* to describe social formations outside India and cross-culturally. In any event, it is certain that the social theory and social structure known as the caste system is still not fully understood, and alternative interpretations will undoubtedly be put forward in the future. *See also* Ambedkar, Bhimrao Ramji; Aryans; Hinduism; Indo-European religion; jajmani system; purity and impurity; Purusha; Reform Hinduism.

castration. *See* eunuch.

casuistry (Lat. *casus*, "case"). **1** A method of reasoning from particular cases to general rules. **2** A pejorative term for specious or petty reasoning.

Judaism: In the medieval Jewish interpretative tradition, casuistry (Heb. *pilpul*, "pepper") is the use of legal and conceptual differentiation to resolve apparent contradictions between talmudic texts. Such analysis assumes that scripture and all later rabbinic texts derive from a single, unitary revelation.

Christianity: Casuistry is a Christian theological method of moral analysis that focuses inductively on the particulars of a specific case. Casuists are suspicious of deductive theoretical approaches to ethics and highly critical of all global deductive pronouncements. At times, casuistry has been negatively understood as a way of making convenient exceptions to general moral norms.

catacombs, underground cemeteries found in Rome, Naples, Sicily, and parts of North Africa, used by Jews and Christians during the Roman period. The artifacts, frescoes, and inscriptions found in these sites are of great importance to historians. The belief that Christians hid in the catacombs to escape persecution or that they worshiped there regularly to escape detection is a nineteenth-century fiction.

catalpa. See bow/catalpa.

catechesis (kat-eh-kee'sis; Gk., "to echo"), the process of instructing new converts in Christianity.

catechism, short manual of instruction used to educate Christians—especially, but not exclusively, Christian youth. Derived from the older tradition of oral instruction, such manuals proliferated after the invention of printing.

Luther's *German Catechism* (1529) and the abbreviated *Small Catechism* (1529), organized around an exposition of the Apostles' Creed, Ten Commandments, and Lord's Prayer, were influential. Other important reformed catechisms were the *Heidelberg Catechism* (1563) and the catechism incorporated into the Anglican *Book of Common Prayer* (1549).

Influential Catholic catechisms were the *Roman Catechism* (1566) mandated by the Council of Trent for the pedagogical use of parish priests, and catechisms written by Robert Bellarmine (1597) for Italy and Peter Canisius (1554) used in German-speaking countries.

Catechisms most commonly use a question-and-answer format. Such manuals were the basic tool of instruction for both Protestant and Catholic youth until very recently. Some catechetical instruction was obligatory before children could enter into the full life of the church. Historically, there was a strong emphasis on the memorization of the catechetical answers.

In the late twentieth century, many religious educators debate the utility of the older format as they attempt to rewrite religious instructional material for contemporary believers. *See also* Bellarmine, Robert; Book of Common Prayer; Canisius, Peter; Heidelberg Catechism.

catechumen (kat-uh-kyoo'men; Gk., "those instructed"), a person receiving instruction prior to the reception of baptism in Christian churches. In the early Roman church the season of Lent marked the period of intense preparation of the catechumens, who were baptized at Easter. *See also* baptism.

Caterina Benincassa. See Catherine of Siena.

Catharism (Gk., "purified"), a Christian dualist movement of the twelfth to the fourteenth centuries. It held that the good god is the source of all good; union with this god stands as the proper goal of human existence. The evil god, controlling the material world, has succeeded in diverting the majority of people from their proper end. Cathars are those who recognize and reject the evil god and who strive to come into the presence of the good god. Avoiding impurity, they abstain from certain foods, especially meat, which is evil, and practice only rites that promote the ascent to the good god. *See also* Albigensians.

cathedral. 1 The principal church of a Christian diocese presided over by a bishop whose teaching authority is symbolized by the chair (Lat. *cathedra*) from which he preaches. 2 A term commonly applied to Christian churches conspicuous for their size or grandeur. *See also* bishop; Christianity (art and architecture).

Catherine of Siena (b. Caterina Benincassa, 1347–80), Italian Dominican lay sister whose mystical writings (especially her *Dialogues*) and ascetic practices were influential throughout medieval Catholicism. She was canonized in 1461 and declared a Doctor of the Church in 1970.

cat-hold doctrine (Skt. *marjara nyaya*), theological doctrine of the Tenkalai ("southern culture") sect of the Shrivaishnavas. Lord Vishnu is said to save the human soul like a mother cat picking up its kitten and taking it to a safe place, without any action on the kitten's part. *See also* Shrivaishnavism; Vaishnavism.

Catholicism (mysticism). In Catholicism, mysticism is the transformation of human consciousness involving a loving awareness of the divine. Early Christianity applied the word *mystical* to the deeper meaning of scripture and to the encounter with Christ in Baptism and Eucharist with the term *mystical body* referring to the Eucharist. Not until the Middle Ages did this phrase refer to the Church. Influenced by the writings of Pseudo-Dionysius (ca. 500), the word mystical also described the personal experience of God. Although later ages read Pseudo-Dionysius in an individualistic sense, his original use of mystical was communal and liturgical. In early Eastern Christianity and in the later Orthodox tradition, mystical theology has connoted the experience of God; in the West, mystical theology has meant systematic reflection on mysticism.

Christian mystical experience is held to be an undeserved, unearned gift, referred to as mysticism's passive quality. Moreover, the experience is ineffable, requiring the mystic to resort to symbols, poetry, etc., to share the event with others. Mysticism involves a knowing even when that knowing is so different from the usual ways of cognition that it is called unknowing. Christian mystical experience culminates in a union with the divine that is a loving knowledge. Mysticism transforms the consciousness of the mystic, elevating the capacity for knowing and loving to new heights where union with the divine occurs. Some modern writers think this experience brings humanity to its fullest perfection possible prior to the beatific vision after death.

Early Christian Interpretations: Origen (d. 254) is often credited with introducing Christianity to a vigorous mystical orientation. Origen articulated the mystical journey of the Church and the soul to loving union with God as an interpreter of scripture. In particular, Origen turned to the marital language of the Song of Songs as the supreme expression of this mystical journey. The allegorical interpretation by Origen of the Song of Songs and other scriptures created an approach to mysticism that deeply affected the understanding and expression of Christian mysticism, leading, at times, to an overly spiritualized mysticism that has not done justice to the human body.

Origen's mysticism did not emphasize the incomprehensibility of God. Some who followed this orientation were Evagrius of Pontus (d. 399), Symeon the New Theologian (d. 1022), and Gregory of Palamas (d. 1359). Eastern Christianity also articulated a mysticism of darkness. Gregory of Nyssa (d. 395) elaborated a mysticism that culminated in a darkness of the mystery, transcendence, and incomprehensibility of God. The mysticism of darkness is called apophatic or negative because the journey to union with God is an ascent that takes one beyond all knowing.

This unknowing is not an agnosticism, but a darkness in which there is a loving union with God.

The crucial voice in this apophatic tradition was that of Pseudo-Dionysius, who was probably a Syrian monk. He described a process wherein all creation became united with God through the created order made divine. Dionysius's *Mystical Theology* presented an ascent of the soul to the dazzling darkness of God. In this journey all that is not of God is left behind through purification, and all ordinary knowing ceases. This apophatic ascent contrasts with the revelation of the divine that descends from God through creation and the sacraments—known as the cataphatic experience. Dionysius has especially affected Christian strains of mysticism in which the mystery and incomprehensibility of God predominate. His impact may be easily discerned in Maximus the Confessor (d. 662), Meister Eckhart (d. ca. 1328), and in the fourteenth century English classic *The Cloud of Unknowing*. Few Christian mystical writings have been untouched by Dionysius's influence, direct or indirect, but Eastern Orthodox Christianity has been the principal proponent of apophatic mysticism.

Not everyone considers Augustine of Hippo (d. 430) a mystic, but his impact on Christian mysticism is undeniable. Augustine used Neoplatonic categories to express his spiritual message, adding an emphasis on the weakened and frail human condition that accentuated the radical need for grace in the mystical life. Augustine also rooted union with God in the experience of the Holy Trinity.

Patristic Interpretations: Gregory the Great (d. 604) was an important link between the mysticism of the patristic era and the monastic world of the Middle Ages. Through Gregory, a doctrine of contemplation became prominent. Later, Thomas Aquinas (d. 1274) taught that the goal of human life is to know God (a seeing with the mind). This Thomistic teaching supported a Dominican doctrine that contemplation is the natural fruition of the life of grace. Out of the patristic era emerged the three ways or stages of the mystical life: the purgative, illuminative, and unitive ways.

The twelfth century witnessed a creative renewal of mysticism. Major leaders were Cistercians such as Bernard of Clairvaux (d. 1153) and William of St. Thierry (d. ca. 1147). Bernard, in particular, gave a new impetus to bridal mysticism. The emphasis on the humanity of Jesus in the twelfth century, especially by Bernard of Clairvaux, issued in a Christ-centered mysticism that flourished especially among the Franciscans of the later centuries. This Christic mysticism was lived by Francis of Assisi (d. 1126) and reflected on by Bonaventure (d. 1274). Later Teresa of Avila (d. 1582), in reaction to overly abstract approaches to mystical prayer, reaffirmed the crucial role of the humanity of Christ in prayer.

In the twelfth century the Victorines at Paris prepared the way for systematic reflection by medieval scholastics. In the thirteenth century Bonaventure provided a theological foundation for effective Franciscan mysticism, while Thomas Aquinas gave primacy to the intellect in the experience of God. Aquinas's defense of the friars' way of life led to his conviction that the fullest expression of the Christian life is to share with others the fruits of contemplation.

The Dominican Meister Eckhart, following Aquinas, gave the intellect the preeminent place in mystical experience. In both vernacular and Latin sermons Eckhart spoke daringly of a oneness with God. Subsequent Rhineland mystics such as John Tauler (d. 1361) and Heinrich Suso (d. 1366) disseminated many of Eckhart's ideas in a modified form. Jan van Ruusbruec (d. 1381) had an Eckhart-like concern with divine union, situating contemplation in the experience of the Trinity, but he wrote in the less complex style of the *devotio moderna* movement, which emphasized the connection between love and contemplation and took a simpler approach to the mystical life than did the Rhineland mystics.

Four English writers of the fourteenth century have received much attention during the modern retrieval of the mystical tradition: Richard Rolle (d. 1358), the unknown author of *The Cloud of Unknowing* (ca. 1370), Walter Hilton (d. 1396), and Julian of Norwich (d. 1416). While Rolle and Hilton also wrote in Latin, all four wrote in Middle English. They demonstrated the power that a malleable language has in the hands of a mystic seeking to communicate mystery. These English writers are down-to-earth, warm, direct, with an interest in solitude and the power of God's love.

Two late medieval figures had important roles in speculation about the mystical tradition. Jean Gerson (d. 1429) reminded readers that in Christian mysticism the soul in union with God does not lose its identity. Nicholas of Cusa (d. 1464) kept before western minds the incomprehensibility of God.

Sixteenth-century Interpretations: Catholic reform in sixteenth-century Spain turned to the mystical tradition. Ignatius of Loyola (d. 1556), founder of the Jesuits, was manifestly more mystical than early commentators pictured him.

Teresa of Avila, the first woman Doctor of the Catholic Church, in her efforts to reform the Carmelites, retrieved the order's original emphasis on solitude and its late medieval mystical inclinations. Teresa wrote vividly and warmly about her mystical experience in *The Interior Castle, The Book of Her Life*, and other writings. She taught her followers a contemplative way of life as preparation for God's mystical graces. She also made clear that God could do what humans were unable to do on the mystical journey. To reform the Carmelite men, Teresa enlisted the help of John of the Cross (d. 1591). Some of John's poetry (for example, "Dark Night") were reports of his mystical experiences. Written for those for whom he acted as spiritual director, his commentaries are explanations of his poetry. John of the Cross's doctrine was little heeded during the centuries when much of Catholicism neglected its mystical tradition. In the twentieth century, Spanish poets rediscovered John of the Cross's poetry. The fourth centenary, in 1991, of his death, has been an occasion for a retrieval of John's mystical doctrine.

Seventeeth- and Eighteenth-century Interpretations: Seventeenth-century France witnessed an intense interest in mysticism. Benedict Canfield (d. 1610), Madame Acarie (d. 1618), Francis de Sales (d. 1622), and Pierre de Berulle (d. 1629) were major figures in this renewal. However, the seventeenth century also gave birth to movements that ran counter to mysticism. Jansenism, with its pessimism about human potential and its harsh rigorism, left little space for a mysticism of love. Quietism's distrust of human effort took passivity to the extreme. The Enlightenment of the eighteenth century and subsequent rationalism drove mysticism into the background of Catholic life.

Recent Interpretations: The post–Vatican II Catholic mystical revival has recognized that the Bible must play a more foundational role in the development of mystical theology. Not only certain biblical experiences like the theophanies to Moses and Elijah but the whole biblical message must be brought to bear as a primary context for spiritual and mystical experience. Christian mysticism has not always kept itself centered on Christ. A vital liturgical life is also necessary to keep mysticism rooted in the life of the church and connected with the sacraments, especially baptism and the Eucharist. Since Neoscholasticism failed to integrate its mystical doctrine with patristic theology, the foundational mystical teachings of the Fathers must also be recovered.

Women's mystical experience has been an integral but sometimes neglected part of the

Christian tradition. However, the women's movement has given an impetus to study more closely the mystical experience of women. In addition to the women mentioned earlier, attention has turned to women such as Elizabeth of Schonau (d. 1164), Hildegard of Bingen (d. 1179), Hadewijch of Antwerp (thirteenth century), Mechthild of Magdeburg (d. 1282/1298), Mechthild of Hackeborn (d. 1299), Gertrude of Helfta (d. ca. 1302), Angela of Foligno (d. 1309), Bridget of Sweden (d. 1373), Catherine of Siena (d. 1380, who was the second and last woman declared a Doctor of the Church), Catherine of Genoa (d. 1510), Mary Magdalen de Pazzi (d. 1607), Jeanne de Chantal (d. 1641), Marie of the Incarnation (d. 1672, who spent thirty-two years in North America), Therese Martin (d. 1897), Elizabeth of the Trinity (d. 1906), and Edith Stein (d. 1942, martyr at Auschwitz). These are only some of the women who have left reports of their mystical experiences or who have explored the meaning of mysticism in the Christian life. When the experience of these female mystics has been more fully investigated, the mystical tradition will be richer and may contain elements that can, from a mystical perspective, creatively address doctrinal and ethical issues.

In the 1960s a desire arose for a more contemplative and mystical life. Many turned to oriental mystical traditions. Thomas Merton (d. 1968) signaled a new era. He introduced English-speakers to a forgotten mysticism and to the importance of dialogue between Christian and non-Christian mystical traditions. The most influential Catholic theologian of the twentieth century, Karl Rahner (d. 1984), not only argued that theology needs mysticism as a resource but that "the devout Christian of the future will . . . be a mystic." *See also* Bernard of Clairvaux; Bonaventura; Bridget of Sweden; Catherine of Siena; Eckhart, John "Meister"; Francis of Assisi; Hildegard of Bingen; Joachim of Fiore; John of the Cross; Julian of Norwich; Lull, Raymond; Molinos, Miguel de; mysticism; Ruusbruec, Jan van; Suso, Heinrich; Tauler, John; Teresa of Avila; Therese of Lisieux.

Catholicism, Roman, the largest of the three major Christian subdivisions (Catholicism, Protestantism, and Orthodoxy). Prior to the mutual bans exchanged by Latins and Greeks in 1054, there were no such subdivisions (though there were many tensions). The Protestant Reformation of the sixteenth century established divisions in the Western church, leading eventually to the designation of those who remained loyal to the pope as "Roman Catholics." This term *catholicism* designates a general ideal of the entire Christian religion expressing its desire for wholeness and community in virtue of which it tries to live. For Roman Catholicism, such wholeness centers in the historic community of Rome, with its leader the pope (thought of as the successor of Peter). While there is debate, in general terms Roman Catholicism adheres to the organization and interpretation of Christian tradition in which the Bishop of Rome is the paramount Church authority.

Early History: New Testament scholars point to indications that early Christians struggled with matters of doctrine, morality, and authority. In writings such as the second-century Pastoral Epistles, the later followers of Paul stressed the office of the presbyter (priest-bishop) as the authoritative voice for settling church disputes. In the early Christian centuries, the role of the bishop, around whom the community usually gathered, was significant. The bishop presided over the weekly Eucharist, served as an official teacher, and maintained the community's continuous link to the disciples of Jesus ("apostolic succession"). Bishops were elected by the entire community, but had to be consecrated by fellow bishops.

Church centers such as Jerusalem, Rome, Antioch, and Alexandria gradually came to be Christian capitals in their geographical areas. The heads of those churches were consulted in matters of dispute, and their teachings carried special weight. The tradition that Peter and Paul, working to establish a Christian community at the center of the first-century world, had died in Rome helped to give the Roman church a special cachet. In the doctrinal debates of the fourth and fifth centuries, the opinion of the heads of the Roman church carried special force, and a consensus developed that the Roman church had the leading reputation for solid faith (orthodoxy). From the respect and deference that the Roman bishops garnered over the centuries, the medieval popes (perhaps beginning with Gregory I at the end of the sixth century) began to assert widening claims to jurisdiction over the whole Church. By the time of the schism between East and West in the eleventh century, these claims, along with numerous differences in ecclesiastical style, history, and cultural conditions (for example, the rise of Islam), persuaded many Easterners (Byzantines) that their collegial traditions were threatened by Roman monarchical views of the papacy.

Post-Reformation: During the Protestant Reformation of the sixteenth century, the moral squalor attached to the papacy of the prior two centuries turned many Westerners away from loyalty to the pope. Martin Luther and others saw the pope as the Antichrist, and even those who did not accept this charge could find religious or political reasons for separating from allegiance to Rome.

Roman Catholicism reformed itself during the Council of Trent (1545–63), and since that time some of its distinctive features have reflected its competition with Protestantism and, to a lesser extent, Eastern Orthodoxy. In doctrinal matters, Roman Catholics have followed Thomas Aquinas (ca. 1225–74) and Trent, qualifying the Protestant Reformers' attacks on reason, works, monasticism, the sacrifice of the Mass, the system of seven sacraments, and the organization of the Church as a hierarchy, with the pope and bishops at the top and the laity at the bottom.

Roman Catholicism became even more monarchical during the nineteenth century, when the special prerogatives of the pope were defined at the First Council of the Vatican (1869–70) to include infallibility (under restricted circumstances). On the whole, the Roman Catholic posture during the seventeenth through nineteenth centuries was strongly conservative, regarding modern scientific and political developments as more harmful than beneficial. Only at the Second Council of the Vatican (1962–65) did Roman Catholicism, under the leadership of Popes John XXIII and Paul VI, initiate officially a dialogue with the modern world. The implications of this Council are still felt throughout Roman Catholic churches.

Roman Catholicism in the Twentieth Century: In the late twentieth century, Roman Catholicism continues to be distinctive for advocating the primacy of the Bishop of Rome over the entire Christian community, although ecumenical discussions with various Protestant and Orthodox groups have produced considerable agreement about the terms under which such primacy might be acceptable to those other groups. Virtually all participants agree that Jesus gave Peter a special place in the "college" of the apostles. Beyond that scholars must consult subsequent history to find indications of how the ministry of Peter would continue through his successors at the head of the Church in Rome. There is much agreement that the high visibility of Pope John Paul II (1978–) gives the Church a natural spokesman. What authority such a spokesman ought to have in a reunited Church is still under debate.

With Eastern Orthodoxy, Roman Catholicism stresses a sacramental view of church life, the position that grace perfects a good human nature, and the legitimacy of the monastic vocation. The modern popes, through their encyclicals on social issues, have made Roman Catholicism both internationalist and committed to a middle way between socialism and capitalism. With Eastern Orthodoxy, Roman Catholicism continues to deny priestly ordination to women. Its moral teachings on sexual matters, including abortion, tend to be more restrictive than those of other traditions, but many Catholic laity increasingly feel they have the right to make their own decisions on such matters. *See also* Counter-Reformation; Orthodox Church; papacy; Protestantism; sacraments and ordinances (Christianity); Scholasticism; tradition; Vatican Council, Second.

Catholicism in Korea, Roman. *See* Korea, Roman Catholicism in.

catholicity, in Christian creeds, one of the characteristics of the church ("I believe in the one, holy, catholic, and apostolic Church"). The term signifies that the church has a universal mission to preach to the whole world; that all people are called upon to hear the gospel; that the church transcends all social and national limits; and that the church is present in the whole world.

Catholic Workers, a social reform movement founded by Dorothy Day and Peter Maurin in New York City in 1933. The movement is best known for its commitment to pacifism; its support for the working class; its establishment of "Houses of Hospitality," which feed, clothe, and shelter the poor; and its monthly paper, *The Catholic Worker*, which examines issues in social justice.

Cayce, Edgar (1877–1945), a famous American healer and prophet, believed to have a remarkable medical diagnostic ability in trance. A devout Christian, Cayce also presented teaching concerning Atlantis, reincarnation, and coming catastrophic changes in the Earth. The Association for Research and Enlightenment was founded in 1932 to preserve and transmit his teachings.

C.E. *See* B.C.E./C.E.

Celestial Masters Taoism. *See* T'ien-shih Taoism.

celibacy, remaining unmarried as part of a religious vocation. Most frequently celibacy is required for priesthood or membership in religious associations. *See also* abstinence; asceticism; bhiksu/bhiksuni; Brahma Kumari; chastity; monasticism.

Christianity: Being unmarried, as well as abstaining from all sexual relations, is a requirement of male and female Christian monastic life. Roman Catholic parish priests are celibate; Orthodox priests are not. However, in the Orthodox Church and the Eastern rites of the Catholic Church, bishops are chosen from monastic (i.e., celibate) clergy only. *See also* clergy; monasticism.

Celtic church, the Christianity that existed among the Celtic peoples of Britain and Ireland from the second century prior to the Synod of Whitby (664), at which Celtic Christians in Britain submitted to Roman ecclesiastical authority and custom. Distinctive Celtic liturgical uses persisted in parts of Ireland and Scotland until the eleventh and twelfth centuries.

Celtic religion. The Celts were speakers of a family of Indo-European languages distributed in the late centuries B.C. across much of western and central Europe; however, in the first centuries A.D. they were confined primarily to the British Isles and France. The surviving Celtic languages are Welsh, Breton, Irish, and Scottish Gaelic; Manx and Cornish died out in the recent past.

Sources: There are extensive material remains, but it is difficult to reconstruct religion on this basis. Several dedicatory inscriptions have been recovered, but their detailed interpretation remains uncertain. Apart from contemporaneous statements by Greek and Roman authors, scholars depend primarily on sources subsequent to the conversion of the Celtic peoples to Christianity—literature from the medieval period and oral traditions collected over the last few centuries. Such material is abundant, and clearly preserves much from the pre-Christian past. This is particularly the case in Ireland, where the compilation of antiquarian lore was one of the main preoccupations of the learned classes and where pre-Christian beliefs and practices continued at every level of society. Evidence of this kind must, however, be treated with caution, for it reaches us through the medium of a new religion in a culture exposed to many foreign influences.

Rituals: Bodies of water, groves, islands, and elevations (natural or artificial) were all used as cult sites by the Celts and have retained potent supernatural associations in later tradition. Many deposits of precious objects in lakes and rivers have been recovered, indicating that water

was an important channel of communication with the gods; indeed, many European river names can be shown to have been originally the names of Celtic goddesses. According to the classical authors, human sacrifice was a widespread and highly regarded practice, employed both to propitiate the supernatural and to foretell the future.

Sacrifices were performed by the *druids,* members of a priestly class that also included poets, legal experts, and diviners. These professionals preserved among themselves an extensive body of memorized esoteric lore and were regarded as authorities on such subjects as myth, prophecy, and the afterlife. There is less clear evidence concerning the rest of the population. Some votive inscriptions seem to reflect the activities of groups outside the druidic hierarchy. In later times, popular cults and practices survived long after the official suppression of the druids.

Beliefs: As noted above, a close connection existed between the gods and prominent features of the landscape. This is reflected in folklore concerning the special properties of places frequented by the fairies. In Ireland the gods were especially associated with burial mounds (Old Irish, *side,* sing. *sid*), and came to be referred to as "the people of the sid." The fertility of the land was held to depend upon friendly relations with the supernatural; this idea is embodied particularly clearly in the belief, attested in various forms among all the Celtic peoples, that a ruler was confirmed in his kingship by mating symbolically with the goddess of his territory.

The gods were also considered to be the sources of all skill and knowledge. The first-century B.C. Roman leader Julius Caesar stated that the principal divinity of the continental Celts was regarded as "the inventor of all the arts." This is evidently a reference to the god Lugus/Lugh, the only deity known under the same name throughout the Celtic world. Various sources mention more specialized figures: gods of poetry, metallurgy, medicine, etc.

The most famous druidic doctrine concerned the immortality of the soul, and the medieval evidence reflects various beliefs concerning the afterlife: there are traces of an idea of reincarnation, but also references to an eternal realm inhabited by the dead and visited sometimes by the living. Grave goods from the early period, such as aristocratic ornaments, weapons, and feasting equipment, suggest that the Celts imagined an afterworld not very different from the life they knew.

Significance: The literature of the medieval Celts exercised considerable influence on that of Europe generally. This was especially true in the case of the Arthurian legend cycle. In this way, many themes traceable ultimately to Celtic religion found their way into the mainstream of Western culture. Considered for their own sake, the Celtic traditions are particularly remarkable for their antiquity, versatility, and cohesion: the complex interplay of native and foreign elements over many centuries is a rich and rewarding field of study. *See also* druid; Indo-European religion; Tain.

cemetery. *See* grave, graveyard.

centaur (sen'tawr), a Greek mythological creature, half man, half horse. Centaurs are typically wild and lustful, but an exception is Chiron, educator of heroes.

Cerberos (suhr'buhr-uhs), the mythological three-headed dog who guards the entrance to the Greek underworld, preventing the dead from leaving or the living from entering. *See also* Hades.

ceremony. *See* ritual.

Ceres (seer'eez), the Roman goddess of grain, analogue of the Greek goddess Demeter.

chai (j*i*; Chin., "fast"). **1** In Taoism, rites of fasting, repentance, or purification. The term refers to rites on behalf of the living and the dead, including exorcism, protection from illness, securing houses, and recitations for salvation. Unlike related folk rites involving animal sacrifice and alcohol, the Taoist rite stresses the offering of petitions and confessing of sins. *See also* fasting. **2** In Chinese Buddhism, a vegetarian meal celebrated on festal occasions such as the Buddha's or the emperor's birthday. It is frequently offered to the monastic community by lay donors in order to make merit, which is often then transferred to deceased relatives. *See also* almsgiving; merit; ritual; Sangha; vegetarianism. **3** Buddhists use the term for the periodic *upposadha* (Skt.) rites at which lay Buddhists assemble to confess sins and recite the precepts.

chakras (chuhk'ruhz; Skt., "wheels", "circles"), in Indic systems, vortexes of energy in the subtle (non-physiological) body. In Hindu and Buddhist Tantrism, *chakras* lie along the spine on three entwined channels of vital energy. One scheme counts six chakras: base of the spine, *mulad-*

hara; genitals, *svadhishthana*; navel, *manipura*; heart, *anahata*; throat, *vishuddha*; and between the eyebrows, *ajna*. The seventh or transcendent chakra above the head (*sahasrara*) is the terminus for the subtle energy, called *kundalini*, that ascends from the muladhara up through the various chakras. Each chakra is likened to a lotus with a set number of petals and is associated with a deity, Sanskrit alphabetic sounds, and geometric shapes and colors. *See also* kundalini; Tantra; Tantrism (Buddhism).

Chalcedon, Council of, the fourth Christian ecumenical council, convened by the emperor Marcian in 451 to abate christological controversies and bring political peace to the Christian Roman Empire. Chalcedon's christological decree employed novel, nonbiblical terms to exclude rival views and carve out a middle ground for an orthodox understanding of Christ. Excluded was the unqualified statement that the Logos assumed a complete human nature, a view that could suggest there were two Sons; also rejected was the simple assertion that the Logos assumed human flesh, such that the human would disappear in the power of the divine nature. Between these extreme views, Chalcedon asserts the existence of one Person (Gk. *prosopon*) or substance (*hypostasis*), acknowledging the existence of two natures united without separation but also without confusion. The Chalcedonian definition set the standard for most orthodox Christology down to the present day. *See also* Christology.

Chaldeans, Semitic-speaking people of the first millennium B.C., renowned in Western tradition for their astrological and occult wisdom.

chalice, in Christianity, the wine cup used in the eucharistic service. *See also* Eucharist, Christian.

Chang Chueh (jahng jweh; d. 184), the leader of the T'ai-p'ing Tao movement, important in the rise of religious Taoism. *See also* T'ai-p'ing Tao.

Chang Hsiu (jahng shyoh; d. ca. 188–191), an important figure in the early history of the Five Pecks of Rice movement. *See also* Wu-tou-mi Tao.

Changing Woman, figure common to Apache and Navajo (Native North America) mythology and ritual. The Apache alternatively call her White Painted Lady. In both cultures, Changing Woman is born after the mythic ancestors complete their journey through the lower worlds and emerge onto the present earth's surface. Changing Woman, sometimes with a twin sister, is impregnated by the rays of the sun and by water dripping into her vagina. She gives birth to twin sons, Enemy Slayer and Born for Water. These warrior twins want to know the identity of their father, but Changing Woman refuses to tell them. Long story cycles describe the journey of the twins searching for their father, the sun. When they arrive at Sun's home, he tests the boys to determine that they are his sons before he equips them as warriors. They return to the Earth to slay the monsters, preparing the way for human habitation.

Changing Woman is the creator of the first Navajo ancestors. She is synonymous with time and seasonal cycles in that she progressively moves through her life cycle. She is wholly benevolent and the central figure in the most common of Navajo ceremonials, Blessingway. In both cultures Changing Woman serves as a model for women. She is central to girls' puberty rites, and she is relevant to all matters of creativity. *See also* myth; North America, traditional religions in; twin myth.

Chang Lu (jahng *loo;* fl. 184–220), figure associated with the Five Pecks of Rice movement, important in the early history of religious Taoism. *See also* Wu-tou-mi Tao.

Chang Po-tuan (jahng bwoh-dwahn; 983–1082), Chinese writer on "inner alchemy" and reputed founder of the "Southern Lineage" of Taoism. *See also* alchemy; Taoism.

Chang San-feng (jahng sahn fuhng), a legendary figure, canonized in 1459, known as a Taoist internal alchemy master who performed magical feats and created the *t'ai-chi ch'uan* martial art system. He is associated with a spirit medium cult and a collection of revealed writings. *See also* alchemy; t'ai-chi ch'uan.

Chang Tao-ling (chahng dou-ling), a famous exorcist who founded the Five Pecks of Rice movement in western China. Claiming revelations (ca. 142) from T'ai-shang Lao-chun (Lao-tzu), he established a magico-religious healing cult that led to the Celestial Master (T'ien-shih) school. Today most Taoist priests consider Chang Tao-ling their founder and patron. *See also* Taoism; T'ien-shih Taoism.

Chang Tsai (jahng-dyi; 1020–77), a co-founder of Neo-Confucianism; he is remembered for his studies of the virtue of self-realization (*ch'eng*) and the cosmological theory of vital energy (*ch'i*). *See also* ch'i; Hsi-ming; Neo-Confucianism.

Chan-jan (jahn-rahn; 711–782), sixth patriarch of Chinese Buddhist T'ien-t'ai school. He nuanced the classification of Buddhist teachings by distinguishing between method, content, and chronology of doctrines. *See also* T'ien-t'ai school.

Channing, William Ellery (1780–1842), perhaps the best-known American Unitarian theologian and minister. *See also* Unitarianism.

Ch'an school (chahn), indigenous Chinese Buddhist movement traced to the late seventh and early eighth centuries. *Ch'an* is the transliteration of the Sanskrit term *dhyana,* which refers to meditative exercises aimed at tranquilizing the mind. Due to the importance of meditation in Buddhism, dhyana texts had existed since the fourth century. The interest of Ch'an, however, was more in elaborating a new doctrinal orientation than with Indian meditative practices as such. Arising partially out of intra-Buddhist sectarian arguments, Ch'an embodied a reaction against dualistic doctrinal formulations—especially regarding enlightenment and nonenlightenment.

Ch'an affirmed the innate enlightenment of all beings, which was endowed by their inalienable Buddha-nature. As a result, it eschewed all traditional textual, institutional, and ethical guides for the attainment of Buddhahood in favor of the practice of cultivating the original purity of one's mind. This original mind was believed to be ineffable and inconceivable. Hence Ch'an practice disparaged discriminatory thought and resorted to the methods of silence, negation, deliberate inscrutability, and even physical violence to achieve spiritual breakthrough. Ch'an attained true institutional and literary presence in the Sung dynasty (960–1279) with the standardization of its literature and practices. Some seminal texts include the *kung-an* (paradoxical teaching that transcends logical or conceptual thought) collections of the *Blue Cliff Record* and the *Gateless Barrier* and the lineage text *The Transmission of the Lamp.* The last is an eleventh-century Ch'an history that records legendary fare such as the transmission of Ch'an from India to China by Bodhidharma and the verse composition battle between Hui-neng and Shen-hsiu for the position of sixth patriarch. *See also* Blue Cliff Record; Bodhidharma; China, Buddhism in; Gateless Barrier; Hui-neng; kung-an; Shen-hsiu; Zen.

chant, a form of ritual speech; a repetitive, rhythmic vocalization. *See also* Japji; mantra; nembutsu.

Chanukah. *See* Judaism (festal cycle).

Ch'an-wei (chahn-way; Chin., "Apocryphal Texts"), speculative pseudocommentary on the Confucian Classics, popularly believed to illuminate the esoteric meaning of the canonical literature; it was highly influential in the political manipulation of portents at court from mid-Han times (beginning of the first century) until proscribed in the seventh century. *See also* Confucianism (authoritative texts and their interpretation).

chaos. 1 In Greek mythology, the yawning gap that separated sky and earth at the beginning. 2 The notion of a primordial state of disorder before divine creative activity. Actual cosmogonies suggest that this scholarly construct is problematic; most creation myths narrate the superseding of one form of divine order by another. *See also* ages of the world.

chaos, return to, a scholarly term for those elements in ritual scenarios, especially associated with new year rites, that feature disorder, reversals, and license. *See also* carnival; chaos; new year festivals; ritual.

chaplain, a Christian ministerial worker assigned to a specific place (e.g., a hospital), or group (e.g., the military), or person (e.g., a monarch) to perform rites or provide counsel.

charism (Gk. *charis*, "gift" or "favor"), in Christianity, the blessings that God bestows on the believer for the sake of a vocation. More narrowly, it applies to the special gifts of the spirit given for the sake of the community described by Paul (1 Corinthians 12.8–11). Such gifts include wisdom, knowledge, faith, miracles, the discernment of the spirit, the gift of tongues, and the discernment of tongues. *See also* gifts of the Spirit; glossolalia; Holy Spirit.

charisma (kahr-iz'muh; Gk. *charis*, "gift" or "favor"), an extraordinary power of leadership, often regarded as supernaturally bestowed, capable of arousing special loyalty or enthusiasm in followers. In the New Testament (especially 1 Corinthians 12–14) Paul presents a charism as a divine bestowal of power not capable of being induced by human effort. It manifests itself in spiritual gifts (*charismata*) such as prophecy, healing, and speaking in tongues (*glossolalia*). This use of the term is appropriated by the modern Christian charismatic movement, whose members claim to reproduce these powers.

The German sociologist Max Weber (1864–1920) expands this concept into a theory of leadership, both religious and secular, distinguishing charismatic authority from traditional and rational/legal authority. The former is found in the inherited office of kings, the latter in the legally defined and purposive bestowals of power characteristic of constitutional democracies. The rational/legal and traditional types rely for their authority on extrinsic factors such as the inheritance of position or rationally justified powers of office; charismatic authority rests on the unique attributes of the leader. This individualistic quality results in the leadership of charismatic leaders being a stimulus to dramatic cultural change. *See also* charismatics; power; religion, sociology of.

charismatic leadership, appointment by virtue of inherent qualities understood as from the god(s), or direct appointment by the god(s). It is the opposite of dynastic leadership. *See also* dynastic leadership.

charismatics (Gk. *charismata*, "gifts"), a term referring to those Christian individuals, groups, sects, assemblies, or churches who place a central emphasis upon the role of the spirit in the Christian life and who seek to demonstrate its presence through the attainment of the baptism of the spirit as evidenced by the presence of such spiritual gifts as *glossolalia* (speaking in tongues).

Until about 1960 what is now known as charismatic religion was largely restricted to the Pentecostal tradition. After 1960 "Pentecostal" emphases began to take root in some congregations within traditional non-Pentecostal denominations, a phenomenon that has been referred to as the neo-Pentecostal movement. By the early 1970s, the term *charismatic* was being used widely to refer to all, without denominational distinction, who emphasized through ecstatic behavior the presence and power of the Holy Spirit in their lives. *See also* charism; charisma; Pentecostalism.

charity. *See* almsgiving.

charm (from Lat. *carmen*, "song," "incantation"). 1 A verbal formula believed to confer power upon an individual or object or to direct power against an individual or object. 2 In popular usage, an object upon which a formula has been recited or, more generally, any object that possesses beneficent power. *See also* amulet.

chastity, sexual abstinence in order to obtain religious purity. In ascetic traditions, chastity may be a lifelong condition. Temporary sexual abstinence is common among warriors, hunters, and individuals undertaking vows. *See also* celibacy.

chegwan. *See* shamanism.

Ch'eng-Chu school (chuhng-joo), Neo-Confucian School of Principle, also called Li-hsueh, founded in the Sung dynasty (eleventh–twelfth centuries) by Ch'eng I and Chu Hsi. It stressed the "investigation of things" (Chin. *ko-wu*) in order to discover the principle of the ultimate good and taught the perfection of the mind in order to serve society and transmit the true Confucian Way. *See also* ko-wu; Neo-Confucianism.

Ch'eng Hao (chuhng hou; 1032–85), elder of the Ch'eng brothers and a founder of Sung-dynasty Neo-Confucian philosophy; he was known for his compassion and humor and the philosophic cultivation of the mind. *See also* Ch'eng I; Neo-Confucianism.

Ch'eng-huang Shen (cheng-hwahng shen; Chin., "wall and moat god"), a kind of Chinese city god who supervises life within the city walls and escorts the souls of the dead to the netherworld. *See also* Chinese myth; civic cults.

Ch'eng I (chuhng ee; 1033–1107), younger of the Ch'eng brothers and the founder of the Neo-Confucian School of Principle; he sought to discern the principle of the good through the reverent examination of things. *See also* Ch'eng-Chu school; Ch'eng Hao; Li-hsueh; Neo-Confucianism.

Cheng-i Taoism (juhng-ee; Chin., "Orthodox Unity"), a sect of liturgical Taoism that flourished under imperial Chinese patronage from the eleventh to eighteenth centuries. Centered at Mt. Lung-hu in south China, the sect was led by hereditary clerics who claimed to be the direct successors of the Celestial Masters (T'ien-shih) of Late Antiquity. In reality, there is no evidence of this. Up to the tenth century, the acknowledged leaders of Taoism were the Shang-ch'ing masters of Mao-shan, and imperial recognition of the Lung-hu clerics only emerged gradually from the eleventh to fourteenth centuries. In 1016 an emperor endowed this seat with the name *Hsin*

Cheng-i, "New Orthodox Unity" (from the formal name of the original T'ien-shih organization, *Cheng-i Meng-wei Tao,* "the Way of Orthodox Unity with the Authority of the Covenant"). Later, this sect was given formal jurisdiction over all Taoists in the south, and the present Taoist canon (the *Tao-tsang*) was compiled under Cheng-i auspices in the fifteenth century. However, the Ch'ing court lost interest in Cheng-i Taoists in the mid-eighteenth century, and early Western references to them as Taoist "popes" were greatly exaggerated. Although Cheng-i Taoism is still practiced (e.g., in northern Taiwan), the sect's authority has been negligible in modern times. Cheng-i priests specialize in ritual exorcism and protective rituals and, unlike the aristocratic, meditative Taoism of the earlier Shang-ch'ing tradition, Cheng-i has always appealed primarily to the masses. *See also* Lung-hu Shan; Shang-ch'ing Taoism; Taoism; Tao-tsang; T'ien-shih Taoism.

Ch'eng-kuan (cheng-gwahn; 738–839), fourth patriarch of the Chinese Buddhist Hua-yen school. He is noted for his monumental commentary to the *Hua-yen Sutra* and for elaborating the four-fold *dharmadhatu* (*fa-chieh*) theory. In the *Hua-yen Sutra,* "dharmadhatu" means "dharma-realm," "dharma-element," and "dharma-cause." The "dharma-realm" is the world of enlightenment, whose essence is the "dharma-element," which acts as the "cause" for the enlightenment of all beings. The dharmadhatu is realized in enlightenment, but is inherent in all beings as their essence or element. The fourfold dharmadhatu elaborates different perspectives from which the dharma-realm can be viewed. Ch'eng-kuan used the concepts of "principle" (*li*) and "phenomena" (*shih*) to frame these perspectives. The dharmadhatu viewed as shih is the ordinary world of differentiated phenomena. The dharmadhatu as li is the true, undifferentiated nature of all dharmas. The unobstructed interpenetration of li and shih, or of the absolute and phenomenal (*li-shih wu-ai*), emphasizes that all phenomena are based on the one true dharmadhatu. Finally, the interpenetration of each and every phenomenon (*shih-shih wu-ai*) teaches the interdependence of all phenomena. These interpenetrating worlds of the fourfold dharmadhatu earned Hua-yen doctrine the nomenclature "teaching of totality." *See also* China, Buddhism in; Hua-yen school.

chen-jen (juhn-ren; Chin., "True Person," "Veritable One," "Perfected One"), a Taoist term for someone who has achieved the highest ideals. First found in the *Chuang-tzu*, in the *T'ai-p'ing ching*, it is the person charged with transmitting Heaven's salvific scriptures from the Celestial Master to a worthy ruler. In Shang-ch'ing Taoism, it refers to the heavenly beings who reveal the nature of reality and the methods for ascending to the heavenly spheres. *See also* Chuang-tzu; Shang-ch'ing Taoism; T'ai-p'ing ching.

Chen-kao (jen-gow; Chin., "Declarations of the Perfected"), an edition of the *Shang-ch'ing ching* (Scriptures of Supreme Purity), which were the focus of the southern branch of Taoism centered on Mt. Mao, edited about 499 by the Taoist scholar T'ao Hung-ching. The first six books contain T'ao's edited versions of dictated texts and transcribed conversations from a series of visits by heavenly Taoist immortals ("the perfected") to the visionary and calligrapher Yang Hsi between 364 and 370. The seventh book is a detailed history of the religious movement that began with Yang Hsi's visions and provides invaluable documentation of a formative moment in the Taoist tradition. *See also* Mao Shan; Shang-ch'ing Taoism; T'ao Hung-ching.

Chenrezig. *See* Avalokiteshvara.

Chen-yen. *See* Esoteric Buddhism in China.

cherub/cherubim. 1 In the Hebrew Bible, a supernatural winged beast that guards the divine throne or the ark. 2 In later Jewish and Christian tradition, a rank of angels. 3 In Christian iconography, small winged children (Ital. *putti*) with innocent expressions.

Cherubim and Seraphim Society. *See* Africa, new religions in.

chesa. *See* ancestral rites.

ch'i (chee; Chin., "ether," "matter-energy," "vital energy," "material force"), an important and multifaceted term in Chinese religion, philosophy, and science, the root meaning of which is "moist vapor" or "breath." Early Chinese teachers spoke of *ch'i* as a vital spirit or energy that animated living beings. As such, it had to be properly nourished. For Confucians, that required moral cultivation so that one's ch'i, undistracted by external things, would conform to the dictates of will. For Taoists, it required mastery of the self through meditation, breath control, diet, yoga, and other techniques so as to harmonize one's ch'i with the material force of the universe ordered by the Tao

(undifferentiated unity). Traditional Chinese medicine attributed illnesses primarily to imbalances in the ch'i that pulsed through the body. Acupuncture, moxibustion (placing burning cones made of the dried leaves of the Artemisia moxa plant on the patient's skin), and other techniques helped to restore its balanced circulation. Ch'i was also an important concept in the correlative philosophy that blossomed in the early Han dynasty (206 B.C.–A.D. 8) systematizing the correspondences between like things that explained their mutual interactions.

In the Neo-Confucian metaphysics of the Northern and Southern Sung dynasties (960–1279), all phenomena were said to be manifest through the intrinsic relation of principle (*li*) and material force (ch'i). Li constituted the essential, unchanging, perfect nature of all things, while ch'i represented their corporeal, transitory, and potentially flawed aspect. Individuals were instructed to perfect their humanity, to purify and harmonize their ch'i with their true Heaven-endowed nature through the external investigation of things and mental introspection. *See also* Chinese medicine; Confucianism; cosmology; li; Neo-Confucianism; physiological techniques, (Taoism); Taoism.

chiao (jou; Chin., "offering," "sacrifice"), a major Taoist ritual in which the priest renews a community's relationship with the Three Pure Ones (San-ch'ing), supreme Taoist deities and source of revitalizing energy and blessings. In contrast to rites addressed to less elevated spirits, this sacrifice utilizes only "pure" offerings of wine, cakes, fruit, or tea and is conducted before a select audience in the closed-off temple; those types of *chiao* commonly offered today are for peace, disease, general blessings, fire disasters, and for the erection or renovation of a temple. At the heart of the rite, the priest and his entourage make offerings that include petitions of forgiveness and renewal of the covenant linking the gods and community. *See also* Chinese ritual; San-ch'ing; Taoism.

chi-chiu (jee-jyoh; Chin., "libationers"), a term for religious practitioners or priests within the Taoist Five Pecks of Rice movement. *See also* Wu-tou-mi Tao.

chien-hsing. *See* seeing the nature.

Chih-i (juhr-ee; 538–597), founder of the Chinese Buddhist T'ien-t'ai school, named after the mountain residence where he spent his latter years. A significant contributor to the *p'an-chiao*

Taiwanese Taoists performing the central nonpublic acts of meditation combining dance, recitation, music, and meditation in the ritual of cosmic renewal (*chiao*), which periodically realigns body, community, temple, and cosmos with the Tao. This ritual used to be performed only once every sixty years, but today a term of ten or twelve years is more common.

system, he classified all Buddhist texts into the framework of Five Periods and Eight Teachings and upheld the *Lotus Sutra* as the consummate and final teaching. *See also* China, Buddhism in; doctrinal classification; T'ien-t'ai school.

chih jen (juhr ren; Chin., "Perfect Person"), one of the *Chuang-tzu*'s terms for a person at one with true reality; it is occasionally used in later Taoism. *See also* Chuang-tzu.

chih-kuai (juhr-guay; Chin., "accounts of the strange"), a genre of Chinese literature consisting of short, usually narrative items of discourse arranged, often topically, in lists. The genre arose in the first centuries of the common era and continued into the eighteenth century. Its hallmark is its exclusive focus on all manner of phenomena deemed "strange" or anomalous relative to the taxonomies and cosmologies dominant in Chinese culture. These include appearances of ghosts, demons, and deities; shamans' and priests' exploits; abnormal animals and plants; distant and fantastic lands and peoples; and numinous mountains and rivers. *See also* Chinese language and literature, religious aspects of; typology, classification.

Chih-yen (juhr-yen; 602–668), second patriarch of the Chinese Buddhist Hua-yen school, who developed a classification scheme that divided Buddhist texts into gradual, sudden, and perfect teachings. He believed that the teachings were the same in content, but that the lesser teachings were expedient techniques aimed at beings of lesser understanding. *See also* China, Buddhism in; doctrinal classification; Hua-yen school.

ch'i-kung (chee-goong; Chin., "energy working"), Chinese exercises combining Buddhist and Taoist elements that focus on developing the body's vital energy (*ch'i*) and aiming toward optimum health by strengthening ch'i and directing it throughout one's body or into another's, particularly to weakened areas. Relaxed postures, regulated breathing, and mental control are paramount features coordinated within the varied practices. *See also* ch'i; Chinese medicine.

childhood. *See* life-cycle rituals.

Children of God, a term first applied by a Washington, D.C., reporter to a religious community begun in 1969 by David Berg, a former Pentecostal youth minister considered the

Moses and prophet of the group. By 1970, the community had adopted the name as a self-designation alongside the alternative, the Church of God. Originally closely associated with similar Jesus People groups, the Children of God established a separate identity under Berg, who led his followers on an Exodus-inspired trek out of the earthquake-threatened environment of California.

The church affirms evangelical views of Christian scripture and a millennial eschatology, expecting an imminent end of the world through a global conflagration during the battle of the forces of good and evil. The central doctrines of personal salvation through total commitment and the inevitable degeneration of Western society are framed in the prophecies and instructions of Berg, known as "Mo Letters," which supplement the conservative traditions of Christianity. Berg calls for the establishment of a utopian communal society, patterned after early Christian groups, under conditions that might allow members to survive the chaos of the impending Last Days. The Church of God became controversial for its advocacy of sexual freedom among members, extending in the late 1970s to its alleged luring of new members through sex and support for polygamy.

Under personal and legal threats in the United States, Berg moved the group's headquarters to Switzerland, changing its name to "Family of Love." Extensive reorganization in the 1980s to prevent sexual misconduct and strengthen the loyal families supportive of the church has consolidated membership but not prevented its overall decline.

chiliasm, the Christian millenarian belief that Christ will return and rule a thousand years. *See also* millenarianism; millennialism; Second Coming.

ch'i-lin (chee-lin; Chin., "unicorn"), in Chinese tradition, auspicious mythical animal with a leonine head, cervid body, bovine tail, and a single fleshy horn.

Ch'ilsong. *See* astral spirits (Korea).

China, Buddhism in. Chinese Buddhism is a form of Mahayana with Theravada elements and forms the basis for Buddhism in Korea, Japan, and Vietnam. Imported from Inner Asia and the Indian subcontinent by at least the first century (the exact date of introduction is unknown, but it is recorded at the imperial court in 65), it transformed Confucianism and Taoism at the same time as it was transformed by them and developed its own lineages between the fourth and sixth centuries to become established as one of the Three Teachings (San-chiao).

Interaction with Taoism and Confucianism: Buddhism was at first thought to be a form of Taoism, and Chinese interest focused upon meditation techniques as a way of obtaining immortality without resorting to Taoist elixirs, which, if taken incorrectly, were poisonous. Until the fourth century, when Buddhism developed its own vocabulary, Buddhist ideas were expressed in Taoist terminology, and, while Taoists assumed that the Buddha had been a disciple of Lao-tzu, Buddhists taught that Lao-tzu had been a disciple of the Buddha. This controversy, which was often so heated that the emperor had to ban it, caused Chinese Buddhists to set an early date for the birth of Shakyamuni (the Buddha) in order to establish his superiority. Buddhism, especially the Ch'an school, accepted many philosophical ideas from Taoism but placed them in a wider context. For example, Taoist immortality was reinterpreted as *nirvana* (liberation). The doctrinal, institutional, and textual cohesiveness of Buddhism stimulated Taoism to develop similar structures.

Confucianism regarded the Buddhist doctrine of rebirth (*samsara*) and the practice of monastic celibacy as threats to ancestor veneration and the integrity of family life, and the traditional freedom of Buddhist monastics from control by the sovereign as an insult to the emperor and a danger to national unity. It also objected that Buddhism was nowhere mentioned in the Confucian classics and was therefore unsuitable for Chinese. Buddhists wrote spirited replies to these attacks and won many concessions from the emperors, some of whom took Buddhist vows, but on three occasions (452–466, 574–578, 845) Buddhism was violently suppressed, monasteries were destroyed, texts burned, images melted down, and monks and nuns killed or forced to return to lay life. In the eleventh and twelfth centuries, so-called Neo-Confucianism borrowed meditation practices and philosophical principles from Buddhism, while at the same time condemning Buddhism as un-Chinese. Chinese Buddhism adopted many Confucian organizational features: a Chinese monastic is accepted into the order (Sangha) as into a family and becomes a "younger brother" of the Buddha, the head of a monastery is treated as a father, the former head as a grandfather, and the founder of a lineage as a patriarch. (Male terms are used for both monks and nuns.)

In general, Buddhism offers the Chinese a

worldview even grander than that of Taoism and a way of escaping the Confucian family structure. A woman, for example, who does not wish to be a housewife can become an autonomous individual, respected in the community, by taking monastic vows, leading services, and perhaps becoming an abbess.

Lineages: Chinese Buddhist lineages (sects) can be divided into imported and indigenous. The imported lineages were Chu-she, or Abhidharma, introduced by Paramartha (449–569) and organized by Hsuan-tsang (596–664); San-lun, or Madhyamaka, introduced by Kumarajiva (344–413) and organized by Tao-sheng (ca. 360–434); and Fa-hsiang, or Yogachara, introduced by Hsuan-tsang. All three lineages, the first of which is Theravada and the latter two Mahayana, died out as they became the basis for the four indigenous lineages, of which two are comprehensive and two are specialized. The comprehensive lineages are the T'ien-t'ai and the Hua-yen.

T'ien-t'ai was named after a sacred mountain in Chekiang where Chih-i (538–597), T'ien-t'ai's founder, arranged, during an extended retreat, all the texts, doctrines, and practices that had until then arrived in China haphazardly into a system that balances doctrines and practices and grades them from elementary to advanced according to a scheme that was developed into the Five Periods and Eight Teachings.

Hua-yen, founded by Tu-shun (557–640), describes reality on the basis of the voluminous *Hua-yen ching* (Flower Garland Sutra), according to which samsara and nirvana interpenetrate in what Fa-tsang (643–712) called the nonobstruction of phenomena and phenomena. T'ien-t'ai, which survives in a reduced form, was at one time the largest and most powerful lineage. Hua-yen was, and is still today, more important as a philosophy.

The specialized lineages are Ch'an and Ching-t'u. Ch'an, best known in English under its Japanese name, Zen, was introduced by Bodhidharma (ca. fifth century), a semilegendary figure supposedly from the southern Indian subcontinent, of whom many bizarre stories are told. Ch'an objects to what it regards as the unnecessary complexity of lineages like T'ien-t'ai, saying that since the Buddha reached enlightenment by sitting in meditation, that is all that is required, but it must be done in earnest. Bodhidharma is said to have sat for so long that his legs dropped off. While being in no way anti-intellectual (as it is sometimes misunderstood to be in the West), Ch'an also eschews extensive study in favor of questions (*kung-an*) intended to effect a direct mind-to-mind transmission independent of the scriptural tradition. Debates over the relative importance of sitting and kung-an and whether enlightenment is attained suddenly or gradually resulted in the division of Ch'an into the Lin-chi and Ts'ao-tung schools.

Ching-t'u was founded by Hui-yuan (334–416) and established by T'an-luan (476–542). The name means "Pure Land," an extra-samsaric paradise presided over by the Buddha Amitabha whose bodhisattva vow has arranged the fruiting of *karma* (the consequences of meritorious or demeritorious actions) such that any being who relies upon him will be reborn in the Pure Land and thus escape samsara. The principal Ching-t'u practice of *nien-fo*, invoking the name of Amitabha, assists practitioners to rely on the purified karma of Amitabha (*t'a-li*, other-power) rather than on their own defiled karma (*tzu-li*). Nien-fo is popular with working laypeople, since it may be said while one performs one's daily tasks, whereas Ch'an sitting is more suitable for monastics and leisured laypeople. However, Chinese Buddhist monastics today usually practice both Ch'an sitting and Ching-t'u invocation.

Vajrayana Buddhism was introduced to China in the eighth century by a succession of three masters from the Indian subcontinent, but it did not survive their deaths, although it passed to Japan where it flourished as the Shingon school. Between 1280 and 1368 China was ruled by the Mongols who reintroduced Vajrayana, in its Tibeto-Mongolian form, which the Chinese incorrectly called Lamaism (Lama Chiao). Supported by the court until the end of the last dynasty, elements of Vajrayana are now found alongside Ch'an and Ching-t'u.

Distinctive Features of Chinese Buddhism: The most astonishing achievement of Chinese Buddhism is that it is Chinese. The Chinese subcontinent has been very resistant to foreign religions, and although some, such as Islam and Christianity, have gained a foothold, only Buddhism has actually been incorporated into the Chinese worldview and given rise to the phrase "The Three Traditions are a harmonious unity" (*san-chiao ho-i*). This is perhaps due to the Buddhist principle of skillful means (Skt. *upaya-kausalya*) according to which the teaching must be adapted to the audience. In China, this meant that a way had to be found to play down, while not ignoring, the otherworldly features of Buddhism and emphasizing world-affirming features. Indian Mahayana began to do this by teaching the nonduality of samsara and nirvana. Chinese Mahayana continues the process by a combination of selection and innovation. The *Vimalakirti Sutra* is popular because it depicts a married layman whose achievements are superior to those of the celibate monks. The *Hua-yen Sutra* is used to explain emptiness not as the devaluing of ordinary reality but as the vibrancy of the scintillation of myriad Buddhas in every speck of dust. The *Awakening of Faith*, attributed to Ashvaghosa but probably written in China, depicts the pure Buddha Mind as, somewhat like the Tao, mysteriously moving into and pervading the defiled mind. The notion of One Mind, originally no more than a teaching on the primacy of thought, has been given a quasi-monistic twist and allied with the Tathagata-garbha, the doctrine that reality is the womb (Skt. *garbha*) of the Buddha (*Tathagata*) and that, as Confucianism and Taoism both teach, the inner nature of things is fundamentally good. Ch'an can then be both Buddhist and Chinese when it speaks of "seeing the nature." It is then a short step to saying that inanimate things possess the Buddha-nature and that, in the babbling brook, one hears "the preaching of non-sentient beings."

Despite all this, Buddhism has often been regarded by the Chinese as world-denying, unfilial, and traitorous. Its incorporation into the general culture as a third tradition, in addition to Confucianism and Taoism, remains ambiguous. *See also* Buddhism; Ch'an school; Esoteric Buddhism in China; Fa-hsiang school; Hua-yen school; Hung-chou school; kung-an; Lin-chi school; Neo-Confucianism; Northern school; Ox-head school; Pure Land school (China); San-chiao; San-lun school; seeing the nature; Silk Road; Southern school; Taoism; Three Stages, Teaching of; T'ien-t'ai school; transformation texts; Ts'ao-tung school; Tun-huang; Vajrayana; Vinaya school; Yun-kang.

China, Christianity in. The story of Christianity in China, beginning in the seventh century, is a complex and continuing one. Ah-lo-pen, a Syrian Nestorian monk, was the first Christian to enter China. Imperial approval to build Nestorian monasteries came in 635. Nestorians cooperated with Buddhists, incorporating Chinese features into their theology and liturgy. Dispersed under imperial persecution in 845, their predominantly foreign communities numbered three thousand.

Roman Catholicism: After centuries of minor contacts, Catholic Jesuit missionaries entered southern China in the 1670s. They maintained spiritual disciplines under assigned directors and strict papal loyalty. Matteo Ricci (1552–1610) was the first permitted to reside in Peking in 1601. He promoted medieval Western theological learning in contrast to current Confucian, Buddhist, and Taoist concepts. Other Catholic monks questioned the Jesuit strategy of accommodation, which supported rites they claimed were mixed with idolatrous superstitions. Papal authority was invoked to resolve this "rites controversy." By 1800 nearly five hundred priests were in China, nearly one-fifth of whom were Chinese, but the Catholic communities were suffering greatly from persecution.

Protestantism: Robert Morrison, the first Protestant missionary, entered China in 1807. He and other Protestant missionaries came through the efforts of denominational and inter-denominational missionary organizations. The Opium War (1840–42) created conditions for colonialists to take up residencies in China, including many missionaries. By 1860 over two hundred male Protestant missionaries had come, most serving as evangelists, medical missionaries, Bible translators, or educators. Foreign and Chinese women filled roles as teachers in girls' schools and as "Bible women," sometimes working in places men could not go. After 1860, Catholic missions also received treaty protections, sending many new orders of brothers and sisters into previously weakened Catholic mission fields. In 1865 Hudson Taylor established the China Inland Mission, which by 1882 had over six hundred missionary evangelists spread throughout China. In this later period American missionaries also began building what became major Christian universities.

Restrictions: The T'ai-ping Rebellion (1843–64), begun by an eclectic Chinese Christian cult, and the Boxer Rebellion, antiforeign riots stimulated by the Empress Dowager in 1900, caused great loss of life. In response, even more growth in missionary and Chinese Christian communities occurred, including the widespread impact of Young Men's/Women's Christian Association organizations. The 1911 Revolution also involved many Chinese Christians, including Sun Yat-sen, the leading revolutionary. New political influences led in the late 1920s to antireligious campaigns. Most Christian universities were judiciously shifted to Chinese Christian leadership. Other situations threatened many Christians, but the victory of Chinese Communism in 1949 stimulated the largest changes. Many Chinese Christians fled overseas, but the majority stayed. "House churches" were formed to avoid persecution, persisting today in many areas. Some Chinese Christian leadership accepted the Communist takeover as a judgment against corruption and foreign imperialism, helping to establish in the 1950s Protestant and Catholic patriotic church movements. These were disbanded during the Cultural Revolution (1966–76), but reopened afterward.

Protestant churches are nondenominational, supported by thirteen seminaries, and led by women and men pastors. Catholics have been split between patriotic churches and those loyal to Rome. After the demise of Western Communism in 1989 and 1990, Chinese officials initiated another period of general religious restrictions. There are no reliable figures for the number of Christians in China. The best estimate (1985) is that they comprise between 1 percent and 1.5 percent of the total population. *See also* Boxer Rebellion; China, Nestorianism in; Chinese rites controversy; T'ai-ping Rebellion; term question.

China, Islam in. Expansionist Islamic proselytizers made extensive use of various caravan routes through Central Asia to reach China in the eighth century. In the major towns along these routes they were received primarily without resistance and grew to be a large and integral part of the population. In these remote regions of China's Central Asian frontier, mosques were constructed, schools were organized, and copies of the Qur'an were printed. Generally, people were allowed to practice their religious rites without interference.

Muslims also reached China by sea, entering the major ports of southeast and east central China. Beginning in the T'ang dynasty (618–907) they made converts and established religious communities in such cities as Canton and Hangchou. By the Sung period (960–1279) these communities in the major urban centers along the coast were large enough to construct mosques and schools, much as the Muslims of the Inner Asian frontier had done. One area in China to develop a sizable Islamic community recently is the island nation of Taiwan. The community of believers now numbers over fifty thousand.

Islam's rigid monotheism, its general intolerance toward other religious systems, its dietary laws, and its demand that its holy book, the Qur'an, remain in Arabic suggest some of the reasons Islam has remained a peripheral and minority religion in China. Islam is primarily important among minority peoples who live in the border areas and autonomous regions that make up Chinese Inner Asia. There are no reliable figures for the number of Muslims in China. The best estimate (1985) is that they comprise 2 percent to 3 percent of the total population.

China, Judaism in. Jews were first recorded in China in 718 during the middle years of the T'ang dynasty. In the centuries that followed, small communities of Jews were found in widely scattered Chinese cities. The Jewish community located in the city of Kaifeng, capital of the Northern Sung dynasty, is the best known of these far-flung communities. It was founded by Jews who migrated to China by way of the Inner Asian Silk Road during the period of the Five Dynasties (A.D. 951 is given as the year of settlement). Stelae and other evidence suggest that the Jews mostly maintained their traditions, kept the Sabbath, and followed the Jewish festival year. The West first learned of this community from Jesuits who discovered it in the early seventeenth century and who studied the community firsthand.

Between 1938 and 1941, the Jewish population of China was radically increased by European Jews fleeing Nazism, and by the deportation of Japanese Jews to China. Between twenty thousand and twenty five thousand of these new immigrants settled largely in the Shanghai area and left China at the conclusion of World War II. There are no reliable figures on the present Jewish population in China; in 1968, there were 230 Chinese Jews residing in Hong Kong.

China, Nestorianism in. Nestorian Christianity was the first form of Christianity to enter China. Modern evidence for Nestorians in China depends on the discovery of the "Illustrious Religion" (Keng-chiao) monument in 1625. This stone monument (completed in 781) includes doctrinal and historical records in Chinese, eulogies to various Chinese emperors, and notes in Syriac. Syrian monks adopted some Buddhist and Taoist terminology and coined terms for God, the Messiah, and the Trinity. Nestorians thrived until dispersed under imperial persecution in 845. Thirteenth-century Nestorian churches in China were unconnected with the original communities. The Chinese Buddhist canon includes the monument text with two *Keng-chiao* manuscripts. *See also* Nestorianism.

China, new religions in, innovative religious systems, normally based on the inspiration of a founder, which self-consciously interpret elements of mainstream Chinese religions, sometimes also incorporating Islamic or Christian elements. The traditional Chinese state classed such movements as heterodox teachings, saw them as rebellious, and sought to suppress them.

New Religions and History: The historical record

in China tends to confound two analytically separable entities: religious societies, often driven underground and occasionally leading to rebellion, and rebellious societies, sometimes concealing themselves in religious garb. Modern scholarship has sought to distinguish between them. The White Lotus Sect (*Pai-lien chiao*), founded in the twelfth century, is frequently regarded as the exemplar of the dissenting religious society, although it was associated with an uprising between 1796 and 1804. The exemplar of the religious political organization is the Triad Societies (*Huang Men*), which came to prominence during the Ch'ing (Manchu) dynasty as anti-Manchu movements and which continue to constitute a problem for police. (Although some of the Japanese new religions, notably Tenrikyo and Omotokyo, have won Chinese converts, it is more useful here to class them with foreign missions in China, for on Chinese soil they lack most of the characteristics of indigenous Chinese new religions.)

There is evidence of innovative religious movements in China from the first centuries, but best historical records date from the late 1500s to the present. Chinese new religions have been associated on the basis of dynastic historical materials with periods of political or economic uncertainty and generally explained as a reaction to social stress. Thus it appears that the fall of the Ming dynasty and establishment of the Ch'ing in 1644, the dislocations associated with the Manchu domination of China throughout the Ch'ing, and the intellectual and emotional pressures created by growing contact with the West stimulated the growth of countless religious societies over the last several centuries. After 1912, limited legal tolerance both encouraged such groups and improved the historical and ethnographic record of them. Most such organizations were small and short-lived, and knowledge of them is from occasional surviving tracts or police reports. Many probably had no more than a dozen members and left no historical trace.

Ethnographic evidence now suggests new movements may be a fairly routine feature of Chinese religiosity at all periods, combining the availability of a large repertoire of traditional beliefs and practices with the leadership inclinations of particular individuals.

Liturgy and Divination: In the English technical literature, contemporary Chinese new religions are often referred to as "sects," but in Chinese they usually call themselves "teachings" (*chiao*) or "ways" (*tao*). All claim to be syntheses of "the three religions": Taoism, Confucianism, and Buddhism. (In some cases "the three" are ex-

panded to include Islam and Christianity, but normally with little effect on practice.) With respect to religious praxis, it is convenient to separate the new religions into two broad categories: those dominated by liturgy and those dominated by spirit-writing divination.

The eclectic liturgy of the new religions usually features long gowns patterned on Confucian or Buddhist models and involves the presentation and removal of offerings of food, flowers, tea, and sometimes wine. Many groups feature chanting of scriptures (their own or traditional—especially Buddhist—ones) by one or more cantors, combined with the reading of petitions from the assembly or individuals in it. Some groups practice purification of the meeting hall by spells or hand gestures. All of these practices are found in mainstream Confucian, Buddhist, or Taoist contexts and are self-consciously patterned on them. Many of these elements are limited to specialists in the primary traditions, however, and the new religions can be seen as democratizing them. Arguably an important motivation for participation in new religions is the opportunity to participate in rituals that are understood as meritorious but normally available only to specialists. Popular rites such as firewalking or purification by moving objects through smoke are also added. Many sectarians maintain that incorporating practices from all religions renders their sects more efficacious than any of the individual traditions.

Many new religions engage in spirit-writing divination, producing texts by automatic writing that range from general moral injunction, through mythological visions, to specific instructions (even medical prescriptions) directed to individual petitioners. Whole scriptures can be produced in this way, which can subsequently be chanted in rituals. (Many groups practice nonwritten divination as well, but it is important to distinguish new religions from the personal following of a popular spirit medium. It is extremely rare for a new religion to center on a nonwritten oracle.) Written revelations are nearly always in nonobsolete Literary Chinese, associating the sect directly with a prestigious element of Chinese cultural tradition.

Organization: New religions vary widely in organization, but many practice explicit initiations into membership and incorporate their members into an elaborate hierarchy of offices, so that each member has both specific obligations to perform and group recognition of his or her importance to the group. When a divinatory oracle is present, there is sometimes tension between the vision of the medium and other powerful members (such as a major contributor or a member who owns and lends use of the hall). Chinese new religions are less often organizationally centered on the founder or on the genealogical descendants of that individual. Instead, authority rests with titled elders, a class to which a member may be promoted by a written revelation in some groups or informal acknowledgment of seniority in others.

Many accounts of Chinese new religions, particularly Chinese accounts from the Ch'ing period, confound religious styles and religious organizations. Most new religions are quite small, with a tendency to fragment into yet smaller groupings. Large organizations with multiple local congregations exhibit only very loose centralized control over local praxis or doctrine. At the same time, the self-consciously innovative character of new religions invites constant interchange from one group to another, and a term like *White Lotus* more often designates a religious style than a religious group.

Cosmology, Theology, and Morality: Many groups loosely described as part of the White Lotus tradition subscribe to a broad mythological charter centering on the Queen Mother of the West (Hsi Wang Mu), who is known in sectarian circles under a variety of names. The Queen Mother, it is said, created humanity and was subsequently grieved at her children falling into evil ways, so she sent a series of Buddhas to save them. The last of these was the historical (Sakyamuni) Buddha, and the next is to be the Maitreya Buddha. Depending upon the group, the Maitreya Buddha of world salvation may be about to arrive, recently arrived, or associated with the group leader. The succession of Buddhas is a standard Buddhist belief, and the cult of the Queen Mother is itself widespread. What is innovative is the linkage of these two to render traditional Buddhism logically inferior to the Queen Mother cult and permitting the argument that Buddhist clergy and believers are practicing an outmoded faith by failing to recognize the immediate presence of Maitreya. Some sects (such as the modern Unity Way) associate with this myth a "celestial mandate" (*t'ien ming*) passed through several ancient religious figures and ending in the leaders of their sects.

An important motif in most new religions is morality and moral renewal. Society is seen as degenerate or materialistic, and participation in the group is believed to be merit-gaining. Nevertheless, the group accepts such traditional Chinese moral values as filial piety, loyalty, sincerity, and benevolence, and with symbolic representations of commitment to moral life (such as abstaining from alcohol and full or partial vegetarianism).

The same emphasis on merit (borrowed in part from Buddhism) is harmonic with the notion of initiation and individual membership and contrasts with much community religion, in which the individual's religious act is undertaken on behalf of family or community.

Recent ethnographic work has shown that members of new religions often have discrepant interpretations of the religious world that the societies create. It now appears that for many members a new religion amplifies their tendency to interpret everyday life events in a religious idiom but does not necessarily channel such interpretations to align with the beliefs of sect leaders. A new religion may be a stage on which different believers present quite different religious dramas to themselves, even though all are linked through the use of a common repertoire of Chinese religious symbols.

Examples: Because of strict laws against religious societies during the communist period, openly operating societies are centered today in Taiwan, Hong Kong, or overseas Chinese communities. The societies mentioned here as representative of the range of contemporary new religions all function openly in Taiwan today.

The Compassion Society (Tsi-huei Tang) was founded in eastern Taiwan in 1949 with a series of planchette revelations from the Queen Mother. The society organized itself into a central temple and local congregations, which now number more than two hundred and are found throughout Taiwan. Most practice their own planchette divination but also encourage members in meditation and chanting scriptures.

The Court of the Way (Tao Yuan) was founded in 1916 or 1917 in Shantung province in response to experiments with planchette divination. (A better-known offshoot, the Red Swastika Society [Hung Wan-tzu Hui], was spawned in 1922 for disaster relief and other public good works.) Only mediums trained at the central temple in Shantung are permitted to manipulate the planchette, and society activities have shifted away from planchette writing in many local congregations since such ordinations have been discontinued. A distinctive liturgy and burial rites exist, along with a distinctive pantheon of deities, which includes deceased sect leaders.

The Celestial Virtue Teaching (T'ien-te Chiao) was founded to be a moral force in the world. Believers are encouraged to meditate on a design composed in part of twenty characters representing names of virtues. Acknowledging the difficulty of being a virtuous person, each believer at initiation selects one of these virtues as a lifelong project, seeking to become a living manifestation of that virtue. Although believers describe this as a religion, the focus is on private meditation and morality, without significant local congregations.

The Unity Way (I Kuan Tao), claiming a celestial mandate dating back to the sages of antiquity and including the Ch'an patriarchs, apparently was organized in modern form in 1928. The planchette revelations, tracts, and scriptural commentaries produced by this sect make it one of the most articulate modern inheritors of the old White Lotus cosmological system centering on the worship of the Queen Mother and the advent of the Maitreya Buddha. The Unity Way is organizationally separate (and much fragmented), however, and emphatically dissociates itself from the White Lotus sects in its documents and initiation oaths. Operating openly in Japanese occupied parts of China during World War II, it was condemned as collaborationist for many years and legalized in Taiwan only in 1987. In common with most sects, the Unity Way stresses moral life, good works, preferential vegetarianism, and adherence to the sect's simplified Confucian-style liturgy, consisting of presentation of offerings. Many popular rites are condemned as superstitious, but participation in them is not prohibited, so that Unity believers are able to take part in community religious festivals, while privately regarding them as a religiously irrelevant concession to still underrefined community mores.

Unity Way apostates sometimes make use of liturgical or cosmological elements of the Unity tradition to found tiny sects of their own, meeting in their founders' houses or hastily constructed outbuildings or in local public temples. Nearly all such efforts are short-lived. *See also* China and Taiwan, new religions in; Chinese popular religion; Chinese sectarian religions; new religions.

China and Taiwan, new religions in.   A variety of religious organizations and systems of belief have emerged on the Chinese mainland and on the island of Taiwan during the twentieth century. One reason for the development of such new religions was China's increasing contact with the West, a contact often manifested in the form of expansionist Christian missionary enterprises. As a result of these efforts, mainstream Catholic and Western-centered Protestant communities developed throughout China, though in numbers far less than the missionaries had hoped for. Numerous independent Chinese-run churches also emerged and often had greater viability and strength than the Western-centered churches. Such churches adhered to more accul-turated and indigenized forms of Christianity, forms of belief that were more acceptable to Chinese accustomed to the highly eclectic and syncretistic universe of Chinese popular religion. A number of churches can be categorized under the rubric of "new religions." One is Watchman Nee's Assembly Hall Church, a church that was begun in the 1920s when Nee, a native of Fukien, fell under the influence of the Plymouth Brethren. The church is now based in Los Angeles but has an actively evangelistic community of believers in Taiwan. A second such church is the True Jesus Church, which began in northern China in the 1910s and reached Taiwan, its present-day center, in 1927. A third such indigenous church is the New Testament Church, based in Taiwan and Hong Kong. Though small in size, this radical Pentecostalist church has gained recognition as a religious body that is willing to confront earthly governments in preparation for a Dispensationalist "End of Days."

A second category of new religions includes groups that have emerged out of mainstream Chinese religious traditions or out of the complex universe of the Chinese sectarian tradition. While many of these groups have been suppressed on the mainland, they flourish in the more open religious climate of Taiwan, fueled by the wealth of the Taiwanese "economic miracle." One prominent example is the I Kuan Tao ("Path of Unity"). This religion began on the Chinese mainland in the 1920s as a variant of the sectarian and militantly millenarian folk Buddhist tradition of the White Lotus sect. A branch began on Taiwan in the late 1940s. While suffering persecution from the Communist regime on the mainland, it was finally legalized on Taiwan in the late 1980s.

The I Kuan Tao, now estimated to have two million adherents, contends that it melds together the "Three Teachings," Confucianism, Taoism, and Buddhism, as well as Islam and Christianity. At the heart of this movement is a combination of folk Buddhist elements with practices of the shamanistic possession sects that have long been a part of Chinese religious life. I Kuan Tao has proven most attractive to a wide range of Taiwan's citizens in both the countryside and the cities by providing them with a Chinese-centered belief system that allows them to confront the stresses of an increasingly secularized and Westernized East Asian society. *See also* China, new religions in; Chinese popular religion; Chinese sectarian religions.

Chinese language and literature, religious aspects of.
Folk religion, Confucianism, Taoism, and Bud-

dhism have all played a significant role in the formation and development of both the written language and literature of China.

Ancient Writings: The earliest-known forms of Chinese writings are those from the Shang dynasty (fourteenth century B.C.) inscribed on ox scapula, tortoise shells, and ritual vessels that speak of divinations and oracular pronouncements. In the Chou dynasty (ca. 1122–221 B.C.), the *Book of History*, the *Book of Rites*, the *Book of Poetry*, the *Book of Changes*, and the *Spring and Autumn Annals* appeared and formed the basis for the principles of Chinese literature that have continued into the present. Those principles emphasized moral rectitude over aesthetics, the concept of retribution, and the ultimate triumph of the upright. Of the numerous other schools of philosophy that blossomed in the Chou dynasty, only Taoism produced texts, the *Tao-te ching* and *Chuang-tzu*, which had a widespread and lasting effect on later literature.

Literary Developments: In the Han dynasty (206 B.C.–A.D. 220), historical scholarship flourished and myths and legends from popular religions and local cults are preserved. In the third and fourth centuries, Taoism took shape as a religion and Buddhism began to take root in Chinese culture. Both religions produced an abundance of sacred texts, revelatory scriptures, and commentaries as well as didactic tales and allegories. Moreover, because Buddhism brought with it new philosophical and religous concepts, vocabulary created for translation was infused into the Chinese language.

The golden age of Chinese poetry occurred during the T'ang dynasty (618–907). Both Buddhism and Taoism, often enjoying official patronage, exerted great influence on verse of that period. The short stories (*ch'uan-ch'i*) that also evolved during this period incorporated elements of Buddhism, Taoism, folk religion, and various supernatural phenomena.

Drama, which became immensely popular during the Yuan dynasty (1279–1368) had its origins in the exorcist dances of the shamans from the Chou dynasty. The novel first appeared during the Ming dynasty (1368–1644) and proliferated in the Ch'ing (1644–1912). Within the Confucian tradition fiction, based on fabrication and creation rather than on the transmission of historical events, was considered to be lowly and subversive. Nonetheless, the novel evolved into an extremely popular literary form. Although the subject matter varied, Taoist, Buddhist, and Confucian themes were woven into the fabric of the texts. Some novels, like the allegorical *Journal to the West* and the masterpiece *Dream of the Red Chamber*, dealt with religious themes di-rectly, while others, like *The Water Margin*, relied more on devices such as satire to make statements about religion. However, the Confucian theme of moral retribution can be seen even in erotic novels such as *Chin p'ing mei*. The rewarding of virtue and moral vindication are themes that are still traceable in much of the literature of modern China. *See also* ch'uan-ch'i; Ch'un Ch'iu; Chuang-tzu; Confucianism (authoritative texts and their interpretation); Hsi-yu chi; I-ching; Taoism (authoritative texts and their interpretation); Tao-te ching.

Chinese medicine. A fundamental affirmation in traditional Chinese religion and philosophy has been that the eternal quest to maintain harmony between heaven, earth, and humankind is a quest for health and happiness. Disharmony is productive of human illness and sorrow. By attending to the rhythms of cosmic and social order, the ancient sages were able to remain free from diseases and misfortunes.

Recognizing the difficulty in reestablishing harmony and healthy function once impaired, the Chinese have emphasized the prevention of disease. As expressed in *Huang-ti nei-ching* (The Yellow Emperor's Classic of Internal Medicine), the most important early Chinese medical text, "To cure an illness that has already developed is like starting to dig a well after one is already thirsty, or forging one's weapons after the battle has already begun." When illnesses have been experienced, the Chinese have sought restoration primarily through the practice of traditional medicine or the healing arts of ritual specialists.

Traditional Medicine: Diagnosis and therapeutic prescription in the context of traditional Chinese medicine have required an understanding of the dynamic interplay of the internal systems of the body and of the important correspondences between related orders of reality, described by reference to standard cosmological categories such as *yin* and *yang*, the four directions, the five elemental phases (*wu-hsing;* wood, fire, earth, metal, water), etc. Basing judgments not on the sciences of anatomy and histology but rather on direct observations of various bodily functions, Chinese doctors have sought to detect systemic imbalances negatively affecting health. By taking the pulse and checking such things as skin color, temperature, odor, and quality of the voice, doctors have attempted to diagnose excesses or deficiencies in an individual's vital energy or *ch'i*, yang in nature, which surges through the body along special energy pathways, just as blood, yin in nature, flows through blood vessels. Therapy has included the dispensing of pharmaceutical preparations, acupuncture, moxibustion, and other means to restore normal balances to affected internal systems. Medications, from a wide variety of materials, largely herbal, have been prescribed for their efficacy in altering realities of the same cosmological type. Acupuncture has utilized needles to penetrate specific points along the energy pathways to rearrange the distribution of ch'i. Moxibustion has employed the heat produced by the burning of a moistened cone made of Artemisia moxa leaves placed on the skin above critical points in the energy pathways to induce a healing influx of ch'i to a deficient functional region.

Ritual Specialists: In cases where traditional medicine has not been effective or deemed appropriate, many Chinese have consulted technicians of the sacred. Ritual specialists have helped to determine the true cause for an illness—e.g., improprieties offending ancestors or other deities, demonic possession, soul loss—and have employed prayers, charms, purification rituals, exorcisms, and other religious actions to effect a cure.

In the contemporary Chinese context, Western medicine, traditional medical arts, and ritual methods of healing are often understood as complementary sources of aid. *See also* body;

ch'i; Chinese ritual; healing; Huang-ti nei-ching; medicine and religion; physiological techniques (Taoism); wu-hsing.

Chinese myth. The earliest texts preserving traces of ancient Chinese myths generally date after the sixth century B.C. Other sources are limited to the oracle-bone and bronze inscriptions from the Shang (ca. 1766–1122 B.C.) and Western Chou (ca. 1122–722 B.C.) periods, which provide only hints of the archaic Chinese stories about the ancestors and gods. The Shang ruling class apparently worshiped many gods associated with natural phenomena and a supreme deity, the High God (Shang-ti), who was also identified with the Shang tribal ancestor. Gods bestowed fortunes and misfortunes and could be appealed to indirectly through deceased ancestors in heaven. The Western Chou people inherited the Shang pantheon and equated the deity T'ien (Heaven) with the Shang High God. The relation of the Chou ruling house to the High God was established by the mythically based theology of history known as the Mandate of Heaven (T'ien-ming).

More complete sources for Chinese mythology (e.g., the *Shan-hai ching,* the *Ch'u-tz'u,* and the *Huai-nan-tzu*) dating to the Eastern Chou

Taoist priest performing a healing ritual in a T'u-ti kung (earth god) temple in Sanhsia, Taiwan. The priest is not affiliated with the temple, but pays a portion of his fee for its use.

(722–255 B.C.) and early Han (206 B.C.–A.D. 220) periods, record and modify fragments of the ancient myths. Reconstruction of original myths sometimes requires a deconstruction of the process by which many mythical deities had been transformed into historical figures. Despite the problematic nature of the ancient mythology, several typological categories can be determined.

Creation: Chinese mythology generally lacks a Creator myth. Instead, there is a self-existing cosmic lump of nondifferentiated stuff (*hun-tun*) from which heaven and earth and eventually all things were spontaneously generated. This theme was later synthesized with the myth of P'an-ku, the cosmic man, who was born from the cosmic egg or from the gourd of hun-tun, and grew so tall that heaven and earth were eventually pushed apart. Some myths specifically concern the origin of the human race: the goddess Nu Kua molded clay into human beings and initiated the practice of marriage. In other versions, Nu Kua and Fu Hsi were depicted as world parents, with intertwined serpentine tails, from whom the human race was born.

Shape of the Cosmos: Heaven and earth were once connected. The High God planted a tree at the center of the world through which deities could descend to earth and humans could climb to heaven to appeal for relief from earthly sufferings. In other stories, the K'un-lun mountain in the far west sustains heaven, and its peak leads to the gate of heaven. Another myth tells that the High God, angered by the violence of some southern tribe on earth, destroyed the connection between heaven and earth. Some myths explain the position of the stars. The High God Chuan Yu once tied all the heavenly bodies to the northern pole with ropes. One rebellious deity, Kung-kung, smashed the western mountain holding up heaven and broke the cords that tied the heavenly bodies. Heaven therefore tilted toward the northwest and the earth sank in the southeast. This made all the major rivers in China run eastward and the heavenly bodies begin to move.

Cosmic Disasters and Human Saviors: Several myths describe floods on earth. Kung-kung, when breaking the heavenly pillar, caused all the water above the clouds to pour down. Another myth describes a catastrophic scene of flood, fire, and monstrous animals on earth; Nu Kua, the maker of humans, smelted stones of five colors to patch the heaven and killed the frightful animals. In other stories, Yu, a compassionate dragonlike deity, with the help of the High God and many other deities, finally stopped the flood by

reshaping mountains and rechanneling rivers. There were also myths concerning drought. The wife of the High God gave birth to ten suns, who bathed in the eastern ocean behind the mulberry trees and took turns traveling across the sky. One day, however, the ten suns decided to appear together and caused a serious drought. Yi, the great archer, shot down nine suns, but was punished by being made a mortal.

The World of Gods, Wars, and Rebellions: The High God reigns over other deities in a loose hierarchy. Deities, often in human-animal hybrid forms, govern heavenly regions and natural phenomena. The throne of the High God is succeeded in a patrimonial pattern, and many deities have blood relationships. Thus, wars and rebellions occur in the heavens. Kung-kung broke the heavenly pillar in his rage against the High God, and Ch'ih Yu waged an epic war against Huang-ti, then the High God. Hsing-t'ien was another deity that challenged Huang-ti. He kept fighting after losing his head, using his nipples as eyes and his navel as a mouth. K'ua-fu was the famous deity who tried to capture the sun and died of thirst during his long chase. K'un stole the magic soil from the High God in order to block the flood on earth and was executed. His corpse remained undecayed for three years; it gave birth to Yu, who finally won the sympathy of the High God and stopped the flood. The archer Yi shot down nine suns, knowing they were the sons of the High God.

Heroes and Ancestors: Many myths explain the origin of certain clans. The Shang ruling class recounted that once a tribal prince, Chien Ti, swallowed the egg of a dark bird (who was identified with the High God) and gave birth to their first ancestor. The Western Chou rulers spoke of how Chiang Yuan stepped on the footprint of the High God and gave birth to their first ancestor. Following the decline of the Eastern Chou ruling clan, similar origin myths flourished among minor clans, often with genealogies relating to mythical deities who had been transformed into humans. *See also* Chou religion; cosmogony; cosmology; hun-tun; K'un-lun; myth; Nu Kua; P'an-ku; Shang religion; Shang-ti; T'ien-ming.

Chinese popular religion. The popular (or folk) religion of China has suffered from neglect, not only by Chinese intellectuals who considered it mere superstition, but also by many Western scholars, who were more attracted to the lofty teachings of Confucianism, Taoism, and Buddhism. Popular religion, however, is the common religion of the Chinese people. It may in fact be considered the ancient matrix from which Confucianism and Taoism arose and to which Buddhism adapted itself.

Self-identity: Mistakenly considered a chaotic amalgam of the "Three Teachings" (Confucianism, Taoism, and Buddhism), popular religion has its own identity and autonomy that can be defined in relation to its myth (or worldview, doctrine, theology), ritual, social expression, and norms of living.

The mythical element of Chinese popular religion is not systematic but includes various common principles: a belief in Heaven as the highest principle; acceptance of fate, dictated by Heaven; the omnipresence of *yin* and *yang* (the complementary principles), operating via the five agents (*wu-hsing*); and a belief in *shen* ("spirit," "soul") and the afterlife. Most of these tenets belong to the common heritage of China and are neither Taoist nor Confucian. The views about the afterlife have been greatly modified and amplified by Buddhist cosmology. What is perhaps at the heart of popular religion is the belief in the supernatural world of gods, ghosts, and ancestors.

There are large numbers of popular gods and goddesses and they are distinct from Taoist deities and the Buddhas and Bodhisattvas. The people interact with these deities through sacrifice, prayer, divination, and mediumistic seances. The popular pantheon is not clearly differentiated and many individual deities do not have strict boundaries. Thus, Kuan-yin is of Buddhist origin but in Taiwan is always found in Ma-tsu temples. Kuan-ti has no fixed "abode" so he is sometimes claimed by the Confucian tradition, popular religion, and sectarian movements. This fluidity of the deities is one reason why popular religion has eluded identification.

The ritual component is very pronounced in popular religion. But popular rituals must not be confused with the rites of the Three Teachings. The only overlap is when the community invites Taoist and Buddhist specialists to perform their liturgy in the community temple.

The social expression of popular religion is centered around the community temple and in private homes (occasionally in the ancestral temple of the clan). But other aspects of a social nature include the priesthood and scriptures. The "priesthood" is less structured than in Taoism or Buddhism (candidates are not formally trained in seminaries) but includes different types of spiritual practitioners such as diviners, fortune-tellers, mediums, exorcists, so-called *fa-shih* (ritual specialists), geomancers, and "red-head" Taoists (a popular shamanistic version of Taoist priest). Although it has been stated that

popular religion has no scriptures, it is clear that, besides oral tradition, there are also written scriptures. These are the widely disseminated "precious scrolls" (*pao-chuan*) and "morality books" (*shan-shu*).

Ethical norms are strongly present in the popular tradition. It is often said that they were borrowed from Confucianism, which is partly correct, but it must be remembered that Confucius and his followers also borrowed from the ancient tradition and its emphasis on transactional reciprocity.

Ritual Practices: Two major types of rituals constitute popular religion in action: clan rituals, addressed to the ancestral spirits, and communal rituals, honoring the community deities.

Ancestor Cult Rituals: Ancestors are the spirits of deceased family members. In an extended family there are a great number of them, but the males in direct patrilineal descent (together with their spouses) are the most important ancestors.

The relationship between the living and the dead expresses the deep-seated belief that the two realms are not completely separate. There is an ongoing exchange of "services," between the two worlds, at least between the living and remembered ancestors. Remote ancestors tend to become anonymous and less vital.

The origin of ancestor veneration goes back at least to the Shang period (ca. 1766–1122 B.C.). Already in Shang times, a two-way relationship existed between the royal house and deceased kings. The living king consulted his ancestors to gain advice in state matters or family affairs and also to secure their assistance. The dead received offerings such as animal sacrifices and great amounts of wealth. Mutual benefit was the first motivation for these practices. Moreover, deceased ancestors had the power to harm or curse their descendants. To counteract this threat, conciliatory sacrifices were offered. The need for clan or family cohesion after a great leader's death was another motivation. Finally, wailing as an outlet for grief was a related motivation. A complex ritual system provided rules for correct behavior in times of loss, so much so that the Confucian master Hsun-tzu considered this social function of ritual of paramount importance. He felt there were no spirits to receive the offerings, but the rituals were necessary for the living. For the people, however, the spirits were real and their well-being after death had to be secured. With the coming of the Buddhist belief in *karma* and reincarnation and the Buddhist vision of hell with all its terrors, new rituals were created in order to bring solace to those suffering in the netherworld. The Ghost Festival is a public expression of this concern.

The practices of the ancestor cult are very complex: appropriate rituals have to be performed before and right after death; other rites

In Taiwan, a paper "spirit house" is burned forty-nine days after an individual's death, marking the transition from spirit to identification with the ancestors.

relate to the encoffining, the choice of a date for the funeral, the funeral rites, and rituals after the body has been cremated or buried. After the funeral, a tablet (*shen-chu*) is installed on the home altar, and regular offerings of food and incense are made to keep the memory of the deceased alive. All important family matters are decided in front of the home shrine, and all decisions are communicated to the spirits. During wedding ceremonies, the young couple kowtows in front of the tablets. Around the time of burial, families purchase a small "house" made of paper and bamboo: the burning of it transfers it to the spirit world to be used by the deceased. Also, "spirit money" is burned in great quantities, and at regular intervals more money is

"sent" to the afterworld for the daily needs of the ancestor. To ensure the happiness and prosperity of the living, the dead have to be buried in an ideal geomantic spot, where the cosmic energies flow in abundance. *Feng-shui* masters are consulted, and if a good spot is found and purchased, the family's well-being is automatically guaranteed.

Communal Worship: The center of community life in traditional China was the community temple. The center of all social interaction, it was both the geographic meeting point and the symbol of community solidarity. The deity enthroned there, chosen by the people, unifies the community and provides security.

Each family contributes funds for the building or restoration of the temple. A temple committee of laypeople chosen by the deity (through divining blocks) is in charge of all religious activities and runs all temple affairs. Some temples own land to secure a regular income. A Chinese community temple is therefore an independent, autonomous entity, publicly owned and controlled by the people, not by any body of religious specialists.

Temple worship is of two major kinds: personal or community-oriented. People go to the temple whenever the need arises. The temple stays open until late at night, with a caretaker in charge. Usually worshipers have a particular goal in mind: to consult the deity concerning some major life concern such as health, marriage, business, birth, study, or travel. After a stereotyped routine of offering incense and bowing before the central altar, they consult the temple oracles, to be found in all community temples, and receive the deity's message. After the ritual is over, spirit money is burned in a furnace outside to thank the god or goddess. This daily ritual can be seen in most temples. Some temples, however, are more famous and attract hundreds of worshipers every day. The presiding deity is believed to possess extraordinary potency, or *ling*.

Several times during the year, there are great community rituals. Most important is the yearly celebration of the deity's birthday. All families visit the temple and honor their protector god or goddess. Food offerings are brought in special ritual baskets and presented to the deity. Wine is also important. The food offered is raw (in contrast to food offered to ancestors, which is always cooked). After the deity has finished dinner, the food is packed again and taken home where it will be served for supper. The gods only take in the spiritual essence of the food.

During the birthday celebration, the deity's

statue is placed in an ornate sedan-chair and paraded around the community with musicians and devotees following. This is an inspection tour that serves as an occasion for the deity to bless the people. In the afternoon and evening there usually is opera or a puppet show performed on a stage facing the temple. Performances are meant as much to amuse the deity as the people.

Of special significance is the "rite of cosmic (or community) renewal." It used to be held only once in sixty years, but nowadays a term of ten or twelve years is more common. It is connected with the rebuilding or redecoration of the community temple and is a sacramental act of renewal. The rich liturgy (performed by Taoist priests, rarely by Buddhists) symbolizes and effectively realizes a cosmic and moral renewal of the community. The people participate through acts of repentance and worship, but the focus is on Taoist rituals: canons of repentance, audiences with the Three Pure Ones, and the purification of the temple premises.

The community temples also organize pilgrimage tours to related temples and temples are often the scene for mediumistic seances or spirit-writing cults. Last, temples are the meeting places of the people, both young and old. Under the smiling glance of the deity, the drama of life goes on. *See also* ancestral rites; chiao; Chinese ritual; geomancy; kuei; popular religion; shamanism; shen-chu; spirit money; temple; wuhsing; yin and yang.

Chinese religions (art and architecture).

Certain Chinese art forms are clearly religious in purpose. One example is archaic funerary art, such as the renowned bronze vessels made to accompany the royal dead to the otherworld from the Shang and early Chou period (eighteenth–eighth centuries B.C.). Another clear example is Buddhist sculpture, its three-dimensionality and emotional directness reflecting its Indian origins. The sinicization of this style can be best traced at the Yun-kang and Lung-men cave sites, where a deeply pious Buddhist faith was eventually given expression in strongly linear Chinese style. A final example is the overtly religious paintings, in which the subjects are the deities, spirits, Buddhas, and Bodhisattvas of the Taoist and Buddhist traditions.

Implicitly Religious Art: Religious and spiritual themes are often implicit in certain artistic genres that may not at first seem religious at all. A prime example is Chinese landscape painting (*shan-shui*), which has Taoist spiritual foundations. Nearly all examples of this genre have

Gazing at a Waterfall by Li T'ang (fl. ca. 1080–1130), one of the major Sung-dynasty Chinese landscape painters.

both elements for which it is named, mountains (*shun*) representing *yang* and waters (*shui*) *yin*, the two cosmic forces that are the first expression of the unseen Tao. Humans, when present, always occupy a humble place in the total scheme of things. These paintings provide an accurate understanding of Taoist views of nature and the human place within it.

Buddhist monks of the Ch'an (Zen) school, such as Mu Ch'i (fl. 1200–1255), painted what appear to be "secular" subjects like monkeys, persimmons, and flowers, yet in so doing expressed their highest religious belief, that the sacred (Buddha-nature) was to be found precisely in the ordinary, or more accurately, that there should be no discrimination between the two.

With the performing arts, most religious themes are implicit. Music had an almost mystical power for Confucius. If the ruler could govern by music and ritual (*li*), society would be civilized and harmonious, without need for the use of force. Music, chanting, and even forms of dance were an important part of all religious ceremonial practices, Taoist, Buddhist, and imperial.

Drama and theater follow local traditions, Peking opera being perhaps the best known. Usually the themes are not religious but stories of love and heroism, although the *Hsi-yu chi* (Journey to the West), with its Taoist and Buddhist themes, is a popular source of operatic scenarios. Dramas were often performed in conjunction with temple festivals, and although they did not usually have religious themes, their purpose was to entertain the deity.

Architecture: Explicitly religious architecture, such as the Buddhist pagoda and certain imperial altars, is relatively rare. The forms of Chinese architecture do not show a sharp distinction between secular and sacred. Chinese temples, homes, and public buildings all replicate the same modular, axial pattern. Courtyards, one following another on an ideal north-south axis, were the basic building blocks of all Chinese architecture, and it was only through the iconography that specific religious traditions found expression. *See also* bronze vessels (China); Ch'an school; Hsi-yu chi; li; temple.

Chinese religions (festal cycle). The religious and social celebrations of the Chinese festal cycle follow the traditional lunar calendar. Originating

A puppet of General Hsie, a member of the divine retinue of the city god (Ch'eng-huang Shen), being carried in a procession in Hsin-chu, Taiwan. In the Chinese lunar calendar, the seventh month is the period of the return of "orphaned spirits," or "hungry ghosts," of the dead who have not been properly cared for. As part of the rituals of control, a procession is held of the city god and his generals and soldiers, who purify and protect the city.

in the religious concerns of early agricultural society, the majority have become secularized by the mid-twentieth century. Most significant were the six national festivals beginning with the lunar New Year, the beginning of spring and a period of renewal before agricultural work began in earnest. The other festivals include the Lantern Festival (fifteenth day of the first month), when brightly colored lanterns were hung from the eaves of homes, shops, and temples marking the end of the New Year's celebration; the Dragon Boat Festival, when the boat races took place (fifth month, fifth day); the Ghost Festival, which occupied the entire seventh lunar month but culminated on the full

moon (fifteenth day) with elaborate offerings made to the wandering ghosts; the Mid-Autumn Festival (eighth month, fifteenth day), when people celebrated the completion of the harvest and focused on the harvest moon and its deity; and finally, one solar celebration, the Clear and Bright (Ch'ing Ming) Festival (106 days after the winter solstice), a time of spring outings to clean, decorate, and offer sacrifices at the ancestral graves.

Birthdays of the Deities: Less universal but still significant for specific groups and particular localities were festivals focused on a single deity. Some examples were Buddhist festivals commemorating important days in the life of Shakyamuni (birthday, fourth month, eighth day; the day he left householder life; the day he entered nirvana) and the birthdays of Kuan-yin and other Bodhisattvas. There were also festivals of Taoist origin (birthdays of, e.g., Lao-tzu, Chuang-tzu, Hsi Wang-mu, and the Jade Emperor), birthdays of popular gods such as Kuan Kung (god of war), Ts'ai-shen (god of wealth), T'ai-shan (god of the Eastern Peak), and the festival of the tragically separated lovers, Cowherd and Weaving Woman (seventh month, seventh day). These last two figures are identified with stars on opposite sides of the Silver River (Milky Way). On this one day each year the decree of the Jade Emperor allowed them to be together.

State Cult: In the calendar for imperial worship, the most important days were the winter and summer solstices. During these times the spirits of Heaven and Earth were worshiped through elaborate sacrifices at the imperial altars. Next in order of importance were the rituals at the imperial ancestral temple and the altar of land and grain, the spring plowing ceremony, and sacrifices to the deities of sun and moon.

Shared festivals were an important integrating factor in Chinese life. Centered around the extended family, they were times of fun and solidarity, when the spirit of the traditional patriarchal family was renewed. The six national festivals provided an occasion when families all over China felt the same sentiments and engaged in the same activities. There was also an integration between upper and lower strata of society, as many of the deities of Heaven and Earth, sun and moon, mountains and rivers were worshiped by emperor and the masses, though in different ways. *See also* ancestral rites; Chinese ritual; Ch'ing ming; Double Yang Festival; Dragon Boat Festival; Ghost Festival; New Year (China); state cult, Chinese.

CHINESE RELIGION

he term *Chinese religion* embraces a very broad spectrum of religious experience, from organized religions (Buddhism, Taoism) to state-sponsored rites (Confucianism) to diffuse and sometimes highly localized cults and practices. Chinese religion as such (also Chinese popular religion or popular Taoism) is often used specifically to denote the diverse, syncretistic, largely indigenous popular religion(s) of China. The beliefs, divinities, forms of worship, institutional structure, and other aspects of Chinese religion have varied over time and from place to place. Chinese religion is widely considered an unsatisfactory term, but it remains in use for want of a better one. Some scholars reject the term altogether, insisting that it is too amorphous to be useful. As a near synonym for "Chinese popular religion," it is a portmanteau term defined largely by what it is not: Chinese religion embraces religious aspects of China not otherwise clearly assignable to institutionalized religions such as Confucianism and Neo-Confucianism (in their religious guises), Buddhism, (religious) Taoism, and imported minority creeds such as Islam and Christianity, but also partly overlapping with some or all of them. But in the broader sense of religion in China, Chinese religion embraces both popular and local beliefs and practices and the various organized and sectarian religions of China.

If the term Chinese religion has any validity, it is because virtually all religions practiced in China share an ancient and somewhat inchoate substrate of beliefs.

ANCESTOR VENERATION

Ancestor veneration is the true bedrock of religious belief in China. Evidence of such devotion can be found even in the burial practices of the Neolithic period. Further evidence accumulates throughout the early historical period; the ancestral cult is one of the few constants of Chinese civilization from earliest times to the present.

Little is known of the rites (if any) performed by commoners for their ancestors in ancient China, but at the elite level the worship of ancestors was a powerful force. The kings of the Shang and Chou dynasties (ca. 1766–221 B.C.), as well as all emperors thereafter, buried their ancestors in great splendor, fur-

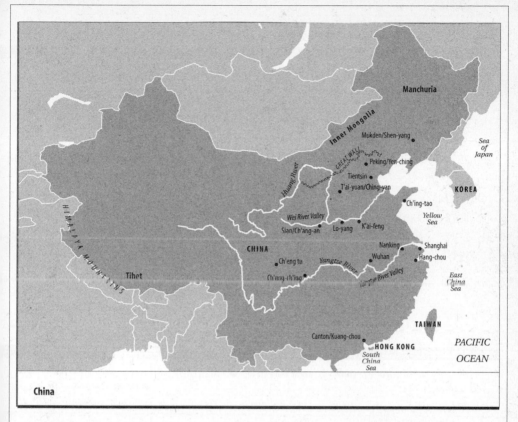

China

nished their graves with real or simulated sacrificial victims and sets of cast bronze vessels and other goods, treated the ancestors as divinities, and routinely consulted them on state affairs through divinatory practices. By the late Chou period if not before, people at all levels of society participated in ancestor veneration with whatever degree of elaborateness their means permitted.

Chinese culture characteristically has been patriarchal, patrilocal, and patrilineal. Authority within the family rests with the eldest male and, through him, with deceased male ancestors. Women marry into their husbands' families and live with their husbands' parents. The most important duty of a married couple is to produce a male heir; the second most important duty is to give a proper funeral to the husband's parents and observe the proper forms of ritual mourning. Ancestors in the male line are held to be conscious and active on the family's behalf; they must be treated with dignity and respect, given offerings on appropriate occasions, consulted in matters of importance to the family, and provided with heirs to continue these duties.

Accordingly, every Chinese home until recent times was equipped with an ancestral shrine containing the spirit tablets (*shen-chu*) of ancestors, where offerings were made and rituals conducted from time to time. Family graves were located in sites said to possess beneficial spiritual properties and were carefully tended on holidays devoted to that duty. The various rites performed on behalf of deceased ancestors overlapped to some extent with other religious manifes-

China*

ca. 3500–1000 B.C.	1000–500 B.C.	500–400 B.C.
Earliest city in China, Liang-ch'eng chen (Lung-shan culture) (ca. 3500)	*I-ching* (ca. 700–600)	Tseng-tzu (ca. 505–436)
Yang-shao culture (ca. 2500)	*Shih-ching* (ca. 600)	Tzu-ssu (ca. 492–431)
Shang (Bronze Age) culture, first distinctively Chinese (ca. 1766–1122)	Lao-tzu, quasi-historical sage; for some, a deity (6th century?)	Warring States Period (481–221)
Chinese writing developed (ca. 1500)	K'ung Fu-tzu (Confucius) (ca. 551–479)	Mo-tzu (ca. 479–381)
Shang oracle bone inscriptions (ca. 1500–1100)		Yang Chu (ca. 440–360)
Chou dynasty (1122–221)		
Duke of Chou dies (1094)		

100–1 B.C.	1–100	100–200
First attempt to suppress shamanism by court officials (99)	Wang Mang, the Usurper, Hsin dynasty (9–23)	Formation of first organized Taoist communities (2nd century)
Yang Hsiung (53 B.C.–A.D. 18)	Late (Eastern) Han dynasty (23–220)	Earliest extant alchemical treatises (140–150)
Huan T'an (43 B.C.–A.D. 28)	Wang Ch'ung (27–ca. 97)	Earliest surviving inscription deifying Lao-tzu as a creator god (165)
	Buddhists enter China (65)	Formation of T'ien-shih Tao (or Wu-tou-mi) and T'ai-p'ing Tao (the "Yellow Turban" movement) (late 2nd century)

* See also the timeline that accompanies the feature article "Buddhism."

tations; with the partial exceptions of Buddhism, Islam, and Christianity, all Chinese religions have accommodated themselves to the cult of ancestors.

MULTIPLE DEITIES

Another aspect of the religious substrate of China was the plurality of the religious imagination on levels ranging from the imperial to the popular. At various times imperial sacrifices were offered to such divinities as the High God of Heaven (T'ien/Shang-ti), the Queen Mother of the West (Hsi Wang-mu), the god of the soil (T'u-ti), the gods of the four quarters, and the deified spirit of Confucius in addition to the imperial ancestors. At the popular level, gods in-

400–300 B.C.	300–200 B.C.	200–100 B.C.
Meng-tzu (Mencius) (ca. 372–289)	Hsun-tzu (ca. 312–230)	*Li chi* (ca. 2nd century)
Chuang-tzu (ca. 369–286)	Han Fei-tzu (ca. 280–233)	Worship of spirit of Master Confucius incorporated into state cult (2nd century)
	Tao-te ching (ca. 250), attributed to Lao-tzu	Chia I (201–169)
	Chin dynasty (221–207)	Tung Chung-shu (179–104)
	Government anti-Confucian campaign (213)	Emperor Wu (140–87)
	Han dynasty (206 B.C.–A.D. 220); early (Western) Han dynasty (206 B.C.–A.D. 8)	*Huai-nan-tzu* (ca. 139)
		Confucianism proclaimed state ideology (136)
		Han armies in Central Asia, Korea, and Vietnam (135–100)
		State university founded to teach the Five Classics: *I-ching, Shu-ching, Shih-ching, Li chi, Ch'un Ch'iu* (125)
		Opening of "Silk Road" across Central Asia linking China and Rome (ca. 112)

200–300	300–400	400–500
"Period of Disunion," approx. 25 kingdoms and dynasties (220–581)	Huns invade China (304)	Strongest development of Chinese Buddhism combined with Hsuan-hsueh (early 5th century)
	Tao-an (312–85)	Strong conflicts between Taoists and Buddhists for state recognition (5th–7th centuries)
	Pao-p'u-tzu (320)	
	Hui-yuan (344–417)	Lu Hsiu-ching (406–477)
	Kumarajiva (344–413)	Taoism state religion in Wei kingdom (424–452)
		Buddhism proscribed in Wei kingdom (446–454)
		T'ao Hung-ching (452–536)

cluded agricultural deities; gods and goddesses of mountains, rivers, and other topographical features; and household gods such as those of the door, the stove, and the silkworm-rearing frame.

Some local deities, such as the goddess of the Hsiang River, eventually rose to national prominence through the attention of poets and scholars who found beauty and romance in their mythologies. The cult of the mother goddess Matsu, protectress of fishermen and seafarers, originated in coastal communities on the South China Sea and later won recognition from the imperial government as an orthodox religion allied with religious Taoism. Still other deities, such as the lord of the soil and his consort, were worshiped throughout China

China

500–600	600–700	
Zoroastrianism introduced into China (early 6th century)	Hung-jen (601–674)	Beginnings of Chan (Jap. Zen) Buddhism (ca. 640)
Reign of Emperor Wu (Liang dynasty), Buddhist patron and opponent of Taoism (502–549)	Beginning of Chinese cultural influence on Japan (607)	Fa-tsang (643–712)
	T'ang dynasty (618–907)	Ssu-ma Ch'eng-chen (647–735)
Chih-i (538–597)	T'ang law code, lasts in China, with revisions, through the 14th century; model with adaptations for Japan, Korea, and Vietnam (624)	Maximum extent of Chinese power in Central Asia (Afghanistan, Kashmir, Sogdiana, Oxus Valley) (650)
Sui dynasty (581–618)		Dominance of (Empress) Wu (655–705)
	Journeys of Hsuan-Tang (ca. 629–645)	Creation of system of imperialism-sponsored Buddhist and Taoist monasteries (666)
	K'uei-chi (632–682)	
	First Nestorian Christian missionary to China (635)	First document for Manichaeism in China (694)
	Islam enters China (638)	

in small shrines located in fields and rice paddies; such deities could be described as being national in distribution but entirely local in effect.

With the advent of Buddhism and religious Taoism, various Buddhas, Bodhisattvas, and Taoist divinities were added to the popular pantheon. Conversely, many local popular deities were added to the pantheons of Buddhism and religious Taoism from time to time. The pantheons of those religions were large, diverse, and elaborately organized to reflect the bureaucratic hierarchy of Chinese civil government. Indeed, the bureaucratization of the Buddhist pantheon was a characteristic of Chinese Buddhism at the popular level.

SACRIFICE

Chinese religions of all types tend to be transactional in nature; that is, deities are offered sacrifices in the hope of obtaining from them benefits of various sorts, whether immediate and specific or long-range and generalized. Official rites in ancient China included blood sacrifices and the ritual offering at altars of meat, grain, and wine; royal and aristocratic funerals routinely involved human and animal sacrifices. Ceramic and paper images gradually displaced living victims in funeral rites, while under the influence of both Buddhism and Taoism blood sacrifices were abandoned for all but high state rites and replaced by offerings of fruit, wine, and other foods. But the principle still held that ancestors required the sustenance of sacrificial food, while other divinities could be bribed with offerings of various sorts.

In the formative centuries of religious Taoism during and just after the Latter Han dynasty (first–third centuries B.C.), a key criterion according to which a local cult was accepted into the religious Taoist community as orthodox or rejected as heterodox was the absence or presence in the cult's rituals of blood sacri-

700–800	800–900	900–1000
Reign of emperor Hsuan-tsung, strong patron of Taoism and cult of Lao-tzu; greatest period of T'ang prosperity (712–756)	*The Platform Sutra of the Sixth Patriarch* (820)	Period of the Five Dynasties and Ten Kingdoms (907–960)
Pai-chang Huai-hai (720–814)	Earliest surviving Chinese printed book, a copy of the *Diamond Sutra* on a 16-foot-long roll (868)	Sung dynasty (960–1279)
Printing invented (ca. 730)		
Defeat of Chinese army at Talas River establishes boundaries between China and Muslim Abassid empire with the result that Chinese and Buddhist influence in Central Asia is replaced by Islam (751)		
Paper taken from China to Muslim countries, eventually to Christian Europe (751)		
Han Yu (768–824)		

fice. Many local popular religions in China have continued up to contemporary times to offer blood sacrifices as part of religious observances, despite the disapproval of more orthodox religions.

TEMPLE-BASED WORSHIP

A further common characteristic of Chinese religions, flowing from its commitment to sacrifice, was the localization of worship at temples and shrines. These ranged from the imperial ancestral shrines and state altars to the shelflike ancestral shrines found in the simplest homes. Every administrative center in imperial China, from the metropolis to county seats, was supplied with temples to Confucius and to the god of war. These were supplemented with privately founded (but sometimes also publicly supported) Buddhist and Taoist temples and temples devoted to local deities. State temples tended to remain vacant except on days specifically devoted to their use, while temples of more popular religions served as social centers and community-service institutions as well. Given the transactional nature of Chinese religion, temples were (and are) used on a regular basis by worshipers making offerings to the divinities, using fortune-telling facilities provided by the temples, and performing acts of worship for essentially private purposes. Buddhist, religious Taoist, and popular-cult temples also, of course, held festivals on designated days, for which the resources of both temples and communities of worshipers were mobilized and in which large numbers of worshipers might participate.

OCCULT PRACTICES

Incorporated into or existing alongside organized religions were various religious or quasi-religious popular occult practices, such as divination and

China

1000–1100	1100–1200	1200–1300
Rise of neo-Confucian thought (11th century) with major figures such as:	Mao Tzu-yuan (1086–1166)	Mongol conquest of China (1215–79)
	Reign of emperor Hui-tsung, patron of Taoism (1101–26)	Ch'uan-chen Taoism receives special benefits from Mongol government (1223)
Shao Yung (1011–77)	First Chan Buddhist monastic codes (1103–1104)	Taoists and Buddhists debate one another in Mongol court (1251–81)
Chou Tun-i (1017–73)	Hu Hung (1105–55)	
Chang Tsai (1021–77)	Wang Che (1112–70)	Tibetan Buddhist monks begin control of Chinese Buddhist monasteries (1260–64)
Ch'eng Hao (1032–85)	Chu Hsi (1130–1200)	
Ch'eng I (1033–1107)	Chang Shih (1133–80)	Yuan dynasty, established by the Mongols. During this period (1279–1368):
	Lu Tsu-ch'ien (1137–81)	
	Wang Ch'u-i (1142–1217)	Confucian scholar/bureaucrats replaced by Mongol and other non-Chinese civil servants
	Ch'en Liang (1143–94)	
	Chin-su lu (1175)	
	Imperial support begins for Ch'uan-chen Taoism (1187)	

fortune-telling, the use of amulets and talismans, shamanism, and even black magic.

Divination was central to state religious practices in ancient China. In the Shang period, questions were posed to gods or ancestors and answered by means of cracks made in ox scapulae or turtle plastrons by the application of heat. Ritual specialists were employed to perform these operations and interpret the results. Scapulomancy, as this type of divination is called, declined in the Chou period and was replaced thereafter by the casting of yarrow stalks to derive the hexagrams of the *I-ching* (Book of Changes). Divination declined in importance at the state level during the imperial period, but was never abandoned.

At the popular level, meanwhile, divination exerted a powerful appeal; no visit to a temple was complete without the casting of yarrow stalks or, especially, the throwing of two crescent-shaped blocks, the configuration of which was held to yield answers to questions posed to the gods.

State astrology relied on reading the positions of the sun, moon, and visible planets (especially Jupiter) in designated regions of the sky and on the interpretation of such portents as eclipses and comets. On the popular level, horoscopic astrology flourished, especially under the influence of Buddhism. In addition, there existed a wide range of fortune-telling practices such as palmistry, physiognomancy, and the reading of moles and other distinctive physical features.

One of the characteristic duties of priests, especially at the temples of Taoism and local popular cults, was the writing of talismans (*fu*) and the dispensing of amulets to prevent or cure disease, promote fertility, ward off malicious spells, and the like.

	1300–1400	1400–1500
Taoism and Buddhism favored by Mongols	Yuan-chang (1328–98)	Wu Yu-pi (1391–1496)
Tibetan Buddhism introduced, with rise of Chinese Tantrism as a result	Imperial edict that civil examinations be based on the *Five Books* and the *Four Classics* (1333)	Hsueh Hsuan (1392–1464)
Mongol court ritual, when not indigenous, is largely Buddhist-Lamaistic	Ming dynasty, return to native rule between Mongol and Manchu periods (1368–1644)	New Taoist canon *(Tao-tsang)*, still in use today; reprinted in 1926 (1406–45)
Major influx of Muslims during this period, with major settlements in western provinces	Ts'ao Tuen (1376–1434)	*Yung-lo ta-tien* (1407)
Nestorian Christianity revived		Chien Hsien-chang (1428–1500)
Marco Polo (1254–1324) arrives in China (1275)		Hu Chu-jen (1434–84)
		Lo Ch'ing (1443–1527)
		Wang Yang-ming (1472–1529)

Shamanism, the use of spirit-mediums to communicate with divinities and the spirits of deceased ancestors, was widespread in Chinese popular religion. Scholars disagree about the antiquity and geographical distribution of shamanism in ancient China, but most authorities allow that shamanism had become prominent at least in coastal regions and the Yangtze River Valley by the time of the Warring States period (481–221 B.C.). Shamanism as such played at best a minor role in the officially sanctioned and orthodox religions of imperial China, but on local and popular levels it remained a significant influence.

The theme of spirit possession, usually through the medium of a recognized adept, played an important role in village-level religious observances for such purposes as communication with divinities and ancestors, the identification and exorcism of malevolent spirits, and the transmission to worshipers of specific instructions from local gods (e.g., the requirement to make particular types of sacrifices in local temples, or to plant or refrain from planting a particular type of crop).

Mediums and adepts, in the guise of witches and sorcerers, occupied a darker niche in Chinese popular religion. Official national and local histories from ancient to modern times detail many instances of black magic, such as the casting of hexes and spells. Allied to the belief in black magic was a set of folkloric beliefs in malicious sprites, fox-fairies, and the like, minor deities that could set traps for the unwary, particularly by luring them into sexual misconduct.

These negative manifestations of divine influence could be countered through the use of mediums who had the ability to identify and exorcise them. Faith healing, and in particular the casting out of demons or the neutralization of spells or spirit possessions, was a recognized function of the leaders of local religions.

China

1500–1600	1600–1700	1700–1800
Wang-chi (1497–1582)	Ku Yen-wu (1613–82)	Hui Tung (1697–1758)
Lin Chao-en (1517–90)	Yen Yuan (1635–1704)	Tai Chen (1723–77)
Li Chih (1527–1602)	Manchu Ch'ing dynasty (1644–1912)	T'ien-ti hui founded (1775–76)
Mongol and Japanese incursions (1550)	Roman Catholic "Chinese Rites contro-	White Lotus Rebellion (1796–1804)
Portuguese establish Macao (1557)	versy," in which ceremonies honoring	
Mattaeo Ricci's mission to China (1583–1610)	Confucius and the ancestors were deter-mined incompatible with Christian beliefs and could not be practiced by Chinese Christians (1645–1742)	

LONGEVITY AND IMMORTALITY

The cultivation of physical longevity and physical or spiritual immortality emerged as a principal goal of Chinese religious practice during the Warring States period; the degree to which the roots of this religious goal extend further back into antiquity is unknown. Various techniques were developed to promote longevity and/or immortality, including abstention from grain and other foods that were held to nourish the "worms" of mortality; yogic breath-control exercises and sexual regimens, collectively known as "nourishing the vital essence"; the ingestion of alchemical elixirs of immortality; and visualization exercises designed to produce elixirs within the body of the adept.

Longevity and immortality, as religious goals, were often conflated and seldom precisely defined. *Immortality* embraced a spectrum of meanings ranging from the attainment of extreme old age to an ability to shed the "husk" of the physical body in order to free the spirit to wander at will to the ability of the soul or spirit to live on as a new member of the pantheon after death. Immortality in the sense of deification after death was a specific goal of religious Taoism.

In the broadest sense, the cult of immortality merged with the bedrock cult of ancestors in Chinese popular religion. To the extent that one can speak of a theology of the ancestral cult, that theology held that the soul of a deceased ancestor persisted for an indefinite period of time in a sentient condition, able to enjoy the sacrifices and veneration offered to it and to intervene in the mundane world to confer benefits on worthy descendants.

This view further intersects with the belief that the souls of the dead were judged by the lord of the underworld and his attendant deities and either allowed to enjoy the status of enshrined ancestors or consigned to eternal perdition. This in turn adumbrates the transactional nature of Chinese religious

1800–1900

T'ien-li chiao revolt (1813)	Muslim rebellions in northern and western provinces (1855–73)	Severe famine in northern provinces (1877–79)
Hung Hsiu-chuan (1814–64)	Treaties of Tientsin (1858)	Sino-French War (1883–85)
British establish Singapore (1819)	K'ang Yu-wei (1858–1927)	Sino-Japanese War (1894–95)
Opium War (1839–42)	Anglo-French military campaigns (1858–60)	Taiwan under Japanese control (1895–1945)
Collapse of Manchu (Ch'ing) empire due to European establishment of "spheres of influence," internal dissension, and independence of former possessions (1842–1911)	Treaty of Peking (1860)	"Hundred Days Reform" (1898)
	"Self-strengthening" period of rapid industrialization (1861–94)	United States announces "Open Door Policy" (1899–1900)
Treaties of Wanghia and Whampoa (1844)	T'an Ssu-t'ung (1865–98)	
T'ai-ping Rebellion (1850–64)	Sun Yat-sen (1866–1925)	
Nien Rebellion (1853–68)	Tientsin massacre (1870)	
Hakka-Cantonese War (1855–57)	Liang Ch'i-ch'ao (1873–1929)	

observances; sacrifices, funeral rituals, and other acts of worship were designed in large part to permit the souls of the dead to avoid consignment to the underworld. In true bureaucratic fashion, the lord of the underworld and his minions could be bribed with appropriate offerings or coerced through the intervention of more powerful deities to release souls that fell into their clutches; souls, or descendants acting on their behalf, could negotiate with the divinities of death to protest against wrongful or premature death or unjust consignment to the underworld.

In Sanhsia, Taiwan, a geomancer scatters rice grains and seeds (symbolizing fertility), nails (indicating a son), and coins (for wealth) on a new grave (1970s).

MESSIANISM

According to ancient and widespread belief, civil authority in China was held by rulers by virtue of a Mandate of Heaven (T'ienming) conferred upon the founder of a dynasty and held in trust by his descendants for so long as they ruled in conformity with Heaven's precepts. Accordingly, a popular perception that a dynasty had ceased to possess the Mandate of Heaven provided the occasion for dynastic rebellions, during which new claimants to the mandate would arise. Messianism in Chinese religion can thus be seen as an extreme manifestation of a broadly accepted political

China		
1900–		
T'ai-hsu (1889–1947)	May Fourth Movement (1919)	People's Republic of China (1949–)
Mao Tse-tung (1893–1976)	Taoist canon *(Tao-tsang)* reprinted under state sponsorship (1923–26)	Tibet absorbed by China (1951–53)
Fung Yu-lan (1895–)		13 state-sponsored conferences on role of Confucius and neo-Confucian thought in Marxist society (1960–62)
Hsiung Shih-li (1895–1968)	Chiang Kai-shek (1887–1975); Northern Expedition (1926–28)	
Boxer Rebellion (1900–1901)	Nationalist (Kuomintang) regime (1928–37)	Fung Yu-lan issues state-sponsored new edition of *History of Chinese Philosophy* from Marxist perspective (1962–64)
Tibetan independence from China (1911)		
Every province declares independence (October 1911–March 1912)	Japan occupies Manchuria (1931)	
	"Long March" (1934–35)	Cultural Revolution (1966)
Emperor abdicates; Sun Yat-sen proclaims Republic (1912)	Sino-Japanese War (1937–45)	Uprising at Tienanmen Square (April–June 1989)
Yuan Shih-k'ai suppresses Republic (1912–16)	Civil war (1945–49)	
Japan cedes dominance in Shantung, Manchuria, and Inner Mongolia at Versailles (1915).		

principle, the difference being that instead of claiming the mandate, the leader of a messianic movement would proclaim that civil authority as such was about to be swept away and replaced by a new era of direct theocratic rule. Because of its almost inevitable association with rebellion, messianism was generally feared by the civil authorities in China and ruthlessly suppressed. Messianic movements in China arose from a variety of wellsprings in popular religion, most especially from splinter groups associated with religious Taoism or with Maitreyan Buddhism, and found concrete expression in secret organizations such as the White Lotus Society. The vast and catastrophic T'ai-ping Rebellion of the mid-nineteenth century was a late manifestation of a long tradition of Chinese messianism; it combined an innovative pseudo-Christian ideology with the ancient doctrine of the era of Great Peace (*t'ai-p'ing*) that would arise upon the overthrow of secular authority.

ORGANIZED RELIGIONS

Religious organizations in China existed sometimes as beneficiaries of state patronage, sometimes with the tacit approval of the state, and sometimes beneath its lofty notice, but seldom, and never for very long, in the face of its active opposition. With the partial exception of Buddhism from the Northern Wei through the mid-T'ang periods (386–845), no organized religion in China ever succeeded in establishing itself as a center of power, prestige, and authority that could rival the state itself.

From ancient to modern times, organized religion in China existed primarily in the form of the "Three Teachings"—Confucianism, Taoism, and Buddhism.

CONFUCIANISM

Most scholars agree that Confucianism was primarily a system of moral and ethical philosophy, rather than a religion as such. The term *Confucianism* is sometimes used loosely to refer to a set of family-centered beliefs and practices the religious manifestation of which was the cult of ancestors, but that usage obscures more than it illuminates. Recognizably religious aspects of Confucianism as such took two quite disparate forms.

State Confucianism arose during the Han dynasty (206 B.C.–A.D. 220) and was characterized by the establishment under government auspices of official Confucian temples and the conducting of rites of Confucian civic religion. Confucian temples enshrined, in the form of inscribed ancestor tablets, the spirits of Confucius and his principal disciples. Sacrificial rites, modeled more or less accurately on the rites of the Chou dynasty, were conducted at those temples on designated holidays, such as the birthday of Confucius, and on such occasions the emperor or his deputies would deliver public homilies on such Confucian virtues as filial piety or propriety. The state rites to Confucius were revived by the government of the Republic of China after the fall of the last imperial dynasty in 1911 and continue to be practiced on Taiwan in part as an emblem of the Nationalist government's commitment to traditional Chinese values.

State Confucian temples were also on occasion used for private worship in imperial times, for example, by candidates praying for success in the official civil service examinations.

The other religious manifestation of Confucianism, associated particularly with Neo-Confucianism of both the Chu Hsi and the Wang Yang-ming schools, involved personal introspection, meditation, and self-cultivation. This was essentially religious in both form and motivation but had as its goal the attainment of sagelike wisdom, goodness, and tranquillity in the present world, with little or no reference to the transcendence of death by an immortal soul. However, it is safe to assume that practitioners of this form of personal, religious Confucianism also attended to the Chinese cult of ancestor veneration, and indeed the primacy of the family line expressed as a continuum of ancestors extending into the past and descendants extending into the future was one of the fundamental assumptions of Confucianism itself.

TAOISM

Taoism arose during the Warring States period as a rather disparate philosophical school that stressed the importance of acting in accordance with the Tao, "natural process," rather than according to the contingent interests of individual persons. By the early Han period it had come to be associated also with cosmological theory, the cult of immortality, and the ideal of religious transcendence.

Taoism as a term denoting an organized religion should, strictly speaking, be limited to the religion founded by the patriarch Chang Tao-ling near the end of the Late Han dynasty. Religious Taoism, in this strict sense, takes Lao-tzu as its founding sage; finds doctrinal truth in a set of canonical scriptures (collected in the *Tao-tsang,* or "Taoism Patrology") revealed to Chang Tao-ling, the Mao-shan (or Shang-ch'ing) patriarchs, and their successors; relies on the direct transmission of doctrine through a line of ordained priests; and takes the cultivation of immortality—that is, transcendence of death to become one of the members of the Taoist pantheon—as its fundamental religious goal. Taoism in popular parlance tends to be used in a much looser sense, embracing everything from the philosophical works of Lao-tzu and Chuang-tzu to the beliefs and practices of Chinese popular religion to doctrines and practices more properly associated with Ch'an (Zen) Buddhism. Particularly in popular works on Chinese philosophy and religion by Western writers, many practices and attitudes are described as "Taoist" that would not be recognized as such by the ordained clergy of religious Taoism.

BUDDHISM

Buddhism reached China from India via the oasis cities of the Silk Road in the first century. After a centuries-long period of preparation and acculturation, Buddhism emerged in the Northern and Southern Dynasties period (221–589) in distinctively Chinese forms. The transactional nature of Chinese religion may in part explain the appeal in China of such schools as Pure Land Buddhism, which offered salvation in a Western Paradise through the intervention of the Bodhisattva Amitabha. Ch'an ("meditation"; Jap. *Zen*) Buddhism represented a radical Chinese reinterpretation of Buddhist doctrine, discarding scriptural authority in favor of enlightenment through meditation and the systematic elimination of mental impediments to direct religious inspiration. Buddhism contributed importantly to the metaphysics and religious attitudes of Neo-Confucianism; Buddhism was itself strongly influenced by native Chinese religious beliefs, as, for example, in a tendency on the popular level to conflate the goddess Ma-tsu with the feminized Bodhisattva Kuan-yin.

Buddhism was subjected to a series of devastating purges motivated in part by political and economic considerations in the mid-ninth century and declined in importance at the elite level thereafter, though it has maintained both organizational strength and doctrinal orthodoxy into modern times. Lamaism, the national Buddhist religion of Tibet and Mongolia, received imperial patronage from the Manchu rulers of the Ch'ing dynasty (1912), but declined in importance in China proper after that dynasty's collapse.

MINOR RELIGIONS

Nestorian Christianity was introduced into China from Central Asia in the eighth century, if not before. It received official state recognition as a religion, but won relatively few converts except among minority peoples such as Khitans and Turks. Nestorianism received some patronage from the Mongol emperors of the Yuan dynasty in China, but declined in importance thereafter and disappeared by the fourteenth century. Catholic missionaries reached China in the late sixteenth century, and Protestant missionaries in the early nineteenth century; neither form of Christianity ever rose above marginal status in China.

Islam was introduced into China in the eighth century by Arab and Persian merchants, who built mosques for their own use in the capital at Ch'ang-an as well as in a number of coastal trading cities. Islam became of greater importance in China after the Yuan dynasty when many minority peoples, especially Uighurs and Kazakhs in Chinese Central Asia and Miao in Yunnan, converted to Islam. A scattered population of Chinese converts to Islam, known as Hui but ethnically indistinguishable from other Chinese except in religious matters, continues to exist in China today.

Colonies of Jewish merchants were formed in Kaifeng and other Chinese cities during the Sung dynasty (960–1279) and gradually became part of the larger Chinese community through intermarriage. A small and religiously vestigial community of Chinese Jews continued to exist in Kaifeng until recent times.

Among the diverse minority peoples of China, many became substantially acculturated to Chinese norms and accepted many of the beliefs and practices of Chinese religion. Some form recognizable religious communities, such as the aforementioned Muslim ethnic groups or the Theravada Buddhist Dai of the southwest. Others, such as the Yao and the Chuang, practice indigenous religions generally, but inadequately, described as animist.

THE RELIGIOUS EXPERIENCE IN CHINA

A famous cliche holds that the Chinese are practitioners of several religions simultaneously; a Chinese official might be a Confucian in public life, a Taoist in private, and a Buddhist in attitudes toward death and rebirth. Like many cliches, this contains an element of truth. The recognized, organized religions of China tended not to emphasize religious exclusivity of belief, though it was generally expected that ordained religious personnel of Buddhism or Taoism would devote themselves exclusively to their own faiths. In general, however, Chinese religion embraces a broad spectrum of beliefs and practices and can only provisionally and imperfectly be sorted into distinct creeds.

Religion in traditional China offered a great variety of possible expressions, from the pomp and splendor of imperial rituals to eremitic mysticism, from vague agnosticism to fervent personal faith, from academic theology to village-level credulity. It is possible to deal quite precisely with various aspects of religion in China, with the doctrines and practices of particular Chinese religions limited as to time and place, and with the religious beliefs of particular Chinese individuals. Chinese religion as such, however, is a term of such wide scope and amorphous reference that it inevitably evokes much while explaining little.

Chinese religions (life cycle). Ceremonies and practices connected with the major life transitions for Chinese people (especially men), or rites of passage, show a gradual crescendo of importance from life's beginning stages to its culmination at death.

Birth: Traditionally, there were a number of practices meant to protect a healthy pregnancy and to deal with the dangerous period before and after birth. Ceremonies recognized the child's first full month and/or the first one hundred days.

Capping and Marriage: Confucian society celebrated the maturity of a young man, at about the age of twenty, with a "capping" ceremony, now long discarded. The transition to full human status, however, came only with marriage, which was essentially an agreement between families, not individuals. The wife left her birth family to be incorporated into her husband's, her status there to be determined by whether she produced a son to continue the patriarchal line. Engagement and marriage were complex and ritualized events, though the wedding ceremony itself was rather simple, including a formal introduction to the bridal chamber and a joint worship of the groom's ancestors. A feast followed to celebrate the union, looking forward to the inception of a new branch of the family.

Death and Burial: Death rituals mark the final and most important life-cycle transition, especially for the male, who would assume his place of power and honor among the patriarchal ancestors. There are many regional variations of death rituals, but all included the choice of an auspicious time for burial, the careful geomantic placement of his grave, and the summoning of Taoist or Buddhist clergy to chant for the welfare of the soul. Offerings included food, flowers, incense, and a whole array of paper goods to be sent along for the use of the departed in the next world. The dead person was placed in a wooden coffin and taken to the place of burial with a grand procession, including music, dancing, actors, and ritual expressions of grief. On all important family occasions thereafter, the ancestors, up through five or six generations, would be ritually informed, fed, and revered.

Overall, Chinese life-cycle rituals reveal that, religiously and socially, the Chinese person grows gradually from the status of nonperson at birth to personhood at marriage and the birth of a son. Finally, at death, persons realized their place of highest importance when they were elevated to the powerful status of revered ancestor. The patriarchical hierarchy was maintained throughout life and canonized in death. *See also* ancestral rites; Chinese ritual; life-cycle rituals.

Chinese religions (thought and ethics). Within the Chinese classical tradition, the terms *tao-te* and *li-hsueh* are used to refer to ethics. The most commonly used modern term is *lun-li*. For most of the premodern Chinese tradition the distinctions between religious and philosophical ethics, common in the modern West, do not apply. Virtually all of classical Chinese thought is at its core ethical. Chinese ethical theory compares to that of the West in that both traditions involve a range of approaches including appeals to virtue, metaphysics, and reason. The principal difference can be seen by the fact that Chinese moral laws are not classically derived from a notion of a "high god"; nor does China develop a tradition of individualism and rationalism such as is found in the post-Renaissance and post-Enlightenment West. Chinese ethics always consider the individual as part of larger aggregates (family, community, empire, nature, cosmos).

The two most important traditions, Confucianism and Taoism, share a common heritage. This includes texts such as the *I-ching;* terms such as the *Way* (*Tao*); and ideals such as harmony (*ho*) and virtue (*te*).

Confucianism is the best-developed expression of a virtue or character ethics in Asia. It has exerted tremendous influence over the development of moral and political life throughout Asia. It is perhaps best compared to the Aristotelian tradition in the West. At the heart of the tradition are the cardinal virtues of *li, jen, chih,* and *i;* a concern for placing the individual within community beginning with the immediate family, then the extended family, community, nation, and finally the cosmos; and the ideal of the perfected human as gentleman or sage. Confucianism views the community in terms of a variety of social rituals (li). All social relations have a formal aspect involving rules that govern decorum or propriety. This formal structure becomes morally charged by a sense of respect, love, benevolence, or reciprocity (jen) guided by wisdom (chih) and righteousness (i). Major figures of the later tradition such as Mencius, Chu Hsi, and Wang Yang-ming developed these basic ideas by adding important metaphysical dimensions.

Taoist ethics usually refer to the tradition that developed from the writings collected in the *Lao-tzu* and the *Chuang-tzu.* Taoism takes a more "natural" approach to ethics than does Confucianism. Taoists are often viewed as escapists who avoid involvement in social life (and are thus seen as nonethical), but in fact they are very concerned with teaching a style of social existence that places its emphasis upon non-willful action (*wu-wei*) and natural spontaneity (*tzu-jan*). Taoism rejects the need for formal rules and structures, pursuing instead a kind of "natural anarchy" that trusts in the inherent goodness of people. People and government should try not to exert their will on people and things. This is nonaction or non-willful action. Taoism seeks to free the mind of formal constraints so that persons are able to follow their own true nature, which corresponds to the true Way (*Tao*). *See also* Confucianism; i; jen; li; Taoism; tzu-jan; wu-wei.

Chinese rites controversy, debate over participation in indigenous rituals by Asian Christians. Primarily a question of religious purity within Catholic communities, it also has been a general problem for Protestants, occurring in Chinese, Japanese, and Korean communities. Refusal to participate in non-Christian rites often stimulated political persecution, while participation in them threatened ecclesiastical excommunication.

Earlier, Nestorian Christians in China performed regular services for the dead and rituals before imperial images. Later, Jesuits were informed by Confucian scholars that rites honoring Confucius and ancestors were merely civil ceremonies. Dominican and Franciscan Catholic missionaries disagreed, claiming that common people who participated in temple rites or worshiped before home altars with spirit tablets believed many idolatrous superstitions. In 1645, guidance from Rome was formally requested. Questions regarding levels of participation (passive/active) in various rites were raised, including details regarding titles and names for God, Confucius, and spirits of the dead. In 1700 a statement from the emperor K'ang Hsi (r. 1662–1722) interpreted the rites as merely civil acts of reverence. Roman authorities disagreed, demanding in 1715 and 1745 that all Catholic missionaries take oaths against participating in superstitious rituals. Converts were taught these restrictions also.

After 1865, Japanese Christians' participation in imperial Shinto rituals forced further confrontations. Protestant missionaries and believers also faced similar problems. In addition, Bible translators struggled to find appropriate names for God in Chinese, Japanese, and Korean. Twentieth-century political changes promoted religious freedom and prompted more lenient interpretations of the rituals, so that in 1939 Rome no longer required the oath against practicing these rites. *See also* China, Christianity in; Korea, Roman Catholicism in.

Chinese ritual. Ritual is a major dimension of the religious and cultural life of the Chinese people, with archaeological evidence for continuous ritual practices dating back to 3500 B.C. To the Chinese, adherence to correct ritual is what has distinguished their cultural identity from that of surrounding "barbarians"; ritual action presumes a single cosmological order in which everything is composed of the same basic ethers (*ch'i*), but polarized according to the principles of *yin* and *yang* and governed by the dynamic succession of the five phases (*wu-hsing*). In China, the invisible world, composed of ancestors, ghosts, and gods, roughly mirrors the organization of the visible world of the living, and these two worlds are bound together by the reciprocal exchange of offerings for blessings; formally coded hierarchies of rites, specialists, and appropriate deities have long enforced some government control over popular worship; and ritual experts are trained professionals hired to perform specific rites and usually do not engage in any additional pastoral or missionary work. Finally, while the written ritual traditions of Taoism, Buddhism, Confucianism, and the imperial cult have variously distinguished themselves from the primarily oral traditions of local folk religion, there has always been a great deal of interaction and dependency among subtraditions.

Traditional and Imperial Rites: Archaeology testifies to a prehistoric cult of the dead involving grave gifts for use in the otherworld and symbols of enduring life such as red ocher or jade. There is also evidence for divination and offerings to enhance the fecundity of the land. Historical records testify to the development of rituals to legitimate the central rule of a conquering king. The elevation of royal ancestors resulted in a divine hierarchy presided over by a High God, identified with Heaven (T'ien), that served to unify and subordinate other gods. The king consulted his ancestors through divination, primarily using oracle bones or tortoise shells, on political, military, or ritual matters. Similarly, offerings to the ancestors and to gods associated with the powers of nature, frequently accompanied by formal petitions, made the king the prime ritual mediator of the invisible and visible worlds. He controlled seasonal rites, codification of the almanac, and supervision of the heavens for portent and signs. The ritual authority of the king and emperor was distinguished from that of traditional shamans (*hsi* and *wu*), men and women who became possessed by spirits in order to heal, bring rain, or exorcise harmful forces.

The emperors of the early Ch'in (220–206 B.C.) and Han (202 B.C.–A.D. 220) dynasties further elaborated an imperial cult in which they presided over a growing systemization of shrines that included city gods and important local deities. The rites of the wind and mountain (*feng* and *shan*), offered by the first Ch'in emperor alone on the top of Mt. T'ai, and repeated by various others, symbolized the approval of the gods. Han emperors adopted a reinterpreted Confucianism (as in the writings of Tung Chung-shu) as a state religion, which led to the emergence of a government Board of Rites and the spread of state-supported temples where rites to Confucius became the focus of the scholar-official class. Confucius (ca. 551–479 B.C.) himself taught ritual (*li*) as proper social relations and behavior in accord with both tradition and moral virtue. As such, ritual included both reverence for the ancestors as well as the conventions of social etiquette. For Confucius, ritual was a moral ordering of human affairs, the very opposite of chaos. As such it had little to do with the appeasement of spirits, elaborate display, or the trading of offerings for divine favors.

Taoist and Buddhist Ritual: Sectarian Taoist movements of the second and third centuries developed complex communal rites involving confession, healing, the salvation of ancestors, and sexual practices to promote immortality. Fourth- and fifth-century Taoist sects added rites of meditation and visualization, also refining local rites of animal sacrifice into bloodless offerings of petitions, incense, and prayers (e.g., *chai, chiao*) in return for the descent of the renewing ethers (ch'i) of the highest heavens. By the ninth century, Taoist ritual was a coherent synthesis of folk religion, court ritual, and Buddhist practices that was further developed by subsequent movements such as the twelfth-century Total Perfection (Ch'uan-chen) sect. The distinguishing feature of Taoist ritual has been its focus on the human body as a microcosm of the macrocosmic universe. Echoing the long-lived shamanic traditions with which it has remained closely connected, Taoist ritual expertise involves the internalization of successive cosmic deities that are then called forth in communal rituals to help summon the life-renewing ethers.

Buddhist ritual included practices of meditation, visualization, recitation of scriptures, fasting, and public confession. Central to Buddhist rites for the lay community is the Ghost Festival (*p'u-tu* or *yu-lan-p'en*), regularly offered for the salvation of the numerous hungry ghosts and the release of the dead imprisoned in the ten courts of purgatory. This ritual of general deliverance introduced important themes of salvation and universality into Chinese ritual life.

Popular Religion: Most ritual in Chinese communities centers on the home and local temple. Domestic rites include offerings to ancestors and household gods such as the gate gods and the kitchen god. The two most important life-cycle rites, weddings and funerals, occur for the most part in the home. Local temples include more than one deity and it is routine for a visitor to acknowledge them all with a bow and incense stick. Offerings of food and money differ for ancestors, ghosts, and gods; and it is said that a steady diet of the offerings intended for a god can convert a ghost into finer stuff. The requests brought to such deities frequently concern the prevention of illness, healing, economic woes, protection of property and family members, prayers for children, and the transfer of merit to ancestors. Various forms of divination (moon blocks, numbered sticks, etc.) are used at local temples. Local temples hold at least one major festival a year, usually on the god's birthday, but many will also celebrate other traditional holidays of the ritual year. Various types of spirit mediums or cults centered on spirit-writing may also be based in local temples. Most common among traditional ritual instruments are firecrackers to warn away harmful forces, musicians and performers to entertain the gods, incense to carry prayers up to heaven, and various denominations of spirit money burned to buy pardons and pay bribes among the heavenly bureaucracy. Especially since the twelfth century, a self-conscious divide has distinguished the decorous rites of elite religion (mainly Neo-Confucianism and some forms of Taoism and Buddhism) from the more colorful rites of popular religion, which China's rulers are still apt to consider no more than superstition. *See also* Buddhism; ch'i; chiao; Chinese popular religion; Chinese religions (life cycle); Ch'uan-chen Taoism; Confucianism; divination; feng-shan sacrifices; geomancy; kingship, sacred; li; ritual; sacrifice; shamanism; state cult, Chinese; Taoism; Tung Chung-shu; wu-hsing; yin and yang.

Chinese sectarian religions. In addition to the observance of lineage and family ancestral rites, the worship of various deities in Chinese popular religion, and the support of state-approved institutional religions like Buddhism or Taoism, laypersons in China have frequently been attracted to voluntary religious societies and organized sectarian movements. Most local societies have had limited goals; religious sects have claimed to offer a uniquely effective means for universal salvation. The government has viewed such groups with suspicion and has often actively suppressed them.

Chinese religious sects can be traced back in history to the period of the Yellow Turbans and the Celestial Masters, sects of the second century associated with Taoism. The majority of sects, however, have been related to folk Buddhism. Often syncretistic in belief and practice, such sects have developed their own organizational structures, congregational liturgies, membership rites, and leadership patterns.

Sects may be distinguished from secret societies in China because of the primacy given by sects to transformative religious visions in which social, economic, and political norms are grounded. Secret societies, in contrast, have tended to support such predetermined norms with elements of religious practice. Moreover, members of religious sects have sought to share their salvific vision openly whenever possible, secrecy being adopted only under circumstances of persecution. Some Chinese sects, like those related to the White Lotus Society, have held millenarian views that have justified messianic warfare against the state, such as occurred with the White Lotus Rebellion (1796–1803) and the Eight Trigrams Uprising of 1813. *See also* church/sect; Huang-chin; Ti'en-shih Taoism; White Lotus Society.

ching (jing; Chin., "classic," lit., "warp"), term first applied to the authoritative Confucian classics and eventually extended to authoritative Taoist and Buddhist works. *See also* Confucianism (authoritative texts and their interpretation).

ching (jing; Chin., "seriousness," "reverence"), Confucian attitude and practice of integrity, single-mindfulness, and reverential self-cultivation. An essential trait for the preparation of the mind in order to achieve sagehood. *See also* Confucianism.

ching (jing; Chin., "seminal essence," originally, "highly polished rice for offerings"), a Taoist term that came to denote subtle and vivifying concentrations of *ch'i* (vital energy) in any of a variety of forms. In physiology, *ching* might refer to a variety of essential bodily fluids and energies, e.g., semen in males and vaginal fluid in females. In the macrocosm, it denoted the essential stuff of stars or spirits, benevolent and malevolent. Since seminal essence represented the form in which life-giving energy could be transmitted, the term often figures in Taoist physiological practices. *See also* ch'i; physiological techniques (Taoism).

Ch'ing ming (ching ming; Chin., "Clear and Bright"), the second most important festival in the Chinese religious year. Occurring in the third lunar month, the festival is dedicated to visiting ancestral tombs. Family members attend to required maintenance, share in an elaborate sacrificial meal, and offer money and other gifts to important ancestors. *See also* ancestral rites; Chinese religions (festal cycle).

chingo-kokka (chin-goh-koh-kah; Jap., "protection of the state"), early Japanese belief that a state-supported Buddhism would use its ritual power to ensure the peace and prosperity of the country.

Ch'ing-t'an (ching-tahn; Chin., "Pure Discussions"), new mode of discourse among a certain group of Chinese literati in Wei-Chin, China (221–420) who cultivated an artistic language associated with three "abstruse" works, the *I-ching*, the *Lao-tzu*, and the *Chuang tzu*. It involved conflicts and reconciliations between Confucian ethics and the Taoist way of life and reflected the religio-philosophical shift from the Han (206 B.C.–A.D. 220) Confucian cosmology of micro-macrocosmic correspondence to a new ontology of being and nonbeing. Its linguistic forms greatly influenced Chinese literature and art, and its practitioners' unusual life-style influenced a tradition of "unconventional scholars." *See also* Chinese language and literature, religious aspects of.

ching-tso (jing-dyoh; Chin., "quiet-sitting"), form of Neo-Confucian meditation used to calm the mind in order to achieve self-realization and Confucian sagehood. Quiet-sitting is practiced in a chair or sitting on the floor. *See also* meditation; Neo-Confucianism.

Ching-t'u. *See* Pure Land school (China).

Ch'ing-wei Taoism (ching-way; Chin., "Clarified Tenuity"), a complex of Chinese ritual traditions founded ca. 900 and codified, in part, in the fourteenth century. Its "thunder rites" allow a priest to internalize the spiritual power of thunder to facilitate meditative union with the Tao (undifferentiated unity). *See also* Taoism.

Chinnamasta (chin-nah-mah'stah; Skt., "she whose head has been cut off"), a Hindu goddess popular in Tantrism. Holding her severed head in one hand and a bloody sword in the other, she stands on the copulating bodies of the love god and his consort. She represents the cyclical rhythms according to which life feeds upon death. *See also* Shakti; Tantra.

Chin-su lu (jin-*soo* loo; Chin., "Reflections on Things at Hand"; 1176), anthology of the writings of Chou Tun-i, Chang Tsai, Ch'eng Hao, and Ch'eng I compiled by Chu Hsi and Lu Tsu-ch'ien. Defining orthodox Neo-Confucian religious and philosophic principles, it expounds metaphysics, cosmology, ritual, and ethics along with recommendations for methods of scholarly study and self-cultivation. *See also* Chang Tsai; Ch'eng Hao; Ch'eng I; Chou Tun-i; Chu Hsi; Neo-Confucianism.

Chin-tan Taoism (jin-dahn; Chin., "Golden Elixir"), a Taoist system of spiritual refinement through meditation, otherwise known as "inner alchemy." An ideal more than a sect, it offers methods of achieving perfection through cultivating spirit (*shen*) and vital energy (*ch'i*). It is popular in the San-chiao ("Three Teachings") synthesis of Chinese religions. *See also* alchemy; ch'i; San-chiao; shen.

Chinul (chin-ool; 1158–1210), Korean Buddhist monk and philosopher. As an ordained monk in the Ch'an (Kor. *Son*) tradition, Chinul rose to the rank of National Teacher (*kuksa*) during the period of the Ch'oe military rule (1170–1258). This same military had promoted and supported Son Buddhism over the teachings of sects that had been supported by the monarchy it had displaced and the aristocracy and civil bureaucracy that it had oppressed.

As a philosopher, Chinul is most noted for his incorporation of Hua-yen Buddhist theory, as explicated by Li T'ung-hsuan (635–730), into Son Buddhism and his attempt to unite all the sects of Korea (teaching and meditative) into a single Korean sect (the Chogye sect). Half a century before, the royal monk Uich'on, with the backing of the throne of his father and three brothers, had decimated the ranks of the Son sects by establishing a meditative T'ien-t'ai sect with the primary emphasis on T'ien-t'ai scholasticism and ritual. Chinul's response was to reverse this synthesis by placing primary emphasis on individual instantaneous enlightenment achieved through meditation on the "living phrases" (*hwadu*) of Ch'an koans (para-doxical teachings that transcend logical or conceptual thought) followed by the study and understanding of Buddhist doctrine as enunciated in the Hua-yen school.

Chinul's reform of Buddhism was important for the period because it defined Buddhism primarily as a practical tradition for the enlightenment of people, without reference to the state-sponsored paradigm of Buddhism as an institution for obtaining blessings and warding off disasters. It was also important as a reform of meditative Buddhism, which previously had sponsored geomantic and prognostication services for the state. Finally, in line with his emphasis on meditation as the primary focus of Buddhism, Chinul established lay meditation and scripture study societies, where ritualism, geomancy, prognostication, the seeking of fame and wealth, all mainstays of Koryo state Buddhism, were shown to be illusory and inferior to the realization of innate Buddhahood. *See also* Chogye Buddhism; Hua-yen school; hwadu; T'ien-t'ai school.

Chinvat (chin'vaht; Avestan, "separator bridge"), the Zoroastrian judgment site after death. The bridge is wide for the good souls, narrow for the evil. *See also* afterworld; Zoroastrianism.

Ch'iu Ch'u-chi (chyoh choo-jee; 1148–1227), poet, Taoist priest, and disciple of Wang Che, the patriarch of Ch'uan-chen Taoism. Ch'iu Ch'u-chi (also known as Ch'iu Ch'ang-ch'un) founded the sub-tradition Lung-men of the Ch'uan-chan school. Courted by several rulers, he was patronized by Genghis Khan, the Mongol general. This led to the rapid growth of Ch'uan-chen Taoism. *See also* Ch'uan-chen Taoism; Wang Che.

Chiu-hua Shan (jyoh-hwah shahn), one of the "four famous mountains" of Chinese Buddhist geography; it is located in Anhwei and is home to the Bodhisattva Ti-tsang. *See also* mountains, sacred; O-mei Shan; pilgrimage; T'ien-t'ai Shan; Ti-tsang; Wu-t'ai Shan.

Chogyam Trungpa (choo'gyahm troong'pah; Tibetan, 1940–87), Tibetan teacher noted for his propagation of Tibetan Buddhism in North America. Trungpa was recognized as the eleventh Trungpa *tulku* ("incarnate lama"), an important line of Kagyu tulkus who presided over the Surmang monasteries in eastern Tibet. He was found and enthroned when he was eighteen months old, was subsequently ordained, and received the rigorous training reserved for high tulkus. He fled Chinese-occupied Tibet in 1959, first working in India under appointment by the Dalai Lama, then traveling to England in 1963, where he relinquished his monastic vows, married, and taught Tibetan Buddhism and its contemplative practices to Westerners. Arriving in the United States in 1970, Trungpa spent the next seventeen years teaching, writing, founding contemplative centers, and inaugurating various organizations, including the Vajradhatu association of (Tibetan) Buddhist churches (Halifax, Nova Scotia, Canada), the Naropa Institute, an upper division accredited college (Boulder, Colorado), the Nalanda Translation Committee (Halifax and Boulder), and Shambhala Training, a nonsectarian program in meditation. Trungpa was known for his innovative, sometimes unconventional approach to transmitting Buddhism to the West and for his insistance that meditation is the cornerstone of Buddhism. *See also* Kagyu-pa.

Chogye Buddhism (chohg-yeh), a unified order of several Korean Buddhist meditative schools during the period of Ch'oe military rule (1170–1258) and in modern times the largest order of celibate, Ch'an (Kor. *Son*) practitioners in Korea. In the Koryo period (918–1392) Nine Mountain Schools of Ch'an had existed, but under the influence of Chinul Pojokuksa (1158–1210) they formed a single school. Though small schools of Northern and Southern Ch'an Buddhism continued to exist until the end of the Koryo period, by the fifteenth century their differences ceased to exist.

Chinul's Chogye school taught that sudden enlightenment occurred through meditative insight into the *koans* (paradoxical teachings that transcend logical or conceptual thought) of the Ch'an tradition (*kanhwa son*) and should be followed by gradual cultivation of the mind through the study of Buddha's teachings. Meditation and quiescent insight were the beginning of learning, not its conclusion. This method also incorporated Pure Land practices as an aid to faith.

Though Buddhism was disestablished in the Neo-Confucianized Choson period (1392–1910), Chinul's perspective on Ch'an Buddhism became mainline practice. In the sixteenth century, the monk Hyujong Sosantaesa (1520–1604) expanded on this perspective by incorporating Neo-Confucianism and Taoist philosophy into Chogye Buddhism. He was also able to reestablish the monk examinations and obtain royal help in the preservation of Ch'an temples.

During the Japanese colonial period (1910–45), the Japanese reestablished Buddhism as a state religion, but, following Japanese Rinzai Buddhist practice, introduced a married clergy. This new sect of Buddhism was called the T'aeko order, after the late Koryo period Imje (Lin-chi) Master Po'u T'aeko (1301–82) and was meant to unite all Buddhist clergy and temples into a single church. In response, the celibate clergy united under the banner of the Chogye order, and after liberation in 1945 it began its long struggle to regain control over the temples given to the T'aeko order. Today both orders exist in Korea, though their life-styles are quite different. The Chogye order is noted for its maintenance of the Vinaya rules, its comprehensive training in both Ch'an and Hua-yen traditions, and its attempts to rid Buddhism of its long-standing folk practices, while the T'aeko order continues its married clergy, hereditary ownership of temples, and its accommodation to popular lay practice. *See also* Chinul; Haein Temple.

Ch'ondogwan. *See* Korea, new religions in.

Ch'ondogyo (chuhn'doh-kyoh; Kor., "teaching or religion of the heavenly way"), one of the first new religions to appear in Korea in the nineteenth century. The Religion of the Heavenly Way was established by Ch'oe Che'u (1824–64) under the name Eastern Learning (Tonghak), a name deliberately chosen by Ch'oe to indicate that his movement was meant to be an alternative to the then current Western Learning (Sohak), or Roman Catholicism. Though opposed to Catholicism, Ch'oe's Tonghak owes much to Roman Catholic doctrine, practice, and organization.

Founding: The founder, Ch'oe Che'u, was a provincial scholar who fell ill and received a vision of the Lord-on-High (Sangje) in 1860. The Lord on High commissioned Ch'oe with a talisman in twenty-one characters to cure people's illness and revealed to him the potions and incantations that would bring about a tranquil age. The creedal base of this new religious movement was a mixture of Neo-Confucian ideas about self-cultivation and the ability of moral discipline to change the political and economic order, Roman Catholic beliefs in the personal protection of a heavenly lord who would help his followers to usher in a new kingdom, and Korean folk beliefs about healing, the use of talismans, and medicine. Ch'oe identified himself with the Lord on High and taught a form of incarnationism to his followers. Because of its similarity to Roman Catholicism, Ch'oe efforts at propagation were suspect and he was arrested for propagating Western Learning and superstitious doctrine. He was beheaded in 1864 during the Second Catholic Persecution.

His group was later led by his nephew Ch'oe Sihyong (1827–98), who further developed the concept of egalitarianism that was a part of the doctrine that heaven and humans are one. Tonghak continued as an underground movement until the 1890s. Thereafter Tonghak leaders led an armed insurrection in 1894 against the government in order to redress social and economic oppression.

Schism: In 1905 a schism in the movement split Tonghak into the Religion of the Heavenly Way (Ch'ondogyo) and the Religion of the Guardian of Heaven (Cich'ongyo). The Religion of the Guardian of Heaven was further divided into the Religion of the Heavenly Ruler (Sangjegyo). Son Pyonghi (1861–1922), the third patriarch of Ch'ondogyo, instilled a sense of patriotism and nationalism in his group during the period of the Japanese occupation by emphasizing education as a means of liberating Koreans from foreign rule. He was also a member of the committee that drafted the Declaration of Independence from Japan and had the honor of reading the declaration on March 1, 1919, at Pagoda Park, a date that is still celebrated by Koreans as their national independence day. Of the nineteen signers of the declaration, thirteen were members of this church.

Chief among the doctrines of this religion is the belief in a supreme being (Sangje), the identification of the faithful with that supreme being, and the belief in the creative and restorative power of the twenty-one syllable talisman given to the religion's founder. This religion also teaches that the paradise of the supreme being will be created on the earth, since that supreme being is already present in the membership.

In daily and Sunday worship services believers pray for oneness with their deity: a bowl of pure water is placed on the altar as a symbol of purity. *See also* healing; Korea, new religions in; millenarianism.

ch'ongbin. *See* village recluses (Korea).

chongmyo. *See* shrine.

Chong Tojon (chuhng to-juhn; d. 1398), Korean Neo-Confucian scholar, military commander, and key player in the military coup that ended the Koryo kingdom and established the Choson kingdom (1392–1910). Though born of lower-class status, Chong Tojon rose to become honored as one of the non-royal founders of the Choson kingdom.

Chong Tojon served as the director of the revived National Academy in the late Koryo period (918–1392). Based on his studies of history and Neo-Confucian teachings, he became the champion of a new rising elite class of bureaucrats who favored breaking relations with the Mongols and establishing formal relations with the Ming. When his friend Yi Songgye refused to attack the Ming over the establishment of a Chinese commandery at Chollyong Pass and returned to the capital to effect a coup d'etat in 1388, it was Chong Tojon who was his protector and ally in the capital.

Chong Tojon was also responsible for enunciating an exclusivist understanding of Confucian values in government that would, four years later, help to bring down the Koryo ruling house and its Buddhist establishment and lay the groundwork for Choson-period Neo-Confucian orthodoxy in the year ahead. Chong Tojon became the ideological spokesman for a complete reform of law, economics, education, and government organization along exclusive Neo-Confucian lines and through his students and academy colleagues began the statewide disestablishment and oppression of Buddhist, Taoist, and shamanist institutions that was to continue in the years ahead.

Chong Tojon's writings against Buddhism and Taoism are especially noteworthy. Unlike the polemical literature of the late Koryo, which urged the disestablishment of the Buddhist and Taoist institutions for the sake of economic and political gains, Chong Tojon's writings, based solely on Neo-Confucian metaphysical theory, argue that Buddhism and Taoism are completely false because they are extreme, one-sided (*idan*) misinterpretations of physical and metaphysical truth. In such treatises as *Simmun ch'ondap* (The Mind Inquires and Heaven Responds), *Simgiri p'yon* (Chapters on Mind, Body, and Principle), and *Pulssi ch'app'yon* (Assorted Discussions of the Buddhist Clan), Chong Tojon refutes the validity of Buddhist and Taoist claims by demonstrating how each contradicts the other and how both reduce the broad, public-minded (*kong*) nature of reality to a selfish pursuit of one's own likes and dislikes. The success of his writings is demonstrated by the fact that later responses by Buddhists and Taoists started with a discussion of Neo-Confucian metaphysics and ended by appealing for accommodation of Buddhism and Taoism within Neo-Confucian terms. *See also* Neo-Confucianism.

chosen people, the people of Israel as elected to a unique role in the service of God. The idea that one people was chosen out of all humanity as

God's special servants is rooted in the Bible and persists throughout later Jewish thought. Created in God's image, initially all humanity has a special role in relation to God. God communicates with and commands only human beings.

In the biblical account of history, humanity rejects its special mission and thus makes itself unworthy of its special status. Distressed with this failure, God decides to destroy the world except for the family of Noah. This family and its descendants also fail to live up to the high challenge God has set before them. After ten more generations, Abraham appears on the scene of history. He lives a life of exemplary devotion to God and God's teachings. Abraham's descendants, the people of Israel, are bound to God by an everlasting covenant and are designated God's chosen people.

"Now then, if you will obey Me faithfully and keep My covenant, you shall be My treasured possession among all the peoples. . . . You shall be to me a kingdom of priests and a holy nation" (Exodus 19:5–6). These key words, which are echoed in many other places in the Bible, designate the people of Israel as having special obligations and a special role in human history. The consciousness of that role is reflected in many aspects of Jewish religious life and practice. A familiar liturgical formulation states explicitly, "You have chosen us from among all the peoples." That chosenness is directly associated with receiving the Torah, which defines specifically what is asked of the people of Israel.

Scripture stresses that Israel was chosen not because of any special natural merit but because of God's love. The tradition reflects the idea that if the people of Israel had any merit that explained why they were chosen, it was that they alone accepted the Torah and committed themselves to its observance without any hesitation. Once chosen, the obligation rests upon them permanently, and they are subject to especially rigorous divine judgment. God says to them, "You alone have I singled out of all the families of the earth, that is why I call you to account for all your iniquities" (Amos 3:2). Chosenness implies special obligation, not special privilege.

The role assigned to the people of Israel is to bear witness to the truth of God, to God's presence in the world, and to God's never-wavering concern with all human beings. "My witnesses are you, declares the Lord, My servant whom I have chosen. . . . So you are my witnesses and I am God" (Isaiah 43:10, 12). When the Jewish people fail to bear witness to God, they betray their trust. They profane the name of God who chose them and assigned them their special role in history. This doctrine is held in most forms of contemporary Judaism, except Reconstructionism. *See also* election; Israel (land, people, state).

Chou i ts'an-t'ung ch'i (joh ee tsahn-tohng chee; Chin., "Concordance of the Three According to the Book of Changes"), a second-century Taoist alchemical treatise. *See also* alchemy.

Chou Kung (joh guhng; Chin., "Duke of Chou"; fl. mid-eleventh century B.C.), son of the Chou dynastic founder, King Wen, and younger brother and chief adviser to Wen's successor, King Wu, who overthrew the Shang; he was chief apologist for the doctrine of the Mandate of Heaven and a paragon of virtue in Confucian tradition. *See also* Chou religion; Shang religion; T'ien-ming.

Chou religion (joh), state cult of ancestor veneration practiced by the Chinese ruling elite during the Chou period, usually dated ca. 1122 to 221 B.C.; some recent scholars, on the basis of archaeology, propose differing dates for the beginning of the period, ca. 1112 B.C. or 1051 B.C. or 1027 B.C.

Derived from the earlier Shang practice of divining ancestral approval through oracle bones, the Chou practice was to report military and ritual activities to ancestral spirits through inscriptions cast inside bronze sacrificial wine and food vessels. They sought spiritual reconfirmation of the Heavenly Mandate (*T'ien-ming*) as accorded by Heaven to the founding Kings Wen and Wu. Ritual conquest was expressed in an archery ritual of hunting birds and catching fish while boating on the Pi-yung Pool, followed by a "tasting" rite held in the king's private temple. The Chou believed they descended from Hou-chi ("Lord Millet") and an altar of soil and millet, set up in each Chou city-state, symbolized the local leader's right to rule.

By the eighth century B.C., the Chou became increasingly concerned with prayers to a pantheon of ancestral and astral spirits for blessings of fertility, good fortune, and long life. Harvests were celebrated with gatherings of kinsfolk and spirits, lavish feasts, drink, and the music of bells and drums. A *shih* ("corpse") personator, a descendant of the ancestor, "hosted" the "guest," or visiting spirit, during the ceremony.

Chou rites were later idealized and codified by Han Confucian scholars in a set of ritual texts revered by emperors up to modern times. *See also* Confucianism; Hou-chi; Shang religion; T'ien-ming; Wen Wang and Wu Wang.

Chou Tun-i (joh duhn-ee; 1017–73), the first great Sung Neo-Confucian; he developed the cosmological doctrine of the Great Ultimate (*t'ai-chi*) as the highest good and taught the cultivation of profound reverence leading to self-realization. *See also* Neo-Confucianism; t'ai-chi; T'ai-chi t'u shou.

chrism, a blessed oil used in the Christian rites of baptism, confirmation, anointing of the sick, ordination, and the consecration of monarchs. *See also* anointing.

Christ Apostolic Church. *See* Africa, new religions in.

Christ for All Nations. *See* Pentecostalism.

Christian Crusade for Truth, a contemporary Christian Identity ministry pastored by Earl F. Jones of Deming, New Mexico. Jones's ministry is somewhat specialized in that his messages, through his *Intelligence Newsletter* and via cassette tapes, as well as through his frequent appearances at Christian Identity retreats, tend not to dwell on the theology of Christian Identity. Rather, Jones is engaged in an ongoing, and increasingly complex, quest to unravel what he believes to be the conspiratorial nature of history. In this, he goes well beyond the theories of Jewish conspiracy central to the theology of Christian Identity, claiming instead that the Jewish people are but one facet of a complex web of overlapping, multigenerational, occult-centered conspiracies, whose machinations explain virtually every event that occurs in the world today. *See also* Identity Christianity.

Christian Foundation. *See* Jesus people.

Christian Identity. *See* Identity Christianity.

Christianity, major forms of. *See* Catholicism, Roman; Orthodox Church; Protestantism.

Christianity (art and architecture). The basic relationship of Christianity and the visual arts (painting and sculpture) is rooted in Christology and incarnational theology, whereas Christianity and architecture have depended upon perceptions of God and the aesthetic and spatial requirements of the liturgy. This relationship is both pragmatic and theological. The history of Christian art and architecture is directly connected to changing interpretations of the human person and of the theology of the human body in Christianity.

Early Christianity: From the beginning, the relationship between Christianity and the arts has been one of action and controversy. The ac-

ceptance of art in the early church helped differentiate Christianity from Judaism. Initial discussions centered on the Hebraic injunction against images and the constant threat of idolatry in religious worship. Some early church fathers saw the problem of images within the framework of Christianity's two foundations: the Hebraic and the Greco-Hellenistic traditions. This basic discussion revolved around the dialectic of the power of images versus the fear of images.

The early church recognized the importance of the visual not only as a primary means of human perception but also as a didactic vehicle. Early Christian art was understood as the visual narration of events to edify with examples rather than as the direct presentation of divinity, which would have been idolatry. Thus, one was initiated and nurtured into Christianity not simply by the word, but by visual images as well.

Earliest Christian art found in the catacombs and house churches make minimal use of representational forms. This symbolic emphasis reflects the concern of Christian artists and theologians with idolatry. Artists depict the stories and teachings of Jesus through the use of classical mythological or Hebrew scriptural figures, thereby avoiding any anthropomorphic depiction of the divine.

Similarly, the earliest examples of Christian architecture are not single buildings dedicated to religious worship or activities. The earliest communities attended to basic worship and rites in synagogues. The only special Christian architectural requirement was a dining room for the celebration of both the Eucharist and the agape meal. Thus, specific rooms were set aside in house churches for these two functions. However, by the third century, entire houses were donated for worship, especially among wealthier communities.

The Constantinian Transformation: In the fourth century, the emperor Constantine irrevocably transformed Christian art and architecture. Once he declared Christianity the official religion of the Roman Empire in 435, Constantine changed the artistic and liturgical requirements for Christian worship. This transformation, centered on the figure of Christ the king, resulted in the stylistic development of Byzantine art and architecture. Just as the costumes, gestures, and rituals of the Byzantine court tradition reshaped the Christian liturgy, and the political prestige of the state religion changed the economic and social status of Christianity, so too the visual image of Jesus became that of an imperial Christ garbed and posed as the victorious warrior-emperor; the visual image of Mary paralleled in gesture, pose, and costume the Byzantine empress. Their forms were depicted in a static and frontal manner, denying the physicality of their natural beings, but in line with the contemporary incarnational and christological teachings.

As Christianity had become the state religion, some form of permanent building was required both for liturgical activity and to substitute for the temples of pre-Christian state religions. In a letter to Macarius, bishop of Jerusalem, Constantine described his plans for the site of the Holy Sepulchre and ordered the construction of a basilica. This classical Roman style of public building became the monumental edifice for worship in the new state religion. A basilica, or "hall of the emperor," consisted of a circle in a square with a nave that was flanked with side aisles leading toward a triumphal arch and a semicircular apse. The triumphal arch, derived from the classical Roman architecture that glorified the military conquests of generals and emperors, was transformed by the Christian tradition to signify Christ's victory over death. In the center of the apse was the cathedra, or bishop's chair of authority. The altar, enframed by the triumphant arch, signified the meeting place of heaven and earth. The altar stood like Christ as a mediator between God and human beings. The basic character of the basilica's interior was that of a path leading Christians from all directions toward the altar.

This development of the first formal Christian architecture was analogous to the initial development of Christian art—adaptation of earlier forms of art and architecture into the needs of the new state religion. This Byzantine style of art and architecture required luminosity brought about by architectural design as well as by the inlaying of precious metals and of mosaics glowing with gold and brilliant color. The simple facades of these earliest basilicas were deceptive, for the interiors were brilliant and glowing, signifying the presence of the heavenly Jerusalem.

The Iconoclastic Controversies: The role of art in Christianity was never simple, clear, or consistent. As the christological and liturgical controversies of the fourth through the eighth centuries brought about creedal and doctrinal definition, the role of images and the theology of the human body was at the center of the discussion. Images were to narrate visually events like the nativity or the crucifixion in a manner appropriate for both theologians and the laity.

The iconographic controversies of the eighth and ninth centuries were a critical period for Christian art. At the heart of these tensions was the dialectical foundation of the Christian tradition: the Hebraic injunction against images and the Greco-Hellenistic appreciation of the beautiful. A new element in the discussion was the emerging influence of Islam with its ban against the veneration of images. In 730, Leo III issued a decree forbidding the veneration of images and forcing the removal of images from churches and monasteries. In 754, the Synod of Constantinople (the Iconoclastic Council) declared all those who venerated or produced religious images to be excommunicate and anathema. Paintings of Christ, the Virgin, and the saints were condemned as blasphemy, while profane images, including portraits of the emperor and the imperial family, were permissible. These controversies eventually were resolved by the Second Council of Nicaea (787) and an Eastern Church Synod of 843 in which the distinction between idols and images made by John Damascene (ca. 675–749) was accepted in conjunction with regulations as to the choice of subject and style of execution of visual images. Idols misled the minds of the faithful through superstition and had no referents other than themselves, while images were adornments and illustrations of the faith and had referent to something other than themselves. The decisive argument was the incarnation of Jesus, for as John Damascene indicated, God used the fullest image possible to present his promise of salvation. Thus, the rehabilitation of images was completed. As a result, the canonical role of the visual was clearly stated and restored within the daily life of the church. However, the image-destroying tendency would resurface sporadically throughout the history of Christianity.

Medieval Christianity: During the medieval period, the visual arts and architecture were nurtured and flourished in their relationship to and with the church. This was the Age of Cathedrals, which were simultaneously the cultural, economic, political, religious, and social centers of cities. The visual modality played a major role in medieval Christian theology. The development of major pilgrimage churches and the Black Plague gave rise to a Christian devotionalism that found helpmates in the visual arts and architecture, such as the didactic visual narratives that adorn the walls of cathedrals, the mystical piety of devotional images, and the glorious enameled cases that preserve treasured pilgrimage relics. In terms of Christian art and architecture, the medieval synthesis reflects a complete integration of the arts when architecture, dance, drama, music, painting, poetry, sculpture, and textile arts worked in unison to produce aesthetic settings that opened the way to religious experience. During the medieval period, all Christian art and architecture was created "for the greater glory of God." In medieval Europe, God and therefore Christianity was the center around which the world revolved. Art was interpreted by Christian theologians as a handmaiden of theology.

The major stylistic developments in Christian art and architecture in the medieval period are the Romanesque and the Gothic. In order to meet both the liturgical needs of the Christian community and the growing number of Christian pilgrims, medieval architects transformed the basilica into a cathedral by extending the nave and expanding the size of the side aisles. These wider side aisles with their accompanying side chapels permitted a flow of pilgrims who came to adore or meditate upon the cathedral's relics while the community could attend a liturgical service at the high altar undisturbed. The earliest architectural style of the medieval cathedral was the Romanesque, which was based upon the imperial Roman architecture of monuments. Thus, the Romanesque in both the visual arts and architecture emphasizes massiveness and monumentality. The Romanesque cathedral is characterized by its thick walls, minimal use of windows or natural lighting, and Roman arches. Romanesque sculpture and manuscript illuminations are equally monumental in their presentation of the human body, deemphasizing its physicality by highlighting static stability and massiveness.

The move toward the Gothic in both Christian art and architecture derived from changes in theological attitudes toward the humanity of Christ and theologies of revelation in the twelfth century. The abbot Suger's (ca. 1081–1151) desire to create a light-filled worship space to signify the soul's ascent to God resulted in his dispatching of architects to study the Byzantine basilicas of Ravenna, Italy, and of Hagia Sophia in Constantinople. These architects returned with a new sense of a liturgical environment that transforms the monumental Romanesque cathedral into the light-filled elegance of Gothic cathedrals such as St. Denis and Chartres. The architectural development of the flying buttress, which took the weight of the building's roof, permitted the construction of thin exterior walls with open space for enormous windows. Gothic artisans filled this new space with stained-glass windows in which geometric and human forms depict the stories of the Christian tradition. The thinner walls also allow the Gothic cathedral to be taller than earlier ecclesiastical edifices. These new tall buildings filled with light symbolize the medieval belief in a transcendent God. Similarly, Gothic sculpture, manuscript illumination, and painting emphasize lightness, new spatial relationships, and elegance. Gothic artists created human bodies that appear to breathe and move,

The Roman Catholic cathedral at Chartres, France. One of the greatest examples of Gothic architecture, it was begun in 1194 and completed in the mid-thirteenth century.

especially as a result of the S-curve in the posture of both Christ and the Virgin.

Renaissance and Reformation: With the Renaissance in fifteenth-century Italy, the center of the world began to shift away from God to the human person, and as a result the role of art and architecture was no longer simply that of a handmaiden. During the Renaissance, the arts flourished and many of the finest works of Renaissance art and architecture, such as Michelangelo's ceiling of the Sistine Chapel (1508–13), were created for the church. However, the revival of classical Greek and Roman philosophy led to a growing interest in classical architecture, art, and mythology. The styles and themes of the visual arts changed dramatically, and even much religious art created for the church was criticized as being too "humanistic" or "secular" or "pagan," and therefore not Christian. One example of this tendency within Renaissance art is Michelangelo's *David* (1504), which is as much a study in the classical beauty of the human body and in human anatomy as it

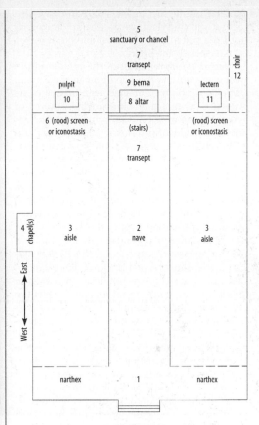

5
sanctuary or chancel

7
transept

choir
12

pulpit
10

9 bema

lectern
11

8 altar

6 (rood) screen
or iconostasis

(stairs)

(rood) screen
or iconostasis

7
transept

4 chapel(s)

3
aisle

2
nave

3
aisle

East

West

narthex

1

narthex

Christian church

Christian churches take many forms, from a plain meeting room to a complex Gothic cathedral. This diagram illustrates some of the architectural features typical of "high" churches. The building is oriented on an east-west axis. The transverse entry space is called (1) the narthex. This opens to a central corridor, (2) the nave, often flanked by (3) side aisles, sometimes with small (4) chapels. The focal point, where most of the ritual is conducted is (5) the sanctuary, or chancel. It is often set apart by stairs and by (6) a screen, or iconostasis, in Greek Orthodox buildings. The sanctuary has a transverse corridor, (7) the transept, in two possible locations, across which the ritualists move. At the center front of the sanctuary is (8) an altar, often on a raised platform, (9) the bema. There is also (10) a pulpit from which the sermon is delivered; there may be (11) a separate lectern for scripture reading. In some churches, separate seating is reserved for (12) the choir (along with musical instruments, if employed). In some churches, there is a container of holy water close to the entrance or a baptismal font near the sanctuary (older churches had a separate building called the baptistery).

is a representation of a scriptural story. The church was both benefactor of these developments in the arts through the patronage and support of Julius II (1443–1513) and critic through the sermons and writings of Savonarola (1452–98). The medieval synthesis was shattered in the Renaissance, and a new way of understanding the role of Christian art and architecture came into being.

Among the causes of the Reformation was hostility to the Italian Renaissance and its arts. The celebration of beauty in nature and the human body that the Renaissance fostered and introduced into Christian worship was incompatible with the Reformers' emphasis on original sin and human finitude. The Reformers also sought a purification of the church, and the mediation of visual images in liturgical worship and devotional piety was seen as a hindrance to direct contact with God. The Reformers' rejection of images cleansed the walls of their churches, changed the role of art and artist in their society, and moved the emphasis in liturgical worship to the Word. Therefore, music and poetry flourished in the Protestant traditions and in their liturgical worship.

In this renewed conflict between the image and the Word, the Protestant traditions not only displayed their interpretation of the Hebraic tradition but also the traditional iconoclastic fear of images. Artists in the Protestant countries sought new patrons to replace their loss of church patronage. As a result the themes of northern art changed. Where northern artists before the Reformation painted in a style similar to those of the South and emphasized the same devotional and scriptural themes, sixteenth- and seventeenth-century northern artists developed a secular style of art that favored realism over idealism and profane subjects over religious ones. Northern artists now painted portraits, genre themes, still lifes, landscapes, and an occasional history painting.

Northern architects, however, found themselves with renewed careers in the building or renovations of churches. These renovations were not simply the removal of visual images from the church building. The Protestant emphases on the fellowship of the Eucharist and the centrality of preaching resulted in new architectural requirements. In those churches that were renovated at this time, the rood screens separating the altar from the congregation were destroyed, allowing visual and physical access to the altar for the Communion service. The pulpit was moved from its earlier position in the front of the church to a position that symbolized the centrality of the Word. Overall, the architectural emphasis of the Protestant churches favored centralization to signify the importance of the gathered congregation as opposed to the Roman Catholic emphasis on the priest as the celebrant of the Mass.

Counter-Reformation and the Baroque: The Roman Catholic Church responded to the Reformers' iconoclasm by defending and redefining the role of art in the Christian faith. In the Twenty-fifth

Session of the Council of Trent (1563), a decree was promulgated with the official rulings concerning liturgical art. This decree had both positive and negative effects upon the future of the visual arts in Roman Catholicism. The next official documents on the role and purpose of art in Catholicism would be issued in the middle of the twentieth century.

The Decree of the Council of Trent indicated that images were to be created by Christian artists and placed in the church for didactic purposes. This type of liturgical art had two functions: first as a visual narration through images whose significance lay not in themselves but in the event they depicted; and, second, as instruction in the articles of faith through images whose meaning lay outside of themselves. Thus, the intrinsic value of the work of art as art was negated. The decree also listed a series of criteria for art appropriate to a religious environment; for example, the use of the nude human figure was banned, leading to many Renaissance masterworks being corrected by Baroque artists. On a more positive note, the Counter-Reformation gave rise to a revival of Christian symbolism in the arts. A new Christian iconography developed as a visual expression and defense of the teachings of Rome, most especially of those teachings criticized by the Reformers, such as the Seven Corporal Works of Mercy, the sacrament of penance, and the role of the Virgin Mary. The fundamental characteristics of Baroque art, that is, chiaroscuro (shadowy light), asymmetrical composition, and dramatic subject matter supported the visual theatricality of this new Roman Catholic iconography.

Architects of this same period found new opportunities in designing churches for the triumphant church following the Council of Trent (1545–63). The medieval cathedral was replaced by a new style of architecture that conveyed ecclesiastical self-assurance and authority, symbolizing the power and exuberance of Roman Catholicism. The facades of these churches had a propagandistic function, to simultaneously proclaim the confidence of the Catholic faith and to persuade or entice those who saw them to enter. The interiors of these Baroque churches were also created to impress the community and to serve the new liturgical needs of the Tridentine worship services. The basic floor plan was that of an oval, which both centralized all movement within the building and created a dynamic thrust forward, allowing no repose or visual rest as had been afforded in the medieval cathedral's side aisles and chapels. The high altar, which was visible throughout the church, now had a new central focus: a tabernacle or re-ceptable for the sacrament. This Baroque architecture and liturgical design was influenced by both the state (imperial coronations) and theater (especially the opera).

Modern Developments: Until the middle of the twentieth century, the role of art in the Roman Catholic Church remained confined to the sixteenth-century guidelines of the Council of Trent. There was not much room for artistic creativity to flourish in terms of Christian art and architecture or liturgical commissions and patronage. As a result, from the Baroque period until the 1940s and 1950s, the finest artists created art for patrons other than the Church. Christian art and architecture that was created for Protestant churches during this same two-hundred-year period (that is, the rococo style of the eighteenth century and the artistic pluralism of the nineteenth century) might best be categorized as sentimental and imitative. For example, the nineteenth-century Gothic Revival was an architectural attempt to revive and parallel the thirteenth-century Age of Faith, which was nostalgically interpreted as the spiritual and theological ideal. The contemporary Episcopal emphases on spirituality, sacramentality, ritual (as opposed to preaching), and the use of visual and decorative elements in worship supported its attempted identification with the superordinate Christian style of the Gothic. Similar nostalgic revivals in the visual arts in the nineteenth century attempted to retrieve not merely the art of the Italian Primitives for the Pre-Raphaelites or the medieval artisans for the Pre-Nazarenes, but also their theology and liturgical practices.

Twentieth-century attempts at Christian art and architecture have also suffered from the loss of a unified religious center and dominant artistic style. Further divisions are recognized between modern artists whose personal art derived from Christian inspiration, and an officially inspired Christian art and architecture effectively created for ecclesiastical needs. One result of the destruction caused by both world wars was the need for new church buildings, especially in Britain, France, and Germany. During the liturgical renewals (or revivals) that occurred in both the Protestant and Roman Catholic traditions in the 1920s and the 1950s, outstanding architects designed new churches, such as Notre Dame du Raincy, in France, and the Reformed Church in Alstetten, Germany, as well as the renovation of damaged buildings such as Coventry Cathedral in England. The critical and influential texts of Jacques Maritain and A. M. Courturier argue for the development of sacred art and architecture that will admit the creative experience of modern art and architecture into

Characteristically plain meetinghouse-style Protestant church, Meota United Church, United Church of Canada (a denomination formed in 1925 by the union of Methodists, Congregationalists, and most Presbyterians in Canada), Saskatchewan, Canada.

Christianity. The Protestant theologian Paul Tillich supports careful theological examination of modern art as a leading source of the existential questions of contemporary Christians. Further, Tillich recognizes the importance of a Christian art and architecture that springs naturally from the contemporary culture.

In his encyclical, *Mediator Dei* (1947), Pius XII urges a qualified acceptance of modern architecture and art within Roman Catholicism. Artists need to steer a middle course between the exaggerations of contemporary realism and symbolism and traditional Christian art. The building and decoration of several "modern" Roman Catholic churches in France such as Notre-Dame-du-Toute-Grace, Assy; Notre-Dame-du-Haut, Ronchamp; and Chapel of the Rosary, Vence, stirred controversy. In 1952, the Congregation of the Holy Office issued the *Instructio de arte sacra*, which summarizes existing laws and gives direction on the building of churches and their ornamentation, but does not set styles for art. The role of art in Roman Catholicism was reviewed by the Second Vatican Council with the Document on the Church and Culture (1965), which opens the door for the acceptance of "modern" art in the Church. In 1973, Paul VI established the Museum of Modern Art,

Vatican Museums, with the gift of his personal collection of twentieth-century art. The American Bishops' Committee on the Liturgy issued *Environment and Art in Catholic Worship* (1978), which established a series of guidelines for art in the liturgical environment and a receptive attitude toward contemporary art.

The current discussion and role of Christian art and architecture is at an impasse. The focus of the discussion has shifted away from the creative dialogue to pragmatic and ethical concerns. The questions of decoration and/or redecoration of the ecclesiastical environment are based upon a nostalgia for representational art and traditional architecture that are comfortable to the eye and nonthreatening to the religious psyche. Ethical concerns about the appropriateness of both the cost and the aesthetic pleasures afforded the worship environment by Christian art and architecture conflict with the plight of human suffering and starvation in the modern world. The fundamental issues of the role and purpose of Christian art and architecture have retreated from the forefront of discussion and activity in the West, although there is vigorous new thinking about art in the churches of the non-European world. *See also* altar; architecture and religion; art and religion; basilica; iconoclasm.

239

CHRISTIANITY

hristianity is the religion that honors Jesus Christ as its founder and as the object of its worship. Its foundational document is the Bible, which is divided into the Old Testament and the New Testament.

Christianity is the largest of the world's organized religions, with particular strengths in Europe, the Americas, and Africa, but it is represented in most parts of the world. It represents just under a third of the world's population with roughly 1.5 billion adherents.

The three largest branches of Christianity, in order of their numerical strength, are traditionally given as Roman Catholic, Protestant, and Eastern Orthodox, although within those broad categories there are numerous denominations.

HISTORY

Christianity traces its origins to small assemblies of believers, largely (but not exclusively) Jewish in makeup, which arose in Roman Palestine and around the Mediterranean in the second quarter of the first century. These groups preached belief in Jesus Christ (the Greek word *Christ* translates the Hebrew *Messiah,* which means the "Anointed One"), who had been executed in Jerusalem but who, according to this belief, rose from the dead to be exalted in heaven. These early Christians saw Jesus as the fulfillment of the messianic promises contained in the Hebrew Bible. Christianity, then, has intimate ties with Judaism, the religion from which it springs.

Although it is difficult to reconstruct exactly the character of these early congregations, there are hints in the sources (especially the Letters of Paul) that can help understand their broad shape and polity. Their initiation rite, called baptism, represented a symbolic death and rebirth by which the old person was put away in favor of a new state of being. The death and rebirth motif was also reflected in their language, which both described their peculiar inclusive character (e.g., the "saints" or the "elect"), as opposed to those who were not part of the community (the "unrighteous" or the "nonbelievers"). The celebration of a symbolic meal (called the Eucharist, "Thanksgiving") memorialized the risen Christ and his sacrificial death.

Early Christianity slowly separated from its roots in Judaism, but its increasing appeal to the gentile population of the Roman Empire did not exclude it from official suspicion. Indeed, the first four centuries of Christian growth were

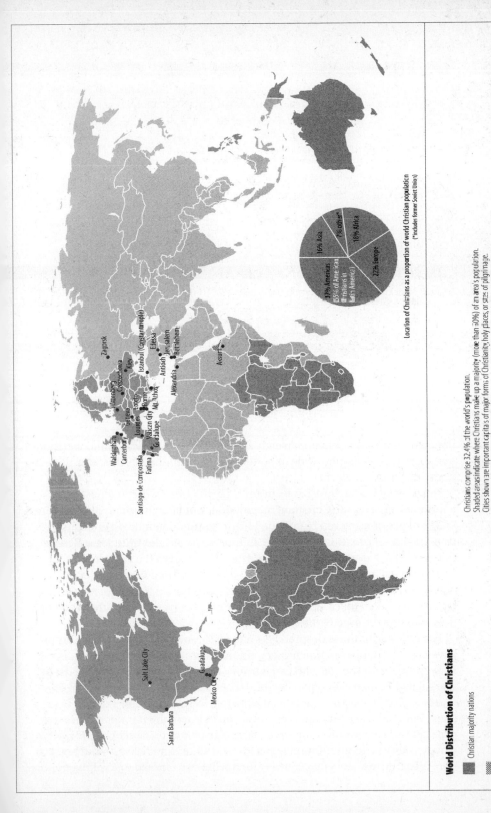

World Distribution of Christians

Christians comprise 32.4% of the world's population.
Shaded areas indicate where Christians make up a majority (more than 50%) of an area's population.
Cities shown are important capitals of major forms of Christianity, holy places, or sites of pilgrimage.

Christian majority nations

divided Christian/ Muslim

Location of Christians as a proportion of world Christian population
(*includes former Soviet Union)

7% other*
18% Africa
22% Europe
37% Americas
(55% of Americas Christians in Latin America)
16% Asia

Zagorsk
Istanbul (Constantinople)
Eleosa
Jerusalem
Bethlehem
Antioch
Wittenberg
Kiev
Czestochowa
Assisi
Geneva
Loreto
Rome
Alexandria
Canterbury
Lourdes
Vatican City
Mt. Athos
Walsingham
Santiago de Compostela
Fatima
Guadalupe

Salt Lake City
Guadalupe
Santa Barbara
Mexico City

Aksum

Christianity

1–100	100–200	200–300
Crucifixion of Jesus (ca. 33)	First Roman account of Christians (110)	Beginning of Coptic Christian era (284)
Beginning of Greek Christian literature (ca. 40)	Roman Empire at greatest extent (117)	"Great Persecution" (297–311)
Paul's letters (ca. 50–56)	Formation of New Testament (ca. 125–130)	
Destruction of Temple in Jerusalem (70)	Early Christian Gnostics (fl. 135–140): Basilides, Satornilos, Valentinus, Marcion	
Four Gospels (ca. 70–125)	Montanism (ca. 172)	
First Roman Pope (ca. 91–101)	Beginning of Latin Christian literature (ca. 190)	

500–600	600–700	700–800
Benedictine Rule, Monte Cassino founded (ca. 525)	Byzantine Empire begins (610)	Muslim invasion of Christian Spain (711)
	Beginning of Muslim conquest of Christian Asia Minor and North Africa (632–718)	

punctuated by outbreaks of persecution, although contrary to popular estimation there was no empire-wide or systematic persecution of Christians until 250 under the emperor Decius.

However sporadic these persecutions may have been, they exercised an enormous force on the Christian imagination. Christian martyrs' shrines were places of pilgrimage even before the fourth century. Their death anniversaries were memorialized (thus giving rise, in time, to a complex liturgical calendar that noted both events connected to Jesus Christ and to the sufferings of the martyrs) and churches were built over their tombs. Their courage seemed to have had a positive impact on the growth of the church; the North African theologian Tertullian (d. ca. 220) is famous for his observation that "the blood of the martyrs is the seed of the church."

The reasons for the widespread growth of Christianity in the Roman Empire have been the subject of much speculation. How a religion honoring an executed provincial criminal who came from a religion (Judaism) that was itself marginal in Roman eyes could become so entrenched that by the end of the fourth century it became the official state religion of the empire is hard to explain. Part of the explanation is external and cultural: the Roman Empire was at peace; it had a common commercial language (common Greek), a safe system of roads, and a tolerance for religious ideas despite its reflexive acts of persecution. All of those factors made it easy for a religion to spread to a willing popula-

300–400		400–500
Armenia becomes first Christian state (301)	Beginning of Ethiopian (or Abyssinian) Christian Church (ca. 350)	Non-Christian religions outlawed, Theodosian Code (410)
Donatist churches in North Africa (fl. 4th–8th centuries)	"Barbarian" invasions of Roman Empire (ca. 375–568)	Beginning of Nestorian Syriac Christianity (ca. 450)
Christianity becomes legal religion in Roman Empire (313)	Jerome's Vulgate (ca. 385)	Council of Chalcedon (451)
Beginning of Christian monasticism, Egypt (ca. 320)	Christianity becomes state religion of Roman Empire, heresy legally defined and prohibited (393)	
Council of Nicaea I (325)		
Constantinople new capital of Roman Empire (333)		

800–900	900–1000	1000–1100
Charlemagne crowned first Holy Roman Emperor (800)	Monastery of Cluny founded (909)	Beginning of schism between Greek and Latin churches, establishment of Russian Orthodox Church (1054)
	Christianity introduced into Russia (ca. 988)	Beginning of conflict between Roman Empire and papacy (1073)
		First Crusade, capture of Jerusalem (1099)

tion. To that must be added a yearning for monotheism among certain classes, the availability of entrance to the religion by all classes and both sexes, the mechanisms for excising remorse or guilt, and a moral and social code that stressed mutual aid and a strong sense of personal ethics.

From the evidence of early Christian history, it seems clear that the religion grew largely through the growth of small communities that then split off to found others. For the first four centuries Christianity's greatest growth occurred in the cities in the Roman Empire and in those places with which Rome had trade or colonial outposts. Indeed, the word *pagan* originally meant a non-city dweller, which, in context, meant one who was not Christianized.

Christians were granted toleration by the emperor Constantine by the Edict of Milan in 311, and Christianity became the official religion of the state by proclamation of the emperor Theodosius in 381. This official recognition had profound implications for Christianity.

Leaving its status as an illegal sect, it now enjoyed the patronage of the state. Inevitably, it absorbed both the sociolegal structures of the larger culture and many of its ideas. Christian communities became designated by geographical areas (parishes and dioceses) overseen by bishops and priests who were aided by deacons and deaconesses who ministered to the social needs of congregations. Large-scale building programs developed and the imperial court took an increasing interest in the social and doctrinal affairs of the church. The social

Christianity

1100–1200	1200–1300	1300–1400
Albigensians (ca. 1165–1375)	Beginning of Mongol invasion of Christian eastern Europe (1239–1478)	Western "Great Schism" (1378–1417)
Saladin conquers Crusader kingdoms (1188)	Inquisition established (1242)	
Catholic Scholasticism (12th–13th centuries)	Death of Thomas Aquinas (1274)	

development of Christianity brought with it an inevitable growth in differentiated social roles. By the fourth century there was a clear distinction between laity and clergy, with the latter enjoying an ever-increasing prestige and power.

By the fourth century Christianity was represented in urban settlements as far north as Roman Britain and south as Roman Africa; west to the Iberian Peninsula and east to Byzantium (Constantinople) and Roman Syria. In fact, the Syriac Church made incursions, over the centuries, as far east as India as well as possessing a toehold in China. With Constantine's edict of toleration in 311, Christianity absorbed large doses of Roman culture under official patronage. Ecclesiastical districts followed Roman administrative divisions; the legal code of the church reflected Roman jurisprudence; and the state involved itself more in church matters. The simple worship service of the Christians grew increasingly more complex and formal even though its bare outline of the celebration of the Word (i.e., the reading of scripture and preaching about it) and the Sacrament (the celebration of the sacred meal of bread and wine representing the body and blood of Christ) was still discernible.

A further development involved the church's efforts to state its belief in a manner that was coherent and faithful to the original intentions of its founder and his first disciples. This effort involved judgments about what was appropriate and inappropriate (with the inevitable distinction between orthodox and heretical teaching) as well as official statements of the former and condemnations of the latter. These controversies raged in the first five centuries of the church's life and were settled by various councils of bishops (some convened by

1400–1500	1500–1600	1600–1700
Portuguese Catholics begin exploration of Africa (1415)	Beginning of Renaissance (ca. 1500)	Formation of Baptists (1609)
Constantinople captured by Ottoman Turkish Muslims (1453)	Anabaptist groups (ca. 1500)	Formation of Society of Friends (ca. 1665)
End of Byzantine empire (1453)	John Calvin (1509–64)	
Gutenberg Bible (1453)	Beginning of Reformation (1517–21)	
Martin Luther (1483–1546)	Beginning of English Reformation, Anglicans and Puritans (1534)	
Muslim Moorish kingdom ends in Spain (1492)	Beginning of Unitarianism (ca. 1538)	
Jews expelled from Spain (1492)	Establishment of Reformed Church, Geneva (1541)	
First voyage of Columbus (1492)	Beginning of Counter-Reformation (1545)	
	Council of Trent (1545–63)	
	First Catholic mission to Japan (1548)	
	Formation of Scottish Presbyterianism (1560)	
	First Catholic mission to China (1582)	
	Beginning of Congregationalism (ca. 1582)	

the emperor) that were considered ecumenical (i.e., universal). The first eight of these ecumenical councils still stand as a source of special authority in the churches of the East and the West. The net result of these controversies was a series of fundamental doctrinal positions that characterize historic Christianity to the twentieth century: a belief in a trinity of Persons (Father, Son, and Holy Spirit) in one God; a belief that Jesus was born fully human and fully divine but was only one person; a canon of authentic books that make up the New Testament portion of the Bible; the place of bishops as the authentic teachers and pastors of the church.

Christianity's emergence as the religion of the Roman Empire coincided with the slow decline of that empire. Barbarian invasions from the North battered the western empire (the city of Rome was sacked in the early fifth century), and the Eastern empire with its center at Constantinople became increasingly separated from the West and developed its own theology and liturgical practice. Those divisions, centuries in the making, would end in a schism between the two churches in the eleventh century creating a division that has existed to the twentieth century between the Orthodox Church in the East and the Roman Catholic Church in the West.

One form of resistance to Roman culture, discernible from the late third century, was the exodus of religious seekers who fled urban areas for the deserts in order to live a more perfectly religious life. These desert dwellers were the seedbed from which monasticism evolved as they regularized their lives by specific rules and by rigid codes of moral conduct. Monasticism exerted an

Christianity		
1700–1800	**1800–1900**	**1900–**
Formation of Morovians (1722)	Formation of Disciples of Christ (1811)	Martin Luther King, Jr., leads non-violent protests against racial segregation in the U.S.A. (1950s–60s)
Formation of Shakers (1747)	Formation of Church of Jesus Christ of Latter-day Saints (Mormons) (1830)	Pope John XXIII (1958–63)
Formation of Methodism (1784)	Formation of Seventh Day Adventism (1844)	Vatican Council II (1962–65)
	Formation of Christian Science (1879)	"Billy" Graham crusades in North America and elsewhere (1950s–90s)
	Formation of Jehovah's Witnesses (1881)	

enormous influence on the shape of Christianity, especially in Syria, Roman Palestine, North Africa, and the Byzantine world. The monastic ideal of a celibate life, of a regular daily round of prayer, of self-denial and asceticism, and of an intense yearning for salvation would leave its mark on later Christianity. Many of the disciplinary practices of the Roman Catholic clergy (e.g., celibacy) have roots in the monastic and ascetical practices of early Christianity.

In the West, when urban life went into decline after the fifth century, the monastic life provided missionaries both to the Germanic countries and to Ireland. In the East, monasteries were centers of religious life in places such as Constantinople and the source for bishops of the church, since bishops were by law celibate. That is still the practice of the Orthodox world in the late twentieth century.

Monasticism (and other, more informal forms of ascetic life) was not the singular domain of men. From the earliest days, there were women ascetics. Organized monasteries of women grew in both the East and the West. In Anglo-Saxon England, for example, these establishments wielded enormous influence on church affairs in the seventh century. Religious orders of women have played an enormous role in the Christian world, especially in Roman Catholic circles, where they have provided not only the personnel for many of the church's social programs but also many of its greatest mystics and spiritual mistresses.

The whole concept of a religious rule of life (Lat. *vita regularis*), characteristic of monasticism, would take on different colorings in the history of Christianity with the rise of religious orders of men and women. Such orders flourished in the West in both the Middle Ages and after the Reformation, where in both eras they were often agents of renewal and reform in the church.

The rise of Islam in the seventh century radically changed the geographical face of Christianity. The traditional Christian strongholds of greater Palestine, Egypt, and North Africa fell to Islam with further Islamic incursions into the Iberian Peninsula in the West and Anatolia in the East. While, in later centuries, there would be pockets of toleration between Islam and Christianity and a fair amount of mutual cultural influence, the response of Christianity was, by and large, hostile. The medieval Crusades were a series of attempts, with varying degrees of success, to wrest the Christian holy places in Jerusalem from the "infidel" intruders. Armed struggles between Islamic cultures and Christian Europe persisted well into modern times, as the nineteenth-century Greek revolt against the Ottoman Turks attests.

By the early Middle Ages (roughly after the year 1000) Christianity had spread northward in Europe, balancing the loss of the Islamic South and East. Russia was evangelized from Constantinople at the end of the tenth century, giving it an Eastern form of worship and polity. In time, the Russian Church would see itself as an autonomous "Third Rome," standing as an equal with the patriarchs of ancient Rome and Constantinople. Missionaries from the West evangelized the Scandinavian countries and the rest of Eastern Europe, which was not under the direct influence of Russia or Constantinople.

With the reemergence of urban life in the Middle Ages, cities took on a more important part in the development of religious life. The rurally oriented monastic centers gave way to the preeminence of episcopal life centered around cathedrals. Schools and, eventually, universities were founded in cities. New religious orders such as the mendicant orders of Franciscans, Dominicans, Augustinians, and Carmelites ministered to urban populations. The papacy became increasingly bureaucratic and took to itself more centralized powers of administration and jurisdiction. Forms of devotional life (the cult of the Virgin, pilgrimage, popular devotions, etc.) multiplied, and religious ideals had an enormous impact on the emerging vernacular literatures (e.g., Dante and Geoffrey Chaucer). Intellectual life was robust, partially because of the rediscovery of Greek learning, which came to the West from Islamic sources, influencing both Christian and Jewish thinkers of the period. The fecund blend of Greek philosophy and Christian theology gave rise to a new synthesis of Christian learning called Scholasticism, a theology of the schools (i.e., of the medieval universities) that supplanted the older monastic theology of the late patristic and early medieval periods.

The eminence of Christian ideas and institutions in the Western medieval world was also its greatest weakness. Repeated attempts to reform the corruption in institutions or to disengage secular control of church life (and wealth) either by official church action (e.g., reforming councils) or charismatic leaders foundered on the embedded self-interest of those who flourished by a lack of reform.

The late fifteenth and early sixteenth centuries were times of convulsive religious change. In 1453, Constantinople fell to the Ottoman Turks. The city that had been the center of Byzantine Christianity now became an Islamic stronghold, and its premier church of Holy Wisdom (Hagia Sophia) was turned into a mosque. In time, the Turks would control many of the traditional Byzantine strongholds, including Greece itself, and would maintain that control until the collapse of that empire's power beginning in the nineteenth century.

The flight of Greek scholars to the West at this time abetted the humanist learning of the Renaissance both in Italy and in the North. Many humanist scholars (preeminently in the North) saw the rise of this "new learning" as one possible vehicle for the reform of Christianity. Although that vision was not to be realized, these humanists did give the Christian world many of the intellectual tools (Bible translations, critical editions of the patristic period, etc.) that would aid the Reformation, both Protestant and Catholic. The humanist emphasis on interior piety and ethical conversion was a direct reaction against the more externalized religion of the medieval world.

The sixteenth-century Protestant Reformation, triggered by the efforts of Martin Luther, a German Augustinian friar, fractured the religious unity of Western Europe. Luther was excommunicated by papal edict in 1521. By the middle of the century, the religious map of Europe was totally changed. Reformers such as John Calvin, Martin Bucer, and Huldrych Zwingli brought the Reformed movement to Switzerland. England broke from Rome under the monarchy of Henry VIII. Scotland and Scandinavian countries participated in the Reformation, as did large segments of Northern Germany and parts of what in the 1990s was Czechoslovakia. Besides the classical reformers such as Luther and Calvin, more radical reform movements emerged as diverse sectarian movements that attempted to reconstitute a primitive form of Christianity based on literal readings of the Bible and an adamantine resistance to secular power and privilege.

The Protestant Reformation brought in its wake many cultural changes. It shifted religious sensibility away from the old Catholic sense of the iconic and sacramental toward a renewed interest in the Word of God enshrined in the scriptures. With that shift, vernacular translations of the Bible became crucial as did the concomitant need for greater literacy. The reformers also put great emphasis on music as a vehicle for worship, so that the tradition of vernacular hymnody as well as other musical forms (e.g., the chorale) flourished.

The Catholic response to the Reformation (the Counter-Reformation) took many forms. New religious orders such as the Jesuits attempted to reform the religious life of the Catholic Church. Authoritarian measures such as the Roman Inquisition, the censorship of books, and strong clerical discipline attempted to stem the spread of Reformed ideas in traditional Catholic countries. The Council of Trent, meeting sporadically from 1545 to 1563, defined its doctrine and practice in strong reaction to Reformation theology and practice. The increased centralization of Catholic polity at this time would distinguish modern Catholicism even until the watershed events following the Second Vatican Council in the 1960s.

Catholic missionary ventures were launched both to the New World of the Americas and, less successfully, to India and the Orient in the aftermath of the great period of Renaissance exploration. Similarly, Protestant churches expanded into the New World as a result of the colonizing impulses of England and Holland in the seventeenth century. Both Catholicism and Protestantism made further incursions into countries both in Asia and Africa as a result of colonial expansion that lasted into the early twentieth century.

The rise of the empirical sciences as well as the sociopolitical revolutions attendant on the European Enlightenment lessened the hold of traditional religion, whether Protestant or Catholic, on the minds of eighteenth- and nineteenth-century Europeans. Political revolutions in the United States (1776) and

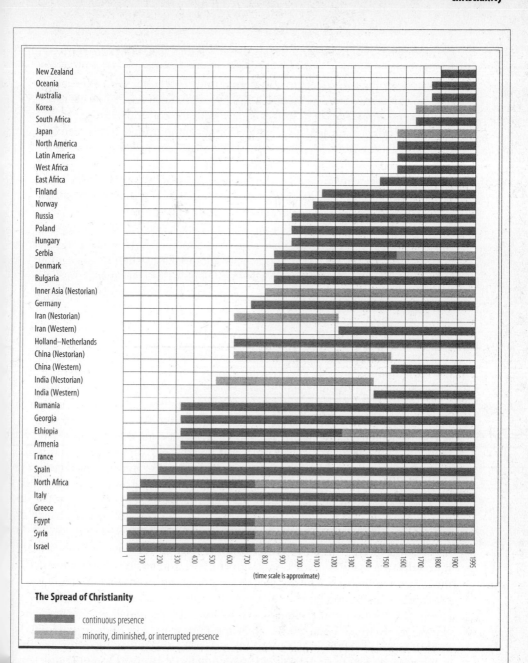

The Spread of Christianity

continuous presence

minority, diminished, or interrupted presence

France (1789) triggered new understandings of the relationship of the church to the state. The rise of scientific historical studies and the sharpening of philosophy as an autonomous discipline eroded the eminence of theology both as an academic discipline and as an overarching framework for human understanding. This process (called secularization) brought about both new attempts on the part of the churches to invigorate themselves and a more noticeable shift of religion away from public power to the private sphere.

Looking back on the twentieth century, it is easy to see a series of shifts in the fortunes of Christianity. After long periods of persecution, Christianity seems to be undergoing a resurgence in Eastern Europe in its offer of an alternative meaning system to a discredited Marxism. Western Europe still reflects the secularizing tendencies of its inherited past with the continual erosion of church attendance. Christianity is still vigorous in the United States, a country that the English writer G. K. Chesterton (1874–1936) once characterized as a "nation with the soul of a church." The traditional Catholicism of Central and Latin America is being invigorated by liberation theology, but significant numbers of Catholics are also joining Protestant churches, especially those with a strong charismatic and evangelical tone. In the non-Western world, Christianity shows exceptional strength in places such as black Africa (where it competes with Islam), parts of India that have a historic Christian presence (e.g., Kerala), and newly independent countries such as Indonesia. Christianity's growth in these areas of the world is inevitably reshaping how Christianity looks as it acculturates itself in places less touched by European cultural modes of thought and action.

SPIRITUAL CHARACTER

As a total phenomenon, Christianity seems so complex in its history and practice one can forget that, at its core, Christianity is based on a simple premise. Christianity asserts that human beings exist in a state of alienation; that alienation (from each other, from God) has been healed through the life and saving deeds of a single person, Jesus of Nazareth. Christianity, then, has at its heart not an idea but a person. Since Christianity further asserts that this person is both fully human and fully divine, it is clear that this person, Jesus Christ, stands as the paradigmatic figure against which all human effort must be measured. Thus, Jesus does something for humanity and is something for humanity.

There are two traditional modes of assertion of these convictions in Christianity. First, there is the preaching of the Word both as an evangelizing technique and as a practice within worship. Second, there is the memorializing of these truths through symbolic actions or rites, (e.g., sacraments, ordinances). It is broadly true that Reformed Christianity puts a stronger emphasis on the first mode (with its insistence on the scriptures, preaching, evangelizing, singing, etc.) and Orthodox and Roman Catholic Christianity assert the latter more strongly, as its more conspicuously sacramental, iconic, and liturgical character shows. Some church bodies (e.g., Anglicans, Lutherans) that have strong roots in both traditions often attempt a middle course between the two emphases.

Because of Christianity's insistent claim that Jesus was truly human there is an inevitable element of imitatability in Christianity; i.e., Jesus, as known through the New Testament, is offered to the believer as a model to imitate. Many scholars have insisted that each Christian generation has found a model of Jesus congenial to, or appropriate for, its own cultural era. Indeed, histories of Christianity tracing the changing models of Christ have been frequent in modern times. In times of persecution, churches would emphasize that Jesus suffered persecution and death, just as Byzantine emperors or medieval kings would find the triumphant Christ who "holds all things in his hands" (the Pantocrater of Byzantine mosaics) a congenial model to worship. In the late twentieth century the image of Jesus as lover and liberator of the poor has had an enormous impact on Christian preaching among the civilly deprived (South African blacks and, in the recent past, African Americans) and the socially marginalized (the *campesinos* of Central and Latin America).

This powerful notion of the imitation of Christ (Gk. *christomimesis*) not only derives from the desire to imagine who Christ is and how he might relate to human life, but also forms the foundation of how people should live; i.e., there is a correlation between christomimesis and Christian ethics. Christianity not only inherits the moral formulations of the Hebrew scriptures (e.g., the Ten Commandments) and the ethical ideals of the ancient Greco-Roman philosophical world (e.g., Stoicism), but also attempts to construct an ethics based on the life and teachings of Jesus. While this ethics is often more honored in theory than in practice, Christianity did (and does) attempt to live out an ethic based on selfless love, care for the poor and the dispossessed, forgiveness of sin, and nonviolence, which Jesus preached as part of his own understanding of those teachings that came from the great classical prophets of ancient Israel.

The complex historical evolution of Christian caregiving institutions (orphanages, hospitals, leprosaria, schools for the poor, etc.) must be seen as attempts to provide instrumentalities for the execution of the command of Jesus to care for "the least of the brethren." Similarly, both historic movements and persons who served the poor and/or attempted betterment of their condition root themselves in this same impulse. Indeed, some commentators have insisted that the early successes of Christianity in the Roman Empire are partially explicable because of the strong commitment of the early Christian communities to provide such aids at a time when social services were rudimentary or nonexistent.

Because Christianity grew largely through the multiplication of communities it was inevitable that the relationship would arise of these communities to the larger culture in general and the state in particular. Christianity went through three great macrodevelopments: from persecution, to establishment (i.e., enjoyment of full state support), to separation from the state and an autonomous existence in most parts of the world. That large picture, however, does not do full justice to the complexity of the issue.

Christianity holds a linear view of history: the world comes from God; history unfolds; and, finally, history will come to an end with the Second Coming of Christ. Inevitably, there is both a yearning for the "not yet" and a concomitant sense of the impermanence of earthly realities.

Historically, Christians of differing times and persuasions have given different emphases to this large worldview. There is a Christian strain of sectarianism that is profoundly ambivalent about "this world," shunning it as temporary and evanescent (e.g., in Catholic monasticism, in sectarian Protestantism) and placing a strong emphasis on the age to come. Another strain sees the coming kingdom as already present, and insists on human work in this world as the establishment of the kingdom in the here and now and as part of God's ultimate plan for the world and humanity.

Many contemporary debates in Christianity (about the role of Christians in the sociopolitical order, for example) ultimately root themselves in the emphasis one chooses to make about the nature of this world in relationship to the end of history. Everything from Third World liberation theology and the aftermath of the Second Vatican Council (1962–65) in Catholicism to the world-affirming Social Gospel or the strong apocalyptic character of some forms of Protestant fundamentalism may be seen as attempts to come to grips with what Augustine (d. 430) called the "two cities" of the world and God.

PROBLEMS AND PROSPECTS

As Christianity begins its third millennium, it is faced with serious challenges both in terms of its own self-understanding and in relation to those who do not share its beliefs.

One demographic fact seems inescapable: the greatest growth in Christianity occurs today outside of Western Europe, which has been the historic intellectual center of both Catholic and Reformed Christianity. With that demographic shift comes new expressions of Christianity that are acculturated into new patterns and symbols. The implications of this shift are profound, since these newer centers of Christianity will inevitably provide a new vocabulary and sensibility to Christian self-understanding. The great task of the future will be to hold in balance the essential Christian proclamation while doing justice to the new insights that derive from cultures other than European ones. As the theologian Karl Rahner (d. 1984) has noted, the day when Christianity can be viewed as an "export item" from the West seems largely over. Only the future will tell what shape African or Asian or Oceanic Christianity will look like.

From its beginnings, Christianity has had divisions and schisms within its own body. Only the most utopian of twentieth-century thinkers hopes for a totally undivided Christianity; more realistic commentators hope, and work for, a lessening of tensions and an increase of cooperation between diverse bodies who commonly profess faith in the person of Jesus Christ. Such internal ecumenism could palliate antagonisms between warring Christian bodies (e.g., Protestants and Catholics in Northern Ireland; Catholics and Orthodox in the Ukraine) as well as lessen the competition between Christian bodies where cooperation (e.g., in social work) would benefit all. This is the task of both the organized ecumenical movement in Christianity and the myriad attempts of Christian groups to grow in mutual trust and to work on common projects. Such trust and cooperation is of paramount importance, since many episodes in Christian history bear witness to how lethal a combination religious zealotry and national identity can be.

Although the foundational Christian documents proclaim the equality of all persons as a root belief springing from the doctrine of the Incarnation, it is only through long meditation, and many false starts, that Christianity has overcome its toleration of slavery, its acceptance of class distinctions, and its passivity in the form of racism. Too often in the past the Christian church was one more vehicle for colonial expansion as, for example, the modern history of Christianity in both Latin America and Africa attest. Current debates about the place of the emarginated and the emergence of Christian feminism indicate how slowly organized Christianity comes to grips with inequalities within its own ranks.

The relationship of Christianity with other faiths has not always been pacific, as, for example, the long history of Christian anti-Semitism demonstrates. With a rising sense of the complex diversity of religious sentiments in the world (brought to the fore by the globalization of information technologies), dialogue with the world's religions is an urgent task calling both for a greater appreciation of those religions and a lessening of the triumphalism endemic to certain forms of Christian proclamation.

Those same information technologies illustrate the vast inequalities in standards of living and the destitution of immense populations either through natural forces or indifferent political forces. Increasingly, Christian bodies have concerned themselves with the struggle for civil rights and for the amelioration of degraded living conditions. Nothing in current history indicates that such struggles are over.

That Christianity has not matched its own rhetoric with perfect performance should surprise no one, least of all Christians. Its founder asserted that the "wheat and the weeds" would coexist until the end of history. Authentic Christianity is not a perfectionist religion but one living in the ambiguities and disappointments of history. This fact does not absolve it from the need to realize the kingdom envisioned by Jesus of Nazareth, but it does mean that, for the Christian believer, the perfection of what Jesus was and what he preached will only come to full realization in the consummation of history. That point was made by Augustine of Hippo in his monumental work *City of God* (413–426): "For the City of the saints is up above, although it produces citizens here below, and in their persons the City is on pilgrimage until the time of its kingdom comes."

Christianity (authoritative texts and their interpretation). *See* Bible, Christian; Bible, interpretation of the Christian; Bible, translations of the Christian; exegesis.

Christianity (festal cycle). In the Catholic Church, the liturgical year begins with the season before Christmas (Advent), which is followed by the Epiphany season, Lent, Easter season, Pentecost (fifty days after Easter), and the post-Pentecost season. This calendar had a slow evolution deriving mainly from the annual celebration of Easter. In addition to this annual cycle there is also a sanctoral cycle that fixes the days for the observance of feasts of the saints. This same twin cycle is followed, with modifications, by the Church of England. The practice of Protestant denominations varies widely, with some (e.g., Methodists, Lutherans) adhering to a liturgical cycle with fixed readings from the Bible, and others (e.g., Baptists) following the civil calendar but with special emphasis on Christian feasts such as those of Easter and Christmas. A basic rule of thumb is this: the more liturgical the tradition, the more fixed the church calendar and its observances.

The Orthodox tradition distinguishes the movable feasts, which are set according to the date of Easter (the *Kanonarion*), and the fixed feast days and saints' days (*Synaxarion*). Since most Orthodox still use the Julian civil calendar rather than the Gregorian one used in the West, there is no sure synchronicity between Western and Eastern feast days. Indeed, there is even a difference in reckoning between the Byzantine and Armenian traditions. The Orthodox tradition uses a book (*Typikon*) containing all feasts, movable and immovable, along with liturgical instructions for proper celebration. Such books differ according to whether the *Typikon* is for monastic or cathedral usage.

In addition to the general calendar of the church in the West, there are also calendars that reflect local interests, or that incorporate certain civil holidays that have a religious resonance, like Thanksgiving in the United States. *See also* calendar (Christian); periodic rites.

Christianity (life cycle). Christian rituals mark the various stages of an individual's life from birth to death.

Birth: In the early centuries of Christianity the only religious ceremony that seems to have accompanied childbirth was a ritual purification of the mother, inspired by Old Testament prescriptions that regarded a woman who had given birth as unclean and required her to make a sacrificial offering (Leviticus 12). The Christian rites consisted chiefly of a series of prayers, which included thanksgiving for deliverance from the dangers of childbirth. This custom later became widely established, being known in England as "churching." Although still practiced in some Eastern churches, it has almost entirely died out among Western Christians today, as a result of changing attitudes toward childbirth.

After the practice of infant baptism became widespread in the fifth century, it effectively functioned as a rite of passage in connection with birth, especially as infant baptism came to be performed very soon after birth, usually in the presence of only the immediate family, and also included the giving of a name to the child, a relic of the time when adult candidates for baptism came with non-Christian birth names. Indeed, in most countries the church's baptismal register was the only way in which any birth was formally recorded until recent centuries.

While infant baptism still continues to function as a rite of passage for many families, in Baptist churches (which have always practiced only believers' baptism) there is a special rite of infant dedication; and in some other churches that are now seeking to distinguish more clearly the process of becoming a Christian from the celebration of birth or adoption, the attempt is made instead to provide a service of thanksgiving and blessing to meet this latter need, not always with much success. In a few cases a service is also offered for use after a stillbirth.

Puberty: Christianity did not originally have any puberty rite, and this is still the case in the Eastern Orthodox Church. However, the development in the medieval West of a rite of confirmation separated from baptism by several years and the deferral of admission to Communion until what was considered "the age of reason" indirectly gave Western Christians a way of marking the transition from childhood. The precise ages at which confirmation and admission to participation in the Eucharist have been practiced have varied in the different Western Christian traditions. In Protestant traditions the service of confirmation, where it has been retained, tends to function as the rite of admission to the Eucharist itself, and is often deferred until early teenage years. Some churches, however, have recently begun to admit very young children to the Eucharist, without any special ceremony, and to defer confirmation until later teenage years, so that the candidates may then make a "mature profession of faith," thus turning it into a rite of passage to adulthood. In the Roman Catholic tradition confirmation and ad-

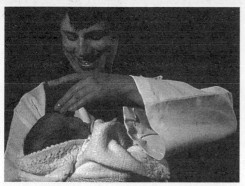

The ritual of Christian baptism (performed here in the United Church of Canada, Calgary, Alberta) takes two major forms. On the left, an infant is being baptized by being sprinkled (aspersion) with holy water from a baptismal font. On the right, an adult is being baptized by total immersion in a natural body of water ("living water"). Infant baptism was not common in early Christianity; it became prevalent after the sixth century when the majority of Christians were no longer adult converts, but born of Christian parents. Adult baptism became an issue after 1517 with the rise of Anabaptist groups who required a second, adult baptism confirming infant baptism once a Christian was conscious of being saved and freely chose to be baptized.

mission to Communion have not always taken place at the same time, and at the beginning of the twentieth century it was decided to lower the age for admission to Communion to seven years. "First Communion" therefore marks an important point of transition in Roman Catholic communities. In many parts of the world, however, including the United States, confirmation continues to be deferred until several years later, on the grounds that it demands a certain maturity. Thus, it keeps its place as a puberty rite.

Marriage: Early Christians seem at first to have followed contemporary local practice with regard to the rituals of betrothal and of marriage. Gradually, however, these two rites began to take place before the local Christian community and were presided over by ordained ministers, though they still included many ceremonies of non-Christian origin as well as Christian prayers. The betrothal commonly included such things as the joining of the couple's hands, the giving of a ring to the bride, and the veiling of her head. The marriage rite involved a celebration of the Eucharist and a special blessing of the couple, or in some places of the bride alone. Eventually the two rites took place on one day and were ultimately united in a single service, and in most Christian countries a church wedding became the only recognized legal form of marriage until recent centuries.

The later rites of the Eastern Orthodox Church focus on praying for God's blessing, and embody a positive attitude toward marriage as part of God's purposes in creation and a strong sense of mutuality in the act of marrying, as for example in the exchange of rings between the couple. A crowning of the couple is also included. This ancient custom is non-Christian in origin, and for that reason was at first opposed by some Christians, but it was defended by others on the grounds that it symbolized victory over passion. The Orthodox Church allows second or third (but not fourth) marriages, whether after divorce or the death of one partner, but in both cases a special rite is used that contains penitential prayers, since it is seen as a departure from the ideal of one marriage that is not even broken by death.

Medieval Western rites, on the other hand, were strongly shaped by the practice of the church at Rome, and made the expression of consent to marry their central feature. Hence in traditional Roman Catholic theology the couple themselves are regarded as the ministers of this sacrament. The rites also reflect a somewhat more negative spirit, with marriage spoken of as a remedy against fornication, and lack the mutuality evidenced in the East: the bride was "given away" by her father to the groom; she alone received a ring; she had a blessing of her own in addition to that of the couple; and sometimes she was required to express wifely obedience. There were many regional variations in the ceremonies that surrounded the rite, according to the dictates of local custom, often of non-Christian origin. These sometimes included the ritual blessing of the couple in their marriage bed. A new Roman Catholic marriage rite introduced in 1969 retained many traditional practices, but attempted to give greater expression to a more positive concept of the married state and to increase the element of mutuality in the symbolic actions. Roman Catholicism allows the remarriage by the same rite of those whose first marriage-partner has died, and of those whose first marriage was annulled, but does not believe that the bonds of marriage can be dissolved by divorce.

Many of the medieval customs survived in the marriage practices of the churches of the Reformation, although some Protestants rejected such ceremonies as the joining of hands and the giving of the ring, on the grounds that they were not commanded in the Bible, and the celebration of the Eucharist generally disappeared from the rite. More recent revisions of the marriage rite in all churches have moved in the direction of expressing a more positive concept of marriage and of its mutuality, although the strong conservatism with regard to the ceremony felt by many families has ensured the survival of a number of traditional features. Most Protestant churches allow remarriage after divorce or the death of the first partner.

Sickness: The custom of praying over those who were sick, laying hands on them, and anointing them with oil was an early Christian practice. The action was often understood as also conveying the forgiveness of sins, since, in the ancient world, sickness was commonly understood as connected with sin. Later practice employed oil blessed by a bishop or priest, and then given to the sick so that they might anoint themselves with it as they felt necessary. Apparently it was sometimes consumed as well as being applied to the body. The clergy were also expected to visit the sick regularly, praying over them and anointing them; and consecrated bread from the church's Eucharist was brought to the sick so that they might continue to share in Communion.

In the medieval West the action of anointing of the sick became restricted to the clergy alone, using oil previously blessed by the bishop. It was generally performed only when the person was close to death. It thus came to be seen as part of the "last rites," conveying forgiveness of sins and preparing the recipient for death rather than promoting healing, and for this reason was eventually known as "extreme unction." The administration of Holy Communion in such cases was also viewed as giving the communicant spiritual food for the journey from life to death, and so was given the Latin name *viaticum*.

The sixteenth-century Reformers abolished the unction of the sick because it was understood in a superstitious way, and they rejected the practice of bringing consecrated bread from the Eucharist to the sick, because they did not accept the existence of Christ's presence in the eucharistic elements. Thus, the ministry to the sick in the Reformation churches has mostly lacked any fixed ritual forms and been informal, with the minister reading Bible passages and saying prayers.

The twentieth century has seen some significant changes in traditional practices. In the Roman Catholic Church the rite of unction has been restored to its former significance as a sacramental expression of the healing power of Christ, and Holy Communion is regularly given to the sick for their spiritual strengthening and not just prior to death, although there is also still a special rite of viaticum. Because the laying on of hands and anointing with oil are found in the New Testament, some Protestants have begun to make use of them in their ministry to the sick.

Death: Early Christians employed burial as the normal means of disposing of the dead, and accompanied this act with prayer, and later with psalms and hymns. Spices appear to have been used to prepare the body for burial, and the Eucharist was celebrated both on the day of the funeral and on the anniversary of the death, expressing the belief that both living and departed were still joined in Communion. Attempts were made by the clergy in the fourth century to dissuade Christians from adopting such contemporary customs as wailing and wearing dark mourning garments, since these implied a lack of faith in the Christian hope of the resurrection of the dead: white garments were to be preferred. They were also instructed not to indulge in the usual sumptuous funeral pomp and lavish trappings, but to give alms to the poor as a memorial of the dead. All these battles, however, were eventually lost.

Later funeral rites of both East and West differ in details but are broadly similar in their general style. They usually begin with prayers and psalms in the home of the deceased, sometimes accompanying the preparation of the body for burial. There is a procession to the church, again accompanied by appropriate chants. At the church there is a service of readings, psalms, and prayers, and, in the West, the Eucharist is usually celebrated. A procession to the grave follows, and the burial is accompanied by prayers of commendation, and ritual acts of farewell and committal, such as the sprinkling of earth on the corpse, which is usually buried with feet toward the east, the direction from which the return of Christ on the day of resurrection was traditionally expected (clergy, however, are buried toward the west, facing their people). These rites, especially in the medieval West, lay greater stress on the fear of judgment than on the joy of entry into paradise that was characteristic of earlier times.

The churches of the Reformation simplified the rites they inherited, and in particular purged them of all reference to any possible intermediate state of purgatory after death, since they believed that the New Testament taught that the fate of the deceased was irrevocably determined at the moment of death: neither prayers nor the offering of the Eucharist could therefore alter that. Indeed, the extreme Reformers refused to allow any rites at all to accompany the utilitarian act of burial, for fear that it might imply belief that the actions of the living could affect the dead. Most churches, however, retained a service that included the preaching of the Christian hope of resurrection and prayers for the mourners, but not for the departed. Recent revisions of funeral rites in Protestant churches have sometimes included a limited element of prayer for the departed, and the new Roman Catholic rites incorporate a more positive note of hope and trust.

When the practice of cremation began to be adopted in Western countries in the nineteenth century, it was at first opposed by most Christians as being incompatible with belief in the resurrection of the body, but in the course of the twentieth century it has become more widely acceptable. It is generally preceded by a funeral service in church or in the crematorium chapel, and sometimes followed by a later interment of the ashes in a family grave or a special burial place, accompanied with appropriate prayers. *See also* baptism; confirmation; life-cycle rituals; marriage; sacraments and ordinances (Christianity).

Christianity (thought and ethics). Reflection on the forms and bases of the Christian life is a special branch of theology, the reflection on the faith and practice of the Christian community. Christian ethics also signifies the more general Christian response to such questions as, What is a good life? or How does one distinguish between good and evil, right and wrong? Christian ethics is an attempt by Christians to contribute to the religious, moral, and political life of humanity.

Any contemporary examination of Christian ethics must discuss a variety of writers and movements, texts, and contexts. At first, it is difficult to think of this variety as a tradition, since consistency is not its chief virtue. Further reflection, however, indicates a degree of unity in the recurrence of certain issues: What are the authoritative sources for Christian judgment? How do revealed sources relate to insights that are natural or common to humanity? What is the relationship of the Christian community to the world? What is the relation of Jesus Christ to the life of humanity?

The New Testament: The significance of such questions and the variety of possible answers is already apparent in the Christian scriptures. Matthew's Gospel presents Jesus as the supreme rabbinic authority. Jesus' disputes with the scribes and the Pharisees do not establish a new religion, distinct from the Judaism of the first century. Instead, they point to Jesus as the "new Moses" who comes "not to destroy the law, but to fulfill it"—that is, to uncover the true meaning of Torah. The Christian community is thus the "true Israel," distinguished not from the world in general, but from the pseudo-Israel (the synagogues) of the Pharisees; and its authoritative source is the Torah as written by Moses and interpreted orally by Jesus Christ.

Paul's Letters reflect a different understanding. The Corinthian correspondence, while concerned with the relationship between the Christian community and the synagogues, also deals with the relation between Christians and non-Jews. In discussions of marriage between believers and unbelievers; questions about divorce, remarriage, and the value of celibacy; or in diatribes against various forms of "immorality" and discussions of the "cleanness" of food offered to idols, Paul responds to questions arising from life in a first-century Hellenistic city. Paul's answers reflect a diverse set of authorities for Christian ethics, including the Torah, sayings of Jesus, his own wisdom based on the Spirit of Christ, common morality, conscience, and agape (love), proposed as the "more excellent way" and chief norm for Christian life. Whether agape, for which the primary example is the sacrificial behavior of Christ, constitutes a foundational principle to which all saints aspire, or a rule having premier status is not finally clear in Paul's writings. Neither is the precise relation of Christian ethics to common morality or to the Torah. Perhaps 2 Corinthians 3:18 provides a clue in speaking of the way that believers "beholding the Christ with unveiled face . . . are being transformed from one degree of glory to another. . . ." Agape then is a norm that ultimately transforms all others by placing them in a new context. Even so, Christian ethics ultimately transforms other systems of practical judgment by referring them to "the surpassing value of Christ" (Philippians 3:18).

Early Christian Writers: The early diversity of Christian ethics is further apparent in the Johannine corpus, the Pastoral Epistles, or such extracanonical writings as the Shepherd of Hermas, the *Didache*, or Gnostic texts. In some respects, the strict moralism of Hermas's vision or the Gnostic ideal of the wise person are reflected in the work of numerous second- and third-century Christian authors. In *On the Crown* and *Against the Pagan Shows*, for example, the North African Tertullian (d. ca. 220) sets forth a notion of the Christian life radically different from the standards of Roman society. There can be no compromise between the external and blessed way of Christ and the temporary, damnable way of Caesar. Tertullian's *Apology*, however, sets forth a more moderate view, arguing that Roman society has nothing to fear from Christians; Christ's teaching serves only to make people good citizens. Whether such distinctions primarily reflect different contexts or different audiences is not entirely clear.

Two other authors demonstrate the possibilities of a more complementary relationship between the Christian community and Roman society. Clement of Alexandria (d. ca. 215) presents the teaching of Christ as true philosophy, which instructs the untutored concerning basic morality, and provides insight into the excellence that the learned aspire to. The slightly younger Origen (d. ca. 254) of Alexandria also illustrates this line of thought, although his works on *Martyrdom* and *Against Celsus* indicate a greater tension between Christ and Caesar than is characteristic of Clement. The latter work in particular argues that followers of Christ cannot participate in rituals of service to the emperor or in wars that Caesar deems just. Such conscientious refusal sets Christians apart as models for Roman citizens, because they never violate norms crucial to Roman social life, and they carry out a special vocation by praying for the empire's peace and security. Christians help to preserve common morality and simultaneously show humanity a more perfect way of life.

Only with the fourth- and fifth-century authors does the outline of an emerging consensus on ethics appear. The context for this consensus is the establishment of Christianity as the state religion of Rome. In the Eastern empire, such establishment was seen as partial fulfillment of God's plan to establish the unity of humankind through the unity of faith. The interrelationship of church and empire would confirm, extend, and transform common morality, particularly as the former served to demonstrate the true origin and destiny of humanity as "partakers of the divine nature" (2 Peter 1:4). Through the centuries, the various Eastern (Orthodox) communities took their mission service as a kind of "leaven" by which human society would be transformed,

the true nature of human beings realized in communion with the Trinity.

In the West, such writers as Ambrose (d. 397) and Augustine (d. 430) took the new situation to call for new types of Christian responsibility. Reflection on war, for example, proceeds differently following Constantine's legitimation of Christianity. Ambrose and Augustine both justify Christian participation in war. According to Ambrose's *On the Duties of the Clergy*, such participation is justified because virtue requires preventing injury to innocents. In Augustine's *City of God* (413–426), the relative peace and order of earthly communities must be preserved, by force if necessary. Only in the city of God will there be secure peace. Ambrose and Augustine make use of a number of distinctions that preserve the ultimate significance of gospel teaching, while simultaneously respecting the insights of common morality and the Old Testament. Thus, Jesus' sayings against the use of force are relevant to defense of self, while force used for the public good may be justified. Similarly, Jesus' sayings refer to dispositions, common justice to actions. Finally, the gospel teachings constitute a norm of aspiration, while the morality of Roman society or of the Old Testament represent a lesser, albeit valid standard for behavior in an imperfect world. In the end, Ambrose and Augustine exemplify the emerging consensus that the Christian community should recognize two states or levels of Christian vocation, each with its special responsibilities and type of perfection: on the one hand, the vocation of the religious; on the other, the various occupations of the laity.

As Augustine makes clear in his work *On the Good of Marriage*, the goods of lay existence are related to the goods of the religious life as the imperfect to the perfect. The metaphor is useful for understanding a number of aspects of ethics in the medieval church: its emphasis on monasticism as the paradigmatic Christian life; its understanding of the relations between ecclesiastical and temporal authority; and ultimately, its response to classical learning, especially those portions of Aristotelian philosophy communicated to Christendom via Islamic civilization.

Medieval Thinkers: Thomas Aquinas's (ca. 1225–74) discussion of moral virtue presents a good example, as does his discussion of the relations between the various types of law. In the former, Aristotle's (d. 322 B.C.) understanding of the virtues as dispositions to behave in ways that accord with wisdom, courage, temperance, and prudence is taken to reflect the perfection characteristic of natural existence, while the theological virtues (faith, hope, charity) are reserved to the life of grace, which surpasses the natural as the perfect does the imperfect, or the whole does the part. As to law, the metaphor of perfect to imperfect, whole to part applies to the relation of divine and natural law. The latter indicates that portion of eternal law (God's wisdom) known to human reason as such. Divine law, corresponding to the revelation in scripture and the teaching of the church, confirms and extends the natural law, ultimately showing the "more excellent way" to which humanity ought to aspire.

Thomas Aquinas's thought eventually comes to dominate Catholic discourse on ethics, as on theology per se; in particular, the Spanish moralists Francisco de Vitoria (1483–1546) and Francisco Suarez (1548–1619) would develop their understanding of the application of natural law to the discovery of the New World in conjunction with their studies of Aquinas. By the late nineteenth century, Pope Leo XIII could declare the study of Aquinas's works a required part of priestly formation. Yet medieval discussion continues to demonstrate the diversity of Christian ethics. In particular, Duns Scotus (1265–1308) and William of Ockham (1285–1348) argue that the commands of God in scripture have priority over natural knowledge of the good. At the same time, such writers participated in movements that sharply delimited the civil authority of the church, and could suggest that Christian ethics stands alongside common standards of judgment, each having its own set of authorities and spheres of influence. Such contradictory positions give rise to the charge that Ockham in particular advocated a theory of "double truth," in which reason and revelation constitute distinctive yet parallel authorities.

Reformation: For Martin Luther (1483–1546), the priority of justification by faith alone is established by the free will of God declared in Christ. That a human being grasps this fact is similarly a free act of God, and is established by revelation. In matters not related to the priority of faith in salvation, however, there is no special wisdom given by revelation—insofar as scripture or the church teaches on morals or politics, it serves only to confirm what human reason is taught by natural law: that human beings exist in a network of relations in which obedience to authority is required to preserve order in a fallen world.

John Calvin's (1509–64) *Institutes of the Christian Religion* (1536) presents a more dialectical view of the relationship between revealed and natural sources of ethical judgment. Calvin's position, in general, is that the scriptural law, especially the Decalogue, is simply the natural law "writ large." By including statements on religion and morality in scripture, God intends to confirm the law of creation and to motivate human beings to obey it. The fallen condition of humanity, however, affects human motivation (even those who outwardly conform to moral law do so for the wrong reasons) and understanding. In particular, fallen human nature perceives its duty to worship, but knows nothing of proper worship. The commands stipulating the oneness of God, proscribing idols, and the like (the "first table" of the Decalogue) are known to fallen humanity only through revelation. Obligations to humanity (the moral commandments of the "second table"), however, are known, at least in their negative form, by all thinking beings. Proscription of murder, theft, and the like is part of the morality common to humanity as such. Yet the teaching of Jesus shows that proscription is not all there is to the moral life. Each negative command carries with itself a positive obligation—for example, "do no murder," viewed in the light of gospel teaching, also means "do everything possible to preserve and protect the life of a neighbor." In this way, revelation serves not only to strengthen but to perfect understanding of the obligations implicit in common morality.

In the sixteenth century, the term *Anabaptist* ("rebaptizers") covers a multitude of groups and a highly diverse set of approaches to Christian ethics. In time, however, the movement came to be identified primarily with the "peace churches"—Mennonites, Amish, and others who held that the "new law" brought by Christ was absolutely obligatory for the Christian community. That common morality or even the Old Testament might justify wars, for example, is no argument for Christian participation in violent activity. The Christian community is set apart by its witness to the standards exemplified in the life and teachings of Jesus.

Post-Reformation: The development of Christian ethics since the Reformation has been profoundly affected by developments in European and American culture. This is so even for the various Orthodox communities, particularly insofar as portions of their membership have migrated to North America. But the process is most clear with respect to the Western church. Protestant denominations, for example, generally present themselves in ways that suggest their debt to one or another Reformation tendency. "Lutheran," "Calvinist" (or "Reformed"), and

"Anabaptist" function as loose indicators of their approach. That Presbyterians are "Reformed," for example, indicates ties to Calvinism, with its historic emphasis on scripture confirming and extending common understandings of morality. It does not indicate that modern Presbyterians follow Calvin's particular moral judgments.

Roman Catholic ethics is also more diverse than commonly thought. Catholic unity exists in the heritage of Thomism, in the great theme of a hierarchy of values and institutions, in the manuals of moral theology meant to guide priests in the legal function created by the sacrament of penance, and in the prominence given to the teaching authority of the papacy. Yet each of these is also a source of diversity. While Thomism does provide a common heritage in modern Catholic ethics, debates concerning the meaning of terms, the priority of various themes in Aquinas's thought, and the revisionist Thomism of Karl Rahner (d. 1984) and others suggest that this heritage is as much a source of diversity as of unity. Changing notions of penance limit the "legal" role of the priest, thus lessening the importance of moral manuals and other traditional sources of guidance. Most important, the prominence given to conciliar authority by Vatican II (1962–65) and the active role taken by national conferences of bishops provide a new context for the exercise of papal authority. In short, Roman Catholic ethics, like its Protestant equivalents, has a rather loose relation to its historic tradition. To say that a particular movement or writer is "Catholic" does not always indicate a precise position in matters of ethics.

Christian ethics thus finds its unity in the questions it asks and the sources to which it must appeal. Christian movements and writers respond to the Christ event. They raise questions about the relationship of that event to other revealed sources, as well as to the common moral sense of cultures like the Roman Empire or the modern West. From the earliest writings Christian reflections illustrate a diversity of understanding concerning such questions. Perhaps Christian ethics is less a tradition of shared judgments than a conversation occurring in many distinctive contexts, and involving many voices—including, in increasing numbers, the voices of feminists and Christians from the Third World. *See also* Christian theological systems.

Christianity (worship). Christian worship is the public and ritual honor given to God in the name of Jesus Christ. According to Paul (Romans 12:1–2) the basic form worship takes is the offering of a person's self to God. Thus, the whole of Christian life can be considered an act of worship. In practice, however, worship has come to mean the formal and visible acknowledgment of God in what is usually called liturgy.

The word *liturgy* is the English equivalent of the Greek *leitourgia*, a compound word from *laos* (people) and *ergon* (work). In secular usage the word meant a benefaction or public service. Inherent in its Christian usage is the interplay between God's service to humankind and humankind's service to God. Thus, an act of worship can be understood as God's service to human beings before it is a human response to God. This accent is found particularly in the attitude of the heirs of the sixteenth-century Reformation, who insist on the priority of God's activity in worship.

Essential to any definition of Christian worship is its christological character. Although the earliest Christians may have continued to worship in the Temple in Jerusalem and in the synagogues, their distinctive worship was always qualified by a christocentric focus. Formal Christian prayer was addressed to God through Christ in the Holy Spirit. Christians were thus able to adapt prayer and ritual forms from their own cultures, but with a new focus—the person of Jesus Christ. In addition a complex interplay can be perceived between Christian belief and worship, as in the traditional adage *lex orandi/lex credendi* (Lat., "the rule of prayer"/"the rule of belief").

Christian worship consists of words (prayers and other ritual formulas) and acts. Sacramental worship emphasizes the use of material objects and physical actions in the process of worship, although not all Christian ritual acts are considered sacraments. In general, churches in the tradition of the Reformation recognize two sacraments based on the witness of the New Testament: Baptism and the Eucharist (or the Lord's Supper). The Roman Catholic and Eastern Christian churches accept seven sacraments: baptism, confirmation (Eastern Christians—chrismation), Eucharist, penance, anointing of the sick, marriage, and holy orders. The churches of the Reformation have tended to stress the verbal aspect of Christian worship over and against sacramental activity. Hence preaching has often predominated in traditions of Protestant worship.

Traditions of Worship: The major scholarly advance of twentieth-century liturgical study has been the recovery of Jewish traditions at the root of Christian worship. Since Christianity was from the beginning a missionary movement Christian faith took root in a number of cultures.

From these cultures came diverse styles and traditions of worship. Jewish Christian worship probably relied heavily on Temple and synagogue, adapting various elements like the *tefillah* (or eighteen benedictions), the *kedushah* (*sanctus* or threefold Holy), blessing (*berakah*), and thanksgiving (*todah*) prayers to Christian purposes. Although none of these traditions survives in its original Aramaic or Hebrew usage, traditions of worship in Syriac and Armenian have retained a number of Jewish Christian elements.

By far the most significant language for the spread of Christianity throughout the Mediterranean world was Greek. A number of Greek-speaking Jewish Christian and purely Hellenistic elements combined to influence the development of Christian forms of worship. A third major cultural and linguistic influence on the development of Christian worship was to come with the composition of Latin liturgical texts beginning in the third century in North Africa and spreading to Rome.

It is difficult to discern the patterns and content of Christian worship up to the fourth century, since very few texts were written. One can only piece together hypothetical reconstructions of Christian worship services from letters, sermons, apologetic and other treatises, and practical handbooks (early church orders such as the third-century *Apostolic Tradition*, ascribed to Hippolytus of Rome).

Two major changes accompanied the legalization and widespread acceptance of Christianity in the fourth century. First, the diverse traditions of Christian worship began to converge under the influence of major urban centers such as Jerusalem, Antioch, Alexandria, Edessa (in East Syria), Caesarea in Cappadocia, Rome, and eventually Constantinople. This convergence was the seed of what later came to be considered the major rites of Christian worship: in the East, Byzantine (from the combined influence of Jerusalem, Caesarea, Antioch, and above all Constantinople), Alexandrian or Coptic, East Syrian, and Armenian; in the West, the Roman (which came to predominate in the Middle Ages), the Gallican (French), Mozarabic (Visigothic or Spanish), and Ambrosian (Milanese or Northern Italian). Various local usages were related to each of these rites, since standardization was difficult in a pre-printing era that relied on the transmission of tradition orally and via handwritten manuscripts.

The second major change in Christian worship in the fourth century is the production of written liturgical prayer texts. Prayers that were originally improvised came to be written down mainly for two reasons: a greater concern for verbal orthodoxy stemming from the various theological controversies of the fourth and fifth centuries, and for the increased number of leaders of worship.

Although the major lines of the various forms of Christian worship had been set by the sixth century, considerable development in the diverse rites took place in the course of the Middle Ages. These developments were related to the growth of the liturgical calendar, the disposition of liturgical space, and the specific needs of the cultures in which Christians found themselves. By far the most significant developments were the retention of a sacral language (Latin) in the West and the separation of officiants (clergy) from participants (the laity) signaled by both architectural developments and the tendency of major prayers to be said in silence.

The gradual dominance of the Roman rite in the West can be attributed to the influence of Rome as a symbolic center for Christian faith, although this rite underwent considerable change in the seventh through ninth centuries when it was imported North of the Alps and eventually returned to Rome in the tenth through eleventh centuries when the fortunes of the city were at an ebb.

In the East, the Byzantine rite became predominant because of the influence of Constantinople, though this rite experienced adaptation when it was translated into Slavonic with the Christianization of Russia and other Slavic lands.

The Reformation of the sixteenth century signaled a watershed in the development of Christian worship. The most significant change was the translation of worship texts into the various languages of the Reformation churches. Also important was the attempt (with varying intensity) to return to the (supposed) worship practice represented in the New Testament. With the invention of movable type in the fifteenth century it became possible for both the Reformation churches and the Roman church to standardize liturgical texts. Apart from these common denominators it is more difficult to describe the development of worship in the Reformation churches homogeneously. The Lutheran churches tended to retain many of the externals of Roman worship, though with a new evangelical spirit and an accent on the reading and preaching of the scriptures. The Calvinist or Reformed churches attempted a more radical return to New Testament practice in a style more severely iconoclastic than the Lutheran reforms. The Anglican Church tended to combine elements of Roman ceremonial with a Reformed bent in theology. The churches of the Radical (often Anabaptist) Reformation sought more freedom in liturgy and moved away from liturgical formulas to improvised prayers. Historical circumstances (e.g., the movement to the frontier in the United States) and movements of thought (the seventeenth- and eighteenth-century Enlightenment and Pietist and Methodist reactions) prompted significant changes in the traditions that developed in the sixteenth century.

The modern liturgical movement, beginning with the nineteenth-century Romantic reaction to the Enlightenment and the industrial revolution, has seen the recovery of the value of the sacramental dimension of worship among the churches of the Reformation and an increased concern with active participation by laity and the centrality of the Bible in the Roman Catholic Church. In the wake of the Second Vatican Council (1962–65), the Roman church revised its liturgical books, and a number of other churches have followed suit. A significant convergence on the meaning of worship and ministry was reached in the World Council of Churches' Faith and Order Commission document, *Baptism, Eucharist and Ministry* (1982).

Forms of Worship: From its earliest days Christianity has known distinctive forms of worship. Even when Christians borrowed elements of worship from Judaism or other local practices they put their own stamp on them, transforming them in a christocentric fashion. Among the most important ritual practices of Christians throughout the centuries have been those associated with initiation.

Baptism and Confirmation: The ritual bath called baptism has been the central focus of initiation rites. While there is considerable debate about the immediate antecedents of this ritual bath, about whether infants were baptized as well as adults in the primitive church, and about whether the word *baptism* connoted other ritual actions like anointing and the imposition of hands, it is clear that Christians universally baptized in water either in the name of Jesus or of the Trinity and that this action was the visible symbol of conversion to Christian faith. By baptism all Christians were considered to receive eschatological outpouring of the Holy Spirit. The rich symbolism of the water bath could be interpreted in various ways, e.g., a bath of cleansing and purification, rebirth to new life, and participation in the death and resurrection of Jesus. The sacramental act of baptism culminated a period of preparation by prayer, fasting, and instruction and by the third century took place at the Easter Vigil (Holy Saturday) to emphasize the candidate's participation in Christ's death and resurrection.

Baptism was considered a once-for-all event. After some controversy between the Roman and North African churches in the third century it was decided that apostates would be readmitted to Christian fellowship (Communion) by the liturgical gesture of the "imposition of hands" rather than by being rebaptized. The historical relation between the imposition of hands, various anointings, and the water bath is a very complex one. The early East Syrian rite placed an anointing before the water bath and seems to have emphasized its character as a participation in the royal messianic mission of Jesus. Other rites eventually employed several anointings. For the majority of the churches from the fourth century on, the clean ritual sequence of initiation consisted of water bath, anointing (also called chrismation), and Eucharist. Thus, participation in the eucharistic meal culminated the initiatory pattern. By the fourth century, preparation for this complex of ritual action could take several years and was intensified in the period of Lent, which preceded Easter. With the triumph of Christianity in the fourth century, the initiation of converted adults became less an issue than the Christianization of society. Thus, infants were baptized, and the original sequence of rites gradually took on a different character.

Baptism was performed by a bishop as the focal figure of the church's unity. It was he who blessed the waters of the baptismal font and the chrism (oil) for the anointing. As the churches expanded both within and beyond the cities, presbyters (priests) were also deputed to baptize. In the East the unity of this act with the church was symbolized by the use of chrism that had been blessed by the bishop. In the West, however, the bishop symbolized this unity in person and the postbaptismal anointing and imposition of hands were performed by him in person. Thus, what came to be called confirmation was gradually severed from its immediate initiatory connection to baptism. In theory, if not always in practice, this confirmation preceded participation in the Eucharist.

The churches of the Reformation reevaluated the practice of confirmation, questioning the New Testament roots of anointing and, since most people had been baptized as infants, requiring a rudimentary knowledge of Christian doctrine for confirmation and admission to communion. Most churches are in the process of reviewing their theology and practice of initiation today, profiting from anthropological studies on the rites of initiation and appreciating anew the classic integral pattern of baptism-chrismation-Eucharist.

Eucharist: The ongoing aspect of initiation among Christians is a sacred meal that has variously been called Eucharist, the Lord's Supper, Holy Communion, the Mass, and the Divine Liturgy. Patterned on accounts of Jesus' Last Supper with his disciples in the Synoptic Gospels and Paul (1 Corinthians 11), Christians recognize Christ's presence among them in the sharing of bread and wine that have been prayed over in this meal. By the second century the meal-ritual was preceded by a service of the Word, which included prayer, readings from the scriptures, preaching, and the singing of psalms. From this time the Eucharist was also considered to be a sacrifice, but how precisely it relates to the sacrifice of Jesus has been a matter of ongoing controversy, as has the relation between the bread and wine and the presence of Jesus.

As with baptism, the immediate antecedents of the Christian Eucharist are debated. It is not clear whether the supper of Jesus was a Passover meal, but most scholars agree that it was at least a festive Jewish sacred meal. The origins of the central or eucharistic prayer have been sought in both Jewish meal blessings (the *berakah*) and thanksgiving prayers (the *todah*), though the search for a single original eucharistic prayer has been largely abandoned. Different liturgical traditions produced eucharistic prayers that varied in structure though containing most of the same elements: the expression of praise and thanksgiving, the memorial (Gk. *anamnesis*; Heb. *zikkaron*) of Christ's activity—including an institution narrative of Jesus' actions at the Last Supper, and an invocation (Gk. *epiklesis*) of the Holy Spirit upon the communicants and the gifts.

The adaptation of Christianity to more favorable circumstances (especially to large public worship spaces called basilicas) in the fourth century led to a greater elaboration of the liturgy. In the course of the Middle Ages as participation in Communion among the laity became less and less frequent, more attention was paid to dramatic elements in the Eucharist, especially the elevation of the Host at the beginning of the institution-narrative. The Reformation signaled two major changes in eucharistic practice. On the one hand the reformers insisted on the Communion of the faithful and not only the priest. On the other, increased attention to the proclamation of the Word and preaching, as well as the people's reluctance to communicate frequently, led to lessening frequency of celebration among the churches of the Reformation. In some churches this meant that the Eucharist was celebrated four times a year. In the course of

Protestant minister blessing the bread and wine at the altar in a eucharistic service; United Church of Canada, Ontario.

the twentieth century, Roman Catholics (encouraged by Pope Pius X in 1906) began to receive Communion more frequently. The Roman Eucharist was reformed both in language and structure after the Second Vatican Council. Many other churches have reformed their eucharistic practice along more classical lines and increased the frequency of the Eucharist, a common ideal being weekly celebration.

Prayer: Christian worship is not exhausted by sacramental activity. From earliest times Christians also simply prayed together. Various times were recommended throughout the early centuries for common prayer: morning; midday; evening; the third, sixth, and ninth hours; bedtime; midnight; cockcrow. The Jews prayed the Shema (Deuteronomy 6:4 with several other scripture passages and blessings) twice a day and the Tefillah (or Eighteen Benedictions) three times a day. The earliest Christian handbook, the *Didache* (second century?), stipulates that the Lord's Prayer be said three times a day.

By the fourth century, Christians were praying together publicly, and the main hours of prayer seem to have been morning and evening. This public daily prayer consisted of hymns and psalms as well as intercessory prayer, led by a clerical officiant and employing a good deal of ceremony (e.g., lights, incense, processions). This form of prayer has been called the Cathedral Liturgy of the Hours. The men and women who took to the Egyptian and Syrian deserts also prayed together, but their prayer was characterized more by a contemplative listening to scripture. This form has been called the Monastic Liturgy of the Hours. Increased contacts between the monks and the urban populations created a hybrid of these two forms of worship. With the clericalization of worship in the Middle Ages, the Liturgy of the Hours came to be the preserve of clerics and monks. It became possible for clerics to pray the Liturgy of the Hours in private using shortened forms of the books (breviaries). They thus assumed an obligation to pray the Liturgy of the Hours (also called the Divine Office) daily. Public daily prayer was preserved by the Anglican tradition, and recent reforms in many Christian traditions have sought to restore the public and communal nature of this form of worship. *See also* Byzantine liturgy; hymnody, Christian; Mass; sacraments and ordinances (Christianity).

Christianity in Armenia. *See* Armenia, Christianity in.

Christianity in China. *See* China, Christianity in.

Christianity in Islam. *See* Islam, Christianity in.

Christianity in Japan. *See* kakure kirishitan; Kyodan, Nihon Kirisuto; Mu-kyokai; Uchimura Kanzo.

Christianity in Syria. *See* Syria, Christianity in.

Christian Science, a religious philosophy and organization founded by Mary Baker Eddy (1821–1910) based on the premise that disease and death are the result of incorrect understanding. Following a healing experience in 1866, Eddy translated her experience into a philosophical system known as Christian Science, the principles of which were set forth in her *Science and Health with Key to the Scriptures* (1875). Eddy claimed to have discovered the key to the correct interpretation of the Bible and that her teachings, properly applied, would lead to a correct knowledge of the Ultimate and, when put into practice, bring an end to disease, suffering, and even death.

Christian Science took institutional form in 1879 in Eddy's Massachusetts Metaphysical College and then in the Church of Christ, Scientist, which still maintains international headquarters in Boston. Eddy maintained firm control over the organization during her lifetime, and several former disciples left to found movements of their own, mainly of the New Thought variety. Christian Science, however, differs from similar "harmonial" movements in its insistence on an explicitly Christian character and its strict organizational system.

Christian Science Sunday worship focuses on readings from the Bible and *Science and Health,* with other services based on testimonials to its effects delivered by believers. The church licenses practitioners, teachers, and readers, and maintains reading rooms in commercial areas as evangelistic devices. It publishes the well-known, award-winning *Christian Science Monitor* as well as educational literature at its Boston headquarters. Membership statistics are not made public; estimated figures for the 1970s are 475,000 in the United States and another 150,000 elsewhere. *See also* Eddy, Mary Baker.

Christian Socialism, a movement that seeks to realize the Christian vision of the kingdom of God through democratic socialist political work. Christian Socialism is found in many developed countries of the Western world, notably France and Italy, in Eastern Europe, but especially in the so-called underdeveloped countries of Latin

America, Africa, and Asia. One of the more political goals of Christian socialists is worker code-termination and self-control. The worker, seen as created in the image of God, becomes a full human being in creating through labor. Neither the state-centered economies of Eastern Europe and the former Soviet Union nor the market-centered economies of the Western world have been effective in realizing the full democratization of work, and both are critiqued by Christian socialists.

Christian socialists have been criticized for being "Marxists in sheep's clothing" in capitalist societies, and for being "bourgeois idealists" in Marxist societies. In the 1990s socialism is undergoing worldwide reevaluation as an economic theory, and for its inattention to environmental concerns.

Christian Socialism has declined in recent decades in Europe and the United States even as it has gained affiliates in Latin America and Africa. *See also* liberation theology.

Christian theological systems. In Christianity, systematic theology is an orderly account of Christian belief; an ordering of Christian belief that occurs in the context of Christian community and practice.

Contemporary Suspicions of "Systems": In late-twentieth-century settings, especially in postmodern North Atlantic societies, the notion of a Christian theological system, or of systematic theology, has become problematic in three senses. First, a general antisystematic temper has been embraced by many academics. Many philosophical and cultural forces have come together in the postmodern age, generating suspicion about anything that universalizes. The particular and the discrete are the order of the day. Reflections not only from Nietzsche, but also from philosophers such as Kierkegaard, Wittgenstein, Heidegger, and Derrida reinforce the suspicion of systems and of the universals or essences upon which many systems have been built.

Second, past theological systems are often described as systematically distorted. Marxist scholars, along with African-American, Latin American, and feminist ones, have exposed many of the great systems to critique, laying bare these systems' rationalization of the oppression of diverse groups. Feminist theologies, for example, write about "androcentrism," a systemic distortion in theological systems of North Atlantic cultures that marginalizes women and reinforces patriarchal structures.

Third, late-twentieth-century societies feature a proliferation of the Christian practices within which Christian belief dwells and from which theological systems might be crafted. This plurality makes it difficult to develop theological systems that possess the comprehensiveness and general applicability usually thought to be traits of a theological system. Contemporary literary criticism and hermeneutics inform many that all writing is limited to one's social location, shaped by factors of economic and political status, sexual orientation, gender, or racial or ethnic heritage. In such contexts, theological systems are less likely to be formulated than are short essays and forays that are occasional, exploratory, situational—accenting the short message, the brief narrative. There have always been critics of systems and systematizers, but today's critics have had a greater impact on theologians. While it is true that fewer systematic theologies have actually been produced in the late twentieth century, it would be premature to say that no systematizing efforts will emerge in the future.

Ordering Theological Reflection: In spite of the problematic nature of theological systems, one can identify distinct resources for ordering theological reflection, influential both in the history of theology, but also in the less systematic, even antisystemic, age of the late twentieth century.

Creedal resources have long given a distinctive shape to Christian theological systems. Such creeds include the "rules of faith" by Irenaeus (d. ca. 190) and Tertullian (d. ca. 220), the Apostles' Creed, the Creed of Caesarea, the Definition of Chalcedon, the Augsburg Confessions, and many others. These creeds may be viewed as closely linked to Christian liturgy and Christian practice, and hence as clarifying expressions of the beliefs present in Christian communities.

Traditionally, the three "articles of the creed" (respectively, God the Father, the Son, and the Holy Spirit) have provided a key structure, crystallizing central scriptural points for subsequent ordering of theological reflection. Much of the early history of theology was structured by creeds, and even when Christian thinkers moved beyond them, their influence was strong. To a significant degree, Thomas Aquinas's *Summa theologiae* (1266–73) are based on the words of the creed. The four "books" of John Calvin's *Institutes of the Christian Religion* (1559) are also structured in terms of the three articles of the creed.

Another mode of ordering Christian theological systems has focused on doctrinal loci, a set of received topics in Christian belief that highlight certain subject matters. This set of topics usually includes the three articles of the creed, but others as well, so that the topics might include a set of ordered notions like the following: revelation, God, creation, providence and evil, anthropology (doctrine of human nature), sin, Jesus Christ, Holy Spirit, the Church, eschatology. Here the resources for ordering are less the creedal givens or articles of faith, and more these articles as they are reflectively developed into a set of topics that have become doctrines, i.e., what the Church believes, teaches, and confesses. Christian systematic theology often understood itself as the development of these topics individually and, especially, in relation to each other. Theology and its history is not reducible to these interrelated topics, since other factors influence theological reflection (context and interests of theologians, philosophical reflection, insights from contemporary disciplines, etc.), but the topics have provided a useful device for ordering Christian theological systems. The topics as used in both Protestant and Roman Catholic Scholasticism are occasionally criticized as constituting a schema of categories that make it difficult for theologians to respond creatively to the needs of a particular age. Even when theologians break free from a slavish schematization of the topics, however, Christian theologians often return to these topics to order their reflections on the nature of Christian belief and practice.

Studies of narrative provide another resource for ordering Christian theology. Here, a structure of theology emerges by viewing theology's scriptural texts with the aid of narrative theory. Narrative is one of several genres in the Bible (including proclamation sayings, epistles, wisdom sayings, etc.). However, the entire biblical text of Hebrew and New Testament scriptures can be viewed as a narrative. It is a grand epic or saga of God's dealing with people. The narrative develops key characters' identities, gives plot by sequencing key events, develops tensions as characters' identities and plots conspire to create the world of the Bible. The literary properties of this biblical world, which structure Christians' own living, also structure theological reflection about that living. The Bible's themes have always been key sources for theological systems, influencing those systems through creeds, doctrinal loci, and other means. By highlighting the Bible as narrative, however, another kind of structural resource for ordering theology emerges, i.e., one that forms theology in accord with the Bible's literary structure. Theological ordering in terms of narrative studies of scripture are markedly evident in the great Protestant theologian Karl Barth's (1886–1968) notion of narrative as the

authoritative aspect of scripture. Roman Catholic theologies during this same period also show the importance of narrative theory for ordering theology, as displayed in the works of Karl Rahner (1904–84) and Johann-Baptist Metz (b. 1928).

Finally, resources for ordering emerge from different types of situational analysis. Three of these may be identified. Each type has in common the trait of making some reference to theologians' situations, and then using that reference to structure theology in a distinctive way. Several theologians, Protestant and Roman Catholic, combine these types in different ways to structure their theologies.

Correlational approaches are marked by a tendency to think in terms of two principal sources for theology: Christian texts and traditions, and interpretations of human situations. Here the primary concern is to refer to key traits of the human situation (anguish, joy and wonder, fundamental trust, systematic injustice) and then bring these into correlation with Christian texts and traditions. This gives theology an apologetic temper that is not simply a recent development. Among twentieth-century theologians, however, Paul Tillich's (d. 1965) "method of correlation" gave this approach a notable prominence, and subsequent theologians have challenged, revised, and qualified Tillich's correlational strategy even while they make their own use of it. The key principle for ordering theological reflection is the correlational activity, moving back and forth between interpretation of human situations and interpretation of traditions.

Hermeneutical and pragmatist approaches question the two-pronged character of correlational approaches, and present a more fluid type of structure for theology. These approaches find it difficult to distinguish texts and traditions from their situations, arguing that these are always in mutual interplay. Hence, the emphasis falls on theology understood as always under hermeneutical, i.e., interpretive, reconstruction within specific communities of practice. Some theologians stress the continual play ongoing between theological tradition and contemporary interpreters, that constant movement between tradition and experience that makes it impossible to separate them. Others accent more the fact that this play occurs within practical settings, demanding pragmatist analysis of how interpretations and theological claims are generated in radically different, often seemingly incommensurable, communities of discourse. In whatever way the emphasis is made, the salient features of this ordering of theological reflection lies in the continuing exchange of question-and-answer in the play of conversation (David Tracy), or as a reflective equilibrium in which there is a "systematic rechanneling of initial commitments in such a way that each act is judged in terms of all the others" (Francis Schussler Fiorenza). Perhaps this is furthest away from traditional understandings of systematic theology in the sense of an arrangement of creedal articles, loci, or narrative forms. But there is a systematic interest, although it is focused on a continual "rechanneling" of the many initial and different starting points that Christians occupy.

Liberation approaches give primacy to the theme of liberating praxis in theology. Theology here may be diversely structured, but it has an identifiable ordering principle in that all its parts (analytic theory, biblical interpretation, symbolic revisioning, doctrinal reconstruction) are related to peoples' needs for liberation from cultural and political oppression: e.g., from racism, classism, militarism, sexism, heterosexism, exploitation of the environment, ethnocentrism. In 1969, the works of Gustavo Gutierrez and Rubem Alves launched Latin American liberation theologies as reflection that claimed to be a "second act," ordered to and occurring after peoples' praxis of liberation. At about the same time, James Cone's black liberation theology presented theological reflection ordered to the theme of emancipation for African Americans resisting white supremacism in the United States. Shortly thereafter, through the 1970s and 1980s, a number of North American women (Rosemary Radford Ruether, Elisabeth Schussler Fiorenza, Sallie McFague, and others) formulated Christian feminist theologies consonant with the long-standing drive for women's emancipation. Theologies especially attuned to women's need for emancipation were, by the late twentieth century, becoming a worldwide phenomenon.

The diverse liberation approaches hardly display anything that might be called a system in the traditional sense. To the contrary, even in their most rigorous and persuasive forms, they draw from diverse sources to create new emancipatory visions and practices. Even so, there is a distinctive ordering orientation marked by a practical and theoretical commitment to the values of deliverance, liberation, and emancipation—an orientation that increasingly provides a center to worldwide effort of networking, connecting, and reconnecting different liberation struggles.

In spite of the decrease of interest in system-atic theological efforts in the late twentieth century there are diverse resources available for ordering theological reflection. Further developments will clarify whether they will issue in new Christian theological systems. *See also* apologetics; Christianity (thought and ethics).

Christmas, the Christian feast celebrating the birth of Jesus Christ on December 25. First mentioned in Rome in the middle of the fourth century, the date was a Christian replacement for the Roman celebration of *Sol Invictus* (Lat., "the Unconquered Sun") at the winter solstice. The observance of the date spread from Rome to the East, although some churches (e.g., the Armenian) celebrate Christ's birth on January 6.

Over the centuries, many customs, not all of them universally observed, became attached to this day. The erection of the Christmas crib (creche) began with Francis of Assisi, who made the first one in Greccio, Italy, in 1223. Use of Christmas greenery (trees, wreaths, etc.) was an adaptation of pre-Christian customs that began in Germanic countries but spread to England in the nineteenth century through the influence of Queen Victoria's husband, who was German. Santa Claus (Saint Nicholas), Father Christmas, and Father Frost are all adaptations of European folk customs celebrated in the winter season. Christmas carols began as a wider custom of singing popular religious songs (as opposed to liturgical hymns) on seasonal feasts but, over the years, increasingly became identified with this season. Midnight services derive from the Western liturgical custom of celebrating three Masses ("Christmas" is from the Old English meaning "Christ's Mass") on the day at midnight, dawn, and midmorning. The seasonal exchange of gifts is connected to an imitation of the Magi as gift-bearers to the Christ child and to the custom of giving children gifts on the feast of Saint Nicholas, who was honored earlier in the month. In many countries it is still customary for gifts to be given on January 6, which is the day of the Magi.

The "twelve days of Christmas" marks the period between Christmas Day and the Feast of the Epiphany (January 6), with New Year's Day marking the midway point of the festal period.

The mixture of Christian piety and popular custom on this day explains why the seventeenth-century Puritans attempted, with scant success, to abolish the feast. *See also* calendar (Christian).

Christology, critical reflection on the person of

Jesus as the Christ. Christology seeks to understand and explain the confluence of God's presence in the full humanity of Jesus' life and death. *See also* Adoptionism; Apostles' Creed; Arianism; Chalcedon, Council of; Docetism; Ephesus, Council of; Gnosticism; Jesus Christ; Monophysitism; Nestorianism; Trinity.

Christopher (Gk., "Christ bearer"), an early Christian martyr and saint. A late legend describes him as a ferryman who once carried the infant Jesus over a river; hence his designation as a patron of travelers.

Chrysostom, John (kris'uhs-tuhm; Gk., "golden mouthed" 347–407), early Christian preacher and homiletician associated first with Antioch (Syria), later becoming patriarch of Constantinople (398–403), a position from which he was expelled as a heretic. In addition to his expositions of biblical texts, he is best known for his early treatise *On the Priesthood*.

chthonic (thon'ik; Gk., "under the earth"), technical term describing gods and spirits of the underworld.

Ch'uan-chen Taoism (chwahn-jen; Chin., "Complete Perfection"), a school of Taoism that started during the early Ch'in dynasty (1115–1234). Its founder was Wang Che (1112–70; religious name: Wang Ch'ung-yang). He claimed, at the age of forty-eight, to have received a revelation from supernatural beings. His doctrinal position is a syncretistic blending of the "three teachings," with the *Tao-te ching* (Book of the Way and Its Power), the *Heart Sutra*, and the *Hsiao-ching* (Classic of Filial Piety) as the main scriptures. In its early history, the school practiced celibacy and an ascetic life-style in solitude. They had no use for "registers and talismans" (*fu-lu*) or for rituals.

Founder Wang attracted seven disciples, including one woman, who propagated the teachings. Each of the seven eventually started his or her own subsect. Together they are called the "Seven Perfected of the Northern School." The most famous disciple was Ch'iu Ch'u-chi, the founder of the Lung-men sect. Today the school is still active in China and in Hong Kong. *See also* Ch'iu Ch'u-chi; Hsiao-ching; Taoism; Tao-te ching; Wang Che.

ch'uan-ch'i (chwahn-chee; Chin., "transmission of the unusual"), a genre of fiction from the T'ang dynasty (ca. 618–907). Written in literary Chinese, these short stories draw upon elements of romantic love, the supernatural, adventure, and satire. *See also* Chinese language and literature, religious aspects of.

Chuang-tzu (jwahng-dyuh; ca. 369–286 B.C.), ancient Chinese philosopher and purported author of the Taoist classic of the same name, which, along with the *Lao-tzu*, figures as the defining Taoist philosophical discourse of ancient times. The fragmented nature of the *Chuang-tzu*, a one-hundred-thousand-word book of fables, anecdotes, and discussions, reveals it to be the composite work of various writers. The pervading themes of the book are freedom, naturalism, and spontaneity. It advocates discarding conventional values and freeing oneself from worldly attachments as a means of dealing with an absurd and chaotic society. The *Chuang-tzu*'s esoteric, mystical approach to life contrasts, perhaps intentionally, with the strong-minded political philosophy of Confucius (551–479 B.C.).

The *Chuang-tzu* uses fanciful stories and paradoxical humor to further its philosophical agenda. It advocates "doing nothing" as a means of achieving oneness with the natural world. This does not involve withdrawal from society, but is instead action unmotivated by desire for personal gain. One's actions should be mindless, like the skilled artisan who performs his craft without thinking and still succeeds.

The *Chuang-tzu* frequently employs contradiction and apparently nonsensical remarks as a way of showing the inadequacy of language. Value judgments, such as distinctions between good and bad, lack any basis in reality. *See also* chih-jen; Taoism.

Chu Hsi (joo shee; 1130–1200), greatest of the Sung Neo-Confucian masters and considered second in influence only to Confucius. His teachings of the School of Principle (Li-hsueh) are based on the investigation of things in order to appropriate the principles and norms of universal creativity and goodness. His teachings are framed in a subtle cosmology making use of the notions of vital energy (*ch'i*); principle (*li*); the normative nature of the Supreme Ultimate as the principle of the highest good; the cultivation of mind (*hsin*); and the perfection (*ch'eng*) of human nature (*hsing*) by means of a disciplined spiritual and intellectual way of life.

Chu propounded the Confucian Way not only to enlighten the individual mind but also to serve the entire world. He was an accomplished civil servant and beloved teacher. His commentaries, recorded conversations, and correspondence with friends and students provided a normative model for the Neo-Confucian spiritual and intellectual path. Along with teaching a model of self-cultivation, Chu wrote historical studies and commentaries on the entire range of the Confucian tradition and coedited the quintessential Sung anthology, *Chin-su lu* (Reflections on Things at Hand). Above all else, he anthologized the Four Books (*Ssu-shu*)—the *Analects, Mencius, Great Learning, Doctrine of the Mean*—as the classical canon of Confucian learning necessary for understanding human reality and the realization of ethical values. *See also* Ch'eng-Chu school; ch'i; Confucianism (authoritative texts and their interpretation); hsin; hsing; li; Li-hsueh; Ssu-shu.

Chu Hsi studies (Korea) (*joo* shee). Chu Hsi studies (Kor. *Chujahak*) is the term Koreans apply to the tradition of scholarship on the writings of Chu Hsi (1130–1200) and his Northern Sung teachers in the late Koryo period (918–1392) and throughout the Choson period (1392–1910). It is also the term applied to all Confucian writings written from the perspective of Chu Hsi's understanding of Confucian doctrine and ritual. Chu Hsi is what Westerners broadly call Neo-Confucianism, though not all forms or developments of Neo-Confucianism were accepted or allowed to be studied in Korea. Korean notions of Chujahak are very narrow and very orthodox, so that even the Northern Sung Masters Ch'eng Hao and Ch'eng I are criticized for not being in conformity with their later disciple, Chu Hsi, on certain points. This same sense of orthodoxy is applied to Korean interpreters of Sung Neo-Confucianism, who had to reconcile all disputes according to the writings of Chu Hsi. The most prominent defender of this orthodoxy in Korea was the scholar Yi Hwang (1501–70), whose disciples and supporters accorded him third place in the transmission of the Orthodox Way (Ch'ongdo) after Chu Hsi and Confucius. Later scholars made this explicit by saying that those who wished to understand the teachings of Yao, Shun, and the Duke of Chou should first study the *Analects*, but in order to study the *Analects* one should first study Chu Hsi, and in order to study Chu Hsi one should first study Yi Hwang. *See also* Ch'eng Hao; Ch'eng I; Neo-Confucianism; Yi Hwang.

Chu-hung (*joo*-huhng; 1535–1615), Ming-dynasty monk who dominated the late-sixteenth-century trend toward unifying the Ch'an and Pure Land schools and encouraging the growth of lay Buddhism. A monastic reformer, he established the Yun-ch'i Temple in Hang-chou, where he stressed strict adherence to Vinaya rules of monastic discipline. *See also* Ch'an school; China, Buddhism in; Neo-Confucianism; Pure Land school (China).

Chu-lin ch'i-hsien (*joo*-lin chee-shehn; Chin., "Seven Sages of the Bamboo Grove"), a group of Chinese Ch'ing-t'an intellectuals in third- and fourth-century China, including Hsi K'ang (223–262) and Juan Chi (210–263). The "Bamboo Grove" is not a real place but is an image derived from Buddhist texts. The term *Seven Sages*, originating in Confucius's *Analects*, alludes to those who shun the world to keep their purity. Refusing to cooperate with the new usurping rulers of the period, the Seven Sages advocated a naturalistic Taoist lifestyle in opposition to formalist Confucian ethics. *See also* Ch'ing-t'an; Hsi K'ang; Hsuan-hsueh.

Ch'un Ch'iu (chuhn chyoh; Chin., "Spring and Autumn [Annals]"), a classic attributed to Confucius briefly documenting incidents involving rulers in his home state, Lu (722–481 B.C.). *See also* Chinese language and literature, religious aspects of; Confucianism (authoritative texts and their interpretation); Confucius.

Ch'un-ch'iu fan-lu (chuhn-chyoh fahn-loo; Chin., "Luxuriant Gems of the Spring and Autumn Annals"), key text of Confucian syncretism, ca. 105 B.C., by Tung Chung-shu. *See also* Confucianism; Tung Chung-shu.

chung (juhng; Chin., "loyalty"), the Confucian virtue and disposition of loyalty, which demands the utmost faithful exertion in the performance of one's duty. *See also* Confucianism.

Chungsankyo. *See* Korea, new religions in.

Chung Yung (johng yohng; Chin., "Precisely Correct in Everyday Affairs"), *Doctrine of the Mean*, a classic of later Confucianism. Originally the thirty-first chapter of the *Book of Rites*, it was first given prominence by Han Yu (768–824). It locates personal equilibrium in a state before emotions are active, claiming harmony of life results from first gaining equilibrium. Portraying the inner life of sageliness, the last sections culminate in elevating Confucius as the partner of Heaven. Chu Hsi (1130–1200) edited it, considering it the most spiritually demanding of the basic texts of Neo-Confucian orthodoxy, the Four Books (*Ssu-shu*). *See also* Chu Hsi; Neo-Confucianism; Ssu-shu.

chun-tzu (juhn-dyuh; Chin., "profound person," "gentleman," "noble man"), a person seeking to realize the highest Confucian ethical standards. By study and self-reflection one practices the virtues of humaneness, righteousness, ritual, wisdom, and faithfulness. *See also* Confucianism.

church and state, the problematic relationship between Christian churches and the state. The issue of church-state relationships is which loyalty is more important and how the two institutions relate to and affect each other.

Jesus was asked about which was more important, loyalty to the state or to God (Mark 12:13–17). Similar questions arose as Christianity developed. The Romans believed the emperor was divine and insisted that citizens of the empire demonstrate their loyalty to the state by worshiping the emperor. When Christians refused, the Romans became hostile toward Christianity. The church was faced with the question of what its attitude to the state should be. The New Testament does not advocate any form of government. Christians are to be loyal and obedient to the state. But the New Testament also insists that civil rulers are not divine and their rule is not absolute but given by God. One's ultimate loyalty is to God, not to the state.

In the fourth century, Christianity was given equality with other religions and, by the end of that century, became the official religion of the empire. For the next fourteen centuries there was an attempt to create a Christian society through the cooperation of church and state. It was assumed that society should be unified and the state church should be the unifying influence. The stability of the social order demanded the religious solidarity of the people. But the question arose as to which institution was to predominate. This question led to the development of four principal models of church-state relationships.

State Domination of the Church: In this case, the state regards itself as the protector and overseer of the church. Civil authorities have the power to make rules for the church, including doctrine and the appointment of ecclesiastical officials. Furthermore, the state has the authority to punish anyone who does not conform to the state's conception of the church. Examples are the church in the eastern portion of the Roman Empire in the Middle Ages and the Church of England from the sixteenth through the nineteenth centuries.

Church Domination of the State: In this approach, the church is responsible for the salvation of everyone, even kings. Since civil rulers are subordinate to the church in this area, it follows that they also should be subordinate in the area of civil rule. Spiritual power is superior to civil power, so the leaders of the church should predominate over civil authorities. The church should not only decide its own leadership and doctrines, but have the power to discipline civil authorities if they do not conform to their roles as the church defines them. Examples are the Roman Catholic Church (in the western portion of the empire) in the Middle Ages, sixteenth-century Calvinism, and the seventeenth-century Massachusetts colony.

In either pattern, only one form of Christianity was given legal recognition and dissenters were forced to conform to the recognized church or were executed. This kind of denial of human rights in the name of governmentally sponsored religion finally caused many to argue for the separation of church and state.

Toleration: After the Protestant Reformation in the sixteenth century fragmented Christianity, nations found it difficult to maintain religious uniformity by permitting only one religious group to exist. In recognition of the variety of Christian groups, the plan of toleration developed. There is one official church, usually financially subsidized by the state, but other groups are allowed to exist and to worship freely. One group is officially recognized by the state; the others are tolerated. Examples are contemporary England, where the Anglican Church is officially recognized, and the Scandinavian countries, where Lutheranism is the state religion.

Separation: The separation of church and state is chiefly an American pattern. As settlers began to colonize the New World, they brought their ideas on state churches with them. Several colonies had an official church and no dissent was allowed. Rhode Island and Pennsylvania were the principal exceptions to this pattern. In reaction to their perception of the history of the union of church and state, the drafters of the United States Constitution included religious freedom by legally separating church and state.

The original Constitution contained only one reference to religion, Article VI: "No religious Test shall ever be required as a Qualification to any Office or public Trust under the United States." No person can be given or denied public office because of religious belief or lack of it. This was an advance of religious liberty over any arrangement in which one could serve in public office only by belonging to the official religion. Later, the First Amendment went further: "Congress shall make no law respecting an establishment of religion, or prohibiting the free exercise thereof. . . ." These two clauses create the separation of church and state. This was the first time in history that a nation included religious freedom in its legal structure. *See also* state religion.

Churches of Christ. *See* Campbell, Alexander.

Church of All Worlds, an eclectic Neo-Pagan organization begun in 1967 by Tim Zell (also known as Otter G'Zell) and inspired by the science-fictional church in Robert Heinlein's *Stranger in a Strange Land* (1961). Celebrating nature and worshiping the Earth Mother and her consort, the Horned God, members seek advancement of personal spiritual awareness through ritual practice, individualistic philosophy, and intense study. After a period of rapid expansion of the centers or "nests" in the 1970s and brief renewal as part of the New Age movement, the church has declined to comprise only a few focus groups in U.S. cities. *See also* Neo-Paganism.

Church of Armageddon, a communalistic and apocalyptic sect founded in Seattle, Washington, in 1969 by Paul Erdmann (Love Israel). Also called the "Love Family," its close bonding and belief that within the group all men are married to all women have attracted controversy.

Church of Christ, Scientist. *See* Christian Science.

Church of Circle Wicca. *See* Wicca.

Church of God. *See* African Americans (North America), new religions among.

Church of God and Saints in Christ. *See* African Americans (North America), new religions among.

Church of Israel, a contemporary Christian Identity ministry located in Schell City, Missouri. Under the leadership of Dan Gayman, the Church of Israel is one of the leading centers of theological research on questions related to Identity dogma and ethics in the world. Its current outreach, through the *Watchman* periodical, occasional studies on scriptural questions, and a cassette tape ministry is international in scope, reaching Western Europe, South Africa, and Australia. Gayman, once noted for his militance in support of the racialist and anti-Semitic doctrines of Christian Identity, has in recent years moderated his message to stress submission to legal authority, although without compromising the apocalyptic millenarianism and conspiratorial view of history typical of Identity ministries. *See also* Identity Christianity.

Church of Jesus Christ Christian. *See* Aryan Nations.

Church of Scientology, an American religion founded in 1953 by L. Ron Hubbard (1911–86). In 1988, it claimed some seven million members worldwide.

Scientology is a technique for enabling the true self (the "Thetan") to recall its identity over successive incarnations, and for "clearing" the self of those involuntary defense mechanisms preprogrammed by the "reactive mind" that reduce human capacities for stimulus response. *See also* North America, new religions in.

Church of Scotland, the established Presbyterian Church in Scotland.

Christianity in Scotland since the sixteenth-century Reformation has undergone numerous changes, yet Presbyterian strength has been a consistent factor. The Reformed Church of Scotland was established in 1560, with deference to John Knox and presbyterial polity. In the seventeenth century, the Stuart kings sought to restore episcopacy and liturgical order to Scotland so that the northern and southern realms of British would reflect uniformity.

The resultant conflict led to the Scottish revocation of episcopacy (1638). Presbyterianism was imposed throughout the British Isles during the period of the Puritan Commonwealth. After a brief return to episcopacy with the Restoration of English monarchy (1660), the Church of Scotland became Presbyterian again in 1690. Those who adhere to episcopacy have since that time comprised the Episcopal Church of Scotland. *See also* Knox, John; Presbyterianism.

Church of the Creator, a church founded in the early 1970s by Pontifex Maximus Ben Klassen in Florida to disseminate a racialist and anti-Semitic doctrine whose central tenet holds that because Jesus was a Jew, Christianity must be Jewish and should thus be eliminated in favor of Creativity. Creativity's dogmatics are derived from Klassen's books: *Nature's Eternal Religion, The White Man's Bible, Salubrious Living, Building a Whiter and Brighter World,* and *RaHowa! The Planet is Ours.* The latter volume is an anagram of RAcial HOly WAr and spells out Klassen's dreams for bringing about "a whiter, brighter world" through revolutionary means. The essence of Creativity is a syncretic blend of rewritten Christianity, health faddism, conspiracy theories, and histrionic racism. Structurally, the church features a universal priesthood of its primarily young, male adherents.

Church of the Eternal Source. *See* Neo-Paganism.

Church of the Twelve Apostles. *See* Africa, new religions in.

church/sect, a sociological distinction that defines "church" as a mode of religious organization in which membership is based on birth, that is inclusive, and that accommodates itself to the world and to society and its institutions. "Sect" is defined as the opposite: its membership is voluntary; it is exclusive; it is characterized by separatism from the world and hostility toward existing social institutions. *See also* religion, sociology of.

Church Universal and Triumphant, an American movement established in Washington, D.C., in 1958 as the Summit Lighthouse by Mark Prophet and renamed by his widow, Elizabeth Clare Prophet, in 1974. In the tradition of Theosophy and especially the I AM Activity, it presents ongoing messages from Ascended Masters on reincarnation, spiritual practices, and American patriotic themes. *See also* I AM Religious Activity; Theosophy.

Ch'u religion (choo), a set of Chinese beliefs associated with the late Eastern Chou–period state of Ch'u (formally extinguished in 223 B.C.).

The mythic ancestor of the Ch'u was Chu Rung, "Blessed Melded Harmony," a Han fire god and a son of the sky god, Kao Yang, "High Sun [principle]."

Shamans sought trysts with water goddesses and sky gods while performing ritual circuits in a boat or in a dance on land and went on spirit journeys accompanied by the protective deities of Wind, Rain, and Thunder, and by supernatural intermediaries such as dragons, phoenixes, and tigers.

The Ch'u were concerned with exorcising evil and achieving immortality: they prayed for long life and good fortune while sacrificing to the spirits of former kings and remote "ancestors." They used tortoise and stalk divination to seek the protection of astral and nature spirits as well as of spirits governing places of human habitation or passage (e.g., the household, the grave, the gateway, and the pathway).

In the Ch'u tombs are found apotropaic monsters with wide eyes, antlers, and long exposed tongues as well as images of hybrid animals, snakes, and birds and pictures of deceased souls as winged creatures or half beasts. *See also* Ch'u Tzu; shamanism.

churinga. *See* tjuringa.

Churning of the Ocean, Hindu myth in which gods and demons jointly churn the ocean of milk to produce the nectar of immortality. The demons lose their share through the trickery of the god Vishnu. *See also* Vishnu.

Ch'u Tzu (choo-dyuh; Chin.,"Words of Chu"), a collection of Chinese shamanistic songs, many with political overtones, by the late Warring-States-period Ch'u state minister Ch'u Yuan (ca. 343–289 B.C.), the Ch'u poet Sung Yu, and several Han imitators. The songs became metaphors for scholarly frustration and Taoist retreat. *See also* Ch'u religion; shamanism.

cinnabar. *See* tan.

circumambulation, the practice of walking around a sacred place or person prior to any ritual performed facing it. It is understood variously as a purification of the individual, as protection of the sacred place or person, or as a gesture of respect. *See also* pilgrimage; ritual.

Buddhist monk circumambulating the *stupa* (reliquary mound) constructed in the fourth century B.C. by the emperor Ashoka marking the site of the delivery of the Buddha's first sermon in Deer Park (Sarnath), Banaras (Varanasi), India.

Hinduism and Buddhism: For Buddhists and Hindus, the site to be circumambulated can be as small as a single image or as large as an entire geographical region; with the latter, the process of circumambulation becomes a complex, multistaged pilgrimage. *See also* devotion (Buddhism); Hinduism (worship).

circumcision, ritual removal of the foreskin from the penis. Widely practiced, it forms a central part of some male rites of passage; elsewhere it is a mark of membership in a religious group or guild. *See also* Australian and Pacific traditional religions; clitoridectomy; initiation rituals; ordeal; puberty rituals; ritual; subincision.

Judaism: Circumcision (Heb. *brit milah*, "covenant of circumcision") was first required of Abraham. Circumcision signifies the covenant between God and the Jewish people (Genesis 17:10–14). A *mohel* (Heb., "circumciser") circumcises infants on the eighth day after birth and proselytes upon conversion to Judaism. Blessings are recited, and the Hebrew name is given. The celebration ends with a festive meal. *See also* Judaism (life cycle).

Islam: Circumcision (Arab. *tahur*, "cleansing," "purification") is a rite of passage for men in all Muslim societies. For women, an analogous practice is largely confined to southern Egypt, the Sudan, Somalia, Ethiopia, and West Africa. Most Muslims consider circumcision an obligation imposed by the Prophet Muhammad. For boys, it usually occurs between the ages of two and seven, although the modern trend is to perform the operation at a younger age. Purificatory rites, along with sacrifice and a feast, accompany male circumcisions, with more modest celebrations for girls. *See also* Islam (festal cycle); Islam (life cycle).

circumpolar religions, the religions of the Eskimo people living in Alaska, Canada, Greenland, and the Arctic region of the former Soviet Union. Circumpolar peoples are highly diverse, often differentiated by linguistic and geographical characteristics. Characteristic religious phenomena include *angakkut* (shaman) journeys, masking, dancing and song festivals, storytelling, reliance upon helping spirits, honoring the souls of game animals, using amulets, and naming practices.

Religious Activity: Religious activity is intricately tied to a subsistence life-style that relies primarily on sea and land animals. Animals are understood to have humanlike qualities and behaviors. Animals have families, live in groups, and are capable of emotions. Eskimos under-stand themselves to be *Inuit* (true human beings). Reciprocity governs all relationships in the diversely inhabited circumpolar world. The rules for human interaction with animals are often dictated by age, gender, and season of the year. Rituals and festivals establish relationships with subsistence animals, the dead, creatures such as giants and dwarfs, helping spirits, and breaches of taboo.

Inua: All living things, plant and animal, as well as mountains, bodies of water, air and earth, have *inua*—an independent humanlike quality, sometimes described as spirit—which enables them to take on a variety of physical forms. An inua may manifest itself as a humanlike face on the back, breast, or eye of an animal. This form is often seen in Alaskan Eskimo masks and artwork. Inua are honored along with other guests during festivals and feasts.

Angakkut: All Eskimos are responsible for maintaining reciprocal balance with the inua. The *angakkut* (shamans), assisted by helping spirits, often diagnose and remedy situations in which reciprocity has been violated. During a seance they may journey to appease angered Moonman or to the bottom of the sea to appease Sedna, the two principal supernatural owners of the animals. To cure an illness the angakkut often retrieve a human soul (which the Eskimo recognize as residing in bone joints) that has been lost or stolen.

The angakkut initiation often requires lonely wanderings, during which the helping spirits might claim the initiate. Angakkut training periods are kept secret until the first public seance is performed. The knowledge given by the helping spirits is meant to be used in a public way, usually at a community seance. Violation of secrecy can end the initiate's training and prevent the initiate from becoming a full angakkut. Only a fully initiated angakkut can fly, a skill necessary for journeys to Moonman and to the end of the horizon. Sometimes, particularly with women initiates, angakkut training is made public and secrecy is violated to stop development of the initiate's powers. If the angakkut do not honor the helping spirits, the spirits can trouble or even abandon the angakkut.

Community: *Ilisiinneq*, which means "to get rid of one's ignorance, to become an expert," is the socially acceptable yet secret way of rehabilitating a person who might be dangerous to community. Publicly confessing the breach of a taboo (such as violation of reciprocity) is encouraged; going public deflates the (usually negative) power of the secret act. Loners or highly secretive people are considered "not proper human beings," not Inuit, and therefore, under great suspicion by the community. Morality is defined within the parameters of positive, public generosity. If someone is ill, gifts to their village might bring a recovery. All forms of stinginess are discouraged.

Masking and Dancing: In Canada and Greenland the primary religious activity is the seance, with purposes ranging from crisis-resolution to entertainment. Masking is rare in Canada and Greenland. In Alaska the Bladder Festival and Inviting-In Feast are performed annually with singing, dancing, and masking. The most diverse and oldest masking and dancing activities in the circumpolar area are performed in Alaska. Sedna is honored annually in a winter ceremony at Baffin Island and North Labrador. The Igulik and East Greenland Eskimos practice communal masking during the shortest days of the year. The Copper Eskimos of Canada have intricate poetry and song feasts to encourage successful hunting or prevent famine. Dancing, singing, and masking remain an important part of Alaskan Eskimo culture in the 1990s. *See also* Bladder Festival; fishing rites/whaling rites; hunting, religious aspects of; Sedna; shamanism; traditional peoples, religions of.

Cistercians, a Christian monastic order, also known as the White Monks because of their plain, unbleached habits. Repelled by the lavishness of much of contemporary monasticism and desiring to live in stricter conformity to the Rule of St. Benedict, Robert of Molesme and his followers founded in 1098 the monastery of Citeaux (Lat. *Cistercium*), just south of Dijon, France. By the mid-twelfth century the order numbered over 350 houses, many located in remote parts of Europe. The rapid growth and popularity of the order was stimulated by the charismatic figure of Bernard of Clairvaux (ca. 1090–1153). The Cistercians aimed at cohesiveness and uniformity and to this end created a strong centralized system of government.

The Cistercians have suffered serious decline since the Middle Ages in both numbers and prestige, although there was a brief resurgence with the founding of the Trappists, a Cistercian offshoot in 1664. *See also* Benedict of Nursia; Bernard of Clairvaux; monasticism.

city god, Chinese. *See* Ch'eng-huang Shen.

civic cults, rituals ensuring the well-being of a city incumbent on all citizens. *See also* Greek religion; ritual; Roman religion; state cult, Chinese.

civil religion, the set of religious or quasi-religious beliefs, myths, symbols, and ceremonies that unite a political community and that mobilize its members in the pursuit of common goals. The eighteenth-century philosopher Jean-Jacques Rousseau proposes the creation of a single, overarching civil religion as a way of re-inforcing the loyalty of citizens to the democratic state.

In the twentieth century, the sociologist Robert Bellah argues for the existence of an elaborate civil religion in the United States that draws on, but is independent of, the discrete religious traditions to which Americans belong. Based on a belief in America's unique destiny as God's "new Israel," this civil religion provides a transcendent goal for the American political process. It contains a pantheon of saints and martyrs (including Washington, Jefferson, and Lincoln), an annual festival calendar, and a central ritual event in the quadrennial inauguration of a president. Distinctive civil religions have been identified in cultures as diverse as Israel, Japan, South Africa, and the former Soviet Union.

Scholars remain divided on the religious and moral significance of civil religions. Some regard them as pale imitations of transcendent religious traditions and as dangerous warrants for aggressive nationalism. Others believe that civil religions are more complex realities. Although subject to abuse, they can inspire positive national accomplishments, contain sources of moral judgment, and serve to correct nationalistic pretensions. *See also* religion, sociology of.

Clare of Assisi (1194–1253), Italian Christian contemplative, disciple of Francis of Assisi, and foundress of the Order of Poor Clares (or Clarissines). *See also* Poor Clares.

Clarissines. *See* Poor Clares.

classification. *See* typology, classification.

clean and unclean. *See* purity and impurity.

Clement of Alexandria (ca. 150–215), leader of the Christian catechetical school at Alexandria, Egypt, and important early theologian who reconciled hellenistic Neoplatonic thought to a new system of Christian knowledge (*gnosis*) in his enormous work *Stromateis* (The Miscellanies).

clergy, that body of Christians who are ordained as preachers or priests and are thus distinguished from the laity. *See also* laity; priest-hood.

clitoridectomy, the ritual removal of the clitoris, less frequently of the labia, from the vagina. In some traditions it forms a central part of women's rites of passage and is considered a prerequisite to marriage. *See also* circumcision; infibulation; initiation rituals; Islam (festal cycle); Islam (life cycle); ritual.

clowns, comic ritual figures who typically engage in contrary and/or scatological behavior. *See also* carnival; Hamatsa; heyoka; reversal; ritual.

Colette of Corbie (1381–1447), French Christian abbess who reformed the Order of Poor Clares, instituting a more rigorous discipline as the result of a vision of Francis. She was canonized in 1807. *See also* Poor Clares.

Cologne Mani-Codex, a tiny (3.5 by 4.5 centimeters) fifth-century Manichaean book in Greek from Egypt containing twenty-three lines per page. Severely damaged, the entire text could not be fully restored. Bearing the title *On the Becoming of His Body*, the book tells of Mani's life among his fellow Elchasaites and his break with that sect. The book gives information about Mani as the last in a long line of prophets and his visitations by his heavenly Twin and contains heavily anti-Elchasaite polemics. *See also* Elchasai, Elchasaites; Manichaeism.

color symbolism, the capacity of colors to condense ideas, summarize principles, or accrue moral meanings. Like shape, size, position, and other qualities of objects, colors often assume symbolic meanings when they appear in ritual and mythic contexts. Employing colors to suggest moral or cosmological meanings may be a universal practice. But the association of particular colors with specific meanings varies from culture to culture. One violates cross-cultural complexity by treating color symbols as if they had one, or even a few, universal meanings.

Among Navajos, for example, the following associations are common but not standard: white / east / male / dawn; blue / south / female / daylight; yellow / west / female / twilight; and black/north/male/night. But these associations vary from the stereotypical Euramerican ones: male/daylight/east/yellow [or red] versus female/night/west/black. Even within a single culture the meanings of colors are contextual. For Navajos white may suggest maleness in one context, femaleness in another. It may be associated with the east in one context, the north in another.

The relativity of color symbols is obvious when one tries to separate meaning and effect. For example, it is uncertain whether Western culture associates red with warmth because it makes Westerners feel warm or because they conventionally associate red with fire or the sun. Cross-cultural study suggests that effect follows from meaning more often than we suspect.

Commandment Keepers of the Living God. *See* African Americans (North America), new religions among.

commandments, rules given by a deity governing divine and human relations. *See also* covenant; mitzvah; 613 commandments; Ten Commandments.

commensality. *See* eating together.

communes, communal living groups sharing expenses and resources under a common philosophy or religious vision, especially those organized since the 1960s.

Contemporary communes may be related to early Christian or South Asian monastic orders or, more directly, the utopian groups of the nineteenth century. Inspired by their ideal of shared work and rewards, American communal societies flourished briefly at New Harmony, Indiana (1814); Hopedale, Massachusetts (1841); and Oneida, New York (1840s), while Hutterites, the Amana Society, and the Shakers have successfully continued communal structures. Since the 1960s, communes comprise both experimental living groups challenging the traditional patriarchal family and religious cooperatives enacting their shared beliefs.

communion. *See* Eucharist, Christian.

communitas. *See* community, communitas.

community, communitas.

Problems of Definition: The notion of community is difficult to define without confronting abstractions and misunderstandings. A community is often thought of as a group or a collectivity, but how does one define a group or collectivity? One strategy is to define the difference between a collection and a collective. A collection is a set of things. Collection *A* and collection *B* are identical collections if they include the same number of the same things. When items are added to or subtracted from a collection it is no longer the same collection. This is not true of a collective or a community. A community is not just an aggregate, or a collection of things, even though a community is composed of individuals. A nation or college, for example, can grow or diminish in size, and one can still talk about the nation or college as the same community it was one hundred years before. Thus, a community has an autonomy of its own.

A community is more than the sum of its members. A community is like a sentence. Although a sentence is composed of words, the meaning of a sentence is more than the sum of the words that constitute it. The relationships that words enter into determine the meaning of a sentence. Similarly, the relationships individuals enter into determine the meaning of community. Just as individual words do not determine the meaning of a sentence, individuals in a community do not determine the relationships they enter into. The relationships are determined by rules that are nomic (lawlike). One stops at a red light, drives on the right side of the road, shakes hands as a greeting, accepts the Supreme Court as an authority, and accepts a common ideology. All communities are constituted by systems of beliefs and practices that define and identify the relationships individuals enter into.

Religious Communities: Religious communities have a specific characteristic that marks them as religious. The beliefs and practices that constitute a religious community are directly related to superhuman beings. Superhuman beings are beings who can do things humans cannot do; they include ancestors, spirits, gods, goddesses, and religious heroes such as Moses, Jesus, and the Buddha.

The beliefs and practices of a religious community are usually studied in the context of the rituals of the community. Rituals are verbal and nonverbal interactions with superhuman beings. They often mark patterns of passage, often called rites of passage, for individual members of the community. Most religions have rituals for conception, naming, initiation into the community as an adult, marriage, and death. All of these rituals constitute the passage of a person from one state or social position into another state or social position.

The great collective rituals of a community usually define the sacred space and time of the community. Such rituals provide the community with specific temporal and geographical orientations.

Finally, religious communities are systems of classification that are constituted through ritual. Rituals define the members and nonmembers of a community. The caste system in India, which includes the rite of the twice-born; bar mitzvah in Judaism; the initiation into the *sangha* in Theravada Buddhism; and baptism in Christianity are examples of classification through ritual. All rites of passage are also rites of classification.

Communitas: Some scholars prefer *communitas* rather than *community* as the proper term for religious community. Communitas is defined as collective life that is opposed to structure. Communitas is often described as antistructure, in opposition to hierarchy and other social structures that cause tension, separation, and alienation. Communitas emphasizes brother and sisterhood, equality, freedom, egalitarianism, and the breakdown of social class. Communitas is the experience of ambiguity and the indeterminate, in opposition to order. Rituals emphasize communitas. There is some truth to this description of communitas, but it cannot be considered a universal for all religious communities.

Communitas may well be in opposition to social hierarchy, and yet entail a specific structure of its own. Many communitas are not antistructure, but, in fact, are clearly structured in opposition to the secular or profane domains of life.

Many ascetic communities emphasize egalitarian structures where all members are equal and thus in opposition to dominant social structures. There are also religious communities that do not demonstrate communitas. The caste system, based upon ritual rules with regard to the pure and the impure, and the Roman Catholic Church are examples of religious communities that exhibit rigid hierarchies. *See also* religion, anthropology of; religion, sociology of; ritual.

Community of True Inspiration. *See* Amana Society.

comparative religion, a systematic study of the commonalities and differences among the religions of the world that proposes and employs categories and principles to aid in understanding, historically and systematically, the universal and the particular features of these religions.

Universal Categories: Beginning in eighteenth-century Europe, the comparative study of religion grew out of the attempt within Western culture to understand the religions of the world, apart from the religions of the West, particularly Christianity. This impetus was motivated by irenic, competitive, and apologetic concerns.

These concerns led scholars to view Western religions, particularly Christianity, as the source of the basic categories and principles of such comparative study. Comparative religion, from its very inception, saw the religious world from a Western point of view.

Though dominated by categories taken from Christianity, comparative religion, a product of the Enlightenment, contained a measure of hostility toward Christianity. But even with this hostility, Christianity was still viewed as the paradigmatic religion, providing the most adequate conceptual resources for producing an understanding of other religions.

Because these conceptual resources were vast, having been honed in centuries of theological debate about cultural life and thought, they were assumed to be completely adequate for an interpretive and explanatory understanding of other religions in other cultures. Eventually these categories and principles were used to describe Christianity itself. For example, the category *myth*, which was initially applied to the sacred narratives of other religious traditions, was eventually applied to biblical narratives as well.

These categories, which were treated as universal and regarded as applicable to all religious traditions, provided both the form and the content of other religions. The categories of salvation, soul, God, worship, prayer, sacrifice, and mysticism, which applied to the contents of Christianity, were used to describe other religious traditions no matter how poorly the categories fit. Even when the fit was acknowledged as problematic, the categories were employed as a standard against which both the "religiousness" and the truth of other religions could be measured and judged. Some comparativists talk about better and worse religions, about one religion "completing" another religion, and even about one religion being truer than another.

Mysticism and theism were particularly important interpretive categories and played important roles in these comparative endeavors. Mysticism, despite its focus upon personal religious experience in Western religions, was a category thought by many to point to a religious form at the heart of religion in many if not all religious traditions.

Theism played an equally determinative role in classifying the religions of humankind. The theistic element provided a model for arranging the religions of the world into theistic types such as monotheism, polytheism, and henotheism, along with additional types such as animism. Textbooks in comparative religion frequently employed these types as the taxonomy that could identify both the similarities and differences among religions. One result of this approach was an emphasis upon similarities and differences in religious beliefs and a neglect of ritual action. The effect of treating these categories as the basis for understanding other religions was that the religions of the world were filtered through a highly constraining mechanism.

Classifying religious traditions in these terms did not serve simply as a method of differentiation, because it was often coupled with theories about cultural evolution that encouraged diachronic analyses about how earlier forms of religion developed into radically different and even superior forms. For example, much debate centered around whether monotheism was the earliest (and truest) religion or whether monotheism was the culmination of a long and progressive set of religious insights and discoveries capable of supplanting and replacing earlier forms of religion. Sometimes Christianity was viewed as the culmination of a long development out of earlier and less complex forms of religion. But even Christianity was refracted through the categorical prism by arguments about whether it extended or obstructed genuine enlightenment.

Because of the power of evolutionary thinking, which was applied to other cultural phenomena besides religion, this state of affairs might have continued indefinitely were it not for two factors. First, as more information about other religions became available through the studies of historians (who were primarily interested in the roots of Western religions) and anthropologists (who were mainly interested in the religions of other cultures, particularly so-called primitive religions), it became increasingly clear that such categories had limited applicability and often provided distorted pictures of the thought and practices of other religions. It also became obvious that the expected sequences of development did not always occur. Furthermore, there was no obvious development from simpler forms of religion to more complex forms.

Second, as more sophisticated theories were developed by historians and anthropologists, both about the religions that contributed to the development of Western religions and about the religions of Asia, Africa, and the Americas, it became apparent that such local categories left out too much, referred to the wrong entities, or misnamed important features of religion.

Persistent dissatisfaction with this hegemony

of interpretive categories eventually led many scholars interested in, and knowledgeable about, other religious traditions to reject such comparative provincialism outright. The reaction was severe and gave rise to a range of alternative approaches, from the denial of the possibility of comparison to the development of new comparative techniques.

Critique of Universal Categories: Some scholars in the history of religions began to argue for the conceptual and behavioral uniqueness of every religious tradition. Underlying this reaction was a radical view about the variability of culture. This approach insisted upon detailed work focusing upon specific traditions. In extreme form this approach enabled comparativists to carve each tradition into smaller and smaller parts, thus limiting comparison to the relationships among the parts of the tradition as a whole. One unintended consequence of this approach was to encourage the student of religion to know more and more about less and less. This does not deny that many fine studies emerged of particular features of particular religious traditions. Nor did comparative judgments cease to be made. In fact, this reaction increased the sensitivity of scholars to the integrity of religious traditions and forced them to recognize the danger of superficial comparisons.

The reaction against provincial and superficial comparison by emphasizing the uniqueness of each tradition mirrored attitudes and ideas in the larger academic world, especially in anthropology. Cultural anthropologists, in particular, began to make a case for cultural relativism, which argued against any attempt at identifying universal features of cultural systems, religious or otherwise. These anthropologists treated similarities among cultural systems as superficial and accidental features that obscured the deep differences about how different societies organized their lives and viewed the world. This methodological move was from the universality of one set of categories derived from Western culture to the relativity of all cultural categories, with no possibility of generalization across cultural systems.

This radical move promised so many gains in specificity that it prevailed among the human sciences, and remains in the 1990s the dominant approach in the study of human cultures in general and of religions in particular. When cultural relativism was coupled with functionalist considerations intent on identifying the role that religious systems play in the larger social systems, scholars of comparative religion could claim that they possessed a method free from superficial cross-cultural generalizations.

Another approach, characteristic of theologically and religiously motivated historians of religion, focused upon the role of universal religious forms. These forms were regarded as largely if not completely inaccessible to scientific discovery and description. Instead, they could be apprehended only by suspending empirical assumptions about the nature of "the sacred." These theological forms lacked scientific motivation; they were based upon certain metaphysical assumptions about what is true, real, and of value. These theologically motivated comparativists argued for universal, or nearly universal, revelatory structures that were supposed to take particular forms in particular religious traditions. The most important category employed was the concept of the sacred or the holy, either of which was thought to disclose itself in social forms and personal religious experience. This theological approach attempted to transcend the provincialism of the earlier approach but at the cost of imposing a universal theological category. It purchased universality at the expense of scientific plausibility.

Languagelike Structures: A revolution in the scientific study of cultural systems (emerging out of a concern with the complex and close relationships between cognitive and cultural phenomena) has recently forced comparativists to rethink their provincialism, their cultural relativism, and their theological universalism. The power of this new approach lies in its ability to demonstrate that cultural systems of any kind are neither as monolithic nor as variable as they were thought earlier to be. A culture can be conceived of as a number of sets of activities, each having a systematic character and each capable of being interpreted and explained by special methods available in the cognitive and cultural sciences. Each culture can therefore be analyzed by significant comparative procedures.

The study of language as a cultural system, which exemplifies many of the problems and properties of religion as a cultural system, provided a significant test of whether unique systems were subject to cross-cultural generalization. Language, which is obviously a cultural system, would seemingly be incapable of supporting significant cross-cultural generalizations because no two languages are alike; each employs different phonological, syntactic, and semantic rules. Nevertheless, scholars were able to demonstrate that languages are indeed susceptible to rule-governed descriptions that are linguistically generalizable.

The new scientific study of language disclosed an intricate system of relationships containing a variety of linguistic properties capable of theoretical analysis and identifiable across languages. At the highest level of abstraction, all human languages seem to be constrained by certain fundamental principles. While grammar differs from one language to another, one can identify formal, substantive, and functional universals that have application to each specific language at the appropriate level of analysis. The uniqueness of each language did not prevent theoretical linguists from identifying candidates for universality of a highly abstract nature across cultural systems. Structuralists, on the basis of their knowledge of recent theories of language, were in the forefront in suggesting new ways for the study of other cultural systems, such as myth and ritual, which acknowledged the uniqueness of mythic and ritual systems but also showed promise for identifying their common features.

One stumbling block to this new comparative work, which attempts to identify the common and the unique elements of each religious system, has been the recently proposed view by hermeneutically inclined scholars who insist upon reading whole cultures (and likewise whole religious traditions) as texts. The metaphor of culture as text has had the unintended consequence of imposing a greater unity on religious traditions than is warranted by historical knowledge of the complex transformations that religions undergo in time. Religions are far more like performances in time than they are like texts in space. A religious tradition is something like a group of second-rate musicians performing a poorly remembered symphony without a score and without a conductor. Music gets played, there is some continuity, but attempting to reconstruct the symphony from the performance will hardly disclose an unambiguous structure.

Prospects: In the 1990s, the key question in comparative religion is, What is being compared when religious traditions are examined alongside each other? If it is specific conceptual, symbolic, or ritual content, then context will always be a stumbling block, because taken out of context any item will fail to support significant generalizations. If it is religious form, then such comparison will only be as good as the conceptual source that generates the form. If it is underlying principles, comparison will only be as good as the theory that underwrites the principles. If it is general categories, such categories will have to be motivated both methodologically and theoretically, and it is at this level that comparative religion reveals its weak spot. While the work of scholars in comparative religion has been rich in description, the attempts to show correlations among different sets of descriptions

are unconstrained by any disconfirmable theory. One is left with little more than the hope that their intuitions do convey significant information about religions, other than the information one can gather about any religious tradition by reading that tradition's literature or by perusing ethnographic documents.

Comparative religion can fulfill its task of identifying the similarities and differences among the religions of humankind, but only if it becomes sensitive to the need for categories and principles that can accomplish that objective. *See also* religion, phenomenology of; religion, the study of; science of religion; typology, classification.

compassion (Skt. *karuna*), in Buddhism the earnest wish to relieve the suffering of all living beings. Compassion is a feeling and state of mind cultivated through the practice of meditation. In Mahayana Buddhism compassion takes a central role as the fundamental motivation behind the vows and saving practices of *bodhisattvas* (Buddhas-to-be). *See also* Avalokiteshvara; bodhisattva; Kannon; Kuan-yin.

comprehensive Buddhism (Kor. *T'ongpulgyo, Ilsung Pulgyo*), name given by nineteenth- and twentieth-century Korean Buddhist scholars to any native formulation that sought to unite all forms of Buddhist doctrine and practice into a single teaching and all institutions based on the piecemeal adherence to those doctrines and practices into a unified cult. The term is most often given to the work of the Buddhist monk Wonhyo of the Unified Silla period (seventh century), who attempted, in such writings as *Simmun hwajaengnon* (The Harmony of Disputes of the Ten Gates) and the *Pophwagyong chongyo* (Essentials of the Lotus Sutra) to spread the view that all the teachings and vehicles (*yana*) of Buddhist practice and their separate institutions, if properly understood, form a single vehicle of Buddhism (*Ilsung Pulgyo*) leading to enlightenment.

This view was in large part a product of Wonhyo's own enlightenment experience. Like many of his contemporaries, Wonhyo traveled to China to study Buddhism in the belief that China was the repository of an orthodox, comprehensive understanding of Buddhism that had yet to be brought to Korea. While traveling he experienced enlightenment and realized that there was no need to seek abroad what was already obtainable at home. Though Wonhyo established a sect of Buddhism he called the Korean Sect (Haedongjong), it never succeeded in replacing the multiple sects of his own and later days. In the context of the Unified Silla and Koryo periods, when royal, aristocratic, and provincial gentry patronage and staffing of multiple sects was a matter of political importance and prestige, unification of sectarian Buddhism was neither desired nor practical. Later leaders of the sectarian schools, including the Hua-yen, T'ien-t'ai, and Ch'an schools, also attempted to unify the sects from their own sectarian tradition, but without success.

By the thirteenth and fourteenth centuries cross-fertilization of practices and doctrines had occurred, so that what remained was only the difference between doctrinal approaches and meditation approaches. With the establishment of the Choson kingdom (1392–1910) and the disestablishment of Buddhism as a national, government-supported religion, institutional difference gave way to a generalized meditative approach that combined the study of scriptures and doctrine with a regimen of meditation and Pure Land ritualism. Today the new Chogye Son order claims that what it teaches is comprehensive Buddhism. *See also* China, Buddhism in; Chogye Buddhism; Wonhyo.

conciliarism, Roman Catholic theory affirming the primacy of Church councils in ecclesiastical affairs. Developed in the late fourteenth and early fifteenth centuries, its greatest accomplishment was the Council of Constance (1414–17), which restored the single papacy, established the supreme authority of councils, and decreed that councils would meet at regular intervals.

Cone, James Hal (b. 1938), leading African-American theologian, held by many to be the first to introduce black theology as a separate field of Christian inquiry. *See also* black theology.

Confessing Church, World War II German church movement. After Adolph Hitler incorporated German churches into the Nazi Party with the creation of the German Christians, the Confessing Church resisted through the Barmen Declaration (1934), which denied that the church was an organ of the state.

confession (Lat. *confiteri,* "to speak," also "speaking out" in the sense of revealing, admitting, avowing). **1** A personal and/or communal statement of beliefs, as in the primitive Christian confession that "Jesus is Lord." Later, the concept was elaborated into longer, more cognitively detailed statements of belief on the theological level. **2** A verbal avowal of personal misdeeds. In the Christian era, a ritualized group avowal of sin as part of Sunday worship. In Judaism the parallel phenomenon

developed communally in the annual congregational confession of sins on the Day of Atonement (Yom Kippur). In Eastern and Western Christianity there also developed the individual confession. *See also* absolution; ritual.

confession (Christianity) (Lat. *confessio,* "declaration"), in Christian traditions, to profess publicly one's faith either as a single act or in a corporate act of worship; to acknowledge one's sin before a congregation or minister as prelude to an act of faith and/or baptism; a shorthand term for the sacramental rite of penance performed in the churches of the Catholic tradition.

In the Roman Catholic Church confession is only one part of the entire sacrament of penance (also known as the rite of reconciliation) that leads up to the act of absolution (forgiveness).

Confession and absolution are part of the regular sacramental life of both the Orthodox and Roman Catholic churches, while the Anglican Communion makes provision for it in *The Book of Common Prayer* (1549). *See also* absolution; penance.

confessor. **1** In early Christianity, an honorary title for one who openly professed the faith during persecution. **2** A priest who hears confessions of sins in church.

confirmation, initiation ritual for a Christian, usually consisting of an anointing with oil and/or a laying on of hands.

In early Christianity part of a single ceremony that included baptism with water followed by an imposition of hands in which the newly baptized received the gift of the Spirit, it is observed as a separate rite in many Christian traditions.

The ritual signals the initiation of the baptized into full and responsible church membership and into a personal mature acceptance of the faith. By the Middle Ages, both Catholics and Orthodox recognized it as one of seven sacraments, complementing and completing the Christian initiation begun with baptism.

Most Protestant denominations do not consider the ritual a sacrament, but view it as a rite of initiation into full Christian discipleship. *See also* anointed in the Spirit; anointing; born-again Christian; Christianity (life cycle); Christianity (worship); initiation rituals; sacraments and ordinances (Christianity).

Confucianism. *Confucianism* is an English term denoting a range of diverse Chinese schools of thought, including the School and Teachings of

The beginning of a Confucian state festival at the National Confucian Academy, Seoul, South Korea. The first participant is carrying the traditional gift of silk from a student to a teacher.

the Literati (Ju chia and Ju-chiao), the Teaching of the Way (Tao-hsueh), the Schools of Principle (Ch'eng-chu or Li-hsueh) and Mind (Hsin-hsueh), and the School of Evidential Learning (Han-hsueh) of the Ch'ing dynasty. The most inclusive defining characteristic of Confucianism is that it embraces all the various East Asian traditions inspired and dedicated to the thought and practice of Confucius, the First Teacher, as he is known throughout the ages. While the Confucian Way has been dramatically and repeatedly transformed in its modes of action, ritual, and scholarship up to today, there always remains a focus on the way of life first expressed by Confucius and the other early masters of the Chou dynasty.

Periods of Confucian Learning: Confucianism has undergone at least six major transformations. First, there is the classical era beginning with Confucius in the sixth century B.C. The classical founders include Confucius (551–479 B.C.), Mencius (372–289 B.C.), and Hsun-tzu (fl. 298–238 B.C.). Also crucial to Confucian self-definition were some other ritual and historical works and smaller religio-philosophic treatises such as *Doctrine of the Mean* and *Great Learning*. Second, there is the Confucian synthesis of the Han dynasty, giving rise to a state-supported imperial Confucian orthodoxy. Tung Chung-shu (ca. 179–104 B.C.) and Yang Hsiung (53 B.C.–A.D. 18) represent Han Confucian scholasticism. Third, there is a long middle period beginning with the fall of the Han dynasty (220) extending to the end of the T'ang dynasty (907). This is also the golden era of Buddhism in China. While it is inaccurate to say that Confucianism was unimportant during this long middle period, it is true that most acute religious and philosophical Chinese intellectuals were involved in the elaboration of Buddhism and the efflorescence of the Taoist religion. Nonetheless, scholars such as Han Yu (768–824) and Li Ao (fl. 798) are revered as the most important of T'ang Confucianists, preserving and defending Confucianism during its time of spiritual slumbers. Fourth, there is the great Northern and Southern Sung revival of Confucian learning and piety known in English as Neo-Confucianism, with Chu Hsi as the greatest representative of the Neo-Confucian renaissance. The Neo-Confucian period extends from the eleventh century to the beginning of the twentieth century. This is also the period in which the revitalized and expanded Confucianism spread into Korea, Japan, and Vietnam, becoming the dominant intellectual force in all of East Asia. Fifth, there is the School of Evidential Learning (Han-hsueh) of the Ch'ing dynasty (seventeenth–early twentieth centuries), which empirically challenged the previous forms of Confucian metaphysics. The work of scholars such as Wang Fu-chih (1619–92) and Tai Chen (1723–77) exemplify this creative expression of the Confucian Way. Sixth, there is the modern transformation and reformation of Confucianism called the New Confucianism. Tracing its inspiration to Hsiung Shih-li (1885–1968), the New Confucianism seeks to describe and commend the Confucian Way as a viable tradition for the creation of a universal modern and ecumenical civilization. The development of the Confucian Way also continues in the work of Japanese and Korean scholars who help to define the multinational nature of the cumulative tradition.

Themes of Confucian Learning: Confucianism perennially focuses on the question of the ultimate values of human life. Confucianism always asks, What makes life worth living? What are the virtues and methods of self-discipline needed to create a humane civilization worthy of esteem? Because Confucianism focuses on questions of ultimate life values, it includes both the religious and philosophic dimensions of human life. For example, Confucians have probed the transcendent dimensions of what it means to understand the will of Heaven and to explore questions of ontology and cosmology. Confucians have sought to fathom the workings of the ceaseless creativity of the Tao (undifferentiated unity) engendered by the alternation of the *yin* and *yang* forces (complementary principles). In their personal moral cultivation, they have tried to find the balance between the Great Ultimate of relational being and the Non-Ultimate of the infinite, the ultimate ground of what is and what is yet to be as the highest human good.

Two key features of the Confucian concern for ultimate life values are found in the realization of the intersubjective, relational, and creative qualities of human nature and the quest for an autonomous morality informed by the insights of Confucian sages and worthies. The realization of intersubjectivity and autonomous morality is always perceived as the aim of human life, the effective moral and individual unity of lived experience within the ceaseless cosmic creativity of the Tao. The traditional symbolic expression of this fusion of cosmological creativity, individual ethics, and social perfection is disclosed in Confucius's concept of *jen*, humanity or humaneness, as the highest human virtue.

The search for ultimate life values is always balanced between cosmological understanding of and individual reflections on the meaning of creativity itself. Cosmic and moral creativity is expressed as the Way of Heaven. This cosmic vision is conjoined with ethical concern for others as expressed in the classical inventory of specific Confucian individual and social virtues. The four cosmological and individual elements are the Will of Heaven, the virtue of humanity, the mind-and-heart of the profound person, and human nature.

The manifestation of the Mandate or Will of Heaven (*t'ien-ming*) as cosmic creativity and the humane concern for self and others is best expressed by Confucius's notion of *jen* as humanity. Jen is the final and proper response of the person to the Will of Heaven; it is textually defined by Confucius in the *Analects*.

For the moral person, the primal virtue of humanity (jen) always lures one onward to greater feats of ethical creativity and self-realization. One becomes a timely agent of the bipolar yin and yang forces; this facet is recorded in the appendices of the *I-ching*, the *Doctrine of the Mean*, and the *Analects*.

The human mind-and-heart (*hsin*) is the agent needed to fuse and cultivate human virtue and the cosmic creative forces. This is achieved by attention to the experiential unity of the mind-and-heart as the balance between cosmic creativity and personal integrity. This mind-and-heart expresses its relational concern by seeking humanity in the midst of other persons. The book *Mencius* best expresses this key elaboration of Confucius's insight into the nature of human ethical perfection and the creation of a civilized society.

According to Mencius and the *Doctrine of the Mean,* the fundamental moral mind can come to manifest the essence of human nature (*hsing*) through moral practice. The key to human nature (hsing) is active creation of new values for a fiduciary community. While building on the traditions of the past, human nature can never be constrained by any previous perfections. Human nature is the heavenly birthright of every human being. Through careful moral and intellectual cultivation of the mind-and-heart, humanity can always be realized in a social setting. Human nature is best defined in the *Mencius* and the *Doctrine of the Mean*.

The Confucian sense of concern for self and others was further specified in a series of universal ethical norms. These consisted of jen as humanity; *i* as righteousness or propriety; *li* as ritual action; *chih* as wisdom or discernment; and hsin as faithfulness. Along with the five virtues, the tradition always emphasized the role of *ch'eng,* or self-realization in action and wisdom, as the proper way to make concrete these cardinal virtues. In terms of how these virtues are lived out, Confucianism always placed a special emphasis on the role of the family as the locus of fiduciary community. While recognizing that individual families may be tragically flawed, the tradition argues for the irreducible nature of the role of the family in the generation of humane human values. It is upon these proper family values that society can be organized in a harmonious and civilized fashion. Hence the family is always the first educational and spiritual matrix, or school, for Confucian virtue.

Universalizing the value of primordial family ties, Confucianism always recognizes a justified social hierarchy. Reciprocity (*pao*), filial piety (*hsiao*), and deference to proper authority and wisdom are key methods for ethical socialization. The Confucians were aware of the tension between the emotional particularism of the family and the drive to universalize these virtues for broader levels of society and the state. The Confucians struggled to find a balance between the threat of nepotism and the recognition that persons learn to be humane in the context of the family. Yet the Confucians firmly held that without a proper recognition of the role of the family and its humane hierarchy, there is categorical confusion of social values and the loss of the humane civilization. Confucians were quick to point out that each person moves chronologically between different family roles, from being a child to being a parent and finally to becoming a respected elder. Each station of life demands appropriate ethical conduct and self-discipline, with all such transformations conformed by the norm of norms: jen as humanity guided by righteousness, ritual, wisdom, and faithfulness.

The Confucian Classics and Authoritative Texts: Another distinctive feature of the Confucian tradition has been its appeal to and veneration of certain classics. If one chooses the Confucian Classics rather than Taoist or Buddhist texts, then membership in the Confucian Way was assumed. Much of the learning and piety of the Confucian tradition was devoted to the careful study of and commentary about these Classics. The precise definition of what was canonical or even important as a canon within a canon changed from period to period. Yet certain works remained central to the tradition. For instance, it would be impossible to conceive of the Confucian Way without Confucius's *Analects* or the *Mencius*. The New Confucianism continues this engagement with the Classics by means of historical studies, commentaries, and philosophic discussions of the application of the tradition to the new features of modern life.

As a social and religious construction of reality, the Confucian religio-philosophic vision is expressed, remembered, and studied by the appropriation of a series of Classics. They have provided a movable historical, philosophic, and spiritual feast for Confucians down through the centuries. The foremost set of Classics includes works such as the *Lun Yu* (Analects), the *Mencius* (*Meng-tzu*), the *Shu-ching* (Book of History) and its major ancient commentaries, the *Shih-ching* (Book of Poetry), and the ubiquitous *I-ching* (Book of Changes). The exact number of Classics has varied from five to thirteen. The second classical set are the great ancient Chou- and Han-dynasty ritual texts, which always have been considered guides to proper conduct. The third division of Classics includes important independent philosophic works by thinkers as diverse as Hsun-tzu, Tung Chung-shu, Han Yu, Chu Hsi, Wang Yang-ming, and Tai Chen.

Chu Hsi, the most important of the Sung-dynasty Neo-Confucians, redefined Confucian discourse by selecting the *Analects*, the *Mencius*, the *Great Learning*, and the *Doctrine of the Mean* as the epitome of the tradition. As glossed by

Chu Hsi, these texts, now called the Four Books (*Ssu-shu*), became the basis for the imperial civil service examinations as well as the medium for Confucian scholarship from the Sung dynasty down to the modern New Confucian movement. Along with the Four Books, Chu Hsi's own anthology of his Northern Sung Neo-Confucian masters, *Chin-su lu* (The Reflections on Things at Hand), and Wang Yang-ming's *Instructions for Practical Living* serve as the secondary classics of Neo-Confucianism. These two works of Chu Hsi and Wang Yang-ming are key to understanding the School of Principle and the School of Mind. Later philosophic texts such as Tai Chen's *An Evidential Study of the Meaning of Terms in the Mencius* demonstrated the difference between the Han Learning and Chu's School of Principle or Wang's School of Mind.

Thus, the Confucian Way is transmitted from generation to generation, from school to school, always seeking to achieve moral, spiritual, and intellectual perfection. Confucianism, always transformed and renewed, lives in the constant study of the Classics and their application to those things that are near at hand to all people, the search for humanity in service to a civil society. *See also* Chin-su lu; Chu Hsi; Confucianism (authoritative texts and their interpretation); Confucius; Han Yu; hsiao; hsin; hsing; Hsin-hsueh; Hsiung Shih-li; Hsun-tzu; i; I-ching; Japan, Confucianism in; jen; li; Li Ao; Lun Yu; Mencius; pao; Shih-ching; Shu-ching; Ssu-shu; Tai Chen; Tao; T'ien-ming; Tung Chung-shu; Wang Fu-chih; Wang Yang-ming; Yang Hsiung; yin and yang.

Confucianism (authoritative texts and their interpretation). The Confucian Classics (*Ju-ching*; Chin., "Confucian scripture"), the authoritative texts of Confucianism, are traditionally the Five Classics (*Wu-ching*) and the Four Books (*Ssu-shu*). Early traditions associated Confucius (551–479 B.C.) with each scripture, either directly or indirectly. The formation of the canon occurred through a process of scholastic development ending in the imperial designation of texts as scripture, *ching*.

The Five Classics: Unlike other religious traditions, canonization of texts in Confucianism has involved a relatively open process, with additions, new emphasis, and scholarly counter-traditions. The Confucian canon of the Five Classics was determined three centuries after Confucius's death in 136 B.C. by Emperor Wu of the Han dynasty, under the influence of the Confucian scholar Tung Chung-shu (179–104 B.C.). One of the five, the *Shu-ching* (Book of History), was important because of its focus on the history of sagely and wicked rulers of previous dynasties, presenting theories why the decree of Heaven supported or opposed their rule. Confucius claimed gentlemen were stimulated by poetry and established through practice of the rites, thereby giving grounds for legitimizing the authority of two more, the *Shih-ching* (Book of Poetry) and *Li chi* (Book of Rites). The *I-ching* (Book of Changes) had been a major interest of Confucius; according to tradition he had written its commentaries. Mencius (372–289 B.C.) claimed Confucius wrote the *Ch'un Ch'iu* (Spring and Autumn Annals), the last of the five, making its terse chronological comments on the rulers of Confucius's home state, Lu, worthy of inclusion in the canon.

The Thirteen Classics: To the canon that included the Five Classics were later added two rites texts (*Chou-li*, Rites of Chou; *I-li*, Book of Etiquette, together with the *Li chi*, Book of Rites); and three commentaries to the *Ch'un Ch'iu* (*Tso-chuan*, *Ku-liang-chuan*, and *Kung-yang-chuan*). Emperor Wen Tsung (827–840) ordered twelve *ching* to be etched into stone: *I-ching*, *Shu-ching*, *Shih-ching*, the three rites texts, *Ch'un Ch'iu* with its three commentaries (counted as three), *Lun Yu* (Analects), *Hsiao-ching* (The Classic of Filial Piety), and the *Erh-ya [Erya]* (a classical philological dictionary). Only during the reign of emperor Kuang Tsung (1190–94) was *Meng-tzu* (Mencius) canonized, completing the so-called Thirteen Classics.

The Four Books: The unique scholarly efforts of Chu Hsi (1130–1200) created the emphasis on the Four Books. *Lun Yu* had been canonized and

Meng-tzu would be canonized later in Chu's career. The *Ta-hsueh* (Great Learning) and *Chung Yung* (Doctrine of the Mean) were originally only chapters in the *Li chi* (Book of Rites); Chu gave them new status as independent texts. Chu considered these four texts the essential teachings of traditional Confucianism. The Jen Tsung emperor (1312–20) of the Mongolian Yuan dynasty was convinced to use the Four Books as the basis for imperial examinations. From 1315 until 1905, the Five Classics and the Four Books were the fundamental texts of Confucianism and its examination system. *See also* ching; Chu-Hsi; Ch'un Ch'iu; Confucianism; Han religion; Hsiao-ching; I-ching; Li chi; Lun Yu; Mencius; Neo-Confucianism; Shih-ching; Shu-ching; Ssu-shu; Tung Chung-shu.

Confucianism (thought and ethics). The principal teachings of Confucius (551–479 B.C.), as contained in the *Analects*, emphasized the practice of moral virtues, especially humaneness or love (Chin. *jen*) and filiality (*hsiao*). These were exemplified by the "noble person" (*chun-tzu*) and expressed within the five ethical relations, namely, between parent and child, ruler and minister, husband and wife, older and younger siblings, and friend and friend. Mencius (372–289 B.C.) further elaborated the importance of individual morality in establishing "benevolent government." He affirmed human nature as being good and having the potential for realizing the four virtues of humanity, righteousness, propriety, and wisdom. The *Great Learning* suggests

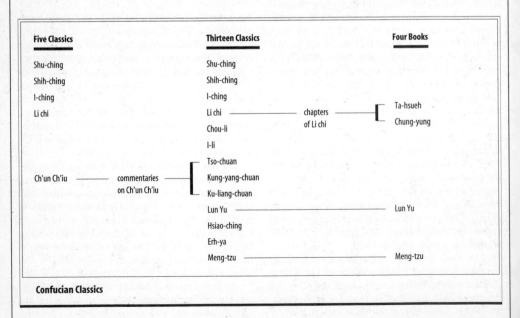

Five Classics		Thirteen Classics		Four Books
Shu-ching		Shu-ching		
Shih-ching		Shih-ching		
I-ching		I-ching		
Li chi		Li chi ———— chapters	——	Ta-hsueh
		Chou-li of Li chi		Chung-yung
		I-li		
		Tso-chuan		
Ch'un Ch'iu —— commentaries ——		Kung-yang-chuan		
on Ch'un Ch'iu		Ku-liang-chuan		
		Lun Yu ————————————		Lun Yu
		Hsiao-ching		
		Erh-ya		
		Meng-tzu ————————————		Meng-tzu

Confucian Classics

that all individual ethical practice effects order in the family, the society, and the nation. Chu Hsi's (1130–1200) Neo-Confucian synthesis was based on a balance of religious reverence, ethical practice, scholarly investigation, and political participation. Chu gave a metaphysical framework to Confucian thought, developing the idea that moral cultivation in harmony with change in the universe allowed the individual to "form one body with all things."

Confucian Ethics in Japan: In Japan, Confucian ethics of harmony and decorum were promulgated in Shotoku's Constitution of 604. Confucian morality was studied by the Zen monks during the medieval period. The spread of Confucian ethics in the Tokugawa period (1600–1868) came through the efforts of Confucian scholars; setting up schools, lecturing to the land-holding magistrates (*daimyo*), and writing ethical treatises (*kunmono*) in a simplified Japanese. Even in the twentieth century Confucian ethics continue to be an important basis of individual, family, and social relations. *See also* Confucianism; Japan, Confucianism in.

Confucianism in Japan. *See* Japan, Confucianism in.

Confucius (Chin. *K'ung Fu-tzu,* "Master K'ung"; 551–479 B.C.), the most famous philosopher of ancient China. Author of the *Ch'un Ch'iu* (Spring and Autumn Annals) and possible compiler of some early poetry, Confucius denied contemporary claims of his sageliness. The most reliable historical source regarding Confucius is the *Lun Yu* (Analects).

Transmitter of the rites and culture of earlier sage-kings, Confucius aimed to counteract the militarism of his day through training prospective leaders in humane government and gentlemanly arts. Ironically, no ruler fully accepted his teachings or employed him in high office. Religious issues were generally secondary to his ethical and political lessons but were expressed through his ritual piety. Sacrifices were properly performed to ancestral spirits at appropriate times during meals and after receiving certain gifts.

Confucius frequented the ancestral temple, presided in exorcism rites, and visited the Grand Temple of the great Duke of Chou. This sagely predecessor had stabilized the kingdom through unselfish service and religious mediation, securing the Mandate of Heaven (T'ien-ming). Confucius's concern to understand the Mandate of Heaven in his day was fulfilled when he was fifty. He anguished over the early death of his best disciple, Yen Yuan, yet pursued a mission he believed was willed by Heaven.

Later Chinese generations claimed Confucius to be the perfect sage, honoring him in temples erected throughout China. The *Chung Yung* (Doctrine of the Mean) calls Confucius the "partner of Heaven and Earth." *See also* Ch'un Ch'iu; Chung Yung; Confucianism; Lun Yu; T'ien-ming.

Congregationalism, a form of Protestantism characterized by a belief in the autonomy of the local congregation. Developed by the Anabaptists in the early sixteenth century, it evolved most fully among the Separatist movement within the Church of England in the latter part of the sixteenth century. The first Congregational Church was established in 1567 in London. Robert Browne (1550–1633) is often called "the father of the Congregationalists" because of his book *Reformation Without Tarrying for Any* (1581), which argues that the local congregation is independent of any civil or ecclesiastical authority.

The story of Congregationalism is intertwined with the controversies that mark British civil and religious history in the sixteenth and seventeenth centuries. Puritans, Separatists, and Independents of various persuasions opposed the idea of a national church. Because of persecution some Independents (another name for Congregationalists) fled to Holland in 1609, and in 1620 moved to America with the *Mayflower* delegation, which founded the Plymouth Colony in Massachusetts. Those who remained in England eventually had their greatest influence under Oliver Cromwell, who became Lord Protector in 1653. That influence rapidly diminished with the death of Cromwell in 1658 and the Restoration of the monarchy.

Congregationalism remained a small but impressive stream of Protestantism within Great Britain. Its greatest strength was in Wales, but it also spread to Scotland and to the large urban areas. Congregationalists founded Mansfield College at Oxford in 1886. Declining numbers and resources in the twentieth century led to the union with Presbyterians in 1972 to form the United Reformed Church.

Congregationalism has had its greatest success in the United States. It flourished in the early American colonies and eventually became the established church of Connecticut and Massachusetts. In 1734 Jonathan Edwards, a Congregational minister in Northampton, Massachusetts, precipitated the First Great Awakening in America with his evangelistic preaching. Congregationalists undertook mission work with the Native Americans and were a part of the westward expansion of the frontier. Congregationalists entered into a "Plan of Union" in 1801 with Presbyterians regarding mission work in the West; this lasted until 1852, when it was repudiated by Presbyterians because of internal doctrinal controversies. In New England Congregationalists had other difficulties. They eventually lost a third of their congregations to Unitarianism, a movement born in the early nineteenth century over disputes about the doctrine of the Trinity.

Nonetheless, the Congregationalists grew and organized for mission work in the nineteenth century. In 1810 they organized the American Board of Commissioners for Foreign Missions, and in 1862 formed the American Home Missionary Society. In 1871 the first National Council of Congregational Churches was held in Oberlin, Ohio. In 1931 the Congregational churches merged with Christian churches to form the Congregational-Christian denomination, and that body merged with the Evangelical and Reformed Church in 1957 to form the United Church of Christ. In 1991 the church reported a membership of 1,605,614 and 6,327 congregations, with headquarters in Cleveland, Ohio.

Theology and Polity: Congregationalists have been on the liberal side of the Protestant spectrum. They share with the broader Protestant family convictions about the sovereignty of God, God's actions in history as recorded in scripture, the Lordship of Jesus, justification by grace through faith, the redeeming and nurturing power of the Holy Spirit, the efficacy of the sacraments of baptism and the Lord's Supper, and the church as the gathered community. Distinctive to Congregationalism, however, are deep convictions about the sufficiency and autonomy of the local congregation, the rejection of creeds, and the role of the individual conscience.

Congregations are traditionally formed by a group of people framing a covenant statement of belief and purpose; one becomes a member by profession of faith in Jesus Christ and by affirming the covenant of the local church.

In this polity the annual meeting of the congregation is central. This tradition has been on the forefront of women's rights and of ordaining women for church leadership. Congregationalists have championed rights of minorities, from their active role in the Abolitionist movement and founding of black colleges in the nineteenth century to their support of the Civil Rights movement in the 1960s and 1970s. Local congregations call their own ministers; the denomination is organized into Associations, Conferences (presided over by Conference Ministers), and a General Synod, which meets every two years.

Congregationalists were at the forefront of work in critical biblical scholarship in America. Yale Divinity School, Harvard Divinity School, the Oberlin School of Theology, Andover-Newton Theological School, and the Hartford Seminary Foundation were centers of congregational influences. Most Congregational churches still reflect a liberal theological perspective, with stress on Jesus as a teacher and example, and strong social ministries. Congregationalism has been broadly reformed, but its non-creedalism and fluidity about doctrinal propositions distinguish it from other reformed churches.

Congregationalists have been, and continue to be, ecumenical in spirit. The United Church of Christ, which is the primary denominational expression of this tradition in the United States in the 1990s, has been a consistent supporter of the National Council of Churches and the World Council of Churches, and a participant in the Consultation on Church Union. Since the mid-1980s long-term merger discussions have been going on with the Disciples of Christ (Christian) Churches. There are newly formed national churches of South India, the Philippines, Japan, Australia, and Canada.

Worship: Worship patterns of the Congregational tradition are structured and formal but not highly liturgical. As with most of the Reformed tradition, the sermon is the focal point. Hymns are sung and there is usually a corporate confession of sin with an assurance of pardon. Various contemporary confessions of faith are used. Infants are baptized and the Lord's Supper is celebrated quarterly. The Reformed sense of the Lord's Supper as manifesting spiritual presence and of the Supper as a memorial prevail among Congregationalists. *See also* Browne, Robert; Protestantism; Puritans.

consecration, the ritual setting apart or dedicating of persons, places, or things as sacred. *See also* himorogi; ritual; sacred, profane; shimenawa.

Conservative Judaism, a movement in modern Judaism, founded in the late nineteenth century, that attempts to combine tradition and change. Known as "Historical Judaism" in Europe, the movement developed in the United States, where it occupies the middle position between Reform and Orthodox Judaisms.

Its center is the Jewish Theological Seminary of America, New York City, with satellite schools in Los Angeles and Jerusalem. Its federation of synagogues is the United Synagogues of America, and its clerical organization is the Rabbinical Assembly, the International Association of Conservative Rabbis. In 1990, approximately a thousand synagogues in North and South America, Europe, and Israel and a like number of rabbis are identified with Conservative Judaism.

History: Despite the efforts of such influential rabbinical leaders as the reformer Isaac Mayer Wise (1819–1900) and the traditionalist Isaac Leeser (1806–68) to forge a single American Judaism, nineteenth-century American Jewry was unable to achieve religious unity or uniformity. As the gap between reformers and traditionalists widened, members of each group found common cause in the view that neither radical Reform Judaism nor insular Orthodoxy could supply the authenticity and vitality to ensure the viability of Judaism in America. In 1886 the Jewish Theological Seminary of America was founded by Orthodox rabbis Sabato Morais (1823–97), H. Pereira Mendes (1852–1937), and Bernard Drachman (1861–1945), who joined with rabbis Alexander Kohut (1842–94), Marcus Jastrow (1829–1903), and others who served moderate Reform congregations but were committed to "positive historical" Judaism. Formulated by Zechariah Frankel (1801–75), head of the Jewish Theological Seminary of Breslau, the "positive-historical" school views Judaism as the product of historical development and calls for an attitude of reverence toward the entire Jewish spiritual tradition and adherence to its legal system, as well as the unfettered pursuit of truth using the methods of the Western scientific tradition. It affirms that authentic Judaism is marked by a dual loyalty to "tradition and change."

The chief architect of Conservative Judaism was the rabbinic scholar Solomon Schechter (1847–1915), who, during his presidency of the Jewish Theological Seminary (1902–15), placed the synagogue at the center of the movement's religious enterprise, established the United Synagogue of America, and bound Conservative synagogues to order and decorum at services, sermons in English, methodical instruction in the religious schools, and selection of rabbis and teachers trained in universities and professional institutions. As goals, he proposed to provide religious instruction for women and opportunities for them to participate in the work of the congregation, to rejuvenate the Jewish home by fostering observance and ceremonies, to use Hebrew in school and synagogue, and to conserve the Sabbath and dietary laws.

The movement's most influential ideologist has been Mordecai M. Kaplan (1881–1983), whose formulation of Judaism as "the evolving religious civilization of the Jewish people" has come to be accepted as "normative" in Conservative Judaism.

Some Conservative Emphases:

The Jewish People: Kaplan's emphasis on the peoplehood component of Judaism (in the triad of God, Torah, and the People of Israel) had already been anticipated by Schechter, who devised the notion of "the collective conscience of Catholic Israel" as the final arbiter of belief and practice.

Revelation: A wide range of views on revelation is found in Conservative Judaism, from those who view it as historic fact to those who consider it a theological concept. The regnant view is that revelation is from God but works through people and is therefore a never-ending process.

The Bible: The record of and guide for the relationship of God and Israel. It is to be read not for scientific or historical truth but for religious instruction.

Jewish Law: All generations of Israel share a common legal tradition, which continues to evolve. The process for change is built into and mandated by the tradition itself. The corpus of law is binding, as is the mandate to give it viability through ongoing renewal.

Ritual: A body of action symbols of commitment to God, who is the source of holiness. Conscious association with the source of holiness confers holiness. A symbol that has become associated with a holy people attains sanctity. Of highest worth are rituals that celebrate historic memories and enhance ethical and aesthetic sensitivity.

Culture: The sense of kinship with the Jewish people past and present is enhanced through shared experiences. It follows that Conservative Judaism, which places such special emphasis on Jewish peoplehood, should place special stress on what strengthens the bonds of community: literature, arts, music, institutions and organizations, and most especially shared language (Hebrew), prayer, and ritual. *See also* Orthodox Judaism; Reconstructionism; Reform Judaism.

Constantine (d. 337), the first Christian emperor whose Edict of Milan (313) brought an end to the persecution of Christians in the Roman Empire. He summoned the First Council of Nicaea in 325 to put an end to the Arian controversy, thus establishing a precedent for imperial leadership of the church.

Constantinople. *See* Byzantium.

contagion, the transfer of power by contact or proximity. Contagion is most often associated with sacred objects or pollution. *See also* ritual; sacred, profane.

contagious magic, the belief that objects in contact with one another will continue to influence one another even when separated, so that what is done to one will affect the other.

contraception. *See* birth control.

contrition, in Christianity, an expression of sorrow for the commission of sins and the resolution to sin no more either because of the fear or love of God.

convent, a dwelling place for nuns. The term is also used, less frequently, for houses of male members of religious orders.

conversion (Lat. *conversio*, "to turn around"), a formal change of adherence from one religious system to another. Conversion is possible only in those religions that understand themselves to be voluntary associations and define themselves by creedal formulations, in contradistinction to the large majority of religious traditions that view membership as conferred solely by birth. *See also* apostasy; mission or missionary movements; voluntary association.

Judaism: In the Jewish worldview, religious conversion (Heb. *tshubah*) supersedes ethnic identification. Today, a person of any ethnic group may convert to Judaism but following conversion is expected to make Judaism—its history, people, and destiny—the matrix of personal identification. Because Jewish law codes regard anyone born to a Jewish mother as Jewish, even if the father is gentile, the requirement of conversion falls only on those born to a gentile mother.

Conversion in the Talmud: The earliest sustained discussion of the process of conversion appears in the Talmud (*Yevamot* 47a, b). For men, the first step of the process is circumcision, a sign in the flesh of God's ongoing covenant with the Jewish people. The essence of the ritual for both men and women is immersion in a *mikveh* ("ritual bath"). The Talmud describes in detail how immediately prior to this act an attempt is made to dissuade the potential convert from embracing Judaism. One is warned of the difficulties of being Jewish—of tying one's fate to a persecuted people and of accepting an exacting set of ritual requirements and moral standards. If not deterred by these admonitions, the individual enters the mikveh. Men monitor the immersion of men, and women the immersion of women. Upon emerging from the water, the individual is a full-fledged member of the Jewish people, obligated to perform the same ritual acts as other Jews, eligible for the same synagogue honors, and able to marry another Jew.

Conversion Today: Conversion today differs from the talmudic description mainly in terms of the period of intellectual and emotional preparation. Individual rabbis, as well as centers for conversion, all require the potential convert to participate in a multifaceted course in basic Judaism lasting about a year. During this time the potential convert learns about Jewish beliefs, values, and practices, starts to observe commandments, develops ties to a specific Jewish community through synagogue attendance and home hospitality, and begins to identify with the State of Israel, the center of Jewish hopes and aspirations.

At the end of this period, a male convert undergoes ritual circumcision. Although usually a minor surgical procedure performed on the eighth day after birth, circumcision of an adult is conducted under anesthetic in a hospital setting. Even a man who has been routinely circumcised as an infant upon conversion to Judaism must undergo a procedure called *hatafat dam brit*, "drawing the blood of the covenant." This act transforms the earlier circumcision into a covenantal affirmation. A simple procedure that does not require hospitalization, it is usually performed immediately prior to the formal conversion.

Potential converts are escorted by their mentor to a mikveh. Upon entering the water they are asked questions by a panel of three, usually composed of rabbis. The answers must indicate that the individual unequivocally rejects any other religion of which he or she may have been a part and accepts without hesitation the basic principles of Judaism. The individual then immerses three times, reciting two blessings after the first immersion: one sanctifying the act of immersion and the other thanking God for bringing the individual to this point in life. Some rabbis then take the convert to a synagogue where a formal declaration of faith is recited and friends gather to congratulate and welcome the new member of the Jewish community.

Conversion in the Various Denominations: Denominational differences have led to the abandonment of a single standard for conversion. The Reform rabbinical association voted in 1892 to permit conversions without any formal rite whatsoever, provided the individual was properly schooled in the precepts of Jewish practice, renounced his or her former faith, and declared belief in the Jewish God. In 1982, partly in response to the high rate of intermarriage, the Reform movement decided to recognize patrilineal Jews, those born to a Jewish father and a non-Jewish mother. Such persons need not undergo any rite of conversion but are accepted as Jewish if raised as Jews and given a Jewish education.

The Conservative and Orthodox movements conduct conversion rites in the manner outlined by the Jewish codes of law, differing somewhat on the level of prior commitment to observe commandments they require of the convert. However, many Orthodox rabbis in the United States are reluctant to accept students for conversion, and in some other countries, the Orthodox rabbinate has established a policy of refusing all requests for conversion.

Motives for conversion are expected to be pure. A person who converts for the sake of marriage to a Jewish partner is not initially regarded by some as a proper convert but is accepted by most rabbis after the fact, upon demonstrating commitment to living a Jewish way of life.

Converts and Jewish Law: Jewish law views conversion as a radical break with one's past and goes so far as to deny kinship ties between a convert and his or her former family. Thus, if the gentile parent of a convert dies, the convert is not expected to observe the set of Jewish mourning rites for parents. Similarly, when a convert is called for a synagogue honor and needs to be identified by patronym and matronym, he or she is routinely designated "the son/daughter of Abraham our father and Sarah our mother," a reference to the biblical figures judged by Judaism to be the first Jews by conviction.

Conversion of Children: Children born to converts after conversion need undergo no conversion ritual and are regarded as Jews by birth. If Jewish parents adopt a non-Jewish child or if non-Jews convert to Judaism and wish to convert their young children as well, the boys must undergo circumcision and both boys and girls must be immersed in the mikveh after the age of five months. In these cases, the child must affirm, upon attaining religious majority at twelve or thirteen, that Judaism is the religion of choice. *See also* Judaism (life cycle); mikveh.

Islam: Conversion is the public recognition of an individual's submission to the faith. After performing the greater ablution, the convert recites the two testimonies before two Muslim witnesses, that there is no God but Allah and that Muhammad is the Messenger of God. (If the convert is Jewish, the testimony that Jesus is a Messenger of God is added.) *See also* Islam (festal cycle).

Christianity: *See* baptism; born-again Christian; catechesis; mission or missionary movements; testimony.

Convince. *See* Afro-Americans (Caribbean and South America), new religions among.

Coptic church, the autonomous Christian church in Egypt.

According to tradition, the Coptic church was founded in the first century by Mark the Evangelist, who became the first bishop of Alexandria.

The separation of the Coptic church from Roman Christianity was the result of combined political and theological tensions. The theological controversy climaxed at the Council of Chalcedon (451) and centered on the union of the divine and human natures in Christ, with the Coptic church arguing that there is one nature after the union (Monophysitism). The patriarchal succession in Alexandria was split in 450 when the Melkites (Greek loyalists of the Byzantine emperor) installed an Orthodox patriarch to replace the exiled Monophysite, Dioscorus, and attempted to force the Copts to accept the Chalcedonian decrees. The Egyptians responded by electing a native Coptic patriarch, Timothy Aelurus. Relief from Byzantine persecution was provided by the Persians in 619, and this was followed in 642 by the Arab conquest of Egypt.

In the twentieth century, the Coptic hierarchy is led by a patriarch with the title of "Pope of Alexandria and Patriarch of the See of St. Mark." The patriarch is elected by lot from a short list of candidates, each of whom must be a lifelong celibate monk and at least fifty years old. Other members of the hierarchy appointed from the monastic ranks include the archbishops, bishops, and the abbots of the Coptic monasteries. Secular priests are permitted to marry, but must do so before ordination.

There are three liturgies used by the Copts. The Liturgy of St. Basil is generally celebrated. At Christmas, Easter, and the Epiphany, the Liturgy of St. Gregory is used, while the Liturgy of St. Mark is celebrated mainly in the monasteries on the Friday before Palm Sunday. The ancient Coptic language continues to be used sparingly in liturgical settings alongside Arabic, although Arabic has replaced Coptic in everyday life.

The Coptic church in Ethiopia is an independent but daughter church of the Egyptian Coptic church.

corn ceremonies, green, rituals performed by the

Seminole, Cherokee, Choctaw, Chickasaw, and Yuchi (Native North Americans of the Southeast) marking the ripening of corn and the beginning of a new year.

The green corn ceremonies—a complex cluster of agriculture-based rituals that vary over time as well as from people to people—serve to renew the whole community, indeed the whole world. Typical of calendrical rites of passage, these rituals effect a cosmic change. The old time (old corn, old fire, old community divisions) is left behind; ahead is the new time of beginnings.

To make real this movement, the community first separate themselves from the time that would be left behind. Public places and residences are cleaned, all the fires are put out, the old food is eaten, followed by fasting. This threshold time between old time and new is full of unusual possibilities; broken friendships are mended and moral infractions—even serious ones short of murder—are cleared. Finally, the ritual performance establishes the new year. In absolute silence, a priest kindles a new pure fire into which the first of the ripening corn is offered. From this fire each family makes its new hearth fire. To celebrate the newness of things and the bounty of life, the people dance and feast. *See also* busk; new year festivals; North America, traditional religions in.

Corpus Hermeticum, Greek and Latin texts from the second to fourth centuries attributed to or associated with the ancient Greco-Egyptian deity Hermes Trismegistos. The basic collection contains seventeen tractates reflecting a mixture of Platonic, Pythagorean, Stoic, and Jewish/Christian philosophical and religious speculation of the type often associated with Gnosticism in Late Antiquity.

cosmogony, myth of the origin of the world. *See also* Australian and Pacific traditional religions; Chinese myth; Earth Diver; Egyptian religion; Gnosticism; high god; Indo-European religion; Japanese myth; myth; Zoroastrianism.

Hinduism: The Hindu myth of creation is described in a number of Sanskrit texts called Puranas; it is the model of which other accounts are but variants.

There is no original cosmogony, no absolute once-and-for-all creation, since time, according to Hindus, is cyclical, without beginning or end. Both the world and the individual go through repeated rebirths. The time cycles of the cosmogonic myth are two-tiered, parallel to the life of the supreme deity, Vishnu (or secondarily Rudra-Shiva). Vishnu is the Purusha, the primordial

Male or Man, conceived as a cosmic *yogin* (Skt., "yoga practitioner") going through alternate periods of expansion and world resorption. This outward and inward movement at the ultimate level is identified as an ever-recurring life and death, each of equal duration, of the god Brahma.

Brahma's life lasts a hundred Brahma years of 360 Brahma days each. A day of Brahma is a *kalpa*, the time unit of the second tier of creation. It is measured by one thousand repeated units called *mahayugas*, which do not command any new pattern of cosmogony. Each mahayuga has four *yugas* of decreasing length and lasts for 4,320,000 years. This fantastic duration makes the cosmogonic myth quite irrelevant to human life. Nonetheless, the two-tiered structure expresses values that have a direct bearing on Hindu society and give it its ideal foundation.

At the ultimate level, the supreme Purusha manifests different stages of being that correspond to the stages of individual yogic experience as given in one early Upanishad, but in an inverted way. Whereas the yogin ascends a kind of ladder to reach transcendent experience, the Purusha, as it were, climbs down it to reach a stage of being called the "egg of Brahma." In terms of Hindu values, this means that the discipline of yoga and its social consequences of world renunciation are the ultimate model of Hindu life, though not the most frequently followed one. Renunciation is supposed to give *moksha*, final liberation from repeated rebirth, as the ultimate goal.

The second level of cosmogony does not show any continuity with the first. Its overall frame is mostly borrowed from myths of the Vedic ritual texts clad in Upanishadic imagery. It starts with cosmic flood and night, in which the earth and all living beings have disappeared. On the water is Narayana, the yogic form of Vishnu, who presides over the cosmic night asleep. Upon waking, he becomes Brahma and starts creation. In the form of a boar he dives into the deep and brings the earth back to the surface. The boar is identified with "Sacrifice," the eternal act of Vedic worship. In fact he is both Sacrifice and the Veda, "act" and "knowledge." Brahma then creates ignorance before emitting creatures, plants, animals, gods, and finally humans. Humans are those who start acting under the sting of pain.

This cosmogony thus leads to organized life on earth. Vedic lore and practice encompass it, but ignorance, coming between sacrifice and concrete life, suggests that life in the world is possible only if people forget their origin from the Purusha and the values attached to him.

Only then can they start acting, performing rites, and following societal rules, the goals of which are desire (mainly sexual), wealth and material interests, and social order, *dharma*. The cosmogonic myth reinforces these goals without mentioning them. On the contrary, when the sting of pain is mentioned, it implies that one may wish to terminate pain by forsaking acts that lead to rebirth and seeking moksha through renunciation.

One part of this cosmogonic myth must deal with the inward movement back to the Purusha. The choice between rebirth and final moksha in this life implies the possibility of individual liberation. But individual moksha cannot be dissociated from the cosmic movement, and the liberated soul will have to follow the same time cycles that will lead to the end of one Brahma life and the total disappearance of the cosmos into the supreme Purusha.

The end of a Brahma day starts with a cosmic fire, after which heavy rains flood the remnant of creation and prepare the scene for the next recreation. In the fire, all living beings are cremated and kept for the recreation, whereas those who are in heaven may escape to a higher sphere, the liberated ones going up to Brahmaloka to await the end of Brahma's life. All others will renew their cycle of individual rebirths at the dawn of the next Brahma day. Ultimately, there is a second tier of world resorption, the exact reversal of the primary creation process from Purusha, which brings the universe back into Purusha. *See also* Brahma; cosmology; four goals of life (Hinduism); liberation; Narayana; Purusha; Veda, Vedism; Vishnu; yoga.

Japanese Religion: Japanese cosmogony is a largely procreative process involving ritual propriety and purification. As described in the *Kojiki* (712) and *Nihonshoki* (720) the primordial phase of creation involved the emergence of various *kami* (divinities, divine presences), two of them associated with *musubi*, the generative force of the universe. The last of these initial kami, Izanagi and Izanami, were ordered to "solidify" the phenomenal world. They did so by stirring a spear in the cosmic ocean. The spear's drippings formed an island, upon which they bore as children the islands of Japan and various kami. Their descendants include the sun goddess, Amaterasu, and the first emperor. *See also* Amaterasu; cosmology; Izanagi and Izanami; Japanese myth; kami; Kojiki; Nihonshoki.

cosmology, the most general understanding of the overall structure of the universe; the picture of the world held by a particular people. *See also* ages of the world; agriculture, religious aspects of; antediluvian/postdiluvian; chaos; chthonic; color symbolism; cyclical time; directional orientations; dualism; ecological aspects of traditional religions; evil; fatalism; fate; golden age; heaven and hell; hunting, religious aspects of; light and darkness; macrocosm, microcosm; mountains, sacred; orientation; right, left; sacred, profane; sacred space and sacred time; salvation; shamanism; sky.

Hinduism: All the classical forms of Hindu cosmology may be characterized as containing a belief in a soul that is "fallen," either because it is individualized or ignorant or in bondage to a body, but that, when liberated or enlightened or universalized, enjoys this state eternally. The universe is the stage for this drama and in some cases instrumental to it.

Spatial Construction: Vedic mythology speaks of Father Sky (Skt. *Dyaus Pitar*) and Mother Earth (*Prithivi*). Sometimes three realms are cited: *bhur* ("earth"), *bhuvah* ("air"), and *svar* ("sky" or "heaven"). The *agnicayana* (building of the fire altar) described in the *Shatapatha Brahmana* is a ritual construction of the cosmos. Two hymns in the *Rig Veda* illustrate philosophical refinement in cosmogonical speculation. One employs negative terminology: "Then, even nothing was not, nor existence" (10:129). Another portrays the universe as a Cosmic Man (Purusha; 10:90).

The Upanishads expand the three Vedic worlds into seven realms correlated with the stages of liberation. At death, the soul is said to leave the funeral pyre and to take, depending on its *karma* (meritorious and demeritorious actions), one of two paths: the path of the gods (*devayana*) or that of the fathers (*pitriyana*). Following the devayana, the soul enters the flames, then the day, then the bright half of the month (waxing moon), the bright half of the year (ascending sun), the sun, the moon, the lightning, and finally the *brahman* and liberation. Following the pitriyana, the soul enters the smoke rather than the flame, then the night, the dark half of the month (waning moon), the dark half of the year (descending sun), the world of the fathers, the *akasha* (space), and finally the moon prior to rebirth.

Cosmology, including the divisions and actions of time, is at the heart of the Puranic vision. The Puranic cosmograph of the *Vishnu Purana* (fourth century) consists of the flat disk of the earth composed of seven concentric islands that double in size as one moves from the center to the perimeter. The islands are separated from each other by oceans, each of which is the width of the island it encircles. In the center of the innermost island, Jambudvipa, is the great golden Mt. Meru, conical in shape and pointed downward. Other mountain ranges divide Jambudvipa into nine *varsha* (regions). The southernmost varsha is Bharata, the only *karmabhumi* ("karma realm"); only there is salvation possible. The outermost island is divided in half by the circular Manasottara ("mind-surpassing") mountain. The vertical divisions are those of the Upanishads. The first three—*bhurloka*, *bhuvahloka*, and *svarloka*—are *kritika*, "transitory" or "made"; they are renewed with every cosmic age (*kalpa*). *Maharloka* is considered a mixed realm because it is deserted by beings at the end of a kalpa but is not destroyed. The three highest realms—*janaloka*, *tapoloka*, and *satyaloka*—are *akritika*, "unmade." They perish only at the end of the life of Brahma (*mahakalpa*).

Divisions of Time: Fifteen twinklings of the eye (*nimesha*) make a *kashtha;* thirty kashthas, one *kala;* thirty kalas, one *muhurta;* thirty muhurtas, a day and night of mortals; thirty such days make a month divided into waxing and waning halves; six months form an *ayana* and two ayanas compose a year. The southern ayana is a night and the northern a day of the gods. Twelve thousand divine years, each comprising 360 such days, constitute the period of four *yugas* (*caturyuga*). The *kritayuga* consists of four thousand divine years; the *tretayuga*, three thousand; the *dvaparayuga*, two thousand; and the *kaliyuga*, one thousand. The yuga is preceded by a dawn and followed by a twilight; each lasts for as many hundred years as there are thousands in the yuga. A thousand caturyugas comprise a kalpa. Fourteen Manus reign within that term during a period known as a *manvantara*. A kalpa constitutes a day of Brahma. At the end of a day of Brahma, the universe is consumed by fire. Brahma sleeps for a night of equal duration, at the end of which he creates anew. Three hundred and sixty such days and nights constitute a year of Brahma and one hundred such years equal the life of Brahma (*mahakalpa*). One *parardha*, or half his life, has expired.

A doctrine of descents, or *avataras*, is joined to the doctrines of time in the *Bhagavad Gita*. Here Krishna states: "For the protection of the good, And the destruction of the evil-doers, To make a firm footing for the right, I come into being in age after age (*yuge yuge*)" (4:8). **See also** Bhu/Bhudevi; Brahma; cosmogony; devayana/pitriyana; Hinduism (thought and ethics); Purusha.

Buddhism: The Buddha is well known for his refusal to speculate about the beginning and end of the world, but he was interested in describing the structure of the world, both as a means of understanding the nature of reality itself and as part of his presentation of the process of salvation. Subsequent Buddhists have followed the Buddha's example, preferring to concentrate on the order of the world in connection with salvation and avoiding speculation about the origins of the cosmos. Buddhists did, however, tend to accept that the world was subject to a process of devolution, a theme that was emphasized in broader currents of Indian mythology.

Buddhist cosmological systems fall into two groups: those that take the world as a single world and those that acknowledge the coexistence of multiple world systems. These two representations of the world are associated, respectively, with the Theravada schools and the Mahayana.

A Single-world Cosmology: In the single-world cosmological system, the world is literally a universe. It is a single, integrated system that consists of a hierarchy of six realms, with the realm of hell dwellers at the bottom, then the realm of suffering ghosts, that of animals, that of *asura*s (semidivine, semidemonic beings), that of humans, and finally the heavenly realms. These various realms are further subdivided hierarchically. There are various heavens of increasing subtlety and pleasure and hells of increasing pain. Human social stratifications fit within and are confirmed by these structures.

Theravada texts in both Pali and Sanskrit employ another cosmological system organized around Mt. Meru. There are seven concentric circles of mountains surrounding this mountain, with a range of iron mountains at the perimeter; this range of iron mountains gives this cosmological system its most common name, *cakravala*. Four continents are located in the ocean that lies in between Mt. Meru and the circles of mountains. One of these continents, or "islands," is Jambudvipa, "The Rose-Apple Island," on which human life takes place. Superhuman beings live on the other islands. Above Mt. Meru, three levels of heavens stretch: those heavens that remain in the "realm of desire," a realm to which the beings of hell, animals, suffering ghosts, and humans have access; the seventeen heavens of "the realm of form," in which beings still have a remnant of material qualities; and those heavens that constitute a "realm of nonform," consisting of four spheres, in which beings have no material characteristics. Access to the realms of form and nonform is only possible through meditation.

Like everything that exists in the universe, the world system itself is subject to change and decay. Thus, it too comes to an end, only to be replaced by another, which will begin the process of cosmic devolution again.

The Coexistence of Multiple-world Systems: Mahayana conceptions of the Buddha accepted the existence of multiple Buddhas, each of which occupied a "Pure Land" or "Buddha-field." Thus a conception of an innumerable number of world systems, one for each Buddha, displaced the conception of a universe found in the Theravada.

The Mahayana tended to arrange these world systems not hierarchically but spatially. The different paradises or Pure Lands of the various Buddhas were arrayed throughout the directions. The Pure Land of Amitabha, for example, is found to the west. The power of these great celestial Buddhas, occupying their individual realms, made it possible for beings to have access to them through devotion and meditation.

Cosmology and Salvation: The different Buddhist cosmologies are not simple descriptions of the nature of the world. In fact, Buddhist intellectuals had other conceptual schemas they preferred for explaining the way things really are. In the Mahayana, reality is best understood within a rubric of emptiness, not by the cosmology of the multiple-world systems. The cosmologies might best be understood as part of the conceptualizations of salvation produced by the different Buddhist schools. In the single-world system, the workings of rebirth are prominent; one can avoid hell and attain heaven by doing meritorious deeds in this life. *Nirvana* is salvation from this single-world system, although sometimes nirvana is represented as being above the formless heavens.

In the cosmology of multiple-world systems, salvation is conceived quite differently. Here salvation is to be reborn in one of the celestial Buddha's Pure Lands. This birth will be one's last, but one is able to enjoy bliss and hear the teaching of a Buddha before attaining emancipation.

Under the impact of science, Buddhists in the modern world have tended to treat the traditional cosmologies only as imagery and symbolism, and cosmologies have lost some of their power to structure perceptions of the social world. It is thus rare, for example, to justify the hierarchical organization of society by reference to cosmological structures. There is a possibility too that they will lose their heuristic value for understanding the processes of salvation, and this will dramatically alter many aspects of Buddhist thought and practice. *See also* Bodhisattvas; Buddhism; Mahayana; Pure Land; Theravada.

Chinese Religion: Unlike the ancient Mesopotamians, whose conceptions of the cosmos are accessible through their epic and omen literature, the cosmology of the ancient Chinese must be reconstructed from the archaeological record and from the complex amalgam of regional myths and legends first committed to writing during the last few centuries B.C. In China the task of conceptualizing the cosmos and of locating human activity within the world was from the first the province of court astronomers and diviners.

Early Models: Distinctive models of jade turtles with two-part shells found in high-status Neolithic burials suggest that the dome of the heavens and the plane of the earth's surface may already have been thought analogous to the animal's vaulted carapace and squarish plastron, the latter being a preferred material for inscription and ritual divination. This early model of the round sky and square earth so typical of later cosmology and cosmography perhaps inspired the early Chinese to discern in the natural markings of this revered creature a replication of the celestial and terrestrial analogues as well as a correspondence of number and pattern. Thus, for example, an early cosmogonic myth concerning the Hsia dynasty founder Yu the Great's successful taming of the chaotic waters of the primieval flood describes his gouging out of the watercourses that drain the nine regions of habitable dry land; the undulating surface and vaguely cruciform shape of the turtle plastron comprises nine distinctly delineated plates whose irregular sutures resemble meandering streams.

The movements of the sun, moon, and planets were closely followed, and by Shang times (ca. 1766–1122 B.C.) a close correlation between celestial events and dynastic affairs was evidently assumed, even though the comprehensive scheme of correspondences between asterisms and geographical regions of China, and between the celestial pole as the abode of the high god (Shang-ti or T'ien) and that of the king or "Son of Heaven" in his palace, did not appear in the literature until much later.

Correlative Cosmology: The mature conception of a correlative cosmos that derived from centuries of accumulated observational experience was catalyzed in classical times by the inspired notion that phenomenal change is ultimately analyzable in terms of a set of prime categories denoting functional qualities or processes, and not constituent elements. These include the binary pair *yin* and *yang* and the Five Phases (*wu-hsing*). Implicit in the idea of a bipolar, dynamic complementarity (male/female, light/dark, hot/cold, dry/wet) symbolized by the prime correlates yin and yang is the conception that both principles are a physical manifestation of *ch'i*, the omnipresent material vapor that pervades the universe, while change itself is a function of the primordial Tao, which lends order to and animates the cosmos. The sequence of Five Phases, perhaps initially correlated with the seasons, was later subsumed under the yin-yang complementarity and served as a means of conceptualizing and organizing all other manifestations and interactions within nature, from the physiological workings of the internal organs to the vicissitudes of the historical process. *See also* ch'i; Chinese myth; Shang-ti; wu-hsing; yin and yang; Yu (the Great).

Japanese Religion: The classical myths (in *Kojiki* and *Nihonshoki*) present no unified worldview. However, a vertical structure dominates in which three realms are distinguished: the celestial realm, home of heavenly deities (*ama tsu kami*); the earthly realm, home of earthly deities (*kuni tsu kami*), including humans, plants, and animals; and an underworld called Yomi. Amaterasu is the sovereign of heaven, the most prestigious realm, while Izanami is queen of Yomi, a place of pollution where the dead dwell. Most Shinto rituals call "down" these deities into wands, trees, or staffs and the end-posts of ancient shrines represent a connecting link between the realms. There is also an undersea world presided over by a dragon king, and an "eternal land" (*tokoyo no kuni*) across the sea, whence come benevolent divine visitors (*mare-bito*). *See also* Amaterasu; cosmogony; demon; Japanese myth; Yomi no kuni.

councils (Buddhism), actions taken by individuals and groups to preserve and, if necessary, restore the legacy of the Buddha, both his teachings and the monastic institutions he established. The First Council, paradigmatic for all subsequent ones, was held shortly after the Buddha's death (ca. 486 B.C.). Five hundred enlightened monks gathered to recite together the teachings of the Buddha; the various canons preserved by different Buddhist traditions are usually traced to this First Council. We can see the First Council as a model for subsequent efforts both to preserve the knowledge and spiritual practices received from the Buddha and to maintain the collective mechanisms necessary for the transmission of his teachings.

A Second Council, said to have been held one hundred years after the Buddha's death, was particularly concerned with these latter mechanisms. It clarified monastic practice and attempted to restore the communal harmony of Buddhist monastic order. Sectarian trends continued, however, so that by the time of the Third Council (250 B.C.) sectarian divisions could not be removed, but were instead confirmed doctrinally and practically with the help of the Buddhist emperor Ashoka.

The Buddhist councils have been used as punctuation points in traditional histories of Buddhism, marking transitions and typically emphasizing the cooperation between political leaders and monks in the task of preserving the Buddha's legacy. Thus, a great council is said to have been held in 100 under the sponsorship of Kaniska, ruler of the Kushan empire. This council committed to writing the commentaries of the Sarvastivada school of Buddhism. Theravada Buddhists variously count nine and six councils. The Thai king Rama I sponsored a ninth council that corrected the text of the Pali canon in the eighteenth century, while the newly independent Burmese government sponsored a council, known in their reckoning as the Sixth Council, to edit Buddhist texts in 1954. *See also* Buddhism (authoritative texts and their interpretation).

Counter-Reformation, the effort of the Roman Catholic Church in the sixteenth and seventeenth centuries to combat the Protestant Reformation. It should be distinguished from the Catholic Reformation, a movement for reform of the Catholic Church that began before the Protestant Reformation and continued alongside it.

The Counter-Reformation included the Church's attacks upon Protestant doctrine and its efforts to extend its sway by reversing Protestant advances in Europe and by missionary activity elsewhere. Included in these efforts were the canons and decrees of the Council of Trent (1546–63) against Protestant teachings, missionary activities of Jesuits and Franciscans in Asia and the Americas, and the establishment of the Roman Inquisition and the Index of Prohibited Books to combat heresy. Results for the Church were renewed vitality, restoration of authority in parts of Europe, and establishment of a presence in mission lands around the world. *See also* Reformation, Protestant; Trent, Council of.

coven (kuv′en), an assembly or meeting of witches. In contemporary Neo-Pagan Witchcraft, the coven is the basic organizational unit of the religion. Although in popular literature, a coven has traditionally had thirteen members (twelve members and a leader), modern covens can have anywhere from three to twenty members.

Entry into a coven comes after a period of

training, traditionally a year and a day. Most covens follow a particular tradition with its own rules, ethics, liturgy, procedures, and training methods. Not all modern witches join covens, and there are probably many more solitary witches than members of groups. *See also* secret societies; witchcraft.

covenant, a formal compact between two unequal parties, divine and human, governing their mutual relationships.

Covenant, the Sword and the Arm of the Lord, or CSA, an important Christian Identity compound until its 1985 demise as the result of a raid by U.S. federal agents. Located near the Arkansas-Missouri border, the compound represented the most violent elements of Identity's survivalist fringe. Founded in 1976 by James D. Ellison, an idiosyncratic, unordained Identity theorist, the CSA became widely known in Identity circles for its ability to supply weapons and paramilitary training. The Covenant, the Sword and the Arm of the Lord shared with other Identity churches a strongly dualistic vision of the world, including the identification of the Jews as the "seed of Satan," but CSA added a cult of personality around Ellison (who once proclaimed himself King of the Ozarks) and a commitment to violence rare in Christian Identity. In 1987 Ellison testified as the government's chief witness against other right-wing thinkers at a Fort Smith, Arkansas, sedition trial, and another CSA member, Richard Snell, was executed in 1995. *See also* Identity Christianity.

Covenant of the Goddess. *See* Wicca.

Covenant of Unitarian Universalist Pagans. *See* Neo-Paganism.

cow (Hinduism), veneration of. The cow is sacred for Hindus, who will not willfully kill one or eat its meat. At festivals, cows may be auspiciously garlanded, decorated, and painted. The belief that the cow symbolizes the Indian motherland sustains cow veneration in modern India.

In Vedic India (ca. 1400–400 B.C.), the cow was favored as a standard of wealth and sacrificed. Not sacred in this period, it slowly becomes so as the concept of noninjury (Skt. *ahimsa*) gains prominence. After ca. 500 B.C. cow sanctity can be recognized in the *Mahabharata* and increasingly in the Puranas.

Coyote, the protagonist of extensive story traditions among Native North American peoples, especially in the western United States. Coyote, manifesting both animal and human characteristics, is often classified by scholars as a trickster figure, based on his gross sexuality (indicated by his long penis that is carried in a pack on his back), his insatiable appetite (he will do anything for a meal and will eat anything, including his own children), and foolish actions (he tries to make fools of all he encounters, and is often made the fool by them). It is not uncommon for Coyote to act as culture hero (in introducing sexuality, stealing light from a malevolent one, or teaching humans how to hunt). *See also* culture hero; trickster.

crane (Chin. *he*), Chinese *yin* symbol of longevity, vehicle of Hsi Wang-mu and the Eight Taoist Immortals (Pa-hsien), and conveyor of the soul to the Western Paradise. *See also* Hsi Wang-mu; Pa-hsien; yin and yang.

Crazy Wisdom Fellowship, the religious group begun by Da (Bubba) Free John (formerly Franklin Jones) in 1970, also called the Dawn Horse Fellowship, the Free Primitive Church of Divine Communion, Johannine Daist Community, and Free Daist Communion. Through its leader, the Fellowship sought to establish a basic loving relationship that, more than any single doctrine or practice, might enhance spiritual growth.

creation. *See* cosmogony.

creationism, an American movement teaching that humanity was created by a discrete act—implicitly or explicitly divine—and did not evolve from other forms of animal life. Creationism, or creation science, emerged in the 1970s in the context of an upsurge of conservative Protestant sentiment in the United States. Attempts to mandate its teaching as a scientific alternative to evolution were passed by several state legislatures, particularly in the South. A series of court cases, especially the "Scopes II" decision rendered by a federal judge in Arkansas in 1982, undermined the movement's legal footing, and subsequent attempts at including creationist material in textbooks were often firmly resisted at the state level. *See also* Scopes trial.

creation out of nothing, a philosophical and theological concept of a deity creating out of the void in which it exists. There is no prior matter. Though prevalent in speculative traditions, the notion is rare in mythic materials. *See also* cosmogony.

creche (kresh; Fr., "manger," "crib"), an artistic representation of the birth of Jesus Christ. The tradition can be traced back to a creche erected in 1223 at Greccio, Italy, by Francis of Assisi. *See also* Christmas.

creed, a formal statement of fundamental beliefs. *See also* usul al-din.

Judaism: Neither the Hebrew Bible nor the talmudic literature presents encompassing creedal statements. Only in the tenth century, in response to internal pressure from the Karaite movement and corresponding to theological discussions then occurring within Islam, did Jewish thinkers begin to formulate statements on Jewish belief. Referred to as "obligations of the heart," "primary principles" (Heb. *hatkhaloht*), "cornerstones," and, most frequently, "foundational beliefs" (*ikkarim*), these creeds attempted to express comprehensively the content of Jewish belief.

Maimonides: Although not the earliest such formulation, the thirteen principles of Maimonides (1135–1204) are among the best known and most important of all Jewish creeds. Presented in the context of his commentary to Mishnah Sanhedrin, chapter 10, Maimonides's principles define the "epikoros" who, according to the Mishnah, has no share in the world to come. In the thirteen principles, Maimonides accordingly proposed to delineate the beliefs that are necessary and sufficient to assure an individual's salvation.

According to Maimonides, Judaism's fundamental principles are (1) God exists and (2) is uniquely unitary; (3) God is not corporeal and cannot be accurately described in anthropomorphic terms; (4) God is eternal and (5) alone is to be worshiped; (6) God designated prophets, (7) the greatest of whom was Moses, who (8) received the entire Torah; (9) the Torah cannot be abrogated or in any way altered; (10) God knows people's deeds and (11) rewards or punishes them as appropriate; (12) the Messiah will come, and (13) the dead will be resurrected.

Maimonides's thirteen principles became central in Judaism when, by about 1300, they were formulated as a hymn ("Yigdal"), which appears in almost all forms of the Jewish daily liturgy. By the mid-sixteenth century, these principles circulated in a clearly creedal formulation, introduced with the statement, "I believe with perfect faith that ..."

Crescas: Among the major critics of Maimonides's formulation, Hasdai Crescas (d. 1410) had the most enduring impact on the later development of Jewish creeds. Crescas defined the formulation of a creed as a philosophical task involving the logical ordering of beliefs so that basic axioms could yield secondary conceptions. Crescas additionally introduced the notion of intentionality, defining heretics not by what they believe but by the perceived source of their belief. A heretic holds beliefs, whether right or wrong, that are viewed as independent of the teachings of the Torah. According to Crescas, but contrary to Maimonides, one who understands one's beliefs to derive from the Torah cannot be called a heretic, even if those beliefs are in fact false.

At the foundation of Crescas's creed are the notions of God's (1) existence, (2) unity, and (3) incorporeality. Six pillars stand on these root principles: (1) God's knowledge of people's deeds, (2) divine providence, (3) God's omnipotence, (4) the appointment of prophets, (5) free will, and (6) the role of the Torah in assuring eternal happiness. These pillars lead to eight additional beliefs that Crescas sees as characteristic of Judaism but not fundamental: (1) God's creation of the world, (2) human immortality, (3) divine retribution, (4) resurrection, (5) the immutability of the Torah, (6) Moses as the greatest prophet, (7) the divine origin of priestly instruction, and (8) the coming of the Messiah.

Abravanel: Isaac Abravanel (1437–1508) devoted an entire treatise to the formulations of Jewish belief of Maimonides, Crescas, and Joseph Albo (ca. 1380–1444). Though he raised numerous objections to Maimonides's thirteen principles, Abravanel ultimately allied himself with Maimonides, defining heresy, for instance, on the basis of the content of one's belief without regard for the perceived source of the specific beliefs. At the same time, Abravanel broadly rejected the claim that any narrow selection of beliefs can accurately encompass the content of Judaism. He held, rather, that, because the Torah was divinely revealed, everything it contains must be accepted; no hierarchy of belief is possible. The rejection of any Jewish belief is heresy and denies the individual a place in the world to come.

Abravanel's unique attitude may result from his having composed it just two years after the expulsion of the Jews from Spain. The declaration that Jews must accept all aspects of Jewish belief possibly was intended to prevent any lessening of Jewish commitment. In Abravanel's view, Jews must accept the entirety of Judaism's beliefs, because all the tenets of Judaism have equally salvific value.

Modern Creeds: The modern period in the formulation of Jewish creeds was heralded by Moses Mendelssohn (1729–86), who argued that Judaism, unlike Christianity, contains no dogmas. Judaism's truths, rather, are identical with the eternal truths discoverable through reason, independent of revelation. These truths are (1) that God, who created and rules all things, is one; (2) that God knows all and metes out reward and punishment through natural and supernatural means; and (3) that God made his will known through scripture. In Mendelssohn's view, these truths, which represent the content of all natural religions, are to be distinguished from Judaism's ritual laws, the only part of Judaism that depends upon revelation rather than reason.

Affected by Immanuel Kant's critique of rational religion, later Jewish thinkers largely rejected Mendelssohn's approach. Reformers in particular have worked to offer clear guidance regarding the essential beliefs that derive from the writings of Judaism. By defining what Jews must believe, the reformers countered traditional Judaism, which focused rather upon the rituals that Jews must practice. For these thinkers, however, the concept that Judaism is an evolving religion has led to only broadly defined tenets, e.g., in the Reform movement's Pittsburgh Platform (1885), which defines Judaism as "ethical monotheism."

This approach stands in contrast to that of Orthodox thinkers, who continue to define Judaism through its ritual, as exemplified in the writing of Samson Raphael Hirsch (1808–88), the first spokesman for a modern Orthodoxy, who proposed that "the catechism of the Jew is his calendar." *See also* Samaritans.

Christianity: Although there are rudimentary creeds in the New Testament (1 Corinthians 8:6), the majority developed in the context of the baptismal liturgy, where candidates were expected to profess their faith before baptism. Other creeds came from church councils and were designed to serve as statements of orthodox faith against the heresies of the day. *See also* Apostles' Creed.

cremation, disposal of the dead by burning. Cremation and burial are the two most common methods of treating a corpse. *See also* afterlife; Hindu domestic ritual; ritual.

crisis cults. *See* revitalization movements.

criticism, higher, nineteenth-century term for literary and historical studies of the Bible, often used pejoratively by conservative Christians. *See also* Bible, interpretation of the Christian.

criticism, lower, nineteenth-century term for textual studies of the Bible. *See also* Bible, interpretation of the Christian.

cross. 1 A sign composed of the intersection of vertical and horizontal lines, variously depicted but widely employed in the history of religions to express the structure of the cosmos. 2 An instrument of execution, used by the Romans, reserved for the punishment of slaves and foreigners. Christian scriptures record the death of Jesus on the cross. Early Christians regarded the cross as an instrument of salvation and celebrated the mystery of God's compassionate incarnation. Early Christian writers interpreted the cross through the symbolism of Hellenistic and Hebraic traditions. They celebrated the cross of Christ as the cosmic tree, which centers creation; they compared the cross to a military banner, symbolizing Christ's power of redemption; and they read Hebrew scriptures in light of Christ's crucifixion, seeing references to trees and wood as prefigurements of the cross.

crozier (kroh'zhur), a staff carried by a Christian bishop as a sign of his pastoral authority.

crucifix, a representation of the Christian cross, frequently including an image of the crucified Jesus. *See also* cross.

crucifixion. 1 A mode of capital punishment by means of nailing, binding, or impaling on a cross. 2 The death of Jesus. *See also* cross.

Crusades, a series of Christian military expeditions (1096–1270), proclaimed by popes, to recover the Holy Land from Muslim control. Participants were promised a variety of temporal and spiritual rewards, including the remission of sins.

crystals, New Age ritual objects thought to contain or focus cosmic energy. Used in healing ceremonies or as protective amulets, quartz and other semiprecious stones are credited with restoring well-being, removing barriers to success, and stimulating visions because of their natural crystalline resonance or occult powers preserved from the primeval past. *See also* New Age movements.

cult (Lat. *cultus,* "adoration," "devotion," "veneration," or "worship"; *colere,* "to cultivate"), a collective veneration or worship, in anticipation of bettering life in this world or the next, in which the collectivity is defined and united by its common devotional practice.

Cult as Religion: For those traditional cultures

in which separate ideas of religion and society are not differentiated, cult is virtually synonymous with culture. Vestiges of this categorical synonymy remain in such larger-scale cultures as those of the Roman Republic, for which the ruler was also *pontifex maximus* (chief priest), traditional Islamic culture, and parts of Chinese Taoism and Confucianism and Japanese Shintoism. In this technical sense, cult always retains a nuance of collective practice or ritual over ideation or belief.

Cult as a Subspecies of Religion: For those cultures in which religion has become distinguished from society, preeminently in modern Western culture, "cult" is understood as a subspecies of religion. In these cases, in which distinct religious and social ideologies of authority are formulated, cults are popular religious practices devoted to a specialized aspect of a larger liturgical system or to a specific figure that is sanctioned by an inclusive religious institution, for example, the cult of the Sacred Heart, the cult of the saints in Roman Catholicism, or the veneration of relics of the Buddha in Theravada Buddhism.

Cult as a Negative Term: Groups that have departed from religiously or socially sanctioned practice or belief are properly designated as sects (sectarianism), a designation often confused with cult in contemporary usage. In these cases, cult is most often employed as a pejorative label for new religions.

Usage by Historians and Phenomenologists of Religion: Since the late nineteenth century, scholars in the history and phenomenology of religion have generally employed "cult" as a designation for the external forms of religious expression. In this usage, cult does not refer to some specialized aspect of religious practice but to the historical and cultural manifestations of the situationally transcendent sacred, the phenomenological essence that religion is presumed to be. The manifestations of the sacred in cultic practice include not only such practices as prayer, ordeals, purifications, festivals, and sacrifice, but also circumstances of place, time, and image.

In such studies, the cultic forms and practices are arrayed according to an assumed development from their primitive manifestations, wherein they are often compared with magic through the personalization of the sacred among the so-called higher religions, to the modern emphasis upon transpersonal religious experience.

While the sacred is always understood by such scholars as manifest in historically and culturally specific ways, the most authentic relationships to this presumed essence of religion are those least encumbered by the external trappings of cult. The emphasis upon an inward grace in distinction from its outward signs reveals an essentially Protestant cultural bias: one of the central characteristics of the Protestant Reformation was its fierce repudiation of such Roman Catholic practices as the cult of the saints.

Social Science Usage: Social scientists have attempted a more objective definition of "cult" as a religious grouping defined by typological rather than cultural and conceptual criteria. When used of primitive or preliterate religious systems, cult is a social type defined in contrast to modern or literate religious systems. When used of modern groups, cult designates an often nonexclusivistic social type tolerated by larger, established religions. In such social science typologies, cults are classified by their distinctiveness of practice, of mentality, or of geographical and social location with reference to dominant or normative religious systems. The distinctiveness of cults is characterized as their marginality, alienation, or anomie. Such deviance from the norm is generally explained by extraordinary social, economic, political, or intellectual circumstances with reference to an established religious system, which, as normative, requires no such explanation. Such typologization of cults as deviant religious groups has its basis in Western cultural concerns with theological orthodoxy and exclusive religious membership. These concerns may be contrasted, for example, with the tolerance and inclusivity associated with hierarchical social organizations such as may be found, for example, in Hinduism or Taoism.

Whether a subspecies of religion, the externalities of religious expression, or peripheral religious groups, cult has become the designation for nonnormative religious practice, at least in the West. Such definitions overlook collective practices as potential contributors to as well as protestors against existing religious systems. By overlooking the innovative aspects of cult, religious and social orthodoxies have contributed to the view that new religious movements are dangerous and unwelcome developments.

culture hero, scholarly term for a character found in oral traditions throughout the Americas, Africa, and Southeast Asia. The culture hero may take diverse forms and is often identified as a trickster. Most have proper names and distinct transformational abilities.

Great Hare is the culture hero of the Northeastern Algonquian; the Crow (northern Plains)

Detail of an ancient Mesopotamian cuneiform relief in Iraq.

talk of Old Man Coyote, the Cree of Wesucechak, and the Mandans (northern Plains) of Only Man. Saya is the culture hero of the Beaver Indians (western Canada), and for the Ojibwa (Great Lakes) it is Wunzh. Ananse is the spider-trickster of the Ashanti (Ghana).

Primarily a wanderer, the culture hero is able to talk with and transform living things into animals as well as change the shape of the landscape. In North and South America culture heroes often have fierce appetites for sex, food, and gambling. Some culture heroes may have animal siblings such as wolf or moose. For example, in many Northwest Coast tribes, the culture hero is a raven or a giant who puts on a raven coat. Raven steals fire, daylight, sun, and water. He also sets game animals free, kills monsters, and founds laws and ceremonies. *See also* Coyote.

Cumina religion (koo'mee-nah), a new movement among the African population in Jamaica. Singing, drumming, dancing, and jumping are the essential physical manifestations of religious ceremonies centered on ancestor reverence that take place at important moments in the life cycle. During the rituals, ancestral spirits possess and transform the participants, some of whom pay homage by speaking in tongues. *See also* Afro-Americans (Caribbean and South America), new religions among.

cuneiform (kyoo-nee'uh-form), the ancient Near Eastern writing system employed by the Sumerians, Babylonians, Akkadians, Hittites, and others. Cuneiform used patterns of wedge shapes to denote specific syllables. *See also* Ebla; Hittites; Mari; Mesopotamian religion.

curate, in the Roman Catholic and Anglican churches, a title for either the pastor or assistant pastor of a parish church.

curia, in Roman Catholicism, the complex of offices that provides administrative support for either the papacy or for a local bishop.

curing. *See* healing; medicine and religion; tobacco and hallucinogens.

curse, powerful verbal formula designed to direct misfortune against persons or things. *See also* anathema.

Cybele. *See* Attis; Magna Mater.

Cycladic religion. The distinctive religion of the Cyclades, a group of twenty-four islands in the Aegean Sea, above Crete, between mainland Greece and present-day Turkey. Although often influenced by its dominant neighbors, Asia Minor and Crete, in the Bronze Age (ca.

Cycladic Neolithic stone figure playing a musical instrument; from Cyprus.

Characteristic Cycladic marble statuette of a female figure (ca. 3000–2500 B.C.), possibly the goddess of death and regeneration, with the head as a schematized mask, the arms in rectangular shape, and an incised vulva. Usually thought of today as white, these statuettes were originally painted in bright colors.

2800–1200 B.C.) the Cyclades developed an autonomous culture and religion.

The religious practices of the period are very poorly documented. There are no written sources; the archaeological evidence does not help much. The few excavated habitations have yielded no identifiable shrines.

Our main source for religion of the Early Bronze Age is in the form of artifacts, most of them found in graves. Attention has focused on the "Cycladic idols," slender marble figures of varying sizes and degrees of stylization. The most abstract version (also the earliest) resembles a violin. More elaborate and naturalistic are the "Keros-Syros" figures. They depict females with slightly bent knees and arms folded on the chest. The pubic triangle is clearly indicated. Male figures are very rare but include male musicians—seated harpists and a standing flutist. Although the figures are now totally white, traces of pigment indicate that details such as eyes as well as facial makeup or tattoos were once painted.

The figures were found mostly in tombs, rarely in settlements. There are a few possible cult sites. At an apparently open site on Keros figurines had been deliberately broken as part of a ritual. The majority of the figures are small amulets. A larger variety (close to three feet, very few life-size) could have been figures for worship.

The female form most likely represents the image of a "mother goddess" who guarantees continuity of life and regeneration. The presence of the figurines both in tombs (as protection) or in settlements (for worship) can thus be easily explained. Most of the figures cannot stand on their own, but were made for lying on their backs. This fits grave use: the female is represented as asleep or dead.

Other cultic equipment also points to the female sphere. A class of terra-cotta objects is popularly known as "Cycladic Frying Pans" because of their resemblance to the modern utensil. They are shaped like a round dish with two small legs projecting at one side. It is difficult to see how they were used. They have no traces of burning (therefore they cannot have been used for cooking) and no means of suspension (therefore they could not have been hung on walls). Their incised decoration, always on the underside of the "pan," is their most striking feature: ships, fish, stars, and interconnected spirals, the latter probably representing the sea. Next to the legs, a pubic triangle is often incised. The Frying Pans are most likely cosmic symbols with special reference to the things important to the Cycladic seafarers: the sea, ships, and stars. The cosmic symbol is cast in a rounded female form, and the pubic triangle is probably a regenerative symbol. It is likely that these objects were offering vessels that contained agricultural products.

Another utensil, common in the Middle

Bronze Age (ca. 2000–1600 B.C.), is a clay pitcher with protruding nipples, decorated with plant or bird motifs, clearly a libation vessel cast in female form.

In the early and middle periods, religious expressions were dominated by a female divinity who ensured success in planting and fishing and regeneration in the afterlife.

The Minoan Period of the Cyclades (ca. 1600–1400 B.C.): By the beginning of the second millennium Crete became a formidable maritime power dominating the Aegean. Many scholars believe that Cycladic civilization retained its cultural and religious autonomy even when it was overpowered by the expanding power of Minoan Crete. A fundamental stratum remained purely Cycladic, but it was overlaid by the official religion of Minoan Crete, which was used to enforce cultural/political control over the Cyclades.

The strongest influence was felt by the island of Thera situated closest to Crete. It adopted Minoan type shrines, symbols, and cult equipment. Paintings show a strong influence of Minoan iconography. Most important among these is an image of a Minoan goddess seated on a Minoan type of structure. Other iconographical features of Minoan derivation are sacred horns and emblems of naval power such as ships' cabins rendered in stylized form in paintings.

Minoan religious features (paintings and a pillar crypt shrine) are attested also at Phylakopi on Melos. At Ayia Irini on Keos, female figures with Minoan-style dress have been found in a building taken to be a temple.

Minoan religion is notorious for its preoccupation with goddesses. Since the purely Cycladic religion also emphasized female divinities, the takeover of features of Minoan religion must have been relatively easy. At any rate there was a Minoan-Cycladic syncretism. Popular cult forms must have remained purely Cycladic, whereas the official religion became Minoanized.

The Mycenaean Period (ca. 1400–1200 B.C.): When the palatial system on Crete collapsed, the Cyclades were incorporated into the Mycenaean empire based on mainland Greece, resulting in a new syncretism.

Phylakopi on Melos has furnished a double shrine with benches and niches. On the benches were found Mycenaean-type figures and figurines, some male, some female, but placed on different benches, suggesting differentiation of genders within the shrine. Animal figurines and a figurine of a "smiting god" of the Near Eastern type also occur as well as a round stone placed at the intersection of the entrance axes of the two shrines. This shrine shows how strong the influence of Mycenaean religion was on one

Cycladic island. *See also* Minoan religion; Mycenaean religion.

cyclical time, the widespread notion that time is a repetitive structure moving from creation to destruction to new creation. It is often, but improperly, identified as characteristic of mythic thought, nature worship, and agricultural religions. *See also* ages of the world; new year festivals; yuga.

Cynicism (sin'ee-siz-em; from Gk. *kuon,* "dog"), a Greek philosophical movement composed of the followers of Antisthenes and Diogenes of Sinope (fourth century B.C.–A.D. sixth century). More a life-style than a philosophical system, Cynicism took its title from Diogenes's nickname, acquired by leading an unconventional life "according to nature." There was no fixed doctrine on what this was, but Cynics in general held that human unhappiness is the result of our bondage through ignorance, desire, and indulgence to the unnatural values fostered by conventional society. These lead us to seek precarious external goods such as wealth, health, and reputation. Happiness, therefore, is found in freedom from unnatural values, achieved through an inner struggle that aims at radical "self-sufficiency": an ascetic renunciation of conventional goods in favor of an independent life of virtuous action founded on self-examination. This is a life that is animal-like in needing nothing and godlike since lacking nothing.

Cynics favored action rather than theoretical argument, and since they saw the artificial constraints of society as the enemy, this tended toward deliberately shocking and antisocial extremes of speech and behavior; e.g., Peregrinus Proteus, a convert from Christianity, burned himself to death before the crowds of an Olympic festival. The Cynics aimed to liberate not only themselves but others by serving as "scouts and heralds of God."

Cyril of Alexandria (sir'uhl; ca. 375–444), early Christian controversialist. A representative of what would come to be called Monophysite Christology, he argued that Christ's divine and human aspects formed one indivisible nature. His chief opponents were the Nestorians. *See also* Monophysitism; Nestorianism.

Cyril of Jerusalem (sir'uhl; ca. 315–386), bishop of Christian Jerusalem, best known for his twenty-three lectures (the *Catecheses*) to adults in preparation for baptism, which are among the earliest sources for elaborated early Christian ritual.

A B C D E F 
G H I J K L
M N O P Q
R S T U V
W X Y & Z

daivas (day'vaz; Old Persian, "evil gods," "demons"), Iranian divinities opposed to the high god. A collective term for archaic Indo-European divinities, it was demonized by the Zoroastrian tradition. *See also* deva; Zoroastrianism.

dakini (dah'kee-nee; Skt.), a female spiritual being in Buddhist Tantrism. Two major types are mentioned, worldly *dakini*, representing non-Buddhist values, and supermundane dakini, who protect and convey the wisdom of enlightenment. Levels of supermundane dakinis include feminine embodiments of Buddhahood itself; their retinue of active manifestations; and their messengers, who may appear to people at any time. Dakinis are both purely spiritual beings revealed in visions and human women. They are frequently depicted as dancing in Tibetan iconography. *See also* Tantrism (Buddhism).

dakshina (dahk'sheen-uh; Skt.), a gift given to officiating Hindu priests for services rendered at a Vedic sacrifice. It was regarded as complementing the offerings to the gods. *See also* sacrifice; Veda, Vedism.

Dalai Lama (dahl'ee lahm'ah; Tibetan *dalai*, "ocean," suggesting oceanic goodness and wisdom; *lama*, "no one is superior to"), spiritual leader of Tibetan Buddhism, considered an emanation of Avalokiteshvara, an enlightened being who embodies the compassion of past, present, and future Buddhas. Each Dalai Lama, regarded as a reincarnation of the previous one, is identified through a combination of oracles, dreams, and visions.

The present and fourteenth Dalai Lama, born in eastern Tibet in 1935, has lived in exile in India since 1959, nine years after the Chinese takeover of Tibet. He received the Nobel Peace Prize in 1989 for peaceful efforts to preserve Tibetan culture in his homeland and among refugee communities. He has worked to democratize the Tibetan government in exile, and is considering new methods for choosing the next Dalai Lama. *See also* Buddhism (thought and ethics); Tibetan religions.

damnation, condemnation to everlasting punishment in the afterlife for sins committed while alive. *See also* afterlife; hell (Christianity); Day of Judgment (Islam); limbo; purgatory, the Roman Catholic.

Tenzin Gyatso (b. 1935), the fourteenth Dalai Lama, receiving the Nobel Peace Prize for his leadership in the peaceful resistance to the 1950 Chinese takeover of Tibet. He accepted the award from Egil Aarvik, chair of the Norwegian Nobel Committee, in Oslo, Norway, on December 10, 1989. In exile in India since 1959, the Dalai Lama has worked to preserve Tibetan Buddhist culture.

dance. In all human societies ideas and institutions are expressed through culturally appropriate affective behaviors such as dancing, singing, playing, orating, narrating, enacting, and reenacting. They are organized as rites, celebrations, spectacles, and entertainment. Through these activities a culture's intangibles are metamorphosed as tangible realities.

A dance performance demands both psychological and physical preparation. It can stimulate all the senses, especially visual, auditory, and kinesthetic. Dancers and observers are transformed through extraordinary uses of time, space, and energy that trigger neurochemical reactions and emotions.

Dance is an admirable vehicle to express and extend religion. As religion provides the rationale and sanctions for dance, so dance quickens religious ideas. Because dance performances are experientially potent, compelling, and memorable, both dancers and observers are spiritually empowered.

Dance in Myths: Dance is a major metaphor in many myths. In Hindu mythology the progenitor/destroyer of life is Shiva, the Lord of the

Tenth-century Chola-dynasty Tamilnadu bronze statue of the Hindu god Shiva as Nataraja (Skt., "lord of the dance"). Encircled by a ring of flames, Shivas's front right hand makes the gesture (*mudra*) "Fear not." His hair flows out in the form of the sacred river and goddess, Ganges, while his right foot crushes the dwarf Apasmarapurusha (Skt., "human ignorance"), Los Angeles County Museum of Art.

Dance. As Nataraja, the Cosmic Dancer, he uses movement to create cosmic harmony. To actualize Hindu mythology, the traditional temple dancers of India were formally trained to express adoration of Krishna, the eighth avatar of Vishnu. Classical Indian solo dances dramatize the milkmaid's love for Krishna, the divine cowherd. The expression of love is a metaphor for the devotee who seeks, awaits, and yields to the divine.

In Japan, the sun goddess Amaterasu, offended by the outrageous acts of her brother, hides in a cave, and the world becomes dark and plagued by evil spirits. To lure Amaterasu out of self-exile, the deities hang a mirror on a beautifully decorated tree, and the goddess Amano Uzume invents dance. When the deities laugh uproariously at her lewd but comical dancing, curious Amaterasu peeks out. She sees her radiant image in the mirror. Stepping out farther, she is captured by another deity who prevents her from returning to the now barricaded cave.

For the Hopi Indians of northern Arizona, the central myth is their emergence from below the earth to this, the fourth world. After emergence, the animal or plant first encountered becomes the eponym for a man, his sister, and her children, thus establishing matrilineal clans. The newly emerged clans promise Maasawu—Lord of the Earth, God of Life and Death—that they will accept the mission to provide moisture for the world. They also agree to be stewards of the sacred center of the world, the place of emergence (Grand Canyon) and the home of the deities (San Francisco Mountains).

To find ritual medicine for controlling moisture, the clans embark on a great diaspora. After returning from their quest each clan establishes a ceremonial society to provide ritual sanctions for the medicine. Each society, in turn, yearly presents a public ceremony. The ceremony is danced, promoting good thoughts and embodying prayer. The gestures, paraphernalia, clothing, and body paint add potency to the prayers. For the Mamzrau women's healing society the women's bare legs are painted as prayersticks; the prayers are literally danced.

Half of each year the *katsina* spirits, powerful interactive supernatural messengers, allow themselves to be embodied by ritually purified men who belong to the Katsina Society. As temporary vehicles for the katsina friends, the dancers enliven the earth and sky by their rhythmic movements. To lend one's body to a katsina friend is a profound experience, and dancers prepare themselves spiritually as well as instrumentally. During the remaining half of the year other ceremonial societies demonstrate their medicine with dances. The observers are not considered to be audience. As nondancing participants they must keep their focus on dance as religious work. The dances help this concentration by pleasing the observers—the dances may be beautiful, funny, or awe-inspiring. The dance work enjoins dancing and nondancing participants to be happy, have good thoughts, and think single-mindedly about moisture and harmony, with mental images of clouds and fertile cornfields.

Traditional Hawaii is a stratified society. Spiritual power (*mana*) is proportionate to an individual's status. The highest ranking of the aristocracy are revered, but their powers are feared by the commoners. A pleasing chant/dance that honors the aristocrats by recounting their exploits and genealogical credentials helps guarantee the aristocrats' benevolence. At the same time, the magic utterances and performances of chants/dances are enhanced by the aristocrats' powers and fertility. Magical chants/dances for engenderment are composed and performed for a royal child at birth as if generative potency were a fait accompli.

Chanters' and dancers' compositions and performances combine one to three levels of meaning: the evocative poetic image, the double entendre, and the esoteric "soul" that is known by a select few. In order to assume this awesome responsibility, the hula people are trained and initiated guild members with their own deities and altars.

In contrast, the Washo Indians of Nevada dance to honor a young woman after her menarche. Requiring no training, no rehearsing, the tight ring of side-by-side dancers circles slowly all night for this solemn yet joyous celebration. The dance's simplicity and mesmerizing quality refocus values of religious significance. In this egalitarian society, everyone has equal access to the divine and everyone in the community dances.

Among the San (Bushmen of the Kalahari Desert), the healing trance dancers are men who, in a single-file circle, shuffle determinedly with widened glazed eyes. Only some of the men achieve the trance necessary to be conduits for the spirits, and they are valuable as healers and religious models. Trancing comes with dedication but not necessarily by honing dancing skills. In contrast, the Bhutanese Buddhist priests practice to produce a polished performance. The wheeling masked dancers, who represent converted evil spirits, require great dexterity and balance.

Dance and Innovation: Religious dances vary in forms and styles. Some dances require special training and practice, while others are performed without training or rehearsing. Some are

Confucian dancers perform the Civil Dance at the National Confucian Academy, Seoul, South Korea.

by or for a selected group of persons only, while others are communal. Some are transmitted from one generation to the next with little variation, but many are newly composed or even improvised. All embody religious metaphors and transform the performers and the observers.

All societies are dynamically experienced. They are not static, reduplicated mindlessly, or untouched by contact with other societies. Both internal and external circumstances require continuous cultural reinvention. Societies are adept at finding ways to persevere. Because of the reintegration of religion and dance, many religious dances do not disappear. Dances are kept viable by retentions, reinterpretations, and transmutations.

For example, Arabic brotherhoods, such as those of the so-called whirling dervishes, apply pre-Islamic traditions to their expression of Islam. The most renowned of the contemporary dervish groups is that devoted to Rumi, the thirteenth-century Turkish poet and mystic. Their movements and use of space are profound religious metaphors. As an illustration, the outstretched arms, with right palm facing toward heaven and left palm facing toward the earth, form the words *la* and *lila* in Arabic script to represent the unity of God.

Ancient beliefs about *jinn* (spirits) continue in the Arab world. Upon hearing the signature drum rhythms of a jinn, individuals who are possessed by that spirit are powerless to resist dancing. Jinn are also formally honored. The Moroccan community of Jahjouka brotherhood produces an annual ritual dance-drama that features the dangerous female jinniya, Aisha Qandisha, who is danced by an adolescent boy. She interacts with a Pan figure, an unruly black goat-man, in a Dionysian dance prefigured in ancient Anatolia.

The raison d'etre of Pueblo dancing in New Mexico has been reinterpreted. Incorporating the Christian calendar, dances are scheduled on patron saints' days, Christmas, Epiphany, and Easter. Before the dances begin, a mass is conducted and the dancers are blessed at the altar. A processional from the church after mass to a shrine in the dance plaza and back to the church after the day of dancing allows an altar icon to watch the dances.

Yaqui Indians of Sonora, Mexico, and Arizona have syncretized Roman Catholicism with their traditional religion to create Yaqui Catholicism. Their major religious festival, that of the passion of Christ, encompasses the entire forty days of Lent. Performed as a morality play, it represents the struggle of good against evil.

Dancing masked figures called *chapayeka*, transmuted from pre-Christian figures into doltish Roman soldiers, are the dancing clowns among the forces of evil. Other pre-Christian figures are the Deer Dancer and his retinue, who, identified as forces of good and dedicated to the Virgin, help defy the forces of evil. The society of the *matachinis* was introduced by medieval Spanish clerics. As interpreted by the Yaqui, the matachinis represent the disciples of Christ who pay penance to the Virgin for having forsaken her son in the Garden of Gethsemane. Their European folk-derived dances are performed on the eves of Palm and Easter Sundays. Facing the altar, they dance for Mary, represented by an icon, their only relevant audience. Even when no other observers are present, the matachinis continue to dance late into the night.

Groups that depart from orthodoxy are catalyzed by charismatic leaders. The Shaking Quakers, or Shakers as they came to be known, followed Mother Ann Lee from England to North America in 1774. Dedicated to purity, expressed by chastity and simplicity, they established self-sufficient communities and waited for the millennium. In groups separated by gender, they danced their worship. For the first few years they danced with ecstasy and spoke in tongues, but later the dance exercises were subdued by strictly enforced choreographic figures.

The Japanese Dance for the Dead is held every summer to honor and entertain visiting ancestral souls. Brought by Japanese immigrants to Hawaii and California, the festival maintains old functions, but new ones are added. In America the Obon is a season of several weeks' duration instead of only one night. On successive weekends dancers go from courtyard to courtyard of temples and Young Men's Buddhist Associations to participate at sites where none of their own ancestors is enshrined. The serial festival attracts teams of visiting dancers who wear matching costumes and demonstrate group dance styles. Persons who are neither Japanese nor Buddhists are invited to attend, buy food and souvenirs, and sometimes join in the dancing. A 1990 Obon held on the pier in San Francisco attracted thousands of observers. Nevertheless, for those who honor deceased loved ones and for the priests who follow age-old rituals, the religious intent is intact.

Negative Attitudes toward Dance: Christianity is often held to be antithetical to dance. Only in sects that deviate from the mainstream or develop in non-European cultures is dance a part of Christian worship. Some argue that the sensuality of dance makes it an anathema to a tradition in which the flesh is denied. But there is nothing in the New Testament that explicitly forbids dancing, and the Old Testament sanctions it. Indeed, Psalm 149 is a reading in many Christian services, in which the prophet exhorts "Let them praise His name with dancing" (verse 3). A movement to do that has gradually emerged during the twentieth century. Perhaps the most renowned dancer to dance her worship publicly was Ruth St. Denis (d. 1968), who dreamed of establishing a "Church of Divine Dance." More recently, the first International Christian Dance and Movement Conference was held in Australia in 1988. Ecumenical in composition and philosophy, the weeklong gathering attracted four hundred Christians from ten countries. *See also* Amaterasu; Apsaras; devadasi; emergence; Ghost Dance; Hamatsa; Hinduism (performing arts); kachina/katsina; mudra; Nataraja; nembutsu odori; Obon; rain dance; ritual; Santeria; Shakers; Shiva; Sufism; Sun Dance, Sun Dance religion.

danka system (dan-kuh), the system, established in 1635, that required all Japanese to register at a Buddhist temple to ensure that they were not Christians. The system was successively strengthened so that temples were responsible for registering marriages, conducting funerals and memorial services, and performing various bureaucratic tasks. In return, parishioners (Jap. *danka*) were required to make contributions to the temple, visit it on certain days, and employ its priests to perform specified rituals. People had little say about which temple they belonged to and could not easily switch temples if their beliefs changed. Although the system was abolished in the late nineteenth century, Japanese families are often affiliated with certain temples that they expect to perform funerals, in many cases, having few other connections to the temple. As a result, such practices were referred to as "funerary Buddhism" (*soshiki Bukkyo*). *See also* Japanese religion.

Dar al-Islam (dahr ul-is-lam'; Arab.,"abode of Islam"), the Islamic world or, more narrowly, those territories guided by Islamic law. The term *islam* is derived from the Arabic word for peace, protection, and security. Islam is a system that promotes social justice and, as a result, is believed to guarantee social solidarity and political stability. The abode of Islam, therefore, connotes the positive conditions enjoyed by those who accept Islam. It is contrasted with the *Dar al-Harb* (abode of war), territories not guided by Islamic law and therefore in constant turmoil.

This terminology is based on tradition, rather than scripture, and is closely related to Muslims' duty to expend all efforts to spread Islam. The terms *Dar al-Islam* and Dar al-Harb are most frequently found in medieval legal texts debating proper relations of the Islamic state with neighboring territories: whether or not to declare war, under what conditions to conclude a truce, etc. The application of this terminology varied with historical circumstances. It generally referred to those areas that either implemented Islamic law; protected the rights of Muslims and their client communities, such as Jews and Christians; and/or did not interfere with Muslims' implementation of Islamic law or practice. Its use had all but disappeared until its revival by some of the more militant contemporary Islamic activists. *See also* Islamic law; Islamic political theory.

Darby, John Nelson (1800–1882), early member of the radical Christian reformist group, the Plymouth Brethren. In 1847, Darby split and became leader of a stricter group of Brethren called Darbyites. Darby's dispensationalist teachings, his criticism of established churches, and his program of regular Bible study have had deep influence on twentieth-century American Protestant fundamentalism. *See also* dispensationalism; fundamentalism.

darshana (Buddhism) (dahr'shuh-nuh; Skt., "vision"), a religious experience or state of awareness in the forms of a vision: a pilgrim's vision of a holy site, a practitioner's vision of a celestial Buddha or Bodhisattva, or a philosopher's analysis of the Buddha's insight. *See also* Buddhism (thought and ethics).

darshana (Hinduism) (duhr'shuh-nuh; Skt., "seeing," "viewpoint"). 1 The viewing of an icon in Hindu worship. 2 In Hinduism, a philosophical system. *See also* Hinduism (worship); images, veneration of; six systems of Indian philosophy.

Dasam Granth (duh'suhm gruhnth; Punjabi or Hindi, "the book of the tenth [Guru]"), the volume of Sikh works attributed to Guru Gobind Singh collected after his death in 1708. Much of it appears to have been written by his followers. *See also* Adi Granth; Sikhism; Sikhism (authoritative texts).

datura (deh-toor'eh; Nahuatl and Span.), jimson weed or thorn apple, used for medicinal and ritual purposes by indigenous peoples from Andean South America north through the Great Plains of

North America. These plants are toxic and psychoactive when ingested, due to large concentrations of scopolamine, atropine, and other alkaloids. Their hallucinogenic properties have been exploited to induce or intensify trance by, for example, Aztec priests and diviners, shamans in the southwestern United States, and in the rites of initiatory cults in native central and southern California. *See also* psychoactive plants; tobacco and hallucinogens.

daven (dah'vuhn; Yiddish, "to pray"), in Judaism, a traditionalistic prayer mode involving highly personal rote recital of prayers *sotto voce*, often while swaying back and forth. *See also* Judaism, prayer and liturgy of.

David, in the Hebrew Bible, king of Israel and Judea, founder of the Judean royal dynasty. In Jewish and Christian tradition, the Messiah will be from the lineage of David. *See also* Messiah.

Davidian Seventh-Day Adventist Association. *See* Branch Davidians.

Day of Judgment (Islam) (Arab. *Yawm al-Akhira*), a Muslim eschatological term for the time of final recompense. The Qur'an affirms that all people will be judged for their beliefs and actions in the world. On the Day of Judgment, signaling the

end of human history, resurrected bodies will appear before God for consignment to eternal bliss in the gardens of paradise or damnation in the fires of hell.

dead, rituals with respect to the. Most religious traditions have means for disposing of the corpse (most commonly by burial or cremation) or preserving it, depending on a particular tradition's view of the afterlife; methods for purification from corpse pollution; rites to protect the living from the return of the dead, including means of guiding the spirits of the dead to their proper place; and procedures for the care and feeding of the dead, for their commemoration and memorialization. *See also* afterlife; ancestral rites; Buddhism (life cycle); burial; Canaanite religion; Chinese religions (life cycle); Christianity (life cycle); cremation; death; Etruscan religion; Garifuna religion; Hindu domestic ritual; Islam (life cycle); Judaism (life cycle); life-cycle rituals; ritual.

Dead Sea Scrolls. *See* Qumran.

death, the cessation of ordinary human existence. Questions concerning the origin of death and the destiny of the dead, as well as rituals regarding the dead, are elements in all religious traditions. *See also* afterlife; afterworld; body;

A Sisala tribal funeral in Tumu, northwest Ghana (1976). In the foreground is the large funerary stool, made more than sixty years ago, on which is displayed a cloth assemblage serving as a surrogate corpse for most of the ritual activities.

dead, rituals with respect to the; life-cycle rituals; resurrection; soul.

Islam: In Islam, death is the common destiny willed by God for all living things. Death is a transitory state for human beings between worldly existence and eternal life.

The onset of death is traditionally conceived in terms of a personal encounter with an angel of death dispatched by God. Prevailing Islamic doctrine conceives of death as an agonizing disengagement of the soul from the body, the outward sign of which is the cessation of breathing. This event marks the end of the predetermined period of mundane life that is to be accounted for at the last judgment, the Day of Judgment, when body and soul are again reunited and resurrected for consignment to the splendid gardens of paradise or the torturous fires of hell. Between death and resurrection, individuals are subjected to a preliminary trial in the grave by the angels Munkar and Nakir and given a preview of their destiny in the hereafter. Prophets, saints, and martyrs acquire special status in the afterlife, which includes the power to convey blessing and intercede on behalf of the living. Such beliefs have prevailed in most Sunni and Shiite communities, but occasionally they have had to contend with dissenting doctrines of transmigration, reincarnation, denial of bodily resurrection, and philosophical refutations.

Islamic jurisprudence sets guidelines for funerary and mourning practices. In general, these require that the body be completely cleansed with water and wrapped in a shroud. Men promptly perform funerary prayers in the presence of the body, usually at a nearby mosque, then convey it to the cemetery, where it should be buried in a freshly dug, unembellished grave, facing toward the Kaaba. Burial at sea is permitted only if it is unavoidable, and prayers should be said even when the body has not been recovered. Martyrs are interred unwashed in their bloodstained garments, without funerary prayers. People should mourn in dignified calm for only three days because death should be accepted as the result of God's will. The living are advised to visit cemeteries to remain mindful of God and their common destiny.

Actual Muslim funerary beliefs and practices commonly differ from guidelines set forth by jurists, however. Besides being an expression of God's will, death is seen as a contagious threat to household prosperity, emanating from forces of envy and malevolent spirits that need to be repelled.

Local cosmographies of the afterlife sometimes diverge quite markedly from normative Islamic ones. Muslims from North Africa to Indonesia have customarily interred the dead in elaborate tombs and mausoleums and performed sacrifices and offering rites for the benefit of the deceased. Mourning routinely entails displays of profound grief, especially by women, and extends from three days up to a year. People visit the tombs of the "very special dead" to seek their blessing and support in confronting worldly problems. *See also* Day of Judgment (Islam).

Japanese Buddhist: Funerary rites are conducted by a family with the assistance of a Buddhist priest in order to transform the deceased into an ancestor. The family washes the body and lays it out with the head to the north, a taboo in ordinary life. The household "god shelf" (Jap. *kamidana*) is covered to prevent pollution. When the coffin is ready, the body is placed in it, dressed as if for travel, and the coffin becomes part of an altar before which a priest chants a formal service. For this, family, friends, and associates of the family offer incense to the deceased. After being opened for a last view of the body, the coffin is nailed shut with blows of a stone from each family member. The body is then taken to a crematorium in an elaborate hearse. After cremation, the family members pick out the remaining bones, put them in an urn, and take this home until interment. From then on, the deceased is represented in ancestral rites by a mortuary tablet inscribed with a posthumous Buddha-name and placed in the home Buddhist altar (*butsudan*). The traditional mourning period is forty-nine days.

Japanese conceptions of death are more notable for their variety than their commonality. This is represented not only by the move from early burial practices to later cremation practices, but in the variety of religions that have contributed to these conceptions. Some common beliefs, however, are that death is a transition into another state of being—whether as a spirit that can annually be called back or honored, or as an occupant of the land of the dead beyond the sea or in the mountains (early Shinto), or as a being reborn in some Buddhist hell or paradise.

Decalogue. *See* Ten Commandments.

deconstruction, a literary-critical and philosophical approach that holds that language does not have any transcendental meaning. Deconstruction evolves out of the post-Nietzschean discussion of the end to metaphysics and refers especially to the poststructuralist and postphenomenological expressions of that discussion.

Deconstruction is a philosophical critique of language as a medium for determinate meaning and thereby is a denial of epistemological certainty. According to the deconstructionist view, language does not have any transcendental meaning, that is, to any set of referents external to language itself, but refers rather to other signs within its own linguistic system. Linguistic signs have meaning in their difference from and hence in relation to the other signs within that system. Rather than seeing language as reflecting or expressing experience, deconstructionists understand language as an autonomous system of self-referential signs constituting and articulating experience and mediating comprehension and cognition. Meaning, in this view, is nonfoundational, deferred from linguistic sign to sign, and finally absent.

Based upon the linguistic deferral of meaning, deconstruction is a recognition of linguistic conceptions as historical constructs. All disciplines are understood to be rhetorical systems, discursive formations with their own history. Any context or any system of reference that might clarify the meaning of a particular text is itself understood to be a construct of history. Deconstruction, then, is a rejection of the controlling nature of language, of the repression of rhetoric that constitutes inherited modes of thought and dominant ideologies.

dedication. *See* consecration.

Deer Park, in Buddhism the site in northern India, near the city of Varanasi (Banaras), where the Buddha is said to have preached his first sermon. *See also* Bodh Gaya; Buddhas.

defilement. *See* purity and impurity.

Degenerate Age of the Dharma (Chin. *mo-fa;* Jap. *mappo*), the third and final period in the mythic history of Buddhism, after which the Buddhist community is expected to die out. The belief that two distinct historical periods—the "Age of the Good Dharma" and the "Age of the Reflection of the Good Dharma"—would follow the death of Sakyamuni Buddha seems to have gained currency in Indian Buddhism no later than the first century. The idea of a third "Degenerate" Age, however, is known only in East Asia. The duration of the first two periods varies from five hundred to a thousand years each; the third period is generally considered to last for ten thousand years and more. Because East Asian Buddhists believed that the Degenerate Age had begun as early as 552, a major issue in East Asian Buddhism was the necessity of finding an optimal way of practicing the Buddha's teachings during this age of limited human capacities and adverse environmental conditions. This idea was particularly influential in the Chinese T'ien-t'ai and Pure Land schools, and in Japanese Tendai, Pure Land, and Nichiren Buddhism. *See also* ages of the world; Buddhism; mappo; Nichiren; Pure Land; Tendai school; T'ien-t'ai school.

deification, the elevation of a human to the rank of a god. It is most commonly achieved after death. *See also* afterlife; apotheosis; Caitanya; euhemerism; Lao-chun; Lao-tzu; Li Hung.

Deima Church (dy'mah; "holy water"), a church established in 1942 by Marie Lalou (1915–51) in the Ivory Coast. Inspired by a series of dreams, she dedicated herself to spreading Christian teachings and healing the sick. The Deima Church prohibited traditional religious practices and forced marriages of women and offered protection against witchcraft. *See also* Africa, new religions in.

Deism, a Christian theological position that asserts that God is the creator of the universe, but does not thereafter exert providential or sovereign control over it. Developed first in England in the late sixteenth century and in France in the eighteenth century, it was an outgrowth of the thinking that propounded natural religion, which was juxtaposed to traditional Christian support of the notion of revealed religion.

The influence of Deism was greater in France and Germany than it was in England. In the United States, some of the drafters of the Constitution, particularly Thomas Jefferson and Benjamin Franklin, were deists. The rise of Deism spurred such counterdevelopments as Pietism, which emphasized religious feeling as being of greater import than right thinking, thus deemphasizing the importance of reason in religion and thereby discounting the thinking of persons such as the deists. *See also* natural religion.

deity (Lat. *deus,* "god"), general term for a god or goddess; in modern Indo-European languages, a synonym for god. In Western semipopular and philosophical usage "the Deity" often denotes the monotheistic God, with "deities" signifying a plurality of polytheistic gods.

Delaware prophets, a series of religious leaders who were active in the Native American Delaware tribe ca. 1745 to 1805. Four of the six known figures—Papounhan (whose career may have begun in 1752), Neolin, the "old priest," and Wangomen—were active during the decade of the 1760s, when the Delaware had been displaced from their eastern homelands to the Allegheny and Ohio River valleys and were caught up in the conflict between the French and the British. The impact of Neolin, in particular, extended beyond his own tribe to the Shawnee, Ottawa, and other tribes in the Ohio country.

All claimed to have had a visionary encounter with a deity that directed and shaped their religious activities. The underlying theme of their various messages was that the present hardships suffered by Native Americans were the result of their having been corrupted by elements of European culture, especially liquor, and that the remedy lay in a return to some version of the old tribal ways. Neolin promised that the Master of Life would send a plentiful supply of game animals once his people abandoned white ways and made certain reforms in their social structure, including the abolition of polygamy and cessation of "the medicine song"—an apparent reference to witchcraft. Missionary reports indicate that Papounhan's preaching transformed his village into an orderly and sober settlement.

The "old priest," Neolin, and Wangomen all made use of a so-called Indian bible. Descriptions of Neolin's "book" indicate that it was a chart showing the physical relationship of earth, heaven, and hell and revealing that the Europeans had blocked the Native Americans' old, easy path to heaven. Neolin sold copies of his chart to his followers for one buckskin or two doeskins each. The "old priest" is reported to have read "like mad" from his "book" every morning; its content is not known. In addition, Neolin claimed that the Master of Life gave him a stick, upon which symbols representing a prayer were carved, and instructed him to have the people repeat this prayer morning and evening. Kenekuk, the Kickapoo prophet, used similar diagrams and prayersticks fifty years later.

The last known figure in this series of Delaware prophets was a Munsee (subgroup of the Delaware) woman whose visions formed the basis for a new religious ceremony, the Big House. *See also* Big House movement; Native Americans (North America), new religions among; Neolin; prophecy in traditional religions.

Delphi (del'fi), a Greek city near Mt. Parnassos and site of Apollo's oracle, considered by some ancients the center of the earth. The sanctuary held temples, a theater, and a stadium where the Pythian games occurred every four years. The Pythia (priestess) sat on a tripod uttering prophecies inspired by the god. *See also* Greek religion; oracle.

deluge. *See* flood stories.

Demiurge, the Gnostic derogatory term (derived from Plato's *Timaeus*) for the creator God of biblical tradition. *See also* Gnosticism.

Democritus (dem-ahk'ri-tuhs; ca. 460–360 B.C.), a Greek philosopher from Abdera; only fragments of his work remain. Like other atomists, Democritus identified atoms with "what is," the void as "what is not," yet insisted that void existed. Invisible atoms move through void, colliding and temporarily forming macroscopic objects. Spherical soul atoms are spread throughout and control the body. Atomic images of divinity surround us. Because all nature is governed by necessity, the fundamental ethical good derives not from will, but from a soul undisturbed by fear or other emotion.

demon (Gk. *daimon,* "power"), a superhuman being midway between humans and gods. The category can include both beneficent and maleficent beings. *See also* angel.

Hinduism: Hindu demons belong, like Hindu humans, to many different castes, and some are hard to tell from Hindu gods. In the *Rig Veda,* the Sanskrit term *asura* (from *asu,* "life") designates a certain group of gods. But in later Hinduism, asura comes to mean antigod, and the term *sura* is coined for "god," as if the initial letter of asura were a privative. Thus, the Vedic gods become post-Vedic demons. Other Vedic families of antigods are the *daityas* (sons of Diti) and *danavas* (sons of Danu, of whom Vritra, enemy of Indra, stands out).

Below these celestial demons are earthbound demons who are antihuman, more precisely anti-Brahman; they steal or defile the sacrifice and plague human sacrificers. These "night-wanderers" include the *rakshasas* (most famous is Ravana, enemy of Rama) and *pishachas* (flesh-eaters). Demons mirror the four human classes (there are Brahman asuras and Brahman rakshasas) and mirror human behavior. Three of the eight classical forms of marriage in *dharma* texts (Dharma sutras and Dharma shustras) are named after the asuras, rakshasas, and pishachas. There are also *yakshas* (mischievous, transformative genies) and *guhyakas* (mountain goblins).

Some demons pose a moral dilemma: they

are "good" in terms of ethical standards that transcend caste law—they may offer sacrifice (to the Vedic gods, their enemies), or engage in ascetic heat (*tapas*), renunciation (*sannyasa*), or devotion (*bhakti*) to a particular god. But they are "bad" in terms of their demonic caste, which dictates that they should steal and kill. Prahlada (a role-model for Mahatma Gandhi) and Bali are exemplary "good" demons. *See also* asura; caste; guardian deities, Hindu; yaksha.

Japanese Religion: Japanese demonology is extensive. In myth, the aboriginal inhabitants of Japan were demonized as "earth-spiders," while a number of "unruly deities" were either placated or exorcised, a practice institutionalized in Shinto ritual. Folk religion knows especially the *yamauba* (or *yamamba*, "mountain hag") who preys upon children to slake her cannibalistic appetites. The related Amanokaju especially preys upon young women. The *tengu* is a phallic demon with a red face and long nose, while the generic *oni* (demon) may work any kind of mischief. Demons are fierce, ugly, and foul-smelling in their true appearance, although many can take any convenient temporary shape. They usually inhabit lonely places, especially mountains. Buddhist temple guardians often are demonic in appearance. *See also* cosmology; insects (Japan); Japanese folk religion; Japanese myth.

demonic possession. *See* possession.

demythologization, a method of interpretation practiced by Christian theologian Rudolf Bultmann (1884–1976) to free the New Testament of first-century mythical concepts and discern its essential message (Gk. *kerygma*). As a theologian, Bultmann affirmed that Christianity is based on the Christ of faith and not on the Jesus of history. As a German pastor, he was concerned that the essential proclamation of that faith be preached in ways that twentieth-century persons could appropriate. Thus, demythologization entailed eliminating such prescientific concepts as a three-story universe (sky, earth, and underworld) and miraculous healings and replacing them with contemporary concepts. *See also* Bible, interpretation of the Christian; Bultmann, Rudolf; exegesis.

Denkart (deen'kahrt; Pahlavi, "established religion"), ninth-century Pahlavi encyclopedic text in nine books containing a summary of Sassanid Zoroastrian orthodoxy. *See also* Sassanids; Zoroastrianism.

depravity. *See* original sin (Christianity).

deprogramming, the practice of intensive counterindoctrination or information-giving aimed at convincing a devotee to relinquish a commitment to a religious group. Coercive deprogramming involves forcible abduction and confinement of the devotee. In the 1970s, such actions were often legalized through temporary conservatorships or guardianships granted to parents of devotees by judges. Such court orders were less frequent in the 1980s.

descent of the Spirit. *See* Pentecost.

descent to Hades, Christian tradition that Jesus, between his death and resurrection, rescued those who died prior to his coming. Some Christian writings emphasize the descent as demonstrating Christ's victory over Satan. *See also* harrowing of Hell.

descent to the underworld, widespread mythic motif of a deity, hero, or other individual journeying to the realm of the dead. In some traditions, there is no escape; in others, there is either a triumph over the powers of death or a partial freedom that allows the figure to spend part of the year among the living and part among the dead. *See also* Adonis; descent to Hades; journey to the otherworld; Kore; Orpheus; Orpheus stories in traditional religions.

destiny. *See* fate.

determinism. *See* fate; free will.

deutero-canonical. *See* Apocrypha; pseudepigrapha.

deva (day'vuh; Skt., "god"), the standard term for a deity in Vedic and later India, especially a celestial divinity. *See also* asura; devayana/pitriyana; Veda, Vedism.

devadasi (day-vuh-dah'see; Skt., "female servant of the deity"), in India, a dwindling institution of women dedicated to temple service who danced and sang in the daily ritual, remained unmarried but sexually active, and embodied auspiciousness. *See also* auspicious, inauspicious (Hinduism).

devayana/pitriyana (day'vuh-yah-nuh/pi'tuhr-yah-nuh; Skt., "path of the gods"/"path of the ancestors"), in the early Vedas of ancient India the paths to and from the world of the gods, also the route of sacrificial offerings, and the path of Death to and from the world of ancestors or "Fathers." Later Vedic texts describe two routes for the self after death of the body: certain ascetics and knowers of the mystical identity of self (*atman*) and absolute (*brahman*) go by way of the moon to the world(s) of the gods and do not return; performers of sacrifices and good works join the ancestors and then return from moon to earth to be reborn as humans, animals, or lower forms of life according to their *karma*. *See also* afterworld; ancestors; cosmology; karma; liberation.

devekut (dev-eh-koot'; Heb., "attachment," "communion," or "union"), term used in Judaism to refer to adhering or holding fast to God.

The biblical injunction to cleave to God was interpreted in various ways by rabbinic authorities. Two main lines of orientation may be distinguished: either adhering or cleaving to God is interpreted in terms of performing pious deeds, or the injunction is to be taken literally, i.e., cleaving to God involves intimate contact.

Philosophy and Mysticism: In medieval philosophical and mystical sources the term *devekut* took on new meanings. In the case of the former, we may further distinguish between an Aristotelian and a Neoplatonic usage. Under the influence of Aristotelian epistemology, devekut was used to indicate a state of intellective conjunction. In this state the perfected intellect is identified with the agent intellect, though not completely united with it. By contrast, for Jewish Neoplatonists devekut denoted the state of union between the human intellect and Mind (*Nous*), the second hypostasis that emanates out of the One. In some cases devekut is also used to indicate union of the human soul and the World Soul, the third hypostasis in the ontological chain.

The philosophical usages influenced the mystical literature, where devekut refers to a unitive experience between the soul or intellect and the divine Thought. This sense was promulgated, e.g., by Isaac the Blind, the Provencal kabbalist, and by his disciples, the Geronese kabbalists Ezra ben Solomon and Azriel ben Menahem, active in the first half of the thirteenth century. Specifically, prayer was treated by these theosophic kabbalists as a contemplative ascent of the soul resulting in the cleaving of thought (*mahshavah ha-deveqah*) to its supernal source, the divine mind. The function of devekut had a decided theurgical connotation as well, insofar as the cleaving to the higher entities in the divine realm facilitated the descent of these powers to benefit the lower world. Still other medieval kabbalists, such as

Nahmanides and the author of the *Zohar*, emphasized that the object of devekut was not the highest emanations but rather the last of them, i.e., the divine Presence (Shekhina), the feminine aspect of God. An important feature of communion with God, which had a profound influence on subsequent mystical and pietistic literature, was expressed by Nahmanides in his commentary on the biblical injunction to cleave to God in Deuteronomy 11:22. Nahmanides emphasized that one must perpetually cleave to God even in such mundane acts as walking, sleeping, or rising. Even social contact should be an occasion for devekut. Another distinctive use of devekut can be found in the ecstatic kabbalah of the thirteenth-century Spanish mystic Abraham Abulafia and his disciples. In this case the Aristotelian model was critical, for Abulafia characterized the mystical experience as the union of the human intellect with the agent intellect or even with God. Abulafia promulgated specific techniques to induce the separation of the intellect from the body resulting in a state in which any barrier separating the mind and the divine intellect is broken down. These techniques consisted of letter-combinations, breathing, chanting, and various meditative postures. Another important kabbalistic aspect of devekut is the notion of cleaving to God by means of contemplating the letters of the divine name with the mind's eye.

Hasidism: The concept of devekut in all its varied nuances continued to have a profound influence on Jewish mysticism, culminating with the widespread use of this term in the Hasidic literature of the eighteenth and nineteenth centuries. From one perspective there is a popularization of the idea of devekut in Hasidism, for communion with God is held out as an ideal for all people. To achieve that end Hasidism taught that any mundane act, even if profane, can become a means for attaining a state of cleaving to God. On the other hand, the Hasidic masters often made a distinction between different types of devekut, with some reserved only for the spiritual elite. *See also* Hasidism; Judaism (mysticism).

devil. *See* demon.

Devil. *See* Satan.

devil's advocate, a once popular name for the person who argued against, or investigated arguments against, a person's being considered for canonization as a saint in the Roman Catholic Church. This office is also called the "Promoter of the Faith."

devil worship. *See* Satanism.

devil worshipers, a derogatory term for the Yezidis. *See also* Yezidis.

Devi Mahatmyam (day'vee muh-haht'm*i*-ahm; Skt., "The Glorification of the Goddess"), Sanskrit text also known as *Durga Saptashati* (Seven Hundred [Verses] to Durga). Its narrative and hymns comprise the earliest comprehensive textual account of the Hindu goddess Durga (sixth century). *See also* Durga; Goddess (Hinduism).

devotio moderna. *See* Ruusbruec, Jan van.

devotion. 1 In ancient Roman religion, the dedicating of an individual to a destructive deity. 2 In general religious discourse, the practice of withdrawal from worldly concerns in order to contemplate divinity.

devotion (Buddhism). Strong feelings of piety toward the objects of Buddhist worship play an important part in cultic practices throughout the Buddhist world. Although Buddhism is technically a nontheistic religion, the religious life of a practicing Buddhist includes many explicit acts of reverence before sacred objects, as well as clear statements and gestures of intense religious emotion.

Early Forms: The earliest Buddhist cult included the age-old Indian customs of prostration, and salutation with the palms of the hands joined. Worship was directed at objects symbolic of the Buddha's presence or ministry: the Tree of Enlightenment, the Buddha's footprint, the Wheel of Dharma, and relics of the Buddha Sakyamuni, one of his immediate disciples, or a former Buddha. Buddhist worship belongs to the general Indian concept of *puja* (Skt.), a term that may be translated as "worship" or "devout offering," but that concretely refers to the pious presentation of offerings before representations of divinity. Mahayana scriptures often list the articles offered in an act of puja, including the traditional Indian offerings of incense, flowers, banners, and parasols. These practices appear in reliefs found in the earliest Buddhist monuments. The faithful offered garlands of flowers and traveled in pilgrimages to distant sites where some symbolic trace of Buddhahood remained.

Developments in Mahayana: Although the cult of relics and *stupas* (reliquary mounds) continued to be an important focus of Buddhist devotion, the appearance of Buddha images in the first and second centuries marked the beginning of a more personal conception of the sacred object of veneration. Eventually, partly under the influence of the Bhakti movement that spread over India in the fifth and sixth centuries, personal devotion to Buddhas and Bodhisattvas became a common element of Buddhist worship. By the second half of the seventh century, Buddhism, especially Mahayana, had developed a complex liturgy, and its literature attested to the greater emotional intensity of Buddhist worship. Litanies to Avalokiteshvara that sang of his miraculous interventions to save living beings were probably chanted at the shrines where the faithful came to ask for assistance before the image of the savior Bodhisattva. Even highly abstract notions such as emptiness could be the object of devotional hymns, as in Rahulabhadra's hymn to the Perfection of Wisdom.

With increased devotion came a greater emphasis on faith and on the saving powers of Buddhas and Bodhisattvas. Although the Buddhist ethic of self-effort remained, reliance on the power of celestial Buddhas and Bodhisattvas became the most popular belief.

East Asia: Buddhism in East Asia continued many of the practices of Indian Buddhism: pilgrimage, cult of the relics, faith in the Bodhisattvas. Hope of rebirth in the Pure Land, through the grace of Amitabha, developed into one of the most influential beliefs in East Asia. In China, the recitation of the name of Amitabha became the common ground for popular devotion and monastic meditation. The chanting of short sacred texts (*sutras*), especially at major pilgrimage sites in the cult of Avalokiteshvara (Chin. *Kuan-yin;* Jap. *Kannon*), also marks popular devotion throughout East Asia. *See also* Bodhisattvas; Buddhism; Buddhism (festal cycle).

Dhammapada (daham-mah-pah'dah; Pali, "Dhamma Verses" or "footsteps of Dhamma"), Buddhist verse anthology containing 423 stanzas on a variety of topics; some are doctrinal, but many are gnomic or moral verses. It is often considered, especially in the West and in Theravada countries, one of the most representative Buddhist texts, although it contains many stanzas found elsewhere in non-Buddhist Indian literature and barely touches on some of the central doctrines and beliefs of Buddhism. Its popularity in antiquity, however, seems attested by the number of recensions that have survived in different Buddhist languages, including Pali, "Hybrid" Sanskrit, Gandhari, Prakrit, and classical Sanskrit. *See also* Buddhism (authoritative texts and their interpretation); Dharma/dharma.

dharma (dahr'muh; Skt.), in classical Hinduism the

action a person should do to "maintain" or "uphold" the proper functioning of the world and everything in it for the welfare of its inhabitants. Kinds of dharmic action include (1) the wide variety of ritual actions that are sanctioned by Brahmans, the Hindu priestly class; (2) the duties, observances, and customs proper to the different kinds of people in India (*varnadharma*, class dharma; *svadharma*, personal dharma); and (3) broad ethical principles common to all people (*samanyadharma*), such as proscriptions of lying and stealing and prescriptions of virtues like self-control and forbearance.

Throughout the history of Brahmanic thought, Brahmans have undertaken repeatedly to state dharma more or less exhaustively in various types of compendia (Dharmasutras, Dharmasmritis, *nibandhas*) and, in the influential philosophical school of Purva Mimamsa (or Karma Mimamsa, "exegesis of the Veda to determine right action"), to ground the idea of dharma critically in a philosophy of Vedic revelation and Brahmanic culture. As this philosophical school recognizes, authority within the Brahmanic tradition is distributed among all communities of Brahmans with a grounding in Vedic tradition. Thus, the dharma even of learned Brahmans varies frequently between regions and between different Brahman *jatis*, or subcastes.

Dharma was recognized as varying further according to the four ages (*yugas*) of cosmic time, in which it declines, and the four phases of individual life (*ashramadharma*): adolescent studentship; responsible adult "householding"; retirement (in old age) from mundane responsibilities for study, meditation, and asceticism; and finally a life of complete renunciation in pursuit of liberation (*moksha*).

The term *dharma*, with the meaning of normative human action, is prominent too in Buddhism. But the differing ethical assumptions of Buddhist discourse subtly alter the term's sense: there Dharma comprehends both the path to *nirvana* (liberation) and the understandings, the truths discovered and taught by the Buddha, that guide persons on that path. *See also* Brahmanism; caste; cosmology; Dharma/dharma; Hinduism (thought and ethics).

Dharma/dharma (dahr'muh; Skt., "supporting principle," "ultimate principle"; Pali *dhamma*), proper course of conduct, norm, the Buddhist religion, ultimate realities, ultimate principles. Dharma has been called "the central conception of Buddhism"; and the expression "the Dharma," or "Buddha-Dharma," is often used to mean Buddhism as a system of thought and practice. The term, however, is elusive, being used in so many different ways that even traditional Buddhist exegesis never offered a single definition. "Translations" are inadequate, but some English equivalents are religion, truth, law, norm, doctrine, righteousness, element, ultimate constituent, phenomenon (phenomena), and nature.

Overview of Meanings: Dharma is derived from the Sanskrit root *dhr-*, "bearing, carrying, supporting, upholding" (related to the Lat. root of Eng., "firm"); hence, Dharma is "that which is a foundation, a first principle." But Dharma is also "that which is held, possessed, or structured" (related to "form"); hence, "that which appears," "characteristic property," "the true form of phenomena." At the same time the term refers in Buddhism, as in other Indian contexts, to religious belief and practice in general (the norm and ideal). The meanings shared with non-Buddhist systems also include those of "social and moral order," "right conduct," or "what is right and proper," as well as the common usage of Dharma to refer to worldly laws. The Indian Buddhist scholar Vasubandhu (fourth century) recognized ten meanings of the word *Dharma*: (1) elements or basic constituents of existence, (2) mental objects, (3) circumstances or conditions of life, (4) impermanence, (5) the Buddhist Path, (6) the goal of the Path (namely, *nirvana*), (7) the Buddhist Doctrine, (8) virtue or virtuous conduct, (9) principles of conduct or religious vows, and (10) worldly laws and justice. In some of these meanings, particularly the first three, the word was often used in the plural, English "dharmas." Uppercase, singular "Dharma" is reserved in English for Dharma as the Buddhist teachings, ultimate truth, etc.

Buddhist Teachings: Dharma can stand for both established order and desirable order. In the second sense the term refers to Buddhist teachings as prescriptions for order—intrapsychic and social. Specifically, Dharma is the teaching of self-cultivation, truth, and liberation in contrast to the rules of conduct taught by the Buddha to his monks (Vinaya). But less technically, Dharma is Buddhist teaching in general and can mean the Buddhist scriptures. The teaching, however, embodies the experience of a Buddha and the universal truths he perceived and revealed. The Buddha Sakyamuni, therefore, attained enlightenment when he perceived or experienced the Dharma. Thereupon, with his first sermon, he "turned the Wheel of Dharma," that is, he set in motion the Buddhist tradition and created the Buddhist community.

Basic Constituents of Existence: Buddhist scriptures also speak of "dharmas" meaning either Buddhist principles (in the plural) or events, phenomena, things as they appear or occur. The boundary between these two meanings tended to be diffuse, because Buddhist doctrines were supposed to reflect reality accurately. Early lists of dharmas made no distinction between the two meanings. Canonical *Sutras* (scriptures, e.g., *Dasottara Sutra*) divided these lists of dharmas by numerical categories. Eventually, such canonical accounting of dharmas led to the formulation of systematic Dharma theories, which attempted to account for rebirth, *karma* (consequences of meritorious or demeritorious actions), the Path, and liberation with a finite number of dharmas.

Scholastic traditions such as that of the Sarvastivada school formulated complex Dharma theories, defining the exact number of categories of dharmas that could be shown to be real—that is, not reducible to more elementary entities. A finite number of these—seventy-five in the mature Sarvastivada system—were supposed to suffice to explain the empirical self, showing how in reality there was no self (*atman*) but a causally connected series (*santana*) of discrete, impersonal dharmas. It was claimed that all seventy-five dharmas had been taught by the Buddha and could be derived from the scriptures. A number of overlapping categories were used to classify the seventy-five dharmas: conditioned and unconditioned, pure and impure, good and bad. For instance, three dharmas were unconditioned (space, nonconscious extinction, and conscious extinction). The seventy-two conditioned dharmas were divided into eleven material dharmas, the one dharma of mind or consciousness, forty-six dharmas associated with mind, and fourteen dharmas not associated with mind.

Dharma theories became the object of criticism of schools such as Sautrantika, Lokottaravada, and Prajnaptivada, which presaged Mahayana views. These schools questioned the reality of many, if not all, of the entities purported to be ultimate realities in earlier dharma theories. These criticisms culminated in Mahayana schools such as Madhyamaka and Yogachara that criticized the concept of dharma as something that remains the same, retains the same character, or can be the permanent property of an entity.

Ultimate Truth and the Ultimate Goal: As a profound experience of the ultimate reality of all things, Dharma is the universal truth that is the object of the full enlightenment of Buddhas. In this sense, Dharma is often used synonymously for the general principles underlying the process of life and existence. This truth is often summa-

rized in the phrase "dependent origination" (*pratitya-samutpada*). This is the natural law of causality, which is beginningless and without a creator, ruler, or controller, hence a law that is independent of human knowledge and will. Buddhas discover and reveal this law; they do not create or affect it in any way. Thus, it is said that whether or not Buddhas appear in this world, the fundamental principle of Dharma (Dharmata) persists.

Since the condition of being a Buddha (Buddhata) embodies the true nature of Dharma and of all dharmas (Dharmata), the term Dharma also designates the reality of Buddhahood. As the human expression or historical manifestation of Dharma, a Buddha's person is said to be "a body of Dharma" (Dharmakaya). A Buddha thus both embodies and knows the reality of all dharmas. His person is the essence of reality and acts in the sphere of the Dharma (Dharma Dhatu). A Buddha embodies the emptiness (sunyata) and the "suchness" (tathata) of all dharmas. *See also* Abhidharma; Buddhas; Buddhism; Buddhism (authoritative texts and their interpretation).

Dharma Dhatu (dahr'mah dah'*too*; Skt., "sphere of the truth"). **1** In Buddhism, the ultimate principle or totality of reality, known perfectly only by the enlightened ones. **2** In contemporary Western Buddhism, regional centers of the association of Tibetan Buddhist churches, founded by Chogyam Trungpa. *See also* Chogyam Trungpa; Dharma/dharma.

Dharmashastras, Dharmasutras (dahr-muh-shas'truhz, dahr-muh-*soo*'truhz; Skt., lit., "law guides"), texts containing the classical Hindu teachings pertaining to the proper conduct of virtually every aspect of human life including life-cycle rituals, correct livelihood, the order of society, statecraft, and law. The earliest may date to ca. 400 B.C. *See also* dharma.

Dharmasutras. *See* Dharmashastras, Dharmasutras.

dhikr (th'ikr; Arab., "remembrance" or "mention"), the Islamic rite of repeating a name of God or a quranic phrase, either vocally or silently, so as to become aware of God.

dhimmi (*th*im'mee; Arab., "member of a covenanted community"), Christian, Jewish, or other protected religious community within the Abode of Islam (Islamic sovereignty). Because they were regarded as People of the Book, the *dhimmis*, though subjected to a poll tax and certain restraints on the practice and propagation of their faith, were guaranteed religious peace and political security under Islam. Their actual treatment varied from ruler to ruler and place to place, but generally the dhimmi communities fared well under Islam, and individual dhimmis often rose to high political positions. *See also* People of the Book.

dialogue, a process of interreligious understanding that demands mutual respect and the requirement that a description of another's religion be affirmed by the member of that religion.

Diamond Society of the Faith Tabernacle Church. *See* Africa, new religions in.

Diamond Sutra, a Mahayana Buddhist scriptural text that expounds the doctrine of the Perfection of Wisdom. The *Diamond Sutra* was written in India in Sanskrit, then carried into East Asia, where it was translated into Chinese (ca. 400) and became one of the most revered summaries of the teachings of Mahayana Buddhism. The text belongs to the body of literature known as the Perfection of Wisdom Sutras, and expresses the central teaching of the Perfection of Wisdom in the paradoxical claim that a *bodhisattva* (Buddha-to-be) should resolve to lead all the beings in the universe to *nirvana* (liberation), while understanding that no beings at all are led to nirvana. *See also* Mahayana; Perfection of Wisdom.

Diana (di-a'nah), ancient Roman deity worshiped in wooded areas and in the city of Rome; she was related to human fertility, childbirth, and children.

diaspora. 1 The religion and culture of any group apart from its homeland. 2 Most commonly refers to the Jewish dispersal in gentile lands. *See also* galut.

diffusion, the process by which elements of a religion spread from one culture to another. Theories of diffusion attempt to account for similarities by postulating borrowing in opposition to those theories that stress independent invention.

Digambara. *See* Jainism.

diksha (dik'shuh; Skt.), a Vedic rite designed to consecrate a sacrificer for performance of the *soma* sacrifice. In later Hinduism, the term is used to describe various initiatory rites. *See also* consecration; sacrifice; soma; Veda, Vedism.

diocese, the geographical area over which a Christian bishop presides. In the Orthodox Church the term is restricted to the area governed by a patriarch.

Dionysius the (pseudo-) Areopagite (di-oh-ni'see-uhs air-ee-op'ah-jit; fl. ca. 500), anonymous Christian Neoplatonic author, named for Paul's Athenian convert (Acts 17). The four works attributed to pseudo-Dionysius have each been influential on later Christian mysticism and angelology: *The Celestial Hierarchy* (angelology), *The Divine Names* (on the attributes of God), *The Ecclesiastical Hierarchy* (on the sacraments), and *The Mystical Theology* (on the ascent of the soul). *See also* Neoplatonism.

Dionysos (di-uh-ni'suhs), a major Greek god, the son of Zeus and Semele. He was the patron of wine and drama and generally of those experiences that transported one beyond the normal human condition. He was worshiped publicly and in private mystery cults concerned with the worshiper's fate after death. In art, he was shown accompanied by wild, half-human satyrs and ecstatic females (Maenads). *See also* Bacchae; Bacchus; Greek religion; mystery religions; Orphism; Zagreus.

Dioscuri (di-aws-kyoor'ee), Castor and Polydeuces (Pollux for the Romans), twin sons of the ancient Greek god Zeus. They were horsemen and protectors of seafarers.

directional orientations, the assignment of meaning to cardinal and semicardinal directions, zenith, nadir, and center. Creation stories and cosmologies are given concrete reference by directional orientations.

Ritual is enacted within directional orientations. Many tribal peoples have extensive local terminology for directional orientations. *See also* orientation; Peking; qiblah; ritual.

disciple. 1 Learner or pupil; one attached to a specific teacher or way of life. 2 In the New Testament, any follower of Jesus, either male or female. The limitation of the term to the Twelve Apostles is a later development. *See also* apostle.

disciple of a sage (Heb. *talmid hakham*), one who has studied the Bible and rabbinic literature under a rabbinic master. In the Talmud, a disciple is also characterized by social, ethical, and ritual attainments, including piety, modesty, a moderate sexual life, and impeccable etiquette and dress. *See also* rabbi.

Disciples of Christ. *See* Campbell, Alexander.

disciplina arcani (Lat., "hidden practice"), the early Christian practice of not explaining the full meaning of rituals until after an individual was baptized and thus fully accepted into the church. *See also* baptism; catechumen; mystery.

disease. *See* healing.

dispensationalism, a Christian theological view that divides history into several periods, or dispensations. The view holds that a specific way is provided for humans to relate to God in each era. Premillennialism, the most noted form of dispensationalism, argues for seven dispensations from Innocence in Eden to the Kingdom in the millennium. *See also* ages of the world; millennialism.

Divali (dee-vah'lih; Hindi, from Skt. *dipavali,* "necklace of lamps"), Hindu festival of lights, occurs on the new moon between October 15 and November 14. A new year rite in some parts of India, it is a time for firecrackers, new clothes, and decorating houses with lights. *See also* Hinduism (festal cycle); new year festivals.

divination, the universal profession of determining the hidden significance of events by a variety of techniques. Though often limited in popular discourse to the future, divination is concerned with the entire temporal range, divining causes (past) as well as relationships between present occurrences. *See also* augurs; Etruscan religion; geomancy; -mancy (suffix); medium; Mesopotamian religion; omen; oracle; ritual; Roman religion; Santeria.

Chinese Religion: Divination is one of the best attested early expressions of Chinese religion, documented clearly on the oracle bones used by Shang (ca. 1766–1122 B.C.) royalty when they sought the guidance of the spirits and ancestors. Their questions and the answers received were recorded on the scapulae of large animals and the lower shells (plastrons) of turtles. The questions were framed to seek a positive or negative response.

The Chou (ca. 1122–221 B.C.) devised a more sophisticated form of divination using milfoil (yarrow) stalks, a method later enshrined in the *I-ching,* the "Book of Changes." The stalks were ritually manipulated and counted in a certain way to produce numbers that indicated one of two types of lines, the unbroken (*yang*) line or broken (*yin*) line. When three lines were thus obtained the diviner had produced one of eight possible combinations, the eight trigrams (*pakua*). Then, in the same manner, another trigram was obtained that was placed above (and posterior to) the first to form a hexagram, of which there are a total of sixty-four. These sixty-four symbolic figures form the basic structure of the *I-ching.* Each has an oracular statement, to which, in the late Chou dynasty, commentaries were added, including one attributed to Confucius. At that point the text became fixed, but the oracles and commentaries were flexible enough that they could be applied to almost any situation. The *I-ching* has remained one of the most influential of Chinese classics and is still used today. Many educated Chinese scorn it while others see it as expressing the essence of traditional wisdom. Today, for example, some Chinese interpret the fundamental negative-positive lines as the basic electromagnetic forces of contemporary physics.

There are many other types of divination: geomancy (*feng-shui*), whose purpose is to divine the play of cosmic powers at any given point in the landscape; the traditional almanac, which indicated favorable and unfavorable days for important events; the activities of spirit mediums or shamans who sought to understand and remedy current problems through contacting the spirits or ancestors; fortune-telling of various kinds, physiognamcy, palmistry, analyzing Chinese characters, dream interpretation, throwing the prayer blocks (*chiao*), and using the bamboo slip oracle. Taken together, these methods testify to the Chinese belief that the ancestors, spirits, and cosmic powers can be contacted and their intentions known about contemporary events and concerns.

Today all forms of divination are stigmatized by the rulers of the People's Republic as "superstition," but complaints about these activities in daily newspapers attest to their continuing popularity among many people. *See also* almanac (China); Chinese popular religion; geomancy; I-ching; oracle; oracle bones; pa-kua; shamanism; yin and yang.

Japanese Religion: In Japan, divination is classically performed by specialists in Chinese *yin-yang* lore or by shamanistic practitioners who learn the divine will in a trance or dream. Animal messengers have also provided portents of the future. At Shinto shrines, worshipers shake a stick from a slotted container to get the number of a printed fortune, or simply use a vending machine. At night, on the streets of urban entertainment areas, one finds specialists in the *I-ching*, palmistry, astrology, etc. In village festivals, various contests of chance or athletic ability are used to foretell what the coming year will bring. *See also* I-ching; Japanese folk religion; shamanism; yin and yang.

divine combat, a type of creation myth in which one deity defeats another and gains control or kingship over the cosmos and the gods. The victor constructs the world in a form different from that of the predecessor deity. Combat is often intergenerational, with a younger god and allies defeating an older deity. *See also* Chinese myth; Enuma elish; Hesiod; Mesopotamian religion; myth.

divine king. *See* kingship, sacred.

Divine Light Mission, a religious movement founded by Shri Hans Maharaj Ji (d. 1966) in the early 1960s in the Hindu Sant Mat tradition. His son, Guru Maharaj Ji (b. 1957), succeeded him as the spiritual mentor, was widely heralded as the "teenage *guru*," and acquired a following among many thousands of young people after his move to the United States in 1971. Maharaj Ji was considered a perfect master, able to perform an initiation called "giving knowledge" that wakened disciples to awareness that all is one and all is divine. Initiates, called "premies," often lived communally and devoted much time to the work of the mission.

The mission suffered a financial setback due to an unsuccessful rally in the Houston Astrodome in 1973, and the next year Maharaj Ji disconcerted many by disavowing celibacy to marry his American secretary. A rift with his mother divided the movement, and the bulk of its adherents had fallen away by the end of the decade. *See also* Maharaj Ji, Guru.

divine man, a specific Late Antiquity Mediterranean figure whose legendary biography includes supernatural birth and childhood, miracles and secret teachings, and a mysterious mode of death. *See also* Apollonius of Tyana; aretology; holy person; Jesus Christ; Pythagoras.

divine right, the claim to absolute authority by virtue of a privilege granted by the deity. Divine right is most commonly asserted by monarchs. *See also* kingship, sacred.

divinity, general term for a god or goddess.

divorce, the termination of a marriage. Though marriage is usually marked by ritual, divorce rituals, beyond the use of a prescribed formula, are rare. Divorce is an important topic (closely related to property rights and inheritance) in religious systems of law. *See also* annulments (Christianity); marital; gender roles; get; Judaism (life cycle); marriage.

divorce (in Judaism). *See* get.

do ut des (doh ut deez; Lat., "I give in order to get"), formula used to interpret sacrifice as a gift to the god(s) with the expectation of a return. *See also* sacrifice.

Docetism, an early Christian belief that Christ's incarnation in human form was a mere appearance. Frequently expressed in Gnostic Christian literature, docetic Christologies assume a strict dualism of divine spirit and the material world, making anything more than an apparent incarnation unthinkable and inappropriate for divinity. Some docetic writings deny Jesus a real physical body while others acknowledge his bodily reality but maintain his spiritual transcendence to the agony of the cross; still others posit two Christs, one who suffers and dies and one who effects the redemption of spirit from matter. Later Christologies are labeled docetic insofar as they deny the real humanity of Jesus. *See also* Christology; Gnosticism.

doctrinal classification (Chin. *p'an chiao*), Chinese technique for ordering divergent Buddhist teachings into progressive and chronological revelations of simple to ultimate doctrines. *See also* Chih-i; Chih-yen; China, Buddhism in; Fatsang; T'ien-t'ai school.

Doctrine of the Mean. *See* Chung Yung.

Dogen (doh-gen; 1200–1253), founder of the Japanese Buddhist Soto school. As a youth, he studied Tendai, but he later practiced Zen under Eisai in Kamakura. In 1223, he traveled to China with Myozen, Eisai's successor, and eventually realized enlightenment under Ju-ching. Returning to Japan, he lived in Kyoto, but later founded a center of practice called Eiheiji in the mountains of Echizen. His major work is a collection of essays called *Shobo genzo* (Treasury of the Eye of the True Dharma). Dogen, who is considered a saint or *bodhisattva* by Buddhist schools in Japan, advocated objectless sitting in meditation (*shikan taza*) and the identification of authentic meditation with enlightenment and

Buddhahood. *See also* enlightenment; Soto school.

dogma (Gk., "opinion," "judgment"), a theological truth stated as a proposition that is held to be an essential part of Christian belief and derived from God's revelation.

dojo (doh-joh; Jap., "practice hall"), Japanese hall or room used either for martial arts such as judo, or for religious purposes, especially in Buddhism and also in a number of new religions. *See also* martial arts.

Dome of the Rock, an octagonal domed shrine built by the Umayyad Muslim Caliph Abd al-Malik in 691 on the sacred place in Jerusalem known as the Haram al-Sharif. Enshrined beneath the dome is an outcropping of the bedrock atop the biblical Temple Mount. The shrine was built to symbolize the commonality yet dominion of Islam over the two other monotheistic religions that regard Jerusalem as a sacred city. For Muslims, the rock under the dome marks the terminus of the Prophet Muhammad's night journey from Mecca to Jerusalem and from thence into the Seven Heavens (Qur'an 17:1). *See also* ascension; Jerusalem.

domestic ritual, rites performed by family members in the home rather than in public consecrated space. They are the most common form of ritual activity. *See also* ancestral rites; Birth Grandmother; Chinese ritual; Hindu domestic ritual; Japanese folk religion; Judaism, prayer and liturgy of; kamidana; kosa; Lares; Roman religion; Sabbath; seder.

Dominicans, popular name of the Roman Catholic Order of Preachers (O.P.). Founded by Dominic of Osma in 1215 to convert the Cathars of Southern France, the Dominicans received papal recognition as an order in 1216 and shortly after embarked on a universal ministry. Dedicated to missionary and pastoral work in Europe and eventually in the Near and Far East, the Dominicans numbered over ten thousand priests in the order by the end of its first century.

One of the great mendicant ("begging") orders, Dominicans share with Franciscans a commitment to a life of poverty. The distinguishing mark of the order is its devotion to preaching and learning enabled by a comprehensive system that attracted some of the finest minds of the Middle Ages to the order, including Thomas Aquinas (ca. 1225–74). Their training made Dominicans ideally suited to staff papal Inquisitions that from the 1230s until well into the modern era were designed to safeguard the intellectual purity of the Church. *See also* monasticism.

Dominic of Osma (ca. 1170–1221), Spanish Catholic monk, founder of the Dominican order (the Order of Preachers) in 1216. *See also* Dominicans.

Donatists, a schismatic group in the African church that in the fourth century broke from the Roman Catholic Church by refusing to accept a particular bishop (Caecillian) because he had been consecrated by an individual accused of having surrendered the Bible to Roman persecutors. A rival lineage of bishops was consecrated; Donatus, for whom the schism was named, was the second of this line. Insistence upon the purity of the clergy from any compromise with persecutors or heretics was a major tenet of the Donatists. Subsequently the Donatist debate was engaged by Augustine (d. 430) over the point of whether the sacraments were valid if administered by an unworthy priest. The Donatists took the view that unworthy priests invalidated the sacraments, with the inference drawn that Baptism must be readministered if it became known that the priest was impure. Augustine argued that the sacraments are valid independently from the moral character of the priest, a position later termed the *ex opere operato* (by the work done) theory of the sacraments. The Donatists survived until the seventh century, when Muslims destroyed the African church in all its forms.

Don Juan (don'hwan), also called Don Juan Matus de Sonora, a shaman and Mexican mystic that author Carlos Castaneda says initiated him into the religious secrets of Yaqui Indian shamanism through drug-induced visions and out-of-body experiences. Through Don Juan's appearance in several popular books, Castaneda created an imaginative metaphysics rooted in sources as diverse as Greek Neoplatonism and Asian meditative traditions, with terminology borrowed from anthropological accounts of indigenous Mesoamerican religions. *See also* Castaneda, Carlos.

dorje (dor'jay; Tibetan, "diamond,""thunderbolt"), in Buddhism, Tibetan term for the Sanskrit *vajra*. *See also* vajra.

Dosojin (doh-soh-jeen; Jap., "ancestral way deity"), Japanese folk deity of boundaries. Dosojin stones represent human couples and are honored as guardians of marital harmony and human fecundity. *See also* Japanese folk religion.

Double Yang Festival, a celebration on the ninth day of the ninth lunar month in the Chinese religious year, called "double yang" because the unbroken *yang* lines in the *I-ching* (Book of Changes) are termed *nines*. It is a day for avoiding evil influences, especially by hiking into the hills. *See also* Chinese religions (festal cycle); I-ching; yin and yang.

doxology, praise or glorification of a deity. *See also* aretalogy.

Dragon Boat Festival, a celebration on the fifth day of the fifth lunar month in the Chinese religious year, prominent for its proximity to the summer solstice. In South China, boats with dragon heads, representing forces responsible for rainfall, compete in races, reenacting the search for an ancient poet who drowned himself. *See also* Chinese religions (festal cycle).

drama and religion. "Drama," typically, has a double reference. Be it tragic or comic, serious or lightly entertaining, drama is both a quality of action, typically involving conflict and resolution compressed in time, and a mode of presentation: actors performing an action or story, especially live actors before a live audience.

The drama of the European medieval stage represents the Christian drama of redemption. In churches and town plazas, one could watch players interpret a cosmic drama, wherein the world is a stage upon which people struggle to attain integrity. In their behalf, God, in Christ, acts redemptively against the devil, sin, and death. At worship, this cosmic drama is enacted in the ritual drama of the liturgy. There, the witnesses are also participants who receive transforming grace.

These double references—to drama as action and performance, to the mundane world and the supernatural or sacred world, and to the audience as witnesses and as participants in the drama—have counterparts in many cultures and make the intersections of drama and religion especially complicated and interesting.

Histories of Drama and Religion: The arts have developed coextensively with the mythology, teaching, ritual, and communal practice that comprise religious traditions. Western drama has its origins in Greek religion. From Aristotle's *Poetics*, and from other sources, we learn that tragedy began with both the dithyramb, a choral song praising Dionysos, and the comic satyricon, precursor to the satyr plays. Satyrs were phallic, goatlike demons; since the word *tragedy* derives from the Greek word for "goat song," one can speculate that Greek drama grew from rituals in which dithyrambs were sung and goats sacrificed. As the masked singers separated themselves from the chorus and addressed one another through dialogue and action, the dramatic form developed. During the fifth to fourth centuries B.C., tragedies were regularly offered in competition at springtime festivals for Dionysos. Yet the plays were not solely related to Dionysos. Any episode from mythology could provide the dramatist with material; only rarely was Dionysos a subject.

The idea that Greek drama is rooted in ritual has been developed in numerous directions, beginning with Friedrich Nietzsche's *The Birth of Tragedy* (1872), wherein tragedy is revelatory of the Dionysian spirit, and followed by James Frazer, who considered drama to have developed out of imitative magic and fertility and purification rituals. Ritual can be crucial for understanding the effects of dramatic performances. What is in contention, here, is whether the historical relation of ritual to drama reveals the nature of drama itself.

The contemporary scholar Rainer Friedrich claims that Greek drama came into its own when it ceased to be ritual. Similar dissociations are evident in other traditions. One may seek the beginnings of Japanese drama in dances (*kagura*) that reenact Shinto myths, including one in which the sun goddess, who has gone into hiding, is enticed from her cave by a comic and erotic dance performed by other deities. Noh plays (fourteenth–sixteenth centuries) and Kabuki theater (seventeenth century) also reflect religious origins in many of their subjects (e.g., Buddhist priests, Shinto deities, exorcisms) and in certain purposes (e.g., to tell Buddhist stories, to please Shinto gods). Zen Buddhism informs the writings of Zeami (1363–1443), a founder and the major theoretician of Noh. But as other cultural material comes to dominate these plays, religious content becomes but another aspect of their cultural background, and entertainment their larger purpose.

In Europe, drama reemerges in the church itself, but how this was so is not certain. Some twentieth-century literary historians propose that European drama evolved from the Latin mass (much as Greek tragedy from dithyrambs). Choral embellishments of the mass, known as tropes, could be divided among singers into a king of dialogue. The tenth-century choral passage *Quem Quaeritis* (Lat., "Whom seek you"), associated with Easter, is the celebrated example. Other theories hold that theater in Europe evolves from liturgical dramas that eventually become separated from the Latin mass, to the mystery plays performed by trade guilds, to allegorical morality plays such as *Everyman* and to secular theater. Realistic and comic elements are introduced—as in the "Second Shepherd's Play" of the Wakefield mystery cycle—which became interesting apart from the religious content.

But developmental theories are disputed for their uncritical Darwinian view of history, for distorting the chronology of the manuscript data, and for failing to treat the plays aesthetically. Among recent scholarship, V. A. Kolve's work on medieval English mystery cycles, performed during the festival of Corpus Christi, sets aside questions of historical influence and examines how audiences might have enjoyed the plays' entwined purposes of reverence, religious instruction, and festive entertainment. O. B. Hardison thinks the *Quem Quaeritis* dialogue derives not from an embellished trope but a ceremony—essentially a drama—performed during the baptismal rites of Easter vigils. The implications are that such drama predates *Quem Quaeritis* and that drama and liturgy arose independently and were mutually interactive.

For some, the archetypal pattern of Christian redemption underwrites the development of medieval drama and the secular theater that followed. But even in the medieval church, and certainly later, the bearing of art upon established tradition could be ironic, viewing religion from unfamiliar angles. The evidence is debatable as to whether Christian doctrine or rite significantly informed Shakespeare. To most, *Hamlet* is a revenge play; to some, it closely reflects Christian attitudes against revenge. To some, *Measure for Measure* is an allegory of providential judgment and mercy; to others, its relation to Christian doctrine is inexact, and the alleged Christ-figure, the duke, is an unworthy manipulator. Again, after the conquest of Mexico, Franciscans mounted dramatic festivals, using native people as players. Some of these productions could be implicitly critical of the conquerors, as in a *Conquest of Jerusalem,* where the Christians were played by Amerindians and the Turks were costumed as conquistadors.

The historical interstices of drama and religion entail contention as well as cohabitation. In the fourth century B.C., Plato thought poets lied about the divine and dangerously aroused people's passions. And many contemporary studies of Greek tragedy view drama as a form of critical inquiry, testing the limits of a culture's religious and ethical frameworks. Christianity has period-ically been antagonistic to the content and the culture of the stage, for historical as well as formal reasons. Early Christians looked upon the spectacles of Roman theater with horror. Their content was deemed frivolous, immoral, and sometimes satirical of and dangerous to Christians (who might find themselves "on stage," martyred). Tertullian (d. ca. 200) called theater the devil's church, and Augustine (354–430), who once loved Roman tragedy, later confessed the hypocrisy of weeping over an actor playing Dido (from Virgil) instead of weeping for his own soul. In the West, critical tension has been the dominant relationship between drama and religion. Theaters were closed in England during Puritan times, and since then critics of many moral persuasions have decried the licentiousness, violence, and ideologies of stage, film, and television. Yet the functional and hermeneutical intersections of drama and religion remain important to the institutions of religion and the stage.

Functions of Drama: At the festival of Purim, Jews, especially children, perform *Purimspiel.* While the content can vary, the performance celebrates the biblical Queen Esther, whose courage and acumen defeated Haman's plot to massacre the Jews of Persia. Purim plays can be noisy, exaggerated, carnivalesque rituals. Roles and status are parodied or reversed, and one may witness a new generation learning the spirit of resistance against historical evil. Balinese dance festivals demonstrate the ritual power of drama, both to interpreters of religion and reformers of theater. The Balinese Hindus view as participants the antagonism of witchlike Rangda and the monster Barong. Both performers and witnesses are literally entranced.

Rituals transform. They may change social boundaries or alter states of consciousness and people's sense of identity and community. The Balinese view of ordinary reality is formed, in part, by such ritual excursions into the extraordinary; presumably this also is a major difference between ritual and theater. But throughout the twentieth century, avant-garde theater directors have returned to ritual in order to create effects that might indeed transform one's worldview. Antonin Artaud (French) imagined, though never fully realized, a theater based on gesture and spectacle rather than verbal language, which would conjure a sense of primordial, metaphysical conflict. Peter Brook (British) employs ritual and mythic traditions to elicit from the stage an ephemeral sense of the numinous, and Richard Schechner (American) uses ritual in performance to effect an awareness of psychological, social, and natural environments. Jerzi

Grotowski (Polish) would eliminate the boundary between audience and performers altogether in elaborate, ritual-like "paratheatrical projects."

The transforming function of drama is not exhausted by ritual. The spectacle of live performance—its multiplying images, its moving bodies immediately seen and heard, its music—is viscerally powerful. Performers only pretend. But their embodied pretenses can effectuate, or make present, the performances of life. On stage, a murder is not a real murder, but a kiss can be a real kiss. The players perform, the audience acknowledges, and something more has transpired than imitation. A kiss has transpired, the effects of which may transcend aesthetic control. Similarly, dramatic dialogue: the to-and-fro of statement, gesture, and silence can transcend the script and catch players and audience in an interplay of different voices and perspectives. The actors, then, interpret their parts hermeneutically: they bring new understanding and invite the audience to join this dialogue. Dialogue of this kind was the point of the epic theater of Marxist Bertolt Brecht. He sought to expose the artifices of theater and use the real situation of distance ("alienation") between actors and audience to didactic advantage, to change minds and change the world. Nigerian writer Wole Soyinka creates a transformational theater based on what he regards as a distinctly African worldview. Borrowing from Brecht, Nietzsche, and Yoruba mythology (which he regards as inherently revolutionary, involving the dissolution and restitution of selves), Soyinka creates drama that would transform awareness of the social, natural, and spiritual forces that bound human life.

Drama shares with narrative literary forms the function of storytelling. And the religious entailments of story are manifold: the defining of traditions in myths and sacred narratives, the transmission of values and beliefs, their transformation and criticism in works of literature, and the capacity of stories to reflect moral, religious, or spiritual concerns in a secular or pluralistic culture. Drama can do all of that and should be so interpreted. But if there are religious dimensions distinctive to drama or which drama is peculiarly suited to explore, they may well be sought where story—or dramatic action—is conjoined with performance—or dramatization. If a play is fully realized as an aesthetic object only when performed, then the dynamics of performance as well as those of dramatic conflict must figure in any religious interpretation of drama.

Most conflicts of good and evil, or the appearances and withdrawals of deities, or the attempts of persons to discover their roles in history and community typically turn on the issue of a character's integrity. The character may be a god or hero, a villain or victim, or Everyman. Integrity, here, is more than characters' honesty or constancy. It is, foremost, their becoming integrated, both within themselves and in their communities. It is their connecting who they were with whom they have become, and with what they must do. One thinks of Achilles or Antigone, Samuel Beckett or Thomas More, Lear or Cordelia, or any character in the plays of Ibsen, for whom problems of selfhood are paramount.

The conflicts of integrity in which such figures perform are not individual only, but communal as well. The city of Thebes witnesses and depends upon the integrity of Oedipus; the poor of Canterbury have tied their fate to Thomas à Becket's. These conflicts are performed, as in life, typically in public. Rarely do classical figures attain to be true to themselves privately, which is why Polonius's advice to Laertes in *Hamlet* ("To thine own self be true") rings hollow. The modern character, who may lack awareness of community, may nonetheless be groping for it, seeking it—if nowhere else—in the audience. The tramps in Beckett's *Waiting for Godot*, the doctor in Peter Shaffer's *Equus*, and the celebrant in Leonard Bernstein's *Mass* ask us, in effect, to validate their absurdity and displacement. If integrity in life has a public and performative dimension, then theater recapitulates and explores that dimension. Its players create and interpret their characters before one another and before us. Drama shares a function of ritual, as a passage wherein performers and audience are invited to participate in the disintegration or reintegration of persons in community, bounded by gracious or threatening horizons. *See also* literature and religion; ritual.

Dravidian, the world's fourth largest language group; it includes twenty-five languages spoken as a mother tongue by approximately 180 million people in South Asia. Tamil, Kannada, Malayalam, and Telegu comprise the four largest. Tamil, with approximately 50 million speakers, traces its sophisticated literary development to the third-century B.C. inscriptions in Brahui script, developing a distinctive orthography by the third century A.D. The rise of classical secular court literature attests to Tamil's maturation in the early centuries A.D. The earliest inscriptions in Kannada are from 450. Linguists hypothesize that the first migration of Dravidian speakers from the mountains of eastern Iran into the Indian subcontinent occurred around 3500 B.C. Attempts to interpret the term *Dravidian* as referring to specific racial features have proven unsuccessful.

dreadlocks, the physical expression of the Jamaican Rastafarian pride in African hair. The hair is grown in its natural form with long flowing locks, uncombed and untreated after washing. Numbers 6:5 provides biblical justification. *See also* Rastafarians.

Dreaming, the, English expression adopted by Australian Aborigines to convey ideas that, though related in their thought, are not usually denoted by a single word in any of their languages. One sense is that of a primordial epoch, the Dreaming or Dreamtime, when beings with remarkable powers arose from the ground, descended from the sky, or appeared from over the horizon. They gave the earth its shape by creating physical features (often from parts of their own bodies), fixed life in species form, established human culture, and gave everything its name. These creative beings, who in their totality are the ultimate explanation of all things, are themselves called Dreamings (roughly equivalent to the anthropological term *totems)*. Their significance to the Aborigines is not merely historical but personal and social, for each individual and group gains a distinctive identity through its association with one or more Dreamings. In many regions it is held that such beings reincarnate themselves as humans, or that they left relics behind that, to this day, are sufficiently potent to impregnate women. This sense of oneness, in which past and present, spirit being and human being, are somehow fused, is also seen in ceremonies in which the actors wear designs and make movements symbolic or mimetic of what the Dreamings did in the Dreamtime. By extension, from these two senses of Dreaming, the Aborigines form other expressions, such as Dreaming-place (a site at which a Dreaming was active and left something of itself) and Dreaming-track (an imagined path along which a Dreaming traveled from place to place in the primordial epoch). Contrary to what is sometimes suggested, the term has no necessary connection with the verb *to dream*, even though present-day revelations to humans by Dreamings normally occur while the recipient is in a dream or trance state. *See also* ancestors; Australian and Pacific traditional religions; totem.

dreams, visions, auditions, and other sensations experienced during sleep. In various religious traditions dreams are seen as direct divine messages. They convey information about future events or carry instructions about things to accomplish or how to behave. The prophetic dream is a near-universal phenomenon.

Japanese Religion: In Japan, dreams are used by deities and the dead to communicate with humans. Dreams have been important in the founding of religious groups, have explained the causes of catastrophes, possession, and illness, and have served shamanistic initiation. Often, the message of the dream is confirmed by an object discovered upon waking. *See also* Japanese folk religion.

Drew, Timothy (1886–1929), known as Prophet Noble Drew Ali, founder of the Moorish Science Temple in Newark, New Jersey, in 1913 and an African-American advocate of Islam. *See also* African Americans (North America), new religions among.

druid (dru'wid; Celtic, "true seer"), a member of the priestly and intellectual elite of the Celts. Druids were the religious and legal authorities in Gaul before its conquest by the Romans (51 B.C.) and were celebrated for their esoteric knowledge. The druid survived as a stock figure in medieval Irish literature. *See also* Celtic religion.

Druids (modern), members of various new religious traditions that attempt to incorporate the insights of ancient Druidism, Celtic history and lore, and romanticized notions of the ancient Druids formed in the eighteenth century. In England today, there are the Order of Bards, Ovates and Druids, and the Ancient Order of Druids, among others.

While there is no scholarly connection between the Druids and Stonehenge, the Ancient Order of Druids used Stonehenge for their rituals until instances of vandalism by the curious closed the ancient site. In the United States, the Reformed Druids of North America (RDNA) began in 1963 as a satirical protest against required attendance at chapel at Carleton College in Northfield, Minnesota. The RDNA developed rituals and lore from Celtic history, poetry, and anthropology, and the movement continued and became more serious, even after the chapel attendance requirement was dropped. The RDNA considered Druidism a philosophy of life, not a religion. In 1966 the New Reformed Druids of North America (NRDNA) reformed Druidism as a Neo-Pagan religion. A few chapters of both groups still exist. Other current American Druidic groups include Ar nDraiocht Fein ("Our

Own Druidism"), founded by Isaac Bonewits in 1983. Currently the largest American revivalist Druid organization, it sees itself as a Neo-Pagan religion based on the beliefs and practices of the ancient Indo-Europeans but adapted to modern needs and sensibilities, such as the preservation of the earth and excellence in arts and scholarship. *See also* Neo-Paganism.

drum, musical instrument most commonly employed in ritual.

Druze/Druse (drooz'; Arab.), adherents of a heterodox Ismaili Shiite sect, called Duruz after Muhammad al-Darazi (d. ca. 1919), an Ismaili missionary. Founded in 1017 in Egypt, the Druze community was oppressed by the larger group of Ismaili Shiites, the Muslim Fatimid dynasty that ruled Egypt and North Africa. The Druze sought refuge in the mountains of Syria-Lebanon, where they since have played a historic role.

Professed monotheists, the Druze hold the Fatimid Caliph al-Hakim (r. 996–1021) to be the sole incarnation of divinity, appearing in all ages. Al-Hakim is believed by the Druze to have created five cosmic principles or ranks: the Intellect, Universal Soul, Word, Preceder, and Follower, which were incarnated in five Druze missionaries. Baha al-Din al-Muqtana (the Follower), who occupies the lowest rank in this cosmic hierarchy, was the author of most of the Druze scriptures, known as the Epistles of Wisdom.

Faced with serious problems of schism led by ambitious missionaries, in 1333 Baha al-Din closed the door of initiation. The Druze have since remained a closed community. Below the five incarnate principles are the fully initiated leaders and then the larger community of ordinary Druze believers. In opposition to these are evil principles representing the darker side of the cosmic order. At death, human souls are immediately reborn in human form. At the end of time al-Hakim, along with one of the incarnate principles (Hamza, who is in occultation), will return to usher in the end of this age and a new messianic era. *See also* Ismaili Shia.

dualism, a term coined in the mid-eighteenth century denoting philosophical theories of two distinct states of ultimate reality, neither one of which is reducible to the other. In Western metaphysics, dualism signifies a permanent distinction between the material and the immaterial, matter and spirit, body and mind (or body and soul), good and evil, or light and darkness. These distinctions are set up in opposition to monisms, viewpoints that unify everything into a single ultimate reality. A semipopular use of "dualism" signifies a view of the world or of history as sharply divided between forces of good and forces of evil. *See also* light and darkness; purity and impurity; right, left; sacred, profane; universal and particular.

Dualism, a racialist religious sect propagated in the early 1970s by Ku Klux Klan leader Robert Miles through his Mountain Church in Cohactah, Michigan. Based on an imaginative hermeneutical approach to Genesis 6:1–4, the Book of Jubilees, and the intertestamental Enoch literature, Dualism posits its adherents as an elite core of the white race who descended from the intercourse of angels with the daughters of men. Although these elites are no longer the physical giants they were in the beginning, they nonetheless carry the genetic inheritance of the angels and have only to realize their ethereal natures to escape the darkness of the earth and return to the light. Miles's inspiration for Dualism stems from his fascination with the twelfth-century French neo-Manichaean Cathari. Dualist dogma contains elements of Gnosticism, the Manichaean dualist heresies of the Middle Ages, contemporary Neo-Paganism, and Christian Identity theory. The primary outreach for Dualism is through a prison ministry. *See also* Catharism.

Duke of Chou. *See* Chou Kung.

Duns Scotus, John (duhnz skou'tuhs; ca. 1266–1308), Scottish Catholic theologian and major critic of Thomas Aquinas, best known for his divorce of faith from reason, and therefore, of theology from philosophy.

Durga (door'gah; Skt., "the inaccessible one" or "she who deals with adversity"), Hindu goddess especially renowned for slaying the buffalo demon, Mahisha, and often associated with royalty. Her worship climaxes annually in the autumnal festival of Durga Puja. *See also* Hinduism (festal cycle); path of devotion; Shakti.

Dutthagamani (duh-thuh-gah'mahn-ee), a king who unified the island of Sri Lanka under Buddhist rule in the second century B.C. and who has been elevated in Sri Lankan tradition to the status of an ideal Buddhist king. Like Ashoka in India, he showed great ferocity in establishing his kingdom, but also great piety in his support of Buddhist institutions and great remorse over the destruction wrought by his military victories. *See also* Ashoka; kingship, sacred.

Dvaita Vedanta (dvī'tuh vay-dahn'tuh), "dualistic" as opposed to "nondualistic" (Advaita) Vedanta, a Hindu philosophical school founded by Madhva (1238–1317). Vedanta (Skt., "the conclusion of the Vedas") is the classical system of Hindu philosophy.

Epistemologically, Dvaita posits three sources of knowledge: perception, inference, and scripture. Knowledge is self-luminous and intrinsically valid. Ontologically, there are ten categories: substance (Skt. *dravya*), attribute, action (*karma*), universality, particularity, specification, wholeness, similarity, force (*shakti*), and nonbeing. There are twelve substances: God (Vishnu), the Mother Goddess, souls, matter, space, time, the universe, ignorance, speech sounds, darkness, mental impressions, and reflection. Reality is characterized by difference, which is thus not mere appearance.

Theologically, Dvaita is theistic. Vishnu is the supreme lord of the universe, approachable only through his son, Vayu, the wind god. Other deities are ranked below Vayu. Creation occurs when God wills matter to evolve. However, space, time, and individual souls are coeternal with God. Souls are subject to reincarnation because of beginningless ignorance, but each soul is unique in essence, possessing the attributes of pure existence, consciousness, and bliss in varying degrees. Souls are of three types: eternally saved, saved, and bound, and the bound are further subdivided: those to eventually attain salvation, those to forever undergo reincarnation, and those working toward eternal damnation. In the state of salvation there is a gradation in the enjoyment of spiritual consciousness and bliss, each soul experiencing these to its fullest natural potential. *See also* nondualism, Hindu; six systems of Indian philosophy; Vedanta.

dvija (dvi'jah; Skt., "twice born"), a term applied to those classes (the three upper castes) in ancient Indian society who are eligible for and have undergone the initiation ritual (*upanayana*). *See also* caste; sacred thread ceremony.

dynastic leadership, the hereditary right to office, common in kingship and priesthood. *See also* charismatic leadership.

ABCD**E**F
GKL
MPQ
RSTUV
WXY&Z

Ea (ay'ah; Akkadian, "the Living One"?), the Babylonian creator god, identified with the Sumerian Enki, god of subterranean waters, magic, and manual skills. *See also* Enki; Mesopotamian religion.

earlocks, peyyot (pay-ohte'; Heb., pl., "corners"), sidelocks. Because scripture forbids rounding off the side-growth of the head and beard (Leviticus 19:27), perhaps in response to pagan practices, the males of a number of Jewish sects grow their beards and sidelocks long. Jewish law understood this commandment to mean that shaving sidelocks with a blade is prohibited but cutting them with a pair of scissors or an electric razor is permitted.

Earth Diver, theme in creation stories connected with the creator twins among North American tribes; the Chukchi, Yukaghir, Mongolic, Turkic, and Finnish tribes of Asia and Europe; the Negritos people of the Malay peninsula in Southeast Asia.

In these stories the original world is water; there is no land. The Earth Diver attempts to find a bit of soil by diving to the bottom of the water. It is often a contest among many animals, such as Loon, Muskrat, Beaver, or Turtle, with only one succeeding. In the Iroquois origin story, various animals (with Turtle succeeding) try to bring up some soil to support the Woman Who Fell from the Sky. Among the Blackfoot (northern Plains), many animals try, but only Muskrat returns to the surface with mud under his claws. In the Beaver (western Canada) version of the story, when Muskrat surfaces with a speck of dirt under his claws he commands it to grow.

In some Siberian versions the Old Creator sends four creatures to look for earth in the bottom of the waters; only one (usually Turtle) succeeds. In Siberian Altaic stories First Man dives into the water at the request of the creator, gathers earth, and then tries to conceal a small amount for himself in his mouth. In Southeast Asia, the dung beetle forms land from mud. *See also* cosmogony; emergence; myth.

Earthmother. 1 Feminine goddess, partner in a divine pair with father sky. 2 The earth as an object of ritual and adoration. *See also* All-Mother; cosmogony; Goddess (Hinduism); Goddess religions (contemporary); Mother Earth; Mother Goddess; myth.

Earth People. *See* Afro-Americans (Caribbean and South America), new religions among.

Easter, the central feast of Christianity celebrating the resurrection of Jesus Christ from the tomb on the third day after his crucifixion. Until the sixth century, both Western and Eastern churches celebrated a night vigil before Easter Sunday at which converts were received in the church by baptism.

Today's popular customs of Easter eggs, rabbits, new clothes, the use of flowers, etc., reflect lingering pre-Christian customs celebrating the coming of spring. The English word *Easter* seems to derive from Eostre, the name of the Anglo-Saxon goddess of spring. *See also* calendar (Christian); Holy Week; resurrection.

Eastern Learning (Kor. *Tonghak*), Korean religious movement founded in 1860 by Ch'oe Che-u (1824–64), based on the revelation of the "heavenly way" (*ch'ondo*). The original name contrasted with the term for Catholicism (*Sohak*, "Western Learning"), which previously had entered Korea. In 1905 the name was changed to *Ch'ondogyo* (teaching or religion of heavenly wisdom). *See also* Ch'ondogyo; Korea, new religions in.

eating together, a central mode of human and of religious association. It is above all an establishment of social boundaries: those with whom one is permitted to eat and those with whom one is not. In religious associations the community established by the meal may be extended to include both supernatural beings and the dead. All elements of the meal, dietary regulations, etiquette, and so forth, continue this rule-governed process of marking off a group constituted by exclusion and inclusion. *See also* community, communitas; food.

Ebla, the ancient name of Tell Mardikh, Syria. The city was occupied in antiquity from prehistoric times through the first millennium B.C. and is primarily known as a result of the discovery of archives of cuneiform texts from ca. 2450 B.C. The remains of approximately twenty-five hundred clay tablets were mostly administrative in nature and written in a Semitic language (Eblaite). A small number of literary texts were written in Eblaite, Sumerian, and possibly Akkadian. Administrative lists and personal names employing gods' names provide some information on religious activities. The pantheon included well-known Semitic deities as well as hitherto unattested ones such as Kura.

Ecce homo, Latin phrase meaning "Behold the

man," from Pontius Pilate's address in the New Testament (John 19:4–6) declaring Jesus' innocence. In Christian art it denotes representations of Jesus wearing the crown of thorns.

ECKANKAR, the contemporary American group based on the teachings of Paul Twitchell (d. 1971), offering spiritual awakening to divine reality. Related to Hindu and Sikh traditions, ECKANKAR trains devotees in ecstatic techniques as the means to tap the "cosmic current" (ECK) contained in sound energy; progress is made in stages, from lower astral levels to the upper reaches of awareness through "soul travel." *See also* North America, new religions in.

Eckhart, John "Meister" (1260–1327), German Christian mystic. A Dominican, Eckhart was a powerful preacher and mystical author, in both Latin and German, who was suspected of heresy toward the end of his life. Although many of his writings have been lost, his thought is constantly being rediscovered by diverse groups of Christian thinkers. Although he found new vocabulary for describing the traditional stages of the soul's ascent to God, he was unusual in that he both affirmed a close identity with God (third stage) and suggested a fourth stage beyond God to an experience of the Godhead. Influential on a contemporary group of Rhineland mystics, Eckhart has been considered a source of nearly every subsequent Christian movement from Protestant Pietism to religious existentialism.

ecological aspects of traditional religions, the relationship of religion to the natural environment. The natural environment influences the development of cultures by offering possibilities and setting limits for sustenance activities. The major options, hunting-gathering and farming, as well as the specific animals and plants available for use, depend upon topography and geographic location. However, choices about the use of resources are never simply pragmatic. They are bound up with a given culture's understanding of the meaning of human existence in the world. Elements of the environment, from the regularities on which sustenance activities are based to unusual occurrences (e.g., geyser basins in Yellowstone, which many Native Americans believed to be inhabited by spirits and therefore avoided) are interpreted by means of a people's worldview.

The influence of ecological factors on traditional religions is apparent in two areas. The first is the contents of myths and rituals, which often reflect local flora, fauna, and geography (e.g., stories about the origin of corn and rituals associated with cultivating it in areas where it is a staple crop; buffalo dances in tribes who lived on or near the Great Plains; four sacred mountains of Navajo myth, identified with specific peaks of their homeland). The second is the way a culture structures its social world, calendar, and religious ceremonies. Where resources are dispersed (e.g., the North American Plains), successful hunting and gathering requires a degree of nomadism. These cultures tend to have small community groups and to emphasize the acquisition of spiritual power by individuals. The relationship between humans and animals is a dominant theme of ceremonialism; there is no fixed cycle of rituals. Where resources are concentrated (e.g., coastal regions of the Pacific Northwest), hunting-gathering cultures developed larger, permanent communities and a fixed yearly cycle of rituals. In cultures where the main livelihood is farming (e.g., the Pueblos of the American Southwest), settlements are permanent; priests and religious societies are the main possessors of spiritual power; and close attention is paid to a calendar and a sequence of ceremonials geared to the yearly agricultural cycle. The very ancient circumpolar bear cult and the respect typically shown by hunters toward their prey, often expressed in special treatment for the bones of the dead game animals, illustrate the similarities that can exist across broad regions among cultures that have similar adaptations to their environment.

The worldviews of traditional cultures often posit a harmonious relationship between humans and their natural environments, and their sustenance activities tend toward conservation of the resource base. In hunting cultures, for example, there are frequently injunctions against killing more animals than are required for survival. Because of this, some have spoken—anachronistically—of traditional peoples as "natural ecologists." It is more accurate and appropriate to say that they recognize their dependence on the natural world and understand their relationships to the powers that govern that world as personal and characterized by mutual obligations. *See also* agriculture, religious aspects of; hunting, religious aspects of; traditional peoples, religions of.

economy (Lat. *economia*, "administration"), in Christian theology, a term used to designate God's unfolding redemptive work of Christ in history, as in the phrase "the economy of salvation."

ecstasy, a state of either extreme association or

disassociation. Ecstasy is a widespread and extremely diverse experiential phenomenon in which the self is expanded beyond its normal range of experience to contact another (e.g., mysticism) or in which the self is lost by being taken over by another (e.g., possession). *See also* altered states of consciousness; Bacchae, Dionysos; ECKANKAR; hitlahavut; Holiness churches; Holy Rollers; Holy Spirit movements; mysticism; possession; revelation; shamanism; trance.

ecumenism (Gk. *oikoumene*, "the whole of the inhabited world"), the quest for Christian unity through dialogue and collaboration among diverse Christian groups. The term is sometimes used to refer to interreligious dialogue between Christianity and non-Christian religions.

Historical divisions have always existed in Christianity, but in the twentieth century a conscious movement for unity developed. The Edinburgh Missionary Conference (1910) between Anglicans and other Protestant denominations acknowledged the scandal caused by divisions. Three organizations were later established to address the issue: the International Missionary Council (1921), the Life and Work Conference (1925), and the Faith and Order Conference (1927). These coalesced in 1948 into a single organization, the World Council of Churches (WCC), headquartered in Geneva, Switzerland. The WCC consists of mainline Protestant churches and Orthodox churches. Emphasis is given not only to dialogue on doctrinal differences and church government, but also on cooperation on issues of social justice. Interdenominational work among theologians is common. National Councils of Churches have been established as local versions of the WCC.

The Catholic Church does not belong to the WCC, but Catholic observers are present at WCC meetings and engage in discussion with their non-Catholic counterparts. Pope John XXIII (1958–63) promoted Catholic openness to the ecumenical movement and established a Secretariat for Christian Unity in 1960. WCC observers were invited to the Second Vatican Council (1962–65) in Rome. Dialogue among Catholic, Anglican, Lutheran, Presbyterian, Orthodox, Methodist, and Baptist groups has resulted in a variety of documents on major doctrinal issues such as baptism, eucharist, and orders (ordination), although fundamentalist groups have resisted such initiatives. *See also* catholicity; dialogue; World Council of Churches.

Edda (ed'ah). 1 The *Poetic Edda* (or the *Elder Edda*), a collection of poems from thirteenth-

and fourteenth-century Iceland. The *Poetic Edda* contains poetry of two kinds, mythic and heroic. The mythic poetry describes the gods, the heroic poetry treats heroes like Sigurd and Helgi. The poems of the gods are either narrative or didactic. They reveal the mystery of origin, of the universe, gods, and humankind. Most renowned of the lays are *Voluspa*, the prophecy of the sibyl; *Havamal,* the "Tale of the High One" (Odinn); and *Skirnismal,* which tells about the wooing of the god Freyr. 2 The *Prose Edda,* a handbook in *scaldic* (poetic) art written about 1220 by the learned Icelander Snorri Sturluson, who wanted to keep the old art alive. The *Prose Edda* is a rich, medieval source of pre-Christian mythological traditions. It consists of four parts: the Prologue, *Gylfaginning, Skaldskaparmal,* and *Hattatal.* The Prologue is different from the rest of the book and brings old mythology in line with medieval European learning. *Hattatal* gives examples of a hundred different forms of verses. *Gylfaginning* and *Skaldskaparmal* present old myths as a world history from the origin of the universe until the last, cosmic destruction, Ragnarok. *See also* Nordic religion; saga.

Eddy, Mary Baker (1821–1910), American founder of Christian Science. She is best known for her work *Science and Health with Key to the Scriptures* (1875). *See also* Christian Science.

Eden, in the Hebrew Bible, a garden planted by God and containing the tree of knowledge of good and evil and the tree of life. Adam and Eve, first man and first woman, lived in Eden until their disobedience and expulsion (Genesis 2–3). *See also* Adam and Eve; Fall; paradise.

Edict of Milan, statute by Constantine and Licinius (313) granting religious freedom to Christians in the Roman Empire.

Edwards, Jonathan (1703–58), leading New England theologian, major influence on the Great Awakening. *See also* Great Awakening.

ee-ja-nai-ka (e-jah-n*i*-kah; Jap., "Isn't it okay?"), riotous singing and dancing that broke out in Japanese urban areas in 1867 and 1868. In part prompted by expectations of talismans falling from the sky, the movement had millenarian overtones during Japan's transition to a modern state. *See also* Meiji Restoration; millenarianism.

egg, cosmic, a cosmogonic motif in which all things are contained in potential form within a single primordial egg. *See also* Chinese myth; cosmogony; myth; P'an-ku.

Eglise de Dieu de Nos Ancestres. *See* Africa, new religions in.

Eglise de Jesus-Christ sur la Terre par la Prophete Simon Kimbangu. *See* Africa, new religions in; Kimbanguist Church.

Egyptian Book of the Dead, a collection of over two hundred prayers, spells, and illustrations from the second millennium B.C. believed to ensure a joyous afterlife for the souls of the dead. Knowledge or possession of these spells facilitated a verdict of innocence of earthly sins in postmortem judgment and provided protection against divine punishment. *See also* afterlife; afterworld; Egyptian religion.

Egyptian religion. The native religious traditions of Egypt flourished from ca. 3110 B.C. to A.D. 550, after which they were largely supplanted, first by Coptic Christianity and then by emergent Islam.

  Continuity and Change: Most of the essential aspects of ancient Egyptian religion were already well defined in prehistoric times. There were numerous local deities and a few gods that had achieved prominence over the whole area that the Egyptians encompassed, i.e., the fertile Nile Valley up to the first cataract at modern Aswan. Common experience and common beliefs, together with a common language, united this Nilotic culture well before ca. 3110 B.C. when a king (Menes) of Upper Egypt (the south) defeated a king of Lower Egypt (the northern Delta area), founded a new dynasty (later known as the first dynasty), established a new administrative center (Memphis), and built a new place of worship (the temple of Ptah). The Egyptians had every reason to be confident in and grateful for their gods' control of the forces of nature, from which they benefited. They also had good reason to want to continue their existence after death much as it had been in life. Preserving the bodies of the deceased, greatly helped by the dry heat of the desert beyond the narrow strip of cultivation, was deemed necessary for the desired afterlife, and provisions of food and drink were also considered logical accompaniments.

  From later periods we have ritual texts that would bring the deceased back to life to be able to partake of these offered provisions, but already the prehistoric burials indicate the belief that return to life was possible and should be provided for. How much more can be learned

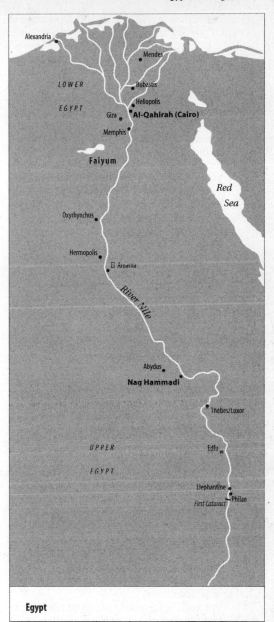

Egypt

from these early burials—from the position of the bodies, orientation of the graves, types of objects and their decoration—is open to speculation. While some would see the practical or sentimental nature of the objects buried with loved ones, others would seek to ascribe ritual significance or a religious purpose to almost everything. Speculation concerning the position and orientation of traditional burials may have some validity, however, as later texts provide reasons for choosing a fetal position with head south and facing west or, alternatively, with head to the north. Such burials were connected with being born again in the womb of the sky goddess, Nut, setting in the west with the sun god, Re, and at the same time looking toward the Field of Offerings, or paradise of the god of the dead, Osiris. Burials with head to the north, on the other hand, are common at certain sites and may indicate a desire to join the "imperishable stars" in the "cool region" or an essentially astral or lunar orientation.

Many deities were represented in prehistoric times, but it is only after real writing occurs in the first dynasty that the association of names and forms become established and we can begin to assess not only the number of gods and the connections between them, but also the religious preferences of individuals in their use of names and titles. The frequency of theophoric names and the number of offices with gods' names or religious sites in them attest to the religiosity of the Egyptians in general. Only much later, with ample documentation, is it possible to assess the impact of this apparently long and profound religious background on Egyptian piety, ethics, and worldview. While there is ample evidence for some continuity in Egyptian beliefs and practices for over three thousand years, there is also evidence for considerable variation in degree of commitment by individuals of any one period and place. While much information is available on the close connection between temple and state in ancient Egypt (this fact had its effect on the populace in general for better or worse), one occasionally discovers unusual figures: a truly penitent king, a very pious priest, an impious drunk, or a woman who would steal from a temple. We know that the Egyptians were human, but to read about the actions of individuals is often more informative than to list their criteria of morality, their ideals in the present and future life, or their terminology and definitions.

The ancient Egyptian religion or religions attempted to describe deities, the creation of the world, the nature of humankind, eternity, and the afterlife in many ways. These beliefs were often placed side by side (even if contradictory) as speculative or descriptive options or as syncretized constructs. The Egyptian word for "god," *ntr,* applies to the great chthonic deities representing aspects of the universe and the natural elements of our world as well as to the anthropomorphic deities—ancestors of the kings, the kings themselves living and dead, and some deified humans whose exceptional achievements led to their apotheosis. Ntr was also occasionally applied to lesser individuals who died and were buried properly, equipped with guidebooks to the beyond and spells for transformations, protection, and provisions.

Mythology in Old Kingdom Pyramid Texts (ca. 2686– 2160 B.C.): The Egyptian pantheon has many generations of gods, most of whom would have been originally separate. Because the kings achieved so much power and wealth, the priests of different cults would have seen the advantage of developing mythologies that linked their chief gods directly to the king. Many royal temples and tombs covered with texts indicate these connections, but the original theological works from temple libraries have generally perished, and it is mainly from these temple and tomb propaganda pieces that we can reconstruct the essentials of each religion. Enough mythological allusions to reconstruct the mythology of different religious systems occur at the end of the fifth dynasty in ca. 2475 B.C., and by this time several different religions had already been subsumed under the myth of divine kingship. A priest or the priesthood of Re, the sun god whose cult center resided at Heliopolis, included the king in his religious system, but, at the same time, maintained the integrity of Re's superior position. In the resulting Pyramid Texts we find the essentials of earlier cosmogonies from Heliopolis, Hermopolis, and Memphis, but the emphasis rests on the relationship between the king and Re. The early Heliopolitan doctrine had Atum, "the Complete One," produce by himself Shu and Tefnut (air and moisture) by spitting, vomiting, or masturbating. This male-female pair in turn produced Geb and Nut (earth and watery sky), and the next generation consisted of two couples, Osiris and Isis, Seth and Nephthys, with the brothers involved in mortal combat for the rule of the world (Geb's legacy). The elder Osiris was killed by the stronger Seth, but Seth in turn was defeated by Osiris's posthumous son by Isis, Horus, who lost an eye in the conflict but avenged his father's death. Horus's sacrifice becomes symbolic and emblematic: the living king is his embodiment, the king at death becomes Osiris, ruler of the dead in a form of cyclical renewal, and Isis becomes a model for the loyal wife and loving mother. The nine gods (or Ennead) preceeding Horus serve chiefly to provide his genealogy; Atum, who should have been supreme, is merely old and distant.

At Hermopolis elements of precreation chaos were described as four pairs (the Ogdoad) of male and female deities ranging from Amun/ Amaunet (hiddenness), Kuk/Kauket (darkness),

Huh/Hauhet (formlessness), to Nun/Naunet (watery abyss). These elements produced an egg from which sprang a creation god who proceeded to produce everything else. Logically, this creator should have been Thoth of Hermopolis, but Atum's name occurs in the Heliopolitan version of the story that survives. The two cosmogonies are neatly tied together in this way, and the Horus-king is still dominant. The relationship of the Horus-king to the Memphite theology is rather self-evident, though the text that describes it is much later in date (from ca. 700 B.C.). This text, known as the Shabaka Stone, records that Ptah of Memphis as Ptah-Nun/Ptah-Naunet, an androgynous link between the eight deities of the Hermopolitan Ogdoad and the nine gods of the Heliopolitan Ennead, conceives in his heart and speaks on his tongue the name of the creator god, Atum. Since Memphis (the capital of Egypt through most of its history) and Ptah's temple were founded by Menes (Narmer or Aha) of the first dynasty, this link to both earlier mythology and the doctrine of divine kingship is to be expected. The really new development in the Pyramid Texts seems to have been the prominence given to the sun god, Re, by the Heliopolitan priest and the apparent acceptance of a slightly diminished role for the king as the sun's son who serves him both in this life and in the next. Re is placed anterior to Atum, and Re's apparent consort and Horus's mother is Hathor ("the House of Horus"), who personifies the entire Ennead.

Middle Kingdom Coffin Texts (ca. 2040–1786 B.C.): The Pyramid Texts also stress the role of Osiris as dead king-god, which makes sense because mortuary literature is designed for the king's afterlife. What is more striking is how soon texts originally compiled for royalty were being copied on the insides of nobles' coffins (men's and women's), how they were adapted, and how the borrowing was explained. Coffins from throughout Egypt dating from the First Intermediate Period (ca. 2160–2040 B.C.) and the early Middle Kingdom contained Pyramid Texts, while coffins from one site in middle Egypt, El Bersheh, contained at least three original books describing in some detail various aspects of the beyond: *The Field of Offerings*, where the deceased would serve Osiris but also live on quite well in the afterlife; *The Book of Ship's Parts*, necessary information for an adherent of the solar cult planning to spend eternity guiding the barque of the sun god; and *The Book of the Ways of Rosetau*, now known as *The Book of Two Ways*, an illustrated guidebook to the beyond. One version of the last book ties together material from three religions, the Osirian, the Solar (Re), and the Lunar (Thoth), and places them in relation to one another. Not too subtly, this book argues that through knowledge of all the texts in it one reaches the highest goal, joining the sun god, Re, in his voyage through the day and night skies. This text draws connections between the common person's goal of becoming a star in the sky with the moon god, Thoth, and the noble's goal of joining Osiris. Obviously, the royal goal of guiding the solar barque of Re would have greater appeal once the book had become available (or affordable) through personalized copies of the texts. The hereafter was thus democratized, and from this point on individuals generally tended to emphasize either the Solar or Osirian aspects of the afterlife and sometimes both, while they, like the king, could devote their energies to one or the other or all of countless national, regional, and local cults.

New Kingdom (ca. 1570–1085 B.C.): Egyptian religion was basically polytheistic. However, many individuals and at least two kings seem to have devoted their energies to one god to such an extent that they came very close to monotheism. References to "god" or "the god" are frequent in literary texts from all periods. The tenth-dynasty instruction for King Merikare provides a unique philosophy and theology of the Re religion in capsule form that is very monotheistic.

The king most associated with monotheism was Akhenaton (r. ca. 1350–1334 B.C.) of the eighteenth dynasty, who changed his name to reflect his new interest in a single generally nonanthropomorphic aspect of the sun god, the sun disk itself, the Aton. Akhenaton's own hymn to the Aton denies the existence of any peer of his god, which itself can be understood in different ways. While it is generally assumed that Akhenaton did not intend to attack all other gods, he attacked many, principally Amun-Re of Karnak, the chief national god of the Theban twelfth and eighteenth dynasties. The subsequent reaction to what Akhenaton had done made him appear more heretical than he was. Tutankhamon's restoration stele typically exaggerated previous neglect of the temples, but in the nineteenth-dynasty Ramesside Period (ca. 1310–1085 B.C.) all those kings associated with Akhenaton and his immediate successors were purged from the records and construction at all the cult centers of Egypt reached a new high level.

During the New Kingdom, between the eighteenth and twentieth dynasties, the royal mortuary literature consists of variants of the illustrated guidebook to the beyond—*Amduat, The Book of Gates,* and *The Book of Caves*—while the texts of those commoners who could afford texts were *Spells for Going Forth by Day*, also known as *The Book of the Dead*, which includes varied selections copied on papyrus rolls from one to more than a hundred feet in length. These texts continue to be addressed principally to Re or Osiris, and one of the most interesting chapters is a judgment scene with a "negative confession" or protestation of innocence before forty-two judges, and the weighing of the heart of the deceased against the feather of Maat (Truth). For the ancient Egyptian, the heart was the seat of intellect and will. Death occurred when the *Ba*-soul left the body, and the *Akh*-spirit is what survived in the afterlife, capable of interacting with both living and dead for good or evil. To continue existing, a person's body or substitute should be preserved together with his or her name—thus the importance of mummi-fication and autobiographical texts, conversely of attacking burials, images, and names of ene-mies in texts, and providing pseudonyms for condemned criminals.

Hymns to many gods survive from the New Kingdom and tend to show much more piety and appreciation of creation than does the mor-tuary literature. The decoration of nobles' tombs shows a distinct shift from mostly secular and biographical scenes in the eighteenth dynasty to predominantly religious scenes in the nine-teenth. Not much of eighteenth-dynasty litera-ture survives, but Ramesside (nineteenth and twentieth dynasties) literary texts all have a strong religious or mythological component that seems to be neither proselytizing nor pedagogic.

Throughout the New Kingdom the political and economic strength of the priesthood of Amun-Re had grown, and so by the end of the twentieth dynasty it is not surprising to see a priestly family usurping royal prerogatives and eventually taking over the royal throne. These priest-kings had to face wholesale tomb rob-beries at home as well as loss of prestige in west-ern Asia. Instability, foreign conquerors, and occasional attempted revivals characterize the Late Period, which also includes the religiously motivated intervention of the Nubian king Piye (Piankhy) and considerable temple construction in the following native twenty-sixth dynasty. A royal daughter appointed as Divine Adoratress of Amun supercedes the high priest of the Kar-nak temple, and successors to this position are adopted. Under Persian, Greek, and Roman domination temples, shrines, and kiosks con-tinue to be erected, generally at the traditional cult sites, and even after conversion to Chris-tianity the temple of Isis at Philae was one of the last outposts of non-Christian religion in the Roman Empire. *See also* Akhenaton; Aton; Ba; Egyptian Book of the Dead; Hathor; Hermes Tris-

Egyptian funeral procession with female mourners and slaves bearing household objects. Wall painting from tomb 55 at Thebes, the tomb of Ra-mose ("son of the deity Ra"), a late-eighteenth-dynasty court official (fl. ca. 1365 B.C.).

megistos; hieroglyph; Horus; Isis; Ka; kingship, sacred; Nephthys; Osiris; Ptah; pyramids (Egyptian); Re; Rosetta Stone; scarab; Seth; Thoth.

Eightfold Path. *See* Four Noble Truths; Path (Buddhism).

Eight Immortals. *See* Pa-hsien.

eight trigrams. *See* pa-kua.

Eisai (ay-ee-sah-ee; 1141–1215), also Yosai, reputed founder of the Rinzai Zen Buddhist school in Japan. Originally a Tendai monk, Eisai traveled to China in 1168 and 1187, partly to bring back stricter monastic practices to reform Tendai. On his second trip his enlightenment was approved by a Chinese Ch'an master. He advocated a mix of monastic discipline, Tantric Buddhism, and meditation, eventually establishing an independent Zen school. Among his works are the *Kozen gokoku ron* (Treatise on the Propagation of Zen and the Protection of the State) and *Kissa yojoki* (Record of Tea-drinking and Nourishing Life). *See also* Ch'an school; Rinzai; Tendai school.

Eizon (ay-ee-zon; 1201–90), a Japanese Shingon Buddhist monk who helped revive the Risshu school, which specialized in monastic discipline and ordinations. Although the Risshu was regarded as one of the conservative Nara schools by performing ordinations for commoners, outcasts (*hinin*), and reestablishing an order of nuns, Eizon led the Risshu to adopt a more progressive social position than Tendai and Shingon. *See also* Ganjin; Nara schools; nun; Risshu; Shingon-shu.

El. *See* Canaanite religion.

Elam (ee'lam), a region and culture of the ancient Near East. Situated between the Tigris and Karun rivers, Elam was closely related to the various cultures of the Iranian plateau. The early history of Elam suggests that tribal groups consolidated into a central political entity around 4000 B.C. with Susa as its capital. The closeness of ancient Sumer stimulated Elam to develop its own writing system, Proto-Elamite. Competition over land and trade between Mesopotamia and Elam led to conflict. With the emergence of the Ur III dynasty in Mesopotamia (ca. 2100 B.C.) Elam was absorbed into this Sumerian state but regained its independence and eventually destroyed Ur around 2000 B.C. The next five hundred years were marked by a strong central administration at Susa under a line of rulers called *sukkalmah* (grand regent). Elamite diplomats and merchants were active across the Near East. Later, Elam was to see a briefer period of extended influence from 1200 to 1100 B.C. and again from ca. 750 to 650 B.C. The language of Elam has no linguistic relationship to other Near Eastern languages. The Elamite religion is only indirectly evidenced and appears to have comprised a pantheon of gods headed by a mother goddess. Most localities seem to have had a patron deity, and larger cities possessed extensive temple complexes with towers similar to the Mesopotamian ziggurats. By the time the Persian Empire emerged (ca. 540 B.C.), Elam was reduced to an administrative district and never again possessed cultural independence. *See also* Mesopotamian religion.

Elan Vital. *See* Divine Light Mission.

Elchasai, Elchasaites (el-kee'say, el-kee'say-*its*; probably from Aram., "hidden power"), a Jewish-Christian prophet (or the divine power that possessed him) and his followers. Elchasai arose ca. 101 in Syria declaring the imminent end of the world and viewing himself as "the Seal," i.e., the last one in a series of prophets. Elchasai had a book named after him, of which only fragments preserved by Christian church fathers survive. His vision of a ninety-six-mile-high Christ/God/Elchasai accompanied by an equally gigantic female Holy Spirit gained a certain notoriety.

Keeping many of the Jewish laws, the Elchasaites nevertheless shunned the institution of priesthood, sacrifice, and the element fire (associated with sacrifice). Their main ritual was repeated self-baptism, which provided forgiveness of sins. While in the water, the person would call on the seven witnesses: heaven, water, the holy spirits, the angels of prayer, oil, salt, and earth.

Thanks to the Cologne Mani-Codex, it is now known that Mani, founder of the Iranian religion Manichaeism, grew up among the Elchasaites, in Babylonia. The codex provides valuable information on the sect's rituals and organization. The Elchasaite missionary Alcibiades came to Rome ca. 220 and convinced the Roman bishop that a second baptism would atone for sins committed since the first one. Arab writers in the tenth century testify to a remnant of the Elchasaites. *See also* baptism; Manichaeism; prophet.

Elchasaites. *See* Elchasai, Elchasaites.

elder, a common translation of the Greek word in the New Testament (*presbyteros*) to refer to a person ordained for teaching or governance in a Christian church.

election, in Christian theology God's act of choosing a people or an individual for a special task or destiny. Jews and Christians have ascribed election to the Jewish people as recipients of the Torah, and Christians have applied the term to those predestined for eternal salvation. *See also* chosen people; predestination.

Eleusinian Mysteries (el-yoo-seen'ee-uhn), a Greek initiatory cult honoring Demeter and Persephone celebrated in the town of Eleusis from prehistoric times through the fifth century. *See also* Greek religion; Kore; mystery religions.

Elijah (ee-lie'juh), in the Hebrew Bible, an Israelite prophet renowned for miraculous deeds. He did not die but was taken up to heaven in a whirlwind with a chariot and horses of fire (2 Kings 2:11). A late prophecy promises his return (Malachi 3:23), giving rise to the tradition that Elijah will be the future forerunner of the Messiah. *See also* ascension; Messiah.

Elohim (e-loh-heem'; Heb., pl. form, "gods"), in the Hebrew Bible, divine name translated as "God" in English. *See also* Judaism, God in.

emanation, a cosmogonic motif in which the universe and all living things are derived from successive outflowings from the godhead. *See also* cosmogony; Gnosticism; Plotinus.

embryonic breathing. *See* t'ai-hsi.

emergence, story theme in which the origin of human beings is explained by their emergence from worlds below the present one. The theme is found in parts of South America, Africa, Melanesia, and New Hebrides. In North America the theme is sometimes connected with Earth Diver stories and themes of birth and journey. The first humans are often described as incomplete creatures living beneath the surface of the earth. They become complete (that is to say, assume their present form) only upon emerging onto the surface of the earth. The place of emergence is specially marked as a locus of ritual.

Many tribes in the American Southwest have emergence stories. For the Zuni, people were led from dark corners within the earth by warrior twins. Zuni know themselves as the daylight people, those who emerged from the earth. For some, like the Navajo, the emergence place is considered the center of the earth. Others, like the Zuni, tell stories of their long search after emergence for the middle place, where the present village was established. The Hopi have a similar pattern.

Navajo emergence stories constitute a virtual catalog of mistakes that produce a background of chaos and corruption against which plans were made and carried out to create the present Navajo world. The lower worlds remain associated with witchcraft and death.

Among South American tribes the culture hero Karusakaibo finds people in the earth. With the help of Armadillo he midwifes their emergence. *See also* anthropogony; Changing Woman; Earth Diver; myth; twin myth.

emic, etic, a distinction between an act of cultural understanding by the actors themselves (emic) and an understanding of that culture by trained outside observers (etic). *See also* understanding.

emigrants (Arab. *muhajirun*), term designating those devout Muslims who emigrated with Muhammad on the Hijra from Mecca to Medina in 622. *See also* Hijra.

Emin, esoteric religio-philosophic group founded in England in the 1970s by Leo (Raymond Armin or Scherlenlieb) to advance self-realization and wholeness through the study of astrology, the tarot, and massage techniques. Part of the Human Potential movement, Emin spread to other English-speaking countries in its early history. *See also* Europe, new religions in; Human Potential movement.

emotions, in the study of religion both the vehicle and the content of religious behavior. As the vehicle, emotions demonstrate the profound significance of religious attachments; as the content they demonstrate the uniqueness of religious experience, which distinguishes it from all other types of experience.

The reason for views emphasizing the emotive meaning of religious thought and action lies in the strong bias in the history of Western thought that regards systems of religion as irrational and devoid of genuine cognitive content. This persists despite available evidence that reasoning takes place within religious systems and that, at least from structuralist and cognitive perspectives, religious systems are "systems of reasons." *See also* feeling.

empathy (Gk. *empatheia*, "to feel in"), the claim that the proper way to understand another religion is to experience it, to whatever degree possible, as its adherents do. Developed in the late nineteenth century to assert the distinctiveness of understanding (Ger. *Verstehen*) in the human sciences from explanation in the natural sciences, empathy, in the study of religion, has been held to be an autonomous, intersubjective method that is neither theological, nor humanistic, nor social scientific. The view is that religious referents have special properties that require the services of a privileged methodology. However, no coherent justification for such a privileged approach has ever been successfully argued, nor has an adequate method for empathy been proposed. Furthermore, since empathy requires introspection, that is, one experiences what another believer experiences only by finding parallels in one's own experience, empathy is the application of knowledge already possessed. Rather than serving as a principle of discovery, it can, at best, only confirm what one already knows. *See also* dialogue; emic, etic; understanding.

empiricism, the doctrine that all knowledge either originates in or is verified by experience. Appeal to experience cannot be advanced apart from some particular theory as to the nature of experience. Two chief theories of experience appear in modern empiricisms. First, classical British and logico-linguistic empiricism from David Hume (1711–76) to A. J. Ayer (b. 1910) defines experience in terms of discrete data derived from the five senses. Emphasis is placed on induction from clear and distinct sensations. Empiricism of this type died out by 1960, due largely to growing recognition of the theory-ladenness of observations. Second, radical empiricism, especially in William James (1842–1910), John Dewey (1859–1952), and Alfred North Whitehead (1861–1947), along with its variants in phenomenology, maintains that particular actualities, their relations and qualities, are the concrete data of bodily experience, not sense-data. Emphasis is placed on the objective status of affectional and volitional qualities. Versions of Jamesian and Deweyean empiricism continue to exert influence in the philosophy of religion. *See also* experience; religion, philosophy of; science and religion.

emptiness (Skt. *shunyata*), the nature of reality as it is understood in Mahayana Buddhism. To know emptiness and embody that knowledge in practice is the principal goal of the Mahayana Path.

Emptiness in the Mahayana Scriptures: Some Mahayana scriptures approach the doctrine of emptiness in a negative way and portray it simply as the denial of any real distinction between two things. *The Perfection of Wisdom Sutras* say that a *bodhisattva* (Buddha-to-be) should lead all beings to *nirvana* (liberation), and also realize that there are no beings at all to be led to nirvana. Texts in this tradition often compare reality to an illusion (*maya*), a magic show, or a dream. Other Mahayana scriptures use a positive approach and focus not simply on the denial of duality but on the reality that is left behind. Texts in this tradition speak of emptiness as the gold out of which the substance of this world is fashioned, as a jeweled net in which every element reflects the light of everything else, and as the Buddha-nature, or the potentiality for Buddhahood, that lies concealed in every sentient being.

Emptiness in Mahayana Philosophy: The philosophers of the Indian tradition tried to explain emptiness in a way that would do justice to both its positive and negative aspects. Nagarjuna and his followers in the Madhyamaka school insisted that emptiness be understood through a doctrine of two truths. When reality is viewed from the ultimate perspective, by asking whether anything has an identity (*svabhava*) of its own, everything is seen as empty. When reality is viewed from the conventional perspective, from the point of view of ordinary, unanalyzed experience, things can serve a useful function. The combination of these two perspectives constitutes the "Middle Path" that gives the Madhyamaka ("Middle") school its name. Taken together, the two perspectives allow a person to recognize that reality is only illusion and, at the same time, to enter that world of illusion and guide it toward a positive end.

The Yogachara school, with its doctrine of mind-only, made more explicit use of the positive scriptural images of emptiness. In Yogachara texts, reality, as a transformation of consciousness, is pictured as the ocean disturbed by waves. To know emptiness is either to calm the waves or to understand that the waves are, in reality, nothing but ocean.

Emptiness and the Buddha: The concept of emptiness plays an important role in Mahayana speculation about the Buddha. From an early time, Buddhists distinguished between two aspects of the Buddha: the Buddha's physical or Form Body and the Buddha's Dharma Body. The Dharma Body could be equated either with the Buddha's teaching or with the distinctive understanding that was embodied in the Buddha's teaching. In the Mahayana, the Buddha's understanding was equated with emptiness. It is common, therefore, for Mahayana literature to equate emptiness with the Buddha himself; to know emptiness is to know the Buddha and vice versa.

Emptiness in Tibet and East Asia: The Tibetan Buddhist tradition has generally followed the Madhyamaka interpretation of emptiness, but not without significant variation. A school of Tibetan philosophy known as the Jonan-pa developed the view that all things are empty not of "self," as in the Indian view, but of "other." Their understanding of emptiness came very close to the monism of the classical Indian Vedanta.

In China and Japan, discussion of emptiness was strongly influenced by the Taoist understanding of Tao as nonbeing. In the meditative traditions of East Asia, especially Ch'an in China and Zen in Japan, the moral and intellectual cultivation of emptiness that was so common in the Indian tradition was also enriched by a practical contemplation of nature. *See also* Buddhism; Buddhism (thought and ethics); Mahayana.

Enchin (ayn-chin; 814–891), the fifth head of the Japanese Buddhist Tendai school. Enchin studied in China from 852 to 858, mastering Tantric Buddhism. He was both a prolific scholar and an able administrator; his followers dominated the Tendai school for several generations. His monastery, Onjoji or Miidera, became the headquarters for the Jimon, one of the two major factions of the Tendai school. *See also* Tendai school.

energies, divine, technical Greek Orthodox term signifying the exterior manifestation of God in the world. The distinction between God's essence or nature and the divine energies goes back to the fourth-century Cappadocian Fathers; however, it was developed systematically only in the fourteenth century by Gregory Palamas as part of his defense of Hesychast (Gk. *hesychia,* "quietness") claims to experience with their bodily eyes the divine light of God. Palamas asserted that, while the divine essence is totally unknowable and incommunicable, a direct and unmediated union of love between an individual and God remains possible through the uncreated divine energies that enables both God's self-revelation to humanity and humanity's participation in the divine life. Palamas is credited by the Orthodox Church with supplying Christian mystical experience with its dogmatic foundation. *See also* Orthodox Church; Palamas, Gregory.

engi (en-gee; Jap., "connection-arising," equivalent of Skt. *pratitya-samutpada,* "interdependent origination"), key Buddhist teaching that things exist through the interaction of causes and conditions. The real-

ization of this truth was held to be the focus of Siddhartha Gautama's enlightenment. *Engi* in Japanese has also come to mean the origin of some thing or event, legends surrounding a shrine or temple, and omens or portents. *See also* Dharma/dharma.

Engi-shiki (en-gee-shee-kee; Jap., "Procedures of the Engi Era"), in Japan, a collection of supplemental governmental administrative and ceremonial procedures compiled between 905 and 927, revising and supplementing the earlier legal codes. Considered a sacred scripture of ancient Shinto, its first ten chapters prescribe the procedures for Shinto national festivals, shrines, and ceremonies. *See also* Shinto.

Enki (en'kee; Sumerian, "Lord of the Earth"), identified with Babylonian Ea, a god belonging to the supreme triad of male deities in the ancient Mesopotamian pantheon. *See also* Ea; Mesopotamian religion.

Enkidu (en-kee'doo), companion to Gilgamesh. In the Sumerian epic traditions he is a subject sharing in his master's adventures; in the Babylonian traditions he is first primitive human but then, civilized, he becomes his master's closest friend. His death sends Gilgamesh in search of immortality. *See also* Gilgamesh; Mesopotamian religion.

enlightenment (Skt. *bodhi,* "awakening," "understanding"), in Buddhism the experience of knowing the nature and the causes of sorrow; in the case of "fully enlightened Buddhas" this understanding is part of a more comprehensive form of enlightenment that includes full knowledge of all causes and effects. A person who has followed the arduous path to enlightenment throughout many lifetimes reaches the condition of awakening when all veils of illusion are removed. In the case of Buddhas, this important sacred event is said to take place under the Bodhi Tree. The archetype for this process is Sakyamuni Buddha, who attained full enlightenment under the Bodhi Tree in Bodh Gaya, India (ca. 530 B.C.).

Levels of Enlightenment: Although enlightenment or awakening is characteristic of a Buddha, others who follow the Buddhist Path can attain enlightenment of different degrees or qualities (e.g., the *bodhisattva*). The highest level is that of perfect, full awakening (*samyak-sambodhi*), which is attained by perfect, full Buddhas (*samyak-sambuddha*), such as Sakyamuni. Four other paths and fruits of Buddhist practice lead to an awakening into the nature and cause of suffering: the paths and fruits of entering the stream, of returning once to human birth, of not returning to human birth, and of perfect sainthood (the condition of an *arhat*).

Mahayana texts describe enlightenment as a process of personal growth in which one attains insight of increasing depths. Thus, the *Ta-chih-tu-lun* attributed to the third-century Indian philosopher Nagarjuna recognizes five degrees of enlightenment: the first intuition arising when the bodhisattva makes the solemn determination to follow the quest of enlightenment (*bodhicittotpada*); the insight that accompanies training in the Path and purifying the mind; the insight resulting from the bodhisattva's service and training under the myriad Buddhas of the universe, by which one begins to see beyond the afflictions; the attainment of an insight free from even the most subtle afflictions (enlightenment proper); and the perfect, unsurpassable enlightenment (*anuttara-samyak-sambodhi*) of a perfect Buddha. Mahayana also makes a general distinction between the enlightenment of disciples (*sravaka*), that of solitary or self-made Buddhas (*pratyeka-buddha*), and that of perfect Buddhas. The enlightenment of the first two is a vision freeing one from sorrow. The second group, in addition, has full insight into dependent origination. But only full Buddhas have omniscience.

Mahayana Concepts of Enlightenment: Mahayana Buddhist apologetics exalt the ideal follower of the Mahayana, the bodhisattva, and reject the *nirvana* (liberation) of arhats and pratyeka-buddhas. The bodhisattva gives rise to the determination to attain the enlightenment of a perfect Buddha, so as to gain possession of the marvelous saving powers of Buddhas, and seeks an enlightenment that is motivated by "great compassion."

In Mahayana texts, enlightenment (*bodhi*), is identified with the wisdom that perceives ultimate reality, the wisdom of emptiness, the knowledge of all things (omniscience), and the marvelous powers that allow Buddhas to come to the aid of those who invoke them. According to some scholastic treatises, this knowledge is reserved to perfect Buddhas: Bodhisattvas do not possess full enlightenment; but the bulk of Mahayana literature presents the Bodhisattva as virtually a Buddha, perhaps lacking in omniscience but possessing the wisdom and insight that gives Buddhas their freedom and power. Bodhisattvas, in fact, go through all but the last stage in the path to Buddhahood. They gain the full insight into emptiness that characterizes Buddhas and attain skillful means (*upaya*) and

the knowledges or supernal skills (*jnana*) used by Buddhas to rescue living beings.

Bodhisattvas also possess the insight into emptiness or "suchness" that, according to Mahayana apologetics, separates full Buddhas from arhats and pratyeka-buddhas. This is the knowledge that all things are empty of self-existence. The state of enlightenment and its object are both defined by the epithets that, according to Mahayana, describe the ultimate reality of all things: inconceivable, ungraspable, without defining characteristics, luminous, and serene. Since the same can be said of all things, including enlightenment and nirvana, the sphere of liberation is not something separate from the world of rebirth and suffering (*samsara*): samsara is nirvana, and nirvana is samsara.

Tantric Notions: Two important dimensions of Mahayana conception of enlightenment played an important role in the development of Tantric doctrine: the identification of enlightenment with knowledge of things as they are and the association of enlightenment with extraordinary powers and magical illusion. Thus, Tantric Buddhism adopts the equation "samsara is nirvana" in the form "the afflictions are enlightenment" (*klesa* is *bodhi*). This human body is the body of a Buddha. As a powerful wonder-worker, the Tantric Bodhisattva is a master of esoteric knowledge, and the path to enlightenment is thus overlaid with ritual and magical symbolism.

The concept of "enlightenment in this body" or in the here and now sometimes is taken to imply a shortcut to enlightenment. This so-called sudden path was central to Indian traditions that had a significant impact in Tibet, especially in the Nyingma and Kagyu traditions. The distinction between sudden and gradual approaches to enlightenment was an important point of contention between various schools in Tibet and China during the eighth century and was crucial in the development of Zen Buddhism in China (Ch'an).

Enlightenment in East Asia: In East Asia, Indian conceptions of enlightenment were adopted and studied, but transformed in the process of translation. With the use of the Chinese word for "path" or "way" (*tao*), for instance, as an equivalent for enlightenment, the ideas of means, goal, experience, and realization were fused into one. This change cannot be separated from the acceptance of theories of sudden or nonmediate enlightenment. These theories, which became the core of Ch'an (Zen) doctrine, asserted that enlightenment is present even in a deluded mind, and that the full practice of all aspects of the path is attained directly in the experience of the nonconceptual, ungraspable reality of enlightenment. Enlightenment was no longer seen as an extraordinary attainment and was seen as synonymous with different degrees of insight or understanding (*chih; hui*). Thus, in Japanese Zen the preferred word for enlightenment, *satori*, simply means insight or understanding, and Zen teachers allow for different degrees of understanding. In this manner, notions of gradual enlightenment are incorporated, paradoxically, into a doctrine of sudden enlightenment. *See also* bodhisattva; Buddhas; Mahayana; nirvana; Path (Buddhism); Tantrism (Buddhism).

Enlil (en′lil), early head of the ancient Mesopotamian pantheon; he was worshiped at Nippur, in the Ekur, at one time Sumer's central sanctuary. *See also* Mesopotamian religion.

Ennin (ayn-nin; 794–864), the third head of the Japanese Buddhist Tendai school. Ennin traveled and studied Tantric Buddhism in China from 838 to 847. His mastery of Tantric Buddhism enabled Tendai to compete with Shingon monks for patronage, but led to the eventual downgrading of exoteric doctrine in Tendai. Ennin also introduced the Pure Land practice of uninterrupted *nembutsu* (recitation of the Buddha's name) into Japan. Besides several important commentaries on Tantric Buddhist scriptures, Ennin wrote a diary of his travels in China that serves as a major primary source for studies of medieval Chinese Buddhism. Ennin's faction of Tendai, known as the Sanmon, later opposed the Jimon faction made up of those in Enchin's lineage. *See also* Enchin; nembutsu; Pure Land; Shingon; Tantrism (Buddhism); Tendai school.

En-no-gyoja (en-noh-gyoh-jah; Jap., "the ascetic En"), name of the legendary founder of Shugendo (eighth century). He combined indigenous Japanese notions with Taoist concepts and Buddhist practices to form a distinctive movement of asceticism and religious life on sacred mountains. *See also* asceticism; mountains, sacred; Shugendo.

Enoch (ee′nock), shadowy figure in the Hebrew Bible, taken up to heaven while still alive (Genesis 5:18–24). In later tradition, many books containing heavenly journeys and secret teachings are attributed to him. *See also* ascension.

enthusiasm. *See* ecstasy.

Enuma elish (ay-noo′mah ay′leesh; Babylonian, "When on high"), the opening words, now used as the title, of a Babylonian myth exalting Marduk, the chief god of Babylon. It is a poem of more than a thousand lines, written in a learned, archaizing language that evokes a sense of great solemnity. It is preserved on seven tablets: (1) introduction, emergence of the gods from chaotic waters, tension between old and young forces; (2) first confrontation, Ea kills Abzu (one body of chaotic waters); (3) second confrontation, Ea's son, Marduk, kills Tiamat (the other body of chaotic waters); (4) Marduk creates the universe; (5) Marduk organizes the universe, ending with the creation of humankind; (6) exaltation of Marduk by the gods; and (7) epilogue, directions that poem be memorized and repeated throughout all generations.

This story is a radical revision of traditional belief. The traditional Mesopotamian pantheon had at its head the triad of An(u), Enlil, and Enki (Ea). Other, younger gods might perform works of valor, be duly honored, and granted an earthly supremacy, but ultimate, celestial authority remained with the triad. *Enuma elish* undoes all this. By the end of the myth, of the ancient triad only An(u) is left, and he is a remote figure. Marduk becomes the only effective divine authority.

Behind this new conception of the pantheon lay the emergence of national gods of unrivaled power and a movement in the late second millennium B.C. toward henotheism (the centrality of one deity among many). Enuma elish was probably composed in the reign of Nebuchadrezzar I (1125–1104 B.C.), a time of Babylon's resurgence and new literary activity. *See also* Marduk; Mesopotamian religion.

Ephesus, Council of, the third Christian ecumenical council, summoned by the emperor Theodosius II in 431 to settle the christological controversies caused by Nestorius, bishop of Constantinople. Led by the bishop, Cyril of Alexandria (ca. 375–444), the council reaffirmed the Nicene Creed, approved Cyril's letter to Nestorius that maintained belief in "one Christ and Lord" without a conjunction of natures, and condemned Nestorius's Christology emphasizing the two natures of Christ. Nestorius's response to Cyril was rejected as blasphemous. Four days after Nestorius's excommunication, the Syrian delegation arrived and deposed Cyril and his supporters. Later, the Roman legates arrived and gave Pope Celestine's support to Cyril, partly because Cyril condemned Pelagianism as well. Ephesus proclaimed Mary *Theotokos* (Gk., "bearer of God" or "Mother of God"), which Nestorius had questioned, and thus gave impetus to the nascent cult of Mary. A second council at Ephesus, the so-called Robber Synod (449), strengthened the hand of Cyril's monophysitic successors. *See also* Christology; Nestorianism.

Ephraem Syrus (ee'fra-em si'rus; ca. 306–373), Christian theologian and poet best known for his liturgical hymns and biblical homilies. Perhaps the most important source for fourth-century Christianity in Edessa, one of the two major Christian centers in Syria.

epic, an extended narrative celebrating heroic traditions. Epic is usually oral and highly formulaic.

epiclesis (ep-ik'lay'sis, Gk., "invocation"), that part of the eucharistic prayer of the Christian liturgy that invokes the Holy Spirit to transform the bread and wine into the body and blood of Christ so that the congregation may worthily partake of the Eucharist.

Epictetus (e-pik-tee'tuhs; ca. 55–135), a Greek Stoic philosopher. Born a slave in Hierapolis (Asia Minor), he was later freed, taught in Rome, was banished (89 or 92), and continued teaching at Nicopolis (northwestern Greece) until his death.

He wrote nothing for publication but was an influential teacher. One student collected his lectures, some of which constitute his *Discourses* and *Handbook*. Epictetus was primarily a moralist, teaching that things external to us are not our affair, but that how they affect our judgments and actions is. Since all external events are ordained by divine providence, virtue, wisdom, and happiness consist in a tranquil acceptance of these things.

Epicureans (ep-i-kyoo-ree'uhnz), followers of the Greek philosopher Epicurus (341–270 B.C.). The Epicurean school in Athens consisted of a number of people living together in accordance with the master's teachings. Most of our knowledge of these teachings comes from Diogenes Laertius's *Lives of the Philosophers* and Lucretius's *On Nature.*

Epicurean physics derived from the atomism of Democritus: there exists nothing but atoms moving in void, and their rearrangement accounts for all change. Our cosmos is one of many such temporary arrangements of atoms, brought into being by purely natural forces. Our souls are also perishable collections of atoms, perceiving the world by means of the atoms emanating from the surfaces of objects. Perfect, imperishable, blessed gods exist, but, contrary to popular opinion, their perfection entails that they cannot have any projects or concerns and so do not intervene in our world. It is good for human beings to respect and admire these beings but not to expect rewards or punishments from them.

Epicureanism was concerned, above all, with ethics, with providing a practical guide to living a happy life. Notoriously, Epicureans saw this as a matter of fulfilling the natural human desire for pleasure. But contrary to the ancient prejudices against them, they did not advocate a life of reckless, sensual pleasure seeking. Rather, they recommended only those pleasures caused by the satisfaction of natural, necessary desires (e.g., for food) and not those that are unnecessary or involve pain (e.g., desire for delicious but unhealthy food). The ideally happy life was one of bodily health and "freedom from anxiety."

epiphany, general term for the manifestation of a deity.

Epiphany, a Christian feast, observed on January 6, commemorating in the Eastern Church the baptism of Jesus and in the West the visit of the Wise Men from the East to the infant Jesus. *See also* calendar (Christian).

epiphenomenon, the theoretical consequence of arguing that religion is the secondary product of a primary cause. *See also* reductionism; religion, explanation of.

Erasmus, Desiderius (ee-raz'muhs; 1466–1536), Dutch humanist who anticipated the Reformation in many aspects of his thought, but remained a staunch Catholic and Augustinian priest. Erasmus is best known as a brilliant satirist and controversialist against aspects of Catholic devotion (e.g., the cult of the saints, monasticism), as a student and editor of both classical and patristic authors, and as the editor of the first printed edition of the Greek New Testament (1516).

Erhard Seminars Training. *See* EST (Erhard Seminars Training).

Esagila (es-uh-gee'lah; a Babylonian name meaning "temple that lifts its head [high]"), the main temple complex in the center of ancient Babylon, dedicated to its city god, Marduk. *See also* Marduk; Mesopotamian religion.

Esalen Institute, an eclectic New Age educational center near Big Sur, California, begun in 1962 by Michael Murphy and Richard Price. Part of the Human Potential movement, the institute has offered consultation, communal retreats, and a wide range of instruction in Asian practices of meditation and contemplation, emphasizing the divergent paths to spiritual enlightenment. *See also* Human Potential movement; North America, new religions in.

Esarhaddon (es-ahr-had'duhn), king of Assyria (681–669 B.C.) who rebuilt Babylon following its destruction by Sennacherib. *See also* Mesopotamian religion.

eschatology, general term for teachings concerning the "last things," the end of the world and processes of salvation. *See also* ages of the world; afterlife; Ahriman; Day of Judgment (Islam); Gesar/Geser; messianic; millenarianism; paradise; Ragnarok; resurrection; savior.

Christianity: Eschatology includes teachings concerning death, judgment, heaven, hell, and the return of Christ (Gk. *parousia*). The term itself was first used in the nineteenth century with the rise of critical biblical studies. One significant early finding was that both Jesus and the apostle Paul seemed convinced that God would terminate history soon. Studies of Jesus' use of "the reign of God" and of Paul's treatment of the return of Christ brought a reevaluation of the relations between the end of history and the new era that Jesus had ushered in.

For current Christian theology, eschatology raises important issues about history. If Christian faith says that the crucial victory occurred in Christ's death, resurrection, and sending of the Holy Spirit, what value should believers place on temporal matters? The mainstream of theologians seems to have reached a consensus that both the New Testament and subsequent faith seek a balance between "now" and "not yet." The substance of salvation (God's forgiveness and eternal life) is available now, in virtue of Christ. But the full expression of salvation can only occur beyond history, where God is all in all, and so does not yet exist. *See also* Antichrist; apocalypticism; Armageddon; chiliasm; Gog and Magog; kingdom of God; Last Judgment (Islam); Messiah; millenarianism; millennialism; New Jerusalem; Second Coming; 666.

Eskimo, name designating the inhabitants of the circumpolar Arctic, believed to have originated with the Montagnais in northeastern Canada.

The most widespread self-designation used by Eskimo speakers (*inuk*; pl. *inuit*) means simply "person, people" in West Greenland and Canada. The Central Siberian Eskimos call

themselves Yupik (*yuk*; pl. *yup'ik*), meaning "real, genuine person."

Eskimo is the word the indigenous people of the Western Arctic largely prefer. The term *inuit* has been largely misused by English speakers. Regional groups have specific names for themselves such as the Inupiat of northern Alaska, the Inuvialuk of Mackenzie Delta, and the Kalaallit of Greenland. *See also* circumpolar religions.

Esoteric Buddhism in China. *Esoteric Buddhism* (*Chen-yen* or *Mi-chiao*) is a Chinese term coined both to include Vajrayana and other modes of Tantric Buddhism in China, and, at the same time, to distinguish the Chinese practice from the Indo-Tibetan Vajrayana.

Esoteric Buddhism flourished in the eighth century under the leadership of Subhakarasimha, Vajrabodhi, and Amoghavajra, all Tantric masters from India. It was heavily patronized by the Chinese emperors due to its reputation for wielding occult powers, such as healing and bringing rain.

True to its Tantric Indian origins, Esoteric Buddhism offered a potent shortcut to enlightenment with practices and secrets that were revealed only to initiates. Its practices included the use of *mantras* (Skt.), or magical prayers capable of breaking one's enchainment in *samsara* (the cycle of rebirth); *mudras*, or sacred gestures associated with particular deities; and *mandalas*, cosmographic diagrams thought to be inhabited by a vast array of Buddhas and Bodhisattvas. The *Mahavairochana Sutra* (Great Sun Sutra), with its womb-element mantra (*garbhadhatu*), was the central text of the school. Initiation ceremonies included sexual rites enacting the belief that enlightenment was attained by the union of wisdom, which was female, with compassion, which was male. It is unclear to what extent sexual practices were actually carried out in China, given the strength of its puritanical Confucian culture. The existence of indigenous Taoist sexual rites that may have had prior links with Indian yogic traditions suggests China's openness to erotic practice. The absence of Chinese translations of sexual Tantric texts, which may or may not be accounted for by the censoring hand of Sung Neo-Confucianism, renders the question inconclusive. After the eighth century, Esoteric Buddhism declined in China, but its vestiges survived in Tibet and in the Japanese Shingon school. *See also* Shingon; Tantrism (Buddhism); Vajrayana.

esoteric movements, religious and philosophical groups centered on knowledge or experience accessible only to those who have received a special initiation or attained a special level of spiritual awareness. Esoteric refers to what is "inner," restricted to persons or groups who are in some way on the "inside" of a secret or process.

Esotericists believe they are custodians of an important truth about reality that is unknown to most people either because it has been intentionally concealed or because by its nature it is unknowable without special training or induction into its mysteries. In this context, initiation or induction implies a set of experiences designed not only to convey knowledge but also to induce an intuitive awareness of unfamiliar dimensions of reality.

Esoteric wisdom characteristically concerns little-known laws of nature, extraordinary psychic and spiritual abilities latent in human beings, and superhuman hierarchies of gods, spirits, and masters.

Because of the cognitive and initiatory emphases, esoteric movements are likely to employ study more than devotion, the lecture more than the devotional sermon, and tightly controlled initiatory scenarios more than devotional practice. Precision of information and technical skill in the use of esoteric knowledge are significant, for these features conform the objective nature and practical importance of its insights.

Esoteric movements in the West have flourished at least from Hellenistic times down to the present. Rosicrucian groups are an early modern example; more recent ones are the Order of the Golden Dawn and, in a broader sense, groups such as Theosophy and Scientology. *See also* Bailey, Alice; Gurdjieff, Georgei Ivanovitch; Hermetism; occult, the; Rosicrucians; Theosophy.

essence (Lat. *esse*, "to be"), a term usually taken to mean what a thing "is" intrinsically, what attributes or characteristics must be found in a particular thing if it is to belong to a certain kind, genus, or species. Essence is distinguished from accidental attributes, which may be absent and are thus "inessential." Platonism and medieval realism conceive of essences as single common natures existing in things of particular species and genera. This view was rejected by Aristotelians, for whom all reality is individual and essences exist as common natures only in intellectual abstraction. Nominalists from Ockham to the contemporary analytic philosophers view essences as merely names applied to individuals bearing "family resemblances."

Essenes (eh-seenz'), an early Jewish sect (second century B.C.–A.D. first century) known for their communism, apparent celibacy, and concern for purity. Their identification with Qumran is controversial.

EST (Erhard Seminars Training), a therapeutic movement founded by Werner Erhard (Jack Rosenberg), a salesman, and based on consciousness training programs and psychology-of-success literature. EST was incorporated as an educational corporation and employed techniques drawn from Scientology, Zen, Dale Carnegie, and humanistic psychology; thus it accommodates elements associated with oriental mysticism to the American success ethic. EST was widely criticized for sanctifying selfishness and for abrasive and traumatic training sessions. Highly successful in the late 1970s, EST was later officially discontinued and replaced by a new organization, the Forum. *See also* North America, new religions in.

eternal, a divine attribute; without beginning or end, unaffected by time, outside time.

eternity. 1 Infinite, endless time. 2 Especially in Christian usage, an afterlife without end.

Ethical Culture, Societies for, a religious association largely active in the United States and England. Founded in 1876 by Felix Adler in New York City, the movement sought to remove the supernatural from Judaism and Christianity and focus on ethical development. It is best known for its social work and educational programs.

Ethiopian churches, independent churches that broke away from mission churches to assert African control over their own religious institutions through Africanization of personnel more than innovations in doctrine or ritual. First developed in the late nineteenth century, these churches are particularly common in southern Africa and Nigeria, areas heavily proselytized by Protestant churches whose missionaries translated the Bible into African languages. In both areas, racism within church hierarchies and among colonial authorities gave added impetus to the drive for church autonomy.

One of the first independent churches, founded by Mangena Mokone, a South African Wesleyan minister, was called the Ethiopian Church. Established in 1892, it took its name from Psalm 68:31, "Ethiopia shall soon stretch out her hands unto God." Mokone stressed self-determination for African Christians and organized a multiethnic church that gained a considerable following among African workers in the gold mines.

In Nigeria the earliest Ethiopian churches were established after the Church Missionary Society arbitrarily removed Bishop Samuel Ajayi Crowther, the first Anglican African bishop, in 1890. Within a few years, Ethiopian churches began to be established and grew rapidly during the period up to World War I, including the African Church movement, made up of disaffected Anglicans, and the pan-Africanist West African Church, inspired by the African Protestant theologian E. W. Blyden (1832–1912). *See also* Africa, new religions in.

ethnoastronomy. *See* starlore and ethnoastronomy.

etic. *See* emic, etic.

etiology, technical term used by scholars to describe a myth that narrates the origins or causes of some (usually physical) phenomenon. *See also* myth.

Etruscan religion (ee-truh'sken). Evidence concerning the religion of the north-central Italian Etruscan cities (ca. 1000–100 B.C.) comes from archaeological, epigraphic, and literary sources. The latter are all Greek and Roman authors: no Etruscan literature survives. The Romans characterized the Etruscans as a most religious or "superstitious" people who excelled in omen reading. Except for funeral rites, little is known archaeologically of religion in the prehistoric Villanovan period (900–700 B.C.). In the early historic period (700–600 B.C.), inscriptions mention native divinities like Aisera Turannuve (*aiser* means "god"; *turan* is Aphrodite/Venus, the goddess of love), Usel (Sun), Thesan (Dawn), and Mamarce (Mars).

Images of gods rarely occur, but artistic monuments record early beliefs and rituals. A monsterlike death demon is represented together with warriors and farmers on a bronze urn from Bisenzio, and scenes relating to fertility and war appear on the decoration of a jug from Tragliatella (near Cerveteri). In the Tomb of Five Chairs at Cerveteri, enthroned male and female statues of the deceased testify to the importance of an ancestor cult, as do statues from a building at Murlo (near Siena).

Development of the Tradition: The Etruscan pantheon developed gradually: its stratified structure resulted from the successive introduction of Greek, Italic, and Roman divinities. Excavations at Gravisca, the harbor of Tarquinia, have proven the coexistence of the cult of Greek Aphrodite and Etruscan Turan, Greek Hera and Etruscan Uni (Latin Iuno), and Greek Demeter and Etruscan Vei. A temple at the sanctuary of Pyrgi, the harbor of Cerveteri, was dedicated to Uni, equated with Phoenician Astarte. A cult statue of a naked goddess from Orvieto may also reflect the worship of goddesses like those of the Phoenicians.

Italic gods like Uni and Menerva are named in inscriptions and represented on engraved mirrors produced between ca. 550 and 150 B.C., together with Greek mythological figures such as Herakles (Etruscan Hercle), Dionysos (Fufluns), Artemis, and Apollo (whose popularity may be explained by Etruscan contacts at the sanctuary of Apollo at Delphi). The artists of mirrors, vases, and sculpture were inspired by imported Greek works of art, chiefly Attic vases. Dedicated to the god Vertumnus, the federal sanctuary, the Fanum Voltumnae at Volsinii (modern Orvieto), was of great importance.

The end of the fifth century B.C. brought a period of political tension and wars against Celts and Romans; artistic monuments (especially from tombs, built and furnished for the afterlife like the houses of the living) give a more pessimistic view of the underworld, showing gods like Charun, who holds a hammer; Vanth, the beautiful angel of death; and the underworld couple, Aita (Hades) and Persipnai (Persephone).

Religious Practices: By the third century B.C., the Etruscans had codified the basics of religious learning, the *etrusca disciplina* (Lat.), which before had traditionally been revealed by prophets like Tages, a boy who was also an old man, and the nymph Vegoia (Begoe, Vecu). Books taught soothsayers, diviners, and priests how to interpret signs sent by the gods through thunderbolts and portents and the livers of sacrificed animals. Hepatoscopy, the consultation of entrails, an Etruscan specialty, is attested by mirrors showing people reading a liver as well as a bronze model of a sheep's liver, the Piacenza liver (ca. 100 B.C.).

According to the Etruscans' belief that world ages, or *saecula* (Lat.), were allotted to each nation, the Etruscan nation was to end after the tenth age (the ninth ended in 44 B.C.). A fatalistic mentality was also reflected by such representations as the goddess Athrpa (Greek Atropos) hammering the nail of Fate.

Gods were worshiped at sanctuaries where terra-cotta votive statuettes or, in the case of healing sanctuaries, images of body parts were offered. In northern Etruria votive bronze figures have been found. Altars and temples, often tripartite, were built after ca. 500 B.C. with a prevalently south or southeast orientation. The form of the Italic temple survived in Roman architecture. The longest Etruscan ritual text (two thousand words), a linen book from the second century B.C. accidentally preserved as mummy wrappings, contains a ritual calendar with instructions for offerings to be made to various gods. Although Etruscan civilization ended about 30 B.C., Etruscan priests (haruspices) were consulted in the Roman world until late antiquity. *See also* Roman religion.

Eucharist, Christian

Eucharist, Christian (yoo'kah'rist; Gk. *eucharistia,* "thanksgiving"), the principal act of worship of the Christian religion, otherwise known as the Divine Liturgy, Holy Communion, Lord's Supper, or Mass. This name has been used from at least the second century, and comes from the thanksgiving prayer that constitutes a principal element in the rite.

Origins: According to Christian tradition, the Eucharist traces its roots to the narrative of the last supper eaten by Jesus with his disciples on the night before he died, when he performed a Jewish grace-ritual before the meal (taking bread into his hands, saying a short blessing of God for it, breaking the bread, and sharing it with those present) and the customary festal thanksgiving prayer over a shared cup of wine at the end of the meal. He is represented as having given these actions a new significance in relation to his imminent death, interpreting the bread as his body "given for you" and the wine as his blood, and as having instructed his disciples to perform them in future in remembrance of him. The eucharistic observances of the earliest Christians were more than a memorial meal: in some traditions believers claimed to experience the living presence of the resurrected Christ in these communal gatherings.

It is generally agreed that these celebrations at first included a complete evening meal, with each participant bringing food to share with the others. But by the middle of the second century they had been reduced to a repetition of the key actions of Jesus—taking bread and wine, saying a thanksgiving prayer over them that recalled all that God had done through Christ, breaking the bread, and sharing the bread and wine. They were now also usually held early on Sunday mornings in conjunction with a worship service involving scripture reading, preaching, and intercession. A vital requirement of these weekly assemblies was that all members of the church should participate, the bread and wine even being carried to those who through sickness or imprisonment were unable to be present.

Later Developments: Along with the stress on the community event as the means of experiencing continuing relations with Christ, there was a growing emphasis on the bread and wine themselves as the locus of his presence, and consequently on their consecration, effected by the recitation of the eucharistic prayer, as the means by which this was realized. This development became stronger in the period after the fourth century when there was a great increase in church membership and a consequent loss of consciousness of the local church as a tight-knit community. Sacrificial language was increasingly applied to the Eucharist. The precise nature of the eucharistic sacrifice, and its relationship to the sacrificial death of Christ, as well as the exact mode of Christ's presence in the bread and wine, would continue to be matters of intense debate among theologians for many centuries.

In time, the eucharistic ritual became more formalized and elaborate and was increasingly an action performed by the clergy for the people. The clergy also began to stress the need for a proper interior disposition before receiving the bread and wine, which had the unintended effect of discouraging their frequent reception, as people judged themselves unworthy to be communicants. Thus, by the end of the Middle Ages people still attended the rite every Sunday, but only received Communion once or twice a year, after making a confession of their sins, and even then, in the West though not in the East, were given only bread and not wine, for fear that the latter might be accidently spilled.

The Eucharist came to be seen by ordinary believers not as a communal meal, nor as heavenly food or the medicine of immortality, as in earlier times, but principally as an object of devotion: it was thought that through the action of the priest in reciting the words of the eucharistic prayer the bread and wine became Christ's body and blood, to be worshiped from afar but not approached, and that in the rite Christ's sacrifice of himself was offered to God the Father so that its benefits might be appropriated by those for whom it was offered, whether present or absent, whether alive or dead. Indeed, while in the Eastern Orthodox Church the Eucharist continued to be celebrated only on Sundays and feasts, in the West it took place regularly on weekdays, often with only the priest present and with the intention of applying its benefits to the faithful departed.

The Reformation: The sixteenth-century Reformation in the West rejected the idea that Christ was in any sense offered in the Eucharist, and most Reformers also denied that a transformation took place in the bread and wine. Instead they generally believed that Christ was present spiritually only to the worthy recipient of Communion. They therefore insisted that those attending the rite should always receive bread and wine, but because people still judged themselves unworthy to participate in the Eucharist frequently, it came to be celebrated only a few times a year in most Protestant churches, and was replaced by a preaching service on other Sundays.

Contemporary Practice: Many churches have returned to the practice of the frequent participation in the Eucharist as a vital part of the Christian ritual in recent years: the Eucharist takes place every Sunday, and is regarded as a corporate event and not just as an opportunity for the individual reception of the sacrament. Roman Catholics too now use a revised rite that involves more congregational participation, and receive Communion on every occasion, often with wine as well as bread. *See also* agape; anaphora; bread and wine; chalice; Christianity (worship); consecration; disciplina arcani; epiclesis; ex opere operato; Grail, Holy; host; Last Supper; Mass; sacraments and ordinances (Christianity); transubstantiation.

euhemerism (yoo-he′mair-iz′uhm), a method of interpreting myth that assumes a kernel of historical fact in mythic expression. It is named after Euhemerus of Messene (ca. 340–260 B.C.), whose philosophical romance, *Sacred History*, theorizes that the deities of Homeric tales had actually been great kings worshiped as gods by their people.

Euhemerism was a popular mode of explanation in medieval and Renaissance history. Eighteenth- and nineteenth-century critics and students of religion proposed theories of religion founded upon the assumed historical distortion of ancestor veneration or upon the deification of tribal warriors or rulers.

Early Christian apologists used Euhemerus as their authority to argue that pagan deities were but mortals. Nineteenth- and twentieth-century biblical theologians, accepting the mythological character of biblical narratives, presented programs for interpreting the mythic elaborations in order to reveal their assumed historical core.

Euhemerism is a rationalistic, religio-historical method for ridding mythic expression of what is judged to be its fantastic distortions in order to reclaim a putative actual history. The term designates any theory of myth as historical distortion or of the transformation of history to myth, theories that still underlie much contemporary religious thought and scholarship. *See also* myth; origin of religion.

eunuch, a castrated male. Voluntary castration is associated either with ascetic vows, resulting in permanent celibacy, or with some forms of priesthood. *See also* Attis; celibacy.

Euripides (yoo-rip′uh-deez; ca. 485–406 B.C.), youngest of the great Athenian tragedians and most popular in antiquity; he was known for his intellectual treatment of unusual themes and questioning attitude toward received beliefs. Eighteen plays survive, more than the combined extant dramas of Aeschylus and Sophocles; we know titles of another sixty plays now lost. His first tetralogy (set of four plays for the annual competition) was produced in 455 B.C. in Athens, the year after Aeschylus's death. His first surviving play comes from 438, the *Alcestis*. In this tale of a woman who chooses to die in her husband's place can be found most characteristics of Euripides's later dramas: attention to extreme situations, frequent paradoxes, a plot dependent on coincidences, the mixture of serious and comic elements (such as the burlesque Herakles figure), a focus on the household, a last-minute rescue, opposing set speeches debating a general topic with new rhetorical techniques, an interest in depicting the emotions of women, and the realistic, psychological presentation of ancient mythology.

On one hand, Euripides's blurring of dramatic genres shaped the formulaic plots of romantic drama in Greek New Comedy (fourth century B.C.) and Roman imitations. Already in the fifth century, the comic poet Aristophanes, who was his younger contemporary, seems to have learned from Euripidean technique even as he parodied innovations like dressing a king in rags (as in the lost *Telephus*), musically innovative arias, monologues on everyday affairs, and the constant Euripidean play between reality and illusion. On the other hand, Euripides can be said to have redefined the realm of the tragic; instead of dramatizing the clash between mortals and Fate, society, or the gods (as had his predecessors), he brought on stage characters struggling with internal contradictions and irrational impulses.

Medea, in the tragedy named after her (431 B.C.), is a good example of the type: barbarian but hellenized, witch but Greek wife, she verbally defeats her estranged husband, Jason, kills his new bride, then murders her own children out of revenge after an agonized monologue. His fascination with such powerful female characters earned Euripides the reputation of misogynist in antiquity. At the same time, the moral relativism of the end of the *Medea* (the murderess is rescued from punishment by her divine grandfather Helios) was felt by some to mark all his work. He was associated with the paid teachers of wisdom called the "sophists" and the professional debunker Socrates (even though he implicitly criticized Socratic belief in the *Hippolytus*). It is said that the philosopher Protagoras first publicly read his work, which was skeptical of the gods, at Euripides's house. The *Hekabe,* the *Hippolytus,* and especially the *Trojan Women* contain scenes in which some character questions the traditional Greek gods. Apollo, throughout the *Ion,* is subjected to intense scrutiny—so much that nineteenth-century critics read the play as an attack on Delphic religion. But the god is shown ultimately unscathed by human criticism. Furthermore, the appearance of controlling deities in Euripides's famous prologues, his frequent use of *deus ex machina* (in which a god's epiphany puts all right), and his concern to connect his dramatic myths with actual worship practices make Euripides's religious stance more complicated than rationalist atheism.

It has been noted that Euripides's radical thought occurs within old-fashioned conventions of dramatic form. In a typically archaizing way, Euripides also goes back three centuries to the Homeric mode of presentation of divinity. He shows conflict between the gods themselves (the contest between Artemis and Aphrodite for Hippolytus) or collusion (e.g., between Athena and Poseidon over Greeks leaving Troy). The new element in Euripides's view of the gods is his psychological presentation of the motivations that cause them to intervene in mortal affairs.

This unique vision is best seen in his last play, the *Bacchae,* celebrating both the danger and complete otherness of the wine god Dionysos and the similar capacity of theater to break down human barriers. Dionysos in disguise returns to his birthplace, Thebes, intent on punishing those who deny his unusual nativity. The city's ruler, his cousin Pentheus, relies on tyrannical orthodoxy in attempting to resist the stranger. Dionysos arranges for Pentheus to view and be captured by ecstatic female followers of the god driven to madness by the king's voyeurism. As the god stages the death of the unbeliever Pentheus to manifest his own divinity, so the playwright frames his drama to acknowledge the blessings of an irrational, emotional spectacle, one that probably provided the distant ritual origin of Greek drama. **See also** Dionysos; Greek religion.

Europe, new religions in. Europe has witnessed the rise of new religious movements during several periods of its history—in, for example, northern and central Europe in the 1530s and in England from 1620 to 1650 and around the turn of the nineteenth century. As in the United States, Canada, New Zealand, and Australia, the present wave became visible to the general public toward the end of the 1960s, although several of the movements (such as SUBUD, Vedanta, and Scientology) had been present in Europe for some time. Often syncretistic in nature, and unlike earlier movements that had been derived almost entirely from the Judeo-Christian culture, many of today's groups can trace their origins to a variety of sources, including both religious traditions (such as Hinduism, Buddhism, Islam, Shintoism, and paganism) and more secular practices and ideologies (such as psychoanalysis, hedonism, existentialism, Marxism, business management, and science fiction).

The majority of contemporary new religions reached Europe by three main routes: first, immigrants bringing their religion with them, as in the case of several Hindu and Islamic sects and the numerous West Indian Holiness and African independent churches; second, Europeans returning from other countries in which they were converted, for example, to the Rajneesh sect in India or to Nichiren Shoshu Buddhism in Japan; and third, the efforts of foreign missionaries, as in the case of the Unification Church, whose missionaries had been converted by Koreans in the United States. There are, however, a number of indigenous movements, such as the Aetherius Society, the Emin Foundation, and the Findhorn Community that originated in Britain, the Raelians and Alliance Universelle in France, Nonsiamosoli and Damanhur in Italy, Opus Angelorum in Austria, Orden Fiat Lux in Switzerland, the Anand Ashram in Denmark, and the Lou movement in the Netherlands.

Due to lack of reliable data, the distribution of the movements is difficult to assess accurately, but work carried out by the Institute for the Study of American Religion suggests that Europe has hosted a relatively larger number of new religions than has the United States. The concentration seems to be particularly high in predominantly Protestant countries such as Germany, Switzerland, England, and Holland; but numerous movements are to be found in

France and Italy, with somewhat fewer in Spain, Portugal, Ireland, Finland, and Greece. Even before 1989, some of the movements had a few members in the Eastern Bloc countries—most were underground (Krishna devotees were imprisoned in the former Soviet Union), but some were openly practicing their beliefs (several Buddhist and Human Potential groups were officially registered in Poland, for example). Since 1989, there has been a veritable flooding of groups into Eastern Europe, offering not only spiritual benefit, but also more secular skills. The Unification Church, for example, offers English-language courses and visits to the West, and Scientology and other self-development movements provide courses and techniques that claim to facilitate the acquisition of skills necessary for success in a capitalist environment.

The actual number of movements depends on what definition is used. If movements from within the Christian tradition (such as Opus Dei and the Restoration movement) and "self-religions" (such as Life Training and Movement for Inner Spiritual Awareness) are included, the total in Europe might be about one thousand; it could be more if individual house churches, New Age groups, and covens were counted separately. Membership figures vary even more according to the definition of what counts as membership. Throughout the entire continent, a million or so individuals may have attended some New Age meetings, been initiated into the practice of Transcendental Meditation, or taken a course in Scientology, EST, or ECKANKAR; but there are very few new religions that have more than a thousand fully committed members (there are about a thousand "Moonies" in the whole of Europe), and a considerable proportion of the movements have well under a hundred followers. Statistically, it would be hard to argue that such religions are responsible for the pan-European drop in church membership in recent years; a necessarily crude calculation of the situation in Britain indicates that less than 5 percent of the half-million loss of membership from the mainstream churches between 1975 and 1980 could be accounted for by people joining an alternate religion during the same period. It is probable, however, that tens of millions have been affected to some degree by either the movements or the ideas that they have helped to popularize: for example, according to the 1990 European Values Survey, 20 percent of Europeans now believe in reincarnation.

Characteristics: Some new religions have attracted an enormous amount of attention in some parts of Europe, while others remain unknown to few but their members. What is clear, however, is the enormous variety to be found in the beliefs, practices, and organization of the movements. While the Unification Church has a remarkably comprehensive theology based on its founder's special interpretation of the Old and New Testaments, the Children of God (Family of Love) have accumulated vast collections of "Mo letters"—comic strips in which the movement's leader, David "Moses" Berg, uses biblical references to support his grossly unconventional views on such subjects as politics, sex, and child-rearing. While the International Society for Krishna Consciousness (ISKCON) relies on its founder's interpretation of the *Bhagavad Gita* and other Hindu scripture, the Rajneeshees are taught to reject all formal teachings but follow a vast collection of talks on tape and in books. While members of the Great White Brotherhood communicate one set of truths through Ananda Tara Shan to her followers near Copenhagen, the "Ascended Masters" send a slightly different set of messages to Elizabeth Clare Prophet for her to relay to communicants of the Church Universal and Triumphant. While some religions, such as Ananda Marga and the Church of Scientology, are highly organized, the New Age movement is a loose network of different groups that may keep in touch through personal contacts, festivals, magazines, newsletters, and mailings. The Brahma Kumaris advocate celibacy for their more committed members and ISKCON prohibits sex except for purposes of procreation within marriage. The Children of God indulged in "flirty fishing" (providing sexual favors in order to obtain money and/or new members), while the Rajneeshees celebrate as broad a diversity of sexual experiences as their stringent precautions against AIDS and other sexually transmitted diseases will permit.

Membership: Generally speaking, those attracted to the new religions have been drawn disproportionately from the young of the middle classes. There are exceptions, such as the working-class blacks who predominate in the Rastafarian movement in England. It should, however, be recognized that, with the passage of time, not only has the core membership of new religious movements grown older, with an increasing number of children being born, but many of the founders (such as Anandamurti, L. Ron Hubbard, Meher Baba, Prabhupada, Bhagwan Shri Rajneesh, and Wierwille) have died, and the movements have adapted many of their earlier practices to their changing circumstances.

Political and Religious Responses: Reactions to the

new religions have varied from outraged protest to tolerance, though rarely enthusiastic, acceptance. The media in the Nordic countries, Belgium, the Netherlands, and Luxembourg have paid only minimal attention to the movements, but certain sections in, for example, France, Germany, England, and Spain have publicized sensationalist and vitriolic reports of abusive and antisocial episodes. Anticult groups, which are to be found in most European countries, differ in the concerns that they express, in their composition (some, for example, are formed by concerned parents, others by evangelical Christians), and in the lengths to which they are prepared to go in combating the movements. Several forcible deprogrammings have been effected, frequently by American or British "professionals" who may charge several thousand dollars for their services, and whose sole qualification is that they themselves were once members of a new religious movement.

While some politicians and religious leaders have expressed concern over the activities of cults, West European governments and churches only occasionally have taken action to curb cult activities. In the late 1970s, the Federal Republic of Germany's Ministry for Youth, Family and Health funded an extensive research project into such groups in Germany, the United Kingdom, the United States, and the Netherlands. This played down many of the alleged dangers of the movements and, recognizing some of the needs that they meet, placed the whole phenomenon in the wider context of social problems facing young people. A report commissioned by the prime minister of France in 1982 and a resolution, passed by the European Parliament in 1984, both calling for stricter controls over new religious movements, have been largely ignored. Around the same time, the Dutch government commissioned a study of contemporary new religions that concluded that no action should be taken. In Britain the government and mainstream churches have, since 1988, been supporting an independent charity, INFORM, which aims to help the general public by providing objective information about the movements. Also in 1988, the Centro Studi Sulle Nuove Religioni (CESNUR) was founded in Italy for the purpose of analyzing and publishing scholarly information about new religions. *See also* Aetherius Society; Ananda Marga; Brahma Kumari; Children of God; Church of Scientology; Church Universal and Triumphant; ECKANKAR; Emin; EST (Erhard Seminars Training); Great White Brotherhood; Holiness churches; Human Potential movement; International Society for Krishna Con-

sciousness (ISKCON); Moonie; New Age movements; Nichiren Shoshu; Opus Dei; Rajneesh Foundation International; Subud; Transcendental Meditation; Unification Church; Vedanta Society.

Eusebius (ca. 260–340), the most important early Christian church historian, best known for his *Ecclesiastical History* and a *Life of Constantine*.

Evagrius Ponticus (ee-vag'ree-uhs pon'tee-kuhs; 349–399), Christian contemplative best known as the first monk to write extensively on the nature of monastic life and to collect the wise sayings of the desert ascetics (a literary form that became increasingly popular in the fourth and fifth centuries). *See also* monasticism.

Evangelical Christian Catholic Church. *See* Africa, new religions in.

evangelical counsels, life practices, stemming from the Gospels, that form the basis of the vows of Christian religious life in nearly all its forms. Also known as the counsels of perfection, they involve poverty, or renunciation of personal property; chastity, or complete abstention from sexual relations; and obedience, or submission of the will in all things but sin to a religious superior. *See also* monasticism; vow.

evangelicals a family of Protestant Christians found in a number of denominations. Evangelicals have taken, and been assigned, a name that actually is as old as the Protestant movement. In Germany the church that claims the heritage of Martin Luther (1483–1546) is called the *Evangelische Kirche*. The term has acquired a more specific reference, over time, to describe a particular company of Protestant Christians, typically conservative. Its emergence as an ascribed, later proudly claimed, title arose in England to identify the spiritual descendants of the Wesleyan movement of the eighteenth century. These Christians emphasized the classic doctrines of personal salvation (justification, regeneration) and sanctification, the power of the Holy Spirit acting within a person's life to transform and empower. This "witness of the Spirit" set off Evangelicals from "Churchmen" who relied more on grace through sacraments than on grace personally experienced. Also the latter had no aspirations to (or illusions about) a profound sanctification wrought by the Holy Spirit, that is, being made holy, or even morally perfect, as some evangelicals were to claim.

In England, the evangelical community stood alongside the establishment, the Church of England, although evangelical Anglicanism has enjoyed some strength from around 1825 to the late twentieth century. In nineteenth-century America, evangelicalism was the mainline religion. It was the form of Christianity practiced by the prominent popular denominations: Methodist, Presbyterian, Baptist, and Congregational (by contrast with Lutheran and Episcopal). Thus the bulk of American church people were evangelical (until Catholics became numerous by 1850). The evangelicals believed forthrightly in supernatural truth and power, the biblical message as divinely inspired, not humanly contrived or naturally explicable. Conversion, forgiveness, the gift of eternal life in this life and in heaven were preached and believed. Prayer was practiced as a real conversation with a living God who could and did respond by using governance over creation to accomplish ends, often in cooperation with faithful followers and in line with their petitions.

"Evangelical" in America in 1810 or 1830 or 1850 was synonymous with orthodox Protestant Christian. Liberals belonged to Deist circles or to Unitarian congregations, and they were a small minority. There were traditionalists, a third category, who were variously Episcopalians and Lutherans, and Roman Catholics. The remaining options were comparatively few.

From the 1870s, major changes accompanied the trend in the churches to subscribe to emergent new perspectives. Evangelicals challenged, and often resisted, those new developments: in particular, higher biblical criticism, theological modes conditioned by evolution and scientific naturalism, and the Social Gospel that concerned itself more with the amelioration of public conditions than with personal piety. These developments had antecedents and earlier counterparts, but after 1900 they struck as an avalanche, taking much of the leadership of the mainline, hitherto evangelical churches with them into a new, though not typically extreme, liberalism.

Evangelicalism is "conservative," in the sense of grounding everything in biblical authority, and being firmly authority-minded. Taking that position requires evangelicals to resist compromise with the standards of the world, no matter how attractive and popular they may be. The innovative teachings and perspectives that were grounded in human inquiry and in "proofs" provided by science, history, textual analysis, and ethical theory had to be rejected.

American Evangelicalism: In this way, American evangelicalism came into being. A movement that stood outside the cultural and religious mainstream from around 1880 to the 1970s, it has acquired following, recognition, and respect, as well as some notoriety since the late 1970s. Its authority-mindedness serves well its passion to grow and wield influence. Often the old mainline ("liberal") churches, in their concern with being responsive to modern currents of thought and social understanding, have yielded solid teaching. The evangelical churches have held firm against compromise and dilution. For many, that sturdiness, clear sense of identity, and commitment make them appealing. Their recent growth and wide acceptance have had other consequences as well: infusing the old mainline churches with a quickened sense of propriety and rectitude; creating a wedge between themselves and other Christian bodies; rendering Christianity irrelevant to modernity-conscious people; and luring evangelical people and churches into the public arena through political involvement and an ethical urgency they yearn to see the whole society adopt.

Fundamentalism is one proportionately small (perhaps 15 percent) branch of the evangelical community. It understands the Christian message in propositional and serial terms. The Bible is taken as having not only infallible authority but inerrant textual precision as well. Independent Baptists, themselves of many varieties, comprise its largest constituencies. Other rationalist bodies belong in this classification, for example, the Churches of Christ, Bible Churches, and the Orthodox Presbyterian Church.

Conversionist and Confessional Approaches: Evangelicalism has two principal ways of approaching Christian meaning and practice, the conversionist and the confessional. The first stresses the conscious personal experience of conversion, by which one's life course, orientation, and destiny are completely changed. Doctrinal emphasis is given to those biblical texts and theological teachings that portray and generate the experience. Thus, doctrine mostly urges people to "accept Christ." Confessional forms of evangelicalism live by a more comprehensive vision of their responsibility. They too are committed to evangelism, converting the world to Christ; but they also interpret, systematize, and formulate Christian meaning. Both groups are totally committed to biblical authority. Representative conversionist groups are the Southern Baptist Convention and the various Pentecostal bodies; confessional groups include the Reformed bodies and such Lutheran communions as Missouri Synod and Wisconsin Synod.

This diversity can obscure the substantial unity that makes evangelicalism an identifiable family within the larger Protestant framework. One element found everywhere is the supernatural grounding and revelation. Another is the certainty that divine power is available to direct lives and history, to heal from all manner of imperfection, and to empower Christ's followers toward genuine righteousness. All truth is referred to biblical teaching and the entire human enterprise is referred for its true nature and course to God's revelation and his will for the created order.

A short list of doctrines is basic: the triune God is gracious and active; Christ died for the sins of all and all must seek and find forgiveness in him, toward a godly life here and eternal life hereafter; the Christian life entails genuine righteousness in thought and deed; the Bible is God's holy Word.

While the black church is evangelical, it has developed its own blending of worship, moral life, and the status of doctrine. It does hold to orthodox Christianity. But response to God's truth is lived out more in joyous worship and in serving human needs than in insisting on assent to doctrine. The disposition to charge heresy, strong among fundamentalists, is quite weak among black Protestants—and recessive but not irrelevant to most other evangelicals.

Popular parlance speaks of evangelicals as *born-again Christians*. But that term is simplistic and the evangelical community resists such generalizations. These Christians are certain of their identity and responsibility because they are certain of the truthfulness and ultimacy of the divine revelation in Christ through the Holy Scriptures. Large and growing, evangelicals are the most visible, and probably the most influential, sector in Protestant Christianity in America in the late twentieth century. *See also* Protestantism.

evangelist (Gk. *euangelion,* "good news"), one who proclaims the Christian gospel. **1** A traveling missionary in the New Testament. **2** Each author of a New Testament Gospel—Matthew, Mark, Luke, and John. **3** A minister who holds no regular charge, but preaches to various groups in revivals or special crusades.

Eve. *See* Adam and Eve.

evil, the antithesis of the good and beneficial, whether perceived as a cosmic power or as a human inclination. *See also* morality and religion; theodicy.

evil eye, the belief in several traditional cultures that certain persons or spirits could cause harm to others simply by looking intently at them. It is often related to envy.

evolution of religion. *See* animism; magic, science, and religion; origin of religion; religion, anthropology of.

ex cathedra (Lat., "from the chair"), a phrase used in Roman Catholicism to describe solemn papal teachings that are uttered, symbolically, from the chair (i.e., the seat of authority) of the pope in Rome. *See also* papacy.

excommunication, a religious sanction that removes an individual from the ritual and social community.

Judaism: Because Judaism has no central authority, excommunication, forced isolation from the Jewish community to punish improper behavior or belief, is usually decreed by a local rabbinical court and applies primarily within that community. There is no formal court procedure or presentation of evidence for excommunication, and any rabbinical court can lift a decree.

Under the ordinary form of excommunication, called *nidduy* (Heb.), the excommunicant behaves like a mourner (except for the ritual tearing of clothes), lives only with family, is shunned by others, and is not counted for the quorum required for worship. The excommunicant's coffin is stoned at burial. Nidduy is announced by the head of the court.

A more severe form, called *herem* ("devoted thing," something forbidden for common use) requires, in addition, that the excommunicant study alone and make a living only from a small shop. The procedure for decreeing a herem entails a proclamation in the synagogue either before the open ark or with Torah scroll in hand, the sounding of the *shofar* (ram's horn), the congregational extinguishing of candles, and the recitation of biblical curses against and warnings about associating with the excommunicant.

In medieval times, the excommunicant was treated as a non-Jew. That status often was extended to the excommunicant's spouse and children, who might also be ostracized.

Talmudic and medieval rabbinic literature lists various reasons for excommunication. Among other causes, a person could be ostracized for causing the public profanation of God's name, ignoring prescribed religious behavior or hindering the public performance of it, incorrect business practices, breaking a vow, improper sexual conduct, violating the Torah on the basis of spurious analogies, insulting a scholar, or decreeing excommunication without sufficient reason.

Over time, particularly in Orthodox communities, excommunication was applied so routinely and automatically to any unacceptable behavior that it lost its punitive and coercive effect.

Christianity: Excommunication in the Christian tradition is an action taken by church authorities by which a person is cut off from participation in the worship life of a congregation because of some serious fault or breach of church discipline. Most commonly, the individual is barred from the sacraments. In certain communities such persons are also socially ostracized in a practice called "shunning."

exegesis, general term for the interpretation of texts. *See also* Abhidharma; abrogation; aggadah; allegory; alphabet mysticism; Bible, interpretation of the Christian; Buddhism (authoritative texts and their interpretation); Confucianism (authoritative texts and their interpretation); criticism, higher; criticism, lower; demythologization; gematria; halakah; hermeneutics; Hinduism (authoritative texts and their interpretation); holy books; homiletics; homily; inerrancy, biblical; Islam (authoritative texts and their interpretation); Islamic law; Judaism (authoritative texts and their interpretation); midrash; Mimamsa; New Text school; Old Text school; typology.

existentialism, a complex movement in twentieth-century continental philosophy and literature, which flourished in Europe after World War I and in the United States after World War II. Religious existentialism is usually thought to begin in the nineteenth century with Soren Kierkegaard ("leap of faith"), and antireligious existentialism with Friedrich Nietzsche ("death of God"). All existentialist authors presuppose the priority of existence over essence and emphasize the distinctive humanness of the person, arguing that human nature has no essence but only a history. They select as most characteristic of the human condition such categories as anguish, contradiction, nothingness, and absurdity. Typical existentialist themes include the anxiety of decision, the radical nature of freedom, the tragic sense of life, the objectifying tendency of thought, the human invention of values forged in freedom, the difficulty of achieving authentic existence, and the importance of subjectivity and individuality as a protest against the claims of universal reason and conformity to the crowd. *See also* literature and religion; religion, philosophy of.

ex nihilo. *See* creation out of nothing.

Exodus, in the Hebrew Bible, the narrative of the Israelites' escape from Egypt under the leadership of Moses, and their wandering in the wilderness before their entry into the promised land of Canaan. *See also* Moses.

ex opere operato (eks-oh'pair-ay ah-pair-ah'toh; Lat., "from the action performed"), a phrase used to describe the efficacy of Christian sacraments as derived from the correct performance of the rite and not *ex opere operantis*, "from the worthiness of the minister." *See also* Donatists; sacraments and ordinances (Christianity).

exorcism, ritual expulsion of demons or evil spirits from an individual or place.

Christianity: In the New Testament, exorcisms are a central part of the public ministry of Jesus. Christianity has utilized exorcisms in a variety of ways: as an integral part of baptismal liturgies in which prayers and rites are used to symbolize the person's departure from sin and entrance into the body of Christians; as blessings to separate material things from profane use in order to dedicate them to divine use (e.g., the exorcism of water used in baptism); and as a rite to free persons from demonic possession. In the Roman Catholic Church this rite can only be done with episcopal authorization. Fundamentalist and Pentecostal churches attempt to drive out the demonic with sessions of prayer, the laying on of hands, and the reading of scripture.

In some forms of early Christianity there was a separate clerical office for the exorcist.

Japanese Religion: Exorcism (Jap. *harai*) is a fundamental concept in Japanese myth and Shinto ritual. In the myth of the primordial parents, Izanagi purifies himself after contact with death in a ritual of washing with water, the prototype of a rite that is repeated every time one enters the precincts of a Shinto shrine. The underworld deity Susano-o undergoes harai after his rampage in heaven in a rite that involved the cutting of his hair and nails as well as his banishment. The list of his "sins" (*tsumi*) reveals a concept of pollution that contains both overt transgressions and accidents in which the one polluted is a victim rather than a transgressor. This breadth of meaning continues in modern Shinto, although the moral dimension is more prominent than in ancient times. In classical Japan the Great Purification, or Great Exorcism (*oharai*), was held twice a year to decontaminate the imperial court and by extension the entire nation, and a version of it today forms the beginning of every Shinto ritual. The ritual text (*norito*) for this alludes to the Susano-o myth and describes the ritual transfer of tsumi into sticks and reeds that are cast into a river, carried away, and lost in the sea by various water deities. Other norito rites were used to banish "unruly deities" to far places; they are without mythic allusions and seek to placate the deities with gifts. Such rituals were performed in times of crisis. When this failed in ancient times a shaman was sought to discover a more particular remedy in the will of the *kami* (divinity, divine presence). *See also* Gion Shrine; Japanese folk religion; norito.

experience, the awareness of direct or repeated contact with some aspect or aspects of one's environment, whether external or internal. While this definition captures the everyday use of the term, it obscures the fact that, in order to investigate the nature of experience, one must use experience as a basic investigatory tool.

The French mathematician Rene Descartes (1596–1650) asks how one is able to distinguish between sensations and images produced by corresponding aspects of the environment and those that are in some way illusory (as, for example, in dreams). In *Meditations on First Philosophy* (1641), he challenges the reader to discover a criterion with which to distinguish objective from illusory experience. Descartes has become best known for establishing the problem of skepticism, the claim that one cannot distinguish between objective and illusory experience based on the content of any particular experience.

Descartes adopts the first-person point of view; he reflects on the character of his own experience. This starting point has been disputed at least from the time of the English empiricist and political philosopher John Locke (1632–1704). In *An Essay Concerning Human Understanding* (1689), Locke assumes what has come to be known as the naturalistic or third-person standpoint: by observing the interaction between a human subject and the physical environment, Locke tries to say how experience is in fact produced. But, as he admits, his empiricism cannot account for such apparent—though unperceivable—features of human experience as, for example, causality and substance. The German philosopher Immanuel Kant (1724–1804) takes up Descartes's challenge. In the *Critique of Pure Reason* (1781–87), Kant argues that even a simple awareness of one's own power of thought requires the existence of objects outside oneself in space and time. This, according to Kant, guarantees that experience puts people in contact with an external world of objects, though it does not guarantee the truth of any given judgment about them.

Both the first- and third-person standpoints have found recent and able defenders. For the American mathematician Charles Sanders Peirce (1839–1914), experience is marked by an external intrusion into a person's ongoing thought. One judges that a shrill noise has been caused by a whistle. The experience is objective—and the judgment true—just in case it is or would be confirmed by sufficient inquiry. By contrast, the contemporary American philosopher of science W. V. O. Quine has urged that, "What to count as observation now can be settled in terms of the stimulation of our sensory receptors, let consciousness fall where it may" (*Ontological Relativity and Other Essays*, 1969). The contemporary American philosopher and psychologist Donald Davidson has brought Descartes's skeptical question full circle by charging that Quine's naturalism has skeptical consequences: How, asks Davidson, can we move from knowledge of our sensory surfaces to knowledge of those (presumably) external *sources* of stimulation?

Recently, philosophers and social scientists have asked whether and to what extent a person's experience depends upon beliefs, posits, and theory of the world. The question is debated to what extent one can isolate religious or aesthetic or moral experience from a theoretical and conceptual background. *See also* empiricism; religion, philosophy of; religious experience.

expiation, the ritual process of removing the consequences of some offense against divinity.

expressive. *See* instrumental and expressive.

ex voto. *See* votive offering.

Ezra, in the Hebrew Bible, a central figure in postexilic Jerusalem. In later tradition, Ezra is often depicted as the author or editor of the Pentateuch.

ABCDE F
G L
M Q
RSTUV
WXY&Z

Fa-chia (fah-jyah; Chin., "Legalist School"), Chinese philosophical school of the Warring States period (481–221 B.C.). Shang Yang (d. 338 B.C.), founder of the Legalist school, denied the validity of both virtue and historical precedent in statecraft. His ideas were extended by Han Fei-tzu (d. 233 B.C.), who saw rewards and punishments as the means of controlling the subjects of a state. Shen Pu-hai (d. 337 B.C.) emphasized administrative methods rather than punitive law. Discredited by the harsh government of the Ch'in dynasty (221–206 B.C.), Legalism declined as a school thereafter.

Fa-hsiang school (fah-shahng), Chinese branch of Yogachara Buddhism founded by Hsuan-tsang and his disciple K'uei-chi in the seventh century. Although Yogachara was introduced to China by Paramartha a century before, a desire to clarify doctrinal problems prompted Hsuan-tsang's journey to India, where he studied the teachings of Asanga and Vasubandhu at Nalanda. Its doctrine that the world is a projection of consciousness earned this school the designation "consciousness-only" (Chin. *wei-shih*). It divided the mind into eight levels of consciousness, of which the last, *alayavijnana* (Skt.), or "storehouse consciousness," was believed to hold the seeds of discriminatory mental phenomena. *See also* China, Buddhism in; Hsuan-tsang; six systems of Indian philosophy; Yogachara.

faith, common Christian synonym for religion (as in "the Buddhist faith," "the Muslim faith") that reduces religion to a set of beliefs.

faith, Christian, the act or virtue or spiritual disposition by which people accept the reality, promises, and love of God. Theologians have proposed many distinctions concerning faith. The term *faith* can refer to what one believes, or the power by which one believes, or the state of soul that belief creates. In the New Testament of the Bible, faith is the attitude necessary to enter the reign of God as well as the precondition that Jesus requires, if he is to work striking signs that God's reign is dawning (cures, exorcisms, acts controlling nature). Catholic theology has stressed the intellectual side of faith: the doctrines that commitment to Christ and the Church entail. Protestant theology has stressed personal trust: making God one's rock and salvation. In the Catholic understanding, faith perfects reason. In the Protestant understanding, faith can call reason into question. Eastern Orthodox theology has insisted on linking right faith with right worship: one only believes correctly when drawn by God's Spirit into prayer.

In a secular culture, the concept of faith carries a certain militancy: believers oppose the outlook and values of those who concentrate on "this world" and neglect God.

faith healing, a term usually limited to the Christian practice of restoring health by means of prayer, a transfer of divine power, or the intervention of the Holy Spirit. *See also* healing; medicine and religion.

faith, hope, and charity. *See* cardinal virtues.

fakir (fuh-kihr'; Arab., "poor man"), a wandering religious mendicant, particularly one who exhibits supernatural powers. Originally applied to Muslim (Sufi) mystics, the term took on its broader usage in India. *See also* asceticism.

Falashas (Amharic, "exiles"), Jewish ethnic group originating in Ethiopia that follows a form of Judaism based upon the Bible, certain books of the Apocrypha, and other religious writings. In 1975 Falashas began to emigrate to Israel, where a large community now resides.

Ethiopian Jewish tradition traces the group's origin to dignitaries from Jerusalem who accompanied the Queen of Sheba back to Ethiopia after her visit with Solomon (1 Kings 10). Ethnographers hold that the group descends from the Agau tribes and was converted by Jews in southern Arabia or in Ethiopia before the fourth century, when the Askum dynasty converted to Christianity. The Falashas' numbers may have been augmented by Jewish captives brought to the area in 525.

The Falashas' religion is based primarily upon scripture, which they have in the Geez translation used by the Ethiopian church. The Falashas believe that there is one God, who chose Israel and whose Messiah will lead the people back to the Holy Land. They observe the pentateuchal laws concerning clean and unclean animals and other matters of ritual purity. They wash their hands before eating and recite blessings before and after meals. Boys are circumcised on the eighth day. The Falashas observe the Sabbath and other festivals, including a variation of the fast of Av but excluding Purim and Hanukkah. Burial is on the day of death and is followed by seven days of mourning.

Religious life centers on the *mesgid* (synagogue), which is divided into two halls. One of these, the "holy of holies," contains a handwritten parchment Pentateuch, bound as a book.

Only the priest and *dabtara* (religious teacher) may enter this room. An altar in the synagogue's court is used for the Passover sacrifice. Prayers are recited in Geez.

Several of the Falashas' observances do not derive from Judaism. Their priests (*kessim*) claim Aaronide descent, but upon ordination by the high priest, any educated man can assume priestly functions. The Falashas also have monks and nuns, who live in monasteries or in seclusion outside the villages. Circumcision of females is practiced, as in many parts of Africa. The Falashas share the Ethiopian belief in spirits and use amulets, charms, and incantations.

In 1975 the Israeli rabbinate affirmed that Falashas were Jews, and a program of bringing them to Israel began. From 1984 to 1985, a secret Israeli airlift code-named Operation Moses brought eight thousand Falashas to Israel. In 1989, an estimated twelve thousand to seventeen thousand remained in Ethiopia, subjected to conditions of famine and anti-Semitism.

Despite its earlier determination that Falashas are Jews, the Israeli rabbinate wants to convert them formally to Judaism and refuses to recognize marriages performed by the Falashas' priests. Within the Israeli Falasha community factions argue for and against accommodation to Israeli orthodoxy.

Fall, in the Hebrew Bible, the narrative of the disobedience and expulsion of Adam and Eve from Eden (Genesis 2–3). Later Christian understandings see in this narrative the Fall of all humankind into sin and death. *See also* original sin (Christianity).

Fallen Angels, postbiblical Jewish, Christian, and Muslim legends concerning the rebellion of Satan/Lucifer/Iblis and his band against God, usually prompted by the creation of the first human being in the divine image and the command that the angels give it homage. In punishment, they are expelled from heaven. *See also* Iblis; Lucifer; Satan.

falsafa. *See* Islamic philosophy.

false face, the common English term describing wooden or cornhusk masks of the Iroquois tribes, principally of western New York State and Canada. The wooden hand-carved masks are frequently characterized by distorted visages, which emphasize askew, prominent noses and mouths. They are usually slightly larger than a human face and often have long hanks of hair made from buffalo mane or horsetail attached to the top. Historically, they were shaped in accordance with a dream, resulting in an array of facial expressions. The wearers of false faces belonged to medicine societies that had calendrical ritual functions. They could be called upon to cure a person afflicted with any of a variety of diseases, from trembling hands to insanity. Calendrical rituals of masked dance, song, and the burning of tobacco were performed to appease the spirits who controlled matters such as high wind, epidemics, and bad luck. Cornhusk masks, called the "bushy heads" due to the fringe of unwoven husk around a tightly woven face, are primarily used when they announce the arrival of the false faces. There is a general connection between wooden masks and hunting and medicine, and the cornhusk masks with agriculture and fertility. The false-face figure appears on stone and pottery pipe artifacts as well as on dolls and miniature masks, which are often attached to a standard-sized mask. Many Iroquois artisans have recently produced both wooden and cornhusk faces as objects of Native American art.

familiar, a guardian spirit, usually in animal form. *See also* guardian spirit; jaguar (South American religions).

Family of Love. *See* Children of God.

fanatic, pejorative term for someone perceived as having excessive religious zeal.

fang-chung shu (fahng-joong shoo, Chin., "arts of the inner chamber"), early Chinese term for private physiological practices designed to preserve sexual vitality; it was occasionally used in later Taoism. *See also* physiological techniques (Taoism).

fang-shih (fahng-shuhr; Chin., "masters of techniques"), magicians in early China who rose to prominence in the northeastern states of Ch'i and Yen in the fourth century B.C. and became widespread and often powerful during the Ch'in and Han dynasties (221 B.C.–A.D. 220). Claiming the ability to produce elixirs of immortality, transmute base metal into gold, and cast magical spells, prominent masters were sometimes patronized by rulers seeking physical immortality. The masters were condemned by Confucianists, who accused them of fraud, sorcery, black magic, and encouraging heterodox beliefs. Some elements of *fang-shih* practice were subsumed into religious Taoism. *See also* alchemy; immortality.

Fan-wang ching (fahn-wahng jing; Chin., "Brahma's Net

Sutra"), scripture used for ordination of Chinese Buddhist monks that forbade killing of all human beings and doing obeisance to laypeople. *See also* bodhisattva precepts; monasticism; ordination.

Fard, Wallace D. (b., d. unknown), known as Master Wali Farrad Muhammad, founder of the Nation of Islam in Detroit in 1930. *See also* African Americans (North America), new religions among; Nation of Islam.

Farrakhan, Louis (b. Louis Eugene Wolcott, 1933), African-American leader of the Nation of Islam since 1975, who advocates economic uplift and the original teachings of Wallace Fard and Elijah Muhammad. *See also* African Americans (North America), new religions among; Fard, Wallace D.; Muhammad, Elijah; Nation of Islam.

fasting, abstinence from food for a length of time. A common ascetic practice, it is also a widespread mode of purification with respect to ritual activities or the restoration of health. *See also* asceticism; food; purification; ritual.

Native American Religions: Fasting is one of a number of institutionalized religious behaviors that prepare individuals for interaction with transcendent powers. Native American fasting may involve food as well as water deprivation and may also be connected with abstinence from sexual contact and other restrictions on behavior. Fasting may be associated with an individual religious activity, such as the quest for a vision or a guardian spirit, accompanied by other institutionalized activities, such as the sweat lodge, or practiced in connection with shamanistic healing or in preparation for raiding or warfare. In some instances on the Plains, fasting may be connected with important life stages such as puberty or other ritual acts such as offering smoke. Participants in the sacrificial features of the Sun Dance fasted; often the individual pledger of the dance and his wife fasted as a part of their preparation. Fasting can thus be connected with an institutionalized ritual position or role, such as shaman, as well as with ritual leaders, such as priests and bundle owners. While there is no set of meanings that would characterize the understanding of all groups on the Plains, the general significance of fasting, along with other institutionalized practices, seems to be related to the belief that humans must demonstrate in a dramatic manner, through sacrifice and cleansing, that they are seriously seeking the aid of transcendent powers. Only in this manner, it seems, will the powers that are implored take note of the human supplicant. Despite tribal variations, in each culture fasting exhibits a set of typical forms and is surrounded by a number of shared cultural expectations. *See also* bundle; guardian spirit; pipe, sacred; shamanism; Sun Dance, Sun Dance religion; sweat, sweat lodge; vision quest.

Christianity: In Christianity fasting derives from the example of Jesus, who both fasted and recommended the practice. Partial or total abstinence from food and drink was institutionalized in early Christianity for certain days. Today in Roman Catholic and Orthodox churches there are seasons of fasting before Christmas and Easter and, in some traditions, a day of fasting before participating in the Eucharist. *See also* Lent.

Islam: Muslims in good health must observe a daytime fast (Arab. *sawm*) during the month of Ramadan by abstaining from food, drink, smoking, and sexual activity. In the evening, a meal is eaten and many attend the mosque for seasonal litanies. A light meal is eaten before daybreak. *See also* Ashura; Five Pillars; Islam (festal cycle).

fatalism, the view that all events are irrevocably predetermined with the result that human effort is irrelevant.

fate, the notion that there is an inevitable necessity that controls everything. Conceptions of fate vary widely: it may be understood as impersonal or personal, malevolent or beneficent, knowable or unknowable. Religious traditions that emphasize salvation often promise liberation from fate. Other traditions advocate submission to fate.

fate (Hinduism), a term commonly used to translate the Sanskrit *daiva* (lit., "that which pertains to the gods"), but this is problematic. In the Upanishads, epics, and Puranas, daiva and *karma* (the consequences of meritorious and demeritorious actions) are sometimes equated, sometimes counterposed. Further, in *bhakti* (devotional) literature the supreme *deva* (God) is capable of overturning karma and daiva alike, while elsewhere, devas, like humans, are considered subject to both forces. A consensus in the literature seems to be that daiva and human effort (*purushakara*) together constitute the primary causes of human events. The unacceptability of a "fatalistic" viewpoint in classic tradition is evident in the rejection of the Ajivikas, known for their doctrinaire ascription of all events to *niyati*, "inevitable necessity"— perhaps the best definition for "fate."

In several regions of India today, "headwriting" is a popular belief: when one is still in the womb, the deity writes on one's head certain immutable qualities and/or parameters of the life to come. In popular belief as in classic literature, there seems to be general acceptance of human responsibility, although people tend to suspect witchcraft, angry deities, or ritual errors as causes for mishaps. Daiva seems to be an explanation of last resort. *See also* Hinduism (thought and ethics); karma.

father. 1 A common biblical title for God. 2 A title of respect for a Christian priest. 3 A title for the abbot of a monastery.

Father Divine (b. George Baker, ca. 1880–1965), African-American minister and founder of the Peace Mission movement in Sayville, New York, in 1932. Son of ex-slaves, Divine developed a theology comprised of elements of African-American Christianity, Methodism, Catholicism, Pentecostalism, and the power-of-positive-thinking ideology, New Thought. He taught that he was God and encouraged followers to channel his spirit to achieve health, prosperity, and salvation. An integrationist, Divine attracted both blacks and whites and campaigned for Civil Rights. During the Depression, disciples opened businesses offering low-priced goods and services, and Peace Missions provided social assistance to the poor. *See also* African Americans (North America), new religions among.

Fatima (fah'ti-mah; ca. 605–633), favorite daughter of Muhammad; wife of fourth Caliph Ali ibn Abi Talib, the first Imam of the Shia; mother of Imams Hasan and Husayn; ancestor of all of Muhammad's descendants. Distinguished by her piety, poverty, and special purity, and known as "the Radiant One," "the Virgin," and "Chief of Women," she is venerated by Muslims, especially the Shia. *See also* Mary; Shia.

Fatima, Shrine of, located in central Portugal, an important Christian pilgrimage site where, it is held, the Virgin Mary appeared to three children on May 13, 1917. *See also* Mary (pilgrimage sites).

Fatimids (fah'ti-midz), a North African dynasty that began as an Ismaili Shia movement in the tenth century. After defeating the Abbasid governor in Tunis, Ubayd Allah, the first Fatimid ruler, was proclaimed the Mahdi in 910. The first four Fatimid caliphs ruled an expanding North African empire, and in 969 their forces conquered Egypt, where they built the new city of Cairo as their capital. Fatimid power reached a peak during the reign of al-Mustansir (1036–94). Control of the state was taken over by military commanders in the mid-eleventh century, and conflict with European crusaders and the rising power of Sunni sultans to the East challenged the Fatimids. In 1171, a Sunni commander, Salah al-Din (Saladin), proclaimed the end of Fatimid rule and established the Ayyubid state. *See also* Ismaili Shia.

Fa-tsang (fah-dzahng; 643–712), most noted systematizer of the Chinese Buddhist Hua-yen school and its third patriarch. His contributions centered chiefly on his use of the doctrinal classification scheme, which he parlayed into an argument for the superiority of the *Hua-yen Sutra*. His prolific writings include a commentary on the *Awakening of Faith*. *See also* Awakening of Faith; doctrinal classification; Hua-yen school.

fatwa (fat'wuh; Arab., "legal opinion"), a formal opinion or decision, treating a moral, legal, or doctrinal question, issued by someone recognized as knowledgeable in the juridical sciences of Islam. While it has no binding force, it is regarded as an authoritative interpretation. A *fatwa* may serve to guide the decisions of judges or rulers in the exercise of official functions. Other persons may rely on such pronouncements for direction and counsel in civic, business, or private affairs. *See also* Islamic law.

fear, the cause of religious belief, according to early theories of religion. *See also* origin of religion.

feasts. *See* festal cycle.

feeling, a psychological term meant to identify either the nonrational vehicle or content of religion. The concept of "feeling" has played a key role in many theories of religion that disparage, ignore, or trivialize the cognitive content of religious systems. On the other hand, in some systems of theological thought it has played an apologetic role designed to entice the "cultured despisers" of religion into granting it serious consideration. Thus, the nineteenth-century German theologian Friedrich Schleiermacher proposed the "feeling of absolute dependence" as the key concept for identifying both the form and content of religious consciousness.

Motivating both of these approaches to religion are a number of factors: first, an insistence upon the irrational or nonrational quality of religion; second, a desire to defend (or attack) religion because of its putative emotive quality; and third, a conviction that whatever meager cognitive content religion might have is peripheral to its social and/or psychological functions. *See also* emotions.

felix culpa. *See* Fortunate Fall.

fellowship. *See* brotherhood.

feminism, belief system centered on the concept of women's equality with men. Although originally developed as a political ideology, feminism has had a notable impact on both the study of religion in the academic world and the practice of religion in America. Feminist thinkers in religion have provided a critique of the role of women in various religious traditions, and have speculated about larger patterns of women's oppression and religious systems.

Feminism brings to the study of religion the basic insight that religion has provided rationalization and justification for the oppression of women. This can be seen in the overwhelmingly male character of the foundation and hierarchy of most religious traditions; it is evident in the religious proscriptions that limit women's autonomy and circumscribe women's lives. The feminist critique of religion has convinced many women to abandon traditional religion as hopelessly pernicious because of male dominance. In the opinion of the late-twentieth-century feminist philosopher Mary Daly, all religions are simply justifications for patriarchy, which is the true dominant religion of our planet.

But many feminist thinkers in the twentieth century are dedicated to reinterpreting their traditions to make a better world for women. Christian feminists Phyllis Trible and Elisabeth Schussler Fiorenza have contributed to new understandings of biblical texts traditionally used to restrict women's roles, while theologians such as Rosemary Radford Ruether, Letty Russell, Sallie McFague, and Nelle Morton have provided new models for Christian understanding of God and human society. Jewish feminists such as Judith Plaskow and Ellen Umansky have suggested ways of redirecting and reinterpreting their tradition. Fatima Mernissi has reinterpreted for Islam, as have Rita Gross, Diana Paul, Sandy Boucher, and others for Buddhism. The general approach of these thinkers has been reinterpretation of sacred texts, and reevaluation of the roles of women in specific religious traditions. This analysis has been accepted by many in the mainstream traditions.

In the 1980s there developed a critique of feminist work in religion from women of color and women of non-Western cultures. These thinkers, generally known as womanist or *mujerista* theologians, include Katie Geneva Cannon, Gloria Anzaldua, and Jacquelyn Grant. Their analysis emphasizes the cultural insularity of much feminist thought in religion as stemming from white, middle-class, Western, educated university traditions. Drawing on poetry and storytelling, womanist thought has forced feminist thinkers to be more aware of their own cultural context. This development will certainly have a significant impact on the future of feminist thought in religion. *See also* androcentrism; feminist theology; gender roles; patriarchal; sexuality and religion.

feminist theology, thinking about God that considers female human experience as significant a source for systematic reflection as male human experience.

The first phase of feminist theology began with nineteenth-century American suffragist women such as Elizabeth Cady Stanton. A second phase began in the mid-1960s when Valerie Saiving Goldstein asked whether sin should be defined the same way for women as for men. Feminist theology in its second phase appears in Christianity as Catholic (Rosemary Radford Ruether) or Protestant (Letty Russell), and in Judaism (Judith Plaskow), Hinduism/Buddhism (Rita Gross), and Islam (Riffat Hassan).

Catholic feminist theology has criticized the Church's refusal to ordain women to the priesthood and offers new definitions of sin, salvation, the nature of Christ, and life everlasting. Protestant feminist theologians work on these topics as well as on making the language of worship, including the words of scripture, more inclusive. Catholic feminists also innovate in this area. The absence of profound differences among Catholic and Protestant feminist theology makes it truly ecumenical.

Jewish feminist theology articulates the being of women in that tradition as both female and Jewish. Writing *midrash* (commentary) from a female perspective and constructing rituals that honor young women's coming of age (bat mitzvah) as well as young men's (bar mitzvah) are two examples of Jewish feminist theology.

Hindu and Buddhist feminist theology started more recently (after 1970), stimulated both by Western women interested in the Goddess worship of these religious, and by Hindu and Buddhist women seeking to understand the oppression of women in Asia in light of their own religious traditions.

Islamic feminism has even more recent origins as Muslim women seek to define themselves as distinct from Western women, while seeking an authentic place for themselves in male-dominated Islam.

Some women have left their religious traditions to better critique their basic androcentrism. They recover women's lost religious traditions in Goddess worship (Carol Christ), or construct new religious rituals and themes (Starhawk, Mary Daly). Naomi Goldenberg calls this movement feminist "thealogy," i.e., reflection on the Goddess.

The word *women* covers a variety of female human racial and social locations, and new words have emerged to stand alongside feminist. Black women use the term *womanist,* coined by Alice Walker to mean "black feminist" or "feminist of color." Ada-Maria Isaisi-Diaz uses "Mujerista Theology" to describe her work of God-talk from Hispanic women's experience. *See also* feminism; Goddess religions (contemporary); women-church.

feng-huang (feng-hwahng), the Chinese "phoenix," an auspicious mythical bird and *yin* symbol in yin and *yang* pairs. *See also* yin and yang.

feng-shan sacrifices (fuhng-shahn; Chin., "wind and mountain"), suburban sacrifices to Heaven and Earth that symbolize a Chinese emperor's Mandate from Heaven; they were instituted in the Han dynasty by Emperor Wu (140–86 B.C.), who performed a *feng* ritual himself on Mt. T'ai, while select officers performed a corresponding *shan* rite at the foot of the mountain. *See also* state cult, Chinese; T'ien-ming.

Feng-shen yen-i (fuhng-shuhn yuhn-ee; Chin., "Investiture of the Gods"), a Chinese novel written in the late Ming period (sixteenth century), perhaps by a Taoist priest. It explores the relationship between self-cultivation and cosmic order and the nature of Taoist orthodoxy by mythologizing the ancient story of how the Chou dynasty conquered the corrupt Shang.

feng-shui. *See* geomancy.

fertility rites, outdated term for some agricultural rituals. *See also* agriculture, religious aspects of; sexuality and religion.

festal cycle, the sequence of major public and communal ritual activities, often beginning with some sort of new year celebration. Termed *intensification rites* by scholars, they constitute the religious calendar of a given tradition. *See also* Buddhism (festal cycle); calendar (Christian); Chinese religions (festal cycle); Christianity (festal cycle); Greek religion; Hinduism (festal cycle); Islam (festal cycle); Judaism (festal cycle); Korea (festal cycle); periodic rites; ritual.

festivals. *See* festal cycle.

fetish (derived from a Portuguese word for medals and crucifixes worn by sailors and extended by them to amulets used by Africans; first used as a generic term by Ch. de Brosses in 1760). 1 An article of paraphernalia used in religious practice, or a physical object representative of religious authority. Fetishes commonly are misunderstood to be objects accorded magical or supernatural powers by their users. Objects such as the perfect ear of corn or Corn Mother, important in religious practices of Pueblos (American Southwest), medicine bundles of various North American tribes, and objects that represent the religious authority of clans in Native American communities are often referred to as fetishes. 2 Small carved stone objects and feather arrangements, with no religious significance, manufactured for commercial sale by modern Native American peoples.

Feuerbach, Ludwig Andreas (foi'er-bokh; 1804–72), German philosopher who, in his influential work, *The Essence of Christianity* (1841), introduced philosophical anthropology to the study of religion. Feuerbach was one of the first to argue a projection theory of religion: that transcendence is best understood as an outward projection of human inner nature and needs. Not only important to Marxist thought, Feuerbach's work stands as the foundation of any secular theory of religion. *See also* projection.

Ficino, Marsiglio (fee-chee'noh; 1433–99), Italian humanist who, through his translations and commentaries, was responsible for the Renaissance rediscovery of Plato. Ficino was the architect of the fusing of Christian and Neoplatonic thought that became central in Renaissance Hermetism resulting in a distinct school of thought different from the Aristotelianism of Catholic Scholastic philosophy. *See also* Hermetism; Neoplatonism.

fideism, a theological position that asserts the primacy of faith over reason.

filha de santo (fee'lya ji sahn'too; Portuguese, "daughter of the saint/deity"), medium and priestess of Afro-Brazilian religions, especially of Candomble. Initiated after lengthy training, each medium experiences possession by an intermediary divinity whose temporary incarnation allowed direct communication. Her male counterpart, rare until the 1960s, is called *filho de santo* ("son of the deity"). *See also* Afro-Brazilian religions; Candomble.

Finnish religion. Our knowledge of pre-Christian Finnish (and neighboring Karelian) religion is based on archaeological, linguistic, and literary sources. The oldest sources are rock paintings, which date back perhaps as early as the fifth millennium B.C. The major literary sources are Mikael Agricola's list of deities (1551), Christfrid Ganander's *Mythologia Fennica* (1789), and the epic songs and incantations written down from illiterate singers and healers during the eighteenth, nineteenth, and twentieth centuries. The religious beliefs of the Finns do not fall into well-defined categories. There are specific spheres of activity for most of the deities, but these do not form a hierarchical system.

Finnish religion is, for historical reasons, syncretistic; that is to say, the Finns have always been influenced by neighboring peoples and their religions. The ancient Eurasian foundation was first influenced by the Indo-Europeans, then by Baltic and Germanic peoples in the west, and Slavic people in the east. Byzantine influence and Orthodox Christianity reached Karelia and eastern Finland as early as in the ninth century. The Crusades brought Roman Catholicism to western Finland in the twelfth century. Both of these major churches created a more or less symbiotic relationship with the ethnic belief traditions. But since the mid-sixteenth century, Protestant Lutheranism has become the dominant religion and it has gradually uprooted the non-Christian traits in religious beliefs and practices.

Cosmology: In vertical cosmography, the world is divided into three levels. The upper level is the abode of the gods in heaven. The middle level is the human world, while the lower level is the underworld, the realm of the dead.

According to another concept, the earth has a celestial lid, the canopy of the sky, that is either fixed around the North Star or is supported by a gigantic pillar that reaches up from the center of the earth to the sky. Instead of a world pillar there may be a gigantic world tree, or mountain. This world mountain can also be placed horizontally in Pohjola, the North Land, which is the realm of the dead. It lies beyond the river of Tuonela (the World Beyond), across which the deceased travel. In the southern horizon, at the intersection of earth and sky, live the tiny *lin-tukotolainen* people, the inhabitants of the land of birds.

Gods and Culture Heroes: According to some Scandinavian sagas, the Karelians in Bjarmia, on the coast of the White Sea, worshiped a god that bears a resemblance to the Scandinavian thunder god, Thor. In Novgorod, the same god was called Perun, which among Finns later came to denote the devil (*piru*). In a similar way, the Baltic thunder god, Perkuons (Latvian) or Perkunas (Lithuanian), has given the Finns the name Perkele, which stands for the devil.

The Karelians in Bjarmia named their thunder god Jomali, from which is derived the Finnish word for god (*jumala*). The Finns and Karelians also called their Jumala, Ukko. The epic songs and incantations often refer to these as being synonymous. Ukko's derivative is *ukkonen*, the Finnish word for thunder, and as such, Ukko is an epithet for Jumala, the high god of heaven and thunder, who controls the weather.

Another deity ruling over the atmospheric phenomena is Ilmarinen, whose name is derived from *ilma* ("weather," "air"). In epic songs, Ilmarinen is presented as a culture hero, a smith who has forged the canopy of the sky. Another creator or demiurge is Vainamoinen.

The Spirits and the Dead: The Finns believed that the dead continue living in their burial ground, in a village of the dead. The extended family included both the living and the dead, and during commemoration events the dead were either given offerings at the sacred grove or they were believed to return—in bird form or formless—to their former homes as dinner guests.

The dead controlled and protected the living members of their family. Similar functions were given to various spirits that possess natural elements (fire, wind), natural areas (forest, water), and cultural domains (dwelling, cattle shed, sauna). Cultic behavior aimed at securing the benevolence of the spirits and, thus, the luck and prosperity that the spirits provided for the living.

In prehistoric times, the mediation between the living and the dead was conducted by the shaman (Finnish *noita*), who was also a healer and the leader in bear-hunting rites. *See also* Baltic religion; Kalevala; Nordic religion; shaman; shamanism.

fiqh. *See* Islamic law.

fire, one of the four basic elements. Because of its central role in human culture, fire has been utilized by religions to provide a variety of symbols and rituals. As a source of light and heat, fire is the focus of most domestic rituals of "hearth and home." Fire is seen also as a means of purification (the "refiner's fire"), and that view is extended, especially in cultures that employ cremation, to the notion of fire as a means of rejuvenation or of gaining immortality. Sacred fires are a feature of many religions. Myths about the origin of fire are universal. *See also* cremation; domestic ritual; fire ritual (Japan); firewalking; Hindu domestic ritual; Hinduism (festal cycle); Holi; light and darkness; purification; sacrifice; Shingon-shu.

fire ritual (Japan), the Hindu Vedic fire sacrifice performed by the monks of the Japanese Shingon school of Buddhism to achieve both exterior (worldly) and interior (spiritual) benefits. Laypersons participate by inscribing their names and wishes on sticks to be burned at the altar. *See also* Agonshu; sacrifice; Shingon-shu; shrauta rites.

firewalking, a ritual means of demonstrating an individual's possession of extraordinary powers by appearing unharmed after walking barefoot over a series of fires or across a bed of hot coals. Firewalking serves as a religious ordeal or test, distinguishing those who truly have superhuman power from false claimants.

Japanese Religion: Walking over hot coals is a major regimen of the Japanese lay mountain ascetics (*yamabushi*), who demonstrate their spiritual control through this ordeal. Devotees participate by inscribing their names and wishes on sticks that are burned on the coals.

firmament, in Mediterranean cosmologies, a dome that separates sky from earth or upper from lower waters. *See also* sky.

First Amendment. *See* law and religion (in the United States).

firstfruits ritual. *See* harvest rituals.

fishing rites/whaling rites, rituals in traditional societies done to ensure the right relationship between the game, its spirit guardian, the fishers or whalers, and their community.

Rituals connected to activities like fishing and whaling, which are necessary to sustain life, may be difficult to understand. A superficial reading of these rituals would take their central act—often a sacrifice of fish or whale meat—as a simple act of barter. Ritual events like the sacrifice of certain parts of the salmon catch to the spirit guardian of the fish, or giving the

choicest part of the whale to the mistress of sea animals, might be seen as payment made for services rendered. Matters are not that simple. Relationships between fish and families, between the mistress of the sea animals and whalers, like any complex relationships, are reciprocal, with duties and obligations on both sides. Right relationship depends on behavior that signals mutual respect. For example, once a year the Inuit return the seal bladders (wherein dwell the souls) to Sedna, mistress of the sea animals; the Saami (Lapps) make tobacco offerings when passing sacred rocks; the coastal people of Japan honor proscriptions against taking female whales with calves; and the Quileute whalers give a potlatch in honor of the slain whale.

When human behavior demonstrates a lack of respect, the guardian of the fish or the mistress of sea animals may take offense. As a result of this breakdown in relationship, the fish or whale may not be released to the offender's nets or harpoons or to those of the family or community. At this juncture a shaman may intervene to visit the spirit realm to repair the damage done. Thus, in Greenland, among the Inuit, the shaman visits Sedna in her realm to comb out her hair, which had been matted by human transgressions transformed into dirt.

Frequently the specialness of the fishing or whaling rites is amplified by their timing: they are often done at the beginning of a new year. Among Native Americans of the Northwest Coast the new year begins with the return of the salmon to the rivers and a ritual in which certain parts of their catch are returned, setting right their relationship to the spirit guardian of the salmon.

These rituals are not merely a religious justification for a primarily economic activity. Exchange of food among family members is more than merely economic; these exchanges help one learn who one is and where one belongs within a community of persons. Fishing and whaling rites are often used to create community meaning, but the community of persons includes spirit beings, sea animals, and fish. *See also* Bladder Festival; circumpolar religion; hunting, religous aspects of.

fish symbol, an ancient Christian sign for Christ. The first letters of the phrase "Jesus Christ, Son of God, Savior" in Greek spell out the Greek word for fish (*ichthys*).

fitna (fit'nuh; Arab., "strife"), civil uprising in Islam over questions of religious leadership. The first *fitna* occurred following the murder of the third caliph, Uthman (656). In 680, the murder of Husayn, leader (*Imam*) of the Shiites, brought on the second fitna. The third fitna began in the second quarter of the eighth century as a revolutionary movement that by 750 had toppled the Umayyad caliphate and brought the Abbasid caliphs to power. The fomenting of fitna within the Muslim community is an issue in Islamic law and plays an important role in Muslim discussions about contemporary reform movements.

Five Classics. *See* Confucianism (authoritative texts and their interpretation).

Five Flavors, parable in the *Nirvana Sutra* likening the progression of Buddhist teachings to the successive refinement of milk into ghee.

Five Houses (Chin. *wu-chia*), the five sects of Chinese Sung-dynasty (960–1279) Ch'an Buddhism: Ts'ao-tung, Lin-chi, Yun-men, Fa-yen, and Kuei-yang. *See also* Ch'an school; Lin-chi school; Ts'ao-tung school.

Five Ks, the five items, each beginning with "k," that Sikhs initiated into the Khalsa must wear:

Sikh merchant, at a house of worship (*gurdwara*) in New Delhi, India, displaying steel bangles (*kara*), one of the Five Ks of Sikhism.

the *kes* (Punjabi, uncut hair), *kangha* (comb), *kirpan* (sword or dagger), *kara* (steel bangle),

and *kachh* (short pants). *See also* Khalsa; Sikhism.

Five Ms (Skt. *panchamakara*), in Indic systems, five elements whose names begin with the letter "m": *madya* (wine); *matsya* (fish); *mamsa* (meat); *mudra* (parched grain); and *maithuna* (sexual intercourse). In Hindu and Buddhist Tantras, these are main elements of the transgressive ritual known as the "worship in a circle" (*chakrapuja*), which deliberately employs what is ordinarily forbidden. While interpreted metaphorically in less extreme, "right-handed" Tantric groups, for "left-handed" groups they form the antinomian core of a highly controlled ritual for the alteration of consciousness. *See also* Tantra; Tantrism (Buddhism).

Five Pecks of Rice. *See* Wu-tou-mi Tao.

Five Periods and Eight Teachings (Chin. *wu-shih pa-chiao*), T'ien-t'ai classification scheme that divides Buddhist doctrines into five periods of revelation corresponding to eight substantive teachings. *See also* T'ien-t'ai school.

Five Pillars (Arab. *al-arkan al-Khamsa*), devotional acts required of all Muslims. These are discussed in Islamic law as *ibadat* ("religious duties"). They include the following duties: (1) *Shahada:* "witnessing" to the oneness of God and the messengerhood of the Prophet Muhammad. (2) *Salat:* "prayer service" performed five times daily (dawn, noon, afternoon, sunset, evening). Each salat is preceded by the call (*adhan*) and purification (*tahara*). The salat contains prescribed words and postures (standing, bowing, prostration, sitting). Salat may be performed alone, but worshiping with others is recommended, and the Friday noon salat must be in congregation, with a sermon. (3) *Sawm:* "fasting" during daylight in the month of Ramadan by abstaining from food, drink, and sensual pleasures. A breakfast is enjoyed in the early evening, followed by traditional litanies in mosques. Before daylight a light meal is taken before resuming fasting. (4) *Zakat:* "almsgiving," based on a percentage of one's wealth (provided a minimum is owned), paid at each year's end. Zakat is not considered as charity but a form of worship and a kind of loan to God that will be repaid multifold. (Charity should be dispensed continuously, as need arises.) Zakat purifies the wealth remaining to the giver and aids various classes of recipients, such as new converts needing support. (5) *Hajj:* "pilgrimage" to Mecca, if possible, once in a Muslim's life, during the annual season. A frequently mentioned sixth pillar is *jihad*, "exertion" in the way of God. Jihad may take various forms, including armed conflict in defense of the Muslim community (lesser jihad) and in the improvement of one's spiritual and social being (greater jihad). *See also* Islam (festal cycle).

Near Eastern Muslim woman at daily prayer, fulfilling one of the five required Pillars of Islam.

Fiver. *See* Zaydi Shia.

Five Viscera. *See* wu-tsang.

flagellation. **1** In the Christian tradition, self-inflicted whipping as a ritual of purification or penance. **2** In other traditions, being whipped is part of the ordeals associated with rites of passage.

flamen (flah'men), a priest in ancient Rome engaged in burning sacrifices. *See also* Roman religion.

flight. *See* ascension rituals.

flood stories, a common mythic motif in which waters cover the world by divine directive. Flood stories are most often associated with themes of punishment, population control, and the end of the world or return to chaos. *See also* antediluvian/postdiluvian; ark in the Hebrew Bible; Noah.

folklore, generally refers to popular learning. In its form of expression and transmission, folklore is often distinguished from the education offered in schools. Folk learning is frequently oral rather than written, and closely tied to labor, craft, or trade.

Folklore studies gather and examine poetry in local dialects, popular dance, music, food preparations, dress, art, games, medicinal remedies, technologies, tools, beliefs, superstitions, and tales. In the nineteenth and early twentieth centuries, folklorists viewed themselves as collectors of the remnants of humanity's past, as these remnants were imagined to be fossilized in the communities marginal to urban civilizations. In 1846, William Toms coined the term *folklore* as the study of the customs and manner of "olden time." Recently, attention has widened to include not only peasants, rural populations, and agricultural communities, but also elements of contemporary popular culture: city dwellers, urban slang, beauty queens, and criminal behavior.

Accounts of the origins of the systematic study of folklore vary widely, perhaps because of the shifting definitions of the field of study. Giuseppe Cocchiara begins his 1954 history of the study of folklore in Europe with Michel Montaigne's *Essays* (1580–95), which intuit a common humanity at work in popular European poetry and in the songs imported from recently encountered nonliterate tribes in Brazil. Other historians of folklore have pointed to Giambattista Vico (1668–1744), Johann Gottfried Herder (1744–1803), or Jean-Jacques Rousseau (1712–78). Contemporary historians of the field of folklore studies frequently trace its development from the Grimm brothers' study of folktales in early-nineteenth-century Germany. The Grimms tied together the three strands—ethnography, linguistics, literature—that folklorists have struggled to undo or refasten ever since.

At the origin of folklore studies there exists an irony not unlike the one central to religious studies. The subject matter, as a distinct category for study, comes into existence in the Enlightenment academy after European contact with peoples who seem not to recognize the distinction. Folklore is conceived of as a separable fragment within European literate culture at the very moment when Europeans encounter cultures whose folklore was deemed identical with culture. "Religion" also comes to denote a realm of belief and behavior separable from culture when Europeans come into contact with communities in the world whose religious life appears inseparable from their cultural existence. This coincidence of the discovery of peoples and the invention of categories renders these central categories both suspicious and intriguing. As a category, folklore succeeds in recognizing common human ground with newly encountered peoples, even as it allows those who study them to distance themselves from their contemporaries, at home and abroad, through the invention of dichotomous terms: primitive/civilized; folklore/literate culture; profane culture/religion.

In his studies of musical cultures, the contemporary American scholar Lawrence Levine has criticized the tendency to treat folklore as the shadow of a more illuminated culture or to consider folklore to be filtered down from hierarchically superior knowledge that is more precise, more technical, or more creative.

Despite the early propensity to study folklore as a search for common humanity, modern folklore studies often point to the distinctiveness of separate groups. Whether folklore studies ought to concentrate on differences or similarities among cultures has been an issue of energetic debate. In the 1950s, Matti Kuusi aimed to discover the Finnish national character through a study of Finland's folklore. Such a view presupposes that folklore accumulates over time in groups that share a distinct ethnic heritage, language, economic practices, religious beliefs, and geography. Kuusi's view that folklore is rooted in communities is widely shared, even though notions of tradition and community have been variously grounded in race, ethnicity, culture, language, and land. In fact, folklore studies have at times been pressed into the service of racialism, ethnocentrism, and nationalism—depending on how one chooses to define "folk."

The contemporary American scholar William A. Wilson, among others, challenges the emphasis on the study of separate groups of folk, arguing that folklore is studied, not on the basis of ethnic membership but because of common humanity and common human interest.

The truth is that many folklorists prefer to straddle lines important to other disciplines. In 1988, the centennial issue of the *Journal of American Folklore* emphasized with approbation that there is no group of theoretical models that encapsulates the field. Just as the definitions of "folk" and "lore" have shifted perceptibly in single and over multiple generations, other key distinctions have been left inexact. For example, there is no consensus on whether the discipline of folklore studies is better situated in the humanities or in the social sciences. One might say that folklore studies exist between the lines drawn by other fields in the academy.

Folklore studies have made a lasting and stirring contribution to the study of religion, by attending to all manner of verbal expressions and behaviors that were often excluded or trivialized in scholarly circles because they defied adequate categorization.

font. 1 A receptacle, usually of stone, for the water used in Christian baptism. 2 A small receptacle (also called a stoup) for holy water found at the entrance of a Roman Catholic Church.

food, central to human existence, food provides religions with a complex vocabulary for symbolism and ritual. Both the partaking of food and the abstaining from eating are central ritual activities. In different religious traditions, some foods may be strongly marked as sacred, others as prohibited. *See also* eating together; fasting; kosher; vegetarianism.

foot washing, a mode of ritual purification.
  Christianity: Based on a New Testament story (John 13:14–17) the ritual of foot washing is observed on Holy Thursday in the Roman Catholic and Orthodox churches and more frequently in certain Protestant churches. It bears a range of symbolic referents, from an expression of humility to a gesture of reconciliation or service.

Forbidden City, central section of the Chinese city of Peking, where imperial audience halls and residential palaces were located. Ordinary people, even ministers, were normally prohibited. The official name is "Purple Forbidden City," after the polar constellation, where Shang-ti, the heavenly deity, was thought to dwell. *See also* Peking; Shang-ti.

Fortunate Fall, or *felix culpa*, the Christian assertion that the Fall of Adam and Eve was beneficial because it necessitated the coming of Jesus Christ. *See also* Fall.

Forum, the. *See* EST (Erhard Seminars Training).

foundation rites, rituals connected with building, often including divination to determine the site, consecration of the site, and purification of the building materials.

foundation sacrifice, the offering made when beginning or concluding construction of a building. It often involved human sacrifice.

founded religion, a nineteenth-century taxonomic term of dubious merit distinguishing those religions that had individual historical founders from those that are collective and traditional. *See also* typology, classification.

Four Books. *See* Ssu-shu.

four goals of life (Hinduism), formulation, dating from the time of the Upanishads, (ca. 700–400 B.C.) of the four *purusharthas* (Skt., "human goals"). The four goals are: *kama* (desire, especially for sexual fulfillment); *artha* (activity oriented toward mundane goals); *dharma* (religion; the harmonization of social and cosmic orders); and *moksha* (liberation from mundane existence into union with the Absolute).

The purusharthas are arranged hierarchically according to their ethical and soteriological import. Seemingly incompatible, they are in fact complementary, maintaining the life of both the individual and society. With the first three, one moves from the subjective and individual to more objective and social concerns; at the same time, one mounts the hierarchy of the Hindu social pyramid.

The individual desires covered by kama range from erotic love (the satisfaction of which is a woman's duty in this male-dominated tradition) to the desire for heaven that impels humans to sacrifice, thereby upholding the universal order. Artha (for which the ends always justify the means) is the special prerogative of princes for whom worldly gain, on behalf of their subjects, is the highest good. Dharma, maintenance of human order in the light of the universal order, is the special concern of the highest, priestly class.

The fourth goal of moksha (liberation), a return to a self-interest of sorts, is a late addition to the three original purusharthas. This goal arose out of a rethinking, in the time of the Upanishads, of the notions of life and afterlife. Previously, the generally mundane goals of kama, artha, and dharma, realized through procreation, economic activity, and sacrifice, were thought to be sufficient to the good life. These become devalued in favor of a withdrawal from mundane existence into a realization of perfect union with the divine essence, individual self with universal Self. This entails withdrawal from the networks of social interdependence and the first three goals. *See also* ashrama/ashram; caste; dharma; Hinduism (thought and ethics); liberation.

Four Noble Truths (Skt. *aryasatya,* "noble truth"), the essential teaching of early Buddhism. According to tradition, after attaining enlightenment, the Buddha proclaimed his liberating insight into the nature of existence in his first sermon through the topic of the Four Noble Truths. The first truth (Suffering) declares the nature of all phenomena comprising ordinary unenlightened experience as suffering, impermanent, and lacking in any enduring or substantial self or essence. The second truth (the Origin of Suffering) states that suffering has a cause, namely, craving. Within this truth is subsumed the fundamental doctrine of conditioning, or dependent origination, which operates both generally and in the moral arena of reward and retribution through transmigration. The third truth (the Cessation of Suffering) asserts that despite the fact of universal suffering in a totally conditioned universe proclaimed by the first two truths, there is liberation through the Cessation of Suffering, which is the *nirvana,* experienced by the Buddha. The fourth truth (the Path leading to the Cessation of Suffering) proclaims that this liberation is accessible to all who follow the way set forth by the Buddha. The fourth truth inaugurates Buddhism as a religion and is the legitimation and touchstone for all Buddhist practice. *See also* Buddhism (thought and ethics); nirvana; Path (Buddhism); suffering.

Four-Seven Debates, sixteenth-century Korean metaphysical and ethical debates about the nature of the four primary, innate emotions (humane empathy, the sense of justice, deference, or propriety, and discrimination of the truth) and the seven temperamentally derived feelings (joy, anger, sorrow, pleasure, love, hatred, and desire) and the role they play in the development of sages and well-ordered societies. These debates were carried on between Yi Hwang (1501–70), Ki Taesung (1527–72), and later, Ki's disciple, Yi Yi (1536–84).

According to Chinese classical and Neo-Confucian writings, the four primary emotions, since they are a part of human nature, are always good. Expression of them keeps people in concert with Heaven. The seven derived feelings, though, arise from the material conditions of the body and environment and thus, without the oversight of a disciplined and educated mind, the expression of these feelings may be bad and do harm to one's nature.

The metaphysical and cosmological theory that underlies these debates had important political and social consequences. Without a set of absolute principles (*li*) by which emotions and feelings could be ordered, it was assumed that every human act and judgment would become its own absolute and ethics, social and political structure, law, and human virtue would be relativized. Korean scholars who defended the notion of innate and derived emotions tended to be politically and socially conservative, while their opponents, who saw all emotions as innate or all emotions as derived, tended to be pragmatic and progressive. During most of the Choson period (1392–1910), it was the conservative interpretation that was in force. *See also* Yi Hwang; Yi Yulgok.

Fox, George (1624–91), founder of the Society of Friends (Quakers), best known for his autobiographical *Journal of George Fox*. *See also* Friends, Society of.

Franciscans, popular name of the Roman Catholic Order of Friars Minor (O.F.M.). Founded by Francis of Assisi (ca. 1181–1226), its Rule received final papal approval in 1123. Thousands joined the first order of Franciscans, which eventually became clericalized, as well as the second order of nuns, the Poor Clares, and the third order of laypeople, who received spiritual guidance from the Franciscans. Subsequent Franciscan history is marred by frequent skirmishes among Franciscans and between some Franciscans and the papacy. For Francis, discipleship to Christ required the complete renunciation of worldly goods, trusting in God to provide for all his needs. As the order grew, many Franciscans perceived a need to modify the vow of poverty. Bonaventure, Minister General from 1257 to 1274, distinguished between ownership and use, holding that while Franciscans could never own any goods, they could have the use of goods held for them by papally appointed agents. This solution, advocated by the Conventuals, was rejected by the Spirituals, who insisted on strict adherence to original practices. The Conventuals and Spirituals split by the end of the first quarter of the fourteenth century. *See also* monasticism; Poor Clares.

Francis de Sales (1567–1622), Roman Catholic Church official and theologian best known for his focus on the possibilities of lay spirituality in his central work, *An Introduction to the Devout Life* (1608).

Francis of Assisi (ca. 1181–1226), Roman Catholic saint, founder of the Franciscan order. The subject of many legendary biographies, including the *Fioretti* (The Little Flowers of St. Francis). *See also* Franciscans.

Frankists, the followers of Jacob Frank (1726–91), a Jewish pseudo-messiah in Poland and the Ukraine. The Frankist movement represents the most extreme culmination of the antinomian forces unleashed by the messianic upheaval surrounding Shabbetai Tzevi in the seventeenth century.

An ambitious despot, Frank emerged as the leader of the Polish Shabbateans and taught that he was the reincarnation of the soul of Shabbetai Tzevi. Frank also condoned a thorough libertinism, and the Frankists were notorious for conducting ritualized orgies. Facing severe opposition from the Jewish rabbinic leadership, Frank sought protection under the bishop of Kamanetz-Podol. Frank adjusted many of his teachings to curry the favor of Christian authorities. With their support, he twice instigated public disputations against the Jews. The Kamanetz disputation of 1757 resulted in the burning of thousands of volumes of the Talmud throughout Poland. The Lvov disputation of 1759 to 1760 centered on the blood libel against the Jews, which the Frankists affirmed. The Lvov disputation also resulted in the mass conversion of thousands of Frankists, including Frank.

The Frankists nevertheless maintained an isolated existence inside the Catholic Church, marrying only among themselves. They survived as a separate group into the nineteenth century. *See also* Messiah; Shabbetai Tzevi.

fravashis (fre-vah'shiz; Avestan, "protecting spirits"), in Zoroastrianism the souls of the heroic dead, a component of every individual. They receive offerings to provide protection and rain. *See also* Zoroastrianism.

Free and Accepted Masons. *See* Freemasonry.

Freemasonry, the world's largest secret society, with its greatest strength in Britain and North America. Though its history may be traced back to the medieval masonic and building guilds, its first formal organization was the chartering of the Grand Lodge (London) in 1714.

To become a Mason one does not have to be a Christian but must acknowledge belief in a supreme being and in the immortal soul. Masons advance through a complex system of degrees correlated to a symbolic spiritual initiation advancing from darkness to full consciousness.

Since 1738, Roman Catholicism has officially condemned Freemasonry as do many Protestant denominations. It is outlawed in several countries, and anti-Masonic sentiments have played an important role in American religious history. *See also* secret societies; Shriners.

free will, a philosophical and theological notion affirming the power of human choice to affect an individual's destiny. Free will is usually contrasted with determinism. *See also* fate.

Freyja (fray'uh), in Norse mythology, the goddess of fertility, sister and wife of Freyr and daughter of Njordr. *See also* Nordic religion.

Freyr (fray), in Norse mythology, the god of fertility, brother and husband of Freyja and son of Njordr. *See also* Nordic religion.

friar, a title for a member of one of the Christian mendicant (i.e., begging) orders who are not properly monks because they are not confined to a monastery.

Friends, Society of, better known as Quakers, an Anglo-American pacifist sectarian movement originating in the religious confusion of the English Civil War and Commonwealth era (1640–60).

George Fox (1624–91), a "seeker" discontented with both the Church of England and the Puritan and other sectarian alternatives that flourished during the period, attracted a radical group of followers through his prophetic words and deeds. According to one tradition, Fox and his followers became known as Quakers when, refusing to swear oaths or otherwise respect the status of the law courts, they urged magistrates to tremble before God rather than the law. More correctly known as the "Society of Friends [of Truth]," they distinguished themselves theologically from other Christians through their doctrine of the "Inward" or "Inner Light," the manifestation of the divine within each individ-

ual that, when recognized and nurtured, inevitably led to religious truth.

Friends in Britain flourished despite adversity. Many were jailed for their pacifist and other nonconforming ways, while others organized their resources to alleviate these sufferings until relief came in the form of the Toleration Act of 1689. Barred from the universities and professions, they benefited from their reputation for honesty and hard work and often were successful in business. Friends rejected hierarchy and churchly authority, organizing instead according to local weekly meetings for worship and progressively less frequent and geographically more encompassing regional meetings for governance. Weekly meetings were not led by ministers, but a clerk was present to record their proceedings. Worship was conducted in silence in a bare meeting house, with individuals speaking only when prompted by the Inner Light.

The "friendly persuasion" was transplanted to the New World in 1682 by William Penn, an aristocratic convert who secured a royal land grant in payment of debts owed his family. The Pennsylvania colony was based on Quaker principles of consensus and fair dealing in its governance; its capital, Philadelphia—"the city of brotherly love"—reflected in its name and spacious layout Penn's hopes for a peaceable society. English demands for support in the French and Indian Wars, however, led to a series of compromises and finally, in 1756, the renunciation of governmental power by the Quakers, who nevertheless continued to constitute a commercial elite in the region.

Quakers in the new American nation continued to cope with the problems engendered by their pacifism, which led to suffering but also proved instrumental in securing governmental recognition of the rights of conscientious objectors. Quakers pursued a peacemaking role by opposing both violence and the injustices that provoked it. Their Inner Light doctrine was incompatible with social inequality, so that women enjoyed equal status to men. Quakers such as John Woolman, Anthony Benezet, and, later, Levi Coffin, were active in the late-eighteenth- and early-nineteenth-century campaign against slavery. Many contemporary British Quakers also became active in reform causes. Their plain speech and dress, modified over time, were also manifestations of this egalitarianism.

Internal divisions manifested themselves early in the nineteenth century in the United States, when social and geographical divisions expressed themselves in theological forms.

From 1826 to 1827 followers of Elias Hicks (1748–1830) near Philadelphia rejected the local elite's embracing of evangelical Protestant tenets and symbols, and called for a return to early Quaker practice. Joseph John Gurney (1788–1847), an English Friend, pressed the evangelical cause further, while John Wilbur's (1774–1856) followers tried to combine the two emphases. Richmond, Indiana, emerged, in the first half of the nineteenth century, as a focus of Gurneyite settlement that was later influenced by the Holiness movement. In the twentieth century, the Philadelphia Meeting—part of the larger General Conference—became the center for Friends concerned with philanthropic and peacemaking activity, while the Friends United Meeting (Richmond, Indiana) and Evangelical Friends Alliance (Cleveland, Ohio) represented more evangelical strains.

In the 1990s, Friends in the United States of various affiliations numbered in excess of one hundred thousand; this was somewhat over half of the worldwide membership, with roughly 20 percent of the remainder in Britain. *See also* Fox, George; Gurney, Joseph John; Hicks, Elias; Inner Light; pacifism, Christian.

Frigg (frig), in Norse mythology, a goddess, wife of Odinn and mother of the gods. Her name is etymologically preserved in "Friday." *See also* Nordic religion.

fu. *See* amulet.

fu-chi (foo-jee; Chin., "spirit-writing planchette"), a Chinese divination instrument used by a possessed medium who holds a wooden branch and writes a message from a deity. *See also* divination.

fudoki (foo-doh-kee; Jap., "topographical accounts"), written records concerning the lands, peoples, and traditions of certain locales in eighth-century Japan. The *Izumo fudoki* (Fudoki of Izumo Province) is the only complete fudoki extant and is an invaluable early historical record of Shinto beliefs and practices. *See also* Shinto.

Fu Hsi (foo shee), ancient Chinese god and "sage-emperor," one of the "three sovereigns" (along with Chu Jung and Shen Nung). He is a cosmogonic symbol, often shown holding a framing square. Fu Hsi and Nu Kua together are a primal couple, usually depicted as serpent-bodied figures with entwined tails. *See also* astronomy; Chinese myth; cosmogony; Nu Kua; San-huang; Shen Nung.

Fuji, Mt. (foo-jee), one of many Japanese sacred mountains. Praised in the earliest poetry and eventually depicted in almost every art form, Fuji was seen both as divine in itself and as the abode of *kami* (divinities, divine presences) and Buddhas. The earliest record of worship at Fuji is from the foot of the mountain, but under Buddhist influence in medieval times there arose the practice of climbing Fuji as a form of asceticism. From late medieval times hundreds of pilgrimage associations formed to worship Fuji and its divinities and to make annual ascents during July and August. Fuji has become a symbol of Japanese identity; today recreational climbers and tourists greatly outnumber religious pilgrims. *See also* kami; mountains, sacred.

Fukuzawa Yukichi (foo-koo-zah-wah yoo-kee-chee; 1835–1901), educator and journalist who fostered knowledge of the West in Meiji Japan. He studied Dutch and English, traveled abroad, and founded Keio University in Tokyo.

functionalism. *See* ideology and religion; religion, explanation of; religion, the study of.

fundamentalism. 1 In its strictest sense, the rejection by a given religious group of the results of historical-critical study of their sacred texts. 2 In a broader sense, the struggle against modernism by religious groups who claim the continued relevancy of earlier time periods for models of truth and value and reject what they perceive as forms of secularism. Such groups are often characterized by a strict authoritarianism that disallows individual variation from the defined (scriptural) norm of faith.

Christianity: Fundamentalism is a Protestant view that affirms the absolute and unerring authority of the Bible, rules out a scientific or critical study of the scriptures, denies the theory of evolution, and holds that alternate religious views within Christianity or outside are false.

A Bible conference of conservative Protestants at Niagara, New York, in 1895 affirmed five doctrinal points that were later named the "five fundamentals": the verbal inerrancy of scripture, the divinity of Jesus, the virgin birth, the substitutionary atonement, and Jesus' bodily resurrection and physical return. Although these points do not include all the elements of Protestant fundamentalism, they are regularly present in fundamentalist views.

A series of volumes entitled *The Fundamentals* by American, Canadian, and British writers (1910–15) carried the discussion further by attacking Catholic doctrine, Christian Science, Mormon teachings, Darwin's theory of evolution, and liberal theology's critical study of the Bible and denial of miracles. In 1920 C. L. Laws used the term *fundamentalist* in the Baptist *Watchman-Examiner* to identify these views.

In the North during the 1920s and following, Presbyterians and Baptists, among others, were torn by controversies over fundamentalism. From this struggle came institutions like Westminster Theological Seminary (1929) and new denominations such as the Orthodox Presbyterian Church and the Conservative Baptist Association of America (1947). Interdenominational organizations were also formed, e.g., the American Council of Christian Churches (1941, to offset the National Council of Churches) and the National Association of Evangelicals (1942).

By the 1950s, Neo-Orthodox theology with its emphasis on biblical revelation had changed the theological situation from a standoff between fundamentalists and liberals by developing a middle ground between them. Since the more militant fundamentalist leaders had settled into their own organizations by then, the basis for intragroup fights lessened, and the controversy waned.

With the political swing to the Right in the 1980s fundamentalist voices found new support. Attacks on evolution and liberal scholarship fell into the background as some fundamentalists emphasized more positive themes such as conversion, personal and social morality, and a right-wing political agenda. In other groups, however, attacks on nonfundamentalist scholarship came with new vigor.

Fundamentalism is characteristically evangelistic. Some ministries combine evangelism with healing. Premillennialism, the view that Jesus will return to earth in visible form and establish a thousand-year kingdom, has frequently been an aspect of the fundamentalist movement. Finally, since the Scopes trial (1925) fundamentalism has waged a war against contemporary science, particularly the theory of evolution. Scientific creationism is one form of the attack. In an attempt to harmonize Genesis 1 and certain scientific arguments, this school holds, for example, that the geologic layers of the earth cannot be used to support the vast time sequences of standard earth science because the catastrophic flood of Noah's day was the source of much of the layering. *See also* evangelicals.

Islam: Fundamentalism is a contemporary category of scholarly comparative analysis referring to those ideologues who advocate a mythic view of Islamic values and seek to restore the timeless fabric of holistic law. They oppose the secular ethos that, in their view, characterizes not only the non-Muslim West but also putatively Muslim nation-states. Islamic fundamentalists are largely drawn from male groups who have experienced colonial rule as disruption and alienation and postcolonial independence as acculturation and hypocrisy. They resent the economic forces that produced urbanization. They protest the absence of divine mandates in the public sphere of sprawling cities. They reject the modernist hegemony, equating pluralism with relativism and atheism. Instead, they uphold radical patriarchy, for which they find sanction in both scripture and history.

Islamic fundamentalists, like other fundamentalists, are modern without being modernist. Whether accepting oil export revenues or using clandestine bank accounts, they benefit from the capitalist-driven world system, despite their official opposition to both capitalism and communism as Western ideologies. They also understand the power of modern technology. They resort to modern media (newspapers, radio, television, cassettes) and, when necessary, they use state-of-the-art weapons (car bombs, Sten guns, plastic explosives) to achieve short-term objectives. Masters of the communications revolution, they often project their message better than do their adversaries.

Yet only a few Islamic fundamentalists are terrorists, and not all Arab terrorists are fundamentalists. It is important to distinguish fundamentalists from other political or social reformers. The late-nineteenth-century activists Jamal ad-din al-Afghani and Muhammad Abduh used Islamic symbols to mobilize powerful anticolonial movements, yet they did not perceive less fervent fellow Muslims as their enemies.

Sunni and Shiite fundamentalists differ from one another, especially in their attitude toward the state. Neither Sayyid Qutb (1906–66), founder of the Muslim Brotherhood, nor Abul-Ala Mawdudi (1903–79), founder of the Muslim League, believed that the nation-state, itself a truncated residue of colonial rule, could become the vehicle for inscribing Islamic values or pursing Islamic ideals. By contrast, their Shiite counterparts had faith in the state, provided it had adopted an Islamic constitution.

Shiite fundamentalists have openly employed the range of Western worldviews, from Marxism to just-war theory to creation science. Ideology itself has been embraced as voluntary religion. Unlike customary religion, ideology requires collective ideals to be translated into reality through concerted action.

Islamic fundamentalists have captured a major state (Iran in 1979), they have assassinated a bold Muslim statesman (Anwar Sadat in 1981), and they have marshalled sporadic public support in Pakistan, Bangladesh, Malaysia, and, most recently, Jordan. However, they remain a minority viewpoint among all Muslims.

funereal rites. *See* burial; cremation; dead, rituals with respect to the; death; life-cycle rituals.

Fu-shen (*foo*-shen; Chin., "god of happiness"), one of three stellar deities in Chinese popular religion; a deified civil official, he is often pictured in mandarin robes accompanied by a child. *See also* Chinese popular religion.

future life. *See* afterlife.

Fylgja (filg′jah), a guardian spirit in Norse mythology who appears as a female being or as an apparition in animal form. *See also* Nordic religion.

ABCDEF
G HIJKL
M OPQ
R UV
WXY&Z

Gabriel, in Jewish and Christian sources, an archangel, best known in Christianity for the announcement to Mary that she was to bear Jesus.

Islam: Gabriel (Arab. *Jibril*) is the angel who conveys God's messages to humans, especially prophets. The Qur'an (26:193) calls him "the trustworthy spirit" for being a faithful messenger. The Qur'an was brought down by him. Islamic tradition represents Jibril as having appeared in human form and conversed with Muhammad, in order to instruct Muslims in matters of religion, and as having guided Muhammad during the latter's journey through the heavens. *See also* angel; archangels (Judaism and Christianity).

Galilee, northern province of Roman Palestine. In the New Testament of the Bible, it was the home and locale of the early ministry of Jesus.

galut (gahl'oot; Heb.), exile and diaspora. *Diaspora* signifies dispersion, while *exile* signifies ejection from one's homeland and loss of sovereignty. The two terms are used interchangeably because in Jewish history exile was always accompanied by dispersion. But this need not have been the case; the nation could have been exiled to one specific country. Conversely, part of the nation could have been dispersed in different countries while another part retained sovereignty in the homeland (this actually occurred in the Maccabean period and also today). Of the two, it is the notion of exile that signifies the more radical crisis in the life of the nation.

Three Historical Exiles: Signifying ejection from the homeland and loss of sovereignty, exile is clearly a category of history—an occurrence in time affecting a national collectivity. In Jewish history it has occurred three times, first when Assyria destroyed the northern kingdom in 732 B.C. In this instance, as in so many others in the history of the ancient Near East, national identity could not be preserved in the circumstances of exile (the loss has generated many legends about the "ten lost tribes of Israel").

The second exile occurred when Babylonia destroyed Judah in 586 B.C. In this case, however, part of the nation returned to the homeland seventy years later (the substantial part, though, remained in Babylonia, thus constituting the first diaspora). In the homeland, internal autonomy was gradually gained, culminating in sovereignty under the Maccabees in 170 B.C. Sovereignty, however, did not last for very long, being progressively eroded by the rising Roman Empire and eventually abrogated altogether, leading to the third exile.

The third exile began with the defeat of Judea and the destruction of Jerusalem by Rome in 70. It is by far the longest exile, lasting until the reestablishment of the state of Israel in 1948. It was during this period that the phenomenon of exile in all its devastating power, painful consequences, and debilitating effects was fully and protractedly experienced by the nation. Also, it was during this exile that the widest scattering occurred. Thus, it is this exile that has come to represent the phenomenon in Jewish consciousness.

Explanations for Exile: Clearly, exile signals a catastrophic event in the nation's life and cries out for explanation and justification. Not surprisingly, any number of explanations were put forth. The most common and widespread, the quasi-official explanation, maintains that exile represents divine punishment for the nation's sins, its severity commensurate to that of the nation's sins. Thus, divine providence is exonerated. Indeed, when the punishment has run its course (or alternatively, when the people fully repent), God will redeem the nation (i.e., reinstitute the Davidic monarchy and the Temple worship as of old).

The other attempts at explanation utilize every facet of human reason and imagination. Thus, e.g., the pain and suffering of exile are likened to the heat of the furnace that purifies metal; or they are seen, if only they be appropriated by the nation willingly, as providing God the justification to bestow prosperity upon the nation in the future; or, as a variation on the foregoing, they are to be taken by the nation as an opportunity for sanctifying the name of God; finally, they can be seen as a necessary stage in the process of growth toward full maturity—the seed that must fall into the ground if it is to grow into a mature tree (e.g., Judah Halevi). All these explanations revolve around the same concern focused upon the first, namely, the pain and suffering of exile. Still, in contradistinction to it these explanations are future oriented and not past oriented: the pain and suffering of the exile come about not to settle accounts for past sins but to provide justification or preparation for the acts of kindness to be bestowed upon the nation in the future.

Aside from this class of explanations formulated in terms of the needs and/or interests of the Jewish nation, there is another formulated in terms of the needs and/or interests of the nations of the world. Whereas the former is self-centered, the latter is altruistic. The most prominent explanation in the latter class is the one that adopts deutero-Isaiah's "suffering servant" motif. The Jewish nation undergoes the pain and suffering of exile to atone for the sins of the nations of the world and thus redeem them. But though an instrument of redemption, exile is still viewed here negatively as a source of pain and suffering. There is, however, another explanation that views exile in positive terms: the Jewish nation is dispersed in order to facilitate its vocation of missionizing to the nations of the world. Understandably, this affirmative evaluation of exile had particular appeal in the context of emancipation in the modern era, but it is interesting to note that it already had been formulated by the sages.

Lastly, there is yet another kind of explanation, encountered in the mystical tradition, which is radically different. For, notwithstanding their many differences, all the foregoing explanations share in viewing exile as a historical category. Jewish mysticism, however, breaks through this historical framework and moves to the metaphysical-ontological domain. The real event of exile results from a shattering in the divine being when part of the divine, the Shekhina, is driven away and alienated from its true place. The historical exile of the Jewish nation is but a reflection of the cosmic exile of the divine (incidentally, this mystical formulation is but an inversion of the rabbinic tradition whereby the Shekhina goes into *historical* exile to be with the people in their wanderings). Clearly, this explanation of the historical misfortunes of exile in terms of a divine-cosmological misfortune has a tremendous comforting impact psychologically. How valid this is, however, in terms of the theological orientation of mainstream Judaism is a different question. *See also* Babylonian Captivity; Shekhina; theodicy.

gandharva (gan-dahr'vuh; Skt., cognate with Lat., "centaur"), in Hinduism and Buddhism, a semidivine, semiequine celestial musician invoked for fertility.

Gandhi, Mohandas Karamchand (gahn'dee, moh-hahn'-duhs Kah'ruhm chahnd; 1869–1948), best known by his title, Mahatma (Skt., "great soul"), social reformer and leader of India's nationalist movement. Gandhi advocated a chaste, modern Hinduism that rejected priests, caste, and deities and focused on Truth (Skt. *satya*) as God. Gandhi's idea of self-sacrifice and asceticism (*tapasya*) was based on the *Bhagavad Gita*. With nonviolence (*ahimsa*) as his ideal, Gandhi developed the technique of *satyagraha* as a virtuous form of conflict resolution and political engagement. *See also* Reform Hinduism; satyagraha.

Ganesha (guh-nay'shuh), the elephant-headed deity, son of Shiva and Parvati, worshiped since the medieval period in Hinduism as the remover of obstacles and bringer of success. His mythology and festival were effectively utilized during the British period to resist colonial authority in the name of a revitalized Hindu tradition. *See also* Shiva.

Ganga, Ganges (guhn'gah, gan'jeez; Skt., Hindi; Eng.), a holy river of India. The principal river given this name originates in the Himalayas, flows past Hardvar, Prayag (Allahabad), Varanasi (Banaras), and Gaya, and empties into the Bay of Bengal at Gangasagar. This Ganga is said to have come from the feet of the Hindu god Vishnu and to have landed first on the matted hair of the god Shiva, where it aroused the jealousy of Shiva's wife. It is also called Bhagirathi and Jahnavi. Other Gangas include a Ganga in the sky (Akashaganga, the Milky Way), a Ganga in the underworld (Patalaganga), and numerous replicas of the Ganga on earth. *See also* ancestors; Hinduism (worship).

ganja, the marijuana plant (*cannabis sativa*) used, albeit illegally, for both spiritual and medicinal purposes in Jamaican society. *See also* Rastafarians.

Ganjin (gahn-jin; 687–763), the founder of the Japanese Buddhist Risshu, the Vinaya school that conducted ordinations and taught monastic discipline. Orthodox ordinations were not performed for the first two centuries of Japanese Buddhism because ten properly ordained monks had never assembled in Japan to perform them. In 742, Ganjin (Chin. *Chien-chen*), a Chinese Vinaya master, was invited to Japan by the emperor's court. After five unsuccessful attempts, Ganjin finally brought fourteen Chinese monks and three nuns to Japan in 754 and established an orthodox ordination tradition. *See also* Risshu.

gaon (gah-ohn'; Heb., "genius"), title bestowed on Babylonian Jewish religious leaders, particularly in the eighth through eleventh centuries, who compiled the first known comprehensive prayer books.

Gardner, Gerald B. (1884–1964), an amateur English anthropologist and folklorist whom many consider the person most responsible for the revival of witchcraft as a Neo-Pagan religion. After his retirement in 1936, Gardner moved to the New Forest area of England, where he became

Riverfront of the Ganges, India's holiest river, as it flows through the sacred city of Banaras (Varanasi).

involved in an occult society, The Fellowship of Crotona. There, he said, he met a more secret group that claimed to be hereditary witches and after the last witchcraft acts were repealed in Britain in 1951, Gardner founded his own coven. Gardnerian Wicca, one of the most important traditions of Neo-Pagan Witchcraft, which many modern Wicca groups have unknowingly assimilated, includes the Goddess as the preeminent deity, the circle as a place to contain magical energy, ritual work done in small intimate groups, and the idea that the priestess of the coven becomes the Goddess through a ceremony known as "drawing down the moon." *See also* Neo-Paganism; Wicca; witchcraft.

Garifuna religion (gah-ree'*foo*-nah; Central American Carib), an integrated set of rituals and beliefs in spirits that incorporates elements from Amerindian, African, and European sources and that distinguishes the Garifuna as a postcontact New World culture.

Origins: An Afro-Indian people, the Garifuna (also known as the Garinagu or Black Carib) originated in the seventeenth century on the West Indian island of St. Vincent, where escaped African slaves intermarried with native Carib Indians. French missionaries had converted them to Roman Catholicism by the eighteenth century, but without eliminating their ancestral rituals and related beliefs about the dead, which derived from Carib Indian and African sources. The British, who gained control of St. Vincent from the French in 1763, finally defeated the Garifuna in 1796, took their land, and deported them to an island off the coast of present-day Honduras. From there, the Garifuna established more than fifty settlements along the Caribbean coast of Central America, extending from Belize to Nicaragua.

In 1840, a British visitor to these communities found that the Garifuna identified themselves as Catholics and went to great lengths to see that their children were baptized. But he also witnessed *dugu*, the paramount ancestral ritual, which was not sanctioned by the church.

Contemporary Practice: Today, Garifuna women have a prominent role in all of the traditional rituals for the dead, which range from burial and novenas to dugu. While outsiders might distinguish between "indigenous" rites such as dugu and Christian ceremonies such as novenas, the Garifuna do not. In their view, the rituals form a whole and share the same purpose: they provide for the needs of the dead and thereby protect the living from harm (illness, other misfortune, even death) at the hands of a neglected and angry ancestor.

Some of the rituals are obligatory and routinely held, while others may be requested by spirits of the dead. A wake and burial, followed by a ninth-night wake, must be held after the death of any adult. Three other ceremonies sometimes follow these. *Tagurun ludu* ends the period of formal mourning by close kinswomen of the deceased; *amuidahani* is the ritual "bathing" of the spirit; a requiem Mass may also be celebrated. Each of these is followed by a small feast. People typically receive requests for amuidahani and a requiem Mass through dreams, in which spirits of the dead can speak to the living. Finally, an ancestor may also ask for two other rituals, *chugu* and dugu, but usually does so by speaking through a shaman.

Few religious roles are restricted to men or to women only, and women can become shamans if they are sought by the spirits. Shamans usually identify themselves as Catholics, as do most older women, who are notably active in the whole range of religious activities, from organizing ancestral rituals to attending church and celebrating Catholic feast days. *See also* Afro-Americans (Caribbean and South America), new religions among.

Garuda (guh-roo'duh; Skt., "devourer"), bird mount of the Hindu god Vishnu; he is the enemy of serpents and is associated with the theft of *soma*, solar myths, Agni, and snakebite remedies. *See also* Agni; soma; Vishnu.

Garvey, Marcus M. (1887–1940), founder of the Universal Negro Improvement Association in Jamaica in 1914. A black Jamaican, Garvey migrated to the United States in 1916. His Back to Africa program promoted black pride and capitalism. Garvey's religious teachings anticipated global unification of people of African heritage under a black God and a Christian-based black theology. *See also* African Americans (North America), new religions among.

Gateless Barrier (Chin. *Wu-men kuan*), collection of forty-eight Chinese Buddhist *kung-an* (riddle, conundrum) with commentary and verse composed by Wu-men Hui-k'ai (1183–1260). *See also* China, Buddhism in; kung-an.

Gathas (gah'thuhs; Avestan, "songs"), seventeen hymns in *Yasna* (a section of the Zoroastrian scriptures) ascribed to Zoroaster, the holiest words in the tradition. *See also* Avesta; Yasna; Zoroastrianism.

Gaudapada (gow-duh-pah'duh; ca. seventh century), Hindu nondualist theologian, reputed author of a verse commentary on *Mandukya Upanishad,* and grandteacher of the Indian philosopher Shankara. *See also* six systems of Indian philosophy.

Gautama (gow'tuh-muh; Skt.), the family name of the Buddha. There is no certainty about the century in which the historical Gautama lived. Buddhists in various parts of the world date the life of the Buddha to either 624 to 544 B.C., 448 to 368 B.C., or 566 to 486 B.C. According to Buddhist biographies, Gautama was born the son of a king in Lumbini, now in Nepal near the modern Indian border. He was raised in luxury, but left home at age twenty-nine in search of "the Deathless." He spent six years after this "Great Renunciation" following the spiritual practices of other ascetic teachers and then experimenting on his own. At the age of thirty-five he attained enlightenment, rediscovering Truth (Dharma) and thus becoming worthy of the epithet "Buddha," or "Awakened One." Out of compassion, he spent the next forty-five years teaching what he had rediscovered, and each of the different Buddhist traditions traces its doctrine to his career. He died at the age of eighty. *See also* Buddhas.

Gayatri mantra (gah'yuh-tree mahn-truh), basic Hindu prayer from the *Rig Veda* (3.62.10) addressed to Savitar, the sun; it is the first mantra learned by twice-born Hindus and is recited at dawn and twilight by Brahmans today as a request for illumination and inspiration. *See also* Brahman; caste; mantra.

Geluk-pa (geh-luhk'puh; Tibetan, "Followers of the Virtuous Way"), dominant Tibetan Buddhist sect since the seventeenth century, also known as Yellow Hats. It was founded in the fifteenth century by Tsong-kha-pa; his writings, *Lam Rim* ("Stages of the Path"), are the focus of meditative training. *See also* Black Hat; Red Hats; Tibetan religions.

gematria (geh-ma'tree-ah; Heb., from Gk. *geimetria,* "measure"), in Judaism, a method of interpreting or decoding Scripture according to either (1) the numerical value of the letters of the Hebrew alphabet, hence of words or phrases, or (2) various systems that substitute Hebrew letters for one another. It is particularly useful in esoteric or mystical exegesis. *See also* alphabet mysticism; exegesis; Hebrew language; Judaism (authoritative texts and their interpretation).

gender and religion. The analysis of gender as a societal variable important to the understanding of religious teachings has long been a part of the sociology and anthropology of religion, but the importance of gender-based analysis of religion has become far more widespread with the development of the more recent feminist critique of religion. Feminism's focus on the subjection of women by the hierarchical systems of major religious traditions has brought increased attention to the interaction of gender and religion.

Partly because of the influence of feminist thought, explorations of gender and religion have tended to focus more on women than on men. Many books about women and religion, or women in specific religious traditions, were published in the 1970s and 1980s. These works tend to raise four very broad issues: the relationship of theology to women's experience, the weight of the past on the religious future of women, the reconstruction of traditions, and the creation of new traditions.

Many theological systems, notably the thought of Emmanuel Swedenborg (an eighteenth-century Christian visionary) and Carl Jung (an early twentieth-century psychologist), have elaborate schemes of relation, dependence, and complementarity between male and female powers. Nevertheless, the relationship between the theological systems of major religious traditions and the religious experience of women is tenuous at best. Since the foundational revelations of most religions have been mediated through an exclusively male hierarchy, definitions of humanity are often based on male experience. For example, in Judaism, at the moment of the giving of the Torah, "the people of Israel" are commanded "do not go near a woman" (Exodus 19:15). Obviously, this prohibition assumes a male definition of humanity and makes an examination of women's relation to the covenant an exploration of silence.

Christian thinkers have been equally concerned about theological statements that claim to speak for all humans, but are clearly gender-marked as male. The Christian Bible, including the appropriation of the Jewish scriptures, sets a conflicting standard of gender analysis. Although the concept of humans made "in God's image" found in Genesis 1:27 explicitly refers to male and female, more Christian theology of gender has been based on the creation story of Genesis 2:21–23, in which the woman is formed from the rib of the man. The gender equality of creation proposed in Genesis 1 is further undermined by the curse of Eve after the eating of the forbidden fruit: "Your desire shall be for your husband, and he shall rule over you" (Genesis 3:16).

The submission of women to men is more elaborately formulated by the "household codes" of the Christian New Testament, such as that found in Ephesians 5:22–23: "Wives, be subject to your husbands, as to the Lord. For the husband is the head of the wife as Christ is the head of the church." The apostle Paul is even more explicit, giving an exclusively male reading of Genesis 1: "For a man ought not to cover his head, since he is the image and glory of God; but woman is the glory of man" (1 Corinthians 11:7).

The concept of the subordination of women to men was codified by medieval Christian authors, as it is in the *glossa ordinaria* (a standard commentary) to the *Decretals* of the thirteenth-century pope Gregory IX: "A woman . . . is not made in the image of God, but man is the image and glory of God, and the woman should be subject to the man, and should be his handmaid."

This insistence on the subordination of women is complicated by the traditional Christian understanding of the fall of Adam and Eve as the "original sin," from which humans can only be saved through the incarnation (becoming flesh), the death, and the resurrection of Jesus. Since Genesis 3 says that Eve first accepted the forbidden fruit from the serpent, she (and by extension, every woman) becomes the cause of sin. Tertullian, a Christian author who lived in North Africa at the turn of the third century, gives a classic statement to this concept: "And do you not know that you are an Eve? The sentence of God on your sex lives in this age; the guilt must live too. You are the devil's gateway; you are the unsealer of that tree; you are the first deserter of the divine law: you are she who persuaded him whom the devil was not valiant enough to attack. You destroyed so easily God's image, man. On account of what you deserve— that is, death—even the Son of God had to die." (*De cultu feminarum* 1.1). The way Christian symbolic thinking has linked sin with the female and Christ with the male is an obvious problem for women.

Much of the late-twentieth-century literature about gender and religion has centered on reassessment of the proscriptions and prohibitions relating to women in sacred literature of various traditions. Within the Jewish and Christian traditions, a good deal of scholarly attention has been lavished on a number of problematic texts. These include Genesis 1–3 (creation and the fall); stories of exceptional women (Sarah, Hagar, Deborah, Ruth, Esther); tales of abused or sacrificed women (Jeptha's daughter, the Levite's concubine in Judges 19, Tamar); accounts of the women around Jesus (Mary the mother of Jesus, the Magdalene, Mary and Martha); and the passages from the Christian Epistles that proscribe women's role and behavior (1 Corinthians 11:3–16) and the "household codes" (Colossians 3:18–4:1; Ephesians 5:22–6:9; 1 Peter 2:18–3:7; 1 Timothy 2:11–15; 5:3–8; 6:1–2;

Titus 2:2–10; 3:1–2). The focus has been on historical contextualization of biblical passages, emphasizing human fallibility over divine egalitarianism. From this point of view, Jesus seems much more supportive than Christianity of women, and some have even gone so far as to assert that "Jesus was a feminist."

In the case of Islam, similar attention has been focused on the companions of the Prophet Muhammad, especially the Caliph (head of the Muslim community) Umar, as the source of the oppression of women. Here again, as in the argument from Christianity, the tradition is understood to have dissolved an original, divinely ordained equal role for women. Imposition of human gender hierarchy on divine egalitarianism is thought to be the result of deeply flawed but essentially human motivations: lust for power, fear of change, and desire for control.

An interesting contrast to the problem of gender and religion in Judaism and Christianity can be found in a consideration of Buddhism. In the context of the Mahayana tradition, wide acceptance of Buddhism as it spread throughout Asia can be correlated with an increase in egalitarian teachings. In other words, Buddhism spread more quickly as it made more places for women. Fundamental Buddhist doctrines, such as compassion, the unity of all things, and the emptying of the mind (including emptying of notions of sexuality), all deemphasize gender. Perhaps for this reason, women figure prominently among Buddhist teachers and leaders in the newest area of the growth of Buddhism, North America. Some have suggested that the female Buddhist leaders of North America are forerunners of significant changes in Buddhism worldwide.

The movement of North American women into Buddhism can be seen as part of the alternative of creating new religious traditions in a search for gender equality. Many other women, particularly in America and Europe, are turning instead to ancient religious traditions, especially those that have female deities, to find a viable religious option. Worship of the Goddess, usually seen as a combination of goddesses of many traditions (Isis, Athene, Astarte, Diana, Inanna), is understood as a celebration of the creative principle of life. Devotion to the Goddess has become a notable movement among white, educated, North American women.

Much of the analysis, including the overall focus on major religious traditions, has reflected the dominance of white, educated, North American women in the study of the relationship between gender and religion. The major religions,

as traditions of nationhood, empire, and power, have often assisted the oppression of women. But in alternative religions (animist and ecstatic traditions, religions of Africans and Native Americans), the question of gender may look very different. Rather than struggling over inclusion in or separation from their religions, women in these traditions have often been an essential part of religion as it is based in society. Women figure prominently among the leaders of Haitian Voodoo and the shamans of Korea. The ancient Greek dramatist Euripides portrayed women as adepts of deep, ecstatic powers that must ultimately triumph over male rationality.

Some Native American traditions even reject the notion of dual genders, allowing a place in society for an "intermediate" gender type, the *berdache*, who were thought to be connected to divination and magical powers. The religious power of nondualistic sexuality has also been a part of twentieth-century spiritual teaching among gay men and lesbian women.

Feminist analysis of gender and religion, with its stress on equality for men and women, can easily reveal the implicit biases of its white, academic, European cultural context. Among African-American women, a perspective known as "womanist" has tried to redress some of these cultural assumptions by stressing the importance of community and the theological power of storytelling as an alternative to any type of gender analysis, even feminist analysis. A nascent men's movement has also taken up the question of gender from the experience of individual men, rather than from the perspective of a male-dominated hierarchy. These new modes of reflection may well reformulate the question of the relationship between gender and religion. *See also* body; feminism; feminist theology; gender roles; separation of sexes (mythic theme); sexuality and religion.

gender crossing, also referred to as *berdache* (bardash; Fr., "male prostitute"), the appropriation, by anatomical males and females, of the dress, occupations, and behavior of the opposite sex. This activity is culturally defined, and has been reported to some degree in almost every culture area of North America.

Gender crossing among Native Americans usually conformed to a social rather than an anatomic heterosexuality. The sexual partners of berdaches were always non-berdaches. Berdache marriages were usually secondary, in addition to the marriage with a heterosexual partner. In the sexual division of labor there is strong association of gender with occupational specialization. In some of the northern Plains cultures "manly hearted women" achieved the same prestige as successful men. In some Native American cultures, the female sphere was perceived as leading to prosperity and distinction. Some men were attracted to the female sphere; they quit the battlefield and became very successful women. Yurok (California) men crossed gender to become shamans, which were very lucrative positions for women.

Male gender crossers were anatomically male, but by occupations and dress they were women. Among the Navajo (Southwest), Cheyenne (northern Plains), and Mohave (southern California), male berdaches were matchmakers, love magicians, and healers of sexual diseases. Navajo berdaches could do the work of both sexes. Special tasks, such as healing, were reserved for berdaches. Among the Yokuts (California), berdaches were the corpse handlers; in Crow (northern Plains) society they were responsible for cutting the ritual lodgepole; among the Papago (American Southwest) and Cheyenne (Plains) they officiated at scalp dances.

Women who gender crossed were not reclassified in a special category, as were the men who crossed. Rather, the women were recognized and honored by their community. These women often experienced transformation visions, sometimes involving other-than-human females, such as the moon. A woman might experience a dream or series of dreams that resulted in her crossing gender boundaries. In most of these situations, her father and/or husband encouraged her to learn male skills and act in the place of male family members in curing, ceremonial, or war activities. These experiences often resulted in very complex and variable behavior; sometimes the women acted and dressed like men and at other times they did not.

Women also crossed the gender boundary out of economic necessity, to hunt and raid in order to support themselves. *See also* gender roles.

gender roles, the assignment of different roles to men and women in the religious and social realms. *See also* gender and religion; men's houses; separation of sexes (mythic theme).

Judaism: Judaism is a patriarchal religion. It views men as independent beings who have freely entered into a covenant with their Creator; in exchange for their loyalty and devotion, God promises them security and prosperity. Because women, gentile slaves, and minors are tradition-

ally regarded as economically dependent upon and socially subordinate to the men who serve as their husbands, masters, and fathers, they are not principal parties to the covenant and, as a result, not obligated to fulfill the same acts of piety. Even so, these groups are bound to the covenant through the men in their lives, who are responsible for monitoring the religious and social behavior of all members of their household.

Men's Roles and Responsibilities: Classical Jewish texts assign men the key role in religious ritual and marriage. It is they who are required to pray three times daily; don phylacteries; recite biblical passages that accept the oneness of God and the yoke of the commandments; observe all holiday rituals, such as dwelling in thatched huts on the Sukkot, the Festival of Booths; and study Torah, expound it, and teach it to others. Moreover, it is men who take women in marriage and who unilaterally may decide to terminate the relationship with a divorce.

Women's Roles and Responsibilities: Rabbinic law codes assign women ritual obligations, but not as many as men. The codes exempt women from fulfilling most positive, time-bound commandments, such as hearing *shofar* blasts on Rosh Hashanah, on the grounds that their time is not their own. Although obligated to pray (Mishnah *Berakhot* 3:3), women are excluded from equal participation in public prayer because only independent individuals of like status can form a prayer module. Women do not lead the grace after meals because that might affront the dignity of the men present, as stated explicitly in the Babylonian Talmud (*Megillah* 23a) in reference to the practice of barring women from reading the Torah scroll in public.

In the codes, for the duration of her marriage a woman surrenders control of her real assets to her husband and is required to turn all income over to him, both earned and unearned. In exchange for these benefits and others, he is obligated to support her.

In the world that produced classical Judaism, the social expectations for women were marriage, motherhood, and managing domestic affairs. Women prepared the food, cared for the home, made the clothes, and nursed the children. Even so, women were not cloistered. They went to the market to shop, occasionally ran a home-based business such as an inn, attended popular lectures by rabbis, consulted with them on legal matters, visited parents on festivals, and actively participated in wedding festivities and funeral rites. Public and private were not different worlds, as they are today, but intersecting spheres.

Ritual Impurity: Women's lesser social status did not lead to viewing them as sources of impurity. Their exclusion from full participation in synagogue ritual is expressed solely in terms of social status; namely, that a man would find himself personally diminished if publicly represented by someone who was his social inferior. No suggestion is made that a woman is excluded because she is a source of pollution. In fact, Mishnah *Niddah,* the tractate dealing with menstruants, focuses primarily on one issue, which pertains only to the domestic sphere: at what point in her cycle does a woman become ritually unclean and as a result forbidden either to engage in sexual relations with her husband or prepare ritually clean food for him?

Study of Traditions: Another limitation placed on women was that they could not join the disciple circle of a master, could not study the religious traditions, and therefore could not graduate to position of rabbi. Passing reference is made to the fact that one does not teach a woman Torah because of her frivolous nature (Mishnah *Sotah* 3:4), but the underlying reason seems to have been that it was not desirable to have women mingle freely with men because of men's easily aroused sexual lust.

Filial Devotion: In one area alone women achieved parity with men: honor due parents. No distinctions are made between the honor due fathers and that due mothers, either in their lifetimes or after death. If necessary, personal dignity had to be set aside when caring for parents, whether fathers or mothers.

Contemporary Implications: The gender-based hierarchy sanctioned by the Talmud remained in place for centuries. Only with the advent of secular feminism in the 1960s has this system become a subject of debate. The perplexing issue is, are the social mores of the rabbinic era inextricably bound up with the basic institutions of religious practice, thus making change impossible, or can one keep the religious institutions intact but open them up to egalitarian application?

Different segments of the Jewish community have responded to this challenge in different ways. The Orthodox rabbinate has stated its opposition to all change, asserting that Jewish law—Torah and even Talmud—is God-given, hence immutable. The Conservative movement, which holds that Jewish law is binding but contains within itself mechanisms for change, as well as the Reform movement, which subscribes to personal autonomy, have embraced change rather willingly. Both have decided to admit women to their rabbinical and cantorial schools, and most affiliated synagogues have become ei-

ther fully or partly egalitarian. As for a woman's inability to initiate a divorce, the Conservative movement has taken a variety of steps to ensure that no woman remains an *agunah* (Heb., "deserted wife"), chained to a man with whom she no longer lives with but who refuses to write her a bill of divorce. This problem does not affect women in the Reform movement because it accepts civil divorce as sufficient for the closure of marriage. But Orthodox *agunot* wait interminably for a Jewish divorce.

The issue of exclusionary language in the prayer book has been addressed only by the Reform and Reconstructionist movements. They have published prayer books in which the Hebrew texts and English translations avoid phrases such as "God our King" and instead employ neutral terminology such as "God our Redeemer." In addition, in the appropriate places, the revised liturgies make reference to the matriarchs as well as the patriarchs. *See also* Judaism (life cycle).

Christianity: *See* feminism; feminist theology; gender and religion; marriage.

Hinduism: *See* Shaktism; women's rites (Hinduism).

Islam: In Islam, the complex set of relations and obligations associated with gender is designated by the Arabic term *jins.*

The Qur'an ascribes to men and women a common origin (4:1), assigns them similar religious duties, and promises them the same rewards and punishments in consequence of their faith and deeds (33:35; 9:71), although women do not participate in war (*jihad,* 4:98–99). The Qur'an banned the pre-Islamic Arabian practice of female infanticide (16:57–59) and granted women the right to life and to possession and control of wealth. Nonetheless, men are assumed to be the financial supporters of women and, in virtue of this, are granted guardianship of women. Men are allowed to take measures to ensure the obedience of women (4:34). Women generally inherit only half the inheritance of a male in comparable relation to the deceased (4:7–12). Men are permitted to marry up to four wives, provided they treat them with justice (4:3), and may marry Jewish or Christian women. Muslim women may marry only Muslim men and do not have the right of polygamy. Men may also have sexual relations with their female slaves. Marriage in the Qur'an is regarded as a contract between the spouses, sealed by the man's gift of a dowry to the woman (4:4). The man's right to divorce is unqualified, although he should let her go with kindness and not take back the dowry (2:229, 4:21). The wife may redeem herself from an undesirable marriage by returning the dowry, with the husband's agreement. After divorce, the husband should provide for his ex-wife during a "waiting period" of three months (2:241), after which he may take her back if he desires (2:228). During this period the woman should not remarry. If the woman is found to be pregnant or has a nursing infant, the man should support her for the duration of pregnancy and nursing, which is specified as until the child is two years old (2:233). Marriage is strongly approved in Islam, and the spouses are intended to mutually comfort each other; God placed love and compassion between them (2:187; 30:21). In sum, the Qur'an says, "Women shall with justice have rights similar to those exercised against them, but men have a rank above them" (2:228).

Modesty applies to both men and women in the Qur'an (24:30–31), but greater attention is given to requirements for women. However, ambiguity remains: women are "not to show their adornment (or beauty) except that which is apparent" and they are to "draw their head shawls over their bosoms" (24:31). The typical interpretation is that women should cover everything except their faces and hands. Some later scholars also demanded that women cover the face. This reflects an increase in the segregation of the sexes and the veiling and cloistering of women, practices that reached their peak in Ottoman times. The Qur'an also enjoins Muhammad's wives to stay in their homes and not display themselves (33:32–34) and tells believers not to speak to their wives except from behind a curtain (33:53).

Women in Islamic History: Muslim traditions (*hadith*) indicate that there was a great deal of mixing between men and women in the days of the Prophet (d. 632). Women prayed in the mosques behind the men; they personally gave Muhammad their oaths of allegiance and even their offers of marriage; and Muhammad provided them with separate lessons. Women, both in pre-Islamic Arabia and in early Islam, treated the wounded and thirsty soldiers on the battlefield, and a few women distinguished themselves in combat. After Muhammad's death, his youngest wife, Aisha, was frequently consulted about details of his life and behavior. However, women were relegated to a separate room in the mosque during the reign of the Caliph Umar ibn al-Khattab (634–644) and were discouraged, sometimes even banned, from mosque attendance. Despite a prophetic hadith that education was a duty for every Muslim, both male and female, literacy was increasingly restricted to

men, to the extent that the Qur'an exegete Zamakhshari (d. 1144) held that literacy, like prophethood, was one of the ways in which God favored men over women (*Al-Kashshaf* 1:505).

Early Sufism attracted a number of prominent women, the most famous of whom is Rabia al-Adawiyya (d. 801), but later Sufism has few female names in its roster of saints, although even in Mamluke and Ottoman times some Sufi orders did initiate women. Although poor and peasant women, of necessity, worked outside the home, wealthier urban women were increasingly cloistered in a separate world, due to the high cultural priority given to the chastity of women, the maintenance of which was held to be the responsibility of men.

Modern Islamic Thought and Social Change: The Modernists, who sought to reform Islam according to its original intention, rather than its later legal development, first began to challenge this state of affairs in the late nineteenth century. They declared that Muslims had, in the name of religion, denied women rights guaranteed them by the original religion of Islam. In 1899 Qasim Amin of Egypt published *The Emancipation of Women*, in which he argued that men had denied women their full humanity and had corrupted their ethical and intellectual nature by forcing them to lead unnatural, cloistered lives. He advocated the removal of the face veil and practices of segregation, allowing women to seek education and employment in the public sphere. He also advocated severe limitations on the practice of polygamy, based on both its social evils and the quranic stipulation that it was to be allowed only if the husband was able to treat his wives equally (4:3), a stipulation considered by some to be impossible in light of verse 4:129, which says, "You will never be able to treat your wives equally, even if you try." He also proposed a revision of divorce procedures to make them more equitable for women.

Amin's book prompted an enormous and continuing controversy among Muslims, which is also fueled by Western criticisms of Islam on the basis of its treatment of women and by recent social developments in the West: the "sexual revolution," rising divorce rates, and increasing numbers of children born to single women are regarded with horror by Muslims and are used by such writers as the highly influential Abul Ala Mawdudi of Pakistan (*Purdah and the Status of Woman in Islam,* trans. 1972) and Muhammad al-Bahi of Egypt (*Al-Islam wa ittijah al-mara l-muslima l-muasara* [Islam and the Direction of Modern Muslim Women], 1979), among many others, as evidence of the inevitable social diasters wrought by women's liberation. These conservative writers advocate strict segregation of the sexes and Islamic modesty norms for women. Although the pursuit of education is now generally acknowledged as commendable for women, many conservatives hold that women should work outside the home only in cases of dire necessity and that women should devote themselves exclusively to being wives and mothers. This point of view is supported by a prevalent idea that men and women are differentially endowed, though equal in humanity, and should have different though complementary social roles.

Nonetheless, women's social roles have undergone considerable change in the twentieth century. Education is compulsory for girls in most countries, and at the university level women constitute one-third of the students in Egypt and even more in Kuwait. Although the situation varies considerably, in many countries women have entered into most professions, particularly white-collar professions. Legal codes drafted in the post-independence states typically placed some restrictions on polygamy and made divorce through the courts mandatory, while they expanded women's rights to seek divorce. These liberalizing trends are challenged again by the rise of conservative political Islamic movements among young people in most countries since the 1970s. Ironically, these movements attract many highly educated women, especially students in the fields of science, engineering, and medicine, who nonetheless endorse the point of view that a woman's place is primarily in the home.

The same paradigmatic Islamic figure might be used to support opposing points of view on the social roles of women. Ali Shariati (d. 1977), who inspired many young people during the Iranian revolution, presented Muhammad's daughter Fatima as strong, courageous, rebellious against unlawful authority, and struggling publicly on behalf of Islam. This same figure was depicted in public speeches by the Ayatollah Khomeini (d. 1989) as the ideal gentle mother and modest, supportive wife. The issue of women's social roles is one of the most heated and frequently debated in contemporary Muslim society. *See also* Islam (life cycle).

General Convention of the New Jerusalem. *See* Swedenborg (Svedberg), Emmanuel.

Geneva gown, a loose-fitting black gown worn by preachers in Reformed Christian churches to distinguish their garb from the vestments of Catholic priests. *See also* cassock.

genie. *See* jinn.

geniza (ge-nee-zah'; Heb., "storehouse," "archives"), a room, usually in a synagogue, for storing disused holy writings and Jewish ritual objects, which may not be destroyed because they contain the name of God.

Genshin (gen-shin; 942–1017), an eminent Japanese Tendai Buddhist scholar best known as the author of the *Ojoyoshu* (Essentials of Salvation), a work on Pure Land Buddhism that influenced both monks and lay believers. For Genshin, Pure Land practices were meditative, but he also guided lay believers in devotional practices. *See also* Pure Land; Tendai school.

Gentile, term used in English Bible translations to denote non-Jewish peoples.

Gentiles, righteous (Heb. *hasidei umot haolom*, "pious ones of the nations of the world"), those Gentiles whom Judaism considers to be worthy of life in the world to come. The concept appears in the earliest rabbinic texts and is discussed by many medieval Jewish philosophers. Most commonly, righteous Gentiles are held to be those who follow the seven commandments given to Noah, ardently seek God and desire to worship God, and accept the divine origin of Moses' prophecy. The term is also applied to Gentiles who helped Jews to escape Nazi persecutions. Those whose names are known are honored at Yad VaShem, the Holocaust shrine-museum in Jerusalem. *See also* B'nai Noah; Holocaust, religious responses to the; Judaizers.

genuflection, the custom of briefly kneeling onto the right knee before the altar as a sign of respect in a Roman Catholic church. In the Eastern church, the custom is a deep bow.

geomancy (Gk., "earth divination"), a widespread system of divination either by means of designs drawn randomly on the ground with sand, pollen, or other similar powders or by detecting, through calculations and signs, the hidden forces present in the landscape. *See also* divination.

Chinese Religion: Chinese geomancy (*feng-shui*, lit., "wind and water") is an ancient system of site analysis to determine its suitability for grave, home, or temple. Diviners often used a special compass (*lo-p'an*) that indicated the main cosmic factors impinging upon a site. In a "lair" (a hollow), in front of a hill, or behind a body of water were the most desired locations. Geomancy is best understood as an ancient method of harmonizing humans and their works with the terrestrial and celestial powers that might bring good or bad fortune to those who wished to build. *See also* lo-p'an.

Korean Religion: Geomancy describes the beliefs and practices associated with the selection of auspicious habitation sites for the living and the dead. Geomancy (*p'ungsu* or *p'ungsu jiri*) was and continues to be especially important for the siting and orientation of houses, palaces, graves, temples, shrines, cities, and even marketplaces in accordance with features of the natural landscape, especially mountains, above- and below-ground watercourses, and wind patterns. Koreans affirm that the natural landscape and the spirits that inhabit it generate positive energy in the form of fortune and prosperity and this energy can be channeled to the descendants of the dead, individually and collectively, through the bones of ancestors. Though habitations for the living can benefit from an auspicious site, the siting of graves was and is considered a more effective means for extrac-

tion of land energy for the prosperity of the living.

The introduction of geomancy may date to the earliest cultural contacts between Korea and China in the first centuries of the common era, but it was primarily at the hands of Buddhist geomancer monks in the Unified Silla and Koryo periods (seventh–fourteenth centuries) that geomancy became widely practiced. The use of geomancy by Buddhist monks first occurred during the seventh century when Ch'an monks brought it with them after study in South China. *Stupas* (shrine mounds) and temples were built by the government to improve and secure geomantic power for the state, and Buddhist ceremonies were created to transfer that power to the ruling family. Buddhist monks taught that evil persons find or may be directed to inauspicious sites as an act of revenge, while compassionate people are rewarded with auspicious sites.

Though propagated by Buddhists, geomancy was also known and practiced by Confucian bureaucrats, Taoists, and village magicians. Its popularity and the seriousness with which it was taken can be seen in the continual shift in capital sites or in the refurbishing of capital walls, which acted as artificial mountains, throughout

At a Taiwanese burial, a practitioner of geomancy (*feng-shui*) determines the precise alignment of the coffin using a compass marked with concentric rings, each bearing a different system of directional designations.

the Silla, Koryo, and Choson periods (up to 1910).

Professional Geomancy: With the disestablishment of Buddhism at the beginning of the Choson period, geomancy was taken over by the government and an Office of Geomancy, Astronomy, and Divination (*So'un'gwan*) was created and staffed by Confucian bureaucrats. Later, there arose a whole class of professional geomancers who belonged to the middle class (*chungin*), though scholars of the noble class (*yangban*) continued to be well versed in the tradition. Geomancy became so closely identified with bureaucratic class status that one of the most widespread sayings of the Choson period was that an auspicious burial of ancestors would produce high government officials. Middle- and upper-class families were especially careful not to allow villagers to do anything that would harm selected gravesites.

Along with geomantic sitings, geomantic prophecy also became widespread in Korea. It became especially popular among provincial families who saw at each new government crisis evidence that the geomantic power of the nation was waning and with it the power of the ruling house. Both the Koryo and Choson kingdoms were founded by provincial families whose rise to power had been prophesied by geomantic experts. Upon their accession to power the first order of business was the selection of a new, geomantically more powerful capital. Geomantic prophesy and prognostication thus became a tool of many peasant rebellions and was used by provincials to express dissatisfaction with the entrenched aristocratic elite of the capital.

Geomancy is still widespread in modern Korea. House sites, gravesites, even new towns are selected according to geomantic principles. Geomancy has also influenced the way modern Koreans think about their own culture on the peninsula, that is, that the spirit of the Korean people comes from the spirit of the land and the spirit of the land is geomantically superior to that of other lands.

African Traditional Religions: While Islamic forms of geomancy employing sand drawings have influenced the divinatory practices of many African cultures, there are indigenous forms and adaptations. Perhaps the most elaborate is the *Ifa* system of the Yoruba of southwestern Nigeria, in which nuts or shells are systematically tossed to the ground, forming one or more of a set of 256 recognized patterns. Each of these patterns is associated with an oral text the diviner has memorized. When these verses are interpreted, the causes of a client's present predicament and its solutions are revealed.

Germanic religion. *See* Nordic religion.

Gesar/Geser (Tibetan/Mongolian), a divine hero-king who is revered in Tibet and Mongolia. According to Tibetan Buddhist tradition, Gesar will return at the end of time to lead a decisive battle against the forces of evil. In the nineteenth century, Gesar was identified with the Chinese war god Kuan-ti, the protector of the Manchu dynasty. *See also* Shambhala; Tibetan religions.

Geser. *See* Gesar/Geser.

Geshe (Tibetan, "virtuous spiritual friend"), degree offered by monasteries in the Geluk-pa and non-Buddhist Bon traditions upon completion of studies emphasizing textual study, philosophical debate, ritual arts, and traditional sciences. The program can take twenty years. The Geshe degree is considered equivalent to the Western Ph.D or Th.D. *See also* Bon; Geluk-pa.

get (Heb., "[divorce] document"), a unilateral declaration of dismissal by the husband of the wife; effects Jewish divorce. It is commissioned by the husband, handwritten by a scribe, and delivered to the wife in the presence of two witnesses. Either she or the rabbinical court must keep it as proof of her marital availability. Without a *get*, even a woman who has been divorced civilly may not remarry under Jewish law.

Ghazali, Abu Hamid Muhammad ibn Muhammad al-Tusi (ga-zah'lee; 1058–1111), Islamic theologian, legalist, philosopher, and mystic. Al-Ghazali is most remembered for his synthesis of orthodox Sunni legalism with an increasingly heterodox Islamic mysticism, revivifying the former and bringing the latter firmly under orthodox control. He also excelled as a philosopher (referred to in medieval Christian texts as Algazal) and theologian, yet after his conversion to Sufism in 1095 he seems to have rejected these disciplines. His *Refutation of the Philosophers* reflects the declining place of philosophy in the Islamic East. Ghazali was also a prodigious expositor of Islamic law. *See also* Islamic philosophy; Sufism.

ghee (gee; Hindi *ghi*, from Skt. *ghrita*, "sprinkled"), clarified butter, common as a ritual offering in Vedic and later India; it was poured into fire to be conveyed to celestial gods by smoke. *See also* sacrifice; Veda, Vedism.

ghetto (geh'toh; possibly from Ital., "foundry"), section of a city or town into which Jews were forcibly settled. *Ghetto* was first employed to describe the walled-in area near a Venice foundry that, in

1516, was designated as the only section of the city in which Jews could dwell. Ghettos were usually walled off from the rest of the urban area, and movement in and out was limited to a small number of gates that were generally bolted at night. Jewish ghettos in the technical sense are limited to Christian lands and were most prominent in medieval Europe and areas under the rule of Nazi Germany *See also* anti-Semitism.

ghost, the appearance of a dead person, usually thought of as a disembodied spirit. *See also* afterlife; demon; Ghost Festival; goryo; Halloween; lemures; revenant.

Korean Religion: In Korea ghosts (Kor. *kwisin*) or wandering spirits are malevolent spirits of those who have died without fulfilling themselves, including unmarried women, young boys, and victims of accidental drowning. Though the spirits of the dead may sometimes communicate with and haunt their descendants in dreams, visions, and shamanic possessions, such hauntings are only occasional and are easily remedied through the performance of expiatory rituals and meritorious acts. Wandering spirits, on the other hand, are nameless, lack knowing descendants, and therefore have not been properly settled in the grave. The highly unusual nature of their death is powerful enough to give them the ability to assume any form, human, animal, or monster, and through these forms they seek revenge on the living. While wandering spirits may be held in check or warded off through the use of amulets, talismans, spirit posts (*changsung*) and various Buddhist and shamanic rituals that invoke the power of higher, more powerful spirits, they cannot be eliminated. A less malevolent form of ghost are the nameless, implike beggar spirits (*tokkaebi*), which are said to hide household items, frighten people unaware in the house, break household objects, steal food, and hover about the back of a household compound near the latrine.

Ghost Dance, a new religious movement among Native Americans of the western United States. The Ghost Dance had two distinct phases, both of which originated in the visions of a Paiute shaman living in western Nevada.

The Ghost Dance of 1870: Wodziwob (d. ca. 1872), the prophet of the 1870 dance, proclaimed that the world would soon be destroyed, then renewed; the dead would be brought back to life and game animals restored. He instructed his followers to dance a nocturnal circle dance. This dance was similar to both older Paiute traditions and an earlier regional movement, the Plateau

Prophet Dance, but it addressed very present conditions of deprivation resulting from white incursions into tribal territories. It spread to California, Oregon, and Idaho but, with the death of Wodziwob and the nonfulfillment of his prophecies, died out within a few years. The Shoshone and Bannock of Fort Hall, Idaho, however, continued to perform the Ghost Dance at least intermittently up to 1890.

The Ghost Dance of 1890: Wovoka (ca. 1856–1932), a Paiute Native American prophet, inaugurated the Ghost Dance of 1890 on the basis of a vision he had received during a total eclipse of the sun. His message was in direct continuity with the 1870 dance: there was to be an imminent renewal of the world in which dead Native Americans would be resurrected and the living would no longer be subject to sickness and old age, game animals would be restored to their former abundance, and the old way of life would once more flourish. Euro-Americans, by this time firmly in control, would be eliminated by supernatural means, such as a flood or earthquake. It is uncertain whether Wovoka announced a specific date for these events, but many expected them in the spring of 1891. Wovoka's message also contained ethical admonitions (e.g., members of different tribes should live in peace with each other; they should cooperate with, not war against, the whites).

In anticipation of the great event and to speed its arrival, Wovoka instructed his followers to perform circle dances periodically. They did so in large numbers, and (especially among Plains tribes) dancers often fell into trances, subsequently reporting that they had visited the spirit world and spoken with dead relatives, who were living a life like the one that had flourished before the coming of the whites.

The 1890 dance spread mainly eastward along the length of the Rocky Mountains and Great Plains. In some tribes (e.g., Paiute, Cheyenne, Shoshone, Pawnee) acceptance was almost unanimous; in others (like the Sioux) only segments of the population became believers. No Pueblo (except at Taos) or Navajo accepted it, the latter because of a culturally conditioned aversion to ghosts.

As news of the Paiute prophet Wovoka began to spread, tribes sent delegations to the Walker Lake Reservation in western Nevada to see him. They returned with versions of his teachings that were sometimes shaped by the particular needs of their tribe. Among the Pawnee, the dance provided the basis for an important cultural renewal, for the visions of the dancers made possible the revival of old ceremonial activities that had fallen into disuse because knowledge of their correct performance had been lost. The Sioux, who had a number of current grievances against the government (e.g., loss of reservation lands, cuts in rations), altered Wovoka's message in the direction of greater hostility toward the whites. Delegates like Short Bull and Kicking Bear advocated the use of "ghost shirts" (special garments that were supposed to make the wearer invulnerable to bullets) and spoke of the possibility of armed conflict with the government soldiers. During 1890, newspapers around the country carried often sensational stories about the "messiah craze" (Wovoka was often called the "Indian messiah") and the possibility of renewed warfare with the Sioux. Violence did erupt in December: during an attempt to arrest him, Chief Sitting Bull was shot to death, and Chief Big Foot and almost three hundred of his band were massacred by the cavalry at Wounded Knee. These events were more the result of government blunders than of a Sioux outbreak.

Later Developments: Following the violence among the Sioux and the failure of the expected transformations the next spring, the popularity of the dance began to fade. However, it did not die out altogether. Wovoka remained active, but shifted his message in the direction of ethical admonitions. As late as 1896 some Kiowa were still dancing, and one of the early Northern Cheyenne delegates, Porcupine, led a brief revival of the dance in 1900.

The movement continued elsewhere in a more substantive way. In the first decade of the twentieth century, Fred Robinson, an Assiniboin who had been instructed in the Ghost Dance by Kicking Bear and had corresponded with Wovoka, brought the dance to a small community of Sioux living in Saskatchewan. Combined with a traditional Medicine Feast, apocalyptic elements disappeared and the themes of ethical admonition and community solidarity predominated. Among the Wind River Shoshone (Wyoming), the Ghost Dance apparently combined with an earlier ceremony (the Father Dance) of thanksgiving to God for food. As a result, the annual renewal of nature took on a cosmic dimension: shamans reported dreams in which they saw the dead assembled in heaven waiting to return to earth at some unspecified time in the future. The people on earth anticipated this event and performed a dance thought to imitate that of the dead. In both these places the Ghost Dance continued to be performed into the 1950s. In the 1970s the dance was revived by the activist American Indian Movement.

Even among persons and groups who no longer practice it, knowledge of the Ghost Dance has not died out and lessons are still derived from it. Thus ca. 1970 the Sioux medicine man Lame Deer reinterpreted an old Ghost Dance song about straightening arrows and killing and butchering buffalo to mean that individuals must live upright lives in order to help bring about a new earth. *See also* Native Americans (North America), new religions among; nativistic movements; prophecy in traditional religions; Prophet Dance; shaman; Wovoka.

Ghost Festival (Chin. *yu-lan p'en*), the Chinese festival of food offerings and prayers for ghosts (*kuei*) focused on the fifteenth day of the seventh lunar month. Originally a Buddhist festival, it displayed sentiments that coincided with Chinese concerns about potentially harmful ghosts who had no one to care for them. *See also* Chinese religions (festal cycle); kuei.

gifts of the Spirit, the Christian apostle Paul's notion of believers being variously equipped by God for service in the world through the presence of certain divinely granted capacities such as teaching, prophecy, healing, or apostleship (1 Corinthians 12:8–11). *See also* Pentecostalism.

Gilgamesh (gil'gah-mesh; Sumerian, meaning uncertain), the legendary king of the Sumerian city-state Uruk (biblical Erech) ca. 2650 B.C. Of the man and his actual achievements nothing certain is known, but within a century of his death he had become a god residing in the underworld, a king and judge. Until the end of Mesopotamian civilization he remained associated with the cult and care of the dead.

Gilgamesh also lived on as a great hero of legendary exploits. Five or six tales were committed to writing ca. 2100 to 2000 B.C. in the Sumerian language. Around 1800 the Sumerian traditions were united in a single work, written in Babylonian, of at least a thousand lines. This version spread across the Near East, at times translated into Hittite and Hurrian. Finally, in the late second millennium, it was edited in a standard form of about three thousand lines.

In this form, the epic has been transformed into a wisdom tale. It is addressed to a reader who is urged to read and ponder the story of a great man's struggle with life and the human condition. It is structured around three weeklong rites of passage: rites conferring humanity, rites rejecting humanity, and rites restoring humanity.

At first Gilgamesh would overcome death by

the immortality of fame. This he achieves by slaying the monster Huwawa. But his dearest friend, Enkidu, dies, and fame becomes worthless. Now he will be satisfied only with the transcendence that belongs to the immortal gods and the one man who shares in this immortality, Utnapishtim, the Babylonian Noah and sole survivor of the Flood; hence the journey to this unique figure. But Gilgamesh learns that this distinction is due to divine caprice, never to be repeated. At last Gilgamesh accepts his mortality and regains his humanity. At the end, pointing to the city Uruk and its mighty walls, he shows a sense of human achievement as well as human limitation; "He was weary but at peace." *See also* flood stories; immortality; Mesopotamian religion; ordeal.

ginseng, root of *Panax schinseng* honored in Chinese lore for its curative, rejuvenating, and aphrodisiacal powers. The name in Chinese refers to the root's humanlike shape, which is traditionally said to indicate its significance for curing human infirmities. *See also* Chinese medicine.

Gion Shrine (gee-ohn), a Shinto shrine in Kyoto, Japan, enshrining Gozu Tenno, a god of pestilence, and other deities. It is famous for its annual summer festival parade of Yamaboko floats instituted in 869 as a rite of exorcism to placate the gods believed responsible for a major epidemic. *See also* exorcism; Japanese religions (festal cycle).

Giovanni di Fidanza. *See* Bonaventura.

giri (gee-ree), Japanese concept of social obligations in contrast to human feelings (*ninjo*). Reciprocal obligations to repay favors (*on*) between *samurai* and lord still operate in contemporary Japanese society. *See also* bushido.

Gita Govinda (gee'tah goh-vin'duh), "Song of the Cowherd Lord," a twelfth-century erotic Sanskrit lyric poem by Jayadeva depicting the love of lord Krishna for the cowherdess Radha. *See also* Krishna; path of devotion; Radha.

glory, luminous quality, frequently a divine attribute.

glossolalia (Gk. *glossa,* "tongue," and *lalein,* "to speak"), the act of speaking in a "language" either unknown or incomprehensible to the speaker. This practice may have played a significant role in

early Christianity. In the late twentieth century, a similar phenomenon is practiced in certain Pentecostal and charismatic traditions. *See also* charismatics; Cumina religion; Pentecostalism.

Gnosticism (nos'ti-siz-uhm; from Gk. *gnosis,* "knowledge"), a term used for a category of religions that emphasize knowledge as essential to salvation. Gnosticism appears in the early Christian centuries, but its origins and age are much debated, and at the present state of research it can hardly be proven to exist prior to Christianity. Neither unequivocally Christian, Jewish, Greek, nor Iranian, Gnosticism is not a clearly delineated religion, but rather a specific religious interpretative perspective. Gnosticism lives mainly in or on the edges of Christianity and Judaism and it bears a number of philosophical, astrological, and magical marks loosely belonging in the Near Eastern and Inner Mediterranean areas.

Cosmologies: Common to many Gnostic texts and systems are an emphasis on dualistic speculations (e.g., light vs. darkness, good vs. evil, the earthly realm vs. the heavenly world, or the Lightworld); a reevaluation of many biblical traditions (especially Genesis and the New Testament) so that the Old Testament God, for instance, becomes an inferior figure ignorant of Lightworld entities above and prior to himself; and a keen interest in the salvation of the human soul, which, due to its Lightworld origin, is opposed to the body it inhabits and possesses a superior knowledge. Gnostic mythologies offer intricate, detailed speculations on cosmic geographics, provide emotional descriptions of the fate of the soul in its material prison, and, in frequently impressive poetry, describe the soul's journey back to its lofty home. In brief, Gnosticism exemplifies the common religious and creative response of Late Antiquity to a feeling of alienation toward bodily, material, even social existence, and a burning interest in arriving at a higher, more authentic level of life. Far from leading to paralytic pessimism, this orientation caused Gnostics to create mythologies, ideologies, rituals, and organized communities. Subversive Gnostic interpretations, especially of the biblical traditions, elicited horrified, swift denunciations from the early fathers of the church, who rightly perceived the Gnostics as a menace to the budding Christian orthodoxy.

Much of what we know about Gnostic doctrines and practices comes from these church fathers, but their accounts are unavoidably colored by a strong hostility toward Gnostics. Direct Gnostic testimonies are available from numerous sources: the Nag Hammadi texts (a cache of fifty-odd documents unearthed in Egypt in 1945); manuscripts found or bought by European scholars in recent centuries; and voluminous texts from two Gnostic groups—the Manichaeans (whose system became a "world religion" stretching from North Africa to China) and the Mandaeans (a still-extant community of Gnostics in Iran and Iraq). Various Gnostic texts show strong affinities with Greek philosophy, Syriac Christianity, and Iranian traditions.

Cosmogonies: Gnostic speculations tend to pose a "prehistory" to the creation accounts in Genesis, imagining a number of Lightworld angelic (aeonic) beings emanating or springing from one or more original, ineffable entities. A progression of male and female emanations eventually result in the lowest levels of aeons where the Old Testament God belongs. Ignorant of—or rebelling against—his more elevated predecessors, this god (sometimes called Samael, "the blind one") creates the visible, material world, the human body (an androgynous Adam or the pair Adam and Eve), and imprisons the human soul in it. Having thus separated the supreme god from the creator god, Gnostics give a negative evaluation of the latter and his minions. In parallel, heroic figures in the Bible turn into villains and vice versa, so that the serpent in paradise and Cain become principles of the light and of *gnosis*, while Noah turns into a collaborator with the ignorant creator. Gnostic ideas about Jesus tend toward splitting his personality, with Christ, the Lightworld aspect of Jesus, escaping crucifixion, while the bodily Jesus, a mere shadow of his real self, is destroyed on the cross.

The principle of evil originates within the Lightworld itself, results unavoidably from the emanation process, or exists as a separate, anti-Lightworld entity from the beginning of creation. Personified (or hypostasized) evil is in many Gnostic myths portrayed as a tragic figure: he (it is usually male) knows of his wrongdoing and ignorance but seems unable to act differently, though he still hopes for his own, final redemption and return to home in the upper worlds. His mother, personified Wisdom or Error, is likewise tragic, but possesses more insight than her son. Human responsibilities include knowledge about the good and evil principles, the numerous aeonic beings populating the spheres between earth and Lightworld, and a firm sense of cosmic geography so that the ascending soul may know its way home. Anthropological models often correspond to cosmic maps: the upper human component is the spirit, the mid-level is the soul, and the material body roughly correlates with the macrocosm.

Rituals: Gnostic religions undoubtedly possessed a rich cultic life alongside the mythological/speculative component, but except for Manichaeism and Mandaeism—and a few scattered texts from other, less delineated traditions—we have only hazy evidence of the intricacies of Gnostic rituals. Initiations, baptisms, sacred meals, rituals for the dead, and techniques for ecstatic experiences are attested in various traditions. Community ethics, class divisions based on levels of gnosis, and aggressively polemical interests against "normative" Christianity and Judaism testify to organized Gnostic schools and groups eager to define themselves against outsiders and against one another.

Gnosticism is also loosely used to indicate phenomena outside of late antiquity, e.g., Sufism, medieval European systems such as those of the Bogomils and the Cathars, William Blake's philosophy, and numerous New Age–related religions. Strictly speaking, however, the term ought to be reserved for the category of religions in Late Antiquity. With very few exceptions, these religions were overrun by Christian orthodoxy and early rabbinic Judaism and disappeared after the fifth and sixth centuries. **See also** Abraxas; Achamoth; Auditors; Barbelo; Basilides; Cainites; Carpocrates; Cologne Mani-Codex; Demiurge; Herakleon; Kephalaia; Mandaeans; Manichaeism; Marcion; Markos; Naas; Naassene Hymn; Nag Hammadi Library; Ophites; pleroma; Poimandres; Ptolemy; Sabaoth; Satornilos; Simon Magus; Sophia; Valentinianism.

Gobind Singh (goh'bind sing; 1666–1708), tenth Guru of the Sikhs. Gobind Rai (later Gobind Singh) was the only child of the ninth Guru, Tegh Bahadur. He inherited the title when his father was executed by the Moghul ruler Aurangzeb in 1675 and ruled the state of Anandpur on the northeastern border of the Punjab, India. Efforts were made by a combination of neighbors and Moghuls to defeat him and in 1704 he was compelled to evacuate Anandpur, losing all four of his sons during the withdrawal. Following the death of Aurangzeb he joined Aurangzeb's successor, Bahadur Shah, and died in the Deccan following an assassination attempt.

Guru Gobind Singh is important for establishing the order of the Khalsa in 1699, confirming the militant posture of his followers, a reputation that made them much feared, and announcing just before he died that he would be the last of the personal Gurus. Instead, the functions of the Guru would pass to the scripture (the Guru Granth) and the corporate community (the Guru Panth). *See also* Adi Granth; Khalsh; Sikhism.

god, common term for a male deity.

G-d, Jewish circumlocution in written English to avoid using the name of God. *See also* Judaism, God in; Tetragrammaton.

God, Goddess common term for the supreme deity. *See also* term question.

goddess, common term for a female deity.

Goddess (Hinduism), feminine deity in the dominant religious tradition of India. Whether Hindu Goddess worship is a unitary phenomenon or a plural one is much debated, by scholars on historical grounds and by Hindus on theological ones.

The Prehistoric Period: Archaeological evidence from northwest India suggests links between the Indus Valley civilization (2500–1750 B.C.) and older traditions of goddess worship in western Asia. The Indus evidence is ambiguous, but widely distributed terra-cotta female figurines show reverence for the powers of fertility, if not specific goddesses. Soapstone seals portraying animals, the plant world, and humans (both male and female) in varying forms of interaction have recently been interpreted as indicating fundamental Goddess power, which is made accessible to male rulers through animal sacrifice. Further interpretation remains tentative here, as does the relationship between the Indus figures and the goddesses of later Hinduism.

Vedic Goddesses: The Indo-European entry into India toward the end of the second millennium B.C. brought a pantheon dominated by gods. Vedic literature, with its sacrificial context, contains some hymns to goddesses, but they are of minor stature. Like Vedic gods, they are often closely identified with natural phenomena—Prithivi with earth, Ratri with night, Vak with speech, Ushas with dawn, Sarasvati with a river—although the maternal Aditi and the horrific Nirriti seem independent of nature.

Hindu Goddesses and the Great Goddess: Although the devotional movement known as *bhakti* (Skt.) was first directed to male deities, by the first centuries there is evidence for Goddess worship as well. At first she is a marginal, bloodthirsty figure, described in the *Mahabharata* as "fond of liquor, flesh, and beasts." But by the time of the *Devi Mahatmyam* (sixth century) she is called "mother of the universe" and understood to intervene in human affairs as the great protectress from adversity. Henceforth goddesses abound in Hinduism, sometimes paired with a god as his consort or power-essence (*shakti*), sometimes as independent, specific deities, sometimes as the Great Goddess (*mahadevi*) from whom all existence comes forth. Worship of these forms varies greatly according to calendar, caste, sect, region, and personal preference.

Parvati is Shiva's consort; her rich mythology shows deep ambivalence about whether power is maternal or ascetic in nature. Shri, or Lakshmi, is Vishnu's consort, associated with fertility and riches, particularly during the festival of Divali, and often understood as mediator between humans and her regally aloof consort. Sita is Rama's devoted wife, a role she definitively models in the *Ramayana* epic. Radha's sensuous relationship with Krishna conveys a subtle theology of eroticism, much developed in poetic expression. Independent goddesses include Durga, vanquisher of the buffalo demon, Mahisha; the gruesome Kali, who frequents cremation grounds and is garlanded with human skulls; the Matrikas ("Mothers"), a collective, euphemistic name for inauspicious, hostile spirits; and many others.

Worship of the Great Goddess is most apparent in the esoteric ritual integration of doctrine and praxis known as Tantra. Though details vary greatly, the goal here is to transform the devotee's body through sacred sound (*mantra*) and sight into the dwelling place of the Goddess, thus coming to know her monistic and universal reality through personal experience.

It is not possible finally to enumerate all manifestations of the Hindu Goddess, for sharply delineated textual figures shade off into countless manifestations at the village level, where she is both ubiquitous and the dominant religious presence. *See also* Bhu Bhudevi; Durga; Indus Valley civilization, religion of; Kali; Mother Goddess; Parvati; Radha; Shakti; Shri-Lakshmi; yoni.

Goddess religions (contemporary), decentralized religious movements that seek to revive, reconstruct, and invent a spirituality that emphasizes the divine feminine. This movement of women (and some men) uses the ancient Goddess religions as inspiration and as models for female power. For some women, contemporary goddess spirituality is a new religion; for others, feminine symbols and deities are sources of renewal within liberal traditions of Judaism and Christianity.

The contemporary movement of Goddess spirituality was born out of feminism. Its small-group focus was inspired by the experiences of feminist consciousness-raising groups of the 1970s, which revealed that personal experiences were to be trusted and acted upon as a foundation for political action.

It was a short step then to the perception that spiritual experiences should also be trusted and that a small, intimate, nonauthoritarian group was most appropriate for religious and psychic exploration.

Many women felt that the images of women prevalent in modern society were so tainted by patriarchal attitudes that it was necessary to search in history and myth for more appropriate images of female strength. In looking for strong, powerful female images that were not defined by men, women came upon two ancient archetypes: goddesses and witches. The goddesses in ancient religions and mythology presented images of women far stronger than most in modern society. The witch, although often a symbol of ugliness and evil in popular culture, long has been an image of feminine power, the symbol of a strong, self-defined woman who lives in deep and loving relationship with the natural world.

Goddess Figure: Women who searched the texts of history and anthropology also found controversial theories promoting the idea of an ancient matriarchal society and began exploring the concept of a feminine deity.

Many of those involved in contemporary Goddess religions do believe in a prepatriarchal age when women held more power and goddesses were venerated. The idea of a universal matriarchy is disputed by most scholars, although there is mounting evidence of some ancient cultures where egalitarianism prevailed. Whether or not a prepatriarchal golden age ever existed, women involved in feminist spirituality view the idea of such an age as a vision and ideal, as part of their fight for a society where women have more freedom and power.

Witch Figure: In 1971, Z. Budapest, a Hungarian-born feminist, started the Susan B. Anthony Coven No. 1, and soon there were similar groups in many states. There are many different traditions of feminist or Dianic Witchcraft, all of which emphasize the Goddess, and most of which (but not all) exclude men. Dianic Wicca, like all forms of Neo-Pagan Witchcraft, focuses on seasonal celebrations, reverence for nature, and personal empowerment through ritual and celebration.

In 1979, Starhawk's *The Spiral Dance* was published, a book of feminist Wiccan ritual and philosophy that may have led to the formation of hundreds of Goddess-oriented ritual groups. In addition, the Goddess spirituality movement began to influence women in mainstream liberal churches and synagogues. The Unitarian Universalists published a study guide for women and religion, which included Goddess-oriented materials, including rituals. Jewish women began to study about the Shekinah (the feminine immanent presence of God) and to look into the history of older pre-Canaanite goddesses such as Ashera and Anath. These women began holding moon circles and trying to find the prepatriarchal roots of Judaism. The United Church of Christ and several other denominations published prayer books and liturgies with language that described God in both male and female terms. Many Roman Catholic women who were fighting to be priests left the Catholic Church and founded Womanchurch congregations where rituals were led by women. And noted theologians such as Matthew Fox talked of God as feminine.

But other women insisted that implicit in Jewish and Christian theology was the notion of God as male, with a resulting legitimization of male authority. These women believed that only by leaving the patriarchal institutions behind could they truly create a spiritual movement that would empower women to feel whole and sacred. Some of these new spirituality groups consider themselves witches; others do not.

Goddess Spirituality: Women's spirituality magazines continue to proliferate, and a few of the many books published with this point of view have become best-sellers. Within the lesbian community, Goddess spirituality has become the dominant religion, as evidenced by the use of symbols, ceremonies, art, and musical offerings at the large annual women's music festivals in Michigan, Indiana, and elsewhere. Workshops devoted to women's rituals and psychic exploration are a common addition at most New Age conference centers.

Goddess spirituality groups differ in size, form, and structure: eclectic groups that hold spontaneous rituals; formal Dianic covens, with a structure and training program; study and ritual groups within mainstream churches; and large, organized festivals where hundreds, even thousands, may gather. Most groups are decentralized, antiauthoritarian, and even somewhat anarchistic.

The Goddess as an image and idea is seen differently by diverse groups and people. Many women found that the idea of a female deity freed them from their own prejudices against their female body. For some, the goddesses are seen as Jungian archetypes, powerful images and potencies that can be used for psychological development. Others see the Goddess as the ravished earth, or as the creative life force both within each individual and of the universe as a whole. For these women, the Goddess is the mystery of life, the power of birth, life, death, and regeneration. Some women see the great Mother Goddess as a beneficent and omnipotent deity, but most reject this view of a transcendent deity and see the Goddess as immanent in all nature. Like Neo-Paganism, Goddess spirituality tends to be nondogmatic, based on poetic inspiration and artistic sense rather than a literal set of doctrines or scripture.

Although Goddess spirituality is a growing movement in the United States and Canada, it is impossible to give precise figures for the number of adherents. However, many authorities believe that, in North America, more than 100,000 people currently are involved in the movement. *See also* feminist theology; Neo-Paganism; Wicca; witchcraft.

godhead,   abstract term for deity.

Gog and Magog,   in Western apocalypticism, the last great world power that must be defeated before the coming of the kingdom of God. *See also* apocalypticism; eschatology.

golden age.   1 In Greek and Roman tradition, the first age of the world. 2 More generally, a utopian period in the past. *See also* ages of the world.

golden calf,   in the Hebrew Bible, "idol" fashioned by Aaron and the people of Israel at the foot of Mt. Sinai during the Exodus. It was the cause of Moses' smashing of the original tablets of the law (Exodus 32).

Golden Dawn,   a hermetic order founded in 1888 and the most famous of modern initiatory occult organizations. Its heyday was the 1890s, when its London lodge was famous for both the literary figures it attracted, such as W. B. Yeats, and the scandals and upheavals that devastated it at the end of the decade. Though the Golden Dawn divided and dwindled in the twentieth century, its ritual practices and elaborate system of grades, each requiring significant esoteric learning and accomplishment, have served as models for many later occult orders in the Western tradition. *See also* Hermetism; occult, the; secret societies.

golden rule,   in its narrow meaning, the teaching of Jesus: "Do to others as you would have them do to you" (Matthew 7:12). Variants of the rule have been claimed for all of the world's major religions.

"Golden Temple,"   a name for the *Darbar Sahib* (Punjabi, "the divine court"), the best known

The "Golden Temple," Harimandir ("Temple of God") or Darbar Sahib ("Divine Court"), the chief house of worship (*gurdwara*) of the Sikhs of India and their central pilgrimage place. Constructed in Amritsar, Punjab, ca. 1589–1603, it was rebuilt during the reign of Maharaja Ranjit Singh (d. 1839). At the front is the Amritsar ("Pool of Nectar").

center of Sikh worship and pilgrimage, established between ca. 1589 and 1603 in Amritsar, northern India. The present marble structure, capped with a massive dome covered in gold leaf, hence the name Golden Temple, dates to the reign of Maharaja Ranjit Singh (d. 1839). *See also* Sikhism.

golem (goh'lehm; Heb., "embryo"), in Jewish mysticism and folklore, an animated humanoid fashioned by a rabbi who had mastered the "secrets of creation." The most famous golems were those created by Loew of Prague, Elijah of Chelm, and Jaffe of Poland.

Golgotha. *See* Calvary, Mt.

Good Friday, holy day celebrated on the Friday of the Christian Holy Week honoring the crucifixion and death of Jesus. *See also* calendar (Christian); Holy Week.

good news. *See* gospel.

Good Samaritan, a New Testament parable (Luke 10:30–37) in which a Samaritan, a member of a despised religious group, is the only one to come to the aid of a man who had been beaten and robbed.

Good Shepherd, a title for Jesus, based on a parable (Matthew 18:12–14) in which the good shepherd leaves his flock to search for a single animal that is lost.

gopi (goh'pee; Skt.), in Hinduism, one of the cowherding girls or women of Braj who epitomize intimate devotion to Krishna. There are some sixteen thousand *gopis*, all sharing in Krishna's dance, but he makes himself present to each as if she were trysting with him alone. *See also* Krishna; path of devotion.

Gorakhnath (goh-ruhk'naht), a legendary *yogin* famous throughout North India for both magical feats and writings on yoga. Said by some to be physically immortal, he probably flourished in the eleventh century. *See also* yoga.

goryo (goh-ryoh; Jap., "honored spirit"), malevolent spirits of the dead in Japanese popular religion. Especially in the Heian period (794–1185), their anger and jealousy over past wrongs were thought to cause natural disasters and by possession inflict illness and death on the living. They were exorcised primarily by Buddhist priests chanting scriptures and inducing them to possess a temporary host. *See also* Japanese folk religion.

gospel (Gk., "good news"). **1** The announcement of the birth, appearance, and death of Jesus and the salvation it brings. **2** A written narrative of the life of Jesus. *See also* aretalogy; Jesus Christ; New Testament.

gourd/calabash. *See* hu-lu.

Gozan (goh-zahn; Jap., "five mountains"), the medieval temple system of Rinzai Zen Buddhism. The term also designates the culture of those temples from the fourteenth through sixteenth centuries. *See also* Rinzai.

grace, a Christian theological term denoting divine gifts without which human salvation would be impossible.

Grace, Charles Emmanuel "Daddy." *See* African Americans (North America), new religions among.

grace at meals, a short prayer, either a formula or extemporaneous, said by Christians before meals.

Graces, the, in Greek mythology, charming and beautiful daughters of Zeus who find joy in nature and in service to other deities, giving physical, intellectual, and aesthetic favors. Their names indicate their qualities: Aglaia (Gk., "radiant"), Auxo ("grower"), Euphrosyne ("joy"), Kale ("beautiful"), and Athaleia ("flowering").

gradual cultivation (Chin. *chien-hsiu*), in Ch'an Buddhism, a graduated series of religious practices that often followed the experience of initial insight (*chieh-wu*). Continued religious effort was believed necessary in order to eradicate the deeply rooted presence of delusion acquired by past karmic actions. *See also* Ch'an school; karma; Northern school; sudden-gradual controversy.

gradual enlightenment (Chin. *chien-wu*), Chinese Buddhist term for attainment of insight through a graduated series of meditative states. *See also*

Ch'an school; Northern school; sudden-gradual controversy.

gradual teaching (Chin. *chien-chiao*), Chinese Buddhist teachings believed to have been preached by the Buddha that employ expedient means in order to convey difficult concepts. While the method of exposition differs, the content is purported to be the same as the advanced teachings.

Graham, William (Billy) Franklin (b.1918), American Christian evangelist best known, since 1954, for his international revivalist activities, the "Crusades," sponsored by the Billy Graham Evangelistic Association. *See also* revival.

Grail, Holy, in Christian legend, the cup that Jesus used at the Last Supper and that caught his blood when he was crucified. The quest for the Grail was combined with the Arthurian romances to produce a complex series of medieval texts and traditions.

granthi (gruhn'tih; Punjabi,"keeper of the *Adi Granth*"), the official who cares for a Sikh house of worship (*gurdwara*), where the scripture is housed, and who leads the daily worship. Any member of the community can perform these duties. *See also* Adi Granth; gurdwara; Sikhism.

grave, graveyard, a burial site, often the location of commemorative rituals in behalf of the dead. In some traditions, a grave is a dangerous location due to the presence of the spirits of the dead. Graves of holy persons become the objects of pilgrimage and places with miraculous powers, especially healing. *See also* afterlife; shrine.

graveyard. *See* grave, graveyard.

Great Awakening, a Christian revivalist movement that swept the American colonies from 1725 to 1760. In experiences of ecstatic joy and release, converts "awakened" to Christ and knew him experientially. By 1730, Theodore J. Frelinghuysen, a Dutch Calvinist, and Gilbert Tennent, a revivalist Presbyterian, had begun the Awakening from their churches in New Jersey. In 1734, Jonathan Edwards, the most formidable apologist for this experiential religion, witnessed to the "surprising work of God" in his Congregationalist church at Northampton, Massachusetts. British evangelist George Whitefield toured the colonies between 1738 and 1740 lending impetus and cohesiveness to the movement. Itinerant revivalists carried the Awakening to the South. Its distinguishing characteristics included the insistence on the personal nature of conversion to Christ, itinerant ministry, and a novel preaching style appealing openly to the emotions. Mobile ministry and individual conversion tended to undermine the parish structure of the old tax-supported churches and led to a proliferation of separate and voluntary ones. The revivalists succeeded in revitalizing colonial Protestantism by a typically modern appeal to individual experience. They accommodated New World Calvinism and Anglicanism to conditions of dramatically expanded personal liberty. *See also* Edwards, Jonathan; revival.

Great Learning. *See* Ta-hsueh.

Great White Brotherhood, in Western occult and theosophical movements, a collective term for adepts who have concluded their cycles of reincarnation and have ascended to a higher place of spiritual existence while retaining an active role in the collective and individual salvation of human beings. *See also* Church Universal and Triumphant; I AM Religious Activity; Theosophy.

Greek and Roman philosophy. The various writings of the Greek and Roman philosophers are often concerned with religious matters ranging from mysticism to atheism. As there are relatively few primary religious documents from either Greece or Rome, philosophical works become an important resource for the reconstruction of Greco-Roman religious beliefs and practices. *See also* Apuleius; Aristotle; Cynicism; Democritus; Epictetus; Epicureans; Heracleitus; Neoplatonism; Parmenides; Plato; Plotinus; Presocratics; Seneca; skepticism, ancient; Socrates; Stoics.

Greek religion. A ritual-based and highly flexible set of beliefs and practices, Greek religion lacked most features that characterize modern religions: it made no claims of universality, did not proselytize, had no regular clergy, hierarchy, sacred texts, revelation, or any moral code backed by religious teaching. With the exception of marginal cults and perhaps the "mysteries" for initiates, theology had no place. Rather, the individual learned about the many gods and lesser divinities from a number of channels. Representations in Homer's poetry and later in state-sponsored drama, stylized depictions in vase paintings or monumental sculpture, along with a rich oral tradition and participation in numerous religious festivals gave worshipers, from a young age, their framework for religious thinking. Most striking is the way Greek religious practice penetrated ethics, aesthetics, and cosmology as well as the conduct of everyday life.

"Greek religion" covers an area both greater and smaller in scope than would have been recognized by inhabitants of Greek lands in archaic and classical times (ca. 800–300 B.C.). On one hand, *ta hiera* (Gk., "holy things")—the nearest native equivalent to the Latin-derived term *religion*—referred mainly to sacred objects and rituals, and not to ethics or metaphysical speculation about the bonds between humans and gods. On the other hand, consideration of the divine entered every aspect of Greek life, from arrangement of the home to dining practices, civic organization, gender and power orderings, agriculture and war. Moreover, while religious concerns were at the core of the Greek *polis* (city-state), shaping every citizen's life, a further common recognition of certain gods, customs, and key sanctuaries forged one of the few bonds that connected the hundreds of quite different city-states existing in Greek-speaking lands from the western Mediterranean to western Asia. Therefore, it is essential that Greek religion be described on two levels.

On the local level, festivals and rites connected with cycles of the year or human life stages predominated. The honoring of local heroes by means of annual cult practice played an important role, as did dedications and sacrifices to the chief gods of the city-state. Such occasions differed widely from one city-state to another; geographical isolation and inherited local traditions ensured that each adopted its own set of laws, spoke a unique dialect, minted its own coinage, developed its own art forms, and followed a distinctive calendar. Our knowledge of local religion in Greece depends largely on archaeological remains, allusions in nonpoetic literature or ancient literary commentaries, and the invaluable work of the educated travel writer Pausanias (second century).

Meanwhile, from the eighth century B.C. on an evolving "Panhellenic" tradition of poetic narratives encapsulated what local communities held in common regarding the Olympian gods and well-known heroes. This conscious poetic trend subordinated age-old local cult-related traditions in favor of more abstract thought about the problematic relationship between divinity and mortals. Our main sources for this view are Homer's *Iliad* and *Odyssey* and Hesiod's *Theogony* and *Works and Days*. In addition, the works of the praise-poet Pindar (fifth century B.C.) and classical Athenian drama show us local religious lore being integrated with a Panhellenic perspective on the gods. This sort of synthesizing explains the surprising assertion by the historian Herodotus (fifth century B.C.) that Homer and Hesiod first created the story of the

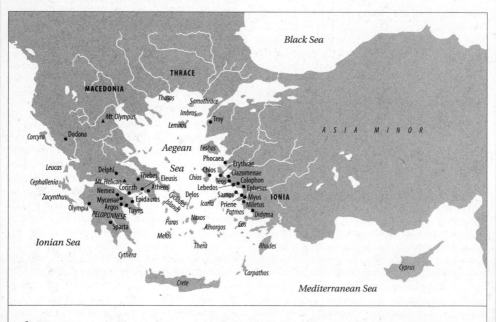

Greece

gods' origins, powers, titles, and forms (*History* 2.53). His comments imply that at least by the fifth century the "Greekness" of any religious belief depended, in the interpretation of the natives, on whether it was known to have a wider domain than the individual city-state. Meanwhile, local religious practices continued, which encouraged some fifth-century philosophers to adopt relativism toward all beliefs. This tendency encouraged the onset of an individualization of religious practices in the postclassical and late antique periods.

The Olympian Gods: The list of twelve Olympian gods provides a nice example of the interplay between Panhellenic ideals and local variations in Greek religion. The number does not change; they can even be known as "the Twelve"; yet different gods were included in this canonical set depending on local worship. At Athens, the Twelve had an archaic altar in the marketplace: included in their corporate worship were, it appears, Zeus, Hera, Demeter, Poseidon, Apollo, Artemis, Athena, Ares, Aphrodite, Hermes, Hestia, and Hephaistos. Later, the representation of the Twelve on the Athenian Parthenon substituted Dionysos, god of wild growth and wine, for Hestia, goddess of the hearth. At Olympia in the Peloponnese, the older gods Kronos and Rhea were included in the Twelve at the expense of Demeter and Hephaistos. The popularity of the latter god at Athens probably reflects the political strength of craft guilds.

The Greek divinities were from the earliest times depicted as human (though they could occasionally assume animal guise). This distinctive anthropomorphism went further than mere personification of mental concepts or physical forces, even if, from the sixth century B.C. on, some Greek thinkers interpreted Homer's gods allegorically. First, the Olympian gods have memory and history; early Greek poetry preserves a sophisticated mythic intuition according to which the present power alignment is shown to be shaped by three generations of psychological conflicts in the family of the gods. As the poet Hesiod narrates in his *Theogony* ("Birth of the Gods," ca. 700 B.C.), the Olympian gods descended from an original couple, Gaia ("Earth") and Ouranos ("Sky"). Kronos, a son of this pair, castrated Ouranos at Gaia's instigation, thus producing the Furies, Giants, ash-tree nymphs, and Aphrodite. Kronos in turn was defeated by his son Zeus, who through a series of marriages and alliances gained lasting control of Olympos (the northern Greek mountain depicted as inaccessible abode of the gods). He has power over his siblings (including his sister/wife Hera, Demeter, Poseidon, Hades, and Hestia) and offspring (the twins Apollo and Artemis, Athena, Ares, Hermes, Dionysos, and Hephaistos).

Second, the Olympians function in Greek thought as an extended Mediterranean family, with the result that control of the cosmos is modeled after a well-known human institution, even in its shifting patterns of alliance and subordination. The Greek gods are not just humanized individuals; they are preeminently social beings, upholding a systematically organized universe through their interlaced desires and aptitudes.

Two crucial functions underlie this polytheism. Through the gods, Greek religion explains human success or failure. When the mythical hero Pelops prays to Poseidon, god of the sea, earthquakes, and horses, he wins a chariot race and a bride (and also becomes an emblem, in mythic tradition, of successful god-hero interaction). Furthermore, the existence of many gods explains human conflicts. When the young man Paris chooses Aphrodite as the fairest goddess in the famous judgment that led to the Trojan War, he gains skill in her special field, sexual attraction, and wins Helen—but at the cost of spurning two other goddesses, Hera and Athena, and turning them into enemies of his doomed homeland. Polytheism, in short, represents the Greek universe as something requiring constant skillful negotiation and balancing of interests on the part of humans in their relation with the divine. Such myths as the story of Hippolytos, who pays with his life for refusing to "honor" Aphrodite while showing excessive respect toward Artemis, articulate the need for flexibility, even cunning, when dealing with gods. Not to recognize the divine is just as bad, as we see in the myth of Dionysos's fatal revenge on the resistant Pentheus, king of his birthplace, Thebes (dramatized in Euripides's *Bacchae*).

The division of powers among Greek divinities can be interpreted as matching to some extent social stages and spheres within Greek culture. In other words, the myths about divine conflict may be serious but symbolic representations of more pragmatic events. Thus, the existence of two goddesses, Artemis and Aphrodite, can represent a division between adolescence and maturity, for both sexes. In this regard it is noteworthy that young women reaching marriage age would dedicate girlhood articles to Artemis as they left her domain for Aphrodite's sexuality. On a wider plane, the distinction between Artemis and Aphrodite recalls the clear-cut Greek division between activities of the civilized center—the polis—versus all that is outside this space: in social terms, the space inhabited by noncitizens, barbarians (Artemis was said to be worshiped by the mythical Amazons), women, and men not yet holding full citizenship responsibilities. In more obvious spatial terms, Artemis embodies the wildness of woods and mountains, the noncivic spaces, while Aphrodite is at home in the domestic center of the city, with such "civilizing" arts as seduction and persuasive speech.

A similar divide characterizes the relations of Hermes—god of flocks, messenger of the dead, and patron of luck and trade—to Apollo, his older brother and god of oracles, colonization, music, purification, plague, and healing. These diverse activities might seem to have no underlying logic. But when we imagine the gods more abstractly, their modes of action seem opposed: Hermes, the circuitous crosser of boundaries, vs. Apollo, who establishes bounds by segmenting out sacred space (whether of the city or of his oracle site, Delphi) and by separating the pure from the impure. On the social level, Hermes, operating outside and on the margins, is a model for the preinitiatory young men who carry on secret nighttime raids or border patrolling, while Apollo, situated at the world's center (Delphi), is the god who welcomes the young into civic society, especially in his role as Phratrios, god of clans.

Polytheism does not rely solely on binary oppositions: Aphrodite, for example, can be contrasted also with Athena, the virgin goddess of crafts and warfare; or with Hera, who shares with her the role of civilizer, only within marriage, whereas Aphrodite is goddess of all attractions. The pairing of Ares and Aphrodite as spouses or lovers expresses the goddess's ambivalent nature, as also an intuited kinship between uncontrollable passions of love and war. At another turn, Ares contrasts with Athena, as she presides over war as systematic craft, he over chaotic slaughter. Much work remains to be done in integrating this recent, structuralist interpretation of polytheism, largely Panhellenic in scope, with the other productive strain in the study of Greek religion, the careful study of cult worship in its various forms on the local level.

The desire for foreknowledge, aid, and protection spawned many specialist gods. Apart from the twelve major Olympians, there existed a realm of minor sea gods (such as Nereus and his daughter Thetis); nymphs of wood, tree, and mountain, often accompanied by Pan, the goat-god, and the hybrid satyrs and centaurs; the

Muses; the Moirai (Fates) Hecate, Hades, and minor "chthonic" (underworld) gods; divinized abstractions such as Aidos (shame) and Nemesis (retribution), and the goddess of childbirth, Eileithyia. Greeks could speak more generally of *to theion* (the divine) or of *daimones* (divinities) in prayer, discussion, or dedication; often sacrifice was made simply "to all the gods." Dedications attest to nearly one thousand cult epithets among the major gods. For instance, Zeus was worshiped by many other names, some of which point to his function as sky god—Ombrios (bringer of rain), Hypsistos (highest)—others to his role as head of a cosmic society. Both of these aspects appear to be inherited from the time of Indo-European cultural unity (about 3000 B.C.), since cognate expressions for "Zeus father" exist in Greek (*Zeu pater*), Latin (*Iuppiter*), and Sanskrit (*Dyaus pitar*). Etymologically, his name is related to a root meaning "clear sky." Some Greek rituals for Zeus still exhibited features of weather magic in classical times, but the sometimes violent sky god who can see all things on earth slowly evolved into an upholder of cosmic justice (Dike) and established order (Themis) in Greek religious thought.

Hera, Ares, Hestia, Ouranos, the Dioscuri, and Helen (worshiped as a goddess in Sparta) have some claim to be partly inherited divinities with Indo-European etymologies. But most of the Greek gods were shaped by contacts with early civilization in at least two other cultural areas, the Aegean and the Near East. Most striking are the many details shared between the *Theogony* succession myth and various "Kingship in Heaven" texts from Anatolia, Egypt, and Mesopotamia. A later wave of Near Eastern influences brought to Greece the worship of such divinities as Adonis, Attis, Bendis, Sabazios, the Phrygian Great Mother and the Egyptian Ammon, Isis, and Serapis.

Minoan-Mycenaean Gods: Within the Aegean area, the pre-Greek Minoan civilization, centered on Crete in the second millennium B.C., left traces of religious activity (offerings of figurines, characteristic double axes, and weapons) in shrines within caves and on mountain peaks often topped by distinctive "horns of consecration." Both places for shrines were popular in Greek worship of later times, but continuity of cult at specific sites from the Minoan period is rare (an exception: the peak sanctuary of Apollo Maleatas near Epidauros). From frescoes, statuettes, and signet rings of the Minoan period, it appears that processions and dances took place in honor of divinities near tree-shrines, and there are hints of sacred kingship, as cult seems to be centered around the great Cretan palace complexes.

Thanks to the decipherment of Linear B writing in 1952, the second or Mycenaean phase of religious activity in the Aegean is now known to have been introduced by early Greek speakers (ca. 1600–1100 B.C.). At Mycenae itself is a shrine with idols and masks (thirteenth century B.C.). Tiryns and Athens later saw temples built atop Mycenaean palace sites. The myths about Herakles and the Trojan War period have been shown to center around sites prominent chiefly in Mycenaean times, and it is this period that brings the first recognizably Greek religious institutions. Texts found on Crete and the mainland refer to the Fury (Erinys), Eleuthia (later Eileithyia), dedications to "all the gods," and particularly to Zeus, Hera, Poseidon, Artemis, Athena, Hermes, and Ares. Surprisingly, there appears this early the name of Dionysos, thought for a long time to be an imported Asian deity.

Sanctuaries: The primary Panhellenic sites for worship and festival—Olympia, Corinth, Nemea, Delphi—helped spread common practices in the period of renewal after the eighth century B.C. The focus of each site, as of nearly every Greek sanctuary, comprised the sacred precinct (*temenos*), outside altar (*bomos*), and cult statue. That in the temple of Zeus at Olympia by Phidias was colossal; sites without Panhellenic aspirations sometimes revered less elaborate wooden models or even nonrealistic images. Statues such as that of Athena in Troy (the Palladium) often had a magical protective power, and some were ritually washed and clothed each year. Within sacred precincts births and deaths were forbidden. Temples served primarily as houses for the gods' images, sometimes as treasuries (housing the various precious objects often dedicated to the gods), never as shelter for collective worship. Instead, the altar formed the center of activity, where meat sacrifice, the essential Greek rite, occurred.

Sacrifice: The ideology of sacrifice as given in the Hesiodic myth of Prometheus and Pandora relates it to the invention of agriculture and origin of marriage: all are institutions made necessary by a primeval break between gods and powerless humans. By sacrificing a domestic animal—sheep, pig, goat, cow, cock, or bull—the individual and polis attract the favor of the divine, "feeding" the gods with savory smoke and inedible thighbones wrapped in fat while at the same time reasserting community through distribution and eating of meat. Chosen beasts were led in procession (often crowned and adorned), purified with water, sprinkled with barley, consecrated, and killed with a butcher knife (*makhaira*); special parts were given to the presiding priest or to the public treasury. Other sacrificial practices for such occasions as truces or dedications to the dead included bloodless offerings (firstfruits, libations of wine, water, milk, honey, unguents) and holocausts, in which all animal parts were burned. Prayers and hymns accompanied sacrifice or the performance of other ritual acts, such as dances, processions, and perhaps early forms of drama. The Cretan *Hymn to the Kouros* (300 B.C.) bids its singers to "leap" for the fertility of herds and fields. At the opposite extreme of ritual enactment was human sacrifice, traces of which from Mycenaean times were found at Anemospilia, Crete, in the 1970s. Myth imagines it as a possibility, but classical history knows only one or two instances.

Oracles: Oracles, whereby one might seek out the will of gods, existed at several places, notably Dodona in northwest Greece, Didyma near Miletus, and Delphi. They may be seen as an extension of widely practiced divination (through casting lots, observation of animal victim at sacrifice, or augury). Delphi became internationally influential by the sixth century B.C. and was consulted on questions of statecraft, religion (e.g., purifications and establishing new cults), and personal affairs. The god Apollo told Zeus's will by inspiring a chosen priestess, the Pythia, to utter prophecies that were then often put into verse by temple officials. The oracle's popularity is attested by dedicatory offerings until the fourth century A.D., when emperor Theodosius I proscribed pagan cults.

The Heroes: A special category were the famous long-ago dead whose alleged gravesites became worship places. The heroes received markedly different sacrifices, done in a pit (not altar) at evening, with blood and libations, imagined as a means of communication with these dead, directed into the ground. Odysseus and other figures of Homeric epic were thus worshiped in various places, as were about eight hundred others, some of whom functioned as mythical semidivine ancestors for aristocratic families, others as patrons of guilds (of heralds, cooks, craftsmen). The hero's bones possessed protective power and thus became political prizes: Athens had the bones of Theseus brought back from Skyros, Sparta those of Orestes from Tegea. This notion underlies Sophocles's play *Oedipus at Colonus*. Heroization continued sporadically into the fifth century B.C.: Sophocles himself was honored with a shrine and cult title after death because he had sheltered the sacred snake of

Asclepios when the cult of that healer-hero first came to Athens (420 B.C.).

Religion and the Polis: A distinctive Greek trait is the organization of religion by and for the city-state. One who wanted to join in worship even at a Panhellenic sanctuary did so through the offices of a local citizen. In a polis, those with highly individual views on the gods (e.g., Anaxagoras, Socrates, Pythagoras) were just as liable to be prosecuted for impiety (*asebeia*) because their questionable belief was felt to threaten the state's survival, analogous to the way in which pollution threatened the sanctity of a sanctuary. The gods and heroes protected the state in crises and gave victory in war, as Theseus was said to have done at the battle of Marathon. In Sparta, kings were also priests of Zeus cults; in democratic Athens, the religious functions of a sacral sovereign were continued by an official called the "king" magistrate. Our main source, Athens, in the sixth and fifth centuries, witnessed change from religious to secular law, from notions of generational guilt and divinely sponsored revenge for homicide to judicial condemnation and personal responsibility. But in most regards this progressive polis still resembled other Greek states, deeply embedded in traditional religious practices.

The Athenian assembly meetings opened with pig sacrifice and prayers; agreements with other states included vows for certain sacrifices. Athenian magistrates had religious duties and all swore to keep the good will of gods, uphold oaths, not neglect festivals and processions, and not tolerate religious pollution. Young Athenian males entering military service swore similar oaths. The goddess who shared a name with the city and whose house dominated its central hill was especially, but not exclusively, revered. Alongside Athena on the Acropolis the mythical king Erechtheus had an archaic shrine; in the marketplace below, tribal heroes and the twelve gods were commemorated. Because the polis evolved from earlier clan groups, it embraced a variety of divine cults. Each district of the city-state was full of its own shrines to gods or heroes, such as the obscure Akademos, whose worship site lent its name to a philosophic school in the vicinity. The assembly voted on new cults, thus controlling the divine canon to some extent.

As a rule, each polis, like each home, was built around a common hearth, located in Athens in the agora. Here citizens could consult the religious calendar, cult rules, and oracle replies recorded on stone. The polis maintained a board of professional interpreters of religious law, the exegetes. In addition, cult officials were paid by the state for overseeing festivals. Priests and priestesses, really administrators rather than holy persons, were originally chosen by clan groups (e.g., those of Poseidon, Erechtheus, and Athena Polias always were Eteobutadae members), but under the democracy were usually appointed by lot for set terms. Any individual could offer private sacrifices at family shrines without a priest. Freelance oracle-mongers, shamanic purifiers, and "initiators" were also known and often despised.

Local religious calendars detailed sacrifices to be made nearly every day, with important festivals every month, among them the Thesmophoria (women's fertility celebration), Anthesteria (feast of new wine and of the dead), Apatouria (clan membership festival), and Dionysia (honoring the wine god). Prominent in classical Athens was the celebration of the mysteries at nearby Eleusis. Here private devotion and public cult to Demeter and her daughter converged: hundreds were "initiated" each year in a weeklong series of processions, sacrifices, and fasts. For those who completed the witnessing of certain (still secret) revelations, the afterlife was thought to bring happiness (rather than the gloom usual in Hades) and in the present, prosperity. **See also** Apollo; Artemis; Asclepios; Athena; Bacchae; centaur; Cereberos; Cycladic religion; Delphi; Diana; Dionysos; Dioscuri; Eleusinian Mysteries; Euripides; Graces, the; Greek and Roman philosophy; Hades; Hekate; Helen of Troy; Helios; Hellenism; Hephaistos; Hera; Herakles; Hermes; Hesiod; Homer; Hydra; Iliad; Indo-European religion; kingship, sacred; Knossos; Kore; Labyrinth; Maenad; Minoan religion; Minotaur; Muses; Mycenaean religion; mystery religions; Narcissos; Odysseus; Olympic games; Olympos; Orpheus; Orphism; Pan; Pandora; Penelope; Perseus; Poseidon; Prometheus; Roman religion; Sophocles; Tartaros; Titans; Zeus.

Gregory I, the Great   (ca. 540–604), Roman Catholic pope (590–604), best known for his activities in centralizing papal administration, for his commissioning of the first successful missionization of England, and for his sponsorship of liturgical reforms. (While both Gregorian chant and the Gregorian Sacramentary are named in his honor, his role with respect to them remains uncertain.) His most influential work, *Liber regulae pastoralis* (Book of Rules for Pastors, ca. 591), became the handbook for medieval bishops.

Gregory Nazianzus.   *See* Cappadocian Fathers.

Gregory of Nyssa. *See* Cappadocian Fathers.

grotto/cave (Chin. *dung,* "cavern"), liminal zones between the mundane and heavenly worlds in Chinese lore. Grottoes were the dwellings of Taoist hermits and immortals (*hsien*), doorways to mystical journeys, or entrances to a paradisiacal world. Above, grottoes connected with the sky, below, with the subterranean world, the Yellow Springs (*Huang-ch'uan*). *See also* Huang-ch'uan; myth.

ground of (all) being, abstract term for divinity.

Guadalupe, Shrine of, a popular Christian pilgrimage site northwest of Mexico City where the

The interior of the Shrine of Our Lady of Guadalupe, Mexico City. A central focus of Catholic pilgrimage, the church displays, above the altar, the miraculous sixteenth-century image of the Virgin on Juan Diego's cloth mantle (*tilma*).

Virgin Mary is said to have appeared, in 1531, to a peasant, Juan Diego, and miraculously imprinted her image on Diego's serape. *See also* Mary (pilgrimage sites); pilgrimage.

guardian angel, a supernatural being that acts as a guide and protector for individuals or nations. *See also* familiar; guardian spirit.

guardian deities, Hindu, figures who guard a village, its fields and boundaries, the four or eight directions, the door of a temple, or the main deity of a shrine. The term is applied to Kshetrapala, the fierce deity believed to protect a village and its environs by making nightly rounds on horseback accompanied by attendants. His temple is usually outside the settled area as opposed to that of the village guardian (Gramadevata), whose temple is within the settlement.

The deity's representations vary from a stone, tree, termite mound, or wooden post to a sculpted image often located in the open, guarded by other deities and votive offerings. Some guardian deities are deified ancestors, warriors, or heroes. Nonvegetarian offerings are made to them, and purity rules are strictly observed. Some guardians do not allow women in their presence. They are prayed to for rain, a good harvest, and general welfare of the village.

The guardian deity of a main temple deity is a figure fiercer, larger in form, and lower in status than the main temple deity. This deity is offered meat, alcohol, marijuana, and leather sandals.

Guardians of both types have a Shaiva rather than Vaishnava cult (even if they are Vaishnava deities). *See also* Hindu domestic ritual; Hinduism (temple art and architecture); Hinduism (worship); Shaivism.

guardian spirit, a supernatural helper. *See also* familiar.

Native American Traditions. A being of power that establishes a special relationship, sometimes lasting a lifetime, with a person as a consequence of a vision experience. Among the Plains tribes, there are vision experiences that give persons access to transcendent power but do not involve the relationship of a guardian spirit. In the case of the guardian spirit relationship, the person's identity is shaped in a special manner, sometimes taking on the qualities of the being who appeared in the vision experience. In some groups, the guardian spirit appears in connection with the passage from puberty to adulthood; the individual receives powers and insight that guide future life. Sometimes the acquisition of a guardian spirit involves the symbolic embodiment of power in material form, a bundle, accompanied by special songs and ritual processes. In some Plains tribes, such as the Omahas, individuals who have experiences of the same guardian spirit form societies that share symbols and ritual processes. In the majority of instances, however, the acquisition of a guardian spirit is an individual matter and is central to the developing identity of the person. Appeal is made to the power of the guardian during times of danger or stress. Persons become confident that they will be successful in important activities such as hunting and war, and that they will be protected against natural disaster and disease. If the outcome is successful, the person attributes this consequence to the guardian; if the result is failure, the person may look for a ritual or behavioral error. In extreme cases, such as the onslaught of epidemics, guardians as well as other elements of the religious system are severely strained. *See also* bear ceremonialism; bundle; fishing rites/whaling rites; hunting, religious aspects of; jaguar (South American religions).

guilt. *See* original sin (Christianity).

guna (goo'nuh; Skt., "quality," "characteristic"), in Hinduism, a property or constituent of nature or of substances, in particular the three features of materiality: goodness (*sattva*), activity (*rajas*), and torpidity (*tamas*). *See also* Hinduism (thought and ethics); six systems of Indian philosophy.

Gurdjieff, Georgei Ivanovitch (guhr-djeye'ef; ca. 1877–1949), Russian-born spiritual teacher and a major influence on twentieth-century alternative spirituality. He is best known for the community of disciples, which included well-known literary figures, that he established in Fontainebleau, France, in the 1920s. His basic teaching was that human beings are asleep and need to be awakened, so that instead of acting merely out of mechanical habit they can truly control their lives. Gurdjieff strove to awaken his pupils through seemingly erratic demands, rapid changes of activity or circumstance, sacred dance, and self-observation. Some groups in the Gurdjieff tradition still operate. *See also* esoteric movements; Human Potential movement.

gurdwara (goor'dwah-ruh; Punjabi, "house of the Guru,"), a Sikh house of worship. It includes a room where people listen to scriptural recitation. Used for social activity, it has a community kitchen offering free meals attached to it. *See also* Golden Temple; Sikhism.

Gurmat (goor'muht; "teachings of the Guru"), central teachings of the Sikh tradition as contained in the *Adi Granth*. *See also* Adi Granth; Sikhism.

Gurmukhi (goor-mook'hih; "from the mouth of the Guru"), the script containing forty-two characters in which the *Adi Granth* and other Sikh texts are written; it is also the standard script for modern Punjabi. *See also* Adi Granth; Sikhism.

Gurney, Joseph John (1788–1847), English Quaker theologian, one of the founding figures of the conservative evangelical wing of Quakerism.

Gurpurab (goor'poor-uhb), occasions associated with the lives of Sikh Gurus celebrated by the community. The births of the first and the tenth Gurus attract the greatest communal attention. *See also* Sikhism.

guru (goo'roo; Skt., "grave person," "venerable person"), a Hindu spiritual mentor or head of a sect, order, or institution. Traditionally, the *guru* is the oral teacher of revelation and ancillary disciplines. In Tantrism the guru initiates disciples into the secret teachings of his particular order, thereby incorporating his followers into his spiritual lineage.

Guru (Sikhism), title first given to ten leaders of the Sikh faith (sixteenth–seventeenth centuries) and then invested in the Sikh community and its scriptures. According to the Sikh faith the Guru, prior to the coming of Guru Nanak (1469–1539), was not a person. Guru Nanak taught that his Guru was the inner "voice" of God. By meditating on the divine Name and listening to this voice every person could discover the way of liberation. Because Nanak embodied these teachings he came to be recognized as Guru by the Sikhs.

The "voice," or Word, of God accordingly took human form and the status of Guru was passed to each of Nanak's nine successors in turn. Shortly before his death in 1708 the tenth Guru, Gobind Singh, announced that when he died the line of personal Gurus would end. The functions of the Guru would pass to the scripture (the Guru Granth) and the corporate community (Guru Panth). The eternal Guru would remain to guide the Sikhs through the words of the scripture and the decisions of the community. *See also* guru; Sikhism.

Gush Emunim (Heb., "Bloc of the Faithful"), movement representing the Israeli Jewish adherents of the settlement of the full biblical patrimony promised by God to the Jewish people in the Old Testament. Although Gush Emunim was not officially formed until 1974, its roots may be traced on the secular side to the Land of Israel movement of the 1950s. Among the Orthodox, the movement goes back to the graduates of the

B'nai Akiva religious youth movement and the nationalists who opted to enter Yeshiva Mercaz Herav in Jerusalem in the early 1960s. Mercaz Herav was founded by the visionary first Ashkenazi Chief Rabbi of Palestine, Abraham Isaac Kook (1865–1935), and taken over at his death by his son Zvi Yehuda (1891–1982). To the elder Kook's faith in the transcendent holiness of secular Zionism, the younger Kook contributed a messianic faith in the inherent sanctity of the full land of Israel. The teachings of the Rabbis Kook constitute the core of Gush Emunim's strongly messianic ideology.

The Israeli victory in the 1967 Six-Day War marked the beginning of Gush Emunim's active phase on two levels. Ideologically, a speech by Rabbi Zvi Yehuda appeared to prophesy the return of the biblical patrimony months before the war. In the messianic excitement that followed the victory, 1967 was posited as the opening of the era of messianic redemption, which would end with the imminent return of Israel to Jewish control. The benefits of the culmination of the messianic epoch were believed to be universal. On a practical level, the capture of the West Bank, the Golan Heights, the Sinai, and East Jerusalem, made the era of settlement possible. The first act of settlement, the occupation of the Park Hotel in Hebron by Gush Emunim Rabbi Moshe Levinger and a handful of followers in 1968, would set the pattern for future actions, whereby a group within Gush Emunim would grow frustrated with endless debate, move to establish an illegal settlement, and force the movement to support the action in response to the opposition of many Israelis. Usually, the Israeli government would ratify the settlers' action.

Even after the formal birth of Gush Emunim in 1974, its structure would remain informal, with any Israeli sharing its ideals or living in the occupied territories accorded a voice in decision-making. In practice, however, Gush Emunim is controlled by a core of rabbinical leaders, most from Mercaz Herav, and their immediate cadre of loyalists. This core leadership, however, composed of such personalities as Moshe Levinger, Hanan Porat, Yoel Bin-Nun, and Eliezer Waldman, was fractious and deeply divided over short-term tactics, if not long-term goals. As a result, there would be a constant falling away and returning to the movement by core leaders who would either enter parliamentary politics through the National Religious Party or through a personal party vehicle, or leave the political stage altogether to return to the yeshiva world as teachers. These founding fathers would return to exert influence on Gush Emunim only when the movement, in their view, had adopted too confrontational a stance with the government or appeared to be without clear direction.

The apex of Gush Emunim's influence came with the Likud Coalition's electoral victory in 1977. Prime Minister Manachem Begin stimulated the settlement of the occupied territories by providing financial incentives to Israelis to move into the settlements, which themselves were being transformed from pioneering enclaves into agricultural communities with individually owned farms and communities from which residents could commute to work in Israeli cities. This institutionalized settlement but at the cost of diluting the messianic ideology of Gush Emunim. The return of the Sinai under the Camp David accords (1979) was a further shock to the movement, but this was rationalized as evidence of the redemptive era, constituting the expected "birth pangs of messiah."

With the defeat of Likud in the 1992 elections, Gush Emunim was at a crossroad. Committed to the redemption of the land, the most motivated settlers, particularly those at Kiryat Arba in Hebron, Ofra near Ramallah, Ariel near Nablus, and at a handful of other religious settlements, having weathered the height of the Palestinian *intifada* (Arab., lit., "shaking off"), showed no signs of acceding to Palestinian control. However, Gush Emunim's greatest achievements were in the spheres of religious theory and of parliamentary action rather than in the economic development of the settlements under their control. After eighteen years of formal existence, and a quarter century of settlement activity, no settlement appeared able to survive without government assistance, and Gush Emunim found itself without the significant reservoir of support among Israel's secular majority that would assure a continuation of funding.

gymnosophists (goom-nah'sof-ists; Gk., "naked philosophers"), Hindu, Jain, or Buddhist ascetics as represented in Greek literature after Alexander the Great's Indian journey (327–325 B.C.).

Gyogi (gee-yoh-gee; 668–749), a wandering Japanese Hosso Buddhist monk famed for his proselytizing among the masses and for leading social welfare activities such as bridge building. Gyogi was called "bodhisattva" by many commoners. Although the imperial court attempted to suppress his activities, he was eventually recognized and awarded the highest rank the court could bestow on Buddhist monks. Gyogi serves as a model for many later recluse monks who rejected careers as officially recognized monks for a life of helping the masses. *See also* bodhisattva; Hosso school.

A B C D E F
G I J K L
M N Q
R S V
W X Y & Z

Hachiman (hah-chee-mahn; Jap., "eight banners"), one of the most popular Shinto deities, commonly identified as the spirit of Emperor Ojin, a kind of culture hero. Although an agricultural goddess may form the ancient core of his cult, he early on became a protector of Buddhism and was identified as a Bodhisattva. Today he is usually seen as a god of war and national protector. *See also* Shinto.

Hades. 1 The brother of Zeus and god of the underworld in ancient Greek belief. 2 A name denoting the underworld itself, "house of Hades," where the powerless dead lead a bleak existence. Hades contains punishments for only a few, mythical offenders of the gods, e.g., Sisyphus, Tantalus, and Tityus. *See also* afterworld; Greek religion; underworld.

hadith (hah-deeth'; Arab., "tradition"), narrative report of what Muhammad, or his companions, said and did; the most authoritative Muslim teaching after the Qur'an. The science of *hadith* is the critical study of these originally oral materials.

Since the first Islamic century (the seventh century), hadith have been essential to quranic exegesis, contextualizing given revelations, clarifying and expanding their content, and answering lexical questions. However, most hadith aim to perpetuate Muhammad's way of life. In thousands of hadith, reports of the Prophet's performance of religious rituals and observances, his views on moral and theological matters, etiquette, and proper conduct, have been piously preserved as normative guidelines for behavior.

Over time, hadith multiplied, often reflecting the positions of partisan groups. With the need to authenticate reports, scholars began to evaluate the chain of authorities (*isnad*) linking a hadith's content to the Prophet. Based on criteria such as the number and reliability of individual transmitters, hadith were classified as sound, good, or weak, and these reports were collected and codified in works such as al-Bukhari's still canonical *al-Sahih*. *See also* Islam (authoritative texts and their interpretation); Islamic law; Muhammad; Sharia; Sunna; tradition.

Haein Temple (Kor. *Haeinsa,* "Ocean Seal Temple"), a large temple-monastery established by the Korean Hua-yen patriarch Uisang (625–702) in the seventh century. It is located on Mt. Kaya, not far from the modern city of Taegu. Haein (also Hain) Temple today serves as one of the chief training monasteries of the Chogye order of Buddhism and as the repository for the Tripitaka Koreana, a thirteenth-century collection of woodblocks for the printing of the Koryo Buddhist canon.

The name of the temple, "Ocean Seal," is taken from the Hua-yen tradition, where it refers to the nature of the vast, oceanlike consciousness of the innate Budda Mind, in which all phenomena are reflected or stamped without contradiction or obstruction. Though established as a Hua-yen monastery, Haein Temple now serves the needs of Chogye order, which bases itself on the integration of Southern Ch'an meditation and scriptural study using Hua-yen hermeneutics. *See also* Chogye Buddhism; Hua-Yen school; oceanic reflection; Tripitaka Koreana; Uisang.

haftarah (hahf-tah-rah'; Heb.), a selection from the Prophets or Hagiographa read in the synagogue on Sabbaths, festivals, and fast days, following the reading from the Pentateuch. *See also* Judaism, prayer and liturgy of.

Haggadah (hah-gah-dah'; Heb., "telling"), the Hebrew text read and discussed at the Passover meal, the seder. Evolved for the purpose of fulfilling the Torah's command to recount the Exodus (Exodus 13:8), the Haggadah contains passages from the Bible, Talmud, and Midrash that elaborate the story and explicate the meaning of the seder rituals and foods. It closes with prayers, psalms, and hymns. *See also* Judaism (festal cycle); seder.

Hagia Sophia (Gk., "Holy Wisdom"), sixth-century Christian church designed by Isidorus of Miletus and Anthemius of Tralles for Justinian in Constantinople. Originally decorated with glowing mosaics, Hagia Sophia fell victim to both Christian and Muslim iconoclasts. It is now a mosque.

hagiography, biographies and legends of holy persons. *See also* aretalogy; Buddhas; hadith; holy person; Janam-sakhi; Jataka; legend; lineage; miracle plays; saint.

Taoism: The biographical tradition concerning Taoist adepts serves both commemorative and didactic purposes. The biographies draw upon oral tradition as well as revelatory visions. Epitaphs, eulogies, and official decrees bestowing titles were often used to supplement the orally transmitted portions of the biographies. These formulaic, and often composite, accounts range from theogony to brief historical sketches and incorporate both Buddhist and local traditions. Focusing on the predestined earthly and otherworldly role and talents of their subjects, these texts often recount a divine birth and youthful precocity while omitting specific personality traits. The writing style of these sketches tends toward unadorned narrative usually set in parallel prose. Most hagiographies were products of specific revelatory traditions, as is evidenced by their emphasis on the texts and practices followed by their subjects. This type of hagiography documents entire lineages of masters who followed a certain sect, while others concentrate on regional lineages or on a certain individual. Beginning in the Sung dynasty (960–1279) there was an increase in ritual and contemplative guides, and the state, which sanctioned the worship of certain deities, began officially promoting the production of these hagiographies. Early examples of biographic collections include the *Lieh-hsien chuan,* the *Sou-shen chi,* and the *Shen-hsien chi.* Although hagiography is a separate entry in Taoist collections, these biographies can also be found in virtually every other genre of Taoist writings. *See also* Chinese language and literature, religious aspects of; Lich-hsien chuan.

Haile Selassie (hi'lee se-la'see; Amharic, "Might of the Trinity"; 1892–1975), ruler of Ethiopia (1930–74). Known as *Ras* ("prince") Tafari, he was crowned King Negus Negusta and assumed the throne name of Haile Selassie I, King of Kings and Lord of Lords, and Conquering Lion of the Tribe of Judah. He traced his lineage from biblical monarchs Solomon and Sheba and was head of the Ethiopian Orthodox Church.

When Italy invaded in 1935, he went into exile in Britain. Supporters in Jamaica regarded him as not only a tireless worker for African independence but also a religious messiah. He returned to Ethiopia in 1941 and was deposed in a revolution in 1974. *See also* Africa, new religions in; African Americans (North America), new religions among; Afro-Americans (Caribbean and South America), new religions among; Rastafarians.

Hail Mary. *See* Ave Maria.

Hajar (Islam) (hay'jahr; Heb. *Hagar*), mother of Ismail (Ishmael) by Ibrahim (Abraham), and matriarch of the Arabs of the northern Peninsula. Hajar was sent to Mecca with her infant son Ismail after being expelled by Sarah. The legends of Hajar and Ismail are associated with the Kaaba and its immediate surroundings in Mecca, where Hajar is said to be buried. Thus, Hajar is remembered in the symbols and rituals of the lesser and greater *Hajj* ("pilgrimages") to Mecca. *See also* Abraham; Mecca; pilgrimage.

Hajj. *See* pilgrimage.

Hako , elaborate pipe ritual known and practiced by many Plains tribes. The Hako may have originated among Native Americans of Caddoan linguistic stock. Popularly known as the Peace Pipe or Calumet ceremony, the term *Hako* was given to the Pawnee ritual by Alice Fletcher (an early-twentieth-century anthropologist). The Pawnee ritual focuses on important symbolic objects: an ear of corn, representing Corn Mother, and two hollow pipe stems, one of which was male and the other female. Among the Pawnees, the pipe ritual establishes kinship relations between two groups, either exogamous bands within the tribe or between two unrelated tribal groups. A special ritual leader along with his assistants leads "fathers" who bear the special pipe stems to the camp of "sons" with whom the kinship relation is to be established. The Pawnee ritual is dense with fertility symbolism relating to the earth and its creatures; other important elements center on a child who becomes a symbol of fecundity and hope for the future increase of the group. Within trading contexts, these pipe rituals help establish peaceful relations among groups. While during the historic trading period the various pipe rituals observed by whites may have facilitated the exchange of goods, these rituals are often rooted in older layers of cultural tradition relating to themes of cultural and world renewal. *See also* North America, traditional religions in; pipe, sacred.

Hakuin Ekaku (hah-koo-in ay-kah-koo; 1686–1769), a Japanese Rinzai Buddhist monk who revived his school with a system of *koan* (a paradoxical teaching that transcends logical or conceptual thought) practice. He was also famous for vivid writings on Zen topics, ink paintings on a variety of Buddhist topics, and sermons for commoners. *See also* Ch'an school; kung-an; Lin-chi school; Rinzai.

halakah (hah-lah-khah'; Heb., "the way," "Jewish law"), the total body of Jewish law.

Scope: The *halakah* includes all aspects of law as formulated, codified, and applied by the recognized Jewish authorities. Under the rubric of halakah there is civil law, criminal law, public law, national and international law, determinations of the scope of political power and authority, issues of war and peace, law of personal status dealing with such subjects as marriage and divorce, and the vast body of legislation dealing with purely religious matters. This latter includes everything from patterns of divine worship and observance of the festivals to laws regulating diet, modes of dress, and marital relations.

Source and Authority: Jewish doctrine understands the halakah to be divine in origin. It is the product of the two Torahs, the written Torah (the Pentateuch) and the oral Torah. The latter consists of the sacred tradition of interpretation and legislation transmitted orally but believed to be given at Sinai as part of the divine revelation. The ultimate ground on which the law rests is its self-representation as God's teaching. It is permanently binding in all times and places.

Codification: According to Jewish tradition the written Torah contains 613 commandments, 248 of them positive injunctions and 365 negative prohibitions. It is immediately evident that the text of the Torah cannot by itself be the totality of the law. It often speaks in general terms that must be made specific for actual practice. For example, although labor is prohibited on the Sabbath, almost nothing is said about what activities constitute forbidden labor. It is the work of the oral Torah, i.e., the entire developing legal tradition, to settle these matters.

The developing law was codified first in the Mishnah, which was put into final form ca. 200. As legal discussions continued, new, more comprehensive codes began to appear. The most important of these are the code of Maimonides (twelfth century), known as the *Mishneh Torah*, and the code of Joseph Karo (sixteenth century), known as the *Shulhan Arukh*. In these codes the 613 commandments of the Torah are expanded to thousands of specific rules. The codifiers culled their material from the Talmud and the later legal literature to produce comprehensive compendia of what they judged to be the settled law. The effect of these codes was to organize halakic study and regularize Jewish halakic practice by setting down fixed rules.

Very quickly the codes themselves became the subject of legal analysis and generated vast literatures of commentary. Although the authors of the codes generally claimed to be providing guidance for people whose learning was insufficient to consult the primary sources, they soon became texts used primarily by highly trained jurists.

The Responsa as a Source of Halakah: Parallel to the activity of codification was an ongoing process in which difficult questions of Jewish law were sent to outstanding scholars for resolution. The answers that they wrote (responsa) were usually treated as public documents rather than private correspondence with the questioner. The rulings in these responsa were often widely accepted and became part of the official body of halakah.

The responsa literature begins in Late Antiquity and continues to the present day. It is the device by which the law is kept current. As the world changes due to advances in technology or medicine or to changes in modes of economic and social organization, new questions arise that require resolution. In contemporary times problems about the permissibility of organ transplants or issues concerning the exact determination of death occupy the attention of the Jewish decisors. Does the use of electricity constitute the forbidden act of generating fire on the Sabbath? Such questions involve matters with serious practical consequences.

The Decision Process: Jews who continue to believe that God's law should guide their behavior in all matters seek the teaching of experts in the halakah to determine their practice. Their questions evoke responses that are circulated and debated until finally some fixed decision is reached. The process involves determining which general principles should be applied to the cases in question and determining what the facts are to which these principles are applied. *See also* aggadah; exegesis; Torah.

Hallelujah (Heb., "Praise God"), a biblical acclamation from the Psalms often used in prayers and hymns in Christian churches especially on festal occasions. It is also spelled (h)alleluia.

Hallelujah Movement, a native/Christian movement among Carib-speaking people in Guyana, Venezuela, and Brazil that arose out of contact with Anglican missions. The movement originated between 1845 and 1885 when a Makusi man named Bichiwung said he had ascended to heaven in a dream. There God gave him directions for Hallelujah: some writing on paper, medicinal knowledge, and a way to gain wealth for his people. *See also* Native Americans (Central and South America), new religions among.

Halloween, a shortened form of "All Hallows Eve" (i.e., the eve of All Saints' Day) celebrated on October 31. The custom of fun, masks, and trickery, peculiar to the British Isles and North America, may have roots in an old Celtic feast celebrating the onset of winter. *See also* All Saints' Day; ancestors.

hallucinogens, a variety of naturally occurring plant substances that have the capacity to alter

halo

consciousness. They are often used in rituals to
obtain visions or other paranormal experiences.

The most common ritual hallucinogens include peyote, various fungi, hemp, sage, and, in
large quantities, tobacco. *See also* Native American Church; psychoactive plants; shamanism;
soma; tobacco and hallucinogens.

halo, light, usually in the shape of a circle,
around head of a supernatural being or holy
person. *See also* glory.

Hamatsa (hah-mah'tsah; Southern or Northern Kwakiutl),
Cannibal Dancers inspired by a powerful man-
eating spirit and featured in the Winter Ceremonials of the Kwakiutl Indians of British
Columbia. The Hamatsas are the most prestigious group of dancers belonging to the shaman
section of the Seal society, the spirit-influenced,
highest-ranked Kwakiutl dance society. The
Hamatsas are served by the lower-ranked Fool
dancers, who are their messengers.

The Hamatsa dance is regarded as typical of
the Winter Ceremonials. As in the dances of the
other shaman groups, a cyclic drama is portrayed in which a protagonist encounters a spirit
that instills him with power, then returns to the
village where the protagonist slowly returns to
normal consciousness, repeating the experience
of the ancestor from whom he inherited the
right to the performance.

Hamatsas are exclusively male and inherit
the privilege of membership in this secret society through parents or fathers-in-law. At the
time his initiation, the novice runs out of the
dance house and into the woods where he is
possessed by the Cannibal Spirit (Bakbak-
walonooksiwae) and with great difficulty is
brought back into the house by society members. In a destructive, cannibalistic ecstasy or
frenzy, the new member dances and "bites" flesh
from the arms of spectators (as carefully
arranged beforehand). Other Hamatsas also
dance, eat "corpses," and take part in complex
theatrical performances involving members of
other dance groups. Hamatsa performances,
like other winter dances among the Kwakiutl, involve elaborate stagecraft, props, and costumes,
and evoke terror, suspense, even laughter, all
held in careful dramatic balance. Despite this
theatricality, the Cannibal Dancers are deeply
involved in socially and religiously complex action, reflecting profound concerns with spirit
protection, the metaphysical interplay of creation and destruction, and the cosmographic
symbolism of the forest. *See also* cannibalism;

initiation rituals; North America, traditional religions in; secret societies; shamanism.

Hammurabi (hahm-moo-rah'bee; Amorite, meaning and
reading of name disputed), king of Babylon ca. 1792 to
1750 B.C. The name is borne by other, more or
less contemporary rulers in Syria, but it is the
Babylonian who is renowned. Hammurabi was
the sixth of his family to rule in the area of Babylon. They had acquired power in the previous
century, but only under him did Babylon become a major power. At his death, Babylon's
control extended from the Persian Gulf into the
east Tigris country, northward into Assyria, and
westward along the Euphrates into Syria. His
most famous achievement was his so-called law
code, a misnomer because Mesopotamian law
was never codified. The laws, engraved on a
stone stele, are a collection of customary law,
difficult cases, clarifications and refinements of
existing law, and some theoretical expansions
covering a range of public and private issues.
Their importance for judicial practice is dubious. In forming such a collection, the work of
chancery scribes, Hammurabi was following a
tradition of half a millennium.

A prologue and epilogue, in contrast to the
laws themselves, are written in a solemn, highly
stylized language. They frame the laws and give
them their religious context. The latter is
reaffirmed by the representation on the stele of a
god, probably Marduk, giving Hammurabi symbols of his authority as legislator and judge. The
prologue itself tells of the choice of Hammurabi
by the gods "to make equity appear in the land."
He is presented as an ideal king, a righter of
wrongs, and a judge called to defend the poor
and the helpless.

The laws engraved on the stone stele comprise a majestic document, and it was copied for
over a thousand years, even outside Babylonia.
See also Mesopotamian religion.

Hanafite (ha'nuh-fīt; from Arab. *Hanifa*), of or pertaining to the school of Islamic law or legal interpretation that originated in Kufa, Iraq, and takes its
name from Abu Hanifa (d. 767). The Hanafi
school grew out of the impressive accomplishments of two of Abu Hanifa's companions, Abu
Yusuf Yaqub (d. 795) and Muhammad ibn al
Hasan al-Shaybani (d. 805), whose writings on
the foundations of private and public interrelationships became standard legal texts.
Although the three founders were closely associated, their doctrine often varied significantly.

Central to the legal methodology of early

Hanafi jurists was the use of human reason in the interpretation of Islamic law. Reliance on the personal opinions or legal reasoning of jurists, as well as local practice, accounted for many Hanafi doctrines, as well as differences among legal experts and schools of law.

The growth and development of the Hanafi school was greatly assisted by imperial patronage during early Abbasid times (750–900) and later under the Ottoman Empire (1500–1900). The Hanafi school spread from Iraq and Syria to Central and South Asia as well as China. Under the Ottomans, it was the official law school of the empire. As a result, the Hanafi school became the official interpretation of Islamic law in much of the Middle East and South Asia. *See also* Islamic law.

Hananim. *See* Hanullim/Hanunim.

Hanbalite, of or pertaining to the classical Islamic law school founded by Ahmad ibn Hanbal (d. 855) in Baghdad. A well-known theologian and expert on the traditions of Muhammad, Ibn Hanbal was the author of an encyclopedic collection of such traditions. In contrast to members of the Hanafi and Maliki law schools, the Hanbalites were traditionists who preferred to base their legal rulings on the Qur'an and the words and deeds of the Prophet. The Hanbalites deemphasized the role of reason, whether it be the independent reasoning of the individual jurist or the more restricted analogical deduction from established principles in the Qur'an and prophetic tradition.

Hanbalite jurists exercised religious and social leadership and mobilized popular support. The Hanbalite distinction between political (caliph) authority and religious (scholars of Qur'an and *hadith*) authority legitimated their activist attempt to enforce their interpretation of Islam and to oppose political leaders, as well as other law and theological schools. Hanbalite religious zeal and commitment were epitomized by Ibn Hanbal, who was imprisoned during the inquisition of the Caliph al-Mamun (d. 833). The conservative reformism of Hanbalism was championed by Ibn Taymiyya (d. 1328), the great Syrian scholar-activist.

Hanbalite decline after the fourteenth century was somewhat reversed with the rise of the Wahhabi movement in eighteenth-century Arabia. Hanbalism was a major influence on the revivalist vision of the founder of this movement, Muhammad ibn Abd al-Wahhab. Hanbalism remains important as the official legal doctrine in modern-day Saudi Arabia, while the thinking of Ibn Taymiyya has had a major impact across the Muslim world on contemporary Islamic activists. *See also* Islamic law.

hands, laying on of, in Christianity, the widely used gesture of placing the hands on a person's head, signifying blessing, healing, transmission of the power of the Holy Spirit, exorcism of demonic powers, ordination to a church ministry. *See also* ordination.

Handsome Lake (d. 1815), a Native American prophet of the Seneca tribe. His visions (1799–1800) formed the basis for the "Good Message," which he carried to the Iroquois nation, whose traditional culture was being undermined by contact with Europeans and confinement to reservations. At first apocalyptic in tone, his preaching soon came to stress reforming Native American life (e.g., he urged temperance and the return to older values in social relationships) and a limited adoption of elements from European culture (e.g., he accepted farming and selective education). He gained a following during his lifetime, and shortly after his death his teachings were formulated into a Code, the recitation of which is central to the Longhouse religion. *See also* Longhouse religion; Native Americans (North America), new religions among; prophecy in traditional religions.

Han Fei-tzu (hahn fay-tsoo; ca. 280–233 B.C.), Chinese Legalist philosopher and disciple of Hsun-tzu; he wrote a handbook of administrative behavior. *See also* Fa-chia; Hsun-tzu.

haniwa (hah-nee-wah), small clay figures found in burial mounds dating from the Tomb period in early Japanese history (ca. 300–552). These figures, representing people, animals, and artifacts, are thought to have been placed in graves to accompany the deceased into the next life. *See also* Japanese religion.

Han religion (hahn), a system of late Chou Taoist, Confucian, Legalist, and local practices in ancient China (206 B.C.–A.D. 220). While the Han government was ordered along Legalist principles and peopled with Confucian-educated officials, the emperors, originally from the southeast, often employed shamans, pursued Taoist recipes for immortality, and went on pilgrimages to propitiate deities of former states and nature spirits. Court astrologers and influential Confucians, such as Tung Chung-shu, followed *yin-yang* and *wu-hsing* theories of the macrocosm to interpret portents and ritual codes. During Wang Mang's interregnum (8 B.C.–A.D. 22), Confucianism became the orthodox ideology and Taoism was marginalized into local shamanistic cults and the practice of medicine, although both Confucius and Lao-tzu were worshiped as gods by this time. By the first century, however, Buddhists began establishing followings at local feudal courts, and by 140 both Buddhist and Taoist ceremonies were performed in the palace.

In the Latter Han period (23–220) discoveries of "old texts" (texts written in ancient script before the Ch'in book burning of 218 B.C.) created a rivalry between an Old Text school and a New Text school (following the Former Han period transcriptions) that revolved around the legitimate interpretation of the Confucian *ching* (canonized classics). Scholars of the Old Text school rejected the New Text school's works of numerology and prognostication derived from the *I-ching*. *See also* Chinese popular religion; Confucianism; Fa-chia; New Text school; Old Text school; Taoism; Tung Chung-shu; wu-hsing; yin and yang.

Han-shan Te-ching (hahn-shahn duh-jing; 1546–1623), Chinese Ming-dynasty reformer and activist who espoused the unity of Buddhism, Taoism, and Confucianism.

Han thought (Kor. *han sasang*), the system of values and practices Koreans are thought to have possessed before the introduction of Chinese civilization and culture. A nineteenth-century nationalist formulation of Korean uniqueness that was later taken up by philosophers and intellectual historians in the twentieth century, Han thought refers to the primal Korean understanding of unity (*han*) in the cosmos and its reflection in all social events. Evidence of this understanding is taken from an analysis of Chinese and Korean texts about the beliefs and practices of the Korean tribes before the advent of Chinese civilization and the establishment of centralized monarchies. The most important source in this formulation is the foundation myth of Tan'gun, in which a natural unity between heaven and earth, gods and humans, husbands and wives, rulers and their people, the living and the dead is an important theme.

Proponents and defenders of this primal worldview argue that the Korean people are properly called the Han people, or the People of Unity, and that all later religious, philosophical, and cultural developments in the peninsula, even when those developments have foreign sources, are adopted and understood by Koreans as part of this innate sense of the unity of things. In the twentieth century this formulation of the nature of perennial Korean consciousness has served in the creation of new religious cults and the development of ethnocentric schools of philosophical and religious interpretation and criticism, and even a shared emphasis in government and economics that Korean ways are better. *See also* Korean foundation myths; Tan'gun wanggom.

Hanukkah. *See* Judaism (festal cycle).

Hanullim/Hanunim (hahn-*ool*-lim/hahn-*oo*-nim; Kor., "the Sky Worthy"; also Hananim, "the One and Only Worthy"; Sangje, "the Emperor Above," "the Lord on High"), Korean sky god, seen as progenitor, ruler, benevolent teacher, and chief tutelary of the Korean people. In some traditions this sky god inhabits the Pole Star (Paeksong) while his human descendant, Tan'-gun, inhabits the Big Dipper (Ch'ilsong). Confucian tradition, with its nonanthropomorphic conception of heaven, also honored the sky, and in dynastic periods kings were expected to acknowledge their sonship before heaven.

This sky god is most often worshiped at the village level in the form of the local mountain spirit, because the first divine ruler of Korea, Tan'gun, changed himself into a mountain spirit and is omnipresent on every mountain.

Christian, Islamic, and the new religious traditions have adopted the name and sometimes the character of the Korean sky god and fused it with the creator-savior-spirit character of their own supreme being.

Koreans still share the belief that the spirit personalities of the dead ascend into the sky as the abode of justice and order, and if those ancestors are piously remembered and sufficiently fed, they will eventually join with the sky as a power over the earth. *See also* Korean foundation myths; sky.

Hanuman (huh'*noo*-muhn), in Hinduism, the monkey god born of Vayu, the Wind, and the nymph Anjana. Hanuman, also known as Hanumat or Mahavira ("great hero"), is Rama's chief agent in the Valmiki *Ramayana* and is later portrayed as Vishnu-Rama's paradigmatic devotee. Characterized by strength and the ability to leap or fly and change form and size, he appears in classical and folk traditions throughout South and Southeast Asia. *See also* Ramayana.

Hanunim. *See* Hanullim/Hanunim.

Han Wu-ti nei-chuan (hahn woo-dee neh-jwahn; Chin., "Intimate History of Emperor Wu of Han"), a third-century Taoist text concerning the Han emperor Wu, who received immortality drugs from the goddess Queen Mother of the West (Hsi Wang-mu). *See also* Hsi Wang-mu.

Han Yu (hahn yoo; 768–824), a Chinese T'ang-dynasty Confucian advocate who established the orthodox line of Confucianism through Confucius and Mencius. In stylish essays, he opposed Buddhism and Taoism, promoting worship of heaven, sacrifices to ancestral spirits, and a doctrine of three levels of human nature. *See also* Confucianism.

Haoma (hou'meh; Avestan), Zoroastrian sacred drink and deity (the same as Indian *soma*). The twigs of ephedra bush are pressed in the *Yasna* ceremony to produce the drink. *See also* soma; Yasna; Zoroastrianism.

happy hunting ground, an inappropriate popular phrase for the Native American view of the afterlife. It does not correspond to native tradition.

harai (hah-rah-ee; Jap., "purification"), the Shinto ritual of purification. As a ceremonial purification, usually by water but also by other means such as priests waving purification wands (*harai-gushi*), it removes pollution and prepares worshipers for close relationship with the *kami* (divinities, divine presences). Most Shinto ceremonies and festivals involve rituals of *harai*. Traditionally, the Great Purification (*oharai*) was performed every six months by government officials. Harai also refers to acts of atonement or penance. *See also* exorcism; Shinto.

Hare Krishna movement. *See* America, Hinduism, in.

Harijan (hah'ree-juhn; Hindi, "people of God"), a term applied to Indian untouchables, coined by Mohandas K. Gandhi (d. 1948) to ennoble them. *See also* caste; Gandhi, Mohandas Karamchand; Reform Hinduism.

Harranians (hahr-ayn'ee-uhnz), third-century, planet-worshiping inhabitants of Harran, near Turkish-Syrian border. Trilingual (Greek, Syriac, Arabic) Neoplatonists, these people translated Greek philosophy into Arabic and were adept at medical and other sciences. After 831, Harrani-ans hid under the name Sabeans, one of three tolerated religious groups under Islamic rule. *See also* Aramaean religion; Neoplatonism.

Harrist movement, a religious movement in Ivory Coast and Ghana, inspired by William Wade Harris (ca. 1860–1928). A Grebo from Liberia, Harris received visions of the angel Gabriel calling him to teach. In 1913, Harris entered the French Ivory Coast and initiated the most dramatic campaign of religious proselytization ever experienced in West Africa. Dressed in white robes, he traveled from village to village preaching the rejection of traditional religions and strict adherence to Christian teachings. Though he did not start his own church, in less than two years he had generated such enthusiasm for Christianity that 120,000 converts flooded the few existing Catholic and Protestant missions. In 1915, the French deported Harris, despite his lack of political agenda, and destroyed many churches built by his followers.

While many Harrists joined mission churches, others kept alive oral traditions concerning the mission of the prophet. In 1923, Methodists visited the Ivory Coast and were stunned to find thousands of Harrist Christians seeking ministers. One missionary visited Harris in Liberia and returned with a letter from the prophet urging people to become Methodist and avoid Catholicism and African religions. Concerned by the authoritarian structure of the Methodist mission, its insistence on tithing, and its condemnation of polygyny, John Ahui led a Harrist delegation to Liberia in 1926 and returned with Harris's last will and testament, which supported independent churches. Freed from persecution after 1945, Harrist churches became a major religious force in Ivory Coast and Ghana. *See also* Africa, new religions in.

harrowing of Hell, archaic phrase for Christ's descent into Hades. *See also* descent to Hades.

haruspices. *See* Etruscan religion; Roman religion.

harvest rituals, celebrations of agricultural production. In these widespread rituals, special focus is given to either the first or the last individual of each species gathered.

Hasan, al- (627–669), grandson of the Prophet Muhammad and second *Imam* of the Shia in 661, he abdicated to his younger brother Husayn. *See also* Shia.

Hasan al-Basri (d. 728), famous Muslim Iraqi

teacher, preacher, and pious ascetic. Among his circle of students were the founders of the Mutazilite school of theology. *See also* Mutazila.

Hasidism (Heb. *hasid,* "pious" or "pietist"), a Jewish popular religious movement that emerged in the second half of the eighteenth century beginning in Podolia in the Ukraine and then spreading to other parts of eastern Europe, including central Poland, Galicia, Hungary, and Belorussia-Lithuania. The founder of the movement is considered to be Israel ben Eliezer Baal Shem Tov, known as the Besht, whose life is embellished by many legends attributing to him extraordinary spiritual powers. In fact, the Besht appears to have been one of several itinerant exorcists and/or preachers characterized by ecstatic behavior and possessing the ability to perform miracles through use of the divine names.

The emergence of Hasidism as a socioreligious movement has to be seen in the context of eighteenth-century Poland-Lithuania. Kabbalistic ideas had already begun to spread in the seventeenth century, taking the form of more popular moralistic or pietistic works. The ground for Hasidism was prepared by the formation of various mystic circles characterized by a distinctive pattern of religious asceticism, in some cases establishing their own form of prayer in independent synagogues. From these small ascetic groups Hasidism grew into a major social movement.

The period of the most intense flourishing of Hasidism was between 1773 and 1815, when the disciples of Dov Baer of Mezhirech, successor to the Besht, helped to spread the movement by establishing centers throughout eastern Europe, thereby assuring its victory over its opponents (*mitnaggedim*). Hasidism provided an alternative way of religious leadership in the form of the *tzaddik* (righteous one) whose charismatic personality made him the sole authority in religious and mundane matters for a given community.

The unique feature of Beshtian Hasidism was the emphasis on the positive value of life, including its most mundane aspects. Contrary to early forms of pietism that stressed the necessity to avoid worldly pleasures and retreat from society, the Besht and his followers taught that one must have an optimistic and joyous orientation in this world and that the higher form of communion (*devekut*) with God is realized in the context of social relations. This is expressed in sundry ways in Hasidic literature, including the famous formula *yeridah le-zorekh 'aliyyah,* "descent for the sake of ascent." Although this formula was interpreted in different ways, it is meant to affirm the necessity of the spiritual master (tzaddik) to descend to the depths of impurity in order to raise fallen souls or holy sparks of divine light that are trapped in the corporeal shells. One finds, therefore, an important transvaluation of religious values in Hasidism: an individual's private communion with God must be interrupted for the sake of responding to some social or communal need. The master on the highest level maintains his communion by means of acting in the social arena. The positive attitude toward life is epitomized as well in the doctrine of corporeal worship, the claim that one must worship God through physical acts such as eating, drinking, and sexual relations.

Underlying the Hasidic ethos is a metaphysics that sees God as the sole reality filling all worlds, where reality is but the veil or garment of the divine light. In some Hasidic texts, this monistic tendency comes very close to denying the independent existence of the world vis-a-vis the divine. *See also* Baal Shem Tov; devekut; Judaism (mysticism); Lubavitch; Mitnaggedim; Tzaddik.

Hasmoneans. *See* Maccabees.

hatha yoga (hah'tuh yoh'guh; Skt., "yoga of violent effort"), Hindu system of rigorous bodily postures and breathing techniques designed to reverse the processes of aging and death and render the body immortal and invulnerable. *See also* asana; breath; chakras; kundalini; yoga.

Hathor (ha'thohr; Gk., from Egypt., "mansion of Horus"), the ancient Egyptian goddess of love and inebriation, daughter and wife of the sun god, Re. She was a protectress of the dead and destroyer of sinners. *See also* Egyptian religion.

Hayashi Razan (hi-yah-shee rah-zahn; 1583–1651), Confucian adviser to the Tokugawa shogunate for over fifty years. He drafted legal codes, edited a Japanese history, and founded the Hayashi College in Tokyo.

healing, diagnosis of the cause of physical or mental illness and development of techniques for curing. Every religious tradition engages in healing practices, especially blessings, exorcisms, and rituals of purification. Most have developed elaborate theories about the origin of illness: the influence of or possession by spiritual powers; human malevolent activities (sorcery, witchcraft); or violation of a religious proscription or commission of a ritual offense by the afflicted individual. *See also* affliction; Chinese medicine; Christian Science; faith healing; medicine and religion; new religions; possession.

Japanese Religion. The prevention or healing of physical, mental, and spiritual afflictions has been prominent in Japanese religion from ancient times to the present, in organized religion as well as folk religion and in new religions. Amulets from Shinto shrines, Buddhist temples, and new religious centers ward off illness; votive tablets are left at such sites to seek specific cures. Some Buddhist divinities are specialists in healing; Buddhist rituals have been used for specific purposes such as ease in childbirth or for exorcism of the cause of physical and mental problems. Popular practitioners combined Buddhist, Taoist, and folk practices to cure; in recent times charismatic founders and leaders of new religions have been active in healing. *See also* amulet.

Healthy–Happy–Holy Organization, or 3HO, an instructional group founded by the Indian Sikh Dharma Yogi Bhajan in Los Angeles, California, in 1968 to promote holistic well-being through kundalini yoga. Flourishing during the period of most intense international interest in Asian meditation techniques, the 3HO taught a simplified or neo-Hindu practice for awakening the psychic energy believed to lay dormant within the human body. *See also* Sikhism in the West.

hearth rituals. *See* domestic ritual.

Heart Sutra, a Mahayana Buddhist scriptural text that expounds, in condensed form, the doctrine of the Perfection of Wisdom. The text is Indian in origin and achieved its greatest popularity in China and East Asia. Its best-known teaching is the claim: "Form is Emptiness, and the very Emptiness is Form." *See also* Perfection of Wisdom.

heathen, derogatory term for a religion that is neither Judaism nor Christianity.

heaven (Christianity), the dwelling place of God, gods, or other spiritual beings such as angels, and the abode of the redeemed in the afterlife. The term also designates the celestial sphere or sky in contrast to the earth. In the Christian tradition, heaven expresses the final fulfillment of human existence, the reward of the redeemed, in contrast to hell, the punishment of the damned. *See also* afterlife; afterworld; eschatology; sky.

heaven and hell, in Western religious discourse, the places of reward and punishment after death. *See also* afterlife; afterworld; cosmology; sky.

Heavenly Masters Taoism. *See* T'ien-shih Taoism.

Hebrew Bible, preferred English term for (Christian) Old Testament. *See also* Apocrypha; Torah.

Hebrew language, principal liturgical language of Judaism. Hebrew (*'ivreet*) is an alphabetic language of the Semitic family, consisting of twenty-two consonants, six principal vowels, and diphthongs. From approximately 400 B.C. (see Nehemiah 13:24) until 1881, Hebrew was strictly a literary language, confined to religious, liturgical, and other official usages. Its limited vocabulary is constructed out of triliteral "roots" in conjunction with various prefixes, suffixes, and infixes. Thus, the triliteral root *s-p-r* in its assorted permutations may denote the verbs "to count" and "to tell," as well as the nouns "story," "scribe," "book," "number," and "counting."

There are four stages in the history of the Hebrew language, each bearing a distinctive vocabulary, grammar, and syntax. They are (1) Biblical Hebrew, as represented in the Hebrew Bible, the oldest portions dating back over three thousand years; (2) Rabbinic Hebrew, as represented in Second Temple Jewish texts, primarily the Mishnah; (3) Medieval Hebrew, as represented in a body of legal, homiletic, poetic, and philosophic literature during the Middle Ages; and (4) Modern Hebrew, as represented in religious and non-religious literature since about 1780, and the primary vehicle of communication in the modern State of Israel. Hebrew functioned as a spoken language of everyday use only through the biblical period and since 1881, corresponding to a revival movement in pre-state Palestine.

Hebrew is regarded in postbiblical Judaism as a holy tongue (*leshon ha-kodesh*; lit., "language of holiness")—it is not only the literary medium of sacred texts, but a sacred vehicle itself: "Just as the Torah was given in *leshon ha-kodesh*, so the world was created with *leshon ha-kodesh*" (*Genesis Rabbah* 18:4). Hebrew is also regarded as one of the distinctive traits of Israel's chosenness, providing it with a national identity.

Great care is to be taken when speaking or writing Hebrew. The vocation of sacred scribe is revered as one of the most holy professions in Jewish life. The warning to a scribe by the second-century sage Rabbi Ishmael is instructive: "Be vigilant in your occupation, for your labor is the labor of heaven. Were you to diminish or add even one letter, you would destroy the entire universe" (BT *Sotah* 20a).

An extreme veneration of Hebrew is found in the medieval philosopher Judah Halevi and in Jewish mysticism. Halevi's characteristic chauvinism maintained that Hebrew, the language of God and the angels, was transmitted, in its perfection, to the Jews as a gift.

In utilizing Hebrew as a symbol for the mysteries of the Godhead and the unfolding of Being, the mystics attached three connotations to Hebrew: a numerologic, an aural, and a graphic significance. The fourth-century *Sefer Yetzirah* (Book of Creation) teaches a morphological creation theory, in which God "spins" the twenty-two letters into 231 building blocks out of which the universe was formed. Numerology (gematria) uncovered a deeper sense of meaning and associations between Hebrew words. Some mystics meditated upon the visual shapes and aural qualities of the letters. The most profound use of Hebrew is found in the ecstatic mysticism of Abraham Abulafia (ca. 1240–91), who used the combination of letters as a meditative technique for achieving mystical union with God. *See also* alphabet mysticism; gematria; language, sacred; Semites; Torah scroll.

hegira. *See* Hijra.

Heian period (hay-ahn; 794–1185), a Japanese era dominated culturally and politically by the aristocracy that saw the founding of the Shingon and Tendai sects of Buddhism and Buddhism's mutual accommodation with worship of native *kami* (divinities, divine presences). *See also* Shingon-shu; Tendai school.

Heidelberg Catechism, a Protestant confession of faith compiled in Heidelberg (1562) and promulgated a year later as the standard of faith for the Palatinate region. It combines a primary Calvinist theology with Lutheran influences that mark it as one of the most interesting efforts to blend Lutheran and Reformed theologies. *See also* Calvinism; Lutheranism.

Heimdall, the mythological Scandinavian god who was the son of nine giant-mothers, guardian of the world, and the father of humankind. *See also* Nordic religion.

Hekate (he′kuh-tee), the ancient Greek goddess of pathways and crossroads and associated with sorcery and the moon. *See also* Greek religion.

Hel (heh′l). **1** A Norse mythological being,

daughter of Loki and queen of the realm of death. **2** The name of the realm of death. *See also* afterworld; Loki; Nordic religion.

Helen of Troy, in Homer's *Iliad* and *Odyssey* the wife of Menelaus, whose flight from Greece to Troy with Paris caused the Trojan War. *See also* Homer.

Helios (he′lee-os), the ancient Greek sun god, with a significant cult only in Rhodes. From the fifth century B.C., he was identified with Apollo. *See also* Greek religion.

hell (Christianity), the final abode or state of everlasting torment for the damned; a place or state of being that separates evil from good. Hell is viewed as the ultimate dwelling place of the damned after a final judgment. Derived from an Anglo-Saxon word meaning "to conceal" or "to cover," hell originally referred to the dark regions of the underworld or punishment by fire. Hell is now often reinterpreted as endless separation from God's presence, self-chosen by the unrepentant. *See also* afterlife; afterworld; damnation.

Hellenism (hel′en-iz-uhm; from Gk. *hellenizo,* "I speak Greek," "I learn to speak Greek"), the process by which non-Greek peoples learned Greek language, culture, thinking, and customs.

After Alexander the Great of Macedonia had defeated the Persian Empire in 333 B.C., he decided that his soldiers should adopt some of the customs of the more sophisticated Persians, while at the same time advocating and advancing Greek culture and language for all of his conquered peoples. The process was continued throughout Roman times, when Greek was the major language of the eastern Mediterranean basin.

Because Hellenism was a process of mutual influence, Hellenistic culture did not greatly resemble that of classical Greece. Alexander left the world with a larger and more unified political and social organization than had existed until that time. Hellenism was characterized by grand imperial states—the Ptolemies ruling Egypt, the Seleucids ruling Syria, the Antigonids ruling Greece, and then, later, the Romans ruling all. They all had standing armies and large systems of imperial and state farms. Along with the adoption of Greek language, trade developed to new heights, facilitated by the invention of gold currency in Lydia, a technical advance that quickly swept through the Greek-speaking world.

Hellenism was first characterized by cosmopolitanism and individualism. Cosmopolitanism in this context was taken directly from the meaning of the two Greek words *cosmos* and *polis:* a citizen of the world, characterized by a new universalism. Hellenism was mainly an urban phenomenon, as those educated for trade and the traditional aristocracies learned Greek faster than the peasants. In Egypt, the ruling family, the Ptolemies, originally Greek, adopted many Egyptian customs but never gave up their Greek identity or language. Thus, the famous Cleopatra VII of Egypt, a lover of both Caesar and Mark Anthony, may be considered Greek by origin, though she was obviously Egyptian by nationality. None of the Ptolemies appear to have cultivated any knowledge of the native Egyptian language.

Religion: During Hellenistic times, the power of traditional national religions was quickly attenuated by the new relativism. Gods of one land could be identified with gods of another on the basis of similar characteristics and functions. Thus, Aphrodite of Greece could be identified with the Syrian goddesses and Isis of Egypt and was worshiped under various names in different places. Similarly, though keeping his name, the originally Jewish Jesus was easily exportable.

Traditional priesthoods of various countries received Greek educations and tried valiantly to make their traditional religions understandable in the new Greek garb. The priest Manetho in Egypt went so far as to visit Athens and become initiated into the Eleusinian Mysteries. He brought back to his Isis temple in Egypt a Greek understanding of his own religion, which was subsequently reformulated as a Greek mystery cult. In this form, the religion of Isis became extremely popular throughout the ancient world, stressing Isis's power to save from the troubles of life rather than her influence over the flooding of the Nile, which had been her importance in traditional Egypt.

The process of hellenization was not always smooth, as is illustrated by the famous Maccabean Revolt of 168 to 165 B.C. in the land of Israel. After Israel had been ceded by the Egyptian Ptolemies to the victorious Seleucids ruling out of Antioch, Syria, trouble began to brew in the country. The Seleucids were extremely zealous Hellenizers and appear to have stimulated a small but very hellenized party among the aristocracy in Jerusalem to act against the native Jewish traditions. A civil war ended with the reinstatement of a native dynasty, the "Maccabees," descendants of rural priests and aristocrats who ruled in shaky independence until the arrival of Pompey at the head of a Roman army in 65 B.C. Contrary to popular opinion, the Maccabees were not religious reformers who kept hellenization out of the land of Israel. They were as interested in hellenization as were other native rulers. The religion of Israel, however, made simple hellenization impossible, because the Hebrews could affirm only one God and the primacy of the Torah and other scriptures. Still, some of the most important contributions of the rabbinic movement—namely, the establishment of an aristocracy based on education and training and the use of the oral law, which made the traditional Torah amenable to change and reinterpretation—can be seen as native interpretations of themes that were under way in other countries in Hellenistic times as well.

Helpers (Arab. *Ansar*), Muslim converts of Medina who sheltered and aided Muhammad and his followers when they emigrated from Mecca beginning with the Hijra (622). *See also* Hijra.

Helwys, Thomas (ca. 1550–1616), English Christian Separatist, one of the early British supporters of adult baptism. He was excommunicated and joined the first Baptist community in Amsterdam, later founding the first Baptist congregation in England in 1612.

Hemerken, Thomas. *See* Thomas a Kempis.

henotheism. *See* polytheism.

Hephaistos (he-fay'stos), the ancient Greek god of fire, son of Zeus and Hera, and husband of Aphrodite. A lame blacksmith, he is patron of craftspeople. *See also* Greek religion.

Hera, an ancient Greek goddess presiding over marriage and the lives of women. She is the daughter of Kronos and Rhea and the sister and wife of Zeus. *See also* Greek religion.

Heracleitus (hair-uh-kli'tuhs; ca. 540–480 B.C.), a Greek philosopher from Ephesus who wrote in an obscure and oracular style. Heracleitus identified the sole deity variously as Zeus, Thunderbolt, War, and perhaps Fire. Although everything is in flux, all things are one. Only divine judgment is inerrant and sees that all is good; humans are woefully confused. Heracleitus rejected religious anthropomorphism and ridiculed the mythographers. The afterlife would not be what we expect; Heracleitus did not say, however, what it would be.

Herakleon (hair-ak'lee-ahn), late-second-century Valentinian Gnostic; he used allegory in writing the earliest exegetical commentary on the Gospel of John. *See also* Gnosticism.

Herakles (hair'ah-kleez), in Greek mythology the son of Zeus and Alkmene. A great hero, he was deified after his death. *See also* Greek religion.

Hercules. *See* Herakles.

heresy (Gk. *hairesis*, "taking for oneself"), in early Greek usage, opting for one philosophical doctrine or school rather than another. In early Greek Christian usage "heresy" came to mean an arbitrary choice, either rejection of doctrines taught by communal authority in the church or a choosing of a doctrine or an interpretation of a doctrine opposed to the authoritative teaching of the church.

The concept of heresy finds its strongest meaning in Christianity because of the very high level of speculative teaching taken over from various strands of Hellenistic philosophy.

Outside Christianity the concept of heresy, though present, is less sharply defined. In Judaism and Islam it often blends into questions of the correct observance of law and custom rather than categories of proper belief. There have been exceptions: the Kairite rejection of the oral law, various messianic claims and types of rationalism—Aristotelian or Spinozan—have been condemned in Judaism. And in Islam the Sunni and the Shiites have disagreed over questions of office, succession, and communal authority.

Zoroastrianism, in its dispute with Manichaeism over the true nature of the cosmic dualism, exhibits a clear example of orthodoxy and heresy in conflict within one tradition.

The closest parallel to heresy in Asian religions might be the conflict between Hinduism and Buddhism over the self versus the non-self, though that is not a dispute within a single tradition. The latter may be found in Buddhism where the various schools disagree over the concepts of the Buddha-nature and appropriate means of attaining enlightenment. But the very strongly Western concept of heresy, with its connotations of central authority and persecution, should be extended only with great caution to non-Western religious traditions. The more neutral term *opposition* is a more prudent usage. *See also* nastika.

Judaism: *See* excommunication.

Christianity: Roman Catholic doctrines have provided the most frequent instances for denial or doubt by those whom the Church has judged to be heretics. Catholicism claims authority to define and teach true doctrine. From that claim arises the responsibility to condemn theological errors, i.e., heresies. The word has been used within other Christian denominations to indicate teachings that differ from the official teaching of any particular religious institution. By extension heresy is any departure from the established views of any kind of institution.

Islam: Because membership in the Muslim faith is achieved by assenting to a set of statements that define Islam and by observing its rituals and rules of conduct, heresy is effectively any assertion or practice contrary to these statements, rituals, and rules. With no hierarchically organized clergy to create dogma and administer belief, the validity of a religious act or concept is determined by a consensus, understood as infallible, among the qualified members of the community, i.e., those whose religious knowledge has earned them the respect and obedience of the congregation.

Heresy lies on a continuum between absolute unbelief and simple heterodoxy. At one extreme, to deny the oneness of God and the prophethood of Muhammad constitutes unbelief, *kufr* (Arab., "ingratitude," hence "refusal to acknowledge God"). To hold such a position is to cease to be a Muslim at all. Many other acts, such as failing to pray or to give alms, moral lapses such as lying and bearing false witness, or crimes such as stealing and murder, may also be considered evidence of unbelief. In extreme cases, the perpetrator may be excluded from the community in this life, as well as be judged as condemned to eternal damnation in the next. On a more abstract level, certain medieval Muslim philosophers were declared unbelievers for maintaining the eternity of the world (as opposed to its divine creation *ex nihilo*) and denying both the bodily resurrection and God's knowledge of particulars.

There was, nevertheless, considerable disagreement on less fundamental matters, generally called *bida* (Arab., "innovation"), a term that is highly revealing of the Muslim concept of orthodoxy, where all departures from the recorded actions and words of the Prophet are treated with utmost suspicion. Even to question the literal meaning of the Qur'an was regarded as innovation contrary to faith by some theologians. Muslims nonetheless have adopted practices that at first had been rejected, turning a "bad" innovation into a "good" one. Examples include publicly celebrating the Prophet's birthday, establishing hospitals, teaching grammar, and a host of other activities that only came to prominence long after the Prophet's death and were, therefore, not historically part of the original religion. Many technical breakthroughs have had to pass through this process before they could be incorporated into the Islamic way of life. All forms of electronic media, for example, initially met with disapproval but were eventually accepted as "good" innovations and are now exploited with great enthusiasm in reporting Islam's holiest ceremonies, such as the pilgrimage to Mecca.

In sum, true heresy, i.e., manifestations of unbelief that threaten the survival of Islam or the state, are taken very seriously and can be severely and violently suppressed. The notion of innovation, however, enables Islam to adapt its medieval doctrinal, legal, and ethical codes to the requirements of modern life, thereby preserving seventh-century religious values under twentieth-century conditions.

hermeneutics (her-me-nyoo'tiks; Gk. *hermeneuein,* "to interpret," derived from the messenger-god, Hermes), the general theory and applied practice of interpretation. Originally concerned with interpreting revered texts, the term now refers to interpretive understanding in general. Hermeneutics seeks to clarify the interpretation of the meanings of any manifestation, expression, or human trace: textual, verbal, visual, logical, unconscious, conventional, and so on. Formerly an adjunct of theology, it encompasses other areas of binding meaning, such as law, art, history, philology, and the humanities.

It is a term at once specialized and technical, yet as ubiquitous and manifold as communication itself. There is hardly a major thinker or intellectual movement that cannot be linked to hermeneutics. Viewed as a method in a specific discipline, or more broadly as the human way of being-in-the-world, hermeneutics remains a notion that changes with its setting. It has connections to philosophy, linguistics, literary criticism, rhetoric, semiotics, cultural studies, anthropology, the social sciences, and even the physical sciences.

Hermeneutics is deeply enmeshed with broader issues concerning the modern condition, if not the human condition as such: these include humanism, the transformation of core beliefs (whether religious, metaphysical, or ideological), the sociocultural processes of secularization and modernization, the tension between the "two cultures" of the natural sciences and humanities, as well as differences among historic cultures. Hermeneutics has been applied to such a wide range of signification that its original locus in textual interpretation is often obscured. Friedrich Nietzsche's observation that "all knowledge is interpretation" is often repeated to underscore the omnipresence of hermeneutics.

The Hermeneutic Situation—Basic Distinctions: Hermeneutics becomes crucial wherever or whenever meanings become problematic, attentuated, or unintelligible. This situation may come about in various ways: through the passage of time, through cultural or linguistic differences, through changes in mental habits or conditions of life, or simply a sense of distance or unfamiliarity. Modern hermeneutics posits or presumes such enveloping mental frameworks as cultures, worldviews, life-worlds, and language-games, stressing the need to mediate between them. Such terms suggest that meanings transpire within the global structures humans inhabit before they are in a position to isolate, ascertain objectively, or even think reflectively about them. There is a circularity and holism here, which may be regarded either as fruitful or vitiating with respect to knowledge. Hermeneutics challenges the belief in strict scientific knowledge (and its twin, epistemology), on the premise that meaning is a broader frame of reference than what usually qualifies as valid scientific knowledge.

Several crucial and interrelated distinctions are often made regarding hermeneutics and its scope. The first concerns the difference between general and special hermeneutics. The former addresses the conditions of meaning more generally or fundamentally, as distinct from meaning as constituted in discrete subject areas, disciplines, or methods of inquiry—juridical, literary, archaeological, theological, and so on. Allied to this distinction is that between ontological and methodological approaches. The former views hermeneutics to be a step beyond epistemology and science, out of the subject/object (or subjectivity/objectivity) distinction, beyond categorical thinking altogether and toward matters deemed more fundamental than strict knowledge. The methodological approach sees hermeneutics as more limited in scope and defined by a set of given concepts and objects.

What constitutes the primary aim or object of interpretive understanding? Is it to apprehend a self-contained "idea" of pure meaning, an individual mind or mind-set, a collective worldview, a culture, a life-world, a way of life, a moment in time, or something timeless? A key issue concerns not only the degree of self-consciousness on the part of the interpreter but also the self-awareness of the producer of the artifact. Methodical interpretation is usually directed toward a meaning that is itself already an interpretation. To what degree must the methodical interpretation of some belief do justice to the believer's own point of view? Some meaningful manifestations are not intended to impart meaning. It is arguable whether one can appeal to a correct or authentic meaning, even if one assumes that intended meaning characterizes most human manifestations.

With its sense of moving between the "letter" and "spirit" of the word, hermeneutics can be regarded either as more semantic or more syntactic in emphasis: that is, concerned with the contents of mind or "spirit" or with the formal, structural, and analytic elements thereof. Interpretation connotes both a process and an outcome, and there have been two strands within interpretative theory, sometimes opposed but also intertwined. The first is more mimetic and objective, concerned with fidelity to an intended original meaning. The second is more subjective and transformative—denying such definite, intentional meaning, and insisting that all meaning is changed in its very transmission, so that the real effect of interpretation is to transform the one who interprets. The former strand can be regarded more conservative and custodial; the latter more liberal and creative.

History of Hermeneutics: The history of hermeneutics can be read as an index of major transformations in Western civilization.

In classical antiquity, hermeneutics arose in a word-centered culture, which for all its insistence upon the power of *logos* and reason, nonetheless remained conscious of differences between the forms of mind and the "really real." Hermeneutics supplemented Socratic injunctions to "know oneself" and to "know what one does not know" by reflecting upon how the interpreter understands textual sources. Aristotle (d. 322 B.C.) wrote a short treatise, *On Interpretation*, that fitted this endeavor into the larger edifice of knowledge applying to different levels of being. Patristic and scholastic thought continued this effort, linking hermeneutics to logic, grammar, and rhetoric.

The rise of empirical natural science altered hermeneutics. The philosopher Benedict de Spinoza (1632–77) acknowledged that his method of interpreting scripture did not differ widely from the method of interpreting nature. The Enlightenment generally endorsed naturalism against the ingrained spiritualism that permeated theological hermeneutics. Giambattista Vico (1688–1744) countered by distinguishing between knowledge of what is found in nature as fact and of what is made by mind as deliberate act: nature and culture could not to be equated. This distinction between physical nature and human culture would later be elaborated into a methodological opposition between the explanation of causes (Ger. *Erklaren*) and the understanding of meanings and purposeful action (Ger. *Verstehen*).

The nineteenth century applied hermeneutic tenets to the study of history, society, art, and cultural artifacts. Interpretation theory mingled with historical consciousness to stimulate much applied research. The German idealists and romantics (Johann von Herder, Wilhelm von Humboldt, Friedrich von Schlegel) held that hermeneutics could be a path beyond (or "within") the visible to sublime, originary, or unconscious meanings. From the premise of a surplus of meaning, it was possible, even necessary, to understand an author (or culture) better than that author or culture understood itself.

Friedrich Schleiermacher (1768–1834) attempted a broad and systematic hermeneutics on idealist premises. He argued that religious faith—and receptivity to all meaning—was primarily inward, personal experience rather than avowal of doctrinal content. As "divinatory" and "reformatory," interpretation penetrates to the inner spiritual core of the text, but in a way that is inevitably dialectical, shuttling between part and whole, text and context, individuality and totality. All human meaning is mediated by language and shared spiritual forms, but its effect is individual.

Wilhelm Dilthey (1833–1911) is called the father of modern hermeneutics for his efforts to establish methodical understanding (*Verstehen*) as the cognitive procedure of history and the other human sciences (Ger. *Geisteswissenschaften*). Following Schleiermacher, he insisted that "human understanding of things human" was valid empirical cognition, grounded in lived experience, language, and the intersecting coherences of individual and collective life. He portrayed *Verstehen* as empathic re-experiencing or "re-living" of expressions of life. An objective approach to cultural phenomena must respect the relational, "for-us" character of meaning given in human experience as purpose and intention. For Dilthey objectivity becomes an externalized intersubjectivity refined over time: the human mind cannot go behind life and lived experience to ground its knowledge, for it remains within a circle of interpretation transpiring in history. Knowledge of others is the path to self-knowledge, through the recovery of the "I" in the "thou."

Drawing upon Dilthey but even more upon

Martin Heidegger (1889–1976), recent hermeneutics has struggled to avoid the pitfalls of earlier positions, including alleged fallacies of scientism, subjectivism, psychologism, historicism, and the assumption of a universal human nature, and to employ hermeneutics to challenge prevailing models of knowledge, reason, and language. Human existence (and experience) is not a discrete, circumscribed datum but a dynamic openness suffused with meaning and proto-interpretive structures. Language preforms the world we live and understand. Understanding cannot be construed as empathy, coexperiencing, or the merger of minds or selves, for such is ruled out by temporality and historicity; it is rather a fusion of traditions or life-forms set down in language.

In the study of religion, recent hermeneutics has both broadened and retrenched the domain of inquiry. For some, it works to restore religious phenomena to an originary religious essence; for others, it serves to link religious life to other fields or disciplines. For more radical Heideggerians, hermeneutics serves as an ultimate path beyond methodical knowledge, beyond conventional thinking, even beyond human being. The history of hermeneutics seems to have come full circle to the question of being as such.

The Conflict of Interpretations: The conflict of interpretations (whether among parties, ideologies, religions, or epochs) makes the need for hermeneutics urgent. Yet there is presently not much agreement on the proper scope and procedures of hermeneutics. With a kind of fitting irony, interpretation itself has become a prime subject of interpretation. This state of affairs may represent the height of critical self-consciousness or the denial of the preconditions of human meaning. Because it dwells so intently upon meaning, hermeneutics seems always to promise a way of making or keeping the world meaningful and worthy of awe. *See also* religion, philosophy of; understanding.

Hermes (huhr'meez), in Greek mythology son of Zeus and Maia. He was the messenger god, a friend of humans, and associated with trickery, herds, the lyre, and the dead. *See also* Greek religion.

Hermes Trismegistos (huhr'meez tris-me-gis'tohs; "Thrice-Greatest Hermes"), a Greco-Egyptian deity of the Hellenistic period (third century B.C.–A.D. third century), associated with mystical and Gnostic revelations.

Hermetism, philosophical and religious practices and speculation associated with the

Hellenistic Greco-Egyptian deity Hermes Trismegistos, preserved primarily in the *Corpus Hermeticum* (second–fourth centuries). *See also* Agrippa of Nettesheim, Heinrich Cornelius; Bruno, Giordano; Hermes Trismegistos; Nag Hammadi Library; occult, the; Poimandres.

hermit, a solitary ascetic, voluntarily removed from society.

hermit (Christianity) (Gk., "desert dweller"), a Christian ascetic who lives a solitary life instead of in a monastic community. Also called an anchorite or anchoress.

Hernandez, Jose. *See* Afro-Americans (Caribbean and South America), new religions among.

Heschel, Abraham Joshua (1907–72), the most influential twentieth-century theologian of Judaism. Author of ten books on philosophy of religion, Judaism, rabbinic theology, and Hasidism, he took an active part in the civil rights movement and marched with Martin Luther King, Jr., in Selma, Alabama.

Hesiod (hee'see-od), a Greek poet who lived ca. 700 B.C. In the *Theogony* he describes the genealogy of the Olympian gods, of whom Zeus was king, and how they came to power and suppressed revolts against their authority. After praising the muses, divine patrons of the arts, the poet describes the origin of the universe in terms of mating and procreation. The first ruler of the gods was Ouranos ("Sky") and Gaia ("Earth"). Ouranos was overthrown by his children, the Titans, led by Kronos, who castrated his father. Kronos swallowed his own children by Rhea, until she tricked him by giving him a stone to swallow in place of the infant Zeus, who grew up to overthrow his father. The succession of dynasties clearly reflects the succession myth known in the ancient Near East. For Hesiod, Zeus is not only the ultimate victor in the struggles between the gods but the guarantor of justice and human morality.

In *Works and Days,* the poet presents arguments for a life of hard agricultural work while being mindful of the gods and especially of Zeus, who supports the moral order. The story of the opening of Pandora's jar (not yet a box) is told as one explanation for the presence of evil in the world. The decline in the quality of humankind and the loss of happiness is described through the sequence of races, from Golden through Silver and Bronze to the present wretched age of the men of Iron. (The race of

Heroes interrupts the decline, being placed before the Iron race.) The poem concludes with a list of lucky and unlucky days. *See also* ages of the world; divine combat; golden age; Greek religion; world parents.

Hesychasm (hez'ih-kaz-em; Gk. *hesychia*, "quietness" or "silence"), method of prayer practiced by the Orthodox monks of Mt. Athos. Central to this method is the Jesus Prayer, in which the name of Jesus is repeatedly invoked as part of a brief formula, e.g., "Lord Jesus Christ, Son of God, have mercy on me." By the thirteenth century Hesychasm had adopted certain physical techniques, including the use of posture and breathing exercises, as external aids to prayer. The goal is to achieve pure, apophatic (imageless) prayer, and to experience the uncreated divine light that the disciples saw at the transfiguration of Jesus. *See also* energies, divine; Orthodox Church; Palamas, Gregory; Philokalia.

heterodoxy, an unorthodox belief. In general usage, it is a less condemnatory term than "heresy." *See also* heresy; orthodoxy, orthopraxys.

hexagram, six-pointed star formed by two equilateral triangles superimposed one on the other with one inverted, common in western magical praxis. It is the modern symbol of Judaism. *See also* Magen David/Star of David.

heyoka (hay-yoh'kah), Lakota (Native North America) classification for a human being who, because of a dream or vision of Thunder Beings, acts in ways contrary to normal behavior. The *heyoka*, who are powerful medicine people, must follow reversed behavior for a specified period of time, usually a year or more. Such behavior may include wearing their shoes on the opposite feet, riding a horse sitting backward, going nearly naked in winter while dressing heavily in summer, and speaking the opposite of their intentions. This behavior reminds people of the meaning of the practices and behaviors they take for granted. The heyoka are sometimes thought of as clowns. *See also* clowns; North America, traditional religions in; reversal.

Hezbollah. *See* Party of God.

Hicks, Elias (1748–1830), American Quaker theologian and prominent abolitionist. Hicks was an early supporter of the doctrine of progressive revelation and attacked the proposal to adopt a creed and other initiatives toward orthodoxy that were put forth by the evangelical wing of Quakerism. After the schism of 1827 to 1828, the liberal Friends were called Hicksites by their opponents. *See also* Friends, Society of.

Hidden Imam, a messianic deliverer; rightful heir to leadership of the Islamic world. Rooted in early Shia movements, the idea achieved fullest development with the Twelver Shia (or Imamis) after the tenth century in Iraq, Iran, Syria, and Lebanon. Convinced that the world cannot exist in the absence of a designated *imam* from the house of the Prophet Muhammad, Twelver Shia maintain that when the twelfth Imam disappeared in 874, he entered divine concealment, or occultation. They believe he will arise in the end time as the *Mahdi* to inaugurate an era of universal justice. The Hidden Imam stands in contrast to most temporal rulers in the Islamic community. *See also* Ismaili Shia; Ithna Ashari Shia; Mahdi; occultation.

Hiei, Mt. (hee-ay), the site of Enryakuji, the major Tendai Buddhist monastic complex in Japan. It was founded by Saicho in the early ninth century and by the eleventh century was a major educational institution. Politically powerful, Enryakuji had major landholdings, fielded warrior monks, and counted many Japanese nobility among its patrons. Its power ended when Oda Nobunaga burned it in 1571. *See also* Saicho; Tendai school; warrior monks.

hieroglyph (Gk., "sacred carving"), a pictographic character in the ancient Egyptian writing system, invented before 3000 B.C. *See also* Egyptian religion; Rosetta Stone.

hierophant. *See* mystagogy.

hierophany, general term for the manifestation of the sacred.

hieros gamos. *See* marriage, sacred.

High Church, Low Church, in the Anglican or Episcopal Christian church, terms used to distinguish traditions that emphasize either its Catholic and liturgical heritage (High) or its evangelical roots (Low). *See also* Anglicanism.

high god, term for one type of supreme deity, once the creator but now utterly removed from the world. As a hidden (otiose) deity, the high god is rarely the object of ritual. Myths of high gods focus on the motivation for their withdrawal. *See also* Chinese myth; Chinese ritual; Japanese myth; Shang-ti; term question.

hijiri (hee-jee-ree; Jap., "holy person," "saint"), a pre-Buddhist term in Japan that, by the Heian period (794–1185), referred to Buddhist itinerants, mountain ascetics, shamanesses, magicians, reciters, Taoist wandering saints, and fortune-tellers. All these popular practitioners who resorted to Buddhist rituals and formulas, Taoist purifications, and the like went directly to the people to meet various religious needs. In medieval times groups of *hijiri* developed, often organized by great temples to travel through the countryside preaching, distributing talismans (*ofuda*), and raising funds for the temple. They passed on temple legends through drama and music and helped to establish popular literary and performing arts. *See also* Japanese folk religion.

Hijra (hij'ruh; Arab.,"emigration"), Muhammad's emigration from Mecca to Medina in 622. For years, Muhammad had preached to the Meccans with little success, losing the essential support of his own clan. Yet, Muhammad's moral prestige and statesmanship impressed Medina's wrangling tribes, who agreed to defend him and his followers if he would arbitrate their disputes. The persecuted Muslims then emigrated from Mecca, followed by Muhammad, with his confidant Abu Bakr, who left secretly to avoid ambush. In Medina, Muhammad quickly attained sovereignty. In Muslim historiography, 622 equals A.H. 1 (*anno Hegirae*). Since then, occasional calls for hijra have been made by Muslims advocating emigration from infidel lands. *See also* Muhammad.

Hildegard of Bingen (hil'de-gahrt; 1098–1179), German Catholic Benedictine abbess and mystic, known as the "Sibyl of the Rhine." Her dictated visions were unusually vivid and, beginning during her lifetime, have been the subject of powerful illustrations by the nuns of her order. She is also known for her writings on medicine and for her musical compositions.

himorogi (hee-moh-roh-gee), upright *sakaki* (evergreen) branches hung with streamers and cordoned off with hemp rope to create a space for the temporary dwelling of Shinto *kami* (divinities, divine presences). *See also* Shinto; shrine.

Hinayana (hin-ah-yah'nah; Skt., "Inferior Vehicle"), a pejorative term used by some members of the schools comprising the Mahayana ("Great Vehicle") wing of Buddhism to refer to the practitioners, practices, and scriptures of their non-Mahayana counterparts. The term should be avoided except in citations of polemical writings. *See also* Mahayana; Nikaya Buddhism; Theravada.

Hindu domestic ritual. Hindu domestic ritual centers on the concerns of married householders and their family members living among their household deities. Families perform rituals and vows in accordance with sectarian and personal schedules. Ritual activities of long-standing tradition have been characteristic of Hindu hearth and home.

Tradition: Each of the many Vedic branches or schools in ancient India generated ritual manuals (*sutras*) for domestic (*grihya*) worship as well as for corporate, high-priestly (*shrauta*) sacrifices. Grihya sutras determined the character of domestic ritualism during the Vedic period (1400–400 B.C.) by identifying the householder as a fire-sacrificer with responsibilities linking him and his wife to the macrocosmic sacrificial system, including its great *soma* rituals. With the emergence of classical Hinduism in the late first millennium B.C., domestic rituals gradually achieved independence from the shrauta schedule and became simpler yet also more varied, attention being paid to class, caste, stage of life, local custom, and particulars such as family and personal deities, fasts, and vows.

Practice: Although no single ritual template applies to the complex span of Hinduism today, certain patterns are evident. According to the Dharmashastras, authoritative Sanskrit texts of religious law, every householder is responsible for five "great sacrifices": simple daily offerings to gods, ancestors, humans, spirits, and *brahman*, or "sacred power." Strict Brahmans as well as others follow relatively detailed procedures with food and water for the first two "sacrifices," but flexibility pertains to both offering substances and definition of recipients for the other three. Grains of rice for a beggar, crumbs for crows, or a few sacred syllables will suffice as minimal offerings.

A household's gods and goddesses receive attention in *puja* (worship) according to the degrees of elaboration practiced by family members. In a few homes morning worship might be performed by the male head of household for one to three hours beginning at dawn, with small images of deities installed in a special shrine area. Rarely, a family priest (*purohita*) might be employed for such routine *devapuja* ("god-worship"). In many homes it may be the wife who worships a picture or image of Rama, Krishna, Shiva, and Parvati, or a local deity in the kitchen, locus of the hearth, where she prepares the food that unites the family with its ancestors and gods.

With exceptions for impure rites of first tonsure and disposal of the deceased, life-cycle rituals are also performed in the home, either with the family priest or another knowledgeable person supervising. These include observances prior to birth and continue with rituals such as name-giving and first-solid-food rituals. Initial tonsure for a boy or a girl is often performed in the family's ancestral village or some important temple visited on pilgrimage. Marriages are conducted at night in the home of the bride. Upon a death, after preparation of the body in the place of death, usually the home, cremation or burial is performed in a special riverside area, where postfunerary ancestral rituals may also occur under priestly direction.

When a married couple builds or enters a new house a special purification ceremony (*vastushanti*) focuses, like its Vedic prototype, on the family fire, although the modern form may be just an oil lamp. Concern for constant purity in the home is also demonstrated by elaborate white powder designs made daily on thresholds and floors by the women of the house. Meditation, fasting, celibacy, and various other vows (*vratas*) are subtler ritual practices within domestic boundaries, as are numerous practices that link each home to village or town shrines, deities, festivals, and sacred rivers and trees. *See also* ancestors; Hinduism (worship); puja; sacrifice; soma.

Hinduism (authoritative texts and their interpretation).

Hindu culture has produced rich and diverse literatures in many languages. Much of this material has been transmitted and interpreted in writing in a fashion that resembles the treatment of authoritative books elsewhere. But Hindu culture has also exhibited a deep suspicion of written materials and so invites enlargement of the concept "book" to include words that have been transmitted and interpreted orally.

The Social Context and Criterion for Authority: The dominant fact of Hindu social and cultural life for over two thousand years has been caste. This multifaceted, ritualized, hierarchical pattern of behavior and attitude produces one Hindu criterion for the authoritativeness of books. The Sanskrit texts known as Vedas, consisting chiefly of hymns composed between ca. 1200 and 900 B.C. for use in a polytheistic sacrificial setting, are understood as the verbal form of ultimate reality, and the Brahman caste serves to embody and interpret this reality. There are four Vedas: the *Rig, Sama, Yajur,* and *Atharva*. The interpretation they received in the five hundred years after their composition—in texts known as

Brahmanas, Aranyakas, and Upanishads—emphasized proper ritual performance of the sacrifice and used this concern as the starting point for speculation about the nature of the universe, culminating in the declared mystical identity of the individual soul (*atman*) and the universal spirit (*brahman*). Later systems of philosophy, known as the Vedanta, have sought to expound the Vedic corpus in commentaries and independent works with two chief goals: specification of proper ritual behavior and explication of the mystical experience of liberation (*moksha*). Other schools—the Samkhya, Yoga, Nyaya, and Vaisheshika—have pursued parallel questions of ontology, epistemology, and soteriology by commenting upon compilations of aphorisms.

Shruti, Smriti, and Bhakti: From the last centuries B.C. onward, new works, virtually all by unknown authors, came to prominence in Hindu culture. From the perspective of the Vedas, whose authority consists of having been "heard" (*shruti*) by gifted poets, these new works appear secondary, for they have been merely "remembered" (*smriti*). The earliest instances of smriti literature are lawbooks, the Dharmasutras and Dharmashastras. Their concern for moral and social order (*dharma*) also pervades the two Hindu epics, the *Ramayana* and the massive *Mahabharata*, whose hundred thousand verses constitute a virtual encyclopedia of cultural life between 400 B.C. and A.D. 400. In the late Upanishads, however, a new devotional impetus (*bhakti*) emerged, and many smriti texts introduce a new, experiential criterion of authoritativeness: a loving and reciprocal relationship between deity and individual human beings. This impetus reached its earliest full statement in the portion of the *Mahabharata* known as the *Bhagavad Gita* ("Song of the Lord"), and books that attest to such a relationship have been among the major landmarks in Hindu culture over the past two thousand years. Throughout that period texts have woven together the concerns for dharma and bhakti in a variety of ways.

Compositions in Sanskrit include eclectic popular material in the Puranas (such as the *Bhagavata*), exquisitely refined religious poetry (the *Gita Govinda*), hymns and theological treatises from varied sectarian perspectives, and esoteric instruction in the Tantras. Interpretive strategies vary greatly.

Authoritative books in the Dravidian languages of South India have been composed from the early centuries A.D., and in the regional Indo-European languages of North India from roughly 1000. Early Tamil poetic anthologies established literary norms that were subsequently adapted to devotional expression, as in the poetry of the Alvars and Nayanars. The bhakti movement also undergirded most literary expression in the north, and such works as Tulsi Das's sixteenth-century recomposition of the *Ramayana* in Hindi remain powerfully influential in Hindu life today.

In recent centuries, chiefly in response to Western and Christian notions of books and scriptures, many Hindu texts have been edited, published, and translated, often (as in the case of the *Rig Veda*) for the first time. Certain of these have been represented as the authoritative books of "Hinduism." But the authoritativeness of Hindu books continues to vary according to caste, sect, and region, with nuanced and diverse balancing of moral, devotional, and philosophical concerns.

Mantra, Recitation, and Performance: Much Hindu interpretation of these works and others consists of exegesis, either orally or in writing. But a significant part of Hindu engagement with words and books proceeds in a very different direction and emphasizes their form rather than content. This approach characterizes engagement with both oral and written material.

What is important from this perspective is not words' meaning, but their sound. They are understood as eternal, as embodiments of power that is accessible through verbatim utterance. Such words are called *mantras*. The hymnic verses of the Vedas are regarded as mantras, but so are many phrases and compositions from later times, and they are often the heart of religious practice, transmitted from *guru* (spiritual leader) to disciple. The mode of engaging such intrinsically potent sound forms is by reciting them. Understanding them is fundamentally irrelevant, and mantras are often semantically meaningless.

This attitude extends beyond formal mantras to other words and books, so that recitation becomes the characteristic Hindu verbal activity. Meticulous attention to detail has produced patterns of astonishingly stable transmission across time and space, without recourse to writing, even of lengthy compositions. The purposes for which recitation is done are various. They include the search for mental and bodily health, the desire for wealth and worldly success, pleasing a deity, and aspiration to individual liberation. Contemporary study of this diversity of Hindu practice correspondingly runs from the familiar humanistic examination of textual content to anthropological inquiry into the function of texts in performance and festival. *See also* Aranyakas; Atharva Veda; Brahmanas; Dharmashastras, Dharmasutras; Goddess (Hinduism); Hinduism; Mahabharata; Purana; Ramayana; Rig Veda; Sama Veda; Veda, Vedism; Yajur Veda.

Hinduism (festal cycle). The Hindu festival cycle is generally organized around four concerns that often overlap: chronometric cycles of sun, moon, and constellations; the ecology and rhythm of seasons (monsoons, planting, and harvesting); celebration of the careers of the deities and other sacred figures; and the moods and needs of the people.

Festival Chronometry: Especially crucial in the sequence of festivals is the chronometric rhythm of the lunar-solar year. The solar year is

South Indian temple cart of the goddess Minakshi, bride of Shiva, at the Hindu festival of Cittarai, April to May, at Madurai, Tamil Nadu.

divided roughly by the solstices into the "northward journey" of the sun shortly after the winter solstice and the "southward journey" shortly after the summer solstice. Because the solar cycle is said to be equivalent to a "day in the life of the gods," many of the auspicious festivals, such as those celebrating the careers of the gods, fall during the "light half" of the earth's journey around the sun (the northward journey). In some states, in addition, months are marked by the sun's entry into each of the twelve zodiacal signs (Skt. *samkranti*).

The festival year is also marked by the lunar cycle, in which the new moon and the full moon mark the beginning and the end of fortnights. In some states, the start of the month is marked by the new moon; in others by the full moon. The fourteen stages of the fortnight are known as *tithis* and are occasionally viewed as corresponding to the careers of the deities. The waxing of the moon is most commonly thought to be auspicious for festive celebration.

A third element of chronometry is the constellational house through which the moon is said to pass in its orbit. There are twenty-seven such houses, each of which is ascribed mythological significance in the life of the gods.

Another element in the ritual calendar, but probably less ancient in India, is the *vara* (week) with its seven days named for the sun, moon, and five planets. Particularly auspicious for worship are Tuesday and Friday, the days of Mars (*mangala*) and Venus (*shukra*), respectively.

These cycles of time operate within larger cycles expanding out into *yugas*, or cosmic eons, and telescoping into smaller and smaller ones in such a way as to suggest a concentric cyclicality corresponding to the rhythm of the cosmos itself.

When one or more of these measures of time conjoin, they are know as a *yoga*, or conjunction. Such conjunctions may end or begin one or more chronometric cycles at once and so have become particularly poignant occasions for the practice of ritual. All such chronometric units are carefully calculated each year and published in a *panchanga*, or ritual calendar; this almanac becomes the basis for all temple ritual, especially for the festival calendar.

Types of Festivals: Texts refer to at least two types of festal activity, the *utsava* and the *vrata*. The utsava is a festival, generally hosted by a temple, lasting five or more days and celebrating the career or special event in the life of the deity. Utsavas are usually observed at the appropriate conjunction of constellation, full moon, and solar cycle. The utsava has retained many of the elements of kingship (e.g., flag raisings and processions), because, in pre-modern times, kings were frequently the patrons of festivals, and because the deity's life and exploits were perceived as corresponding to a king's.

The vrata, on the other hand, is often observed by families and individuals in ways that involve fasting, purification, the keeping of vows, and other special rituals. Vratas are generally performed at times of chronometric transition

or potential trauma, for example, at the first new moons following the winter and summer solstices or at other of the "dark" times in the lunar-solar calendar. Shivaratri, or the "night of Shiva," in the month corresponding to February and March, is one occasion on which vratas are performed, invoking Shiva's saving of the faithful.

The Festival Sequence: The "light half" of the year begins with the first month following the winter solstice and is generally homologous to the six sacred hours (*muhurtas*) of the ritual day, from sunrise to noon. This period is also often seen as corresponding to the career of the deities and to the ecological rhythms of the land: January through February, for example, is marked by rituals welcoming the return of the sun to its northward journey and, in some regions as well, the harvest of rice (e.g., Ponkal in Tamil Nadu); festivals, especially in Shaiva temples, celebrate the god's youthfulness and virility.

March through April is marked as the occasion for love, marriage, fertility, and new growth. Throughout North India, for example, the festival called Holi is climaxed at the full moon of March–April by the kindling of bonfires, which, among other things, replicates the burning of the demoness Holika; the love-play of Krishna and the conquest of good over evil are also reenacted. Not coincidentally, in such regions as northcentral India, the beginning of the agricultural year is celebrated. On the ninth day of the waxing moon, Rama's birthday is commemorated, especially in parts of North India. In the south, gods and goddesses are given in marriage as an expression of the creativity of the season.

By May or June, the hot season, festivals act out the powerful warriorlike, even terrifying, aspects of the divine. Parashurama's appearance, for example, is celebrated on the third tithi of the bright half of the lunar cycle. Parashurama is the avatar, or incarnation, of Vishnu, who appeared in order to avenge the stealing of a cow by Kshatriyas from his Brahman father.

The first month following the summer solstice marks the beginning of the "dark half" of the solar cycle and the cooler portion of the year. As in the first few hours of the afternoon in the ritual day, there is a period of general ritual abstinence or of divine "absence" or latency. This solstice also coincides with the coming of the southwest monsoon in much of India. There are agricultural festivals of planting or transplanting (e.g., Atippuram in Tamil Nadu) and also occasional theological festivals commensurate with the season. For example, the eleventh day of the bright fortnight of July to August marks the occasion when Vishnu goes to sleep for four months.

On a square of cow dung, small lamps are lighted during the Hindu Festival of Lights (Divali) in a house in Karimpur, Uttar Pradesh, India (1984). Divali, held during the dark-moon half of the lunar month corresponding to September and October, is often thought of as the Hindu New Year ritual.

Intimations of the restoration of the socio-cosmic order occur by the time of the autumnal equinox, which is generally seen as corresponding to dusk of the ritual day. Krishna's birth, for example, is celebrated on the eighth day of the dark fortnight of August to September. During this month, especially in rural settings, festivals are held celebrating the implantation of the earth, betrothal of the Goddess, worship of the *nagas*, or snake deities, and other rites suggesting fecundity.

Festivals occurring after the autumnal equinox tend to be festivals of the nighttime. Particularly full is the lunar cycle of September through October. Navaratri (lit., "nine nights"), also celebrated in some regions in the spring, is commemorated for the first nine days of the bright half of this lunar cycle. This period recalls Durga's slaying of the buffalo demon. Since the fifteenth century at least, a number of kings and regional potentates especially in the South India were patrons of the Navaratri and, thereby, were seen as the conquerors of evil, corresponding to the deeds of the Goddess. Also during this cycle, Dassehra commemorates Rama's slaying of Ravana, especially in north-central India. The waning fortnight of this lunar month is climaxed at the next new moon by Diwali, the festival of lights, falling at the ritual midnight of the year, when ancestors revisit their kin and are returned to their ancestral home by the burning of lights and exploding of firecrackers. In parts of the south, the October and November new moon also marks the coming of the northeast monsoon and starts the festival of Skanda Shashti, the birth of Skanda and his conquest of evil.

Festal events throughout November and December move toward preparation for the "dawn" of the ritual year. December through January is often marked by the enhanced significance of predawn rituals in temples.

This cycle, measured as it is by several astronomical markers, acts out the rhythm of the cosmos' waxing and waning. At the same time, it celebrates the careers and exploits of the deities as well as the moods and patterns of the seasons. People who participate, therefore, understand the cycle's significance in many different ways, not least of all as expression of the trials and triumphs of personal, communal, and cosmic life. **See also** auspicious, inauspicious (Hinduism); cosmology; Divali; Hindu domestic ritual; Hinduism (worship); Holi; Kumbha Mela.

HINDUISM

About 80 percent of India's approximately 800 million people would either call themselves Hindu or be classified as Hindu by one definition or another. There are in addition about 20 million Hindus in other parts of the world, most having left India during the colonial period or since Indian independence (1947), but some, as on the island of Bali in Indonesia, tracing their history back to the earlier expansion of Indian culture (both Hindu and Buddhist) through Southeast Asia (ca. 100–1400). The considerable population of Hindus among the approximately one million South Asians in North America has been increasingly active over recent years in temple building, cultural outreach, support for India, and promotion of ecumenism with other non-Hindu South Asian religious communities.

HINDUISM AND ORIENTALISM

Probably no other religious tradition, however, has been more closely scrutinized for its fissures than Hinduism. Put simply, as early as the 1960s, and with increasing intensity since the emergence in the 1980s of a scholarly discourse on orientalism, it has become fashionable to argue that Hinduism is but a Western orientalist invention. On the other hand, the same period has also seen a resurgence of Hindu identity in the political sphere. In such circles, Hinduism is a contested but very real entity: a source for reclaiming India's most ancient heritage from Western and Islamic influences and a world religion with its own diaspora and missions.

There is some sense to recent claims that early European orientalists in effect invented what has come to be recognized as Hinduism. A great legacy of the Indology of the late eighteenth through early twentieth centuries is the homage it paid to Hinduism as one of the world's most ancient creeds, a religion, however, whose noble beginnings were alleged to have soon fallen victim to processes of decadence and fission. The first generation of Indologists, the orientalist founders of the Asiatic Society of Bengal and the College of Fort William in Calcutta, were reared on Enlightenment ideals of natural religion, tolerance, and classicism and known as orientalists for their attempt to appreciate Indian culture, or at least the "best" of it, as a spur to its own inner renewal.

Among them, William Jones in 1786 established the place of Sanskrit in the family of Indo-European languages, underlining a link between Europe and Asia and a rational unity beyond cultural diversity. Others sifted through Hindu literatures to determine their chronology, finally identifying the *Rig Veda* (ca. 1400–1000 B.C.) as Hinduism's oldest textual source. The result was not only the discovery of a history to Hinduism but the promotion of the idea that, at its roots, Hinduism had a Vedic golden age.

Moreover, this golden age could be the source of a "Hindu Renaissance." Were Hinduism only to cut away such "medieval" accretions as polytheism, idolatry, mysticism, widow self-immolation (*suttee*), the complications and in-equities of caste, and fertility rites linked with goddess worship and Tantrism, it could recover, among other orientalist fancies, a lost Vedic monotheism and social egalitarianism.

Later generations, inspired mainly by the work of the German philologist Max Muller (1823–1900), acclaimed the Vedic source for their vigorous male pantheon of so-called nature deities: for example, Agni, god of fire, and deities associated with the dawn (Ushas), sun (Surya, Savitar), moon (Chandra), rain (Parjanya, Indra), the cosmic order called *rita* (Varuna), and an intoxicating juice extracted from a plant called *soma* that inspired the visionary poetry of the Vedic poet-sages (*rishis*). The Aryan authors of the *Rig Veda* composed much of their poetry to praise these and numerous other gods, none of whom were sim-ply *nature deities*, despite the continued use of the term in textbooks.

Most prominently worshiped was the war and rain god Indra, who was laud-ed for enabling the Aryans (a term that probably carried the connotation "those who are noble") to defeat a people dubbed Dasas or Dasyus, basically "slaves." Nineteenth-century Indology assumed that the Dasas were non-Aryan, but re-cently this has been contested by an argument that they were an earlier wave of Aryans who did not use soma.

By the mid-nineteenth century, the Indo-European linguistic affinities lent themselves not only to studies in comparative Indo-European mythology and ritual, but—through a ready parallelism between the Aryan and colonialist "conquests"—to the newly emergent theory, linked with Darwinian ideas, of master (also called martial or masculine) and subject (also called effeminate) races. Tribal, caste, and linguistic affinities were thus linked with race, and In-dian populations were classified according to whether they resisted the British with weapons, in which case they were martial, or with literary and economic means, in which case they were effeminate.

Against this background, the religion of the *Rig Veda* was now construed to combine an intuitive feel for nature with a triumphant, beef-eating, and origi-nally Indo-European warrior culture. Along with such "positive" images of early Vedic religion, however, Western Indology, with its linear model of evolutionary decline (rather than Western progress) ready at hand, was quick to trace the seeds of degeneration and fission that were supposedly already latent in the *Rig Veda* itself. The mythological and polytheistic aspects of the *Rig Veda* were said by Muller to have resulted from a *disease of language*, a term he coined to explain how the original poetic intuition of the "Infinite" through nature, and especially through observing the dawn and sunrise, deteriorated into fanciful mythmaking about anthropomorphically divinized natural forces. Then the latest books of the *Rig Veda* introduced strains of henotheism (praising the god one worships for the moment as being all other gods in one), pantheism, skepticism, a charter for the caste system, a search for the ultimate unity (a monistic absolute) beyond the multiplicity of polytheism, and eventually, as others rounded out the theory, a moribund, religiously dominated civilization of navel-gazing passivity and fatalism.

This was a two-way mirror held up to reflect the tastes and self-images of Western romanticism, social Darwinism, and imperialism (rather than just colonialism) justified by a confidence that modernization was equivalent to Westernization (including the spread of Christianity and science through the use of the English language), and the strident anti-Hindu polemic of many missionaries. The past glories of Hinduism—much less generously portrayed than by the previous generation of orientalists—were not so much a source of renewal for Hindus as a justification for their subjugation. Since Indians could not, in British eyes, return to those glories on their own, imperialist intervention was justifiable.

VEDIC RELIGION AND RELIGIONS

While the religion of the *Rig Veda* could thus be treated as a unified development, the term *Vedic religion* was susceptible to other usages that have never attained scholarly consistency. The *Rig Veda* is the oldest of four Vedas, a grouping that grew to reflect the systematic ordering of Vedic sacrificial ritual. Each Veda became the province of one class of specialist priests. Thus one usage has been to treat Vedic religion as constituted by the religion of the three oldest "liturgical" Vedas (the *Rig Veda*, the *Sama Veda*, and the *Yajur Veda*), or by the four Vedas (the three plus the "magical" *Atharva Veda*). Some have also used the term to identify an original Rig Vedic religion.

Over a period of close to a thousand years (ca. 1400–400 B.C.), however, these four specialist priestly classes each developed three types of further literature that were the output of their respective schools: Brahmanas (ca. 1100–700 B.C.), a literature that systematized and carried forward the Vedic sacrifice; Aranyakas (ca. 800–600 B.C.), treatises on forest life, involving an inward, meditative alternative to the outward performance of sacrifice; and Upanishads (ca. 700–400 B.C.), varied and largely unsystematized teachings about ultimate reality and its experience through self-knowledge.

This corpus of literature, from the four Vedas to the Upanishads, can also be called *Veda* (Skt., "knowledge"). That is one of the two main terms used for it by later Hindus when they claim "the Veda" as their source of authority. The other term, *shruti,* means literally "that which is heard," but is usually translated as "revelation," conveying the sense that Veda constitutes for Hindus the authoritative source of revealed knowledge, as distinct from ancillary or later texts classified as *smriti,* "tradition" or "memory." Veda or shruti can thus also refer to the tensions and harmonies that nevertheless cohere within this vast textual corpus. When Hindus speak of the Vedas as their source of revelation, some such inspired coherence is assumed. One can thus also refer to "Vedic religion" with this implication.

Mid- and late-nineteenth-century Indology, however, spent much of its

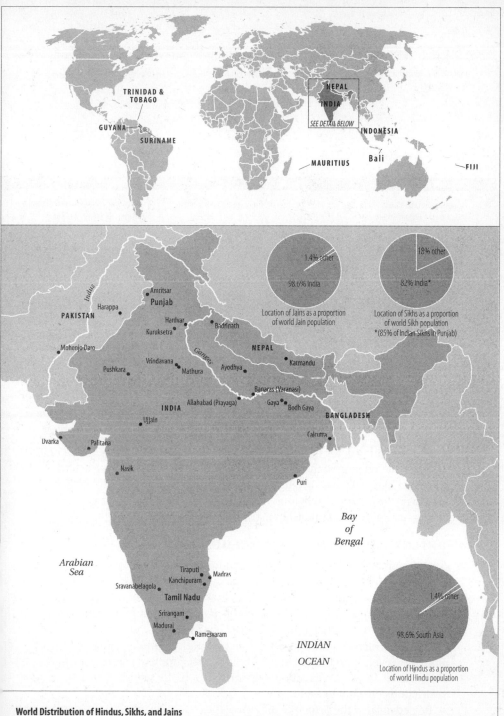

TRINIDAD & TOBAGO

GUYANA

SURINAME

NEPAL

INDIA

SEE DETAIL BELOW

INDONESIA

MAURITIUS

Bali

FIJI

Indus

Amritsar
Punjab

Harappa

PAKISTAN

Hardvar

Kuruksetra

Badrinath

Mohenjo Daro

Vrindavana

Pushkara

Mathura

NEPAL

Katmandu

Ganges

Ayodhya

Banaras (Varanasi)

INDIA

Allahabad (Prayaga)

Gaya

Bodh Gaya

BANGLADESH

Ujjain

Dvarka

Palitana

Calcutta

Nasik

Puri

Arabian
Sea

Tiraputi

Kanchipuram

Madras

Sravanabelagola

Tamil Nadu

Srirangam

Madurai

Ramesvaram

Bay
of
Bengal

INDIAN
OCEAN

1.4% other

98.6% India

Location of Jains as a proportion
of world Jain population

18% other

82% India*

Location of Sikhs as a proportion
of world Sikh population
*(85% of Indian Sikhs in Punjab)

1.4% other

98.6% South Asia

Location of Hindus as a proportion
of world Hindu population

World Distribution of Hindus, Sikhs, and Jains

Hindu majority areas

Hindus comprise a plurality (25%–49%)

Hindus comprise 13.5% of the world's population. Dark shading indicates where Hindus make up a majority (more than 50%) of an area's population; light shading indicates where Hindus are 25–49% of an area's population. Sikhs comprise .34% of the world's population; they are largely concentrated in the Punjab. Jains comprise .07% of the world's population; they are largely concentrated in India. Cities and other geographical features shown are important Hindu, Sikh, or Jain holy places or sites of pilgrimage.

India*

3000–2000 B.C.	2000–1000 B.C.	1000–800 B.C.
Indus Valley civilizations (ca. 2750–1750)	Indigenous Ganges cultures (ca. 1800–1200)	*Brahmanas* (ca. 1000–700)
	Indo-Europeans (Aryans) enter northern India (ca. 1550)	
	Rig Veda (ca. 1400–1000)	

500–400 B.C.	400–300 B.C.	300–200 B.C.
Ramayana and the *Mahabharata*, including the *Bhagavad Gita* (ca. 500 B.C.–A.D. 400)	Alexander the Great reaches north India (327)	Mauryan king Ashoka becomes patron of Buddhism (reigned 272–236)
Panini (fl. 500–400)	Mauryan empire (ca. 322–185)	*Laws of Manu* (ca. 200 B.C.–A.D. 200)

100–300	300–400	400–500
	Early Tantrism (300–500)	Patanjali (fl. 2nd century B.C. or 3rd to 5th centuries A.D.)
	Gupta empire (ca. 320–480)	*Puranas* (ca. 400–1200)

* Indian dates until the 13th century are particularly difficult to fix with any precision. Contemporary scholars propose dates for the same individual or work that may differ by centuries.

energy assigning dates to this literature and inventing further "subreligions" such as "the religion of the Brahmanas" (unfavorably dubbed "priestcraft") and the more highly regarded "religion (better, philosophy) of the Upanishads." In any case, these varied "religions"—including "Vedic religion" in all these forms—are indeed orientalist constructs.

ORIENTALISM AND HINDU REFORM MOVEMENTS

Such orientalist inventions and reinventions of Hinduism provided nineteenth-century movements with terms and motivations for Hindu reform. Exemplary in this regard were two movements: the Brahmo Samaj, founded in 1828 by Rammohun Roy (1772–1833), which reflected the earlier, more generous period, and the Arya Samaj, founded in 1875 by Swami Dayananda Sarasvati (1824–83), which reacted against the second period's unflattering portrayals. Both, however, shared the critique of polytheism, idolatry, caste, and such other social ills as suttee (widow self-immolation), female child marriage, and restrictions on women's education.

Roy advocated the principle that the Vedas could be turned to selectively and looked primarily to the Upanishads; but he also looked to Islam and Christianity to establish a congregational form of worship new to Hindus and to support

800–700 B.C.	700–600 B.C.	600–500 B.C.
Indo-Europeans occupy south India (ca. 800)	*Upanishads* (ca. 700–400)	Siddhartha Gautama (the Buddha) (ca. 566–486)
Aranyakas (ca. 800–600)	*Dharmasutras, Dharmashastras* (ca. 400 B.C.–A.D. 400)	Vardhamana Mahavira, traditional founder of Jainism (d. ca. 527)
		Gandara region of north India conquered by Achaemenid empire (519)

200–100 B.C.	100–1 B.C.	1–100
Kanada (ca. 200 B.C.–A.D. 100)	Jain split into Digambara and Shvetambara (79)	Kanishka, Kushan emperor, gains control of north India (78–102)
Hellenistic kingdoms established in northwest India (185)		
Earliest surviving Sanskrit inscription (ca. 150)		

500–600	600–700	700–800
Pallava Tamil dynasty in south India (575–900)	Bhakti begins in south India, the Alvars and Nyanmars (600–700)	Muslims occupy Sind region (712)
	Gaudapada (ca. 7th century)	Shankara (ca. 8th century)

his conviction that all religions taught the same underlying personal divine unity. Dayananda advocated a strictly orthodox Vedic religion, rooted especially in the four Vedas, and sought to refute Islam and Christianity and to counteract their missions by aggressive reconversion tactics of his Samaj. While the Brahmo Samaj has left only small ongoing offshoots, its liberal idealism has inspired other movements. The Arya Samaj remains highly active and has also provided inspiration for other late-nineteenth- and twentieth-century Hindu self-strengthening movements, from regional and pan-Indian forms of nationalism to Hindu "fundamentalist" political movements.

FROM EARLY TO LIVING HINDUISM

If reform carried the implication of going back—in whatever fashion—to the Vedas, this was largely because post-Vedic Hinduism was viewed by the orientalist "inventors" of Hinduism as having generated the bewildering complexity that was reflected in the current-day nineteenth-century Hinduism that was alleged to be in such desperate need of reform. Colonialist administrators, missionaries, and armchair scholars of Sanskrit texts who (like Muller) never visited India all concurred from their different perspectives on this negative representation of living Hinduism and its indiscriminate sources.

India

800–900	900–1000	1000–1100
Manikkavacakar (fl. 9th century)	Matsyendranath (fl. 10th century)	Gorakhnath (fl. ca. 11th century)
Nammalvar (fl. 9th century)	Kapalikas and Kalamukhas (fl. 10th or 11th centuries)	Ramanuja (1017–1137)
Rajput dynasties dominate north India (800–1569)	*Bhagavata Purana* (ca. 900)	
Yamuna (919–1038)	*Tevaram* (ca. 900)	
	Cola Tamil dynasty in south India (900–1300)	
	Abhinavagupta (fl. 975–1025)	
	Muslim military actions in India (986–1018)	

1400–1500	1500–1600	1600–1700
Kabir (ca. 1440–1518)	Portuguese establish Goa (1510)	British East India Company (1600–1874)
Mira Bai (ca. 1450–1547)	Mughal dynasty; Muslim control of large part of India (1526–1857)	*Adi Granth* compiled by fifth Sikh guru, Arjun (1603–1604)
Nanak, first Sikh guru (1469–1539)	Tulsi Das (ca. 1532–1623)	Gobind Singh (1666–1708)
Vallabha Sampradaya (1479–1531)	Reign of Akbar, Mughal emperor (1555–1605)	Formation of Sikh Akalis (ca. 1690)
Vasco da Gama, first European to reach India by sea (1498)	Amritsar, Sikh holy place founded (1577)	Calcutta established by British (1690)

The topic of post-Vedic Hinduism has thus been equally problematic, depending on whether the stress is on continuities or discontinuities. But the most conventional practice is to contrast Vedic religion, either in its more extensive sense (from the Vedas to the Upanishads) or in its phases and subreligions, with Hinduism proper. The latter can then be seen either as a melange of adventitious divergences and convergences or as a development from within one continuous tradition, one that claims the Vedic heritage as in some sense its own but departs from it as well in significant ways. Scholars of both persuasions, however, usually divide post-Vedic Hinduism into historical phases, the most typical being a division into epic, classical, medieval, and modern eras.

These periods have been loosely, and often confusingly, defined. "Epic" is used to cover the broadly agreed-upon period of the composition of the two epics, the *Ramayana* and the *Mahabharata,* ca. 500 B.C. to A.D. 400. The latter text includes the *Bhagavad Gita,* with its seminal enunciation of a hierarchical and reciprocal relationship between the three "paths" of *karma yoga, jnana yoga,* and *bhakti yoga:* the disciplines (*yogas*) of action, knowledge, and devotion. The same period also embraces the codification of many of the most

1100–1200	1200–1300	1300–1400
Nimbarka Sampradaya (12th or 13th centuries)	Muslim sultanate of Delhi established (1206)	Vijayanagar Tamil dynasty in south India (1300–1700)
Kampan (12th century)	Madhva (1238–1317)	Mongols, under Timur, invade India, sack Delhi (1398)
Muizzuddin Muhammad founds first Muslim empire in India (1175)	Vedanta Desika (1238–1369)	
Gita Govinda (ca. 1180)	Pillai Lokacharya (1264–1369)	

1700–1800	1800–1900	
Maratha Hindu confederacy (1707–1818)	Balak Singh (1797–1862)	Vivekananda (1863–1902)
Ramprasad Sen (1718–75)	Expansion of British control (1818–59)	Mahatma (Mohandas K.) Gandhi (1869–1948)
Decline of Mughal power (1748–1857)	Brahmo Samaj founded (1828)	Sri Aurobindo (1872–1950)
Failed French attempt to gain presence in India (1751–57)	Dayananda Sarasvati (1824–83)	Bhakti Siddhanta Sarasvati (1874–1937)
Rammohun Roy (1772–1833)	Ramakrishna (1836–86)	Arya Samaj founded (1875)
	Keshah Chandra Sen (1838–84)	Queen Victoria proclaimed Empress of India (1877)
	Bal Gangadhar Tilak (1856–1920)	Ramana Maharshi (1879–1950)
	Sepoy rebellion (1857)	Indian National Congress founded (1885)
	British assume control of India's government (1858)	
	Radhasoami Satsang founded (1861)	

prominent manuals on Hindu law (Dharmashastras, Dharmasutras), statecraft (Arthashastra), and philosophy (the *sutras* of most of the six "orthodox" Hindu *darshanas*, or "viewpoints"), as well as the earliest known developments in Shaivite and Vaishnava sectarianism, temple building, iconography, and pilgrimage.

The classical period, which some scholars extend back to include the later epic period, takes in the expansion of Hindu *bhakti* ("devotional") mythology from the epics to the earlier Puranas, and royal patronage of great temples in North India; further Shaivite and Vaishnava sectarian developments, including the codification of manuals (*agamas, samhitas*) on temple ritual, architecture, and iconography; and the emergence and henceforth pervading influences of Tantrism, with its sexual rites and imagery (ca. 500).

The medieval period, beginning by convention in the early eighth century and continuing into the seventeenth, launches the development of vernacular saint-singer bhakti traditions that spread throughout India—starting with the Vaishnava Alvars and Shaivite Nayanmars (ca. 600–1000) of the Tamil country—stressing a highly emotional, ecstatic, and sensual bhakti. In counterpoise,

Shankara, the eighth-century philosopher, articulates a normative Smarta orthodoxy based on a nondualist (Advaita Vedanta) interpretation of the Upanishads, advocating the path of knowledge, with recognition of the empirical world as *maya*, illusion. Institutionally, Shankara stressed the dharmashastric social norms of caste (*varna*) and life stage (*ashrama*) and reserved a subordinate place for devotion to bhakti deities (*saguna brahman*, "the absolute with qualities") as a concession to women and non-Aryan Shudras (workers and servants) and as a prelude to knowledge of the impersonal and qualityless absolute (*nirguna brahman*). From the early eleventh century, encountering increasing Islamic hegemony over most of the subcontinent, medieval Hinduism is then marked by continued developments in royally sponsored temple building, especially in South India beyond immediate Muslim sway; the composition of later Puranas; a proliferation of new Vaishnava, Shaivite, and now Shakti (goddess-worshiping) sects throughout the subcontinent; mystical Sant movements striving for a rapprochement with Islamic Sufism; the enrichment of distinctive regional bhakti traditions by songs of devotion, local Puranas for major temples, and versions of the classical epics composed in vernacular languages; the development of regional festivals often linked with newly developed forms of dance-drama (in the north, called *lilas*) based on these vernacular traditions; and "new" regional folk epic, drama, and mythological traditions concerned with local deities, especially goddesses and male guardian deities, unknown in the Vedic-classical continuum.

INTERPRETING HINDUISM'S DIVERSITY

The image of rampant Hindu diversity has been protracted through these periods chiefly by scholarly attention to the development of vernacular traditions and the history of different *sampradayas,* or "sects" (the term *denominations* would be better), centered on Vishnu, Shiva, and the Goddess, and in the classical and medieval periods also on the sun god Surya and the elephant-headed god Ganesha. Such emphases have exaggerated the degree to which major devotional texts such as the epics and Puranas, which have a popularity beyond the sects, were inspired by sectarian rivalries. In recent centuries new and often nonsectarian sampradayas have also formed around the teachings of charismatic *gurus* (spiritual leaders).

The study of post-Vedic Hinduism has also divided itself into areas of specialization, many of which have produced rich scholarly literatures. In particular,
the areas of Dharmashastra, the six philosophical darshanas, sectarian cult and
theology, vernacular poetry, temple and domestic cult and ritual, kingship,
caste and kinship, folk Hinduism, and even, notwithstanding reservations
about its sexual rites, Tantrism are ones in which scholarly idiosyncracies have
usually been checked by the need to correlate textual translation and exegesis
with knowledgeable Indian authorities or observable conditions. Probably the
major area in which orientalist scholarship has downplayed Hindu categories
and sensibilities in favor of its own, however, is in dealing with bhakti mythological traditions.

It is not possible to discuss in short compass the free rein with which scholars
have mirrored their own varied fancies in studying the vast field of Hindu
mythology. Exemplary, however, are two themes that are significant for their
representation of normative Hindu concepts: *avatarana*, or divine descent, and
the *trimurti*, or "three forms" of the absolute brahman.

Whether motivated by comparison with Christianity or by other humanizing,
historicizing, or psychologizing impulses, the Hindu mythology of divine incarnations, or *avataras*, has, until only recently, been denied any Hindu theological significance. In particular, the two most important (because they are the
most worshiped) of Vishnu's divine descents, or avataras, those of Krishna and
Rama, are explained away as results of massive interpolations into the *Mahabharata* and the *Ramayana*, the epics that first tell their tales.

In each case there is a double argument. First, it is alleged that Krishna and
Rama were originally only heroic human beings who were divinized by Vaishnava sectarian designs. Second, it is argued that their stories are only composites, fusions of the humanly plausible narrative segments (Krishna's alliance
with the five Pandava brothers and participation in the *Mahabharata* war;
the palace intrigue that leads to Rama's banishment) with fanciful mythic or
romantic themes (Krishna's childhood with the cowherd women, or *gopis*;
Rama's miraculous birth, forest idylls, monkey allies, and fights with demons).
It is becoming increasingly recognized that the texts do not support these de-
constructions.

Similarly, the trimurti concept of Brahma as creator, Vishnu as preserver, and
Shiva as destroyer has been downgraded as a supposedly late (sixth century)
and relatively meaningless construct, sometimes contrasted in this light with
the Christian Trinity. Overlooked is the fact that it functions as an important
structuring principle in epic and Puranic cosmology and mythology and in popular Hinduism more generally.

Also, from the late nineteenth century on, archaeological and anthropological studies have introduced further entries into the Hindu composite. The remains of the Indus Valley civilization, discovered and first excavated between
1922 and 1931 by the Archaeological Survey of India under the directorship of
Sir John Marshall, opened up a prehistory of Hinduism that had previously
been unsuspected. It introduced a pre-Vedic, goddess-worshiping Indus Valley
culture that was not only, in all likelihood, non-Aryan, but probably domi-

nated by speakers of a proto-Dravidian language akin to living South Indian Dravidian languages.

This probability (Indus Valley writing has not been deciphered, so its linguistic identity remains uncertain) has been seized upon by scholars of varying persuasions, most notably those who would argue for the antiquity and grandeur of South Indian Dravidian culture in relation to North Indian Aryan culture. Others have turned the Indus Valley evidence into arguments for an ancient materialist-spiritualist dualism, for the primacy (and implied nonmartial character) of goddess worship versus the martial triumphalism of the Vedic Aryans, for a pre-Vedic and thus pre-Aryan cult of Shiva, and for continuities between Indus Valley religion, popular village Hinduism, and the religions of South Asian Dravidian- and Munda-speaking tribes.

These arguments, however, are all fragile and invariably impute one or another fundamental and irreconcilable "dualism" to Hinduism and Indian culture. Anthropologists, for instance, have drawn upon the hypothesis of a pre-Vedic Dravidian culture to stress the autonomy of the "living" and often oral "little" village or tribal traditions they have studied, often assuming them to be unaffected by or resistant to Aryan, Brahmanical, or Sanskritic influences. Or where parallels are evident, their tendency is either to argue that the village or tribal tradition represents the "original" (as with post-shaped deities in Andhra Pradesh villages and among tribes in Orissa, Gujarat, and Bihar, whose iconography may recall the Vedic sacrificial post), or that the tribes or villages register the great tradition's influences only by a thin veneer (as with tribal usages of the Hindu name Bhagavan for their "high god"). Competing romanticizations of the Vedic, the village, and the tribe, not to mention the pastoral and the agricultural, and the Aryan and the Dravidian, have made it virtually impossible to get a clear sense of the complexities that lie behind more than three millennia of familiarity and interactions between these varied populations.

The origins and nature of Hindu goddess worship have also been the subject of controversy. While some have argued for a direct continuity from Indus Valley religion through ancient village goddess traditions surviving into recent centuries, others have argued for aboriginal, tribal, ancient Near Eastern, and Vedic origins. Similarly, while Hindu Shaktism regards the goddess as a unified figure under such names as Mahadevi or Parashakti, with many "forms," or avataras, there is no consensus among scholars as to whether to begin an interpretation of the goddess from such a unified standpoint, which is the usual Hindu perspective, or to take each goddess as a separate individual personality.

DISINVENTING HINDUISM

Clearly, those who have recently argued that there is no such entity as Hinduism have ample ammunition in the arguments of earlier generations of Indologists and in the problems raised by recent archaeological and anthropological studies. But recent arguments also have something new about them. They reclaim the banner of Hinduism's alleged incoherence but draw attention as well to the fact that "Hinduism"—its very name—is not a native concept. It has, in other words, been invented by outsiders: first by Muslims, then by the

British. It is not just the history of Hinduism that has been invented but its very identity. And if history can be put to both good and bad uses, the usage of the name, according to certain scholars, has become pernicious.

The most repeated arguments against Hinduism as a meaningful ensemble are as follows. First, the process of naming religions was itself part of an early-nineteenth-century trend toward reification in the concept of "religion." Second, *Hinduism* is but an umbrella term for a vast melange covering everything from elite Sanskritic philosophies to tribal *animism*—itself a term of Western coinage that was put into service to classify Indian religions in the colonialist project of the Indian census. Third, attempts at definition of the "essentials" or "norms" of Hinduism routinely overstress the "high" classical Brahmanical doctrines of the Vedas as the source of eternal knowledge, of *dharma* (moral and social order), *karma* (law of moral causation), transmigration, caste (*varna*), life stage (*ashrama*, including renunciation, or *sannyasa*), and of liberation (*moksha*). There are no essentials that all Hindus would accept. Finally, the concept of Hinduism derived from early orientalists has been fostered in India itself, through the modern period, not only by major reformers but by upper-caste, mercantile, and landed elites who have learned to use the legal and political routes opened up under British and post-independence laws to "reform" Hinduism, to link it with nationalist aspirations, and, mainly over the last half century, to construct a highly politicized antisecular "syndicated Hinduism" based on the artificial census-derived notion of a "Hindu majority."

There is much to reckon with in these arguments. Hinduism is one of many religions that were reified in late-eighteenth- and early-nineteenth-century discourse. Hinduism is diverse. Essentialist definitions of Hinduism are unpersuasive. And the modern politicized and "syndicated" Hinduism is a reality and is different from what proceeded it and what surrounds it in its contemporary milieu. Its inroads into rural, popular, and sectarian forms of Hinduism are increasingly evident. It has developed not only against a background of the colonialist "invention" of Hinduism and Hindu reform movements challenged by this "invention," but in a geographical context permeated by assertions of religious identity by other communities (Christian, Muslim, Sikh, Buddhist) in various parts of South Asia. In postindependence India, the political ideal of secularism has also stimulated Hindu reaction and fostered attempts to forge pro-Hindu political movements. This does not mean, however, that these arguments are either singularly or collectively convincing.

CONTINUITIES AND UNITIES

It is of course true that the term *Hindu* (Arab., lit., "one living near the Indus River") does not appear prior to the Muslim period. But there are still numerous ways in which the tradition, whatever one chooses to call it, has affirmed its continuities, its unity, and its differences from other traditions, before the modern period.

One was the notion, articulated in the epic period, that the current of teachings and practices carried on from shruti through smriti traditions was the *sanatana dharma,* "eternal dharma." Another is the classical philosophical opposition between *astikas,* "those who affirm that 'it is'" (Hindus) and *nastikas,* "those who say 'it is not'" (materialists, Buddhists, Jains). Hinduism is precisely the dharma that affirms: the Vedas, the *atman,* brahman, God, etc. Another was the attempt of Shankara to revive this eternal dharma under the umbrella of Smarta orthodoxy, encompassing the paths of action and devotion under that of knowledge and establishing a Vedantic philosophical-theological discourse in which later sectarian theologians would have to participate, even while disagreeing with him. Another is the role that pan-Indian routes of pilgrimage played in balancing the rise of regional and vernacular sectarian traditions.

In the modern period, reformers such as the Bengali ecstatic Ramakrishna Paramahamsa (1836–86), his activist disciple Swami Vivekananda (1863–1902), the pacifist Mohandas K. (Mahatma) Gandhi (1869–1948), the militant agnostic Hindu nationalist Vir Savarkar (1883–1966), and the philosopher-statesman (former president of India) Sarvapalli Radhakrishnan (1888–1975) each promoted competing visions of a unified and unifying Hinduism. But most central through all these periods is the regard that Hinduism has held for the Veda.

VEDA AND HINDUISM

The closure of the Vedic corpus as a body of "revelation" would seem to have been set by about the fourth century B.C. Within the early works on Dharmashastra and in the Mimamsa and Vedanta, the most orthodox of the philosophical schools, a post-Vedic doctrine soon developed that this Vedic revelation is eternal and *apaurusheya,* "not authored by a person." It is likely that these doctrines were in part designed to assert the superiority of the eternal, unauthored Veda over the "authored" and thus "historical" canons of Buddhism and Jainism, which launched their rival movements in the centuries just preceding this closure. The original oral character of Vedic teaching was also felt to be superior to the written canons of these rival movements. Alternately, devotional texts such as the epics and Puranas regarded the Vedas as a primordial teaching of the god Brahma, renewed at the beginning of each cycle of four ages (*mahayugas*) by the seven Vedic rishis.

It is often pointed out that the six "orthodox" philosophical schools of Hinduism apply the principle of the authority of the Veda either very selectively or merely pay it lip service. Various other smriti texts are prone to claim that they are "equivalent to the Veda," based on some "lost Veda," or are themselves "fifth Vedas." Similarly, numerous vernacular works are said to be equal to the Veda. Such claims are usually regarded as superficial: as signs, if anything, that Veda survives only as a term of prestige, its original meaning depleted, with the Veda itself superseded by later texts that can be about virtually anything. But the Vedas are not as irrelevant as these assertions suggest.

The *Mahabharata* (500 B.C.–A.D. 400) presents the most instructive case of a "significant" fifth Veda. In probably being the first text to refer to itself as such, the "great epic" incorporates countless allusions to Rig Vedic *mantras* and peoples, Vedic sacrificial practices (it refers to its great war as a "sacrifice of battle"), and Upanishadic ideas and symbols. Most of the Vedic gods take human birth to enter into the epic crisis.

Certain scholars regard the epic as a devotional (bhakti) rereading of the Vedic revelation. It can, in any case, be regarded as one of the foundational texts for the classical consolidation of Hinduism, that is, as one of the means through which the tradition aspired to be a unity in the face of the challenges of the non-Hindu "heterodox" movements such as Buddhism, Jainism, and materialism. It also served to buttress this consolidation against the political and religious instability brought about in the northwest by foreign intrusions, from the invasion of Alexander the Great (327–325 B.C.) through the rule of the Kushanas (second century). Indeed, both epics—the *Ramayana* and the *Mahabharata*—project the image of a pre-Buddhist and pre-Jain pan-"Hindu" South Asian subcontinent, still peopled by Vedic rishis and practices and extended in the *Ramayana* even to Sri Lanka.

According to the *Mahabharata* myth, the goddess Earth appeals to Vishnu, the supreme deity of the text, to rescue her from the demons who oppress her and who threaten to submerge her in the cosmic ocean. Vishnu incarnates himself as Krishna and, along with the other incarnate Vedic gods, participates in the crisis that builds up to the epic's great battle that rescues and renovates the earth and institutes our present age, the Kali Yuga, or Age of Discord, as one in which bhakti—devotion to the gods—is proclaimed by Krishna himself as the ideal religious path for both genders and all castes.

The *Bhagavad Gita*, which text-critical Indologists have persistently sought to isolate from the rest of the *Mahabharata* as an interpolation (usually with interpolations of its own), is arguably the centerpiece of the whole. Indeed, it can be regarded as an early attempt to unpack the hierarchical interrelationships, from a bhakti standpoint, of the various ritual, social, philosophical, cosmological, and soteriological strains of the tradition and thereby assert and display its underlying unities.

Just before the battle, Krishna tells the exemplary warrior-prince Arjuna why it is his duty (dharma) to participate in the battle and not to give way to his "compassionate" impulse to drop his weapons and retreat from the fight like a renouncer (*sannyasin*). Krishna teaches Arjuna that in order to discipline his mind as a warrior-yogin, Arjuna must come to recognize his true foe as his own "compassion": it is but a form of attachment or desire that he must discipline himself to overcome so that he can act without desire for the fruits of his actions, thereby freeing himself from bondage to their results and making them an offering to Krishna as God.

Moreover, Krishna asserts his supremacy over all other gods. He outlines the various religious paths or yogas of action, knowledge, and devotion that lead to him as well as the dharmic order that sustains both social and individual life. It is this order that ultimately he sustains, even through a cataclysmic battle, for "the welfare of the world," a world of imperiled dharmic order whose cosmological situation Krishna unveils against the background of a divinely ordered bhakti universe of vast temporal cycles (*kalpas*), ages (*yugas*), divine births, and reformulated concepts of space and matter.

But post-Vedic Hinduism's allegiance to the Veda is not just a matter of doctrines and texts. The notion that it is so is precisely the heritage of the "narrow"

Indological orientalism that has attempted to recover the history of Hinduism through its texts alone and its "definition" or "essence" in some kind of orthodoxy of Brahmanical doctrine or basic beliefs. For one thing, Vedic thought is expressed in a style that remains distinctive to Hinduism: that of forging *bandhus*, networks of hidden and often symbolic connections or resemblances. This is seen not only in the epics, but with a special force in Hindu Tantric texts. These acknowledge the authority of the Veda and affinities with it, while also asserting various ways in which Tantra is superior to Veda, such as the insistence that Tantric initiation (*diksha*) is required even for those from upper castes who have the entitlement (*adhikara*) through Vedic initiation to hear the Veda.

Nor is Veda simply a preserve of Sanskritic or Brahmanical strains of Hinduism. The *Basava Purana*, a virulently anti-Brahmanical Telugu text (thirteenth century) of the reformist Shaivite Lingayat sect of Andhra Pradesh and Karnataka, is full of Vedic quotations.

REDEFINING HINDUISM

Countering attempts at a postorientalist deconstruction of Hinduism, the anthropologist Gabriella Eichinger Ferro-Luzzi argues that one need not abandon the term Hinduism or deny it the status of a religion. She turns helpfully to the philosopher Wittgenstein's discovery that concepts may be held together by a "family resemblance," by complicated networks of overlapping and crisscrossing similarities. Hinduism, she argues, is just such a concept, a current term for which is *polythetic*, indicating a concept that cannot be defined but only exemplified.

She further introduces the concept of "prototypes" in Hinduism, referring to those features combining high frequency and prestige that are recurrently replicated in its crisscrossing and overlapping network. Pilgrimage, asceticism, and vegetarianism are good examples that she cites, to which might be added yoga. Not all Hindus participate in such practices, and they are not unique to Hindus. But whether an individual does them or not, or believes in such "high" doctrines as karma or a nondualistic brahman, or for that matter in the Veda, they have a distinctive frequency, prestige, and style within the Indian context that marks them as Hindu.

Another significant prototype in Hinduism is sacrifice. Not all Hindus perform sacrifice. The vegetarian, ascetic, and even pilgrimage strains of Hinduism in fact stand against animal (and of course human) sacrifice, though one could show that they each involve sublimations of it. Moreover, an argument can be made for regarding sacrifice as one of the main threads that link Vedic religion to post-Vedic Hinduism.

It has often been pointed out that the main bhakti deities of post-Vedic Hinduism—Vishnu, Shiva, and the Goddess—appear in relatively few hymns in the *Rig Veda* as compared, for instance, to Indra, Varuna, Agni, and Soma. In the Brahmanas, however, these future bhakti deities are singled out for highly prominent roles in the Vedic sacrifice. One hears repeatedly that "Vishnu is the sacrifice." He measures the sacrifice from within by his "three steps," a theme already present in the *Rig Veda*. Rudra-Shiva, on the other hand, is associated with impure and dangerous dimensions of what goes on at the periphery of the sacrifice. A Brahmanical litany of a hundred names, the *Shatarudriya*, praises him as the lord of outsiders: thieves, pilferers, cut-purses, etc. The goddess of prosperity (Shri), the chief "fruit" desired in many sacrifices, is represented in the Brahmanas, among other things, in the high altar (*uttaravedi*) that, in one myth, turns into a lioness that stands between the gods and *asuras* (enemies of the gods) before siding with the gods and bringing them prosperity (*shri*), her blessings. These traits anticipate those of the lion-riding goddess Durga, who in Puranic myths saves the gods from defeat by the asuras. It is thus from within the matrix of the Vedic sacrifice that the gods of bhakti and Hindu sectarianism first take on their definitions and their preeminence.

These same deities then take on incarnations in the *Mahabharata*, whose "sacrifice of battle" is clearly modeled on the Vedic sacrifice, in which the sacrificial implements are already referred to as weapons. Vishnu in the epic incarnates himself in Krishna; a portion (*amsha*) of Rudra-Shiva is embodied in the destructive figure of Ashvatthaman; and Shri incarnates herself in the chief heroine, Draupadi. The *Mahabharata* war is fought to relieve the burden of the goddess Earth, who receives the blood of the slain warriors, whom the text compares to animal victims.

Animal sacrifices, with major changes but also likely continuities, have been performed at royal festivals from Vedic through modern times. On the popular level, they are also performed for regional, caste, village, and temple deities, and especially goddesses, throughout India. One will read repeatedly that such goddesses are "bloodthirsty." But that is just another piece of unexamined colonialist and missionary rhetoric, or at least an idea that is in conflict with the Hindu view that deities (including not only Krishna, but Shiva and various goddesses) are the models for those who would act without desire (or thirst) for the fruits of their actions.

Throughout the transformations of the sacrifice from Vedic to post-Vedic times, it is also not just a question of live victims but of their "vegetarian" substitutes. The offering of coconuts is a conventional substitute for the offering of the human head. Pumpkins filled with red powder are cut, simulating the cutting of flesh. The lighting of camphor on a tray with offerings to wave before a temple deity replicates the role of the Vedic Agni, god of fire, as the medium through whom sacrifices are offered to the gods.

Moreover, it is not just a matter of the practice of making sacrificial offerings, but of distinctively Vedic continuities in the forms and apparatus of the sacrificial cult. Vedic religion is often stated to have been "aniconic," to have used no images of its deities, in contrast to the iconic worship of later temple Hinduism. But this is an oversimplification. It does seem that no icons were used in the worship of the Vedic gods. But the shapes of the Vedic sacrificial terrain, of the altars (square, circular, half-circled, tapered, and trapezoidal) upon it, and of ritual implements like the sacrificial post and the Vedic chariot, are visualized forms—envisioned, that is, by the Vedic sages or rishis, and thus "revealed" no less than their poetry and knowledge.

It has been argued that these forms persist in popular temple, folk, and even tribal Hinduism as a continuing legacy of the Vedic revelation. Temple Hinduism, even where it does not include blood sacrifice in its high Brahmanical tradition, would also incorporate transformations of the Vedic sacrifice in its geometric temple plans, tapered altars, temple chariots, Shiva-lingams (designed like the Vedic sacrificial post), and other implements and rites of worship (*puja*).

NEO-HINDUISM

Finally, there would seem to be a growing recognition that modern scholars make a precarious double claim when they argue, on the one hand, that their orientalist predecessors colluded with Hindu reformers to invent Hinduism (as if Western scholars could ever have had such impact), and, on the other hand, that current "postorientalist" Indologists are now positioned to undo the damage. As if in recognition of this immodest predicament, certain scholars have preferred to use the terms *neo-Hinduism* or *neo-Vedantic Hinduism* to describe many of the same reform movements. This terminology implies that there was indeed Hinduism prior to its alleged "invention."

Such scholars note that this neo-Hinduism builds upon ancient Hindu traditions while also transforming them. Thus Sarvapalli Radhakrishnan, for example, advocates a universalization of the Vedic principle of entitlement to receive Vedic teaching (thus no longer restricting it to upper-caste males), claims for Hinduism an impulse to social reform and an all-inclusive tolerance of other religions, and finds in ancient Hindu philosophical traditions a principle of harmonization (*samanvaya*) that can be extended to all the religions of humankind.

The claims that Hinduism is highly tolerant and that it offers unique possibilities for ecumenical dialogue are part of modern Hinduism's image as a world religion and are not without their complications for other religions that are to be tolerated. What is important here, however, is that these principles, drawn from within the tradition's own pasts, are ones by which Hinduism has recurrently sought to tolerate its own diversity and to harmonize itself.

Hinduism (life cycle). *See* four goals of life (Hinduism); Hindu domestic ritual; Hinduism (thought and ethics); Hinduism (worship); Kanyadana; sacred thread ceremony; women's rites (Hinduism).

Hinduism (mysticism). Hinduism is one of the most mystical in emphasis of the major religions because of the high value it places on interior experience. The interior dimension in the Hindu tradition might be said to have begun ca. 800 B.C., when it became accepted that the rewards of the Vedic sacrifice could be gained not only by full performance of the rites, but also by a mental performance of the rite's essentials. This turn led to an inward search for the deeper powers and realities within the human person that ran parallel to the outward search for the dominant realities and correspondences in the universe.

Wisdom Mysticism: It was largely from these two searches that Hindu wisdom mysticism was born, especially the varieties witnessed in the texts called Upanishads. The inward search terminated in *atman* (Skt., "self"), a person's permanent, irreducible essence. The outward search ended with *brahman,* the absolute reality, described down through the ages as "Being," "Consciousness," and "Joy." The supreme "correspondence," realization of which confers ultimate freedom, is that "this atman is brahman" (*Brihadaranyaka Upanishad* 4.4.5, and elsewhere). The fundamental reality of the human microcosm is thus seen to be the essence and source of the world-at-large, the macrocosm.

Knowledge gained through meditation or conferred by a wise teacher (*guru*) was the means to realization. Two tendencies well known in mystical literature pervade the Upanishads: the Absolute (brahman) is viewed as all, and brahman is viewed as emphatically One. Further, though one's own meditative and other effort is strongly required, effort will not suffice of itself: "This Atman is not to be obtained by instruction, nor by intellect, nor by much learning. He is to be obtained only by the one whom He chooses; to such a one that Atman reveals His own person" (*Mundaka Upanishad* 3.2.3). Other characteristically mystical images abound in the Upanishads, notably that of selves/souls as sparks from the divine Fire and that of atman as "smaller than a grain of rice" yet "greater than the sky" (*Chandogya Upanishad* 3.14.2).

Yoga: Yoga, a "discipline" whose forms are manifold and whose origins reach back to very ancient India, is defined by Patanjali as "the cessation of the movements of the mind" (*Yogasutras* 1.1.2). But far from seeking to obliterate consciousness, the yoga practitioner (*yogin*) masters both conscious and subconscious to attain what has been called "transconsciousness." Yoga brings to bear a moral, physical, respiratory, and mental discipline of a thoroughness unparalleled in human history upon its goal of liberating the "person" from "nature," or "matter," into his or her proper (and permanent) state. Yoga meditation causes the repeated, mutual deepening of knowing and being that characterizes authentic mysticism. Both the intensity of dedication and the relentless interiority of yoga discipline, as well as the meditative experiences generated, merit the name *mysticism*. But so also does the renunciation of the magical powers such as feather-lightness and disappearance, which are mastered as by-products of the ever deeper meditative process; these are cast off so that the yogin can go "naked," as it were, into eternity.

Advaita Vedanta ("Nondualism"): The eighth-century philosopher-mystic Shankara established Advaita Vedanta as the dominant wisdom interpretation of the Upanishads. Brahman as "One" is seen to be so much more real than brahman as "Many" that the material universe itself is declared to be an "illusion" (*maya*) by comparison with brahman. A disciple, whose desire to break free from the world must exceed the desire to get out of a burning house, will then be guided—by the right guru—through constant "hearing" of the Upanishads, "thinking" about them and the commentaries on them, and, finally, "deep, repeated meditation" until saving wisdom dawns. There is then no more birth; the realized atman becomes brahman.

Love Mysticism: The Hindu tradition's first and greatest synthesis of "devotion" (*bhakti*) with both Upanishadic and yogic wisdom is the *Bhagavad Gita* (ca. 200 B.C.–A.D. 200). In the *Gita* Krishna is the supreme object of yoga meditation, the supreme model for performance of duty, the "Supreme Self," the "Supreme Brahman," and the grace-giving "Supreme Person" who "loves well" and thus urges his beloved to attain definitively to him by devotion. The *Gita*'s mysticism is thus decisively theistic and is probably the first kind of Hindu mysticism that can be practiced realistically by a householder who remains in the world.

A bhakti much more emotional—thus more often defined simply as "love"—arose in South India in about the sixth century. Passionate love for the deity—Vishnu/Krishna for many, Shiva for many others, the goddess Durga/Kali for some—became both the means and the end. Ecstasies resulting from possession by the deity or other types of love madness were adornments rather than defects for these love mystics. Tamil-language poetic conventions were used to create heart-rending songs of separation from the deity as well as celebrations of union, as happened later in Persian and Spanish mysticism. And imaginative meditation was used to project oneself into the deity's scriptural games and exploits.

Vaishnava Mysticism: Two varieties of love mysticism can be seen in the South Indian tradition of Ramanuja (eleventh century): the *Gita*'s bhakti as described above; and absolute "surrender" to Vishnu, whose grace is so plentiful and freely given that no prerequisites (such as learning, discipline, or eligibility by caste, all of which are required for the *Gita*'s path) can stand in its way. This distinction between step-by-step devotion according to scriptural law and ecstatic love in response to Vishnu/Krishna's grace, lavished on those he chooses, is important for other Vaishnava traditions as well, especially those of Vallabha (1479–1531) and Caitanya (1486–1533). In these last two another important path is added: an aesthetic/theological mysticism in which the devotee, or her or his guru, chooses a person from Krishna's scriptural games as a model. By conforming oneself imaginatively in meditation to this model, one deepens one's love for Krishna, usually according to one of four relationships: servant/Master, friend/Friend, parent/Child, or beloved/Lover. Such love is rewarded upon death by entry, in a form like that of one's model, into Krishna's Eternal Game. This deliberate meditative worship has been called "an aesthetic yoga."

Shaiva Mysticism and Name Mysticism: The Tamil Shaiva and Virashaiva systems most emphasize love of Shiva. One Virashaiva teaching echoed in all other Hindu systems—indeed in mysticism generally—says that, to the movement of constant expansion and engagement that is Shiva's creation, brought about by his power of "magic" or "illusion" (*maya*), the sole sufficient countermove is the disengagement brought about by Shiva's power of bhakti and his grace.

A further characteristic of Hindu love mysticism is constant recitation of and meditation on the name or names of the deity. In this, even those who emphasize the deity's namelessness call out to "Name" (Hindi *nam*), while lovers of a very specific god sing, for example, "The Thousand Names of Vishnu."

Tantric Mysticism: Certain Shaiva and Goddess-worshiping (Shakta) traditions place significant emphasis on bhakti and wisdom, but are really best described as Tantric. Tantric mysticism goes to great lengths to complete the microcosm/macrocosm equivalence mentioned above by actualizing not just the soul (atman), but the entire human body as a detailed microcosmic version of the universe. In this sense Tantrism completes an implicit mystical synthesis of Indian religion. Hindu Tantrism accomplishes this chiefly by means of a rigorous physical, psychological, symbolic, and mystical yoga in which, through advanced breath control and deep meditation, the Goddess-power (*kundalini*) is caused to ascend along a path roughly parallel to the spine and finally to unite with the God-power (Shiva) in the brain. This union is experienced as a resolving and nullifying of all opposites, even that of subject and object. *See also* atman; brahman; maya; path of devotion; six systems of Indian philosophy; Tantra; Vedanta; yoga.

Hinduism (performing arts). The dazzling variety of forms and traditions in Indian dance, drama, and music reflects India's cultural diversity. Like other Indian phenomena, even closely related forms in the performing arts are distinguished from each other on the basis of language, conventions, the socioreligious identity of the performers, the audience, the arena, and context of performance. Nevertheless, music, dance, and drama form a coherent system in which all three arts are intrinsically linked to one another and share certain fundamental aesthetic and cultural assumptions. The Indian performing arts have at least three characteristics in common. First, the boundaries between classical and folk elements, between the elite and the popular, have always been fluid; the various traditions have continually interacted with each other and enriched each other, creating fresh syntheses. Second, the development of the performing arts at all levels has been profoundly influenced by a unified classical aesthetic theory formulated early in their history. Last, although the arts have been important in all the major Indian religions, they have been shaped above all by Hinduism in terms of their cultural function as well as of their content. This has meant that music, dance, and drama have always been connected with sacred matters either directly, through their content and function, or indirectly, through the conception of artistic performance as a transcendent activity.

Drama: Classical Sanskrit drama is the logical starting point for a discussion of the Indian arts, for it is the original locus of a general aesthetic for all the arts, including literature. According to the oldest and most authoritative text on classical drama, the Sanskrit *Natyashastra* of Bharata (ca. third century B.C.), the aim of the performing arts is to evoke in the viewer or reader an aesthetic experience that is really a psychological state, the artistically refined counterpart of eight (later nine) basic human emotions (*bhava*). By describing, enacting, or otherwise suggesting these emotions in their several contexts and developmental phases, the corresponding aesthetic mood or flavor (*rasa*, "essence," "juice") is created in the audience. Drama (*natya*) is the most complete of the arts, since it is here that rasa can be evoked at its best, through a combination of means, which the *Natyashastra* characterizes as the four kinds of *abhinaya* (expressive enactment) relating to speech, physical movement and gesture, cos-

In Brindavan, India (1976), Krishna's home and the site of his romance with Radha, a young Brahman boy assumes the role of Krishna in the drama (*rasalila*) of the loves of Krishna.

tume and makeup, and the expression of emotion. Poetry, dance (*nritya*), and music (*samgita*) are thus intrinsic aspects of dramatic performance.

The *Natyashastra* presents classical drama as a creation of the gods; modern scholars have suggested that it developed in the context of particular Vedic sacrifices. Whatever its origin, the earliest fully developed classical plays in Sanskrit available to us reflect the sophisticated culture of the Gupta court (fourth–seventh centuries) and show that such plays were written and performed for the entertainment of a courtly audience. The ten types of plays are defined and described in the tenth-century treatise *Dasarupaka* of Dhanamjaya.

The *Shakuntala*, of Kalidasa, preeminent dramatist and writer of the Gupta age, is the most beloved of Indian plays, celebrated for its evocation of aesthetic mood. *Shakuntala* is also the classic exemplar of the themes, structure, and conventions of the Sanskrit theater. Taking a tale from the older epic *Mahabharata*, Kalidasa masterfully depicts the course of the love between King Dushyanta and the beautiful Shakuntala. The king and the girl meet at her adoptive father's hermitage, are doomed to separation and suffering by a sage's curse, and are reunited when the king's memory of Shakuntala is restored by the recovery of the ring he had given her. Every aspect of the play contributes to the evocation of the dominant rasa, the erotic: the tightly structured plot unfolds in stages as a map of the emotional states of the characters, the beauty and valor of the girl and the king, their characteristic virtue, the setting, language, imagery, mime, even the clown's (*vidushaka*) wit. Poetic description and mimed action combine in the depiction of the king chasing a deer or of Shakuntala taking leave of her friends at the hermitage. Elegant Sanskrit verse alternates with plainer prose, and with speech in the Prakrit vernacular. The happy ending of the *Shakuntala* is typical of Sanskrit drama: the absence of tragedy reflects an important way in which the principles of *karma* (the consequences of meritorious or demeritorious action) and cyclical time are put to work in the classical literature to present an ideal world. Most Sanskrit plays focus on the erotic and the heroic moods, reflecting the preoccupations of the courtly civilization.

Despite their orientation to an audience of elites, the Sanskrit treatises on drama are fully aware of the diverse popular theatrical styles that have continued to develop and flourish in the various linguistic-cultural regions of India. The regional traditions contain much that can be identified as folk, yet have sophisticated conventions and classical traits of their own; they also share some of the stylistic devices of Sanskrit drama, such as the role of the *sutradhara*, the stage manager (lit., "he who holds the strings"). Composed in the spoken regional languages and dialects, the traditional theaters are among the chief means through which the masses of India encounter the narratives of the gods and heroes from the Puranas and the epics *Ramayana* and *Mahabharata*. The regional drama articulates a wide range of cultural experience: Yakshagana, the theater of rural Karnataka, presents pan-Indian myths in the context of spirit cults and ritual peculiar to the region; the Gujarati Bhavai pays little attention to the epic and Puranic tradition; the Hindi Rasalila of Vrindavan focuses entirely on the mythology of Krishna. Each regional theater makes selective and creative use of the expressionistic possibilities of theater: color symbolism, costumes and makeup, staging, narrative techniques, and music and dance. Owing to their strong emphasis on expressive mime, music, and dance, a number of traditional dramatic styles such as Kathakali are classified as dance rather than as theater. Modern Indian playwrights and directors have imaginatively incorporated aspects of the traditional theaters into their plays to create a vital Indian theater for the modern age.

Dance: Classical dance is depicted in Buddhist, Hindu, and Jain art and sacred and secular literature, including sculpture, stories, plays, and treatises from the earliest times onward. From these sources we learn that dance was at once a sacred and a secular activity. Courtesans who are skilled in the art of dance are important characters in the *Mricchakatika*, a Sanskrit play of the Gupta era, and in the Tamil national epic *Cilappatikaram* (sixth century). The Hindu god Shiva is Nataraja, king of dancers, the god who dances out the creation and destruction of the universe, and the lord of the drama and dance. The ancient institution of female temple dancers continued until recently in the Bharata Natyam and Odissi traditions of southern and eastern India. In these and other forms we see the systematic development of the elaborate language of abhinaya in dance, consisting of facial expression depicting bhava; hand gesture (*hasta*); and stances (*karana*) and body movement (*angahara*) described in the *Natyasastra*. Particularly in the solo dance styles such as Bharata Natyam the dancer explicates the erotic rasa in the dual contexts of earthly love and devotion to God (*bhakti*) through the depiction of the heroine (*nayika*) in the various phases of love. The different styles place varying emphases on lyricism, narrative, and drama: the Odissi dance focuses on the love of Krishna and

Radha as portrayed in the twelfth-century Sanskrit lyric poem *Gita Govinda;* Bharata Natyam pieces are directed to various Hindu gods, while the North Indian Kathak relates to vernacular lyrics on the loves of Krishna.

Music: Music has ancient sacred associations in Indian civilization. It is associated with the Vedic chant as sacred sound in its musical aspect (*saman*). In the indigenous pre- and non-Vedic religions of India, music, drumming, and dance have always been used as means for access to and control of the sacred. The devotional song continues to be an important lyric form in popular (*bhajan, kirtan*) as well as classical music (*dhrupad, kriti*). The diverse regional styles of Indian music continue to share the basic principles described in classical treatises such as the *Natyasastra:* the primacy of melody and melodic line (and a corresponding absence of harmony); the notions of *shruti, raga,* and *tala;* improvisation; and an oral pedagogic tradition. The raga is a scale type consisting of five to seven specific notes differentiated by microtonal pitch (shruti). Most Indian ensemble performances are devoted to solo vocal or instrumental (flute, veena, sitar) improvisation on specific ragas, followed by short compositions and solfeggio improvisation within the boundaries of a well-defined cycle of beats (tala); the instrumental accompanists, including the important percussionist (mridangam, tabla drum), follow, echo, and respond to the lead performer in complex rhythmic and textural counterpoint.

After the thirteeth century, Indian classical music split into the Hindusthani (North Indian) and Carnatic (South Indian) traditions. Each tradition has its own ragas, talas, forms, and conventions. Hindusthani music flourished under the patronage of North Indian rulers, both Muslim and Hindu, at centers such as Lucknow. The golden age of Carnatic music is embodied in a devotional compositional form (*kriti*) developed by Tyagaraja and others in Tanjore during Maratha rule (seventeenth–nineteenth centuries). Hindusthani music reflects Perso-Arabic and Islamic religious and courtly influences, while Carnatic music has retained its Hindu orientation. The Hindusthani tradition has systematically refined the ancient associations of ragas with particular moods, times of day, and seasons. Both traditions reflect the vast lyrical output of the poet-saints in the various regional languages in the devotional movements all over India, beginning with the Tamil Nayanars and Alvars in the seventh century, whose hymns are used in temple ritual and personal devotion.

Bengali drummer in Brindavan, India (1976), participating in ritual singing (*kirtan*) of the names of Krishna and Radha, a mode of worship established by the ecstatic poet Chaitanya (1486–1533).

Hinduism (poetry). Poetry plays an important, central role in the Hindu religious tradition. The Sanskrit *mantras* (sacred utterances) that comprise the hymns of the *Rig Veda* (ca. 1200 B.C.), praising the gods and accompanying the sacrificial ritual, are forms of *vac*, sacred speech, itself a manifestation of primeval sacred sound. The *rishi*, the Vedic seer-poet who intuitively received and transmitted the hymns, is also the prototype for Valmiki, author of the epic poem *Ramayana* (500 B.C.–A.D. 400). Spontaneously expressing his compassion for a bird whose mate was killed by a hunter, Valmiki is said to have given birth to the *shloka* meter and the art of poetry (*kavya*) in Sanskrit, becoming *adikavi*, the first poet. The epic poem is also a sacred narrative resulting from the seer-poet's meditative vision of the deeds of prince Rama, Vishnu incarnate, born a warrior to destroy demons who are threatening the cosmic moral order.

In the *Ramayana* and in Vyasa's *Mahab-harata*, the two Sanskrit epics of oral traditional origin, heroes shade off into gods, and gods rub shoulders with men. If the *Ramayana's* hero is a divine incarnation, Krishna, another incarnation of Vishnu, takes an active part in the central action of the *Mahabharata*, the great war between the Kuru princes. Kampan's *Irama-vataram* (Descent of Rama, twelfth century) and Tulasi Das's *Ramacaritmanas* (Holy Lake of the Acts of Rama, sixteenth century), beloved versions of the Rama narrative in vernacular languages (Tamil and Hindi, respectively), reflect a growing emphasis on the divine aspects of Rama's persona, to which the other characters, as well as the audience, are expected to react in a devotional mode. Yet Rama's "human" appeal as a model for *dharmic* (ethnical-social) role-playing is very much the concern of these *bhakti* (devotional) *Ramayanas* as well.

The conjunction of human-divine relationships, and of models for ethical behavior, finds its quintessential expression in the *Bhagavad Gita, The Song of the Lord,* located in the *Mahabharata's* sixth book. The *Gita* has been the seminal textbook of Hindu faith and practice, offering a creative synthesis of fundamental concepts such as *yoga* (discipline), *karma* (the consequences of meritorious or demeritorious action), class *dharma* (social responsibility), and bhakti (devotion). Over the centuries successive interpreters, including Mahatma Gandhi (d. 1948), have drawn upon the *Gita's* poetic language and metaphors in responding to its complex ethical message.

In India, not all verse is poetry, and classical poetry (*kavya*) includes drama and prose. According to the classical poetic theory, the only true poems are those works whose primary aim is aesthetic response. *Alamkara*, figures of speech, dominate the classical poetry addressed to kings and connoisseurs, and serve as the prime examples in poetic theory. In the religious context the focus on poetry as ornate speech has been most productive in the genre of the *stotra*, poems (mainly in Sanskrit) praising specific Hindu divinities. The classical aesthetic categories of *dhvani* (suggestion) and *rasa* (aesthetic flavor), on the other hand, have been transformed by the poetry of emotional bhakti (devotional) poetry. Kalidasa (fourth century), India's most famous classical poet, is primarily a "court" poet, yet his work is suffused with a consciousness of the sacred and pervaded by the central themes of Hindu myth and ethics. In the drama *Shakuntala*, Kalidasa explores the relationship between sacred duty and desire, while he devotes the long poems *The Birth of Kumara* and *The Dynasty of Raghu* to the contemplation of the marriage of Shiva with Parvati and the sacred dimensions of kingship, respectively.

The lyric impulse has been the moving, expressive force in the popular devotional movements that swept India between the sixth and seventeenth centuries. Prototypical of the bhakti hymns are the songs of the Tamil saint-poets (the Nayanars and Alvars, ca. sixth–eighth centuries) dedicated to Shiva and Vishnu in the temples of South India. The Tamil saints' songs are revered in their sectarian canons as equal to the Vedas in sanctity. Spanning all the regions of India, bhakti poems—hymns, *bhajans*, and *kirtanas*—reflect the range of bhakti religiosity, from the celebration of the mythic and iconographic forms of God to the fierce iconoclasm and reformist devotional fervor of the South Indian Virashaiva poets (twelfth century) and the North Indian antisectarian saint Kabir (fifteenth century). Bhakti songs have in common an emphasis on emotional devotion, on the saint-devotee's relationship with God, and on the saintly persona as much as on the deity.

The bhakti poets sing of the bond between devotee and god in metaphors of diverse human relationships, settling on the relationship between lovers as the definitive model capable of fully expressing the anguish as well as the ecstasy of devotional love. Over and over, they use the metaphors and conventions of courtly love poetry in the context of sacred love—the woman pining for her absent lover, the many moods of the relationship, the joyous but all too brief union of the lovers. In relation to the deity, the bhakti saint is the female lover. In this respect the women saints, active in one of the few arenas in which we hear women's voices in Indian literature, clearly had the advantage: in the passionate love songs that the North Indian woman poet Mira-Bai (sixteenth century) addressed to Krishna we may discern psychological authenticity, attested by their enormous popularity.

Saints of either gender had access to the archetypal myth of divine love, the passion of the cowherd Krishna and the milkmaid Radha. The most complete bhakti narration of the myth is Jayadeva's (twelfth century) lyric-dramatic poem in Sanskrit, the *Gita Govinda, Krishna's Love Song.* But the genius of later bhakti songs is also captured in the vignettes of the changing moods of Radha and Krishna's love, offered, for example, in the songs of the Bengali Vaishnava poets (sixteenth century). The Bengali Vaishnava teacher Caitanya (sixteenth century) used an approach far removed from that of Abhinavagupta (tenth century), the renowned classical authority on aesthetic philosophy who argued that the

aesthetic response to poetry (the rasa experience) was a legitimate form of the ultimate religious experience of transcendence. Caitanya transformed the classical rasa doctrine with his theory of the enjoyment of Radha-Krishna love as the ultimate aesthetic experience, manifesting itself as a new rasa called *madhurya,* "sweet delight." Hindu lyricism continues to flourish in such different areas of Indian literature and art as the song repertoire of North and South Indian classical music, and the poems of twentieth-century writers Rabindranath Tagore (Bengali) and Subramaniya Bharati (Tamil). *See also* Alvar; Bhagavad Gita; Caitanya; Gita Govinda; Mahabharata; mantra; Nayanar; Ramayana; Rig Veda; Tulsi Das.

Hinduism (temple art and architecture).

Brahmanic Hindu temples are usually dedicated to the worship of one of the three main divinities of Hinduism: Shiva, Vishnu, or the Goddess (Devi). Each is the chief divinity of a major Hindu sect. Occasionally, Brahmanic temples are dedicated to other deities: e.g., the sun god Surya (at Konarak, Orissa, built on the plan of a solar chariot, and at Martand, Kashmir) or the demiurge Brahma.

The essential components of a Hindu temple are few, in spite of the many ancillary shrines and chapels that can be added, in time, to its basic plan. Most important is the sanctuary, called the womb chamber (Skt. *garbha griha*).

Architecturally, the womb chamber, also called a womb house, is small (usually square), without windows, dim, and deep inside the temple complex. It contains the temple's most sacred image, representing, generally, the cosmic nature of the temple's divinity. The garbha griha of a Shiva temple will contain the *linga,* sign of Shiva's transcendental nature and creative power. Often the sanctuary has no further imagery or decoration.

Theologically, the divinity's energy radiates from the womb chamber, creating the forms of other deities seen on the walls of the temple, particularly along the lines of the four directions and their interstices. Divine forms found at the centers and corners are imbued with special potency. Divine forms aligned most directly in relation to the womb chamber are the most important.

The womb chamber is fronted by one (later, several) pillared porches (*mandapas*), the second essential component of the temple. Dance performances and recitations honoring the presiding deity take place in a mandapa. The doorway connecting the mandapa to the garbha griha can be decorated with auspicious symbols.

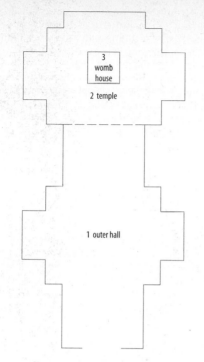

Hindu temple

While Hindu temples may be small buildings or immense complexes covering many square acres and soaring up many stories, covered with statuary and pierced with windows and doors, their basic underlying structure is simple. After circumambulating the outside of the building the worshiper enters, frequently through (1) an outer hall (*madapa*) or a series of antechambers until (2) the sacred temple proper (*prasada*) is reached. At the exact center of the prasada is (3) a square inner chamber, the "womb house" (*garbha griha*), containing the central sacred object. The garbha griha is not only the central, innermost part of the temple complex, it is also roofed with the highest tower (*shikhara*). The various buildings and rooms of the temple (and temple complex) provide a series of ambulatories so that the process of circumambulation can continue in interior space.

Doorways, critical points of transition, are adorned with symbols that confer blessings on the devotee: e.g., a vase brimming with vegetation (a life symbol), amorous couples (symbolic of fecundity), and vegetal and floral scrolls (suggestive of abundance). The main doorway often shows two females carved on either side: anthropomorphic representations of the Ganges and Jumna rivers, which purify the devotee entering the sanctum.

The temple, which can be made of stone, wood, or brick, usually faces east. In this way, the god of the sanctuary can arise with the first rays of dawn as they stream through the complex.

A Hindu temple is the temporary residence on earth of the transcendental god, who descends into the icon properly consecrated for his occupancy. Ostensibly a god manifests himself in an apprehensible form to provide humans a means for worship. Clockwise circumambulation (*pradakshina*) of the object or the temple itself is done for veneration. Ambulatories allow for circumambulation around the sanctuary and around the temple in wide courtyards.

The plan of a Hindu temple, together with the measurements of its structural components, are subject to specific rules to ensure that the temple achieves its purpose, which is to replicate some metaphysical person or place. The temple may be the house and body of the indwelling god. It may also be conceived of as the world mountain or the cosmic axis. Choice of temple sites and architectural terminology demonstrate these intentions. The name given to the temple tower is *shikhara*, "mountain peak." Some temples are called Meru, the mountain at the center of the universe, or Kailasa, the mountain residence of Shiva. Sometimes grottos resembling mountainous caves were cut out of the rock to become Hindu shrines.

To ensure that a temple will be built in harmony with the cosmos that it replicates, its ground plan includes a geometric diagram (*mandala*) upon which the temple is erected. The diagram is usually a square divided into smaller squares; it may contain the drawing of the Universal Man, Purusha, arranged diagonally in such a way that each small square contains a part of his body. This diagram is called the Vastupurusha Mandala.

These considerations did not restrain the production of rich and varied architectural styles. Temple styles can be divided into three categories based upon three distinctive temple towers. First is the Nagara or northern type with its characteristic curvilinear spire, emphasizing a continuous vertical profile. Second is the Dravida or southern type, whose tower achieves height by means of a series of ascending horizontal terraces. The third is the barrel-roofed Vesara type, largely restricted to central and western India. Other distinctions can also differentiate one "order" from the other. Styles overlap and borrowing occurs, so regional differences are not absolute.

Hindu Temples in North India: The Dashavatara, a sixth-century Vishnu temple at Deoghar (Madhya Pradesh), begins to show the distinctively convex northern superstructure. The cubical sanctuary, facing west, is entered through an intricately carved portal composed of a series of projecting lintels and cornices decorated with auspicious symbols. On the center plaque over the door appears an image of Vishnu on the serpent to show the sanctuary is his. The sanctuary's three other outer walls display large carvings of scenes from Vishnu's legends.

The grottolike Shiva temple on the island of Elephanta (in Bombay harbor) is extraordinary for its high-quality sculptures and its innovative biaxial plan to accommodate two main icons. The western end of the east-west axis contains the linga in the garbha griha. The southern end of the north–south axis features a large torso with multiple heads of Sadashiva (17 feet, 10 inches) representing god in the process of manifesting himself.

Temples in Orissa from the seventh to the eleventh centuries exhibit stages in the development of northern style's elegantly curved spire, or shikhara. The seventh-century Parashurameshvara Temple to Shiva in Bhuvaneshvar displays the early Nagara profile. Rising above the sanctuary (as do all Hindu temple towers), it has four sides, each composed of a central vertical projection and two lateral projections, in lower relief, to the right and left of the central projection. The main western side, on its central projection, shows the unfolding of Shiva from subtle to manifest form. The largest relief, the lowest one that terminates the unfolding process, illustrates Shiva's triumph over the demon Ravana shaking Mt. Kailasa: a divine *lila* (act of creative play), it displays a more material form than the subtler forms that precede it. The shikhara's capping stone, a large ribbed ring-stone (*amalaka*), is repeated in smaller versions at the corners of the spire's successive stories. Repetition of forms where they become smaller and ornamental is an essential schema in the development of the temple tower and accounts for an internal logic and organic rhythm in its elevation. On the three outer walls of the sanctuary appear images of Shiva's family.

Perhaps the climax of the soaring northern temple tower is the eleventh-century Kandariya Mahadeo Temple at Khajuraho. Its shikhara rises 102 feet. Its ground plan, expanding by a succession of halls unified to the sanctuary by a common podium and by a series of roofs connected to the main roof (over the sanctuary), simulates smaller mountaintops leading up to the main peak. The pradakshina path, included in the temple structure itself, resembles a path cut into the mountain. *Kandariya* means cave and refers to Shiva's Himalayan home on Mt. Kailasa.

Hindu Temples in South India: The southern and central styles are both incipient at Mamallapuram, on the seacoast south of Madras. Five temples called Rathas ("chariots"), cut from granite

boulders in the late seventh and early eighth centuries, document the early Dravida and Vesara styles. The Bhima Ratha is a long building with the barrel roof. The Dharmaraja Ratha reveals a pyramid-shaped shikhara, attaining height by three horizontal terraces, each shorter than the one below. The tower, capped by a bulbous dome (*stupika*), already contains the main elements of the southern "order."

The first southern structural temple, the Shore Temple of the eighth century, also stands at Mamallapuram. This granite temple has three sanctuaries and two towers resembling attenuated versions of the Dharmaraja Ratha's tower. Repetition of architectural elements also occurs in the Dravida tower; at the Shore Temple, smaller versions of the crowning stupika recur in successive terraces. An internal passageway for circumambulation goes around the main shrine.

Forty miles from Mamallapuram, further evolution of the Dravida style can be seen in the eighth-century Kailasanatha and Vaikunthaperumal temples, both at Kanchipuram. The Kailasanatha, a Shiva temple, has an elaborate enclosing wall pierced by gateways surmounted by the Vesara roof that is reminiscent of the form seen on the Bhima Ratha. Gateways (*gopuras*), huge in size, become characteristic of late South Indian Hindu temple architecture.

During the same period, intense activity also occurred in central India. Perhaps the most spectacular achievement was at Ellora (Maharashtra), where the largest rock-cut temple was executed in a continuation of the southern style. The Kailasa Temple at Ellora is about 276 feet in length by 154 feet in width and 100 feet high. Typical southern architectural components include a molded base on which rests the temple wall, which is punctuated by deeply recessed reliefs framed by slender pilasters; the overhanging eaves; and a tower composed of a series of diminishing terraces that display reduplication of larger architectural forms. Cut from living rock are not only the temple proper, with its sanctuary and shikhara, and the pillared mandapa fronted by a porch, but also the entire temple precinct, including a shrine to Shiva's bull, Nandi; gigantic free-standing pillars on either side of Nandi's shrine, and an elaborate entrance portico; five small chapels around the temple's main sanctuary; and subsidiary shrines in the surrounding rock wall connected by bridges to the main temple. Sculptural reliefs introduce the element of drama into narrative art, using light and shade to enhance impact.

A culmination of Dravidian temple architecture is found at Madurai. In the seventeenth century, the great Madurai Minakshi temple expanded so much that it resembles a city. Its courtyard is filled with ancillary shrines, a temple tank for ritual ablutions, dance halls, pillared pavilions, priests' quarters, and stalls selling food and flower offerings. A boundary wall surrounding the entire compound is punctuated by four monumental gopuras that overshadow the tower of the main shrine. The gopuras are entirely covered with brightly painted stucco deities. Gigantic in scale, the temple nevertheless is linked closely in its architectural details to preceding developments in the Dravida style. *See also* circumambulation; guardian deities, Hindu; Hinduism; Hinduism (worship); Jainism; mandala; temple.

Hinduism (thought and ethics). Hindu ethics encompass the aims of life, the norms of conduct, and the virtues and vices that have evolved in Hindu life, thought, and practice over three millennia. Hinduism does not have any formal treatises on ethics, but according to the Hindu ethicists (Skt. *dharmashastrins*), the sources of Hindu ethics are revealed and nonrevealed scriptural literature (*shruti* and *smriti*), established usage and examples of saints and sages, and approval by one's inner conscience.

Aims and Stages of Life: The "aims of life" (*purushurthas*) consist of wealth and statecraft (*artha*), pleasure and happiness (*kama*), duty and virtue (*dharma*), and liberation (*moksha*) from earthly existence. Moksha is the highest and is variously described as a state of unalloyed bliss, the self's absorption in the absolute, and enjoying the beatitude of the deity's presence. The first three aims of life are empirical, but moksha is transcendental. The pursuit of moksha, according to some ethicists, requires one to undergo the life stage of an ascetic (*sannyasin*). Hindu thinkers have divided human life into four stages (*ashramas*). The first stage is that of the student (*brahmacharin*), in which religious and spiritual education is pursued. The second is that of the householder (*grihastha*), in which the individual is married and discharges familial and social obligations. The third stage is that of a forest dweller (*vanaprastha*); the individual retires to a forest to meditate on the spiritual truths. The last stage is that of an ascetic who has renounced the world and is free from social and ritualistic obligations. The first three stages of life are governed by dharma, but the ascetic stage is beyond dharma.

Dharma and Karma: Dharma, which is the nearest equivalent to modern conceptions of morality, has only an empirical reality. Moksha is the

transcendental reality and is beyond good and evil. Some ethicists maintain that the first three human aims, especially dharma, are necessary conditions for the attainment of moksha. Though dharma has no transcendental reality, it is metaphysically related to *karma*, or the law of moral causation. According to the law of karma, every deed, including moral deeds, binds the individual to the empirical world and determines one's moral status. We are, according to karma, what we have done in the past, and we shall be in the future what we do now. Moral freedom and moral determinism are thus combined in karma. Good deeds bring into one's life good effects and bad deeds bring bad effects. Since the fruition of these effects takes more than one lifetime, rebirth doctrine became a necessary corollary to karma to assure that death is not the end of all moral action. The enjoyment and suffering of the fruits of one's actions presuppose an appropriate body, self, and social group in which this takes place. The caste system provides the social groups in and through which the law of karma operates. A person's birth in a specific caste also indicates a measure of moral progress achieved in previous lives.

Norms of Conduct: Dharma in Hindu ethics imposes duties on the individual. Rights and entitlements are given secondary status. Hindu ethicists divide an individual's dharma or duties into specific dharma (*visheshadharma*) and general dharma (*sadharanadharma*). Specific dharma consists of an individual's duties to one's caste (*varnadharma*), duties appropriate to one's stage in life (*ashramadharma*), duties specific to the role one is playing (a father, mother, etc.). General dharma imposes duties equally on all members of the community irrespective of caste, role, and stage of life. Though dharma is conceived as eternal, exceptions can be made when dealing with difficult situations (*apaddharma*). Hindu thinkers also maintain that dharma changes with changing times.

Virtues and Vices: The virtues and vices (*guna-gunas*) are not specific to one's caste or role but general norms of conduct everyone ought to pursue. Early Hindu sacred literature recognizes three cardinal virtues, namely, self-control (*dama*), charity (*datta*), and compassion (*daya*). Other prominent virtues include nonviolence (*ahimsa*), truthfulness (*satya*), non-stealing (*asteya*), nonpossession (*aparigraha*), purity (*shaucha*), detachment (*vairagya*), fortitude (*virya*), and fearlessness (*abhaya*). Of all these, nonviolence is considered the most important. It is not just a negative injunction against killing, but a positive prescription to treat all life, not merely human life, as sacred. The vices recognized in Hinduism include lust (*kama*), anger (*krodha*), greed (*lobha*), delusion (*moha*), pride (*mada*), and malice (*matsarya*) and should be avoided in thought, word, and deed. **See also** ahimsa; caste; dharma; four goals of life (Hinduism); karma ; liberation.

Hinduism (worship). In the Hindu tradition, worship takes many forms, among which are recita-

The bride's brother is pouring offerings of rice, symbolizing progeny, from a winnowing fan onto the outstretched hands of the Brahman bride and groom at a rural Hindu wedding in Karimpur, Uttar Pradesh, India.

tion of the name of the deity (Skt. *namajapa*), congregational singing (*samkirtana, bhajana*), night vigils of prayer and song (*jagarana*), oblations and fire sacrifices (*homa, yajna*), meditation (*dhyana*), and pilgrimage (*tirthayatra*). *Puja*, a ritual offering of hospitality to a god as a most welcome and honored guest, is one of the most popular forms of worship. Ritual bathing (*snana*) can be a form of worship in itself, but it also precedes most rites of worship as well as

life-cycle ceremonies (*samskara*): purity of mind and body are important prerequisites for Hindu worship. Gift giving (*dana*) and vows and fasts (*vrata*) may be undertaken to attract a god's attention and favor. In life-cycle ceremonies, memorial rites (*shraddha*), and rites of expiation (*prayashcitta*) the favor of the deity is sought through prayers and invocations. Festivals (*utsava, yatra*) are grand occasions for worship. One may witness several forms of worship in one festival, be it a one-day or month-long festival. All these forms of worship praise the deity while purifying the devotee.

Individual prayer is more prevalent than congregational forms of worship. A worshiper may concentrate on a mental image of a god or pray before a physical image (*murti*). A Hindu can worship daily or occasionally before the

A group of Hindu women from several households belonging to a Brahman lineage in Karimpur, India (1984), have prepared a mound of cow dung pierced by straws with cotton balls attached, which represents Lampblack Mother (Siyao Mata), the auspicious sign of the unity of their lineage. The winnowing baskets containing offerings are symbolic of the households' prosperity. The bundle of straws in the central basket will be used later in the ritual as a broom, sweeping poverty out of the women's path while sweeping sons under their upheld saris.

home shrine and never set foot in a temple. However, many do flock to temples, especially on festival days, for *darshana*, the sight of the divine image that brings auspicious blessings.

Sectarian Worship: The deity worshiped varies according to the sectarian and personal beliefs of the devotee. The major sectarian groups are the Vaishnavas, devotees of Lord Vishnu; the Shaivas, followers of Lord Shiva; and the Shaktas, worshipers of the Goddess. The image in which a deity is represented varies widely; however, there are some traditional pan-Indian forms. Vishnu is popularly depicted in the form of one of his incarnations, such as Rama or Krishna, who are traditionally flanked by their respective consorts, Sita and Radha. Shiva is worshiped in the form of the phallic-shaped *linga*. The Goddess, often symbolized by a triangle or a trident, is typically portrayed in a specific manifestation such as Kali, Durga, or Shri-Lakshmi. At the beginning of a worship service, the deity is invited by the devotee or priest to enter these images.

A home altar is generally crowded with images, pictures, and statues of many different deities and revered teachers, with the family deity (*kuladevata*) presiding from a central, slightly elevated position. Each deity receives attention, although the family deity or the deity whose feast day it is receives special offerings. Temples, though designed around one particular deity, also house many side altars to other deities, usually but not always within the same sectarian family. Each deity has a divine vehicle (for Shiva, the bull Nandi; for Vishnu, the eagle Garuda), which a devotee honors before entering the sanctum. If the temple is not centered around the elephant-headed Ganesha, one will often find him near the entrance, as he is the god of thresholds and obstacles. When visiting temples, devotees bring flowers, incense, sweets, pieces of clothing, and other offerings to please the deity. Each deity has preferred colors, flowers, leaves, scents, and foods, and vendors outside temples prepare platters of offerings that conform to the deity's tastes. Devotees hand their offerings to the priest or place them at the deity's foot. They may stay for a worship service scheduled for a particular time, sit in the temple hall reading devotional literature, listen to the singing of a local *bhajana* group, or make a private tour of the temple's shrines, offering a prayer and a flower to each deity.

Puja: The most visible form of Hindu worship in India today, found in both homes and tem-

Hindus performing devotion (*puja*) at the temple of Shiva Jaqqernath, Puri, India, by placing flower garlands on the image (1975).

ples, is *puja*. Puja is a worship service that honors a deity as a respected guest. In temples, daily pujas are performed by trained priests who are responsible for the waking, feeding, bathing, clothing, and praising of the deity. In households, both men and women conduct pujas before the home shrine. On special occasions they may call upon the expertise of the family priest

South Indian Hindu male carrying food offerings to Murukan, the most popular Tamil deity, in Paini, Tamil Nadu.

to direct the puja. Despite large crowds at a temple service eager for a glimpse of the deity and for a share of the blessing (*prasada*), puja is not a communal service of worship in the fashion of the Christian liturgy. It is a personal ritual of devotion in which the devotee offers service, prayers, and comforts to the god in exchange for the god's blessing. These offerings (*upacara*) have a set number and a ritually prescribed order. The sixteen-step puja is common in many temples and is performed on special occasions in the home, where the five-step puja is the daily norm.

The sixteen-step puja entails an invitation (*avahana*) to the deity to enter the image or place of worship and offering the deity a seat (*asana*) and water to wash his or her feet (*padya*), followed by a libation (*arghya*) and water for sipping to cleanse the mouth and lips (*acamana*). The image is then bathed (*abhisheka, snana*), dried, and presented with pieces of cloth or clothing (*vastra*) and a sacred thread (*yajnopavita*). Gifts of perfume or fragrant ointment (*gandha, anulepana*), flowers (*pushpa*), and incense (*dhupa*) are proffered to the deity and then placed at his or her feet. Oil lamps (*dipa*) and a meal of the deity's favorite foods (*naivedya*) provide the comforts of home in this ritual of hospitality. After the feasting of the deity, the worshiper circumambulates the image (*pradakshina*) and respectfully bows (*namaskara*) before the deity. Repeating the deity's holy name, the devotee throws flowers on the image (*mantrapushpa*) as the final offering. Waving of lamps (*arati*) accompanied by a devotional hymn often follows the puja. Food and flowers that have been received and blessed by the deity during the service are then shared among the devotees, who in partaking of the food partake of the god's grace and favor.

Puja in its simplest form is the welcoming and succoring of a most desired guest, the deity. This personal relationship with the deity that it seeks and cultivates is characteristic of most forms of Hindu worship, which developed within a climate of devotional fervor (*bhakti*). **See also** domestic ritual; Goddess (Hinduism); guardian deities, Hindu; Hinduism (festal cycle); puja; Shaivism; Shaktism; Shrivaishnavism; Vaishnavism.

Hinduism in America. *See* America, Hinduism in.

Hindu Renaissance, collective designation for various socioreligious movements that arose in India under the leadership of Hindu intellectuals in the nineteenth century. The Renaissance movements were initiated by upper-class Hindu men who were reacting to Western education (introduced among elites by the nineteenth century British colonial regime) and to British criticism of Hindu practices. Drawing selectively on sacred texts and other aspects of earlier Hindu traditions, Renaissance leaders constructed visions of a Hinduism that was both rooted in a glorious past and ready to move into a progressive future purged of long-standing social ills. Among the targets for reform were the caste system, polytheism, image worship, and oppression of widows.

The starkly monotheistic Brahmo Samaj movement led the way in Calcutta, seat of colonial government, under the leadership of Ram Mohun Roy (1772–1833), followed by Debendranath Tagore (1817–1905) and Keshhub Chunder Sen (1838–84). Most influential was the Arya Samaj movement in the Punjab, founded by Swami Dayananda Sarasvati (1824–83), an ascetic teacher who reformulated the "Aryan" Vedic religion in modern terms. Swami Vivekananda (1863–1902) extolled Vedanta philosophy in America and elsewhere and established the Ramakrishna Mission, a monastic organization dedicated to serving and educating disadvantaged groups in Indian society. *See also* Arya Samaj; Brahmo Samaj; Hinduism; Reform Hinduism.

hinin (hee-neen; Jap., "nonperson," "the misguided"), a Japanese term for beggar, outcast, or criminal. Of Buddhist origin, it originally referred to a demonic dragon or evil spirit.

Hippocrates (hip-pok'ruh-teez; 460–390 B.C.), celebrated Greek physician regarded as the father of scientific medicine; he is noted for having discounted the supernatural explanation of disease.

Hiranyagarbha (hi-ruhn'yuh-gahr'buh; Skt., "Golden Embryo"), in Vedic and later India, the first created being and source of all other creatures, he is identified with Prajapati in Vedic and with Brahma in later Hinduism. *See also* Prajapati; Veda, Vedism.

Hirata Atsutane (hee-rah-tah ah-ts*oo*-tah-nay; 1776–1843), scholar of the National Learning school (Kokugaku) who asserted the supremacy of Shinto. While rejecting Buddhism and Confucianism, he valorized and popularized the values of Japan's archaic past. *See also* Kokugaku; Shinto.

Hirsch, Samson Raphael (1808–88), important German Jewish author, essayist, and prayer book and Bible commentator, and a prominent pulpit rabbi in Frankfurt am Main. Hirsch's *The Nineteen Letters* and *Horeb* popularized the notion that strict adherence to Jewish law could be combined with an affirmation of secular culture. His teachings continue to guide Jewish Neo-Orthodoxy today. *See also* Orthodox Judaism.

historical religion, a type of religious system associated with linear time and most frequently attributed to Israel, in contrast to systems associated with cyclical time attributed to Near Eastern myth. This influential theoretical distinction, first made by the Pan-Babylonian School in the nineteenth century, was soon extended by scholars to include a distinction between a Hebraic historical consciousness and a Hellenic preoccupation with categories of space and an ahistorical structure of cyclical time. Subsequent historians of religion have appropriated and universalized the distinction between historical religion as the primary characteristic of the Judeo-Christian tradition in contrast to an "archaic ontology" of myth based upon an ahistorical "eternal return." Theologians have exploited this distinction to argue for the truth of a historically based biblical religion, in contrast to the mythic nature of non-Western religions. This distinction disregards the evidence that all religious systems employ both "historical" and "mythic," "linear," and "cyclical" concepts in their religious expressions. *See also* typology, classification.

historicism, the view that human beings are exclusively historical beings and that all human ideas, institutions, and ideals are historically contingent constructs that have significance only for their positions in place and time.

Historicism and Nineteenth-century Thought: Although the contextual understanding of human events has been documented since the seventeenth century, historicism emerges as an intellectual movement only in nineteenth-century German scholarship, especially in the areas of law, economics, and the humanities. Historicism was defined first by analogy with, and then as an alternative to, naturalism, the scientific, generalizing approach to nature promulgated by Enlightenment thinkers.

The law of existence, according to the historicists, is change, whether structured by the materialism of a particular culture or by a theory of developmental process such as evolution. Historicism is an extension of the secularization and naturalization of existence associated with Enlightenment thought, in which the measure of an assumed universal human nature became atomized into an infinite array of situated realities. It stands in opposition to any transcendental norm of religion or any metaphysical absolute of philosophy that holds human existence to be more than its circumstances. In opposition to the Enlightenment faith in reason to direct history, historicism represents the Romantic view of the autonomy of history, which understands reason itself to be a historical construct, meaningful and valid only in its setting. Reason itself, in this view, is located in the process upon which it reflects.

Perhaps most disturbing to both the Western religious and humanistic traditions, historicism temporalizes and thus relativizes the atemporal character previously attributed to moral judgments. As historical reflection is determined by its historical situation, so human values, according to this view, are rooted in the conditions of social existence, and are appropriate only to the historical and cultural contexts of their formulation. Value, in other words, becomes subject to historical explanation. The famous historicist manifesto to reconstruct the past "as it actually was" (Ger. *wie es eigentlich gewesen*) was intended to emphasize that history did not, like philosophy, properly make prescriptive or normative judgments. However, the nineteenth-century ascendency of the scientific ideal reshapes this disclaimer into the positivistic goals often attributed a more narrow "science" of history by which, it was held, the past might be definitively reconstructed. This objective view of historiography contributes to the establishment of history as a field of inquiry independent of philosophy and literature.

The new discipline of history was abetted by a nineteenth-century rise of nationalistic sentiment that supported collections of state records in national archives. This new availability of national historical materials, together with historicism's own emphasis on situational uniqueness and thus on cultural particularity, fostered a view of history as political process that established the agenda for much subsequent historiography.

Historicism is associated with a descriptive rather than with a theoretical orientation. Historicism rejects, in other words, the validity of theory, whether the Enlightenment theory of natural law or of generalizable political norms, or any construct of values—whether taken to be of divine or human origination—held to be applicable to the diversity of human societies.

A so-called crisis of historicism occurred

during the first part of the twentieth century, as two world wars shattered historicism's generally benign, even optimistic, view of the historical process. An emergent philosophical and literary pessimism that questioned the validity of historically formulated and culturally transmitted values was reinforced by methodological doubt about the possibility of historical certainty that fostered a subsequent intellectual and moral skepticism. The legacy of historicism is the problematic, born of the autonomy of history, of the validity of situational norms.

Historicism and the Study of Religion: Historicism was formative in shaping the contemporary study of religion. Its historical method was taken over by biblical scholars and historians of religion. These scholars, along with the historicists, were concerned not only to establish the most accurate record of religious expression, but to locate these texts and their subsequent commentaries in their appropriate historical contexts.

The historical-critical authentication of biblical texts and the restriction of their meaning to their historical context challenged the transcendental authority traditionally attributed these texts by those that held them to be authoritative. Thus many conservative theologians rejected this method as a reduction of revealed religion to human construction. Under the influence of post–World War II existentialism, liberal theologians rejected what they perceived to be a historical determinism by which human meaning is bound to the conditions of the time in question. They argued, rather, in favor of the positivity of every historical situation as providing the possibility for decision.

Those historians of religion who had embraced the historicist method of a value-neutral descriptive phenomenology argued ironically that a historically contingent or existentially situated view of religious phenomena cannot explain their "essence"—the transhistorical reality that they supposed religion really to be. They regarded the history of specific religious meaning to be part of the transhistorical nature of the human spirit. These historians of religion joined the theologians in rejecting historicism, along with psychologism and sociologism, as "reductionistic."

The New Historicism: During the final quarter of the twentieth century, a loose coalition of historical scholarship has emerged in France and the United States that has been called the "new historicism." This new movement shares with the old historicism the fundamental premise that all human events and expression are histor-

ically and socially constituted. It emphasizes, however, the situated role of the historian over that of historical event, radically subjecting the past to the present. Since it views all historical knowledge as relative to the standpoint of the historian, self-critical reflection is central to its historical enterprise. Whereas theory was rejected by historicism in favor of the positivity of the situated past, history, for the new historicists, is inseparable from theory. Temporality, apprehended by theoretical awareness, explicitly replaces the situationally transcendent norms of Enlightenment appeal while addressing the problematic of judgment posed by the old historicism.

Although historicism had understood human ideas and ideals to be historically constituted and had rejected idealistic abstraction for an emphasis upon situated fact, its view that history was the key to knowledge tended to be all-encompassing. In contrast to the lingering Enlightenment ideal of universal human values implied in this totalizing project of the old historicism, the new historicism emphasizes a local politics of value—including that of the historian. Historical objectivity, in the view of the new historicists, cannot imply social or political neutrality.

The focus on the theoretical and political orientation of the historian by the new historicists emphasizes the situated character of past formations as "other" to the present, in contrast to the historicist view of a past contingent with the present through some specified law of causal change. The new historicists have become allied thereby with those social science theorists who are concerned with issues of the validity and propriety of Western categories in the study of other cultures. With these social scientists, the new historicists understand human acts and expressions to be embedded in the material practices of their cultural context. The distinctions between the literary texts that so preoccupied the historicists and the nondiscursive practices observed by social science fieldworkers are thereby dissolved. In contrast to the political and diplomatic concerns that dominated the work of the old historicism, the new historicism is concerned more with social and cultural histories, with histories of everyday life, in addition to intellectual history, and with rhetorical analyses of historical writing itself. The new historicism understands itself as a cooperative project in which traditional disciplinary boundaries are blurred in a collaborative historical project of the human sciences.

The increasingly theoretical concern of the

new historicism with issues of explanation, understanding, comparison, and expression, with its reflective recognition of "others"—whether in historical or geographical remove, with everyday expressions and practices as well as with those of the elite—parallel the traditional concerns of religious studies. Although religious expressions and practices are a central concern of the new historicism, the response of religious studies, with its own legacy of transhistorical values, to this new historically oriented human science remains an open question. *See also* science of religion.

history, Western view of, a socially constructed form of knowledge that attempts to order human activities in time. The word *history* is used, often ambiguously, to designate not only accounts of human actions but also the events themselves. The historical relics upon which such knowledge is constructed survive, however, only in compositions of interpretive historiography, selections of museum collections, or fortuitously preserved archaeological remains. Because such interpretative frameworks are themselves historical constructs, the most interesting history is the history of history.

For classicists the paradigm of historiography is the reflective inquiries of the ancient Greeks. For others, it is a secularized version of the Hebraic eschatological pattern. For the Greeks, historiography was a broad search for determinate knowledge; only with Aristotle in the fourth century B.C. did the word history become associated with narrative as opposed to the inquiry that preceeded it. For the Jews, history originated as narrative situated with reference to a future, that is, a recognition of indeterminate possibility neglected by Greek and Roman historiographers.

With the rise of Christianity to cultural dominance in the West, the Hebraic legacy of divine providence as the governing principle of historical order was reemphasized by such influential writers as Eusebius (d. ca. 339) and Augustine (354–430). Against this theistic guaranty of temporal order that came to dominate medieval historiography, the Renaissance return to the ideals of classical antiquity affirmed human agency and emphasized the human social and political capacity to form one's world. By the nineteenth century, the principle of evolution, the impact of individual "great men," and the effective forces of the material world had completely replaced providence in the agenda of a scientific historiography.

Twentieth-century historians understand history primarily as the temporal coordination of relationships rather than the objective ordering of events. Since social awareness presupposes prior social existence, all societies preserve statements of some kind about past events, and the awareness of these statements of origin play some part in their present. The principles and categories of this view of history are no more fixed than the social relationships they express.

Social identity, according to contemporary social historians, is affirmed by collectively remembering an identifying past. Collective memory operates by locating identity in defining images of the past. The technique whereby these images are located is commemoration, ritualized mnemonic practices that clarify the paradigmatic designs of the collective memory. In rites and rituals, commemoration fixes memory in the midst of change and stabilizes the collective identity.

Historiography has always assumed a defining system of ideas that identify a social present by interpretively ordering and selectively preserving a reconstructed past. The goal of even the most positivistic historian can never be historical certainty, but the approximation of probability in the face of human possibility.

history of religion(s), a widely used term designating the academic study of religion from either a comparative, a phenomenological, or a historical point of view. *See also* comparative religion; religion, the study of; science of religion.

hitlahavut (Heb., "fervor" or "enthusiasm," from a root meaning "flame"), in Judaism, a term used in Hasidic literature to characterize the state of ecstasy of the soul in its constant attachment to the spirit of God. *See also* Hasidism.

Hittites (hit′tītz), a people of Anatolia in the second millennium B.C., and a general designation for various first-millennium peoples of southern Anatolia and northern Syria who shared the legacy of second-millennium Anatolian traditions. Vacillation between these two connotations is responsible for some confusion in biblical references.

Origins and Affiliations: The term *Hittite* is associated with the language, people, and civilization of a kingdom ruled from the city of Hattusha (Boghazkoy) in central Anatolia (modern Turkey). The Hittites were not politically unified until the seventeenth century B.C., although aspects of their culture, particularly art and religion, were rooted in earlier Anatolian traditions. The Hittite language, belonging to the Anatolian group of Indo-Europeans, was spoken in Asia Minor before the late third millennium, and possibly much earlier. However, Hittite speakers were but one of several peoples living in a matrix of small, competing kingdoms when literacy was first brought to Anatolia by Assyrian merchants in the first centuries of the second millennium.

One of these early polities, Kanesh (modern Kultepe), harbored the most important of the Assyrian trading colonies and stood out as a center of native political power. Later, in calling their own language "the language of Kanesh," the Hittites implied that this city was their original home. Although an obscure interval intervenes between its destruction and abandonment in the eighteenth century and the rise of a unified Hittite monarchy, Kanesh was remembered in Hittite writing.

History: The political history of the Hittites is divided into two periods of unity, the Old Kingdom and the Empire, with an intervening period of weakness and confusion. In the seventeenth century, the first monarchs of the Old Kingdom quickly consolidated power on the Anatolian Plateau, undertook military operations in northern Syria, and even launched a celebrated raid on Babylon. Although little archaeological evidence dating to this period has been recovered, Hittite writing begins in this period, providing us with key documents such as the Hittite law code.

The fourteenth and thirteenth centuries were the heyday of the Empire, when Hittite control stretched over virtually all of Asia Minor and most of Syria. This was an age of diplomacy and conflict between great powers, wherein Egypt, Mitanni, and eventually Assyria represented the primary opponents of the Hittites in the Levant.

Art and Literature: The ruins of Boghazkoy, with fortifications enclosing an area of 168 hectares, more than thirty temples, and an elaborate palace complex, bear witness to the prosperity of the imperial capital. The architectural sophistication of the Hittites, particularly in stoneworking, is manifest both here and at other sites. Reliefs of rulers and anthropomorphic deities were carved on rock faces throughout Anatolia, the most elaborate series of which are found in the open-air shrine and funerary monument of Yazilikaya.

The cuneiform archives of Boghazkoy are the richest source of information on the Hittites of the second millennium. The majority of these were written in Hittite, which scholars have

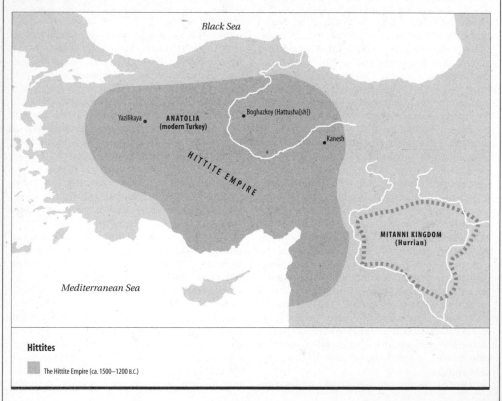

Hittites

The Hittite Empire (ca. 1500–1200 B.C.)

been able to read since B. Hrozny's decipherment in 1917. Hittite scribes also copied documents in Akkadian, Sumerian, Hattic, Hurrian, Luwian, and Palaic. These tablets, belonging to temple and palace archives, focused on the concerns of the administrators of the great institutions of the state: historical texts, treaties, laws, royal correspondence, protocols, hymns, prayers, myths, rituals, oracles, vocabularies, and inventories. The Hittites also developed a quite different, hieroglyphic, script that they used primarily on seals or in association with rock reliefs.

Religion: The polytheism of the Hittites is remarkable, and their texts refer to a "thousand gods" of the kingdom. The acquisition of foreign deities appears to have been a feature of imperial policy. Cult images captured in war were removed to the capital where their worship was maintained. One reason for the unusual richness of the Boghazkoy archives is that they contained many rituals and cultic texts in the native languages of imported gods. These included not just those of Anatolian peoples, such as the non-Indo-European Hattians who had lived in the area of Boghazkoy prior to the arrival of the Hittites, but Hurrian and Mesopotamian gods as well.

The pantheon of the core Anatolian area appears to have been assembled from local cults, with little syncretism. For example, there were numerous storm gods, each associated with a different city. While it was recognized that these gods shared common attributes, they were often invoked separately in such documents as political treaties.

The most exalted deity was the sun goddess of Arinna, whom one text states was worshiped elsewhere as Hepat, chief goddess of Hurrians. Beside the storm god, other deities that figure prominently in Hittite mythology are Telepinu, a vegetation god; a male sun god; and a goddess of both war and sexuality analogous in many ways to the Akkadian Ishtar.

The Hittite king devoted much of his time to maintaining cults and participating in an annual cycle of religious festivals. Hittite kings were deified after death, but while living were essentially high priests responsible for preserving the favor of the gods toward the kingdom.

"Hittites" of the Iron Age: The Hittite Empire was obliterated in the chaos that afflicted all of the Near East ca. 1200 B.C. Anatolia was plunged into a dark age from which it did not begin to recover for four centuries, during which the Hittite language disappeared.

Some of the traditions of the Empire, sculptural style and the hieroglyphic script in particular, were adopted by city-states that sprang up in southern Anatolia and northern Syria in the centuries between 1200 and 700 B.C. Although the Israelites, Assyrians, and Urartians called the inhabitants of these cities Hittites, important distinctions separate them from the Hittites of the Empire—not the least of which is their language, which is a dialect of Luwian written in hieroglyphs.

Biblical References: The term Hittite in the Bible is problematic, particularly when given as a name for an aboriginal population dwelling in the promised land prior to the arrival of the Israelites. Because the southern Levant was unquestionably in the Egyptian, rather than Hittite, sphere of influence, it has been suggested that in these cases Hittite should be read "Hurrian." *See also* Boghazkoy; Hurrians; Indo-European religion.

hocus-pocus (ho'kis-po'kis), incomprehensible formulas used in magical procedure. Some argue that the term is a corruption of the central words of institution in the Catholic Mass, "this is my body" (*hoc est enim corpus meum*).

Hodr (hoo'duhr), a Norse mythological figure who killed Baldr by shooting him with a mistletoe. *See also* Baldr; Nordic religion.

Hoguk Pulgyo. *See* National Protection Buddhism.

Hokke genki (hohk-kay gen-kee; Jap., "Record of Miracles Concerning the *Lotus Sutra*"), a collection of Japanese Buddhist tales compiled in the middle of the eleventh century that illustrate the miraculous power of the *Lotus Sutra. See also* Lotus Sutra.

Holi (hoh'lee; Hindi), Hindu spring festival widely celebrated in rural North India, featuring a carnival-like reversal of social roles. It is associated both with the god Krishna and with the destruction of the demoness Holika. *See also* Hinduism (festal cycle).

Holiness churches, those Christian churches tracing their origin to a mid-nineteenth-century American Protestant movement originally within Methodism that focused on "experience" of the Christian life.

The Holiness movement generally claims biblical authority for its understanding of Wesleyan perfectionism. It sought to develop its ecclesiastical forms in keeping with its interpretation of apostolic Christianity. Consequently, its first and primary goal was to restore the church to its proper primitive New Testament standards. The emphasis among the Holiness churches was the call for members to experience again God's Spirit, so that the church could recover its basic vision. Their quest for total sanctification sets them apart from those within Methodism and eventually led to the creation of "Holiness churches," and the formation of the National Holiness Association (renamed, in 1971, the Christian Holiness Association). The Holiness movement claims a regular membership of almost two million in the United States alone, but the effective membership is probably double that number. *See also* African Americans (North America), new religions among; Methodism; Nazarene, Church of; Protestantism.

Holiness Tabernacle Church. *See* Jesus people.

holocaust, a sacrifice in which the offering is wholly destroyed by fire.

Holocaust, religious responses to the. *Holocaust* is a biblical term derived from the Septuagint's translation of the Hebrew *olah* into the Greek *hololcauston.* It suggests "a whole burnt offering" or sacrifice made to God. It has come to be used to describe the death of an estimated six million Jews as part of a program of attempted genocide by the Nazis between 1933 and 1945. Alternatively, this event is referred to as the *Shoah,* or time of desolation.

The near annihilation of the "eternal people" by the Nazis and the extensive cooperation of Christians raise profound questions that have generated a significant body of post-Holocaust theological writings in both Judaism and Christianity. Despite considerable diversity, this literature regards the Holocaust as an event of such cataclysmic proportions that it forces a rereading and reinterpretation of religious meaning and challenges some of the most fundamental religious convictions of each tradition. The problem of faith after Auschwitz (one of the extermination sites, now in Poland, used by the Nazis) is different for Judaism than for Christianity. For Judaism, it is God's presence in history and the reliability of the covenant promises that are in question; for Christians, it is their own credibility and that of their tradition. For the first time in two thousand years, Christians are acknowledging the legitimacy of the Mosaic covenant. Paradoxically, they do so precisely when Jews are calling this covenant into question.

Jewish Responses: Although the Holocaust has generated a wide variety of Jewish responses, five characterize most post-Holocaust Jewish theologians: (1) The Holocaust is identified as a unique event of such tragic proportions that (2) God's justice and faithfulness are called into question, and, as a consequence, (3) the covenant is also called into question and redefined in such a way as to (4) allow a place for both the secular and the religious Jews within the covenant. Finally, (5) the existence of the State of Israel is taken as a sign that God's saving presence can still be experienced in history after the Holocaust.

Such figures as Ignaz Maybaum, Richard Rubenstein, Emil Fackenheim, Elie Wiesel, Irving Greenberg, Eliezer Berkowitz, and Arthur Cohen acknowledge that although there have been other great traumatic events or ruptures that have threatened to submerge Jewish faith in an abyss of meaninglessness, the Holocaust is more devastating and therefore requires a more drastic response. Arthur Cohen, for instance, argues that when the Temple was destroyed, meaning was restored by proposing that its destruction was a punishment for failing to keep the covenant. In the case of the expulsion from Spain, meaning was restored by seeing this as the beginning of a new era of mystic gnosis. With the Nazi death camps the abyss opened once more, and "one-third of the Jewish people fell in." This time neither guilt nor mystic hope was able to provide a meaning for this event. Thus the Holocaust remains a rupture, or caesura. It is like an open wound—a gaping abyss of meaninglessness that there can be no question of closing. At best one can hope to build a bridge over it, allowing life to go on even as the wound remains exposed.

Thus, though there is some continuity with the tragedies of the past, the scope and magnitude of the Holocaust is such that the old arguments will not work to reestablish confidence in the biblical God of the covenant. Emil Fackenheim has made this point by arguing that the overwhelming majority of Jews who perished were not nonobservant Jews but precisely the most observant Jews from the villages of eastern Europe. Consequently, Jews have found themselves compelled to question the justice and faithfulness of God—where was God during the Holocaust? A variety of answers has been proposed by Jewish post-Holocaust theologians. The most extreme have been offered by Richard Rubenstein, who argues that the prophetic God of history died at Auschwitz, and there is no reason to look with hope toward this God, whom Judaism will have to forgo.

Other post-Holocaust theologians have refused to take this dead-end path. Irving Greenberg, for instance, responded to Rubenstein by arguing that after Auschwitz there must be no final solutions, not even theological ones. Instead, Greenberg affirms "momentary faith." There are moments when it is possible to experience faith in God's saving presence in history, and other moments when such faith is overwhelmed and blotted out by the smoke of Auschwitz; neither is capable of canceling out the experience of the other. For Emil Fackenheim, God's saving presence might not have been experienced at Auschwitz, but God's commanding presence was. After Auschwitz, the line between sacred and secular in Judaism seems to have collapsed. The amazing thing is that even secular Jews have refused to abandon their identity as Jews. This proves, he argues, that both religious and nonreligious Jews have responded to God's silent yet commanding voice from Auschwitz, a voice that forbids them to grant Hitler a posthumous victory. Thus, rather than being destroyed by the Shoah, the covenant is redefined. In his own way, Elie Wiesel, as a survivor of Auschwitz, provides a similar response. He suggests that God has broken his covenant promises and that, therefore, the covenant is no longer binding on the Jewish people. Yet, he argues, Jews continue to keep the covenant of their own free volition because being a Jew means refusing to give up hope even in the face of despair. It also means engaging in a continuous wrestling match with God in which, like Job, one puts God on trial and calls God into question. Wrestling with God is a theme that is central to the work of Eliezer Berkowitz as well, who describes post-Holocaust Jews as "Job's brothers" who seek to understand God's hiddenness during the Holocaust.

All these Jewish theologians share an understanding of faith as wrestling with God (Genesis 32:23–32). This theme provides continuity with pre-Holocaust Judaism. It is rooted in an understanding of the covenant as an intimate two-way relationship in which God as well as human beings can be called to account. In the tradition of Abraham, these theologians have had the *chutzpah,* or audacity, to demand that the Judge of all also be just (Genesis 18:25). Like Jacob, Job, and the rabbis of the Talmud, they understand arguing and wrestling with God as itself a form of faith—perhaps the only form possible after Auschwitz. The exception to this model that proves the rule is Richard Rubenstein, who has not been able to construct a bridge of continuity between "pre" and "post" Shoah Judaism.

Finally, it is commonly held, with the exception of Rubenstein and Maybaum, that if the

Holocaust suggests the absence of God in history, the emergence of the State of Israel suggests God's returning presence to history. In fact, the event that seems to have constellated Jewish post-Holocaust theology is the 1967 war of Israel with Egypt. Jews everywhere experienced that war as a return of the threat of total annihilation. Once again the world stood by and did nothing. That Israel was not annihilated but instead soundly and swiftly defeated its enemies was spontaneously experienced as miraculous. The conclusion seemed inescapable to many—this unlikely outcome signaled the return of God's saving presence to history.

Though the development of post-Holocaust theology has become a major influence in contemporary Judaism, it has provoked criticism as well. Some, such as Michael Wyschogrod and Jacob Neusner, argue that the Holocaust and the emergence of the State of Israel are events that the Torah's theology of Israel and its history can accommodate in familiar structures. Marc Ellis, who seeks to build a Jewish alliance with Christian liberation theology, argues that the "excessive" emphasis on the State of Israel has transformed Holocaust theology into an establishment theology that justifies everything the State of Israel does, even when its behavior toward the Palestinians violates the prophetic ethical tradition at the heart of Judaism.

Christian Responses: If the defining moment of Jewish post-Holocaust theology was the 1967 war, Christian post-Holocaust theology may well have been defined by the calling of the Second Vatican Council (1962–65) by Angelo Roncalli, then newly elected as Pope John XXIII. During World War II Monsignor Roncalli, as apostolic vicar and delegate to Turkey and Greece, had been instrumental in saving thousands of Jewish lives by issuing false baptismal certificates. As pope, he appointed Cardinal Augustin Bea to shepherd through the council a document on the church's relationship with the Jews. John XXIII died in June of 1963, before the council had finished its work. However, under Cardinal Bea's guidance, and despite significant political obstacles both from within and outside the church, the Vatican II declaration *Nostra Aetate* finally appeared in October of 1965. The declaration began a tide of change in the Christian churches, both Catholic and Protestant. In the decades that followed, most of the major Christian denominations (Lutheran, Calvinist, Methodist, Episcopal, etc.) in Europe and America have followed suit, inaugurating a new day in Jewish-Christian relations.

What is striking about this change is that

unlike other revolutionary changes in the churches, it came from the top. The challenge for the churches is to bring this change in orientation to the level of the average Christian in the pew. At least three things have been accomplished by the Vatican declaration and its Protestant counterparts. For the first time in two thousand years (1) the churches have publicly acknowledged their guilt in fostering the teachings of contempt and the role that these teachings played in making the Holocaust possible; (2) the churches have acknowledged the ongoing legitimacy of the Mosaic covenant; and (3) the churches have set an agenda of changes to be instituted in Christian teaching, preaching, and liturgy whose purpose is to eradicate anti-Jewish stereotypes that have been fostered by Christianity.

The impact of the Holocaust on Christian thought and teaching has been extraordinary. For almost two thousand years Christians preached the message of supersession, the doctrine that Christians have replaced Jews as the chosen people of God, even as their new covenant replaced the old. Never in two thousand years had the churches admitted that any covenant other than the one inaugurated by Jesus of Nazareth was efficacious for salvation. Now, for the first time, Christians have to rethink the meaning of virtually every Christian doctrine in the light of this recognition of the Jewish covenant.

These new church declarations leave a host of unanswered questions that shape the agenda of post-Holocaust Christian theology. Three key issues have emerged: (1) What is the relationship between the two traditions and how can it be expressed in a way that undoes the teachings of contempt and of supersession? (2) If the Mosaic covenant is valid in its own right, in what sense is Jesus the Messiah and Savior?

A third question emerged from the ongoing dialogue between Jews and Christians, in which Christians have been asked to recognize the significance the State of Israel has for many Jews. Consequently, a number of Christian post-Holocaust theologians have asked (3) whether or not a theological transformation of Christianity can really be sincere and complete if it does not lead to political support for the State of Israel, seen by so many Jews as absolutely essential to Judaism's post-Holocaust survival.

The Vatican II declaration *Nostra Aetate* denied the myth of supersession and affirmed the validity of the covenant of Judaism by appealing to Paul's letter to the Romans, which compares the gentile church to a wild olive branch grafted onto the natural olive tree of Judaism (Romans 11:16–18). Writing before the destruction of the second Temple, Paul did not subscribe to the supersessionist mythology, which interpreted the Temple's destruction as a sign of the rejection of the "old covenant." Paul's grafting model represents a suppressed tradition—a road not taken that is now being explored. Almost all post-Holocaust Christian theology tries to account for the relationship between Judaism and Christianity by appealing to this Pauline model.

Paul's model, however, leaves a number of unanswered theological questions about the relation between Jews and Christians. Was Paul suggesting that the grafting on of the Gentiles to the natural olive tree of Judaism through faith in Jesus constituted a second covenant, or was he saying there was just one covenant in which the followers of Jesus were the newest members? How is the relationship between Jews and Christians to be understood, and what are its implications for other Christian beliefs? As a result of this ambiguity a number of alternative interpretations have been put forth. The complexities of these interpretations do not fit neatly into any easy classification scheme. However, for the sake of simplicity the interpretations of Monika Hellwig, A. Roy Eckhardt, and Paul Van Buren may be classified as one-covenant theories, while those of James Parkes, Franklin Littell, Clemens Thoma, John Pawlikowski, and Rosemary Ruether could be called two-covenant theories. What is at stake in this discussion is whether Christianity is to be understood simply as an extension of Judaism for Gentiles (single covenant) or whether it has a distinct religious vision of its own to offer (double covenant). This question also has a bearing on Christian beliefs concerning salvation—whether salvation is the result of being grafted onto the holy root of Israel through faith in Jesus or whether a separate path of salvation is offered through faith in Jesus. Consensus on these issues is unlikely.

Though there is great diversity of opinion on the above questions, on the question of the messiah Christian post-Holocaust theologians are virtually unanimous in declaring that Jesus is not the messiah expected by the Jews. Since Christianity is thought to be founded on this claim, its denial would appear to present extreme difficulties for the future of Christianity. Some, such as Ruether, have suggested that Christian experience has so "spiritualized" the term that what Christians mean by *Christ* is radically different than what Jews mean by *messiah*. Others, such as Hellwig, prefer to emphasize that the title messiah is an eschatological term that can only be affirmed when Jesus returns, bringing a new heaven and a new earth. On this model, Jesus is "not yet" messiah, and both Jews and Christians are still awaiting the messiah's coming. Because, in fact, much of the New Testament literature insisted that a return of Jesus would be necessary for the complete fulfillment of the messianic hope, this type of claim is less than radical. The affirmation of Jesus as messiah would simply be restricted to the realm of faith and hope, where it belongs, rather than of fact. Finally, there is virtually unanimous agreement among post-Holocaust Christian theologians on support for the State of Israel. The great ethical failure of Christianity during the Holocaust was its failure in word and deed to protect Jewish lives. In a world where the continuance of Jewish life is still seen as precarious, support for the State of Israel and its right to self-defense is seen as something of a litmus test of Christian seriousness about a new age of post-Holocaust Jewish-Christian relations.

As with their Jewish counterparts, Christian post-Holocaust theologians have their critics. Evangelical and Fundamentalist theologians tend to share the affirmation of support by post-Holocaust Christian theologians for the State of Israel. But, at the same time, most continue to affirm the myth of supersession. Moreover, they reject all attempts to modify the concepts of covenant, messiah, and salvation. Many Protestant and Catholic theologians (especially liberation theologians), out of sympathy for the Palestinians, tend to reject the support for the State of Israel offered by post-Holocaust Christian theologians. Yet many are cautiously open to reconsidering the meanings of covenant, messiah, and salvation. And they seem to be willing to replace supersessionist theology with Paul's grafting model. Virtually all Christian theologians reject the worst stereotypes of the teachings of contempt, such as deicide, but many remain insensitive to the subtler stereotypes, such as the portrayal of the Pharisees (and hence Jews) as legalists. As with their Jewish counterparts, Christian post-Holocaust theologians have an unfinished agenda whose outcome is still in question. *See also* anti-Semitism; theodicy.

holy. *See* Sacred, the.

Holy Alamo Christian Church. *See* Jesus people.

holy books, texts marked as authoritative and sacred. Several patterns predominate: the books are old; they are given by the gods; they are written by holy persons; they were given through inspiration; they were lost and recovered. *See also* Babism; Baha'i; Bible, Christian; Bon; Buddhism (authoritative texts and their interpretation); canon; ching; Confucianism (authoritative texts and their interpretation); Druze/Druse; Engi-shiki; Hinduism (authoritative texts and their interpretation); Islam (authoritative texts and their interpretation); Jainism; Judaism (authoritative texts and their interpretation); Kanjur; Shrivaishnavism; Sikhism (authoritative texts); Tao-tsang; Zorastrianism.

Holy Communion. *See* Christianity (life cycle); Eucharist, Christian.

Holy Ghost, archaic Christian term for Holy Spirit.

holy/Holy. *See* sacred, profane; Sacred, the.

holy of holies, the innermost and most sacred room of the Jewish temple, restricted to all but the high priest on the Day of Atonement. *See also* temple.

holy person, one who serves as an exemplar of virtue and an embodiment of sacred power. The holy person lives according to the highest ideals of a religious tradition. Such a life might involve rigorous asceticism, profound exposition of doctrine, prophetic or mystical experiences, or martyrdom. The result of such a life is the achievement of the ultimate goal as defined by that tradition, such as salvation for a Christian or *nirvana* for a Buddhist.

As one who has followed the teaching and fulfilled the spirit of a religious tradition, the holy person can become an example for others as to how to live their lives. But as one who has thus become a "friend of God" (an Islamic designation) the holy person has also acquired miraculous powers, such as the ability to heal the sick, experience visions of the divine, levitate to the heavens, or serve as an intercessor. The aid of the holy person is therefore sought by ordinary believers, either personally during the holy person's lifetime or posthumously by means of their relics or shrine. The holy person thus becomes not only an exemplar of the sacred, but a source of supernatural power in the profane world.

The Attainment of Holiness: The means to the attainment of holiness vary considerably from one religious tradition to another. Confucian sages, Buddhist monks, Indian gurus, and Christian visionaries can in different ways become holy people. What elevates holy people above other ascetics, teachers, or healers is the heroic level of their achievement. Miracles often serve as verification of such extraordinary stature.

The holy person should be distinguished from several other categories of sacred individuals. First, the holy person is human and should where possible be separated from any form of divinity. Second, the holy person should be differentiated from the founders of religious traditions, such as the Buddha or Confucius, or other figures, such as the Virgin Mary. Finally, while a holy person often holds an office—such as priest or shaman—that is invested with sacred power, the holy person is one whose virtue surpasses that conferred by the office itself.

A holy person is thus an individual human being who has attained a close personal relationship with the sacred, which is both remarkable and worthy of imitation. That attainment, however, is not unique. Part of what makes a holy person an exemplar is the fact that that person's virtue is modeled on that of earlier holy people and can in turn be shared by later devotees. The means by which the holy person relates to the sacred and the nature of the sacred itself are both particular to that person's religious tradition. No single definition can be universally applied.

The use of the term *holy person* in contemporary religious studies is designed to avoid the use of a term drawn from a single religious tradition. The term, however, is indirectly derived from the Christian term *saint,* which has its roots in a Latin word (*sanctus, -a*) meaning a holy person. Other religious traditions have their own precise terms for which holy person is but an analogue.

Cross-cultural Perspective: Early Christians honored as saints specifically those persons who were thought to have earned immediate entrance to the kingdom of heaven after their death. In practice only a limited number of people were so venerated. The first to be so recognized were martyrs, who had died for their witness to the name of Christ. With the end of persecution, monks who endured the symbolic martyrdom of rigorous self-denial came to be officially honored as saints. Still later bishops, teachers, visionaries, and others were included in the possible ranks of the saints. As residents of the court of heaven, saints were capable of working miracles, and their prayerful intercession could help ordinary Christians gain salvation. The veneration of these saints was central to the practice of medieval Christianity, and continues to be important in modern Orthodoxy and Catholicism, although it was rejected by the Protestant reformers.

Both Islam and Judaism are religions that, out of fear of idolatry, reject the use of any image of the divine or of any human intermediary with the divine. Nonetheless, rabbinic Judaism of the classic period gave reverence to a large group of exemplary biblical heroes. Medieval Jewish communities compiled lists of martyrs whose example served as instruction in the need for steadfast faith. Since the eighteenth century, various rabbinic schools have extended veneration to the *zaddikim* or *hasidim,* the "disciples" of various important masters who embody the power of mystical teachings. Still, the holy person has always remained of marginal importance in Judaism. Islam, on the other hand, has developed a number of centrally important categories of venerated figures whose importance is widely accepted. A *shahid* is a martyr who has died for the faith. The *awliya,* or "friends of God," are teachers and ascetics who have earned a close relationship to the divine and thus wield miraculous powers, particularly at their tombs. A number of historical *imams,* or leaders of the community of Muslims, are revered by Shiites.

In Hinduism it is not always possible to make precise distinctions between holy persons and the anthropomorphic appearances of divinities. The range of types of people who over the course of history have been thought to embody holiness is immense, but focuses on three categories: those who have had close relationships to divinities, such as the *rsis* or sages of the Vedas; those who have achieved some form of spiritual liberation (*siddha* or "perfected one"), and thus amassed miraculous powers through accumulated austerity; and great gurus or teachers, of whom Shankara (eighth century) was apparently the first accorded posthumous veneration.

Buddhism and Jainism define holy people more exclusively within the context of the attainment of enlightenment. Jainists venerate *tirthamkaras,* those historical figures who taught the Jainist path and achieved enlightenment, as well as more recent monks of particular piety who are known as *sadhu,* or "spiritually great souls." For Theravada Buddhists, an *arahant* can be either a historical disciple of Buddha or a more recent monastic "worthy" who has achieved the highest stage of spiritual development. In addition to the wisdom and virtue they attain on the path to enlightenment, they also can perform miraculous and magical feats. For the Mahayana, a *bodhisattva* is a "Buddha-to-be," someone who will achieve enlightenment in the current lifetime and can transfer merit to fellow humans, thus speeding fellow human beings on their own paths to enlightenment. The former ideal is specifically confined to monks, while the latter is open to all. These concepts all betray a basic tension between the ideal of enlightenment as a pure state of being and the practical reality of the great powers that are believed to accompany its attainment.

Elsewhere persons who hold sacred offices can transcend them through the unique holiness of their actions or instruction. A Confucian teacher, for example, can become a *sheng*, or venerated sage. Similarly, various Native American and African shamans have become leaders of large-scale movements. The devotion of their followers marks them as holy persons.

This list by no means exhausts the possible analogues to "holy person" in the world's religions. Nor is an analogue present in all traditions. Protestant Christians reject the cult of saints and use the term *saint*, if at all, to refer to all true members of their community. Similarly some rigorist interpretations of Islam, Judaism, and Buddhism avoid the veneration of any human being.

The Holy Person, Power, and Society: There is a tension present in the concept of the holy person. In the eye of the believer the holy person has inherently become an exemplar of how to live one's life and has thus become an embodiment of sacred power. In practice, however, a person cannot attain holiness in isolation; achievement must be recognized by a community of fellow believers. These are the disciples of a living teacher or the pilgrims who flock to the shrine of a martyr. Without such an audience the holy person could not serve as an exemplar and there would be no clientele for miraculous powers. The example and sacred powers of the holy person are in fact social constructs, which are informed and constrained by their humanity and their gender, by their life and their death, as well as by institutional considerations.

People become holy in different ways than do places, or totemic animals, or ritual objects. A sacred mask, for example, confers holiness upon the dancer who wears it, but that dancer does not become inherently holy in the manner of a martyr or an ascetic monk who has attained enlightenment. The holiness of the dancer is evanescent, that of the holy person enduring. The masked dancer is a ritual performer, the holy person has become a living embodiment of the sacred, an actual piece of the kingdom of heaven or of nirvana. As a human being, the holy person transmits sacred power in ways that are quintessentially human. Devotees gather to hear the sermons of a great teacher, bring gifts to the shrine of a saint or bodhisattva, or build geneologies to demonstrate their descent from a martyr or imam. The veneration of holy people implies that sacred power can be dispersed not only through rituals or sacraments, but through social relationships.

The construction of holiness is also constrained by gender or, more accurately, by the cultural construction of gender. A medieval Christian woman, for example, could become a saint as a visionary or martyr, but not as a preacher or bishop (offices from which they were excluded). Confucianism restricts teaching, and thus sagehood, to males. While there have historically been monastic orders for women in both Buddhism and Jainism, they have produced few figures of widespread veneration. Just as the power wielded by holy people necessarily reflects its social and cultural context, so too the ways in which women have attained positions of veneration as holy people (notably in Christianity, Hinduism, and Islam) also reflect the historic misogyny of the world's religions.

The holy person becomes an exemplar for others as a result of the way in which he or she has lived. For an exemplar to have meaning, however, it must be disseminated beyond the circle of those disciples or students who have intimate knowledge of that particular person. Written or oral legends (known under the general heading of hagiography) serve to transmit that example and play a vital role in the construction of holiness. This literature follows traditional forms and is intended to convey a moral message rather than historically accurate biography.

While the power of a holy person begins during his or her lifetime, miracles are performed not only by the living, but also (and perhaps most often) posthumously, usually in relation to physical objects known as relics. Corpses are the favored relics and tombs the preferred sites of shrines in Christianity and Islam, but teeth, clothing, statues, and books can all serve as relics. These act as the continued physical presence in the material world of the holy person after the holy person's death. They should not be regarded as symbols, but as an actual extension of the holy person's charismatic power. The miracles performed by holy people and their relics include such visible marvels as cures and exorcisms, but also invisible acts such as the remission of sin or the transfer of merit.

The institutional hierarchy of a religious

tradition often seeks ways to control the power of the holy person, declaring its right to validate a person's holiness through such processes as that of canonization in Catholicism. Through investigation the example provided by a holy person comes to be approved and the sacred origin of miracles verified. Most religious traditions have categories such as witch or heretic that serve as the antithesis of the holy person. They, too, can perform wonders, but their powers are opposed to the correct practice of religion and have their origin in an evil debasement of a correct life. *See also* asceticism; deification; hagiography; miracle; mysticism; relics; saint.

holy persons, religious specialists. *See* abbess/abbot; acharya; acolyte; Akali; Alvar; anchorite; apostle; archbishop; archimandrite; arhat; augurs; ayatollah; babalawo; baul; beadle; Berserk; bhiksu/bhiksuni; bishop; biwa hoshi; Black Head Taoist; bodhisattva; Bon; Brahman; Buddhas; cantor; cardinal; chaplain; charismatics; chi-chiu; clergy; confessor; curate; Dalai Lama; devadasi; disciple; divine man; druid; elder; evangelist; fakir; fang-shih; flamen; friar; gaon; guru; gymnosophists; hijiri; hsien; Hujjat al-Islam; hungan; imam; Ise Virgin; kannushi; kataribe; lama; Levi; Madhi; mahasiddha; martyr; medium; Messenger of Allah; Messiah; metropolitan; minister; muezzin; mulla; murid; National Shaman; National Teacher; Nayanar; nazirite; novice; nun; Panchen Lama; pastor; patriarch; Pir; pope; preacher; prelate; presbyter; priest/priestess; prophet; Prophet, The; rabbi; rishi; sadhu; sage; saint; savior; scribe, in Judaism; shaman; shaykh; sheng; Skinwalker; snake handlers; son of God; staretz; Sufi; swami; tulku; Tzaddik; ulama; Vestals; vicar; village recluses (Korea); wali; witness (Islam).

Holy Rollers, popular name for ecstatic American Christian groups (most frequently Methodist) who manifest experience of the Spirit by jumping and rolling on the ground.

Holy Sepulchre, Church of the, a Christian church in Jerusalem at the traditional site of Christ's grave; a major Christian pilgrimage site. Constructed at the command of the emperor Constantine by the architect Zenobius, it was dedicated in 336. Burned by the Persians in 614, a new church was constructed by 626. This was destroyed by Muslims around 1009 and was replaced by a larger Crusader church around 1130. Partial remodeling has occurred since, with the present church largely the result of a major reconstruction in 1810 following a disastrous fire.

Christian pilgrims approaching, through the Greek Orthodox shrine, the tomb of Christ within the Church of the Holy Sepulchre, Jerusalem.

Holy Spirit, literal English translation of the Greek *pneuma hagion*, which is first used to render the Hebrew *ruach elohim* ("spirit [or breath] of God") in the Greek translation of the Hebrew Bible, the Septuagint. "Holy Spirit" is widely employed in the New Testament and later Christian literature.

Judaism: In Judaism the holy spirit is the divine power through which the prophets receive and transmit their message. The rabbis taught that when the age of prophecy ended, the holy spirit departed from Israel. *See also* revelation.

Christianity: The Holy Spirit is the third "Person" in the Christian understanding of divinity as a trinitarian community. The basis of Christian faith in the Holy Spirit lies in both parts of the Christian Bible. The Old Testament speaks of the breath of the Lord, which expresses the divine presence and power. In the New Testament, Jesus is led by the Spirit throughout his ministry. At his resurrection, the Spirit comes to the followers of Jesus (most dramatically at Pentecost). Johannine theology speaks of believers' abiding in the Spirit, as in the Father and Son. Pauline theology leaves the distinction between the risen Christ and the Spirit unclear.

Subsequent Christian theology has stressed the charismatic effects of the Spirit. The gifts of the Spirit, from prophecy to speaking in tongues, are powers intended to build up the church. The Spirit is a presence in Christian prayer, both communal and private. The Spirit is a deposit on eternal life and the defender of believers against all spiritual threats. Some theologians speak of the Spirit as God-given and received. In the Trinity, the Spirit is the mutual love of the Father and the Son (the Western view) or the Father's love (the Eastern Orthodox view). *See also* anointed in the Spirit; charism; gifts of the Spirit; Trinity.

Holy Spirit Association for the Unification of World Christianity. *See* Unification Church.

Holy Spirit movements, Melanesian Christian renewal movements, active since the 1960s, that emphasize experience of the Holy Spirit. Some Holy Spirit movements have remained within mainline churches. Others, in the postmission period, have become independent churches.

Holy Thursday, (or Maundy Thursday, after the command [Lat. *mandatum*] of Jesus to do these things), the day of the Christian Holy Week that commemorates the institution of the Eucharist at the Last Supper. The rite of washing the feet is also observed. *See also* calendar (Christian); Eucharist, Christian; Holy Week; Last Supper.

holy water, water consecrated by the blessing of the priest in certain Christian churches for use upon entering a church and in ceremonies. The water and its use symbolize purity and regeneration. *See also* ablution.

Holy Week, the remembrance of the passion, death, and resurrection of Jesus celebrated annually in Christian churches. Palm Sunday marks the beginning of the week, followed by Holy Thursday, Good Friday, the Easter Vigil on Saturday evening, and Easter Sunday. This complex of feasts began, probably, in fourth-century Jerusalem. *See also* calendar (Christian).

Homer (hoh'muhr), legendary Greek poet who probably lived around 700 B.C. Nothing certain is known about him, but ancient tradition viewed him as a blind poet from Chios or Smyrna who traveled around the Greek world composing songs about great heroes. His name was attached to a number of hymns and epic poems (now lost) in antiquity, but only the *Iliad* and *Odyssey* are now attributed to him. By the end of the sixth century B.C. a guild of singers called the *Homeridae* (Gk., "sons of Homer") were active on Chios, reciting these epics and stories about the life of "Homer."

The Homeric poems were composed and chanted in hexameter verse by a single performer to the accompaniment of a stringed instrument such as the lyre. The *Iliad* and the *Odyssey*, each twenty-four books long, probably came at the end of a long oral tradition. Homer is credited as the master poet who shaped their final form, although some believe different poets composed each work.

Both poems reflect important conceptions of religion. Unlike those of later Greek religion, Homer's gods live together on Mt. Olympos in a unified society like the early Near Eastern gods and they interact at will with mortals. They are anthropomorphic and live at ease, feasting and meeting in assembly with their king, Zeus, god of the sky. Hades and Persephone rule the underworld, and minor gods or nymphs inhabit rivers and mountains.

For some, Homer's gods appear too comical to be taken seriously. When they enter the battle in *Iliad* 5 and whine at minor wounds while mortals fall in death, or when Aphrodite's husband, catching her in a lover's embrace, calls the other gods to watch in *Odyssey* 8, the effect is humorous. But the gods can suffer too, as when a weeping Zeus must watch the death of his son in *Iliad* 16.

The gods also drive the action in the poems. The *Iliad* begins with a plague sent by Apollo against the Greeks in answer to the prayers of his priest and ends with Hermes leading one enemy to reconcile with another. In the *Odyssey*, a hostile Poseidon delays Odysseus before Athena finally effects his safe return. In each poem mortals make careful sacrifices, conduct funeral rites, and consult prophets about the will of the gods. *See also* Greek religion.

homiletics, field of study focusing on the preparation and delivery of sermons.

homily (Gk., "discourse"), an address given during the Christian liturgy, often synonymous with sermon (Lat., "speech"). In Catholic usage, the short explanation of the Gospel given by a priest or a deacon during the celebration of the eucharistic liturgy, required at each public Mass on Sunday and recommended at each weekday Mass.

homosexuality, sexual relations between members of the same gender. Religious traditions place both negative and positive value on homosexuality as a boundary-crossing activity. For some, the power to invert culturally sanctioned relations is a mark of, or a means to acquire, supernatural power; for others, it is a forbidden activity.

Temporary homosexual relations are frequently found in both male and female puberty initiations, in male-bonding activities within warrior groups, and as part of a series of reversals in carnivals, usually by adapting some mode of transvestism. *See also* gender crossing; reversal; sexuality and religion.

Honen (hoh-nen; 1133–1212), founder of the Jodoshu (Pure Land school) of Japanese Buddhism. Ordained a Tendai monk on Mt. Hiei when he was fourteen, Honen during his youth traveled to temples in Nara and Kyoto searching for a practice that was appropriate to his abilities. At forty-two, he came across a passage written by the Chinese Pure Land master Shan-tao that convinced him that salvation during the cosmic period of degeneration (*mappo*) could be gained by the sole practice of *nembutsu* (chanting Amida Buddha's name). In Kyoto he began speaking to groups of laypeople about nembutsu. Criticisms by Tendai and other monks about the exclusive focus on nembutsu practice eventually led to Honen's exile. His major work is the *Senchakushu* (Treatise Selecting the Nembutsu of the Primordial Vow). *See also* Jodoshu; mappo; nembutsu; Shan-tao.

hongaku (hohn-gah-koo; Jap.,"innate or primordial enlightenment"), in Japanese Buddhist terminology originally the quality of all phenomena that enabled people to realize enlightenment. However, in medieval Tendai documents, it sometimes came to refer to teachings that claimed that ordinary people, without any practice, were Buddhas or that this world, just as it is, was a Pure Land. Although such teachings were often considered degenerate, they influenced many of the Kamakura schools. *See also* enlightenment; Kamakura schools; Pure Land; Tendai school.

Honganji (hohn-gahn-jee; Jap.,"Temple of the Primordial Vow"), the site in Japan of Shinran's mausoleum and today the headquarters of the Jodo Shinshu. *See also* Jodo Shinshu; Shinran.

honji suijaku (hohn-jee sooee-jah-koo; Jap.,"fundamental basis,""manifest trace"), a Buddhist-Shinto theory in medieval Japan relating specific Buddhist figures (celestial or symbolic Buddhas and Bodhisattvas) to specific Shinto *kami* (divinities, divine presences). The Buddhist figures were seen as the fundamental basis, while the Shinto kami were understood as the manifest traces of that basis. This theory is an example of a larger phenomenon in Japanese religious history in which Shinto and Buddhism mutually influenced each other. *See also* Bodhisattvas; syncretism (Japan).

Hooker, Richard (1553–1600), one of the chief Anglican apologists. His treatise *Of the lawes of ecclesiasticall politie* (1594–97) was a powerful defense of the Church of England against both Puritan and Roman Catholic criticisms. *See also* Anglicanism.

horoscope, astrological chart, especially of heavenly conjunctions at an individual's birth. *See also* astrology.

Horus (hohr'uhs), the ancient Egyptian falcon god, son of Isis and Osiris. His incarnation in the pharaoh of Egypt marked the victory of cosmic order over the forces of chaos. *See also* Egyptian religion.

Ho-shang Kung (huh-shahng gohng; Chin., "Venerable Gentleman of the River"; ca. first–second centuries), pseudonym of the earliest Taoist commentator on the *Tao-te ching* (mid-fourth century B.C.); he opposed Confucian thought, which parted with the Way of nature. *See also* Tao-te ching; Taoism.

Hosso school (hoh-soh), school of Japanese Buddhist thought introduced in 653 by Dosho and based on Indian Yogachara and Chinese Fa-hsiang teachings. Partly because of the Fujiwara clan's patronage of its headquarters at Kofukuji in Nara, it was the dominant school during the eighth and ninth centuries and one of the most important schools through the eleventh century. Its teachings that Buddhahood required three incalculable eons and that some people lacked the potential ever to realize Buddhahood prevented it from enjoying wide popularity. *See also* Fa-hsiang school; Kofukuji; Yogachara.

host, a common designation for the thin, usually round, wafers of unleavened bread used for Communion in the Roman Catholic Church.

hotoku (hoh-toh-koo; Jap.,"returning virtue"), Japanese concept of repaying what is received from heaven, earth, and humans by sincerity and diligence. Ninomiya Sontoku (1787–1856) and his followers formed societies around this idea. *See also* Ninomiya Sontoku.

Ho-t'u, Lo-shu (huh-*too*, lwaw-shoo; Chin., "Yellow River Diagram," "Lo River Writing"), cosmological diagrams. In Chou mythology, the Ho-t'u was revealed to Fu Hsi by a "dragon-horse" from the Yellow River; he used it to create the eight trigrams (*pa-kua*). The Lo-shu was revealed to Yu the Great on the back of a turtle from the Lo River. Extant diagrams date from the early Sung Neo-Confucianists in the tenth century but probably originated in third-century B.C. numerology. They comprise grids of numbers from one to ten (Ho-t'u) or from one to nine (Lo-shu); the latter is equivalent to the Magic Square of Three. *See also* Fu Hsi; pa-kua.

Hou-chi (hoh-jee; Chin., "Lord Millet"), Chinese agricultural deity and divine ancestor of the Chou people. *See also* Chou religion.

house of study (Heb. *bet midrash*), rabbinic center for study and prayer. Through the talmudic period, the *bet midrash,* under exclusive rabbinic control, was distinct from and deemed by the rabbis to be holier than the community-run synagogue. In medieval times, the bet midrash often was merged with the synagogue but retained its distinctive character as a place primarily for study of rabbinic texts and Jewish law, rather than for prayer. In contemporary usage, the term refers either to an academy of rabbinic study or to the area within such an academy designated for study of rabbinic texts. *See also* Torah study.

Houteff, Victor T. *See* Branch Davidians.

hsiao (sheeou; Chin., "filial piety"), Confucian virtue of properly serving one's parents. Confucius (551–479 B.C.) considered it a child's natural obligation to both living and dead parents. Filial reverence was extended by analogy to political submission and was a conception expressed both in ancestral rituals and imperial worship of Heaven and Earth. *See also* Confucianism; Hsiao-ching.

Hsiao-ching (shahoh-jing; Chin., "Book of Filial Piety"), one of the central books of Confucianism used to train children in respect for elders and proper action (*li*) in all public and private relationships. *See also* Confucianism; li.

hsien (shen; Chin., "immortal"), in Chinese traditions, a human being who has achieved immortality through certain transformations after a long refinement of the soul and body. Such a transformation enables the *hsien* to possess magic powers and roam in heavenly realms, unlike the spirits of the dead, who are usually subject to the judgment and control of the subterranean bureaucracy. The Chinese concept of immortality appeared as early as the eighth century B.C. Only after the fourth century B.C. was a cult of hsien mentioned, which grew tremendously popular in the Han dynasty (206 B.C.–A.D. 220). Immortals in the Han were envisioned as dwelling on the elusive eastern isles or on the western K'un-lun peaks and as freely bestowing drugs of deathlessness.

Religious Taoism in the Six Dynasties (220–581) systematized and elaborated hsien techniques to include dietary, respiratory, and gymnastic methods; alchemical and sexual practices; and the visualization of the deities abiding in the body as well as the macrocosm. Degrees of refinement might allow one to become either a celestial hsien (complete purification of both soul and body, achieved during one's lifetime) or a terrestrial hsien (deliverance of soul from body only after death). The former abide in celestial realms while the latter dwell in the holy mountains and secret caverns of the world. The hsien ideal gave rise to a vast body of Taoist and folkloric art throughout Chinese history. *See also* alchemy; immortality; K'un-lun; physiological techniques (Taoism).

Hsi K'ang (shee kahng; 223–262), a member of the Taoist "Seven Sages of the Bamboo Grove" (Chu-lin ch'i-hsien) who insisted that one should follow one's heart instead of conventional Confucian norms. *See also* Chu-lin ch'i-hsien; Hsuan-hsueh.

Hsi-ming (shee-ming; Chin., "Western Inscription"), a writing by the Neo-Confucian philosopher Chang Tsai interpreting the Ch'ien (father) and K'un (mother) hexagrams from the *I-ching* (Book of Changes) and using them to express the relationships among humanity, nature, and heaven. *See also* Chang Tsai; I-ching; Neo-Confucianism.

hsin (shin; Chin., "heart-mind"), a central concept in the classical Chinese philosophical tradition. It refers generally to the seat of intelligence, emotion, and wisdom.

hsing (shing; Chin., "human nature"), according to the Confucian *Chung Yung* (Doctrine of the Mean), what heaven imparts to human beings for their moral cultivation and perfection. Human nature is manifested through the five constant virtues of humanness, righteousness, ritual propriety, wisdom, and faithfulness. For the Neo-Confucians, human nature is a species of heavenly principle found in every human being. Following Mencius, most Confucians hold that human nature is fundamentally good, although human beings can only realize the good if they correctly cultivate their nature through study and service to others. *See also* Chung Yung; Confucianism; Neo-Confucianism.

Hsin-hsueh (shin-shweh; Chin., "School of Mind"), the second most important Neo-Confucian religiophilosophic movement, founded by Lu Hsiang-shan (Lu Chiu-yuan, 1139–93) and revived by Wang Yang-ming (1472–1529) in the mid–Ming dynasty. In contradistinction to the School of Principle (Li-hsueh), it taught that moral and cosmic principles are to be found by the examination of mind and not in external things. It is also known for the doctrine of the unity of knowledge and action. *See also* Li-hsueh; Lu Hsiang-shan; Neo-Confucianism; Wang Yang-ming.

Hsiung Shih-li (shuhng shuhr-lee; 1885–1968), twentieth-century reformer of idealistic Neo-Confucianism; he eclectically combined elements from Wang Yang-ming, "consciousness-only" Buddhism, the *I-ching*, and Western philosophy. *See also* I-ching; Neo-Confucianism; Wang Yang-ming.

Hsi Wang-mu (shee wong-moo; Chin. "Queen Mother of the West"), Chinese Han (206 B.C.–A.D. 220) goddess of death, immortality, and the Western Paradise. Pictured with a leopard tail, tiger teeth, and a spool-like headdress, she sat on K'un-lun mountain by a sacred tree and was accompanied by the jade hare preparing immortality drugs, the three-legged bird (sun symbol), the toad (moon symbol), the nine-tailed fox, and sometimes an armed guard. She presided over peach feasts with immortality seekers. Her less popular male counterpart was "King Lord of the East" (Tung Wang-gung). *See also* crane; Han religion; K'un-lun; Mu T'ien-tzu chuan.

Hsi-yu chi (shee-yoh jee; Chin., "Journey to the West"), a Chinese novel written in the late Ming period (sixteenth century) and commonly attributed to Wu Ch'eng-en. By a fanciful and elaborate retelling of the historical story of the monk Hsuan-tsang's seventh-century pilgrimage to India in search of Buddhist scriptures, the novel explores basic Chinese religious themes such as the Buddhist ideas of emptiness and nonduality, Taoist self-cultivation through internal alchemy, Confucian moral order, and the syncretic harmony of these three traditions. Hsuan-tsang's westward journey, assisted by a semidivine monkey and other companions, becomes a subtle allegory for the religious quest. *See also* Hsuan-tsang.

hsu (shoo; Chin., "vacuity," "emptiness"), a term often used in Taoist texts to describe the mystical state of oneness with the Tao. *See also* Tao.

hsuan (shwahn; Chin., "dark," "mysterious," "occult"), a key term in Chinese religious and philosophical writing applied, often adjectivally, to metaphysical entities.

Hsuan-hsueh (shwahn-shweh; Chin., "Abstruse Learning"), a Chinese religio-philosophical movement that developed in the third and fourth centuries as a reaction against the formalist ritualism and artificial cosmology of Han Confucianism. This movement is basically syncretic and is focused on an awakening of the self. Primary concerns involve the relationship between being and nonbeing, language and meaning, and Confucian ethics and Taoist philosophy. All three of these issues are centered on the problem of defining the personality of a sage. According to Wang Pi, the root of the world is nonbeing, which refers to an undifferentiated state from which all things spontaneously emerged. Nonbeing per se is unutterable and must be expressed through beings. Similarly, in the human realm nonbeing must be realized through rituals and moral codes. Whoever spontaneously responds to the world in accord with these principles is a sage. Therefore the thought of Confucius and of Lao-tzu become one. Hsi K'ang, who emphasized spiritual freedom, turned to Chuang-tzu. Insisting that one should be true to one's inner feelings, he rejected Confucian ethics. Kuo Hsiang argued that only those who harmonize with things within the human realm can achieve spiritual freedom beyond it. Hence, a sage is a Taoist who observes moral codes, or a Confucian who attains spiritual transcendence. *See also* Hsi K'ang; Kuo Hsiang; Wang Pi.

Hsuan-tsang (shwahn-dzahng; 596–664), T'ang monk whose pilgrimage to India is celebrated by the popular Chinese novel *Hsi-yu chi* (The Journey to the West). Noted for his extensive translations of Yogachara scriptures into Chinese, he was also the founder of the Fa-hsiang school. *See also* Fa-hsiang school; Hsi-yu chi.

Hsun-tzu (shuhn-dyuh; ca. 312–230 B.C.), Chinese Confucian philosopher (fl. 298–238 B.C.) famous for his belief that human nature is evil until cultivated through the practice of *li* (ritual). He believed that true rulers should be educated sages who have gained the moral insight and popular support necessary for effective leadership. He condemned the mysticism and the mockery of Confucian ritual by Mo-tzu and Chuang-tzu, as well as the ethereal Confucian idealism of Mencius. His text, known as the *Hsun-tzu*, consists of thirty-two sections, some in fragments and not all by his own hand. *See also* Chuang-tzu; li; Mencius; Mo-tzu.

Hua-hu ching (hwah-*hoo* jing; Chin., "Conversion of the Barbarians"), an anti-Buddhist text compiled by the Taoist Wang Fou in the early fourth century and later expanded; it is now lost. The text pictured Buddhism as merely a debased form of Taoism taught to Indian "barbarians" by Lao-tzu, hence unfit for Chinese. *See also* China, Buddhism in.

Huai-nan tzu (hw*i*-nahn dzuh; Chin., "The Master of Huai-nan"), syncretistic Taoist text compiled at the court of Liu An, king of Huai-nan, around 139 B.C. It includes chapters on astronomy, astrology, statecraft, and other philosophical topics and represents a summary of Huang-Lao Taoist teachings of the early Han period. *See also* Huang-Lao Taoism.

Huang-chin (hwahng-jin; Chin., "Yellow Turbans"), a Chinese Taoist politico-religious uprising of A.D. 184 that helped to end the Han dynasty. Persuaded that the "yellow heaven" would replace the "blue heaven," they wore yellow turbans as their symbol. *See also* Chinese sectarian religions.

Huang-ch'uan (hwahng-chwan; Chin., "Yellow Springs"), the Chinese underworld in the first millennium B.C., dark underground waters where earthworms drink and people meet again after death. *See also* afterworld; Chinese myth.

Huang-Lao Taoism (hwahng-lau), the earliest documentable Taoist movement, originating on the eastern coast of China around the third century B.C. Its devotees venerated Lao-tzu, teacher of self-cultivation and perfect government through inaction, and Huang-ti, a legendary king who was considered the ideal ruler and patron of immortality practices. Among the ruling elite, Empress Dowager Tou became its most famous promulgator. When she died (135 B.C.), Huang-Lao Taoism was displaced by Confucianism at the imperial court, though its political ideals and esoteric arts continued to be influential in organized Taoism. *See also* Huai-nan tzu; Huang-ti; Lao-tzu; Taoism.

Huang-tao (hwahng-dou; Chin., "the Yellow Way"), Chinese term for "the ecliptic," the apparent path through the twenty-eight lunar mansions traced by the sun, moon, and planets. *See also* astrology.

Huang-ti (hwahng-dee; Chin., "Yellow Emperor"), ancient god, mythical sage-ruler, and one of the "five emperors." A cosmogonic deity, he is god of the intersection of heaven and earth and all associated images of centrality (earth, yellow, the imperial metropolis, etc.); he is also the inventor of metallurgy and other civilizing arts. *See also* Chinese myth; Fu Hsi; Huang-Lao Taoism; Huang-ti nei-ching; sang-huang; Wu-ti.

Huang-ti nei-ching (hwahng-dee nay-jing; Chin., "Inner Classic of the Yellow Emperor"), oldest and most influential treatise on Chinese traditional medicine. Written as a conversation between the legendary Yellow Emperor and his physician, it pictures the human being as a microcosm of the universe and discusses ethics, religion, and life regimens. *See also* Chinese medicine.

Huang-t'ing ching (hwahng-ting jing; Chin., "Yellow Court Scripture"), important scripture of Shang-ch'ing Taoism written during the fourth century and consisting of an "inner" and "outer" canon. Based on ancient traditions, it describes the visualization of various gods inhabiting the body as a means to longevity, even immortality. *See also* body; Shang-ch'ing Taoism.

hua-t'ou (hwah-toh; Chin., "head of speech"), Chinese Buddhist technique derived from the *kung-an* (a paradoxical teaching that transcends logical or conceptual thought) and used to clear the mind of conceptualizations and produce meditative calm. *See also* Ch'an school; kung-an; meditation.

Hua-yen school (hwah-yen; Chin., "Flower Garland"), indigenous Chinese school originating in the sixth century that represents the development of autonomous Buddhist thought in China. Named for the *Avatamsaka*, or "Garland Sutra," the Hua-yen claims that this text contains the Buddha's superlative teaching. Hua-yen lore states that the Buddha preached the *Avatamsaka* immediately after his enlightenment. His followers were unable to comprehend it, however, so the

Buddha resorted to simpler, then increasingly advanced, teachings until they were able to grasp the perfect teaching of the *Avatamsaka*. The centrality of doctrinal classification in the Hua-yen school is evident in its fivefold classification scheme, articulated primarily by Ch'eng-kuan and Fa-tsang. This scheme posits three levels of "gradual" teachings, followed by the "sudden" and "perfect" teachings. The Hua-yen school is often identified with the "teaching of totality," which refers to its most distinctive doctrine. Hua-yen posits that all *dharmas* (events) have two states: principle or noumenon (*li*) and phenomenon (*shih*). Li is the static and essential condition of all things, whereas shih represents their dynamic state, which gives rise to phenomena. Although li and shih articulate dualistic categories, Hua-yen teaches that the two completely interpenetrate each other (*li-shih wu-ai*). Thus, it was possible to hold that the deluded mind in its phenomenal state still had the purity of noumenon intrinsic to it. It also teaches that all phenomena interpenetrate each other (*shih-shih wu-ai*), building on Buddhist theories of causality that claim that all events arise codependently. *See also* Ch'eng-kuan; Chih-yen; China, Buddhism in; Fa-tsang; Haein Temple; Tu-shun.

Huguenots (hyoo'guh-nots; Fr., origin disputed), the name given to French Calvinist Protestants. At first subject to persecution, they were granted limited toleration by the Edict of Nantes (1598), banished from France in 1685, and granted full political rights in 1789.

Hui-neng (hway-nuhng; 638–713), the purported sixth patriarch of Ch'an Buddhism who rose from a simple rice pounder to defeat Shen-hsiu for the position after composing a poem demonstrating his superior understanding. He is credited with founding the Southern school, distinctive for its emphasis on instantaneous enlightenment and iconoclasm toward traditional Buddhist rituals, figures, and texts. *See also* Ch'an school; Shen-hsiu; Southern school.

Hui-ssu (hway-suh; 515–577), northern Chinese Buddhist monk whose teachings formed the precursor of the T'ien-t'ai school. Known for his adeptness at meditation exercises, he was also the teacher of Chih-i, who was the founder of T'ien-t'ai. He first articulated the premise that the *Lotus Sutra* contained the highest Buddhist teaching. *See also* Chih-i; Lotus Sutra; T'ien-t'ai school.

Hui-yuan (hway-yooan; 344–416), Chinese Buddhist monk noted for the religious community he founded at Lu-shan. He focused on the *prajna* (Skt., "wisdom") texts, often explaining them through Taoist terminology, and promoted the translation of *dhyana* (meditation) texts. He organized the first recorded Amitabha cult and is thus considered the first patriarch of Pure Land Buddhism. *See also* Pure Land school (China).

Hujjat al-Islam (hooj'at el-is-lahm'; Arab., "Proof of Islam"), a title designating a learned authority. Hujjat al-Islam, in Shiite Iran, was a *mujtahid* (religious authority) with political prestige. Now that religious and political authority are intertwined, Hujjat al-Islam is a member of the religio-political establishment below the rank of mujtahid.

hu-lu (hoo-loo; Chin., "calabash," "gourd"), a gourd with twin bulges and a constricted middle (*Lagenaria siceraria*) or a similarly shaped pot or vase. A traditional decorative motif, it refers in Taoism and popular Chinese religious lore to the mythological themes of a miniature paradise world or a container that holds the elixir of life.

Human Potential movement, a term used to designate the loosely affiliated contemporary groups promoting the release of the innate human capacity for creativity through self-realization practices.

Related to the teachings of G. I. Gurdjieff (ca. 1877–1949) on the untapped potentials of the human mind and to efforts begun by psychologist Abraham Maslow on group awareness, the movement expanded during the 1960s and 1970s to comprise numerous autonomous institutes, communities, and study groups. Popular practices include Asian-influenced yoga and meditation, holistic medicine, encounter groups, and controversial psychological techniques such as primal scream therapy and rebirthing. Participants in the movement hope to experience a fuller life, heightened perception, and spiritual well-being. *See also* Gurdjieff, Georgei Ivanovitch.

hungan (huhn-gahn'), or *oungan*, male ritual specialist, according to traditional Voodoo or Vodou terminology. Synonymous with "papa-loa" or "male master of the gods," this title has its origins in African Fon religion, and in Haitian religion identifies a complex role of priest, visionary, and counselor. *See also* Voodoo.

Hung-chou school (huhng-joh), ninth-century Chinese Ch'an Buddhist sect founded by Ma-tsu and predecessor of the Lin-chi school of the Sung dynasty. It stressed that all mental and physical actions were manifestations of Buddha-nature and sought to collapse the dualism between delusion and enlightenment by emphasizing the intrinsic purity of mind, which was manifest in all spontaneous expressions of feeling. It also supported the technique of "sudden enlightenment," which eschewed the need for arduous self-cultivation in favor of an instantaneous realization of one's originally pure nature. The Hung-chou line survived its rivals, but often came under attack for its antinomian tendencies. *See also* Ch'an school; Lin-chi school; Ma-tsu; sudden enlightenment.

Hung Hsiu-chuan (huhng shoh-jwan), the founder of the T'ai-ping movement, an eclectic Christian-Chinese cult that rebelled against the Ch'ing dynasty in 1849 to 1864.

Hung (1814–64) underwent a religious episode in 1837 and seven years later interpreted his dreams as a call from God to convert to Christianity and to evangelize among the Hakka people of South China. After studying the Bible and the doctrines of Baptist Christianity, he finally rejected formal denominational Protestantism and developed his own sectarian tradition.

In this new religion, Hung combined Confucian elements and his own Jehovah-centered version of Christianity. He also developed outlines for a radical new society based upon the laws found in the Pentateuch and those found in traditional Chinese works. This society was intended to live by a strict code that stressed adherence to a rigid morality and was intended to cure the evils of life in the late Ch'ing. *See also* China, Christianity in; T'ai-ping Rebellion.

Huns, an inner Asian people of the south Russian steppe and central Europe during the third to the fifth centuries; they are best known under the rule of Attila from 434 to 453 for perturbing both Roman and Christian political and religious control. *See also* Inner Asian religions.

hunting, religious aspects of. While the religious practices and beliefs of hunters and gatherers vary widely, hunting as a ritual activity shares a common ideology among diverse groups, especially among circumpolar peoples. Within the hunt, which usually is undertaken only by initiated males, the worlds of animals, of humans, and of supernatural beings are brought together in complex structures of reciprocity. The hunter leaves behind the human world of the settlement and enters the "wild" worlds of the animals and supernatural beings. With skills that are often understood to be gifts from the spirits, the hunter seeks to kill the animal (also a supernatural gift), which is represented as an offering to the supernatural realm. The meat meal is seen as a dinner with the animal as host, and humans and supernatural beings as guests. Great ritual care is taken by the hunters to return the spirit of the animal to its supernatural home or owner, eventually to return again as a game animal. *See also* Ainu religion; Australian and Pacific traditional religions; bear ceremonialism; Bladder Festival; Finnish religion; fishing rites/whaling rites; master/mistress of the animals; North America, traditional religions in; South American religions, traditional; traditional peoples, religions of.

hun-tun (huhn-duhn; Chin., "chaos"). **1** Ancient Chinese mythological term for a figure or undifferentiated condition associated with the creation of the world. **2** Technical term in Taoism for a state of undifferentiated consciousness. *See also* Chinese myth; cosmogony.

huppah (khoo-pah'; Heb., "covering"), the canopy under which the Jewish wedding ceremony is performed. Usually made of a prayer shawl or other fabric draped over four poles, it symbolizes the home in which the couple begins married life. *See also* Judaism (life cycle).

Hurrians (hurr'ee-uhnz), a people who formed a major part of the population of eastern Anatolia, northern Syria, northern Iraq, and northwestern Iran in the second millennium B.C. The Hurrian language, known from cuneiform inscriptions, is neither Semitic nor Indo-European, having close affinities only with Urartian. A common origin for Hurro-Urartian and East Caucasian languages still spoken in the former Soviet Union has been suggested but not proven.

Hurrians appear in northern Mesopotamia at least as early as the mid-third millennium, and later inhabited an arc of territory from Alalakh and Ugarit on the Mediterranean coast to Nuzi in northeastern Mesopotamia, largely in societies in which they formed only one element of a polyglot population. They constituted a substantial majority in the kingdom of Mitanni, which dominated northern Mesopotamia and Syria in the middle of the second millennium, but even in this case the ruling elites belonged to another, Indo-Iranian–speaking group. Hurrian traditions, particularly myths and rituals, were extremely important in the Hittite Empire, many of whose kings bore Hurrian names before ascending to the throne.

Hurrian diffusion and assimilation complicate the discussion of Hurrian religion, which cannot be treated as a unified or consistent system. Hurrian myths and rituals are best documented at the Hittite capital, Boghazkoy, but elsewhere such fundamentals as the rank of gods differ. In most cases the head of the pantheon is the Teshub, a weather god often depicted astride a bull or in a chariot drawn by bulls. Also important are the goddess Hepat, a solar deity who serves as Teshub's consort in the west, and Shaushga, who combines the attributes of a war goddess with authority over sexuality and passion.

Scriptural references to "Horites" (Hurrians) as one of the preconquest populations of the promised land probably have some validity, as does the suggestion that many biblical references to Hittites would make more sense if this were merely a corruption of the word for Hurrian. *See also* Hittites.

Hus, Jan (huhs; Ger. pron., hoos; 1372–1415), Bohemian Christian reformer, early supporter of John Wyclif. Hus (also Huss) is best known for his attacks on the immorality of clergy and indulgences, for his valuing of scripture over tradition, and for his argument that the Roman Catholic Church was only one branch of the church militant. His advocacy of distributing both wine and bread to the laity resulted in his followers (Hussites) being known as Utraquists (Lat., "each of two"). Hus was burned as a heretic.

After Hus's death, his followers formed their own group, the Unitas Fratrum ("Unity of the Brethren"), refashioned, in 1727, as the Renewed Unitas Fratrum or Moravian Church.

Husayn ibn Ali (hoo-sayn' ibn ah'lee; b. 626), grandson of Muhammad by his daughter Fatima and third *imam* of the Shii Muslim community. Tradition abounds with tales of the Prophet's love for Husayn and his elder brother, Hasan, whom Muhammad called "the two masters of the youths of Paradise." Husayn's fame, however, rests on his religio-political opposition to Umayyad rule, which finally cost him his life.

In answer to the repeated entreaties of the followers of Ali and his descendants in Iraq, Husayn agreed to lead them in *jihad* (armed struggle) against the Umayyad ruler Yazid. Accompanied by his family and a small band of supporters, Husayn set out for Kufa, the district capital of Iraq and center of Shii activism.

Husayn and his seventy-odd armed men were intercepted by a large army, which included many of his alleged supporters. He was forced to encamp at a spot called Karbala on the banks of the Euphrates. After a week of inconclusive negotiations, matters were brought to a head on the day of *ashura*, 10 Muharram (October) 680. Husayn, his sons except one, and all his male followers died in the uprising, and the women were taken captive. This tragedy and the events leading to it provided the context for the Shii ethos of suffering and martyrdom and an inspiration for poetry and drama, liturgy, and devotion. *See also* Ashura; Shia; Taziyah.

Hussites. *See* Hus, Jan.

Huter, Jacob (d. 1536), also Hutter, Moravian Christian Anabaptist leader, executed as a heretic, whose communal followers became known as Hutterites. *See also* Hutterites.

Hutterites also called Hutterian Brethren, an Anabaptist group of Moravian origin taking its name from Jacob Huter (martyred 1536). After years of enforced migration through central and eastern Europe, the Hutterites finally abandoned the Ukraine to settle in the northern American prairies in the 1870s. Hutterites differ from other groups of Anabaptist origin such as the Amish, whom they resemble in many ways, primarily in holding goods communally. This practice, together with their use of modern farming equipment, has given them an economic advantage often leading to friction with their neighbors and has led in part to their migration from the Dakotas to the prairie provinces of Canada. Currently, there are about three hundred Hutterite colonies, or family-based settlements, in North America. *See also* Anabaptists.

hwadu (hwa-doo), a dialogue technique used by Ch'an (Kor. *Son*) Buddhists in Korea. The *hwadu* is an exchange between a Ch'an master and his disciple in which a series of questions is asked about a story (Chin. *kung-an;* Jap. *koan*) taken from Ch'an history. These stories record a similar exchange between Ch'an masters and their disciples in the past and the answers given by those disciples who were then judged as being enlightened. In Korean practice, the Ch'an practitioner is expected to concentrate on the meaning of the recorded response and demonstrate his own understanding to the master. This practice allows the master to gauge how close the disciple is to his own enlightenment. *See also* Ch'an school; kung-an.

Hwarang Troop (hwah-rang; Kor. *Hwarangdo,* "Flower Youth Troop"), a Korean aristocratic military group of the Silla and Unified Silla periods (sixth–eighth centuries) responsible for the assimilation and practical application of Chinese literature, religion, philosophy, and practical arts to the service of the state. The Hwarangdo was a communal body of unmarried males drawn from native and subjugated aristocratic and royal families in the kingdom of Silla. They lived by a set of rules meant to inculcate absolute loyalty and sincerity to the monarchy, filiality and fidelity in friendship, and courage and compassion in warfare and military service to the state.

This group was established and headed by a Buddhist priest, though there are indications that it had been modeled on a previous group established by and for women mediums and shamanic adepts. Members of the troop made pilgrimages to sacred mountains and streams, conducted singing and dancing rituals, sought the intervention of dragon spirits in human affairs, and studied the traditions of Buddhism, Taoism, and Confucianism. This group was heavily influenced by the then current belief in the imminent descent of Maitreya, since the head of this group and later some of its members were identified as incarnations of the future Buddha. It was also influenced by native and imported Taoist traditions of the transformation of humans into immortals, and several members are said to have ascended into the sky. Several outstanding warriors and statesmen of Silla are said to have come from this troop, and the group itself was instrumental in the unification of the peninsula by Silla and the securing of borders against T'ang incursions after T'ang troops had aided Silla in the destruction of the kingdoms of Koguryo and Paekche. *See also* Kim Yushin; Korea, Maitreyism in.

hyanggyo. *See* academies (Korea), private and public.

Hydra (hī'druh), a Greek mythological monster with many serpent heads, guardian of the spring at Lerna in Greece, who was killed by the hero Herakles.

hymn, song that invokes or celebrates the god(s).

hymnody, Christian, songs for liturgical use. Since the sixteenth-century Protestant Reformation, hymnody has become unison singing by congregations. Earlier, hymns were often sung by an individual or a few voices. Many biblical texts are hymns woven into Gospels or Epistles. The Magnificat (Luke 1:46–55) is the best known; but other examples are Luke 1:68–79; John 1:1–18; and Philippians 2:5–11. Both Byzantine and Western chant and hymnody derive from the Syro-Palestinian liturgy and its roots in Jewish synagogue practice with little unison singing and much improvisation. During the Middle Ages, congregations sang carols, while hymns developed in private devotion and as transitions in liturgies sung by leaders. In Reformation traditions, Martin Luther (1483–1546) encouraged all worshipers to sing hymns with lyrics based on biblical texts and with tunes taken from popular songs. By the mid-sixteenth century, John Calvin had promoted the *Geneva Psalter* (1563) with metrical settings of all 150 Psalms to 125 different tunes; but English Puritans sang psalms to fewer tunes.

Modern hymnody dates from Isaac Watts's *Hymns and Spiritual Songs* (1707), which developed lyrics expressing response to Christian experience. Such developments were expanded with Charles Wesley's (1707–88) lyrics for nine thousand hymns and John Wesley's (1703–91) translations of German hymns. Hymns figured prominently in the Oxford Movement's renewal of Anglican liturgy during the 1830s. In the 1870s, simplified hymns motivated revivals led by Dwight Moody and Ira Sankey in England and America. Liturgical renewal inspired by Vatican II in the mid-twentieth century opened many Roman Catholic churches to hymns sung by congregations. *See also* Calvin, John; Christianity (worship); Luther, Martin; Magnificat; Moody, Dwight Lyman; Oxford Movement; Watts, Isaac; Wesley, Charles; Wesley, John.

hypostasis, the widespread pattern of personifying as a separate deity an attribute or an organ of a divine being, for example, the word of God, divine wisdom. *See also* Logos; Shekhina; Sophia.

A B C D E F
G H I J K L
M N O
R S T
W X Y & Z

i (yee; Chin., "rightness," "appropriateness," "duty"), Confucian virtue of proper self-orientation, the guiding principle that directs people to their duties and restricts impulsive actions. Respectful children and trustworthy officers have variously attained this sense of appropriateness. Mencius considered it one of four basic human virtues. *See also* Confucianism; Mencius.

I AM Religious Activity, the religious movement begun in the United States in 1930 by Guy Ballard (1878–1939) following his encounter with the Ascended Master Saint Germain, an important spirit guide known in Theosophy. The I AM movement is in the theosophical lineage and emphasizes reincarnation, chanting, color, and spiritual ascension as the goal of human life. It inculcates American patriotism, and many members have supported the political right. In 1944 charges against I AM leaders were rejected by the U.S. Supreme Court in a landmark religious liberty decision. *See also* Great White Brotherhood; North America, new religions in; Theosophy.

Ibadat. *See* Five Pillars; Islamic law.

Ibadite (i-bah'd/t; from Arab. *Ibadi*), a member of the Islamic sect that broke away from the Kharijites in the seventh century. The founding of the Ibadites is attributed in traditional sources to Abd Allah Ibn Ibad, who is said to have broken with the more extreme Kharijites, especially over the latter's insistence on the assassination of non-Kharijites for religious reasons. A moderate sect, the Ibadites engaged in religious discussions with other Muslim groups and survive today in small communities in East and West Africa. *See also* Seceders.

Iblis (ib-lees'; Arab., probably from Gk. *diabolos,* "devil"), a complex demonic figure in Islamic religious thought, understood as the fallen angel, the tempter, and the head of the hosts of devils. As an angel, he pridefully refused God's command to bow down before the newly created man Adam and thus was cursed and banished from Paradise. Until the Day of Judgment Iblis will lead the legions of devils in tempting humans to do evil. His major act of cunning was to persuade Adam and Eve to disobey God and eat of the tree of immortality in the Garden, which resulted in their consignment to earthly existence. *See also* Adam and Eve; Day of Judgment (Islam).

Ibn al-Arabi, Muhyi ad-Din (i'bin el-ah'ruh-bee; 1165– 1240), the grand master of Islamic mystical philosophy. Ibn al-Arabi's writings constitute a central moment in Sufism. They place mystical union (*fana,* lit., "passing away") at the heart of medieval Islamic discourse, and are grounded in the Sufi notion of the complete human being. A recurrent image is the human heart as a mirror that, in mystical union, becomes the locus of divine self-revelation. Of the more than two hundred works attributed to Ibn al-Arabi, the best known are *The Interpreter of Desires* (love odes and mystical commentaries on them), *The Meccan Openings* (his comprehensive *summa*), and *The Ringsettings of Wisdom* (a microcosm of his ideas presented as a direct revelation from the Prophet Muhammad).

Ibn al-Arabi's fluid and dynamic dialectic of immanence and transcendence was later systematized under the doctrine of *wahdat al-wujud* (unity of being). Many Sufis consider him to be the "seal of the Muhammadiyyan saints." His tomb in Damascus has become a popular shrine. *See also* Sufism.

Ibn al-Rewandi (ibn ar-ra-wahn'dee; d. ca. 910), ninth-century extreme rationalist Muslim theologian. Apparently originally a Mutazilite, and subsequently accused of some form of Manichaeism, Ibn al-Rewandi's late thought was often represented as opposed to religion. Arguing that "the prophets were all magicians," Ibn al-Rewandi rejected the doctrine of divine revelation, championed the doctrines of dualism and eternity of the world, and attacked the ostensible miracles and other supernatural elements of the Qur'an. By deriding not only Muhammad and the Qur'an, but prophecy and scriptures in general, Ibn al-Rewandi was castigated by Muslim religious thinkers as the archetypal sneering and hyperrationalistic exponent of irreligion. Such notoriety may account for the lack of preservation of his books. *See also* Mutazila.

Ibn Khaldun (ibn' khal-doon; 1332–1406), a Muslim philosopher and historian whose three-volume introduction to world history has had considerable influence on scholarship in both the Islamic and Western worlds. He expounded a theory of cyclical movement in history, in which nations emerge from the communal spirit of tribal solidarity (*asabiyya*) that, in turn, decays once political power and urban luxury are attained. These ideas have earned him the title of the first sociologist. Ibn Khaldun's theory of religion focuses on its superiority over mere kinship and tribal solidarity in social formation. Ibn Khaldun's introduction has been translated into several languages, including English. *See also* Islamic philosophy.

Ibn Taymiyya (ibn' tay-mee'yuh; 1263–1328), an Arab theologian and legal scholar, active in Syria and Egypt, teaching Hanbalite law and other Islamic disciplines. He polemicized against the teachings of the other three Sunni schools of law and opposed the corrupt practices of the Sufis of his day. As a result, his opponents had him imprisoned several times, in Cairo, Alexandria, and Damascus. His writings and reputation for activism have continued to inspire and influence reformers and radicals. *See also* Hanbalite; Islamic law.

Ibrahim. *See* Abraham.

I-ching (ee-jing; Chin., "Book of Changes"), a diviner's manual traditionally ranked first among the Five Classics of Confucianism. It enjoys pride of place within the Confucian canon because its archaic origins may be traced to the ritual divinations of the royal Chou court in the eleventh century B.C. and perhaps even earlier. The method of the *Changes* partially supplanted the Shang-dynasty practice of divining by oracle bones, but may have shared a certain number mysticism with its predecessor.

The oldest stratum of the *Changes* consists of the sixty-four six-line figures, or hexagrams, representing all possible combinations of a basic set of eight trigrams composed of broken and unbroken parallel lines, together with the prognostications associated with the individual lines and with each hexagram as a whole. The appendices known as the "Ten Wings" date from about the second century B.C.; they offer a Confucian exegesis of what was already a most obscure text. In practice each hexagram is built up line by line from the bottom through a procedure involving the arbitrary division and counting off of a handful of yarrow stalks that establishes the numerical value of each line, whether odd (unbroken) or even (broken), changing or stable. When the broken and unbroken lines became identified with *yin* and *yang*, the binary process of building each hexagram seemed to the cosmologists to symbolize perfectly the evolution and numerical structure of the cosmos itself. In the system of the *Changes*, the enigmatic "images" associated with the hexagrams and their various parts are thought to offer instruction about the dynamic potentials of phenomenal circumstances and how to respond to them. *See also* astronomy (China); Confucianism (authoritative texts and their interpretation); divination; yin and yang.

icon (Gk., "image," "portrait"), especially in Byzantine and Orthodox Christianity, a visual representation of Jesus Christ, the Virgin Mary, angels, individual saints, or events of sacred history. Varying in size from small portable to wall-size icons, these sacred images were made of mosaic or painted colors, never carved or sculpted.

Frontal, flat, laconic, and shadowless, the icon was a visual window to the meaning of the event or holy person depicted, not a realistic presentation sacred in and of itself (and, thus, idolatrous).

The legitimacy of the use of icons was affirmed at the Second Council of Nicaea (787) after a protracted battle against their use by the "image breakers" (*iconclasts*). This event is still annually memorialized as the "Triumph of Orthodoxy" in the Eastern liturgies of Christendom. *See also* Christianity (art and architecture); Orthodox Church.

iconoclasm (Gk., "breaking images"), a religious tradition that attacks the use of images in worship. *See also* aniconic; images, veneration of.

Christianity: Within Christianity, various iconoclastic movements have rejected both the anthropomorphic depiction of God and the representation of the human figure and its veneration in art.

Iconoclasm is most often associated with Byzantium, where religious disturbances were engendered by debates on the theology of the icon and the Second Council of Nicaea (787) and the Synod of Orthodoxy (843–847) officially denounced iconoclasm.

Protestant iconoclasm initially reacted violently toward images. John Calvin (1509–64) and Huldrych Zwingli (1484–1531) rejected them; Martin Luther (1483–1546) held a moderate position. Emphasizing the Word, not the image, as the vehicle of revelation, Luther recognized the didactic function of the visual image. His friendship and patronage of the artist Lucas Cranach the Elder led to the establishment of a Protestant iconography. *See also* Christianity (art and architecture).

iconostasis (Gk., "support of image or portrait"), a screen of icons, distinctive to Orthodox Christian churches, separating the altar area from the congregation. Typically, the iconostasis consists of five rows of icons depicting the ways of God in history. *See also* icon; rood screen.

Identity Christianity, a contemporary North American Christian movement named for its identification of the Anglo-Saxon, Germanic, Scandinavian, and other European peoples with the ten tribes of Israel who did not return from the Assyrian captivity of 740 to 721 B.C. Christian Identity evolved in the United States and Canada from British-Israelism. The ideological transformations that would create from the heretofore philo-Semitic theology of British-Israelism the racialist and anti-Semitic doctrines of Christian Identity took place in the interwar years of the twentieth century, primarily in the United States, when profound changes in American social mores, international entanglements, economic disruption, and a massive wave of immigration, particularly of Eastern European Jews, radicalized the movement.

While it is impossible to locate a precise moment in which modern Identity Christianity was born, a key event was a 1930 convention in Detroit that brought together a number of British-Israel adherents, including Howard Rand, the head of the Anglo-Saxon Federation of America, and William J. Cameron, an associate of Henry Ford, Sr., and a driving force behind the publication of the *Dearborn Independent*'s series of anti-Semitic articles, republished for national distribution as the four-volume *The International Jew. The International Jew*, built on the foundation of the spurious *Protocols of the Elders of Zion* (1923–25), won widespread support in the movement, convinced Howard Rand and his more moderate followers of the truth of a Jewish conspiracy theory of history, and was easily combined with the ideas of such racialist British-Israelites as Ku Klux Klan leader Reuben H. Sawyer to lay the foundation for contemporary Christian Identity beliefs.

No systematic dogma is accepted by all Identity Christians; however, there are some constants. From British-Israelism, Identity theorists found in the inerrant Bible sets of "footprints" from a series of forty to fifty passages through which Identity interpretation succeeded in tracing the ten tribes from Palestine to Europe and eventually to North America, identifying in the process the United States as the New Jerusalem. Explicit in this endeavor was the effort to prove through scripture that the divine covenant claimed by the Jews was in reality the most grandiose theft of culture—of identity—in human history, and that the Anglo-Saxon and other European peoples are in fact God's covenant people.

The Jews, shorn of the covenant, were identified as the literal offspring of Eve and Satan (in the guise of the snake) and demonized in scripture as the "synagogue of Satan" (Genesis 2:9, 3:9; John 8:44), whose numbers were swelled by the tenth-century conversion of the Khazar tribe. Additionally, Identity hermeneutics frequently identifies blacks with the "beasts of the field" (Genesis 1:25). Emerging from this hermeneutical process was an intensely dualistic theology characterized by an acute form of apocalyptic millenarianism that would at times catalyze the movement into political action and at other times mandate a selective withdrawal from the surrounding society.

Overlaying the scripturalism of modern Christian Identity are other identifiable strands of belief. From British-Israelism comes a marked strain of occultism, including pyramidology and homeopathy. From the American religious matrix, much of Sacred Name doctrine and a great deal of Mormon influence can be found as well.

Identity praxis, from its inception, has been centered on the imperative to awaken "white Israelites" to their true identity. In Howard Rand's chiliastic formulation, the success of this endeavor would constitute nothing less than universal redemption. Christian Identity, however, has failed to make significant inroads into American consciousness, serving to further fragment an already decentralized movement.

In the decades of the 1940s and 1950s, several key Identity theorists gathered around the xenophobic radio broadcaster Gerald L. K. Smith, learning in the process the techniques of organizing and managing a mass movement of national scope. These individuals, including Wesley Swift, William Potter Gale, Bertrand Camparet, and Colorado anticommunist activist Kenneth Goff, emerged from the Smith movement with a confirmed sense of militancy. They would act as teachers for a new generation of Identity leaders, ordaining men such as Dan Gayman, Richard Butler, and Thomas Robb. These leaders serve to illustrate the compatibility of Identity theology with other belief systems, including the Ku Klux Klan (Sawyer, Swift, and Robb), the antitax Posse Commitatus (Gale), and a number of other right-wing movements.

The Christian Identity movement of the 1960s and 1970s is based on this post–Gerald L. K. Smith model. Ministers locate their churches in a particular area where small, local congregations are formed. These churches tend to be concentrated in the northwestern states, California, and Missouri. From this local base, leading Identity ministers rely on mailing lists to disseminate their teachings via publications and cassette recordings. Radio time has been difficult to obtain, although the late Sheldon Emry of the Heirs of the Promise ministry in Phoenix had a radio network. Dave Barley of Sand Point, Idaho, heir of Heirs of the Promise, sold these radio slots in an attempt to break into satellite television. Identity ministers also utilize summer religious retreats, and some ministries also offer a prison outreach.

Christian Identity today is a deeply divided movement. Like earlier millennial movements, Identity Christians are faced with two choices: withdrawal from society, primarily into survivalism or into isolated compounds, or selective engagement with the dominant culture. While the vast majority of Identity Christians have opted for the latter, a further choice has to be made: heed the council of the radical fringe of the movement and adopt a theology of violence or submit to government authority and maintain their chosen way of life with as much autonomy as is feasible for an unpopular minority religion in the United States. This active/revolutionary vs. withdrawal/submission to authority dichotomy constitutes the primary cleavage among Identity adherents today. Again, almost all Identity Christians have chosen to live within the laws of the society whose core beliefs and values they anathemize. *See also* Aryan Nations; British Israelites; Christian Crusade for Truth; Church of Israel; Covenant, the Sword and the Arm of the Lord; New Christian Crusade Church; Scriptures for America.

ideology and religion. There are two main views of the relationship between religion and ideology: the Marxist view, which sees religion as a case of ideology, and the functionalist view, which sees ideology as a case of religion.

Religion as Ideology: According to Marxists, the economy constitutes the basis, or infrastructure, of society and is composed of two parts: the social relations of production—for example, domination and subordination—and the social forces of production—all the elements involved in the process of production. Politics, law, art, ethics, philosophy, religion, and other noneconomic aspects of society form the superstructure of society.

The Marxist term *ideology* sometimes designates a separate category within the superstructure but more often designates the superstructure as a whole—or better, designates the view expressed by the superstructure. Ideology refers to the way politics, law, art, ethics, philosophy, and religion bolster the infrastructure. Ideology refers not to a single idea but to the whole outlook of a period.

For Marxists, a belief, including a religious belief, can be ideological in any of three ways. Cognitively, a belief is ideological when it is false, thereby blinding one to the truth. More precisely, a belief that is ideological cognitively blinds one to one's true economic interests. Hence religion for Marxists ordinarily diverts

one from worldly, material needs. Genetically, a belief is ideological when it originates as a means of supporting society. Propaganda is the most blatant example of genetic ideology. Functionally, a belief is ideological when, whatever its origin, it serves to uphold society.

Karl Marx (1818–83) himself never assumes that all beliefs are ideological. Science for him is true, originates for wholly intellectual reasons, and has no role in maintaining the economic status quo. But other Marxists, such as Friedrich Engels (1820–95), reduce science to ideology genetically, functionally, and perhaps cognitively. Art for most Marxists can be ideological in one or more senses, but need not be. The same is true of ethics. Both art and ethics will therefore remain in modern socialism, which will be free of the need for ideology but not of the need for art and ethics. Because religion, by contrast, is inherently ideological, at least cognitively and functionally, it will inevitably disappear.

Even though religion, as an expression of ideology, diverts believers from recognizing their real needs, it is not the product of any conspiracy.

On the one hand, no Marxist denies the reality of the superstructure. What is illusory is not the existence but the autonomy of the superstructure. On the other hand, no Marxist denies an intimate tie between the infrastructure and the superstructure. How close the tie is varies from Marxist to Marxist.

Extreme Marxists, including Vladimir Lenin (1870–1924) and sometimes Engels, deem the infrastructure the cause of the superstructure: the economy causes either the form the superstructure takes or the superstructure itself. For example, the infrastructure accounts for the bourgeois form ethics takes in capitalism and accounts for the fact as well as the form of religion in capitalism. The superstructure not only originates out of the infrastructure and mirrors it, but also functions to reinforce it. Protestantism originates out of capitalism, reflects the capitalist notion of autonomous individuals competing freely for success, and serves to justify a kindred economy.

Less extreme Marxists, including Marx himself, grant that the superstructure may arise on its own but insist that it lasts only because it fits the infrastructure, which it both mirrors and reinforces. Protestantism might have arisen for wholly spiritual reasons, but thrives because it matches capitalism better then Catholicism and thereby wins support from capitalism while supporting it. Darwinian-fashion Protestantism survives because it is better suited to its environment.

Ideology as Religion: Religion subsumed under

ideology presupposes a substantive definition of religion: religion is the worship of something supernatural or otherworldly that is in fact the projection of something merely human. By contrast, ideology subsumed under religion assumes a functional definition of religion: religion is whatever set of beliefs and practices stirs a community most deeply. By a functional definition, political ideology, nationalism, and Marxism itself would qualify as religions. Secular humanism, atheistic existentialism, environmentalism, psychoanalysis, feminism, and science might also qualify.

The test is whether a movement garners sufficient loyalty that adherents are prepared to sacrifice themselves for it. The test is also whether a movement provides formal rituals—for example, oaths, holidays, parades, insignia-like flags, founding fathers, martyrs, and revered writings. Belief without practice constitutes a mere philosophy, not a religion.

The French sociologist Emile Durkheim (*The Elementary Forms of the Religious Life*, 1912) pioneers the treatment of ideology as religion. While in places he seems to define religion substantively, he can be viewed as defining the sacred functionally: as whatever moves a society most deeply. In the wake of the decline of Christianity, Durkheim predicts the emergence of a secular religion of the state, a religion akin to the one created during the French Revolution. Alternatively, Durkheim ("Individualism and the Intellectuals," 1898) proposes the creation of a secular religion, one worshiping humanity itself.

The American sociologists W. Lloyd Warner and Robert Bellah follow Durkheim in arguing for a "civil" religion in America. This secular religion, existing alongside Christianity, serves to weld people into a nation. For Bellah, it serves to weld them as a means to a different end: enabling them to serve the national ideals of equality and peace. The fulfillment of those ideals constitutes less a function than a duty.

While anthropologist Clifford Geertz, like Durkheim, refers to the sacred in his definition of religion, he even more clearly than Durkheim defines religion functionally: as whatever "function[s] to synthesize a people's ethos—the tone, character, and quality of their life, its moral and aesthetic style and mood—and their worldview—the picture they have of the way things in sheer actuality are, their most comprehensive ideas of order" (*The Interpretation of Cultures*, 1973). The worldview tells one what to believe, especially about otherwise inexplicable, unendurable, or unjustifiable experiences. The ethos tells one how to act in wake of the worldview. For example, belief in the innate depravity of humanity would explain harm suffered at the hands of others and would make the harm more nearly endurable, whether or not quite justified. The belief would also dictate a more rigid style of childrearing, schooling, and government.

In defining religion by what it does, Geertz allows for secular movements as religions. Those movements must provide practices as well as beliefs, a way of life as well as a set of beliefs, an ethos as well as a worldview. Geertz himself distinguishes ideology as a "cultural system" from religion, but by "ideology" he means political ideology.

There is a difference between an ideology as a secular form of religion and an ideology as a secular counterpart to religion. Many theorists of religion see secular ideology as the modern successor to religion rather than as the continuation of religion. Those theorists who subsume ideology under religion consider ideology a variety of religion, not a substitute for religion.

Whether religion is subsumable under ideology or ideology under religion is an open question. Against the subsumption of religion under ideology one could argue that the extrahuman realm postulated by religion is not reducible to a merely human one. Against the subsumption of ideology under religion one could argue that a secular ideology lacks exactly the extrahuman dimension of religion. *See also* religion, explanation of.

idol (Gk. *eidolon*, "image"), in Western religious discourse, a pejorative term designating, narrowly, any three-dimensional or sculpted figure, or, more broadly, any bas-relief or painting, mosaic, or mural of a figure representing a god or goddess and used in cultic practices. The figure can be in human or animal or other form, including mixed human and animal. Most world religions—ancient and modern, oriental and occidental—view such images as proper representations of divine beings to be worshiped. By contrast, some religions—ancient Hebraism, Judaism, Christianity, and Islam—ban all representation of the bodiless God in any visible form. *See also* Christianity (art and architecture); images, veneration of; Islam (art); Judaism (art and architecture).

idolatry, pejorative term denoting alleged worship of idols. *See also* idol; images, veneration of; Islam (art).

Iglesia Ni Cristo (ee-glay'sy-ah nee krees'toh; Span., "Church of Christ,"), an indigenous Philippine Christian church founded in 1914 by Felix Manalo. This intensely anti-Catholic church has grown rapidly since its founding, to become one of the largest rivals to Catholicism in the Philippines. Manalo, known as "the Angel from the East," initially recruited the poor and uneducated of Manila, who accepted his sole authority over doctrine and all organizational affairs. After World War II, the INC spread throughout the Philippines and began to attract better-educated and more prosperous Filipinos. By obliging members to vote for endorsed candidates in state elections, the organization is politically influential. *See also* Southeast Asian Islands, new religions in.

Ignatius of Loyola (1491–1556), founder of the Roman Catholic Society of Jesus (the Jesuit Order). His manual, *Spiritual Exercises* (1522–41), remains the foundation of most Catholic retreat practice. It is organized as a set of disciplines, visualizations, and meditations that are practiced over a four-week period. Canonized in 1622, Ignatius was designated the patron saint of spiritual exercises in 1922. *See also* Jesuits; retreat; spiritual direction, Christian.

ignorance. *See* superstition, ignorance.

IHC, Christian monogram for the name Jesus.

Ikhnaton. *See* Akhenaton.

Ikhwan al-Muslimin. *See* Muslim Brotherhood.

ikki (eek-kee), local Japanese uprisings, often with a religious base, as in those of the Buddhist True Pure Land school in the fifteenth and sixteenth centuries. *See also* Jodo Shinshu.

I Kuan Tao. *See* China, new religions in.

ilhad. *See* heresy.

Iliad (il'ee-ad), Greek epic poem attributed to Homer telling of Achilles's anger when Agamemnon, his commander, takes away his prize of honor during the Trojan War. Achilles refuses to fight until his best friend, Patroklos, is killed by Hektor. The poem illustrates the glory and suffering of war and of the human condition. *See also* Greek religion; Homer.

Illuminati, the Order of, an organization of the Masonic type concerned with the study of the occult. Established in Bavaria in 1776 by Adam Weishaupt and patronized by the writer Baron von Knigge, it had an elaborate system of degrees and was modeled organizationally on the Jesuits. The order spread rapidly among educated and liberally minded persons until suppressed by the Bavarian government. It was accused of being a secret force behind the French Revolution, and the idea of the Illuminati as a deeply underground cabal continuing to intervene in world affairs resurfaces periodically. *See also* occult, the; secret societies.

ilm, an Arabic Muslim technical term for intellectual understanding, as opposed to experimental knowledge, intuition, or the more gnostic type of wisdom of mystics (Sufis). As a collective noun, *ilm* denotes an organized body of knowledge, sacred or profane, as well as science. Those who profess religious ilm, in particular, are known in Islam as the *ulama*, which in the broadest sense can be translated as "scholars." *See also* ulama.

Ilsung Pulgyo. *See* comprehensive Buddhism.

images, veneration of, ritual attention to images. Though condemned by some aniconic religious traditions as idolatry, the veneration of images is a widespread phenomenon. Understandings of images vary both between and within traditions. For some, an image is the embodiment of the deity; for others, this embodiment lasts only during the ritual. For some, images serve as a focal point for the attention of the devotee; for others, images occasion the recollection of the qualities of the sacred personality.

Within some traditions there are rituals for constructing an image, for consecrating it, or for endowing it with life or power. Other groups see images as possessing miraculous powers, transferred to the devotee either by direct contact or through their veneration.

Beyond these theological and ritual considerations, payment for the construction and maintenance of images is a major mode of religious patronage. *See also* aniconic; art and religion; Buddha image; darshana (Hinduism); devotion (Buddhism); Hindu domestic ritual; Hinduism (worship); icon; iconoclasm; idol; idolatry; linga; Pancharatra; path of devotion; Vaishnavism.

imago Dei (ee'mah-go day-ee; Lat., "image of God"), the notion in the Hebrew Bible, important in both Jewish and Christian thought, that human beings were created in the image of the deity (Genesis 1:26–27). What constitutes the likeness has been the subject of much debate: co-regency, moral qualities, spiritual resemblance. In general, Jewish thought continues to affirm the likeness; Christian thought holds that the image was wholly or partially lost due to the disobedience of Adam and Eve, that is, the Fall.

imam (i-mahm'; Arab., "leader"), leader of Muslim ritual prayers and, occasionally, a title for an authoritative religious scholar. By extension, this quranic term evolved to refer also to the overall head of the Muslim community. While Shia Muslims believe that the Prophet Muhammad designated Ali as the first *Imam*, initiating a tradition of hereditary succession, continuing leadership, and spiritual authority, Sunni Muslims have held to choice by consensus, citing the selection of Abu Bakr as the first caliph. Thus, the two groups have differed in history over the choice of the imam, his status, and the nature of his custodial role. *See also* Islamic political theory; Shia.

Imamate (from Arab., "office of the imam [leader]"), the question disputed between Shiite and Sunni Muslims over whether Ali was the first *Imam* or the fourth caliph. *See also* Islamic political theory; Shia.

Imami, Imamiyya. *See* Imamate; Ithna Ashari Shia; Shia.

iman (ee-mahn'; Arab.), in Islam, faith in Allah (God), his angels, his books, his messengers, and the Last Day. Traditionally, the first pillar of Islamic law, *iman* has always implied a threefold relationship of internal conviction, verbal attestation, and consequent action. Differing schools of theology have stressed one term of the relation more than others. *See also* Five Pillars.

Immaculate conception, a Roman Catholic belief about Mary's sinlessness, declared as a divinely revealed dogma by Pope Pius IX (1854) that she was from conception, by the singular grace of God, because of the merits of Jesus, free from all stain of original sin. The feast day is celebrated December 8. *See also* Mary; original sin (Christianity).

immanence, divine attribute, present in the cosmos and not existing apart from it.

immortality. 1 Not being subject to death. Immortality is a claim made for supernatural beings and, in some traditions, for the soul. It is a promise offered to members of some religious traditions and the goal of some religious disciplines. 2 A gift of eternal life granted by the gods to exceptional humans in the face of the general lot of humanity, which is to die. 3 Having eternal fame, not subject to being forgotten, a claim or gift characteristic of heroes. *See also* afterlife; alchemy; body; Churning of the Ocean; fang-shih; Gilgamesh; Gorakhnath; hsien; Isles of the Immortals; ju-i; Pa-hsien; physiological techniques (Taoism); shih-chieh; shou; soul.

imperial cult. *See* kingship, sacred.

impermanence (Skt. *anitya*, "not permanent"), a fundamental characteristic of existence according to Buddhism. The primary and motivating insight of Buddhism, that existence is suffering, is based on the conviction that existents, lacking an enduring self or essence, are impermanent. Meditation, especially on the repulsive aspects of human mortality, strengthens awareness of impermanence, which helps to sever the craving held to cause suffering. Developing this soteriology, some philosophical schools of Buddhism further radicalize the teaching of impermanence by categorically denying any duration to any phenomena, insisting on an ontology of absolute momentariness of all existents. *See also* Buddhism (thought and ethics).

Inanna (ee-nahn'nah; Sumerian, "Mistress of the Sky"), the Sumerian goddess of love and war, identified with the Akkadian Eshtar (Ishtar). Her name reflects her identity as Venus, both morning and evening star; her father is either the sky god or the moon god, her brother the sun god. Her main cult center was Uruk (biblical Erech), but her worship, as a hymn proclaims, was universal. Her character was complex: bloodthirsty warrior (battle was her dance), willful girl, fickle lover. She is married but also the harlot, and her cult seems to have been in part orgiastic, staffed by eunuchs, transvestites, and homosexuals. *See also* Ishtar; Mesopotamian religion.

Inari shrine (ee-nah-ree; Jap., probably a place-name), shrine honoring a popular Japanese deity of wealth and good fortune. Originally a rice deity, Inari is associated with Ugatama, the Shinto goddess of food and clothing. Flanking the worship center of many Inari shrines are life-size fox statues with phalluslike tails. Most famous is the shrine at Fushimi, near Kyoto, noted for its tunnels of Shinto gates (*torii*). *See also* shrine.

inauspicious. *See* auspicious, inauspicious (Hinduism).

INC. *See* Iglesia Ni Cristo.

incantation, a verbal formula believed to confer power upon an individual or object or to direct power against an individual or object. *See also* charm.

incarnation (Lat., "to be made flesh"), the assumption of bodily form by a divine being or spirit. In Christianity, the incarnation refers to the doctrine holding that God took living form in Jesus of Nazareth to redeem humankind. Controversies flourished in the early centuries of

Christianity, with orthodox trinitarian and christological teachings being formulated in response to what were perceived as misguided understandings of the incarnation. The doctrine of the Trinity, formally pronounced at the Council of Nicaea (325), sought to affirm against docetic views that Christ was of the same substance (Gk. *homoousios*) with God the Father. Orthodox teaching on the "Person" of Jesus, formally pronounced at the Council of Chalcedon (451), sought to mollify the opposing Antiochene and Alexandrian schools of thought by declaring Jesus to possess "two natures in one Person." *See also* avatar; Christology; Jesus Christ.

incense, aromatic plant substances (usually gums or spices) burned as part of a religious ritual, usually for the purpose of purification. *See also* smoke.

Christianity: Incense symbolizes the prayers of worshipers and honor to God as well as serving as an agent of purification.

incest, incest prohibition, sexual relations between partners culturally marked as too closely related; the forbidding of such relations. Incest and incest prohibition remain controversial topics in the study of religion and culture. Most of the scholarship has been on incest prohibitions as cultural products or as rules that mark the beginning of culture and religion. For both Sigmund Freud and Claude Levi-Strauss, prohibition of incest produces kinship systems, since the law against incest produces exogamy. Most theories emphasize a culture's incest restrictions, remaining silent on the subject of incest itself, which is usually viewed as a natural phenomenon. The focus on the taboo rather than the deed has produced a great deal of scholarly confusion. The confusion can be cleared up by noting that incest is cultural and social, not a natural phenomenon; incest prohibitions are not universal; sex and marriage are not related or synonymous; and incest is permitted if not prescribed in some societies. Prohibition against incest cannot be properly understood unless it is analyzed as the negation of incest. Incest as a deed is antisocial, marking disorder, chaos, or power. As a social product it transforms sex into power and powerlessness. The taboo sustains order, unity, and hierarchy. *See also* kinship; sexuality and religion; taboo.

incest prohibition. *See* incest, incest prohibition.

incubation. *See* Asclepios.

independent invention. *See* diffusion.

Indian Shaker Church, a Christian sect stressing healing found among Amerindian tribes of the Northwest Coast, the Plateau, and northern California. The church was one of many syncretic movements that grew out of the visionary experiences of indigenous prophets under the influence of Christian missionaries in North America in the nineteenth century. It incorporates European Protestant and native shamanistic traditions, although outwardly rejecting "Indian" religious beliefs, practices, and paraphernalia. Meetings are held in specially built churches featuring simple altars with white-painted crosses and white candles. Singing and handbells are used to induce trances in which God's power is manifested by physical trembling, called "the shake." This power is used by congregants to heal the sick and to cast out evil through the laying on of hands. Prophecy and mediumship are also important practices. Some congregations revere the Christian Bible, while others have rejected it as suitable only for non–Native Americans.

The church originated in the spiritual experience of John Slocum, a member of the Salish tribe from Puget Sound, who received instructions from God while in a deathlike state in 1881. Slocum's wife, Mary, introduced "the shake" and together they inaugurated the new church. It spread among the Salishan peoples of Puget Sound and eastward into the Plateau region, where it was adopted by Yakima, Umatilla, Wasco-Tenino, Klamath, and, to a lesser extent, Nez Perce tribes. The church reached northwestern California in 1926, and churches have been built there by Yurok, Hupa, and Tolowa congregations. It remains strong today, often accompanying, rather than replacing, indigenous religious practices. *See also* Native Americans (North America), new religions among.

Indo-European religion. Describing the religion of the ancestors of the speakers of Indo-European languages is a major challenge. The existence of an original Indo-European speech community rests exclusively on the assumption that the Indo-European languages are all derived from a common stock reflecting the culture of a prehistoric population living in the fifth millennium B.C. or earlier. Ever since the kinship of these languages was recognized by Sir William Jones in 1786, historical/comparative linguistics has endeavored to determine what the protolanguage looked like and to reconstruct the culture associated with it. However, even nowadays the location of this specific culture and of its bearers remains a matter of dispute among scholars, as practically every tentative association of the earliest Indo-Europeans with a clearly defined archaeological group has been challenged. Some place the Proto-Indo-Europeans in the Near East and even link their diffusion east and west with the spread of agriculture. While there is linguistic evidence of an early practice of agriculture among the Indo-Europeans, a number of scholars emphasize pastoralism as their major economic activity and, accordingly, situate their homeland somewhere in the Eurasian steppes between the Aral Sea and the Pontic plains, where the domestication of the horse provided them with a means to expand over wide territories. Furthermore, the Balkans and northeastern Europe have also been claimed as the areas from which the Indo-Europeans originated.

The location of the Indo-European homeland, its ecology, and the major features of its culture, economy, and social organization have a direct bearing on its religion. Belief systems, ritual practices, and the structure of the pantheon are indeed directly affected by the way of life and the prevailing socioeconomic factors as well as by laws and institutions.

About a decade ago, the historian of religion Bruce Lincoln tried to show that the pastoral economy mainly exemplified by the early Indo-Iranian civilization and religion would account for their fundamental myths describing creation as a sacrifice and accounting for the tensions between priests and warriors. But if the Indo-Europeans were primarily agriculturists, as some archaeologists contend, Lincoln's comparison of their beliefs with those of the East African cattle-raising tribes loses much of its pertinence.

Whatever the case may be, in the absence of direct testimony the tenets of Indo-European cult and religion as well as the structure of its pantheon may only be determined by means of a critical study of the identifiable Indo-European heritage in the beliefs and rites of the historical Indo-European peoples. Such a task is, however, rendered particularly difficult because of all the external influences to which the Indo-European peoples were exposed prior to the appearance of the earliest documents.

Cosmic and Atmospheric Deities: Etymology provides us with a valuable clue, as a number of early Indo-European peoples share the (reconstructed) term *dyews*, which designates the sky god, associating celestial sacrality, i.e., light and transcendence, with sovereignty and creativity. This deity can be identified with Vedic Dyaus pitar, Greek Zeus pater, and Latin Jupiter. In

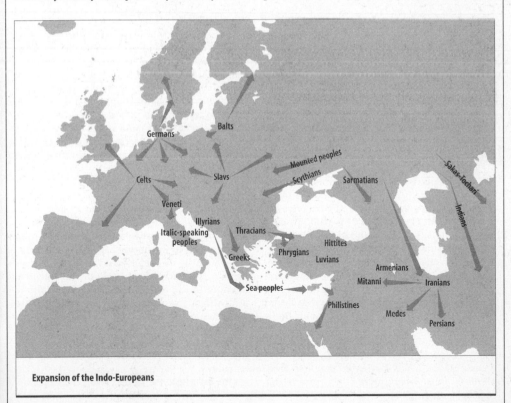

Expansion of the Indo-Europeans

Hittite its name survives in *sius*, "god," whereas the adjective from the same root, **deywos*, "divine" appears in Latin as *divus*, "divine," and designates the Germanic god **Tiwaz* (Old Norse Tyr; Old Eng. Tiw; Old High Ger. Ziu). Unfortunately, this is the only divine name for which a common Indo-European origin can be claimed.

Nevertheless, we must assume the existence of other Indo-European deities connected with nature and the cosmos. The thunder god, for example, gets his name either from the roaring of the thunder (Old High Ger. Donar; Celtic Taranis [also Tanaros]), or the striking of the lightning (Lithuanian Perkunas). Atmospheric deities appear to be associated with the warrior function: as the thunderstorm releases the waters from the heavy clouds and makes rain drench the parched earth, the thunder is the divine champion who breaks the obstacle that retained the waters. Thus, Indra (Skt., lit., "the virile one") slaughters the snakelike monster Vr(i)tra (Skt., lit., "resistance") and "frees" the waters. This "killing of the dragon" is a primordial act described by a formula that appears to be preserved in most of the Indo-European mythological traditions.

Cosmogonic Myths: Whereas Hesiod's *Theogony* depicts the constant intercourse between Ouranos and Gaia, the concept of a hierogamy (sacred marriage) between Father Sky and Mother Earth does not seem to belong to the common Indo-European heritage. The close association of sky and earth as Dyaus and Pr(i)thivi in the Vedic tradition may rather reflect a primal Indo-European androgyne: in a cosmogonic act, Indra, by his strength, separates the sky from the earth, propping up the heavenly vault. In many cases, the earth goddesses of the Indo-European peoples, however, appear to reflect the mother goddess of the pre-Indo-European cultures.

There must have been an Indo-European creation myth relating how the sacrifice of a primal being made it possible to create the world from the dismembered parts of his body: the heavenly vault is made from his skull, his eyes become the sun and the moon, his blood the oceans and the rivers, his hair the plants, etc. There is much evidence of the one-to-one correspondences between the parts of the microcosm (the human) and those of the macrocosm (the universe). However, problems develop when one tries to elaborate on this cosmogonic tradition preserved in ancient India and Iran as well as in Scandinavian mythology to construct an Indo-European myth in which the first priest, called **Manu-*, kills his twin, the first king, **Yemo-*, thus establishing the pattern for sacrificial offerings.

Sociogony—The Origin of Social Classes: From the body of his immolated brother, **Manu-* then fashions heaven and earth as well as the classes of Indo-European society. However, the sociogony described in the Vedic *Purushasukta* (*Rig Veda* 10.90, 11–12), according to which the Brahman came from the mouth of the sacrificed primal being, the Kshatriya (warrior) from his arms, the *Vaishya* ([Aryan] commoner) from his thighs, and the *Shudra* ([non-Aryan] menial laborer) from his feet, cannot be readily paralleled in the other Indo-European traditions. To be sure, according to the Roman historian Tacitus (*Germania*, ch. 2), the three major tribal groups of ancient Germany descend from three heroes who are themselves the sons of the mythical founder of the Germanic people, Mannus, son of the androgynous primal being Tuisto, born from the Earth. But apart from the name Mannus, the Vedic text and the Germanic tradition have very little in common. There is no trace of the alleged sacrifice of the first king, and the tribes issued from the triad of sons of Mannus cannot readily be associated with definite social classes. Only the Ingaevones (near the North Sea) are definitely connected with a fertility deity and could be assumed to represent the class of agriculturists and pastoralists, but similar associations do not apply to the other two groups, the Herminones and Istaevones.

Closer to the Indo-Aryan tradition is the parallelism of an Iranian myth. Here, the first king, Yima, loses his royal glory in three phases. As the king represents the very essence of the social classes, his aura is reincarnated in three mythical entities: his sacral ruling function is taken over by Mithra, his victorious power by the dragon-slaying hero Thraetaona, and his manly courage by the virile Keresaspa. But this transfer hardly reflects the establishment of three basic social levels of Iranian society.

The Iranian myth rather parallels Indra's loss of his majesty to the god Dharma, of his physical force to the divinized wind (Vayu), and of his beauty to the divine twins (Nasatyas) as a result of his sins. The lost attributes of Indra are then reincarnated in the heroes of the *Mahabharata*, the Pandava: the eldest, Yudhishtira, receives Indra's spiritual power (*tejas*); the physical strength of the god is divided between Bhima and Arjuna, the former representing the more brutal aspect of military force (*bala*) while its more chivalrous features (*virya*) are displayed by the latter. Similarly, the beauty of Indra (*rupa*) is divided between the human twins Nakula and Sahadeva.

The Bovine and the Creation Myth: The bovine's role in the reconstructed Indo-European

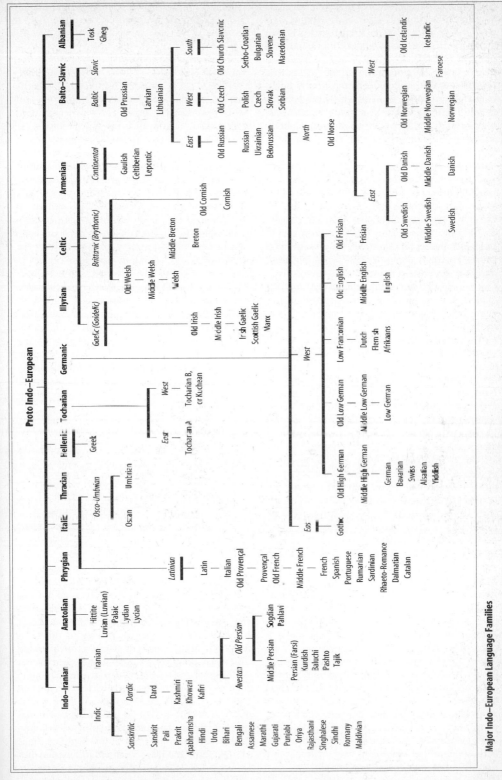

Proto Indo–European

Major Indo–European Language Families

creation myth also creates difficulty. It is indeed assumed that an ox is sacrificed together with the first king in the original Indo-Iranian version of the myth where the ox's body provides the material to create the animals and the plants. In the European version, however, we deal with a primal cow who merely feeds the primal being before the sacrifice, as is shown by the Scandinavian tradition about the cow Audhumla feeding the giant Ymir, whose dismembered body will serve to create the world. Her main function, however, appears to be to lick the grandfather of Odinn out of the primal ice. As for ancient Rome, one can hardly believe that the she-wolf who fed Romulus and Remus represents a transformation of the primal cow because of the martial character of Roman culture.

This brief discussion of the reconstructed Indo-European creation myth (as presented by Bruce Lincoln) illustrates the complexity of deriving the original form of a myth from chronologically and geographically disconnected sources on the basis of apparently related features, modified in their representation by the various Indo-European cultures.

Functional Hierarchy in Society and Pantheon: Nevertheless, at some point in the evolution of their society, the Indo-Europeans must have had a hierarchized social structure that deeply marked their religious ideology. This is what Georges Dumezil demonstrated in numerous works spanning half a century of patient and constructive research in Indo-European myth and religion.

There is no way to prove that the tripartite organization of Indo-European society that he and Emile Benveniste postulated independently in the early 1930s actually reflects the earliest institutional pattern of the Indo-European community. But there is abundant evidence that the functional hierarchization found in the Indo-Iranian society pervaded many of the mythological and religious traditions of the Indo-European peoples. Basically, three functional levels are recognized in Indo-European society: magico-religious sovereignty, with both sacerdotal and juridical aspects; physical strength and military power; and productivity, implying fertility, health, and wealth.

On the societal level, the three functions are represented by the priestly class, the warrior class, and the mass of the agriculturists and pastoralists. When the Indo-Europeans occupy new territories, the subdued non-Indo-European people fall into a fourth class of serfs or low servants deprived of civil and religious rights. This is the system that obtains in ancient India and Iran with their four-tiered social hierarchy:

India	Iran	English Translation
1. *Brahman*	*athravan*	"priest"
2. *kshatriya*	*rathaeshta*	"warrior"
3. *vaishya*	*vastro fshuyant*	"commoner"
4. *shudra*	*huiti*	"menial people"

Parallel Greek tradition, as reflected by Plato's *Critias*, distinguishes *hiereis*, "priests," *makhimoi*, "warriors," *georgoi*, "farmers," and *demiourgoi*, "artisans." As the fourth class is excluded from sociopolitical and religious activities, it is not even mentioned in other contexts, e.g., among the Celts, where Caesar identifies the two privileged classes of the druids and the nobility while the third class represents the bulk of the population. This situation was still found in Ireland at the time of the Christian conversion, when the society ruled by a king consisted of a powerful priesthood, a military aristocracy, and the *bo airig*, "free stock-breeders."

In the pantheon, this organization was reflected by a similar functional tripartition into sovereign, warrior, and essentially fertility gods. In Vedic India these were represented by Mitra-Varuna, who embodied, respectively, the juridical and the magico-religious aspects of the sovereign function; Indra, the divine champion endowed with tremendous power who reflected the warrior function; and the Nasatyas, the divine twins, active as helpers and closely associated with horses.

Georges Dumezil paralleled these with the gods of ancient Rome and Scandinavia:

	Rome	Scandinavia
1. sovereignty (juridical)	Jupiter Deus Fidius	Odinn Tyr
2. war/physical force	Mars	Thor
3. fertility/wealth	Quirinus	Njordr Freyr/Freyja

This system does not, by far, represent the totality of the Indo-European deities. Within definite groups of Indo-Europeans functional shifts may have been taking place, such as in the Germanic pantheon, which is slanted toward the warrior function. Moreover, both in Rome and in Scandinavia the original war god appears to have taken over some aspects of the third function. Actually, in some cases, such as the Celts, it is practically impossible to reconstruct the original structure of the pantheon. When the second-century Greek historian Lucian of Samosata interpreted Ogmios as the Celtic equivalent of Herakles, he obviously considered him the divine champion who appears as Ogma in the Irish epic literature. But as Ogmios drags along a retinue of captive men and women and Ogma is credited with inventing of the *ogham* script, one may draw striking parallels with Odinn's escort of dead heroes, the *einherjar,* and Odinn's invention of the runes.

On the other hand, the Celtic war god appears as Mars Toutatis in Gallo-Roman inscriptions and as the ruthless Teutates in Lucian, and his name designates him as a tribal god. The equivalent of Jupiter is the thunder god Taranis/Tanaros like Donar/Thor in the Germanic world (as the name of the day Thursday [Lat. *dies Jovis;* cf. Ital. *jovedi*] indicates). Another powerful god, cited by Lucian and appearing in the inscriptions of Gaul as well, is Esus, who has been compared with Wodan/Odinn, but the equivalent of this Germanic god is rather Lug, who was equated with Mercury as master of all arts. Protector of the poets and leader of warriors resorting to magic to ensure victory, Lug shares, indeed, many features with Odinn, who is also equated with Mercury (cf. the name of the day Wednesday, from Old Eng. *Wodenes daeg;* Lat. *dies Mercurii* [Fr. *mercredi*]). Moreover, while Caesar states that the Celts worship Mercury as their most important god, Tacitus says the same about the Germanic people, and in his presentation of the Germanic pantheon, the three functions are reflected by the following:

1. magical		
sovereign	Mercury	Wodan/
		Odinn
juridical		
function	Mars	Tyr (cf.
		Tuesday,
		Old Eng.
		Tiw in
		Tiwes daeg)
2. physical		
force	Herakles	Thor
3. fertility	Nerthus (mother	Njordr
	earth of the	
	Ingaevones)	
	Isis (among the	
	Suebians)	
	Alces, the divine	
	twins	

If all this tends to show that if Dumezil's tripartite system does not work smoothly in all the Indo-European traditions, it nevertheless remains an important component of these traditions, as numerous myths are patterned on it.

The "Sins" of the Warrior: When Dumezil describes the trespasses of typical representatives of the warrior function, their transgressions appear to infringe on the ethical rules of the three levels of Indo-European society. Indra's sins, for example, consist of a brahmanicide (killing the three-headed son of Tvastr); a blatant violation of an agreement (breaking a truce with Vr(i)tra to murder him); and taking the shape of Gautama to seduce his wife, Ahalya. The victim of the first crime is clearly a member of the priestly class, the second wicked act obviously breaks the code of honor prevailing in the warrior class, and the third misdeed is an act of lust violating the rules of conduct more specifically relevant to the third function. Similarly, the Germanic hero Starkad commits a regicide when he kills his king, Vikar, in what was supposed to be a sham sacrifice. After that, he wanders about in northern and eastern Europe performing glorious acts of bravery until he commits his second sin by abandoning the battlefield in an unexpected show of cowardice. Ultimately, he kills his trusting former combat companion, King Olo of Denmark, for a sum of money offered by conspiring noblemen. Again, the first crime relates to the sovereign function, the second infringes upon the ethics of the warrior, and the third is an act inspired by greed, which connects the misdeed to the third function.

Primordial Wars and the Structure of Society: In the same way, events in the mythical early history of Rome can be interpreted in correlation with the concept of the hierarchized social tripartition: as Dumezil indicates, the Sabine war illustrates how the three functions become integrated into a well-balanced social organization. The founder of Rome, Romulus, accompanied by brave young warriors, has the protection of Jupiter and, as son of Mars, he is endowed with strong warlike qualities. But for all these advantages, relevant to the first two functions, the new city is poor and without women. So Romulus takes advantage of the festival of the agrarian deity Consus to carry off the Sabine women, forcing the rich Sabine agriculturists to confront him and his troops. In the ensuing war both parties gain a temporary but indecisive advantage, as the Sabines bribe the daughter of the guardian of the Capitol with gold and jewels, and Romulus regains control over his panicking army by calling upon the magical intervention of Jupiter. Ultimately both sides realize that neither can win and they compromise, the wealthy Sabines being integrated in a state protected by the gods and defended by youthful warriors.

Dumezil has shown how strikingly this parallels the story of the war between the Aesir and the Vanir in Nordic myth: the Aesir represent the sovereign and the warrior functions and include such deities as Odinn, Tyr, and Thor; the Vanir are the gods of the third function providing rich crops from the land and the sea and sponsoring wealth and love (they include Njordr and his son and daughter, Freyr and Freyja). The Aesir open the hostilities when Odinn hurls a spear into the Vanic camp. The war remains indecisive until the Vanir send the "witch" Gullveig (lit., "thirst for gold") to their enemies, who try in vain to get rid of her. Neither group succeeds in gaining any major advantage over its adversary and they finally decide to make peace and to exchange hostages. As a result of this truce Njordr and Freyr move to Asgardr, where Freyja also resides, and the community of the gods finds its harmonious balance with the collaboration of the two groups.

Obviously there is a common theme and a parallel scenario in these etiological myths accounting for the structure of the relevant divine and human communities. The gist of this is that the Indo-Europeans must have had a set of shared accounts of the origin of their society as well as of the creation of the world, of which we find only a distant echo in the traditions of the individual Indo-European peoples.

Cult and Religious Concepts: In addition to this mythological lore, the Indo-Europeans also shared a number of cultic practices and religious concepts.

The Latin verb *credo* and the Old Irish *cretim,* "I believe," reflect an Indo-European phrase, **kred dheH-*, "to put one's trust (in someone)," which survives in Vedic as *sraddha-* (also divinized as Sraddha, goddess of offering, as offerings are based on the trust the devotee puts in the deity to return the favor).

Another typical example of ancient religious vocabulary is the Avestan phrase *yaozhda-*, "purify (what has been defiled), consecrate ritually, sanctify," literally, "put in an optimal state." The same idea of fullness of well-being is expressed in Vedic by the phrase *sam yos-*, but the underlying Indo-Iranian noun **yaus* corresponds exactly to Latin *ius*, "justice," which makes one wonder about the semantic link between these terms. The basic concept of ius is to define the maximal domain to which an individual or group can naturally or statutorily lay claim. Just as the Indo-Iranian **yaus* defines the fullness of holiness or well-being, Roman ius determines the maximal area of action juridically recognized and, in a way, "secularizes" the idea of plenitude of sacralization expressed by its Indo-Iranian counterpart.

Emile Benveniste's studies have revealed many further details about Indo-European religious practices such as libations and sacrifices, solemn vows and pledges, prayers and supplications, divination and auguries, and the like. Particularly striking is the twofold designation of the "sacred" that reflects its positive and negative valuation in Indo-European society as "what is filled with divine power" and "what is forbidden to human contact"—a dichotomy illustrated in Avestan by the contrast between *spenta* and *yaozhdata:* the former is etymologically derived from a root meaning "to swell" and expresses the exuberance of supernatural power with which something is loaded, whereas yaozhdata designates "what has been put in a state of ritual purity" and may therefore not be defiled (i.e., is taboo).

Likewise, the Germanic **weihaz*, "consecrated" (Gothic *weihs;* cf. Ger. *weihen,* "consecrate") means "dedicated to the gods as their exclusive possession" (it belongs to the same root as Lat. *victima,* "animal offered in sacrifice to the gods"). It contrasts with **hailagaz,* "holy" (cf. Ger. *heilig*), which derives from a root expressing "physical health" and the well-being it entails (cf. Eng. *hale;* Ger. *heilen,* "cure, make healthy"): it refers to the divine power that ensures the physical integrity, well-being, and good fortune of human beings.

Similarly, in Latin *sacer* reflects the absolute quality of sacredness; it indicates what is consecrated to the gods. The *sacerdos,* "priest," is the one who can communicate with the gods through the ritual, and the sacrifice is the ritual operation by which he transfers the consecrated victim to the divine world, making it sacred. This is why the outcast, severed from human society, is called *homo sacer:* anyone can indeed put him to death because, like the sacrificial animal, he no longer belongs to this world. While sacer denotes, by itself, a specific state, Latin *sanctus* refers to the result of an operation—a prohibition or injunction supported by law (i.e., a sanction that protects it against any kind of infringement).

Roughly equivalent to the contrast between sacer and sanctus is the relationship between Greek *hieros,* designating what is consecrated to the gods ("sacred") or charged with divine presence, and *hagios,* indicating what is protected against any violation.

Where texts are not available, the religious terms thus provide many hints on Indo-European religious life in its various aspects, revealing unexpected correspondences such as the etymological links between Hittite *tallija-*, "call solemnly upon a deity (to do something)" and Old Norse *thulr,* "oral performer of the cult," mediating between gods and humans. Another correspondence is seen between Vedic *brahma,* originally "form, shape, (ritual) formula," the Brahman being a "creator of forms," a poet-singer, and Old Norse Bragi, the Scandinavian god of poetry, manipulator of "taunting words." The poet is indeed censor and praiser in Indo-European society, as Vedic, Roman, and Celtic traditions show, and as the priest recites ritual formulas, he manipulates formulaic phrases, many of which live on in the literature of the Indo-European peoples as, for example, Vedic *sravas akshitam* and (Homeric) Greek *kle(w)os aphthiton*, "imperishable glory," the supreme reward of the hero whose fame will live forever in the writings of the poets. *See also* Baltic religion; Celtic religion; Finnish religion; Greek religion; Hinduism; Iranian religion; Mycenaean religion; Nordic religion; Old European religion; Roman religion; Zorastrianism.

Indra (in'druh; Skt.,"virile power"), god of the sky and king of the gods in Vedism and Hinduism. As the warrior god of the Indo-Aryans in their invasion of the Indian subcontinent, he is the supreme god of the *Rig Veda*, where he is invoked to help his human allies conquer their enemies, called Dasas ("slaves") or Panis, indigenous people assimilated to demons and said to have stolen cows from the Aryans and hidden them in a cave; in retrieving the cows, Indra also finds the sun. As god of rain, with the phallic thunderbolt for his weapon, he kills Vritra, the serpent demon of drought, and he is invoked for the fecundity of humans and animals. In later Hinduism he endures in mythology but is no longer worshiped. *See also* Rig Veda; Veda, Vedism.

Indra's net, metaphor used by the Chinese Buddhist Hua-yen school to visualize totally interpenetrating worlds, akin to the mutually reflecting jewels of Indra's net. *See also* Hua-yen school.

indulgence, in early Christianity, the remission of public penace imposed on a sinner by the church; in later Catholicism, the Church's remission of punishment in purgatory due to sin in view of prayers or good works done by a penitent. Misunderstandings and abuses of this practice were widely noted in the late Middle Ages and became one of the causes of the Protestant Reformation in sixteenth-century Germany. *See also* penance; purgatory; sin.

Indus Valley civilization, religion of. The religion of the agrarian urban culture that emerged in the Indus Valley of western India ca. 3000 to 2500 B.C. and spread to the Ganges Valley and the Deccan before its decline around 1750 B.C. can best be described as goddess-centered. A continuity of village cultures can be traced in the Indus region from at least 6000 B.C., all evidencing goddess worship by the number of clay female figurines created in a variety of regional styles. Similar female figurines were also produced during the Indus urban period, but the most important evidence of Indus Valley religion comes from ritual platforms at various urban sites—especially Mohenjo Daro, apparently the civilization's main ritual center, where several major structures and a large ritual bathing tank occupied the massive brick-encased platform mound—and from engraved soapstone stamp seals found throughout the range of the settlements.

The seals are inscribed with the only known examples of Indus writing, most likely an early Dravidian language, accompanied by a variety of pictorial symbols—most often male animals—and a number of what appear to be mythic or ritual scenes involving a buffalo-horned goddess, trees, and various symbolic animals. Using the evidence of these scenes, the ritual platforms, the related Elamite religion in Iran, and later Dravidian village rituals, we can posit an Indus religion based on blood sacrifices to a goddess who embodies both the life-giving and life-threatening powers of nature. Transmitted through posturban village cultures, this goddess religion became an important component in later Hinduism. *See also* Goddess (Hinduism); Hinduism.

ineffable, 1 Divine attribute, unknowable. 2 Forbidden to be spoken (e.g., name of a deity).

inerrancy, biblical, the Christian belief that the Bible is free from error. In its most extreme form inerrancy insists that although the Bible is not primarily a book of history, geography, or science, when it speaks of these matters it is free from error of any sort. The contention is that if error is admitted at any point a similar claim could be made at every point. Total inerrancy is usually limited, in theory, to the original manuscripts (autographs), but in practice it is often applied to the particular translation used by a community committed to inerrancy, for example, the Vulgate for Roman Catholics until recently, and the King James Version for fundamentalist Protestants.

A more moderate form of inerrancy maintains that freedom of error is limited to matters of faith and practice, allowing for human conditioning with respect to historical, geographical, and scientific details that do not pertain to salvation. Proponents of this position sometimes adopt the term *infallibility* rather than inerrancy. This distinction is not used consistently. The notions of inerrancy or infallibility have direct import not only on theological issues but on the authority of the biblical texts for contemporary ethical and moral issues.

inexhaustible treasury (Chin. *wu-chin-tsang*), surplus Buddhist monastic donations sold or loaned at profit to defray the expenses of temple activities. *See also* China, Buddhism in; merit.

infallibility, Roman Catholic doctrine, proclaimed at the First Vatican Council (1869–70) that an official proclamation directed to the entire Church by the pope on matters of faith and morals contains no errors.

infant baptism, the practice within some Christian groups of baptizing newborn or young children, rather than only adults. When the child reaches the age of accountability, it must vow faith in Christ and commitment to the Christian church. Infant baptism has been a recurrent source of controversy in Christian history, especially during the time of the Reformation. *See also* baptism.

infanticide, the deliberate killing of newborn children. Though sometimes used as a form of population control (females are particularly vulnerable), infanticide is ritually practiced, although more often alleged of a religion other than one's own. Child sacrifice, especially of the firstborn, occurs, as does the killing of twins and deformed children understood to be dangerous or polluted. Exposure is the most common form of infanticide, both in fact and in legends of the threatened childhood of a hero (e.g., Moses, Oedipus).

In some religious traditions, abortion and birth control are condemned as a type of infanticide. *See also* abortion; birth control; purity and impurity; sacrifice; violence and religion.

infibulation, a ritual fastening together of the labia so as to prevent copulation. A feature in women's age-grade ceremonies. *See also* clitoridectomy.

infinite, divine attribute, having no limits. As a substantive, Infinite, it is a name for the divine.

i-nien san-ch'ien. *See* Three thousand worlds in an instant of thought.

initiation rituals, induction into an age group, a secret society, or a religious office or community. These rituals center on an individual's change of status and are usually performed only once in a lifetime. *See also* age-sets; baptism; bullroarer; circumcision; life-cycle rituals; mutilation; ordeal; puberty rituals; ritual; Santeria; secret societies; shaman; shamanism; vision quest.

Inner Asian religions. Inner Asia does not conform to a precise geography. It is often taken as a residual category, namely that central portion of the Eurasian continent that remains when one takes away the civilizations of Europe, the Near East, India, and East Asia, as well as the northern circumpolar region. Projected on a map, this area would be bounded on the north by the south Russian and Mongolian steppes, on the south by the Himalayas, on the east by the border of the Gobi desert and Manchuria, and on the west by the Black Sea. This diversity of geography is matched by the variety of languages. The Altaic family (Turkic, Mongol, and Tunguz language) is the most extensive, with large populations representing the Uralic family (Finno-Ugric and Samoyed languages), paleo-Siberian, Indo-Iranian, and a set of unrelated languages in the Caucasus region. In a like manner, Inner Asia has been characterized by a multiplicity of indigenous religions, together with world religions adopted at various times by the peoples of this vast area.

The most important god among the Turkic and Mongol peoples was Tengri, the sky god. Cosmology and astrological observation were important and many had ritual prayers to the four directions. Divination and scapulimancy (omens based on "reading" the patterns on shoulderbones of sacrificed animals) were practiced. Some tribes had priestly classes (e.g., the Scythians), but most common were shamans who, in their state of ecstasy, intervened between humans and spirits, particularly for the souls of the dead and in medical treatment for the living.

World Religions in Inner Asia: Buddhism was first introduced into central Asia by Kanishka, ruler of the Kushan empire in the first century and patron of Buddhism. Although present in the Turkic Empire (ca. 550–743) and among the Uighurs (743–840) of the Mongolian steppe, Buddhism reached its climax among Turkic peoples during the Uighur kingdom of Kocho (850–1250) in the Tarim Basin. Under the Mongols, the Tibetan monk Phags-pa (1235–80) advanced Buddhism and was ordered by Kublai Khan to create an official script for the court. The Mongol sack of Baghdad in 1258 established the Mongol

Ilkhanid period in Persia, where Buddhism was adopted by Arghun (1284–91) but never gained support among the populace, and under the reign of Gazan (1295–1304) the official religion was changed to Islam. Buddhism declined with the splintering of the Mongol empire, but was revived by Altan Khan, who conferred the title of Dalai Lama on the head of Tibetan Buddhism (Yellow sect) in 1577. Translation into Mongol of the Buddhist canon began in the seventeenth century and was complete by the mid-eighteenth century. The western Mongols also adopted Tibetan Buddhism in the seventeenth century. The incorporation of indigenous deities into this northern Buddhism transformed it into a form unique to Inner Asia.

Manichaeism, propagated especially by Sogdians on the Silk Road, existed in the Turk empire. Manichaean texts have been found, written in Old Turkic, which provide valuable additional knowledge of the religion. In 763, the Uighur ruler Mou-yu (759–780) converted to Manichaeism and for a brief time it was the state religion.

Islam: Arab penetration into central Asia (from the mid seventh century) combined with Turkic forces to defeat the Chinese army at the Battle of the River Talas (751), ending Chinese influence in western central Asia and permitting Islam to penetrate and remain in the region. The northernmost reaches of Islam came with the Volga Bulgars (seventh–tenth centuries); with the Khazars (sixth–mid-tenth centuries), who, when they adopted Judaism, prevented the further spread of Islam; and with the Mongol state of the Golden Horde (mid-thirteenth–mid-sixteenth centuries). The growth of Sufi orders (Yasaviya, Kubraviya, Naqshbandiya) from the Timurid period (late fourteenth century) coincided with the decline of official, institutionalized Islam and brought Islam to the steppe nomads. After the collapse of the kingdom of Kocho in 1250, Islam became the dominant religion in the Tarim Basin and Chinese Turkestan.

Christianity: The Nestorians, traversing Inner Asia, reached China in the late fifth century. Their influence is evident from Nestorian documents written in Uighur Turkic found in Turfan and Tunhuang, and in Turkic inscriptions on Nestorian gravestones in the Semirechiye region from the twelfth to the fourteenth centuries. The Nestorian church reached its height in the fourteenth century under the Mongols until Gazan adopted Islam and the Timurids persecuted the Nestorians. Christianization of some Turkic tribes (Cumans, Pechenegs) occurred during the eleventh to thirteenth centuries. The most important contacts with Christianity came under the Mongols when papal embassies were sent by Innocent IV in 1245 to proselytize and to demand that the Mongols cease their attacks on the West. These were followed by numerous missions to preach Christianity to the peoples of Inner Asia. The conquest of Siberia by Russia (beginning in the mid-sixteenth century) brought the Russian Orthodox Church to the region. Protestant missions sought converts in Inner Asia, establishing missions in China to penetrate the Mongolian and Manchurian areas and missions in Persia to penetrate central Asia, but these met with little success.

The diversity of gods and spiritual elements in Inner Asia contributed toward a general tolerance toward religions from the outside, while its geographic position made it a crossroads for new religious doctrines. *See also* Buddhism; Islam; Manichaeism; Nestorianism; shaman.

Inner Light, concept promulgated by Quaker theologian Robert Barclay (1648–90) in *Apology for the True Christian Religion* (1678). It is the certitude of inward knowledge and confidence in the Holy Spirit within the Christian that negates the need for or authority of external agencies, whether the sacraments, ordained ministry, or the Bible.

Inquisition, a Catholic tribunal that conducted ecclesiastical legal proceedings to identify and punish heretics. The first Inquisition was established in 1229.

Inquisition, Spanish, a series of official Roman Catholic investigations, lasting from 1479 to 1814, to identify and condemn heretics and Jewish or Muslim converts to Christianity who continued to practice their original religion. In the sixteenth century, its scope was expanded to include Protestants.

insects (Japan). In Japanese myth and folklore insects are seen as the spirits of people (usually deceased), monsters, or comical figures. As spirits, they may manifest yearning, sorrow, or lightheartedness. Often they are malevolent (e.g., spiders are seen as goblins, and mosquitoes as *gaki* [hungry ghosts]) and considered sources of *tsumi* (ritual impurity, sin). *See also* demon; Japanese folklore; Japanese folk religion; tsumi.

In Sha Allah (in shah' ahl-lah'; Arab., "if God wills [it]"), common Islamic expression indicating the absolute will and power of God over creation.

insider, outsider. *See* emic, etic.

inspiration, literally, having one's breath taken over by the breath of the deity. Inspiration is always applied to persons and is a positive term for possession. *See also* breath; kami-gakari; Muses; possession.

Christianity: the classic statement of the Christian belief in biblical inspiration is 2 Timothy 3:16: "All scripture is inspired by God [lit., "God-breathed," Gk. *theopneustos*] and profitable for teaching, for reproof, for correction, and for training in righteousness . . ."

The nature and extent of God's role is widely disputed among those who hold some view of inspiration. The position, at one extreme, is that the words themselves are directly inspired. God dictated the words; the biblical authors simply recorded them. This is called verbal or plenary inspiration. At the other end of the spectrum is the assertion that the inspiration of the Bible is no different from the genius that attends great writers, artists, and musicians throughout the ages. A mediating view is that God inspired the authors, but that they formulated their words in terms of their own personalities and historical circumstances. This view allows for levels of inspiration in scripture; that is, some writings more directly reflect their divine source than others.

Discussion of inspiration often extends beyond consideration of the canonical materials to the significance of the inspiration of the contemporary reader.

instrumental/expressive, theoretical terms used in the debate on religion and rationality. The question whether religion is rational or not is directly dependent on how rationality is defined. Rationality is often defined in instrumentalist terms, as a calculation of means to achieve some end. An action is rational if it is taken instrumentally, as a means to achieve a certain goal, or maximizes the satisfaction of one's desire. Thus, if one has beliefs and desires that provide the means for achieving some goal, or that maximize the satisfaction of a desire, then one can consider those beliefs and desires together with the action as rational. For example, if one has well-founded beliefs about a certain medicine and the desire for restoring one's health, then the taking of the medicine, the beliefs, and desire are rational.

This instrumental theory about rationality has been very influential in the study of religion, myth, and ritual. If religious beliefs and practices are instrumental reasons and acts for achieving specific ends, it would seem that some if not all religious beliefs and practices are, at best, false if not irrational. From the instrumentalist point of view, the belief that Nats (Myanmar) or Phi (Thailand) cause illness and that certain rites (acts) in their behalf will restore health is false, and persistence in holding the belief and performing the rites is irrational.

Why do certain societies persist in holding beliefs and practices that are clearly not instrumental in achieving certain goals? The well-known response is that the beliefs and practices although false or irrational also have unintended consequences that are of value to the survival of the society. For example, although the beliefs and practices may not be rational, they may have unintended effects that function to maintain order in a society, or reduce anxiety in times of crisis.

Another solution to the problem is to deny that religious beliefs and practices are instrumental means for achieving certain ends. This alternative does not deny the theory that rationality is best explained in instrumental terms; it simply denies that religion is rational. Religion, myths, and rituals are expressive; like art or dreams, they are symbolic. The task, then, is to decipher religious beliefs and practices as symbolic systems.

The main problem with the instrumentalist theory of rationality is that it is too narrow. One encounters many occasions when there is more than one way to achieve a certain goal, when no one means is the best means, or, one has no way of knowing the best means that would maximize the satisfaction of a desire. The problem with the expressive theory of religion is its vagueness and the lack of agreement on what the symbols mean and why human beings have them. *See also* rationalism, intellectualism; ritual.

integration, religion as a means of. *See* religion, the study of.

Intellectualism. *See* rationalism, intellectualism.

intensification rites, a technical term for repetitive rituals that affect an entire society, most often expressed in terms of the language of natural cycles, e.g., seasons, phases of the moon. *See also* festal cycle; periodic rites.

intention, in religious discourse, the focus of the mind, the sense of purpose that leads to action.

intention (Judaism) (Heb. *kavvanah*), the concept that the meaning and significance of an action are determined by the individual's underlying purpose rather than what he or she physically does or says.

In Scripture: Scripture applies the idea of intention only in a few areas. It distinguishes between intentional and unintentional desecration of holy things (Leviticus 22:10–14) and between homicide and manslaughter (Numbers 35:16–28).

In most areas of ritual and law, however, scripture is unconcerned with intention and understands the significance of an action to be inherent in its outcome. Leviticus, e.g., deems a priest's offering of a sacrifice to be valid as long as he carries out the proper actions, regardless of what he is thinking while he performs them. Comparably, scripture categorizes physical objects on the basis of their appearance, without regard for what people wish to do with them. For most of scripture, classification and proper behavior are determined by the character of the physical world and thus by outward appearances, established by God without regard to human cognition and purpose.

In Rabbinic Judaism: In contrast to this scriptural position, rabbinic Judaism makes intention central in all aspects of law and ritual. The rabbinic view is that physical actions have no inherent meaning and that an action's significance or an object's status can be determined only in light of the actor's intention.

The rabbinic view holds that people inherit an incomplete world that awaits human interpretation and ordering. This is familiar from the Yahwistic creation story (Genesis 2.4–20), in which Adam names the animals and so completes creation. But it is unlike the pervasive priestly conception (see Genesis 1:1 2:3), which understands humankind to have been placed in a completed and perfectly ordered world.

The rabbinic perspective imputes to Israelites the power to determine what is sacred and profane, to judge which actions conform to or break the law, and to establish the status of physical objects. For instance, the Mishnah treats as foods, subject to tithes, only things someone actually intends to eat. If the individual plans to discard even an edible substance, it is deemed refuse and is exempt from tithing. Likewise, a priest—or anyone engaged in a ritual—must intend to perform that act properly. If one intends to do the wrong thing, the act is invalid, even if it conforms to the rules. Human intention and purpose establish the significance and effect of actions and impart meaning to a world that has no inherent order.

In Later Judaisms: In medieval and modern Judaisms, the concept of *kavvanah* developed narrowly and usually denotes a state of mental concentration deemed necessary to fulfill the obligation to pray and carry out other religious commandments. In line with the Mishnah's theory, this later tradition holds that, in prayer and other ritual, it is not enough to say the required words or to perform a set of compulsory actions. Rather, people fulfill their religious obligations only if they first acquire the proper frame of mind, with appropriate cognizance of the sacred nature of their activity.

intercession, the actions taken by one person on behalf of another, usually to rectify some form of religious offense.

International House of Justice. *See* Baha'i.

International Society for Krishna Consciousness (ISKCON). *See* America, Hinduism in.

interpretation. *See* empathy; hermeneutics; understanding.

interreligious understanding. *See* dialogue.

Inter-Varsity Christian Fellowship, an academically oriented evangelical Christian collegiate fellowship organized under its present name at Cambridge, England, in 1927. The movement came to the United States and Canada prior to World War II and is now represented on many campuses. *See also* evangelical.

intrinsic enlightenment (Chin. *pen-chueh*), Chinese Buddhist doctrine that the mind is innately pure even under deluded states of consciousness. *See also* Buddha nature.

Inuit. *See* circumpolar religions; Eskimo.

invisibility, the state of being unseeable, often attributed to supernatural objects in myths and folktales as well as categories of supernatural beings.

invocation (Chinese). *See* nien-fo.

invulnerability, the mythic motif that a supernatural or heroic being is incapable of being wounded or slain. Often combined with the "Achilles's heel" motif that there is a single exception, i.e., if wounded in a secret vulnerable spot, or by a weapon made from a single substance. *See also* Baldr; Krishna.

Ippen (eep-pen; 1239–89), founder of the Japanese Buddhist Jishu Pure Land movement. His central religious experience was a revelation received from a *kami* (divinity, divine presence) thought to be a manifestation of Amitabha Buddha, at Kumano in 1274. The revelation instructed Ippen to distribute amulets (*ofuda*) that established a karmic connection between believers and Buddha. These guaranteed salvation regardless of the individual's beliefs or morality. Every instant the Buddha's name was recited (*nembutsu*) was an instant of salvation. Chanting transformed this world into a Pure Land, and those saved would celebrate by dancing while reciting the nembutsu. *See also* amulet; Jishu; karma; nembutsu; Pure Land.

Iranian religion, a general term denoting either pre-Zoroastrian or non-Zoroastrian Iranian religious phenomena. The question of what phenomena to label as Iranian is made more complicated by the continuing debates over the dating of Zoroaster and Zoroastrianism (beyond the latter's adoption as the state religion of Iran during the Sassanid period, 224–651), the dating of non-Pahlavi Iranian religious texts from which most of the data concerning Iranian religion is derived, and the question of a pre-Zoroastrian or non-Zoroastrian Mazdaism (religion devoted to Ahura Mazda, the "wise lord"). *See also* Ahura Mazda; Zoroastrianism.

Irenaeus of Lyons (*i*-ray-nay'uhs; ca. 130–200), one of the major early Christian apologists. A native of Smyrna, he was bishop of Lyons from ca. 178 to 200. His most famous work, *Against Heresies*, is largely devoted to an attack on forms of Christian gnosticism.

Isa. *See* Jesus Christ.

Ise-ko (ee-say-koh), a Japanese confraternity or pilgrimage association for visiting the Shinto shrines at Ise. From medieval times both spontaneous and organized pilgrimages became popular for common people. *See also* Ise Shinto; Ise Shrine; pilgrimage; Shinto.

Ise Shinto (ee-say), also Watarai Shinto, school of Shinto developed in Japan at Ise Shrine during the medieval period emphasizing the shrine as the source of imperial legitimacy. Under the influence of Watarai Nobuyoshi (1615–91) Buddhist influences in Ise Shinto were replaced by Confucian ones. *See also* Ise Shrine; Shinto.

Ise Shrine (ee-say), the primary shrine of the classical Shinto tradition, located at Ise Bay in southern Honshu, Japan. It enshrines the sun goddess Amaterasu, simultaneously the main *kami* (divinity, divine presence) of Shinto and the ancestral (founding) kami of the Japanese imperial family, and is thought to be the oldest shrine in Japan. Its inner shrine was built in the third century while the outer shrine was built in the fifth century. An ancient tradition of rebuilding the two main structures every twenty years has helped preserve its ancient architectural features. Over the ages Ise has not only been visited regularly by the imperial family but has become an important national pilgrimage site. *See also* Amaterasu; Ise Shinto; Shinto.

Ise Virgin (ee-say), the consecrated ritual presence of the Japanese imperial house at the Ise Shrine. Her service involves divination, pilgrimage, offerings, and purification. *See also* Ise Shinto; Ise Shrine.

Ishmael (ish'may-uhl), in the Hebrew Bible, the son of Abraham and his concubine, Hagar, and ancestor of the Arabs. *See also* Ismail.

ishtadevata (ish-tuh-day'vuh-tah; Skt., "desired deity"), in Hinduism, a personal god chosen or favored by the devotee. It may differ from one's family deity (*kuladevata*) or a village deity (*gramadevata*). *See also* guardian deities, Hindu; Hindu domestic ritual; Hinduism (worship); path of devotion.

Ishtar (eesh'tahr; Akkadian, "goddess"), the goddess par excellence of the Sumero-Babylonian pantheon. She was fused with the Sumerian Inanna, "Lady of Heaven," and with the West Semitic Astarte (and Attar). Sexual and warlike, terrestrial and astral, Ishtar was associated with fertility and identified with the planet Venus. *See also* Inanna; Mesopotamian religion.

Ishvara/Isha/Ishana (eesh'vuh-ruh/eesh'uh/eesh-ah'nuh; from Skt., "lord," "ruler," "master," respectively), names used mainly for the god Rudra-Shiva in Vedic and Hindu literature. *See also* Rudra; Shiva; Veda, Vedism.

Isis (*i*'sis), an ancient Egyptian goddess of great power, wife and sister of Osiris and mother of Horus. After Osiris's murder by Seth, she collected his dismembered body and through her magic restored him to life in the hereafter. She was best known as a protective Mother Goddess, depicted as a falcon or a woman with outstretched wings. *See also* Egyptian religion; Horus; Osiris.

Islam (art). Striving to conform with Islam as religion and to reflect the values of Islam as civilization, Islamic art flourishes from Spain to India from 800 to today. It is essentially an art of decoration, whose main components are calligraphy, arabesque, and geometric ornament.

Calligraphy: Calligraphy is the most original and most important element in Islamic deco-

A verse of the second *sura* of the Qur'an inscribed in the form of a horse; a painting from the sixteenth-century Islamic Moghul Empire in India.

ration. As the art of beautiful writing, it stands at the heart of the Islamic tradition. For Muslims, the Qur'an is truly the revealed Word of Allah (God), his perfect revelation. As that word, given through Muhammad to humankind, the Qur'an is the Word, which is the beginning with God. God is revealed in his Word, and his Word was made writing. In Islam humankind is not born sinful, but forgetful, and the Word of God is a reminder of one's duty and of one's faith. Thus, verses from the Qur'an serve as the central icon of Islam and as the central visual affirmation of the religion. Writing became an art, and Muslim artists have expended energy and ingenuity in developing many beautiful scripts for the Arabic alphabet. Writing is perceived as beautiful quite independently of whether one can read it, and it adorns objects of all sizes and for all purposes. In architecture there is great variety both in the selection and in the placement of quranic verses. Two common verses for religious architecture are (9:18), which invites those who believe to visit the mosques of God, and the Throne Verse, which begins "God, there is no god but He, the Living, the Everlasting" (2:255). The former is usually placed over doors and the latter under or around domes. For small objects, the short chapter (*sura*) 112 is popular.

Arabesque and Geometric Ornament: Origins of arabesque and geometric ornament were pat-

terns that formed part of the rich artistic heritage of the Byzantine and Sassanian empires, into which the Arab nomad tribal armies moved with lightning speed and a minimum of destruction and dislocation in the seventh century. The new Muslim rulers, whose own artistic tradition was aural and poetic and whose possessions were largely practical and portable, at first impressed native craftsmen to build their monuments and decorate their artifacts. The craftsmen used the decorative vocabulary and techniques of the former empires: quartered marble, glass mosaic, the pendentive, the inhabited frieze, geometric patterns from the Byzantine world; sculpted stucco, glazed tile, the squinch, the tree of life, pearl borders from the Sassanian world; and the acanthus, the split palmette and vine ornament from both. Figural art occurs in the iconography of kings—the ruler in majesty, feasting, drinking, being entertained by musicians and dancers, and triumphing in the hunt. This was primarily taken from Sassanian Iran, and the imagery was incorporated into Islamic decorative motifs. But its role was always a subordinate one. Human and animal representations appear primarily on artifacts for court and domestic use, in nonreligious contexts and objects. The Qur'an does not prohibit figural imagery, and Muhammad himself was against idolatry, not images. Figural images have no place in Islamic religious art, however, wherein the Word is God's Word, and wherein arabesque and geometric ornaments, although abstract, have a suggestive, spiritual dimension. Arabesque ornament is based on vegetal forms, which developed from grapevines and split palmettes and acanthus leaves of the pre-Islamic late classical Near East decoration. It is ornament based on a continuous stem that splits regularly, producing a series of counterpoised leafy secondary stems that split again and are reintegrated into the main stem. The governing principles are those of reciprocal repetition in a rhythmic alteration of movement, along with the desire to fill the entire surface with ornament. The twining, coiling, interlacing, overlapping natural forms give the surface a tremendous feeling of movement, of life, of energetic but ordered activity. The patterns are beautiful in and of themselves, but in their abstract arrangement they also impart a spiritual message.

In Islam, nature is one of the manifestations on earth of God's creative activity. The vegetal forms of the arabesque stem, leaf, and flower derive from the most ancient symbols of fertility and abundance. The unbroken stem of the arabesque exemplifies the continuous activity of God. These abstract patterns expand the viewer's vision to the source of life itself. These patterns are reminders. The Qur'an repeatedly makes the point that nature is under God's sovereignty, and that in it humans can see God's activity. It is full of signs: "It is He who sends down to you out of heaven water, of which you have to drink, and of which trees, for you to pasture your herds, and thereby He brings forth for you crops, and olives, and palms, and vines and all manner of fruit. Surely in that is a sign for a people who reflect" (16:10–11; also 6:99). Geometric forms like the arabesque were also derived from the pre-Islamic art of the Middle East and have concrete and abstract forms. They also embody the visual principles of repetition, symmetry, and continuous generation of pattern. The

Characteristic Islamic geometric ornamentation in the Golestan (or Gulistan) Palace, Teheran, Iran.

complex forms are developed from simple shapes such as circles, squares, and stars. Geometric patterns complement those of the arabesque, for they appeal to the intellect rather than to the emotions, and they express crystalline order, clarity, and stability. The art of geometry is related to the study of mathematics and the other sciences, which were keenly pursued by the scholars and philosophers of Islam. Geometry is used in Islamic architecture and art, not only to please the eye but also to entertain the mind. Herein lies the hidden, deeper

level to this ornament. The geometric forms are often based on the circle or the star, both of which have transcendental significance. The circle has no beginning or end; it is infinite. The star, a distant point in the cool night sky, is also a fixed point, a guide to the traveler in the desert and on the seas. The Qur'an frequently refers to stars as proof of God's continual guidance to humankind: "He it is who appointed for you the stars, that you might be guided by them in darkness on land and sea" (6:97). The stars are also guards for humans against evil: "We have adorned the lower heaven with the adornment of the stars, and to preserve against every rebel Satan" (37:6–7).

Artists in Islam: In Islam, God alone is the Creator, the Artist. Muslim architects, craftsmen, and artisans worked by-and-large anonymously. Islam emphasizes tradition and conformity over innovation and originality. There are no Michelangelos in Islamic art. Islamic society did not differentiate the artist from the artisan. In fact, the artist in Islam was rather like a musician playing well-known compositions. One often worked as part of a collective group rather than as an individual. An artist was rarely concerned with developing radically new ways of expression. The concern was to do the same thing, but better than one's predecessors or contemporaries. This overall conformity of theme and purpose gives to Islamic art a calmness, a continuity, a coherence, which constantly affirms the relationship between God and the visible, everyday world.

Segmentary Presentation: Calligraphy, arabesque, and geometry in panels, bands, registers, and friezes cover the surfaces of buildings and objects. The indefinite movement and direction of these undulating and straight lines are limited only by the finite borders of the shapes that contain them. In making visible part of a pattern that exists in its complete form only in infinity, the Islamic artist relates the limited, seemingly definite object to infinity itself. This sense of movement and continuous space is enhanced by the fact that similar patterns occur in different areas, such as floors, walls, ceilings, and from one object to another. With this extra dimension the ornament achieves a sense of fluidity. It is no longer static, confined by frames and borders, but dynamic. At first glance this segmental organization of the surface in exploding, infinitely possible patterns may seem to puzzle the eye. But this is ornament that is not meant to be taken in at a glance. Each section is meant to be looked at and pondered, absorbed individually.

On another level this segmental presentation of themes can be interpreted as a deeper insight into the cosmological mysteries: few things can be grasped in their entirety; they are revealed only in part and only in their relationship with other aspects of God's infinite variety.

Colors: The natural world, comprehended and interpreted by the human intellect, is an important element in Islamic ornament. God's generative and creative powers are described by the quranic verses. Lush arabesque forms and complex geometric patterns beautify and transform the simple structural forms they cover. They also contrast sharply with the sere, stark setting in which they are found. Much of this ornament was crafted in lands that contain vast deserts. Domes are carved, colored, or patterned to define and outline them against the yellow sand and the pale sky. Metallic highlights such as gold on manuscript pages, copper luster on pottery, gilt on glass, and gold and silver on brass enliven and embellish the surface material. Objects lavishly decorated and glowingly accented become gorgeous counterpoints in simple contexts.

Color is another important factor in Islamic art. The first and favorite color is blue—and its variants—a color that appeals for many practical and psychological reasons. Blue is cheaply obtained from copper and sulfate. In the firing of ceramics, blue is a stable and reliable color, yielding satisfactory results under both high and low firing temperatures. Blue is associated with good luck. It is the color of heaven, the color of water—precious and life-giving in much of the Islamic world. It is a cool color and offers surcease from a constant and often harsh sun. Another important color is green, the color associated with the Prophet Muhammad.

Actual elements, such as water and light, are incorporated into Islamic art and become integral parts of it. Water, in static, reflective pools and ponds, or in splashing and sparkling cascades, reminds the viewer of the Qur'an's multiple images of heaven, for example 16:15, 15:45. Decorative architectural elements on Islamic buildings are often shaped so as to refract, reflect, and to be transformed by light and shade. Windows covered with colored glass or wooden and stucco latticed grills reduce and suffuse the glare of the sun. These window grills are ornamental in themselves; they also project new patterns into the environment.

As with the other themes and aspects of Islamic ornament, these elements lead to an aesthetic intuition of God. Light, which helps humans find their way through the physical world and perceive objects more clearly, is a metaphor for God, who guides human beings' spiritual life. Star patterns as the basis of a design are common in Islamic art. A lamp or a can-

A common feature of Muslim Egyptian architecture, the *mashribbya* (often Anglicized as moucharaby) is a projecting second-story window with grills or latticework (Cairo).

dle in a niche is used as a visual metaphor of God: "God is the light of the heavens and the Earth, the likeness of His Light is a niche wherein is a lamp. The lamp in a glass, the glass as it were a glittering star . . ." (24:35). A light guides believing men and women to their destination—heaven (57:12). Less obviously, the Islamic artist forms ornamentation in such a way that its beauty cannot be fully appreciated until light interacts with the object. Shadows and reflections become living forms of decoration: they fill undecorated space, create a sense of mystery, and provide the viewer with a moving, living sign of God.

ISLAM

Islam is an Arabic term meaning "submission" to the will of the one God, Allah. The Arabic root "s-l-m" (like its Hebrew cognate "sh-l-m") means "peace," the peace and human social accord gained by submitting to the will of God. Closely associated with this act of submission is acceptance of the seventh-century prophet Muhammad (ca. 570–632) as the last and final Messenger of God, the "seal of the prophets." Those who submit—who "fear God and obey His messengers," which scripture, the Qur'an, frequently admonishes humans to do—are known as Muslims.

Islam is a global religion. The vast majority of Muslims around the world (about 85 percent) identify themselves as "Sunni," and follow one of the four accepted schools of legal interpretation: Malikite (Africa); Hanafite (Egypt, Turkey, Central Asia); Hanbalite (Arabia, Gulf Arab states); and Shafiite (Middle East, Southeast Asia). A significant minority identify themselves as "Shii" or "Shiites," living primarily in Iran, Syria, and Lebanon. Although both Sunni and Shii Muslims practice their religion in nearly identical ways, their worldviews differ somewhat owing to conflicts that occurred during the first generation after Muhammad's death and about which there are significant differences of interpretation.

Until the latter half of the twentieth century, most North Americans knew little about Islamic religion. Much of the non-Muslim world's sudden interest in Islam has arisen in part as a result of tragic conflict in the Middle East and elsewhere in the Muslim world. That conflict has had many causes, but European colonialism in the nineteenth and twentieth centuries produced many of the conditions and motivations that led to it. News reports and political analysis of more recent disputes involving Muslim populations, such as the Arab/Israeli conflict (1948), the Iranian Revolution resulting in the taking of American hostages (1979), and the U.S.-led Allied war against Iraq ("Desert Storm," 1991), have contributed to a climate of negative information and disinformation about Arabs and Muslim peoples more generally.

In the 1980s, representations of Islamic religion and cultures began to appear more frequently in the media, in public-school history and social studies textbooks, and in university general studies and elective curricular offerings. Yet the common assessment of Muslims and specialists on Islam is that much of the information about Islam that gets published is less than accurate and often misleading. On the other side, exponents of such movements as multiculturalism

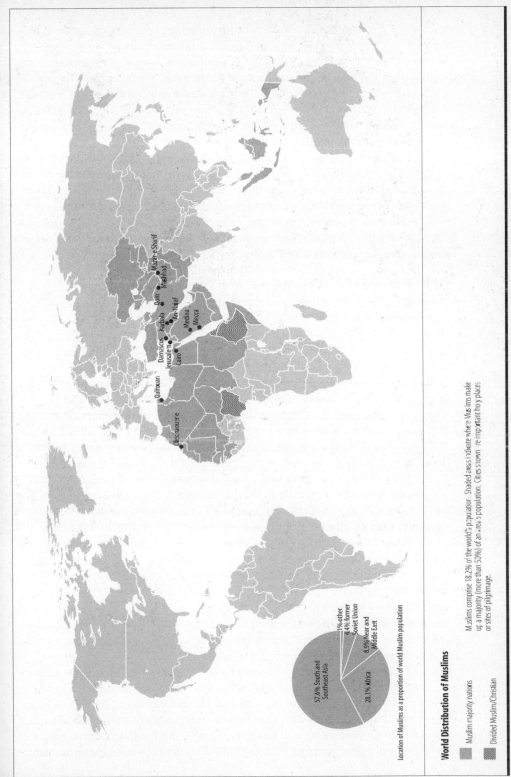

World Distribution of Muslims

Muslims comprise 18.2% of the world's population. Shaded areas indicate where Muslims make up a majority (more than 50%) of an area's population. Cities shown are important holy places or sites of pilgrimage.

Muslim majority nations

Divided Muslim/Christian

Location of Muslims as a proportion of world Muslim population

57.6% South and Southeast Asia

28.1% Africa

8.9% Near and Middle East

4.4% former Soviet Union

1% other

Mazar-e-Sharif
Mashhad
Qom
Karbala
Damascus
Jerusalem
Cairo
An-Najaf
Medina
Mecca
Qairouan
Ouagadougou

have sought to remedy the problem by encouraging public schools and the media to provide unbiased information about Islamic peoples and their cultures. However, raw information about Islamic societies and cultural symbolism without proper analysis of social and cultural systems can also be misleading. An example is the tendency, when conflict has erupted in the Muslim world, to invite specialists to speak in the media or in the schools on the Five Pillars of Islam, as though analysis of the traditional beliefs and practices of a religious community can explain everything that takes place in that society.

There is a need for more nuanced understanding of the increasing amount of information, much of it still inaccurate, about Islam. Speaking and writing responsibly about Islam is a task facing students and teachers, reporters in the print and broadcast media, government officials, international businesses, as well as domestic businesses that operate in markets that include rapidly growing Muslim communities in North America. First, however, some general information and observations about Islamic civilization will be useful.

GENERAL OBSERVATIONS

Islam is the youngest of the major world religions, dating from the seventh century. Historians of religion classify Islam as a universal missionary religion, the second largest tradition belonging to this category. The other two are Christianity (the largest) and Buddhism. A global ethnographic survey of Muslim peoples in 1984 estimated the world population of Muslims at 837 million; in 1992 the Encyclopedia Britannica Book of the Year estimated 950 million Muslims worldwide (as compared to 1.7 billion Christians, 17 million Jews, and 884 million nonreligious peoples). Muslims form the majority in some fifty-six nations and close to 50 percent in four other countries. Most of these countries lie in a belt of economically poorer, less well-industrialized nations across Africa and Asia, the so-called Third World.

A notable exception to this pattern with respect to personal income levels (among the highest in the world in the late twentieth century) is the Persian (or Arabian) Gulf region. Gulf Muslim societies nonetheless exhibit a socio-religious ethos that is among the most conservative, exclusive, and tightly controlled in the Muslim world. Gulf Arab expressions of social and theological conservatism stem from one of the four schools of law to which Sunni Muslims adhere, the Hanbali school, named after the popular legal and religious scholar, Ahmad Ibn Hanbal (d. 855); reformist and "puritanical" expressions of Islam, including the Wahhabi (named after Muhammad Ibn Abd al-Wahhab, 1703–92) movement in Arabia, have frequently come from Muslims who have subscribed to Hanbali interpretations of Islamic law.

A popular image of Muslims in the West is that of camel-driving Arab nomads, the Bedouin. This view is inaccurate in two important ways. First, only a small minority of Muslims are Arabs (and not all Arabs are Muslim). In 1984 the world population of Arab Muslims was estimated to be under 137 million, some 16 percent of the world Muslim population. After Arabs come Bengalis (93 million), Punjabis (57 million), and Javanese (53 million). Persians rank as the eighth largest ethnic group of Muslims at 23.5 million, Kurds as the seventeenth

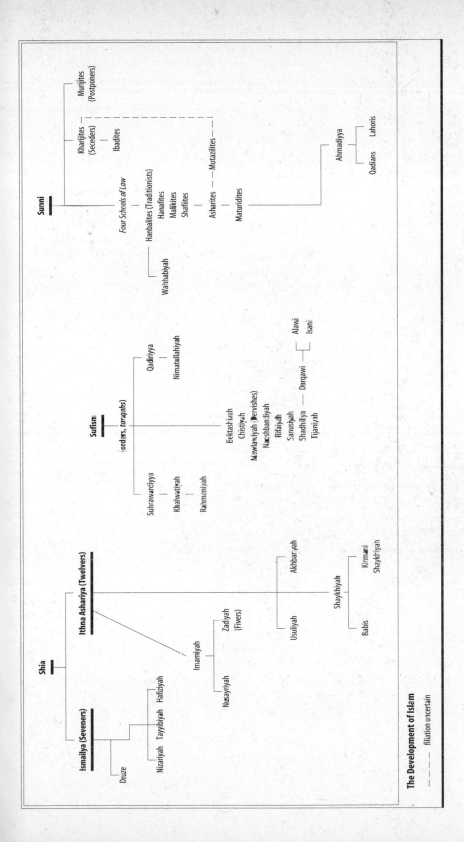

Islam

500–600	600–700	700–800
Muhammad born (ca. 570)	Ali ibn Abi Talib (600–661)	North Africa under Muslim control (700–711)
Abu Bakr (580–634)	Fatima (605–633)	Ibn Ishaq, compiler of first life of Muhammad (704–767)
	Muhammad emigrates to Medina *(hijra)*, founding of Muslim community *(ummah muslimah)*, year one (AH) of Muslim calendar (622)	Invasion of Spain (711)
	Battle of Badr (624)	Expansion to borders of India (Sind) and central Asian steppes (Samarkand) (712)
	Hasan ibn Ali (627–669)	Adawiyah (ca. 715–801)
	Early caliphate (631–661)	Rabia al-Adawiyya (721–801)
	Death of Muhammad (632)	Charles Martel defeats Muslims at Poitiers, halting invasion of France (732)
	Abu Bakr, first caliph (632–634)	Khariji revolt (742–746)
	Rapid Muslim expansion, including Arabia, Syria, Iraq, Egypt, and parts of north Africa (632–641)	Abbasid caliphate (750–1258)
	Basri (642–728)	Cordoba becomes capital of Muslim Spain, Europe's largest city by the 10th century (756)
	Ali assassinated (661)	al-Shafii (767–820)
	Ummayad caliphate (661–750)	Ibn Hanbal (780–855)
	First Muslim (unsuccessful) attack on Constantinople (673)	Muhasibi (ca. 781–857)
	Completion of Dome of the Rock (Jerusalem) (692)	Idrisid dynasty, Morocco (789–926)
		Ibn Anas (d. ca. 795)

largest, at 10.4 million, Somalis as the twenty-first at 7.6 million, and Bosnians (in the former Yugoslavia) as the fiftieth at 2.2 million. Second, the representation of Muslims by Hollywood and the media as camel drivers bears little relation to cultural realities. Only a small minority even of Arab Muslims are nomads. Throughout the diverse ethnic/linguistic and geographic world of Islam, the vast majority—nearly 70 percent—are peasants living in rural areas in an agrarian economy. By contrast, about 30 percent of the world Muslim population lives in urban areas. Only about 2 percent of the Muslims in the world today are pastoral peoples living nomadic lifestyles.

In North America, Islam is estimated by some demographers to become the second largest religious community (after Christianity but ahead of Judaism) sometime early in the twenty-first century. Thus, Islam is not only one of the largest and fastest growing religions in Africa and Asia; it is quickly becoming a major confessional community in North America. Consequently, large Muslim communities thrive in some of the biggest media markets across the United States. Smaller inland cities, such as Cedar Rapids, Iowa, have well-established Muslim communities with mosques, religious schools, and community centers. Muslim children are enrolling in increasing numbers in public schools; Muslim parents are joining parent-teacher organizations and running, often successfully, for local school boards and for political office.

800–900	900–1000	1000–1100
Bukhari (810–870)	Farabi (890–950)	Ibn Hassan (994–1064)
Qushayri (817 875)	Ibn Masarrah (883–931)	Hakim (996–1021)
Tabiri (839–923)	Ismaili Fatamid dynasty in North Africa and Egypt (909–1171)	Baqillani (d. 1013)
Nazzam (d. ca. 840)		Ibn Aqil (1040–1119)
Hallaj (858–922)	Maximum extent of Iranian and Transoxonian Samanid dynasty's rule (913–942)	Seljuk Turks form alliance with Sunni rulers, establish Sunni as international form of Islam (1055–1220)
Kindi (d. ca. 870)		
Ashari (873–935)	Ibn Babawayhi (918–991)	Ghazali (1058–1111)
Muslim control of Sicily (878–1060)	Jabbar (ca. 935–1025)	Berber Almoravid dynasty; Marrakesh is their capital (1058–1174)
Tirmidhi (d. ca. 883–892)	Kulayni (d. 939)	
	Maturdi (d. 944)	Ibn Yasin (d. 1059)
	Tusi (955–1067)	Jilani (1077–1166)
	Cairo founded as Fatamid capital (969–972)	Ibn Tumart (1080–1130)
	Biruni (ca. 973–1055)	First Crusade (1095–1099); Jerusalem captured by Christians (1099)
	Ibn Sina (Lat. Avicenna) (980–1037)	
	Ghaznavid dynasty extends Muslim power in north India (998–1118)	

Despite the smaller percentage of Muslims living in urban areas, the city has always been an essential social environment for Islamic practice. The Muslim place of worship, the mosque (from the Arabic term *masjid*, "place of prostration"), has played an important role in urban centers, where it often serves also as a place for advanced study of the religious sciences. Indeed, the major mosque and gathering place in any predominantly Muslim city is called the *jami* ("congregating"), which in many locales is a work of architectural majesty. Hospitals and schools are often associated with major mosques in Islamic cities. The Friday noon gathering for the most important weekly prayer in Islam is particularly important in cities, where Muslim rulers and distinguished personages often lead the prayer or give the sermon. Among the major cities in the Muslim world today are Cairo, Baghdad, Damascus, Tehran, Lahore, and Yogjakarta.

If Bedouin nomads comprise only a small portion of the world Muslim population, nonetheless the contribution of these Arab pastoral societies and their relation to the urban growth and social ethos in some parts of the Islamic world should not be overlooked. The Muslim philosopher of history and social theorist Ibn Khaldun (1332–1406) argued that the tough self-reliance of nomadic lifestyles, when combined with tribal loyalties, produces an important factor called "group solidarity," or *asabiyya,* in the formation of civilization. In time,

Islam

1100–1200	1200–1300	1300–1400
Ibn al-Arif (1088–1141)	Ibn al-Abbar (1199–1260)	Ibn Khaldun (1332–1406)
Ibn Zur (Lat. Avenzoar, or Abumeron) (1090–1162)	Sultanate of Delhi established (1206)	Ibn Abbad (1333–90)
Ibn Abi Asrun (1099–1189)	Jalal al-Din Rumi (1207–73)	Songhay kingdom in upper Niger (1340–1590)
Ibn Tufayl (1110–85)	Collapse of Almohads, withdrawal from most of Spain (1212–69)	Timur (Tamerlane), Turkish warlord, attacks Muslim centers from India to Syria (1369–1405)
Berber Almohad dynasty (1121–1269)	Some Mongol groups war with Muslims halting their expansion into Europe; western Mongols Islamized by 1295 (1220–1405)	Ottoman (Turkish) Empire (1380–1918)
Sabbah (d. 1124)		
Jawzi (1126–1200)		
Ibn Rushd (Lat. Averroes) (1126–98)	Mali kingdom in upper Niger region of Africa, Timbuktu as capital (ca. 1230–1340)	
Ibn Bajjah (Lat. Avempace) (d. 1139)		
Ghurid dynasty rules eastern Iran and Punjab (1148–1215)	Hajji Bektash (ca. 1247–1338)	
Razi (1149–1209)	Mamluk rule in Egypt and Syria (1250–1519)	
Ibn al-Arabi (1165–1240)	Ibn Ata Allah (1252–1309)	
Ayyurbids restore Sunni in Egypt (1171–1250)	Muslim Mongol Il-Khans begin domination of Shi'ite Islam in Persia (Iran) (1258–1370)	
Muizzudin Muhammad founds first Muslim empire in India (1175)		
Ibn al-Farid (1181–1240)	Ibn Taymiyah (1263–1328)	
Ibn Tufayl (Lat. Abubacer) (d. 1185)		
Saladin recaptures Jerusalem from Christians (1187)		

asabiyya gives way to the social and cultural patterns of higher urban cultures that are less hardy and self-reliant, and thus a civilization will fall back into social conditions for which tribal lifestyles provide more effective means of survival. Ibn Khaldun's theory of the vicissitudes of Islamic history has earned him the title "father of the social sciences." His three-volume *Muqaddimah* (Introduction to History) has been translated into English and has been the subject of several studies by modern scholars.

What the Arab Bedouin did contribute to Islamic religion and society, of significance far beyond the demographic limits of the Arab component in Islamic civilization, was their language, Arabic. Although Persian, Turkish, Indian, Malay, and other ethnic Muslim communities are often critical of the exaggerated role the Arabs have claimed for themselves in the unfolding of Islamic history, all Muslims cherish the Arabic language and try to learn at least some quranic and other religious phrases in Arabic. Today, as in classical times, the religious sciences of Islam (including quranic recitation and commentary, prophetic traditions [*hadith*], law, and theology) are studied and taught in Arabic by Muslims around the world. Indeed, at the beginning of the twentieth century, a revival of Arabic language and literature occurred in Arab lands, leading to the development of a modern standard form of Arabic for the classroom,

1400–1500	1500–1600	1600–1800
Kabir (ca. 1398–1448)	Suleyman (Suleiman) I, most powerful Ottoman ruler (1494–1556)	Taj Mahal constructed by Mughal emperor, Shah Jahan (1632–54)
Malacca state, Malay peninsula (1400–1511)	Forced conversion to Catholicism of Spanish Muslims, beginning of Moriscos (1502–1609)	Shabbetai Tzevi, Jewish messianic figure, converts to Islam (1666)
Jami (1414–92)	Ottoman forces capture Belgrade (1521)	Decisive battle near Vienna ends Muslim expansion north and west into Europe (1683)
Suyuti (1445–1505)	Sunan Bonang (d. ca. 1525)	Ibn Abd al-Wahhab (1703–92)
Constantinople captured by Ottoman forces of Mehmed, the Conqueror; renamed Istanbul (1453)	Mughal dynasty in India (1526–1857)	Shah Wali Allah (1703–62)
Christians conquer Granada, last stronghold of Islam in Spain (1492)	Ottoman armies besiege Vienna for three months (1529)	Muhammad Baqir Bihbihani (1705–90)
	Portuguese conquer Malacca (1551)	Muktar al-Kabir (1728–1811)
	Akbar, Mughal emperor (1555–1605)	Tijani (1737–1815)
	Ahmad Sirhindi (1564–1624)	Decline of Mughal power in India (1748–1857)
	Shirazi (1571–1640)	Beginning of Russian control of Muslim territories (1755)
	"Long War," Habsburgs and Ottomans (1593–1605)	Napoleon I invades Egypt (1798)
	Isfahan becomes Safavid capital in Iran (1598)	

public speaking, and the media. At the end of the twentieth century, the revival of Arabic applies to non-Arab Muslims as well. One of the marks of the modern reassertion of Islamic identity in virtually all parts of the world where significant Muslim communities live has been the study of the Arabic language.

The importance of Arabic as a significant factor in Islamic identity is as much theological as linguistic, and this has been the case throughout Islamic history. It is important to Muslims that Arabic was the language in which the Qur'an was revealed, in stylistic perfection so remarkable that Islam has seen the Qur'an itself as God's miracle through the Prophet Muhammad. By the ninth century, Muslim theologians argued that just as God had given to Moses, as a sign of his prophethood, the power to change rods into serpents and divide the Red Sea; and just as God had given to Jesus, as a sign of his prophethood, the power to heal the sick and raise the dead; so God gave to Muhammad the ability to recite his word in language so beautiful that even the most gifted Arab poets and orators could not imitate it when challenged by Muhammad to do so. Even non-Arab Muslims, most of whom must approach the Qur'an in translation in order to grasp its intellectual content, join Arab Muslims in asserting the ultimate untranslatability of the Qur'an.

Islam		
1800–1900	**1900–**	
Aga Khan I (1804–81)	Ruhollah Khomenei (1902–89)	First Arab-Israeli war (1948–49)
Large portions of Islamic Africa, Eurasia (including Near and Middle East) under European Christian control (1815–1900)	Muslim league founded (India) (1906)	Bangladesh becomes independent (1971)
	Sayyid Qutb (1906–66)	Shah of Iran exiled; Iranian revolution (1979)
	"Young Turk" revolution (1908)	
Sayyid Ahmad Khan (1817–98)	Partition of Ottoman territories among European powers as result of World War I (1915–23)	Hezbollah (Hizb Allah) founded in Lebanon (1982)
Ghulam Ahmad (1835–98)		
Muhammad Ahmad ("the Madhi") (ca. 1840–85)	Long process of independence of Muslim lands from European imperialism (1919–84), beginning with Afghanistan's independence from Britain (1919), accelerating after World War II (e.g., Pakistan, 1947), and drawing to a close with the Sultanate of Brunei's independence from Britain (1984)	Naguib Mahfouz (Egypt) receives Nobel Prize for Literature (1988)
Namik Kemal (1840–88)		New process of independence as Muslim republics of former Soviet Union (including Azerbaijan, Kazakhstan, Kyrgystan, Tajikistan, Turkmenistan, and Uzbekistan) attain self-government (1990–91)
Muhammad Abduh (1849–1905)		
Muslim rebellion in China (1862–78)		
Ibn Abd Allah (1864–1920)		
Suez Canal (1869)		
Muhammad Iqbal (1876–1938)	Formation of Muslim Brotherhood (Egypt) (1928)	
Mustafa Kamal Ataturk (1881–1938)		

HISTORICAL OVERVIEW

Looking at the long expanse of Muslim civilization from the seventh century to the present, Islamic history can be divided into two parts. The question is where to locate the divide. Many contemporary Western historians have seen 1500 as the rough dividing line between traditional Islamic civilization and the rise of modern Islamic societies. In the late fifteenth and early sixteenth centuries, three Islamic empires arose, in Anatolia (Ottoman), Iran (Safavid), and the Indian subcontinent (Mughul). These empires lasted until the beginning of the modern period, when growing European influence and eventually colonialism, among other factors, hastened their collapse. Others have seen 1300 as the major divide between classical and modern Islam, for in 1258 the Mongols destroyed the imperial office of the caliphate in Baghdad, thus bringing to an end the practical hope of a universal Sunni Islam under one Muslim ruler.

By 1200, however, the Islamic religious tradition achieved its present religious institutional forms. The last of the twelve descendants of Muhammad's family through his paternal cousin and son-in-law, Ali son of Abu Talib, to be recognized as *imam* (spiritual leader of the Shiite communities) had disappeared. The twelfth imam, according to the majority of the Shia, was believed to have gone into occultation in the latter part of the ninth century. By the mid-tenth century, the main body of the Shia of Ali declared the Greater Occultation of the Twelfth Alid Imam. For the next three generations, until the mid-eleventh century, Shiite theologians established the main texts and practices of Shiite Islam. The devotees of the seventh imam, Ismail, whom they believed had gone into occultation, became a significant heterodox (and sometimes subversive) sect in medieval Islam. Still another alternative sect of the Shia, the followers of the fifth imam were named *Zaydis* after him. Until 1200, the Zaydis represented a theological posture that was strongly critical of the Sunni caliphate, but that nonetheless accepted more of Sunni doctrine than the other Shia groups.

The four schools of Sunni jurisprudence (Shafiite, Hanafite, Hanbalite, and Malikite), along with the main Shiite tradition in jurisprudence (Jafarite), became entrenched in Islamic society by the end of the twelfth century. Moreover, by this time, Islamic religious thought had become completely identified in method and worldview with jurisprudence, and less so with theological speculation and reflection. Matters of faith and practice were decided, case by case, in written opinions (*fatwas*) according to how the legal scholars interpreted and applied the four roots of law: the Qur'an, *Sunna,* the consensus of the community, and reasoning by analogy from known divine commandments or prophetic practice to newer situations. The primary authority of these four roots had been established by al-Shafii (767–820), one of the founders of the four law schools. These roots of the law combined four sources—divine word, prophetic example, communal precedent, and individual reasoning—with much room for difference of opinion and debate on virtually every issue.

The process of public and disciplined disputation on virtually every point of interpretation in faith and practice is known in Arabic as *khilaf.* Religious and legal disputation became a chief cultural expression, not only among Islamic schools of jurisprudence, but also between Muslim and non-Muslim theological virtuosos and among heterodox sectarians, philosophers, and other factions within Islamic society in the early Middle Ages (until 1100, at least). What united the Islamic world was (and is) far less a single polity (the caliphate was in receivership to local warlords by 950) or a supreme spiritual leader (there was none in Islam) than a set of sources and methods of interpreting those sources (namely, Qur'an and Sunna).

Those charged with carrying on this tradition of education in the religious sciences and interpreting them continually as differences arise are known as the *ulama* ("knowers," "learned ones"). Unlike Christian clergy, who are ordained and who bear sacramental authority, the ulama are men recognized by their communities for their learning in the religious sciences of Islam. The ulama seldom command political power as such. Rather, they are teachers, jurisconsults, and religious intellectuals, situated between the rulers and the ruled in Islamic societies. Historians often note that the major difference between Shiite and Sunni ulama is that the former have tended to take a stance of opposition to Muslim political regimes, while the latter have usually been more accommodating to the wishes of rulers.

Still another social institution of traditional Islamic religion that was well established by 1200 was Sufism, the Islamic form of mysticism. The Sufi worldview was based on the same sources as other Muslims, the Qur'an and Sunna. But the early mystics (and ascetics) stressed spiritual discipline and the inner meaning of the religious duties required by Islamic law. Above all, they pursued methods of attaining union with God. Virtuoso mystics in the early centuries of Islam drew disciples. In time, Sufi brotherhoods, known as *tariqas,* became

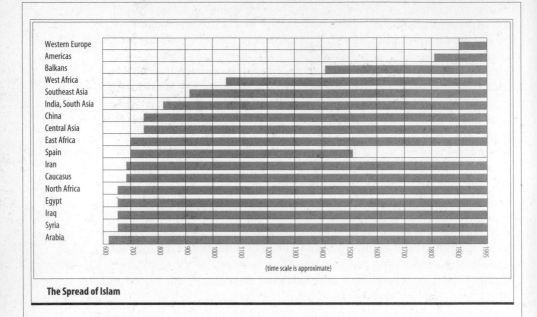

The Spread of Islam

powerful alternative modes of living the Islamic religion. Today, Sufi brother-hoods are still active in the Nile Valley and elsewhere in the Muslim world.

If the major Islamic institutions were established by the year 1200, the symbols and forms they took had been established in the beginning generation of Islam, the time of the Prophet Muhammad and the four Rightly Guided Caliphs, who ruled Islam for the next thirty years.

ISLAMIC BEGINNINGS

The story of its beginnings has been for Islam, as for most religions, an important framework in all ages for self-understanding. A chief concern is for what constitutes the Muslim community, or *umma*. Islam traces its rise to the historical appearance of Muhammad, who later sources say was born ca. 570 in the Arabian trading and pilgrimage shrine town of Mecca. Arabia was dominated by tribal social and cultural patterns, including alliances and conflicts with other tribes. The Quraysh tribe, into which Muhammad was born, had dominated Mecca and its shrine, the Kaaba, and commercial markets (mostly cara-vanserai) for several generations. In Islamic cosmology, the appearance of the Prophet Muhammad among his own Arab people brought an end to a global period of crude human ignorance, or *jahiliyya*. The other "Peoples of the Book" (primarily Jews, Christians, and Zoroastrians), who had preceded the Muslim community, had perverted the scriptures brought to them from God by their prophets. The notion that jahiliyya symbolizes the need for the renewal of true religion has been an important theme for Muslim reformers, especially in modern times.

According to Muslim biographical and historical works in Arabic dating from the ninth century, Muhammad's call to prophethood began when he was forty years old (ca. 610). In a dramatic moment during a night of vigil in a cave in the mountains near Mecca, Muhammad was ordered by the angel Gabriel to "recite in the name of the Lord . . . who teaches man by the pen what he knows not" (Qur'an 96:1–4 passim). Though Muhammad was reported to have been sore afraid and unsure of himself in the first instance, those recitations of God's word in miraculously beautiful Arabic were to continue to come to him throughout his life, until his death in 632. In Mecca during the first years of Muhammad's prophethood, the revelations of the divine word that were "sent down" took the form of strong warnings to Meccan society to repent of social immorality and to give up pagan polytheism. The message was met with derision and scorn on the part of most Meccans.

The entire collection of recitations, forming a book about the length of the Christian New Testament, is known in Arabic as the Qur'an (lit., "recitals"). The cardinal importance of the Qur'an in Muslim life—in educational foundations, legal formulations, moral expectations, social behavior, liturgical practice, artistic performance (chanting and calligraphy), and in everyday speech—is a hallmark of Islam that is at once theological and aesthetic. Islamic societies are infused with the message, as well as the aesthetic appeal, of the Qur'an at many conscious and subconscious levels.

From the beginning, the message of the Qur'an and the moral and spiritual precedents established by the living example of the Prophet claimed authority over all of life, including religious duties, as well as matters pertaining to family, the market, and the state. The revelation of the Qur'an, however, was incomplete when, in 622 (year one in Muslim chronology), after several years of harassment by the elders of the Meccan Quraysh tribe, the followers of Muhammad decided to leave Mecca for an agricultural oasis town called Yathrib, later named Medina (city [of the Prophet]), an event celebrated as the Hijra.

In Medina, Muhammad was recognized as Prophet not only by the Meccan followers who had emigrated with him, known as Muhajirun, but also by the citizens of Medina known as the Ansar ("helpers"), who had invited Muhammad to preside over their tribally divided community in the traditional manner of the Middle Eastern judicious tribal leader. The revelations that were "sent down" to Muhammad in Medina now pertained to his growing community of followers, containing prescriptions for social behavior and ritual performance.

Moreover, what Muhammad said, when asked questions in Medina about religion, or *din,* and what he did in the practice of it became known as *sunna* ("path," "practice"). The Sunna of the Prophet Muhammad became the second major source of scriptural authority after the Qur'an. The Prophet's Sunna, that is, his words and deeds and matters on which he otherwise indicated approval or disapproval, were remembered by his Companions and transmitted by them to subsequent generations. These verbal traditions about the Prophet's Sunna are known as *hadith.* The most authoritative generations of transmitters were the first three, known respectively as the Companions, the Followers, and the Followers of the Followers.

By the ninth century the hadiths numbered in the tens of thousands. Several collections were made and written down, organized either according to the Companions and Followers, etc., who transmitted them, or according to the topics of their content. Six collections, each in several volumes, became known as "The Sound" collections. Of these, the most famous and oft-quoted is that of al-Bukhari (d. 870), which has been printed in many Arabic editions and translated into English.

Bukhari's collection begins with a brief section on the inspiration of the Qur'an. The following sections are on faith, religious knowledge, and purity, including ritual lustrations (baths) after polluting activities, and lesser ablutions performed before the prayer. Among the most polluting substances are semen and blood. Many hadiths in these sections pertain to the need for lustrations following sexual intercourse, as well as for women experiencing postpartum or menstrual bleeding. Many of the hadiths in this section are traced back to Ayisha, the Prophet's youngest and, reputedly, his favorite wife.

Several sections in Bukhari's collection contain prophetic sayings on the religious duties of Islam (prayer, alms, fasting, and pilgrimage). The last few volumes contain hadiths on such topics as *jihad* ("struggle," "effort"), the virtues and merits of Muhammad and other prophets, wills and testaments, inheritance, marriage, good manners, taking and keeping oaths, the divinely set punishments (for stealing, murder, etc.), and the interpretation of dreams. Significantly, the last section of Bukhari's collection is on *tawhid* ("divine unity"), the doctrine that lies at the basis of the Islamic concept of monotheism.

Ten years after the Hijra to Medina, Muhammad died in his own home of natural causes. The Islamic rejection of the doctrine of Jesus' divinity is based on the quranic conviction that Muhammad, like all prophets before him, including Jesus, was a mortal human being. Yet Muslims believe, as Christians do, in the virgin birth of Jesus and in the perfect moral nature of all prophets. Hence, to say that Muhammad and all the preceding prophets from Adam to Jesus were mortal and not divine is not to say that they were merely "ordinary" human beings, in the Islamic worldview. If the central problem of Christology for the church fathers was to resist the attraction of Arianism, which emphasized the humanity of Jesus the Christ to the exclusion of his divinity, the problem surrounding Muhammad's prophethood has been the temptation for Muslims to exalt his extraordinary nature. A ritual and festal occasion for celebrating and remembering the Prophet Muhammad is the *Mawlid* ("birthday") ceremony, which is popular in North Africa, Southeast Asia, and in many other parts of the Islamic world. However, in Arabia, among those Muslims who follow the Hanbali Sunni interpretation of law, celebrating the birthday of the Prophet is forbidden and regarded as *bida* ("[unlawful] innovation").

Muhammad experienced many struggles and conflicts with opponents and enemies during his lifetime. These experiences and the terms for them, along with the struggles for power among various factions after Muhammad's death, became paradigmatic for later Islamic history. The Muslim community's sense of self-identity in relation to non-Muslim communities, as well as its sense of what separates Muslims from non-Muslim peoples, is derived largely from events in the lifetime of the Prophet and of his companions who survived in the seventh century. For example, the message of submission to the one God Allah was sharply critical of Arab pagan polytheism. Islam viewed polytheism from the vantage point of strict monotheism, declaring that the worst form of false belief was to "associate" (*shirk*) other deities with Allah. Shirk is the opposite of the aforementioned *tawhid*. Long after the polytheism of Arabia, and other lands to which Islam spread, was no longer a challenge to Islamic belief, the concept of shirk has remained potent nonetheless. Leaders who do not rule Muslim nations according to Islamic precepts, for example, are often accused of shirk, that is, of not being good Muslim theists; their accusers claim they do not rule according to divine legislation, or *Sharia*. In modern times, those rulers who have sought Western support, and who (in the eyes of their Muslim subjects) have abandoned rule according to the Sharia, are often accused of shirk.

SPEAKING ABOUT ISLAM . . .

A significant problem for those who read, speak, or write about Islamic topics is the cultural stereotypes that many Muslims find offensive. This is not a trivial problem. Those writing for broadcast and print news media, as well as for features and school curricula, now find that what they say about Islam circulates widely in the Muslim world, thanks to modern technology and telecommunications.

For example, despite the above-mentioned statistics about the extent of the world Muslim population, and the fact that Americans have more information about Islam and Muslims than ever before, ignorance and misinformation still exist. According to a survey conducted by a North American professional association of scholars in Middle Eastern studies, in the 1990s, social studies textbooks on the Middle East and other regions that include Islamic societies often still represent Muslims as camel-driving nomads. In fact, as mentioned already, only about 2 percent of Muslims are pastoral nomads.

A related problem for the growing number (and percentage) of writers, teachers, and speakers who deal with Islamic topics is the inevitable ethnocentrism of persons culturally situated in North America. It would not be surprising for a Southern Baptist and an agnostic secular humanist to have quite different conceptions of the significance of religion in American public life. Often, however, little thought seems to be given to the fact that neither the Baptist nor the agnostic will understand religion in public life the way it would be understood by a Sunni Muslim in Egypt or a Shiite Muslim in Iran.

In Western textbooks, the historical encounter with Muslim peoples often has been portrayed primarily in terms of armed conflict motivated by religion—from the defeat by Charles Martel (the Hammer) of the advancing Arab Muslim armies at Poitiers in the eighth century (blocking Arabs from further entry into Europe through Gaul); to the Crusades beginning in the eleventh century (recapturing the Holy Land from Muslim "infidels"); to the Reconquista in Spain in the late fifteenth century (repulsing Muslims from southern Europe altogether); to the struggles between Turks and Europeans in the Balkans (stopping the "Saracen hordes" at the gates of Vienna); down to late-twentieth-century coun terterrorism (protecting North American tourist, business, and military inter-ests endangered by a putative global Islamic threat).

Some measure of understanding the converse experience, the Islamic experi-ence of the West during the past two centuries, is important for those who may seek to understand why many Muslims represent modern Islam in anti-Western dialectical terms. Historically speaking, Muslim encounters with Chris-tian European civilization around the Mediterranean did not much affect the vast majority of Muslim societies in Africa and Asia (including the Middle East, Central Asia, and the Indian subcontinent) until the colonial period. The Islam-ic response to the concept of "the West" (Euro-American civilization; Judeo-Christianity; capitalist-driven colonial subjugation of Muslim societies) did not develop until the nineteenth century. At first, the common image of the West among the Muslim intelligentsia (at least, those writing for and read by Western scholars) was of a society that educationally, economically, and militarily was vastly superior to Islamic civilization; Islam was seen as having fallen into rela-tive impotence since the great achievements of the ages of the Prophet Muham-mad, the conquests under the Rightly Guided Caliphs, and the Golden Age of the Abbasid Empire.

Less visible in Europe and America were indigenous eighteenth- and nineteenth-century Islamic movements to "renew" traditional religion and so-cial systems. These movements are now seen by most historians as a response to the decline of the premodern regimes that once bound much of the Islamic world together in regional empires: the Ottomans in the eastern and southern Mediterranean, the Safavids in Iran and parts of Central Asia, and the Moghuls in South Asia. In the twentieth century, the mood began to shift from admira-tion of Western achievements to resentment of Western colonialism and impe-rialism. Muslim discourses against the West—specifically against secularism, capitalism, and communism as failed systems—intensified during the twenti-eth century.

Those who read and write about Islam today do so not only in the wake of Western colonial (economic and military) control of much of the Muslim world, but also within a Western-constructed discourse about Islam—a discourse that has come to be known as orientalism. Since 1979, when Edward Said published a book titled *Orientalism*, offering a scathing indictment of European studies of Arabs and Muslims, much of earlier Western scholarship on Islam has come under increasing criticism by both Muslim and non-Muslim scholars. Nonethe-less, in the ongoing study of Islam in Western scholarship, contemporary histo-rians, religionists, and social scientists are heavily indebted to the pioneering contribution of previous generations of Arabists and Islamicists.

North American as well as Muslim writers often confuse normative descrip-tions of religious beliefs and practices with historical expression and social be-havior. Under the impact of acceptable argument in the social sciences, some North American writers represent Islam in terms of what they perceive Muslims actually to be doing—in the mosque and home, and in society more generally, in gender relationships, and in the treatment of Muslim sects and non-Muslim minorities. In this view, the adjective "Islamic" qualifies virtually all social behavior observed in Muslim societies. The popular confusion of normative religion with the things religious people actually do, or seem to be doing, can lead to pernicious, self-serving comparisons: "My religion teaches 'thou shalt not kill,' but the people of religion X seem to kill each other all the time." Creedal demand and actual behavior can be two quite different things.

Many Muslim scholars, on the other side, mean by "Islam" a system of beliefs and practices revealed by God in scripture (the Qur'an) and perfectly exemplified in the life of the Prophet (the Sunna). In this latter view, some of what outsiders observe ordinary Muslims believing and doing is regarded as un-Islamic, heretical, or even blasphemous. Thus, Western writers may come under criticism for characterizing observed phenomena within the full range of Muslim social and religious practices in ways that orthodox Sunni or Shii Islam does not recognize as essentially Islamic. One way to avoid potential misunderstanding when writing about Islam (or any religious tradition) is to be clear in the beginning as to whether one is speaking about a normative system of beliefs, ritual performances, and social practices, or whether one is dealing with observed social behavior and the manifestation of culture in actual circumstances.

In comparative religious studies generally, more information and analysis is needed on how Muslims negotiate the disparity between what the Qur'an and Sunna require of them and what they may do in apparent conflict with those ideals. This is a central problem in religious studies more generally. One of the best sources for seeing how Muslims experience and cope with this disparity, found in all religions (and indeed in human existence universally), can be found in the poetry and novels of Muslim writers, such as the 1988 Nobel Laureate, Naguib Mahfouz of Egypt.

Islam (authoritative texts and their interpretation).

The Qur'an (Arab., "recitation," "reading") is the Muslim record of God's revelation to Muhammad.

While recognizing its theological relation to prior forms of revelation, such as the Torah (*Tawrat*) and Gospel (*Injil*), Muslims view the Qur'an as God's full and final disclosure to the last of his prophets, Muhammad. They further understand Muhammad to be the conduit, not the composer, of the Qur'an. As God's very words, which were revealed to his Prophet in the Arabic language, the recited or written Qur'an is itself the temporal reproduction of an uncreated and eternal archetype, "the well-protected tablet" or "mother of the book." To underscore this conception of revelation, it has become a commonplace in works on the comparative study of religious traditions to associate the Qur'an not with the Hebrew Bible or the Christian New Testament but with the person of Jesus Christ as the incarnate Word. Similarly, recitation of the Qur'an has been compared with certain Christian understandings of the Eucharist because a belief in the realized presence of God's Word is central to both.

Muslims find within the Qur'an God's final guidance for humankind in all aspects of human life. This scripture serves as far more than a source of religious inspiration; prescriptions and proscriptions within the Qur'an address the whole range of human personal and social behavior. Therein has God made clear "the straight path" and given explicit expression to the manner in which humans must live in accordance with his will. Because the Qur'an is God's very Word and a graced gift for human guidance, the physical text itself is treated with respect and reverence. Its pages are carefully protected from any sort of dirt or damage. It should not, for example, ever be placed on the ground. Pious Muslims will perform mandated ablutions before handling the Qur'an and will avoid doing so if in an unavoidable state of ritual impurity (e.g., during menstruation or puerperium).

The Function of the Qur'an in Muslim Life: From the seventh through the twentieth centuries the Qur'an has stood ideally as the foundational document in the organization of Muslim societies. Quranic injunctions, in combination with the recorded statements and behavior of Muhammad (*hadith*), have formed the basis for the comprehensive recognition of divine law (*Sharia*) in its jurisprudential particulars (*fiqh*) and as the ground for sociopolitical organization. In its very language the Qur'an has acted as a centrifugal social force throughout the Muslim world. Quranic words and phrases have penetrated the languages of Muslim peoples worldwide, while memorization of the Qur'an, even by non-Arabic-speaking Muslims, has fostered a sense of linguistic fraternity among the whole Muslim community (*umma*). Contemporary militant groups and opposition parties in many Muslim countries draw upon both the legal and linguistic commonality of the text as a means of legitimating their claims for social and political reform.

For Muslims the Qur'an functions first as an oral/aural phenomenon and then as a visual/textual one. Its very name as a "recitation" underscores the primacy of this orality. Muslims liturgically experience the Qur'an in the prescribed cycle of daily prayer (*salat*). During each of the five prayer periods the opening verses of the Qur'an are repeated, as are other portions of the sacred scripture. Every calendrical feast day and life-passage rite in the Muslim world, be it a naming ceremony, a circumcision, a marriage, or a funeral, is marked by the sound of quranic cantillation. The thirty nights of Ramadan, the fasting month, provide a particularly important opportunity for public recitation. The sounds of the recited Qur'an, now often conveyed by broadcast or audio cassette, certainly stimulate religious fervor, but, more important, they function for Muslims as a profound source of blessing (*baraka*), an oral ambient that continually reminds the believer that God is present in his Word.

The opening chapter (*sura*) of the Qur'an often is among the first sounds that a child hears as it is clasped in its parents' arms after birth. Traditionally in the Muslim world, formal education commenced with Qur'an recitation and memorization. The first school a child would attend was, and often still is, a Qur'an school (*maktab* or *kuttab*). This transnational educational experience affords yet another point of commonality for the worldwide Muslim community. The rote recitation learned in such schools becomes, for some students, a prelude to full memorization of the Qur'an. Although Arabic is not the mother-tongue of most present-day Muslims, many people in all Muslim countries continue to learn the entire text by heart as an act of disciplined piety. One who does so acquires the prestige of a *hafiz* (lit., "custodian" of the Qur'an). From the beginnings of Islam such an accomplishment has been a source of honor and esteem.

Yet memorization itself constitutes but one aspect of the fully developed science of quranic recitation (*tajwid*). Long years of tutelage and practice are required to produce a professional standard of cantillation. Those who master the intricacies of this skill are in great demand for both public and private performance. Recent research among the Muslims of Indonesia even reveals the use of such contemporary cultural phenomena as quiz games and stadium competition in the cultivation of this highly regarded capability.

Complementing the pervasive orality of the Qur'an are certain prominent written functions. Architectural calligraphy expresses the visual authority of the text and establishes a dominant graphic motif throughout the Islamic world. Quranic words and phrases embellish the facades and interiors of mosques, shrines, tombs, schools, and public buildings. Manuscript illumination of the quranic text, as recorded in thousands of museum-quality codices, furnishes further evidence of visual reverencing of the word. On a more popular level, this same reverence can assume theurgic dimensions. Appreciation of the text's power is manifest when verses of the Qur'an are worn on the body in amulets, when the text is prayerfully consulted for good omens, or when the ink of its penned verses is dissolved in water and imbibed as a healing potion. The transtemporal power and blessing of the Qur'an finds ultimate attestation in the fact that its recitation is the only religious obligation that will endure in paradise.

Chronologies of Revelation and Codification: Issues of the Qur'an's textual format and formation have presented scholars, both Muslim and non-Muslim, with two predominating chronological concerns. The first centers on the chronology of revelation, while the second concentrates on that of textual fixation. The structure of the Qur'an could be described as an inverted pyramid. Except for the first, its 114 suras are arranged in roughly descending order of length, so that the initial suras are far longer than those with which the text concludes. The suras themselves have come to acquire titles and are prefaced (except for the ninth) with the *basmala,* the prayer formula usually translated as "In the name of God, the Merciful, the Compassionate." In addition to its chapter divisions, the Qur'an has been apportioned into various recitative units, such as seven or thirty parts, to facilitate its complete recitation in a week or a month.

In studying the Qur'an, scholars have attempted to chart the chronology of its revelation through both stylistic and historical analyses. An early consensus about the identification of Meccan and Medinan suras has been maintained with some modification and refinement. Most scholars have accepted the sura as an integral unit of revelation and have confined their analysis to subdivisions within the two basic chronological categories. Differences between these two are often readily apparent, with the terse challenges of the earliest Meccan period gradually shading into the lengthy legal and narrative pronouncements of the late Medinan period. Associating particular historical incidents with certain parts of the Qur'an as "occasions of their revelation" allowed Muslim scholars to tie the chronology of revelation more closely to the biography of Muhammad.

The concerns that propelled such scholarship were not merely academic. Legal consequences were attendant on the order of revelation in those cases where a later disclosure abrogated the legislative force of a former. Theological consistency could also hinge on such historical assessment as in the case of the so-called Satanic verses, where an earlier revelation (ultimately ascribed to Satan), which ostensibly permitted intercessory prayer to certain goddesses, was subsequently divinely corrected.

In addition to studying the chronology of the revelation itself, scholars of the Qur'an charted the various stages of its textual formation. With some exceptions, a consensus eventually emerged among Muslim scholars about this chronology of codification. According to these accounts, Muhammad received the quranic revelations through multiple modes of divine transmission and then repeated them verbatim to his close followers and associates. Orality remained, throughout the Prophet's lifetime, the primary form of conveyance. Although certain narratives mention that quranic verses were recorded on such materials as bones, palm leaves, stones, and bits of leather, apparently no full written version of the Qur'an existed before the death of Muhammad (632).

With the Prophet's death, and the consequent cessation of revelation, the process of textual compilation entered another stage. The accounts differ about whether the first attempt at a full codex was made during the caliphate of Abu Bakr (d. 634) or that of Umar (d. 644). In either case, the endeavor was managed by a group under the leadership of Zayd ibn Thabit (d. 666), formerly a secretary to Muhammad. This codex, which eventually passed to Umar's daughter Hafsah, became but one of a number of written recensions in circulation, to say nothing of the unwritten versions still carried in the memories of many. During the caliphate of Umar's successor, Uthman (d. 656), a group was commissioned—once again under the leadership of

Zayd ibn Thabit—to produce an official text. Concern about the increasing range and diversity of textual and recited variants, as well as about their potential legal implications, apparently prompted this effort. According to traditional accounts, the codex belonging to Hafsah was collated with other codices and recited versions in a process that accorded dialect priority to Quraysh, the Prophet's tribe. Copies of this "Uthmanic" recension were then distributed to the principal metropolitan centers, such as Medina, Kufa, Basra, and Damascus, and attempts were made to suppress variant recensions.

Although these attempts were not entirely successful, the "Uthmanic" codex gradually superseded other transcriptions and eventually achieved canonical status. Considerable assistance in this achievement was provided by the concurrent orthographic development. The earliest codices of the Qur'an were produced with a script that lacked vowel markings and the points necessary to make certain consonantal distinctions. Oral recitation, of course, provided what was missing in this rudimentary script. Within the first three Islamic centuries refinements of Arabic orthography created diacritical marks to distinguish similar consonants and clarified ways of indicating both long and short vowels. With these developments it became possible to fix the range of acceptable textual variation. The man credited with doing so, Ibn Mujahid (d. 936), relied upon an apposite prophetic hadith (saying) as the justification for setting the range of "readings" at seven, although this figure has sometimes been increased to ten or even to fourteen.

While the recorded range of textual variation to be found in the early exegetical works runs to the thousands of elements, the actual import of most of these is insignificant. In fact, the accepted range of quranic readings has come to be regarded as part of the Qur'an's richness and uniqueness. Despite this range, however, one particular line of transmission (that of Hafs on the authority of Asim) has gained primacy in the twentieth century because the 1923 Egyptian edition that reproduces it has become the contemporary standard.

Analysis and Interpretation of the Qur'an: The reverence accorded the Qur'an as God's own Word is also clearly demonstrated in the centuries of analysis and interpretation (*tafsir*) devoted to this text. In the last millennium Muslim scholars have produced thousands of commentaries, most of them in Arabic but others in the principal languages of the Islamic world. The painstaking attention paid to each verse attests to both the authority of the quranic text and its fascination for generations of Muslim intellectuals. Among the earliest efforts at quranic interpretation were rudimentary glosses, which grew from a concern with the linguistic and grammatical peculiarities of the Qur'an. Out of these proto-commentaries can be traced the development of the advanced study of Arabic grammar and lexicography. These early philological investigations were not undertaken as mere intellectual exercises but as a grave and pious charge. Fear of error or of simply being unequal to the interpretive challenge remained a matter of serious concern within the early Muslim community. Nevertheless, the activity of commentary continued, enlarging its scope to include discussion of historical circumstances as well as matters of theological and legal significance. An initial limitation of this exercise to exegetical statements from Muhammad and his companions as the only valid form of interpretation was eventually broadened to incorporate doctrinal and juridical concerns, as well as mystical and allegorical allusions. With the modernist commentators in the early decades of this century, quranic interpretation attended to social and political issues, an orientation that has been greatly emphasized by certain contemporary exegetes.

Quranic Teachings: Given its mode of arrangement by descending sura length, the Qur'an does not divide itself either by theme or by genre. Rather it combines such genres within its suras as admonitory narratives, legal prescriptions, prayers, parables, descriptions of the life to come, polemical addresses, and details of ritual requirements. Additionally, throughout the suras may be traced a number of persistent themes, ranging from a forceful condemnation of idolatry to the legal and ethical injunctions requisite for the proper conduct of human life. Certainly the fundamental teaching of the Qur'an centers upon the doctrine of God. No scripture more emphatically announces the divine uniqueness and unicity. In his omnipotence God creates all things with the simple imperative "Be" (2:117 and passim) and ceaselessly sustains them. Those verses traditionally held to be the first ones revealed underscore God's creative activity: "Recite in the name of your Lord who created, created man from a [blood] clot" (96: 1–2). God's creative power continually expresses itself in the "signs" (*ayat*) with which he has filled the heavens and the earth. The succession of day and night, the rain that waters fields and crops, human mastery of the sea, as well as the processes of physical growth and maturation, all exemplify God's creative and sustaining presence to the pious and perceptive mind.

Assertion of God's unity (tawhid) counts as the primary theological proposition in the Qur'an. Although acknowledging the existence of other spiritual beings, such as angels, demons, and *jinn*, the Qur'an uncompromisingly maintains that "There is no god but God" (37:35 and passim). All forms of idolatry and polytheism are excoriated as *shirk*, i.e., as compromising the divine uniqueness by associating anything with God. Characterizing God as One (*wahid*), however, is not the only way in which the Qur'an depicts the divine. From this scripture, Muslims have culled a long list of epithets with which to exalt God in prayer. Known as "the beautiful names," titles such as "All-Knowing," "Merciful," "Forgiving," "Eternal," and "All-Powerful" create a litany of praise when fingered on prayer beads and offer to Muslim minds a continuous reminder of the divine's multiple attributes.

In his beneficence, God has repeatedly offered guidance to humankind by sending prophets and messengers who could communicate his will. This succession of divine revelations constitutes the quranic understanding of salvation history. While the names of many of these prophets and messengers, such as Adam, Noah, Abraham, Moses, and Jesus, will be recognized by those familiar with the Bible, others are particular to the Qur'an. For Muslims, Muhammad stands as the last or "seal" of the prophets, just as the revelation accorded to him represents God's final guidance for humankind. Because all proceed from the same source, the Qur'an understands itself to be fully consonant with previous divine revelations, as rightly conveyed and interpreted by their recipients. Discrepancies between the Qur'an and previous scriptures, such as the Torah and Gospel, are judged to be the result of deliberate or inadvertent falsification of these latter books by Jews and Christians. Not only are both the Qur'an and Muhammad deemed infallible, the revelation of the Qur'an is regarded as the miracle that ratifies Muhammad's claim to prophethood. Unique in linguistic and stylistic beauty, the Qur'an presents an unattainable idea of perfection.

The response expected by God for the kindness of this consummate revelation is one of both gratitude and obedience. This dual response is most adequately manifest in the basic act of submission (*islam*) that the creature accords the Creator. The God-given faculties of intelligence and perception innately prepare the individual for such submission. The Qur'an also recognizes, however, that many obstinately refuse to accept God's guidance. These it excoriates as ingrates and unbelievers (*kafirs*), liable to the ultimate demands of divine justice. The final judgment, known variously as the End, the Last Day, the Day of Resurrection, the Day of Decision, the Hour, will be the concluding moment in which each individual stands accountable for the response rendered to God's guidance and mercy. The deeds of a lifetime will be weighed in the balance, their preponderance of good or of evil determining an eternity of bliss or tribulation. As the Qur'an graphically describes both the delights of heaven and the torments of hell, it continues to remind the listener and reader that the choices made in this lifetime will have lasting consequences.

To aid humans in making these choices, the Qur'an presents various guidelines for the conduct of human relations and for the ritual behavior required by God. Such prescriptive and proscriptive injunctions eventually were systematized by Muslim jurisprudents, in combination with recorded Prophetic exempla (hadith), as the Sharia. While in no sense a legal code book, the Qur'an nevertheless offers basic guidance about the fivefold religious duty of Muslims, as well as about those aspects of individual and social self-regulation necessary to the righteous life of the community. Prohibitions against usury, alcohol, and gambling are joined with rules for inheritance, for marriage and divorce, and for commercial relations.

Translations of the Qur'an: The quranic text has become accessible to those who speak no Arabic largely as a result of scholarly initiative rather than Muslim missionary zeal. In fact, Muslims have maintained an aversion to translations, maintaining that the inimitable Qur'an is truly itself only in Arabic, the language of God's revelation. Renderings in other languages, therefore, are considered paraphrases or interpretations, an understanding that is reflected on the title pages of most English versions. Nevertheless, translations of the Qur'an have been made into most languages of the Islamic world, although none of them are deemed acceptable for liturgical purposes, i.e., for the prescribed prayer or for public recitation.

The earliest recorded translation of the Qur'an into a European language was the Latin version produced in the twelfth century by Robert of Ketton at the request of Peter the Venerable, the abbot of Cluny. Some three centuries later this translation was published in Basel,

Switzerland, with a preface by Martin Luther, and subsequently disseminated in Dutch, Italian, and German. In the late seventeenth century, a second Latin translation was produced by Ludovico Marraci, with an English one by George Sale following in the next century. Both of these were made directly from the Arabic, with the latter accompanied by a "Preliminary Discourse" that would introduce Islamic belief and practice to several generations of English readers. This century has witnessed a multitude of translation efforts by both Muslim and non-Muslim scholars. (A recent Turkish bibliography of Qur'an translation lists renderings in sixty-five languages.) Prominent English versions include those of a British convert to Islam, Marmaduke Pickthall; of J. M. Rodwell, who presented a chronological rearrangement of the suras; of Richard Bell, who executed an even more elaborate chronological reconstruction; and of A. J. Arberry, who sought to reproduce something of the stylistic power and allure of the original.

Contemporary Scholarship on the Qur'an: In the nineteenth and early twentieth centuries the principal concerns addressed by non-Muslim scholars of the Qur'an, such as G. Weil, T. Noldeke, F. Schwally, I. Goldziher, and R. Bell, were those of chronology, textual criticism, and source analysis. For Muslim scholars, on the other hand, much of this work represents a blasphemous disregard of the Qur'an's divine origin and an unacceptable importation of the historical critical methodologies popular with biblical scholars. More recent studies have concentrated on recension theories, thematic analyses, and structural and semantic investigations. Two British scholars, John Wansbrough and John Burton, published books in 1977 that took issue with the traditional Muslim understanding of the Qur'an's textual codification. That they reached opposing conclusions may be one reason why their work has yet to receive sustained critical refutation or support.

Scholars such as Fazlur Rahman, Toshihiko Izutsu, and Jacques Jomier have concentrated on the holistic exploration of specific quranic themes. While proceeding from very different contextual perspectives, their investigations have opened valuable avenues of synthetic analysis. Attention to the liturgical function of the recited Qur'an has drawn upon literary theory to study the unitary structures of early suras as manifest in their rhythmical patterns. Contemporary literary theory also has provoked investigations, particularly those of Muhammed Arkoun, which explore the semantic cohesion of the Qur'an as expressed in a complex system of internal relations subsequently recast in the major interpretive efforts of the great, classical commentators. *See also* Arabic; Qur'an recitation; Qur'an school.

Islam (ethics). Ethics, which in contemporary English usage indicates the study of practical justification, has no single parallel in Islamic tradition. Instead, one must think of several terms, each of which signifies a discipline developed during the classical period of Islamic civilization (ca. 750–1258). *Ilm al-akhlaq* (science of virtue), for example, indicates a type of discourse centering on the cultivation of a good character. Perhaps the most accessible example is the *Nasirean Ethics* attributed to the Shii scholar Nasir al-Din Tusi (d. 1274).

A related form of discourse is signified by *adab* (letters). Here one finds the reflections of gentlemen at court, learned in the arts of poetry, history, and rhetoric. Such reflections took several forms. Amr al-Jahiz (d. 868), for example, became famous for his satirical talents. In his hands, adab seems to be the discipline of a pundit. Others, for example Nizam al-Mulk (d. 1092), focused on statecraft and produced works in the genre of "mirror of princes" literature, giving advice to rulers on the administration of kingdoms.

Most central to the study of ethics, however, were the three disciplines signified by the terms *falsafa* (philosophy), *kalam* (dialectical theology), and *fiqh* (jurisprudence). The first, associated with such authors as al-Farabi (d. 950), took the available fragments of Greek philosophical works and developed them in connection with Islamic themes. Al-Farabi, for example, held philosophy to be a quest for excellence, especially as related to the intellect and moral character. The quest is open to all who have the requisite intelligence and enough worldly goods to allow time for contemplation—a realistic enough observation, but one that undermines the basic equality of humanity that is central to Islamic revelation. How then does the philosopher reconcile his quest with the message of the Prophet? Essentially, al-Farabi writes, prophecy and philosophy are one, the major difference being that the Prophet perceives the truth suddenly, by inspiration, while philosophers must gain understanding by long and arduous struggle. In addition, the Prophet has the gift of making the truth accessible to those who lack the capacity for philosophy. This he does by means of narratives and commands. For most of humanity, it is the Prophet's commands that constitute the primary criterion for ethical judgment, though the "real" foundation of such judgment is philosophy—not the words of the Prophet.

Kalam begins with a different set of interests and questions. The Mutazila, comprising the earliest identifiable kalam movement, were primarily interested in clarifying the nature of Islamic doctrine, including its relation to notions of justice. According to Mutazili thought, justice has to do with the attribution of praise or blame to agents who perform specific acts. Human beings generally agree about the relation of justice to particular cases: one who performs murder deserves blame, while one who tells the truth deserves praise. But what is the foundation for such judgments? The answer ultimately lies in the fact that God has so constructed the universe as to be governed by moral law. In the end, God will reward the good and punish the evil, according to the standards of this law.

It would be unjust, however, for God to impose such a sanction unless human beings have the ability (1) to discriminate between just and unjust acts; and (2) to choose between the two. According to the Mutazila, human beings do have such abilities. In particular, human beings learn to make discriminating judgments by reflecting on the relationship of particular acts to basic intuitions (e.g., that doing harm without reason is blameworthy). Such intuitions are basic, in the sense that they are not derived from any other beliefs. They are the necessary postulates for moral judgment—even prophets (such as Muhammad) refer to these intuitions in promulgating their message. Ethical judgment, then, does not rest on the Prophet's revelation, but on an independent and universal capacity to know and do justice.

Asharite kalam represents a very different perspective on justice, in which notions of moral intuition and human responsibility are secondary to an emphasis on the overwhelming power of God. According to al-Ashari (d. 935) and his followers, nothing happens apart from God's will. When human beings act in ways that deserve praise or blame, they do so by the will of God. Further, the only way to judge such acts is by referring to texts chosen by God as the means of God's self-revelation: in particular, the Qur'an and reports (*hadith*) of the words and deeds of the Prophet Muhammad.

By emphasizing the importance of revealed texts, Asharite thinkers sought a relation between their kalam and the discipline of fiqh. Translated literally, fiqh means "comprehension," specifically comprehension of divine guidance. As al-Shafii (d. 820) put it in his epistle, the concern is with that guidance "whereby no one who takes refuge in it will ever be led astray."

The primary contribution of al-Shafii and other fiqh scholars was to propose theories as to the ways human beings could comprehend this guidance. In general, their theory of *usul al-fiqh* (the sources of comprehension) referred to a hierarchy of revealed texts and to acceptable modes of reasoning based on the texts. The Qur'an, as the "speech of God," is the basic text of fiqh. The Qur'an is then confirmed and extended by reports of the exemplary practice (*Sunna*) of the Prophet. Qur'an and Sunna can be further extended through various modes of reasoning, the most popular of which came to be known by the term *qiyas* (analogy). Last, the notion of *ijma* (consensus) served as a check on those who would make judgments about specific applications of God's guidance, referring as it did either to the consensus of scholars knowledgeable in the study of fiqh or to the common sense of the community of Muslims.

The subsequent development of Islamic ethics rests in large part on the relationships between falsafa, kalam, and fiqh that developed during the classical period. For Sunni Muslims, the textualist tendencies exemplified in Asharite kalam and in fiqh became primary. Much of Sunni thought came to regard practical judgment as a matter of obedience to God's commands, made known in specific, revealed texts as interpreted by recognized scholars. The emphasis on reason in search of wisdom characteristic of falsafa was relegated to a secondary position. Even kalam eventually became secondary to the work of the scholars of fiqh, whose discussions came to carry so much weight that their work alone became associated with the term *Sharia* (law). By comparison, kalam and falsafa retained a more central role among the Shia, as did ilm al-akhlaq.

In modern times, both Sunni and Shii ethics show the influence of a changing political context. Especially since the abolition of the Ottoman caliphate (1924), Islamic thinkers have focused on the necessity of establishing an Islamic state, and the appropriate means to achieve such a goal. Insofar as such thinkers reflect the traditional disciplines outlined above, fiqh stands out as the most important. Indeed, much of the intellectual effort associated with resurgent Islam deals with issues of political authority, the use of force, and the shape and policies of an Islamic state in terms of fiqh. Currently, Muslim scholars in a number of states are turning their attention to issues of medical ethics and economic reform. What their judgments will be and what role the classical disciplines will finally play in modern Islamic ethics remains to be seen. *See also* Islamic law; Islamic philosophy; kalam.

Islam (festal cycle). Although Islam recognizes only two canonical feasts, the concluding of the Ramadan fasting month and the feast of sacrifice during the pilgrimage month, there are numerous additional festal occasions and observances that have an honored place in Muslim life. It is useful to classify the festivals of Muslims into those that occur on a calendrical cycle and those that are observed according to critical moments in personal or collective life. The first are generally festivals relating to the entire Muslim community, whether *umma* (Arab., worldwide), regional, local, or a combination. An example of the first is the feast of the breaking of the Ramadan fast (*Id al–fitr*), of the second a celebration of the Prophet Muhammad's birthday (observed in some regions but not in others), and of the third a local saint's birthday festival, as in an Egyptian village. All are calendrical and all communal, but only the first is universally observed, because it is obligatory. Life-crisis rites generally pertain to personal life-cycle events like birth, naming, circumcision, initiation (as into a Sufi order), marriage, and death. But auspicious natural occurrences, such as eclipses and earthquakes, as well as humanly caused events like battles, victories, and revolutions, may also be accorded religious value and thus incorporated into an Islamic way of reflecting and evaluating special events. Life-crisis rites—circumcision, for example—may be observed as a communal festival at a significant calendrical point, such as a saint's birthday.

The Islamic Lunar Calendar: Islam recognizes a lunar calendar of approximately 354 and one-third days, divided into twelve months of twenty-nine or thirty days. The calendar began in the summer of 622, the year of the Prophet's Hijra from Mecca to Medina, and is now in its fifteenth century. Traditionally, the calendar was regulated by optical sighting of the new moon at the beginning of each month, but in modern times astronomical calculations are used so that there is a standard calendar for the world's Muslims. Because the lunar year of Islam permits no periodic intercalation (adding days to make it harmonize with the solar year), it amounts to eleven days fewer than the solar year annually. Thus Islamic calendrical festivals and other observances gradually recede through the seasons

so that pilgrimage and fasting, for example, will be during the hot, cool, or moderate seasons on a thirty-three-year cycle, or about twice in an average lifetime. This peculiar circumstance affords Islam a festal cycle that may be thought of as both transcending the natural round, on the one hand, and consecrating it, on the other. (Muslims also use, for agricultural, commercial, and political purposes, the nearly universal solar Gregorian calendar.)

Major Calendrical Festivals: The two festivals mentioned above, namely the Feast of the Breaking of the Ramadan Fast, also known as the "Lesser Feast," and the Feast of Sacrifice, or "Greater Feast," occur in the last quarter of the Islamic year. Ramadan, the ninth month, contains many memories of holy events and is observed by a complete fast during the daylight hours. The first revelations of the Qur'an came down during the last part of Ramadan, and this month is the only one mentioned in the Qur'an.

Sugar dolls for sale in a shop window in northern Egypt; their consumption is a traditional way to end Ramadan, the Islamic holy month of fasting.

The new moon at the close of Ramadan marks the first of the month of Shawwal, and on this day the Feast of Fast-Breaking begins its three-day course. A festival *salat* ("prayer") is performed, often by the whole community in a large open space; a special alms is collected for the poor; and Muslims enjoy favorite foods and exchange gifts and cards.

On the tenth of the last month of the year, *Dhu-l-Hijja* ("Pilgrimage Month"), Muslims around the world perform animal sacrifices in memory of God's sparing of Abraham's son (Isaac in Jewish and Christian traditions, Ishmael in Islam). This "feast of sacrifice" (also known as *qurban bayram* in the Turkish tradition) coincides with the annual pilgrimage to Mecca and is a potent reminder to Muslims of their global fellowship. A special salat is performed in an open place, and then heads of families or other appropriate male adults sacrifice a goat, sheep, or bovine animal. The sacrifice is preceded by naming the sponsor(s) and reciting "In the Name of Allah" and "God is Most Great." With the animal's head pointed toward Mecca, the sacrificer performs the slaughter with a sharp blade, simultaneously severing the victim's windpipe and jugular vein. A female family leader may have the sacrifice performed in her family's behalf by an appropriate male relative or other agent. (As a last resort, she may perform the sacrifice herself.) The meat is typically divided into three portions, with one third for the poor, a third for neighbors and friends, and a third for the sacrificer's household. The festivities connected with the "Greater Feast" go on for three days.

Muslim sacrifice of sheep in Yogyakarta, Indonesia, on the tenth day of the month of pilgrimage, 1970. A central ritual on the last day of the pilgrimage to Mecca is the Feast of the Major Sacrifice (Id al-Adha). For those who cannot undertake the pilgrimage, the same sacrifice is performed on the same day wherever they are, uniting the community of Islam.

Beyond the two canonical festivals, Islam recognizes no other as obligatory. However, observance of certain other events is widespread. Among calendrical events is the Islamic New Year, which falls on the first day of the first month of the Islamic Year, Muharram. The New Year is not a major festival, but the first ten days of Muharram do mark a major period of Shiite observances commemorating the martyrdom of Imam Husayn at Karbala in 680. Passion narratives (*taziya*) are recited or performed and processions held. The tenth of Muharram—Ashura—is the Shiite memorial of martyrdom and redemption, with confession of guilt for abandoning the doomed Husayn and other Imams. The day is often marked by public self-flagellation. Ashura is observed by Sunnis as a minor fast day, in fact a parallel observance with

Judaism, but the tragic events of Shiism play no part.

The Prophet Muhammad's birthday (*mawlid al-nabi*) is commemorated on the twelfth of the

Crowd of Muslims in Indonesia (1978) rushing for pieces of a rice mountain constructed in honor of the Prophet Muhammad's birthday, the Mawlid-al-Nabi, celebrated on the twelfth day of the third lunar month of the Muslim year.

month of Rabi al-Awwal. Although celebrations in the land of Muhammad's birth are forbidden by the Wahhabi code of Saudi Arabia, Muslims in other countries celebrate the day in a wide variety of customary ways, with special foods, processions, the singing of odes and litanies by Sufi fellowships, and enjoying free time where the day is a holiday.

The month of Shaban, just before the fast of Ramadan, contains numerous observances of saint days. In many Muslim lands, persons of marked spirituality may come to be venerated as a special type of human, known as a *wali*. According to the Qur'an (10:63; 4:45; 5:55), a wali is someone believed to be a close "friend" of God, who in turn is wali, "friend," "protector," of the person. A wali is something like a saint, if specifically Christian connotations are excluded. In Egypt, for example, there are many shrines—usually marked by a building topped by a dome, called a *qubba*—scattered throughout the cities, towns, and rural villages. People visit the shrines to receive blessings (*baraka*) and to ask for intercession with God and a host of other things. There is usually an annual mawlid on the wali's birthday, with lesser or greater celebrations, depending on the prominence of the shrine and the means and numbers of its supporters. Major shrines, such as those of Sayyid al-Badawi in Tanta, Sayyida Zaynab in Cairo, and Sidi Abul Haggag in Luxor, host extravagant mawlids, lasting as long as a week and climaxing with a grand procession through the streets. Sufi activities may be associated with mawlids, but not necessarily so. In Tanta, however, the local chapters of major Sufi orders do join the grand procession with flags, ornamented horses, drummers, and chanters. The wali being venerated—Sayyid al-Badawi—was himself a great Sufi master of the thirteenth century. (Significantly, he has more than one mawlid, but the fall one—held according to the solar calendar—is the grand one, perhaps suggesting a pre-Islamic origin in fertility-related beliefs.) The mawlid of Imam al-Shafii in Cairo has no particular Sufi associations. Its wali was a great legal scholar and his spirit is believed by visitors to be capable of interceding, especially in difficult matters connected with crime and justice. People address letters to Imam al-Shafii and drop them in the enclosure under the great qubba sheltering his remains.

Muslim saint veneration is also widespread in North Africa (in Morocco it is known as *maraboutism*), the Levant (including only Yemen and Oman from the Arabian Peninsula), the South Asian subcontinent, and the Malaysian-Indonesian archipelago. In Java the *Wali Songo* (Javanese, "nine saints") are revered as bringers of Islam to the island in the fourteenth and fifteenth centuries. Their mawlids are well-attended, resplendent affairs, combining pan-Islamic symbolism and piety with regional customs and lore.

All Muslims—Sunni and Shiite—may make the "visit" (*ziyara*) to Medina, which they customarily do in conjunction with the pilgrimage to Mecca. (The latter is a duty for those who are able, whereas the former is merely recommended and meritorious.) In Medina, visitors pay respects at the tomb of the Prophet and at many other sites commemorating the early history of Islam and its heroes. Shiites also venerate the holy Imams of their tradition by pious "visits" to their shrines: Ali's in Najaf, Iraq; Husayn's in Karbala, Iraq; and others in Mashhad and Qum, Iran, and other places. Manuals of devotion are used for these visits, which serve to bind together the community of Shiites as a special people who believe and practice at both the umma level and in their own community of memory and salvation.

Life-crisis Rites: The festal cycle of life-crisis rites includes birth, naming, circumcision, religious education, marriage, initiations, and death. As observed above, sometimes such rites are coordinated with calendrical observances, but they do not thereby lose their personal meaning for the celebrant(s).

Birth and Naming Rites: *Hadiths* (traditions) recommend that a male relative or other suitable person utter the call to prayer into the newborn's right ear and the call to rise for the performance of the prayer into the left ear. A morsel of date meat (or suitable substitute) is chewed until soft, then placed into the mouth of the infant, marking the first solid food and the beginning of life outside the womb. The opening *sura* of the Qur'an is recited, and family and friends gather, bearing gifts. Many Muslims also perform an *aqiqa* ("sacrificial victim") ceremony on the seventh day following the birth. The baby's hair is shaved and weighed, whereupon an equivalent amount of silver is given as alms. A sacrifice of two sheep or goats is offered for a boy, one for a girl. Aqiqa is an old Arabian custom. It is compared to the sacrificial ram that Abraham was permitted to offer up in place of his son and thus becomes a consecration of the newborn to Allah.

Naming may be done at birth or at the aqiqa ceremony. Names are taken from a wide variety of sources, and they may be influenced by relatives' names, auspicious events, the seasons, or other things associated with the time of birth. Most Muslims choose an honored, traditional Islamic name for their child, even though other appellations may be included in the full name. The Prophet recommended that such deity-linked names as Abdallah ("Slave of Allah") and Abd al-Rahman ("Slave of the All-Merciful"), as well as the names of the Prophets (e.g., Musa ["Moses"], Ayyub ["Job"], Nuh ["Noah"]), be used. Muhammad also permitted the use of his own name and those of his family and companions (like Aisha, Fatima, Khadija, Ali, Umar, Uthman).

Islamic names include the simple name, such as those given in the examples above. In addition, Muslims use honorifics, such as Abu ("Father of") and Umm ("Mother of"), Ibn ("Son of"), and Bint ("Daughter of"), as in Abu Bakr, Umm Kulthum, Ibn Umar, and Bint Jamila. Other names indicate a trade or other distinctive factor pertaining to an individual. Examples are Musa al-Najjar ("Moses the Carpenter"), Ahmad al-Khabbaz ("Ahmad the Baker"), Zaynab al-Khayyama ("Zenobia the Tentmaker"), and the famous Sufi, Husayn ibn Mansur al-Hallaj ("Husayn son of Mansur, the Carder [of wool; but also of souls]"). Finally, some Muslims have a name associated with a place. Jamal al-Din al-Afghani is the name of a famous modern reformer thought to have come from Afghanistan, while the great medieval theologian Abu Hamid al-Ghazali's place-name appellation probably derives from Ghazala, his hometown in Iran.

New Muslims usually adopt an Islamic name, whereupon they either substitute it for their old name or add it on. Prominent examples of conversion names in recent American life are the basketball player Kareem Abdul Jabbar, formerly Lew Alcindor, and the prizefighter Muhammad Ali, who earlier was Cassius Clay. African Americans who embrace Islam also sometimes adopt a traditional African name (like the Yoruban female name *Ife* ["love"] or the male name *Foluke* ["placed in God's hands"]), as well as an Islamic one. Sometimes the Islamic name is also a traditional African name, adapted from Arabic, such as the Swahili names *Subira* ("patience rewarded") for girls and *Juma* ("born on Friday") for boys, thus affirming identity through a remembering of preslavery roots, which for many were Islamic as well as African.

When a new Muslim pronounces the *Shahada* ("I bear witness that there is no god but God; I bear witness that Muhammad is the Messenger of God"), there is rejoicing among Muslim friends, who may hasten to suggest auspicious Muslim names for their new brothers and sisters in the faith. A national Islamic magazine, published in Washington, D.C., lists new Muslims and their adopted Muslim names alongside their former names. Very often the Muslim name is added to the former one, resulting in hybrids like Ahmad Washington and Fatima Parkhust. Western women who marry Muslims will often take the husband's last name, but this is not necessarily evidence of conversion. Muslim women in traditionally Islamic societies, however, normally do not take their husband's last name but continue to use the family name of their fathers.

Circumcision: Muslims universally agree that circumcision, although not mentioned in the Qur'an, should be performed on males at some point, usually sometime after age seven and before maturity. The operation is known as *khitan*, but is also called *tahara* ("purification"). In Southeast Asia, for example, circumcision often is performed in conjunction with a first public recitation of a portion of the Qur'an. A whole class may be circumcised in the same ceremony, with a panoramic class photo taken in front of the mosque or Islamic school, followed by family and community celebrations featuring festival foods, music, and many guests, as well as a display of the brave young lads (who often undergo a degree of terror before the operation, but must nevertheless deport themselves bravely). When circumcision is performed with such elaborate ceremony it serves also as a form of initiatory passage rite into the responsibilities of adulthood. Circumcisions are often performed at the time of saint festivals, because of the spiritual blessings abounding at those times.

Female "circumcision" (*khafd*) is sometimes practiced by Muslims, but is neither required by Islamic law nor generally thought to be appropriate. It may be a real clitoridectomy or simply a symbolic scarring. Nevertheless, female genital mutilation remains as a pattern of culture in the Nile regions and other places in the Middle East and Asia and is not limited to Muslims. The practice is euphemised as *sunnat* ("recommended") in Southeast Asia, where its practice is in the mild form. No celebrations accompany female "circumcision," for it is a domestic rite associated with female status and the attainment of sexual maturity and responsibility.

Marriage: Islam strongly affirms marriage and producing offspring as early in adult life as feasible. The sexual bond of marriage is part of worship and a foretaste of heavenly bliss, which it most closely resembles. Only in rare cases does Islam consider abstention from marriage to be acceptable. Thus, there is no monasticism in Islam (although there may well be moderate asceticism). Persons who follow rigorous spiritual disciplines, such as Sufis, also marry and have children, as did the Prophet Muhammad, whose example Muslims follow.

The solemnization of Islamic marriage is strictly a legal matter of mutual agreement to a contract and not in itself a festival, although it nearly always provides the occasion for one. The signing of the marriage contract is accompanied by a brief recitation from the Qur'an and remarks about the responsibilities and joys of the married state. The bride is represented by a male guardian (father, brother, or other person), who concludes the agreement on her behalf with the groom. Although arranged marriages among Muslims are still the norm, the potential partners are permitted to see each other and sometimes to converse together in a chaperoned situation before making their own decisions about whether to proceed.

After the legal ceremony, the festivities begin. As they are neither required nor regulated by Islamic law, Muslim marriage celebrations vary greatly from culture to culture. Observant Muslims follow Islamic principles when participating in marriage festivities regarding social relations (especially against mixed dancing), the prohibition of alcoholic beverages, and mixing Islamic and polytheistic symbols and customs. Typical festivities include music and dance—males and females dancing in their separate groups, sometimes within sight of each other, sometimes in separate spaces. Festival foods are served in profusion and many guests will share in the fun. More or less lavish hospitality is a statement of the host's generosity and status, as well as an auspicious sign for the marriage's future. In Java, Muslim wedding festivities are often celebrated by the staging of a shadow puppet play that continues into the wee hours, entrancing children and adults with the mythical stories of heroes and villains, accompanied by the mysterious sounds of the gamelan's gongs and xylophones. In traditional Arab villages, a bloodstained sheet is publicly displayed the morning after the nuptials, testifying to the all-important honor of the bride and her family (and sometimes to the potency of the groom). Upper-class, modernized Muslims in Cairo or Lahore, for example, may hold the wedding festivities in a luxury hotel, wearing Western-style formal wear. There will be no mixed dancing or serving of alcohol, but guests of the highest Islamic respectability of both sexes may socialize easily. Muslim wedding festivities may last only part of a day or night, or they may continue for days, depending on the culture, the region, the social system, and the resources and status of the host. One thing is certain: although the concluding of the legal contract of marriage is all that is necessary, Muslims everywhere would think something was very wrong with a wedding that did not include the best kind of celebration available. Muslim marriage is not just a joining of two individuals—it is also a joyous renewal of kinship ties, friendships, and alliances within a moral community, where custom, status, and harmony are most important.

It should be added that Muslims usually marry within their faith. Muslim women are not permitted to marry non-Muslim men, but Muslim men may marry Jewish or Christian women, with children born of the union brought up Muslim. Finally, although Islamic law permits Muslim men to have up to four concurrent wives, polygamy is generally disapproved and uncommon in most Muslim societies.

Observances Associated with Death: Although death is not a happy occasion and the funeral and committal to the grave not a proper topic in themselves for this article, Muslims do celebrate the memory of their dead in various ways in different cultures. In Southeast Asia, for example, local custom (*adat*) mixes with Islamic practices. In the southern Philippines, among the Sama people of Tawi-Tawi, a cow is often sacrificed on the death of its owner (who bought it for the purpose). People often go into debt providing a yearlong schedule of feasts commemorating the death of a family member. Even among Tawi-Tawi Muslims of reformist opinions condemning such festivities, they nevertheless are observed often for purposes of social status and respectability.

Throughout the Muslim world it is common (although not required) to have some sort of gathering, however modest, on the fortieth day after the death. Litanies may be read and the Qur'an is recited. In Cairo, for example, brightly colored awnings will often be pitched, underneath which are strewn carpets, with gilt chairs arranged along the periphery on all sides. Guests are served coffee and a professional reciter chants passages from the Qur'an. Visitors' names are duly inscribed in a guest book, and people console the bereaved and remark on the merits and goodness of their departed loved one. In addition to the fortieth-day observance, a hundredth-day observance is also widely held, thus completing the schedule of post-death remembrances.

Muslims, especially women, often visit cemeteries on Fridays. In Java, families have picnic outings at the graveyards, remembering departed family members and enjoying a dignified, although not overly solemn, occasion. The following greeting may be addressed to the departed in the cemetery: "Peace be with you, people of the graves. May Allah forgive both us and you. You have gone before us and we follow."

A Modern Muslim Festivity—The Qur'an Chanting Competition: Islam has always encouraged peaceful competition in matters of faith, religious learning, and good works. Because the proper recitation of the Qur'an is so very important, Muslims developed special schools for learning the practice and contexts for enjoying it. One of the modern Islamic world's most enthusiastically followed forms of Qur'an-centered piety is the competition in its recitation. Competitions, called *musabaqa*, are held in the Middle East, Asia, Southeast Asia, and the West, where increasing numbers of Muslims live. Perhaps the most extensively developed competition is the national Musabaqa Tilawatil Qur'an ("The Competition in Recitation of the Qur'an"), held every two years in Indonesia.

Throughout Indonesia, children and adults enjoy Qur'an recitation contests at the local, regional, provincial, and national levels. After a cycle of runoff contests, provincial teams are selected for the all-Indonesia MTQ, as the ten-day event is called. Contestants are divided into classifications of boys, girls, women, men, and handicapped. Contests include memory recitation, specific styles of recitation, and, for youth, lively and popular quiz shows on all aspects of the Qur'an.

The competitive Qur'an recitations in Pontianak, West Kalimantan (on the island of Borneo), in the early 1980s were preceded by a parade through the streets of the host city, with local religious, educational, and cultural organizations participating with drill teams, bands, floats, and singing. In a large university sports stadium, the president of Indonesia, Suharto, presided over the opening events, which included a full review of all the teams as they marched around the track in traditional costumes behind a large brass band playing the competition march. The raising of a special flag alongside that of the Republic of Indonesia, musical renditions by a Christian Chinese choir and orchestra of thousands, several thousand children waving pom-poms on cue from the endzones, and an Islamic dance performance by an 1,100-member troupe of lavishly costumed men and women. The recitation of the Qur'an proceeded from a glass-walled chanting pulpit in the middle of the stadium, with architectural details taken from the traditional buildings of the region, capped by neon calligraphy of the names "Allah" and "Muhammad." Near the stadium was a special pavilion housing a vast display of books, posters, cassettes, pamphlets, and other items pertaining to the propagation of Islam and the Qur'an. On one of the days an Islamic fashion show was held, featuring appropriate attire for men and women made from beautiful Indonesian fabrics.

Prizes were awarded in a variety of categories, with a best provincial team also being recognized. After the days of competition, which were covered each evening on television, there was an elaborate closing program with an awards ceremony, followed by departure for home. The winning team was East Java. On its arrival back in the capital of Surabaya, the team was welcomed by a Muslim musical organization and paraded through the city's streets in a motorcade with the trophies displayed from a decorated truck. The event ended with a reception at the governor's mansion.

Competitions held in other countries include worldwide contests in Kuala Lumpur and Saudi Arabia, where the strong regional cultural aspects of the Indonesian Qur'an competition would not be imitated. The Indonesian Qur'an competition is, as its organizers call it, a "national discipline," and as such is closely related to governmental and Islamic programs of inter-religious, moral, and patriotic harmony in that largest of all Muslim national populations. *See also* Islam (life cycle).

Islam (life cycle). While the notion of life cycle has gained prominence as a term denoting stages of psychological development, an Islamic understanding locates its meaning largely within a framework of traditional rituals. Major life crises are experienced as having religious significance as well as marking personal and social transformation. Other, intermediate transitions may lack public celebration but are, nonetheless, seen as defined and sanctioned by Islam.

Muslim culture is not monolithic. It embraces a rich variety of practices spanning scores of different ethnic and linguistic communities geographically concentrated in the Middle East but found throughout the world. All Muslims accept as preeminent revelation a core of beliefs that stems from its inspired scriptures (Qur'an) and from the normative example of Muhammad and provides the essential features of the worldview and the ritual system that structures a life cycle.

The concept underlying all else is embedded in the term *Islam* itself, meaning submission or commitment to God. Consequently, obedience to the divine will provides the rationale for treating the changes that mark growth in both individual and collective terms. The ritual counterpart to this is the profession of faith in God and his Prophet. Variations and elaborations of this testimony are repeated at all junctures in the life cycle.

Birth: When a child is born into a Muslim family the first sound it should hear is the call to prayer. Customarily, one whispers it into the infant's right ear and then into the left a similar formula that is used to inaugurate the actual praying.

Formal social recognition of the child is marked later by a naming ceremony that may be accompanied by other rites, such as a first haircut. The gathering of family and acquaintances to hear readings from the Qur'an, as well as a procession, a meal, sacrifices, or gifts are frequent components of this occasion. Babies and small children are widely considered to be exceptionally vulnerable to unseen forces. Charms may be employed, designed to protect children against such threats as malevolent spirits or the evil eye.

While circumcision is not explicitly prescribed in the Qur'an, it is regarded as essential for males. In some areas, notably the Nile Valley, a parallel operation, clitorectomy, though now illegal, is performed on females. Although no age is fixed, circumcision normally is performed while the boy is still a toddler. In traditional settings, it is often a festive occasion; whereas in modern contexts, it is performed without celebration at a medical clinic.

Prayer and Fasting: Initiation into the obligatory

duties of daily prayer and ritual fasting during the month of Ramadan often serve as significant milestones in a Muslim's development. Their importance also affects the emergence of gender identity, which increases as a child approaches puberty. Collective prayer involves the segregation of sexes. Hence, as a boy begins to fulfill this duty, around the age of seven, his attendance at congregational rites assists in his incorporation into the public realm of men with the mosque as its symbolic focus.

Girls, as they approach adolescence, eventually come to observe restrictions that qualify their ritual purity and limit their freedom of movement and association. A pattern of constraints on their participation in formal religious observances outside the home coincides with their socialization into roles that center largely on family life. Lately, widespread reactions against these inherited patriarchal conventions have diminished their impact. Muslim women are increasingly obtaining modern education and pursuing related career opportunities.

Fasting also denotes self-mastery and greater responsibility, thus conferring enhanced status. A child begins around the age of puberty to observe the discipline for some days during the sacred month, gradually increasing their number as years go on. The capacity to carry out this obligation is regarded as an attribute of full adulthood.

Marriage and Parenthood: Islam views marriage as the expected state of life incumbent on all who are not physically or mentally impaired. Religiously motivated celibacy has had its proponents among some mystics but was given no approval by Muhammad. Due to the central importance accorded to kinship bonds, marriage is reckoned as the pivotal event in the life cycle. Marriage serves to establish not only a new family, but symbolically to renew and expand the solidarity of the entire community.

The Qur'an details several categories of prohibited unions on the basis of proximity of blood and religious affiliation. For instance, Muslim men may marry Christian and Jewish (but not pagan) women, whereas Muslim women are not allowed to marry any except Muslim men. In practice, in many Muslim societies marriages tend to be arranged by parents or other intermediaries. In tribal settings, certain types of clan cousins are often regarded as the preferred partners. It is expected that a first-time bride is a virgin. Polygyny, one man having up to four wives, is permitted, although in modern times it is rare and has always been hedged by legal stipulations.

Through marriage, numerous rights and du-

ties arise that may directly affect a wide circle of kin, including matters of mutual support, inheritance, and defense. Because almost all Muslim societies are patrilineal, it is usually the woman who undergoes the most radical transition as she changes residence and may enter an established household as a stranger.

Islamic marriage is a bilateral contract. Some elements are fixed, while others are variable and must be agreed upon by the parties themselves. For example, one feature called *mahr* involves a certain sum, in money or kind, usually including gold jewelry, which a prospective groom presents to his intended wife (and sometimes to her father). While the exact arrangements and the amounts concerned vary enormously among different groups and across class lines, the social consequences of this sum contribute to the consolidation of the extended families and the stability of the marriage. A wife retains the mahr, and possibly other property, in her own right as a form of security. In many cases, this sum is delineated in two parts, the second of which is only incurred in the event of divorce. Thus, the prerogative for unilateral divorce, which Islamic law vests in the husband, is counterbalanced by economic as well as moral pressure to preserve the marriage.

The fullness of marriage is achieved only with the birth of a child. A son confers greater prestige. Fatherhood and motherhood of a male are ordinarily marked by a new form of address, a teknonym, the parents being called "father of" and "mother of" followed by the first son's name.

The Pilgrimage (Hajj): The obligation of Muslims to perform the pilgrimage to Mecca at least once in a lifetime does not specify a particular age. Islamic law conditions this duty upon a believer's capacity because the expense and exertion required can make its realization prohibitive for many. By custom, those who undergo this religious journey often do so in their riper years or at a time of personal crisis. Thus, accomplishing the Hajj can fulfill various functions in a life cycle.

Countless other shrines and holy sites, in addition to the principal sacred cities of Mecca and Medina, are recognized as pilgrimage centers. Many of these sites, which mark local or regional saints' tombs or other relics, have considerable significance as points of reference in conjunction with a turning point in a life cycle. At these places the faithful may seek advice, healing, refuge, make vows, or in some cases linger to study or engage in spiritual retreat. For Shiites, the shrines of Karbala in Iraq are sacred. All Muslims revere Jerusalem.

Death: Death leads to the final rite of passage

A Muslim cemetery in Giza, Egypt.

in the life cycle of a Muslim. Preparations for dying normally include reaffirmations of faith. After death, the body of the deceased is washed, wrapped in a shroud, and promptly conveyed to the cemetery for burial. The corpse is turned in the grave to face Mecca in imitation of the posture assumed at prayer. A relatively simple ceremony at the graveside follows. Depending on the stature of the deceased, and varying according to custom, funerary memorials also may occur at intervals after death, seven days, forty days, or a year later. The central feature on these occasions is a recitation of portions of the Qur'an while the bereaved family and friends accept condolences.

Muslims believe in a final judgment leading to eternal reward or punishment and in resurrection. The character of such tenets varies due to differing interpretations of the traditions. Many believe that the soul will undergo an interrogation by two angels, Munkar and Nakir, who will examine a person's faith and weigh out the good and the bad of one's life. While the Qur'an contains many passages that describe paradise as a garden of delights and hell as a pit of tormenting flames, most Muslims understand these images as affecting a resurrected body transformed in ways that eliminate the passions and ambiguities of mortal existence.

Sufism and Ethics: The generalized elements of an Islamic life cycle refer to patterns of growth and change in a chronological perspective. Two important notions of a different sort also deserve mention. First, the tradition of Sufism views the life cycle with an emphasis on trust in God rather than conformity to details of law. Its final objective is the attainment of illumination and mystical union. Key to this system is the strict subordination of the disciple to the religious leader, who provides guidance through stages that strive for absorption into the divine.

Second, *adab* ("social graces") recasts the life cycle in the light of a rich tradition deriving from classical sources on training in the virtues. Reflections on ethical conduct, along with the knowledge and skills appropriate to particular relationships and functions in society, comprise the core of this extensive body of literature.

Islam (thought). *See* kalam.

Islam, Christianity in. Christians, known in Islam as al-Nasara and as al-Masihiyun, have special status, along with Jews and other religious communities, as People of the Book. In one place the Qur'an calls them the People of the Gospel (5:47). The designation *al-Nasara* (Nazarenes) occurs fourteen times in the Qur'an, apparently referring to Christians. The beliefs and practices attributed to the Nazarenes, some of which the Qur'an commends and some of which it criticizes, are typical of the Monophysite, Nestorian, and Eastern Orthodox Christian communities that lived in the Middle East in the seventh century. The attitude in the Qur'an toward Christians is best summed up under two headings, the doctrinal and the practical.

From the doctrinal perspective, the Christian doctrines of the Trinity, incarnation, and historicity of Jesus' death by crucifixion are rejected as out of hand by the Qur'an and Islam. The Qur'an eschews argument about religion and recommends that Muslims and Christians submit themselves and all that is dear to them to the judgment of God (3:61). As for the practical arrangements of daily life, the Qur'an recommends that Muslims take neither Jews nor Christians as friends (5:51). It also calls for Christians and other People of the Book to pay the poll tax, maintain a low social profile, and enjoy the protection of the Islamic community (9:29).

In the course of time, Islamic jurists elaborated a detailed set of conditions in the so-called Covenant of Umar for social and political governance of the protected non-Muslim religious communities. These conditions have been enforced with varying degrees of vigor over the centuries, but for the most part they have remained more theoretical than real restraints on the lives of Christians. Muslim scholars have also discussed the question of whether or not the Nazarenes of the Qur'an are, in fact, the Christians whose several denominations continue to live in symbiosis with Muslims in Islamic lands. In common parlance, most Arabic speakers do not call Christians Nazarenes but simply Christians (al-Masihiyun—from the Semitic term for Messiah).

Until the time of the Crusades (eleventh through thirteenth centuries), Christian communities in the lands governed by the caliphate were large and often prosperous. Thereafter, a decline began that continues today. Many Christians have become Muslim; many others have emigrated to the West. Nevertheless, Christian groups remain influential in the Middle East, and have contributed to such modern movements as Arab nationalism. In the twentieth century, most of the traditional, indigenous Christian groups (Melkites, Syrian Orthodox, Copts, Greek Orthodox, Assyrians, and Chaldeans) have joined together with more recently arrived Roman Catholics and Protestants, collectively to defend their common interests in the Middle East Council of Churches. *See also* dhimmi.

Islam, Judaism in. Judaism is one of the protected religious communities under Islamic rule. Jews existed in Arabia from before the birth of the Prophet Muhammad and are prominently mentioned in the Qur'an and early Islamic literature. With the expansion of Islamic society after the death of Muhammad, the majority of the world's Jewish population lived within Islamic lands as protected (*dhimmi*) subjects. From the eighth through the fifteenth centuries, most Jewish institutions and modes of worship were developed or transformed in symbiosis with or in reaction to Islamic culture.

Most scholars agree that Muhammad's contact with the Jews of northwestern Arabia was formative in religious and political life. Muslim sources represent the Jews among the chief opponents to the new religion of Islam, although it is said that some Jews converted. Chapter (*sura*) 2 of the Qur'an contains a long section on the Jews and their beliefs. Muhammad's basic position was that the Jews, like the Christians, had been the recipients of God's revelations but had corrupted the text and had historically acted in opposition to God's prophets and his laws. Despite this, the Jews were admitted as members of Muhammad's commonwealth in Medina as long as they did not perform treasonous acts, such as aiding Muhammad's enemies. Muhammad's treaties with the Jews of the captured Arabian towns of Khaybar and Tayma form the basis of later treaties of capitulation during the conquests and the treatment of Jews as a protected subject population.

The Islamic conquest of the Jewish communities in Mesopotamia, Palestine, and Egypt released a tension within the Jewish communities that had only been latent under the Sassanian (Persian) and Byzantine empires, and we see the rise of Karaite Judaism as a major challenge to rabbinical Judaism. Other groups, such as the Isawiya, Yudghaniya, and Mushkhaniya—some linked formally or informally to Shiite doctrines in Islam—also developed in this period of religious foment. Intercommunal competition between Muslims and Jews included such issues as whether Ibrahim (Abraham) was a Jew or a proto-Muslim, because he lived before the coming of the Torah. The ultimate result was that Rabbinic Jews became established in the caliph's court through the office of the Rosh Golah (exilarch) and Jews of all varieties lived as tributary citizens with limited but guaranteed rights in Islamic society.

Spain, North Africa, Egypt, the Yemen, Palestine, and Iraq all had flourishing Jewish communities who spoke and wrote in Arabic as well as

Hebrew. Hebrew grammar was based on Arabic models, and many Jewish speculative theologians, such as Maimonides in twelfth-century Spain, wrote in Arabic and were read by Muslims, Christians, and Jews.

In modern times, particularly after the establishment of Israel, Judaism has become equated with Zionism in the minds of many Muslims, who themselves have more recently defined Islam with elements of nationalism. Thus, the clash of Jewish and Muslim nationalisms has revived anti-Jewish interpretation of the Qur'an and classical Islamic texts. *See also* dhimmi; gaon.

Islamic Jihad (ji-had'; Arab., "extreme effort"), an Islamic revivalist group generally held responsible for the assassination of Egyptian President Anwar Sadat in October 1981. A militant offshoot of more moderate Islamic activist groups in Egypt, this group first appeared in the late 1970s in anti-Coptic Christian activities in southern Egypt. Its organization consists of an indeterminate number of semi-autonomous cells. One cell, within Egypt's military, was charged by the central Jihad assembly with executing Sadat, explaining its action in a pamphlet called "The Neglected Duty," saying Muslims must wage armed struggle against un-Islamic leaders and any Muslims who cooperate with them.

Islamic law (Arab. *Sharia*, "path"). The *Sharia* is the sum total of divine categorizations of human acts, a categorization of a human act being its placement in one of five categories: obligatory, recommended, neutral, reprehensible, or forbidden. Among the various ways of defining these categories, a common one makes an act obligatory if its occurrence occasions reward and its nonoccurrence punishment; recommended if its occurrence occasions reward but its nonoccurrence does not occasion punishment; forbidden if its nonoccurrence occasions reward and its occurrence occasions punishment; reprehensible if its nonoccurrence occasions reward but its occurrence does not occasion punishment; and neutral if both its occurrence and its nonoccurrence occasion neither reward nor punishment. Because God is the sole categorizer of human acts, the Sharia is, in fact, both law and moral code.

This conflation of law and morality has not hindered Muslims from believing it to be their special vocation to transform the Sharia into positive law through the erection of Islamic states. Throughout the long development of Islamic political theory, one feature is persistent:

the insistence that a sine qua non of Islamic statehood is the application and enforcement of the Sharia. It is the categorizations of human acts as obligatory and forbidden that most lend themselves to transformation into positive law, because the state is primarily a dispenser of penal sanctions, not of rewards. Rewards tend to be viewed as otherworldly sanctions, while punishments are seen as belonging as much to this world as to the world beyond, even though in the latter they have a more awesome character. Penal sanctions are thus the prime instrument of social control within the Islamic state.

Foundations: It became, by the end of the ninth century, a generally agreed upon principle among Muslim jurists that valid rules of law must be grounded either directly or indirectly in authoritative texts, of which there were two major categories, Qur'an and *hadith*. The Qur'an contained the words that the Prophet Muhammad heard from the angel Gabriel and recited to his contemporaries, while the hadith embraced sayings of the Prophet himself or tales of his deeds. These sayings and deeds delineate for Muslims a corpus of normative custom (*sunna*) and are regarded as constituting, as much as the Qur'an itself, a channel of divine revelation. A rule was grounded directly in the texts if it could be shown to be contained within the meaning of the texts. A rule that had no such grounding, but could be shown to be an analogue of another rule that did, gained equal validity according to the majority of Muslim jurists. Text-based rules and analogy-based rules thus formed the two major types of rules in Islamic law.

Text-based rules were widely acknowledged to be subject to a degree of uncertainty, owing to the difficulties involved in the interpretation and authentication of texts. This was even more the case with analogy-based rules. This uncertainty, however, was by no means detrimental to the enterprise of living according to the law, thanks to the generally accepted principle that a considered opinion as to what constituted a rule of law rendered that rule binding both upon the jurist who held the opinion and upon all nonjurists who chose to follow his doctrine. Opinions necessarily varied from jurist to jurist with the result that, early in the development of Islamic law, variant schools of legal doctrine arose. Of these, four eventually came to be predominant among Sunni Muslims: the Hanafite, Malikite, Shafiite, and Hanbalite schools, each claiming as its eponym a famous master jurist of the classical period. Shiites have, in contrast, insisted upon the greater monolithicity of their legal doctrine, attributing its essential formation to infallible *Imams,* among whom the sixth, Jafar al-Sadiq (702–755), was noted for the abundance of his legal doctrines.

Among Sunnis, the frank acceptance of the diversity of valid legal opinion gave rise to a kind of relativism. Whatever a jurist was led by diligent study and reflection to regard as the law was indeed the law for him and for his followers, no matter how great the discrepancy between his view of the law and that of other jurists. This is not to say that there did not emerge wide areas of agreement. It is often noted that the various schools of law in Islam agree on basics while differing on detail. Nonetheless, what for the external observer might appear to be an issue of mere detail could, for the Muslim jurists, be an issue of great magnitude. In a religious culture that emphasizes conformity with divine dictates in all areas of daily life, detail can be all-important.

The relativism of Sunni juristic thought should not be taken to mean that there was no notion of a single coherent and noncontradictory law of God. The existence of such a law is presumed. But the jurists were fully aware of their fallibility vis-a-vis the complexities of the texts, and the indefiniteness of the boundaries and authenticity of the corpus of hadith texts in particular, upon which the formulation of the law in large part depended. Accordingly, jurists regarded disagreement and diversity of interpretation as inevitable. This was seen to be desirable; a saying of the Prophet affirmed that diversity within the community was a divine mercy.

When disagreement existed, the jurists agreed that dogmatism was not permitted, that toleration of opposing views was mandatory. The most one could claim for one's opinion was probability, but to claim probability was to admit the possibility that one could be mistaken, and this admission opened the door to the possibility that one's fellow-jurist holding a contrary opinion could be right. When unanimous agreement among jurists arose, the situation changed dramatically, for the Prophet was credited with a statement to the effect that the community could never agree upon an error. This was thought by most jurists to amount to an attribution of infallibility to the consensus of scholars. The fallibility of the individual scholar, which disallowed dogmatism, thus was hedged in by an infallible consensus that did warrant dogmatism. Disagreement was a signal to all that none should claim finality for his view, agreement a signal that finality had been achieved. Consensus was reckoned accordingly

as a "source" (*asl*) of law, along with the textual sources, the Qur'an and hadith, and the method of analogical reasoning.

Interpretation: The difficulties involved in the extrapolation of rules from the texts and in the use of analogical reasoning have always been viewed by Muslims in a positive light, because these difficulties make the work of the jurist toilsome and thus enable him to earn a reward in the hereafter. Juristic endeavor is most frequently referred to as "toil" (*ijtihad*). While God could presumably have provided his community with a body of ready-made law, he was believed to have preferred to involve human agents actively in the formulation of law. For this reason he supplied, not the law, but rather the materials (i.e., revealed data) out of which the law was to be constructed and the methods to be used in its construction. It is the human agent, therefore, who must build up the actual law, using the materials and methods given. Arabic provides a word for law considered as a human construction, *fiqh* (understanding), whereas Sharia designates the law considered as what it is in and of itself: the law of God. Fiqh is thus the fallible human understanding of that Sharia as expressed in concrete rules. Because it is these rules that human beings must actually live by, the fiqh may be regarded as law in its own right. It is a humanly constructed positive law that is meant to approximate, as closely as possible, the ideal law of God.

A single example will serve to illustrate the juristic toil that goes into the making of fiqh. The Qur'an states: "Marry those women who are pleasing to you" (sura 4:3). Do these words signify an obligation to marry? Do they merely recommend marriage? Or do they but make marriage permissible? The key element is the imperative verb form, *marry.* Because imperatives abound in the texts, whatever one says concerning the significance of marry! will establish a principle that will be applicable to other texts. The Muslim jurists were well aware that the imperative form could signify a variety of meanings, including obligation, recommendation, and permission. The question was whether any one of these meanings could be regarded as the true literal meaning, as opposed to nonliteral, or figurative, meanings. Some jurists considered obligation to be the literal sense of the imperative and felt that, when presented with a word such as marry, they could make an initial presumption to the effect that marriage is obligatory and then examine the context to see if there were anything in it that warranted setting aside this literal sense in favor of a figurative sense. Upon failing to find any such contextual factor, the jurist was then in a position to transform his initial presumption into a rule of law. Examination of the context was no easy matter because context was defined broadly to include not just the immediate context (for example, the surrounding verses) but the entire corpus of texts inclusive of both Qur'an and hadith. Considering that the corpus of hadith was vast, the search process could seldom lead to absolutely unassailable conclusions; hence, the principle that the jurist should settle for a sense of what was probable.

But many jurists regarded the imperative verb form to be truly ambiguous, ambiguity being defined as the coexistence of two or more literal meanings. Others threw up their hands, refusing to take any position. Their view had the same hermeneutical consequences as the view of the exponents of ambiguity. For both groups, the imperative verb form warranted no initial presumption at all. One had no basis whatsoever with which even to begin the process of constructing a legal rule. Instead, one had to look for more helpful data in the texts, for example, indications that failure to marry occasioned some sort of penalty or justified blame. Debates between exponents of the various approaches to dealing with the imperative verb form themselves occasioned much toil for the jurist, since one should become familiar with all arguments advanced by all parties before coming to an opinion of one's own.

To these hermeneutical agonies could be added, in many cases, agony over the issue of authenticity of the text. Quranic texts were widely regarded as being of unquestionable authenticity. If, however, on discovering that a quranic text did not yield a rule of law, one turned to hadith texts, which raised immediately the authenticity issue. Virtually all hadith materials traditionally have been classified under the heading of "report of individuals" (*khabar al-wahid*), including those assembled in the most widely used hadith collections. The majority of jurists have regarded this category of text, as opposed to the "widely disseminated" (*mutawatir*) quranic text, as being of probable authenticity at the very most. Because probability admits of degrees, the jurist becomes embroiled in the task of weighing hadith passages against each other to determine which enjoy the higher degree of probability as to authenticity.

The consensus, as depicted in the classical theory, has the effect of lifting rules of law from the level of the probable and contestable to the level of the certain and incontestable. A good ex-

ample of its operation relates to the quranic command, "Perform the prayer!" (sura 11:116), *prayer* here being a reference to the ritual prayer that Muslims are to perform five times daily. Here again an imperative verb form is present; but whereas marry must be contemplated within a setting of vigorous disagreement between different viewpoints, "perform the prayer!" is contemplated within the setting of a universal agreement among Muslims reaching back to earliest times that the performance of the ritual prayer is an obligation that rests upon every Muslim. Consensus was erected, in classical Sunni theory, into an infallible indicator of the divine law such that whenever universal agreement arose among Muslims, debate was necessarily terminated, and future generations of Muslims were unable to resurrect debate over issues that the consensus had, at any point in Muslim history, settled. It would be an act of heresy, if not outright unbelief, for any Muslim to suggest that, owing to the ambiguity of the imperative verb form "perform the prayer!", the obligatory character of the ritual prayer may be considered a topic of debate on which a diversity of opinions is allowable.

Common Features: Among the features that unite the various Muslim legal schools, despite their differences, four may be singled out. The first is a strong moralistic bent, something that one would expect of jurists concerned with the expounding of a law that was of divine origin and thus inseparable from morality. This moralism is exhibited in the tendency of the jurists to restrict human freedom in areas in which Western law seeks to facilitate that freedom. Although the Muslim jurists proceeded on the basis of a presumption of freedom, they were primarily concerned to set the boundaries of that freedom, and thus their imposition of the law generally had more to say about duties than about rights, notwithstanding the careful attention given to the latter.

The second feature is their preference for the oral declaration over the written or other kind of instrument. A contract, for example, was never effected by means of a written instrument as such. Nor could a written document stand by itself as evidence of a contract. On the other hand, oral declarations were subject to a rigorous formalism. If the proper formula was neglected, a contract could become null and void.

The third feature common to all legal doctrine in Islam is what may be called its individualism. The Muslim jurists never developed the notion of the corporate person. Only individuals could be bearers of rights and obligations. True, individuals could jointly assume rights and obligations, making possible various types of mercantile partnerships, for example. But in so doing they were acting as individuals in concert, not as agents of an incorporated enterprise. Among the individuals recognized by Islamic law is God, who is, however, a bearer of rights only and who, to some extent, replaces the state or body politic as a bearer of rights. The non-recognition of the state as a legal entity and possible party to disputes helps to account for the absence of a developed criminal law in the writings of the Muslim jurists. Certain of the offenses that Western law counts as crimes are treated as offenses against God, whereas others are treated as injuries of one individual to another and as subject to what amounts to civil action. For example, fornication, false accusation of fornication, theft, and the drinking of intoxicating beverages belong to the former category, while homicide and bodily harm belong to the latter.

The fourth feature is the disproportionate attention, as compared to Western law, given to contracts and other dispositions or transactions. It is in the treatment of contracts, dispositions, and transactions that the moralism of Islamic law is especially prominent. The consideration in a contract must, for example, be well-defined and entirely free of uncertainty. This requirement effectively disallows not only gambling, which the Muslim jurists vehemently abhorred, but virtually all aleatory transactions, including insurance contracts. Where an exchange of items is involved, as in contracts of barter or sale, the jurists show a strong bias against delay in performance. Only under carefully worked out conditions is a delay in delivery of a commodity or payment of a price allowed. Exchanges of interchangeable items—which include monetary exchanges because money is always, in the thinking of the jurists, precious metal—are subject to especially rigorous restrictions. The best known of these is the prohibition against usury, which as traditionally explained amounts to a prohibition against interest in all its forms. In the realm of dispositions of properties, a major provision of Islamic law is its limiting of bequests to one-third of the estate and its distribution of the remainder according to fixed rules largely laid down in the Qur'an. All of these restrictions have a plainly moralistic basis: property is a gift from God that has been entrusted to human beings to assure their well-being, and it should, therefore, not be exposed to risk, exploitation, or human caprice.

These four features pertain to the substantive law expounded by the jurists. On the side of adjective or procedural law, the first thing to note is the Muslim jurists' conception of a court of law. For them a court is nothing more or less than an agency charged with the application of the substantive law that they expound. The judge (*qadi*) single-handedly assumes the responsibility for decision-making. Courts comprised of more than one judge are rare in Islam. Alongside the court of the qadi, called the qadivial court, there existed in premodern Islamic society courts that did not consider themselves bound to apply the law of the jurists. But these nonqadivial courts are never mentioned in the classical works of Muslim jurisprudence.

The qadi was a delegate of the head of the state, from whom his judicial authority derived. Muslim jurists did not envision any sort of separation of powers. This placed qadis in a position of continual subordination to their appointing superior and militated against their autonomy. Furthermore, a qadi's jurisdiction was defined by the appointing superior and could be changed at any time. On the other hand, a qadi's decision, once rendered, was not subject to any sort of formal judicial review. There is no appellate jurisdiction in Islamic law. Because the law that the qadi was to apply was diverse, consisting of a range of juristic opinions, the jurists appreciated the need for consistency in the judicial process and therefore required a judge to make a decision consistent with the decisions of his predecessors in the same region. This requirement amounted to a qualified acceptance of the principle of *stare decisis*. Where two or more schools of law had significant representation among the population, the appointing superior sometimes appointed a qadi for each school.

The rules of evidence worked out by the jurists insisted upon the oral testimony of trustworthy witnesses as the only admissible evidence. In order to prove trustworthy, a witness had to submit to a careful screening process, and qadis commonly kept lists of persons who had been attested as trustworthy. This remarkable feature of the procedural law reflects Muslim thinking about truth: the word of a truly trustworthy person is taken prima facie to be a source of probable truth. Because the possibility of error, lapse of memory, or misperception must always be taken into account, the jurists required two witnesses to establish a fact in most cases.

Litigation always had to be initiated by a private party, public prosecution being unknown in Islamic law. Even in cases of offenses against God, such as fornication or theft, an action had to commence with a complaint by a human party directly affected. All procedure in Islamic law is, therefore, on the order of what in Western law is called civil procedure. Litigants could, if they so chose, be represented in court by deputies. These were not, however, attorneys in the strict sense. They held no license from courts, did not belong to organizations approved by courts, and were not required to have training in the law.

The law worked out by the classical jurists was, both in its substantive and procedural aspects, largely an ideal construction that seldom enjoyed full application. Actual legal life among Muslims has entailed an interplay between ideals and realities, with ideals impinging on the real world in varying degrees. A commonly accepted assessment has it that the law of the jurists was most widely and consistently applied in the area of family and inheritance law and least widely and consistently applied in the area of crimes and torts, with commercial law falling somewhere in between. It is well known that governments in the medieval Islamic world developed criminal codes and procedures and courts for the hearing of complaints that operated independently of the qadivial courts and were not bound to the law developed by the jurists. It is also well known that commercial law developed over time into an essentially autonomous merchant law that coincided with the law of the jurists in regard to certain basic principles but departed freely from it whenever need dictated. Frequently, departures from the strict requirements of the law were justified by means of legal fictions, and a literature expounding these fictions flourished. *See also* hadith; Hanafite; Hanbalite; Ibn Taymiyya; Malik ibn Anas; Malikite; Shafiite; Sharia; Sunna.

Islamic philosophy. *Falsafa* ("philosophy") is the Arabic term for the Hellenistic tradition of rationalist inquiry as pursued in premodern Islamic civilization. Muslim scholars established this field of endeavor by appropriating major elements of the Hellenistic philosophical corpus and then developing this tradition within the Islamic cultural milieu.

This process of appropriation and development was two-sided. On the one hand, falsafa is a clear continuation of and elaboration on Hellenistic philosophy. Technical issues arising in Platonism, Aristotelianism, and Neoplatonism (Stoicism and Materialism play a less important role) are compared, discussed, and reworked in great detail.

On the other hand, Muslim intellectuals pursued philosophy in the historical context of dealing with specific intellectual, religious, and ideological issues that arose at particular times in Islamic civilization. As such, thinkers used the framework of Hellenistic philosophy to formulate and answer questions pertinent to their own culture's intellectual and spiritual needs.

The interplay of these two processes—the technical and the cultural—brought into being philosophical thought of truly impressive brilliance. The resulting corpus of texts represents a tradition of evolving intellectual synthesis that constitutes a major achievement of Islamic civilization.

The Early Cultural Milieu: The Arab invasions of the seventh century brought a new political and cultural hegemony into areas governed for centuries by the Byzantine Greek and Sassanian Persian empires. The early bases of this new hegemony combined the ethos of Arab tribalism with the new and dynamic religion of Islam. The conquering Arab Muslims did not enter a cultural vacuum, however. The power that Islam displayed as a unifying cultural force was amazingly strong, and part of its strength was the extent to which it encouraged creative appropriation of preexisting traditions. The basic dynamic was to include everything that did not directly contradict fundamental tenets of the new religion.

Early Islamic theology was an intense and eclectic affair. Muslim thinkers found themselves confronting representatives of other creeds and strains of thought—Christianity, Judaism, Zoroastrianism, Manicheanism, even paganism and atheism. This encounter forced them to develop theological positions that they, in turn, argued and defended among themselves.

Moreover, the issue of political leadership, that is, the nature of the caliph's political and religious authority, was hotly contested throughout the seventh and eighth centuries. Early Muslim theologians found that they too were forced to adopt political positions, and they defended these positions according to their understanding and interpretation of the foundational texts of Islam, the divinely revealed Qur'an and the hadith, accounts of the Prophet Muhammad's statements and actions regarding religious issues that were thereafter collected and codified.

Early theologians first debated issues by means of oral disputation. Although written tracts also became commonplace by the ninth century, speculative theology became known as *kalam* (speech) and theologians as *mutakallimun* (those who speak or dispute with one another). Early instruction was individual; circles of students congregated around scholars. Theologians attracted followers due to the cohesiveness of the theologians' ideas and the force of their personalities. Although many of these early schools of thought were ephemeral and passed away with their founders, their ideas were often appropriated by movements begun by the next generation.

Prominent among early theological controversies were the disputes between the rationalist Mutazilite thinkers and the literalist traditionalists. Issues were free will and predestination; the nature of God and his relationship to attributes ascribed to him in the Qur'an and hadith, both physical attributes (hand, eye) and notional ones (power, knowledge, will); sin and whether a sinner should still be considered a Muslim; God's omnipotence and justice (could he be just and still omnipotent?); and whether the Qur'an was created or uncreated speech. Also significant were arguments between proto-Sunni and proto-Shii movements over the proper qualifications of the *imam*, or caliph, the religious and political leader of the Muslim community and empire.

Simultaneously, other areas of Islamic religious study evolved: the study of Arabic philology, methods of quranic exegesis, the critical study of hadith, compilation of historical accounts, and the development of schools of Islamic jurisprudence. In these enterprises, scholars sought out whatever tools promised to advance their study. The incorporation of philosophy as such a tool must have initially appeared auspicious. Nevertheless, Hellenistic philosophy comprised a unified and cohesive tradition of thought, and its rationalism threatened theology as much as it seemed to be able to help it. As a result, the extent to which theologians could accept philosophy became a controversial issue. The relationship between reason and revelation remained fraught in the centuries that followed.

Early Translation Movements: Arabic was the religious and governmental language of the new empire. From the middle of the eighth century, it also became the main medium of Islamic philosophy as over the next two centuries much of the Hellenistic philosophical and scientific corpus was translated from Syriac and Greek. The work of translating medical and scientific texts had already begun in the late seventh century. Later the Caliph al-Mansur (r. 754–775) personally encouraged this process. By the reign of his grandson, al-Mamun (r. 813–833), the *Elements* of Euclid, the *Almagest* of Ptolemy, and other works of science, as well as numerous medical and astrological/astronomical works (subjects dear to the hearts of rulers), had been rendered into Arabic. Al-Mamun himself founded a research institute and library, the *Bayt al-Hikma* (House of Wisdom), that supported scholars in their translation efforts. Members of prominent families of governmental ministers (such as the Barmakids and the Banu Musa) also sponsored the work of such noted translators as al-Hajjaj ibn Yusuf (d. 833), Yahya ibn Masawayih (d. 857), and most famous of all, Hunayin ibn Ishaq (d. 873). The process of translation continued into the tenth century with the efforts of Thabit ibn Qurra (d. 901), Ishaq ibn Hunayin (d. ca. 910–911), and Qusta ibn Luqa (d. ca. 912), Abu Bishr Matta (d. 940), Yahya ibn Adi (d. 974), and Ibn Khammar (d. ca. 1017).

The achievement of these scholars was impressive. They translated into Arabic all of the known works of Aristotle (except possibly the *Politics*), as well as commentaries on them by, among others, Alexander of Aphrodisias, Themistius, and John Philoponus. Among Plato's works, the *Timaeus*, the *Republic*, and the *Laws* were available in full; they and some of the dialogues also existed in the form of summaries and commentaries by such thinkers as Galen. Galen's own works were translated, as well as summaries of works or collections of individual quotes, from the full range of the Greek philosophical tradition. Finally, several Neoplatonic tracts were translated. Prominent among these were the *Secret of Secrets, Liber de Causis*, and the *Theology of Aristotle*. All of these were attributed to Aristotle, even though the first is apocryphal, the second adapted from a work by Proclus, and the third consists of selections from the *Enneads* of Plotinus. The attribution of these Neoplatonic works to Aristotle clouded Muslim philosophers' understanding of the significant differences between his thought and that of Plato and Plotinus. Consequently, one task of such philosophers as al-Farabi (Lat. *Alfarabi*) and Ibn Sina (Lat. *Avicenna*) was to attempt to harmonize the ideas of these thinkers. The resulting synthesis led to the development of a distinctly Islamic form of Neoplatonism.

Most of the translators were Christians, although a few Jews or Sabians (members of a non-Muslim sect located in Harran) were among them. In general, they lived in Baghdad and were connected with the intellectual elite of the Abbasid court. They usually translated from Syriac, although a few learned Greek as well. Despite the undeniable importance of their activities, which included composing commentaries and summaries as well as translating, from a larger perspective they mainly served as conduits. In this sense, they resemble the Spanish Muslim, Jewish, and Christian translators who conveyed philosophy from the Islamic world to the medieval West. The great philosophers who made use of their translations, however, were Muslim, and the intellectual context within which they worked was one shaped by early Abbasid Islamic culture.

Early Muslim Philosophers: The first great Muslim philosopher was Abu Yusuf Yaqub al-Kindi (ca. 800–870). Of Arab stock, al-Kindi is often referred to as the "Philosopher of the Arabs." It is more accurate, however, to view him as an important member of the cosmopolitan elite of early-ninth-century Baghdad. He was the associate of two caliphs, al-Mamun (d. 833) and al-Mutasim (d. 842), as well as a tutor of the latter's son. Al-Kindi was well-versed in the theological issues of the time, particularly those between Mutazilites and traditionalists, as well as with contemporary aspects of Persian, Indian, and Greek thought. He himself sponsored translations, commissioning a revised translation of the *Theology of Aristotle* and a version of Aristotle's *Metaphysics*. He composed about 250 works, but only some forty survive; the most important of these is his *On First Philosophy*.

Al-Kindi defended the study of Greek philosophy by saying that human learning is progressive; one must benefit from and build on the discoveries of past generations. He emphasized the importance of logic and mathematics as philosophical tools and outlined the structure of the sciences. Finally, he formulated questions that were to interest philosophers thereafter: the relation between the One and the Many, between the eternal intelligible and the transient material realm, and between divine and human knowledge, that is, between prophetic revelation and rationalist inquiry. In this last regard, as a good Muslim he defended the priority of prophecy over reason. In several writings, he also offered philosophical interpretations of quranic verses. Although al-Kindi continued to be widely read by later generations, his importance rests less on the subsequent influence of his ideas than in his introducing philosophy into the mainstream of Abbasid culture.

Not all early philosophers followed al-Kindi's conciliatory attitude toward Islam. Ibn al-Rewandi (d. ca. 910) was a free-thinker who espoused naturalistic views. He believed in the eternity of the world and may have embraced a kind of Manichean dualism. He also rejected prophetic revelation and the efficacy of mira-

cles; he even apparently composed a parody of the Qur'an.

More famous is Abu Bakr ibn Zakariya al-Razi (Lat. *Rhazes*), who died around 925. Al-Razi is chiefly known as a great physician whose medical compendium, *al-Hawi*, remained a major textbook in the Islamic world and the West, where it was known as *Continens*, until the sixteenth century. In philosophy, al-Razi was influenced by Plato and strains of Pythagorean and perhaps Sabian thought rather than by Aristotle. One of his main sources was Plato's *Timaeus*, and it is probably from his study of this work that he derived his theory of the five coeternal principles: Matter, Space, Time, Soul, and the Creator (or Demiurge). In the eternal continuum in which these principles coexist, the Creator formed the material world in response to the Soul's desire to mix with Matter. Simultaneously, he endowed humans with the faculty of reason so that through its medium, particles of Soul could find enlightenment, leave their material forms, and reintegrate themselves into the eternal Soul. The purpose of philosophy is to facilitate and hasten this process.

This cosmology explains al-Razi's belief in metempsychosis, or the transmigration of souls, because the process of spiritual purification may take many lifetimes. It also explains why he rejected prophetic revelation. Rational thought suffices to redeem humankind; belief in supernatural intervention only hinders the process of spiritual purification. Needless to say, neither Ibn al-Rewandi or al-Razi were very popular with Muslim thinkers.

The Baghdad Philosophers: By the tenth century, philosophy was beginning to enter the mainstream of the intellectual life of the capital. One can obtain a picture of how intellectuals including scholars, poets, theologians, and government officials, incorporated philosophical topics in their evening soirees from the writings of the litterateur, Abu Hayyan al-Tawhidi (d. ca. 1023). Prominent among the Baghdad philosophers were al-Tawhidi's teacher, Abu Sulayman al-Sijistani (d. 1000), known as "The Logician," and the Christian translators Yahya ibn Adi and Abu Bishr Matta. Cosmology and psychology were major interests, as was the issue of the efficacy of logic as an intellectual tool. Al-Tawhidi has preserved a disputation, for example, held in 936 at the home of a government minister in which Abu Bishr Matta debated the grammarian Abu Said al-Sirafi. Abu Bishr was worsted in the debate, but that it occurred at all demonstrates the cultural importance that philosophical inquiry was beginning to assume.

Another well-known Baghdad philosopher was al-Miskawayhi (d. 1030). He was a polymath who wrote literary and historical texts as well as philosophical tracts; he also served as a government minister and librarian for the Buyid rulers who controlled Baghdad at the time. Al-Miskawayhi's cosmology was Neoplatonic in orientation, but he is best known for his ethical treatise, *The Refinement of Morals,* in which he combined Aristotelian psychology with Platonic ethics. The activities of the Baghdad thinkers were important, but they became overshadowed by the thought of al-Farabi and Ibn Sina.

The Great Neoplatonists: The first truly outstanding Muslim philosopher was Abu Nasr al-Farabi (ca. 870–950). Little is known of his life. He was born in Central Asia and appears to be of Turkish origin. As an adult, he lived in Baghdad for many years and died in Aleppo, whose ruler he served toward the end of his life. Al-Farabi was a keen logician and appears to have been the main architect of the Neoplatonic theory of emanation that was elaborated on and refined by Ibn Sina. His most original contribution, however, was his political thought.

Influenced by Plato's *Republic,* al-Farabi devoted several works to developing his vision of the social efficacy of different types of political regimes. At the heart of his theory is the concept of an ideal ruler, the Philosopher/Prophet who would rule over the Virtuous City. Potential ideal rulers, whose intellectual development enabled them to communicate with the Active Intelligence, might exist as individuals in any place and age. But their social beneficence could only achieve its full effect if they became the rulers of a political system. In this case, the ruler would organize society for the good of all, assigning each type of individual his or her appropriate role so that different parts of society would interact to unite in a harmonious whole.

Al-Farabi lived during a period when the authority of the Abbasid caliphate was in decline, and this might have influenced the interest he took in politics. During the life of his great successor, Abu Ali al-Husayin ibn Sina (ca. 980–1037), the political breakup of the empire had reached a state in which political idealism was no longer realistic.

Ibn Sina was a brilliant analytic philosopher, but his real strength was as a systematizer. His remarkably creative mind combined attention to the smallest details of philosophical argument with a unified vision that encompassed the entire philosophical corpus. He has been justly called the "First Scholastic." In his magnum opus, *al-Shifa* ("The Healing"), he organized the philosophical curriculum, beginning with logic, then physics, and then metaphysics, into a format that has been followed in the Islamic world until modern times. Ibn Sina was arguably the greatest Muslim philosopher, and subsequent Islamic philosophy was to a large extent a commentary on the system he built.

Ibn Sina organized his philosophy around the concept of existence. God, whom Ibn Sina termed the *Necessary Existent,* is a pure essence whose existence is necessary. From him emanates spiritual and then material beings whose existence is contingent. Some of these beings, Intelligences and Souls, are eternal; those on earth—minerals, plants, animals, and humans—are transient. Humankind is distinguished from all creation by its ability to use the rational faculty to come into contact with the Divine. Philosophy is the science that trains humans to do so; this is why its study is incumbent upon those qualified intellectually to pursue it.

Both al-Farabi and Ibn Sina hold prophecy and revelation in high regard. Each considers the prophet as someone who first uses his intellect to commune with spiritual representatives of the intelligible universe and then conveys this revelation to others in language that all can understand. For Ibn Sina, prophecy is even a social necessity; society could not cohere without the divine authority that prophetic revelation invests in social legislation. Ibn Sina may be counted as one of the founders of the Islamic tradition of allegory; he composed several short allegories that were very influential.

Speculative Shiism and the Ikhwan as-Safa: The tenth century witnessed the elaboration of speculative Shii thought. Several Shii thinkers were heavily influenced by Neoplatonism and Hellenistic wisdom literature, but most of their writings assume forms that put them beyond the purview of this survey. One exception is the *Ikhwan as-Safa* (Epistles of the Brethren of Purity*)*. This collection of fifty-one treatises was written in Basra toward the end of the tenth century by members of a secret society of thinkers of apparently Ismaili Shii orientation. The *Epistles* combine strains of popularized Neoplatonism and Pythagoreanism and constitute a curriculum that falls into four groups: the mathematical, the physical, the psychological, and theological. Number plays an essential role in the Brethren's thought, as does the idea of correspondence between the cosmic macrocosm and the human microcosm.

The Spanish Tradition: Interest in philosophy began in Muslim Spain (Andalusia) as early as the ninth century. Nevertheless, great philosophers did not emerge until the twelfth century. The first of these was Abu Bakr Muhammad ibn

Bajja (d. 1139; Lat. *Avempace*). Ibn Bajja was deeply influenced by al-Farabi's thought, but his political vision was more pessimistic. In the few works of Ibn Bajja that have survived, he stresses the possibility of attaining human perfection, but through individual study rather than through political association. This viewpoint may have influenced the thought of Ibn Bajja's better-known pupil, Abu Bakr ibn Tufayl (d. 1185).

Ibn Tufayl was an intimate of and chief physician to the Almohad ruler, Abu Yaqub ibn Yusuf (d. 1184). Although Ibn Tufayl may have written on medical and scientific matters, he is mainly known for his allegorical/philosophical narrative *Hayy ibn Yaqzan* (Alive, Son of Awake). This reworking of a treatise of the same name by Ibn Sina explores the potential of human beings for self-perfection. Its protagonist, Hayy, lives alone on a desert island. Through a combination of empirical observation and logical reasoning, he ascertains the structure of the sublunar and supernal realms and ends with obtaining direct communion with the Necessary Existent. After obtaining this measure of perfection, he comes into contact with a community whose members believe in revealed religion. Hayy immediately perceives the congruence of his insights with the teachings of their prophet; but he soon learns that others can only accept these truths through the indirect medium of religious revelation. Dispirited, Hayy returns to his island to train select disciples in obtaining unmediated religious experience.

Ibn Tufayl's student and successor was the brilliant Abu al-Walid Muhammad ibn Rushd (1128–96; Lat. *Averroes*). Ibn Rushd was also concerned with the relation between reason and revelation. In careful terms, he emphasized the harmony between the two by suggesting the efficacy of reason in interpreting revelation. In a similar vein, he composed a refutation of al-Ghazali's attack on the philosophers (see below), defending the orthodoxy of their opinions. Ibn Rushd's own thought was strongly Aristotelian, and many of his commentaries on Aristotle's works were translated into Latin in the major translation movement of the twelfth and thirteenth centuries. Ibn Rushd thus exerted a significant influence on medieval Scholastic thought. Although he also influenced the Jewish philosopher Maimonides (d. 1204), Ibn Rushd was less influential in the Muslim East.

Although not themselves philosophers, two other major Spanish Muslim thinkers were deeply influenced by philosophy. The first was Ibn al-Arabi (d. 1240), whose speculative mystical theories had a tremendous impact on later

Muslim thought. The second was the historiographer Ibn Khaldun (d. 1406), who created a sophisticated philosophy of history.

Al-Ghazali and Later Theology: By the eleventh century theology was ready to come to terms with philosophy. The person who effected the compromise was the Asharite theologian Abu Hamid al-Ghazali (1058–1111). In his revealing autobiography, *The Deliverance from Error*, al-Ghazali tells how he devoted three years to the study of the philosophy of al-Farabi and Ibn Sina, even writing a summary of their main doctrines. Al-Ghazali decided that philosophy itself was true, but that philosophers, through their unreliable rationalistic speculations, had distorted many of its doctrines. In another book, *The Incoherence of the Philosophers* (to which Ibn Rushd replied), al-Ghazali declared logic and much of physics to be theologically acceptable but offered detailed attacks of twenty points of metaphysical doctrine that he considered erroneous.

After al-Ghazali, the study of philosophy, especially logic, and the use of philosophical terminology to address theological issues became common. The theologian Fakhr ad-Din al-Razi (d. 1209) and the Shii thinker Nasir ad-Din al-Tusi (d. 1273), for example, even composed commentaries on works by Ibn Sina.

Later Philosophy: Later philosophy in the East consisted mainly of critiques of and elaborations on the thought of Ibn Sina. Although Abu al-Barakat al-Baghdadi (d. 1116) approached Ibn Sina from an Aristotelian point of view, more typical was analysis of his Neoplatonism from the increasingly prominent perspective of Islamic mysticism, or Sufism.

Shihab al-Din Yahya as-Suhrawardi (d. 1191) developed a philosophical system that combined philosophical speculation with reliance on the experiential techniques of mysticism. He wrote several allegories, but his main work is *Hikmat al-Ishraq* (The Philosophy of Illumination), in which he questioned the validity of Aristotle's categories and posited a cosmic hierarchy of luminous entities. Light, rather than Ibn Sina's Existence, was the basis of as-Suhrawardi's metaphysics. Because of his eccentric personal behavior and unorthodox teachings, he was condemned to death in Aleppo and died at the young age of thirty-eight.

Philosophy after the thirteenth century revolved around creating a synthesis drawn from the Neoplatonism of Ibn Sina, the illuminationism of as-Suhrawardi, and the mystical theosophy of Ibn al-Arabi. Each of these thinkers had focused on how humans could find perfection within the spiritual cosmic hierarchy, and this became the central issue of philosophical inquiry. This tradition has continued to be taught in Iran until the present (the Ayatollah Khomeini, for example, was well-versed in it), but its last great theoretician was Sadr al-Din al-Shirazi, or Mulla Sadra (d. 1641).

The study of philosophy in the modern Islamic world is in a state of flux. The split between adherents of the premodern tradition and of modern Western philosophy is severe and promises to remain so for some time. Nevertheless, although the cosmology of Islamic philosophy is undoubtedly dated, its insights into ethical, political, and spiritual dimensions of human existence are not. Indeed, most universities in the Muslim world have departments of falsafa that study the classical Hellenistic/Arabic tradition, as well as other developments in the history of Western philosophy. *See also* Ghazali, Abu Hamid Muhammad ibn Muhammad al-Tusi; Ibn Khaldun.

Islamic political theory. The central issues that gave rise to the development of Islamic political theory were questions of the nature of the community, who should lead the community, and the discrepancy between a normative ideal and political reality. Islamic political thought was not simply the product of theologians or intellectuals but grew out of the historical experience of a community in which religion and politics were intertwined. From its origins, the Prophet Muhammad guided and governed a trans-tribal, religio-political community in which religious solidarity was to replace tribal ties and loyalties. Under the Prophet, the community of believers existed as a religio-political community whose task was to serve as the vehicle for the realization and spread of God's will—a God-centered and ordained community with a mandate to promote good and prohibit evil.

The integral relationship of religion to politics was rooted in quranic interpretation, the example of Muhammad's religio-political leadership as prophet as well as political and military leader, belief that God's law (*Sharia*) was a comprehensive blueprint for state and society, and a tendency to regard events and actions not simply as political but also as religious issues.

The secession of the Kharijites from the early Islamic community and Sunni-Shii differences over who should succeed the Prophet Muhammed as head of the community were formative influences on the development of Islamic political thought. The Kharijite movement resulted when a group of Muslims in 656 revolted against the fourth caliph, Ali. The caliph

had agreed to arbitration in a dispute with a rebellious general, Muawiyah (who, upon Ali's death [660], became the founder of the Umayyad dynasty). The Kharijites believed that a grave sinner was no longer a Muslim. They condemned both Muawiyah for his rebellion and the Caliph Ali for his compromise, seceded from the community, and waged holy war. Kharijite rejection of the Sunni caliphate, as well as the Shii Imamate (religious leadership), was rooted in their belief that all good Muslims should elect and be eligible for election as ruler.

The division of the Muslim community into its two broad branches, the Sunni majority and Shii minority, is based on competing models of community leadership: the Sunni caliphate and the Shii Imamate. Upon the death of Muhammad, the majority of the community, believing that Muhammad had not designated a successor, accepted the selection, by a group of the Prophet's close associates, of Abu Bakr as caliph (*khalifa*, "successor," "deputy") of the Prophet. The institution of the caliphate, his selection through a process of consultation (*shura*) and consensus (*ijma*), the oath of allegiance (*baya*) sworn by his electors, and the covenant (*ahd*) of the caliph with the community to rule according to Islamic law (Sharia) became the accepted form of legitimate government for Sunni Islam. This vision was contested by the Shii, who rejected the Sunni caliphs as usurpers. The Shii believed that Muhammad had designated Ali, his cousin and son-in-law, to be leader (*Imam*) of the Muslim community and that the senior male descendant of the family of the Prophet (*Ahl al-Bait*) should be the divinely inspired religio-political leader of the community.

The caliphate and the Imamate constitute two contesting visions of community leadership in Islam. In fact, the Imamate remained primarily a theory because Shii were subordinated to Sunni hegemony for centuries. As a result, Shii political thought tended to be characterized by an idealism in which early Shii political revolutionary activism gave way to apolitical withdrawal as Shii awaited the return of the Hidden Imam and with him the restoration of a just order. Meanwhile, Sunni Islamic political theory developed as justifications for a political reality often at odds with normative Islam.

During Abbasid rule (750–1250), Islamic political theory took shape as theologians and jurists, many of whom enjoyed royal patronage, sought to maintain the divine origin and purpose of the community and to legitimate Abbasid claims. This became all the more critical with the progressive disintegration of the Abbasid empire in the tenth century, as the actual power and central authority of the caliph was challenged by sectarian disputes and eroded by the emergence of local sultanate governments.

No single doctrine of the caliphate became universally accepted. For some, the true caliphate was restricted to the first four Rightly Guided Caliphs. Some pragmatically bridged the gap between the caliphate and the dynastic monarchy that prevailed under the Umayyads and Abbasids. Others, such as Hasan al-Mawardi (d. 1058; *Principles of Government*) and Abu Hamid Muhammad al-Ghazali (d. 1111; *The Book of Counsel for Kings*) presented a more theoretical and idealized view of the caliphate or Islamic government. Among its common themes were: God is the absolute sovereign and ruler of the universe, the ultimate authority in the state; through a covenant, authority is delegated to humankind as God's instrument in the world; the institution of the caliphate is based on revelation and not simply reason, the quranic designation to serve as God's representative or viceregent on earth; the caliph is elected by a group of influential community leaders, followed by community acceptance or public acclamation; and the caliph, as the Commander of the Faithful, is the guardian and protector of Islam, whose primary task is to enforce God's law, subject to the following qualifications for office—justice, knowledge to interpret and apply the law, and descent from the Prophet's tribe (Quraysh).

Yet, the idealism of Sunni Islamic political theory was tempered by accommodation to political reality. The disjuncture between what should be and what was, as evidenced by the degeneration of caliphal rule into dynastic monarchy, the ignoble qualities of many rulers, and the reduction of the caliphal office after the tenth century to that of a figurehead raised the question, Were Muslims required to revolt against un-Islamic rulers or usurper governments? The prevailing opinion favored order over political chaos, maintaining that public interest necessitated the acceptance of usurpers, provided these sultans formally acknowledged the caliph as the spiritual and temporal head of the community, mentioned his name in the Friday community prayer, and promised to uphold Sharia rule.

Despite the diversity of Muslim politics and of Islamic political thought, a common denominator emerged: the minimal requirement for an Islamic government was not the religious commitment and moral character of the ruler or government but official recognition of the Sharia that assured the character, unity, and legitimacy of an Islamic state. *See also* caliph; fundamentalism; Imamate; Seceders; Sharia.

Islamic theology. *See* kalam.

Islam in China. *See* China, Islam in.

Islam in Korea. *See* Korea, Islam in.

Islam in North America. *See* North America, Islam in.

islands of the blessed, a widespread mythical motif of a paradisical place (often in the west, where the sun sets) in which the good dead reside. *See also* afterlife; afterworld.

Isles of the Immortals (Chin. *P'eng-lai, Fang-chang, Ying-chou*), in ancient Chinese lore, floating island paradises in the Eastern Sea inhabited by immortals and white fauna, and having mountains shaped like the lidded vases used in alchemy for drugs. Palaces of gold and silver look like clouds when seen by mortals from a distance. If mortals tried to reach the islands, the three (sometimes five) islands sank beneath the sea. Ch'in- and Han-dynasty emperors (second century B.C.–A.D. fifth century) sent expeditions there to seek elixirs, but the boats never returned. *See also* alchemy; Chinese myth; immortality; mountains, sacred; paradise.

Ismail (Arab. *Ishmael*), Ibrahim's (Abraham's) son by Hajar. Thus, Ismail is regarded as the patriarch of the Arabs of the northern Arabian Peninsula and a link to the biblical genealogy. Ismail helped his father establish the Kaaba at Mecca. He is sometimes called *Abu Fida* ("the ransomed one") because Muslims hold that he (and not Isaac, as in the Bible) was the intended sacrificial offering to God. Ismail is said to be buried with his mother and other prophets, near the Kaaba. *See also* Abraham; Ishmael; Messenger of Allah.

Ismaili Shia (is-mah'ee-lee shee'ah; Arab.), a group consisting of those Shiite Muslims who, on the death of their sixth *Imam,* Jafar al-Sadiq, in 765, gave allegiance to a line of his descendants through his son Ismail. Members reflect diverse cultural, linguistic, and economic patterns in daily life and are to be found mostly in Afghanistan, China, East Africa, India, Iran, Pakistan, the former Soviet Union, Syria, and, of late, in the West.

Following an initial period of consolidation, the Ismaili emerged in the tenth century in

North Africa and Egypt to establish a dynasty of Imams who ruled for more than two centuries under the title *Fatimid* (after Fatima, the daughter of Muhammad and wife of Ali, the first Imam). During this period Ismaili influence grew, leading to the development of intellectual, scientific, cultural, and economic activity on a wide scale. Cairo, the Fatimid capital in Egypt, was founded in 969, together with the still famous Al-Azhar University.

The next major phase of activity in Ismaili history occurred in Iran and Yemen. After the death of the Fatimid Imam Mustansirbillah in 1094, the Ismailis split over the succession into two subgroups: the Nizaris followed Nizar, the eldest son, while others accepted a younger son, after whom they are known as Mustalis. The Nizaris established a state in Iran and Syria, subsequently destroyed by the Mongol invasion in 1256. Since then these Ismailis have maintained allegiance to a continuous line of Imams. The present Imam is Prince Karim (b. 1936), also known as the Aga Khan IV.

The Mustalis, on the other hand, believe that during the twelfth century the last Imam went into concealment. His successors, though hidden, guide the community through an intermediary, called *Dai*. The Mustalis built a thriving state in Yemen, but after its eclipse in 1566, moved their headquarters to India, where the present Dai lives.

Like other Muslim schools, Ismailis have developed their own tradition of quranic interpretation, law, and theology, with a strong emphasis on the use of intellectual and philosophical tools. This emphasis relies on the critical role of the Imam, who preserves, interprets, and teaches the quranic message, guiding the community in material and spiritual matters and contextualizing Islam in accordance with changing times and circumstances. Religion and revelation in Ismaili thought are viewed from a dual perspective, an outer significance and meaning reflected in the formal aspect of the faith and an inner esoteric significance for understanding the spiritual dimension. *See also* Fatimids; Hidden Imam.

Isra. *See* ascension.

Israel (land, people, state). In Judaism, Israel refers, first of all, to the children of Abraham and Sarah, Isaac and Rebekah, and Jacob and Leah and Rachel: the holy people. Israel refers to a group, specifically, the holy people whom God first loved and to whom God gave the Torah, the land of Israel, and much else. In the theology and canon of Judaism, the word *Israel* refers to the people and, by extension, may bear such qualifications as "land of . . . ," "king of . . . ," and any number of other subordinate categories. Though in contemporary usage Israel often refers to the State of Israel, in Judaism—Scripture and liturgy alike—the word Israel refers to a supernatural entity, not a this-worldly group. Israel refers to the recipients of God's revelation, the Torah, and God's favor and grace. The issue of who or what is Israel then forms a theological question. When people call themselves Israel and refer to that same group of which the Hebrew Scriptures or "Old Testament" speaks, they claim to embody the Israel chosen by God in the here and now.

To be Israel in that sense generally involves one of three definitions of Israel: (1) the extended family of Abraham, Isaac, and Jacob, who was called Israel, hence Israel as a genealogy; (2) a people that, as a social entity, is unique and has no analogy to any other social entity, hence a social entity that is sui generis, defined by the holy way of life and worldview characteristic of that social entity; and (3) a mixture of the two, Israel both as family and unique or singular nation defined not by genealogy but by taxonomic genus.

In contemporary secular usage, the term Israel denotes the State of Israel and *Israeli*, a citizen of that nation. Israel in common speech also may now refer to a particular place, namely, the State of Israel or the land of Israel. An Israeli is now a citizen of the State of Israel, living in the land of Israel, under the government of Israel; one who goes "to Israel" is going to the land or State of Israel.

Israel in Rabbinic Judaism: Every Judaism uses the word Israel to refer to the social entity that it proposes to establish or define, and all Judaisms deem their "Israels" to form a continuity of the Israel of whom the Hebrew Scriptures ("Old Testament") speak. Some deem the connection to be genealogical and fundamentally ethnic, putting forth a secular definition of their Israel. Rabbinic Judaism defines its Israel in supernatural terms, deeming the social entity to form a transcendental community, by faith. That is shown by the simple fact that a Gentile of any origin or status, slave or free, Greek or barbarian, may enter Israel on equal terms with those born into the community, becoming children of Abraham and Sarah. The children of converts are Israelites without qualification. Because that fact bears concrete and material consequences, e.g., in the right to marry any other Israelite without distinction by reason of familial origin, it follows that the Israel of rabbinic Judaism must be understood in a wholly theological framework. This Judaism knows no distinction between children of the flesh and children of the promise and therefore cannot address a merely ethnic "Israel," because for rabbinic Judaism, Israel is always and only defined by the Torah received and represented by "our sages of blessed memory" as the word of God, never by the happenstance of secular history.

In the Mishnah, ca. 200, Israel may refer to an individual Jew (always male) or to "all Jews," that is, the collectivity of Jews. The individual woman is nearly always called *bat yisrael*, daughter of (an) Israel(ite). The sages in the Mishnah did not merely assemble facts and define the social entity as a matter of description of the given, rather, they portrayed it as they wished to. They imputed to the social group, Jews, the status of a systemic entity, Israel. To others within Jewry it was not at all self-evident that "all Jews" constituted one Israel, and that that one Israel formed the direct and immediate continuation, in the here and now, of the Israel of holy writ and revelation.

Two metaphors, rarely present and scarcely explored in the Mishnah, came to prominence in the Talmuds and formed the definition of Israel in Judaism to this day. These were, first, the view of Israel as a family, the children and heirs of the man, Israel; second, the conception of Israel as sui generis. While Israel in the first phase of the formation of Judaism perpetually finds definition in relation to its opposite, Israel in the second phase constituted an intransitive entity, defined in its own terms and not solely or mainly in relation to other, comparable entities. The enormous investment in the conception of Israel as sui generis makes that point blatantly. But Israel as family bears that same trait of autonomy and self-evident definition.

By claiming that Israel constituted "Israel after the flesh," the actual, living, present family of Abraham and Sarah, Isaac and Rebekah, Jacob and Leah and Rachel, the sages met head-on the Christian claim that there was—or could ever be—some other Israel, of a lineage not defined by the family connection at all, and that the existing Jews no longer constituted Israel. By representing Israel as sui generis, the sages moreover focused upon the systemic teleology, with its definition of salvation, in response to the Christian claim that salvation is not of Israel but of the church, now enthroned in this world as in heaven. The sage, model for Israel, in the model of Moses, our rabbi, represented on earth the Torah that had come from heaven. The sage embodied what Israel was and would be.

The theory of Israel as a society made up of persons who because they constituted a family stood in a clear relationship of obligation and responsibility to one another corresponded to what people much later would call the social contract, a kind of compact that in palpable ways told families and households how in the aggregate they formed something larger and tangible. The web of interaction spun out of concrete interchange now was formed not of the gossamer thread of abstraction and theory but by the tough hemp of family ties. Israel formed a society because Israel was compared to an extended family. That, sum and substance, supplied to the Jews in their households (themselves a made-up category that, in the end, transformed the relationship of the nuclear family into an abstraction capable of holding together quite unrelated persons) an account of the tie from household to household, from village to village, encompassing ultimately "all Israel."

Israelite religion, the religion of ancient Israel of the second and first millennia B.C. as distinguished from the new religion, Judaism, which developed in the Late Antique period (first century).

There are two main sources for the religion of Israel, archaeology and the Hebrew Bible, which cannot be reconciled. Much of the scholarly debate of the 1980s and 1990s has focused on this tension, with the result that a leading formulation speaks of three religions of Israel: the archaeological, the textual, and the one created by modern scholarship in its attempts to synthesize the first two.

Archaeologically, the religion of Israel appears to be a typical Canaanite religion with a variety of deities, sacred places, and ritual functionaries. Sacred kingship and its patronage of civic religion expressed primarily in the practice of sacrifice are most characteristic.

Within the Hebrew Bible, largely composed or edited after the cessation of native kingship (ca. 565 B.C.), these values are displaced. There is a tendency toward a singular deity, a singular temple, and a negative evaluation of sacred kingship. *See also* Canaanite religion; Judaism; Samaritans.

Ithna Ashari Shia (ith'na a'sha-ree shee'uh; Arab., lit., "twelvers," i.e., followers of the twelve *Imams*), a Muslim group also known as *Imamiyya*, the largest group within Shia Islam. In contrast to the larger Sunni branch of Islam, the Shiites hold that the leadership (Imamate) of the Muslim community descended from the family of the Prophet Muhammad (d. 632). The Ithna Ashari Shia, as their name implies, hold that twelve Imams existed on earth. Believing in the necessity and infallibility of the office of Imam, the Shiites regard the Imam as the only person in the community with the authority to interpret religion. During the absence of the Imam, as has been the case since the last (twelfth) Imam, al-Mahdi, went into occultation (874), the Shiites are guided by their scholars, known as *mujtahids* or *ayatollahs*. These scholars are regarded as the Hidden Imam's spokesmen, acting on his behalf and guiding the Shiites in religious, social, and political matters.

The Twelvers developed their own interpretation of religious law, which they adhere to in their religious observances. In addition, the Twelvers express their piety in the annual commemoration of the wrongs committed against the household of the Prophet, especially the murder of their third Imam, al-Husayn, in 680 at Karbala and through pilgrimages to the tombs of their Imams, who were all believed to have suffered martyrdom at the hands of oppressive Sunnite rulers.

The Twelvers' minority status and frequent persecution required them to conceal their true beliefs in order not to arouse the animosity of other Muslims. This was the key to their survival until Twelver Shiism became established as a state religion by the Safavid dynasty of Iran in the sixteenth century. *See also* Shia.

Ito Jinsai (ee-toh jin-sah-ee; 1627–1705), Confucian scholar of the Japanese Ancient Learning school (Kogaku). He concentrated on the original meaning of the classics and emphasized humaneness (*jin*), loyalty (*chu*), and faithfulness (*shin*). *See also* Japan, Confucianism in; Kogaku.

iwakura (ee-wah-k*oo*-rah; Jap., "rock seat"), a stone serving as a temporary "seat" for a deity in some Shinto shrines; it is often the main object of worship. *See also* shrine.

iwasaka (ee-wah-sah-kah; Jap., "rock boundary"), the enclosure marking off the precincts of a Shinto shrine. In ancient times the *iwasaka* probably defined a sacred place without a building. *See also* shrine.

Izanagi and Izanami (ee-zah-nah-gee, ee-zah-nah-mee; Jap., "he who invites," "she who is invited"), the primordial parents of Shinto mythology. The "invitation" is to the sexual creation of the cosmos, beginning with the Japanese islands and including many other deities. Izanami's death in giving birth to the *kami* (divinity, divine presence) of fire makes death a part of life and her the goddess of the land of the dead. *See also* cosmology; Japanese folklore; Japanese folk religion; Japanese myth.

Izanami. *See* Izanagi and Izanami.

Izumo Shrine (ee-z*oo*-moh), one of the oldest Shinto shrines. Located on the southwestern coast of Honshu Island, it has been an important rival Shinto center to the Ise Shrine throughout Japanese history. *See also* Ise Shrine.

A B C D E F

G H J K L

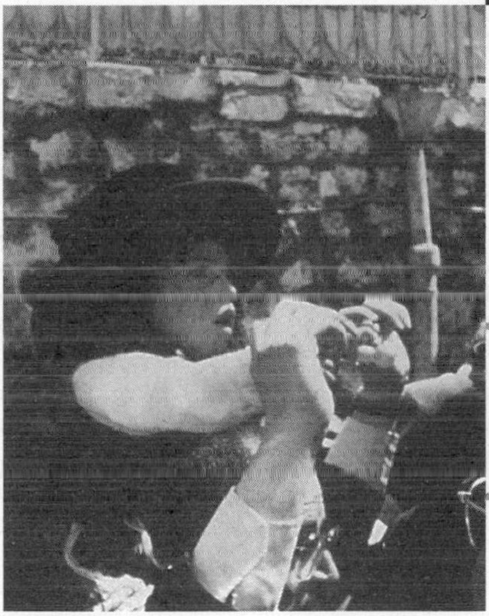

O P Q

T U V

W X Y & Z

Jacob-Israel, in the Hebrew Bible, one of the three patriarchs, father of the twelve tribes of Israel.

Jacob's Ladder, in the Hebrew Bible, the dream of the patriarch Jacob at Bethel of a ladder stretching from heaven to earth with angels "ascending and descending" (Genesis 28:10–22). *See also* Bethel.

jade, a precious mineral (nephrite) shaded dark green to translucent white traditionally honored in Chinese lore for its beauty and its religious, philosophical, and sexual connotations. Jade was placed in the mouths of the dead in ancient times and was carved for other ritual and decorative uses.

Jagannatha (juh-guh-nah'tuh; Skt., "Lord of the World"), in Hinduism, presiding deity of Puri (Orissa), India, a form of Krishna/Vishnu for Vaishnavas, of Kali for Shaktas, and of Bhairava for Shaivas; he is also Vishnu's Buddha avatar. His processional chariot yields the English term *juggernaut. See also* avatar; Balarama; Kali; Vishnu.

jaguar (South American religions), large New World feline appearing frequently in Amazonian mythology as the enemy to be overcome by twin culture heroes. Although jaguars are presented as the ancient enemies of human beings, their power to change form and to cross boundaries is appropriated by ancestral shamans. Because jaguars are both black and sun-colored, they are associated with both night and day. Their powerful voices recall thunder. Because they exist over a wide range of altitudes and are equally at home in water, land, and trees, jaguars are imagined to be masters at navigating boundaries. Jaguars (along with anacondas) are the animals that appear most frequently in visions as the spirit helpers of Amazonian shamans.

Ecuadorian Canelos and Napo Quichua children who are selected to become shamans are fed a small fruit called *puma muyu,* which will allow them to change into jaguar form at will when they become adults. After young men have killed jaguars or acquired jaguar spirit helpers, the jaguar becomes an important part of their identity. Red face paint made from annatto seeds may be applied in jaguar patterns, and jaguar teeth or claws may be worn in necklaces that attribute jaguar characteristics to the wearer. Jaguar images occur frequently on pre-Columbian ceramics from Chavin to the Inca period, from the tenth century B.C. to the fifteenth century A.D. *See also* shaman; shape shifting; South American religions, traditional.

Jahiliyya (jah'hil'lee'yah; Arab.), the period before Islam. Often translated as "Time of Ignorance," Jahiliyya is better described as the period of uncivilized barbarism before knowledge of God's requirements and guidance brought civilization, proper behavior, and peace (lit., *Islam*) to the world. The Jahiliyya is sometimes divided into the period from Adam to Ibrahim (Abraham), and a second period from Isa (Jesus) to Muhammad, the Seal of the Prophets.

Jainism (jī'niz-em; Skt. *jainas,* "followers of, or children of, the victor [*jina*]"), an Indian religion probably founded by Vardhamana Mahavira in the sixth century B.C.

According to Jain tradition, its teachings extend back into the prehistory of this cosmic age, through a series of twenty-four Tirthankaras ("makers of the river crossing"), whose lifetimes collectively stretch over a period of nearly nine million years. Contemporary scholarship offers a different picture, arguing that, as with its contemporary, Buddhism, Jainism emerged out of Brahmanic Hinduism. Accepting the probable historicity of the last two Tirthankaras, Mahavira, the twenty-fourth in the chain, appears to have been a sixth-century northeastern Indian religious leader who developed the teaching of his predecessor, Parshva (fl. ninth century B.C.).

History: Little can be recovered of the early history of Jainism. By the first century A.D., the community had split into two main groups and these remain dominant throughout Jain history, the Digambara (lit., "clad [only] in the four directions," i.e., nude) in southern India and the Shvetambara ("white clad") in western India, signifying a dispute as to whether nudity was a requirement of the ascetic life or whether the wearing of a single garment was a sufficient sign of nonattachment to the body. Each group disputes the legitimacy of the other and the status of each other's canonical texts. In subsequent centuries, a number of sectarian or reformist groups have developed, especially within the Shvetambara. One set of groups seeks to restore ascetic ideals, in particular that of mendicant monks as opposed to temple-dwelling monks, such as the eleventh-century Kharatara Gaccha ("fierce sect"), the thirteenth-century Tapa ("ascetic"), and the eighteenth-century Terapenthins (meaning uncertain). The other set, focusing on ritual reforms, especially the rejection of images, include the fifteenth-century Sthanakavasi ("those who dwell in preaching halls") and the seventeenth-century Adhyamatma ("innermost soul").

Jainism has never left India, except through emigration. In 1994, there were 3,927,000 Jains, nearly 99 percent of whom live in India, largely in the states of Mysore and Gujarat.

Teachings: The Shvetambara and Digambara preserve different versions of the Jain canon (*agama*, "tradition"). The Shvetambara canon, collected in the sixth century, comprises forty-five books largely in Prakrit, a Middle Indo-Aryan language that diverged from Sanskrit. The oldest of these, eleven *Angas* (limbs), purport to preserve the teachings of Mahavira. The Digambara canon collects a group of sectarian writings composed, according to tradition, centuries after Mahavira's death by Digambara sages. The most important of these are the Prakrit *Karmaprabhrita* (chapters on *karma*) and the *Kasayaprabhrita* (chapters on the passions), traditionally dated to the second or third centuries.

Jain mythology and cosmology are largely shared with Hinduism. There are four classes of divine beings inhabiting a three-layered cosmos. However, superior to the gods are the Tirthankaras and other liberated souls (*siddhas*), who are collectively known as the Lords of Gods (*devadhidevas*) and provide models for salvation.

While recognizing the common Indian karmic law of the meritorious and demeritorious consequences of actions, Jainism conceives of karma as a substance rather than a process. The individual's soul-substance (*jiva*) is mingled with karmic substance to produce a person. All actions, good and evil, past and present, produce karmic particles that weigh one down and bind one to endless rebirth. Liberation (*moksha*) consists in freedom from rebirth by halting the influx of new karmic particles and by eliminating those acquired from the past through disciplines of knowledge and ascetic practices. The most famous teaching of Jainism, noninjury (*ahimsa*) to every living being, is based on the notion that all forms of life possess jiva. As extended in Jainism, this not only means restraint from physically injuring any sort of animal, but also the rejection of psychological and intellectual violence, as evidenced in the ethic to respect both sides of any argument.

Community: The Jain community is focused on forms of monastic life supported by laypersons. Monks (and in some sects, nuns) take five vows (to abstain from violence, deceit, theft, attachment to material things, and sex) and practice the Three Jewels (*ratna-traya*) of right belief, right knowledge, and right conduct. In principle, monks adopt a wandering and mendicant way of life, retiring to monastic houses or temples only during the rainy season to avoid injuring small creatures that swarm in mud.

Laypersons accept a modified form of the five monastic vows, adding several other obligations, especially almsgiving. Householders regularly practice meditation, fast twice a lunar month, and publicly confess their faults.

Architecture: Constructed on the Hindu model, Jain temples are distinctive in two respects: the innermost shrine houses an image of a Tirthankara, rather than a deity; and the temple is marked with the central Jain symbol, a swastika surmounted by three dots and a half-moon. In traditional interpretation, the four arms of the swastika represent four levels of life (those born in one of the seven Jain hells; those born as plants, insects, or animals; those born as humans; and those born as divine beings). The three dots symbolize the Three Jewels, the half-moon, and liberation. *See also* ahimsa.

jajmani system (jahj-mahn'ee; Skt.), that aspect of the Indic caste system that entails hereditary division of labor, professional and religious specialization, and interdependence among discrete castes. A *jajman*, or "patron," is one who has a certain domestic service (ritual or mundane) performed by a member of another caste that specializes in that particular service. *See also* caste.

Jamaa movement (jah-mah'; "family"), a movement within the Catholic Church of Katanga, Belgian Congo (now Zaire), beginning in the 1940s but independent by 1953, that established fellowships modeled on relations within the family. The movement was influenced by the European Catholic priest Placide Tempels (1926–77), whose work in the region led him to emphasize the idea of community-based spirituality. *See also* Africa, new religions in.

James, in the New Testament, one of the original apostles. His title, "brother of the Lord," has been troublesome to those Christians who emphasize the perpetual virginity of Mary; they argue that *brother* is a term for cousin or that he is Joseph's son from a previous marriage.

jami. *See* mosque.

Janam-sakhi (juh'nuhm-sah'ki; Punjabi, "birth-testimony"), a traditional account of the life of Nanak (1469–1539), first Guru of the Sikhs. Janam-sakhis first appear in the mid-seventeenth century and are hagiographical narratives formed by stringing together anecdotes about Nanak. *See also* Nanak; Sikhism.

Jansen, Cornelius Otto (1585–1638), Belgian Catholic theologian whose work *Augustinus* (1640) gave rise to the movement called Jansenism. *See also* Jansenism.

Jansenism, a Catholic reform movement identified with the writings of the Belgian theologian Cornelius Otto Jansen (1585–1638), characterized by rigid Augustinianism and moral rigor. Centered in France, Belgium, Holland, and Italy in the seventeenth and eighteenth centuries, the movement sought to preserve a traditional interpretation of grace and free will by accenting the power of concupiscence over free will, affirming the necessity and irresistibility of grace, teaching the absolute gratuity of predestination, and claiming that Christ died only for the elect. Five Jansenist propositions were condemned by Pope Innocent X in 1653. Clement XI renewed the condemnation with the bull *Unigenitus* (1713). Aspects of Jansenism survived into the nineteenth century.

Janus (yah'noos), ancient Roman god of gates and doors, hence the god invoked at the beginning of any undertaking.

japam (juh'puhm; Skt., "muttering"), among Hindus the repetition of a deity's name or a mantra as a spiritual exercise. *See also* mantra.

Japan, Buddhism in. *See* chingo-kokka; danka system; engi; hongaku; Hosso school; Japanese religion; Jishu; Jodo Shinshu; Jodoshu; Kamakura schools; Kegon school; mujo; Nara schools; nembutsu; Nichiren; Obaku Zen; relics; Rinzai; Risshu; Sanron school; Shingon-shu; Soga clan; Soniryo; Soto school; temple; Tendai school; ujidera; warrior monks; Yuzu-nembutsu school.

Japan, Christianity in. *See* kakure kirishitan; Kyodan, Nihon Kirisuto; Mu-kyokai; Uchimura Kanzo.

Japan, Confucianism in. Confucianism in Japan before the Meiji Restoration (1867) falls into three major periods: its introduction, its medieval development, and its early modern phase. The first period, from the fifth to the thirteenth centuries, is the era of the Han and T'ang commentators (*Kanto kunko jidai*). The second period, from the thirteenth to the seventeenth centuries, is the era of Sung learning (*Sogaku jidai*). The third period, from the seventeenth to the middle of the nineteenth century, when various schools flourished, is the era of the learning of Chinese scholars (*Kangakusha jidai*).

The introduction of Confucianism into Japan began in the fifth century with the arrival of Korean scholars. With the gradual centralization of the Japanese state, Confucian philosophy came to play a significant role, as in the *Seventeen Article Constitution* of Prince Shotoku Taishi (574–622), in which Confucian moral values of harmony, order, and consensus are evident. The Confucianism of the Nara period (710–794) included the adoption of a bureaucratic form of government based on T'ang models, the use of divination as derived from Han Confucianism, emphasis on Confucian kinship values, the importance of historical writings as a means of legitimizing authority, and the development of a system of state-sponsored education.

During the Kamakura (1185–1333) and Muromachi (1333–1568) periods there was a shift in emphasis from the role of Confucianism in the court and in government to its adoption as a mode of scholarly learning within the Zen Buddhist monasteries. However, many monks acted as advisers to government officials and, thus, Confucianism continued to play a political role for the Hojo regents and the Ashikaga *shoguns.* Contemporaneously, Neo-Confucianism was introduced by many of the Zen monks in the Gozan temples, some of whom had traveled to China and brought back texts.

In the Tokugawa period (1603–1867), various forms of Confucian thought emerged as significant. These included Chu Hsi Neo-Confucianism (Shushigaku), Wang Yang-ming Neo-Confucianism (Yomeigaku), and the School of Ancient Learning (Kogaku). This period is marked by the transition from the medieval role of the samurai as warriors to their early modern role as scholars, teachers, government advisers, and politicians. Confucianism moved out of the Zen monasteries into the secular arena. Tokugawa Confucianism was more than simply Shogunate orthodoxy or an interest of Zen monks; it was a dynamic plethora of schools, ideas, and individuals. Tokugawa Confucian scholars stressed the importance of education and self-cultivation. Through their teaching and writing they helped to spread Confucian ideas among many classes of people.

The amalgamation of Confucian political loyalism and Shinto nativism eventually led to the Meiji Restoration. Confucianism has had a significant impact on Japanese society, culture, and education down to the present. Mutual reciprocity, respect, and responsibilities in human relations; harmony, consensus, and loyalty in cultural values; and humanistic learning for practical improvement and moral cultivation are key values bequeathed by Confucianism in Japan. *See also* Confucianism; Kogaku; Meiji Restoration; Neo-Confucianism; Shushigaku.

Japan, new religions in.

New religions (*shin shukyo*) constitute the most prominent religious phenomenon in contemporary Japan. Since the mid-nineteenth century many hundreds of new religions, from small local cults centered around one shamanic leader to vast national organizations counting millions of members, huge religious centers, and their own newspapers and publishing services, have emerged in Japan, particularly among the country's growing urban population. Though no definitive figures exist, it is reliably considered that some 20 percent of the Japanese population may be affiliated with one of the new religions.

Members of the Shingon-derived new religion Gedatsukai, performing *ohyakudo* ("hundredfold") walking penance at their "Sacred Land" (Goreichi). Gedatsukai, headquartered in Tokyo, was founded in 1929 and has about three hundred thousand adherents.

The new religions, because of their sheer numbers, represent such a wide and diverse phenomenon that any attempt at classification and categorization necessarily runs into difficulties. Not all new religions are alike, and even those sharing many common characteristics may differ quite strikingly in other respects. However, despite this, there are some generalizations to be made that are essential to any overall understanding of the nature of these new religions.

In particular, there are two interrelated areas of common ground. First, there is the setting within which they have arisen and exist, i.e., the social situation that has conditioned their formation and growth in the context of Japanese religion and society. Second, there are their internal characteristics, in terms of religious content, the general themes they espouse, and what they provide for their members. Although the internal content may vary, there are, amidst the diversities, a number of common themes.

Definitions and Settings: The exact definition of a new religion in Japan is problematic: some religions that are classified as new religions by outside observers may trace their origins to earlier religious traditions and, hence, claim that they are not "new" at all. Adherents of Soka Gakkai, regarded as the largest new religion in Japan, consider themselves to be part of the Nichiren Buddhist tradition that developed about seven hundred years ago, and Tenrikyo, another of the largest new religions, originated more than 150 years ago.

In reality, the term *new religions* stands in contrast with established (*kisei*) religions, for it cannot be fully understood without an awareness of the nature of the established mainstream religions in Japan, Shinto and Buddhism. Each of these has had an accepted place in the social system, connected to the household (*ie*), itself probably the most important institution in Japanese society. Individuals are related to the outside world, and receive their religious affiliation, through the ie, which has traditionally been affiliated with both the local Shinto shrine and the Buddhist temple.

Such affiliation has been largely institutionalized and based on social situation rather than on individual faith. The established religions are, however, perceived to be structuralized, hierarchical, bureaucratic, lacking in spiritual dynamism, and out of touch with the lives and spiritual needs of ordinary people. Identified with the sources of power, patronage, and the status quo in Japan, they have not been forces for change and for the amelioration of the circumstances of ordinary lives.

The appeal of the new religions needs to be seen against this background, for they represent a positive, confident, and continuing attempt to provide an individually based faith of relevance to people in everyday life. Belonging is thus—in origin at least—a matter of conversion and of personal faith rather than of social circumstance. As new religions have grown in size and age, however, they have developed many of the characteristics associated with established religions, and, as a result, the older new religions have lost members to newer, less structured, and more dynamic groups.

Origins and Growth: The new religions have expanded, particularly at times of social unease, and largely amongst Japan's growing urban population. Over the last century or so, much of

Japan's population has moved from rural areas, with their strong frameworks of community and belonging, to urban areas that often lacked these qualities. The new religions have been especially active in providing a sense of belonging and community to people in such circumstances.

The period in the mid-nineteenth century when Japan's feudal society began to fall apart, and when the country was opened up to the outside world, was a time when new religions such as Tenrikyo, Kurozumikyo, and Konkokyo came to the fore, originally out of a Shinto milieu in rural Japan. The period of economic depression following the post–World War I industrial expansion and urbanization was another time of social tension in which new religions such as Reiyukai and Soka Gakkai made their appearance, especially gaining converts among the urban poor of Tokyo and other major cities. In the years after Japan's war defeat in 1945 and during the tumultuous period of the American occupation, new religions grew extensively. Large numbers of new religions appeared each year, and while some quickly disappeared again, many, such as Soka Gakkai and Rissho Koseikai, grew immensely.

Though their pace of growth tended to ease off after the late 1950s, new religions have continued to grow until the present. In the years since the mid-1970s, a period during which the processes of internationalization coupled with growing fears about the future on environmental grounds have caused growing unease in Japan, a wave of new religions, including Mahikari, Agonshu, Shinnyoen, and Kofuku no Kagaku, termed by Japanese analysts *new* new religions (*shin shin shukyo*) has rapidly gained a large following among the educated young and those uneasy at the cultural erosion caused by the rapid Westernization of Japanese society.

Types and Orientations: Rather than presenting new ideas as such, new religions tend to reinterpret and reformulate extant religious ideas within a format relevant to people in contemporary society. The Japanese new religions are, on the whole, eclectic and assimilative in their sources and influences, drawing themes from Shinto, Buddhism, the Japanese folk tradition, and, increasingly, from Christianity.

It is perhaps best to define their orientations by where they place their sources of inspiration, with the folk and Shintoesque new religions usually forming their teachings around revelations from creator deities who, once aloof, are now returning to speak through a chosen prophet and leader in order to save the world from its present morass and to lead humans to the realization of a happy life. Such religions, including Tenrikyo, Konkokyo, and Oomoto, thus tend to focus very much on their inspirational founders as mediums of the divine and to regard their writings as revelatory scriptures.

These religions often have extensive galaxies of spirits and deities of an eclectic variety. It is not uncommon, especially among the more recent new religions, for Buddhist, Shinto, and folk deities to mingle alongside figures imported

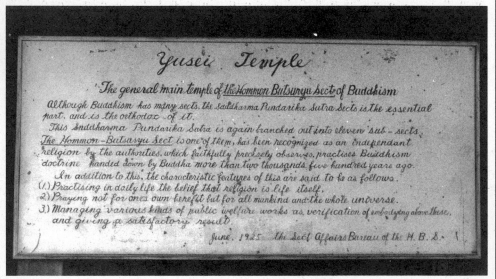

A sign from the Hommon Butsuryu sect of Buddhism. This lay movement was developed in Kyoto in 1857 and currently has over five hundred thousand adherents. On the sign are listed the teachings, which focus on the *Lotus Sutra,* and major features of the sect.

from Christianity and elsewhere. Jesus, for example, appears alongside folk, Shinto, and Buddhist figures in the cosmologies of Oomoto, Mahikari, and several other groups, while Kofuku no Kagaku (founded in 1986) incorporates Jesus, Buddha, Moses, and Confucius, along with the Shinto deity Amaterasu, a previously unknown deity El Ranty, the Greek god Zeus, the Persian Zoroaster, and a variety of guiding spirits, including Isaac Newton, into its pantheon.

New religions related to Buddhism generally are less focused on spiritual revelations than on locating their sources of inspiration in a particular text from the Buddhist canon. Their roots, however, are in the religious inspiration of the founder, who has discovered such new meanings in the text and presented it as a source of religious truth and power. Reiyukai, for instance, established in Tokyo in the 1920s by Kubo Kakutaro and based on his studies of the *Lotus Sutra*, regards that text as its core teaching and provides its followers with an abbreviated version of the sutra for use in rituals and to be recited as an act of spiritual practice.

Other religions with a Buddhist orientation include Agonshu, which uses the early Buddhist *Agama Sutras* as key texts in its ritual performances, and Shinnyoen, which focuses on the *Nirvana Sutra*. It is usually the case in the Buddhist new religions that, although members may study the meanings of the text, the major focus is on the ritual powers and efficacy that are believed to be contained within it. Recitation takes precedence over interpretation.

Reordering the World—the Personal Level: No matter what external form they take, the roots of the new religions, in terms of teaching and practice, may be traced to premodern Japanese religious cosmologies, which are reaffirmed as valid in the modern world. Such reaffirmations point to a latent antimodernism that often has strongly Japanocentric tendencies, asserting Japan's role as a special nation with a spiritual message for the rest of the world. Among the themes constantly reiterated in the new religions are the importance of ancestral and other spirits of the dead, the practice of regarding misfortunes as spiritual events requiring religious and ritual solutions, and the assertion that through techniques learned in the new religion and through the grace of its leaders and deities, people can find liberation, solve their problems, and have a happy life. The new religions, thus, have a this-worldly, positive, and practically ameliorative orientation, often asserting that the aim of existence is to live a good, happy, and positive life on this earth.

New religions tend to exist within a dynamic of problem interpretation and solution on the spiritual level that asserts premodern views of causation over more modern ones. Thus, problems on the material plane have roots in spiritual causes: illness may, for instance, be interpreted as occurring because of a failure to pay homage correctly to the spirits of one's ancestors (in Agonshu), because of malevolent possession by an animal spirit (in Mahikari), or because one's behavior has led to karmic accretions of spiritual dust on the mind, which, in turn, has caused physical upset (in Tenrikyo). Many new religions may use all of these themes together.

Because the problem is located in the spiritual, so must be the answer. This is not to suggest that new religions deny medical healing, but that they consider that this alone is an insufficient answer to the problem, one that treats only the physical symptoms and does not get to the root of the problem. In the Mahikari perspective, for instance, treating the germ is not enough: one needs to placate the unhappy ancestor or exorcize the evil spirit that caused one to ingest it in the first place. Often, self-reflection, repentance, and the recognition of one's own faults are promoted as basic steps in the solution of problems.

New religions thus reaffirm traditional religious orientations, telling their members to take part in such practices as venerating their ancestors, while simultaneously offering new avenues of practice and technique through which to eradicate problems and develop good fortune. Because such practices are generally straightforward and accessible, this has placed control for the personal solution of problems within the scope of the ordinary person.

Most new religions augment their practices with counseling services, whereby members may seek further advice about life-style and other problems from experienced members and officials of the religion. Sometimes, as in Rissho Koseikai, this is done in group discussions, with members sharing their problems (and also their positive experiences) and talking them through with others. Besides helping strengthen the personal faith of the members, this approach gives members a sense of self-worth and makes them feel actively involved in dealing with their lives and those of others.

The focus on practice points to the pragmatic nature of most new religions: the route to conversion usually lies in trying out the practices, rather than through the route of studying doctrinal issues. This, in turn, makes most new

Members of Gedatsukai, a Shingon-derived new religion founded in Japan in 1929; while visiting the religion's "Sacred Land" (Goreichi) they participate in Gedatsukai's distinctive rite of pouring sweet tea over a sacred pillar, a means of memorializing the souls of all dead people.

Such solutions generally center on the use of spiritual techniques for eradicating social problems that so far have been inadequately handled by political and other media and that are made possible due to the new truths articulated by the inspirational leader. At times, world salvation is associated with the rise of a new age and world civilization centered on Japan. This theme, which is found in Kofuku no Kagaku, Mahikari, and many other movements, has become increasingly prevalent in recent years.

Those new religions that preach doctrines of world renewal have always been attractive to disadvantaged members of society who see the new religions as vehicles of hope and salvation in a world that does not offer them much on a material level. Tenrikyo and Oomoto first grew among the rural poor of nineteenth-century Japan, while Reiyukai gained its footing among the urban underclasses in Tokyo in the 1930s. Recent sociological research has shown, however, that the new religions increasingly have appealed to educated and prosperous sections of Japanese society. Education and economic success have, if anything, stimulated the numbers who join these new religions. They present an alternative approach to personal and individual salvation and liberation, as well as appearing to offer their members a means of coping with and overcoming the strains, stresses, and unease of modern society and social change.

The concept of world salvation and the fact that new religions appear as alternatives to the established structures does not mean that these religions are radical or that they seek social change. Because they place their solutions in the spiritual realm, the Japanese new religions are generally rather conservative, socially and politically, and few have worked toward political or economic reform. Indeed, many appear to positively affirm the status quo in social relations: in Reiyukai, for instance, women are enjoined to be humble and to accept their subservient position. Indeed, in many new religions, misfortunes may be attributed to the fact that the normal codes of social relationship (which, in traditional Japanese terms, affirm the existence of hierarchies, of the prevalence of seniority, and of male over female) have been breached.

religions readily accessible, bringing in large numbers of people eager to try out new techniques in the hope of attaining some benefit. A high turnover may result, as some people try a technique and fail to see any benefits.

Reordering the World—World Salvation: Paralleling the theme of self-transformation, many of the new religions have, on the wider level, offered the promise and prediction of *yo naoshi* (reordering the present world and building it anew). This message is often prophetic and millennial, preaching a coming collapse of the existing order while offering salvation from this potential destruction. Implicit in this view is an antimodernism that suggests modern society has lost its way and requires spiritual salvation.

These messages of impending collapse have grown in strength as the millennium approaches, and as gloomy prognoses about environmental problems appear. However, the new religions are not pessimistic as such: rather, their prophecies of doom are underpinned with optimistic messages that the new religions possess solutions to the present human dilemma.

Founders and Charismatic Powers: A predominant theme in many new religions, often crucial to promises of world renewal and personal liberation, is that of a charismatic founding figure, who in life is the central source of teaching and practice and is regarded as an *ikigami* (living deity). After death, too, the founder may still be revered: Tenrikyo, for instance, considers that its founder, Nakayama Miki (1798–1887), did not die but ascended in order to guard spiritually over the religion from above. Often, too, the tomb or memorial of the founder becomes a central focus of unity, worship, and pilgrimage.

Such figures fit into the Japanese religious historical tradition of powerful ascetic and shamanic figures who, through a process of austerities and revelation, acquire powers to heal, to divine, to offer spiritual counseling, and to alleviate the sufferings of others. Many of these figures are female: the shamanic path has always offered an avenue of religious self-expression denied through the male-dominated hierarchies of the established religions in Japan, and, consequently, one finds that many of the founders (and indeed, perhaps a majority of the followers) of new religions have been women.

Such founder figures serve, in the eyes of their followers, as living examples of and metaphors for the possibilities of personal and global transformation. In the folk and Shinto traditions, the founders usually experience revelations from a new or previously unseen deity who gives them a new message and mission for this world. In the Buddhist tradition, it is more often that the founders acquire new insights into Buddhist texts. In either case, the founder becomes a figure of power and transcendence, the spiritual authority and source of the religion with the power to spiritually intervene on behalf of their followers and relieve them of their problems.

A common thread that runs through the lives of many founders is that of personal weakness and failure that is transformed via spiritual practice and revelation into spiritual power. As symbols of weakness who have overcome their own weaknesses, the founders thus exemplify an innate message of the possibilities of self-transformation and salvation to their followers. Thus, Kiriyama, founder of Agonshu, often refers to his own background of failure when talking of the potentiality of self-transformation and urging his followers to overcome their problems and attain their wishes.

Charismatic leadership frequently creates dynasties in the new religions, but the inheritance of charisma may turn out to be problematic, with disputes sometimes breaking out between the family and close disciples.

Lay Orientations and Proselytism: Just as the new religions give their followers a sense of personal control of events, so, too, do these religions give their followers special responsibility for the dissemination and growth of the faith. Surveys have shown that the majority of recruits to new religions have been converted by close friends or family members. Recruiting others enhances members' self-esteem and enables them to feel

they are a valuable part of the religion, actively contributing to its spiritual dynamism.

The ability to spread the word with enthusiasm and to mobilize the lay membership has been a core factor in the growth of new religions, enabling them to reach wide audiences. The language and techniques that they have espoused have further enhanced this process, for the new religions generally express their teachings not in the complex terminology of Buddhist texts or the obscure language of Shinto prayers, but in simple, accessible modern Japanese in pamphlets, broadsheets, books, and, more recently, in films, television advertisements, and videos.

Oomoto, one of the earliest new religions to utilize mass communications techniques, expanded rapidly in the early decades of the twentieth century because its members went out on street corners preaching their faith and because Deguchi Onisaburo, Deguchi Nao's charismatic son-in-law, organized newspapers and broadsheets disseminating Oomoto's teaching. Almost all new religions proselytize vigorously, assimilating all manner of communication techniques. This is especially true of the "new" new religions: Agonshu, for example, uses a telecommunications satellite to simultaneously link its religious centers across Japan, and produces videos explaining its teachings and activities.

Conclusions: The new religions present, through their modern techniques of communications, a new face on many premodern cosmological themes. Their premodern folk themes, such as the prominent role afforded to the ancestors (themselves symbols of tradition and continuity), help to reinforce and revalidate Japanese cultural themes of identity for people troubled by the fast-changing pace and Westernizing trends of contemporary Japanese society. This innate antimodernism is not obscurantist, however, for the modern ambiance of these new religions, their espousal of modern techniques of communications, as well as their futuristic visions of world salvation, serve to assure their members that they are not just in touch with contemporary reality but are, in fact, a means of asserting control over and guiding it in social contexts, just as they are in personal ones.

Because they are able, thus, to provide a viable framework through which to deal with problems on personal and social levels and to offer avenues through which personal and social amelioration and salvation may be accessed, Japanese new religions have continually attracted members in Japan. The continuing emergence of further new religious groups, as with the "new" new religions in recent years, suggests that this process is a continuing one and that the new religions will continue to grow.

Postscript—Japanese New Religions Abroad: Expansion abroad also has begun to some extent. The earliest moves made were among Japanese immigrant communities in Brazil, Hawaii, and the continental United States, but gradually the new religions have moved further afield to non-Japanese audiences. The optimistic and self-affirming Buddhism of Soka Gakkai, for instance, has gathered upwards of one hundred thousand followers in the United States and a smaller number in the United Kingdom, many of them upwardly mobile young middle-class people to whom Soka Gakkai's positive, self-affirming perspectives have an inherent appeal. Mahikari has gained a small number of followers both in the West and more prominently in the Caribbean (especially in Martinique and Guadalupe) and in West Africa, where its focuses on spirit possession, ancestors, and spiritual healing have much in common with indigenous religious traditions. Probably the majority of Japanese new religions now have some form of international profile, maintaining at least one overseas center and counting a small number of non-Japanese followers in their midst. This again is an area of further potential growth, although because of their close roots in the Japanese tradition and because their origins are connected to Japanese circumstances, it is hard to envisage these new religions becoming major or mass movements outside of Japan. *See also* Agonshu; Aum Shinrikyo; Konkokyo; Kurozumikyo; Mahikari; Nichiren Shoshu; Omotokyo; Oomoto; PL Kyodan; Reiyukai; Rissho Koseikai; Shinnyoen; Shushigaku; Soka Gakkai; Tenrikyo.

Japan, Taoism in. Taoism has been a religious influence in Japan, but not a distinct, institutional tradition. Beliefs about Taoist immortals and paradises influenced early Japanese mythology and folklore, and Taoist magic and medicines can be discerned in the earliest Japanese records. Taoist magic has endured in Shinto and in the mountain asceticism of Shugendo. Other Taoist influences have come from the *on'yoji* (*yin-yang* masters), who practiced magic and divination originally at the court and later in their own guilds. The practice of Koshin-machi, a popular all-night vigil for long life, is based on Taoist belief. *See also* Japanese folk religion; Japanese religions (festal cycle); Shinto; Shugendo; Taoism; yin and yang.

Japanese folklore. The study of Japanese folklore properly began with the work of Yanagita Kunio (1875–1962). Among the few translations

of his extensive publications are a fragment of his *Folklore Dictionary* and several collections of folktales. Two notable inheritors of his legacy have been Hori Ichiro, influenced by Mircea Eliade, who concentrated on folk religion; and Seki Keigo, who, influenced by Antti Aarne and Stith Thompson, systematized the study of Japanese folktales. Folktale motifs, many shared with China and some with Europe and India (particularly the divine-spouse type), have been identified as important elements in Japanese mythology as well as in subsequent literature. *See also* Japanese folk religion.

Japanese folklore, insects in. *See* insects (Japan).

Japanese folk religion. Folk religion in Japan, as elsewhere, is characterized by a high degree of local diversity and a lack of any institutional organization able to transcend local boundaries. It is by definition a subordinate part of a larger system of regional, national, or international culture and organization that is recognized as official or dominant. Thus, Japanese folk religion is associated with the Shinto and Buddhist organizations with which it partly shares beliefs and practices.

Although usually thought of as a peasant phenomenon, it is made up of the habitual beliefs and observances of any people, whether urban or rural. The basic social unit of Japanese rural folk religion is the *dozoku*, or extended village, which is composed of a system of relationships among families rather than individuals. Enshrined within the dozoku is its *ujigami*, the deity who looks after the area and from whom the villagers consider themselves to be descended. In addition, one or more Buddhist temples may be present, as well as minor sacred places and shrines. These may be sacred pools or stones, or roadside shrines dedicated to Dosojin or the Bodhisattva Jizo, where only occasional obesience or offerings may be made. The larger shrine has a hereditary priest attached to it and all the members of the dozoku are expected to support it with offerings and labor. This cooperative spirit extends to the agricultural duties of planting, harvest, and maintenance of irrigation works as well as serving the *kami* (divinities, divine presences) at *matsuri* (festival) time. Although most dozoku temples are affiliated with a particular Buddhist sect, sectarian consciousness is muted. And, although Shinto and Buddhist cults have been officially separated for more than a century, in practice there is much mixing of the two systems.

Village and Family Rites: Among the collective religious rituals regularly observed are those that

Young Japanese men storm the gate guarding Toad Rock, an ancient Shinto sacred place in southern Honshu. This ritual combat between the youths and the old men holding the gate closed is part of the Kannokura fire festival held every February 6.

attend the planting, transplanting, and harvesting of the rice crops, and those addressing aspects of the midsummer rite of the dead (Obon). The agricultural rites honor *Ta no kami* (field deity) and *Yama no kami* (mountain deity); the latter looks after the local food crops during the growing season and withdraws to the mountains in winter. Obon is an important part of the Japanese system of ancestral reverence; it consists of welcoming fires leading down into the village from a mountaintop thought of as the land of the dead. The ancestors are fed and entertained and after several days sent away again. Funerals are conducted by the local Buddhist priest. Regular family rites include the ritual meal with the returned dead of Obon and the marking of the new year and Setsubun (end of winter). In many families daily rites of prayer and food-and-water offerings will be made at the two household shrines, the *kamidana* (god shelf) for the native deities and the *butsudan,* a miniature Buddhist shrine that contains the family mortuary tablets. A village might also contain several *ko,* which are voluntary groups organized to honor a particular deity, carry out specific festival obligations, or promote pilgrimages to a distant shrine or temple for its members. If *yamabushi* (mountain ascetics) are active in the area, a lay organization oversees hikes to various mountain shrines and the performance of esoteric rites there. In times past these yamabushi often arrogated to themselves Shinto priestly functions and practiced the healing arts in conjunction with *miko* (female shamans). The shaman would enter into a trance, become possessed by a kami or other spirit, and deliver an oracle that would tell the yamabushi what rite to administer to effect a cure. Shamanism still exists in the villages of Japan, and it is especially associated with crisis situations such as illness. The shamanic tendency can also be observed at the founding moments of many new religions of the nineteenth and twentieth centuries. **See also** animals and birds in Japanese religion; hijiri; Japanese folklore.

Japanese myth. Japanese mythology is found in the *Kojiki* (712) and *Nihonshoki* (720); useful variants can be found in *Kogoshui* (807). The first two texts were compiled by imperial decree, and their weaving together of previously separated traditions reflects the concerns and ideology of the court. The last puts forth fragmentary "corrections" more favorable to the Imbe clan of Shinto priests. The narrative can be divided conveniently into seven parts: (1) prelude; (2) primordial parents (Izanami and Izanagi); (3) Amaterasu and Susano o; (4) Susano o and Okuninushi; (5) descent of Ninigi; (6) Hohoderi interlude; and (7) Jimmu's expedition.

The prelude probably borrows from Taoism; it moves from the oneness of primordial chaos (undifferentiated Tao) to the division of *yin* and *yang,* followed by a stream of vaguely defined creator deities who provide genealogical distance from the point of beginning. The cosmogony is completed by the primordial parents, who sexually procreate producing the Japanese islands and the archetypes of the many natural objects and powers found there, each understood as a distinct *kami* (divinity, divine presence). Eventually the primordial mother, Izanami, dies giving birth to the fire kami. She descends to the underworld and is pursued by the grieving Izanagi, who breaks a taboo and thereby unleashes the powers of death into the world at large. This portion of the mythology has strong Polynesian affinities.

Creation is completed then by Izanagi alone, not by sexual but by ritual means when in the course of purification from the pollution of death many new kami are brought into being. Most important are Amaterasu, whose visible attribute is the sun, and Susano-o, characterized as the storm god. These two indulge in a kind of cosmic sibling rivalry that juxtaposes Amaterasu, as the feminine weaver and proponent of order, to Susano-o, the impetuous male whose undisciplined energy threatens to destroy the world. Susano-o's "sins" (*tsumi*) consist in disruption of rice cultivation and disruption and pollution of rituals, most notably the *niiname-sai* (tasting of first fruits) and a more mysterious weaving ritual. In a scenario resembling Southeast Asian myths, Amaterasu flees, concealing herself in a cave, thus plunging the world into the chaos of darkness, and Susano-o is banished from heaven. The many kami of heaven assemble and by applying many forms of magic draw the sun out of the cave and thus restore order. Decisive are the use of the mirror, ever after associated with Amaterasu, and the shamanic dance of Ame no Uzume, who is possessed (*kami-gakari*) by the goddess.

The fourth part describes Susano-o's heroic adventures on earth, where his now more controlled energy enables him to rescue a maiden from a dragon, marry, and establish a dynasty at Izumo. His descendant Okuninushi ("great land owner") becomes the active ruler of the land. This story is broken into by the descent of Ninigi (part five), the grandson of Amaterasu, who descends to earth to establish the heavenly hegemony of Amaterasu. For this to occur, Okuninushi must be subdued; he accepts subordination by being enshrined at Izumo, where he henceforth "dwells hidden," thus legitimizing this cult center. These descent motifs owe much to both Korean kingship myths and to Malay rice-god myths, while the theme of "pacification" presumably alludes to real events in the long process of political and religious unification of diverse rival clans and power centers. The ideological goals of the court, namely, to give mythic legitimization to the imperial clan's claims to sovereignty, are now nearly fulfilled. It only remains to connect these archetypal events with the time the works were written (ca. 700). The Hohoderi interlude consists of a collection of folktales loosely strung together by genealogy. Finally Jimmu, the first "earthly" emperor, fights his way to the Yamato area with much help from Amaterasu. One of his sons, Yamato-takeru ("the hero of Yamato"), dies at the hands of a vindictive local kami. *See also* Amaterasu; cosmogony; cosmology; Izanagi and Izanami; Jimmu, Emperor; kami; Kojiki; Nihonshoki; Susano-o; yin and yang.

Japanese religions (art and architecture). All the arts have played an important role in the religious life of the Japanese, with Shinto particularly influencing the literary, performing, and architectural arts, and Buddhism particularly influencing the literary and visual arts (especially iconography in sculpture and painting).

The architectural forms of Shinto and Buddhism have not only been influential, but have themselves symbolized the close relation to nature or the characteristics of Buddhist understandings of "salvation." Shinto was particularly important in contributing to the development of poetic traditions expressive of deep feelings about nature and/or the spirits of the departed, while Buddhism influenced much of the literature of the medieval period (tenth to sixteenth centuries).

The Shinto influences on early literature are particularly evident in the seventh- and eighth-century compilations of myth and legend, and in the earliest collection of poetry in Japan, the *Man'yoshu*. Subsequent to that, the Buddhist influences are most evident in literary works such as the *Nihonryoiki* (early ninth century), the poetry collections of the tenth and eleventh centuries, the Noh plays of the fifteenth century, and even many of the novels of the twentieth century.

In the visual arts the iconography of Buddhism has constituted, by itself, a very important artistic tradition expressive of the nature of the Bodhisattva and Buddha path.

The performing arts have been more influenced by Shinto, with its rich tradition of ritual music and dance (*kagura*) and its linkage to the important festival (*matsuri*) tradition in Japan in which drama, costume, and music play such an important part. The Noh drama tradition is, for example, rooted in these ritual performing arts.

Not only did these religions, in their various sectarian and historical manifestations, use the arts as direct expressions of their own ideals and practices, they also contributed to a broader understanding of artistic discipline and production as itself sacred or religious. This has often been referred to in Western scholarship as representing a "religio-aesthetic" tradition in which aesthetic or artistic experience and pursuit were seen as religious, and vice versa.

This latter attitude was born in early Shinto, nurtured by early Buddhism, influenced by incoming Chinese ideals and arts, and deepened by the Zen Buddhism of medieval Japan. Some of the new religions of Japan and individual artists in contemporary Japan have continued this tradition.

Many of these religious art forms are still alive in Japan today not only in their traditional forms but in forms adapted to contemporary ideals. *See also* dojo; kagura; Kojiki; ma; Man'yoshu; Nihonshoki; Noh drama; temple.

JAPANESE RELIGION

apanese religion includes the variety of religious traditions found in the Japanese archipelago, ranging from organized religions (Buddhist sects, State Shinto) and more diffuse systems (Confucianism, Taoism) to localized cults and popular folk practices. *Japanese religion* is often used as a coverall term to indicate the amorphous, shared elements of religious belief and practice in Japan, where the "walls" between religions tend to be porous. While Japanese religious beliefs and practices have been influenced by the cultures of Korea and China since the early centuries of the common era, nativist scholars have often argued for the continuous existence of a distinctive Japanese religion and religiosity (Shinto, "the way of the *kami* [divinities]") associated with the imperial cult. Thus, *Japanese religion* and similar terms are used not only descriptively but also in ideological discourse.

Elements of continuity and change are, of course, found in the history of every religious tradition. There is a danger of essentializing religion, however, by implying that elements of continuity over time have always meant the same thing or functioned in the same way(s) in different contexts and in different constellations or relations with other constituent elements. Given the persistent influence of nativist scholarship in Japan, this danger is especially acute in the modern study of Japanese religion. Nevertheless, if the term *Japanese religion* is at all useful, it is because almost all religions found in Japan have incorporated certain basic beliefs and practices.

AFFIRMATION OF THE NATURAL WORLD

Affirmation of the natural world as good and as a potential locus of spiritual salvation is one of the constants of Japanese religion. The concept of the phenomenal world as somehow corrupt or fallen never really prevailed in Japan, perhaps in part because of the absence of a radical sense of transcendence. While Japanese mythology, found in the *Kojiki* (712) and the *Nihonshoki* (720), suggests a three-tiered cosmology, consisting of the Plain of High Heaven (Amagahara), this world, and the underworld (Yomi no kuni), kami cults focus on the phenomenal world. Thus, whereas Zeus, in ancient Greek thought for instance, was imagined as residing on Mt. Olympus, kami are often identified

RUSSIA

Hokkaido

Sapporo

Sea of Japan

Mito

Honshu

Tokyo (Edo)

JAPAN Mt. Fuji Kamakura

Kyoto Mt. Hiei

Osaka Nara Ise

Kobe Tenri

(Heiankyo)

Izumo

Mt. Koya

Shikoku

Kyushu

Nagasaki

PACIFIC

OCEAN

Okinawa

Japan

with specific natural sites (e.g., the twin peaks of Mt. Tsukuba are considered to be the "kami bodies" [*shintai*] of the divinities Izanagi and Izanami). In Japanese Buddhism the world was frequently viewed as a locus of salvation, while some geographical areas were imagined to be Buddhist heavens and others served as natural mandalas (cosmic diagrams), focal points for meditative practice. Even when viewed in the darkest terms (e.g., in the devolutionary view of the present age in cosmic history as *mappo*, the age of degenerate dharma), the world and the human condition were considered to be redeemable somehow, either through rites of purification or the gracious efficacy of the merit and compassion of a Bodhisattva.

FLUIDITY OF DIVINE AND HUMAN STATUS

Coupled with the affirmation of the phenomenal world, Japanese religion has typically recognized the ontological status of divinity as one in which humans can participate. In the kami cults, this belief has found expression in the assertion that the members of the imperial family were living or "manifest kami" and in the recognition of certain individuals (most recently some founders of new religious sects) as *ikigami*, "living kami." In Buddhism, many figures (e.g., Prince Shotoku and Kukai) came to be understood as human incarnations of one or another Bodhisattva. In the medieval period, other historical figures who had been wrongly executed or

Japan*		
4000 B.C.	**300 B.C.–A.D. 200**	**200–400**
Jomon culture (ca. 4000 or 3000–250)	Yayoi culture, beginning of Sino-Korean influence (ca. 250 B.C.–A.D. 250)	Yamoto period (ca. 250–710) Inner shrine at Ise (3rd century)
400–500	**500–600**	**600–700**
Outer shrine at Ise (5th century)	Korean Buddhism enters Japan (538 or 552) Prince Shotoku (574–622) Buddhism proclaimed official religion of Japan (594)	Buddhist temple, Horyu-yi, constructed in Nara, world's oldest surviving wooden building (607) Hui-kuan, Korean priest, introduces Jojitsu (Satysiddhi) and Sanron (Madhyamika) Buddhism (625) Taika reforms (646–51) Two Japanese priests bring Kusha (Abidharma-kosha) Buddhism from China to Japan (658) Japanese priest, Dosho, introduces Hosso (Yogachara) Buddhism from China (666)

* See also the timeline that accompanies the feature article "Buddhism."

exiled were believed to be transformed at death into *goryo*, haunting spirits, who could be pacified and controlled only through enshrinement (divinization) and subsequent worship. At the popular level, all deceased persons were (and are) frequently referred to as *hotoke*, or Buddhas.

IMPORTANCE OF THE SOCIAL COLLECTIVE

Japanese religion has tended to be organized collectively rather than emphasizing individual faith. In prehistorical and ancient Japan, worship focused on *ujigami*, the kami of extended clans (*uji*), based on social, political, and economic alliances rather than on a sanguinary basis. Later, the family, including both the living and the dead, became the locus of much cultic activity, most importantly of ancestral or memorial rites. In State Shinto in the latter half of the nineteenth and the first half of the twentieth centuries, the emperor was represented as the "father" of the national family, a metaphor extended even to present imperialist designs as benevolent expressions of "world familyism."

EMPHASIS ON LOCAL CULTS

Like Hinduism, Japanese religion finds expression primarily in local or regional rather than national cults. Today, common sites of worship are in the home before the Shinto altar (*kamidana*) or Buddhist memorial alcove (*butsudan*) or at the gravesite of a deceased relative. Communal rites center around local shrine and temple festivals (*matsuri*). Even cults having a national distribution, such as those of the Buddhist Bodhisattvas Jizo and Kannon, involve individual offer-

Japan

700–800		800–900
First Confucian ceremony in Japan (701)	Kegon (Avatamshaka) Buddhism introduced (740)	Saicho (767–822) founds Japanese Tendai Buddhism (805)
Nara period, capital moved from Fujiwara to Nara (710–84)	Buddhist ordination hall established at Nara by Chinese monk (754)	Kukai (774–835) founds Japanese Shingon Buddhism (806)
Kojiki compiled (712)	*Man'yoshu* completed (ca. 769)	Ainu brought under permanent Japanese control (812)
Nihonshoki compiled (720)	Heian period. Capital moved to Heian (Kyoto) (794–1185)	Shobo, systematizer of Shugendo (832–909)
Japanese priest brings Kusha (Abhidharma-kosha) doctrine from China (736)		Ennin (793–864) establishes Tai-mitsu, esoteric Tendai (847)
Chinese priest brings Ritsu (Vinaya) Buddhism to Japan (736)		Enchin (814–91) founds Miidera Tendai (858)
Indian Buddhist monk, Bodhishena, arrives in Japan (736)		Fujiwara regency (897–1185)

ings and prayers based on personal needs before the ubiquitous statues in almost every town and village rather than at a national sacred site. Only a few places, such as the Ise Shrine or, more recently, the Yasukuni Shrine, have attained any national significance.

HISTORICAL OUTLINE

In spite of these general elements of continuity, Japanese religious history has nevertheless been characterized by continuous change.

Prehistorical Japan Very little can be said with any certainty concerning the religious beliefs and practices of prehistorical Japan. Lacking any written sources from Japan before the eighth century, scholars can only draw tentative inferences from the archaeological evidence. Archaeologists divide prehistory in Japan into the Jomon ("cord pattern") period (ca. fifth millennium B.C.–A.D. 250) and the Yayoi period (ca. 250 B.C.–A.D. 250), based on distinctive pottery designs. The Jomon period was characterized by a hunting and gathering culture, while the Yayoi period witnessed the introduction of rice cultivation from the Asian continent. The cultural influences on prehistorical Japan seem to have been varied. In an influential, if disputed, thesis, the Japanese scholar Oka Masao argued in 1933 for five distinctive influences informing ancient Japanese myth, ritual, and social structure, ranging from a South Pacific cultural complex (horizontal cosmology, female shamans, brother-sister deities, etc.) to a Siberian complex (vertical cosmology, descending deities, etc.).

One of the few possible written references to prehistorical Japan is the Chinese dynastic history of the kingdom of Wei (220–265), which reports turmoil in Yamatai, an island kingdom, until a female shaman or divinatory medium named Pimiko (or Himiko) assumed control, ruling from seclusion within a

900–1000	1000–1100	1100–1200
Engi-shiki compiled (905–927) Ryobu Shinto (ca. 970)	Ryonin (1071–1132)	Honen (1133–1212) establishes Japanese Jodo (Pure Land) Buddhism (1175) Eisai (1141–1215) transmits Rinzai Zen from China (1191) Shinran (1173–1262) Kamakura Shogunate; rise of samurai (1192–1333)

heavily guarded palace. A younger brother served as the transmitter and interpreter of her ecstatic pronouncements to the people.

The Kofun ("tumulus") period (ca. 250–600) is so called because of the presence of huge artificial burial mounds in the plains area surrounding present-day Nara. These tombs indicate the development of a hierarchically organized and centrally controlled society, arranged on the basis of religio-political power or charisma. Cultural contact with the Korean and Chinese kingdoms increased greatly in this period, while Confucian, Taoist, and Buddhist concepts and practices were introduced. Worship and cultic practice seem to have been organized along extended clan (uji) lines.

Early Historical Japan Written history in Japan begins in the eighth century in the form of three works commissioned by the central government: the *Kojiki* (712), a redaction of oral myths and legends; the *Nihonshoki* (720), an imperial historical chronicle along Chinese lines covering the period from the time of creation down to the late seventh century; and the *Man'yoshu*, a poetic anthology of over forty-five hundred verses. These texts provide important information on the religious beliefs and practices of the elite in ancient Japan, but less concerning the religious lives of ordinary people. In large measure they were intended to legitimate the power, prestige, privilege, and position of the imperial family and court based on the religio-political ideology of imperial descent directly from Amaterasu Omikami, the sun goddess, the ujigami of the clan that emerged as the imperial clan. With the development of a national consciousness, the cult took on a larger role. According to the *Nihonshoki*, approval to build the first Buddhist temple in Japan was granted to the head of the powerful Soga clan, provided the temple was built on the clan estate where the enshrined Buddha would serve as the ujigami.

Japan

1200–1300	1300–1400	1400–1500
Ise Shinto (ca. 1200)	Koken Shiren, *Genko shakusho* (1332)	Increased influence of Chinese neo-Confucian thought; Shugendo institutionalized as Shugenshu (15th century)
Pure Land Buddhists banished from capital (1207)	Brief return to direct imperial rule (1334–37)	First performance of Noh drama under imperial patronage (1408)
Jien completes *Gukansho* (ca. 1220)	Ashikaga Shogunate (1338–1573)	
Shinran (1173–1262) founds Japanese Jodo Sin (True Pure Land) Buddhism (1224)	Zen temple constructed in Kyoto; imperial patronage of Rinzai Zen (1339)	Yoshida Kanetomo (1435–1511) founds Yuiitsu (also Urabe or Yoshida) Shinto (1484)
Dogen (1200–1253) transmits Soto Zen to Japan (1227)	Edict ranking Gozen Zen monasteries (1386)	Armed conflicts involving True Pure Land Buddhism (1465–88)
Statue of Amida Buddha erected at Kamakura (1238)	Golden Pavilion constructed (1394–97)	Omin civil war (1467–77)
Nichiren (1222–82) founds the Hokke (Lotus), later known as the Nichiren school (1253)		Rennyo (1415–99) "restores" Honganji branch of True Pure Land (1479)
Unsuccessful invasion attempts by Mongols (1274, 1281)		Great Kyoto fire (1489)
Ippen (1239–89) founds Ji Buddhism (1275)		

The introduction of Chinese script opened the world of ideas of greater Asia to the Japanese, including the universal claims and principles of Buddhism, Confucianism, and Taoism. With China's great cultural prestige and Buddhism's proven ability to serve as a unifying religio-political system, it is little wonder that the imperial prince Shotoku (574–622) sought to make Buddhism a national faith. Taking the Sui emperor Wen Ti (r. 581–604) as his model, Shotoku sought to unify the nation and to strengthen imperial power by utilizing Confucian, Buddhist, and Taoist ideas and values in concert with native mythic traditions. Shotoku's ideals were partially institutionally realized in the late seventh century in the Ritsuryo state, or "Imperial Rescript State." This has been characterized as a form of "immanental theocracy," wherein the universal principles of the Tao and the Dharma were identified with the person and will of the sovereign, envisioned as a living divinity in human form. In what was to become a regular pattern in Japanese history, the government sought to control all religions and to organize them hierarchically under court supervision.

Nara, the first permanent capital and modeled on the Chinese capital, was established in 710. It served as both the religious and political center of the country, with the emperor sponsoring the casting and installation of the great bronze Buddha Vairochana in Todaiji, the Great Eastern Temple. The government supported six schools of Buddhism, largely centered in temple and monastery complexes. At the folk level, popular religious figures included mountain ascetics, healers, and magicians who incorporated a variety of Bud-

1500–1600	1600–1700	
Arrival of first (Portuguese) Europeans (1543)	Tokugawa Shogunate (1603–1867)	Ishida Baigan (1685–1744)
Francis Xavier, first Catholic missionary in Japan (1549–51)	First of series of Confucian tutors and advisers to Shoguns (1608)	Hakuin Ekkaku (1685–1768)
Azuchi period (1574–1602)	Nakae Toju (1608–48)	Beginning of the intellectual movement, "National Learning" (Kokugaku) (1688–1703)
Imperial edict (unenforced) banishing Catholic missionaries (1587)	Buddhism de facto religion of Tokugawa Japan (1614)	Expansion of flower arranging, tea ceremony, Kabuki, and Noh (1688–1703)
27 Franciscans and Japanese Christians executed at Nagasaki (1596–97)	Yamazaki Ansai, founder of (neo-Confucian) Suiga Shinto (1618–82)	
	"Great Christian martyrdom," Nagasaki (1622)	
	Yamaga Sokko (1622–85)	
	Europeans expelled from Japan, with exception of Dutch in Nagasaki (1624–41)	
	Matsua Basho, haiku poet (1644–94)	
	Obaku Zen brought from China, only new Buddhist sect of Tokugawa period (1654)	

dhist and Taoist concepts and practices into their own religious world. A part of this folk tradition was later loosely institutionalized as the mountain-centered Shugendo sect. The intermixing of local and imported religious beliefs and practices also found expression in the late eighth century in the amalgamation of shrines and Buddhist temples at the same sites, a pattern that continued down to the late nineteenth century and the forced separation of Buddhism from Shinto by the Meiji government.

With the move of the capital to Heian-kyo (present-day Kyoto) at the turn of the ninth century, two new schools of Buddhism emerged: Tendai and Shingon, founded by Saicho (767–822) and Kukai (774–835) respectively. Both included esoteric practices and encouraged in their own ways the amalgamation of kami and Buddhist cults. Theoretically, this found expression in the philosophy of *honji suijaku*, which asserted that kami were the "manifest traces" (*suijaku*) of the Buddhas, who were the original cosmic realities (*honji*). Saicho also emphasized the centrality of the *Lotus Sutra*, with its universal soteriology, as had Prince Shotoku earlier.

The *Engi-shiki* (927), a record of rules and regulations from the Engi era (901–922), includes details concerning the rituals performed as part of the liturgical calendar of the court. Especially notable are the ritual prayers (*norito*) to kami on various occasions, including an annual rite of national purification. Taoist influence is evident in such things as divination, astrology, directional taboos, and emphasis on the need to establish harmony between *yin* and *yang* elements.

Japan

1700–1800	1800–1900	
Kamo Mabuchi (1697–1769)	Hiroshige (1797–1858)	Meiji restoration and the creation of State Shinto (1868–1912)
Motoori Norinaga (1730–1801)	Gunnai uprising (1836)	
Hokusai (1760–1849)	Tenrikyo, modern Japanese religion, founded by Nakagama Miki (1798–1887) (1838)	Government Department of Shinto established (1868)
Hirata Atsutane (1776–1843)		
Ninomiya Sontoku (1787–1856)		National royalist shrine established in Tokyo (1869)
Kansei reforms (1789–1801)	Opium War (1839–42)	
Shushigaku (Confucian Chu-Hsi) becomes official school of learning (1790)	Kurozumikyo, modern Japanese religion, founded by Kurozumi Munetada (1780–1850) (ca. 1840)	"Great Doctrine," separating Buddhism (the Tokugawa state tradition) from Shinto and requiring the compulsory registration of all households as Shinto (1870–73)
	Tempo reforms (1841–43)	
	First Perry mission (1853–54)	Daisetsu Teitaro Suzuki (1870–1966)
	Rising Sun flag adopted (1854)	Royalist shrine at Kobe (1872)
	School of Western Learning established by shogunate (1855)	State-sponsored cult of proto-emperor Jimmu; current emperor proclaimed a "living *kami*" whose birthday was celebrated as a national religious holiday; Shinto (and some Buddhist) clergy declared "national priests" (1872)
	Konkokyo, modern Japanese religion, founded by Kawate Bunjiro (1814–83) (1859)	

The Heian age (794–1185) also saw the rise of belief in goryo. Rituals of pacification of these spirits developed, based in large part on earlier rites of spirit pacification (*tama-shizume*) coupled with Buddhist elements. At the same time, belief grew that the present age was the "age of degenerate dharma" (mappo), in which the spiritual capabilities of human beings had seriously degenerated. This belief later fostered the rise of a number of distinct religious practices based on the need for seeking salvation through appeal to the power and mercy of others (*ta-riki*), notably Bodhisattvas, since salvation through one's own efforts (*ji-riki*) was no longer possible.

These practices, including the *nembutsu* (recitation of the Buddha's name), the *nembutsu odori* (dance accompanying the nembutsu), and Ippen's use of *ofuda* (prayer strips), became the mainstays of the "New Buddhisms" of the Kamakura period (1192–1333), where simple acts of faith were advocated and the possibility of salvation opened to ordinary people. Creativity in religious beliefs and practices accompanied the decline of the power (military and monetary) of the court and the shift to multiple military rulers (*daimyo*, of whom the *shogun* was supreme commander).

Pure Land Sects Pure Land Buddhism, the Nichiren sect, and Zen all emerged in the Kamakura period. The Jodo (Pure Land) and Jodo Shinshu (True Pure Land) sects, associated with Honen (1133–1212) and Shinran (1173–1262) respectively, advocated the nembutsu, the recitation of the phrase *namu Amida*

1900–		
To keep State Shinto as a national religion, the government created a new category of Sect (*Kyoha*) Shinto, initially recognizing 13 groups (1882–1908)	Russian-Japanese war (1904–5)	Religious Corporations Ordinance (1945)
	Japan annexes Korea (1910)	Emperor Hirohito (1901–89) becomes constitutional monarch (1946)
	"Conference of the Three Religions" (Shinto, Buddhism, and Christianity) (1912)	Post-war formation and expansion of new religious movements (1946–)
Lay movement, "Society for the Establishment of the Great Way," formed to combine elements of Buddhism and State Shinto (1888–89)	World War I (1914–18)	Union of New Religious Organizations in Japan founded (1951)
	Rapid formation and expansion of new religions (1920–30)	End of Occupation (1951)
Meiji constitution (1889)	Reiyukai, modern Nichiren sect, founded by Kubo Kakutaro (1892–1944) and Kotani Kimi (1901–71) (1925)	Soka Gakkai fastest growing religion in world (1952–65)
Imperial Rescript on Education (1890)		
Sino-Japanese war (1894–95)	Soka Gakkai, modern Nichiren sect, founded by Makiguchi Tsunesaburo (1871–1944) (1937)	Soka Gakkai headquarters in United States, first outside Japan, established (1963)
	Religious Organizations Act (1939–40)	Census reports membership in new religions comprise 22.4% of Japanese (1980)
	World War II (1941–45)	
	State Shinto dismantled as national faith by occupation decree, reduced to one of the religions (1945)	

Butsu ("I put my faith in Amida Buddha") as the sole means of salvation in the age of mappo. Nichiren (1222–82) took the *Lotus Sutra* to be the only true repository of Buddhist teachings and established it as an object of veneration.

Zen began as a monastic meditative discipline in Japan, but came to have great cultural influence, especially in the arts. Eisai (1141–1215) founded the Rinzai sect, which emphasized the possibility of sudden enlightenment within everyday life and the use of *koan* (riddles or conundrums). Dogen (1200–1253), on the other hand, advocated seated meditation (*zazen*) and gradual enlightenment in his Soto sect. Zen institutional development received a great boost in 1338 when the shogun ordered the establishment of sixty-six Zen "temples to pacify the country" (*ankokuji*). Significantly, it was in Zen temples that the study of Chinese classics and Neo-Confucianism began in earnest. At the same time, Soto temples inaugurated simple funeral and memorial rites for the people, which continue to be popular today.

Tokugawa Period The Tokugawa period (1600–1867) helped to establish the basis for modern Japanese society. After the destruction by Oda Nobunaga (1534–82) of the institutional power base of the Tendai and Shingon schools, the Tokugawa shoguns supported the reorganization of society and values along Confucian lines. For purposes of social control, all persons were required to be registered as parishioners of Buddhist temples. The "five relations" (Chin. *wu-lun*) of Confucianism were emphasized, with ultimate loyalty being owed to the shogun, or highest national authority. Here, too, the family served as a model for meaningful participation in corporate activities where individual desires and interests were subordinated to the collective good.

The Tokugawa period also witnessed an important restoration movement among Shintoists, who advocated Shinto as a "native" tradition in contradistinction to "foreign" ones such as Buddhism, Confucianism, and Christianity. Figures such as Kamo Mabuchi (1697–1769), Motoori Norinaga (1730–1801), and Hirata Atsutane (1776–1843) argued for a return to a "pure" Japanese religiosity and religio-political order. Special emphasis was placed on the *Kojiki,* the *Nihonshoki,* and the *Man'yoshu* as repositories of the nativist tradition. The movement of nativist scholarship was influential in fostering a renewed nationalism.

Meiji and Modern Japan The Meiji period (1868–1912) is remarkable for the restoration of imperial rule, a sustained attack upon the old regime and Buddhism, the forced separation of Buddhism and Shinto (*shinbutsu bunri*), rapid Westernization and modernization, and the emergence of many new religious cults or "new religions." The attempt to "purify" Shinto and return to an imagined Golden Age when Shinto was distinct from Buddhism led to the establishment of State Shinto. Much of what is commonly represented today as constituting ancient Shinto belief and practice actually dates from this period.

Many new religious movements have appeared in Japan in the nineteenth and twentieth centuries. Commonly referred to as "new religions" (*shinko shukyo,* lit., "newly arisen religions"), they are more properly viewed as religious societies or cults, since few make exclusivistic truth claims or demand their members eschew participation in other religions. These groups, whether Buddhist or Shintoist in emphasis, all originated with a charismatic founder considered to be either divine or divinely inspired who offered new revelations, forms of worship, and objects of veneration. These groups often practice forms of faith healing or offer counseling to parishioners concerning problems in their daily lives. Beliefs and practices are usually a combination of elements drawn from several preexisting traditions such as Buddhism, Taoism, Shinto, folk practice, or Christianity. Strikingly, they tend to appeal, at least in the original generations, to individual faith, although over time this is often followed by the pattern of "inheriting" a faith. "New religions" such as Tenrikyo, Soka Gakkai, Kurozumikyo, Gedatsukai, Mahikari Sukyo, and others are one of the most dynamically growing parts of religious life in Japan today.

Participation in a religion in Japan is rarely exclusivistic. One may be a Christian yet perform memorial rites for one's ancestors, be a member of a Shintoist "new religion" yet have a Buddhist funeral, and so on. Many Japanese today do not think of themselves as religious. In a sense, this is a result of the success of the Meiji government's attempt to identify (State) Shinto with the national essence in the popular imagination and in law. In a recent legal case brought by a Christian widow who sought to block the ritual enshrinement of her husband's spirit (*tama*) by a veterans' group in the Yasukuni Shrine, the Supreme Court ruled that such rites were not religious and, moreover, that the tama of citizens belonged to the nation, not the individuals themselves or their families. The definition of Japanese religion, then, continues to be an important issue in Japanese society, not just in academia. If Japanese religion is not always readily recognizable, this is because religious values are so tightly woven into the warp and woof of Japanese society that they do not stand out as a distinct figure.

Japanese religions (festal cycle). Japanese festivals (*matsuri*) are of two kinds: indigenous and imported. Indigenous folk and institutionalized Shinto festivals are held to ensure the continued material (especially successful harvests), physical (especially freedom from pestilence and natural disasters), and spiritual well-being of people living within a particular community by "entertaining" or "attending to" (*matsurau*) the gods (*kami*) and the souls (*tama*) of the dead. A typical matsuri begins with purification rites (*monoimi*) intended to cleanse the participants of polluting forces; offerings, such as rice cakes (*mochi*), rice wine (*sake*), and other comestibles, and ritual prayers (*norito*) that work to stimulate a favorable divine response; and a communion meal of the offerings (*naorai*) shared by both participants and gods. Other typical features include lively processions of the kami in a portable shrine (*mikoshi*), ceremonial dancing known as *kagura*, and special entertainments such as horse and boat races and tug-of-war contests, all of which increase the vitality of both the local kami (*ujigami*) and the local people (*ujiko*).

The most important festivals are held during the spring and autumn, which mark the two crucial seasonal stages in the agricultural cycle. During spring planting, festivals invoke the blessings of the kami, who have descended from the mountains to the fields. During the autumn harvest, festivals of thanksgiving for a bountiful crop are performed for the deities, who then return to their mountain abodes. Summer and winter festivals are also held to avert natural calamities that would endanger the harvest. From the Heian period (794–1185), summer festivals, such as the Gion festival celebrated every July at the Yasaka Shrine in Kyoto, developed to ward off the many epidemics that plagued city life in the premodern period. With the modern period, many matsuri have either disappeared or lost their religious focus. New secular festivals, such as the famous snow (*yuki*) festival in Sapporo in northern Japan, have appeared as entertaining tourist attractions.

There is also a wide variety of nationally celebrated annual observances (*nenju gyoji*) that originally came from China. Some of these festivals were introduced to the imperial court during the Heian period and, later, after many changes, were made a fundamental part of the Japanese festival calendar. The Obon festival, for example, though related to popular beliefs of the return of ancestral spirits at the end of the summer, was originally a Buddhist celebration. Other such imported festivals that are widely celebrated today are Setsubun (Bean Scattering Ceremony) on February 3 or 4, the Hina Matsuri (Girl's or Doll's Festival) on March 3, the Tanabata Festival on July 7, and the Tango no Sekku (Boy's Festival) on May 5. *See also* Gion Shrine; Japanese folk religion; Obon; Setsubun.

Japanese religions, animals and birds in. *See* animals and birds in Japanese religions.

Japanese religions, sacred music in. In Japan music is linked both to specific religions (Shinto, Buddhism) and to certain quasi-religious traditions or institutions in Japan. Shinto music consists primarily of instrumental music used in ritual performances, while Buddhist music is better represented by chanting practices in monastic settings.

Music has also been associated with folk-religious practices, as well as with theatrical or other entertainment traditions. The music of the imperial court may not be obviously religious, but its status as sacred music is unquestioned. *See also* kagura.

Japji (juhp'jee; Punjabi, "repeat"), the composition by Nanak, the first Guru of the Sikhs, with which the Sikh scripture *Adi Granth* begins. Devout Sikhs repeat it every morning after bathing. The chant affirms Nanak's view of liberation. *See also* Nanak; Sikhism.

Jataka (jah'tuh-kuh), a type of Buddhist literature consisting of stories of the previous "births" of the being who became the Buddha. A collection of 547 such stories is included in the Pali canon. Many of the Jataka tales include ancient folk motifs from pre-Buddhist India. In Buddhist communities, the Jataka tales are often used to teach and reflect upon the virtues of generosity, loyalty, and self-sacrifice. *See also* Buddhas; Vessantara.

Jehovah (juh-hoh'vuh), incorrect reading of the proper name of Israel's deity, joining the consonants of YHWH to the vowels of Adonai. A medieval Christian invention, Jehovah became popular in some traditional English translations of the Bible. *See also* Adonai; YHWH.

Jehovah's Witnesses, a Christian millennialist sectarian group that arose in the United States late in the wake of the "Great Disappointment" that followed the failure of William Miller's prophecies in the 1840s. The Witnesses, called such since 1931, grew out of a movement known as the International Bible Students' Association, organized in 1872 by a Pittsburgh haberdasher, Charles Taze Russell. Russell taught that Jesus had initiated a "Millennial Dawn" in 1874 with his invisible return to earth and predicted that the millennial age would commence in 1914. Although the cataclysmic events of World War I reinforced the hopes of Russell and other millennialists, he and his successor, Judge J. R. Rutherford, continued to adjust the date in the face of repeated disconfirmations.

Despite such disconfirmations and other adversities, the Jehovah's Witnesses have enjoyed enormous success during the middle and later years of the twentieth century. The Witnesses deny the doctrine of the Trinity and restrict the achievement of full sainthood to 144,000 saints. They refuse military service on the grounds that all their members are ministers, refuse blood transfusions, and do not salute the flag. These practices have led to hostility and persecution, but their refusal to salute flag was vindicated by the U.S. Supreme Court in *West Virginia State Board of Education vs. Barnette* in 1943.

The tightly organized Witnesses have their headquarters in Brooklyn, New York, and meet locally in "Kingdom Halls." They are often most visible in their door-to-door evangelism and sale of their magazine, *The Watchtower.* Their membership in the mid-1980s numbered about seven hundred thousand in the United States and nearly three million worldwide. *See also* Adventists; Miller, William; Russell, Charles Taze.

jen (ruhn; Chin., "benevolence," "humaneness"), fundamental virtue of Confucius's teaching in the *Lun Yu* (Analects). After cultivating a consistent attitude of humane concern for others expressed in appropriate rituals involving personal routine as well as matters of great social and political importance, one may be considered a benevolent person. Confucius promoted it by urging officials to love others and teaching responsive students proper attitudes in interacting with guests and commoners. Rituals of Chinese sages were used to express and refine these attitudes. Later Confucians elevated *jen* into the paramount virtue of the gentleman (*chun-tzu*). *See also* chun-tzu; Confucianism; Lun Yu.

Jerome (348–420), also known as Eusebius Hieronymous, greatest of the early Roman Catholic Bible scholars. Jerome was the leading translator of the authoritative Latin translation of the Bible, the Vulgate. *See also* Vulgate.

Jerusalem (jeh-roo'sah-lem; Heb.), a city claimed by the State of Israel as its capital, also an important holy site for Judaism, Christianity, and Islam.

History: Archaeology reveals that Jerusalem was inhabited by 1800 B.C. About 1000 B.C., King David transformed it into the capital of the new nation Israel. After 922 B.C., the kingdom split in two; Jerusalem remained the capital of Judah, the southern kingdom, until the Babylonians sacked it in 587 B.C. Over the following centuries, Judah was a province of various empires: first that of the Babylonians, then the Persians, Alexander the Great, the Ptolemies, and the Seleucids. In 164 B.C., a revolt against the Seleucids established Jerusalem as the capital of an independent kingdom ruled by the Maccabees. In 63 B.C., Israel again became a province, this time of the Roman Empire. The Jews revolted against the Romans in 66. The revolt was crushed, and Jews were banished from Jerusalem and its environs.

Jerusalem was rebuilt by the Romans and then was part of the Byzantine Empire until the Islamic conquest in 638. In 1099, the Christian Crusades succeeded in establishing the Christian Kingdom of Jerusalem. The Christians controlled Jerusalem on and off until 1247, when it was sacked by the Turks. After that, Jerusalem was governed by the Egyptians until 1517, when the Ottomans gained control. In 1948, after a few decades of British rule, the Jews in the region declared Israel an independent state and claimed Jerusalem as its capital. Jerusalem remained divided between the new state and Jordan until 1967. Since then, Jerusalem has been a united city, governed by the State of Israel.

Judaism: For Judaism, Jerusalem has been a holy city since King Solomon built the first temple to Yahweh there around 950 B.C. From that time, the Temple formed the center of Jewish worship for nearly a thousand years, with a brief break between 587 and 520 B.C. The Temple was destroyed by the Romans in 70. After that, Jerusalem assumed a symbolic importance; its holy past was revered and its glorious future as the city of God emphasized. The Temple ruins, most importantly the Western Wall, became a holy site for pilgrimage.

Christianity: For Christianity, Jerusalem is where Jesus spent the last few weeks of his ministry. The places where Jesus performed various acts have taken on a holy status. Among these sites are the Via Dolorosa, the route Jesus walked to his crucifixion, and the Church of the Holy Sepulchre, commemorating the site where Christians claim Jesus was buried and then rose from the dead.

Islam: Jerusalem was taken from the Christian Roman Empire by Muslim armies through a negotiated settlement in 635. For the Muslims, the sanctity of the city was based on its biblical associations, particularly with Ibrahim (Abraham) and the temple of Sulayman (Solomon). It was probably somewhat later that Jerusalem was identified with the "remote place" that was the goal of the Prophet Muhammad's Night Journey, mentioned in Qur'an 17:1. Early on, the Muslims built a shrine, the Dome of the Rock, and Aqsa mosque atop Haram al-Sharif, known to Jews as the Temple Mount.

Known as al-Quds ("the Holy") in Arabic, Jerusalem played no great political role under Islam. Muslim regard for the city was, however, dramatically heightened in the wake of the Crusades, and thereafter, and particularly under the Mamluk sultans (1250–1517), there was continuous and remarkable building activity in the city. Endowed law colleges and Sufi convents crowded around the northern and western sides of the Haram al-Sharif. The old walled city of Jerusalem remained under Muslim sovereignty, with only one or two brief interruptions, until the Israeli occupation in 1967. *See also* Calvary, Mt.; Dome of the Rock; Holy Sepulchre, Church of the; pilgrimage; temple; Via Dolorosa.

Jesuits, a Catholic religious order for men founded by Ignatius of Loyola (1491–1556) in 1534 and approved by Pope Paul III in 1540. The constitution for the community, written by Ignatius and approved in 1550, focused on two tasks: the reform of the Roman Catholic Church, particularly in response to Protestantism, and service in the foreign missions, especially in those areas that had been just discovered. To fulfill these tasks, in addition to the vows of poverty, chastity, and obedience (to one's superior in the order) Jesuits were required to take an additional "fourth vow" of obedience to the pope and were freed of traditional obligations associated with religious life, particularly a distinctive garment and the recitation of the Divine Office, daily prayers at specified hours. The Jesuits were most associated with spiritual revival, especially through the *Spiritual Exercises* (1522–41) of Ignatius, and education. Many of the important theologians of the sixteenth- and seventeenth-century Catholic Reformation period were Jesuits. Although marred by several conflicts during the seventeenth and eighteenth centuries, including their dispute with Jansenism, the Chinese rites controversy, and the suppression of the Society by Clement XIV in 1773 (although later restored by Pius VII in 1814), the Jesuits remain one of the most important orders in the contemporary Church, particularly in the field of education. *See also* Ignatius of Loyola.

Jesus, quest for the historical, the critical evaluation of sources in order to distinguish the probable Jesus of history from the Christ of faith. The phrase comes from the English title of a book (1906) by Albert Schweitzer that reviewed and critiqued a stream of eighteenth-century lives of Jesus from Reimarus to Wrede. Schweitzer's own formulation of Jesus as a disappointed eschatologist has not been accepted, but his illustration of how a description of the historical Jesus reflects the one who creates it has been commonly acknowledged. In the first half of the twentieth century—due partly to the emergence of form criticism, with its stress on the impact of the early church on the Jesus tradition—the quest was largely abandoned by scholars.

In 1953, a new quest began. A set of criteria have been developed for distinguishing "authentic" (i.e., historical) material: appropriateness to the linguistic and environmental context of Jesus, an Aramaic-speaking Jew in first-century Palestine; dissimilarity from Jewish and early church norms, therefore distinctiveness of Jesus (used to include or, narrowly, to exclude material); multiple attestation in various strands of tradition; coherency with material meeting the above criteria; and, most recently, distinctive form—proverb or aphorism and parable. In the late twentieth century some scholars continue the "quest" while others remain skeptical.

Jesus Christ (Gk. form of Heb. *Joshua;* Gk. *christos,* "anointed"), name of the founder of the Christian religion. Christ is a title designating Jesus as the Messiah (Heb., "anointed") of the Jewish people. The expression *Jesus Christ* is shorthand for *Jesus the Messiah,* but early on the title *Christ* came to be used as a name, and the designation Jesus Christ became customary.

Life of Jesus: Jesus was born in Palestine, under Roman occupation, during the reign of Emperor Augustus (27 B.C.–A.D. 14), by modern reckoning in 6 B.C. The earliest sources (written by Christians several decades after his death) give his birthplace as Bethlehem, a few miles south of Jerusalem. His family came from Nazareth in Galilee in northern Palestine, and he passed his early years in Nazareth. In his late twenties he traveled south to the vicinity of Jerusalem and became a disciple of John the Baptist, a Jewish ascetic and prophet who lived in the Judean desert east of Jerusalem preaching a message of

An image of Christ as headman from a Catholic church in Kagua, in the southern highlands of Papua New Guinea (1983).

repentance in preparation for the coming day of the Lord. When John was imprisoned and beheaded, Jesus began an independent ministry centered not in the desert of Judea but in the towns and villages of Galilee.

Jesus addressed his message chiefly, if not wholly, to Jews (Matthew 15:24), and the language, imagery, and ideas that inform his preaching and teaching are thoroughly Jewish. His most characteristic expression, "kingdom of God" (Mark 2:15; Matthew 4:17), had roots in Jewish hopes for the restoration of Jewish political authority in the land of Israel. He called twelve disciples, corresponding to the twelve tribes of Israel, and told them that when the kingdom was restored they would sit on twelve thrones judging the tribes of Israel (Matthew 19:28; Acts 1:6) in their lifetimes (Acts 1:6). The kingdom of God signified the time when Jews would serve God with full and undivided devotion and God's will would be done on earth. Jesus believed that the kingdom would come in the near future, and he linked its arrival to his own person and work (Luke 17:20).

Jesus was a healer and exorcist, and in the Gospels his miracles play a prominent role, especially at the beginning of his ministry (Mark 1:27). He was also a teacher of great spiritual depth who spoke less of doctrine than of a wisdom that gives life value and meaning. Some of his sayings and his parables have passed into common usage, e.g., "Where your treasure is, there will your heart be also" (Matthew 6:21); "Be as wise as serpents and as innocent as doves" (Matthew 10:16); and the parable of the good Samaritan (Luke 10:29–37).

Jesus lived a simple life and moved among men and women of little means and status. He was compassionate to the sick and poor, kind to outcasts, gentle with the handicapped, yet quick and clever in debates with opponents. He liked solitude and sometimes retreated from society to be alone with God in prayer. During the years of his active ministry he gathered a small group of disciples to assist him in his work. After his death these followers, called apostles, and a group of women who were part of Jesus' circle formed the core of the tiny community that would become the Christian church.

After traveling around Palestine for almost three years healing and teaching, Jesus came to Jerusalem, where he was arrested and brought to trial before the Roman authorities. The reasons for his arrest are still unclear to historians, but his teaching about the kingdom of God may have been seen as seditious. He was sentenced to death and hung on a cross to die (hence the prominence of the cross as a Christian symbol). Several days after his death some of his followers reported that Jesus had appeared to them alive, and these appearances were the beginning of the Christian church. His disciples were convinced that God had not abandoned him in death. Because of Jesus' extraordinary life, his closeness to God, his patience and forbearance in suffering, God had raised Jesus from the dead. He was, in the language of Paul of Tarsus, whose Letters written several decades after Jesus' death provide a vivid picture of early Christian beliefs, the "first fruits of those who had fallen asleep," (1 Corinthians 15:20) the beginning of a new way of life that would culminate in the resurrection of all humankind.

Jesus' place in Christian worship and piety and thought, and hence in the history of humankind, is unintelligible without reference to the Christian belief in the resurrection. On Easter (the day of resurrection) Christians greet each other with the words: "He is risen. He is risen indeed. Alleluia." By this greeting they confess that Jesus Christ is not simply a human being who lived an exemplary life, but the divine

Son of God (Romans 1:1). Like other human beings, he had a body, underwent physical and mental growth, felt hunger and pain, knew joy and pleasure, died and was buried in the earth; yet he rose to new life and, according to the Christian scriptures, is Savior, Word of God, Life, Truth, Bread of Life, the First and the Last, the True Vine, the Way, Holiness, Wisdom, Righteousness, and all else that is good and true and noble. In the words of an ancient Christian hymn, "Jesus Christ is the Light of the World; the Light no darkness can overcome."

Jesus as Founder: In many respects Jesus can be compared to Moses and Muhammad, the other two founders of Abrahamic religions. He was a messenger from God, a prophet, who lived in communion with God and taught God's ways to human beings. Yet the differences between Christian conceptions of Jesus and Jewish and Muslim conceptions of Moses and Muhammad are as significant as the similarities. Moses, who received the Torah (Law), God's authoritative revelation, on Mt. Sinai, is considered the teacher par excellence, but he is not considered divine and is not an object of worship. Similarly, in Islamic thought, though Muhammad is revered as the "Messenger of God" who received from Gabriel the words of the Qu'ran and ascended briefly into heaven to behold the divine glory, his life ended with his death and he is not revered as a divine being. Jesus, on the other hand, is believed by Christians to be alive and present in the Eucharist (holy communion), the Christian ritual meal of bread and wine; the Christian community is called the "body of Christ" and has a mystical communion with the living Christ. Even the Christian calendar, in contrast to that of Jews or Muslims, is oriented almost wholly to the events in Christ's life, e.g., his birth, baptism, death, resurrection, ascension into heaven, and final return in glory.

Early Christologies: Early Christian thinkers realized that the declaration that Jesus Christ was divine seemed to compromise their belief that God was one. This led to the most significant theological controversy in Christian history, the debate at the Council of Nicaea (325) over the relation of Christ to God the Creator. When it was over, Christians had formulated a unique understanding of God known as the doctrine of the Trinity: God is conceived as one God, yet within the Godhead there are three distinct Persons, God the Father, God the Son (Jesus Christ), and God the Holy Spirit. In the words of the Nicene Creed (325), the most universally accepted Christian confession: "We believe in one Lord Jesus Christ, the Son of God, begotten from the Father, only-begotten, that is, from the substance of the Father, God from God, light from light, true God from true God, begotten not made, of one substance with the Father, through whom all things came into being, things in heaven and things on earth . . ."

From earliest times, then, Jesus was always seen to present two faces of Christian piety: one human, born like other human beings who ate and drank and slept, who knew sadness and joy, grief and elation; the other the divine Son of God, "one with the Father," the second Person of the Trinity. Because he is a human being, he lived at a particular place and time and shared in human limitations; at the same time he is the divine Son of God whose death has cosmic significance for all of humankind. The traditional Christian formulation (adopted at the Council of Chalcedon in 451) to express this mystery is that Jesus Christ is known "in two natures (divine and human) in one Person." In his Person the divine and human have been joined, so much that it is possible to say that Mary, Jesus' mother, was not simply the mother of Christ, but the mother of God. This formulation rests on the Christian doctrine of the incarnation (becoming flesh) as expressed in the Gospel of John: "And the Word [the divine Son of God] became flesh and dwelt among us, full of grace and truth; we have beheld his glory, glory as of the only Son from the Father" (1:14). According to classical Christian teaching, in Jesus Christ God has taken on human nature and entered fully into human life and history, including suffering and death.

In Christian life, worship, and art, the figure of Jesus has taken many different forms. Early Christians debated whether it was proper to address prayers to Christ since he was a human being. Jesus had prayed to God with the words "our Father," and some Christians argued that prayer should only be addressed to God the Father. In the course of time Christ became the object of prayers and hymns (for example, the traditional liturgical hymn *Gloria in Excelsis* reads "Lord Jesus Christ, only Son of the Father . . . receive our prayer. For you alone are the Holy One, you alone are the Lord . . ."), yet most prayer is addressed to God the Father "through Jesus Christ his only Son our Lord."

Representations of Jesus: The duality of divine and human in one person is evident in Christian art. On the one hand, Christian artists have delighted in the human images of Christ presented in the Gospels: the weak and helpless infant at his mother's breast, Jesus' deep anguish in the Garden of Gethsemane as he realizes his death is imminent, the pathos of his abandonment at his crucifixion (the most popular image of Christ in the West); on the other hand, he is pictured as a glorified and divine figure transfigured on Mt. Tabor (Matthew 17:1–8) or enthroned in power and majesty after his resurrection. Some Eastern Christian icons show Christ sitting on a heavenly throne as the Lord of the universe (Pantocrator, "all powerful"). As Christ lifts his hand in blessing he holds a book inscribed with the words, "Come to me all who labor and are heavy laden . . ." (Matthew 11:28–30). Even in triumph and glory Christ's humanity is clearly evident and he seems to welcome the viewer with tenderness and love. Paintings of Christ's crucifixion display the stark reality of his death as a human being as well as his self-giving love on behalf of humankind. A related image, the Pieta (best known through Michelangelo's 1499 statue, now in St. Peter's in Rome), depicts the Virgin Mary supporting the youthful body of the dead Christ immediately after his death.

Imitation of Christ: From the beginning of Christian history Jesus was seen as an example or model of the Christian life. For some (e.g., early Christian martyrs) this meant a readiness to suffer as Christ had suffered: "A person is approved if, mindful of God, he endures pain while suffering unjustly. . . . If when you do right, and suffer for it you take it patiently, you have God's approval. For to this you have been called, because Christ also suffered for you leaving you an example that you should follow in his steps" (1 Peter 2:19–21). One of the most widely read books in Christian history, written by Thomas a Kempis, bears the title *The Imitation of Christ* (1118). This work takes the form of a meditation on the life of Christ and begins with words from the Gospel of John: "He who follows me can never walk in darkness" (8:12), and continues, "If we want to see our way truly, never a trace of blindness left in our hearts, it is his life, his character, we must take for our model. Clearly, then, we must make it our chief business to train our thoughts upon the life of Christ." Other writers have seen Jesus as a model of virtue in the fashion of the sages of antiquity. His life, writes John Chrysostom (d. 407), serves to "form us in virtue. . . . In order that we may follow him more easily, Christ took on our flesh and our nature, and leads the way and shows how to keep the commandments by his own actions."

Closely related to the idea of imitation is the command to "follow Christ." This injunction has its roots in the words of Jesus to Simon and Andrew, fishermen on the Sea of Galilee: "Follow me . . ." (Mark 8:34). The most significant and enduring form of "following Christ" has been Christian monasticism. According to Athanasius (ca. 296–373), Antony (ca. 251–356), the first monk, had heard the story in the scriptures that the apostles had forsaken everything to "follow the savior." When he heard the words "If you would be perfect, go, sell what you possess and give to the poor, and you will have treasure in heaven," he immediately gave away what he owned to follow Jesus. From this beginning a movement of great power and spiritual depth swept the Christian world, and monasticism, drawing on the words "Follow me," was to become one of the most enduring features of Christian life.

A quite different interpretation of Jesus' command can be seen in Charles Monroe Sheldon's popular American work *In His Steps* (1896). Sheldon built his conception of following Jesus around the question, What would Jesus do in such a situation? Sheldon's Christ had little to do with the suffering Jesus of Thomas a Kempis; his Jesus looked very much like a confident and aspiring American businessman, a teacher of eminent practicality and commonsense rationality. This interpretation of Jesus was as much shaped by the currents fashionable in late-nineteenth-century American life as it was by the historical figure of Jesus or Jesus as interpreted in classical Christian tradition, yet this plasticity in the figure of Jesus has allowed Christians of every generation to find in him a model that fits their own times.

Jesus in Spiritual Tradition: At the same time that Jesus' actions serve as models or examples within Christianity, there is a venerable spiritual tradition centered on the person of Jesus. Here Christ is an object of love and affection, and the language of devotion has a strongly erotic character. In his personal prayers, Anselm of Canterbury (d. 1109), a medieval philosopher and theologian, speaks of Christ as "hope of my heart, strength of my soul, help of my weakness" but then goes on to speak of his desire for Christ: "I thirst for you, I covet you." Similar sentiments are evident in the music of Johann Sebastian Bach (1685–1750). One aria in his *Christmas Oratorio* has these words: "I stand beside your crib, O Little Jesus, my life, I come and offer you what you have given me. Take it. It is my spirit and my mind, my soul and my feeling, take them all and let them please you." Another illustration is the popular Christmas carol "In the Bleak Midwinter": "What can I give him, Poor as I am? If I were a shepherd I would bring a lamb; If I were a wise man I would do my part; Yet what can I give him—Give my heart." One of the most frequent images in Christian spirituality is Christ as the bridegroom and the church as the bride. In the West some Christians offer devotions to the sacred heart of Jesus. In Eastern Christianity, the one-line Jesus Prayer ("Lord Jesus Christ, Son of God, have mercy on me") is repeated over and over until it becomes a spontaneous cry of the heart.

Influence of Jesus: Jesus' influence has not been restricted to Christians (he is revered as a prophet by Muslims and is treated with great respect as a Messenger of God in the Qur'an). Others have admired his teaching while rejecting the claims of the Christian community about Jesus' divinity. As early as the third century, Porphyry, the Greek philosopher and disciples of Plotinus, argued that Jesus' disciples had perverted his message. They fabricated stories about him and "claimed for their master more than he really was." Jesus, according to Porphyry, had not made himself the object of his teaching; his message centered on God and God's relation to human beings.

Later thinkers, following Porphyry's lead, have insisted that the "true" Jesus was a teacher of wisdom. During the Enlightenment, as the Gospels were read outside of the Christian theological tradition, philosophers and moralists turned with fresh interest to the teachings of Jesus. Usually this meant concentrating on the Sermon on the Mount (Matthew 5–7) or certain parables in the Gospels. A striking illustration of this can be found in the writings of Thomas Jefferson (1743–1826). He wrote a book based on the Gospels called *The Philosophy of Jesus of Nazareth*, which "abstracted what is really his from the rubbish in which it is buried." By rubbish Jefferson meant those passages that spoke about the uniqueness of Jesus and lent support to Christian ideas of Christ's divinity. He prepared an edition of the Gospels called *The Life and Morals of Jesus of Nazareth* that excludes all miraculous and supernatural elements.

Drawing on Enlightenment ideas, others saw Jesus as a teacher of conventional wisdom, a civilized, reasonable, high-minded moralist who taught the Fatherhood of God and the brotherhood of humankind. Early in the twentieth century, reformed Jewish thinkers took an interest in this "de-christologized" Jesus whose ethical teachings they could admire. Martin Buber (1878–1965) called Jesus "my great brother," admired him as a teacher who had an authentic relation to God, but at the same time rejected the Christian claim that he was the divine Son of God.

There is also a political Jesus, evident in the "Battle Hymn of the Republic": "In the beauty of the lilies Christ was born across the sea, With a glory in his bosom that transfigures you and me; As he died to make men holy, let us die to make men free, while God is marching on." In the debate over slavery in the nineteenth century, abolitionists invoked Jesus' teaching that human beings should serve no master but God alone. Pacifism, the practice of nonviolence, has been seen as a way of following Jesus. Tolstoy cites Matthew 5:39: "Do not resist one who is evil. But if any one strikes you on the right cheek, turn to him the other also." Jesus' teaching and example made a deep impression on Mohandas K. Gandhi (1869–1948), who believed that nonresistance had been expressed by no one better than Christ. In his struggle for civil rights for American blacks, Martin Luther King, Jr. (1929–68), a Christian clergyman influenced by Gandhi, rested his philosophy on the "overpowering force of the figure of Jesus." In more recent years, Jesus has been claimed as a revolutionary political figure by liberation theologians. In this view Jesus confronted people in power and met his death at the hand of political authorities who resisted his ideas and actions. The kingdom of God, as proclaimed by Jesus, envisions the day when human beings will be free of the domination of other human beings. By his life and teaching Jesus challenges his followers to dismantle the oppressive structures that deprive men and women of freedom and transform the societies in which they live.

Islam: Isa is the Arabic name for Jesus, son of Maryam (Mary), in Islam. Isa is mentioned more than a dozen times in the Qur'an; he is regarded as a man like Adam (3:59), who was the Messiah, a word and spirit from God (4:171), to whom God brought down the gospel as a guidance and an admonition (5:46) for the God-fearing people of his time and place. He was born of the Virgin Maryam, who miraculously conceived him by the action of God's spirit (19:17). At the end of his life on earth, his adversaries neither killed him nor crucified him, according to the Qur'an, but God raised him up to himself (4:157–58). On the day of resurrection, Isa will be a witness against the People of the Book (4:159). During his life, Isa worked signs and miracles by God's permission (3:49), in testimony to the veracity of the divine message he brought. In Islamic tradition Isa, together with Ibrahim (Abraham) and Musa (Moses), is said to have met Muhammad on the occasion of his nocturnal journey (*isra*). In Islamic mysticism (Sufism), Isa is a figure commanding respect, especially for the holiness of his life and his sayings on asceticism. *See also* Christology.

Jesus movement, the cluster of independent religious groups begun in the late 1960s, proclaiming a renewed dedication to the "one way" taught by Jesus and preserved in the Christian Gospels. Often associated with conservative evangelical ministries or with denominational youth ministries, the Jesus movement attracted religious seekers disappointed with or confused by the myriad new and Asian-influenced religions. Participants emphasized their similarities to the early Christian community through a communal life-style, shared property, simplified rituals, and gospel study, while adapting New Age ideas such as boundless love and the transcendent unity of religions. *See also* North America, new religions in.

Jesus people, members of the movement begun in the late 1960s, proclaiming a renewed dedication to the "one way" taught by Jesus and preserved in the Christian Gospels. Offering an alternative to the myriad new and Asian-influenced religions, the Jesus movement inspired a modest resurgence in evangelical ministries among college-age youth. *See also* North America, new religions in.

Jew, originally a term referring to an inhabitant of Judea. Later, it was applied to adherents of Judaism.

Jewels, Three. *See* Three Jewels.

Jews for Jesus, the best-known organization within messianic Judaism. Founded in San Francisco in 1973, the group consists of Jews who believe that Jesus is the Messiah. *See also* North America, new religions in.

Jihad (ji-had'; best known of many words formed from Arab. root j-h-d; "struggle" or "effort"), in Islam, struggle "in the path of God" or to "make God's cause succeed" (Qur'an 9:40). In the Qur'an, *jihad* is connected with the imperative to command good and forbid evil (3:104, 110), especially with reference to the struggle of believers against persecution and idolatry. When this struggle takes the form of warfare, the Qur'an speaks not simply of jihad, but of *qital* (killing). Jihad is, therefore, not simply equivalent to "holy war," though the struggle of believers may include war under certain conditions.

Classical Sunni jurists identified the jihad as a war to expand Islamic territory—not to make converts per se, but to extend Islamic hegemony. To this end, they developed an extensive set of rules governing resort to and conduct of war. Shii jurists, especially the Twelvers, dissented from this judgment, and argued that during the occultation of the Twelfth Imam military activity could only be used to defend established Islamic territory. Contemporary Islamic thought offers two broad interpretations of jihad. One stresses its comprehensive nature as the struggle to command good and forbid evil through self-discipline, education, and social reform. On this interpretation, jihad may include defensive wars, but not wars of expansion. The second interpretation stresses the necessity of struggle to establish an Islamic state and includes discussion of military activity as a means to that end. *See also* Islamic political theory; violence and religion.

Jimmu, Emperor (jeem-moo), legendary first emperor of Japan who subjugated rebellious earthly gods and established his court in the general area of present-day Kyoto. *See also* Japanese myth.

Jingu-ji (jin-goo-jee; Jap., "shrine-temples"), Japanese Buddhist temples built close to or on the grounds of Shinto shrines for the purpose of performing Buddhist rituals (and reading Buddhist scriptures); they were banned by the government in the late nineteenth century. *See also* shinbutsu bunri; syncretism (Japan); temple.

jinn, in Islam, an invisible order of beings, created of fire, who possess extraordinary powers and, like humans, are accountable for their actions. Some *jinn* are good, others evil.

Jishu (jee-shoo), Japanese Buddhist order of itinerant Pure Land proselytizers founded by Ippen (1239–89); it was divided into an ascetic monastic group and lay followers. The Jishu developed into a large and influential order by the end of the sixteenth century, but many of its followers later joined Jodo Shinshu. *See also* Ippen; Jodo Shinshu; Pure Land.

Jiun (jee-oon; 1718–1804), Shingon monk who strove to revive interest in Buddhist morality and monastic discipline among both Japanese laity and monastics. *See also* Shingon-shu.

Jizo (jee-zoh), Japanese Buddhist name for *Kshitigarbha*, the Bodhisattva who saves people from hell. In Japan he is also the guardian of travelers and deceased children. Images are dedicated to him in cemeteries, along roads, and in temples. Certain temples of Jizo are for aborted and stillborn children. *See also* Bodhisattvas; Kshitigarbha; Pure Land.

jnana yoga. *See* path of knowledge.

Joachim of Fiore (yoh'oh-kheem; ca. 1132–1202), Italian Catholic monk, visionary, and apocalyptic exegete. He was most influential because of his development of a threefold pattern of history: the Age of the Father; the Age of the Son, which was drawing to a close; and an immanent third age, the Age of the Spirit, which would last until Christ's return. This last prophetic stage excited a variety of millenarian expectations, spread by pseudo-Joachimite prophecies, and was deeply influential on a number of spiritual revivals, especially within Franciscan circles. *See also* ages of the world; apocalypticism.

Job, both a person and a book in the Hebrew Bible. Job's faith is tested with respect to the question of theodicy, Why do the righteous suffer? *See also* theodicy.

Jodo Shinshu (joh-doh shin-shoo; Jap., "True Pure Land School"), Japanese Buddhist school founded by Shinran (1173–1262). While Shinran considered himself a follower of Honen, his thought and approach to practice differed in important ways. This school was established through the efforts of a number of Shinran's descendants, especially Kakunyo (1270–1351), Zonkaku (1290–1373), and Rennyo (1415–99), who were able to create a hierarchical institution based on the Honganji. Today the Shinshu has more adherents than any other Buddhist school in Japan. *See also* Honen; Honganji; Jodoshu; Pure Land; Rennyo; Shinran.

Jodoshu (joh-doh-shoo; Jap., "Pure Land School"), Japanese Buddhist school founded by Honen (1133–1212). It is based on the teaching that the *nembutsu* (recitation of the Buddha's name) is the sole practice necessary for the salvation of commoners. Bencho (1168–1232) and his disciple Ryochu (1199–1287) played major roles in creating Jodoshu doctrine and establishing the Chinzei faction of the school. In the Seizan faction founded by Shoku (1177–1247), the nembutsu continued as the major practice, although others, such as adherence to the Precepts, were eventually recognized. *See also* Honen; Jodo Shinshu; nembutsu; Pure Land.

John, by tradition the author of the fourth Gospel in the New Testament as well as three epistles.

John Canoe festival, an African-American slave ritual (also known as Kunering), featuring a masked male mock king dancer and carnival activities. Popular in nineteenth-century America, it is practiced today in the West Indies.

John of Patmos. *See* John the Divine.

John of the Cross (1542–91), Spanish Carmelite monk, close associate of Teresa of Avila and together with her a major monastic reformer, one of the greatest Catholic mystics and Spanish poets. John's description of the stages of mystic ascent has been deeply influential on Catholic spiritual literature. His best-known works include *The Spiritual Canticle* (1578–91), *The Ascent of Mount Carmel* (1579–85), *The Dark Night* (1579–85), and *The Living Flame of Love* (1582–91). Each text consists of a poem and a lengthy commentary. *See also* Carmelites; Teresa of Avila.

John the Baptist, a first-century figure who appears in Josephus's *Antiquities*, the New Testament, and later Christian and Gnostic sources, and is seen by Christians as a forerunner of Jesus. Probably aligned with baptist movements in Judaism, John preached the end of time and instituted a baptism for the purification of sins. *See also* baptism; Christianity; Jesus Christ; Mandaeans.

John the Divine, or John of Patmos, author of the Revelation (or Apocalypse) of John, the last book in the New Testament.

Jomon period (joh-mohn), hunting and gathering stage of Japanese prehistory, ca. fifth millennium B.C.–A.D. 250, taking its name from the cord-marked pottery found at most sites. *See also* Japanese religion.

Jonestown. *See* People's Temple.

Jon Frum , a cargo cult movement that existed in the New Hebrides (now Vanuatu). The movement began in 1940 on Tanna, spread to other islands, and had faded by the 1960s. Participants, who were hostile to the paternalism of the Presbyterian mission and the British administration, were led in turn by at least three prophets, each known as Jon Frum and each thought to be a manifestation of the indigenous spirit Karaperamun. Jon Frum encouraged cooperative work and revived kava-drinking and dancing, practices discouraged by the mission. Positive experiences with American troops in World War II led some members to build model airfields and to speak of a Jon Frum, king of America, who would displace the British. *See also* cargo cults.

Jordan River, flows through the Sea of Galilee and ends in the Dead Sea. It was the site of two crossing miracles in the Hebrew Bible (Joshua 3:7–17; 2 Kings 5:1–14) and of Jesus' baptism by John the Baptist in the New Testament.

journey to the otherworld, a widely distributed mythic motif of travel to a supernatural realm: heaven, the underworld, a land or city at the bottom of the sea, paradise (celestial or terrestrial), a mysterious island, etc. Such a narrative often involves a heroic quest or a dangerous journey accompanied by guardian spirits. *See also* ascension; descent to the underworld; Gilgamesh; Isles of the Immortals; paradise.

journey to the underworld. *See* descent to Hades; descent to the underworld.

journey to the upperworld. *See* ascension.

Journey to the West. *See* Hsi yu chi.

Ju (roo; Chin., "scholars," "literati"), group of Chinese scholars interested in rituals and skilled arts prior to the third century. In later traditions, they were identified as having been followers of the Confucian school.

Judaism (art and architecture). When one thinks of Christianity or Buddhism, magnificent works of art and architecture immediately spring to mind. This is hardly the case with Judaism, whose fame is largely linked with its literary contributions. This lack of Jewish artistic masterpieces has been attributed to an inherited congenital incapacity for the visual arts. Many scholars also assume that the collective unconscious of the Jews does not tolerate images; the strict biblical prohibition explicit in the second commandment is taken as operative throughout Jewish history. This commandment, it is argued, was formulated because the Hebrew God was an implacable enemy of images. Theories grounded in Hegelian metaphysical and metahistorical racial formulations, or on the unswerving observance of the second commandment, although still popular, are hardly convincing.

In the Bible itself the clear mandate "You shall not make for yourself a graven image or likeness" (Exodus 20:4–5) is followed eleven chapters later with the story of the desert artist Bezaleel, who was "endowed with a divine spirit of skill, ability and knowledge in every kind of craft" (Exodus 31:1–3) and commanded to fashion the very images condemned in the earlier section of Exodus.

If these conventional explanations are no longer considered adequate explanations, what may have caused the absence of a great artistic heritage among the Jewish people? No doubt a major reason for the lack is that Judaism (unlike Christianity and Buddhism) never conceived of God in physical form, and any representation of the deity was strictly forbidden.

Furthermore, it must be acknowledged that one cannot speak of one second commandment or attitude—of an unchanging concept that never transcended its original biblical confines. In the course of Jewish history multiple understandings of the second commandment developed. Each Jewish involvement with a new society or changing conditions in an older society demanded reinterpretation and reevaluation of the original biblical prohibition.

Friday Evening; painting by Isidor Kaufmann, Jewish Museum, New York (ca. 1920).

Another factor impeding the establishment of a creative and long Jewish artistic tradition is that except for very short periods, Judaism did not flourish within a wealthy, independent, and separate country. Unlike that of other continuous entities, Jewish history developed and evolved primarily within multiple societies, cultures, and civilizations; its art consequently bears the unmistakable imprimatur of this long and diverse multicultural experience. A critical inquiry into all known artistic Jewish remains reveals no isolated, unique thread but, on the contrary, a many-colored thread interwoven into the fabric of Jewish involvement in the larger non-Jewish society. Thus, something as distinctly Jewish as the Temple of Solomon turns out, on close examination, to be an intricate part of ancient western Asian art; the art of the synagogue is not sui generis, but grows out of Greco-Roman art; and the art in medieval Hebrew manuscripts is inseparably linked to the art in medieval Christian and Islamic manuscripts.

Judaism, as a minority religion within major Christian and Islamic countries, had no powerful body like a centralized church or monarchy to sponsor art. Moreover, in Christian countries Jews were barred not only from many occupations but also from the religious guild organizations where they could have acquired the skills needed in sculpture, painting, or architecture. Thus, most Jewish buildings, paintings, and ceremonial objects were the work of Christian artists. Only from the nineteenth century on, with the demise of the Christian guild system and the rise of secular societies, do artists of Jewish birth become acclaimed masters in the realms of painting, sculpture, and architecture.

Probably the most astonishing recent discovery was the synagogue of Dura-Europos in Syria, dated 244 to 245. Its extensive series of images is the first continuous, narrative cycle based largely on the Bible; it appeared two hundred years prior to similar cycles in churches. This unusual find has demanded serious reexamination of long-held theories on the origins of Christian art, the Jewish attitude toward images, and the types of Judaism practiced not only in that Syrian desert town but in the major ancient centers of Judaism in Babylonia and Palestine. *See also* idol; synagogue.

Judaism (authoritative texts and their interpretation).

Judaic interpretation (midrash) of Scripture accomplished one of three goals in the reading of the written Torah: prophecy, paraphrase, and parable. One interpretive interest asked how the ancient Scriptures set forth the pattern of human events in time to come; a second undertook to amplify and explain the simple sense of Scripture; the third provided for Scripture parables and other concrete comparisons drawn from contemporary life for the clarification of God's meaning in revelation. The word *midrash* is generally used in three senses: (1) It may refer to a compilation of scriptural exegeses, as in "the midrash says," meaning, "the document contains the following. . . ."; (2) it may refer to an exegesis of Scripture, as in, "this midrash shows us . . . ," meaning, "this interpretation of the verse at hand indicates. . . ."; (3) it may refer to a particular mode of scriptural interpretation, as in the phrase, "the Jewish midrash holds . . . ," meaning (it is supposed) that a particular Judaic way of reading Scripture yields such-and-such a result; or a particular hermeneutic identified with Judaism teaches us to read in this way rather than in some other.

The three varieties of midrash derive from three distinct Judaisms or Judaic religious systems in antiquity. They involve the interpretation of Scripture in one of three ways: as (1) prophecy, characteristic of the Judaism set forth in the Dead Sea Scrolls as well as of the Judaism laid out by the school of the Gospel of Matthew; through (2) systematic paraphrase, accomplished by the translators of Scripture into Aramaic, the common language of much of the Jewish world, and Greek; and as (3) parable, inclusive of allegory and metaphor, characteristic of the biblical interpretation of the Judaism of the dual Torah. That Judaism, deriving from the rabbis of the Mishnah, Talmuds, and midrash compilations, today defines Judaism. But, as we recognize, there were diverse Judaisms, and no single orthodoxy, in ancient times, and so too there were different approaches to the reading and interpretation of Scripture, as well as to the use of Scripture for the statement of a religious system.

The basis for biblical interpretation in rabbinic Judaism, the Judaism of the dual Torah, is the myth of divine revelation to Moses at Sinai of the Torah in two media, oral and written, hence "dual Torah." The rabbis who stood in the line of tradition from Sinai produced commentaries to the written Torah as follows: *Sifra* to Leviticus, *Sifre* to Numbers, another *Sifre*, this one to Deuteronomy, of ca. 200 to 300; then *Genesis Rabbah, Leviticus Rabbah,* and *Pesiqta deRab Kahana,* of ca. 400 to 500; then *Lamentations Rabbah, Ruth Rabbah, Esther Rabbah,* and *Song of Songs Rabbah,* of ca. 500 to 600.

Paraphrase: A principal interest of the earlier compilations of midrash, in *Sifre* to Numbers and *Sifre* to Deuteronomy, is to join in the discourse of Scripture, meaning to make oneself part of the conversation. This is done by simply bringing to bear the sorts of questions that a listener will direct to the speaker in a dialogue: "Do you mean that in general, or only concerning the specific case? What is the sense of that phrase? In other words, do you maintain . . . ?" and similar matters. Application to the everyday world commences with translation into the framework of the here and now.

Prophecy: In its prophetic mode, midrash turned matters around by explaining the present out of the resources of eternity. Scripture's account of the past instructed sages on how to explain what was happening then and told them also what would happen in times to come. The question of events' meaning was rephrased in terms of the scriptural paradigm. Scripture, the written Torah, defined what an event was and also indicated what happening did not fall into the category of an event at all. Midrash in search of prophecy focused upon history, meaning the representation of intelligible sequences of purposeful events presented as narrative.

This address to Scripture as future history had no precedent in the Judaism of the dual Torah. The Judaism that had been taking shape beginning two centuries before the Mishnah in 200 did not encompass in its canonical writings a single historical work. The writings it did produce, moreover, rarely contained much narrative or even biography of a sustained nature. To define the terms of the crisis that defined the task of midrash as prophecy is simple. Christians saw Israel as God's people, rejected by God for rejecting the Christ. Israel saw Christians, now embodied in Rome, as Ishmael, Esau, Edom: the brother and the enemy. The political revolution marked by Constantine's conversion not only forced the two parties to discuss a single agendum and defined the terms in which each would take up that agendum, it also made each party investigate the entire past in attempting to make sense of the unprecedented and uncertain present. When emperors convert and governments shift allegiance, the world shakes under people's feet. In writings prior to those of midrashic compilations that were brought to closure at the end of the tumultuous fourth century, sages had in general treated scriptural history as typology or, as we say, they simply amplified narratives without yielding pointed contemporary conclusions. No pattern of history emerged in earlier midrash so as to impose articulated meaning on contemporary events. Rather than seeing historical events as patterned and therefore producing unique, yielding lessons on their own, the authors of *Sifra* and the two *Sifres* classified events in accord with the shared taxonomic traits among them. History as a sequence of unique, linear events, coming from somewhere and going to some other goal, played no articulated role in the writing at all.

Parable: Midrash as parable shows how the Judaic sages read the everyday as the metaphor against which the eternal is to be read, and the eternal as the metaphor against which the everyday is to be reenacted. It is exemplified in the powerful reading of Genesis by *Genesis Rabbah*, of Leviticus by *Leviticus Rabbah*, in both cases bringing to Scripture the anguish and the terror of difficult times—and learning from Scripture God's plan and program for all times. The deep structure of human existence, framed by Scripture and formed out of God's will as spelled out in the Torah, forms the foundation of everyday life. Here and now, in the life of the hour, humanity can and does know God. So everyday life forms a commentary on revealed Scripture—on the Torah—and Scripture, the Torah, provides a commentary on everyday life. When the Judaic sages read Scripture as a parable for the ordinary and the familiar, they transform not Scripture into what is commonplace but what is routine into the extraordinary framework of what is not. For example, they teach how to find in the everyday a parable for the transcendent, and so the commonplace turns out to provide a metaphor for the wholly other. Midrash-exegesis therefore mediates between the Holy Scriptures of ancient Israel and the living age. The way of doing so forms a paradigm.

The interpretation of Scripture in the Judaism of the dual Torah has been characterized by William Green as a labor of "writing with Scripture." That is to say, the received Scriptures formed an instrumentality for the expression of a writing bearing its own integrity and cogency, appealing to its own conventions of intelligibility, and, above all, making its own points. Any notion therefore that the authorships of Judaism proposed a systematic exegesis of Scripture conducted in terms of the original or historical program of Scripture, or appealed to Scripture for validation or vindication of doctrine or practice perceived as independent of Scripture, distorts the character of the discourse of Judaism. Scripture formed part of the Torah. The authorships of Judaism, particularly in late antiquity, also participated in the discourse and statement of the Torah. As Green says, they did not write *about* Scripture, they wrote *with* Scripture, for Scripture supplied the syntax and grammar of their thought. *See also* midrash.

Judaism (festal cycle).

Biblical Basis: Continuous but not entirely consistent with its biblical prototype, the Jewish calendar is lunar-solar, with years measured by the sun but months inaugurated by each new moon. Twelve lunar months fall eleven days short of the necessary 365-day solar year, so an extra month, Adar Sheni (Heb., "second Adar") is intercalated seven times every nineteen years. Months are either twenty-nine or thirty days long, in which case, Rosh Khodesh ("new moon" [day])—itself semiholy—lasts two days, the thirtieth day of the previous month and the first day of the new one. Nowadays, the year begins in the autumn with Tishri and continues through Cheshvan, Kislev, Tevet, Shevat, Adar, Nisan, Iyar, Sivan, Tammuz, Av, and Elul. "Days" are charted from evening to evening.

Rabbinic Judaism inherited an agriculturally rooted biblical calendar. At its core were three pilgrimage festivals: Pesach ("Passover"), Shavuot ("weeks"), and Sukkot ("booths"). Pesach, the anniversary of the Exodus, celebrated also the early spring harvest during what was then the first month of the year, Nisan. Seven weeks later, at Shavuot (known also as Pentecost), the grain harvest ripened. The autumn festival of Sukkot marked the final ingathering of the summer crops.

A separate strand of thought produced the weekly Sabbath as well as Yom Kippur ("day of atonement"), described as a "Sabbath of complete rest and self-denial" (Leviticus 16:31), on the tenth day of Tishri, the seventh month. The first day of Tishri—later known as Rosh Hashanah ("new year")—presaged Yom Kippur.

Finally, Zechariah 8:19 refers cryptically to annual fast days in the fourth, fifth, seventh, and tenth months. These are eventually identified as Asarah beTevet ("the tenth of Tevet"), Shivah asar beTammuz ("the seventeenth of Tammuz"), the Fast of Gedaliah (commemorating the death of Gedaliah, governor of Judah, 2 Kings 25:25) on the third of Tishri, and Tish'a be'Av ("the ninth of Av")—all events that constituted stages of the Babylonian siege and destruction of the first Temple.

The unifying principle behind these three calendrical strands is the concept of sacred covenant between God and Israel. God had elected Israel, redeemed Israel from Egyptian bondage, and deeded to Israel its own land where it could expect agricultural fecundity in return for covenantal loyalty. The three harvest festivals combined sacred time and space: time, in that the promised harvest had come due; space, in that appropriate worship entailed offering sacrifices of God's bounty and making pilgrimages to appear personally at the sacred center of the universe, the Jerusalem Temple. The Sabbath signified the sacred status of Israel as covenant partner (Exodus 31:13). It denoted God's rest on the seventh day of creation (Exodus 20:11), which Israel, as God's partner, duly emulated. And it also recollected God's covenantal redemptive act in Egypt (Deuteronomy 5:15). The Day of Atonement restored the covenantal relationship marred by human sin, and other fasts were called *ad hoc* when crops failed, or annually, to commemorate historical instances of divine punishment occasioned by Israel's covenantal lapse. All festivals are thus, above all, *mikra'ei kodesh* (holy convocations), sacred gatherings of the sacred people in its sacred space to mark sacred time.

Rabbinic Adaptations: The rabbis adopted the Bible's presupposition of a covenant but not its root metaphor of agricultural fertility. With increasing hellenization, not agricultural produce but God's Word, Torah, became central. Outfitted as it was with visual reminders of the harvest—a palm branch and a citron and the

Jews gathering for prayer at the Western Wall in Jerusalem, site of the destroyed Temple, during Passover (1970s). In the Bible, Passover is one of three feasts requiring a journey to the Temple in Jerusalem.

sukkot (or harvesting booths) themselves—the ingathering festival of Sukkot largely retained its agricultural cast, though it was increasingly reconceptualized as a recollection of the booths that Israel must have used during its covenant-forming journey from Egypt. Passover lost all agricultural connotation, becoming known instead only as the anniversary of the Exodus. Most striking of all, Shavuot was completely redefined as the time of revelation at Mt. Sinai. Thus, Torah, not the fruit of the land, became the covenantal gift par excellence.

A second rabbinic mutation of the sacred calendar resulted from the rabbis' increasing preoccupation with sin. Originally, confessions had functioned equally as professions. While giving produce to the priests, farmers professed their successes and confessed their failures in serving God adequately (see Mishnah, *Maaser Sheni* 5:10–13). Later practice, however, encouraged only confession of sin. This new emphasis on derogatory human sinfulness heightened the significance of fasts, which multiplied dramatically—some people fasted twice weekly (see Luke 18:12; Mark 2:18). The major annual fasts of Tish'a be'Av and Yom Kippur became more important too.

By now, there were four new-year celebrations in each annual cycle. But the fact that the first day of Tishri introduced the period of introspection leading up to Yom Kippur guaranteed that after the economic situation determining the others had ceased, this single date would be kept by Jews as their sole Rosh Hashanah, or New Year. (A remnant of a second new year, originally the fiscal year for fruit trees, the fifteenth of Shevat is still kept as a tree-planting celebration today.) The entire period between Rosh Hashanah and Yom Kippur became known as the Ten Days of Repentance; and the seven weeks from Passover to Shavuot, originally just the days to count the *omer* (sheaf of barley), that is, to count off the days of the harvest, took on a similar somber cast, redefined now as the *sefirah* (counting) in the dual sense of counting the omer and of reckoning with Israel's own experience of sin and punishment. Except for Lag ba'Omer ("thirty-third day of the omer") the sefirah period is observed in semimourning, in that elaborate festivities like weddings are traditionally prohibited. Also, the three weeks between the seventeenth of Tammuz and the ninth of Av were conceptualized as being *bayn hametzarim* (between two tight places), and outfitted with mourning regulations that lead to the severe fast of the ninth of Av.

The rabbis expanded the calendar in other ways as well. Purim marked the deliverance recounted in the Book of Esther, and Hanukkah commemorated the Hasmonean victory of the second century B.C. Special lections dominated the liturgy of specific seasons and holy days. The *megillah* (scroll [of Esther]) was read at Purim, while four other scrolls (Lamentations, Song of Songs, Ruth, and Ecclesiastes) found a place in the liturgy for Tish'a be'Av, Pesach, Shavuot, and Sukkot, respectively. The *arba parashiyot* (four [special] lections) introduced Purim and Passover: the Sabbath approximately two weeks prior to Purim—Shabbat Shekalim ("the Sabbath of shekels") featured the reading of the biblical command to collect the shekel tax; Shabbat Zakhor ("the Sabbath to remember" [Amalek]) followed, introducing Purim's theme by recollecting the biblical enemy, Amalek; after Purim, Shabbat Parah ("the Sabbath of the heifer") detailed a biblical atonement sacrifice, thereby proclaiming the need to greet the Passover period pure of sin; and Shabbat haKhodesh ("the Sabbath [announcing the new] month") then inaugurated Nisan as the preparatory period for Passover.

Other special Sabbaths, named for prophetic lections, included Shabbat hagadol ("the Great Sabbath") immediately preceding Passover (see John 19:31); Shabbat Shuvah ("the Sabbath of Repentance") in the Ten Days of Repentance; Shabbat Khazon ("the Sabbath of the vision") prior to the ninth of Av, and Shabbat Nakhamu ("the Sabbath of consolation") following the same fast.

Some holidays are kept for an extra day by Orthodox, Conservative, and Reconstructionist Jews living in the diaspora; originally, setting their occurrence depended on visual sighting of the new moon by a central authority. Unable to learn of that decision in time, but knowing that the new moon had to fall on one of two possible days, outlying settlements would observe both days to make sure their observance corresponded with the correct astronomical configuration.

The Annual Calendar Today: Rosh Hashanah and Yom Kippur (late September or October) constitute the "High Holidays" called *yamim noraim* (Days of Awe). The former is characterized by the blowing of the *shofar* (ram's horn), a practice often initiated daily in the preceding month of Elul as a call to repentance. The ceremony of Tashlikh invites people to empty their pockets into a stream of water, symbolic of cleansing their souls of sin. The Yom Kippur service begins with the chanting of Kol Nidre, a favorite prayer, and ends with Ne'illah, a service of "closing of

An American Jewish Passover meal (*seder*), in Kansas City, Missouri (1991). The young woman is lifting up a roasted lamb bone (*zeroa*), symbolic of the Passover sacrifice, from the large plate before her containing four other symbols of Passover: roasted eggs, also representing sacrifice; bitter herbs (*maror*), reminders of Israel's slavery in Egypt; *haroset,* a mixture of crushed fruit, nuts, and wine, interpreted as the mortar the Israelites were forced to make in Egypt; and a plate containing the first vegetable (*karpas*) to be dipped in salt water later in the meal.

the gates," symbolic of the gates of the Temple (once) and of the end of twenty-four hours in which prayer, fasting, and penitence have interceded for the life of human sinners.

Sukkot—beginning only four days after Yom Kippur—lasts eight days and is marked by the building of open-air booths decorated with produce in which families eat and (in some places) sleep. The *arba'ah minim* (four [agricultural] species)—a palm branch (*lulav*), a sprig of myrtle, a willow leaf, and a citron (*etrog*)—are waved by worshipers to acknowledge God who brings forth nature's bounty. The seventh day, Hoshanah Rabbah, is semipenitential in nature and features calls for salvation. The eighth day, Shemini Atseret, concludes Sukkot. The days between the first and last (or, in the diaspora, the first two and last two) days are called *khol hamo'ed* (the profane days [within] the holiday). More sacred than average weekdays, they nonetheless fall short of full sacrality—like Rosh Khodesh—in that work is not prohibited on them.

The day after Shemini Atseret presents Simchat Torah ("the joy of [concluding the reading of] the Torah"). Originally movable, celebrated whenever the Torah lectionary, which lasted about three and a half years, ended, Simchat Torah nowadays accompanies the completion of an annual cycle that terminates at the same time every year. Attendant celebration includes calling everyone to the Torah for the honor of reading a line within it, dancing around the sanctuary carrying Torah scrolls, and beginning the annual reading all over again.

Hanukkah, falling usually in late December, has emerged as the second or third most observed holiday in modern Jewish life and is widely seen as a celebration of freedom. For eight days, candles are lit at nightfall in an eight-branch candelabra known as a menorah, or (in modern Israel) a *khanukiyah*. Families exchange gifts, play games with a dreidel (Yiddish, "spinning top"), sing songs, and eat special foods (potato pancakes and doughnuts). It is a "minor" festival in that work is permitted.

By February or March, Purim arrives, its very month of Adar bringing unrestrained joy. Purim customs include giving gifts to the poor and dressing in costumes. At the *megillah* reading, people drown out Haman's name by twirling noisemakers called *gragers* (Yiddish). Favored foods include the *hamentash* (Yiddish), a dough pocket stuffed with cooked fruit.

Pesach (Passover) falls in the spring. Its first night is marked by the seder, a family feast accompanied by a liturgy called the Haggadah ("the telling [of the Exodus tale]"). Forbidden foods for Passover, called *khametz* (leaven) are removed from the home on the day prior, the last remains ritually hunted down in a ceremony called *biur khametz*, and then burned the next morning. The seder features special foods, including four cups of wine (*arba kosot*), unleavened bread (*matzah*), and bitter herbs (*maror*). A piece of matzah eaten at the feast's conclusion is called the *aphikoman. Me'ot khitim*, a communal charity fund, provides these foods for the poor. Illustrative of Jewish ceremonial creativity today are new Haggadah versions that appear annually, featuring novel prayers for world peace and human freedom.

Seven weeks after Passover, Shavuot commemorates revelation of Torah. Traditionalist communities feature an all-night vigil (*tikkun khatsot*) entailing continual study of sacred texts. Reform Jews, who celebrate confirmation, do so on Shavuot. Favored foods include dairy products.

The weekly Shabbat ("Sabbath") features rest and sanctification. Medieval mystics pictured it as a bride or queen, a personification in time of God's feminine aspect, and recited "[Who can find] a woman of valor . . ." (Proverbs 31:10–31) to greet it. Hasidic circles usher it out also with a *melaveh malkah* (accompanying the queen), a feast lasting late into Saturday night. Older prayers include the kiddush ("sanctification"), which welcomes the Sabbath by acknowledging its sanctity, and the *havdalah* (separation), a concluding rite dividing sacred time from profane.

Contemporary Jews have become history conscious, seeing their essence in their membership in the sacred people, Israel. Thus, historical holidays, especially those that favor celebration over mourning and feasting over fasting—such as Passover and Hanukkah—are growing in popularity. The High Holidays too still carry sacred symbolism to most Jews. By contrast, the historical fasts—such as Tish'a be'Av—and the festivals of Sukkot and Shavuot, once major events for land-conscious Jews, are now often ignored. New holidays too have made their appearance, above all, the springtime Yom haShoah ("Holocaust Day") and Yom ha'Atsma'ut ("[the State of Israel's] Independence Day"). Israeli Jews also keep Yom Yerushalayim ("Jerusalem Day") to mark Jerusalem's 1968 reunification and Yom haZikaron (Memorial Day) for its soldiers lost in battle. Beginning in 1988, there were signs that Kristallnacht was being marked also, in the United States. **See also** Sabbath.

Judaism (life cycle). The life-cycle events of Judaism constitute a coherent ritual exercise over a lifetime. The worldview expressed therein is that regular repetition of ritual acts is an effective way to guarantee that a Jew live in a moral and pious fashion, remembering the covenant made at Sinai and the high-minded principles of Torah.

Rites of Initiation: The act of *brit milah* (ritual circumcision), performed on male infants on the eighth day after birth, places a permanent reminder of the covenant in the flesh of a male Jew. The solemn ceremony is followed by a festive meal for family and friends. Thirty days after birth a second ceremony, called a *pidyon habben*, is held for a firstborn male child. His father redeems him from the service of God by giving five silver coins to a descendant of the priestly line (*kohen*).

Until children reach the age of religious maturity, twelve for girls and thirteen for boys, they are exempt from the obligation to perform ritual acts. However, while still young, they are given extensive training in the performance of these acts and encouraged to engage in them voluntarily. Jewish day and afternoon schools teach children classical Jewish texts and Jewish history, values, and beliefs.

Upon attaining his or her majority, on becoming a bar or bat mitzvah, a young Jew is expected to perform all obligations (*mitzvot*), both acts of piety and acts of lovingkindness. This milestone is celebrated publicly, with the youngster reading from Torah or Prophets and then offering an interpretation.

Celebrating the completion of the Hasidic Jewish haircutting ritual at the tomb of the second-century sage and reputed author of the *Zohar*, Rabbi Simeon bar Yohai, on the anniversary of his death in Meron, Israel. The three-year-old boy, wearing his father's hat, has received his first haircut, with his sidelocks left long. This marks his entrance into the men's community.

Dietary Restrictions: The laws of *kashrut* (dietary restrictions) regularly remind Jews of their relationship with God. Leviticus 11 presents a long list of forbidden species, the most well known of these being the pig. Other verses add other restrictions, such as a ban on consuming the blood of permitted animals (Leviticus 17) and cooking a kid in its mother's milk (Exodus 34:26). The rabbis of the Talmud turned the Torah's guidelines into an elaborate set of rules, stressing certain practices not explicitly mentioned in Torah, such as slaughtering in a pain-minimizing way and absolutely separating all dairy and meat products.

Every time Jews eat, at home or out, they must monitor their actions, making sure that they fall within the prescribed parameters. They may purchase only meat of an animal that was slaughtered by a *shohet* (certified slaughterer) and then soaked and salted to remove most of the blood. An animal that was slaughtered according to Jewish law but upon inspection found to have a defect that would have caused it to die within a year is called *terefah* (torn) and may not be eaten. Kosher butchers do not sell the hindquarter of the animal where the sciatic nerve is located. According to Torah (Genesis 32:33), Jews do not eat this nerve out of deference to the patriarch Jacob.

The term *kosher*, meaning fit, describes food that Jews may eat and utensils they may use to prepare such food. A kosher home, one in which all laws of kashrut are observed, stocks two sets of dishes and cooking utensils, one for the preparation of meat and the other for dairy. Foods that are *parveh* (neutral), such as grains, fruits, and vegetables, may be served on either set of dishes. No food that is *treif* (forbidden by Jewish law), such as pork products or shellfish, may be served in a kosher home.

The prohibition on eating an organ torn from a live animal encourages Jews to behave compassionately toward God's creatures. A portion of bread dough is thrown into the fire, the portion a Jew in Temple times gave to a priest. In all, the wide-ranging rules related to food regularly remind Jews of their divinely mandated social conscience and tribal consciousness.

Rules of Dress: A *kippah* or *yarmulke* (skullcap) is worn by many Jewish men when eating, studying, and praying, and by some Jews all the time. This highly visible head covering serves as a mark of Jewish identification as well as a reminder of the presence of God everywhere.

A *tallit* (prayer shawl), decorated at its four corners with *tzitzit* (fringes), is worn during prayer to help achieve proper concentration. *Tefillin* (phylacteries), small black boxes containing Torah verses written on parchment, are wound around the head and arm during morning prayer, symbolically effecting a betrothal between a Jew and God. The verses found in the tefillin speak of God's oneness and the acceptance by Jews of the yoke of God's commandments. Jews are required to hang a *mezuzah* on the right doorpost of their homes. This tiny receptacle, which, like tefillin, contains key Torah verses written on parchment, serves as a constant visual reminder of the basic principles of Jewish life. Some Jews, on the High Holidays and also under the wedding canopy, don a white *kittel* (caftan) as a sign of purity and the start of a new chapter in life. The Torah forbids a Jew to wear clothing made of *shaatnez*, a mixture of linen and wool.

Marriage: Judaism sees in human relationships a path to the sacred. *Kiddushin*, the Hebrew term for betrothal, means sanctification. Because Jewish authorities consider marriage to be the ideal state for mature adults, the mitzvah of escorting a bride to the wedding canopy ranks high in the rabbinic scheme of things, taking precedence even over burial of the dead.

The Jewish wedding ceremony is composed of two distinct segments, the kiddushin or *erusin* (betrothal) and the *nissuin* (wedding blessings and feast). In rabbinic times these ceremonies used to be separated by twelve months, but because young women sometimes found themselves abandoned by a fiance who left town and never returned, it became routine to perform them both on the same day.

During the entire ceremony the couple stands under a *huppah*, a canopy symbolizing the home they will share. The groom places a ring on the bride's finger, declaring that she is set aside or sanctified for him. A rabbi or other officiant recites the betrothal blessings, and the couple shares a cup of wine. To separate between betrothal and wedding, the *ketubah* (marriage document) is read aloud. The second part of the ceremony consists of seven blessings on the themes of creation as a series of successive separations and marriage as an act of joining together of disparate parts—for now, this man and woman, and in the future, the Jewish people and their land. The couple then sips from a second cup of wine. The ceremony concludes with the groom shattering a glass underfoot, a reminder of past Jewish catastrophes and the need to work for a better world.

Immediately after the wedding ceremony the

couple is required to spend some time together away from the guests, a way of symbolically consummating their marriage. The wedding festivities continue with a feast in celebration of the occasion. It is customary for the guests to entertain the newlywed couple.

Marriage confers upon husband and wife a set of reciprocal rights and responsibilities. Some of these are outlined in the contract, a document that guarantees that property the wife brought into the marriage remain hers and promises her a cash settlement should the husband divorce or predecease her. According to the Talmud, a husband is expected to support his wife, provide her with all the necessities of life, and also meet his conjugal obligations to her. She is expected to prepare the food, make the clothes, care for the children, and run the home. Other stipulations of Jewish marriage, not spelled out in the contract, include medical care, domicile for the widow, funeral arrangements for the wife, and ransom if she is kidnapped or taken captive.

Marriage in the biblical and rabbinic periods was viewed as the acquisition of a wife by a husband. For the duration of the marriage, she was not allowed to engage in sexual relations with any other man, but he was permitted to take a second wife. The corollary of this asymmetrical relationship is that infidelity in the Bible is defined as a wife's act of sexual impropriety with a man who is not her husband. Numbers 5 states that if a man suspects his wife of being a *sotah*, a woman who has strayed from the path of righteousness, he may take her to the Temple and force her to submit to the "water ordeal" (Numbers 5:11–31) to test her innocence.

Judaism has a positive attitude toward sexual pleasure. As long as it occurs in a marital context, no form of sexual expression is proscribed. In monogamous marriage, the social norm since the rabbinic period, the couple is restricted from sexual relations for approximately two weeks of every month, the time corresponding to the wife's menstrual period and the seven "clean" days that follow. After her immersion in a ritual bath (*mikveh*), the couple is permitted to resume sexual activity.

Divorce: Like marriage, divorce is unilateral. Only the husband may decide to terminate the relationship and dismiss his wife; she has no say in the matter. Upon divorcing her, he has to write her a *get*, a bill of divorce, and deliver it to her. If for some reason he dismisses her but does not write her a get, she becomes an *agunah*, a woman tied to a husband she is no longer living with but not free to marry another.

Levirate Marriage: The Torah deems it important that a Jew's name be kept alive through his children. If a man dies childless, his wife is obligated to marry his brother and is considered already betrothed to him upon her husband's death. A child born to this couple bears the name of the deceased brother. Should the brother choose not to marry the widow, he must undergo a ceremony called *halitzah*. By removing a shoe from the brother's foot and spitting on the ground in front of him, the widow dissolves her bond to the family of her deceased husband.

Funerary Rites: In Judaism, funerary rites, like other rites of passage, view each individual as precious to the community. Underlying this set of ritual acts are the concepts of preserving the honor and dignity of the deceased and creation in the image of God. It follows that autopsies are prohibited, unless absolutely necessary for the sake of medical research or the moral functioning of society.

When death seems imminent, a Jew is encouraged to recite a confessional prayer that asks God for forgiveness for past misdeeds and a place with God after death. Starting from the moment of death, the corpse is cared for by a group of community volunteers, who keep a continuous watch over the body, purify the corpse with water, and dress it for burial.

Jews are instructed to rend their garments immediately upon learning of the death of a close relative. From the time of death and until burial is over, the immediate relatives of the deceased—parents, spouse, siblings, and children—are called *onenim*, individuals in a state of deep grief, and are exempt from fulfilling any of the positive observances of Judaism.

The funeral service consists of three parts: readings from Psalms, a eulogy that summarizes the life and accomplishments of the deceased, and the memorial prayer. The mourners and others then escort the corpse to the burial grounds. The Hebrew term for funeral, *levayah* (escorting), refers to this accompanying of the deceased on this final trip. At the cemetery, immediately before interment, either a rabbi or the mourners themselves recite *tzidduk hadin*, a prayer justifying the divine decree.

While burial is taking place, friends of the bereaved family prepare a meal, called the meal of consolation, for the mourners to eat upon their return from the cemetery. The immediate relatives of the deceased "sit *shivah*" (seven). For seven days, starting with the day of burial, they stay in one place, usually the home of the deceased, and receive visits from friends. Shivah is a way of drawing the community into the lives of the grieving family and marking and mourning the death of their precious relative. Jewish law places a number of restrictions on the mourners for the week of shivah: they are not allowed to go to work, bathe for pleasure, anoint the body with oil, engage in sexual relations, wear leather shoes, or study classical Jewish texts. It is customary for the mourners to sit on stools or low chairs. The Sabbath that falls during shivah counts as one of the seven days, but no public mourning observances are allowed on that day. The seventh or last day of shivah is abbreviated, with mourning ending after the morning services.

A less intense period of mourning, called *sheloshim* (thirty), continues until thirty days have passed following the burial. During this time the mourners resume social and professional relationships but are still restricted in several ways. Men may not shave. Neither men nor women may have their hair cut or attend social or religious celebrations. The end of sheloshim ends the period of mourning for a spouse, sibling, or child. For parents one continues to mourn and avoid social gatherings for a full year.

During shivah and afterward, at each of the prayer services, mourners recite Kaddish. This prayer, written not in Hebrew but Aramaic, says nothing about death. It is a doxology, a prayer extolling God, saying that human beings lack the faculties to adequately describe God and God's attributes. Kaddish was not originally composed for mourners but served as a marker between the various sections of the service. As time passed, it became customary for mourners to lead the congregation in this prayer. The reason for this custom is not clear, but some speculate that the prayer's grand language and cosmic perspective comfort the mourners by suggesting that the death of a loved one, as untimely as it may seem, is part of an overall, divinely orchestrated scheme.

Each year on the *yahrzeit* (Yiddish, lit., "time of year"), the anniversary of the day of death as determined by the Jewish calendar, close relatives attend synagogue services, recite Kaddish, are called to the Torah scroll, and, if possible, serve as prayer leader. In the home, an anniversary candle is lit at sundown to burn throughout the following day.

After about a year has passed, it is customary to place a tombstone at the head of the grave. The Hebrew name and patronym, and more recently also the matronym, are engraved in the stone, as well as the day of death on the Jewish calendar. The English name of the deceased and the date of death according to the secular calendar are usually engraved as well.

On the three pilgrimage festivals, Passover, Shavuot, and Sukkot, and also on Yom Kippur, *Yizkor* ("May God remember"), a memorial prayer for the dead, is recited. Charitable donations are pledged in memory of one's deceased relatives, and God is petitioned to care for their souls.

Judaism, particularly from the rabbinic period on, believes in life after death (immortality) for the soul and resurrection of the dead in the time of the Messiah.

Conversion to Judaism: If a Gentile wishes to convert to Judaism, he or she must become a partner in the covenant. For both men and women the first stage of this process is acquiring detailed knowledge of Jewish practices and beliefs by studying Jewish texts, the Hebrew language, and the history of the Jewish people. Men must then undergo ritual circumcision, or if they are already circumcised, blood is drawn. The key acts for both men and women are personal acceptance of the obligation to perform mitzvot followed by immersion in a mikveh. Upon emerging from the waters, the individual is a full-fledged member of the Jewish people. Judaism's willingness to admit converts indicates that it is an open system, one that views the covenant with God as accessible to anyone who is ready to accept its terms.

Gender Issues in Judaism: Judaism, like other ancient religions, is patriarchal: it views men as the primary party to the covenant with God, and hence obligated to engage in numerous acts of piety. Women, who were socially subordinate to and economically dependent upon men, could only enter the covenant through their relationships with men and were therefore not required to perform the same acts of piety. Men had to pray three times daily, don phylacteries, hear the ram's horn blown on Rosh Hashanah, and dwell in thatched huts on the Festival of Sukkot. Women were exempt from all of these positive time-specific acts because their time was not their own. Moreover, even if a woman was competent to execute a certain act of piety, such as reading from the Torah in public, she was not allowed to do so, because her inferior social standing would affront the dignity of the men present.

Women managed all domestic affairs—food and clothing preparation, care of the children and the home. They were required to turn all earned and even unearned income over to their husbands, who then gave them an allowance for household and personal expenses. Women's extensive limitations in both marriage and divorce reflected their lower social standing. The serious contemporary implications of this lower status, in particular women's inability to initiate a divorce, have yet to be fully resolved.

The larger question emerging from a discussion of women's position in Judaism is how their secondary and subordinate status meshes with Judaism's acknowledged affinity for justice and fair treatment. If the life-cycle rituals in Judaism reinforce commitment to the covenant between God and the Jewish people, and if the overriding principles of that covenant are justice and equality in human dealings, then in the area of women's rights and responsibilities, Jewish practice is deficient. However, because responsa throughout the ages have displayed a remarkable aptitude for introducing modifications in Jewish practice while at the same time jealously guarding underlying Torah principles, it should not be difficult for contemporary rabbis to make the ethically mandated changes.

Judaism (mysticism). Judaism may be said to possess a mystical tradition in two senses: (1) since the end of the biblical era, there has been a persistent tradition of esoterica, and (2) a good deal of these secret teachings involve ascent to and unitive experiences with the divine realm. Such experiences are not described in terms of rational, intellectual processes but are usually the result of intense meditative or illuminative preparatory rites. This combination of esotericism and unitive experience lies at the core of Jewish mysticism.

The Hebrew Bible does not know of mysticism in this sense. Prophetism and mysticism are merged only in the later Middle Ages, and though some of the more visionary prophets (Isaiah, Ezekiel) would serve as paradigms for subsequent Jewish mystics, the Hebrew Bible does no more than radiate a sense of mystery concerning the theophanies. There is no evidence for esoteric traditions underlying biblical prophetism; nor is there the suggestion that the Hebrew prophets experienced a mystical union with God.

Merkabah Mysticism: The beginnings of Jewish mysticism can be found in the surviving literature of the first centuries. Within the rabbinic community, exegetical speculation arose concerning two crucial issues that were deemed to have an esoteric nature: ma 'aseh bereshit ("account of creation") and ma 'aseh merkavah ("account of the chariot"). It is the second topic, rooted first and foremost in the puzzling chariot vision of Ezekiel 1, that eventually gave rise to the oldest form of Jewish mysticism, usually designated "merkabah mysticism." Merkabah mysticism flourished for over a thousand years until it was supplanted by the theosophical mysticism of the Provencal-Spanish *kabbalah* in the thirteenth century.

The earliest merkabah speculations were exegetical expositions of the prophetic visions of God in the heavens and the divine retinue of angels, hosts, and heavenly creatures surrounding God. The earliest evidence suggests that merkabah homiletics did not give rise to ascent experiences.

Talmudic interdictions concerning merkabah speculation are numerous and widely held. Discussions concerning the merkabah were limited to only the most worthy sages, and admonitory legends are preserved about the dangers of overzealous speculation concerning the merkabah. According to tradition, the sages Yochanan ben Zakkai (d. ca. 80) and Akiba ben Joseph (d. ca. 135) were deeply involved in merkabah speculation. Rabbi Akiba and his contemporary Rabbi Ishmael ben Elisha are most often the protagonists of later merkabah ascent literature.

Beyond the rabbinic community, Jewish apocalyptists engaged in visionary speculations concerning the divine realm and the divine creatures that are remarkably similar to the rabbinic material. A small number of texts unearthed at Qumran indicate that the Dead Sea community engaged in merkabah speculation. Jewish magical texts also evidence a deep affinity with the rabbinic merkabah homilies. Recently, considerable scholarly attention has been paid to the use of merkabah themes in early Jewish-Christian and/or Gnostic circles.

The merkabah homilies eventually consisted of detailed descriptions of multiple-layered heavens (usually seven in number), often guarded over by angels and encircled by flames and lightning. The highest heaven contains seven palaces (*hekhalot*), and in the innermost palace resides a supreme divine image (God's glory or an hypostatic angel) seated on a throne, surrounded by awesome hosts who sing God's praise.

It is not known precisely when these images were combined with an actual mystical experience of individual ascent and enthronement. Contemporary historians of Jewish mysticism usually date this development to the third century. There is dispute among historians over whether these ascent themes were the result of some "foreign," usually Gnostic, influence or the product of religious dynamics within rabbinic Judaism.

Within the merkabah (heavenly throne, chariot) or hekhalot (heavenly palace) texts, it is possible to distinguish two central elements: the mystical ascent culminating in a visionary experience, and the adjuration of angels. The ascent texts are extant in four principal works, all redacted well after the third but certainly before the ninth century: (1) *Hekhalot Zutarti* (The Lesser Palaces), which details an ascent of Rabbi Akiba; (2) *Hekhalot Rabbati* (The Greater Palaces), which details an ascent of Rabbi Ishmael; (3) *Ma'aseh Merkabah* (Account of the Chariot), a collection of hymns recited by those who ascend to the heavenly throne; and (4) *Sefer Hekhalot* (Book of Palaces, also known as 3 Enoch), which recounts an ascent and divine transformation of the biblical figure Enoch into the archangel Metatron, as related by Rabbi Ishmael.

A fifth work provides a detailed description of the enthroned glory presumably apprehended by the "descenders" to the throne at the climax of their ascent. This work, preserved in various forms, is called *Shi'ur Qomah* (Measurement of the Body) and is thought by some scholars to be rooted in a mystical exegesis of the Song of Songs. The *Shi'ur Qomah* contains measurements of the bones, limbs, and appendages of the Creator on a vast scale. A particular divine or angelic name, usually composed of what appears to be an incomprehensible sequence of consonants, is also attached to each limb. Though some later authorities, e.g., Saadya Gaon (d. 942), accepted the work, advocating a nonliteral interpretation, others, e.g., Maimonides (d. 1204), ultimately concluded that the book was a forgery and that study of it amounted to idolatry. *Shi'ur Qomah* served as an important source for subsequent kabbalistic theosophy.

Though in the merkabah texts themselves the problem of creation was not of paramount importance, the treatise *Sefer Yetzirah* (Book of Creation) represents an attempt at cosmogony from within a merkabah milieu. This text was probably composed during the seventh century and evidences the influence of Neoplatonism, Pythagoreanism, and Stoicism. It features a linguistic theory of creation in which God creates the universe by means of the ten primordial numerals (*sefirot*) together with the twenty-two letters of the Hebrew alphabet.

Merkabah mysticism flourished in the Near East through the tenth century. There is significant evidence for the influence of merkabah mysticism in Islamic thought. Merkabah traditions were transported to the European Jewish communities at a relatively late date, most likely through Italian conduits, around the ninth century. An important source for the preservation and transmission of the documents were groups of German Jewish Pietists active in the Rhineland in the twelfth and thirteenth centuries.

Various older theosophic currents and mystical tendencies converged in the twelfth and thirteenth centuries, which may be considered the period of the richest development of Jewish mysticism. In particular we can speak of three distinct centers of activity: the German Pietists, the theosophic kabbalists, and the ecstatic kabbalists.

German Pietism: Several major groups belonged to this pietistic movement, the Haside Ashkenaz ("German Pietists"). The main circle was led by Judah ben Samuel of Regensburg (d. 1217) and his leading disciple, Eleazar ben Judah of Worms (d. 1240). In addition to preserving the older merkabah texts, the Pietists developed their own theosophy, which combined merkabah mysticism, the philosophy of Saadya Gaon (882–942), the writings of Shabbetai Donnolo (b. 913) and Judah ben Barzillai (late eleventh to early twelfth century), and Jewish Neoplatonism, especially that of Abraham ibn Ezra (ca. 1092–1167).

At the center of the Pietistic theosophy is the doctrine of the divine glory (*kavod*). A lively discussion in Pietistic circles revolved around the question of the nature of the glory. Three distinct approaches were identified: the glory was a created light extrinsic to God (Saadya); it was emanated from God and therefore attached to the deity (Abraham ibn Ezra); the visible form of the glory is an image within the mind of the prophet or mystic and not an entity outside the mind (Hai Gaon [939–1038]). The Pietists reject the first view and waver between the second and third. Following the view expressed by Nathan ben Yehiel of Rome (1035–ca. 1110), itself based on earlier sources, Eleazar of Worms distinguishes between an upper and lower glory. The former is an amorphous light, called the "Presence" (*Shekhinah*) or "great splendor" (*hod hagaddol*), while the latter is the aspect that assumes different forms within the prophetic or mystical imagination. Judah and Eleazar both insist that the Creator is simultaneously outside and inside the image. One can therefore pray to the visible glory, which is an image, for God is present in that very image. The forms that the lower glory assumes are multiple in nature, changing in accordance with God's will and the particular capacity of the given visionary. The most important of these images is the anthropomorphic shape suggested already by prophetic visions, including the chariot vision of Ezekiel. Indeed, the Pietists appropriate *Shi'ur Qomah*, applying the corporeal measurements not to the

Creator (as the text explicitly states) but rather to the form that is constituted within the imagination. By contrast, according to the second major circle of Pietists, known as the Hug ha-Keruv ha-Meyuhad ("Circle of the Special Cherub"), the measurable enthroned figure is the Special Cherub, the anthropomorphic representation of the divine glory.

It must be noted, however, that alongside the exoteric doctrine of the glory the main circle of Pietists developed a more esoteric tradition. The main tenets of this tradition are the identification of the glory with the Tetragrammaton (the four-letter divine name) and the possibility of imaging the letters of this divine name as a human figure. The lower glory, at times identified as a cherub or the image of Jacob-Israel engraved upon the throne, is also characterized as an angel. One may also discern from the Pietistic writings that study of the chariot involved a mystical praxis, whereby the Pietist ascended by means of meditation upon the divine name. Eleazar thus specifies a series of rituals of purification as a prelude to both the study of the chariot and the activity of mentioning the divine name.

Theosophic Kabbalah: The precise origins of kabbalistic speculation remain somewhat obscure, though it is generally assumed that fragments of older documents made their way to central Europe from the East. Rabbinic writings themselves may be viewed as a repository of an ancient Jewish theosophy that has been preserved in a very fragmentary form and that was elaborated into a comprehensive and systematic doctrine by the medieval kabbalists. It is also likely that there was a prehistory to some kabbalistic ideas that were transmitted orally.

One of the crucial problems in the historical development of theosophic kabbalah is the relationship between Gnosticism and Jewish esotericism. Some scholars maintain that the similarities between Gnosticism and kabbalah are purely phenomenological in nature, whereas others insist there is a historical connection as well.

Whatever the relationship between Gnosticism and kabbalah, it is evident that in twelfth-century Provence and northern Spain, a theosophic conception of God began to crystallize in Jewish writings. The main elements of this theosophy include the imaging of God in terms of a male-female polarity and the theurgical understanding of normative religious practice such that fulfillment of the traditional precepts increases the stature of the divine and, conversely, failure to do so weakens the divine. In the first

text dedicated fully to a theosophical-theurgical conception of God, the *Sefer ha-Bahir* (Book of Illumination), and more evidently in the writings of the Provencal kabbalist Isaac the Blind (ca. 1160–1235) and his thirteenth-century Geronese disciples, Ezra ben Solomon and Azriel ben Menahem, the key term employed to describe the ten gradations that collectively make up the divine realm is *sefirot*, a term first used in *Sefer Yetzirah* to designate the primary ciphers employed in the process of creation. The transition from ancient Jewish mysticism to medieval kabbalah can be seen in the critical semantic shift related to the denotation of this term. The sefirot that make up the divine pleroma are depicted in *Sefer ha-Bahir*, and in subsequent kabbalistic texts, either as a cosmic tree or as the primordial man. In the case of Isaac the Blind and his disciples in Gerona, the ten sefirot (emanations) are set against the *Ein-Sof* ("Infinite"). The latter term designates the unknowable, nameless Godhead that projects itself into the ten emanations that comprise the dynamic personality of God. In contrast to the Bahiric symbolism, heavily gnostic and mythological in orientation, the Provencal-Spanish kabbalists introduced Neoplatonic images and terms in order to explain the process of emanation of the sefirot from the Infinite. Utilizing Neoplatonic concepts, these kabbalists also developed a notion of contemplative prayer resulting in the intellectual ascent of the mystic to the divine, culminating in a state of communion (*devekut*). This Neoplatonic terminology became the subsequent heritage of theosophic kabbalah.

As in the case of the German Pietists, the theosophic understanding of God in the kabbalistic sources involved an ecstatic, visionary component. The two main symbolic systems to describe these sefirot were those of light symbolism and name symbolism. Knowing the divine powers, therefore, entailed a state of illumination in which these powers were visualized either as lights or as letters of the divine names. In the history of kabbalistic thought two dominant approaches developed to explain the precise nature of these emanations, the essentialist and the instrumentalist views. According to some kabbalists, the sefirot were considered to be the divine essence itself, whereas others claimed that these attributes were instruments employed by God in the creative process. Each of the sefirotic emanations were given various names principally culled from Scripture. In fact, the ten sefirot were said to be contained within the Tetragrammaton, which in turn was identified as the Torah in its mystical essence. Visualization of the sefirot thus was realized by means of meditative contemplation of the letters of the Torah scroll. The very process of textual study was considered by kabbalists to be an occasion for mystical vision, the Torah being treated as the objectified form of the divine image.

In the thirteenth century, principally in Catalonia and Castile, kabbalistic study and literary activity was limited to small elite circles, though some of the major kabbalists, e.g., Moses ben Nahman (1194–1270) and Solomon ben Abraham ibn Adret (ca. 1235–1310), were leading rabbinic authorities and communal leaders. Theosophic kabbalah reached its most elaborate expression in the crowning work of the period, *Sefer ha-Zohar* (Book of Splendor), a text attributed to the second-century Palestinian rabbi Simeon bar Yohai. In fact, the *Zohar* was composed in stages during the last two decades of the thirteenth century in Castile. Though the leading scholarly opinion is that the *Zohar* in its diverse literary strata was authored by a single hand, Moses ben Shem Tov de Leon (1240–1305), a strong alternative is that parts of this text may have been written by several mystics working together within one circle or fellowship. The composition and dissemination of the *Zohar* represent a critical closure in the history of kabbalistic literature insofar as much subsequent kabbalistic literary activity took the form of commenting upon the Zoharic text. Another important literary genre consists of imitations of the *Zohar*, as in the fourteenth-century *Ra'aya Mehemna* (The Faithful Shepherd) and the *Tikkunei Zohar* (Embellishments of the Zohar), composed by an anonymous Spanish kabbalist.

With the expulsion of Jews from Spain in 1492, the center of kabbalistic activity shifted from there to other countries, including Italy and Palestine. The most significant center to develop in post-Zoharic kabbalah was in Safed in the sixteenth century. Several prominent kabbalists, e.g., Joseph Karo (1488–1575), Solomon Alkabez (ca. 1505–84), Moses Cordovero (1522–70), and his disciple Elijah de Vidas assembled together in Safed. A major innovation in Safedian kabbalah can be traced to the teachings of Isaac Luria (1534–72), based to a great measure on earlier theosophic doctrine, including the thought of Cordovero. The Lurianic kabbalah was disseminated by several leading disciples, including Hayyim Vital (1543–1620), Moses Jonah, and Joseph ibn Tabul. Another version of Lurianic thought, also highly influential in the Diaspora communities, was propagated by Israel Sarug. Some of the most distinguished kabbalists in Italy in the later part of the sixteenth century, e.g., Menahem Azariah da Fano (1548–1620) and Aaron Berechiah of Modena (d. 1639), established a school based on the Sarugian version of Lurianic kabbalah. Sarug also taught Abraham Herrera (ca. 1570–1635), whose *Puerto del Cielo* combines the kabbalistic teachings of his master with Neoplatonic philosophy. A mixture of the traditions of Vital and Sarug is evident in the *Emek ha-Melekh* (1648) of Naftali Bacharach.

Luria's teachings played an important role in subsequent developments in Jewish mysticism, including the pseudo-messianic movement of the seventeenth century, Shabbateanism, and eighteenth-century Hasidism. In addition to formulating a complicated theosophy that was deeply mythological in nature, Luria and his circle in Safed were instrumental in instituting changes in the liturgical and ritualistic life of Judaism that are still intact to this day. These changes assured the continued influence of kabbalah upon Judaism and in many ways brought the mystical tradition into the forefront. The influence of Lurianic kabbalah is also evident in more popular ethical and homiletical literature that served as an important background for the emergence of Beshtian Hasidism.

Ecstatic Kabbalah: Alongside the development of theosophic kabbalah in the second half of the thirteenth century there emerged another type of kabbalah or esoteric tradition, ecstatic or prophetic kabbalah. Its major exponent was the Spanish mystic Abraham Abulafia (b. ca. 1240). Whereas the theosophical kabbalah focused on the inner workings of the God based on the doctrine of the ten emanations (sefirot) and the possibility of human action to affect that structure, ecstatic kabbalah was focused on the attainment of a state of mystical union in which all boundaries separating the self from the God were overcome. The union is so complete in the ecstatic experience that the individual mystic can utter, "He is I and I am He." The ecstatic state of union was characterized by Abulafia as prophecy, which he further described, following Maimonides, as the conjunction between the human and divine intellects. In his understanding of the means to realize this state, Abulafia, however, differs radically from Maimonides, whose rationalistic philosophy was based on the principals of Aristotelian epistemology as transmitted by its medieval Islamic interpreters.

The chief techniques employed by Abulafia and his disciples include letter-combination (identified by Abulafia as the genuine merkabah mysticism) in three stages, written, oral, and mental; recitation of the divine names; and special breathing exercises and bodily motions connected with the chanting of different vocalizations of the names. These techniques were intended to help the individual to free his true self, i.e., the intellectual soul, from the bonds of the body so that he may ultimately achieve a state of cleaving to God (devekut). This union with the divine must be realized, according to Abulafia, through a process called *hitbodedut*, which implies both social isolation and intense mental concentration. Frequently, the object of that mental focus is described as the letters of the Tetragrammaton. The latter are also visualized within the mystical imagination as an anthropomorphic form, at times identified with the demiurgical angel Metatron (the personification of the Active Intellect). In the mystical vision in Abulafian kabbalah, therefore, the letters of the Tetragrammaton have the capacity to appear within the imagination of the prophet-mystic as a human figure.

Abulafian kabbalah had a profound influence on subsequent kabbalah, beginning with a circle established in northern Palestine at the end of the thirteenth century that combined ecstatic kabbalah with Sufism. Ecstatic kabbalah also played a major role in sixteenth-century Safedian kabbalah, in the writings of Moses Cordovero and his disciples as well as in the writings of Hayyim Vital. It was principally through these channels that Abulafian kabbalah had a decisive influence on the Hasidic movement that flourished in eastern Europe in the eighteenth and nineteenth centuries.

Judaism (thought and ethics).

Religious Thought:

The Problem of a Jewish Philosophy or Theology:
Throughout its history, Judaism, like most other religions, has contained within itself certain fundamental ideas about God, humanity, and the world and the relation between them. Indeed, as a religion (particularly, a biblical religion) rather than a philosophy, the central concern of Judaism is focused precisely on the relation between these entities rather than on the entities taken in themselves. Judaism has certainly dealt with these entities taken singly when it considered such issues as which attributes, if any, can be ascribed to God; or whether human beings are a compound of body and soul and, if so, what the relation is between the two; or whether humanity is free and, if so, in what sense and to what extent. Still, Judaism's main concern is with the relational categories linking these entities, such as, e.g., creation and revelation signifying

the relating of God to the world and humanity respectively or prayer and ritual signifying the relating of human beings to God.

But although Judaism has always contained these concepts and categories, it has not always articulated or explicated them in a sustained, systematic, and rational fashion. In other words, Judaism has not always developed an explicit theology or philosophy of religion (what might be referred to as "religious thought"). This is not surprising, because there is no innate reason why every religion must articulate its faith in a theological or philosophical manner. In fact, the extent to which a religion explicitly expresses itself through a philosophical-theological formulation will largely depend on the way the religion in question witnesses to the divine. In those religions whose central mode of witnessing to the divine is by asserting the truth of certain propositional statements—e.g., doctrinal religions such as Christianity—the philosophical-theological expression is indeed an essential aspect of the religion itself. But other religions witness to the divine in other ways; Judaism accomplishes this through the medium of "commandment." Such religions have no built-in need for the philosophical-theological expression to play a central or required role. To put it another way, religions for which the philosophical-theological expression is essential are those that formulate themselves in terms of ontology. That is to say, the philosophical-theological expression is essential to those religions that locate the human predicament in one or another aspect of its being. Religions for which the philosophical-theological expression is not essential formulate themselves in other terms, the most prominent of these being ethical.

Judaism formulates itself in the ethical rather than in the ontological domain. Consequently, its central mode of witnessing is in the observance of commandments instead of the profession of doctrines; its essential expression is not philosophical-theological but rather legal-halakic (the ethical being mediated through the law). This being the case, it should not be surprising to find that the philosophical-theological undertaking is neither essential nor indigenous to Judaism; rather, it is pursued only sporadically—at certain places and at certain times—and even then only peripherally, the main concern always being the legal-halakic. Indeed, the philosophical-theological undertaking does not arise naturally from within Judaism but only in response to challenges from worldviews expressed by other religions and cultures. Left to itself, Judaism does not turn to the philosophical-theological but rather to the legal-halakic mode of expression.

In the long history of Judaism, competing worldviews have challenged Judaism in three major encounters; consequently, there are three instances in which the philosophical-theological undertaking flourished in Judaism. These are (1) in Alexandria from the second century B.C. to the middle of the first century A.D.; (2) in the medieval period, first under Islam from the tenth to the thirteenth century and then under Christendom (but mainly in places around the Mediterranean such as Spain, Provence, and Italy that were in close proximity to the Islamic world) from the thirteenth to the sixteenth century; (3) in the modern era, mainly in Germany, from the middle of the eighteenth century to our day. In each of these instances Judaism comes into close contact with an alternative, competing culture that inevitably challenges its worldview and precipitates for it a "shaking of the foundations." Thus, in Alexandria Judaism encounters the Hellenistic culture, in the Middle Ages the Islamic culture, and in the modern era the European culture. Ultimately, however, in all three instances Judaism actually encounters one and the same alternative, competing worldview, namely, that of Greek culture, of Athens. In Alexandria it is encountered directly, while in the Middle Ages it is mediated through Islam and in the modern era through European, mainly German, culture. In the face of the challenge presented in each instance, Judaism has to reassert and reestablish its validity, and this inevitably calls the philosophical-theological undertaking into play. But beyond these differences in chronology and geographic-cultural mediation, there are three further differences in method (and even in content) of the philosophical-theological undertaking in the three periods. The first revolves around the issue of which specific philosophical system serves as the basis on which the alternative worldview mounts its challenge to Judaism. Thus, in the Alexandrian period it is the philosophy of Plato or Stoicism; in the Middle Ages it is the philosophy of Aristotle or of Neoplatonism; in the modern era it is the philosophy of German Idealism (i.e., Immanuel Kant, Georg Hegel, and Friedrich von Schelling).

The second difference, paralleling the first, revolves around the issue of which philosophical system the defenders of Judaism turn to in order to overcome the challenge and reestablish and reaffirm the foundations of Judaism. Thus, for example, Philo turns to Plato, Maimonides to Aristotle, Ibn Gabirol to Neoplatonism, Her-mann Cohen to Kant, Samuel Hirsch to Hegel, and Rosenzweig to Schelling.

The third and final difference revolves around the issue of which dimension of Judaism's structure of faith (the divine, the human, or the relationship subsisting between the two) is the focus of the philosophical-theological concern. In the Alexandrian period it is the relation between the divine and the human. Thus, e.g., the category of the logos or of wisdom occupies a prominent place in the thought of this period (e.g., Philo, Aristobulus, *Wisdom of Solomon*). Likewise, scripture and ritual laws are very much at the center of discussion. Regarding Scripture, the issue is how it is to be interpreted, specifically whether it should be understood literally or through analogy (e.g., Aristobulus, Philo), whereas regarding ritual laws, the concern is to interpret them as carrying moral signification (e.g., *Letter of Aristeas*). All these categories—the logos, wisdom, Scripture, ritual law—pertain to the relation between the divine and the human. They all signify a bridging of the gap between the two—intermediation or communication between the two.

In the medieval period, by contrast, the focus is the divine dimension. There is a pervasive concern with the various proofs for the existence of God (e.g., Maimonides, Crescas, Ibn Daud); or with the divine attributes, their signification, predication, and multiplicity (e.g., Maimonides, Gersonides, Ibn Daud); or with scriptural anthropomorphism (e.g., Maimonides).

In the modern era, the focus is the human dimension. Most of the fundamental issues or themes in this period revolve around the human predicament as manifested, e.g., in human finitude or existence in the flux (e.g., Rosenzweig, Soloveitchik); unique human capacities, such as freedom (e.g., Samuel Hirsch) or the sense of wonder (e.g., Heschel); the particular human situation, orientation, or striving, as the ethical situation (e.g., Cohen and Lazarus) or the orientation toward community and one's fellows (e.g., Buber) or the striving for maximal self-fulfillment (e.g., Kaplan). Indeed, religion itself is all too often perceived as but a human product—as a manifestation of the human spirit (e.g., Krochmal, Formstecher) or as an expression of culture (e.g., Kaplan, Baeck). Of course, in formulating the solutions to these issues, the divine and the relation between the divine and the human come to the fore, but only as they impinge on the human situation and not in their own terms. In this connection, it may be interesting to note that this shift from the divine to the human pole can be seen in the shift from book titles revolving around God in medieval times (e.g., Gersonides's *Wars of the Lord* or Crescas's *Light of the Lord*) to titles revolving around humanity and religion in modern times (e.g., Formstecher's *Religion of Spirit,* Cohen's *Religion of Reason,* Heschel's *Man Is Not Alone,* Soloveitchik's *Halakhic Man,* and Buber's *Between Man and Man*). It may also be interesting to note that this shift in focus parallels a shift in the nature of the ultimate that Rosenzweig identifies with respect to philosophy's tendency to reduce all of reality to one ultimate entity—to nature in antiquity, to God in the Middle Ages, and to humanity in the modern era.

Thus, the threefold diachronic shift in emphasis in the philosophical-theological domain reflects the threefold synchronic division in the very content that constitutes Judaism's structure of faith—the division between the divine pole, the human pole, and the relation subsisting between the two. This synchronic threefold division is aptly captured in the so-called statement of the Jewish trilogy "God, Israel and Torah are one"; indeed, this statement encompasses all three subdivisions within the structure of faith, with "Israel" representing the human pole and "Torah" representing the relation between the divine and the human. As such, all essential content in the structure of faith is included in this statement. More important, the statement indicates that Judaism does not differ from other religions in the format of its structure of faith, for the structure of faith of practically every religion exhibits a threefold division between the divine, the human, and the relation between them. Rather, Judaism's distinctiveness stems from the content it pours into this uniform threefold format, i.e., by what it has to say about the divine, the human, and the relation between them.

Core Tenets: This content, however, like the content of any historical religion, is by no means monolithic. For it is almost inevitable that a variety and diversity of views should arise in any religion that has managed to endure for a length of time. In Judaism this may be even more pronounced because, as noted earlier, Judaism, unlike Christianity, does not witness to the divine through its tenets of faith; consequently, it can afford to be more "tolerant" or "broad-minded" with respect to variety and diversity in the formulation of these tenets in a way that it could never be about its own mode of divine witness, namely, with respect to the explication of the law.

Still, beneath the great variety and diversity of opinion lies a fundamental core of views on which a general consensus has prevailed through the ages. Indeed, in the same way that there is a "coinage of prayer"—i.e., certain prayers that constitute the very essence of the prayer service—so there is, one may suggest, a "coinage of the religious thought." That is to say, there is a core of tenets of faith amid the great diversity in Judaism's religious thought that remains fairly constant and accepted by most thinkers.

First, the religious thought of Judaism perceives God as exclusively one. This holds true not only in the arithmetical sense of not having any other divine being and in the understanding that there is no multiplicity in God's being but also in the sense of being unique, i.e., of being qualitatively (and not merely quantitatively) different from all other beings. Clearly, such a God cannot be reduced either to the human or to nature (nor can either be elevated to God); neither incarnation nor apotheosis is possible here. This God is by very essence a theistic God. Furthermore, God is endowed with omnipotence and omniscience, which is reflected in God's being a creator and a providential deity. And although rationally (and therefore philosophically) there is a tendency to shy away from such an assertion, the religious impetus in Judaism on this point is too strong for its religious thought not to recognize and somehow accept that its God has to be a personal being in the sense of being a conscious being, a Thou, a God who is aware of and concerned with human beings and their world (even in medieval Jewish philosophy, where the rationalistic orientation is most pronounced and thus the pull to an It-God very strong, the personhood of God cannot be explicitly denied). Lastly, this divine concern with human beings and their world expresses itself essentially in God's unrelenting demand for the pursuit of justice. God is by very essence a just God and God's claim on humanity is essentially that it be likewise just.

Second, paralleling this view of the divine, Judaism's religious thought acknowledges human beings as also conscious beings and consequently beings endowed with freedom. Indeed, it is in these aspects that their likeness to the divine resides, that they are bearers of the divine image. And it is in consequence of this freedom that humans become agents who are accountable and responsible for their actions. As such, they are ethical agents, that is, agents toward whom ethical prescriptions and expectations can be directed. Still, unlike the divine, the human is also part and parcel of nature. Human beings are not only spirit but also matter—body as well as soul. This duality, however, does not mean an ontological duality of substance (the Platonic compound of two distinct entities). Ontologically, the human is a unitary being, a single entity; the duality is a duality of participation—the human as a unitary being participates in two dimensions of existence, that of consciousness and that of power. This carries the further implication that the human being who before was merely given the potential, the capacity, for ethical conduct (by virtue of being constituted as a being-of-consciousness) is now thrown into the continual necessity of actualizing this potential. Human beings are continuously confronted with the necessity of making decisions and choices between two alternatives. It is in the making of such decisions and choices that the ethical is constituted. Thus, for humanity the ethical life is not merely a possibility, it is an inescapable destiny.

Third, following the portrayal of both the divine and the human, the relation between the divine and the human is essentially constituted within the domain of ethics—the divine challenge for justice (and God's impartation of the guideposts that lead to it) and the ongoing, continuous human drama of struggling (and often failing) to respond to this challenge. It should not be surprising to find that this relation (1) refracts itself through the "horizontal dimension," that is, through the world of one's fellow human beings and (2) articulates itself in terms of the law (civil, criminal, international). Indeed, as pointed out earlier, this is most aptly signified in the statement of the Jewish trilogy, where the human pole is represented not by the individual person but by "Israel," i.e., by the national collectivity, and the relation is represented by "Torah," i.e., by the teachings of the law. For the ethical can take place only in the context of the "horizontal dimension," in terms of the relation between fellow human beings, and is most readily objectified in terms of the law.

Ethics:

Theoretical Considerations: In discussions of Jewish ethics the first question is whether there is a Jewish ethic independent of Jewish law. The Jewish law specifies detailed and all-encompassing rules for the conduct of individual and communal life. These rules reflect a value system that is their underlying foundation. That system and the concrete patterns of behavior that flow from it are believed to derive from a divine mandate: God has revealed through his Torah the way God wants the people to conduct their lives. There are, however, those who argue that Judaism recognizes ethical principles that stand outside the law and that may serve as criteria of the moral

acceptability of the law itself. There is evidence to support such a claim, but it is not possible to offer a definitive resolution of this question.

The Biblical Teachings: Elements in the Bible may point to an independent moral law. Cain is condemned for the murder of his brother, and the succeeding generations before the great flood are described as guilty of extreme moral corruption. Yet, at that point in the Bible there are no specific rules about right behavior. Abraham challenges God's justice even though there is not yet a specific rule of justice set forth. The later prophets often chastise the people for conforming to ritual rules while showing insufficient concern for the poor and the downtrodden in society, even though it is not immediately evident that the law puts greater value on the latter.

One explanation offered for all this seemingly extralegal moral material is that it rests on a natural moral law that is known to us independently of revelation. This law is recognized in Scripture, according to this view, and it explains the types of cases just cited. Alternatively, the sages of the Talmud held that from the very beginning of human history God commanded Adam, and then Noah, to observe a set of seven commandments that encompass the basic elements of common morality. These commandments are addressed to all humanity and bind every person. Cain and the later generations were condemned because they violated these commandments. Viewed in this way, Judaism knows no morality other than what derives from God's commandments.

Rabbinic Teachings about Ethics: In the long history of Judaism after the biblical period, the law was elaborated into a vast system of prescriptions for ordering the life of the Jewish community. Though we do not have in the law any clear identification of the specifically moral elements, there is strong evidence that the rabbis were consciously concerned with the ethical dimension of the law. A sharp distinction is drawn between laws that concern our relationship with other human beings and those that concern our relationship to God. Violations of the latter can be atoned for by confession and ritual expiation. No atonement is possible for offenses against other persons until we have first set right the wrong we have done and gained the pardon of the victim of our misbehavior. This suggests clearly a concern with the ethical as a special aspect of the religious life. Loving behavior to others is a necessary condition for true love of God. Here again, however, it can easily be argued that we are dealing with a distinction within the law itself, not with an ethic that is prior to or independent of the law.

A similar point can be made with respect to the other principles of the law that are often construed as evidence of an independent ethic in Judaism. The legal literature includes considerations that are explicitly called rules "that go beyond the line of the law." These rules seem to demand a standard of behavior morally higher and more sensitive than that set down by the law. Other principles seem to point in the same direction. They include, among others, injunctions to follow the way of special piety (*middat khasidut*) or to determine the law in accordance with the principle that the ways of the Torah are ways of pleasantness. Specific rulings are based on these considerations. As we have already seen, these principles may be taken to be ethical rules that stand above the law, or they may be construed simply as rules within the law itself.

Value Hierarchy—The Supremacy of Human Life: Whatever we may say about the presence of an independent ethic in Judaism, it is clear that the law itself rests on a hierarchical value system. A Jew is bound to observe the entire law, but there will always be conflicts within the system that need to be resolved. In the resolution of these conflicts, the law reveals the system of values that governs it. A study of some concrete instances of the operation of this value system is the best way we have to set forth an account of the ethics of Judaism.

The preservation of human life and health is one of the prevailing values in Jewish law. When this comes into conflict with other rules of law, they are regularly set aside in favor of preserving life. Sabbath observance, e.g., is a major duty. It is, in fact, one of the criteria of true membership in the Jewish faith community. Nevertheless, when a human life is threatened by illness or by other dangers, one is required to violate the Sabbath in order to save a life. This is, in fact, not a violation of the Sabbath but the fulfillment of a higher duty that takes precedence over the Sabbath.

We see this same principle operating with respect to abortion. Under most ordinary circumstances Jewish law forbids abortion. However, in a case where the pregnancy or the delivery threatens the life of the mother, it is not only permitted but required to save the life of the mother even at the expense of the life of the fetus.

This very doctrine of the supreme value of each individual human life also imposes restrictions on the sacrifice of one life for another. As the rabbis express it, no person's blood is redder than that of another. That is to say, no one life can be assigned greater value than any other life. Consequently, it is forbidden to take one life in order to save another. As a result, the modern medical technology of organ transplants evokes positive and negative responses in Jewish law. It is a moral duty to save another person's life even with our own organs, but only so long as we can do so without endangering the life of the donor. Each person has the same duty to preserve his or her own life as to preserve the life of another. The blood of the other is no redder than your own. In turn, one may not endanger another human life for one's own benefit.

This regard for human life affects very deeply the way in which Jewish law deals with capital punishment. In the Pentateuch a great many violations are punishable by death, yet in practice Jewish law made it nearly impossible to impose the death penalty. The rules of evidence were interpreted so rigorously that there could hardly ever be sufficient ground for a court to sentence the accused to death.

The Mishnah records that in preparing witnesses who are going to testify in a case involving capital punishment, the judges must admonish them concerning the gravity of their responsibility: "You should know that the laws governing a trial for property cases are different from the laws governing a trial for capital cases. In the case of a trial for property cases, a person pays money and achieves atonement for himself. In capital cases [the accused's] blood and the blood of all those who were destined to be born from him [who was wrongfully convicted] are held against him [who testifies falsely] to the end of time." Testimony in capital cases in a Jewish court takes place in this atmosphere, in which the witnesses are required to be aware of the preciousness of each human life. The effect on the judicial system of this attitude toward human life is made evident in another passage from the Mishnah: "A *sanhedrin* [high court] that imposes the death penalty once in seven years is called murderous." A second sage says that even once in seventy years would make this a murderous court. And two other great sages add, "If we were on a sanhedrin, no one would ever be put to death." We see here how the ethical principle that puts supreme value on human life affects various aspects of the law.

Value Hierarchy—Truth Telling: The law places high value on truth and on keeping one's word. Even in cases where, due to a loophole in the law, one may not be formally obligated to keep one's word, the sages condemn anyone who takes advantage of such a legal technicality. The Torah teaches such high regard for truth that it warns judges against any decision that is motivated either by excessive regard for the wealthy and socially prominent litigant or by excessive concern for the poor, downtrodden litigant. In judicial proceedings truth alone must prevail. As the rabbis teach, the seal of God is truth.

Yet there are many circumstances in which the law specifically permits or even requires the truth to be bent in order to save people from embarrassment. Thus, at a wedding one should always praise the grace and beauty of the bride even if she is ugly. Here the value of human dignity takes priority over literal truth. In similar fashion, truth may be bent in order to preserve harmony within a family. The rabbis note that for this purpose even God bends the truth. When the divine messenger assures Abraham that Sarah will give birth to a son, she privately expresses her doubt. She notes that she has long passed the menopause and adds, "My husband is so old." Yet when reporting her doubts to Abraham, God deletes her statement about the age of her husband. God does so, say the rabbis, to prevent conflict between husband and wife. This is only one of numerous instances recorded in Jewish legal literature in which the ethical value of truth, however highly prized, yields to the even greater values of human dignity and harmonious human relations.

Value Hierarchy—Kiddush Hashem: If there is a single value that stands at the very summit of the entire axiological system of Judaism, it is the obligation of *kiddush hashem*, the sanctification of the holy name of God. Ultimately every Jew is charged to live his or her entire life in such a way as to bring honor to God, whom Jews and Judaism strive to serve. In extreme cases this may be done by way of martyrdom. There is a long history of faithful Jews giving their lives rather than desecrate the divine name or bring dishonor to the God of Israel. Such martyrdom has an exalted place in the hierarchy of Jewish values. A martyr is literally a witness; Jews are required to bear witness to God's truth by the extreme act of sacrificing their lives when called upon. They are required no less to bear witness to God's truth by the way in which they live their daily lives.

The very high value placed on life itself is superseded when what is at stake is the honoring of the divine name. There are three circumstances in which the law requires that life should be sacrificed for the exaltation of God. When a Jew faces a choice between the threat of death and idolatry, murder, or adultery or incest, the Jew must choose to be put to death. Jews may not betray their loyalty to God by worshiping idols, or by murdering human beings, because all are created in God's image, or by dishonoring that divine image through sexual immorality.

The value of kiddush hashem requires that one sacrifice one's own life rather than yield to such immoral demands. True love of God is shown by giving precedence to God's honor even at the cost of one's own life.

There is, however, another dimension of kiddush hashem, which is reflected in the moral quality of ordinary daily human life. As the medieval philosopher Moses Maimonides puts it in his code, "Whoever abstains from a transgression or fulfills a precept, not from any personal motive, not induced thereto by fear and apprehension or by desire for honor, but solely for the sake of the Creator, blessed be He, . . . sanctifies the name of God." Perhaps the highest value in Judaism is to bear witness every day in all of one's dealings to the truth of the presence of God in the world. Jews should always behave in such a way, says a passage in the Palestinian Talmud, that whoever observes them will be moved to proclaim, "Blessed be the God of the Jews."

Whether or not it contains an independent ethic, Judaism rests on a set of values that aim to achieve what is deemed the highest level of human refinement and moral sensitivity. This constitutes the ethics of Judaism, even if there is no formal ethical theory to express it. It is fully embodied in the all-encompassing Jewish law, which defines how Jews are to order their lives in relationship both to God and to their fellow human beings.

Judaism, God in. Over the centuries, Judaism has developed a variety of ways of speaking and thinking about God.

Names of God: *Hashem* (Heb. "the Name") is often used in ordinary discourse as a way of referring to God without using an actual divine name. This is done to conform with the taboo on pronouncing the tetragrammaton, the four-lettered divine name, YHWH. (The more popular transcription, Jehovah, has no foundation.) *Adonai* ("my Lord") is widely used, especially in Jewish liturgy and in the public reading of the Torah, as an acceptable way of addressing or referring to God. Another name for God that has equally wide currency is *Elohim*. Adonai and Elohim are used only in liturgical settings. Hashem has become the common way of referring to God in nonsacred discourse. There are many other terms for God in the Bible and in rabbinic literature to which no taboo is attached, e.g., "The Compassionate One," "The Holy One Blessed Be He," "Master of the World."

The Nature of God: The most fundamental characteristic of God in Judaism is absolute unity. "Hear, O Israel, the Lord our God, the Lord is one" (Deuteronomy 6:4), the Jewish declaration of faith in God's existence and unity, is recited at least twice each day as part of the fixed liturgy. It affirms that God is metaphysically one, that God is unique because there is no other being like God, and thus God is incomparable.

It follows that there can be no likeness or image of God. Judaism prohibits any physical representation of God. God is absolutely incorporeal, without any physical or bodily properties. The Bible often speaks about God in language that suggests corporeality. References to God's eyes, outstretched arm, finger, and other bodily properties are common. In all normative forms of Judaism these are taken to be nonliteral ways of speaking about God's power in the world. There is no language that can express these ideas without the vocabulary of corporeality.

God in Relation to the World: In Judaism, God is first and foremost the creator of the world. God is the source of all being and the ground on which all existence rests. As creator, he is the Lord of nature and of history. God establishes the order of nature but retains the power to intervene in that order. This is attested by the miracles that are reported in Scripture. These divine incursions into the natural order are motivated by God's connection with and concern for humankind.

God's relation to Israel is special, expressed through a covenant in which God seeks the loyalty of the people and they seek divine love and protection. As Scripture makes clear, however, God's presence in history is by no means restricted to one nation. God is the universal God whose love and concern extends to all peoples.

That concern is most strikingly evident in the revelation at Sinai. It is there above all that God emerges as the giver of the Law. Through the divinely given Torah, Jews are taught what it is that God asks of them, what is good and what is evil. God is the ground of all morality, of all true values. Loyalty to God is expressed by observing the divine law. It is in that way that human beings make manifest the presence of God in the world.

Transcendence and Immanence: The God of Judaism is generally understood as a transcendent being. God existed before anything else, and all that exists is dependent on God. Yet, God is also present in the world. Minimally, God is present in the sense in which artists can be said to be present in their creations. The dialectical tension between God's transcendence and immanence is a recurring theme throughout the history of Judaism. Among the philosophers and theologians are found conceptions of God that range from absolute transcendence to pantheistic immanence.

In Judaism, even the conceptions of God that put the greatest emphasis on transcendence still leave place for human beings to elevate themselves to the divine plane. Faith, prayer, and, above all, good works serve to bring humankind ever closer to God. This is the self-transcendence in which human beings break out of their finite limits to achieve fellowship with God. Salvation and redemption occur, according to Jewish teaching, not only in history, but ultimately in the divine realm that stands beyond history. *See also* Adonai; creed; G-d; Judaism; (thought and ethics); revelation; Shekhina; YHWH.

Judaism, music in. In Judaism, prayer, whether public and formal or private and individual, is inconceivable without music. Music is an integral part of Jewish religious life. Prayer, study, and performance of the ritual precepts (Heb. *mitzvot*) in public or private are all carried out with the simultaneous voicing of melodies, tunes, or wordless chants established by long, nearly universal usage.

The Sabbaths, festivals, feast days, holy days, and ordinary weekdays are all symbiotically joined to their individual musical figures, as are the ceremonies of the home and the rites associated with the life cycle. Jewish music represents the surviving heritage of a complex network of groups, communities, sects, and congregations and a kaleidoscopic variety of modes, scales, and styles.

Temple Music: Some musicologists trace the music of Judaism to the First Temple in Jerusalem (destroyed 587/586 B.C.) where music was performed by a caste of temple professionals, the Levites. The Hebrew Bible mentions a range of instruments used in the "Temple orchestra" for both signaling and instrumental purposes, for example, the *nevel* (harp), *kinnor* (lyre), *halil* (double-oboe), *chatsotsra* (silver trumpet), and *shofar* (ram's horn). Only the shofar, a signaling instrument, is still used today. It is sounded during the holidays of Rosh Hashanah (New Year) and Yom Kippur (Day of Atonement). Three kinds of tones are prescribed for the shofar: *tekiah* (a long note), *teruah* (a staccato note or shake), and *shevarim* (a changing note). After the destruction of the Second Temple in A.D. 70, instrumental music ceased to be a part of Jewish public worship and was later explicitly prohibited by rabbinical authorities. Until the nineteenth century, liturgical music in the synagogue—the institution that replaced the Temple as the site of Jewish communal worship—was strictly vocal.

Synagogue Music: The liturgical music of the synagogue falls into two main categories: the chanting, or cantillation, of the books of the Hebrew Bible used in public worship (all books of the Hebrew Bible except Proverbs, Ezra, Nehemiah, and Chronicles); and the melodic recitation of prayers. The chanting of scripture is believed by some scholars to extend back to the early centuries B.C., and it is clear that the Psalms were chanted and that some may have been sung antiphonally. Biblical chanting is indicated by a series of neumes, or accents, called *ta'amim*, written above or below the biblical text. The earliest extant written source for these neumes dates to the ninth century A.D. During worship, the biblical books are never read in plain speech; they are always chanted. The melodic quality of the ta'amim varies almost from biblical book to biblical book. The mode for chanting from books in the Pentateuch, for example, differs from the mode for chanting books from the Prophets—both of which are done weekly. In addition, there are other modes for other books chanted on holidays, for instance, the book of Esther on Purim and the book of Lamentations on the ninth of Av. These modes are ordinarily built on a tetrachordal scale.

It appears that the music for the prayers derives from biblical cantillation, but it has developed differently. The liturgy is composed of diverse musical themes or motives (*nusach*), within which the prayer leader, the *chazzan*, has exceptional musical latitude. The services for weekdays, Sabbaths, High Holy Days, festivals, and other holidays each have distinctive musical themes associated with them. Since the words of the liturgy often are duplicated from service to service, the music historically played an important role in conveying the mood, tone, and sense of the holiday.

In addition to its part in public worship, music plays a key role in the ritual study of biblical and rabbinic texts. A distinct set of melodic phrases, for example, is employed in the study of the Talmud in the synagogue and rabbinic study houses, and the Talmud itself mandates that rabbinic traditions are to be studied musically. The Grace after Meals (*birkat ha-mazon*), Sabbath and festival table songs (*zemirot*), and the Passover Haggadah all bring Jewish religious music into the domestic realm. The traditional liturgical chants of Judaism show the imprint of the music of the countries in which Jews lived. But Jewish religious music did not change very much throughout the 1,500-year period when both European (Ashkenazic) and North African (Sepharadic) Jews were largely isolated from their neighbors.

Musical Developments in the Enlightenment: The most important developments in liturgical music began during the nineteenth-century Jewish Enlightenment (*Haskalah*), with one significant exception. In the seventeenth century an enlightened Duke of Mantua allowed Jews the opportunity to study music and dance. One of these, Salomone Rossi, called "Il Ebreo" (1570–1628), became the court composer. Besides much instrumental and some secular vocal music, he published thirty musical settings for texts from the Jewish prayer book: *Solomon's Songs, Psalms, Hymns and Temple-songs*. The style of these compositions, written for three to eight voices, was similar to that of the other Italian composers of his time and was attacked by the Italian rabbinate, although vehemently defended by the chief rabbi of Venice.

The Napoleonic era, and with it the Enlightenment, brought Jews in contact with their Christian neighbors, and this new relationship profoundly influenced Jewish liturgy. The "reform" of the synagogue service began slowly in Vienna when the great cantor Salomon Sulzer (1804–90) sought to assimilate the contemporary non-Jewish musical style into the music of the synagogue. He composed his own settings of the liturgy for all occasions of the Jewish liturgical year and even asked his non-Jewish friends Schubert, Seyfried, Volkert, and Wurfel to contribute works to his collection *Shir Zion*. The reformers in Germany, especially in Hamburg and Berlin, were much more radical. They introduced prayers and hymns to be sung in German, reorganized the service along the lines of the Lutheran model, and introduced the mixed choir and the organ. However, the mainstream Reform movement developed more carefully. Inspired by the changes of Sulzer in Vienna, the large synagogues of Berlin added choirs (at first all male, then mixed) and in 1866 an organ to their services. The greatest composer in Berlin to follow the favorite Sulzer melodies with his own was Louis Lewandowski (1821–94). This reform spread quickly through Germany, France, the Low Countries, and even into the larger congregations of eastern Europe and the Austro-Hungarian empire. One of the most fertile places for the more radical reforms was the young United States, where the Hamburg German-language hymnal was used in all Reform congregations throughout the nineteenth century. In Europe there was a feverish creation by new Jewish composers writing liturgical music: Naumbourg in France; Aaron Friedmann in Austria; Weintraub in East Prussia; Kirschner, Korniyzer, and Lampel in Germany; and Moritz Friedmann in Hungary, to mention only a few.

The spread of the Reform movement to America brought a great deal of creative activity. It began in the South in the congregation of Charleston, South Carolina, in 1824 and spread to such congregations as Har Sinai in Baltimore, Maryland (1842), and Emanu-El in New York City (1845). Encouraged by the leadership of Rabbi Isaac Mayer Wise (1819–1900), the founder of American Reform Judaism, congregations hired both Jewish and non-Jewish organists and choir directors. The choir became as important as the cantor had been, and music was composed by such men as Sigmund Schlesinger (1835–1906), Edward Stark (1863–1918), and many others. Schlesinger's music and that of many of the non-Jewish musicians commissioned to write services was influenced by Italian, French, and German opera tunes and music of the Protestant church.

The art of the cantor, which developed especially in eastern Europe and was then brought to America, was similarly influenced. In the later part of the nineteenth century, many cantors were exposed to Italian opera. Much of the "newer" cantorial style contained the florid and freely improvisatory ardor of Italian opera, which had great popular appeal. Cantorial concerts were frequent, and the names of such great cantors as Joseph (Jossele) Rosenblatt, Mordecai Hershman, Zavel Kvartin, Moshe Koussevitzky, and many others became revered household names.

Music in the Twentieth Century: The twentieth century brought great change to the development of Jewish liturgical music for four reasons: there was a greater consciousness of tradition; musicologists were studying the various Jewish traditions and trying to separate influences; highly trained and skilled composers were entering a field that was suddenly opening for them; and a musically trained cantorate was available.

In the early part of the century, musicologists such as Idelsohn, Jasser, Werner, and others studied the history of Jewish liturgical music, did comparative studies, and collected great volumes of tunes from all countries. Later in the century, Albert Weisser, Alfred Sendry, Johanna Spector, Judith Eisenstein, Max Walberg, Marko Rothmuller, Israel Katz, and Mark Slobin continued and expanded upon their work. Cantorial anthologies by Gershan Ephross and Chemja Vinaver as well as a book by Isadore Freed on the harmonization of the Jewish modes were of great significance in enriching knowledge about the entire field of Jewish music. These developments led to a heightening of a sense of Jewishness among many young composers who had been excellently trained in music and in the Hebrew language. In Germany such men as Heinrich Schalit, Hugo Adler, Herbert Fromm, Julius Chajes, Herman Berlinsky, and others began to compose music utilizing the newly developed harmonic idioms to create a fresh music for the synagogue. In France it was Algazi; in England, Alman; in Sweden, Rosenblueth; in Italy, Castelnuova Tedesco; in Canada, Ben Steinberg and Saul Glick; and in America, Binder, Zilberts, Weiner, Helfman, Freed, and Saminsky. Even non-synagogue composers of Jewish origin began writing music for the service. The Bloch *Avodath Hakodesh* (Sacred Service) and the Milhaud *Service Sacre* became instant successes as concert pieces as well as liturgical settings. Just before and during World War II most of the aforementioned European composers emigrated to the United States. Encouraged by both Reform and Conservative congregations, they joined their American colleagues in a sustained and most distinguished creative period of liturgical music. They were joined by many composers who had already distinguished themselves in the secular field: David Diamond, Hugo Weisgall, Henry Brant, Joseph Achron, Miriam Gideon, Robert Starer, Leonard Bernstein, Lukas Foss, Jacob Druckman, David Amram, Jack Gottlieb, and Samuel Adler. Younger men and women are constantly entering the field and continuing the tradition; to mention only a few: Michael Isaacson, Simon Sargon, Stephen Richards, Maxine Warshauer, and Benji Schiller. Also, many young, excellently trained cantors are now enriching the liturgy of the synagogue.

In the late 1960s, the liturgical music of the synagogue received a significant setback. Many congregations deemphasized the formal synagogue service, which flourished from ca. 1850 to 1965, and replaced it either with informal services or small groups that meet in homes. The music performed at these services is mostly taken from the camp songs created for youth camps by the Reform and Conservative movements. This has meant the demise of the very sophisticated music written before these movements began to curtail the use of the mixed choir and organ in favor of congregational singing led by the cantor and the guitar. These developments leave in doubt the future of liturgical music for the synagogue. *See also* Judaism, prayer and liturgy of.

JUDAISM

A religious system, Judaism appeals to the Pentateuch, the Five Books of Moses, called the Torah, as the foundational account of God's revelation to humanity through Israel, the holy people. Judaism is a monotheist religion. The word *Judaism* applies to a variety of closely related religions, past and present. A Judaism, or Judaic religious system, is made up of (1) a worldview, which by reference to Torah sets forth the intersection of the supernatural and the natural worlds, accounts for how things are, and puts them together into a cogent and harmonious picture; (2) a way of life explained by that worldview that carries out the concrete laws of the Torah and so expresses the worldview in concrete actions; and (3) a social group, called by a Judaism (an) "Israel," for which the worldview accounts and which is defined as an entity and in concrete terms by the way of life. A Judaic system constitutes an explanation for the group (again: "Israel") that gives social form to the system and an account of the distinctive way of life of that group. A Judaic system derives from and focuses upon a social entity, a group of Jews who (in their minds at least) constitute not *an* Israel but Israel.

There is not now, and never has been, a single Judaism. No Judaic religious system recapitulates any other, and no linear and incremental history of one continuous Judaism is possible. But each Judaism reworks in its own circumstance and context a single paradigmatic and definitive human experience. All Judaisms over time have worked out the pentateuchal pattern of exile and return.

It is an error to view all Judaisms as a single unitary religion and to ignore the profound differences in belief and behavior among the Judaic faithful in times past as much as in our own day.

Through history, diverse Judaisms have won the allegiance of groups of Jews here and there, each system specifying the things it regards as urgent in both belief and behavior. Yet all systems allege that they represent the true and authentic Judaism, or Torah, or will of God for Israel, and that their devotees *are* Israel. Each Judaism ordinarily situates itself in a single historical line—hence, a linear history—from the entirety of the past. How do we distinguish one Judaism from another? We can do so when we identify the principal symbol to which a given system on its own appeals, when we uncover its urgent question, and thus define the answer it considers "natural."

All Judaisms do begin with and refer back to one Judaic system, that of the

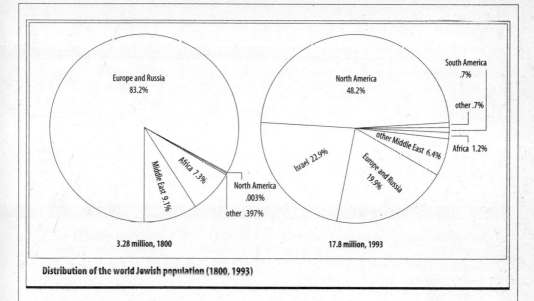

Distribution of the world Jewish population (1800, 1993)

Pentateuch. The first and paradigmatic Judaic religious system, the Pentateuch, ca. 500 B.C., represented the Jews' existence as exile and return. The way of life was one of sanctification of everyday affairs, e.g., eating, drinking, sexual conduct; the worldview stressed God's conditional covenant with Israel, the terms of which are set forth in the Pentateuch. The definition of Israel was genealogical, and Israel was represented as a family descended from a single couple, Abraham and Sarah. Composed in the aftermath of the destruction of the Temple in 586 B.C. and in response to the exile to Babylonia, the Pentateuch selected as its urgent question the conditions under which Israel retains the land of Israel. Hence exile and restoration formed the paradigm for the initial Judaic system.

Because the formative pattern imposed perpetual, self-conscious uncertainty, treating the life of the group as conditional and discontinuous, Jews have asked themselves who they are and invented Judaisms to answer that question. On account of the definitive paradigm affecting their group life in various contexts, no circumstances have permitted Jews to assume their existence as a group. Looking back on scripture and its message, Jews have ordinarily treated as special, subject to conditions, and therefore uncertain what (in their view) other groups enjoyed as unconditional and simply given. Why the paradigm renewed itself is clear: this particular view of matters generated expectations that could not be met, hence created resentment—and then provided comfort and hope that made possible coping with that resentment. Promising what could not be delivered, then providing solace for the consequent disappointment, the system at hand precipitated in age succeeding age the very conditions necessary for its own replication.

Subsequent systems, to be identified by their distinctive framing of their generative symbol, their definition of the canon of writings in addition to the Old Testament, and their definitions of the way of life and worldview that would

Judaism

600–500 B.C.	500–400 B.C.	400–300 B.C.
Destruction of first Temple in Jerusalem by Babylonians (586)	Ezra (ca. 450)	Hellenistic period; Jewish religious literature in Greek flourishes (367–334)
Babylonian exile (or, captivity) (586–538)		
Return from exile; construction of second Temple in Jerusalem (538–515)		
Persian period; most of Hebrew Bible either written or edited (538–333)		

1–100	100–200	200–300
Roman prefecture or procuratorship in Palestine (6–66)	Unsuccessful revolt against Roman rule led by Simon bar Koseba (bar Kokhba). Expulsion of Jews from Jerusalem (131–135)	Parthian Babylonia becomes new religious and intellectual center (3rd century)
Unsuccessful Jewish revolt against Roman rule (66–73)	Mishnah edited by Rabbi Judah the Prince (ca. 200)	
Destruction of second Temple in Jerusalem by Roman armies (70)		
Rabbinic academy at Yavneh (Jamnia) (70–132)		

characterize their Israel, recapitulated that same issue. The recurrent pattern set forth the view that the life of the group is uncertain, subject to conditions and stipulations. Nothing is set and given, all things are a gift: land and life itself. But what actually did happen in that uncertain world—exile followed by restoration—marked the group as special, different, select. With the promulgation of the Pentateuch as the "Torah of Moses" under the sponsorship of Ezra, the Persians' viceroy, ca. 450 B.C., all future Judaisms and their Israels would then refer to that formative experience as it had been set down and preserved as the norm; exile and return then stood for alienation and remission.

The definition and history of Judaism then comprises definitions and histories of Judaisms, all of them responding to a single paradigm, and none of them recapitulating any other. Moreover, none stands in a linear and incremental relationship with any prior one. Each took shape in its own circumstance and in response to its own political and social issues. But all Judaisms have recapitulated that single paradigmatic experience of the Torah of "Moses," the authorship that reflected on the meaning of the events of 586–450 B.C. selected for the composition of history and therefore interpretation. That experience (in theological terms) rehearsed the conditional moral existence of sin and punishment, suffering and atonement and reconciliation, and (in social terms) the uncertain and always conditional national destiny of disintegration and renewal of the group. That moment captured within the Five Books of Moses, that is to say, the judgment of the generation of the return to Zion, led by Ezra, about its ex-

300 200 B.C.	200–100 B.C.	100–1 B.C.
Seleucid period (281–267) Translation of Hebrew Bible into Greek (250 B.C.–A.D. 200)	Maccabaean conflict; Jewish civil war (167) Hasmonean (Maccabaean) "kingship" (163–152)	Rome establishes control of province of Palestine (67–62) Herodian dynasty established by Rome (37 B.C.–A.D. 93)

300–400	400–500	500–600
Beginning of construction of Christian Jerusalem under Constantine (335)	Editing of Jerusalem Talmud (the Talmud of the Land of Israel) (ca. 400)	Editing of Babylonian Talmud (ca. 500) Babylonian gaonate (6th–11th centuries)

traordinary experience of exile and return, would inform the attitude and viewpoint of all the Israels beyond.

Consequently, each Judaism identifies what is wrong with the present and promises to make things tolerable now and perfect in the indeterminate future. A Judaism therefore stands for a situation to escape, overcome, survive. The repeated pattern of finding the world out of kilter ("exile") but then making it possible to live for the interim in that sort of world, that generative paradigm, perpetuates profound resentment: Why here? Why us? Why now? And, to the contrary (and this is the resentment), why not always, everywhere, and forever? A Judaic religious system recapitulates a particular resentment. In this way each Judaism relates to other Judaisms.

Two reasons account for the perennial power of the pentateuchal system and perspective. One is that for many Jews the generative tension precipitated by the interpretation of the Jews' life as exile and return, which forms the critical center of the Torah of Moses, persisted. Therefore the urgent question answered by the Torah retained its original character and definition, and the self-evident answer—read in the synagogue every Sabbath morning as well as on Monday and on Thursday—retained its relevance. But the other reason is that people saw what was not always there because through the Torah of Moses they were taught to.

The second of the two reasons is the more important: the question answered by the Five Books of Moses persisted at the center of the national life and

Judaism

600–700	700–800	800–900
	Beginning of Karaite movement (8th century)	Muslim pact of Omer (800)
	Independent Khazar kingdom (8th–13th centuries)	

1200–1300	1300–1400	1400–1500
Nachmanides (= Ramban) (1194–1270)	Forced conversion to Catholicism of Spanish Jews, beginning of Marranos (1391)	Don Isaac Abrabanel (1437–1508)
Zohar, beginning of kabbalah in Spain and Provence (13th century)		Joseph Caro (1488–1575)
Solomon Adret (= Rashba) (1235–1310)		Expulsion of Jews from Spain (1492)
First Disputation (1240)		Lithuanian Council of Four Lands (mid-15th century–1764)
Abraham Abulafia (1240–91)		

remained, if chronic, also urgent. The answer provided by the Pentateuch therefore retained its self-evident importance. The question persisted because scripture kept reminding people to ask that question, to see the world as the world was described, in scripture's mythic terms, out of the perception of the experience of exile and return. To those troubled by the question of exile and return, that is, the chronic allegation that Israel's group life did not constitute a given but formed a gift accorded on conditions and stipulations, the answer enjoyed the status of (mere) fact.

While Jewish history records a variety of competing Judaisms, from late antiquity to the nineteenth century, a single Judaism predominated, the Judaism of the dual Torah, both written and oral. This Judaism is called, variously, "rabbinic," after its principal authorities; "talmudic," after its authoritative document; "classical," because of its theological standing; or, simply, "Judaism." The histories of Judaisms are to be divided into four periods. The first was the age of diversity, in which many Judaic systems flourished, from the period of the formation of the Hebrew scriptures, ca. 586 B.C., to the destruction of the Second Temple, in A.D. 70. The second was the formative age, from 70 to closure of the Talmud of Babylonia, ca. 600. The third was the classical age, from late antiquity to the late eighteenth century, in which that original definition dominated the lives of the Jewish people nearly everywhere they lived. The fourth is the modern age, from the late eighteenth century to our own day, when an essentially religious understanding of what it means to be Israel, the Jewish people,

900–1000	1000–1100	1100–1200
Sa'adia Gaon (882–942)	"Golden Age" in Spain (11th–13th centuries)	Abraham ben David (= Rabad) (1125–98)
	Solomon ben Isaac (= Rashi) (1040–1105)	Moses Maimonides (= Rambam) (1135–1204)
	Judah ha-Levi (1075–1141)	First blood libel charge, Norwich, England (1144)

1500–1600	1600–1700	1700–1800
Moses Cordovero (1522–1609)	Shabbetai Tzevi (1626–76)	Baal Shem Tov, beginning of Hasidism (1700–1760)
Judah Loew, the Maharel of Prague (1525–1609)	Nathan of Gaza (1643–80)	Moses Chaim Luzzatto (1707–46)
Isaac Luria (1534–72)	Chmielnicki massacre (1648–49)	Ezekiel Landau (1713–93)
Date of Messiah according to Solomon Molcho (1540)	Jews first arrive in North America (1654)	Elijah, Gaon of Vilna (1720–97)
Chaim Vital (1542–1620)		Jacob Frank (1726–91)
		Moses Mendelssohn (1729–86)
		Emancipation period (1740–1878)
		Shneur Zalman (1747–1813)
		Beginning of Haskalah (ca. 1770)

came to compete among Jews with other views and other symbolic expressions of those views.

THE AGE OF DIVERSITY (586 B.C.–A.D. 70)

In the first period there were various Judaisms, that is, diverse compositions of a worldview and a way of life that people believed both represented God's will for Israel, the Jewish people, and defined who is and who is not "Israel," or truly an heir to scripture and its promises and blessings. During that long age, nearly five hundred years, a number of different kinds of Judaisms came into being. Also during that time the Judaism of the dual Torah came into being and competed for Jews' loyalty with those other Judaisms.

THE FORMATIVE AGE OF JUDAISM (70–640)

The first date, 70, marks the destruction of the Temple of Jerusalem by the Romans. The second, 640, refers to the Arab conquest of the Near and Middle East in the early years of Islam. During this period the canon—authoritative writings—of the Judaism of the dual Torah, which became normative, took shape. That canon consisted of "the one whole Torah of Moses, our rabbi," reaching Israel in two forms, that is, through two media. One was the written Torah, which the world knows as the Hebrew scriptures or the Old Testament. During the formative age sages selected those particular books of ancient Israel's library that Judaism would accept. During that same period the part of the Torah

Judaism		
1800–1900		
Moses Montefiore (1784–1885)	Union of American Hebrew Congregations established (1873)	Verein Deutscher Staatsbuerger Juedischen Glaubens established in Berlin (1893)
Samuel Raphael Hirsch (1808–88)	Major Eastern European Jewish emigration to North America (1880–1929)	Dreyfus Affair (1894–1906)
Seesen synagogue established (1810)		
Israel Salanter (1810–83)	First European emigration (*aliyah*) to Israel (1882–1903)	Jewish Workers Alliance (Bund) established in Vilna (1897)
Major German Jewish emigration to North America (1836–60)	"Tref Banquet" (1883)	Union of Orthodox Hebrew Congregations (U.S.) (1899)
Breslau Seminary established (1854)	Pittsburgh Platform (1885)	
Theodor Herzl (1860–1904)	Jewish Theological Seminary established (1887–1902)	
Abraham Isaac Kook (1865–1935)	Central Conference of American Rabbis founded (1889)	
1900–		
Menachem Mendel Schneerson, the Lubavitcher Rebbe (1902–94)	British Palestinian Mandate (1922)	Dead Sea Scrolls discovered (1947)
Kehillah (New York City) (1909)	Reconstructionism begins (1922)	Israel declares independence (May 14, 1948)
Hadassah founded (1912)	Yeshiva University founded (1928)	Excavation and reconstruction of Masada (1965)
United Synagogues of America established (1913)	Nazi Nuremberg laws (1935)	
	World Jewish Congress founded (1936)	Six-Day War (1967)
Balfour Declaration (1917)	Holocaust (Shoah) (1938–1945)	Yom Kippur War (1973)
	United Jewish Appeal established (1939)	

that came to Israel not in writing but orally, through the memory of Moses, the prophets, and the sages, down to the present, also reached definition. The first of the documents that preserved this memorized and orally transmitted Torah in writing was the Mishnah; the last was the Talmud of Babylonia. In between, writings of two kinds reached authoritative status, first, amplifications and commentaries for the Mishnah, and second, the same sort of writing for scripture. So the formative age saw the composition of a single, cogent canon, that "one whole Torah of Moses, our rabbi," that constituted Judaism.

That Judaism took shape in two distinct stages, 70 to 200 and 200 to 600. The first stage is represented by the Mishnah, a philosophical law code, ca. 200, in the consequence of the destruction of the Second Temple and the defeat of Bar Kokhba three generations later, emphasizing sanctification. The question addressed by the mishnaic system was where and how Israel remained holy even without its holy city and temple. The second stage, 200 to 600, is marked by the Talmud of the Land of Israel, also called the Yerushalmi or Jerusalem Talmud, an amplification and expansion of the Mishnah, ca. 400, in the aftermath of the rise to political power of Christianity, presenting a dual emphasis on both sanctification and salvation. The question taken up by the talmudic system—the dual Torah in its first definitive statement—was when and how holy Israel would be saved, even with a world in the hands of the sibling of Israel, Esau, or Christendom (and, later on, in the power of the sibling Ishmael, or Islam, as well). A second Talmud, also serving to explain the Mishnah, took shape in Babylonia and reached closure at ca. 600. This other Talmud, called the Talmud of Babylonia or the Bavli, drew into itself a vast range of materials, treating both the Mishnah and scripture, and presented the definitive statement of Judaism, then to now.

The Judaism of the dual Torah, written (scripture, pentateuchal) and oral (the Mishnah and its exegetical works, as well as the exegetical treatments of scripture called midrashim), confronted the chronic and pressing questions of the Jews' circumstance and provided answers deemed self-evidently valid. It asked the question of the ascendancy of Esau and Ishmael and answered that holy Israel would ultimately find salvation at the end of time through its life of sanctification of the here and now. That self-evidently valid answer to the urgent question of existence is why the system endured from its origin, in the fourth century, to the point, in the eighteenth and nineteenth centuries, at which the original circumstance addressed by that Judaism radically changed. Then new questions, out of phase with the old, would demand new answers.

The Judaism of the dual Torah came into being—at its first stage—as the amalgam of two of the three strands of the period of diversity, specifically, the priestly and the sagacious. Among three main choices we have outlined, the messianic, priestly, and scribal, the Judaism of the two Torahs began with the priestly, now represented by the Pharisees and their method, and the scribal, now in the persons of the scribes, or sages and rabbis, and their Torah teachings. The priestly-Pharisaic strand contributed the method, the emphasis on the sanctification of the everyday. The scribal strand defined the content, the substance of Torah study, with stress on mastery of scripture and application of the contents of scripture to ordinary affairs.

The third, the messianic strand, with its emphasis on history, the nation-society as a whole, and the end of time, would become important as the Judaism of the two Torahs developed in its second stage. But at the outset the definitive documents, the Mishnah and its closest relations, paid slight attention to that theme. It entered the picture when, after the conversion of Constantine in the fourth century, Christianity became the dominant religion of the West. Then the messianic theme demanded attention, since Christianity laid stress on Christ as Messiah. The vast movements of history, culminating in the enthronement of Christ as king of the world in the Roman Empire, demanded a response from Israel's sages. Sages of the time in the Yerushalmi and in *Genesis Rabbah* and *Leviticus Rabbah* framed an appropriate doctrine of history and of the Messiah: the Messiah will come to Israel when Israel keeps the Torah as sages teach it. From Late Antiquity to the nineteenth century, this is the Judaism that predominated.

THE CLASSICAL PERIOD OF JUDAISM (640–1787)

The rise of Islam marks the end of the formative period of the Judaism that would prove normative. The end of the classical period is marked by the American Constitution, drawn up in 1787, which inaugurated the world in which the political and cultural setting for the Jews in Europe and America changed from what it had been under Christendom. In the long intervening age, here called the classical period, a single Judaism, the one teaching the dual Torah of Sinai, came to full definition and predominated. During that time, whatever important ideas or issues developed Jews addressed them within the categories of the Judaism of the dual Torah. For example, a variety of mystical ideas and practices entered the world of Judaism and attained naturalization within the Torah, and a philosophical tradition restated the truths of the Torah in terms of Greek modes of thought represented by Aristotle and Plato as the Muslim philosophical schools transmitted them to the West.

In the mystical tradition, the great work was the *Zohar*, written toward the end of the thirteenth century in Spain, and, in the philosophical tradition, the most important figure was Maimonides, 1135–1204, who restated the whole of Judaic law and theology in a systematic and profoundly philosophical way. Both of these encompassing modes of thought, the mystical and the philosophical, transformed "the one whole Torah of Moses, our rabbi" from a mythic to, on the one side, an intensely felt and profound doctrine of the true nature of God's being, and, on the other side, an intellectually rich and rational statement of the Torah as truth. And both found an ample place well within the received canon, to which each made a massive contribution of new and authoritative writings. The power of the one whole Torah, oral and written, to encompass and make its own essentially fresh ways of thought and life testifies to the classical character of this Judaism, everywhere definitive. So mysticism and philosophy alike made their contribution to the altar of the Judaism of the dual Torah. What is more interesting still, that same original system possessed the power to define its own heresies. This we see in Karaism, the heresy that rejected the myth of the dual Torah, and Sabbateanism, the heresy that rejected the myth of the Messiah as a Torah sage.

THE MODERN AND CONTEMPORARY SCENE (1787–)

In modern times, the diversity characteristic of the period of origins has come to prevail once again. Now the symbolic system and structure of the Judaism of the dual Torah has come to compete for Jews' attention with other Judaic systems, on the one side, and with a wildly diverse range of symbols of other-than-Jewish origin and meaning on the other. What of the Judaism of the dual Torah in relationship to the life of Israel, the Jewish people over time (not to be identified only with the contemporary State of Israel, which came into being in 1948)? That Judaism of the dual Torah endured and flourishes today as the religion of a small group of people.

From 1800 to 1900 a number of other Judaic systems—worldviews, ways of life, addressed to an "Israel"—came into being. These included Reform Judaism, the first and most important of the Judaisms of modern times. The changes deemed reforms involved at first matters of liturgy, then important issues of doctrine. Reform took seriously the political changes that accorded to Jews the rights of citizens and demanded that they conform, in important ways, to the common practices of their countries of citizenship. Reform took shape in the first quarter of the nineteenth century. Some decades later, in the middle of the century, Orthodoxy stated the position that one may observe the law and also enter into the civilization of the West. Affirming the divine origin of the Torah, Orthodoxy effected a selective piety, e.g., affirming secular education in addition to study of the Torah. These are the two modern Judaisms of keenest interest in the spelling out of any theory of the history of Judaism.

The Judaic systems of the nineteenth and twentieth centuries took shape within a span of not much more than a hundred years, from somewhat before 1800 to somewhat after 1900. The weakening of the Judaism of the dual Torah and the development of competing Judaisms find exemplification in two important Judaisms in no way continuous with the received system. Zionism and American Judaism constitute not heresies of the Judaism of the dual Torah but Judaisms in no way defined within the terms and categories of that Torah. They derive from experiences in no way generated by the Torah myth. And yet both Judaisms very clearly and strikingly recapitulate the original paradigm of exile and return—even in America, where that paradigm forms an utterly dissonant conflict with the political and social reality confronting the Jewish group.

It remains to ask, Who is a Jew? The answer to that question, according to Jewish law as codified in the Torah as interpreted by the Talmud and defined by rabbis from late antiquity to the present day, is this: a Jew is a person who was born of a Jewish mother or who has been converted to Judaism. (Reform Judaism now recognizes as a born Jew the child of a Jewish father and a non-Jewish mother.) But not all Jews practice Judaism, and, moreover, those Jews who do practice Judaism interpret in diverse ways the beliefs and requirements of their version of Judaism.

Judaism, prayer and liturgy of. No single conceptual scheme sufficiently describes the entire gamut of Jewish worship through the centuries. One central focus of synagogue worship is the reading and study of Torah, whether that study is conceived as being itself an act of devotion, or as the exegesis of a sacred text in a manner relevant to a contemporary reader. Not every service features reading from the Torah scroll. Study per se, embedded as it is within the prayer book itself, has been viewed as virtually sacramental, salvific in essence. Synagogue and home are the twin focuses for worship, but Jews may pray wherever they find themselves. They pray as individuals, but some prayers require a *minyan* (quorum) of ten adults (for Orthodox Jews, males only). Hebrew is the preferred language of prayer, but Reform Jews often use the vernacular. Music was once primarily the chanting of texts, but Hasidic Jews introduced the *niggun* (wordless melody); German Reform Judaism discovered hymns; Salamone Rossi created high Renaissance court music for prayer. Thus, nearly every general statement about Jewish prayer has its exceptions.

General Characteristics: Jewish worship is liturgical in that it favors fixed literary formulas at precise times. Originally variable, these formulas took on greater and greater fixity until the ninth century, when they were encoded in a *siddur* ("order [of prayer]"; prayer book). As the siddur expanded, its contents were subdivided into other volumes: a *makhzor* (cycle) for holiday liturgy, and the Haggadah ("narration") for the Passover seder service. There are three services daily: *shakharit* (morning), *minkhah* (afternoon), and *ma'ariv* or *arvit* (evening); but the latter two are generally combined at day's end for convenience.

Basic Service Structure and Themes: The shakharit service (which follows) demonstrates the usual liturgical structure, from which minkhah and arvit deviate only slightly.

The central prayers are the Shema ("Hear [O Israel . . .]") and its blessings, and the Tefillah ("the prayer [par excellence]"), which follows it. The former is credal, affirming God's unity and threefold attributes of creator, revealer of Torah, and redeemer. The latter—known also as Shemoneh Esrei ("the eighteen [blessings]") and amidah ([prayer said] "standing")—is largely petitionary, but it includes also the kedushah (sanctification) affirming God's sanctity ("Holy, holy, holy . . .") and the birkat kohanim ("priestly benediction"; Numbers 6:24–26).

Preparatory to these two primary rubrics are the birkhot hashakhar ("morning blessings") and pesukei deZimrah ("verses of song"). The former—originally home devotions but since the ninth century recited also in the synagogue—contains benedictions relevant to beginning the daily cycle (e.g., thanksgiving for one's bodily functions) and fragments of biblical and rabbinic texts for study. Eventually, some well-known poems with traditional melodies were added: notably, *Yigdal*, the Maimonidean principles arranged poetically, and *Adon Olam*, a poem of uncertain origin praising God's eternal nature and protective grace. The "Verses of Song" prepare the worshiping community for its statutory prayers that follow. Composed primarily of the Daily Hallel ("praise"), Psalms 145–50, and intended for communal singing, it ends with the Birkat haShir ("blessing of song"), one version of which (Nishmat) affirms, "The soul of every living creature will praise You!"

From preparatory Morning Blessings and Verses of Song, the community is officially called to prayer by the Barekhu ("Praise [God]!"), after which the Shema and the Tefillah follow. Since medieval times, the Tefillah has been followed by Takhanun, supplications emphasizing human sinfulness and divine grace. Monday, Thursday, and Saturday feature *keriyat hatorah* ([the public] reading of Torah). A continuous lectionary (Genesis to Deuteronomy) assures the reading of the entire Torah annually. (Lections are long, however, and liberal congregations read only part of them.) At each reading, a few worshipers are honored by receiving invitations from the *gabbai*, the synagogue functionary who orders the Torah "service" for an *aliyah* (ascending [to the Torah]). Saturday mornings include also a Haftarah ("concluding [prophetic reading]").

The service concludes with the Alenu and Kaddish, two prayers affirming God's mastery of the universe and ultimate reign. The latter appears also in different formats as a rubric divider throughout the service and is chanted in different melodies, linked to calendrical occasions. Today the Kaddish is regarded primarily as a mourners' prayer.

Sabbath and Holiday Expansions: The core liturgies are expanded thematically for the Sabbath and holidays, and a service called Musaf ("addition"), which still carries echoes of ancient Temple theology, is appended in the morning. It concludes with *korbanot* (texts on sacrifice) and a reiteration of Judaism's monotheistic theme: Ein Keloheinu . . . ("There is no one like our God").

Holiday expansions differ with the nature of the day in question but are marked by complex poetic expansions, going back frequently to the

Byzantine period, called *piyyutim* (sing. *piyyut*), such as the *selikhot* ([poems for] forgiveness) on Yom Kippur (the Day of Atonement). The best known, perhaps, are by Eliezer Kalir (ca. sixth–seventh centuries) and include Geshem ("rain") and Tal ("dew")—prayers for agricultural fertility but symbolic also of the belief in bodily resurrection. Other famous piyyutim include Unetaneh Tokef, a small part of a much larger poem, actually, which images the dread of the days of awe (Rosh Hashanah and Yom Kippur) at which time human behavior is scrutinized and human destiny sealed. Relatively few of the once abundant store of piyyutim have survived in modern-day synagogues, which find the prolix word-plays in these poems difficult to appreciate and impossible to convey in translation.

Other holiday expansions include blowing the *shofar* on Rosh Hashanah while praising God's rule (*malkhuyot*), noting God's covenantal recollection of Israel (*zikhronot*), and acknowledging the *shofar*'s symbolic role as harbinger of the messianic age (*shofarot*). Central to Yom Kippur is the repeated communal confession: Ashamnu ("We have sinned") and Al Khet ("For the sin [which we have sinned against You . . .]"). From Rosh Hashanah to Yom Kippur, the liturgy invokes God's grace in the face of human iniquity, with Avinu Malkenu ("Our Father, our King . . . [have mercy on us]").

Home Prayer: Home prayer too calls for specific prayer texts at specific occasions. Meals are preceded by blessings over the foods to be consumed and followed by the Birkat haMazon, a series of blessings that constitute the Jewish Grace after Meals. The *kiddush* (a prayer introducing sacred time) and *havdalah* (a prayer ending it) are said at home as well. In addition, there are prescribed prayers for such things as passing miraculous sites; retiring for bed; setting out on a journey (*tefillat haderekh*); and observing nature's grandeur—like rainbows or thunderstorms—all of which occur while alone and in no particular place but prompt the recognition of the divine presence in the universe.

Components of Jewish Worship:

Torah: Jewish worship awards centrality to the liturgy of the word. Thus, much Jewish worship revolves about Torah: the *korbanot* in Musaf, for example, or the lectionary itself. A textual homily called *devar Torah* (a word of Torah) often follows the lection, and even rites of passage (coming of age and mourning after a death) traditionally call for study and a learned discourse.

Mitzvah: Jews confront God's word, in its primary form of legal prescription, such that Jews pray out of a sense of mitzvah ("commandment"). *Keva*, prescriptive "fixity," is balanced, however, by the requirement of *kavvanah*, spiritual attentiveness to one's commanded task. Originally, freedom to create differently worded prayers around the prescribed theme provided kavvanah; when fixed wording prevented such continued creativity, piyyutim were created for insertion into the fixed texts; eventually, kabbalists applied the word kavvanah to novel literary introductions to standard prayers, detailing the latter's spiritual intent, directing the worshiper to the prayer's inner meaning. Today, kavvanah may mean any of the above, or just the inner intentionality of saying a prayer, despite its fixed words and prescribed manner, as if it emanated creatively anew from the depth of one's very being.

Peoplehood and Covenant: The theological basis for prayer-as-commandment is God's collective covenant with Israel at Sinai, according to which God lovingly reveals the Torah, including its worship prescriptions. Despite considerable individual piety, therefore, Jews worship first and foremost as members of the people Israel: the fixed confession liturgy enumerates sins of which any particular individual is probably guiltless but that everyone acknowledges anyway; statutory prayer requires the minyan; prayer formulas speak of "we," "our God," and "us"—almost never of "I," "my God," and "me."

Democracy: Because Jews share equally in the covenant, Jewish worship is democratically constructed. Though traditionalists still distinguish people by descent from the Israelite castes—one is a *kohen* (priest), *levi* (Levite), or *yisra'el* (an Israelite), these now are only honorific titles, carrying a few symbolic privileges: the right to bless the people on holidays, or to receive the first *aliyah*. Significantly, the prayer leader—who is designated *sheliakh tzibbur*, "the congregation's agent"—may be any respected and knowledgeable layperson, though frequently is specially trained as a *khazzan* (cantor). Orthodox worship, however, still maintains a gender division, in which women are technically exempt from time-bound positive commandments in general, the three daily prayer services among them. Orthodox women may not serve as sheliakh tzibbur, and, in fact, those who choose to attend services are separated from men by a gallery or a visual barrier (*mekhitsah*).

Berakhah: The literary building block for all Jewish worship is the *berakhah* (blessing, benediction). The rabbis eschewed a purely biblical liturgy. Long biblical citations, like the Shema, are bracketed by blessings, and short ones are inserted into blessings. The Tefillah is called also the Shemoneh Esrei, "the eighteen [blessings]," because structurally, it is just a series of blessings; the marriage rite's central prayer is known as "the seven blessings." Eating food and observing the miraculous in nature evoke blessings also. The creation of new blessings ceased by the ninth century, after which new prayers were framed in other genres. Still, the blessing form of prayer dominates and characterizes Jewish worship.

But Jewish blessings neither "bless God" nor invoke God's blessing on us. Rather, in classical rabbinic theology, blessings are transformational vehicles mediating the human-divine contact. The world's produce is God's, for example: eating it requires a blessing lest one feed off sacred substance while being oneself in a nonsacred state. Similarly, observing a rainbow (the sign to Noah of God's presence) or a world-renowned scholar (a reflection of divine wisdom) calls forth a blessing lest one fail to acknowledge the numinous presence of the divine in nature or the intellect and thus make profane use of the sacred. Judaism posits a primary binary opposition between sacred and profane. It values both, seeing human beings as rooted in both at the same time. But it asks that Jews not mix the categories. Thus, blessings transform objects of enjoyment from their ontological state of the sacred into a sufficiently nonsacred entity available for human use. In their origin, therefore, blessings were the means by which Jews meet the domain of the sacred.

Worship Space: Though prayer may occur anywhere, Judaism establishes sacred sites, both at home and in synagogue. At home it is the table, around which meals are shared and family worship rituals performed. In the synagogue, it is the entire worship space, outfitted above all with one or more Torah scrolls, which are kept in a wall cavity called an *aron hakodesh* (a sacred cabinet), known as an ark. These scrolls are usually decorated with embroidered cloth covers and silver ornaments, including the *yad* (hand), a hand pointer to facilitate reading Torah without losing one's place. A *parokhet* (curtain) covers the ark and opens to reveal the Torah scrolls. The sheliakh tzibbur leads the prayers from the *bimah*, generally a raised platform either in the center or at the front of the sanctuary. Because, traditionally, prayers are often recited facing Jerusalem, the eastern wall may be designated by a decorated object called a *mizrakh* (east). Outside the sanctuary, there may be bins containing *tallit* (prayer shawls) and *kippah* (Heb.) or *yarmulka* (Yiddish, "head covering") for worshipers who neglect to bring their own.

Movement Differences: A Jewish reformation in nineteenth-century Europe and America applied modern Western aesthetics, ethics, and science to worship. Reform Jews translated prayer books, shortened the service, extracted offensive content from ancient prayers, highlighted the sermon as religious instruction, introduced modern musical notation along with mixed choirs and an organ, granted women equality, and no longer demanded traditionalistic prayer garb, which they considered medieval.

Today, there are four recognized Jewish movements in the United States: Reform, Conservative, Reconstructionist, and Orthodox—each with its own subgroupings and unique approaches to liturgical questions. They all are recognizably continuous with classical Jewish worship tradition, and by and large, though members of any single group might disagree with a particular stand taken by the others, all could worship together, conscious of the covenant with God that they share and celebrate as the basic fact of Jewish existence.

Current Trends: Jewish worship since World War II has undergone renewal. New prayer books worldwide reflect on the Holocaust and the State of Israel. Many traditions jettisoned a century ago have been recovered. The trend is toward greater congregational participation, gender egalitarianism, an ambiance of informality and warmth, and an implicit theology of immediate (not transcendent) and intimate (not distant) divine presence, taking place in modest sanctuaries with adjustable spaces that highlight the shared peoplehood of the assembled worshipers.

Judaism in China. *See* China, Judaism in.

Judaism in Islam. *See* Islam, Judaism in.

Judaizers, non-Jews who follow Jewish practices. The term first occurs in Esther 8:17 (Greek text) to refer to Gentiles who became Jews. It is most frequent in early Christian texts, where it refers pejoratively to Christians who adopt, or to Jewish Christians who retain, certain Jewish observances, such as circumcision or food taboos. *See also* B'nai Noah; Gentiles, righteous.

Judas Iscariot, in the New Testament, one of the original twelve disciples; his betrayal of Jesus to the authorities results in the Crucifixion.

Judea, in the Hebrew Bible, the Southern Kingdom ruled by the house of David distinguished from the Northern Kingdom of Israel, or Samaria. The name Jew originally designated an inhabitant of Judea.

Judeo-Christian tradition, recent term emphasizing the kinship of Judaism and Christianity. The notion that these two religions can be melded into a single tradition is without scholarly merit. *See also* Abrahamic religions.

Judgment Day, Christian term, found chiefly in the New Testament, for the imminent last period of world history when Christ, or the Son of Man, will render verdicts of salvation or damnation on all human beings. *See also* apocalypticism; eschatology; Second Coming; Son of Man.

ju-i (*roo-ee*; Chin., "as you wish it"), slightly curved scepter, commonly of jade. A Chinese symbol of immortality, it was carried by Taoist gods and was formerly bestowed on officials as a mark of imperial favor.

Julian of Norwich (ca. 1342–1420), English Catholic mystical writer who took her name from the church of St. Julian in Norwich, where she spent the latter part of her life as a recluse. Her book, *The Sixteen Revelations of Divine Love,* based on two days' experiences occurring on May 8 to 9, 1373, was written twenty years afterward.

Julian the Apostate (331–363), Christian derogatory title for Flavius Claudius Julianus, the last Roman emperor to attempt to displace Christianity as the state religion with an amalgam of Greco-Roman deities and cult practices.

Jupiter (*joo'pi-tuhr*), supreme divinity of the ancient Romans. Originally a native Italian sky god identified with Zeus, Jupiter controlled weather changes, rain, and storms. Maintaining the sanctity of treaties and oaths, he was the chief protector of Rome; he was worshiped by magistrates entering office and by generals returning victorious. *See also* Roman religion.

justification by faith alone, fundamental principle of the Protestant Reformation that salvation depends entirely on the grace of God rather than on human actions. *See also* Reformation, Protestant.

Justin Martyr (ca. 100–165), early Christian apologist. He developed a distinctively Christian reading of the Old Testament and was one of the first to deploy quotations from the Gospels in his arguments with Jews, Greco-Roman philosophers, and other Christian thinkers. His authentic works are the *First Apology* and the *Dialogue with Trypho the Jew.*

ABCDEF
GHI K

PQ
UV
WXY&Z

Ka (kah), in ancient Egyptian religion, one of the three aspects of the soul, a spiritual duplicate of the living person and recipient of postmortem food offerings. *See also* Egyptian religion; soul.

Kaaba (kah'bah; Arab.), the most sacred place on earth in Islam, founded, according to Islamic tradition, by Ibrahim and Ismail. Muslims everywhere face toward this black-draped cubic building—located within the grand mosque in Mecca—during ritual prayers and walk around it during the Mecca pilgrimage. Its eastern corner contains a holy black stone. Some traditions link the Kaaba, also known as "God's sacred house," with a celestial shrine and with the heart of the true believer. *See also* Mecca; pilgrimage.

Muslims bowing toward the Kaaba as part of the ritual circumambulation (*tawaf*) of this holiest of Islamic places during the pilgrimage to Mecca.

kabbalah. *See* Judaism (mysticism).

kachina/katsina, (kah-chee'nah; Hopi), a masked being understood in ethnographic studies of Pueblo (American Southwest) religions as an intermediary between communities and their nonhuman creators. Frequently explained as ancestor spirits, kachinas can be representations of natural forces, birds and animals, aspects of other tribal groups, and figures in intertribal history, among others. Kachinas have power to bring rainfall, among other forms of weather, and to protect the health and well-being of community residents, crops, and livestock. Their annual visits to Pueblo communities are dramatized by members of religious fraternities in the form of masked kachina performances, which conclude with prayers to the kachina and assurances by the community of its continued regard for its capabilities. Believed by archaeologists to predate the arrival of the Spanish into the American Southwest, kachina masking practices are thought to have originated after 900 at Casas Grandes, Chihuahua (in present-day Mexico), and to have been imported from there to the Pueblo community of Zuni in Arizona. In the twentieth century, kachina performances have been documented in a number of Pueblo communities, including Zuni, Hopi, Santo Domingo, Isleta, and Ysleta del Sur (near El Paso, Texas). Public kachina performances have been most elaborated by the Zunis and Hopis; in the latter community, more than 250 different kachinas are recognized. Turtle Dance, believed to be an unmasked kachina performance, occurs at Taos, San Juan, and San Felipe. Navajo and Apache masked performances are thought to be derived from the Pueblos. The human identity of kachina impersonators is kept secret from children before their initiation into religious life. Beginning with the children's witnessing of the unmasking of the kachinas, the long initiation process includes, for Pueblo men, their first participation in a kachina performance. Besides their masked impersonations, kachinas appear also in the form of dolls, constructed of cottonwood and dressed or painted and given to children to acquaint them with various kachina figures. The dolls evidently are used as fertility figures and in Pueblo healing practices. They are also made for commercial sale. *See also* North America, traditional religions in.

Kada Azumamaro (kah dah ah-*zoo*-mah-mahr-oh; 1669–1736), Japanese scholar and poet of the National Learning school (Kokugaku) who urged that a school for these studies be established and that nativism be adopted by the government. *See also* Japan, Confucianism in; Kokugaku.

Kaeryong, Mt. *See* mountains, sacred.

kafir (ka'fir; Arab., "one who is ungrateful"), a legal and theological term in Islam for one who is an unbeliever. The act of unbelief (*kufr*) stands in opposition to *iman* ("belief," "faith") and is treated extensively in Islamic law. In addition to outright unbelief is feigned or insincere belief. *See also* munafiq.

kagura (kah-goo-rah; Jap., "gods' entertainment"), a generic term for Shinto music and dance. Ritual music and dance figure importantly in Shinto mythology and have been central to Shinto practice throughout history. The ritual forms are designed to please the enshrined *kami* (divinities, divine presences) and thereby gain the benefits of their power. *See also* Japanese religions, sacred music in; Shinto.

Kagyu-pa (kah-gyoo'pah; Tibetan, "command lineage"), one of four principal schools of Tibetan Buddhism, renowned for its emphasis on meditation. Originating in India with Tilopa and Naropa, the school was founded in Tibet by Marpa (1012–96), who taught the *yogin* Milarepa. The Kagyu-pa developed several branches, with the Karma Kagyu sect being the largest. The Kagyu-pa incorporated teachings of other schools, particularly of the Nyingma-pa lineage. Originally a school of retreatant meditators, the Kagyu-pa early on took a monastic form, which it maintains to this day while continuing to specialize in meditation and strict retreat. *See also* Karma-pa; meditation; monasticism; Tibetan religions.

Kaibara Ekken (kah-ee-bah-rah ayk-ken; 1630–1714), Confucian scholar who helped spread Japanese Neo-Confucianism through extensive writing and teaching. Philosophically, he emphasized a monism of *ch'i* (material force) while advocating *jitsugaku* (practical learning). *See also* Japan, Confucianism in; Neo-Confucianism.

Kakuban (kah-koo-bahn; 1095–1143), Japanese Shingon Buddhist monk who founded the Shingi Shingonshu, an interpretation of Tantric Buddhism that incorporated Pure Land beliefs and was attractive to the masses. *See also* Pure Land; Shingon-shu; Tantrism (Buddhism).

kakure kirishitan (kah-koo-ray kee-ree-shi-tahn; Jap., "hidden Christians"), Christians remaining in Japan after the Tokugawa prohibition of Christianity (1614) and subsequent persecutions, carrying on their faith secretly until the abolition of Christian prohibition laws in the mid-nineteenth century.

kakure nembutsu (kah-koo-ray nem-boo-tsoo; Jap., "hidden recollection of Buddha"), in Japan, secret Pure Land Buddhist devotions in the Tokugawa period (1615–1868) in areas where the True Pure Land sect (Jodo Shinshu) had been banned. *See also* Jodo Shinshu; Pure Land.

kalam (kah-lam'; Arab.), the technical term for "Islamic theology." In everyday language, the word simply means "speech, talk, utterance." In technical usage, however, it early acquired the connotation of "argument, dispute about theological matters"; therefore, the "science of *kalam*" (*ilm al-kalam*, sometimes abbreviated to kalam) came to signify speculative theology based on rational argument and developed in a dialectical structure that followed the rules of real or fictitious debate. Because the meaning of the term is derived from structure and presentation rather than from content, it does not correspond exactly to what Christians understand by "theology." There were other forms of theological expression in Islam: the creed, the epistle, the juridical expertise (*fatwa*), the apocalypse, the didactic poem, heresiography, and, later on, especially the commentary. There was also, in the beginning, implicit theology, above all in the prophetic tradition (*hadith*). Moreover, rational theology came to be rivaled by Sufism, which expressed its theological ideas in the language of mysticism.

Because of its dialectical structure, kalam could appear eristic to believers of a fideistic type, as *talk* in the sense of "verbiage." Their critique was, however, a formal one, directed against contentiousness rather than against argument. It did not preclude theology as such, although the name of the discipline was changed and the scope of topics decreased. Theology was then called *usul al-din* (basics of religion) instead of ilm al-kalam, and the books produced in the new literary genre were relatively short. In contrast to this, kalam works tended to have *summa* character and could consist of many volumes. It is true that in kalam, too, certain problems were considered to be basic, as compared to others that were subtle (*latif*) or complicated (*daqiq*). But the latter ones tended to attract attention as objects for progressive research and as a means for demonstrating sophistication. This is why early kalam abounds in paraphernalia, especially in the realm of natural science: speculations about atomism, the location of the earth in the cosmos, the elements, etc.

Kalam as a Technique: Dialogue as a literary form and debate as an instrument of dialectics are already found in antiquity and in early Christianity. Since Plato, philosophical problems had been presented in the form of questions and answers. Patristic theology developed, at a later stage, the corresponding literary genre of dialectical argumentation (Gk. *erotapokriseis)*. Rhetorical and juridical training centered around the disputation, where fictitious cases were discussed in order to sharpen the student's dialectical skill. If important enough, real debates were recorded in shorthand and published in a stylized—sometimes adulterated—form. Kalam participates in this tradition. It is, therefore, not improbable that the Arabic term kalam reflects the Greek term *dialeksis*.

As transmitters of the Greek tradition into Arabic, Syriac-speaking Christians have been proposed. It should be remembered, however, that the Arabs had long been in contact with the world of Late Antiquity and that Islam was not only a product of the neophytes. Structures of dialectical reasoning are found abundantly in the Qur'an. There, God instructs his messenger how to deal with his pagan opponents; in doing so he uses the question-and-answer scheme ("when they say . . . then tell them . . ."). In contrast to the Old and to a lesser degree the New Testaments, the Qur'an presupposes the existence of rational and dialectical theology; moreover, the relationship between God and humankind is conceived in juridical terms where God presents an "argument" (*hujja*) that humankind, if intelligent enough and not obstinate, has to acknowledge. Seen this way, kalam is something typically Islamic; in later centuries, even theologians who were opposed to it frequently conceded that most—or all—rules of reasoning could be traced back to the Qur'an (and, thereby, to revelation itself).

Yet, the earliest phase of Islamic theology seems to have preferred the medium of the epistle. It is not until the last years of Umayyad domination (661–750) and the beginning of the Abbasid revolution (first half of the eighth century) that the professional exponents of kalam (*mutakallimun*) appear in our sources. They worked for the opposition movements; their task was propaganda and missionary activity. The Umayyad government had no need for them; for propagating its political ideas in a religious disguise it possessed the institution of the *qussas*, popular preachers who were paid as a kind of clergy. Under the Abbasids (750–1258), however, these qussas quickly lost their influence, and kalam became the main instrument of religious discourse. The mutakallimun were invited to the court of the caliphs at Baghdad. The mutakallimun had to support the state in its persecution of dualist heresy (*zandaqa*) and were frequently asked to discuss controversial issues in the presence of a prince or a governor and in bourgeois circles. When the mutakallimun felt well versed enough they also entered the field of interreligious debate, especially with Christians, less frequently with Zoroastrians and Jews. The spirit of these discussions seems to have been relatively chivalrous, sometimes even relaxed; but the official support and the high social prestige, together with the awareness of representing the victorious side, nourished elitist feelings that did not arouse sympathy among the lower classes and their religious leaders. The mutakallimun themselves finally realized that constant discussion could lead to a dead end and that arguing from a priori premises may result in "equivalence of proofs," whose Arabic term (*takafu' al-adilla*) also has a Greek equivalent (*isostheneia ton logon*). From the tenth century onward, the reservations against kalam became stronger; only in jurisprudence did disputations remain uncontested. But even at the end of the twelfth century, Fakhr al-Din al-Razi (d. 1209) proudly reported on his debates with theological opponents in eastern Iran.

From the late ninth century onward, a special branch of scholarly literature dealt with the rules of debate (*adab al-jadal*). The forensic character of kalam demanded a special kind of logic similar to the one described in Aristotle's *Topics*. In a debate, the syllogism was of no great use; rather, the technique preferred by the mutakallimun was the so-called *muarada* (Lat. *retorsio*), where the counterargument was based on a premise used by the opponent himself. Much attention was paid therefore to analogy (*qiyas*) and its appropriate ratio (*illa*); in this area the interdependence of theological and juridical reasoning was most obvious. But adab al-jadal also included rules of disputational courtesy: who is allowed to ask the questions (asking always being more advantageous than answering), and how one should formulate questions in order to enter into a straightforward dialogue without eliciting mere "statements" from one's opponent. When does one of the partners have to acknowledge defeat, and which consequences are to be drawn from this? Should the loser "convert" to an opponent's view or at least stop expounding one's own ideas?

In the last point, the old relationship between disputational practice and missionary activity comes through, but, of course, usually situations were not understood so strictly. Debates were handled rather like tournaments; in higher teaching they could also serve as a kind of examination. The person who had lost the first round was frequently given the chance to be the questioner in a second one. In interreligious disputes, opinions could be exchanged with relative freedom, at least as long as the cultural setting allowed for it. The Qur'an largely was avoided as an explicit argument in a controversy with non-Muslims, and frequently people conceded that beyond rational provability there was an existential commitment to one's religion that was not necessarily shaken by a verbal defeat. The system favored the display of rhetorical and dialectical skill, but even among those who supported it many remained aware of the fact that carrying one's point did not always mean being right. There could be an arbiter, the prince, for instance; but normally the audience was expected to remain silent and to abstain from demonstrations of sympathy or aversion. The reality was, of course, apt to be different; the treatises on adab al-jadal cannot deny their theoretical and idealistic character.

Kalam as a Discipline: In spite of its dialectic character, kalam was not merely an art of contradiction-making. In its great days, during the first centuries of Islam, it dealt with vital issues, and it used the most modern means of conceptualization, in natural science as well as in textual analysis and in epistemology. The main theological subjects that were discussed in the time when Islam was about to find its identity were freedom and/or createdness of human action, the definitions of faith and belief, the concept of God, especially with regard to anthropomorphism, and the political ways of the early community, especially the first four caliphs (who were later, in a largely successful attempt at harmonization, called the "righteous" ones, *al-khulafa al-rashidun*). For a number of speculations the ground had been prepared by the earlier religions, especially Christianity, and by Greek philosophy in its Syriac as well as its Middle Iranian disguises. But there is still no evidence for a direct influence or dependence. Islam never forgot that it had its own individual approach; this had, after all, been its raison d'etre. The Christian church fathers had been unanimous in advocating free will, whereas in Islam this doctrine, from the beginning, was counterbalanced by a strong trend toward determinism and predestination. Monotheism (*tawhid*) defined itself as an alternative to Christian Trinity and Zoroastrian or Manichean dualism; however, it was not always understood as necessarily involving a transcendental or noncorporeal image of God. The problem of whether belief was a mere act of assent or had to be attested by works had eagerly been discussed in Christianity. But in Islam, the issue seems to have arisen out of the conviction of early Muslims that their community had been chosen by God as the best and only trustworthy recipient of revelation and that, therefore, everybody who joined it by this mere fact deserved paradise. The same incentive appears to have been responsible for the controversy about the appropriate conception of history, which could serve as a criterion for the political decisions made by the early community. History was understood as salvation history, and the discord in the first civil war then came as a shock. Companions of the Prophet had stood on both sides, and people had been killed; this was a sin that called for justification.

The religious evaluation of an a priori, merely political event like the first civil war (*fitna*), which was to be followed by several others, explains why the political groupings that originated at this moment could live on as theological movements until today: the Kharijites, who rejected the caliphate altogether and therefore organized their communities on a "presbyterian" basis; the Shia, who insisted on the priority of Ali, the son-in-law of the Prophet, and therefore had to admit that historical reality had gone wrong since the election of the first caliph; and the great Sunni majority, who accepted the facts as they saw them and believed in a consensus of the community beyond political failure. The spokesmen of the Sunnis thought that the question of who had been the sinner in the civil war had to be left open and that the decision about it had to be postponed until the Last Judgment; after this principle they were called "Postponers" (Murjiites).

However, since these groups understood themselves as religious movements, their political standpoints usually were linked to other issues. Kharijites could appear as adherents of free will or of determinism, as anthropomorphists or transcendentalists. Having seceded from the majority, they were no longer able to admit that membership in Islam was the only or the main criterion of belief but had to stress the importance of righteous action, or works. The Shiites upheld the priority of assent in belief, but they understood it as the assent to Ali and his successors, the other Muslims having gone astray or being ungrateful for God's mercy. The Shiite concept of God mostly tended to a more or less enlightened anthropomorphism. Murjiites believed in free will when, in the eighth century, they founded a school in the Iraqi town of

Basra, whereas in eastern Iran, under Jahm ibn Safwan (d. 745) and his adherents, they followed a rigid determinism. It seems that most of these doctrinal differences grew out of local traditions; Islam had expanded too early and too rapidly to have a firm identity that imposed itself everywhere under the same form. But it also created a huge oecumene where ideas could be freely exchanged. Many alternatives (e.g., free will vs. determinism) were still of equal rank, and there were no universal institutions (councils, synods, etc.) that might have defined or enforced orthodoxy. Something like a uniform theological doctrine took shape only when certain adherents of a rationalist systematization of Islam, the so-called Mutazilites, found the support of the Abbasid government and gained attention by their dominant role at the court (at the end of the eighth century). Dogmatic compromises had been attempted before, in some of the movements mentioned above, but because of their local character these were now looked upon as provincial and labeled sectarian.

The Mutazilite theologian Abu al-Hudhayl (d. ca. 840) defined the platform of his school in five "principles" (usul), which he considered to be indispensable. Some of them turned out to be time-bound and were quickly given up or reinterpreted, but the first two were to become the trademark of the movement: monotheism, in the sense of transcendentalism, and God's justice as the guarantee of humanity's free will. As such, Abu al-Hudhayl's initiative represents the first attempt at sifting out basic issues that could serve as criteria between right and wrong and even between belief and unbelief. From then onward, creeds and catechisms were a rather common phenomenon. Those, however, that have been preserved normally do not follow the Mutazilite line. For soon enough the Mutazilites were confronted by countermovements that either rejected kalam altogether (for instance, the Hanbalites) or used it for defending a position that seemed closer to the Qur'an and to the prophetic tradition. This development was strengthened and, in a certain way, initiated by an event that caused the Mutazila to be suspected of supporting repressive measures taken by the Abbasid government against the religious spokesmen of the lower classes, namely, the so-called mihna ("trial," usually translated as "inquisition"), in which everyone holding a religious office had to declare his loyalty to the government-proclaimed dogma of the createdness of the Qur'an (833–ca. 850). That this seemingly secondary issue could turn into a litmus test was due to its implications: the Qur'an was

considered to be God's own Word, i.e., his speech, which contained the "names" God had given to himself. The createdness of these names, or God's predicates, could be understood as the createdness of his attributes, and the createdness of his speech entailed the temporality of his will, which had been expressed in his revelation. This is why the oldest anti-Mutazilite theology, mainly represented by Ibn Kullab (d. ca. 855), concentrated on the doctrine of attributes and the relationship between God's eternal will and the commandments found in the holy Scripture. Ibn Kullab conceived God's speech on a metalinguistic level, i.e., as the intended meaning formulated only in the revealed text, for example, in Hebrew in the Bible and in Arabic in the Qur'an.

In spite of this opposition, the Mutazila still managed to expand. From the end of the ninth century, most Shiites were gradually won over. The persuasiveness of the Mutazilite approach was grounded on its systematic rigor; the school now entered its scholastic phase. Ibn Kullab's ideas, on the other hand, were taken up in a modified way by Ashari (873–935), who was to become, in later perspective, the founder of the dominant orthodox school of theology. Ibn Kullab had been attacked and persecuted by those who opposed kalam altogether; Ashari, on the contrary, tried to appease these critics by using many of their own fideistic formulations, especially the famous "without qualification" (bila kayf), by which they accepted the anthropomorphisms in the Qur'an. In reality, however, he remained a true mutakallim; he did not shrink from discussing subtle issues, and on many points he differed only slightly from Mutazilite positions. Al-Ashari had his own view of the divine attributes, but in principle he shared the transcendentalist concept of God, which the Mutazilites had elaborated in their controversy with early Shiism and which remained typical for Islam until today. Rather, he clashed with them on the question of free will. It is true that he shared the view held by most of them that human power to act is not a permanent quality but only related to one specific action. Whereas they, however, thought that this power, or capacity, comes into existence at least one moment before the action to which it is related, al-Ashari regarded the capacity as coexistent with the action. Because the Mutazilites had thought that power itself is given by God (and not part of an independent "nature" belonging to humans), al-Ashari's position implied that the action, too, is created by God and can only be "performed" or "appropriated" by a human being. In the view of the Mutazilites, God had shown his justice by leaving human beings alone in their decisions for good or bad and by rewarding or punishing them accordingly. For al-Ashari, God's justice was beyond all human categories and did not restrict his liberty of dealing with humankind as he wishes. Attempts at defining a natural law and rational ethics, which are found in early Mutazilite theology, therefore were not pursued and had no future in Islam once Mutazilism gave way to Asharism.

Due to political and social developments in Iraq, especially in the capital Baghdad, the center of Mutazilite as well as Asharite kalam slowly shifted to Iran. In Asharism this led to a renewed interest in the problem of anthropomorphism. A Sufi movement, which had started in the town of Nishapur and then spread into Afghanistan, the Karramiyya, had won many adherents in the lower classes by rejecting transcendentalism and by building its theology around the concept of a corporeal God sitting in heaven on his throne. In reacting against this, Asharism associated with trends that advocated a reformed and enlightened kind of mysticism appealing to the jurists and the religious circles in the bourgeoisie. The arguments against the "primitive" aspects of anthropomorphism and exegetical literalism were frequently taken from the arsenal of the Mutazilites. Kalam still worked with a common stock.

The mutakallimun were soon confronted with an opponent they had long thought they could neglect: *falsafa* (Islamic philosophy). For generations, philosophy had been the domain of Christians; now, after it had been taken over by Muslims, Aristotelian logic laid bare the weaknesses of dialectics. From the end of the eleventh century onward, especially through the endeavor of al-Ghazali and Fakhr al-Din al-Razi, theological and juridical arguments were put on a new, syllogistic basis. Aristotle's metaphysics, in contrast to logic, had a longer way to go; his "theology" was discredited because of the doctrine of the eternity of the world, which had been attacked by kalam for centuries. The same applied to Neoplatonism; emanationist cosmology was closely linked to the Ismaili Shiite heresy. Al-Ghazali, in his *Incoherence of the Philosophers*, openly criticized the pagan elements in the system of the falsafa. But the philosopher whom he had foremost in mind, Ibn Sina (Lat. *Avicenna*), nevertheless left a strong impact on him and considerably influenced later theological thinking, especially that of Fakhr al-din al-Razi. When Islam, after temporarily having lost its supremacy during the

Mongol invasion in the thirteenth century, recovered in Iran and rebuilt its educational structures, the first manual of theology written in the new era, Adud al-Din al-Iji's *Mawaqif*, devoted only two of its six sections to, properly speaking, dogmatic issues; the rest dealt with epistemological and metaphysical propedeutics.

Besides Asharism, Iran generated a second school of theology, which is connected today with the name of al-Maturidi (d. ca. 944). The school was roughly contemporary, but originated far in the East, in Transoxania, and was closely connected with the tradition of the Sunni jurist Abu Hanifa. From the end of the eighth century, theological ideas that Abu Hanifa had developed at Kufa had been adapted to the intellectual milieu of eastern Iran. Later on, popular catechisms developed on this ground. Al-Maturidi was the first important systematic theologian who worked on this basis in Samarqand; two centuries later Abu al-Muin al-Nasafi (d. 1114) composed his *Tabsirat al-adilla* (Exposition of the Proofs), the most comprehensive summa of the school to be preserved. Unlike al-Ashari, al-Maturidi was for a long time not considered the founder of the school; in Transoxania this honor was accorded to Abu Hanifa. And unlike Asharism, the theology in Samarqand and other eastern towns was not influenced by Aristotelian logic or Ibn Sina's metaphysics until a very late stage, under Taftazani (d. 1390). In the Mamluk age of the thirteenth century and afterward, in the Ottoman Empire, Maturidism could spread to the West together with Hanafite jurisprudence, and al-Maturidi was put on an equal level with al-Ashari.

But kalam had lost its vigor; it had become an affair of textbooks. Disputations about living theological issues no longer took place. Reformist movements such as Wahhabism identified with the antidialectic attitude of Hanbalism; mystical brotherhoods favored interiorized piety and active charity against intellectual brilliancy. It is true that some modernists of the nineteenth century, such as Jamal al-Din al-Afghani (in his *Refutation of the Materialists*) and Muhammad Abduh (in his *Treatise on Monotheism*), took up the kalam tradition and that in twentieth-century Egypt Mutazilite ideas enjoyed a certain revival because of the urge to assert human liberty. But as it seems now, this no longer suits the mood of the time. Liberal intellectuals as well as fundamentalists care about juridical and socio-political problems. The locus of theological speculation is *tafsir* (quranic exegesis); one of the rare classical topics that still attracts attention is *ijaz*, or the miraculous insuperability of the Qur'an. Kalam as a technique may have left its traces in a certain predilection for theological controversy, but it no longer exists as a part of academic training. In Saudi Arabia it is completely forbidden; only in Iran, where Shiism preserved its ancient links with Mutazilite theology, is it still held in esteem. *See also* Asharite; Mutazila.

Kalevala (kah'lev-ah-lah; Finnish), an epic compiled of Finnish and Karelian oral poetry (songs and incantations in trochaic tetrameter) by Elias Lonnrot (1802–84), a Finnish medical doctor and folklore collector. The first edition (12,078 verses) was published in 1835; the second edition (22,795 verses)—the "official" one and the national epic of Finland—was published in 1849.

Lonnrot interpreted the contents of the collected songs historically and compiled them in a way that depicts a plot from the creation of the world to the arrival of Christianity among two neighboring and rivaling peoples, the good Kalevala and the evil Pohjola. This he did in accordance with contemporary Romantic theories, which regarded the epic genre as depicting an unwritten national history. Finnish intellectuals welcomed the epic as giving the Finns a history of their own—and thus, a legitimate proof for being a nation—as well as showing their national character.

Lonnrot compiled the epic using a text-critical method according to which the different variants of the "same" songs were compared to one another and the "defects" of one variant were patched with material from others. This was believed to provide a complete and most original form of a given song. The historical interpretation has often been challenged by a mythological one, according to which the characters are to be understood as pre-Christian gods and other deities. Whatever the reading, the epic has been a significant symbol in Finnish cultural and political history. While some of its materials are believed to derive from pre-Christian times, as a compilation the epic represents the mythologies of Romanticism and nationalism rather than any religion of antiquity. *See also* Finnish religion.

Kali (kah'lee; Skt., "the black one"), Hindu goddess. Fierce and bloodthirsty, she haunts battlefields and cremation grounds, wears a garland of severed heads and a girdle of severed arms, and holds a severed head and bloodied sword. Despite her fierce appearance she is regarded by her devotees as a beneficent mother figure. *See also* Goddess (Hinduism); path of devotion; Shakti.

Kali Yuga (kah'lee yoo'gah; Skt.), in Hindu cosmology, the last of four repeating ages (*yugas*): that of iron in which the law (*dharma*) is like an animal on one leg. In *bhakti* (devotional) texts salvation is only possible in the Kali Yuga. *See also* cosmology.

kalpa (kal'pah; Skt., "divide," "distribute"), a term for Indic ritual or doctrine of ceremonies as well as division of time: a cycle from creation to dissolution. *See also* cosmology; yuga.

kama (kah'muh; Skt., "desire"), one of Hinduism's four goals of life (*purusharthas*), together with *dharma* (religion), *artha* (profit), and *moksha* (liberation). *Kama* incarnate is the god of erotic love, who incites lust by means of arrows made of flowers shot from a bowstring made of bees. Kama once attacked Shiva, the great *yogin*, who used his third, yogic eye to burn Kama to ashes, making him henceforth disembodied, but all the more irresistible. *See also* four goals of life (Hinduism).

Kamakura (kah-mah-koo-rah), capital (located on the central east coast of Honshu Island) of the first ruling Japanese shogun and the name of the period of rule from that city (1185–1333). The period witnessed the founding of Japanese Zen and popular devotional Buddhist sects. *See also* Japan, Confucianism in; Japanese religion.

Kamakura schools (kah-mah-koo-rah), the collective name for six Japanese Buddhist schools (Jodoshu, Jodo Shinshu, Jishu, Rinzai Zen, Soto Zen, and Nichiren) founded during the Kamakura period (1185–1333). Most of the schools share a number of characteristics, such as emphasizing faith, choosing a single practice, and appealing to the masses; as a result, some scholars have referred to the rise of these schools in a short period as the "Kamakura reformation." *See also* Japanese religion; Jishu; Jodo Shinshu; Jodoshu; Nichiren; Rinzai; Soto school.

Kamashastra. *See* Kamasutra/Kamashastra.

Kamasutra/Kamashastra (kah-muh-soo'truh kah-muh-shah'struh; Skt., "treatise on desire, erotics"), Indian text on the arts of love. Written by Vatsyayana ca. 400 it is an exhaustive treatise composed for the edification of both sexes on the theory and practice of *kama*, desire, the first of the four Hindu goals of life. *See also* four goals of life (Hinduism); kama.

kami (kah-mee; Jap., "sacred," "divinity"), the mythological, natural, or human figures worshiped within Shinto. The term *kami* is indigenous to Japan although it came to be written with a Chinese character; it has been compared with the Ainu term *kamui*. Kami refers to what is sacred, pure, and powerful, but it may be a destructive as well as creative force (for example, volcanoes and mountains are kami). Mythological deities, recorded especially in the *Kojiki* and *Nihonshoki* texts, are usually divided into heavenly and earthly kami. Natural forms of kami include mountains, waterfalls, trees, boulders, rivers, and the like. Emperors, as descendants of the sun goddess (Amaterasu Omikami), have been considered manifest kami. Some great human beings have been viewed after death as kami and enshrined in Shinto shrines; in popular belief, charismatic figures such as founders (or foundresses) of new religions are considered living kami (*ikigami*).

Representations of kami in visual, especially plastic, form are rather late. Usually kami are considered to reside in or be called down into an object of worship (*shintai*) within a Shinto shrine and may be sent away after a ritual. Kami are also invoked, customarily with a prayer strip (*ofuda*) in the Shinto-style altar (*kamidana*) in a home. In recent centuries common belief was that every locale had a tutelary kami (*ujigami*). *See also* Ainu religion; cosmology; Japanese folk religion; mountains, sacred; Shinto.

A Shinto priest in Tokyo, Japan (ca. 1980), uses a paper brush to ward off bad spirits from the altar at the ritual presentation of a one-month-old child to its tutelary *kami*. Following the presentation, the infant is considered the kami's child and throughout his or her life will maintain a special relationship to this kami, participating, for example, in the kami's annual festivals.

kamidana (kah-mee-dah-nah; Jap., "god shelf"), a small Shinto shrine or altar found in many traditional Japanese homes. Amulets representing deities important to the family may be found there. *See also* Japanese folk religion.

kami-gakari (kah-mee-gah-kah-ree; Jap., "deity catching"), possession by a *kami* (divinity, divine presence) in Japanese shamanism. A kami takes over the body and mind of a human host (*miko, kuchiyose*), who thereby delivers sacred oracles. An important part of mainstream religion in ancient times, the usually female shaman is now marginalized. Possession has figured in the founding of a number of new Japanese religions. *See also* inspiration; Japanese folk religion; kami; possession; shamanism.

kami-oroshi (kah-mee-oh-roh-shee), descent of a *kami* (divinity, divine presence) into a ritual site at the start of a Japanese Shinto ritual or to take possession of a priestess. *See also* kami; miko.

Kamo Mabuchi (kah-moh ma-boo-chee; 1697–1769), Japanese National Learning (Kokugaku) scholar and *waka* poet (a poet whose works contain fixed line lengths of 5-7-5-7-7 syllables). He wrote massive commentaries on the Japanese classics, particularly the *Man'yoshu*, emphasizing the importance of simplicity and spontaneity. *See also* Japan, Confucianism in; Kokugaku.

Kamo shrine (kah-moh), one of the preeminent shrines in the classical Shinto tradition. The two Kamo shrines of Kyoto, Japan, sponsor the great annual "Hollyhock Festival" (*Aoi matsuri*). *See also* shrine.

kamui (kah-moo-ee), Ainu term (also *kamuy*) for deities or gods, applied to both malevolent and benevolent beings, possibly related to the Japanese term *kami*. *See also* Ainu religion; kami.

K'ang Yu-wei (kahng yoh-way; 1858–1927), a Chinese reformist Confucian, eclectic religionist, and utopian politician. Schooled in classical Confucianism, he adopted an unorthodox Confucianism that characterized Confucius as a political reformer and religious founder. K'ang integrated Buddhist and Christian sources into a national Confucian religion for which he sought imperial support in 1898. In 1902 he wrote unusual Confucian commentaries to five important classical texts. Although he continued promoting Confucianism as a state religion after 1911, K'ang believed that a future world era of scientific progress would ultimately support a universal humanistic religion.

Kanjur (kahn'joor; from Tibetan, *bka'-'gyur,* "translation of the Word [of the Buddha]"), one of the two main divisions of the Tibetan Buddhist canon containing translations of Indian Buddhist texts considered to be the direct teaching of the Buddha or his immediate disciples. Several printed recensions are in existence today, but the original redactions circulated in manuscript form. The earliest *Kanjur* was the Tshal-pa version, which formed the basis of "The Old Narthang." The latter is the source for present day *Kanjurs,* which contain approximately one thousand works in roughly one hundred volumes. The bulk of these works are translated from Sanskrit. The oldest extant printed version is the Peking *Kanjur* of 1411. *See also* Buddhism (authoritative texts and their interpretation); canon; Tibetan religions.

Kannon (kahn-nohn; Jap., "Avalokiteshvara"), in Japanese Buddhism the Bodhisattva who exercises the profoundest compassion. Several popular pilgrimage courses connect temples dedicated to Kannon. In the Middle Ages, people sought Kannon's paradise by heading south in ships, but the paradise was also identified with specific places in Japan. *See also* Avalokiteshvara; Bodhisattvas.

kannushi (kahn-noo-shee; Jap., "Shinto priest"), in ancient times a man who through abstinence (and usually hereditary succession) qualified to mediate between people and *kami* (divinities, divine presences) at large Shinto shrines. *See also* kami.

Kanphata yogins (kahn'fuht; Hindi, "split-eared"), Hindus initiated into the Nath yogic tradition through the piercing of their ear cartilages, a reputed seat of sensual appetites. They are conspicuous by the large earrings they subsequently wear. *See also* Nath; yoga.

kanyadana (kahn-yuh-dahn'uh; Skt., "gift of a maiden"), the Hindu marriage rite in which the father, or his stand-in, gives the bride away to the groom. Other gifts are traditionally presented to the groom as well, and *kanyadana* can in practice entail a dowry.

Kapalika (kah-pah'lee-kuh; Skt., "those who bear a skull"), a medieval Hindu sect of devotees of the god Shiva. In Hindu myth, Shiva quarrels with the god Brahma and beheads him. To atone, Shiva must wander about using the skull of Brahma as a begging bowl. This Great Vow, or Mahavrata, served as the model for the religious vow of the Kapalika ascetics. Otherwise, they seem to have followed the tenets of Hindu Tantrism. Historical evidence suggests that the Kapalikas never became very influential. Nonetheless, Kapalika ascetics are often portrayed as hedonistic buffoons or necrophiliac villains in traditional Indian literature. *See also* Shiva; Tantra.

Kaplan, Mordecai M. (1881–1983), American rabbi, theologian, educator, and founder of the Reconstructionist movement in Judaism. Ordained at the Jewish Theological Seminary, where he taught for over fifty years, he expounded Judaism as the "evolving religious civilization of the Jewish people." He was an architect and critic of Conservative Judaism, and also influenced Reform Judaism. Kaplan advocated a radical, naturalistic theology, but more widely influential was his advocacy of a Jewish communalism, Zionism, Jewish cultural expression in literature and art, and creativity and experimentation in liturgy. The Reconstructionist movement, based on his teachings, has its own rabbinical college and congregational organization. He is the one American Jew to have founded a viable religious movement. *See also* Reconstructionism.

Karaites (from Heb. *qaraim,* kah-rah-im'; "Scripture-reader"), a sect in Judaism formed by Anan ben David ca. 800 that rejected the rabbinic conception of God's revealing to Moses at Sinai an oral Torah in addition to the written one. Karaites maintained that only the Pentateuch, the written Torah, was valid for Judaism. They rejected such nonbiblical customs as Hanukkah and rigidly followed Pentateuchal laws on the Sabbath, ritual cleanness, and consanguineous marriage.

Rabbinic Judaism declared Karaites heretics because of their denial of the dual Torah and banned marriage to them. As opponents of rabbinic Judaism, Karaites achieved influence in Middle Eastern Jewries, and they remained numerous in the Middle East and in the Crimean part of Russia until the twentieth century. In the invasion of the USSR from 1941 to 1944, the Germans classified Karaites as Gentiles and did not send them to the death camps.

Karbala (kar'ba-luh), a Muslim holy place in Iraq, the site of the tomb of Imam Husayn, Muhammad's grandson and the Shia *Imam,* who was killed there in 680, while resisting the imposition

of the rule of Yazid, successor to the first Um-
mayad ruler, Muawiya. Karbala has since become a center for Shia pilgrims, symbolizing
Husayn's martyrdom and struggle against injustice. The commemoration of the tragedy draws
thousands of pilgrims each year for mourning
assemblies and processions during the month of
Muharram. *See also* Husayn ibn Ali.

Kardecism, spiritualist teachings of Allan Kardec (Hippolyte Leon Denizard Rivail, 1804–69)
on the transmigration of spiritual essences in a
hierarchy of cosmic powers.

A leading mystic in the mid-nineteenth-
century studies of magnetism, positivism, and
communications with the dead, Rivail also consulted Christian theology, Hindu philosophy,
and evolutionary theory in his development of a
universalist Spiritist understanding of psychic
and spiritual phenomena. The 1858 volume *Le
livre des esprits contenant les principes de la doctrine spirite* (Book of the Spirits), dictated by the
Druidic spirit Kardec, revealed that each human
soul labors toward spiritual perfection through
successive incarnations, although encumbered
and contaminated by its proximity to material
forms. Kardecism teaches that the incarnate
spirits, lowest in cosmic rank, are aided by the
superior entities—including spirits who are no
longer incarnate, nonincarnate spirits, Jesus,
and the creator God—united in their pursuit of
charity, the highest virtue. The lower disembodied spirits communicate readily through human
mediums to provide spiritual and practical guidance to the living.

Kardecism was briefly popular in Europe, but
received its most substantial support in nine-
teenth- and twentieth-century Brazil, where
Kardecist and Spiritist groups such as *Umbanda*
still thrive. *See also* Afro-Americans (Caribbean
and South America), new religions among; Umbanda.

karma (kahr'muh; Skt., "deed," "action," "ritual," "result"), a
central Indian term with various meanings.

1 Any mental, verbal, or physical action or
intention, especially a morally correct or textually prescribed activity.

2 Ritual activity, particularly the ancient Indian rites propitiating a pantheon of gods as
prescribed in the Vedic texts. Ritual performance might be done to meet religious obligations, such as initiation into the community, to
honor one's ancestors, or to fulfill individual desires such as wealth, progeny, or immortality.
The results of ritual, which are also called
karma, were sometimes interpreted as "unseen"
(*apurva*), that is, postponed or not yet noticeable in order to explain apparently delayed consequences. While all could admit that actions
would eventually bear consequences, the doctrine of unseen results provoked lively debate
and reconsideration of the importance of ritual.

Early Vedic traditions preserved in texts
called Brahmanas (ca. 800 B.C.) suggest that
gods could respond to ritual worship according
to their divine wills. Later Brahmanas, however,
suggest a mechanistic view whereby ritual action controls the gods and brings irrevocable
and irrefragable results to officiants, participants, and patrons, for better and worse. The
mechanisms and results of ritual shape one's
world accordingly.

3 The results or consequences of actions or
intentions.

4 The principle or ethical law, originally developed in South Asian religions, that determines one's past, current, and future existences
as well as commensurate rewards and punishments in accordance with thoughts and practices.

First appearing textually in the Upanishads
(eighth–fifth centuries B.C.), the concept of
karma is a fundamental presupposition of all
South Asian religious systems, with the exception of the materialists, who deny its efficacy.
Going beyond the Brahmana texts' view that
karma refers to ritual activity, the Upanishads
imply that karma refers to all types of action as
well as to a more abstract principle or system of
norms pertaining to action and consequences.
Brihadaranyaka Upanishad (3.2.13) states the
common view that one becomes good by good
action and evil by evil action. The same Upanishad (4.4.5) also says that karma is rooted in
kama ("desire").

The concept of karma, however, may predate
its appearance in Vedic texts and originate in
traditions indigenous to the Indian subcontinent. Jainism, which maintains the view that
karma is a substance from which one must ultimately extricate oneself, may present a more archaic notion than that of the Upanishads.

Across South Asian religions, the notion of
karma implies an utterly consistent and impersonal process of cause and effect that can be
used to describe, explain, or predict the past,
present, and future condition of things. In later
Hindu texts karma is treated as yet another creation of the deity. In the *Bhagavad Gita,* for example, the avatar Krishna restates Upanishadic
views about its independent role in determining
causal material processes and asserts his own
divine prerogative to transcend its effects.

Interpretation of the process of karma and its
implications has preoccupied South Asian reli-

gious, social, and medical traditions. All agree that current situations are partially predetermined by the fruit (*phala*), good or bad, of past sown seeds (*bija*) and that continuing and future effects will be determined by the ongoing accumulation of deeds and intentions. Hindus, Buddhists, Jains, and others all assume karma to be essential to understanding an individual's current life situation and future prospects, as well as his or her moral destiny, suffering, good fortune, and social status. However, differences arise as to the nature of actions, results, and the relationship of the two. All use karma to explain descriptive and normative realities and all consider it a factor in understanding the achievement of ultimate freedom from suffering and rebirth.

While happiness in present and future lives depends on building a store of good merit through conscientious actions or karma, most would concur that no amount of accumulated good deeds is ever sufficient to achieve the highest human goal, that of bringing the cycle of death and rebirth, itself generated and sustained by karma, to an end. Rather, one must reach a point at which one seeks a means by which to free oneself from karma and engage in a discipline, such as the various yogas involving action, knowledge, devotion, and grace, whereby one is no longer subject to either its processes or results. *See also* Buddhism (thought and ethics); Hinduism (thought and ethics); Jainism; liberation; merit; nirvana; path of (ritual) action; Umbanda; yoga.

Karma-pa (kahr-mah'pah; Tibetan, "man of action"; from Skt. *karma*, "action," and Tibetan -*pa*, "man"), the title given in Tibetan Buddhism to each member of the line of "incarnate lamas" (*tulkus*), understood as human embodiments of the Bodhisattva Avalokiteshvara, who have acted as reigning hierarchs of the Karma Kagyu ("Black Hat") school, the largest branch of the Kagyu-pa (Kagyo school). *See also* Black Hat; Tibetan religions.

karma yoga. *See* karma; path of (ritual) action.

Karo, Joseph (1488–1575), lawyer and mystic, author of the *Shulhan Arukh* (Heb., "Set Table"), the most important code of Jewish law from his time to the present. Karo also produced a diary of mystical experiences, *Maggid mesharim* ("Speaker of Uprightness"), which records the revelations he claimed to have received nightly from a heavenly speaker. *See also* Judaism (mysticism); Shulhan Arukh.

Kashmir Shaivism (kazh'mihr shi'viz-uhm), in Hinduism, the teachings of several related lineages of northern Shaivite teachers and philosophers that developed in Kashmir from the ninth through the thirteenth centuries. The most famous exemplars were Abhinavagupta (tenth century) and his disciple Kshemaraja. Based on the anonymous and revealed texts of the Agamas and Tantras, this tradition propounds a Tantric alternative to the restrictive and highly orthodox Mimamsa and elaborates a challenge to the later mainline Vedanta.

Central texts include Vasugupta's foundational *Shiva Sutras* (Aphorisms of Shiva), Kallata's *Spanda Karikas* (Stanzas on Vibration), Utapalacharya's *Ishvara Pratyabhijna Karikas* (Stanzas on the Recognition of the Lord), and Abhinavagupta's *Tantraloka* (Light on the Tantras). The teachings of these authors offer the earliest theoretical bases for a complex and sophisticated Hindu Tantrism based on the notion of Shiva as the paradoxical and all-pervading consciousness and elaborating the ritual and meditative methods for the experiential and blissful recognition of Shiva as the intrinsic self-identity of the practitioner. Highlighting the centrality of the Goddess as the Shakti, or power of consciousness, the tradition propounds the innovative doctrine of the *spanda*, the vibrational nature of consciousness. *See also* Mimamsa; Shaivism; Tantra; Vedanta.

Kasuga Shrine (kah-soo-gah), a Japanese Shinto shrine famous for its connection to the eighth-century Fujiwara family. Its art provides evidence of early Buddhist influences on Shinto. *See also* Japanese religions (art and architecture); shrine; syncretism (Japan).

kataribe (kah-tah-ree-bay; Jap., "reciters"), an early Japanese hereditary association of reciters who recounted important myths, legends, and genealogies at court ceremonies; these were later collected in works of eighth-century chronicle literature such as the *Kojiki* and *Nihonshoki*. *See also* Kojiki; Nihonshoki.

katsina. *See* kachina/katsina.

Kaur (kow'uhr; Punjabi, "princess"), Khalsa title assumed as part of every Sikh female name. *See also* Khalsa.

kegare (kay-gah-ray), Japanese notion of ritual impurity or defilement, mythically traced to Izanagi's journey to the underworld and usually linked with death and blood. *See also* harai; Izanagi and Izanami; tsumi.

Kegon school (kay-gahn), one of the six Japanese Buddhist schools of Nara. Kegon was based on Hua-yen teachings from China. Its influence in the eighth century is reflected by the choice of Vairocana Buddha for the Great Buddha at Todaiji. During subsequent centuries, although able scholars such as Gyonen (1240–1321), Myoe (1173–1232), and Hotan (1659–1738) studied and wrote about Kegon teachings, the school was more important as a source of doctrine than as an institution. *See also* Hua-yen school; Nara schools.

kehillah (keh-hee-lah'; Heb., "community"), Jewish communal government. The *kehillah* governed the lives of the Jews in medieval Europe, collecting taxes and spending them on education, charity, support for the sick, burial of the dead, arbitration of disputes and conflict within the community, governance of the ritual life of the synagogue, and other aspects of the welfare of Jewry as a self-governing entity. Rabbis generally ran the government, because knowledge of the law of Judaism was required for making practical decisions.

kelal yisrael (ke-lahl' yis-rah-el'; Heb., "the whole community of Israel"), also *knesset yisrael* (Heb., "the community of Israel"); the idea, in Judaism, that all Jews together, called "Israel," are held to be responsible for one another and that all may be called upon to suffer on account of the sins of each individual. The theologian of Conservative Judaism, Solomon Schechter, translated the concept into "Catholic Israel." In midrashic literature the community of Israel is personified as the beloved of God. In mystical literature, the community is often personified in dialogue with God. *See also* Israel (land, people, and state).

Kenekuk, a Kickapoo Native American prophet (active 1816–52) who claimed revelations specifying social and ceremonial reforms. *See also* Native Americans (North America), new religions among; prophecy in traditional religions.

kenosis, the Greek christological term in the New Testament (Philippians 2:7) expressing the belief that the preexistent Christ "emptied" or "impoverished" himself in order to become human.

Kephalaia (ke-fah-lay'uh; from Coptic, "chapters"), a fourth-century book containing ninety-five chapters of Mani's instructions and lectures to his pupils. It is uncertain whether Mani himself wrote the book, but in it he converses with his disciples on revelations, mythological and doctrinal matters, and ethical rules. Originally the book contained about 520 pages and was one of the main sources for Manichaean religion. *See also* Manichaeism.

kerygma (kay-rig'muh; Gk., "proclamation"), noun used to refer to the essential Christian "preaching" to elicit the decision of faith, in contrast to "teaching" (Gk. *didache*). *Kerygma* signifies primarily the "gospel," the "good news" of God's redemptive activity through Jesus as the Christ.

ketubah (kuh-*too*-vah'; Heb., "document [of marriage]"), in Jewish law, contract that stipulates the financial obligations of the husband to the wife, should there be a dissolution of the marriage by death or divorce. Its provisions include a lump-sum payment to the wife and the return of her dowry. The *ketubah* is read and witnessed at the wedding and kept by the wife. *See also* Judaism (life cycle).

Khadija (kha-dee'juh; d. 619), foremost wife of Muhammad and reckoned by many to have been the first convert to Islam.

Khalsa (khal'sah; Punjabi, "royal domain"), the order into which committed Sikhs of both sexes are initiated, begun by the tenth Guru, Gobind Singh, in 1699. Not all Sikhs are members of the Khalsa. *See also* Five Ks; Sikhism.

Kharijite. *See* Seceders.

khatib. *See* preaching.

khutba. *See* preaching.

kiddush (kee-dush'; Heb., "sanctification [prayer]"), in Jewish ritual, a blessing properly known as "sanctification of the day," inaugurating holy time, and recited at the onset of Sabbaths and most holidays. *See also* Judaism, prayer and liturgy of.

Kierkegaard, Soren Aaby (keer'ke-gor; 1813–55), Danish philosopher, strong critic of both the state Lutheran church and the Hegelian system. His writings were deeply influential on religious existentialism. Often published under a pseudonym, his best-known works include *Either/Or* (1843), *Fear and Trembling* (1843), *Philosophical Fragments* (1844), *The Concept of Dread* (1844), and *Concluding Unscientific Postscript* (1846).

His multivolume *Journal* is also of importance. *See also* existentialism.

Kija (ki-jah), a legendary founder of an ancient kingdom on the Korean peninsula. According to Korean and Chinese sources, Kija was a minister of the last king of the Shang dynasty who fled China after the Chou conquest. With five thousand followers, Kija established a kingdom in the Korean peninsula in 1122 B.C. This kingdom, called Kija Choson, as opposed to Old Choson (founded by the mythical Tan'gun), is said to have lasted until 196 B.C., when Chinese Han imperial colonies replaced it. Kija is said to have taught the Koreans the laws and customs of China, including the Nine Divisions of the Great Plan (which he created for the instruction of King Wu of Chou), the Eight Punishments for civil offenses, and the practice of rice and barley cultivation.

Later T'ang sources indicate that Kija was regularly worshiped as an ancestral deity of the Ki, Han, and Sonu clans in the state of Koguryo at an altar-shrine set up for this purpose outside the city of Pyongyang. During the Unified Silla period (seventh century), the worship of Kija was not in evidence. In the succeeding Koryo period (918–1392) government worship of Kija as a national ancestor was linked to its claim to be the legitimate successor of Koguryo and in 1102, at a time when Koryo Confucian literati power was at its height, the altar to Kija at Pyongyang was refurbished and a memorial tablet erected. In the Choson kingdom (1392–1910) the political role of state worship of Kija was heightened even further as Choson scholars proclaimed under the banner of Neo-Confucianism that Kija was the first legitimate ruler of Korea, because he was enfeoffed by the founder of the great Chou dynasty and brought Korea to the height of civilization through the practice of the Kingly Way. Kija and Tan'gun were both honored by the Choson government at Kija's shrine, though in 1412, Tan'gun was removed and installed in a shrine of his own. Government worship of Kija continued until 1897.

The Kija tradition is often seen from both Chinese and Korean perspectives as evidence of an early Korean adherence to what would later become classical Confucian tradition. Passages from Chinese dynastic, apocryphal, and Confucian literature are regularly used to indicate that Confucius himself knew of the existence of the Korean people, a people beyond the eastern sea who formed a superior nation, and that Confucius wished to live among them because of their refined customs and unwavering propriety. The

Kija tradition was especially favored and promoted by Confucian literati, ancient and modern, because it tied Korean nationhood and culture to one of the earliest periods of China, yet preserved Korea's independence of China. Kija was and is seen as the great cultural founder, while Tan'gun was and is seen as the ethnic and political founder. The tradition is also creatively reinterpreted in the twentieth century as the basis for the Korean orthodox understanding of and adherence to Confucian tradition because Koreans had early practiced what Confucius was later to teach. *See also* Korean foundation myths.

kije. *See* ancestral rites.

Kimbanguist Church, or L'Eglise de Jesus-Christ sur la terre par le prophete Simon Kimbangu, the largest of a series of churches inspired by the prophetic ministry of Simon Kimbangu (1889–1951) in the Belgian Congo (now Zaire), French Congo, and Angola. Simon Kimbangu was educated in Baptist Missionary Society schools and worked as a catechist. Beginning in 1918, he had visions commanding him to teach and to heal. He resisted this prophetic calling until April 1921, when he began to heal the sick. His spiritual healing and his critique of mission Christianity and BaKongo *nkisi* (powerful medicines, charms) attracted a massive following. His claim of revelation from Jesus brought Christianity directly into the lives of the BaKongo in a way that missionaries could not. Despite the absence of an overtly political message in his teachings, Belgian authorities viewed his mass following with alarm and ordered his arrest. In September 1921 he was sentenced to death, though this was eventually commuted to life imprisonment. After Kimbangu's arrest, other prophetic figures emerged, claiming inspiration from Kimbangu and developing distinct interpretations of the Kimbanguist message.

In the 1950s, Belgian authorities allowed Kimbangu's sons to establish the church and in the postcolonial era it has become the official Kimbanguist church, preventing government recognition of other Kimbanguist churches in Zaire. It has since become the largest independent church in Africa, with some four million members by 1988. *See also* Africa, new religions in; prophecy in traditional religions.

Kim Sisup (kim sisuhp; 1435–93), an early Choson-period Korean Confucian scholar, onetime Buddhist monk, student of Taoist alchemy, and author of romances and fantastic tales. Kim

Sisup is considered one of the Six Confucian Ministers Who Lived (Kor. *yuksaengsin*) because, on hearing the news of the usurpation of King Tanjong's throne by the boy's uncle King Sejo (r. 1455–68), he burned all his books and took up the life of a wandering Ch'an monk. In 1463 he returned to Seoul and, upon the recommendation of the sons of King T'aejong, worked in the palace on the translations of Chinese Buddhist scriptures into Korean, using the recently invented Hangul alphabet. In 1481 he ended his career as a monk to take up the life of a Buddhist layman. Until his death he continued to study the texts of the three traditions—Buddhism, Confucianism, and Taoism—and to write about their unity. Within the tradition of Neo-Confucian metaphysical studies, Kim Sisup stands as an early proponent of *ki*, or material-force, and monism; and in his own studies of religious ethics, rituals, and doctrines he stresses a pragmatic realism. Within Taoist tradition, he likewise stressed the empirical effects of Taoist alchemical meditation (*nedan*) against mystical and religious interpetations. In 1782 Kim Sisup was honored with the posthumous office of Censor and his spirit tablet was installed in the Shrine to the Six Living Ministers at Yongwol, the site of the seventeen-year-old King Tanjong's exile and assassination. *See also* Ch'an school; Confucianism.

Kim T'aegon (kim tagohn; 1822–46), the first Korean to be ordained a priest in and be canonized a saint by the Roman Catholic Church. Kim T'aegon, known by his Catholic baptismal name of Andrea Kim, was converted by his father and baptized by the French missionary Maubant in 1836. After training in the Chinese language he was sent to the Paris Foreign Missionary Seminary in Macao, and later to Manila. He returned to Korea in 1842 but was forced to leave because of persecution. He secretly returned in 1845 and prosyletized in the vicinity of Seoul. Five months later he sailed to Shanghai, where he was ordained a priest in the Paris Foreign Missionary Society. In 1846, upon his return to Korea, he was captured and imprisoned while trying to set up a secret escape route for missionaries. He was subjected to six inquisitions before being given the death penalty. In 1857 the Vatican declared him reverend and in 1925 conferred on him the status of blessed. He was later raised to rank of saint. *See also* Chinese rites controversy; Korea, Roman Catholicism in.

Kim Yushin (kim yoo-shin; 595–673), a member of the Hwarang Troop and a leading military figure in Silla's unification of the Korean peninsula in the seventh century. Kim Yushin had been a member of the former royal house of Pon Kaya, a kingdom that Silla had conquered in 532. With his friend and, later, brother-in-law, Kim Ch'unch'u (604–661), Kim Yushin led Silla troops against Paekche incursions in 629 and 644. In 654 when the Silla queen Chindok (r. 647–654) died without a successor, Kim Yushin and his troops raised Kim Ch'unch'u to the throne as King Muyol (r. 654–661). In 660, with the help of T'ang naval forces, Kim Yushin led fifty thousand troops against Paekche and conquered that kingdom. In 667, again with T'ang reinforcements, Kim was appointed to lead the attack on Koguryo but fell ill. After the fall of Koguryo, Kim led the Sillan troops that ousted the T'ang troops, which had invaded the Koguryo domains. Kim Yushin's tomb is decorated with stone relief sculptures of the twelve animals of the zodiac, all bearing weapons to protect his spirit. He was later celebrated in many battle tales of Silla heroes and after his death was worshiped as a tutelary dragon protector of the Silla state. *See also* Hwarang Troop.

King, Martin Luther, Jr. (1929–68), African-American minister and national civil rights leader. Born in Atlanta, Georgia, King graduated from Morehouse College and was ordained a Baptist minister in 1948. He attended Crozer Theological Seminary, then received a Ph.D. in Systematic Theology from Boston University in 1955. Pastor of the Dexter Avenue Church in Montgomery, Alabama, King was elected president of the Montgomery Improvement Association, formed to protest racial discrimination in public transportation. In 1957 he became president of the Southern Christian Leadership Conference and a year later his *Stride Toward Freedom: The Montgomery Story*, the first of seven books, was published. King articulated a philosophy of nonviolent civil disobedience that drew in part on the techniques taught by Mahatma K. Gandhi (1869–1948). During a protest against segregated eating facilities in Birmingham, Alabama, in 1963, King was arrested, and while in jail wrote his famous "Letter from a Birmingham Jail." In August 1963, King led a massive civil rights demonstration in Washington, D.C., and delivered his "I Have a Dream" speech on the steps of the Lincoln Memorial. He received the Nobel Peace Prize in 1964, and subsequently carried his civil rights campaign to parts of the northern United States. King was assassinated on April 4, 1968, in Memphis, Tennessee, having gone there to assist striking sanitation workers. A national holiday on January 15 honors this internationally recognized

Martin Luther King, Jr. (1929–68), leading the march for African-American voting rights from Selma to Montgomery, Alabama, March 1965. Immediately to Dr. King's left is Rabbi Abraham Joshua Heschel (1907–72), the American Jewish theologian.

champion of human rights. *See also* ahimsa; satyagraha.

kingdom of God, Christian belief, central to the New Testament, that God's rule will be established on earth following the defeat of evil on the day of judgment. The kingdom of God is also a term of contrast to the secular kingdom(s) of the earth. *See also* eschatology; Judgment Day; kingdom of heaven (Judaism).

kingdom of heaven (Judaism), the age of the universal sovereignty of God. According to Jewish teaching, the world begins its history under God's exclusive rule, and the end of history will see the return of God's rule, the kingdom of heaven on earth.

In the Beginning: Nature was created by God and stands permanently under God's rule. God guarantees the stability of the natural order, and God alone performs miracles to change that order. Initially, the order of history is also exclusively under the power of God. Adam and Eve live in an idyllic paradise, and their responsibility lies only in following the divine mandate. The kingdom of heaven is fully manifest on earth.

In the Order of History: When the first human beings sin, they are driven into the order of history as we know it, where the results of human sin are everywhere present. Instead of peace, there is strife; instead of love, selfishness. The perfect reign of God has been replaced by the sinful reign of humanity. God remains king, but now humanity often ignores and rejects God. In Jewish liturgy God is always *melekh ha-olam*, king of the world, but a king who seems to have withdrawn from the world.

The tragedy of history is that humanity has turned away from God. Yet Jewish religious thought stresses that humanity strives to return to the kingdom of God. The central acts of Jewish prayer are called "accepting the yoke of the kingdom of heaven" and "accepting the yoke of God's commandments." Prayer and good works have the power to transform the human condition so as to make human beings again worthy to live in the kingdom of heaven.

Human efforts meet with frequent failure. Nevertheless, the confident hope for salvation persists, certain that human deeds affect the outcome of the historical process. Even if humanity fails, Scripture teaches that God will not permit human wickedness to destroy forever the ideal state of things on earth: "And the Lord shall be king over all the earth; in that day shall the Lord be One and His name one" (Zechariah 14:9).

In the Messianic Age: Judaism teaches that history will be fulfilled with the coming of the Messiah and the institution of a new age. The redemption of the Jewish people will bring about the redemption of all humanity: "And the many peoples shall go and say: 'Come, let us go up to the Mount of the Lord, to the House of the God of Jacob; that He may instruct us in His ways, and that we may walk in His paths'" (Isaiah 2:3).

In that blessed age when all peoples are under the sovereignty of God alone, both history and nature will be transformed. Peace and harmony will replace strife and hatred. Justice will prevail, and no one will suffer poverty or rejection: "The wolf shall dwell with the lamb, the leopard lie down with the kid" (Isaiah 11:6). Under God's sovereignty humankind will return to the original paradise, to the age when the kingdom of God is again the actual state of history and nature. *See also* Judaism, God in.

King James Bible. *See* King James Version.

King James Version, an English translation of the Bible commissioned by King James I of England and published in 1611. Also called the Authorized Version, it was for more than 250 years the unrivaled translation used by English-speaking Protestants. Though later English translations, using better manuscripts and increased knowledge of the cultural world of the biblical periods, are more accurate, the impact of the KJV on English literature remains undiminished. Many conservative Protestant groups still consider it to be the normative inspired text. *See also* Bible, translations of the Christian.

kingship, sacred. *King* is an Old English word closely related to *kin* and connoting the foremost person of a particular clan, but the term now has a technical meaning within the study of world religions. King describes a category of sacred persons who either embody, represent, or personify the divine power(s) that are considered the

source of the prosperity of the community. Unlike the priest, the king does not always perform the rituals that connect the divine with the human world but rather manifests these powers in his own person and then redirects that power to the public. However, kings are not be confused with any persons acting as head of state. While ancient kings often functioned as the pivot of social, legal, or even bureaucratic power, their relationship to divinity remains the defining element in kingship and differentiates the sacral king in the study of religions from a narrow definition of the king as an early head of state.

As a human in direct relationship to the divine, a king's sphere of influence extended beyond the state or the social order. Frequently, the king was perceived by devotees as the ruler of a spiritual kingdom above, beyond, or simply alongside the secular state. It is in this sense that figures such as Jesus and the Buddha were portrayed as kings, although they ruled no earthly domain. The figure of the sacral king exists in the contemporary world with neither land nor political power. The English monarchy still rules the popular imagination, as do the erstwhile maharajas of India. As a genre of modern public culture, the unrecognized but power-laden young king appears in literature and film from the tales of King Arthur to Luke Skywalker of the *Star Wars* film series.

In world history, the sacral king as the embodiment of divine powers is widespread but not universal. The origins of kingship are usually traced to the breakdown of tribal systems and the rise of the city and of the early state. The early anthropologist James G. Frazer concentrated on the primitive origins, drawing his examples from European folklore and the then contemporary tribal cultures for his monumental study of kingship, *The Golden Bough*. Historians, however, derived their definitions of kingship from the study of the ancient cultures of Egypt, Mesopotamia, Israel, Greece, India, and China.

In the context of the study of religions, however, the issue of the relationship of king to the nascent state is not as crucial as delineating the nature of the king in relationship to divinity or sacred power. A typology of this relationship is complex and depends on the nature of deity as well as on the kinds of ritual contact permitted between humanity and divinity in each society. Because no civilization is homogeneous, types overlap in some cases or remain in contention in others. But in spite of the wide variety of kingship and the complex issues that beleaguer any broad comparative scheme, at least four types of sacral kingship appear frequently over a wide range of materials. The king is understood as (1) the servant of the gods in the temple; (2) the living icon who is the embodiment of divine power in human flesh; (3) the sacrificer who kills and offers sustenance to the god(s) for the entire society; or (4) the sacrificial victim or the divine corpse whose dead body becomes the nexus of mortality and immortality.

The Servant: The king had exclusive charge of having the physical images of the gods fashioned. In their iconic form, the gods required elaborate clothing, food, and shelter, which the king provided by constructing state temples to house them and by maintaining a staff of priests to serve their needs. On the walls of Egyptian temples are numerous reliefs of the pharaoh himself ministering to the divine images. In Mesopotamia, the king's ability to protect and serve the divine icons exemplifed his right to rule. A defeated king saw the divine images abducted from his temples and the images of the gods of the victorious king set up in their place. In India, the maharajas continued to prefix their names with the officially recognized title of "Servant of" the tutelary deity of their realms well into the twentieth century. Their exclusive right to provide the food and garments for that divine image was a mark of their right to rule and was protected by local law.

The right to commission sculptural bodies for the gods and the right to protect and care for these divine bodies put the king in a reciprocal relationship with the gods. He gave them an earthly form and they gave him a divine body. This issue of sharing of divinity, however, became problematic in the case of Israel, where kings in the line of David maintained the temple and acted as God's servant but not as his keeper. The injunctions against graven images forbade in theory the imaging of God, so that a reciprocity between God and king never had unequivocal theological sanction. The divinity of the king remained an issue for other monotheistic religions. While some states in the Christian and the Islamic worlds maintained a king as God's chosen ruler, suspicion of the king usurping the supreme power of God remained and erupted periodically, as in the cases of eighteenth-century European and American revolutions or the recent overthrow of the shah of Iran.

The Icon: Kings are more than the divine patron of state temples. Frequently, a king's body is the object of state rituals and is displayed in the same pose and with the same accoutrements as the divine icons of the realm. In modern times, India and Bali provide rich examples of rajas enthroned as living icons whose very countenance brought blessings to all who saw them. Sometimes a sculptural image of the king became a divine icon in his own lifetime or after his death. A king of ancient Assyria records that he set up the image of his divine lord but also set up his own image in the palace of a conquered king. In modern India, there are functioning temples to the images of departed rajas.

The king functioned as an icon under three distinct but sometimes interrelated conceptions of his divinity. Some scholars have suggested that the king's body was the first concrete manifestation of divine power and that later worship of the images of gods was patterned on the model of the king. However, in traditions asserting that the gods were the kings' progenitors, such a notion was unthinkable. In Japan and Assyria, for example, the king was treated as an icon because he was the "son of" the gods. Likewise, as the gods' loyal servant, the king's body functioned as an icon on the logic that a servant is literally a part of his master.

The Sacrificer: There is evidence that the role of the king as the chief sacrificer to the gods was initially unrelated to temples or temple worship and may provide a distinct genre of sacral kingship. In early Chinese records, the king made offerings on an open-air altar and that act of sacrificing appears to define his royal office. Elsewhere, the king often appears in competition with the priestly class for this right. Saul, the first king of Israel, lost his right to rule (1 Samuel 13:10) because he usurped the rights of the prophet-priests by performing a sacrifice to God in the absence of the prophet Samuel. In India, vestiges of an ancient dispute over the rights of kings and priests to perform the sacrifice are preserved in early texts. Some recent theories suggest that the king as sacrificer was a vestige of his much earlier role as killer of men in the ritual of war in which he was not only the slayer but risked being the slain. His divinity thus derived from his dual role as both victim and master of life and death.

India provides the clearest example of the king as analogous to the sacrificial victim as well as the sacrificer. A highly developed perception of sacrifice viewed the body of the victim as the font of all life. In this sense the king's body was analogous to the victim of the first primeval sacrifice that engendered the cosmos. Using the same sacrificial logic that developed in the Mediterranean world, the Gospel of John readily employs the figure of Jesus as the sacrificial lamb as a sign of his divinity.

The Divine Corpse: The close connection of the

royal corpse with divinity is not always bound with the logic of the sacrifice. Ancient Egypt provides the classic example of the royal corpse as the center of state ritual. The early extant temples in Egypt are royal funeral temples and some scholars have suggested that temple ritual derives from the royal funeral rites. In nineteenth-century Bali, the funerals of kings were far more elaborate than their coronations. Frazer, in *The Golden Bough,* provides multifarious examples of the connections between the royal corpse and the fertility of the earth. The theme dominated the study of kingship until the last two decades, in part because of the close association of the dying and rising king with the figure of Christ in early Christianity. *See also* Egyptian religion; Indo-European religion; Mesopotamian religion; Shango.

Roman Religion: The Romans, in particular, often admired leadership to the point of granting kings and emperors divine status. After death, an emperor was granted divine status (Lat. *divus*) by the Senate, which was celebrated in connection with his funeral. Even before his death, however, the emperor seemed to have a special relationship to the gods; the title *Augustus,* first bestowed on Octavian, suggests that the emperor's spiritual power (*numen*) was broadened and amplified beyond the capacity of a mere citizen. Numen related to a central aspect of the emperor's performance, the power to bestow benefits on the empire—military success, fertility of the flocks, safe journeys, lucrative commerce, and freedom from plague and famine are most often mentioned. The abundance of benefits meant the emperor was a savior; the empire received salvation from the gods through his auspices. Part of the emperor's official powers rested on his office as *pontifex maximus,* the chief priest of the Roman state religion. By means of this office he functioned as an intermediary between the gods and the Roman people, channeling numen to benefit the empire. All provinces, particularly those far from Rome, celebrated the emperor's power in local festivals that were coordinated with the official calendar of rites sent out annually from Rome. The synchronicity of these rites created a sense of imperial unity despite the conglomeration of tribes and peoples that entered the Roman orbit through conquest. *See also* ancestral rites; apotheosis; numen; Roman religion.

Hinduism: Monarchy has been the presumed political context for nearly all classical discussions of governance, public righteousness, and proper social order in India. A king, traditionally from the Kshatriya group of castes, was a local or regional monarch (the geographical size of the domain could vary) to whom subjects offered loyalty and taxes in exchange for protection and the maintenance of order.

The Sanskrit term raja ("king") can be traced to the *Rig Veda,* where it is used primarily to refer to various deities, but occasionally designates powerful humans, such as King Sudas (1.11.63). In medieval Hindu epic literature kingship frequently is an office ordained by the deity Brahma at the beginning of the world. Kingship is understood to extend beyond the human realm. Major categories of nonhuman entities often include a figure that occupies the functional equivalent of the human king. Wherever there is order, the assumption is there must be kingship to establish and perpetuate that order. In the Puranic literature, for example, Candra is named the king of the stars and of medicines; Varuna is king of the waters; Valsravana, the king of kings; Himavat, the king of mountains; Garuda, the king of birds; and the tiger, the king of animals.

Royal Politics: Indian political theory is generally synonymous with the theory of proper kingship, righteously and effectively executed according to divinely ordained royal norms (*rajadharma*). Unlike the Greek state (*polis*), which represents the supreme expression of human accomplishment, Indian kingship grew out of a profound sense of imperfectability in this world. Kingship is desirable because it is the only alternative to chaos. Nothing but a powerful king can ensure the preservation of proper order (*dharma*) and the king must act with liberal applications of force (*danda*) in order to be effective. The deployment of spies is not simply tolerated, it is positively enjoined. Indeed, a king should consult his official spies at the start of each day. The *Aitareya Brahmans* first suggests a contractual theory of the state whereby, in exchange for protection, subjects pay taxes. In the coronation oath, however, the king further commits himself to the maintenance of proper order as embodied in sacred law, customary practice, the authority of Brahman priests/advisers, and the need to keep his people happy and prosperous. A kingdom will inevitably flourish if the king rules righteously: rain will fall, crops will grow, peace will prevail. The converse is also true: poverty and hardship among subjects always reflect serious failures on the part of the king. In this cosmic arrangement, the king is father, the earth is mother, and royal subjects are their children. A notable moral lapse on the part of the king could wreak natural havoc and disaster.

Kings and Brahmans: Though a king's powers are absolute, he cannot exercise them arbitrarily. To act in violation of the divinely ordained order (dharma) would be to forfeit any legitimate claim to kingship. Brahman ministers were the final authority as to the appropriate interpretation of divinely ordained courses of action. No king could operate effectively, that is, in accord with dharmaraja, without the legitimacy bestowed upon him by these Brahman priests. This uneasy relationship—that between a king endowed with a monopoly on power and ministers endowed with an essential monopoly on legitimacy—proved time and time again to be the source of extended debate in political manuals. The ambiguous interdependence between Brahmans and kings always made for a dynamic, but never clearly defined, relationship involving tensions and necessary accommodations. This shifting equilibrium tended to check a king's arbitrariness. That the Brahmans were exempt from punishment of any kind was a weight toward their end of this always dynamic balance of power. Still, the major restraints on a king's power were moral rather than constitutional, and the moral power lay primarily with the Brahmans.

Divine Kings: If Brahmans were understood to be the guardians of legitimacy and purity by virtue of their training in sacred texts and their knowledge of tradition, kings were understood to have their unique claim to divinity. The earliest stories of kingship appear in the *Mahabharata's Shantiparvan* (59.6ff.), in which the divine but fragile nature of the office is most striking. These early kings are infused with portions of the gods, particularly of Vishnu, though other texts, notably the *Manusmriti* (ch. 8), assert that kings are born from the shoulders of the deities Indra, Vayu, Yama, Surya, Agni, Varuna, Candra, and Kubera. This divine infusion seems to be recognizably effective only after the king proves himself worthy by performing righteous acts. Any claims the king might make to divine qualities emerge from the office of kingship: functionally speaking, kingship does not, therefore, come from divinity. The first three kings in mythic Indian history who preceded King Prithu deserted their thrones prematurely. They believed there was no way for them to remain in the world as kings without becoming corrupt. Only by retiring were they able to preserve their own sense of righteousness. King Prithu was successful only because he managed to give precedence to Brahman advisers. As king, his authorized function is sacred, and therefore so is he to the extent that he measures up to the performance of those functions. It would probably be accurate to say that traditionally the Indian king has more divine responsibility than he

has divine right. The divine origins of kingship lend legitimacy to the office but not necessarily to the person. Performance alone can do that. Nevertheless, the proper code for conduct in the presence of the king involves dealing with him as though he were a deity, just as dealing with deities often involves treating them like kings. A vivid illustration of this sacred-royal symbolism is found in the temple traditions of India. In several Indian languages the terms *temple* and *palace* are the same word. Images of deities are treated by Brahman priests as though the images were kings and queens in court. Devotees, when making requests, have "audiences" with the deities. It is not unusual to find regional temple histories that trace the lineage of a local dynasty to the deity whose temple that history extols. When a king is installed, the event is both political and religious, for a separation between these two realms was never contemplated. One of the greatest of all Vedic sacrifices, the Hajasuya, accompanies a king's elevation to his new office. The sense that the king embodies divinity pervades the political and religious literature, and he is instructed to perform large, regular sacrifices so that the kingdom will prosper. Still, the tradition also preserves a separate vision of kingship as an entirely human, civil, and secular endeavor. Manu is regarded as the first king, and he assumes office strictly to curb the baser instincts of those he rules.

How a king succeeds to kingship is generally less relevant than the fact that he rules as a righteous king once he has gained the throne. Often the office is hereditary, but it need not be. A corrupt king qualifies for impassioned vilification in the tradition, while a righteous king may rightly assume a place among the deities. **See** *also* Arthashastra; Ashoka; Veda, Vedism.

Buddhism: Buddhism knows several different models of kingship that have variously influenced Buddhist rulers throughout history, including the three related mythic models of the king as "universal monarch" (Skt. *cakravartin*), as "great elect" (*mahasammata*), and as "righteous ruler" (*dharmaraja*); the model of the king as an ideal layman, an incarnational model, and a messianic model.

Mythic Paradigms: Several of these paradigms were formulated or reformulated during the influential reign of the Indian emperor Ashoka (third century B.C.), who did much to establish the relationship of Buddhism to the state and who became exalted throughout Asia as the chief exemplar of Buddhist kingship. But also important were the earlier figures of Bimbisara and Ajatasatru, kings of Magadha at the time of the Buddha, and the many later rulers of Asian

Buddhist kingdoms who became paradigms in their own nations.

According to separate but related myths, the model Buddhist king is a sovereign whose rule both expresses and depends on his righteousness (*dharma*). Thus, the universal monarch owes his legitimacy not to the inheritance of the throne from his father but to his support of Dharma. This is symbolized by his earning, at the beginning of his rule, a mythical Wheel of Dharma, which will guide him throughout his reign and disappear should he slip in his uprightness. The righteous universal monarch's rule, then, is a golden one in which peace, prosperity, and religious practice all prevail.

The great elect, on the other hand, is so called because he is chosen by his peers as one who is best able to maintain order in an age of threatening chaos. He governs in a time of decline, but, importantly, he still manages to do so with righteousness, and he is appointed with the consent and support of the governed.

Both the universal monarch and the great elect are obviously related to a third model of kingship, that of the righteous ruler, who owes his name to his embodiment of the Dharma. He too is one who observes the various duties of the king, including such things as liberality, good conduct, absence of anger, nonattachment, the wise dispensation of justice, etc. More specifically, the righteous ruler supports the Buddhist community of monks materially, militarily, and, if need be, by purging it of heterodox elements.

Kingships and the Lay Order: Implicit in this is the notion that the king should also be a model for all Buddhist laypersons, setting standards for merit making and for cultic practices. Thus, in one of the legends of King Ashoka, what is emphasized is the spiritual quality (as well as the quantity) of the gifts he makes to the monastic order and the fervor of his devotion to the Buddha.

On the other hand, Buddhists also viewed the powers of the king with some ambiguity. Though generally holding kingship in high esteem, they were not unaware of some of its potentially Machiavellian dimensions and did not hesitate to warn against these by recounting tales of (in their view) bad rulers alongside legends of good ones. More anecdotally, they might draw attention to the failings of even model monarchs. Moreover, the king might further be "kept in his place" by being portrayed as spiritually inferior to the Buddha or to Buddhist monks.

This did not prevent the development of what might be called an incarnational theory of Buddhist kingship, whereby rulers were sometimes identified with a god, a Bodhisattva, or even a Buddha. Various Chinese emperors were praised as Buddhas incarnate, and, in Southeast Asia, monarchs were commonly thought to be avatars either of Hindu deities or of Bodhisattvas such as Avalokiteshvara. In Tibet, the figure of the Dalai Lama, though not a king, came to be thought of in a similar fashion.

Messianic Kingship: Finally, it is important to note the messianic dimensions of kingship in Buddhism. According to Buddhist myth, the advent of the future Buddha Maitreya will be ushered in by the reign of a great king, Sankha, himself a universal monarch. Accordingly, various historical Buddhist rulers, especially in Southeast Asia but elsewhere as well, sought to bolster their own kingship and to give it a certain millenarian urgency by identifying themselves with either Sankha or Maitreya himself. *See also* Ashoka; Maitreya; universal monarch.

Chinese Religion: From earliest times, kingship in China was the focus of religious, civil, military, and economic power. The king, or "one man," combined in his person the roles of chief priest and master of ceremonies in the ancestral cult, head diviner, commander-in-chief of the armies, bestower of property and patents of nobility, chief justice, sole intermediary between the temporal and spiritual worlds, and symbol of the state. Traditional accounts of the legendary sovereigns of prehistory depict the king as a fount of sagely wisdom and bestower of all the benefits of civilization. The twelfth-century B.C. dynastic transition from Shang to Chou witnessed a shift away from efforts to absolutize the divine status of the royal ancestors toward a reassertion of the "Mandate of Heaven" (T'ien-ming), the preeminent role of Heaven in conferring the mandate to rule "all under Heaven." This led to a shift in the ideological dimensions of the kingship in inclusive and moral directions, but did not diminish its crucial significance. The fate of the dynasty and the welfare of the state continued in the public mind to depend on the king's exemplary performance of a multitude of secular and religious functions. Centuries later in early imperial times, when it had already become customary for the emperor to delegate all but the most ritually symbolic duties, it was still an article of faith that "the Mandate of Heaven cannot be without its vessel." *See also* Chinese ritual; Dutthagamani; state cult, Chinese; T'ien-ming.

Japanese Religion: The imperial cult surrounding the Japanese emperor emerged in the fourth and fifth centuries and assumed classical form in the seventh and eighth centuries through a synthesis of Chinese and Japanese traditions. The emperor ruled by virtue of being a descendant of the goddess Amaterasu and a manifest *kami* (divinity, divine presence) and combined the roles of chief priest, sacred king, and living kami. The notion of kami should be clearly differentiated from Western, monotheistic notions of God. Though in theory combining supreme religious and political authority, the emperor's power was frequently only titular as imperial power waned throughout the thirteenth to nineteenth centuries. The Meiji Restoration in 1868 was carried out at least partially to restore the emperor's prestige and influence and resulted in the formation of a state religion centered around the emperor. Though connected at this time with a notion of pure Shinto, the imperial cult historically incorporated much from Confucianism, Taoism, and Buddhism. With the end of World War II, the emperor renounced his divine status and state and religion were formally separated. The emperor is constitutionally regarded as the symbol of the unity of the Japanese people and the imperial cult as the private religion of the imperial family. *See also* kami; Meiji Restoration; Shinto.

Mesoamerican Religions: Kingship is a sacred office in which the ruler operates as a conduit for sacred powers, thereby mediating between the human realm and nonhuman realms of the cosmos. By serving to funnel life-giving powers both from and to the nonhuman realms populated by various animistic forces and powerful deities, the entire universe is sustained, and a successful human community is maintained.

Among the Mexica-Tenochca of the Mexican highlands (fourteenth–sixteenth centuries) and the late Classic Maya of the Yucatan Peninsula (fifth–tenth centuries), kingship was structured along kinship lines, which often could be traced to an ancestral deity and/or earlier civilization bearing mythical import. Succession generally followed through the male line, although occasionally women became rulers. Since polygamy was practiced, the pool for heirs was often large, allowing for flexibility in the process and for merit to play a role. Rulers were assisted by lords, who were drawn from or adopted into appropriate kinship lines and who performed a variety of administrative, governmental, and advisory duties.

A parallelism between social, political, and economic levels of existence and cosmic realities characterized the Mesoamerican universe. The king was equated with the sun and other celestial bodies, and his reign was correlated with a complex calendrical system that regulated the cosmos. While the sacred nature of kingship gave rulers extreme powers, the exercise of these powers was also limited both by the inevitability of their own deaths and by the necessity of effectively assuring a satisfactory existence on earth. If the king failed to sustain the cosmos, human life would be adversely affected, and the king could be disposed of.

The Olmecs (1500–50 B.C.) provided both the historical basis for late–Classic Mayan kingship and a mythical background, for Mayan elite genealogical lines were traced back not only to particular deities but also sometimes to the Olmecs. At Cerros (Belize, 50 B.C.), the king was identified with both the rising and setting sun and the morning and evening star. This Olmec cosmic equation was elaborated on at the late–Classic Mayan site of Palenque (Chiapa), wherein the great lord Pacal (603–683) was identified with the sun, and his funerary temple was designed so that a shaft of light thrown by the setting sun at the winter solstice entered the Mayan underworld through his tomb just as he himself must travel through that underworld. On this perilous journey, he was required to defeat numerous evil lords before being reborn as a celestial object.

Mayan and Mexica-Tenochca kings met heavy ritual and governance demands. In order to feed the cosmos and release cosmic powers into the human realm, kings frequently performed rites of personal bloodletting and waged war in order to gain captives for use in communal sacrificial rituals. Warfare was multifaceted and also served as an expansionistic tool, although Mexica-Tenochca kings utilized this tool more than Mayan. In response to a severe drought in the mid-fifteenth century, warfare was increased. This increase precipitated Mexica hegemony in Mesoamerica and coincided with an apparent progressive tightening of the hierarchical structures, thereby making social mobility more difficult.

Mexica-Tenochca kings traced their ancestry to a patron deity, Huitzilopochtli, and to the earlier Toltec civilization represented by the priest-king Quetzalcoatl. At birth the king received the "heart" of his patron deity, Huitzilopochtli, along with other animistic forces from various ancestors endowing him with a simultaneously human and nonhuman nature. His ascension to the throne activated this endowment by opening him to a god assimilated with Huitzilopochtli, Tezcatlipoca; and his own royal activities strengthened it further. These powers were only temporary, however, for when his time had ceased—either due to natural causes or to forces brought on by his own failure to perform his duties—he would, like all other things living on the earth's surface, disappear. *See also* sacrifice.

kingship in heaven, myth of. *See* divine combat.

kinship, the reckoning of social relations and the organization of social groups based on ties of blood and marriage. In many small-scale, traditional societies, kinship represents the primary mode of economic, political, and often religious organization. The importance of this for the study of religion lies in the kinship-based human societies within which religion presumably first emerged, especially with regard to such practices as so-called totemism and ancestor veneration. Although often expressed in terms of a shared substance of blood or bone, kinship involves more than genealogical relatedness. It pertains to a set of culturally defined rights and obligations regarding people and groups, modeled on—but not always limited to—such factors as descent from a common ancestor and alliances to other groups through marriage. The interests and commitments arising from shared residence also play an important role in defining kinship.

Descent, Marriage, and Residence: Kinship in industrial societies differentiates the nuclear family from wider circles of kin: siblings remain distinct from cousins, nephews, and nieces; mother and father from uncles, aunts, and grandparents; and these latter refer indiscriminately to maternal and paternal relatives. In contrast, kinship in nonindustrial societies often emphasizes lineal descent from some ancestor on either the paternal (patrilineal) or maternal (matrilineal) side. The essential unit of kinship is not the nuclear family but the lineage (a group of men and women descended from a common ancestor through known links) or the clan (men and women descended from an ancestor through unspecified but assumed links).

Descent may be unilineal (traced exclusively through either male or female links), double (in which different rights and obligations are passed down each line), or cognatic (any combination of male and female links). Descent groups generally remain exogamous, with rules of marriage specifying either the lineages or clans into which one should marry (prescriptive systems) or those into which one cannot (proscriptive systems). Husbands and wives, by definition, belong to different descent groups. Rather than creating autonomous nuclear families, marriage results in the incorporation (to varying degrees, depending on the culture) of one spouse into the lineage or clan of the other, usually reflected in local rules of residence.

Residence rules may be patrilocal (bride resides with her husband's people), matrilocal (husband resides with wife's people), bilocal (residence with either spouse's people), or more rarely, duolocal (both spouses remain with their own people) or even avunculocal (the couple resides with the husband's mother's brother, which in systems of matrilineal descent enables mature males of the matrilineage to reside together). Line of descent and rules of residence often coincide but need not always, since matrilineal descent can occur with patrilocal residence and vice versa. Also, while lineal descent systems imply exclusive social groupings, individuals retain close ties to several lineages or clans in addition to their own, especially those allied to them by marriage. For example, in systems of patrilineal descent, a person's mother's, father's mother's, and mother's mother's people often remain important sources of support, refuge, and resources. Indeed, in systems of cognatic descent, in which descent can follow any combination of male and female links, individuals hold claims to an array of kin groups, and residence with one group or another most commonly activates potential kin ties.

Far from being a rigid genealogical grid, kinship in these societies precipitates social categories (e.g., friend and foe, coresident and stranger, marriageable and unmarriageable) that define the basic ground rules of social life. Yet people also continually temper the relative importance of these categories through the overlapping, crosscutting, and competing ties of their own personal kindreds (the actual circle of kin unique to any given individual) that arise from the necessities of daily life and the vagaries of individual life history.

Totemism: Kinship-based societies have long been associated with totemism, which posits a sacred link between social groups (especially, but not always, descent groups such as clans) and species of plants and animals. In *The Elementary Forms of the Religious Life* (1915), Emile Durkheim (an early-twentieth-century French sociologist) argues that totemism represented the earliest form of religion because it occurred in what he took to be the most rudimentary of human societies—the Australian Aborigines—where sacred symbols (*tjuringas*) emblematic of certain plants and animals embodied the moral power of the clan over its members. Ethnographically, however, Durkheim erred in presuming a direct correlation between "church" (a congregation of celebrants) and "society" among the Australian Aborigines. In fact, the "clans" that cared for most totems generally lived intermixed with members of other clans in different foraging bands and only came together sporadically to perform their rituals; ritual group and quotidian social group never coincided but crosscut one another. Also, although technologically simple, Australian Aborigine societies evinced extremely complex social systems over which anthropologists still ponder.

French anthropologist Claude Levi-Strauss in *Totemism* (1962) argues that totemism represents not the worship of plants and animals but a system of thought in which distinctions between natural species serve as an analogy for the differentiation of social groups. Totemism exemplifies neither a misguided mysticism of identity between human and animal nor a primitive pragmatism of worshiping things that are "good to eat." Instead, natural species are "good to think" within the social-logic of kinship-based societies.

Ancestral Rites: Ancestral rites reflect more than a memorialism for the dead that denies the finality of death. Ancestors often embody essential moral and sociological principles, whether filial piety or the jural authority of elders over junior lineage and clan members. The presumed presence and powers of ancestors sanctify the rules by which their descendants live. Apical ancestors (the forebears from whom lineage or clan members claim descent) constitute important points in genealogical reckoning that delimit descent groups while also linking them to more distant kin.

Descendants choose their ancestors as much as they passively descend from them, since, not surprisingly, genealogies in nonliterate societies often conform to the current states of affairs between living descent groups as they ally, feud, prosper, or die out. Like totemism, ancestor veneration directly sanctifies the largely kinship-based rationale by which these peoples organize and legitimize their social worlds. *See also* ancestors; incest prohibition; marriage; taboo.

kippah. *See* skullcap/kippah/yarmulke.

Kitano Daimyojin (kee-tah-noh dah-ee-myoh-jeen), spirit of Japanese scholar-poet Sugawara Michizane (845–903), deified at Kitano Shrine as the god of learning to placate his ghost, angry because he was exiled and killed as a result of political intrigue. *See also* shrine.

kiva (kee'vuh; Hopi), semisubterranean, round or rectangular structure, entered by a roof opening and/or a side door, used by Pueblo Indians (American Southwest) for ceremonial purposes, including initiation into religious societies. The *kiva* serves also as a gathering place for discussions of religious matters and other community concerns. *See also* traditional peoples, religions of.

Native American *kiva*, Mesa Verde, Colorado, from the Anasazi culture (ca. 1200), showing the typical arrangement of this subterranean ceremonial building with benches surrounding a small hole (*sipapu*) symbolic of the tribe's mythical place of origin.

kneeling, characteristic posture of submission, common in the presence of deities or monarchs.

Knossos (naw'sohs), the greatest of the Bronze Age palaces on the island of Crete, destroyed in the fourteenth century B.C. Elaborate court rituals and ceremonies, including bull leaping, are likely to have taken place in the Bronze Age palace. Centuries later the Greeks attached a number of stories to the site. A labyrinth was said to have been built by Daedalus for King Minos. In it the king confined the Minotaur, half man, half bull, the offspring of his wife Pasiphae's union with a bull. The monster was killed by the Athenian hero Theseus with the help of the king's daughter, Ariadne. *See also* Cycladic religion; Greek religion; Minoan religion; Mycenaean religion.

Knox, John (ca. 1514–72), Christian Scottish reformer, an ordained Catholic priest who became a Protestant and was an influential and founding figure in the Church (Kirk) of Scotland. Knox wrote or participated in the writing of the *Scottish Confession* (1560), the *First Book of Discipline* (1560), and *The Book of Common Order* (1556–64). He also wrote the *History of the Reformation of Religion within the Realm of Scotland* (first complete edition, 1644). *See also* Church of Scotland; Presbyterianism.

ko (koh; Jap., "lecture"), Japanese fraternal organizations that originated in Buddhist circles but came to be popular among religious groups for devotional and especially pilgrimage purposes; some *ko* were mutual assistance associations. *See also* Ise-ko; pilgrimage.

koan. *See* kung-an.

Kobo Daishi. *See* Kukai.

Ko Ch'ao-fu (geh chahow-*foo*; fl. ca. 397–402), figure associated with the emergence of the Chinese southern Mao Shan school of Taoism (also called Shang-ch'ing Taoism) in the fourth century. Following the popularity of an earlier set of revelations, the *Shang-ch'ing ching* (Scriptures of Supreme Purity), Ko Ch'ao-fu composed the *Ling-pao ching* (Scriptures of the Sacred Treasure) about 397, which he claimed to be the culmination of revelations conferred on his ancestor a century before. These scriptures were important for their personification of the Tao as a trinity of "heavenly worthies" and for their ritual instructions. The liturgical materials in these texts formed the basis for Taoist communal rites in subsequent centuries. *See also* Ling-pao ching; Lu Hsiu-ching; Mao Shan; Shang-ch'ing Taoism.

kodo (koh-doh), the "Ancient Way" advocated by various Japanese National Learning (Kokugaku) scholars. Kodo was depicted as the way of the age of the gods when natural morality prevailed. *See also* Kokugaku.

Kofukuji (koh-*foo*-koo-jee), primary temple of the Japanese Buddhist Hosso school and one of the seven major temples in Nara. It flourished as the temple of the Fujiwara clan and eventually became one of the most important educational and political institutions in Japan, controlling large manors and fielding warrior monks. *See also* Hosso school; warrior monks.

kofun (koh-foon; Jap., "ancient tumulus"), large, mounded tombs that were built for members of the Japanese aristocracy from the fourth to seventh centuries predominantly in the Kanto and Kinai regions and in Kyushu. Funerary goods excavated from the tombs are a major source of information on the religious and sociopolitical life of early Japan. *See also* haniwa; Japanese religion.

Kogaku (koh-gah-koo), Japanese Ancient Learning school; it urged a return to the early Confucian texts such as the *Analects* and *Mencius* rather than the later Neo-Confucian commentaries of Chu Hsi. Leading scholars included the *bushido* writings of Yamaga Soko (1622–85), the ancient meaning commentaries of Ito Jinsai (1627–1705), and the textual studies of Ogyu Sorai (1666–1728). *See also* bushido; Ito Jinsai; Japan, Confucianism in; Ogyu Sorai; Yamaga Soko.

Kogoshui (koh-goh-shoo-ee; Jap., "Gleanings in Ancient Words"), polemical collection of Japanese myths and legends compiled by Imbe Hironari in 807 to further interests of the Imbe clan of ritualists at court. *See also* Japanese myth.

Ko Hung (guh hohng; 283–343), Chinese author of the *Pao-p'u-tzu* (The Master Who Embraces Simplicity)—a compendium of Taoist practice and thought—and compiler of the *Shen-hsien chuan* (Record of Divine Immortals)—a collection of biographies of Taoist saints and immortals. Born into a family of officials, he later spurned political life to become a literary recluse. His writing described and defended Taoist alchemy and other practices for attaining immortality that were popular in southern China but disparaged by the immigrant northern ruling elite. *See also* alchemy; Pao-p'u-tzu.

Kojiki (koh-jee-kee; Jap., "Record of Ancient Matters"), an ancient Japanese collection of myth and legend. Compiled by imperial decree in 712, the *Kojiki* is the most authentic extant source of Japanese mythology, although many of its narratives have parallels in the longer *Nihonshoki* (720). It begins with the cosmogony and tells of an unbroken chain of biological lineage from the divine primordial parents through the early emperors. Although a collection of myths and legends from a number of different regions and clans, it presents a more or less unified picture. Politically and socially it legitimized as the will of the gods both the paramount position of the aristocracy and the claim of the imperial clan to rule. Motoori Norinaga in the eighteenth century made it the cornerstone of his nativist revival (Kokugaku). *See also* cosmogony; Japanese myth; Japanese religion; Kokugaku; Motoori Norinaga; Nihonshoki.

koko. *See* kachina/katsina.

Kokugaku (koh-koo-gah-koo), National Learning school, which focused attention on early Japanese literature as a means of understanding Japan before the entrance of Chinese culture. Also known as the Shinto revival, this nativist movement was launched in the eighteenth century by Kada Azumamaro (1669–1736) and

Kamo no Mabuchi (1697–1769). This was further developed by Motoori Norinaga (1730–1801) and Hirata Atsutane (1776–1843). Keichu (1640–1701), a forerunner of Kokugaku, studied the *Man'yoshu*, emphasizing the pure spirit and emotion of the ancient poets. This philosophical approach was picked up by Kada Azumamaro, who taught Kamo no Mabuchi. They sought to uncover the pre-Confucian and pre-Buddhist Japanese thought expressed in these early texts. The greatest of these scholars was Norinaga, a student of Mabuchi, who compiled studies of *The Tale of Genji* and the *Kojiki*. Atsutane moved Kokugaku closer to a Shinto nationalist ideology with a cosmological basis. In the twentieth century many Kokugaku themes were used before World War II by nationalists to help support an imperial ideology. *See also* Hirata Atsutane; Japanese religion; Kada Azumamaro; Kamo Mabuchi; Kojiki; Motoori Norinaga.

kokutai (koh-*koo*-ti; Jap., "national essence"), the religious, political, and cultural identity of the Japanese people. As used in the nativist movement (Kokugaku) of the eighteenth century by Motoori Norinaga, it meant the values and worldview embodied in Shinto mythology. In the modern period the idea buttressed State Shinto, especially the emperor cult. It has been little used since 1945. *See also* Kokugaku; Motoori Norinaga.

Kol Nidre (kohl need-ray'; Aram., "all vows"), in Jewish ritual, originally a legal formula annulling vows, but now the solemn prayer introducing Yom Kippur. It is known primarily for its distinctive cantorial melody. *See also* Judaism (festal cycle).

Konjaku monogatari (kohn-jah-*koo* moh-*noh*-gah-*tah*-ree; Jap., "Tales of Times Now Past"), a collection of Japanese tales from India, China, Korea, and Japan, probably compiled in the late eleventh or early twelfth century, perhaps as materials for preaching by Buddhist monks.

Konkokyo (kon-kor'kyor), a Japanese new religion with Shinto leanings founded in rural Okayama prefecture by Kawate Bunjiro (1814–83) after an illness in which he was visited by a deity named Konjin. Subsequently, the deity was revealed as Konko Daijin (lit., "great god of golden light") and took over Kawate's mind and body. Henceforth, Kawate acted as a mediator between the human and divine and gathered followers, who organized themselves into the religion Konkokyo in 1885, after his death. Konkokyo claims about five hundred thousand members today

and continues to venerate Konko Daijin. *See also* Japan, new religions in.

Koran, antiquated transliteration of Qur'an. *See also* Islam (authoritative texts and their interpretation).

Kore (koh'ree), an ancient Greek goddess, also known as Persephone (Lat. *Proserpina*); she is the daughter of Demeter and bride of Hades (Pluto), king of the underworld. *See also* descent to the underworld; Eleusinian Mysteries; Greek religion.

Korea, Buddhism in. *See* Buddhas and Bodhisattvas (Korea); Chogye Buddhism; comprehensive Buddhism; Korea, Maitreyism in; National Protection Buddhism; National Teacher; Nine Mountain schools; Pure Land school (Korea); scripture rites, Korean Buddhist rituals including; Tripitaka Koreana; Uich'on; Uisang; Vinaya (Korean Buddhism); Won Buddhism; Wonhyo.

Korea, Confucian virtues in. While the notion of virtue is not necessarily a religious notion or the product of a single religion, Korean understanding of virtue, in theory and practice, assumes a fixed cosmology that may be broadly described as Confucian. The terms used to describe and analyze virtue (*todok, yuli*) in any religious context are drawn from Confucian notions of a priori principles that serve as the basis for and explain the meaning of microcosmic and macrocosmic events. These principles taken together constitute the True Way (the Tao) of things. Korean Confucianism, Buddhism, Taoism, Christianity, and the new religions all recognize and support such basic virtues as integrity-loyalty (*ch'ung*), obedience-filial piety (*hyo*), restraint-propriety (*ye*), and honesty-justice (*ui*) and their application in domestic and social life. All recognize that the exercise of such virtues is a matter of training and education. On the other hand, the lack of such virtues constitutes a lack of knowledge, culture, and, fundamentally, the lack of human status.

In the long history of Korean religions certain virtues have been especially emphasized. Integrity-loyalty combines both the internal and personal devotion to the Tao with the external and social devotion to one's parents, family, and sovereign. Expressions of this loyalty include filial devotion to all older members of one's family and one's family's ancestors and the extension of this filial feeling to older classmates, teachers, supervisors, and government officials. The devotion also demands, even at the cost of one's life, the defense of the integrity of all those to whom one is devoted, and thus exacting vengeance became an important aspect of filial devotion and loyalty.

Restraint-propriety is also an important virtue for Koreans, who consider it to be the chief characteristic of their culture. This virtue combines the internal and personal practice of self-restraint and frugality with the external and social practice of deference and liberality toward others. Like integrity-loyalty, restraint-propriety operates within a hierarchical context. Elders (familial and social) are treated with the highest respect, and one's personal feelings, ideas, and opinions are not allowed to interfere with the expression of that respect or cause disharmony between generations. In a broader context, restraint-propriety means being well-trained and well-disciplined and is synonymous with culture. Those who lack it or do not know how it operates are considered, at the very least, barbarian and, at most, no different from wild animals. *See also* academies (Korea), private and public; An Yu; Chong Tojon; Chu Hsi studies (Korea); Four-Seven Debates; Kija; Practical Learning school; Shrine to Culture; village recluses (Korea); Yi-Gi Debates; Yi Hwang; Yi Saek; Yi Yulgok.

Korea, Islam in. Though present in China as early as the late seventh century, Islam did not become a practice in Korea until the early part of the twentieth century, when a group of Korean settlers in Mukden, China, adopted Islam. This group of Korean Muslims later moved south into the Korean peninsula after World War II. This Korean Muslim community was not widely known until Turkish troops, who served in the United Nations Forces in the Korean War, found them. In 1955 the Korean Islamic Society was founded and a mosque established. In 1967 this society became the Korean Muslim Federation. In 1976, with money from Saudi Arabia, Korean Muslims erected a central mosque in Seoul and seven other mosques in Korea. Since the early 1970s the number of Korean Muslims has increased to over twenty thousand, in large part because of increased cultural and economic exchanges between Korea and the Middle East and conversions to Islam by Korean construction workers and engineers while residing in the Middle East.

Korea, Maitreyism in. Maitreyism, the belief in the coming of the Maitreya Buddha before the end of the present world system, played an important political and nationalistic role in the propagation and final acceptance of Buddhism as a state religion by the ruling houses of the Korean Three Kingdoms period (ca. 57 B.C.–A.D. 668). What appealed especially to those houses was the figure of the righteous universal monarch Sankha, who precedes and creates the causal conditions for the descent of Maitreya from the Tusita heaven into the world, and the notion that such a peaceable and prosperous kingdom (sometimes referred to as the Third Assembly of the Dragon Splendor) then becomes the center and unifier of the world of nations.

In Koguryo, epigraphy on grave stelae indicates a widespread belief in the future establishment of the Pure Land of Maitreya within the Koguryo domains. In the kingdoms of Paekche and Silla, there were many stories circulated and miraculous images discovered that indicated that Maitreya or Maitreya's righteous king had been born into those kingdoms. In some instances successive rulers identified their ancestors with the king Sankha and themselves with Maitreya, or chief ministers of state, including the head of the Hwarang Troop in Silla, were identified with the future Buddha. The belief in Maitreya's Pure Land, where followers of the final Buddha would reside, was always understood as an earthly Pure Land rather than some place beyond this world and the border of death. The political implications of such a doctrine were especially prominent, since the descent of Maitreya into the Korean peninsula meant that Korea had been favored with the appearance of Buddhas in the past and was not dependent on other countries in Asia for its moral and religious standing.

This belief was also supported by the ancillary belief that Korea was the object of the Mauryan king Ashoka's search for a country of righteousness, where the Buddhist law would be preserved during the time of the decline of Buddhism (*malbop*). Discoveries of ancient temple flagstones, gold reliquaries, and wood ash thought to date from the time of the Kasyapa and Kokamuni Buddhas were seen as evidence that Korea had been the favored birthplace of the Buddhas of previous world systems. *See also* Buddhas and Bodhisattvas (Korea); Hwarang Troop; Maitreya; Pure Land school (Korea).

Korea, Neo-Confucianism in. *See* academies (Korea), private and public; Chu Hsi studies; Four-Seven Debates; village recluses (Korea); Yi-Gi Debates; Yi Hwang; Yi Saek; Yi Yulgok.

Korea, new religions in. Diverse in origins, beliefs, practices, and organization, the many religious movements that arose in Korea since the nineteenth century share enough with Korean culture and religion, and with each other, to be considered a common group of religious developments. These new religions may be characterized negatively by what they are not. They are other than indigenous Korean religion, i.e., the philosophical and religious traditions of Taoism and Confucianism from China; Buddhism, which is of Indian origin but was introduced from China; and Christianity, which also came to Korea through China. However, each of these traditions contributed some elements to new religious movements, which were formed as lay religions or voluntary organizations, contrasting with both the diffuse and unorganized indigenous traditions (including shamanism) and the organized religious traditions of Buddhism and Christianity.

The first Korean new religion was Tonghak (Eastern Learning), founded by Ch'oe Che-u (1824–64) in 1860; its name contrasts with Catholicism, known then as Sohak (Western Learning). Ch'oe received a revelation of the "heavenly way" (chondo) from a deity who told Ch'oe to teach the unity of humans with the deity and the equality of all humans. This egalitarian emphasis brought the leader and his movement into conflict with prevailing Confucianism and feudalistic society; Ch'oe was executed, as was the second leader of the movement. The third leader replaced the name Tonghak with Ch'ondogyo ("teaching or religion of the heavenly way"), and the movement became a major Korean religion; it was also a pioneer in social reform and a leading voice in opposition to Japanese colonialism from 1910 to 1945.

Another major new religion is Won Buddhism, founded in 1916 by the son of a farmer, known by his followers as the venerable Sotesan. The movement did not originate directly from Buddhism, but from the inspiration of the founder after reflection and meditation on the meaning of life. Sotesan was critical of traditional Korean Buddhism, centered in remote temples and monasteries and unrelated to the daily life of the common people. He was equally critical of the materialism and selfishness of the people and advocated social reform for women's rights and better educational opportunities. After his enlightenment on these matters, Sotesan came to associate his own experience and message with that of the Buddha and Buddhism. A key notion of Won Buddhism is the perfection of the circle (won), which is the universal Buddha-nature, with preference for worshiping Buddha-mind rather than the literal Buddha

image. The founder advocated not only moral training but also practical activity, such as cooperative ventures for improving farmlands and for mutual savings, insisting that such physical and moral training was integrally related to Buddhist spirituality. With emphasis on equality of lay participants and religious leaders, Won Buddhism also has been involved in educational programs and founded a number of its own schools, including a modern university.

One of the remarkable aspects of Korean new religions is the prominence of Christian or Christian-derived movements. The perception of these groups, inevitably, will differ considerably: their founders and members see themselves as Christian, while many Western (and some Korean) Christians view these groups as marginal or heretical. Apart from the question of their orthodox or unorthodox Christian character, they certainly represent the most vital new religious movements in contemporary Korea. Two of the largest Christian groups, Chondogwan and Tongilgyo, arose after World War II.

Chondogwan, or the Evangelical Church, was founded by Pak Tae-son, who was active in the Presbyterian Church but by the mid-1950s had developed his own charismatic abilities and teachings to the extent that the Presbyterians labeled him a heretic. Nevertheless, despite opposition from established Christian groups and lengthy imprisonment, Pak's following expanded rapidly. His inspiration to found a new religion came from a vision in which he received the blood of Jesus and the ability to transmit its power. Through a special rite of laying on hands he was able to transmit the blood of Jesus directly to people and assure them of forgiveness. In another rite he changed ordinary water to holy water, or the blood of Jesus, with which the believers purified themselves from sin. Church services feature highly dynamic singing and preaching. This group has also been engaged in economic programs, developing several Christian towns with their own factories and housing.

Tongilgyo is known in the West as Unification Church; its adherents were named "Moonies" by detractors who twisted the name of the founder, Moon (or Mun) Sun-myung (b. 1920). He was active in Christianity from his youth, founding a church in Pyongyang, North Korea, after liberation from the Japanese in 1945. Later he was imprisoned by Communist authorities. Moon was also arrested in Seoul, South Korea, but was cleared of charges and his movement quickly grew. Moon had received special revelations that enabled him to give new interpretations to the Bible and Christian history. The major religious

Priestess of Suungyo, a new religion in South Korea that practices healing with cold water drawn from a sacred well. She is pouring the water into cups for use in the ritual; at Kyeryongsan.

tenet of his teaching was that the sin of Adam and Eve was not erased by Christ, who brought a spiritual but not physical salvation. Moon understood himself to be the Second Advent described in the Bible, and, as such, he had discovered the Divine Principle, which explains the complete nature of human history, from Adam and Eve to the present, and offers a complete logical critique of all philosophical systems. Tongilgyo teachings and churches are tightly structured, with the ideal that all peoples and all religions become one family under God. An individual's entire life, even marriage, should be lived according to the divine plan, not according to individual selfish desire. Tongilgyo is involved in a number of industrial and business ventures and has been quite active in Korean and international anti-Communist movements. Whereas Chondogwan is limited to Korea, Tongilgyo, known by various names, has been successful in recruiting members in other Asian countries and in the West.

In addition to these larger and more conspicuous new religions, there are hundreds of smaller movements. For example, the area around Mt. Kyeryong, which has its own mystique dating from eighteenth-century prophecies about imminent renewal there, is a haven for many new religious movements.

The sheer number and great diversity in Korean new religions defies simple generalization, but as a whole they contain the following features: natural affinity with the cosmos as a sacred entity; a close bond between religious salvation and national identity, often in connection with economic programs; orientation of the group around a semidivine or charismatic leader; techniques of healing and divining; Confucianistic ethical codes; Buddhist rituals and images; Taoistic (and Neo-Confucian) forms of geomancy. Each new religion has developed its own distinctive heritage out of this larger Korean context. *See also* Eastern Learning; Religion of the Heavenly Way; Unification Church.

Korea, Protestantism in. The transmission of Protestant Christianity into Korea began in the 1880s through the efforts of Presbyterian ministers working in China near the Chinese-Korean border. As in Roman Catholicism before it, many Protestant conversions took place through the publication and dissemination of religious tracts and the Christian scriptures. Lay converts in China and Japan returned to Korea to spread this form of Christianity and to invite foreign missionaries into the country.

Early Forms: Presbyterianism had been the first form of Protestant Christianity introduced into Korea, but it was soon followed by Methodism and Episcopalianism. By the turn of the century there were Anglo-American, Australian, and Canadian missionaries working throughout the Korean peninsula. The work of these missionaries centered on the establishment of schools, hospitals, and publishing houses. This focus was in large part due to the nature of government ambivalence about foreigners' activities and the contemporary Protestant emphasis on social welfare, cultural progress, and religious education.

The appeal of Protestantism was its support of modernization and democratization, and in the years to follow Korean Protestants fully participated in the reform and independence movements of Korea. Protestant missionaries and lay converts championed the causes of literacy in the Hangul script and a deep sense of patriotism over and against the Japanese presence. Protestant missionaries also used the Hangul script to publish literature. Laywomen were used to proselytize. Many schools, hospitals, and seminaries for the training of clergy were founded by converts rather than missionaries, so that by the end of the first decade of the twentieth century Korea had its own native ministers.

Divisions: In 1907 Korea saw its first Protestant revival and the number of converts increased from two hundred thousand to seven hundred thousand. Most of these conversions came from the working classes, especially from among women. During the Japanese colonial period (1910–45) Protestantism became a form of anti-Japanese nationalism and was identified with proindependence movements. Membership in churches suddenly decreased among men, who were subject to the greatest Japanese surveillance. After the suppression of the March 1, 1919, independence movement, Protestant churches divided along liberal and conservative lines. Conservative churches sought to accommodate themselves to the Japanese presence, while liberal churches went increasingly underground. By 1938 all foreign missionaries were expelled and the churches were closed. Protestant worship continued in homes through Bible reading and the singing of hymns. Toward the end of World War II there was an attempt to unite all churches into a single church, but without success. Churches were again divided at the end of World War II, as the country was split between Russian and American spheres. With the outbreak of the Korean War, Protestant churches were divided by waves of messianic revivalism and fundamentalist conservatism.

Since 1955 the membership in Protestant churches has steadily increased, especially among charismatic and Pentecostal groups. The presence of faith healing, emphasis on the presence of evil spirits, and ritual possession by the Holy Spirit has a unique appeal to Koreans, especially women, who still suffer disdain from a male-dominated society and the church hierarchy. It is estimated that two-thirds of all Protestant Christians are women. *See also* academies (Korea), private and public; Theology of the People.

Korea, Roman Catholicism in. Roman Catholicism was first introduced into Korea in the seventeenth century through contacts between Korean scholars in the annual embassies to the Chinese Ming and Ch'ing courts and Chinese scholars who had converted to or were acquainted with the Catholic teachings of Jesuit missionaries. Brought back to Korea were copies of pamphlets and books written in Chinese by Jesuit missionaries and their followers that included summaries of Roman Catholic doctrine, essays on the moral life, information about Western science, geography and cartography,

astronomy, agriculture, and mechanics. These texts and the knowledge they contained became known in Korea as Western Learning (Sohak).

Early Korean followers of this Western Learning came from royal and aristocratic literati lineages that were associated with Yi Ik's Practical Learning movement (Sirhakp'a). This branch of Neo-Confucian learning showed a keen interest in precise scientific knowledge that could be used to improve the livelihood of the ordinary person and the nation as a whole.

Though initial interest in Catholicism focused on its scientific knowledge, there soon evolved an interest in Catholic religious doctrine. The earliest religious organization evolved when scholars, after their instruction and baptism in Peking, returned to Korea to spread Catholic doctrine, baptize one another, carry out Catholic rituals, and elect their own priests and a bishop. This self-evangelized church remained in force until 1789, when Korea came under the jurisdiction of the bishop at Peking. French and Chinese missionaries from China followed in 1785 and 1795, and conversions continued to increase. When the Jesuit priest Peter Grammont entered the country secretly in 1785, there were less than two thousand converts; when Chou Wen-mu (1752–1801) arrived in Seoul in 1795, there were over four thousand converts, a number that increased to ten thousand by the turn of the century.

Rites Controversy: One aspect of Korean conversion to Catholicism that was to determine much of later history was the question of memorial rites for the dead. Known in China as the rites controversy, this issue not only involved questions about the worship of Confucius and his disciples but also questions about the nature, value, and efficacy of clan ancestral rites. In China and Korea such worship was not only a private act but a public duty enforced by law. Upper classes especially were held accountable for the maintenance of these cornerstones of the Confucian political and legal system. The 1742 papal ruling on the incompatibility of ancestral rites with Catholic belief meant that many who converted came into conflict with the Korean laws on these rites. When King Chongjo (r. 1776–1800) proscribed Western Learning as a heresy in 1785, he was not only maintaining long-standing Korean tradition but also defending the ideological and moral basis of Korean society. But in 1790, the bishop at Peking banned Korean Catholics from participating in ancestral rites, and in 1791 Yun Ch'i ch'ung, Korea's first Catholic martyr, was sentenced to death for not offering rites to his mother.

This controversy, which was not resolved until the twentieth century, was further complicated by the fact that Korean and Chinese Confucian understandings of the nature and efficacy of ancestral rites were changing. A more utilitarian and less religiously ambiguous understanding of these rites had begun to emerge from the study of Confucian classics from a historicist perspective. Han-dynasty traditions of legalism, pragmatism, empiricism, and textual analysis were revived while centuries of orthodox commentary and religious practice were abandoned for the sake of understanding what the classics actually said. Unfortunately this movement, which never questioned the necessity of ancestral rites, was not sufficiently widespread to prevent the clash between Catholic episcopal and papal intransigence on the meaning of ancestral rites and the Korean legal orthodoxy about its necessity.

Political Dimensions: After 1790 Catholic conversions increased among the lower and middle classes (*chungin*). Upper-class conversions continued, but at a slower rate. Political expedience and a more sophisticated distinction between the adoption of Western science versus Western religion may explain this shift. At the same time, the countercultural perspective of Catholicism and its early royal, aristocratic, and scholarly adherence, as well as the technical knowledge and science found in Catholic writings, appealed to middle and lower classes seeking upward mobility. The rapid growth in Catholic conversions (ten thousand converts by 1800) posed a serious challenge to the oligarchic aristocratic society of the time and its increasingly rigid Confucian orthodoxy. The result of the conflict, sparked by the rites controversy, was a series of officially mandated persecutions in 1801, 1839, and 1866.

The 1801 persecution arose from factional strife in the regency of the Queen Dowager Kim. The Pyokp'a, or Old Doctrine Faction, had ties to the Dowager and saw her regency as an opportunity to rid the court of the Southern/Expediency Faction, which had protected Catholics in the previous reign and counted converts among its members. The persecution was intensified when it was discovered that Hwang Sayong had secretly tried to send a letter to the bishop of Peking requesting that Western powers send naval and land forces to compel the government to grant religious freedom to Catholics. Hwang was executed and Catholics were branded as traitors.

With the marriage of King Sunjo to a woman of the Andong Kim clan (many of whom had converted to Catholicism) and the rise to power of Sunjo's father-in-law, Kim Chosun, the persecution of Catholics ended. At this time three French priests entered the country and Catholicism gained wider acceptance.

King Honjong (r. 1834–49), Sunjo's grandson and successor, was the son of a P'ungyang Cho clan woman and during his reign the anti-Catholic Pyokp'a P'ungyang Cho clan came to dominate the court. In 1839 a second persecution resulted in the death of the French priests and many Korean converts; in 1846 Korea's first Catholic priest, Kim T'aegon, was put to death.

During the reign of King Ch'olchong (r. 1849–63), the Andong Kim clan returned to power and the policy of persecution was relaxed. By 1863 there were a dozen French priests working in the country and some twenty-three thousand converts. Most of these converts came from urban and capital commercial classes, as well as from the urban poor and uneducated. Catholic notions of social equality, concern for women, and a final rectification of injustice in the coming kingdom of God certainly appealed to those excluded from political, economic, and social power.

In the next reign, Prince Regent Hungson Taewon'gun, father of King Kojong (r. 1864–1907), embarked on a series of strict reforms to secure direct monarchical control of the government. Fearing the spread of Western ideas, especially among disaffected lower classes, and suspicious of the repeated attempts by Western powers to open trade relations through the sending of warships, Taewon'gun launched a persecution of Catholics in 1866 and established a policy of isolation. Catholicism was proscribed as an outside encroachment and foreign missionaries and large numbers of Korean Catholics were executed.

Modern Developments: After 1876 Korea was forced to sign treaties with Western powers guaranteeing the safety of foreign missionaries. Of the thousands of Catholic clergy and laity persecuted in the nineteenth century, seventy-eight were proclaimed martyrs blessed by the Vatican in 1925. Of these, Kim T'aegon, Korea's first ordained priest, was eventually declared a saint.

In the twentieth century, Roman Catholicism in Korea has continued to grow, despite competition from Protestantism and new religions. Its traditional appeal to the politically oppressed and disenfranchised lower classes has been translated into an appeal for social, democratic, and economic justice. The Catholic Church has spoken out against recent dictatorial regimes and government oppression and corruption, at the risk of imprisonment, and it has protected and defended student and worker protests. The Church continues to remain independent of the government and to give its followers an identity that allows for a critical stance toward the social, political, and cultural institutions of the time. *See also* ancestral rites; Chinese rites controversy; Kim T'aegon; Practical Learning school.

Korea, Taoism in. It is not clear when religious Taoism first entered the Korean peninsula, but mural paintings of flying immortals in Koguryo tombs of the third century assume some Taoist influence. Historical documents indicate that the texts of the Taoist philosophers Lao-tzu and Chuang-tzu were studied in the fifth century and that some Buddhist temples were converted into Taoist abbeys when priests of the Celestial Master sect arrived in Koguryo from China in the sixth century. As part of its diplomatic relations with T'ang China in the seventh century, the Koguryo government further adopted the use of T'ang state rituals (Chin. *chiao*) to heaven and the stars for the protection of the royal family and the state.

Pre-Choson: Paekche records indicate that apart from the study of the *Lao-tzu,* little was known of Taoism, but Silla, from the sixth to the ninth centuries, adopted the worship of Taoist deities, used Taoist literature and philosophy in the training of its Hwarang Troop, saw the appearance of recluse adepts much in the manner of the Seven Sages of the Bamboo Grove, and developed a tradition of inner alchemical studies, especially in the areas around Mt. Kaeryong.

During the Koryo period (918–1392) Taoism continued as an official state cult. Shrines to Taoist astral and mountain deities were established by the government and annual ceremonies to heaven and Taoist retreats (*chai*) were ordered for the protection of the state. Taoist geomancy, calendrical prognostication, dietetics, medicine, and inner alchemy became popular throughout the Koryo period and knowledge of Taoist philosophy, hagiography, and legends is well represented in the poetry and prose of the dynasty.

Choson: In the Choson period (1392–1910), Taoism, like Buddhism, was officially disestablished. The Taoist ceremonies and shrines that had been supported by the government in the Koryo period were abandoned. While public practice of Taoism and the public expression of Taoist ideas was considered heterodox (Kor. *idan,* lit., "strange and extreme") upper- and lower-class private practice continued. Taoist inner alchemy and medicine were especially

well developed by upper-class literati and in the sixteenth and seventeenth century predictions from the eighth century about the flourishing of Taoism in Korea seemed to come true. Scholarly interest in Hsien Taoism, the Taoism of immortality, produced a series of manuals for the practice of inner alchemy and several collections of Korean Taoist biographies, which traced the history of Taoism back to the time of Tan'gun. Taoism and its various disciplines were also of interest to such Practical Learning school scholars as Yun Hyu (1617–80) and Pak Sedang (1629–1703), as it had been to the *ki*-monist Neo-Confucian scholars So Kyong-dok (1489–1546), Yi Yulgok (1536–84), Kim Changsaeng (1548–1631), and Chong Yop (1563–1625).

In the eighteenth and nineteenth centuries, Taoism became a countercultural protest movement as middle- and lower-class scholars, writers, artists, and the founders of new religions satirized the aristocratic (*yangban*) society of their day and espoused a return to the pre-Confucian Korean past. In the twentieth century, interest in Taoist philosophy, meditation, medicine, and even escapist literature continues as part of the revival of traditional Korean culture and as part of the unease with modern, technological society. *See also* alchemy; Chuang-tzu; Lao-tzu; Neo-Confucianism; Practical Learning school; T'ien-shih Taoism.

Korea (festal cycle). Until recently Korea's economy was primarily agricultural and its festival calendar celebrated important turning points in the agricultural and pastoral year, including the solstices, equinoxes, advent and departure of winter cold and summer heat, first plantings, periods of animal grazing and reproduction, and the harvesting of crops. These festivals were not only important for the economic life of the people but also for their social and political life, because it often was at such times that political and social decisions were made.

Agricultural Festivals: In the earliest periods of Korean history, before the advent of Chinese culture, most Koreans lived in clan confederacies over which presided an elected headman or king. Confederacy business and organization followed the agricultural calendar. Among the Puyo people, the Yongoje, or Festival of Agriculture, was celebrated during the fifth month and at the end of the grazing season in the tenth month; at these times, marriages and appointments to public offices were made. In Koguryo the harvest rite was known as Tongmaengje, or Celebration of the Eastern Alliance (with the Sun), and was celebrated in the tenth lunar month. Thereafter royal hunts were conducted and according to the results of the hunt, members of the ruling clans were given offices, ranks, and land allotments. Among the tribes of the southeast (Suro and Silla) a twice-yearly rite called Suritnal, or Day of the Sun, was held to mark the beginning of the grain-planting season in the fifth lunar month and to mark the end of harvest in the tenth lunar month. On these occasions the heads of aristocratic clans would meet to discuss community business and, when needed, appoint a new monarch.

All of these agricultural and pastoral festivals began with religious ceremonies conducted on mountaintops or in groves of sacred trees (*sodo*). These religious sites were marked by special privileges: killing within their precincts was forbidden and they could therefore be used as places to resolve community disputes. The rites were conducted by shamans, shaman kings, or divine men. Though little is known about these rites, the terminology used to describe them indicates that they included drum playing, dancing, and the use of animal totems.

Commemorative Festivals: After the advent of Chinese cultural forms and the reorganization of clan groups into cities nations, these celebrations continued in a new form. The foundation myths of the various ruling houses were wedded to ancestral remembrance rites and the worship of culture heroes. Clan identities gave birth to national identities. Agricultural festivals remained, but they were understood and conducted as occasions for reaffirming the values of the nation-state. In addition, the advent of artisans, city builders, bureaucrats, and even professional religious changed the meaning of the agricultural calendar and added new reasons to celebrate changes in the year. Even in modern, secular, predominately urban Korea the Harvest Night Festival, which marks the beginning of the rice harvest, remains as a celebration of family and clan remembrance and feasting. The solar and lunar New Year festivals likewise combine the functions of community renewal, family remembrance, and the advent of the new agricultural year. *See also* National Protection Buddhism; scripture rites, Korean Buddhist rituals including.

Korean foundation myths. The foundation myths of Korea record the origins of important ruling clans and ancient states. They all share the common feature of describing those origins as a matter of divine action and heavenly descent. The most important of these myths is the Koguryo Tan'gun myth, which tells the story of the first ruler on the peninsula. Tan'gun was born from the union of the Son of the Lord of Heaven (Hwanung) with a human female who had been transformed from a bear. This myth relates that after a fifteen-hundred-year reign in the Kingdom of the Morning Light (Choson), Tan'gun transformed himself into a mountain god (*sansin*) at Mt. Paegak and thus became the tutelary spirit of the Korean people. In Buddhist and folk iconography, Tan'gun is usually represented as an armed general or old man sitting atop a tiger, and his heavenly residence is the Seven Stars, or Big Dipper.

Other important myths include those of the founding of Northern Puyo, where the Ruler of Heaven himself descended to rule; Eastern Puyo, whose descendants came from a golden frog-boy given by the gods of mountains and streams; the myth of Tongmyong (Eastern Light), the founder of the state of Koguryo, who was born from an egg that had descended in the sunlight; the progenitor of the Kyongju Kim clan, Kim Alchi, who descended from heaven as a young boy in a golden box; the progenitor of the Kyongju Pak clan, Pak Hyokkose, born from a luminous, gourd-shaped red egg laid by a heavenly dragon; and the progenitor of the Karak Sok clan, Sok Tarhae, born from a magpie egg that arrived in a boat on the shore of the Silla state.

All of these myths, with their solar, ornithological, and animal symbolism, have important roles in the formation of Korean religious and national consciousness. They are decidedly distinct from Chinese counterparts and bear stronger resemblance to eastern Siberian and Central Asiatic myths, a fact that cultural historians, ancient and modern, are quick to point out. Their recording at the hands of a Buddhist monk during the time of the Mongol invasions (thirteenth century) and their being shunned by Confucian historiographers indicate a Korea-centered consciousness and sense of pride. They serve as the basis for the continued worship of mountain spirits at the village level and the pride Koreans have about the geomantic power of the natural landscape. Their influence can be seen in the solar and light symbolism of the Korean kingdom titles, shamanic and Buddhist rituals, and even the nineteenth-century revival of the Korean national calendar that begins with the birth of Tan'gun in 2333 B.C. They have generated, especially in times of political, economic, and social crisis, renewed affirmations and reappropriations of Korean uniqueness. *See also* Han thought; Kija.

Korean religion. *See* ancestral rites; astral spirits (Korea); geomancy; Hanullim/Hanunim; Kija;

Korea, Confucian virtues in; Korea, Islam in; Korea, new religions in; Korea, Protestantism in; Korea, Roman Catholicism in; Korea, Taoism in; Korea (festal cycle); Korean foundation myths; kosa; kut; shamanism; Tan'gun wanggom.

Koresh, David. *See* Branch Davidians.

kosa (koh-sah), a private tribute offering made by Korean women to household gods, including the House Lord (Songju), the Birth Grandmother (Samsin Halmoni), the House Site Official (Toju T'aegam), the Seven Stars (Ch'ilsong), and the Kitchen God (Chowang). The private offering of *kosa* by women is an important and necessary complement to the public ritual feasting of ancestral spirits by men. Both ensure the protection, prosperity, and continuity of the household. The tribute offering usually consists of bowls of wine and specially prepared rice cakes, which are offered to ensure the gods' blessings or have them remove some evil. The kosa is performed at important times of the year: after the harvest, following lunar cycles (new moon and full moon), after a death in the household, and when major changes, fortunate or unfortunate, occur in the household. Though the performance of kosa to household gods is in no way related to the periodic feeding of ancestors, it is a necessary part of maintaining the good fortune of the household. *See also* astral spirits (Korea)

kosher (Heb. *kashrut,* "fit," "fitness"), the Jewish dietary laws. Jewish religious practice includes a complex set of rules about permissible and forbidden foods. Their origin is biblical, and they are elaborated in postbiblical Jewish law.

The Rules Concerning Animals: The food restrictions apply primarily to the flesh of living creatures and products derived from them, not to fruits and vegetables. The main biblical sources for the restrictions on animals are Leviticus 11 and Deuteronomy 14. The lists given there are extensive but not exhaustive.

Kosher animals are those that have cloven hooves and chew their cud. Lack of one or both of these characteristics renders an animal nonkosher, and its flesh may not be eaten. More than forty such animals are listed in Scripture, of which the best known is the pig. Whether listed or not, any animal that lacks the required characteristics is not kosher.

Scripture also lists permitted and forbidden birds and fowl but does not specify their characteristic features. The Mishnah introduces a general rule forbidding all birds of prey, not only those listed in Scripture. Permitted birds must have three characteristics: an extra talon at the back of the foot, a crop, and a gizzard that peels easily (Mishnah *Hullin* 3:6).

The mark of permissible fish or any aquatic creatures is that they have fins and scales. This excludes shellfish, eels, frogs, etc. The criteria are clearly established, although debates arise over some questionable cases, such as swordfish. In general all insects are forbidden, except for four types of locusts and grasshoppers. Because the tradition of identifying them has been largely lost, they are generally not eaten.

Some portions of kosher animals are also forbidden. These include the sciatic nerve (Genesis 32:33), certain portions of the fat attached to the stomach and intestines, and certain types of fat in the abdomen. Food products derived from nonkosher animals are also prohibited. This includes fats such as lard, as well as the milk or eggs of forbidden animals. All blood is categorically forbidden.

The Preparation of Kosher Meat: For the flesh of permitted animals and birds to be kosher, they must be slaughtered by a specially trained and qualified functionary in accordance with a set of detailed rules. The knife must be perfectly sharpened without even the smallest notch. The trachea and esophagus must be severed in a single stroke, bringing about nearly instantaneous and painless death. The internal organs are then carefully examined for any sign of disease, which would disqualify the animal as kosher. No animal may be eaten whose death has been caused by anything other than ritual slaughter.

Before the meat may be used it must be purged of the internal blood by a process of first soaking it in cold water and then covering it with heavy salt to draw out the remaining blood. Alternately, the blood may be drawn out by roasting the meat over an open flame.

Milk and Meat: Three times, Scripture forbids seething a kid in its mother's milk. Rabbinic law interprets this as a prohibition against cooking or eating together meat and dairy products. The established practice is to maintain in the kitchen and at the table a complete separation. Separate pots and pans, dishes, and cutlery are used for meat and dairy foods. Not only may they not be eaten together, but there is a prescribed waiting time after eating meat before one may eat milk products. The most widespread practice is to wait six hours, but some communities wait only three hours, and in a few places the practice is to wait one hour.

The Reasons for the Kosher Laws: No definitive explanation can be given for the dietary laws in general, and certainly not in all their details. Scripture associates them with the quest for holiness and states without further explanation that whoever eats forbidden foods is defiled. Some claim that these are hygienic rules, which also serve the purpose of separating the Jews from their neighbors, thus discouraging assimilation and protecting the integrity of the Jewish religious community. There is, however, no clear evidence to support these explanations. Most persuasive is the rabbinic teaching that there is no satisfactory account of the dietary rules, and Jews must simply observe them as a divinely mandated discipline that expresses loyalty to God and God's law in even such mundane activities as eating and drinking. *See also* food; Judaism (life cycle); parveh.

Kotani Kimi (koh-tah-nee kee-mee; 1901–71), charismatic cofounder of the Japanese "new religion" Reiyukai. She emphasized honoring ancestral spirits and repentance and attracted many members, especially through healing. *See also* Reiyukai.

kotoage (koh-toh-ah-gay; Jap., "to raise up words"), speaking boldly to or in the presence of a *kami* (divinity, divine presence) in ancient Japan. It is a ritual act that invokes the magical power of words (*kotodama*). *See also* kami; kotodama.

kotodama (koh-toh-dah-mah; Jap., "the spiritual power residing in words"), ancient Japanese belief that beautiful words correctly intoned contained a spiritual potency (*tama*) that could bestow blessings or a desired outcome. *Kotodama* was found in prayers (*norito*), spells (*kotoage*), word charms (*kotowaza*), and popular songs (*wazauta*). *See also* kotoage; norito; tama.

K'ou Ch'ien-chih (koh chyin-juhr; 373–448), a Taoist reformer concerned with social order and ethical behavior. He claimed divine revelations and was declared a "Celestial Master" by a non-Chinese ruler of a state in North China. *See also* T'ien-shih.

ko-wu (geh-woo; Chin., "investigation of things"), the Neo-Confucian theory and practice that teaches how to discover the principles of things by an examination of things and events in the world. It includes the reverential effort to achieve moral insight by means of the study and recognition of things as they really are. The process of *ko-wu* is crucial for the School of Principle because it taught that the world was pluralistic. True wisdom therefore includes the examination of as much of the world as possible in order to ascertain the functioning of the heavenly principle manifest in each thing and person. *See also* Ch'eng-Chu school; Li-hsueh; Neo-Confucianism.

Koya, Mt. (koh-yah), sacred Japanese mountain chosen as the founding site and headquarters of the Shingon Buddhist sect by Kukai (also Kobo Daishi; 774–835), in 816. After Kukai's death, Mt. Koya began to lose much of its influence to other Shingon institutions such as Toji in the capital, Kyoto. About 170 years after Kukai's death, a cult arose around Kukai as part of an effort to revive Mt. Koya; Kukai was said not to have died, but to be deep in meditation as he awaited Maitreya's arrival. Eventually, he was identified as Maitreya or Vairochana and Mt. Koya as his heaven or Pure Land. As a result, pious lay believers made pilgrimages to Mt. Koya and had their graves established there so they might meet Maitreya with Kukai after death. *See also* Kukai; Maitreya; mountains, sacred; Pure Land; Shingon-shu; Vairochana.

kratophany, general term for the manifestation of divine power.

Krishna (kri'shnuh; Skt., "black"), the dark-complexioned god often identified as an avatar (incarnation) of Vishnu, but for many Hindus more important than Vishnu himself. Incarnating divine love (*prema*) and beauty together with a fascinating quality of effortless play (*lila*), Krishna has in recent centuries been worshiped primarily as a mischievous child and peerless lover. In earlier centuries, didactic and heroic aspects were more prominent.

The earlier Krishna is often known by the patronymic Vasudeva, a title he bears as head of the Vrishni lineage of Mathura, a city on the Jumna River. Vasudeva Krishna's principal deeds are to wrest Mathura's throne from Kamsa, a usurping kinsman; to battle Jarasandha, king of Magadha, for control of Mathura (Krishna apparently loses); to move westward to coastal Dvaraka, where he establishes his own dynasty; and to counsel his cousins, the Pandavas, in the epic *Mahabharata*.

Yet Krishna has another side: Gopala ("the cowherd"), a persona that seems quite distinct from Vasudeva Krishna in early texts and sculptures. The texts show how Krishna was born into the Vrishni lineage in Mathura, but go on to explain that he was immediately adopted by the Abhira herders of the surrounding Braj countryside, there to remain throughout his childhood and youth. Krishna's idyllic life in Braj ends only when he returns to Mathura to kill Kamsa; there his maturity begins.

In the *Bhagavad Gita,* a portion of the *Mahabharata,* Vasudeva Krishna is celebrated as the supreme divinity. Joining the *Mahabharata's* battle not as a combatant but as an adviser (to his Pandava cousin Arjuna), he is not implicated in the conflict, but transcends it. Arjuna, by cultivating an equanimity that his reliance upon Krishna makes possible, learns to transcend the world, though his involvement in its struggles continues.

Later, in the *Bhagavata Purana,* another theology of Krishna's supremacy appears, this time in relation to Krishna Gopala. The mischievous, amorous cowherd manifests his transcendence by dancing with all the cowherd maidens (*gopis*) of Braj in such a way that each feels she alone holds his attentions. As with Arjuna, the importance of any worldly involvement is relativized.

Krishna's supremacy has also been experienced as cosmic victor. Since Gupta times (fourth–sixth centuries) one sees this in two images: Krishna lifting Mt. Govardhana to protect his Braj companions from the storms of Indra, captain of the Vedic pantheon, and taming the black snake Kaliya, who infiltrated the Jumna. Indra's threat comes from the waters above, Kaliya's from the waters below. In defeating them, Krishna subjects the entire universe to his control. *See also* avatar; Bhagavad Gita; lila; Mahabharata; Vaishnavism; Vishnu.

Krishnamurti, Jiddu (krish-nah-muhr'tee; 1895–1989), world leader to the Hindu-inspired Theosophists. Disavowing his role as leader and its personal power, Krishnamurti urged followers to transcend the limits of religious doctrines and organizations in their quest for universal truths. Rather than submit to another for spiritual guidance, Krishnamurti taught that each person must begin with a sense of inner freedom and build from intellectual knowledge to limitless and timeless perception. His teachings are not well known, despite their preservation in writing and through a few remaining Krishnamurti Institutes in the United States and the United Kingdom; rather, Krishnamurti has, since his death, become something of a New Age icon: the great leader who declined to benefit from his spiritual mastery. *See also* Theosophy.

Kronos, father of the king of the Greek gods, Zeus, who was overthrown by the latter. Kronos had overthrown and castrated his own father, Ouranos ("Heaven"). The Roman equivalent was Saturn. *See also* Hesiod.

Kshatriya. *See* caste.

Kshitigarbha (kshi-ti-gahr'bah; Skt., "earth-womb"), one of the "celestial" Bodhisattvas of Mahayana Buddhism. In East Asian folk religion, Kshitigarbha (Chin. *Ti-tsang;* Jap. *Jizo*) stands at the gates of hell to guide and console the dead as they suffer the travails of the underworld. He is guardian of crossroads, and hence of travelers and pilgrims. He is also the protector of children. *See also* Bodhisattvas; Jizo.

Kuan-ti (gwahn-dee; Chin., "Emperor Kuan"), deity of martial virtues in Chinese popular religion. A deified third-century hero, he protects against evil spirits. *See also* Chinese myth; Chinese popular religion.

Kuan-yin (gwahn-yin; Chin., "one who hears sounds"), Bodhisattva originally known in Indian texts as Avalokiteshvara and described in the *Lotus Sutra* as a merciful character capable of saving all living beings from suffering and danger. Also known as Kuan-shih-yin, he is a male figure until the T'ang dynasty (618–907), when iconographical images of a white-robed female began to appear. The gender switch was most likely a result of Tantric influence, in which compassion was visualized as a female god. An object of popular devotion and cultic activity, Kuan-yin took on many devotional images and became particularly associated with the power to grant children. *See also* Avalokiteshvara; Bodhisattvas; China, Buddhism in; Miao Shan.

kuei (gway; Chin., "ghost," "demon"), malevolent spiritual entities in Chinese popular religion, contrasted with *shen,* beneficent spirits. The malignant *kuei* are generally believed to be souls that are restless because of untimely or violent deaths, inauspiciously sited graves, or ancestral neglect. While the shen are honored and invoked in worship, the kuei must be propitiated, repelled, or exorcised. They may be responsible for misfortune, illness, or death. One of the most important ceremonies in the Chinese religious year is the Ghost Festival, when the gates of hell are opened and the kuei, free to roam, receive special offerings. *See also* Chinese popular religion; Ghost Festival; shen.

Kukai (koo-kah-ee; 774–835), founder of the Japanese Buddhist Shingon school. Also known as Kobo Daishi, he traveled to China at the same time as Saicho, but Kukai went to the capital, Ch'ang-an, to study Tantric Buddhism, while Saicho went to Mt. T'ien-t'ai. Although Kukai was supposed to study in China for twenty years, he returned to Japan after two and a half years and established Shingon centers at Toji, Todaiji, and Mt. Koya. He eventually won fame for his literary style, calligraphy, and mastery of Tantric Buddhist doctrine and practice. Among his major works are the *Benkenmitsu nikyoron* (Treatise on Distinguishing Exoteric and Tantric Teachings), *Jujushinron* (The Ten Stages of the Development of the Mind), and *Sokushin jobutsugi* (Realization of Buddhahood in This Very Body). *See also* Esoteric Buddhism in China; Koya, Mt.; Shingon-shu; Todaiji.

Kukjagam. *See* academies (Korea), private and public.

kuksa. *See* National Teacher.

Kumano, Mt. (*koo*-mah-noh), site of three Shinto shrines identified in the Heian period (794–1185) with the Buddhist Pure Land and made into a major pilgrimage center. *See also* mountains, sacred; pilgrimage; Pure Land.

Kumarajiva (*koo*-mah-rah-jee'vah; 344–413), Kuchean Buddhist translator who led an extensive translation project in the Chinese capital of Ch'ang-an between 402 and 413. Well versed in doctrine, he preferred Mahayana texts and was responsible for the introduction of Nagarjuna's Madhyamaka teachings to China. The Madhyamaka developed as the San-lun, or "Three Treatises," school, which was carried out mostly by Kumarajiva's disciples and which taught the basic doctrine of emptiness (Skt. *shunyata*). Although the school enjoyed a certain presence during the fifth century, and briefly revived under Chi-tsang (549–623), the dialectical system of Nagar-juna never took firm root on Chinese soil and the school died out. *See also* China, Buddhism in; Madhyamaka; San-lun school.

Kumbha Mela (*koom'buh meh'lah*; Skt., "pot festival"), Hindu bathing fair held every three or four years at one of four places in northern India (Haridvar, Prayag, Vjjain, Nasik) where divine nectar is said to have fallen from a heavenly pot. Occurring once in twelve years, the Maha, or Great Kumbha Mela, at Prayag draws thousands of mendicants and millions of lay pilgrims in the world's largest religious gathering. *See also* ablution; pilgrimage.

kundalini (*koon-duh-lee'nee*; Skt., "coiled one"), in Hindu and Buddhist Tantrism, the latent and highly potent spiritual energy resting at the base of the spine. Often depicted as a serpent sleep-ing coiled three and a half times around a Shiva linga in the *muladhara*, or base *chakra* (energy vortex), this power (*shakti*) is awakened by the initiatory power of the *guru* (spiritual leader) and is said to move upward "like lightning" through the various chakras to reunion with Shiva at the top of the head. The yogic uncoiling of this energy produces the transformative, meditational states of tantric mysticism. *See also* chakras; Tantra.

Kunering. *See* John Canoe festival.

kung-an (*gong'ahn*; Chin., "public case"), anecdotes or stories of question-and-answer sessions between Chinese Ch'an Buddhist masters and their disciples. Devised as pedagogical tools, *kung-ans* pose paradoxical questions or problems, the nonintellectual, nonconceptual resolution of which represents a spiritual breakthrough. Kung-ans were collected and published during the Sung dynasty (960–1279). *See also* Blue Cliff Record; Ch'an school.

kung-fu (*goong-foo*; Chin., "work accomplished"), Chinese term connoting accomplishment or skill resulting from time and effort spent in working toward mastering a specific activity or reaching a particular goal. The term frequently signifies "martial arts" in general, a discipline that often reflects Taoist and/or Buddhist elements. *See also* martial arts.

kungmu. *See* National Shaman.

K'un-lun (*kuhn-luhn*), famous Chinese mythical mountain in the far west that was the paradise abode of the Queen Mother of the West; it is an important symbol in Taoism, equivalent to the Buddhist Mt. Sumeru (Meru), or cosmological "world mountain." *See also* cosmology; Hsi Wang-mu; Meru, Mt.; paradise.

Kuo Hsiang (*gwoh shahng*; d. 312), a figure of the Taoist Hsuan-hsueh movement who combined Taoist naturalism with Confucian ethics. *See also* Hsuan-hsueh.

ku poison (*goo*; Chin., "insanity," "poison"), ancient Chinese term for an especially potent poison made from the distillate of various poisonous insects sealed in a vessel for a year. *See also* shamanism.

Kurozumikyo (*ku-ro-zu-mee-kyor*), a Japanese new religion founded by Kurozumi Munetada, a Shinto priest in rural Okayama prefecture. In 1814, after losing both parents and falling ill,

Kurozumi prayed to the sun deity Amaterasu and had a revelation that the human and divine were one. Out of his teachings developed Kurozumikyo, which sees Amaterasu as the guiding spirit of the universe. *See also* Japan, new religions in.

Kurukshetra   (kuh-ruh-kshe'trah), a town in northern India eighty miles north of New Delhi, the site of the eighteen-day battle of the Hindu epic poem *Mahabharata*. *See also* Mahabharata.

kut   (koot), Korean rituals that fall outside Buddhism, Confucianism, Taoism, and other more traditional religions. These rites are generally called folk rites but are more precisely called shamanic rites (*kut*). The most common are the kut to the tutelary spirits of the mountains and rivers, kut to tutelary spirits of villages and towns, and kut for relief from natural disasters. Also, when a household is plagued by misfortune, a kut can be performed to appease the household god or gods that have been offended.

The occasion for the performance of a kut is some form of pollution, where normal conditions have been disrupted and communication with the spirits will lead to a resolution. The order of the kut involves a cleansing of the ritual space, an invocation of the gods through song, dance, and dramatic narrative (which may also lead to an ecstatic possession of the shaman), an offering of food and wine, an oracular pronouncement by the shaman explaining the causes of the pollution and how it is to be dealt with, and a dispatching of or settling with the gods with assurances that conditions have been resolved.

The most prominent types of kut include the Naerimkut, which is used to inititate a new shaman and cure her of the illness that comes from an unacknowledged possession; the Changsungje kut, which is performed every three years at the New Year to renew the power of the spirit posts (*ch'onha taejanggun*) that protect most villages; the Kolmaegikut, which is performed to rid a house or village of ghosts; the Nokkut, which is used to guide the spirits of the dead into the other world; and the Chesukut, which is used to promote the welfare of the living and to promote village harmony. *See also* shamanism.

Kuttab.   *See* Qur'an school.

Kuya   (koo-yah; 903–972), a wandering Japanese Pure Land Buddhist monk (*hijiri*) who propagated the *nembutsu* (recitation of Buddha's name) in cities, often teaching people to chant while dancing (*nembutsu odori*). Also known as Koya, he was probably the first person to spread the nembutsu among the masses as a simple declaration of faith rather than as a magical formula to vanquish bad *karma* or as an aid to meditation. *See also* karma; nembutsu; nembutsu odori; Pure Land.

Kwanzaa   (kwahn'zah; possibly from Swahili, "firstfruit of harvest"), an African-American holiday celebrated December 26 through January 1. It was created by Maulana Karenga and first celebrated in San Diego, California (1966).

The seven-day family festival centers around seven symbols: a straw table mat (*mkeka*) on which the other objects are placed; fruits and vegetables (*mazao*), which symbolize the results of collective labor; ears of corn (*muhindi*), one for each child in the family; a libation cup (*kikombe cha umoja*) for the ancestors and communal drinking; gifts, to be distributed on the seventh day; and a candleholder (*kinara*) to hold seven candles (*mishumaa saba*), three red, one black, and three green, each signifying one of the "seven principles" (*nguzo saba*)—unity, self-determination, collective work and responsibility, cooperative economics, purpose, creativity, and faith—each featured on one of the days.

Each day, the celebrants greet one another with the question, What is the news? The proper response is the name of the appropriate principle for the day.

The sixth day is the climactic moment of the ritual, with a communal feast; music, addresses, and honoring of elders.

kwisin.   *See* ghost.

Kyodan, Nihon Kirisuto   (kyoh-dahn, nee-hon kee-ree-soo-toh; Jap., "Japan Christian Church"), the united denomination formed of most Protestant denominations in Japan during World War II; after the war some withdrew, but today it remains the largest Protestant denomination in Japan.

Kyoto   (kyoh-toh), ancient capital of Japan in the Heian era (794–1185; then known as Heiankyo) and the home of the imperial court from 794 to 1868; located on the southern part of Honshu Island, it has many historical sites, temples, and shrines and is home to many traditional festivals and arts. *See also* Heian period.

ABCDEF
GHIJKL
M   Q
R   V
WXY&Z

Labyrinth, the maze in which the legendary king of ancient Crete, Minos, kept the Minotaur, who was half man, half bull. The monster was killed by the Athenian hero Theseus, aided by the king's daughter, Ariadne. The plan of the Bronze Age palace of Knossos may have given rise to the story. *See also* Cycladic religion; Knossos; Minoan religion.

Ladino (Lat. *latínus*), language of the Sephardic Jews who have their roots in Spain. It is essentially the Spanish that was spoken in the Iberian Peninsula in the fifteenth century. It serves the same purpose for its speakers as Yiddish does for Ashkenazic Jews in that it is a *lingua franca* and a complement to the native tongue of the country of residence, from which words and phrases are borrowed and integrated into the Spanish base.

The evolution of Ladino is the opposite of that of Yiddish, which started out as a dialectical variant and then developed into a literary language. Conversely, Ladino originated in the rich, cultured idiom of medieval Spain and became impoverished until it reached its present status as a dialect with regional differences.

In Spain Ladino was basically the same language spoken by the Christians interspersed with Hebrew words, especially in matters related to Judaism: holy days, birth, circumcision, marriage, death. Until World War II Hebrew characters were used in writing; today it is written in Latin characters, often transcribed according to the language of the host country. Both Hebrew and Ladino are used in the Sephardic synagogue and for Sabbath prayers. *See also* Sephardi.

laity, those members of Christian churches who are not formally ordained for ministerial positions in the church. *See also* clergy.

lama (lahm′ah), in Tibetan Buddhism anyone regarded as a teacher by virtue of spiritual attainments; or, more broadly, anyone who has completed a specified period of training. A lama need not be a monk or nun, and not all clergy are lamas. *See also* Dalai Lama; Tibetan religions.

Lamb of God. *See* Agnus Dei.

language, sacred, the language used in the primary religious traditions or texts and understood to be that spoken by the god(s). It is employed in rituals, at times in opposition to vernacular speech. *See also* Adi Granth; Arabic; Hebrew language; holy books; Pali; Sanskrit; Shrivaishnavism; vernacular.

Lantern Festival, Chinese festival of the fifteenth day of the first month, marking the end of the New Year's festivities. In recent centuries it became only an opportunity to view and display a wide variety of colorful lanterns. *See also* Chinese religions (festal cycle); New Year (China).

Lao-chun (lou-juhn; Chin., "Lord Lao"), along with T'ai-shang Lao-chun ("Most High Lord Lao"), an appellation of the deified Lao-tzu in the Taoist religion. Lord Lao appeared on earth to transmit texts and authenticate the legitimacy of certain Chinese dynasties. *See also* Lao-tzu; Taoism.

Lao-tzu (lou-dzuh), the patriarch of Taoism, the patron of the Taoist religion and founder of philosophical Taoism, and the author of the *Tao-te ching* (Book of the Way and Its Power, also known as the *Lao-tzu,* mid-fourth century B.C.), one of the preeminent Taoist classics. Whether a historical Lao-tzu actually existed is unknown. He is said to have written the *Tao-te ching* at the request of a border guard as he traveled west out of China. The *Tao-te ching* is a brief, obscure philosophical work stressing acquiescence to the way of nature rather than to society. Some feel, however, that it was meant to influence politics, advocating governance through passive means.

Lao-tzu later (traditionally in 142) appeared in deified form before Chang Tao-ling and transmitted divine revelations that revitalized Taoism. Subsequent second-century texts record his appearances before sage-kings under various names. He was also said to have converted the barbarians to Taoism on his travels west by becoming the Buddha. Other incarnations include Mani (216–274, Persian founder of Manichaeism) and, in one version of his birth, his own mother. His family name, Li, was identical to that of the T'ang-dynasty (618–907) ruling family, helping to put Taoism in favor during that time. *See also* Chang Tao-ling; Taoism; Tao-te ching.

Lares (lah′rays), divinities of the ancient Roman household, who, together with the Penates and Vesta, formed the nucleus of family worship. *See also* Roman religion.

Last Judgment, a nonbiblical Christian term commonly referring to the anticipated judging of peoples or individuals, the living and the dead, by God or Christ at the close of history. The biblical "day of the Lord" or "day of judgment" refers to the (usually imminent) coming of God, the Messiah, or the Son of Man to punish the evil and redeem the righteous. In Christian tradition, Matthew 25:31–46 and the Book of Revelation have influenced poets and artists as well as theologians to elaborate a picture of the end-time apportioning of eternal rewards and punishments. *See also* eschatology.

last sheave ritual. *See* harvest rituals.

Last Supper, the New Testament narrative of the last meal Jesus ate with his disciples prior to his arrest, trial, and crucifixion. It is important for the words of eucharistic institution identifying his body and blood with bread and wine.

Lateran Councils, a series of five ecumenical Catholic councils held at the Lateran Basilica in Rome between the twelfth and the sixteenth centuries. The last two are given special status. The Fourth Lateran (Twelfth Ecumenical) Council (1215) represents the high point in medieval papal legislation. Important decrees include its teachings on transubstantiation, the reform of Church order, and its requirements involving the yearly reception of the Eucharist and yearly confession. The Fifth Lateran (Eighteenth Ecumenical) Council (1512–17) is known for its condemnation of the conciliar decrees of Constance and Basel, which made church councils superior to the pope, and its rejection of the Pragmatic Sanction of Bourges, which made the pope's jurisdiction subject to the will of a king. Although aware of widespread abuse, the Council failed to enact measures that would ensure Church reform and is therefore associated with the conditions that led to the Reformation.

Latter-day Saints, Church of Jesus Christ of, also known as the Mormon Church, or LDS, a Christian body, American in origin but global in constituency, that considers the authority of the church to have been lost from the second century to the 1820s. Basing its teaching and practice on the message of and through Jesus, it believes that the 1820s "latter day" revelation restored the true church.

The signal event of the postbiblical age, the Restoration, occurred through the divine revelation given to Joseph Smith, Jr., in 1820 (when he was fourteen) on his family's farm near Palmyra, New York. He was visited by two divine personages, who announced that he must not join any existing sect and that, by implication, a "sect to end all sects" existed and was emerging. In 1823, the angel of the prophet Moroni (son of Mormon who died about 400) appeared to Smith to tell him that records written on gold plates,

along with two special stones to help in the translation from "Reformed Egyptian," were buried in a nearby hill. He found those stones four years later, discovered (recovered) as the *Book of Mormon*. It was published in 1830, and the new/old church was organized with new adherents almost immediately active overseas as well as at home.

The story within the *Book of Mormon* bridges the faithful, authoritative church of the apostolic age—before the apostasy—and the Restoration in the "latter days" in America. It recounts the history of a tribe of ancient Israelites who sailed eastward to the American hemisphere about 600 B.C. They maintained a civilization in the Americas for centuries and were visited by the resurrected Christ. This civilization came to an end in the time of Mormon and his son Moroni when one of the two peoples, the Lamanites, ancestors of Native Americans, triumphed over the other, the Nephites, the people of righteousness. Moroni buried this sacred history recorded by his father; it remained sealed and hidden in the earth for over fourteen centuries.

Christ, the Bible, and America are basic to Mormon thought. So too is the symbology of Israel, a chosen people who wander, are buffeted, and finally settle. The people to whom this special vision was granted were Israelites. After centuries of tribulations, that vision came into focus through Joseph Smith, the young "prophet, seer, and revelator."

History: The Joseph Smith story is Abrahamic. But Smith, after leading the Saints to Kirtland, Ohio, Jackson County, Missouri, and Nauvoo, Illinois, was murdered by an anti-Mormon mob while in jail in 1844. The "Moses" of the movement, Brigham Young, rallied the Saints and led them to the Salt Lake Valley, which he knew to be "Zion."

Earlier the independent state of Deseret, the Mormon homeland became the American state of Utah in 1896. The original Temple, sacred space to which only members of the church are admitted, and the famous Tabernacle stand on Temple Square in Salt Lake City. As the church's headquarters, that city is the center of education, welfare, and missionary activities, and genealogical research as well, all of them highly organized and extensive.

Latter-day Saints live out of a history and by written authority: biblical history and Restoration history through the Bible and the *Book of Mormon* (also *The Pearl of Great Price* [1842] and *Doctrines and Covenants* [1835]). They are very much a people; the sense of community that binds them is powerful. In 1988, United States membership stood at 4.5 million; outside the land of origin, membership was 2.5 million with most notable strength in Mesoamerica, Asia, the South Pacific Islands, Great Britain, and Scandinavia. At any given time, more than thirty-five thousand missionaries are at work.

Not all Mormons belong to the Utah-based church. The "Reorganized Church of Jesus Christ of Latter-day Saints," with offices in Independence, Missouri, reports a quarter million members. It claims to be the continuation of the original church founded by Smith, all of its presidents having been his descendants. Three smaller bodies also make up the Mormon family: Temple Lot, Bickertonites, and Strangites.

Authority and Ethics: In the Mormon tradition the offices of the First Presidency and the Twelve Apostles, a total of fifteen men, speak for the church and oversee it. The president of the church has the highest rank of "prophet, seer, and revelator"; as such he issues official pronouncements that have a binding quality.

Mormon ethics centers on the family. The role of parents is promoted with the greatest earnestness; children are taught godly ways and discipline. Mormon family units are large. One reason is the theological teaching of premortal existence; existent spirits are waiting to be born.

Marriage has two forms: for time, the conventional Christian marriage that terminates at death; and for eternity. Ideally a couple chooses marriage "for eternity," that is, sealed by the proper ceremony in a temple. This makes the couple eligible for the highest opportunity for salvation. Marriages may also be performed, vicariously, by the living, for those who have died without the opportunity to accept Mormon teachings when alive. Here one encounters another distinctive Mormon teaching, degrees of progression in eternity, ultimately becoming like God himself, a doctrine rooted in the nature of human beings as "gods in embryo."

Bound with these is the issue of Mormon exclusivism. The Saints are vigorous proselytizers. At the same time, the church teaches the eventual salvation of all, a condition facilitated by the opportunity for growth in the afterlife.

Polygamous marriage is largely passe to the church. This practice began with Joseph Smith in 1843, expanded slowly, then was openly acknowledged at a general church conference in 1852. Plural marriage has been forbidden since the Woodruff Manifesto of 1890 (though a very small number still practice it).

LaVey, Anton Szandor (b. 1930), founder of the

Church of Satan, in San Francisco on Walpurgis Night (April 30), 1966, and author of *The Satanic Bible* (1969), *The Compleat Witch* (1970), and *The Satanic Rituals* (1972). *See also* Satanic churches in America; Satanism.

law and religion (in the United States). The interrelationship of law and religion inevitably depends upon their societal context. A given culture necessarily affects both the character of its law, the character of its religion, and the mode of interaction between them. The United States provides an especially valuable microcosm within which to view these two highly visible and influential institutions, first because of the peculiar history of each in American life, and second because developments in recent years are encouraging them to work together in seeking the common good for their society.

Early Developments: The positivistic character of law in the West, which followed from its removal from ecclesiastical control, was from the beginning part of the worldview of American lawyers, trained as they were in the tradition of English common law. British legal philosopher John Austin (1790–1859), who formulated a theory of positivism in the early 1800s, saw law as a brute social fact based on power, which in turn could be exercised for good or ill. For him laws were coercive commands, whether they be wise or foolish, just or unjust. Law did not necessarily serve the common good, nor was it always designed to do so. U.S. Supreme Court Justice Oliver Wendell Holmes, Jr. (1841–1935), who continued Austin's jurisprudence, defined law as prophesies of what the courts will do in fact and nothing more. For legal positivists of the last century, law was thus law as it is, not law as it ought to be: it represented simply what a society was like at any particular time in its history.

The positivists shaped American legal education to correspond with their understanding of law. The result was to produce lawyers who by and large deeply distrusted generalizations and had little or no concern for the larger social issues involved in reaching legal decisions. Legal realists, on the other hand, who became the twentieth-century heirs of the positivists, readily acknowledged that law can never be isolated from economic, political, and cultural developments, but they could see no place in legal education for any critical judgment on the social values responsible for such development, because such values were by definition unanalyzable, nothing more than inscrutable expressions of personal preference. The task of the lawyer was thus to focus exclusively on the data of a particular case, and to analyze, classify, and systematize only these data. This obviously gave lawyers great skill in dealing with complex detail, but it did little to develop social consciousness and concern.

Legal realism has recently generated a more radical form of itself: the critical legal studies movement. Critical legal theory rejects the notion of law as value-free and somehow above political, economic, and social considerations. It insists that law actually embodies the dominant values of society, and only seems to be neutral and independent. It therefore lends legitimacy to whatever values and mores predominate at any given time. This movement underlines what legal historians have been saying for some time: law is a creature of society; when society changes, law changes.

Religion in America, like law, has had its own peculiar history. When the Founders formulated the religion clauses of the First Amendment, religious pluralism had been flourishing for some time in the Colonies. These clauses were conceived as the legal recognition of an actual state of things, as well as an effort to strengthen the new nation by excluding from government concern all religious differences among its people. This legal acceptance of religious pluralism meant that Americans gave up the notion, generally accepted at the time, that a government had to use its coercive power to inculcate whatever shared religious belief it thought essential for its well-being. Rejecting establishment in favor of persuasion thus proved to be an original political ingredient of the new nation. Americans were the first people in history to realize that religious solidarity was not needed to stabilize the social order.

There was an immediate gain for religion here. Law now guaranteed the freedom of every religious group from interference by government as well as by other religious groups. Since no single church was to be established, it was to the self-interest of each to be tolerant of all in order to continue to experience toleration for itself. This meant that the chief characteristic of the churches was their voluntarism. Because the whole strength of an individual church rested upon those people freely consenting to belong to it, its form was usually extremely flexible, reflecting the moods and sentiments of the nation at any given time. Whenever there were shifts in prevailing social attitudes, religious styles and loyalties tended to shift too.

Religious symbols thus became highly adaptable and resilient. Mainline religious institutions could move either toward a more prophetic public stance or toward a more accommodating private stance, depending on the changing moods and disposition of its members and the populace as a whole. Disestablishment and voluntarism meant a pluralism of religious commitments, with no unifying set of beliefs or ideals held by all. Multiple worldviews and multiple value systems could now coexist in peace. This situation is in the 1990s engendering an unusual dynamism in the churches as well as the beginnings of a deprivatizing impulse rarely seen in mainline American religion. It is also making religious leaders aware of the cultural need for religion to take the initiative in its relationship with law.

Contemporary Interaction: Interactions between law and religion were not frequent in America's past. From the time the new nation was founded, religious institutions were generally convinced that their most important public role consisted in exercising the freedom guaranteed them by law to believe, teach, and worship as they chose. In exercising this freedom each church accepted its exercise also by every other church, thereby acknowledging the right of all citizens to be nourished religiously in any way they wished. The resulting pluralism not only individualized religious membership but also privatized religious experience. To guarantee that government would not interfere with such privacy, religious bodies were scrupulous on their part not to interfere with government.

Such infrequent interaction in the past fostered unfortunate presuppositions within both institutions. Religious people usually made the mistake of presuming that church-state separation, or the separation of legal and religious institutions, had to be reflected in a separation of religious and legal values, as well as in the total secularization of legal thought. The corollary of this mistake was another: the failure to distinguish between public order on the one hand, reflecting the coercive aspects of law, and the common good on the other hand, entrusted both to law and to other institutions, an arena where they all interact with each other in a context of pluralism and free public debate.

The legal mind had its own presuppositions. It found it extremely difficult to distinguish moral values from moral absolutes. For positivists, genuinely shared meanings in public life could be reached only by fiat. Hence the entry of religious groups into the civil arena was always equated with an effort to impose some religious policy. For the positivist mind this presented a special danger to government, since by law there was no way to control what any religious group believed and taught. Disestablishment and pluralism thus inhibited both law and religion from even discussing values and commitments that could be shared in the public sphere.

Developments in recent years have begun to change this. Both institutions are now in a cultural transition. Law is becoming aware that issues of justice and equality, which face it on every side, are much more than questions of fair procedure: they involve value choices and moral commitments on the part of the nation as a whole. For the great problem of conscience today is the conflict between the egalitarian tradition and the antiegalitarianism of our economic system. Civil rights, human rights, and economic rights have consequently become the leitmotiv of growing litigation in the courts. Moral discourse is thus finding its way back into legal discourse at the very time that religious discourse is becoming less privatized and more sensitive to the common good.

This growing religious concern for the common good is due chiefly to a widespread recovery of the prophetic tradition. This tradition most often operates at the periphery of American religion, moving toward the center only when some concrete social structure is clearly seen to deny justice to a certain segment of society. This was the case when strong religious support was enlisted for the abolition of slavery in the nineteenth century and for the growth of labor unions in the early twentieth. The tradition fell into decline, however, and remained so until rekindled in the 1960s by Martin Luther King, Jr.'s (1929–68), prophetic call to end racial segregation and to recognize the dignity of all black Americans.

In the 1990s the tradition is making itself felt strongly again, in the sanctuary movement for those fleeing oppression in Latin America; in the advocacy of civil rights for homosexuals and equal rights for women; in denunciation of nuclear arsenals, hard-core pornography, and capital punishment; in national efforts to arouse concern for the plight of the poor, homeless, and elderly. Along with movements on both sides of the abortion question, all these foci of economic and social justice involve law. As a result, advocates of the tradition are finding themselves constantly calling upon law to assert its civic and social responsibility.

Religion's sharpened focus upon the common good has been paralleled by a developing sense of social responsibility on the part of law. While the legal profession has always functioned to some extent as an interactive structure in society, able to influence life in business, govern-

ment, and local communities, legal positivists and realists have never felt at home with concepts like "the common good." While their highly individualistic professionalism argued for law's value neutrality, their skepticism usually looked upon morals as no more than officially established mores. This moral aloofness has been receding for some time. In the face of the nation's moral pluralism, value choices for the larger society have gradually come to be synonymous with legal choices. Whenever customary norms break down, Americans always turn to law, forcing it to fill the vacuum. As other authorities weaken, law by default assumes a commanding importance, the final way out of dilemmas stemming from moral as well as political controversy.

The 1990s present a new phase in the relationship between religion and law in America, wherein both are seeking by civil argument to develop strategies and to support public commitments that are larger than individual preferences. Both are now searching for some new social ethic, for ways to understand anew what is right and wrong for the community as a whole. Perhaps the most important advantage of such civil argument is that religious groups will inevitably become more realistic about the consequences of disestablishment and pluralism. For it is the very nature of a secularized society like the United States to be complex and contradictory in regard to shared meanings.

Precisely because such a society does not respond to any single organizing principle, the differences between religious and legal values will always lack the rigidity implied by terms like *separation of church and state* and *autonomy of the secular*. The capacity of each of these institutions to interact with the other is now high. But religious readings of social reality are still much more likely to be met with sharp critique than with passive tolerance. Hence there can be no simple or completely stable relationship between religion and law, even though in a given situation today the dialogue and its results may be quite satisfying for both. *See also* church and state; state religion.

Law [of Moses]. *See* Torah.

LDS. *See* Latter-day Saints, Church of Jesus Christ of.

lectionary, the fixed cycle of public readings of holy books on ritual occasions.

Lee, Ann (1736–84), woman who brought Shakerism, a Christian communtarian group, from England to America in 1774. Known as Mother Ann, she was believed to be the embodiment of the female principle in Christ, as Jesus was the embodiment of the masculine. *See also* Shakers.

left. *See* right, left.

Legalist school. *See* Fa-chia.

legend, a popular, anonymous narrative. Legend is often distinguished from myth by scholars who claim that it possesses some factual or historical base.

Legio Maria. *See* Africa, new religions in.

Lei Feng (lay feng), young soldier-worker who was a paragon of virtue during the Maoist period (1966–76); he was known for selfless devotion to the Communist party and the people. *See also* Maoism.

Lei-kung (lay-guhng; Chin., "Duke of Thunder"), a fierce deity with drum, mallet, and dagger in Chinese popular religion; he is often associated with the Mother of Lightning. *See also* Chinese popular religion.

lemures (le'moor-ays), ancient Roman ghosts believed to return to harm the living. Three festivals occurred in May to propitiate and honor them.

Lemuria (le-muhr'ee-ah), a lost island said to have existed in the Pacific or Indian Ocean. Similar in image to Atlantis, Lemuria, or Mu, was the home for transcendent beings who now seek to aid human spiritual understanding. Authors since the 1920s have linked it with the biblical garden of Eden and ancient American civilizations. *See also* Atlantis.

Lenshina, Alice Mulenga (len-shee'nah; ca. 1924–78), an African, Bemba woman thought to be a messiah. After a near-death series of visions commanding her to teach an apocalyptic Christian message, she required her followers to abandon all community responsibilities and reject secular authority. The Zambian government imprisoned many of her followers and banned her church. *See also* Africa, new religions in.

Lent (Mid. Eng., "springtime"), the forty days (excepting Sundays) of penance and fasting that precedes Easter in the Roman Catholic, Orthodox, Anglican, and some Protestant churches. *See also* calendar (Christian); Christianity (festal cycle).

Levi (lay-vee'; Heb.), alleged, usually eponymous, descendant of the tribe of Levi. Because Levites served under the priests in ancient Israel, in the synagogue service a Levi is privileged to be called second, after the priest (*kohen*), to read from the Torah scroll and washes the hands of the priests before the priestly benediction. *See also* Judaism, prayer and liturgy of.

li (lee; Chin., "principle," "reason"), a key concept in Neo-Confucian thought. It refers to the metaphysical principles at the foundation of the physical and moral universe. While *ch'i* refers to the "stuff" out of which the universe is formed, *li* is the order and coherence of the universe. The importance of li as a concept reaches its peak in the philosophy of Chu Hsi (1130–1200), who says, "if we are to pin down the word li, neither existence nor nonexistence can be attributed to it. For before Heaven and Earth existed, it already was as it is." *See also* ch'i; Neo-Confucianism.

li (lee; Chin., "ritual," "mores," "ceremony," "propriety"), a central concept in Confucianism. The origins of the term are to be found in reference to religious ceremonies and rites. Confucianism generalizes *li* such that it applies to virtually every aspect of social interaction. In this sense, community is viewed as sacred rite. While li provides the structure or form for social interaction, it is benevolence or reciprocity (*jen*) that transforms that structure into a moral system. *See also* Chinese ritual; Confucianism; jen.

liang-chih (leeahng-juhr; Chin., "innate knowledge"), a Neo-Confucian method of insight into the fundamental mind needed to realize innate knowledge and extend moral action. In the School of Mind (Hsin-hsueh), it reveals the fundamental mind as the unity of knowledge and action and seeks for each individual the extension of the knowledge of the good to the utmost limits of humanity. *See also* Hsin-hsueh; Neo-Confucianism.

Li Ao (lee ou; fl. 798), prominent T'ang-dynasty forerunner of the Sung-dynasty Neo-Confucian revival. He stressed the rectification of the mind by means of self-actualization based on the *Chung Yung* (Doctrine of the Mean). *See also* Chung Yung; Neo-Confucianism.

libation, ritual pouring out of a liquid as an offering.

libationers. *See* chi-chiu.

Liberal Catholic Church, a movement founded in England in 1915 and brought soon after to Australia, New Zealand, and the United States, which combines the Old Catholic emphasis on sacraments and the episcopate with theosophical teaching. The church has more than five thousand members in the United States, many of whom are also Theosophists. *See also* Old Catholic Churches; Theosophy.

liberal Judaism. *See* Reform Judaism.

liberation (Skt. *moksha, mukti*), in Hinduism, release from the cycle of birth and death (*samsara*). Liberation is considered by some traditions the ultimate goal of human life, but there are substantial differences in opinion on the nature of the liberated state as well as the paths that lead to it. While some traditions accept removal of ignorance and self-perfection through knowledge to be the way to *moksha*, others believe in the salvific grace of a loving deity to be the only way by which one is lifted out of the cycles of rebirth. Fundamental to these ideas is the notion of *karma*, or action. Actions, especially those caused by desire, lead to merit and demerit, which bind one to the cycle of life and death. Removal of the karma accumulated over countless lifetimes leads to liberation from the painful cycle of rebirth. Liberation, in some contexts, is also perceived to be opposed to *dharma*, the injunctions of righteous and dutiful actions that maintain the cosmic and social orders but that nevertheless give rise to further karma.

Early Views of Liberation—Vedas and the Upanishads: In the earliest literature of the Vedas (1500 B.C.), the human soul is portrayed as being with its ancestors in the afterlife. Notions of rebirth and liberation are not found in the earliest Vedic strata but appear for the first time in the Upanishads, composed around the sixth century B.C. Here, ideas that are continuous with later formulations of liberation first begin to surface. The soul is considered to be immortal; it is unborn and eternal and does not die when the body perishes (*Katha Upanishad* 1.2.19). Quelling of desires is said to lead to immortality. In a famous passage (*Brihadaranyaka Upanishad* 1.3.28) the petitioner asks to be led from unreality to reality, darkness to light, and death to immortality. The supreme being, *brahman*, is said to be all-pervasive and beyond the senses, mind, intelligence, the great soul, and that which is unmanifest; one who knows this supreme being becomes liberated and immortal

(*Katha Upanishad* 2.3.7–8). Through the phrase *tat tvam asi* ("that you are"), one that reverberates in Indian philosophy for generations, the human soul is considered to be either identical to, sharing the essence of, or being inseparable from brahman. Experiential knowledge of this relationship is considered liberation.

Liberation in the Bhagavad Gita: In philosophical traditions like Samkhya-Yoga that predate the *Bhagavad Gita*, liberation of the soul is through its extrication from primordial matter. In its liberated state, the soul is blissful in its splendid isolation. In later compositions like the *Bhagavad Gita* (200 B.C.–A.D. 2000), the worldview of Samkhya-Yoga is integrated into a theistic worldview. Here, Krishna reveals himself as the supreme deity, and the nature of the human soul and the disciplines to seek liberation are discussed in detail. The soul is described as casting off old bodies and taking on new ones (2:22); the disciplines of action, wisdom, and devotion as leading to liberation are extolled; and in the last chapter (18.66), Krishna assures his cousin Arjuna (and generations of future devotees) that he will liberate from all sins anyone who goes to him for refuge.

Liberation in the Schools of Vedanta: Shankara (ca. 700), a prominent interpreter of nondualistic Vedanta, portrayed this earth and life cycle as having limited reality; once the soul realizes that it is and always has been brahman, this life passes away like a dream. The soul, through the realization of its true nature, is liberated. Liberation is therefore removal of ignorance by knowledge. This can be attained in this life itself and human beings can be liberated while still embodied (*jivan mukti*); final release will come after the death of the body. Those liberated in this life itself act without binding desire and, having "crossed over," help others to achieve liberation.

Ramanuja, the eleventh-century theologian, perceives loving devotion to Vishnu to lead to release from the bonds of life and death. Vishnu, the supreme brahman, pervades all human beings and the entire universe like a soul pervades a body. Since the human soul is the body (*sharira*) and the servant (*shesha*) of the supreme being, liberation is not portrayed as the realization of identity between the two. Rather, it is the intuitive, total, and joyful realization of the soul's relationship with the lord and surpasses a lesser goal called *kaivalya*, where the soul is freed from the cycle of samsara but is aware of bliss in an isolated state. While technically kaivalya is also liberation, one is warned not to be trapped by it, because communion with the deity is said to transcend the rapture of isolation. In the devotional hymns of the Shriva-ishnava community, following the Puranic literature, Vishnu is portrayed as reigning over Vaikuntha, or heaven. The liberated human soul, after cleansing itself in the waters of the river Viraja, which encircles heaven, approaches Vishnu and his consort Shri-Lakshmi, renders loving service, and is never separated from them.

Madhva, a thirteenth-century philosopher, is unique in the Hindu traditions in classifying some souls as eternally bound; and even in liberation, there are different grades of enjoyment and bliss. Caitanya (fifteenth–sixteenth centuries) sees devotion as the only way to liberation, and moksha itself is seen as the enjoyment of an intense, passionate, physical, spiritual love of Krishna that resembles the love that the cowherd girls felt for him. Being with Krishna in the eternal paradise of Vrindavana is considered to be the ultimate goal one can reach.

Liberation in Tantric Literature: Although aspects of Tantric thought and practice are pan-Hindu or even pan-Indian phenomena, Tantric literature distinguishes itself frequently from other schools of thought. Tantrism offers ways to master "supernatural" powers and attain liberation by techniques and rituals that involve both body and mind. An important aspect of Tantric teaching is the acceptance of desire and enjoyment as playing an integral part in the path to liberation. Attainment of powers that lead to enjoyment in this world and beyond are not seen as a digression from the goal of liberation. Tantric texts are usually sectarian and notions of liberation can only be understood in terms of Vaishnava, Shaiva, or preeminently, Shakta doctrines. The Tantric believer lives in a universe filled with energy that must be used in order to attain powers or liberation. This energy, on one level, is seen in the divine potential of a human being, resident in the *kundalini* (spiritual energy at the base of the spine) or in magical diagrams, sounds, and actions. *Mantras*, or verbal formulas that have the potential to liberate, correspond to diagrams that serve as representations of the cosmos; by mental and physical processes these are internalized, meditated upon, and sometimes placed on and integrated into parts of one's body.

With the exception of Tantrism, most schools of thought perceive this world as an obstacle toward moksha. Occasionally, however, in devotional schools worship of the lord enshrined in a temple is said to impart the bliss that is generally thought of as being only available in heaven. Depending on the philosophical, liturgical, or devotional context, liberation in the Hindu tradition may either reject or embrace this world or reject or meditate on a deity outside oneself; a liberated being may still continue to live in this world or only be liberated after death of the physical body. *See also* four goals of life (Hinduism); karma; Krishna; merit; reincarnation (Hinduism, Indian); Tantrism (Hinduism); Vedanta; Vishnu.

liberation theology, thinking about God that finds its source for Christian reflection and action in the faith and life of the poorest people while using the tools of social analysis to illumine the structures of their oppression.

Liberation theology began in Latin America in the late 1960s with the work of such Catholic theologians as Gustavo Gutierrez, Jose Miguez-Bonino, and Leonardo Boff. For Gutierrez (b. 1928) the extreme poverty of Latin America is not a stage on the way to a more developed economy; it is a means to keep already developed countries rich. Therefore, the Christian theologian must begin by unmasking why people are so poor and continue by speaking God's judgment on those responsible for oppression.

The early liberation theologians, mainly European-trained, used Marxist concepts in their economic analysis, provoking criticism from some quarters. Because liberation theologians view history as being in the hands of God, they use Marxist tools for different ends than those of secular Marxists.

Since the 1970s, liberation theology has spread throughout the world. Because it requires close examination of particular social conditions, it takes on a distinct character in each region. In North America, African-American theologians such as James Cone and feminist theologians such as Letty Russell and Rosemary Radford Ruether have used its themes. In South Africa, it has addressed apartheid (the legal separation of races). Asians often call it "Minjung theology," (Kor., "poor-people theology") and value myth and story-telling over discursive argument.

Li chi (lee-jee; Chin., "Book of Rites"), classical Confucian compendium of ceremonial practice dating to the third and second centuries B.C.; it is the authoritative source for orthodox Confucian ritual. *See also* Confucianism (authoritative texts and their interpretation).

Lieh-hsien chuan (leh-shehn jwahn; Chin., "Collected Accounts of the Perfected"), early collection of biographies of Taoists who attained immortality. *See also* hagiography; hsien.

Lieh-tzu (leh-dzuh; Chin.), a Taoist philosophical text (authorship uncertain, possibly written in the third century) that expresses escapist and fatalistic aspects of Taoism. Similar to the *Chuang-tzu* in anecdotal style, the work is distinguished by its emphasis on the illusoriness of the phenomenal world. *See also* Chuang-tzu.

life-crisis rites, an alternative term for life-cycle rituals. *See also* life-cycle rituals.

life-cycle rituals, nonperiodic rituals that mark significant stages in an individual's life: birth, puberty, marriage, death. *See also* age-sets; Birth Grandmother; Buddhism (life cycle); Chinese religions (life cycle); Christianity (life cycle); dead, rituals with respect to the; death; initiation rituals; Islam (life cycle); Judaism (life cycle); marriage; naming rituals; nonperiodic rites; puberty rituals; ritual; Roman religion.

light and darkness, one of the fundamental oppositions or dualisms in religious symbolism. Though the particular identifications vary, light is always positive; darkness, negative.

lights, the use of lamps, candles, and other sources of illumination in ritual contexts. The general symbolism of light equates it with a long list of positive attributes, including life, immortality, and divine presence.

Li-hsueh (lee-shweh; Chin., "School of Principle") also called Cheng-chu, the dominant Neo-Confucian school founded by Ch'eng I and Chu Hsi. It emphasized the investigation of things (*ko-wu*) in order to discover the principle (*li*) of things. Principle itself is contrasted with vital energy (*ch'i*), which forms the material substrata of all things and persons. Li-hsueh is also the main Neo-Confucian school in Korea and Japan. *See also* Ch'eng I; ch'i; Chu Hsi; Hsin-hsueh; ko-wu; li; Neo-Confucianism.

Li Hung (lee hohng), a popular name or title among the medieval Chinese Taoist messianic movements referring to a would-be messiah and incarnation of Lao-tzu. *See also* Lao-tzu.

lila (lee'lah; Skt., "play," "drama, show," "sport," "dalliance"), a theological, dramaturgical, and aesthetic concept associated with Hinduism. It explains why a complete and self-sufficient divinity created the world. In some scriptures, the deity is understood to have been motivated not by any unfulfilled desire or lack, but by a spirit of play comparable to that of a child who becomes absorbed in a game for its own sake. Elsewhere, gods and goddesses are said to have descended to earth in order to act out their playful *lilas*, or dramas. This idea has been most thoroughly elaborated in the cult of the young Krishna, whose lilas include playing tricks on his elders, stealing butter, and enjoying adulterous liaisons with local cowherdesses: such antinomianism has stimulated much theological argument. The lilas of Krishna and other gods are described at length in numerous Hindu scriptures; celebrated by eminent medieval North Indian poets; and represented countless times in South Asian painting, sculpture, and music, and they are the subject of meditational practices wherein devotees seek to visualize, recreate, and ultimately participate in them.

Lilas are also ritual dramas, public and theatrical enactments of events in the lives of incarnate gods, in which the deities themselves are believed to be briefly embodied in the actors upon the stage. *Krishnalila* and *Ramlila* are the best-known such traditions, but dramatizations of other epics, such as the *Mahabharata*, are also found. In colloquial North Indian languages, those who "show off" or "act out" are said to be "showing their lila." The concept is also invoked to explain and compensate for unfortunate situations or events: "What can one do? It is God's lila." *See also* Hinduism (performing arts); Krishna.

Lilith (lill'ith), in Jewish popular tradition, the first wife of Adam and a demonic figure, especially known as a child stealer.

limbo (Lat. *limbus*, lit., "border," "edge"), in Roman Catholicism the place after death containing the souls of those not admitted to heaven through no fault of their own: those born before Christ and infants who died before baptism. *See also* afterlife; afterworld.

liminality. *See* ritual.

Lin Chao-en (lin jou-uhn; 1517–98), a Chinese writer, healer, and religious leader. Known as "Master of the Three Teachings," Lin used Buddhist and Taoist terms and techniques (especially Ch'an and "inner alchemy") to support Neo-Confucian goals like cultivating "the sagely mind." *See also* alchemy; Ch'an school; Neo-Confucianism.

Lin-chi (lin-jee; d. 866), Chinese Ch'an Buddhist

master of Ma-tsu's Hung-chou line who is considered the ancestor of the Lin-chi lineage established during the Sung dynasty (960–1279). He exhorted disciples to "kill the Buddha" if they should meet him in order to emphasize the need to unfetter the mind from attachments and restrictions of orthodoxy and allow it spontaneity of expression. *See also* Ch'an school; Hung-chou school.

Lin-chi school (lin-jee), Sung-dynasty Chinese Ch'an Buddhist sect and descendant of the Hung-chou line that favored the use of *kung-an* (a paradoxical teaching that transcends logical or conceptual thought) and extreme tactics such as shouting and beatings as teaching devices. Its symbolic and physical use of violence emphasized the need to do away with rational, cognitive operations in one's attempt to grasp enlightenment. Its anti-intellectualism stressed that words could not express truth except when used as instruments for the subversion of conceptual thought. This often produced enigmatic, non-sequitur answers to religious questions, or simply wordless expressions or gestures that functioned as triggers to mental liberation. *See also* Ch'an school; Hung-chou school; kung-an.

lineage (Chin. *tsung*), Ch'an Buddhist polemical term referring to the filiation of a school and also its essential teachings. *See also* Ch'an school.

ling (ling; Chin., "spiritual power"), the efficacious inner spirit of a being or thing; in the popular Chinese religious tradition, the term refers to the supernatural numinous power evoked in religio-magical activities. *See also* Chinese popular religion.

linga (ling'uh; Skt., "mark," "sign,"), a widespread Indian phallic figure. In Brahmanic literature *linga* is a subtle, unchangeable sign for the otherwise unknowable. In the *Mahabharata* it is first linked with Shiva not as a sign for his sexuality but as an emblem of his cosmic creative energy.

In the Shaiva Agamas, it is the symbol of the transcendental form of Shiva, called Para Shiva, whose power is cosmogonic and devoid of priapic associations. These texts consider the linga the most fitting representation of Para Shiva's formless aspect beyond all phenomenal distinctions and recommend it as the sanctuary image for all Shiva temples.

The earliest known linga artifacts, dating from the first century B.C. to the third century A.D., are shaped like realistic phalli. Thereafter the shape becomes progressively more abstract. By medieval times, its observable portion, rising from the *yoni* (its feminine base), forms a round block with a domed apex. *See also* Lingayat; Shaivism; Shiva; yoni.

Lingayat (ling-ah'yuh-tuh; Kannada, "abode of linga"), a South Indian Shaivite Hindu sect. The term is derived from the distinctive practice of wearing the *linga*, or *ishtalinga*, a perhaps phallic symbol of the god Shiva. An alternate name, *Virashaiva*, refers to the sect's ardent devotion to Shiva. Basava, a twelfth-century religious and political leader at Kalyana in northern Karnataka, is commonly accepted as the movement's founder. He probably had as precursors the five great *acharyas* (Skt., "teachers")—Revana, Marula, Ekorama, Pandita, and Vishva—who are venerated by some Lingayats. Basava was also assisted in his reform efforts by numerous pious companions, including Allama Prabhu, Cennabasava, and Mahadeviyakka. Their *vacanas*, devotional prose-poems in colloquial Kannada, convey the movement's central teachings: abolition of caste and gender distinctions, nonobservance of Hindu pollution taboos, emphasis on personal relationship to Shiva, and rejection of elaborate temple rituals. The Lingayats' own rituals emphasize veneration of peripatetic teachers and daily personal meditation on the ishtalinga. Today the movement numbers some ten million members, mostly in the state of Karnataka and environs, where it has become a caste in itself and a potent political presence. *See also* Mahadeviyakka; Shaivism; Shiva.

ling-chih (ling-juhr; Chin., "magic fungus"), bracket fungi collected by Chinese on sacred mountains that restored life to the dead. *See also* Chinese popular religion.

ling-pao (ling-bou; Chin., "sacred treasure"), a term originating in ancient Chinese shamanism denoting the descent of spiritual forces (*ling*) into a human being or sacred object (*pao*). *See also* shamanism.

Ling-pao ching (ling-bou-jing; Chin., "Scriptures of the Spiritual Treasure"), a generic term denoting a category of scriptures in the Taoist canon. With the exception of the earliest examples, which deal with Taoist physiological practices, these texts are characterized by an emphasis on communal ritual and universal salvation. *See also* Ko Ch'ao-fu.

Ling-pao Taoism (ling-bou), a school of Taoist practice characterized by communal ritual for the salvation of all and the belief that its scriptures originated in cosmic patterns at the genesis of the world. It originated in the area around the capital of southern China (present-day Nanking) in the early fifth century. Meant as a synthesis of and replacement for all other major religions of the time, it was from the beginning heavily influenced by Mahayana Buddhism and exhibits many of the same concerns, particularly regarding rebirth, intercession, and the salvation of all beings. From other Taoist schools it borrowed methods of ritual practice, concepts of self and the corporeal gods, meditation, and exorcism.

While the Ling-pao scriptures were often at the center of Buddhist-Taoist debate, charges of plagiarism were forestalled through the claim that the Ling-pao scriptures were copies of the "true script" that appeared in the heavens at the birth of the cosmos. All later religious traditions thus represented imperfect understandings of this original script, more perfectly presented in the Ling-pao texts. Even the Buddha, as one of the transformations of the deified Lao-tzu, was a mere foreign disciple of the primordial supreme deity, the "Heavenly Worthy" of the Ling-pao scriptures. The Ling-pao synthesis, constantly renewed throughout the course of history, proved enduring. Most rituals performed by present-day Taoists are known as "Ling-pao" rites. *See also* Lu Hsiu-ching; Taoism.

lip piercing, lip plug, traditional practice and ornament common among traditional peoples as exemplified by native South American peoples, including the Brazilian Kayapo, Nambicuara, and the Ecuadorian Shuar. The lip plug is an important symbol of religious power because it ritually opens and closes the body passage responsible for speech, breath, and alimentation. By controlling entry into the mouth it provides protection from disease spirits. Only children who can control the functions of eating, crying, and speaking become initiated in lip-piercing ceremonies. Lip plugs then become symbols of status. Made of bone, wood, silver, or feathers, the varying styles mark the different qualities of power that distinguish genders or ethnic groups. Sometimes the size and shape of the plug identifies the initiate with the power of the particular animal it evokes. For example, a large circular lip disk may evoke the extended lip of the red howler monkey, a species with a particularly powerful voice.

lip plug. *See* lip piercing, lip plug.

li-shih wu-ai. *See* nonobstruction of principle and phenomena.

litany (Gk., "entreaty"), Christian prayer form in which a series of petitions or invocations are answered by a repeated response.

literature and religion. The association of literature with religion goes back to the dawn of human history when individuals, or more likely groups, first explained the significance of their experience by seeking to narrate it in forms that we now call myths. That association has continued to the present day even though, as in most cultural traditions, literature is no longer considered a medium of revealed truth and no longer serves a ritual function.

Forms of the Relationship: The relations between literature and religion, particularly in the West, have taken three, possibly four, historically periodizable forms. Though one or another of these forms has been predominant in each period, all have made their way into every period in some residual or emergent fashion. In the first, which lasted in the West from classical antiquity to the early modern or Renaissance period (it is sometimes still predominant in the East and Middle East), literature possesses a complementary, often correspondent, relationship with inherited religious traditions and communities. It has served either as an allegorical representation of religious ideas, as in medieval miracle plays like *Mystere d'Adam* and the Chester or Wakefield cycles, or in later morality plays like *Everyman* and *The Castle of Perseverance*, or it has been issued in forms where religious ideas are fused with social, political, and aesthetic beliefs, as in Homer's *Iliad* (mid-ninth century B.C.), Virgil's *Aeneid* (21 B.C.), or Edmund Spenser's *Faerie Queene* (1590, 1596). Such texts have had the effect, if not the intention, of valorizing religious beliefs and values by representing in their structures and their themes both the assumptions of religious faith and the structures of religious experience.

In the second historical period, which lasted from the end of the Middle Ages until the beginning of the European Enlightenment, literature and religion begin to develop more adversarial relations. Evident earliest, perhaps, in the courtly love literature associated with Chretien de Troyes and the new spirit of romance and secular impiety injected by French literature into English in a work like Geoffrey Chaucer's *The Canterbury Tales*, this new, more critical relation between literature and religion, which was also encouraged by the revival of classical learning and the burgeoning interest in geographic and scientific discovery, takes two characteristic forms. In satirical works like Rabelais's *Gargantua and Pantagruel*, the comedies of Moliere, Swift's *Gulliver's Travels*, and Voltaire's *Candide*, in Benjamin Franklin's *Autobiography* and the historical romances of Nathaniel Hawthorne, it precipitated an active criticism and sometimes censuring of orthodox beliefs and practices. In works like Denis Diderot's *Rameau's Nephew* and Herman Melville's *The Confidence-Man*, as well as in Dostoevsky's *Notes from Underground* or Tolstoy's *The Death of Ivan Ilych*, it led to an attempt to subvert and undermine conventional religious feelings and presuppositions.

In the third historical period, the relations between literature and religion would change again. From the Romantic period onward, writers like William Wordsworth in *The Prelude*, Marcel Proust in *Remembrance of Things Past*, and Rainer Maria Rilke in the *Duino Elegies* have exhibited less interest in opposing religion than in discovering some form of substitute for it. The act of writing becomes the act of a mind searching for, as Wallace Stevens remarks in "Of Modern Poetry," "what will suffice." Whether in the tortured, disorienting tales of Franz Kafka or the ironic stories and novels of Ernest Hemingway, the answer is often found, when it is found at all, where Stevens locates it—in the banalities of the commonplace.

In the postwar period, however, as literature turns less against religion than against itself, there has been a withering even of this spiritual expectation. Texts like Jorge Luis Borges's *Labyrinths and Other Writings*, Milan Kundera's *The Unbearable Lightness of Being*, and Don Delillo's *Libra*, leave few if any traces of religion, save possibly the memory that literature once had purposes other than the parody of its own possibilities; that literature once was held responsible for expressing not only the unsaid but the unsayable. In late-twentieth-century writing, the transcendence that formerly was religion has frequently given way to the self-emptying, often self-doubting, immanence that now informs contemporary writing. This is a scene, frequently described as postmodern, that in texts like John Barth's *Chimera* or Samuel Beckett's *Endgame* or Nathalie Sarraute's "The Silence" celebrates not only the death of the author but the disappearance, really evacuation, of all depth of understanding.

There are, of course, exceptions to this schema. Forms like comedy and tragedy have always borne an ambivalent, and often an oppositional, relation to conventional religious meaning and practices, and texts ranging from Aristophanes's *The Frogs* and Ludovico Ariosto's *Orlando furioso* to Camoes's *The Lusiadas*, Thomas More's *Utopia*, and William Morris's *News from Nowhere* have sought to supplant, or at any rate to supplement, them. Nonetheless, for all their limitations, classificatory schemes such as this one can be helpful in delineating tendencies that organize an otherwise vast and complex field.

Modern Study of the Relationship: The modern Western study of the relations between literature and religion can be dated almost literally from the moment when literature ceased to remain a handmaiden of faith and was transformed instead into one of its secular, or at least its heterodox, complements and occasionally competitors. This moment corresponds almost exactly with the publication of the second edition of Giambattista Vico's *The New Science* (1744), where for the first time in the history of the West the imagination is defined as generic to the human mind and truth and poetry described as merely two of its species. Vico's defense of the faculty of the imagination opens up the possibility of reconceiving myth and fable as indigenous to the experience of any people, and within less than a century Johann Gottfried von Herder would argue that poets are the most representative authors of any country and poetry the language most revealing of their humanity. Herder helps clear the ground for a definition of that realm of sense and sensibility that eventually became known as the aesthetic, a realm of experience that was then philosophically installed at the center of human spiritual affairs in a variety of important texts, including David Hume's "Of the Standards of Taste," Immanuel Kant's *Critique of Judgment*, Friedrich Schiller's *On the Aesthetic Education of Man*, Georg Wilhelm Friedrich Hegel's *Phenomenology of the Spirit*, and Samuel Taylor Coleridge's *Biographia Literaria*.

The case for the modern study of literature and religion is probably put most influentially by Matthew Arnold (1822–88) when in "The Study of Poetry" he laments the decline of received religion while at the same time insisting that literature was now in a position to take its place. Correlating the strongest part of Victorian (essentially Protestant) religion with its unconscious poetry, Arnold opens the way for a more disciplined examination of the linkages between literary expression and religious understanding and practice. This examination has to some degree followed the fashions of criticism. Under the influence of the New Humanists in the 1920s, for example, interest in the relations between literature and religion takes a decidedly ethical if not moralistic turn. Thanks to the emergence of the New Criticism a decade later, the study of religion and literature becomes more determinedly aesthetic and formalistic in the 1930s and 1940s. With the development of phenomenology and existentialism in the late 1940s and 1950s, literature and religion studies become more philosophical and metaphysical. In the 1960s, 1970s, and early 1980s, the rise (and sometimes decline) of structuralist and poststructuralist methodologies encourages exploration of the relations between literature and religion to become more linguistic and semiotic. But in the 1980s and 1990s, study of the relations between literature and religion follows the lead of critical schools yet again by turning in directions recently opened up by ideological and cultural criticism involving questions of gender, class, race, and colonial subjugation.

Stages in the Modern Study of the Relationship: Despite these various critical wanderings, one can discern several stages in the organized study of the relations between religion and literature in the twentieth century. During the first stage, which runs from the 1920s to the early 1940s, the central concerns are diagnostic or apodictic. Literature is important to and for an understanding of religion either because it lays bare the existential dilemmas of modern life and faith or because it renders in compelling terms the hazards of trying to survive those dilemmas without faith. In the second stage, which dates from the end of World War II to the middle of the 1960s, the animating motives of this crossdisciplinary, and sometimes interdisciplinary, study become more directly apologetic or historicist. Literature becomes valued either because it gives displaced but enduring expression to some of the abiding themes of the Judeo-Christian tradition or because, in serving as a repository of elements of the Judeo-Christian religious inheritance, it helps restore to some of those elements a portion of their lost historical meaning.

The third and most recent stage of this study begins at the end of the 1960s and continues into the 1990s. A creature of the new immigration of theory from Europe to Great Britain and the United States, this third stage centers around issues that in the broad sense are either linguistic or cultural. Among those concerned with linguistic issues, the religious questions raised by and addressed in works of literature relate to the meaning of language, or with elements that like ritual, the unconscious, or even philosophical reflection, can be construed as a language. Among those concerned with cultural issues, the religious questions posed by and confronted in literature relate to literature's nature and function as part of some larger system of meaning and signification that is not principally linguistic but rather ideological.

Conclusions of Modern Study: The modern study of the relations between literature and religion has yielded several important conclusions. The first has to do with the difficulty of adequately comprehending the diverse history and expressions of either without appreciating their implications for and relations with the other. Just as the literary heritage of any culture can be unintelligible without an appreciation of the ways it has been nourished by its religious heritage, so the religious heritage of most cultures cannot be sufficiently understood without an appreciation of the ways the religious heritage has been transmitted in, and transformed by, that same culture's literary tradition.

Second, if literature and religion have, as in the West, been entangled for so long that it is difficult to study one without becoming involved in the interpretation of the other, one need not be a mere epiphenomenon of the other. Even where literature and religion appeal to the same systems of meaning and signification, they inhabit and employ those systems in somewhat different ways. Literature employs meanings heuristically, even hypothetically, for the sake of showing where they might lead and how they might matter. Religion is predisposed to employ meanings more paradigmatically, to show how they make all else matter because of the order of authority they entail.

Third, the relationship of literature and religion in most circumstances may best be perceived as symbiotic. Religious paradigms help people contain the otherness of their circumstances by providing images of an ideal order with which people can attempt, notionally and ritualistically, to identify or conform. The works of literature that contain the richest and deepest religious resonance tend to explore hidden, often potentially disturbing, dimensions of those religious paradigms or images of ideal order by organizing them into an encompassing verbal structure whose explicit purpose is to delineate, through the light it sheds on their essential nature, the possibility of alternative, and hopefully more constructive, modes of responses to them. Works of literature thus loosen the hold of religious paradigms and at the same time reinforce them, but the reinforcement they afford under such aesthetic conditions often produces as a consequence the beginnings of a revisioning, an extension, of the religious paradigm or idea of order itself. A religious allegory like John Bunyan's *Pilgrim's Progress* (seventeenth century) does not merely re-echo central Puritan tenets of faith but refashions them in the process of submitting them to aesthetic formalization. Even where literature corroborates religious values and truths, it also manages, however subtly, to recreate them in ways that are as often beneficial as they are detrimental to religion itself. *See also* drama and religion.

Liu Hai-ch'an (lyoh hí-chahn; fl. 1031), obscure patriarch of Ch'uan-chen Taoism and reputed teacher of Chang Po-tuan and Wang Che. *See also* Chang Po-tuan; Ch'uan-chen Taoism; Wang Che.

loa (lwah), or *lwa,* a divinity or divine spirit in traditional Voodoo or Vodou terminology. The term has its origins in African Fon religion, and in Haitian religion identifies numerous unseen powers, including African-Christian deities and saints associated with natural phenomena. Worshiped through grand ceremonies and personal devotion, the loa may become present to human communication through mediums in possession trance rituals. *See also* Voodoo.

logical positivism, the view that all statements except those of empirical science, logic, and mathematics are meaningless and devoid of cognitive content. In its pure form, logical positivism was defended during the first third of the twentieth century by those philosophers and scientists who made up the famed Vienna Circle, and was often accompanied by the doctrine that all meaningful statements can be expressed in the vocabulary of physics.

Central Doctrines: In the modern period, the philosophical roots of logical positivism reach to the Scottish philosopher David Hume (1711–76). Like the positivists after him, Hume aimed to overthrow or eliminate traditional metaphysics, including statements about God, a transcendent reality, or being in itself. The contemporary English philosopher Alfred Ayer (1910–89) says that Hume gives "rhetorical" expression to Ayer's "own thesis that a sentence that does not express either a formally true proposition or an empirical hypothesis is devoid of literal significance" (*Language, Truth, and Logic*, 1946).

The positivists drew inspiration from two main sources: first, from those elements of the philosophical tradition that they regarded as antimetaphysical. The early positivists saw themselves as extending a line of thought that, after Hume, had blossomed with the eighteenth-century German philosopher Immanuel Kant (1724–1804) whose *Critique of Pure Reason* (1781–87) criticized the pretensions of dogmatic and speculative metaphysics. Several influential positivist works—including Moritz Schlick's *General Theory of Knowledge* (1918), Rudolf Carnap's *Logical Construction of the World* (1928), and Hans Reichenbach's *Theory of Relativity and A Priori Knowledge* (1920)—may be viewed as addressing the Kantian problem of delimiting the scope of human knowledge.

Second, the early positivists appealed to the spectacular success of modern physics, especially Einstein's special and general theories of relativity. As they saw it, relativity's success illuminated a central tenet of any properly "scientific" philosophy: the rejection of nonobservables. Einstein had noted that we never observe absolute motion; rather the velocity of a given body is always observed relative to the motion of other bodies. When Einstein did away with the notions of absolute motion, absolute space, and absolute simultaneity, he confirmed the positivists' distrust of nonobservational, metaphysical notions. They then set about extending this success, to eliminate—from all domains of human inquiry—excess theoretical structure that "makes no observable difference."

Religious language, especially talk about God, was among the more obvious candidates for excision. The surgical tool quickly became known as the principle of verification: a statement was significant or meaningful if it could be verified. Verification in turn came in two basic forms, logical and factual. Some statements are analytic—true under all empirical circumstances in virtue of considerations of language alone; under this category fell logic and mathematics, as well as such tautologies as "All bachelors are unmarried men"; the rest are synthetic—factual assertions to be verified or falsified according to specific empirical procedures. This distinction between the analytic and the synthetic led the positivists to conclude that natural knowledge has two corresponding elements: a form, which is in some sense conceptual or mind-dependent, and a content, which is contributed by the world or experience.

Since talk about God is apparently not analytically true, and since there do not seem to be specifiable procedures for its verification, the positivists concluded, with Hume, that it should be "committed to the flames" as strictly meaningless. However, as Ayer remarks, the positivist view undermines atheism and agnosticism as well as belief in God. The point was not to deny the absolute possibility of the truth of theological talk; rather, the aim was to show that one cannot speak about or inquire meaningfully into the nature and existence of God. As many of the logical positivists pointed out—and as had Hume before them—there is irony in this position, for it is hard to distinguish it from the strain of orthodox Jewish, Christian, and Muslim belief that holds that God is a mystery that transcends human understanding.

The positivists gave such normative disciplines as ethics and aesthetics only somewhat gentler treatment. Ethical and aesthetic judgments do not express factual truths (in that sense they too are meaningless); they are "partly expressions of feeling," and, in the case of ethics, "partly commands."

Philosophical and Theological Responses: Criticism of the verification theory of meaning soon follows. An initial problem of verification is that counterexamples seem plentiful. For example, how does one verify the assertion, "Caesar crossed the Rubicon"? Surely historical assertions are meaningful, though there is no specifiable procedure for their verification or falsification. And how is the principle of verification to be verified? That an assertion's meaning is its method of verification is not analytic; but, if it is to be synthetic, what observable difference does it make? Critics of positivism also question its antitheoretical stance and its rejection of nonobservables. Perhaps the most telling example comes from a main source of the positivists' own inspiration: as discussion of relativity deepened, it was widely seen to require large doses of theory and to embrace several nonobservable entities. Indeed, the variably curved space-time of general relativity is not itself observable.

A deeper problem with the observational/theoretical distinction is pointed out by, among others, the American logician and philosopher W. V. O. Quine (b. 1908). In "Two Dogmas of Empiricism" (1951), Quine argues for its dissolution on the grounds that changes in theory can alter what counts as observational and nonobservational; put differently, the positivists failed to recognize the "theory-ladenness" of observation. Finally, the positivists' emphasis on observation led philosophers to question their notion of evidence—presumably what observation yields. But, taking perception as a sensation

caused by some event or object, the fact of causality does not itself identify the active event or object; that identification can come only in the form of a belief. But how can one give evidence for that belief except by appealing to a further, supporting belief? Here the positivists face the unattractive prospect of either giving up the evidential force of perception or of accepting a vicious circularity.

Of the several theological responses to logical positivism, two are perhaps most influential. First, many theologians simply ignore the positivist challenge, viewing it as little more than an outburst of antireligious sentiment given philosophical dress. And, as positivism began to falter under the pressure of a variety of philosophical objections, these theologians could claim a measure of vindication. So long as the positivists could not defend such doctrines as verificationism and the rejection of unobservables these theologians felt free to speak of God knowing that their talk could not be verified and that its object could not be observed.

A second line of response concedes that talk about God lacks straightforward empirical significance, but argues that it possesses important noncognitive significance. Thus, much work has been done from the 1950s to the 1990s to show how religious language actually functions in religious communities. Some hold this function to be mainly moral, some mainly aesthetic; others emphasize the metaphorical nature of such central theological statements as "God is love," and still others point out the deep connection between religious talk and human emotion.

While both of these theological responses to positivism have found defenders, many people find them less than satisfactory. As to the first, even if specific positivist proposals are abandoned, it is hard to resist the basic idea that the positivists tried to elaborate, namely, that the meaningfulness of speech depends (in some way) on its empirical content (however that content should be thought of). Indeed, recent years have seen new proposals that seem to improve upon the positivists' verificationism while still rejecting theology as lacking cognitive content. Again, many theologians and philosophers of religion have resisted the noncognitivist response for the following reason: theological statements (talk about God) seem to be intended as factual assertions like those of the empirical sciences. It would appear that most persons who subscribe to the Western monotheisms take themselves to be making as straightforward an assertion when they say, for example, "God is on my side" as when they say, while looking at a cat on a mat, "The cat is on the mat." Noncognitive theories of religious language seem unable to capture this basic self-understanding.

Rather than rejecting theoretical or unobservable entities outright (God, variably curved space-time), one must look for criteria to separate the good from the bad. Thus, the enlightened (post) positivist would challenge theology to show that it is more like (good) general relativistic gravitational theory than like (bad) Newtonian gravitational theory. Such a challenge maintains the traditional positivist insistence that all speech must, if it is to be meaningful, yield or futher some inference, explanation, and confirmation; much contemporary philosophy—as well as a good deal of contemporary theology—would join in this insistence. *See also* empiricism; religion, philosophy of; religious language.

Logos (Gk.,"word"), a Greek philosophical term for the divine creative and controlling power in the universe, adopted in the New Testament as a title for Christ as the "Word of God," and developed in later Christian thought as the designation of the eternal second Person of the Trinity. *See also* hypostasis; Shekhina; Trinity.

lohan (luoh-hawn; Chin., term for *arhat* [Skt.,"worthy"]), a seventh-stage *bodhisattva* in Chinese Buddhism who has attained *nirvana* sufficient for saving himself but not others. *See also* bodhisattva; nirvana.

loka (loh'kah; Skt.), in Hindu cosmology, a "world" or "realm." The Vedas speak of three *lokas* (earth, atmosphere, and heaven), the Upanishads seven. Access to higher realms is gained by sacrifice, austerity, knowledge, and faith. *See also* cosmology.

Loki (loo'kee), a Norse mythological figure who is both a burlesque trickster and a kind of demiurge, the originator of evil. *See also* Nordic religion.

Lollards ("mumblers of prayers"), followers of the Christian scholar John Wycliff in fourteenth- and fifteenth-century England. They promoted the translation of the Bible into English and criticized Catholic doctrines and practices, including transubstantiation, clerical celibacy, prayers for the dead, and ecclesiastical wealth. Although condemned by Parliament's "On the Burning of Heretics" (1401), they thrived until the arrest and execution in 1414 of one of their prominent leaders, Sir John Oldcastle, following an armed uprising led by Lollards. Thereafter, their numbers decreased and they survived largely underground. Their influence can be seen in later Reformation thought and practice. *See also* Bible, translations of the Christian; Wycliff, John.

Longhouse religion, a Native American religious tradition of the Iroquois people, active from 1818 to the present. The central rite is the periodic recitation of the Code of Handsome Lake by recognized preachers during a three- to five-day ceremonial. *See also* Handsome Lake; Native Americans (North America), new religions among.

lo-p'an (luhaw-pahn; Chin., "compass platter"), instrument used by Chinese experts in geomancy (*feng-shui*). It consists of a magnetic needle surrounded by concentric circles arranged with the elements of Chinese cosmology. *See also* geomancy.

Lord of the Flies. *See* Beelzebub.

Lord's Day, a Christian synonym for Sunday. *See also* Sunday.

Lord's Prayer, the prayer that, according to Christian tradition, Jesus taught his followers. Found in Matthew 6:9–13 and Luke 11:2–4, it epitomizes Jesus' teaching concerning the kingdom of God. Matthew's version, appearing with the concluding doxology as early as the *Didache* (ca. 100), has been used extensively in Christian worship.

Losar (Tibetan *lo-gsar*), festival of the New Year celebrated the first month of the Tibetan year (February). Traditionally it is held at the time of the winter solstice. Celebrations include cleansing and purification activites as well as feasting and carnival festivities. Prior to the Chinese occupation of Tibet in 1959 Losar included a complex array of public and private rituals designed to exorcise evil influences and ensure the accumulation of good *karma* (Skt.; lit., "deed") for individuals and the community. *See also* Buddhism (festal cycle); Tibetan religions.

Lo-shu. *See* Ho-t'u and Lo-shu.

Lost Tribes (of Israel), a complex legend concerning the location and fate of ten tribes of Israel who were exiled in 722 B.C. by the Assyrians (2 Kings 17:6; 18:11). In most accounts they are located far away in a mysterious land, ruled by a Jewish king and guarded by the river Sambatyon, which is impassable six days a week but passable on the Sabbath.

Quests for the Lost Tribes motivated travelers, and the existence of the Tribes became an important element in medieval Jewish and Christian millenarianism.

Though many different peoples have been identified as descendents of the Lost Tribes, the most famous identification is with Native Americans, as expressed in Manasseh ben Israel's *Hope of Israel* (1650). *See also* Black Jewish movements; Identity Christianity; Latter-day Saints, Church of Jesus Christ of; Yahweh ben Yahweh.

lotus (Skt. *padma*), aquatic plant and central Buddhist symbol representing the purity of enlightenment appearing in an impure world. Buddhas and Bodhisattvas are depicted as sitting on lotuses, while, in legend, great saints are often born within them. *See also* enlightenment; Om mani padme hum.

lotus posture, Indic seated position in which the right foot is placed on the left thigh and the left foot on the right thigh; it is particularly well suited for yoga and meditation. *See also* meditation; yoga.

Lotus Sutra, a scripture belonging to the Mahayana wing of Buddhism dating from the first century. The text treats the Buddha not as an ordinary mortal, but as an eternally existing being who manifested himself as the historical Buddha Sakyamuni. The text also presents the idea that Buddhist doctrines are not fixed but mutable (according to the principle of "skillful means," the practice of adapting the Buddhist teachings to the needs of one's audience). This scripture is of central importance in the Chinese T'ien-t'ai school and in the Japanese Tendai and Nichiren schools. *See also* Buddhism (thought and ethics); Mahayana; Nichiren; Tendai school; T'ien-t'ai school.

Lourdes, the site in southeastern France of a Christian pilgrimage shrine dedicated to the Virgin Mary, who is reputed to have appeared to a fourteen-year-old peasant girl, Marie Bernarde (Bernadette) Soubirous, beginning in 1858. The spot is marked by a spring whose waters are thought to be curative. *See also* Mary (pilgrimage sites); pilgrimage.

love, Christian the central religious and moral ideal of Christianity.

As interpreted by Augustine (d. 430), love (Lat. *caritas*) is directed first toward God. Human beings are so structured as to find lasting happiness only in God, the highest Good. Human pursuit of happiness by loving what is less than God is futile; the chief purpose of love is to bring one's neighbor into communion with God. True self-love and love for God are coincident or coextensive. Augustine held that the substratum for Christian love is the spirit, rather than the body, the urges of which lead the self away from God.

The medieval Catholic theologians retained the emphasis on love for God. Mystics wrote of the stages through which love for God develops, and understood love for neighbor as assisting others in undertaking spiritual ascent. While emphasis was placed on the divine-human relation, the purpose of love was held to encompass meeting one's neighbor's bodily needs (charity). Self-love was given considerable status, as was love for family and friends (Lat. *philia*).

The Reformation questioned aspects of medieval theories concerning love for God. Martin Luther (1483–1546) saw the striving for happiness through love for God as encouraging selfishness. For Luther, selflessness before God's will in the service of one's neighbor was the only answer to human egocentricity.

In the late twentieth century, discussion of Christian love has concentrated on the degree to which it permits self-love in relation to the neighbor. Feminists, among others, have developed important criticisms of radical self-denial. Some theorists have lamented the deemphasis on love for God and the reduction of the purpose of love to bodily welfare. Others have attacked the dualism between spirit and body, stressing that Christian love must take embodiment and sexual expression into its center. While some theologians have tried to relate Christian love to philosophical positions such as utilitarianism, others have concentrated on what they hold to be the distinctive biblical teaching on love.

Low Church. *See* High Church, Low Church.

lu (*loo;* Chin., "register," "record"), spirit register listing the names of deities used in Taoist ritual and organization. The founder of the second-century Taoist sect of the Celestial Masters (T'ien-shih), Chang Tao-ling, claimed to have received registers from the deified Lao-tzu that established a covenant between heaven and earth. Initiation, advancement, and ordination in the Taoist community has traditionally been accompanied by the reception of graded protective registers (*shou-lu*). *See also* Chang Tao-ling; T'ien-shih Taoism.

Lubavitch, one of the most famous and influential Hasidic dynasties, also known as Habad Hasidism, founded by Shneur Zalman of Lyady (1745–1813), a disciple of Dov Baer, the Maggid of Mezhirech (d. 1772), successor to Israel ben Eliezer Baal Shem Tov (d. 1760). The name Lubavitch is taken from the town in Belorussia that became the center of Habad when its founder moved there in 1813.

Habad Hasidism is distinctive in that it places a high premium on intellectual pursuits (alluded to in its name Habad, an acrostic for *hokhmah, binah,* and *da'at,* i.e., wisdom, understanding, and knowledge) in addition to advocating an enriched pietistic life. The classical works of Habad represent some of the most systematic presentations of Hasidic thought.

In the wake of World War II, the sixth successive leader of Habad, Joseph Isaac Schneersohn (1880–1950), established the new headquarters of the movement in Brooklyn, New York, and in 1948 founded the Kefar Habad in Israel. In the last forty years, under the guidance of the seventh leader, Menahem Mendel (1902–94), son of Levi Isaac Schneersohn, the institutions of Habad have greatly expanded, becoming a dominant force in the dissemination and preservation of traditional Judaism throughout the modern world. *See also* Hasidism.

Lucian of Samosata (ca. 120–180), a Syrian satirist, rhetorician, philosopher. His more than eighty surviving writings in Greek include an expose of religious charlatanism (*Alexander, the False Prophet*), a firsthand description of the cult of Atargatis (*The Syrian Goddess*), and satirical writings mocking traditional religion. *See also* Atargatis.

Lucifer, Christian name for Satan as prince of the fallen angels based on the Latin translation of Isaiah 14:12, "How you have fallen from heaven, O Lucifer," where the name refers to the planet Venus. *See also* Satan.

Lu Hsiang-shan (loo shahng-shahn; 1139–93), founder of the Neo-Confucian School of Mind (Hsin-hsueh) and the great opponent of Chu Hsi. He taught the unity of mind, principle, action, and knowledge as the fundamental source of the human good. Thus, the investigation of the good is simply the investigation and realization of the good mind. *See also* Chu Hsi; Hsin-hsueh; Neo-Confucianism.

Lu Hsiu-ching (loo shyoh-jing; 406–477), foundational figure in the Taoist liturgical tradition. Patronized by rulers in South China, Lu edited the holy texts of the Ling-pao tradition and is credited with formulating the first Taoist canon. He unified various religious strands to establish a set of ritual practices amenable to all levels of society. His liturgies gave coherence to Taoism down to the twelfth century and continue to influence much of Taoist practice today. *See also* Ling-pao Taoism; Taoism.

Luke, by tradition the author of the third Gospel in the New Testament as well as the Acts of the Apostles.

Lull, Raymond (ca. 1232–1316), Catalan Catholic mystic, Neoplatonic religious philosopher, and missionary. His early *Book of Contemplation* (ca. 1272), the first work of medieval theology not in Latin, was originally written in Arabic, then translated into Catalan. Lull was unusually knowledgeable of both Judaism and Islam and viewed them, along with Christianity, as mutually understandable given their shared faith in the unity of God.

Lumpa Church (loom-pah; "highest" church), founded by Alice Mulenga Lenshina (ca. 1924–78) in Northern Rhodesia (Zambia) in 1953. Guided by apocalyptic visions, Lenshina's church avoided social interaction with nonadherents and challenged the right of the Zambian state to exercise authority over church members. Lenshina and many of her followers were imprisoned, and her church was banned. *See also* Africa, new religions in.

lung (luhng; Chin., "dragon"), auspicious mythical animal. With a symbolic repertoire quite distinct from that of Western dragons, dragon imagery pervades Chinese art and religion from antiquity to modern times. The dragon was dangerous but benevolent and auspicious when tamed by a person of spiritual power. It is a symbol of water, both as abyssal depths and as clouds; a symbol of *yang*-within-*yin* and yin-within-yang, hence of creativity; a yang image when paired with the *feng-huang,* phoenix; and a symbol of royal authority, as on imperial "dragon robes." *See also* yin and yang.

Lung-hu Shan (luhng-hoo shan; Chin., "Dragon-and-Tiger Mountain"), a sacred Taoist mountain in Kiangsi province, China, center of the Cheng-i school of Taoism. *See also* Cheng-i Taoism; mountains, sacred.

Lung-men (luhng-muhn), rock caves south of Loyang, China, where thousands of inscribed Buddhist images were carved between the sixth and tenth centuries.

Lung-men Taoism (luhng-men; Chin., "Dragon Gate"), a subsect of Ch'uan-chen Taoism, founded by Ch'iu Ch'u-chi (1148–1227). Summoned by Genghis Khan, Ch'iu Chi-chi became the most famous religious figure of his time and made Ch'uan-chen Taoism the most popular Taoist school. *See also* Ch'uan-chen Taoism.

Lun Yu (luhn yoo; Chin., "Discussed [and Approved] Sayings"), Confucian classic most often called the *Analects* in Western translations recording sayings and actions of Confucius. Although compiled by later disciples of Confucius, it was not considered a classic until the second century. Most of its twenty books describe the sage Confucius as he responds to questions, discusses important themes, and lives out his principles. Several books include sayings of Confucius's most important disciples. The tenth book describes Confucius's personal disposition, ritual expressions, and religious piety. Chu Hsi (1130–1200) elevated it as one of the *Ssu-shu* (Four Books) of later Confucianism. *See also* Confucianism (authoritative texts and their interpretation); Confucius; Ssu-shu.

Lu-shih ch'un-ch'iu (loo-shuhr chwuhn-chyoh; Chin., "Spring and Autumn Annals of Master Lu"), syncretistic Legalist text ascribed to Lu Pu-wei ca. 250 B.C. *See also* Fa-chia, syncretism (Japan).

Luther, Martin (1483–1546), pioneer of the German Reformation and most important of the founders of Protestant Christianity. Born in Saxony, he was educated at Magdeburg, Eisenach, and the universities of Erfurt and Wittenberg. He taught Bible and theology at Wittenberg from 1508 until his death. Theological study led him to challenge much in the medieval tradition, especially with respect to the nature of faith and the Word of God. His theological innovations and his attacks on church practices, together with other factors, led to the establishment of Protestant churches. *See also* Lutheranism; Reformation.

Lutheranism, Christian reform movement stemming from Martin Luther (1483–1546), Augustinian monk and Bible professor at Wittenberg University in Germany. Inspired by Paul's Letters, Luther centered his teaching on justification by grace through faith alone, that people gain favor with God (justification) purely as a divine gift (by grace alone) to those who trust in Jesus Christ (through faith alone). In 1517 Luther began a protest against Roman Catholic practices and teachings that based favor with God partly on good deeds. When Luther's teaching was challenged as inconsistent with traditional Catholic doctrine, he replied that scripture takes precedence over teachings of popes and church councils.

Early History: In those German territories where Lutheran teachings were accepted, a rather conservative reformation in church life was begun. Unlike more radical reform movements, Lutherans generally accepted practices not conflicting with justification by faith. In worship Lutherans followed the Roman liturgy, except for deleting certain parts about sacrifice, simplifying the service, and employing German instead of Latin. Luther pioneered congregational singing of the liturgy and hymns. While recognizing two rather than seven sacraments, Lutherans practiced infant baptism and taught the real presence of Christ in the Eucharist but elevated the importance of preaching on scripture, and discouraged praying to saints. Lutherans retained an ordained clergy, but rejected the requirement of celibacy.

Repeated attempts at reconciliation with Rome failed; in the process Lutherans produced the first Protestant confession of faith, the Augsburg Confession (1530). Lutheranism spread to other territories, but won political protection only in the Scandinavian countries where it became dominant. A war that broke out in Germany between Lutheran and Roman Catholic princes ended in the Peace of Augsburg (1555), which said each prince's religion determined his territory's religion; dissenters could only move.

Later Developments: Internal theological conflicts arose after Luther died in 1546 as the next generation sought to clarify Lutheran teachings. These disputes were settled with the *Formula of Concord* (1577), and further developed in the confessional writings of the *Book of Concord* (1580).

Orthodoxy and Pietism were the two most powerful forces in Lutheranism over the next two centuries. Lutheran Orthodoxy stressed pure doctrine by expounding and defending Lutheran teachings in sermons and theology. The vitality of church life varied in politically fragmented Germany, for each territorial Lutheran church tended to come under the control of its prince. Although some princes had laws requiring church attendance, a distance often existed between university-trained pastors, whose position made them part of the upper class, and most members. Pietism emerged as a renewal movement within Lutheranism in 1675 when Philip Jacob Spener's *Pia Desideria* (Pious Desires) made six proposals for church reform, including use of the Bible in small groups (conventicles) and more emphasis on holy living. After Spener, Pietism was centered at Halle, Germany, under August Francke (1663–1727), who initiated various programs of social as well as church reform. Pietism spread to the Scandinavian Lutheran churches, and a young German Pietist pastor Henry Melchior Muhlenberg came to America and organized some Lutheran congregations into the Pennsylvania Ministerium in 1748.

Lutheranism in America: Lutheranism in America has wrestled with the question, What does it mean to be Lutheran in a pluralistic society? When some regional synods formed the General Synod in 1820, the delegates could agree only upon the name *Lutheran;* the Lutheran confessions were not mentioned. Gettysburg Seminary professor Samuel Simon Schmucker advocated "American Lutheranism," which conformed more to evangelicalism. In 1855 the anonymous *Definite Synodical Platform* even urged revision of the Augsburg Confession to delete "errors" such as the real presence in the Eucharist. However, as increasing numbers of Lutherans immigrated, those who emphasized historic Lutheran teachings gained strength; at the opposite pole from Schmucker was the Missouri Synod's C. F. W. Walther. Charles Porterfield Krauth, seminary professor at Philadelphia, defended Lutheran teachings such as the real presence, and in 1867 the more confessional eastern synods established the General Council. In the Midwest most immigrants formed conservative synods. At first new Lutheran immigrants tended to unite by nationality, location, and theology, so many synods were created. Among those established by Germans were the Missouri (1847), Wisconsin (1850), and Iowa (1854) Synods; by Norwegians the Eielsen (1846) and Norwegian (1853) Synods. The Swedes founded the Augustana Synod (1860), Danes the Danish Church (1878), and Finns the Suomi Synod (1890). As ethnicity, geography, and old theological differences became less significant, many synods merged.

In the twentieth century two issues have divided American Lutherans—views of the Bible and of ecumenical relations. Conservatives have said fidelity to the Lutheran confessions requires saying the Bible is inerrant; they have also been very wary of relations with Christians of different doctrinal positions. The conservative Missouri and Wisconsin Synods have not joined the Lutheran World Federation or the World Council of Churches. Others have held a neo-Lutheran perspective that regards the Bible as the Word of God but resists calling it inerrant; they also have said Lutheran confessional loyalty calls for openness to ecumenical relations. After World War I neo-Lutheran thinking gradually became dominant in the synods that formed The American Lutheran Church (1960) and the Lutheran Church in America (1962). In 1987 these two bodies and a neo-Lutheran group from the Missouri Synod formed the Evangelical Lutheran Church in America. These churches have been active in the Lutheran World Federation, World Council of Churches, and in theological dialogues with Roman Catholics that declared "a convergence [though not uniformity] on justification by faith." Lutheranism has spread throughout the world, with a total membership in 1988 of 59,003,201. *See also* Pietism; Protestantism.

LXX. *See* Septuagint.

A B C D E F
G H I J K L
M N O P Q
R S V
W Z

ma (mah; Jap., "interval"), an important idea in the religio-aesthetic tradition of Japan. In Noh drama, the moments of no action (the intervals in between the actions) are the most important part, for they are filled with the actor's spiritual power. Empty spaces serve similar functions in the arts and architecture of Japan. *See also* Japanese religions (art and architecture); Noh drama.

Maccabees, dynasty of Jewish rulers in second and first century B.C. Also called Hasmoneans, they came to prominence in the revolt against Antiochus Epiphanes (165–164 B.C.), celebrated in the feast of Hanukkah. *See also* Hellenism.

macrocosm, microcosm (Gk., "large world"/"small world"), the widespread notion that there exists a correspondence between the heavenly world and the terrestrial, or between the cosmos and the human body, such that one can serve to model the other. *See also* ages of the world; cosmology.

Macumba (mah-koom'bah, derivation unknown), Brazilian new religion, found principally in southeastern cities, with ritual priests and mediums who accept possession by divine spirits.

One of the older sects drawing on native Brazilian, African, and Christian traditions, Macumba spread from Rio de Janeiro to Sao Paulo and, since the 1970s, throughout Brazil. Although standard treatments may confuse Macumba with formative Umbanda groups, some distinguishing characteristics may be discerned in Macumba, including an emphasis on individual participation through divination consultations, the presence of spirits of the dead in the possession rituals of the (mostly female) mediums, and predominance of men in leadership roles. The urban context has lessened emphasis on African ethnic ties, resulting in the intermingling of religious symbolism and terminology of Angolan-Congolese derivation with popular Roman Catholic theology and—more recently—Kardecism, as well as the broadening of the membership across racial and class lines.

Members suffered severe repression in the 1950s and 1960s at the hands of local, state, and federal governments, but membership only receded in the 1980s owing to the popularity of Umbanda and missionary Protestant evangelical churches.

The term *Macumba* has also served as the generic rubric for all Afro-Brazilian religious groups, and as a specifically derogatory term for evil and secret magical rituals. *See also* Afro-Americans (Caribbean and South America), new religions among; Afro-Brazilian religions; Kardecism.

madhhab (math'hab; Arab., "school"), a viewpoint or way of thinking and arguing in Islamic theology, law, and other religious disciplines. A *madhhab* different from one's own is generally regarded by Muslims as within the acceptable limits of varying interpretations of Islamic belief and practice. Intense devotion to one's madhhab, leading to the rejection of all others, is considered to be fanaticism by most Muslims.

Madhva (muhd'vuh; ca. 1238–1317, or ca. 1199–1278), founder of the Hindu Dvaita Vedanta school. Ordained a monk by a follower of Shankara's Advaita, Madhva dissented with his preceptor's interpretation of the spiritual classics. In two all-India tours, he converted many, including his preceptor. His works include dualistic commentaries on the *Brahmasutras*, Upanishads, and *Bhagavad Gita*. *See also* Dvaita Vedanta; six systems of Indian philosophy; Vedanta.

Madhyamaka (muhd'yuh-muh-kuh), a school of Mahayana Buddhist philosophy. The name Madhyamaka (Skt., "The Middle") identifies the school with the long line of Buddhist philosophers who have attempted to give an intellectual account of the Buddha's Middle Path. An adherent of the school is called a Madhyamika or a Shunyavadin ("One who holds the doctrine of Emptiness").

The school traces its origin to Nagarjuna (second or third century), an Indian philosopher who gave the first systematic account of the Mahayana concept of emptiness. Nagarjuna's most important work, *Mula-madhyamaka-karikas* (The Root Verses on the Middle Way), argues that all the categories of reality, from simple causation to the attainment of *nirvana* (liberation), are empty (*shunya*) of identity (*svabhava*). In addition to *The Root Verses*, Nagarjuna is credited with several important epistemological works and a series of devotional hymns.

As the Indian Madhyamaka tradition developed, controversies arose over the proper application of Nagarjuna's logical method. Buddhapalita (fifth or sixth century) and Candrakirti (seventh century) argued that the followers of Nagarjuna should no longer take their opponents' assertions and reduce them to absurd conclusions and should not maintain independent positions of their own. Their school is known as Prasangika Madhyamaka from the word *prasanga*, which means "absurd conclusion." Bhavaviveka (sixth century), another commentator on the works of Nagarjuna, argued that it was impossible for Madhyamikas to enter into debate without maintaining an independent argument. Bhavaviveka's school is called Svatantrika Madhyamaka from the word *svatantra*, which means "independent."

The Madhyamaka tradition was introduced into China by the great Buddhist translator Kumarajiva (350–409). Under the name of the San-lun ("Three Treatise") school, Madhyamaka enjoyed a brief period of influence at the beginning of the T'ang dynasty (seventh century) and flourished briefly in Japan. Madhyamaka thought had its greatest influence, however, in Tibet. Many of the early missionaries in Tibet were Madhyamaka philosophers from eastern India, and Madhyamaka philosophy was adopted by the founders or leading figures in several of the major Tibetan sects, notably the Geluk-pa (dGe-lugs-pa). Under Geluk-pa influence, Madhyamaka has been the dominant tradition in Tibetan philosophy up to the present day. *See also* Buddhism (authoritative texts and their interpretation); emptiness; Geluk-pa; Mahayana; Tibetan religions.

Madonna (Ital., "my lady"), title of the Virgin Mary, used in English to denote representations of Mary with the infant Jesus.

madrasa (ma'dra-suh; Arab., "place of learning"), places where studies in the Islamic religious sciences were conducted. Since the nineteenth century, the term has been extended to all schools. Religious learning often takes place in Friday mosques, with areas of the courtyard reserved for study at certain parts of the day. Rulers, notables, wealthy merchants, and pious endowments provide lodgings and support for scholars and students. Because of the high community value placed on religious studies, many students begin them, but few secure employment as religious functionaries or advance to higher levels.

mae de santo (maihng' ji-sahn'too; Portuguese, "mother of the saint/deity"), leader and priestess of the traditional Afro-Brazilian religions, especially of *Candomble*. *See also* Candomble.

Maenad (mee'nad), a female follower of Dionysos in Greek mythology; she is represented as in frenzy during his rituals and with long robes, ivy garlands, and carrying a staff tipped with a pine cone (Gk. *thyrsos*). *See also* Bacchae; Dionysos; ecstasy; Greek religion.

magatama (mah-gah-tah-mah; Jap., "curved jewels"), sacred kidney-shaped jewels such as the Yasaka Curved Jewels, one of the three imperial regalia of the Japanese emperor, along with the Yata mirror and Kusanagi, the miraculous sword from the goddess Amaterasu. *See also* kingship, sacred; mirrors, sacred.

Magen David/Star of David (mah'gen dah'vid; Heb., "Shield of David"), the six-pointed star, an important graphic symbol of Judaism. It appears on ritual objects, synagogues, and books—even on the flag of the Jewish state, Israel. Prior to the nineteenth century, however, the Star was neither popular nor specifically Jewish. From antiquity, the Magen David only occasionally decorated Jewish, Christian, and Moslem buildings. It often appeared with other geometric patterns. In medieval times, both Christians and Jews thought the symbol had magical powers against demons. It was during the emancipation of European Jewry, starting in the early nineteenth century, that the Magen David became the widespread symbol of Judaism.

Magi (may'jl, from Old Persian, of uncertain origin), Median priestly caste, later a title for Zoroastrian priests. In the Hellenistic world it connoted figures with wide occult knowledge. *See also* Iranian religion; Zoroastrianism.

magic. *See* amulet; black magic; charm; contagious magic; curse; evil eye; fang-shih; hocus-pocus; incantation; magic, science, and religion; majinai; maya; necromancy; pentagram; phylactery; sorcery; theurgy; white magic.

magic, science, and religion. The question debated by scholars is less whether magic, science, and religion are distinct and more whether or not they are compatible. Nineteenth-century scholars tend to stress their incompatibility. Twentieth-century scholars stress their compatibility.

Edward Tylor: The key nineteenth-century theorists in the debate are the anthropologists E. B. Tylor and James Frazer. For Tylor (*Primitive Culture*, 1871), magic, science, and religion alike are at once explanations of the physical world and, secondarily, attempts to control it. Both magic and science correctly assume that the world operates by natural laws. Magic and science are incompatible because magical laws are false, scientific ones true. By contrast to both magic and science, religion falsely assumes that the world operates by the wills of one or more gods.

For Tylor, "primitives" have both magic and religion; "moderns" have science. How magic and religion are reconcilable Tylor never says; nor does he say how moderns can be simultaneously religious and scientific. More precisely, he never says how scientific moderns can retain religion as an explanation of the world, for he assumes that modern religion is ethics rather than an explanation of the world and so runs on a different path than science. Where religion does survive as an explanation, it is a mere dying relic. Magic that survives is likewise a relic: it is superstition.

James Frazer: While Frazer's (*The Golden Bough,* 1890–1915) views on magic, science, and religion are far better known than Tylor's, Frazer takes most of his views from Tylor. When going beyond Tylor, he pits magic against not only science but also religion. All three systems are mutually exclusive. Earliest humanity had only magic. Later, though still primitive, humanity developed religion—the distinction here between magic and religion is identical with Tylor's. Frazer then proceeds to combine the two in an in-between stage that follows the incompatible stages of sheer magic and sheer religion in which humans, by playing the roles of the gods, magically induce divine behavior.

Bronislaw Malinowski: The principal twentieth-century analysts of magic, science, and religion have been the anthropologists Bronislaw Malinowski and Mary Douglas. Like both Tylor and Frazer, Malinowski ("Magic, Science, and Religion," 1925) assumes that all three enterprises are explanations of the physical world. Like them, he assumes that magic and science postulate impersonal forces and that religion postulates gods. Further, he too assumes that magic and science, though not religion, explain the world in order to control it.

But where for Tylor and Frazer magic and science are redundant efforts, for Malinowski they are not: primitives have so rudimentary a science that magic is needed to supplement it. Tylor and Frazer contend that magic sometimes works because it coincidentally involves scientific techniques—for example, the planting of seeds in the ground. Malinowski asserts that primitives recognize the difference between magic and science and employ magic to shore up their tenuous science. Possessing keener scientific expertise, moderns have scant need of magic.

For Tylor and Frazer, magic and science are mutually exclusive accounts of the world. For Malinowski, the two accounts are neither incompatible nor redundant, though he fails to say how they are compatible. The difference for him is not only that the magical explanation is false and the scientific one true, but also that magic is an emotional as well as a practical activity. It arises in desperation and amounts to wish fulfillment.

Malinowski ascribes to religion a different function from that of magic and science: not to control the world, but to justify a world beyond one's control. Religion alters not the world but one's attitude toward it. Like magic, it alleviates primitives' anxiety over their helplessness before the world. Magic treats immediate anxieties like hunger. Religion treats longer-term ones like death. Religion serves also to unify the community, by justifying the social world.

Malinowski reconciles religion with magic and science in the same way that he reconciles magic with religion: by appealing to the compatibility of the functions served, not to the compatibility of the explanations themselves. For Malinowski, as for Tylor and Frazer, moderns cannot have magic, science, and religion because the effectiveness of their science renders magic unnecessary and religion irrelevant. Primitives can have all three because the limited efficacy of their science leaves room for the other two.

Mary Douglas: Mary Douglas (*Purity and Danger,* 1966) attacks the conventional view, pioneered by the nineteenth-century biblical scholar William Robertson Smith, that primitive religion is magical and modern religion spiritual or ethical. She argues that there is more to primitive religion than magic and more to modern religion than spirituality or ethics. Rather than arguing, like Malinowski, that primitives have both religion and magic, she argues that they have both a nonmagical and a magical side to their religion. Because the two sides are of religion, they are presumably part of a single explanation of the world and so do not need to be reconciled conceptually since their functions are compatible.

For Douglas, as for Malinowski, Tylor, and Frazer, the magical side of religion serves to control the world, though, by subsuming magic under religion, she does not explain how gods are subject to magical manipulation. The nonmagical side of religion, for Douglas the primary one, serves to organize the world by classifying it. A rain dance, for example, serves primarily not to induce rain but to distinguish the rainy season from the dry.

Douglas is equally concerned with reconciling magic with science, and she similarly does so by making them comparable. Spring cleaning, to cite her favorite example, serves less to remove accumulated dirt than to classify the seasons into winter and spring. Like a rain dance, it serves primarily to make a statement, not to affect the world. For Douglas the prime function of magic and religion alike is expressive, not instrumental. *See also* instrumental and expressive; origin of religion.

Magna Mater (mahg'nah mah'tair; "the Great Mother"), a name under which the ancient Romans worshiped Cybele, the mother of the gods, a divinity of Anatolian origin. *See also* Attis; Roman religion.

Magnificat, Latin name for the New Testament hymn uttered by Mary (Luke 1:46–55).

Mahabharata (mah-hah-bah'rah-tah; Skt., "great tale of the Bharatas"), an ancient epic poem composed in India. The 180,000-line poem is the culmination of a long process of oral composition and transmission eventually put in writing apparently before the year 400. Hindu tradition attributes its composition to the sage Vyasa.

The *Mahabharata* tells the story of the heroic Pandava brothers who fought their cousins, the Kauravas, for possession of the Bharata Kingdom. The epic often describes the Pandavas as sons of gods or gods incarnate and the Kauravas as demons incarnate; their battle is depicted as the result of a divine plan to rid the earth of demons. The Pandavas are counseled by their ally Krishna, who is revealed to be an incarnation of Narayana Vishnu.

The *Mahabharata* includes the well-known Hindu scripture the *Bhagavad Gita*, in which Krishna reveals his divinity to his companion Arjuna Pandava and teaches Arjuna the discipline of action (*karma yoga*), the performance of actions without desire for personal gain. The *Mahabharata* also includes a long passage in which Bhisma transmits to Yudhisthira Pandava religious and political teachings to prepare him for kingship and liberation (*moksha*). There are numerous other passages of religious significance scattered throughout the epic.

The *Mahabharata* describes itself as "the fifth Veda." But while the Vedas are concerned with performance of sacrificial ritual, the epic teaches devotion (*bhakti*), particularly to Krishna/Vishnu. Moreover, the *Mahabharata*, unlike the *Vedas*, is explicitly intended for all people, women as well as men, low caste and high. It has been popular for over two millennia as a compendium of wisdom and a source of paradigmatic figures. *See also* Bhagavad Gita; Hinduism (authoritative texts and their interpretation); Krishna; Vishnu.

Mahabodhi Society (mah-hah-boh'dee), a Buddhist association founded by the monk Anagarika

Dharmapala in Sri Lanka in 1891. The principal aim of the society was to restore the temple at Bodh Gaya in northern India, the site at which the Buddha is said to have achieved his enlightenment. *See also* Bodh Gaya; Buddhas.

Mahadeviyakka (muh-hah'day-vi-yuhk-kuh; Kannada, "great goddess sister"), a twelfth-century Lingayat female saint. Her ardent devotion to Lord Shiva led her to reject King Kaushika's marriage proposals, leave her parents, and wander naked singing hymns to and seeking union with her "true" husband, Lord Shiva himself. *See also* Lingayat; Shiva.

Mahanubhava (muh-hah'noo-bah-vuh; Skt., "one who has a great experience"), a Hindu sect founded by Chakradhara in Maharashtra in the thirteenth century. Mahanubhava teachings emphasize strict asceticism, but the group includes laity as well as monks and nuns. All practice exclusive devotion to a single god (Parameshvara), the sole source of liberation, considered to have been incarnated in Krishna, Dattatreya, Chakradhara, Gundama Raula, and Cangadeva Raula. Devotees' recollection (*smarana*) of these incarnations is fostered by pilgrimage, a cult of relics, and a substantial body of literature in Old Marathi, including biographies of Chakradhara and the other incarnations. *See also* asceticism; Krishna; pilgrimage.

Mahaprajapati (muh-hah-pruh-jah'puh-tee), in Buddhism the Buddha's aunt (and nursemaid), who later campaigned for the ordination of women and became a prominent Buddhist nun. *See also* Buddhas.

Maharaj Ji, Guru (ma-ha-raj' jee; Hindi; b. 1957), the religious title and name of Prem Pal Singh Rawat, who succeeded his father, Shri Hans Maharaj Ji, as the spiritual leader of the Divine Light Mission in 1966. *See also* Divine Light Mission.

Maharishi Mahesh Yogi (mah-hah-ree'shee mah'hesh yo'gee; b. 1911), popularizer of Hindu meditative practices in the West through his simplified technique of Transcendental Meditation. *See also* North America, new religions in; Transcendental Meditation.

Mahasamghika (muh-hah-sang'gee-kuh; Skt., "belonging to the majority community"), one of the groups of schools comprising the so-called eighteen schools of Nikaya ("sectarian") Buddhism that emerged in the centuries following the death of the Buddha. The northern wing of the Mahasamghikas, based in northwest India and Afghanistan, portrayed the Buddha as a supernatural being who only appeared to be embodied in this world. The other branch, based in southcentral India, appears to have minimized the attainments of the *arhats* (enlightened followers of the Buddha) and may also have advocated the pursuit of complete Buddhahood by the Buddha's disciples. *See also* Nikaya Buddhism.

mahasiddha (mah-hah-si'dah; Skt., "fully perfected one"; also simply *siddha,* "perfected one"), enlightened ideal of Indian Tantric Buddhism, also important in Tibet. In hagiography, *siddhas* are depicted as ordinary people, frequently of low caste, who, under the demanding tutelage of a *guru,* practice Tantric Buddhist meditation in retreat. Attaining liberation, they are understood as unconventional saints of wisdom, compassion, and virtually unlimited magical power, who are venerated by gods and humans alike. *See also* Tantrism (Buddhism).

Mahavira. *See* Jainism.

Mahayana (mah-hah-yah'nah; Skt., "Great Vehicle"), name applied to the schools resulting from the synthesis of a variety of new ideas and practices that emerged within the Buddhist tradition during the first century B.C. through the third century A.D. Major ingredients in the formulation of this new wing of Buddhism included a reformulation of the understanding of the identity of the Buddha (previously seen as an ordinary mortal who had attained the maximum degree of insight of which a human being is capable, the Buddha was viewed by certain proto-Mahayana thinkers as the manifestation of an eternal Being or entity, and thus in a certain sense beyond the limits of ordinary human capacities); a redefinition of the nature of Buddhist practice (while earlier Buddhist schools had seen the ideal path as an imitation of that undertaken by the Buddha, resulting in a personal experience of enlightenment and subsequently in compassionate activity toward others, Mahayana thinkers emphasized the importance of the exercise of compassion prior to enlightenment, accusing their non-Mahayana counterparts of being concerned only with their own welfare; they also claimed that only practice of this sort could result in full Buddhahood); and an extension of the concept of no-self (while earlier Buddhists affirmed that all compounded things are transitory and must necessarily disintegrate at

some point, Mahayanists viewed even the momentary components of such entities to be insubstantial and thus in a certain sense unreal).

Origins: What came to be known as the Mahayana did not emerge as a monolithic movement; rather, its schools are the product of the weaving together of a variety of elements formulated in a variety of contexts. The concept of the Buddha as a supernatural being was probably developed by the northwest Mahasamghika schools, while the idea that full Buddhahood was a legitimate goal of Buddhist practice appears to have been formulated first in Sarvastivadin circles. The extension of the idea of no-self is more difficult to trace.

The idea that the Mahayana schools were the product of a lay Buddhist environment (in contrast to the "Buddhist elite" of monks and nuns) was once quite influential but has recently been losing ground as scholars have pointed to the primacy of the monastic ideal in the earliest Mahayana scriptures.

Scriptures and Pantheon: Once these three new ideas had been formulated, they were brought together by scholastic Buddhist thinkers in a synthesis that ultimately came to be known as the Mahayana. For most of the laity, adherence to the Mahayana took the form simply of paying homage to several new members of the Buddhist pantheon (in particular, a number of celestial Buddhas and Bodhisattvas) and accepting the legitimacy of the new Mahayana scriptures (*sutras*), composed four or more centuries after the death of the Buddha but attributed to the Buddha himself. Among these scriptures some of the earliest (and ultimately most influential) were the three Pure Land sutras (the larger and smaller *Sukhavati-vyuha* sutras and the meditation on the Buddha of Infinite Life), the *Lotus Sutra,* and the early Prajnaparamita (Perfection of Wisdom) texts, including the *Ashtasahasrika* (Perfection of Wisdom in 8,000 Lines). It is not at all clear that the authors of these various sutras would have considered themselves members of a single school at the time of their composition; in fact, the opposite is more likely, that each of these groups of literature emerged in a separate environment and they were only brought together into the single category of "Mahayana literature" several centuries after the fact.

New members introduced into the Buddhist pantheon fell into two categories: the so-called celestial Buddhas (e.g., Amitabha, Amitayus, and Vairochana) and the celestial Bodhisattvas (e.g., Avalokiteshvara and Manjusri). Scholars have raised questions concerning the geographic origins of virtually all of these figures (suggesting, in particular, that most or all of them may be the result of Iranian influence). Whatever their origins, however, these figures became central to both devotional and philosophical reflection among Mahayana Buddhists.

Philosophy: For the more philosophically inclined, however, it was not sufficient simply to accept these new scriptures as the word of the Buddha or to offer homage to these new members of the Buddhist pantheon. The complexity of the ideas these scriptures contained and the unanswered questions concerning the status of these new Buddhas and Bodhisattvas required a new philosophical synthesis, and ultimately these new notions were solidified into two major schools: the Madhyamaka and the Yogachara. The Madhyamaka school emphasized the interdependence of all phenomena and the absence of an enduring "own-being" (*svabhava*) in any entity. The Yogachara school viewed the Madhyamaka position as dangerously close to nihilism (that is, toward denying the reality of the karmic law of cause and effect in the realm of moral action) and affirmed the reality of a substratum of consciousness underlying the transitoriness of all phenomena. For the Yogacharins even consciousness was viewed as existing in dependence on other phenomena and thus was not ultimately real; it played an important role, however, in explaining both the nature of everyday experience and the structure of the moral law of cause and effect.

Geographical Diffusion: Mahayana Buddhism became the predominant wing of Buddhist thinking in China as early as the third century and played a leading role in Tibet from the seventh century on. In Central Asia, however, it appears to have gained a significant number of adherents only in Khotan, while the remainder of Central Asians gave their allegiance to the Sarvastivada school. In Southeast Asia the Mahayana has risen to prominence in Vietnam (where it was introduced under Chinese auspices), while most other nations fall largely within the Theravada camp. Likewise in Korea and Japan the Mahayana has gained a position of almost exclusive prominence as a result of its introduction from China. *See also* Buddhism; Buddhism (authoritative texts and their interpretation); Madhyamaka; Nikaya Buddhism; Theravada; Yogachara.

Mahdi (meh'dee; Arab., "rightly guided one"). 1 Messianic restorer and bringer of divine justice in Islam. *See also* Day of Judgment (Islam). 2 Epithet for Muhammad Ahmad (1844–81), leader of Sudanese revolt against Anglo-Egyptian rule. *See also* Ithna Ashari Shia.

Mahikari (ma-hi-ka'ree), a Japanese new religion founded by Okada Kotama in 1959 when Su, a hitherto unknown deity, was revealed to Okada as the creator of the universe. The cosmology revealed to Okada resembles other new religions of the Oomoto lineage, such as Sekai Kyuseikyo, of which Okada was a member. Su, according to the revelation, created a benevolent universe with Japan at its center. Gradually the world became polluted by human desires and by evil spirits until Su had to return to save it from destruction through the offices of Okada. Mahikari posits a return to a pristine human glory and teaches that problems come from spirit possession, either by unhappy ancestral spirits or by animal spirits.

The way to rid the person of these spirits is through *okiyome*, radiating rays of divine light from Su mediated through amulets worn by believers and blessed by Okada, who, until his death, was Su's mediator on earth. Mahikari has a strong belief in spiritual healing and in the ability of members to perform miracles and exert control over events through okiyome. It especially attracts young people in Japan but has a high membership turnover, and has, since the death of Okada, split into two rival groups. *See also* Japan, new religions in; Oomoto.

maithuna (mi-toon'uh; Skt., "paired," "coupled"), the practice of ritualized sexual intercourse in the Hindu and Buddhist Tantric traditions. Symbolically replicating the union of Shiva and Shakti, the conjoined pair meditatively bypasses and transmutes ordinary orgasm to stimulate the ascending *kundalini* (energy at the base of the spine) and experience an inner and mystical union. *See also* kundalini; Tantra.

Maitreya (mi-tray'uh), the next Buddha to appear in this world, whose advent is anticipated by virtually all schools of Buddhism. Maitreya is not based on a historical figure, though a disciple with a similar name makes a brief appearance in the Pali canon; it has been argued, but not proven, that Maitreya is a Buddhist version of the Iranian deity Mithra. Maitreya is expected to be born in this world in the distant future (dates range from 540 million to 5.4 billion years from now). Like the historical Buddha Sakyamuni, he will attain enlightenment and lead many followers to liberation. At present he is believed to reside in the Tusita heaven, where he has been visited by Buddhist mystics in visionary trance.

Maitreya is credited with the authorship of a number of Buddhist treatises (belonging to the Yogachara school) that were revealed during such visits. Buddhists have sought communion with Maitreya through vows to be reborn in his Tusita heaven and by attempting to gain sufficient merit to be reborn on earth during his lifetime. In China the figure of Maitreya was assimilated into Taoist mythology, resulting in the expectation of the imminent appearance of Maitreya and a number of revolutionary uprisings in his name. *See also* Bodhisattvas; Buddhas.

Maitreyism in Korea. *See* Korea, Maitreyism in.

majinai (mah-jee-ni), Japanese prophylactic and curative magic, including exorcism, purification, and charms. Some practices have become general custom, such as sprinkling salt on someone returning from a funeral. *See also* amulet; exorcism; Japanese folk religion.

Makhzor (mahkh-zohr'; Heb., "[annual] cycle [of prayers]"), Jewish holiday prayer books as opposed to Sabbath and daily liturgy. *See also* Judaism, prayer and liturgy of.

makoto (mah-koh-toh; Jap., "true sincerity"), proper moral attitude long associated in Shinto with the pure or true heart. The great Shinto scholar Motoori Norinaga (1730–1801) revived interest in this by referring to the "sincere heart" as the spark of the divine in the human. *See also* Motoori Norinaga.

malaika. *See* angel.

Malcolm X (1925–65), foremost spokesperson for the Nation of Islam. He advocated black separatism and self-protection against white violence. In 1964, he broke from the group, returning from a pilgrimage to Mecca convinced that traditional Islam promised interracial harmony. He founded the Organization of Afro-American Unity, a program for African-American liberation. *See also* African Americans (North America), new religions among; Nation of Islam.

Maldevian movement. *See* Afro-Americans (Caribbean and South America), new religions among.

Malik ibn Anas (ma-lik' ib-in' e-nes'; d. 795), renowned Muslim religious scholar of Medina, founder of the Malikite school of religious law. *See also* Malikite.

Malikite (ma'li-kit; Arab.), of or pertaining to the Malikite school of Islamic religious law, predominant throughout North Africa and the Muslim regions of Central and West Africa, as well as in Upper Egypt. This school developed out of the practice of Malik ibn Anas (d. 795) and his followers. *See also* Islamic Law.

mambo (mahm-bow'), a female ritual specialist according to traditional Voodoo or Vodou terminology. Synonymous with "mama-loa" or "female master of the gods," this title has its origins in African Fon religion, and in Haitian religion identifies a complex role of priestess, visionary, and counselor. *See also* Voodoo.

Mamluks (mam'looks; Arab., "owned objects"), military slaves who became an important part of Muslim military forces in medieval times. The Mamluks of the Ayyubid sultans in Egypt took control of the state in 1250 and organized the successful military responses to the European Crusaders and the Mongol invasions of the thirteenth century. Mamluks of Kipchak-Turkish origin controlled the state until 1382, when Circassian Mamluks became the dominant force. Initially, the Mamluks were militarily effective, but by the fifteenth century Mamluk conservatism resulted in an unwillingness to adopt newer military techniques. The Mamluk state was conquered by the Ottomans in 1517.

mana, Melanesian term for an object or person possessing power, either temporarily or permanently, and characteristically found only in relatively complex native societies, where it appears to function as a term of status. Misunderstood as being a general notion of impersonal power, it was widely appealed to by nineteenth- and early-twentieth-century theories of religion as a primitive form of sacrality. *See also* manitou; orenda; origin of religion; Sacred, the; Wakan Tanka.

Manasa (muh-nuh'sah; Bengali), a pan-Indian goddess of snakes, especially cobras, most popular in northeast India and Bangladesh. Called Vishahari, "mistress of poisons," she is propitiated during the monsoon season, especially by snake handlers.

-mancy, suffix signifying a method of divination attached to a noun indicating the object used. Examples include hydromancy (divination by water), oneiromancy (divination by dreams), ornithomancy (divination by the flight of birds). *See also* divination.

Mandaeans (man-dee'uhnz; from Mandaic *manda*, "knowledge"), an extant group of Gnostics living in Iraq and Iran. Possibly as early as the first century, the Mandaeans emigrated from the Jordan Valley area eastward to the riverways of present-day Iraq and then to southeast Iran (Khuzistan). Subjected under Islam since the mid-seventh century, the Mandaeans have survived, at times under duress. Until the Iraq-Iran war of 1980 to 1988, they numbered perhaps fourteen thousand, but at present the size of the population is difficult to estimate.

Literature: Mandaic is an East Aramaic dialect, and the Mandaeans possess a large literature. Myths, liturgies, ritual commentaries, magical texts (some on lead strips and clay bowls), and a book of astrology make up the largest written tradition of any one Gnostic group—with the possible exception of Manichaeism. The *Ginza* (Mandaic, "treasure"), the main collection of texts, is divided into the *Right Ginza* and the *Left Ginza*. The former consists of mythologies, revelations, moral teachings, and apocalyptic texts while the *Left Ginza* contains chiefly hymns. *The Book of John* incorporates several texts, some of them featuring John the Baptist, a prophet "adopted" by the Mandaeans in Islamic times. Parts of the large collection *The Canonical Prayerbook of the Mandaeans* date back at least to the third century.

Mythology: As in most Gnostic traditions, in Mandaean myths light strives with darkness. The dualism is not absolute but allows for a certain uneasy cooperation between light and dark forces. The soul, fallen or sent out from the upper realms, the Lightworld, to dwell in the human being, yearns for its original home. Mandaean poetry reaches its heights in the hymns describing the soul's complaints, hopes, and ascent. Usually, a Lightworld figure, an utra, acts as a revealer and savior to the soul, but in this process he himself may become tainted with matter and evil. Some utras are world creators, such as Ptahil, whose goals become intertwined with those of Ruha, his female opponent, the mother of the planets and the zodiac spirits. However, Ruha is not unequivocally evil, for she hails from the Lightworld and represents the spirit in the Mandaean anthropological model of the human being consisting of body, spirit, and soul (in ascending order).

Rituals: Mandaean ritual life centers on repeated baptism (*masbuta*) in flowing water (*yardna*, "Jordan"). A ritual for the dead, the *masiqta* ("raising-up"), transports each Mandaean soul from the dead body to its Lightworld home, and various meals are eaten for the dead. Complex rituals for initiating priests secure a continued, though small, supply of the lower-level priest class, the *tarmidas*, and, more rarely, the upper-level *ganzibras*. Traditionally, only priests had access to the scriptures, but in recent years concerned Mandaeans have produced books about the religion for laypeople so that not only the learned class, the Nasoraeans, know the traditional teachings. This marks one of several features in a revitalization movement and it promises continued life for a religion that many thought destined for extinction. *See also* baptism; Gnosticism.

mandala (mahn'duh-luh; Skt., "circle"). 1 Elaborate, symbolic geometric design used in Hindu, Buddhist, and Jain rituals. *Mandalas* are complex, multicolored cosmodiagrams representing the totality of the macrocosm in relation to the human microcosm. They provide an ordered, patterned display of the many levels of the sacred inhabited by assemblages of powers and deities. Numerous variants exist, but the geometric arrangement of mandalas typically expands out in layers from a center and is oriented along directional axes. While mandalas are often circular, square mandalas figure prominently in architectural representations of Hindu temples as well as in the design of sites for initiatory rituals in the Tantra. Here they demarcate the sacred terrain within which the deities abide for the space of the ritual.

Buddhism: The mandala is a psychophysical diagram used in Buddhist Tantric liturgy and yoga. From the viewpoint of deluded, egoistic experience, the world and body appear random and chaotic. However, in an enlightened perspective, revealed in the mandala, the world is seen as a divine cosmos and the body as a microcosm. "Mandala" refers in an ideal sense to the nature of reality itself, but also names the particular symbol that represents and liturgically embodies this reality. Within the mandala reside, in the center and concentric arrangements around the center, particular celestial Buddhas, whose number, gender, and identity depend upon the particular Tantric text and tradition with which the mandala is associated. It has a complex symbology with dimensions both cosmological (directions of the compass, colors, elements, times of day, annual seasons) as well as microcosmic (psychological types, emotions, elements of perception, types of wisdom). Physical representations of the mandala, used in liturgy, include two-dimensional depictions and three-dimensional structures. Using them, practitioners mentally create or visualize the mandala and its inhabitants according to textual instructions. The visualized mandala is brought to life through the descent into the visualized image of the living presence of the appropriate deities. The most well-known use of the mandala occurs in the rite of initiation, in which the initiate is led through a complex ritual, the climax of which occurs with the "showing of the mandala" and the entering of the initiate into it. After this, one is empowered to carry out the ongoing practice of the liturgies and thus to visualize and enter the mandala at will. The mandala is also important in Tantric yoga, where ultimate reality is found within the body, which is visualized as a mandala with divine inhabitants. *See also* Hinduism (temple art and architecture); Tantra; Tantrism (Buddhism).

A Tibetan Buddhist *mandala* from the Paro monastery in Bhutan. It is a schematic representation of the cosmos as governed by the Wheel of Time (the various eccentric orbits occupying the center ground of the mandala).

2 A chapter or division of a book. For example, the ten books of the early Hindu scripture *Rig Veda* are termed mandalas, i.e., "circles" of hymns.

Mandate of Heaven. *See* T'ien-ming.

Manichaeism (man-i-kee'iz-uhm; Gk. *Manichaios,* from Aram. *mani hayya,* "Mani, the Living"), religion based on the teachings of the prophet Mani, who was born in Babylonia in 216. His parents were Iranian: his father, Patik, from Hamadan, was a resident of Seleucia-Ktesiphon; his mother was related to the ruling Parthian Arsacides. Mani grew up in a baptist community his father had joined. The tiny Greek Cologne Mani-Codex, "On the Genesis of his (Mani's) Body," identifies the community's founder as Alchasaios, or Elchasai (confirmed by the Arab historian an-Nadim in the tenth century), who flourished ca. 100.

In 228 Mani received his first revelation by an angel, his heavenly twin (Gk. *syzygos*), in "to ransom (Mani) from the error of the sectarians." After a second revelation in 240 he broke in public with the community and moved to the capital Seleucia-Ktesiphon. At issue were the legitimacy of harvesting and the efficacy of rituals. Purity comes, according to Mani, through knowledge, not through bathing. His views were inspired by Marcion and Bardesan and by Jewish, Gnostic, and Encratite groups and scriptures. Mani suffered the death of a martyr during the reign of the Sassanian emperor Bahram I (274–277).

Worldview and Practice: Mani was the author of seven canonical works, preserved only in fragments, written in Aramaic except for the Middle Persian *Shabuhragan,* dedicated to the Sassanid monarch Shapur (ruled 240–273), who supported Mani. These texts teach two doctrines: the existence of two opposing eternal principles, light and darkness, and three stages of a cosmic battle: a preliminary stage, a stage in which both principles become mixed and battle for control of the cosmos, and a final stage in which light will win over darkness. This dualism resembles that in the Zoroastrian battle between light and darkness. For Mani the present world has been created to rescue heavenly light scattered as particles in the world. Human beings recalling the divine origin of their light-selves can help in releasing them.

Mani's doctrine was expressed in different symbolic forms. It was progagated through pictures and scriptures in nearly all known ancient languages and it adopted different religious conceptions (Platonic, Christian, Zoroastrian, Hindu, Buddhist, and Islamic). In contrast, the practice of the adherents was uniform.

The Manichaean Community: The Manichaean church consisted of two classes: the Elects (from Lat. *electus*) and the Auditors (Lat. *auditor,* "hearers"; Gk. *katechoumenos*). Only the Elects were constitutive; Auditors belonged to the church only by serving them. The Elects could fulfill different functions in the clerical hierarchy. Manichaean pictures, found in central Asia, show Hearers kneeling in front of female or male Elects adoring them. The Elects wore white garments and had to observe ascetic rules. Augustine, from 373 to 382 a Manichaean Auditor in North Africa, labeled the rules as the three seals of mouth, hands, and heart. An Elect was to keep his mouth pure and abstain from sexuality and from working. He had no fixed abode and wandered around like a foreigner in an alien world.

Auditors were obliged to serve the Elects through alms and hospitality. By preparing bread they polluted themselves, since agriculture was regarded as hurting the light. By eating the bread and other vegetables the Elects could free the captive light in the food and become "saviors of God." In their daily life the Hearers had to act according to ten commandments and to observe ritual times. They could hope to have a part in the process of salvation.

Spread: After his break with the Elchasaites, Mani was commissioned by his angel with a worldwide mission. At first he went to India. Later, his religion, supported by merchants, achieved missionary success in the Roman Empire. Due to its success it was severely persecuted, first by the Roman emperor Diocletian in 297 and later by Christian rulers. In the West the term *Manichee* was later used by orthodox Christians to designate heterodox groups holding dualistic worldviews (such as the medieval Paulicians, the Bogomils, and the Cathars). In the East Manichaeism was conveyed along the Silk Road. In the eighth century it became the official religion of the central Asian state of the Uigurs, while it was suppressed in the Islamic state of the Abbasids. In China it survived as late as the sixteenth century. *See also* Augustine of Hippo; Catharism; Cologne Mani Codex, Elchasai, Elchasaites; Gnosticism; Inner Asian religions; Kephalaia.

manifest, latent, a distinction often associated with functional theories. Manifest functions are those that are intended and recognized by participants in the system, while latent functions are neither intended nor recognized by the participants. *See also* emic, etic.

Manikkavacakar (mah'nee-kah-vah'sah-gahr; Tamil, "he whose speech is rubies"; ca. ninth century), Hindu poet-devotee who composed Tamil lyrics to the god Shiva. His *Tiruvacakam* is sung during Tamil Shaiva temple ritual. *See also* path of devotion; Shaivism; Shiva.

manitou (man'i-too), designation for sacred power used by Algonquian-speaking Native American peoples. Although the name was recorded in European writings as early as the late sixteenth century, a coherent, bias-free understanding was longer coming.

Manitou is simultaneously all-pervasive and unusual. Any physical form—those obviously alive and those not obviously so—may be manitou, but not all are. Other-than-human persons—spirits—are manitou. According to many of the stories of the Algonquian-speaking people, the being that has power, the manitou, can change shapes easily, especially from human to animal forms. It may be possible by means of rituals, dreams, or visions to become kin to this kind of manitou. Conversely it is possible to offend the manitou and become estranged from it.

Power objects are manitou, and can be used by those who have knowledge and a relationship with them. Some stories indicate that one's supply of power can be used up or wasted.

Manitou is potentially both life-threatening and life-sustaining. Used with harmful intentions, manitou can destroy. With positive intentions, it can be used to heal, to nurture, to affirm life. *See also* mana; North America, traditional religions in.

Manjushri (man'joo-shree; Skt., "charming splendor"), one of the main "celestial" Bodhisattvas in Buddhism. The Bodhisattva of wisdom, he is often represented carrying the sword of wisdom in his right hand and the books of the Perfection of Wisdom in his left. In the scriptures he is the mouthpiece for some of the most radical and critical statements of the teachings of emptiness. In East Asia, Manjushri (Chin. *Wen-shu;* Jap. *Monju*) may appear by himself, sometimes as the main image in Zen temples, or accompanied by figures such as Vimalakirti. In the popular tradition a variety of miracles are attributed to him, many of which are associated with his most famous sanctuary, Mt. Omei in southern China. *See also* Bodhisattvas; Perfection of Wisdom; prajna.

manna, in the Hebrew Bible, miraculous food provided to the Israelites during their wilderness wandering (Exodus 16:2–36).

mansin. *See* shamanism.

mantra (mahn'truh; Skt., "instrument of thought"), yogic meditational device in Hinduism, Buddhism, and Jainism. Mantra most often denotes a sequence of sounds (meaningful or meaningless) made potent by formal initiatory reception from a *guru* (spiritual leader) and used as a tool for meditation. The most famous mantra, *om,* figures in cosmological accounts as the source of creation. Others include *Namah Shivaya,* "Adoration to Shiva," and the Buddhist *Om mani padme hum,* "Om, Homage to thee, O Manipadma." Mantra repetition (whether verbal or mental) is thought to attune and potentize the awareness of the practitioner, disclosing the absolute foundation of consciousness. Mantras are also a central instrument in ritual and magical practices. *See also* Gayatri mantra; Hinduism (authoritative texts and their interpretation); meditation; Om/Aum; Om mani padme hum.

Manu, Laws of (mahn'*oo*; Skt., lit., "man," referring to the progenitor of humankind), an encyclopedic work composed ca. 200 B.C.–A.D. 200 that is perhaps the most important Hindu text on *dharma,* social and religious "duty." Topics addressed in the text include the proper comportment and socioreligious obligations for individuals of the different classes (*varnas*) and stages of life (*ashramas*); how a righteous king should rule; the appropriate relations between men and women; cosmogony, *karma* (the consequences of meritorious or demeritorious actions), and rebirth; rites of passage and other domestic rituals; and how one should conduct oneself in everyday life. *See also* dharma; kingship, sacred.

Man'yoshu (mahn-yoh-sh*oo;* Jap., "Collection of Ten Thousand Leaves"), the earliest extant collection of Japanese poetry; it includes 4,500 poems, primarily *tanka* ("short poems"), written between 600 and 759. Many poems involve a magico-religious context of ritual and *kotodama* (the sacred power of words). *See also* Japanese religions (art and architecture); kotodama.

Maoism (mou-iz-uhm), the quasi-religious cult of Mao Tse-tung (1893–1976), which rose to its zenith in the early years of the Chinese Cultural Revolution (1966–76), then rapidly disappeared. His devoted followers confessed their faults, participated in ritualistic rallies, offered their lives for the victory of the proletariat, and quoted the little red book of Mao's writings as a kind of sacred scripture. The Mao cult was millennial, looking forward to a utopian state with a classless society. It had its saints, martyrs, and heroic figures, such as Lei Feng, and was religiously exclusive, leaving no room for competing ideologies. *See also* Lei Feng.

Maori new religions. For almost two centuries the Maori of New Zealand have been in contact with Europeans (*Pakeha*) and for slightly less than that time they have been involved with representatives of European Christianity. Inevitably perhaps, the temporal proximity of Christianity and colonialism reinforced Maori perceptions of Pakeha power, and the dispossession and despair of the nineteenth century found expression in religious movements employing the symbols of Christianity to explain Maori desolation and to hold out hope for Maori redemption. These movements have persisted into the twentieth century, reflecting the enduring Maori sense of injustice. However, while the Old Testament was the model from which nineteenth-century Maori prophets drew inspiration, the New Testament has been the source for twentieth-century religious leaders.

Suffering the loss of their lands in the nineteenth century, the Maori found Old Testament imagery especially apt; they had prophets in their midst who would lead their chosen people out of exile into the promised land. Indeed, they called themselves *Tius* (Jews), worshiped Jehovah, and celebrated the Sabbath on Saturday. Continuing the metaphor, the colonial government was cast in Pharaonic terms. The Old Testament, made available in its entirety in 1858, a time when metaphors of isolation and dispossession were especially relevant, provided the mythology through which the Maori could distance themselves from the Pakeha intruder. The early concept of charismatic leadership provided continuity; for most Maori, the mantle of prophecy—passed down from one religious leader to the next, from one area of the country to the next—represented an inclusive relationship encompassing all prophetic ancestors. Nineteenth-century prophets, however, with the exception of Te Kooti, whose followers organized the still-thriving Ringatu church, had local followings with no formal organization that could withstand the death of the prophet.

In the twentieth century, Maori responses have become both more formal and more national with the institution of organized churches, and their metaphors now are borrowed from the New Testament. The twentieth century's religious activity probably began on the banks of the Rangitikei River, on the west coast of the North Island, with the prophet Mere Rikiriki. For followers of contemporary movements, her decision to seek the Holy Spirit in the Rangitikei by jumping into the river forty times (reflecting the repeated use of this number in the New Testament) opened a new religious age. Her assertion that the foundations of her movement were Matthew, Mark, Luke, and John clearly indicated the shift in emphasis into the New Testament. For most people, however, she is famous as the aunt of Wiremu Tahupotiki Ratana, whose renown she prophesied.

Ratana began as a faith healer, performing miraculous cures of the desperately ill and crippled. He received his message in 1918, an especially bad time for Maoris, who had been decimated by the influenza epidemic and whose soldiers, returning from World War I, did not find equality in New Zealand society. Drawn by oratory that could not help but move the defeated and the dispossessed, his Maori followers included individuals with tribal affiliations from all over New Zealand. They were called the *morehu* ("survivors") and Ratana was known as the *mangai* ("mouthpiece"), suggesting his role as mediator rather than generator of divine will.

The Ratana pantheon included not only the Father, Son, and Holy Spirit but a number of ministering angels who shared characteristics with traditional Maori and Christian mediators. By advocating the abolition of *tohungaism* (reliance on leaders who employed occult knowledge) and sorcery, Ratana reflected the preoccupations of Maori national leaders, who had reached the decision that accommodation, rather than resistance, was the path to be taken in the twentieth century. In many ways Ratana prepared Maoris to enter the Pakeha world, albeit on their own terms. He turned his attention to politics in 1928, forged an alliance with the Labour Party, and succeeded in effecting a Ratana monopoly of the four Maori parliamentary seats (1943–63). The church still has an active membership today, with a hierarchical clergy recruited from all over New Zealand; its concern with national politics has made explicit the important interrelationship between religious and political action.

In other areas of New Zealand, local prophets continue to have followings. Their gifts are varied; some are faith healers, others are seers; while others maintain contact with areas of Maori culture not respected by the Pakeha majority. In the Maori renaissance of the 1980s, interest in traditional Maori religion and in Maori versions or understandings of Christianity resurged. The history of Maori religious activity since contact demonstrates the particular ability of religious imagery and metaphor to encapsulate the Maori condition and to provide continuity in the face of rupture and dislocation. *See also* new religions.

Mao Shan (mou-shan; Chin., "Mt. Mao"), sacred Taoist mountain in South China and center of Shang-ch'ing Taoism (also called Mao Shan Taoism). *See also* mountains, sacred; Shang-ch'ing Taoism.

mappo (mahp-poh; Jap., "latter law") in Japanese Buddhism an era of degeneration, in which many paths to salvation become impossible. Since this era was calculated to begin in 1052, the idea of *mappo* informed many of the Buddhist reform movements of the late Heian and Kamakura periods (twelfth century) and remains a fundamental doctrine of many sects. *See also* ages of the world; Degenerate Age of the Dharma.

Mara (mah'ruh; Skt., "Death"), the "Evil One" in Buddhism. Mara is a god, the Lord of the Realm of Desire, and the chief opponent of the Buddha and his religion. He endeavors to block Buddhists from transcending his realm by attaining enlightenment. Thus, he hinders the efforts of meditators and preachers and seeks to lead astray celibate monks and nuns. He attacked the Buddha himself at Bodh Gaya and tried to tempt him sexually. Mara is also a symbol for anything likely to keep one under the sway of repetitive material existence (*samsara*), such as delusions and defilements. *See also* Buddhas; samsara.

maranatha (mah-rah-nah-thah'), Aramaic Christian petition, "Lord Come!"

Marcion (mahr'cee-on), a radical ascetic theologian from Sinope on the Black Sea who propounded his Christian Gnostic teachings in western Asia Minor and in Rome ca. 140. Marcion preached grace against law, but sharply distinguished the Old Testament malevolent God from the Christian God who was Jesus' father and who remains wholly alien to humans. Marcion let women teach and baptize. His strict, charismatic movement attracted numerous adherents and produced many martyrs. The first creator of a Christian canon, Marcion forced the orthodox to create something like the present New Testament. *See also* canon; Gnosticism.

Mardi Gras (Fr., "Fat Tuesday"), in Christianity the day before Ash Wednesday, the beginning period of Lent. Mardi Gras is traditionally the final day for eating meat until Easter Sunday. *See also* calendar (Christian); carnival; Lent.

Marduk (mahr'dook), also called Bel ("lord"), god of exorcism and "Lord of Wisdom." As city god of Babylon, he rose to prominence ca. 1800 B.C. The Creation Epic *Enuma elish* gives theological rationale to the political rise of Babylon and tells of Marduk's ascension to power. *See also* Enuma elish; Mesopotamian religion.

marebito (mah-ray-bee-toh; Jap., "stranger"), in Japanese folk religion, deities who mysteriously appear at harvesttime or the turn of the year bringing new life to rice seeds and humans. *See also* Japanese folk religion; Japanese religions (festal cycle).

Mari (mah′ree), an important ancient Syrian city located on the upper Euphrates River. Situated at a point where several trade routes converged, Mari (modern Tell Hariri) has been under excavation since 1933. The archaeological evidence suggests that the city was founded around 2600 B.C. and reached its peak in the period from 2000 to 1800 B.C. as evidenced from an archive found in one palace. Numbering more than twenty-five thousand tablets, the archive consists of letters and administrative records that provide a detailed picture of everyday life. The city was destroyed by Hammurabi, king of Babylon, around 1760 B.C. *See also* Mesopotamian religion.

Maria Candelaria (kan-de-lair-ee′ah), also known as Maria Lopez, a Tzetzal Mayan girl from Chiapas, Mexico, whose vision of the Virgin Mary in February 1712 became the basis of a Mayan separatist movement and holy war. When the Spanish army reconquered Cancun, she escaped and was never captured. Thereafter, she became a folk saint whose pursuit by Spanish "Jews" is recalled in contemporary Mexican carnival dramas. *See also* Mary (pilgrimage sites); Native Americans (Central and South America), new religions among.

Maria Lionza. *See* Afro-Americans (Caribbean and South America), new religions among.

Marie Bernarde Soubirous. *See* Bernadette of Lourdes.

Mark, by tradition the author of the second Gospel in the New Testament of the Bible.

Markos (mahr′kos), a Valentinian Gnostic of the late second century who was active in Gaul (France), was interested in number speculations, and let women prophesy and have priestly functions. *See also* Gnosticism; Valentinianism.

Maronites, name for those predominantly Lebanese Christians who trace their origins traditionally to Maro (350–433). It was only in the seventh century, under John Maron, that the Maronites became a separate ecclesiastical community. Converted by Emperor Heraclius to the doctrine of monotheletism (which held that there was only one will in the incarnate Christ), the Maronites became isolated theologically from both Monophysite and Orthodox churches. Following their excommunication in 680 by the Council of Constantinople, these monothelite Christians began to elect their own patriarch who, for safety, established his seat at Qadisha in the isolated hills of Lebanon.

Since the twelfth century, the Maronite community has forsaken the monothelite doctrine and adopted numerous features of the Roman Catholic Church while retaining many of its Eastern characteristics and prerogatives. Its hierarchy is led by the "Patriarch of Antioch and the East," who is chosen by the Maronite archbishops and bishops, and subsequently approved by the pope. In keeping with Eastern tradition, clerical marriage is still permitted among the lower clergy. The secular priests are selected by their congregations and are responsible for the administration of the sacraments. The liturgy is celebrated in Syriac. The liturgy is a version of an ancient Antiochene rite that has been modified and brought into conformity with the rites of Rome.

Marpa (mahr′pah; 1012–96), major figure in the propagation of Buddhism in Tibet. He visited India three times, receiving teachings from tantric masters Naropa and Maitripa, which he transmitted to his principal Tibetan disciple, Milarepa. Marpa is the first Tibetan member of the Kagyu-pa lineage. *See also* Kagyu-pa; Milarepa.

Marranos (mah-rah′nose, Span., "swine"), pejorative term for Jews forcibly converted to Christianity who continued in secret to practice Judaism. Known also as "New Christians" or Conversos, Marranos first appeared in Spain in 1391, when pogroms forced many Jews to convert to avoid execution. In 1492, when publicly professing Jews were expelled from Spain, Marranos remained behind. Known by their Jewish family origin, however distant, Marranos constituted a distinct group in Spanish society.

The Jews of Portugal were forcibly baptized in 1497, and many became Marranos. During the Spanish Inquisition (1478–1834), which was directed at Christian heretics, not professing Jews, "New Christians" accused of Judaic practices were tried and severely punished or burned at the stake.

Marranos practiced Christianity outwardly and Judaism in secret. This meant preserving certain Judaic customs, e.g., lighting candles on the Sabbath eve and fasting on the Day of Atonement. Many ultimately escaped from Spain and Portugal and reverted to Judaism. They were accepted by the Jewish authorities not as apostates but as forced converts, meaning that they were not deemed sinners but were welcomed back into the community as is. The first Jewish communities of the Western hemisphere derived from Marranos who escaped from Spanish and Portuguese colonies to Dutch and British ones.

marriage, a formal social and legal relationship, governed by rules and established through ritual, that recognizes an enduring sexual union and the legitimacy and status of its issue. *See*

At a wedding in Delhi, India, a Hindu bride and groom are displayed in their traditional wedding dress before hundreds of guests.

also Buddhism (life cycle); Chinese religions (life cycle); Christianity (life cycle); divorce; Hindu domestic ritual; Islam (festal cycle); Islam (life cycle); Judaism (life cycle); kanyadana; ketubah; kinship; life-cycle rituals.

Christianity: Marriage in the Christian tradition held an ambiguous position prior to the Protestant Reformation. Jesus was unmarried, and Paul counseled against it. The dualistic strain in the early church viewed sexual intimacy as a bodily temptation detrimental to the spirit. Augustine (d. 430) justified marriage strictly for the purpose of procreation and rearing children in the faith and expressed reservations about the realities of family life that interrupt the contemplative path. Medieval Catholicism developed a two-tier ethic, namely, an upper tier of celibate men and women, and a lower tier for those who married. Despite these reservations, marriage was considered a Christian sacrament.

Martin Luther (1483–1546) rejected the two-tier ethic, in favor of a single tier in which all persons are called to the special "estate" of marriage, God's holy order of creation.

In current Christian ethics, a few writers have defended "open marriage" in the wake of the sexual revolution. More conservative Protestants have firmly resisted this revisionist trend. Catholicism has struggled to maintain the ideal of faithful marriage against an atmosphere of sexual license. Some feminists have rejected marriage, but more recently leading theorists have come back to an affirmation of family life. Some ethicists have come to doubt whether romantic love is an adequate basis for a lasting marriage, which should be grounded in loyalty and Christian love. The contemporary Christian ethicist James M. Gustafson has argued that recent Christian ethics has not given sufficient attention to the basis of lasting Christian marriage.

Islam: Muslims view marriage as a bilateral contract whose principal elements are prescribed by the revealed law (*Sharia*). Other features derive from custom or are subject to negotiation by the parties concerned. The authority and responsibility of the man are paramount, but the rights and duties of the woman are also defined.

Marriage is regarded as a universal duty, the fullness of which includes children. Celibacy lacks religious sanction. While polygyny, one man having up to four wives, is permitted, it is exceptional and hedged with conditions that specify equal treatment of all wives. The Qur'an specifies categories of persons between whom marriage is forbidden and permitted. Common, especially in clan societies, is the *bint amm* ("paternal cousin") marriage, which serves to bind and extend families. Divorce is permitted; remarriage after divorce is common.

marriage, sacred, ritual sexual relations between a king, understood as in some sense divine, and a goddess. Whether this is done through mimetic activities or with an actual woman playing the role of a goddess varies and often remains obscure. *See also* kingship, sacred; sexuality and religion.

Mars, an ancient Italic god second to Jupiter in importance; a war god identified with Ares, he also possessed agricultural functions. In Rome, his own priest as well as the archaic Arval and Salian brotherhoods performed cult rituals. In mythology, he was the father of Romulus, founder of Rome. *See also* Roman religion.

Martha and Mary, biblical sisters who, in Christian symbolism, represent the active and contemplative life. According to Luke's Gospel (10:38–42), Martha served Jesus in her home while Mary sat at his feet.

martial arts, a set of traditional warrior combat skills transformed into spiritual disciplines.

Hinduism: Considered one of the eighteen traditional branches of knowledge in ancient India, the martial arts were known as the "science of archery" (Skt. *dhanurveda*) since practice with a bow was considered supreme. By birthright teachers of martial arts were either Brahmans (members of the priestly class, the highest of the four castes) or Kshatriyas (members of the second caste, including warriors, princes, and kings), although Shudras (workers and servants) and people of "mixed castes" could be called to combat. Martial artists underwent training in psychophysical and meditational exercises, weapons, and empty-hand combat. Circumscribed by rituals, the lengthy training brings superior self-control, mental calm, and the single-point concentration necessary to "conquer the god of death [Yama]" (*Agni Purana* 250.15).

Chinese Religion: Archaeological evidence demonstrates that, as early as the Chou dynasty (1122–221 B.C.), China had developed the foundations of fighting techniques into true martial arts. Evolved from ancient survival techniques, these systems became spiritual disciplines in their own right.

The religious dimension of martial arts was tempered by many factors. By necessity, fighting arts are an offshoot of the survival instinct of individuals, clans, and even dynasties. Thus, military, social, and political elements were always present, providing the rationale and impetus for the development and evolution of the martial arts.

Of the more than four hundred Chinese martial arts styles existing today, some developed within the ranks of imperial bodyguards, some within small village family clans, and others within the seclusion of temple walls. The philosophic and religious aspects of these systems, in turn, nurtured their physical, mental, and spiritual practices. Confucian, Taoist, and Buddhist elements are present.

Martial arts came to include meditative practices, training the mind to look inward for religious enlightenment. In this tradition, the body was seen as a microcosm of the universe. Schools of boxing developed, founded upon subtle Chinese philosophic principles such as *t'ai-chi* ("Great Ultimate") and *pa-kua* ("eight trigrams"). Within a Buddhist context, the arrival of Bodhidharma (448–527) at the Shaolin Temple in Hunan province started a tradition of utilizing martial arts practices to strengthen body and mind for the rigors of religious discipline. *See also* Boxer Rebellion; pa-kua; t'ai-chi.

Japanese Religion: In medieval times Japanese martial arts (*bujutsu*, also *budo*, "the martial way") included eighteen arts, although in the Tokugawa period (1600–1868) the standard number was seven: swordplay, spearmanship, archery, horseback riding, judo, firearms, and military strategy. Originating in the warrior (*samurai*) class, the martial arts were developed for use in battle or self-defense. Influenced by Buddhism and Confucianism and taught in the context of bushido (the warrior ethical code), the martial arts involve both mastering martial skills (*waza*) and engaging in spiritual discipline. Developing the martial heart (*kokoro*) made the warrior calm and unmoved in the face of danger and death; developing pliancy (*yawara*) allowed the warrior to parry and fight with naturalness and harmony. The techniques and spiritual training have been passed on by masters in various schools. Popular martial arts today are *kendo*, the way of the sword; *kyudo*, the way of the bow; and judo, the way of yielding (wrestling). *See also* bushido.

martyr (Gk., "a witness"), one who dies rather than renounce one's beliefs.

Judaism: In Judaism, the earliest martyrs were those killed by Antiochus IV (175–163 B.C.) when they refused to abandon their ancestral religion. In later texts, perseverance unto death became known as *kiddush ha shem*, "Sanctification of the Name (of God)."

Christianity: Roman opposition encouraged an ideal of martyrdom among some early Christians, especially in the second and third centuries. The veneration of these martyrs gave rise to the cult of the saints.

Islam: In Islam martyr is an honored title borne by one who suffers and dies while engaged in religious struggle (Arab. *jihad*). The Qur'an accords the highest rank to those who relinquish their lives and riches in God's path and gives assurance that they are forever alive and well nourished. Equal in glory to physical martyrdom are sufferings endured in the inner moral struggle of the self over its own base nature. The most celebrated of martyrs in Islam are al-Husayn (d. 680), massacred grandson of the Prophet, and Sufi mystic al-Hallaj (d. 922), executed for claiming unity with the Absolute.

Mary, mother of Jesus Christ, commonly called the Blessed Virgin Mary. Precise historical knowledge about her life is meager. The Gospels give various portraits and weigh her significance differently. The various Gospel scenes have entered the Christian imagination and been frequently depicted in Eastern icons and Western art. Gaps in Gospel portraits of Mary were filled in by second-century apocryphal literature, notably the *Protevangelium of James.*

Subsequent Christian doctrine and devotion maintained and developed her pivotal actions in redemptive history. Through her the Savior was born, irretrievably connected to the flesh of the human race. Through her free cooperation with God's design, the ancient disobedience of Eve was overturned. Later beliefs about her included that she powerfully intercedes for all God's children, especially the weak (mediatrix); that she was graced from the beginning of her existence (immaculate conception); and that she now lives body and soul in heaven (assumption). The Reformation criticized excesses that led to transferring trust from Christ to Mary. Contemporary Catholicism recovered the biblical themes of her faith and discipleship and her membership in the church as its preeminent model.

A popular cult of vast proportions has been directed toward Mary, whom some in the late twentieth century name a female symbol of deity, a loving, powerful Mother present and protective of her children. Shrines such as Our Lady of Lourdes in France and Our Lady of Guadalupe in Mexico draw millions of pilgrims annually. New miracles and apparitions continue to be reported.

Mary in Islam: Maryam (Mary), the mother of Isa (Jesus), appears in both quranic and Islamic lore. Her name means "the pious one" and she is often associated in Islamic piety with Fatima, Muhammad's daughter. Maryam's name appears thirty-four times in the Qur'an; twenty-two times she is mentioned in the phrase "Jesus the son of Maryam." In the Qur'an, Maryam is said to be the daughter of Imran (66:12), the biblical father of Moses, and the sister of Aaron (19:28), thereby belonging to the prophetic family. Islamic tradition records many privileges of Maryam, including the idea that, like Jesus, she was never touched by Satan. *See also* assumption; Fatima, Shrine of; Guadalupe, Shrine of; Jesus Christ; Lourdes; Madonna; Mary (pilgrimage sites); Theotokos.

Mary. *See* Martha and Mary.

Mary (pilgrimage sites), sites of reported appearances of, cures by, and memorials to the Virgin Mary as places of special Christian devotion and pilgrimage. Important sites (with dates of reported appearance in parentheses) include Banneux, Belgium (1933); Bayside, New York (1970s); Beauraing, Belgium (1932–33); Cairo, Egypt (1968–71); Cap de Madelaine, Canada; Czestochowa, Poland; Einsiedeln, Switzerland; Fatima, Portugal (1917); Garavandal, Spain (1961–65); Guadalupe, Mexico City, Mexico (1531); Knock, Ireland (1879); La Salette, France (1846); Le Puy, France; Loreto, Italy; Lourdes, France (1858); Mariazell, Austria; Medjugorge, Bosnia-Herzegovina (1981–93); Montserrat, Spain; Necedah, Wisconsin (1950s); Paris, France (1830); Pellevoisin, France (1876); Pontmain, France (1871); Rocamadour, France; Santo Cerro, Dominican Republic; and Walsingham, England (1061). Not all of these sites have been sanctioned by ecclesiastical authority, but they remain popular focuses of devotion. *See also* Mary; pilgrimage.

Mary Magdalene (mag'dah-leen), the most prominent female disciple of Jesus. In the Christian Gospels, she was healed by Jesus, became his disciple, supported his movement, accompanied him to Jerusalem, witnessed his death, and was the first person to whom the resurrected Jesus is said to have appeared. There is no basis for the later tradition that she was formerly a prostitute.

mashriq al-Adhkar. *See* Baha'i.

masjid *See* mosque.

masks. Although there are definitional controversies, the fundamental notion of a mask is that it conceals the wearer's face so that another visage may be displayed. Within traditional religions (especially in Africa, Melanesia, and North

America), the mask is usually the face of a divinity, an ancestor, or a culture hero. Masks frequently reference mythic events and are used when these events are represented. Within some traditional religions, knowledge of the true meaning of the masks is confined to secret societies; in others, knowledge is sexually differentiated; in others, there are complex layers of exoteric and esoteric understanding. Two popular theories of masks appear to rest on misunderstandings: masks are not chiefly representations of the dead (as they may be in European carnivals), and they are not a means of "mystical identification," where the masked figure becomes the supernatural being referenced by the mask. *See also* ancestors; culture hero; false face; Halloween; secret societies; t'ao-t'ieh; yeibichai.

Masons. *See* Freemasonry.

Mass (Lat. *missa*, "go, it is ended"; the dismissal ending the Roman Catholic liturgy), a term for the Catholic eucharistic rite, also referred to as "the Eucharist" or "the liturgy."

Variations of the rite exist; the Roman rite, used in the West, is the most extensive. Its structure is not dissimilar to Orthodox and Anglican eucharistic liturgies.

Mass begins with a greeting by the presider, a penitential prayer, a hymn of praise (the "Gloria"), and an opening prayer.

The liturgy of the Word follows, consisting of one or two scripture readings and a responsorial psalm. Following an alleluia refrain, a New Testament Gospel reading is done by the presider. A homily is usually given after these readings, followed by a profession of faith (creed) on Sundays and feast days. The segment concludes with general intercessory prayers.

The most important phase, the liturgy of the Eucharist, begins with the preparation of the altar and the presentation of the gifts of bread and wine. The eucharistic prayer or prayer of thanksgiving (traditionally referred to as the "canon") is offered by the presider and includes the consecration of the bread and wine.

The Communion rite follows, consisting of the Lord's Prayer, a sign of peace exchanged among the membership, and the reception of Communion (bread or both bread and wine). A concluding rite of blessing and dismissal ends the Mass. *See also* Byzantine liturgy; Christianity (worship).

master/mistress of the animals, in the traditions of archaic hunting peoples and herders, a supernatural figure with either human or animal attributes. Known by many native titles, master or mistress is the generic name employed by scholars.

Among some groups, the master or mistress rules the forest and is guardian of all animal species. Among other groups, the figure rules over only one species, usually a large animal of economic importance: bear (Eurasian and North American tribes), reindeer (circumpolar), whale, seal, or walrus (northern coastal), beaver, caribou (North American), jaguar, wild pig, tapir (Amazonian).

The master/mistress controls the game animals or their spirits (in herding cultures, by penning them). A certain number are released each season as food for humans. The animal's corpse must be treated with respect, and its soul returned, through ritual, to the master/mistress. *See also* Delaware prophets; ecological aspects of traditional religions; Finnish religion; hunting, religious aspects of; Sedna; South American religions, traditional; traditional peoples, religions of.

matha (muh'tuh; Skt., "hut," "cloister"), a Hindu monastic institution. Typically a center for the teaching and practice of a particular Hindu sect, a *matha* centers on a *guru* (spiritual leader), usually a celibate ascetic. *See also* monasticism.

Ma-tsu (mah-dzuh; 709–788), Ch'an master whose teachings spawned four out of the five schools of Chinese Sung Ch'an Buddhism. *See also* Ch'an school; Five Houses; Hung-chou school.

matsuri-goto (mah-tsoo-ree-goh-toh; Jap., "ceremonial affairs"), traditional Japanese notion of combining government and religion. Centered on the priest-king (emperor), it was supported by myth. *See also* Japanese myth; kingship, sacred; Shinto.

Matsyendranath (muhts-yen'druh-naht; Skt., "Lord of the Fishes"; ca. tenth century), founder of the Hindu Nath sect. In the form of a fish, he overheard Shiva's mystic teachings to the goddess Parvati and transmitted these to his human disciples. *See also* Nath; Shiva.

Matthew, by tradition the author of the first Gospel in the New Testament of the Bible.

matzah (mah-tsah'; Heb., meaning uncertain), unleavened bread. Consumed by Jews during Passover as required by Torah, *matzah* symbolizes liberation and divine redemption. *See also* seder.

Maundy Thursday. *See* Holy Thursday.

Ma-wang-tui (mah-wahng-dway), an archaeological site near Ch'ang-sha, China, with tombs dating to the early second century B.C. containing such things as the earliest copies of the *Tao-te ching* and a silk banner depicting the journey to the afterlife. *See also* Han religion; Tao-te ching.

Mawlid [or Mulid] al-Nabi (mow'lid [or moo'lid] oon-na'bee; Arab., "birthday"), the anniversary of the birth of Muhammad, on the twelfth day of the third month of the Muslim year. *See also* Islam (festal cycle).

maya (mah'yah; often from Skt. *ma,* "to measure or make," but more probably from *man,* "to imagine"), in the Indic Vedas, the magic, mental power of the great *asuras* (gods or antigods, primarily Varuna and Indra) to create real or illusory phenomena; in the plural (where it seems to mean "tricks," "wiles," "magic") it is also attributed to lesser demonic powers. In the epics, *maya* is generally confined to the power of sorcery or art (still both demonic and divine), the prerogative of demigods (such as the *yakshas* who bedevil the Pandavas in the wilderness in the *Mahabharata,* or the great *rakshasa* Ravana who uses maya to abduct Sita and to fight Rama in the *Ramayana*), or of artisans such as Maya, the demonic architect who builds the Pandaras's assembly hall. In Buddhism, maya becomes further demoted to "duplicity," one of twenty-four evil passions. But at the same time, in the philosophy of Samkhya, maya is elevated to a major metaphysical force and is identified with *prakriti* as source of the visible universe. And in Vedanta, maya is the power of illusion with which the deity creates the illusion of the visible universe. Moreover, in the mythologies and theologies of *bhakti,* maya is often identified with another sort of art, *lila,* the metaphysical playfulness in which God indulges in the otherwise meaningless act of creating the illusion of the universe and of lesser illusions within it. Thus, in the *Bhagavata Purana,* when Yashoda, the foster mother of Krishna, experiences an epiphany of her son as the god who embodies the entire universe, Krishna re-deludes her by spreading over her the maya of her belief that he is simply her human child.

Maya in Vedanta: Maya is, for Vedanta, a false image that must be realized and penetrated through correct philosophizing; it is related to but sharply distinguished from *bhrama,* the trick of the senses that leads people to mistake one thing for another. Bhrama can always be corrected through further experience and hence might be called empirical illusion; maya, which is the gap between all experience and the transcendent reality, *brahman,* might be called transcendent illusion, and can never be disproved or verified by any experience.

There are two different degrees of the maya doctrine corresponding to two different degrees of the philosophy of idealism. The more extreme, associated with nontheistic, nondualistic doctrines in both Hinduism (such as the philosophy of Shankara) and Buddhism (such as Nagarjuna's Madhyamaka philosophy), suggests that humans all invent the same mental images (maya) and project them onto an empty reality—for Shankara, empty except for brahman. Maya is the trick of the senses that makes people believe the universe is there at all. The modified form of the doctrine, tempered by the qualified nondualism of philosophers such as Ramanuja, argues that deity projects out of itself the illusory universe, which human sense mistakes for what it is not (as one mistakes a rope for a snake). But this universe, being a part of deity, does exist (just as the rope exists). The deeper reality, however, that underlies the sensible universe, can be sensed in dreams and visions and reached through meditation or the love of the god. *See also* brahman; Madhyamaka; nondualism, Hindu; prakriti; six systems of Indian philosophy; Vedanta.

mazal tov (mah-zahl' tohv'; Heb., "[under] a good zodiac sign"), used idiomatically in Judaism to express congratulations on all joyous occasions.

Mazdak (maz'dak), the founder of a heretical Zoroastrian movement under the Sassanid king Karadh (488–531). Possibly influenced by Manichaeism, Mazdak is best known for his message of property sharing. *See also* Zoroastrianism.

mead, the sacred liquor in Scandinavian myth that Odinn gives to inspire poetry. *See also* Nordic religion.

Mecca (mak'kuh; Arab.), also Bakka (Qur'an 3:96), ritual center and origin point of Islam, located in western Arabia. Muslims assert it was visited by Ibrahim (Abraham). The earliest reference was a second-century Greek one, to Macoraba. By the year 600, Mecca long had been a sacred place (*haram*), and hence a commercial center. After Muhammad's Hijra, Meccans fought eight years against the Muslims, who seized Mecca definitively in 630. While Ibn Zubayr ruled in Mecca as caliph (680–692), the Kaaba was destroyed by Muslim political opponents, the Marwanids. Because of its symbolic importance, Mecca has been seized throughout history by dissident groups, including the

Qaramatians (930) and a modern group that seized the Haram mosque in 1979. Strict Wahhabis from eastern Arabia took Mecca in 1924 and leveled unorthodox popular shrines outside the Kaaba area. *See also* Islam (festal cycle); Kaaba; Medina; Muhammad; pilgrimage.

medicine and religion. The historic interrelationship of medicine and religion is grounded in the fact that both phenomena concern human suffering, illness, dying, and death; medicine deals with these reminders of human fragility empirically, while religion deals with them existentially, on the level of meaning and interpretation. Because many cultures believe that illness is caused by some violation of moral or religious norms, healers, such as shamans and witchdoctors, have been religious figures able to restore the moral or spiritual balance. Historically considered, medicine and religion have been largely inseparable.

Human beings typically turn to religion in their efforts to make sense of disease and suffering. These latter inevitably lead to anxiety, and to religious projection that allows diminishments to be both understood and tolerated. Physicians have classically been people formally linked to religious institutions, as exemplified by the great rabbi-physicians of Judaism, such as Moses Maimonides. All the sacred scriptures of world religions include paradigm stories about individuals who grapple in desperation with suffering and its meanings. Judaism's book of Job, Christianity's suffering Jesus, and Buddhism's many stories of overcoming the inevitable reality of human suffering are all cases in point. Religion might be defined in part as a socially constructed worldview that functions to mitigate the otherwise intolerable reality of human suffering and decline.

Modern empirical medicine can sometimes effectively restore health or relieve physical pain, but it can never change the fundamental frailties that define human finitude and mortality. This is why religion still holds a major place in the health-care setting, since for most people, regardless of their cultural origins, religious interpretations and rites of passage alone serve as adequate coping strategies. While secular psychiatry has emerged as a source of interpretive insight for some people, it has by no means displaced the centrality of religious meanings, nor is it likely to. Contrary to Sigmund Freud's predictions about modern culture, religion has burgeoned rather than disappeared. No caregiver insensitive to the humanistic importance of religion can claim to understand patients as persons.

The Religious Valuation of Medicine: In general, religious traditions have valued medicine highly. However, religious systems have recognized a tension between the presence of disease as divine providence, and human efforts to heal. In Judaism the Karaites, a sect following the teachings of Anan ben David, opposed the use of all medicines, since God alone should be the physician. But the classical approach of Judaism has been to strongly encourage resort to medicine and human ingenuity in healing, with the recognition that behind all healing lies the hand of God. Islam too considers the use of medicine a solemn obligation for the sustaining of invaluable human life. Islam views the medical profession as the most meritorious service in God's sight.

Of the world religions, by far the most complicated respecting the evaluation of medicine is Christianity. While Christian tradition has generally held medicine in high esteem, and has articulated the virtues of the physician consistent with charity and love, its savior figure is a faith healer, and over one-third of the gospel accounts are devoted to stories of healing. Thus, among the early Christians, faith healing was part of the sect's appeal. Christian Science is a prime example of a religious group that rejects modern medicine. Over the last several decades, a considerable number of evangelical Protestant sects have emphasized faith healing over modern medicine. Christian Science can be viewed as an anticipation of this sectarian trend.

Nevertheless, Christianity in its mainstream Catholic and Protestant forms follows the Jewish affirmation of medicine, and appeals to the Hebrew biblical passages that interpret medicine as God's creation and honor the physician. In none of the monotheistic faiths, however, is medicine ever an alternative to prayer and faith, but is understood as an instrument through which God works.

There are numerous instances in which non-Western cultures have resisted medical progress. In Japan, for instance, the reluctance to accept organ transplantation is rooted in Buddhist proscriptions against individualism. Confucian cultures generally look down on organ donation as a violation of filial duties toward one's lineage, and of respect for ancestors. Medical anthropologists emphasize the permanence of indigenous religious values that defy the utilitarian, empirical, and rational system of the Western medical worldview. Others suggest that these indigenous values will eventually give way to "progress."

The Medical Valuation of Religion: Medicine has historically valued religion greatly. However, with the advent of secularization and empirical science, religion has been devalued to varying degrees. A significant development in recent psychiatric ethics is the publication of the American Psychiatric Association's "Guidelines Regarding Possible Conflict Between Psychiatrists' Religious Commitments and Psychiatric Practice" (1990). Prepared by the association's Committee on Religion and Psychiatry, the guidelines begin with the precept that psychiatrists "should maintain respect for their patients' beliefs." If conflict between physician and patient arises regarding religion, the former is to "demonstrate empathy for patients' sensibilities and particular beliefs." The principle of respect for persons and their subjective sources of meaning permeates the Guidelines.

There is no doubt that psychiatric illness can manifest itself in religious expression. It is often difficult for the clinician to determine the relationship between a patient's religious beliefs and the origin and symptoms of a given psychopathology. In some instances, religion may help a person's condition, while in other situations, certain manifestations of religion may be a symptom of a deeper problem. One cannot conclude, however, that religious beliefs and practices are generally indicative of illness. Psychopathology sometimes occurs in the religious context, but religion generally plays a constructive role in human life. While medical practitioners often demonstrate considerable respect for patients' religious beliefs, and hospitals often provide space for pastoral care, there is a significant tension between medicine and religion in the area of psychiatry.

More empirical research needs to be done by medical scientists on the affects of religious belief and experience on mental and physical health. It is problematic that so little serious empirical research is being done by psychiatrists on the relationship between religion and mental health. Research needs to be done in order to ascertain the role of religious belief vis-a-vis health. At the very least, clinicians need to understand objectively the contributions that religious belief can make to mental health. Recent studies indicate that religious belief and practice can contribute to a person's well-being. A study of psychiatric inpatients finds that those with religious beliefs were less prone to depression and anxiety. Another study persuasively indicates that religion is of considerable importance in the ability of adult burn patients to deal with the stress of traumatic injury. As for the importance of religion among the elderly, some systematic studies have started to appear.

The Context of Tension: Biomedicine in general, and psychiatry in particular, have become a dominant framework in Western society for understanding and influencing the human condition. Psychiatry has become particularly influential in America since World War II—so much so, that bias against religion will adversely affect the care and treatment of large numbers of patients. While biomedicine and psychiatry have become more dominant interpretive models for behavior and experience in modern America, eclipsing religion in the academic and intellectual circles that shape the medical culture, religion remains a central framework for understanding the human situation among the wider populace.

Religious attitudes can be a powerful dynamic overlooked by the busy practitioner. This may help explain the surprising interest in alternative medicine in an age of expanding technological sophistication. At least some of this interest can be attributed to the separation of technical and clinical medicine from a more holistic view of humanness that includes the religious component of a person's life.

The problem is at root historical. The Western view of the person has been molded by a history of struggles for ascendancy as scientific views countered historic theologies. The purely rational scientific view eventually won a general acceptance in psychiatric circles in the twentieth century. The tension and suspicion between the two frameworks still remain. From the scientific side this struggle centers on the quest for verification and the ability to quantify and replicate procedures. Since attitudes in general and religion in particular are subjective, the historic separation seemed inevitable. *See also* Ayurveda; body; Chinese medicine; healing; physiological techniques (Taoism).

medicine bundle, among traditional peoples, a collection of objects held to be of high religious significance. An assortment of apparently common objects—plants, stones, crystals, bones, hair, skins, pollen, herbs, masks, and flints—are wrapped together, the whole of which is called a medicine bundle. The bundle itself is often considered medicinally and spiritually potent. For some cultures the bundle contains items integral to their origin and history. The preparation and opening of medicine bundles is usually a religious and often ritualized action. Objects removed from the bundle may be used in medicine rituals. Some bundles are rarely opened. *See also* bundle; North America, traditional religions in.

medicine man, power-user in traditional societies. This outdated label came into use because healing is one of the chief activities of the power-user (*heyoka*, Lakota Sioux; *chimbuki*, Ndembu; *saman*, Yakut) in traditional religions.

Medina (ma-dee'nuh; Arab., "the city [of the Prophet]"), formerly Yathrib, in the northwest (*Hijaz*) of Arabia, an optional pilgrimage site and a sacred place (*haram*). Here was the first Muslim political community, the Prophet's house, and Islam's first mosque. After ceasing to be the Islamic capital in 656, Medina remained a center for the study of *hadith* and law. Medina holds the al-Baqi cemetery with the graves of many early Islamic heroes, including Shiites. Over these had been erected shrines, but in 1804 and again in 1925 after the Saudi conquest, the strict Wahhabi movement destroyed them. *See also* Islam (festal cycle); Mecca; Muhammad; pilgrimage.

meditation, a process of contemplation usually undertaken in a structured manner. *See also* Hinduism (worship).

Buddhism: Meditation serves as a general label for a broad range of consciousness-altering practices described and recommended by Buddhists as instrumental in removing passion and ignorance and in helping the practitioner progress toward *nirvana* (liberation). Nirvana is the religious goal theoretically pursued by all Buddhists; one might expect, then, that all Buddhists would practice meditation as the primary and paradigmatic means of reaching it, but this is not the case. For most of Buddhist history meditation has been something theorized about and (to a lesser extent) practiced almost exclusively by monks; meditation by lay Buddhists has been the exception rather than the rule. Nonetheless, meditation has been and remains a topic to which Buddhist theorists in all cultures have devoted much attention, and there is a large volume of literature concerned with analyzing, categorizing, and defining the kinds and uses of meditation. What follows will provide an introduction to the more important distinctions made in this area by Buddhists.

The Cultivation of Tranquillity: Tranquillity (Skt. *samatha)* is a desirable condition in Buddhist theory. This is because the violence of uncontrolled emotions and the instability and repetitiveness of obsessive patterns of thought are taken to trap the individual in the beginningless round of rebirths and redeaths that Buddhists call *samsara.* Such states must therefore be calmed or tranquillized. Buddhists call techniques designed to bring this about the "cultivation of tranquillity."

Tranquillity is sometimes valued in its own right and is sometimes seen as a preparation for

Chinese Buddhist monks arriving for daily meditation at the Gu-Shan monastery, China (ca. 1970).

the development of insight into reality, the way things really are. In either case, the techniques employed have the same goal: the reduction of effect, or the range and intensity of the practitioner's emotional experience, and the reduction of uncontrolled analytical and discriminative thought.

The practitioner's progress toward tranquillity is most often represented by descriptions of a series of altered states of consciousness called *dhyanas.* This word was later represented in Chinese as *ch'an* and in Japanese as *zen;* these are the names of schools for which the practice of meditation is of central importance. As progress is made through this hierarchically ordered set of altered states of consciousness, the range of states of mind available to the practitioner is gradually reduced. This is true both for emotional and for cognitive states. So, when the first dhyana is attained, the practitioner can still feel joy and happiness, though no longer negative affective states such as grief or suffering. But by the time the fourth dhyana has been reached, no positive or negative emotional states remain: there is only a neutral condition of equanimity (*upeksa*).

Similarly, as the practitioner progresses through the dhyanas, the capacity to think analytically, to form concepts, and to use language is gradually left behind. According to Buddhist theory, this is necessary because continued engagement with them will inevitably lead to a compulsive proliferation of concepts and ideas, a proliferation that makes proper tranquillity impossible.

When both emotions and intellect have been properly calmed in this way, tranquillity has been attained, though the process of reducing the range and tone of the practitioner's states of mind may continue until, in an extreme case, all mental activity of any kind ceases and a condition called the attainment of cessation (*nirodha-samapatti*) is reached. This is an extreme case of the cultivation of tranquillity, and although it is described and recommended in many Buddhist texts on meditation, it has a somewhat ambiguous status since it is not clear just how its relationship to the attainment of nirvana should be understood.

Many stories are told in Buddhist texts to indicate the nature and effects of this altered state. One of the most famous concerns the monk Mahanaga, who, it is said, attained cessation in the meditation hall of a monastery, and while he was still absorbed in cessation the meditation hall caught fire. All the other monks gathered their belongings and fled. But Mahanaga, since he had attained cessation, was not capable of responding to external stimuli, not even to stimuli as urgent as a blazing fire, and so he sat unmoved while the monastery burned around him.

There are many specific practices recommended for developing tranquillity. One of the more common involves the use of a device called a "totality" (*kritsna*). This is a material object, most commonly a clay disk whose color is as neutral as possible and whose surface is as smooth as possible. One sets this disk upon a pedestal at eye level and sits down directly in front of it a short distance away. One then concentrates all one's attention upon it, gradually excluding from one's sensory awareness all other stimuli and all extraneous concepts and emotions. Eventually, after long and hard practice, one is able to form a mental image of the clay disk, an image without any of the small imperfections of shape and color necessarily present in the physical object. This mental image then replaces the physical object as the object of meditation, and the image is then "totalized" (hence the name "totality") or extended, as the tradition puts it, in all directions until (from the practitioner's viewpoint) it fills the whole universe.

The Cultivation of Insight: Tranquillity, once attained, may also be used as the basis for the development of insight (*vipashyana*). This is accurate knowledge of the way things are. Such knowledge is necessary because without it various kinds of ignorance or misunderstanding may occur, and these in turn may cause the practitioner to have inappropriate emotional responses to the objects of such misunderstanding. So, for example, if one thinks (wrongly, according to Buddhist metaphysics) that one is an eternal and continuing soul or self, one is likely to have improper emotional attachments to one's future. Or, if one thinks that the beauty of physical objects is somehow intrinsic to them, one is likely to be inappropriately attached to them or desirous of them.

Various techniques are recommended as a cure for such misunderstandings. Paradigmatic is the process called "mindfulness" (*smrita*). This is close and continuous observation of every process that goes to make up the psychophysical life of a practitioner. One may, for example, apply mindfulness to the breath. In doing so one simply observes, without manipulating, the rhythms and nature of one's breathing. The object is to become aware of every detail of the breathing process that is accessible to close observation of this kind. So one attends to and mentally notes the passage of air through the nostrils and into the lungs, the rise and fall of the chest and abdomen, the exit of air through the mouth. Or, the same kind of observation can be applied to the patterns of thought, feeling, and intention that jointly constitute the mental life. So one might analytically observe the processes by which, in some specific situation, the feeling of fear (or lust, or embarrassment, or indeed anything at all) comes into being, noting the causally connected chain of events that produces the feeling, and noting the fine details and alterations of the feeling itself as it comes into being and passes away.

The goal of these observational practices is always the same: to gain insight into the minute components of processes that usually pass too quickly for anything other than the most general impression of them to be possible. Such insight is in turn supposed to lead to the direct experiential verification of key items of Buddhist doctrine, notably that everything is impermanent, which means that all apparently long-lasting processes or states are in fact made up—constructed by the mind out of minimally short-lived events, each of which ceases as soon as it has come into being and given rise to its successor. Realization of these and associated truths through the cultivation of insight then leads to both accurate knowledge and detachment; and when fully developed these conjointly bring the practitioner to nirvana.

It should not be difficult to see how this remorselessly analytical observation of one's mental life will tend to reduce the power of one's emotional states. If, at the same time as feeling desire for some attractive object or fear of some threatening situation, one applies the cultivated habit of observing and making a mental note of the causal processes by which these states come into being, it will be vastly more difficult to allow oneself to be swept away and controlled by them. Imagine mentally noting "this instance of desire is caused by a pleasurable visual stimulus" at the same time as the desire is being felt. The desire will lose some of its power, and this is part of the point of the practice.

Paths and Stages: Buddhist scholastics devoted an enormous amount of intellectual energy to the creation and elaboration of complete, systematic, and all-inclusive meditational paths. One motive for doing this was to answer a number of difficult questions about the relations between the cultivation of tranquillity and the cultivation of insight; another was to provide a systematic account of the connections between meditational practice and Buddhist doctrine; a third, no doubt, was the urge, present among scholastic thinkers in all traditions, toward completeness and comprehensiveness.

These meditational paths were often of staggering complexity, requiring many hundreds of pages for their exposition. They are elaborated and defended in texts produced by Buddhist thinkers, Mahayana and non-Mahayana, in all the major cultures in which Buddhism flourished. Notable examples are Buddhaghosa's (fourth–fifth century) *Visuddhimagga,* composed in Sri Lanka; Candrakirti's (ca. 600–650) *Madhyamakavatara,* composed in India in the seventh century; Chih-i's (538–597) *Mo-ho chih-kuan,* composed in China; and Tsong-kha-pa's (1357–1419) *Lam rim chen mo,* composed in Tibet. The paths presented in these texts (and in many others like them) differ in many details and are not infrequently incompatible with one another. Such differences arose sometimes from differences in doctrinal commitments and sometimes from differences in practice. But they have in common the attempt to set forth a complete meditational path from the beginning of practice to the attainment of nirvana and to provide a place for every kind of technique valued by the tradition.

A complete meditational path of the kind contained in these texts is typically gradualist and hierarchical in its approach; that is, it is divided into paths (*marga*) or stages (*bhumi*) that must be practiced in due and proper order if progress is to occur; and it is presupposed that progress in such a path will be deliberate and slow. The attainment of nirvana through the removal of all cognitive and affective errors cannot happen quickly because of the complexity of the practices to be mastered and the subtlety of the doctrinal matters to be understood. So, for example, Candrakirti's presentation of the meditational path in his *Madhyamakavatara* is divided into ten stages, each of which is in turn given many subdivisions.

Sudden and Gradual: The gradualist view of meditational practice presented above is not, however, the only one to be found in the tradition. While it was certainly dominant in India, Tibet, and South Asia, it was less so in China, Korea, and Japan. There it was rivaled by the development and defense of the claim that nirvana can be attained suddenly, in the blink of an eye, without the arduous practice of a graded and ordered meditational path. On this view, human persons (and perhaps other sentient beings as well) are already in fact Buddhas; they are prevented from realizing this and from functioning as such only by an illusory veil of ignorance.

Meditation, if necessary at all, is then important only as a tool to allow what is already present in the practitioner to become manifest and active. And such manifestation may happen quite spontaneously, without any formal meditational practice, or with nothing more than a concerted and continuing effort to see one's own true nature, which is the same as the nature of Buddha. Hui-neng (638–713), called the sixth patriarch in the southern tradition of Ch'an (Zen) Buddhism in China, is presented as teaching this view in *The Platform Sutra of the Sixth Patriarch:*

> What is . . . this teaching that we call "sitting in meditation"? In this teaching "sitting" means without any obstruction anywhere, outwardly and under all circumstances, not to activate thoughts. "Meditation" is to see internally the original nature and not become confused (19).

Here, meditation is identified with the absence of confusion that results from not thinking. This absence of confusion is in turn the same thing as one's "original nature," which is simply the fact of one's Buddhahood. The purpose of sitting in meditation—a practice that in Japanese Soto Zen, which originated in Dogen's (1200–53) writings, came to be called *shikan taza,* "just sitting"—is then just to learn how to stop having confused thoughts. And for this purpose the complex paths and stages of scholastic Buddhism are of little use.

Visualizations: The use and recommendation of visualization techniques as part of meditational practice is found in all Buddhist traditions, though it became more prominent with the development of Tantric practices in India after the third century or so. A paradigmatic instance of visualization is the recollection (Skt. *anusmriti*) of a Buddha, the calling to mind of a visual picture of a Buddha, either as he was when embodied and teaching in a world like this one, or as he is in one of his quasi-divine bodies in a heaven, surrounded by Hearers and Bodhisattvas (Buddhas-to-be) listening to his teaching. Texts provide enormously detailed descriptions of Buddha-bodies, and such descriptions are often used as templates for visualization practice. So, for example, descriptions of the thirty-two major marks and eighty minor marks on the body of a Buddha teaching in a world like ours—marks including such things as thousand-spoked wheels on the palms of the hands and soles of the feet—are learned, visualized, and meditatively played with until an eidetic image of the relevant Buddha-body can be called to mind at will.

Buddha-bodies are not the only things whose meditational visualization is recommended. Equally important, especially in Tantric Buddhism in Tibet and East Asia, is the use of *mandalas*, symbolic diagrams of the cosmos with great sacred power. Mandalas may, of course, be actual physical objects, cosmograms made out of colored sands or painted on cloth, but they may also be eidetic images of such physical objects, called to mind by the practitioner at will in the absence of any external stimulus.

Theories surrounding the symbolism of both Buddha-bodies and mandalas are exceedingly complex. They contain, when fully developed, all of Buddhist cosmology and psychology. All that can be said here is that the practice of visualization, whether of Buddha-bodies, mandalas, or some other sacred representation of the cosmos, is taken to be more than a complex feat of memory and control over one's visual images (though it is certainly at least those things). It involves also the gaining of power over oneself and the cosmos, power gained through the homologizing of oneself to the cosmos. This happens because the object of visualization is taken not just to represent the cosmos in its real aspect, but actually to be it; in visualizing it fully and completely the practitioner both enters it and is entered by it. Its power and meaning become the practitioner's, and since its power and meaning are precisely those of Buddhahood, proper visualization too results in the attainment of the desired religious goal. *See also* Ch'an school; mandala; nirvana; Soto school.

Chinese Religion: Meditation has been an important element in Taoist spiritual practice, though its relationship to Taoist thought and doctrine is unclear. There were many different methods of Taoist meditation reflecting different concepts of reality and different soteriological models. In general, Taoist meditation involved psychic purification and spiritual integration, often conceived as "returning to the root," or to the Tao.

While intimated in the *Tao-te ching* and the *Chuang-tzu*, meditational practices are clearly articulated only in later Taoism. In much of early religious Taoism (e.g., in the *T'ai-p'ing ching*), meditation is generally expressed in terms of attaining or retaining Oneness. Other traditions, as seen in fourth-century Shang-ch'ing texts, instructed the adept in visualizing a celestial hierarchy of divinities and drawing them into his own inner universe. Other medieval practices involved the visualization and internalization of stellar divinities. During T'ang times, Taoist meditation was influenced by several Buddhist methods, and the concepts and values of Ch'an color the meditational practices of later Taoism and Neo-Confucianism alike. From the eleventh century, most Taoist meditation was related to the practice of "inner alchemy."

Contemplative practices were often an important element of Neo-Confucian self-cultivation, although they were never as central as in Buddhism or Taoism. These practices were sometimes controversial, since any "Confucian" who advocated them was compelled to distinguish them from Buddhist or Taoist practices. Nonetheless, Neo-Confucian meditation—generally styled "quiet-sitting" (*ching-tso*)—was actually a variation upon the *zazen* of Ch'an Buddhism. Neo-Confucians maintained that "quiet-sitting" was not directed toward achieving "enlightenment," but the same was actually true in contemporary Ch'an. Neo-Confucianism, like Ch'an, saw techniques such as zazen as merely an aid to allowing true human nature to take full effect. What distinguished "quiet-sitting" from other forms of Buddhist or Taoist meditation was the general absence of specific precepts regarding technique.

Chou Tun-i (1017–73) advocated "quiet-sitting" as an aid to centering the self. The goal was to quiet the mind and reestablish a condition of "sincerity" by controlling the thoughts, emotions, and intentions that impede the pure functioning of the "original mind." The intention was not to disengage from the world, for, as Chu Hsi explained a century later, the principle (*li*) of one's mind is identical to the inner principles of all things. "Quiet-sitting" was deemphasized by Wang Yang-ming (1472–1529), but it became very popular among other Ming Neo-Confucians such as Kao P'an-lung (1562–1626). Chu Hsi's explanation of the goal as transforming the ordinary mind into the "mind of the Tao" was perpetuated by later Taoists, such as the Ch'uan-chen master Liu I-ming (ca. 1737–1826). *See also* ching-tso; Chou Tun-i; Chuang-tzu; Chu Hsi; Shang-ch'ing Taoism.

medium, a person who serves as an intermediary between the human world and the supernatural or spirit realm through divination, trance, and/or spirit possession.

Many religions of tribal and traditional cultures in Africa, Asia, Oceania, and the Americas have especially valued mediums for their capacities to receive and interpret direct communication with deities, souls of the dead, and other nonhuman powers. Spirit mediumship specifically assumes not only the existence of independent spirit entities and a distinction between human and supernatural realms, but also the innate or learned ability of some to surrender their bodies to spirit control or incorporation. Mediums, like shamans and prophets, may also diagnose and cure illnesses, locate lost objects, resolve enigmas, and advise on future events.

While religions such as Buddhism, Hinduism, Christianity, and Islam currently reject trance possession for reasons ranging from doubt of its validity to its presumed connection with demonic powers, some pentecostal and evangelical Christian sects encourage prophecy, and glossolalia, or speaking in tongues, and other Western movements have revived the medium's role. In Spiritualism, for example, mediums contact the spirits of the dead and convey messages from wise entities of ancient cultures. New Age movements have also embraced a form of mediumship, trance channeling, for communication with transcendent powers. *See also* divination; New Age movements; possession; Spiritualism; trance.

meeting house, the common designation for the place where the Religious Society of Friends (Quakers) gathers for weekly worship and monthly organizational meetings. *See also* Friends, Society of.

megillah (muh-gee-lah'; Heb., "scroll"). **1** Any of five biblical books (Esther, Ruth, Lamentations, Ecclesiastes, Song of Songs) recited liturgically from a scroll. **2** In common use, only Esther, read at Purim. *See also* Judaism (festal cycle).

Meher Baba (1894–1969), formerly Merwan Sheriar Irani, religious leader and organizer of Sufism Reoriented, a revival Hindu-Islamic movement begun in India. According to his fol-

lowers, Meher Baba was the incarnation of the highest celestial being for his epoch; his dawning awareness of his salvific role led him first to take a vow of silence and later to expound his universalist teachings centered on the experience of pure love. From its Indian base, Sufism Reoriented launched seminars in Western countries and flourished in the United States during the 1970s; its founder's death diminished its subsequent efforts. *See also* North America, new religions in.

Meiji (may-jee), name of both the Japanese emperor (Meiji Tenno, 1852–1912) and the historical period of his reign (1868–1912). Meiji, the first emperor after the demise of military rulers (*shogun*), is revered as the founder of modern Japan and honored with a large shrine bearing his name. *See also* Meiji Restoration; Meiji Shrine.

Meiji Restoration (may-jee), Japanese historical period (1868–1912). The Restoration of 1868 ended rule by military dictators and "restored" the emperor (Meiji Tenno) as official head of state. Together with complex economic and political factors, one of the forces supporting the emperor as the true leader of the country was a combination of Confucian and Shinto ideals. Two results of the restoration were heightened prestige of the emperor as symbolic head of the new nation-state and the short-lived dominance of Shinto in state affairs. *See also* kingship, sacred; Mito school; Shinto; Yamazaki Ansai.

Meiji Shrine (may-jee), monument in Tokyo (completed in 1920) commemorating the founder of modern Japan, the emperor Meiji Tenno. *See also* Meiji Restoration.

Melanesia, new religions in.

The Indigenous Context: Melanesia presents diverse environments within which ideas and rituals introduced since first colonial contact have mingled with traditional ideas and practices. The region includes Irian Jaya (a province of Indonesia), Papua New Guinea, the Solomon Islands, Vanuatu, Fiji, and New Caledonia (a French territory).

Indigenous Melanesian religions focus on relationships to ancestors, land spirits, and other spirits or deities, and on rituals that mediate such relationships. In most Melanesian cultures, a rich mythology discusses beginnings and analyzes the human situation. Ritual is directed toward acquisition of wealth and toward healing, which includes not only restoring the health of the individual but also identifying and healing the fractures of social life. These concerns influence the way that outside religions, particularly Christianity, have been received and modified within Melanesian environments.

Colonialism and New Religions: Christianity, Islam, and Hinduism were introduced into Melanesia during the nineteenth century. Bahai has appeared more recently. Christianity in its several varieties has been the most influential. Today some 90 percent of Melanesians claim to be Christian, but this does not mean that they have abandoned indigenous practices and worldviews. In some areas, Christian missions, expanding westward from already established strongholds in Polynesia, preceded the establishment of colonial administrations. West New Guinea, or Irian Jaya, was claimed by the Dutch in 1828; New Caledonia by France in 1853; Fiji by Britain in 1874; South East New Guinea, or Papua, by Britain in 1884; North East New Guinea, or Kaiser Wilhelmsland, by Germany in 1884; the New Hebrides, now Vanuatu, jointly by France and Britain in 1887; and the South Solomons by Britain in 1893. In all but New Caledonia and Irian Jaya, the path to nationhood has overlapped with the development of local styles of Christianity.

Hinduism and Islam came to Fiji with indentured laborers from India who were recruited by the British between 1870 and 1916 to work on sugar plantations. Today Fijians who are ethnically Indian are divided in religious allegiance. Some are Hindu, some Muslim, and the majority Christian; only a few Melanesians in Fiji have adopted Hindu rituals. In Irian Jaya, the neo-colonial power, Indonesia, has introduced Islam, but it remains largely the religion of non-Melanesian civil servants, businesspeople, and farmers originally from other parts of Indonesia. There is a small Hindu component among these newcomers.

The original colonizing powers were Christian nations, who saw missions as their allies in the spread of civilization. European missionaries brought both Catholic and Protestant Christianity to Irian Jaya from the nineteenth century onward. Europeans, Americans, Australians, and New Zealanders, usually with the cooperation of colonial powers, introduced Catholic, Anglican, Lutheran, and Calvinist forms of Christianity in other parts of Melanesia. Pacific Island missionaries, from places such as the Cook Islands and Tonga, which had been evangelized a generation earlier, were crucial in the early work of the London Missionary Society, an evangelical mission organization with a large Congregational influence. All the denominations trained local catechists, evangelists, and other ministers to carry the gospel further.

Missionary Christianity: Prior to European contact there were both ceremonial exchange networks and long-standing trade arrangements among local groups. Some Melanesians sought to establish similar arrangements with the newcomers, while others deeply resented their intrusion and responded to it with hostility. Unwittingly, missionaries often became involved in conflicts. Those who had worked in the chiefly kingdoms of Polynesia were ill-equipped for encounters with the small-scale, frequently warring, groups of Melanesia. From difficult beginnings in eastern Melanesia in the mid-1800s to post–World War II evangelization efforts in the highlands of Papua New Guinea, missionaries encountered harsh terrain and societies whose members were prepared to assert their will and their dignity against intruders.

From the mid-nineteenth century to the outbreak of World War II, the so-called mainstream churches (Catholic, Lutheran, Anglican, Methodist, Congregational, and local churches resulting from their efforts) were dominant in Melanesia with Baptists, Seventh-Day Adventists, and others in the minority. The relationship between Catholics and others in the early phases of missionization can be described at best as competitive. Today, however, there is a high level of cooperation among the mainstream churches.

As missionaries became more aware of the ritual and mythic traditions of Melanesians, they took one of two approaches. Some, asserting the uniqueness and finality of God's revelation in Jesus Christ, rejected the "magical practices and superstitions" of Melanesians. Others sought to interpret whatever good intentions and aesthetic appeal they could recognize in Melanesian cultures as "seeds of the gospel" to be fulfilled in conversion to Christianity. In both cases, missionaries sought conversion away from traditional Melanesian religions toward Christianity, while Melanesians tended to incorporate Christianity into indigenous ways of life.

Missions, with their schools, hospitals, and development works, were a significant influence in social change, major advocates of a modern scientific worldview, and even agents of secularization. Melanesians, whose religions were oriented toward human well-being, and who had processes such as myth and initiation for transmission of knowledge and ritual processes for healing, could appreciate the educational and health services of the missions. Christianity could be understood as the "law" of Europeans and the mythic and ritual aspects of Christianity could be seen to have the same relationship to European economic realities as traditional myth and ritual had to hunting, gardening, and exchange of valuables.

Following World War II, evangelical and pentecostal missions from Australia and the United States, such as the Assemblies of God and the Foursquare Church, entered Melanesia. Like the mainstream denominations, they established rural mission stations and involved themselves in educational and health services and development projects. They promoted a Spirit-filled Christianity, with ecstatic features such as speaking in tongues, which was in contrast to the more doctrinally and liturgically based approach of the earlier missions. In the 1970s a new band of pentecostal missionaries, many from Scandinavia and the United States, began establishing churches in urban centers. Pentecostal emphasis on the work of the Holy Spirit has had an influence not only in their own communities but also in the development of charismatic groups and Holy Spirit movements among other denominations.

Melanesian Styles of Christianity: As Melanesians became Christians and reflected on Christian stories and rituals in the light of indigenous religious traditions and changing socioeconomic experience they began to produce their own theologies, i.e., their own understandings of the relationship of gospel and culture. Some of these theologies have come dramatically to the attention of the world in their manifestation as cargo cults, while others have informed movements of renewal within the churches or led to the development of independent churches.

From the encounter of Melanesian religions and Christianity have arisen images of Jesus as ancestor of the Christian clan and of Jesus as ideal brother. In the figure of Jesus, many people find it possible to expand notions of clan based on a founding ancestor and to extend notions of brotherly cooperation and exchange. The ideology of universal brotherhood articulated as nation-states developed from colonial territories in the 1970s was frequently linked to the person of Jesus. As ideal brother, Jesus is thought to embody and extend traditional values of siblingship. Hence, the overt political involvement of Melanesian church personnel and the use of Christian rhetoric in political campaigns can be substantiated by appeal to Jesus' concern for his brothers and sisters.

The 1960s and 1970s saw not only movements toward political independence but also movements toward church independence. The major Protestant denominations in the region localized their leadership and decision-making. Autonomous local churches succeeded mission churches. However, most still depend to some extent on overseas mission bodies or partner churches for financial aid and personnel. Catholics were granted their own regional bishops' conferences. Among Catholics, a self-study movement in Papua New Guinea and the Solomon Islands, seeking to implement the insights of Vatican II, took as its slogan, "We are the Church," and emphasized inculturation of the gospel. Catholics remain more dependent on overseas personnel than do other Christian communities.

Christianity has been a catalyst in the recently articulated notion of a "Melanesian way." This notion, which proposes that there are certain understandings of person and behavior common to Melanesia, brings together diverse traditions that, in the past century and a half, have been influenced by the universalistic outlook of Christianity. In becoming part of the tradition of modern Melanesia, Christianity has enabled people to think beyond local loyalties and to forge an identity with a larger group. Ecumenical Christian gatherings have provided opportunity to speak to a biocosmic spirituality, a spirituality rooted in traditional understandings of the relationship of land and community, which can be correlated with the notions of creation and the cosmic Christ expressed, for example, in Paul's Letter to the Ephesians 1:10.

Independent Churches: A number of Melanesian religious and sociopolitical movements, which arose within or around mission churches, have developed into separatist churches. They speak to people's concern for a Christianity that is Melanesian and also to the alienation from the ways of the ancestors that conversion to Christianity has entailed. Among these movements, the Christian Fellowship Church, which separated in 1960 from the Methodist Mission in New Georgia in the Western Province of the Solomon Islands, is the largest. Silas Eto, its founder, who is also known as Holy Mama, believed that he had been designated by the pioneer missionary J. F. Goldie and by the Holy Spirit to form a new church. Christian Fellowship theology is basically that of the Methodists but places greater emphasis on ecstatic states and on the role of the now dead founder, whom some would see as a fourth person in God.

The Hehela Church on Buka Island in the North Solomons was founded by John Teosin in 1960 as an alternative to the Catholic Church and the Australian Administration. The Kwato

Church grew out of the work of an English missionary, Cecil Abel, who originally worked with the London Missionary Society in the Milne Bay area of Papua but separated from it because of his interest in developing an industrial mission. His two sons, who were influenced by the Moral Rearmament Movement, continued his work. Similar to the United Church in theology and liturgy, the Kwato Church rejects hierarchy and insists on congregational decision-making. Other independent churches include the Paliau Church in Manus Province, Papua New Guinea, which separated from the Catholic Church; the Remnant Church in Malaita Province, Solomon Islands; the Congregation of the Poor in Fiji, whose founder advocates a return to the attitudes of the early Christians; the NaGriamel Federation Independent United Royal Church in Vanuatu, which began as a land reappropriation movement; Friday Religion in Bougainville, Papua New Guinea, which separated from the Catholic Church; the Peli Association in the East Sepik Province, Papua New Guinea, which as a cargo movement rejected the Catholic Church and Australian Administration, then became involved with Canadian New Apostolic Church missionaries and now is working on its integration of tradition and Christianity; the Yali movement in Madang Province, Papua New Guinea, which developed out of a multiphase cargo movement in the southern Madang area; the Moro movement of Guadalcanal in the Solomon Islands, which draws parallels between figures of Christian history and theology and figures of Solomon Islands' tradition.

Hinduism, Islam, Bahai: Hinduism and Islam were introduced to Fiji not as missionary religions but as the faiths of nineteenth-century Indian indentured plantation workers and twentieth-century migrants. These two religions have few Melanesian adherents. In Papua New Guinea, Muslims associated with the Indonesian Embassy in recent years have been active in inviting Melanesians to join them in worship and study, and a small number of Papua New Guineans have converted to Islam. In Irian Jaya the presence of Islam is more obvious. Saudi Arabians have financed the building of mosques around the capital, Jayapura, and Indonesian government officials and migrants tend to be Muslim. (Indonesia has the largest Muslim population of any country.) However, Melanesians in Irian Jaya, particularly those who are pro-independence, have not been inclined to convert to Islam. There are some Hindus among the migrants, particularly among the Balinese whose Hinduism incorporates aspects of pre-

Hindu Balinese religion. In recent years, Bahai with its message of peace and its ecumenical outlook has begun to attract adherents in Melanesia, but in the early 1990s its following was still small. *See also* cargo cults; Holy Spirit movements; mission or missionary movements.

Mencius (men'shee-uhs; Chin. *Meng-tzu;* 372–289 B.C.), orthodox Confucian philosopher, second only to Confucius (551–479 B.C.), who systemized Confucius's teaching. Arguing that human nature is inherently good, Mencius identified four germs of human character that, if properly nurtured, mature into the virtues of benevolence, rightness, propriety, and wisdom. Honoring Confucius as the incomparable sage, Mencius claimed all persons in principle could become sages through studying the Classics, practicing moral disciplines, and cultivating natural energies. The book taking his name was probably compiled by him and close disciples. Chu Hsi (1130–1200) made it the third of orthodox Confucianism's *Ssu-shu* (Four Books). *See also* Chu Hsi; Confucianism; Confucianism (authoritative texts and their interpretation); Confucianism (thought and ethics); Ssu-shu.

Mendelssohn, Moses (1729–86), important German-Jewish philosopher, leader in Jewish emancipation and the modernization of Jewish culture and education. His best-known book, *Jerusalem* (1783), presents Judaism as "revealed legislation" and distinguishes Jewish religion from Jewish peoplehood. It argues that basic Jewish religious doctrines, such as the existence and unity of God, derive from reason, not revelation, and are universal. By contrast, Jewish law, revealed at Sinai, applies only to Jews, for community regulation and to strengthen reason. Mendelssohn's mastery of German culture and his friendship with the dramatist G. E. Lessing earned him social acceptability rare for a Jew in that country during the 1700s. His ideas influenced Reform and Orthodox Judaism.

mendicancy (Islam), begging or receiving alms. While not formally sanctioned, mendicancy is governed by other considerations in Islamic law, ritual, and ethos. The Qur'an and *hadith* contain injunctions for and against begging. However, *zakat* ("poor tax" or, more generally, *sadaqa,* "charity") is one of the Five Pillars of Islam and considered a religious duty of every Muslim.

The life of the Prophet Muhammad serves as a model in the development of begging and almsgiving as a source of religious merit and a religious duty. Hadith present the theme of

Muhammad's poverty, which is remembered by those who venerate the Prophet through charity. This theme is also used by those who follow his example of poverty as a sign of devotion to God.

The term *fakir* indicates both one who is impoverished and one who forsakes all worldly attachments for God. Mendicants often find refuge in mosques, which serve as places of prayer and shelter for the needy and displaced. Early Muslim beggars traced their descent to the People of the Bench—a pious group of Muhammad's companions who lived in his mosque. Another mendicant group, the Banu Sasan, were wanderers in medieval Islam, comprising tricksters, magicians, and public preachers. Whether ascetic or destitute, the mendicant may be perceived as a source of blessing (*baraka*) and a symbol of humility. Ethnographic descriptions of the Muslim world show that beggars will use this perception to request alms by calling out the names of God and the Prophet, reminding believers of the incumbent duty of *Zakat*. *See also* almsgiving; fakir; Zakat.

Mennonites, a church of the radical or left wing of the Protestant Reformation. Titles often applied to Mennonite churches are "peace churches" and "believers' churches."

This family comprises several Mennonite bodies, the Amish and Hutterite people, and a few Brethren bodies. They originated in Europe, but most divisions occurred in America. They are called radical since they mean to go to the roots of Christianity by practicing assiduously the teachings of the primitive church. Centrally, they aim to avoid conformity to the world, which may mean a refusal to bear arms or to vote or to take oaths. Some go further, by refusing to send their children to public schools, or to use modern technology, or to dress according to current styles.

Their original name, Anabaptists, was given them by their detractors. Because they regarded the Catholic practice of infant baptism as inauthentic, they were dubbed rebaptizers (in Greek, anabaptists). From the beginning, they have been at odds with prevailing fashion, religious as well as cultural, caring only about conformity with their understanding of what God prescribes. *See also* Anabaptists.

Menno Simons (men'oh sī'muhns; 1496–1561), Dutch Christian reformer. He was the leader of groups of persecuted Anabaptists who became known as Mennonites. *See also* Mennonites.

menorah (meh-noh'rah), seven-branched lampstand first mentioned in Exodus 25:31–40 and 37:17–24; probably stood in the Second Jerusalem Temple. Depicted on the triumphal Roman Arch of Titus of 70, it is a national symbol of modern Israel.

men-shen (men-shen; Chin., "door gods"), printed images of fierce-looking military figures posted on the doors of Chinese homes on New Year's Day; they protect against evil spirits. *See also* New Year (China).

men's houses, structures commonly used by traditional peoples to ritually separate one gender from another. Often located at the center of a village, men's houses serve as sites where rites that must be concealed from the eyes of women are carried out. Within the house, seating arrangements coordinate age-set and clan affiliation with the four cardinal directions and the calendar. Festival masks and instruments are often stored here during the seasons when their use is proscribed. Usually bachelors live in these houses along with married men who are observing temporary sexual abstinence. *See also* age-sets; initiation rituals; secret societies.

menstrual blood, usually understood as a polluting substance. *See also* gender roles; mikveh.

Mercury, the ancient Roman god of commerce. He was identified with the Greek Hermes, appearing in myth often as a messenger. *See also* Hermes.

merit, a basic concept in Buddhist ethics. Merit making is one of the fundamental practices of all Buddhists—both lay and monastic. It is closely connected to the notion of *karma* (Skt.), according to which good (meritorious) deeds will bear positive results in this or a future lifetime and bad (demeritorious) deeds will have negative ones.

Buddhists recognize many different ways of making merit. These are sometimes systematized into formal lists that include such things as observing basic moral precepts, respecting one's elders, listening to sermons, rejoicing at the merit making of others, and practicing meditation. Foremost on these lists, however, is the practice of giving (*dana*).

Giving: Giving can take many forms, but most commonly it refers to the material support offered by laity to the monastic community in the form of food offerings, gifts of robes and supplies, repairs to monastic buildings, funds for ceremonies and festivals, etc.

Several factors can affect the efficacy of an

act of giving in bringing about positive results. The amount one gives and the mind-set with which one gives it may be significant, but most important are the qualities of the "field of merit" in which one "plants" one's gift. Simply put, the more meritorious the field, the more one will reap from one's act. As the above list implies, the monastic community has long been affirmed as one of the most fertile of fields, and this obviously has had important implications for Buddhist ethics; consistently in Buddhist countries the building of a new monastery for monks has been considered more meritorious than, for instance, the construction of a new city hospital.

One of the basic principles of merit making is that merit tends to engender more merit. For example, a monk who preaches a sermon makes merit by "giving" the teaching to the laity; the laypersons listening to him, however, also make merit by hearing him preach. Similarly, a layperson who puts food into a monk's begging bowl makes merit by virtue of that act, but the monk, too, makes merit by providing the layperson with the opportunity to make the offering.

Motives of the Merit Maker: Generally speaking, Buddhists have one or more intentions in mind in performing acts of merit. First, they may simply be interested in obtaining rewards for themselves in a future lifetime. Thus, they may desire, as a result of their good deed, to be reborn as a rich person or as a divinity in heaven or simply to avoid rebirth in one of the lower realms.

Second, they may be interested in escaping entirely from this cycle of rebirth by attaining enlightenment (*nirvana*). It is important to recognize this motivation, because it is sometimes thought that merit makers have essentially given up on the possibility of enlightenment and resigned themselves merely to seeking a better rebirth. They are thus often contrasted with monks actively practicing meditation. In fact, however, acts of merit in Indian Buddhism were traditionally accompanied by a statement of intent on the part of the merit makers to attain enlightenment at some point in the future, and this by virtue of their act of merit. Today, in Theravada countries, such intentions usually take the form of a resolve to be reborn at the time of the future Buddha Maitreya and to reach nirvana under him. In this way meritorious deeds do not necessarily keep one in the cycle of rebirth but represent a viable channel to liberation.

Finally, merit makers may also have as a motivation the alleviation of the suffering of others. This they may accomplish directly (when their act of merit is immediately beneficial) or indirectly by the practice of ritually transferring the merit they make to a relative or friend, especially to a deceased parent. Persons who thus give away their own merit do not thereby deplete their own stock of it, but, in fact, accrue more merit by virtue of their good deed, the transfer of merit being itself a merit-making act.

Such transfers may be theoretically against an individualistic interpretation of karma, but early on they became a common Buddhist practice. Moreover, their logical extension may be found in Mahayana Buddhism in the notion of the *bodhisattva* (Buddha-to-be), who is portrayed as possessing a vast reservoir of merit, which he or she may freely share with all suffering sentient beings. *See also* almsgiving; bodhisattva; Buddhism (thought and ethics); karma.

merkabah. *See* Judaism (mysticism).

Merton, Thomas (1915–68), American Catholic Trappist monk first known for his autobiography, *The Seven Storey Mountain* (1948). Poet, mystic, and journalist, Merton excited interest in monasticism in others and explored the tensions between a contemplative life and an engaged social consciousness in himself. Merton's appreciation of other religious traditions, coupled with his strong ecumenism, made him an important international figure.

Meru, Mt. (may'roo), cosmic mountain at the center of the Hindu and Buddhist universe reaching from earth to heaven. The heavens circulate about Meru, the heavenly Ganges descends from Vishnu's toe to its top, and certain gods reside there. Hindu temples symbolically represent Meru. *See also* cosmology.

mescaline. *See* hallucinogens; Native American Church.

Mesmerism, the practice of inducing trance states, named after Franz Anton Mesmer (1733–1815), the father of modern hypnotism. Believed to facilitate both healing and the development of psychic powers, Mesmerism was influential in the emergence of Spiritualism and several mental science movements. *See also* Spiritualism.

Mesoamerican religion. Monumental ceremonial centers were a major focus of Mesoamerican cities, with their complex religious performances and socially stratified societies. In every case, religious experience and expressions were acted out, symbolized, and concentrated in ceremonial centers of different types and sizes.

A Short History: Mesoamerica was a geographical and cultural area covering the southern two-thirds of mainland Mexico, Guatemala, Belize, El Salvador, and parts of Honduras, Nicaragua, and Costa Rica in which the powerful processes of primary urban generation distinguished Meso-america as a cultural entity, beginning with the emergence of food production during the second millennium B.C. and ending with the Spanish conquest in the sixteenth century. While it appears that human populations entered the New World through the Bering Strait land bridge connecting Siberia and Alaska as early as 60,000 B.C. and reached the Basin, or Valley, of Mexico by 20,000 B.C., the cultural patterns that led to the rise of permanent, monumental ceremonial centers and dramatic public religious performances began with the development of agriculture between 6500 and 2000 B.C. Prior to this development, various peoples speaking many languages migrated into North America and Mesoamerica. Over 250 languages for the area covering Mexico and Guatemala have been identified. These peoples encountered a geography of contrasts and wonders, highlands and lowlands, with an astonishing variety of ecosystems. High mountain ranges, periodically volcanic, form high valley systems and plateaus where major cultural centers developed at different periods in history. These high mountainous areas sweep down on the eastern and western sides into lowland areas that give way to the Gulf of Mexico, the Caribbean Sea, and the Pacific Ocean. The plateaus and high valleys as well as the fertile areas of the lowlands, including dense forests, served as important centers of pre-Hispanic cultures.

The most creative cultural development in pre-urban Mesoamerica was the control of food energy contained in plants. One text, from a much later historical period, shows that the natives compared the creation of the human body with the creation of corn. By 2000 B.C., corn, beans, avocados, squash, cotton, and chilies were domesticated, pottery was made, and ritual burial of human beings was practiced. These plants, artifacts, and the human body were believed to be imbued with sacred powers and came to play important roles in the mythology, ritual speech and costumes, shrines, and performances of Mesoamerican religions. During the last stages of this agricultural development, people created some of the ritual relationships with the human body that eventually became central

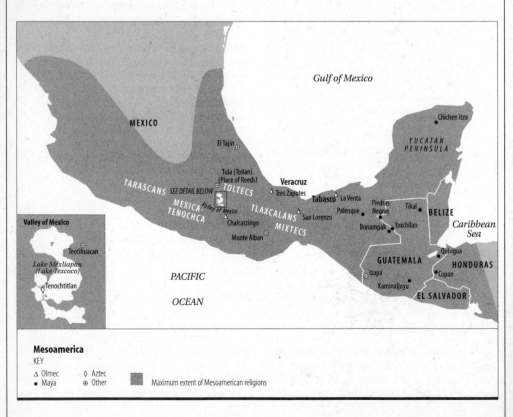

Mesoamerica
KEY

△ Olmec   ◇ Aztec

● Maya   ⊕ Other   ▨ Maximum extent of Mesoamerican religions

to the religions of numerous Mesoamerican peoples. These included special offerings to the dead, the dismemberment of human beings, sacrifice, and cremation. Powerful beliefs in the longevity of the human spirit and an afterlife were present. By 1800 B.C. the stage was set for the development of villages and holy towns in which some of the basic cultural patterns for the next three thousand years were established.

The subsequent periods of development of Mesoamerican society and religion have been divided for practical purposes into three major phases: the Formative, the Classic, and the Post-Classic.

The Formative period (1800 B.C.–A.D. 100) was characterized by the gradual rise of complex ceremonial centers and the appearance of monumental architecture. Hieroglyphic writing and calendrics, the introduction of social stratification, short- and long-distance trade routes, and the first outlines of political statehood also developed in several areas. The outstanding culture in the Formative archaeological record is the Olmec civilization, whose scattered ceremonial centers took shape around 1800 B.C. and collapsed by 300 B.C.

The surviving evidence for the Olmecs consists of stones, sacred stones, ceremonial architecture, pottery, and human and animal bones. Called the Mother Culture of later Mesoamerican religions, the Olmec style of art and architecture rose in a variety of sacred precincts and caves, originating in the lowland regions of southern Veracruz and western Tabasco near the coast of the Gulf of Mexico and spreading to central and southern Mesoamerica.

The most impressive religious expression of Olmec culture involves reshaping the earth. The Olmec media for art and symbolic expression were jade, basalt, clay, and the earth itself in the forms of caves and hills, each of which was transformed to represent the realities of the religious imagination and social hierarchy. Caves became the settings for cave paintings and rituals of mythic events, while cliffs became the sacred sites of carvings of human-animal-earth-spirit relations. Olmec ceremonial centers were assemblages of sacred places made of redesigned earthly materials arranged on and within the earth. One example of the earth reshaped as a religious expression is the bas-relief on a cliff at Chalcatzingo (800 B.C.), where an Olmec ruler or man-god is seated in a cave holding a box surrounded by clouds, water, jade, vegetation, and the natural stone wall representing the earth itself. At another Olmec site large mosaics were laid out to form a jaguar mask buried

in multiple layers beneath the surface of the earth. Even more impressive are the scores of colossal basalt heads, six to ten feet high, representing rulers or gods, carved in Olmec ceremonial centers along the Gulf Coast of Mexico.

San Lorenzo, La Venta, and Tres Zapotes were monumental ceremonial centers with pyramids, temples, altars, and tombs ornamented with a number of fantastic religious motifs depicting animal-human relations. Such combinations as human-jaguar, jaguar-bird, bird-jaguar-caiman, caiman-human appearing along with rattlesnakes and other poisonous snakes such as fer-de-lances, harpy eagles, and monkeys were considered manifestations of the enormous powers of the sky, earth, and underworld. It is likely that these carefully carved, sometimes precious-stone images reflect the belief in spirit helpers who took the form of powerful, aggressive, even dangerous animals used by shamans, priests, and rulers.

The most remarkable intellectual and artistic developments in Mesoamerican history took place during the Classic period, usually dated between 200 and 900. The Classic period resulted in the maturation of the Formative period processes, including the proliferation of ritual and solar calendrical systems, sizable agricultural bureaucracies, and the emergence in several areas of large political units either organized by capital cities—as in the case of Teotihuacan in the central highlands—or characterized by regional centers that competed intensely for access to economic goods and control of political and religious prestige—as in the Mayan regions.

Other important Classic centers included El Tajín along the Gulf Coast, where the cult of the Ball Game, or *tlachtli*, was developed; Monte Alban in Oaxaca, which consisted of a spacious hilltop ceremonial center with temples, courtyards, a ball court, tombs for elites, and astronomically oriented buildings; and Izapa in Guatemala, where complex pictorial narratives were carved throughout an array of monumental buildings. But it was in the Mayan regions of Guatemala and Mexico that the greatest social and symbolic achievements of the Classic period took place.

The style and nature of the Classic Mayan world is well represented in a small jade plaque discovered in 1864 by workers digging a canal in eastern Guatemala. This 8½-inch object, which now resides in Leiden, Holland, contains two typical images of Mayan life. On one side is a Long Count calendar date corresponding to the year 320, while on the other is an extravagantly dressed Mayan lord stepping on a small-sized captive underneath him. This combination of social stratification, warfare, and the sacred calendar carved in jade illustrates the integration of crucial elements of Mayan achievement. In a number of cases elaborately carved and crowded ceremonial centers included steep, high pyramid temples, palaces, ball courts, sweat baths, stelae, and altars facing carefully planned courtyards that were sometimes linked

The great Mesoamerican Mayan ceremonial complex at Chichen Itza (ca. 200–1200), southcentral Yucatan, Mexico. The Castillo (the Great Pyramid) is in the foreground; the Temple of the Warriors is in the background.

to other courtyards and even cities by causeways. Among the over fifty major Mayan sites containing large stelae and associated altars plus carved scenes and inscriptions covered with images of royalty, calendrical notations, and fantastic supernatural figures are Copan, Quirigua, Piedras Negras, Bonampak, Palenque, Kaminaljuyu, Tikal, and Yaxchilan.

The most beautiful and perhaps revealing Mayan ceremonial center was Palenque, where a series of temples known as the Group of the Cross contain interior panels depicting Mayan cosmology interwoven with the ritual performances of Mayan rulers, both male and female. At the center of these cosmological images stands an *axis mundi* in the form of a fantastic tree decorated with corn, blood, mirrors, body parts, gods, serpents, day and night, and other symbolic items. As the narratives on the walls of temples show, the political, dynastic, agricultural, and social life of the Mayan cosmos revolved around and was oriented by this emblematic axis, which took on a number of agricultural forms.

The Classic Mayan cultures suffered a widespread collapse throughout many ceremonial centers between 790 and 889. This is evident because one of the greatest achievements of the Maya, an elaborate Long Count calendar covering millions of years, disappeared from use in the architectural record. Archaeological investigation reveals a rapid decline in population, increased warfare, and ecological depletion, which devastated the powerful Mayan culture.

The greatest Classic imperial ceremonial center of the central highlands was Teotihuacan (Abode of the Gods), located just north of the Valley of Mexico. At its height it was populated by over two hundred thousand people who lived among immense towering pyramids, elaborate ceremonial courtyards, and residential palaces all laid out in the image of a quincunx, or four-quartered design around the axis mundi. The city's cosmological orientation is reflected in the layout of the largest ceremonial structure, the Pyramid of the Sun, whose great stairway faces a westerly point on the horizon where the sun sets directly in front of it on the day of its first passage through the zenith. What auspicious moment in Teotihuacan's schedule of activities this day signified will never be clear, but it is obvious that there was a noble attempt to achieve a harmony between the great pyramid and celestial dynamics.

Teotihuacan's religion was animated by six major cultic forms: fertility, warfare, ball games, dynastic rulers, burial, and titular patrons. The city's symbols and ceremonies were imposed upon and adapted by many other city-states for which it was the center of an expanding, pulsating empire until its rapid collapse sometime in the eighth century.

Other cultures, such as the Toltecs, Mixtecs, Tlaxcalans, and Tarascans, played very significant roles in the history of Mesoamerican religions.

Sacred Centers: When the Spaniards arrived in the Aztec capital of Tenochtitlan in 1519, Aztec religion was based, in part, on the Toltec tradition of the eleventh-century capital Tula, or Tollan (Place of Reeds), where Topiltzin Quetzalcoatl (Our Young Prince the Feathered Serpent) established cosmic harmony, the arts, the calendar, agricultural abundance, eloquent rhetoric, and priestly rituals before falling into disrepute. "From him it began, from Quetzalcoatl it flowed out, all art and knowledge" was one of the refrains sung in Aztec schools. Topiltzin Quetzalcoatl was a priest-ruler, a kind of man-god who represented one of the greatest of Mesoamerican creator gods, Quetzalcoatl. The prolific deity Quetzalcoatl had assisted the cosmic creators, Ometecuhtli and Omecihuatl, organize the original universe. Among the many achievements of Topiltzin Quetzalcoatl, the influence of three may be traced in Aztec religion: the creation of a splendid capital that served as a microcosm of the universe; ritual training focusing on the human body as an image and receptacle of sacred forces and capable of participating in cosmic renewal; and the creation of the arts, especially the speech arts, to acquire profound knowledge.

When Aztec informants spoke to Spanish priests after the conquest about their cultural past, they emphasized that it was the Toltecs "who came to cause the cities to be founded" (*Florentine Codex*). During the reign of Topiltzin Quetzalcoatl, a great kingdom, Tollan, was established, where "squashes were very large, and some quite round. And the ears of maize were as large as hand grinding stones, . . . they could hardly be embraced in one's hands" (*Florentine Codex*). Technological and artistic achievements, astronomy, and feathermaking adorned a capital ordered by a series of magnificent ritual buildings oriented to the four quarters of the world, which demarcated a ceremonial precinct that subsequent rulers would emulate in the construction of their own ceremonial precincts. At the center of this ritual geography stood Crying Out Mountain, from which Topiltzin Quetzalcoatl dispensed laws, customs, ritual procedures, and sacred authority. This sense of centrality and temple order influenced the Aztec conceptions of ceremonial centers when they rose to prominence several centuries after the Toltec kingdom collapsed.

Perhaps the most outstanding monumental ceremonial center of late Mesoamerican history was the Aztec Templo Mayor (1390–1521), called Coatepec, or Serpent Mountain, by the priests. It was the quintessential axis of the Aztec empire, which included over four hundred towns and communities stretching, unevenly, from the Caribbean to the Pacific. This one great temple contained both the symbolism of the cosmos in its architecture, and ritual offerings from throughout the empire buried in its floors. It achieved in one architectural structure what Quetzalcoatl's four temples and sacred mountain achieved in Tollan.

The Aztecs called their world *cemanahuac*, or "land surrounded by water." This land was conceived as having five parts with four quadrants called *nauchampa*, literally the four directions of the wind, extending outward from the central section. At the center stood the city of Tenochtitlan, which was also conceived as the foundation of thirteen celestial levels inhabited by gods, colors, astronomical bodies, and male and female forces. At the exact point of intersection between the horizontal nauchampa and the thirteen vertical levels stood the Aztec Coatepec, Serpent Mountain, the Great Temple. It con-

The Great Temple (Templo Mayor) of Tenochtitlan (Mexico City), the center of the Aztec universe, as depicted by Aztec artists in the sixteenth-century *Codex Duran*. The stepped pyramid is surmounted by twin temples. The shrine on the left (north) was dedicated to Tlaloc, the deity of rain and fertility. The shrine on the right (south) was dedicated to the Aztecs' patron deity, Huitzilopochtli, a figure representing war and the world-sustaining ritual of human sacrifice.

sisted of a huge pyramidal base that supported two major shrines. Two stairways led up to the shrines of Tlaloc (Rain God) and Huitzilopochtli (War God). The south side of the pyramid represented the mythical mountain of Coatepetl, the mountain birthplace of the war god Huitzilopochtli, who rose each day as the sun to dominate the moon and stars, symbols for Aztec enemies. The north side of the temple represented the Mountain of Sustenance associated with Tlaloc's paradise, a lush green landscape that provided the precious rains and moisture that regenerated the agricultural world of the empire. Symbolically, this one building incorporated the ecology and cosmology of the Aztec world and served as the theater upon which religious ideas and commitments could be displayed and acted out.

Another of Topiltzin Quetzalcoatl's achievements was his direct experience of Ometeotl, the Creative Heavenly Pair who dwelt in the innermost part of heaven at the top of the celestial levels. This ecstatic experience was the result, in part, of intense ascetic rituals in which he fasted, did penance, bathed in icy cold waters, and performed autosacrifice, bleeding parts of his body with stingray spines and maguey thorns. In Aztec religion, the most pervasive sacred center where elaborate ceremonies were carried out was the human body. The human body was considered a potent receptacle of cosmological forces, a living, moving center of the world vulnerable to ritual requirements as well as enemies.

The *Codex Fejervary-Mayer* shows a typical image of the Mesoamerican cosmos, which is divided into five sections, with four quarters each

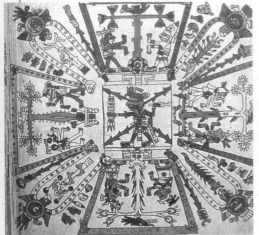

An Aztec ritual calendar from the fifteenth-century deerskin *Codex Fejervary-Mayer.* This representation of the cosmos is organized in the typical center-with- four-quarters pattern (with a pair of gods in each quarter). At the center stands Xiuhtecuhtli, the fire deity and lord of the hearth. At the top left is Piltzintecuhtli, protector of children. Continuing clockwise are Iztli, the personified obsidian sacrificial knife; Mictlantecuhtli, the lord of death; Centeotl, the maize goddess; Chalchiuhtlicue, the water goddess; Tlazolteotl, patron of weavers and midwives; Tlaloc, the deity of rain and fertility; and finally, Tepeyollotl, the "heart of the mountain."

containing a sacred tree with a celestial bird on top, surrounding the central region where Xiuhtecuhtli, the Fire God, is dressed in warrior regalia. His body, a ritually transformed human body, receives the forces associated with the four quarters through blood streams that flow from the dismembered body of the god Tezcatlipoca into the central space he occupies.

In Aztec theories of medicine reflecting the relations of celestial forces, blood, and the ritual transformations of humans, the human body was progressively filled—at conception, birth, first exposure to fire and sunlight, and at points of special achievements in life—with powers originating in the celestial spaces above and in sacred events that took place in mythical time.

Although all parts of the human body were loaded with these special powers, the powers were concentrated in three parts of the human physiology. The head, especially in the hair and in the fontanel area, was filled with *tonalli,* an animating force or soul that provided vigor and the energy for growth and development. The heart received deposits of *teyolia,* which provided emotion, memory, and knowledge to the human. The liver received *ihiyotl,* which provided humans with bravery, desire, hatred, love, and happiness. It was thought of as a luminous gas that could attract and charm other people. These forces or animating entities directed the physiological processes of a human body, gave the person character, and were highly valued by the family and sought after in warfare and ritual sacrifice. Some of these powers could be taken from a human body in sacrifice and either offered to the gods as a form of debt payment or acquired by the person who touched the physical entity in which they resided. Every human being was seen as the living container of these forces, but certain individuals—such as warriors, deity impersonators (*teotl ixiptla,* lit., "images of the deity"), lords, or artists at the moment of creativity—contained extraordinary supernatural powers.

Religious powers were accessible to humans not only through the sacrality of monumental ceremonial centers and the cosmic powers contained within the body, but also through eloquent spoken word. Effective rhetoricians were held in the highest regard because, at least since the time of Topiltzin Quetzalcoatl, eloquent speech forms and metaphors were used as vehicles to bring the divine into the social world.

Among the Nahuatl-speaking Aztecs, verbal arts were vehicles for the sacred and were taught by a group known as the *tlamatinime,* or "knowers of things." Called "a stout torch that does not smoke," the tlamatinime were trained at *calmecacs,* or schools of higher learning, to preserve honored traditions, produce and read painted manuscripts, and develop refined metaphors and poems to probe the foundations of human existence. Central to their craft was the memorization and cultivation of *huehuetlatolli,* or the ancient word. These ancient sayings and ethical traditions also enabled speakers to break out of illusion and penetrate the true foundation of the universe. This craft utilized *in xochitl, in cuicatl* ("flowers and songs"), artistic expressions in the forms of words, songs, and paintings that connected the human personality, referred to as "face and heart," with the divine. Nezahualcoyotl, the Fasting Coyote, ruler of the Aztec ceremonial city of Texcoco, wrote about "flowers," or poetic truth, which travels into the celestial sphere,

> Even though flowers on earth
> may wither and yellow,
> they will be carried there,
> to the interior of the house
> of the bird with the golden feathers.
> (*Native Mesoamerican Spirituality*,
> Miguel Leon Portilla)

This method of seeking the interior of things through language reached its highest form in the huehuetlatolli—florid, elegant metaphorical speeches that were memorized and presented at ceremonial occasions such as the coronation of a ruler, the entry of youth into the calmecac, undertaking the work of a midwife, or a marriage ceremony. A central idea in this art form was the expression and union of dualities—language and social dualities that approximated and replicated the divine duality, Ometeotl, the Dual God, who dwelled in the highest part of the cosmos and whose nature penetrated all levels of reality.

Sacrifice and the Underworld: In both stereotype and historical fact Mesoamerican religions were heavily sacrificial. Many sacrifices were performed in public ceremonies, recounted in song, painted and carved in artwork, and even performed by gods, ancestors, and the dead. While it is clear that Mesoamerican sacrifices involved gift exchanges between gods and humans (the Aztecs called them *nextlaoaliztli*, or debt payment) as well as offerings to gods, it also appears that human sacrifices were ceremonial techniques involving terrible ordeals and the cunning sacrifices of gods in order to defeat the finality of death.

Appreciating the cosmic forces at work in the human body, the complicated and varied ceremonies of human sacrifice can be understood as methods of accessing and renewing sacred powers encapsulated in the human physique. Guided by detailed ritual calendars, Aztec ceremonies of ritual killing of animals and humans were carried out during every month in the eighteen-month ritual year. Whether ensuring cosmic creativity; restoring powers of fertility to the sky, streams, mountains, fields, and women; or nourishing the sun to ensure the stability of the empire and capital, blood sacrifices were carried out by priestly orders specifically trained to dispense the victims swiftly, and rejuvenate, through violent release, the divine powers within them.

These methods involved different types of sacrifice of captive warriors and purchased slaves, including women and children. Though a variety of methods of ritual killings were used—including decapitation, burning, hurling from great heights, strangulation, and arrow sacrifice—the typical ritual involved the dramatic heart sacrifice and the placing of the heart in a ceremonial vessel (*cuauhxicalli*) in order to nourish the gods. Amid the drums, conch shell trumpets, rattles, and other musical instruments that created an atmosphere of dramatic intensity, blood was smeared on the face of a deity's image and the skulls of some victims were placed on the giant skull rack (*tzompantli*), which held scores of head trophies.

Since Aztec sacrifice has been widely discussed, the following will focus on Mayan sacrifices during the fabulous journey of the Hero Twins, Hunaphu and Xblanque, through Xibalba (the Quiche Maya underworld) as recorded in the *Popul Vuh*, or Book of Council, an 8,500-line document discovered in the beginning of the eighteenth century in a Quiche Mayan community in Guatemala.

In the Classic Mayan world, humans and gods had relationships based on mutual care and nurturance. The gods created humans, who were therefore in their debt. The ongoing existence of human life depended on the generous gifts of life, which the gods continued to dispense through children, germination, rain, sunshine, the supply of animals and objects of power. But the gods also depended on humans to care, nurture, acknowledge, and renew their powers. One mythic account of the Maya states that the "Maker, Modeler, Bearer, Begetter" created humans so they would give praise, respect, and nurturance to the gods. This sense of reciprocity was acted out in ritual sacrifices. However, the relationships of humans to divinities is more complex and problematic in the Mayan conception of the underworld where ordeals, torture, and sacrifice continue to take place after death.

Carved on the sarcophagus of the seventh-century ruler of Palenque, Pacal, or Lord Shield, is a vivid image of a Mayan lord at the moment of his death and descent into the underworld. The image shows Pacal, with a small bone attached to his nose at the moment of death, representing the seed of rebirth, falling into the gaping jaws of the underworld, which is pictured as two huge skeletal dragons joined at the chin to form the U-shaped opening representing the passage into Xibalba. The ordeals the king will face are similar to those reported in the *Popul Vuh*, which contains creation myths, sacred histories, and descriptions of ritual performance representing a long tradition of Maya religious thought.

Quiche cosmology is characterized as a long performance of "sowing and dawning," that is, planting and harvesting, burial and rebirth, sunset and sunrise, repeated in cycles of cosmic creations and destructions and the adventures of heroes who face ordeals and transformations. In a relevant episode the Hero Twins, Hunahpu and Xblanque, play a game and disturb the Lords of Death in Xibalba by stomping around and bouncing the ball loudly. One Death and Seven Death summon the Twins into the underworld to play a game. The boys go into Xibalba, cross Pus River and Blood River and see the Black Road, White Road, Red Road, and the Green Road. With the help of a mosquito the Twins learn the names of the Lords: One Death, Seven Death, House Corner, Blood Gatherer, Pus Master, Jaundice Master, Bone Scepter, Skull Scepter, Bloody Teeth, Bloody Claws. The Lords put the Twins through many ordeals including a series of nights in houses designed to destroy them. First they are forced into the Dark House and given a torch and two cigars and told they must return them unconsumed in the morning. The Twins take the tails of macaw birds, which look like torches, to the sentries and put fireflies on the tips of the cigars, giving the false appearance of having them lit all night. The next night they are tested in the Razor House and survive by persuading the knives to put down their points. Then they survive the Cold House, the "jaguar-packed home of jaguars," the Fire House, and finally the Bat House, where "monstrous beasts, their snouts like knives, the instruments of death," decapitate one of them. The other Twin rejoins the head to his brother's body, regenerating his human form. They jump into an oven and the Lords of Death grind their bones into powder, and throw it into the water believing the Twins destroyed. They regenerate as catfish in the water, and reappear as human vagabonds and magicians. When they perform a human sacrifice without killing the victim, the Lords of Death command one Twin to sacrifice and regenerate the other Twin. When this is achieved successfully, the Lords exclaim, "Do it to us! Sacrifice us!" Having taken the game to this crucial point, the Twins sacrifice the Lords but do not bring them back to life.

The Twins declare that the remaining Xibalbans will only receive offerings of plant and animal incense in the future and must limit their attacks on the weak and guilty. Then the boys ascend out of Xibalba, straight into the sky, and become the sun and moon.

In this mythic tradition, sacrifice takes on a different meaning than what we might have expected. The Twins suffer the tortures of the underworld, gain knowledge of self-transformation, and overcome the final static condition of death through cunning, trickery, and the death of gods. It is not the gods who are renewed, but human lives, which are transformed into other forms of nature. It is not gift exchange that is experienced in this particular Mayan sacrifice, but the limiting of death as an ultimate reality. The Twins kill the gods of the underworld instead of each other and ascend into the celestial levels to become a permanent pattern of renewal, a mythic model for certain ceremonial performances in Mayan religion.

This engaging story helps clarify the meaning of the cosmic scene of Pacal's tomb. His descent marked the beginning of another ceremonial career in another set of ceremonial centers, in the underworld and eventually the celestial sphere. His new career after death involved the struggle to overcome the Lords of Xibalba with the same cunning, courage, and self-transformation of the Twins. And like them, Pacal rose to become, through continued sacrifices both above and below ground, the Sun, rising above the horizon, passing regularly across the heavens, giving the Maya a celestial performance of regeneration. *See also* cannibalism; kingship, sacred; pictorial writing systems; sacrifice; Sahagun, Bernardino de; Sun Stone; Templo Mayor; Tenochtitlan.

Mesopotamian religion.

Third Millennium B.C.: The earliest written source materials for early Mesopotamian (Sumerian) religion are not continuous. One may roughly define two large textual groups: cuneiform tablets from the end of the Early Dynastic period (ca. 2700 B.C.) and two distinct traditions from the old Babylonian period (ca. 1720 B.C.), an earlier one that consists primarily of school exercises from southern Mesopotamia (Sumer) and a slightly later one from central Mesopotamia (Babylonia). There are scattered finds of documents from the intervening periods but they are limited at present. The original context of the later material is not known but some of the texts may have originated from temple environments. The recovered Early Dynastic materials from Sumer were written almost exclusively in the Sumerian language; this remained the language of literature and liturgy in Old Babylonian times, when Sumerian was no longer spoken. High forms of Akkadian (Babylonian), a Semitic language, were also used sporadically. There is also a small but significant group of early texts written in two or more Semitic languages or dialects.

Other sources for the study of religion, such as architecture and the plastic arts, have also survived.

The first literary texts from Sumer, indeed the earliest literary texts in the world, come from the cities of Fara (ancient Shuruppak), Abu Salabikh, Adab, and Nippur and are primarily religious in character. It must be stressed that our ability to understand these early texts is still very limited. The myths and magical incantations are particularly difficult. Nevertheless, it is possible to discern that many early narratives, while different from later texts, described the origins and lives of major deities. Some of the compositions begin with cosmological introductions such as "after the heavens had been separated from the earth, when the earth was separated from the heavens," in order to establish a sacred space and time for the narrative that follows.

Pantheon: In early Mesopotamia power was locally centered in independent city-states, but there were strong elements of common religious traditions. Each city had a major deity, and these deities were organized in family groupings hierarchically ordered along kinship lines. The top deity in this hierarchy was technically An, the sky god, god of the city Uruk; in practical terms it was Enlil (Illil), god of Nippur, but Nippur was never the seat of kingship. Most deities had temples and chapels in the various cities of Sumer, although certain local traditions can be observed and some deities appeared under slightly different guise in different locales.

Early Syncretism: Third-millennium Mesopotamia was inhabited by different peoples living in close proximity, and as a result one can observe religious syncretism. For example, Semitic deities such as Su-en and Shamash, the moon and sun, became identified with Sumerian Nanna and Utu. The Sumerian gods were both male, while in certain Semitic religions the sun and moon were opposite in gender. In fact, in some Akkadian personal names one can still trace the original feminine sun goddess. The Semitic goddess Ashtar (later Ishtar) was partly identified with Sumerian Inanna. Although in many Semitic religions there was a pair Ashtar/Ashtarat, masculine and feminine, in Mesopotamia Inanna/Ishtar (Venus) embodies a complex set of masculine and feminine features, sometimes portrayed as the morning and evening star. It has also been observed that early Mesopotamian Semitic personal names include, with minor exceptions, only two deities: Ilum ("the god") and Ashtar. This changed around 2400 B.C. when a different set of Semitic dialects, dubbed Old Akkadian, appeared on the scene.

Worship: The official religion was part of the ideology of the state and private individuals participated only in large public festivities, not in everyday rituals in the temples. Private worship of gods or of ancestors was conducted within the house, at a shrine or a small chapel, depending on the wealth of the individual. There were, however, public cult places for the worship of the dead belonging to the highest members of society, including high priests and priestesses, kings and queens. Ceremonial meals were taken by the living even as the dead were offered food and water. Each person had a personal deity who interceded on his or her behalf with the higher gods. Communication with the divine was done by diverse channels. One could pray to one's personal deity, pay a priest to pray to a deity who was responsible for a specific area, present a votive object, or commission a letter to be deposited in front of a divine statue. On very rare occasions (in the early second millennium), the gods sent letters to priests and kings with answers or even queries. More often elite individuals commissioned specialists to read the omens. The omens were sought primarily in the livers and entrails of sheep, but smoke, oil, astronomy, and other phenomena were also analyzed for divine answers. The diviner performed an elaborate rite just before sunrise in which he invoked the gods of the night to "put truth" (later "write") in the organs of the sheep that he was about to sacrifice. He then searched the liver for certain marks good and bad. An adding up of positive and negative features resulted in the appropriate answer to the supplicant's question.

Religion and the State: One of the characteristic features of the earliest large cities in Mesopotamia was the central complex of temples and shrines, and the very scale of the architecture testifies to the social importance of the temple as an ideological and economic institution. The theory that the first city-states were governed by the religious sector is no longer maintained, but the undoubted economic power of the temples is well attested. Economic documents and artistic representations testify to the existence of elaborate public sacred celebrations.

A momentous change in religious thought came about in the later half of the third millennium when the king Naram-Sin (ca. 2254–2218 B.C.) pronounced himself divine. This was an attempt to center religious and secular power in one person and to provide a new form of royal legitimacy. Naram-Sin's presumption of world dominance and his use of the title "King of the Four Corners of the Universe" show the simultaneous centering of universal dominion with a

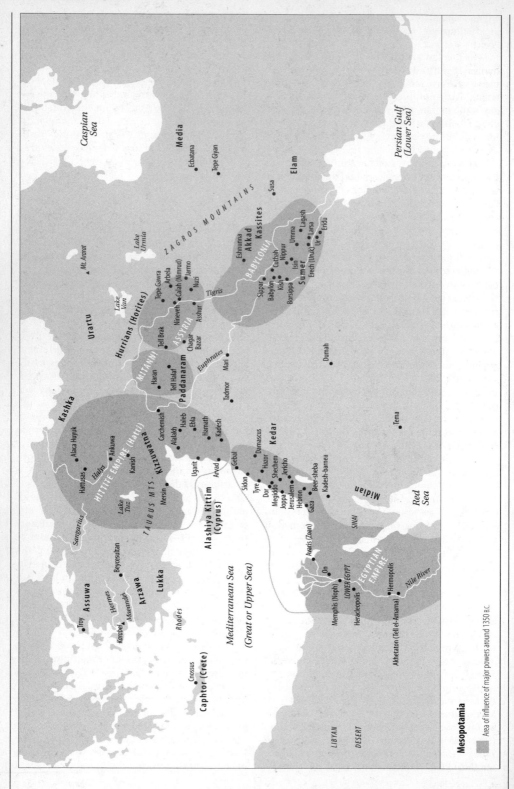

Caspian Sea

Media

Ecbatana

Tepe Giyan

Persian Gulf (Lower Sea)

Elam

Susa

ZAGROS MOUNTAINS

Kassites

Eshnunna

Akkad

BABYLONIA

Sumer

Lake Urmia

Sippar

Cuthah

Nippur

Umma

Lagash

Larsa

Erech (Uruk)

Ur

Eridu

Babylon

Kish

Isin

Borsippa

Tepe Gawra

Arbela

Kalah (Nimrud)

Jarmo

Nuzi

Nineveh

ASSYRIA

Asshur

Tigris

Lake Van

Hurrians (Horites)

Urartu

Mt. Ararat

Tell Brak

Chagar Bazar

MITANNI

Haran

Tell Halaf

Paddanaram

Euphrates

Mari

Tadmor

Dumah

Kashka

Alaca Huyuk

Ankuwa

Kizzuwatna

Carchemish

Alalakh

Ebla

Haleb

Hamath

Kadesh

Damascus

Kedar

Hattusas

Ilahs

HITTITE EMPIRE (Hatti)

Kanish

Lake Tuz

TAURUS MTS.

Mersin

Ugarit

Arvad

Gebal

Sidon

Tyre

Dor

Hazor

Shechem

Megiddo

Jericho

Joppa

Jerusalem

Hebron

Beer-sheba

Gaza

Kadesh-barnea

Midian

SINAI

Red Sea

Tema

Sangarius

Beyesultan

Assuwa

Hermus

Karabel

Maeander

Arzawa

Lukka

Troy

Rhodes

Alashiya Kittim (Cyprus)

Mediterranean Sea (Great or Upper Sea)

Avaris (Zoan)

On

LOWER EGYPT

EGYPTIAN EMPIRE

Memphis (Noph)

Heracleopolis

Hermopolis

Akhetaton (Tell el-Amarna)

Nile River

Cnossus

Caphtor (Crete)

LIBYAN DESERT

Mesopotamia

Area of influence of major powers around 1350 B.C.

change in the concept of kingship. The dynasty in power collapsed soon after the reign of Naram-Sin, but the idea of divine kingship was taken up again by the rulers of the next central dynasty, the Third Dynasty of Ur, beginning with the second king, Shulgi (ca. 2094–2047 B.C.). The worship of the king allowed the crown to consolidate power over the large temple estates of the time. Moreover, in these centralized states religion and royal power were fused by installing royal children in the highest priestly offices.

Mythology: The literary texts of the early second millennium preserve a number of mythical narratives. These are primarily concerned with the major deities Enlil, Enki, Inanna, and Ninurta. In almost all of them the primary motif is the contrast between order and disorder. One can almost posit an underlying structure to most of these texts: order is disrupted and must be reinstated, and the process results in a new reality. Order is symbolized as an abstract function of hierarchical power—it is in the hands of the top deities—and as an object—there is a tablet of destinies that can be stolen by liminal figures such as the lion-headed Anzu (Zu) bird. Also, order is reified in a set of principles, both abstract and concrete, especially the Sumerian *me* (Akkadian *parsu* [*partzu*]). The Sumerian noun, but not the Akkadian, is derived etymologically from the verb "to be." Each entity, including abstractions such as "kingship," had its *me*. These abstract principles are sometimes represented metaphorically as physical objects; they could be set in a corner or stolen, as in the example of Zu's thievery.

Although the matter of order/disorder is always there beneath the surface, a variety of subjects are treated in the myths. These texts cannot be read alone, but must be interpreted within the confines of the whole tradition. This is particularly evident in the case of two distinct stories about the marriage of Enlil and Ninlil. They differ in almost all details and yet are complementary rather than contradictory. The same can be stated about creation stories that may appear to be irreconcilable and yet must be read together. Another set is composed of myths concerning the most ambiguous of Mesopotamian deities, Inanna/Ishtar. She was the goddess of violence, war, and sex but not of procreation, and despite what is often stated she had nothing to do with the various manifestations of the Mother Goddess. Inanna constantly disrupted world order, as in a myth in which she decided—incongruously because she incarnates life—to take over the netherworld, the domain of her sister Ereshkigal. She died there and could be re-

Statuette of a supernatural lion-headed eagle from Mari (Syria), ca. 2500 B.C. to 2350 B.C.

deemed only when her lover Dumuzi replaced her in the netherworld. The passions that led to this affair could only be put to rest by means of a sacrifice, one that resulted in a new reality.

The Cult: In addition to myths there are cultic compositions, primarily from northern Babylonia, that provide a closer view of the everyday cult in the temples, where the gods lived. These texts were sometimes spelled out in syllabic orthography that allowed those with limited knowledge of Sumerian to pronounce prayers and laments. A handful of administrative ritual texts provides additional information on the cult, as do texts from temples' archives. Cult statues were treated as incarnations of divinities and were clothed and fed each day, with special celebrations reserved for specific festivals. Feast days were often arranged according to the phases of the moon. The goods and the food offered to the gods were actually distributed to temple personnel and dependents, who thus partook of the divine table.

Second and First Millennia B.C.: Many essential features of the last phase of Mesopotamian religion have roots in earlier periods. The emergence of the national gods Marduk and Assur together with their cults; the concern with death, witchcraft, and sorcery; and the emerging importance of the astral aspect of the divine realm seen in the spread of celestial divination may, however, be singled out for focus.

Cosmic Gods: A cosmic triad of gods was associated with parts of the universe: Anu with heaven, Enlil with air, and Ea with the waters around and below the earth. Anu was the head of the pantheon in genealogical terms, but he had an adversarial relationship with humankind. Enlil had a special relation to demons and the netherworld and played the role of the punishing god with respect to humanity, sending the enemy to inflict defeat (in "The Curse of Agade") or sending the Flood to destroy the human race (in "Gilgamesh" and "Atrahasis"). In contrast to Anu and Enlil, Ea, known as the patron god of exorcism and wisdom, was considered a friend and helper of humankind.

Astral Gods: A celestial triad of gods was associated with the brightest heavenly bodies, the moon, sun, and Venus. The beneficent (except when eclipsed) moon god Sin, son of Enlil and father of the sun god Shamash, was symbolized by the bull. Shamash brought light and equity, judged heaven and earth, and protected the destitute and maltreated. Venus was deified as the goddess Ishtar and depicted as the eight-pointed star.

National Gods: The states of Babylonia and Assyria each promoted to national level the cult of the divine patron of its respective capital city, Marduk of Babylon and Assur of Assur. The Marduk cult was legitimized by the *Enuma elish* text, repeated every year as part of the New Year celebration. Assur's worship was limited to Assyria, whereas Marduk continued to have a following in Assyria as well as in Babylonia.

Other Gods: Enlil's son Ninurta, worshiped in his father's city of Nippur, was associated with fertility as well as with war and hunting. Ninurta appears chiefly as the hero of the story about the theft of Enlil's Tablet of Destinies by the demonic bird Anzu. Marduk's son Nabu became the patron god of scribes and had his temple in Borsippa. The first millennium saw a dramatic rise in the popularity of the Nabu cult, particularly in Assyria.

The chief deities of the netherworld and of death, the pair Nergal and Ereshkigal, were both worshiped in Cutha. Other gods were Gula, the goddess of healing, the fire god Nusku, or Girra, and the storm god Adad.

Institutions: The site on which the temple stood was fixed from very early times, and the temple of a particular city functioned as the household for the deity (or deities) associated

Votive statue from Ninni Zaza temple, Mari (Syria), 2000 B.C. to 1000 B.C.

with that city as its patron. The raised foundation platform (later a staged tower structure called a ziggurat) symbolized a mountain reaching the heavens and became the characteristic architectural feature of the Mesopotamian temple. The royal house had the responsibility for the building of temples and support for their treasuries. Important temples in Assyria were those for Assur in Assur, Ishtar and Nabu in Nineveh, and Ninurta in Calah (Nimrud). In Babylonia, the major temples were of Marduk in Babylon, Anu in Uruk, Enlil in Nippur, Nabu in Borsippa, Sin in Ur (and Harran), and Shamash in Sippar.

From the earliest times the temple exercised land ownership, trade, and money lending, as well as establishing standards of weights and measures (the latter attested only in Old Babylonian). Until the Achaemenid period (538–331 B.C.), the temple received revenue in the form of taxes (tithe), paid in silver, barley, wool, livestock, and other goods. From King Nabonidus

(555–539 B.C.) onward, the state seems to have interfered increasingly in temple affairs. In the late Arsacid period (second century B.C.), when Babylon was no longer the cultural or commercial center of Mesopotamia, the Babylonian temple was the single institution of Mesopotamian civilization preserving such activities as cuneiform writing and law, cult, and the science of astronomy.

Cult: The city cult belonged to the city's patron deity and was situated in the city temple. Except for the occasional public festival involving the procession of the god or gods outside the temple precinct, the city god's cult was the exclusive domain of priests (and sometimes the king). The deity, represented by and physically embodied in the anthropomorphic image of its statue, was attended to in accordance with a ritual care-and-feeding schedule that filled the calendar year. All this was predicated on the assumption that human beings were created to serve and care for the gods. Prayer, fasting, and other observances seem to have been a royal obligation, not practiced by the population at large.

Reconstructed ninth-century B.C. head of a royal man-bull from Nineveh (Iraq).

The Babylonian state cult of Marduk, originally the patron god of the city Babylon, was instituted relatively late, during the reign of Nebuchadnezzar I (1126–1105 B.C.), but continued to the very end of native Babylonian rule of Mesopotamia. Indeed, the existence of the Babylonian temple is attested in cuneiform documents as late as the first century A.D. and was known to outsiders (e.g., to Pliny, d. 79) as the site of Chaldean astronomy. By the mid-first millennium, the cult of the divine scribe Nabu rose in significance alongside that of his father, Marduk. An Assyrian statue is inscribed with the admonition: "In Nabu confide, trust not in another god!" and Nabu was still the object of prayer for the Seleucid king Antiochus I Soter in the third century B.C.

While the official state cult did not repress the worship of other deities, some virtually henotheistic theological texts refer to Marduk as the all-embracing manifestation of divinity, absorbing within himself all those aspects formerly represented by other gods in the pantheon. But seemingly monotheistic tendencies are attested for other gods as well (e.g., the hymn to Ninurta in which parts of his body are identified with various gods).

Popular participation in the wider city cult was limited to festivals in which the divine statue was carried out into the community in procession, such as in the New Year's festival or the festival to consecrate the sanctuary. Ceremonies for ritual mourning (such as that for the eclipse of the moon) also included the participation of the community.

Administrative records from temple archives reveal an organized priesthood in each of the chief city temples. The temple was the workplace not only of "priests," for which there was no general Akkadian term, but also of others such as exorcists or craftspeople (carpenters, jewelers, seal cutters, and smiths). All temple personnel, i.e., those with access to restricted temple areas, were termed *temple enterers*.

Literature: Prayer was the literary medium for addressing the deity with complaints, requests, and thanks. Some prayers were accompanied by food or incense offerings. Extreme exaltation of deities (particularly Ishtar/Inanna, Marduk, Shamash, and Sin) found literary form as well. The religious poem entitled "Let Me Praise the Lord of Wisdom," in praise of Marduk, sees him as the god of exorcism and healing. The poem, formulated as a first-person narrative of someone afflicted by divine wrath, tells of the blessings Marduk gives to the undeserving sufferer.

Ritual and magic comprise a standardized and serialized literary corpus. The various ritual

713

series refer to ceremonies performed by the king, such as *bit rimki*, "house of ablution," where the king is ritually bathed. The two major magical textbooks were compiled for incantation priests to relieve suffering by appeal to Marduk or directly to the fire god, respectively. In both, evil is dispelled by burning. Another important ritual of appeasement was performed by the lamentation priest in the case of lunar eclipses, understood to be of particular danger to the king. Perhaps of greatest significance for the cult and the cultic calendar was the text *Enuma elish*.

Of the well-preserved Akkadian mythological texts, the one most familiar to the West is undoubtedly the Gilgamesh epic. Another account of the mythic Flood is given in "Atrahasis," or "Exceedingly Wise," from the epithet for the sole survivor of the Flood. Like Utnapishtim in the Gilgamesh version, Atrahasis escapes the waters of the Deluge in an ark.

One myth that shares with Gilgamesh the theme of the human hero's contact with the divine concerns Adapa, the servant and fisherman of Ea in his temple at Eridu. While Adapa was fishing, the South Wind caused Adapa's boat to capsize. For this, Adapa "broke the wing" of the wind and stopped it from blowing, an act perceived by the gods as a cosmic crime. When, however, he appeared for judgment before Anu, king of heaven, he was favored by Anu and, instead of punishment, was offered the bread and water of life. Because Ea had counseled Adapa not to eat or drink, fearing it would be the bread and water of death, Adapa wasted his chance to attain the immortality possessed only by the gods.

Other mythological subjects deal with relationships among the gods, such as the "Descent of Ishtar (Inanna)."

Mesopotamian theological writing can best be described as a branch of the literate scholarship of the scribes in which, ostensibly for the purpose of scribal training, the world and all its phenomena were classified, organized, and presented in the form of word lists. Divine names and scholarly explanations of the names are included in this scholastic enterprise. The lists of gods (entitled An, which indicates Anum), which are attested from the third to the first millennia, give an idea as to the organization of the pantheon as well as the history of its development.

Divination can justifiably be brought within the broad definition of religion as the sole area in which contact is thought possible between the otherwise separate realms of divine and human. The importance of the Mesopotamian astral deities Shamash, Sin, Ishtar, and the storm god Adad comes to the fore in celestial divination, which enjoyed high prestige during the Sargonid rule of Assyria. The sun god and storm god played major roles in providing oracles and omens, acting as intercessors between the human and divine realms, especially in the field of extispicy (entrail divination). In Mesopotamia, divination became a literate and scholarly pursuit, which, particularly in the first millennium, encompassed elements that would later overlap with "science," according to our modern notions. This can be seen in the close relation between astrology and astronomy after ca. 500 B.C. The first millennium development of "judicial" astrology, based on astral signs from gods, and its dependence on knowledge of heavenly phenomena and on an ability to compute those phenomena with great sophistication became one of the major legacies of Mesopotamian civilization to the West. *See also* Akitu; Astarte; Berossus; cuneiform; Ea; Ebla; Elam; Enki; Enkidu; Enlil; Enuma elish; Esagila; Esarhaddon; Gilgamesh; Hammurabi; Inanna; Ishtar; kingship, sacred; Marduk; Mari; Mother Goddess; Nergal; Ninlil; Ninurta; Oannes; priest/priestess; Sargon; temple; Tiamat; ziggurat.

Messenger of Allah (Arab. *rasul allah*), a title of the Prophet Muhammad. The Qur'an mentions many prophets, of whom Muhammad was the last (seal), but only seven besides Muhammad are accorded the title of *messenger:* Nuh (Noah), Lut (Lot), Ismail (Ishmael), Musa (Moses), Shuayb, Hud Salih, and Isa (Jesus). *See also* Ahmadiyya; Babism; Baha'i.

Messiah (Heb. *mashiah,* "anointed with oil"), a figure marked as a holy person by virtue of being anointed. In the Hebrew Bible, the term *messiah* is most commonly applied to priests, with kings comprising the second most frequent category. There are no references to an eschatological figure called Messiah in the Hebrew Bible. In the Greek translation of the Hebrew Bible, the Septuagint, *mashiah* is translated by the secular Greek term *christos* ("oiled"), providing the English "Christ." In some postbiblical Jewish texts and throughout Christian literature, Messiah is used as an eschatological title, although the references in Jewish writings to priests as "messiahs" remain dominant. In scholarly literature, the term messiah has been extended to refer to saviors outside the Jewish or Christian traditions, although this modern usage is frequently softened by using an adjectival form, e.g., "messianic figure."

Judaism: In Judaism, the Messiah is the eschatological redeemer of the Jewish people and, secondarily, of all humanity. The Messiah and the epoch he heralds are conceived as an end to the interminable exile and as a time of the ingathering of the Jews to the promised Holy Land. Along with this politico-nationalistic theme is a religious and universal one. The Messiah signals the end of the present order and inaugurates the final age, "the world to come."

Messiah in Ancient Judaism: Judaism did not always possess a messianic concept in this eschatological and redemptive sense. The Messiah doctrine in Jewish thought emerges clearly during the period of Roman rule over Palestine in the last few centuries B.C. In the Hebrew Bible, the "Lord's anointed" is never an eschatological figure and "Messiah" usually refers to an anointed king of the descendants of David. The promise of a restoration of the Davidic monarchy by later prophets never implied the arrival of a miraculous or metahistorical figure who would physically and spiritually redeem Israel. These more intricate attachments to the term Messiah came only later.

Under the oppressive Roman regime during the Second Temple period, nascent political hopes for a return to Davidic rule apparently developed into a belief in a redemptive figure. When exile and banishment from the land of Israel became a hard historical reality, the national hopes for a miraculous return to Davidic monarchy were raised to heightened levels.

Messianism first appears in some prerabbinic varieties of Judaism. Jewish apocalyptists and the Qumran sect exhibit strong messianic tendencies, with an admixture of political and more miraculous themes. In the first century, Jesus of Nazareth became a redemptive figure for some Jews, both in the land of Israel and the diaspora. The razing of the Second Temple in 70 accelerated messianic speculation among Jews, as did the failed Bar Kokhba rebellion against Rome in 135.

Varieties of Messianic Teaching: The literature of rabbinic Judaism supplies no uniform teaching about the Messiah or the signs of the messianic age. In the Mishnah, the figure of the Messiah as redeemer is negligible. In the Talmuds, more attention is paid to the "days of the Messiah" and the epoch of the "birth pangs of the Messiah" than to the actual characteristics of an individual Messiah. The messianic age will be marked by an end of exile, an ingathering of the dispersed Jewish people to the land of Israel, and political independence under a Davidic descendant. In diverging rabbinic traditions, the messianic age will be brought about either through a gradual improvement of the human condition or through a cataclysm. One set of traditions draws a distinction between two messianic figures: the Messiah son of Joseph (or Ephraim), who is the harbinger of the messianic age and is fated to die, and the Messiah son of David, the redeeming Messiah (Babylonian Talmud *Sukka* 52a).

With the emergence of Christianity and its rival messianic claims, more attention was given to the actual figure of the Messiah and the precise events surrounding his appearance in order to distinguish Jewish beliefs from the focused speculations about Jesus.

By the Middle Ages, the various rabbinic teachings about the Messiah had been instituted into a set doctrine. The catastrophic eschatology became more pronounced. Medieval tracts go into great detail concerning the signs of the messianic age, most of which are of a cataclysmic nature. Momentous historical events such as the Crusades or the Mongol invasion were interpreted by contemporaries as marks of the messianic end.

Some medieval thinkers, particularly the Jewish mystics, stressed a spiritual dimension to the messianic age. The Messiah would not only restore Israel to political ascendancy, but would end spiritual exile from God.

In general, Jewish leaders preached a passive anticipation of the Messiah. Warnings were issued against calculating the end time or using astrology to predict the messianic age. Furthermore, Jews were cautioned to do nothing to upset God's preordained redemption or to elicit the messianic epoch before its time.

This quietist pose was not uniformly enforced. The history of Judaism is replete with messianic pretenders and movements. Most were localized outbursts and short-term novelties. In the Middle Ages, Abu Isa of Isfahan, Solomon Molkho, Shabbetai Tzevi, and Jacob Frank are among the most famous and successful messianic pretenders. Tzevi's messianic claim, first declared in 1665, was the most tumultuous and far-reaching.

Modern Messianism and Zionism: Modern Jewish religious movements have tended to downplay the role of messianism. The liberal movements (Reform, Conservative, and Reconstructionist) either ignore or revalorize messianism into a nationalist-humanist hope of moral and spiritual salvation. The Nazi genocide in Europe and the creation of the State of Israel, however, have prompted a reevaluation of the role of messianism in contemporary Judaism. The Zionist enterprise was interpreted by some theologians as a secular fulfillment of an otherworldly messianism in the plane of contemporary politics. In traditionalist religious circles messianism is a live issue, and the establishment of the State of Israel is deemed the "beginning of the flowering of our redemption." Religious Zionists tend to gravitate toward a resurgent messianism, though very few have either claimed that the messianic age is at hand or identified a particular individual as the promised Messiah. More quietistic ultra-Orthodox Jews tend to regard the establishment of a modern nation-state as "forcing God's hand" and a transgression against the promised eschatological design. *See also* anointing; redemption (Judaism); Shabbetai Tzevi.

Christianity: The Greek translation of the Hebrew term Messiah, "Christ" is the common title for Jesus among Christians. While often used as if it were Jesus' surname, it is best translated as a royal title, Jesus the King, bearing the sense of his being the eschatological savior who will rule the new world order. *See also* Jesus Christ.

messianic, a term with specific reference to Jewish and Christian traditions but extended to include any religious tradition focused on a belief in the immanent appearance of a saving figure. *See also* eschatology; Gesar/Geser; Ghost Dance; Mahdi; Maitreya; millenarianism; prophet; T'ai-p'ing Tao; Wovoka.

metamorphosis. *See* shape shifting.

metasomatosis (Gk., "from one body to another"). *See* afterlife; metempsychosis; rebirth; reincarnation.

metempsychosis (me-tem-*sí*-koh'sis; Gk.), the concept that after death the soul, or essential living principle, of a person or entity is reborn in a new body. Generally, the rebirth is held to correspond to one's deserts, good or bad, or to be part of an overall cosmic plan; thus, existence may be conceived to be a very long, perhaps infinite, chain of such incarnations. Belief in metempsychosis is a staple of Eastern religions, where the goal usually is ultimate liberation from the chain of rebirths. Belief in metempsychosis also occurs in Western Platonism and its occult and theosophical progeny. *See also* afterlife; occult, the; soul; Theosophy.

Methodism, a form of Protestant Christianity that emerged in England out of the teachings of John Wesley (1703–91). Wesley was an ordained Anglican priest who, while a fellow of Lincoln College, Oxford, joined a student Bible study group known as the Methodists, or the Holy Club. (The title *Methodist*, while clearly applied derisively, is of uncertain derivation.) Following a period in the American colonies (1735–37), Wesley returned to England where, on May 24, 1738, he had a decisive spiritual experience that convinced him of the personal relationship to the savior that one obtained when being saved by faith alone. Becoming a circuit preacher, Wesley was responsible for many Christians "converting" to a more intense mode of Christianity featuring mutual confession and rebuke. In 1743, Wesley drew up the *Rules* governing such associations. In 1784, Wesley ordained preachers in his movement, thus making it functionally independent from the Church of England, although Methodism remained, technically, a "society" within the church until 1794. Wesley's *Sermons* (1744–60), his *Explanatory Notes Upon the New Testament* (1755), and his 1784 abridgment and emendation of the Thirty-nine Articles of the Anglican Church remain the central documents of Methodism.

In North America, Methodism had a somewhat different history and evolved distinctive social forms that have remained influential. The Methodist Episcopal Church was founded as an independent religious organization in Baltimore in 1784. The conference system of government (developed out of Wesley's British practice), with a hierarchy extending from the local church to the general (national) level, is responsible for all matters of church discipline, and the regional level, the annual conference, appoints the ministers in the area. Ministers are itinerant, traveling within an area's churches for a year (the origin of the "circuit preacher" tradition in America). They are assisted by ordained and lay preachers who are members of local churches.

The episcopal Methodist tradition recognizes the power of the bishop to appoint ministers. Led by the Methodist Episcopal Church, and joined by the Methodist Episcopal Church South, the United Brethren in Christ, the Evangelical Association, and the Methodist Protestant Church, they merged in 1968 to form the United Methodist Church. Those Methodist churches that do not accept the bishop's authority and vest more power in the laity include the Congregational Methodist Church and the First Congregational Methodist Church of the U.S.A. A third group largely rejects what they see as the liberalism of the larger Methodist organizations and, since 1939 or 1940, have joined together in the Bible Protestant Church, the Methodist Protestant Church, and the Fundamental Methodist Church.

Since 1787, there has been a strong African-

American presence within Methodism. The African Methodist Episcopal Church was founded in 1816 and was joined by others such as the Reformed Zion Union Apostolic Church, the Reformed Union Episcopal Church, and the Christian Methodist Episcopal Church.

In 1992, Methodism was the third largest affiliated Christian denomination in America, with 13,265,748 members and 52,216 churches. *See also* African Methodist Episcopal Church; perfectionism; Protestantism; Wesley, John.

metropolitan, a Christian ecclesiastical title for a bishop who has jurisdiction over a province with more than one diocese. In the Greek church the title is used for diocesan bishops.

Miao Shan (mee-ou-shahn), Chinese tale of a princess who became a Buddhist nun despite the king's objections. When her father falls ill, Miao Shan gives her own flesh to cure him. The legend was connected to cultic centers devoted to the worship of the Bodhisattva Kuan-yin, of whom Miao Shan is a manifestation. *See also* Avalokiteshvara; Kuan-yin.

michi (mee-chee; Jap., "way"), the word most often used in Japanese to indicate a path, process, tradition, or "Way" of religious significance. Also termed *doh*, this concept seems to have come to Japan with Chinese influences in the early historical period when Buddhism was referred to as the "Way of the Buddhas" and Shinto the "Way of the Gods."

Subsequently, the concept has become ubiquitous in Japan for indicating a tradition of practices and sacred ideals or goals—whether understood as a religion (as in reference to Taoist or Confucian teachings and practices) or simply as religious in significance (as in reference, for example, to the "Way of the Warrior" in Japan).

Beyond this, many of the fine arts and martial arts have also been understood as Ways of religious significance: from the "Way of Poetry" in the twelfth century to the "Way of Archery" in the fifteenth century, these master/disciple artistic traditions have been important expressions of Japanese religious life. *See also* Japanese religion; Tao.

Mi-chiao. *See* Esoteric Buddhism in China.

microcosm. *See* macrocosm, microcosm.

Mid-Autumn Festival, a Chinese celebration on the fifteen day of the eighth lunar month fo-

cused on the moon, and in former times on the lunar deity popularly known as Ch'ang O. Moon-shaped cakes are eaten and people go out to enjoy the full harvest moon. *See also* Chinese religions (festal cycle).

Middle Way. *See* Four Noble Truths; Path (Buddhism).

Midgardr (mith'gahr-thruh; Norse, "the home of the middle"), in Scandinavian mythology, the dwelling place of humankind. *See also* Nordic religion.

midrash (mee-drahsh'; Heb., "interpretation," "study"), rabbinic Bible interpretation. The term may be used three ways: (1) the interpretation of a single verse of Scripture in Judaism, as in "the midrash of a verse," (2) a compilation of exegeses of Scripture, or (3) the method or process of exegesis characteristic of rabbinic Judaism. Because no manner of reading and interpreting Scripture is common to all types of Judaism or unique to any of them, the most precise usage is the second: a compilation of scriptural exegesis by the sages of Judaism.

Midrash compilations produced in Judaism's formative period, the first seven centuries A.D., are of three kinds: verse-by-verse readings, discursive presentations of viewpoints, and large-scale theological essays in exegetical form. The verse-by-verse compilations, produced first from ca. 200 to 400, addressed Leviticus, in *Sifra*; Numbers, in *Sifre* to Numbers, and Deuteronomy, in *Sifre* to Deuteronomy, with stress on legal passages in those books; and Exodus, in *Mekhilta*, attributed to R. Ishmael. The discursive presentations, produced in the late fourth and the fifth centuries, present through scriptural commentary propositions on the social and theological-historical laws that govern the life of Israel. The principal compilations of this type took up Genesis, in *Genesis Rabbah*; Leviticus, in *Leviticus Rabbah*; and the sacred calendar's lectionary cycle, in *Pesiqta deRab Kahana*. The third type of midrash compilation set forth fundamental theological propositions expressed in elaborate articulation through repetition, in a different language, of a single point. Compiled in the sixth and early seventh centuries, they treat Lamentations, in *Lamentations Rabbah*; Esther, in *Esther Rabbah I*; Ruth, in *Ruth Rabbah*; and Song of Songs, in *Song of Songs Rabbah*. The midrash compilations at the end of the formative age set forth in vast detail the fundamental structure of the theology of Judaism. *See also* exegesis; Judaism (authoritative texts and their interpretation).

miko (mee-koh), Japanese female shaman who acts as a spiritual medium for messages from the dead, fortune-telling, and healing. Mikolike figures are found from Empress Jingu in the *Nihonshoki* (Chronicles of Japan, 720) to Nakayama Miki, the founder of the nineteenth-century new religion Tenrikyo. Today *miko* also refers to young priestesses with no shamanic powers who dance and assist in ceremonies at Shinto shrines. *See also* Japanese folk religion; Nihonshoki; shamanism.

mikveh (meek-veh'; Heb., "gathering [of water]"), Jewish ritual bath. Immersion in a *mikveh* for purposes of ritual cleanness is required of married women after their menstrual period and of proselytes as part of the conversion process. A mikveh should be filled with approximately five hundred liters of "natural water," such as rain, but may contain drawn water if connected by pipes to a store of rainwater. *See also* ablution; conversion; Judaism (life cycle); menstrual blood.

Milarepa (mee-lah-ray'pah; 1040–1123), Tibetan holy man, disciple of Marpa, and second Tibetan member of the Kagyu-pa lineage. Milarepa overcame early adversity, spent much of his life in solitary retreat, and became Tibet's greatest saint and the archetype of the meditator hermit. *See also* Kagyu-pa; Marpa.

millenarianism (from Lat. *mille,* "thousand"; *annus,* "year"), the apocalyptic belief in a one-thousand-year kingdom to be established by Jesus at the end of historical time. Related to Zoroastrian and Jewish concepts of divine chronology and other Mediterranean cosmologies of serial world ages, the Christian origin of millenarianism is found in a brief passage in the canonical book of Revelation (20:1–10). That passage foretells the imprisonment of the devil for a period of one thousand years while resurrected Christian martyrs reign with Jesus; following the holy epoch, a great battle and cataclysm bring the end of the world and the resurrection of the remainder of humanity for the Last Judgment. The term has lost its precision in recent years because of its application to widely disparate utopian or eschatological beliefs, as well as to heterodox, reforming, and insurgent religious movements.

History: Christians have interpreted the passage in Revelation concerning the millennium both symbolically and literally. The dominant theologians, especially since Augustine (d. 430), have supported belief in the eventual and redemptive end of historical time but have viewed the prophecy as part of an extended allegory on the culmination of divine and human conflicts. Consequently, the prevailing Christian teachings have declared the church to be the embodiment of the millennial kingdom, separated personal from universal fate, and indefinitely postponed Jesus' return and the final cataclysm. Since the second century A.D., however, a few Western European theologians, prophets, messiahs, and their followers have taken the prophecy literally and expected not only the thousand-year reign but also the complete enactment of the apocalypse on earth with the reappearance of Jesus in his Second Coming. The association of the figure of Jesus with numerous messianic and utopian hopes—otherwise unconnected with canonical Christianity—undoubtedly fueled such developments. "Premillennialists" have placed the Second Coming of Jesus before the paradisiacal millennium, emphasizing a sudden cosmic transformation and the survival of a triumphant few, while "postmillennialists" (also simply called "millennialists") expected Jesus' return and the final battles of good and evil after the thousand-year span of a global Christian community established by determined proselytization.

The Montanists, an early Christian dissident group in Phrygia, based their expectations of the Second Coming and the New Jerusalem not only on sacred scripture but also on new revelations. Such augmentation of the canon marked the European millennial tradition until the 1600s; visionaries also consulted Christian and Jewish Apocrypha, the *Sibylline Oracles,* and the augurs of local astrologers in order to fix the date of the Last Days. Millennial hopes soared again in Europe in the Middle Ages, especially as the calendar approached mystical numbers in the years 666 and 1000, and new expectations of the impending end of the world were ignited by the thirteenth-century prophetic writings of Joachim of Fiore. Messianic movements and elaborate legend cycles arose in the wake of the deaths of great rulers such as Frederick I (Barbarossa), Frederick II of Germany, and Sebastian of Portugal, connecting royal resurrection and imperial triumph with the millennial age.

Early modern Protestant groups of the Radical Reformation reasserted the imminence of the millennium, but recentered the prophecies on canonical sources through their emphasis on scriptural authority. While the Anabaptists of Munster proclaimed the inauguration of the millennial kingdom with their community, most Reformers expected merely to contribute to its arrival through preaching the Christian "Word." Dispensationalists, such as the Plymouth

Brethren in England, reckoned historical events as fulfillment of biblical prophecy and configured the world's eras in seven dispensations, including the ultimate millennium.

Modern Millenarianism: Revivalism and evangelical Christianity in the United States have renewed sectarian efforts to calculate the end of the world through literal interpretations of the Revelation text. Seventh-Day Adventists, despite the disappointment of two failed prophecies based on the biblical visions of Daniel, have spread worldwide their belief that a pivotal era began in 1844 and the millennium is near. Similarly, Jehovah's Witnesses insist that because God as absolute ruler demands unquestioning obedience, the biblical text is an infallible guide to human history. They await the approaching battle of Armageddon and the subsequent millennial reign of Jesus among the saved on earth, even though their hopes have been repeatedly dashed by unfulfilled prophecies of its advent. In the mid-twentieth century prophets cast anti-communist sentiment in an apocalyptic light, taking their script from the more popular passages of the book of Revelation and the cryptic writings of Nostradamus (Michel de Notredame, 1503–66, French physician and seer), and interpreting all manner of international conflict as auguring the Last Days. It is to be expected that the approach of the year 2000 will precipitate additional millenarianism among those conversant with the Christian belief.

Millenarian-type Religious Movements: The designation *millenarian* has been extended to a wide variety of dissident religious movements that do not, in fact, hold any belief in the thousand-year apocalyptic kingdom. This debasement of terminology is not uncommon in comparative studies in religion, where many typologies derived from Christian theology are uncritically applied to diverse phenomena. Thus, spontaneous or revolutionary religious movements, occasionally independent of direct Christian influence, that anticipate an imminent transformation of social relations or of the cosmic order initiated by divine or superhuman agency are called "millenarian" or "messianic movements," or simply "crisis cults."

The non-Christian "millenarian" examples commonly include Chinese Taoist revolutionary movements such as the Yellow Turbans, certain Theravada Buddhist sects expecting the imminent appearance of the Buddha Maitreya, and Hindus calculating the approach of the great cataclysms concluding the cosmic cycle, or *kalpa*. While such groups certainly share specific elements—notably social criticism and imminent eschatology—with other millenarian-type enthusiastic movements, they do not mirror the core beliefs originally attached to the category. A wider range of insurgent religious groups that emerged during the attempted proselytization of colonized peoples by Christian missionaries are more appropriately labeled millenarian because they exhibit clear use of the Christian apocalyptic traditions in combination with local beliefs in cyclic transformations. Examples of these are the cargo cults of New Guinea, new prophetic churches in Africa, the Ghost Dance among native North Americans, and the shaman-led migrations among the Tupi-Guarani in South America, which followed decades of mission activities. *See also* Africa, new religions in; Afro-Americans (Caribbean and South America), new religions among; Age of Aquarius; apocalypticism; cargo cults; Chinese sectarian religions; Ch'ondogyo; ee-ja-nai-ka; eschatology; Ghost Dance; Joachim of Fiore; Korea, Maitreyism in; Maoism; messianic; nativistic movements; new religions; okage-mairi; revitalization movements; secret societies; White Lotus Society.

Chinese Religion: Perhaps the first millenarian movement in China can be said to be the Way of Great Peace (T'ai-p'ing Tao) movement in the second century. The members of this movement revered Huang-ti and Lao-tzu, patrons of immortality and perfect rulership through inaction. Believing that the reign of Great Peace would come soon, they rebelled against the Han dynasty in 184. A messianic movement, the Way of Celestial Masters (T'ien-shih Tao), appeared in the west also in the second century. An affinity with Taoist ideology and a subversive inclination were persistent characteristics in many messianic movements during the medieval period. Many worshiped Lao-tzu (often incarnated as Li Hung) as the messiah who would deliver the elect into the land of immortals or initiate a new reign on earth. There were also Buddhist forms of messianism, many of them centered around the Buddha Maitreya, who was to come imminently and transform the world order. Another messianic tradition in China was Manichaeism, which advocated the coming of the third and final state of cosmic history in which Light will overcome Darkness. In the fourteenth century the White Lotus Society, an influential, syncretistic messianic tradition, became the label for all messianic groups. It preached the imminent cataclysm and the deliverance into a paradise of emptiness through the agency of an Eternal Mother. The T'ai-ping Rebellion, starting in 1850, is a more recent, and a very dramatic, example of a Chinese messianic movement. *See* *also* China, new religions in; T'ai-ping Rebellion; T'ai-p'ing Tao; T'ien-shih Taoism; White Lotus Society.

Japanese Religion: Millenarian movements appeared as early as the seventh century in Japan, but are best represented by the "world renewal" (*yonaoshi*) movements of the Edo period (1615–1868). These included popular uprisings, mass pilgrimages to the Ise Shrine, riotous dancing in urban areas (*ee-ja-nai-ka*), and religious responses to great earthquakes. Some saw the advent of Miroku (Maitreya) Buddha. The restoration of the emperor to power in 1868 represented to many a return to a paradigmatic past. Millenarian expectations have since been channeled into many of the "new religions," which see themselves as harbingers of a new age for humanity. *See also* Japan, new religions in.

millennialism (Lat. *mille*, "thousand," and *annus*, "year"), the Christian belief in the thousand-year reign of Christ and his saints on earth as described in Revelation 20:1–10. Premillennialists interpret the thousand years as a literal future time when Jesus will return and reign in Jerusalem prior to the final judgment. Postmillennialism and amillennialism view the thousand years as symbolic, the former of a future time of peace and harmony, the latter of the spiritual presence of the kingdom in the believer's heart. *See also* Adventists; Antichrist; chiliasm; eschatology; Jehovah's Witnesses; Judgment Day; rapture.

Miller, William (1782–1849), American preacher active in upstate New York who announced in 1831 that the world would end with the advent of Christ in 1834. Discredited by the failure of its specific prophecy, the Millerite movement disappeared after 1845 and led to a general suspicion of millenarian predictions among American Protestants. However, Millerite elements regrouped, forming the Advent Christian Church (1860) and the Seventh-Day Adventists (1863). *See also* Adventists.

Mimamsa (mee-mahn'sah; Skt., "inquiry"), Hinduism's school of ritual theology. Originally a mode of oral argumentation, Mimamsa achieved its enduring form in Jaimini's *Purva Mimamsa Sutras* (100 B.C.), a comprehensive but extraordinarily terse analysis that systematized and reinterpreted the canon of older texts and rituals known as the Veda. Mimamsa's methods and supporting doctrines were elaborated and refined in the authoritative commentary of Shabara (after 200), in the rival schools of Kumarila Bhatta and Prabhakara Mishra (both

eighth century), and thereafter in a series of ever more elegantly argued treatises. Among Mimamsa's distinctive contributions are sophisticated grammatical and epistemological strategies by which textual and ritual meaning could be ascertained without reliance on historical context and authorial intention; a subtle analysis of the interdependence of language and action and the consequent judgment that all knowledge is inherently practical; and an exhaustive defense of tradition, which nevertheless transformed it by deemphasizing mythological and supernatural elements. Mimamsa influenced almost every area of Hindu learning; its most important religious heir, the Vedanta, extended Mimamsa's framework to include, and thereby legitimate, the later meditational and speculative texts known as the Upanishads. *See also* six systems of Indian philosophy; Vedanta.

Mind, School of. *See* Hsin-hsueh.

mind-only (Skt. *citta-matra*), a central doctrine of the Yogachara school of Indian Buddhist philosophy. In the works of Asanga and Vasubandhu (ca. fourth century), the earliest authoritative interpreters of the Yogachara tradition, the doctrine of mind-only is presented as a form of idealism. The world is considered nothing but mind or, in another common phrase, nothing but consciousness (*vijnaptimatra*). The doctrine of mind-only is often explained by saying that ordinary images of reality are like the images someone sees in a dream. The images themselves are illusory, but the mind in which the images occur is real.

The doctrine of mind-only need not be interpreted as a form of idealism, however. In an important early scriptural text, *Dasabhumika* (The Sutra on the Ten Stages), the claim that "this world with its three realms is mind-only" is interpreted as meaning that there is no permanent self that serves as the subject of experience. This interpretation of mind-only was used by the Madhyamaka opponents of the Yogachara to deny the reality even of the mind itself. *See also* Buddhism (thought and ethics); Yogachara.

mind-to-mind transmission (Chin. *i-hsin chuan-hsin*), Chinese Ch'an Buddhist method of enlightenment conferred directly from master to disciple with no reliance on scriptural teachings. *See also* Ch'an school.

Minerva (mi-nuhr'vah), a native Italian goddess of handicrafts (identified with Athena); together with Jupiter and Juno she was one of the three chief ancient Roman divinities. *See also* Athena.

ming (ming; Chin., "fate," "destiny"), an important term in Chinese religio-philosophical thought often referred to as "Heaven's Mandate," *T'ien-ming.* While historically the Chinese have entertained both fatalistic and antideterministic views, the dominant Confucian perspective has always affirmed sincere moral cultivation while "waiting for destiny," something ultimately beyond human control. *See also* T'ien-ming.

Ming T'ang (ming tahng; Chin.,"Bright Temple"), an ancient Chinese royal building that incorporated cosmic symbolism, glorifying the ruler as the representative of Heaven and the pivot of time and space. There are many early literary descriptions, but no archaeological evidence. The Temple of Heaven in Peking was built as a kind of latter-day Ming T'ang. *See also* Temple of Heaven.

miniature garden (Chin. *p'en-tsai, p'en-ching,* "vegetation in a container"), Chinese horticultural, religious, and aesthetic practice going back to the seventh century that involves the construction of miniature landscapes and microcosmic perfect worlds; it forms the basis of the more widely known Japanese bonsai tradition.

minister. 1 One who performs any of a number of Christian church functions. 2 The title for a preacher or pastor in most Protestant churches.

Minjung Sinhak. *See* Theology of the People.

Minoan religion, the Aegean religion of the third to second millennium B.C., largely centered on the island of Crete; it is often distinguished from the neighboring Cycladic religion.

Minoan religion (its name derived from the legendary King Minos) is only known from archaeological remains. What written (Eteocretan) texts exist that can problematically be identified with it have remained undeciphered.

Minoan religion was centered on the worship of powerful goddesses, frequently depicted as accompanied by subordinate male consorts. The double ax (Gk. *labrys*) functions as a sign of divinity, occasionally appearing as a separate object of devotion. In addition to mountains, caves, and gravesites—the prime centers of Minoan sacrificial ritual—there appear to have been buildings with religious functions. *See also* Cycladic religion.

Minotaur (min'uh-tor; Gk., probably from *Minos,* king of Crete, and *tauros,* "bull"), a legendary Cretan monster with a bull's head and a man's body confined in a labyrinth and killed by Theseus. *See also* Knossos; Labyrinth.

Mira Bai (mee'rah bi; ca. 1498–1547), a Hindu poet-saint in Rajasthan, India. A Rajput princess, she left her husband's palace to live an ascetic life and compose songs praising the god Krishna. *See also* Krishna.

miracle, occurrence or capacity of supernatural origin.

Christianity: In the Bible, miracles are acts of God that testify to the divine concern and solicit faith. For example, the Exodus, in which God led Moses and the people who became Israel out of Egypt, became the great Old Testament paradigm of why Israel should trust the Lord. In the New Testament, the intent of the miracles of Jesus is clearest in the Gospel of John, which considers them "signs" of who Jesus is and what authority he possesses.

Most Christians accepted miracles with little question until the modern era, when science and critical philosophy called them into question. In the modern debates, miracles are often reduced to natural prodigies: things apparently breaking or suspending the ordinary laws of nature.

Islam: The most significant term for a divine sign is the Arabic, quranic term *aya,* which means "sign of God" generally, "verse of the Qur'an" in particular. Another term, *mu'jiza,* means an extraordinary act or event believed to be wrought by God through his messengers and prophets that proves the truthfulness of their mission. Isa (Jesus) raising the dead, Moses parting the Red Sea, and the unlettered Muhammad given the Qur'an are examples. The miraculousness of the Qur'an was believed to consist in its inimitability and revealing of things unseen. Still another term, *karamat* ("miracles of grace"), designates another type of sign wrought by God through a Sufi saint, including healing, the saint's knowledge of unseen things, and speedy flights to distant places. *See also* aya.

miracle plays, popular dramas focusing on the life, deeds, and death of holy persons. *See also* hagiography.

miraj. *See* ascension.

mirrors, sacred, usually polished metal mirrors

found in early Japan and showing Chinese influence. Some were regarded as a seat for and as a channel of communication with the gods; others were used to ward off spirits. The most famous is the Yata Mirror, one of the three imperial regalia along with the Yasaka Curved Jewels and Kosanagi, the miraculous sword from the goddess Amaterasu. *See also* magatama.

Mirza ali Muhammad. *See* Babism.

Mirza Husayn ali Nuri. *See* Baha'i.

Mishnah, the (meesh-nah'; Heb., "repetition," "teaching"), a six-part rabbinic code of descriptive rules issued ca. 200. Because the document takes for granted paramount events of the second century, e.g., the defeat of Bar Kokhba and the end of the Temple in Jerusalem, it was brought to closure after ca. 135.

The Mishnah presents a profoundly philosophical system that employs numerous cases to make the single general point that all things are one, complex things yield uniform and similar components, and there is a hierarchy of being to be discovered through the proper classification of all things. This philosophical representation of the theology of the one and singular God is presented as a law code and represents the thinking of Jewish sages who flourished in the middle of the second century in the land of Israel.

The document is divided into six divisions, subdivided among sixty-three tractates. The six divisions are (1) agricultural rules; (2) laws governing appointed seasons, e.g., Sabbaths and festivals; (3) laws on the transfer of women, and property along with women, from one man (father) to another (husband); (4) the system of civil and criminal law (corresponding to what we today should regard as "the legal system"); (5) laws for the conduct of ritual and the Temple; and (6) laws on the preservation of ritual purity both in the Temple and under certain domestic circumstances, with special reference to the table and bed. The principal interest of all but the third and fourth divisions is in the Temple, cult, priesthood, and sacred calendar and offerings. In the aftermath of the war against Rome from 132 to 135, with the Temple declared permanently prohibited to Jews and Jerusalem closed off, the philosophers addressed issues of cult, temple, holiness of people, land, food, and the like through the laws of the Mishnah. Moreover, the fourth division, on civil law, presents an elaborate account of a political structure and system of Israelite self-government. The Mishnah employs a profoundly priestly and Levitical conception of sanctification.

Tradition attributes the Mishnah to Judah, patriarch of the Jewish community of Palestine ca. 200, but its authorship is unknown. The Mishnah does not imitate the Hebrew of Scripture, assign its sayings to biblical figures, or claim to emerge from a fresh encounter with God through revelation. The Holy Spirit is not alleged to speak here.

The Mishnah's tractates are divided topically. Their subdivisions are marked by the confluence of theme or subject matter and form or patterning of language. When a new theme or topic commences, a fresh formal pattern is used.

The completed Mishnah was represented as the part of the "whole Torah of Moses, our rabbi," which had been formulated and transmitted orally, so it bore the status of divine revelation alongside the Pentateuch. The claim in the tractate Abot of a chain of oral tradition from Sinai to the Mishnah made it a principal holy book of Judaism. The Palestinian and Babylonian Talmuds, formed around, and shaped in part as commentaries to, the Mishnah, form the center of the curriculum of Judaism as a living religion.

The tractates of the Mishnah are:

Agriculture: Berakhot, blessings; *Peah*, the corner of the field; *Demai*, doubtfully tithed produce; *Kilayim*, mixed species; *Shebiit*, the laws of the seventh year; *Terumot*, food in the status of the priestly ration; *Maaserot*, tithes; *Maaser Sheni*, second tithe; *Hallah*, dough offering; *Orlah*, the disposition of the produce of a fruit tree in the first three years after planting; *Bikkurim*, firstfruits.

Appointed Times: Shabbat, the Sabbath; *Erubin*, the meal of commingling; *Pesahim*, Passover; *Sheqalim*, the shekel offering; *Yoma*, the Day of Atonement; *Sukkah*, the Feast of Tabernacles; *Besah*, conduct on the festival day; *Rosh Hashanah*, the new year; *Taanit*, fasting days; *Megillah*, the festival of Purim; *Moed Qatan*, conduct on the intermediate days between the first and final holy days of the festivals of Passover and Tabernacles; *Hagigah*, the festal offering.

Women: Yebamot, levirate marriages; *Ketubot*, marriage contracts; *Nedarim*, vows; *Nazir*, the Nazirite vow; *Sotah*, the wife accused of infidelity; *Gittin*, writs of divorce; *Qiddushin*, betrothals.

Damages, Civil Law: Baba Qamma, Baba Metsia, and *Baba Batra*, civil damages; *Sanhedrin*, the institutions of government, penalties inflicted for crime or sin; *Makkot*, flagellation;

Shabuot, oaths; *Eduyyot*, testimonies; *Abodah Zarah*, relations with idolators; *Horayot*, instructions of the court; *Abot*, the Founders and their sayings.

Holy Things: Zebakhim, the conduct of animal sacrifices; *Menakhot*, the conduct of meal offerings; *Khullin*, unconsecrated food and the rules affecting it; *Bekhorot*, firstborn; *Arakhin*, pledges of one's value made to the Temple; *Temurah*, the disposition of a beast that has been declared a substitute for a beast that has been consecrated; *Keritot*, the penalty of extirpation; *Meilah*, sacrilege; *Tamid*, the daily whole offering; *Middot*, the architecture of the Temple; *Qinnim*, bird offerings.

Purities: Kelim, the uncleanness of utensils; *Ohalot*, the uncleanness of a corpse; *Negaim*, the uncleanness of the leper; *Parah*, the offering of the red cow and preparation of purification water; *Tohorot*, rules of uncleanness governing unconsecrated food; *Miqvaot*, ritual baths; *Niddah*, the uncleanness of the menstruating woman; *Makhshirin*, rendering produce susceptible to uncleanness; *Zabim*, the uncleanness of flux; *Tebul Yom*, the uncleanness of one who has immersed and awaits sunset for the completion of the process of purification; *Yadayim*, the uncleanness of hands; *Uqtsin*, uncleanness of parts of produce in relation to the produce as a whole. *See also* Judaism (authoritative texts and their interpretation); Talmud.

Mishneh Torah (meesh neh' toh-rah'; Heb., "review of the Torah"), Maimonides's code of Jewish law, compiled in 1180, also called *Ha-Yad ha-Khazakah* ("the mighty hand"). The philosopher Maimonides (1135–1204) addressed the need to provide a comprehensive code to order and systematize the vast and diffuse materials of the Jewish legal system. Since the compilation of the Mishnah (ca. 200), sporadic attempts at codification of the law had been partial and largely unsystematic.

Maimonides decided to compile a comprehensive code that would serve as an authoritative source for legal decisions. He dealt with the whole range of Jewish law, including those areas that were no longer operative after the destruction of the Temple and the exile.

Written in Arabic, the Mishneh Torah is organized in fourteen books, each with numerous sections and subsections. Unlike other codes, it also treats the basic principles of Jewish faith and the account of the messianic age as topics appropriate to a code of Jewish law.

Despite the enormous respect for Maimonides's work, his code evoked intense contro-versy. He was attacked for failing to include the sources for his legal decisions and criticized by those who viewed his philosophic principles as a threat to religious orthodoxy. Nevertheless, the Mishneh Torah has survived as the supreme example of Jewish legal codification. *See also* Torah.

Mission des Noirs. *See* Africa, new religions in.

mission or missionary movements, the organized effort to propagate one religion among adherents of another. *See also* Africa, new religions in; Afro-Brazilian religions; America, Hinduism in; Australian and Pacific traditional religions; China, Buddhism in; China, Islam in; China, Nestorianism in; China and Taiwan, new religions in; conversion; Inner Asian religions; Korea, Islam in; Korea, Protestantism in; Korea, Roman Catholicism in; Melanesia, new religions in.

mistress of the animals. *See* master/mistress of the animals.

miter (mi'tuhr; Gk.; Lat., *mitrah* "head band"), the characteristic headdress of Christian bishops. In the East, it is crown-shaped; in the West, it is in the form of two inverted shields.

Mithra (mith'rah; from *mithra*, Old Persian, "contract"), an ancient Iranian god of Indo-Iranian origin designating "social relationship" or "compact." Mithra is often represented with solar associations. *See also* Indo-European religion; Mitra.

Mithraism (mith'ruh-iz-uhm), ancient Roman mystery cult, known in antiquity as the Mysteries of Mithras, that flourished throughout the Roman Empire from the first through the fourth centuries. The most important centers of the cult were in and near the city of Rome itself and in the provinces where Roman legions were garrisoned, especially along the Rhine and Danube rivers. However, remains of the cult have been found in every part of the empire. The cult groups met in small temples (Lat. *mithraea*) often constructed underground because they were designed to imitate caves. Cult members included soldiers, state bureaucrats, and merchants; women were excluded. Like other mystery cults, Mithraism kept its doctrines and practices strictly secret, revealing them only to initiates. There were different grades of initiation, and in the most well-established groups their number became standardized at seven. As a result of Mithraism's secrecy its teachings were not recorded in writing by cult members, but some fragments are preserved in the writings of outsiders like Christian church fathers, Neoplatonic philosophers, and practitioners of magic.

In the absence of literary evidence, scholars attempting to reconstruct the nature of Mithraism have had to rely chiefly on the abundant and elaborate iconography that decorated the mithraea. The most important element here is the tauroctony, or bull-slaying scene, in which the god of the cult, Mithras, is shown in the act of killing a bull. This image was located in the central cult-niche in every mithraeum and thus must embody in pictorial form the central belief of the cult. Some scholars have argued that because the name of the god of the cult, Mithras, is the same as the name of the ancient Iranian god Mithra, Mithraism must have derived from the Iranian worship of Mithra, and therefore Mithraic iconography should be interpreted by finding parallels to its elements in ancient Iranian myth. But the Iranian worship of Mithra shows none of the characteristics essential to the Roman cult of Mithras, and the Iranian god Mithra was never involved with killing a bull. Therefore, it seems more probable that the origins of Mithraism lie not in ancient Iran but in the Greco-Roman world.

Because Mithraic iconography contains a large amount of astronomical symbolism, most of those who see Mithraism as Greco-Roman in origin regard the cult as having been based on Greco-Roman cosmological or astrological beliefs. In particular, it seems likely that the killing of the bull by Mithras represents the end of the Age of Taurus caused by the precession of the equinoxes, an astronomical phenomenon that was discovered shortly before the cult's origins; alternatively it has been argued that the tauroctony is a pictorial representation of certain Greco-Roman beliefs about the journey of the human soul through the heavens.

Mithraism succumbed to the spread of Christianity by the fifth century. The anti-Christian emperor Julian in the mid-fourth century professed a Platonized form of Mithraism, but soon after his death Christian authorities began to act forcefully against Mithraism. After the edicts of Theodosius at the end of the fourth century prohibited all pagan worship, Mithraism quickly disappeared, although it no doubt survived in isolated pockets into the fifth century. *See also* mystery religions.

Mithras (mith′rahs), the god of the ancient Roman mystery cult of Mithraism; he is most typically portrayed killing a bull (the "tauroctony"). *See also* Mithraism.

Mitnaggedim (Heb., "opponent" or "adversary"), the term designating the official Jewish opposition to Hasidism in Lithuania led by Elijah ben Solomon Zalman, the *gaon* of Vilna (1720–97). Himself an accomplished kabbalist, the Vilna gaon perceived the new movement as a threat to traditional authority. The Hasidic emphasis on ecstatic prayer and adherence (*devekut*) to God through mundane acts was perceived as a challenge to Jewish values, according to which the intellectual study of Torah was considered to be the highest path to God. The opposition movement also objected to changes in ritual, as well as to the introduction of new customs. *See also* Hasidism.

Mito school (mee-toh), a school of Japanese thought that developed in the Mito domain (now Ibaraki) and became a formative influence on the nationalist ideology of the Meiji Restoration. The Mito lord, Tokugawa Mitsukuni (1628–1700), founded a historical research institute (Shokokan) to compile the *Dai Nihon Shi* (History of Great Japan). Mito nationalism was promoted in the nineteenth century by Aizawa Seishisai, Fujita Toko, and Fujita Yukoku, who urged the preservation of the "body of the nation" (*kokutai*). Thus, the slogan "Revere the emperor, expel the barbarians" (*sonno joi*) became a rallying cry for meeting foreign threats by restoring the emperor. *See also* kokutai; Meiji Restoration.

Mitra (mi′truh; Skt., "Alliance"), god of Vedic and later India, ordinarily paired with Varuna. Mitra was later identified with the sun. *See also* Varuna; Veda, Vedism.

mitzvah (meets-vah′; Heb., "commandment"), in Judaism, a religious duty. The plural, *mitzvot*, encompasses all biblical and rabbinic law and refers to the complete system of Jewish religious, ethical, and social practice.

The Talmud states that there are 613 mitzvot: 248 positive responsibilities and 365 prohibitions. Attempts to list the commandments in conformity with these numbers have yielded inconsistent results. Rabbinic sources also distinguish biblical commandments from rabbinic ones and isolate important commandments from less significant ones (even while emphasizing that all must be equally followed). In the medieval period, Jewish philosophers sought a reason for each commandment. They distinguished rational commandments from revealed ones.

Jews become obligated to observe the

mitzvot at the age of majority. Traditionally, this is thirteen for boys and twelve for girls. In contemporary practice, thirteen is used for both. Rabbinic law exempts women from positive precepts that must be performed at a fixed time, for example, statutory prayer. In Conservative and Reform practice, this distinction between men and women increasingly has been abolished.

Jews frequently use the term *mitzvah* simply to refer to a good deed. This usage is presaged in the Talmud, which applies the term to meritorious acts that are not legal or ritual obligations. *See also* Torah.

Miwa, Mt. (mee-wah), Shinto sacred mountain in Nara prefecture, Japan, regarded as the *shintai* (object embodying the god) of the god Omononushi enshrined in the Omiwa Shrine. *See also* mountains, sacred; Omiwa Shrine; Omononushi.

Mizrachi Party (miz-rah-khee'; abbrev. of Heb. *mercaz ruchani*, "spiritual center"), a Zionist religious pioneering movement, founded in 1902. In 1956 it merged with its labor wing, Hapoel Hamizrachi, to create the Israeli National Religious Party. *See also* Zionism.

mizuko (mee-zoo-koh; Jap., "water child," "child that does not see"), in Japan, an aborted fetus, stillborn child, or child who dies shortly after birth. Special Buddhist rites and temples are dedicated to *mizuko*, generally invoking the Bodhisattva Jizo, guardian of deceased children. *See also* Jizo; mizuko kuyo.

mizuko kuyo (mee-zoo-koh koo-yoh), Buddhist rituals performed by modern Japanese to ask the Bodhisattva Jizo (Kshitigarbha) to care for aborted children. *See also* Bodhisattvas; Jizo; Kshitigarbha.

mock king, a widespread figure in carnivals exhibiting characteristic role reversals. Most frequently, a slave or individual of low social status would play the role of king for the duration of the festival. *See also* carnival; John Canoe festival; Pinkster festival; reversal; Saturnalia.

modernism. 1 A term used in Pope Pius X's encyclical *Pascendi* (1907) to denounce the "synthesis of all heresies." The encyclical was aimed at European Catholic theologians, but suspect Americans included faculty at St. Joseph Seminary (Yonkers, New York), whose journal, *The New York Review,* was closed in 1908. 2 A term applied by fundamentalist Protestants to their liberal opponents' views during the post–World War I controveries over evolution. Liberal theologian Shailer Mathews adopted the term in *The Faith of Modernism* (1924). As a politicized, externally imposed label more than a self-designation, modernism eludes strict definition. Liberal theologians to whom it was applied shared an openness to modern science and culture and a developmentalist worldview. They rejected the Scholastic method, applied historical method to biblical studies, and tried to rethink revelation and doctrine in terms of divine immanence and historical development.

modernization, term used to describe the complex series of changes in economic, social, and cultural life by which less developed societies acquire characteristics common to more developed societies. Among these characteristics are industrialization; self-sustaining economic growth; enhanced social mobility; the spread of literacy, education, and communication; national unification; and the expansion of popular participation in the political process.

Historically, the concept of modernization was linked to the industrial revolution in England in the seventeenth century. This process spread quickly from England to Europe, and eventually to the North American continent. Following World War II, the modernization process extended to large parts of Asia, Africa, and Latin America.

The study of modernization has involved all branches of the social sciences—anthropology, sociology, psychology, economics, geography, and history. Some have argued that modernization is a chief reason that the social sciences as such came into being. Key theoretical concepts in the social sciences, for example, Henry Maine's (1822–88) distinction between "status" and "contract" as the basis of human relationships, Ferdinand Tonnies's (1855–1936) contrast between a social organization based on rational self-interest and choice (Ger. *Gesellschaft*) and one based on biological solidarity and tradition (Ger. *Gemeinschaft*), and Max Weber's (1864–1920) treatments of the rise of capitalism, were initially advanced to help explain the modernization process.

Religion and Modernization: Within the wide-ranging literature dealing with modernization, not all authors considered religion in their analyses. However, the general tendency among social scientists assessing the process of modernization, from Karl Marx in the nineteenth century to American writers in the post–World War II era, has been to view religion as a negative factor. These writers have generally seen religion as posing a series of obstacles to modernization.

In this literature, religion is viewed as hindering modernization in at least four different ways. First, at the doctrinal and ethical level, religions are viewed as encouraging attitudes of "otherworldliness" or "fatalism" within their adherents. It is argued that Christian notions of an afterlife, Hindu conceptions of caste, the Buddhist and Hindu idea of *karma,* or popular Muslim concepts of fate have contributed to the weakening of adherents' resolve to strive and innovate. Some commentators add religious teachings that oppress women or promote large families and other teachings that oppose usury to the list of specific doctrinal or ethical obstacles to development. Second, religious practices are seen as diverting the faithful from more economically productive efforts: ceremonies, feasts, and spending for the construction or endowment of religious buildings consume income that could be used for education, housing, or economic investment. Third, religious functionaries are viewed as not being economically useful members of the community. They are also seen as obstructing change by often siding with conservative social classes. Fourth, religion is a source of division in society. Religions, it is said, contribute to intolerance and thereby impede the national integration, social mobility, and collective action that are crucial to modernization.

The work of Max Weber is often viewed as running counter to this generally negative appreciation of the role of religion in modernization, but in some ways Weber's work fits within this paradigm. In *The Protestant Ethic and the Spirit of Capitalism* (1904–1905) Weber seeks to prove that religion played a key role in at least one historically successful example of modernization in the West. Weber argues that ascetic Protestantism, especially Calvinism, through its concept of "the calling," fostered the attitudes of striving and rational planning that led to material accumulation and industrialization. Yet Weber's wider work serves to confirm the negative role played by religion elsewhere. In Weber's view, Asian religions tended to stifle whatever buds of capitalist development appeared in their societies. By fostering magical practices, they made the world into a "great enchanted garden" where systematic, rational effort could find no place. In general, Weber views religion as opposed to the kind of "means-ends" rationality essential for science and economic modernization.

Modernization and Secularization: If, within this tradition of thought, religion has been viewed as an obstacle to modernization, modernization has also been viewed as inimical to religion. Many theorists of modernization argue that modernization leads inevitably to secularization and the decline of religious influence in society. The processes that lead to modernization, it is argued, contribute to the loss of power by religious leaders, a decline in loyalty to sacred dogma, or a weakening of religious values. According to this body of theory, therefore, if religion poses an obstacle to modernization it is, at best, a temporary one, since religion declines as modernization moves forward.

Recent theoretical and empirical studies of modernization challenge this tradition of thought in various ways. Some scholars accuse this tradition of being Eurocentric and prejudiced in favor of Western models of development. They point out that many of the leading sociological theorists of modernization, from Weber through Talcott Parsons (1902–79), had little or no firsthand knowledge of the less developed societies they were describing. These societies, it is argued, are complex and bring many resources, religious and nonreligious, to bear on modernization. In some cases, these scholars point out, religion has played a major role in fostering the kind of national integration that is believed essential for modernization. Religion has also provided complex incentives for group unity and economic striving among religious subgroups in these societies. One example is the important role of immigrant Hindu, Muslim, and Confucian communities in capitalist development in many Afro-Asian polities. Some scholars have also discovered analogs of Weber's ascetic Protestantism in traditions as diverse as Japan's Samurai culture or religiously inspired movements for social change in India.

Recent events have also thrown open to question the evolutionary model implicit in much modernization theory, according to which societies inevitably progress from traditional-religious status to secular orientations. The rise of fundamentalisms of various sorts in the Middle East, Latin America, and the United States has challenged both the claim that modernization leads to secularization and the claim that traditional religious orientations are incompatible with economic development. More deeply, these developments have challenged the simple equation between rationality, secularism, and modernization that has often been implicit in modernization theory. In the face of diverse religious movements promoting different programs and visions of economic development, it is increasingly difficult to sustain the view that there is only one model of social transformation to modernity and that it involves only the kinds of secularism and economic rationality that historically characterized the West. *See also* religion, sociology of; secularism.

Moghul Empire (moh'gal), established Muslim control over most of the Indian subcontinent. It was begun by Babur (d. 1530), a Timurid prince who gained control of northern India early in the sixteenth century. During the long reign of Babur's grandson, Akbar (1556–1603), a complex imperial administration was created. Some Moghuls, such as Awrangzeb (1618–1707), emphasized the Islamic character of Moghul rule, while others stressed pluralistic policies. Although the Moghuls faced many wars of dynastic succession and revolts by different subject groups, the empire remained dominant in India until the establishment of British control in the eighteenth century. The empire formally ended when the British abolished the position of emperor after the revolution of 1857. *See also* Akbar (the Great); Hinduism.

Mohammedan, improper and insulting designation for a Muslim.

Mohammedanism, improper and insulting designation for Islam.

mohel (moh-hel', Heb., "circumciser"), an observant Jew who is trained in the necessary surgical procedures and is well versed in the ritual requirements of the *brit milah* (circumcision) ceremony. The Talmud obligates a father to circumcise his son but permits him to delegate this task to a *mohel. See also* circumcision; Judaism (life cycle).

Mohism (moh'iz-uhm), Chinese philosophical school founded by Mo-tzu and flourishing ca. 400 to 200 B.C. The Mohists rejected the hierarchical loyalties and extravagant ceremonials characteristic of Chinese society as detrimental to a morally based social order. They advocated instead universal love and frugality; they rejected aggressive warfare but upheld the right of national defense. Mohists sought truth in the physical world; the Mohist canon contains works of scientific interest. While Mohism had little influence on Chinese moral philosophy, individual Mohists attained influence as specialists in defense, numerology, and other technical subjects. *See also* Mo-tzu.

Molinos, Miguel de (moh-lee'nuhs; ca. 1640–97), Spanish Catholic mystic, best known for his *Spiritual Guide* (1675). He was condemned for the heresy of "Quietism." Molinos taught that the soul attains perfection when it abandons all effort to achieve union with God. In 1685, when the nuns for whom he was spiritual director, understanding their actions as consonant with his teachings, gave up their rosaries, recitation of the Divine Office, and confession, Molinos was sentenced to life imprisonment. *See also* Quietism.

monasticism, a specific form of religious social organization governed by strict rules and ascetic disciplines and aimed at attainment of individual salvation. *See also* asceticism; bhiksu/bhiksuni; celibacy; hermit; Jainism; Jishu; Kagyupa; monk; novice; nun; ordination; Sangha; vihara; Vinaya; wat.

Christianity: Monastics (Gk. *monos*, "alone"), or monks, are those Christians who have separated themselves from worldly concerns, devoting their lives to the service of God in order to win salvation. There are two principal types of Christian monasticism. In eremitical or anchoritic monasticism, a monk lives in complete isolation from other people and usually engages in strict ascetic practices. In cenobitic or common life monasticism, groups of monks live together, following a common rule.

The origins of monasticism are shrouded in mystery, beginning, apparently, with Antony of Egypt (ca. 251–356). Although eremites flourished from the third century through the medieval period and were acknowledged, even by cenobites, to have adopted a more demanding form of monasticism, it is cenobitic monasticism that has played the more important role in the history of Christianity. In the East, the first cenobite was Pachomius (d. 346), whose monasteries dotted the Nile Valley. The dominant form of Eastern cenobitism follows the Rule of St. Basil (d. 379). The West soon developed its own indigenous brands of cenobitic monasticism. Eventually, the Rule of St. Benedict of Nursia (d. ca. 550) came to the fore and after the Carolingian period most Western monks were Benedictine in allegiance.

Throughout the early and medieval periods, monks often dominated the Christian scene. In the East, monks safeguarded theological orthodoxy, as the great christological and trinitarian controversies show, as well as provided bishops to the church. In the West, monasteries were important oases of culture during the centuries of repeated invasions, preserving the works of classical and early Christian authors for posterity. As they prospered and grew wealthier through the generous donations of lay patrons, Western monasteries came to play an integral role in feudal society. In more recent centuries, however, monasticism has suffered serious decline. Nevertheless, monks throughout the Catholic and Orthodox worlds continue their pursuits, and through the writings of such monastic authors as Thomas Merton (1915–68), challenge other Christians to deepen their own spirituality. *See also* abbess/abbot; Anthony; Benedictines; Benedict of Nursia; Carmelites; celibacy; Cistercians; convent; Dominicans; Evagrius Ponticus; evangelical counsels; Franciscans; hermit; Jesuits; novice; nun; Orthodox Church; Pachomius; Poor Clares; Taize.

monk, male member of a monastic community. *See also* bhiksu/bhiksuni.

monkey-hold doctrine (Skt. *markata nyaya*), theological doctrine of the Hindu Vatakalai ("northern culture") sect of the Shrivaishnavas. Vishnu saves the human soul by seeing its act of surrender as an occasion for the release of salvific grace. The soul clings to the lord's grace like a baby monkey clinging to the mother. *See also* cat-hold doctrine; Shrivaishnavism.

mono no aware (moh-noh noh ah-wah-ree; Jap., "the wonder/pathos of things"), a Japanese term, important especially in twelfth-century literature and aesthetics, that represents the growing Buddhist influences on refined (aesthetic) sensibilities in early Japan. *See also* Japanese religions (art and architecture); Motoori Norinaga.

Monophysitism (Gk., "one nature"), the fifth-century christological position that there was only one nature, wholly divine, that assumes and dominates the flesh of Jesus Christ. With its roots in Cyril of Alexandria's formula of "one nature after the union" and in Cyril's more extreme successors, Eutyches and Diascorus, Monophysitism flowered in various forms as a persistent rejection of the Chalcedonian decree of Christ's two natures, human and divine, in one Person. In the sixth century, a final break with the Chalcedonians occurred with organization of Monophysite Christian churches. These churches exist today in Syria, Armenia, Egypt (among the Copts), and Ethiopia. *See also* Christology.

monotheism (Gk. *monas,* "one" and *theos,* "god"), a belief that there exists only one divine being. In a broader sense monotheism may also denote belief in only one high or ultimate god (sometimes termed *henotheism*) with a plurality of lesser and nonultimate deities under the high god's authority, or a plurality of lower manifestations of that ultimate god. In strict monotheism there are no lesser deities, though there are angels or demons of a superhuman nature. These often function analogically to the lesser deities in the broader type of monotheism, as intermediaries between God and the world.

monsters. **1** Powerful supernatural beings who violate native taxonomic categories. Often represented as composite figures, monsters bring together human and animal characteristics (the latter may be drawn from several species). Combat with monsters is a frequent episode in cosmogonies and hero tales. **2** Deformed humans whose birth is often considered portentious.

Montanus (fl. 150–175), a Phrygian Christian apocalyptic prophet who, together with two prophetesses, claimed passive verbal inspiration for a series of charismatic revelations, including the coming of a new Jerusalem in Phrygia.

Moody, Dwight Lyman (1837–99), American evangelistic preacher. After leaving a successful business career, Moody became active in the Sunday School movement and the YMCA. He first came to national prominence as a result of a successful evangelical tour of England (1872–75), traveling with Ira David Sankey, with whom he composed the Sankey-Moody *Hymn Book* (1873). Moody anticipated many of the tenets of later Christian fundamentalism, most particularly its antipathy to "higher criticism" of the Bible. This later concern was institutionalized in 1889 in Moody's Chicago Bible Institute, now known as the Moody Bible Institute.

Moon, Sun Myung (b. 1920), the Korean founder of the Unification Church, believed by his followers to be the Messiah. *See also* Korea, new religions in; Unification Church.

moon blocks, small crescent-shaped wooden blocks, flattened on one side, popularly used in Chinese divination; the answer is determined by which sides are showing after a pair of blocks is thrown. *See also* divination.

Moonie, a popular name for members of the Unification Church, founded by Sun Myung Moon (b. 1920) in Korea. *See also* Unification Church.

Moorish Science Temple, religious movement founded by Prophet Noble Drew Ali (Timothy Drew) in Newark, New Jersey, in 1913. Ali contended that African Americans were actually Moors or "Asiatics," their true homeland Morocco, and their original religion Islam. The cursed descendants of Ham, the white race, had conquered Moorish Americans by enslaving them and robbing them of their heritage. Liberation demanded the rejection of white religion, Christianity, and separation from Euramericans. By embracing Islam, Moorish Americans would achieve unity and return to power. Followers refrained from alcohol, drugs, and cigarettes. Symbolizing their Islamic commitment, men wore red fezzes and women wore long dresses. *See also* African Americans (North America), new religions among; Drew, Timothy.

morality and religion. Morality may be defined as the set of culturally transmitted norms governing the conduct of human beings with one another, whereas religion may be thought of as involving norms, beliefs, and practices governing the relationship between humans and supernatural beings. Conceived in this way, morality primarily concerns the horizontal plane of human experience, while religion relates to a more vertical dimension that points toward transcendent realities. While it is possible to distinguish morality and religion conceptually in this way, in most cultures throughout history, the two have been closely connected.

Religions have related to human moral conduct in four different ways. First, religions identify moral norms by means of explicit teachings or through the character ideals or moral exemplars they hold up for imitation. These norms typically include basic standards of morality incumbent on all persons as well as distinctive forms of supererogation—conduct "above and beyond the call of duty"—valid only for adherents to the religion or, even more narrowly, for an elite group of persons within it. Second, religions serve to legitimate these norms by tracing their source to sacred (or supernatural) realities. Third, religions help reinforce moral conduct by affirming the reality of moral retribution: the belief that the righteous are rewarded and the wicked are punished. Finally, religions provide ways of responding to the sense of guilt or worthlessness people experience when they fail to obey moral norms or to fulfill higher moral ideals.

Moral Norms: Virtually all the world religious traditions embody specific codes of moral conduct. Among these are the Ten Commandments of Hebrew faith, Jesus' Sermon on the Mount, the various requirements of *dharma* in Hinduism's Code of Manu, the Precepts of Buddhism, and the Islamic decalogue (sura 17:22–39) in the Qur'an. In addition to these relatively brief codes, religions usually develop elaborate bodies of normative instruction keyed to circumstances of time and place and often having the force of law in their respective religious communities. Examples include Judaism's extended tradition of Torah commentary (forming *Halakhah*, or Jewish law), St. Paul's letters, or the extensive body of Islamic jurisprudence (*Shari'ah*).

Normative teachings of this sort do not usually make sharp distinctions between moral and religious obligations. Religious and ritual obligations to supernatural beings exist alongside norms governing conduct among people. The side-by-side prohibitions of idolatry and murder in the Ten Commandments are an example, as is Confucius's emphasis on *li* (proper ritual behavior) along with obligations to one's parents in the *Analects* (8:2; 12:1; 15:17). Nevertheless, it would not be correct to say that religions are unfamiliar with the distinction between religious and moral norms. In the teachings of many traditions one finds criticisms of purely ritual efforts to please God or the gods at the expense of equal or more stringent obligations to one's fellow human beings. The biblical prophet Amos, for example, condemns the purely ritualized and immoral behavior of his contemporaries: "I hate, I despise your feasts, and I take no delight in your solemn assemblies. . . . But let justice roll down like waters, and righteousness like an ever-flowing stream" (5:21, 24). Confucius criticizes members of the Chinese elite who believe that Heaven is satisfied with outward displays of piety and ritual in lieu of sincere efforts at righteousness and benevolence: "A man who is not Good, what can he have to do with ritual? A man who is not Good, what can he have to do with music?" (*Analects* 3:3). The Qur'an (sura 2:172–77) insists that being upright is not a matter of "turning your faces to the East or to the West" (i.e., performing superstitious rites to ward off evil powers), but believing in Allah and in "bestowing one's wealth . . . on the orphans and the unfortunate."

In their moral teachings, religions sometimes emphasize and sometimes soften the line between ordinary and supererogatory behavior. Many traditions espouse two codes of ethics, one for laypeople and another for a religious elite. The Buddhist distinction between the Five Precepts for householders and a more stringent code of Ten Precepts for monks is an example. The former prohibits obvious moral wrongs like murder, adultery, or theft while the latter holds up a higher standard of celibacy and material austerity. The Roman Catholic distinction between the Evangelical Precepts and Counsels parallels this. In some cases, the higher standard is open to all members of the religious community as they struggle toward moral perfection. Examples are the Talmud's idea of behavior beyond what the law stipulates (*lifnim mishurat hadin*) and Islam's moral-legal category of behavior recommended for but not required of all believers. In some traditions, an effort is made to hold all adherents to a single, demanding standard of conduct. The Protestant Reformers' insistence on the "priesthood of all believers" and some Protestant sectarians' insistence on pacifism or celibacy for all believers illustrate these dynamics. In general, whenever religious moral obedience becomes lax or corrupted, there is a tendency for reform movements to arise that insist on the the highest standards of moral-religious conduct and that emphasize the tradition's supererogatory components.

Legitimating the Norms: Religions not only identify moral norms, they play an important role in legitimating morality by tracing its norms to a sacred source. In theistic traditions such as Judaism, Christianity, Islam, or Confucianism this source is usually the will of God. In nontheistic or polytheistic traditions, morality may be rooted in an impersonal sacred cosmic order to which even the gods are beholden. The Hindu and Buddhist concepts of dharma, the classical Greek conception of justice (*dike*), and the Taoist concept of "the way" are all examples. Sacred appeals lend morality an authority it may otherwise lack. Although moral conduct (as opposed to unbridled egotism) usually contributes to human welfare, the sacrifices that morality may require can sometimes utterly frustrate individuals' pursuit of happiness. Seeking to justify morality simply in terms of its contribution to human welfare, therefore, can be problematic. When moral norms are justified solely in terms of human reasoning, moreover, differences of opinion in the interpretation or understanding of moral norms can lead to strife and conflict. By tracing morality to a sacred source and by placing it beyond human control, religions respond to both these problems. As a result, even in the 1990s many people who are uncomfortable with the supernatural components of religion believe that morality requires a religious foundation.

Moral Retribution: Morality is also powerfully supported by religious affirmations of the reality of moral retribution. In worldly affairs, there often seems to be no connection between moral striving and the individual's fate. Not only do righteous people frequently suffer while the wicked flourish, but righteousness may actually enhance suffering, and wickedness can contribute to worldly success. Against these observable facts, religions almost always affirm the ultimate proportionality of moral reward and punishment. They usually rely on various transcendent states or supernatural agencies to effect this proportionality. Jewish, Christian, and Muslim notions of heaven and hell or "the world to come" are familiar examples. Here God assures proportionality between moral striving and its reward. In other religious traditions, different beliefs, states, or agencies may be involved. Among the traditions of Africa, retribution is often effected by lower classes of spiritual beings. A murderer, for example, may find himself pursued by the angered spirit of his victim, and one who mistreats a co-wife risks exposing himself to a witch's curse. In traditions deriving from India, retribution is usually effected by the nonpersonal law of *karma* according to which deeds in this life naturally generate consequences for the individual either immediately or in future reincarnations. Karma affects even the gods, and it is remorseless in its operations: the *Dhammapada* tells us that one cannot escape it "even in the clefts of the mountains" (9:27). Karma is also consummately just, fitting the punishment to the crime: the alcoholic is likely to be reborn as a mental defective; in a future life, the thug or robber will fall victim to criminal violence.

Since retribution is certain, the demands can be great, and few human beings are ever able to live perfectly blameless lives, religions also provide means for easing guilt and the moral despair arising from a sense of inevitable punishment. Rituals, including means of penance, sacrifice, and pilgrimage, play an important role in this aspect of religious life. Beliefs about supreme and sacred moral realities are also important. In theistic traditions, God is usually portrayed not only as just, but as merciful, and the resources of mercy are said to outweigh those of justice. In the Talmud, God's justice is identified with his left arm; his mercy with his right arm. Mercy is the stronger limb "so that it may be able to suppress the arm of justice." In Christianity, divine mercy expresses itself in the sacrificial death of Christ, which at once upholds justice (the punishment merited by human sin) while sparing sinners the full consequences of that punishment. Asian traditions offer transcendence of an otherwise pitiless karmic justice in various ways. Among the devotional (*bhakti*) traditions of India, for example, there is the promise of instant release from one's sin through loving adoration of the God. Among religious adepts, similar release from karma and sin may be pursued by the disciplined paths of meditation and breath control (yoga), leading to knowledge (*jnana*) and liberation (*moksha*). Religions' promises of forgiveness of sin often stand in tense relationship with these same religions' insistence on moral striving and the reality of reward and punishment. Frequently, efforts are made to reduce this tension by insisting that strenuous repentance for wrongs must precede forgiveness, and that forgiveness should be exhibited by believers in a life of purified and renewed moral exertion.

Criticism: In the course of history, religions have displayed concerted attention to facilitating and enhancing moral conduct. Beliefs and rituals have been elaborated that assist in this fourfold effort of identifying, legitimating, rewarding, and renewing moral conduct in the face of worldly adversity and inevitable human failures. Sometimes, however, these efforts have given rise to less-than-moral or even immoral religious teachings and practices. The effort to ground morality in a divine command, for example, can lead to inflexible and authoritarian approaches to the moral life. The emphasis on reward and punishment has sometimes produced an attitude of crass egotism, with moral performance measured solely in terms of its likely religious benefit. And the possibility of forgiveness has sometimes led to a slackening of moral striving and a passive reliance on grace.

Throughout the ages, religious and nonreligious thinkers have raised voices of caution or protest against these tendencies. As early as the Euthyphro dialogue, Socrates is presented as criticizing various immoral conceptions of the gods and the unreasoning reliance on the divine will as a guide to the moral life. In the modern period, voices of criticism have become even more pronounced. Following the religious wars of the sixteenth and seventeenth centuries, thinkers of the Enlightenment sought to develop nonreligious rational groundings for morality in the quest for a moral order that could rise above sectarian differences. The great moral system of Immanuel Kant (the eighteenth-century German philosopher), with its emphasis on rational autonomy, and of the English utilitarians, with their stress on morality's promotion of happiness, are examples. Eighteenth- and nineteenth-century thinkers went further. Not only did they regard religiously based ethics as replaceable, but some espoused the view that they are morally pernicious. In different ways, thinkers such as Karl Marx (1818–83), Sigmund Freud (1856–1939), or Friedrich Nietzsche (1844–1900)

argued that religion leads to immoral conduct, hypocrisy, and injustice.

In the twentieth century, thinkers have become less certain about these criticisms. Sociologists such as Max Weber, Talcott Parsons, or Robert Bellah have identified the crucial role played by religious ethics in the development of moral attitudes. Philosophers as diverse as G. E. M. Anscombe or R. M. Hare have asked whether morality without religious support makes sense. Although these debates are far from being resolved, the question of the relation between morality and religion remains as lively and as important as ever. *See also* Buddhism (thought and ethics); Chinese religions (thought and ethics); Christianity (thought and ethics); Confucianism (thought and ethics); Hinduism (thought and ethics); Islam (thought and ethics); Judaism (thought and ethics).

Moral Rearmament, interdenominational religious movement begun in the 1930s and connected closely with the career of the American Protestant clergyman Frank Buchman (1878–1961). It stresses spiritual awakening and the pursuit of four absolute moral principles—honesty, selflessness, purity, and love. *See also* Buchman, Frank.

Moravian Church. *See* Hus, Jan.

Mormons. *See* Latter-day Saints, Church of Jesus Christ of.

Moroni (moh-roh'nĩ), in Mormon tradition, the last of the Nephite prophets who, in resurrected form, as an angel, informed Joseph Smith of the golden plates of the Book of Mormon on September 21, 1823. Moroni had buried the plates fourteen centuries earlier. After Smith completed their translation, Moroni bore them away. *See also* Latter-day Saints, Church of Jesus Christ of.

mortal sin, in Roman Catholic theology, a serious offense against God that, unrepented, merits damnation. Three conditions create such a sin: a serious offense in itself; knowledge of that seriousness; and a free act of the will to commit the offense. *See also* sin.

Moses (Heb. *Mosheh*), the towering figure in the narrative of the Hebrew Bible who led Israel out of Egypt and transmitted God's commandments.

Judaism: Jewish tradition regards Moses as he is described in Deuteronomy 34:10, a prophet of unparalleled intimacy with God and the transmitter of the divine law; he is so celebrated in a widely sung synagogue hymn, "Yigdal." Jewish liturgy does not lionize Moses, lest he be adored. Rabbinic tradition holds that Moses, called "Moses, our rabbi," handed down not only the written Torah but a comprehensive interpretation of it (oral Torah) that would be spelled out in the later rabbinic codes and commentaries. Yet a paradoxical legend shows Moses puzzled by what later sages would make of his teaching. *See also* Samaritans; Torah.

Islam: Moses (Arab. *Musa*) is depicted as a prophet in the Qur'an and revered in Islam as "one who conversed with God." The Qur'an narrates his confrontation with Pharoah, an exodus from Egypt, and the revelation at Sinai. Orthodox Muslim theologians agree that God spoke directly to Musa, though the authority of Musa's Torah is abrogated by the subsequent revelation of the Qur'an. Musa and his Torah are recognized, nonetheless, as the first instance of an apostle of God receiving a divine law. Likewise, the relationship of Musa to his brother and deputized successor Harun (Aaron) is seen, especially by Shiite Muslims, as the model for the delegation of authority from Muhammad to Ali. *See also* Messenger of Allah.

mosque (mosk; from Arab. *masjid,* "place of ritual prostration"), a site of assembly and worship for Muslims. Although there are thousands of mosques, Muslims assign highest status to those of Mecca, Medina, and Jerusalem. Additionally the Shia revere the mosque-shrines of Karbala and Najaf in Iraq and Mashhad and Qum in Iran.

Origins: The earliest Islamic sources employ the term *mosque* with sketchy detail as to appearance. As a ritual space for assembly and worship, the mosque has its origins in two kinds of places: the precincts enclosing the Kaaba (i.e., the Sacred Mosque in Mecca), and the houses of the first generation of Muslims. The Sacred Mosque served as a plaza for prayer and circumambulation about the Kaaba. In houses, a room or a corner of a courtyard was set aside for worship by individuals and small groups of Muslims. Prayer at home brought God's blessing to the inhabitants, plus it allowed Muslims to congregate and fulfill their religious obligations when access to the Sacred Mosque was not possible. After the Hijra to Medina (622), Muhammad's domestic compound served as the chief mosque for the community, with others distributed among the outlying houses of his followers. Eventually the Mecca Mosque became the orientation point (*qibla*) for all outlying mosques, while the Prophet's house-mosque served as their prototype.

Forms and Embellishments: The architectural form of mosques varies according to time and

mosque

Muslims gather in a mosque for the required five daily prayers. No other Muslim ritual is performed in a mosque. Before entering a mosque, one washes (often in a fountain in the mosque's courtyard) and removes one's shoes (racks are usually provided). The (1) prayer hall proper is without seating, its floor is often covered with rugs. There are no images or other ritual objects. A central feature is (2) an arch (*mihrab*) that orients the congregation toward Mecca. To the right of the arch is (3) a raised platform (*minbar*) that serves as a pulpit from which prayers are led and, especially on Fridays, sermons delivered. In large mosques, the minbar bisects the prayer hall to make it possible for everyone to see and hear. Women are in a segregated section of the hall.

Some mosques have other structures attached to them, such as a tower (minaret) from which the summons to prayer will be chanted, a school, or a scholarly library.

place. As a rule, mosques consist of indigenous architectural elements that are modified and combined so as to create buildings that look strikingly new. The most typical features—columns surmounted by arches, rectangular porticoed courtyards, qibla niches (*mihrabs*), minarets, domes, vaulted portals (*iwans*)—first achieved prominence in Arab and Persian Muslim environments, based on Hellenistic/Late Antique antecedents.

Other common mosque features are the pulpit (*minbar*), located to the right of the mihrab, a fountain for required ablutions, latrines, and shoe racks near the entrance. Floors are covered with carpets; they are not to be tread upon by shoes. Many mosques contain clocks to help worshipers keep to their prayer schedule. Mosque walls can be plain, but in many instances they are decorated with beautiful marble or glazed tiles bearing bright geometric and floral patterns, mirrors, Arabic inscriptions, and stained-glass windows. Ceilings can be equally ornate.

Functions: The principal function of a mosque is to provide a sanctified place for the fulfillment of Muslim prayer obligations, especially for males. Women usually pray at home, or at the mosque in a segregated area. Select mosques (*jamis*) serve as places for collective Friday prayer. Since the time of the Prophet, such mosques have served as urban centers of governmental control and of public welfare. Islamic colleges (*madrasas*) incorporate mosques, as do Sufi convents and royal palaces. Many mosques are also mausoleums and pilgrimage centers because they contain the remains of influential and saintly individuals. Moreover, according to one widely circulated tradition, anyone who builds and cares for a mosque will gain a dwelling like it in paradise. Besides prayer, many Muslims today turn to mosques for health and child care services, food, shelter, and money in times of need. *See also* Islam (art).

Mother Ann. *See* Lee, Ann.

Mother Earth, figure, goddess, archetype, or concept commonly thought to be widespread and having great antiquity among religions the world over. Scholars have proposed that the earth was understood as a mother even before the rise of fertility goddesses during the development of agriculture, but Mother Earth was displaced by goddesses of vegetation and harvesting. Alternatively, scholars have identified Mother Earth as characterizing the cosmic dualism of agrarian peoples, which sets in opposition the celestial male elements and the earthy or underworld female powers. Here the marriage or sexual union of Father Sky and Mother Earth is essential to fertility and life. A statement attributed to a Native North American named Smohalla (Wanapum, Plateau area) exemplifies this characterization: "You ask me to plow the ground. Shall I take a knife and tear my mother's bosom? You ask me to dig for stone. Shall I dig under her skin for bones? You ask me to cut grass and make hay and sell it, and be rich like white men. But how dare I cut off my mother's hair?" Contemporary Native peoples of both North and South America know her as *pachu mama*, and Mother Earth helps articulate a common native spirituality and ethos that stands in contrast to that of European-Americans. Admiration and respect for the earth may demonstrate a spiritually based ecology.

The term *Mother Earth*, designating a ubiquitous and ancient figure or concept, originated with the rise of the comparative study of religion and culture in the late nineteenth century and was not widely used by Native North Americans until well into the twentieth century. Mother Earth appears to be a very modern concept used by both scholars and Native peoples to draw together a variety of religious figures and concepts. *See also* Afro-Americans (Caribbean and South America), new religions among; Earth-mother; Prithivi.

Mother Goddess, a generic term for the female deity of the earth, fertility, and creation. In ancient religions goddess figurines associated with fertility have been found in sites of human habitation going back to the second half of the fifth millennium B.C. These figurines are most commonly made of clay, sometimes of stone. They have often been found at ritual sites such as altars and may be miniature replicas of larger statues placed in temples. These representations of divinity show exaggerated female sex characteristics (pubic triangles, breasts, buttocks, and thighs) and sometimes combine zoomorphic characteristics such as the head of a snake, bird, or fish. Geometric patterns replicating designs from or recalling the goddess figurines have been identified on a large variety of earthenware bowls and other (largely ceremonial) objects dating from the late fifth to the beginning of the third millennium B.C.

Two aspects of the ancient Mother Goddess have been suggested by scholars: she is at once "the Giver of All" (life, water, food, happiness) and "the Taker of All" (i.e., death). She was most likely associated with cycles of death and rebirth, such as those of the moon, the tides, the agricultural year. This close symbolic linking of the goddess with life cycles is further strengthened by other, related, designs found in ancient cult sites that also suggest birth and life in transition: crescents, uteri, caterpillars, and butterflies.

These most ancient representations of the Mother Goddess show the early development of major aspects of goddesses known from historical periods. Texts from the second millennium B.C., for example, tell of the descent to the underworld of the Sumerian goddess Inanna. Inanna's journey to hell and back was undertaken in order to secure the return to life of her husband, the shepherd Dumuzi. Echoes of this story, a female goddess' search for her own or a partner's immortality, are found in the legends of Isis in Egypt and Kore (Persephone) in Greece. The Babylonian goddess Ishtar, whose consort was named Tammuz, was the version of Innana known to the ancient Israelites: the prophet Ezekiel decries the women of Jerusalem he found "weeping for Tammuz" at the north gate of the temple (Ezekiel 8:14).

Examples of the goddess of life, often associated with power over death, are found in many cultures. The original Mother Goddess of the Greeks was Gaia (or Ge), whose very name means "earth." The name of Demeter, the mother of Kore, may be derived from the Greek *ge meter*, which literally means "earth mother." The Greek goddess Artemis (the Roman Diana) was associated with the waxing and waning of the moon. The Hindu goddess Kali, seen as capable of enormous compassion and horrifying destruction, is the mistress of both life and death. The female protagonist of the Song of Songs, a poetic book of the Hebrew Bible, is described in similar double-edged metaphors: "You are beautiful as Tirzah, my love, comely as Jerusalem, terrible as an army with banners" (Song of Songs 6:4).

There are also many mother goddesses in Native American cultures, including the Shawnee "Our Grandmother," the Corn Goddess of the Iroquois and Hopi, and the Hopi Spider Woman, from whom all flesh was born. The goddess Yemaja of the African Yoruba people is a creator from the sea who brings life and rebirth. Yemaya is also worshiped in Brazil and the islands of the Caribbean, where aspects of her cult have mingled with the cult of the Virgin Mary.

Elements of these manifestations of the ancient mother goddesses can also be seen in the Christian cult of the Virgin. Mary, who is called Queen of Heaven, is associated with the moon and is the virgin mother of an incarnate god who dies and is reborn. After the triumph of Christianity in the Mediterranean world of the fourth century, Ephesus, a Greek city in Asia Minor that had been dedicated to Artemis or Diana, became famous for the cult of "Mary of the Ephesians." In Mexico, the apparition of the Virgin Mary at Guadalupe developed into a cult that took over the site and some aspects of the Aztec goddess Coatalcopia.

In Contemporary Thought and Practice: All of this evidence suggests that many manifestations of the Mother Goddess, patron of birth and rebirth, figured in the religious life of the ancient world and that the importance of the Mother Goddess reaches even into modern religious traditions. Reflecting on the antiquity of this religious image, nineteenth-century anthropologists suggested that the Mother Goddess was the original concept of divinity known to humans, an expression of the power of the holy that was suppressed by the increasingly patriarchal, or male-controlled, nature of society. This idea of an ancient, lost, female power was joined with the idea of the Eternal Feminine propagated by European Romanticism to inspire many thinkers of the early twentieth century. Both the poet Robert Graves and the psychoanalytic theorist Carl Jung were fascinated by the idea of an ancient, archaic, repressed, but still powerful principle of female divinity.

In the later part of the twentieth century, feminist thought has done much to reclaim, but also revise, the figure of the Mother Goddess. There are two major reasons why this array of goddesses from the ancient world and non-European cultures has informed feminist spirituality. One is the readily apparent fact that male-imaged divinities reinforce male supremacy and do not represent women's special spiritual concerns; the other is that the mother goddess imagery, because it focuses on giving life, is a type of divinity that relates more directly to women's experience than do the transcendental gods of Western religious traditions, who tend to reinforce male alienation from concrete, everyday reality.

Some contemporary goddess worshipers center their rituals around figures such as Isis, Inanna, Yemaja, or Spider Woman; but more commonly, the characteristics of these and other specific goddesses are merged into a composite character known simply as the Goddess. Twentieth-century followers of the goddess tradition, from Robert Graves to the feminist author Carol Christ, assume that behind all of these manifestations of female divinity is a single creative principle: that Inanna, Isis, Gaia, the Magna Mater of the Romans, all the goddesses of creation, are one. Although some participants in the goddess movement have complained that this monotheistic conception of the goddess mimics patriarchal religion, the notion of the Goddess as a fusion of all female creative power has become a standard part of New Age spirituality and Wicca (feminist witchcraft). Wiccan circles are cast in the name of the Goddess. A spirituality of ecology has interpreted Gaia, the ancient Greek Earth Mother, as the living principle of the earth itself and so has extended goddess spirituality out of the strictly religious into a realm of ecological activism.

Goddess spirituality has also influenced mainstream Judaism and Christianity through incorporation of the Goddess into prayer and liturgy. Protestant Christians have developed theology and ritual centering on Sophia, the principle of wisdom found especially in Wisdom, one of the biblical Apocrypha. Jewish women have infused the traditional ceremonies of Rosh Hodesh (the new moon) with symbolism from ancient cults of the Goddess. In the Orthodox and Roman Catholic traditions of Christianity, of course, the figure of the Virgin

Mary has always been powerful; but it is striking that more men than women writers from these traditions try to claim Mary as a manifestation of the ancient Mother Goddess. This may be related to the way the cult of the Virgin has functioned as a part of traditional, patriarchal Christianity.

But perhaps the most widespread manifestation of the cult of the Mother Goddess in the twentieth-century is a broadly diffused, but only tangentially religious, concept of the Goddess as a means of spiritual awakening and self-knowledge for women. As the poet Ntozake Shange puts it: "I found God in myself and I loved her fiercely." The insight here is that women's creative spirituality is strong and closely linked to the ultimate powers of life. This movement turns to the archaeological evidence, the ancient figurines of the Mother Goddess, to argue that there was once a time when women were not subject to men or male concepts of divinity. This "golden age" of matriarchy has been subject to vehement criticism on the grounds that the surviving evidence does not support the claims. Those who find the Goddess a source of spiritual strength counter with the argument that evidence for her cult may have been destroyed by millennia of patriarchal suppression. Besides, they argue, the historical fact does not matter nearly as much as the spiritual reality of a female divine principle of life, an ancient, enduring aspect of human religiosity. *See also* Baltic religion; Cycladic religion; feminist theology; Mesopotamian religion; Minoan religion.

motif, the smallest unit of meaning in a tale that has the power to persist in tradition. Scholars classify motifs in world folk literature as well as in specific cultures according to the numerical system of Stith Thompson, *Motif-Index of Folk Literature* (2d ed., 1958). It is a general assumption of folklorists that the presence of the same motif in two or more tales does not imply genetic relations. *See also* folklore; tale type.

Motoori Norinaga (moh-toh-oh-ree noh-ree-nah-gah; 1730–1801), Japanese scholar of the National Learning (Kokugaku) school. To understand Japanese thought before Chinese influence he advocated studying early Japanese literature and wrote a major commentary on the *Kojiki*. In his work on *The Tale of Genji* he highlighted the literary and aesthetic idea of *mono no aware,* a deep empathy for the transiency of life. *See also* Kokugaku; makoto; mono no aware.

Mo-tzu (mwaw-dzuh; ca. 479–381 B.C.), also Mo Ti, opponent of Confucius and founder of the Mohist philosophical school. Mo-tzu criticized luxurious ceremonies, family-based loyalty, and aggressive warfare; he advocated frugality, universal love, and warfare for defensive purposes only. *See also* Mohism.

mountains, sacred, mountains to which holiness has been imputed, often because of their height (nearness to the sky dwelling of the gods) and inaccessibility (remoteness from humankind). *See also* Athos, Mt.; Meru, Mt.; Olympos; pilgrimage; shrine; Sinai; South American religions, traditional; Zion.

Chinese Religion: Mountains are the most important features of Chinese spiritual geography. Attested as sacred places in the earliest Shang inscriptions (fourteenth century B.C.), mountains have retained their sacral aura throughout subsequent history.

Myth and History: The numinous quality of mountains is clear from Chinese landscape painting, poetry, garden design, imperial worship, monastic religion, and pilgrimage. Chou (ca. 1122–221 B.C.) emperors sacrificed to four sacred mountains as abodes of the gods and ancestors and the sources of rain and fecundity.

A myth in the book of *Lieh-tzu* describes mountains as pillars that uphold the sky. It tells of how Kung-kung, a monster, demolished one of these pillars and how it was restored by the creatrix Nu Kua, who seated it on the back of a mythic tortoise for stability. This myth is repeated in the architecture of many temples whose pillars rest on tortoise bases.

Under the influence of "five phase" (*wu-hsing*) thinking in the Han period (206 B.C.–A.D. 220), the number of specifically revered mountains was increased to five, which became standard for imperial worship from that period up to the twentieth century. The five were T'ai in the east (Shantung), Heng in the south (Hunan), Hua in the west (Shensi), Heng in the north (Shansi), and Sung in the center (Honan). By the Ch'ing dynasty (1644–1912), two other sets of five mountains were added to the worship of the spirits of the earth by the emperors.

Buddhists often chose to build their monasteries on mountains, because of both the seclusion and the numinous connotations. Among their most important mountains were Wu-t'ai in Shansi, O-mei in Szechuan, Lu in Kiangsi, Chiu-hua in Anhwei, and T'ien-t'ai in Chekiang.

Mountain lore was very important in Taoist traditions, which considered them the mysterious dwelling place of the immortals. Caves and grottoes dotted their higher elevations, monasteries and hermitages were built where *ch'i,* cosmic breath, coursed most strongly. Among the

Sacred Mountains of China, Japan, and Korea

most important mountains to the Taoists were O-mei and Lu, already mentioned, as well as Kuai-chi south of Hangchou, T'ai Po near Ch'ang-an, Ma Ku in Kiangsi, Lo Fou east of Canton, and Mao between Lake T'ai and Nanking.

Mountains of the Imagination: Equally important were the mythic mountains K'un-lun and P'eng-lai. The former was described as a nine-story mountain in the northwest, a cosmic axis, and the center of the world. It was equivalent to Sumeru of the Buddhist tradition but was early incorporated into Chinese mythology as the dwelling place of Hsi Wang-mu, the Queen Mother of the West, a paradise of immortality.

P'eng-lai was the most famous of three Isles of the Immortals said to be located somewhere in the eastern sea off the coast of China. The first Ch'in emperor sent an expedition to find these islands and bring back their secrets of immortality. Later, the emperor Han Wu-ti built replicas of them in his imperial park. From that time on, the wealthy built miniature mountains in the lakes and ponds of private and imperial gardens to recall this myth of immortality. **See also** ch'i; Chiu-hua Shan; grotto/cave; Isles of the Immortals; K'un-lun; Lieh-tzu; Lung-hu Shan; Mao Shan; Miao Shan; O-mei Shan; T'ai Shan; T'ien-t'ai Shan; wu-hsing; Wu-t'ai Shan.

Japanese Religion: From ancient times many Japanese volcanoes and mountains such as the well-known Fuji were not only praised in poetry but also venerated as the dwelling places of *kami* (divinities, divine presences) and as objects of worship. The earliest religious activities related to sacred mountains took place at the base or lower slopes, but due to the influence of Taoist notions of mountain wizards and especially the influence of Buddhist ascetic practices, religious specialists came to climb sacred mountains as a spiritual exercise. In conjunction with ritual and ascetic practice on sacred mountains, Buddhist temples and Shinto shrines were built there. Shugendo ("the way of mastering power" on sacred mountains) was the main movement institutionalizing practice on sacred mountains. From medieval times not only religious specialists and nobility, but many laypeople, made pilgrimages to sacred mountains.

A number of folk beliefs and practices are associated with sacred mountains. Spirits of the dead (ancestors) are thought to go to sacred mountains and reside there; some mountains are special sites for enshrining and memorializing spirits of the dead. Fertility and water link mountains to agriculture, especially rice cultivation. A widespread belief is that the rice kami dwells in the rice field during the growing season, ascends to the nearby mountain in the fall as the mountain kami, and once more descends to the rice field in spring as the rice kami. Some seasonal rituals, especially in spring, celebrate this movement of kami. The mountain kami is considered female, but until the late 1800s women were forbidden to climb most sacred mountains. *See also* Fuji, Mt.; Gozan; Hiei, Mt.; Japanese folk religion; kami; Koya, Mt.; Kumano, Mt.; Miwa, Mt.; Shugendo.

Korean Religion: The worship of mountain spirits as well as the association of mountains with many religious and miraculous events throughout Korean history is ancient and long-standing. Certain mountains are associated with all the religious traditions and with the mythic history of Korea. Beginning with the descent of Tan'gun, the legendary founder of the first Korean state on Mt. Paekdu and his final apotheosis on Mt. T'aebaek, the descent of Avalokiteshvara on Mt. Sorak, and Manjusri on Mt. Odae, mountains have been the place where Buddhas and Bodhisattavas have descended to Korea (many peaks still bear their name), where Taoist immortals have ascended into the sky, and where hidden prophetic books and oracles have been found. Mt. Kaeryong is especially important in regard to geomantic prophesies, since it was on its slopes that the prophesies about the found-

ing of the Koryo kingdom were heard and the book containing the prophesies about the successor to the Choson kingdom was found. It is also at Mt. Kaeryong that most of the nineteenth- and twentieth-century new religions had their start. The most common use of mountains is as the site of graves and as the dwelling place for village tutelary spirits. *See also* Buddhas and Bodhisattvas (Korea); Tan'gun wanggom.

mourning, rituals and customs that formally and publicly express grief at a death. Though most often carried out by relatives, friends, and neighbors, they may be the responsibility of professional mourners or burial guilds. *See also* dead, rituals with respect to the.

Movement of Spiritual Inner Awareness (MSIA). *See* ECKANKAR.

mudanq. *See* shamanism.

mudra (mood'rah; Skt., "seal"), a symbolic hand gesture used in Buddhist and Hindu art and ritual practice. Highly codified configurations of the palm and fingers of one or both hands, *mudras*

Ninth-century bronze Buddha from Kashmir, India; his hands make the *mudra* ("gesture") Varada, calling on the cosmos to witness his Buddha hood, Los Angeles County Museum of Art.

are visual "seals" of invocatory mantras or attributions of divine character. Mudras are most prevalent in the statuary of deities as signifiers of their acts of grace (e.g., dispelling fear, imparting instruction, fulfilling vows) or as abbreviated references to mythic narrative (e.g., the Buddha's calling Earth to witness his enlightenment). The Buddha shows the gesture of fearlessness (*abhaya-mudra*), for example, by extending his hand vertically with its palm facing outward, or the gesture of meditation (*dhyana-mudra*) by placing both hands together in his lap. The symbolic language of gestures in Indian culture has been elaborated with greatest complexity in the tradition of Indian dance, where the combination of hand gestures (*hastas*) and movements is said to yield more than a million variations. *See also* dance; Hinduism (performing arts).

muenbotoke (m*oo*-en-boh-toh-ke; Jap., "unconnected spirits"), in Japanese tradition, the spirits of those who have no descendants to perform ancestral rites. In periodic rites, they are given offerings in addition to those for ancestors. *See also* ancestral rites.

muezzin (moo-uh-*th'thin*; Arab.), Muslim crier who calls the faithful to the five daily (*salat*) prayer services. The call is chanted in a clear, loud voice from atop a minaret or other appropriate position. The call magnifies God, testifying to his oneness. Muhammad's apostlehood is remembered and the believers are beckoned to hasten to prayer and success.

mufti. *See* fatwa; Islamic law.

muhajirun. *See* emigrants.

Muhammad (moo-ham'mad; Arab., "praised one," ca. 570–632), the founder of Islam. Muhammad was born in the Arabian city of Mecca. Orphaned early, he grew up in poverty in the Hashimite clan of the dominant Meccan tribe, the Quraysh, who controlled the polytheistic religious sanctuary, the Kaaba, as well as dominating commercial and political life in western Arabia. He overcame his low social standing through hard work, a pleasing personality, and his marriage to the rich widow Khadija. His contemplative nature prompted him to seek the source of his good fortune through religious devotion. His prophetic career started when he was about forty years old when he experienced his first revelation. After an initial period in which only his family knew of his religious experiences, he started a public career in Mecca as a prophet and reformer. He met with increasing hostility from the establishment in Mecca in particular. He moved from Mecca to Medina in 622. This move (*Hijra*) enabled Muhammad to establish his new community on a firm political and spiritual foundation during the decade before he died. The Hijra of 622 was later marked as the beginning year of the strictly lunar Muslim calendar. The record of Muhammad's life and prophetic activity is found only partly in the Qur'an, which Muslims hold to be the Word of God. The more complete record of his life is found in two posthumous sets of traditions of sacred biography, the *Sira* and the *Sunna*. The latter, composed of small descriptions of events in Muhammad's life called *hadith*, became the basis for Islamic law. Muhammad's actions and sayings thus became models for proper Muslim behavior. Muslims regard Muhammad as the Seal of the Prophets, the last in the line of prophets partly shared by Judaism and Christianity that began with Adam. The Qur'an, God's message to humankind through Muhammad, is regarded as the final revelation before the Day of Judgment.

Birth: The biographical sources, the majority of which are posthumous, indicate little that is certain about Muhammad's years before he publicly became a prophet. The traditional year of his birth, 570, is associated with the Ethiopian Christian general Abraha's unsuccessful attempt to capture Mecca using an army equipped with a war elephant. The year is thus linked to *sura* 105 of the Qur'an, and the year is called the Year of the Elephant. In reality, however, that event must have taken place earlier, and the description in Qur'an commentary of Abraha's attack can be understood as portraying Mecca as the new Jerusalem by paralleling the event with descriptions of Sennacherib's siege of Jerusalem. Muhammad's birth is linked with other miracles in the sources. Muhammad's mother is said to have been told of his birth by a heavenly voice and to have had a light shine from her womb as far as Syria. The miracles are not necessary for Muslim belief but have become part of the popular celebration of the Prophet's birthday in some communities.

Muhammad's father, Abdullah ibn Abd al-Muttalib, died before Muhammad was born, and his mother, Amina, died shortly after. Muhammad was first under the protection of his grandfather, Abd al-Muttalib, and then his uncle, Abu Talib, who became like a father to Muhammad.

Early Life: Sura 93:6–8 summarizes the important part of Muhammad's early life: "Did He not find you an orphan and give you a home; find you in error and guide you, and find you impoverished and enrich you?" Because of God's beneficence, Muhammad was enjoined to act justly and tell of God's goodness, just as Muhammad's tribe, the Quraysh, were enjoined to worship God and practice social justice because of what he had given them. The sura reports that Muhammad was sent to live among the Banu Sad ibn Bakr, thus linking Muhammad to a noble bedouin ancestry. The story of the opening of Muhammad's breast and the cleansing of his heart is associated with this tradition, reflecting later apologetic interpretations of sura 94. In the popular imagination, the removal of the black dot from his heart allowed Muhammad to be the immaculate model for Muslims.

Muhammad's material success in this part of his life is attributed to his commercial association with the rich widow, Khadija bint ("daughter of") Khuwaylid, and his later marriage to her. It is not clear whether she or any in her family provided Muhammad with any religious instruction or encouragement, but she was related to the Christian scholar, Waraqah ibn Nawfal. She did give Muhammad social standing and considerable personal support during his early religious experiences. She was the mother of all of Muhammad's children except Ibrahim. His three sons by her, al-Qasim, al-Tayyib, and al-Tahir, died in infancy, as did Ibrahim. His daughters, Zaynab, Ruqayya, Umm Kulthum, and Fatima, all played important roles in the early Muslim community. Muhammad's new social status enabled him to assume a central role in the rebuilding of the Kaaba, although the particulars of the story have been embellished by later narrators. Muhammad's change of fortune seems to have produced a religious crisis in which he sought the source of the good he received. If some Western analyses of the Qur'an are correct, he looked first to the religious traditions around him for the answers. Muhammad was not alone in his search for religious truth. Muslim tradition tells of at least four men who broke with polytheism and adopted some form of monotheism just before or during Muhammad's time. The four, called *Hanif*, were Waraqa ibn Nawfal, Khadija's cousin, who converted to Christianity; Ubaydallah ibn Jahsh, who converted to Islam after the beginning of Muhammad's mission, but later became a Christian; Uthman ibn al-Huwayrith, who went to the Byzantine court, became a Christian, and received high office; and Zayd ibn Amr, who, unconvinced by any available organized beliefs, remained an unaffiliated worshiper of God. In addition to polytheism, the presence of an active Jewish community and several proselytizing Christian groups contributed to a charged religious atmosphere in Arabia in the early seventh century.

Revelation and Early Mission: In the period prior to the beginning of Islam, Muhammad seems to have practiced an annual religious withdrawal and devotion in the caves around Mecca. Little is said of the actual practice, but it lasted for a month each year. During one of these devotional retreats on Hira, a mountain near Mecca, Muhammad received his first visit from a figure later tradition identifies with the angel Gabriel. Opinions differ about which sura, or chapter of the Qur'an, represents the first revelation. The majority says that sura 96:1–5 is the first, while a minority places sura 74 in that position. The experience came on Muhammad suddenly, frightening him to the point that he contemplated killing himself to avoid being thought either insane or a *kahin* (a mantic seer), which his detractors called him anyway. Gabriel dissuaded him, and when Muhammad returned to Khadija, she helped persuade him that he had had a true revelation from God. The first revelations were in the form of inspirations during which Muhammad was sometimes wrapped in his cloak (sura 74). According to some analysts, this was an inducement for the reception of revelation, but Muhammad could not control or predict the events, as embarrassing periods of God's silence testifies. When revelations did come, Muhammad would undergo physical changes evident to those around him. His detractors accused him of fits or epilepsy, a charge eagerly taken up by Western critics of Muhammad.

While it is difficult to make a definitive chronology of Muhammad's reception of the Qur'an, both Muslim and Western scholars have been able to place the portions of the Qur'an in a rough historic order. This order, it should be noted, differs from the normal order of the verses of the Qur'an and relies heavily on extraquranic interpretations. Accordingly, the first messages of the Qur'an emphasize Muhammad's relationship to God, what he received from him, his goodness, and Muhammad's obligations because of his relationship to God. Similarly, God pointed out to Muhammad what he had given Muhammad's tribe in wealth and privilege, making them responsible both to worship God by giving thanks and to practice social justice by sharing their bounty with those less fortunate than they. This, then, is the foundational message of Islam found in the earliest portions of the Qur'an: God, the creator and owner of everything, has been gracious enough to provide humankind with both necessities and a surplus. Humans must be thankful to God and worship him exclusively, and they must share their surplus with those who have less.

God is represented as a good, merciful, giving God, the creator (sura 96), the controller of the universe (sura 55), the provider for all his creation (sura 80). Humankind's response should be a sense of gratitude and humility, a servant or slave to God. But humans are termed ungrateful, *kafir*, which generally means unbelief because it implies a denial of God's beneficence and power (sura 96:6). Humans also have an obligation to their fellows and to the other creatures of God. One should not oppress the weak or waste God's gifts (suras 93:6–11; 92:5–11). Many interpreters see Muhammad's early life experiences in the quranic social and religious message. Responsibility goes beyond the individual and extends to the whole of the community (*umma*). God, for example, provided the Quraysh with their worldly success as seen in sura 106: "Because of the protection of the Quraysh, their protection of the Winter and Summer caravans, let them worship the Lord of this house (the Kaaba) who fed them in hunger and kept them safe from fear." Failure to show gratitude would invite calamity in this world and the next, because, as the Qur'an states in numerous places, all returns to God. The ultimate return is the Day of Judgment, at which time the heavens will split, the earth will spread out, and the sinner will be cast into Hell's fires (sura 84). The righteous will receive rewards in Paradise, described as a pleasant celestial garden.

Muhammad saw himself as a "warner" to remind his fellow humans of their obligations to God, to prevent disaster and to bring as many as possible to the straight path. The Qur'an is filled with stories of past prophets and their attempts to warn. The stories of Lot and Noah, for example, are recalled for what can happen to sinful people. Even in Muhammad's early career, he appears to have seen himself linked to the prophetic traditions of Judaism and Christianity. These themes form the basis of the earliest message of Islam. Muhammad the Warner and the Prophet, made aware of what he had received from God, is told of his obligation to God and to humanity. These obligations apply to all who have received God's blessing and who wish to avoid damnation. Failure to heed the warnings results in dire consequences on the Day of Judgment or before. Muhammad's earliest message was aimed at the Arabs around him. Some analysts contend that Muhammad was preaching only to the Arabs and that Islam became a universal religion only after Muhammad's death, but there is nothing in these early passages that precludes a more universalist interpretation.

Meccan Reaction and Muhammad's Response: Muhammad seems to have enjoyed initial success in persuading a few to follow his message. Most sources agree that Khadija was the first to convert to Islam, probably along with her daughters. There is no agreement, however, about who was the first male to convert. Shiite Muslims assert that Ali ibn Abu Talib, who would have been about nine years old and was Muhammad's cousin, was the first. Some Sunni traditions hold that the first male convert was Zayd ibn Haritha, a manumitted slave, while other Sunni traditions claim that Abu Bakr, Muhammad's first successor, was the first. Except for Abu Bakr, the first converts outside of Muhammad's family were not the most influential members of Meccan society, so his preaching seems to have caused little concern. There is some indication that they thought Muhammad to be an ecstatic seer who would help them find lost animals, act as a dowser, and most important, settle disputes. But, as Muhammad's mission became more defined in their minds, the Meccans began to realize that his call to worship only one God would undercut their religious, and hence economic, hold on western Arabia. They began to taunt and jeer at Muhammad and make it difficult for him to preach, particularly in the market on Friday at midday when crowds would be gathered around. The opposition stopped short of violence at first because harming Muhammad would have brought about civil war. But the opportunities for Muhammad and the nascent community to practice Islam were limited. About this time, Muhammad sent a group of his followers to Abyssinia. The reasons for this "little Hijra," as it came to be known, are obscure and may be based on the economic ties between Mecca and that part of Africa. Muslim stories report that the Abyssinian ruler received the Muslims warmly, but evidently not warmly enough for Muhammad to shift his mission to Africa. This period of Muhammad's career ends with the deaths of his two main supporters, his family protector, Abu Talib, and his wife, Khadija. Muhammad's social standing in the community worsened, and the Meccans tried an economic boycott of Muhammad's Hashimite clan, who supported him more out of clan loyalty than from belief in his mission. The exception was Abu Lahab and his wife, who strongly opposed Muhammad and are mentioned in sura 111 as consigned to Hell. While the boycott was a failure, it was clear that Islam could not easily expand in the hostile Meccan atmosphere.

Muhammad began to seek other places in Arabia for his new religion and community.

Muhammad's Night Journey, Ascent, and Other Miracles: Many versions of Muhammad's early life associate miracles with him that have become part of popular Muslim piety. Muhammad is said to have fed all the workers in Medina from a handful of dates and dissolved a rock with his saliva. Probably the most famous and completely elaborated miracle is Muhammad's night ride from Mecca to Jerusalem on the back of a marvelous mount called Buraq, and his ascent from Jerusalem into heaven to the throne of God. This story became part of a collection of stories about Jerusalem known as *Fadail al-Quds* (The Virtues of Jerusalem). The journey is supposed to have taken place in one night. From an early date, Muslim authorities differed in their reaction to the story, some contending that it was only a vision or spiritual journey, others that it was a physical journey. All authorities link the story to sura 17:1. Later versions of the Night Journey and the Ascent (*Miraj*, "ladder," possibly linked to Jacob's Ladder in the Bible) exhibit parallels with Jewish and Christian ascent stories. Many scholars see this tradition as influential on Dante Alighieri's *Commedia* (The Divine Comedy). Most Muslims do not regard a belief in miracles associated with Muhammad as necessary to the faith.

The Hijra: After twelve years of preaching and recruiting new followers to his religion, Muhammad had failed to stem the growing animosity of the Meccan establishment, so he turned to other venues for his message. He seems to have tried to move to other towns within the Meccan confederation, the most prominent being Taif. Finally he met a delegation from the city of Medina, ancient Yathrib, who invited him to come to their city both for his message and for his skills as a mediator. During the negotiation period from 621 to 622, the main outlines of Muhammad's role probably were worked out. Codified later in a collection of agreements known generally as the Constitution of Medina, Muhammad and his followers became part of the political construct of the city. Muhammad was to be the arbiter of all disputes in the city, which was divided not only between Arabs and Jews but also within each of the groups over limited agricultural resources. Muhammad recognized the legitimate autonomy of both Muslims and Jews and declared them to be one community. The Constitution of Medina anticipates many of the later patterns of relationships between Muslims and the People of the Book: Jews, Christians and, later, Zoroastrians.

Most of the Meccan followers of Muhammad who could leave preceded Muhammad to Medina. Muhammad and Abu Bakr were the last to leave after an attempt on Muhammad's life by a coalition representing most of the tribes. The Meccans pursued Muhammad and Abu Bakr, who hid in a cave until the raiding party passed. According to the biographies, a spider spun a web over the entrance, deceiving the Meccan pursuers. When Muhammad arrived in Medina around September 22, 622, he and his followers were aided by those Medinans who had converted earlier. These, and later all Medinan converts to Islam, were called Helpers (*ansar*), while those who made the migration with Muhammad, and later all Meccan Muslims, came to be known as the Emmigrants (*Muhajirun*), a distinction that perpetuated the pre-Islamic South Arab–North Arab dichotomy in later political disputes. Arrayed against him in Medina were tribes of Jews and their Arab allies, who seemed to control major areas of the Medinese economy. Medina had tribes of Jews, tribes of Arabs, but mostly tribes of both Jews and Arabs. All of these elements of the city were in conflict, and it was Muhammad's task to turn them into one community and fend off Meccan military attacks.

The Establishment of the Community at Medina: While Muhammad had been placed in the center of the politics of Medina, his followers were living off the charity of the Helpers. As part of a plan to resist and defeat Meccan economic and military strength and to provide sustenance for his Muslims, Muhammad instituted a series of raids on Meccan trade caravans. The first raid took place in a month in which there was a kind of truce that was, nevertheless, tied to pagan practices and Meccan interests. The rich booty from the raid partly allayed the unease among some of his followers about the timing of the raid, and sura 2:217 settled the issue. This raid led to a retaliation by the Meccans, who were defeated at the Battle of Badr, the first Muslim military victory. Badr attracted attention in Arabia to Muhammad and his skill as a military leader, and more groups began to ally themselves with him and become, at least nominally, Muslim. The continued Muslim threat led the Meccans to launch another offensive in 624 or 625. The forces met near a hill called Uhud, and in spite of early Muslim successes, the Meccans succeeded in wounding Muhammad and forcing the Muslim force to flee and regroup on the hill. Many have regarded this battle as the first Muslim defeat. In reality, the Meccans were unable to follow up on their advantage and did not succeed in getting rid of Muhammad and the Muslim threat. The Meccans made one last attempt to defeat Muhammad by besieging the city of Medina. But Muhammad had fortified its exposed flank with a trench, hence the battle was called the Battle of the Trench. Unable to succeed or lure enough forces into defecting, they had to withdraw. This last effort marks the end of Meccan domination of western Arabia, and by January 630, the Muslims had conquered Mecca and established Islamic worship around the Kaaba.

Muhammad's battles with the Meccans were directly related to his expanding influence in western Arabia. More and more tribes joined him and became Muslim, at least nominally. But there were groups both in Medina and in the surrounding areas that offered open or covert resistance. Some of the leading Jewish tribes, but not all of the Jews, openly opposed Muhammad and were expelled from the city, still leaving a number of individual Jews. Some of the Arabs who had converted to Islam secretly aided Muhammad's enemies and are soundly condemned in the Qur'an. Khaybar, a fortified Jewish city, was the center of military resistance to Muhammad, and Muhammad conquered it in 628. The defeated inhabitants were allowed to remain on their land by paying an annual capitulation tax of half of the annual harvest, but they were allowed to retain their religion and community structure. This is a continuation of the principles of the Constitution of Medina and forms, along with other similar actions, a basis for Muslim treatment of subject peoples when the Islamic empire formed after the death of Muhammad.

The End of Muhammad's Career: In 630, Muhammad had been so successful as a religious leader and a general that he was able to march into Mecca virtually unopposed. By this time, the basic formation of Islam as a religion had taken place. The rites of the five daily prayers (*salat*) had been instituted, and the direction of prayer fixed toward the Kaaba in Mecca. Muslims were supposed to pay a portion of the surplus of their wealth as charity (*Zakat*), and the earlier twenty-four-hour fast of Ashura, parallel to the Jewish Yom Kippur fast, had been replaced by the month-long daylight fast of Ramadan (*Sawm*). The testimony of faith (*Shahada*) had probably grown out of oaths of fealty to Muhammad and his religion. But the one institution, the annual pilgrimage to Mecca (*Hajj*) was not instituted fully until March of 632, when Muhammad performed a model pilgrimage around a cleansed Kaaba, setting the pattern for all future Muslims to do so once in their lives. After what became known as the Farewell Pilgrimage, Muhammad

became ill and died in June of 632 in the arms of his favorite wife, Aisha, the daughter of Abu Bakr. After some confusion, Muhammad was buried in Aisha's apartment. Many had expected Muhammad to live until the Day of Judgment, and Muhammad had not provided a successor. Muslim doctrine holds that he is the last of God's prophets and can have no true successor, but a series of temporal successors, called caliphs, starting with Abu Bakr, carried on the task of expanding what Muhammad had built.

Muhammad in Muslim Piety: Muhammad's life is a model for Muslims to follow. His words and actions, codified in Islamic law, form a precedent (*Sunna*) against which any act can be judged. Unlike Christian views of Jesus, Muhammad is viewed as only human, not divine. He is held to have been guided by God, and a minority contends that Muhammad's human propensity toward sin was removed from him. Some Muslims regard Muhammad as the locus of special miracles (*Karamat*) or blessings that are thought to originate with God. In some areas of the world, Muslims celebrate Muhammad's birthday (*Mawlid*) with elaborate festivities. Feasting, parades, fairs, and other entertainments accompany recitations of Muhammad's life and deeds, often in poetic form set to music. For some, the recitation of those poems actually invokes Muhammad's presence and his attendant blessings. Such views and practices are vigorously condemned by those who find no quranic basis for the celebration and regard it as an innovation in the religion. All Muslims, however, are brought up to love and revere the Prophet, so that slights to him or mockery made of him are often regarded as more serious in the popular imagination than more serious theological deviations.

Western Views of Muhammad: Until modern times, Western views of Muhammad have, with rare exceptions, been hostile. The tendencies of Islamic biographies to portray Muhammad as a spiritual parallel to various prophets, including Jesus, have been seized on by Western polemicists to say that Muhammad was merely a deceiver, and even the Antichrist. This bias is so pervasive that the Western reader must be cautioned about finding it in much material available in Western languages. Another favorite theme for Western writers has been the number of Muhammad's wives. Often cited as an indication of Muhammad's worldly excess, such views are entirely absent from even the most extreme ascetic Muslim writers and are a product of the Christian celibate tradition. Some recent Western biographies deny that we can know the historical Muhammad and contend that all of his biography is a hagiographic fiction. *See also* Islam.

Muhammad, Elijah (1897–1975), leader of the Nation of Islam. A disciple of Marcus Garvey and Wallace Fard, he advocated Islam and black separatism. *See also* African Americans (North America), new religions among; Nation of Islam.

Muhammad, Wallace D. (b. Warith Deen Muhammad, 1933), son of Elijah Muhammad and founder of the American Muslim Mission, an interracial sect with ties to Sunni Islam. *See also* African Americans (North America), new religions among; American Muslim Mission; World Community of Islam.

Muhammadiyah, (moo-ham'ma-dee'yuh; Indonesian, "the way of Muhammad"), the largest and oldest modernist Islamic organization in Indonesia. Its theology combines modernism, i.e., individual interpretation of scripture, with fundamentalism. Muhammadiyah seeks to purify Islam by eliminating mysticism, saint cults, and other practices not mandated by Muhammad. Two significant achievements are the development of leadership roles for women and the provision of advanced theological instruction for lay Muslims.

Muhammadiyah also runs theological and secular schools, hospitals, and women's and youth organizations. The organization's nonpolitical character enabled it to survive the Dutch colonial period and since then to adapt to the changing political contexts of independent Indonesia. *See also* Southeast Asian Islands, new religions in.

Mujahidin. *See* Mujahidun.

Mujahidun (moo-ja-hid-oon'; Arab., "those who undertake jihad"), contemporary Muslim activists engaged in the struggle to resanctify Islamic society. Various groups appropriate the name, for example, the Afghani rebels fighting Soviet influence in the late 1980s.

mujo (moo-joh; Jap., "impermanence"), a key concept brought into Japan by Buddhism. All things are radically impermanent, and the recognition of that fact helps decrease one's attachments. In some parts of the tradition, the "feeling" of *mujo* was tantamount to Buddhist enlightenment. *See also* enlightenment; samadhi.

Mu-kyokai (moo-kyoh-kai; Jap., "no-church"), Japanese Christian movement beginning around the turn of the twentieth century that rejects denominational and institutional forms, focuses on independent Bible study groups, and emphasizes personal religious experience and honest work. Led by Uchimura Kanzo (1861–1930), Mu-kyokai Christians have sought a Japanese form of Christianity free from foreign structures. *See also* Japan, new religions in.

Mu-lien (moo-leein; Chin. *Maudgalyayana*), Buddha's disciple and subject of popular tales that recount his journey to hell to rescue his mother.

Mulid. *See* Mawlid al-Nabi.

mulla (Arab., "master"), a Muslim title for local clergy among the religious leaders of the Ithna Ashari Shia.

mumin (moo'min; Arab., "believer"), one who holds the articles of Islamic faith (*iman*). "Mumim" is often distinguished in Islamic discourse from "Muslim." *See also* iman; Muslim.

munafiq (moo-na'fik; Arab., "backslider," "hypocrite"), a term in Islam for those who say they accept Islam but fail to live up to their obligations. Referring originally to some converts in Medina, the *munafiqun* (pl.) are seen in the quranic cosmology as particularly dangerous because their feigned belief constitutes a threat to the stability of the Muslim community. Early Muslim theologians (*mutakallimun*) and jurists (*fuqaha*) debated extensively whether ultimately a munafiq was a believer (*mumin*) or an unbeliever (*kafir*). *See also* heresy; kafir; ridda; shirk.

munmyo. *See* Shrine to Culture.

Mun Sonmyong. *See* Moon, Sun Myung.

Munsu Posal. *See* Buddhas and Bodhisattvas (Korea).

muqri. *See* Qur'an recitation.

murid (moo-reed'; Arab., "aspirant"), a novice of a Sufi order, disciple of a *shaykh*.

Murjiite. *See* Postponers.

murti (moor'tih; Skt., "material form"), Indic term for anything with definite shape or limits. Mediating invisible realities to normal perception, *murtis* represent gods, demons, souls, mantras (sacred utterances), *brahman* (ultimate reality) or Buddha-nature in literature, ritual, meditation, paintings, sculptures, and icons. A murti can be a stone, tree, book, picture, teacher, or imagined image; commonly it is a multiple-armed human figure holding weapons, gestures, and postures of esoteric meanings. Sacralized murtis embody that which they represent and reside in shrines, temples, or homes for blessings and protection.

Murukan (moor'oo-guhn), ancient Tamil deity, also called Ceyon, Cevvel, and "the Red"; he is the prototype of masculine prowess and youthful beauty. First mentioned in "Cankam" poetry of the first millennium, he was identified with Skanda-Kumara, son of Shiva and the goddess Parvati. Husband to Devasena, "the Army of the gods," he also marries a Tamil bride, Valliyamman. Murukan rides the peacock. His spear destroys ignorance. He defeats the demon Cur/Surapadma, cut down in the form of a mango tree in the sea.

Muses, in Greek mythology, the nine beautiful daughters of Zeus and Mnemosyne (Memory): Calliope, Clio, Erato, Euterpe, Melpomene, Polyhymnia, Terpsichore, Thalia, and Urania. They sang and danced at the gods' festivals. Throughout antiquity they were celebrated as the inspirational deities of literature, poetry, music, dance, and all intellectual endeavors.

Music Square Church. *See* Jesus people.

Muslim (moos'lim; Arab., "one who submits"), one who submits to the will of Allah (God). As distinct from the term *mumin*, which refers to one who holds the Islamic faith, *Muslim* denotes one who submits to the will of Allah and to the practice of Islam in daily life. *See also* Dar al-Islam; mumin; umma.

Muslim Brotherhood, the oldest, most popular and influential movement in the contemporary Islamic resurgence. Founded in 1928 in Egypt by Hasan al-Banna, the organization gained broad grassroots appeal through its advocacy of simple Islamic life, careful organization in small cells of family units, and concern with all aspects of social organization, including education and health, legal, and financial services. Having abandoned the revolutionary activities that have kept the group technically illegal since the 1950s, the Brotherhood now participates in Egyptian elections through other political parties. Active Brotherhood branches exist throughout the Arab world.

Mutakallim (moo-ta-kal'lim; Arab., "Muslim theologian"), one who practices the religious science of *kalam* and investigates the fundamentals of religion using dialectical reasoning. *See also* kalam; usul al-din.

Mutazila (moo-uh-ta'zi-luh; Arab.), a rational school of theology in Islam. It was first connected with the names of Wasil ibn Ata (d. 748) and Amr ibn Ubayd (d. 761), who taught in the city of Basra, Iraq. A second group of Mutazilites flourished in Baghdad. Each group had its successive disciples and distinctive, subtle differences on points of doctrine. The controversial issue that led them to isolate themselves (Arab. *itazala;* hence the name Mutazila) from other theologians was whether the grave sinner was to be considered a believer or an unbeliever? Wasil's answer was that the grave sinner was neither a believer nor an unbeliever but was in an intermediate position: a reprobate. By ca. 900, the Mutazila—who referred to themselves as "The People of Justice and Unicity"—had come to express their doctrine in five fundamental principles, affirming (1) the unicity of God, (2) God's justice, (3) God's commitment to carrying out His threats of punishment to the wicked and promises of reward to the faithful, (4) that the grave sinner is neither a believer nor an unbeliever, but in "an intermediate position," and (5) commanding the good and forbidding the evil.

Discussion of the first principle logically led the Mutazilites to deny that God has essential attributes and affirm that God is living, all-knowing, all-powerful, willing, speaking, etc., in virtue of his essence. Consequently, the Qur'an is not uncreated, as mainline theologians held, but created. The principle of God's justice led them to reject the doctrine of predestination and affirm human free will and an individual's power over one's actions. Furthermore, the adherence of the Mutazila to human free will and personal responsibility and accountability, and to the fifth principle (above) led them to espouse the political view that a sinful caliph should be deposed, and if he resists then rebellion against him is lawful and so is killing him.

The Mutazilite doctrine of the created Qur'an was upheld by three Abbasid caliphs: al-Mamun, al-Mutasim, and al-Wathiq (who ruled in succession from 813 to 847). They attempted to enforce Mutazilite doctrine on society by compelling the leading religious thinkers to subscribe to it. Resistance led to an inquisition, which caused many uncompromising scholars suffering and imprisonment. The most famous example is Ahmad ibn Hanbal (d. 855). This episode ended when al-Mutawakkil succeeded to the caliphate in 847; persecution then was reversed and traditionalism restored. The Mutazila were weakened but continued to produce great scholars such as Abd al-Jabbar (d. 1025) and al-Zamakhshari (d. 1144). Although Mutazilism seemed to collapse by the time the Mongols sacked Baghdad in 1258, Mutazilite doctrines (with the exception of their doctrine regarding the caliphate/imamate) were adopted by the Zaydiyya branch of the Shia, which flourished in Yemen, where it still survives. Although the Mutazilites are often characterized as heterodox thinkers, their attempt to place Islamic religious belief on a rational basis in conjunction with revelation has found some support among twentieth-century Muslim intellectuals. *See also* kalam.

Mu T'ien-tzu chuan (moo teein-tsoo juhahn; Chin., "Account of Emperor Mu"), an anonymous historical romance about the travels of Emperor Mu, considered to be the earliest piece of Chinese fiction. The original text (probably written ca. 300 B.C.) covered the journeys to the four corners of the kingdom, but the only extant section is on the western journey. The best-known passage is the emperor's meeting with the goddess called Queen Mother of the West (Hsi Wang-mu), with whom he exchanges verses and to whom he pledges his vassalage. *See also* Hsi Wang-mu.

mutilation, various operations performed on the human body for ritual purposes, including expiation, mourning, initiation, and asceticism. Sometimes mutilation is a mark of social and religious status. *See also* body; circumcision; clitoridectomy; flagellation; infibulation; Kanphata yogins; lip piercing, lip plug; ordeal; penile bloodletting; subincision.

Mycenaean religion, the religion of mainland Greece and Aegean, with the exception of Crete, during the Late Bronze Age (ca. 1500–1100 B.C.). It is known chiefly from archaeological remains, from texts written in Linear B (the oldest surviving form of the Greek language, first successfully deciphered in 1952), and from scholarly reconstructions out of later forms of Greek religion.

While clearly a form of Indo-European religion, Mycenaean religion closely parallels aspects of contemporary ancient Near Eastern religion, most particularly in its focus on sacred kingship and on the palace as a prime religious center. The goddess-centered religion of the earlier Minoan period (ca. 3000–1200 B.C.) has been replaced by a male-dominated pantheon, although the religious iconography largely remains Minoan in character. *See also* Greek religion; Indo-European religion.

Myoe (myoh-ee; 1173–1232), Japanese Buddhist cleric famous for his attempts to revive Kegon teachings by combining them with Tantric practices. He was renowned for his ascetic life-style, his desire to travel to India to visit Buddhist sites, and his criticisms of Honen's Pure Land movement. Among his works is a dream diary. *See also* Honen; Kegon school.

mystagogy (Gk. *mystagogia*, "initiation" or "instruction"), a technical term used by Hellenistic mystery religions to refer to their secret rites of initiation. Mystagogy was used by early Christians for the introduction of catechumens to baptism and the Eucharist, the details of which were kept hidden from those who were not baptized. Toward the end of the fourth century, the explanation of the liturgy took the distinctive form of mystagogical homilies that were delivered privately to the neophytes following baptism. *See also* catechumen; disciplina arcani.

mystery (Gk. *mysterion*, "secret"), that concerning which one must be silent.

In Greek religious usage, as in the Eleusinian Mysteries, the term *mysterion* meant the secret words and ceremonies taught to initiates who were then forbidden to speak of them to outsiders. The same rule was found in later mystery cults of the Greco-Roman era. Aristotle (d. ca 322 B.C.) speaks of the initiates as "suffering" or undergoing emotional experiences, rather than acquiring information or learning in the narrowly cognitive sense.

In New Testament Greek *mysterion* is given a new meaning by Paul (Romans 16:25) to describe the risen Christ. Mystery was subsequently reapplied more narrowly to the basic Christian rituals—initiatory baptism and the Eucharist. The philosophical-theological meaning of mystery, as something cognitive but paradoxical, begins with Alexandrian Christians such as Clement and Origen (ca. 200). In this speculative sense, mystery comes to mean supernatural or suprarational information imparted by God to the human mind. *See also* mystagogy; mystery religions.

mystery play, medieval Christian dramatization of a biblical narrative. Plays were often grouped together and performed in cycles by laypersons in the vernacular.

mystery religions, secret cults in the Mediterranean world during the Greco-Roman period.

In spite of their numerous differences, these cults are discussed together because they represented a similar form of religion. Commonly originating in ancient tribal and perhaps even fertility rituals, the mystery religions emphasized salvation for individuals who decided, through personal choice, to be initiated into the secret rites of certain gods or goddesses in order to feel close to each other and to the divine.

General Characteristics: In contrast to the official, public religions, in which people were expected to show outward allegiance to the divine, the mystery religions manifested inwardness and privacy of worship. Those who participated in these private religions ordinarily shared, as well, in the public festivities (with music, dance, parades, processions, sacrifices, and rituals of purification). The initiates took vows of silence to ensure that the holy secrets revealed in the private ceremonies would not be divulged to profane outsiders, and as a result comparatively little is known about specific features of these ceremonies. In descriptions of the Eleusinian Mysteries it is said, in general, that the private ceremonies included "things recited," "things shown," and "things performed," and presumably such observances may have been typical of other mystery religions as well. Usually a sacred meal was shared by those initiated into the mysteries. At least some of the participants in the secret ceremonies claimed to have undergone an extraordinary experience that could be described as death and rebirth.

Greek Mystery Religions: The mystery religions celebrated in ancient Greece included the Eleusinian Mysteries, the Andanian Mysteries, and the Mysteries of Dionysos, as well as the Mysteries of the Kabeiroi (or Cabiri, the great gods) at Samothrace. The most influential of the Greek mystery religions were the Eleusinian Mysteries, observed at Eleusis near Athens and devoted to the worship of Demeter, the "grain mother," and her dying and rising daughter Kore, the "maiden." From early times a public, civic agricultural cult at Eleusis glorified the fertility and life of grain; the later Eleusinian Mysteries used similar rituals to celebrate the transformed lives of people. The Mysteries of Andania in the southwestern Peloponnesus were dedicated to Demeter, Hermes, Apollo Karneios, Hagne, and the great gods. The Mysteries of Dionysos were apparently as diverse as this Greek god of animal maleness, wine, drama, and ecstasy. Ancient sources portrayed the followers of Dionysos sometimes participating in his wild power with mad abandon; sometimes indulging themselves in the sexual libertinism of the Bacchanalia or in more domesticated sexuality; and at other times enjoying the Dionysian pleasures of eating, drinking, and drama. Among the Orphics the wilder side of Dionysian worship was rejected, and the practice of tearing flesh and consuming it raw became the original transgression for those who wished to live the life of purity and Dionysian bliss.

Mystery Religions of Middle Eastern Origin: During Hellenistic and Roman times mystery religions with roots in the Middle East became increasingly popular among people of the Mediterranean world. Often colorful and exotic in character, these mystery religions advocated the worship of the Great Mother Cybele and Attis from Asia Minor, the Egyptian deities Isis and Osiris, and a Roman adaptation of the Persian deity Mithra, as well as the Syrian goddess and the slain youth Adonis, and other deities.

The mysteries of the Great Mother and her dying paramour Attis developed from the fierce religious traditions of Phrygia and rose into prominence in the Roman world after the Great Mother was formally welcomed into Rome in 204 B.C. These mysteries were renowned for unusual festivals, such as the *taurobolium* (Lat.), or ritual bath in the blood of a sacrificed bull, and flamboyant followers, such as the *galli*, or self-made eunuchs in transvestite garb. The Greco-Roman mysteries of Isis and Osiris (or Osiris-Apis, "Sarapis," Osiris joined with the Apis bull) are not to be equated with classical Egyptian mystery plays of succession and funerary rituals of mummification. The Greco-Roman mysteries are best known from the vivid account of Apuleius, who provided a detailed portrayal of the preliminary festivities as well as a guarded description of the private rite of initiation as an experience of darkness, death, and perhaps also rebirth. Devotion to Mithras ultimately derived from Persian religion, but the mysteries of Mithras developed within the context of the Roman Empire into a mystery religion with astronomical and astrological interests.

The Mystery Religions and Early Christianity: Ancient and modern interpreters have tried to account for the obvious similarities between the mystery religions and early Christianity in several ways. Some modern scholars have maintained that the mystery religions and early Christianity were dependent upon each other, and that Christianity in particular borrowed from the mysteries. Balanced interpretations avoid simplistic conclusions about dependence and acknowledge the parallel development of the mysteries and Christianity. The mysteries and early Christianity were Greco-Roman religions, and as such they often addressed similar social and religious needs and offered their devotees similar ways of salvation and transformation. *See also* Dionysos; Eleusinian Mysteries; Mithraism; Orphism.

mysticism. Although etymologically related to the notion of *mysteria* found in the mystery religions of the Greek world, known only to initiates (*mystai*), and later applied to Neoplatonic conceptions of nonverbal contemplation and early Christian understandings of the deeper meanings of scriptural revelation, the term has come to mean a variety of things. Most modern meanings are linked by the assumption that the term refers to a special, immediate (though not necessarily unmediated), metanormal, and usually though not always transcendental experience in which ordinary epistemological, logical, and ontological categories are challenged, if not transcended.

No single definition of the term can cover its multiplicity of uses. The common definition that locates the concept in "the desire for unity with God" is flawed, because not all theistic mystics would accept this characterization of their activity and intentions, e.g., most medieval Jewish mystics (*kabbalists*) would reject this description, while religions such as Buddhism have no God with whom to become unified. Buddhism denies the ontological existence of a "self" thus making the notion of union between a self and God, or the loss of self in God, the traditional meaning of *unio mystica*, altogether anachronistic. Again, so-called nature mystics do not seek union with God, but blissful integration with nature. Thus, rather than erroneously seeking one monolithic definition, it appears best to recognize the diversity of experiences, doctrines, communities, and teachers identified as mystical—bound together by "family resemblances," i.e., some aspects in common, some very different, all bearing an emphasis on the experiential element in knowing, on what philosophers call "knowledge by acquaintance" rather than "knowledge by description," and the transcendence of more ordinary categories of knowing during such experiential states. At the same time, the ultimate reality with which mystics of diverse traditions become acquainted appears not to be a single object, at least not insofar as their reports and descriptions mean anything at all.

Language and Description: It is customary to identify mysticism with ineffability. Most mystics, across traditions, agree that at the ultimate level their experience is indescribable and transcends exact linguistic formulation. However, as evidenced by the libraries of mystical writings, individual mystics and mystical traditions do not altogether eschew language. They employ language in a variety of ways—in prayer, teaching, magical acts, scriptural interpretation, metaphysical descriptions, poetry, biography, aphorisms, autobiography, magic, ascent texts, and as techniques of meditation and transformation—all of which indicate that language is not altogether alien to or inimical for mystical purposes. The exact view of how language fits within and works upon the mystical journey varies from tradition to tradition, probably finding its most negative evaluation in various Neoplatonic streams of Christian mysticism, and certain broad currents in Hindu and Buddhist teaching, and its most positive evaluation in Jewish kabbalah.

"Common Core" Claims: For the past century, in particular since the pioneering work of American philosopher William James in his classic *Varieties of Religious Experience* (1902), many students of mysticism have sought to identify a "common core" of attributes that would identify experiences as authentically mystical. One will find such lists, in some form or other, in the work of such distinguished scholars as Evelyn Underhill, Walter Stace, and R. C. Zaehner, among many others. These lists usually are variations of James's original effort in which he identified mystical experience as possessing four basic characteristics: ineffability, a noetic quality, transiency, passivity. While these terms individuate certain forms of experience as mystical, they are not sufficient in every instance because not all mystical experiences contain all four, and more important, these characteristics, on close review, turn out to be vague. James and the others who follow his lead are here misled by the surface grammar of the mystical reports they study. What appear to be similar-sounding descriptions are not similar descriptions and do *not* indicate the same experience because language is itself contextual and words have meaning only in contexts. The same words— *beautiful, sublime, ultimate reality, ineffable, paradoxical, joyful, transcending all empirical content*—can apply and have been applied to more than one object. The nature of the experience, the nature of the referent, and the comparability of various claims are not assured by this seemingly common verbal presence alone.

Choosing descriptions of mystic experience out of their total context does not provide grounds for their comparability but rather severs all grounds of intelligibility, for it empties the chosen phrases, terms, and descriptions of definite meaning. This logical-semantic problem plagues all the attempts that various scholars, from William James on, have made to provide a common phenomenological description of mystical experience. Thus, such efforts, such lists of putatively common elements, turn out not to establish anything like a common core to all mystical experiences.

Epistemology of Mystical Experience: In most treatments of mysticism, it is assumed that there is a common, transdenominational, transcultural X, which lies at the center of mystical experience. All, or at least most, mystics are said to experience this X. Transcending biology, culture, history, language, religious authority, and tradition, mystics are seen as directly and unmediatedly experiencing the reality beyond all appearances. Only after their peak experiences, returning to their earthbound habitats, their native historic and religious communities, do they find the need to label, describe, and interpret their experiences. Then they can only employ the language, symbols, and theology of their own religious traditions. This postexperiential activity, now situated within particular historic and doctrinal contexts, alone accounts for the wide diversity of mystical reports and the dissimilarity of mystical doctrines and traditions.

This epistemic model has been strongly challenged by Steven T. Katz and others, who argue that there are no pure (i.e., unmediated) experiences. Neither mystical experience nor more ordinary forms of experience give any indication, or any grounds for believing, that they are unmediated. All experience is processed through, organized by, and makes itself available in extremely complex epistemological ways. The notion of unmediated experience seems, if not self-contradictory, at best empty. This epistemological fact seems to be true, because of the sorts of beings humans are, even with regard to the experiences of those ultimate objects of concern with which mystics have intercourse. This mediated aspect of all experience seems an inescapable feature of any epistemological inquiry, including the inquiry into mysticism, which has to be properly acknowledged if any investigation of experience, including mystical experience, is to get very far.

A proper evaluation of mediation leads to the recognition that in order to understand mysticism, one must not just study the reports of the mystic after the experiential event but must acknowledge that the experience itself as well as the form in which it is reported is shaped by concepts that the mystic brings to, and which shape, his or her experience. For example, the Hindu mystic does not have an experience of X that is then described in the familiar language and symbols of Hinduism, but rather the mystic has a Hindu experience, i.e., an experience that is not an unmediated experience of X but is itself the preformed, at least partially, anticipated Hindu experience of brahman. Again, the Christian mystic does not experience some unidentified reality, which the mystic then conveniently labels God, but rather has the at least partially prefigured Christian experiences of God, or Jesus, or the like. The significance of these considerations is that the forms of consciousness that the mystic brings to experience set structured and limiting parameters on what the experience will be, i.e., on what will be experienced, and rule out in advance what is "inexperienceable" in the particular context. For example, the nature of the Christian mystic's premystical consciousness informs the mystical consciousness such that he or she experiences the mystic reality in terms of Jesus, the Trinity, or a personal God, rather than in terms some nonpersonal entity or state. Furthermore, close attention must be paid to the organic changes in ideology and historical development that specific traditions undergo, and how these changes affect the mystical experiences of mystics in each tradition. This process of differentiation of mystical experience into the patterns and symbols of established religious communities is experiential, and does not take place only in the postexperiential process of reporting and interpreting the experience itself: it is at work before, during, and after the experience.

Mysticism and Religious Traditions: Mysticism is usually depicted as an autonomous realm of experience that uneasily fits in with more traditional and widespread religious beliefs, practices, and communities. The mystic is portrayed as that rare soul whose life soars above dogma and community, leaving the sober majority behind to its mechanical, if irrelevant, religious teachings and practices. Moreover, it is claimed, at the exalted level of the mystic experience, the specificity of given religious systems is transcended in a sense of absolute oneness that is common to all true mystics. All true seekers come to know—to feel—the sameness that is the ultimately real. Tragically, the mystic must descend from this height and then, caught up again in tradition and history, space and time, he must express what is truly inexpressible in the inadequate symbols and syntax of a particular faith community.

This common understanding, however, is as suspect as it is widespread, for it may well be a fundamental error to juxtapose the mystic and the tradition, the mystic individual and the socioreligious environment. In order to understand mysticism it is necessary to ground the mystic in context so that one comes to realize the necessary connection between the mystic's way and the mystic's goal; the mystic's problematic and the mystic's solution to this problematic; the mystic's intentions and the mystic's actual experiences.

Mystical experiences are the result of traversing the mystical ways, whatever specific way one happens to follow. What one reads, learns, knows, intends, and experiences along the path creates to at least some degree the anticipated experience made manifest. There is an intimate, even necessary, connection between the mystical and religious texts studied and assimilated, the mystical experience had, and the mystical experience reported. In each mystical tradition, as in each of the larger religious communities in which the mystical traditions inhere, there is an inherited theological-mystical education that is built upon certain agreed sources. For this reason the proper, detailed study of mysticism must be historicized, localized, and contextualized. This means that the significance of such central phenomena as the role of religious education, the nature of mystical texts and their peculiar forms of interpretation, the status of meditation and its diverse explanations and contexts, the function of a mystical teacher and guide, the implications of tradition and religious law, and the role of mystical communities, among many other subjects, must all be taken into account in deciphering the nature of particular mystical experiences. *See also* Catholicism (mysticism); empiricism; Hinduism (mysticism); Judaism (mysticism); meditation; religion, philosophy of; religious language; Sufism.

myth. Myth is a much misunderstood and misused word that requires a precise definition. A myth is a story that is transmitted orally; has a beginning, a middle, and an end; and narrates the deeds of superhuman beings. Superhuman beings can do things humans cannot do; they need not have qualities or properties of human beings. They may, for example, be formless spirits that affect the lives of human beings or other superhuman beings.

No story about superhuman beings, no myth. Fiction is not myth even though it may be about superhuman beings. The assertion "That is just a myth," meaning "That is false, unreal, or imaginary," is a misuse of the word, even though myths may be false or imaginary, depending

upon the theory one adopts for explaining myths.

Most scholars agree that we cannot take the existence and actions of superhuman beings literally. Once scholars agree on this the meaning of myths becomes problematic; this leads to the need for a theory that will explain their meaning.

Theories of Myth: There are six major theories of myth.

Historical Theory: This theory explains myth by tracing its history. It often looks for the first appearance of a myth and then attempts to describe the myth's development through history. The meaning of a myth is its history. This approach is highly dependent upon philological methods of study. The basic problem with this theory is its assumption that meaning (semantics) is essentially historical. The theory, if true, is limited, since it would work best in cultures that have produced written texts that contain the history of particular myths.

Rationalist Theory: This theory is also known as the "intellectualist" theory. Its basic premise is that myths are attempts to explain the world and humans' experience of the world. Thus, myths are similar to modern scientific theories. The difference is that mythical accounts of the world are false. Scholars who use this theory of myth emphasize that to say myths are false explanations of the world does not entail that those who believe in myths are irrational. A theory may well be false yet rational as an attempt at explanation. The history of Western science, for example, includes numerous theories that have been shown to be false, yet, one does not on this account conclude that this history is a history of irrationality. One problem of this theory is that it does not provide an adequate answer to why societies, including Western society, persist in believing what is false.

Another version of this theory avoids this problem. This version agrees that myths are attempts to explain the world, but it does not conclude that such explanations are false. According to this version the concepts "true" and "false" are relative to a particular culture's worldview. Furthermore, what is real and what is unreal is given meaning in particular languages. Thus, the truth value of myth is relative to the particular culture in which it is found. The basic problem with this version is that it seems to be self-contradictory. By asserting its truth for all cultures, relativism becomes the only proposition that is not relative to a specific culture and language.

Functionalist Theory: This theory is the most

popular; it is well known in anthropology, psychology, and sociology. It has been called the essential theory of the social sciences. If one wants to discover the meaning of a myth one must look for its use. The meaning of a myth is found in what the myth does. Myths function to satisfy essential needs of societies and individuals. This function also explains why myths persist. Although there is no agreement on what the basic needs are, scholars have attempted to demonstrate that the needs are biological, psychological, sociological, or a combination of all three. The problem with this theory is the vagueness of the term *need* and the logic of the premises that are used in the theory.

Symbolic Theory: This theory is often tied to the functional theory of myth. It denies that myths are false attempts to explain the world. In fact, myths are not explanations of anything. They are symbolic representations of abstract meanings, psychological repressions, complex collective structures, metaphysical archetypes, or a transcendent reality that is often defined as "wholly other" or "the Sacred." The basic assumption in all of these variations on the theme that myths are symbolic is that myths have a hidden meaning that must be deciphered or decoded. The task, then, is to disclose this hidden meaning. The problem with this theory is that it does not explain why societies and individuals persist in speaking in a coded language. This problem becomes more troublesome when one remembers that the people who use this coded language are not aware of the real meaning of myth, since this meaning remains hidden.

Scholars often use myth as a symbolic representation of social structures. Thus, if one has a set of myths from a culture, one should be able to deduce the social structure from them. This would be particularly valuable for societies no longer living. Myths do use geographical places, kinship terms, and the like in unfolding the story. Great caution, however, must be used in reading myths as maps of a social terrain, since they often depict the reverse of the actual social structure of the society in which they are found.

Structuralist Theory: The structuralist theory of myth usually denies that myths are explanations or false descriptions of the world. It also denies that myths function to satisfy needs. Structural studies of myth are indebted to developments in modern linguistics. Thus, just as the history of the English language is not equivalent to its meaning, the meaning of a myth is not equivalent to its history. Myths are cognitive structures through which people think. The task, then, is to explain the basic structure of myths, to show the logical system on which myths are based. This system is usually described as a system of relations that are oppositional or binary. The emphasis is on describing the various oppositional relations that the elements of a myth enter into. It is this syntax that constitutes the structure of myths. Thus, the meanings of myths are not to be found on the surface but in the set of oppositional relations that constitute the logic of the myths.

The problems with this theory are similar to those found in approaches to myth as symbolic representations. Structuralist theories of myth obviously view myths as having hidden meanings. Furthermore, the meanings of myths are often described as identical with their structure. If this is true it would be a unique feature of myths. Many scholars doubt that this is the case, since in linguistics, syntax (structure) may well be necessary for producing a meaningful sentence, but syntax and semantics are not identical. For example, "Green ideas sleep furiously" is a well-formed sentence, syntactically, but it is meaningless as an utterance in common English. Structuralist approaches to myth will have to demonstrate why this is not the case in the language of myth. Although the use of linguistic models in the study of myth has been quite useful, and the stress on the relations of elements in myth rather than on the elements themselves is an important correction, the meaning of myth remains illusive. What is needed is a well-formed semantic theory of myth that can use structuralism as its base.

Eclectic Approaches: Eclectic approaches to myth are really not theories of myth, since these approaches deny that there is a single theory of myth that can be used for explaining all myths. Myths are complex. Some may be attempts to explain, others may satisfy certain human needs, symbolize something, consist of binary structures, or communicate hidden meanings.

The basic problem is knowing how to go about selecting the proper method for explaining a particular myth. This decision is not an empirical one, since the meaning of a myth does not rest on its surface, or else there would not be widely different approaches to the study of myth. Finally, how does one avoid incoherence given the fact that the various theories of myth are often incompatible if not contradictory?

Myth and Ritual: At one time many scholars thought that myth was the libretto for ritual. Myth was "the thing said" over "the thing done." This approach to myth became known as the Myth-Ritual school, and was popular for a time in the early twentieth century. If true, this approach to myth would have been very helpful in reconstructing rituals for societies no longer living. Given the vast corpus of myths from many cultures, this approach to myth is false. Most myths cannot be explained as the libretto for a ritual.

Myth and rituals do have one characteristic in common: the actions of superhuman beings. This does not mean that a ritual is an imitation or the acting out of a particular myth. The opposition of human and superhuman beings is the essential characteristic for defining myths in all cultures: no superhuman beings, no myths. **See also** All-Father; All-Mother; androgyny; antediluvian/postdiluvian; anthropogony; Changing Woman; chaos; cosmogony; cosmology; Coyote; creation out of nothing; culture hero; death; descent to the underworld; divine combat; Dreaming, the; Earth Diver; Earthmother; egg, cosmic; emanation; emergence; etiology; flood stories; folklore; golden age; high god; invulnerability; islands of the blessed; journey to the otherworld; legend; master/mistress of the animals; monsters; Mother Earth; Mother Goddess; motif; oral tradition; Orpheus stories in traditional religions; paradise; rainbow snake; religious themes in the literature of traditional societies; ritual; saga; separation of the sexes (mythic theme); sky; storytelling; tasks, heroic; tests, heroic; trickster; twin myth; vagina dentata; world parents.

ABC E

GHI L

M N OPQ

RSTUV

WXY & Z

Naas (nah's; from Heb. *nahash*, "serpent"), one of the three revered original principles according to Gnostic groups such as the Naassenes. *See also* Gnosticism.

Naassene Hymn (nah-seen'), a Gnostic text that describes Christ as a redeemer who descends to save the imprisoned soul and reveal secret knowledge. *See also* Gnosticism.

Nabataean religion. The Nabataeans, originally a nomadic people from Arabia, first appeared at Petra, in southern Jordan, in 312 B.C. The beginning of their history remains obscure. When the first Ptolemies of Egypt began to stimulate the exploration of Arabia, the Nabataeans were already present; they had abandoned their local dialect and accepted Aramaic as their official language. From their kingdom of Petra some tribes moved northward subduing the land as far as Damascus. These Nabataeans detached themselves from their Arabian origins and worshiped the deities who secured their new agricultural life. This explains the coexistence in the inscriptions of two religious trends: the cult of Dushara, the national god of caravaners, patron deity of the royal family, styled the god "who separates night from day," and the cult of Baal-shamem (Aram., "the Lord of Heaven"), with whom the Nabataeans became acquainted while living on the fertile soil of southern Syria. At the spacious sanctuary dedicated to Baal-shamem at Sia, a hallowed place in the Hauran, the god's epithet was "Lord of the World." Dionysos was revered and his gifts cherished in the Hauran, while Shaial qaum ("the One who leads the people") is described in the inscriptions of the nomads as the god "who does not drink wine." Another major god is Qos, who had his sanctuary at Khirbet Tannur, in Transjordan, where he was represented holding in his left hand a multibranched thunderbolt, the symbol of the lord of rain. Among the female deities of the pantheon the most prominent was Allat, the goddess of ancient Arabia, who assumed indistinctly the features of the Greek Athena and of the Phoenician Astarte.

Paramount among the Nabataeans was the cult of altars and of dressed stones (*baetyls*), a ritual that to some extent was carried out by all the Semites in the Middle East. The popularity of the baetyl as the residence of the deity remained alive until Christian times. Nabataean burial customs stand out in the entire ancient Middle East: the Nabataeans practiced both direct and second burials. The outstanding monuments of Petra and of Hejaz bear witness to Nabataean funerary ceremonies.

naga (nah'guh; Skt., "snake"), in Hinduism, a supernatural being in the form of a snake, or half human, half snake, that resides in the nether regions.

Nag Hammadi Library (nahg hah-mah'dee), a collection of ancient codices discovered in 1945 at Nag Hammadi in Egypt that has permanently and significantly altered the shape of knowledge about Gnosticism. This is because the library is an assembly of primary texts. Preserved in Coptic, the language of Christian North Africa, it has also expanded awareness of the use of the Coptic language and its dialects and contributed to knowledge about ancient libraries.

The library contains fifty-three texts, some of which are duplicates (indicating their importance). Among the non-Gnostic texts are a translation of a fragment of Plato's *Republic* and three Hermetic texts: *Asclepius*, the *Discourse on the Eighth and Ninth*, and the *Prayer of Thanksgiving*. The *Sentence of Sextus* and the *Teachings of Silvanus* are Christian wisdom texts. Different genres in the Gnostic texts include: apocrypha (three versions of *The Apocryphon of John*), apocalypses (*The Apocalypse of Peter; Zostrianos; Marsanes; Allogenes*); revelation dialogues (*The Sophia of Jesus Christ*); and Gospels (the *Gospel of Truth;* the *Gospel of Philip;* the *Gospel of Thomas*). There are also non-Christian Gnostic texts: the *Paraphrase of Shem;* the *Apocalypse of Adam;* and *Eugnostos the Blessed.*

The diverse forms of Gnosticism are reflected in the variety of texts. Scholars have provisionally identified two main branches: Sethianism and Valentinianism. Future investigations will test the adequacy of these categorizations. Scholarship on the texts has moved away from the question of Gnostic origins toward assessment of the phenomenon of Gnosticism itself. The prominent role of female figures and imagery in Gnostic texts continues to be explored. Previous assumptions are being questioned: Are the texts best described as ascetic? Is location within philosophical systems the best way to study Gnostic texts? What weight should be given to ritual and magical elements in many texts? *See also* Christianity; Gnosticism; Hermetism; Valentinianism.

Nakatomi clan (nah-kah-toh-mee), the most important lineage of Japanese Shinto priests. A branch, the Fujiwara, politically dominated the

Ritsuryo period (645–1191) by marrying their daughters to emperors. *See also* Ritsuryo; Shinto.

Nalanda (nah-lahn'dah), famous Buddhist monastic university in northeastern India that flourished from the fifth through the twelfth centuries.

Namdhari (nahm-dah'rih), the largest and most prominent among the modern Sikh sects. Namdharis trace their origins to Balak Singh (1799–1862), but it was only under his charismatic successor, Ram Singh (1815–85), that they acquired considerable popularity, particularly in the rural areas of the Punjab. Ram Singh insisted that his disciples follow a strict religious regimen. They were to rise at three in the morning and spend the early hours remembering the divine name and readings from the Sikh scriptures. Unlike orthodox Sikhs, Namdharis recognize a line of living Gurus and the present head of the sect is Baba Jagjit Singh. *See also* Sikhism.

naming rituals, public conferring of a name, usually on newborn children but also at important changes in an individual's status (e.g., entering a religious community, being crowned king or queen). *See also* Christianity (life cycle); Hindu domestic ritual; Islam (festal cycle); Islam (life cycle).

Nammalvar (nam-ahl'vahr; Tamil, "our alvar," "our saint"; ca. ninth century), title given to Sathakopa, the most important Tamil poet-saint of the South Indian Shrivaishnava tradition. By the eleventh century, the Shrivaishnavas considered his four Tamil poems (especially the *Tiruvaymoli*) to be "revealed" and equivalent to the four Sanskrit Vedas. Images of Nammalvar are installed in almost all Shrivaishnava temples and selections from his poems are recited daily in temple and domestic worship. In liturgy and theology, Nammalvar is considered to be a mediator between Vishnu and the devotee. *See also* Alvar; Shrivaishnavism; Tiruvaymoli.

Nanak (nahn'uhk; 1469–1538), first Guru of the Sikhs. Nanak was born in the Punjab, India. After his childhood in the village of Talvandi he took employment as a steward in Sultanpur Lodhi. There he underwent a mystical experience and spent several years visiting the sacred places of the Hindus and Muslims. Returning to the Punjab he took up residence in the village of Kartarpur, where he attracted a growing number of disciples. These disciples or Sikhs (lit., Hindi

from Skt., "disciples" or "learners") were the beginnings of the Sikh community (Panth).

Although he was born a Hindu, the message Nanak preached transcended differences between Hindus and Muslims; however, it is not merely a blend of the two. Nanak's doctrine was drawn largely from Hindu origins, the principal source being the Sant tradition of northern India, with some features coming from the Nath tradition. During its subsequent history the Panth has progressively undergone changes that have resulted in the Sikhs becoming clearly distinct from Hindu society.

Nanak taught that religion must be practiced within a person, the only true pilgrimage center being the human heart. Humankind seeks freedom from the bonds of transmigration. For Nanak the path to liberation was the divine Name and following that path could be achieved through the discipline of *nam simran*, or "meditation on the Name."

The *nam*, or "Name," is a summary term that comprises the whole nature of Akal Purukh, or God, gathering into a single word all that constitutes the divine. Akal Purukh, through the "voice" of the mystical Guru uttered within, communicates the *Shabad* or "Word" to the receptive person. That person, ideally in the quiet of the early morning, applies the mind to meditation on the Name. By means of regular reflection on the nature and being of Akal Purukh, one's eyes will be increasingly opened to the wonder and the peace all around.

In the world around and within, the devout will perceive a divine order. Bringing oneself into ever closer harmony with this divine order, one will perform the deeds that carry a person progressively to higher and yet higher levels of spiritual perception. Eventually one attains to *Sach Khand*, "the Realm of Truth," the condition surpassing all human telling. There the spirit unites with Akal Purukh and in that union of perfect peace the last shackles of transmigration finally fall away. Although Sikhism has acquired many other features in succeeding centuries it has neither lost nor modified Nanak's teaching concerning the divine Name as the way of liberation. *See also* Akal Purukh; Sikhism; Sikhism (authoritative texts).

Nandi (nahn'dee; Skt., "happy"), a humpbacked bull on which the Hindu god Shiva rides. Women who wish to conceive touch his statue in Shiva temples. *See also* Shiva.

Nara (nah-rah), the first permanent capital of Japan (located on the southern part of Honshu) and the period of rule from that city (710–784). During this period, Buddhist doctrines and images symbolized imperial power. *See also* Japan, Confucianism in; Japanese religion; Nara schools; Todaiji.

Nara schools (Jap. *Nanto rokushu*), six Japanese Buddhist academic traditions typical of the study groups formed during the Nara period (710–784) at Todaiji: Hosso, Sanron, Kegon, Risshu, Kusha, and Jojitsu. Although they are called schools, they were different from the exclusive traditions that emerged in later Japanese Buddhism. The last two groups were based on Abhidharma texts. The Kusha (based on Vasubandhu's *Abhidharmakosa*) and the Jojitsu (based on Harivarman's *Tattvasiddhi*) were never independent groups. The *Abhidharmakosa* has traditionally been studied by monks from a variety of Japanese schools. *See also* Hosso school; Kegon school; Risshu; Sanron school; Todaiji.

Narayana (nah-rah'yuh-nuh; Skt., "the place where humans go"), a complex Hindu deity, identified in different traditions as a manifestation of either Vishnu, Krishna, Brahma, or Purusha (the primordial human). In some traditions, Narayana is another name for the archaic deity Vasudeva, variously identified with Vishnu and with Vishnu's manifestation, Krishna. Within Vaishnavism, Narayana is that form of Vishnu that lies sleeping on the serpent Sesha, enclosed within his own uterine waters, emanating the cosmos, enclosing and pervading all beings. *See also* avatar; cosmogony; Vishnu.

Narcissos (from Gk. *narke*, "numbness," "stupor"), in Greek mythology a youth who so loved only his own reflection that he pined away, died, and was turned into the flower that bears his name.

naskh *See* abrogation.

nastika (nah'sti-kuh; Skt., "atheist," "nihilist," lit., "one who says 'it is not'"), Hindu term for the "unorthodox," those who reject the authority of the Vedas, the existence of God, or the doctrine of rebirth; frequently applied in philosophical texts to Buddhists, Jains, and the Charvakas (Materialists).

Nataraja (nuh-tuh-rah'juh; Skt., "king of dancers"), an epithet of Shiva, the dancing Hindu god of creation and destruction. More widespread as a visual image than as a subject in texts, it acquired definitive form in Tamil Nadu during the eleventh century. Typically, a Nataraja icon, in bronze, depicts Shiva with four arms dancing on a sprawling dwarf (personifying ignorance) and surrounded by an aureole of flames. A whirring drum in his upper right hand connotes the first emanation of life while a flame in his upper left heralds final conflagration. *See also* Shiva.

Nath (naht; Hindi, "master"), a tradition of yogis still widespread throughout North India. With origins as early as the eighth century, this heterogeneous group including both ascetics and householders flourished in early Indo-Islamic times, ca. 1100 to 1400. Many Naths are distinguishable by thick earrings worn in holes pierced through their ear cartilages. Nath ascetics with intact cartilages are known as *aughars*. Frequently identifying their ultimate object of worship as Shiva, Naths have nevertheless differed from most other Shaivites in looking to a physically conceived immortality, which can lead them to hatha-yogic and alchemical practice. Great magical feats are told of the legendary "nine Naths." Of these, different lists usually include Matsyendranath, Jalandharnath, Kaniphanath, Dharamnath, Gopi Chand, and, most notably, Gorakhnath. *See also* Shaivism; Shiva.

National Protection Buddhism (Kor. *Hoguk Pulgyo*), the term used to describe the relationship between Buddhism and the ruling houses of the Korean Three Kingdoms, Unified Silla, Koryo, and, to a lesser extent, the Choson periods. Buddhism had from the period of its introduction (late fourth century) appealed to the ruling houses of the Korean peninsula as a teaching that could ritually cure disease and ward off disasters. Buddhist institutions, ceremonies, and clergy were understood as aids to those ruling houses in the protection and even advancement of their political systems.

In Koguryo and Paekche, Buddhist monks were at the complete service of the state, acting as ambassadors, spies, and officiants at national ceremonies for the protection of the king and state in the forms of the P'algwanhoe (Eight Vow Assembly) and Paekkojwahoe (Hundred Seat Assembly). In Silla, monks proclaimed the Silla to be the land of previous Buddhas and apotheosized Silla monarchs as incarnations of the Righteous King that precedes the advent of Maitreya, the Buddha of the Future. Silla monks also served as recruiters of military forces and led monk troops into battle. They inspired the creation of the nine-story pagoda at Hwangyongsa to repel Koguryo invaders and establish Silla as the center of the nine surrounding nations. In Unified Silla, monks conducted protecting *dharma* assemblies for the recitation of Buddhist texts based on the teachings of the *Golden Light Sutra*, the *Sutra on Benevolent Kings*, and the *Lotus Sutra* to cure illnesses, stop astronomical irregularities and provincial revolts, and celebrate the protection of tutelary dragon spirits. Temples, like Pulguksa and the Sokkuram Grotto, were built to ward off invasions and make Unified Silla the object of worship by the surrounding nations.

In the Koryo kingdom, the Wang royal family had similar temples and pagodas built to guarantee the safety of the peninsula. It also established a system of national protection temples (*p'ibo myongdang*), which were meant to correct the faults in geomantic power and ensure the prosperity and power of the Koryo state. Buddhists served as teachers and chaplains of the royal family and held large dharma assemblies reciting Buddhist texts for the edification and protection of the state.

With the advent of the Choson period (1392), though, Buddhism was disestablished and replaced by Neo-Confucian orthodoxy. Buddhist institutions and clergy remained, but they were no longer assured the financial and moral support of the government. Despite oppression and even disdain, Buddhists continued to seek some place within the Choson kingdom polity, but their services to the state were reduced to serving in guerrilla bands during the Japanese and Manchu invasions or acting as country tutors in classical Chinese literature. *See also* Buddhas and Bodhisattvas (Korea); Comprehensive Buddhism; geomancy; Uich'on; Uisang; Uiyon.

National Shaman (Kor. *kungmu*), a Korean public office and a title created in the late Koryo period (918–1392) and maintained in the Choson period (1392–1910). Despite Confucian protests against the appointment of a national shaman, Koryo and Choson kings continued to appoint them and give them access to the royal family. They were maintained at government expense and their duties were to assist the monarch and his family with domestic problems. Choson-period national shamans also combined with their manipulation of the spirits a deep knowledge of folk herbal medicine and thus acted as doctors as well as mediums. This practical aspect is what probably assured their employment in the palace in spite of continued Confucian criticism. *See also* kut; shamanism.

National Teacher (Kor. *kuksa*), a Korean Buddhist office and title from the seventh to the early twentieth centuries. The *kuksa* was the chief adviser of the government on Buddhist affairs and nominally the head of the Buddhist church, though he exercised no direct control over individual clergy or monasteries. Appointment to this office was by royal prerogative and, with the establishment of an examination system for Buddhist clergy in the Koryo period, those chosen for this office were usually drawn from the ranks of the examination monks. The kuksa also served as a court counselor for national rituals, ordinations, the study of monks abroad, and the awarding of ranks to monks, and many came from royal and aristocratic families. This office was paired with another office, that of royal preceptor (*wangsa*), an honorary title given monks of unusual ability and reputation. *See also* National Protection Buddhism.

Nation of Islam, American religion founded in 1930 and also known as the Lost-Found Nation of Islam.

Origins: A yard-goods peddler whose background remains unknown Wallace Fard (Master Wali Farrad Muhammad) organized the Nation of Islam in Detroit during the Depression. Fard claimed to be a prophet from Mecca, bearing a message from Allah to black Americans. His teachings rested on the concept that Islam was the only true religion of African Americans, who in reality were descendants of "Asiatic black men," the original human race who had brought civilization to the world. Fard established the University of Islam to provide classes on his philosophy and Islamic tradition. He also organized the Fruit of Islam, a paramilitary group of young men, trained in the use of weapons and charged with the protection of the Nation of Islam and its members.

Growth: In 1934 Fard disappeared, and Elijah Muhammad (formerly Elijah Poole, 1897–1975) assumed leadership. Under Muhammad's guidance the movement slowly began to gain converts, finally booming in membership in the 1950s and 1960s, much due to the recruiting efforts of Malcolm X, a converted ex-convict who had become the group's major spokesperson. Muhammad focused on economic advancement, encouraging followers to open and patronize black businesses. He insisted that followers adhere to strict Islamic dietary, dress, and social codes. He demanded abstinence from alcohol and drugs. Many disciples changed their names, adopting Arabic or African names. Muhammad also proposed complete separation of blacks and whites and the establishment of a black state in the southern United States. In Muhammad's view, whites were an inferior race, devils created by experiments in genetic muta-tion conducted by an evil scientist, Mr. Yacub. God had permitted whites to dominate people of African heritage as a test of the black race. He predicted that African Americans would soon reclaim their power, ending white domination and Christianity.

Much of the controversy surrounding the Na-tion of Islam concerns Elijah Muhammad's in-terpretation of Islam. Critics charged that he distorted the teachings of Allah and the Qur'an. Malcolm X, after returning from a trip to Mecca, came to question the authenticity of Elijah Muhammad's teachings and the legitimacy of his leadership. Despite Malcolm X's defection and opposition from other public figures, the group survived and gained converts.

Division: Upon the death of Elijah Muhammad in 1975, the Nation of Islam split into several fac-tions. One, led by Elijah Muhammad's son Wal-lace (b. 1933), and known as the American Muslim Mission, admitted whites to its ranks. Affiliated with Sunni Islam, the sect promotes cooperative capitalism and secured business contracts from the United States government. Another faction, led by Minister Louis Farrakhan (a.k.a. Abdul Haleem Farrakhan; b. Louis Eugene Wolcott), seeks to preserve the orthodox teach-ings of Elijah Muhammad and is highly critical of the United States government. Farrakhan pro-motes black enterprise and has called for a war against drugs and poverty. Demanding repara-tions by the American government to people of African descent for their ancestors' sacrifices while enslaved, he is also an advocate of black separatism who envisions African Americans re-turning to Africa. *See also* African Americans (North America), new religions among; Fard, Wal-lace D.; Farrakhan, Louis; Muhammad, Elijah; Muhammad, Wallace D.; North America, Islam in.

Native American Church, the name under which the peyote religion was incorporated in 1918. Use of the small spineless cactus, *Lophophora williamsii*, called *peyotl* by the ancient Aztec, has been dated as early as 8000 B.C. and reported sporadically from A.D. 1600 to 1918. Historical reports place its origin in religion among the Huichol and Tarahumara peoples in Mexico, and it has spread to most western Amerindian tribes in the United States and south-central Canada.

Peyotists, not infrequently participants in other Christian or native religions, accept a monotheistic deity shaped by Christian trinitar-ian terms and invoke peyote as the mediator of human-divine interaction. The noncreedal faith is supported by personal psychic experiences of the supernatural, induced by the hallucinogenic cactus, and its ethical norms, based on Christian moral values, demanding intra-group generos-ity, chastity, family solidarity, and abstinence from alcohol.

The principal ceremony is an all-night ritual and consists of praying, singing, preaching, tes-timonies, and ingesting pieces of the peyote cac-tus. Sponsored by a person troubled about health or a case of illness in the family, this ritual is believed to offer curative powers of both botanical and spiritual medicines.

While peyote theology and ethics are satu-rated with Christian ideology and represent the acceptance of new social values, the rituals that remain the core of the cult are entirely native. *See also* Native Americans (North America), new re-ligions among.

Native Americans (Central and South America), new religions among, a set of religions, sects, and movements whose origins lie at the intersection of indigenous beliefs and practices and the colo-nizing cultures or evangelizing religions of West-ern Europe.

Categories: In Latin America, defining an in-digenous religious movement as "new" is itself a religious, often polemical, and sometimes a legal act. After campaigns to introduce Chris-tianity and enforce orthodoxy among the native population failed, seventeenth-century Catholic bishops such as Pena Montenegro of Quito used loopholes in canon law to avoid prosecuting na-tives for heresy. In this legal maneuver, most tra-ditional aspects of native religion were redefined as *costumbre* ("custom"), leaving only the stan-dard Catholic aspects under the legal definition of religion. Unless they explicitly defied the au-thority of church or king, emerging religious movements could, thereby, be ignored as mere custom.

This state of affairs endured until the twenti-eth century, when liberal governments through-out Latin America opened tribal areas to Protestant missions. In order to recognize tribal peoples as a legitimately non-Christian mission field, Protestants redefined native Catholicism as "Christo-paganism," a Catholic veneer over an eclectic remnant of animistic superstition. Viewed through this lens, all of native Christian-ity became a new religion. Without resorting to confessional definitions of what does or does not constitute a "new" religious movement, it is possible only to survey the patterns of religions that emerged from contact, focusing on those movements that in some way defined them-selves as new.

Andean Traditions: Even before Christianity entered the scene, native religions throughout the Americas had well-established ways of recognizing religious diversity and periodic change. In the Andes, for example, distinct ethnic groups, each with their own religious songs and dances, were paired as *hanan* ("dominant") and *hurin* ("subordinate"). At the *pachacuti,* or turning of each solar age, groups that had been in the dominant hanan position became hurin, and those that had been in the subjugated hurin position became hanan. It was within this interpretive framework that Andeans made sense of the Christian invasion.

In the sixteenth-century Conquest, Christ and the European Christians were believed to have risen from the hurin into the hanan position, deposing Inca religion back into the hurin position. The deposed Inca, thereby, was paired with the European Christ as a kind of hurin "Indian Christ" who would return to the dominant hanan position at the turning of the next world age. This was the origin of the *Incarri* ("Inca king") myth that provided a general formula for new religions. Every few decades, native prophetic movements would emerge, claiming to embody the return of the ancient Inca dead and their deities. These movements were accommodative because in order to share in the return, the prophets not only preserved the religious markers of their present native, hurin identity, but also took over prominent symbols of the hanan, or white Christian, identity.

The earliest example of an Andean Christian movement patterned on the hanan/hurin scheme is the Taqui Onqoy, or "sickness chant," movement of the 1560s. In response to a devastating smallpox epidemic, the Quechua prophet Juan Chocne announced the turning of world ages and took on the name of San Juan. Two of his associates took the names Santa Maria and Santa Maria Magdalena. Although it was these Christian saints who were to preside over the return of the native world, they called on their followers to gather on the mountaintops, the ancient sacred places of the Andean people. There they were to dance in the new age by performing the Taqui Onqoy, or sickness dance. All dancers were to abandon the dress and food associated with European Christianity. The hurin was becoming hanan, and those who continued to identify with the powerful Europeans would become animals and would walk upside-down when the reversal of fortunes occurred.

In 1742 Juan Santos, an Andean Quechua who had studied under the Jesuits, appeared on the Rio Shimaqui in eastern Peru and announced himself to be the returning Inca king. He claimed that at the moment God created the sun he also created the Inca Huaina Capac to embody the sun. Because this creation took place on the second day after the death of Jesus, Huaina Capac was actually the Holy Spirit, the replacement of Jesus. Seeing the great injustices committed by the Spanish, God had decided to destroy the earth with fire and had sent Juan Santos, Huaina Capac's heir, to punish the Spanish and to restore the divine law. To his Christian names, Juan Santos, he added the messianic title Atahualpa, the name of Huaina Capac's son, the last Inca ruler, whose decapitated body is believed to be regenerating underground and who will return at the end of time.

The Amuesha, Campa, Shipibo, Conibo, and other east Peruvian tribes heeded the call to revolt, and the Spanish presence was wiped out in their territories. Juan Santos was never apprehended by the Spanish opposition. His tomb became the site of Campa worship, in which a new tunic was laid out annually for 150 years in the messianic hope that Juan Santos would return to wear it.

After the 1780 revolt of Tupac Amaru II, all symbols associated with the Inca king cult, such as the *maskaypacha* (Inca crown), were strictly outlawed. But less visible messianic movements have continued in the Andes until the present time. After tribal reservations were dissolved under Colombian law early in the twentieth century, Paez prophet Manuel Quintin Lame (d. 1967) had a vision of the returning "Indian Christ" that he experienced as a call. According to Lame, Christ had announced that the age of white domination that had begun in 1492 was at an end. The son of a native woman would sit on the throne and whites would become the servants. From 1924 to 1931 the town of Llanogrande, renamed "San Jose de Indias," became a religious center in which Lamista dramas of the native king were performed on major fiestas. In 1931 San Jose de Indias was destroyed by local landowners, and Lame was jailed.

The movement then entered a more clandestine phase that peaked in 1939. On December 31, 1938, Lame declared tribal lands reconstituted. To assist him in governing the new age, he appointed a native government of twelve men modeled on the apostles. In the year that followed, he wrote a third testament that he titled *Thoughts of the Indian Educated in the Colombian Forest.* The book, which combines Paez tribal notions of time and sacrifice with Christian symbols, was intended as a riddle that whites could read but not decipher. Its publication was a shamanic act designed to bring about the definitive end of white rule. The Lamista movement was crushed during the Colombian civil war of the 1940s but was reconstituted shortly after Lame's death. His manuscript continues to be respected by modern Lamistas as "the doctrine and the discipline."

Mesoamerican Traditions: Like the Andes, Mesoamerica also has a long tradition of separatist native/Christian movements roughly based on the turning of world ages in native calendars. In February of 1712 the appearance of the Virgin Mary to Maria Candelaria (Maria Lopez) in Cancuc, Chiapas, triggered a Mayan holy war. The ancient Mayan world was to replace Spanish Christianity, which, in turn, was identified with the Jews. In each town of the region a native vicar, identified as the son of the town's patron saint, replaced Spanish priests. God the Father was to be replaced by the Virgin. The Spanish king was declared dead and three native kings were inaugurated to replace him. When the Spanish army came to put down the revolt, four native women identified with earthquake, lightning, flood, and wind were carried to the river to unleash these elements against the Spanish "Jews" who came to persecute the cult of the Virgin. The Cancuc movement was defeated, but related movements have appeared periodically.

In 1867, for example, a Chamulan Maya girl had a vision of three stones dropping from the sky. The stones were venerated and the girl, Augustina Gomez Chebcheb, was given the titles "Mother of God" and "Santa Lucia." When white priests sought to suppress the cult, a local Mayan prosecuting official, Pedro Diaz Cuscat, exhorted local tribal people to stop venerating white saints. In place of the white Christ, an "Indian Christ" was created by crucifying an eleven-year-old boy named Domingo Gomez Chebcheb. The uprising inspired by this cult was called the War of Santa Rosa.

South American Traditions: Coastal Brazilian tribes also responded to years of Jesuit missionary and colonial presence with new religions, two of which have left little documentation. In Jaguaripe, Bahia, Portuguese immigrants, native Brazilian Indians, and biracial colonists joined in the movement known as *Santidade* ("holiness"). Guided by leaders called "Pope" and "Maria" or "Mother of God," the community expected an imminent cosmic cataclysm. Their worship centered on an unshaped stone, and ritual use of rosaries and crosses augmented the "drinking" of tobacco smoke to induce visions. Jesuit records similarly describe mass migrations among Tupi-Guarani tribes, led by prophets and seeking a "land without evil" to the east. Occasionally analyzed as an indigenous phenomenon, the dating and all other evidence

points to these utopian quests as the result of native/Christian contact.

In the Amazon basin and savannahs the tradition of shamanic contests and spirit journeys provided additional vehicles for the development of new religions. The understanding that spiritual power is a scarce commodity over which tribes compete gave rise to the idea that whites had originally stolen Christian rituals from the Indians. Shamans could recover these stolen songs and dances by journeying directly to heaven in ecstatic flight.

According to Akawaio tribal accounts of the Hallelujah cult, a nineteenth-century Makusi shaman named Bichiwung journeyed to England where he discovered that the whites were deliberately hiding the way to God. Bypassing the missionary, Bichiwung journeyed directly to God's secret home in England through spirit flight. There God gave him medicine, secrets for trading with whites, and extraordinarily productive crops to plant. He also gave him some writing identified as an "Indian Bible" and the spirit chants called "Hallelujah."

As presently practiced, Hallelujah is a body of spirit songs and dances revealed to a succession of prophets during shamanic spirit journeys. Each Hallelujah village is guided by a lifetime leader (*ebulu*) who is assisted by helpers (*baidolu*). Meetings are held in church buildings, but at least some dances are carried out in the open air. Although much of the content of the Hallelujah movement is based in Christianity, it retains a clearly antiforeign bias. Christianity and its wealth are said to have been stolen from native people, and Hallelujah is a way of getting it back. According to one account, God is said to have told the Hallelujah prophet Able to hide certain Hallelujah revelations from the whites so that they would not steal them as they had stolen the English language.

During the same time period, another group of messianic movements emerged, partly in response to widespread debt peonage in the northwest Amazon. A Baniwa shaman named Venancio Kamiko identified himself with "Christu" or Christ and claimed the power to release tribal people from their debts. Like Bichiwung and the Hallelujah prophets, Venancio is said to have made periodic spirit journeys to heaven, where he received revelations. As the movement reached its peak, he prophesied that the white world and all those identified with it would end in a cosmic fire on Saint John's Day (the June solstice) 1858. To escape the conflagration, the Baniwa and neighboring peoples were to abandon their crops and perform continuous dances.

Brazilian troops crushed Venancio Christu's original movement in 1858, but in that same year the dancing spread to the Vaupez River where a Tukano named Alexandre Christu predicted that natives and whites were about to switch places. Evidence of the enduring effects of the movement lie in the fact that stories of Venancio's supernatural contests with later rubber barons and white soldiers continue to be told.

In the mid-twentieth century, the rise of Protestant fundamentalist and pentecostalist missions contributed still more to the emergence of new religions. Missionary preachers called for a complete change of life in preparation for the return of Christ. And they advocated the independent interpretation of the Bible by tribal people. In the process of this biblical interpretation, indigenous visions of the end were almost necessarily combined with those from the book of Revelation. The resulting change of life often took unexpected turns.

In 1956, for example, Ezequiel Ataucuzi Gamonal, a Seventh-Day Adventist convert, had a vision in the village of Picoy in Tarma province, Peru. Ezequiel claimed to have been taken up into the third heaven, where he saw the heavenly father write the "Ten Commandments, the Ten Words of the Covenant" on a blackboard. Ezequiel was commanded to copy the writing on a piece of cardboard, which became a sacred text for the new sect he founded: the Israelitas del Nuevo Pacto Universal. According to the teaching of the Israelitas, the messiah had already been born in Peru. In the earlier stages of the movement the Peruvian jungle was proclaimed as the promised land, and thousands of people left their homes and farms in the sierra and migrated to jungle areas such as the Zamaya valley to wait for the messiah. Later the promised land was reinterpreted as the person of the founder.

The influence of Protestantism on new religious movements extends well beyond the direct converts of Protestant missions, however. After the Wycliff Bible Translators had worked among the Shipibo and Conibo, for example, an itinerant Catholic layman called Hermano Jose Francisco wandered up the Peruvian rivers from Brazil preaching and planting crosses. The new religious movement that emerged as a result of his preaching in the 1970s is called the Cruzada Catolica Apostolica y Evangelica de la Cruz, the name itself combining both Catholic and evangelical elements.

Like evangelical missionaries, the Hermanos de la Cruz, as members call themselves, stress lay interpretation of the Bible, but only of the old Nacar-Colunga Spanish version. Because that translation is no longer preferred by the Catholic Church and is not used by Protestants, it is increasingly difficult to acquire. As a result, white Catholic priests are suspected of hiding the real text of the Bible in order to circulate their own. In addition to the Bible, the Hermanos have a special scripture called the "Hidden Treasure," believed to have been written by the founder himself. Despite their biblicism, the Hermanos de la Cruz have incorporated many elements of native Amazonian religion. In language reminiscent of Ge tribal quests for the land without evil, native people are warned to flee to certain utopian communities in the jungle where the cross is set up in the center of the village. There they expect to escape the cataclysmic judgment of the world and to enjoy fabulous harvests.

Like Venancio Christu, the itinerant Hermano Jose Francisco is identified with Jesus but has many characteristics of a native culture hero. He is said to age and to be reborn with each daily journey of the sun. And he undertakes spirit journeys to heaven at crucial junctures in the liturgical year, such as Christmas Eve.

The religious movements surveyed up to this point have all centered around shamans or prophets who sought the healing of whole societies. But another important cluster of religious movements centers around the healing of individual bodies. In these healing movements the vehicle of religious change is often the traditional practice of integrating recently deceased shamans into the corps of a living shaman's spirit helpers. In addition, folk healers weave elements taken from Euroamerican medicine into their practice. Contemporary shamans from the Quito area, for example, call their mountain spirit helpers on celestial telephones and compare divination by guinea pig entrails to hospital X rays and the sucking out of sorcery to surgery. Upon their deaths these modern healers often gain the status of ancestral curing spirits, and their innovations gain religious authority. Representative of this pattern of healing in the modern period is Jose Gregorio Hernandez, a Catholic surgeon who introduced the microscope to Venezuela and then died in a car accident in 1919. Once dead, he became the center of a spiritualist healing movement that spread throughout Venezuela, Colombia, and Ecuador. In rooms adorned with the symbols of medical science, folk healers draw on shamanistic traditions. But instead of sucking out pathogens in the traditional manner, healers possessed by Jose Gregorio are said to perform a spirit version of modern Western surgery. The practitioners show many of the signs of a new religious group but do not challenge the authority of the Catholic Church. Hence, the Hermano Jose Gregorio can be tolerated as a folk saint. As of 1989 there was even a small altar to the surgeon at the rear of the Santo Domingo Church in Quito.

The new religious movements surveyed have emerged out of certain potential openings for independence in the various religions brought together by the Conquest. This means that in Central and South America, at least, the typology of so-called new religious movements is ambiguous. Prophets such as Juan Santos Atahualpa, Venancio Christu, Alejandro Christu, or Manuel Quintin Lame understood their movements to be new only in the sense that they believed themselves to be inaugurating the prophesied return of the old ways. For them, as for many missionaries, the act of recognizing, or refusing to recognize, the traditional in the novel was itself a religious act. *See also* Maria Candelaria; new religions; Santidade.

Native Americans (North America), new religions among, a variety of efforts to refocus and assert traditional religious understandings of the world and the group's place in it in response to changes in the social and historical situation.

Problems of Definition: Native North Americans typically did not understand religion to be a separate, identifiable entity within their larger culture, but any movement in which claims about the nature of the world and the Native Americans' place in it are a central concern may be considered "religious." These religions are "new" with respect to cultural patterns existing in the group at the time they come into being. Frequently, they identify with an (often idealized) older stage of the culture. But while they resemble the traditional religious system in fundamental ways, it is of more importance that they achieve a new synthesis that revisions life in a changed social and historical environment. The "new" that they advocate is typically not progress toward assimilation.

Because the new religions about which there is information emerged after contact with the Christian West, the question arises of the extent of their dependence on Christian ideas and rituals. Elements reminiscent of Christian teachings are not difficult to find (e.g., Handsome Lake's references to heaven and hell; apocalyptic predictions in Handsome Lake [d. 1815], the Plateau Prophet Dance, and the Ghost Dance; "books" used by Delaware prophets; the use of Bible and cross in some peyote rituals). Handsome Lake reported a conversation with Jesus during one vision, and whether Wovoka (ca. 1856–1932) claimed to be or not, many Indians

and whites thought of him as the messiah. It is important to note, however, that Native Americans typically did not share the European-Americans' assumption about the need for exclusive religious loyalty. Christian elements, as well as other aspects of white culture, could be taken up (sometimes, as in the case of the Plateau Prophet Dance, even before direct contact with whites) into a movement that aimed to revise traditional (i.e., authentically native) culture. Even when Native Americans converted to Christianity, they often appropriated the Old World faith in their own way, so that in some sense a "new" religion resulted. The Yaqui are a good example. Converted by Jesuit missionaries, their church preserves many Catholic elements but weaves them into a ceremonial system that expresses a uniquely Yaqui worldview. Rites are conducted by lay leaders called *maestros;* there are no priests, and the church is not recognized by Rome. Indian Shakers, though they consider themselves a Christian sect, insist they are a distinctly native religion.

Overview: The underlying dynamic in the development of new religions among Native North Americans is the necessity of cultures to adapt to the changing circumstances of their world. New religions tend to arise in times of crisis and generally are motivated by both a sense of deprivation and a desire to achieve specific benefits (e.g., effective medicines, items necessary for sustenance, trade goods).

Most often, the crisis has been associated with the encroachment of European-American culture. The history of individual tribes (e.g., the Delaware prophets) and the fact that the earliest movements were in the East and Southwest suggest that new religions tend to occur when white encroachment is of sufficient duration and intensity to constitute a serious threat to the viability of native cultures.

Most new religions began with the activity of a prophet. Some of these remained the sole or chief leader (Handsome Lake, Kenekuk, Wodziwob of the 1870 Ghost Dance, Wovoka); in other cases there was a succession of prophets, some of which were better known than others (Neolin among the Delaware; Smohalla in the Plateau Prophet Dance). On the other hand, the origin of the peyote religion is traced to visionary experiences of ordinary tribal members. In both cases, however, there are visions that give the movement supernatural sanction. One can also see lines of influence between prophets: Kenekuk's prayersticks resemble those used earlier by Neolin, and there is striking similarity in doctrines among the Prophet Dance and the two Ghost Dances.

The new religions of the postcontact period arose primarily from the need to reassert, redefine, and invigorate traditional cultures threatened by assimilation into a dominant and intrusive foreign culture. But the indigenous tradition was not essentially unchanging until threatened by white colonialism. For example, after the Navajo migrated from their northern homeland and settled in the Four Corners region of the Southwest (ca. 1500), they developed, before direct contact with Europeans, a significant new religious pattern (the nine-night curing chant) as a result of contact with their new neighbors, the Pueblo Indians.

Once established, new religions may become traditional—as in the case of the Longhouse religion—and are themselves subject to change and renewal. Such change may be gradual and not greatly affect the overall thrust of the movement, but circumstances may lead to more dramatic and rapid changes.

Responses to Crises: New religions originate in situations perceived by their followers as a crisis in the life of the group. Generally, the crisis is precipitated by contacts between two cultures. Sometimes the effects are positive; contact opens new possibilities when the old culture is ripe for change. The Yaqui invitation to Jesuit missionaries to work among them and the Navajo gradual adoption of a more settled existence illustrate this pattern.

But mostly the impact is negative. Old worldviews prove unable to explain present conditions, and alternatives have to be found (the Indian Shakers, for example). The influence of white culture resulted in disruptions and pathologies in tribal societies, one of the most notorious being alcohol abuse. The Code of Handsome Lake, for example, begins with a graphic description of the havoc caused in an Iroquois village by a party of drunken men. Handsome Lake's visions were simultaneously the cure of his own alcoholism and the beginning of his prophetic career, and the very first element in his teaching was that the creator was saddened by his people's use of "whisky" (similarly, Delaware prophets; Kenekuk).

As tribes were forced out of their original homelands and, later, confined to reservations, the crisis could be perceived in terms of lost possibilities: to control their own territories, to move about freely for hunting and raiding, and (as fertile lands and major fisheries fell into the hands of whites and animals like beaver and buffalo became increasingly scarce) to provide for their own sustenance. These were important factors in the rise of the 1870 and 1890 Ghost Dances among the Paiute of Nevada and in the

spread of the latter movement throughout the Rockies and Plains (also, Smohalla, who opposed the sale of Indian lands; the Redbird Smith movement among the Cherokee). Tenskwatawa, the Shawnee prophet, was one of those who saw the Native Americans' miserable condition as punishment for their having accepted elements of white culture and advocated a return to primitive purity.

Sometimes the crisis was precipitated by direct and brutal oppression. Thus, attempts to suppress Pueblo religion by floggings and destroying cultic paraphernalia and *kivas* stimulated Pope, a visionary from San Juan Pueblo, to lead an uprising against the Spanish in 1680. Sometimes protection of vested interests is an important concern. For example, in 1801, a Chumash prophet near Santa Barbara reported that the god Chupu had spoken to her promising death to non-Christian Native Americans who submitted to baptism and to Christian Native Americans who did not give gifts to him.

The teachings of new religions commonly harken back to a past era in the people's history. In some cases the intent is to restore a "real" past: after driving the Spanish from New Mexico, the Pueblos quickly destroyed the missions, rebuilt the kivas, and reinstated traditional religious practices. Other teachings anticipate a return to an idealized past. Wovoka promised ghost dancers that when the world was renewed there would be no more whites, game animals would be abundant again, dead Indians would return to life, and people would live the old life in a world free of disease and old age. His admonition that Native Americans live at peace with one another introduced a major modification in traditional values.

Some movements undertake an alteration and refocusing of old traditions. Among reservation Shoshone and Utes, the Sun Dance lost its connections with warfare and hunting and focused, instead, on empowering individuals to embrace native values and live productive lives within their communities. Similarly, elaborate mythologies and rituals centering on peyote are very old in Mexico, and from the American Southwest there is documentary evidence of peyote use in divination as early as 1720. But beginning at the end of the nineteenth century, a transformed peyote religion, incorporating traditional native elements (visions, curing, seeking power through ordeals) and Christian ones (references to Jesus, use of the Bible and symbols like the cross) spread among North American tribes. Peyote rites differ from tribe to tribe and even within tribes, but in general this religion provides believers with a way of affirming their native identity—the focus is "pan-Indian"—and a rationale for living at peace in the wider society.

Some of these movements were of short duration (Spanish attempts to reconquer New Mexico began in 1681, and by 1694 were successful) and others endured (the Longhouse religion of Handsome Lake; the Native American Church, a federation of peyote groups). In some cases the need that stimulated the movement remained, but the new religion proved inadequate to meet it (the failure of apocalyptic promises to materialize was a factor in the rapid decline of the Ghost Dance after 1892) or was overwhelmed by other forces (the Pueblos soon lapsed into fighting among themselves and were unable to maintain a united front against the Spanish). Sometimes the crisis itself was redefined. The negative impact of white encroachment on Native North Americans did not diminish, but after a time the problem was understood less in terms of getting rid of whites and reestablishing the old life and more in terms of maintaining indigenous values and identity over the long haul. The prophet Handsome Lake recognized this need and soon abandoned the apocalyptic in favor of a program geared toward defining authentic Iroquois existence in a changed world; his Longhouse religion remains a force in Iroquois culture down to the present. Where the Ghost Dance survived, its focus became a quest for good health (Shoshone) or guidance for living an upright life (Saskatchewan Sioux). But for the most part, the Ghost Dance was replaced by peyote religion, which emphasized strength for coping over time.

Differing reactions by state and local governments also had an effect on the duration of some of these movements. Handsome Lake received a letter from President Thomas Jefferson in 1802 advising the Iroquois to listen to and follow him, and this enhanced his reputation and strengthened his hand against the opposition he encountered on some reservations. The tragic massacre of Sioux at Wounded Knee in December 1890 convinced some to abandon the Ghost Dance and seems also to have motivated Wovoka to modify his teachings in the direction of ethical admonition. Finally, despite years of persecution and white hysteria over drug use, a series of state laws permitting the ritual use of peyote laid the foundation for the continued existence of the Native American Church. *See also* Black Elk; Delaware prophets; Ghost Dance; Handsome Lake; Indian Shaker Church; Kenekuk; Longhouse religion; Native American Church; new religions; Neolin; North America, new religions in; North America, traditional religions in; Prophet Dance; Smohalla; Wovoka.

nativistic movements, a designation loosely applied to a wide range of religious and social movements that seek to reestablish or continue all or some portion of their indigenous religious beliefs and practices.

The term has enjoyed extended usage in ethnographies and theoretical sociological studies adopting an unstated disdain for nonwhite cultures and their rejection of Eurocentric values or Christianity. Twentieth-century anthropologists have applied the rubric to conquered or colonized tribal peoples undertaking the preservation of their own culture in a conscious, organized fashion, particularly when essential political, economic, and religious changes threaten the traditional identity of the community. In such cases, the movements reportedly will select distinctive elements that especially symbolize an independent or traditional heritage and thereby attempt to recreate the past—living as the ancestors did in order to avoid progress. Some further distinctions are made on the basis of the type of elements selected: magical nativistic movements center their efforts on the perpetuation of religious and symbolic culture, while rational movements preserve or reinstitute social and political structures. As the distinction suggests, scholars may view the former as "irrational flights from reality."

Religious movements that have occasionally been labeled "nativistic" include the cargo cults of New Guinea and the nineteenth-century Native American Ghost Dance. Ethnocentric revivals among the Irish Celts, Pueblos of the southwestern United States, and the Japanese, as well as the American Know Nothing movement, have also been called "nativistic." The pejorative overtones of the term render it useless for modern discussion; it reveals more about the user than about the phenomenon so labeled. *See also* acculturation; Boxer Rebellion; Delaware prophets; Ghost Dance; mission or missionary movements; revitalization movements.

natural law, the Christian belief that God implants in creation a moral law that can be detected by human intelligence apart from revelation.

natural religion, a term used to mark a distinction among religions: natural versus supernatural religions, or natural versus revealed religions. The distinction here is between religious thought that arises from unaided human reason, hence "natural," and that which is dependent on divine revelation. This distinction is often linked to an evolutionary theory that began with natural religion. In most instances, the contrast is used to mark, improperly, evaluative or polemical judgment. *See also* Deism; supernatural religion; typology, classification.

natural theology, the body of theological thinking that derives from the employment of natural human capabilities and knowledge. Traditionally, it has been contrasted with revealed theology. Based upon unassisted human reason and imagination, the very possibility of natural theology is debated based on varying estimates of the extent, power, and reach of natural human capabilities. Within the spectrum of Christian theologies, Roman Catholic and liberal Protestants have held human nature in higher esteem and thus have been more receptive to and supportive of the idea of a natural theology than have conservative Protestants. In some taxonomies of human thinking, natural theology is equated with philosophy of religion. Natural law, arguments for the existence of God, the knowledge of God discernible through the universe, the human soul, human freedom, and immortality are among the topics frequently included in natural theology. In the study of comparative religion, natural theology is a major issue when the religions that claim to be based on revelation (e.g., Christianity, Islam, and Mormonism) are placed alongside others that are not primarily based upon such claims. In contemporary discussions a more dynamic idea of natural theology is being formed in which the distinction between natural and revealed theology is less useful. *See also* natural religion; revelation.

nature-origination (Chin. *hsing-ch'i*), Chinese Huayen Buddhist doctrine articulating how the conditioned mind and phenomenal realm arise from the state of original purity. *See also* Huayen school.

nature worship, the worship of natural forces and objects. Nature worship was often viewed by scholars as the first stage of religion; gods and goddesses of mythology were explained as personified natural phenomena. In recent scholarship, this outdated evolutionism has been rejected in favor of a more cognitive approach, which emphasizes thinking with (rather than about) natural objects and categories. *See also* origin of religion.

Nayanar (nah'yuh-nahr; Tamil, "leader, lord"), a saint in the Tamil Shaiva canon. The sixty-three Nayanars (Tamil pl., Nayanmar) are the early leaders and cult figures of the Tamil Shaiva sect, a Hindu sect localized in the Tamil-speaking area of South India. Along with the Vaishnava Alvars, the Nayanmar were the first saintly personalities venerated in a Hindu *bhakti* (devotional) cult.

Especially revered among the Nayanars are Nanacampantar, Appar, and Cuntaramurtti (ca. 550–750), poets who made pilgrimages to shrines of Shiva and sang hymns to the god. Collectively known as the *Tevaram,* the 796 hymns of the three poet-saints constitute the first seven books of the Tamil Shaiva canonical texts and are sung during temple ritual.

The *Periya Puranam* (The Great History) of Cekkilar (ca. 1135) is the definitive hagiography of the Nayanmar. The list of sixty-three represents a cross-section of Tamil society in the period between 500 and 750, during which time the historical figures among the saints appear to have flourished. Included in the group are kings and farmers, Brahmans and low-caste men, a woman, even a converted Buddhist monk. In contrast to the traditional Hindu hierarchies of caste and gender the saints formed an ideal community of devotees (*atiyar*) of Shiva.

The saints' lives offer powerful examples of the central values of the sect, unswerving devotion to Shiva and acts of service to the god and his devotees, ranging from offering ritual worship to sacrificing one's own life. The veneration of the Nayanmar continues to be an important part of Tamil Shaiva practice. *See also* Shaivism.

Nazarene, Church of the, an indigenous American Protestant denomination, established in 1895, that stands in the Holiness tradition. Its heritage is Wesleyan, a fact best seen in its concern for Christian perfection. Focusing on the moral life, it affirms that spiritual power as a work of grace is available to accomplish entire sanctification (freedom from original sin and a state of total devotion to God). Divine healing is affirmed but alongside medical means. This church had a national membership of 550,000 in 1988. *See also* Holiness churches; perfectionism.

Nazareth, town in southern Israel (Galilee), in the New Testament the home of Jesus.

nazirite (na'zuh-rit; from Heb. *nazir,* "consecrated one"), in Judaism, one dedicated to God by a vow to abstain from intoxicants, haircuts and shaving, and contact with a corpse.

necromancy. 1 Divination by calling up the spirits of the dead. 2 In Christian texts of the medieval period, a general term for sorcery.

needs, religion as a satisfaction of. *See* ideology and religion; religion, explanation of; religion, the study of.

nei-kuan (nay-gwahn; Chin., "inner observation"), a Taoist term denoting meditation methods for envisioning and nourishing the gods residing within the body. *See also* Amitabha; physiological techniques (Taoism).

nei-tan (nay-dahn; Chin., "internal alchemy"), Taoist term for procedures of internalized mystical transformation that use an alchemical vocabulary of refinement. *See also* alchemy; physiological techniques (Taoism).

nembutsu (nem-boo-tsoo; Jap., "invoking the Buddha"), central practice in Japanese Pure Land (Jodoshu, Jodo Shinshu) Buddhism of invoking the Buddha Amida, also called Amitabha, through repetition of the formula *Namu Amida Butsu* ("I take refuge in Amida Buddha") with the hope of rebirth in Amida's Pure Land paradise. *See also* Bodhisattvas; Jodo Shinshu; Jodoshu; Pure Land.

nembutsu odori (nem-boo-tsoo oh-doh-ree; Jap.,"dancing nembutsu"), Japanese joyful dance accompanying the Buddhist chanting of Amida (Amitabha) Buddha's name, reputedly started by the monk Kuya (903–972) and popularized widely by Ippen (1239–89). *See also* Amitabha; Bodhisattvas; Jodo Shinshu; nembutsu; Pure Land.

Neo-Confucianism, an English neologism used to designate the great Northern Sung revival of Confucian learning begun by Chou Tun-i, Chang Tsai, Shao Yung, Ch'eng I, and Ch'eng Hao. Historically divided into the School of Principle (Li-hsueh) and the School of Mind (Hsin-hsueh), Neo-Confucianism was the dominant East Asian religio-philosophic system from the twelfth to the early twentieth century in China, Korea, Japan, and Vietnam. The two greatest figures were Chu Hsi for the School of Principle and Wang Yang-ming for the School of Mind. The Neo-Confucians developed and perfected the earlier Confucian roots of metaphysics, ontology, cosmology, epistemology, ethics, and literary and historical theory. *See also* Chang Tsai; Ch'eng Hao; Ch'eng I; Chin-su lu; Chou Tun-i; Chu Hsi studies (Korea); Confucianism; Hsin-hsueh; Li-hsueh; Shao Yung; Wang Yang-ming.

Neo-Confucianism in Korea. *See* Chu Hsi studies (Korea); Four-Seven Debates; village recluses (Korea); Yi Hwang; Yi Saek; Yi Yulgok.

Neolin (nee'oh-lin), a Native American prophet of the Delaware tribe. Beginning about 1762, he exhorted the Delaware to renounce European trade goods and return to aboriginal customs. In preaching he utilized a chart showing the obstacles by which Europeans had made Native American access to heaven difficult. The Ottawa chief Pontiac appealed to Neolin's teachings to gain support for an attack on the British at Detroit. *See also* Delaware prophets; Native Americans (North America), new religions among; prophecy in traditional religions.

Neo-Manichaeans. *See* Albigensians.

Neo-Orthodoxy, Protestant theological movement after World War I, a reaction against liberal theology. Major emphases include God's transcendence instead of liberalism's focus on God's presence within culture, God's self-revelation rather than human discovery of God in religious experience, and the seriousness of sin as rebellion against God in contrast to liberalism's confidence in overcoming mere ignorance. *See also* Barth, Karl.

Neo-Paganism, an eclectic, decentralized religious movement with more than one hundred thousand adherents in the United States and Canada. Inspired by the pre-Christian nature religions of Europe, Neo-Pagans creatively combine ancient pagan ideas with insights and practices of present-day tribal peoples and romantic ideas drawn from science fiction and fantasy.

Neo-Pagan religions include revivals and reconstructions of Egyptian, Celtic, Norse, and Greek paganism as well as Neo-Pagan Witchcraft (Wicca) and contemporary Goddess religions. Although these groups are diverse, autonomous, and even somewhat anarchistic, they share eight general principles. First, Neo-Pagan groups share a reverence for nature and an emphasis on rituals based on seasonal celebrations—the solstices, equinoxes, solar and lunar rites, planting, fertility, and harvest festivals. Neo-Pagan groups also are polytheistic, believing in a multiplicity of deities and that there are many spiritual pathways to the divine. These groups are pantheistic, seeing deity as immanent and alive in everything, as opposed to transcendent. Sacred space, however, is defined as a particular spot, region, or land, or a place created through ritual. Neo-Paganism considers experience to be more important than belief. The emphasis is on participation and creativity in ritual and a thirst for ecstatic experience. Adherents may use written liturgies, but there are few dogmas and no sacred scripture, prophets or *gurus,* and little proselytizing. Neo-Pagans do share beliefs in reincarnation and goddesses, who are equal with gods, or primary in Goddess religion groups. Finally, Neo-Paganism promotes an ethic of personal responsibility, sometimes expressed as, "An ye harm none do what ye will."

Neo-Pagans have reclaimed the word *pagan,* based on its Latin root *paganus* ("country-dweller"). They regard the common usages of pagan (e.g., "worshiper of false gods," "idolater," "one who is nonreligious") as the sorrowful legacy of Christianity's persecution of pagan beliefs. Like present-day tribal religions, Neo-Pagans seek to attune themselves with the cosmos and the seasonal cycles of nature. Neo-Pagans emphasize oral tradition over revealed scripture and focus on ceremonies for birth, death, initiation, coming of age, and community bonding.

History: Several different political and philosophical traditions helped create the Neo-Pagan movement in the 1960s and 1970s: an awakening to a sense of planetary ecological crisis and a belief that most monotheistic religions place humans above nature, encouraging them to exploit the natural world; the rise of the feminist movement and a search for a spiritual dimension that would include a divine feminine; and certain aspects of the Human Potential movement and the counterculture of the 1960s, in particular the belief in self-actualization and the innate sacredness of the human body and mind. The Neo-Pagan movement has also been influenced by science fiction and fantasy writers.

Several early groups helped establish the philosophical basis of Neo-Paganism. Feraferia, founded by Fred Adams in 1957, was a group with intricate, artistic rituals that advocated a return to a pre-industrial, vegetarian society. The Church of All Worlds, founded by Otter Zell in 1967, was based on Robert Heinlein's vision in the book of the same name, with a dose of the thought of Ayn Rand and Abraham Maslow. The Church of All Worlds became influenced by ecology, tribal religions, and the idea of the Mother Goddess. Zell put forth an idea similar to the Gaia hypothesis several years before the idea became popular through the work of James Lovelock. The Church of the Eternal Source, founded by Harold Moss, revived worship of the ancient Egyptian gods, and the Pagan Way, a loose grouping of groves, provides an entry point for those interested in Wicca. Later these groups were joined and influenced by the explosion of contemporary Goddess spirituality and by the work of feminist activists such as Starhawk.

Neo-Paganism is decentralized and contains hundreds of autonomous groups. Groups and individual members communicate with each other through more than one hundred newsletters, magazines, and computer bulletin boards. There are also scores of festivals and gatherings where different groups and individuals come together to share teachings and rituals. While the tendency toward fierce individualism remains, in the last decade there has been a trend toward more institutionalization, with Neo-Pagans fighting for the same rights guaranteed to other religions. Some Neo-Pagan groups have incorporated and won legal recognition as churches: they have opened seminaries, performed legal marriages, and established nature sanctuaries. A few of the larger and better known Neo-Pagan organizations include The Covenant of the Goddess, Circle Sanctuary, The EarthSpirit Community, The Church of All Worlds, and The Covenant of Unitarian Universalist Pagans (CUUPS), a group of Neo-Pagan congregations and groups operating within Unitarian Universalism. *See also* Asatru; Church of All Worlds; Druids (modern); Goddess religions (contemporary); North America, new religions in; Wicca.

neophyte (nee'oh-fit; Gk., "newborn"), in Late Antique mystery cults and in Christianity, a new initiate, a new convert. *See also* catechumen; rebirth.

Neoplatonism, a school of Greek philosophy in late antiquity whose dominant characteristic is a speculative development of the transcendental and psychologically transformative aspects of Plato's philosophy. Many of its aims and methods are taken up by Jewish, Christian, and Islamic thinkers. Its deductive metaphysics and rationalistic principles surface in modern philosophers from Spinoza to Hegel. The sacred space of the Gothic cathedral is configured by the Neoplatonic metaphysics of light. Connections between different orders of reality and experience owe much to its tradition of allegorical interpretation. The Neoplatonic heritage is rich and, arguably, still alive.

Chief Schools and Figures: The seminal thinker in this diverse and resilient tradition is Plotinus (d. 270). With striking originality, he refashioned ideas inherited from earlier Greek philosophers, expressing them with a new power and clarity. His chief pupil and editor, Porphyry (d. 305), published the *Enneads*, the movement's first and most important body of writings. In the fourth century Iamblichus (d. 326) and the Syrian school articulated both a more conventionally religious and a more rigidly rationalistic version of this revived Platonism, trends that continued during the fifth and sixth centuries in the Athenian school under its most famous heads, Syrianus (d. 437) and Proclus (d. 485). The contemporary Alexandrian school is important for scholarly commentaries on Aristotle's works, especially the logical treatises. Neoplatonic ideas entered the Christian tradition with Augustine and Gregory of Nyssa in the fourth century (through Plotinus and Porphyry); influenced Boethius, Pseudo-Dionysius, Scotus Eriugena (Proclus); permeated medieval thought both through earlier Christian Platonists and the *Theology of Aristotle* (Plotinian writings erroneously ascribed to Aristotle); and spurred the Renaissance Platonic revival.

Basic Ideas: Pagan Neoplatonists shared the Platonic view that philosophy is a way of life, a twofold path in pursuit of goodness and truth. Progress is possible, they believed, only when theory is combined with practice, moral purification with rigorous thought. Transcendental realities are not, ultimately, abstract, for they are accessible to those who experience them. The states of consciousness correspond directly to metaphysical realities, which constitute three levels: the One or Good; the intelligible world of the Forms (the paradigms of material things); and Soul, both cosmic and individual, which straddles the boundary between the intelligible and sensible worlds.

The purpose of human existence is to ascend the hierarchy of being, to achieve ever greater degrees of unity and thus of perfection. A basic principle of Neoplatonism is that each human being is capable of realizing the true self, which transcends the limited empirical ego. This self-transformation begins with meditating on the order and goodness of the external world or by turning within. Because the cosmos is a theophany, or manifestation of God, it can call the soul back to its source "above" or "within." Significantly, the trajectory of this "ascent within" impelled Neoplatonists, notably Plotinus and Augustine, to embark on the deepest explorations of human subjectivity before the modern era. On the question of spiritual methods, some (Plotinus) thought that reasoning and purification were sufficient to awaken the true self; others (Iamblichus, Proclus) thought divine grace, prayer, and theurgy, a form of ritual purification and magic, were necessary for salvation, a position analogous to that of Christians like Augustine.

Mysticism: Realization of the true self culminated in divinization, variously defined. The most extreme examples was, perhaps, Plotinus's doctrine of mystical union with the One. Not surprisingly, most Neoplatonists specified lesser degrees of attainment as the ultimate goal. Plotinus's pagan successors deemphasized mystical union with the One: the highest experience pertained to the intelligible, not to the supreme, sensible world. Similarly, for many Christian Platonists the goal was the celestial-angelic world. Thus, "union with God" could not be the utter emptying of the human self, with the rather too complete divinization envisioned by Meister Eckhart, because such a transformation threatened divine uniqueness and transcendence. Mystical experiences of divine presence animated the various Neoplatonists' dialectical investigations of the problem of divine transcendence and immanence, absence and presence, stimulating both religious and metaphysical solutions.

Doubts about the intelligibility of all discourse and experience are raised by Neoplatonic negative theology—without falling into nihilism. Because the One, or God, is absolutely transcendent, neither language nor thought can grasp its reality. Even the intelligible realm of metaphysical essences transcends rational understanding. Neoplatonism thrives on this fertile tension between a transcendental, realist metaphysics that demands conceptual precision and a mystical spirituality emphasizing ineffability and direct experience. *See also* Bruno, Giordano; Catholicism (mysticism); Dionysius the (pseudo-) Areopagite; Ficino, Marsiglio; Gnosticism; Hermetism; Islamic philosophy; Lull, Raymond; occult, the; Plato; Plotinus; Porphyry; theurgy.

Nephthys (nef'this; Gk., from Egypt., "mistress of the house"), an ancient Egyptian goddess who facilitated the daily rebirth of the sun god, Re. She and her sister Isis brought their brother Osiris back to life. *See also* Isis; Osiris.

Nergal (nuhr'gahl; Sumerian, "Lord of the 'Big City' [the underworld]"), the divine king of the underworld, worshiped principally at Cuthah in northern Babylonia. *See also* Mesopotamian religion.

Nestorian Christianity (China). *See* Nestorianism.

Nestorianism, a Christian movement following the teaching of Nestorius (d. ca. 451), a fifth-century Antiochene monk and Bishop of Constantinople. Known for his oratorical skills and theological interests, Nestorius became a persecutor of heresies upon becoming bishop. As part of his campaign, he delivered a sermon against the use of *Theotokos* (Gk., "bearer of God") as a title for Mary. For Nestorius, Mary might be called *Anthropotokos* ("bearer of the Man") or, better, *Christotokos* ("bearer of Christ"), but she could not be the mother of God, since the divine Logos preexists the incarnation. Such an assertion countered popular piety in which Mary was venerated as the mother of God; it also rankled Cyril of Alexandria and Celestine, the Roman pope, both of whom already harbored suspicions of Constantinople's orthodoxy and ecclesiastical pretensions. A Roman synod condemned Nestorius's teachings in 430, and Cyril launched an offensive against Nestorius, culminating in the Council of Ephesus (431). Nestorius stood squarely in the christological tradition of Antioch, which emphasized the dual natures in Christ. Within this framework, Nestorius legitimately could hold that scriptural references to Jesus' development in wisdom and stature (Luke 2:52) and to his suffering properly apply only to the human nature. Nestorius's motive was to protect the dignity of the divine nature, while insisting on Jesus' full humanity, for redemption of humanity can only be accomplished through a real human being. Nestorius's opponents, however, misrepresented him to mean that Christ was merely an inspired man or that there were two Christs, one divine and one human. Consequently, he was excommunicated at the Council of Ephesus and exiled to Egypt in 436. After the Council of Ephesus, a Nestorian party continued to exist in eastern Syria around the theological school of Ibas of Edessa. Expelled from Edessa in 489, the Nestorians emigrated to Persia. Nestorian churches continued to flourish despite persecution under the Sassanids and the Turkish and Mongol invasions and extended, through missionary efforts, their presence from Arabia to India, Tibet, and China. Since the sixteenth century, several Nestorian churches have reunited with Rome, notably those of Malabar in southern India. In modern times, the Nestorian communities in northern Iraq claimed this territory as their ancestral home, suffering political persecution in their quest for an independent state. In the late twentieth century the Nestorian churches persist largely in the West, especially the United States. *See also* Christology.

Nestorius (d. ca. 451), Syrian Christian theologian, best known for his critique of the veneration of Mary as the "mother of God" (Gk. *Theotokos*).

Nestorius was condemned as a heretic at the Council of Ephesus (431). Syrian Christians who did not accept his banishment formed the Nestorian Church. *See also* Nestorianism; Theotokos.

neti neti (nay'tee nay'tee; Skt., "neither this nor that"), the Hindu Upanishadic doctrine in which absolute reality is said to transcend all categories of experience. *See also* brahman; Upanishads.

New Age movements, the cluster of autonomous groups and related philosophies originating in the 1960s that collectively advocate an expanded notion of human spiritual potential linked with hopes for social and planetary renewal.

Since the 1800s the term *New Age* has been part of the vocabulary of occult and Spiritualist groups, which have optimistically proclaimed an evolving higher consciousness in humankind. The New Age movement revives the trends present in America since the Transcendental movement that began in the mid-1830s, integrating the Hindu concepts of the self and the cosmos and the Western esotericism associated with the ancient wisdom of Egypt or Greece with the modern emphasis on individualism, material success, and simple problem-solving. With the rediscovery of old truths, human society is thought to be on the brink of a new era of spiritual transformation.

The divergent individuals, attitudes, arts, and associations now identified as part of the New Age movement emerged from the counterculture of the 1960s and its fascination with Asian religions and the universalist perspectives on spirituality that challenged the traditional Western monotheisms. Rather than conform to a single creed or follow a single teacher, New Agers cultivate a spirit of experimentation, stitching together a patchwork quilt of beliefs in reincarnation, *karma*, disembodied spirits, paranormal powers, holistic medicine, pantheism, and the underlying unity of all religions with the hope for a coming great spiritual leader. The New Age synthesis, a progressivist myth heralding the cumulative improvement of humanity, reveres ancient and tribal traditions as well as the modern technologies that preserve and link them. New Age philosophies ground their diversity in the truth to be found in immediate personal experience, seeking the spiritual transformation that will shatter the limits of mundane life, initiate a new awareness of the bonds among individuals, and enable the creation of an enlightened global community fully integrated with its earthly environment.

The focus of the New Age movement has exhibited several shifts since the 1970s. The earlier interest centered on Asian or Asian-trained spiritual leaders or *gurus* offering simplified versions of Hindu, Buddhist, and Sikh meditative or other practical techniques to attain enlightenment. That trend has gradually incorporated or given way to the revived Western occult traditions, including Witchcraft and communication with the spirit world or with extraterrestrial beings through channeling or visions. On the more practical end of the New Age spectrum has been the development of alternative medicines, therapies, and holistic healing, including psychic surgery, new dietary schemas such as macrobiotics, the study of biorhythms, and use of crystals. The most recent dimensions of New Age spirituality began exploration of elements of African or Native American tribal religions, especially shamanism and trance induction. In sum, an earlier interest in Transcendental Meditation and the Rajneesh Foundation has shifted through EST and psychic research to Sun Bear and Lynn Andrews.

In the 1990s, the New Age movement encompassed an eclectic assemblage of apparently separable beliefs and practices. While an individual group might center its efforts on a particular path for spiritual enhancement, participants typically try several distinct programs or techniques simultaneously or serially, in hopes of finding the most suitable combination. Communication and coherence has been built through a network of conferences, periodicals, and popular publications. The current widespread familiarity in Western countries with terms such as *reincarnation, astrology,* or *channeling* suggests an expansion of New Age influence, but the limits of its philosophy may be seen in the increasing scientific and skeptical challenges posed to the more extreme claims of psychic powers and the novel reinterpretations of religious traditions. Evangelical churches in the United States and Europe have denounced the movement as antithetical to traditional Christian values, with some even prophesying that its popularity augurs the end of the world. Ethnic traditionalists have decried the selective borrowings of tribal religious practices from their natural contexts as a subtle form of racism or imperialism, while scholars place the movement within the late-twentieth-century quest for renewed religious meaning in the wake of modernist fragmentation. *See also* Age of Aquarius; North America, new religions in.

New Christian Crusade Church, a contemporary Christian Identity church formed in 1971 in Metairie, Louisiana, and pastored by James K. Warner. Warner is less noted among Christian Identity adherents for his contributions to the development of Christian Identity doctrine than he is for his extensive connections with the often conflicting elements of the American radical right wing. Before accepting the Identity message, Warner was a member of the neo-Nazi movement of George Lincoln Rockwell and, with David Duke, of the Knights of the Ku Klux Klan. Warner's New Christian Crusade Church has an active publication arm but is best known for its mail-order book catalog, which features texts of interest to readers sympathetic with any right-wing cause. *See also* Identity Christianity.

New Covenant. 1 Christian claim to supersede Israel based on a prophecy in Jeremiah 31:31–33. 2 Alternative title for the New Testament.

New Jerusalem, Jewish and Christian apocalyptic belief that the present Jerusalem will be replaced by a city under divine rulership. *See also* apocalypticism; eschatology.

New Jerusalem, Church of the. *See* Swedenborg (Svedberg), Emmanuel.

Newman, John Henry (1801–90), British Christian apologist and historian. Originally a member of the High Church Anglican tradition, in *Tracts for the Times* (1841), number 90, Newman ably defended the Church of England as mediating between Roman Catholicism and Protestantism. In 1845, Newman converted to Catholicism, later becoming a cardinal. He became Catholicism's most effective English apologist in works such as *Essay on the Development of Christian Doctrine* (1845), *Apologia pro vita sua* (1864), and *A Grammar of Assent* (1870).

New Testament, the collection of materials written by the early Christians (ca. 50–150) and later canonized as scripture; together with the Hebrew Bible, or Old Testament, it constitutes the Christian Bible. Earliest are the Letters (Epistles) of Paul; Pauline authorship is generally uncontested for seven, in probable order of their composition (1 Thessalonians; Galatians; 1, 2 Corinthians; Philippians; Philemon; Romans) and debated for three (2 Thessalonians, Colossians, Ephesians). The Letters address specific problems in churches known to Paul. Four anonymous Gospels—the synoptics (Matthew, Mark, Luke) and the fourth Gospel (John)—narrate the "good news" of God's activity in Jesus' life, death, and resurrection. Acts of the Apostles (volume 2 of Luke) continues the story of the development of the early Christian movement. Revelation, an apocalypse, narrates a vision of the end-time reflecting the despair and hope of the persecuted. The Pastorals (1, 2 Timothy; Titus) are almost universally regarded as second century and attributed to Paul pseudonymously. The "catholic" (or "universal") Letters (James; 1, 2 Peter; 1, 2, 3 John; Jude) include reflection on earlier writings and address issues of the second century.

In 367 these twenty-seven books and no others were listed by Bishop Athanasius of Alexandria as officially accepted (canonical). All were originally written in *koine* Greek, the common language of the ancient eastern Mediterranean world. No original "autograph" exists; all the books are known from copies of copies of copies of manuscripts. *See also* Bible, Christian.

New Text school, reformist-minded Confucian scholars (such as Tung Chung-shu), dominant in the former Han dynasty (206 B.C.–A.D. 8), who considered authoritative the received texts of the Confucian Classics, rather than a different "old text" version in archaic characters of dubious provenance. *See also* Confucianism (authoritative texts and their interpretation); Old Text school.

New Year (China) , the most important celebration in the Chinese religious year, traditionally observed on the second new moon after the winter solstice. The festival period lasts a full month, beginning in the middle of the twelfth lunar month and extending to the fifteenth day of the new year. Sacrifices on the twelfth day of the twelfth month to T'u-ti kung, the local earth god, initiate the holiday period. On the twenty-third or twenty-fourth day of the twelfth month, a feast is held to honor Tsao-chun, the god of the family hearth. Feted with sweets, he departs to make his annual report on the family to Yu-huang Shang-ti, the Jade Emperor, who rules the bureaucratic pantheon of deities recognized in Chinese popular religion. The household is then thoroughly cleaned in preparation for the arrival the next day of celestial deities, who watch over events until the return of the terrestrial deities.

Prior to the central feast on New Year's Eve that celebrates the unity of the family, sacrifices are offered to ancestors, tutelary deities, and restless spirits. Following the elaborate family meal, members socialize until midnight, when traditionally they prostrate themselves, in order of precedence, before their elders and joyously greet the new year. The god of the hearth is wel-

comed back on the fourth day of the first month. The festivities conclude on the fifteenth day, with sacrifices to the Agent of Heaven, a Taoist deity, and the Lantern Festival's lights, dragon dances, and fireworks. *See also* Chinese religions (festal cycle); Chinese ritual; T'u-ti kung.

new year festivals, a major category of ritual commemorating the cosmogony and bridging the transition between the old year's order and the new. Scholars distinguish between two phases: rituals of elimination, which dispose of the exhausted elements of the past year, and rituals of commencement, which celebrate and incorporate fresh elements of the new. The two phases are often separated by an interregnum characterized by ritual license and reversals. *See also* Big House movement; chaos, return to; Divali; festal cycle; Lantern Festival; Losar; periodic rites; rebellion, rituals of; Rosh Hashanah; sacred space and sacred time.

Balinese New Year's festival in the village of Paksabali. A procession carries the statues of the gods to the river to be washed. Following this cleansing, the statues will be tied to long bamboo poles and a battle of the gods will be staged, with the celebrants attempting to knock one another's deities to the ground.

1 The Great Sphinx (Egypt. *Harmakhis*) at Giza, on the west bank of the Nile River, erected by the fourth-dynasty Egyptian pharoah Khafre (Gk. *Chephren*) ca. 2650. Approximately 240 feet long and 66 feet high, the Sphinx is an expression of sacred kingship; its face is a portrait of the king. In the background is the pyramid of Menkaure (Gk. *Mycerinus*), constructed as a royal tomb. **2** Cuneiform (Gk., "wedge-shaped") writing, made with a reed stylus on a clay tablet. Read from left to right, it was the system with which most Mesopotamian texts were written from the third millennium to the first century B.C. Of the thousands of tablets that have survived, the majority concern business, legal, and governmental matters; fewer than 2 percent are primarily religious. **3** The west face of the Parthenon, the chief temple dedicated to the goddess Athena, the Virgin (Gk. *parthenos*), on the sacred hill of the Acropolis in Athens, Greece. Constructed 447 to 432 B.C., it was a major center of civic religion, celebrating Athens's divine patroness. Devotees would circumambulate the building several times before entering the sanctuary. **4** Samaritan priests embrace after sacrificing the Passover lamb at Mt. Gerizim, Israel. Unlike the Jewish Passover meal, in which the sacrifice is wholly symbolic, the Samaritans retain the actual sacrificial killing. Samaritanism, along with Judaism, Christianity, and Mandaeanism, is one of the few Late Antique religions to continue into the late twentieth century. **5** Second-century sculpted head of Medusa, one of the monstrous Gorgons of Greek myth, employed as a guardian at the Temple of Apollo in Didyma, Turkey. **6** Cernunnos, a Celtic deity known only from artistic representations and one Latin inscription. In this relief, from a second-century B.C. silver ritual basin, discovered in Gundestrup (Jutland), Denmark, the only depiction of Cernunnos from outside the region of the eastern Celts, he is shown in typical form: stag antlers emerging from his head (Cernunnos in Celtic means "crown of the head," not "horned one," as previously thought), a cross-legged posture, wearing a tunic and carrying a heavy gold neck-chain (torque) in his right hand and a ram-headed serpent in his left. His worship has been revived by contemporary Neo-Pagan groups.

1

2

3

4

5

6

1

7

8

9

7 Anonymous etching of a young Jew being instructed, before ritually assuming his adult role (Heb. *bar mitzvah*), in fastening his phylacteries (*tefillin*), two small leather boxes tied to the forehead and left arm before the morning daily prayers. The phylacteries contain four biblical passages handwritten by a scribe on parchment in fulfillment of the commandment in Deuteronomy 6:8. **8** Jews offer prayers and petitions at the Western Wall in Jerusalem (known before the establishment of the State of Israel as the Wailing Wall), by tradition a part of the destroyed Temple structure. The left side is restricted to men; the right, to women. The Muslim Dome of the Rock and the al-Aqsa mosque are visible in the background. **9** Many Jewish homes can be recognized by the *mezuzah* (Heb., "doorpost") affixed to the right side of their doorposts in strict fulfillment of the commandment to write Yahweh's words on "the doorposts of your house" (Deuteronomy 6:9; 11:20). The mezuzah is usually a cylinder containing the first two verses of the Hebrew prayer, the Shema, handwritten on parchment by a scribe. The mezuzah on the outer door is often kissed upon entering or exiting the house. **10** Jewish students, at Stern College, New York, celebrate the 1995 wintertime feast of Hanukkah (Heb., "dedication") by lighting candles in an eight-branched candelabrum (*menorah*), with an additional candle used to light the others, one candle each night for eight nights, to celebrate the miraculous rededication of the Temple in Jerusalem in 165 B.C. A blessing is said as the candles are lit, often followed by singing the hymn *Maoz tzur* ("fortress of rock").

10

11

13

12

11 Platter containing the five central symbols of the Jewish Passover displayed at the seder meal: a roasted egg and lamb bone symbolic of the Passover sacrifice; bitter herbs (Heb. *maror*), reminder of Israel's slavery in Egypt; the vegetables (*karpas*) to be dipped in saltwater later in the meal; and a mixture (*haroset*) of crushed fruit, nuts, and wine, representing the mortar that the Israelites were forced to make. In the center of the platter is a wine cup that will be filled and set aside for the return of the prophet Elijah. To the far right of the platter is a covered dish, containing unleavened bread (*matzah*). **12** A Yemenite rabbi reviews a marriage contract (Heb. *ketubah*) prior to the wedding service. Written in Aramaic, and containing the financial obligations of husband to wife, the ketubah is read aloud and witnessed at the ceremony and kept by the wife. **13** Exterior of the Altneuschul (Ger. Yiddish, "old new school") synagogue in Prague, Czech Republic, the oldest functioning synagogue in Europe, most

14

15

recently refurbished by the state in 1966 and 1967. Constructed in its present form ca. 1280, with numerous fifteenth- and sixteenth-century additions, it served the large medieval Jewish quarter ("Old Town") on the right bank of the Vltava River. It is a gray stone building with a main room for the men and a set of annexes, a vestibule in the south and a women's section in the north and west. The lower clock, visible to the right, is part of the eighteenth-century Jewish government hall, giving the time in Hebrew numerals with its hands rotating counterclockwise. **14** A nineteenth-century Yemenite shofar, a ram's horn instrument, blown on the Jewish New Year (Heb. *Rosh Hashanah*) and at the conclusion of the Day of Atonement (Yom Kippur) in three sound patterns: a sustained single note (*tekiah*), three broken notes (*shevarim*), and a set of staccato notes (*teruah*). The fish design is unusual. **15** Holocaust memorial in Lincoln Park, San Francisco, California, displays sculptures of concentration camp victims by George Segal (b. 1924).

16

17

20

18

19

16 The Black Madonna (or Black Virgin), a wooden statue that has been an object of Christian pilgrimage since the fourteenth century. Presently housed in a nineteenth-century chapel at the Benedictine abbey in Einsiedeln, Switzerland, its coloration is often explained as being the result of smoke from candles burned before it across the centuries. **17** The basic elements in the Christian ritual of the Eucharist. The bread represents the body of Christ. The wine represents the blood of Christ. **18** Congregants receive the eucharistic bread and wine from an ordained woman minister and her assistant, United Church of Canada, Ontario. **19** Nigerian Christian pilgrimage group, in the 1970s, carries a cross on Good Friday to the site of Jesus' crucifixion in Jerusalem. **20** Two male adults being baptized by total immersion in living water by a Baptist minister, Pirate's Cove, Newport Beach, California (1991). **21** St. Thomas Day procession of the priest and members of the Anglican Church of Papua New Guinea at Uiaku in 1981. **22** Area of the sanctuary in St. Paul's, London, cathedral of the Church of England and parish church of the British Commonwealth. Designed in the Baroque style by Christopher Wren, it was constructed between 1675 and 1710, replacing Old St. Paul's, destroyed in the Great Fire of 1666.

22

21

23

26

25

24

23 Roman Catholic pilgrims light candles at the Shrine of Guadalupe, a central pilgrimage site northwest of Mexico City where Mary is said to have appeared in 1531 and imprinted her image on a serape. **24** Fourteenth-century stained-glass windows from the lower Rhineland Roman Catholic parish church of St. Maurice in Mutzig. Christ's crucifixion is depicted at the center of the large window and is framed by images of Adam and St. John in the narrow windows to the left and right, suggesting the Christian belief that the crucifixion is the midpoint of human history. **25** Ethiopian Christian church of Biet Maryam ("House of Mary") in the pilgrimage center of Lalibela (or Roha), Ethiopia, carved from a solid rock face in the late twelfth or early thirteenth century, and famous for its frescoes. The various rock churches of Lalibela are presently administered by priests of the Coptic Church. Christianity in Ethiopia dates back to the early fourth century. **26** Fresco of Mary and the infant Jesus from the Orthodox Assinou church in Cyprus. Roman Catholicism and the Orthodox Church are distinctive within Christianity for their emphasis on the saving role of Mary. In Orthodox Christianity, this is summarized by her title, Theotokos (Gk., "god bearer"). **27** A pilgrim makes an ascent on her knees while holding candles to be offered during a 1987 votive pilgrimage to the Orthodox Church of the Madonna of the Annunciation (Gk. *evangelistra*) on the Cycladic island of Tinos. The church displays an icon of Mary miraculously discovered in 1823.

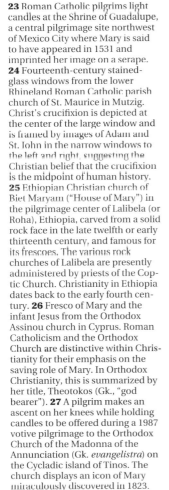

27

28

29

30

32

31

28 The Taj Mahal is a tomb complex, including a mausoleum and mosque, constructed by the Muslim Mogul emperor Shah Jihan in commemoration of his wife, Mumtaz Mahal (from whom the site derives its name), outside of Agra, India. Completed in 1654, it is both an architectural masterpiece and a pilgrimage site. **29** Muslim pilgrims circumambulate the Kaaba, the central shrine at Mecca in Saudi Arabia, seven times, in a counterclockwise direction, during the pilgrimage (Arab. *hajj*). This pilgrimage (the one pictured here was made in 1974) is required of all Muslims at least once in their lifetime, unless circumstances make it impossible, and dates back to Abraham and Ishmael. **30** Contemporary mosque in Pattani, southwestern Thailand, ca. 1985. The large pool is used for ablutions prior to entering the mosque. While Muslims comprise only 4 percent of the total, largely Buddhist, Thai population, they are an overwhelming majority in Pattani and other cities close to the Malaysian border. **31** A painting on the outer wall of an Egyptian house memorializes the inhabitant's pilgrimage experience, by train and boat to Mecca, with the Kaaba and the Grand Mosque (Arab. al-Masjid al-Haram). **32** Chinese Muslims at daily prayer in the Niu Jie mosque in Peking (Beijing), People's Republic of China. Dated by tradition to the tenth century, the mosque is probably later than the thirteenth.

33

34

35

33 The Dome of the Rock in Jerusalem, one of the three central mosques of Islam, constructed by Caliph Abd al-Malik in 691. Built on the site of the biblical Temple Mount, in Islamic tradition it marks the place where Muhammad began his ascension (Arab. *miraj*, "night journey") to the seven heavens. **34** Interior of a contemporary European mosque, constructed in the 1970s in Munich, Germany. Its most prominent feature is the large niche (Arab. *qiblah*) that orients the worshipers toward Mecca. **35** A Persian miniature (1504) depicts Muhammad's ascent (Arab. *mihaj*) through the seven heavens on the back of the supernatural animal Buraq. As elaborated by tradition from the terse description in the Qur'an 17:1 2, the Prophet experienced a nocturnal visionary journey from the mosque at Mecca, to the Temple Mount in Jerusalem (later the site of the Dome of the Rock), and then through the heavens, encountering angels and prophets, until he stood before the throne of Allah.

36

37

38

39

36 Alaskan Eskimo shaman's mask. The shaman (Eskimo-Aleut *angakok* or *angalkuq*) has powers of healing, by removing impurity or recovering souls that have been stolen; weather control; and assuring the continuity of game animals by a spiritual journey either under the waters or into the sky to interact with the master or mistress of the animals, aided by animal guardians, techniques for achieving ecstatic states, and ritual equipment such as masks. **37** Navajo sandpainter uses crushed minerals to fashion figures and patterns to be used in a healing Holyway ritual in Four Corners, Arizona, 1982. The person to be cured sits in the center of the painting and the powers of the Holy People (Navajo *ye'ii*), represented by the elongated humanoid forms, are transferred to that person by having materials from the painting applied to his or her body, thereby destroying the painting. **38** The founding of the Aztec city of Tenochtitlan in Diego Duran, *Historia de las Indias di Nueva-Espana e islas de tierra firme* (completed in 1581, first published 1867–80). Although clearly imposing European styles on native pictorial tradition, Duran has the central elements of the foundation myth, continued to this day on the flag of Mexico. After the Aztecs emerged from the Seven Caves, their patron deity, Huitzilopochtli, commanded their shaman-priest to lead the people to a place where the god would appear in the form of an eagle perched on a blooming nopal cactus growing from an island in the middle of a lake. They should construct their first city at that spot. **39** Masked Karaja men perform a ritual dance personating fish spirits. The middle figure holds a rattle, their only ceremonial musical instrument. The Karaja are a small South American tribe, belonging to an independent language family, living along the Araguaia River near Bananal Island in central Brazil. Fish are their major food source. Karaja masked rituals are strictly limited to initiated males and are of two kinds, those personating animal spirits and those personating the powerful dead.

40 West African Yoruba masked dancer personates the powerful ancestor Jenju (Yoruba, "he devours in the bush") at a 1974 Engungun ritual devoted to the collective spirits of the patrilineal ancestors. The elaborate cloth construction worn by the dancer is topped by a display of skulls of sacrificed animals.

41 An adolescent Ndembu girl in Zambia, 1985, performs the coming-into-adulthood (Ndembu *kwidisha*, "bringing out") dance as part of her puberty initiation. After spending three months in a seclusion hut, she dances before the villagers, adorned with a string of sacred white beads that symbolize her future children and carrying a switch in her right hand that represents adult authority. At the conclusion of the dance, she will join her future husband in his hut. **42** A ritual specialist (Sinhalese *kapurala*) manipulates fire as a sign of his power during a healing rite in Sri Lanka, 1969. A young woman is suffering from stomach pains caused by the offended spirit of her dead grandmother. The spirit will be attracted to the "temple" of banana stalks and leaves, on the left, and be appeased. Buddhism and Hinduism in Sri Lanka coexist with indigenous Sinhala religion; for example, the closely related ritual activity of fire-walking was first brought to Sri Lanka by Tamil Hindus and is now largely practiced by Buddhist ecstatics. **43** Ilahita Arapesh men's house (Pidgin Eng. *tamburan*), Maprik subdistrict, Papua New Guinea, 1961. The entrance is through the hole in the lower right. Men's houses are characteristic of many traditional societies. Entrance is restricted to initiated males who use the house as a ritual center, a place for transmitting secret traditions and storing or displaying sacred objects, as well as a site for making political decisions.

44 Offerings being presented to the gods at a Balinese New Year festival, Paksabali, ca. 1970 to 1985. Bali's synthesis of Hinduism, Buddhism, Tantrism, and indigenous traditions, called Agama Tirtha (Skt., "religion of holy water"), stands in sharp contrast to the rest of Muslim Indonesia.

40

41

43

42

44

45 *Kali* (Skt., "black"), the destructive manifestation of the Great Goddess, tramples the inert body of Shiva in a Kali-festival statue from Bihar, India. This scene, frequently depicted in Indian paintings and statues, represents the power (*shakti*) Shiva depends on, without which he is but a corpse (*shava*).

46 A Shaivite Hindu wandering ascetic, a holy person (Skt. *sadhu*) or renouncer, who has left home and ordinary society to focus on physical and spiritual disciplines. Both his facial markings and the trident he carries indicate his devotion to Shiva.

47 Image of Hanuman, the Hindu monkey deity, on Chowpatty Beach, Bombay, India. A central figure in the classic epic the *Ramayana*, he is portrayed in devotional Hinduism as Vishnu-Rama's exemplary disciple and is celebrated in folk tradition as a patron of bodybuilders (his celibate retention of semen yields great strength) for his shape-shifting abilities and his powers at defeating evil spirits.

45

46

47

48

49

48 Kashmir Shaivite devotion to the presence of Sharika Devi, Srinagar, India. Since the eleventh century, Sharika Devi, a local family goddess, has been identified with the major Tantric goddesses, Tripurasundari or Shrividya, and ultimately with Mahadevi, the Great Goddess, whose power (Skt. *shakti*) is manifested in these more local forms.

49 Hindu woman performing ablutions in the river Ganga (or Ganges). The river is not only a prime means of ritual purification but is also a goddess who is worshiped by bathing in her waters.

50

51

52

50 A Hindu woman draws auspicious rice powder designs (Tamil *kolam;* Hindi *rangoli*) in front of her house in Gokarna, India. The daily preparation of these designs is the major responsibility of women and an important aspect of daily domestic ritual. **51** Seventh-century South Indian Hindu temple at Mahabalipuram, Tamilnadu, India. One of five standing monolithic temples from an original group of seven at this important coastal site. **52** Tantric cosmic diagram (Skt. *mandala*) of the Hindu deity, Vishnu, from Nepal, ca. 1420. In this somewhat atypical representation, Vishnu is shown in a seated position, holding his four attributes, one in each arm, and surrounded by a twelve-petal lotus, each petal depicting one of his various manifest forms (avatars), more usually numbered as seven or ten. On the right is seated Narasimha, Vishnu's man-lion avatar. On the left is Krishna, one of Vishnu's preeminent avatars.

53 The contemporary Tulsi Manas Temple, the second largest temple in Banaras (now Varanasi), constructed in the mid-twentieth century in honor of Tulsi Das (ca. 1532–1623), the Mughal-period North Indian Hindu poet-saint whose retelling of the *Ramayana* in Hindi (*Ramcaritmanas,* Hindi, "Lake of Rama's Deeds") is a holy book. Along with scenes from the epic, the temple features an animated plastic statue of Tulsi Das turning the pages of his manuscript and chanting Rama's name. **54** A Hindu devotee, at the conclusion of his act of worship (Skt. *puja*) receiving from the Brahman priest food offerings (*prasada*) that have been consecrated to and by the deity in a temple devoted to Shiva and Vishnu in California (1980s). Prasada usually consists of food and/or flowers and is understood to be partaking and sharing of the god's grace and favor.

53

54

55

56

57

58

59

55 Tibetan Buddhist mural from the Himalayan Rangdum monastery at Ladakh, in northwest India. A cosmic diagram (Skt. *mandala*), it depicts the earthly paradise of Shambhala, which holds the hidden teaching of the Wheel of Time (*kalachakra*) in the form of an eight-petal lotus blossom. In the center is Gesar, the enlightened future king who will defeat the forces of evil and establish the Buddhist golden age. **56** Japanese Shingon Buddhist pilgrim offers water at a grave shrine on Mt. Koya, the sacred mountain in the Wakayama Prefecture of Japan, revered as the founding site (816) and headquarters under Kukai (774–835) of Shingonshu. Kukai was identified with the messianic Buddha, Maitreya, and Mt. Koya with the paradisical Pure Land. Consequently, many Shingon Buddhists are buried on Mt. Koya so that they might meet Maitreya with Kukai after death. **57** Ordination of a Theravada Buddhist monk in Sri Lanka (1969). After his ritual head shaving, the young man is purified with a water libation. In most Theravadan Buddhist countries, ordination is a rite of passage for all males who become novice monks for a short period of time. This practice is uncommon in Sri Lanka. **58** Statue of the Reclining Buddha, with a *stupa* (Burmese *hpaya*, "lord") in the background, at Buddha Park, Yangon (Eng. Rangoon), Myanmar (formerly Burma). Yangon is a religious as well as a political capital; its Shwe Dagon pagoda is the center of Burmese Buddhism. The Buddha Park, which also contains the World Peace pagoda, an immense artificial grotto that serves as an assembly hall, and the campus of the International Association for Advanced Buddhist Studies, was constructed in 1952 in preparation for the convening of the Sixth Buddhist Council (1954–56), part of the celebrations of the 2500th anniversary of the founding of Buddhism (Buddha Jayati). **59** Buddhist relic mound (Skt. *stupa*) at Sanchi, Madhya Pradesh, India. The three stupas at Sanchi (third century B.C.–first century A.D.), associated with King Ashoka (r. ca. 272–232 B.C.), constitute one of the earliest surviving Buddhist ceremonial complexes in India. To the left is the ceremonial gateway (*torana*) carved with scenes of the Buddha's previous lives taken from the *Jataka* ("Birth") tales.

60 Cambodian Theravada Buddhist presenting gifts to monks at the annual New Robes ceremony, San Jose, California, in 1989. This festal-cycle ritual marks the close of the monastic rain retreat and is the occasion for laypersons to partici-pate in the merit generated by the monks' rigorous ascetic practices during the retreat. **61** Chinese women pilgrims offering incense at a mountain roadside shrine associ-ated with Kuan-yin, the Bodhisattva of compassion, during the spring pilgrimage season (mid-February to mid-April) in the Hangshow region, People's Republic of China, 1989. This is the most basic ritual act as expressed in the Chinese term for pilgrimage, "paying one's respect to a mountain and offering incense" (*ch'ao-shan chin-hsiang*). The women carry incense in their shoul-der bags, which will be stamped with names of the shrines they vis-ited. When they die, they are cre-mated in their pilgrimage clothing and shoulder bags; the stamps serve as passports to the Western Paradise.

60

61

62

63

64

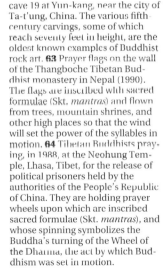

62 Colossal seated Buddha from cave 19 at Yun-kang, near the city of Ta-t'ung, China. The various fifth-century carvings, some of which reach seventy feet in height, are the oldest known examples of Buddhist rock art. **63** Prayer flags on the wall of the Thangboche Tibetan Bud-dhist monastery in Nepal (1990). The flags are inscribed with sacred formulae (Skt. *mantras*) and flown from trees, mountain shrines, and other high places so that the wind will set the power of the syllables in motion. **64** Tibetan Buddhists pray-ing, in 1988, at the Neohung Tem-ple, Lhasa, Tibet, for the release of political prisoners held by the authorities of the People's Republic of China. They are holding prayer wheels upon which are inscribed sacred formulae (Skt. *mantras*), and whose spinning symbolizes the Buddha's turning of the Wheel of the Dharma, the act by which Bud-dhism was set in motion.

13

65

65 Colossal stone statue of Lao-tzu in Ch'uan-chou, a city in the eastern coastal province of Fukien, People's Republic of China. Separate sculptural representations of Lao-tzu are uncommon. He is more often depicted as one member of the triad of the Three Pure Ones (San-ch'ing): T'ien-tsun, Ling-pao, and Lao-tzu.

66

67

66 A 1979 portrait of Confucius, above an altar with ritual vessels, facing the front entrance of the Ta-cheng tien (Chin., "Hall of Great Accomplishment"), popularly known as the Temple of Confucius, the central sacrificial hall of the temple complex in the pilgrimage town of Ch'u-fu, Confucius's birthplace in the Shantung Province, People's Republic of China. The temple complex, begun in the fifth century B.C. and constantly rebuilt through the latter part of the twentieth century, consists of 466 buildings with 54 gates, laid out in a compound two-thirds of a mile long. Ch'u-fu also contains the Residence of Confucius's Descendants and the Tomb of Confucius (along with the graveyard for his descendants), both continually used by members of the Confucian lineage through the 1990s. **67** Taiwanese Taoist altar prepared for the central ritual of cosmic renewal (Chin. *chiao*), an esoteric rite that periodically realigns the body, community, temple, and cosmos with the Tao. In its full form, this ritual is performed once every sixty years; a less elaborate form, every twelve or twenty years. **68** Chinese domestic altar, Taiwan (1970s). A characteristic focus of ritual in every Chinese household, the left half of the altar is devoted to the ancestors; the right, to the gods. On the right wall, behind the large, square incense burner, is a scroll depicting five popular deities: Kuan-yin, the Buddhist Bodhisattva of compassion; Kuan Yu, a Taoist deified martial lord; T'ien-shang Sheng-mu (known on Taiwan as Ma-tsu), the virgin protectoress of seafarers; Tsao-shen, the Lord of the Hearth; and T'u-ti kung, the earth god. On the left side of the altar, behind the ancestral incense burner, is the ancestor's portrait. The scroll on the left wall displays the Chinese character for longevity written in a hundred different ways. **69** Display of a ritually slaughtered pig at a temple of Ch'ing Shui Tsu Shih Kung on Taiwan in the 1970s, celebrating the local deity's birthday on the sixth day of the first lunar month, a festival that, along with the "big pig" sacrifice, often includes ritual firewalking. The pig, having been stabbed in the heart with a purified knife, is shaved, except for a patch along the spine that is inscribed with an auspicious character, and displayed with a bunch of bananas in its mouth and a live fish tied by a thread to its nostrils. The other decorations, including money, plastic flowers, the Nationalist flag, and dolls, are at the option of the donor family.

68 69

70 Workers and civic officials perform a foundation ritual at the construction site of the Hong Kong Academy of the Performing Arts. With a geomancer (Chin. *feng-shui*) in attendance, incense sticks, ripened fruit, roasted hens, and a pig are offered as sacrifices to ward off evil spirits and bless the building (ca. 1980s). **71** Young Japanese males push to break down a ritual gate (Jap. *torii*) as part of the Shinto *kannokura* fire festival, held every February 6 in Southern Honshu, Japan. The gate guards a sacred presence (*kami*) in a large boulder called Toad Rock. Older males seek to prevent the young men's passage in a form of initiatory ordeal. **72** A mountain ascetic (Jap. *yamabushi*), an initiated member of a secret society within esoteric Shingon Buddhism, participates in a religious procession at a small shrine in Kyoto, Japan. The yamabushi are laypersons engaged in secular pursuits, except for certain times of the year when they go on pilgrimages and conduct secret rituals on sacred mountains. **73** Korean female shaman (Kor. *mansin*), in the 1980s, dancing in a possession trance as part of an elaborate ritual (*kut*) most often performed for healing or on behalf of the dead. **74** Small Japanese Shinto domestic shrine with offerings to the divine presence (Jap. *kami*) who protects children. **75** Ritual orchestra preparing to perform during the Offerings of Tribute and Sacrificial Food (Kor. *chonp'ye*) portion of the Confucian state *sokchon* ("dispense the libations") rites at the National Confucian Academy (*Songgyu'gwan*, "Hall for the Establishment of Balance"), Seoul, Korea. Sokchon is a ritual offering of food and drink before the images, portraits, or spirit tablets of Confucius and other Chinese and Korean sages. It has been continuously celebrated at the Academy since the fourteenth century. Confucian state ritual is more highly elaborated in Korea than anywhere else.

71

72

74

73

75

76 Two members of the Afro-Brazilian Candomble religion, having been possessed, are costumed and ritually assume the persons of two gods, each originally an African Yoruba deity, the male, Oshun, and the female, Yemanja. **77** *Goddess*, a drawing in pencil and casein by Robin Samuel Sierra © 1986. The rediscovery of the ancient Goddess worship is a prominent feature of various feminist and Neo-Pagan new religious movements. Here the artist recaptures the characteristic form of the paleolithic European and neolithic Old European and Cycladic divine woman statuettes, a figure lacking head and arms, with prominent vulva and hips. **78** A Hare Krishna devotee in Stockholm, Sweden, in 1992 beats a drum accompanying chanting in praise of Krishna. The International Society of Krishna Consciousness (ISKCON), a missionary form of devotional Hinduism, was first brought to the United States by A. C. Bhaktivedanta Swami Prabhupa (1896–1977) in 1965, and spread from North America to Europe, with more than two hundred centers worldwide. **79** Thousands of members of the Soka Gakkai International (SGI) gathered in Hokkaido, Japan, in 1983 for the Third World Peace Youth Culture Festival. Such gatherings offer opportunities for cultural exchanges among young people from around the world as part of the SGI's programs for peace, culture, and education. **80** Members of a Voodoo (Vodou) "family" in Haiti, 1989, at a ceremony invoking Danbala Wedo, originally an African Dahomean ancestral spirit, the most ancient and respected of the Voodoo spirits, whose form is that of a serpent and rainbow and who is associated with St. Patrick. The sacred center pole is the chief means for the spirits to travel between their subterranean home and the land of the living. Called the "doorway of Danbala" (Haitian Creole *poto-Danbala*), it is surrounded by a cornmeal diagram (*veve*) used to invite the spirit and illuminated by a candle.

76

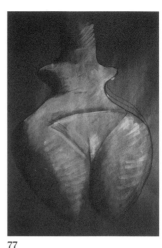

77

78

79

80

NEW RELIGIONS

A new name for a centuries-old phenomenon, *new religions* is the recently coined term for independent groups that have arisen from the encounter of existing religious traditions, particularly through the latter part of the postcolonial period. Such new movements offer their participants an original religious complex, born of selected old and new elements and interpretations of the sacred in life and ritual, which not only validates a transformed worldview but also enhances their spiritual experience.

TERMINOLOGY

The term *new religions* is a broadly inclusive one, replacing a bewildering variety of labels, many of which have been extended far beyond their original and particular use. The oldest set of identifying terms emphasizes the unusual qualities of new religions. Thus, terms such as *nativistic, revival,* or *revitalization movement,* often employed to identify groups arising in opposition to oppressive colonial cultures, stress the reactive rather than creative aspects of those groups. In so doing, they may reduce the religious content to aspirations for later political movements. Similarly, the overgeneralized and often pejorative *crisis cults* or *syncretistic movements* suggest that the religious communities so named are merely derivative of more thoughtful or less precipitous religions, while the vocabulary of *charismatic cults* portrays their participants as confused and gullible masses subject to a powerful leader.

Another type of terminology, extended from the analysis of Western traditions, identifies the religious focus of the new groups but may fail to note their value or originality. The limited schema of *denomination, sect, cult,* and so on, for example, is based in Christian ecclesiology, and its adoption by social scientists perpetuates the perception that none but Christian communities are *churches,* that is, respectable traditions. More specific terminology, such as *millennial, prophetic,* or *messianic movement,* has lost considerable impact in its extension to religious groups that have no doctrines concerning the Last Days, a thousand-year kingdom, messengers revealing divine words, or anointed saviors. The innovative, spontaneous, and controversial features of many new groups have led a large number of scholars to identify them as simply cults or

Devotees of the International Society for Krishna Consciousness (ISKCON) chanting in procession in front of a chariot containing an image of Krishna in Boston, Massachusetts, in the 1970s. A missionary form of devotional Hinduism, ISKCON was first brought to the United States by A. C. Bhaktivedanta Swami Prabhupada (1896–1977) in 1965. In 1990, ISKCON claimed three thousand American initiated members and 500,000 lay members who visit their temples at least monthly.

movements. Those terms may reflect a sense that these are not true religions, but their systemic viability and distinctively spiritual nature leads to the recognition that these, too, may be so designated. The use of the term new religions, then, indicates that these independent groups, while novel, may be taken seriously for study as complex worldviews that offer a significant experience through integrated beliefs and practices.

THEORIES OF NEW RELIGIONS

A wide range of movements may fit into the category of new religions; this very diversity has given rise to different approaches attempting to comprehend the contexts in which new religions occur and how their principal elements may be typed or categorized. Since the 1950s, scholarship on new religions has generally employed four strategies, focusing analysis primarily on the context in which new religions emerge, their relations with the dominant religious tradition or normative culture, the evolution of an internal social structure for the group, or its distinguishable religious features. The first three analytic strategies depend on sociological perspectives, and, if used exclusively, may disregard the religious content of the movements.

The first type of explanation focuses on the context of new religions, stressing the unstable conditions of the contemporary society, the marginal status of participants, and the impermanence of the nascent movement as social change proceeds. The emphasis on such disruptive conditions, presented as causal factors in the creation of new religions, spotlights the practical concerns of the groups and links them to revolutionary political movements but may not explore the sacred dimensions or spiritual claims. Approaches following the second explanatory strategy center on the relations with the dominant political or religious institutions and usually characterize new religions as accommodating, reinterpreting, or rejecting the mainstream traditions. Accordingly, accommodative new religions may make consolidated efforts to fit into a changing society. Other new religions experience the dominant religion as too inclusive, too formal in its institutional functions, or as having compromised with an ide-

Members of the Japanese new religion Gedatsukai honoring the symbol of the rising sun during a festival at their sacred headquarters in Tokyo. This Shingon-derived Buddhist sect was founded in 1929 and has about 300,000 adherents.

ology too alien to the older ways of that community, and so attempt to transform the manner in which value and power is perceived or withdraw from the system entirely. The distinctiveness of new religions, then, lies in their break with usual patterns of authority or legitimacy and repudiation of moderation and cooperation. Scholars using either of these first two strategies may also advance the psychological perspective that new religions fill an emotional need and suggest that either "relative deprivation" (the feeling that reasonable material needs are not being met) or "cognitive dissonance" (the feeling that a valued belief system cannot explain current events) propels the members into participation. The third strategy examines the internal social organization of new religions, with the presence of a charismatic founder, initial small size, or limited locale of the community, and loose or informal social bonds. Although this perspective was once used to suggest that new religions were of little historical consequence, recent studies analyzing social organization utilize extensive comparisons with other, nonreligious group and leadership styles and reveal a wider variety of organizational models among new religions. Finally, many contemporary scholars have adopted a fourth strategy, analyzing new groups in terms of their religious content. These scholars have noted such distinguishing characteristics as esoteric or novel theologies, the emphasis on individual quests for mystical experience, simple rituals promoting personal well-being, and communal if not mass meetings.

CHARACTERISTICS OF NEW RELIGIONS

While religious movements that call for reform or revival may occur within a single religious tradition as part of the normal process of change, new religions are those that have emerged from the encounter of two or more religious traditions. The processes through which they are formed may be categorized in three patterns: new religions emerge in the context of conquest and colonization during the prolonged contact of two or more traditions or through the creative interpretation of a perceived harmony among existing traditions. The collision of colonial powers with indigenous cultures has produced many new religions, especially since the sixteenth-century conquests by Western Christian powers. Under visionary leaders, dissident communities in Africa and the Americas found the power, identity, and meaning in the religious sphere that had eluded them in the political, economic, or cultural spheres of their rapidly changing societies. New religions, while thus expressing the problems of the oppressed, nevertheless used the religious symbolism of the oppressors, especially the Christian motifs of salvation fused with local beliefs in cosmic transformations. New religions have also developed without the immediate pressures of religious conflicts, through the prolonged interaction of religious traditions such as has occurred on the Asian mainland and islands. While the emergence of a single new group may be related to political reversals, social chaos, or economic upheaval, studies over time suggest that the new groups arise periodically, reinterpreting the indigenous and imported religions or revitalizing local folkways with the valued symbols and expressive modes of the national religions. Finally, new religions of the modern era, especially New Age groups, have resulted from the deliberate interrelation of several religions. Since the 1960s in Europe and North America, some religious seekers have envisioned the fundamental unity of sometimes quite alien religious traditions as well as a sort of universal interpretation of symbols and their deeper meanings; their insights have resulted in the rebirth of occult dimensions of Western religions mingled with ancient and Asian concepts of reality and the afterlife.

Recent scholarly efforts to characterize other, more specific dimensions of new religions, while necessarily reducing their exuberant variety, contribute a valuable overview of their similar causal factors, religious beliefs and practices, and social organizations. Occult or exotic features do not, however, dominate the list. While each new religion begins in a significant parting from the existent traditions, it must—whether rejecting or reinterpreting—remain meaningful in terms of those traditions and may continue familiar relational structures, concepts, symbols, or ritual elements alongside its more innovative features.

No single causal explanation may suffice for all new religions; still, several contributory factors may be observed in varying degrees, including political oppression, extensive economic disruption or deprivation, social stress, crises in community health or the environment, cultural disintegration, unresolved moral dilemmas, and an unresponsive or rigid religious institution. Not surprisingly, the existence of a dissident religious tradition may be the most important factor in the appearance of new groups in any region, under any other stressful circumstances. The worldviews of new religions combine old and new elements in a unique panorama, offered as a universal perspective for the broader community, superior to or even prior to any previous understanding of reality—recapturing a primordial truth. Most new religions generously recommend practical means for spiritual advancement and personal problem-solving. Individual visionary experiences or the learning of magical techniques may open vistas for personal empowerment and a sense of self-worth. Similarly, simplified rituals and communal sharing may enhance the spiritual value gained in the new commitment. A smaller percentage of new religions aims at exclusivity and so emphasizes secret doctrines or esoteric studies, followed by elaborate initiations, in order to gain extraordinary powers. In inaugurating a new association, many new religions rely on a charismatic founder, whose spiritual experience provides both legitimacy for personal authority and a model for devotees. While some communities are initially egalitarian, others begin in a more or less rigid hierarchy; the pattern for internal management may be significantly related to the dependence on the leader. Still, new religions emphasize voluntary membership and may celebrate individuality in their doctrines and rituals.

REGIONAL PATTERNS

The study of new religions may be undertaken through many meaningful perspectives, and different cross-cultural views on their shared patterns of emergence and characteristics present valuable insight into human spirituality. In order to adequately portray the widespread presence of new religions without removing them from ongoing religious life, the following survey has been organized by geographic region; within each region, religions are identified by their special features and in chronological order.

Africa Sub-Saharan Africa has been home to thousands of individual new religions since the mid-1800s, most of which have sprung from contact between traditional religions and the introduced forms of Christianity. A small number of new groups focus, however, on Islam or the indigenous religions themselves. Linked with the disruptive processes integral to the colonial encounter or, more directly, resultant from the domination by the alien institutions of European governments and Christian churches, new religions reclaim the indigenous power to explain new conditions or find meaning in them.

The breadth of new religions in Africa mirrors the diversity of the mostly Protestant Christian missions established there. Failure on the part of separate Christian churches to accommodate traditional beliefs and open church leadership to Africans inspired the formation of new groups professing not only more suitable Christian doctrines but also African control of the institutions themselves. From this beginning, new religions have moved in two directions, either toward separatist denominational churches, or toward prophetic communities that supersede denominational affiliation. Separatist religions began in the nineteenth-century Ethiopian churches and continue with later groups that integrate traditional African religious elements, including the Catholic-based Legio Maria and Jamaa movements and the Protestant-based East African Revival. Independent new religions have followed a charismatic or prophetic leader whose revelatory experience both shapes the institutional mode and balances old and new religious insights. The model for leadership, however, varies; it may modernize Judeo-Christian prophetic, messianic, or apostolic ideals or synthesize a substitute. Many religions of this type, including the Harrist and Aladura movements and the Zionists of South Africa, have cooperated to a greater or lesser degree with the Christian churches and the respective colonial governments. Islamic-inspired movements may also draw on prophetic revelations to introduce a new relationship between God and the world. Rather than form new churches, however, such groups are absorbed by existing Islamic brotherhoods or shrine associations. A few new religions seek to restore the power and prestige of indigenous traditions and the value of ancient lifeways. In their renewal of traditional religions through more universal interpretations, such groups may prove more responsive to a modern pluralistic society.

The Americas and the Caribbean The new religions of Central and South America developed in two strands, the first integrating indigenous and Christian religious elements and the second further influenced by African and, later, spiritist beliefs and practices. The two strands similarly expressed resistance to the catastrophic invasions by European Christians and the enslavement of indigenous peoples at their hands. The earliest new religions among native peoples—perceived as heresies by Catholic clerics—adopted Christian symbols of throne, Bible, and mystical meals and merged common spiritual perceptions across the religious boundaries. The native belief in periodic renewals of the world corresponded with the Christian teachings on Jesus' Second Coming, and visionaries either fused or paired the Messiah Jesus with their hoped-for redeemer. Announcing the return, then, of Jesus, the Holy Spirit, or the Inca king to reverse the colonial dominance by the Spanish or Portuguese, male leaders among Peruvians and coastal Brazilian communities assimilated priestly, prophetic, papal, or messianic roles in new religions beginning in the 1500s. Mesoamerican groups reflected the regional importance of the Catholic cult of the saints and centered their hopes on incarnations of the Virgin Mary, such as Maria Candelaria, or other saintly female leaders. In coastal Honduras, the Afro-Indian Garifuna have established an independent religion whose rituals, led by women, bespeak Amerindian, African, and Roman Catholic sources. Other new religions, such as the Hallelujah movement, began with shamans' journeys not to the spirit world but to Christian otherworlds and claimed transcendent power through the revelations or even texts collected there. Twentieth-century religions, centered variously in new scriptures or spiritual healing, reflect not only the changing perspective of the indigenous peoples but also their late encounters with Protestant evangelical missions.

A different type of new religion, found primarily in Brazilian cities, developed from the contact between Brazilindian, Roman Catholic, and African religious traditions. Rooted in the covert practices of slaves, Afro-Brazilian religions identified individual Catholic saints with the ancestral divinities of Africa and America and contacted them in elaborate trance possession rituals. Once closely related to African rituals and beliefs, most communities have restructured in the late twentieth century under spiritist teachings to offer a more universal or modern religious path and call upon the higher spirit beings to solve spiritual and material problems.

In North America three categories of new religions emerged from the encounter of cultures, the first two represented in the exclusive new religions among Native Americans and African Americans and the third including the new groups since the 1960s. Native American new religions were distinctive local attempts to recapture meaning in lives radically disrupted by European and Euro-American conquest. Guided by prophetic leaders and their visions, each group incorporated elements from Christianity—a revealed text, angelic or divine inspiration, biblical history, or the teachings of Jesus —but reflected the indigenous conviction that religion must be interwoven with other life experiences. Despite constitutional guarantees of religious freedom, native religions were deliberately suppressed in the United States until the 1970s, and new pan-Indian movements, such as the ghost dances begun among Plains Indians in the 1890s and the Native American Church, which continues sacramental use of peyote, were especially targeted for their defiant efforts to recover tribal traditions. Since the 1960s, however, New Age spirituality has embraced Native American perspectives on the effectiveness of ritual in shaping human identity and the necessary relationship between humans and their natural environment.

New religions among African Americans have unified their participants in protest against the injustices of slavery and subsequent discrimination and in confirmation of ethnic identity and self-worth. The most widespread innovations are in the independent Christian sects that, strongly shaped by African religious heritage, undertook positive programs toward self-determination after the U.S. Civil War. Drawing on the liberating teachings of Jesus and the American social gospel movement and influenced by the black-pride sentiments of Marcus Garvey, black Holiness churches and Pentecostal sects, as well as independent African-American branches of Christian denominations, have significantly contributed to the development of American Christianity. Other African Americans rejected Christianity as alien or irredeemably involved with the institution of slavery; they have, instead, supported the Islamic- or Jewish-derived religions. Islamic groups, such as the Moorish Science Temple and the Black Muslim movements, identified African heritage with Islamic civilization; once only superficially associated with Arabic Islam, most such religions have overtly established relations with Sunni Muslim groups since the 1970s. Black Jewish groups concluded that enslaved Africans, like the lost tribes of Israel, were chosen people held temporarily in bondage until divine history restored them to glory and power; contemporary groups, such as the followers of Yahweh ben Yahweh, have varying degrees of adherence to mainstream Judaism.

The Euro-American culture of North America has supported waves of interest in alternative spirituality, beginning in the colonial period. The opportunity for religious freedom and the exploration of humanistic concepts, the immigration of religious minorities from around the world, and the accompanying curiosity about non-Christian spiritual insights has provided both fertile ground and diverse resources for the development of new religions. A fascination with

European magic and the occult, founded in Neoplatonism, grew alongside Christian revivalism in early U.S. history and engendered not only intellectual and humanistic religious philosophy, such as transcendentalism, but also the esoteric groups based in Freemasonry and later Spiritualism. The heirs to the nineteenth-century Theosophy and Rosicrucians became publicly active in the 1960s, rejecting traditional Christian denominations and seeking a renewal of personal or unmediated spiritual experience through universal religious truths. Since then, the trends in significant new religions have been varied: some have announced communications with otherworldly powers, such as Spiritual Masters or mysterious alien beings; some rely on intense and secret training, as in groups inspired by G. I. Gurdjieff (ca. 1877–1949); some—the Neo-Pagans and modern Witches—recall ancient European nature religion; and others have either established American groups affiliated with new religions of Japan or Korea or—in the case of New Age groups—eclectically combined elements of Asian religions, such as yoga, meditation, chanting, and reincarnation with ancient Egyptian or Greek religious symbols and Native American spirituality.

African (Yoruba-Oya) Ergungun dancing at a ceremony on the island of Itaparica, off Salvador, Bahia, Brazil, January 1983. The Ergungun cult of representing the collective patrilineal Yoruba ancestral spirits with elaborate cloth constructions was brought by African slaves to Brazil in the early nineteenth century.

Caribbean new religions are surprisingly numerous and strong; some of the better known, such as Vodou or the Rastafari movement, have influence far beyond their places of origin. Religious creativity on the islands is connected historically with oppressive political or economic situations, but more recent developments express the diverse religious needs of the diverse population. Most new religions reveal a combined African-Christian heritage in differing proportions. One type of new religion emphasizes a reconnection with Africa in order to find meaning in the experience of Africans in the New World; new groups such as the Rastafarian offer both a coherent view of enslavement and a related ethics system, while providing a political base for community building. A second type—including Vodou in Haiti and Santeria in Cuba—integrates the complex Roman Catholic and West African religious systems. Centered in rituals for African deities and spiritual healing, these new religions recently reached new members in cities in the United States and Canada. A third type of new religion has renewed elements from the Christian evangelical and African traditions in their rituals and church institutions; the many separate communities are identified according to the prophetic leader whose guidance they follow. Asian traditions, present in the

Caribbean since the nineteenth century, have recently flourished through devotional groups alongside newly popular Islam-inspired movements.

Asia The rich and multifarious traditions of Asia have periodically engendered new religions, which freely intermingle the older indigenous symbols and rituals with the institutional interpretations of Taoism, Shinto, Confucianism, and Buddhism. Islam and Christianity, more recently, have contributed to the pattern of religious renewals. Because new religions may arise in connection with internal changes in the social, economic, or political order, or with the need to enact moral and spiritual reforms, the causal factors are more difficult to identify across the region and its history.

Innovative religions have been documented in China since the 1500s, although some older forms may date to the preceding millennium. Associated with the social and economic stresses of dynastic change or contact with Western powers, and drawing on the complex resources of local beliefs, rituals, and leadership roles, new religions are a recurrent aspect of Chinese religious life. The new "teachings" or "ways" may harmonize the mainstream traditions of Taoism, Confucianism, and Buddhism; restore specific elements of folk practice; and claim the nominal influence of Islam and Christianity. While the individual groups are small or short-lived, they may participate in larger dissident traditions; characteristically, they integrate members into a hierarchical organization directed by elders respected for their teaching or divination skills. That class of elders offers access to esoteric elements of Chinese cultural traditions, either to rituals preserved by adepts or revealed scriptures or to divinely inspired oracles of mythological and personal import. Within the wide range of Chinese new religions, the Compassion Society, the Court of the Way, and the Celestial Virtue Teaching, among others, have coalesced to form the White Lotus tradition centered on the divine Queen Mother of the West, whose salvific revelations descend through incarnate Buddhas and individual sect leaders; other groups, such as the popular Unity Way, propound the renewal of moral values usually identified with Neo-Confucianism, while still others renew ancient Taoist symbols in newly revealed heavenly mandates. In the late twentieth century, these new religions thrive only in Taiwan or in diaspora Chinese communities.

Korean new religions, present since the mid-1800s, have similarly created an original spiritual response to social, political, and religious change through the intertwining of indigenous divination and healing traditions with nonindigenous religious elements, including Taoist cosmology, Confucian ethics, Buddhist rituals, and Christian redemptive theology. Numerous groups, guided by charismatic leaders and often propounding nationalist ideologies, not only exalt the sacredness of their homeland but also seek universal renewal; only one group—Tong'ilgyo, or the Unification Church—has successfully recruited other Asian and European and American members.

New religions in Japan have drawn millions of participants since their inception in the mid-1800s, particularly in the 1950s and again in the 1980s. While a small number trace their lineage to older established sects, most new groups renovate mainstream Shinto and Buddhist concepts, assimilate selected elements of Christianity, and create modernistic perspectives and practices. Rejecting the dominant factions as outmoded in their bureaucratic hierarchies and devoid of true spiritual value, new religions offer communities of faith and personal growth for the increasingly urban population. While the charismatic founders of Shinto-related groups such as Tenrikyo and Konkokyo promulgate divinely inspired revelations and renew the sacrality of daily life, Buddhist-related groups such as Reiyukai, Soka Gakkai, Rissho Koseikai, and Agonshu

Contemporary altar painting with a central panel containing a representation of Kwanum (Kannon), the Buddha of Infinite Compassion (Avalokiteshvara). The painting is located at Kyeryongsan in the temple of The Infinite Heaven Way, a new Japanese religion.

reinterpret classic texts as modern practical guides or sources for ritual power. Contemporary groups may revitalize the premodern reliance on ancestral aid for spirit sicknesses, offer self-realization through problem-solving techniques, or proclaim salvation for a doomed modern life. Since the early 1980s, enthusiastic laymembers have spread the unique view of the "new new" religions Agonshu and Mahikari further, inviting young Japanese to try out their alternative spirituality; many groups have extensive membership in the Japanese immigrant populations in the United States and the United Kingdom but draw few non-Japanese participants.

In the Southeast Asian islands, new religions have also responded to the disruption of economic, political, and cultural life caused by colonial domination. Rebellions against Spanish oppression in the Philippines found expression in the convergence of Christian millennial imagery, rituals, and leadership titles with indigenous magic in local peasant groups. While the older groups increasingly militarized and politicized, the more recent religious trend has seen the birth of indigenized and independent Christian Philippine churches such as the popular Iglesia ni Christo, whose followers may also be found in the United States. Similarly, anticolonial sentiment in Indonesia found early expression in messianic movements merging Muslim and Hindu-Javanese elements; twentieth-century religions maintain fewer ties to Islam, and newer groups revitalize Hindu, Buddhist, or Javanese mystical traditions for personal spiritual advancement. Government regulation of new religions has compelled nominal affiliation with mainstream traditions, overt emphasis on Indonesian nationalism, or, more recently, the ideological identification of alternative religions as "faiths." Little is known about regional new religions on the continent other than the Vietnamese new religion of Cao Dai, whose discipline and traditions blend Buddhism, Taoism, and Confucianism in the worship of the Mother Goddess.

Europe While revolutionary religious movements have been a recurrent factor in European history, only in the late modern period have groups emerged that embrace a diverse, even global, religious heritage. The most recent of the new religions have emerged since the end of the 1960s, appearing in the predominantly Protestant Western European nations before spreading gradually but persistently into Eastern Europe. The religious movements, drawing primarily the disaffected and unchurched young people of the middle class, cannot be said to be ignited by religious, social, or even natural catastrophes; instead, their rise may be connected with the increased numbers of immigrants in Europe, the conscious efforts made by Asian new religions to expand their reach, the global travels of Western Europeans themselves, or simply the attractions of exotic teachings and practices for modern religious seekers. While the dissident movements of previous eras stayed within the bounds of Jewish or Christian traditions, new religions incorporate Asian, African, Native American, or Neo-Pagan insights along with perspectives from more secular philosophies.

European countries, as a whole, host an especially wide variety of new religions, exceeding the diversity found in the United States; each group, however, may have fewer than a thousand members. The most popular individual religions are the Unification Church, the Children of God, the International Society for Krishna Consciousness, and the Great White Brotherhood—all text-centered communities. The New Age groups, although not an organized religion, may be the most influential phenomenon, reaching a wide audience through festivals and popular publications. From these sources, many of the teachings of new religions, such as reincarnation, meditation, nature reverence, and the prophetic interpretation of traditional scriptures, are familiar and even positively received by a significant percentage of Europeans. In the 1970s and 1980s, however, sensationalist accounts of the recruitment of members and secret practices of new religious communities engendered not only virulent attacks on individual groups but also another anticult movement. More recent efforts in response to new religions have included mainstream church-supported research and its dissemination and the modernization of Christian practices themselves.

Oceania and Australia The diverse island cultures of Melanesia in the 1800s experienced several waves of colonization by European countries supported by the missionary work of Protestants and Catholics, with rival denominations and governments dividing the territories. Early missions were drawn into local hostilities or faced violent rejection when their collaboration with colonial oppression was recognized. When Christian evangelists, as well as the colonial government officials, failed to enter into the expected and divinely sanctioned trade relationships with Melanesians, the indigenous communities tried, through ritual means, to get the hidden European wealth or "cargo" that might revive the proper exchanges. Most such "cargo cults" were short-lived, although they may have inspired later political rebellions. While a few later missionaries suggested superficial parallels between Melanesian culture and the new Christian message, the usual introduction of Christianity emphasized its unique salvation necessitating the abandonment of old ways. The association of later missions with improved education and health facilities added to its appeal, but Melanesian Christians have preferred to reinterpret the imported religion in Melanesian terms, portraying Jesus, for example, as a clan ancestor or ideal brother supportive of traditional cooperative values. The result has been the rise of independent churches organized by Melanesians, as well as a renewed effort at accommodation by international missions. Hinduism, introduced in Fiji by immigrants, and Islam, followed by Indonesians residing in Papua New Guinea, have drawn few Melanesian followers and, apparently, inspired no new religions.

Since the nineteenth century, the Maori—dispossessed by colonial powers in New Zealand—have adapted Christian symbols to envision their own emancipation. Reviving rituals and images from the Old Testament, the new religious groups of the 1800s followed charismatic leaders who communicated with Maori ancestral spirits and prophesied a return from their latter-day Babylonian exile. Mere Rikiriki and Ratana, prophets in the early twentieth century, supported Maori nationalism, rejected indigenous rituals, and worshiped the Christian Trinity as well as native spirit powers, with the New Testament providing not only theological legitimacy but also the models for hierarchical organization. During the 1980s, however, the development of independent Maori-Christian churches was counterbalanced by a resurgence of local traditions.

Australian Aborigines have, since the early 1900s, responded to the havoc wreaked by Western domination in new religions, transforming traditional practices with novel Christian perspectives. Christian influence is seen in millennial movements promising miraculous deliverance from Europeans or restoration of native wealth and in revival groups that await religious reciprocity from the Christian church powers for their sacred revelations. While some smaller groups in the north and west anticipate a cosmic resolution through a new Captain Cook, southern coastal Aborigines have more recently offered a universalized interpretation of ancient healing for modern spiritual ills.

See also Africa, new religions in; African Americans (North America), new religions among; Afro-Americans (Caribbean and South America), new religions among; Afro-Brazilian religions; Afro-Surinamese new religions; Australia, new religions in; China, new religions in; China and Taiwan, new religions in; Europe, new religions in; Identity Christianity; Japan, new religions in; Korea, new religions in; Maori new religions; Melanesia, new religions in; Native Americans (Central and South America), new religions among; Native Americans (North America), new religions among; Neo-Paganism; New Age movements; North America, new religions in; Southeast Asian Islands, new religions in.

Nichiren (nee-chee-ren; 1222–82), the Buddhist priest whose teachings formed the basis of several Japanese Buddhist sects that bear his name. He maintained that the *Lotus Sutra* was the only teaching that would lead to salvation during the period of the end of the Dharma (*mappo*). He admonished the government several times, hoping to gain support for his views and have those with differing views suppressed, but he was exiled twice. The persecutions strengthened Nichiren's faith, leading him to feel that he was "living the *Lotus Sutra*" and was identified with several of the Bodhisattvas mentioned in the text. Nichiren advocated chanting the title of the *Lotus Sutra* (*daimòku*) so that the practitioner could turn this world into a paradise. After death, believers might hope to be reborn on Vulture Peak (Ryosen), where Sakyamuni eternally preached the *Lotus Sutra*. Among his major works are the *Rissho ankokuron* (Establishment of the True Teaching and Protecting the Nation), *Senji-sho* (Determining the Time), and *Kaimoku-sho* (On Opening the Eyes). Nichiren's beliefs and practices are the basis of several of the more important new religions of Japan, including Soka Gakkai, Reiyukai, and Rissho Koseikai. *See also* Lotus Sutra; mappo; Reiyukai; Rissho Koseikai; Soka Gakkai.

Nichiren Shoshu (nee-chee-ren; Jap., "the true teaching of Nichiren"), a name under which the Japanese Buddhist new religion Soka Gakkai is known outside of Japan, as with Nichiren Shoshu America (NSA). The name is taken from the Buddhist sect from which Soka Gakkai developed in Japan. *See also* Japan, new religions in; Soka Gakkai.

Niebuhr, Reinhold (nee'boor; 1894–1962), American Protestant theologian best known for his writings that seek to relate Christian social teachings to contemporary political and social issues, including *Moral Man and Immoral Society* (1932), *Interpretation of Christian Ethics* (1935), and *The Nature and Destiny of Man* (1941).

nien-fo (neein-fooaw; Chin., "invoking the Buddha"), Chinese meditation practice of uttering the Buddha's name in order to attain rebirth in a Pure Land. *See also* China, Buddhism in; nembutsu; Pure Land; Pure Land school (China).

Nihang (ni'huhng), a militant order of Sikhs. Members dressed in distinctive dark-blue robes and sporting an assortment of weapons are commonly seen outside Sikh shrines. Fiercely independent, the Nihangs are organized into loosely knit roving bands headed by a nominal chief. *See also* Sikhism.

Nihon ryoiki (nee-hohn reeoh-ee-kee; Jap., "Miraculous Stories of Karmic Retribution in Japan"), a collection of 116 Buddhist tales compiled around 823 by the monk Kyokai demonstrating the efficacy of *karma* through tales set in Japan. *See also* karma.

Nihonshoki (nee-hohn-shoh-kee; Jap., "Chronicle of Japan"), compiled in 720, the first of six official histories of Japan; also known as *Nihongi*. Along with the *Kojiki* (Record of Ancient Matters, 712), it provides a chronicle of Japan that presents Shinto myth, legends, and early history while legitimating the line of sovereigns. *See also* cosmology; Japanese myth; Kojiki; Shinto.

Nikaya Buddhism (nee-kah'yuh; Skt., "school," "sect"), a generic name assigned to the various schools (traditionally counted as eighteen) that emerged within the Buddhist community during the first several centuries after the death of the Buddha (ca. 486 B.C.). These schools shared two features: the refusal to accept the so-called Mahayana scriptures, composed four or more centuries after the death of the Buddha, as having the word of the Buddha himself and the refusal to accept the various celestial Buddhas and Bodhisattvas (likewise introduced under Mahayana auspices) into the Buddhist pantheon. The various Nikaya schools thus accept only the Buddha Sakyamuni, the future Buddha (now still a *bodhisattva*, or Buddha-to-be) Maitreya, and the so-called "Buddhas of the past" (believed to have lived prior to Sakyamuni), who were the objects of veneration in the pre-Buddhist period, as valid objects of reverence.

While in the period immediately following the death of the Buddha the Buddhist community appears to have remained largely intact (comprising the period of "primitive" or presectarian Buddhism), within approximately a century and a half the Buddhist community began to divide over a variety of issues. The earliest disagreements appear to have been over matters of monastic rule (Vinaya), while later dissension centered around doctrinal issues.

Early Sectarian Divisions: The cause of the first-known schism, which resulted in the separation of the Mahasamghikas ("Majority-ists") from the Sthaviras ("Elders"), is itself a matter of dispute. According to Mahasamghika sources a disagreement arose because certain non-Mahasamghika Buddhists were altering (i.e., adding to) the original list of monastic rules. According to sources emanating from descendants of the Sthaviras, the disagreement concerned the status of those who had attained the final stage of enlightenment, *arhats*, with the Sthaviras claiming that an arhat was exempt from regression and from worldly faults, while the Mahasamghikas contended otherwise.

Divisions within the Sthavira Group: Subsequent splits clearly centered on matters of doctrine. Some two centuries after the death of the Buddha a group known as the Vatsiputriyas separated from the Sthavira wing, contending (in contrast to both the Sthavira and the Mahasamghika schools) that a quasi-soul, the *pudgala* ("person"), transmigrated from one existence to the next. Soon afterward the Sarvastivadins ("those who claim that all exists") separated from another Sthavira group, the Vibhajyavadins ("those who make distinctions"), with the former claiming that the past and future, as well as the present, can legitimately be said to "exist," while the latter held that only the present (and, according to certain Vibhajyavadin subschools, those past actions that have not yet borne karmic fruit) can be said to have any reality. Around three centuries after the death of the Buddha a division occurred within the Vibhajyavadin group over the issue of the relationship between the Buddha and the monastic community, yielding two schools known as the Mahisasakas (who claimed that the Buddha formed part of the monastic community) and the Dharmaguptakas (who claimed that he did not). This issue, though partly doctrinal, had considerable economic overtones, for the underlying question was whether laypeople could make greater merit by contributing to the upkeep of the monks and nuns or to the flourishing cult of the burial mound (*stupa*) containing the relics of the Buddha or other venerated teachers.

Divisions within the Mahasamghika Group: The causes of subdivisions within the Mahasamghika group are less clear. If the Mahasamghika sources themselves are to be believed, an intragroup schism took place over the degree of perfection attained by the arhat, with the northern schools (including the so-called Lokottaravadins, or "Transcendentalists") asserting that the arhat was incapable of imperfection or relapse, while the southern Mahasamghika schools relegated him to a more human level. What is certain, however, is that the Lokottaravadins eventually came to hold a supermundane view of the Buddha, claiming that he was far above the level of ordinary mortals and had only "appeared" in this world to save human beings. The southern Mahasamghika schools, by contrast, appear to have maintained a far more human view of the Buddha.

Geographical Diffusion and Current Status: Of the various Nikaya schools that emerged in the centuries following the death of the Buddha, only the Theravada ("teaching of the Elders") survives today, holding sway in Sri Lanka and most of Southeast Asia. During the early centuries A.D., however, the most influential Nikaya schools appear to have been the Mahasamghikas and the Sarvastivadins, both of which flourished in northwest India. The predominant school throughout Central Asia appears to have been the Sarvastivada, which maintained its dominant position in this region until at least the ninth century.

Literary Remains: While a complete Theravadin canon has been preserved in South and Southeast Asia, the writings of many of the other Nikaya schools have been lost. Only a few Sarvastivadin and Mahasamghika works have survived in their original Indian languages, while a somewhat larger number (together with a few Dharmaguptaka works) have been preserved in Chinese translation. Several texts of the Mulasarvastivada school (an offshoot of the Sarvastivada) survive in Tibetan translations. Only two or three texts belonging to the Vatsiputriya group (long considered heretical by other Buddhist schools) have been preserved in Chinese translation. *See also* Buddhism; Buddhism (authoritative texts and their interpretation); Mahasamghika; Mahayana; Sarvastivada; Theravada.

Nimbarka Sampradaya (nim-bahr'kuh suhm-pruh-dah'yuh), a sect founded by the Vaishnava saint Nimbarka in the twelfth century in North India. Nimbarka is credited with the philosophical position called Bhedabheda Advaita, which connotes simultaneous "difference" between the soul and God and "nondifference." This attempts to resolve the paradoxical interpretations of the nature of the divine-human relationship set forward by competing Vedanta schools of Hindu philosophy by situating the primary theology of North Indian Vaishnavism squarely in the Radha-Krishna relationship. Nimbarka's theory and devotion possibly influenced the supreme master of late Sanskrit poetry, Jayadeva, the author of the erotic love poem on the Radha-Krishna relationship, the *Gita Govinda*. *See also* Gita Govinda; Vaishnavism; Vedanta.

nimbus, circle of light around the head of a supernatural being or holy person. *See also* glory.

Nine Mountain schools, Korean form of Southern Ch'an Buddhism in the late Unified Silla period (seventh century). These schools had been brought from China by Korean monks who had studied with the disciples of the Southern Ch'an masters Matzu Tao-i and Pai Chang. Though we know little about the actual practice within these schools and how they differed from their Chinese counterparts, we know that each school constituted in Korea a separate lineage. Each lineage was located on a separate mountain with one main temple whose name was either taken from the mountain or whose name became the mountain name.

The Nine Mountain schools marked a departure from all previous Buddhist institutions on the peninsula because they were deliberately established outside the capital and far from support of royal and aristocratic clans. They appealed to the provincial gentry's notions of individualism and regionalism and gave heightened status to those families excluded from participation in capital government. It was the sons of the provincial gentry who founded these schools and who filled their ranks. The doctrine of innate Buddhahood without reference to class status, taught by the Ch'an schools, helped to move Buddhism beyond the aristocratic and ceremonial elitism that had characterized its life in the capital. *See also* Ch'an school; National Protection Buddhism.

Ninigi (nee-nee-gee), also known as Ninigi-no-mikoto; Shinto deity sent by the sun goddess Amaterasu to pacify and rule Japan. He was the grandfather of the legendary first emperor, Jimmu. *See also* Amaterasu; Japanese myth.

Ninlil (nin'lil, Sumerian, meaning uncertain), a goddess, the wife of Enlil or of Assur; she was known to the Greeks as Molis (Muleta, Mulitta) and identified with Aphrodite. *See also* Mesopotamian religion.

Ninomiya Sontoku (nee-noh-mee-yah sohn-toh-koo; 1787–1856), a practical and moral Japanese philosopher who advocated agricultural revitalization and the repayment of virtue (*hotoku*) through cooperation, thrift, diligence, and local self-help. *See also* hotoku.

Ninurta (nin-*oor*'tah; Sumerian, "Lord of the Producing Earth"), Sumerian god of fertility in fields and flocks. Also a war god, he was the son of Enlil. *See also* Mesopotamian religion.

Nirankari (nihr-uhn-kahr'ih), a reformist Sikh sect founded by Baba Dayal (1783–1855) to protest against the theology and religious practices of dominant Sanatan Sikh tradition. Sanatan Sikhs believed that God periodically reincarnates. Baba Dayal denied this and proclaimed that God, as conceived by Guru Nanak, was *nirankar* (Skt., "formless"); consequently the sect came to be called the Nirankaris. Although Baba Dayal and his successors had only a small following within the Sikh community, their teachings and efforts at reform proved significant when Sikhism came to be redefined at the turn of the century. The present head of the sect is Gurbakhsh Singh and his headquarters are in Chandigarh. *See also* Nanak; Sikhism.

nirguna/saguna (neer'guh-nuh/sah'guh-nuh; Skt., "without qualities"/"with qualities"), Hindu philosophical distinction, beginning in the Upanishads, between the two modes of the absolute *brahman*, absolute reality. *Nirguna* defines brahman as transcending qualification; *saguna* defines the lower, immanent brahman often identified as a personal god. *See also* brahman; path of devotion; six systems of Indian philosophy.

nirvana (nihr-vah'nuh; Skt., "blowing out"; Pali *nibbana*), the ultimate religious goal in major forms of Hinduism and all forms of Buddhism.

Hinduism: In the religion of the Brahman priesthood in India a dichotomy had evolved in religious goals and attitudes toward time. Producing continued life in time by sacrificial-ritual action (the first sense of the word *karma*) had formerly been desirable, but it now came to be seen as an inevitable and undesirable form of suffering, since it meant subjection to "repeated dying" in a sequence of lives. It was possible to be reborn in the sequence of lives as an animal, as a human being at different levels of the Brahmanic social hierarchy, and as one of the many gods inhabiting the universe. Such gods were not immortal; their lives, however long, would end in death, as did all lives in time. Thus the round of rebirth (*samsara*) was "world without end"—but that was the problem, not the solution. The highest goal, the attainment of *nirvana*, was to achieve, by ascetic withdrawal from society, a timeless union of microcosm and macrocosm, to realize the essential identity of the self (*atman*) and the universe (*brahman*).

Buddhism: Early Buddhism accepted the Hindu general understanding of nirvana and the monastic ideal but rejected the Brahmanic notion of the unity of atman and brahman.

Theravada Buddhism: The early Buddhist doctrine of no-self declares both the individual being and the sequence of such beings in rebirth to be a causally connected but ever-changing stream of events, with no "self" as what Brahmanic texts had called its "inner controller." Religious action (karma now in a generalized and ethicized sense) can produce good rebirth, accepted as a lesser goal. The highest goal is the conquest of time, death, and suffering in timeless nirvana. This nirvana is not a state of the self, there being no such thing; it is, rather, the complete realization of selflessness. But neither is it equivalent to nothingness; it is, one might say, a "peace which passeth all understanding." Many epithets are applied to it in texts, both positive and negative: it is the "going out of the flame" (the literal sense, from the root *nir-va*, "to go or blow out"); the highest happiness; the further shore beyond the ocean of suffering; a calm, peaceful, and stable realm of safety; a city; and so on. But none of these epithets is taken to do more than point toward the reality of nirvana, in itself indescribable.

In understanding nirvana and the changes the idea underwent, it is vital to see that the words nirvana and *parinirvana* can be used to denote two related but obviously different events. The first is the "blowing out" of the flames of greed, hatred, and delusion, as was achieved, for example, by the Buddha at the age of thirty-five under the Bodhi Tree. This is called (pari-)nirvana, but also *bodhi*, rendered in English as "Enlightenment" or "Awakening"; this term is derived from a root meaning "to be or become awake," as is the word *buddha*, "the Awake(ned)." This first sense of nirvana is described in primarily psychological terms. The second realization of nirvana, final nirvana—the word parinirvana has sometimes been used in only this sense—is when the enlightened person "dies" (the texts usually use a verb, "to nirvanize"), as did the Buddha at the age of eighty. This second sense of nirvana, the eschatological, does not play a role in all forms of Buddhism. Those traditions that accept the idea of a final nirvana have resolutely refused to elaborate on it: it is not the return to a primordial cosmogonic reality, not the realization of the true (universal) Self; it is, simply, indescribable.

Mahayana Buddhism: What seems to have been for the most part a minority movement in South and Southeast Asian Buddhism but is almost universal in Tibet and East Asia, the Mahayana, or "Great Vehicle," depicted what it took itself to be superceding as the Hinayana, "Lesser Vehicle." Modern scholars often use a less pejorative term, *Theravada*, or the *Sravakayana*, "Disciples' Vehicle." The idea of nirvana in the Greater Vehicle underwent many radical changes; discussions of Buddhism in Western scholarship are often obscured by not making this clear. The proponents of the Greater Vehicle claimed that the Disciples' nirvana was not the highest goal. It is sometimes said that they saw attainment of it by an individual disciple as "selfish"; this cannot be right (and represents no indigenous Buddhist term), since nirvana is, after all, the attainment of selflessness. What they did claim was that it was a restricted, lesser goal, when compared to the *bodhisattva's* vow to help enlighten all living beings. This vow, however, is to be seen against a new understanding of nirvana: Greater Vehicle texts concentrate almost wholly on the first sense, that of enlightenment. The idea of a final nirvana, a definitive exit from the realm of suffering temporality, is rejected in favor of an endless concern with the enlightenment of all beings. In some texts the nirvana of a Buddha is called *apratisthita*, "unestablished"; that is to say, a Buddha is not "in" the round of rebirth, since he has realized the highest enlightenment; but neither is he "in" nirvana, seen as a separate and unconnected ontological state.

Further developments, particularly important in East Asian Buddhism, make the picture yet more complex. Ideas of the Buddha-mind or Buddha-nature, explicitly said in both traditional and modern traditions to be the True Self, seem to return, if only analogously, to the pre-Buddhist Brahmanic picture. That is to say, enlightenment is the realization of one's true identity as Buddha-mind, a return to the ground of all being (an idea that often goes along with a more or less direct form of philosophical idealism). Modern forms of such Buddhism, both in Asia and the West, clearly prefigured by the Greater Vehicle's emphasis on the first, psychological sense of nirvana, tend toward demythologization: nirvana and samsara become states of mind, ways of being in the suffering world rather than ontological accounts of it and eschatological hopes to be free from it. *See also* Bodhisattvas; Buddhism (thought and ethics); Four Noble Truths; liberation; suffering.

nisa, al- *See* gender roles.

niyya (nee'yuh; Arab., "intention"), prayer offered by individual Muslims at the beginning of important rituals.

Njordr (ne'ord-uh), in mythology the Norse god of

fertility and richness, fishing and shipping, father of Freyr and Freyja. *See also* Nordic religion.

Noah, in the Hebrew Bible, a righteous man, saved, along with his family, from the Flood (Genesis 6–9). *See also* ark in the Hebrew Bible; B'nai Noah; flood stories.

Islam: Noah (Arab. *Nuh*) is the first prophet bringing punishment for the sins of humankind, according the Qur'an and Islam. Postquranic commentary embellishes the story of Nuh and knows of a fourth son, Canaan or Yam, who is drowned. The quranic story of Nuh is often recited by Muslims when they are about to set out on a potentially perilous journey, such as the pilgrimage to Mecca (*Hajj*). *See also* Messenger of Allah.

noble savage, primitivist term referring to a member of a tribal culture, particularly directed to highly regarded qualities that were thought to stem from living in a natural state. The term must be used with great caution because it values people of a given culture according to the norms and beliefs of another, unrelated culture. This reference to the "noble savage" dates from at least the late sixteenth century, reached its most widely recognized exponent in the eighteenth century in the works of Rousseau, and is by no means absent from twentieth-century thought.

Noble Truths, Four. *See* Four Noble Truths.

Noh drama, Japanese lyric dance-drama, still performed today, that attained classical form in the fourteenth century largely through the efforts of Kan'ami (1333–84) and his son Zeami (1363–1443). Noh is sometimes performed as an offering to the gods and is accompanied by comic performances called *kyogen* ("mad words"). Divided into plays about gods, ghosts of warriors, ghosts of women, living people, and demons, Noh provides a panoramic view of the medieval Japanese synthesis of Buddhism and Shinto. The best-known type of play involves the encounter between a wandering Buddhist monk and a ghost in search of salvation. *See also* Japanese religions (art and architecture); ma.

no-mind (Chin. *wu-hsin*), the severing of thought and dispensing of words that is the goal of all Chinese Ch'an Buddhist meditative practice. *See also* Ch'an school; meditation.

nonconformist, a term first applied to those religious groups who dissented from the disciplines and authority of the Church of England; now a general term for a variety of Protestant denominations. *See also* Separatist.

nondualism, Hindu. Characterizing nondualism is problematic. One cannot conceive of or describe nonduality; if one conceives of or describes "it," it is not nondual. Further, since nonduality is always interpreted and in a context, one must speak of various nondualisms (union, identity, substantial, qualitative, etc.), which is certainly true of Hindu nondualisms. Still, all believers in nonduality share the notions that multiplicity arises from a single basis that appears in different modes or states, and the everyday dualistic experience of the "I" and the world is ultimately false. The knower/subject and known/object are not truly separate.

Perhaps the best-known Hindu nondualisms are those of Vedanta and Tantrism. The Vedanta tradition is based on the Upanishads, sacred texts investigating the nature of ultimate reality (Skt. *brahman*). In numerous places, the Upanishads assert that the true self (*atman*) is identical with brahman and that all appearance is truly nondual. Shankara, the best-known eighth-century proponent of Advaita (nondual) Vedanta, held that brahman is qualityless (*nirguna*) and identical with the eternal partless self. He argued that due to beginningless ignorance (*avidya*), we superimpose illusory phenomenal manifestation (*maya*) on the changeless nondual self/brahman (and vice versa). Overcoming this ignorance brings liberation.

Tantrism held that one must dissolve all apparent dualities such as matter/consciousness, microcosm/macrocosm, and male/female by reintegrating these manifestations into a higher nonduality. Tantrics were often followers of Shiva. For example, in the Kashmir Shaivism of Abhinavagupta (tenth century), all is ultimately Shiva, pure being and consciousness, cause and substance of all phenomena. The world (including souls) is Shiva's self-manifestation, a freely assumed self-limited appearance eventually coming to self-recognition. The world and objects are not illusory since ultimately they are Shiva, whose consciousness contains multiplicity in his (veiled but pervasive) unity. This understanding that all multiplicity is projected from yet contained in a single divine being also holds for certain followers of Vishnu/Krishna, such as Vallabha (1479–1531) and some in the Caitanya (1486–1533) tradition. *See also* Dvaita Vedanta; liberation; maya; Shiva; six systems of Indian philosophy; Tantra; Vedanta.

nonliteracy, an essential characteristic of traditional religions stressing the oral nature of religious actions and symbols.

When all important transactions of a culture are oral, the continuity of values depends on the individual memories of the elders of a society. While Westerners might consider that nonliteracy makes a tradition vulnerable, it also provides resilience and strength, and, at the same time, creative adaptability. Throughout their histories, traditional religions have encountered new situations, new peoples, new ideas—frequently with tension between the new and the traditional cultural values. It is here that oral traditions can be far more creative and versatile than written traditions. What is no longer meaningful can, over time, be forgotten; what becomes meaningful can be incorporated into the oral lore. *See also* oral tradition; storytelling; traditional peoples, religions of.

nonobstruction of phenomena and phenomena (Chin. *shih-shih wu-ai*), Chinese Buddhist doctrine holding that because all phenomena arise in interrelation, each is organically a part of the whole and they all mutually reflect each other.

nonobstruction of principle and phenomena (Chin. *li-shih wu-ai*), Chinese Hua-yen Buddhist teaching that all phenomena are permeated by principle because they arise from the intrinsically pure mind. *See also* Hua-yen school.

nonviolence. *See* ahimsa; Gandhi, Mohandas Karamchand; Jainism; King, Martin Luther, Jr.; pacifism (Christian); satyagraha; vegetarianism.

Nordic religion. To delimit Old Norse religion in time and space is not an easy task. The period ends with the victory of Christianity during the tenth and eleventh centuries. It is much more problematic to decide when it started. The sources disclose no decisive breaks in the religion of the north until the coming of Christianity. Archaeology tells us that there were major political and social upheavals in the periods before the Viking Age, which started around 800, but these do not automatically correlate with any significant changes in the religious outlook of the people involved.

However, it seems reasonable to assume that a group settled in Northern Europe during the third millennium B.C., and that the sources of the later periods often reflect their religious ideology. Linguistically the Scandinavians belonged (and belong) to the Germanic-speaking peoples, of which they make up the northern branch. It is likely that the whole of the Germanic area, until the coming of Christianity, had a common religious ideology, although minor differences occurred, just as they do inside the Nordic area. When we speak of "Nordic religion" instead of "Germanic religion," it is due to historical circumstances: Christianity spread much sooner in the southern parts of the area than in the north. Our sources for the pre-Christian religion of the south are few, and they do not allow us to draw a picture of the religion proper.

Concerning the north, the situation is very different, and we have many sources giving us detailed information on both religious ideology and practice, at least for the later parts of the pre-Christian period, i.e., the Viking Age. This, then, is the time and space for known "Nordic religion": the Scandinavian countries and Iceland in the period from ca. 800 until the coming of Christianity.

The Sources: Our information on Nordic religion has come down to us through many different sources that must be evaluated separately. We must first differentiate between the archaeological record and the texts. The first category gives us some information about burial forms and other cultic practices but very little about their meaning and significance. In order to incorporate this information into the religious system we therefore depend heavily on the written sources. These we can divide into contemporaneous and later sources. Among the first, there are runic inscriptions and some of the so-called scaldic poetry. Although we do get some important information from these texts, it is still so scant that we must also include the later texts in order to understand the religion. Some of these sources are very difficult to date, for instance, one of the most important text groups of all concerning the mythology: namely, the so-called *Elder Edda*. This contains a lot of poems concerning gods and heroes of pre-Christian times. Scholars have disagreed a great deal about the source value of these poems, primarily because they dispute their dating. Some would place most of them in pre-Christian times, whereas others tend to regard them as composed in Christian times by Christian poets. Since they are all anonymous there is no way to determine exactly when and for what purpose they were written. The content, however, seems for the most part to be of old origin. Other works, in prose, also give important information, such as the *Younger Edda* (or *Prose Edda*), written by the Icelander Snorri Sturluson around 1220, which contains much mythological information. Both the *Younger Edda* and Snorri's other great work, *Heimskringla,* are problematic sources, because they were written so long after the introduction of Christianity. But several scholars have nevertheless been able to show that Snorri must have had some older, to us unknown, written or oral sources at his disposal. The same type of problem applies to the different genres of Icelandic sagas: they are all written from the twelfth century onwards, and it is difficult to distinguish between the author's own imagination and the knowledge that he may have had of the period he describes.

Myths: The early Scandinavians believed in a polytheistic system of gods, much like the Greeks and many other peoples. The two families of gods, Aesir and Vanir, lived in Asgardr (the world of the Aesir) situated somewhere in the middle of the world where the world tree, Yggdrasill, was (or, according to some sources, in heaven). Most of the gods were related to each other, and the most powerful figure, seen as father of many of the other, was Odinn. He was primarily the god of the kings and nobles, and his most characteristic trait was his magical ability. He was able to intervene in the wars of humans, to teach humans various kinds of sorcery, and of course to practice it himself. Most famous among his skills was a certain kind of sorcery called *seidr,* which was nevertheless looked upon with much skepticism, because males could not practice seidr without being accused of *ergi* ("unmanliness"). Odinn was also the king of Valhall, where the dead warriors came after having fallen in battle, as decreed by Odinn himself. He was, moreover, associated with the poetry that played a role in many kinds of magic, just as he was the god of the runes (lit., "secrets"). His magic was primarily used in connection with war, but he also ruled over the wind and other natural phenomena. Odinn, or at least a god of the Odinn-type, is probably very old and dates back to Indo-European times.

Another very early god is Tyr, whose name is derived from an Indo-European word for the sky (*dyauh*) but whose position in the Viking Age seems to have been of minor importance, although there is some evidence for his connection with the *thing* (Old Norse, "assembly of warriors") and consequently law and the taking of oaths.

The most famous of Odinn's sons was Thor, very different from his father, who was the intellectual god par excellence. Almost all the myths in which Thor plays the main role emphasize his physical strength. He was constantly fighting the giants living far from the center of the earth, in Utgardr (the outer world). Nevertheless, they were always threatening both the gods and humans who lived in Midgardr (the middleworld). In this way Thor was primarily the defender of cosmos against the power of chaos. Using his hammer as a weapon, he also created thunder and lightning and eventually rain, and was thus connected with the fertility of the soil. A group of gods not part of the Aesir family were the Vanir. They consisted of only three members said to have been given as hostages to the Aesir after a war between the two groups. Njordr was father to Freyr and Freyja, and they were all first and foremost connected with fertility. Their cult was characterized by the use of phallic symbols and obscene songs and acts.

Another god was Baldr, said to be the purest of all the gods, but he was accidentally killed by the ill advice of Loki. Loki was the trickster of the Norse pantheon who in the last phase of the world's development (Ragnarok, "the fate of the gods") supported the giants, although according to the myths, he lived among the gods.

Gods with only a few or no myths at all are Heimdall, Hermodr, Hodr, Ullr, and several others, while among the goddesses are Frigg (the wife of Odinn), Sif (the wife of Thor), Skadi, Nanna, Gefjun, and Idun.

The overall view of the Scandinavians seems to have been that immediately after the creation of the world, there was a period that may be characterized as a golden age, but after that everything went downhill until the present time, which is the time after the killing of Baldr and just before Ragnarok. The gods did not set the good examples they should, and among humans moral and social rules tended to break. This course of events was due to fate, more powerful than even the gods. This concept played a major role in the beliefs of the Viking Age. During Ragnarok all gods, human beings, and giants will be killed and Yggdrasill destroyed. Afterward, however, a new world will be created, inhabited by the sons of the old gods and a new generation of human beings.

Rituals: The cult of the Scandinavians can be divided into public and private types. Of those in the first category we have many descriptions. One of the most detailed is the one by the German canon Adam of Bremen who described the cult in Uppsala, which was said to have been common for all the peoples of Sweden. Adam's reliability has been questioned (he writes shortly after 1070), but much of his information seems to be quite plausible. He describes a temple with statues of Odinn, Thor, and Freyr, and tells how they were worshiped with both human and animal sacrifices. It is also clear from Adam and many other sources that the king, or the political leader, played a major role in the public cult. We are less well informed about the private cult, but there is no doubt that especially the fertility aspect was focused on in it.

Major rituals were carried out in connection with war, the agricultural cycle, and in times of crisis. Also, funerals had an elaborate system of rites, including sacrifices. The most detailed description of such a funeral is that of the Arab writer Ibn Fadlan, who actually saw a Viking funeral in 922. Whereas the mythological sources give us a good deal about beliefs in connection with the fate of the dead (most important is that the dead warriors or those who are initiated to Odinn go to Valhall, whereas those who die of old age go to Hel, the gloomy place in the netherworld), Ibn Fadlan's testimony is one of the few that gives us detailed information about the rites. Other "rites of passage" existed, such as initiations into the warrior bands under the protection of Odinn, but unfortunately information is scant on these matters.

The End of Nordic Religion: At the end of the tenth century Christians succeeded in converting the Danes and, soon after, the Norwegians and the Icelanders; the Swedes were only converted during the late eleventh century and even later. How much the new religion actually meant to the individual is difficult to imagine, in that many were forced to undergo baptism. But from the twelfth century onward only scattered remnants of the pre-Christian religion were left in folk belief. These, on the other hand, have existed up until the present century. *See also* Aesir; Asgardr; Baldr; Berserk; Edda; Freyja; Freyr; Frigg; Fylgja; Heimdall; Hel; Hodr; Indo-European religion; Loki; mead; Midgardr; Njordr; Odinn; Ragnarok; Thor; Valhall; Valkyrja; Vanir; Vikings; Voluspa; Votan; Woden; Yggdrasill.

norito (noh-ree-toh; Jap., "ritual words"), ancient Shinto ritual prayers. Accompanied by music, dancing, and food and drink offerings, the *norito* formed the core of the rituals of official, or court, Shinto. Primarily found in the tenth-century *Engi-shiki*, the most important ritual texts are the *oharai* ("great purification"), held on the last day of the sixth and twelfth months, and the *toshi-gohi* (spring rice-planting festival). There are also a number of exorcisms, thanksgivings for harvest, and prayers to accompany political ceremonial. The norito are formulaic and usually contain a contract with the gods ("If you do this, then we will do that"); they also contain frequent allusions to mythic events and many bolster the legitimacy of the imperial polity. *See also* Engi-shiki; exorcism; Japanese religions (festal cycle); Shinto.

North America, Islam in. The first identifiable individual Muslim to have come to North America is one Estevanico, a navigator with Marcos de Niza in 1539. Thereafter, some African slaves brought over to work the southern plantations and adventurers such as Hi Jolly constitute the earliest Muslim presence on the continent.

Ross, North Dakota, is the site of the first recorded organized Muslim prayer (1900), and the first convert to Islam was an American consul in Manila, Mohammed Alexander Russel Webb, who became Muslim in 1887. Cedar Rapids, Iowa, has had a continuous Muslim presence since early in the second decade of this century and is reputed to have built the first mosque, in 1934. However, the proto-Muslim Noble Drew Ali, a black prophet, founded a Moorish Science Temple in Newark, New Jersey, in 1913, and he instilled important features of Islamic belief in his followers.

The Canadian census of 1871 recorded thirteen Muslims in Canada, all in Ontario, but immigration from the Middle East expanded rapidly after the turn of the century. Forty percent of the Muslim population in Manitoba is said to have died fighting for Canada in World War I.

Since these foundational days, immigration has expanded enormously the number of Muslims in both countries, an indigenous Islam has developed in the United States, and there have been conversions through Sufi (mystical) associations. Each group has grown in distinctive ways. Among the first group, the primary institutional action was to establish a mosque, of which the original mosque in Edmonton, Alberta, is the best known. Immigrant groups have constructed mosques wherever their numbers have made it viable, and the mosque has become a symbol of Muslim permanence in North America. Arabic teaching during "Sunday school" classes and Muslim cemeteries are also marks of local Islamic institutional forms, while national organizations such as the Federation of Islamic Associations in the United States and the Council of Muslim Communities of Canada give voice to Muslim concerns. At one time, differences between Sunni and Shia Muslims were blurred as intermarriage occurred and the lack of sufficient numbers militated against strict sectarianism. This now has been largely

North American Muslims gather after prayer services outside the Islamic Center, Cedar Rapids, Iowa (1976).

modified by the influx of migrants from all major Muslim sects.

More dramatically, the second group, indigenous Muslims, has made a significant impact on the religious makeup of North America. Under the leadership of men such as Elijah Muhammad and his son, Warith Deen Muhammad, many Americans have joined the Black Muslim movement, which in recent years has moved closer to mainline Islamic beliefs. The original Black Muslim movement has been split, with part of the group following Minister Louis Farrakhan in his allegiance to Elijah's early doctrine.

Nevertheless, programs designed for upgrading inner-city blacks, prison programs, economic restructuring, and self-help organizations within the movement have made Islam nationally and internationally recognized as a religious force to be reckoned with in North America. Finally, Sufi groups have also played a role in bringing Muslim religiosity to seekers in college and intellectual circles, and permanent Sufi dance associations exist in many cities across North America.

North America, new religions in, new or unconventional religious movements begun since European settlement, in both sectarian forms of the predominant Christian religion and other, largely non-Christian activities. The prolifera-

tion of new religions in English-speaking North America can be attributed to several causes: the immigration from many places of people of ethnic and religious minorities seeking freedom of expression; conditions of oppression such as often generate novel religious responses, as among African Americans and Native Americans; the frontier with its psychological pressures and its opportunities for experimentation; the idealism of a new society, which suggested fresh and even utopian spiritual possibilities; and the existence of relative religious freedom itself.

The recent development of North American civilization coincided with the emergence of modern science and technology, producing in its wake the great religion versus science controversies, which led to many religious results both orthodox and unconventional. Hardly less important was the Euro-American "discovery" of Asia and its spiritual heritage in the same centuries. Finally, there was the cumulative cross-fertilization impact of the meeting and mixing of many spiritual strands, including the Native American with its shamanism and the Asian, due to immigration and the westward movement of peoples across the continent.

Historical Outline: The history of non-Christian or marginally Christian religious movements in North America may be divided into several great epochs. The first, from colonial times to the commencement of Spiritualism in 1848, may be thought of as a period of European esotericism and gradually increasing Eastern intellectual influence. The establishment of a Rosicrucian fraternity in Pennsylvania in 1694 and, on a darker note, the Massachusetts witchcraft trails of the 1690s, reveal an early awareness in the New World of an alternative spiritually embedded in Christian Europe. The heir of Neoplatonism, it embraced the Jewish (and increasingly Christian) *kabbalah*, theurgy, and such auxiliary practices as astrology and evocational magic. Its fundamental pillars were ptolemaic cosmology, the doctrine of correspondences (e.g., belief in relationships susceptible to magical usage between planets, gemstones, the organism of the human body, etc.), and the "great chain of being" (i.e., a hierarchy of angelic or quasi-divine beings between humanity and God).

This worldview, sometimes labeled Rosicrucianism, had undergone a great revival in Renaissance science and occultism (finely reflected in much Elizabethan literature) but, after the new science of Copernicus and Newton, had become increasingly discredited in the eyes of intellectuals. Yet as it declined it fragmented, so that thinkers might hold to certain tenets but not to others, as did Benjamin Franklin, who ridiculed astrology but exalted the great chain-of-being concept. This made the "spiritual" aspects of the alternative reality, divorced from the obsolete scientific side, accessible to seekers.

There were those for whom the spiritual signs and concepts of the old wisdom remained significant. First, Freemasonry in the eighteenth century revamped and revived much symbolism from the other tradition in its quest for alternatives to clericalist Christianity. Then two new figures, Emmanuel Swedenborg (1688–1772) and Anton Mesmer (1733–1815), provided new garments for the traditional wisdom. Swedenborg reinvigorated the doctrine of correspondence and spoke to the sensitivities of a new age by offering a therapeutic, rather than forensic, vision of the other world. Mesmer, the father of modern hypnotism, taught that trance states opened one to occult knowledge of transcendent realities. Both presented anew the great virtues of the alternative tradition, its sense that the universe as a whole, like a human being, is a complex intermingling of spirit and matter, and that through intrapsychic means one can gain intimacy with the infinite universe on all its levels.

Both Swedenborg and Mesmerism were popular in America in the first half of the nineteenth century. They were flint and tinder for the new movement that marks the second epoch, Spiritualism. That faith began as a lively frontier amalgamation—under some influence from Native American shamanism—of Swedenborgian theology and the Mesmerist trance, which became mediumship. The Spiritualist epoch (1848 until the founding of the Theosophical Society in 1875) was marked by enthusiastic but diverse and decentralized practice; much the same could be said about its excited but unwieldy intellectual expression (by Andrew Jackson Davis, Allan Kardec). The emphasis was on the rapport of Spiritualism as an optimistic, humane new religion with the new emergent scientific and democratic world; many Spiritualists were active in such radical causes as abolition of slavery, women's rights, socialism, and prison reform. At the same time, thus far on a purely intellectual level, something else harbinging the future entered the discourse: the East. Transcendentalists such as Henry David Thoreau and Ralph Waldo Emerson were talking of Brahma, the Buddha, and the *Bhagavad Gita,* and hinting that here lay a wisdom beside which all the proud works of the West were but puny and ephemeral toys.

The great achievement of the Theosophical Society, founded in New York in 1875, was to combine the East and the esoteric West as two expressions of what it called "Ancient Wisdom." On the practical level, its strong orientation toward verbal expression—books and the lecture hall—together with an Eastern aperture characterized the third epoch in American new religious movements, 1875 to 1960. This was the era not only of Theosophy and its devolutions, from Krishnamurti to I AM, but of other Eastern movements, especially those derived from the famous World's Parliament of Religions in Chicago in 1893, the Vedanta Societies, and Western Zen. Of a more indigenous flavor were the New Thought movements, emphasizing positive thinking, such as Unity and Religious Science, and a few Western occult movements like Rosicrucianism. Though some, like the thus-far very small Zen centers, certainly did not overlook practice, third-epoch groups were basically linear-thought adventures, with books to read, classes to attend, speakers to hear. But as the twentieth century went on, into the twenties and finally the fifties, the weight begin to shift: more is heard about charismatic leaders, Krishnamurti or Yogananda of the Self-Realization Fellowship, and about the increasingly widespread actual practice of yoga or Rosicrucian esoterica.

Then, in the 1960s, a new style of alternative spirituality, together with a whole congregation of new groups, burst in. Essentially, the new people of the sixties—mainly young, alienated, and, above all, initiated by the psychedelic drug experience to want nondrug equivalents of the pharmacological "high"—were in no way content with the verbalism and intellectualism of the older alternatives. These people wanted experience and a total life-style to go with it; beyond that they often wanted a community in which to live it, with a charismatic leader and a band of disciples. In other words, they demanded not only the ideas of India or Japan, but also the food, the dress, the language, the temple-incense smells, and the authentic *guru* or *roshi* from those lands of exotic spirituality. Rather than the reassuring symbols of continuity with Sunday morning in a liberal Protestant church, which were all too apparent in the Vedanta Society or the theosophical lodge, people in the sixties, in their bells and beads, were ready for symbols of discontinuity with virtually anything except Shangri-La or Xanadu. Out of their quest came, or greatly exfoliated, a number of new movements that have dominated the scene since. Nearly all form a definite community, though it may be tightly or loosely structured, and center on a definite spiritual technique, such as a certain method of chanting or meditation, which adherents find offers fairly immediate, direct results. Most also in some way recapitulate the basic features of the ancient alternative spirituality tradition: mentalism, immanence, correspondences, and intrapsychic means of realization.

Major Forms: Five major forms of North American new religious movements presented themselves through these four epochs.

The first are groups in the Rosicrucian and theosophical tradition, the most direct heirs of the Renaissance revival of occult Neoplatonism. As we have seen, groups styling themselves Rosicrucian existed in colonial America, and the oldest extant group, the Fraternitatis Rosae Crucis, was founded in Pennsylvania in 1868. The largest and best-known is the widely advertised Ancient and Mystical Order of the Rosae Crucis, established by H. Spencer Lewis in 1915 and now headquartered in San Jose, California. (It emphasizes that it is not a religion.) Rosicrucians generally teach that little-known facts and laws of the universe, which may include reincarnation and occult kinds of cause-and-effect relationships, shape our destinies and can be mastered by techniques best taught in a lodge setting.

The Theosophical Society was founded in New York in 1875, principally by the colorful Helena Blavatsky (1831–91), a widely traveled woman of Russian aristocratic antecedents, who would become a prolific occult writer, and her companion Henry Steel Olcott (1832–1907), a lawyer and journalist interested in Spiritualism. Theosophists shared with Rosicrucians an interest in half-forgotten ancient wisdom and occult laws of nature. But the former drew not only from Western sources like the Gnostics and the Rosicrucians themselves, but soon perceived the Eastern religions also as reservoirs of that much-needed legacy. The journey of Blavatsky and Olcott to India in 1879, and the subsequent establishment of the society's international headquarters there, typify this move. Theosophy also made itself dramatic—and controversial—by stressing the role of hidden but living "masters of the wisdom," largely esconced in Tibet, with whom Blavatsky and others claimed to be in communication.

The Eastern connection and the role of the masters have been at the root of certain schisms Theosophy has undergone and have also presented the basic problems and opportunities dealt with by devolutions of Theosophy. These include the Liberal Catholic Church, closely related to "Adyar" Theosophy, which endeavors to express the Ancient Wisdom through the forms of Catholic liturgy; Anthroposophy, founded by the German sometime-Theosophist Rudolf Steiner (1861–1925) to inculcate a style of occultism keyed to Western culture; the Full Moon Meditation Groups and other activities related to the voluminous writing of Alice Bailey (1880–1949), believed to mediate teaching from a master called "The Tibetan," which puts special emphasis on group meditation as preparation for a New Age; and the I AM Activity, founded in the 1930s by Guy Ballard (1878–1939) on the basis of revelations of the master Saint Germain, whom Ballard said he had encountered on Mt. Shasta, and other "Ascended Masters." All of these groups, deriving from the opening decades of the twentieth century, suggest a desire to reexperience the theosophical mystique in the context of vivid worship, fresh charismatic personalities, or new contacts with the masters. This might be expected as the third phase advances toward the sixties' spiritual awakening, when features like those were greatly sought.

The next cluster of alternative groups, the Spiritualist, dates to the second phase. In the first decades after the Fox sisters reported rappings in 1848, Spiritualism was a yeasty but inchoate activity in America. It boasted a number of "circles," traveling lecturers, mediums, and publications, but no real center or institutional structure. Further, it contained a deep, though often unrecognized, split between two agendas: scientific research into psychic phenomena and Spiritualism's meeting of religious needs. By century's end these two objectives had received increasingly divergent institutionalization, the former in such organizations as the American Society for Psychical Research (founded in 1884 on the model of the British 1882 Society for Psychical Research), the latter in the formation of Spiritualist churches, generally with structure and liturgy on a broadly Protestant model, in the 1890s. The oldest and largest Spiritualist denomination, the National Spiritualist Association of Churches, was established in 1893. In Spiritualism, however, denominational ties are characteristically tenuous. Many churches have been independent or have shifted allegiances frequently, and numerous ephemeral denominations or associations have risen and fallen. Inevitably, the important thing to Spiritualists is not a church's affiliation, but the charisma of a particular medium/minister who ordinarily generates a following on his or her own. From the beginning, Spiritualism has played a special role in providing women opportunities for spiritual leadership.

An interesting twentieth-century movement that seems to have significant roots in Spiritualism is that of UFO cults. Virtually from the onset of the modern "wave" of reported sightings of unidentified flying objects or "flying saucers" in 1974, individuals have appeared to claim the status of "contactees," persons contacted by the extraterrestrial navigators of those ships. In the 1950s, particularly, those aliens were portrayed as wise, benign, virtually godlike beings—"technological angels," in Carl Jung's phrase—who had invested their chosen earthling with a message, generally of warning and hope couched in quasi-religious terms. While the contactee's initial engagement with the space beings was often a true initiatory adventure, involving direct conversation and a ride in their marvelous craft, subsequent communication generally was subjective, not seldom in a small group, highly suggestive of mediumship and Spiritualist circles. Indeed, it frequently transpired that contactees had a background in Spiritualism or similar activities. A few religious groups from that era, such as the Aetherius Society, have survived, but contactee UFO religion at the end of the twentieth century is not what it was. Yet popular books and movies suggest that general interest in UFO angelology and demonology remains high.

A third category of new religious movements are what, for want of a better term, may be called *initiatory groups*. These groups specialize in offering programmatic experiences believed to result in inner awakening and transformation. Examples are groups in the following of G. I. Gurdjieff (1872–1949), the Russian magus well known for his work in France between the world wars. Proclaiming that humanity is asleep and must awaken to activate higher centers of power and autonomy, he taught techniques to sound that reveille, from sacred dance to self-awareness practices. A number of groups of various names, often under the guidance of students of Gurdjieff, continue his approach.

A different example of initiatory religion is Scientology, founded by L. Ron Hubbard (1911–86) in the early 1950s, first as Dianetics. Its complex and frequently changing ideology can be summarized in the concept that human beings are essentially spirit (the "thetan") entrapped in the world of matter, energy, space, and time through "engrams," the psychic residue of past fears and traumas; these can be "cleared" by Scientological "processing" or counseling. Scientology has engendered fierce controversy and criticism for its financial and religious practices, but it remains one of the most visible of the postwar new religious movements.

Nowhere is the postwar, and especially sixties, spirit of flamboyance and participation more evident than in the Neo-Pagan movement and its allies. In that era a number of persons sought fresh religious perspectives in the revival of the pagan faiths of pre-Christian Europe. Revivalist pagan groups practice modern versions of the faiths of the ancient Egyptians, Greeks, Celts, or Norse, often complete with colorful costumes and theatrical rituals. Others, sometimes identifying themselves as followers of "Wicca" or benign Witchcraft—viewed as a general continuation of the Old Religion—put together contemporary expressions of the pagan spirit. The growing trend seems to be toward finding new ways to articulate the essence of paganism, its sensitivity to both male and female spiritual power, to nature and to the inner meaning of polytheism. The feminist spiritual quest, often culminating in a felt need to name and worship the Goddess, has become an important asset to Neo-Paganism. So has a renewed interest in Native American religion, especially shamanism; the search for pagan resources has now moved well beyond the ancient Mediterranean and European world to embrace Africa, Asia, and pre-Columbian America. Groups practicing ceremonial magic, another resource, also continue, though fairly small in numbers.

Groups of Eastern background may be conveniently divided into those of Indian derivation, and those based in the Buddhist, Islamic, or East Asian traditions. Indian—that is, Hindu—institutional work in the West began around the turn of the twentieth century with the Vedanta Societies of the Ramakrishna Mission, concerned chiefly with teaching the nondualist Vedanta philosophy. It was supplemented by the Self-Realization Fellowship of Yogananda Paramahansa in the 1920s. Later movements, mostly flourishing in the sixties, have included the Maharishi Mahesh Yogi's popular Transcendental Meditation, a number of new yoga schools and groups, and, on the side of *bhakti* (devotional Hinduism), the colorful International Society for Krishna Consciousness, the "Hare Krishnas." Other groups have centered around particular gurus or teachers, often believed by their devotees to be *avatars* ("divine incarnations"), the adherents of Satya Sai Baba, Meher Baba, Rajneesh, and Anandamayi Ma, for example.

Buddhism for Westerners in North America has four major aspects: Zen, much publicized through its association with "beat" writers in the 1950s and now practiced in a number of centers; Vajrayana or Tibetan Buddhism, which burgeoned in the 1960s, both because of the opportune arrival of *lamas* exiled from Tibet and because its unparalleled flavor of magic and mystery appealed to the 1960s mood (e.g., the almost psychedelic vistas unveiled in the immensely popular *Tibetan Book of the Dead*); Nichiren Shoshu, a Japanese Buddhist denomination (strongly promoted by Soka Gakkai, a lay Nichiren missionary organization that grew spectacularly in post–World War II Japan) centered on chanting, whose simple practice and extraversive spirit brought many converts from the 1960s on; and groups centered on Theravada Buddhism, especially its meditation techniques—this quieter practice came late, but there were those who found its psychological subtlety very helpful.

Other East Asian religions include the Unification Church (popularly known as the "Moonies"), the unconventional and controversial version of Christianity presented by Sun Myung Moon of Korea; and several of the new religions of Japan, such as Mahikari and Seicho-no-Ie, which have won both occidental and Japanese-American adherents. From lands of Islamic cultural heritage have come Baha'i, brought to the United States in 1893 and established institutionally in 1907 as a new universal religion believing that the Persian Baha'u'llah (1817–92) was the prophet and religious founder for this age; Subud, a free spiritual practice of Indonesian Sufi background; and, of course, the Black Muslim movement, now growing very close to conventional Sunni Islam.

As the twentieth century ends, North American society shows every sign of becoming increasingly pluralistic in ethnic, cultural, and spiritual terms. This can only presage a bright future for new and unconventional religious movements. *See also* Aetherius Society; African Americans (North America), new religions among; Age of Aquarius; America, Hinduism in; American Muslim Mission; Anthroposophical Society; Aquarian Gospel of Jesus Christ; Arica; Aryan Nations; Asatru; astrology; Baba Ram Dass; Black Israelites; Black Jewish movements; Black Muslims; B'nai Noah; Branch Davidians; Buddhism; Cayce, Edgar; Children of God; Christian Crusade for Truth; Church of All Worlds; Church of Armageddon; Church of Israel; Church of Scientology; Church of the Creator; Church Universal and Triumphant; communes; Covenant, the Sword and the Arm of the Lord; Crazy Wisdom Fellowship; crystals; cult; deprogramming; Divine Light Mission; Don Juan; Druids (modern); Dualism; Eastern Learning; ECKANKAR; Esalen Institute; esoteric movements; EST (Erhard Seminars Training); Goddess religions (contemporary); Golden Dawn; Healthy-Happy-Holy Organization; Human Potential movement; I AM Religious Activity; Identity Christianity; Jesus movement; Jesus people; Krishnamurti, Jiddu; Meher Baba; Moorish Science Temple; Neo-Paganism; New Age movements; New Christian Crusade Church; new religions; North America, Islam in; occult, the; People's Temple; psychics; pyramids (New Age); Rajneesh Foundation International; Rosicrucians; satanic churches in America; Scriptures for America; Self-Realization Fellowship; Sikhism in the West; Spiritualism; Subud, Synanon; Theosophical Society; Theosophy; Transcendental Meditation; Unification Church; Universal Peace Mission; Urantia Book; Vedanta Society; Way International, The; Wicca; witchcraft; World Community of Islam; World Plan Executive Council; World's Parliament of Religions; Yahweh ben Yahweh.

North America, traditional religions in. These comprise the indigenous life orientations to overlapping and sometimes internally differentiated ecological areas. Ecology, distinctive views of cosmos and culture, ritual, and history have shaped North American religions.

Ecology: Ecology affects the ways in which traditional religions posit transcendent others that give the world its particular character, recognize that the world is reconstituted in human ritual action, and renegotiate religious truth in interaction with other cultural views of reality in order to adapt to ecological and technological change.

North America

Tribal name (culture area, language family)

Abnaki (IX, Algonkian)
Achomawi (V, Hokan)
Acolapissa (X, Muskogean)
Acoma (VII, Keresan)
Ahtena (II, Athabascan)
Aleut (I, Eskimo-Aleut)
Algonkin (IX, Algonkian)
Alsea (III, Yakonan)
Apalachee (X, Muskogean)
Arapaho (VIII, Algonkian)
Arikara (VIII, Caddoan)
Assiniboin (VIII, Siouan)
Atakapa (X, Tunican)
Attiwandaron (IX, Iroquoian)
Baffinland Eskimo (I, Eskimo-Aleut)
Bannock (VI, Uto-Aztecan)
Beaver (II, Athabascan)
Bellabella (III, Wakashan)
Bellacoola (III, Salish)
Beothuck (IX, Beothukian)
Biloxi (X, Siouan)
Blackfoot (VIII, Algonkian)
Caddo (VIII, Caddoan)
Cahita (VII, Uto-Aztecan)
Cahuilla (V, Uto-Aztecan)
Calusa (X, ?)
Caribou Eskimo (I, Eskimo-Aleut)
Carrier (II, Athabascan)
Catawba (X, Siouan)
Cayuse (IV, Penutian)
Chakchiuma (X, Muskogean)
Chastacosta (III, Athabascan)
Chehalis (III, Salish)

Cherokee (X, Iroquoian)
Cheyenne (VIII, Algonkian)
Chickasaw (X, Muskogean)
Chilcotin (II, Athabascan)
Chimariko (V, Hokan)
Chinapa (VII, Uto-Aztecan)
Chinook (III, Chinookan)
Chipewyan (II, Athabascan)
Chiricahua (VII, Athabascan)
Chitimacha (X, Chitimachan)
Choctaw (X, Muskogean)
Chumash (V, Hokan)
Coahuilteco (X, Hokan)
Cochimi (V, Hokan)
Cocopa (VII, Hokan)
Coeur d'Alene (IV, Salish)
Columbia (IV, Salish)
Comanche (VIII, Uto-Aztecan)
Comox (III, Salish)
Concho (VII, Uto-Aztecan)
Conestoga (IX, Iroquoian)
Coos (III, Penutian/Coos)
Copper Eskimo (I, Eskimo-Aleut)
Costano (V, Penutian)
Cowichan (III, Salish)
Coyotero (VII, Athabascan)
Coyukon (II, Athabascan)
Cree (IX, Algonkian)
Creek (X, Muskogean)
Crow (VIII, Siouan)
Cusabo (X, Muskogean)
Dakota, see Eastern Dakota; Western Dakota
Delaware (IX, Algonkian)
Diegueno (V, Hokan)

Dogrib (II, Athabascan)
Eastern Dakota (VIII, Siouan)
Eastern Greenland Eskimo (I, Eskimo-Aleut)
Eastern Sioux (VIII, Siouan)
Erie (IX, Iroquoian)
Flathead, see Salish
Fox (IX, Algonkian)
Gabrielino (V, Uto-Aztecan)
Gosiute (VI, Uto-Aztecan)
Gros Ventre (VIII, Algonkian)
Guasave (VII, Uto-Aztecan)
Haida (III, Na-Dene/Haida)
Halchidhoma (VII, Hokan)
Han (II, Athabascan)
Hare (II, Athabascan)
Havasupai (VII, Hokan)
Hidatsa (VIII, Siouan)
Hitchiti (X, Muskogean)
Hopi (VII, Uto-Aztecan)
Huma (X, Muskogean)
Hupa (V, Athabascan)
Huron (IX, Iroquoian)
Iglulik Eskimo (I, Eskimo-Aleut)
Illinois (IX, Algonkian)
Ingalik (II, Athabascan)
Iowa (VIII, Siouan)
Iroquois (IX, Iroquoian)
Isleta (VII, Tanoan)
Jemez (VII, Tanoan)
Jicarilla (VII, Athabascan)
Jumano (VII, Uto-Aztecan?)
Kalapuya (III, Penutian/Kalapuya)
Kalispel (IV, Salish)
Kamia (V, Hokan)

Kansa (VIII, Siouan)
Karankawa (X, Hokan)
Karok (V, Hokan/Karok)
Kaska (II, Athabascan)
Kawaiisu (V, Uto-Aztecan)
Kickapoo (IX, Algonkian)
Kiowa (VIII, Aztec-Tanoan)
Kiowa Apache (VIII, Athabascan)
Klallam (III, Salish)
Klamath (V, Penutian)
Klickitat (IV, Sahaptian)
Kutchin (II, Athabascan)
Kutenai (IV, Kutenian)
Kwakiutl (III, Wakashan)
Kwalhiokwa (III, Athabascan)
Labrador Eskimo (I, Eskimo-Aleut)
Lake (IV, Salish)
Lakota, see Eastern Dakota; Western Dakota
Lillooet (IV, Salish)
Lipan (VII, Athabascan)
Luiseno (V, Uto-Aztecan)
MacKenzie Eskimo (I, Eskimo-Aleut)
Mahican (IX, Algonkian)
Maidu (V, Penutian)
Malecite (IX, Algonkian)
Mandan (VIII, Siouan)
Manso (VII, Tanoan?)
Maricopa (VII, Hokan)
Massachuset (IX, Algonkian)
Menomini (IX, Algonkian)
Mescalero (VII, Athabascan)
Metoac (IX, Algonkian)
Miami (IX, Algonkian)
Micmac (IX, Algonkian)

Missouri (VIII, Siouan)
Miwok (V, Penutian)
Mobile (X, Muskogean)
Modoc (V, Penutian)
Mohave (VII, Hokan)
Mohegan (IX, Algonkian)
Molala (IV, Penutian)
Monacan (X, Siouan)
Mono (VI, Uto-Aztecan)
Montagnais (IX, Algonkian)
Mosopela (X, Siouan)
Nabesna (II, Athabascan)
Nanticoke (IX, Algonkian)
Natchez (X, Muskogean)
Navajo (VII, Athabascan)
Netsilik Eskimo (I, Eskimo-Aleut)
Neutral, see Attiwandaron
Nevome (VII, Uto-Aztecan)
Nez Perce (IV, Sahaptian)
Nicola (IV, Athabascan)
Nicolino (V, Uto-Aztecan)
Nootka (III, Wakishan)
Northern Alaska Eskimo (I, Eskimo-Aleut)
Oglala (VIII, Siouan)
Ojibwa (IX, Algonkian)
Okanagon (IV, Salish)
Olamentke (V, Penutian)
Omaha (VIII, Siouan)
Opata (VII, Uto-Aztecan)
Osage (VIII, Siouan)
Oto (VIII, Siouan)
Ottawa (IX, Algonkian)
Paiute (VI, Uto-Aztecan)
Pamlico (X, Algonkian)

Panamint (VI, Uto-Aztecan)
Papago (VII, Uto-Aztecan)
Passamaquoddy (IX, Algonkian)
Paviotso (VI, Uto-Aztecan)
Pawnee (VIII, Caddoan)
Pennacook (IX, Algonkian)
Pensacola (X, Muskogean)
Pima (VII, Uto-Aztecan)
Piro (VII, Tanoan)
Polar Eskimo (I, Eskimo-Aleut)
Pomo (V, Hokan)
Ponca (VIII, Siouan)
Potawatomi (IX, Algonkian)
Powhatan (X, Algonkian)
Quapaw (VIII, Siouan)
Queres (VII, Keresan)
Quileute (III, Chimakuan)
Quinault (III, Salish)
Sahaptin, see Nez Perce
Salina (V, Hokan)
Salish (III, Salish)
Sanpoil (IV, Salish)
Santee (VIII, Siouan)
Sarsi (II, Athabascan)
Satudene (II, Athabascan)
Sauk (IX, Algonkian)
Sekabi (II, Athabascan)
Seminole (X, Muskogean)
Seri (V, Hokan)
Serrano (V, Uto-Aztecan)
Shasta (V, Hokan)
Shawni (IX, Algonkian)
Shoshoni (VI, Uto-Aztecan)
Shuswap (IV, Salish)
Siuslaw (III, Yakonan)

Slave (II, Athabascan)
Snuqualmi (III, Salish)
Southampton Eskimo (I, Eskimo-Aleut)
Southern Alaska Eskimo (I, Eskimo-Aleut)
Spokane (IV, Salish)
Susquehannock, see Conestoga
Tahltan (II, Athabascan)
Takelma (III, Penutian/Takelman)
Tamaulipeco (X, ?)
Tanana (II, Athabascan)
Tano (VII, Tanoan)
Taos (VII, Tanoan)
Tarahumara (VII, Uto-Aztecan)
Tenino (IV, Sahaptian)
Teton (VIII, Siouan)
Tewa (VII, Tanoan)
Thompson (IV, Salish)
Tillamook (III, Salish)
Timucua (X, Timucuan)
Tlatskanai (III, Athabascan)
Tlingit (III, Na-Dene/Tlingit)
Tolowa (III, Athabascan)
Tonkawa (X, Hokan)
Tsetsaut (II, Athabascan)
Tsimshian (III, Penutian/Tshimshian)
Tubatulabal (V, Uto-Aztecan)
Tunica (X, Tunican)
Tuscarora (IX, Iroquoian)
Tutchone (II, Athabascan)
Twana (III, Salish)
Umatilla (IV, Sahaptian)
Ute (VI, Uto-Aztecan)
Waicuri (V, Hokan?)
Wailaki (V, Athabascan)

Walapai (VII, Hokan)
Wallawalla (IV, Sahaptian)
Wappo (V, Yukian)
Washo (VI, Hokan)
Western Alaska Eskimo (I, Eskimo-Aleut)
Western Apache (VII, Athabascan)
Western Dakota (VIII, Siouan)
Western Greenland Eskimo (I, Eskimo-Aleut)
Western Sioux (VIII, Siouan)
Wichita (VIII, Caddoan)
Wind River (VI, Uto-Aztecan)
Winnebago (IX, Siouan)
Wintun (V, Penutian)
Wishram (IV, Chinookian)
Wiyot (V, Macro-Algonkian/Wiyot)
Yahi (V, Hokan)
Yakima (IV, Sahaptian)
Yamasee (X, Muskogean)
Yana (V, Hokan)
Yankton (VIII, Siouan)
Yaqui (VII, Uto-Aztecan)
Yavapai (VII, Hokan)
Yazoo (X, Tunican)
Yellowknife (II, Athabascan)
Yokuts (V, Penutian)
Yuchi (X, Uchean)
Yuit (I, Eskimo-Aleut)
Yuki (V, Yukian)
Yuma (VII, Hokan)
Yurok (V, Macro-Algonkian/Yurok)
Zuni (VII, Zunian; Uto-Aztecan?, Penutian?)

The various cultural areas (excluding the Arctic and urban areas of Mexico) represent different patterns of adaptations to natural regions. Ecology affects relations between humans, plants, and animals and shapes adaptations to the land, the development of material culture, and social organization.

Subarctic peoples from the eastern seaboard to west of the Great Lakes, and in the Canadian west and Alaska, relied upon hunting and gathering and developed distinctive tools, including snowshoes, toboggans, and canoes as winter-summer adaptations to lake, river, and seashore. Harsh winters precluded agriculture, and Subarctic peoples lived in family bands of ten to thirty people. Plant and fish resources made it possible for these bands to aggregate into groups similar to tribal units during the summer.

South of the Great Lakes, and from New England to the Gulf of Mexico, eastern peoples hunted and gathered, but agriculture made town life possible. Many of these groups developed matrilineal clans reflecting women's vital agricultural role. Complex economic, political, and religious alliances among clans extended kinship identity to create tribes and tribal confederacies. The best known are the Huron and Six Nations confederacies in the Northeast, and the Five Civilized Tribes

in the Southeast, each tribe an alliance of independent but culturally similar towns.

Since the eighteenth century, distinctive Plains cultures developed from Canada south to the Mexican border, bounded on the west by the Rocky Mountains. These peoples hunted buffalo and so were organized in highly mobile bands that coalesced into tribal confederacies for summer hunting. Since many Plains people were actually migrants from the East, the Great Basin, and the Plateau, their nineteenth-century cultures balanced a number of ecological and technological influences. Even indigenous agriculturalists such as the Mandans and Hidatsas were profoundly affected by the horse and gun.

The Southwest, including New Mexico, Arizona, northern Mexico, and parts of California, also had indigenous and intruding peoples. Inmigrating hunting and gathering tribes, the Navajo and Apache, interacted with the sedentary agriculturalists of New Mexico and Arizona, and some shifted from band to clan social organization. The Spanish brought the Pueblos horses, guns, cattle, sheep, and new plants, and thus strengthened reliance on agriculture and made possible the raiding and herding cultures of the Apache and Navajo. By contrast, Piman-speaking peoples of the Sonoran Desert relied mostly on gathering and hunting, though they practiced floodplain agriculture where possible.

Embodying the overall ecological challenge of the West, California overlaps four contiguous cultural regions. The peoples of the Colorado River share the desert-riverine adaptations of the Southwest Pimans. In California proper, acorns supplemented small game and fish on the coast and in the north. Ample resources supported the formation of confederacies of small, sedentary tribelets. The peoples of the Mojave Desert and those east of the Sierra Nevada share the gathering life-styles and small band organization of the arid Great Basin region. The cultures of northeast California blend into the hunting and fishing cultures of the Plateau. Finally, the coastal peoples of northern California merge into those of the Pacific Northwest, where plentiful salmon made social hierarchy, large villages, and confederacies possible.

Cosmos and Culture: Mythology has had a far greater impact than ecology on Native American religions. Western Europeans who settled in North America separated the human-made cultural order from god-given nature and, consequently, differentiated between human and divine nature. Native Americans' creation stories show how their particular cultures came from the caring gifts of great, powerful others; they do not distinguish between the ecological, political, economic, social, or the religious. Expressing everyday enactment of transcendent realities, their cultures are microcosmic performances of both cosmic order and disorder. The creation myths that establish the religious challenge of everyday life also declare that transcendent realities are not superior to the human realm. Rather, the myths show that each cosmic domain has a reciprocal relationship to all others. Each class of beings affects the well-being of others for good or ill, depending whether they compete or cooperate.

Stories of the beginning declare that all sentient beings share the same personal nature. What Western Europeans categorize as supernatural (gods, spirits), natural (animals, plants, weather, seasonality), and cultural (humans), Native Americans hold as essentially similar because, as persons, they all share intelligence, will, and voice. As persons, they all affect the world. Myth recognizes that these others are powerful, dangerous, and sometimes helpful. Reflecting awareness that power can be used in antisocial ways, creation stories balance violence and moral order. The coming-into-being of cosmic realities is a deeply personal process marked by emotions that suggest the range of religious intentions all persons share—pain,

pride, joy, envy, viciousness, generosity—on a scale that suggests a range of responsibility toward others. Ecological factors might limit the kinds of people living in a given region, but myth regulates their interaction. Since the great others' gifts inform each culture, mythology stresses that cooperative relations engender cosmic and cultural order. Creation stories recount the interaction of entities from various cosmological dimensions, each with good and evil motives. Native American religions can thus be understood as interpersonal systems characterized by reciprocity, cooperation and competition, trust and suspicion.

Few of the mythic others have the cosmos-centering functions of gods. The creators have great power, but their sculptural gestures—modeling, blowing, stretching, defecating, stamping, etc.—are human gestures. Some Native American traditions, among them the Plains Pawnee, the southwestern Pueblos, southern Californians, and the Beaver in British Columbia, say that creator figures brought the cosmos into existence. The Pawnee creator, Tirawahat, established heaven and then positioned in it a hierarchy of powers: Sun, Moon, Morning and Evening Star, and the constellations. These secondary powerful persons struggled, achieved solidarity, created the earth, and populated it with humans. Tirawahat reentered the scene and in primordial acts of thinking, gesturing, breathing, lightning, and thundering vitalized the entire cosmos. Tirawahat's ritual role makes him an exception: such creators are seldom addressed in ritual, and when they are, they are only one of many powerful persons in a cosmos shaped by reciprocal cooperation rather than hierarchical superiority.

More commonly, Native American myth concerns itself with the nature and the workings of the cosmos, rather than its origin. These stories take the world as preexisting but unfinished, and so tell of cosmic struggle. In the widespread Earth Diver myth, primary others assisted the creator. They dove into chaotic waters for a bit of mud that the creator extended and formed into the earth's surface. The story recognizes that the cosmos comes into being through acts of self-sacrifice, because the animals often died in their efforts to grasp substance from chaos.

An Iroquoian variant of the Earth Diver myth reports that Sky Woman fell from a preexisting sky dimension. Birds rushed to ease her fall and settled her on the back of Turtle, who now supports the land Sky Woman brought into existence. Sky Woman's daughter gave birth to the twins, another common mythic theme. The Good Twin was born naturally, but his brother sliced through his mother's flesh, killing her. In an account characteristic of the Southeast, corn, beans, squash, and tobacco grew from her buried body. Then, in a typical contest of power, the Good Twin vanquished his brother, and the Evil Twin pledged to help humans cure the diseases he had created. In Navajo and Apache myth, the twins Monster Slayer and Born for Water (figures adopted from the Pueblos) overcame numerous obstacles to win power from their father, the sun. They then set about destroying monstrous others who attacked people. Because they recognized the constructive moral challenge of adversity, they also permitted several monstrous others to live, among them Sickness, Lice, Poverty, and Old Age. A similar Pacific Northwest story recounts Raven's theft of fire from selfish Sun so that people might have light and heat.

All over the continent powerful heroes brought people the culture they needed in order to survive in a cosmos of potentially hostile others. They created tools, adjusted ecology, instituted kin and social organization. The heroes transformed a disordered cosmos only to a degree. They left behind a cosmos of violence and struggle. Their acts also empowered people to engage adversity. They provided the rituals that reciprocally channel power among humans, plants, animals, and themselves. On the Plains, White Buffalo Woman gave the Lakota the Sacred Pipe, which when properly smoked draws the pity of the great others. In the Navajo Southwest, naive heroes-in the becoming set out on great adventures, paid for their ignorance with pain and death, benefited from assistance given by powerful great others, proved their ethical transformation in trials and power contests with the great others, and so won healing ceremonies for their people. Widespread trickster figures also express the dangers of moral ignorance. Engaging in outrageous burlesques of ethical wisdom, they reveal how selfish folly results in selfishness, unbridled lust, and violence.

Ritual and History: No matter how imagined and symbolized, creation stories establish what is and ought to be, who is responsible, the comparative power and responsibility of the great others, animals, plants, and human beings. The myths also explain how power circulates among them, the inescapable fact of violence, the central value of kinship as well as analogous forms of solidarity in marriage, friendship, tribal, and confederated life. If confronting and dealing with friendly and dangerous others defines the religious challenge, then Native Americans extend the sociology of religion beyond the human community to create and maintain solidarity with plant, animal, and natural others. Attempting to work constructively with all sorts of other-than-human beings leads to various forms of behavior: avoidance, smoking tobacco, fasting, singing and dancing, sexual abstinence, and making offerings when gathering plants, hunting animals, and fishing. Native Americans use these acts to win friends and influence enemies, to express need and sorrow, and to seek assistance. Above all, these rituals express human responsibility in the cosmic scheme of things.

Ritual links the present and the mythic age of origins. Each Native American group (some 250 languages are still spoken) performs rites given by the great others, and modified in the present through dreams and visions in which the great others empower individuals to serve their communities. Religious specialists include dreamers, diviners, shamans, medicine men and women, singers, dancers, lineage leaders, and highly trained priests. Since Native American traditions are nondogmatic and performed in song and dance, each religion varies from person to person according to sex, age, experience, training, and gifts of power. These differences are often acknowledged in ritual performances of significant life-cycle changes. While some people have power and influence with the great others and some do not, community opinion has shaped religious innovation over the centuries. In powerful religious acts, the people themselves legitimate the religious guidance of their specialists.

Among the Algonquian-speaking peoples of the Subarctic, Catholicism has had a major impact on traditional religions in reaffirming the core values of sharing, cooperation, and solidarity with plants and animals. In the original notion of power imaged in the culture hero's altruistic acts, *kitchi manitou* of the Ojibwa Nanabozho and *kuta'hando* of the Abenaki Gluskap, power to the highest qualitative, ethical degree has partially merged with the missionaries' image of God as He Who Made All. This being has come to unify the great cosmic powers as a Master of Creation and, sometimes, Keeper of the Game. But in adapted mythological accounts, this great spirit is often the equal of the culture hero and requires his assistance, a mythological balance between old and new that is common throughout North America. In addition to Christian prayer and worship, dreams and visions continue to channel power to humans, especially to counter the baleful impact of witches and demons. Thus, a native reinterpretation of Christianity in light of the revealed truths of creation mythology has led to a conservative religious adaptation.

On the Canadian and American reservations of the Iroquoian-speaking Six Nations, social crisis and prophetic call to ritualistic renewal remain closely related. Before European settlement, when the tribes suffered from interclan violence, a prophet, Deganawidah, showed the Iroquois how to extend the Longhouse rafters and thus kinship to other nations. The ritual installation of the forty-nine named chiefs, and their ritualized discourse, has actively worked toward the mythic ideal of intertribal solidarity. Specifically, the Longhouse religion instituted by the nineteenth-century prophet Handsome Lake preserves tradition in the face of Euramerican culture and Christianity. In a vision, Handsome Lake was acknowledged by Jesus as his moral equal. Under the prophet's guidance the Six Nations continue to perform the ancient cycle of Thanksgiving directed toward the great cosmic others, "Our Life Supporters": the Midwinter Ceremony, a series of world-renewal rites; Ohgiwe, a ritual honoring the dead; and festivals addressed to Maple, Strawberry, and the Three Sisters: Corn, Beans, and Squash. Under Christianity's influence, the Good Twin, the culture hero Tarachiawagon, has become somewhat godlike, and is addressed variously as the Master of Life, Our Creator, the Great Spirit, and, sometimes, as God. Performed by the masked False Face Society, the subdued power of the Evil Twin, now rechanneled for human welfare, still purifies the community and cures sickness.

As in the Subarctic and Northeast, the religions of the Southeast have adapted ancient tradition. Their eighteenth-century religions preserve to various degrees the core symbols of ancient Mississippean cultures: they uneasily balance a perfect sky realm against a chaotic, threatening underworld. Respectively symbolized by fire and water, the sun above and evil monsters below struggle in the human domain; depending on how they act, humans throw their weight toward one side or other. Southeastern peoples stress that daily acts of personal purification, and seasonal acts of communal and cosmic renewal, are religious duties. The annual green corn ceremonial draws together everyday acts of cleansing, curing, planting, war, and hunting to reciprocate the assistance of, and to harmonize relations with, the great others. Variously affected by Christianity and forcibly moved to Oklahoma in the 1830s, Southeastern peoples carry with them the fire symbolizing cosmic interdependence. In the 1990s, many Southeastern peoples in the East and Oklahoma are Christian, but healers continue to cure and the people renew themselves

in gathering, hunting, and corn ceremonialism. A partially secularized Stomp Dance still draws people together, balances male and female, and mediates distance between the clans.

Plains religions gradually formed in the eighteenth century and reached a mid-nineteenth-century climax in rituals for buffalo hunting, horse raiding, and warfare, only to be suppressed by the United States. Despite the end of

Native American Shoshoni tribal painting of the Sun Dance, the most characteristic Plains religious ceremony. Within the lodge (represented by the circle) figures dance around a sacred pole.

the interdependence between buffalo and the tribes, Plains Indian religions weathered the subsistence shift and official opposition. At the height of the crisis, the late-nineteenth-century Ghost Dance (which originated in the Far West) reasserted solidarity between the living and the dead to renew reciprocal ties within the tribes and between them and the great others. Even in the darkest years, individuals sought the assistance of the great others in frequently performed pipe ceremonies; in the activities of medicine men, shamans, and medicine societies; in renewing private and public medicine bundles; in using the sweat lodge to purify themselves and to prepare for vision quests; and, above all, in performing the tribal Sun Dance. Once concerned with success in hunting and war, the Sun Dance went underground against a hostile American response only to reemerge in the more sympathetic 1930s. Because of its acts of privation and self-sacrifice, the Sun Dance has evolved into a celebration of reciprocal relations between the people and the Sun, along with those many great others the Lakota call "all my relatives." Individuals also use the ritual to pursue power for themselves and their relatives and to heal disease. In the

1990s, personal religious needs are balanced against the Sun Dance's concern for communal well-being. Some Plains individuals have also forged relationships with the great figures of Christianity, and many others follow the road to self-understanding and healing provided by the Native American Church, an incorporated institution that is now a major force in sustaining a pan-Indian, religiously grounded ethnicity.

Ancient ceremonies that produce tribal identity by renewing ties of reciprocity with the great others remain especially visible in the Pueblo and Navajo Southwest. Pueblo ritual cycles keyed to winter, summer, agriculture, hunting, rain, and curing endure despite centuries of Spanish, Mexican, and American opposition. The Pueblo Revolt of 1680 closed a period of religious oppression and marked the long-range adaptation that led the New Mexican Pueblos to keep traditional and Catholic ritual practice separate. The Zuni and Hopi Pueblos have remained even more closed, and have maintained ritual solidarity in the face of Catholic, Protestant, and Mormon missions whose success has, until recently, been confined largely to outmigrating individuals. Neighboring Navajos have developed an extensive religious pluralism that juxtaposes traditional chants and rites (which derive from an encounter with Pueblo mythological and ritual forms) with Catholicism, evangelical Protestantism, Mormonism, and the Native American Church. Each addresses some of the varied needs of the people. Blessingway rites still ensure peace and harmony, and Enemyway protects against dangerous outsiders and has become the major ritual means of mediating distance and resolving distrust among more than sixty clans.

Because of dispersed settlement patterns, arid floodplain agriculture, and less cohesive ceremonial systems, religion has played a less noticeable role in the adaptation of the Pima and Tohono O'odham of southern Arizona and the Yuman-speaking peoples of the Colorado River. Dreams remain important as channels of power given in songs, summer rains are celebrated in cactus wine rituals, and the dead are placated in now-modified funeral rites. Among the Tohono O'odham, Catholic rites, saints, and prayers have been integrated with tradition to produce what is called Sonoran Catholicism (the refugee Arizonan Yaqui practice is an older and more complex variant). At the same time, tradition has held off intruding Hispanic and American cultures, as in the distinction made by Piman medicine men between indigenous disease (Staying Sickness) and the infectious diseases of outsiders (Wandering Sickness). In this way, the Pimans maintain a ritual practice aimed at placating and renewing reciprocity with the offended great others in order to cure disease. Particularly displaced by the American commercial economy, and suffering adversely the loss of water resources, the Pimans of central Arizona have absorbed many of the cultural implications of Presbyterian Christianity, including religious, social, economic, and political institutions. Tradition nevertheless still survives in the ideal of tribal well-being.

California stands at the center of historical forces propelling changes in ritual practice throughout the Great Basin, Plateau, and into the Pacific Northwest. Throughout the region's diverse ecological areas Christian missions led to reinterpretations of ceremonial life. In coastal California, Spanish and then Mexican intolerance during the Mission period (1769–1836) forced compliance, but did not stop either traditional religious practice or the ongoing need to assess Catholic claims against tradition. While southern Californian societies were uprooted and reconstituted in the missions, an indigenous movement, named Chingichngish after the Gabrielino culture hero, has preserved traditional rituals concerned with rites of passage and the transmission of ritual knowledge. Catholic rites now include harvest ceremonies, processions in thanksgiving for crops and prayers for rain.

Northern California shares the broad patterns by which the interior tribes of the Great Basin, Plateau, and the tribes of the Pacific Northwest reacted to the sudden intrusion of Americans. Throughout these regions, prophets commonly anticipated the invasion in dreams and visions. Ritualistic affirmations of tribal solidarity and revitalized relations with the dead emerged in the California and Great Basin Ghost Dances of 1869, 1870, and 1890. Precursors of pan-Indian movements, these rites promised a rejuvenated cosmos with either Americans eliminated or harmoniously embraced. In the Great Basin, the late-nineteenth-century Bear Dance and Sun Dance reaffirmed ties with nature, and in the twentieth century the Traditional-Unity Movement has joined tradition with pan-Indian religious rites, including the sacred pipe, sweat lodge, and peyote.

Throughout the nineteenth century, prophetic dreamers of the Plateau variously stressed a nativistic rejection of American ways of life, competing versions of which were presented by fur traders, missionaries, the military, and territorial administrators. The prophets urged a revitalistic return to old rhythms of reciprocity with a myriad of spirit helpers, and thus

Native American Pomo woman in traditional dress carrying two healing staffs, Sonoma County, California (1960). In 1970, there were some nine hundred Pomo remaining in northcentral California.

stressed that world order depended on a carefully executed relational ethics. The Idaho Nez Perce were factionalized before these nativistic, revitalistic, and acculturative options. Nativist Nez Perce met military defeat. Accommodationists preserved and strengthened kinship affiliations in exploring Presbyterianism, Catholicism, and, in the twentieth century, Pentecostalism as new, and competing, channels of power to the people.

On the Pacific Coast, Salish peoples followed the prophet John Slocum, whose mediation between spirit dancing, Protestantism, and Catholicism became incorporated as the Indian Shaker Church, which is now found from northern California to British Columbia. Characteristic Northwest rituals—the spirit dancing of the Salish, the Winter Ceremony and potlatches of the Kwakiutl and their neighbors, and mortuary rites maintaining continuity between people and their clan ancestors among the Tlingit and Haida—retreated, adapted in ways distinctive of each tribe, and survived. All faced opposition

from Protestant, Catholic, and Russian Orthodox missionaries, and some rituals were outlawed by American and Canadian authorities. Many rites went underground until the post–World War II period, when they were reestablished to revitalize bonds of reciprocity between the peoples and their respective great others.

In the post-contact era, ecological and technological change has been the order of the day: elimination of once pivotal plants and animals; land loss; population depletion; economic marginalization; individualistic adaptation to a cash economy; bureaucratic, authoritarian political institutions; and, increasingly, the urbanization of Native American populations have been major forces of secularization. Such cultural shifts in the lives of each tribe have undercut relations with the great others; at the same time they have undermined each tribe's distinctive social structure.

In every instance, including conservative estimations of Christianity, achieving revitalized cosmic relations and renewing tribal ethnicity has also countered challenges deriving from the nature of tribal life itself. Religious change has meant different things to different people depending on age; sex; expertise in language and ritual knowledge; leadership in band, clan, and tribe; and degree of identification with dominant cultures. Many religious movements, including the Sun Dance, the Native American Church, the Indian Shaker Church, and contemporary spirit dancing, have addressed these tribal divisions by strengthening the power of individuals, trusting that their well-being would vitalize whole communities. Each movement has thus aimed to achieve an ongoing microcosmic cultural replication of mythically derived macrocosmic order. The successful history of ritual adaptation to cultural adversity testifies to the realistic sense of struggle channeled to the present through tradition. In the beginning, and in the present, the great others (now sometimes including the great others of Christianity) exemplify the challenge of adversity. They continue to empower the people with the rituals necessary to their survival as distinctive tribes. *See also* American Indian; Big House movement; Black Elk; Bladder Festival; bundle; busk; Changing Woman; circumpolar religions; corn ceremonies; green; Coyote; culture hero; Earth Diver; emergence; false face; fishing rites/whaling rites; gender crossing; guardian spirit; Hako; Hamatsa; happy hunting ground; heyoka; kachina/katsina; kiva; manitou; medicine bundle; medicine man; Mother Earth; orenda; Orpheus stories in traditional religions; pipe, sacred; pollen; potlatch; powwow; prayerstick, prayerfeather; rain dance; road of life; sandpainting; Selu; Sipapu; Skinwalker; soul; Sun Dance, Sun Dance religion; sun worship; sweat, sweat lodge; sweet grass; totem pole; twin myth; vision quest; Wakan Tanka; winter count; yeibichai.

Northern school (Chin. *pei-tsung*), Chinese Ch'an Buddhist sect associated with Shen-hsiu. It thrived under imperial patronage throughout the eighth century but was later denounced on doctrinal and lineage grounds. Sung-dynasty historiography replaced Shen-hsiu with Hui-neng as the sixth patriarch of Ch'an and criticized the school for its "gradualistic" practices. *See also* Ch'an school; Hui-neng; Shen-hsiu.

no-self (Skt. *anatman;* Pali *anatla*), Buddhist doctrine positing the lack of an indwelling individual essence. Like most Indian religion, Buddhism draws a contrast between the state of imprisonment in a sequence of rebirths (*samsara*) stretching from the beginningless past and freedom from rebirth in a timeless state of bliss called "liberation" (*moksha*) or, more usually, *nirvana*. The Buddhist doctrine of no-self is held to constitute its unique and definitive access to truth and salvation.

In opposition to other ideas, such as the Brahmanic doctrine of the individual/universal Self (*atman*), no-self holds that continuity within one life and between lives is not due to an indwelling individual essence, but to relations of conditioning that arise between earlier and later parts of an impersonal series of psychophysical events. The moral conditioning of *karma* ("deed") is the most religiously important kind, but it coexists with other kinds of causation (e.g., physical). This doctrine became very complex, but the basic idea is simple: what appears as a unitary agent and subject of experience is in fact a collocation of psychophysical events, and the goal of meditation is to "realize" the truth of self-lessness, both to understand it and to make it real. This is not a deterministic view: by no means all of the constituents of personality are effects of past causes; and the operation of the mind includes active elements such as initiative and effort, which are nonetheless "not-self."

A number of different analyses of what appears as a "self" or "person" were made. One of the most frequent analyses, shared by all schools, is division into five "constituent elements" (Skt. *skandha;* Pali *khandha*): rupa, form or body; *vedana*, feelings, affective reactions to experience; *samjna* (Pali *sanna*), perceptions and ideas (the mind is regarded as a sense, and so samjna refers to the objects of all six senses, when apperceived in determinate linguistic form); *samskara* (Pali *sankhara*), a heterogeneous category often translated as "mental formations," most but not all members of which are volitional; and *vijnana* (Pali *vinnana*), consciousness. Consciousness was further subdivided, producing ideas that resemble Western notions of an unconscious mind. In a sequence of rebirth, the most important constituent is consciousness. From moment to moment in one life, consciousness is a constantly changing conditioned factor; from one life to the next the same kind of conditioned change exists, but it is associated with two different bodies. The point of such analyses is that there is no self, no unconditioned and therefore unchanging autonomous center to all this; nor indeed does it make any sense to speak of a self outside of the constituent elements.

Later philosophy, often reacting against earlier Buddhist scholasticism, developed the idea further into a denial of all essences, in things as in persons, sometimes to the point of extreme nominalism. Here the idea of no-self was subsumed under the wider category of "emptiness" (*shunyata*), which denies the existence of inherent existence (*svabhava*, lit., "own-being") in all things, including the constituent factors posited by Buddhism itself. *See also* aggregates; Buddhism (thought and ethics); Dharma/dharma; emptiness; Four Noble Truths; impermanence.

no-thought (Chin. *wu-nien*), Chinese Ch'an Buddhist meditation technique that emphasizes nondiscrimination as the appropriate method for directly apprehending one's true nature. *See also* Ch'an school; meditation.

novena, a Roman Catholic devotional practice, common since the Middle Ages, of observing nine days or weeks of prayer either privately or publicly.

novice, a candidate for membership in a religious community. During the training period the candidate is taught about the practices of the community under the direction of a novice master or mistress.

nudity, appearing naked in cultures where being clothed is the norm. Ritual nudity strongly marks an individual as being temporarily different. *See also* gymnosophists; Jainism; Mahadeviyakka.

nuke-mairi (noo-kay-mah-ee-ree; Jap., "runaway pilgrimages"), type of Japanese pilgrimage (*okage mairi*) to the Ise Shrine in the eighteenth and nineteenth centuries in which pilgrims left to go on pilgrimage without permission from their local government officials. *See also* okage-mairi; pilgrimage.

Nu Kua (nyoo gwah), ancient Chinese cosmogonic goddess. She is the consort of Fu Hsi, with whom she is depicted as a serpent-bodied deity holding a drawing compass. *See also* Chinese myth; Fu Hsi; mountains, sacred.

number symbolism, the belief that numbers are a code that, when deciphered, reveals deeper meaning. *See also* Pythagoras.

numen (noo'men; Lat., "to nod," i.e., the will of god), originally the visible evidence of the power of the ancient Roman gods but used in comparative religion as the European equivalent of *mana* (Polynesian, impersonal religious power). *See also* kingship, sacred; mana; Roman religion.

numinous, primary datum of religious experience, an overwhelming sense of the holy. A term developed by the German theologian Rudolf Otto in *The Idea of the Holy* (1917). *See also* Otto, Rudolf; religious experience.

nun, female member of a monastic community. *See also* monasticism.

Christianity: Roman Catholics, Eastern Catholics, the Orthodox, and Anglicans have communities of nuns. Some Protestant denominations, e.g., Lutherans, have sisterhoods or communities of deaconesses. In Catholicism, *nun* is a popular term referring to any woman who, as a vowed member of a religious congregation or order, lives the evangelical counsels of poverty, chastity, and obedience. Those under simple vows are properly called sisters and are normally not cloistered and are involved in active work in the wider world. Nuns are technically only those women religious under solemn vows who live a life of self-denial and prayer in cloistered convents.

Nuns have existed in Christianity since the early fourth century. Although nuns lived strictly secluded lives, convents and monasteries offered women an alternative to marriage and the possibility of education generally denied other women.

Vatican II (1962–65) modernized the way of life of nuns. Nuns totally dedicated to contemplation are still governed by the rules of enclosure, but many no longer wear the traditional robe and veil. They continue to see their life of prayer as the primary reason for being in community. *See also* abbess/abbot; Carmelites; convent; Poor Clares.

Buddhism: Although nuns formed a part of the early Theravadan Buddhist religious community (Sangha), they disappeared as an institution by the tenth century. (In the latter part of the twentieth century, there is a modest revival of Theravadan nuns in Taiwan.) However, the institution continued in Mahayana Buddhism, especially in China, Tibet, and Japan. For example, the first Japanese ordained as Buddhist monastics were women. Nuns (Jap. *ama*) continued to play a major role in Japanese Buddhism through the eighth century, but the validity of their ordinations and their participation in court-sponsored rituals were called into question and their status declined by the early ninth century. Afterward, women were ordained as nuns in private ceremonies by monks using a variety of precepts. As a result, they were not considered the equals of monks. During the thirteenth century, orders of nuns were reestablished by monks from the Risshu and Zen schools. *See also* bhiksu/bhiksuni.

Nyaya (nyah'yuh; Skt., "logic," "method," "correct judgment"). 1 The science of logic reputedly established by Gautama (ca. sixth century B.C.). One of six Hindu philosophical systems, it is distinguished by its epistemology and use of logical methods and proofs to obtain knowledge about the objective world, the soul, and God (Ishvara). *Nyaya* defines ultimate liberation as the cessation of suffering brought about through the acquisition of knowledge by four means: perception, inference, analogy, and testimony. Knowledge arrests suffering and rebirth by dispelling the misconception that the eternal soul is bound to the ephemeral body. 2 A maxim illustrative of a logical principle. *See also* liberation; six systems of Indian philosophy.

Nyingma-pa (ni-ing-mah'pah), known as "the Ancients," oldest order of Tibetan Buddhism. It originated in the eighth century based on the teachings of the Indian Tantric master Padmasambhava. Nyingma-pa organize Buddhist teachings hierarchically into nine vehicles culminating in the Great Completeness traditions, which highlight techniques for experiencing the mind's primordial purity. Not necessarily monastic, the order maintained about one thousand monasteries in Tibet. *See also* Padmasambhava; Tibetan religions.

nymph (nimf), in Greco-Roman mythology, a female spirit inhabiting waters or trees.

A B C D E F

G H I J K L

M N O P Q

T U V

K Y & Z

Oannes (oh'ahn-es), in the third-century B.C. Greek historiographical work *Babyloniaka* by Berossus, the name of a mythological fish-man. He also appears in a Babylonian tradition of pre-Flood sages. *See also* Berossus; Mesopotamian religion.

Obaku Zen (oh-bah-koo), a Japanese Zen Buddhist school founded by the Chinese monk Yin-yuan Lung-ch'i (Jap. *Ingen Ryuki*, 1592–1673) with its headquarters at Mampuku-ji, near Kyoto. Although Ingen was from the Lin-chi (Jap. *Rinzai*) school, the architectural style of the Obaku school's monasteries, the robes of its monks, ritual implements, ceremonies, style of chanting, and clothing all differed from the Rinzai school because Obaku was brought from China centuries after Rinzai had been established in Japan. Obaku also allowed for the mixing of Pure Land elements with meditation. Although the Obaku school did not boast large numbers of adherents, it influenced Japanese culture in a variety of ways. *See also* Lin-chi school; Rinzai.

Obon (oh-bohn), also Urabon, a Japanese Buddhist festival in which offerings are made to the spirits of the deceased, usually on the fifteenth day of the seventh month. The Buddhist service is based on the *Yu-lan-p'en ching*, a text that relates Maudgalyayana's attempts to save his deceased mother who had been reborn as a hungry ghost. It was first performed in 657. *See also* ancestral rites; Ghost Festival; Japanese religions (festal cycle).

occult, the, practices and beliefs relating to "hidden" spiritual truths or esoteric insights essential to fully understand the inner workings of the universe on the divine and mental, as well as physical, planes. These truths and insights may be deemed occult because they have been deliberately concealed (perhaps to maintain them as the possession of an elite) or because, by their nature, they are unknowable apart from special preparation and initiation; in any case, they generally are regarded as powerful. Characteristically, the occult concerns such areas as subtle features of human psychospiritual anatomy; the naming and petition or evocation of invisible hierarchies of gods, angels, or spirits between heaven and earth; and the veiled laws of nature underlying psychic phenomena and the effects of magical operations.

The associated doctrines of Hellenistic Neoplatonism about macrocosm/microcosm, planetary spirits, and theurgy, or the practice of magical evocation, laid a foundation for the Western occult view that the universe results from the thorough intermingling of material substances and "finer" ones whose nature resembles the human mind and soul. In the Neoplatonic occult world, virtually everything is humanly significant and subject to human control on the mental, as well as the physical, plane.

This tradition endured a long quasi-underground life during the Middle Ages and emerged as a powerful intellectual force in the Renaissance. The underlying worldview of the occult, including Ptolemaic astronomy and Galenic medicine, was basic to pre-Copernican and pre-Newtonian science and made the occult dimension of that science less at odds with accepted cosmology than it later became.

By the eighteenth century, the Neoplatonic worldview was well separated from science. But it sustained itself, as occultism, particularly among those who wished to accept its spiritual premises in the context of a newly emergent scientific world. In this manner, the occult has continued to flourish, though often against the grain of its surrounding intellectual culture, down to the late-twentieth-century New Age movement. The central appeal of the occult has been the sense of personal power, together with access to significant wisdom, that it affords the individual in a mechanistic universe and anonymous mass society, in which conventional religion also seems alienating.

An essential point of the occult perspective is the concept of correspondences, which postulates the interaction of specific entities of the macrocosm and the human microcosm, as between astrological signs, gemstones, days and hours, and organs of the body or particular human endeavors. The complex correspondence systems validate astrology, an important wing of occultism, and magic of various kinds.

The occult notion of cosmic hierarchies, sometimes spoken of as the "great chain of being," suggests a rich, personalized, spiritual universe around and above (and, on its dark, demonic side, below) the human level. Theurgy, broadly understood, entails the possibility of channeling wisdom and power from those entities through magic and mediumship. The dramatic arts of ritual or ceremonial magic, culminating in the evocation of spirits, also have long been a mainstay of occultism. At the same time, the occult sense of a universe of profoundly interlocking material and spiritual agencies supports its emphasis on the mental components of healing and achievement.

Occultism has been continued in the modern Western world, sometimes openly, by a variety of groups and movements. These include, on the ritual and initiation side, the Order of the Golden Dawn and the Ordo Templi Orientalis. The Liberal Catholic Church, several Rosicrucian groups, and more recently the Wicca (modern "white" Witchcraft) and Neo-Pagan movements have presented important occult themes amid varying degrees of ritual, initiation, and secrecy. Theosophy, Anthroposophy, and related groups have taught occult ideas openly in a largely lecture-hall setting. Traditions comparable to Western occultism have existed in non-Western cultures as well. *See also* Castaneda, Carlos; esoteric movements; Freemasonry; Golden Dawn; Illuminati, the Order of; Liberal Catholic Church; Neoplatonism; Rosicrucians; secret societies.

occultation, to disappear from view, to be hidden; often occultation is understood as being taken up while alive to the divine realm. *See also* Druze/Druse; Elijah; Enoch; Hidden Imam; translation.

oceanic feeling, sensation of being connected to the eternal realm or to the entire world. A term coined by the twentieth-century French author Romain Rolland and picked up by Freud, it is used as a characterization of the subjective affect of religion. *See also* emotions; feeling.

oceanic reflection (Chin. *hai-in*), Chinese Buddhist deep meditation wherein the mind attains a state of unitary consciousness (Skt. *samadi;* Chin. *sanmei*) and mirrors all phenomena, past, present, and future, as in a great ocean. *See also* meditation.

Oceanos (oh-see'an-os), in Greek mythology the embodiment of the ocean, regarded as a great cosmic power and an early ruler of the gods. *See also* Greek religion.

Oda Nobunaga (oh-dah noh-*boo*-nah-gah; 1534–82), powerful Japanese military leader who played a leading role in Japan's reunification in the sixteenth century after years of strife; he is also known for destroying the power base of the Tendai Buddhist sect. *See also* Tendai school; warrior monks.

Odinist. *See* Asatru.

Odinn (*oo*'deen), in Norse mythology the father of the gods. He was worshiped as the god of fate, war, human sacrifice, poetry, shamanism, magic, and secret knowledge, and was the lord of the aristocratic warriors' realm of death (Valhall). His name is etymologically preserved in "Wednesday." *See also* Asatru; Indo-European religion; Nordic religion; Woden.

Odysseus (oh-di'soos; Gk., "Trouble"), ancient Greek hero. Known for his cunning intelligence and a favorite of the goddess Athena, Odysseus is credited with the idea of the wooden horse that ended the Trojan War. Afterward he spent ten years returning home to his wife, Penelope, and son, Telemakhos, on Ithaca. Portrayed by Homer as a self-reliant and versatile man with great powers of rhetoric, endurance, self-control, and guile, Odysseus was treated more harshly by later tradition. There he symbolized variously the unscrupulous politician, the comic glutton, the exile yearning for home, the eternal wanderer, and the quintessential searcher for knowledge. *See also* Greek religion; Homer.

Odyssey (od'i-see), Greek epic poem attributed to Homer telling of Odysseus, the resourceful "man of many turns" and his adventures returning home after the Trojan War. Beginning in the tenth year after the war, the first four books set the scene of turmoil on Ithaca, where his wife's suitors have overtaken Odysseus's palace. These books introduce the theme of hospitality and portray Odysseus through the eyes of others, as Telemakhos, his son, travels to Pylos and Sparta for news of his father. Odysseus appears first in the fifth book, stranded for seven years on the hidden island of the goddess Kalypso, who finally agrees to release him. After a storm sent by Poseidon destroys his raft, Odysseus washes up on the island of the Phaiakians and tells the story of his wanderings. Books 9–12 detail his adventures in distant, sometimes savage lands, his trip to the underworld to receive a prophecy from Tiresias, and the loss of all his comrades. In the second half of the poem Odysseus returns to Ithaca and, with Athena's help, tests the loyalty of his family, friends, and servants. Disguised as a beggar, he tells several lies about his life that reveal important aspects of his real character while helping to conceal his true identity. Finally, having killed the suitors with his bow, he is himself tested by Penelope and ultimately reunited with his father. The epic adapts a common folktale plot (the hero's return), suppressing its magical elements and showing a world where the gods work justice in human affairs. *See also* Homer; Odysseus.

O.F.M. *See* Franciscans.

ofudesaki (oh-*foo*-day-sah-kee; Jap., "tip of the writing brush"), a name given to sacred scripture in the Japanese new religions Tenrikyo and Omotokyo, indicating they were written down as revelations. *See also* Omotokyo; Tenrikyo.

Ogyu Sorai (oh-*gyoo* soh-rah-ee; 1666–1728), Japanese scholar of the Ancient Learning (Kogaku) school who wrote *Bendo* (Distinguishing the Way) and *Benmei* (Distinguishing Names), calling for a return to the original Confucian classics. *See also* Kogaku.

oil. *See* anointing; chrism.

ojoden (oh-joh-den), biographies of those reborn in the Buddhist Pure Land. The earliest Japanese text of this genre was the *Nihon ojo gokurakuki* (Record of Japanese Reborn in Paradise), compiled in 984 by Yoshishige Yasutane. Other collections were compiled as late as the mid-nineteenth century. They were an important source for proselytizing among the masses and for delineating the balance between faith and practice that might lead to favorable rebirth. Although rebirth in the Pure Land was originally a step toward final salvation, in many of these texts it is seen as the final goal. *See also* Bodhisattvas; Jodo Shinshu; Jodoshu; Pure Land.

okage-mairi (oh-kah-gay-mah-*i*-ree; Jap., "thanksgiving pilgrimage"), spontaneous mass Shinto pilgrimages to the Ise Shrine during the Tokugawa period (1600–1868). The largest of these pilgrimages took place in 1830, after word that amulets from the shrine were falling from the sky. For some, pilgrimage was a way of conveying thanks to the sun goddess, Amaterasu, for her blessings; for others it was an expression of millenarian expectation with wild singing and dancing (*okage odori*). *See also* nuke-mairi; pilgrimage.

Okina (oh-kee-nah; Jap., "venerable old man"), legendary godlike figure in Japan who appears in folk performances and the Noh play of the same name. *See also* Japanese myth; Noh drama.

Okinawa, religion of. Okinawa is both the name of the main island of the Ryukyu archipelago, which runs between Kyushu and Taiwan and contains over 140 islands, and the name of the Japanese prefecture embracing all of the islands. Though sharing cultural and linguistic roots with Japan, Okinawan culture developed largely outside the direct sphere of influence of the Japanese imperial system and also absorbed considerable cultural and religious influence directly from China.

Traditional Okinawan religion is centered on a belief in *kami* (divinities, divine presences), similar to that found in Japan, who are connected with the sea, mountains, groves, fields, springs, and the hearth. The annual cycle of festivals traditionally followed the Chinese lunar calendar and is centered on farming, fishing, and ancestors. As exemplified by the priestess who served with the traditional Okinawan king, religious ritual duties are performed primarily by women in Okinawa. Priestesses were also the primary religious specialists at the regional, village, and family group levels and served to mediate between their group and kami. Another female religious specialist is the shamaness who works independently and serves primarily to diagnose and cure various types of illness. Okinawan religion shares many features with Chinese and Japanese folk religion and shows the influence of Confucianism and folk Buddhism. State Shinto was introduced with the annexation of Okinawa by Japan in 1879. Christianity entered in 1846 and expanded with the American presence after World War II. Many Japanese new religions have also enjoyed success in the postwar years. *See also* Chinese popular religion; Japanese folk religion; kami.

Okuninushi (oh-koo-nee-noo-shee), Shinto deity who helped bring civilization to Japan. He was a powerful regional deity who submitted to the central authority of the sun goddess Amaterasu. *See also* Amaterasu; Japanese myth; Shinto.

Olcott, Henry Steel (1832–1907), cofounder (with Helena Blavatsky) and first president of the Theosophical Society, as well as prominent American advocate of Buddhism. *See also* Theosophical Society.

Old Believers, Christians who split from the Russian Orthodox Church in opposition to Patriarch Nikon's demand in 1652 that Russian liturgical practices conform completely to those found among the Greek patriarchates. Eventually condemned in 1666 and 1667 and severely persecuted, they split into two main groups, the *Popovtsy*, who retained a priesthood, and the *Bezpopovtsy*, who rejected the priesthood. *See also* Orthodox Church.

Old Catholic churches, a group of national Christian churches that split off from Roman Catholicism over issues unrelated to the sixteenth-century Protestant Reformation. The first Old Catholic church, the Church of Utrecht (Netherlands), rejected the 1713 papal condemnation of Jansenism, consecrating a bishop independent of Rome in 1723 and becoming a fully separate church in 1873. The majority of Old Catholic churches were formed in protest to the 1870 declaration of papal infallibility at the First Vatican Council. Most Old Catholic churches look to Utrecht as their center and are in communion with the Anglican Church. Of the estimated 549,000 Old Catholics, some 350,000 are members of the Polish National Catholic Church of America. *See also* infallibility; Jansenism.

Old European religion. The Goddess-centered religion of pre-Indo-European, prepatriarchal Old Europe (ca. 6500–3500 B.C. in southeast and ca. 4500–2500 B.C. in western and northern Europe) had its beginnings in the Paleolithic. Its emergence must have reflected the existing human social structure. The worship of female deities is connected to a mother-kinship system and ancestor veneration in which woman as mother is the social center. Woman's ability to give birth and nurture new life from her body was seen as the ultimate divine metaphor. There are no traces in Paleolithic or Neolithic art of a father figure.

The invention of ceramics, ca. 6500 B.C., marked the appearance of thousands of figurines and vases, temples and their miniature models, wall paintings, reliefs, and countless ritual articles, providing abundant data for the reconstruction of Neolithic religion. The richest finds are from southeastern and Danubian Europe and from the Aegean and Mediterranean islands.

An iconography of the Goddess comprises several kinds of abstract or hieroglyphic symbols: X's, V's, triangles, meanders, and the like; representational images such as vulvas, breasts, and birds' feet; and animal symbols representing various aspects of the Goddess and embodying her power. The iconography that persisted for thousands of years, in combination with postures, gestures, and costume, makes it possible to decipher the types and functions of deities.

Deities: Old European deities can be described in four main groups: (1) the Goddess who personifies the generative life-giving forces of nature; (2) the Goddess who personifies the destructive forces of nature; (3) the Goddess of regeneration, who controls the life cycles of the natural world; and (4) the prehistoric male deities, who make up only 3 to 5 percent of the corpus of neolithic sculpture.

The Generative Goddess is represented under three aspects: life or birth giving, fertility, and life protection and healing. The Life or Birth-giving Goddess creates life out of herself. Her symbols are her generative body parts—vulva, breasts, and buttocks. The Birth-giving Goddess, shown in birthing posture, has an enlarged, swollen vulva. Vulva and seed patterns depicted alone may have represented her or had an amuletic quality. In zoomorphic form, this Goddess is the deer, elk, and bear.

The Pregnant Goddess is fertility incarnate. From the Upper Paleolithic, the Goddess' fertility was expressed by a naturalistic nude with hands placed on her enlarged belly. At the beginning of the Neolithic, this ancient deity was transformed into an agricultural Goddess, the protectress of grain and bread. Sculptures of the Pregnant Goddess were decorated with spirals, snakes, rhomboids, and four-corner signs. Special altars were built for her next to the bread ovens. For at least eight thousand years, her sacred animal was the pig.

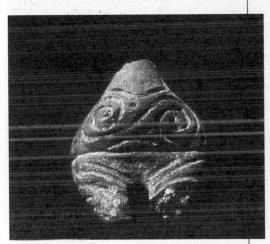

"The Fat Lady of Sitagroi," Macedonia, ca. 4500 B.C., a statuette of a pregnant goddess with two snakes (spirals) incised above her belly, from the Karanovo-Gumelnita culture of Thrace and Macedonia (ca. 5500–4500 B.C.).

The Goddess of life protection and healing appears in many forms. The Bird Goddess appears with a beak or a pinched nose, a long neck, female breasts, and wings or winglike projections, often with a special hairdo or crown. As a waterbird (duck, goose, swan with a human mask, or a woman with a bird's mask) she was a nourisher and increaser of goods. As a spring bird, she assured the eternal return of life energy. Her images are marked by meanders, "beak-and-eyes," chevrons, V's, and zigzag lines.

She often has a V-collar and diagonal lines or bands across her cheeks. As a protectress of the family and village, she was worshiped in temples from the seventh millennium B.C. onward. The sacred animal of the Bird Goddess was the ram.

A small figurine (7.2 inches high) of the "Bird Goddess" from the central Balkans ca. 4500 B.C.; she was the primary divinity of the Vinca culture (ca. 5000–4000 B.C.).

The Snake Goddess was worshiped in temples and at home to ensure the well-being of family life, fertility, and regeneration through harmony with the cycles of nature. The hibernation of the snake is analogous to death, while the shedding of old skin represents rebirth or immortality. Its return in springtime signifies the rebirth of the natural world. The Snake Goddess was portrayed crowned in a cross-legged pose, usually with snakelike hands and feet. In her crown are sometimes found a whole nest of snakes.

The Death Goddess is commonly figured as a bird of prey. Images of vultures and owls found in temples and tombs are expressions of the neolithic Death Goddess. Wall paintings from Catal Huyuk in central Turkey (seventh millennium B.C.) show vultures attacking headless bodies, depicting the widespread practice of excarnation (defleshment of corpses). In western Europe the Owl Goddess is found engraved on menhirs (upright stones) at the entrances to megalithic graves or within the graves themselves. The round eyes of this goddess, sometimes joined with beak and eyebrows, are found in megalithic temples such as Newgrange and Knowth in Ireland, while the Owl Goddess of southeastern Europe appears in the form of urns.

The anthropomorphic Stiff Nude, found in graves in every culture of Old Europe, is best known from the Aegean Cycladic marble figurines of the third millennium B.C. She is carved of bone, marble, alabaster, or light-colored stone because death was envisioned as a white, bonelike form. She is rendered in a stiff pose, nude, usually without breasts, with tapered legs, hands either on her chest or extended along her sides. Her large pubic triangle expresses the promise of regeneration. In the Aegean and Mediterranean regions she wears the mask of the Bird Goddess with no mouth, whereas the figurines from eastern central Europe wear the masks of snakes, with a long mouth, fangs, and round eyes.

The Goddess of Regeneration, who represents rebirth, appears in forms related to female generative organs: the pubic triangle—expressed as triangles and hourglass shapes; the vulva—as seed and bud shapes and as eggs, often painted red; the uterus—expressed as fish or hedgehog, as well as fetuses shown as frogs or hares. She is also rendered as a bee, butterfly, moth, or other insect. These symbols are often combined with the features of the Vulture Goddess.

The female womb with its fallopian tubes resembles the shape of a bull's head with horns, an image found for millennia throughout Old Europe, Anatolia, and the Near East. The most magnificent representations of bull heads are from Catal Huyuk temples in wall paintings and reliefs of the seventh millennium B.C. The bull-head motif in the hypogea (subterranean tombs) of Sardinia is predominant as a sign of regeneration. The so-called horns of consecration, characteristic of the Minoan culture of Crete of the third and second millennia B.C., continue this symbolism.

Male deities are rare in the sculpture of Old Europe. One type, found in various culture groups between the seventh and fourth millennia B.C., sits on a chair with hands on knees or supporting his chin. He may represent dying vegetation, analogous to the historically known flax god Linos, who spends winter as a seed, is born in spring, dies in summer, and returns to earth again. Young males in ithyphallic (sexually excited) posture and those wearing he-goat or ram masks most likely express the potency of springtime fertilizing powers. Phalli and standing ithyphallic men are perhaps prototypes of the Greek herms and god Hermes. Centaurs with the body of a bull and the head of a man are known from the Vinca culture in former Yugoslavia dating from the fifth millennium B.C. and from Cyprus during the fourth millennium B.C. These were stimulators of the fertility of Mother Earth and the regeneration of the dead. Male gods could also have been the guardians of forests and wild animals, since this motif has survived in folklore and in the customs of northern Eurasia. There is a seated sculpture holding a hook, from the Tisza culture in Hungary, that may be ancestral to the historically known Silvanus, Faunus, and Pan.

Temples: The earliest temples in southeast Europe date from the second half of the seventh millennium B.C. These resemble houses and are always found within clusters of dwellings. Exterior and interior decorations such as wall paintings and reliefs distinguish temples from regular houses. Inside are found sculptures, figurines, exquisite vases, altars, small sacrificial tables, libation vases, ladles, and other ceremonial equipment. The Sesklo temples in northern Greece from 6500 to 5500 B.C. are of two rooms. The smaller was a workshop in which ritual ceramics, figurines, and garments were made; the larger room held an altar. Excavations at Achilleion, near Farsala in Thessaly, have shown that temples were dedicated to specific goddesses. In certain temples only Bird Goddess figurines and beaked heads were found. In other temples the Snake Goddess was worshiped. Other temples were appropriated to the themes of death and regeneration and were abundantly decorated with bullheads, horns, triangles, uterine and aquatic symbols, eggs, life columns, upwardly winding snakes, lizards, and dogs. Reliefs and wall paintings in Catal Huyuk temples represent the Goddess in two aspects: death in the form of vultures and regeneration in the shape of frogs.

The triangular-shaped temples at Lepenski Vir, from ca. 6500 B.C. to 5500 B.C., discovered on the bank of the Danube near the Iron Gate in northern former Yugoslavia, were clearly dedicated to the theme of death and regeneration. These small sanctuaries form a semicircle with entrances facing the Danube. After excarnation, the bones of the dead were gathered, then buried beneath temple altars accompanied by rites of regeneration. More than fifty temples have been excavated. At the center of each temple were the remains of a rectangular stone altar surrounded by V-shaped flat stones set on edge in a pattern of continuous triangles. At the head of the altar were one or two oval statues of red limestone, up to fifty or sixty centimeters high. Some exhibit anthropomorphic features, faces and breasts, or fishes' mouths and eyes. Several sculptures appear to comprise three manifestations of the Goddess of Death and Regeneration: those of woman, fish, and predatory bird. Many were carved with labyrinth motifs and painted with red ocher. Symbols of regeneration are dominant: the egg, the fish, the labyrinth, and the red color. The floor plan of these temples is apparently in the shape of the female pubic triangle. The bones of fish, red deer, dogs, and wild boars (animals symbolizing death) were excavated from the altars.

The temples of Malta in the central Mediterranean are also sanctuaries of regeneration. They began as egg-shaped underground tombs that evolved, during the fourth and beginning of the third millennia B.C., into anthropomorphic expressions of the Goddess with enormous egg-shaped arms and buttocks. This image is also repeated in numerous stone sculptures. Symbols found on ceramics, reliefs and wall engravings, stone blocks and altars (bulls, horns, phalli, rising snakes, lizards, budding and branching plant shoots, and animal processions) speak the same language of regeneration. The pubic triangle of the Goddess is repeated in various places—carved from large stones and erected with the narrow end downward, like altars.

Hundreds of miniature clay temples from the seventh through the fourth millennia B.C. convey significant information about the architecture and purpose of temples. These models, about twenty-five to fifty centimeters in length, are often decorated with symbols and signs or even a bust of the Goddess for whom the model was made. Roofless models usually portray bread ovens, platforms, large vases, and figurines grinding grain in preparation for the baking of sacred bread. The model of a two-story temple from the Cucuteni culture of the fifth millennium B.C. was found near Kiev, at Rozsochuvatka. The lower level was a workshop, while the main shrine was on the top level surrounded by a terrace. A full-scale two-story temple from about 5000 B.C. was excavated in Radingrad, northeast Bulgaria, proving that models were true replicas. In the lower level were found tools for decorating ceramics, small dishes for grinding ocher, palettes for paints, as well as a big oven. In the upper level was an altar with a loom beside it for weaving.

Burial Practices: Symbols of regeneration—the egg and the regenerative organs of the Goddess (pubic triangle, uterus, belly, buttocks)—are the basis of Old European tomb shapes manifested in the architectural forms of western European megalithic graves and earthen long barrows that are triangular or trapezoidal. The inner tombs have passages into chambers, symbolic of a vagina and uterus, or the tombs have "courts" in the form of open legs leading to the inner chambers. Occasionally, these tombs are anthropomorphic, in the shape of the body of the Goddess. Long barrows are also bone-shaped, symbolizing death. Elsewhere in Europe, the egg is the dominant shape of graves, often seen as simple egg-shaped pits or rock-cut tombs in which the dead were placed in a contracted fetal position and sprinkled with ocher. The dead, especially newborn babies, were also buried in egg-shaped pots. Egg-shaped halls and niches of subterranean tombs are painted in red, the color of womb blood, considered necessary for rebirth.

In northern and central Europe, individual burials prevailed. In the fifth millennium B.C., in the Dnieper-Donets culture, collective family burials were practiced, and in western and Mediterranean Europe communal collective burials in megalithic graves and underground chambers were the rule. Collective burials of members of extended families continued in Crete throughout the third millennium B.C.

In Neolithic Europe, both individual and communal burials are encountered. Between 7000 and 5000 B.C. cemeteries are not known. Babies, youngsters, and women were buried beneath the floors of houses. Although formal disposal areas emerged in southeast and Danubian Europe around 5000 B.C., the two-stage burial (excarnation and reburial) continued, as evidenced by disarticulated bones found in the communal burials of western European megaliths. Complete skeletons, with rare exceptions, are not found in megalithic graves. In some megalithic tombs where cremation was practiced, as in Newgrange, Ireland, unburned bones were broken into small bits and scattered throughout the passage, chamber, and recesses. Such practices may indicate the desire to promote a faster disintegration into the realm of the ancestors.

The Old European burials are entirely distinct from the Indo-European burials that supplanted them. These dissimilar practices represent totally different ideologies. The Old Europeans emphasized cyclic regeneration from the body of the Great Mother, whereas the Indo-Europeans emphasized a lineal continuity of the importance of powerful individuals.

The civilization of Old Europe disintegrated as a result of invasions by patriarchal Indo-European-speaking tribes (ca. 4500–2500 B.C.) who brought a pastoral economy, a patriarchal social structure, and a male-dominated pantheon of gods. The millennial traditions of Old Europe became the rich substratum for the development of subsequent European cultures. The Minoan culture of Crete and Thera continued the Old European religion and worldview into the second millennium B.C. *See also* Baltic religion; Cycladic religion; Indo-European religion.

Old Testament, the common Christian designation for the books of the Hebrew Bible. To avoid invidious comparison between Old and New, the terms *Hebrew scriptures* or *Tanakh* (an acronym derived from the three divisions of the Hebrew Bible) are increasingly used. *See also* Bible, Christian.

Old Text school, rationalist Confucian scholarly tradition dominant from the Late Han dynasty 23–220) on; it considered authoritative archaic "found" versions of the Classics purportedly deriving from Confucius's own hand and criticized the reformism and speculative excesses of the New Text school. *See also* Confucianism (authoritative texts and their interpretation); Han religion; New Text school.

Olympic Games, a festival held every four years in the precinct of Olympia, the main sanctuary of Zeus. According to tradition, the games were founded in 776 B.C. by Herakles (or Pelops) in honor of Olympian Zeus and abolished by Emperor Theodosius I in 393 during his campaign against paganism. Initially, the games included only one day of running and wrestling. But after their reorganization in 472 B.C., they lasted five days and featured jumping, footraces, wrestling, boxing, horseraces, and the pentathalon. Religious sacrifices began and ended the games, with crowns of wild olive and a final evening banquet for the victors.

Olympos (oh-lim'pohs), the highest mountain in Greece, located in Macedonia. It figures prominently in ancient Greek religion and mythology as the home of the gods. *See also* mountains, sacred.

Om/Aum (ohm/oum; Skt.), the most sacred Hindu monosyllable; it begins and ends recitations from Vedas and prayers and is considered the "seed" of all *mantras* (sacred utterances). In Upanishadic mystical analysis, "o" can be thought of as the diphthong "au," revealing three sounds in one ("a," "u," "m"), representing the three worlds (earth, air, sky) as one. *See also* mantra; Om mani padme hum.

omega. *See* alpha and omega.

O-mei Shan (oo-may shahn), mountain in Szechuan Province, China, one of the "four famous mountains" popular as pilgrimage sites for Chinese Buddhist laypeople. *See also* Chiu-hua Shan; mountains, sacred; pilgrimage; T'ien-t'ai Shan; Wu-t'ai Shan.

omen, in divination, a favorable or unfavorable sign. *See also* divination.

Omiwa Shrine (oh-mee-wah), one of the oldest Shinto shrines in Japan, near the ancient capital of Nara; it is famous for having, in place of a constructed main sanctuary, Mt. Miwa itself as the sacred object of worship. *See also* Miwa, Mt.

Om mani padme hum (ohm mah'nee pahd'may hoom), a Buddhist mantra, or a series of sacred syllables, used to invoke the power of Avalokiteshvara, the Bodhisattva of compassion. In India, it first seems to have meant, "O thou with the jeweled lotus," with *manipadme* functioning as a single word. In Tibet, *mani* and *padme* were treated as separate words, meaning "O the jewel in the lotus." The meaning of the mantra, however, lies less in the significance of the individual words than in its religious function. Tibetan Buddhists chant the mantra, carve it on rocks, print it on flags, and spin it in prayer wheels to ward off danger and fill the world with the power of Avalokiteshvara's compassion. *See also* Avalokiteshvara; lotus; mantra.

omnipotence, divine attribute, the possession of unlimited power.

omnipresence, divine attribute, the capacity to be in all places simultaneously. *See also* bilocation.

omniscience, divine attribute, the capacity to know and see everything.

Omononushi (oh-moh-noh-*noo*-shee; Jap., perhaps "great sword-ruler"), the Shinto *kami* (divinity, divine presence) worshiped at Mt. Miwa. He takes the shape of a snake and is renowned in folk legend as a great womanizer. *See also* Miwa, Mt.; Omiwa Shrine.

Omotokyo, the older name of the new Japanese religion Oomoto. *See also* Oomoto.

One Mind (Chin. *i-hsin*). 1 In Hua-yen Buddhism, the belief that all phenomena, both absolute and relative, have the Mind as their one essence, 2 In Chinese Buddhism a mind concentrated on religious practice, free from distractions. *See also* Hua-yen school.

Ontake-kyo (on-tah-kay-kyoh), a Japanese religious movement, formerly part of Sect Shinto, named after the sacred mountain Ontake (or Mitake) and noted for pilgrimage and trance experiences. *See also* pilgrimage; Sect Shinto.

ontological argument, the popular designation for the reflections on God by Anselm of Canterbury (d. 1109) in his *Proslogion* (1078–79). Taking as his starting point his belief in God as "that than which nothing greater can be thought," Anselm observes that it is greater to exist in both reality and understanding than in understanding alone. Thus, God truly exists in both reality and understanding. There are various ways of being in reality. Some exist now but will cease to exist. Others do not now exist but will come into existence in the future. The greatest way of being is to exist and not be able not to exist. Thus, as "that than which nothing greater can be thought," God must exist in such a way that God's nonexistence is inconceivable. Anselm's reflections have occasioned a great deal of philosophical interest, and some continue to view them as an argument bearing demonstrative force. However, in all likelihood Anselm himself intended his comments as a meditative exercise, designed to bring his monastic readers to a deeper grasp of their God. *See also* Anselm.

Oomoto (oor-moh-toh; Jap., "the great origin"), a Japanese new religion derived from revelations made by the deity Ushitora no Konjin to the illiterate peasant woman Deguchi Nao from 1892 onward. Deguchi had suffered numerous misfortunes prior to her possession by the deity; afterward she acquired, according to followers, healing and divinatory powers and recorded, in automatic writing, the teachings in which Ushitora revealed himself as the creator of the world and promised the creation of an ideal society in the present. Deguchi's son-in-law, Deguchi Onisaburo (d. 1948), himself a shamanic religious practitioner who received revelations from various spirits, extended Oomoto's spiritual healing techniques, and developed the religion as a mass movement through extensive proselytism and use of mass media.

By the 1920s membership in Oomoto was in the millions, and it engendered several other new religions of similar style, many seceding from Oomoto. Its prominence, coupled with Onisaburo's aggrandizing style, led it to its suppression by the Japanese government in the 1920s and 1930s. After 1945 Oomoto reorganized but since the death of the charismatic Onisaburo has never recovered its earlier dynamism. It continues to preach religious tolerance, to foster ecumenical worship, and to assert the value of artistic expression as a spiritual practice. *See also* Japan, new religions in.

O.P. *See* Dominicans.

Ophites (oh'fíts; from Gk. *ophis,* "snake"), a Gnostic cult venerating the snake as the chief spiritual principle; it is attested by second- and third-century Christian authors. *See also* Gnosticism.

opium of the people, a phrase employed by Karl Marx in *Contributions to the Critique of Hegel's Philosophy of Right* (1844), referring to religious belief as consoling the socioeconomically oppressed with promises of justice and bliss in the afterlife. This sort of hope, Marx argues, defuses the legitimate anger and energy of the oppressed, thus preventing them from taking appropriate action in this world against their oppressors. Marx sees religion—especially Judaism and Christianity—as a mental and emotional narcotic useful to the oppressing classes. Opium does not cure an illness but merely dulls its pain. When what the Marxists view as the correct solution is applied, oppression ends, and with it the pain of the once oppressed classes. The need for religion as an illusory cure becomes superfluous, and religion, in this view, will inevitably disappear.

Opus Dei (oh'pus day'ee; Lat., "the work of God"), secretive, conservative Roman Catholic lay organization established by Jose Maria Escriva de Balaguer in Madrid in 1928. Opus Dei gained papal approval in 1950.

oracle. 1 A message from god(s), usually of a divinatory nature. 2 The shrine where such messages are received. 3 In extended usage, any divine message or revelation, usually transmitted by a prophet. *See also* Delphi; divination; Greek religion; Shang religion.

oracle bones, bovine scapulae and turtle plastrons used extensively in Chinese royal divinations on a variety of topics during Shang and early Chou periods (ca. 1766–722 B.C.). The appearance of these oracle bones (called "dragon bones") in apothecaries in the 1890s led to the discovery of the royal Shang ritual complex. Intense heat applied to oval gouges in the bone caused distinctive cracks to appear on the reverse; incised alongside, using the earliest Chinese writing, would typically be the diviner's name, divination charge, the king's prognostication, and, exceptionally, verification of the outcome. Over one hundred thousand inscribed oracle bones have been discovered. *See also* Chou religion; divination; Shang religion.

oral tradition, the portion of a culture that is tradition and knowledge passed on by word of mouth. Speech-related acts—riddles, songs, stories, proverbs, prayers, jokes, epics, chants—are the most obvious forms of oral tradition. Other forms include practice of architecture, dance, directional orientation, performance, making of tools and ritual objects, rituals themselves.

A central characteristic of oral tradition is its immediacy. All exchanges are face-to-face. It matters not only what is learned or taught, but also where, when, and from whom. In trying to understand oral tradition one must pay attention to the context in which the information is conveyed. Since most oral traditions now come to scholars in the form of written texts that are neither oral nor traditional, attending to performative contexts means being suspicious and tentative about many of our findings. *See also* storytelling.

orant (aw'rant), characteristic posture of devotion with arms raised over the head. Orant is common in early Christian art and in contemporary enthusiastic Christian groups to indicate both supplication and experience of the Spirit.

ordeal. 1 The ritual infliction of pain, most commonly as part of initiation. 2 A juridical procedure to determine guilt or innocence requiring divine intervention to rescue the individual from harm if innocent. *See also* flagellation; initiation rituals; mutilation.

ordinances. *See* sacraments and ordinances (Christianity).

ordination, the formal procedure by which an individual is licensed as a religious practitioner. *See also* Buddhism (life cycle); monasticism; priest/priestess; sacraments and ordinances (Christianity); Sangha; Santeria.

Judaism: In Judaism, *semikah* (Heb., "laying on of hands") is the rite that confers leadership and the authority to perform judicial functions. The concept derives from Numbers 27:22–23, where, at God's command, Moses lays hands on and thus transfers some of his divine spirit to Joshua. Rabbinic sources claim an unbroken chain of ordination, hence authority, from Moses through early rabbinic times.

Beginning in the fourth century, the practice was generally replaced by documents of appointment, which certified the individual's legal knowledge. Contemporary American and Israeli Orthodox rabbinical academies use the traditional form of laying on of hands, as does Reform Judaism. *See also* rabbi.

Christianity: From early times the appointment of those who were to occupy positions of leadership within the Christian community was accompanied by religious rites. By the middle of the second century three levels or "orders" of ministers were established—bishops, presbyters, and deacons—together with a varying number of minor orders appointed for specific subordinate functions. At first the rites for the three orders consisted of two parts, the election of the ministers by the whole assembly and then the community's prayer that God would bestow on them the gifts needed for the effective exercise of their ministry. Later, however, the practice of popular election declined, and the rites centered around the act of prayer accompanied by the laying on of hands, which came to be viewed as the ritual means by which God made someone a minister. The ordained ministry was now understood as constituting a priesthood acting on behalf of the members of the church, and consequently medieval ordination rites became much more elaborate and included the bestowal of symbols representing the priestly nature of the office and of the sacred vestments that would be worn by the new minister. In the West the hands of the newly ordained were also anointed, and eventually their permanent celibacy was required.

The churches of the Reformation understood the Christian ministry differently, not as serving as a sacrificial priesthood but primarily as preaching God's work, and so they rejected all the medieval ordination ceremonies as misrepresenting its true nature. Some Christian groups abolished a separate ordained ministry altogether, viewing every member of the church as a minister, but most retained a single order of ministers of the word in place of the earlier hierarchical structure and returned to simple services of prayer accompanying their appointment, sometimes preceded by a public election of the candidates.

More recent revisions of ordination rites have seen a considerable convergence of understanding of the nature of ordination and ministry. Catholics now stress the centrality of prayer in the act of ordination, and Protestant rites often include the handing over of appropriate symbols of office. Laypeople now also frequently exercise functions (e.g., the reading of the Bible in church services and the distribution of the eucharistic elements) that were formerly restricted to the clergy. Although all Christian traditions in the past ordained only men, many Protestant churches have now begun to ordain women.

Consecration to Religious Life: While from the beginning of the second century women were not ordained to positions of leadership within orthodox Christian communities, those who were widows were accorded a special place of honor. They were not only recipients of the church's charity, but also appear in some places to have exercised certain ministerial functions, especially with regard to other women, where propriety prevented men from undertaking such activities. This latter role was later assumed in Eastern churches by specially appointed women known as deaconesses.

Also among early Christians were some who voluntarily chose a life of poverty and sexual abstinence as an expression of their religious commitment, and their numbers grew considerably from the fourth century onward. Organized communities or orders of such men and women were formed, living together under a common rule of life, with formal rites marking the various stages of admission into this particular form of religious life and of appointment to offices within it. A central feature of the rites of admission is the self-offering or consecration of the person to that way of life as a permanent state, expressed in vows of poverty, chastity, and obedience. Since such communities were later marked by the particular form of dress they wore, the clothing of a new entrant, the habit, also came to form part of the rites.

Japanese Buddhism: Although Japanese Buddhist ordinations (Jap. *jukai*) are often similar to those practiced in other Buddhist countries, important differences exist. The Nara schools used the *Ssu-fen lu* (*Dharmaguptaka Vinaya*), a version of the traditional *Vinaya*. However, Saicho used the Mahayana *Fan-wang ching* to ordain Tendai monks. As a result, the Kamakura schools have developed a variety of ordinations influenced by the Tendai tradition. Although ordination as a monk originally included renunciation of the world, from the eleventh century onward becoming a monk was also a way for nobles to advance their careers. As a result, some monks withdrew from the large monasteries to become recluses (*tonseso*) and live in hermitages far away from increasingly politicized and secularized monasteries. In addition, ordinations were often performed on the sick and dying in hope that the karmic merit would help them either recover, be reborn in the Pure Land, or obtain a good rebirth. These changes led to lax views on monastic discipline. As a result, Japanese monks today marry, eat meat, and drink alcohol. *See also* Kamakura schools; Nara schools.

orenda (oh-ren'dah; Huron), power or force innate to all Iroquoian objects, from stones to hurricanes to deities. Comparable concepts held by other Native North American tribes are designated by *wakan* (Sioux), *manitowi* (Algonquian), and *pokunt* (Shoshonean). The root *ren* is associated with the power of song, a principal vehicle of contact between the Iroquois and their spiritual world. *Orenda*, a deciding factor of superiority, accounts for a hunter's success or a warrior's victory. Orenda is generally conceived as beneficent. Malefic power, such as that used to invoke a spell, was called *ot'gon*. It could only be dispelled by a shaman with greater orenda than the curse. One's orenda could be influenced and weakened in the dream state. A warrior could dream of approaching, or being approached by his opponent's orenda, and the ensuing struggle between orendas could determine victory or defeat for the warrior in actual battle. Early missionaries to the Iroquois equated orenda to the Christian concept of soul mainly due to its life-energizing properties and due to the missionaries' misunderstanding that one's orenda passed on to the Iroquois life after death. Contemporary references sometimes equate orenda to a Great Spirit, but this notion is removed from the original, individualized, personal notion of orenda. *See also* mana.

Organization of Afro-American Unity. *See* African Americans (North America), new religions among; Malcolm X.

orgy, ritual characterized by frenzy and featuring singing, dancing, drinking, and sexual activities. Originally associated with Greco-Roman Dionysiac cults, it has become a generic term.

orientation, the use of the cardinal directions in order to place religious activities or buildings. Frequently associated with the notion of auspicious and inauspicious directions: east being most frequently the favored direction; north, the most dangerous. *See also* directional orientations.

Origen (or'ee-jin; ca. 185–254), Greek Christian theologian, later condemned as a heretic. Origen is best known for his biblical studies, especially the *Hexapla*, which set forth various versions of the Bible in parallel columns; for his apologetics, especially the treatise *Against Celsus;* and for his early presentation of Christian systematic theology, *De Principiis.*

Original Hebrew Israelite Nation. *See* African Americans (North America), new religions among; Black Israelites.

original sin (Christianity), offenses against God and God's creation, transmitted to all human beings as a result of the actions of Adam and Eve. While pride was the cause of original sin, sin was particularly present in sensuality. Prior to the Fall, human beings were able not to sin; after the Fall, they were unable not to sin. Augustine (d. 430) held that prior to sinning, Adam and Eve were in a state of perfect communion with God. Pelagius (d. ca. 418) argued that all human beings are able not to sin and rejected the notion of transmitted original sin. Irenaeus held that Adam and Eve could not have been in a state of spiritual perfection prior to the Fall, since then they would never have fallen, the joy of communion with God being so great. Thomas Aquinas (ca. 1225–74), like Irenaeus, held that after the Fall human beings were not totally depraved.

The Protestant Reformation returned to Augustinian pessimism. Martin Luther (1483–1546) argued for total depravity and the damnable nature of all human beings. The Renaissance and Enlightenment rebelled against this pessimism and celebrated the natural goodness of human nature. More recently Social Gospel theologians and Christian Marxists have held that sin is not inherent to human nature, but rather results from unjust social structures. *See also* Fall.

origin of religion. The question of the origin, together with that of the function of religion is twofold: Why does religion originate, and how does religion originate? The "why" is concerned with the recurrent origin of religion. That origin is usually formulated as being a need, which religion continually arises to fulfill. The need can be for anything—for example, for food, health, security, or justice. It can be on the part of either individuals or society. The why question does not assume that religion is the sole possible way of satisfying the need; it argues only that whenever religion arises, it arises in response to a need.

The "how" is concerned with the initial origin of religion. The answer is historical. The how question asks not what causes religion to emerge whenever it does but what caused religion to emerge when it first did.

It is often said that classical theorists of religion are most concerned with the origin, if also the truth, of religion and that contemporary scholars are most concerned with the function, if also the meaning, of religion. This characterization is simplistic. Contemporary theorists remain as concerned as their classical counterparts with the recurrent origin of religion. Indeed, the function of religion is invariably held to be the fulfillment of the need that gives rise to religion: the why of the function and of the origin are the same. To assert that religion arises to satisfy a need for food is to assert as well that religion functions to satisfy that need. Even the meaning of religion is tied to the why of the origin. To assert that religion arises to satisfy a need for food is inevitably to translate religious talk into talk about food. Gods become gods of vegetation.

The difference between present-day and earlier theorists of religion is that present-day theorists have largely, though not uniformly, abandoned the quest for the historical origin— the how—of religion. The quest has been abandoned not because the answer has been found but because the answer will never be found: scant evidence survives of the invention of religion. It is not that earlier scholars placed the origin later than present-day ones and so expected to be able to discover historical artifacts. Earlier scholars typically considered religion to be as old as humanity. The earlier scholars freely speculated; contemporary ones are more cautious.

Edward Tylor: The exemplar of the nineteenth-century quest for the historical as well as recurrent origin of religion is the anthropologist E. B. Tylor (*Primitive Culture*, 1871). He reconstructs the historical origin in the absence not only of direct evidence of the origin but even of direct evidence of the earliest form of religion. Assuming that religion arises to satisfy a sheer intellectual need for explanation, Tylor (1832–1917) imagines that "primitives" first postulated souls in an effort to explain two observations: the contrast between the mobility of the living and the immobility of the dead, and the appearance of human shapes in dreams and visions. Primitives hypothesized that souls give life and motion to otherwise dead and inert bodies. Primitives then ascribed souls to all of nature (animism). Eventually, they personified the souls, which thereby became gods inhabiting and controlling all phenomena save humans themselves. Religion thus arose from a scientificlike combination of observation, inference, and generalization. In answering how religion arose, Tylor is not answering when it arose. He is speculating on how religion arose whenever it arose.

James Frazer: For anthropologist James Frazer (*The Golden Bough*, 1890–1915), religion arises in reaction to primitives' dismay at the failure of magic. Where magic assumes the capacity of humans to manipulate the world directly, religion defers to the powers of gods, who can be beseeched and pressured but never forced. Frazer (1854–1941) suggests that magic came first and that, in despair at its impotence, primitives conceded their incapacity to control the world. More cursorily than Tylor, Frazer suggests how they proceeded to postulate gods in place of the magical laws of nature. When religion began Frazer does not say. Why it began he is certain: religion arises to satisfy a need for basic necessities, the satisfaction of which requires an explanation of the operation of the world.

Emile Durkheim: Like Tylor and Frazer, the sociologist Emile Durkheim (*The Elementary Forms of the Religious Life*, 1912) reconstructs the historical origin of religion. Durkheim (1858–1917) argues that religion originated in the gathering of the totemic clan. Ordinarily, members of the clan lived apart. Whenever they gathered, their sheer contact with one another created an extraordinary feeling of energy and power. They felt infused, uplifted, omnipotent. Knowing that individually they lacked this power, they ascribed it not to themselves collectively but to possession by something external. They fastened on the totemic emblem, which they knew was a symbol of their totem yet which they nevertheless took as the object of worship. They even valued it above the totem itself. Because the supernatural power that they ascribed to the totemic emblem was in fact their own collective power, the true origin of religion was their experience of themselves.

For Durkheim, there is no why of origin because religion arose accidentally—as the false ascription of power to the emblem, which thereby became a god. Durkheim is explaining the origin of religion; the origin is simply unintentional. Religion did not arise in order to serve a need, as if society were a thinking entity that had created it in order to win loyalty. Rather, religion began serving society, and serving society indispensably, once it arose.

Sigmund Freud: Sigmund Freud (*Totem and Taboo*, 1913) provides the most daring theory of the origin of religion. Freud (1856–1939), a neurologist and the founder of psychoanalysis, argues that religion arose in response to the guilt that primitive sons felt for having killed their fathers, who had barred them from sexual access to the women of the primal horde. Totems and then gods were postulated to enable the sons to alleviate their guilt by obeying their now deified fathers, whom they had earlier failed to obey. Like Tylor and Frazer, Freud provides a why as well as a how of the origin: religion arises to satisfy the need to relieve guilt over oedipal deeds.

Max Weber: Where for other theorists the why of religion is the same wherever there is religion, for Max Weber (*The Sociology of Religion*, 1922) the why changes. Initially, religion arises for the same end as for Frazer: to provide physical necessities. Eventually, religion comes instead to provide meaning. Weber (1864–1920) does not explain how religion arose in its original, magical form. He does explain how the why of religion changed.

The magician, according to Weber, was originally self-employed and was therefore hired anew each time. Consequently, he developed no systematic doctrines, only concrete techniques. Not until there emerged a stable clientele of worshipers—a congregation, or cult—did a priesthood emerge. Not until priests succeeded magicians did metaphysics—a comprehensive explanation of the world—emerge in place of mere technique. Likewise not until priests arose did ethics—ends achieved through obedience—emerge in place of coercion—ends achieved through technique. The combination of metaphysics and ethics made religion rational rather than ad hoc and constituted the stage of religion after magic. Finally, not until a cult emerged did the concept of a fixed god—singular, named, personal, and involved—emerge in place of the magical concept of multiple, weak, nameless, impersonal, and uninvolved fleeting gods.

Only with the development of rationalized religion did there develop a desire to resolve systematically a discrepancy between expectation and experience. That desire was for meaning: the demand for a coherent explanation and justification of experience. According to Weber, suffering was the experience that most needed justification. A sufficient explanation for the failure of magic was that the technique had been misapplied. But rationalized religion had to explain the failure of the gods to respond to the behavior they themselves had dictated. Because their failure meant their failure to prevent or withhold suffering, the explanation sought was a theodicy. The theodicy ultimately involved the provision of salvation.

Since all human beings for Weber recognize the discrepancy between their expectations and their experience, all harbor the potential yearning for meaning. But its emergence depends on rationalized religion, the emergence of which itself depends on a particular kind of religious leader—a priest—whose emergence depends in turn on a particular kind of social organization—a cult. Weber claims not that every cult produced a priesthood but only that every priesthood required a cult. He claims not that every cult produced a fixed god but only that a fixed god required a cult. His historical explanation is more modest than that of other theorists because he claims to be giving only necessary, never sufficient, causes.

Clifford Geertz: The origin that contemporary scholars provide is largely recurrent rather than historical. Social theorists such as Clifford Geertz, Mary Douglas, Victor Turner, Robert Bellah, and Peter Berger are primarily concerned with the why, not the how, of religion. The how that they consider is not how religion arose, but how it functions.

Clifford Geertz (*The Interpretation of Cultures*, 1973) argues that religion arises to provide the same need as Weber—meaning—though for Geertz it is the original as well as the subsequent need fulfilled by religion. Rather than explaining how religion arose to satisfy that need, Geertz explains how religion, once established, satisfies it.

As an example of what Geertz calls a cultural system, religion provides meaning by telling both what to believe and how to act in the wake of the beliefs. A cultural system provides not only a conception of reality but also an accompanying way of life. Religion in particular provides not only a worldview but also an ethos. A cultural system meshes the conception with the way of life. In the case of religion the worldview makes the ethos natural, and in turn the ethos provides a concrete, living manifestation of the worldview.

Like Geertz, other contemporary theorists of

religion ignore the how and the when of the origin of religion and focus on the why. The why is usually, as for Geertz, a need for meaning. From such a perspective contemporary theorists are far less concerned with the origin of religion than most classical theorists. *See also* religion, the study of.

origin story. *See* etiology.

orisha (aw-ree-shah'; Yoruba, "head source"), a spiritual being honored in the religions originating among the Yoruba people of present-day Nigeria and Benin.

Yoruba stories speak of a primordial time when Orisha was a single being who was struck by an enormous stone and shattered into millions of pieces. Many of these fragments were gathered together in ceremonial vessels, but most remain unrecognized amid the objects of the world. Orishas can thus be manifest as stones, plants, rivers, and other natural and human-made objects; as forces of nature such as thunder and wind; as musical sounds and human gestures in ceremonies; and as invisible anthropomorphic personalities whose intercession is sought for all manner of human problems.

Orishas are honored and petitioned in ceremonies of praise and sacrifice. The most dramatic of these invoke the orisha to "mount" the "head" of an initiated medium so that the personality of the orisha enters the human community to dance, speak, and, ultimately, prophesy and heal.

During the slave trade, priests and priestesses of the orishas were taken to the Americas where they established religious communities throughout the Caribbean and, more recently, in the United States. There are now more devotees of the orishas in the New World than in the Old. *See also* Africa, traditional religions in; Afro-Americans (Caribbean and South America), new religions among; Afro-Brazilian religions; orixa; Santeria.

orixa (oh-ri-shah', from Yoruban *orisha*, "deity"), god or goddess in African-linked religions of the Americas, usually in an intermediary position between the creator deity and lesser spirits. *See also* Afro-Americans (Caribbean and South America), new religions among; Afro-Brazilian religions; Santeria.

Orpheus (or'fee-uhs), Greek hero, patron of the arts, and reputed founder in the sixth century B.C. of Orphism reform of Dionysian excesses. *See also* Greek religion; Orphism.

Orpheus stories in traditional religions, stories with a motif parallel to the Greek story of Orpheus, who went to the land of the dead to retrieve his wife. The motif is widespread in North America, Siberia, Greenland, Africa, and Melanesia. The journey to the land of the dead, undertaken by a relative in search of a deceased family member, usually requires permission from the supernatural guardian of the realm of the dead and some prohibitions, such as not looking at or touching the dead person or looking back on the return trip. The inevitable violation means failure and the prohibition of the dead ever returning to life. It accounts for the permanence of death.

In one example (Blackfeet, northern Plains) a young man goes in search of his deceased wife. He is instructed by an old woman, who supplies him with powerful medicine and a pipe to communicate with the spirits in the land of the dead. The spirits eventually return his wife to him. The couple is instructed to sweat thoroughly in a sweat house outside the village before seeing anyone. The husband is given a warning against meanness toward his wife. After a number of years, when one day the husband threatens to burn his wife with fire, she vanishes and is never seen again. *See also* afterworld; descent to the underworld; journey to the otherworld.

Orphism, the first Greek religion claiming a founder, Orpheus, whose life, descent to the underworld, and death by dismemberment was recounted from the sixth century B.C. Orphism is first documented in Attica, whence it spread to southern Italy. Orphic literature, however, is considerably later. It focuses on the overlapping themes of gods, world, and humans. Their unity is summarized in the Orphic principle, "All things proceed from unity and are resolved again into unity" (Diogenes Laertius *Prologue*. 3). In myth, the Titans, offspring of Earth and Heaven, dismembered, roasted, and devoured the young Dionysos-Zagreus, son of Zeus and Persephone. Zeus incinerated the Titans and from their ashes arose the human race, constituted thereby from the evil nature of the Titans, but also from the divine Dionysos whom the Titans had eaten. To regain one's true nature, one must flee the Titanic in order to save the Dionysian, a process that included teachings concerning the transmigration of souls (Gk. *metempsychosis*) and punishment in the underworld, as well as salvation. Whether Orphism was an organized culture tradition is disputed. Though there are documented examples of local Orphic groups, recent studies speak increasingly of an Orphic attitude conducive to an ascetic life-style that permeated ancient and Hellenistic thought. Both the restructuring of traditional Greek myth in Orphic literature and its ascetic life-style suggest a sociology of renunciation with respect to the ideals of Greco-Roman social life. *See also* Dionysos; Greek religion; metempsychosis; mystery religions.

Orpingalik (ohr-pin-gah'lik), well-known Netsilik (Canadian) Eskimo *angakkok* (shaman), hunter, singer, and poet who shared information with the Danish explorer Knud Rasmussen during the Fifth Thule Expedition of 1921 to 1924. *See also* circumpolar religion; shamanism.

Orthodox Church, a fellowship of Christian churches that has developed historically from the Church of the Byzantine Empire. There are currently fifteen self-governing ("autocephalous") churches, including the four ancient patriarchates of Constantinople, Alexandria, Antioch, and Jerusalem. The See of Rome, which is the fifth Patriarchate in the system of Pentarchy established at the Council of Chalcedon (451), separated from the Orthodox Church. The Patriarch of Constantinople, known as the Ecumenical Patriarch, is given primacy of honor within the Orthodox Church but has no authority comparable to that of the pope. The system of patriarchs does not undermine the equality of bishops. Conciliar authority is held to be superior to that of the patriarch. Thus the unity of the Orthodox Church does not reside in the primacy of a single individual or in a centralized administration, but in a common faith defined primarily through the seven ecumenical councils and in sacramental Communion. Of the other eleven self-governing churches, those of Russia, Serbia, Georgia, Romania, and Bulgaria are also headed by patriarchs, while the churches of Greece, Cyprus, Albania, Poland, former Czechoslovakia, and America are led by metropolitans or archbishops. In addition there are "autonomous" churches in Japan, Finland, and Crete that are not fully independent.

History: The Orthodox maintain that the ecumenical councils of Nicaea I (325), Constantinople I (381), Ephesus (431), Chalcedon (451), Constantinople II (553), Constantinople III (680) and Nicaea II (787) provide an infallible guide to Christian doctrine and church organizations. They do not recognize as ecumenical any council held after Nicaea II. The christological definitions reached at Ephesus and Chalcedon resulted in a lasting separation of the Orthodox Church from other Eastern churches who rejected these settlements. These churches, who also refer to themselves as Orthodox, include a once vigorous Nestorian church centered in Persia, and the Monophysite churches of Syria (Jacobite Church), Egypt (Coptic Church), Ethiopia, Armenia, and India.

The schism between the Byzantine Church in Constantinople and the Church of Rome developed gradually from causes that were theological, cultural, and political. The use of the title *Ecumenical Patriarch* of the Patriarch of Constantinople, the coronation of Charlemagne by Pope Leo III as emperor of the Holy Roman Empire in opposition to the Roman Emperor of Byzantium, the dispute over the use of leavened or unleavened bread in the Eucharist, debates over clerical celibacy, the papal excommunication of the Orthodox in 1054, and finally the sack of Constantinople by the Crusaders in 1204 and the subsequent installation of a Latin patriarch in the Great Church, Hagia Sophia, all exemplify the deteriorating relationship between the Orthodox and Western churches. Yet the Orthodox perceive the fundamental issues underlying the lasting schism to be chiefly two: the development of the claim for papal primacy over all bishops including those in the East, and the Western introduction of the *filioque*, the claim that the Holy Spirit proceeds from the Father and the Son, into the Nicene Creed. Political expedience led emperors to seek union at the Council of Lyons (1274) and Council of Florence (1438–39), but these unions were renounced by the Orthodox Church.

Expansion of the Orthodox Church was achieved by missionary activity among the Slavs in the ninth century. Cyril and Methodius developed a Slavonic alphabet and provided the people with the liturgy in the vernacular. Church Slavonic remains the liturgical language of the Russian church. Russia itself became Orthodox in 988 after the conversion of the Kievan prince Vladimir I. The fall of Constantinople to the Turks in 1453 left the task of preserving and developing Orthodox traditions primarily with the church in Russia. The Russian church gained independence from the Patriarch of Constantinople in 1448, when Russian bishops first elected their own metropolitan, and was recognized as a new patriarchate in 1589. Other autocephalous Orthodox churches were established as national churches in the Balkans following the collapse of the Ottoman empire in the nineteenth century.

Church Structure and Worship: The Orthodox claim to be the one true, visible church. The structure of the Orthodox Church is guided by the Byzantine *nomocanon*, a collection of traditional regulations from various sources including the ecumenical councils, the final form of

orders within the Orthodox Church, are typically married men. However, the decision to marry must be made prior to ordination since the Orthodox forbid marriage after an individual's ordination.

Seven sacraments are recognized by the Orthodox Church: baptism, chrismation (confirmation), Eucharist, confession, holy orders, marriage, and anointing of the sick. Orthodox children are initiated by infant baptism, which includes a triple immersion in water. Chrismation, in which the priest anoints the child with oil (chrism), immediately follows baptism and is believed to confer the Holy Spirit. After baptism and chrismation children are allowed to partake of Holy Communion. The sacrament of confession is provided for the remission of sins committed after baptism and typically an Orthodox will go to confession prior to Communion.

The heart of Orthodox worship is the divine liturgy (Mass). There are four different eucharistic liturgies, the most common being the Liturgy of St. John Chrysostom. Typically the liturgy is presented in the vernacular and it is always sung a cappella either by the choir alone or, occasionally, with the congregation.

A distinctive feature of Orthodox worship, both public and private, is the use of icons. An icon is a flat picture bearing an image of Christ, the *Theotokos* ("Mother of God") (lit., "Bearer of God"), or a particular saint. In venerating an icon, honor is given to the person represented in it. Veneration of icons was attacked during the iconoclastic movement of the eighth and ninth centuries. Behind this controversy over liturgical art was a theological dispute concerning the doctrine of the Incarnation and the relation between divinity and humanity. The victorious Orthodox faith affirmed that the image of Christ reveals God who became visible in the Incarnation, and the images of the *Theotokos* and the saints reveal the deification of humanity, which God makes possible through Christ.

Monasticism: Monasticism has been an important element in Orthodoxy since the fourth century. Unlike monasticism in the West, Orthodox monasticism has never developed religious orders, each devoted to a special service such as education or missionary work. Orthodox monasticism exhibits a greater degree of individuality. Each Orthodox monastery is a separate foundation governed by its own rule, and in addition to cenobitic (communal) monasticism the Orthodox have both preserved the original eremitic (solitary) form and developed idiorhythmic monasticism that allows for greater individual freedom within a communal context. Advocates of these forms have occasionally

Pilgrims making their way on their knees to the Orthodox Church of the Madonna of the Annunciation, on the Greek island of Tinos in the Cyclades. The church is one of Greece's foremost pilgrimage sites because it houses a miracle-working icon of the Annunciation of the Virgin.

which is attributed to Photius, a ninth-century patriarch of Constantinople. However, the church is understood to be first and foremost a eucharistic community, not an institutional organization, and it is according to this self-understanding that the *nomocanon* is interpreted. The Orthodox believe that the church is the body of Christ through which a Christian participates in the divine life and finds salvation. Each local community of Christians gathered around its bishop and sharing in the Eucharist is the whole body of Christ uniting heaven and earth.

The structure of the visible church is hierarchical. The highest office is that of the bishop, who is responsible for teaching the faith and celebrating the sacraments in his own community. Bishops are believed to stand in the apostolic succession; responsibility for appointing bishops to vacant Sees generally falls to the General Synod of each autocephalous church. Bishops are drawn from the monastic clergy who, having taken monastic vows, are not permitted to marry. Priests and deacons, the other two major

Greek Orthodox bishop celebrating the liturgy at a meeting of the World Council of Churches in Canada (Vancouver, British Columbia).

come into conflict, as in the violent dispute between the Possessors and Nonpossessors in Russia during the sixteenth century over questions of monastic property and the relationship between the Church and society. The Possessors emphasized the social responsibility of the Church and hence the need for large monastic revenues, whereas the Nonpossessors, who were mainly hermits, emphasized poverty and the life of prayer. Despite the victory of the Possessors in this instance the primary aim of monasticism remains the individual monk's pursuit of the contemplative life in prayer; consequently, the active service does not receive the same emphasis in Orthodox monasticism as it does in the West.

Monasticism has been influential in the development of the Orthodox spiritual tradition, a distinctive element of which is Hesychasm. Hesychast spirituality centers around the Jesus Prayer and has its roots in the spirituality of Evagrius Ponticus (a fourth-century monk) and the Macarian Homilies. Hesychasm reached its height during the fourteenth century among the monks of Mt. Athos in Greece, which had been the center of Orthodox monasticism since the tenth century. Attacks on Hesychasm by Barlaam the Calabrian brought forth the fullest theological defense of Hesychast practices and Orthodox beliefs concerning the divine light and divine energies by Gregory Palamas, a monk of Athos. Hesychasm was officially confirmed as Orthodox teaching at the Councils of Constantinople in 1341 and 1351. *See also* Athos, Mt.; Hesychasm; icon; Monophysitism; Nestorianism; Philokalia; Photius; Theotokos.

Orthodox Judaism, one of the divisions of the modern Jewish religious community.

Historical Background: Although Judaism has always been characterized by internal divisions of various kinds, the modern period brought a new dimension to these divisions. Social and political emancipation allowed European Jews to enter into the mainstream of the life of the general community. This brought with it a desire on the part of many Jews to adapt their life-styles and even their religious practices to the norms of the world in which they were living. Forces within the Jewish communities began to press for religious reform or even for the secularization of Jewish life. The former became identified in the early nineteenth century with Reform Judaism. The latter generated a variety of Jewish political movements, most prominently political Zionism.

Orthodox Judaism was the response of the traditional religious community to the threats of Reform and secularization. It was a conscious ideology formulated as a reaction to the new historical circumstances, and it claimed to represent authentic classical Jewish religion against the changes instituted by the various types of reform. To the present day, Orthodox Judaism continues to define itself, on the one hand, in opposition to the non-Orthodox religious movements and, on the other hand, in relation to the ancient Jewish tradition.

Doctrine and Practice: There was no absolutely fixed body of doctrine in early Judaism. Until Maimonides (1135–1204) formulated a set of thirteen articles of faith, there was no single authoritative Jewish creed. Although the creed of Maimonides became widely accepted over the centuries, it never achieved exclusive formal status, and a number of versions of the principles of Jewish faith were developed by thinkers of later times. Identity as a faithful, practicing Jew was determined not so much by formal professions of faith as by conformity to the law. In an important sense this continues to be the case, so that the term *orthodoxy*, suggesting commitment to correct doctrine, is viewed by many as misleading.

It is, however, the case that the challenge of religious reform evoked a theological response. The newly named Orthodoxy defined itself as affirming that divine revelation included the whole Torah, written as well as oral. The belief that the Torah in our hands was given by God through Moses at Sinai was now articulated as the basic criterion of Orthodox Judaism. The term *Torah* was taken to include not only the text of the Pentateuch but the entire subsequent tradition of Jewish law and practice as set forth in the Talmud and codified by the later authorities. All is considered binding; all is considered to carry with it an absolute divine mandate.

From this perspective, the role of the teachers of Torah is not to make law, but only to interpret the received law. Orthodox Jews understand themselves as those who affirm the divine source of the entire Torah and who conduct their lives in accordance with the law as interpreted by recognized authorities. The creedal dimension and the dimension of practice are the fixed criteria of Jewish Orthodoxy.

Contemporary Orthodoxy and Its Divisions: Though these criteria apply to all forms of contemporary Orthodoxy, this does not mean that there is simple uniformity within Orthodox Judaism today. One finds, rather, a diversity of social and intellectual settings in the various Orthodox communities. There is a generally accepted distinction between "modern/centrist" Orthodoxy and "rightist/ultra" Orthodoxy. Both recognize the same Torah and follow essentially the same set of religious practices, but what separates them is no less important than what unites them.

The ideology of the Orthodox right basically denies any intellectual or spiritual validity to non-Orthodox forms of Judaism and to the non-Jewish world in which Jews live. This view leads to a deliberate policy of withdrawal and separatism in all matters. Distinctive "Jewish" styles of dress and even of language are elevated to the status of religious imperatives. Secular education is rejected as having no intrinsic value. It may be acceptable to acquire the education needed to pursue a career or practice a profession, but anything more is a rejection of the supreme worth of the study of Torah. In this view all wisdom and all truth derive from the canonized texts of the Jewish tradition as they are interpreted by the true Torah scholars of each generation. It is in that social and intellectual milieu that a faithful Jew should live, limiting contact with the general society only to what is practically necessary.

In sharp contrast, modern Orthodoxy affirms the positive value of much in the contemporary social and intellectual world. It seeks to remain loyal to the principles of faith and the rules of practice dictated by the Torah; however, it seeks to do so while living actively in the context of modern society. It finds in that society much that can enhance and deepen Jewish faith and Jewish self-understanding. This kind of Orthodox Judaism sees secular learning in a positive light. It is not just a practical necessity to be grudgingly accepted, but an important way to enhance and deepen the quality and substance of Jewish religious life. Yeshiva University, the main institution of higher learning of modern Orthodoxy, has as its motto "Torah Umadda" ("Torah and Knowledge"), that is, a deliberate marriage of Torah and secular learning. Modern Orthodoxy lives fully within the social and intellectual realities of its contemporary society.

Against Reform and Conservative Judaism, modern Orthodox Judaism continues to define itself in the same terms as the religious Right. These forms of Judaism are rejected because they deny or question that the Torah and the legal tradition are the revelation of God's teaching as received at Sinai. A practical consequence of this doctrine is that the law is no longer viewed as binding in its totality. For modern Orthodoxy this rejection of the law robs non-Orthodox forms of Judaism of religious validity. Rejection of the law, in practice as well as in theory, is construed as a denial of the very foundations on which Jewish faith rests. *See also* Conservative Judaism; creed;

Hasidism; Reconstructionism; Reform Judaism; Torah.

orthodoxy, orthopraxy, respectively, correct doctrine and correct practice or ritual. The terms are often used to distinguish or classify various religions. Christianity is said to emphasize orthodoxy while Hinduism stresses orthopraxy. The distinctions are probably based upon the fact that Christianity has a defined scripture (a canon) while Hinduism does not. Nevertheless, such labels distort the religions to which they are applied. Beliefs and rituals are necessary and equally emphasized elements in all religions. *See also* typology, classification.

orthopraxis. *See* orthodoxy, orthopraxy.

orthopraxy. *See* orthodoxy, orthopraxy.

O.S.B. *See* Benedictines.

Osho Foundation International. *See* Rajneesh Foundation International.

Osiris (oh-sī′ris), in myth the Egyptian divine king and judge in the netherworld. Following his death at the hands of his brother, Seth, Osiris fathered the royal god Horus. In funerary ritual, the dead became Osiris. First limited to the royal dead, from the beginning of the Middle Kingdom (2052 B.C.) this hope was extended to all the deceased. *See also* Egyptian religion; Horus; Isis; Seth.

Ostia, the port city of ancient Rome. It is the site of numerous temples of Roman gods, deified emperors, and foreign deities.

otiose deity. *See* high god.

Otto, Rudolf (1869–1937), German Protestant theologian best known for *The Idea of the Holy* (1917), which locates religious experience as a sense of the "numinous." *See also* numinous; religious experience.

Ottomans. The Ottoman Empire began in the thirteenth century as a Muslim warrior state on the frontier between Islam and the Byzantine Empire. It combined the warrior spirit with a tolerant style of rule and patronage of learning and arts. It rapidly expanded during its first three centuries, conquering Constantinople in 1453 as well as most of the Arab world and North Africa. By the end of the reign of Sulayman the Lawgiver (1520–66), most of the Balkans were also under Ottoman control. Seiges of Vienna in 1526 and 1683 mark the Ottomans' farthest expansion into Europe. By the eighteenth century, they had begun to lose territories in the face of local revolts, nationalist revolutions, and European expansion. During the nineteenth century, Westernizing reforms transformed many Ottoman institutions. The empire formally came to an end after it joined Germany and was defeated in World War I.

Owner of the Animals. *See* master/mistress of the animals.

Oxford Movement, an Anglican High Church reform movement centered at Oxford University between 1833 and 1845, prompted by a general decline in religious life, fear of liberalism, and anxiety caused by political changes in England. It began with John Keble's sermon on "National Apostasy" in 1833, and relied heavily on the series *Tracts for the Times* (1833–41) to garner support for its positions, which included the claim that the Church of England was a divine institution based on apostolic succession, that liturgy was central to the church's life, that ministry was for service, and that *The Book of Common Prayer* was the rule of faith. Although strongly criticized by the liberal party, particularly after the departure of several of its leaders into the Roman Catholic Church, the movement gained considerable support and had a lasting effect on the Church of England. *See also* Anglicanism.

Ox-head school (Chin. *Niu-t'ou tsung*), an early school of Chinese Ch'an Buddhism named after its headquarters on Ox-head Mountain; it contributed to the final form of Ch'an by reconciling the opposing positions that had polarized the Northern and Southern schools during the controversy over sudden or gradual enlightenment. *See also* Ch'an school; Northern school; Southern school; sudden-gradual controversy.

ABCDEF
GHIJKL
MNO**P**Q
RS T UV
WX Y & Z

Pachomius (pa'koh-me-yuhs; ca. 290–348), Egyptian Christian monk, founder of communal (ceno-bitic) monasticism. After a period spent with a company of solitary (anchoritic) monks, Pa-chomius established the first monastery gov-erned by a Rule, which combined physical work with prayer and a system of discipline. *See also* Coptic church; monasticism.

pacifism (Christian), term first used to charac-terize the sentiments of disarmament advocates in Europe in the early years of the twentieth cen-tury. It is in the late twentieth century used to classify any number of persons or groups who resist or oppose war and participation in war. Mohandas K. Gandhi (1869–1948) and Martin Luther King, Jr. (1929–68), may be described as pacifists, as are Mennonites, Amish, and by some accounts, the Christian church prior to the time of Constantine. Contemporary discussion focuses on distinguishing types of pacifism, dis-tinguishing cases of opposition to war based on a particular group's sense of vocation (Mennon-ites) from others in which criticism of war refers to humanitarian principles and the hope for world government, or to concerns about the de-structive potential of modern weaponry. While most Christian groups do not officially advocate pacifism, they do identify resistance to war as a legitimate option for their members. *See also* ahimsa; Amish; Friends, Society of; Jehovah's Wit-nesses; Mennonites.

Pacomania. *See* Afro-Americans (Caribbean and South America), new religions among.

Padmasambhava (pahd-mah-sahm'bah'vah; eighth cen-tury), Indian holy man instrumental in the early propagation of Buddhism in Tibet; he is famed for quelling demons and helping establish Tibet's first monastery. Padmasambhava is re-garded as the founder of the "Old School" (Nyingma-pa) of Tibetan Buddhism but is revered by all schools of Tibetan Buddhism. *See also* Nyingma-pa.

pagan, a derogatory term designating a person who is not a member of a dominant religion such as Christianity or Judaism, usually connot-ing negative personal and cultural qualities.

The term, often employed synonomously with "uncivilized," "hedonistic," or "primitive," derives from *paganus*, Latin for "villager," "rus-tic," or "civilian." An etymological parallel to "heathen" (originally meaning "rustic" or, per-haps, "ethnic") was built on its supposed con-temptuous application by early urban European Christian converts to unconverted peasants. The earliest extant use, however, is ca. 202 by the Christian apologist Tertullian, who contrasts the "soldier" of Christ with the unfaithful "civilian."

In a deliberate attempt at redefinition, new religions in Europe and North America have re-cently adopted the word *Neo-Pagan* for their na-ture-centered and pantheistic membership. *See also* Neo-Paganism.

Pagelanca. *See* Afro-Brazilian religions.

pagoda. *See* architecture and religion; stupa.

Pa-hsien (bah-shen; Chin., "Eight Immortals"), a famous group of legendary Taoist sages believed to have reached immortality. They were first grouped to-gether during the Sung dynasty (960–1279). Their popular stereotyped images are seen in paintings, embroidery, woodcarvings, ivory, and on chinaware; their presence is an omen of hap-piness. They represent various stations in life (young, old, male, female, rich, poor) and are usually listed in fixed order with certain per-sonal emblems. The traditional listing is:

1. Li T'ieh-kuai, who carries a crutch and magic gourd;
2. Chung-li Ch'uan, who holds a fan;
3. Lan Ts'ai-ho, who is either a woman or a her-maphrodite and carries a flower basket;
4. Chang-kuo Lao, an old man and recluse with magic powers whose emblem is a bamboo tube with two beating rods;
5. Ho Hsien-ku, the only female of the eight, who is identified with a lotus flower;
6. Lu Tung-pin, a scholar turned recluse who holds a fly-whisk and magic sword;
7. Han Hsiang-tzu, who fell from a peach tree to become an immortal and whose emblem is the flute; and
8. Ts'ao Kuo-chiu, military commander and brother of an empress whose emblem is a pair of castanets.

See also hsien; immortality.

Pai-chang Huai-hai (bi-jong hwi-hi; 720–814), a Chi-nese Ch'an Buddhist monk, author of a highly influential Ch'an monastic code (*Ch'ing-kuei*, Pure Rules). *See also* Ch'an school; Pure Rules.

pai-pai (bi-bi; Chin., "clap hands," "worship"), in China a term with the literal meaning of bringing the hands together and bowing to express ritual re-spect. In Taiwan, it refers to worship of the gods, especially at the grand festivals held on their birthdays. *See also* Chinese ritual.

Pai-yun Kuan (bí-yuhn gwahn; Chin., "White Cloud Monastery"), a Taoist monastery in Peking. Its origins go back to the eighth century, but it became famous as the center of Lung-men Taoism in the thirteenth century. It is now the center of the Taoist Association of China. *See also* Lung-men Taoism.

paksu. *See* shamanism.

pa-kua (bah-gwah; Chin., "eight trigrams"), symbolic figures formed of three lines, each either unbroken or broken. They combine to form the sixty-four hexagrams of the *I-ching* used in divination. The eight trigrams were thought to embody mystical properties and also to define eightfold cosmological categories (directions, winds, etc.). *See also* divination; I-ching.

Palamas, Gregory (pal'ah-mas; ca. 1296–1359), Greek Orthodox Christian mystical theologian and defender of the Hesychastic traditions of contemplation and their belief in a physical vision of divine light. *See also* Hesychasm.

Pali (pah-lee; Pali, "texts"), a language of Theravada Buddhism used for liturgical and scholarly purposes in Sri Lanka, Burma (Myanmar), Thailand, Laos, and Cambodia. The name *Pali* was used originally by Theravada Buddhists to refer to the works in their scriptural collection, usually known as the Pali canon. Modern scholars, however, generally use Pali as the name of a language: the language of the texts found in the Pali canon. This language functioned in Theravadin history as the equivalent of church Latin, an elite language of scholars who otherwise used vernacular languages, but it always had ceremonial uses as well, and thus it is frequently chanted in Theravada Buddhist rituals.

Pali is an Indo-Aryan language related to the ancient languages of India, including both Vedic and classical Sanskrit, as well as modern languages of South Asia, such as Hindi, Bengali, and Sinhala; it is distantly connected to English as an Indo-European language.

The date and place of origin of the Pali language are obscure. It seems likely that Pali is a refined and composite literary language that was developed out of various vernacular languages of ancient North India, but it was also heavily influenced by Sanskrit; the process of its development began near the time of the historical Buddha, sometime close to the fifth century B.C.

Pali literature falls into a variety of divisions. Most important are the canon, considered to be the authentic teachings of the Buddha, and the commentaries on the canon. The language has also been used for historical, poetic, and scientific works. *See also* Buddhism (authoritative texts and their interpretation); language, sacred; Theravada.

Palm Sunday, the Sunday before Easter and the opening day of Holy Week. A Christian feast day, it commemorates Jesus' entry into the city of Jerusalem accompanied by crowds who "took palm branches and went out to meet him" (John 12:13). *See also* calendar (Christian); Holy Week.

Pan, a rural divinity in Greek myth associated with wild nature. He sends madness ("panic") but is also a bucolic musician, inventor of the "Pan pipes."

Pan-Babylonian, a late nineteenth- and early-twentieth-century theory that all religion is essentially astrological and that all ancient mythology diffused from Babylonia. It is important for having introduced the notions of worldview (*Weltanschauung*) and the cyclical nature of mythic time. *See also* astrology; cyclical time; starlore and ethnoastronomy.

Pancharatra (puhn-chuh-rah'truh; Skt., "five nights"), Hindu sect glorifying Vishnu's power to bestow salvation on the faithful who worship his gracious presence in sacred images.

The Pancharatra principles for private worship of the divine form at home shrines are passed on through initiation and instruction by hereditary preceptors, while for public adoration at temples the same is done through priestly liturgies. The basic principles were set down in Sanskrit texts referred to collectively as the *Pancharatragama* (reputed to number 108, but actually comprising over 200, only a few of which are extant in their original forms).

Once widely dispersed throughout India, the Pancharatra sect survives most notably in Tamil South India alongside a similar group called Vaikhanasas. Both are known as Shrivaishnavas because of the prominent place they give to the goddess Lakshmi, or Shri, in theory and practice. Unlike the Vaikhanasas, Pancharatra priests do not supervise worship in as many Vishnu temples; they purposely incorporate into normative, Sanskritic styles of worship evidences of their Tamil devotional heritage; they accept all devotees, including women and low-status *shudras* for initiation; and they stress surrender (*prapatti*, "to fall at someone's feet") to the deity. *See also* Shri-Lakshmi; Shrivaishnavism; Vaikanasa.

Panchen Lama (pahn'shen lahm'uh; Tibetan, "great scholar"), title first given to Tibetan Buddhist abbots of Tashilungbo monastery, the most powerful Geluk-pa institution in Tsang and later seat of the Panchen Lamas. Panchen Lamas are chosen by being recognized as the reincarnation of their predecessors.

The most recent Panchen Lama, chosen without traditional testing through the involvement of Chinese Nationalists and Communists, spent his life in China. He died in 1989. *See also* Geluk-pa; Tibetan religions.

Pandava (pahn'dah-vah; Skt., "descendant of Pandu"), patronymic for five sons of Pandu, heroes of the Hindu epic *Mahabharata*. Married to Draupadi and depicted as sons of gods, they represent order and good. *See also* Mahabharata.

Pandora (Gk., "all-gifts"), in Greek myth the first woman, made from earth and imbued by all the gods with various charms (hence her name). Sent by Zeus in revenge for Prometheus's theft of fire, she unlocked evils for mortals by opening a fatal jar (later, "Pandora's box"). *See also* Hesiod.

Panini (pahn'i-nee; ca. 500–400 B.C.), the renowned Indian author of a grammar, the *Ashtadhyayi*, describing the Sanskrit of his time and archaisms in Vedic. Grammar is one of the Vedangas, works associated with the Vedic scriptures; Panini's is the model grammar in India. This, together with discussions in Patanjali's (second century B.C.) *Mahabhashya*, served as the basis for associating grammar with more philosophical inquiry. *See also* Patanjali; Sanskrit; Veda.

P'an-ku (pahn-goo), Chinese mythological cosmic giant figure born from the cosmic egg whose dismemberment gives rise to the human world. *See also* Chinese myth.

Panth (puhnth; Punjabi, Hindi, "path"), the Sikh community. The Panth constitutes "a people who stand together." All Sikhs belong to the Panth as opposed to the narrower initiatory order, the Khalsa. *See also* Khalsa; Sikhism.

pantheism (Gk. *pan*, "all" and *theos*, "god"), the concept that all that exists is, in some way, ultimately identical with the divine reality. In some forms of the doctrine the universe is derived from the being of God; in other systems the universe in all its parts constitutes the divine reality as its sum total.

pao (bou; Chin., "retribution," "recompense," "reciprocity"), the pan-Chinese response or reciprocity appropriate to social standards and authentic human ritual action. The assumption is that every social action requires a response, a return of meaning or merit, and the bipolar balancing of the cosmic rhythms of *yin* and *yang*. *See also* yin and yang.

pao-chuan (bou-jwahn; Chin., "precious scrolls"), a type of popular Chinese literature that usually deals with topics in Taoism, Buddhism, or folk religion. The long, prose texts are often used to disseminate the teachings of various sects, but the format was sometimes used for stories with no apparent religious significance. *See also* Chinese language and literature, religious aspects of.

Pao-p'u-tzu (bow-poo-dzuh; Chin., "The Master Who Embraces Simplicity"), a Taoist treatise in defense of the possibility of attaining transcendence and immortality, written by Ko Hung (283–343). The work is divided into inner and outer sections. The former includes discussions of operative alchemical techniques, herbalism, sexual practices, charms, and meditation. The discussions in this section are based on earlier texts, many of which are now lost. The outer, "Confucian" chapters deal with politics and social issues. Ko connects the two sections with an argument advocating hermeticism in times of social upheaval. *See also* Ko Hung.

papacy, a collective noun describing the power of the Roman Catholic pope. The word can mean a range of things: the historical reality of the central office of power of the Roman Catholic Church; the official attitude of the popes on a certain issue or doctrinal question as seen in their writings and speeches (e.g., the modern papacy has written much on the social question); as a shorthand term for the entire ensemble surrounding the papal office that would include, at least, the working of the papal bureaucracy. In that last sense, the word is a synonym for the term *Vatican*.

The long presence of the popes in Rome has led to common periodizations of the papacy, especially after the centralization of its power in the early medieval period: historians may speak of the papacy as medieval, Renaissance, post-Reformation (or Tridentine), modern, and contemporary.

Discussion on the contemporary papacy orbits around two crucial issues: first, the relationship of papal authority to the teaching authority of the bishops and, second, the impact and scope of papal claims with respect to ecumenical discussions about Christian unity. Both issues are complicated by the 1869 definition (at the First Vatican Council) of the infallibility of the pope when he teaches on faith and morals in a manner declared to be infallible. *See also* conciliarism; Gregory I, the Great; infallibility; pope.

Paracelsus (b. Phillipus Aureolus Theophrastus Bombastus von Hohenheim; pa-ra-sel'sus; 1493–1541), a Swiss physician, considered a father of modern medicine; a major figure in the occult tradition. His extensive writings contain, in a manner typical of his time but with creative personal flair, much use of alchemy, astrology, and the power of mystical imagination. *See also* occult, the.

paraclete (pair'-uh-kleet; Gk., "mediator, intercessor"; Lat. *advocatus*), a technical Christian term used primarily in the New Testament for Jesus as "advocate" with God on behalf of humankind, or for the Holy Spirit, his replacement (1 John 2:1; John 14:16, 26; 15:26; 16:7). It is used rarely outside Christian sources.

paradise (Persian, "garden"). 1 General notion of a postmortem abode of the blessed, often perceived as celestial. *See also* afterlife; afterworld; Aksobhya; Amitabha; Amoghasiddhi; Brahma Kumari; Ch'ondogyo, death, eschatology, Hsi Wang-mu; hu-lu; Kannon; Pure Land; Shambhalah; Tokoyo. 2 In Western religious discourse, a synonym for the Garden of Eden.
Islam: Paradise, a heavenly realm generally referred to as "the garden(s)," is both the primordial home of Adam and Eve before their sin and expulsion and the eternal abode of those who earn it through virtuous living. The garden is said to be of four or seven levels and to contain rivers and flowing fountains, shade trees and fruits, jeweled couches, and all things conducive to the bliss and peace of its inhabitants. At the uppermost level is the Throne of God, under which the faithful will sit. Opinions vary among Muslim scholars as to whether the detailed descriptions of Paradise are literal or symbolic.

Paramahansa Yogananda (par-ah-mah-hans'ah yog'ah-nan-dah; 1893–1952), born in India as Mukunda Lal Ghosh, a teacher of yoga who came to America in 1920 and established the Self-Realization Fellowship in 1935. His *Autobiography of a Yogi* (1946) is widely read. *See also* Self-Realization Fellowship.

Paramartha (pah-rah-mah-ahr'tah; 449–569), Indian who came to China and produced the earliest translations of Sanskrit Yogachara Buddhist texts into Chinese. *See also* China, Buddhism in.

parapsychology, investigations into occult subjects such as extrasensory perception, mental telepathy, psychic healing, or spirit communication, in order to provide scientific proof for religious or metaphysical beliefs. The term was popularized by J. B. Rhine in the 1950s for his work "alongside of" orthodox psychology.
Studies and testing begun by the English Society for Psychical Research (founded in 1882) and members of the American Society of Psychical Research (1884) and advanced at American universities such as Stanford and Duke failed to confirm that some individuals receive the directed thoughts of others beyond the limits of ordinary probability or coincidence or affect physical objects without some direct, if hidden, means. Also, the Committee for Scientific Investigation of Claims of the Paranormal has debunked psychic phenomena, and renowned magicians have challenged paranormal claims as fraud. Despite such opposition, the fascination with non-Western and nontraditional religions during the 1960s and the subsequent rise of the New Age movement have reinforced beliefs that such extraordinary abilities are innate but as yet undeveloped in the human mind. *See also* occult, the; religious experience.

Parham, Charles Fox (1873–1929), founder of the American Christian pentecostal movement based on an experience of glossolalia while being "baptized with the Holy Spirit," on January 1, 1901. *See also* glossolalia; Pentecostalism.

parish, an area whose inhabitants are under the care of a Christian priest or pastor. In Roman Catholicism, a parish may be organized ethnically or for a given clientele, but the normal basis for a parish is geography.

Parmenides (pahr-men'i-deez; ca. early fifth century B.C.), a Greek philosopher from Elea who anticipated and influenced Plato's dichotomy between being and becoming. *See also* Plato.

Parousia. *See* Second Coming.

Parshva. *See* Jainism.

Parsi, Indian form of Zoroastrianism. *See also* Zoroastrianism.

particular. *See* universal and particular.

Party of God (Arab. *Hizb Allah* or *Hezbollah*), an Islamic revivalist movement in Lebanon that emerged from among that country's roughly one-third Shiite population after Israel's invasion of Lebanon in 1982. Closely aligned with Iran, the movement calls for Islamic government in Lebanon.

Parvati (pahr'vah-tee; Skt., "the mountain-dwelling one"), a Hindu goddess associated with the god Shiva and counterbalancing his antisocial tendencies to make him accessible to the social order. *See also* Shiva.

parveh (origin uncertain), in Judaism, foods classified as neither dairy nor meat. Rules of *kashrut* prohibit eating dairy and meat products together. Parveh foods, such as eggs, grains, fruits, and vegetables, may be eaten with either. *See also* kosher.

Pashupata (puh-shoo'puh-tuh), a Hindu sect of devotees of the god Shiva as Pashupati (Skt., "Lord of mortal souls"), founded or reorganized by Lakulisha in the second century. An offshoot of the Pashupatas, the Kalamukhas, became quite influential in medieval South India. Today few if any Pashupatas exist. Pashupata texts discuss the universe as effect, the deity as cause, union (*yoga*), religious observances, and salvation. They also specify five stages of spiritual development. In the second stage, the devotee courts dishonor by feigning disreputable behavior in order to transfer religious merit from those who scorn him to himself. *See also* merit; Shaivism; Shiva.

Passion, Christian term for the sufferings of Jesus during his final week, especially the agony in the garden of Gethsemene and the Crucifixion.

Passover. *See* seder.

pastor. **1** In Christianity, the title for the priest who heads a parish. **2** The title for a Lutheran minister in parochial work. **3** A general designation for a member of the clergy.

Patanjali (puh-tuhn'juh-lih), most likely a collective pseudonym for a number of Hindu authors responsible for writing the *Yogasutras* between the second century B.C. and the third to fifth centuries. Traditionalists identify Patanjali with the Sanskrit grammarian (ca. second century B.C.)

who is believed to have been a manifestation of the serpent king Ananta (or Shesha), an incarnate Vishnu and keeper of secret traditions, such as yoga. In 195 pithy aphorisms, Patanjali defines and describes the physical and meditative disciplines intended to yoke body and mind and ultimately effect the liberation of the soul. *See also* yoga.

path (Skt. *marga*), in Hinduism, one of the major methods for obtaining liberation. Three paths are traditionally enumerated: the path of (ritual) action (*karma marga*), the path of devotion (*bhakti marga*), and the path of knowledge (*jnana marga*). These three may also be designated as the three *yogas*, or disciplines (*karma yoga, bhakti yoga, jnana yoga*). Most Hindu discussions of the three paths have been deeply influenced by their detailed comparison in the *Bhagavad Gita* (200 B.C.–A.D. 200). *See also* liberation; path of devotion; path of knowledge; path of (ritual) action.

Path (Buddhism) (Skt. *marga*), the basic practice of Buddhism. The last of the Four Noble Truths, which are the essential teaching of Buddhism, declares that there exists a path leading to *nirvana,* the cessation of the universal suffering characterizing the ordinarily experienced conditioned universe. The Path thus inaugurates Buddhism as a religion and is the legitimation and touchstone for all Buddhist practice. Throughout the development of Buddhism, the Path integrates all sanctioned forms of practice that are ultimately directed to this end of liberation. Therefore, descriptions of the Path vary greatly among Buddhist groups of different periods and cultures.

The early characterization of the Buddha's teaching as the Middle Path stresses the preeminently practical and ethical aspect of his teaching: the extremes of either libertarianism or asceticism are to be eschewed in favor of a focused and moderate approach that optimizes purity and awareness. For in Buddhism, liberation from suffering is achieved not by intellectual or by ritual or ascetic accomplishments, but by replicating the liberating experience of the Buddha that occurs through insight into the abandonment of defilements, or alternatively, into the causal mechanism underlying the universe of suffering existence. Intellectually, therefore, Buddhism is the Middle Path because it emphasizes the only practical method of liberation and refuses to become sidetracked by vain philosophical debates.

The indispensable basic practices conducive

to liberation were codified by the early Buddhist tradition as the Eightfold Path, including right or correct: views, intention, speech, action, livelihood, exertion, mindfulness, and concentration. These eight can be grouped into three general ethical and religious principles: morality, concentration, and insight. By the repeated practice to perfection of these three, one frees oneself from the defilements of phenomenal and conditioned existence and obtains liberation from suffering epitomized by death and rebirth. Practicing morality entails the conscious and intentional avoidance of all misconduct by body, speech, or mind, e.g., theft, slander, and greed. Concentration involves the performance of a series of mental exercises that enable one to successively master the defilements associated with different levels of existence and to attain certain supernormal powers. At the highest level of concentration, all conception and feeling are eliminated and the final and most subtle variety of defilements are abandoned in a state approximating nirvana. Acquiring insight leads one beyond ordinary intellectual assent to the truth of the Buddhist teaching to the replication of the Buddha's enlightenment experience and its liberating insight into the nature of existence.

Later Indian Buddhist Abhidharma teachers incorporate virtually all early Buddhist practices of morality, concentration, and insight into a complex and intricate Path structured hierarchically according to successive stages in the abandonment of defilements and the cultivation of insight. Progress along this Path is marked by the attainment of specific religious fruits culminating in the final goal of the *arhat*, who attains both complete freedom from defilements, or nirvana, and perfect insight, or enlightenment. *See also* Buddhism; Four Noble Truths; nirvana.

path of devotion (Skt. *bhakti marga*) a number of ways in Hinduism to permanent union with a deity (especially Vishnu/Krishna, Shiva, or Durga/Kali). The dominant characteristic is *bhakti* (Skt., "devotion [to the god believed supreme]"), but with a flavor in the early period (300 B.C.–A.D. 500) of "loyalty, dedication" and in the middle and later periods (500–present) of intense "love."

Early Devotion: India's epics (*Ramayana* and *Mahabharata*) and Puranas ("Antiquities") are the prime scriptures of devotion. The first great synthesis occurs in the *Bhagavad Gita*, "The Song of the Blessed Lord" (ca. 150 B.C.). Krishna, an incarnation (*avatara*) of Vishnu, teaches a path that combines the paths of detached performance of duty (*karma marga*), meditative

wisdom (*jnana marga*), and devoted worship (*bhakti marga*). Devotion is the culmination, for even after one has mastered duty and wisdom, one "attains the highest devotion to me," says Krishna to his disciple Arjuna, because "I love you well" (18.54, 64). Thus, the ideal of early devotion is a disciplined sage who loves.

South Indian Devotion to Vishnu and Shiva: A more emotional devotion originated in the Tamil-language areas in the sixth to ninth centuries. There the twelve Alvars ("those deeply immersed") sang the glories of Vishnu and his incarnations, while the sixty-three Nayanars ("Leaders") praised Shiva in poem and story. This Tamil expression of devotion was soon imitated in all the vernaculars of India. The Tamil poetic conventions portraying love in separation as well as union are now used to describe love of God in works by Nammalvar and the Alvar poetess Antal; the *Tevaram* poems of three Nayanars; and, in Sanskrit, the *Bhagavata Purana*.

Devotion to Vishnu, Krishna, and Rama: Probably the largest group of Hindu devotees is the Vaishnavas, i.e., worshipers of the Supreme God Vishnu and his most famous incarnations. There are today four major traditions (Skt. *sampradaya*), with different founders and initiation rites, centers of worship, and theologies. The Shrivaishnava tradition, with Ramanuja (1017–1137) as its chief theologian, is found throughout South India. The tradition of Madhva (1238–1317) is centered in the Shri Krishna Temple in the coastal Karnataka town of Udupi. The tradition of Vallabha (1479–1531), which, like the next tradition, accepts Krishna as the supreme Name and Form of God, counts many followers in northwest India. The tradition of Chaitanya (1486–1533), paragon of ecstatic lovers of Krishna and his consort Radha, flourishes in Bengal and Orissa.

The epic hero Rama is Supreme God for many North Indian devotees. Prominent in this development was the poet-saint Tulsi Das (1532–1623), who retold the great epic in Hindi. People of all castes and strata worship Rama—a mark of most devotional movements early on, but not always thereafter.

Devotion to Shiva: Of the many traditions for whom Shiva is Supreme God, two South Indian movements may be singled out: Tamil Shaivism and the Virashaivas ("heroic followers of Shiva"). Tamil Shaivism is exemplified by the poet Manikkavacakar (ninth century) and the huge temples of Madurai and Tanjore. And in Karnataka, the twelfth century saw Basavanna consolidate the egalitarian Virashaiva movement.

Devotion to Durga/Kali: Worship of the Supreme

Goddess is important in Bengal. Mother Kali's foremost devotee was the ecstatic mystic Ramakrishna (1836–86).

Devotion and Attributes: Particularly in poetry, devotion to a god described graphically in terms of color, bodily marks, clothing, etc., is distinguished from devotion "without attributes," i.e., to a god no further described. In the fifteenth and sixteenth centuries, the poet Surdas and the princess Mira Bai exemplify the first, with their intentness on every detail about Krishna; the sharp-tongued weaver Kabir and Nanak, founder of the Sikh religion, sing passionately to a God sometimes called only "Name."

Two Patterns of Paths of Devotion: The "Path of Grace" marked out by Vallabha details a Vaishnava pattern. Nine scriptural "parts" of devotion lead to four final stages. One practices "hearing (of the Lord), glorifying (him in song), remembering him, attendance at his feet, worship, adoration, servanthood, friendship, and offering oneself (to him)" (*Bhagavata Purana* 7.5.23). One has thus attained "love," which intensifies into "passionate attachment" and even "obsession." One begins to see Krishna everywhere; the sign that the final stage, "Total Love," has arrived. In Total Love, one first sees Krishna in everyone and everything and then loves him by means of all one's senses and every part of one's body, mind, etc. When such a lover dies, he or she enters immediately into Krishna's Eternal Game.

A good example of growth in love of Shiva is the six-phase Lingayat path. "Devotion" is marked both by attempts to love Shiva and difficulty in detaching oneself from the world. "Discipline" brings with it ordeals and temptations, along with an intolerance of other gods and their followers. In "receiving," the devotee dedicates the action of each sense to Shiva, simultaneously realizing Shiva's presence in each sense. In "experiencing" one feels Shiva still more inwardly, as one's very breath; external worship here fades from importance. "Refuge" features a love so intense that the devotee manifests symptoms of madness at still being in the body. In "unity," Shiva and his beloved become inseparably one.

As to the final status of persons: Vaishnavism and Tamil Shaivism teach a continued communion of love between God and devotee, while the other systems teach final union, as above.

Worship: Images of Krishna/Vishnu are consecrated for both temples and homes of Vaishnavas, while for Shaivas the cylindrical stone *lingam* embodies Shiva's presence. Modes of worship vary, but one widespread principle is "as with (one's) body, so with the god," i.e., one worships the image of one's god in the manner and with the accoutrements one would prefer for oneself in the best circumstances. *See also* Alvar; Bhagavad Gita; Bhagavata Purana; Goddess (Hinduism); Hinduism (worship); Krishna; linga; mysticism; Shaivism; Shaktism; Shiva; Vaishnavism; Vishnu.

path of knowledge (Skt. *jnana marga*), one of Hinduism's three principal methods to end worldly suffering and liberate the soul from death and rebirth: the paths of knowledge, (ritual) action (*karma marga*), and devotion (*bhakti marga*). The subjects of knowledge and epistemology should not be confused with the knowledge path.

First elaborated in the *Bhagavad Gita* (ca. first century), the path of knowledge is taught as a *yoga*, or discipline, capable of dissolving primordial misconception (*avidya*) that is caused by the ill effects (i.e., the *karma*) of actions and intentions performed in past and present births. The text assumes that knowledge refers only to valid cognitions and that such cognitions are liberative. The goal of the knowledge path is to realize the correct relationship between the individual self (*atman*) and the universal self (*brahman*) or god. The *Bhagavad Gita* also suggests the so-called combination doctrine known as *jnana-karma-sammuccaya-vada*, in which knowledge must combine with selfless dutiful action to be complete. Proper action is said to culminate in knowledge (6.33), while rejecting action altogether is hypocritical (3.6), antisocial (3.16), and impossible (3.33). Knowledge purifies (6.38) and purges the effects of karma (6.37); while it requires sensual control (6.39), it brings the greatest peace (6.39).

The knowledge path is expounded primarily by the Vedanta school, which concerns itself with the exegesis of the end or consummation (lit., -*anta*) of the Vedas, that is, the Upanishads, *Bhagavad Gita*, and *Brahmasutras*. The foremost proponent of the knowledge path is the eighth-century theologian Shankara, who rejects the notion that action (or devotion) must combine with knowledge to bring an end to suffering and cyclical rebirth on the grounds that the results of all actions are impermanent. A direct and unmediated comprehension of the ultimate is the sole cause of final liberation. Further, the knowledge by which one identifies the individual self (atman) with ultimate reality (brahman) is obtained only from scripture (*shruti*), though logic (*tarka*) supports this view. The path of knowledge requires a familiarity with scriptural revelation that culminates in a personal revelation. Other Vedantins, such as Ramanuja (eleventh century) and Madhva (thirteenth century), dispute Shankara's uncompromising nondualism and subordinate the path of knowledge to the path of devotion.

The knowledge path is also central to esoteric Tantric traditions that root themselves in the texts called Tantras and Agamas. Tantrics, like the nondualistic (*advaita*) Vedantins of Shankara's school, give the knowledge path priority over the paths of dutiful action and devotion but usually argue in favor of the combination of knowledge and ritual action. *See also* Bhagavad Gita; nondualism, Hindu; Vedanta; yoga.

path of (ritual) action (Skt. *karma marga*), one of the three traditional Hindu methods for achieving liberation. As early as the Vedic period (ca. 1400–400 B.C.), the path of ritual action received its primary formulation as the performance of the world-maintaining rituals of sacrifice. Sacrifice strengthened the cosmic order, maintained the bonds between the gods and humans, and ensured one's destiny in the future life. On this sacrificial base, the ideology of which continues to be enacted in the daily acts of domestic devotion of Hindus and in their more elaborate rituals and festivals, rests all of the various elaborations and modifications of *karma marga*. Three main reinterpretations of the sacrificial component have been most influential: the domestication of the ritual as an affair of householders rather than priests and kings; the interiorization of sacrifice, so that it becomes a spiritual discpline in which one offers up oneself through austerities (*tapas*, lit., "heat"); and the extension of ritual to include every sort of human social and religious action and duty, understood to contribute to liberation if one "sacrifices" self-interest by performing the deeds without attachment to the fruits of one's work. Thus, it was possible for Mohandas Gandhi (1869–1948) to interpret his nonviolent resistance to the British as an instance of karma marga. *See also* ahimsa; liberation; sacrifice.

patriarch. 1 A historical title for the bishops of the ancient Christian cities of Rome, Alexandria, Antioch, Constantinople, and Jerusalem. 2 The title assumed by the heads of certain independent Orthodox churches.

patriarchal, a descriptive term for any aspect of a religion that is male dominated. *See also* androcentrism.

patriarchal succession, line of twenty-eight Indian patriarchs from the Buddha to Bodhi-

dharma and six Chinese patriarchs from Bodhidharma to Hui-neng acknowledged by the Chinese Ch'an Buddhist tradition. Each patriarch transmitted enlightenment directly from his mind to his successor's, providing a basis upon which to claim authority and authenticity "outside of words and scriptures." *See also* Ch'an school; China, Buddhism in.

patriarchs, in the Hebrew Bible, Abraham, Isaac, and Jacob.

Patrick, a fifth-century Christian missionary and saint who evangelized Ireland. His feast day, March 17, is celebrated as a day of national pride.

Pattini (pah'ti-nee; Sinhala, from Skt. *patni*, "wife," "lady"), a goddess prominent among Buddhists in southwestern Sri Lanka. Although historically her cult originated in South India, she is considered by Sinhala Buddhists to be a guardian of the Buddhist religion. She is an idealized mother figure, and her cult includes many curing rites.

Paul, a first-century Jew who experienced himself called by God to be an apostle (messenger) of Jesus Christ to the Gentiles (non-Jews) to assure them of their acceptance by God. Paul dominates the New Testament. Much of the traditional "life of Paul" derives from the Acts of the Apostles, a secondary source dating from the 90s: his instruction under the Pharisee Gamaliel, his Christian "conversion" on the road to Damascus, his three missionary journeys. Primary sources are seven Letters generally regarded as authentic and written in the 50s: 1 Thessalonians; Galatians; 1, 2 Corinthians; Philippians; Philemon, Romans. These present Paul's response to specific problems of congregations he established or knew. The authenticity of three Letters (2 Thessalonians, Colossians, Ephesians) is disputed. The Pastorals (1, 2 Timothy, Titus) are generally regarded, on the basis of second-century language and concerns, as pseudonymously attributed to Paul. Hebrews has long been recognized as non-Pauline.

Paul's understanding of faith has been of immense importance throughout the centuries, and he has been both heralded as "the second founder" of Christianity and maligned as the perverter of Jesus' teaching. *See also* New Testament.

Peace Mission. *See* Afro-Americans (North America), new religions among; Father Divine.

peach (Chin. *t'ao*), Chinese symbol of longevity,

immortality, paradise, and sexuality. Peach wood is used in the automatic writing trance ritual and as an amulet to drive away evil. The garden of the Queen Mother of the West (Hsi Wang-mu) has peaches that confer immortality. *See also* Hsi Wang-mu.

Peking, also Beijing, most recent and final imperial capital of China during the Ming (1368–1644) and Ch'ing (1644–1912) dynasties. The city was built in its present form in the early Ming on a site used as a capital by earlier Tartar and Mongol rulers. It had a mythic claim to pre-eminence as the location of the capital of the Yellow Emperor (Huang-ti). The plan of the city conformed to the perfect royal capital first described in the *Chou Li* (Rituals of Chou) and later incorporated into such cities as Loyang and Ch'angan. According to dynastic myth, the emperor was the Son of Heaven and Pivot of the Four Quarters of the Earth. The Chinese capital was therefore built in the "center of the world" on a direct line drawn south from the North Star, where Shang-ti, the heavenly deity, was believed to dwell. Conforming precisely to these requirements, Peking was a city of concentric squares surrounded by walls and moats and oriented to the four cardinal directions. By the early sixteenth century the Chia Ching emperor had completed the classical arrangement of its altars: the altar of Heaven to the south, earth to the north, sun and moon to the east and west, respectively. The imperial ancestral temple (east) and the altar of land and grain (west) straddled the axial way just south of the Forbidden City (imperial palace complex). *See also* directional orientations; Forbidden City; Shang-ti; Temple of Heaven.

Pelagius (pee-lay'ji-uhs; ca. 354–420), Christian theologian and expelled heretic, condemned for teaching that humans are capable of choosing the good. In his formulation, he did not deny the postulation of original sin, but he was quickly associated with such a denial. *See also* original sin (Christianity); Pelagius.

penance, a penalty for a violation of religious law. *See also* absolution.

Penelope, the wife of Odysseus in Homer's *Odyssey.* She represents the ideal of a faithful wife in Greek literature. *See also* Homer; Odyssey.

penile bloodletting, causing blood to flow by the insertion of a sharp object into the urethra. It is a male initiatory ordeal, especially in Pacific island cultures. *See also* initiation rituals; ordeal.

penis-sheath, feature of adult male dress for various traditional peoples. Like the enclosing of women at first menses, sheathing the penis ritually controls chaotic procreation to ensure a mature world. In some groups, the person who first sheathes the penis of the initiate becomes a kind of godfather or ritual sponsor. *See also* gender roles; initiation rituals.

pentagram, the five-pointed star used extensively in ceremonial magic and occultism. It is said to represent the human form, the five senses, and the star of the magi, among other meanings. Tracing the pentagram allegedly has great power in banishing spirits. The inverted pentagram, with two points up, is a token of Satan and evil. *See also* occult, the; Satanism.

Pentateuch, the first five books of the Hebrew Bible: Genesis, Exodus, Leviticus, Numbers, and Deuteronomy.

Pentecost, the fiftieth day after Easter, a Christian celebration commemorating the "pouring out" of the Holy Spirit described in the biblical book of Acts (2:1–42).

Pentecost (Judaism). *See* Shavuot.

Pentecostalism, a Christian religious movement originating in the United States at the turn of the twentieth century based on the restoration of the "gifts of the Holy Spirit," traditionally first bestowed on the day of Pentecost, to Christian worship and practice. The roots of modern Pentecostalism lay in the Holiness movement, which emerged during the nineteenth century among Methodists who believed that John Wesley's (1703–91) teachings on "entire sanctification" or "the second blessing" were not being given proper centrality within that tradition. It was within the matrix of the splitting off of Holiness churches from Methodism during the late 1800s that Pentecostalism had its immediate origins.

Early History: The earliest Pentecostal history is shrouded in legend, but the excitement attendant on events occurring at the Bethel Bible College conducted by Charles Fox Parham (1873–1929) in Topeka, Kansas, are commonly cited as the movement's beginning. Here, on January 1, 1901, Agnes Ozman, one of the Bethel students, is said to have "spoken in tongues" (glossolalia). Pentecostalism regards the occurrence of speaking in tongues as initial evidence of "baptism in the Holy Spirit," a crucial event for Pentecostals. Other "gifts" of the Holy Spirit are healing, prophesying, and the interpretation of prophecy (see 1 Corinthians 12:8–10).

Parham spread word of these events and influenced William J. Seymour, a black Holiness preacher whose Los Angeles congregation became the setting for another classic occurrence of the descent of the Spirit. The Azusa Street revival, which ran under Seymour's guidance from 1905 to 1913 at the Apostolic Faith Mission, drew worshipers and visitors from many races and was representative not only of the prolonged enthusiasm characteristic of the early days of the movement but also of its racial inclusiveness. Other outbreaks took place in Tennessee and North Carolina, so that the movement rapidly took on a national character.

The early days of formative Pentecostalism were characterized by a sense of a return to the apostolic age; the intervening centuries of history were collapsed into an ongoing Spirit-filled present. The Bible was taken as a literal account of that age, which was not to be interpreted historically but experienced as still, or again, occurring. This effervescence resulted in the founding, and soon also the splitting, of many new churches embracing Pentecostal teachings. With denominationalization came an end to the movement's initial racial inclusiveness, and the groupings that emerged strictly followed racial lines. Similarly, though women such as Aimee Semple McPherson (1890–1944), founder of the International Church of the Foursquare Gospel, played prominent roles as preachers in early years, women were often restricted to subordinate roles as the movement became routinized and reflected social norms.

The Assemblies of God brought together in 1913 several localized groups sharing origins in the Reformed rather than the more dominant Wesleyan tradition; though initially opposed to creeds, it was soon compelled to take a stand against advocates of the "Oneness" position— also known as the "Jesus Only" or "New Issue" movement—who denied the Trinity and demanded rebaptism in the name of Jesus only. The Church of God (Cleveland, Tennessee) grew out of an earlier Holiness group founded in 1886 and experienced repeated splits. The Church of God in Christ, the largest black Pentecostal denomination today and now based in Memphis, was founded in 1907 when Charles H. Mason broke with fellow leaders of an earlier Holiness group after his conversion at Asuza Street.

Aimee Semple McPherson's International Church of the Foursquare Gospel was organized around that evangelist's Angelus Temple (Los Angeles) in 1923.

New Pentecostalisms: Pentecostalism and other similar strains of Protestantism went into something of an eclipse during the 1920s and subsisted primarily in the smaller towns of the South and Southwest. Following World War II, a new emphasis on faith healing arose, manifested in the work of tent evangelists such as A. A. Allen and William M. Branham. Their work was taken into new dimensions by Oral Roberts (b. 1918) , who expanded his ministry into radio and television. Roberts ultimately left the Pentecostal Holiness Church, a coalition of groups of Wesleyan Holiness origins, for the United Methodist Church. Oral Roberts University (1965) in Tulsa, Oklahoma, with its accompanying Prayer Tower and City of Faith medical complex, is testimony to his organizational ability and personal charisma as well as the emergence of Pentecostalism into the social, economic, and cultural mainstream.

The Pentecostal movement enjoyed a vast new popularity during the conservative Protestant resurgence of the 1970s and 1980s; membership in the Assemblies of God, for example, rose from some 500,000 to over 1.1 million between 1960 and 1982. Also successful were "televangelists" Jim and Tammy Bakker, Jimmy Swaggart, and Pat Robertson, who enjoyed wide television followings during the early 1980s. Jim Bakker and Swaggart, however, ran afoul of the Assemblies of God, with which they were affiliated, for sexual transgressions, and Bakker was sentenced to prison for financial misdealings. Robertson, who is affiliated with the Southern Baptist tradition, ran unsuccessfully for the Republican presidential nomination in 1988. Like Oral Roberts, both Robertson and the Bakkers developed large-scale physical plants around the CBN broadcasting system and university in Virginia and Heritage Village, U.S.A., in South Carolina respectively.

The Pentecostal impulse was also spread in later years by organizations of like-minded believers that transcended denominational boundaries, such as Women's Aglow Fellowship (1967) and Demos Shakarian's Full Gospel Business Men's Fellowship (1951). Another channel was the "charismatic movement," which spread Pentecostal practices throughout the Roman Catholic and mainline Protestant denominations and took on major proportions at a series of Catholic college campuses beginning in 1967.

Pentecostalism has probably been the

fastest-growing Christian religious movement during the twentieth century and has found a particularly receptive audience in Latin America, Africa, and Oceania. Worldwide membership in Pentecostal denominations in 1980s was estimated at 175,000,000—6.7 million in the United States—with millions more identifying with various charismatic movements. *See also* Assemblies of God; Holiness churches; Parham, Charles Fox; Protestantism.

People of the Book (Arab. *Ahl al-Kitab*), the Muslim term for religious communities with scriptures. The phrase occurs some fifty-four times in the Qur'an. It designates the Christians, the Jews, and the Sabeans, who are named together in the Qur'an (2:62) as those people who "believe in God, the Last Day, and act virtuously." Some authorities also counted the Zoroastrians among the People of the Book. In early and medieval Islam, all peoples to whom God had sent a scripture were accorded protection in Islamic law in return for paying a poll tax (*dhimmi*). A covenant attributed to the Caliph Umar set out the conditions under which the People of the Book could live peaceably under Islamic rule; these conditions were elaborated in Islamic law (*Sharia*) by the mid-ninth century. The Covenant of Umar made non-Muslim religious communities living under Islamic rule responsible for upholding their own religious duties and laws. The formal conditions also included dress codes, numerous prohibitions, and rules for dealing with Muslims; they forbade non-Muslims from propagating their faith among Muslims. In fact, however, the Covenant of Umar, in its idealized form, has never been fully enforced. Nonetheless, its principles have informed Muslim thinking about non-Muslim communities living in Islamic societies, and it continues to frame some Muslim discourse about relations with non-Muslims today. *See also* dhimmi.

People's Temple, a movement led by Jim Jones, originally a minister of the Disciples of Christ. In the 1960s Jones developed an interracial ministry in Indianapolis and received favorable attention for his work for racial equality. Influenced by the black prophet Father Divine (d. 1965), Jones gradually transformed his congregation into a social movement in which socialist and antiracist themes increasingly displaced Christian theism.

Jones relocated his community to California and developed a program of social service. In the late 1970s Jones relocated his movement again, this time to the nation of Guyana where he envisioned a farming community at "Jonestown." Jones's worldview became increasingly dualistic and messianic as he began to see himself as a savior embodying divine socialism and liberating humanity from the symbol of the Judeo-Christian "sky god," allegedly used by capitalism to justify the oppression of blacks, poor people, and women. Jones anticipated a nuclear holocaust and genocide against blacks. Growing opposition mobilized by former temple members precipitated a fact-finding visit to Jonestown in November 1978, during which Congressman Leo Ryan and several of his group were murdered by Jones's guards. Anticipating the imminent destruction of the community by government forces, Jones had poisoned fruit-flavored drink served in a previously rehearsed mass suicide ritual; more than nine hundred people perished with Jones through suicide and murder.

perennialism (Lat. *philosophia perennis*, "perennial philosophy"), the view—popularized though not originated by Aldous Huxley in *The Perennial Philosophy* (1944)—that there is a universal core of religio-philosophical truth, chiefly of a meditative-mystical and/or ethical sort, common to all the great religious traditions. The perennialists hold that religious traditions differ only in their outer doctrinal, legal, liturgical, and institutional manifestations, which constitute the mere surface levels of religious and ethical experience. Hence, they maximize the similarities between the mystical and ethical cores of the world's religions. As a corollary they minimize the importance of the differences and historical-cultural specificities of particular religious traditions.

perfectionism, a Christian religious ideal chiefly associated with the teachings of John Wesley (1703–91) and Methodist theology. Within general Christian teaching, notions of human perfection and perfectability are always qualified by the postulation of original sin and the need for an extraordinary act of grace. Wesleyan thought held that perfection is possible. At some point after conversion, believers instantaneously experience "the great salvation," which results in the conviction that sin had been completely and permanently removed from them. Those who have had this experience are restored to the original human condition of being the "image of God" (Genesis 1:26–27) and are to live out their lives in a continual state of prayer and devotion. *See also* Methodism.

Perfection of Wisdom, the nondualistic awareness that is considered the goal of the *bodhisattva* (Buddha-to-be) path and the principal subject of the *Perfection of Wisdom Sutras,* the fundamental scriptures of Mahayana Buddhism. The term *Perfection of Wisdom* (*Prajnaparamita*) can be used in a variety of ways in Mahayana literature. Dignaga, a fifth-century Mahayana commentator, explained that the term has five distinguishable meanings: it can refer to the nondualistic awareness that constitutes the Buddha's awakening, to the Buddha himself, to the goal of the bodhisattva path, to the bodhisattva path, and to a body of scriptural texts. The relationships among these meanings give a good illustration of the way the concept of nonduality ties different aspects of the Mahayana Path together. Nondualistic awareness is the understanding that all things are empty of identity: there is nothing to distinguish them or make them "two." This understanding is what makes the Buddha a Buddha, so it is, in Dignaga's second meaning, identical to the Buddha himself. As the Buddha's enlightenment, this understanding is the goal of the Path, and because the goal, when viewed from the point of nonduality, is not different from the Path used to reach the goal, the Perfection of Wisdom also is the Path. The term can also be used to name not only the Path used to attain the goal, but the body of literature used to express it.

The Perfection of Wisdom literature emerged in India in the first century B.C. As the Mahayana tradition developed in India, the Perfection of Wisdom literature grew from a brief series of verses to *The Perfection of Wisdom Sutra in One Hundred Thousand Lines.* The basic text was elaborated in narrative form, summarized in verse, and finally, in the Tantric period (after the seventh century), condensed into the single syllable "a." In Mahayana ritual, the text of the Perfection of Wisdom was considered a substitute for the Buddha and was treated as an object of worship. *See also* Mahayana.

Perfect Liberty Kyodan. *See* PL Kyodan.

Pergamon, a Greek city in western Asia Minor (now part of Turkey) that became the capital of the kingdom of the Attalid dynasty in the third and second centuries B.C. While the kingdom was relatively small, the city was built up as one of the richest and most beautiful of the time. On its citadel a monumental altar to the god Zeus was decorated with high reliefs depicting the battle of the gods and giants. It is now reconstructed in a museum in Berlin. Outside of the town lay a famous sanctuary of the healing god Asclepios.

periodic rites, regular communal rituals, most often those associated with significant events in the culture's existence, such as planting and harvest or the anniversary of the community's foundation. *See also* festal cycle.

Persephone. *See* Kore.

Perseus (puhr'see-uhs), the Greek hero whose feat of securing the head of Medusa is an example of the combat theme common to myths of the eastern Mediterranean region. Associated by the Greeks with the Persians, Perseus was the reputed founder of Tarsus in Cilicia, a center of his cult.

pesantren (pe-sahn'tren; Indonesian), an Indonesian Islamic religious school. The *pesantren* resembles a Middle Eastern Islamic school (Arab. *madrasa*). Subjects taught include Qur'an exegesis and recitation, Arabic, *hadith,* law, philosophy, and mysticism. Many pesantrens now teach secular subjects and have become involved in rural development projects. *See also* madrasa; Qur'an school.

Petro, one of the two major pantheons or "nations" of divinities in traditional urban Voodoo in Haiti. The name probably derives from an early priest in Haitian religion and now designates spirits who are characteristically "hot" and powerful and worshiped with spirited rhythmic dancing. Its counterpart is the pantheon of compassionate Rada spirits. *See also* Voodoo.

petroglyph, pictograph, a drawing on stone that is carved, pecked, scratched, abraded, or created by a combination of these techniques (petroglyph), or painted (pictograph). Described commonly as rock art, petroglyphs and pictographs appear as human and animal figures and as abstract forms throughout the world; notable examples include the cave paintings at Altamira in Spain and Lascaux in France, the Tassili drawings in the Sahara Desert, and the *wondjina* paintings in northwestern Australia. In North America, petroglyphs, the more common form, and pictographs have been discovered on nearly every part of the continent; however, they exist in greatest number in the Great Basin and Southwest regions, in California and on the Columbia Plateau, occurring rarely on the Great Plains and east of the Mississippi. Believed to be

Petroglyphs of hands, figures, and geometric designs from the Native American Anasazi culture (600–1200), Mesa Verde, Colorado.

the creations of indigenous peoples, petroglyphs and pictographs have been tentatively identified by archaeologists as documents of human migrations, hunt kills, commemorations of events such as warfare and astronomical phenomena, and records of designs used in textiles and ceramics. Others may have been created as part of a religious practice or a hunt ceremonial. It has proven nearly impossible to accurately date and culturally identify North American rock art. Although many examples are thought to predate European conquest, others are identified as modern. The term *gravel petroglyph* refers to the enormous gravel outline figures of spirals, spread-eagle humans, and four-legged animals found on the lower Colorado River in southeastern California. A similar example, the Nazca lines, occurs in Peru. The most highly elaborated North American examples of pictographs are the polychrome paintings of the Chumash people in southern California, and other culturally unidentified examples found in the Four Corners region and in western Texas. Common design motifs of North American rock art include the human hand, bear track, thunderbird, mountain sheep, shield figure, feathered serpent, and humpbacked flute player.

peyote. *See* hallucinogens; Native American Church.

peyyot. *See* earlocks, peyyot.

phallic worship, an outdated term for a form of nature worship focused on devotion to representations of the sexual organs. *See also* images, veneration of; nature worship; sexuality and religion.

Pharisees (fair′i-seez; from Heb. *perushim,* "separate ones" or "interpreters"), a group of especially observant and influential Jews, mainly in Palestine. The Pharisees were a reform group that was socially and politically active in Jewish society during the Hasmonean period (140–63 B.C.) and the Roman period until the destruction of the Temple (63 B.C.–A.D. 70). Their program included the observance of priestly rules of ritual purity with respect to food and interpersonal contact both within their group and among the people whom they could influence. They also stressed strict observance of Sabbath and of tithing of crops. This program of sanctification of the people and daily life was based on ancient Israelite covenant traditions and strove to establish a secure Jewish identity in the face of Hellenism, the dominant cultural force of the period.

The Pharisees' reform program caused them to strive for political power, which reached its height under Queen Alexandra (76–67 B.C.), who gave them direct political control over some domestic affairs, and its nadir under King Herod (37–4 B.C.), when numerous Pharisees were executed for plotting with members of Herod's family over the dynastic succession. The Pharisees were clients and allies of the governing class and served as officials, educators, and experts. They were influential with the people and noted for their accurate interpretation of the law, simple standard of living, and harmonious relations with others. The first-century Jewish historian Flavius Josephus compares them to a Greek philosophical school and attributes to them belief in both divine providence and free will, life after death (a claim also found in the New Testament), and reward and punishment for human actions. He also claims that they possessed their own, nonscriptural traditions. Many of the conflicts between the Pharisees and Jesus recorded in the Gospels concern the Pharisaic reform agenda of tithes, Sabbath, and purity. The Gospels' accounts of the Pharisees as culpably blind, legalistic hypocrites and opponents of Jesus must be read as early Christian polemics against Jewish and rabbinic leadership.

The Pharisees as an organized and active social and religious group ceased to exist in 70 with the destruction of Jerusalem and its governing institutions. It is doubtful that the Second Temple sages of rabbinic literature were Pharisees. But the Pharisaic program and mode of organization greatly influenced the post-70 rabbinic movement, which gradually gained dominance among Jews during the next three centuries. *See also* Sadducees.

Philo (fi'loh; ca. 20 B.C.–A.D. 50), Jewish exegete and philosopher of Alexandria. Especially known for his use of allegory, he wrote commentaries on various sections of Genesis, as well as treatises on Jewish laws, cosmology, and such biblical figures as Abraham and Moses. He exhibits knowledge and appreciation of Hellenistic and Platonic thought. *See also* allegory.

Philokalia (fi-loh-kay'lee-uh; Gk.), an eighteenth-century collection of Greek Christian writings from the fifth to the fifteenth centuries that focus on spirituality and mysticism. It is mainly concerned with the practice of the prayer of quiet (Gk. *Hesychasm*) and the use of the Jesus Prayer (the constant repetition of the phrase "Lord Jesus Christ, Son of God, have mercy on me") to attain that quiet. *See also* Hesychasm.

Phoenicians (foh-nee'shuhnz), a Semitic people who inhabited the towns of the eastern coast of the Mediterranean, a stretch of land about two hundred miles long running from Tartus in the north to Jaffa in the south. The Homeric epic calls the inhabitants of Sidon Phoenicians and describes them as craftsmen and navigators. However, the origin of the word *Phoenician* remains uncer-

tain: the term *ponike* that occurs in the Mycenaean texts of the fourteenth century B.C. to describe the color "purple," a "spice," or the "date palm" does not imply any ethnic entity. In the second millennium B.C. the Phoenicians could not be differentiated from the Canaanites, who are known to us through their archaeological artifacts, monuments, and cuneiform texts. Sometime after 1200, the Phoenicians adopted a system of writing consisting of twenty-two consonantal signs that is considered the ancestor to the Greek alphabet.

The most important Phoenician cities were Aradus, Byblos, Sidon, and Tyre. Byblos has yielded archaeological material furnishing evidence of its connections with Egypt starting in the third millennium. The two cities Tyre and Sidon developed friendly relations with the Aramaean kingdoms of the Syrian inland and with the royal houses of Judea and Israel. Architects and craftsmen of Hiram, king of Tyre, worked on the construction of the temple of Jerusalem, while Phoenician architects were responsible for buildings in Samaria, the capital of Israel. From Cyprus to Spain, the Phoenicians established a series of satellites.

Very few religious inscriptions have been found, but the composite character of the Phoenician cults is evident in Babylonian, Egyptian, Hebrew, and Greek sources. Baalat, the divine Lady of Byblos, was identified with the Egyptian Hathor. Melqart, the main deity of Tyre, was assimilated by the Greeks as Herakles. He became the overall god of the Phoenicians. His cult appears in Gades (Cadiz in Spain), where an early tradition places it in the twelfth century B.C. Melqart's counterpart at Sidon was Eshun, a god who presided over health, soon identified with Asclepios. Astarte, called Aphrodite Urania by Herodotus, was a prominent figure of the Phoenician pantheon and her occasional title "Name of Baal" clearly indicates that she was believed to be a personification of the divine power. The cult of the goddess Tanit, once a minor deity in the Phoenician homeland, acquired a prestige at Carthage and in its colonies matched only by that of Baal Hamon (Kronos/Saturn). In the Carthagean empire both of these divine names frequently figured on the stelea offered to the gods. New archaeological studies coupled with a fresh reading of the literary sources prove conclusively that stories of infant sacrifice to Baal Hamon, mischievously attributed to the western Phoenicians by Greek and Roman authors, should be dismissed. Neither in their daily religious practices nor in their funerary rites did the Phoenicians differ from their Semitic neighbors. Their gods, however, were worshiped as "Lords" of the urban settlements and not as the ancestral protectors of the tribe. *See also* Aramaean religion; Canaanite religion.

Photius (foh'shee-uhs; ca. 820–891), Greek Orthodox patriarch of Constantinople. When the Roman church objected to his appointment, this precipitated the Photian Schism, the progenitor of the ultimate split (1054) between Western and Eastern Christianities. Photius was a prolific writer. His *Bibliotheca* (Library), which describes and quotes from several hundred books, both exhibits his wide-ranging knowledge and serves often as the only source of information for many of these texts that have been otherwise lost. *See also* Orthodox Church.

phylactery. 1 An amulet containing a written text believed to possess protective power worn or carried by an individual. 2 In the plural, the usual translation of the two boxes, *tefillin*, containing small pieces of parchment with scriptural quotations bound by leather straps to the forehead and left arm of devout Jewish males during daily morning prayers, in fulfillment of Deuteronomy 6:4–9. *See also* amulet.

physiological techniques (Taoism), methods intended to achieve either physical longevity or postmortem immortality. While procedures vary, all include a meditative component and are based on traditional Chinese ideas concerning the nature of the human body. According to these ideas, human life depends upon the ephemeral coordination of a multiplicity of organic and spiritual functions. In addition to various vital forces, there are at least two sorts of soul, the *hun* (volatile in nature) and the *p'o* (aqueous in nature). When any one of these components is harmed, illness and eventual death result. Immortality was possible only if all the body's constituents remained intact.

In Taoism, each human body part and function is governed by a spirit. There are, for instance, gods of the hair, of the liver, and of the "nine palaces" of the brain. In addition, there are three hun souls and seven p'o souls. Some of the body's components, such as the p'o souls and the "three worms" (*san-ch'ung*), demonic essences who thrive on grain, desire the death of their human host. The goal of physiological practice is to rectify, strengthen, and eventually transform these corporeal gods. Transformation of the body converts it into a durable yet subtle form like that of Taoist divinities, so that one might freely roam the hidden places of earth, ascend to heaven, or live among the stars.

Methods: The simplest methods of longevity, often used to supplement more difficult procedures or to extend one's existence on earth for the completion of transcendent practices, are dietary and gymnastic. Dietary injunctions include the avoidance of grain and the substitution of various "pure" foods and herbs, such as pine nuts, atractylis, and calamus root. Gymnastic practices generally include breathing exercises and are used to guide pure breath, including astral essences, to the various bodily organs and energy centers.

Other sorts of breathing exercises are more contemplative, although the goals are similar. Such methods of "inner observation" (*nei-kuan*) depend upon envisioning the astral breaths to be ingested as deities, as fire, or as a heavenly beverage. These breaths are then observed through meditation as they descend into the body to strengthen and transform the appropriate bodily organ. Sometimes the goal is described as nurturing an inner "embryo," a perfect being to replace the body, which might then be discarded like a cicada's husk. This and similar methods are called "liberation from the corpse."

Sexual practice was important in early Taoism, though it was later deemphasized and discouraged in favor of "inner observation" practices. Known as "joining the breaths," Taoist sexual rites, which taught *coitus reservatus*, were to replenish missing *yin* in the male and *yang* in the female, restoring both to balance. Alchemy, too, was always carried out in conjunction with meditation and dietary practices. By at least the tenth century, operative alchemy was almost entirely replaced by "inner alchemy," the transmuting of corporeal spirits through meditation, envisioned as an alchemical process occurring within the closed furnace of the body. *See also* alchemy; body; yin and yang.

pictograph. *See* petroglyph, pictograph.

pictorial writing systems, systems of notation characterized by an effective and often sophisticated use of pictorial elements and the employment of conventionalized signs with little obvious reference to the natural world. Often utilizing phonetic signs, these systems have been described by a confusing array of technical terms, such as *ideographic, ikological, semaisographic*.

Mesoamerican: Mesoamerican writing systems are recorded in many media (including stone, mural painting, ceramics, painting on paper) and address diverse topics ranging from geographical, genealogical, and historical to calendrical and cosmological subjects. Many pre-Hispanic manuscripts are painted on a paper made from a type of tree bark. Ritual, calendrical, and genealogical manuscripts tend to be screenfold in format, while others (especially maps and tribute records) often are produced on unbound single sheets.

The interpretation of Mesoamerican writing is challenging, for nowhere does a Rosetta stone exist, and colonial sources often give faulty information. Originally, "reading" probably included the oral recitation of complex material only partially represented by the written texts. Decoding usually relies on combining approaches, such as the rendering of careful comparisons between a wide range of archaeological materials and sixteenth-century ethnohistorical sources; the drawing of analogies between modern cultures and indigenous languages; and the attempt to locate a given code's inner structural coherency.

The beginnings of conventionalized writing can be traced as early as the Olmec and related cultures along the Gulf Coast of Mexico (Preclassic: 1500–100 B.C.). One of the earliest examples appears on a stone stela at the site of Tres Zapotes in Veracruz. Here a date corresponding to the year 31 B.C. is recorded, using what was to become a widespread notational system in which numbers are represented by series of bars and dots. The passage of time was calculated with extreme precision by all preconquest Mesoamericans.

One of the most developed writing systems was used by the Classic Mayan elite in northern Guatemala (300–900). Historical, political, and religious matters were recorded on stone stelae, reliefs, and murals. Portrayed are the careers and concerns of an aristocracy in which the lives of male and female leaders were closely linked with temporal-cosmological conceptions.

The Spanish almost totally destroyed the late preconquest evidence because they recognized its inseparability from indigenous religious orientations. Only a limited number of manuscripts are now available—for instance, only four Mayan, several Mixteca, and no clearly preconquest Aztec examples exist.

A number of postconquest manuscripts, prepared under the direction of the Spanish, form an important codical corpus. Painted on both native and European papers, these manuscripts frequently display altered forms of many elements found in earlier writing traditions. One representation of this cultural blending is the *Codex Borbonicus*, a collection of Mexica-Tenochca calendrical manuscripts. The first portion is a divinatory calendar skillfully done in a pre-Hispanic style related to Mixtec traditions and may be preconquest in origin. The remainder, while indigenous in flavor, clearly show the effects of Spanish influence. *See also* Mesoamerican religion.

Pietism, a movement in German Lutheranism that began in the seventeenth century under the leadership of Phillip Jakob Spener (1635–1703) and August Franke (1663–1727) in reaction to the emergence of Protestant Orthodoxy with its rationalistic emphases. It emphasized the whole person—affect, emotion, experience—in combination with rationality. Often criticized for its irrationality, subjectivism, and emotionalism, the movement nonetheless has exerted significant influence. Defenders argue that it restores the proper relation between the dimensions of lived experience that has always characterized Christian faith. After the seventeenth century, it helped shape much of English Puritanism, French Quietism, and Methodism. Friedrich Schleiermacher, a nineteenth-century German theologian of major influence on the development of Protestant liberalism, identified himself as within the pietistic strand of Protestants. Some of its major emphases have been ethics, the importance of praxis, and missionary outreach. *See also* Lutheranism; Methodism; Puritans; Quietism; Spener, Phillip Jakob.

pilgrimage, a round-trip journey undertaken by a person or persons who consider their destination sacred. Pilgrimage is a subcategory within the larger category of religious journey. It is distinguished from religious journey by two premises: first, it makes a consistent distinction between "home" and "destination"; and second, although pilgrimage is transformative, its focus is not a permanent change of status. Instead, pilgrimage is open-ended; it is a locus of negotiation between the known and the unknown, the familiar and the unfamiliar, and the individual and the collective. Pilgrimage has more elasticity in this negotiation than other religious rituals, simply because resolving issues in a permanent way is not a characteristic of pilgrimage.

The cognitive aspects of pilgrimage are underdeveloped in scholarly theories. By using a definition of pilgrimage that emphasizes the pilgrim's role in making a place sacred, one acknowledges the importance of cognition in pilgrimage. That a place may be sacred is not a "given"; a place must be constituted as such by believers. At least initially, many places of pilgrimage are not uncontroversially labeled as "sacred"; who considers a place as sacred and why determine over time the level of controversy surrounding a place of pilgrimage.

A pilgrim praying at the Shrine of Our Lady of Guadalupe, Mexico City. The major Catholic pilgrimage site in North America, the church displays, above the altar, the miraculous sixteenth-century image of the Virgin on Juan Diego's cloth mantle.

Both topographically and cognitively, pilgrimage is a decentralizing phenomenon. It requires leaving, then returning, home. Religiously, home is a place where one has established access to worship. Structures are built to maintain this access, ranging from a special corner or room within a residence to a building specifically for worship, such as a church, mosque, or temple. All of these are special places that maintain one's sense of the unknown in the midst of one's familiar social world. In contrast, a place of pilgrimage may not initially be a place of established access to worship and may even stand outside of the social world. If a structure is present, it usually has been added later and in any case does not itself confer sacrality on the site. Instead, the focus of pilgrimage is on the actions of divine beings or those who are specially connected to divine beings. Pilgrims tell of these often strange actions through story, painting, and other arts. In their attempts to understand these divine actions pilgrims use known elements from home; for example, describing the vision of a holy woman as an appearance of Mary, drawing upon known pictorial representations of her; praying at the site with prayers learned at home; and leaving objects from home at a pilgrimage site. At home, things familiar are made unfamiliar; at pilgrimage sites, things unfamiliar are made familiar.

Pilgrimage is also decentralizing with regard to time. At home, a sense of liturgical time governs the attention given to the unfamiliar in the midst of the familiar. A liturgical calendar maps out a sequence of religious time in minutes and hours as well as in days, months, and years. This order constitutes appropriate times for worship. One can go to a church, mosque, or temple at any time, but one cannot hear a liturgy at any time; similarly, a worship room is always inside the home, but the attention to prayer is given only at certain times. Time, as well as place, distinguishes the unfamiliar from the familiar. In the case of pilgrimage, the sense of timing is diverse, and it runs on a scale larger than daily ritual time, for there is no guarantee that one will be able to undertake a pilgrimage more than once in one's life. A comparative review of times appropriate for performing pilgrimage suggests a continuum of possibilities. At one end of the continuum are spontaneous visits, inspired by specific and individual reasons for undertaking the pilgrimage, such as personal illness, the performance of cremation rituals, or the fulfillment of a vow. In the middle of the continuum are visits to pilgrimage places occasioned by anniversaries of historical events, such as visiting Bethlehem on December 25, the day Christians consider Jesus' birthday, or Canterbury Cathedral on an anniversary of December 29, 1170, the date of the murder of Thomas a Becket. At the other end are pilgrimages performed at specific ritual times, such as the Islamic *Hajj*, the pilgrimage to Mecca required of all Muslims at least once in their lives that takes place during the twelfth lunar month. Time distinguishes the Hajj from an ordinary visit to Mecca. If a Muslim goes to Mecca outside of the Hajj ritual time, then the visit cannot be considered as Hajj; correspondingly, non-Muslims are forbidden to go to Mecca during the Hajj. The temporal structure of the Hajj suggests that although the pilgrimage site may be accessible to nonmembers, pilgrimage as ritual is performed by members.

Yet the sum of pilgrimage is greater than its decentralizing parts of place and time. At its core are stories of high drama and religious efficacy. The experiences of pilgrimage, whether described in story, poetry, song, or image, are highly personal narratives, often related in the first person though sometimes in the third person. The force of these narratives is testimonial to the efficacy of being religious at an unfamiliar place: they bring the experiences of pilgrimage home. The narratives are a way for pilgrims to negotiate known and new ways of being religious, and they are a means for this negotiation to be heard by the pilgrim's family, friends, and acquaintances. This hearing is crucial because pilgrimage to a given place cannot be maintained by any single pilgrim, due to the hardship and expense of travel. Instead, the narratives work by engaging the hearers and encouraging them to perform pilgrimage to that place. Within the structures of place and time, the pilgrim's round-trip journey and subsequent narratives are the lifeblood of pilgrimage. *See also* Amritsar; Bodh Gaya; Deer Park; devotion (Buddhism); holy person; Kannon; mountains, sacred; pilgrimage, theories of; relics; ritual; sacred space and sacred time; shrine.

Hinduism: Pilgrims journey to sites where divine power is especially accessible to human beings. Hindus travel to shrines, temples, riverbanks, lakes, and mountaintops seeking relief from afflictions, visions of the gods, removal of sins, and detachment from worldly concerns. Many pilgrims also travel to perform rites on behalf of recently deceased kin and ancestors. In pilgrimage centers, guided by local priests, pilgrims worship, bathe in sacred waters, visit temples, make offerings, and perform charities.

Hindu pilgrims in Brindavan, India, the home of Krishna, shower his statue with liquid *panchamrit,* a mixture of milk, curds, ghee, water from the nearby Jumna River, and other substances. Watched over by a Brahman priest, the liquid flows from Krishna's head to his feet, where it will be collected and taken home by the pilgrims.

They also obtain mementos such as pictures of the deities or foods offered to them that may be shared with relatives and neighbors upon returning home. Presently and increasingly popular throughout modern India, the Hindu practice of pilgrimage is rooted in ancient mythic and scriptural charters.

The earliest reference (ca. 1000 B.C.) to pilgrimage in Hindu scriptures, according to textual scholars, is found in the *Aitareya Brahmana* of the *Rig Veda* (7.15), where the "wanderer" is praised and the wanderer's sins are said to be destroyed. Numerous later texts, including the epic *Mahabharata* (500 B.C.–A.D. 400) and several of the mythological Puranas (ca. 400–1200), elaborate on the virtues of particular places and river waters not only to destroy sins but to grant boons including health, wealth, and progeny in this life, as well as deliverance after death.

The Sanskrit and Hindi word for a pilgrimage center is *tirtha,* literally a ford or place of crossing. The concept is associated with pilgrimage centers not simply because many are on riverbanks, but because they are metaphorically places for transit—either to the other side of particular worldly troubles or beyond the "ocean" of human existence conceived of as endless cycles of birth and death.

Pilgrimage is often advertised in classical Sanskrit texts as well as present-day vernacular tracts as an "easy" and populist practice. It thus contrasts with fire sacrifice, prescriptively undertaken by wealthy, high-born males, as well as with yoga or asceticism, for which only the spiritual elite have the requisite inner strength.

The institution of pilgrimage is an integrating force among the linguistically and culturally diverse Hindu peoples of the Indian subcontinent. For example, one widely recognized set of sacred centers are the "four places" founded at sites in the four cardinal directions. These are Badrinath (north), Puri (east), Rameshraram (south), and Drarka (west). A pilgrim who visits all four of these sites circumambulates India. At most sites periodic religious fairs, or *melas,* mark auspicious astrological moments or important anniversaries. Fairs mean not only an increased influx of pilgrims, but flourishing trade and a profusion of artistic productions and cultural performances.

The Hindu concept of pilgrimage extends beyond literal earthly travels. It becomes a symbol for other valued religious and spiritual practices. In some esoteric yoga teachings the human body is a microcosm within which the adept directs the breath on pilgrimage from one spot to another. Reformers such as Guru Nanak

(1469–1539), founder of Sikhism, and Dayananda Sarasvati (1824–83), founder of the Arya Samaj, both denounced the practice of pilgrimage as wasteful and devoid of religious meaning, but spoke of inner pilgrimages to inner "crossing places" represented by truth and knowledge.

Ideas surrounding Hindu pilgrimage sustain a tension between belief in external ritual action and conviction that inner realities take priority. For those with pure hearts, proverbs assert, any water is sacred Ganges water; by the same token, fish who swim in the Ganges River do not go to heaven. Nevertheless, that more than twenty million Hindus each year expend time, effort, and cash to journey on the earth testifies to the persistent power of Hindu pilgrimage traditions and to the multiple divine, natural, and social attractions found in pilgrimage sites. *See also* Banaras; circumambulation; Ganga, Ganges; Hinduism (worship); Hinduism (festal cycle); Kumbha Mela; Mahanubhava; Ramana Maharshi; Seven Holy Cities.

Christianity: In Christianity, pilgrimages to Jerusalem became popular in the time of Emperor Constantine (306–337), when he with his mother, Helena, attempted to locate places traditionally associated with Jesus and often initiated the construction of shrines and churches on these sites. Almost equal in importance to religious journeys to the Holy Land were visits to Rome. By the end of the fourth century, pilgrimages to places associated with Christ, Mary, the apostles, or martyrs were commonplace and accepted as part of Christian devotion. From the eighth century, the practice of imposing a pilgrimage as an act of penitence increased the number of pilgrims. Because of growing devotion to saints and relics, medieval pilgrims were also attracted to local shrines and the tombs of saints. Provided for by ecclesiastical and civil legislation, pilgrimages flourished in the Middle Ages. Sixteenth-century Protestant Reformers criticized commercial and spiritual abuses associated with them and effectively abolished pilgrimages in most forms of Protestantism, seeing such journeys as neither a Christian duty nor a devotional act with spiritual benefit. In modern times, sites connected with reported apparitions of Mary, such as Guadalupe (Mexico), Lourdes (France), and Fatima (Portugal), have become significant centers of pilgrimage for Roman Catholics. *See also* Fatima, Shrine of; Guadalupe, Shrine of; Jerusalem; Lourdes; Mary (pilgrimage sites).

Islam: The pilgrimage to Mecca, or the Hajj, is required of every physically and financially ca-

Priests in procession (background) on the way to give a benediction to the pilgrims (foreground) at the Roman Catholic shrine at Lourdes, France, in the 1970s.

pable adult Muslim once in a lifetime. It is one of the Five Pillars of Islam and is enjoined in the Qur'an: "And pilgrimage to the House is a duty unto Allah for mankind, for him who can find a way thither" (3:97). The Kaaba, the large black cube in Mecca, was a pilgrimage site before the rise of Islam. At the close of his life, Muhammad claimed the pilgrimage site for Muslims from pagan tribes and abolished the idols. In the latter part of the twentieth century, each year roughly one and a half million Muslims undertake the journey to Mecca during the last month of the Islamic calendar. *Ziyara* (Arab.), or visitation to saints' shrines, is another form of pilgrimage, but unlike the Hajj, it is not formally prescribed.

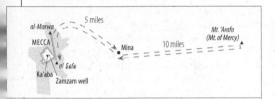

The Hajj

The Hajj must be performed during a specific period and entails a number of collective and individual rites. The first stage is a ritual cleansing that enables one to enter the sacred space of Mecca and separates the pilgrim from previous roles and associations. A white, seamless garment for men, a ritual cleansing, and an inward statement of one's intention to perform the Hajj accomplish this "ritual purity." Women do not wear the white garment of the men but may wear a white dress that fully covers their body except the hands and face. Often, instead of plain white, women wear their own customary regional dress, which displays the various cultures meeting in Mecca. The sameness of the men's dress emphasizes their equality as Muslims and the unity of the Muslim community.

After attaining the state of purity, the pilgrim enters Mecca and begins the rites of the Hajj, often accompanied by a guide. The pilgrim first may perform a "lesser Hajj" (*Umra*) before undertaking the full Hajj. This "lesser Hajj" involves circumambulating the Kaaba, a canonical prayer, and "Running" (*sa'y*) between two hills. This "Running" rite recalls the desperate route taken by Abraham's wife, Hagar, in search of water. The "Running" concludes the "lesser Hajj" and begins the further rituals of the full Hajj.

The most important moment of the Hajj occurs on the day of the "Standing" (*wuquf*) ritual on Mt. Arafa. Improper performance of the "Standing" leaves an individual's entire Hajj invalid. The pilgrims assemble on Mt. Arafa at midday and are led in collective and individual prayer until sundown. After sunset, the pilgrims spend the night in a locale on the road back to Mecca. Here they find pebbles for tossing at three pillars symbolizing the devil. The following day is the "Stoning" of the devil and "Sacrifice," which celebrates Abraham's sacrifice of a ram to God instead of his son, Ishmael. The "Feast" following the "Sacrifice" lasts three days and both the "Sacrifice" and the "Feast" are celebrated by Muslims throughout the world, not only by the pilgrims in Mecca. Following the Sacrifice, the pilgrim cuts or shaves his or her hair and may assume regular dress again. Often the pilgrims will close the Hajj by another circumambulation around the Kaaba and a final stoning of the devil.

The pilgrim's safe return home is met with celebration. He or she reenters the world with new status and respect and a new appellation of *Hajji*. The pilgrim is considered by some to be a source of blessing. The Hajj rituals dramatically emphasize key aspects of Muslim devotional life. A continual assertion of God's unity punctuates the Hajj performance. The notion of membership in an inclusive Muslim community is dramatically enacted as the pilgrims dress in the white garment and collectively follow the steps of the Hajj. The notion of prophethood is celebrated as the Hajj rituals recall both Muhammad's retaking of the city from pagan tribes and Abraham's covenant with God.

Each year the Hajj assembles people from throughout the world and thus provides an important means of communication and exchange. This aspect was especially significant before the rapid air, land, and sea travel of the modern era. Pilgrims often made their trip in caravans, traveling with other pilgrims from their region. A pilgrim might stay in Mecca following the Hajj to engage in trade or study. The Hajj has, in large part, been possible only for elites due to the financial strain of traveling the long, arduous route to Mecca. As transportation becomes faster and easier, the Hajj is becoming accessible to larger segments of the population. *See also* Islam (festal cycle); Islam (life cycle); Jerusalem; Kaaba; Karbala; Mecca; Medina; Qom; Taj Mahal; Umra.

Japanese Religion: Based upon the prestige of imperial pilgrimage, miraculous accounts of holy men, or the biographies of sectarian founders, a great variety of pilgrimage traditions had become popular in Japan by the Edo period (1615–1868). Chief among these were pilgrimages to: the eighty-eight temples of the island of Shikoku, associated with the life of Kukai (Kobo Daishi, 774–835), the founder of the Shingon sect; the thirty-three temples of Saikoku (west country), dedicated to the Bodhisattva Kannon; and the Ise Shrine, enshrining Amaterasu, the sun goddess and ancestor of the emperor. There were many others, including local imitations of the more prestigious pilgrimages and those to sacred mountains.

Pilgrims generally wore special coats or hats and had each temple's seal stamped in a book or on their coat or staff. In return, they attached slips of paper with their name and hometown on the temple's pillars and walls. They also sang the special hymn of each station. Some financed their own travel; others lived by alms or with the support of a local devotional group they represented.

The number of pilgrims was quite large in the Edo period; those going to Ise periodically numbered in the millions for a single year. Pilgrimage led to the development of institutions of travel, including transportation, guidebooks, inns, and souvenirs. Much of Japanese tourist behavior has its roots in pilgrimage. All the major pilgrimage traditions continue today, aided by modern transportation. *See also* Ise-ko; Ise Shrine; ko; mountains, sacred; nuke-mairi; Ontake-kyo.

pilgrimage, theories of.   There are three general approaches to or theories about pilgrimage. The first is typological, the second views pilgrimage as a rite of passage, and the third attempts to explain pilgrimage as a satisfaction of certain needs.

Typological Theories of Pilgrimage: Most typological theories of pilgrimage construct a hierarchical framework that is applicable across religions and will help classify the vast diversity of pilgrimages. For example, the typology can be based on specific sites: shrines for a superhuman being, sites connected with the actions of a superhuman being, natural sites as sacred space (a river, mountain, or a natural or geographical object).

Typologies of pilgrimage are often arranged on the basis of a higher/lower hierarchy. Thus, pilgrimages can be described as encompassing a single major tradition, e.g., pan-Hindu or pan-Muslim, versus those that are sectarian. Another typology might describe pilgrimages according to their universal, regional, or purely sectarian significance. Variations on this approach often use terms such as *great* versus *little* tradition or *orthodox* versus *heterodox* as models for a typology.

Typological approaches for classifying and describing the complexity of pilgrimages are highly individualistic; thus, no single typological classification has been settled on as the most adequate approach. In fact, all such approaches usually break down after careful scrutiny and use.

Pilgrimage as a Rite of Passage: Pilgrimage is often viewed as a rite of passage. This approach emphasizes pilgrimage as the liminal phase of a ritual, as expressing community versus structure, equality versus inequality. Pilgrimage from this point of view is an opposite social structure: it emphasizes the immediate, the unstructured, spontaneous, and creative experiences as opposed to the structured, rule-governed, and institutionalized nature of regular social life.

It seems obvious that all pilgrimages consist of a preliminal (beginning), liminal (middle), and postliminal (end). There are, however, two fundamental flaws in this approach to explaining pilgrimage. The first is that most pilgrimages are not rites of passage that transform an individual from one mode or state of being into another—from single to married, child to adult, prince to king, human to ancestor, and the like. In brief, most pilgrimages are not in and of themselves transformative. Some pilgrimages are mandatory, others voluntary. Pilgrimages are often taken out of devotion to some superhuman being (a saint, hero, ancestor); others are taken as a means to some end (the achievement of health or gaining of merit). Thus, one cannot universalize this theory for all pilgrimages. A change of status from sickness to health may indicate that a particular pilgrimage can be explained as a rite of passage, but not all pilgrimages fit this model.

The second flaw in this theory is the notion that pilgrimage expresses communitas in opposition to social structure and classification. A limited number of pilgrimages may confirm moments of liminality and the experience of communitas, but other examples of pilgrimage emphasize structure, inequality, and hierarchy. In India most pilgrimages are performed with strict caste observance and the rule of pure/impure is not abolished.

Functional Theories of Pilgrimage: Most explanations of pilgrimage are functionalist in their structure. This theory asserts that the best approach to explaining pilgrimage is to demonstrate that it satisfies some need. Functionalist explanations of pilgrimage answer the question, Why do people perform pilgrimage? Thus, pilgrimage as a rite of passage can also be viewed as a functionalist explanation in that pilgrimage is held to satisfy the need for communitas.

There are at least three different functionalist models for explaining pilgrimage as satisfying needs. The first model attempts to demonstrate that the essential need fulfilled is that for social integration. The second model places the emphasis on the need for the reinforcement of existing patterns of behavior and social relations. The third pattern is more individualistic: it emphasizes that the basic need fulfilled by the practice of pilgrimage is the development and maintenance of values and ideals in individuals that are essential for the welfare of the individual and society. These models are not contradictory; in fact, they are often combined to form a more complex model that explains pilgrimage as fulfilling both social and individual needs. Functionalist explanations always insist that both the individual and the society have certain needs that must be satisfied and that the satisfaction of these needs is necessary for the survival of the individual and the society. Pilgrimage is a cultural trait, institution, or unit that fulfills these needs.

Although this explanation has become widespread in the academic study of religion, it is seriously flawed. Critics have demonstrated that functional explanations are, at best, heuristic devices that are neither falsifiable nor verifiable, yielding conclusions that are at best trivial in value.

One alternative for explaining pilgrimage practices would be to place them in the semantic field or cognitive system of which they are an element. Most explanations of pilgrimage omit this important part of the pilgrimage system. Pilgrims go on pilgrimages because of the belief system they share with others. In order to explain the practice, this approach has to place pilgrimage in relation to the cognitive or propositional attitudes serving as the truth conditions that constitute the practice as a rational act. From this point of view pilgrimage is only one element in a complex system of cognitive relations. The study of pilgrimage in isolation from this system produces a distortion of its meaning. Complete studies of pilgrimage taking this theoretical position have yet to be undertaken. *See also* pilgrimage.

Pimiko Queen (pee-mee-koh), also Himiko, female shamanistic ruler of the Yamatai region ca. 200. She consolidated political power after a period of unrest and established relations with China. *See also* Japanese religion; shamanism.

Pinkster festival, an African-American slave ritual, lasting seven days and featuring a mock king and other carnival activities. It was most popular on the East Coast of North America in the nineteenth century. *See also* mock king.

pipe, sacred, ritual object widely used in many contemporary Native American and pan-Indian religious activities in North America. Archaeological evidence documents pipes in North America from four thousand years ago. However, the earliest recorded use of pipes is in 1575 in Eastern Canada. The Lakota (Plains) introduced the pipe to many tribes in the 1870s. Increasing ritual use of the pipe, particularly as a separate rite, has occurred in nativistic as well as pan-Indian movements. Pipes were used to welcome seventeenth-century missionaries in eastern North America. Pipe ceremonies are used for healing, to promote intertribal relations, and blessing in the subarctic, Plains, Iroquoian, Pacific Coast, and Southwest tribes.

There are different tribal accounts of the origin of the pipe. In some stories, pipes were given during creation, in others for healing. For example, the pipe is found in the creation stories of the Ojibwa, Iowa, and Blackfeet with special relationships to clan animals. Among the Blackfeet, Bear gave its skin for the wrapping of the medicine pipe. White Buffalo Calf Woman gave the Bison Calf Pipe to the Sioux (Lakota).

The pipe stem and bowl are usually kept separate and only joined for use in a specific ritual event. One-piece tubular pipes of bone in the Pueblo Southwest and the Plains are the only tubular pipes still in use.

Pipes are understood to be powerful in and of themselves, and for this reason they are kept and cared for by men and women who have been chosen and initiated to be keepers of the pipe. *See also* Hako; Native Americans (North America), new religions among; North America, traditional religions in; smoke; tobacco and hallucinogens.

Pir (peer; Persian, Hindi), title commonly given to leaders of Muslim mystical orders in South Asia. *See also* Sufism.

pitriyana. *See* devayana/pitriyana.

Platform Sutra of the Sixth Patriarch (Chin. *Liu-tsu t'an ching*), a scripture of the Ch'an school of Chinese Buddhism attributed to the sixth patriarch,

Hui-neng (638–713). It contains his autobiography, sets forth the Southern school's "sudden" teaching, collapses the distinction between meditation and the attainment of wisdom, and recommends the practice of "no-thought." *See also* Ch'an school; Southern school.

Plato (play'toh; ca. 428–347 B.C.), close associate of Socrates, celebrated Athenian philosopher, and founder of the Academy. Twenty-five of his dialogues and the *Apology* survive, as well as other writings of less reliable authenticity. The early dialogues are imaginative recreations of Socrates's life and views, with the later dialogues the primary source for Plato's own original and vastly influential thought.

Plato was skeptical of the capacity of the written word to express philosophic truth and his thinking exhibits continual development, but his characteristic view of things is roughly that there are two worlds, this one—deficient in reality, full of change, revealed by perception, and an object of mere opinion—and another, divine realm of real, immutable, mind-independent Forms that are the proper objects of knowledge. The things of our world have their properties by participating in Forms and so depend upon them for what they are (but not vice versa); e.g., particular triangles have the properties of triangularity by participating in Triangle-itself. The creator god of the visible universe (Demiurge) used the Forms as patterns, imposing them on preexisting chaotic matter, and thus it is from Forms such as Beauty-itself and the Good that the universe derives its beauty, goodness, and law-governed order.

Human beings are eternal, reincarnating souls, temporarily lodged in bodies, having three parts—the appetitive, spirited, and rational elements—with happy, virtuous souls being those governed by their reason as it apprehends the Forms of virtue (e.g., Justice-itself). But although a soul comes to know the entire hierarchy of Forms prior to its incarnation and birth, the body proves a hindrance to the knowledge of these innate truths. Hence, it requires extensive philosophical investigation to "recollect" these eternal truths, motivated by an innate longing for mystical association with the Forms, a desire manifested in the experience of the erotic love of beauty. *See also* Neoplatonism; Socrates.

plausibility structure, a sociological term for the religious legitimation of a worldview by claiming a base in cosmic reality. *See also* projection.

pleroma (ple-roh'mah; from Gk., "fullness"), a central Gnostic concept denoting the condition or locale of otherworldly bliss; it is contrasted with *kenoma*, the "empty" material world. *See also* Gnosticism.

PL Kyodan (kee-yoh-den; Jap.), also "Perfect Liberty" Kyodan, a Japanese new religion founded in 1946, venerating the sun as the source of all being. Emphasizing that humans are one with the divine, PL Kyodan affirms the importance of art and human creativity as avenues of religious expression and fulfillment. *See also* Japan, new religions in.

Plotinus (ploh'tin-uhs; 205–270), Greek Neoplatonic philosopher. In his *Enneads* Plotinus forged diverse philosophical and religious doctrines into a systematic but vital whole. His account of the structure of reality can be viewed from both the metaphysical and individual perspectives. Plotinus's universe comprises three levels: the One or Good, the Transcendental Absolute; Intellect, the universal Mind, which eternally contemplates itself as a realm of pure, immaterial essences; and Soul, a manifold reality that includes both the World-Soul and individual, embodied human souls. All existing things are constituted from the One through its ceaseless, spontaneous overflowing—first, the intelligible Forms, which are the archetypes of all lower realities, and then individualized souls, which enmesh themselves in the material world. The structure extends from absolute unity to the dispersed multiplicity of matter. But from a human perspective Plotinus's universe seems less a multileveled, hierarchical structure than a dynamic scale of degrees of consciousness. Transcendence means interiority. Though as good as they can possibly be, the material world and the life lived in it are insubstantial, unsatisfying, and constricting for the human soul, whose true self is the supraindividual Intellect and whose ultimate goal is the One. The most personal and dynamic aspect of Plotinus's thought focuses on the soul's mystical return to the One by means of moral purification, introspection, intellectual contemplation, and love for the One's reality, which transcends all description and understanding. *See also* emanation; Neoplatonism.

pluralism, religious, the problem and opportunity of the simultaneous presence of different religious traditions within a single society. Religious pluralism is held by some scholars to be a distinctly modern phenomenon.

Pluto (ploo'toh), the ancient Greek and Roman

god who rules the underworld (also known as Hades and Dis) together with his abducted queen, Proserpina. *See also* Hades.

Plymouth Brethren, Christian Congregational group founded in England in 1831 by A. N. Groves. *See also* Darby, John Nelson.

pneuma (noo'mah), spirit in Hellenistic anthropology.

Poimandres (poi-mahn'drehs; Gk., possibly "shepherd of humankind"), the name or title of a deity in Tractate 1 of the *Corpus Hermeticum* (second–fourth centuries) associated with Hermes Trismegistos and Thoth or Tat. Poimandres comes to the author of the text and reveals all the secrets of the universe, especially the origins and purposes of humankind. *See also* Gnosticism; Hermetism.

Polish National Catholic Church of America. *See* Old Catholic churches.

pollen, dust of seed plants, used as a means of prayer practices of Navajo and Pueblo (American Southwest) peoples. Flower pollens are important in the nonpublic religious performances of certain Pueblo communities, including Hopi. Among the Hopi, pollens are used in the preparation of prayerfeathers, themselves intended as prayers for health and fertility. Among the Navajo, pollen is used in healing performances as an ingredient in the bundles of healers. Flower pollens sometimes are used to construct the sandpaintings that figure importantly in Navajo healing practice. Corn pollen, as well as pollens from wild plants, is used in the Navajo ceremonial, Blessingway, to bless all participants as well as the ceremonial paraphernalia and lodge. Navajo rituals conclude with the passing of a sack of pollen to all observers, each of whom uses a pinch to form a communal prayer. Some of the pollen is placed in the mouth and on top of the head; the rest is scattered upward while speaking a short prayer. Anthropomorphized in Navajo religious traditions as Corn Pollen Boy and Corn Ripener Girl, pollen represents life and fertility. *See also* medicine bundle; prayerstick, prayerfeather; sandpainting.

pollution. *See* purity and impurity.

polytheism (Gk. *poly,* "many" and *theos,* "god"), the belief in a plurality of gods. Polytheism has several varieties. It may posit a number of relatively co-equal deities. Or the gods may coexist under one or more superior divinities with authority over them. The latter pattern is sometimes termed *henotheism.*

Poor Clares, a Catholic order of contemplative sisters founded by Clare of Assisi between 1212 and 1214 under the inspiration of Francis. The two branches of the order are the Urbanists, who abide by a more moderate rule proposed by Urban IV in 1264, and the Colettines, who adopted the original Rule of St. Clare following its restoration in the fifteenth century under the leadership of Colette of Corbie. Their commitment to the daily recitation of prayers at fixed hours (the Divine Office), contemplative prayer, penance, manual labor, and strict enclosure makes them one of the most austere women's orders in the Roman Catholic Church. *See also* Clare of Assisi.

pope. 1 In Roman Catholicism, a title of the Bishop of Rome as head of the Church. 2 A common term for a parish priest in the Orthodox Church.

popular religion, religious beliefs and practices that are the opposite of elite or official religious forms. Popular religion became an important subject in the study of religion during the Enlightenment. Many scholars write about popular Taoism, which is in opposition to philosophical Taoism. Popular Hinduism is in opposition to Yoga or Indian asceticism, and Buddhism is often divided into meditational asceticsm and popular Buddhism.

The concept has also been used to study the religion of a people or folk and is directly related to the early academic interest in the origins of religion and the religion of nonliterate ("primitive") religion. The concept is also used to mark a distinction between "great" and "little" traditions in a religion, or "higher" versus "lower" religions, that is, distinguishing levels of religion that are abstract and metaphysical from levels of religion that are more concrete and rich in myth and symbol. *See also* typology, classification.

Porphyry (por'fee-ree; 232–304), Neoplatonic philosopher, the most effective opponent of early Christianity, against which he wrote some fifteen books.

Poseidon (poh-say'duhn), an ancient Greek god associated with the sea and navigation, horses, and earthquakes (hence the title *earthshaker*); he was the son of Kronos and brother of Zeus. *See also* Greek religion.

po-shan lu (boh-shahn *loo;* Chin., "hill-shaped incense burner"), Han-dynasty (206 B.C.–A.D. 8) bronze miniature mountain paradise on a pedestal, used in ancient Chinese ritual. *See also* paradise.

possession, a ritual trance state, learned through extensive training and achieved in religious ceremonies, during which individuals are said to experience the indwelling presence of powerful spirits. Possession may be an involuntary condition or one deliberately sought. It may be a peripheral experience, judged negatively by the culture, for which an expert in curing (exorcism) is required. It may be the central experience of a religious group, highly valued and desired, for which an expert guide sometimes serves as an enabler. Possession is a relatively widespread phenomenon found in religions ranging from Shinto to Santeria, but the experience of or belief in possession occurs only under specific conditions. Possession trance cannot occur unless the religious community acknowledges both the independent existence of spirits and the reality of possession. Other factors supportive of possession include a high degree of rigidity and differentiation in social roles outside the religion, the acceptance of psychological vulnerability for the sake of wisdom, and a religious worldview including multiple spirit worlds.

The traditional Christian and popular Western view of possession limits it to the unwanted presence of demons and evil spirits who maltreat the human host, although glossolalia, or speaking in tongues, and the experience of being "moved by the Spirit" are related phenomena. Other religions, with more flexible understanding of the varieties of divine powers, encourage the direct communication with them that possession rituals allow; possession is thus an important element in many indigenous religions of Africa, Asia, and the Americas, as well as in the African-influenced new religions of Umbanda, Santeria, and Voodoo. In those communities, greater and lesser spirits are worshiped directly when they descend into the bodies of devotees or specially trained mediums; once among their followers, the spirits transform the behavior and appearance of the one possessed and offer transcendent advice for the spiritual and material problems of their congregations.

Beyond its religious context, the possession trance has been described in physiological terms, which emphasize the trembling, sweating, radical changes in alertness, and other visible bodily effects that accompany it, and in psychological terms, noting the alteration in thinking, emotional control, perceptions, and

suggestibility that identify the possession trance as an altered state of consciousness. In other studies, sociologists suggest that possession has an adaptive function within a particular religion, temporarily allowing the expression of otherwise inexpressible ideas and providing the motivation for social change both within and without the organization. Not surprisingly, some have emphasized the connection between spirit possession cults and economic deprivation or social oppression, especially during periods of devastating social changes, such as urbanization, transformations in class structure, and the weakening of traditional family and personal supports. Under such burdens, the deprived and oppressed—especially women—may use possession trance to improve both personal position and community fortunes. In religious terms, the role of medium is undertaken by those who seek further spiritual commitment to their religion, who are advised that their illnesses or recurring problems stem from the inborn but undeveloped potential for such contact with the spirit world, or who spontaneously enter trance or experience possession during the rituals.

As an element in religious belief, the possession trance allows the religious community to act out its understanding of the result of contact between the human and superhuman worlds. The physiological and psychological changes that characterize the trance state, as well as the visible empowerment of the possessed individuals, represent the impact on a mere mortal when the door to otherworldly communication is opened. *See also* affliction; altered states of consciousness; Candomble; ecstasy; exorcism; filha de santo; inspiration; kami-gakari; loa; medium; new religions; Shanga.

postdiluvian. *See* antediluvian/postdiluvian.

Postponers (Arab. *al-Murjia*), a theological movement of early Islam. A controversial issue arose concerning the judgment of the sinner. Members of this movement opted to leave the judgment to God, therefore postponing it to the hereafter. The Murjiite view that Islam is an internal matter of faith and not external deeds has been accepted by many later Muslim theologians. *See also* kalam; Seceders.

postures, religious. *See* genuflection; hatha yoga; Hesychasm; kneeling; lotus posture; mudra; orant; prostration.

potlatch (pot'lach; Chinook), any of a variety of ceremonials in which property is ostentatiously and dramatically distributed as gifts or destroyed, performed among the Native peoples of the Northwest Coast of North America. Potlatches are found from the Tlingit of coastal Alaska in the north to the Lower Chinook at the mouth of the Columbia River in the south and among the Haida, Tsimshian, Bella Coola, Kwakiutl, Nootka, and Salish. The ceremonial distribution of property, accompanied by feasting, dancing, singing, and oratory, is enacted toward various ends: as a means of validating a hereditary claim to a fixed, ranked, and named social position; to save face in the wake of an accident or embarrassment; as a mode of competition between one kingroup, represented by its chief, and another; and as an aspect of ritual mourning following the death of a chief. Tlingit potlatches are most closely associated with memorial feasts, those of the Tsimshian and Haida with the elevation of new chiefs, the Bella Coola and Nootka's with legitimizing the claims of younger people to new statuses. Face-saving potlatches are most commonly found among the northernmost groups, while competitive gifting and the destruction of property are characteristic of the Southern Kwakiutl.

Anthropologists have provided a number of interpretations for these events. These include views of potlatches as means of social integration, of ecological adaptation through redistribution of resources, as efforts to define and strengthen group relations based on marriages, and as primarily religious events celebrating and clarifying the symbolic relationships between spirits, animals, and living and dead human beings. Recent analyses stress the religious dimensions of potlatches, suggesting mortuary and memorial functions of the rituals. *See also* North America, traditional religions in.

power. 1 Perhaps the most general characterization of the sacred. 2 In the plural, a common designation for supernatural beings.

powwow (Algonquian), gathering associated with shamanistic healing practices, or dancing that took place before a hunt or other important event. In English the term came to refer to a conference or meeting, and is sometimes associated with popular healing rituals. Contemporary Native American gatherings are often referred to as "powwows." Usually a central element of these events is a range of competitive dances, featuring elaborate and often expensive costumes. Dancing was forcibly repressed by the United States government, but preconquest dancing was ubiquitous in North America, associated with ritual processes relating to important life activities such as hunting, healing, warfare, fertility, and other occasions when communication with transcendent powers was required. In this sense dance was a deeply religious expression. After the conquest and the establishment of reservations, some dances began to express a more general pan-Indian identity. To identify powwows exclusively with pan-Indianism, however, obscures their other important features. Such gatherings may strengthen important elements of tribal identity during periods of cultural renaissance within particular groups. Particular tribal traditions are enacted, revivified, and sometimes transformed through contemporary Native American dancing. However they are interpreted, powwows must be seen as an expression of a continuing Native American presence, having both continuity and discontinuity with the past. *See also* dance; North America, traditional religions in; shamanism.

Practical Learning school (Kor. *Sirhakp'a*), Korean Confucian school, begun in the seventeenth century, that went beyond the theory of Confucian metaphysics and philosophy to utilitarian concerns. Indebted in some part to the Western learning that had been introduced from China and contemporary Chinese empirical studies of history and textual criticism, the Practical Learning school rejected the dogmatic stance of orthodox Confucian learning and took up the cause of finding solutions to problems of productivity, national defense, agriculture, trade, and the general welfare of the people. Partisans of this school tended to be skeptical of the theory and practice of national rituals, including ancestor veneration, preferring to look at the utilitarian effects rather than the supposed metaphysical realities that underlay such rituals. They were also aware that aristocratic class interest was at the heart of the orthodoxy they rejected and had been the cause of most of the social ills they wished to solve.

The Practical Learning scholars took as their point of departure the investigation of things as they actually are, not as they represent some reflection of an ideal and unchanging truth. They investigated history, social science, natural science, agriculture, mechanics, and even linguistics. If they could not verify a view of things, they rejected it. At the heart of their investigations was a deep insight that Korea's conditions had changed while its ideology had not. Thoroughly Confucian in their orientation toward the world, the Practical School scholars were able to demonstrate historically why Confucian ideology had failed. *See also* Confucianism.

Prajapati (pruh-jah'puh-tee; Skt., "lord of creatures"), the Vedic deity of creation, often identified with other creator gods such as Purusha (the "Cosmic Man"). In the later Vedic sacrificial literature, Prajapati rises to a prominent position in the pantheon and is depicted as the cosmic totality in both the spatial and temporal senses. Prajapati produces the cosmos by an act of "emission" or emanation, and the Vedic ritual is often conceived as a restorative act that reunites Prajapati's dispersed parts, the manifest universe, into a constructed whole. *See also* cosmology; Veda, Vedism.

prajna (prahj'nah; Skt., "wisdom," "knowledge"), in Buddhism the knowledge or insight that is associated with the Buddha's enlightenment. The term is applicable to a wide range of conceptual and nonconceptual understandings, as indicated by the triad of the wisdoms that consist of hearing, thinking, and meditating. The first and second have to do with various levels of conceptual insight; the third with a nonconceptual experience associated with considerable concentration.

As a technical term, *prajna* occurs in a variety of contexts; in Indo-Tibetan Buddhist literatures two of the most significant are Abhidharma (exegesis of doctrine) and related analyses of mental functioning and elaborations of the *bodhisattva* (Buddha-to-be) path.

Abhidharma generally describes fifty-one mental factors and includes wisdom among the five "determining factors" that accompany every virtuous mind. In this context wisdom is characterized as a mind that individually differentiates the faults and qualities of an object. The function of such wisdom is to overcome doubt regarding behavior toward and perception of that object.

The bodhisattva path is often described in terms of ten stages, each associated with a particular perfection. In the first stage, simultaneous with the initial direct cognition of emptiness, one has the prajna that realizes emptiness; in the sixth stage this wisdom, now fully enhanced, is known as the Perfection of Wisdom. The four remaining perfections, of method, prayerful aspiration, power, and insight, are subdivisions of the perfection of the sixth. In this gradualist view of the Path, insight is a special form of prajna and the function of this wisdom is to overcome ignorance.

Much of the Zen tradition in China, Japan, and Korea favors a model of sudden discovery over a model of gradual development. *See also* Abhidharma; bodhisattva; enlightenment; Perfection of Wisdom.

prakriti (pruh'kri-tih; Skt., "matter," "nature"), in Hinduism, the primal source of the material world, juxtaposed to *purusha*, or spirit. *See also* cosmology; purusha.

pralaya (pruh'luh-yuh; Skt., "dissolution"), period of dissolution of the bond between soul and body on the individual level, and of the universe, understood as the body of the deity, on the cosmic level. Four types are distinguished: *nityapralaya*, individual physical death; *atyantikapralaya*, end of rebirth (*moksha*); *prakritapralaya*, dissolution of the material universe at the end of a *mahakalpa*, or life of Brahma; *naimittaka-* or *avantarapralaya*, intermediate dissolution, following a day of Brahma, integrating individual acts with the cosmic drama engaging the supreme deities (Vishnu, Shiva) in the lower worlds' (earth, atmosphere, and heaven) periodic incineration and dissolving into water. *See also* cosmology; kalpa.

prasada (pruh-sah'duh; Skt., "serenity," "favorable disposition"). **1** Flowers and food offered to Hindu deities and then shared among devotees as "grace." **2** A prominent term within the Hindu devotional tradition for divine favor in grace, kindness or blessing. *See also* Hinduism (worship).

praxis, a general term for practice, often used in religious scholarship to refer either to ritual action or ethical conduct.

prayer, direct address to the god(s), especially in the form of petition or praise. *See also* devotion (Buddhism); Gayatri mantra; Hinduism (worship); Judaism, prayer and liturgy of.

Christianity: Christian prayer has four major dimensions, each of which may predominate in a given situation. The first is speaking to God. Jesus continued Jewish practice in addressing God. In the Lord's Prayer, Jesus taught his disciples to address God as "Our Father in Heaven," using *abba* (Aram.), the intimate word for father. Another dimension is listening to God. Speaking to God is a response to God's prior address. Prayer that focuses on listening to God is also called meditation. A third involves attention to God's presence. A sense of communion with God often accompanies speaking or listening to God, but prayer centered mainly on attention to the divine presence is often called contemplation. Christian mystics have distinguished different levels of contemplation or degrees of unity with God. A fourth dimension is communion with other people. Prayer with others is basic to Christian worship, and prayer for others (intercession) is common; yet private prayer also takes place within the context of some supportive Christian community. *See also* Christianity (worship).

Islam: Known as *salat* (Arab., "prayer"), Islamic prayer is a short, highly formalized worship service required five times daily (at dawn, noon, mid-afternoon, sunset, and evening). Salat is performed in a clean, quiet place after undergoing ritual purification. Because the prayer service requires total prostration with forehead touching the floor, the surface must be free of impurity carried by shoes or other means. Thus, shoes are never worn in the prayer place. Although it is permissible to perform the salat alone, it is recommended that it be observed with others in a congregation, however small. The Friday noon salat, which features a sermon, must be performed by a congregation in order to be valid.

Muhammad declared that, while prayer is the key to paradise, purification is the key to prayer. Muslims perform two types of ablution, depending on whether they have experienced minor or major impurity. Minor impurity can be removed by a regulated washing of the hands, arms, feet, ankles, face, ears, nostrils, and mouth, with the rubbing of a moistened hand over the hair. This ablution (*wudu*) removes impurity caused by sleep, using the toilet, fainting, and certain other things. Major impurity is caused by such things as seminal emission, sexual intercourse, menstruation, and postpartum bleeding. Major impurity is removed by a thorough, ritualized bathing (*ghusl*) of the whole body including the hair.

The salat is announced by the call to prayer (*adhan*), which is chanted in a traditional manner. Once the individual or congregation is prepared, a briefer form of the call summons the worshipers to rise up for the immediate performance of salat. The worshipers face Mecca, which in a mosque is marked by a niche (*mihrab*) in the wall. The direction of prayer is called *qibla*, and it must be ascertained as accurately as possible for the salat to be valid. (Travelers often use compasses, and hotels in Muslim lands often have qibla markers in guest rooms.)

In congregation, one person serves as prayer leader (*imam*) by standing alone at the front and center, serving as a model for the rest to follow in regimented fashion. The imam does not need to be a religious professional but may be any respected adult who knows the procedures and can recite suitable passages of the Qur'an from memory. Males serve as imams for male and mixed congregations, whereas females may lead only other females in salat. Males occupy the front of the prayer space, nearest the imam, while females occupy the rear, separated from the males by a space or partition, or they may worship in a separate room or building. Regardless of whether the congregation is single sex or mixed, both males and females have an equal obligation to perform the salat. Only males, however, are required to observe the Friday noon congregational salat in a public mosque; females may observe that salat validly at home.

The congregation lines up in neat rows behind the imam and follows uniformly and simultaneously right after the imam initiates a motion. The motions of prayer involve both spoken formulas and varied bodily postures and gestures. The basic ritual unit is called a *raka* ("bowing") and consists of standing, bowing, sitting in a semi-kneeling position, and full prostration with the forehead touching the clean floor or ground. Different daily salats require differing numbers of rakas—two, three, or four—but additional rakas are recommended either before or after the required ones for all the daily salats. In any event, performance of the salat does not take more than seven to ten minutes, although it should not be hurried and the worshiper should not depart with unseemly haste afterward.

The salat is immediately preceded by framing one's sincere intention (*niyya*) and mentally rehearsing what is about to be performed. This *niyya* is indispensable; without it the performance is invalid. It is an effective way of separating one from the mundane affairs of the day and entering into a mood of composure, clarity, awe before God, and spiritual spontaneity.

The Friday congregational salat, especially, reinforces Islam's strong community-mindedness. Throughout, the worshipers face straight ahead, emphasizing the vertical relationship of creature and Creator and symbolizing the worldwide unity and strength of the Muslim community (*umma*) as it focuses on the holy Kaaba in Mecca, where heaven and earth are believed to touch.

Besides the formal prayer service of the five daily salats, there are also special salats for the two yearly festivals (ending the Ramadan fast and observing the Feast of Sacrifice), funerals, and eclipses. Muslims also practice personal, spontaneous prayer, known as *dua* ("invocation," "calling upon"), which includes petition, intercession, and confession of sins, as well as seeking of forgiveness. Dua is usually practiced immediately after the salat, but it may be offered at any time. The posture is sitting, with hands held open in front of the breast, with palms up and eyes focused straight ahead. Afterward, God is praised and the palms are drawn gently over the face. Some Muslims use prayer beads to help them remember sequences and cycles of personal prayer, with traditional texts collected in devotional manuals. Muslims also pray by calling down God's blessings on Muhammad, his family, and companions. Finally, there is a form of prayer, known as *dhikr,* that centers in ritualized remembering of God and his holy names as contained in the Qur'an. The Sufi mystics of Islam have developed dhikr into advanced meditation practices. *See also* ablution; Allah Akbar; basmala; dhikr; mosque; niyya; Sufism.

Shinto: In Shinto, prayer is associated closely with rites of purification and offerings. They provide an ongoing sense of being in a sacred community with the *kami* (divinities, divine presences). *Norito* are stylized ritual prayers in ancient poetic language chanted as part of sa-

cred rites such as national purification and harvest festivals. Private prayers usually concern this-worldly benefits such as health or educational success. They are performed by clapping hands and bowing, accompanied by monetary donation at a shrine or food offerings at the home altar. *Ema,* wooden tablets on which one places a personal petition, can be left at a shrine. *See also* norito; Shinto.

prayer beads (Islam) (Arab. *subha*), strings of eleven, thirty-three, and ninety-nine beads used to facilitate Muslim devotions, including reciting and meditating on the "Ninety-Nine Names" of God. Beads made of amber and sandalwood are especially prized, although such an aid is neither required nor universal in Islam. *See also* prayer.

prayer breakfast, a religious meeting characteristic of conservative Christians combining breakfast and extended group prayer.

prayer flag, a flag used in the practice of Tibetan Buddhism to invoke the power of sacred syllables. Flags are inscribed with sacred syllables and flown from trees, mountain shrines, or other physical structures so that the wind will set the power of the syllables in motion. *See also*

Tibetan Buddhist prayer flags over the Tsang-po (Brahmaputra) River in 1987.

devotion (Buddhism); prayer wheel; Tibetan religions.

prayerstick, prayerfeather, single feather, or feathers together with other materials such as wood, stone, and wild plants, used as forms of prayer in religious practices of Pueblo and Navajo cultures (American Southwest). Varying widely in size and complexity, these religious objects are referred to as prayersticks in the ethnographic literature of the Navajo and Pueblo groups and as prayerfeathers in the literature of the Hopi. Among the Zuni, prayersticks are placed at shrines on various occasions during the ceremonial year as prayers for the well-being and fertility of Zuni people, crops, and livestock. Among other occasions, they are made as part of the annual late autumn Shalako performance concerned with successful hunting and agriculture. Among the Hopi, prayerfeathers are used in all religious performances and are included in some as part of the dress of participants; they are also used in the ceremonial first planting of crops and placed at the shrine in every Hopi field. During Soyal, the Hopi winter solstice performance, prayerfeathers are made for all of the villagers, their fields, and animals as prayers for the physical health and general well-being of all. Among the Navajo, prayersticks are included in the medicine bundles of Navajo healers and are used in Navajo healing performances.

prayer wheel , a wheel used in the practice of Tibetan Buddhism to invoke the power of certain sacred syllables, notably the mantra *Om mani padme hum.* Prayer wheels vary in size from small objects that can be held easily in the hand to large cylinders that are permanently fixed inside the structure of a temple. The sacred syllables are inscribed on the outside of the wheel and are set in motion by spinning the wheel. The origin of the Tibetan prayer wheel is obscure, but its significance as a devotional object is clearly related to other symbolic complexes in Buddhist culture. The spinning of the wheel reflects the Buddha's turning of the Wheel of the Dharma, the act by which the Buddhist tradition was set in motion. And the syllables themselves reflect a general Indian reverence for sacred sounds either as expressions of power in their own right or as means to invoke the power of important deities. In Tibetan Buddhist practice the syllables om mani padme hum are associated with the Bodhisattva Avalokiteshvara and are used to invoke Avalokiteshvara's compassion. *See also* Avalokitesh-

Buddhist prayer wheels at the Kumbum monastery, Quinchai, China.

vara; devotion (Buddhism); Om mani padme hum, Tibetan religions.

preacher, a Protestant clergyman.

preaching, the delivery of a sermon or religious instruction.

Islam: Preaching in Islam has its origin in the practice of the Prophet Muhammad, who established the sermon as the central feature of the congregational prayers held in major mosques at Friday noon. Ordinarily delivered in Arabic by the leader (*imam*) of prayer, the formal elements of the sermon (*khutba*) include an initial praise of God, the profession of faith, an exhortation, and concluding blessings and supplications for those in need. The sermon also contains an invocation that mentions the ruler by name. Hence this ritual oratory may provide the public setting for religious leaders to pronounce on the legitimacy of secular powers.

Beyond the mosque, the rhetorical skills of popular, itinerant preachers and storytellers are widely attested in the Middle Ages. In modern times, some Muslim preachers enjoy extensive influence through the broadcast, recording, and publication of their sermons.

Precepts (Five, Eight, and Ten), the moral observances undertaken by Buddhists. For laity, there are five: not to take life, steal, engage in sexual misconduct, lie, or use intoxicants. Vowing to undertake these five precepts along with refuge in the Three Jewels is a formal sign that an individual is a Buddhist.

Laypeople are encouraged to keep four more precepts on the quarter days of the lunar month. For a night and a day they should refrain from eating after midday, using ornaments, watching entertainment, and using luxurious beds. Counting the second and third of these as one, they add up to eight. In addition, the precept about sexual misconduct is extended to all sexual activity.

Ten precepts are observed by novices entering the monastic order and today by laywomen leading a renunciant life. These ten observances are those found in the Eight Precepts with the addition of a prohibition against the use of money; the prohibitions against ornaments and entertainment, which counted as one precept in the list of eight, here count as two. Fully ordained monks are bound not only by the Ten Precepts, but by more than two hundred rules found in the *Vinaya*, the section of the Buddhist scriptures concerned with monastic discipline. *See also* Three Jewels; Vinaya.

predestination, the Christian doctrine holding that God chooses in advance those who will be saved. Approaches to the doctrine are many but can be reduced to two general ones: that God predestines the elect on the basis of foreknowledge that they will respond to the offer of grace or that God predestines those who will be saved apart from foreknowledge and then effects their response to grace. The second position has been a distinctive feature of many Calvinist or Reformed Protestant confessions. In other major Christian denominations the doctrine has usually received less emphasis and less precise definition. *See also* Arminius, Jakob; Calvinism; salvation.

preexistence, the widespread notion that a divine being or a human spirit or soul existed in a previous state before becoming incarnate in its present form. *See also* soul.

prelate, a designation for high-ranking Chris-tian clerics. In the Anglican Church it refers to bishops alone; in Roman Catholicism the term also applies to certain officials of the Vatican curia.

prema (pray'muh; Skt.), among Vaishnava Hindus, supreme love, love of the self-giving sort that is its own end, unlike *kama*, which is founded on desire and yields progeny. *See also* karma; Vaishnavism.

presbyter (Gk., "elder"), in the New Testament a person who advised on the governance of a Christian church. Originally, presbyter was a synonym for *episcopos* ("overseer"), but by the second century distinct offices had evolved; episcopos was the office of bishop and presbyter that of priest.

Presbyterianism (Gk. *presbyteros,* "elder"), a form of church government within the Reformed tradition. Theologically derived from John Calvin (1509–64), Huldrych Zwingli (1484–1531), Martin Bucer (1491–1551), and John Knox (1514–72), Presbyterianism came to designate the Reformed churches of Scotland and the British Isles.

Critical for the Reformed understanding of the church was the joint governance, and a graded system of governing bodies called presbyteries, synods, and a General Assembly. The term *Presbyterian* began to be used in the first half of the seventeenth century in Scotland to refer to the Reformed churches who preferred a polity based on the shared power of governing bodies, as opposed to the other Separatist groups (Congregationalists and Baptists), who retained a Reformed theology but stressed the autonomy of the local congregation.

Presbyterianism had its beginnings in Scotland but moved quickly across the Atlantic, with the first American Presbyterian Church founded on Long Island (1644) with subsequent churches established in the Midwest and South. A number of the signers of the American Declaration of Independence were Presbyterians, and the Presbyterian form of church government was a model for the framers of the United States Constitution. Later international missionary efforts created a strong Presbyterian presence in Korea, Brazil, the Middle East, Mexico, and Africa.

Doctrine: Presbyterians affirmed the major tenets of Martin Luther's treatises of 1520, but their ecclesiology and doctrinal priorities were shaped more by the beliefs of Calvin and Zwingli. Presbyterians affirmed the sovereignty of God, the Lordship of Jesus Christ, the authority of scripture, justification by grace through faith, the priesthood of all believers, and the efficacy of only two sacraments, baptism and the Lord's Supper. Presbyterians were distinctive in their belief that God is sovereign over all of creation; hence their interest in all structures of civil order; that God has specially called some people to be elected servants; that the Lord's Supper is characterized by Jesus' spiritual presence and is essentially a memorial service, and that church polity should be based on a system of graded courts that are representative assemblies. The historical confessions of Presbyterianism have included the Apostles' and Nicene Creeds, the Scots Confession (1560), the Heidelberg Catechism (1563), the Second Helvetic Confession (1566), and the Westminster Confession (1645). In 1967 the United Presbyterian Church in the United States of America adopted a more contemporary confession, and the recently created Presbyterian Church in the United States of America, formed in 1983 by the merger of the (northern) United Presbyterian Church in the United States of America and the (southern) Presbyterian Church in the United States, adopted a new statement of faith in 1991. Presbyterians have historically affirmed the parity of all ministers and the right of congregations to call their own pastors.

Worship: Worship in Presbyterian churches is structured and modestly liturgical. The sermon remains the focal point of worship. The Lord's Supper is normally celebrated on the first Sunday of the month, although some churches observe this only quarterly. Infants are baptized by sprinkling, as are adults who have not been previously baptized. Virtually all Presbyterian churches observe the seasons of the church year.

Varieties of Presbyterianism: Presbyterian churches in Great Britain have steadily declined in membership in the twentieth century; this led to the union with Congregationalists in 1972 to form the United Reformed Church. The Presbyterian Church of Scotland remains the national Church of that land but attendance and influence are diminishing. Over the years, the diverse streams of Presbyterian churches in the United States have merged to form more inclusive bodies; the major body, the Presbyterian Church in the United States of America, had 2,856,713 members in 1991, with 11,501 churches and 20,338 ministers.

Headquarters of the Presbyterian Church in the United States of America are in Louisville, Kentucky. Presbyterians have been active in ecumenical circles. Presbyterian churches in Canada merged with Methodists and Congregationalists in 1925 to form the United Church of Canada, and Australian Presbyterians joined in a similar union in 1977 to form the United Church in Australia.

A number of smaller Presbyterian churches in the United States have broken away from the larger bodies over the years. From 1741 to 1768 the controversy over revivalism eventually led to the founding of the Cumberland Presbyterian Church in the mid-South. Controversy over doctrinal and ecclesiastical issues produced the "New School–Old School" controversies from 1837 to 1869. The slavery issue split the church north and south in 1861; the reunion of those two bodies did not occur until 1983. The Modernist-Fundamentalist controversy created deep divisions from 1895 to 1925; the residues of that debate about scripture are still found within the church. The Presbyterian Church in America was founded in 1973 to affirm the inerrancy of scripture, as well as to protest the ordination of women and other social action issues endorsed by the Presbyterian Church in the United States of America.

Mission interests of northern Presbyterians after the Civil War created a number of black Presbyterian congregations and colleges in the South, and the assimilation of those congregations into the newly formed Presbyterian Church in the United States of America has been a high priority. Missionary work with Hispanics, Native Americans, and Asian peoples have given today's Presbyterian Church a diverse membership. *See also* Campbell, Alexander; Knox, John; Protestantism; Reformed churches; Westminster Confession.

pre-Socratics, a group of Greek philosophers, most of whom were before the time of Socrates (470–399 B.C.), though some (e.g., Philolaus and Democritus) were actually contemporaries of, and others (e.g., Archytas) were even later than, Socrates. Their writings are preserved only by quotation in works by later authors. Most lists of pre-Socratic philosophers include the following: among the early Ionians (from Asia Minor and the eastern islands) are counted the Milesians Thales (early sixth century B.C.); Anaximander (early to mid-sixth century B.C.), and Anaximenes (mid- to late sixth century B.C.), said to be Anaximander's student; Xenophanes of Colophon (mid-sixth century B.C.), who settled and taught in Sicily; and Heracleitus of Ephesus (late sixth to early fifth century B.C.). A second group, Greek colonists in southern Italy, include Pythagoras of Samos (late sixth century B.C.), who settled in Croton and whose followers—the Pythagoreans—included perhaps Alcmaeon of Croton (early fifth century B.C.), an early medical writer, and certainly Philolaus (mid- to late fifth century B.C.) and Archytas (late fifth to mid-fourth century B.C.), both of Tarentum; the Eleatics, namely, Parmenides (early fifth century B.C.), said to be a student of Xenophanes, and Parmenides's student Zeno (mid-fifth century B.C.), known for his paradoxes; and others said to have been Parmenides's students, Empedocles of Acragas (mid-fifth century B.C.) and Melissus of Croton (mid-fifth century B.C.). A third group of later figures from Ionia and the mainland include Diogenes of Apollonia (early to mid-fifth century B.C.); Anaxagoras of Clazomenae (early to mid-fifth century B.C.); Archelaus of Athens (mid-fifth century B.C.), said to be Anaxagoras's student; and the atomists, Leucippus of Miletus (mid-fifth century B.C.), and Democritus of Abdera (late fifth century B.C.).

Relation to Other Early Thinkers: Scholars generally distinguish the pre-Socratics from the Sophists, although their writings reflected similar interests and viewpoints. These groups are not distinguished in Aristophanes's *Clouds* (423 B.C.) and seem to have been combined in popular prejudice by the time of Socrates's trial in 399 B.C. Scholars also often compare the opinions of the early medical writers—called "Hippocratics" as followers of Hippocrates of Cos (mid-fifth century B.C.)—to those of the pre-Socratics and Sophists, with whom they share many doctrines.

Religious Innovations and Influences: The pre-Socratics who wrote about religion offered a great variety of opinions that cannot be simply classified. Many were daringly revisionary. At least four categories of innovation may be identified. The first is the replacing of mythological explanations with naturalistic ones. Especially in the philosophies of the Milesians, Anaxagoras, the atomists, and some Sophists, meteorological, astronomical, and other common phenomena were explained as the effects of natural forces and not traditional divinities. The early thinkers often explicitly identified these forces as "gods," however. This sort of early natural science is parodied in Aristophanes's *Clouds*. Intellectuals thought to engage in natural science (e.g., Socrates) were later (apparently falsely) branded as atheists. In a similar vein, the early medical writers posited natural (as opposed to divine) causes and cures for diseases.

The second category of innovation was the moral critique of traditional religion. Especially in the surviving fragments of Xenophanes and Heracleitus, we find criticisms of certain religious practices and of the mythographers' immoral and anthropomorphic depictions of the gods. Similar moralizing doubts about traditional conceptions of the gods are expressed by some Sophists and various characters in the works of the Athenian dramatists, who were perhaps influenced by the pre-Socratics' arguments. The medical writers' insistence on the natural causes for disease may also have flowed from their rejection of the traditional idea that the gods could cause evil. Socrates, Plato, and Aristotle—to one degree or another—followed this way of thinking as well by arguing for the moral perfection of god or the gods.

Third, the pre-Socratics were involved with unusual cults and conceptions of the afterlife. Especially among the Greeks in Italy, one finds a strong, but unusual, religious element. The Pythagoreans in particular are associated with Orphic cult and are said to have practiced vegetarianism for religious reasons and to have believed in reincarnation.

And finally, certain passages from the works of a number of pre-Socratics strongly suggest inclinations toward monotheism; some almost certainly constitute direct affirmations of it. Suggestive passages may be found here and there in a number of the fragments of the Ionian naturalists and the Eleatics, but especially in the moralizing works of Xenophanes and Heracleitus. Such thinkers may well have influenced Plato and Aristotle, both of whom explicitly endorsed monotheism in their later works. *See also* Greek religion.

priesthood, holy persons by virtue of professional office; individuals, often belonging to a hereditary caste and usually male, who are formally inducted into the service of the god(s) in a holy place.

priest/priestess (*presbuteros;* Gk., "elder"), ritual specialist who normally performs, leads, or assists in religious rituals with community support.

Issues of Definition: Priests and/or priestesses sometimes officiate at ceremonies conducted for the benefit of the community at large. At other times they perform rituals for specific individuals or family groups. In both cases they usually express widely diffused and socially sanctioned religious sentiments and ritual commitments, and so may be said to function on behalf of a community of worshipers. Those whom they serve as ritual practitioners, moreover, tend to deem them masters of ritual knowledge and often of cosmological, theological, and moral knowledge as well.

While the above characterization of the

priest or priestess serves for general orientation, two considerations need to be taken into account. First, persons whose major social identities are other than those of priest or priestess sometimes discharge what can be regarded as priestly duties. In some traditional African societies, for example, monarchs and chiefs are invested with religious responsibilities, and they perform animal sacrifices and preside over agricultural and other rituals on behalf of their subjects or followers. Roman emperors performed animal sacrifices. In many societies, heads of families or of larger genealogical clusters lead prayers, offer up sacrifices, or perform other religious rituals on behalf of their kin.

Second, within a given society religious practitioners whom we might call priests overlap in their public activities with other religious figures whom, on the basis of certain criteria, we may prefer to term *shamans, medicine men, witch doctors, magicians,* or *prophets.* While scholars have expended a good deal of ink in efforts to separate conceptually different types of religious specialists, sharp distinctions among them may be hard to sustain when confronted by the complexities and subtleties of social life in different parts of the world.

In light of both complexities within cultures and differences between cultures, perhaps the best way to conceive of priests and priestesses is by reference to relatively clear cases of what is generally meant by those terms, what many speakers of English are likely to judge good exemplars of the category. From there the terms *priest* and *priestess* can be extended to other cases by analogy. However, one must pay close attention to the ways in which those other cases may diverge from the type cases. In many societies no sharp line is drawn between "religion" and other aspects of culture. All societies do not divide up and categorize the realities they recognize in quite the same ways. Facile applications of one culture's category labels to another may severely distort the descriptions of peoples' perspectives and institutions.

The exemplars that most English speakers would probably judge to fit the category best are various sorts of Christian priests. Some might also regard the Jewish priests who officiated at the temple in Jerusalem as good exemplars, and perhaps also (though allowing for great diversity) Greek and Roman priests, especially as they are associated with sacrifices.

Christian Priests: In the New Testament Jesus is described as "a great high priest, that is passed into the heavens" (Hebrews 4.14). In mainstream Christian traditions Christ is the high priest of the New Covenant who gave himself as a sacrifice for the redemption of humankind. This sacrifice is viewed as a salvific act that makes possible a new relation between the human and the divine, just as by assuming human nature, many Christians affirm, Christ joins divinity and humanity. Christ is thus the unique *pontifex* (Lat.), or "bridge-builder," who mediates between human beings and God.

Roman Catholics recognize a corps of priests whom they regard as distinctively participating in Christ's priesthood. Through the sacrament of ordination, their church teaches, priests are endowed with a special power and grace in a chain of ordinations that goes back to Jesus, who ordained his apostles priests at the Last Supper. The Last Supper is regarded as a sacrificial meal, and Jesus is held to have commanded his apostles and their successors to offer his sacrifice. In this perspective, the priest, in celebrating the Mass, presides over a sacrifice in which Christ is present. The priest, moreover, can grant absolution for sins and perform other cultic acts. His duties also include proclaiming and teaching the gospel and he is often entrusted with other pastoral duties as well.

Protestants generally accept Christ as priest. But instead of supporting a special corps of priests who repeat (rather than merely commemorate) Christ's sacrifice as encoded in the Eucharist, many Protestants follow Martin Luther, the sixteenth-century Protestant Reformer, in affirming "the priesthood of all believers." Most Protestants deny that the Eucharist is a sacrifice and that there is need for a distinctive cultic priesthood to preside over sacrifice and to dispense other sacraments. At the same time, however, many support religious specialists who proclaim and teach the gospel and otherwise minister to the needs of congregants. Most Protestants—Anglicans/Episcopalians excepted—call their religious specialists "ministers" or "pastors" (Lat., "shepherds") rather than priests, thus stressing pastoral rather than cultic functions. The various Eastern Orthodox confessions recognize a priesthood with both cultic and pastoral duties.

The Jewish Priesthood: Our understanding of the development of the Jewish priesthood is incomplete in various respects. Among the problems not fully resolved is that of the origins and responsibilities of the Levites and their relationship to persons denominated *kohanim* (Heb.), generally rendered into English as "priests." Major biblical traditions indicate that the Levites constituted a priestly tribe with no territory of its own, that Levites were entrusted with the care of the ark of the covenant, and that certain descent lines within the tribe of Levi—that of Aaron (brother of Moses) and, later, that of Zadok (priest in the time of David and Solomon)—emerged as the accepted kohanim. At the same time, however, certain biblical passages suggest that the development of the priesthood in ancient Israel may have been rather more complex.

Originally the ancient Israelites sacrificed at numerous shrines. Sacrificial rites, however, were eventually centralized at the temple in Jerusalem. Priests (kohanim) officiated at the altar, taught and worked to maintain ritual purity in keeping with the precepts of Mosaic law, and engaged in oracular pursuits by casting lots. Priests also played important political roles both before and after the Babylonian captivity (ca. 598–536 B.C.). Levites fulfilled a number of less prestigious but still highly valued roles at the temple: they were singers, musicians, gatekeepers, and the like.

With the destruction of the temple in 70 A.D. and the abandonment of animal sacrifice, the priesthood lost most of its functions. Kohanim and Levites, however, enjoy limited liturgical honors today. They are given precedence, for example, in the order of persons called to say blessings over the scrolls of the law. Among Orthodox Jews, moreover, kohanim must obey certain special restrictions (a *kohen*, for instance, cannot marry a divorced woman). Ritually observant Jews are expected to know if they are kohanim or Levites by descent, and public recognition is facilitated in some cases by the bearing of certain patri-surnames, most saliently those of Cohen and Levy.

Greek and Roman Priests and Priestesses: Among the ancient Greeks and Romans women often played important roles as priestesses, especially (but not exclusively) in the service of goddesses.

In Greece, a priest or priestess served a particular god or goddess and was normally associated with a specific temple or shrine. Priestly service, generally speaking, was open to citizens, though in some places special qualifications were imposed. In certain shrines, for example, the priests or priestesses publicly identified with the local cults were supposed to be prepubescent boys or girls, in others mature men or women. In some shrines the priests were obligated to be celibate, in others not. In different places people acceded to the priesthood in various ways, such as buying offices, being entitled to them through family ties, or election. Members of the priesthood were not obliged to teach morality or dogmas. They were expected to discharge cultic duties associated with their specific shrines. Those duties usually included the intoning of invocations to the gods and officiating at sacrifices (in some shrines special slaughterers actually killed the victims).

Priesthood among the Romans was also diverse and complex. Certain priestly offices were as much civil and political offices as religious ones. In 63 B.C., for example, the politically powerful Julius Caesar increased his power by being elected chief priest (Lat., *Pontifex Maximus*, "the Greatest Bridge-Builder") of the major state cult in the declining Republic. Later, when the empire was established, the emperor sacrificed and performed other priestly functions as part of his imperial prerogatives and duties. *See also* Brahman; clergy; Indo-European religion; ritual; Roman religion; sacrifice.

primitive religion, religion of traditional peoples. The term is common but inappropriate. *Primitive* gains its meaning from its contrast to *civilized* or *advanced*. When restricted to technological aspects of culture, primitive may accurately reflect cultural differences. As an adjective for religion, it likely reflects values projected on traditional cultures by modern Western self-definition. *See also* typology, classification.

Prithivi (puhr'ti-vee; Skt., "broad one," "earth"), deified Earth, goddess of Vedic and later India. She is characteristically paired as Mother with Father Heaven (Dyaus). Separating Heaven and Earth was a primal cosmogonic act. *See also* cosmogony; world parents.

process thought, a broad movement in modern philosophy and in philosophical theology that emphasizes an evolutionary worldview and the temporal flow of experience. In contrast to classical modes of thought, process thought regards being as an abstraction from becoming, and replaces the idea of solid substances with the more dynamic categories of process and constitutive relations. The term *process* refers to the becoming or the emergent occurrence of novel instances of energy-events, taken as the most concrete facts of nature. The primacy of relations is asserted as constitutive of these processive unit-events on the basis of a descriptive generalization of the scientific principle of relativity. Metaphysically, it represents a form of naturalism that understands nature as self-sufficient and self-explanatory, a dynamic and organic web of events rather than a mechanistic or deterministic scene of independent substances. Theologically, it entails an extension of the properties of process and temporality to the notion of the divine. Ecologically, it emphasizes continuity between human and subhuman processes of life that form social patterns of greater or less intensity. Epistemologically, it is distinguished by attention to a prelinguistic and bodily mode of causal perception that provides an elemental basis for knowledge of other actualities. Ethically, it advances an understanding of the communal self and of altruism that is very close to the Buddhist understanding of no-self and of compassion. Its main representatives have been Anglo-American thinkers, especially Alfred North Whitehead (1861–1947), the British-American philosopher and mathematician, and Charles Hartshorne (b. 1897), a North American process philosopher. *See also* religion, philosophy of.

profanation, the act of desecrating objects or space set apart as sacred.

profane, contrast term to sacred, that which is forbidden to come in contact with the sacred. *See also* sacred, profane.

Progressive Judaism. *See* Reform Judaism.

projection, the objectification of internal experience in the external world. It is a term used to explain the origin of religious beliefs and practices. Although the term is seldom defined, explanations of religion that use the mechanism of projection agree that a religion is based upon actual experience. What that experience is depends upon the particular theory. For example, Sigmund Freud (1856–1939) argues that religion is a projection of repressed psychological experiences. For Ludwig Feuerbach (1804–72), religion is a projection of human qualities, "all theology is anthropology." For Karl Marx (1818–83), religion is a projection of political or economic experiences. Rudolf Otto (1869–1937) thinks that religion is a projection of the experience of the "numinous" and Emile Durkheim (1858–1917) explains religion as a projection of collective experiences.

All of these projection theories agree that religious beliefs and practices cannot be taken literally; they must be viewed as symbols that must be decoded in terms of the basic experience from which they are projected.

The basic weakness with all of these theories is the difficult task of explaining why projection into religion of basic human experiences is necessary, and why believers take their beliefs and practices literally rather than symbolically. The-

ories of projection are forced to admit that all religious practitioners are ignorant of the real, hidden meaning of their beliefs and practices. *See also* Feuerbach, Ludwig Andreas; ideology and religion; origin of religion; Otto, Rudolf; plausibility structure; religion, psychology of; religion, sociology of.

Prometheus (proh-mee'thee-uhs; Gk., "forethought"), in Greek mythology a trickster and culture hero who deceived Zeus and stole fire for humankind. *See also* Greek religion.

promised land, in the Hebrew Bible, the land of Canaan to which Israel returns following the exodus from Egypt (esp. Deuteronomy 8:7–9). In Christian allegorical interpretation, it is often understood as heaven.

prophecy. *See* prophet.

prophecy in traditional religions, a mode of communication between a divine reality and a human audience. In cultures that believe such contact to be possible, this communication takes the form of a dialogue: messages in both directions are channeled through individuals who are recognized by others in the society as qualified to perform this function. Those who play this role have been called by a number of terms, including *shaman, conjurer, spirit medium,* and *prophet.* These figures are present in a variety of times and places, and their words and actions display significant cultural differences. In terms of social dynamics, however, all are examples of prophecy.

It is assumed that prophets have had direct contact with a deity and that the particular messages they convey are based on that contact. Recipients often interpret their initial experiences as indications that a deity has selected them to assume the role. Such contact is essentially a private matter and cannot be directly confirmed by members of the audience, although there are ways of signaling its occurrence (e.g., trances, narrative accounts of revelatory experiences, and rubrics like "Thus says . . ."). On the other hand, the prophets' public performances are directly accessible, and audiences evaluate them on the basis of how well they conform to cultural expectations (the content of the message must be acceptable; the performance must include specific features—e.g., a trance, a verbal account of the deity's wishes—and must be fluent) and how effective they are in dealing with the current situation (e.g., whether a cure occurs or instructions for coping with a current crisis seem cogent). Whatever the response, it has the potential to influence the prophets' future activities. Prophecy exists only when at least some members of the audience affirm that the performance fits the expected pattern. The function of acts of power (sometimes referred to as "tricks") attributed to prophets is to provide members of the audience with direct supernatural confirmation of the prophets' authority.

Prophecy tends to occur in conjunction with crises, which may vary greatly in scope. Some basic types are fundamental disruptions of native cultures caused by European colonialism (e.g., Handsome Lake, Wovoka, and founders of Melanesian cargo cults); relations within or between local groups (e.g., spirit mediums in Zimbabwe adjudicating a succession to chieftain; Siberian shamans combating disruptive spirits sent by another clan); and the threats to everyday life caused by violent weather, illness, or the temporary disappearance of game animals (shamans and spirit mediums generally). In the first type of crisis, the prophetic message often contains new rules of behavior and elements of apocalyptic. Such figures are reminiscent of biblical prophets, and it is tempting to limit the category "prophet" to them; but for persons in other types of crisis, communication with the divine is equally crucial. The connection with crisis and the fact that not every crisis situation occasions such a response mean that the prophetic role, while it may remain latent within a given culture, is not exercised continuously. *See also* cargo cults; Delaware prophets; Ghost Dance; Handsome Lake; Kenekuk; Kimbanguist Church; Native Americans (North America), new religions among; Neolin; prophet; Prophet Dance; shaman; Smohalla; Wovoka.

prophet (Gk., "speaking for [a deity]"), a specialist in divine-human communication. The prophet is a highly variegated figure. Within some cultures, prophets are professionals, salaried members of a guild well integrated into the political structure; in others, prophets are individuals, voluntarily or involuntarily capable of prophecy, who are marginal figures. Some prophets are ecstatic, others are not. Some serve public forms of religion; others establish their own cults. *See also* Babism; Baha'i; divination; Elchasai; Elchasaites; Messenger of Allah; Muhammad; prophecy in traditional religions; revelation.

Prophet, The, standard appellation for Muhammad. *See also* Messenger of Allah; Muhammad.

Prophet Dance, a religion that emerged among several Native American groups in the central and southern Plateau region of North America during the 1830s, before the coming of Christian missionaries to the area. Inspired by reports of Christian teachings from elsewhere and by life at Hudson's Bay Company trading posts, the Prophet Dance incorporated an indigenous round dance form and openness to revelations received in trance but added songs celebrating God the creator, observance of the Sabbath every seventh day, the use of crosses as talismans, flagpoles, and leadership by secular chiefs rather than shamans. *See also* Native Americans (North America), new religions among; new religions; prophecy in traditional religions; revitalization movements; shaman.

Prophets, the second major section of the Hebrew Bible.

proselyte, a religious convert.

prostration, characteristic posture of submission, common in the presence of deities or rulers.

Prostrate pilgrims circle Mt. Govardhan, India (1975), until reaching the town of Jatipura.

Protestantism, a term first employed in Germany in 1529 to denote those princes and cities who issued protestations against a ban instituted by the Diet of Speyer, an assembly of the Holy Roman Empire, on each principality or city determining its own faith. The term was rapidly taken up by both supporters and opponents of those religious groups that grew out of, or held allegiance to, the controversies and doctrines associated with the Reformation, and gave rise to another early generic term, *Reformed Christianity*.

While generalization is difficult—there are more than two thousand Protestant groups in

---

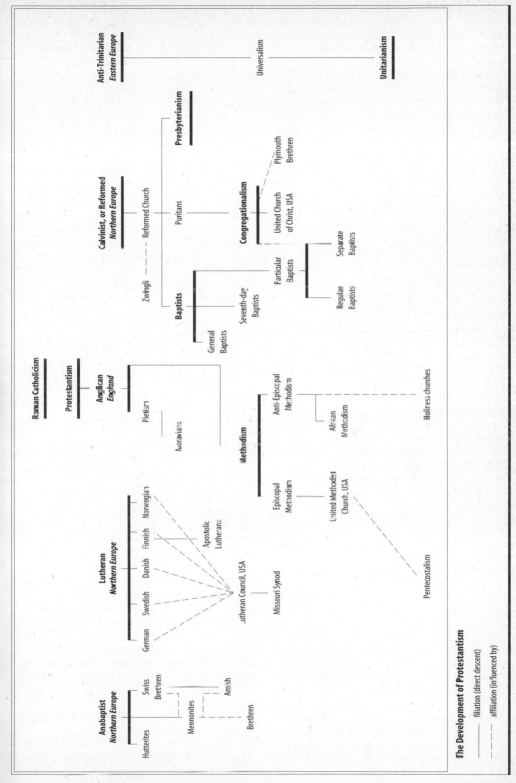

The Development of Protestantism

— filiation (direct descent)

- - - affiliation (influenced by)

Roman Catholicism

Protestantism

Anglican *England*
- Pietism
  - Moravians

Lutheran *Northern Europe*
- German
- Swedish
- Danish
- Finnish
- Norwegian
- Apostolic Lutherans
- Lutheran Council, USA
- Missouri Synod

Anabaptist *Northern Europe*
- Hutterites
- Swiss Brethren
- Mennonites
- Amish
- Brethren

Methodism
- Episcopal Methodism
- Anti-Episcopal Methodism
- African Methodism
- United Methodist Church, USA
- Holiness churches
- Pentecostalism

Baptists
- General Baptists
- Seventh-day Baptists
- Particular Baptists
  - Separate Baptists
  - Regular Baptists

Calvinist, or Reformed *Northern Europe*
- Zwingli
- Reformed Church
- Puritans

Congregationalism
- United Church of Christ, USA
- Plymouth Brethren

Presbyterianism

Anti-Trinitarian *Eastern Europe*
- Universalism
- Unitarianism

the United States alone—those denominations that owe their origin to the Reformation often share broad creedal formulations, such as justification by faith alone; an emphasis on the supremacy of scripture over tradition; the primacy of two sacraments, baptism and the Eucharist; a rejection of the papacy; and an insistence on the "priesthood of all believers."

The major families of Protestantism are Anabaptist, Anglican, Baptist, Congregationalist, Fundamentalist, Lutheran, Methodist, Pentecostal, Presbyterian, Reformed, and Unitarian. *See also* Adventists; Anabaptists; Anglicanism; Baptists; Congregationalism; evangelicals; fundamentalism; Holiness churches; Lutheranism; Methodism; Pentecostalism; Presbyterianism; Reformation, Protestant; Reformed churches; Unitarianism.

Protestantism in Korea. *See* Korea, Protestantism in.

providence, benevolent care and direction of the world and all beings by a deity.

Judaism: Throughout the Bible, the behavior and the personal concerns of human beings occupy God's attention. God also controls the fate of entire nations. Some later rabbis taught that God controls even the smallest events on earth, claiming that "a person does not bruise his finger on earth unless it has first been decreed in heaven." God is the judge of all, dispensing reward and punishment while leaving humanity free to choose its own way. Even the sophisticated theories of later philosophers have sought to preserve these basic biblical claims. *See also* Judaism, God in.

pseudepigrapha (Gk., "false writing"). **1** A general term indicating the judgment that a work was not written by the attributed author. **2** A collective term for postbiblical Jewish writings that are not included in the Protestant Apocrypha. For those that are found as a part of some Christian Bibles, the preferred term is *deuterocanonical*. *See also* Apocrypha.

pseudo-Dionysius. *See* Dionysius the (pseudo-) Areopagite.

psyche (psou'kay), soul or self in Hellenistic anthropology. *See also* soul.

psychedelic substances (Gk., "soul-manifesting"), refined chemicals that have the capacity to enable ecstatic experience. Though some are based on the active agent in psychotropic plants (e.g.,

mescaline), others are laboratory products (LSD). In the 1960s, based in part on the works of Aldous Huxley and Timothy Leary, there was much exploration of psychedelic experience. For some, it became a form of religion; for others, it was used as an explanation of the physiological basis of mystical experience. *See also* psychoactive plants.

psychiatry and religion. *See* medicine and religion.

psychics, individuals believed to have extraordinary mental abilities, including extrasensory perception, clairvoyance, and telepathy. Some, including self-realization proponents, argue that all humans have the innate capacity for mental communication, for seeing into the future, or perceiving hidden objects, and thus, by extension, for psychic healing and spiritual transformation. The Human Potential movement similarly supported claims for paranormal powers latent in the human mind, while several scientific institutes are studying such phenomena. Skeptics, however, maintain that telepathic skills are rare, the results of ordinary coincidence and thus illusionary or the product of fraud. *See also* parapsychology; Spiritualism.

psychoactive plants, plant species that have the capacity to enable ecstatic experience. Patterns of usage vary widely: in some cultures they are used only by holy persons (shamans, curers) and in others, by members of a secret society; in still others, they are in general use. Collection of the plants is almost always a highly ritualized activity, and the plants themselves are usually understood to be a divine gift or a divinity. Methods of ingestion vary widely and include smoking, snuffing, chewing, drinking, and rectal insertion. The best-known psychoactive plants include species of *Datura* (esp. *D. innoxia* and *D. stramonium*), marijuana or hashish (*Cannabis sativa*), various mushrooms (esp. *Amanita muscaria, Psilocybe mexicana, Stropharia cubensis*), peyote (*Lophophora williamsii*), tobacco (*Nicotina rustica, N. tabacum*), yaje (*Banisteriopsis caapi*), and the mysterious soma. *See also* ecstasy; Native American Church; psychedelic substances; Rastafarians; shamanism; soma; tobacco and hallucinogens.

psychotropic substances. *See* psychoactive plants; tobacco and hallucinogens.

Ptah, the ancient Egyptian creator god of

Memphis, who created the world by thought and word. *See also* Egyptian religion.

Ptolemy (tol'uh-mee), writer of treatises and letters explaining Valentinianism, a Christian Gnostic sect. He may have died as a Christian martyr in second-century Rome. *See also* Gnosticism; Valentinianism.

p'u (*poo;* Chin., "uncarved block"), Taoist term that refers to the unsullied condition of union with the Tao. *See also* Tao.

puberty rituals, a class of initiation rituals, or rites of passage, that pertain not to biological maturation but to socially defined passages from childhood to adolescence and adulthood. Arnold van Gennep (an early-twentieth-century French sociologist) first distinguished physical puberty from social puberty in his book *The Rites of Passage* (1909). He noted that although often associated with sexual maturation, initiation rituals in many cultures can occur well before adolescence or extend long after. So-called puberty rituals thus serve to formalize sociological rather than biological changes in the human life cycle. The rituals dramatically or symbolically separate initiates from their childhood existence, usually through physical seclusion, then instruct them in the formal requisites of their new status, and finally mark the resulting transformation overtly, whether through behavioral changes in dress or privileges, or physically through bodily mutilation, scarring, or circumcision. *See* bar mitzvah/bat mitzvah; Buddhism (life cycle); initiation rituals; Judaism (life cycle); life-cycle rituals; men's houses; mutilation; ordeal; penis-sheath; ritual.

puja (*poo'jah;* Skt., "worship"), worship of the deity or a spiritual teacher especially at a home shrine, one of the most significant ways in which Hindus express devotion. Many households set aside some space where pictures or small images are enshrined. *Puja* may involve simple acts of daily devotion, like lighting oil lamps and incense sticks, reciting prayers, or offering food to the deity. Usually all members of the family can participate, but more elaborate or specialized rituals of worship may involve a priest or special personnel. *See also* domestic ritual; Hindu domestic ritual; Hinduism (worship); path of devotion.

Pukkumina (Jamaican, "a little madness"), also Pocomania, a Jamaican religious group that incorporates both African and Christian practices. *See*

also Afro-Americans (Caribbean and South America), new religions among.

p'ungsu/p'ungsu jiri. *See* geomancy.

Punjab (puhn'jahb; Persian, "five waters"), the area of northwestern India where the Khyber Pass opens onto the plains. Hinduism was established here with the invasion of the Aryans and, much later, Islam. Later still, from the sixteenth century, it became the homeland of the Sikhs. *See also* Sikhism.

punya (poon'yuh; Skt., "merit"), in Indian religions, the meritorious (such as almsgiving or performing *pujas*) deeds or intentions accumulated or transferred that advance well-being. *See also* karma; merit.

Purana (poo-rah'nuh; Skt., "ancient"), a compendium of Hindu mythology, history, philosophy, ritual, and much else. The eighteen "great" Sanskrit Puranas (variously listed) were composed from about 400 to 1200, but innumerable "sub" Puranas continued to be composed in Sanskrit and vernacular languages for several more centuries. No Purana can be accurately dated. Many were originally oral in composition and continue to be performed orally, though most are now available in written texts.

A Purana is traditionally said to treat five topics: cosmogony, subsequent creation and destruction, genealogy of gods and sages, reigns of the Manus, and the dynasties of the solar and lunar kings. But most Puranas are devoted to other subjects, particularly the myths and rituals of the great sectarian gods, Vishnu, Shiva, and the Goddess Devi, as well as lesser gods like Ganesha and Samba. Many discuss technical subjects such as architecture, ethics, and medicine (human and veterinary). *See also* Bhagavata Purana; Hinduism (authoritative texts and their interpretation).

Pure Land (from Chin. *ching-t'u;* Jap. *jodo,* "purified field"), also Pure Lands, in Mahayana Buddhism, a world system purified by the power of a Bodhisattva's solemn vow and virtuous practices. Originally the term *purified field* referred to a world where a Buddha or Bodhisattva had appeared. Later the term came to refer to those world systems that had been made pure by the power of a Bodhisattva's vows and his subsequent attainment of full enlightenment. Although the purification of a world system is the work of only one Bodhisattva, and there can be only one Buddha presiding over a Pure Land,

Mahayana tradition states that there are as many Pure Lands in the universe as there are grains of sand in the Ganges River.

Although the Pure Land is given a concrete location and physical characteristics, metaphoric interpretations are common in the exegetical literature. Critiques of the otherworldly character of the belief also occur within as well as outside of Pure Land traditions. Some texts reject the notion of a distant Pure Land and emphasize the importance of "purifying" or transforming the present world. Others equate the purification of one's own mind with the purification of the world, so that the world becomes the Pure Land. These views were particularly important in the development of Chinese Ch'an as a tradition fusing meditation with faith in the Pure Land, and in Japanese Zen critiques of Pure Land belief.

Amitabha's Pure Land: By far the most influential of these conceptions is that of Amitabha's Pure Land, Sukhavati, which is today synonymous with Pure Land belief. The Buddha Amitabha (Jap. *Amida*) obtained this Pure Land as the result of the solemn forty-eight vows he made when, as the Bodhisattva Dharmakara, he promised to seek enlightenment in order to create a paradise where those who heard his name and believed in him could be reborn. The doctrine of Mahayana Sukhavati, like that of other Pure Lands, is firmly grounded in generalized Mahayana beliefs such as the Bodhisattva vows, the saving powers of Buddhas and Bodhisattvas, the belief that Bodhisattvas visit distant Buddha-fields to worship myriad Buddhas, and the power of the transfer of merit. Sukhavati is depicted as a "paradise," i.e., a gardenlike enclosure, the inhabitants of which know nothing but beauty and bliss. In marvelous gardens and groves birds and plants preach the Dharma (the ultimate truth according to Buddhist teachings), and the presence of the Buddha Amitabha is accessible to living beings in varying degrees. Living beings from impure lands who hear the name of the Buddha Amitabha and have faith in his vows can be reborn in his Pure Land.

East Asian Developments: Such beliefs originated in India and then spread to East Asia, where they have become a major influence in the development of Buddhist piety. Chinese Pure Land teachings developed in the context of T'ien-t'ai and Ch'an doctrine and practices, and in this form had a major influence in Korean, Vietnamese, and Japanese Buddhism. But Pure Land Buddhism in Japan eventually became a self-sustaining system of beliefs forming independent denominations of Pure Land believers, the strongest among which are the Jodoshu and the two branches of Jodo Shinshu. East Asian tradition also speaks of the Pure Lands of Bodhisattvas, such as Maitreya's Tusita Heaven and Avalokiteshvara's Potala. Graphic representations of different Pure Lands played an important role in East Asian iconography and religious architecture. *See also* Buddhism (authoritative texts and their interpretation); Jodo Shinshu; Jodoshu; Pure Land school (China).

Pure Land school (China) (Chin. *Ching-t'u tsung*), a school of Chinese Buddhism that established rebirth in a Pure Land as an intermediate goal on the way to *nirvana*. Mahayana Buddhism teaches that there are a number of Buddhas, each of whom presides over a Pure Land that is free from all worldly taints. In East Asia, the most popular of these Buddhas is Amitabha, whose Pure Land is located in the west. As an aspirant to enlightenment, he vowed that if he attained Buddhahood he would utilize his accumulated merit to create a Pure Land to which any being who sincerely called upon his name would go. The fact that he is now a Buddha indicates the fulfillment of his vow.

Believers who lack the opportunity or talent to take up the rigorous practices necessary to attain enlightenment can call on Amitabha, who will come at the time of death and take them to be reborn in his Pure Land. Once there, all their needs will be automatically supplied, and they will have all the time, intelligence, and skilled teachers needed to engage in religious practices and eventually gain enlightenment.

The Pure Land school itself developed under a series of masters beginning with Hui-yuan and culminating with T'an-luan, Tao-ch'o, and Shan-tao. After the persecution of 845, Pure Land teachings became the property of all Chinese Buddhists. Today, calling upon Amitabha's name in the hope of rebirth in the Pure Land constitutes a "way of faith" available to all. *See also* China, Buddhism in; Hui-yuan; Pure Land; Shan-tao; T'an-luan; Tao-ch'o.

Pure Land school (Japan). *See* Genshin; Jishu; Jodo Shinshu; Jodoshu; Kumano, Mt.; Kuya; nembutsu; ojoden; Yuzu-nembutsu school.

Pure Land school (Korea). Korea never developed a separate Pure Land school, as in other countries of Asia, but Pure Land practices, scriptures, and traditions were adopted by all the text and meditation schools at an early age. During the pre–Unified Silla period (ca. 356–676), belief in the Pure Land of Maitreya had been widespread and had been used by Silla monarchs as a means of enhancing the status of Silla as the Pure Land of the Buddha. In the Unified Silla period (seventh to ninth centuries) the *Amitabha Sutras* were introduced and became very popular both among aristocratic and gentry monks. Pure Land practices tended to satisfy both the need for meditation and for ritual practice. As in other North Asian countries (China, Japan), Pure Land practices appealed to rural classes and were propagated among them by wonder-working monks. With the introduction of Ch'an Buddhism in the ninth century, Pure Land practices were incorporated into Ch'an practice as an aid to faith, just as they had been incorporated into the dominant Hua-yen school two centuries before. Since the ninth century the recitation of Pure Land *sutras* and the invocation of Amitabha's name (*yombul*) have become a part of every temple regime and form the core of most lay worship. *See also* Bodhisattvas; Buddhas and Bodhisattvas (Korea); Korea, Maitreyism in; Pure Land.

Pure Rules (Chin. *Ch'ing-kuei*), a code of Chinese Buddhist monastic rules composed by Pai-chang in the eighth century and still binding upon Ch'an monasteries. *See also* Pai-chang Huai-hai.

purgatory, the Roman Catholic belief in a temporal place or condition for souls who, after death, need purification before entering heaven. This doctrine holds that sinners who die are subject to punishment for those sins, venial (minor) and mortal (grave), which, while forgiven, are still in need of expiation. The residue from the sinful choices still inhibits the individual from the full vision of God. The purifying punishment is usually described as an intense fire, either in a literal or figurative sense.

The teachings were defined at the Church Councils of Lyons (1274) and Florence (1439). Practices evolved of offering Mass for the souls in purgatory along with private prayers and works of piety (e.g., indulgences, almsgiving, fasting) on their behalf.

Protestant denominations do not accept the doctrine; Eastern Orthodox Christianity accepts it with some differences from Roman Catholicism. *See also* afterlife; afterworld.

purification, the ritual process by which a person, object, or place is made clean from pollution. *See also* harai; purity and impurity; sweat, sweat lodge.

Purim (poo-reem'; Heb., "[casting of] lots"), a light-hearted holiday (14 Adar) that commemorates the deliverance of the Jewish community of Persia, as recorded in the Book of Esther. Observances include reading the Book of Esther in the synagogue, parading in costume, exchanging Purim delicacies, and giving charity to the poor. *See also* Judaism (festal cycle).

Puritans, members of the Church of England in the sixteenth and seventeenth centuries who called for a purification of the established church's morals, theology, and worship along lines established at Geneva, Switzerland, by John Calvin (1509–64) and his followers. Originating among scholars in the 1570s at Cambridge University, the movement encountered persecution under the early Stuarts at the beginning of the seventeenth century, then emerged as momentarily influential during the years of the English Civil War and Interregnum (1643–60) after acquiring sympathy in Parliament. Other Puritans, such as the Pilgrims of 1620 and the 1630 expedition led by John Winthrop, established four "Holy Commonwealths"—Plymouth, Massachusetts Bay, Connecticut, and New Haven—in New England, free from English interference. In England, Puritans merged into the broader category of Protestant Dissent following the Restoration of the Stuarts in 1660. In America, New England Puritans gradually became transformed into the Congregationalist denomination, named after their distinctive polity, by the time of the Declaration of Independence in 1776. *See also* Anglicanism; Congregationalism.

purity and impurity, a set of conceptions that vary in content from one religious tradition to another but that generally involve three, often closely related, matters: the separation of the sacred from the profane, especially through taboo; ideas about dirt and its relationship to patterns of cultural classification; and the human body and social control of its potentially polluting excretions and imperfections. *See also* caste; harai; Indo-European religion; kigare; kut; tsumi.

Sacred and Profane: Religious notions of purity and impurity commonly concern the status of persons, things, and acts relative to the sacred. In his classic work *The Elementary Forms of the Religious Life* (1915), the early-twentieth-century French sociologist Emile Durkheim defines the sacred as that which religions protect and isolate from everyday, profane things. Sociologically, the essence of the sacred lies not in any intrinsic or universal property of religious things themselves but rather in the social interdictions or taboos (rules of conduct) that by definition always hedge religious acts, objects, and ideas around with restrictions. In contrast to other customary or legal rules, taboos remain absolute and unquestioned, evidenced by the spontaneous public reprobation as well as inevitable divine retribution that sacrilege always provokes. Durkheim sees in this imperious, inviolable quality of the sacred a symbolic expression of the moral, rule-governed nature of society itself and of each human individual's dependence on the collective social order.

Such a definition of the sacred suggests that religious purity and impurity, in inferring relative proximity to the sacred, depend closely on individual conformity to rules of ritual conduct. This is not to say that the sacred simply corresponds to that which is pure and the profane to that which is impure. The sacred encompasses unclean as well as holy things, since taboos restrict profane contact with both; profane things in turn imply no inherent impurity, only that they must obey taboos. In this regard, any contact with the sacred demands that profane communicants observe the proper restrictions, or "negative rites" as Durkheim calls them. These at once substantiate the boundary between the sacred and the profane, while also outwardly demonstrating the deference that enables profane beings to approach and commune with the sacred, what Durkheim means by "positive rites." Similarly, violation or neglect of taboos unequivocally distances mortals from the sacred. The defilement of sacrilege applies automatically and irrevocably to transgressors, regardless of intent or motive. Taboos thus engender fixed ritual procedures that themselves become a de facto model for, if not outright expression of, individual moral worth, public social order, and eternal cosmic truth. Purity and impurity betoken the extent to which individuals conform to this order. At the same time, however, this ritual order only serves as a means to the sacred; it never constitutes the sacred itself. Indeed, the very restrictions that ritual by definition imposes on its participants opposes them to the sacred, even as it constitutes their principal means of attaining communion with it. Purity and impurity thus characterize the conditions of contact between the sacred and profane but do not alone define the essential opposition between the two.

Dirt: In addition to this association with ritual injunctions sanctified by the sacred, religious purity and impurity also often evoke seemingly more mundane matters of physical cleanliness.

The twentieth-century social anthropologist Mary Douglas has effectively argued in her landmark book, *Purity and Danger* (1966), that cleanliness involves not just hygiene but, more fundamentally, respect for conventions. Even in contemporary Western societies where bacterial contagions define hygiene, ideas of cleanliness have as much to do with purely conventional standards of orderliness as they do with pathogens. What people define as clean originates in the "cherished classifications" that they use to give shape and permanence to otherwise shifting perceptions of the world around them. Individuals build up such classifications from their own experience and from each other, informed by, but not limited to, shared patterns of language and custom that they come to internalize.

Conversely, dirt represents matter out of place that contravenes these cultural schemes. More than simply a residual category, dirt's very existence presumes an active violation of other categories. Dirt threatens orderliness in two ways. First, it results from any unseemly crossing of category boundaries, for example, dried food left over on a supposedly clean plate. Second, and more intractably, dirt results from inadequacies in categorization itself. Because natural classes exist only inasmuch as they shade unevenly into one another, no single system of classification ever achieves total consistency or comprehensiveness. Exceptions continually challenge category boundaries. People may choose either to deny these anomalies, to explain them away as in fact part of their system of classification, or to prohibit them explicitly as unclean. This last, for example, is how Douglas interprets the dietary laws in Leviticus and Deuteronomy. Far from unclean in any hygienic sense, those animals forbidden to the Hebrews belied God's creation of creatures belonging properly to land, air, and water.

Such an understanding of dirt clarifies three points about purity and impurity. First, it reinforces suggestions that purity and impurity relate more to relationships between things than to the nature of things themselves. Neither disguised nor misguided attempts at hygiene, things become pure or impure in relation to one another and to the particular system of classification that differentiates them in the first place. Second, dirt as either systemic ambiguity or anomaly remains intrinsic to the act of classification itself. Given the impossibility of unequivocally classifying everything, all categorizations constantly create their own dirt from those things that fall outside, or between, their bounds. Consequently, conventional categories demand continual reaffirmation and reconstitution. Things at their margins can serve as powerful instruments for both, although ambiguities and anomalies as such need not always become dirty. They do, however, provide ready exceptions that, when explicitly imbued with danger, can reaffirm the very categories that they confound. This suggests why otherwise unclean things such as blood often acquire crucial symbolic value in religious rituals. Third, dirt as a byproduct of classification demonstrates that purity and impurity, and the taboos that they presuppose, relate directly to more general patterns of symbolic order that make up any culture. They are neither merely arbitrary nor exclusively concerned with the sacred. Indeed, even the sacred itself may be seen as a particular kind of category that by its very isolation from other categories actually helps to sustain them. By conforming absolutely to its proper place, by remaining forever holy in the sense of being whole and complete, the sacred epitomizes the possibility of proper categories. In purely conventional fashion, it belies the shortcomings intrinsic to mundane classifications.

The Body: The human body often serves as both the subject and the source for modeling ideas of purity and impurity. On one hand, the body pertains to individuals, yet on the other, individuals exist only as social beings, subject to the collective norms (standards) and values (morality) of the society to which they belong. Consequently, proper treatment of the body and control of its functions express the literal internalization of cultural categories and conventions by the individual. Here again, matters go well beyond simple hygiene.

For example, women in many societies observe menstrual taboos. In some cases, they are tabooed from normal social life during their menses and must live in special houses. Although originally thought to express local beliefs about the polluting nature of women, recent studies suggest that such taboos simply dictate that menstruating women behave appropriately, and that as long as they do so, they are no more polluting than anyone else. Menstrual taboos may imply women's inferior social position, but they can also constitute the basis for women's counterinterpretations of themselves as the moral pillars of society precisely because they uphold the taboos. Similarly, ideas of bodily purity and pollution inform the caste system in India. There, social position relates ideologically to containment of the inevitable impurities of organic life through appropriate ritual acts and avoidances. Occupational specialization and marriage within one's own caste, however, have transformed purity and impurity from concerns about passing individual contaminations into permanently ranked social distinctions of a rigid, if finely gradated, economic, political, and cosmological hierarchy.

Purity and impurity only exist conditionally in the taboos separating sacred from profane, in the vagaries of cultural categories, in the social forms imposed on individual bodies. One unavoidably engenders the other. *See also* body; dualism; sacred, profane.

Hinduism: The terms *purity* and *impurity* gloss Sanskrit and vernacular terms such as *shuddha, pavitra, shaucha,* and *sattva* and their opposites *ashuddha, apavitra, ashaucha,* and *asattva.*

The principle of the pure and impure is particularly relevant in the spheres of intercaste relationships and bodily states. One modality of intercaste relationship, hierarchy (two others are reciprocity and centrality), is articulated in terms of purity and impurity, and castes are considered low and high relative to each other. Transactions flowing from low to high castes are greatly restricted since the low would pollute the high. Castes are kept separate and hierarchized by such restrictions. However, transactions flowing from high to low castes are not similarly restricted. According to legal texts (Dharmashastras), high-caste men can marry lower-caste women, their offspring constituting a new category ranking somewhere between the father and the mother. Access to occupations as well as wealth follows the same logic that evinces the greater power of the purer castes.

At the bodily level, unbounded and disarticulated states are impure. The body's boundaries are protected in the same way as the boundaries of a caste; what is hierarchically high must be protected from what is low. Overflows, such as bodily effluvia, that cross the bodily boundaries render it impure. Such impurity is removed both by ritual ablutions and the passage of time. Unbounded states such as flowing hair signify a state of impurity; bounded or articulated states such as bound hair signify a state of purity. *See also* caste.

Judaism: Uncleanness, or ritual impurity (Heb. *tumah*), is the concept that a person or object can be in a state that precludes contact with the Temple or ritual. This condition of uncleanness is transferred to other persons or objects in a variety of ways, including contact, supporting the weight of an unclean object, or being under the same roof with it. Although the state of uncleanness is unrelated to any tangible condition, e.g., being physically dirty, it is corrected primarily through bathing, which renders the individual clean (*tahor*) until uncleanness again is contracted. These rules originate in Hebrew scripture, which only explains their general motivation: because the people of Israel are consecrated to God, who is holy, they too must be holy (see Leviticus 11:43–47). Uncleanness is understood to be the opposite of holiness.

Scripture lists three primary sources of uncleanness: (1) certain emissions from human sexual organs, including menstrual blood and ejaculate from the penis; sexual intercourse renders both the man and the woman unclean (Leviticus 15:18); (2) human corpses and the carcasses of animals other than those that may be slaughtered for food (Leviticus 11:24–30); and (3) a disease conventionally translated as "leprosy," which affects people, clothing, and buildings (Leviticus 13:45–46).

Scripture further differentiates levels of uncleanness. Corpses are the most virulent, rendering unclean everything in the same room with them. People rendered unclean by a corpse remain unclean for a week and must undergo a detailed purity rite (Numbers 19:11–22). They transmit a lesser level of uncleanness to other people, who are made unclean until the evening, when they must bathe. Comparably, menstruants, who are themselves unclean for a week, render other people, utensils, and clothes they touch or sit upon unclean until the evening.

The mishnaic rabbis, perhaps following the Pharisees, extended scripture's notion that purity applies primarily in the Temple. They hold that all food should be eaten as though it were a sacrifice to God. This means that Israelites, the foods they consume, and the dishes on which the foods are prepared and eaten must conform to the requirement of cleanness. In this way, all the people of Israel will live and eat as though they are priests at the altar of the Jerusalem Temple, i.e., as a holy nation of priests.

To develop scripture's system, the Mishnah details sources of uncleanness, objects susceptible to uncleanness, and modes of purification from uncleanness. Numerous laws clarify the practical implications of these matters. Along with a general prohibition against imparting uncleanness to foods, the rabbis legislated against prayer and study of religious texts by individuals in a state of uncleanness. However, the people probably never meticulously followed these laws. The rabbinic sources speak of a small group of individuals, designated "associates," who are distinguished by their consumption of common foods in a state of cleanness. Addition-

ally, many rabbinic laws refuse to segregate the unclean or even to deny them the right to participate in the synagogue or academy.

By medieval times, the extension of the purity laws to common foods and the notion that Israelites must avoid contact with unclean things were largely rejected. Today, only certain laws of cleanness are observed. Within Orthodox Judaism, the rules for the menstruant and sexual relations are preserved. Many of priestly descent still avoid corpse uncleanness, e.g., by refusing to enter a cemetery. Ritual washing of the hands before meals, intended to prevent contamination of the food, still is practiced.

Islam: Purity is a state of ritual preparation encompassed by the rules of *tahara* (Arab., "purity"). Muhammad considered purity half of faith and the gateway to prayer. Different types of ritual impurity are classified as major or minor. The former are caused by such things as sexual activity, menstruation, and childbirth, while the latter are brought about by natural evacuations and sleep. Minor impurity is removed by ablutions of hands, arms, feet, ankles, face, mouth, ears, and hair. Major impurity is removed by a full bath in clean water. In the absence of water, pure dust from the ground or other surface may be substituted in an abbreviated, yet fully efficacious, ablution. The Prophet taught that no Muslim is ever polluted per se.

purusha (poo-roo'shuh; Skt., "human being," "person"), in the Samkhya and Yoga philosophical systems, soul, spirit, or consciousness as opposed to materiality (*prakriti*). *See also* prakriti; Samkhya; yoga.

Purusha (poo-roo'shuh; Skt., "human being," "person,"), In Indic tradition, the primal "Man" (*Rig Veda* 10.90, known as the *Purushasukta*) out of whose sacrifice by dismemberment the universe is created. Originally thousand-headed, thousand-eyed, and thousand-footed, by his sacrifice he creates all beings from only one-fourth of himself, while three-fourths constitutes "what is immortal in heaven." Among the ordered and interconnected taxonomic sets generated from his dismemberment, most noteworthy is the creation of the four *varnas*, or classes: the Brahmans from Purusha's mouth, the Kshatriyas from his arms, the Vaishyas from his thighs, the Shudras from his feet. As the oldest mention of the four-varna scheme, the text sanctions the varna system as both divinely instituted and organically founded in this prior "personal" unity. While Purusha remains both transcendent and immanent, the sacrifice (*yajna*) is instituted as the foundation of all "laws" (*dharmas*).

The term *Purusha* remains a prominent name for the transcendent aspect of male divinity, whether Shiva or Vishnu, in late Upanishadic and epic-Puranic Hinduism. *See also* caste; cosmogony.

Purushottama (poo-roo-shoht'tuh-muh; Skt., "supreme male"), name recalling Pursuha of the *Rig Veda*. In theistic yoga, it denotes the supreme divinity (Vishnu, Shiva), who governs the cosmic rhythms by emerging from and reentering yogic concentration. *See also* Purusha; yoga.

pyramids (Egyptian), royal tombs of the Egyptian Old and Middle Kingdoms. Egyptians built two types of pyramids, step and true, mostly in northern Egypt. The oldest pyramid is the step pyramid of Djoser (ca. 2650 B.C.), built of a series of stone mastabas, or bench tombs, set on top of one another. The first true pyramid dates to the fourth dynasty (2614–2502 B.C.), and it and later pyramids incorporate the step pyramid in their construction. Usually associated with the rise of the sun god Re, the best-known pyramids are those of the fourth-dynasty kings Cheops (Khufu), Chephren (Khafre, and its sphinx), and Mycerinus (Menkaure) on the Giza plateau, each of which has subsidiary pyramids. Late Old Kingdom pyramids (ca. 2400 B.C.) contain the oldest Egyptian mortuary texts, the Pyramid Texts, which are spells to help the deceased make a successful journey to the netherworld, some of which incorporate the sun imagery of the pyramids themselves.

The twelfth-dynasty kings and several of their thirteenth-dynasty successors (1991–1650 B.C.) built pyramids in Upper Egypt across the Nile from Thebes, but no later rulers did so until the eighth century B.C.

The exact manner of building the pyramids continues to fuel discussion, though some kind of ramp system is generally assumed to have been used. In all times, devious plans were conceived to thwart prospective tomb robbers, but although every pyramid was intended to be impenetrable, virtually none remained inviolate, even in its own day. *See also* Egyptian religion.

pyramids (New Age), structures thought to concentrate beneficial cosmic energy within their space, according to New Age views. Relating their powers to a purported significance in ancient Egypt, modern users claim that pyramids not only preserve food and sharpen knives but also, on a larger scale, provide more healthful living quarters. *See also* New Age movements.

Pyrrhonism. *See* skepticism, ancient.

Pythagoras (pi-tha'gor-ahs; ca. 580–500 B.C.), Greek teacher from Samos who traveled to southern Italy where he founded a religious society (or philosophical school) at Croton around 531 B.C. Very little is known of his life, except that he was a follower of Apollo and was himself identified as a god by some. Pythagoras left no written work, imparting his teachings orally and apparently emphasizing secrecy within his community of followers. By tradition, all discoveries in the school were attributed to its founder, so a history of Pythagoreanism is difficult to uncover.

Pythagoras taught that the soul was immortal and bound to a cycle of reincarnations that imprisoned it in the bodies of plants, animals, and men. Believing this cycle could be broken only by a purification best achieved through study, Pythagoras taught a way of life devoted to the study of nature and the cosmos. His philosophy thus became a religion, open to men and women alike, whose aim was the salvation of the soul. His followers were said to live in silence, avoid eating meat, and believe that numbers were the real nature of things.

Pythagoras's discovery that the basic intervals in a musical scale (fourth, fifth, octave) could be expressed by numerical ratios between the smallest whole numbers (4:3, 3:2, 2:1) led to his doctrine that the nature of the universe lay in numbers, the study of which would reveal the harmony of the whole. The number 10, as the sum of the numbers in these ratios (1, 2, 3, 4), became central and was represented by the tetractys, an equilateral triangle with four units on each side:

This symbol represented the unity of ten opposites (limited/unlimited, odd/even, one/many, etc.) that made up the universe and that, as a unity, was divine. Whether the source of the universe was generated from this One or from the pair Limited/Unlimited is unclear. *See also* divine man; metempsychosis; mystery; number symbolism; vegetarianism.

A
E F
G
L
M N O P
Q
R S T U V
W X Y & Z

qadi (kah'dee; Arab.), a Muslim judge appointed by the ruler, responsible for the application of Islamic law in such matters as personal status, inheritance, and religious endowments.

qiblah (kib'luh; Arab.), the direction in which Muslims offer ritual prayer. Jerusalem was the original direction. Seventeen months after Muhammad's migration to Medina (622), the Kaaba in Mecca was appointed the new and final *qiblah* (Qur'an 2:143–44, 149). Mecca is faced in performing certain other ritual acts, for example, in animal slaughter.

Qom (gom; Persian), the sacred pilgrimage and university city of Twelver Shiite Muslims south of Tehran, Iran, site of the shrine of Fatima, sister of the eighth *Iman*. The mosque-university at Qom is the preeminent theological institution for training Shiite *ulama*.

Quakers. *See* Friends, Society of.

Quds, al-. *See* Jerusalem.

Queen Mother of the West. *See* Hsi Wang-mu.

Queen of Heaven, common epithet of a powerful goddess.

Quietism, Italian and French heretical Catholic movement inspired by Miguel de Molinos (1628–96), who taught that union with God is gained by removing all mental images. When passive union with God is attained, Molinos believed that sin is impossible.

Qumran (koom'rahn), the Transjordanian site of the discovery of the Dead Sea Scrolls, a collection of manuscripts containing 520 identifiable Jewish texts from the third century B.C. through the first century A.D. Of these, 157 are biblical texts constituting the oldest recovered manuscripts, with crucial import for textual criticism and transmission. The remainder are a variety of forms of literature, including Hebrew and Aramaic manuscripts of apocryphal writings formerly known largely in Greek and a large collection of previously unknown texts. The identification of the site and the connection with the Essenes is controversial. *See also* Apocrypha; Essenes.

Qur'an. *See* Islam (authoritative texts and their interpretation).

Qur'an recitation. The Arabic word *qur'an* means "recitation" and designates the revelations recited by Muhammad and accepted by Muslims as the verbatim speech of God. Although a consonantal text of the Qur'an was compiled shortly after Muhammad's death (632), oral tradition retained primary authority. Later, acceptable variant readings were codified to ensure the religious efficacy of ritual and worship. Recitation in Arabic of quranic verses is required during daily prayers, and recitation of the entire Qur'an remains a central feature of Islamic festivals and holidays. Similarly, quranic recitations celebrate family occasions, such as marriages and births, while comforting believers in times of crisis, especially death. The importance of this spoken divine word in Muslim life is underscored by the written Qur'an, with its clear liturgical divisions for recitation.

Most public recitations of the Qur'an are performed by professional chanters who have memorized the Qur'an under the direction of recognized teachers in the oral tradition. Through years of study and practice, students, usually male, master the quranic language and the rules and etiquette of recitation—its sounds, nasalizations, assimilations, pauses, and starts. In a state of ritual purity, a chanter recites in one of two styles. *Tartil* ("slow, distinct chanting") stresses accurate pronunciation and intonation, thereby promoting religious reflection and edification. In contrast, the more popular *tajwid* ("euphonious recitation") is highly stylized and embellished with distinct cadences and periods of silence that aim to evoke feelings of awe and reverence.

Qur'an school (Arab. *kuttab*), place for the study of the proper recitation of the Qur'an. Instruction

Young East African Muslim boys and girls pose with their teachers at a Qur'an school (*madrasa*) at the Pangani Mosque, Kenya.

takes place in mosques, special buildings, private homes, and open spaces. The emphasis on memorization and recitation in these schools is sometimes so great that literacy is not acquired even after years of attendance. Attrition due to economic factors is high. Until the age of seven or eight, boys and girls often attend mixed classes, although they are later separated. Once a prerequisite for higher Islamic learning, Qur'an schools now often serve as de facto preschools.

rabbi (ra'bi; Heb., "my master," "my teacher"), from Late Antiquity to modern times, the intellectual and spiritual leader of the Jewish community. The term *rabbi* was first used following the destruction of the Jerusalem Temple in A.D. 70. It referred to sages ordained through the laying on of hands, which was performed only in the Land of Israel. In Babylonia, the term *rav* ("master," "teacher") was employed. In medieval times, the designation *ha-rav* indicated scholarly standing, while rahv frequently was used simply to mean "mister." In the modern period, rabbi again is used for an individual ordained by a Jewish seminary.

The office of rabbi embodies the social and religious ideology first expressed in the Mishnah and the talmudic literature. These documents derive from a class of scholars and teachers who were authorities in a tradition of scriptural interpretation and religious thought and practice that they called the oral Torah. As sole spokesmen for the oral Torah, rabbis increasingly became the central religious and legal functionaries of the Jewish community. In addition to their preeminent religious activity, study of Torah, in the talmudic period (fifth–sixth centuries) rabbis began to serve as judges, to fix the calendar, to administer the community's system of social welfare, and to promote religious observance. These rabbis functioned much like other contemporary holy men and magicians and were understood to have a particularly close relationship to God and therefore to possess special powers, including the ability to curse or to bless. Rabbis used their position to reshape the lives of common Jews in the image defined by the oral Torah.

In the talmudic period, rabbis generally supported themselves from a trade at the same time that they performed rabbinical duties. By the twelfth century, the rabbi became a full-time religious functionary, often remunerated as an employee of the self-governing Jewish community. The rabbi then acquired a broad range of responsibilities and powers. Based upon his study of Torah, he rendered legal decisions on issues ranging from ritual practice to business law; he officiated at marriages and funerals, slaughtered animals according to ritual standards, performed circumcisions, and acted as scribe.

The medieval rabbi preached in the synagogue at least twice a year, and, in some locales, more regularly. But he was not a synagogue director or prayer leader. His primary affiliation remained the local rabbinic academy (yeshiva), the head of which often served as the community's chief rabbi. Since the beginning of the nineteenth century, this situation has changed. The dissolution of the self-governing Jewish community and the emergence of Reform and Neo-Orthodox Judaism quickly created a need for a rabbi who would resemble the Protestant minister, serving the needs of an individual congregation. The rabbi now had to assume a broad range of pastoral responsibilities as well as lead prayer, preach, and direct congregational social, educational, and philanthropic activities. In this setting, rabbinic training necessarily was broadened to include areas of secular learning ranging from psychology to business administration.

Though contemporary rabbinic authority increasingly derives from skills not associated with traditional learning and knowledge, modern rabbis struggle to maintain an identity based upon their mastery of rabbinic texts and their embodiment of the values of the Torah, to remain Jewish role models, distinguished from other teachers, social workers, and counselors.

The contemporary rabbinate also struggles with other current political and social issues, including sexual equality. The Reform, Reconstructionist, and Conservative movements now ordain women as rabbis despite the talmudic rule, largely rejected in these movements, that a woman may not serve as a witness or judge, two of the rabbi's central functions. The conflict over ordination of women underlines the fragmentation of the contemporary Jewish community and highlights the extent to which the rabbinate's continuing leadership depends largely upon its ability to mediate between tradition and the needs of the modern Jewish community. *See also* ordination; synagogue; Torah.

rabbinical court (Heb. *bet din*, "house of judgment"), a Jewish court of law. Rabbinic sources assign Jewish courts of three and twenty-three judges jurisdiction in civil and criminal matters, respectively, and attribute to the "Great Sanhedrin" of seventy or seventy-one judges vast legislative, administrative, and judicial powers. Because Jewish governments in antiquity had limited autonomy, Jewish courts probably exercised few of these functions. The *bet din* was central to the self-governing medieval Jewish communities and had broad responsibilities. In modern times, the bet din usually is a religious court, dealing with such matters as divorce, conversion, and dietary laws. In Israel, the rabbinical court has jurisdiction over Jews in matters of personal status as well.

Rada (rah'dah), one of the two major pantheons or "nations" of divinities in traditional urban Voodoo in Haiti. The term probably derives from a Dahomean place name and now designates spirits who are characteristically "sweet," wise, and generous, such as the snake spirit Damballah. Its counterpart is the pantheon of forceful Petro spirits. *See also* Voodoo.

Radha (rahd'hah; Skt., "desired object"), in Hindu mythology, Krishna's favorite among the cow-herding women (*gopis*) of Braj. She is regarded by many Vaishnavas as equal in status to Krishna, since the love they share is divine. For some she is even higher, because she feels this love more constantly and intensely than he. *See also* Bhagavad Gita; Krishna; path of devotion; Vaishnavism.

Radhasoami Satsang (rah'dah-swah'mee suht-suhng'; Hindi, "the true fellowship of Radha's Lord"), a movement founded by Swami Shiv Dayal Singh in Agra, North India, in 1861. Each of twenty branches is led by a spiritual master (*guru*). The largest, at Beas, claims over a million adherents worldwide.

Radhasoami teachings, derived from Kabir, Nanak, and other medieval Hindu saints, hold that the soul, trapped within matter and time, is liberated through *surat sabd yoga* (the discipline of uniting one's soul with the divine sound current) and through *bhakti* (love) of the master.

Radhasoami has experimented in religious socialism and influenced such Western movements as ECKANKAR and the Divine Light Mission.

Radio Church of God. *See* Worldwide Church of God.

Ragnarok (rahg'nah-rok; Old Norse, "the fate of the gods"), in Norse mythology the final battle between the gods and the forces of evil leading to the destruction of the world. *See also* Nordic religion.

rahit-nama (rah-hit'nahm'uh; Punjabi), document defining the code of conduct of the Sikh Khalsa. From the early eighteenth century *rahit-namas* were standardized, and in the 1930s they were approved for general use by the Shiromani Gur-

dwara Prabhandak Committee, the preeminent Sikh religious body, in the text called *Rahit Maryada*. *See also* Khalsa; Sikhism.

Rahner, Karl (1904–84), German Catholic theologian. He interpreted Scholastic philosophy in existentialist terms, and systematically reinterpreted authoritative Church teachings for contemporary Catholicism in a lengthy series of essays collected in the more than twenty volumes of *Theological Investigations* (1954–).

rainbow snake, spirit being having the form of a snake, widely reported in Australia, associated with water, and appearing in the sky as a rainbow. It is variously represented as male, as female, and as sexually ambiguous; the female version is identified, in parts of Australia, with the All-Mother. In some regions there appears to be one rainbow snake; in others there are many. Especially in monsoon areas, with their alternation of wet and dry seasons, there is a clear connection between the rainbow snake and the seasonal cycle. Rainstorms can be destructive, but they also revivify the earth. Rainbow snakes are commonly regarded as dangerous to people: many myths tell of humans who were swallowed and regurgitated (dead or alive); it is accepted that the same fate could befall people today. But the myths may also be regarded as culturally creative, for example in establishing major ceremonies, in which the symbolism of swallowing and regurgitation may be dominant. A natural process, observable in the behavior of real snakes, is here used as a model for a cultural process of initiatory advancement. Similarly, many magicians owe their powers to an experience of possession by a rainbow snake. Images of rainbow snakes are common in aboriginal art, including rock art and the body art of ceremonies. The basic snake design is often embellished with eggs or splashes of rain, which bring out the association of the rainbow snake with fertility and revivification. In some regions rainbow snakes are identified with the spiritual essence of life, for a female must be entered by one if she is to have a child. *See also* All-Mother; Australian and Pacific traditional religions.

rain dance, common generic term for religious performances, particularly summer dances of Pueblo (American Southwest) peoples, sometimes extended to Native Americans generally; used by Native and non-Native Americans to denote the performances' single function as rainmaking. Contrary to this interpretation, Native American religious performance practices are complex and variable in form, concept, and intent. Public summer dances, although conducted by the Pueblos with the express purpose of encouraging rainfall sufficient to support successful crops in an arid environment, form part of elaborate systems of religious practice, which are ongoing throughout the year. The dances have multiple significances. They may function to control weather or to restore health to community residents, crops, and livestock; they may serve also as a means of initiation or as a reenactment of part of the community's religious history. A single dance can engage many concerns: to communicate community prayers for rain in a dry season, to express communally held social and religious values, to publicize recent lapses in a community member's behavior, to satirize idiosyncrasies of other tribal and Euramerican peoples, to restore productivity of fields and livestock, to heal an ill member of the community, and, in the form of public giveaways, to provide to all residents and visitors a share in the community's economic prosperity. In every case, *rain dance* connotes more than simply the performance of some narrow or superficial primitive superstition. *See also* dance; North America, traditional religions in.

Rajneesh, Baghwan Shri. *See* Rajneesh Foundation International.

Rajneesh Foundation International, neo-Hindu religious organization founded in Poona, India, by Baghwan Shri Rajneesh to promote the pursuit of spiritual enlightenment through the adoption of a disciplined, communal life-style.

Inspired by aspects of Hindu and Tantric concepts of personal dedication to spiritual advancement, the Rajneesh Meditation Center was begun in the 1960s and drew international adherents attracted to its simplified practices of "dynamic" or no-effort meditation and receptivity to momentary impulses. Communal as well as devotional life in India centered on Rajneesh himself, considered to have been incarnate divinity. The leader subsequently expanded his teachings to emphasize the necessity of commitment to an enlightened leader, reunification of spiritual and material life, and intense meditative efforts in order to achieve personal transformation. In the early 1980s, Rajneesh led a group of initiated followers, mostly North American converts, to establish Rajneeshpuram, a commune near Antelope, Oregon. Criticisms of his intrusion into rural life, forays into local politics, munificent life-style, and sexual immorality ended with his indictment and deportation in 1985 for immigration fraud.

While the organization persists both in India and in independent centers in the United States and Europe, the foundation has declined since the death of its founder in 1990.

Rama (rah'muh; Skt., "charming"), the hero of the Hindu epic *Ramayana,* who is believed to have lived in the remote past. The eldest of four princely brothers and rightful heir to the throne of Ayodhya, Rama calmly accepts a stepmother's demand for his exile and spends fourteen years in the wilderness, accompanied by his wife, Sita, and brother Laksman. There he protects sages from marauding demons, only to suffer the abduction of Sita by their lord, Ravana, the ten-headed king of Lanka. Aided by an army of monkeys and bears, Rama constructs a bridge to the demons' island citadel, slays Ravana in fierce battle, and recovers Sita. His exile completed, he returns to Ayodhya to commence an exemplary reign. In some versions, he is later forced by public pressure to banish his wife, whose twin sons become in time the first reciters of the epic story.

Revered throughout India for his steadfastness, compassion, and valor, Rama is also worshiped by many Hindus as the seventh incarnation of the world-protecting god Vishnu. Today his name serves, especially in North India, as a common nonsectarian designation for the supreme being. *See also* avatar; Hinduism (poetry); Ramayana.

Ramadan. *See* fasting; Five Pillars; Islam (festal cycle).

Ramakrishna (rah-muh-krish'nuh; 1836–86), Hindu mystic and inspiration for the various Ramakrishna movements founded by Swami Vivekananda: the Vedanta Society (New York, 1895) in the West; the Ramakrishna Mission and the Ramakrishna Order (1897) in India. Ramakrishna was a priest at the Dakshineshwar Temple outside Calcutta, devoted to the goddess Kali. Almost illiterate and strictly ascetic, he taught "God-realization" and renunciation of "women and gold." Uninterested in the intellectual aspects of religion, he was a devotee who believed he had attained the experiences at the heart of all religions and that they were the same. The movements that followed changed his emphasis on devotion into social relief activities. *See also* America, Hinduism in; North America, new religions in.

Ramana Maharshi (rah'muh-nuh muh-huhr'shee; 1879–1950), the most famous Hindu monist saint of the twentieth century. In adolescence he underwent an experience of psychological (spiritual) unity with Shiva and afterward fled his home in Madurai for Arunachala (southwest of Madras) to live a life of asceticism. There his ashram eventually became a center of spiritual pilgrimage. *See also* asceticism; pilgrimage.

Ramanuja (rah-mah'noo-juh), foremost interpreter of Hindu theistic Vedanta for Shrivaishnavas of South India. Although traditional dates given to Ramanuja are 1017 to 1137, others suggest 1077 to 1157. Born in Shriperumbudur, he spent most of his life in Shrirangam. He fled to the Hoysala kingdom (modern Karnataka) to avoid persecution by the Chola king, but returned to Shrirangam a few years before his death. In commentaries on the *Vedantasutras, Bhagavad Gita,* and in independent treatises, he proclaimed the supremacy of Vishnu-Narayana and emphasized that devotion to Vishnu leads to liberation. He challenged the eighth-century philosopher Shankara's interpretation of scripture, especially his concept of *maya* (mental projections taken as/for reality) and belief that the supreme reality (*brahman*) is without attributes. Shrivaishnavas revere Ramanuja as a savior of the community. His images are found in many temples. *See also* liberation; mysticism; path of devotion; Shrivaishnavism; six systems of Indian philosophy; soul; Vedanta.

Ramayana (rah-mah-yah'nuh; Skt., "the acts of Rama"), a Hindu epic tradition. Its earliest literary version is a Sanskrit poem of some twenty-four thousand couplets attributed to the sage Valmiki. It is believed by many scholars to date to around 500 B.C. to A.D. 400, though Hindu tradition places its composition in the far more remote past. Recounting in seven books the life story of Prince Rama of Ayodhya, the epic contains passages of great beauty and is revered as the archetype of poetry. At the same time, its principal characters present ideal models of personal, familial, and social behavior and hence are considered to exemplify *dharma,* the principle of moral order. Preserved through various recensions, the Sanskrit text became an inspiration for later storytellers and poets and its title a generic name for several hundred literary retellings in the regional languages of South and Southeast Asia. From about the tenth century onward, the religious worship of Rama as an incarnation of Vishnu gave rise to influential devotional versions that emphasized the divinity of the hero and heroine and reinterpreted many events of the story. Notable examples include the Tamil version of Kampan (ca. eleventh century), the Bengali of Krittibas Ojha (fourteenth century), and the Hindi of Tulsi Das (sixteenth century). Such regional versions of the *Ramayana* also gave greater theological importance to the monkey Hanuman, Rama's friend and helper.

The influence of the *Ramayana* early spread beyond the Indian subcontinent to become an important component in the literatures and visual arts of Southeast and East Asia. In contemporary India, the *Ramayana* tradition continues to inspire fervent devotion as well as ongoing performance through recitation, storytelling, folksong, annual cycles of pageant plays, film, and (during 1987–88) a phenomenally popular television serialization. *See also* Hinduism (poetry); Rama.

rapture (Lat. *rupere,* "to seize"), a term employed in the New Testament of the Bible to refer to the eschatological event during which Christians who are living on earth will be "caught" up to meet the Lord in the air (1 Thessalonians 4:17). Often disregarded by mainline Protestantism as an indication of an obsolete early worldview, the concept is often given prominent attention in conservative or evangelical circles where it becomes focused in the debate over premillennialism and postmillennialism. *See also* millennialism.

rasa (rah'suh; Skt., "juice," "flavor"), in Indian aesthetics and, by extension, in certain devotional contexts, the sentiment or emotional response that art, or the divine, may produce in an audience. As enumerated in the "fifth Veda," Bharata's *Natyashastra,* a treatise on dramaturgy (before the fourth century), there are eight primary *rasas:* love, heroism, disgust, anger, humor, fear, pity, and astonishment. Later theorists debated whether "peace" should be added as a ninth or defined as the rarified absence of all sensuality. Some Vaishnava theologians employ the term to classify five varieties of love for Krishna: tranquil, servile, comradely, parental, and erotic. *See also* Hinduism (performing arts); Hinduism (poetry).

Rashi, popular acronym for Rabbi Solomon Isaac (1040–1105) of Troyes, France, author of the most influential commentaries in Judaism to the Hebrew Scriptures and the Babylonian Talmud. On the Hebrew Scriptures his commentary is eclectic, gathering and arranging rabbinic exegetical comments into a collage of authoritative interpretation. On the Babylonian Talmud the commentary is pedagogical and analytical, explaining the sense of words and the meaning of passages. Because Rashi's commentaries are the point-by-point departure for all religious study of these documents, he defined the religious world of Judaism from his time to the present. *See also* Judaism (authoritative texts and their interpretation).

Rashidun. *See* Rightly Guided Caliphs.

Rastafarians (ras-tah-fair'ee-uhns; from Amharic *Ras* ["Prince"] *Tafari*), members of a cultural and spiritual movement, the Ras Tafari, centered on Ethiopian ruler Haile Selassie (1892–1975). It developed in the Jamaican countryside and has become a major political and religious force in the life of the Caribbean and among Africans in the New World. Its roots lay in the different forms of ancestral beliefs among rural Jamaicans, which were submerged during the period of slavery and colonialism. The Rastafarians emerged following the Garvey movement in the 1920s, when African identification flourished in the Western world. Drawing inspiration from the positive references to Ethiopia in the Bible, such as in Psalms 68:5, the early members proclaimed that they were true Africans and that Haile Selassie, ruler of Ethiopia, was their king and spiritual leader. For some, this meant not only identification with independent Africa but also embracing the beliefs of the Ethiopian Orthodox Church.

When Haile Selassie, who traced his lineage from the Biblical monarchs Solomon and Sheba, was crowned emperor of Ethiopia in 1930, some early Rastafarians saw him as the new African messiah and took his common name, Ras Tafari, for their movement. In the period following the Italian invasion of Ethiopia and during his exile in Great Britain, Haile Selassie formed the Ethiopian World Federation, which developed the first links between the Ethiopian monarch and his supporters in Jamaica.

After the liberation of Ethiopia in 1941, some Rastafarians sought repatriation back to Africa. A few moved to Ethiopia and were settled on land granted by the ruler in Sheshame, in the Shoa province. The great majority of Rastafarians remained in Jamaica and formed a major source for cultural protest against Eurocentrism in Jamaican society. Through their songs of racial memory and pride and social protest, the Rastafarians brought world attention to their ideas of African redemption. Spokespersons such as Bob Marley, Peter Tosh, and Bunny Wailer brought this new music—called "reggae"—to a wide audience and in the process popularized some of the views on Africa and religion that were intrinsic to the beliefs of the Rastafari movement.

Through the efforts of the movement, the Ethiopian Orthodox Church became one of the official religions in Jamaica. The Rastafarians also introduced into Jamaica the Orthodox Christian view that Jesus Christ, as God, was both divine and human. The Rastafarians generally eschew formal means of worship, and different groups among them hold differing beliefs. For example, some believe that Haile Selassie was a representative of God on earth, while others do not; some do not believe in organized religions at all.

Rastafarians can be distinguished by their dreadlocks and use of the colors of African liberation: red, green, and gold. Some smoke marijuana (*ganja*) as a holy sacrament and as a result are harassed by law enforcement agencies. Members do not eat pork, and many are vegetarians as well. Though they believe in and make use of the Christian Bible, they hold that the King James Version is a tool for Western expansion and domination.

Since the death of Haile Selassie in 1975, the movement has grown substantially, and there are now Rastafarians wherever people with African roots reside. *See also* African Americans (North America), new religions among; Afro-Americans (Caribbean and South America), new religions among; dreadlocks; Ethiopian churches; ganja; Garvey, Marcus M.; Haile Selassie.

Rasul Allah *See* Messenger of Allah; Muhammad.

rationalism, intellectualism, an approach to religion that assumes religion to be a cognitive rather than a psychological, sociological, or economic phenomenon. Religion, it is maintained, arises and functions to serve some cognitive end—most often, explanation. In the social scientific study of religion the intellectualist approach was initially dominant during the late nineteenth and early twentieth centuries, then was long dismissed as artificial, and only in the last few decades has made a comeback.

Edward Tylor and James Frazer: The classic exponents of the intellectualist approach to religion are the anthropologists Edward Tylor (*Primitive Culture*, 1871) and James Frazer (*The Golden*

Bough, 1890). For both, religion arises and functions to explain the physical world. One or more gods are postulated as the direct causes of events in the world. For Frazer, explanation is a means to control: knowing, for example, that gods determine the weather enables one to secure from them the proper amount of rain for crops. For Tylor, a purer intellectualist, explanation is an end in itself: whatever practical use is made of the knowledge that gods determine the weather, the prime payoff is the knowledge that they do so.

The term *rational* is notoriously difficult to define. Minimally, it means noncontradictory. More fully, it means systematic and comprehensive.

Religion for both Tylor and Frazer is scrupulously rational. It provides a consistent and complete account of all phenomena in the external world. Religion is the primitive and ancient counterpart to modern science. It rests on the scientificlike procedures of observation, generalization, and hypothesis, though not ordinarily on testing. "Rational" does not mean "true." Both Tylor and Frazer take for granted that religion is rational yet false. Religion is false because there are no gods in the world. But religion remains fully rational because the belief in gods is a coherent and systematic one. Religion becomes irrational only once modern science arises. Even then, religion itself is not irrational. Only the retention of religion alongside modern science is irrational, for the two are incompatible sets of belief.

Bronislaw Malinowski: The classic critics of a rationalist and intellectualist approach to religion are the anthropologist Bronislaw Malinowski ("Magic, Science and Religion," 1925) and the philosopher Lucien Levy-Bruhl (*How Natives Think*, 1910). Both are certain that Frazer and especially Tylor misconceive the nature of religion, and do so because they misconceive the nature of believers. For Malinowski and Levy-Bruhl, no less than for Frazer and Tylor, religion is a premodern phenomenon: believers are "primitives" and ancients. But Tylor and Frazer purportedly err above all in seeing primitives as akin to moderns—intellectual, reflective, scientific.

According to Malinowski, primitives are practical rather than intellectual in nature. They busy themselves in the world rather than speculate about it. Preoccupied with survival, they have neither the luxury nor the inclination to philosophize.

Religion for Malinowski arises and functions neither to explain nor even to regulate the physical world but simply to endure it. Religion emerges not out of scientificlike detachment but out of desperation. Anxiety, not Aristotelian wonder, impels it. Religion arises at the limits to human endurance. It serves neither to explain how crops grow nor even to make them grow but to cope with the prospect of failed crops—and of hunger and deprivation. Operating above all through myth, religion for Malinowski reduces anxiety by justifying what cannot be altered. Myth states that death, disease, and natural catastrophes exist because a long time ago some event introduced them forever into the world. These woes can never be eradicated, only understood and so better endured. Strikingly, religion for Malinowski, no less than for Tylor and Frazer, offers an explanation of the world. But that explanation is only a means to a non-intellectual end: the reduction of anxiety. Malinowski's view of religion is still uncompromisingly anti-intellectual even if for him religion works by explanation.

Malinowski's view is most keenly anti-intellectual because for him primitives possess science alongside religion. Science arises and functions to explain and control the physical world. Religion justifies what cannot be controlled. Rather than the primitive forerunner of modern science, religion coexists with primitive science exactly because the two serve different ends.

In contrast to Tylor and Frazer, Malinowski is uninterested in the contents of the explanation provided by religion. He is concerned only with its psychological efficacy. He is therefore uninterested in the logic, coherence, or comprehensiveness—in short, the rationality—of religious belief. Malinowski's very indifference to the issue evinces his anti-intellectualist stance.

Lucien Levy-Bruhl: If at one end of the theoretical spectrum Malinowski rejects the intellectualist approach to religion because it makes primitives too otherworldly, at the other end Lucien Levy-Bruhl rejects the intellectualist approach because it makes them insufficiently otherworldly.

For Tylor and Frazer, primitives differ from moderns in degree only. Like moderns they are innately intellectual. Their capacity to think is merely weaker than that of moderns. For Levy-Bruhl, primitives differ from moderns in kind. They are emotional rather than intellectual in nature. They seek to commune with the physical world rather than to explain it. Religion is, as for Malinowski, the product of feeling rather than of thinking. For Levy-Bruhl, as for Malinowski, religion coincidentally provides an explanation of the world, but it scarcely arises to do so. It arises instead to rekindle mystical oneness with the world.

According to Levy-Bruhl, primitives do not believe that all natural phenomena harbor individual gods but rather that all natural phenomena, including humans, partake of an impersonal, mystic realm. The sharing of mystic properties enables phenomena to become one another yet remain what they are: humans become birds yet still remain humans. Levy-Bruhl calls this belief "prelogical," for it violates the fundamental law of noncontradiction: the belief that something cannot simultaneously be both itself and something else. For Levy-Bruhl, then, primitives do not think rationally.

Claude Levi-Strauss: More than any other thinker, the structural anthropologist Claude Levi-Strauss (*Introduction to a Science of Mythology*, 1964–71) has been responsible for a revival of the intellectualist view of religion. While he limits himself to myth, he deems myth a primitive phenomenon, thereby countering Malinowski, Levy-Bruhl, and others who dismiss the intellectualism of primitives.

Levi-Strauss castigates Malinowski for deeming primitives wholly practical in nature. Primitives, he insists, are as concerned as moderns with explaining the physical world. Similarly, Levi-Strauss berates Levy-Bruhl for deeming primitives entirely emotional in nature. Primitives, he again insists, are as concerned as moderns with explaining the world around them. They, too, can detach themselves from the world and think about it. When, in *Myth and Meaning* (1978), Levi-Strauss states that primitives are moved by a need or desire to understand the world and that they proceed by intellectual means, exactly as a philosopher, or even to some extent a scientist, can and would do, he seems indistinguishable from Tylor and Frazer. Yet he is severely critical of Tylor and Frazer—not because they regard primitives as less intellectual than moderns, but because they regard primitives as intellectually inferior to moderns. For Levi-Strauss, primitives are intellectually different rather than inferior.

Primitives approach the world concretely; moderns, abstractly. Hence, myths deal with particular characters—for example, with Oedipus, not with every human being—and with particular events—with Oedipus's marrying Jocasta, not with all sons' marrying their mothers. Primitives treat phenomena qualitatively; moderns, quantitatively. Primitives focus on the observable, sensible, secondary qualities of phenomena; moderns on the unobservable, insensible, primary ones. Yet myth for Levi-Strauss is no less scientific than modern science. It is simply the science of the concrete rather than of the abstract. Myth is primitive science, but it is not therefore inferior science.

If myth is an instance of mythic thinking because it deals with concrete, qualitative, and observable aspects of phenomena, it is an instance of thinking, modern or primitive, because it classifies phenomena. According to Levi-Strauss, human beings think in the form of classifications and project those classifications onto the world. Human beings think, specifically, in the form of oppositions. Myth is an exquisitely rational as well as intellectual enterprise because it arises not merely to explain the world but to resolve the oppositions, or contradictions, that have been cast onto it.

The fundamental contradiction projected onto the world is that between nature and culture. Humans experience themselves as at once animal-like (nature) and uniquely human (culture). The recurrent oppositions found in myths between raw and cooked food, wild and tame animals, and incest and exogamy exemplify the opposition of nature to culture. Because the basic opposition expressed by myth is that between nature and culture, the true subject of myth is not the world itself but the resolution of the contradictory relationship humans have to the world.

Because myth concerns the place of humans in the world rather than the world itself, it would seemingly have existential or emotional import, as myth does for Malinowski. Yet Levi-Strauss treats myth as a coldly intellectual phenomenon: the oppositions it expresses constitute logical puzzles rather than existential or emotional predicaments. Even in resolving contradictions, myth for Levi-Strauss does not serve to make humans feel better, as it does for Malinowski. The satisfaction is austerely intellectual.

With Levi-Strauss the intellectualist view of myth and religion reaches its apogee. Myth is not merely an inferior forerunner of modern science but a different kind of science of equal stature. As rigorous, as precise, and as comprehensive as modern science, myth is no less rational. *See also* magic, science, and religion; myth; religion, anthropology of; religion, the study of; ritual.

Rauschenbusch, Walter (rou'shen-bush; 1861–1918), American liberal Protestant theologian best known for his espousal of the "social gospel." His best-known work is *Christianity and the Social Crisis* (1907). *See also* Social Gospel.

Re (ray; Egypt., "sun"), the ancient Egyptian sun god, who died every evening at dusk and was re-born each dawn. He was often depicted as the winged sun. *See also* Egyptian religion.

rebellion, rituals of, institutionalized occasions within stable societies that burlesque or reverse social norms and behaviors, permit usually pro-hibited actions, and flout or mock established figures of authority. *See also* carnival; reversal.

rebirth. 1 A state achieved by virtue of ritual death. 2 Synonym for reincarnation. *See also* af-terlife; initiation rituals; reincarnation; samsara.

Reconstructionism, a modern movement of Ju-daism in North America and, to a lesser extent, in Israel. Reconstructionism is the formal name for the movement inspired by the American the-ologian and rabbi Mordecai Kaplan (1881–1983). He taught on the faculty of Conservative Ju-daism's Jewish Theological Seminary from 1909 to 1963 and had an enormous influence on two generations of Conservative rabbis. While at the seminary, Kaplan led a group of like-minded colleagues in laying the foundation for a new movement, beginning with the establishment of the Society for the Advancement of Judaism in 1922 and culminating in the creation of a formal organized movement in 1940.

Judaism as Civilization: Reconstructionism be-gins with Kaplan's formulation of Judaism as a social phenomenon rather than a spiritual ori-entation. Kaplan's thought, still central to today's Reconstructionism, exhibits the profound im-press of American civic life and the thought of Emile Durkheim and John Dewey. Judaism is defined as an evolving civilization: the corporate beliefs, actions, and institutions of the Jewish people. As an ever-changing civilization, little of Judaism is timeless and eternal, except the con-tinuity of peoplehood and the desire for moral perfection.

Kaplan rejects as senseless any notion of tra-ditional theism and decries all religious claims of supernaturalism and transcendentalism. God is conceived as a force in the universe that makes for goodness, justice, mercy, and truth. Prayer is therefore the subjective human reflec-tion on moral salvation, and the significance of prayer is in the affect it creates within the indi-vidual.

Chosenness and Community: Kaplan rejects the supernatural attribution of chosenness to the people of Israel on two counts: it contradicts a naturalist reading of human history, and it is of-fensive to notions of equality and democracy fostered in modern society. As a nationalist, Kaplan affirms the uniqueness of the Jewish people, but he rejected all claims of superiority and exclusivity. All references to the "chosen people" doctrine are expunged from the Recon-structionist liturgy, or otherwise interpreted in light of this teaching.

While rejecting the chosen people doctrine, Kaplan affirmed the centrality of community in Jewish civilization. He thought that the syna-gogue should provide a full range of cultural and social services for the community. Thus, he pre-ferred the model of community center, with full facilities for a wide range of leisure-time activi-ties, over the traditional Jewish house of prayer.

Kaplan affirmed a commitment to Jewish law, but rejected all authoritarian claims of Torah. For Kaplan, Jewish law was a *sanctum* to be experimented upon and reconstructed to co-incide with the actual values and interests of the people. In general, traditional practices were in-vested with new meaning, most often of a socio-logical nature. An openness toward ritual innovation and creativity is fostered in Recon-structionism.

Kaplan was one of the first Jewish theolo-gians to call for thorough equality of women in Jewish life. He was also a convinced Zionist, who saw in the rebirth of Jewish national aspirations the transformation of a medieval messianism into a worldly yearning for salvation.

The Reconstructionist Movement: Kaplan's socio-logical and historical orientation appealed to myriad Jewish intellectuals, who, though at-tracted to his ideals, remained mostly in the Conservative camp. It was not until the fledgling movement established its own seminary that Reconstructionism became an established and vital movement of mass appeal.

The Reconstructionist Rabbinical College (RRC) was founded in 1968 in Philadelphia. The movement distributes a magazine, *The Recon-structionist*, which has been published since 1935. By 1990, approximately sixty-five congre-gations belonged to the Reconstructionist movement (organized under the Federation of Reconstructionist Congregations and Havurot), and approximately two hundred rabbis are members of the Reconstructionist Rabbinical Association, founded in 1975. Reconstruction-ism is thus the smallest of the four organized movements in contemporary North American Judaism, alongside Orthodox, Reform, and Con-servative Judaism.

Reconstructionism has passed through two distinct phases. The first phase was based on an unwavering commitment to Kaplan's teaching, from the founding of the movement until the mid-1980s. The second phase commences with Rabbi Arthur Green's (1941–) appointment as dean of the Reconstructionist Rabbinical College and his ultimate elevation to president. Green, ordained as a Conservative rabbi and a distinguished scholar of Hasidism, has shifted away from the antisupernaturalism inherent in Kaplan's formulation toward a more spiritualist reading of Judaism. But the principles of Reconstructionism remain intact: a recognition of constant change in Jewish life and an enduring commitment to Jewish continuity, social action, and the values of democratic society. *See also* Conservative Judaism; Orthodox Judaism; Reform Judaism.

Recusants, Roman Catholic dissidents during the reign (1558–1603) of Elizabeth I who resisted royal attempts to integrate English religious practice by uniform use of *The Book of Common Prayer*. *See also* Book of Common Prayer.

redeemer. *See* savior.

redemption. *See* salvation.

redemption (Judaism) (Heb. *geullah*). 1 As a theological category, the saving of Israel from disaster here and now and from its political condition at the end of time. Redemption is collective and concerns the entire people, Israel. It is carried out at the end of time by God or by the Messiah. God is called redeemer (Job 19:25: "I know that my redeemer lives") when he saves his people. God appears as redeemer of Israel in the liturgy, and divine action in removing Israel from Egypt is one definition of redemption. God as redeemer is represented as repeating what was done when the Israelites were saved from Egyptian slavery. Redemption is associated with the figure of the Messiah, who is called the redeemer and who in his person will effect redemption.

Rabbinic Judaism contains two views on the character of redemption. One deems the sole important change to be Israel's freedom from gentile rule. The other expects a complete revision in everyday reality. Reform Judaism affirms not the personal Messiah but the messianic age and teaches that humanity must bear responsibility for helping to bring redemption. Because its theory encompasses the language of redemption, modern Zionism, a political movement, is characterized as a secularized restatement in

political terms of the category of redemption. *See also* galut; Messiah; Zionism.

2 As a legal category, the transformation of the status and condition of an individual, e.g., the restoring of freedom to a slave, and of the entirety of Israel, e.g., from subjugation to self-government. The "redeemer" could be one who ransomed a kinsman or restored to its original ownership property that had been inherited and then sold. The act of redemption then carries out familial responsibilities, in which one member of a family is responsible to save or redeem another person or property belonging to that same family.

Red Hats (Tibetan *zhva-dmar*), name given to an important lineage of the Buddhist Kagyu-pa incarnations founded by and closely associated with the Black Hat, or Karma-pa, lamas. Typically, the Karma-pa recognizes and trains the new Red Hat lama as his regent. When the Karma-pa dies and the next Karma-pa incarnation is found, it is the responsibility of the Red Hat lama to educate the child in the traditions of his predecessor, the previous Karma-pa. The term *Red Hat* is sometimes used by Westerners to refer to schools of Tibetan Buddhism that are not "Yellow Hats," i.e., the Geluk-pa lineage. *See also* Geluk-pa; Kagyu-pa; Karma-pa.

Red Sea (Sea of Reeds), crossing of the, in the Hebrew Bible, a miraculous parting of the waters that allowed the Israelites to escape while the pursuing Egyptians were drowned (Exodus 14).

reductionism, the practice of giving an account of a social phenomenon (belief, action, experience, practice, institution) in terms that differ from those employed by the agent to which the belief or action is ascribed, or by the culture of which that practice or institution is a part.

A reduction is a purportedly exhaustive translation of a theory or description of a phenomenon in terms that differ from those in which the theory or phenomenon has been identified. The term comes from the philosophy of science. Some philosophers of science have distinguished between theoretical statements and observation statements, and then attempted to translate, or reduce, theoretical statements to statements about observables.

In the study of religion, reductionism has become an epithet used of any attempt to describe or explain a religious phenomenon in nonreligious terms. Much depends, of course, on how one draws the boundary between religious and nonreligious terms. It has become common to criticize psychological, sociological, economic, or even historical accounts of religious phenomena as reductionist. For example, a psychoanalytic explanation of Paul's conversion experience or of the mystical experience reported by Teresa of Avila, or an economic explanation for the Reformation might be criticized as reductionist.

In fact, reduction is an ordinary product of explanation. The steam rising from a kettle may be redescribed in terms of the motion of water particles in air, or in terms of the molecular and atomic structure of those particles, depending upon the purpose of the inquiry. Both redescriptions employ the language of physics. Sometimes reductions cross disciplinary boundaries. Biological phenomena are described in cellular or molecular terms, and understood as chemical processes. Those processes may be explained within the language of physics. Early in this century, some philosophers of science embraced the goal of a unified science, in which all scientific theories would be reduced to one canonical set of terms and laws, usually thought to be those of physics. Most now doubt the possibility of a single unified science, and reject it as an ideal.

Religion includes beliefs, emotions, actions, practices, institutions, and other social phenomena. For the study of religion, a distinction must be drawn between descriptive reduction and explanatory reduction. The former is illegitimate, but the latter is not.

Descriptive Reduction: The objects of the human sciences differ from those of the natural sciences in that they are identified by a description. Any action, attitude, emotion, practice, or product of human activity must be so identified. A single event may be described in several different ways: flipping a switch, turning on a light, signaling by a prearranged code, alerting a burglar, or by any one of a number of descriptions. The appropriateness of the description depends upon context. When describing an action, one must identify it with a description that captures the intention of the agent. The agent intended to turn on the light, so one can ascribe that action to the agent. The burglar was alerted, but the agent did not intend or try to alert the burglar.

Similarly, an experience is identified by a description. Paul experiences the risen Jesus on the road to Damascus. A Sufi mystic describes his experience as total absorption in Allah, a kabbalist as *devekut*, or adhesion to God, a Madhyamaka Buddhist as *sunyata*, or emptiness. These descriptions, with their references to the cultural systems in which these terms have their meaning, are intrinsic to the experience.

Descriptive reduction is illegitimate. An accurate account of an action, experience, or practice must identify it using the description employed by the actor or the person who has the experience. William James, the nineteenth-century philosopher, quotes Sarah Edwards on her experience of a "constant, clear, and lively sense of the heavenly sweetness of Christ's excellent love." She writes, "I seemed myself to perceive a glow of divine love come down from the heart of Christ in heaven into my heart in a constant stream, like a stream or pencil of light" (William James, *The Varieties of Religious Experience*, 1902). To describe this experience as simply one of a stream or pencil of light would be to lose the experience that Edwards reports.

An experience must be identified with a description that can be ascribed to the person who had that experience. An action must be identified with a description that can be attributed to the agent. In order to understand a belief, action, experience, practice, or institution, one must master the language, the cultural symbols, and the grammatical rules that govern linguistic and social behavior in the culture in which the action, experience, or practice is ensconced. To understand the experiences reported by Teresa of Avila, one must learn the concepts, beliefs, assumptions, and practices of sixteenth-century Spanish Counter-Reformation Catholicism. Ignorance of this context leads to descriptive reduction, the failure to capture the grammatical structure and conceptual relations that are constitutive of those experiences.

Explanatory Reduction: While a belief, action, experience, or practice must be identified using a description that is couched in the language of the agent or culture to which it is attributed, this restriction does not hold for an explanation of that belief, action, experience, or practice. After describing Teresa's experiences in the language of her culture, one might go on to offer a psychoanalytic hypothesis to explain those experiences. Or the explanation might be couched in the language of social psychology, or of economics, or theology. These explanatory hypotheses need not be restricted to the concepts and beliefs that were available to Teresa. One can speak about economic and social strata in fifth-century Athens, and cognitive dissonance among Jesus' disciples after his death, even though these concepts and the theories associated with them were not available in Athens or Jerusalem. Explanatory reduction is legitimate and is a normal part of explanation. Regardless of the form of explanation, whether a narrative is constructed or reference is made to covering laws and initial conditions or to structural relations or other kinds of causes, that which is explained is set in another, more comprehensive, context. The explanation is usually and properly formulated in terms that differ from those in which the phenomenon is described.

The theorist has no obligation to restrict the terms of his explanation to those that would be understood by the agent or culture he is studying. The adequacy of the explanation is judged by its comprehensiveness and its plausibility with respect to the beliefs and assumptions of the theorist, and not those of the culture under study.

Concern about reductionism in the study of religion is often part of an apologetic strategy designed to show that there is a religious dimension of human experience that cannot fully be accounted for in naturalistic terms. Confusion between descriptive and explanatory reduction often leads to the citation of examples of descriptive reduction, and the inference from those examples to the conclusion that reduction is illegitimate. That conclusion is then erroneously extended to all social, scientific, and historical explanations of religious beliefs, acts, experiences, and practices. *See also* religion, explanation of; religion, the study of.

Reformation, Protestant, a movement of religious reform in the sixteenth and early seventeenth centuries that created deep and lasting divisions within Western Christianity. Beginning as an effort to purify the life and teachings of the Catholic Church, the movement eventually produced separate churches that constituted a third major strand of Christianity alongside Eastern Orthodoxy and Roman Catholicism.

The label *Protestant* had its origin in a document presented to imperial assembly, the Diet of the Holy Roman Empire, meeting at Speyer, Germany, in 1529. Three years earlier the Diet had granted a measure of toleration to the followers of Martin Luther (1483–1546). When in 1529 the Diet and emperor rescinded that toleration, representatives of twenty principalities protested the action. Opponents spoke of those who made the protest as Protestants.

Gradually the name Protestant was applied more broadly and included not only the followers of Luther but also those of the Swiss reformers Huldrych Zwingli (1484–1531) and John Calvin (1509–64)—the so-called Reformed or Calvinist tradition. Anglicans called themselves Protestants during much of the Reformation era.

In the modern world the term is often used to include nearly all Western Christians who are not Roman Catholics.

By any but the narrowest of definitions the Protestant Reformation included people who were diverse in their patterns of religious life and thought. Disagreement and even hostility often existed, for example, between Calvinists and Lutherans. Yet there were unifying themes: an emphasis that people are justified before God by faith alone, not by works of love; the affirmation that all are equal before God, a theme expressed especially in attempts to narrow the gap between clergy and laity; appeal to the unique authority of the Bible; and rejection of the authority of the Roman hierarchy and, especially, the papacy.

While the churches of Protestantism continue in the present, the period of the Protestant Reformation may be said to have ended in the mid-seventeenth century, when the movement ceased expanding and the religious situation became more stable with the restoration of the monarchy in England (1660) and the end of the Thirty Years' War on the continent (1648). At that time the Lutheran tradition dominated in eastern and northern parts of the Empire and in Scandinavia, while the Reformed tradition was strong in Switzerland, some southern parts of the Empire, France, Holland, England, and Scotland.

In addition to the Lutherans and Reformed Protestants, other European Christians separated from Rome in the sixteenth century. Anabaptists and other sectarian groups came into being. If one defines as Protestants only the followers of Luther, Zwingli, or Calvin, these sectarians were not Protestants, for they often differed sharply from those Reformers in theology, religious practice, and social attitudes. But if one enlarges the definition to include all sixteenth-century Christians who broke with the Catholic Church in the name of religious reform, then these groups too belong to the Protestant Reformation. *See also* Protestantism.

Reformed Christianity. *See* Protestantism.

Reformed churches, denominations derived from the Reformed (Calvinistic) stream of the Protestant Reformation. As that tradition spread into Switzerland, France, Germany, Holland, England, Scotland, and Hungary, it produced national churches. French Protestants, called Huguenots, were subject to persecution during the wars of religion. They remain a miniscule presence in France.

Reformed people emigrated to America,

where they established churches. In 1628 Dutch settlers established the Reformed Church in America (RCA) with the organization of the Collegiate Church in New York. A second wave of Dutch emigrants came to America in the 1840s and founded the Christian Reformed Church (CRC). These people settled in western Michigan, and after a series of controversies with the RCA, decided to remain an independent denomination.

Within the Dutch Reformed communities in America, a controversy erupted in 1924 that led to the formation of the Protestant Reformed Churches of America. The theological debate emerged over "Common Grace," whether God extends grace to all persons, not just the elect, and hence whether unregenerate persons are capable of civic good. The Protestant Reformed Churches of America left the CRC over this issue in 1926 and still advocate a more open and flexible understanding of grace.

German Reformed people began to emigrate to America in the early eighteenth century. They organized the German Reformed Church in Philadelphia in 1747 and settled in Pennsylvania, North Carolina, and the Midwest. In 1863 that body changed its name to the Reformed Church in the United States (RCUS). It merged with the Evangelical Synod of North America (also a strongly German group) in 1934 to form the Evangelical and Reformed Church; that body merged with the Congregational Christian churches in 1957 to form the United Church of Christ. The Hungarian Reformed Church in America (HRCA) was formed in 1904 under the care of the Reformed Church of Hungary. In 1924 the HRCA agreed to join the RCUS and to preserve its ethnic identity by being called the "Magyar Synod." A small number of congregations dissented from that merger and voted to continue in association with each other by continuing the name of the Hungarian Reformed Church in America.

All Presbyterian churches are a part of the broader family of Reformed churches. Issues that have divided the Reformed churches are the interpretation of scripture, the authority of the historic confessions, interpretations of predestination, cooperation with other churches, and how to cope with intellectual developments of the modern world. Although most Presbyterian bodies still endorse the Westminster Confession of 1645, they differ markedly in their interpretation of its authority.

The various Reformed churches are loosely affiliated with the World Alliance of Reformed Churches and are also known as the World Presbyterian Alliance. Founded in 1975, it is head-

quartered in Geneva. It is made up of 173 churches from 86 countries, representing over seventy million people. The Alliance meets about every seven years and is advisory in nature. *See also* Calvinism; Protestantism.

Reform Hinduism, a number of influential movements and individuals in nineteenth- and twentieth-century India that effected significant changes in the Hindu tradition.

By the early nineteenth century, British power had spread throughout India. The encounter of Indian traditions with Western religion and culture provided the context for religious change. The British brought with them military might and technology and introduced an educational system incorporating ideas about equality and science.

Although initially they did not intend to interfere with religion, in time Christian missionaries criticized certain widely held ideas and practices. In *Indian Thought and Its Development* (1936), Albert Schweitzer argued that when the influential eighth-century Hindu philosopher Shankara held that the world was "illusion," he undercut the basis for ethics and social concern. Indian thought was world- and life-negating. This critique was echoed by missionaries who also criticized the use of images, child marriage, suttee, polygamy, dowry, and the low status of women.

As they reformulated Hindu belief and practice, Reform Hindus did not accept and reject such criticisms uniformly. As early as 1828, with the founding of the Brahmo Samaj by Ram Mohun Roy (1772–1833), radical changes were initiated. Perhaps less radical but no less involved in religious and social change were the Arya Samaj, founded in 1875 by Dayananda Sarasvati (1824–83), and the Ramakrishna Mission, founded in 1898 by Vivekananda (1863–1902) in the name of his spiritual preceptor Sri Ramakrishna (1836–86), the Bengali mystic. Rabindranath Tagore (1861–1941), the literary giant, and Mohandas K. Gandhi (1869–1948), who led India's fight for independence, also made a significant impact. Individual thinkers such as Aurobindo Ghose (1872–1950), who worked for Indian independence before retiring at Pondicherry in South India, and S. Radhakrishnan (1888–1975), who had a distinguished academic career and served as president of India, had a strong influence on religious change.

Religious Thought: An important issue was religious authority. Ram Mohun Roy held reason to be a test to which any religious idea or practice must conform. Attracted by Christianity and

Unitarianism, he held the ethics of Jesus in high regard, but could not affirm the doctrine of the Trinity because he considered it irrational. Dayananda Sarasvati reaffirmed the authority of the Vedas and found many modern technological inventions prefigured in the Vedic texts. Perhaps the most influential view, however, was that religious experience was the final authority. Ramakrishna had numerous mystical experiences on which he based his affirmation that all religions are true. In prison for activities related to the independence movement, Aurobindo experienced the entire world as part of Krishna. This vision made him reluctant to see the world as less than real. In his mature thought, he built an imposing system on his mystical experience and extrapolations from it. Radhakrishnan also held that religious experience was fundamental and doctrine was simply reflection on that experience. If the Upanishads held a special place, it was because of the experience of which they were expressions. All of these thinkers interpreted received texts in the light of religious experience and overrode those texts if religious experience demanded it.

Another issue was the nature of ultimate reality. In the face of criticisms against idolatry and the Christian promotion of monotheism, both Dayananda Sarasvati and Ram Mohun Roy affirmed one God. Roy held that this was taught in the Upanishads, while Dayananda found it in the *Rig Veda*. Although the *Rig Veda* contains hymns to a variety of deities, Dayananda held that it taught one God under a variety of designations. While Radhakrishnan held that ultimate reality was beyond personality and that the personal deity was a lower level of spiritual perception, Ramakrishna sought to hold to both the personal and the impersonal. Having claimed experiences of both, he could maintain that both were a necessary part of ultimate reality. The Brahmo Samaj and the Arya Samaj opposed the use of images. Radhakrishnan was less radical, holding that they were useful for persons of lower spiritual attainments. Ramakrishna, however, was a temple priest and found the use of images no barrier to spiritual experience.

The value and reality of world are affirmed by most Reform Hindus. Radhakrishnan, following Vivekananda, argued that while the world was not ultimately real, it was relatively so, and while it remained, activity was mandated. Arguing against the criticism of missionary theologians and Schweitzer, he sought to find a foundation for ethics and social action. Even the doctrines of *karma* (the consequences of meritorious and

demeritorious action) and rebirth, which were frequently given as a reason for fatalism, were seen as offering opportunity for free choice. Karma was like a hand of cards dealt to individuals at birth that could be played poorly or well. On that one's future depended and in that consisted one's freedom. Ram Mohun Roy and Dayananda Sarasvati also affirmed the world, as did Aurobindo, whose evolutionary system sought to perfect and divinize the world rather than to transcend it. Gandhi's work for independence and his social concern would never permit him to deny the reality of the world, and Rabindranath Tagore's more aesthetic approach to religion was predominantly affirmative.

Most Reform Hindu thinkers and movements held to some form of universal religion in the face of Christian exclusivism. Ram Mohun Roy was convinced that everyone would accept the monotheism he found in the Upanishads. Radhakrishnan argued that the religion of the Spirit was universal and was the spiritual trunk from which all religions branched. By placing the emphasis on religious experience rather than doctrine or ritual he, and thinkers such as Aurobindo and Ramakrishna, could affirm that experience as basic to all faiths. Universality and tolerance were commonly affirmed, with the exception of Dayananda Sarasvati, who sought to convert Muslim and Christian converts back to Hinduism.

Many Reform Hindus also demonstrate an apologetic thrust. In the face of apologetic Christianity, they learned to defend their faith with equal vigor. They held that their faith was scientific (based on experience) and that there was no room for the kind of hostility between science and faith that Christianity had experienced. Moreover, Radhakrishnan held that Hinduism was quite modern. The caste system provided the possibility for all people to realize their spiritual potential and thus it embodied a spiritual democracy. Emphasizing tolerance, Radhakrishnan held that for true Hindus there were few places dedicated to God in which they might not worship and few prayers in which they might not reverently join. The Ramakrishna Mission continues to this day to celebrate Christmas along with Hindu holidays.

Social Issues: Perhaps more striking than the ideological ferment were the questions about the social dimensions of traditional religion. Some of the issues opposed by the Brahmo Samaj from its inception were also opposed by other groups. Several such issues impinged on the status of women. There was strong opposition to child marriage, which, because of the proscription against widow remarriage, was particularly hard on young widowed girls. Polygamy seemed to make women more property than partners. Suttee, the practice of a widow throwing herself on the funeral pyre of her husband, was opposed. The Arya Samaj allowed widows to remarry if they were not past a certain age and favored divorce under exceptional circumstances. They also opposed the practice of dowry whereby the bridegroom demands a fixed sum from the bride's father at the time of marriage. When Reform Hindus accepted caste, it was based on character and qualities rather than on birth. Even Gandhi supported some form of caste, but he rejected the notion of untouchability, calling untouchables Harijans, or "children of God." Untouchability and proscriptions against interdining and intermarriage were often seen as accretions that had attached themselves to an originally pure arrangement. On the positive side, female education was supported and women were permitted to read the Vedas, a prerogative previously reserved for males of the three upper classes.

Reform Hinduism effected changes, but it was not discontinuous with its religious past. However radical the Brahmo Samaj might be viewed, Ram Mohun Roy believed that his monotheistic view was to be found in the Upanishads, Dayananda Sarasvati accepted the Vedas as the foundation of his teaching, and Radhakrishnan firmly believed that he was simply expounding the misunderstood views of the influential eighth-century philosopher Shankara. Radhakrishnan wrote commentaries on the Upanishads, *Brahmasutras*, and *Bhagavad Gita*. Worship of the Mother Goddess was important to Ramakrishna, and Aurobindo wrote essays on traditional texts. While these thinkers were intent on making changes, they were equally confident that they were not leaving their tradition.

Embodying a new Hindu self-consciousness, these reformers were, in a sense, formulating rather than reforming Hinduism. While defending Hinduism, Radhakrishnan was also defining the "Hinduism" that he was willing to defend.

Whatever village Indians thought and practiced, and whatever the texts of previous ages might be taken to mean, Reform Hindus of the twentieth century were optimistic. Karma and rebirth were not the basis for fatalism but of hope for the future. Radhakrishnan's definition of Hinduism was so persuasively presented that he convinced many Hindus and Westerners alike that Hinduism was what he said it was, that is, that the real thing did indeed resemble his

ideal system. *See also* Arya Samaj; Brahmo Samaj; caste; Gandhi, Mohandas Karamchand; Hinduism; Hindu Renaissance; Shri Aurobindo; Vivekananda.

Reform Judaism, a modern movement growing out of the eighteenth-century European Jewish experience of political emancipation and intellectual participation in the Enlightenment. It is also known as progressive or liberal Judaism.

Reform Judaism is both an attempt to adjust classical Judaism to changes in its external situation, especially those elements leading to increased social and cultural integration, and an effort at internal self-criticism of the received tradition.

German Reform: Reform Judaism may be understood as an attempt, within German Jewry, to convert Judaism from an ethnic identification to a voluntary association, from a total way of life to a religion defined by a set of beliefs. As such, early Reform represents the reconstitution of Judaism according to contemporary Protestant models. Saul Ascher (1767–1822) in his work *Leviathan* (1792) rejected adherence to the totality of the law (Heb. *Torah*) as the prime characteristic of Judaism, delimiting a set of beliefs (e.g., God of love) and practices (e.g., circumcision, Sabbath observance) as constituting essential Judaism and leading to an internal spiritual fulfillment of the individual.

The earliest efforts at reform focused on the liturgy. In the German kingdom of Westphalia, Israel Jacobson (1768–1828) experimented, from 1808 to 1813, in creating a synagogue that was solely devoted to worship (analogous to a Christian church), eliminating "oriental" elements from the service (especially modes of chanting) and introducing a rite of confirmation adapted from Lutheranism. In 1813, Jacobson moved to Berlin and established a synagogue that featured a rabbi in vestments giving sermons in German on the Christian model, vernacular hymns, a boy's choir, and an organ. In 1817, the "New Temple Association" of Hamburg was formed. Implicit in the title is the rejection of the hope for the rebuilding of the Temple in Jerusalem as well as the notion that the synagogue is an interim institution, serving only until the Temple is rebuilt. The Hamburg *Prayerbook* (1819) gave expression to this acceptance of life apart from the land of Israel by removing references to the Temple and the return to Zion and by excising particularist passages concerning Israel's election.

The somewhat eclectic experiments in liturgical reform that characterized this movement in the early nineteenth century soon yielded to a more thoroughgoing and systematic effort. A generation of German rabbis, trained both in traditional seminaries and in secular universities, brought the historical-critical methods of scholarship, central in Protestant studies of the Bible and church history, to bear on both the Hebrew Bible and the totality of rabbinic tradition. This approach, the *Wissenschaft des Judenthums* (Ger., "science of Judaism"), is associated with figures such as Abraham Geiger (1810–74) and Samuel Holdheim (1806–60), who would come to be seen as the founders of Reform Judaism, as well as Zacharias Frankel (1801–75), who would be identified with Conservative Judaism.

For Geiger, both the written and oral Torah was to be understood as a progressive, ever-changing body of tradition shaped by historical contingency. This provided one criterion for reform. If the historical conditions have changed, the law no longer applies or must be reformulated to be adequate to the present. A second criterion is the nature of Judaism itself. As did Saul Ascher, Geiger held that Judaism is not to be defined by adherence to traditional law but is, rather, a spiritual "essence," a revelation of "ethical monotheism" that was expressed, in timebound fashion, in its laws and rituals. Laws and rituals that no longer express this essence must be abandoned or refashioned. Holdheim represents a more radical impulse toward reform. Using the same sort of historical scholarship, he defined the present in terms of German Protestantism. Hence, in Holdheim's synagogue, the specific commandments were abrogated, the traditional liturgy was abbreviated and recited, with a few exceptions, in German, and the Sabbath was transferred to Sunday. He redefined the essence of Judaism to be a messianic universalism.

From 1844 to 1846, some forty German rabbis, influenced primarily by Geiger, met in three conferences to consolidate reform. While their plans for a revised prayer book and for undertaking radical reforms such as the full participation by women in religious services were not realized, their decisions provided a checklist of practical items that would become hallmarks of Reform Judaism: the voluntary use of Hebrew in the liturgy and the elimination of all particularism, especially prayers for the return to Zion, the rebuilding of the Temple, and the reinstitution of the sacrificial system.

From 1850 on, Reform Judaism became an effort of increased organization until, by 1870, it became the dominant mode of Judaism in Germany. While never effective in eastern Europe, reform movements spread throughout western Europe and England, culminating in the establishment of the World Movement for Progressive Judaism in London in 1926.

American Reform: With the immigration of German Jews to the United States beginning in the early nineteenth century, Reform Judaism began its American phase. The Har Sinai (Heb., "Mt. Sinai") Congregation in Baltimore, Maryland, founded in 1842, is the first successful Reform synagogue in North America. The Pittsburgh Platform (1885), written under the leadership of Kaufmann Kohler (1843–1926) and Isaac Meyer Wise (1819–1900), formulated the classical expression of American Reform Judaism. Judaism is a religion progressing in accord with reason, not a nation. Its beliefs are centered in the moral laws of Torah and its mission was one of social justice. All commandments not in accord with this ethical imperative and with the spirit of the times are to be rejected. Along with the platform, this first stage of American Reform generated a number of organizations that still play an important role: the Union of American Hebrew Congregations (1873), Hebrew Union College (1875), and the Central Conference of American Rabbis (1889).

While the commitment to social justice and the ethical interpretation of the Jewish tradition remain central features of American Reform, subsequent generations, especially as evidenced in the Columbus Platform (1937), prepared under the leadership of Samuel Cohon (1888–1959), were more encouraging toward the use of Hebrew and traditional symbols and rituals. The platform also supported Zionism for the first time as a desirable goal for Reform Judaism.

In the 1990s, Reform Judaism is most dominant in North America, with over one million members. While there is a small but active Reform movement in Israel, Reform Judaism, as well as Conservative and Reconstructionist Judaism, is not recognized by the Orthodox Israeli rabbinate. *See also* Conservative Judaism; Judaism, prayer and liturgy of; Orthodox Judaism; Reconstructionism; Wissenschaft des Judenthums; Zionism.

reincarnation, belief in the rebirth of the soul in successive life forms. *See also* afterlife; metempsychosis; rebirth; soul; Umbanda.

reincarnation (Indian), the notion that life does not end at an individual's death but is transformed into other forms. Reincarnation in India is probably as old as the agricultural ethos of the

Neolithic period (ca. 2300–1500 B.C.). Later, the idea finds possible expression in Vedic songs (twelfth century B.C.), in which the spirit enters onto either the "path of the gods" or the "path of the fathers," the latter possibly a reference to the human world. It also finds implicit expression in rites said to ensure the sacrificial patron's future existence with the gods. Upanishadic, Buddhist, Jain, and Yogic philosophers subsequently generalized that the way to avoid repeated death was to avoid rebirth. All types of behavior, including thoughts and especially desires (because desires lead to thoughts, which lead to actions), constituted ethical and psychological seeds, the fruits of which would be borne in future lives. Hindu and other teachers cosmologized this system of rebirth: pure, unselfish acts lead to life in the realm of the gods; emotional acts to a return to life in the human world with its social gradations; and impure, selfish acts to rebirth as an animal, plant, or even mineral. *See also* devayana/pitriyana; karma; liberation; merit.

Reiyukai (rei-yoo-kai; Jap.), a Japanese new religion preaching the value of the Buddhist *Lotus Sutra* and the importance of venerating one's ancestors. Teaching the consequences of neglecting ancestral spirits, Reiyukai asserts that all problems are manifestations of one's own shortcomings. It strongly affirms respect for the ancestors, elders and seniors, and the duty of the wife to honor and obey her husband.

Reiyukai developed during the 1920s in Tokyo from the teaching of Kubo Kakutaro, Kotani Yasukichi, and his wife, Kotani Kimi. Kotani Kimi's charismatic personality was the mainspring around which the movement developed, but it also proved a hindrance to greater expansion as Kimi was unable to accept divergence from her own prescribed teachings. One prominent member who was forced to leave Reiyukai was Niwano Nikkyo, who departed in 1938 to establish Rissho Koseikai, which reflected many of the themes of Reiyukai but rapidly overtook it in size. *See also* Japan, new religions in; Lotus Sutra.

relativism, the view that knowledge and morals are relative to historical epoch, to society, to conceptual scheme, to scientific worldview, or to personal conviction. Relativism is often contrasted with absolutism, the view that there are criteria or standards by which claims can be fairly, neutrally, or objectively judged and assessed. Most philosophers have rejected relativism (at least about knowledge) on the basis of

arguments reaching back to Socrates; but the view does seem to have the support of common sense, and so continues to find defenders.

Versions of Relativism: One may begin with relativism about knowledge. Here one may contrast "strong" with "weak" relativism. According to Socrates (ca. 470–399 B.C.), Protagoras holds that "Each one of us is a measure of what is and of what is not. . . . To the sick man his food appears sour and is so; to the healthy man it is and appears the opposite. Now there is no call to represent either of the two as wiser—that cannot be—nor is the sick man to be pronounced unwise because he thinks as he does, or the healthy man wise because he thinks differently. . . . In this way it is true . . . that no one thinks falsely" (*Theaetetus*). Thus, for Protagoras, a statement or belief is true whenever someone holds it; it is true if it seems true.

A weaker relativism merely claims that the adjudication of truth is impossible. In this view, there may in fact be an objectively correct position and one that is objectively false; but the claim is that one can only bring one's own criteria to bear, while the person holding an opposing view can only bring his or her criteria to bear. In this view, truth is objective, while its criteria are subjective. Thus, the strong relativist would hold that it may be true (for most Westerners) that parrots are not persons, but also true (for certain Brazilian tribesmen) that parrots are persons. The weak relativist would hold that, objectively speaking, either persons are or are not parrots; however, it is fruitless to ask who is right, for one can only appeal to one's own standards of justification.

Similar positions have been defended with regard to moral claims or beliefs. "Strong" moral relativism says that moral truth is relative to such factors as the attitudes of the speaker, the age or society in which the moral claim is made, the laws and agreements under which people live, and the like. The weaker relativism merely denies that there can be a rational choice between competing moral beliefs; it does not deny that there is an objectively right (or at least best) course of action, but only that one could ever be in a position to know that one had found it.

Moral relativism has often seemed attractive to persons who reject a relativism about knowledge. To such persons, it seems a matter of brute or objective fact (not just "for me" but for all knowers) that either a parrot is or is not a person; but whether, for example, children have a duty to support their aged parents is a matter (so it is said), of convention, or of emotion, or perhaps of economic utility. Often such persons are moral relativists because they hold that moral sentences by their very nature cannot be true or false. And, since they cannot be true or false, one cannot determine which of two contradictory moral judgments is true and which is false.

Relativism and Religion: Relativism has found defenders both among those concerned with the scholarly or academic study of religion and, for different reasons, among believers themselves. Many in the first group are attracted to relativism, first, because it seems to respect the dramatic degree of divergence among the religions; under the term *religion* one must accommodate traditions ranging from ancestor worship to ethical monotheism to human sacrifice. Second, relativism seems to recognize that religious conceptual schemes or frameworks often organize the cognitive and moral experience of its practitioners. Relativism thus appeals to those who doubt or deny that one can adjudicate claims between conceptual frameworks—whole systems of religious belief—that have little or nothing in common. In such cases, there seems little basis for comparison, let alone adjudication.

Relativism has often seemed attractive to believers as an apologetic strategy. One way to insulate or protect traditional religious claims from, for example, scientific criticism, has been to segregate the two in a relativistic way: empirical or scientific truth is restricted to the natural world, while religious truth pertains to matters spiritual. In this way, a single statement—say, God created the universe in six days—can be both true (in a religious framework) and false (in a scientific one). There is, of course, a tension between this strategy and the traditional claims of religions for absoluteness and universality. To claim for one system of belief that it is true for all persons and for all times is the antithesis of all relativistic standpoints.

Criticisms of Relativism: Since Socrates, most philosophers have rejected relativism about knowledge on the grounds that it is self-refuting. If, as Protagoras maintains, knowledge is relative to the perceiver, then how can Protagoras defend one theory of knowledge over any other competing theory? For if knowledge is relative, then the task of judging claims to knowledge—as well as theories of knowledge—is pointless. Three contemporary American philosophers—W. V. O. Quine, Hilary Putnam, and Donald Davidson—have written influentially on behalf of Socrates's charge of incoherence. Whereas Quine's and Putnam's arguments aim to reveal an internal inconsistency in relativism—either that, if truth is culture bound, then the relativist ought to assert the absolute truth of that culture,

rather than relativism; or, that the relativist's claim (that assertion is impossible) undercuts what the relativist is doing (asserting the truth of relativism)—Davidson in 1973 or 1974 first develops a general theory of linguistic interpretation and then argues that relativism (about knowledge) cannot be right because it is incompatible with that theory. Davidson argues that interpretation is holistic; that, when one identifies another speaker's words, one presupposes that that speaker believes much that is true about what those words represent. For example, one cannot take someone who says "It is raining" to be talking about rain unless one also takes that person to believe what one believes about clouds, water, puddles, wetness, and so on. If, then, one claims to have interpreted much of another's vocabulary, the scope of presupposed agreement must be correspondingly enlarged. In this way, Davidson tries to cast doubt upon the idea of a conceptual framework that might be alien or radically different from one's own. When shorn of the idea of an alternative conceptual framework, relativism about knowledge comes down to the simple—and philosophically uninteresting—observation that no two persons have exactly the same web of belief.

The question arises whether any of these arguments are effective against moral relativism or against relativism concerning religion. Currently, it is hard to find much agreement on these questions among moral philosophers and theologians. The answer depends, of course, upon how one construes moral and religious judgments and beliefs. If one takes them to express factual, empirical claims, then the above arguments bear as much on morals and religion as they do on ordinary natural knowledge. If, on the other hand, one takes moral judgments and religious beliefs to be in some way noncognitive—if, for example, they are not empirical truths but disguised commands or expressions of emotion or aesthetic preferences—then the arguments seem misdirected. However, there is a price to be paid for this immunity. Once the relativist denies that moral or religious beliefs express (true) empirical claims, then any relativism about morals or religion becomes uninteresting. For, having ruled it irrelevant, the relativist can no longer claim that truth—or knowledge of it—is relative. *See also* religion, philosophy of.

relics, objects considered sacred because of their close association with holy persons. *See also* holy person; pilgrimage; shrine.

Christianity: Relics are things considered sacred by reason of their association with the saints. One may distinguish three classifications: actual physical remains in whole or part; things closely identified with saints such as clothing or personal possessions; and mementos touched to the bodies of saints or places sacred to them, most frequently tombs. *See also* martyr; miracle; pilgrimage; saint; shrine.

Buddhism: Relics, the venerated remains of the Buddha and of various other Buddhist saints, have been the object of worship in Buddhism throughout its history. Objects thought to have been part of the Buddha's body (bones, teeth, ashes, hair), his personal belongings (begging bowl, robe), or traces of his presence (footprints, shadows) have long attracted pilgrims throughout the Buddhist world.

According to one legend, the first venerators of the Buddha's relics were not his disciples but eight North Indian kings. Each received a share of the cremated remains, which he enshrined in a funerary monument (*stupa*). Later, these eight shares were retrieved by King Ashoka and redistributed into eighty-four thousand stupas all over his empire.

This intimate connection with kingship was to remain a feature of Buddhist relics. Possession of the Buddha's tooth, for example, often served as a legitimation of sovereignty in Sri Lanka; in China in the 1950s, another tooth of the Buddha (currently enshrined just outside of Peking) was sent on a great propaganda tour of South and Southeast Asia.

The veneration of relics by lay Buddhists has a more directly spiritual significance. Though denied by some, there is much evidence to suggest that the Buddha himself is thought to be "present" in his relics and so encounterable by devotees. At the same time, the relics, being dead bones, serve as powerful reminders of the truth of impermanence, one of the cardinal doctrines of Buddhism. *See also* devotion (Buddhism); impermanence; Tooth Relic.

Japanese Buddhism: The most notable relics in Japan are the cremated remains of Sakyamuni Buddha (*shari*). They have been known in Japan since 584 and large quantities were brought from China in the eighth century. Other relics have been discovered through dreams or other miraculous intervention. Generally the size of rice grains, they are kept in many prominent temples and are the objects of special services. Nevertheless, relics have never attained the religious and political importance they have had in much of the rest of the Buddhist world. Far more prominent have been the graves and artifacts of Japan's own sectarian founders and holy men. In modern times, Southeast Asian countries have donated relics to Japanese Buddhist organizations.

religion. *See* religion, definition of; religion, the study of.

religion, anthropology of. A field of study concerned with the lived significance of religious ideas, experiences, and institutions, and which formulates general propositions about the role of religion in human existence. Rather than attending strictly to doctrine or devotions, anthropology treats religion as a part of culture—that is, as integral to the common understandings, activities, and circumstances that shape a people's way of life. Heavily influenced by Emile Durkheim (an early-twentieth-century French sociologist), the anthropology of religion had traditionally investigated the ways in which sacred rites and representations foster social solidarity and shared sensibilities within communities of celebrants. Since the 1980s, attention has turned to the ideological uses of religion in legitimizing differences in status, power, and interests within and between social groups. Such holism enables anthropologists to compare religions across cultures to ascertain how and what different religions (or the same religion in different times and places) contribute to the personal, social, and political life of human individuals and groups.

When the anthropology of religion began in the nineteenth century, if focused largely on questions of origins and evolution. Taking religion to be a human universal indicative of the "psychic unity" of humanity, theorists such as Herbert Spencer, Edward Tylor, and Sir James Frazer argued that the apparent diversity of religions reflected the evolutionary stages through which human religion as a whole had developed. Tripartite sequences such as magic, religion, and science, or animism (belief in spiritual beings), polytheism, and monotheism were proposed. Although these sequences culminated ethnocentrically in European Christian civilization, the evolutionists laid the basis for further scientific studies by identifying cross-cultural similarities in religious beliefs and practices.

The difficulty of verifying the general origin or evolution of religion leads twentieth-century anthropologists to study the role of religion in specific tribal (kinship-based) or folk (highly insular, localized) societies. Particular attention is paid to the bearing that ritual practices and beliefs had on the social organization or psychological orientation of the society in question. Beginning in the late 1950s, the structuralism of Claude Levi-Strauss (a twentieth-century French anthropologist) and the symbolic studies of Anglo-American anthropologists such as Victor Turner, Edmund Leach, Mary Douglas, and Clifford Geertz begin to address less the social or psychological functions or religion than the intrinsic nature of religion itself, especially through the analysis of ritual and sacred symbolism.

Ritual: Whether ostentatious public ceremony or solitary private prayer, some form of ritual characterizes all religions. Anthropologists have variously proposed that ritual renews individual commitments to the moral and social order, focuses people's attention on matters of collective importance, allays anxiety in the face of uncertainty, establishes a personal sense of transcendent order in a disorderly world, sanctifies ideologies of rule and resistance. As a type of social behavior, ritual minimally involves the performance of specific acts and utterances, which, unlike habits, the performers themselves do not create but must follow according to publicly recognized canons. In discussing these "obvious aspects of ritual" in *Ecology, Meaning, and Religion* (1979), American anthropologist Roy A. Rappaport points out that invariance in ritual's form establishes a certainty of behavior, and therefore a kind of "truth"; ritualists must then enact—if not actually internalize—this truth by performing the ritual, for no ritual ever occurs without performance. Whatever its other ostensible goals, ritual's formalism precipitates fixed patterns of mutual, unambiguous conduct that can sanction further social coordination, cooperation, and trust among its participants. These formal patterns need not always imply formality, since rituals can dictate license and revelry as easily as dignity and restraint.

The overall structure of ritual also sets it apart from ordinary behavior. French sociologist Arnold van Gennep notes in *The Rites of Passage* (1909) that ritual generally exhibits a three-stage process of separation, transitions, and reincorporation: first, preliminal rites such as washing or other acts of purification separate participants from the mundane world; second, liminal rites work some kind of change or transformation in the performers or in the world around them (often a symbolic death and rebirth); and third, postliminal rites such as meals reincorporate ritualists back in everyday affairs. Sociologically, ritual tends to reduce the different social statuses and roles of participants to what Victor Turner (a twentieth-century British social anthropologist) calls *communitas*, a generalized bonding between individuals as whole persons. Behaviorally, ritual restricts conduct to the dictates of ritual elders vested with the authority—and authoritarian power—to preside over it. In

this sense, ritual appears to serve two contradictory ends. Because it constitutes a moment "in and out of [social] time," when individuals commune directly with one another freed from the normal constraints of society, Turner likens communitas to an "anti-structure" that renews the flexibility, creativity, and sense of personal transcendence essential to human cultures. At the same time, ritual is highly regulated and normative. Ritual embodies the tension found in all human sociality between individual willfulness and collective convention, the immediacy of interpersonal communitas and the need for social order. Because it establishes a purely conventional form that simultaneously enjoins otherwise autonomous individuals to conform to it, ritual is "the basic social act."

Symbolism: The sociological and behavioral formalism of ritual often contrasts with the richness of its symbolism. Symbols, because they are by nature things that stand for something else, beg definition—religious symbols doubly so because ritualists can often offer little explanation of their meaning beyond the need to use them in a ritually specific manner. Anthropologists generally attempt to discern the cultural—as opposed to personal or theological—significance of sacred symbols. They attempt to find in ritual objects, acts, and utterances evidence of a people's way of classifying (and thus thinking about) reality or of the way they organize, legitimize, and rationalize their society and themselves. This cryptographic approach assumes that religion represents a kind of language and ritual a mode of communication that together convey essential messages to those who accept their validity. In seeking to decode the multiple meanings presumably hidden in ritual symbols and performances, this approach demonstrates that sacred symbols relate systematically to social realities and that symbols can only be understood in relation to other symbols within a given culture and the social circumstances that precipitate their use. The question remains, however, if ritual symbols communicate such important information about the world, society, and self, why do they often do so in such obtuse or extravagant fashion? Is religion nothing more than a society's self-mystification by its own symbols?

Faced with such questions, some contemporary anthropologists such as Fredrik Barth, Dan Sperber, Roy Wagner, and Roger Keesing, among others, argue that sacred symbols carry no intrinsic meaning of their own but instead evoke personal meanings from individuals. The purpose of symbols lies less in conveying specific information than in bringing individuals together in what they take as intrinsically meaningful social action. Sacred symbols do this by reaffirming the motivated as opposed to arbitrary nature of symbolic meanings in general. That is, in any symbolic system, no necessary connection ties a given signal (word, act, object) to its referent (what it means or represents); instead, definitions must be agreed upon and learned by users of that particular language or culture. This otherwise arbitrary relation between symbol and meaning, sender's intention and receiver's understanding, undergoes constant relativization (loss of certainty) through idiosyncratic use, misuse, or outright lying. In the face of such indeterminacy, the enigmatic nature of sacred symbols provides a constant point of reference—what the contemporary American anthropologist Roy Rappaport calls "sanctity"—by associating concrete acts and objects with transcendent (and therefore absolute, unfalsifiable) propositions—e.g., "God is great"; "Ancestors punish transgressions." Since no one can categorically disprove the existence of God, ancestors, or the like, the validity of sacred postulated depends on the degree to which they are accepted rather than on objective proof. Once accepted, however, the purely conventional association between sacred symbol and transcendent referent becomes an enduring paradigm for symbolic associations in general. At the same time, the intrinsic vagueness of sacred symbols also means that the social precepts they embody remain eminently contestable, thus revealing their ideological as opposed to purely theological nature.

Because it seeks general propositions about the nature of religion in human societies, the anthropology of religion demonstrates more than the social, psychological—or even ecological—functions of religion. It also suggests that, far from needless mystification or extravagant afterthought, religion stands at the heart of our capacities as symbol-using—thus truly human —social beings. *See also* animism; ideology and religion; magic, science, and religion; origins of religion; religion, the study of; ritual; symbol.

religion, definition of. Defining religion is often held to be difficult. Introductions to the study of religion routinely include long lists of definitions of religion as proof of this. However, these lists fail to demonstrate that the task of defining religion is so difficult that one might as well give up on the task. What the lists show is that there is little agreement on an adequate definition.

A specific definition of religion usually comes from a particular discipline or theory of religion. Thus, definitions that refer to religion as social representations are rooted in sociological explanations of religion, and definitions that refer to religion as symbolic of some mental or unconscious reality are based in psychology. Although some definitions place theoretical limitations on what the term *religion* means, there is nothing inherently invalid or false about such definitions.

Inadequate Definitions: There are definitions of religion, however, that are troublesome. The source of the trouble is the definitions' vagueness and ambiguity. Definitions of religion as "ultimate concern," "worldview," or "the sacred" are examples. Such definitions are not only vague but also far too wide in meaning. For example, if religion is defined as "ultimate concern," then what prevents a concern for staying out of prison for being taken as religion? Moreover, such definitions often demand further definitions; one now needs a definition of "ultimate concern," or "worldview." Religion, given these kinds of definitions, could be just about anything. The same can be said of definitions of religion that define the term as a certain kind of experience, for example, "an oceanic feeling," or "the feeling of absolute dependence." Such definitions are of little use because of the vagueness of the terms *experience* or *feeling*.

There are also definitions of religion that are too restrictive or limited. Religion as "belief in God" is a good example. Although this definition would include all monotheistic religions, it would exclude all polytheistic religions, or religions without any god at all. This demonstrates that there is empirical evidence that can be used to test the adequacy or inadequacy of a definition of religion.

An Adequate Definition: One may clarify the term religion by defining it as a system of beliefs and practices that are relative to superhuman beings. This definition moves away from defining religion as some special kind of experience or worldview. It emphasizes that religions are systems or structures consisting of specific kinds of beliefs and practices: beliefs and practices that are related to superhuman beings. Superhuman beings are beings who can do things ordinary mortals cannot do. They are known for their miraculous deeds and powers that set them apart from humans. They can be either male or female, or androgynous. They need not be gods or goddesses, but may take on the form of an ancestor who can affect lives. They may take the form of benevolent or malevolent spirits who cause good or harm to a person or community. Furthermore, the definition requires that such superhuman beings be specifically related to beliefs and practices, myths and rituals.

Defining religion as a system of beliefs and

practices relative to superhuman beings excludes Nazism, Marxism, or secularism as religions. This definition also excludes varieties of nationalism and civil quasi-religious movements. *See also* religion, the study of.

religion, explanation of. An explanation is a description that allows one to understand something, or understand something at greater depth. All explanations entail truth conditions, e.g., that the explanation is correct or true. Explanations differ depending on situations. An explanation, for example, of the doctrine of *karma* will differ depending upon whether one is talking to a class of ten-year-olds, senior citizens with little formal education, or a university seminar consisting of graduate students in South Asian studies. Since the 1920s the term *explanation* has been given a restricted definition as an account of why some object, event, or state of affairs occurs. Explanations have to do with causes, laws, and predictions. Given this narrow meaning many scholars of religion think that any attempt to explain why religions exist and persist is a contradiction in terms. This conviction is a central theoretical issue in the study of religion. One of the reasons for the conviction is based upon the view that an explanation, in science, is best defined as a "deductive-nomological" process (nomological, from Gk. *nomos,* "law," means to place something under a law). In other words, scholars who insist that explanations cannot be applied to religion are assuming a specific theory of explanation.

The Deductive-nomological Model of Explanation: Although the deductive-nomological model was well known throughout the Enlightenment, it was refined in the twentieth century by scholars such as Carl Hempel, Rudolph Carnap, and Karl Popper. Following Hempel, an explanation consists of two parts. The *explanandum* is a description of the events or objects to be explained. Such events, objects, or states do not always entail why they occur, but often cover cases in which one explains why an event or state fails to occur. The *explanans* consists of premises that are made up of laws (or "lawlike" propositions) and the factual conditions in which the explanandum occurs. An explanation is a logical deduction of an event by subsumption under certain laws and factual conditions. A deductive-nomological explanation is an argument in which the explanandum deductively follows from certain premises in the explanans.

The assumption that scientific explanations entail the use of laws was in place long before Hempel produced the model that became definitive for such explanations. Laws of nature were necessary to explain and predict the origin and occurrence of events. The nineteenth-century philosophers John Stuart Mill and Auguste Comte are two examples of this "modern" approach to explanation that became known as positivism. Positivism contains three essential principles. First, although there are many intellectual disciplines and a diversity of research interests, there remains only one unified method that can be identified as science. Second, among the disciplines, mathematics and physics are the model, or standard, for defining scientific method. Third, scientific explanation is basically causal and consists of the subsumption of particular events under universal laws. Any attempt to explain events or actions by means of intentions, purposes, or goals is thus ruled out as unscientific. The scientific task is to discover the laws and the facts that will causally explain intentions, actions, and human aims. The continued existence, withering criticism notwithstanding, of behaviorism and sociobiology and the emergence of what has become known as cognitive science provide ample proof that the principles of positivism remain active.

The Functionalist Explanation of Religion: Functionalism has been identified as the primary theory of the social sciences and has become a commonsense theory of religion. It has also been described as a type of causal explanation.

The basic thesis of functionalism is that religion functions to fulfill certain needs in the society and in the individual. Religion functions to unify, integrate, maintain, or reduce anxiety in the social or personal system.

Although the theory remains popular, it is bankrupt. Most persons quickly find that the following type of explanation is fallacious:

1. The Indian social system is functioning adequately in a specific setting and time.

2. The society functions adequately only if certain needs (integration, maintenance, etc.) are satisfied.

3. If the Hindu pilgrimage to Banaras is present, then as an effect the needs will be satisfied.

4. Therefore, the pilgrimage is present in the specific setting and time.

The fallacy, of course, is a simple one. It is called the fallacy of affirming the consequent. It argues something like this: 1. If Mary oversleeps, she will be late for church. 2. She was late for church. 3. Therefore, she overslept. Many different things can be placed in number 2: she decided not to go; she became ill; had an accident. The only way this type of explanation can be made into a valid argument is by making premise 3 a necessary condition by asserting:

3. Only if the pilgrimage is present, then as an effect the needs will be satisfied. The problem, of course, is that this turns the explanation into an argument that is true by definition. Furthermore, no one would want to argue that an individual cultural trait, unit, or element is necessary to the maintenance or integration of a social system. The best that can be done with this kind of argument is to conclude that something or several things are functioning to fulfill the needs, but they cannot be identified. Or one can conclude that it is highly likely that the pilgrimage is functioning to fulfill the needs. Conclusions that argue that something is highly likely are neither true nor false.

Critiques of Positivism: Many scholars, especially in the cultural sciences, find the basic principles of explanation as defined by positivism far too restrictive (if not unattainable) in the study of human nature and history. The notion that explanation seeks causes and universal, predictable events was rejected as the standard for the study of history and culture by early-twentieth-century scholars such as Max Weber, Georg Simmel, Wilhelm Dilthey, and Benedetto Croce. The study of human nature, of history, seeks to understand what is unique and individual. Intentionality, morality, religion, all human institutions are not explainable by subsumption under universal laws.

This dualist point of view became a powerful force in the study of culture and religion. It split the scientific enterprise into two domains—the natural and the cultural. The two domains required two types or sets of explanations, which the Germans called *Naturwissenschaft* (natural science) and *Geisteswissenschaft* (cultural science). By the beginning of the twentieth century this dualism between nature/culture, fact/value, explanation/understanding, law/ideology became fully systematized in the work of Wilhelm Dilthey and Max Weber. The dualism is presupposed by scholars of religion who identify the study of religion as belonging to the broad discipline known as *Religionswissenschaft* (the science of religion).

The power of this dualistic approach to science and its influence on the intellectual development of the modern West cannot be overestimated. The basic thesis is that things human cannot be explained by natural law. For example, one can consider a common event, the crash of a commercial airplane. Experts, after careful sifting of the facts, together with the knowledge of certain laws, can explain why the crash (event) occurred. In fact, this causal explanation can also be used to predict the occurrence of such events. As a consequence all

planes of a certain type are grounded for careful inspection. Hempel's refined model of scientific explanation seems to describe this process of explanation perfectly. Yet Weber would point out that this kind of explanation is not an adequate account of the total event. The subsumption of the event under the cover of certain facts and laws does not and cannot explain the event as the tragic loss of life and suffering, loss of income to the airline, new regulations, loss of jobs, lawsuits, etc. The deductive-nomological model may well explain the physical, natural event of the crash, but it cannot explain the crash as a cultural or religious event. This is the domain of the cultural sciences, the domain of meaning, of action, intentionality. It demands a unique theory of understanding, empathy, or sympathetic participation in order to grasp, not the cause of the event but its meaning. In brief, cultural and religious events (actions) cannot be reduced to natural causes. Religion cannot be explained in the positivist sense of explanation. Meaning and value are not natural facts or events.

Most scholars of religion who agree with the above usually view the academic study of religion as antipositivist. Most of the scholars who agree with this theory, for example, Dilthey, Weber, Croce, and Otto, are positivists. Although they disagree with the first premise of positivism—that science is a unified, single method—not one of them rejects the notion that explanation in the natural sciences is best described by the deductive-nomological model. Where they do disagree is with scholars who think that this model can be used in a straightforward way for explaining cultural actions and events, including religion. Scholars such as Sigmund Freud (psychology), Emile Durkheim (sociology), Robin Horton (anthropology), E. O. Wilson (sociobiology), or Paul Churchland (cognitive science) who believe that the principles of positivism remain true for both nature and culture are simply viewed as reductionists.

The Demise of the Deductive-nomological Model: The assumption that the deductive-nomological model is the ideal standard for explanation is no longer viable in the 1990s. Philosophers of science have shown that the model is neither necessary nor sufficient for satisfactory explanations in science. Moreover, it is not the case that every satisfactory explanation need entail a law or a lawlike proposition. For example, take "Why did Jones get a rash?" as the explanandum. The explanans, "Because he was injected with penicillin," provides a satisfactory explanation for understanding why he got a rash. No law is needed. Much depends upon the situation or context. There may be situations in which some version of a covering law is needed for an adequate explanation, but this is not the case in all situations. Finally, there seems to be very little agreement on the nature of law. What is a law and what is an adequate description of "lawlike"? Are they universal? Are they general descriptions? Are they necessary? There is little agreement on questions such as these. The fact that there are no laws or lawlike propositions to explain why religion exists, or what it is, does not mean that an explanation of religion cannot be provided. This can be done in many different ways. Following Peter Achinstein (*Laws and Explanations*, 1971), each of the following items can be classified as explanations of the Hindu pilgrimage to Banaras: 1. A description of the actual event itself. 2. The fact of the pilgrimage in Hinduism. 3. The structure of the ritual event as a rite of passage as a state of affairs. 4. The propositional (semantic) attitudes that constitute the ritual. 5. The ritual as a cause of what certain Hindus believe and how they behave. The situation, the specific questions that define how deep, comprehensive, or complete an explanation will be, will provide a correct and proper understanding.

Religion as Worldview: The rise and the fall of the deductive-nomological theory of explanation has led many scholars to believe that it is vain, if not ethnocentric, to think that anyone could come up with an adequate explanation of religion. Explanations, like religions, are theory-laden, relative to a specific time and culture. One must think of religions as worldviews. Worldviews are neither true nor false; they are the frameworks from which people talk about what is true or false. There are neutral explanations. Thus, what is true or false is given in the framework of a particular worldview, lived-world, or form of life.

This approach to religion assumes that truth is relative to a specific culture or worldview. This popular approach can be classified as cognitive, or conceptual, relativism. Cognitive relativism assumes that assertions and observations about the world are relative to a specific conceptual scheme. This is not the obvious assertion that Australian religions will not have myths that include terms such as *snow* or *polar bear*. From the relativist point of view, the religions of the world cannot contradict each other because the concepts in one religion have different meanings than the concepts in other religions. In brief, the meanings of religions are incommensurable. This approach, however, is never pressed to its final consequences simply because they lead to incoherence.

Taken literally, conceptual relativism leads to the following conclusions. If it is true that what is meaningful, true, or real is given in the sense of a conceptual scheme, language, or religion, then:

1. There can be no genuine disagreement among religions.

2. In order to understand Buddhism or Judaism one would have to become a Buddhist or Jew, but how?

3. There can be no genuine translation of one religion or language into another—translation becomes impossible.

4. Finally, how would one go about confirming this explanation of religion?

If taken literally, relativists must somehow rise above all worldviews in order to make the assertion. But in doing so they would contradict themselves. Is the assertion "All religions are relative to a specific conceptual scheme" a universal assertion, or is it also relative to a particular worldview?

Explanation and Theory: To explain religion presupposes some theory about religion. To have a theory of religion is to have some notion about what the object of religion is. The object of religion is not empirically given but theoretically constructed. The explanation of religion is a theoretical enterprise; it is the production of knowledge. What does it mean to have a theory about some subject?

1. To have a theory about some subject is to have a set of propositions about the subject that one does not know to be true but believes to be plausible or true.

2. One does not know that the propositions are false; on the contrary, one believes them to be true or at least plausible.

3. One believes that the theory will provide a better understanding of the subject by explaining, interpreting, providing causes, or solving puzzles that have blocked competing theories.

4. One believes that the theory consists of propositions that assert what is the case, and that these propositions contain at least the central and distinctive assumptions of the theory.

5. One believes that there is no more fundamental theory from which these propositions can be derived.

6. Finally, the theory is not a set of rules but may contain certain rules.

See also reductionism; religion, the study of; theory.

religion, phenomenology of (Gk. *phainomenon*, "that which appears"), a branch of religious studies that focuses on descriptive rather than historical or causal understanding of religious expressions.

Phenomenology is the investigation of that which is observable—as distinguished from an explication of causes that lie behind appearances. As a general form of study it limits itself to describing rather than explaining experience. Applied to religion, phenomenological method takes many forms but always concentrates on exposing the specific nature and structure of religious experience.

Background: The phenomenology of religion is ordinarily understood in contrast to the history of religion, and together they comprise the two traditional divisions of the field of religious studies, formerly called "the science of religion" (Ger. *Religionswissenschaft*). As such they are both distinguished at least in principle from the normative, metaphysical approaches of theology and the philosophy of religion and are intended to represent an unbiased, descriptive method of construing religious subject matter.

These distinctions were set forth by the Dutch scholar P. D. Chantepie de la Saussaye in his *Manual of the Science of Religion* (1887). The phenomenological part of this work identified and described classes of typical religious forms found cross-culturally, such as sacrifice and prayer, the veneration of stones and trees, sacred times and places, scriptures and myths. Many religion scholars in Europe continued to use this inventorial style, but by the time of Gerardus van der Leeuw's *Religion in Essence and Manifestation* (1933) the method of the phenomenology of religion had developed from the earlier classificatory, taxonomic approach to a richer, more complex one that emphasized a special role and process of "understanding" (*Verstehen*).

Van der Leeuw's work brought together several features of method that are still associated with the movement: first, the need for a suspension of the phenomenologist's own preconceptions about whether the described religious phenomena refer to anything real or unreal, in order to, second, perceive the essential character of religious experience on its own terms; third, the use of comparative parallels to help disclose what is central about any given type or pattern of religious life; and fourth, the importance of understanding as a process that involves the interpreter's capacity to reconstruct the meaning of religious expressions.

Other notable figures associated with this "science of religion" tradition are the Scandinavian W. Brede Kristensen (1867–1953) and the Rumanian-born Mircea Eliade (1907–86).

Sometimes phenomenological approaches to religion derive not from the enterprise of comparative religion but from the philosophical tradition of Edmund Husserl (1859–1938) and Martin Heidegger (1889–1976). Each advocated that the task of philosophy is to attempt a systematic, faithful description of how humans experience the world, though Husserl carried this out in formal terms analyzing the structure of consciousness, and Heidegger demonstrated it through an analysis of "lived" meanings and ways that the world "discloses" its nature.

Common Features: Religion is a realm of human experience that constitutes a subject matter not just for belief and speculation but for description and understanding. Like any form of culture, e.g., art or the economy, religion has its own unique categories through which it perceives the world. By temporarily setting aside (i.e., bracketing) the biases of one's own interpretive position and by paying close attention to the special functions and organizing qualities of those religious categories—like ritual and myth —one can gain access to how religious symbols and practices function for the believer and thus constitute a "world." Evaluations about whether religious expressions ultimately refer to anything true or untrue are temporarily set aside in this process—the suspension of judgment that phenomenologists designate by a technical term, *epoche* (Gk., "to hold back").

In attempting to do justice to the character of religious life phenomenologists avoid describing their subject matter in terms that reduce it to other than religious factors. The phenomenon of religion, it is held, is precisely its religious meaning to participants, the lived, engaged relationship of humans with what is sacred to them, and therefore it is that relationship—the point of view of the insider—that should be the irreducible object of analysis.

A distinctive feature of religious experience is that it presupposes the existence of a power or presence that is other than human or that transcends ordinary life. Phenomenologists have used terms such as *the Sacred* or *the Holy* to designate this class of transhuman objects and focal points around which so much religious life revolves. To believers the Sacred may be manifest in a variety of ways, e.g., at holy places, in revered ancestral objects, through words of scriptures and names of gods, or even as an indwelling spirit within oneself. In *The Idea of the Holy* (1917) the German theologian Rudolf Otto presents what some consider a classic account of the multiple, nuanced aspects of religious experiences of "the wholly other"—unique feelings that he termed "the sense of the numinous."

Finally, for phenomenologists of religion the many behaviors and representations through which religious life is expressed reveal common, cross-cultural patterns, such as myths of origin and rites of purification, and these form parts of a general language of religion. The supposition is that comprehension of this language can help clarify the function of otherwise obscure images and behavior met in cultures other than one's own. Thematic material thus gives intelligibility and generic context to specific cultural variations.

Issues and Criticisms: The phenomenology of religion has been surrounded with controversy. One objection is that while the method claims a certain objectivity, it has in practice shown decided ideological positionings on the part of its expositors. Phenomenologies, it is argued, are always carried out in the service of particular interpretive purposes. Early versions tended to represent religious patterns in terms of a Western-oriented, evolutionary scale that reflected a commitment to the superiority of Christianity. Many phenomenologies use the concept of the Holy/Sacred in a reified, religious way, as though "the Sacred" were an actual ontological referent synonymous with "the Divine," and in these cases what was supposedly a descriptive enterprise becomes an implicit form of theology.

Conversely, other critics have taken the view that the phenomenology of religion is in fact too neutral or value-free, and argue that, because it fails to address directly the issue of religious truth, it is not fully capable of understanding or doing justice to religious experience.

Both versions of this debate—that phenomenology either over-interprets religion or underinterprets it—have shown the importance of how differences in theory determine differences in what counts as religious data and have thus served to advance methodological awareness in religious studies generally.

Another common criticism is that the phenomenology of religion deals too much in abstract, ahistorical ideal types and removes itself from the cultural and historical contextuality of religious life. The meaning of myths and rites, the argument goes, always reflects specific social locations and purposes, but these the phenomenologists typically ignore. Too often phenomenology posits or relies on uncritical, timeless typologies that are neither informed by nor applicable to culturally diverse settings. A related charge is that phenomenologists speak about the meaning of religious forms in general while overlooking what those forms mean in the lives of actual participants.

The phenomenological claim about the irreducibility or autonomy of religious subject matter has not gone unchallenged even within the field. Critics have held that in opposing reductionism phenomenology has itself reduced religion to a purely ideal religious level and has thereby insulated religion from all other forms of description and explanation. Partly as a corrective response, many modern religion scholars are investigating explanatory and interpretive frameworks that will create linkages with the social sciences.

To some, classical phenomenology of religion is an anachronism, living off the conceptual frameworks of previous eras and unable to offer clear criteria for what would count as a valid interpretation of religious material. To others pursuing versions of a more integrative, contextualist phenomenology that would overcome some of these criticisms, the movement is still a valid, ongoing attempt to describe religious worlds. Whatever the future of the phenomenology of religion, some of its features have, by assimilation, become premises of the larger, modern field of religious studies, particularly the idea of religion as a subject matter that can be investigated dispassionately, with comparative perspective, and without theological presuppositions. It is in this sense that the phenomenological standpoint has sometimes served as a general rallying term for an academic approach to religion that seeks to establish itself in the context of humanistic studies and secular university education. *See also* comparative religion; religion, the study of; typology, classification.

religion, philosophy of, in Western tradition, the discipline for the analysis and assessment of cognitive meaning in particular religious traditions. As a critical practice, it is at least as old as the ancient Greek posing of questions to Hebrew texts. As a distinct discipline within the study of religion, however, it emerges as the Enlightenment ushers in the new burdens of proof associated with Western modernity, and the Age of Faith yields to the Age of Analysis. In its Western setting, philosophy of religion is usually associated with the belief structure of the Judeo-Christian tradition, and bound up with the attempt by biblical religions to reinterpret their myths and symbols in light of the challenges occasioned by changes in intellectual culture and secular experience. In North America in the latter part of the twentieth century, philosophy of religion entails intellectual reflection on the meaning and truth of religious claims, principally oriented to a public, usually academic, audience.

It has been common until recently to distinguish philosophy of religion from the discipline of theology, understood as the systematic expression of the faith of a particular church-related or ecclesiastically rooted community. However, in view of the work of such philosophical theologians as Robert Neville, David Tracy, and Schubert Ogden, who urge the importance of public criteria in theology and its responsibility to the academy and the public, it has become increasingly difficult to make hard and fast distinctions between theology and the philosophy of religion.

In the 1990s, most practitioners either of philosophy of religion or of philosophical theology agree that their discipline cannot be limited simply to a sociological assessment or confessional narrative of what a particular religious group believes to be true, without consideration of whether those beliefs are in fact meaningful or true. Because philosophy of religion is philosophical, it can take as primary neither the self-authenticating datum of revealed scriptures nor the self-privileging endeavor of intratextual theologics. Because it is philosophy of religion, a subject matter that encompasses a broad array of cross-cultural material, it cannot serve simply as a prolegomena to Christian theology alone. But neither can the philosophy of religion presume that religion exists as some common universal underlying all religions; only positive religions exist, as Friedrich Schleiermacher argues in his 1799 critique of the Enlightenment's concept of natural religion, and the concept of religion itself needs to be recognized as a modern and Western concept, as Wilfred Cantwell Smith shows in *The Meaning and End of Religion* (1963).

Classical Sources: Early landmarks in the philosophy of religion include Benedict de Spinoza's *Theologico-Political Treatise* (1670), John Locke's *The Reasonableness of Christianity* (1695), and Gottfried Leibniz's *Theodicy* (1710). But it is principally in the work of David Hume, Immanuel Kant, and Georg Wilhelm Friedrich Hegel that philosophy of religion emerges in the early modern period. More than any other philosopher of religion, David Hume (1711–76) inaugurates the shift from the Age of Faith to the Age of Analysis; his versatile investigation of religion adds up to a devastating critique of any religion founded on revelation (*The Natural History of Religion*), miracles and prophecy (*An Enquiry Concerning Human Understanding*), or reason (*Dialogues Concerning Natural Religion*).

The problem of evil, which preoccupies a great deal of contemporary philosophy of religion, receives its classical formulation in the famous challenge to theistic belief that Hume issues in the *Dialogues:* "Epicurus's old questions are yet unanswered. Is he willing to prevent evil, but not able? Then is he impotent. Is he able, but not willing? Then he is malevolent. Is he both able and willing? Whence then is evil?" For the next two hundred years, religious piety enters into a fateful alliance with philosophical skepticism and becomes characteristic of a deep tendency of Protestant religious thought. Another Humean strain in philosophy of religion surfaces among twentieth-century analytic philosophers who stress the noncognitive nature of religious language while promoting its conative or expressive meaning.

Immanuel Kant's (1724–1804) contribution to philosophy of religion serves both to extend and deepen Hume's critique of speculative reason and to pose the possibility of establishing religion on the practical grounding provided by morality. On the Kantian thesis that knowledge extends no further than to mathematics and science, the classical arguments for the existence of God are shown to illicitly transcend the limits of human understanding. Historically, the impact of *The Critique of Pure Reason* (1781–87) has been to widen the gap between knowledge and belief. Because of the dualism between the noumenal realm of "things-in-themselves" and the phenomenal world of "appearances," Kant can consider the ideas of God, immortality, and freedom only as ideally regulative of human thinking, never constitutive of actual human knowledge. Even though Kant wishes to ground religion in belief rather than in knowledge, he considers these beliefs rational and fully defensible. In *Religion Within the Limits of Reason Alone* (1793) he argues that the experience of being obligated to obey moral law is unavoidably represented by the human imagination as though it is imposed by a divine lawgiver and thus moral reasoning leads directly to religion. Religion, however, does not occupy an autonomous space or claim a cognitive domain of its own, underived from the moral life. The revolution Kant introduced reverses the expectation that morality revolves around belief in God and substitutes the theory that belief in God revolves around morality.

Responses to the Kantian critiques generally

determine the various directions of philosophy of religion throughout the nineteenth and into the twentieth century. The efforts of G. W. F. Hegel (1770–1831) to abolish the Kantian ontological and epistemological dualisms resulted in a view of reality as constituted by the process of Absolute Spirit coming to gradual self-consciousness through a dialectical unfolding in history. The religious implications of this philosophical position are apparent in Hegel's *Lectures in the Philosophy of Religion* (1827), which depict his view of a dialectical progression in the history of religion, leading up to and culminating in Protestant Christianity. Religion for Hegel has unsurpassable content, but philosophy possesses the highest form; what religion must express figuratively and parabolically through symbols, philosophy can say literally and directly. In contrast to Kant, who claims he wants only "to eliminate knowledge in order to make room for faith," it can be said that Hegel removes faith in order to make room for knowledge.

Among those unwilling to follow either the Kantian relocation of religion within the limits of reason alone, or the imperialism of the Hegelian speculative system, is Soren Kierkegaard (1813–55), whose existentialist valorization of subjectivity becomes most influential, not in the nineteenth century, but in the twentieth, with its post-Holocaust distrust of reason and scientific progress. Accentuating the "absolute paradox" at the heart of the Christian religion's claim that the eternal has entered time, Kierkegaard stresses religion's role as "offense" and articulates the meaning of faith as lived from within the primacy of an individual's existence. His *Concluding Unscientific Postscript* defines truth equivalently with faith as "an objective uncertainty held fast in an appropriation process of the most passionate inwardness."

The young Hegel could trumpet forth the Promethean desire "to vindicate at least in theory the human ownership of the human treasures formerly squandered on heaven," but it is Ludwig Feuerbach (1804–72) who overcomes Hegel's oscillation between the human-subject and the God-object by coming down squarely on the side of the human. In *The Essence of Christianity* (1841) Feuerbach produces a new form of religious humanism that celebrates the truth of the divine predicates (love, justice, mercy, etc.) severed from any divine subject. Feuerbach sees the truth in religion as consisting in the relation of humankind to itself, and its untruth as an alienated product of projecting that nature outside itself.

Despite Feuerbach's infusion of materialist and naturalistic themes into philosophy of religion, idealism continues as the most influential philosophical view of religion throughout the nineteenth century. Whether among British idealists such as Thomas H. Green, F. H. Bradley, and Bernard Bosanquet, or in the work of the American Josiah Royce, the presence of philosophical idealism colors the selection of questions to ask and the ideas about what is problematic, e.g., how to reconcile the distinctiveness and freedom of the individual with the all-inclusive "absolute." Nineteenth-century exceptions to the rationalist temper of idealism include Rudolf Otto (1869–1937), who locates the basis of religion in the sense of the holy or the numinous, and Friedrich Schleiermacher (1768–1834), who grounds it in the "feeling of absolute dependence." Others, such as Albrecht Ritschl (1822–89), accept both the first and second of Kant's critiques and further refine the basis of religion in morality, while Friedrich Nietzsche (1844–1900), the evangel of the death of God, promotes the view that religion is a slave morality.

The American spirit in philosophy of religion, chiefly in the works of William James, Charles Sanders Peirce, and John Dewey, contributes a new form of pragmatic empiricism in philosophy that has important consequences for religious thought. James's classic *The Varieties of Religious Experience* (1902) draws upon widespread testimony by "sick-souls" and "healthy-minded souls" alike to reach the conclusion that "the conscious person is continuous with a wider self through which saving experiences come." Dewey's *A Common Faith* (1934) proposes that the "religious" be studied apart from existing forms of institutional religion and that "God" be used to designate the active relation between ideal ends and actual conditions. American radical empiricism and pragmatism represent a constructive alternative to positivist empiricism and the linguistic veto throughout much of the twentieth century.

Perennial Problems: Among the problems considered by philosophers of religion are the existence of God, as well as the coherence of any attributes predicated of deity; the validity of religious knowledge claims; the question of theodicy; the meaning and truth of religious language; the hope of immortality; the relation of faith and reason; the relation between religion and science; evaluation of the nature of religious or mystical experiences; and, more recently, the relations among world religions and the implications of religious pluralism. Given the prominence of ethical monotheism and the Western,

Eurocentric cast of philosophy, the topic of theism has been centerstage in most philosophy of religion. Arguments for the existence of God can therefore be taken as a kind of prism through which to view all the overlapping topics such as religious language, mysticism, immortality, theodicy, etc., in the successive historical stages of philosophy of religion.

Since their first formulations in the ancient period, theistic arguments show a history of evolution, with the ontological argument dominating until the Middle Ages, the cosmological and teleological arguments coming in for most scrutiny until the early modern period, and moral arguments receiving most interest since the late eighteenth century and Kant. Since the 1970s, all of these arguments, as well as other issues in religious epistemology, have taken on considerable intricacy and renewed philosophical interest. The ontological argument, which is an a priori mode of reasoning based on the concept of necessary existence, aims to show that the concept of God is such that God could not fail to exist, that is, that divine existence entails a necessary, rather than a merely contingent, mode of existence. Cosmological arguments, of which in the medieval period Thomas Aquinas (ca. 1225–74) offered three, dealing with change, causation, and contingent being, aim to show that there must be a "first cause," variously understood, to account for that which requires explanation. In recent versions, which exploit the sense of awe or wonder that anything should exist rather than nothing, even an infinite series of contingent causes requires an explanation in terms of a first, or highest, cause that is itself necessary or self-existent. Teleological or design arguments, in their post-Darwinian form, aim to show that theistic explanations are more probable than nontheistic explanations, either for individual cases of adaptation in nature or for the conjunction of these cases constituting the world as a whole. Moral arguments for the existence of God point to a supreme being as implicated in the fact of moral obligation, at least for any rational agent who acknowledges such obligation as having an absolute and unconditional authority. While all of these arguments fall short of proof, and each gives rise to important philosophical as well as religious objections, the discussion continues to supply relevant clarifications of the underlying issues.

For many philosophers of religion the fundamental problem for theism is the logically prior question of whether a coherent conception of God can be developed. In what has come to be known as process philosophy, based largely on the work of Alfred North Whitehead (1861–1947) and Charles Hartshorne (b. 1897), the alleged incoherence of traditional conceptions of God prompts the need for critically assessing the overall epistemic status of classical theism. Process philosophers of religion argue that temporality, becoming, and internal relations are just as definitive of deity as they are of creatures. Rather than make God an exception to metaphysical first principles, as classical theists did, process philosophers conceive God as their chief exemplification. By recommending the "principle of dual transcendence," Hartshorne shows that God contrasts with "creatures" not as an abstract infinite over and against the finite, but as a concrete unity inclusive of both the infinite and the finite. Conceived as a creative process at work immanently in all actualities, luring them toward self-transcendence, the divine power is regarded as persuasive, not coercive, and the standard notion of omnipotence gives way to a new understanding of relational power. The implication of this reasoning for the theodicy issue leads process thinkers to conclude that the "problem of evil" represents a refutation only of the utterly transcendent, completely omnipotent creator depicted by classical theism, and not of an evolutionary divinity in a pluralistic world of other self-determining creatures without beginning or end.

Contemporary Issues: With an increasing realization of the way in which thought and belief are shaped by language, philosophy of religion in the twentieth century has taken the form of inquiry into the type of utterances that express religious belief, as an attempt to make explicit the logic of religious discourse. As the problem of God has shifted from the ontological to the linguistic level, questions as to the truth of various religious beliefs have been transposed into considerations of the justification of convictional utterances and requisite conditions for a "happy speech-act." Considerable debate has surrounded such questions as, What are the logical relations between religious statements and statements in other areas of discourse? Are there special ways in which terms are used in religious utterances? To what extent should religious statements be construed as expressive of feelings and attitudes or as directions to action, rather than as factual claims? How is the nature and function of religious symbolism best understood?

Contemporary philosophy of religion encompasses two distinct but related tasks: the first deals with issues of justification and the rationality of religious belief; the second has to do with hermeneutical attempts to elucidate the distinctive character and meaning of religious practices, beliefs, and experiences. Those philosophers of religion whose interest is in questions of justifiability typically concentrate on the belief aspect of religion, with the apparent assumption that the elucidation of other elements of a religious system, such as ritual, moral choice, cosmology, etc., is ultimately related to the justifiability of some belief or set of beliefs. Some interpret the task of justification narrowly to consist in showing the rational defensibility of various religious beliefs, as though a minimal not-yet-proved-false defense could serve as a positive recommendation. Others maintain that sheer defensibility should not be confused with plausibility and that a stricter account of plausibility conditions also needs to be provided. Hermeneutical efforts in contemporary philosophy of religion usually focus on disclosing some common core or essence of religion, or exhibiting the distinctive grammar and rules of religious "forms of life." Purely descriptive accounts that aim only to elucidate the meaning and structure of religious life often circumvent the difficult justifiability and rationality debates, but at the expense of incurring the criticism that they harbor apologetic purposes. Both tasks, involving explanation as well as understanding, are essential to any fully adequate philosophy of religion. However, one of the recurring dilemmas of philosophy of religion is that elucidation alone is insufficient, while neither justification nor refutation is ever conclusive.

The contemporary recognition that a philosophical understanding of any one religion requires seeing it in relation to other religions has led to the growth of comparative studies. New calls for the creation of a comparative philosophy of religions share a concern that the discipline become more global in its orientation, comparative in its methodology, and empirical in its inquiry into the differences between specific religions. The comparative philosophy of religions is necessarily interdisciplinary, making as much use of history of religions and cultural anthropology as previous practitioners have made of speculative metaphysics and hermeneutical phenomenology.

Philosophy of religion in the 1990s is entering not only an emerging global era, with a new opening to the religious worlds of the East, but also a changed cultural situation summarized by the many meanings of "postmodernism" now proliferating in the West. Insofar as philosophy of religion studies the strictly intellectual interpretations of any religious tradition, it encounters beliefs, symbols, and ideas that are embedded in specific sociocultural power relations. Insofar as the discipline faces the challenge of encounter with traditions expressing practices and beliefs that are not predominantly associated with European, white, male modes of understanding, it will be required to elaborate new models of interpretation, a broader theory of evidence, a cross-cultural conception of human rationality, and a more complex appraisal of the norms applicable to cases of divergent, rival claims on comparative topics. *See also* agnosticism; atheism; belief; deconstruction; emotions; empathy; empiricism; essence; existentialism; experience; feeling; fideism; hermeneutics; instrumental and expressive; logical positivism; magic, science, and religion; modernism; mysticism; myth; natural religion; pantheism; process thought; projection; rationalism, intellectualism; reductionism; Relativism; religion, definition of; religion, explanation of; religion, phenomenology of; religion, the study of; religious experience; religious language; science and religion; symbol; theism; theodicy; theology; theory; understanding; universal and particular.

religion, psychology of, the description, explanation, and/or interpretation of religious phenomena by the application of psychological methods and theories.

Early Studies: Wilhelm Wundt (1832–1920) initiates the psychological study of religion in his Leipzig laboratory during the late nineteenth century. His approach, focused on collective expressions of religion in the distant past, did not survive him.

Wundt's student, G. Stanley Hall (1844–1924), transports the new discipline to America where he refocuses its attention to the experience of contemporary individuals, especially those converted in Protestant revival meetings. Hall's redefinition of the emerging field is echoed in the writings of his most prolific students, James H. Leuba (1868–1946) and E. D. Starbuck (1866–1947). Leuba relies primarily upon personal interviews for his data, while Starbuck combines interviews with questionnaires to gather self-reported introspective data. Starbuck's *The Psychology of Religion* (1899) is the first book-length study published in the field. In its focus on individual experience, especially conversion, Starbuck's book makes the religious values of Protestant America central to the psychological study of religion and also sets much of its agenda for the first half of this century.

Classic Works and Issues: The classic work of this early period is William James's *The Varieties of*

Religious Experience (1902). James (1842–1910) excludes all cultural dimensions of religion—myths, rituals, institutions, and social interactions—thus limiting religion to the feelings, acts, and experiences of individuals. He draws his sources from the diaries, letters, and occasional interview reports of those creative, if neurotic, personalities he called "religious geniuses." James's occasional efforts to construct a psychological theory adequate to explain religious phenomena were of little consequence for the field. However, his descriptions of discreet religious phenomena, especially his definition of mysticism and his narratives of conversion, have been used throughout this century.

In contrast with James's descriptions of religious experiences, Sigmund Freud (1856–1939) uses psychoanalytic theory to explain the origins and consequences of religion as both an individual and a cultural phenomenon. His writings on religion span virtually the whole of his professional career, from "Obsessive Acts and Religious Practices" (1907) through *Moses and Monotheism* (1939). In *The Future of an Illusion* (1927), Freud explains the origins of belief in God the Father as a projection created out of an adult's experience of helplessness and the childhood memory of a godlike father. He identifies such a belief as an illusion with harmful consequences for psychological development; it is regressive, trapping individuals in a lifelong posture of infantile dependency.

Freud's *Moses and Monotheism* appears to present a second, quite different, psychology of religion. In contrast with a God imagined as an external object of dependency, "the religion of Moses" promotes the internalization of paternal authority, thus providing the basis for the renunciation of instinctual gratification and illusion while furthering moral growth and intellectual development. However, Freud clearly distinguishes "the religion of Moses" from Judaism, and some recent scholarship suggests that his book on Moses is not really about religion, but part of the early-twentieth-century discussion concerning the distinctiveness of the Jewish people.

Recent feminist analyses of Freud's work have identified the pervasiveness of gender bias in his writings. Though much criticized, his developmental, dynamic, and structural models still serve as theoretical foundations on which others build alternative interpretations of religion.

Among religionists, Carl Jung (1875–1961) is probably the favorite of all psychologists: for example, his writings are cited extensively by Roman Catholics, New Age enthusiasts, and feminist advocates of a new spirituality. Unlike Freud's critique of religion, Jung identifies immediate religious experiences as essential to psychological health.

Jung's primary contribution to the psychology of religion is his theory that individuals are psychologically grounded in an unconscious not confined to themselves, but common to humanity, a "collective unconscious." For him, it is not religion that is an illusion, but rather the Enlightenment belief that each person is a rational and self-contained individual ego, with no connections to older cultures or life-forms of earlier evolutionary stages. According to Jung, both psychoanalytic therapy and religious experiences enable people to confront the otherwise repressed archetypes of their own unconscious. Archetypes are primordial potencies common to the human species but disclosed only through some particular symbolic expression: e.g., for many Christians, the Virgin Mary expresses the archetype of "the benign woman."

Unlike the work of Freud and the early Americans, Jung does not focus his attention on, or limit his sources to, the Western religions of Christianity and Judaism. As he finds the dreams of his patients to express religious symbols from Buddhism or Ancient Egypt, Jung begins a systematic study of Asian and archaic religions. In the myths and images of these culturally alien and long-forgotten religions, he finds most clearly expressed the wide range of archetypal symbols that animated the psyches of his mid-twentieth-century Zurich clients.

Gordon Allport (1897–1967) suspected that psychoanalytic psychologies of religion, Freud's in particular, are not valid in their conclusions because of the nature of their database. Their sample populations of patients are too limited in number and too psychologically abnormal to provide the basis for a psychology of religion. In *The Individual and His Religion* (1950), Allport sought to write a psychology, not a psychopathology, of religion. For this purpose, he constructed an elaborate questionnaire administered to a sample population of students at Harvard College. In a later study, also dependent on questionnaire data, he examines how prejudice is related to religious practices and beliefs.

Allport's method of inquiry has two distinct advantages: it expanded the database of earlier psychoanalytic studies and included the societal and cultural resources of adult religion. His survey instruments asked respondents to identify their denominational affiliation, frequency of participation in religious activities, creedlike beliefs, and similar items constitutive of religion as a social factor. In spite of his intention, however, Allport's theory is not adequate for integrating such objective social variables with the subjective attitudes and experiences of individuals.

In contrast, the primary contribution of Erik Erikson (1902–94) is a theoretical model able to accommodate both early interactions of an infant with parents and the cultural forms constitutive of an adult religious life. Erikson expands Freud's psychosexual model to require a consideration of societal institutions and cultural resources at each developmental stage. Parents and their children do not repeat the same script in every generation and culture, but parents mediate the changing demands and possibilities of their societies to their offspring. Erikson also extends Freud's five developmental stages beyond puberty to an additional three stages of adulthood. As a result, he formulates a psychology of religion in which the earliest ego strengths of the individual are repeatedly tested by the crises of adult life even as they are renewed and transformed by the religious resources of society. Conversely, the religious images and stories that nourish a mother's sense of basic trust also play a vital role in the development of her infant's earliest ego strengths.

Erikson's *Young Man Luther* (1958), while originally praised for its initiation of psychohistory, was later valued for its psychosocial developmental model in which early childhood experiences are repeatedly intersected by formative religious resources of adulthood. Erikson depicts Martin Luther's religious crisis as simultaneously a struggle with his own father, the Holy Father (the pope) in Rome, and the Heavenly Father. Luther's resources for healing included his mother's affection for him as an infant, his gentle confessor, Dr. Staupitz, the "maternal theology" of Augustine, and the Bible as "the mother he could at last acknowledge."

In Erikson's psychosocial developmental model, psychology of religion cannot confine itself to the interior experience of the individual (James), the earliest experiences of childhood (Freud), or the myths, creeds, and behaviors of adult religious communities (Allport). Instead, the field must focus on all of these as they interact with each other.

After Erikson, others have taken up his task of tracing religious development through adult stages. Paul Pruyser and William Meissner have been two of the most productive twentieth-century authors in this endeavor. James Fowler (b. 1940), in addition to Erikson, has also drawn on the work of Jean Piaget (1896–1980) and

Lawrence Kohlberg (1927–87) in his studies of "faith development" patterns. Fowler uses structured interviews for gathering data from participants in Asian, as well as Western, cultures. He seeks to identify a fixed sequence of faith stages that is not culture-dependent but universal, analogous to the order of stages in psychosocial, cognitive, and moral development.

In contrast with those who have focused on adult developmental stages, Ana-Maria Rizzuto, in *The Birth of the Living God* (1979), has directed her clinical and theoretical attention to the formation of religion in the earliest stages of childhood. Like D. W. Winnicott (1896–1971) and other psychoanalysts from the British object relations school, Rizzuto replaces Freud's categories of instinctual energies with the language of relationships. Like Erikson, she finds pre-Oedipal infant-mother relations to be more decisive for the formation of religion than the father-son conflict of the Oedipal crisis. According to Rizzuto, "God-representation" has its origins in the primary object representations of the pre-Oedipal child, but it is continually reinforced and modified by the growing child's observations of parental participation in religious rituals. For Rizzuto, this God-representation is neither an internal nor an external object, but something in between: as an object, God is most like the beloved blanket or teddy bear of the young child, a transitional object that enables the growing child to negotiate transitions between self and others.

While interpretations of religion that include societal and adult dimensions emphasize the positive consequences of religion, none of them ignores its destructive potential, for instance, as a moralism generating hatred for self and others as well as an inhibition to maturation.

Other Applications: Psychology of religion has not been confined to psychological theorists working in clinical or academic contexts, but has also influenced several related fields.

In the history of religions (or phenomenology of religions), Jungian psychology has consistently played the most prominent role. Because of Jung's early exploration of universal archetypes in Asian and archaic religious materials, others studying the same subjects found it natural to adapt some of his basic concepts (such as archetypes or collective unconscious) for their own work. This is apparent in the scholarly works of Mircea Eliade (1907–86) as well as in the more popular writings of Joseph Campbell (1904–87).

In the study of theology, Paul Tillich (1886–1965) is best known for his extensive appropriation and revision of Freudian insights in his own distinctive form of Protestant theology. Among Jewish theologians, Richard Rubenstein (b. 1924) has most frequently used Freudian materials, for instance, in his theological interpretation of the Holocaust. In feminist theology, Catherine Keller (b. 1953) merges process theology with a modified Jungian psychology, stressing its emphasis upon the connectedness of all human beings and corresponding denial of the separated ego as an adequate psychological model.

Finally, the field of pastoral psychology or pastoral counseling has been indebted to the theoretical work of psychology or religion since its inception. Oskar Pfister (1873–1956), Swiss Lutheran pastor and lifelong friend of Freud, is one of the earliest pioneers in this work. American publications in this field extend from a 1936 volume by Anton Boisen through the mid-century works of Seward Hiltner to the writings of Don Browning at the end of the century. Other indicators of the continuing importance of this field are the many clinical pastoral education programs for the education of clergy; journals and professional associations; and the recent emergence of pastoral counseling centers.

Psychology as Religion: Beyond all academic boundaries, psychology of religion has often been translated directly into the practice of religion through religious or quasi-religious movements. Jung's psychology has been the most frequently used resource in the service of spirituality. Other examples are the Gestalt psychology of Fritz Perls and the self-actualization psychology of Abraham Maslow (1908–70) as used in conjunction with Asian religions in the growth centers of the 1960s and 1970s. Robert Ornstein's psychology of meditation, with its use of biofeedback technology, and Stanley Graf's pharmacological studies of drug-induced religious experiences, were also appropriated in quasi-religious movements. In the 1990s, *Common Boundary: Between Spirituality and Psychotherapy* is both a magazine and a movement extending psychology into spirituality. The popular Twelve-Step Program, originally derived from Alcoholics Anonymous, is now available for an almost unlimited variety of addictions: e.g., Overeaters Anonymous, the St. Augustine Society for the Sexually Addicted. At this point, the interaction of psychology and religion in America has come full circle: William James's description of conversion experiences were used in the original formation of Alcoholics Anonymous; through the Twelve-Step Program, the conversion narratives he reported from the be-

ginning of the century have been recycled back into the practice of religion, only now in hotel ballrooms rather than in tent meetings.

Conclusions: From this review of a century's work in psychology of religion, a few conclusions do emerge.

First, psychology of religion is best understood as a particular hermeneutical (interpretive) theory, analogous to other methods of interpretation in the humanities, and not a science. Claims concerning the capacity of the discipline to deliver scientific explanations of religious phenomena, subject to empirical verification, have been shown to be false. From James and Freud through Erikson and his intellectual heirs, the primary contributors to the psychology of religion have provided insightful interpretations of religious phenomena.

Second, like other schemes of interpretation, psychology of religion needs to be suspicious of the religious particularity of its cultural context. Only in America would religion be conceived in the individualistic terms of James, and only in America would the study of religion give such prominence to conversion experiences. This Protestant bias of the field was as apparent in the 1950 publications of Allport, with questions for all respondents concerning their belief in Christ and view of the church, as it was in James. Similarly, gender bias is not limited to Freud, but contaminates both psychological theory and religious imagery.

Third, psychology of religion has yet to recognize that its categories are culturally conditioned, hence historically limited in their application. Many theories still presume a universality for their psychological models that historical inquiries do not confirm. For example, a developmental framework is not constitutive of childhood in all cultures. However, psychohistorical studies of past religious heroes, such as Martin Luther (1483–1546) or Augustine (354–430), have yet to appropriate the historical mode of inquiry long prevalent in other forms of religious scholarship, such as biblical studies.

religion, sociology of. Sociologists regard religion as an institution, a stable cluster of values, norms, statuses, roles, and groups developed around a basic social need. Their goal is to explain religious behavior by reference to broad theoretical propositions about the needs of social systems and how religious behavior helps meet them. To some sociologists, the connection between society and religion is so strong as to suggest that the very constitution of society is a religious process. The distinction between sacred and profane, which lies at the heart of all religions, serves as a symbolic reminder and celebration of individual and collective subjection to society: the attitude of awe and reverence attached to sacred objects is nothing but the sentiment inspired by society in its members, projected outside of consciousness and objectified. Religious life thus thickens and solidifies community life, inducing a sense of attachment to the community and its values.

Sociologists assume that the expression of religious sentiments must be embedded in social forms. Sociology is the geometry of social life, searching in the content of material reality for the pure relational forms underlying it. Form might be social structure (e.g., authority relations) and content might be a specific set of beliefs (e.g., those of Mormons concerning their charismatic founder, Joseph Smith). Form might be function (e.g., reaffirming a community's sexual ethics) and content might be a particular ritual (e.g., Jewish marriage vows). When considering religious practices (e.g., choosing a spouse from within one's own group of believers), sociologists are less interested in the specific religious injunctions being followed than in the form of relation (e.g., exclusivism, or sectarianism) those practices reveal. Sociologists are particularly interested in the interaction between form and content, such as when the mundane features of a religious organization (the content) become affected by a sense of sacredness (the form), such that matters of expediency (e.g., selecting leaders) become sanctified. Religious beliefs, rituals, proscriptions, ecclesiastical forms —all religious phenomena—are for the sociologist a point of departure, data to be observed, analyzed, and explained. The sociologist is not concerned with testing the truth of belief, determining the efficacy of rituals, judging the correctness of ethics, or providing the warrant for a kind of church. The sociological standpoint is one of sympathetic detachment, an empathic understanding of the beliefs and practices of others without, however, making a commitment to religion itself. Professional detachment is not the only reason the sociologist must resist becoming immersed in any particular religion. The sociological version of the scientific experiment is controlled comparison. The significance of the religious factor in social life can only be determined if it is possible to hold other factors constant, and this requires comparing situations that are similar in all respects except the religious phenomenon of interest. A comparative perspective on religion is thus an intrinsic feature of sociology.

Differentiation: Modern sociology is best understood as a response to the problem of order created at the beginning of the nineteenth century by the collapse of the old regime caused by industrialism and revolutionary democracy. Both industrialism and revolutionary democracy in their own ways furthered the process of structural differentiation, whereby the major institutional spheres of society become disassociated from one another, attached to specialized collectivities and roles, and disembedded from kinship, territorial, and other ascriptive units. Largely autonomous economic and political systems emerge, no longer under the control of the church, containing their own values and own sources of legitimation. While some sociologists believe structural differentiation inevitably weakens the ties between religious and other roles and statuses, and diminishes the cohesive properties of religion, others see in functional specialization a means whereby religious institutions gain strength and vitality: a religious institution specifically oriented to the satisfaction of spiritual needs is better adapted to a society where all roles and statuses have become highly differentiated. Others see in differentiation merely a reassignment of functions: while older religious structures (such as established churches) might be crumbling, other social forms, less conventionally churchlike (e.g., televangelism, patriotic celebrations), have replaced them. The task of sociology is to locate and account for them. All sociologists agree, however, that it is important to avoid thinking about structural differentiation as an abstract process over which human agents have little control: the boundary dividing religion from the rest of society is contested terrain, located in classrooms, courts of law, and city council chambers. This way of thinking allows for the possibility of de-differentiation. Under conditions of perceived national crisis or international conflict, political issues reassume a religious aspect and the churches become prominent in political campaigns.

In the United States, at least, differentiation has not marginalized religion, although some sociologists would say that it has privatized it, relegating it to the level of a personal concern and sundering its links to community. There are patterns of difference in religious activity among the population (it is conventional for young adults to disavow or show little interest in the religious commitments of their parents) and levels of religious observance have fluctuated somewhat, but, as measured by repeated survey data, religiosity remains steady despite the rapid pace of technological and economic change and equally disruptive changes in urban forms and styles of living, which have virtually destroyed the neighborhoods and communities that sociologists once believed were the necessary foundation for religious institutions.

Most people acquire their religious identities through their families. Especially where family pressures are reinforced by religious schooling, children will adopt the religion of their parents, or, when they marry, change their religion to make the marriage religiously homogeneous. The interweave of family and religious roles means that demographics has a significant impact on patterns of religious observance: churchgoing tends to be lowest in those periods when a higher proportion of the population is single and rises when many families have young children. The wife and mother is expected to be the principal carrier of the religious obligations of the family and in most denominations is the chief conduit through which religious inheritance passes. Conversely, family roles and interactions are shaped by religious preference and level of commitment: sex-role attitudes, age at marriage, choice of spouse, number of children, methods of socialization, level of marital satisfaction, and likelihood of divorce all vary by denominational membership and, to a lesser extent, level of religious commitment.

Contrary to the expectations of some sociologists, religion and politics in the United States remain closely intertwined. Party affiliation and church membership are conjoint measures of social integration. They tend to weaken simultaneously if the population's trust in social institutions declines, and they both tend to be neglected by young adults whose level of integration is typically low. Religion is a more powerful influence on party preference in the United States than social class. Recent studies also indicate that religious ferment within a society (e.g., people leaving liberal for more conservative denominations, church leaders becoming embroiled in single-issue politics such as abortion, increasingly bitter conflicts over church-state issues such as prayer in schools) rises and falls in association with political conflicts caused by economic and social changes.

Rationalization: Besides their interest in the consequences of structural differentiation for religion, sociologists are also drawn to the study of religion because of their assumption that people need to symbolize, codify, experience, and celebrate their place in the social world. Human beings must make sense of those occurrences, such as death, innocent suffering, and of random fortune, that appear unfathomable. Human beings' need to interpret their conditions of existence, construct an identity for themselves, and impose order on their environment calls for some philosophy of moral meaning, or theodicy.

Theodicies furnish widely different answers to problems of meaning. Some relativize the good things of life and encourage resignation. Others insist that the world be brought into accordance with religious ethics and demand activism. Sociologists expect there to be an "elective affinity" between the type of spirituality and religious duty emphasized by a religion and the manner in which social groups must work and reproduce themselves. This assumption underlies sociological studies of the relation between religious ethics and economic behavior and attitudes, most notably the argument that a link exists between the Protestant ethic (of hard work and asceticism) and the spirit of capitalism (wherein time is money and profits are not to be squandered on consumption), an argument that has guided many sociological studies of the relation between religious identity and economic status.

For sociologists who emphasize the cosmological aspect of religion, its ability to make sense of the social world, the inescapable topic of study is the trend known as rationalization. Interpreted narrowly, as the methodical attainment of a given end by means of a precise calculation of adequate means, this process would appear to be corrosive of religious thinking. People would become more concerned with how things shall be done than with what shall be done. Interpreted more broadly, as an increasing theoretical mastery of reality by means of increasingly precise and abstract concepts, it can be applied to religion itself and represents not a decline but a change in religious practice and belief corresponding to changes in society at large. Furthermore, few sociologists would argue that rationalization colonizes the entire social world or deny that many forms of rationalization (e.g., impersonal organizations) create their own forms of irrationality that, in turn, pose new problems of meaning.

To the extent that religion satisfies the desire for meaning, it can be both world-maintaining and world-destroying. While the privileged elaborate doctrines that emphasize their being, the deprived fashion religions that legitimate what they will become, and these religions might well call for a rejection of the world. Religion can therefore be a source of disorder and change as well as of order and continuity, of challenge as well as comfort. Attention is thus drawn to the social conditions that might spark religiously in-spired renewal. These include major demo-graphic shifts in the population (e.g., more young people), economic deprivation (e.g., falling crop prices), and political crises. A paral-lel line of investigation, at the individual level, seeks to determine the characteristics of those drawn to new religious movements (e.g., the so-cially mobile, the alienated), the processes whereby they become converted to these move-ments (e.g., through networks of friends and acquaintances or prior organizational member-ships), the inspirational role played by prophets or charismatic leaders, and the features of reli-gious organizations that bind converts to their new identities (e.g., initiation rituals).

Sociologists have developed elaborate con-ceptual schemes for thinking about the various forms religious organizations have assumed. Some organizations are world-affirming, and develop elaborate and formalized structures suitable to this accommodationist stance. Oth-ers are world-denying, and seek an organiza-tional form resistant to encrustation and compromise. Most sociologists assume that even the most vehement religious rejections of the world must eventually make some compro-mise because they must meet the functional im-peratives of any modern organizational form (e.g., fund-raising, proselytizing, office mainte-nance, record-keeping). Consequently, all reli-gious organizations can be expected to exhibit some tension between their spiritual and their rational, administrative aspects. This tension is often revealed in factionalism within the church, in the development of separate lines of adminis-tration, one priestly and charismatic, the other administrative and rational, and in the strain ex-perienced by the religious professionals who seek to combine them.

Critical Issues: Not all the theoretical and methodological tools available to sociologists have been applied with equal vigor or success to the subject of religion. While some of the founders of the discipline were hostile to reli-gion, most of those subsequently drawn to its study were more sympathetic, in large part be-cause they subscribed to the view that society cannot exist without religion of some form. The exception is those sociologists who draw heav-ily on the theories of Karl Marx, the nineteenth-century German political philosopher. Marxist critical theory argues that the human author-ship of culture and society is concealed by reli-gion in favor of false notions about the dependence of humans on external supernat-ural and sacred powers. It seeks to transform

directly the pattern of exploitative social rela-tions to the point where alienation would no longer be experienced and, consequently, reli-gious distortions of reality would supposedly become unnecessary. Modern Christianity, with what Marx called "its cultus of abstract man," was a precondition for the development of the abstract and universal market relations of capitalism. Many sociologists side with Marx in seeing religious privatism as part of a larger complex of changes, including mass con-sumerism, atomized leisure activities, attenu-ated versions of family intimacy, and a reluctance to become involved in politics. However, they have rarely conducted analyses of particular instances of religious mysti-fication or attempted to show in detail how new types of religion are linked to new types of alienation.

An enduring debate within the discipline of sociology has to do with the appropriateness of applying the methods of discovery and explana-tion of the natural sciences to the social world. This debate spills over into the sociology of reli-gion, where the problems are more acute than in any other sphere of investigation. Sociology seeks to generalize, to distill a mass of data into a few abstract categories. For example, all vari-eties of and reasons for church attendance are distilled into a single category and used for pur-poses of analysis, for instance to help explain how people deal with stressful life events. Masses of data must be gathered by impersonal and highly simplified means, such as question-naires. Responses to these questionnaires are summed, averaged, and submitted to various other quantification procedures. These proce-dures would appear to trivialize and distort reli-gious phenomena because the procedures must limit themselves to simple and crude statements of belief and the most superficial reports of reli-gious observance and practice. Methods of gath-ering more qualitative data, those that explore the nuance of language and permit the expres-sion of sentiment, such as in-depth interviews and participant observation, are necessarily time-consuming, and because the database is correspondingly narrow, many sociologists re-gard them as providing an insecure foundation for generalization and therefore question their utility.

Religion of the Heavenly Way.   *See* Ch'ondogyo.

Religionswissenschaft.   *See* comparative religion; religion, the study of; science of religion.

THE STUDY
OF RELIGION

The study of religion in a nontheological, academic setting is a modern phenomenon. It has its roots in the Enlightenment, the development of the physical and cultural sciences, and the discovery of other cultures. It was born in an ethos that allowed scholars to study religion from an observer's point of view, a point of view that was not necessarily religious or antireligious. The goal was to describe, compare, and explain the history and evolution of religion, its diversity, and its persistence in all cultures.

This new effort at explaining religion also established such academic disciplines as anthropology and sociology. With the exception of the so-called phenomenology of religion, this interest in religion also prompted the quest for new theories of religion. Since this quest is seldom described, one can raise the questions: What is a theory? What does it take for someone to have a theory about something?

WHAT IS A THEORY?

Classically, a theory is a set of hypothetical-deductive premises that interpret theoretical terms or statements that are connected to observational statements by means of correspondence rules. This has become known as the logical positivist model of theory, and has been thoroughly refuted by philosophers of science.

Peter Achinstein's work (1968) on theory is a good example of the contemporary view that took hold after the demise of logical positivism:

1. The construction of a theory is a highly cognitive enterprise; it is the engine for the production of knowledge. It is cognitive because it entails holding certain propositional beliefs concerning the theoretical object of our study or explanation.
2. Someone who has a theory about religion, for example, does not know that the theory is true, but does believe the theory to be plausible if not true.
3. Someone who has a theory does not know that the theory is false, but on the contrary believes it to be true or plausible.
4. A theory provides a better understanding of something. The theory provides

a better explanation or interpretation; it removes something puzzling, indicates causes, or supplies reasons.

5. A theory consists of propositions that assert what is the case, and contains at least the central and distinctive assumptions of the theory.
6. A theory entails the belief that one does not know of any more fundamental theory from which the propositions can be derived.
7. Finally, a theory is not a set of rules, but may contain rules.

BASIC APPROACHES

Origin Theories of Religion The quest for the origin of religion was of central importance to early scholars because they assumed that if the origin of religion could be explained, one could then go on to interpret its meaning and evolution in history. There are many variations on this approach to the study of religion, but three stand out as having a profound influence on the contemporary study of religion.

The Intellectualist/Rationalist Approach E. B. Tylor's *Primitive Culture* (1871) remains the classic inquiry into the origin of religion from an intellectualist, rationalist approach. Tylor (1832–1917) defines religion as "the belief in spiritual beings." The task is to investigate the causes that produced religion and then explain its evolution. This approach is explanatory, Tylor thought, because the lower stages of religion would become explanations for higher stages.

The single most important principle in this work is the idea of the psychic unity of mankind as a rational unity. Without this rational unity, comparison and evolutionary analysis would be impossible. With this principle in mind, Tylor presents a theory that explains not just how the belief in spiritual beings came about but also demonstrates the essential rational continuity of religious belief throughout history. The theory posits animism as the first, "primitive," stage in the evolution of religion. Animism refers to the notion of a ghost-soul animating man in the body, and appearing in dream and vision out of the body. Thus, the most primitive religious belief in ghosts or souls is based upon empirical experience: i.e., dreams, sleep, and trances, the distinction between a live and dead body. Animism is a rational attempt to explain certain kinds of experiences. Animism, the primitive conception of the human soul, becomes the model for other spiritual beings whose purpose is to explain nature on a very primitive level. The history and evolution of religion is an ever more abstract attempt at explaining experiences, moving from animism to the personification of nature, polytheism, monotheism, and metaphysics. This evolution of thought reaches its highest level in the nineteenth century with the separation of scientific explanation from ethics and morality.

Tylor emphasizes that although religious explanations of nature are false they are not, therefore, irrational.

The Tylorian view of religion as rational or intellectual remains a vital theory in the contemporary study of religion, as can be seen in the publications of such scholars as Robin Horton and Melford Spiro.

The Sociological Approach Emile Durkheim's *The Elementary Forms of the Religious Life* (1912) remains the classical source for the sociological origins of religion. Durkheim (1858–1917) rejects Tylor's theory of animism on three grounds. First, animism cannot explain how the projected soul becomes a sacred cult object, the cult of the ancestors. Second, even if true, animism is a late stage in the evolution of religion, since most primitive religions do not have ancestral cults. Finally, the theory, if true, turns religious beliefs into hallucinatory representations that have no objective basis at all. For Durkheim, all religious beliefs are true once one discovers that they are symbolic representations of the collective life. Religious beliefs and practices are symbolic of social facts. The totem as the god of the clan, for example, "can therefore be nothing else than the clan itself, personified and represented to the imagination under the visible form of the animal or vegetable which serves as totem." Furthermore, religious beliefs separate everything that is known into sacred and profane things, and rituals express the rules of conduct while in the presence of sacred objects. Thus Durkheim defines religion as "a unified system of beliefs and practices relative to sacred things, that is to say, things set apart and forbidden—beliefs and practices which unite into one single moral community called a Church, all those who adhere to them." The object of religion is a collective reality, a symbolic representation of collective life, and its origin is found in totemism, which represents the most simple form of collective life. Durkheim never doubts that the collective consciousness is as real as individual experience and therefore provides us with an objective reference for explaining religion as the moral and cognitive force that binds groups together. The notion that religion is a preeminently social phenomena is fundamental to contemporary studies of religion.

The Psychological Approach Although Sigmund Freud (1856–1939) agrees that the origin of religion begins with totemism, he radically disagrees with both Tylor and Durkheim. From Freud's point of view religious beliefs and practices originate in deep psychological repression. They are basically illusions, symbolic projections, based upon desires. Freud's theory is based upon a hedonistic view of human nature; the purpose of life is to maximize pleasure and avoid pain.

The origin of religion, according to Freud, is a specific act. Using Charles Darwin's theory of the horde, Freud, in *Totem and Taboo* (1913), constructs a story in which young males gather together in order to mate with females who are kept by the oldest, most powerful male. To do this they kill him. Feeling remorse and guilt, they then contract never to kill again and create a remembrance feast with the corpse as the meal. This deed locates the origin of culture and religion, the origin of kinship systems, totemism, and the taboo on incest. Henceforth, the satisfaction of desires will be severely restricted by religious prohibitions (beliefs), but the pain caused by these taboos will be lessened by periodic ritual practices that symbolically reenact the original deed.

The origin of religion is based upon individual psychological experiences, the satisfaction of individual instincts. Although Freud never discusses Durkheim's sociological theory, it is clear that he would have nothing to do with collective effervescence as the basis for explaining religion. Durkheim can be identified as a methodological holist in his approach to religion, while Freud's approach is a clear case of methodological individualism.

Freud is fully aware that the story is speculation but never doubts that the beginning of culture and religion must have something like incestuous violence as its cause (the beginning of the Oedipus complex). Variations on this heuristic hunch remain popular with many contemporary scholars of religion, for example, Rene Girard (*Violence and the Sacred*, 1972).

Functionalist Theories of Religion Origin theories of religion soon lose their importance, because there simply is no way one can confirm or disconfirm their truth. Nevertheless, both Freud and Durkheim insist on a second important assumption. Once the origin of religion was in hand, both Freud and Durkheim had to explain why religion persists on such a universal scale. Why, for Durkheim, do human beings persist in taking symbolic representations literally? Why, for Freud, do human beings persist in believing what is in fact an illusion? The answer in both cases is that religion persists because it functions to fulfill basic needs in human beings. This is the basic premise of all functionalist approaches to the study of religion. It was once the primary theory in the social sciences and remains the most widespread approach to the study of religion.

A. R. Radcliffe-Brown (1881–1955) explained it this way: the functional method of interpretation rests on the assumption that a culture is an integrated system. In the life of a given community each element of the culture plays a specific part, or has a specific function. The function of a ritual or ceremonial is to express and thereby maintain sentiments that are necessary for social cohesion.

Over the decades scholars have committed themselves to this approach to the study of religion because it seems to be empirically testable. The slogan became "religion is what religion does." Functionalism brings together a large number of scholars who disagree on some fundamental issues concerning religion. For example, Bronislaw Malinowski (1884–1942) thinks that the basic needs that religion satisfies are biological in nature. Radcliffe-Brown, following Durkheim, believes that the needs are basically social. This feud is finally settled by George Homans's 1941 assertion that both are right: religious beliefs and practices function to satisfy both individual biological and collective group needs for the reduction of anxiety.

A second example can be taken from the contemporary anthropological debate between Melford Spiro (b. 1920) and Edmund Leach (b. 1910). Spiro thinks that certain beliefs, such as that water spirits cause pregnancy, should be taken literally as rational, though false, explanations. Leach thinks that, on the contrary, such beliefs are not to be taken as false explanations but as symbolic expressions that reinforce existing social institutions.

A final example can be found in the writings of contemporary Africanist J. H. M. Beattie's 1964 argument that rituals and religious beliefs are essentially expressive, while Robin Horton (b. 1932) thinks they are fundamentally cognitive, rational attempts to explain the world. Victor Turner (1920–83) resolves this apparent conflict by insisting that religious symbols as units of meaning have emotive, cognitive, and physical value. It is a mistake, therefore, to insist on one or the other.

Despite the disagreement, all endorse some version of Radcliffe-Brown's description of functionalism as the most adequate theory for the study of religion. Functionalism attempts to explain why religious institutions and beliefs come into existence. Functionalism explains why and how religion functions and persists, and shows what role religion plays in an integrated social system.

Most contemporary theories of functionalism insist that the functions of religion are unintended consequences of the presence of religion. Thus believers may indeed take their religious doctrines literally—the gods exist for them—but that is not of central concern or debate to theorists. The theorist wants to explain how religious beliefs in a specific social setting have unintended consequences that satisfy real social needs. Many scholars are convinced that functionalism does just that. Unfortunately this theory is seriously flawed.

Critiques of Functionalism Criticism of functionalism comes in a variety of models. The simplest remains the work of the contemporary philosopher of science Carl Hempel. The premises of this theory follow.

1. X (a society) is functioning adequately in a setting of kind C.
2. X functions adequately only if a functional requirement Z is satisfied (let Z stand for reduction of anxiety).
3. If Y is present in X, then as an effect Z would be satisfied (let Y stand for a particular ritual).
4. Hence, Y is present in X. This conclusion is invalid. It asserts that "If Y, then Z; Z, therefore Y." It commits the logical fallacy of affirming the consequence. The logic of the argument can be corrected by adding "only if" to premise 3.

Thus, only if Y were present in X, then as an effect Z would be satisfied. One can now conclude: Y is present in X. But this is true by definition. No one wants to argue that cultural units or elements, like religious belief or ritual, are necessary for the satisfaction of needs. Indeed, one may ask how would one go about empirically demonstrating that this is the case? This revision asserts that nothing else could satisfy the need.

The best revision of the model is to revise premise 3 once again: if Y or its functional equivalent is present in X, then it is highly likely (very probable) that Z is satisfied. The conclusion now becomes: Y or its functional equivalent is present.

The argument remains invalid, and has become trivial. Anything could satisfy the need. In any case, "highly likely" or "very probable" are arguments that are neither true nor false.

Attempts to construct a more sophisticated model have also failed. For example, John Elster in 1980–82 proposes the following model. A cultural institution or element X is explained by its function Y for a group Z, if and only if,

1. Y is an effect of X,
2. Y is beneficial for Z,
3. Y is unintended by actions producing X,
4. Y (or at least the causal relation between X and Y) is unrecognized by actors in Z,

5. *Y* maintains *X* by a causal feedback loop passing through *Z*.

This more complex model is too powerful. It claims that *X* is explained "if and only if" *Y* is an effect of *X*. Using the earlier example, this model asserts that "if and only if" a particular ritual is present then as an effect anxiety will be reduced, and that anxiety reduction maintains the ritual via a feedback system through the group. Thus the rituals or beliefs of a society must be necessary and sufficient causes. There cannot be any functional equivalents or other kinds of elements that could serve as substitutes. No social scientist would make this claim. Furthermore, the notion of a feedback system as a social mechanism must be used in a metaphorical way. The usual example of a feedback system is a thermostat in a heating system. The point to be stressed here is that this holds true only for closed systems. No social scientist would want to argue that a group or specific society is a closed system. Finally, premise 5 cannot be derived from any of the other premises.

Elster notes that in virtually all attempts to use this model one or more of the five premises is lacking. Furthermore, it is impossible to come up with an example where the presence of all the premises are demonstrated. Once again, this is not surprising given the strong "if and only if" clause in the model. How could anyone claim that an institution or behavioral pattern *X* is explained by its function *Y* "if and only if" *Y* is beneficial for *Z?* Finally, nothing can be inferred from the presence of premises 1, 2, and 3, and it would be fallacious to conclude the presence of 5 from the presence of premises 1 through 4.

One can only conclude that functionalism is at best a heuristic device for talking about religion. Heuristic devices are neither true nor false; they are hunches or guesses.

Phenomenology and History of Religion Functionalism becomes popular because of anthropological studies of societies that are not literate. Such societies lack written traditions that are crucial evidence for historians. The history of religions is important because it provides the content or material for understanding and interpreting religions. Histories of religion are descriptions of the beliefs, practices, art, and drama of religion as well as its interrelations with economics, politics, ethics, and geography. The history of a religion is not a complete study of religion. The history of a religion does not provide its meaning.

The phenomenology and history of religions as disciplines in the study of religion are more than just historical descriptions of religions. The development of the phenomenology and history of religion is essentially European. The term *phenomenology* in this approach to the study of religion has nothing in common with the term as it is used in philosophy, especially as it is used in the philosophical phenomenology of Edmund Husserl (1859–1938) and his followers.

The phenomenology and history of religions arise out of theological concerns. Most of the early scholars who identify themselves as adhering to this approach—Rudolf Otto, C. J. Bleeker, Joachim Wach, and Gerardus van der

Leeuw—are theologians who became interested in religions other than Christianity.

Two basic assumptions run through the history of this approach to the study of religion. The first is that the history of religion is the history of the manifestation of the sacred. The sacred is often described as ultimate reality, the real, the absolute, and is in all cases viewed as a transcendent reality. Rudolf Otto (1869–1937) asserts that it is "wholly other" and Mircea Eliade (1907–86) often describes it as "opposite the profane," which is contingent, arbitrary, the domain of becoming as opposite to Being.

This approach to religion usually constructs various typologies of religion, the types representing ways in which the sacred has manifested itself in the history of religion. The emphasis is not so much on history as it is on the various typologies of the sacred. The phenomenology and history of religion could be viewed as the modern version of a natural theology or metaphysics divested of its monotheistic properties.

The second assumption in this approach is its rejection of all theories that explain religion from sociological, psychological, sociobiological, or political/economic points of view. All such approaches to the study of religion are charged with being reductionistic. Religion is *sui generis*, literally, "of its own kind"; it is unique, thus it cannot be explained by terms from another domain. To explain religion as fulfilling social or psychological needs misses the one crucial point—that the essence of religion is its representation of the sacred.

One consequence of this approach to the study of religion was that it gave scholars a reason for the creation of departments of religion as independent disciplines in colleges and universities. If religion needs its own methodology, it can join other academic disciplines that have specific methods for inquiring into subjects not reducible to other departments.

The term *reduction* is never adequately defined by historians and phenomenologists of religion. The assertions "This approach is reductionistic" or "Levi-Strauss is a reductionist" dismiss other methods and theories of religion without further argument. Unfortunately, this kind of dismissal is false. One usually reads that a sociological or psychological explanation of religion is reductionistic because it explains away religion; it reduces religion to something else. This is not true. Reductions are related to explanations and explanations are theory-laden.

Reduction in most sciences is the explanation of a theory in one area of research by a theory used in another area. Theoretical reduction provides the possibility of more powerful explanations that have greater simplicity and are broader in their capacity to explain. Reduction does not falsify theories. Reduction takes place when, given two theories, one of the theories is found to be more comprehensive and explains more than the reduced theory, while including the data of the reduced theory. Reduction, properly understood, entails theories, not data.

It is important to understand fully the drastic consequences of this approach for the study of religion. If religion refers to the sacred, a reality that is sui generis, then it becomes impossible to explain what religion is. The sacred is not a theoretical object or a theoretical term. The sacred is a transcendent reality that manifests itself in history as religion. How does one know this? How can one confirm or disconfirm that this is so? The answer is clear—one can't. At this point one must leave the study of religion and must turn to theology or faith for the answer.

Structuralist Theories of Religion Structuralist theories of religion are the most recent development for the study of religion. Structuralism has been used successfully in such disciplines as anthropology, sociology, comparative literature, music, and film. It has not attracted many scholars in the study of religion. This resistance can be understood once structuralism is seen in all of its revolutionary force. Its major premises reject most of the basic assumptions of both functionalist and phenomenologist approaches to the study of religion.

Although many scholars think of Claude Levi-Strauss as the major author of structuralism, structuralism actually has its beginnings in linguistics and the work of Ferdinand de Saussure (1857–1916). Saussure realized that a science of linguistics did not exist; no one had worked out the nature of its object of study.

The question What is the object of our study? is clearly a theoretical one. The first, crucial premise is that whatever the concrete entities of language are, they are not directly accessible. The object of linguistics is not immediately given. The application of this premise to the study of religion would reject all notions of religion as sui generis, as something given in immediate experience, such as a numinous experience, or as the satisfaction of a set of given needs.

The second premise of structuralist theory is that language (or religion) is a system of signs. A sign is made up of a signifier (sound image) and signified (concept), and the relation between the two is the signification of the sign. This theory of language excludes the notion of reference as a necessary term for explaining language. This rejects an essential premise in both functionalism and the phenomenology of religion. Functionalism clearly assumes that the meaning of religion can be explained by reference to basic needs. Phenomenology attempts to explain the meaning of religion by reference to the sacred.

For Saussure and other structuralists, signs or elements in a system are arbitrary. What then defines a sign or an element in a particular system? Since there are no fixed universal essences, or givens, signs are purely relational. The relation between terms or elements in a system defines them. This emphasis on relations demonstrates the holistic nature of structural theory. Elements, signs, or symbols in themselves are meaningless. The significance of signs and symbols is thus established only by the total network of interrelations in a particular system.

A third important premise of the theory is that one must distinguish between language, which is a system of structure, and speech, which is performance or act. Language is a system; speech is use of the system—I speak a language. This distinction is compatible with Noam Chomsky's separation of language into competence and performance as a means of specifying the proper object of linguistics. To use this theory for the study of religion, one must make a distinction between religion as a system or a structure and the practice or performance of religion in the daily lives of believers. It will do little good to ask performers to describe this system, for they are for the most part unaware of what the system is, just as most English-speaking persons are unaware of the syntax and semantics of English. The discovery or construction of this system is a theoretical enterprise that is not given in the empirical data.

The distinction between synchronic and diachronic analysis is a direct consequence of the third premise. Diachronic, historical, or evolutionary stages are irrelevant to structural (synchronic) explanations of religion. For example, the structuralist would argue that the structure and meaning of Buddhism is not the sum of its history, nor is it found in the stages of its development.

Levi-Strauss recognizes the importance of this theory for anthropology and the study of myth and totemism. The errors of past studies consist in concentrating on the history of a myth or a specific god or the search for a reference for the specific names of deities or totems. Totemism, once believed to be the origin of religion, is now viewed as the imaginary product of the academic mind. The contemporary Indologist Louis Dumond applies the theory to the study of the Indian caste system as a structure of relations constituted by the ritual opposition "pure/impure" and the anthropologist Stanley Tambiah successfully applies the theory to a study of Theravada Buddhism in Thailand. The use of structuralist theory for explaining religion tells scholars that to discover the significance of Theravada Buddhism and Hinduism, for example, one must begin with a defined set of oppositional relations between two important elements in both religions: renouncer (ascetic)/householder.

The structuralist approach and the impact of new developments growing out of the cognitive sciences have yet to be fully applied to the study of religion. One of the great gaps in the study of religion is the lack of a well-formed theory of semantics that will explain the meaning of religion on both levels of belief and practice.

religious experience, an experience or aspect of experience that is believed to have religious significance.

The term refers to reports of experiences of God or of other objects or powers considered divine in different religious traditions. Theologians and theorists of religion during the past two centuries speculate as to whether or not religion is universal in human experience, taking different forms in different cultures. Some argue that a religious dimension of experience is the ground for the beliefs and practices that constitute different religious traditions. Much depends on how "religious experience" is to be understood.

History: The term *religious experience* has been prominent in the study of religion since the writings of the American psychologist and philosopher William James (*The Varieties of Religious Experience*, 1902). But the idea figures importantly in Christian thought during the nineteenth century, both in Protestant theology and in attempts to found a science of religion. Both these endeavors are strongly influenced by the work of Friedrich Schleiermacher (early-nineteenth-century German theologian and philosopher), who advances a theory of religion as a distinctive moment that pervades all of human experience, and employs that theory in a systematic redescription of the chief doctrines of Protestant theology.

Though the concept develops in the nineteenth century, it is employed by Schleiermacher, James, and others to identify a dimension of experience, or a kind of experience, that is taken to be widespread across different cultures and historical periods. Religious thinkers and scholars of religion have thought that if the religious moment in experience, or the distinguishing marks of religious experience, could be identified, one could identify the distinctive character of religion. Some appeal to religious experience to ground or justify religious belief and practice in the face of skepticism about appeals to metaphysical arguments, revelation, or ecclesiastical authority. Often these descriptive and justificatory programs are combined.

Reports of mystical experiences, of powerful emotions of joy and of sadness, of perception of spiritual beings, of moments of great calm, of disorder and order in one's life, of sickness and of healing, of special insight and blind faith, are all included under the rubric "religious experience." They are identified as such if the experience is judged, by the one who has it or the one who cites it, to have religious significance. That judgment depends heavily on how one defines religion.

Schleiermacher holds that the religious component of experience is a feeling or intuition that is qualitatively distinct from other kinds of feeling, though it is never found in isolation from them. In his early work he refers to it as a "sense and taste for the infinite" (*On Religion*, 1799), and later as a "feeling of absolute dependence" (*The Christian Faith*, 1821–22). James denies that there is anything psychologically distinct about religious feeling. Religious feelings draw from a common storehouse of human emotions. Religious love is love directed to a religious object, as is religious joy or sadness. Both, however, identify the core of religious experience as a sense of some reality that is not exhausted by the world of natural causes.

William James: James defines religion as "the feelings, acts, and experiences of individual men in their solitude, so far as they apprehend themselves to stand in relation to whatever they consider the divine." James does not claim that this formulation captures the essence of religious experience. Religious experience, for instance, is not always solitary. But the formulation calls attention to something important that James does not sufficiently exploit: feelings, acts, and experiences must each be identified under a description. In describing experience, reference must be made to, first, how one apprehends oneself to stand in relation to, second, what one considers to be divine. The object of the experience, and the experienced relation between the subject and the object, must be described in the language of the subject, and from that point of view. The same event may be perceived, and therefore experienced, quite differently by two people, whether they are participants or observers of the event.

James proposes a typology of religious experience that focuses on a sense of wrongness and a need for transformation. He also considers the value of such experiences, both as they contribute to or detract from a healthy human life and as a source of knowledge. The examples he considers are nearly all drawn from Christian culture, and show a distinct Protestant and antiecclesiastical bias. But the philosophical issues he raises are instructive.

To identify an experience in this way requires what the twentieth-century anthropologist Clifford Geertz calls "thick description," an elucidation of the relevant cultural context, in which reference is made to the concepts, beliefs, rules, and practices that would be assumed by the person to whom the experience is attributed. A vision of the Virgin in fifteenth-century Castile differs from a vision of the Madonna in early-twentieth-century Italian Harlem. To describe both only as experiences of Mary, or visions of a holy woman, misses much of what is experienced in each case. A Tibetan monk reaching a summit in Ladakh and a Native American of the Northwest Coast reaching the summit of Mt. Tahoma (now Mt. Rainier) may each experience a heightened sense of the unity and the vastness of the universe, but their experiences may be very different.

Ambiguity of "Experience": An experience is always an experience of something, or about or with respect to something: I saw *X*, she was surprised at *Y*, he was happy about *Z*. The terms by which this object is characterized are crucial for the identification of the experience. To take a simple perceptual example, imagine a hiker noticing a bear on the trail ahead and running for the nearest tree. From the safety of his perch, the hiker sees that it is not a bear, but a log that the hiker mistook for a bear. What did the hiker experience? The hiker could not have experienced a bear, because there was no bear to experience; but the hiker must not have experienced a log, because that would not have caused anyone to turn and run. The experience is identified differently if the object is described from the point of view of the subject having the experience, or from that of an observer.

One might say that the hiker experienced the log as a bear. But that is not quite accurate. One might experience one's home as a prison or a refuge, but the hiker experienced a bear. If one is interested only in what is on the trail, one will attend to the best explanation: it is a log. But if one is interested in the experience, in order to understand it, to study it, or to explain it, one must identify it with a description that captures the way the subject conceived of the object and how the subject apprehended himself to stand in relation to it.

Ambiguity of "Religious": Different religious traditions provide the concepts and beliefs that inform people's experiences. People experience a vision of Jesus, love of Krishna, devotion to Torah, a sense of God's providence, a foretaste of liberation from suffering and rebirth, or insight into the truth of the Buddha's teaching. They don't usually have a "religious experience." That description comes into use after James. Some people might identify their experiences as religious, without explicit reference to different religious traditions. Since 1969, the Religious Experience Unit at Mansfield College of Oxford University has been collecting such experiences. But most experiences that might be identified as religious are Christian, Hindu, Nuer, or Jewish

experiences that are not detachable from the language of a specific tradition.

In that case, the identification of the experience as religious is not internal to the experience, but is made from outside. How is it that certain experiences are selected as religious? Reports of experience whose content is given by traditions considered religious (e.g., Buddhism, Judaism, Christianity, Islam) are included. But religious content is not enough. An appreciation of Giotto's frescoes in the Arena Chapel in Padua, Italy, or the Buddhist ceremonial complex at Borobudur, or Brahms's *German Requiem* need not be a religious experience, though it may be. Whether or not it is religious depends on what James describes as how subjects apprehend themselves to stand in relation to the religious object.

The adjective *religious* can classify the experience in terms of its content, or judge the significance of the experience. Religious experiences, in the first sense, are those that make reference to religious subject matter, or to conceptions of gods or parallels in other traditions. This is what James refers to as "whatever they may consider the divine." Religious experiences, in the second sense, are those judged to be perceptions of, encounters with, or participation in the divine. James refers to the way people apprehend themselves to stand in relation to whatever they take to be divine. Two people may engage in the same spiritual exercises, including manipulation of mind and body (fasting, learning to control breathing and other automatic functions, meditating on a particular image or sound), and experience states that can be described in similar terms (calming of the mind, sense of oneness with the universe, peace, bliss). One person might understand this state to be the consequence of the physical and mental regimen, and to be explicable in naturalistic terms. The other might understand the regimen to be a catalyst that helped achieve a mystical experience that cannot wholly be accounted for in such terms. Or, two people witness a dramatic cure at Lourdes, and both are amazed. One assumes that some psychological and physical forces are at work that cannot yet be understood, but that the event must be explicable in terms of natural causes. The other believes a miraculous cure has occurred. In each of these examples, the second person experiences the state or event under a religious description, and the first does not. The two differ in the kind of explanations they assume are appropriate for the experience, or in the way they apprehend themselves to stand in relation to what they have experienced.

Protests against reductionist accounts of religious experience often reveal that what is significant about such experiences is that they cannot be fully accounted for in naturalistic terms. To explain Paul's vision and voices on the road to Damascus as resulting from cortical lesions (James's example), or a moment of Buddhist insight as the appropriation and internalization of the doctrines of the tradition in which the adept has been nurtured, is to offer a psychological or sociological account that fails to capture the religious significance of the experience. By judging any such account to be reductionist, a religious experience is defined in such a way as to ensure that it transcends any natural explanations.

Conclusion: Study of religious experience can illumine the varieties of religious life. People interpret their experiences by means of the concepts, beliefs, assumptions, and images that are available to them. The images, narratives, rituals, and doctrines of religious traditions shape the experiences of people in those traditions. One's experience of the death of others, and of the prospect of one's own death, will differ in theistic and nontheistic traditions, from one theistic tradition to another, and within different strands of that tradition.

Attempts to identify a core religious experience, or a few types that are invariant across cultures but interpreted differently in different cultures, are unpromising. Such a procedure leads to descriptive reduction, or to the loss of the experience as it is understood by the person to whom the experience is attributed.

The apologetic use of religious experience as a locus of authority to which one can appeal in the face of skepticism about the authority of traditional scriptures, councils, rabbis, *gurus,* and philosophical argument has not been successful. Religious experience cannot alone provide a justification for religious doctrine and practice. It is itself a product of religious traditions, doctrines, and practices. *See also* emotions; experience; feeling; mysticism; religion, philosophy of; religion, psychology of; Schleiermacher, Friedrich Ernst Daniel.

religious language, the use of meaningful utterances, inscriptions, or signs in a religious context. While language is central to any theory of religion, at least three problems prohibit a unified account of religious language. The first problem is that the field of semantics—the theory of linguistic meaning—is in the 1990s quite unsettled. Philosophers and linguists are far from consensus over the question of what constitutes meaningful use of language. Second, the many thousands of religious traditions put language to such an array of uses that it may not be possible to bring them into a unified form. Third, the notion of religious language raises a difficult question in interpretation theory: Are there discrete forms of language (religious, moral, scientific, aesthetic, etc.), or are linguistic transactions essentially alike in kind, differing mainly in context?

Theories of Linguistic Meaning: A theory of meaning is a theory that tries to specify the knowledge necessary for the mastery of a language. Perhaps the most long-lived twentieth-century theory of meaning is verificationism. Originally developed around 1930 by the logical positivists in Vienna, verificationism proposes that a sentence is meaningful if and only if it can be empirically tested, at least in principle. An empirical test would be the conceivable experiences that confirm or disconfirm the claim. The meaning of a sentence (spoken or written) is given by laying out the conditions of its verification or falsification. For example, the meaning of "This diamond is hard" is given in the experience of being unable to scratch it. This theory accords well with the intuition that language must have some empirical content or anchor. However, criticisms were advanced early on. For example, the verifiability requirement apparently rules out all sentences of universal form, for their verification would require an infinite set of observational data. The same holds true for the falsification principle: no finite number of observations could falsify "There exists at least one fire-breathing dragon," and yet one knows quite well what the sentence means.

The early 1960s, primarily in the United States and Britain, saw the rise of "truth-conditional" semantics, the leading idea of which is that one gives the meaning of a sentence by giving the conditions under which it would be true. Knowledge of the truth conditions of sentences for a language suffices, on this account, for linguistic understanding. For example, the words *il pleut* are true in French if and only if it is raining (then and near the speaker). By itself, this will appear a trivial result; however, knowledge of many such truth conditions enables observers to see how the recurring, component words of a sentence contribute to its meaning. And such knowledge offers the kind of linguistic mastery that a theory of meaning aims to deliver. While empiricist in orientation, truth-conditional semantics is clearly less restrictive than verificationism, since it merely asks what would make the sentence true.

Among the more serious criticisms of the truth-conditional approach are the following. First, there are questions about its scope, for significant portions of natural languages seem not to have truth values. For example, it is not clear what condition would make "Murder is wrong" true, or "Close the door" false. Second, the threat of regress arises when one asks, In what does the knowledge of truth conditions consist? If not in further truth conditions, then linguistic meaning is ultimately not truth-conditional after all; but if in further truth conditions, there then arise difficult questions about how language-learning is possible.

A third approach to semantic theory holds to the slogan "Meaning is use." In this view—associated with, among others, the twentieth-century Austrian philosopher Ludwig Wittgenstein—one determines the meaning of an expression by discovering what its role is in a given community's linguistic activity. The idea is that every so-called form of life or language game has its own rules and logic, and that one must enter into the form or game before attempting to evaluate it. Thus, the philosopher's primary job is to eliminate confusions that result from misusing or misunderstanding the rules that govern a particular language game. Critics of this approach allege that it exaggerates the conceptual distance between different linguistic communities. If one, for example, comes upon a people who think the earth is flat, rather than impute to them a language game on which it is true that the earth is flat, one would conclude that they mean something very different by "earth." A related criticism is that the form of life associated with, for example, magic and fairies can be criticized from the outside. To think that it cannot endorses a relativism in which all beliefs are equally true.

Challenges to Religious Language: Defenders of verificationist and truth-conditional semantics usually find talk about an abstract God meaningless. Advocates of the meaning-as-use approach typically see such talk as equal to other speech.

The verificationist and truth-conditional challenges are easily stated. How does one verify or falsify that, for example, "God is a loving father," or that "God created the world," or that "The Son of God raised the dead"? One has no public access to the religious entity in question. And neither can one say what would make any of these true—what does God look like such that he can be recognized? Some believers speak of God as masculine, but what biological structure licenses such talk? Problems and questions such

as these have convinced most contemporary philosophers that religious language is cognitively empty and meaningless.

Besides these semantically motivated challenges, the late nineteenth and twentieth centuries provide what might be more neutrally termed *empirical* challenges to the meaningfulness of religious language. For the nineteenth-century German social theorist Karl Marx, religious language is a vehicle for repression, a means for the ruling economic elite to obstruct the improvement and development of the masses. For Marx, the real meaning of talk about a perfect God, about heaven and hell, about sinfulness and redemption has to do with diverting the believer's attention from unnecessarily harsh earthly suffering. And for Emile Durkheim (the early-twentieth-century French sociologist), religious language expresses the worship of society; society is the suprapersonal reality to which talk of God really refers. Durkheim bases this claim on his observation that talk about God is produced by a person's interaction with society. Durkheim believes that religious symbols had been necessary for the stable functioning and reproduction of society. But he foresees a day when people will be mature enough to face the unvarnished (unsymbolic, literal) truth.

Like Marx and Durkheim, Sigmund Freud also believes that religious people are generally unaware of the true meaning of their religious language. In *The Future of an Illusion* (1927), the Austrian psychoanalyst argues that language about, for example, the benevolent rule of divine Providence really expresses the continuation into adulthood of the child's terror, helplessness, and desire of protection by a powerful father. Freud holds that religious language is illusory in expressing beliefs for which there could not be adequate evidence, and that are held merely because they satisfy a wish.

Defenses of Religious Language:

Cognitive Theories: Cognitive theories of religious language are designed to meet the charge of meaninglessness on its own terms. They aim to vindicate the idea that statements about God and salvation do seem to describe aspects of the world and to make truth-claims about it. To meet the verificationist and truth-conditional challenges, the contemporary British philosopher John Hick argues that the believer may actually meet God in an afterlife and may then be in a position to verify religious beliefs (and/or to specify their truth-conditions). While some theologians have taken up Hick's notion of eschatological verification, it is not without difficulties. An immediate problem is how one would recognize God as such; since one has no definite image of the deity, how could identification take place?

A second cognitive theory of religious language has lately been advanced by the American philosopher Alvin Plantinga. His idea is that language expressing belief in God is, under certain conditions, "properly basic"—that is, natural, spontaneous, even self-evident. Defenders of this view argue that such utterances, like those describing current perceptions and recent memory, carry their verification and truth conditions with them. A virtue of this approach is its willingness to take seriously the common report that belief in God can be irresistible or overpowering. However, its defenders have not yet been able to provide criteria of what is "properly basic."

Finally, James F. Ross, also a contemporary American philosopher, has revived the medieval view that talk of God gets its cognitive content by analogy. Ross argues that analogy is a systematic and universal feature of natural language, and is crucial to understanding it. The religious person, says Ross, typically takes ordinary words such as *forgives, loves, is powerful*, and *knows*, and uses them analogically of God. There is no problem assigning meaning to such words in ordinary, nonreligious contexts; Ross's idea is that, when applied to God, one understands these words by preserving while extending their sense by a rule of proportionality—they are true of God as they are true of humans, but in proportion to God's greater perfection. One issue here is the extent to which such words can be exported into abstract contexts; for example, many philosophers have argued that such words can be applied only to agents that have physical bodies.

Noncognitive Theories: Supporters of noncognitive theories of religious language concede that religious language is not empirically or cognitively meaningful. They argue that it is wrong to think of religious language as purporting to represent reality at all, that its import or significance lies elsewhere. Thus, for Immanuel Kant, the eighteenth-century German philosopher, religious language is disguised moral talk. In professing belief in God, the moral lawgiver, the religious person is really cementing a resolve to act morally well. Kant holds that talk about immortality, too, has moral import: since one apparently cannot perfect oneself in this life, language about the hereafter really expresses the hope of continued moral progress. Concerned that Kant's view reduces religion to morality, the Moravian pastor Friedrich Schleiermacher seeks to provide religious language with its own au-

tonomous domain: the expression of religious feeling. By "feeling," Schleiermacher means neither passing sensations nor emotions. Rather, in *Speeches on Religion* (1799), he argues that religious language attempts to capture what the religious person will recognize as the "intuition of the universe"—"the acceptance of everything individual as part of the whole." Both Kant's and Schleiermacher's influential views foreshadow those of the twentieth-century positivists, who, having proved talk about God to be cognitively meaningless, saw it as "attitudinal," as expressing a sentiment or desire.

Another view of religious language that continues to find defenders holds that religious language tries to say what cannot be said. According to this view, as long as no one tries to say these things there is no problem. Trouble arises when someone insists on doing what cannot be done, that is, to give expression to the inexpressible. In the hands of most mystics, and some philosophers, the recommendation is to retreat into silence. This is not a popular option among professional theologians. However, many theologians defend religious language on the grounds that it is the best that one can do given the inexpressible nature of its subject matter. The twentieth-century Protestant theologian Paul Tillich at times promotes this view. Tillich recognizes that Christianity is full of words—hymns, sermons, theological books, even the Bible. But he holds that at the core of Christianity (and other religions as well) is a nonrational element that is not capable of being conceptualized. For Tillich, the term *God* does not name an entity or even an identifiable theistic conception; rather, God stands for "the ground of Being," the object of our ultimate concern. The one who sees religious language as cognitively meaningless can have no objection.

Finally, recent years have seen the emergence of so-called metaphorical theology. The associated view of language may be thought of as a radicalization of the analogical thesis. Rather than seeing the religious, analogical use of language as dependent upon its ordinary, literal employment, the claim is made that all language is metaphorical; there is no literal meaning of the sort that verificationist and truth-conditional semantics presuppose. Thus, religious language cannot be justly criticized for failing to achieve it. As many of its proponents have recognized, there is here the danger of inconsistency or even self-refutation. Is the claim that all language use is metaphorical itself metaphorical? It would seem that the very idea of metaphor depends upon that of literality.

The claim that all language use is metaphorical is often based on the thesis of semantic holism, the idea, negatively expressed, that no term in a language possesses its content or meaning independently. Positively, the holist says that words are given meaning by their location in the wider linguistic network. Thus, one can only talk meaningfully of prayer candles if one can also talk about heat, light, solidity, color, weight, and so on. Semantic holism does seem to capture a deep truth about language and interpretation. But it does not favor the language-as-metaphor view. It may be, for example, that verification- and truth-conditions come holistically. Holism bears on religious language in one further respect: if words stand together in one holistic continuum, then there is an incoherence in the very notion of a discrete sphere of religious language, just as there is in that of political or economic or scientific language. It is because words stand together that they are then available for such diverse duty. *See also* belief; religion, philosophy of; symbol.

religious themes in the literature of traditional societies.

The oral traditions that maintained the resilient complexities of group identity in traditional societies into the twentieth century are often set in opposition to the educational policies of colonizing governments. Out of these encounters between traditional and colonizing societies has come writing, often in the language of the colonizing powers, that shows the power of literary technique to mediate between oral and written, local and intercultural, sacred and worldly. Writers fuse personal experiences of threat into represented struggle to emerge from it, and religious structures often provide needed themes and images.

Words, with their power to bind and sever ties between humans and spirits and among members of the terrestrial community, exist not just as the medium of traditional literature but as its subject. Questioning how language works is a fundamental literary theme, because the origins of indigenous literatures derive from the ways historical events superimposed on traditional societies new languages and worldviews while subverting the associative networks within aboriginal languages that link verbal meaning to social interactions. In most traditional communities in the 1990s, oral literary genres continue as powerful adaptive forces helping to channel cultural resources into the network of linguistic representability; writing echoes the role of the oral traditions.

Colonization of traditional peoples undercuts language itself, giving rise, in indigenous literatures, to references to silence in the face of this threat that seems to overwhelm all available cultural resources. Various thematic clusters take on their unique tonalities within the overarching concern to maintain the networks of meaning that together channel cultural resources into linguistic representations. Even a casual reading of the major novelists and poets from traditional societies leaves one with a sense of an array of characters who enjoy few privileges. One hears the voices of the dispossessed for whom questions of survival are so immediate that the rhetorical forms of their expression can never be overused. But such literature is far from defeatist. The characters find ways to claim their places in a heritage of communal relationships and perceptions that are the gift of endurance. The characters have a hardy mentor in the traditional trickster figure, whose stories play a crucial role in maintaining a sense of cultural continuity. Trickster highlights human fallibility and motivates the search for its remedy. Humor permeates the written literature.

As modern technology threatens the earth itself, indigenous writers bind the force of their historical struggle for survival to that of planetary survival. Although some traditional peoples have experienced forced geographical relocation, they have nurtured a precisely remembered awareness of a homeland that gives them identity. Now many indigenous writers are uniting to use their awareness of exile and their loyalty to their historical sense of place to warn against global environmental decline. *See also* myth; nonliteracy; oral tradition; storytelling.

remnant, in the Hebrew Bible, the small subportion of Israel that will be redeemed.

Remonstrants. *See* Arminius (Hermandszoon), Jakob.

Rennyo (ren-nyoh; 1415–99), the eighth head of the Japanese Buddhist Honganji sect of Jodo Shinshu when it was moribund and when Shinran's successors had split into several groups. In order to revive the Honganji and unify Shinran's followers, Rennyo wrote letters (*Ofumi*) to explain Shinran's teachings in a forceful but simple manner. He also compiled sets of rules (*okite*) to rid the school of heresies and systematized the liturgy, making ample use of hymns. A skillful politician, Rennyo used his twenty-seven offspring to unify the Jodo Shinshu by appointing sons to key posts at associated temples and marrying daughters to important Pure Land leaders. *See also* Jodo Shinshu; Pure Land; Shinran.

renunciation. *See* asceticism.

repentance, the self-conscious rejection of a previous mode of life, now considered evil, and the promise to undertake new proper modes of behavior. *See also* penance.

Repentance (Chin. *ch'an-hui*), Chinese Buddhist monastic service held fortnightly in which participants confess violations of monastic discipline.

responsa (Heb. *sheaylot uteshuvot*, "questions and answers"), the recorded answers of rabbinic authorities to questions about Jewish law.

The Nature and Origin of the Responsa: The Talmud and the subsequent codes, vast as they are, are insufficient to deal with every question of Jewish religious practice and cannot anticipate every legal problem that requires decision. As a result of social, economic, political, and technological change, new problems arise that are not dealt with in the older legal literature. Through the centuries individual Jews turned to their rabbis for guidance about such new problems, and local rabbis frequently directed these questions to the outstanding Jewish jurists of their age. The responsa are the vehicle for the solutions the Torah must provide to every problem of law and practice.

The Legal Technique of the Responsa: Although each legal authority has his own style, they share a common method. They first determine what the facts are in the case before them. They then determine under which legal categories this case falls and which general principles apply. They search the literature for precedents that might shed light on the present case. With or without a precedent, the respondent constructs an argument that shows how the general principles apply to the particular case. He then draws a conclusion that specifies what the law is in the case before him. The written response does not always record this complex process of legal research and analysis; responsa exist of every length and degree of elaboration.

History of the Responsa Literature: As early as the compilation of the Talmud there are instances of questions being directed to various authorities for resolution. The genuine form of responsa literature begins, however, with the leaders of the Babylonian academies, especially from the middle of the eighth to the middle of the eleventh centuries. Their responsa not only deal with purely legal questions but also often take up theological questions and questions of textual exegesis. From the twelfth century on, legal authorities in all Jewish centers were writing responsa that were widely distributed and studied, and the process has continued without interruption to the present. In the twentieth century there are large numbers of responsa written in Europe, Israel, and America that reflect the new circumstances of life in those places. It is estimated that there are well over three thousand volumes of published responsa, plus large numbers of unpublished manuscripts.

The Responsa as a Source for Jewish History: From the questions that are asked we learn much about the life of the Jews in different times and places that is not readily available through archives or other standard historical sources.

Maimonides is asked whether Karaites may be counted among those who constitute the required prayer quorum of ten men. From the question we learn that despite deep religious differences with the Karaites, many Jews still considered them part of the Jewish community. Maimonides's response reinforces this view. He answers that they may not be counted toward the prayer quorum, because they deny the validity of this law; however, they may be treated as legitimate Jews with respect to all those matters in which they agree with the rabbis. Thus, we learn about the status of the Karaites in the twelfth century.

From questions concerning proper practice at meals we learn about the foods that were eaten as well as the customs surrounding dining. Elementary questions about religious practices show that the ritual was not absolutely fixed. They also tell us about the low level of learning and observance in the community that raised such questions. Issues arising out of problems concerning ownership and transfer of property, as well as other issues of commerce, teach us about the nature of housing, the modes of property division, business relations between Jews and non-Jews, currency rates and values, and the extent to which Jews in a non-Jewish society retained judicial autonomy.

Contemporary responsa address issues arising out of technological and social change. They deal with the status of electricity in Jewish law, for example. There are ongoing discussions about the use of electric lights, telephones, automobiles, etc., on the Sabbath. The student of these responsa in a future age will discover a rich picture of the way technology transformed daily life and became a problem for Jewish religious observance in the twentieth century.

New medical technology has generated questions about such issues as artificial insemination, organ transplants, and conditions for legitimate abortion. The widespread practice of adopting infants whose natural parents are unknown raises questions about the status of those children within the Jewish community and the relation in law between these children and their adoptive parents.

The establishment of the State of Israel created new circumstances that generate legal problems. May a young man or woman choose to settle in Israel against the explicit wishes of parents who reside elsewhere? How does one conduct a defense establishment in accordance with Torah law? How shall dairy farmers deal with milking their cows on the Sabbath? These are only some of the many problems that are posed by Jews seeking to apply Torah law to life in a modern Jewish state.

Perhaps the most striking instance of how responsa preserve historical reality is in the questions and answers generated by the circumstances of Jews under Nazi persecution during the years of the Holocaust. The questions reflect the bitter reality of the oppressed. Consider how much is contained in the following questions: Because we are slave laborers, is it proper for us to recite in the morning liturgy the benediction praising God "who has not made me a slave"? Is it permissible to try to save one's life by assuming the identity of a non-Jew? History, theology, social reality—all come together in just one such question. The Holocaust responsa teach us about a dimension of the horrors of those years that no historian can reconstruct from the usual sources of history. *See also* mitzvah; rabbi; rabbinical court, Talmud, Torah.

resurrection, rising from the dead, either collectively or individually. Although the form of the body may change, the personhood remains intact. *See also* afterlife; rebirth; soul.

Judaism: Resurrection is the belief that at the end of time God will restore the dead to bodily life. There is little clear evidence in the Hebrew Bible to support this doctrine, and numerous passages seem to be outright denials of the possibility of bodily resurrection. "If a man dies can he live again?" (Job 14:14; cf., e.g., Job 7:9; 2 Samuel 14:14). Of the few passages that seem to affirm resurrection, the strongest states, "Many of those that sleep in the dust of the earth will awake, some to eternal life, others to reproaches, to everlasting abhorrence" (Daniel 12:2; cf. Isaiah 26:19). Although the exact meaning of these passages is in dispute, they are widely treated as teaching the doctrine of the resurrection of the body.

Resurrection in Law and Liturgy: The dominant trend in rabbinic Judaism considers resurrection to be a fixed dogma. A passage in the Mishnah rules that one who denies that the Torah teaches the resurrection of the dead will be excluded from the world to come, i.e., such a one is a heretic. In this way the doctrine is given the strongest possible official support. In addition, three times each day, in the statutory Jewish prayers, there is the affirmation that God will bring the dead back to life, thus providing powerful reinforcement of the doctrine.

Although the tradition views the belief in resurrection as mandatory, there is no agreement as to the nature of resurrection, its time, or its relationship to such other eschatological states as the days of the Messiah or the world to come. Various views are expressed about how and when the dead will come to life. It is also not clear whether the resurrected bodies will remain alive forever or whether their return to life is temporary.

What seems to unify the various views about resurrection is the conviction that body and soul are equally part of human nature. Neither can act without the other. Resurrection implies that at the end of time, when all humanity is to stand in final judgment, whole persons will be judged, not soulless bodies or disembodied souls.

In Later Jewish Thought: Most of the Jewish philosophers and theologians of the Middle Ages considered resurrection to be a fixed article of faith, no matter how they differed in their accounts of the nature of the event. The most prominent Jewish thinker of the medieval period, Moses Maimonides (1135–1204), developed what he considered to be an absolutely binding set of thirteen articles of faith. He included in them the bodily resurrection of the dead, although he considers it to be a concession to the popular incapacity to conceive of nonbodily existence. He teaches that the resurrection will be a temporary state followed by a purely spiritual eternal life.

The doctrine is still affirmed today in very traditional Jewish circles, but it is openly rejected by most liberal Jewish religious thinkers. They tend to conceive of human immortality in purely spiritual or even metaphoric terms. Even when rejected, the doctrine of resurrection is one of the most intense human protests against the frightening finality of death. *See also* creed; eschatology.

Christianity: Throughout most of the Hebrew Bible, life is assumed to end with death. In Jewish apocalyptic literature (second century B.C.) the idea of resurrection appears as God's vindication of the elect at the end of history. Against this background Christian beliefs developed in the resurrection of Jesus as the eschatological act of God and the promise of the resurrection of all believers. To the early traditions of the "appearance" of the risen Jesus (e.g., 1 Corinthians 15:3–8) were added traditions of the "empty tomb" (e.g., Mark 16:1–8). Only later did Christianity combine the idea of the resurrection of the body with the Greek idea of the immortality of the soul. *See also* eschatology; immortality; Jesus Christ.

retreat, a Christian term for a place for or the act of retiring for a period of contemplation and prayer, either under a director or on one's own. *See also* spiritual direction, Christian.

retribution (Judaism), divine. The claim that God rewards good and punishes evil arises from the concept that one God created a perfect and just world, demands that people adhere to a system of laws and practices deemed just, and rewards those who do and punishes those who do not follow the divine will.

According to the Hebrew Bible, divine reward and punishment occur in this world (see Exodus 20:12; Leviticus 26). The prosperity of the wicked is seen as temporary (Psalm 92:8), just as the suffering of the righteous is understood invariably to come to an end. The latter concept is illustrated by the righteous Job, whose suffering was compensated when, by the end of his life, he received a twofold replacement of everything God had taken from him, including his first wife and children.

Talmudic rabbis and medieval Jewish philosophers move beyond this simplistic perspective by positing final retribution and reward in a coming world. In this view, the wicked are compensated in their current life for any good they might do, while, in the coming world, God will severely punish their evil deeds. The righteous, by contrast, suffer in this world for slight infractions they commit; in the coming world, they will be rewarded for their pious deeds.

A second approach to divine retribution, which first appears in the talmudic literature, holds that good deeds are their own reward and that one must serve God without regard for any potential reward (Mishnah *Abot* 1:3). This view, developed in the philosophy of Maimonides (1135–1204), Gersonides (1288–1344), and others, sees retribution as a natural process primarily affecting the sinner's rational self and having much less effect on his or her body or external circumstance. This view rejects the notion of bodily resurrection and holds that retribution in the coming world applies only to the rational soul. In the world to come, only righteous people, who, because of their righteousness, have acquired self-knowledge, will achieve immortality.

In contemporary Jewish thinking, the credibility of Judaism's doctrine of divine retribution has been challenged by the Holocaust, leading some liberal Jewish thinkers, notably Richard Rubenstein (1924–), to reject completely the traditional doctrine that God acts in history so as to reward proper behavior or to punish evil. *See also* Judaism (thought and ethics); Judaism, God in; theodicy.

revelation, the transmission of knowledge from the divine to the human. *See also* divination; Hinduism (authoritative texts and their interpretation); inspiration; Islam (authoritative texts and their interpretation); oracle; Sharia.

Judaism: In Hebrew, the term *mattan torah,* "the giving of the Torah," refers to God's self-revelation and the transmission of divine teachings to the people of Israel. According to Judaism, the paramount revelation of God to the Israelite people occurred at Sinai, when God communicated to Moses a detailed system of laws intended to govern the Israelites' individual and corporate existence. Revelation accordingly comprises the physical act through which God called upon Israel to be the covenanted people. In keeping with this view, rabbinic Judaism holds that a Jew who denies that the law (Torah) derives from revelation loses the possibility of life in the world to come (Mishnah *Sanhedrin* 10:1), and one who deems so little as a single rule not to derive from God is called a despiser of the Torah (Babylonian Talmud *Sanhedrin* 99a).

The rabbis hold that, at Sinai, God transmitted to Moses the entirety of the divine law, encompassing the content of both prior and subsequent acts of communication with human beings (see *Exodus Rabbah* 29:6). When rabbis speak of mattan torah, they therefore refer to this event in particular, in which, they hold, Moses beheld God as in a translucent mirror (Babylonian Talmud *Yebamot* 49b). All other experiences of revelation are of lesser importance, reflected by the fact that, at these times, God appeared with less clarity, e.g., to the prophets, who saw God as though through dark glass (Babylonian Talmud *Yebamot* 49b), or to other individuals who saw God in dreams.

In scripture, revelation routinely is marked by God's physical manifestations (see Genesis 12:6–7 and numerous instances in which God "appears" to an Israelite progenitor or prophet). Rabbinic Judaism understands the period of

God's physical participation in revelation to have ended with the prophets. The rabbis see revelation in their own day as resulting from human interpretation of the laws and other information received at Sinai. In this view, knowledge of God no longer results from God's self-revelation; it depends, rather, upon humanity's proper grasp of the Torah. By thinking about Torah, the rabbi participates in revelation, making manifest God's thought in God's own words.

In this process of revelation, God does not physically self-reveal to any person. Indeed, even if God chooses to self-reveal, e.g., through a heavenly voice (*bat qol*) or by disrupting the natural order, such divine intercession is rejected as immaterial to the determination of the law (Babylonian Talmud *Baba Metzia* 59a–b). Such decisions are in human hands alone. The rabbis' own deliberations and legal discussions disclose aspects of the divine will that have an authority and status equal to that which God made known in the revelation at Sinai.

The rabbis thus develop a concept of revelation entirely unanticipated by scripture. They hold that, at Sinai, Moses actually received two distinct aspects of the revelation, the written law, embodied in the text of the Pentateuch, and an oral law, transmitted only by word of mouth. While the written component of revelation had always been accessible to all of the people of Israel, the oral part was transmitted only to successive generations of sages so as to have reached the hands of the rabbis alone.

In the second century, to assure that this oral revelation would not be lost as a result of war or other physical or intellectual calamity, the rabbis began to codify and preserve it in written form. The oral Torah thus was encompassed by the Mishnah, completed in the third century, and by subsequent documents of rabbinic Judaism, concluding with the Babylonian Talmud, completed in the sixth century.

Medieval Jewish philosophers and later thinkers developed the biblical and rabbinic conceptions of revelation in directions compatible with ideologies current in their own day. Following an Aristotelian concept of revelation, Maimonides (1135–1204) understood revelation to be a natural phenomenon, the result of the interaction of the human rational and imaginative faculties (*The Guide of the Perplexed* 2.36). In this approach Maimonides differed from Judah Halevi (ca. 1075–1141), who held that revelation, which derives directly from God, is superior to reason, which has a human source and so is subject to doubt.

Contemporary Orthodox thinkers continue to develop the rabbinic understanding of revelation as a historical event through which God related specific commandments to humanity. Liberal thinkers, by contrast, increasingly have understood revelation to be part of a continuing process through which humans become aware of the divine. Hermann Cohen (1842–1918) rejected the notion of an opposition between reason and revelation, arguing that God is revealed in the creating of humans as rational beings. Revelation thus is a trait of humankind, not the result of a special mode of cognition or the product of any historical event. Other contemporary Jewish thinkers, especially naturalist philosophers, have rejected the notion of revelation as a divine gift given by God to an essentially passive humanity. Instead, they propose a doctrine of inspiration in which human beings are the primary actors and in which, as a result, revelation comprises a purely subjective experience that may change from age to age. *See also* Judaism, God in; Torah.

Revelation, Book of, the central book of Christian apocalypticism and millenarianism. Written in the first century by John of Patmos, it is the last book in the New Testament. *See also* apocalypticism; John the Divine.

revenant, an individual returned from the dead. *See also* ghost; spirits.

Reverend, an honorific used as a title for a Christian cleric.

reversal, a characteristic element within some forms of ritual in which the ordinary taxonomies, rules, conventions and norms are inverted. Reversal is an expression of the extraordinary period of time defined by ritual and the separate nature of the ritual community in opposition to the everyday or profane. *See also* carnival; heyoka; Holi; John Canoe festival; rebellion, rituals of; Saturnalia; Skinwalker.

revitalization movements, a designation, popularized by sociologists and anthropologists, loosely applied to religions that seek to revive all or a select portion of their traditional beliefs and practices when essential political, economic, and religious changes threaten the identity of the community.

Although concerns for renewal and reform exist at the heart of most religions, the identification of such efforts as revitalization movements has generally been limited to studies of conquered or colonized tribal peoples undertaking the reestablishment of their own culture in a conscious, organized fashion. In such cases, scholars emphasize extreme deprivation, economic exploitation, or pervasive cognitive dissonance as the chief factor in the crisis provoking the revitalization attempts. Religions that regularly have been labeled "revitalization movements" include the cargo cults of Melanesia and the nineteenth-century Native American Ghost Dance, as well as prophetic movements in West Africa and among Native American tribes.

The popularity of the term in the mid-twentieth century is connected with two recurrent prejudices among scholars: first, simple xenophobia, expressed in disdain for nonwhite cultures and their rejection of Eurocentric values or Christianity, and, second, a resistance to extension of the rubric "religion" to non-Western or non-Christian groups. Its pejorative connotations and irresolvable imprecision leave *revitalization movements* a term to be avoided. *See also* nativistic movements; new religions.

revival, a Christian religious service aimed at bringing about an intense emotional experience of conversion in those attending. Revivals have their roots in the piety of John Wesley's Methodist movement in England and the Great Awakening in the American colonies in the mid-eighteenth century. *See also* Graham, William (Billy) Franklin; Great Awakening; Methodism.

Revival Zion. *See* Afro-Americans (Caribbean and South America), new religions among.

ri (ree; Chin. *li*), in Japanese thought, principle in contrast to material force (Chin. *ch'i;* Jap. *ki*). The Chinese Neo-Confucian Chu Hsi (1130–1200) emphasized the interaction of *ri* and ki as constituting the metaphysical structure of the universe. Ri is multivalent and includes the source of life, the ordering principles of natural law, and the organizing principles for social ethics. *See also* ch'i; Chu Hsi; li; Neo-Confucianism.

ridda (rid'duh; Arab., "apostasy"), the blasphemous act of rejecting Islam by those who once claimed faith. *See also* apostasy; blasphemy.

right, left, a primary opposition in bodily orientation much elaborated and assigned value in cultural systems. When one compares religions, one finds that, almost universally, the right is sacred, the left is profane; the right is auspicious, the left inauspicious. In India, the right hand is pure, the left impure, but ascetics receive food with the left hand. One circles a sacred object clockwise, that is, from the right side. Right is male, left is female; people shake hands with their right hands. The Buddha entered *nirvana*

resting on his right side. As Robert Hertz points out in "The Preeminence of the Right Hand" (1909), this classification is not natural but cultural. The dominance of the semantics of the right is not because the left hand is weak. The left hand in some cultures is often mutilated, because the right hand is the ideal to which all must conform. It is the opposition between the moral and the immoral, life and death. "The right hand of the Lord hath the preeminence" (Psalm 118:16).

The right side often represents transcendence. In paintings of the Last Judgment, Christ's right hand is raised, indicating paradise for the elect, while the left hand is lowered, pointing toward the hell of the damned.

The right hands are joined in marriage; the right hand takes the oath and concludes contracts. The left hand is the hand of sorcery, perjury, and death. But this set of oppositions must not be taken as absolute. In China, the connotations may be reversed. Right and left in traditional China, although unequal, are also relative to the circumstances. Although obligatorily right-handed, in the classification of all things into *yang* and *yin*, the left is yang and male, while the right is yin and female. The Chinese tradition also speaks of a Tao that is left, heterodox, and magical, while the Tao of the right is orthodox, ritual, and legal.

Right and left are often assimilated with the cardinal points of space. In Arabic and Hebrew, for example, left is associated with the north, and right is associated with the south. In China, yang/left and yin/right also signify east and west.

The opposition of right and left signifies a highly complex cognitive system of classification that becomes part of the religious language for ordering the world. *See also* directional orientations; dualism; typology, classification.

Rightly Guided Caliphs (*al-khulafa al-rashidun,* Arab.), the first four caliphs, or successors, to the Prophet Muhammad. Often referred to simply as the Rashidun, these four men were close associates of Muhammad and related to him by blood or marriage. On the death of Muhammad in 632, Abu Bakr was first chosen to lead the Muslim community in prayer and battle; he consolidated the confederation of Arab tribes that Muhammad had begun. When Abu Bakr died in 634, Umar ibn al-Khattab took the position and supervised the massive Arab conquests. In 644, Uthman ibn Affan succeeded Umar. Uthman's reign was marred by problems of corruption that led to his assassination in 656. Ali ibn Abi Talib then took office, but his authority was challenged, and he too fell victim to murder in 661. It has become an article of faith in the creeds of the Sunni (traditionalist) majority that the Rightly Guided Caliphs were the best of Muslims after the Prophet, and that they succeeded in the order of their religious virtue. During their rules, the Qur'an was standardized and the Islamic religious sciences established. The Sunnis regard this period as second only to Muhammad's as a golden age in Islamic history. In contrast, Shiite Muslims regard the first three caliphs as usurpers of the right of Ali, who alone, in their view, was entitled to succeed. *See also* Islamic political theory; Shia; Sunni.

Rig Veda (rig vay'duh; Skt., "knowledge of verses"), a collection of 1,028 hymns addressed to various deities, to be recited during ritual, that is the oldest text of India and traditionally Hinduism's most sacred, the fundamental revealed (*shruti*) text. Composed in archaic Vedic Sanskrit by a number of professional bards (*rishis*) or bardic families in poetry of deliberate complexity over a period of several hundred years (ca. 1500–1000 B.C.), the text was meticulously preserved by oral tradition and written in medieval times. It is divided into ten books (*mandalas*, lit., "circles").

Books 2–7, the core of the oldest *Rig Veda*, constitute the Family Books, each attributed to a different bardic family. Book 8 contains smaller family collections. All of these books contain hymns to a variety of gods, especially Agni and Indra. Book 9 contains hymns addressed solely to the god Soma Pavamana, the deified intoxicating drink. Books 1 and 10 contain smaller collections and also some miscellaneous appended material, including hymns with apparently secular character and others of philosophical and cosmogonic speculation. In later Vedic ritual, the *Rig Veda* serves as the manual for the Hotar priest and is widely quoted in the other Vedas. *See also* Hinduism (authoritative texts and their interpretation); Veda, Vedism.

Rinzai (rin-zah-ee), Japanese Zen Buddhist school based on the Chinese Lin-chi school of Ch'an. Although Eisai (1141–1215) is often regarded as the founder of the school, important roles were played by Enni Ben'en (1201–80) and several Chinese masters such as Lan-hsi Tao-lung (1213–78). The school was patronized by the military rulers, resulting in a hierarchical classification (*gozan*) of temples. Art such as poetry and calligraphy flourished in many of these temples. Eventually a number of masters spoke out against the secularization that accompanied government patronage. The most famous of these is the eccentric Ikkyu (1394–1481). Although the vitality of Gozan art declined, Zen influence on the arts was continued by such figures as the tea master Sen Rikyu (1522–91) and the swordsman Takuan (1573–1645). Modern Rinzai practice of the *koan* (a paradoxical teaching that transcends logical or conceptual thought) was influenced by Hakuin (1686–1768). Later Rinzai adherents such as Shaku Soyen (1856–1919) and D. T. Suzuki (1870–1966) were responsible for the early spread of Zen in the West. *See also* Bankei Yotaku; Ch'an school; Eisai; Gozan; Hakuin Ekaku; Lin-chi school; Suzuki, Daisetsu Teitaro.

rishi (ri'shi; Skt., "seer"), one of the inspired poets of Vedic India who composed the Vedic hymns. Seven are commonly enumerated; they were later revered as semidivine figures. *See also* Rig Veda.

Rissho Koseikai (ri-shor kor-say-kai; Jap.), a Japanese new religion that seceded from Reiyukai under the leadership of Niwano Nikkyo in 1938. Its membership is about two million. Taking its name from Nichiren's treatise of 1260, the *Rissho Ankokuron* ("the treatise on establishing true Buddhism to establish peace in Japan"), it teaches members to develop their own enlightenment in fellowship with others. It runs special discussion groups (*hoza*), during which members discuss personal problems and issues of faith and receive advice on how to deal with these in line with Buddhist principles. It also preaches the importance of world peace and maintains an active peace foundation. *See also* Japan, new religions in; Nichiren; Reiyukai.

Risshu (rees-shoo), one of the six Japanese Buddhist Nara schools. Founded by Ganjin (687–763), the school advocated observance of the traditional 250 *Ssu-fen lu* (*Dharmaguptaka Vinaya*) precepts for monks, but interpreted them through the threefold Mahayana precepts (prohibiting evil, promoting good, and benefiting sentient beings). Although the school declined during the Heian period (794–1185), it was revived by Eizon. As a result, two factions of the school arose based at Saidaiji and Toshodaiji. *See also* Eizon; Ganjin; Nara schools; ordination; Vinaya.

rita (ri'tuh; Skt., "truth"), in Vedic and later India, the expression of the real nature of things and the proper relations between beings. Formulating such truth conveys supernatural power and maintains cosmic order. Guarding *rita* is the god Varuna's special province. *See also* Varuna.

rite. *See* ritual.

rites de passage, category of ritual first proposed by Arnold van Gennep (1909). *See also* initiation rituals; pilgrimage, theory of.

Ritsuryo (ree-tsoo-ryoh; Jap., "law and regulations"), the constitutional law that governed the period (645–1191) when the Japanese political, economic, and social systems were modeled directly on Chinese prototypes. Previously the hereditary clans, each with its own priesthood and religious cult, had been paramount; with the institution of Ritsuryo a centralized monarchy dispensed government offices, established social status, and regulated religious affairs. Shinto was organized and gained official status. *See also* Nakatomi clan; Shinto.

ritual. The term *ritual* needs a precise definition because of the widespread misuse of the word. Ritual is a system of actions and beliefs that has a beginning, a middle, and an end, and is directly related to superhuman beings. Superhuman beings are beings who can do things humans cannot do. These beings do not necessarily have the qualities and properties of human beings; they may, for example, be formless or take the form of monsters or animals.

This definition of ritual excludes such things as routines and habits. Talk about the rituals of bees, fish, birds, and animals is at best metaphorical if not anthropomorphic. What makes ritual action unique to human beings is the relation it has with superhuman beings. This relation is usually expressed through the language of ritual belief. It is this relation that constitutes ritual. Thus, ritual is made up of act and belief.

Ritual as System: Rituals have a specific system or structure that involves passage from one mode of existence to another. This structure has three stages that can be identified as follows: the preliminal stage, the liminal stage, and the postliminal stage. All rituals, or rites of passage, consist of this threefold structure that marks the beginning, the middle, and the end of a ritual.

The preliminal stage marks a separation of the initiate from the present mode of existence. It marks, by ritual action, separation from family, the end of childhood, single status, the present year, month, week, or day, or passage into a new community. The preliminal rite of separation often involves a last meal with kin, change of clothes, shaving of hair, or an ordeal of some kind symbolizing death.

Liminality, the second stage, is the crucial stage of a ritual. It is in this stage that rebirth, transformation, or recreation takes place. For example, the ritual that transforms all Hindu boys of the three upper castes into adults is called "the twice born" (*dvija*) ritual, and many Christians speak of themselves as "born again" Christians. The ritual action in this stage often dramatizes death, a return to the womb, or the beginning of time. Status and gender are usually abolished.

Liminality is "communitas," where all those gathered together are equal, where social stratification and hierarchy are done away with. Words such as *sisterhood* or *brotherhood* are often used to define this liminal community. Liminality is classless, atemporal, and often uses the culture's cosmology to signify a new beginning or a rebirth. The initiates are often referred to as infants, or as neither male nor female. Normal social structures are often suspended in orgiastic activity or its opposite, an ascetic mode of life. Thus, liminality often appears to be lawless in its opposition to the states of existence both before and after its performance.

In the liminal stage of a ritual, sacred objects are shown, and myths and other important traditional knowledge are repeated by those who conduct the ritual. Thus, liminality is both creative and preservative of tradition.

The postliminal stage of a ritual marks the ritual's end. It marks the transition into a new mode of existence by means of giving gifts, offerings, benedictions, celebrations, or a brief withdrawal of the initiate before full entrance into the new mode of existence. (The Western tradition of the honeymoon after the wedding ceremony is an example.) Celebrations of the beginning of a new time (day, week, month, or year) signify the end of time and the beginning of a new era or time.

When rituals are examined by means of this tripartite structure it becomes clear that although liminality mediates between the old and the new existence, it is also in opposition to both.

In the life span of an individual, especially in traditional cultures, most if not all significant human events—birth, naming, initiation into adulthood, marriage, death, construction of buildings, wars, entrance into professions, education, and the very structure of time and space—are all marked by ritual. Thus, all significant acts can be defined as ritual acts. Art, music, and drama also find their origin in ritual.

Theories of Ritual: Scholars are in agreement about the structure of rituals as rites of passage. There is, however, little agreement on the meaning of rituals. This situation is primarily due to the seemingly odd nature of many ritual practices and beliefs. To Westerners, rituals of other cultures often appear unintelligible.

The Rational Theory: The theory that rituals are

rational actions, instrumental means for achieving specific goals, was at one time the most popular theory of ritual, and continues to be defended by many scholars against sustained criticism. The theory defines rational action as a means for achieving an end. Ritual acts, according to this theory, are performed as a means for achieving a goal. In general terms, rituals are performed for the satisfaction of some desire. The difference between ritual acts and other kinds of rational action is that the beliefs that are related to all rituals are false. Scholars who adhere to this theory point out that a false belief does not entail irrationality. The history of modern science is riddled with theories that turned out to be false, yet neither the history of science nor those that held the beliefs are labeled irrational. Nevertheless, this theory has always faced a crucial question: How does one account for the fact that societies persist in believing what is false? This question does not just arise for those societies that are labeled as nonliterate. It can be raised for any society in which rituals are performed. In brief, why do most individuals persist in believing what is false?

Scholars who adhere to what has often been called the rationalist or intellectualist theory of ritual have spent a great deal of time resolving this problem. One solution asserts that no ritual belief is false, since no one could survive by persistently believing false propositions about themselves and the world. What one needs to do is find the correct referent of ritual beliefs. The solution is to see that the truth value of ritual beliefs, the reasons for ritual action, does not rest in unverifiable statements that seem nonsensical, but refers to social relations, social order, and cohesion, which are both intelligible and empirically verifiable. This solution produces a theory that is an objective and rational account for why rituals are performed.

The problem with this explanation of ritual is that our informants will have nothing to do with it. A Burmese Buddhist who performs rituals to ward off the negative effects of Nats (spirits), a Hindu who worships Shiva, or a Christian who participates in the ritual of the mass would take little comfort in being told that what he or she is really doing is uttering symbolic statements and maintaining social order by performing rituals. This solution must account for why people do not know what they are doing.

A second solution relativizes the truth conditions of beliefs. To say that ritual beliefs are false, or not in accord with reality, is to make an ethnocentric mistake. What is true, what is false, what is real or unreal, is given in the sense of a specific language. Thus, truth conditions are relative to the rules of particular languages. The rationality of ritual beliefs is relative to the truth conditions that are constituted by the language of a particular culture. The problem with this solution is that it cannot be asserted as a universal rule without contradiction. The relativity of truth conditions, if true, would make religious conversion and linguistic translations impossible.

The Expressive Theory: The expressive theory of ritual is a direct outcome of the attempt to solve the problems produced by the rational theory of myth. It solves the problem by asserting that ritual practices and beliefs are not rational as a means for achieving an end. This is not a negative judgment concerning ritual. It is made to avoid the conclusion that ritual beliefs are false. One avoids this conclusion by denying that rituals have a truth value.

Ritual beliefs are not informative; they do not entail a truth value, as do other propositions. Furthermore, ritual acts are not instrumental, a means for achieving some end. Ritual beliefs and acts are ends-in-themselves; they are expressive like music and art. In the strict theoretical sense, rituals are nonrational.

When ritual beliefs are taken literally, as common propositions involving truth conditions, one is confronted with nonsense. The meaning of ritual acts and beliefs, therefore, can best be explained as symbols or metaphors that must be interpreted as codes or representations of biological, sociological, psychological, or metaphysical realities. Some scholars use a combination of these referents as the most adequate approach for explaining ritual.

The problem with this approach, however, is that one can never know which interpretation is the correct one. What is worse, it would seem that any apparently nonsensical ritual could be taken as code or symbol for some hidden meaning. Finally, how does one account for the fact that those who perform the ritual do not see that what they are doing is indeed something symbolic, containing a hidden meaning? One finds the same problem as with the rationalist theory of ritual; people who perform rituals do not really know what they are doing.

A more adequate approach to explaining ritual may develop through the use of contemporary models in linguistics, the philosophy of language, and the cognitive sciences in general.

See also ablution; age-sets; agriculture, religious aspects of; ancestral rites; anointing; apotheosis; apotropaic ritual; ascension rituals; atonement; baptism; bear ceremonialism; belief; burial; cannibalism; carnival; chant; chaos, return to; circumambulation; circumcision; civic cults; clitoridectomy; clowns; confession; consecration; corn ceremonies, green; cremation; curse; dance; dead, rituals with respect to the; directional orientations; divination; domestic ritual; drama and religion; drum; eating together; excommunication; exorcism; fasting; festal cycle; fire; firewalking; fishing rites/whaling rites; flagellation; food; foundation rites; foundation sacrifice; gender crossing; grave, graveyard; harvest rituals; healing; holocaust; homosexuality; hunting, religious aspects of; images, veneration of; incense; infibulation; initiation rituals; instrumental and expressive; intensification rites; intercession; libation; life-crisis rites; life-cycle rituals; lights; lip piercing; lip plug; marriage; marriage, sacred; masks; meditation; men's houses; mock king; mourning; mutilation; naming rituals; necromancy; new year festivals; nonperiodic rites; nudity; ordeal; ordination; orgy; penile bloodletting; periodic rites; pilgrimage; pipe, sacred; possession; potlatch; prayer; prayerstick, prayerfeather; puberty rituals; purification; purity and impurity; rain dance; rationalism, intellectualism; rebellion, rituals of; rebirth; religion, anthropology of; religion, definition of; repentance; reversal; rites de passage; sacred space and sacred time; sacrifice; sanctification; sandpainting; secret societies; sexuality and religion; shamanism; smoke; subincision; Sun Dance, Sun Dance religion; sweat, sweatlodge; symbol; taboo; temple; tjuringa; tobacco and hallucinogens; transvestism, ritual; vision quest; votive offering; vow.

road of life, designation, common in Native American religions, for proper moral and ritual conduct. While the image is a recurring one, the shape of the image is varied: for the Delaware-Lenape the white road begins in the east and moves in a circular movement to the west; for the Navajo the road of life is a broken circle; for the Pima and Papago it is a complicated circular maze, the proper navigation of which depends on divine help; for the Oglala Sioux the red road runs from north to south, along an axis marked by purity and life.

The rituals that mark that road are, for the most part, rites of passage. They are highly varied rituals that mark and make real the passages or life crises of a person. *See also* North America, traditional religions in.

Roman religion. Roman religion was broadly regulated by the ancient Roman state, from those practices belonging to its early history as a rural community to those developed during its expansion as an empire; Roman religion came to an end as the state gradually adopted Christianity during the fourth century.

The primary objective of Roman religion was to maintain good relations or "peace" between the gods and the citizens of Rome (Lat. *pax deorum*). The Romans believed that such peace was necessary for the safety and prosperity of the state and of individual Romans. The chief means for meeting this objective was an elaborate system of rituals performed and regulated by both religious and civil officials. Roman religion imposed no demands on individuals to observe a code of ethics or to profess a personal faith. As contrasted with the varied religions of individual Romans, Roman state religion was primarily a communal phenomenon observed in social units ranging from the family to the state; individual practices were of concern only to the extent that they affected the community. For modern readers, the most striking characteristic of Roman religion is likely the omnipresence of the state and its officials in all areas of cult: as regulators, performers, and beneficiaries. The ancient Romans drew no rigid boundaries between "church" and "state"; the two spheres were inextricably bound.

Divinities: Roman religion was a polytheistic system of native and acquired divinities. The earliest divinities generally lacked the anthropomorphic characteristics associated with classical Greek religion. The Romans developed no extensive mythology; they borrowed most such stories from the Greeks. Tradition attributes even the introduction of roofed temples and images of the gods to foreign influence; Etruscans were responsible for the first temple and cult statue in Rome, that of Jupiter the Best and Greatest, the chief god of state (late sixth century B.C.). Also characteristic of this nonanthropomorphic perspective was the worship of groups of undifferentiated beings such as the spirits of the storeroom (Penates), the benevolent dead (Di Manes), and the hostile dead (lemures). Another widespread tendency of early Roman religion was the narrowly functional character of many divinities; there was a god of mildew, which attacks grain (Robigo), and a god of the boundary stone (Terminus). Even a being that had manifested itself only once might be the object of cult. Aius Locutius, for example, was the supernatural voice that once warned of the approaching Gauls. Finally, the occurrence of divinized abstractions, mostly political in nature, is noteworthy; among them were Victoria (Lat., "victory"), Fides ("trustworthiness"), Concordia ("concord"), and Salus ("well-being"). In contrast to these rather narrow divinities, others such as Jupiter had wide-ranging competencies from the earliest times.

Expansion of the Roman pantheon, always

under state control, occurred in response to varied concerns, including politics, war, famine, and epidemics. During the Etruscan domination of Rome (late sixth century B.C.), the cult of Jupiter the Best and Greatest was associated in a tripartite temple with the cults of the goddesses Juno and Minerva—a novel triad that introduced elements of Italic, Hellenic, and Etruscan cults to Rome. Vows, made in times of crisis, frequently account for the introduction of divinities. At the battle of Lake Regillus, for example, the commander A. Postumius vowed a temple to Castor, the Greek god of horsemen, for his aid in the conflict (499 B.C.). Just prior to that campaign, a grain shortage had motivated official consultation of a collection of Sibylline oracles. As a result, the same Postumius vowed a temple to Ceres, the goddess of grain, with Liber and Libera, a group that represented under Latin names the Greek triad of Demeter, Dionysos, and Kore. Later consultations of these Sibylline oracles in other crises led to the introduction of many foreign deities such as Asclepios, the Greek god of healing in 293 B.C. following an epidemic. Evocation was another practice that brought foreign deities to Rome: a commander, before attacking a foreign city, summoned its protective deity to abandon the city for a better cult among the Romans.

An important factor in expansion of the Roman pantheon was syncretism, the mingling of elements of different religions. Thus, the association of the Roman goddess Ceres with Liber and Libera introduced the Greek Demeter with her elaborate myth. As Rome expanded its presence throughout the Western world, the process of syncretism also affected foreign cults. Foreign deities were identified with Roman counterparts and received appropriate names and attributes; for example, the Phoenician-Punic god Baal in Carthage was equated with Saturn or Jupiter.

Although the Roman state was generally open to the expansion of its pantheon, under certain circumstances it was quite hostile to foreign cults. In 205 B.C., after frightening prodigies led to consultation of the Sibylline books, the Senate officially received the Anatolian cult of the Great Mother, Cybele. After fuller acquaintance with its orgiastic practices, especially the self-castration of priests, however, the state severely restricted the cult by forbidding citizens to observe its rituals or serve as priests. A similar concern for public order and morality played a part in the governmental suppression of the oriental mystery cult of Bacchus (186 B.C.), although the god had early received official acceptance under the latinized form of Liber (493 B.C.). Fears of political conspiracy increased the severity of the response to the cult that, according to the historian Livy, had large numbers of servile and foreign members, foreign leadership, and nocturnal meetings involving secrets and oaths. Out of their omnipresent desire to avoid angering any divinity, however, the Romans did allow small groups to observe necessary rituals under strict supervision.

The first three centuries A.D. saw the growing popularity and official acceptance of oriental cults, often in the form of mysteries, throughout the empire. Prominent among these were the cults of Egyptian Isis and Persian Mithra. Under Claudius, the Great Mother's consort Attis was officially recognized and the priesthood opened to citizens. Other important oriental deities of the empire were Sabazios and Jupiter Dolichenus. In contrast, Christianity often encountered a hostile reaction, for the monotheistic Christians were thought to pose a threat to the integrity of the state. One reason for this suspicion was their refusal to invoke the emperor or his guardian spirit when swearing oaths, especially in the army.

Imperial Cult: A prominent element of imperial cult was the divinization of the emperor at his death by senatorial vote. The Greek-inspired prototype for such apotheosis was that of Rome's legendary founder Romulus. Julius Caesar (d. 44 B.C.) was the first Roman to receive this honor; his successor Augustus, second. For some unpopular rulers (e.g., Nero), however, the Senate denied apotheosis. The practice of granting divine honors to living emperors probably derived from the Greek cult, which honored rulers and military leaders, including victorious Roman generals. In Rome and Italy, Augustus restricted official worship to his family's procreative spirit (Lat. genius) in combination with the spirits of crossroads (Lares Compitales). In the provinces, he also limited worship to some degree by linking his cult with that of the goddess Roma. Augustus encouraged the perception of himself as primary mediator between the human and divine, a role symbolized by his accumulation of priestly offices and perhaps also by his chosen name (augustus may indicate the recipient of favorable auspices). The encouragement of personal divine honors in Rome and Italy varied among his successors. As the imperial cult diminished in the third century, the tendency was to view the emperor as divinely chosen and protected rather than personally divine.

Priesthoods: Roman religion supported a complex hierarchy of religious personnel who served

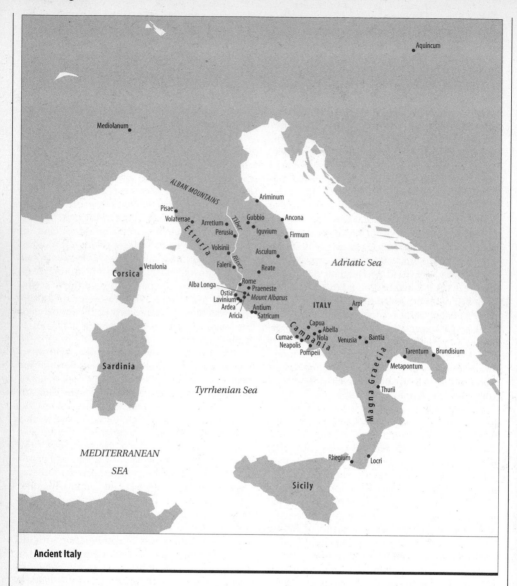

Ancient Italy

both as experts and as practitioners of the cult, the latter role often shared with civil officials. Very few religious officials devoted themselves full-time to religious duties; most served in public office as well. Like magistrates, by the first century B.C., the members of the most important priesthoods were elected. The priestly group having the broadest control over religion was the college of Pontiffs (*Pontifices*), which consisted of the King of Religious Rites (*Rex Sacrorum*), Pontiffs (whose number gradually grew to sixteen), including the Chief Pontiff (*Pontifex Maximus*), fifteen priests of individual deities (*Flamines*), and finally, six Vestal Virgins.

The Rex Sacrorum carried out various religious duties the king had performed under the monarchy. Although the Pontiffs also performed some ritual duties no one else could, their more important roles were administrative and advisory. They regulated certain religious activities of individuals, including rites for the dead and tomb law. They also kept the calendar, which indicated days for religious observances, legal business, and electoral or legislative assemblies. In addition, the Pontiffs, at the request of the Senate, gave advice on religious matters that concerned the state. The Senate itself, in Republican times, retained the final authority to issue appropriate decrees. The priests for individual deities included three major priests, who served the chief archaic gods: Jupiter, Mars, and Quirinus. The priest of Jupiter (*Flamen Dialis*) is noteworthy because he was bound by numerous archaic taboos, including prohibitions against touching a she-goat, raw meat, ivy, beans, or the dead. The twelve minor priests represented archaic divinities, most of whom are virtually unknown. The Vestal Virgins were the priestesses of Vesta, the goddess of the hearth fire; their primary task was to tend the fire of the state hearth. In addition, they prepared sacrifices for certain state rituals. The second most important priestly college was that of the Augurs (their numbers grew to sixteen). The primary ritual function of this college was to inaugurate certain places within the city for the observation of divine signs by magistrates. An inaugurated location was also necessary for meetings of the Senate. Augurs alone could interrupt a civil assembly in progress by announcing the observation of bad omens. Concerning matters of divination, the Augurs, like the Pontiffs, served as advisers to the Senate. In addition to these two oldest colleges, another important priestly college was the Fifteen Men (their numbers increased from two), who administered cults of foreign origin and, when ordered by the Senate, consulted and interpreted the oracular Sibylline books. Other priestly groups were involved with individual deities or specific rituals. The Salian brotherhood, dedicated to Mars as god of war, performed various rites, including ritual dancing, in March and October, the beginning and end of the season of war. The Fetial priests were in charge of rituals pertaining to international relations: making treaties, demanding reparations, and declaring war. In the imperial period, priestly orders were selected or instituted to serve the cult of the emperors, including the Masters of Urban Regions (*Vicomagistri*) and colleges of freedmen (*Augustales*).

Divination: In a religious system whose objective was to maintain good relations with the gods, much emphasis was necessarily placed on divination, the attempt to ascertain divine will. The Roman state undertook no major political or military action without first consulting the gods to determine their approval or disapproval. Before every meeting of the Senate and every legislative or electoral assembly, officials took the auspices. Sometimes this was done by observing the flight of birds from a place especially inaugurated for that purpose. Another method (*tripudium*), also used on the battlefield, involved the observation of chickens that were kept caged for this purpose. If they ate hungrily, dropping crumbs, the signs were positive. A more common method of divination was extispicy, the examination of the entrails of sacrificial animals. Specialists (*haruspices*) in this art learned from the Etruscans read the entrails at most public sacrifices. Blemishes or irregularities, indicating divine displeasure, necessitated the repetition of the ritual. In addition to these rituals, observed before important undertakings, other practices sought the means of averting divine anger. In the event of prodigies such as unusual weather phenomena, deformed births, or miraculous occurrences, which warned of future disasters, the Senate, after accepting the reports, might seek the expert advice of haruspices or the college of Fifteen Men. On other occasions, including epidemics, famines, and major military defeats, the Senate might order the college of Fifteen Men to consult the Sibylline books. This collection of Greek oracular verses, traditionally acquired under the monarchy, sometimes advised the introduction of new deities or rituals.

Rites and Ceremonies: To assure continuing good relations with the gods, the Romans instituted a large number of public religious observances ranging from simple sacrifices for individual divinities to great games extending over several days and honoring many gods. The civil calendar, regulated by the Pontiffs, designated the days set aside for these observances. Most took place annually on fixed dates; some, however, were movable rites whose dates the Pontiffs determined each year. Other extraordinary rites were performed in response to specific situations such as crises or prodigies indicating the need for expiation.

One common characteristic of Roman rituals was a seemingly obsessive concern with precision. Although ritual actions and words developed and changed over the years in response to varying needs, there was a strong tendency to preserve the forms that had proven to be effective over time. Some of the prayers preserved in Republican cult were no longer comprehensible even to the priests themselves. The concern for precision also manifested itself in the practice of *instauratio*, the repetition of a ritual observance, in part or in whole, if any word or action was omitted or incorrectly spoken or performed. For this reason it was customary for a Pontiff to dictate to the officiating magistrate the appropriate ritual formulas, which were preserved in priestly books. Further evidence of precision appears in the traditional language of the prayers that accompanied all religious rites. Particular care was paid to the invocation, which named the divine recipient. It included the divine name, sometimes followed by the phrase "or by whatever name it is proper for you to be called." If the name was unknown, the generic formula "whether god or goddess" was substituted. Frequently invocations concluded with a general address to "all gods and goddesses" after the naming of specific deities.

At the heart of every ritual was a sacrifice. It could be a simple vegetarian offering, often grain cakes, with a liquid offering of milk for certain rustic or archaic divinities. More frequently the offerings were animals and wine. Detailed prescriptions regulated the selection of animals: usually male victims for male gods; female for female; light-colored animals for celestial deities; dark for chthonian; particular species for certain deities. After the ritual killing, haruspices examined the entrails for signs of divine approval. If they were acceptable, attendants cooked the entrails separately and then the officiating person, not necessarily a priest, burned them with a few slices of meat on the altar. The remaining meat was consumed by participants in the ritual. The officiant performed his duties with head covered and to the accompaniment of a flute, attempts to avoid the sight or hearing of bad omens. (In cults performed according to the Greek rite, the officiant sacrificed bare-headed.)

In addition to the sacrifice, most ceremonies included a procession of participants along with the sacrificial victims. Processions of an encircling form were characteristic of a purificatory rite, such as that described by the Roman author Cato (234–149 B.C.). Participants led the sacrificial animals, a pig, sheep, and bull (*suovetaurilia*), around the fields to be purified. Perhaps the best-known procession was the triumph of a victorious military commander, an honor granted only by decree of the Senate. A lengthy procession that included the commander (dressed to resemble the statue of Jupiter), his soldiers, senators, magistrates, captives, and sacrificial animals entered the city and advanced to the temple of Jupiter the Best and Greatest, where the commander sacrificed the animals. A rather different type of procession was involved in a supplication, which some scholars consider a native Roman ritual. Men, women, and children processed from temple to temple, supplicating the gods with prayer and offerings. The state could order this ritual on occasions of either joy or distress: in response to prodigies, war, or victories. Under the emperors, this ritual became primarily a vehicle for honoring the imperial family on occasions such as birthdays.

Under Greek influence, the Roman public cult took on a more anthropomorphic and emotional character. In 399 B.C., after consultation of the Sibylline books concerning an epidemic, the Senate ordered the first performance of a *lectisternium* in Rome. Twelve deities were represented in Greek fashion by statues resting on ceremonial couches before a banquet. In 217 B.C., to expiate a prodigy of an androgynous birth, the Pontiffs ordered for the first time a procession in Greek style in which a chorus of young girls presented ritual dances and a hymn to Juno.

The Romans also honored certain deities with festival games (*ludi*), consisting primarily of chariot racing with additional performances of trick riding, wrestling, and boxing. For the first time in 240 B.C., the Roman games in honor of Jupiter included the performance of a play. From the late third century B.C., dramatic performances occurred regularly at games for various deities.

Private Cult: The primary focus of the private cult was the household and its dwelling. Here several deities received worship, sometimes under the collective name Lares, which included Vesta, the Penates, and the Lar of the household. Vesta was the spirit of the hearth fire; the Penates of the family's storeroom. The Lar of the household, according to one widely held theory, derived from spirits that protected the farmland (Lares); he then entered the domestic cult through the household servants. It was the responsibility of the male head of household to see that all of these divinities received daily offerings and prayer. Each household had a shrine (*lararium*) that contained statuettes of the Lares and sometimes other divinities especially honored by the family. Another household spirit was Janus, who dwelt in the doorway; his image displays two faces looking in opposite directions. Finally, each household honored the *genius,* the procreative spirit of the family, residing in the male head of household. The genius received offerings on the birthday of the head of household and on other family holidays. All of these divinities of the private cult had parallels in the public cult. The state Vesta had her own temple and priestesses, the Vestal Virgins, who tended the public hearth fire. There was also a temple to the Public Penates. At crossroads, the Lares Compitales received worship and, during the empire, also the genius of the emperor. In the forum stood a large free-standing gate, the Janus Geminus, which, according to tradition, stood open when the state was at war and closed only when the state was at peace.

Members of each family also observed various rites of passage. At birth, there were rituals of purification and name giving. When he was about seventeen, an adolescent boy ceremonially dedicated to the Lar of the household the protective amulet of childhood, set aside his childhood clothing, and put on the toga of manhood. A girl usually set aside her childhood belongings the day before she married. For the wedding, a bride observed ritualistic methods of dressing and fixing her hair. A procession accompanied her to the house of the bridegroom, who carried her over the threshold. To assure her welcome, she made propitiatory offerings to the deities of her new home. At death, various rites propitiated the spirit of the deceased so that it would not return to harm the living. Funerals sometimes involved elaborate processions leading the dead outside of the city where cemeteries were located. Banquets were held there at the tomb on the day of burial and at periodic commemorations. Since maintaining peace with the spirits of the dead concerned the whole community, the civil calendar designated a nine-day period in February (*Parentalia*) for visiting tombs and making offerings to each family's dead. On the day following this observance, families gathered to celebrate continuing kinship ties (*Caristia*). In May, another public observance (*Lemuria*) propitiated the spirits of the malevolent dead. An account of a private ritual of the Lemuria tells how the head of household arose at midnight to expel these spirits with incantations, apotropaic gestures, and an offering of black beans spit from his mouth.

A New State Religion: By means of a series of decrees in the fourth century, Christianity officially replaced native religion in the Roman Empire. Beginning in 341, laws prohibited sacrifices, closed public temples, removed the altar of Victory from the Senate house, prohibited the private cult, removed privileges from priests, and destroyed temples. The replacement process was slow and not without resistance and occasional retreat. *See also* Aeneid; apotheosis; Apuleius; Ceres; devotion; Diana; Edict of Milan; Etruscan religion; flamen; Indo-European religion; Janus; Jupiter; kingship, sacred; Lares; lemures; Magna Mater; Mars; Mercury; Minerva; Mithraism; mystery religions; numen; Ostia; priest/priestess; Rome; Saturn; Seneca; Sibylline oracles; Venus; Vergil.

Rome, a city on the Tiber River in west-central Italy. The ancient city was settled, according to tradition, in the eighth century B.C. but was probably inhabited as early as the tenth century. It was the location of one of the earliest Christian communities and is now the seat of the pope, the head of the Roman Catholic Church. The pope's residence, since 1929, forms an independent city-state known as Vatican City. Rome and the Vatican maintain many ancient Christian monuments as well as those of the Roman Empire, which antedated Christianity.

rood screen (Old Eng.), support for the large cross (*rood*) at the entrance to the chancel of medieval churches. Its function was to separate the laity from the sanctuary and to elevate the crucifix. *See also* Christianity (art and architecture); iconostasis.

rosary, a counting device, usually made of either a knotted cord or a string of beads, used as an aid in repetitive prayer.

Rosetta Stone, an ancient Egyptian black basalt stone inscription, discovered in 1799 by a French captain of the Napoleonic force in the Delta region near Alexandria at a site near Rosetta (Arab. *Rashid*). Now in the British Museum, the text, in Greek and two versions of Egyptian, one hieroglyphic and one demotic (a later cursive form of Egyptian writing), provided the key to the decipherment of Egyptian hieroglyphics by Jean-Francois Champollion in 1822. The inscription, written in 197 B.C., commemorates Ptolemy V Epiphanes's accession to the throne and proclaims support of Egyptian traditional religion. *See also* Egyptian religion; hieroglyph.

Rosh Hashanah (rohsh hah-shah-nah'; Heb., "the beginning of the year"), the Jewish new year, a two-day solemn occasion (1–2 Tishri), the beginning of a ten-day period of introspection and repentance. Blasts from the ram's horn (*shofar*), a wordless form of prayer, punctuate lengthy synagogue services. Home rituals include dipping apples in honey for a sweet year. *See also* Judaism (festal cycle).

Rosicrucians (ro-ze-kroo'shen; Lat., "rosy cross"), groups in the Western occult tradition that practice an esoteric mix of alchemy, astrology, Theosophy, and kabbalistic interpretation of scripture. The term emerged in 1614 or 1615 with the appearance in Germany of three anonymous publications about a secret Rosicrucian order of adepts. Though these writings were likely hoaxes or allegories, the term persisted.

In England, Rosicrucian speculation was associated with such seventeenth-century luminaries as the Cambridge Platonists and the hermeticist Robert Fludd (1574–1637). The term has been kept alive by several nineteenth- and twentieth-century American orders, as well as in Masonic usage. The best-known modern group is the Ancient and Mystical Order Rosae Crucis, of California, founded in New York City in 1915. *See also* occult, the; secret societies.

routinization.   *See* charisma.

Rudra (rood′ruh), an ambivalent Hindu deity linked with uncontrollable natural forces, harming, and healing. Gaining prominence in later Vedic religion, he receives the remainder of sacrificial offerings and comes to be lauded as "the One" unbegotten, unexcelled creator of all, the "auspicious" (*shiva*) liberation-bestowing supreme deity in *Shvetashvatara Upanishad*. Henceforth a name for Shiva. *See also* Shiva.

Rumi, Jalal al-Din (ja-lahl′ e-deen′ roo-mee; 1207–73), great Persian mystic poet and inspiration for the Mevlevi dervish order. Rumi lived in Konya, Anatolia, where he received a traditional religious education, married twice, and had four children. A prolific poet, he composed more than three thousand poems while his seventy-one discourses form a frequently studied mystical compendium. *See also* Sufism.

runes.   1 Signs of divination and magic. 2 The characters of the fourth-century Scandinavian alphabet associated with the secret knowledge of Odinn. *See also* antiquity, religions of; Nordic religion.

rusalka (roo-sahl′kah; Russ.), in Slavic folklore a female spirit, the victim of suicide, drowning, or unbaptized death, who lives in woods, fields, and waters luring men to doom.

Russell, Charles Taze (1852–1916), American conservative Christian who devoted his substantial fortune to founding the International Bible Students Association, out of which developed the Jehovah's Witnesses. In 1879, he began publishing *The Watchtower*, and in 1884 he formed the Watch Tower Bible and Tract Society. His own millennialist writings have been largely collected in the six volumes of *Studies in the Scriptures*. *See also* Jehovah's Witnesses.

Ruusbruec, Jan van (rois′brock; 1293–1381), Flemish Catholic mystic best known for his work *The Spiritual Espousals* (1350). He was most influential on the form of late-fourteenth-century Catholic spirituality known as *devotio moderna* (Lat., "modern devotion"), which focused on individual meditation on the life and death of Christ and resulted both in classic texts such as Thomas a Kempis's *The Imitation of Christ,* and the establishment of lay associations such as the Brethren of the Common Life.

Ruysbroeck, Jan van.   *See* Ruusbruec, Jan van.

Ryobu Shinto (ryoh-boo shin-toh; Jap., "dual Shinto"), a form of Shinto that first arose ca. 970 to harmonize Shingon Buddhism and the Ise shrines. The main *kami* (divinity, divine presence) of Ise, Amaterasu Omikami (the sun goddess) was equated with Dainichi (the sun Buddha); the inner and outer shrines of Ise were seen as the two aspects of Dainichi in complementary fields of cosmic force (*mandalas*). This kind of syncretic thought influenced later Shinto schools and popular belief and practice. *See also* Ise Shrine; Shingon-shu; Shinto; syncretism (Japan).

Ryogen (ryoh-gen; 912–985), a monk who revived the Japanese Buddhist Tendai school from a period of decline and helped make it one of the most powerful political and economic institutions in Japan. *See also* Tendai school.

Ryokan (ryoh-kahn; 1757–1831), a Japanese Soto Buddhist monk whose poetry is renowned for its sensitivity and Zen sentiments. *See also* Soto school.

Ryonin (ryoh-nin; 1071–1132), founder of the Japanese Buddhist Yuzu-nembutsu sect. *See also* Yuzu-nembutsu school.

A B C D E F
G H L
M N Q
R S T U V
W X Y & Z

Sabaoth (sah-bay-oth'), a Hebrew name for God, used by Gnostics to indicate the chief world creator and ruler. *See also* Gnosticism.

Sabbath (Heb. *shabbat,* "cessation [of labor]"), a religious day of rest. In the Hebrew Bible, the importance of abstention from secular pursuits is highlighted by the inclusion of the Sabbath, but no other ritual observance, in the Ten Commandments and by the claim that the origin of the day was to be found in God resting on the seventh day of creation, understood in the Jewish calendar as extending from sundown Friday night to sundown Saturday night.

Judaism: The Sabbath is a regular reminder of some basic theological and moral principles of Judaism. Scripture calls this day a "Sabbath for God," suggesting that just as God engaged in creative endeavor for six days but rested on the seventh, so too should human beings (Exodus 20:10–11). Elsewhere it notes that the Sabbath recalls God's intervention in behalf of the Israelites, freeing them from slavery in Egypt and providing them the opportunity to become an independent nation (Deuteronomy 5:15). Frequent reference to this transformative event in the weekday and Sabbath prayers reminds Jews of their obligation to show loyalty to God and compassion for humanity.

Sabbath Observance: Aside from stating that the Sabbath is a day of cessation from work, scripture does not set forth clearly how the Sabbath is to be observed. A few injunctions are mentioned: no kindling of fire, no going about to collect manna, no plowing or reaping. That serious consequences ensue when one breaks Sabbath law is made clear by the imposition of a death sentence on a man caught gathering kindling on the Sabbath (Numbers 15:32–36). But aside from Temple offerings, no positive Sabbath observance by the community or individual is mandated. Even the prophets address only the restrictive aspect of Sabbath observance, chastising the people for conducting business on the Sabbath and transporting goods from place to place.

Only in the period of the Mishnah (ca. 200) are the contours of positive, personal Sabbath observance sketched in. For the first time, specific acts are prescribed for the home and synagogue. The key elements of Sabbath ritual are *kiddush* (Heb., "sanctification"), a declaration of the onset of Sabbath holiness, to be recited at sundown Friday night and followed by a festive Sabbath meal; special Sabbath prayers; public readings from Pentateuch and Prophets; study of Jewish texts; and *havdalah* (differentia-

tion)—a declaration of "separation" to be chanted at sundown Saturday night, proclaiming that the period of holiness has ended. The practice of lighting oil lamps (or candles) for the Sabbath, probably to eat the evening meal by, also originates in Mishnah. These lamps later became part of the sanctification ritual and a powerful symbol of the tranquillity of the Sabbath.

As for the restrictive aspect of the Sabbath, rabbinic law codes promulgate a list of thirty-nine forms of labor forbidden on the Sabbath, including such activities as plowing, reaping, baking, hammering, and sewing. Most of the proscribed actions relate directly to the preparation of food, the production of clothing, and the construction of shelter. To lower the likelihood that any of these rules would be violated on the Sabbath, the rabbis erected "fences" around the law, prohibiting, for instance, moving scissors from place to place lest one forget and use them to cut. As a result of these manifold legal developments, by the end of the rabbinic period, the Sabbath became a day of physical restoration, spiritual nourishment, and intellectual stimulation.

Later Developments: Some striking developments in Sabbath observance in posttalmudic times occurred during the period of flourishing mysticism in Safed in the sixteenth century. The Qabbalat ("welcoming the Sabbath") service, recited before Friday evening prayers, originated with these men who would greet the Sabbath "Queen" by reciting in "her" honor a series of psalms and their own poetry. The custom of singing *zemirot* (table hymns) at each of the Sabbath meals is also associated with this group of mystics, who did not originate the idea but made it standard practice.

Sabbath in Contemporary Times: Today, the Sabbath is probably the most important spiritual and social force in the lives of observant Jews. Through its prescriptions and proscriptions, the Sabbath brings families and communities together for a day of prayer, study, conversation, eating, singing, and relaxation. Synagogue services in all branches of Judaism attract more worshipers on the Sabbath than any other day except for the High Holidays; rabbis preach on this day; and most bar and bat mitzvah ceremonies are held in the synagogue on the Sabbath. Because of the ban on Sabbath travel, still observed by most Orthodox and some Conservative Jews, many families choose to live within walking distance of the synagogue.

Christianity: The Christian Sabbath is a weekly holy day observed by worship and abstention from unnecessary work. Most Christians observe Sunday as their Sabbath. A small number of denominations, such as the Seventh-Day Adventists, follow the Jewish practice and observe Saturday as their Sabbath. *See also* Lord's Day; Seventh-Day Adventists; Sunday.

Sabeans. *See* Harranians.

sacerdotal, synonym for priestly. *See also* priesthood.

sacraments and ordinances (Christianity), communal ritual acts, instituted by Christ or the church, which communicate the presence and grace of God to believers. A sacrament employs specific words, gestures, and physical elements such as bread, wine, oil, or water, as a means of divine-human encounter. Ordinances are, in general, practices commanded by God via the Bible. Hence *The Larger Catechism* (1529) speaks of the "outward and ordinary means, whereby Christ communicates to his church the benefits of his mediation," which are "his ordinances, especially the Word, sacraments, and prayer." Some biblically oriented Protestant denominations refer to the ordinances of the New Testament such as baptism, the Lord's Supper, and footwashing not as sacramental means of grace but as obedient acts of remembering of what God has done.

Origins and Early History: The term *sacrament* derives from the Latin *sacramentum,* which in common usage meant an oath of military allegiance or a pledge of fidelity enacted publicly with some visible sign. The early apologist Tertullian (d. ca. 200) first used the term to refer to baptismal rites in which new Christians pledged their faithfulness to Christ. Sacramentum was used to translate the earlier Greek word *mysterion,* which denoted invisible realities or particular sacred rites such as were practiced in the mystery religions. Paul, writing in the New Testament, uses mysterion to refer to divine secret wisdom beyond human reason, which God chooses to reveal to human beings. Paul also uses the term to refer to Christ, as well as to apostolic preaching and to ecstatic utterances "in the Spirit." As used in the Eastern Church's sacramental theology, the term highlights God's mysterious self-disclosure in liturgical rites—most especially in the Eucharist.

While there is no single definition or "theology of sacraments" in the New Testament and the earliest Christian writings, the centrality of rites of initiation (baptism) and Eucharist is undeniable. Various meanings of sacrament may be discerned in the teachings and disciplines surrounding Christian initiation, the eucharistic meal, rites of forgiveness and healing, and burial. All point to God's saving purposes for the world revealed in Jesus Christ.

Responding to misunderstandings and heresies in the second and third centuries, the fourth-century church generated a wide range of theological reflection on sacramental practices. Augustine (d. 430) contributed several important definitions, including the idea of a sacred sign that represents what it signifies, "the visible form of an invisible grace." A sacrament, he contended, results when the Word of God is added to the appropriate physical element. In response to the Donatists in North Africa, who claimed that only morally good celebrants could perform beneficial sacraments, Augustine asserted that the sacraments depend solely upon God, not on human goodness.

Early theologians did not develop a systematic interpretation, nor was there a specific number of sacraments. The practices of Christian initiation (baptism) and the celebration of the Eucharist every Lord's Day (Sunday) were assumed and experienced as enactments of what Christians believed about God and Jesus Christ. "Proclaiming the mystery of Christ" was enacted as well as preached, and Easter was its fullest celebration.

Medieval Developments: Building upon distinctions and concepts found in the first six centuries of Christian thought, the twelfth century saw a dramatic development in sacramental theology. Until then there was considerable latitude in doctrine, number, and variety of liturgical styles of celebrating according to the diverse cultural contexts. Debates over the nature and meaning of the Eucharist occurred in the mid-ninth century and continued through the eleventh century. Questions were raised concerning how and in what manner Christ was present in the physical elements.

All the while, popular piety and local sacramental practices were changing. From the seventh century onward, penance (the rite of forgiveness of sins) shifted from a public ritual focused on severe sins to a private one required of all believers. Rites of healing gradually became focused narrowly upon dying and death, hence the sacrament of extreme unction. The Eucharist became more clergy-dominated with less communing by the people; and private Mass, celebrated by priests alone for specific intentions, became widespread.

Scholastic theologians of the twelfth and thirteenth centuries sought to interpret and systematize the church's approach to sacraments. Peter Lombard's *Sentences* (ca. 1150) specified seven "dominically instituted" (commanded by Christ) sacraments and summarized the definitive earlier teachings of the church about them: baptism, confirmation, the Eucharist, penance, extreme unction, ordination and marriage. Lombard, following Augustine, claimed that a sacrament is properly so called because it is a sign and an expression of the invisible grace of God, so that "it bears its image and its cause."

The Council of Florence (1439) declared the Roman Catholic Church to have these seven sacraments, which both "contain grace and confer it upon all who receive them worthily." Sacraments had become a whole system in which each stage of human life was cared for: birth, human growth, marriage, sickness and death, and ordination to the priesthood. By the end of the fifteenth century this "sacramental system" provided a comprehensive pattern of pastoral care for all in the Church. Heavily juridical in interpretation and application, it was, in many respects, riddled with abuse. Increasing unrest with the whole system resulted in attempts at reform in preceding centuries, but conditions were especially ripe for Martin Luther's protest early in the sixteenth century.

The Reformation and Enlightenment: The attack upon the theology and Roman Church's practices of the sacraments by the Reformers (Martin Luther, John Calvin, Martin Bucer, Huldrych Zwingli, and others) resulted in simplified rites in vernacular languages, congregational singing, biblical preaching, and an attempt to train and involve the laity in sacramental participation. The number of sacraments instituted by Christ was reduced from seven to two: baptism and the Lord's Supper. A wide variety of theological interpretations of what the sacraments do and signify sprang up among varying Protestant movements. While some, like Luther, maintained a strong sense of "real presence" in the Eucharist, others made stronger distinctions between the physical and spiritual aspects of the sacraments. Philosophical viewpoints departed radically from the tradition using Aristotle's (d. 322 B.C.) thought, in Thomas Aquinas (ca. 1225–74) and official Roman teachings. Protestant Reformers stressed biblical criteria, the centrality of preaching, and faith of individual believers in their drive to simplify and to reform and purify the sacramental practices of the Roman tradition. Consequently, the Eucharist itself became more penitential and was eventually lost as the principal Sunday service. Counter

to Protestant reforms, the Council of Trent (1545–63) reiterated the truth of seven sacraments, while recognizing some need for pastoral changes.

During the eighteenth century and the Enlightenment, the theology of sacraments shifted among many Protestants to moral influence and matters of experience, and especially to human action in the sacraments. Part of the legacy of this period is a diminished sense of mystery and of God's acting in the sacraments as "means of grace." The American frontier brought a still more experiential and pragmatic set of attitudes that shaped evangelical traditions.

Twentieth-century Reform and Renewal: The twentieth century has witnessed remarkable ecumenical and liturgical developments that have reformed and renewed sacramental life in Protestant, Anglican, and Roman Catholic churches. Anticipated by earlier movements such as the Wesleyan reforms of the eighteenth century, the Oxford Movement of the nineteenth, and Benedictine liturgical reforms, sacramental theology and practice have reclaimed the primacy of Sunday and of Easter and the eschatological dimension of sacramental worship. The promulgation of the *Constitution on the Sacred Liturgy* of Vatican II (1963–65) restored many important Reformation and early church insights as well as contemporary concerns for the life context of the church. While the traditional seven principal sacraments are retained, the notion of multiple presences of Christ—in the people's assembly, in the Word read and preached, in the prayers—now enriches the mystery and meaning of sacramental presence and the benefits of participation.

From the 1970s on, nearly every major Protestant denomination has undertaken liturgical revision and renewal of sacramental practice. The reformed rites of Christian initiation and Eucharist, along with rites of reconciliation, healing, marriage, and burial, have attempted to anchor their theology in a unitive sacramentality, relating all to Christ the "primordial sacrament." At the same time, new appreciation for cultural diversity and indigenous patterns of faith experience and style of worship have allowed various liturgical families to respect and learn from one another. A distinctive ecumenical consensus has generated several important bilateral agreements on the meaning of the sacraments. Twentieth-century renewal of sacraments thus is profoundly ecumenical and theologically oriented toward basic questions of human existence.

Despite new understandings of sacraments

as God's self-communication, deepened by insights from history, ritual studies, and the social sciences, Christians remain divided over such issues as frequency of communion, the character of God's action, scriptural obedience, and especially the question of church authority and the order of church ministry. Yet converging baptismal and eucharistic practices among Christians promises an unprecedented framework for sacramental life and theology. *See also* anointing of the sick; baptism; Christianity (life cycle); Christianity (worship); confirmation; Eucharist, Christian; marriage; ordination.

sacred, profane, respectively, persons, places, or things set apart or having some religious significance, and so accorded worship, veneration, or respect; and persons, places, or things held to be incompatible with or thought to desecrate those things having positive religious significance. While both terms figure prominently in the modern study of religion, they have proved difficult to define with precision and are of mixed empirical utility. A central question in the study of religion has been whether these terms identify objective properties of things or whether they are terms of classification.

Emile Durkheim: In the modern social scientific fields, especially sociology and anthropology, use of the distinction between the sacred and the profane can be traced to the French sociologist Emile Durkheim (1858–1917). In *The Elementary Forms of the Religious Life* (1912), Durkheim writes that "the division of the world into two domains, which include everything that is sacred in one and everything that is profane in the other, is the characteristic feature of religious thought." Durkheim defines the terms *sacred* and *profane* by associating each with a specific form of human behavior: "Sacred things are those which are protected and isolated by prohibitions; profane things are those to which the prohibitions apply, and they must keep their distance from sacred things." By this behavioral approach, he could render his distinction exhaustive: "All that exists" is either sacred or profane. Further, he insists on the "absolute heterogeneity" of the sacred and the profane. All religions employ some version of this dichotomy, which they take to represent "two worlds which have nothing in common." Whereas such seeming oppositions as health/illness and good/evil have, in fact, common elements (life, morality), the sacred and the profane "radically exclude each other."

For Durkheim, the terms sacred and profane serve as classificatory concepts; they do not stand for intrinsic properties of persons, places, or things. By defining them in terms of the behavior of religious persons, he refuses to admit them as qualities of events or objects discoverable through empirical inquiry; rather, they are "superadded" and "superimposed" upon their objects.

Criticisms of Durkheim: Durkheim's view, while influential, has been sharply criticized. One common criticism is that the two terms are not mutually exclusive. W. E. H. Stanner (b. 1905) notes the ritual use of such mundane things as water, fire, musical instruments, and cosmetics; these things are often neither protected nor proscribed, and so—on Durkheim's own terms—can be considered neither sacred nor profane. In addition, says Stanner, both terms admit of degrees; persons, places, and things can be sacred or profane to greater or lesser extents—that is, they can be protected or proscribed more or less vigorously ("Reflections on Durkheim and Aboriginal Religion," 1967). Durkheim briefly acknowledges this point, but seems to miss (Stanner says "suppress") the empirical and logical problems that it entails.

The empirical problem is that, to the extent that the sacred and profane admit of degrees, dichotomy is rendered—as a classificatory scheme—less precise and so less helpful. The English anthropologist E. E. Evans-Pritchard remarks that Durkheim's distinction does not "aid in a classification of observed facts" (*Theories of Primitive Religion*, 1965). The difficulty is not that religious people do not display the "setting apart" and "proscriptive" behaviors upon which Durkheim's definitions depend; the trouble is that the behaviors take so many different forms and come in so many different strengths that no single descriptive term can cover them.

Evans-Pritchard also finds that the ethnographical evidence "does not support the rigid dichotomy [Durkheim] makes between the sacred and the profane," and that the distinction does not "permit testing by observation in the field." Here Evans-Pritchard seems to be pointing out a logical or conceptual weakness in Durkheim's theory: by insisting on the absolute heterogeneity of the sacred and the profane, Durkheim cannot accommodate objects and events that seem to house them in some combination. For example, what status can Durkheim accord the pollution of a sacred object? In this instance, a distinction is needed between the impurely sacred and the profane; and many cases seem to call for distinguishing between sacred and profane profanations. But given the radical dichotomy with which Durkheim begins, it is hard to see how he could make these distinctions. Durkheim could have avoided this problem had he kept to his strictly behavioral criteria; the needed distinctions would then come by noting the differences in the way that religious persons act toward, say, sacred versus profane profanations. But this would be to give up the absoluteness of the distinction and, in any case, would still leave Durkheim open to the empirical objections discussed above.

Mircea Eliade: After Durkheim's, perhaps the most influential work on this topic is that of the Rumanian-born historian of religion, Mircea Eliade (1907–86). His monograph, *The Sacred and the Profane* (1957), gained a wide audience in the United States during the 1960s and 1970s. Like Durkheim, Eliade places the sacred/profane distinction at the center of this theory of religion. For Eliade, *homo religiosus*, or religious man, is defined by the tendency "to live as much as possible in the sacred or in close proximity to consecrated objects." And like Durkheim, Eliade insists that the sacred and the profane are "wholly other"; the sacred "is of a wholly different order, a reality that does not belong to our world, in objects that are an integral part of our natural 'profane' world." However, Eliade breaks with Durkheim over a central issue.

Durkheim's picture is of the human mind at work classifying its physical environment; for Durkheim, the sacred is not an intrinsic property of things but is rather a title bestowed by human beings on other persons, places, or things. Eliade reverses this relationship. For him, it is the sacred that acts upon the human subject: "Man becomes aware of the sacred because it manifests itself, shows itself, as something wholly different from the profane. To designate the act of manifestation of the sacred, we have proposed the term *hierophany*. . . . It expresses no more than is implicit in its etymological content, i.e., that something sacred shows itself to us."

The sacred for Eliade is an active property of things. As for what shows or manifests itself, the sacred is "equivalent to a power, and . . . to reality. The sacred is saturated with being." Again, it is real. By contrast, the profane is unreal and chaotic. A prime function of the sacred is to "found the world," to provide a point of orientation. To take two of Eliade's best-known examples: from a purely physical standpoint space and time are homogeneous. No region of space nor single moment of time can be distinguished, by some intrinsic physical property, from any other region or moment; all regions and moments are, in that sense, alike. But an irruption

of the sacred "detaches" a part of space and/or time from its surrounding parts, making it qualitatively different. Thus, the temple, basilica, birth, or ecstatic vision can give the religious person's world a center, a point of passage between the profane existence and the other world of sacred space and time.

Criticisms of Eliade: Because Eliade, like Durkheim, finds the sacred to be wholly different from the profane, he too cannot account for their joint appearance in a single object or event. Eliade calls this problem "the paradox represented by every hierophany."

Perhaps the most important and controversial criticism of Eliade's view is the following: Durkheim interprets a religious person's actions, worldview, etc., based on what the person seems to hold or believe to be sacred (or profane). Eliade undertakes that interpretation by appealing to a sacred or profane property of some thing. The former interpretation is a part of an encompassing theory of the human person. But the latter, because it affirms the existence of sacred things that can act in virtue of their sacred property, has seemed to many to be itself a religious undertaking. This affirmation no doubt accounts for the wide appeal of Eliade's view among those who think that religion is best understood in its own terms or, as Eliade puts it, "on its own level." On the other hand, to those inclined to a more social scientific point of view, Eliade's work has often seemed a kind of protective strategy, a way of defending the autonomy of religion in the face of other, profane explanatory strategies. *See also* religion, definition of.

Sacred, the, term for the object of religious worship, often associated with a view of religion as the experience or feeling of an immaterial, awesome, overpowering impersonal realm or force that is at once intimidating and alluring and is the opposite of everyday, profane reality, yet may manifest itself in profane reality.

Religious Studies: Both religionists and social scientists trace the notion of the sacred to the analysis by R. H. Codrington, a nineteenth-century missionary, of the primitive Melanesian idea of an impersonal supernatural force, mana. Religionists maintain that the only possible source of an experience so out of the ordinary must be a sacred reality itself. For some religionists, the sacred manifests itself directly to humans, but even for those religionists for whom the sacred manifests itself through the profane world, the sacred transcends that world.

The German theologian Rudolf Otto (*The Idea of the Holy*, 1917) provides the classic religionist analysis of the sacred, or "holy." He introduces the idea of opposition between the holy and the nonholy. Because humans, he argues, experience the holy directly, they feel humbled rather than elevated by the encounter, which therefore argues further for the uniqueness of the entity experienced. Otto also introduces the idea of opposition within the holy, which at once attracts and repels humans.

Even religionists for whom the sacred manifests itself through the profane world pit the sacred against the profane—and do so for apologetic ends. Hence Rumanian-born historian of religions Mircea Eliade (*The Sacred and the Profane*, 1957) argues that the sacred coexists paradoxically with the profane, to which it is scarcely reducible.

Social Sciences: Some social scientists seek only to characterize religion as the worship of the sacred, not to account for the sacred itself. The Scottish biblicist William Robertson Smith (*Lectures on the Religion of the Semites*, 1889) describes opposition not only between the sacred and the profane but even more within the sacred. Smith divides the sacred into attractive and repellent halves. He pits the sacred against the profane in stressing the taboos restricting contact with either the attractive or repellent half.

French sociologist Emile Durkheim (*The Elementary Forms of the Religious Life*, 1912) provides the classic sociological explanation of the sacred: group euphoria. The opposition between the sacred and the profane is really that between the group and the individual. While projected onto physical entities of various kinds, the sacred for Durkheim is really society itself.

The classic psychological explanation of the sacred is Carl Jung's (*Psychology and Religion*, 1938). Adopting Otto's description of religious experience, Jung attributes that experience to the "collective unconscious."

In the 1990s, many scholars of religion urge the abandonment of the concept of the sacred on both logical and empirical grounds: the concept neither makes sense nor fits the data. In addition, the concept has been used by religionists to mystify the object of religious worship and thereby keep it from being explained at all— an even more desperate alternative than claiming that an object so mysterious can only be explained religiously. *See also* mana; religion, definition of.

sacred books. *See* holy books.

sacred heart. 1 A Roman Catholic devotional practice developed in the eighteenth century centered on the physical heart of Jesus. 2 The image of the wounded heart of Jesus, usually with a crown of thorns encircling it.

sacred space and sacred time, fundamental patterns in religious life and basic concepts in the cross-cultural study of religious worlds.

Sacred spaces and times are among the most common, visible forms of religious expression. Clearly delineated from ordinary or profane space and time, they are the major external matrices and foci through which religious systems make contact with what is deemed holy.

The idea of sacred space and time as important categories in religion has been basic to the cross-cultural, phenomenological perspective in modern religious studies. The notion emerged in the writings of late-nineteenth-century comparativists, and was given further development in the French school of sociology, the European history and phenomenology of religion tradition, and especially the works of Mircea Eliade (1907–86). A major effect of these approaches has been to show that religiousness is not just a matter of beliefs but also of observance and ritual participation.

The adjective *sacred* connotes both dedication to a transhuman purpose, and powerful, in the sense that participants acknowledge a superhuman connection at these specially defined junctures. *Profane,* the antonym of sacred, in its Latin original means literally "outside the temple" (*pro* and *fanum*) so that profane space and time are thus equivalent to routine, unconsecrated life. Space can have a sacred aspect in an even more elemental, territorial sense by virtue of the intensity and strategicness of the social boundaries it signifies, e.g., hearths, thresholds, homes, villages, or "the motherland."

Forms of Sacred Space: Sacred space is formed in different ways according to various types of cultures. In small-scale societies for which the encompassing natural world is experienced as a medium of revelation, powerful parts of the environment such as certain mountains, bodies of water, or caves are regarded with reverence. In more complex city-state cultures, where centralized political authority is of supreme, even cosmic importance, the gods are conceived more in terms of rulership, majesty, or patronage and given residency in temples and grand-scale ceremonial centers. In both instances religious life gives focus to places where the supernatural appears to be most present and active.

Sacred space sometimes forms around places that are associated with great events in the memory of the community. Scriptures, myths, and legends recount sacred histories that tell of the miraculous or world-founding deeds of gods and ancestors performed at certain sites. Thus, Israel is the Holy Land in Judaic and Christian traditions, as is Vrindaban in India to devotees of Krishna, and the areas of Mecca and Medina to Muslims. Tribal cultures typically regard features of their immediate landscape as corresponding to the activities of ancestral beings in mythic times. In all traditional religions, geography and mythology are intertwined. Often one's whole land is understood to be divinely ordained. Birth or burial places of saints and founders become pilgrimage sites. Just as the great mosque at Medina is built over Muhammad's tomb, St. Peter's Basilica in Rome rises over the remains of its patron namesake.

Sometimes sacred space is created by an act of ritual. Cultures with little or no permanent religious architecture may construct focal points for communication with the gods each time the need arises. In the annual Plains Indian Sun Dance rites, a lodge is built to encircle a tree that has been chosen, cut, positioned, and sanctified for the occasion and that then represents the center of the world. In this way, a single sacred object, altar, or image can form a fixed point around which a religious space rises up. The Christmas tree—selected yearly, set up, and decorated in Christian households—establishes a ceremonial center around which certain traditional religious behaviors may then take place.

Obvious examples of sacred space are the permanent shrines, temples, churches, or other buildings constructed to provide dwelling places for superhuman beings or their manifestations in relics, saints, or sacraments. A shrine may be small and domestic, such as a "god shelf" in the corner of a home, or it may be a conspicuous, public center such as a cathedral, laden with political, economic, and aesthetic prestige. The temples of ancient city cultures with their hierarchical systems of professional priesthoods, offerings, and sacrificial performances, altars, and inner sanctums formed the prototype of liturgical Christian churches in the Roman Catholic and Eastern Orthodox traditions.

Jewish synagogues, Muslim mosques, and many "plain style" Protestant churches embody a different concept of space—not the classical concept of the temple as the splendid abode of the god (within which there is a "holy of holies"), but rather the idea that a religious building is essentially a place for the congregation of believers to manifest their faith collectively. The focal point is not an altar at which offerings are made, but more typically a pulpit or reading stand from which scripture is recited. There is no special category of priesthood or intermediary here, no special interior zone where officiants but not laity can enter (though the Torah scrolls of Judaism are housed in a centralized "ark"), and no images of deity.

Functions of Sacred Space: Sacred space has many general functions. It can create a stable orientation in the midst of a changing world and a visible center around which religious life can express itself—many cultures signify this with terms such as *the heart of the world, the center of the world,* or *the navel of the universe*. It creates an opening, a gate of access to the sacred realm. It gives intensified meaning to all actions and objects within it, providing a framing, sanctifying context for ritual. Usually the process of entering sacred space requires a state of readiness and purification—figuratively, and sometimes literally, one's profane shoes must be left at the door. The nature of the space imposes requirements on those who would enter it, and it is this state of consecration that allows the possibility of contact with the transformative power of the holy. Finally, while sacred space can enhance definition of status and membership it can also dissolve structured social roles.

The holy shrine at Mecca, the Kaaba, represents all these functions. In Islam it is acknowledged as the place on earth ordained by God as the focal point of communication with the divine. All Muslims throughout the world face toward it in their daily prayers and aspire to make a pilgrimage to its precincts at least once in their lives, an event that requires extensive acts of self-purification. Non-Muslims are excluded from its territory, but the believers who make the journey experience a human unity that transcends racial and economic differences.

The Symbolism of Sacred Space: Sacred space is often constructed in a symbolic way. Gothic cathedrals feature verticality and majestic power, thus showing a contrast between the heavenly glory of God and the small, creatureliness of humans. Hindu temples often emphasize the presence of divinity within a dark, mysterious "womb" of interiority. Shintoism typically honors the connection of gods with nature in the open, gracious lines of simple wooden shrines set within the rhythm of local landscapes. Hopi ceremonial kivas are built beneath the ground, showing respect for the earth as the underlying source of fertility. The enormous Buddhist ceremonial pyramid in Borobodur, Java, is shaped in ascending levels of terraces, representing stages in the journey of human consciousness toward supreme enlightenment. The unpretentious Puritan or evangelical meetinghouse signifies that true religiousness is a matter of faith, not institution.

Sacred Time: Sacred space and sacred time overlap in many of their features. Where one frames an opening to the superhuman in the midst of the visible world, the other does so in the midst of the temporal. Like space, consecrated time has the character of something that can be approached, entered, participated in, and exited. The observance of sacred space and time are usually linked, as in traveling to a pilgrimage site or attending a particular church.

In the believer's mind sacred time opens onto and participates in the reality of that which it honors. Any festival or holy day embodies the spirit of its object: it is a time of the Buddha's Enlightenment, of the Hebrew Exodus from slavery, of the resurrection of Christ. Sacred time is thus charged with the power of the gods and paradigms that it celebrates. One of its functions is to make present a mythic time of origins—the time of superhuman ancestors and teachers or other world creators—and bring this to bear on contemporary life. This typically takes place through recitation of the holy words and cosmogonic accounts of scriptures or their oral equivalents in myth.

As with space, sacred time comes in many forms. A period each day set aside for prayer exemplifies it, but so does the entire holy month of Ramadan, during which Muslims fast from dawn until dusk. Sacred time can have any content: depending on the occasion, it can be anything from celebrative and ecstatic to solemn and mournful. It can be calendrically fixed or it can be performed only on special occasions as the need arises. The first, periodic, type is illustrated by weekly sabbaths and Sundays, and by annual holy days such as Yom Kippur or Easter; the second type is seen in onetime rites of passage such as baptisms, marriages, initiations, inaugurations, or funerals.

Periodic Sacred Times: Every traditional culture renews the foundations of its world periodically through special festivals and rites. The forces upon which its existence depends—e.g., crops or herds, the institutions of kingship or social exchange, or the specific beliefs of religious traditions—are then regenerated. For societies where survival is directly linked with the contingencies of the food supply, ritual often coincides with pertinent points of seasonal passage, e.g., solstices and equinoxes, times of planting and harvesting, animal migrations, and other economic rhythms.

As nature is recreated annually, so too is the world of moral purity and social values. While the festivals of the relatively modern world religions usually remain linked to seasonal junctures, the sacred focus of their renewal is more on the enduring power of scriptural teachings and paradigms. In repeating the same holy days year after year religious communities place upon the world of ordinary history and change their own calendars of spiritual order.

Whether periodic sacred times come in annual or in shorter cycles, the renewal is cyclical in the sense that within any week, month, or year time seems to return to its own foundations—an "eternal return" to the primal realm of superhuman origins and truths. These occasions both recall and reinvigorate the powers that typically are neglected or diminished during the course of ordinary, routine time when people are necessarily more preoccupied with mundane affairs. By regularly resorting to the realm of religious power, for example, the sacrifice of Christ in the Christian liturgy or the teachings of the Buddha, life is returned to its true basis.

Great annual regenerative times bring all normal business to a halt and involve the entire community. Lasting several days, they include major feasts, the intensification and renewal of key social bonds, public displays that celebrate the ideals of the occasion, and full-scale purifications of various kinds. In order to form a new, fresh world it is necessary to dissolve the old order of worn-out structures and moral faults. It is a time when religious communities show themselves in their most exemplary form. It is also a worldwide pattern that annual times of renewal often involve or are preceded by times of license and chaos—for example, Carnival (or Mardi Gras), which precedes the forty days of Lenten fasting that culminate in Easter.

Smaller cycles of time also keep the community in regular contact with the sacred. The sabbath day is a prime example. In biblical tradition, the "seventh day" is ordained from the time of creation to be kept separate from the other six. Christians converted this into the idea of "the Lord's Day," or Sunday, commemorating the day of Jesus' resurrection. While Muslims observe Friday afternoon as a time of special collective prayer, they are also expected to engage in prayer at five specified times throughout each day, showing that not only in the course of the year but also in the cycle of a single day the return to the sacred can be regularized.

Sacred Times of Passage: The second, or noncalendrical, type of sacred time sanctifies moments of transition. These are the occasions when significant changes in collective and individual life need to be brought into contact with super-human power, e.g., when a child is named and brought into community membership, when a person is initiated into adult or religious respon-sibilities and knowledge, when marriage is ef-fected, when leaders are inducted into office, or when the disruption of death occurs. At all these times a new identity needs to be made sacred—in many cases it is the rite itself that creates the status—and a special time is designed expressly for that purpose.

Sacred times magnify both to the insider and to students of religion the specific values of the religious communities that perform them. Thus, the East Asian new year showcases the centrality of family and filial piety; annual Southeast Asian festivals highlight the sacred relationship be-tween laity and monastics; certain tribal soci-eties periodically emphasize the value of male prowess; and the High Holy Days of Judaism show the primacy of ethical responsibility. Even secular nation-state cultures observe important anniversaries, such as their founding revolu-tions.

Sacred Space and Time as Categories of Comparative Study: The concepts of sacred space and time are linked to comparative perspective in the study of religion. Since there are multiple, coexisting versions of the center of the world and of the holiest day of the year, each religious universe constructs space and time around its own sa-cred absolutes. Understanding the general func-tions of these categories lends a certain intelligibility to behaviors and beliefs that might otherwise seem odd, foreign, or inscrutable.

While these patterns share many features across cultures, religious systems are each made up of unique historical and cultural matrices—so that the form, content, and style of sacred space and time will differ from setting to setting and be shaped by sociological variables. Some mystical types of religion reject the dichotomy of sacred versus profane altogether, maintaining that ultimate reality is ubiquitous and not just particularized at certain points.

The broad use of these concepts requires caution about taking one version as the stan-dard for describing all others, and needs to take account of local contexts and nuances of mean-ing. So employed, the categories become useful tools for exploring both the common and differ-ent ways religious people inhabit their worlds. *See also* architecture and religion; cyclical time; do-mestic ritual; Dreaming, the; ecological aspects of traditional religions; festal cycle; life-cycle rituals; Mesoamerican religion; mountains, sacred; myth; new year festivals; pilgrimage; ritual; sacred, pro-fane; temple.

sacred thread ceremony (Skt. *yajnopavita*), part of the Hindu *upanayana* (initiation rite), in which a *guru* invests the student-initiate with a thread to be worn always over the left shoulder except in calls of nature or rituals concerning ancestors or *rishis* (Vedic bards). Formerly it was reserved for the three twice-born classes; now it is some-times adopted by other communities. *See also* caste; dvija; sacrifice.

sacred time. *See* sacred space and sacred time.

sacrifice (Lat., "to make sacred"), preeminently the ritual slaying of an animal and the transference of all or part of the corpse to the divine sphere. By extension, bloodless sacrifices may involve vegetables or cultural products.

This simple model implies that every sacrifice has four points of focus: the one who sacrifices, the sacrifice itself, the mode of trans-ference, and the recipient of the sacrifice. These vary from culture to culture and from ritual to ritual, but no description of sacrifice is complete without specifying these four elements and the relations among them.

Native and academic explanations of sac-rifice abound. Any explanation of sacrifice is, in fact, a theory of religion in miniature. Sacrifice has been categorized as a gift (an offering), a means of communication between the profane and the sacred, an attempt to establish reciproc-ity between the human and the divine realms (most often expressed by the formula, "I give in order to get"), an expiation, a substitution, and a reenactment of primordial events. Each of these understandings can find examples or native statements to support it. One cannot decide be-tween explanations of sacrifice at the level of data; a decision will only be persuasive at the level of theory. *See also* bear ceremonialism; Celtic religion; Indo-European religion; Islam (festal cycle); Roman religion; Santeria.

Aztec Religion: The ritual sharing of a variety of plant, animal, and human edibles in a feeding exchange between human and nonhuman enti-ties was undertaken in order to sustain the cos-mos in a state of ordered existence. The foodstuffs of sacrificial rituals ranged from the blood and body parts of various animals and hu-mans to figurines made of amaranth and honey. All sacrifice has a lengthy history throughout Mesoamerica, although extreme forms of human sacrifice (including cannibalism) probably were practiced most extensively by Nahuatl-speakers of the Mexican Highlands (the Aztecs) from the mid-fifteenth to early sixteenth centuries.

Varied forms of Aztec sacrifice (nonhuman and human) were performed in many different contexts. Quail, jaguars, crocodiles, ducks, salamanders, and amaranth cakes were among the nonhuman offerings used. One of the most widespread practices was human autosacrifice. Involving limited ritual bleeding, these rites were enacted on numerous occasions ranging from royal coronations to the naming of newborn babies. Different techniques were utilized in the more extreme forms of human sacrifice, including decapitation, drowning, and heart extraction. These rituals were associated with both war and the agricultural cycle and included willing (and sometimes unwilling) participants drawn from many segments of society. Offerings were shared with not only celestial entities (such as the sun) but also earthly recipients.

Written resources on Aztec sacrifice were collected by their Spanish conquerors in primarily the sixteenth century and probably overemphasize the quantity and violent nature of the sacrifice. Moreover, the Spanish never understood its full significance. They were inclined to explain it as coming from the devil, as similar to Christian penitence, or as mere superstition.

Modern explanations for sacrificial rites vary, though most agree that these rites involved some sort of feeding exchange. Some see sacrifice as a prescientific stage in a human evolutionary process. Others suggest that it served as a means of population control, a dietary supplement providing protein, an effective and/or maladaptive route to political expansion, or a way for the elite to maintain hegemony. Others attempt to uncover the religious logic structuring sacrificial practices. Many of these theories lack satisfactory support and by themselves each is insufficient to explain such a complex and widespread phenomenon.

From a religious perspective the exchange of sacrificial edibles among the animated elements in the universe maintains cosmic balance. It is likely that the overriding logic was that if one wanted the cosmos to provide food, one also had to feed the cosmos. Death and destruction were seen as necessary correlates to life and creation, for one cannot eat without also killing.

An extension of this theory suggests that the cosmos was viewed as being governed by a concept of motion (Nahuatl *ollin*): existence characterized by a continually destructive-creative process of transformation. By linking all sacrificial rites with an intricately precise calendrical system, this process of transformation could be kept alive and moving on an orderly path. *See also* cannibalism.

Hinduism: The pre-Vedic Indus Valley religion (ca. 2300–1500 B.C.) probably practiced sacrifices connected with goddess worship. Reconstructions of a presystematized Vedic sacrifice, which may have included buffalo sacrifices, the victim's beheading at the sacrificial stake (Skt. *yupa*), agonistic opposition between double sacrificers, and violent social instability, are controversial. It is Vedic ritual's systematization that is decisive for understanding sacrifice in Vedic and post-Vedic Hinduism.

Vedic Sacrifice (ca. 1400–400 B.C.): Definition of Vedic sacrifice (*yajna*) turns on the Sanskrit verbal root *yaj*, "to offer." The Purusha hymn in the *Rig Veda* (10.90) tells how the manifold world and the first institutions (*dharmas*) were produced: by sacrificing Purusha ("Man"), "the gods sacrificed the sacrifice by the sacrifice." The three derivatives from yaj suggest the unity of sacrificer, sacrificial act, and victim.

Substances (*dravya*) suitable for sacrifice include animals, the divine *soma* plant, grain and milk products, and speech (recited Vedic verses, *mantras*). Purusha is the exemplary animal victim (*pashu*), since he alone can both sacrifice and be sacrificed. The four other suitable victims (horse, bull, ram, he-goat), substitutes for Purusha, are classified among domesticated village animals, but Purusha is "of the forest."

Vedic sacrifice has two aspects. *grihya*, "domestic," and *shrauta*, "connected with *shruti* [Vedic revelation]," often called "solemn." Grihya rites are based on *smriti*, tradition, rather than shruti. The main distinction is that whereas grihya sacrifice requires one fire, shrauta requires three. Many rituals, such as the *agnihotra* (dawn and evening milk libations into fire), have both grihya and shrauta versions.

The grihya fire should originate from the wife's paternal home, brought to the couple's new household after marriage. It should be tended for family ceremonies (*samskaras*) until its last service at the husband's cremation. The householder must also perform five daily "great sacrifices" (*mahayajnas*): to *brahman* (offering mantra), ancestors, gods, other "beings," and humans (hospitality rites).

Although shrauta rites are the focus of the older ritual texts (Brahmanas [ca. 1100–700 B.C.] and *Shrauta Sutras* [ca. 800–300 B.C.]), rituals of the later *Grihya Sutras* (ca. 600–100 B.C.) are described or presupposed in the Brahmanas. Entitlement for shrauta sacrifice presumes the prior grihya rites of *upanayana* (initiation rite that includes the sacred thread investiture making one twice-born) and marriage. A special shrauta rite, *agnyadheya*, "establishment of the fires," allows one to perform shrauta sacrifices and become an *ahitagni*, one "having established fires." In contrast to the grihya fire, the first shrauta fire, the *garhapatya* ("householder's fire"), must be lit by churning firesticks. But in continuity, these should first be warmed over the grihya fire.

Entitlement to perform either schedule is open only to married "twice-born" men: Brahmans, Kshatriyas, Vaishyas. Ahitagnis must always have been a wealthy and punctilious minority. Grihya rites can be performed by the householder himself, or with a domestic priest. Shrauta rites require the sacrificer (*yajamana*) to enlist from one to seventeen priests drawn from the schools that specialized in the ritual use of the four Vedas. While the priests served the sacrificer and received honoraria (*dakshinas*, cows or gold), the sacrificer alone, with his wife, reaped the desired benefit. The ultimate fruit of sacrificial work (*karma*) is heaven, but specific sacrifices target food, cows, sons, victory, etc.

One classification mentions yajnas of three types, each with a prototype and six others, totaling twenty-one. First are *pakayajnas*, "sacrifices with cooked offerings," typified by the evening agnihotra and designating grihya rites generally. Second, having the agnyadheya as prototype, are *haviryajnas. Havis*, oblatory material, denotes mainly milk, ghee, and grain (cakes and gruel) offerings, but also animal organs. Third are *somayajnas:* pressing soma and filtering its empowering and poetry-inspiring juice. The prototype here, *agnishtoma*, "praise of Agni," is the most aspired-to rite of nonroyal ahitagnis: a five-day spring rite with fourth- and fifth-day goat sacrifices and three soma pressings on the fifth.

Animal sacrifices fall into the first two categories. Typical domestic ones were hospitality rites. A controversial grihya rite, performed yearly in autumn or spring, was the offering, northeast of the village, of a "spit ox" (*shulagava*) to Rudra.

Complex Shrauta Rites: The shrauta animal sacrifice (*pashubandha*) requires the same type of additional altar—a *mahavedi*, "great altar"—as the soma sacrifice, so the two are often combined. Three ambitious royal rites involved both: *ashvamedha* (horse sacrifice), *rajasuya* (royal consecration), and *vajapeya* (drink of strength). Possibilities for combination are infinite, and the priests' art was to "see" and "know thus" as to the transcendent order of connections and equivalences (*bandhus*) that make ritual karma take the desired "unseen" (*adrishta*) effect for the yajamana. Most complex was the *agnicayana* (piling up of [the brick] fire [altar]), by which the sacrificer attained immortality by surpassing the year and the worlds embodied in the altar identified with Prajapati, god of the sacrificial life-death round.

The shrauta sacrifice's primary ritual ground (*devayajana*), with its three fire altars, was suitable for dairy and grain oblations. The garhapatya, round like the earth, is the main cooking fire. Here the sacrificer's wife sits silently, or occasionally cooks. The two other fires, lit from the garhapatya, are the *dakshinagna* and *ahavaniya:* the "southern fire," a south-facing semicircle, linked with the atmosphere and positioned to defend against nefarious forces of the south, realm of the dead; and the fire "to be offered into," square like heaven, which receives most of the offerings. Between the garhapatya (west) and ahavaniya (east) is the *vedi*, an hourglass-shaped pit or elevation on which purificatory grass is strewn as a seat for the invoked gods and a place for sacrificial utensils.

The additional mahavedi required for animal and soma sacrifices extends east of the devayajana as an eastward-tapering trapezoid. An axis extends from the garhaptya through the vedi and ahavaniya to a "high" or "further altar" (*uttaravedi*) on the mahavedi, and finally to the yupa on the mahavedi's eastern boundary. Fire transferred from the ahavaniya and placed on the uttaravedi's "navel" becomes the mahavedi's new ahavaniya for animal or soma sacrifices, while the original ahavaniya becomes the new garhapatya. While the devayajana represents the fixed order of the three worlds or the fortified immobility of the *asuras* (supernatural enemies of the gods), the mahavedi, shaped "like a chariot," connotes movement and communion with the transcendent mobility of the soma-drinking, chariot-riding gods.

In the pashubandha, though the animal is first tied to the yupa, signifying submission, it is later slain northeast of the mahavedi at the shed of a shadowy priest, the *shamitar*, who kills it bloodlessly in an "unharmful" manner by suffocation or strangulation. The animal is then "revived" by washing so it can attain heaven. The shamitar then dismembers it. The Brahmanas are obscure on treatment of the head, but prolific in attributing power to the "head of the sacrifice" in myths. The true offering (*ahuti*) consists of the destruction of the fatty omentum in the new ahavaniya: a gift to the gods, or a demonstration of the sacrificer's abandonment (*tyaga*) and disinterest before distributing sacrificial shares. The sacrificer and priests then share food portions, but with no banquet such as occurs in grihya rites.

Several strains run through shrauta rites. "Man" is the measure of sacrifice. The first and exemplary sacrifice is of "Man." The yupa is normally measured by the yajamana's height. Through bandhus, he is identified with the victim, with his fires, and, through Prajapati, with the entire macrocosm.

Spatially, the sacrifice is portable and mobile: the site is variable and not reused; altars and yupa are abandoned. There are no fixed temples or altars on high places. It is aniconic: deities are invoked through speech rather than embodied in images.

Contests are arranged so the yajamana wins, with rivals often represented by priests. Sacrificial implements are regularly compared with weapons. Magical rites (*abhicara*) are designed to harm or kill a rival.

A sacrificer must begin with *shraddha*, "confidence" in the rite's efficacy and the trustworthiness of his priests, who can deliberately turn the rite against him. Confidence prepares him for *diksha*, "consecration," whereby he offers himself (his *atman*) by becoming an embryo that is reborn through the rite. This prepares him to make the yajna proper, which redeems his self from the gods by the substance offered. As one who amasses power through diksha, he then disperses it as dakshinas to the priests. Finally, yajamana, wife, and priests bathe to disengage themselves from the sacrifice, disperse portable implements by depositing them in water, and reenter the profane world.

Ultimately, the knowledge of equivalents points toward the "mental sacrifice" (*manasa yajna*) and "sacrifice to the self" (*atma-yajna*) of the Aranyakas and Upanishads, in particular the "oblation in the fire of the breaths" (*pranagnihotra*) of the forest dweller and renunciant. Here offering food into one's own inner fires (breaths) becomes a sacrifice equivalent and means to self-realization.

Post-Vedic Sacrifice (after ca. 600): Aside from justifications for sacrifice in the Mimamsa philosophical system, post-Vedic traditions designate yajna as the religious virtue of the age previous to our Kali Yuga ("age of discord"), which is characterized by "giving." Puranic texts indicate that the twice-born no longer perform sacrifice, leaving it to Shudras and others of low birth. Nonetheless, sacrificial concerns and imagery pervade the law books, epics, Puranas, Agamas, and many hagiographies.

The war in the *Mahabharata* epic is a "sacrifice of battle." In the *Bhagavad Gita* Krishna says that brahman is "established in sacrifice" (3.3), which exemplifies the reciprocity between gods and humans whereby each acts for the "welfare of the worlds" without desire for personal fruits. The Purusha of the *Rig Veda* becomes the model for the primary cosmogony, with the supreme Purusha as *yogin* animating the evolution of nature. For secondary creation, to retrieve the earth from the waters, Brahma becomes the "sacrificial boar" (*yajnavaraha*) whose body parts are aspects and implements of sacrifice. The periodic dissolution of the triple world by fire is analogous to a funerary sacrifice. The Hindu temple is built upon a diagram that recalls the sacrifice of the "Purusha of the site" (*vastupurusha*).

In popular Hinduism, especially in goddess worship, blood sacrifice through beheading characterizes village buffalo and goat sacrifices, and medieval royal Dasara sacrifices. Vows taken for folk deities, e.g., self-impalement with needles, hook-swinging, or firewalking, also have sacrificial connotations of self-offering. The question of continuities with Vedic weapons, posts, and fires is debated. *See also* Goddess (Hinduism); Hindu domestic ritual; Hinduism (worship); path of (ritual) action; Veda, Vedism.

Chinese Religion: In China, offerings of grain wines, slaughtered animals (colts, oxen, sheep, pigs, or human victims), jade, silk, and prepared dishes have been made to the seasons, legendary or ancestral founders of dynasties, and to deities of particular stars, mountains, rivers, and regions of celestial governance. Since Neolithic times, the dead have been feasted, particularly just before burial, with a vast array of food and drink presented in ritual vessels. Emperors since the Han period (206 B.C.–A.D. 220) have worshiped heaven and earth in secret *feng-shan* (wind and mountain) rituals at Mt. T'ai and during the Suburban Sacrifice in the "Hall of Numinous Light" (Ming T'ang). *See also* ancestral rites; Chinese ritual; feng-shan sacrifices; Ming T'ang.

sacrilege. *See* profanation.

sadaqa. *See* almsgiving.

Sadducees (sad'yoo-seez; from Heb. *tzaddikim*, "righteous ones"), an upper-class religious, social reform, and political interest group in Palestinian Judaism from the second century B.C. to the late first century, usually contrasted with Pharisees. The first-century Jewish historian Flavius Josephus claims the Sadducees rejected immortality of the soul, attributed all human activity to free will and none to fate (or providence), and rejected customs and traditions not explicitly stated in Scripture. He also says that they recruited members from the upper classes, including priests, were boorish and conflictual in their social interactions, were strict interpreters of "the law," and were disliked by the people. Sadducees in the New Testament of the Bible accord with Josephus's account. In rabbinic literature, which champions the Pharisees, the Sadducees are treated as adversaries and even heretics. *See also* Pharisees.

sadhana (sah'duh-nuh; Skt., "effective"), in India, one of a variety of practices said to lead to liberating perfection: contemplation, asceticism, worship of a personal deity, and ethical living. *See also* asceticism; dharma; liberation; meditation; yoga.

sadhu (sah'doo; from Skt., "to go straight to the goal"), a male ascetic in Indian religions. The corresponding feminine form is *sadhvi*. Hindu *sadhus* are identified by their *parampara*, the succession from the founder of a sect or order in the Vaishnava or Shaiva traditions. "False" sadhus may be vagrants disguised as religious seekers. *See also* asceticism; Shaivism; tapas; Vaishnavism.

Safavid, the Islamic Shiite dynasty that ruled Iran from 1501 to 1779. The movement actually began with Safi al-Din (1252–1334), a popular Sufi *shaykh*, or "master," who called for the reform and purification of Islam. In 1501 Shah Ismail (1487–1524) proclaimed himself to be the manifestation of the Alid line of *Imams* from early Islam. This combination of Sufism and Shiism evolved into a powerful state for several centuries, as a political and theological counterpoise to the Sunni Ottomans of Anatolia and the Moghuls of India. What Shah Ismail began in 1501 reached its height under Shah Abbas (1588–1629). The Safavid capital at Isfahan became renowned for its architectural monuments and patronage of the arts and learning. This was also the period when much of the population of Iran converted to Twelver Shiism, which helped to consolidate Safavid authority over their subjects. Diplomatic and economic relations with Europe increased under the Safavids. They also fomented conflict with Sunni Islam and the powerful Sufi brotherhoods. By the eighteenth century the Safavids irreversibly began to lose control of the military and the central government to regional challengers. *See also* Shia.

saffron robe, the distinctive garment of Bud-dhist monks and nuns. A variety of robes are permitted in different Buddhist communities, and the yellow-orange robe is typical of only Theravada monks. Robes were originally made of discarded rags, but new robes are now given ceremonially to monks by laity. *See also* bhiksu/bhiksuni; Sangha.

saga (Icelandic, related to Old Norse *segja*, "to say"), an account or narrative. As a technical term it designates the medieval Icelandic literary narratives written in the Norse language during the period from the late twelfth century to the first half of the fourteenth century.

The sagas are divided into Family sagas (or sagas of Icelanders), sagas of Old Times, sagas of the Bishops, and sagas of the Kings. The Family sagas deal with persons and events during the "saga age," the time of the early settlement of Iceland (ca. 930–1050). Among other Family sagas, *Egils saga* and *Njals saga* are best known for their literary qualities. The sagas of the Old Times take place in a time before the settlement of Iceland. They contain fantastic adventures, supernatural happenings, and battles with ghosts and were sometimes referred to by the Icelanders as "Lying sagas." The sagas of the early Bishops (Iceland was converted to Christianity in the year 1000) consist of both hagiographical and historical accounts. Some were written in Latin and then translated into Icelandic. They treat the period ca. 1000 to 1340 and were written down ca. 1200 to 1350. To the sagas of the Kings belong anonymous works such as *Fagrskinna* and *Morkinskinna* and the well-known *Heimskringla* by Snorri Sturlusson (1178–1241), which treats a time span from mythical beginnings to 1177. *Heimskringla* was composed ca. 1230.

The historical value of the sagas is a point of debate. Earlier it was believed that they represented an unbroken, historically true oral tradition of past events until the moment they were written down. Today even the historically "realistic" sagas are looked upon as historical novels, as literary creations of artistically gifted authors. The sagas represent the knowledge of their own time, and the gap between the "saga time" and the time the saga was composed has been filled with folklore materials suited to the interests and aspirations of the saga writer. Nevertheless, the sagas are still indispensable to our knowledge of Old Norse history, church history, politics, and pre-Christian religion. *See also* Edda; Nordic religion.

sage, a category of holy person. *See also* holy person.

saguna. *See* nirguna/saguna.

Sahagun, Barnardino de (sah'ah-goon; ca. 1499–1590), Franciscan missionary to Mexico who compiled vast records on the Aztecs. Born in Leon in Sahagun, Spain, he studied at the University of Salamanca and arrived in Mexico in 1529. His major work, *A General History of the Things of New Spain,* or the *Florentine Codex,* is a twelve-volume collection modeled after medieval European encyclopedias. Using sophisticated interviewing techniques, he recorded information in Nahuatl, Spanish, and Latin on topics ranging from religion to natural history. Despite Sahagun's use of European categories and his goal to promote conversion, his work remains among the most important resources on Aztec life and thought. *See also* Mesoamerican religion.

Sahajdhari (sah-haj-dahr'ee; Punjabi), a Sikh who believes in the Sikh Gurus and their teachings in the *Adi Granth,* but who has not been initiated into the Khalsa and does not follow its code of conduct. *See also* Khalsa; Sikhism.

Saicho (sah-ee-choh; 767–822), posthumous title Dengyo Daisha, founder of the Japanese Buddhist Tendai school. After being ordained at Todaiji with the *Ssu-fen lu* precepts, he broke with tradition to climb Mt. Hiei to practice austerities. While in seclusion on Hiei, he became interested in the Chinese T'ien-t'ai tradition, and several years later he was able to travel to China to obtain better texts. There he met the eminent T'ien-t'ai monks Tao-sui and Hsiug-man, as well as representatives of Ox-head Ch'an and Tantric Buddhism, and obtained a Mahayana *Fan-wang* precepts ordination. After he returned to Japan, he found the court much more interested in Tantric Buddhism than in Tendai. To ensure the institutional independence of Tendai, he asked that Tendai monks be ordained with the *Fan-wang* precepts instead of the *Ssu-fen lu* precepts traditionally used in East Asia. Permission was granted one week after his death. Among his major works are *Sange gakusho shiki* (Regulations for Tendai Monks), *Kenkairon* (Treatise Revealing the Precepts), and the *Shugo kokkai sho* (Essay on Protecting the Nation). *See also* Tendai school; T'ien-t'ai school.

Saigyo (sah-ee-gyoh; 1118–90), Japanese Shingon Buddhist monk who was considered one of the great poets of the thirty-one syllable *waka.* His poems on impermanence and loneliness reflect his Buddhist aesthetics. *See also* Shingon-shu.

saint, a category of holy person. *See also* holy person; relics; Santeria; South American religions, traditional.

Christianity: In Christian tradition, the term *saint* bears several meanings. 1 A person conspicuous for holiness or sacred power who is venerated in life and after death. 2 A term used in the Christian scriptures, mainly by Paul, to designate a member of the Christian community. 3 In the Roman Catholic and Orthodox churches, a person who is publicly venerated in the liturgy as an intercessor in heaven and a model of Christian virtue. In these churches, there is also a veneration of saints' remains ("relics"), and places identified with them are maintained as shrines. In both churches, their feast days are kept on stipulated dates. The calendar of these feasts is called the sanctoral cycle in the West and the menaion in the East. The process by which these churches identify and designate such persons for inclusion in the list (canon) of the venerated is called canonization. *See also* calendar (Christian), martyr; miracle; relics; pilgrimage; shrine.

Islam: Cults of saints exist in virtually all Muslim countries, with many local variations and customs. The Arabic term for saint (*wali*) means a friend or client, based on the quranic expression "the friends of God" (10:62). Saints are popularly believed to continue in their graves to act as mediators and intercessors on behalf of their devotees in both spiritual and temporal matters. A living saint, known as a *shaykh* or *pir,* may function as a spiritual guide, teacher, and healer. While there is no official body or process in Islam that determines individual sainthood, some Muslims rank saints below the level of prophets and believe that saints possess divine inspiration and are capable of manifesting signs (*karamat*) of grace that may border on the miraculous. *See also* baraka, Islam (festal cycle); miracle; Sufi; wali.

sake (sah-kay), a popular Japanese rice wine used as an offering at Shinto altars and as a sacred drink in weddings.

Sakya-pa (sahk'yah-[pa]), one of four major schools of Tibetan Buddhism. The Sakya-pa originated in India and is renowned for its teachings on the Hevajra Tantra. The Tibetan originator of Sakya-pa, Drogmi (992–1074), taught Konchog Gyaltsan, founder of the Sakya (Tib., "gray earth") Monastery (1073), central seat of the school and source of its name. The Sakya-pa played a key political role in developing the priest-patron relationship with the Mongols in the fourteenth century by which the Sakya-pa became, in effect, regents of Tibet.

Succession of rulership is by family, with nephew succeeding uncle. *See also* Geluk-pa; Kagyu-pa; Nyingma-pa; Tibetan religions.

Saladin (from Arab. *Salah al-Din,* 1138–93), Kurdish Muslim general who replaced Shii Fatimid dynasty in Cairo with his own Sunni Ayyubid dynasty (1171–1250), extending his power to Syria in 1174. His victory over the Crusaders at Hattin (near Lake Tiberias) led to Jerusalem's restoration to Muslim control in 1187, thus triggering the Third Crusade. *See also* Crusades.

salafiyya, al-. *See* fundamentalism.

salamu alaykum, al- (as-sa-la'moo a-lay'koom; Arab., "peace be upon you"), universal greeting among Muslims, to which the reply is *"wa alaykum al-salam"* ("and upon you be peace").

salat. *See* prayer.

salvation, the belief that human beings require deliverance. A distinctive trait of some religions, it is a notion almost entirely absent in others. *See also* enlightenment; liberation; salvation, religions of; savior.

Christianity: Christians through the centuries have generally agreed on the three main features of salvation. First, while the initial fruits of salvation may be experienced in the present life, its full realization is delayed until the next. Only in heaven, in the immediate presence of God, will people's deepest desires for peace, justice, and fulfillment be completely satisfied. Second, there are numerous obstacles in the present life that make attaining heaven difficult, and of themselves people are incapable of salvation. It is only by the grace of God that these obstacles are overcome and people are made worthy of God. And third, Jesus Christ is absolutely decisive for salvation, for it is principally through Christ's work that God has made available the grace required to resolve the problems and contradictions of human existence.

Variety of Approaches: Within this broad consensus, there has been considerable variety in approaches to the question of salvation (soteriology). There is no agreement among Christian theologians, for example, about the precise nature of the obstacles hindering the attainment of heaven. For those influenced by Augustine (d. 430), sin disqualifies one from salvation. With sin, the self is thrown into confusion and is unable to perform the acts that God requires of the saved; with sin, one has put oneself at enmity with God, and thus cannot expect God to bring one into heaven. For others, such as the early Greek church fathers and some of the Scholastics such as Thomas Aquinas (ca. 1225–74), the emphasis lies elsewhere, on the qualitative and ontological difference between people and God. Salvation means to live God's own life, to know and love God directly as God knows and loves God. But people are not God and so cannot of themselves achieve the life appropriate to God.

Disagreement about the human predicament leads in turn to differing descriptions of the grace that meets these obstacles. In the Greek fathers and Aquinas, grace has a primarily elevating function. Grace raises one above one's natural powers, making it possible to perform actions pleasing to God and readying its possessor for entry into the divine inheritance in the next life. Among those who focus on the problem of sin, however, grace can be perceived in two basic ways. For Martin Luther (1483–1546), grace means forgiveness. People are always sinners, both before and after the reception of grace. The difference is that by grace God has imputed God's own righteousness to the believer, thus disregarding that person's sin. In Augustine, however, grace works not only for forgiveness of sin but for a real transformation in its recipient as well, enabling the person to perform the morally good actions that God seeks from those who will attain heaven.

Divergent views of the human situation and of grace lead similarly to distinctive analyses of the work of Christ. For the Greek fathers, the incarnation is tied directly to the elevating capacity of grace: "God became human so that people could become God" was a favorite way of stating the significance of Christ. For those who place more emphasis on the devastating effects of sin and its destruction of community with God, considerable effort has been devoted to portraying the precise manner in which Christ conquers sin and makes grace available. Perhaps the most famous example in the West is found in the *Cur Deus Homo* (Why God Became Human) of Anselm of Canterbury (ca. 1033–1109). For Anselm, people have been called to the transcendent destiny of life in heaven with God. To attain this good, people must perform actions perfective of human nature. By these actions, people concomitantly offer the honor that is owing to the Creator. But, by sin, people have defected from the path that leads to God and, moreover, have failed to give to God the honor owing to God. It is impossible for people of themselves to return to the correct path to God or to restore to God the honor removed by previous sin. Whatever good people might subsequently do would simply give to God the honor associated with that act, not make up for the dishonoring of previous sin. Hence, people owe a debt to God, but cannot make good on this debt. Through sin, finally, death has entered the world, as a punishment imposed by God as the consequence of human sinning. At this point the importance of Christ for Anselm becomes apparent. Jesus Christ is both human and divine. As human, he possesses everything that is essential to being human. But sin is not essential to being human; it is a corruption introduced to the nature by people themselves. Hence, Christ is completely innocent of sin, and all his acts offer, as they should, complete honor to God. Nor did Christ have to die; death, after all, is a punishment imposed by God on sinful people. Hence, when Christ died on the cross, he did this voluntarily, and moreover went beyond the call of his duty to God, offering to God in his innocent death something not owed to God. Jesus Christ is fully God as well, and so whatever he did was of infinite significance, applicable to all those who share his human nature. Thus, by his voluntary death Christ has satisfied for the debt owed by sinful people to God and has cleared the way for those who belong to Christ to attain heaven.

Recent Concerns: Recent discussions of salvation have sought to bring into prominence the communal character of salvation, in the process paying greater attention to the social structures that promote sin and the effectiveness of God's Word in transforming sinful society, as well as certain aspects of the biblical message, such as the kingdom of God, that have been relatively neglected in traditional teachings. Similarly, theologians have been stimulated by the pluralism of the modern world to consider more closely the salvific possibilities of non-Christians, asking, Is there salvation apart from Christ? *See also* eschatology; grace; Jesus Christ; Messiah; savior; sin; soteriology.

salvation, religions of, the class of religions that evidence a sense that the present world and human beings are not as they should be. In contrast to religions of sanctification, they teach that struggle against, and transcendence of, the structures of the world is a worthy goal. *See also* sanctification, religions of; typology, classification.

Salvation Army, a Christian semimilitary organization founded by William Booth in England in 1878 and devoted to nondenominational evangelization and social service.

samadhi (suh-mah'dee; Skt.,"concentration,""absorption"), Indic philosophical term. 1 Meditative concentration on a single object, gradually calming the mental whirlwind. 2 The last of three stages in yoga (after *dharana* and *dhyana*), ultimately culminating in an immutable concentration in which all mental activities cease and the mind becomes totally absorbed in its object. 3 In Buddhism, a state of consciousness leading to higher forms of meditation (dhyana) that finally result in nondualistic consciousness. *See also* meditation; yoga.

Samantabhadra (sah-mahn-tah-bah'drah; Skt., "perfect goodness"; Chin. *P'u-hsien;* Jap. *Fugen*), in Buddhism the Bodhisattva of virtuous action, who embodies the vows and ideal conduct of all Bodhisattvas. *See also* Bodhisattvas.

Samaritans, the community that worships on Mt. Gerizim just south of Nablus, the major urban center in central Palestine. After the Assyrian conquest of the northern kingdom of Israel in 722/721 B.C., the name of the capital, Samaria, was extended to the entire land, now made an Assyrian province. The Bible (2 Kings 17) relates that the inhabitants were deported and the country repopulated with people from different parts of the Assyrian Empire. These people allegedly grafted a superficial Yahweh cult upon their own religion in order to "appease the God of the country" (v. 26). Also appearing in 2 Kings 17 is the first mention of the name Samaritans (Heb. *Shomerim*), giving it a strong connotation of paganism and idolatry. This picture is a polemical Judean description. According to the Assyrian annals, 27,290 people were exiled, which would amount to no more than 5 to 15 percent of the population.

Instead of referring to themselves as Samaritans, the descendants of the inhabitants of the northern kingdom emend the Hebrew *Shomerim* to *Shamerim,* "keepers" or "observers (of the law)." Their religion is a Yahwism based on the five books of Moses (Genesis–Deuteronomy), the sole canonical scripture of the Samaritans. Devotion to the law is the second article of the Samaritan creed, which also demands faith in God, Moses, Mt. Gerizim, and the last day and the resurrection. Except for the fourth item (Mt. Gerezim), the creed contains tenets central to all Jews. At some time between 400 and 200 B.C., the Samaritans built a temple on Mt. Gerizim, claiming it was the place of the desert tabernacle of the Hebrews after they arrived in the Holy Land. About 130 B.C., John Hyrcanus, the military leader of the Judeans, demolished the

Samaritans at Mt. Gerizim, near the west bank of the Jordan river, light fires to roast the Passover lambs they have just sacrified. Unlike the Jewish Passover meal, in which the sacrifice is wholly symbolic, the Samaritan ritual retains the actual sacrificial killing.

Samaritan temple, but the Samaritans continued to worship there. Even today they sacrifice the Passover lamb on their holy mount according to the regulations in the law.

Moses occupies a place in Samaritanism surpassing that in Judaism. In the period of Samaritan revival in the third century, from which the earliest extrapentateuchal literature of the Samaritans derives, the theologian Marqah wrote an extensive commentary on the career of Moses in which he is said to have obtained divine nature. Both Marqah and his colleague Amram Darah wrote hymns in which Moses is praised alongside God. In the medieval additions to the liturgy, preexistence is ascribed to Moses.

The expected savior in Samaritanism is the "Prophet like Moses" (Deuteronomy 18:15, 18). Some say it is Moses himself who is to return. He is the *Taheb*, a title interpreted as "the Returning One" or "the Restorer" of the golden age and the tabernacle, which God removed when some of the Hebrews disrupted the cult on Mt. Gerizim and went south. Originally, the Taheb seems to have been an ideal type of the community repenting and returning to God.

Sama Veda (sah'muh vay'duh; Skt., "knowledge of chant[s]"), a sacred Vedic Sanskrit text, the manual of the Udgatar priest, containing verses almost entirely extracted from the *Rig Veda* and arranged for chanting at the *soma* ritual. **See also** Rig Veda; soma; Veda, Vedism.

Samkhya (sahng'kyuh; Skt., "enumerating"), name of one of the six systems of Hindu philosophy, founded by the sage Kapila (550 B.C.) and linked ideologically to Patanjali's Yoga. Samkhya's goal is to dispel the ignorance that causes one to confuse materiality (*prakriti*) with eternal consciousness (*purusha*); its method involves enumerating categories. The first category of twenty-five principles, consisting of twenty-four forms of materiality and one ubiquitous consciousness, provides the basis for the second, consisting of eight intellectual dispositions. The third category of fifty intellectual patterns is created by the interaction of principles and dispositions.

In Samkhyan dualism, consciousness is a permanent, passive witness to the transformations that occur in the twenty-four principles of manifest materiality, which evolve from the one original (or unmanifest) materiality. All things, including ourselves, are transformations of the one materiality and therefore preexist in manifest causal antecedents, just as fire is potential in wood or yogurt in milk. Confusion must also be rooted in materiality since consciousness is utterly inactive. While Samkhya fails to explain how consciousness and materiality become confused or how they might interact, it asserts that systematic enumeration methodically dispels primordial confusion and frees one from the delimiting conditions of material causality. *See also* six systems of Indian philosophy.

samsara (sahm-sah'ruh; Skt., "flowing together"), an Indic term for the cycle of birth and death, the phenomenal realm of flux, that is, the "ordinary" spatio-temporal world. More narrowly, it is the cycle of "rebirth" (and redeath) governed by *karma* (the consequences of meritorious and demeritorious actions) and experienced by all living beings. There are various Hindu, Buddhist, and Jain "paths" for gaining liberation from samsara. *See also* karma; liberation; nirvana; Path (Buddhism); reincarnation.

Samsin Halmoni. *See* Birth Grandmother.

sanatana dharma (sah-nah'tah-nah dahr'mah; Skt., "eternal law, duty, religion"), Hindu self-designation for Hindu religion and culture, referring to them as unchanging and divinely sanctioned. *See also* dharma; Hinduism.

Sanbo ekotoba (sahn-boh ee-koh-toh-bah; Jap., "Paintings and Explanations of the Three Treasures"), Japanese handbook to Buddhist personages and festivals compiled by Minamoto Tamenori in 984.

San-chiao (sahn-jeou; Chin., "Three Teachings," "Three Religions") 1 A general expression for the three traditions of Confucianism, Taoism, and Buddhism. 2 A technical term for a form of Chinese religion that combines Confucianism, Taoism, and Buddhism. There is a long history of syncretistic thought in China, but it reached its peak in the sixteenth and seventeenth centuries with *San-chiao ho-i*, "the union of three teachings in one." This movement either emphasized different elements of each tradition or held that any of the three Ways could lead to enlightenment. 3 In the Ch'ing dynasty (1644–1912), a term used to refer to Christianity, Buddhism, and Confucianism. *See also* Chinese religion.

San-ch'ing (sahn-cheeng; Chin., "Three Pure [Ones]"), triad of high Taoist deities originally associated with the Ling-pao tradition. *See also* Ling-pao Taoism.

san-ch'ung (sahn-chuhng; Chin., "three worms"), Taoist term for three principles or entities in the body that inhabit the cinnabar fields and cause disease, old age, and death. *See also* physiological teachings (Taoism).

sanctification, the ritual process of purification, the procedure for making a person, place, or thing sacred.

sanctification, religions of, the class of religions that evidence a sense that the present world and human beings are as they should be. In contrast to religions of salvation, they teach that active maintenance of the structures of the world is a worthy goal. *See also* salvation, religions of; typology, classification.

sandpainting, ritual designs usually constructed by strewing variously colored crushed mineral or vegetal materials on the ground. Also called drypaintings, sandpaintings are found in religions worldwide, notably Hindu *mandalas*, Australian aboriginal totem emblems, and in Native American cultures particularly in the Southwest. The most widely known are those made by Navajos (American Southwest) integral to certain forms of healing ceremonials. During the daytime of some Navajo healing rituals, the paintings are constructed on the floor inside the ceremonial hogan (lodge). Sandpaintings depict, as elongated humanlike forms, Holy People (ye'ii), figures identified with the life force and with the inner life forms of all living things. In this way their powers are made present. These paintings are commonly surrounded by a guardian rainbow, also humanlike in form, with an opening aligned with the door of the lodge, which is always to the east. The person whose illness is being treated sits in the center of the painting and, in a prayer ceremony, is identified with the figures in the painting by having materials from the painting applied to corresponding body parts from the feet to the head. Navajo sandpaintings, though elaborate and aesthetically pleasing, are destroyed in their ritual use. The destruction designates that the powers of life present in the design have been internalized by the suffering person who, through this ritual, is made into a beautiful, healthy human being, reflecting the surrounding world. Reproductions in any form are discouraged, though there exist permanent craft and fine art forms, usually for sale, that reproduce elements of these designs. Not used as an instrument of cure, these art and craft forms are not considered religious, except in the most

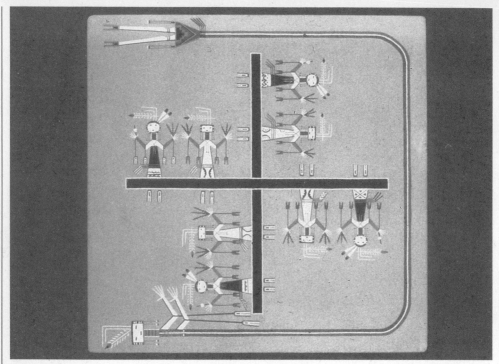

Native American Navajo "whirling logs" sandpainting from Arizona used in a healing ceremony.

general sense. *See also* mandala; North America, traditional religions in.

Sangha (sahn'guh; Skt., Pali, "group"), the Buddhist monastic order. An essential aspect of a Buddha's career as a religious teacher is the establishment of a monastic order that will be able to preserve his teaching and provide a social context for its practice. Since the time of the Buddha, the Sangha has played a central role in almost all aspects of Buddhist practice. Members of the Sangha have been teachers, exemplars for others, and recipients of honor and offerings.

The Sangha as a Collective Body: The Buddhist monastic order is divided into separate but parallel male and female branches. A further distinction is made in the Sangha between novices and those who have undergone a higher ordination. The terms *monk* (Skt. *bhiksu*) and *nun* (*bhiksuni*) are technically reserved for those who have received higher ordination. A novice, whether male or female, is obligated to observe the Ten Precepts, while a monk after higher ordination is expected to observe over two hundred rules, and a nun more than three hundred. The precise number of rules varies according to the Vinaya text preserved by different Buddhist schools. Although the specific details of the regulation of monastic behavior vary, there is a common pattern to Buddhist monastic life, which is all the more remarkable given the cultural and doctrinal diversity found in the Buddhist world.

The Sangha is an autonomous body that is, ideally, self-regulating. The governance as well as the ritual activity of the Sangha is based locally, and there is no individual or collective body that can make decisions for the Sangha as a whole. This preference for the local has permitted, if not encouraged, divisions within the Sangha and today a variety of monastic traditions and lineages exist. These can prevent the monks belonging to the different groups from performing certain monastic actions together.

The ordination traditions of nuns in South and Southeast Asia ceased at some point in the medieval period; the reasons for this disruption are not completely clear, but possible reasons include sexist attitudes within Buddhist society and the destruction accompanying the Muslim invasions of North India at the beginning of the second millennium.

The History of the Sangha: The Sangha is probably the oldest monastic community in the world. It is thought that originally the Sangha was a community of wandering ascetics, and this might help to explain the absence of large-scale institutional structures in the Buddhist monastic order. But early in the history of Buddhism, monks and nuns began to live in monasteries, some of which became economic and cultural centers; it is not uncommon for Buddhist monasteries to have economic resources at their disposal, and in some countries, monasteries became major landowners.

The history of the Sangha is in many ways one and the same as the history of Buddhism. Buddhism has spread through Asia with the establishment of local Sanghas. Theravadin texts speak of the Buddha's tradition only taking root when there is a Sangha with native-born members who can recite the Vinaya. It is only with the transmission of Buddhism to North America and Europe that Buddhists have come to envision the possibility of a Buddhist community without a Sangha.

The Ritual Activities of the Sangha: All members of a local Sangha must gather for collective activities such as confession ceremonies and regular recitation of the monastic code. The Sangha is also responsible for the initiation of new members in the different ordination rituals.

Other religious activities of the Sangha fall into two divisions. On the one hand, some monks and nuns, usually the majority, are heavily involved in the religious life of the wider Buddhist community. Members of the Sangha serve as ritual specialists and officiate at various ceremonies. They give sermons, chant texts, participate in offerings and other merit-making rituals for important occasions in the life of the laity, and are present at funerals.

On the other hand, some members of the Sangha focus on the cultivation of their own individual spiritual life and place a great emphasis on asceticism, moral purity, and rectitude as well as on meditation. These activities are often seen to be typical of the Sangha at its best, and those monks and nuns who live such disciplined lives within the Sangha are widely admired.

The Sangha is a "field of merit" for the laity. Gifts of the material necessities of the Sangha, from buildings to robes and bowls (and in the modern world pens and electric fans), bring merit to the donors greater than if the same objects had been given to others. But monks do not only passively receive such gifts. In return, they give back the Buddha's teaching to their benefactors. They are thus thought to return a superior gift.

The Noble Community: A distinction is made between the Sangha of those who are merely ordained and the more precious noble community of the spiritually advanced, although the members of the latter frequently belong to the former. It is especially this noble community that is venerated in the third of the Three Jewels in which Buddhists take refuge. *See also* almsgiving; bhiksu/bhiksuni; merit; monasticism; nun; Three Jewels; Vinaya.

Sanhedrin (Heb. and Aram. loanword, from Gk. *synedrion*, "assembly, council, court"), the supreme Jewish religious, judicial, and political body in the land of Israel from 63 B.C. until the fifth or sixth century. Allegedly composed of seventy or seventy-one members, it was called by some rabbinic sources the "Great Sanhedrin." The historian Josephus and the Gospels portray it as a judicial and political council headed by the high priest or king and convened in various places to promote political programs. By contrast, the Mishnah describes it as a legislative body in the Jerusalem Temple, headed by the foremost rabbinic authority and dealing primarily with religious issues. Scholarly efforts to reconcile these contradictory descriptions have not succeeded. Consequently, historical knowledge of the Sanhedrin remains uncertain. *See also* rabbinical court.

San-huang (sahn-hwahng; Chin., "Three August [Ones]"), three mythic Chinese sovereigns, Fu Hsi, Shen Nung, and Huang-ti, who function as legendary culture heroes. They were all divinely conceived, and their civilizing contributions prior to the founding of the Chinese polity include the calendar, music, manufacturing, boats and wheeled vehicles, and the art of government (Huang-ti); plowing, animal husbandry, herbal medicine, and markets (Shen Nung); writing, the sexagenary cycle, divination, hunting, fishing, and cooking (Fu Hsi). Though they are not mentioned in the earliest reliable texts and were largely ignored by Confucians, increasingly elaborate popular legends about the three proliferated from the late Chou period (ca. 1122–221 B.C.) on; ultimately they became enshrined as important deities in the Taoist pantheon. *See also* Fu Hsi; Huang-ti; Shen Nung.

Sankey, Ira David. *See* Moody, Dwight Lyman.

San-lun school (sahn-luhn; Chin., "Three Treatises"), Chinese Buddhist school that specialized in Madhyamaka teachings. Through a rigorous analysis of phenomena, they sought to demonstrate that things cannot be proven to exist or not to exist, thus steering a middle path between the twin fallacies of absolutism and nihilism and establishing the truth of emptiness. They took their name from their three fundamental texts, two by Nagarjuna and one by Aryadeva. Kumarajiva founded the school in the early fifth century, but it faded in importance after the death of its last great thinker, Chi-tsang, in 623. *See also* China, Buddhism in; Kumarajiva; Seng-chao.

Sanron school (sahn-rohn), one of the six Japanese Buddhist Nara schools. Sanron was based on Indian Madhyamaka and Chinese San-lun teachings. The school was influential until the ninth century. *See also* Nara schools.

Sanskrit (Skt. *samskrita*, "perfected," "polished"), an ancient Indo-European language formed on the Indian subcontinent by the convergence of numerous dialects of Old Indo-Aryan (ca. 1500 B.C.). The earliest surviving Sanskrit inscription is dated ca. 150.

Hinduism: The Sanskrit language is sacred to Hindus because of its use in holy texts, because many consider it a language befitting the gods, and because its use has been restricted to elite groups of specialists, especially priestly Brahman castes, who claim privileged knowledge and authority on the basis of their familiarity with the language and the materials composed in it.

Eventually codified and standardized by the grammarian Panini (ca. 400 B.C.) and succeeding commentators Katyayana (ca. 300 B.C.) and Patanjali (ca. 200 B.C.), the earliest Sanskrit is called Vedic, the first extant representation of which is the *Rig Veda*. A collection of 1,028 hymns primarily describing an evolving pantheon of gods, the *Rig Veda* is followed by other Vedic texts, including prose works called Brahmanas, which present the details of sacrificial rituals, and the mystical, speculative Upanishads. Vedic texts, organized primarily by ritualistic principles, are sacred in word as well as in sound; many are recited as part of rituals in which semantics become subordinated to the rules of performance. Regarded as a source of eternal knowledge, many Hindus hold Vedic texts to be authorless (*apaurusheya*) revelation originally "heard" (*shruti*) by sages; in contrast, all other Hindu religious texts are classified as "recollection" or "remembrance" (*smriti*) with respect to Vedic revelation.

The classification of non-Vedic texts as remembrance does not necessarily diminish a given text's sacrality or religious importance. The *Bhagavad Gita*, for example, is treated as both sacred words, in the sense of enshrining divine teaching, and as religiously authoritative. While most Hindus would agree that the Sanskrit language is sacred, not all texts in San-

skrit are sacred, religiously authoritative, or important for all Hindus: much depends on the status attributed to the voice within the text and on the persons who judge the text's significance.

Non-Hindu religions, including Buddhism and Jainism, have employed Sanskrit as a scriptural language but do not ordinarily regard the language itself as sacred. *See also* Buddhism (authoritative texts and their interpretation); Hinduism (authoritative texts and their interpretation); Rig Veda; Veda, Vedism.

Buddhism: Although Pali is the chief sacred language of Buddhism, Buddhist Hybrid Sanskrit, a variety of the Sanskrit language, is used in several important early Mahayana scriptures. The language is a hybrid of classical Sanskrit and the Indian vernacular languages, or Prakrits, that were popular from approximately 100 B.C. to A.D. 300 in the early stages of the development of the Mahayana. As Mahayana literature evolved, it lost many of its vernacular features and adhered more closely to the model of classical Sanskrit. The texts originally written in Buddhist Hybrid Sanskrit, such as the *Lotus Sutra* and the *Perfection of Wisdom Sutras*, are among the most influential Mahayana scriptures in Asia. *See also* Mahayana; Pali.

Santa Claus, legendary Christian figure identified as a children's gift giver who comes on Christmas Eve. The name is a corruption of "Saint Nicholas," whose feast was marked by the giving of gifts to children (December 6). The Nicholas story blended with a non-Christian European figure of Winter. Similar figures are known in Europe as Father Christmas or Father Frost. *See also* Christmas.

Santeria (sahn-teh-ree'ah; Span., "the way of the saints"), an African-derived religion developed in Cuba and spread throughout the Caribbean and the United States by Cuban exiles.

History: Santeria comes from the ritual life of the Yoruba people of present-day Nigeria and Benin. Brought to Cuba as slaves in the late eighteenth and early nineteenth centuries, the Yoruba reconstructed their religious identity in response to the Catholicism of their captors. Often replaced by *Lucumi* (the Yoruba self-designation) or *la regla de ocha* (order of the *orishas* [Yoruban "spirits"]) the word *Santeria* recalls the correspondences made by devotees between the saints of Cuban Catholic folk piety and the spirits carried from Africa. While the relationship between the African and Christian elements of Santeria are complex, they are unified in a ritual system of communication with the orishas and personal spiritual growth.

Ritual System: The basic unit of the Santeria community is the *ile*, an autonomous organization that means at once "house," "community," and "family." Over each ile presides a priest or priestess, who acts as a godparent by initiating "godchildren" into the rites sacred to the spirits. The godparent gives birth to the spirit in the godchild. Ideally all are united by filial ties of mutual love and respect.

The Santeria priesthood is conferred in a ceremony called *asiento*, in which a particular orisha is "seated in the head" of a devotee. With the power of the *orisha* to heal and bring success in life, the initiate, now properly called a *santero* or *santera*, is capable of giving birth to godchildren and establishing an independent ile. While individual iles may include from a handful to hundreds of active devotees, the number of initiates is usually no more than 10 to 20 percent of the ile. Asiento ceremonies are expensive, and the commitment to serve an orisha in this way is said to require the seriousness and solemnity of a marriage contract.

Gradual commitment to the life of the ile can be marked by a series of lesser initiations, in which the devotee receives specially consecrated necklaces or elementary symbols of certain orishas. Some male devotees are called to a special track of spiritual progress in divination that can culminate in the most respected priesthood in Santeria, that of the *babalawo* ("father of the mystery").

Santeria may be seen as a system of ritual communication between orishas and their devotees. When devotees experience problems in life they seek out a diviner, usually their Santeria godparent (perhaps a babalawo if the problem is sufficiently grave), to determine the spiritual cause of the problem. Frequently divination reveals that an orisha has caused the problem in order to gain the attention on which the spirit depends for sacrifice and praise. The diviner will diagnose the problem, identify the orisha or orishas who are behind it, and prescribe a set of sacrifices that will resolve the situation. Thus, the orishas communicate their needs to human beings.

Human beings respond by offering to the spirits a variety of vegetable and animal sacrifices as prescribed by divination and carried out according to an elaborate code of symbolic ingredients and ritual steps. These sacrifices strengthen the orishas and dispose them to act on the devotee's behalf in meeting the challenges that the devotee faces. The sacrificial relationships may be characterized in some cases as ones of fearful respect and in others as relationships of loving affection.

The most dramatic form of communication between orisha and devotee occurs in ceremonial dances called *bembes*, where the community gathers to praise a spirit with drum music, feasting, dance, and song. The orisha may call specifically for a bembe or it may mark a calendrical observance of special days of initiation in the ile. An orchestra of three drums and a vocal soloist are retained to produce the rhythms and songs that will call the orishas to the feast. It is hoped that one or more orishas will manifest themselves by "mounting" trained mediums and directing their bodies as riders command horses. Through the medium, an orisha will dance, sing, and feast with the congregation and will offer healing advice and prescriptions. The bembe brings together the communication of divination and sacrifice into an actual dialogue with the orishas, present as personalities incarnated in the bodies of medium priests or priestesses.

Modern Developments: Since the Cuban revolution of 1959, nearly one million Cubans have left the island to settle in South and Central America, the Caribbean, and the United States. Thousands of them were devotees of the orishas, and the religion has been a focal point of their immigrant experience. Santeria has been described as a social force to acclimate Cubans to new and sometimes hostile environments by offering familiar cultural exchanges and access to hopeful spiritual power.

It is difficult to estimate the numbers of devotees because the religion has no formal organization beyond the individual ile. Devotees also have had to be discreet in professing a non-Christian religion that practices the sacrifice of animals. It is likely that initiated priests and priestesses in the United States number in the tens of thousands, and active devotees could be counted in the hundreds of thousands. The religion is growing in the United States. More devotees openly profess it, and some have founded public organizations to promulgate it, following ecclesiastical or academic models, either as churches or research institutes. *See also* Afro-Americans (Caribbean and South American), new religions among; babalawo; orisha.

Santidade (sahn-tih-dah'jih; Portuguese, "holiness"), religious movement of sixteenth-century Brazil combining indigenous and Roman Catholic elements; the word *santidade* had apparently been applied by Jesuit missionaries to the ritual practices of native Brazilians.

Portuguese immigrants, native Brazilians, and biracial colonists, led by a "pope" and "Maria" or "Mother of God" prophesying a cosmic cataclysm, joined in the worship of an unshaped stone. Ritual use of rosaries and crosses augmented the "drinking" of tobacco smoke to induce visions. Following the suppression of Santidade by the colonial government, a handful of participants confessed to the visiting Portuguese Inquisition of 1591 to 1593. Santidade and other similar movements laid the foundation for later Afro-Christian groups of the inland northeast of Brazil. *See also* Native Americans (Central and South America), new religions among.

Saosyant (soush'yent; Avestan, "the Future Benefactor"), in Zoroastrianism the title of the third son of Zoroaster, who will inaugurate the final renovation of the world. *See also* Zoroastrianism.

Sarasvati (suh-ruhs'vuh-tee), a goddess of Vedic and later India. Originally a deified river name, she became identified with Vak, "Speech," and was later interpreted as the goddess of eloquence. *See also* Veda, Vedism.

Sargon, the name borne by two major kings of Mesopotamia. 1 Sargon I of Akkad (ca. 2350–2279 B.C.), the first Semitic king over a unified lower Mesopotamia. His fame became the basis of several later legends regarding his rise to power. 2 Sargon II (721–705 B.C.), king of Assyria, who led several successful military campaigns in Palestine and Syria.

sarim. *See* village recluses (Korea).

Sarvastivada (sahr-vahs-tee-vah'duh; Skt., "the doctrine that everything exists"), an early Indian Buddhist sect. Prevalent in the north and northwestern Indian subcontinent and in Central Asia, the Sarvastivadins possessed, by the first century, a complete canon of scriptures written in Sanskrit, noteworthy for a set of Abhidharma treatises (doctrinal exegeses) that examine all aspects of Buddhist doctrine. Through the position that "everything exists" they claim that all constituent factors of existence can exert causal effects from all three time periods, the past, present, and future. The elaboration of Abhidharma became the basis for the later development of this sect, the focus of controversies with related and rival schools, and the impetus for many later developments in Indian Buddhist thought. *See also* Abhidharma; Buddhism (authoritative

texts and their interpretation); Nikaya Buddhism; Sautrantika.

Sassanids (sa-sa'nidz), imperial Persian dynasty from western Iran who ruled Iran from 224 to 651. The period saw the establishment of Zoroastrian state orthodoxy. *See also* Achaemenid; Zoroastrianism.

Satan (Heb., "opponent," "adversary"), personification of evil in the religions of the West. Satan appears as an angelic being in the Hebrew scriptures. *See also* Iblis; Lucifer.

Christianity: In the New Testament, Satan is the enemy of God, a fallen angel whose power over humanity is only broken by Jesus' acts of healing, exorcism, and ultimately death on the cross. In medieval Catholicism Satan first emerges as a popular image of folklore. The familiar portrait of the devil with horns, cloven hoofs, and tail seems to be a compendium of traits ascribed by the European populace to ancient fertility spirits, such as the Greek god Pan or the satyrs of mythology.

Islam: Satan (Arab. *Shaytan*) is identified with Iblis, chief of the legions of devils who try to lead humans astray. He is responsible for the seduction of Adam and Eve and appears in the hearts of people tempting them to disobey the commands of God. Satan is to be destroyed by the savior to come (Mahdi), whose appearance will signal the arrival of the Day of Judgment. Devilish or satanic creatures are said to be able to appear in human form so as to confuse and mislead their victims. Hosts of satans will serve as tormentors in the fires of hell.

satanic churches in America, organizations from the 1960s counterculture and the 1980s New Age movement that are explicitly devoted to the devil. The best known is the Church of Satan, established in San Francisco in 1966 by Anton LaVey (b. 1930). A longstanding interest in occultism and psychic phenomena brought LaVey toward the realm of alternative spirituality and an affirmation of Satan as a personification of the full range of natural human feelings and drives. The desire to express avarice, gluttony, lust, and anger at those who block one is normal in humans, LaVey insisted, and should not be confounded by guilt as it is in most religions. While condemning drugs and criminal or sadistic activity, the Church of Satan exalts hedonism and positive self-affirmation. Its often-dramatic rituals assert, at base, the innocence of appetite and permit the ventilation of rage against one's enemies.

The Church of Satan's presumptive elitism and the strong character of its founder have led to schisms. The most important was the Temple of Set, founded in 1975 by Michael Aquino, which moved in an occultist and ceremonial magic direction. The Temple of Set reached a high point in the late 1970s before suffering its own tensions. Other Satanist groups include the Brotherhood of the Ram, the Church of Satanic Brotherhood, and the Ordo Templi Satanis. *See also* North America, new religions in; Satanism.

Satanism, the worship of the principle, personified as Satan or the devil, seen in the Jewish and Christian traditions as the direct adversary of God and the embodiment of absolute evil.

Satanism has a necessary conceptual relationship to those monotheistic religions. It should not be confused definitionally with paganism, including contemporary Neo-Paganism and Wicca ("white" Witchcraft), or with occultism. The real Satanist in some sense accepts the biblical worldview but chooses to honor what stands in opposition to its deity.

Although it may have tangled roots in the extreme dualism of ancient and medieval Manichaeism and in survivals of pre-Christian religion—or in popular perceptions of these cults—the true background of modern Satanism lies only in the late medieval and early modern eras, with their rising spiritual tension, heightened sense of cosmic drama, and, above all, grim atmosphere of witch hysteria. Virtually all the accounts of Satan worship, pacts with the devil, etc. extracted under torture—in these periods are false. The witchfinders' imaginations constructed a satanic mythology that some later chose to actualize. Thus, by 1680 a major Satanist scandal shook the court of Louis XIV of France, as Madame de Montespan, the king's mistress, was accused of participating in black Masses and the sacrifice of babies to hold the affections of her royal lover. Subsequent discussion of serious Satanism has, whether appropriately or not, tended to draw on these rites and Abbe Guibourg, who performed them, as prototypes.

The late nineteenth century saw a revival of interest in the tradition, especially in France, where theatrical satanic rites matching the decadent fin-de-siecle mood were widely reported. In England in the early twentieth century, the notorious magician Aleister Crowley, though not a Satanist, attracted attention for his flouting of conventional morality and his self-designation as "The Great Beast 666." Devil worship had been recognized and, indeed, was a feature of folklore in America, as in England, at least since the days of the witch trials. But the tense post–World War II era in America, especially the 1960s counterculture, seemed a milieu in which Satanism could flourish.

In the mid-century and later atmosphere of rock music, psychedelia, and occultism, groups professing Satanism arose. They ranged from the much-publicized Church of Satan in San Francisco to clandestine if not criminal coteries such as the Manson family. Then, as always, isolated sociopaths also claimed satanic inspiration and displayed satanic symbols such as the double horns or inverted pentagram. Perhaps chiefly for shock value, symbols and sometimes lyrics capable of satanic interpretation were flaunted by popular heavy-metal rock groups. This new rise of Satanism provides a counterpoint to the much-heralded rise of evangelical Christianity in the 1970s. As in the days of the witch trials, charges and lurid accounts of satanic doings in America often exceed provable or probable reality.

The best-documented instances of modern Satanism involve teenage dabblers in the satanic arts. In this construction, youthful dabblers are invariably white, middle class, and acting out some form of rebellion against their parents. Lacking a coherent theology, these adherents often invent rituals based on a combination of a literal reading of Anton LaVey's *The Satanic Bible* (1969), interpretations of certain heavy-metal rock lyrics, popular press coverage of the alleged activities of multigenerational Satanists, and frequently the use of psychedelic drugs and alcohol. While these activities are often harmless, occasionally they have resulted in tragedies, up to and including murder. Ironically it is at the level of teenage dabblers that evangelical and fundamentalist Protestant members of anticult groups and concerned law enforcement officers become involved in efforts to combat Satanism. These groups often posit the existence of a multigenerational satanic conspiracy as the root cause for young people to be drawn into Satanism. The publicity attracted to this anticult movement serves to further reinforce the public perception of the pervasiveness of modern Satanism at all levels of involvement. *See also* satanic churches in America.

satchidananda (suht-chid-ah'nuhn-duh; "Being-consciousness-bliss"), term used in Hindu Vedanta literature to indicate the positive attributes of nondual *brahman*, the cosmic substratum. *Sat* is pure distinctionless being, *chit* is unconditioned, self-luminous consciousness, and *ananda* is unqualified, bliss (beyond temporary human pleasures). *See also* atman; brahman; Vedanta.

Sati (suh'tee; Skt., "good woman"). **1** Hindu goddess, wife of Shiva, who placed herself in her father's sacrificial fire when he refused to invite her husband to partake of the ritual. **2** In Hinduism a morally exceptional married woman, one who is filled with *sat*, or power flowing from virtue. **3** The Hindu practice (Eng., "suttee") of a married woman immolating herself on her deceased husband's funeral pyre. Persuaded such sacrifices were involuntary, the British criminalized the practice in 1829, and it has occurred rarely since. *Sati* immolations in recent times have received extensive media attention and have become a volatile symbol for the conflict between a nostalgic traditionalism and secular modernism in India. *See also* Reform Hinduism; Shiva.

Satornilos (sa-tor'nee-los), also known as Saturninus, an ascetic Gnostic teacher who was active in second-century Syria; he was a pupil of Simon Magus or Menander. *See also* Gnosticism; Simon Magus.

Saturn, the ancient Roman god identified with the Greek Kronos and generally associated with sowing. His festival (December 17) was the Saturnalia. *See also* Kronos.

Saturnalia, a Roman holiday (December 17 or 22) that featured a variety of ritual reversals. Today it is often used as a generic term for rituals of rebellion, carnivals, and return to chaos. *See also* carnival; chaos, return to; mock king; rebellion, rituals of.

satyagraha (suht-yuh-gruh'huh; Skt., "truth-grasping"), a term coined by Mohandas K. Gandhi (1869–1948) from the Sanskrit words for "holding firmly" and "truth" to describe his nonviolent method of social struggle and conflict resolution. *See also* ahimsa; Gandhi, Mohandas Karamchand; Reform Hinduism.

Satya Sai Baba (suht'yuh sah'ee bah'bah; b. 1926), a modern Hindu religious leader. Born in South India and reputed author of many miracles, he is regarded by his followers as a reincarnation of Sai Baba of Shirdi (a similar but earlier figure from Maharashtra) and as an earthly manifestation of Shiva and Shakti.

satyrs (say'tuhrz), wild, lustful creatures, half man, half ass, who formed the retinue of the Greek god Dionysos. Satyrs were figures of myth, not cult. *See also* Dionysos.

Sautrantika (sow-trahn'ti-kuh; Skt., "those who rely upon scriptural discourses as authoritative"), an early Indian Buddhist doctrinal school. As an opponent of the dominant Sarvastivada sect, the Sautrantikas assert the strict momentary existence only of present factors that exert causal efficacy through serial dependence. *See also* Sarvastivada.

savior, supernatural being able to effect salvation. *See also* Bodhisattvas; Buddhas; Buddhas and Bodhisattvas (Korea); Gesar/Geser; Jesus Christ; Korea, Maitreyism in; Saosyant.

sawm (or siyam). *See* fasting; Five Pillars.

scapegoat. **1** One of two goats the Israelites chose by lot at the Day of Atonement, driven into the wilderness to carry off the sins of the people as part of a purgation ritual. **2** By extension, an innocent victim onto whom blame is transferred.

scarab, an Egyptian amulet seal in the form of a beetle, associated with the morning sun and representing renewal for the bearer. *See also* Egyptian religion.

scarification. *See* mutilation.

Schechter, Solomon (1847–1915), president of the Jewish Theological Seminary of America from 1902 to 1915, scholar of rabbinics, and architect of Conservative Judaism in America. Born in Romania, he studied Jewish texts traditionally in Galicia, received scholarly training in Vienna and Berlin, and was Reader in Rabbinics at Cambridge University. The uncovering of the manuscripts at the Cairo *genizah* (storehouse for discarded manuscript pages) brought him international notice and an invitation to head the reorganized Jewish Theological Seminary, which in his day, he fashioned into the preeminent institution of higher Jewish learning in America. He gave early shape to Conservative Judaism and was the founder of the United Synagogue of America. *See also* Conservative Judaism.

schism, a formal division in a religious body caused by a disagreement over polity, governance, or more commonly, doctrine.

Schleiermacher, Friedrich Ernst Daniel (shli'er-mah-kher; 1768–1834), the most influential nineteenth-century German Protestant theologian. His early work, *On Religion: Speeches to Its Cultured Despisers* (1799), introduced the role of intuition and feeling in religious belief. In his best-known work, *The Christian Faith* (1821–22), this was developed into a definition of religion as "the feeling of absolute dependence."

Scholasticism, a form of Roman Catholic theology first taught in medieval universities. From the time of its origins in the twelfth century, Scholasticism has generated and encouraged disagreement over a broad spectrum of issues. Philosophically, the most bitter disputes have been over universals, with realists affirming and nominalists denying the extramental reality of ideas. Theologically, Scholastics have disagreed over such questions as the precise manner in which salvation occurs, and the possibility of making meaningful statements about God. There is, however, a general agreement among Scholastics about the goal and methods of theology. The aim of Scholasticism is the systematic ordering and investigation of the truths of the Christian faith, employing to this end the tools and concepts of philosophy, including but not exclusively the thought of Aristotle (d. 322 B.C.). Among the great Scholastics of the Middle Ages were Albert the Great (ca. 1200–1280) and Thomas Aquinas (ca. 1225–74) from the Dominican order, John Duns Scotus (ca. 1265–1308) and William Ockham (ca. 1285–1347) from the Franciscan. *See also* Albertus Magnus; Aquinas, Thomas; Catholicism, Roman; Duns Scotus, John.

School of Principle. *See* Cheng-Chu school; Li-hsueh.

Schweitzer, Albert (shwī'tser; 1875–1965), German Nobel Peace laureate (1952), musician and musicologist, Bible scholar, Christian theologian, and medical missionary in Lambarene, Africa. Schweitzer's most enduring intellectual influence is his dissertation *Von Reimarus zu Wrede* (1906; translated into English under the title The Quest for the Historical Jesus, 1910). In this work, Schweitzer reviewed and effectively ended the nineteenth-century liberal views of the life of Jesus by emphasizing that Jesus could not be understood apart from his eschatological beliefs in the imminent end of the world. This results in Jesus being a "stranger" to our time. *See also* Jesus, quest for the historical.

science and religion. Both science and religion are cognitive and cultural systems that claim to possess the intellectual means and the institutional resources for acquiring, analyzing, representing, and communicating knowledge about what is real, important, and true. The problem for scholars is to clarify the nature of the relationships between these forms of knowledge. Of particular interest is the question of whether they are congruent or incongruent with each other.

The Underlying Debate: Historically, issues about the relationship between science and religion have exercised Westerners, but they have been acknowledged and discussed in many other cultures as well, increasingly so in the twentieth century as the achievements of the natural sciences have spread across the globe.

Although some of the debate about the relationships between science and religion takes place within the particular sociocultural frameworks of scientific and religious institutions and involves arguments between scientists and religious thinkers, others (especially historians and philosophers of both science and religion) are eager and willing participants in the conversation.

All participants in the debate, regardless of their institutional context, seem to recognize that nothing less is at stake in these inquiries than determining the shape of knowledge.

In Western thought, particularly, historians and philosophers of both science and religion call attention to issues about what counts logically, and has counted historically, as scientific and religious knowledge. In addition to focusing upon such epistemological issues, historians and philosophers of science and religion also force people to pay attention to the institutional context in which candidates for knowledge are proposed, their point being that candidates for knowledge reflect the interests and concerns of the scientific and religious institutions involved.

The debate about the determinants of the shape of scientific and religious knowledge has been contentious. For example, early in the attempt to confront and resolve the issues about the relationships between science and religion in Western thought it became apparent that there is much disagreement about the epistemological status not only of religious knowledge but of scientific knowledge. Many historically and philosophically oriented participants in the debate were not willing to concede that scientific knowledge occupied an especially privileged epistemological position; scientific knowledge, too, had to establish its epistemological credentials. They could not simply be taken for granted.

Despite such problems, however, historians and philosophers of both science and religion seem willing to concede that scientific knowledge, though not privileged, is nevertheless an admirable form of knowledge that has as its goal the development of an explanatory understanding of the social and natural worlds. They also seem willing to agree that such explanatory understanding is marked by its empirical tractability or independent testability. Some historians and philosophers of science interested in the relationship between science and religion argue for a line of demarcation between scientific and all other forms of knowledge, including religious knowledge.

The line of demarcation proposed by such thinkers consists in distinguishing candidates for knowledge by their ability to conform to the principles of verifiability or falsifiability. Such demarcation principles proved to be extremely controversial in both the philosophy of science and the philosophy of religion, because they either exclude candidates for knowledge such as mathematics or include candidates for knowledge that the contenders were attempting to exclude. They also proved problematic for those cognitive scientists engaged in explanatory theorizing about religion itself, because these cognitivists were unwilling to exclude arbitrarily from their theorizing the possibility that religious knowledge might count as a form of knowledge. Whether or not the religions of humankind possess a form of knowledge about what is real, important, and true is itself a matter of empirical inquiry that can only be decided by systematic and independently testable theories. Few were willing to concede that such issues could be decided in an ad hoc manner. From their point of view, the job of the scientist interested in developing an explanatory understanding of religion is to explain how what appears to be a candidate for knowledge is or is not what it claims to be. The issue is seen as being empirical and not merely logical.

The issue about the relationship between science and religion is not only an issue in Western thought but is a global issue. Some form of religion and some form of science appear to exist in most, if not in all, human societies. Some scholars in the intellectualist tradition argue that underlying the apparent idiomatic differences between scientific and religious knowledge there lie fundamental similarities, and to such an extent that they are virtually the same theoretical enterprise, both are capable of producing knowledge about the world on the basis of unobservable entities.

Whether or not the intellectualists make a plausible case for their view of the relationship between science and religion, it is difficult to ignore the fact that thinkers in every religious tradition have had to wrestle sooner or later with the problem of the relationship between what they know religiously and what scientists claim that people do and can know about the natural and social worlds.

Religious thinkers within the same culture have by no means adopted the same approach to specifying the relationship between science and religion. Even within each religious tradition, perspectives about this relationship vary, so, for example, the theory of evolution has been both accepted and rejected by different religious groups within the Christian religion, and first rejected and later accepted by others.

Whether the issue of the relationship between science and religion is Western or global, scholars in Western intellectual history who argue for the validity of religious knowledge seem to agree that such knowledge consists in the development, explication, application, and defense of the categories and conceptual systems that emerge from within a religious tradition.

Religious knowledge not only represents the specific cognitive contents of a specific religious tradition but permits and even encourages the making of judgments about other forms of knowledge, even the specific knowledge claimed in other religious traditions. Not only do scientists claim to possess a theoretically based and an empirically tractable knowledge about religion, but representatives of specific religious traditions generate views about the epistemological status of their own religious knowledge, about scientific knowledge, and about the cognitive contents of other religious traditions.

In any given cultural context, one can expect provocative views both about the relationship among religious cognitive systems and about the relationship between scientific and religious cognitive systems as defined by the religious system in question. One cannot assume that in these different cultural contexts the same stance is adopted toward either science or religion. It is certainly the case that within the history of Western thought unanimity about the relationship between scientific thought and religious thought has been impossible to achieve.

A Cognitive View: The cognitive approach to religion focuses upon the cognitive categories people employ in religious and nonreligious contexts and upon the cognitive process that leads to judgments about what is real, important, and true. Of particular interest to cognitivists are the problem of human bias in all of cognitive traffic with the world, the role theory plays at the deepest levels of human perception, the extremely complex nature of the reference of human concepts, and the intricate relationships between interpretive and explanatory activities. Cognitivist inquiries lead to the conviction that a much richer theory of human rationality is required than any presently possessed.

A cognitive approach to religion starts with an examination of the problems that lead to the discernment of the shape of knowledge itself. Cognitivists argue that when religious knowledge and scientific knowledge contend for the title *knowledge* then one should investigate the properties of such knowledge and how they are acquired. Cognitivists seek a science of knowledge, a cognitive science empirical in nature, that can clarify, systematize, and adjudicate the various claims made about epistemological issues in general, about the epistemological status of religious knowledge, and about the congruence of scientific and religious knowledge.

When cognitivists pursue such lines of investigation and research, some surprises are in store about the nature of rationality itself. Bias is seen as a key issue. Some of the most interesting work in the cognitive sciences, some of it cross-cultural, focuses on the nature of the formation and employment of categories employed by human beings in their cognitive traffic with the world. Getting a fix on category formation and employment permits cognitivists to elucidate important aspects of human bias.

Whereas in earlier theories bias is identified with the emotive, the irrational, and the nonrational, cognitivists show that bias is endemic in human reason and has positive as well as negative qualities.

Fundamental to the cognitive approach is the view that in any attempt to discover and elaborate the nature of human rationality one is not doomed to a simple choice between logic and irrationalism. Cognitivists show that human reasoning is a far more complicated process than many have been willing to acknowledge. They show that human reason employs patterned cognitive activities such as heuristic strategies, models, and prototypes in the process of acquiring and instantiating human knowledge. Even syllogistic reasoning itself, the traditional paradigm of rationality, seems to be underwritten by a nonsyllogistic pattern of cognitive activity. To require that rationality conform to the standards of syllogistic reasoning does not account for why logicians make mistakes and excludes some of the most important features of explanatory understanding, especially the human ability to make viable judgments about problematic features of the world without having to engage in deductive logic.

More important is the insistence of cognitivists that the notion of theory needs to be extended to show how commonsense judgments, though deeply entrenched, are in fact revisable and can be replaced by more adequate, powerful, and coherent theories of what is real, important, and true. Rather than limiting theoretical activity to specialized activity among the scientific elite, cognitivists extend the notion of theory to the very heart of perceptual and conceptual processes themselves. Scientific theories become special cases of a general human ability.

Even the notion of reference (the direct mapping of concepts onto the world) has not escaped criticism and emendation. Nor has the division between interpretation (the kind of knowledge valued in the humanities) and explanation (the sciences).

A key organizing concept in discovering and constructing the shape of knowledge is the insistence by cognitivists that knowledge of the world is mediated by theories of the world. It is not as if some forms of knowledge are especially privileged and therefore incapable of revision. Wherever human beings attempt to develop explanatory understandings of the world, a process that commences at birth and continues throughout people's lives, one will find explanatory theorizing at work. So while the intellectuals overemphasize the human interest in explanation, they do see that human beings are fundamentally theoretical in their interactions with their social and natural environments.

This is a far broader view of theory than many philosophers and scientists are willing to concede, but it is a view that is beginning to establish a considerable body of scientific achievement. At least some aspects of the problem of the congruence between science and religion seem to await the results of such cognitivist inquiries. *See also* magic, science, and religion; religion, philosophy of.

science of religion, the field within religious studies that purports to provide a scientific explanation of religion. Despite the claim inherent in the term *science*, practitioners of the field often offer only a description, not an explanation, of religion. The fact that the term *science of religion* is used interchangeably with the term *phenomenology of religion* confirms its often descriptive character. The science of religion amasses and classifies data about religions throughout history and the world, but it does not always account for the data amassed and classified. Out of wariness that any explanation of religion is inherently nonreligious, or reductive, practitioners often refrain from explaining it. They typically invoke arguments used against the possibility of a scientific explanation of human behavior generally.

Alternatively, the science of religion proposes explanations of religion, but the field fails as science because it does not presume an open, critical attitude toward the subject matter. To be scientific is not merely to provide some explanation of religion but to take into account other possible explanations, to test them all, to accept the best explanation, and at the same time to continue to seek still better explanations.

Testing can take either strictly explanatory or, less ideally, merely interpretive form. Taken as explanation, testing usually means prediction. However, prediction is not the sole possible test. Applicability, or interpretability, is another. An interpretation is testable with respect to translatability.

A critical, scientific attitude toward religion dictates the testing of not just one explanation or interpretation but its rivals as well. A critical attitude also dictates the search for new, superior explanations and interpretations.

The science of religion as it has been widely practiced is uncritical and thereby unscientific because it permits only an irreducibly religious explanation and interpretation of religion. The science of religion is unscientific because sociological, anthropological, and psychological explanations and interpretations are barred. Any testing that is allowed is intramural; it occurs only within an irreducibly religious framework.

According to some practitioners, the field of the science of religion was founded by the Victorian Indologist Friedrich Max Muller. Muller goes beyond a description of religion to an explanation and interpretation of it. But his explanation and interpretation are irreducibly religious. He defines religion as the experience of the infinite, which gets experienced through natural phenomena like the sky but which is not reducible to those phenomena. By defining the object of worship as other than natural, Muller rules out any naturalistic, or reductive, explanation or interpretation of religion.

What is true of Muller is also true of subsequent practitioners of the science of religion—among them Nathan Soderblom, Rudolf Otto, Gerardus van der Leeuw, Joachim Wach, Geo Widengren, Raffaele Pettazzoni, and Mircea Eli-

ade. Indeed, the field has long pitted itself against the sociology, anthropology, and psychology of religion—each of which proposes, in its view, too scientific an approach to religion. The science of religion begins only after the social scientific study of religion has been excluded. No social scientific explanation or interpretation of religion can possibly succeed when built into the identification of the subject of study is an irreducibly religious way of explaining and interpretating it. In a truly scientific approach to religion, *religion* would be only the provisional, not the final, term for the subject. *See also* comparative religion; religion, phenomenology of.

Scientology. *See* Church of Scientology.

Scofield, Cyrus I (1843–1921), American Christian dispensationalist. A St. Louis businessman, Scofield, under the influence of Dwight Moody's preaching, became a Congregationalist minister and an advocate for the sort of dispensationalism advocated by John Nelson Darby and the Plymouth Brethren as set forth in Scofield's *Rightly Dividing the Word of Truth* (1888). In 1902, Scofield began to edit the *Scofield Reference Bible* (1909), which became the text of dispensationalist fundamentalism. *See also* Darby, John Nelson; dispensationalism; Moody, Dwight Lyman; Plymouth Brethren.

Scopes trial, the 1925 trial of a high-school biology teacher, John Scopes, for violating a Tennessee statute prohibiting the teaching in public schools of the Darwinian theory of evolution. Known as the "Monkey Trial," the trial resulted in Scopes's conviction (later overturned) but helped discredit the Christian fundamentalist opposition to evolution as contrary to a literal reading of Genesis 1. *See also* creationism.

scribe (Judaism) (Heb. *sofer*), a term that refers to various individuals and groups with specialized literate skills. The term has different, sometimes divergent, meanings in different texts and periods.

In the Hebrew Bible figures called scribe include a muster officer (Judges 5:14); Baruch, who recorded Jeremiah's prophecies (Jeremiah 36:32); and Ezra, the sixth-century B.C. Persian government officer and Israelite priest who brought the "book of the law of Moses" (Nehemiah 8:1) from exile and read it to the population of Jerusalem. Later Jewish tradition depicts Ezra as a significant transmitter of tradition and precursor of rabbis.

The book of Ecclesiasticus, written ca. 180 B.C. by Jesus ben Sira, portrays the scribe as a sage: a man of culture, an expert in Scripture, and an adviser to the government. In 1 and 2 Maccabees scribes are presented as a political group allied with pietists, but in Josephus the scribes are village and court officials or bureaucrats with no distinctive religious ideology or expertise. In the New Testament the scribes oppose Jesus and appear as a learned group, perhaps teachers, affiliated with political power groups.

In the Mishnah and the Talmuds scribes fill four roles. They are (1) interpreters of Scripture and (2) a source of oral Torah (religious teaching), as in rabbinic references to "the words of the scribes." The term also refers (3) to a writer of documents and letters and to the (4) copyist who produces the Torah scroll.

Only the last definition persists in modern Judaism. The scribe, who writes Torah scrolls and phylacteries, receives special training and is viewed as performing an essential religious duty. *See also* phylactery; Torah scroll.

scripture rites (Korean), Buddhist rituals including the Lantern Festival (Kor. *Yondunghoe*), the Assembly of the Eight Vows (*P'algwanhoe*), and the Hundred Seat Assembly (*Paekkojwahoe*). All of these Buddhist scripture rites were based on passages in the Mahayana scriptures that promised to confer blessings and eliminate disasters for those who recited, adorned, celebrated, or caused others to recite, adorn, or celebrate these scriptures. These rites were celebrated at state expense by the governments of the Three Kingdoms, Unified Silla, and Koryo periods (ca. 57 B.C.–A.D. 1392) and functioned as national protection rituals.

The Lantern Festival on the fifteenth day of the first lunar month was based on a passage in the *Lotus Sutra*. It combined the function of a New Year's festival and a Buddhist community renewal festival by celebrating the enlightenment of the Buddha. Of the three main scripture rites, the Lantern Festival is still the most popular and is celebrated at New Year's and on the Buddha's birthday in April.

The Assembly of the Eight Vows was celebrated on the fifteenth day of the eleventh lunar month and was based on the Middle, or Medium, Agama Sutra (*Madhyagama*). It was first celebrated to propitiate and honor the spirits of the warrior dead. Later it became a ceremony for use during times of drought and other natural disasters.

The Hundred Seat Assembly, based on the Sutra on Benevolent Kings (*Jen-wang ching*), was used to entreat the Buddhas and the spirits of heaven and earth to bring tranquillity to the nation. It was especially in the Koryo period (918–1392), during the Jurched and Mongol invasions, that the Hundred Seat Assembly was held.

All three scripture rites were held on a large scale, involving thousands of monks simultaneously in the capital and provinces. Even though the purposes of these rituals were many, the form of the rituals was the same. It included an assembly of large numbers of Buddhist clerics and lay supporters to chant publicly and give honor to Buddhist Mahayana texts and doctrines, followed by a Dharma Oration or Sermon to the assembled participants, and finishing with vegetarian feasts for all participants. The expense of these rites, which were sometimes celebrated monthly, was borne by the government. In modern times they are paid for by private contributions and the selling of religious objects. *See also* National Protection Buddhism.

scriptures. *See* holy books.

Scriptures for America, a contemporary Christian Identity ministry centered in LaPorte, Colorado. Pastored by Pete Peters, Scriptures for America is among the most outspokenly militant exponents of a racialist and virulently anti-Semitic form of Identity theology. While among Identity adherents Peters is not noted as an outstanding scripturalist, he is a dynamic speaker. The organizer of the most successful Identity religious retreats, he draws believers from around the country to Colorado in a revival-meeting atmosphere. Peters has been instrumental in seeking to bring together leading Identity pastors in an attempt to give Christian Identity an increasingly sectarian form. *See also* Identity Christianity.

seasonal rituals. *See* intensification rites.

Seceders (Arab. *al-khawarij*), a branch of Islam, so called for seceding from the Shiite party of Ali in 658 because Ali accepted the suggestion to submit to arbitration the armed conflict regarding Uthman's murder. In contrast to the Postponers, the Seceders held that overt sins are grounds for expulsion from the Muslim community. The Seceders split into several subgroups of which only the Ibadiyya of Oman survived. *See also* Islamic political theory; Postponers.

Second Coming, belief that Jesus Christ will

come again at the close of the age to judge the wicked and vindicate the righteous. The term developed from the New Testament term, the *parousia* (Gk., "presence," "coming," or "arrival") of the Lord Jesus (1 Thessalonians 2:19) or the Son of Man (Matthew 24:27, 37, 39). The New Testament never refers to the Second Coming, but in John 14:3, Jesus says he will "come again," and Hebrews 9:28 affirms that Christ "will appear a second time." Some passages suggest (2 Thessalonians 2:1–12) and others deny (Mark 13:32–33) that there will be discernable signs of the coming. Most passages assert the coming to be imminent (Matthew 10:23), although some deal directly or indirectly with the problem of its delay (2 Proverbs 3:1–10). Some Christian groups continue to read the "signs" of the times (especially interpreting the book of Revelation) and set a date for the Second Coming. *See also* Adventists; chiliasm; eschatology; millennialism.

Secret of the Golden Flower. *See* T'ai-i chin-hua tsung-chih.

secret societies, voluntary associations whose existence or whose rites and teachings are unknown to the general public. Entrance is often by means of some initiatory procedure that strongly marks off those inside the secret society from those outside. *See also* Freemasonry; kachina/katsina; mystery; mystery religions; Opus Dei; voluntary association.

Chinese Religion: Clandestine associations have played a significant role in Chinese society. They have offered individuals without position or hope in the established order an alternative world of meaning, encompassing religious, political, and social reality. Throughout Chinese history, therefore, secret societies have been perceived as potential threats to the mandate of dynastic rulers. Suppressed by Chinese authorities, many have been based on revolutionary and utopian ideologies. Such societies, which some date as early as the Late Han dynasty (23–220), have commonly emphasized secrecy; elaborate initiations incorporating Buddhist, Taoist, and popular religious elements; esoteric signs and symbols; blood oaths; and harsh penalties for those who forsake their commitments. The designation *secret society* has often been employed ambiguously in Western literature. However, these characteristics may serve to distinguish such societies from peasant movements and sectarian religions in China, such as the millenarian White Lotus sect, which did not, except when persecuted, enjoin secrecy.

The most important secret society in Chinese history has been the Triad Society, so called because of its emphasis on harmony between heaven, earth, and humankind. Founded in the seventeenth century by loyalists who sought to overthrow the Ch'ing dynasty (1644–1912) and restore the Ming (1368–1644), the Triad, as most secret societies, was loosely organized in autonomous lodges. Since the republican revolution of 1911, to which it contributed, the Triad has been increasingly linked to criminal activities. Other secret societies in modern Chinese history include the Association of Elder Brothers, the Green Band, and the Red Spears. *See also* Chinese sectarian religions; Triad Society; White Lotus Society.

sect. *See* church/sect.

Sect Shinto (Kyoha Shinto), a term created by the Japanese government (1882–1908) initially designating thirteen Shinto groups as sects on the basis of each having a founder; thus distinguishing them from Shrine Shinto, or State Shinto, which has no founder. Sect Shinto groups generally do not maintain shrines. The government action was undertaken to preserve State Shinto as a national way of life rather than as a religion. *See also* Shinto; Shrine Shinto (Jinja Shinto).

secular humanism, a term, often pejorative, used to describe the belief that ultimate values reside solely in the human individual and possess no supernatural origin or grounding. Since the later nineteenth century, the humanist movement in the United States, expressed in the programs of the Ethical Culture Society and the nontheistic wing of Unitarianism, has existed primarily among groups of intelligentsia and has resulted in "Humanist Manifestoes" issued in 1933 and 1973. Shaped primarily by Enlightenment rationalism, Darwinian science, and later, by Freudian and post-Freudian psychologies, humanism is a highly diffuse force in American culture. Its influence as an organized conspiracy rather than a widespread climate of opinion was alleged by the "New Religious Right" during the 1970s and 1980s as evidence of the moral deterioration of the United States, particularly in the secularization of public education.

secularism, term that ascribes to human actions, thoughts, or institutions the properties of worldliness. The term expresses either a theological or a political judgment about specific actions, thoughts, or institutions that are in contrast to the religious sphere. Theological assessments involving the ascription of the term *secularism* to various sociocultural forms function as ideological epithets rather than as theoretical categories capable of identifying and explaining human behavior. Its use signifies the postulation of a fundamental split between the secular and the religious.

Theological and political debates employ the term secularism in three major ways: the exclusionary, the hierarchical, and the integrative. In the exclusionary approach, secularism signifies an explicit and radical disjunction between the secular and the religious, which then calls for specific actions, attitudes, and structures on the part of either the religious or the secular. For example, from a religious perspective secular values might be regarded as threats, which require not only exclusion from the religious sphere but active resistance to secularism. In such a view the world is at odds with, and inimical to, the religious sphere. It invites and requires a vocabulary of contention.

From the secular point of view the exclusionary approach presumes that it is precisely the religious that represents the menace to the social order and, therefore, needs to be constrained, institutionally, philosophically, and behaviorally.

Such exclusionary perspectives are difficult to maintain in actual social situations and for extended historical periods. Therefore exclusionary rhetoric, both theological and political, often becomes transformed into alternative formulations that suggest a continuum rather than a radical disjunction between the secular and religious spheres. In effect, a hierarchical system of assessment comes into play. It is equally likely, for example, that secular values will be viewed as subordinate rather than as disjunctive to religious values. The image is hierarchical because it presents a ranked set of ideologically circumscribed territories that consist of distinct but related levels of influence with their own special spheres of activity and obligations.

Finally, it is also possible from some religious perspectives for secular values to be thoroughly integrated into the religious sphere, not in the subordinate sense but in the sense of domains that possess special functions. The metaphor is a division of labor to get a job done.

The political use of the metaphor of secularism may assume either positive or negative forms. Used to show approval, secularism implies that there is an acceptable form of religious behavior that enables the right exercise of political power and authority. Here the view is that a well-functioning society permits and encourages differences among cultural systems to exist but insists that the role of the religious must be supportive of the social order. But secularism can also involve a system of valuation in which religion is viewed as undercutting or constraining the positive role of secularity. Here the sphere of the religious is viewed negatively.

From a theoretical perspective, secularism does not have explanatory content. Its use requires either a theological or political conceptual scheme that is itself in need of explanation. Such an explanation is possible only after theological and political discourse are recognized as being internal to theoretically defined cultural systems. Secularism has a place in theological and political language; it has no role to play in any scientific language that attempts to account for such systems. *See also* modernization.

seder (say′dehr; Heb., "order"), the Jewish Passover eve home ritual. Its liturgy, or ritual script, the Haggadah, was largely compiled by the end of the second century but received considerable elaboration thereafter: in third- to tenth-century Babylonia; in post-Crusade northern Europe; and in our time, particularly in America. Illuminated Haggadot appeared in Europe (fourteenth to sixteenth centuries); movable type resulted in artistically embellished printed Haggadot, a tradition continuing to this day.

Early Developments: The seder arose out of a biblical tradition to rehearse the Passover experience in an annual meal featuring the eating of the paschal lamb (the *pesakh*). Influenced by first-century Greco-Roman symposium banquets, tableship groups (*khavurot;* sing. *khavurah*) met to celebrate the seder. The Gospels of Mark, Matthew, and Luke, which assume Jesus' Last Supper was a seder, and such ancient Jewish sources as Josephus testify to the seder's popularity but allow no definitive reconstruction of its contents. However, it is likely to have included (1) a meal, including prayers welcoming sacred time, or otherwise setting the stage for the ritual, followed by symbolically significant foods, especially *matzah* (unleavened bread), *maror* (bitter herbs), four cups of wine, and (before 70, and in Jerusalem) the pesakh itself; (2) rhetorical questions about the evening's uniqueness; (3) a ritualized answer incorporating the Exodus experience; and (4) *hallel* ("praise [of God the redeemer, via psalms]"). Theologically, the night recollected God's past redemption of Israel from Egypt and posited hope for final redemption from history, yet to come.

The Mishnah (ca. 200) reflects a further stylization of the rite, including suggested questions, a specific midrashic text for answers, and explicit recitation of the food symbolism. Moreover, by then (with the Temple's destruction), the Passover offering had ceased, the meal had been moved to the end of the evening, and other symbolic foods had emerged: notably, *kharoset*, a thick condiment made by mixing fruit with wine; cooked dishes as stand-ins for the defunct sacrifices; and a final piece of matzah called *afikoman.*

Later Developments: Contributions up to the tenth century included, particularly, the expansion of the stage-setting, which now included a third-century debate over the essence of servitude, and the "four-children narrative," a tannaitic text positing four ways in which children understand the Exodus tale. The answer was outfitted with a listing of the ten plagues and a poem (*Dayyenu,* "it is enough for us") asserting that any one of the events constituting the Exodus would have been "enough" to warrant hallel, "praise" to God.

Further alteration came in Europe in the centuries following the massacre of Rhineland Jewry by Crusaders and under the influence of Christian postmillennial piety. Expecting the imminent arrival of the Messiah, Jews added an after-dinner "chapter" to the seder. Opening the door for Elijah, who was to herald the Messiah, they called for revenge on their enemies and petitioned to be transported themselves for "next year, in Jerusalem." In fervent anticipation, a fifth cup of wine—eventually renamed "Elijah's Cup"—was held ready for consumption as a symbol of ultimate deliverance. The seder's focus shifted to this after-dinner period, which was then outfitted by later generations with a variety of folk songs to end the evening.

Seder spirituality in the rabbinic period thus revolved about the collapsing of time. It was prompted by food symbols such as wine and unleavened bread, which were seen as pointing to salvation past and future. By contrast, post-Crusade spirituality substituted a specifically messianic myth, centered in Elijah and paralleling the Christian medieval anticipation of a Second Coming.

The Seder Today: Today, a third spiritual focus is evident: the seder as celebration of Jewish peoplehood. Following the Holocaust and the birth of the State of Israel, Jews have popularly redefined Jewish history as a recurring instance of near-destruction followed by miraculous survival. New Haggadot thus emphasize the Jewish people's miraculous continuity and reaffirm the

American Jewish seder in Kansas City, Missouri (1991). Reading from the traditional ritual book (the Passover *Haggadah*), the young man is lifting a small plate of bitter herbs (*maror*) and interpreting them as reminders of Israel's slavery in Egypt. On the large platter in the foreground are four other symbols of Passover: a roasted lamb bone (*zeroa*) and roasted eggs, symbolic of the Passover sacrifice; *kharoset,* a mixture of crushed fruit, nuts, and wine, interpreted as the mortar the Israelites were forced to make in Egypt; and a plate containing the first vegetable (*karpas*) to be dipped in saltwater later in the meal.

vision of universal freedom as the rationale for Jewish survival. They draw especially on Holocaust literature, as on writers who capture the Jewish vision of a better tomorrow despite the tragedies of today, and they posit the State of Israel as a symbol of continued near-destruction on the one hand, but of tenacious continuity toward a glorious messianic age of peace and harmony on the other. *See also* Judaism (festal cycle).

Sedna (sed'nah; Baffin Island, "one down there"), Sea Woman, the keeper of game animals, from Greenland west to Alaska, also known as Nuliayuk (Netsilik, "the lubricious one") and Nerrivik (Polar, "the meat dish"). She lives under the sea in various dwellings or at the horizon (Greenland) of sea and sky where the dead live. The Siberian Chuckchi have a similar figure known as mother of the walrus.

Seasonal rituals were often performed to appease Sedna so she would release underwater game animals. *See also* circumpolar religions; fishing rites/whaling rites; hunting, religious aspects of; master/mistress of the animals.

seeing the nature (Chin. *chien-hsing*), in Chinese

Ch'an Buddhism, a technical term for enlightenment, i.e., seeing one's own true nature. *See also* Ch'an school.

Self-Realization Fellowship, a Vedanta association founded by Paramahansa Yogananda (1893–1952) in 1935 on the basis of work he had done since arriving in the United States from India in 1920. The fellowship was the second major Hindu Vedanta group in America after the Vedanta Societies, oriented primarily toward the spiritual needs of persons of occidental background. Its activities include yoga classes (emphasizing a "kriya yoga" technique taught by Yogananda), religious services, and the distribution of literature. Leadership is exercised by a monastic order including both monks and nuns. Headquarters are in Los Angeles; centers can be found in most major cities. *See also* America, Hinduism in; North America, new religions in; Paramahansa Yogananda; Vedanta.

Selu (see'loo; Cherokee, "corn"), a Corn Woman present in many (Southeast) North American tribes, similar to figures found broadly where maize is grown in North America. She is sometimes referred to as Agawela, "The Old Woman." In stories, Selu is murdered, sometimes decapitated, her body dragged about a field; her blood originates the first corn plants. Sometimes she is First Woman married to First Man. Among the Iroquois (Northeast) her counterpart is one of three sisters responsible for corn, beans, and squash. Selu also appears as a single green stalk of corn that, before transforming into a beautiful woman and disappearing, teaches hunting secrets and the importance of generosity. *See also* agriculture, religious aspects of; North America, traditional religions in.

semiotics, the study of signs, usually undertaken on the basis of some linguistic theory. *See also* symbol.

Semites, peoples speaking one of the Semitic languages, including Akkadian, Hebrew, Phoenician, Aramaic, Arabic.

Seneca (sen'uh-kuh; 4 B.C.–A.D. 65), Roman statesman and noted Stoic, for a time tutor and adviser to the emperor Nero. Seneca's numerous essays, plays, and letters are powerful exhortations to adopt the Stoic way of life by valuing only virtue and putting the individual will into harmony with the divine will. *See also* Stoics.

senet (sen'et; Egypt., "passing"), an ancient Egyptian board game of thirty squares. Originally secular, it was later associated with death and the afterlife. *See also* Egyptian religion.

Seng-chao (seng-jou; 374–414), the second great master of the San-lun school of Chinese Buddhism after the founder, Kumarajiva. He wrote three treatises setting out the school's philosophy systematically. His use of current Chinese philosophical concepts hastened the adaptation of Indian Buddhist teachings in China. *See also* China, Buddhism in; San-lun school.

separation of church and state. *See* law and religion (in the United States).

separation of sexes (mythic theme), common image for the division of the cosmos in the creation myths of traditional peoples. Frequently, the reason for separation is incest. In the Ecuadorian Quichua version of a widespread Amazonian myth, for example, a girl marks the face of her unknown lover with paint only to discover that he is her brother. Out of shame, the brother rises into the sky to become the moon while the girl becomes the Jilucu bird. Their star children flood the world with tears, and the ordered world arises out of the flood. In other groups, the myth of separation frequently centers around a battle between the sexes in which men take control of sacred objects and rites that had previously belonged to women.

Separation myths vary greatly from culture to culture, but in each case they provide models for the specialized gender roles recognized by a people. Because the order of the entire community is thought to depend on the periodic performance of these myths, festivals often orchestrate a breakdown of separation rules followed by a return to order. Indiscriminate sexual encounters may be encouraged during such festivals, masked dancers may cross-dress, and battles between the genders may be staged before order is renewed. *See also* gender and religion; gender crossing; gender roles; myth; sexuality and religion.

Separatist, a term first applied to Congregationalist groups that dissented from the disciplines and authority of the Church of England; now a general term for a variety of Protestant denominations. *See also* Anglicanism; Congregationalism; nonconformist; Puritans.

Sephardi (seh-fahr-dee'; Heb.; pl., Sephardim), a Jew descended from a family originating in Spain or Portugal. The name Sepharad (Obadiah 1:20) came to apply to Spain. After their expulsion from Spain in 1492 and from Portugal in 1497, Sephardi Jewry settled in North Africa and the Middle East. Sephardi Jews spoke Ladino, based on medieval Spanish, and developed their own religious practices. *See also* Ashkenazi; Ladino.

seppuku (sep-*poo*-koo; Jap.,"cutting the abdomen"), also *harakiri*, Japanese ritual suicide by self-disembowelment. As an honorable death for *samurai* (warrior class), it involved careful preparation for a ritual slashing of the abdomen, followed by beheading by an assistant. *See also* bushido.

Septuagint, the earliest known Greek translation of the Hebrew Bible. A translation of the Pentateuch, the first five books, according to Jewish tradition, was made in Egypt around 250 B.C. and it is probable that the other books were translated no later than the first century. The legend that the translators were isolated and produced versions that coincided word for word was designed to establish the divinely inspired nature of the translation. The Septuagint, often abbreviated LXX, was the Bible of the early Christian church. *See also* Bible, translations of the Christian.

Sermon on the Mount, in the New Testament Gospel of Matthew (5–7), a lengthy sermon attributed to Jesus understood to contain the core of his teaching. *See also* Beatitudes.

Servetus, Michael (sir-vee'tuhs; 1511–53), Spanish Catholic theologian and physician who was condemned for heresy and burned in effigy by Catholic authorities, and tried and burned in actuality by Calvinists. A brilliant anatomist, credited with discovering the pulmonary circulation of the blood, Servetus's theological writings were instantly controversial. In his *De Trinitatis erroribus libri VII* (The Errors of the Trinity in Seven Books, 1531, supplemented by two additional books, 1532) he appeared to deny the separation of the three Persons. In *Christianismi restitutio* (The Restoration of Christianity, 1546), he attacked Calvin's *Institutes.*

Seth, the ancient Egyptian god of disorder and confusion manifested in the elemental forces of nature. He was vilified as the murderer of Osiris and archenemy of Horus. *See also* Egyptian religion.

Setsubun (say-tsoo-boon; Jap.,"division of the season"), a Japanese domestic celebration of the end of

winter. Soybeans are thrown into and out of the house to ward off bad spirits and bring good luck. *See also* Japanese religions (festal cycle).

seven deadly sins, the classification of faults lethal to the Christian spiritual life. Although early writers proposed differing lists and enumerations, that proposed in Gregory the Great's *Moralia* (sixth century) became standard and traditional: pride, envy, covetousness, anger, sloth, lust, and gluttony. *See also* sin.

Sevener. *See* Ismaili Shia.

Seven Holy Cities (Skt. *saptapuri*), seven of the oldest sacred cities of India, considered to be gateways to liberation (*mokshadvara*). They are traditionally designated as Ayodhya, Mathura, Dvaravati (or Dvaraka), Kashi (also known as Banaras), Avantika (better known as Ujjain), Maya (modern-day Hardvar), and Kanchi (Kanchipuram or Conjeeveram). *See also* liberation; pilgrimage.

The Seven Holy Cities of India

Seven Mothers, a group of Hindu goddesses usually associated with important male gods: Brahmani (associated with Brahma), Maheshvari (associated with Shiva), Kaumari (associated with Karttikeya), Vaishnavi (associated with

Vishnu), Varahi (associated with Vishnu's boar incarnation), Narasimhi (associated with Vishnu's man-lion incarnation), and Aindri (associated with Indra). Their main function is to protect the stability of the world against demons. In early literature, groups of goddesses called "mothers," usually numbering more than seven, are also described as dangerous and the cause of disease. *See also* Goddess (Hinduism).

Seven Rishis (ri'shiz), seven Indic sages, usually Atri, Bharadvaja, Gautama, Jamadagni, Kashyapa, Vasishtha, and Vishvamitra, who were the poets of *Rig Veda* "family books" and, later, stars of the Big Dipper, whose proximity to the north star connects them with the salvific northern "path of the gods." Six of their wives, stars of the Pleiades, symbolize marital instability, while the seventh, Vasishtha's Arundhati, beside him in the Big Dipper, represents fidelity. The seven plus Agastya, the southern star Canopus, are the eponymous ancestors of the eight lineages in the Brahman system of exogamy. *See also* Brahman; devayana/pitriyana; Rig Veda; rishi.

Seventh-Day Adventist. *See* Adventists.

Seven Wonders of the Ancient World, outstanding sights of art and architecture in the Hellenistic world listed as early as the mid-second century B.C. They include the pyramids of Egypt; the hanging gardens of Babylon, terraced gardens attributed to Nebuchadnezzar II; the statue of Zeus at Olympia, a gold and ivory cult statue by Phidias; the temple of Artemis at Ephesus; the tomb of Mausolus, ruler of Caria; the Colossus at Rhodes, a bronze statue of Helios overlooking the harbor; and the Pharos, or lighthouse, at Alexandria, on Pharos Island.

sexuality and religion. As a primary human activity, sexuality is both celebrated and controlled by religion.

Religions celebrate sexuality through life-cycle rituals, through agricultural and hunting rituals that focus on plant and animal fecundity, through a variety of orgiastic rituals, and by utilizing sexual intercourse as a spiritual discipline.

Religions control sexuality through marriage rituals and by means of a variety of ascetic practices. *See also* agriculture, religious aspects of; androgyny; asceticism; bodily secretions; body; celibacy; dance; devadasi; gender crossing; gender roles; homosexuality; incest, incest prohibition; kama; kundalini; lila; linga; maithuna; marriage; marriage, sacred; mutilation; orgy; physiological techniques (Taoism); rasa; separation of sexes

(mythic theme); Shakti; Shaktism; Shiva; Tachikawa-ryu; Tantra; transvestism, ritual; vagina dentata; world parents; yoni.

SGPC, abbreviation for Shiromani Gurdwara Prabandhak Committee, the elected board established by the Indian government in 1920 to oversee all of the principal Sikh houses of worship (*gurdwaras*). *See also* Sikhism.

Shabbetai Tzevi (shab'ti tsvi; 1626–76), messianic pretender and central figure of Shabbateanism, the messianic movement. Tzevi was born in Smyrna, Turkey, where he received a rabbinic education laced with *kabbalah*. His libertine behavior resulted in banishment from Smyrna in 1654. He declared himself Messiah in 1665 and was imprisoned by Ottoman authorities the following year. Facing a death decree, Tzevi converted to Islam in September 1666. He continued to practice Judaism secretly and never renounced his messianic claim.

Tzevi enjoyed a large following. Even after his apostasy, many refused to renounce his claim. Some Shabbateans, known as the Donmeh, emulated the Messiah's conversion to Islam; the group survived into the twentieth century. *See also* Frankists; Messiah.

Shafiite (sha-fi'it; Arab.), of or pertaining to the Shafiite school of Islamic religious law, predominant in Lower Egypt, the Hijaz, and throughout the Muslim parts of Southeast Asia. An outgrowth of the legal doctrine and theory of Muhammad ibn Idris al-Shafii (d. 820), Shafiite writers, in subsequent generations, played a major role in the development and refinement of the methodology governing the formulation of the religious law. *See also* Islamic law.

shah (shah'; Persian, "king"), originally the title of the ancient kings of Persia.

shahada. *See* martyr; witness (Islam).

Shaiva Siddhanta (shi-vuh sid-duhn'tuh; Skt., "the established doctrine of Shaivism"), a system of Hindu theology, the dominant form of Shaivism in Tamil India. Its canonical texts are the Sanskrit Shaiva Agamas, which regulate ritual worship; the twelve-part Tamil *Tirumurai*, consisting of devotional poetry and hagiography; and the fourteen *Meykantashastras*, a set of Tamil doctrinal treatises. Shaiva Siddhanta ontology posits three realities: God, souls, and bondage. The dynamics of the system revolve around how souls move from a situation where they are defined by bondage to a state of being in intimate communion with God. This transformation is effected by Shiva's grace. *See also* Shaivism; Shiva.

Shaivism (shiv'iz-uhm), the religious practices, beliefs, and institutions associated with the Hindu deity Shiva.

History and General Features: Although the roots of Shaivism are probably very ancient in India, the literary appearance of the deity Shiva first occurs in late Vedic literature where Shiva is identified with the Vedic storm god Rudra. From his initial mention, Vedic Rudra is an uncanny deity. His cult seems to have been associated with people on the margins of Vedic society, and there always remains an element of outsidership in this god and his ways. Indeed, Shiva has long been connected with ascetics and asceticism, and in the later Hindu pantheon Shiva is the archetypal *yogin* dwelling on the periphery of civilized life.

Paradoxically, of all the major Hindu gods Shiva is also the one most enmeshed in family relationships, since later myths recount how he marries the goddess Parvati and has two sons, the elephant-headed Ganesha and the youthful warrior Skanda. Shaiva mythology, in fact, is a rich source of Hindu thinking about sexuality, social relations, ritual, cosmic process, and metaphysics.

One of the later old Upanishads, the *Shvetashvatara,* takes the important step of identifying Shiva with the cosmic absolute—the supreme, universal *brahman*—thus doing for Shiva what the *Katha Upanishad* and *Bhagavad Gita* accomplished for Vishnu and Krishna. Eventually, in the early centuries of the common era, Shaiva sects emerged—the Pashupatas, Kapalikas, and Kalamukhas. But it was in the Tamil-speaking areas of South India that Shaivism developed into a popular cult. There between the years 600 and 900 a group of poets called Nayanar flourished who sang Tamil hymns addressed to Shiva, typically praising the god in the forms in which he had manifested himself at various locations now marked by temples.

The conjunction of popular devotion directed to Shiva with a cult centered on temples, each containing a central icon of Shiva and each claiming special myths recording the god's action at that place, gained for Shaivism an ascendancy in South India that it has never lost. Diverse philosophies and movements, all within the Shaiva orbit and most of them originating in the southern regions of the Indian peninsula, came into being. These spanned the Hindu social-philosophical-ritual spectrum from Shankara's monistic and Smarta Brahman-oriented Advaita Vedanta to the theistic and largely non-Brahman Shaiva Siddhanta to the reformist and anti-Brahman Virashaiva ("heroic Shaiva") sect of Karnataka and the Telugu country.

Iconography: While there are numerous myths about Shiva, many represented iconographically, Shiva's most common icon is the *linga,* his stylized phallic emblem. A particularly striking and complex icon of Shiva is that of Nataraja (Skt., "king of the dance"), representing Shiva's cosmic dance of creation, preservation, and destruction. The cult of Shiva as Nataraja is centered at the great temple at Chidambaram in Tamil Nadu. Shaiva art reached its zenith when the Chola dynasty (ninth–thirteenth centuries) dominated much of South India and sponsored the building of large stone temples and the fashioning of exquisite bronze icons used in temple ritual.

Literature: Important Shaiva texts include the Sanskrit epics and Puranas that recount widely known myths about Shiva; the mainly ritual texts called the Shaiva Agamas stating norms for worship in temples and at home; devotional works of numerous saints, from Sanskrit hymns of praise to the poems of the Tamil Nayanamar to the pithy, direct sayings (*vacanas*) in Kannada of the early Virashaivas; a myriad of local Puranas recording the exploits of Shiva at particular temples; and philosophical-theological treatises, especially those of the Tamil Shaiva Siddhanta and of Trika or Kashmir Shaivism (in Sanskrit). *See also* Kapalika; Kashmir Shaivism; linga; Nataraja; Nath; Nayanar; Pashupata; path of devotion; Shaiva Siddhanta; Shiva.

Shakers, Christian sect founded in Manchester, England (1747), by Jane and James Wardley, demanding celibacy of its followers and believing in Christ's Second Coming in female form. They were known originally as "shaking Quakers" because of wild displays of religious ecstasy during worship, including dancing, speaking in tongues, stamping, and trembling of the body. Migrating to the United States, they settled throughout much of the Northeast. Their chief charismatic leader, a blacksmith's daughter named Ann Lee, led the movement from 1753 and came to be called "Mother Ann," or "Mother Spirit in Christ." In the 1990s they are almost extinct. *See also* Lee, Ann.

Shakti (shuhk'tee; Skt., fem., "energy," "power"), Indic sacred, active power personified as a goddess, the female principle of the universe, or the Absolute. Her manifestations include Chinnamasta, Durga, and Kali. As a goddess, Shakti represents the creative consort of any god, but she is especially associated with Shiva. Shiva-Shakti indicates the divine union of opposites: male–female, quiescence–activity, soul–matter. In Shakta sects (worshipers of Shakti), Shakti herself is the transcendent One, worshiped as the *yoni* (vulva, vagina). In popular Hinduism, the faithful wife is the Shakti for her family, providing prosperity and progeny and avenging wrongs. *See also* Goddess (Hinduism); sexuality and religion; Shaktism; Shiva; yoni.

Shaktism (shuk'tiz-uhm), that aspect of Hinduism pertaining to the mythology, philosophy, and worship of *shakti*, a Sanskrit term that means "power" and refers to the creative, active aspect of the divine. This power usually counterbalances a passive, aloof aspect of the divine. In most cases the active principle is perceived as female and the passive aspect as male.

By extension, then, Shaktism has come to refer to Hindu Goddess religion in all its diversity and complexity. There are innumerable goddesses in Hinduism and they range in type over a wide spectrum. Many are associated with and subservient to powerful male gods and play primarily domestic roles, while others are independent and play a range of roles that are often atypical for females in Hindu culture. The goddess Durga, for example, is a cosmic queen and a great warrior, while Kali drinks blood, haunts cremation grounds, and often threatens the stability of the world by her violent dancing.

Shakti is also associated with a dynamic energy called *kundalini* that is pictured as a serpent residing at the base of the spine. Kundalini is aroused in certain forms of yoga and can bring about differing states of consciousness by traversing the central bodily axis that runs along the spinal column. In this aspect, shakti refers to an intrinsic, vital aspect of all human beings.

Shaktism is closely associated with Tantrism in Hinduism. Tantric texts and Tantric spirituality often accentuate, favor, or otherwise privilege the divine feminine. In some Tantric texts and circles sexual rites are stressed as a means of arousing or affirming the inherent power of shakti, and many Tantric texts take pains to assert the superiority and inherent sacrality of women. Some Tantric texts place goddesses in the role of teacher and expounder of religious and philosophical secrets; others promote the worship of virgin girls.

Hindus particularly devoted to goddesses are called Shaktas, and along with the Shaivas (those partial to the god Shiva) and the Vaishnavas (those partial to Vishnu or one of his incarnations) they constitute one of the three main devotional accents in the Hindu tradition. Despite the great diversity found in Hindu Shaktism, nearly every facet of it is characterized by the idea of the divine or ultimate reality expressing itself in dynamic fashion. This emphasis counterbalances a strong theme in other areas of Hinduism teaching the aloof, unchanging, static nature of ultimate reality. *See also* Goddess (Hinduism); kundalini; Shaivism; Shakti; Tantra; Vaishnavism.

shalom (shah-lohm'; Heb., "peace"), in Judaism, the ideal state of human life and society, the realization of total harmony in all spheres. So central is peace that it is one of the Hebrew names of God. The standard Jewish greeting is "Peace be with you." *See also* salamu alaykum, al-.

shaman (shah'men, shay'men; Russian or Tungus), a religious healer and diviner in tribal societies. Shamans are distinguished by creative rituals that alter their normal consciousness and evoke transformative powers in the form of spirits who are often associated with the local landscape.

A shaman's ritual performance creates complex symbol systems derived from dream or vision experiences and from socially recognized religious practices. Objects seen in a dream, such as stones, bones, or animal skins and feathers, may be ritually manipulated while the shaman performs intricate songs associated with dream or vision states of consciousness. The dramatic ritual actions may be accompanied by preparation of herbal recipes for healing. As corporate personalities, shamans embody local community interests and direct their practices to pragmatic concerns such as discovering the causes of illness, locating animals for hunters or making rain for agriculturists, and guiding members of the community through difficult life passage moments such as birth and death.

The idiosyncratic expressions of the shaman are different from those of religious figures involved in institutionalized multicommunity religions. Yet the shaman brings the local community into a relationship with culturally recognized supernatural powers. As a religious personality, the shaman is a guide for the community in its encounter with the powers of the spirit world.

Formation Patterns: Shamans are often initiated into their vocations by a visionary call in which spirits communicate with the future shaman. Spirit presence is validated for tribal audiences by the shaman's altered psychic state and by the efficacy of the ritual that gradually coalesces after the call. The specific features of the formative call provide the impetus for shamans to create rituals that are believed to summon the spirits and their powers.

Sickness and the resulting treatment by a shaman may bring on the initial contact with spirits for some initiates. For others the trauma of spirit contact may cause physical sickness or dreams of bodily dismemberment by ancestral shaman spirits. Shamans' sicknesses follow cultural patterns and often reflect explorations into prohibited or contrary behavior. For many shamans the practice of the ritual imparted to them by the spirits leads to their cure and defines their community roles as healers, ecstatic guides, and spiritual mediums.

The emergence of shamans may be marked by an initiation ritual conducted by a society of shamans. Often the emergence of a shaman is validated by the first cure or by the successful entry into a trance or possession state that demonstrates the presence of spirits. Such techniques of ecstasy bring the shaman, the ritual suppliant, and the broader community into imaginative and controlled experiences with culturally recognized spirits.

Function: Cosmology refers to the traditional beliefs by which people think about their physical bodies and animating souls, and place themselves in their surroundings and in the origins of the perceived universe. Shamans ritually reenact their initiating experiences in the context of the tribal cosmology. The personal symbols of many Siberian shamans are sewn onto their coats, in association with the cosmic tree, which is believed to span the layers of the universe. The drums and rattles of Amazonian shamans are ritually crafted to instill in them the transformative sound of the shamans' power, which is linked to the sonic powers of the rain forest as cosmos. These symbols function as an organized system that informs the patient and community of the powerful cosmic forces associated with the shaman.

During the ritual performance many shamans recover lost souls or seek information about pragmatic concerns by means of a spiritual journey. This ecstatic journey often depends on a determination of the cause of the soul loss. Shamans may travel to the underground habitations of the dead in search of lost souls or to the realms of the sky to petition the powers that control the animals and the weather. By connecting their communities to cosmological forces shamans sustain hope in the confrontation with the terrors of life.

During ritual performances, through use of cultivated imagery, shamans create an intense expectation among the participants for the imminent arrival of spirit forces. During this ritual process shamans often exhibit investigative skills when they interview patients. By evoking the spirits through song, rhythmic percussion, or bodily exertion, the shaman brings the patients' concerns into the imaginative realm associated with the spirits. The shaman may withdraw into subliminal states in which the images drawn from personal visions and from the tribal cosmology are controlled and intensely focused. The shaman's control and focus may be transmitted to the patient and audience through rigorous bouts of sweating, singing, massage, fire-manipulation, or sucking out a supernatural source of illness with bones. Often shamans structure experiences in which normal perceptions are confounded by sleight of hand or synesthetic confusion. Thus, the shaman engages the patient and participants in the transformative purposes of the ritual.

Community approval is a factor in a shaman's ability to heal sickness in individuals and communities. By perceiving illness in cultural, rather than merely physiological, terms shamans help patients redefine their sickness in the harmonious images of the cosmology. Such action is subject to scrutiny by the community. Negative criticism of shamans is couched in the language of witchcraft. The shaman's inner mental states are guardedly subjective and yet visible for public scrutiny. Shamans have described their inner mental states in relation to their formative call experiences. The altered mental state of a shaman can be understood as a return to that initial liminal experience. The shaman's trance and resulting spiritual journey engage a cognitive map of the cosmos first revealed in the call experience and developed through years of ritual practice. The "map" followed in the trance journey may also be understood as a path of thought on which the shaman arranges symbols according to a personal imaginative logic. The shaman's thought process in the ritual performance provides novel ways of organizing and thinking about the world. *See also* Ainu religion; ascension rituals; circumpolar religions; dead, rituals with respect to the; Finnish religion; healing; holy person; initiation rituals; jaguar (South American religions); journey to the otherworld; possession; shape shifting; soul-loss; trance.

shamanic rites (Korea). *See* kut.

shamanism (Tunguz *saman,* "shaman"), those practices and beliefs that center on communication with the spirits of nature and the spirits of the dead through the ritualized possession of a shaman who serves as a spirit medium. In its narrowest sense, shamanism is confined to the northern circumpolar region and, through diffusion, to areas such as China, Japan, Korea, and North and possibly South America. *See also* Ainu religion; Finnish religion; Hamatsa; Japanese folk religion; kami-gakari; miko; South American religions; traditional.

Chinese Religion: In Chinese shamanism, possibly derived from Shang and Chou (ca. 1766–221 B.C.) divination rites to ancestral spirits, *wu* (Chin., "female shamans"), *chu* ("those who invoke"), or *hsi* ("male shamans") contacted the spirit world through a trance induced by chanting and dancing to drum music. Shang oracle bones and Eastern Chou textual evidence suggests the use of wu for exorcism, dream interpretation, and curing illness. During a drought, they were exposed to the sun or burned at the stake to elicit spiritual empathy and bring rain. Although shamans have been employed in rain rituals up through medieval times, clay frogs eventually replaced human sacrifice and exposure. In exercises of spirit control stemming from the late Chou period, shamans performed ecstatic ritual dances involving spiritual flight, sexual liaison, and spirit possession. Later, shamans' powers depended on special guardian spirits, often those of famous historical personages or of nature deities, associated with local temples or cult centers. While possessed of these spirits' powers, they could command *shen* (deities), kill *kuei* (ghosts), and communicate with specific spirits of the recently deceased. In trance they would perform miracles as evidence of their powers: mutilate themselves without consequence, walk through fire, spirit-talk, or ghost-write. The writing and blood, especially from their tongues, was used to make amulets.

Since the first century, when Confucianism was the orthodox religion, and later, when Taoism struggled for orthodoxy, shamans, although still occasionally employed officially, were considered socially marginal characters and treated with suspicion. In sporadic government purges, female shamans were accused of sorcery (e.g., enslaving souls and black magic) and male shamans (especially those with large cult followings) of plotting rebellion. Witch-hunts focused on the use of *ku* poison, a form of black magic since the Chou period associated with female control and sex; both a love potent and a deadly poison, it was made by putting poisonous insects and snakes together in a pot until they bit each other to death and putrefied into a dark gooey essence of evil that was then used to kill or seduce men.

While in traditional China the role of the shaman was often hereditary, in modern southeastern China, a *tang-ki* ("divining youth") is believed to be chosen by the deity itself. The deity possesses and protects the human subject through an ecstatic trance involving a theatrical scene of self-mortification; the man whacks his back and forehead with weapons, such as a "ball of nails," a "seven-star sword," the saw of a sawfish, a spiked club, or a large "moon axe." Shamans are presently used in Buddhist purification rituals; in exorcisms to cure illness, spirit possession, and infertility; and to drive evil out of villages or homes. *See also* Chinese ritual; kuei; ku poison; ling-pao; shen; Yu-pu.

Korean Religion: Shamanism is often seen as Korea's indigenous religious tradition and the template of Korean consciousness upon which other religious traditions have been built. It is also seen as the heart of folk religion and therefore that orientation toward the world least affected by modernization and Westernization.

Korean shamans act as prophets, physicians, and priests, helping to restore health, promote the financial welfare of clients, aid in conception and child-rearing, and alleviate the misery of the common people. Korea recognizes both female (*mudang*) and male (*paksu*) shamans, though female shamans predominate. Female shamans have the ability to invoke gods and spirits of the dead through song and dance, to be ecstatically possessed by familiar spirits or the spirits of the dead, and to communicate (*kongsu*) to clients information from the world of spirits.

Shamans are generally divided between hereditary or trained shamans (mudang, *sesupmu*) and possessed shamans (*mansin, kangsinmu*). The hereditary shamans, mostly in the southern provinces and almost all women, are usually the daughters of shamans who have voluntarily take up the shaman life and are trained by their mothers to invoke the spirits. The hereditary shamans tend to perform very dramatic and colorful rites (*kut*) and are expert storytellers.

The possessed shamans, mostly in the northern provinces, find their identity after experiencing a long illness or calamity (*sinbyong*, "god disease"). To be cured of this disease they must go to another shaman who will force the spirit that caused the disease to take possession of her.

Once possessed, the new shaman must be taught how to control the possession and how to end it. The rite she goes through is a long, arduous initiation rite (*naerim kut*) that names the possessing spirit, determines why the spirit is interested in this woman, and finally dispatches the possessing spirit. With the removal of the spirit the woman is cured of her disease. At this point she may or may not choose to live the life of a shaman. She can always be possessed if she wants, but she need not be. If she takes up the life of the shaman, then she must learn to control her possession and put it to use. Both types of shamans can invoke spirits, but only the mansin can bear the spirits within her own body.

A third type of shaman is the *chegwan*, or ritual leader, a temporary function that is bestowed on a villager who will carry out some rite on behalf of the village. Though not possessed, chegwan must follow a ritually pure life-style prior to the rite so that they can successfully invoke the local tutelary spirit.

Because shamanism is the vehicle of many ancient Korean practices, there is much interest in it today. It is studied for its songs, dances, costumes, and perspective on the world. In more recent times interest has grown further, since many Koreans are uneasy with modernization and they believe they were forced to give up shamanism by the Japanese in the colonial period (1910–45) and during the Pak regime (1961–80) without having first had a chance to understand it. There are today about forty thousand registered shamans in Korea. *See also* kut; National Shaman.

Korean shaman in front of an elaborate altar with food offerings to ancestral spirits, in Seoul. In Korea, most shamans are women.

Shambhala (shahm-bah'lah; Skt.), an important earthly paradise in Tibetan Buddhism. Hidden by the snow mountains north of Tibet, Shambhala is said to hold the mystical doctrine of the Wheel of Time. An enlightened king (Gesar) is prophesied to come out of this sanctuary to defeat the forces of evil and establish a golden age of Buddhist teachings. *See also* Gesar/Geser; paradise; Tibetan religions.

Shang-ch'ing Taoism (shahng-ching; Chin., "Highest Purity," "Highest Clarity"), important early school of religious Taoism arising in the fourth century.

Between 364 and 370, Yang Hsi, a visionary or medium, received nocturnal revelations from a group of immortals led by Lady Wei Hua-ts'un, who had died in 334. The revelations written down by Yang, perhaps via automatic writing, consisted of thirty-one sacred volumes called the *Scriptures of Supreme Purity.* Collected by T'ao Hung-ching (456–536), these works became the nucleus of the first Taoist canon, which was divided into three parts, or grottoes. The Shang-ch'ing scriptures were collected in the first part, called the *chen-tung,* or "grotto of perfection."

The new movement based on these scriptures was named Shang-ch'ing Taoism, or Maoshan Taoism, and became the most significant Taoist school in medieval China. It developed the theories and meditative practices of the *Huang-t'ing ching* (Yellow Court Scripture) centered on meditation through inner visualization in order to enhance spiritual and physical health by preservation of one's *ching* (seminal essence) and the purification of *ch'i* (vital energy). *See also* Chen-kao; ch'i; ching; Huang-t'ing ching; Maoshan; T'ao Hung-ching; Taoism; Ta-tung Chenching; Yang Hsi.

Shango (shahn'go; Yoruban), legendary African king divinized as the spirit of thunder, lightning, and force.

Oral tradition places Shango as the fourth king of Oyo, the political center of Yorubaland in Nigeria during the seventeenth and eighteenth centuries. His father was Oranyan, the founder of Oyo, and his grandfather Oduduwa, the progenitor of the Yoruba people.

Shango was a sorcerer as well as a monarch, and his ruthless use of force raised opposition within Oyo. He abdicated the throne for the isolation of the forest and vowed to rule invisibly. His enemies reported that the king had hanged himself, but his loyal followers replied that he had ascended into heaven as an *orisha* (divine spirit).

Shango became the patron of subsequent kings of Oyo, and his cult spread throughout Yorubaland. During the slave trade many of Shango's priests and priestesses were taken to the Americas, where they established him as one of the most popular African spirits now venerated in Brazil, Trinidad, Haiti, and Cuba. His legends can be found in various guises in African-American folklore. In the last thirty years, Latin and Caribbean immigrants have reestablished Shango's worship in American cities, especially Miami and New York.

Shango's aid is sought in all matters of personal and communal concern, especially those that might require strength and courage. While Shango may be consulted privately, he has a famous appetite for feasting and large ceremonies are often held in his honor. Strict rules govern the kind of foods, songs, dances, and instruments Shango "likes" and are likely to coax his presence.

The high point of these ceremonies is when Shango "descends" to "ride" a medium priest or priestess specially trained to be his "horse" on ceremonial occasions. Seated in the "head" of his medium, Shango will dance, sing, eat, and drink with his followers, offering advice and blessings to petitioners. *See also* Africa, traditional religions in; Afro-Americans (Caribbean and South America), new religions among.

Shang religion. The extensive oracle-bone divination records of the latter half of the Shang dynasty (second millennium B.C.) provide a wealth of information on the religious and cultic practices of the Shang elite. In the inscriptions the royal ancestral cult figures most prominently, since the Shang king sought to communicate with his deceased ancestors by divination. The ancestors were enlisted to predict the outcome of military ventures, the king's illnesses, royal journeys, the harvest, and natural disasters and to resolve even the minutest issues of a purely ritual character: which sacrificial rite(s) would achieve the desired result, how many victims to offer, which kind (including human), which colors, which sex, on which day of the sexagenary cycle, and so on. By the end of the dynasty the royal ancestors and the obligatory rites dedicated to them had proliferated to the extent that the ritual cycle of sacrifices had expanded to approximately a full calendar year.

Since the spirits of the royal ancestors were expected to intercede with the high god Ti (later Shang-ti) and with the powerful spirits of localities, mountains, and rivers, a fragmentary picture also emerges of a temporal landscape frequently intersected by the sacred realm. This other realm evidently shared many of the strongly hierarchical characteristics of the Shang, with a supreme ruler who "commanded" dedicated minions, natural spirits, wind, and

weather, who "sent down" aid or misfortune, and to whom sacrifices and entreaties could only be indirectly communicated via intermediaries. *See also* ancestral rites; Chinese popular religion; divination; myth; oracle bones; Shang-ti.

Shang-shu. *See* Shu-ching.

Shang-ti (shahng-dee; Chin., "Highest Lord"), supreme deity in ancient Chinese religious tradition; "God" in popular usage. It first appears as Ti ("Lord") in Shang-dynasty (fourteenth century B.C.) oracle-bone inscriptions, then as Shang-ti from early Chou (twelfth century B.C.) on (synonymous with T'ien, "Heaven"). Shang-ti is the supreme arbiter of phenomenal existence who possesses power to "command" what is beyond human control: the weather, natural disasters, lesser spirits, dynastic fortunes, harvests, etc. Shang-ti was initially unapproachable except when the spirits of the royal Shang ancestors were enlisted as intermediaries; under the empire, in the mid-seventeenth century, Shang-ti/T'ien became the object of grand sacrifices at important seasonal junctures and on state occasions. *See also* term question; T'ien.

Shan-hai ching (shahn-hi jing; Chin., "Classic of Mountains and Seas"), a magical Chinese geography written ca. third–first century B.C. and attributed to Yu, the legendary controller of water and land. The first five chapters, the "Book of Mountains," describe the flora, fauna, minerals, and spirits of the four directions. Other sections include the "Book of Lands Beyond the Sea," "Book of Lands Within the Sea," and "Book of the Great Wilderness," which describe spirits, required sacrifices, exotic tribes, tales of creation and transcendent beings, and divine genealogies. *See also* Chou religion; Han religion; Yu (the Great).

Shankara (shuhn'kuh-ruh), also Shankaracharya, a highly influential figure in Indian religious thought to the present day; he is the best-known exponent of Advaita (nondualistic) Vedanta. The traditional dating is 788 to 820; others suggest 700 to 750.

According to tradition, Shankara was born a Brahman in Kaladi, South India, renounced the world in his youth, lived in Banaras, and traveled extensively. He showed great skill in disputation and founded a monastic order and monasteries throughout India. He is best known for his independent *Upadeshasahasri* and commentaries on the *Brahmasutras*, major Upanishads, and *Bhagavad Gita*.

According to Shankara, these latter texts

teach that knowing the true self (Skt. *atman*) to be identical with changeless ultimate reality (*brahman*) brings liberation (*moksha*) from bondage to transmigratory existence (*samsara*). Ritual action or worship of gods leads to better rebirth or the world of the gods, but full liberation comes only from removing ignorance (*avidya*), i.e., the superimposition of illusory diversity on qualityless (*nirguna*) brahman. *See also* Hinduism (thought and ethics); liberation; mysticism; path of knowledge; six systems of Indian philosophy; Vedanta.

shan-shu (shahn-sh*oo*; Chin., "good books," "morality books"), a variety of popular Chinese books addressing common themes of social morality, including handbooks on moral edification, religious tracts, stories of retribution for good and bad deeds, ledgers for calculating merits and demerits, popular operas, Buddhist scriptures known as "precious scrolls" (*pao-chuan*), and "spirit-writing" (*fu-chi* or *pai-luan*) texts that record the revelations of various deities. They draw on a synthesis of Buddhist, Taoist, and Confucian ideas, particularly belief in karmic retribution and in an alloted span of life that is shortened by evil deeds. *See also* Chinese language and literature, religious aspects of; fu-chi; pao-chuan.

Shan-tao (shahn-dou; 613–681), early master of the Chinese Pure Land school; he expedited the school's transition from a way of discipline to a way of faith by making *nien-fo* (chanting the name of the Buddha) the preeminent practice and popularizing it among the masses. He retained but downplayed the school's other, more strenuous disciplines. *See also* nien-fo; Pure Land school (China).

shanti (shahn'tih), a Sanskrit term that signifies the "cooling, bringing to rest" of a thing or situation that is "overheated or threateningly out of order" and the state of "quiet, calm, or peace" that then results. *Shanti* serves as the generic name for a large class of Hindu rituals applied in a host of ominous, uncertain, or dangerous situations. In various yogic religions it designates a profound quieting of the body and mind that occurs through the practice of sitting, concentrative meditation. Some aestheticians asserted that shanti, inner quiet or calm, could be a *rasa*, an effect of a literary work. *See also* meditation; rasa.

Shao Yung (show-yuhng; 1011–77), one of the five Northern Sung-dynasty Neo-Confucian masters credited with the revival of Confucianism. He was later considered heterodox because of his interest in a cosmology linked to mystical numerological speculations. *See also* Neo-Confucianism.

shape shifting, the capacity to change bodily form at will. It is a common characteristic of gods, spirits, and religious functionaries (e.g., shamans). In folklore, magical objects can shape shift. *See also* Hanuman; jaguar (South American religions); shaman; tanuki.

Sharia (sha-ree'ah; Arab., "path"), the religious law of Islam. This law embraces the entire body of rules and moral directives that God has ordained. In essence, a moral law by which human beings are to be judged in the hereafter, the Sharia may become part of the actual judicial apparatus of an Islamic state. *See also* Islamic law.

shaved head, part of a Buddhist monk's or nun's expected appearance. Shaving the head is a climax of the Buddhist ordination ceremony, indicating indifference to sexuality and conventions of attractive appearance. *See also* bhiksu/bhiksuni; Buddhism (life cycle); Sangha.

Shavuot (shah-voo-oht'; Heb., "weeks"), a Jewish holiday (6 Sivan), called Pentecost in English, that falls seven weeks after Passover. Originally an agricultural event to mark the spring wheat harvest and the bringing of the first ripe fruits to the Temple, the holiday was given new meaning by talmudic rabbis, who suggested, after a close reading of biblical verses, that Torah was given at Sinai on Shavuot. *See also* Judaism (festal cycle).

shaykh (Arab., "an elder"), an Islamic term of respect used to designate a tribal chief, head of family, or respected Islamic religious figure, in particular, the leader of a Sufi order. *See also* Sufism; tariqa; ulama.

Shaytan. *See* Iblis; Satan.

she-chi (shuh-jee; Chin., "soil and millet"), altar to the spirits of the soil and grain, and the conventional term in Chou texts for agricultural rites associated with their worship. Hou Chi ("Lord Millet") was the legendary progenitor of the Chou people; the earthen altar-mound (*she*) was sacred to the local spirit of the soil. *See also* Chou religion.

Shekhina (sheh-khee-nah'; Heb., "dwelling"), in Judaism, God's indwelling presence, the this-worldly manifestation of God, especially in contexts of revelation or in the perceived sanctification of specific objects, people, or locations.

First found in early postbiblical texts, the term roughly corresponds to the use of "Logos" or "Holy Spirit" in early Christian thought. In Aramaic translations of the Hebrew Bible, the Aramaic equivalent of Shekhina is used for such expressions as "the face of God" and "the glory of God." The Targums thus avoid attributing blatantly anthropomorphic features directly to God. In rabbinic texts the term is used more broadly, both to designate the physical manifestation of God and, on occasion, simply as another word for God.

Talmudic rabbis appear to have understood the Shekhina metaphorically and not to have viewed the Shekhina as a real, physical aspect of God. The talmudic literature presents descriptions of conversations between God and the Shekhina and images of the Shekhina's presence within this world, especially in the form of light (e.g., Exodus Rabbah 32:4). But such passages often are introduced with the caveat "as if it could be," making explicit their metaphorical weight.

Medieval Jewish philosophers avoided all possibility of anthropomorphism by describing the Shekhina as an independent entity created by God rather than as a physical representation of God or as an aspect of God's essence. Saadiah Gaon (882–942) followed by Maimonides (1135–1204) identifies the Shekhina as the intermediary between God and humans that accounts for prophetic visions. Following this same view, Judah Halevi (ca. 1075–1141) holds that the Shekhina and not God appeared in prophetic visions. According to Halevi, this same visible aspect of the Shekhina dwelled in the Temple in Jerusalem; it is separate, however, from an unseen, spiritual Shekhina that dwells with every righteous Israelite.

Kabbalists most frequently defined the Shekhina as the sphere closest to the empirical world, of which it is the sustaining force. Representing the feminine principle, the Shekhina was held to have no light of its own but to receive divine light from the other spheres. In the mystics' view, through prayer and observing the commandments, Jews assist in reuniting the Shekhina with the heavenly masculine principle. By following the Torah, they work to restore the original unity of God, which was destroyed by the people's sins, by evil powers, and as a re-sult of the Jews' exile. *See also* anthropomorphism; hypostasis; Logos; Judaism (mysticism); Judaism, God in.

Shema (shuh-mah'; Heb.,"Hear O Israel ..."), daily prayer in Judaism affirming monotheism, accompanied by blessings affirming God's creative, revelatory, and redemptive roles. In popular usage it denotes only the biblical verse (Deuteronomy 6:4) that begins the prayer. *See also* Judaism, prayer and liturgy of.

shen (shen; Chin., "spirit," "deity"), in Chinese tradition, the heavenly aspect of the soul (*hun*) as differentiated from the earthly (*p'o*) aspect, when it escapes from the corpse of a sage, powerful historical figure, or religious adept; or a natural, astral, or distant ancestral spirit; or, a god as opposed to a *kuei* (ghost). *Shen* are usually housed in temples where they are offerd prayers, incense, and food sacrifices for protection from the myriad forms of evil worked by demons, unhappy spirits of the dead, or nature sprites such as foxes. Miracles are the work of shen. *See also* kuei; physiological techniques (Taoism).

shen-chu (shen-jew; Chin., "spirit tablet"), in Chinese ancestor veneration, a wooden tablet displayed on the altar of a home or ancestral hall, in which the heavenly aspect of an individual's soul (*hun* or *yang*) permanently resides. *See also* ancestral rites.

sheng (sheng; Chin., "sage," "saint"), in Chinese tradition 1 a mortal with supernatural powers gained through self-cultivation, one who could hear the gods, understand the Tao, and he in harmony with the cosmos. 2 An exemplary figure such as one of the legendary sage-kings or Confucius.

Shen-hsiao Taoism (shuhn-shyou; Chin., "Divine Empyrean"), a liturgical tradition established at the court of the Sung emperor Hui-tsung (early twelfth century). It revised the *Tu-jen ching* (Scripture of Salvation) and depicted Hui-tsung as a divinity. *See also* Cheng-i Taoism; Tu-jen ching.

Shen-hsiu (shuhn-shyoh; ca. 606–706), the foremost Ch'an Buddhist monk in T'ang-dynasty China. After his death the Southern school targeted him as an exponent of gradual enlightenment during the sudden-gradual controversy. His reputation faded and he lost his position as sixth patriarch in favor of Hui-neng. *See also* Ch'an school; Hui-neng; sudden-gradual controversy.

Shen-hui (shen-hway; 684–758), an obscure Chinese Ch'an Buddhist monk until 732, when he launched the attack upon the Northern school of Ch'an that precipitated the sudden-gradual controversy. He later gained imperial patronage, which hastened the Southern school's victory and the election of his teacher Hui-neng as the sixth patriarch. *See also* Ch'an school; Hui-neng; sudden-gradual controversy.

shen-jen (shuhn-ren; Chin., "spiritual person"). 1 One of the terms in the *Chuang-tzu,* a fourth-century B.C. Taoist classic, for the ideal person. *See also* Chuang-tzu. 2 The "Celestial Master" who brings salvation in the first-century *T'ai-p'ing ching* (Scripture of Great Peace). *See also* T'ai-p'ing ching.

Shen Nung (shen nuhng; Chin., "divine farmer"), ancient Chinese god, inventor of agriculture. He is one of the "three sovereigns" (San-huang), along with Fu Hsi and Huang-ti. *See also* Chinese myth; San-huang.

Shesha (shay'shah; Skt., "remainder"), the serpent of infinity in Hinduism. When the universe is flooded at the end of an eon, Vishu sleeps on Shesha's coils. *See also* cosmogony; Vishnu.

Shia (shee'uh; Arab., "a separate or distinct party of men who follow or conform with one another, [though] not all of them agreeing together"; applied to one or many, male or female, without variation). When used in a specific sense of "partisans" in the domain of religion, the term denotes a large group of different Muslim schools of thought that believe that Ali ibn Abi Talib, through a specific designation (*nass*) by Muhammad, inherited not only his political but also his religious authority, immediately following the Prophet's death in 632. As such, Ali was the legitimate head of the Muslim polity and ultimate authority on questions of law and doctrine in Islam. As a corollary to this tenet, the Shia refused to acknowledge and regard as legitimate the first three caliphs, Abu Bakr, Umar, and Uthman, whom the Shia considered usurpers of the leadership that rightfully belonged to Ali and his descendants.

Origins: The historical origins of the Shia are difficult to reconstruct because of the controversial presentation of their views by the Sunnite authors and propagandistic reporting by later Shiite authors. Modern Islamicists, depending on Sunnite majority sources, have generally regarded the Shia as having diverged from the Islamic norm, having begun as followers of a political leader who was gradually transformed into a religious figurehead. An objective evalua-tion of the early Islamic community in the light of the Qur'an and its attitude toward the caliphal office is indispensable for understanding the genesis of the Shiite movement.

Muhammad's message, as embodied in the Qur'an, provided immense spiritual, as well as sociopolitical, impetus for the establishment of the ideal community (*umma*) of Islam. Muhammad himself was not only the founder of a new religion but also the custodian of a new social order. Consequently, the question of leadership was the crucial issue that divided Muslims into various factions in the years following his death. The compromise reached at that stage, that leadership belongs to the Meccan member of Quraysh, the Prophet's tribe, is a clear indication that as the leader of the umma, the caliph's authority was founded on religious legitimacy and practical considerations. The early years of Islamic polity were characterized by a constant succession of victories of the Muslim army under the first three caliphs. But as this period reached its end and civil wars broke out in 656 under Uthman, the third caliph, contention arose over the necessity of a qualified leadership to assume the office of *imam*. Most of these early discussions on the leadership took at first sight political form, but eventually the debates focused on the connection between divine guidance and the creation of the Islamic world order. The tension occasioned by the existence of injustice in the Muslim polity gave rise to two distinct, and in some ways even contradicting, attitudes among Muslims: quietist and activist. Both these attitudes had sanction in the Prophet's life and teaching. However, the exponents of a quietist posture were also the supporters of authoritarian politics, giving unquestioning and immediate obedience to almost any Muslim authority who publicly agreed to uphold Islamic norms. The exponents of an activist posture supported radical politics, which taught that there was no obligation of obedience to corrupt and wicked rulers and that it was necessary to remove an unjust authority from power. Gradually the quietist and authoritarian stance toward the Muslim rulers, whether just or unjust, became associated in varying intensity with the majority of the Sunnite Muslims. The activist and radical stance, in the early centuries, became the attribute of Shiite Islam.

The rise of several individuals as imams, and the sympathetic, even enthusiastic, following that they attracted shows the anxiety that was felt by religiously oriented Muslims in the awareness that the Islamic ideal lacked actualization in the external world and that the qualified imam could and would further the formation of a just society with a fitting political organization.

Development of Shiite Doctrine: Early conceptualization of the Prophet's leadership and the intricate relationship between his political and religious authority determined the attitude of many a Muslim who believed the legitimate head of Islamic polity to hold both spiritual and temporal power. The Prophet's spiritual authority included the power to interpret the message in the Qur'an without corrupting the revelation. Islam, in order to continue its function of directing the faithful toward the creation of a just and equitable order, was in need of a leader who could perform the Prophet's comprehensive role authoritatively. The exaltation of the Prophet and his rightful successor gave rise to the concept of an infallible Imam from among the descendants (*ahl al-bayt*, "people of the house") of the Prophet who could create an ideal Islamic community. The entire doctrinal edifice of the Shia was, thus, constructed on the concept of *wilaya* (authority, loyalty) of Ali, who became the first Shiite Imam. In fact, among the Shia, Ali's wilaya became the sole criterion for judging true faith.

The Shiite concept of Imam, which heightened the religiopolitical sense of the legitimate head of state as God's deputy (*khalifa*) on earth, was bound to meet with much resistance because it not only demanded the recognition of Ali and his descendants as the Imams with real control of the entire Muslim polity, it also was a challenge to the rule of the Umayyad caliphate and a rallying point for all who felt discriminated against or maltreated by the ruling house. Consequently, from its inception Shiism emerged as an opposition party. Nevertheless, Ali was deprived of his political power and was passed over for succession three times in a row. Almost a quarter century after the Prophet's death, the caliphate was assumed finally by Ali in 656. But Ali's leadership was marred by political turmoil in Muslim polity. After a brief and contested rule he was murdered and his son and designated successor, Hasan, became the caliph. Hasan's caliphate had lasted for less than six months, when circumstances forced him to abdicate in favor of Muawiya, a member of the Umayyad clan whose enmity toward the Prophet and his Hashimite clan was well known. However, Hasan continued to be acknowledged by the Shiites as their second Imam. Under the impact of historical circumstances during these formative years of the Shiite ideology, leadership of the community was divided into a temporal and spiritual sphere. The former was regarded as usurped by the ruling dynasty, which in theory

required proper designation by the Prophet, but was tolerated as long as its sphere of action was limited to the execution of the law. The spiritual sphere likewise required a clear designation, also by the Prophet. However, the spiritual authority with the right to demand obedience was not contingent upon the Imam's being invested as the ruling authority who could enforce obedience. In this sense, spiritual authority resided in Ali from the day the Prophet died. After Ali the position was transmitted from one legitimate Imam to his successor through the process of special designation, which also guaranteed authoritative transmission of the knowledge about Islamic revelation through these rightful and infallible Imams.

After Hasan, his brother Husayn became the third Imam of the Shiites. However, Husayn revolted against the Umayyad state, based in Damascus, in response to the political situation created by the ascension of Muawiya's son, Yazid. Husayn undertook a journey to Karbala in southern Iraq in 680. On the tenth of Muharram, known as the day of Ashura, Husayn and his family and friends were killed by Umayyad troops. Husayn's death was a turning point in the Shiite religious ethos and introduced into Shiism the element of passion and highlighted the quranic ideal of martyrdom suffered in the path of God. The Shiites preserved this day in their salvation history through annual commemoration (*Taziya*) as a tragic event reminding humanity of the sullied nature of power and the way righteous ones suffer in the world. Although for the greater part of Shiite history, the memory of Karbala has been tempered by the tradition of political quietism, there were times when the episode was used to encourage activism to counter injustice in society. The most recent examples of the activist interpretation of the Karbala episode occurred during the Islamic revolution of Iran from 1978 to 1979 and radicalization of the Lebanese Shiites since the 1970s.

Against this political undoing of the Shiite leadership in the early history of Islam, the Shiite creed did not regard it necessary for the Imam to be invested with political authority in order to be considered as the Imam. The position of Imam became defined in theological terms, needing only the designation from the legitimate Imam to his successor. This method of succession guaranteed the delegation of the spiritual authority of the Prophet to the Alid Imam. Both Hasan and Husayn held a special status in Muslim popular piety because they were the Prophet's grandsons through his daughter Fatima. The popular veneration of the Prophet's family was common among Muslims in general. However, in Shiism, the Prophet's family members were regarded as the bearers of authentic Islam. Accordingly, all the Imams were required to be the descendants of Ali and Fatima.

Several protest movements arose under a wide range of leaders from among Ali's descendants, who were able to arouse in their followers a genuine religious urge to achieve sociopolitical goals. However, the Shiite attempts at direct political action were met with brutal resistance from the ruling dynasty, and very early their efforts met with failure. The resultant frustration produced further Shiite factions. The radical factions insisted on armed resistance to the oppressive rule of the caliphate. These were also known as *ghulat* (zealots, extremists) because of the extravagant claims they made for their imams. The ghulat attributed communications dealing with prophetic revelations about future uprisings and seditions to the Imams, thus endangering the very survival of the Shiite movement. The moderate factions, having experienced the futility of direct political action, were prepared to postpone indefinitely the establishment of true Islamic rule under their Imam. More than any other factor, it was the tragedy of Karbala in 680 and later the failure of the revolt of Zayd, Husayn's grandson, in 739, which marked the turn toward a quietist attitude by these factions, who until then had been willing to fight for their ideals.

But Shiite efforts, until the time of Abbasid victory in 750, were still lacking in a well-formulated doctrine of the Imamate. It was then that the great Imam Jafar al-Sadiq (d. 765), who had been largely responsible for the moderation and discipline of the radical elements, provided Shiism with the basic conceptions of the creed. In the political turmoil of the eighth century the Alid Imams had the opportunity to propagate Shiite viewpoints without inhibition and modify the revolutionary tone of early Shiism into a more sober and tolerant school of Islamic thought. The Shiite leaders encouraged and even required the employment of precautionary dissimulation (*tagiyya*) of their faith so as to avoid pressing for the establishment of the Alid rule and the overthrow of the illegitimate caliphate. Tagiyya-oriented life also signified the will of the Shiite minority to continue to strive for the realization of the ideal by preparing the way for such an insurrection in the future. Al-Sadiq's contribution in shaping the religious and juridical direction of Shiism was central. He was acknowledged by all the Shiites as their Imam, including those of radical leaning who led the revolts to establish Alids as the legitimate head

of state. He was also recognized as an authentic transmitter of the *hadith* in the Sunnite compilations. It was almost certainly under his leadership that moderate Shiism, with its veneration of the Prophet's family, came to be sanctioned by the Sunnite majority as a permissible expression of Islamic piety. More significantly, the moderate Shiite school of law was named after him as the Jafari rite and was tolerated as a minor deviation along with the four major schools of Sunnite law. In addition, for the majority of the Shiites, his attitude toward politics became the cornerstone of their political theory, which, in the absence of the imam's political authority, did not teach its followers to overthrow tyrannical rulers and replace them by the imam. In fact, as the doctrine of the Imamate taught, although the imam was entitled to political authority, his Imamate was not contingent upon his being invested as the wielder of actual power. Moderate Shiites continued to uphold the leadership of the descendants of Ali and Fatima through Jafar al-Sadiq until the line reached the twelfth Imam, Muhammad al-Mahdi (b. 873), who was believed to be the last and the living Imam. He was also the promised Mahdi of the Muslim tradition and the Hidden Imam, whose return as the messianic reformer they awaited. These were the Imamiyya Ithna Ashariyya or "Twelvers." The disappearance of the last Imam is designated as the doctrine of "occultation" (*ghayba*). The occultation is divided into two forms: "The Short" and "The Complete." According to this division, during the Short Occultation, which lasted for about seventy years (873–941), the last Imam appointed some of his prominent followers as his special deputies to carry on the function of guiding the community in its religious and social affairs as functional imams. However, during the Complete Occultation (941–present) the learned jurists (the *mujtahid,* see below) among the Shiites were believed to have been appointed by the last Imam as his general deputies pending his return at the end of time. This belief made it feasible for the emergence of Ayatollah-like leadership in Twelver Shiism.

Political Struggles under Radical Shiism: Radical Shiites had become so strong by the middle of the eighth century that one of their factions was able to organize an Abbasid revolution, which successfully established their dynastic caliphate. The Abbasids, however, following the consolidation of their power, turned against their Shiite supporters by abandoning their revolutionary expectations and adhering to Sunnism. The idea of the Mahdi as a future conqueror who would set things right was already in circulation in Medina around 680. The belief became greatly accentuated with the disintegration of the caliphate, both Umayyad and Abbasid. The rise of the messianic Imam was expected by all those who had been deprived of their rights under the existing regimes. It was believed that the Mahdi, being endowed with divine knowledge like that of the Prophet himself, would launch the revolution to rectify the unfavorable condition of the community at the suitable time. Consequently, the belief in the savior Imam, Mahdi, had become a rallying point for the discontented, religiously oriented circles, including the militant Shiite factions. Ambitious persons among them found that they could manipulate genuine religious devotions of ordinary men in the name of the descendants of Ali. However, the ensuing struggle to install a legitimate authority led to the murder of several Shiite leaders and the failure of the revolts to redress the situation. This apparent setback, provoked by the atrocities of the ruling house, was explained by means of two interrelated beliefs about the Mahdi: the concealment (ghayba) and the return (raja) of the messianic Imam at the appropriate time. Whereas the belief in the concealment of the legitimate Imam signified the postponement of the establishment of the Islamic order, the belief in his eventual return helped the Shiites to persevere under difficult circumstances and to hope for reform pending the return of the messianic Imam.

Main Forms of Shiism: In the course of history three main forms of Shiism survived (although on account of different beliefs, the three divisions broke into many subdivisions).

The Zaydiyya, who supported the revolt of Zayd in 739 and acknowledged him as their imam, were closest to the Sunnites. During the latter part of the ninth century they had established small principalities in the Caspian region of Iran as well as in the Yemen. They insisted that the imam from among the descendants of the Prophet, as his rightful successor, had to rise and undertake direct political action to replace a usurpatory rule and that both employment of precautionary dissimulation and belief in the concealment and ultimate return of the Mahdi were contrary to the very essence of Shiism. Shiism, according to them, was associated with the real control of the Muslim world, which had to be attained with the sword of the imam established by the community as part of their religious obligation. Nevertheless, like the Zaydi Shias of Iraq in the ninth and tenth centuries, who had to adapt themselves to the existing adverse conditions, the Zaydiyya did not hesitate to employ taqiyya.

A second group, the Ismailiyya—who traced the Imamate through al-Sadiq's son Ismail and whose several subdivisions, such as the Druze, the Nusayris, and Ali Ilahis, formed the bulk of the radical group called ghulat—adopted a radical posture and led the most successful revolutionary movement in Islam. During the tenth century, the leader of the Ismaili movement, Ubayd Allah al-Mahdi, established the Fatimid caliphate and proclaimed himself the caliph of the entire Muslim world. The Fatimids built up a large empire stretching from North Africa and including Egypt and several other parts of the Muslim world including Yemen. The fundamental belief among the Ismailis was the distinction between the *zahir* (exoteric) and the *batin* (esoteric) aspects of Islamic revelation. The exoteric aspect was the apparent meaning of the revelation and its application in the praxis, which changed with the emergence of a new prophet. The esoteric aspect consisted of the inner meanings of the revelation, which remained unchanged and the interpretation of which was available to the infallible Imam as the political and religious leader of humankind. The Ismailis aimed at abrogating all the religious laws and believed that at the advent of the Mahdi, a new religious era with a universal religion would be instituted.

A third group, the Imamiyya, or the Twelvers, formed the majority of the Shiites and the appellation of the Shia generally applies to them. Their doctrinal position in relation to the other two groups is regarded as intermediate and their religious and historical works are the most accessible of all the Shiite literature.

Shiite Theology and Jurisprudence: Fundamental principles of Shiism consist of five tenets: (1) the affirmation of the unity of God; (2) belief in the justice of God; (3) belief in prophecy; (4) belief in the Imamate; and (5) belief in the Day of Judgment. In four of these principles, that is 1, 2, 3, and 5, Shiites in general share a common ground with the Sunnites, although there are differences on points of detail. The belief in the justice of God is similar to that of the Mutazilites. In the ninth and tenth centuries, when the theological exposition of the Shiite school was being worked out, its theologians adopted an essentially Mutazilite rational theology in which reason was prior to both sources of revelation, the Qur'an and the Sunna. Accordingly, reason guides a person to ethical knowledge and asserts that good and evil are rational categories, independent of whether or not revelation declares them as such. The fourth principle, the Imamate, the Sunnites do not consider as a fundamental principle of religion, while the Shiites make it their central and cardinal principle.

Shiite jurisprudence confers on reason the priority in accord with its rational theology. The comprehensiveness of Islamic revelation had to be discovered, interpreted, and applied by use of reason. Accordingly, in their legal theory, alongside the Qur'an, the Sunna, and the consensus (*ijma*) of the jurists, which were admitted as sources for deducing rulings of the Sharia by the Sunni legal scholars, the Shiites included reasoning as the fourth source. However, it was not for just anyone to undertake the rational interpretation of the revelational sources. Only a religiously qualified person could assume the authority (wilaya) that accrued to the imam as the rightful ruler in Islam. This authority in Shiism was invested in a mujtahid (jurisprudent) who applied *ijtihad* (independent reasoning) in issuing judicial decisions (*fatwa*). Moreover, the Shiites included the communications of their Imams as part of the Sunna, and although the Sunnites admitted little substantive variation from the Sunna in juridical content, the Shiites had their own compilations of hadith. After the Middle Ages, it was not until recently that religious-legal practice based on the Shiite school of law was formally acknowledged as valid by the Sunnite scholars in Egypt. *See also* Alids; Ali ibn Abi Talib; Hidden Imam; Husayn ibn Ali; imam; Imamate; Ismaili Shia; Ithna Ashari Shia; Sunni; Zaydi Shia.

shih-chieh (shuhr-jyeh; Chin., "deliverance from the corpse"), a miraculous mode of Taoist ascendance to immortality in medieval China. Insufficiently perfected to achieve simultaneous liberation with the spirit, the adept's body disappeared and observers found only clothing or other personal effects in its place. *See also* body; physiological techniques (Taoism).

Shih-ching (shuhr-jing; Chin., "Book of Poetry/Songs"), anthology of the earliest surviving Chinese religious hymns and poems in archaic language whose editorship is traditionally ascribed to Confucius; it is one of the Five Classics and source of much literary allusion. Compiled ca. sixth century B.C., it consists largely of ancient ceremonial songs originally performed to musical accompaniment during the court rituals of the early kings of the Chou dynasty; to these were added the "airs of the principalities," topically more varied, and lyrical love songs and popular refrains evocative of village life and nature. *See also* Confucianism (authoritative texts and their interpretation).

shih-shih wu-ai. *See* nonobstruction of phenomena and phenomena.

shimenawa (shee-may-nah-wah), Japanese sacred rope made of twisted straw with zigzag paper streamers used in Shinto to demarcate sanctified space or objects and to ward off evil influences. *See also* shrine.

shinbutsu bunri (sheen-boo-tsoo boon-ree; Jap., "kami-Buddha separation"), a Japanese government policy initiated in 1868 separating Buddhism and Shinto. The purpose was to establish Shinto as a state institution in service to the building of a modern nation. Shinto shrines, clergy, and rituals were separated from Buddhist temples, personnel, and rites, and the complex associations of Shinto gods with Buddhas and Bodhisattvas were nullified. The imperial household no longer participated in Buddhism. This government action precipitated unofficial physical attacks on Buddhism. In a process extending from 1882 to 1908, the state categorized Buddhism as a religion and Shinto rituals as nonreligious, obligatory rites of the state. *See also* shinbutsu shugo.

shinbutsu shugo (sheen-boo-tsoo shoo-goh; Jap., "kami-Buddha syncretism"), the Japanese assimilation of native Shinto with Buddhism, involving the identification of *kami* (divinities, divine presences) with various Buddhas and Bodhisattvas; this amalgamation was widely influential in Japan up to the Meiji Restoration, when Shinto was officially separated from Buddhism. *See also* Meiji Restoration; shinbutsu bunri; syncretism (Japan).

Shingon-shu (shin-gohn-shoo; Jap., "True Word Sect"; Jap. for Chin. *chen-yen,* trans. of Skt. *mantra*), sect of Japanese Buddhism devoted exclusively to Tantric practice. It was founded in Japan by Kukai (774–835; posthumous title, Kobo Daishi; also known colloquially as O Daishi Sama) at the beginning of the ninth century following his initiation in China in 805 by Hui-kuo. Kukai also became the successor to Hui-kuo shortly thereafter.

The main focus of the sect is Tantric ritual practice. Shingon practices were organized into a unified system by Kukai out of what had been two separate ritual traditions, Hui-kuo having been initiated into both of them. These two ritual traditions are in turn linked to two *mandalas* (cosmogonic diagrams) and two texts. The Taizo (Jap., "womb-repository"; Skt. *garbha*) mandala symbolizes enlightenment in the form of compassion. The main textual source for this mandala is the *Dai-nichi kyo* (Great Sun Sutra; Skt. *Mahavairochana Sutra*). The Kongo-kai (Jap., "vajra realm"; Skt. *vajradhatu*) mandala symbolizes enlightenment in the form of imperishable wisdom. The main textual source for this mandala is the *Kongo-cho gyo* (Vajra Crown Sutra; Skt. *Vajrashekhara Sutra*). The central deity of both mandalas is Dainichi (Great Sun Buddha; Skt. *Mahavairochana*), who is considered by the Shingon tradition to be the *dharmakaya* (Skt., "body of dharma"), the Buddha Body of Truth. The connection between Mahavairochana as the Great Sun Buddha and Amaterasu as the sun goddess provided one of the stimulants for the spread of Shingon in Japan.

In Shingon ritual, as in both Hindu and Buddhist Tantrism generally, practice is centered on recognition of the identity of the practitioner and the chief deity evoked in the ritual performance. Training in the sect involves the performance of four rituals in sequence over a period of one hundred days. This Training in Four Stages (Jap. *shido kegyo*) culminates in one of the most typical Tantric rituals, the *goma*. In this ritual, offerings are made into a fire built in a hearth on the altar. In keeping with the practice of ritual identification, the mouth of the hearth is visualized as simultaneously being the mouth of the Buddhas, Bodhisattvas, and other deities evoked in the ritual, as well as the practitioner's own mouth.

Two of the main centers of Shingon in contemporary Japan are the temple complex on Mt. Koya and Toji temple in Kyoto. *See also* fire ritual (Japan); Koya, Mt.; Kukai; mandala; Saigyo; Tachikawa-ryu; Tantrism (Buddhism).

Shinnyoen (shin-nyo-en; Jap.), a Japanese new religion founded by Ito Shinjo (1906–89) and his wife, Tomoji, in 1936. Using esoteric Shingon Buddhist rites and themes, Shinnyoen has, from the mid-1970s, developed into a mass movement, claiming by the late 1980s more than two million members. It takes as its sacred text the *Nirvana Sutra,* which it sees as teaching the way for all living creatures to realize their potential Buddhahood. Two of Ito's sons who died (Chibun, aged three, and Yuichi, aged fifteen) are venerated as having sacrificed themselves to alleviate the sufferings of others and to act as guides and guardians in the spirit world. *See also* Japan, new religions in.

Shinran (shin-rahn; 1173–1262), founder of Japanese Buddhist Jodo Shinshu ("True Pure Land" school). Shinran spent twenty years as a Tendai monk on Mt. Hiei but abandoned Tendai practices to follow Honen. When Honen was exiled to Shikoku, Shinran was exiled to Niigata prefecture, where he married Eshinni and proselytized. His marriage established the precedent of a married clergy for Jodo Shinshu and eventually led to the hereditary structure of Jodo Shinshu leadership. He later went to Ibaragi prefecture to teach and finally retired to Kyoto to write his major work, *Kyogyoshinsho* (Teaching, Practice, Faith and Enlightenment). Throughout his life, Shinran stressed the importance of reliance on the power of Amida (*tariki*) rather than one's own power (*jiriki*). He considered faith to be the primary cause of salvation, but he argued that it was given by Amida rather than developed by the believer. According to Shinran, Pure Land teachings were primarily for every person no matter how evil or corrupt, an interpretation that won many converts from the lower classes. *See also* Hiei, Mt.; Honen; Jodo Shinshu; Pure Land; Tannisho.

Shinto (shin-toh; Jap., "way of the *kami* [divinities, divine presences]"). Shinto arose in ancient Japan around the worship of *kami*, later interacted with Buddhism and Chinese traditions, and has continued as a major religious force up to the present. Shinto was not founded, but emerged gradually out of the myths, beliefs, and rituals of prehistoric Japan. Local mythical traditions were unified and codified in the eighth-century *Kojiki* and *Nihonshoki* (*Nihongi*), which blended the accounts of many kami into a central tale of creation of the Japanese islands and descent of the emperor (considered a kami) from the sun goddess (Amaterasu). Although these writings record the "age of the gods" (and court chronicles), they are not considered scriptures in the sense that other religions use the term (e.g., for the Vedas, Qur'an, or Bible).

The indigenous religious heritage in Japan was local in nature and not highly organized until about the middle of the first millennium, when Buddhism and Chinese influence entered Japan; at this time the earlier Japanese religious beliefs and practices received the name Shinto and came to be more formally institutionalized and codified, partly in reaction to and also in relation to Buddhism, Taoism, and Confucianism. The most distinctive feature of the prehistoric heritage that continued within Shinto is the belief in and worship of kami. The term kami (sing. or pl.) refers to the sacred, pure, or powerful and can be expressed in a number of different forms: as mythological kami (usually distinguished as heavenly and earthly), as local forces of creation and nature (such as sacred mountains, waterfalls, rivers, trees, and boulders), emperors (manifest kami), and even powerful human beings.

In the earliest times kami were apparently worshiped at ritual sites in natural surroundings. Later, wooden shrines were built to house

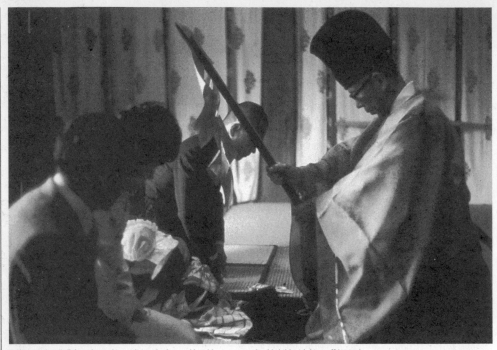

A Shinto priest in Tokyo, dressed in traditional robes and hat, blesses a month-old child with his staff (1980s).

such ceremonies, but kami were not considered to permanently reside in the shrines; rather, they were temporarily invoked for ceremonies of prayer and offerings and then "sent away." Rituals have been closely associated with seasons and growth, such as spring planting and fall thanksgiving, the new year, and periodic purification rites. In general, the Shinto tradition and participants in Shinto have assumed the presence of kami in the natural setting, and there has been no strong theological tradition to demonstrate the existence of kami; nor has there been creedal affirmation of belief in kami. On the local scene, to be a member of a village meant to participate in the annual festivals of the local Shinto shrine as a matter of course. In fact, it can be argued that the heart of Shinto is in the variety of local traditions and general assumption of the presence of kami in the life of nature and the nation. Until late medieval times shrines did not have specifically named kami, and local people worshiped their tutelary kami rather than a particular mythological kami.

From the time Buddhism and Chinese culture entered Japan, Shinto was directly influenced by these traditions and was practiced in close connection with them, especially with Buddhism. Shinto continued its ancient priestly customs of abstinence and purification as a precondition to ritual, but Shinto became intertwined with Buddhism (and Taoism); Buddhist priests served Shinto shrines, Buddhist scriptures were recited, and Buddhist rituals were performed at Shinto shrines. A common practice was to build Shinto shrines and Buddhist temples next to each other.

In recent and modern times two dates are of crucial significance for Shinto: 1868 and 1945. In 1868 the Meiji Restoration not only "restored" the emperor to rule (in place of the military ruler, or *shogun*), but also forcibly separated Shinto from Buddhism and at least temporarily made Shinto a primary force in the government of the nation-state; this practically made Shinto the established religion. With 1945 came not only the end of World War II, but a new era for Shinto—the victorious Allied forces brought about the emperor's renunciation of divinity and the disestablishment of Shinto. Since 1945, Shinto is one among a number of religious options for the Japanese people, and although some country shrines have fallen into disrepair and disuse, famous old shrines and large city shrines have flourished with many visitors during their seasonal festivals. *See also* Engi-shiki; Ise Shinto; Japanese religion; Japanese religions (festal cycle); kami; Ryubo Shinto; Sect Shinto (Kyoha

Shinto); shrine; Shrine Shinto (Jinja Shinto); Yuiitsu Shinto.

shirk (Arab., "associating"), a form of disbelief in Islam. Originally referring to polytheism, the term refers now to any religious and political belief deemed un-Islamic.

Shiromani Gurdwara Prabandhak Committee. *See* SGPC.

Shitala (shee'tuh-lah; Bengali, "the Cool One"), the northeast Indian goddess of pox, especially smallpox; pockmarks are euphemistically labeled the "grace of the Mother."

Shiva (shi'vuh; Skt., "auspicious"), one of the great pan-Hindu gods. His name in Sanskrit is a hopeful euphemism, since many of his aspects are inauspicious. He is often linked with Vishnu and Brahma in a trinity in which Shiva plays the role of destroyer. This aspect is traceable to a Vedic god, the uncanny, liminal, and wild Rudra, who is mentioned only briefly and uneasily in the *Rig Veda*, but is praised in the "hundred names of Rudra" (*shatarudriya*) of the *White Yajur Veda* and is worshiped with devotion in the *Shvetashvatara* Upanishad.

The epics tell how Shiva destroys the universe by dancing his *tandava* dance or by transfixing three demonic cities with a single arrow. He also destroyed the sacrifice of his father-in-law, Daksha, to which he had not been invited, after Sati, Daksha's daughter and Shiva's wife, killed herself in what becomes the paradigm for suttee. Shiva beheaded Daksha but then restored him with the head of a sacrificial goat after he had been mollified with hymns of praise. Shiva also cut off one of the five heads of Brahma to punish him for committing incest with his (Brahma's) daughter, the Dawn. The head stuck to Shiva's hand as he wandered through India, until it fell in Banaras at a spot henceforth known as "The Release of the Skull" (*kapalamocana*). Shiva's devotees, including Kapalikas ("skull-bearers"), who carry skulls in emulation of him, regard Banaras as Shiva's sacred city.

Linga: Shiva is also god of the erect phallus (*linga, lingam*). Some have traced this aspect to the ithyphallic figure who appears on a single seal from the Indus Valley civilization (and who may also be seated in a yogic position, another characteristic of Shiva) or to phallic images found more generally in prehistoric India. Other sources of Shiva's phallicism are the Vedic gods Indra (who, like Shiva, is castrated in epic mythology) and Agni (who, like Shiva, gives his fiery seed to the Ganges). The epics and Puranas also tell how a great pillar of fire appeared from the cosmic waters, and from this flame linga Shiva emerged to claim supremacy and worship over Brahma and Vishnu. And when Shiva seduced the sages' wives in the pine forest and they castrated him, all procreation ceased until they established the worship of his linga.

Shiva is also worshiped as the husband of Parvati, daughter of the mountain Himalaya (and reincarnation of Sati). He is father of Skanda, general of the gods, and stepfather of Ganesha, whom Parvati created by herself and whom Shiva beheaded and then restored with an elephant's head. Shiva's "vehicle" is the bull Nandi, which often lies devotedly before his temples.

Yogi: Shiva is also the god of *yogins* and ascetics; he meditates in the Himalayas, draped with snakes and smeared with the ashes of corpses. As a yogin, he is emulated by ascetic sects such as the Naths and Aghoris in North India and the Virashaivas in South India. With his *tapas* (inner heat generated by yogic praxis), Shiva released a flame from his third eye and burned to ashes Kama, god of erotic love, when Kama shot a fiery arrow of passion at Shiva in a vain attempt to force him from his meditations. But Shiva revived Kama in a disembodied form even more powerful and pervasive than it had been before. Shiva thus expresses not only his own ambivalence (as phallic god who is the ally of Kama, and yogin who is Kama's enemy) but a more profound and widespread tension between the fires of asceticism and eroticism.

Unlike Vishnu, Shiva does not ordinarily have avatars (incarnations); but he has manifested himself in various forms, and his epiphanies are memorialized in the local texts of shrines ranging from the great temple complexes of Khajuraho in the north and Madurai in the south to simple mounds of clay, honored with a few flowers or fruits, beside sacred trees and ponds. *See also* linga; Lingayat; Shaivism; Shakti.

shofar (shoh-fahr'; Heb., "ram's horn"), instrument blown liturgically on the Jewish holy day Rosh Hashanah and at the conclusion of Yom Kippur. *See also* Judaism (festal cycle).

Shoghi Effendi Rabbani. *See* Baha'i.

shogun (shoh-guhn; Jap., "generalissimo"), Japanese imperial military title assumed by a succession of leaders of military governments (*bakafu*) from Minamoto Yoritomo (1192–99) to Tokugawa Ieyasu and his successors (1603–1867). *See also* Meiji Restoration.

Shotoku, Prince (shoh-toh-*koo*; 574–622), second son of Emperor Yomei and regent for Empress Suiko, who played a major role in establishing Buddhism in Japan and encouraging the active acquisition of Chinese culture. Commentaries on Buddhist works are attributed to him. Later, various legends about him contributed to a flourishing cult. At times he was identified as an incarnation of Kannon (Avalokiteshvara) or Sakyamuni or as the reborn Chinese T'ien-t'ai master Hui-ssu (515–577). *See also* Soga clan.

shou (show; Chin., "long life"), Chinese ideal of longevity. The goal of preserving life was fundamental throughout Chinese tradition. Many felt it vital to seek either prolonged life in the present body or continued spiritual existence as a *hsien*, or immortal. *See also* hsien.

Shou-hsing (shoh-shing; Chin., "star of longevity"), a stellar deity in Chinese popular religion. Pictured with white beard, staff, and peach, he determines the date of each person's death. *See also* Chinese popular religion.

shou-i (shoh-ee; Chin., "preserving the one"), Taoist term for mystical technique of returning to, and maintaining, unity with the Tao. *See also* Tao.

shraddha (shruhd'dah; Skt., "trust"), in Vedic and later India, an abstract noun expressing trust, especially in the efficacy of ritual and teaching. It was sometimes deified as a goddess, Shraddha. *See also* sacrifice.

shrauta rites (shrow'tuh; Skt., from *shruti,* "what is heard," i.e., the Vedas), Vedic sacrifices (*yajnas*) performed by a consecrated sacrificer (*yajamana*) employing as many as seventeen priests. As early as ca. 800 B.C., textual branches of the Vedas called *Shrauta Sutras* were compiled, manuals detailing elaborate schedules of sacrifices accompanied by *mantras* (sacred utterances) to various deities. Basic offerings (*homas*) into the altar fires included milk in the fundamental shrauta rite, the *agnihotra*, twice daily to Agni; grain cakes of rice, barley, millet; domestic animals; juice of the *soma* plant; water, butter, honey, and *sura*, a grain beverage. Great soma rituals such as the royal consecration or horse sacrifice extended for two or three years. *See also* sacrifice.

Shri Aurobindo (shree ohr-oh-bin'doh; 1872–1950),

Hindu leader who taught "Integral Yoga." After leading extremist nationalists (conceiving the independence struggle as "yoga"), he retired in 1912 and combined Eastern and Western ideas to view reality as a spiritual/physical evolution of the Absolute, best understood through a consciousness that transcends reason. *See also* Reform Hinduism; yoga.

Shri-Lakshmi (shree-luhk'shmee; Skt., "the auspicious one"), a Hindu goddess associated with wealth, royalty, good luck, and auspiciousness; she is the consort of the god Vishnu. She is associated with the lotus and the fertility, growth, and vigor of the world. *See also* auspicious, inauspicious (Hinduism); Vishnu.

Shrimala (shree-mah'lah; Skt.), queen of Ayodhya, the main character in the *Shrimala Sutra,* a Mahayana Buddhist text teaching the One Vehicle and the Tathagatagarbha ("Buddha-essence"). *See also* Mahayana.

shrine, a sacred place usually commemorating a holy person by housing relics or being constructed over the tomb. *See also* holy person; pilgrimage; relics; stupa.

Christianity: A shrine is a sacred place marked off as a monument or sanctuary to which pilgrims come for prayer, devotion, or in expectation of supernatural intervention.   *See also* Fatima, Shrine of; Guadalupe, Shrine of; Lourdes; Mary (pilgrimage sites); pilgrimage; relics; saint.

Interior of the Roman Catholic shrine at the Jasna Gora Monastery, Poland, containing the portrait, traditionally ascribed to St. Luke, of the Black Madonna of Czestochowa. The shrine is a major pilgrimage site, and the Black Madonna is considered the patron queen of Poland. In recent years her image has been depicted on badges of the Polish Solidarity movement.

Islam: Shrines are usually centered around tombs, graves, or courts of sacred persons. An important exception, since it is not a grave site,

graves. Annual festivals are held to commemorate the death anniversary (*urs*) of the saint, and these are occasions for rituals that may include poetry and music recitals, even at bazaars and places of entertainment. Muslim purists, such as the Wahhabis of Saudi Arabia, condemn many aspects of shrine visitation as being innovations not practiced by Muhammad and as continuations of pre-Islamic practices, (e.g., the veneration of sacred trees).

Many of the shrines are considered to be places of spiritual power (*baraka*), where the sick or mentally ill can be brought for cure. Thus, the reasons for visiting shrines may vary, from the seeking of worldly gains, such as having a child or passing an examination, to the attaining of the spiritual benefits of communing with the spirit of the saint through intuitions, visions, or dreams. In some countries, shrines are presided over by the descendants of the saint entombed there, while in others the government has appointed civil servants as custodians because these shrines may be political power bases and important sources of revenue. *See also* baraka; Ibn al-Arabi, Muhyi ad-Din; Islam (festal cycle); Kaaba; Karbala; Mecca; Medina; pilgrimage.

Japanese Religion: In the earliest times, *kami* (divinities, divine presences) were worshiped in natural settings, with a specific area set aside as sacred. From early historic times there arose an architectural style of shrines of thatched buildings on raised pillars. Kami either resided in the shrine within a sacred object (*goshintai*) or were invoked through prayer, offerings, and rituals, and then sent away. Only rarely do Shinto shrines (*jinja*) house sculpture and paintings (which is a common feature of Japanese Buddhist temples).

Shinto shrines vary considerably in size, style, and local tradition, but some general hallmarks may be offered. Usually the approach to a shrine is signaled by the presence of a *torii*, or sacred archway. After passing through this archway, a devout visitor proceeds then to a *temizuya*, which provides running water for rinsing hands and mouth (for purification), then climbs the steps of the *haiden* (hall of worship). There the person rings a bell by swinging a rope, places money in an offering box, claps hands and bows, perhaps sending up a silent prayer. The *honden*, or main hall, is reserved for purified priests who present offerings and prayers on special occasions. *See also* Gion Shrine; himorogi; Honganji; Inari shrine; Ise Shrine; iwakura; iwasaka; Izumo Shrine; Japanese religions (art and architecture); jingu-ji; Kamo

The Mosque of the Prophet in Medina, Saudi Arabia, the second holiest city in Islam. This mosque is second only to the Great Mosque at Mecca in sanctity. By tradition, Muhammad worked on the construction of the original place of worship; his tomb is within the building, as are those of his early followers Abu Bakr and Umar.

is the main shrine of Islam, the holy Kaaba at Mecca, which marks the direction of prayer for Muslims and is the goal of the annual Hajj (Arab., "pilgrimage"). The tomb of the Prophet Muhammad (d. 632), which is housed in the mosque of Medina, Saudi Arabia, is also a site of pilgrimage for Muslims, who traditionally spend eight days (forty prayers) in the city so as to complete their visitation cycle to the shrine.

Pilgrimages are made by Shiite Muslims to the tombs of the descendants of the Prophet and his family, whom Shiites regard as the heirs of the Prophet's charisma. The major Shiite shrines are at Karbala and Najaf in Iraq and at Mashhad in Iran. All over the Muslim world the tombs of Sufi saints are sites for visitation.

Shrines that develop around tombs are often the sites of vowing behavior, which is evidenced by pilgrims tying strings to the latticework of the shrine or to nearby trees, and by donating gifts to the shrine, such as cloth mantles to cover the

shrine; Kasuga Shrine; Kitano Daimyojin; Kumano, Mt.; mountains, sacred; Omiwa Shrine; Shinto; Sumiyoshi shrine; torii.

Miniature Shinto *kami* ("sacred presence") shrines at Mt. Koya, one of the holy mountains of Japan.

Korean Religion: The national shrines of Korea include all the dynastic shrines (Kor. *chongmyo*) of the various ruling houses, the Shrine to Culture (Munmyo) maintained at the National Academy in Seoul (Songgyun'gwan), the altars to heaven and earth, and the altar to the god of land and grain (*sajidan*). One could also include all government-sponsored temples (Buddhist and Taoist) during the Koryo and Choson periods (918–1910), the shrines to Tan'gun and Kija (now located in North Korea), and the memorial shrines to the Korean War dead and General Yi Sunshin, a defender of Korea during the seventeenth century. At one time each of these shrines had its own regularly scheduled ceremonies that were carried out at government expense and according to law. Today the Korean government maintains these shrines as cultural properties, but worship is voluntary or is carried out by private associations. *See also* academies (Korea), private and public; Haein Temple; Shrine to Culture; Sokkuram Grotto.

Shriners, or the Ancient Arabic Order of the Nobles of the Mystic Shrine, an American parallel organization of high-degree Freemasons devoted to secular activities such as clowning, parades, and philanthropy. *See also* Freemasonry.

Shrine Shinto (Jinga Shinto), the worship of *kami* (divinities, divine presences) at local shrines, distinguished from Sect Shinto by having no founder. *See also* Sect Shinto (Kyoha Shinto); Shinto.

Shrine to Culture (Kor. *Munmyo*), one of the oldest religious institutions on the Korean peninsula.

Dedicated to the spirits of Confucius and his worthy Chinese and Korean disciples, it has been and continues to remain the locus of spring and autumn feasting rituals (*sokchon*) that celebrate and promote Korean adherence to Confucian values.

The first Shrines to Culture were established in the Three Kingdoms period (57 B.C.–A.D. 668), when each state established an educational institution for the training of bureaucrats in the Confucian tradition and it was at these schools that statues and portraits of Confucius and his disciples were first honored. In the succeeding Unified Silla (668–935), Koryo (918–1392), and Choson (1392–1910) periods, a single National Academy (Taehak) was established in the capital and on its grounds was erected a Shrine to Culture. With the establishment of public academies in provincial capitals (*hyanggyo*) during the Choson period, smaller versions of the Shrine to Culture were likewise erected.

It was in the Koryo period that the kings first began to honor Korean scholars as models of learning and virtue by installing their spirit tablets in the Shrine to Culture. The first Korean spirit tablets to be placed in the shrine were those of Ch'oe Ch'iwon (858–895) and Sol Ch'ong (ca. 661–700). Later the number of Korean scholars so honored was raised to eighteen. By the eighteenth century the spirit tablets of 113 Chinese and eighteen Korean scholars were enshrined and by the beginning of the twentieth century there were over 208 tablets enshrined. Today only the tablets to Confucius, the Four Assessors, the Ten Philosophers, the Six Sung Sages, and the Eighteen Korean Scholars are enshrined in the main hall.

Though Confucianism today is no longer a state religion, private Confucian societies continue to maintain the order of rites (sokchon) at the Shrine to Culture. These rites are religious banquets for the spirits of the enshrined and are offered at the spring and autumn equinoxes. The order of the rite includes the advent of officiants, the welcoming of the spirits, the offering of food, three offerings of wine, three ritual prostrations, the removal of food vessels, and the ritual dispatching of the spirits. While this is being done, traditional music and ritual dances are performed in the courtyard in front of the shrine hall. The music and dances performed during the sokchon are derived from Sung and Ming sources but were revised in the fifteenth century by King Sejong. The costumes of the officiants, musicians, and dancers follow Ming-dynasty style. *See also* academies (Korea), private and public; shrine.

Shrivaishnavism (shree-vish-nahv'iz-uhm), name given to the Hindu community that worships Vishnu and his consorts Shri-Lakshmi, Bhu (the goddess Earth), and Nila. Although the word *Shrivaishnava* occurs in inscriptions in the Tiruvengadam (Tirupati) temple around the tenth century, the community became organized around the time of the eleventh-century theologian Ramanuja, whom they consider to be their principal teacher and interpreter of scripture.

The Shrivaishnava community differs from other Hindu traditions in that it considers not only Sanskrit texts such as the Vedas, the *Bhagavad Gita,* and the epics as sacred, but holds the Tamil compositions of the twelve poet-saints (Alvars) as revealed and on par with the Sanskrit Vedas. Specifically, the *Tiruvaymoli* (Sacred Utterance) of Nammalvar is considered to be the Tamil or Dravida Veda. The Shrivaishnava community refers to its scriptural heritage as *ubhaya vedanta,* or dual Vedic theology. The Alvars are honored in the Shrivaishnava temples. The community also considers the 108 temples that the Alvars glorified to be heaven on earth; worship in these Vishnu temples is conducted with selections from Sanskrit and Tamil scripture.

While Ramanuja held both devotional praxis (*bhakti yoga*) and surrender to Vishnu as ways to liberation, in later generations the community became divided over this issue. The subsects came to be called the Vatakalai ("northern culture") and Tenkalai ("southern culture"). While these names are of later origin, the philosophical differences can be traced back at least to the thirteenth-century writings of Vedanta Deshika and Pillai Lokacharya, the leading teachers of the Vatakalais and Tenkalais.

Although many of the spiritual teachers of the community are Brahmans, Shrivaishnavas may be from of any caste, including the so-called outcasts. Members of this community are primarily from the southern states of Tamil Nadu, Karnataka, and Andhra Pradesh, but their temples, especially those in Tiruvengadam and Shrirangam, and more recently the temple in Penn Hills, Pennsylvania, are popular centers of pilgrimage in the larger Hindu tradition. *See also* Alvar; cat-hold doctrine; Dravidian; monkey-hold doctrine; Nammalvar; Pancharatra; path of devotion; Ramanuja; Tiruvaymoli; Vaikhanasa; Vaishnavism.

Shroud of Turin, the purported burial cloth of Jesus preserved since late medieval times in a chapel adjacent to the cathedral in Turin, Italy. This cloth, because of a stained image that in photographic negative reveals the clear outlines of a man, has been the object of pious attention. Recent tests (1988) suggest that the relic is no older than the late medieval period. *See also* relics.

shruti. *See* Hinduism (authoritative texts and their interpretation).

shu (shoo; Chin., "forbearance"), Confucian virtue of consideration for others; it involves restraining one's responses to others on the basis of the restraint one seeks from them. Acting this way makes rulers respectable and prepares one for humane interaction. Confucius summarized his teaching as "faithfulness (*chung*) and forbearance." *See also* Confucianism.

Shu-ching (shoo-jing; Chin., "Book of History," also known as *Sheng-shu,* "Book of Documents"), compilation of the oldest transmitted historical documents in the Confucian canon, dating from the ninth to the sixth centuries B.C. Deriving from the royal court, the documents consist largely of political harangues, religious exhortations, and ritual texts resembling in language and tone the patents of investiture and other records of a commemorative or archival character inscribed on the ritual bronze vessels. Among the authentically early texts are speeches attributed to the duke of Chou (Chou Kung) that set forth the doctrine of the Mandate of Heaven (T'ien-ming) and the Chou indictment of Shang misrule. *See also* Chou Kung; Confucianism (authoritative texts and their interpretation), T'ien-ming.

Shudra (shoo'druh), lowest of the four traditional Hindu social classes, or *varnas.* Shudras, traditionally excluded from participation in Hindu rituals and study of the Veda, have as their sole religious duty serving members of the higher classes. *See also* caste.

Shugendo (shoo-gen-doh; Jap., "way of mastering power"), a distinctive Japanese form of ascetic practice on sacred mountains. Combining indigenous Japanese notions of *kami* (divinities, divine presences) residing in Japanese mountains with Taoist concepts of mountain wizards and Buddhist practices of mountain ascents, the legendary founder En-no-gyoja (En-no-shokaku) pioneered a form of asceticism and religious practice developed on many mountains from medieval to early modern times; some groups are still active today. *See also* asceticism; En-no-gyoja; kami; mountains, sacred.

Shulhan Arukh (shool-khahn' ah-rookh'; Heb., "set table"), the code of Jewish religious law by Joseph Karo. Published in 1565, the work covers (1) ritual obligations of everyday life from dawn to dusk, including blessings, prayers, and observances of Sabbaths and festivals (*orakh khayyim*); (2) laws governing the conduct of life and life passages, dietary laws, mourning, ethics, piety, and religious virtues, respect for parents, charity (*yoreh deah*); (3) laws of marriage, divorce, and other questions of personal status (*ehven haezer*); (4) civil law and institutions of the community of Judaism (*khoshen mishpaht*). The *Shulhan Arukh* has been translated into the languages of all the places Jews live and is consulted for everyday guidance. *See also* Karo, Joseph; mitzvah; Torah.

Shun. *See* Yao, Shun, and Yu.

shunning, Christian denominational practice of forbidding social contact with members who have breached church discipline or committed immoral acts. *See also* excommunication.

shunyata. *See* emptiness.

Shushigaku (shoo-shee-gah-koo), Japanese Neo-Confucianism of the tradition of the Chinese philosopher Chu Hsi, which was introduced via Zen monasteries during the Kamakura period (1185–1333) and flourished in the Tokugawa period (1600–1868). Metaphysically it stressed the interaction of principle (*ri*) and material force (*chi*); politically it advocated "benevolent government"; and ethically it stressed the importance of self-cultivation. *See also* Chu Hsi; Japan, Confucianism in; Neo-Confucianism; ri.

Shvetambara. *See* Jainism.

Sibylline oracles (si-bil-een'), in Greek and Roman tradition ecstatic prophecies attributed to an aged woman called the Sibyl. Fragments of Roman, Jewish, and Christian collections survive, containing oracles from the fourth century B.C. through the fourth century A.D. *See also* Roman religion.

Siddhartha (sid-hahr'tah; Skt., "He whose aims are fulfilled"), the given personal name of the Buddha in later Buddhist traditions. *See also* Buddhas.

siddhi (si'dee; Skt., "accomplishment"), either of two kinds of attainment gained by the Buddhist saint; wordly *siddhi* includes various supernormal powers, and supreme siddhi is the attainment of enlightenment. *See also* enlightenment.

Siddur (see-door'; Heb., "order [of prayers]"), in Judaism, daily and Sabbath prayer book, first compiled in the ninth century. *See also* Judaism, prayer and liturgy of.

sign of the cross, a Christian ritual gesture practiced since the late second century of tracing a cross on the forehead with the thumb of the right hand or touching the forehead, chest, and both shoulders. The sign is usually made by both Catholic and Orthodox Christians before prayers are said. The gesture is also in the liturgy, especially at the mention of the three Persons of the Trinity and by clergy when blessing persons (e.g., at baptism) or things.

Sikh Dharma. *See* Healthy-Happy-Holy Organization; Sikhism in the West.

Sikhism (sik'iz-uhm), a religious tradition that originated in the Punjab region of North India and encompasses over sixteen million people, most of them Punjabis, who live in India and around the world. They revere a lineage of sixteenth- and seventeenth-century Gurus, respect a book (the *Adi Granth*) that contains the Gurus' teachings, and possess a strong sense of communal identity symbolized by the characteristic turbans and beards worn by Sikh men.

Early Sikh History: The ten Gurus dominate the first phase of Sikh history (sixteenth–seventeenth centuries), in which a small religious fellowship swelled into a significant movement. The Sikh tradition began with the teachings of Guru Nanak (1469–1539), who was considered by many scholars to have been a *sant*—one of the poet-singers of medieval India who preached the need for loving devotion (Skt. *bhakti*) to a formless, nonanthropomorphic God. He urged his small group of followers to meditate on the divine name (Punjabi *Nam*), and anyone who absorbed his teachings was called a "learner"—a *sikh*.

After Guru Nanak's death, most Sikhs felt that his spiritual authority had been transferred to one of his disciples, Angad (1504–52). A few Sikhs regarded Guru Nanak's son as his real successor, and they formed a separate community, the Udasis. The main community of Sikhs grew over the years as each Guru was succeeded by another, and more disciples were brought into the fold. Guru Angad compiled Guru Nanak's hymns, adopting for liturgical purposes a distinctive script, Gurmukhi ("from the mouth of the Guru"). His successor, Guru Amar Das (1479–1574), divided the growing community into specific congregations. His son-in-law,

Guru Ram Das (1534–81), succeeded him and founded a city that came to be known as Amritsar and that is regarded as the sacred center of the faith. Succeeding him was his son, Guru Arjan (1563–1606), who is credited with creating the Sikh's sacred book, the *Adi Granth*, by compiling the poetry of the Sikh Gurus and such medieval sants as Kabir, Ram Das, and Namdev. Guru Arjan constructed the Sikhs' main pilgrimage center in Amritsar, Harmandir ("Temple of God"), or Darbar Sahib ("Sanctuary of the Lord"), also known by its English name, the Golden Temple. Guru Arjan found himself increasingly occupied with fending off the Moghuls' attempts to control his community. His son, Guru Hargobind (1595–1644), who succeeded him, developed the military strength of the community and advanced the concept of *miri-piri*, the notion that Sikhs follow both secular and sacred swords of leadership. Guru Har

A Sikh family on pilgrimage to the "Golden Temple." Constructed ca. 1589 to 1603 and rebuilt during the reign of Maharaja Rajit Singh (d. 1839), it is the Sikhs' chief house of worship and place of pilgrimage. The Amritsar ("Pool of Nectar") lies before the temple.

Rai (1630–61) was only fourteen when he succeeded Guru Hargobind, his grandfather; his reign was preoccupied with the Moghul threat. He was succeeded by his son, Guru Har Krishan (1656–64), who became the Sikhs' master when he was only five and died of smallpox a few years later. His successor was his great uncle, Guru Tegh Bahadur (1621–75), a son of Guru Hargobind; he is remembered for his travels and his martyrdom at the hands of Moghuls. He is said to have been executed because he refused to convert to Islam.

Guru Tegh Bahadur's son, Guru Gobind Singh (1666–1708), was the last in the Sikh lineage, and many regard him second in importance only to Guru Nanak. He turned the Sikh fellowship (*panth*) into a brotherhood (*khalsa*). During the fall festival of Baisakhi in 1699, Guru

Gobind Singh is said to have instituted the Khalsa, imposing several requirements on the faithful: an initiation rite involving nectar (*amrit*) stirred with a double-edged sword; the wearing of five symbols—uncut hair, a comb, a steel wrist bangle, a sword, and short breeches—that begin (in the Punjabi language) with the letter *k*; and the adoption of his own name, Singh ("lion"), as the name for each man in the Khalsa, and Kaur ("princess") for each woman. Guru Gobind Singh, whose four sons had been killed in skirmishes with the Moghuls, is also said to have proclaimed that with him the line of Gurus had come to an end. Instead, the authority of guruship was to be conveyed through the Khalsa as a whole and through the writings of the *Adi Granth*, which has henceforth come to be called the *Guru Granth Sahib*. Guru Gobind Singh's own writings in the *Dasam Granth* are also highly revered.

Sikh Kingdoms in the Eighteenth and Nineteenth Centuries: The second stage of Sikh history (eighteenth to mid-nineteenth centuries) was dominated by the leadership of powerful Sikh princes and military commanders. After the death of Guru Gobind Singh, many Sikhs rallied behind Banda Singh, one of his disciples, in a rebellion against the Moghuls. With the disintegration of the Moghul empire in the mid-eighteenth century, a number of Sikh military groups, or *misls*, staked claims to parts of the Punjab. As these groups and their leaders established control, the popularity of Sikhism in their areas expanded enormously. Eventually, the leader of the misl in Shukarchakia, Ranjit Singh, emerged as dominant among his peers, and after conquering Lahore in 1799, he ruled as maharaja of the whole region, where he became known as the "one-eyed lion of the Punjab."

Maharaja Ranjit Singh had to confront a new enemy, however. The British had effectively replaced the Moghuls as imperial rulers, and in 1806 the Maharaja signed a treaty that for a time kept the British safely in Delhi and out of the Punjab. Soon after Ranjit Singh died in 1839, the British reasserted their territorial interests, and in 1846, at the conclusion of the first Anglo-Sikh war, they conquered Lahore and what was left of Ranjit Singh's kingdom. The Punjab had been the last independent kingdom in India to be conquered by the British.

Modern Movements and Organizations: The third stage of Sikh history (mid-nineteenth century to the present) was characterized by organizations that have brought definition to the faith and political power to the community. The most influential movement was the Singh Sabha, which began to form chapters in Punjabi cities in the 1870s and 1880s. The Sabha was the creation of a developing urban elite within the community who wanted a Sikh response to the challenges from Christian missionaries and the urban Hindu reform movement, the Arya Samaj, which claimed Sikhs as their own. The slogan of the Singh Sabha was *Hum Hindu Nahin Hain* ("We are not Hindus"). To prove the point, the Sabha began to legislate on matters of faith and custom, providing for the first time an orthodox standard for Sikh beliefs and practices. In 1902 the Chief Khalsa Diwan was created as an umbrella entity to govern all Sikh groups, one that would serve as the final arbiter in religious and organizational disputes. Sikhism as an "organized religion," therefore, can be said to have begun at the turn of the twentieth century.

As a result of the interest in maintaining a Sikh orthodoxy, a number of Sikhs attempted to assert control over their shrines and *gurdwaras* (places of worship, lit., "the thresholds of the Guru"), which had come to be managed by Udasis, Hindus, and other nonorthodox Sikhs. The movement crystallized in 1920 with the establishment of a Shiromani Gurdwara Prabandhak Committee (SGPC, "Central Gurdwara Management Committee"). In the same year a militia was formed to seize control over the gurdwaras: the Akali Dal ("army of immortals"). In 1924 the government acceded to its demands, turning the gurdwaras over to SGPC control, and creating a government-supported system of elections to select representatives to the SGPC. The Akali Dal was the major faction within the SGPC. During the independence movement it often supported Gandhi and the Indian National Congress; later, after India's independence in 1947, it emerged as a political party and became the major rival to the Congress Party in the Punjab.

When the Punjab was partitioned at the time of independence, the Sikhs in West Punjab migrated to the Indian side, many of them encamping for a time in Delhi. The creation of Pakistan inspired many Sikhs to demand a homeland for themselves. The first movement in this direction was the demand for a Punjabi Suba—a Punjabi-speaking state—where Sikhs would be in the majority. The movement was supported by the Akali Dal and the SGPC, and led by Master Tara Singh in 1961, and by Sant Fateh Singh, who underwent a protest fast, in 1966. The prime minister, Indira Gandhi, acceded to the Sikh demands, and a new Sikh-majority Punjab, along with a Hindu-dominated Haryana and Himachal Pradesh, were created out of the old Indian Punjab.

In the late 1970s a new demand arose for an independent Sikh homeland, Khalistan. This goal—along with the desire to purify Sikhism of its compromises with modern secularism and the urge to stand up to the rising power of Hindu politics in India—fueled an angry new militant movement led for a time by Jarnail Singh Bhindranwale. He was killed in 1984 in Operation Bluestar, the Indian army's attempt to rid the Golden Temple of militants. To avenge that act of desecration, Prime Minister Indira Gandhi was assassinated by her Sikh bodyguards in November 1984, and thousands of Sikhs were killed in ensuing riots. Unrest persisted in the Punjab well into the 1990s, as Sikhs throughout the world increasingly regarded their religious community as separate from Hinduism and free from its cultural ties to India.

Sikh Beliefs and Religious Practices: Although the Sikhs have a legitimate claim to comprising an autonomous religious community, their beliefs and practices display many of the elements of the cultures that have influenced the tradition over its five-hundred-year history. Like most Indians, including Hindus and Buddhists, Sikhs accept the idea of the karmic cycle of births and rebirths; the notion that the world is veiled in *maya*, "illusion;" and the importance of *dharma* (righteous behavior) in achieving spiritual merit. Sikhs, however, are likely to use the Muslim term *hukam* to refer to the divine order underlying all reality; and their dharmic obligations are prescribed in their own texts, the *Rahit-namas*. The Sikhs' definitive code of proper behavior and spiritual practice, the *Rahit Maryada*, was compiled in 1945.

Like India's medieval *sants*, Sikhs believe that God cannot be perceived in human or any other form; only the divine name (Nam) can be perceived, and therefore revered. Like Nath yogis, Sikhs attempt to become aware of the "unstruck sound" (*anahad shabd*) that lies at the heart of creation and to achieve more and more rarified inner states of consciousness. Unlike the Naths, however, Sikhs eschew any form of yoga. They regard meditation, communal worship (*kirtan*), and concentration on the divine name as sufficient means of achieving the highest state, Sachkhand, "the realm of truth."

The Sikh obeisance to the Guru goes beyond anything in the normative Hindu tradition: the Sikh Guru is the mediator of divine grace, the closest embodiment of divinity that can be known. The phrase *Wahi Guru* ("Praise to the Guru") has come to be a Sikh term for God. Sikhs believe that all ten of their founding Gurus were of the same divine essence, and for that reason popular Sikh art often portrays them looking substantially the same. The main holidays of Sikhism (*gurpurabs*) are the birthdays of Guru Nanak and Guru Gobind Singh, and the martyrdom day of the fifth Guru. Since the power of gu-

Treated as a living Guru, the Sikh holy book *Adi Granth* ("Original Book") is wrapped up for the evening and ritually opened and read in the morning. Compiled by the fifth Sikh Guru, Arjan, at Amritsar in 1603–04, it is the central object in all Sikh houses of worship (*gurdwaras*).

ruship is invested in the *Adi Granth*, the book is sometimes treated as a person: it is consulted for advice, and the names of children are usually determined by opening the *Adi Granth* soon after birth and beginning the child's name with the first letter that appears on the left-hand page. For special occasions, the whole of the *Adi Granth* is read out loud, an event that is called Akhand Path ("unbroken reading") and takes two days and two nights to complete.

In many ways the book is an object of devotion and functions, like a *murti* (image of god) in a Hindu temple. The *Adi Granth* occupies the place of honor on a raised platform in a gurdwara; it is garlanded, fanned, and covered with a cloth at night. Adherents bring to it offerings

and leave with *prasad* (blessed food, often a solid porridge made of honey and wheat, and a puffed rice candy). Unlike Hinduism, however, the faithful receive not only the sight (*darshan*) of the divinity, but also the sound, conveyed by the musical reading of the verses of the *Adi Granth* from a cantor known as a *granthi*. For pilgrimage, the Sikhs have special gurdwaras, including the Golden Temple in Amritsar and Guru Gobind Singh's Anandpur Sahib in the Himalayan foothills.

The Changing Sikh Community: Considering the Muslims' attempts to conquer them and the Hindus' efforts to absorb them, Sikhs have been understandably attentive to the need to preserve their distinctive identity. They greet each other with a unique salutation, "*Sat Sri Akal*" ("the true timeless Lord"), a phrase that is sometimes given in response to the cry, "*jo bole so nihal*" ("the one who speaks [this] will be blessed"). They frequently display the symbol of the two-edged sword surrounded by a circle, or even more frequently the *ekankar* symbol taken from the first phrase of Guru Nanak's morning prayer, the Japji, which is regarded as the "root *mantra*" (*Mulmantra*) of Sikhism. Even more striking are the symbols worn by Sikh men who observe the five Ks, especially the carefully groomed beards and long hair tied in colorful turbans.

A Sikh meditating at the "Golden Temple," Amritsar, Punjab. More than 80 percent of the world's Sikh population lives in India, most concentrated in the Punjab where there are more than one thousand Sikh houses of worship.

Not all Sikhs are strict in observing these practices, and a distinction is made within the Sikh community between the *keshdhari* (the long-haired ones) and the *sahajdhari* (the "path of simplicity" ones). The former are also known as *amritdhari*, those who have received the amrit (nectar) in the Sikh initiation rites. Increasingly the keshdhari standard is the one that is followed. As Sikhism develops a more rigid orthodoxy of thought and practice, a number of religious movements that once flourished under the Sikh umbrella have become peripheral to the Sikh mainstream. Among these are the Namdhari movement, the Radhasoami Satsang, and the Nirankaris. It was conflict between Jarnail Singh Bhindranwale and the Nirankaris in 1978 that began the spiral of violence that climaxed in the assassination of Indira Gandhi.

Other differences among Sikhs stem from caste. There are no priests and no priestly caste within Sikhism. Instead, two large caste groups have vied for leadership: urban merchant-caste Khatris and rural land-owning Jats. The ten founding Gurus were all Khatris: the first three were from the Bedi, Trehan, and Bhalla subcastes, respectively, and the other seven were members of the Sodhi subcaste. Before the end of the seventeenth century large numbers of Jats had joined the fold, and by the end of the eighteenth century they clearly dominated it. Many merchant-caste Sikhs reverted to Hinduism or became active in Namdhari, Nirankari, and Radhasoami movements. In the nineteenth century the Singh Sabha helped to make Sikhism respectable among members of urban castes, but the Sikh political entities of the twentieth century, including the Akali Dal and the SGPC, were again dominated by rural Jats. Increasingly many Jat Sikhs have moved from agriculture to positions in the army, police, and transportation services. Administrative, educational, and modern business positions, however, were largely occupied by Khatris and other urban castes. The militant movement led by Jarnail Singh Bhindranwale was supported primarily by rural Jat youth, many of whom felt excluded from what they regarded as their birthright: leadership in modern Punjab society.

Other Sikh caste groups, including the Tarkhans (carpenters, also known as Ramgharias), Aluwalias (brewers), and the so-called untouchable castes, Chamars (leatherworkers) and Chuhras (sweepers), have allied with one side, then another, in the Jat-Khatri competition. Chamars who are Sikhs are called Ramdasias, a name associated with the fourth Guru (Ram Das) and also with a medieval Marathi sant (Ramdas). Chuhras who are Sikhs are called Mazhabi, which means "the faithful," and sometimes serve as *granthis* in gurdwaras. In the 1920s and 1930s many Sikh members of untouchable castes broke away to form their own faith, Ad Dharm (Original Religion), as a way to avoid being used as pawns in the competition between castes and religions.

Sikhs from all castes are highly mobile people, and in the United States, the United Kingdom, Canada, Kenya, Fiji, and many other parts of the world, Sikhs comprise a disproportionately large percentage of the immigrant Indian community. In the United States, Caucasian Americans have joined what they call the Sikh Dharma Brotherhood. Increasingly, Sikhs abroad regard their faith as a world religion. Like their fellow Sikhs in the Punjab, they have begun to question to what extent their faith is linked to Indian culture and to what it extent it is part of an independent, global tradition. *See also* Adi Granth; Akali; Akal Purukh; Amritsar; Five Ks; Gobind Singh; Golden Temple; gurdwara; Gurmat; Gurmukhi; Gurpurab; Guru (Sikhism); Janamsakhi; Japji; Kaur; Khalsa; Namdhari; Nanak; Nihang; Nirankari; Panth; Punjab; rahit-nama; Sahajdhari; SGPC; Sikhism (authoritative texts); Sikhism in the West; Singh; Singh Sabha; turban; Udasi.

Sikhism (authoritative texts). The supremely authoritative text in the Sikh religion is the *Adi Granth,* or *Guru Granth Sahib.* Shortly before his death in 1708, Guru Gobind Singh declared that the status of Guru would be conferred on the scripture and the community. Throughout the eighteenth century the Sikhs placed the *Dasam Granth*—the writings of Gobind Singh and other materials—alongside the *Adi Granth,* treating the two as Guru. In the two hundred years since then, however, the *Dasam Granth* has receded, leaving the *Adi Granth* as supreme.

In interpreting the *Adi Granth* the devout Sikh treats it as the Guru personified, with every word treated as literally true. This does not create the same difficulties as a fundamentalist approach to the Christian Bible, for the *Adi Granth* consists overwhelmingly of songs in praise of God and of the way to achieve liberation. It does, however, serve as a caution to the scholar and may be one reason why interpretation of the *Adi Granth* is still a guarded enterprise. Several commentaries on the *Adi Granth* exist, but these go little further than explaining context and meaning.

The *Dasam Granth* still retains the title of Guru even though its actual status today is clearly well below that of the *Adi Granth.* Some of the works it records are attributed to Guru Gobind Singh and these compositions clearly rank with those of the *Adi Granth* as *gurbani* ("the Guru's word"). A substantial proportion of the *Dasam Granth* consists, however, of mythological stories that seem clearly to have come from retainers of the Guru. These compositions create problems, and the response over the last hundred years or more has been to put them aside. The works attributed to Guru Gobind Singh receive as much attention as those of the *Adi Granth*, but the remainder of the *Dasam Granth* is largely ignored. Language further compounds the problem as the Braj of the *Dasam Granth* is now little understood.

While two substantial scriptures are both regarded as the Guru, another category of text is occupied by the poems of two of the Gurus' followers, Bhai Gurdas and Bhai Nand Lal "Goya," whose works are approved for recitation in *gurdwaras* (Sikh houses of worship). Bhai Gurdas was a prominent Sikh, a relative of the third Guru and amanuensis for the fifth Guru when the *Adi Granth* was being compiled. In Punjabi he wrote 39 or 40 lengthy poems called Vars, and in Braj 556 brief poems. Bhai Nand Lal was a poet of Guru Gobind Singh's court, and he wrote his *Divan* and *Zindagi-nama* in Persian. Except for the Vars of Baih Gurdas, very little attention is paid to the poets' works. Language difficulties partly account for this.

These collections constitute the whole of the Sikh canon. Although other works have a conspicuous religious content, none of them can claim formal religious authority. *See also* Adi Granth; Dasam Granth; Gobind Singh; Guru (Sikhism); Sikhism.

Sikhism in the West. Since the early twentieth century, there has been an immigrant Sikh community in North America. In 1968 Yogi Bhajan (b. 1929), a Sikh from Delhi, began teaching in Los Angeles. Gathering an American following, he founded the Healthy Happy Holy Organization (3HO) in 1969. In 1971, Yogi Bhajan was recognized as the chief authority for the Sikh Dharma in the Western world, with 3HO as its educational bureau. This marks the first time in Sikh history that a group of people not of Punjabi descent and culture have adopted the Sikh faith. The number of Westerners in the Americas and Europe embracing the Sikh religion has grown to an estimated five to ten thousand. Western Sikhism is headquartered in Los Angeles, with a sizable population in northern New Mexico, were Sikhs gather at the time of summer solstice. Sikh ashrams exist in most major North American cities, many named after Guru Ram Das (1534–81), the fourth Sikh Guru and one for whom Western Sikhs have a particular affection. Adherents do not cut their hair, smoke, eat meat, or drink alcohol. Both men and women tie turbans and often dress in Eastern styles, preferring white cotton clothes. The majority have

identified themselves as Khalsa, an order established by Gobind Singh, the tenth Sikh Guru, in 1699. Their spiritual leader is Harbhajan Singh Khalsa Yogiji (Yogi Bhajan) who teaches kundalini and white Tantric yoga. *See also* Healthy-Happy-Holy Organization; Sikhism.

Silk Road, the ancient and medieval trade route that stretched from India through Afghanistan, Central Asia, and Xinjiang (Hsin Chiang) to China, with additional branches reaching as far as Persia and Rome in the West. It was along this road that Buddhism was first exported from India to East Asia (second to first centuries B.C.), taking root in a number of oasis communities along the way.

Buddhism along the Silk Road (a region also known as Central Asia, in contrast to Inner Asia, which applies to all of Central Eurasia, including Tibet and Mongolia) appears to have been quite conservative, rejecting the innovations introduced by the Mahayana schools (except in the city of Khotan) and preferring to transmit the Buddhist scriptures in their Indian originals rather than in local vernaculars. After the sixth century, however, Indian influence gradually yielded to that of China in the eastern part of this region, resulting in the widespread adoption of Mahayana Buddhism. Meanwhile, Islam had made significant inroads. By 1000, Khotan fell to the Muslims, and by the close of the Mongol period (1368) the entire region had shifted its allegiance from Buddhism to Islam. The importance of the Silk Road as a trade route diminished with the development of sea trade after the fifteenth century. *See also* Buddhism; China, Buddhism in; inner Asian religions.

Simon, Richard (1638–1712), French Catholic biblical scholar whose *Critical History of the Old Testament* (1678) was the first work to advance criteria for determining sources in the Pentateuch.

Simon Magus, also Simon the Magician, a controversial figure who was reviled as "the father of all heresy" by early Christian writers. Active in the mid-first century, Simon hailed from Gitta, Samaria, and traveled about as a miracle worker and as an incarnation of the "One God." Ever-present, Simon claimed, "In every heaven I took on a different form" (Epiphanius *Adversus Haereses* 21). Simon's partner was Helen (an incarnation of, among others, Helen of Troy), whom he had rescued from a brothel and who represented "Thought," the first female Gnostic principle that emanated from the "One God."

Lost in the deepest levels of material creation, the soul-symbol Helen was restored by her Christlike savior. Simon claimed that his grace provided salvation—there was no need to listen to the (biblical) prophets or to rely on good deeds.

Various Christian sources testify (more or less spuriously) to Simon's activities: he is portrayed in the New Testament (Acts 8) as a fake convert to Christianity and in the Pseudo-Clementine writings as a preacher and miracle-man competing with Peter (Peter wins). Hippolytos says that Simon tried to fly (an attempt at resurrection) but had a bad fall and later died. Another account states that a three-day stay in a grave killed him. Historically, not much is certain, but Simon probably founded a Gnostic group in Samaria. His self-description as an embodiment of "the highest power" and as "the Standing One" reflects a Samaritan-Jewish background. *See also* Gnosticism.

sin, an offense (usually deliberate) against a religious or moral law.

Judaism: In Judaism, sin is a violation of the stipulations of the covenant with God. Hebrew scripture uses a number of terms to signify sin, chief among them *het,* designating a failure to carry out a duty; *avon,* which refers to crookedness or transgression; and *pesha,* a serious breach of covenantal responsibility. Later rabbinic Judaism most commonly uses the general term *averah,* from a root meaning "to pass over." The rabbis thus convey their perception that a wrong deed is a sin insofar as it transgresses God's will as laid out in divine revelation.

The rabbinic literature distinguishes sins of commission, in which one does that which is expressly prohibited, from sins of omission, in which one fails to do what is required. Because they involve the individual's conscious action, sins of commission generally are considered more serious. The gravest of these are murder, idolatry, and sexual impropriety. These are the only sins that one may not commit under any circumstance, even if one is threatened with being killed (Babylonian Talmud *Sanhedrin* 74a).

The rabbis comparably distinguish intentional misdeeds (*zadon*) from actions that are unintentional (*shegagah*). Both categories of sin require expiation through appropriate punishment and/or payment to the injured party or, in the case of sins against God, sacrifice or (after the destruction of the Temple) prayer. Other things being equal, intentional actions, and especially intentional crimes against God, are the most severe types of sins, while unintentional wrongs against individuals are the lightest. Alongside this general perspective, however, the rabbis are cognizant of the context in which any particular act is performed: an otherwise minor infraction performed in public explicitly to disparage Judaism is of greater weight than a more serious infraction committed in private with no communal significance.

In line with Genesis 8:21, rabbinic Judaism holds that people are by nature inclined to sin. This evil inclination, the *yetzer ha-ra,* is perceived as an integral aspect of the human condition, a temptation to which all people are subject. The rabbinic notion of the evil inclination differs, however, from the Christian concept of original sin. According to Judaism, although subject to temptation, a heinous force that must constantly be fought, people do not have an inherited, corrupt nature. Death exists because of Adam's sin, and all people suffer for that first misdeed. But the death of each individual results from his or her own actions. Although death was instituted with Adam, human beings die as a consequence of their own sins (Tanhuma *Bereshit* 29; Tanhuma *Hukkat* 39).

Some rabbis even see in the temptation to sin one of life's motivating powers. Upon capturing the evil inclination for three days, the men of the great synagogue are said to have discovered that productive activity no longer took place (Babylonian Talmud *Yoma* 69b). *Genesis Rabbah* 9:7 similarly argues that, were it not for the evil inclination, people would not marry, raise a family, construct a house, or engage in business. In this view, human aspiration and productivity result directly from people's need to constantly overcome their tendency toward evil.

To avoid falling into sin, people must recognize the ever-present eyes and ears of God (Mishnah *Abot* 2:1), who will make public even that which is done in private (Babylonian Talmud *Sotah* 3a). More than anything else, study of Torah and practice of the law are held to ward off the temptation to sin (Babylonian Talmud *Sotah* 21a). Upon a person's entry into a house of study, the inclination to sin is said to dissipate completely (Babylonian Talmud *Kiddushin* 30b). God is held to have said, "My children, I created the inclination to sin, but I created the Torah as its antidote. Therefore, if you occupy yourselves with the Torah, you will not be delivered into [sin's] hand!" (Babylonian Talmud *Kiddushin* 30b). *See also* Judaism (thought and ethics); retribution, divine (Judaism); yetzer ha-ra, ha-tov.

Christianity: Sin is any action or habit detrimental to the spiritual progress of the self, or to moral interrelations. New Testament Greek calls sin *harmartia,* a missing of the mark or a wandering from the path. Theologically, sin is rebellion against God that results in spiritual regress and harms against self or neighbor. Augustine (d. 430) defined sin as "any transgression in deed, word or desire of the eternal law," indicating that sin, consistent with the teachings of Jesus in the Sermon on the Mount, can be a matter of thought or intention alone, as well as of action.

Roman Catholic moral theology recognizes various classifications of sin (e.g., original or personal, formal or material, habitual or active). The most important practical distinction is between mortal (or grave) and venial (less grave) sin. Thomas Aquinas (ca. 1225–74) defined a mortal sin as one that turns the soul from God, depriving it of grace and of eternal happiness. To be mortal, Aquinas held that a sin must cause grave injury to the self, the Christian community, or to God and divine purposes; and issue from a moral agent who is fully aware of the wrongness of the sin and acts intentionally.

Classically, all personal sins were thought to be rooted in seven tendencies (pride, gluttony, sloth, covetousness, anger, lust, and envy). Pride, for example, gives rise to obstinacy and disobedience, while gluttony gives rise to drunkenness and impurity.

Protestant ethics rejected the distinctions between mortal and venial sins, since all sins are equally damnable, and all point equally to the need for God's grace. Distinctions between individuals as relatively more or less sinful gave way to the Protestant notion that all persons are wholly sinful and can be justified only through faith. Some nineteenth-century Protestant thinkers viewed sin as the result of unjust social structures rather than as a disorder within the self. In recent Catholic thought, liberation theology has also emphasized this view. *See also* absolution; Confession (Christianity); contrition; grace; mortal sin; original sin (Christianity); penance; salvation; seven deadly sins.

Sinai, in the Hebrew Bible, the mountain where Moses received the divine law. Its geographical location is uncertain.

Singh (Punjabi, "lion"), Khalsa Sikh title assumed as part of every male name, symbolizing courage and daring. *See also* Kaur; Khalsa; Sikhism.

Singh Sabha (sing suh-bah'), a wide-ranging Sikh religious movement, active from 1873 to 1920, that as a result of the social and cultural forces unleashed by British rule in India greatly transformed the tradition and gave rise to a highly systematized modern Sikhism. Singh Sabha leaders endowed the Sikhs with texts, histories, symbols, festivities, a ritual calendar, sacred space, and life-cycle rituals that were intended to leave no ambiguity in defining what it means to be a Sikh. The innovations not only led to the dissolution of diversity within the Sikh community but also permanently distinguished its constituents from all other religious communities in South Asia, particularly Hinduism. *See also* Sikhism.

Sinification, the process whereby the Chinese adapt imported ideas to fit their own temperament and outlook. Buddhism interacted with the native Chinese philosophies of Confucianism and Taoism and, under their influence, received new ideas as well as reinterpretations of many of its existing teachings. For example, whereas a Buddhist monk in India left home and severed all family ties, the Chinese Buddhist establishment, under pressure from Confucianism, reinterpreted monastic ordination as an act of family loyalty. By making such adjustments, Buddhism became more acceptable to the Chinese people.

Sipapu (see-pah'poo; Pueblo; specific language unknown, "earth navel"), a precise geographical location important in Pueblo (American Southwest) traditions that attests to the peoples' emergence from within the earth into the present world. Sipapu refers also to a cavity dug in the kiva floor as a representation of these underworld origins; as such, it figures importantly in reenactments of emergence history. *See also* emergence; kiva; North America, traditional religions in.

sister. *See* nun.

sisterhood, a characteristic term of voluntary association among women where social language replaces that of biological kinship.

sistrum, an Egyptian musical instrument; shaken, it makes rasping sounds for use in the ancient rituals of Hathor and related goddesses.

613 commandments, in Jewish tradition the total number of commandments in the Hebrew Bible (613 is the numerical value of *torah,* "law"). The traditional enumeration lists 248 positive and 365 negative commandments. *See also* mitzvah; Torah.

666, in the New Testament book of Revelation, the "number of the Beast" who is the archenemy of Christianity (Revelation 13.18). Though originally most likely the numerical value of "King Nero" written in Hebrew letters, the figure has been constantly reidentified throughout Christian history. *See also* eschatology.

six systems of Indian philosophy (Skt. *shad darshana,* "six views"). The six systems articulate theories of logic, ontology, knowledge, and scriptural interpretation foundational to Hindu theology and secular Indian thought. Transmitted largely in Sanskrit, the philosophical discourse propounding these theories is dominated by the priestly intellegentsia (Brahmans).

All six systems assume a stance with regard to the canon known as the Vedas limited to Hindus: the Vedas are the authorless revelation by which one obtains ultimate validity for knowledge. All six systems assert there is an eternal soul that must be liberated from the cycle of death and rebirth, though they do not necessarily agree on methods or theories.

Individual systems produce texts and commentaries, though traditionally the six are treated in pairs. The order of pairings implies an evolving intellectual heritage and, to a lesser extent, dependent conceptual relations. The first pair, Nyaya (Skt., "rule," "logic," "analysis") and Vaisheshika ("distinction," "characteristic"), provides methods and ideologies to which the second, Samkhya ("number, "enumeration") and Yoga ("effort," "discipline," "joining"), responds; the third pair, Mimamsa ("investigation") and Vedanta (lit., "the end or culmination of the Veda"), builds on issues raised by both preceding pairs. The history of the six systems involves adoption, adaptation, and rejection of methods, concepts, and structures between and within systems.

The Logic and Distinct Characteristics Systems: Nyaya, or Logic, founded by Gotama (ca. third century B.C.), and Vaisheshika, or Distinctive Characteristics, first expounded by Kanada (ca. third century B.C.), rely more on argument than on scripture to establish positions. Nyaya's interests are primarily in theories of argumentation and epistemology, while Vaisheshika focuses on descriptive ontology.

Nyaya deems rational inquiry necessary to investigate objects and to obtain knowledge of the soul. There are four means for obtaining knowledge: sense perception, inference, analogy, and testimony. Sense perception produces immediate knowledge when contact between sense organs and objects is error-free. Inferential knowledge mediated by logical relations re-

quires that in statements such as "there is fire on a mountain," the subject (the mountain) is connected to the thing to be proved (fire) by a connector (such as smoke); the connector must belong to the subject (smoke observed on the mountain) and must pervade the thing to be proved (all smoky things are fiery). Analogy produces valid knowledge through comparison of something unknown with something already known. Testimony refers to any authoritative statement that passes test of certainty.

Nyaya affirms a plurality of souls belonging to both humans and nonhumans that suffer due to past and present ignorant actions and are freed only by obtaining valid knowledge. Nyaya is also interested in proving God's existence. Since the universe is beginningless and without material origin, God is not the only eternal entity but an omniscient soul who is the necessary efficient cause of creation and destruction.

By the fifth century, Nyaya is paired with Vaisheshika, whose name, "Distinctive Characteristics," reflects its primary interest: the identification and classification of reality's essentials. These essentials are divided into six basic categories that exist as real phenomena apart from human conceptualization. They are substance, quality, motion, universality, individuation, and inherence. Substances consist of collections of invisible atoms, are permanent, preexistent, and characterized by various qualities. Vaisheshika also asserts that negative entities such as "absence" and "difference" are substances. Thus, the "absence" of a pot is a substance of no less ontological value than the pot itself. While a substance's material essence does not change, its qualities may. Qualities are properties born by individual substances. For example, a substance appearing as an unbaked clay pot may have the quality of appearing brown before being fired and red afterward. The particular brownness of a clay pot belongs only to that pot and can change, as it does after being fired. Further, the particular brownness of a given pot is an entity within the class of the quality "brown."

Similarly, the category *motion,* defined as the causative force of any movement, is also a plurality that inheres in individual substances, albeit momentarily. The category of universals is an independent entity to which individual substances, qualities, and activities belong; universals form a plurality of genera, such as the "potness" of all pots or the "cowness" of all cows. In contrast to universals, the category *individuation* designates the category by which other categories, such as "potness," may be related to more inclusive genera, such as "clay-object-ness." Inherence is that which binds and sustains relations between substances.

Nyaya's logical methods and epistemology and Vaisheshika's realist, pluralist ontology establish positions to which others feel obliged to respond. Further, both create methodologies and theories that stand apart from particular doctrinal arguments, thus setting precedents for philosophical discourse.

Systems of Enumeration and Discipline: Samkhya, or Enumeration, founded by the sage Kapila, which appears nascently in the Upanishads (ca. 600 B.C.–A.D. 100), is treated systematically first by Ishvarakrishna in the *Samkhyakarikas* (ca. 350–550). Samkhya enumerates categories and principles (*tattvas*) in order to describe reality's essences. The first category of twenty-five principles (twenty-four material and one of ubiquitous consciousness) forms the basis for the second, made up of eight intellectual dispositions; the third category of fifty intellectual patterns arises from the relationship of principles and dispositions.

Samkhya is dualist inasmuch as consciousness is a permanent, passive witness to the changes that occur in the twenty-four material principles that evolve from one original, unmanifest materiality. Since all things are transformations of one material and preexist in casual antecedents, just as fire inheres in wood and yogurt in milk, confusion too is rooted in materiality. Samkhya's goal is to dispel the ignorance that causes one to confuse the principles of materiality (*prakriti*) with the principle of eternal consciousness (*purusha*), though it does not explain how consciousness and materiality were originally confused or how they interact. Samkhya theories appear practically dependent on techniques and methods developed in the sibling system, Yoga.

Yoga expands Samkhya metaphysics by a twenty-fifth principle, God (Ishvara), and suggests a split between theistic and nontheistic tendencies within the larger tradition. Yoga's most important contributions involve methods for acquiring control over materiality and liberation of the spirit.

First systematized in the aphoristic *Yogasutras* (ca. third century) attributed to the sage Patanjali, so-called royal or *Raja Yoga* has eight hierarchical stages of practice. In the first two stages one is purified and prepared for higher physical and mental practices that lead ultimately to a state of single-pointed concentration (*ekagrata*), in which an individual's eternal spirit is disentangled from matter and reunited with God. Both Samkhya's metaphysics and Yoga's meditative disciplines exert tremendous influence on Indian religion beyond the limited scope of philosophical discussion.

Systems of Investigation and the "End of the Veda": Mimamsa, or Investigation, is better known as Earlier, or Purva, Mimamsa in contrast to its sibling, Vedanta, called Uttara, or Later, Mimamsa because of its focus on the later Vedic texts (the Upanishads) and subject matter (absolute reality or *brahman*). Both systems are preoccupied with interpretation of scripture rather than establishment of independent methods or philosophies. Their primary subject is duty (*dharma*), including religious and ethical actions, as enjoined by the Vedic texts. Originating in response to challenges to Vedic authority and scriptural consistency, Purva Mimamsa is first systematized in the *Mimamsa Sutras* (ca. first century B.C.) attributed to the sage Jaimini and later divides into two subschools emerging from the works of Kumarila Bhatta and Prabhakara (ca. 600–700).

Purva Mimamsa claims that Vedic scripture alone is the self-evident authority for correct knowledge of duty and that the Vedas' essence pertains to matters of transcendence, knowledge about which is not obtainable by such means as perception, inference, or analogy. Since the Vedas are regarded as eternal and uncreated, their truths cannot be empirically refuted; Vedic authority rests not on divinity but on such transcendent realities as duty and liberation (defined as the fulfillment of duty).

Though it is preoccupied with scriptural injunctions, Purva Mimamsa's sophisticated theories of language deeply influence other systems. The Vedanta, or Uttara Mimamsa, adds the *Brahmasutras* (ca. third century B.C.) and *Bhagavad Gita* (ca. second century B.C.) as textual foundations (*prasthana*) beyond the Vedas.

Vedanta evinces less interest than Purva Mimamsa in fulfilling scriptural injunctions, focusing instead on the inquiry into absolute reality (*brahman*) and the relation of the soul (*atman*) to God. Schools within Vedanta dispute matters of epistemology, ontology, and practice and become associated with particular scriptural interpretations and theological movements. While all would agree the ultimate objective is liberation of the soul from cyclical death and rebirth, methods and theories differ significantly. Some, such as Gaudapada (ca. seventh century), Shankara (788–820) and their followers, espouse theories of absolute nondualism (*kevaladvaita*), in which all perception of difference is ultimately rooted in ignorance (*avidya*). Divinity is a relatively insignificant topic. Others, such as Bhaskara (ca. 850), position themselves between monism and ontological pluralism, maintaining that absolute reality is both the formless, causal principle and the manifest reality of material effects. Ramanuja (1017–1137) reconciles personal devotion centered on the god Vishnu with an absolutistic philosophy; his school is called qualified nondualism (*vishishtadvaita*). Madhva's (1238–1317) theological dualism is reminiscent of Samkhya; all reality, including matter and individual souls, is finite and dependent on the one infinite, omniscient God who personifies as Vishnu in the form of Krishna.

While all six systems remain intellectually active to some degree, from about the seventh century on Vedanta gained influence and popularity that far exceeds others. *See also* maya; Mimamsa; Nyaya; Samkhya; Vedanta; Yoga.

sixty-year cycle, Chinese calendrical enumeration by means of the Ten Heavenly Stems and Twelve Earthly Branches; it uses the series of sixty unique combinations of the twenty-two signs. *See also* calendar (China); Ten Heavenly Stems and Twelve Earthly Branches.

siyam. *See* fasting; Five Pillars.

S. J. *See* Jesuits.

Skanda (skuhn'duh; Skt., "Effusion," "Destruction"), the son of the Hindu god Shiva. Also known as Murugan and Kataragama, he is one of the most popular gods in present-day South India and Sri Lanka. His cult is often seen as quintessentially Tamil, but he is a popular deity among Sinhala Buddhists who consider him a Buddha-to-be and a guardian of Buddhism. Possession is often associated with Skanda's cult.

There are various myths about Skanda's origin, including that he is the son of Shiva and his goddess-consort, Parvati, or that he is born of the sparks emanating from Shiva's brow. Skanda is also said to be the leader of Shiva's armies, and his martial and romantic exploits are extolled in mythology and celebrated in festivals at places sacred to him. *See also* Shiva.

skandhas. *See* aggregates.

skepticism, ancient (from Gk. *skeptomai*, "to investigate," "to inquire"), "Pyrrhonism" or its offspring, "academic skepticism," a Greek philosophical movement (fourth century B.C.– A.D. second century) characterized by its attacks on the dogmatic, theoretical knowledge claims of competing schools (e.g., the Stoics). Founded by Pyrrho (ca. 362–272 B.C.), Pyrrhonism offered equally persuasive arguments on both sides of any issue,

yielding "suspension of judgment" on the matter. As a result, skeptics make no assertions on any topic but only acknowledge how things "seem." This was thought to yield a happy life free of the anxiety that plagues those who make fixed theoretical commitments.

Skinwalker, among the Navajo and other Southwest tribes, a malevolent male witch (Navajo, *yenaldlooshi*) who wears coyote skins and practices rituals that reverse normal conventions (cannibalism, necrophilia).

skullcap/kippah/yarmulke, head-covering of various types worn by Jewish males in prayer and religious ceremonies to exhibit reverence for the presence of God. Many Orthodox Jews always keep their heads covered as a testimony that God is ever-present. Reform Judaism makes head-covering optional.

sky. 1 The abode of the god(s). 2 A deity identified with the sky, usually masculine and associated with all-seeing powers. 3 One of the primary cosmogonic elements, usually requiring separation from earth so as to allow room for the rest of creation. 4 The goal of ascension rituals. 5 In some traditions, the location of the land of the dead or a paradisical locale. *See also* afterlife; afterworld; ascension; ascension rituals; cosmology; firmament; Hanullim/Hanunim; heaven (Christianity); high god; Indo-European religion; Indra; Shang-ti; Takamagahara; term question; T'ien; world parents.

smarta (smahr'tuh), in Indic traditions, a text or custom sanctioned by tradition (*smriti*). The term is also used for orthodox Brahmans, especially followers of the eighth-century Hindu philosopher Shankara, and for the teachings of nondualist Vedanta. *See also* Hinduism (authoritative texts and their interpretation); Vedanta.

Smith, Joseph (1805–44), founder and prophet of the Church of Jesus Christ of Latter-day Saints. His revealed writings, along with the Bible, constitute the Mormon canon. *The Book of Mormon* (1830), translated from hidden golden plates, extends the narrative of the Hebrew Bible to America. His other writings are collected in *Doctrine and Covenants* (1835) and *The Pearl of Great Price* (1842). *See also* Latter-day Saints, Church of Jesus Christ of.

Smohalla (ca. 1818–1907), a Native American prophet of the Wanapum tribe of the Columbia/Snake River region in the present state of

Washington. In the manner of leaders of the Plateau Prophet Dance, he "died" (about 1860) and returned to life with a message concerning the imminent destruction of the world, the resurrection of the dead, and the need to return to old customs. Insisting that God intended all to share the resources of the earth, Smohalla opposed the division and ownership of land, the reservation system, and the White work ethic. *See also* Native Americans (North America), new religions among; prophecy in traditional religions.

smoke. 1 A widespread form of ritual connection between the terrestrial and celestial realms, especially in sacrifice, where the smoke transports the food from the altar to the god(s). 2 A frequent means of purification of both persons and places. 3 In smoking rituals, the major means of ingesting psychoactive plant substances. *See also* fire; ghee; pipe, sacred; psychoactive plants; sacrifice; sweet grass; tobacco and hallucinogens.

smriti. *See* Hinduism (authoritative texts and their interpretation).

Smyth, John (smith; ca. 1554–1612), British nonconformist minister. He established the first congregation of English Baptists. *See also* Baptists.

snake handlers, members of independent Christian Pentecostal churches, mostly in Appalachia in the United States, who take literally Mark 16:18 as a mandate for handling live poisonous snakes during worship services as a sign of invulnerability to physical harm conferred by the Holy Spirit. Such groups are small in number and their activity generally illegal. *See also* Pentecostalism.

Social Gospel, a Christian social reform movement among liberal American Protestants that flourished from 1880 to 1918. The movement's best-known theologian was the German-born Baptist Walter Rauschenbusch. Commitment to social reform had long been part of Protestant America's evangelical mainstream. The Social Gospel movement refocused this commitment on the plight of impoverished urban workers and their families. The Social Gospel integrated work for progressive social reform into the optimistic, postmillennial view of the kingdom of God typical of American Protestants. Contributing to the coming kingdom through social reform required concerted Christian advocacy. The movement generated a national interdenominational cooperative agency known as the Federal Council of Churches of Christ in America founded in 1908. *See also* Rauschenbusch, Walter.

society and religion. Society and religion represent two interdependent and reciprocally related aspects of human experience. Although religion has a profoundly personal dimension, the desire to communicate and share religious experience invariably gives rise to communities of religious believers. In time these communities often become religiously based social and political orders. Societies have consistently turned to religion to provide a basis for their common life. Together these two ideas, the essentially social nature of religion and the intrinsically religious nature of society, comprise key aspects of the study of society and religion.

Historical Overview: Not only have all the great historical religions given rise to specific communities of belief and practice, over time these communities have also usually evolved into comprehensive societies basing their political, economic, social, and cultural life on religious foundations.

The major traditions deriving from the Bible—Israelitic religion, Judaism, Christianity, and Islam—clearly evidence this pattern. In each case, religious revelation beginning with an individual or small group of individuals soon takes the form of an expanding community of believers who eventually seek to establish a sacred political state based on this revelation. The Israelite nation, for example, is conceived of as a divinely ordained society. When historical events impeded Israelite nationhood, the aspiration to a religiously constituted social order lived on in the various messianic and nationalistic movements of, first, Hebrew and, later, Jewish faith.

Islam displays a similar pattern. Beginning with the revelation received by the Prophet Muhammad, Muslim faith has produced a world-embracing, transnational religious community, the Islamic *ummah*. But Islam has also given rise to a series of sacralized theocratic states, the political, legal, economic, and social structures of which have been derived from Islamic teaching. For many Muslims, social life is unacceptable without an Islamic foundation.

The vigor of its many early local church communities testifies to Christianity's strong social impulse. However, Jesus' apparent disinterest in political power (Matthew 22:21) has led some observers to conclude that Christianity has a primarily spiritual rather than political or juridical character. Whether or not this was the case,

Christianity eventually gave rise to a series of states or empires tracing their origins and institutions to Christian revelation. Medieval society as a whole had an essentially religious basis, with its political, economic, and social hierarchies conceived to be rooted in God's ordinances. This pattern continues even after the breakup of medieval civilization. Even though Protestantism is sometimes associated with religious individualism and the primacy of individual faith, the Protestant Reformers strongly affirmed the ideal of a Christian society. Calvinism provides an illustration. Whenever Calvin's followers were ascendent, they sought to establish church-ruled and theocratic societies.

These two dynamics—religion's tendency to take social form and the reciprocal tendency of societies to establish themselves on a religious basis—are also evident in Eastern religions. In both China and Japan the leading indigenous religious traditions not only take social form as communities of adherents, they also provide powerful undergirding for society as a whole. From its inception, Confucianism seeks to provide moral teachings and methods of personal cultivation leading to a harmonious social order. Although Chinese society often strayed from this ideal, its political life has always shown a strong Confucian imprint. In Japan, Shinto exemplifies the interdependency of the spiritual and temporal realms, with the two united in the religiously conceived role of the emperor as a divine personage.

The traditions of India, particularly Hinduism and Buddhism, are sometimes thought to contradict the claim that there is a reciprocal relationship between society and religion. Hinduism is often viewed as involving more a mode of individual consciousness than a religious community. Although Buddhism often takes social form in monastic communities, its ideal is seen to be the solitary mendicant wandering in the quest for personal salvation.

Both views, however, miss the deeply social dimension of these faiths. If orthodox Brahmanical Hinduism has not usually given rise to specific religious communities or churches, it has tended to perceive and shape Indian society as a whole in religious terms. In turn, over the centuries, Indian society has found in Hindu sacred teachings means of understanding and justifying its principal political, economic, or social institutions. For example, Vedic teachings provide a mythological basis for the caste order by tracing its inception to a primordial act of divine sacrifice (*Rig Veda*, 10.90).

Buddhism, too, incorporates a powerful soci-etal impulse in its conception of kingship. From the time of King Ashoka, Buddhist teaching places the individual and monastic quest for salvation within the context of a social order governed by Buddhist ethical and religious ideals. In the Theravada Buddhist lands of Southeast Asia, where historical conditions have sometimes permitted the working out of this ideal, societies with distinctive Buddhist political, economic, and social institutions have emerged.

The Study of Society and Religion: The reciprocal relationship of society and religion was observable long before it became an object of scholarly study. In the nineteenth century, however, with the emergence of both the critical study of society and the analytical study of religion, attention focuses on explaining why society and religion are so commonly linked in these ways.

Karl Marx: One of the earliest and most influential explanations of the sociality of religion and the religiousness of society is offered by Karl Marx (1818–83). Like other thinkers of his era, Marx seeks to explain the persistence of religion despite the waning credibility of its metaphysical or supernatural claims. The solution to this puzzle, Marx argues, lies in understanding that the primary role of religion is to justify and uphold society's economic and political structures. Since Marx believes that economic exploitation and oppression underlies all previous and existing societies, this means that religion serves to glorify and reproduce oppressive social orders in symbolic form. For example, claims for the religious sanctity of political rulers, in Marx's view, are nothing more than efforts to buttress these rulers' power and authority. This often hidden social agenda explains religion's persistence. It also leads Marx to believe that religion would vanish once social oppression is eliminated by communism.

Emile Durkheim: Later in the nineteenth century, Emile Durkheim (1858–1917), a founding figure of the sociology of religion, offers a different explanation of the reciprocal relationship between society and religion. In his classic work, *The Elementary Forms of the Religious Life* (1912), Durkheim seeks to understand the basis for the important religious distinction between the sacred and the profane. Durkheim traces the power of the sacred and the veneration accorded religious objects to human beings' dependence on society and worship of it. Divinity, he concludes, is nothing more than society "transfigured." Durkheim further argues that this eminently social basis of religion explains the importance of religious rites, which, in his view, represent efforts by society periodically to reaffirm the bonds attaching individuals to it. Because Durkheim sees religious belief and practice as essentially social, he believes that religion would not vanish with the growth of scientific knowledge nor would it disappear, as Marx believes, if social oppression ends. As an expression, celebration, and reinforcement of human beings' sociality, religion would persist in societies whatever their specific state of development.

Max Weber: The work of Max Weber (1864–1920) represents a third major approach to the study of society and religion. Weber, like Durkheim, views religion as having a powerful relationship to social facts, but he traces its origin to the conceptual and psychological needs of human individuals faced with the perennial problem of meaning posed by suffering, death, and injustice.

Because of its relation to individual emotional and cognitive need, religion for Weber is a keystone that locks all the other features of human culture into place. This gives religion an independent role versus social fact. Without denying Marx's claim that the economic or material substructure powerfully influences the religious superstructure, Weber argues that religion could be an independent as well as a dependent variable in social, economic, and political life. Weber dedicates much of his specific historical research to showing the unique role played by biblical faith in general and Calvinist Protestantism in particular in contributing to the emergence of capitalist civilization.

Modern Views: Students of society and religion since Marx, Durkheim, and Weber build upon the work of these thinkers and apply it to emerging features of religious life. Marxist theorists, for example, try to understand the persistence of religion in ostensibly socialist or communist societies and the revolutionary and transformative role of popular religion in some social settings. Drawing on suggestions in Marx's work, thinkers such as Antonio Gramsci (1891–1937) and Louis Althusser (1918–90) emphasize the role of religious belief and practice not just as a reflection and support of oppressive structures but as a protest against these structures by persons denied alternate means of expression. Within the framework of Marxist theory, this understanding gives religion a continuing and sometimes positive role in social change.

Scholars influenced by Durkheim and Weber seek to develop and apply both thinkers' insights to the complex situation of secularized or secularizing societies. Given the importance of religion for society on both thinkers' views, one challenge posed for theorists is understanding society and religion in the face of the declining vitality of many formal religious organizations today.

Responding to this phenomenon, some scholars in the Durkheim tradition argue that the progressive differentiation and complexity of modern societies eliminates the possibility of a single, unifying religious culture for society as a whole. In different ways, contemporary sociologists such as Thomas Luckmann or Richard Fenn argue that while secularization does not mean the end of religion in modern society, it does foster less social and more privatized forms of religious expression.

Somewhat opposing this view is Robert Bellah's (b. 1927) argument that there exists a vigorous civil religion at the core of American society by means of which citizens of the United States conceive of their nation in transcendent terms and celebrate its common life. Since Bellah first introduced this idea, similar civil religions have been identified in a variety of other modern societies from the former Soviet Union to South Africa.

Secularization is not the only distinctive feature of modern religious life. Also important is the appearance of religious fundamentalism in the midst of secularized or secularizing societies. Some scholars interpret these movements in Durkheimian terms as a reaction against the anomie or normlessness of societies deprived of traditional religious support. For these thinkers, the absence of a unifying religious culture in modern societies sometimes fosters the aggressive quest for a reintegration of religious and social life that fundamentalism represents. The emergence of religious fundamentalism has also called to mind Weber's understanding of the important role of charismatic religious leaders. By drawing on or adapting a religion's enduring solutions to problems of meaning, and by mediating these to a loyal band of followers, charismatic leaders are often at the center of social change.

Religion is undeniably a social phenomenon. Not only do religions invariably take social form in the varieties of fellowship characteristic of religious communities, they usually seek to transform society as a whole by bringing it into conformity with their religious teachings and ideals. Over time, few societies have escaped this process of religious transformation or have done without an identifiable religious base. Seeking to understand this recurrent reciprocal relationship between society and religion, some theorists follow Marx in seeing religion as little more than a "mask" concealing the real material forces of social continuity or change. Others, in the tradition of Durkheim, emphasize the social origins of religion but differ from Marx in seeing religion as a necessary and irreplaceable feature of social life. Finally, thinkers in the tradition of Weber view religion as a symbolic cultural resource of independent significance but one that nevertheless interacts powerfully with aspects of social life. *See also* civil religion; community, communitas; ideology and religion; modernization; religion, sociology of; secularism.

Socinus, Faustus (soh-si'nuhs; 1539–1604), anti-Trinitarian theologian whose writings were influential on Unitarianism. He was active especially in Poland. *See also* Unitarianism.

Socrates (sok'ruh-teez; 470–399 B.C.), famous Athenian philosopher. He wrote nothing, and thus what we know of him concerns mostly his later life as portrayed in a variety of somewhat divergent accounts: primarily Plato's dialogues, Aristophanes's *Clouds*, Xenophon's writings, and passages in Aristotle's works. Socrates was apparently a genial, humorous man of remarkable intelligence and courage. He was interested primarily in ethical issues, relentlessly pursuing them through the cross-examination of those with pretensions to moral knowledge. His success at this, as well as his personality, moral character, and views, drew a number of admirers to him, several of whom became founders of schools of philosophy (e.g., Plato). The fact that these discussions are generally shown as failing to produce an adequate answer to the question at hand (e.g., "What is piety?") and Socrates's own frequent professions of ignorance have led some to suppose that Socrates had no positive doctrines of his own. But it is more commonly thought that he developed a revolutionary moral theory, according to which the happy life we all desire requires knowledge of the virtues. From this Socrates drew startling conclusions; e.g., that our souls are harmed by vice, that no one does wrong knowingly, and that it is always worse to do harm than to suffer it. These views, the "Socratic method" of cross-examination, and the moral example set by Socrates had a tremendous impact on the subsequent history of Western philosophy.

Scholars have seen Socrates as a profoundly religious figure, pursuing philosophy in obedience to a god-given command, while others have found him a merciless critic of religion. Both are partially correct. Socrates was a man of his own time; he acknowledged the existence of gods and the private divinatory "sign" that warned him away from danger. But he was also a reformer of Greek tradition, especially in his insistence that the gods would never commit injustices of the sort portrayed by the poets.

Nonetheless, it would have been easy enough to mistake Socrates for an atheistic Sophist. For this reason, and possibly others, he was brought to trial on a charge of atheism and corruption of the youth. He was found guilty and, refusing a chance to escape, committed suicide by drinking hemlock. *See also* Plato; pre-Socratics.

Soga clan (soh-gah), powerful Japanese family in the Yamato court of the sixth and seventh centuries whose members were the first great patrons of Buddhism in Japan; under the leadership of Soga no Umako (d. 626), they helped the imperial Prince Shotoku establish a strong central government. *See also* Shotoku, Prince.

Sohak. *See* Korea, Roman Catholicism in.

sojae. *See* academies (Korea), private and public.

Soka Gakkai (soh-ka gak-kai; Jap., "value creation society"), the largest Japanese new religion, founded by Makiguchi Tsunesaburo (1871–1944) in 1928 as an educational society designed to propagate Buddhist values. A distinct religious body since 1937, it formerly acted as a lay branch of the Nichiren Shoshu Buddhist sect in Japan, although frequent tensions have developed with its parent sect. Proscribed during the war (Makiguchi died in prison), it grew rapidly afterward through aggressive proselytism that has at times led it into controversy in Japan. Under its present leader, Ikeda Daisaku, who became president in 1960, it has developed an international presence with a small following, especially among young urban professionals in the United States and United Kingdom.

It advocates a state based on Buddhist principles and established a political party, *Komeito* ("clean government party") in Japan for this purpose. Though now officially separate, religion and party retain close links.

Regarding the latter half of the *Lotus Sutra* as the essence of all Buddhism, Soka Gakkai identifies Nichiren himself as the source of salvation for the present world. It regards the invocation *Namu Myoho Renge Kyo* ("hail to the wonderful law of the lotus") from the *Lotus Sutra* as encapsulating the essence of Buddhist power, and followers chant this before a *gohonzon* (a scroll depicting Nichiren's sacred calligraphy). It is believed that such chanting can improve one's life, bring happiness, and lead to the development of a better society. *See also* Japan, new religions in.

Sokkuram Grotto (suhk-koo-rahm), a Korean Buddhist grotto, or artificial cave shrine, constructed of pure granite in 751. This grotto, one of the greatest cultural and engineering achievements of the Unified Silla period (seventh–ninth centuries), was constructed under the authority of the prime minister Kim Taesong (701–774) on the side of Mt. T'oham overlooking the East Sea for the purpose of protecting the state from foreign invasion. Built in three sections—an entrance chamber, a connecting corridor, and a domed, circular chamber—the grotto was made first of finished granite and then covered with earth to simulate a natural cave.

The entrance chamber has a series of eight larger-than-life guardian figures carved in high relief on granite slabs. The short, connecting corridor has the images of the Four Heavenly Kings similarly carved. The domed chamber is faced by a stone arch resting on two octagonal pillars. Flanking the arch and extending in a circle around the chamber are relief sculptures of Brahma, Indra, Manjusri, Kshitigarbha, and ten disciples of the Buddha. The last relief sculpture located at the far end of the chamber is that of an exquisite eleven-headed Avalokiteshvara. In the center of the chamber is a massive, seated image of Vairochana Buddha with a large lotus nimbus carved into the dome wall at its back. The dome of the chamber rests on a series of ten niches, carved as a series of lotus petals, in which are found various types of seated Buddha images.

The style of the carvings, including the lotus-petal and lotus-leaf ornaments on the pillars, wall supports, Vairochana pedestal, and the draperies on the carved figures, is reminiscent of T'ang Chinese style. The grotto is completely surrounded by a retaining wall and intervening dead-space corridor, which has helped to keep the shrine in nearly perfect condition. Like many of the temples, shrines, and *stupas* (reliquary mounds) of the Unified Silla period, the grotto constitutes a powerful *mandala* (center of cosmic forces) for the protection of the state and draws upon the teaching of Esoteric Buddhism for its inspiration and construction. *See also* Esoteric Buddhism in China; grotto/cave; National Protection Buddhism; shrine.

sokushin jobutsu (soh-koo-shin joh-boo-tsoo; Jap., "realization of Buddhahood with this very body"), in Japanese Buddhism, Tendai and Shingon theories about

how Buddhahood might be quickly realized. The Shingon position explained how ritual practitioners could call forth their innate Buddhahood through Tantric rituals. Tendai arguments were initially based on the story of how the eight-year-old dragon girl in the *Lotus Sutra* realized Buddhahood, but they later also incorporated Tantric teachings. *See also* enlightenment; Shingon-shu; Tendai school.

sola scriptura (Lat., "scripture alone"), phrase used by Protestant Christians to deny that extrascriptural tradition is a source of divine revelation. The Catholic Church rejected the phrase. *See also* Reformation, Protestant; tradition.

Solomon, in the Hebrew Bible, king of Israel, son of David, responsible for the construction of the Temple in Jerusalem and renowned for his wisdom. Ancient scholars attributed four biblical books to him: Song of Songs, Proverbs, Ecclesiastes, and Wisdom of Solomon.

soma (soh'mah), body in Hellenistic anthropology.

soma (Hinduism) (soh'muh), in the *Rig Veda* a hallucinogenic plant, the expressed juice of which is ritually ingested by the priests (inspiring them to compose Vedic hymns) and offered to the gods. Invoked as a god, *soma* later becomes the moon, where the juice is stored for the gods to drink. *See also* psychoactive plants; Rig Veda; sacrifice; Veda, Vedism.

Songgyun'gwan. *See* academies (Korea), private and public.

Soniryo (soh-nee-ryoh; Jap., "Rules for Monks and Nuns"), Japanese Buddhist monastic rules based on Chinese regulations. The extant set of rules was part of the Yoro code, compiled in 757, but similar rules were probably part of the Taiho code of 718. The rules restricted monks and nuns from freely ordaining others, traveling, proselytizing, practicing divination, eating meat, and drinking alcohol. Although some rules were based on traditional Buddhist ideals of monastic discipline, many of the restrictions limited the freedom of monks and nuns, treating them as ritual specialists whose main duty was protecting the state. *See also* Sangha; Vinaya.

son of God, individual standing in a special relationship to the deity. 1 Title most usually assigned to sacred kings throughout the ancient Mediterranean world. One becomes a son of God either by divine choice or by divine-human sexual intercourse. *See also* kingship, sacred. 2 An early royal title for Jesus. In later Christian literature, Son of God is contrasted with Son of Man, with the former indicating Jesus' heavenly nature and the latter his earthly embodiment. *See also* Christology; Jesus Christ; Son of Man.

Son of Man. 1 Hebrew or Aramaic expression with a range of meanings, from a synonym for humankind or the first person pronoun *I*, to an apocalyptic figure expected as judge between the righteous and the wicked at the end-time. 2 A title used in the New Testament of the Bible, both by and of Jesus; later writers sometimes improperly took the title to refer to Jesus' earthly appearance, as opposed to the heavenly Son of God. *See also* son of God.

Sophia (soh-fee'ah; Gk., "Wisdom"), the female creator in some Gnostic systems; in others, the fallen aeon who initiates material creation. *See also* Aion/Aeon; Gnosticism.

Sophocles (sah'fuh-kleez; ca. 496–406 B.C.), a Greek tragedian. Of 123 plays, seven survive (*Ajax, Antigone, Oedipus Tyrannos, Trachiniai, Electra, Philoctetes,* and *Oedipus at Colonos*). Athenian audiences apparently preferred his traditional religious attitudes to the skepticism of his contemporary Euripides. After his death, he received heroic honors for introducing the cult of Asclepios to Athens. *See also* Euripides.

sorcery, the use of supernatural or magical power to bring about a cause-and-effect relationship on objects and people. In general, sorcerers practice their trade with evil intent. A sorcerer's knowledge may be learned from experience or learned from a teacher; therefore it is available to anyone. It is not considered an inheritable trait, as contrasted to witchcraft, which is frequently inherited. It is virtually indistinguishable from witchcraft in all other respects. *See also* witchcraft.

soteriology, doctrines and beliefs concerning salvation.

Soto school (soh-toh), Japanese Zen Buddhist tradition based on the Ts'ao-tung Ch'an Buddhism brought to Japan by Dogen (1200–1253). After Dogen's death, many of the school's monks departed from his austere teachings to follow the lead of monks such as Keizan (1268–1325) in developing teachings for the commoners. Among the rituals used were funerals and ordinations, while meditation was neglected. Soto became one of the most popular Buddhist schools in Japan. Efforts were made at Dogen's temple, Eiheiji, to preserve Dogen's teachings and practices, but the temple declined for a time until restored by Giun (1252–1333). *See also* Dogen; Ryokan; Ts'ao-tung school.

soul, animating force conjoined with the body in a human being but capable of separation at death and under other circumstances such as dreaming. In many religious traditions, the soul is understood as preexistent to any particular incarnation and as immortal once detached from the body. In dualistic anthropologies, the soul is that part of the human constitution related to the divine, in opposition to the body. *See also* abortion; afterlife; animism; Ba; body; breath; dualism; fravashis; immortality; Ka; metampsychosis; psyche; shen; soul-loss; tama.

Indian Religions: All Indian religions and philosophies, including Buddhism but excepting materialists who consider humans merely aggregated matter, propound theories of a soul.

Vedic and Hindu Views: Hindu theories vary but generally agree that the soul is autonomous, spatially unmeasurable, objectively real, and ultimately unaffected by *karma* (the consequences of meritorious and demeritorious actions); that it survives physical death; and that it is distinguishable from what is unintelligent, insentient, or impermanent. Different terms introduce subtle conceptual distinctions as to the soul's ontological and epistemological status.

The most ancient sources, the Vedas (ca. 1500 B.C.), acknowledge a distinction between the physical body (e.g., *deha, kaya*) and the soul, the latter being ultimately "unborn" (*ajobhaga*) and "deathless" (*amartya*). An individual and independent entity, it animates the body and is separated from it at death or sometimes temporarily in such states as sleep, religious ecstasy, or unconsciousness. At death the soul flies like a bird either to the world of ancestors (*pitriloka*) or gods (*devaloka*), depending on the adequacy of one's earthly ritual. In later portions of the *Rig Veda* (ca. 1000 B.C.), *Purusha,* or "person," refers to the primordial universal soul in whom all souls originate.

Later Hindus consolidate and elaborate such views. The idea of a universal soul or *paramatman* as the source of everything (including individual souls) is advanced in diverse Upanishadic teachings (ca. 900–200 B.C.). Here the soul, usually called *atman* or purusha, is described as bearing qualities (*saguna*) in relation to god, and impersonally as qualityless (*nirguna*). It is also called existent (*sat*), intelligent (*cit*), and blissful (*ananda*) in nature. Residing in the heart, it is identical with creation's ultimate source, *brahman*. Realizing its nature confers immortality or union with god. The Upanishads also contain the nascent Samkhya school's absolute distinction between matter (*prakriti*) which includes intellect (*buddhi*), ego (*ahamkara*), and mind (*manas*)—and purusha as soul or spirit.

Later Upanishad exegetes disagree on the soul's relationship to the body and its identity with absolute reality, or god. Influential interpreters include Shankara (eighth century), whose monism identifies the individual and universal soul and establishes the soul as the only true reality; Ramanuja (eleventh century), whose qualified nondualism asserts relationships of difference and identity between the supreme soul and individual souls; and Madhva (fourteenth century), whose absolute dualism posits ontological distinctions between matter, souls, and god.

Other Views: Buddhists reject the notion that any entity can be eternal or unchanging and teach that there is "no-self" (*anatman*), that is, no transmigrating soul. However, a conventional self is said to function in dependent relationships and to bear the consequences of actions and intentions that determine consecutive lives. Liberating knowledge distinguishes the conventional self—aggregated of elements drawn together by the moral force of previous deeds and desires—from the misconception of an immutable, substantial, and eternal soul.

Jains posit a soul (*jiva*) separable from matter, but prior to liberation coextensive with the body it occupies and susceptible to pain and binding discoloration from bad karma. Ajivikas posit souls that encompass yet extend far beyond the bodies they occupy. *See also* aggregates; atman; Hinduism (thought and ethics); karma; six systems of Indian philosophy.

Judaism: The soul is the animating element of living things contrasted to the physical body, which is the soul's vehicle. The Hebrew words generally translated as "soul" (*nefesh, neshamah,* and *ruakh*) refer to breath. This accords with the fact that in the Hebrew Bible and later Jewish writings the soul is associated primarily with respiration, narrowly signifying the life force. This view differs from that of other Near Eastern cultures, which associate the soul more broadly with power, destiny, and appearance.

Talmudic rabbis neither conceived of the soul's immortality as separate from that of the body nor imagined the transmigration of the soul from one body to another. Body and soul, rather, were understood to be separate

only in origin, with the body deriving from human parents and the soul originating with God, to whom it returns when the body dies. Later, at the time of the resurrection of the dead, the soul will be restored to that same body (see Jerusalem Talmud *Kilaim* 8:4, 31c; Babylonian Talmud *Berakhot* 60a).

According to talmudic Judaism, all human souls were brought into existence at the time of creation, having been aspects of the spirit or wind (*ruakh*) of God referred to at Genesis 1:2. The Messiah will come either when all of these souls have been used or, alternatively, when God has finished creating all of the souls intended from the beginning (see, e.g., Babylonian Talmud *Abodah Zarah* 5a).

Accompanied by divine messengers and conscious of its origins, the soul enters the womb at the time of conception (Babylonian Talmud *Berakhot* 60b). When people sleep, the soul ascends to heaven, returning renewed in the morning (*Genesis Rabbah* 14:9). Although the soul protests its birth into the world, it also protests the body's death. It lingers near the body for three days, hoping that it will return to life (Tanhuma, *Miqetz* 4; *Pequdei* 3). After three days, the soul returns to God to await the time of resurrection (Babylonian Talmud *Sanhedrin* 90b–91a). During the first twelve months after death, the soul remains in contact with the disintegrating body (Babylonian Talmud *Shabbat* 152b–153a). After this, the souls of the righteous go to paradise (*gan eden*, the Garden of Eden) and the souls of the wicked, to hell (*gehinnom*).

Medieval Jewish philosophers associated souls with all living things, including animals and plants as well as humans. But they disagreed about the nature of the association between the soul and the physical entity. Those who followed Plato (e.g., Solomon Ibn Gabirol, 1021–58) generally treated the soul as a distinct entity conjoined with the body. Those who followed Aristotle (e.g., Abraham Ibn Daud, 1110–80), by contrast, treated the soul as an aspect of the body, responsible for the body's ability to engage in independent activity. In this latter view, unlike in the earlier talmudic perspective, body and soul can have no existence independent of each other.

In keeping with the earlier rabbinic view, medieval Jewish philosophers rejected belief in the transmigration of souls, a concept they saw as incompatible with the more fundamental doctrine of resurrection. In this, Jewish philosophy differed from kabbalistic mysticism, in which the doctrine of transmigration is central. *See also* resurrection.

Traditional Religions: Ideas about spiritual entities or forces that animate living beings, providing movement, power, consciousness, and personhood, are widely distributed throughout traditional religions. No one set of concepts prevails, even in a given community. Life is a cojoining of souls and bodies, with an in-standing soul (as the Navajos say) providing life to the body (as wind gives life to the world), manifesting itself in breath, prayer, and song. Human and other forms of life depend upon this spiritual force for their existence. Efforts are taken to maintain the soul-body union, since soul-body separation implies death.

Ideas about health, sorcery, medicine, and shamanism are formulated with reference to concepts of soul. For the Ojibwas, health is a stable communion between soul and body. Sorcery may involve damage or theft of a soul. Medicine includes rebalancing of soul-body relations, and shamanism attempts the recovery of lost or stolen souls. The body's dependence on the soul represents the material world's dependence on the spiritual realm. Souls are often said to be dynamic, vital forces. For the Lubas, one's life project is to augment one's vital force, in order to increase potency in oneself and in one's community. At death a potent vital force will become a powerful ancestor and perhaps receive homage from the living and be reincarnated into future members of the lineage.

Alternatively, each person may possess multiple souls. The dual-soul concept is widespread in North America. Each soul represents an aspect of life functions, such as foresight or strength, or a part of the body. If one soul animates the body while a second, free soul travels far and wide in dreams and visions, such spiritual entities enhance communication with the spiritual world through ecstatic (out-of-body) experiences. The way in which one lives a life is related in part to the condition of the soul beyond death. The soul, however, does not constitute the real person apart from the physical body, nor is the soul valued above life itself. Rather, souls are viewed as crucially supporting means of life, not ends in themselves. The Igbos posit a multiple self, with three spiritual aspects: *obi* (breath, vital force, animation, consciousness), *chi* (emanation of the supreme god, one's personal destiny), and *eke* (reborn spirit of an ancestor, a guardian spirit). None of these souls is the complete person; neither is the combination of the three. They are the spiritual dimensions of human personhood that make life possible. Souls are not thought to be the exclusive property of humans and deities (spiritual beings). Humans live in an animate world inhabited by ensouled beings, a concept sometimes referred to as *animism.* Human beings owe both practical and ethical attention to all ensouled beings, including animals, plants, clouds, and mountains. *See also* shamanism; soul-loss.

soul-loss, absence of soul from a living body, cause of sickness and death. Though the soul may be lost through dreaming or expelled by sneezing, most usually it has been stolen by sorcery. A religious specialist (frequently a shaman) is required to locate the soul and return it to its owner's body. *See also* shaman; shamanism; soul.

South American religions, traditional. The Amazon drainage basin alone is inhabited by hundreds of tribes speaking diverse languages: Arawakan and Cariban on the Northern tributaries; Tupian and Ge on the Southeastern rivers; Jivaroan (Shuar), Tucanoan, Quichua, and Panoan in the west, etc. The religions of these Indian nations are not voluntary associations with creeds or charters that members subscribe to; one would not label oneself a member of a South American Indian religion. Nor can anyone articulate a standard set of beliefs that the tribe subscribes to. Most of the people who could be identified as practicing an indigenous religion are also members of some Christian church. Even the medicine people, who might be identified as the ritual leaders of indigenous religions, frequently identify themselves as Catholics. Despite Christian influence, however, millions of native people throughout South America continue to maintain the distinctive ceremonies of their respective nations.

To skim the surface of these many South American traditions briefly highlighting common denominators would reduce them to trivia. Rather, we shall look in some detail at representative rituals from two culture areas: the closely related Shuar and Quichua cultures of the Ecuadorian Amazon and the Inca/Quichua of the Andes.

The Amazon: The purpose of Napo Quichua and Shuar religion is to court intimate relations with the spirit persons (*supay runa* or Shuar *arutam*) that inhabit the rivers, cliffs, forests, and manioc gardens. These spirits are the humanlike ancestors of the present plant and animal species. Each of these spirits has its own history. According to Napo tradition, armadillos, for example, are the descendants of people who survived a forest fire. In the process of surviving that fire the armadillo people received certain skills or gifts. Their armor is the hardened remains of the blankets that people rolled them-

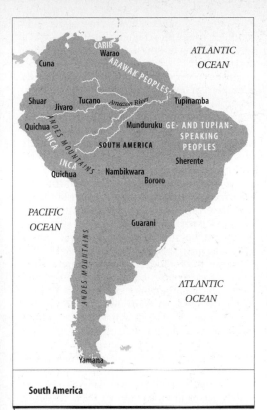

South America

ate some of that attractive power for themselves. Relations with the anaconda people center on the specific cliffs where the game is kept. At puberty Shuar boys fast at these locations in search of visions. If their quests are successful, the anaconda spirit women come to them as helpers. They "marry" the boys, giving them the attractive power of the anaconda people. Throughout their lives these boys seek to deepen their relations with their anaconda spirit helpers.

Before major hunts, medicine men make spirit journeys to the homes of their anaconda in-laws to negotiate the release of game. As these men sing, their animal spirit wives open the doors of the pools and the fish swim out. They open the doors of the mountains and the peccary run out. When the hunters go out at dawn, the animals come to them because the men have the attractive power of the anaconda spirit people.

Drawing game from the hill houses is not a one way movement. To replenish their storehouses the anaconda people are said to take human lives, transforming them back into animal form. For hunters without special relations to the anaconda people, walking along the riverbanks is dangerous. The anacondas may appear as beautiful girls to lure hunters into their underwater home. If the hunter fails to recognize the anaconda in her human guise, he may be seduced and turned into an animal himself.

In recent decades significant numbers of Amazonian hunters have become evangelical Christians. The converts often identify the yacu runa as devils and traditional shamans as witches. But conversion does not mean a complete break with the religious world of the hill houses, because converts still hunt the animals released by traditional shamans. "When the witches ask the devils to release an animal for them," one man said, "we steal it from the devil just like you might steal a chicken that has been let out of someone else's house."

While men hunt, traditional Quichua and Shuar women spend much of their time preparing manioc. Like the animals, manioc plants are believed to be transformations of ancient human life. According to Shuar myth, a poor woman with no knack for growing crops once saw manioc peelings coming down a stream she thought was uninhabited. She followed the stream upriver until she came to a beautiful manioc field. It was the home of Nunghui, Manioc Woman, the mother of manioc. Nunghui took pity on the woman and gave her a holy baby who was really Manioc Woman's sister, or double. As long as the manioc baby was respected and cared for she sang spirit songs that

selves in. Their digging skills were learned while escaping the fire. Although they are no longer visible as people, the human ancestors of the armadillos and other animals are still present as supay runa, or spirit people, governing the special gifts of their descendants. These spirits are the object of Quichua and Shuar religion.

Like the armadillos, each species with its unique gifts is a particular transformation of human life. If the specialized skills of the animals represent transformations of ancient human life, living people may acquire these skills as well, and they do so by entering into special relationships with the animal spirit persons. Among the most important of the animal spirit people in the Napo and Shuar worlds are the large predators: jaguars, harpy eagles, and anacondas. The anacondas, called *yacu runa*, or water spirit people (Shuar *tsungui*), are especially important because they are persons transformed in ways that allow them to attract game. The yacu runa lock all the game animals they attract inside their anaconda houses—cliffs and whirlpools that serve as reservoirs of game. Hence they are said to be the owners of game.

To be successful, native hunters court the favor of the yacu runa, and if possible appropri-

miraculously produced large quantities of manioc. But one day the woman grew careless and left the manioc baby alone with her other children, who threw dirt in the baby's eyes. In anger the holy child withdrew, transforming herself back into the ground. But as she sunk into the manioc field she left special stones, manioc plants, and manioc-growing songs that were remembered by the poor woman.

The earth into which Nunghui's daughter disappeared, the plants, and all the things she left behind, are the living remains of Manioc Woman. Her life is in them. Traditional Shuar women spend their lives cultivating close relations with Nunghui as she appears in the form of these living remains. They feed the stones as they would feed the child of Nunghui. They treat the plants and earth tenderly, observing their growth, singing to them as they would sing to the child of Nunghui. As they do so, they become the women of Nunghui, women with hands specially gifted for raising manioc and a wide variety of other plants.

Andes: The Andes was one of only a few areas in the world where city-states evolved independently. Some observers claimed that the Incas, in the city-state of Cusco, introduced a new religion of the sun. Unlike previous Andean religions, Inca religion was classified as an imperial religion, which, like the religions of Rome or Japan, unified the state by identifying the emperor with the sun.

The Incas simply adapted pan-Andean patterns to suit their particular needs. As in the Amazon, Andean religion centers on a sacrificial exchange with local mountains and pools believed to be the spirit reservoirs of game, crops, and rain. As in the Amazon, these reservoirs are owned by spirit people who take the form of the great predators: the condor, the puma, the anaconda (*amaru*). The Inca cult differs from other Andean religions in that it subjects the old Andean exchange with the mountains and lakes of sustenance to an elaborate system of state control.

Like other Andean peoples, the Incas identify local mountains both as places of emergence for local tribes and as the houses out of which the sun rises. It is said that at the dawn of the age, the Inca ancestors emerged from a cliff in Tampu T'oqo mountain and ascended to the city of Cusco, which means Zenith. This emergence of the Incas from the inside of a mountain to the Zenith is identified with the ascent of a new sun, which inaugurated a new age. According to Inca myth, when a new sun emerges it incorporates the remnants of the previous age into

a new reign. The Inca campaign to integrate surrounding tribes into the nascent Inca state is a way of carrying out these solar acts of subduing and ordering.

At the center of the Inca state is Qorikancha, a temple that housed a huge gold disk of the sun. According to the chronicler Garcilasso de la Vega, Qorikancha (the Temple of the Sun) had adjacent gardens outfitted with gold images of maize fields and other crops. Modern Andeans say that the interiors of mountains are similarly outfitted with gold maize fields and storehouses of crops and animals. Thus, Qorikancha, the man-made "Sun House" at the center of Cusco, may have been intended to mirror the mountains of sustenance that housed the sun—perhaps even Tampu T'oqo, the mountain out of which the Incas themselves had emerged.

At the heart of Inca religion is a system of exchange between this central "Sun House" and cults to local mountains throughout the Andes. Radiating out from Qorikancha like a sundial were four principal roads to the four quarters. At intervals of every hundred miles or so along these rays, the Incas constructed administrative centers, each with a temple of the sun and a granary. Each of these temples and storehouses would have mirrored both Qorikancha in Cusco and the local mountain houses of the sun, which were spirit storehouses of grain and animals. By putting Incas in control of these administrative centers and temples, the Inca state centralized control of commerce with all local hill houses. Offerings and sacrifices to local mountains were now collected by the state and redistributed to the various spring or mountain shrines. The resulting gifts of animal and crop fertility that were drawn from the mountain lakes were then mediated back to local people through the Inca state. The Inca elite did indeed identify themselves with the sun, whose home was inside these mountains. But their identity was by no means exclusively solar. They also took names such as Poma (Jaguar) or Tupac Amaru (Great Anaconda), names that identified them with the animal spirit owners of game inside the mountains.

With the execution of the Inca Atahualpa in 1536, Christianity replaced Inca tradition as the religion of state. Centralized control over the spirit storehouses was broken, but despite persecution, native Andean religion adapted and survived. The approximately six million Quichua-speakers and two million Aymaras now living in the Andean region constitute the largest surviving native culture in the Americas. Until the 1950s nearly all native Andeans identified themselves as Catholics. Many modern Andean people are devoted to local saints. Pervasive pictures of saints and pilgrimages undertaken to visit them give the impression that modern Andean religion differs little from Spanish popular Catholicism.

On closer examination, however, native Andean veneration of the saints turns out to be inseparable from the cult of mountains. The most prominent local virgins and saints are believed to have emerged out of the mountains just as the Incas did. In the Quito area, for example, the Virgin of Quinche was born out of a boulder near Mt. Oyacachi on the eastern horizon, the Virgin of Banos was born out of a spring in the side of the mountain mother Tungurahua to the south, and so on. San Ignacio and San Antonio de Pichincha emerged out of Mt. Lulubamba. The insides of mountains from which the saints came are described as containing churches or as having gold walls like churches. When the saints emerged from their mountain homes they were said to have been "caught" and housed inside the gilded walls of churches that, like the Inca temple Qorikancha, look like the insides of mountains. For native Andeans, churches, like mountains, are centers of concentrated power from which to draw blessing for plant and animal fertility.

While some myths tell how the saints emerged from the mountains, others tell how the mountains and lakes arose from the deeds of the saints. In the Quito area it is said that in ancient times the Virgin and a male saint (often called Taita Dios or Nuestro Senor) were starving. In their hunger they journeyed to the great wealthy estates to beg a little food from the stockpiles of maize. They were turned away. The saints then punished the hacienda owners by turning their whole estates, complete with chapels, into the mountains (Mt. Imbabura, Cerro Chivo) or lakes (San Pablo) of sustenance in northern Ecuador. There is thus an inseparable connection between the insides of churches with their saints and the insides of mountains with their mountain spirit people.

During times of abundance, water, as well as plant and animal life, is drawn out of these mountains to sustain human needs. But as with the hill houses in the Amazon, the depleted mountain reserves must then be replenished. The mountains are believed to become killers. They create mirages that lure travelers to their deaths in canyons. They appear to cowboys or truck drivers as beautiful women to lure them inside the mountains from which they never return. At high altitudes, hail and frost suck the life

out of the crops, drawing the sap back into the mountains. In drier, lower altitudes the mountain spirits ride dust dervishes into the communities, sucking water from the fields. When these winds blast children or other persons whose vital power (*suerte*) is weak, they get wind sickness or fright sickness (*susto*). Their depleted life force replenishes the mountains.

Andean shamans are frequently understood to be pious Christian people who mediate the circulation of sustenance and blessing between the mountains and human communities. In the Quito area higher-level curers are said to be ritual kinsmen (*compadres, comadres,* or spouses) of the mountain spirit people. In nocturnal curing ceremonies they lay out an altar to the mountains called a mesa. Mesas vary across the Andes, but in the Quito area they contain stone ax heads representing the body parts of various mountains or petrified animals found in the springs. After these medicine stones are laid out and surrounded with flowers, the mountains are summoned in song. When they appear in little winds, the shamans feed them rum, tobacco, and food in exchange for returning the blood or soul of the sick.

It is within the broader context of commerce with the mountains that the Andean fiesta system is best understood. During the fiestas of the saints huge quantities of chicha, hominy, potatoes, or llama meat are prepared. Neighbors from distant mountains or from other parts of the same mountain are given lavish hospitality. In hosting them people are said to host the mountains from which they come. In the community of Juncal, Ecuador, masked men representing mountains dance from house to house consuming the food. Through all this drinking and eating the mountain storehouses are replenished for another season.

In the 1990s the fiestas are generally sponsored by the community as a whole. But before the 1970s individual couples sponsored a series of fiestas as a way of establishing their own special relations with the saints and the mountain spirit people. After having passed through a standard series of fiesta sponsorships providing music, dancers, and huge quantities of food and drink, the husband and wife became completed persons (*pasado runacuna*). By that time they were often deeply indebted, but their credit with saints and with the mountain spirit reservoirs was strong.

To lift out any general principles from these few examples risks reducing the South American traditions to a caricature, and has been done only to provide some preliminary orientation for further journeying into the rich complexity of the South American traditions. At the heart of all native South American religions is the desire to maintain intimate relations with the plant and animal spirit people on whom life depends. The power of these spirit persons tends to be concentrated in local mountains and lakes from which life emerges. Present human life is linked to these mountains in a closed economy. The spirit people give game, manioc, maize, rain. In return they also take life. By tuning human life to the seasonal movements of the holy people, rituals help to regulate this exchange. Christianity has not brought an end to exchange with the mountain spirit people; instead it has been adapted to fit this basic pattern. *See also* agriculture, religious aspects of; guardian spirit; hunting, religious aspects of; jaguar (South American religions); Mesoamerican religion; mountains, sacred; shamanism; temple.

Southeast Asia, religions of. The mainland countries (Thailand, Myanmar, Cambodia, Laos) emphasize Buddhism, while the island countries (Indonesia, Malaysia, southern Philippines) emphasize Islam. These world religions tend to dominate the lowland, irrigated rice areas. The so-called animistic religions dominate the remote tribal areas such as the highlands on the mainland and the interior jungle of the islands. ("Animism" refers to religions that emphasize the spiritual animation of material objects and locales: spiritual essences in sacred graves, weapons, amulets, or graves, for example.) Aside from these Buddhist, Islamic, and animistic areas, Confucian and other Chinese religions exist (in Vietnam, Singapore, and in Chinese minority communities throughout the region). Christianity is prominent in the Philippines, in areas of Indonesia such as the Toba Batak of Sumatra, the Minahasans of Sulawesi, and the Ambonese of the Moluccas, and in Chinese and other middle-class groups throughout the region. Small but old Jewish communities are to be found in some urban areas, as are other faiths associated with particular ethnic groups, and new cults and movements not directly associated with the historic world religions continue to emerge.

In the religions of Southeast Asia, one finds rich and varied religious experience. Whether Buddhist, Muslim, or other, Southeast Asian religions tend toward a kind of animism. The earliest religious pattern of the region is animistic,

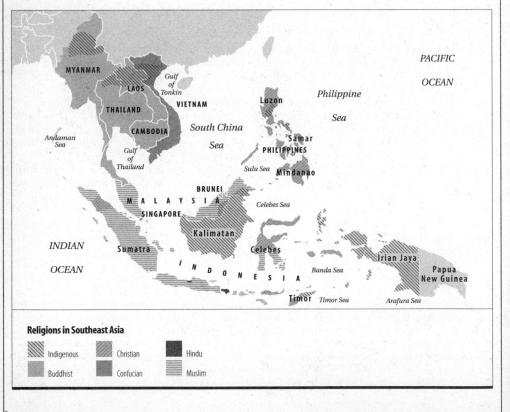

Religions in Southeast Asia

Indigenous | Christian | Hindu
Buddhist | Confucian | Muslim

and this remains the most pervasive. The world is experienced as a field of spiritual energy that pervades all of life and can become concentrated in almost any form. For those of a purist inclination, these energies are seen as concentrated in some single entity, such as God. For those of a mystical inclination, the energies are more pervasive and can be discovered through meditation and other exercises that unite self and cosmos. All three orientations (animist, purist, mystic) are found among Southeast Asians professing all the major religions, notably Buddhism or Islam.

Hindu influences become apparent by the second century, and gain expression in the great Hindu empires such as Angkor Wat in Cambodia and Majapahit in Java during the period from the seventh to the fifteenth centuries. The spread of Theravada Buddhism on the mainland and Islam in the islands, beginning around the fourteenth century, adds a new culture, which is followed soon after by the arrival of Western cultures and Christianity. As each new wave of religious and cultural influence spreads, the older ones are not eliminated but contextualized—coming to represent a certain level or domain within the total religious experience. Thus, a single shrine may include figures representing Buddhism, Islam, Christianity, and animism; a person may be primarily Buddhist but also profess Islam; a prayer may be directed to deities or figures of all of these faiths; and a person may practice magical animistic ceremonies in some circumstances, Hindu astrology in others, and follow Buddhist principles in another. *See also* Southeast Asian Islands, new religions in.

Southeast Asian Islands, new religions in.

Sectarian religious movements, drawing on both world religions and indigenous beliefs, have been a prominent feature of life in the Southeast Asian Islands throughout the colonial period and have continued into the republican period. During the colonial periods in both the Dutch East Indies and the Philippines, such movements commonly were vehicles for protests against foreign rule, with its accompanying economic disruption and oppression. However, in neither region can all movements be traced to political or economic distress. Rivalries among social groups with different cultural allegiances in the nineteenth and twentieth centuries have also contributed to sectarian activity, along with cultural alienation brought about by intensifying Western influences.

Philippines: Anticolonial rebellions on a small scale, the *tumultos*, occurred at regular intervals throughout the period of Spanish colonialism and from very early on were shaped around Christian millenarian imagery. One of the earliest, in Panay in 1663, was led by a sorcerer named Tapar, who claimed to be "God Almighty." Every twenty years or so the Spanish faced outbursts led by individuals who styled themselves as God, Jesus, or the pope and offered their bands magical protection in the imminent end of the world.

The first coordinated rebellion of more than local dimensions was the uprising of Apolinario de la Cruz in 1841. This movement frustrated the desires of the Catholic Church to infiltrate the indigenous population. Cruz, denied entrance into a Catholic order on racial grounds, founded his own lay brotherhood, the Cofradia de San Jose, but was refused recognition by the archbishop of Manila. This sparked a rebellion joined by elements of the rebuffed native intelligentsia as well as economically oppressed peasants. Armed suppression forced the increasingly heretical Cofradia underground, and survivors moved to mountain hideouts. In the ritual life of those mountain refugees are the historical origins of the *Colorums*, sectarian groups and cults that patronized pre-Christian religious sites identified with sites in the Christian Holy Land.

In the last decade of the nineteenth century and the first decade of the twentieth, the revolution against the Spanish and the upheavals associated with American intervention unleashed a spate of peasant religious movements. Among these was the Guardia de Honor, a lay association founded by Dominican friars in the mid-nineteenth century to promote devotion to the Virgin. In 1890, when the friars attempted to turn it into a counterrevolutionary force, the Guardia began to escape control of the Church. By 1894, it had metamorphosed into a heterodox peasant movement. The little town of Cabaruan in Pangasinan became the center of sect activities, growing from a population of about five hundred to twenty-five thousand at its peak in 1901. Uneasy with this aberrant society and complaints of pillage of neighboring lands, the American forces occupied the town and an offshoot center, Santa Ana, in 1901 and dispersed the population. By 1910, police actions against remnants had ceased.

During the time the Guardia de Honor was active, other sectarian groups also emerged, some peaceable and others rebellious. Among these were the Santa Iglesia ("Holy Church"), Dios-Dios, Colorados, the Pulajanes ("Red Shirts") and the bands of Papa ("Pope") Isio and Papa Faustino. A lull in new activity followed in the decade after 1910. This was broken in the 1920s by millenarianistic uprisings—identified with Colorums—in northeastern Mindanao. These were inspired by religious revolts in Nueva Ecija in 1925 and Iloilo and Negros Occidental in 1927, and by the major Colorum movement in 1931 in Tayug, Pangasinan, just twenty miles from the onetime center of the Guardia de Honor, Cabaruan. Between 1932 and 1952, however, sectarian movements receded, giving way to secular protest movements: the peasant Sakdal uprising of 1935, socialism, and communism.

While the militaristic millenarian movements of the early 1900s inevitably attracted suppression, and millenarianism itself suffered an eclipse during the period of secular protest, movements for a naturalized Church bore more enduring fruits. The most prominent of these fruits are the Iglesia Filipina Independente (The Philippine Independent Church) and the Iglesia Ni Christo (The Church of Christ). The Iglesia Filipina Independente was founded in 1902 by Gregorio Aglipay, a Philippino Catholic priest who served as chaplain general to the revolutionary forces of Aguinaldo and was excommunicated by the Spanish ecclesiastical hierarchy. The Iglesia Ni Cristo was founded in 1914 by Felix Manalo, a self-taught student first of Catholicism and then of Protestant Christianity. The Philippine Independent Church and the Iglesia Ni Cristo are today substantial religious forces in the country, with almost mainstream profiles. Together with about 350 other Protestant churches or sects, many of them strongly naturalized, they account for approximately 20 percent of the Philippine Christian population.

Alongside the Catholic, Protestant, and naturalized Philippine Christian churches in the postcolonial Philippines, millenarianist groups once again have appeared, belying both the thesis that millenarianism is exclusively a response to colonialism and that protest movements follow an irreversible evolutionary trajectory from supernatural to secular as regions encounter the industrial and technological world. In the wake of failed secular protest movements and in a world severely disrupted by war and accelerating capitalist expansion and Westernization, numerous new sects and some revitalized prewar sects have appeared on the Philippine scene since the 1950s. Sambahang Rizal (Rizal Church), Bathalismo, the Adarnistas, the Divine Crusaders of Christ, the Iglesia Sagrada ng Lahi (Pride of the Blood Church), and the Iglesia Watawat ng Lahi (Pride of the Race Church), as well as a number of Colorum groups claim

memberships ranging between 7,000 and 125,000. Like prewar millenarian movements, they draw on both Christian and indigenous beliefs and center around leaders believed to have supernatural stature and powers. Unlike the prewar movements, however, they have substantial urban as well as rural followings, and all worship national heroes, particularly Jose Rizal, the nineteenth-century novelist, physician, and nationalist executed by the Spanish in 1896.

Indonesia: As in the Philippines, millenarianism has been endemic in the Indonesian islands throughout the colonial period and is still part of the religious scene. In areas of the Dutch East Indies where there existed an Islamic population (mostly peasant areas on the island of Java) religiously inspired protest movements were almost invariably messianic. (The nativistic and anti-Muslim Samin movement most active in central Java between 1904 and 1915 is a notable exception.) Messianic beliefs derived both from Islamic culture, with its tradition of the return of the Imam Mahdi, and from Hindu-Javanese culture with its beliefs in a Ratu Adil ("Just King"). Whatever the cultural idiom, the Messiah was expected to establish an archetypal "just" kingdom in which right order and prosperity would prevail.

Regardless of the degree of emphasis on indigenous elements, millenarianist protest movements in the Java prior to the twentieth century remained self-consciously Muslim. This derives from the cultural gap between the rural religious leadership and the aristocracy, who accepted the role of intermediaries for Dutch rule. Islam was practiced in court circles in a lax and highly Java-centered form. Much of the peasantry did the same, but independent Muslim community leaders in the countryside (Arab. *ulama* or Javanese *kiyayi*) of a stricter bent were often able to brand both local princes and the Dutch as *kafirs* (Arab., "unbelievers") and thereby rally disgruntled subjects against colonial oppression.

Non-Muslim millenarian movements erupted after the turn of the century in tribal areas in the islands beyond Java when direct colonial administration was introduced. Among the Toraja, a traditional pattern of temporary withdrawal from society, called *mayapi*, took an unexpected form between 1902 and 1908, when disgruntled successionists awaited an unprecedented opening of the world of the ancestors to the living. Similar movements among the Dayaks, called *nyuli*, occurred first in the late 1880s, but the major outbreaks were in the 1920s. In the Batak areas of Sumatra, messianism developed around the figure of a legendary priest-king, Si Singa Mangaraja, who was expected to save believers from a millennial cataclysm. One sect organized around these beliefs, the Pormalin group, still attracted members in the republican period. Another manifestation was the Parhudamdam movement, active between 1915 and 1930. This movement actually claimed the status of a "new religion" (*agama baru*) and displayed a degree of conscious competition for legitimacy—on the terms of the world religions—not seen in the outer islands until much later in the century.

Intensifying contacts with Near Eastern Islamic reformism and the spreading of bureaucracy into all areas of life in Java ushered in a new era of religious innovation after the turn of the century. Those committed to the Hindu, Buddhist, and indigenous elements of their religious heritage found it difficult to maintain an allegiance to Islam. At the same time, the increasingly popular mode of association—formal organization—required that commitments be stated with a new specificity and identified with a distinctive name. Under these circumstances, inspired teachers began to identify their teachings as something other than Islamic, whether "Javanese Islam" (*Islam Jawa*) or more Hindu-Buddhist in character. The majority of these were mystical (*kebatinan*) and occultist groups, though some were more concerned with ethics and psychological well-being. Some of the groups perpetuated Javanist messianism.

After independence, such groups proliferated dramatically and began to attract the epithet *new religions*. The term reflected, on the one hand, the desirability of formal recognition as a religion (*agama*) under the 1945 constitution, which committed Indonesians not only to a belief in God, but to a belief that the nation should support religions. On the other hand, the term reflected the hegemony of the monotheistic religions, according to which the only true revelations were old ones. Sectarian groups thus believed they needed government legitimation. To achieve this, many attempted to gain recognition as religions, either individually or categorically. Numerous sects featured the term agama in their names (e.g., Agama Islam Sejati Republik Indonesia [The True Islamic Religion of the Republic of Indonesia], Agama Adam Makrifat, Agama Sapta Darma, and Agama Islam Hak [The Rightful Islamic Religion], whose members prayed facing the ancient Buddhist temple of Borobudur, where the spirit of the Prophet Muhammad was thought to have descended). As in the Philippines, a nationalistic

element was common in the names and teachings of the sects. In Indonesia, this most commonly took the form of references to the *Panca Sila* (Five Pillars) of nationhood in the preamble to the constitution.

Fears of communist influences in the mystical groups, as well as strict Muslim objections to the proliferation of heresies in the highly unstable political and economic environment of the early sixties, were behind the major setback for mystical and other groups arising out of the native genius. Sukarno's Presidential Decision No. 1 of 1965 (later made into law by the Suharto government) identified only six religions of "world" stature as deserving of support under the constitution. New religions were henceforth illegal and many were disbanded, some violently, as in the case of Mbah Suro's sect, where communist affiliations or anti-Muslim sentiment was suspected.

Mystical and other independent spiritual groups were never again able to insist on recognition as religions. In the 1970s, however, the patronage of the Javanist Suharto regime secured for them legitimation as *faiths* (*kepercayaan*), a term also found in the constitution in a context suggesting equivalence, if not identity, with religion. New spiritual groups thus remain active today and attract from a few hundred to many thousands of members. The largest are Subud (the only Javanese faith to have overseas branches), Pangestu, Sumarah, and Sapta Darma. Some outer island tribal traditions have also achieved acceptance as named faiths alongside the Javanese mystical groups.

Despite the many similarities in the histories of sectarianism in the Philippines and Indonesia, it is remarkable how differently indigenous syncretic movements have been treated under their respective republican governments. In the Philippines, where Catholicism has been discredited for its role in Spanish colonialism, naturalized Christianity and even Rizalista extrapolations from Christianity have suffered no legal restriction as long as they refrained from armed conflict with the state. In Indonesia, however, the role of Islam in the nationalist movement and the need to make limited concessions to substantial Christian ethnic minorities have made for a hegemonic alliance of "world religions" and a long, only partially successful struggle on the part of indigenous spiritual groups to escape persecution and second-class status. *See also* Iglesia Ni Cristo; Muhammadiyah; Southeast Asia, religions of; Subud.

Southern school (Chin. *Nan-tsung*), name taken by

the school of Chinese Ch'an Buddhism that championed the teaching of sudden enlightenment. After winning the sudden-gradual controversy, its position became normative for all subsequent schools of Ch'an and Zen Buddhism, although the school itself died out after the persecution of 845. *See also* Ch'an school; Northern school; sudden-gradual controversy.

Sowon. *See* academies (Korea), private and public.

space. *See* sacred space and sacred time.

Spener, Phillip Jakob (1635–1703), German Lutheran theologian, a key figure in the growth of the Pietist movement through his organization of "schools of piety" and his major work, *Pia Desideria* (Pious Desires, 1675). *See also* Pietism.

spirit. *See* soul.

spiritism, term meaning both belief in or a system for communication with the spirits of the dead, based in the tradition that human beings are composed of separable body and spirit and that the latter survives death as a personal entity. Formerly used to identify all such phenomena of other-worldly interchange, the term has been superseded by more precise designations, such as Spiritualism, connoting modern efforts and organizations descendant from the nineteenth-century phenomena of Europe and the Americas; shamanism, tribal practices centered on individual gifted seers who communicate with the spirit world; and mediumship or trance-mediumship. The origin of the term *spiritism* has been (questionably) attributed to Allan Kardec (1804–69), to whose religious cosmology, Kardecism, the name spiritist is still applied. In Brazil, where Kardecism remains a vital religious principle, national spiritist congresses have been held twice since the 1940s, and spiritism is identified with spirit-possession of trained mediums in new religions of varying African and Christian heritage. *See also* Afro-Brazilian religions; Kardecism.

spirit money, a generic term for an extensive class of imitation banknotes burned during popular Chinese rituals as offerings to gods and ancestors; it is also called ghost money or mock money. Burning transfers the money to the spirit world, where gods and ancestors can use it for their living expenses.

The variety is immense: large sheets decorated with gold are offered to heaven and higher deities; smaller sheets are presented to lower-

ranking gods; silver sheets tied together in thick bundles are offered to ancestors. *See also* ancestral rites; Chinese popular religion; Chinese ritual.

spirit possession. *See* possession.

spirits, general term for minor supernatural beings, especially disembodied ghosts.

Spiritual Baptists. *See* Afro-Americans (Caribbean and South America), new religions among.

spiritual direction, Christian practice in which one receives guidance on the journey to holiness. Christians see Jesus as the guide of the disciples, and the Christian tradition considers the Holy Spirit the primary guide of the community and the individual. Directors facilitate the action of the Holy Spirit.

The monastic experience gave birth to personal spiritual direction, as neophytes needed the counsel of experienced elders. A refinement of spiritual direction came with the Jesuits of the sixteenth and seventeenth centuries who applied the *Exercises* of Ignatius of Loyola (d. 1556) to the spiritual direction of Jesuits and others.

Direction is no longer closely associated with the sacrament of penace. Modern directors are aware of psychological insights, and assume a less authoritarian role. *See also* Ignatius of Loyola; monasticism; retreat.

Spiritualism, the belief that the spirit component of the human individual survives bodily death and that it is possible to communicate with spirits of the departed. Spiritualist churches offer spirit "readings" as a part of worship services, endorse psychic phenomena, and on occasion present trance-mediumship.

Origins: The origins of modern Spiritualism can be traced to the Fox sisters, Margaret (ca. 1833–93) and Catherine (1839–92), who in 1848 reported hearing a series of rappings in their farmhouse near Rochester, New York. Their announcement that the mysterious sounds were messages from a departed spirit stirred tremendous publicity and ignited a wildfire Spiritualist movement. Lectures, circles, and mediumship sprang up in the northeastern frontier areas. Debunkings, then as later, only succeeded in swelling interest.

The remarkable interest in Spiritualism, fired by the Fox sisters' revelations of 1848, can be explained only in terms of prior preparation. The tinder for that flame was the Swedenborgianism and Mesmerism popular in the United States of the 1830s. The combination of Swedenborg's concept of the afterlife with mesmeric trance in the experimental atmosphere of the young republic supported mediumship and Spiritualism. Also influential were the examples of Native American shamanism and the sentimental focus on death and dying in vogue in those years. More concretely, the way had been prepared by a trance-delivered 1847 book by Andrew Jackson Davis (1826–1910), *The Principles of Nature*, which was largely Swedenborgian in content. Davis subsequently became known as a major theoretician of Spiritualism.

The American Setting: Spiritualism moreover answered to an apparent need for a new religion felt by some in the new republic. Aware of the novelty of the democratic experiment, they yearned for a faith capable of expressing its fresh values. For a time, Spiritualism served. It was said to be the most democratic of religions because it did not depend on the authority of the past or of an entrenched hierarchy; instead, the role of medium was open to all. Women especially found in Spiritualism a faith that not only seemed particularly sensitive to their feelings and concerns but also afforded them opportunity to exercise spiritual leadership—if only by giving voice to spirit mentors—then denied them in almost all other religions.

Early Spiritualism was articulate on reform. Spirits discoursed eloquently through entranced mediums on behalf of abolition of slavery, prison reform, the rights of women, and the protection of workers against exploitation. Proponents of Spiritualism also claimed it to be the most scientific of religions—if also "the oldest religion in the world" because of its lineage to the paleolithic shaman—because it based its beliefs on empirical evidence, the extraordinary happenings of the seance room.

Spiritualism was transmitted to England in the 1850s, whence it was carried to Australia, New Zealand, and South Africa, where it has probably had more adherents per capita than elsewhere in the English-speaking world.

On the European continent, such envoys as the celebrated Scottish-American "physical medium," D. D. Home, made table-turning and spirit-rapping the midcentury talk of the highest circles, including the courts of the French emperor and the Russian czar. Spiritualism also spread to Latin America, especially Brazil, where, in interaction with African-Brazilian cults, it has been a powerful spiritual influence with followers in the millions. It also has affected such new religions of Japan as Oomoto.

Worship: In the Anglo-American realm, Spiritualism faded as a vogue but has sustained an ongoing life. By the end of the nineteenth century, the mediumistic faith had made a transition from home circles, stage demonstrations, and experimental sittings to ecclesiastical life. Spiritualist churches, with altars, choirs, and ministers, had become the norm by the 1890s. Services characteristically follow a typical Protestant format, with hymns, inspirational texts, and sermon, but climax in the unique Spiritualist feature, readings by a medium. Standing at the front of the church, the medium will address particular members of the congregation, giving each person messages from spirit friends and information on future events. Spiritualist churches with their medium-ministers are generally independent, with only tenuous loyalty to the several Spiritualist denominations.

Popular interest in Spiritualism has waxed and waned. There was, for example, an upsurge in the 1920s following the tragic loss of life in World War I; it was abetted by vigorous worldwide lectures on behalf of the faith of its most famous convert, Arthur Conan Doyle (1859–1930), creator of Sherlock Holmes. In the late twentieth century the New Age interest in channeling seemed in some respects to be but Spiritualism under another name. *See also* medium; Mesmerism; North America, new religions in; parapsychology; psychics.

spirituality, Christian, in Roman Catholic devotional writing, the piety, the religious sensibility or insights of an individual, usually a saint. By extension it can refer to the traditional ambience of a particular Roman Catholic religious order. This ambience shapes the orders' communal life, and is also a guide for members of those orders who preach, write, and counsel individuals on the spiritual life of prayer and devotion.

spirituals, deeply emotional religious songs developed as African-American black slaves identified with stories of Israelite exodus from Egypt. Lyrics were sometimes coded to signal escape times and routes, with Canaan meaning Canada and Satan standing for slave masters. Spirituals' musical structure, style, and content are traced to both Africa and nineteenth-century Protestant American camp meetings.

Spring and Autumn Annals. *See* Ch'un-ch'iu.

Ssu-ma Ch'eng-chen (soo-mah chuhng-juhn; 647–735), the most celebrated Taoist leader of the T'ang dynasty. Of noble birth, he was a writer and artist as well as patriarch of the Shang-ch'ing lineage. He was honored as a wise and reliable counselor to several Chinese emperors. Several meditation texts attributed to him present a "gradualist" process of mental purification that results in union with the Tao and immortality after death. *See also* Shang-ch'ing Taoism.

Ssu-ming (soo-ming; Chin., "controller of fate"), god of longevity in Chinese popular religion; he is commonly identified with Tsao-chun, the kitchen god, who records human deeds. *See also* Chinese popular religion; Chinese ritual; New Year (China).

Ssu-shu (soo-shoo; Chin., "Four Books"), a Confucian canon determined by Chu Hsi (1130–1200) consisting of the books ascribed to Confucius and Mencius: *Lun Yu* (Analects), *Meng-tzu* (Mencius), *Ta-hsueh* (Great Learning), and *Chung Yung* (Doctrine of the Mean). Neo-Confucians refer to the Four Books and the Five Classics as the roots of Confucianism. *See also* Chu Hsi; Chung Yung; Confucianism (authoritative texts and their interpretation); Lun Yu; Mencius; Ta-hsueh.

staretz (stah'rets; Russ., "elder"), in Orthodox monasticism, a monk who, after a lengthy period of ascetic retreat, functions as a spiritual master. In the Greek Church he is called a *geron*. *See also* Orthodox Church.

starlore and ethnoastronomy, the knowledge of the stars, particularly as it is communicated verbally, through stories and tales, through ritual expertise, or through apprenticeship in the crafts or arts. Ethnoastronomy is the study of astronomic systems as they are envisaged in diverse cultural communities around the globe. The two terms are nearly synonymous. They emerge from a growing awareness of the role that astronomic knowledge has played in human history, in the organization of society, and in the development of fundamental concepts in culture.

The awareness that religious worldviews are involved with astronomic systems and symbolism is not new among students of religion. Apart from suggestive references in earlier authors, in 1798 Charles Francois Dupuis argued that all myths and fables were distorted attempts to speak of the regular movements of the stars. Observation of the starry night was the basis of a universal religion. Dupuis sketched the major constellations of this worldwide religion by guiding his readers through the mythologies of peoples around the globe, demonstrating how the irrational thought of myth might be de-coded with reference to the rational science of astronomy.

At the beginning of the twentieth century, the study of starlore played a large part in the study of Ancient Near Eastern religions by the so-called Pan-Babylonianists such as Hugo Winckler, Alfred Jeremias, and Eduard Stucken. They considered nearly all myths to be star myths, especially describing the triumph of astronomic order over chaos. They believed that social life and relations were modeled on the orderly relations perceived to exist among heavenly bodies. The appointments of religion—the structure of the temple, surrounding city precincts, and the social order revolving around them—reflected the order of the stars. They also held to the narrow view that astronomy began in the ancient Near East—especially Babylon and Assyria—and spread outward from there, becoming more confused and mystified as starlore moved outward into world populations.

Since the appearance of *Hamlet's Mill*, a global study of astronomy and mythology by Giorgio de Santillana and Hertha von Dechend in 1969, more careful attention has been given the ethnoastronomy of contemporary peoples as well as ancient systems, known mostly through archaeoastronomy.

Several sources currently fuel the study of starlore and ethnoastronomy: the decoding of the astronomic values of archaeological sites, including some going back to megalithic times; the discovery that astronomic observations among nonliterate populations are precise and complex; and the richness of the mythology associated with the observed movements of the stars as it is linked, in systematic ways, with knowledge of natural history, social organization, growth through the life cycle, agricultural or economic activities, and symbolic systems. Not to be discounted as a motive for the study of starlore is the new relationship of contemporary people to stars, provoked by space travel and astrophysical explorations via satellite.

Present efforts seldom try to reduce all religious symbolism to the literal movement of stars. Anthony F. Aveni has been a major stimulus for the exploration of astronomic systems and their relation to religious life, whether in his own work on the archaeology of sacred sites and the structure of calendars, or in his coordination of multidisciplinary teams of researchers to investigate horizon-based astronomies in the tropics. David Ulansey has applied the study of astronomy to the Hellenistic mystery religions of the eastern Mediterranean; Rubellite K. Johnson has presented important work on native Hawaiian astronomy, as it was enfolded in priestly knowledge. Studies such as those by Gary Urton and R. T. Zuidema of communities in the South American Andes demonstrate that starlore can best be understood as one aspect of the many processes drawn together to form a world by mythic and religious imagery. More balanced and comprehensive, these approaches contend that astronomic orders embellish, in distinctive ways, the fabric of perceptible orders in the universe, whether in human life or the natural history of plants, animals, or weather patterns. The procession of stars in the Milky Way, for example, is interlocked with the biorhythms of diverse species in the eco-niche as well as with the shifting rains, winds, and rainbows, which change as the sun courses back and forth between the solstice points.

In many traditional religions, the coordination of astronomic observations with ritual life grounds calendrical systems, which are sometimes simple and oftentimes complicated. Calendars not only mobilize social groups around points of the astronomical year but allow communities to evaluate their existence in time from distinct points of view. Recurrent appearances of stars allow communities to muse on the contradictions inherent in the passage of time and to puzzle out the existence of conjunctions among historical events, cosmic phenomena, and human life cycles that might otherwise pass unrelated. Megalithic peoples in Europe may have integrated into their astronomically oriented structures the cult of the dead, the experience of ordered space, the sacredness of stone, and the centrality of a female divinity. In other places on the globe, alignments on recurrent appearances of stars have generated long-counts and multiyear megacycles extending over periods of 16, 18, 52, or even 256 years, as in the Inca, Aztec, and Maya calendars. Such long time frames permit human life to be recast, allowing a community to resituate itself and reevaluate its activity and destiny in temporal terms that are more elastic than the individual human life span. *See also* astronomy (China).

Star of David. *See* Magen David/Star of David.

stars and constellations (Taoism). In China, the most powerful cosmic forces were frequently associated with the heavenly bodies, interpreted from ancient times as either beneficent or maleficent influences. Vitally concerned with achieving and maintaining cosmic harmony, Taoists assumed the traditional governmental responsibility of ritually managing the cosmos.

In certain rites, the priest symbolically traverses and unites the heavenly spheres. The precise visualization of the stellar divinities was also basic to many meditative processes. The practitioner could acquire protection from maleficent influences or nourish his spiritual essence by internalizing the luminous power of the stellar divinities. *See also* astronomy (China).

state cult, Chinese, the annual calendar of ritual obligations assumed by Chinese sovereigns. Shang (ca. 1766–1122 B.C.) rulers already considered themselves as both political leaders and high priests. Sometime in the Chou period (ca. 1122–221 B.C.), dynastic apologists developed the ideology of the Mandate of Heaven (T'ien-ming), which stated that the rulers were divinely appointed but must govern justly, with zealous concern for the welfare of the people. As religious functionaries, rulers were also required to offer regular sacrifices to the spirits of Heaven and Earth, to dynastic ancestors, and to the spirits who controlled the success of agriculture.

Each year, officials on the Board of Rites calculated times for the annual ritual calendar. The emperor himself officiated at the most important sacrifices; the rest were carried out by duly appointed deputies. The greater sacrifices were quite elaborate, with some, such as the sacrifices to Heaven and Earth at the winter and summer solstices, requiring many days of preparation and large numbers of officials, ministrants, musicians, dancers, and sacrificial animals.

Next in importance were the sacrifices to the dynastic ancestors at the imperial ancestral temple and those at the altar of land and grain. These latter rites, as well as the emperor's yearly spring plowing ritual at the Altar of the First Farmer, were performed to ensure the success of agriculture, on which the welfare of all China depended. There were also lesser rituals offered at many other sites in and around the capital. *See also* calendar (China); Chinese ritual; kingship, sacred.

state religion, a religion established by law as the single religion of a nation. In the 1990s, thirty-eight nations had state religions. Buddhism is the state religion of Bhutan, Myanmar, Sri Lanka, and Thailand; Christianity (Orthodox), of Bulgaria and Greece; Christianity (Protestant), of Denmark, England, Norway, Scotland, and Sweden; Christianity (Roman Catholic), of Argentina, Bolivia, Costa Rica, El Salvador, Malta, Paraguay, and Vatican City; Hinduism, of India and Nepal; and Islam, of Algeria, Bahrain, Bangladesh, Brunei, Comoros,

Iran, Iraq, Jordan, Kuwait, Malaysia, Maldives, Mauritania, Morocco, Oman, Pakistan, Saudi Arabia, Tunisia, and the United Arab Emirates.

State religion needs to be distinguished from state-subsidized religion, which is a far more widespread phenomenon. States may support one or many religions. For example, Iceland subsidizes the religions of all of its citizens, including those who have revived the ancient Norse religion of the Aesir gods. *See also* Christianity; church and state; Edict of Milan; law and religion (in the United States); matsuri-goto; Roman religion; Shinto; voluntary association.

State Shinto. *See* Shinto.

stations of the cross, fourteen plaques or pictures found in many Roman Catholic churches depicting incidents from Jesus' last days. Devotees move to each in succession meditating and praying. Especially popular during the Lenten season and Holy Week, this practice began in Europe in the late Middle Ages and was vigorously promoted by Franciscan friars. *See also* pilgrimage.

Steiner, Rudolf (1861–1925), an Austro-German modern mystic concerned with the interaction of science and spirituality, a prolific lecturer and writer, and founder of the Anthroposophical Society in 1912. *See also* Anthroposophical Society.

stigmata, the imprint of wounds on the hands, feet, and side resembling the wounds of Christ that have been experienced by certain Christian mystics beginning with Francis of Assisi (1181–1226). The Roman Catholic Church is cautious about the phenomenon since some well-studied cases are almost surely hysterical or psychosomatic. *See also* crucifixion; Francis of Assisi.

Stoics (stoh'iks; from Gk. *Stoa Poikile,* Athens' "Painted Porch"), a major Greek philosophical school, beginning with Zeno's classes held on the Painted Porch (ca. 300 B.C.). The movement is generally divided into the Early Stoa of Zeno, Cleanthes, and Chrysippus (ca. 300–150 B.C.); the Middle Stoa of Panaetius and Posidonius (second and first centuries B.C.); and the Late Stoa of Seneca, Epictetus, and Emperor Marcus Aurelius (first and second centuries A.D.). Their views had a profound impact on the social and political life of Rome and were an important influence on later Neoplatonism and Christianity.

The Middle and Late Stoics revised the philosophical system laid down by the Early Stoa, but the most essential elements of the Stoic system persisted. It was sometimes portrayed as a tree enclosed by a wall: logic (epistemology, logic, rhetoric) is the wall that protects the rest of Stoicism by spelling out the rules for discovering its truths; physics (ontology, physics, theology) is the tree that displays the structure of the cosmos; and ethics is the fruit, the practical guide to a happy life lived in harmony with the cosmos.

Logic: Stoic logic made important advances, including a sophisticated analysis of language into sound, significance (Gk. *lekton*), and thing signified, a systematic truth-functional analysis of propositions (including the material "if-then" conditional), and an account of deductive argumentation in terms of five elementary patterns of inference. The Stoics analyzed empirical knowledge as an acquisition via perception of an accurate mental representation of an object that coheres with the rest of our knowledge. This account was effectively criticized by various Skeptics.

Physics: The Stoics were materialistic pantheists, holding the formative, guiding principle of the cosmos to be a reason identical to the one God (Zeus). Individual things more or less closely approximate this rationality, with humans and gods the most rational. The history of the universe is cyclical and deterministic, beginning as a manifestation of the ruling part (*to hegemonikon*) of the cosmos, an intelligent creative fire, passing into an organization of four elements, and returning by divine providence to its original position in a fiery conflagration. Each cycle is an "eternal recurrence" of the events of the preceding cycle. As materialists, the Stoics analyzed the soul as corporeal breath, and so saw it as subject to generation and destruction.

Ethics: Human happiness is a tranquil state of the soul, whose motions are rationally harmonized with those of the divine order of the universe and thus undisturbed by the turbulence of the irrational emotions. This is the condition of the Stoic sage, and it is unaffected by the loss or gain of any external factors such as wealth or health. Rather, happiness depends solely on possessing knowledge of virtue, the only real good. The sage is perfectly brave, then, by knowing what is really good and bad; he knows pain and death are not real evils and thus fears neither. An influential corollary of this is the conviction that regardless of race, rank, or nationality, all human beings possess the divine spark of reason and must be treated accordingly and that it is our duty to promote a rational world order.

storytelling, the oral narration of story and tradition, an important aspect of religious traditions worldwide. Storytelling creates bonds, heals, clarifies identity, celebrates life paradoxes, and entertains. It presents, maintains, remembers, and critiques history.

Stories may originate through dreams or from spirit helpers. Stories, often considered property, may be bought or received as a gift. Apprenticeship with recognized storytellers is often needed to learn accurately the extensive and often highly complicated story traditions. Some stories are told as an essential part of ritual, and thus must be told with precision, and are often dramatically performed. Yet individual storytellers may delight in producing rich variants of often-told stories.

A good storyteller has the ability to develop and use the many voices in a story, performing the story while telling it. Storytelling is an activity that continually creates as well as preserves.

In many traditions there are men's and women's stories. Often storytelling is restricted to certain seasons or times of day. Most cultures have designations of various story types in elaborate typologies, including such distinctions as true and false stories, anecdotes, and origin stories.

Storytelling is an important activity to religions worldwide but is essential to traditional religions where there is an absence of writing. Virtually the entire tradition and heritage of these cultures are borne by storytelling, the essential act of cultural continuity. *See also* oral tradition.

structuralism. *See* religion, the study of.

stupa (stoo'puh; Skt., "crown of the head," "top"), a Buddhist monument, generally dome-shaped with towerlike structures on top. The practice of building *stupas* goes back to burial mounds of pre-Buddhist India.

The primary significance of the stupa has generally been connected with the Buddha and carries a number of distinctively Buddhist interpretations. It can be a reliquary, that is, a monument that contains traditional relics of the Buddha, his mortal remains, and objects he used. At times, copies of Buddhist scriptures—his teachings—were put in stupas. Symbolically, the stupa commemorates the Buddha's achievement of enlightenment. Other symbolic interpretations of the parts of the stupa also turned it into a concrete representation of Buddhist cosmology and doctrine. As both reliquaries and symbolic representations, stupas occupy central places in the ritual and art of most Buddhist communities. They are important objects of worship and have frequently been built at pilgrimage sites. *See also* architecture and religion; devotion (Buddhism); pilgrimage; relics.

Women circumambulating the Bodhnath *stupa* in Kathmandu, Nepal (1987). Especially revered by Tibetan Buddhists, the *stupa* is approached by climbing some six hundred steps.

subha. *See* prayer beads (Islam).

subincision, a ritual slitting of the underside of the penis, frequently accompanied by the use of ashes or other irritants to produce a prominent scar. Subincision is an element in some male rites of passage. *See also* circumcision.

Subud, an Islamic- and Hindu-influenced religion begun in Java in 1933 by Muhammad Subuh. Worldwide attention began in the 1950s with Subuh's extensive traveling and lectures and subsequent international congresses for adherents, who recognized Subuh as the mysterious Indonesian teacher foreseen by Georgei I. Gurdjieff (1877–1949). The core teachings of Subud demand that each person surrender completely to the divine will in all aspects of life. Drawing on popular ecstatic rituals and traditional Sufi practices, Subud eschews superficial intellectual redirection and centers the human relationship with the divine power in sex-segregated services called *latihan*, through which individuals may freely experience direct communion with God. *See also* Gurdjieff, Georgei Ivanovitch; Southeast Asian Islands, new religions in.

succession myth. *See* divine combat.

sudden cultivation (Chin. *tun-hsiu*), in Chinese Buddhism, religious practice that aims directly at highest enlightenment with no intermediate goals. *See also* Ch'an school; Southern school; sudden-gradual controversy.

sudden enlightenment (Chin. *tun-wu*), in East Asian Buddhism, an abrupt and total attainment of enlightenment with no necessary prior cultivation. *See also* Ch'an school; Southern school; sudden-gradual controversy.

sudden enlightenment followed by gradual cultivation (Chin. *tun-wu chien-hsiu*), the Chinese Ch'an Buddhist teaching that sudden enlightenment must be subsequently deepened by gradual cultivation. *See also* Ch'an school; Southern school; sudden-gradual controversy.

sudden-gradual controversy, a controversy between the Northern and Southern schools of Chinese Ch'an Buddhism over the issue of whether enlightenment required gradual cultivation or was already present and needed only to be realized. In 732, Shen-hui, an obscure Ch'an monk, launched an attack upon the line of Ch'an monks then enjoying imperial patronage, asserting that they taught gradual enlightenment. He claimed that the lineage of his own teacher, Hui-neng, which he called the Southern school, had preserved the orthodox teaching of sudden enlightenment. Shen-hui's paradigm of sudden enlightenment controlled all subsequent Ch'an discourse. *See also* Ch'an school; Hui-neng; Northern school; Shen-hui; Southern school.

sudden teaching (Chin. *tun-chiao*). **1** In T'ien-t'ai Buddhism one of Buddha's teaching methods in which he preaches the highest doctrine with no preparatory instruction. **2** Buddhist teachings that propound sudden enlightenment. *See also* sudden-gradual controversy; T'ien-t'ai school.

suffering, the experience of pain that, when apparently unmerited, raises acute questions for religious systems concerning the nature of the universe and of human existence. *See also* theodicy.

Judaism: According to Judaism, human suffering proves neither that God is evil and desires that creatures suffer nor that God is less than all-powerful and able to prevent such suffering. Suffering rather is viewed as a punishment for sin, with evil actions returning evil upon their perpetrators. This theory, which has its foundation in scripture (see, e.g., Leviticus 26, on communal punishment), is expressed succinctly in the Babylonian Talmud: "If a person sees that sufferings afflict him, let him examine his deeds" (*Berakhot* 5a).

To account for the apparently unjustified suffering of righteous adults or of innocent children and to explain the frequent prosperity and success of the wicked, rabbinic Judaism posits final retribution and reward in a coming world. The wicked, in this view, are repaid in their current life for any good they might do, but in the coming world God will severely punish them. In their present life, by contrast, the righteous suffer for slight infractions they commit, but they can look forward in the coming world to a complete reward.

In the talmudic literature, suffering thus reflects God's special love for the people of Israel. It is an aspect of the process of purification through which individuals and the nation atone for sins and become closer to God. In the Talmud, human affliction accordingly is defined by its technical name, "chastisements of love" (Heb. *yisurim shel ahavah*), and is seen as an aspect of the nation's atonement that assures that God's loved ones will merit eternal reward.

While generally proposing that suffering helps maintain the proper relationship between the people and God, the talmudic literature also evidences a very different view, that suffering may not be deserved and that those who suffer have reason to reproach God. In this perspective, the reasons for suffering are beyond full human comprehension. The Mishnah accordingly states that one should not rejoice when one's enemy suffers, for the one who rejoices may soon be subject to a similar misfortune (*Abot* 4:19). Comparably, the Babylonian Talmud depicts Moses' viewing of the torture and death of Rabbi Akiba (*Menahot* 29b). When Moses protests, "Master of the Universe, is this the Torah and this its reward?" God responds simply, "Be silent, for this is the way I have determined it."

In this view, God suffers along with his righteous creatures. The Babylonian Talmud states, "When the Holy One, blessed be he, reflects that his children are plunged in distress among the nations of the world, he drops two tears into the Great Sea, and the sound is heard from one end of the world to the other" (*Berakot* 59b).

Medieval Jewish philosophers uphold the notion that God is completely just. Maimonides (1135–1204) accordingly holds that suffering always punishes a previously committed sin (*Guide of the Perplexed* 24). If suffering appears to be unjustified, it is because people mistakenly believe that God created the universe for their sake. In Maimonides's view, by contrast, suffering that appears contrary to human interests in fact benefits the world as a whole. Because people are unable to comprehend the ultimate purpose and meaning of that world, they are unable properly to understand what happens to them. But this is a failure of human intelligence, not a reflection of any imperfection in God or in God's larger plan.

Maimonides's explanation of suffering influenced Baruch Spinoza (1632–77), who proposed that suffering is only apparent and that, through a life of science, people can come to understand God's will and, hence, combat their perceived afflictions. This claim, that God is thoroughly just but that people fail to comprehend his ways, largely dominated the Jewish philosophical approach to suffering until the Holocaust. That apparently inexplicable event has led many contemporary Jewish thinkers to replace traditional understandings with a range of interpretations that include a rejection of the previously central view, rooted in scripture, that it is in God's nature to protect God's people or to control the events of history at all.

Buddhism: According to Buddhism, suffering (Skt. *duhkha*) is a fundamental characteristic of existence. Existence is characterized by early Buddhism as impermanent, suffering, and non-self: that is, existents occur as impermanent or temporary aggregates of phenomena, devoid of any enduring or substantial self or essence; if they are mistakenly sought as lasting, they inevitably result in suffering. The insight that existence is suffering is established by tradition as the first of the Four Noble Truths and becomes the starting point and cornerstone of all Buddhist teaching and practice. While ordinary persons may view the obvious afflictions and mortality of human existence as suffering, in Buddhism suffering is seen as a necessary by-product of the process of transmigration (*samsara*) and indeed of all ordinary experience. The inevitability of suffering in unenlightened experience precludes the attainment of heaven and the like as the objective of religious practice. Instead, the ultimate goal is *nirvana*, or the extinction of suffering through the removal of its

cause, craving. The elimination of suffering provides the motivation for the Buddha's own practice and for sharing his teaching with others. It remains a fundamental concern throughout the complex historical development of Buddhist doctrine and practice. Thus, in later Buddhism, the centrality of suffering is represented by the figure of the Bodhisattva ("being of enlightenment") who, directed by universal compassion, delays his nirvana through a vow to alleviate the suffering of all sentient beings. *See also* Bodhisattvas; enlightenment; Four Noble Truths; nirvana.

Suffering Servant, in the Hebrew Bible, a figure of redemptive suffering (Isaiah 42:1–4; 49:1–6; 50:4–9; 52:13–53:12). Though the recitation of trials is largely in the past tense, the text has generally been interpreted as prophetic: by Jewish tradition, of Israel; by Christian tradition, of Jesus.

Sufi (soo'fee; Arab., "wearing wool," the traditional garment of prophets), an Islamic mystic. The Sufi movement is based on intensive devotion to Muhammad and the Qur'an. Through master-disciple relationships, Sufi orders have played important roles in the political, cultural, and religious histories of Islamic countries. *See also* Sufism.

Sufism, term generally applied to mystical currents in Islam. The word is derived from *suf* (Arab., "wool"), pointing to the woolen frocks of Middle Eastern ascetics; an etymologically incorrect derivation is from either *safa* ("purity") or from the Greek *sophos* ("wise").

Early Movements: The first ascetic movements began in the early eighth century when the Muslims were conquering large areas between southern Spain and the Indus Valley. Pious preachers tried to remind the Muslims of the dangers of worldliness, and small groups of men and women devoted themselves intensely to nightly vigils, fasting, and meditation on the Qur'an. Fear of God and eternal punishment loomed large among these ascetics. A woman, Rabia of Basra (d. 801), introduced the concept of pure love of God: one should act without hope for paradise or fear of hell, only out of love. This new emphasis on love grew into the central concept of Sufism. Ascetic currents existed in eastern Iran, Iraq, and in Egypt. It is likely that they had contacts with Buddhist and even more with Christian anchorites and monks: in early Sufi texts, Jesus appears as the ideal representative of renunciation, love, and divine joy.

During the ninth century different aspects of Sufism developed. In Egypt, Dhual-Nun (d. 859), credited with the introduction of the concept of *marifa* (nonintellectual knowledge), was the first to speak in his prayers of the hymns he heard from everything created, an experience based on the quranic statement that everything is created to worship the creator. The world, considered by the ascetics to be "a dunghill" or "a rotten carcass," thus gained a new religious dimension, and later Sufis translated the silent praise of trees and flowers into poetry.

At about the same time, Bayazid Bistami (d. 874) lived in northern Iran; he was a lonely seeker who tried to reach God by stripping off all his human qualities and undertaking long spiritual flights. Bayazid's quest is expressed in paradoxical statements in which absolute self-effacement, deification, and sometimes the feeling of disappointment appear side by side. His exclamation *Subhani* ("Praise be to me!") has been quoted thousands of times by later Sufis who wanted to express their complete union with God. Bayazid's contemporary, Yahya ibn Muadh of Rayy, Iran, was called "the preacher of hope." To him, Sufism owes some of its tenderest prayers, in which the tension between human sinfulness and hope for grace is expressed poignantly.

The main development of early Sufism is connected with Baghdad, the Abbasid capital, where Muhasibi (d. 857) developed a refined system of psychology in which even the slightest movements of the soul were scrutinized, ideas about the mutual love between humans and God were discussed, and the emphasis on God as the One and Unique was succinctly expressed in the phrase, "Only God has the right to say 'I,'" which remained a central point in all Sufi movements. The sober Baghdadian trend culminated in Junayd (d. 910), whose cryptic letters show his attempts to hide the great mystery of a human being's return "to the state as he was before he was," that is, to the point before God's primordial covenant with humanity in which human beings acknowledged Allah as their Lord. Such mysteries were never to be divulged to outsiders. It was the "divulging of the secret" that led one of Junayd's junior colleagues to death: Al-Husayn ibn Mansur al-Hallaj was executed in 922 allegedly for saying *anal-haqq* ("I am the Creative Truth," that is, "God"). However, the reasons for Hallaj's execution were actually his attempts to introduce reforms and reach a complete interiorization of the faith. Combining strict asceticism with burning love of God, he often called people to kill him so that the "I," which separated the eternal from the created being, would be removed. His "redemption of Satan" shocked many, but remained alive in some later Sufi circles. His *Kitab at-tawasin* contains the parable of the moth and the candle, one of the favorite symbols in Sufi literature.

The Path: In the tenth century, theories of sainthood were developed, a hierarchical structure of the "friends" of God (*auliya*) culminating in the *qutb* ("pole" or "axis"), around which everything turns. Later Sufis often claimed to be the qutb of their time, and the different degrees of saintliness, as well as the question of miracles, were to play an important role in Sufi thought. The mystical path was elaborated: it begins with repentance and leads the striving disciple (*murid*) through a lengthy range of stages, the exact sequence of which depends on God's grace. Every step had to be controlled by the master (*murshid; shaykh*, Arab.), in whose hands the disciple is "like a dead body in the undertaker's hand." The most important aspect of the path (*tariqa*) is the constant struggle against the *nafs* (lower soul): this is the "greater Holy War." By means of fasting far beyond the prescribed times, by getting little sleep, and by avoiding anything legally doubtful, Sufis undertook a hard spiritual training. *Tawakkul* (absolute trust in God) and *faqr* ("poverty"), in the sense of feeling a poor human being before the eternally rich God, are some of the central concepts for the Sufi. One must "polish the mirror of the heart" by the constant recollection of God (*dhikr*), based on the quranic statement (13:28), "Verily by the recollection of God the hearts acquire peace." Dhikr consists of the manifold repetition of the word *Allah* ("God") or of the profession of faith or another religious formula. The master has to find the formula that is appropriate for the disciple's spiritual state. At the end of the path, love and/or gnosis can be experienced, and the hope of the seeker is to reach *fana* ("annihilation") in God and to attain *baqa* ("eternal life") in God.

Listening to music, which could lead to ecstatic dance, was first a kind of relaxation; it was frowned upon not only by the orthodox but also by many Sufis. However, the mystical concerts (*sama*) with whirling dance became part and parcel of a considerable number of Sufi fraternities, although they were institutionalized only in the Mevlevi order.

The Sufi strove to "die before death" and slowly to replace lowly human qualities with divine ones. Helpful rules to guide the outward behavior were written in a number of books from the late tenth century onward; the most comprehensive work is Ghazali's *Ihya ulum ad-din* (The Revival of the Religious Sciences), which completes the Sufis' attempt to prove that Sufism and orthodox Islam are not at all different, and which teaches the type of moderate Sufism that largely formed later Muslim piety.

Sufi Fraternities (Tariqas): The founders of the first orders, the Suhrawardiyya, composed important works on Sufi education in the latter part of the twelfth century. About the same time the Qadiriyya order appeared, based on the teachings of Hanbalite preacher Abdulqadir Gilani (d. 1166). The Qadiriyya spread between West Africa and Indonesia, while other orders remained restricted to their original areas (thus, the Chishtiyya to India, the Mevleviyya to Ottoman Turkey). Through the writings of these orders, Sufi thought became known not only to the actual disciples of the master but also to a great number of lay members who were attached to them. The originally elitist quality of the Sufi was slowly lost. The lay members received spiritual guidance from the master and experienced emotional fervor during meetings on the death anniversary of the founder of the order or of a former master. The tombs of Sufi masters developed into places of pilgrimage where visitors (who came in the hundreds of thousands during the annual festivities) hoped for help in worldly and otherwordly matters. The Sufi orders catered to the spiritual needs of millions and contributed to the expansion of Islam in many areas, especially as their leaders sometimes used the regional languages instead of the quranic Arabic or the Persian of high literature, and thus helped various idioms, particularly in the Indian subcontinent, to develop literatures of their own.

Theosophical Traditions: At the same time that the first fraternities were founded, a mystic from Iran, also called Suhrawardi (d. 1191), developed a light-mysticism, weaving together Greek, Hermetic, and ancient Iranian ideas. Suhrawardi spoke of the soul's return from the "Western exile" to the Eastern spiritual home in highly technical Arabic and in short, delightful Persian parables. Slightly later, the man appeared to whom later Sufism owes most of its teachings: Ibn Arabi (d. 1240), from Mrucia, Spain. His system, usually called *wahdat al-wujud* (the unity of existence) is contained in his immense *Futuhat al-makkiyya* (The Meccan Revelations) and his prophetology in the *Fusus al-hikam* (The Facets [Bezels] of Wisdom). His theosophic teachings have been considered by many Muslims, and by the majority of earlier Western scholars, to be sheer pantheism. However, Ibn Arabi held that the divine essence remains hidden and never becomes part of creation. Rather,

it is through the divine names working in the created universe that humans can reach an approximation of the unknowable God. The fullness of the names are manifested in Muhammad, who thus becomes the perfect man (*insan-i kamil*), the boundary between the divine and the created. In the course of time, the historical Prophet of Islam had been surrounded by veils of light; he appears as the cause and goal of creation, light from the divine light, beloved of God. But he remains always a creature created by, not born from, God even though his light precedes everything. While classical Sufis hoped for annihilation in God, later seekers thought of the way in terms of stages of the different prophets and hoped for final union with the *haqiqa muhammadiyya* (archetypal Muhammad).

Ibn Arabi's ideas were adopted by almost every later school of Sufism. Arabi's teaching was, however, often understood as meaning *hama ust* ("Everything is He"), and in this form permeated the ecstatic utterances of innumerable mystical poets who claimed to have experienced the essential unity of God and creature. One can say that Ibn Arabi's systematization of the mystical experience and the structure of the world largely replaced the early voluntaristic approach to the divine by a gnostic-intellectualistic view.

Poetic Traditions: In the meantime, Sufism had taken a firm root in Iran, where it found its most beautiful expression in poetry. Arabic Sufi poetry has only one major representative in Egypt, Ibn al-Farid (d. 1235). In Iran, however, the Sufis invented new forms of expression, especially the *mathnawi*, a poem in rhyming couplets that could be extended at will and became the vehicle of instruction from the days of Sanai of Ghazna (d. 1131). His *Hadiqat al-haqiqa* (The Orchard of Truth), with its mixture of anecdotes and didactic verses, is the model for all later Sufi mathnawis. The second major mathnawi poet in eastern Iran was Fariduddin Attar (d. 1220), who not only wrote a Persian hagiographical work but also several mathnawi, among which *Mantiq ut-tayr* (The Language of the Birds) is well known. It tells of the journey through seven valleys of the soul-birds and their discovery that they themselves, being *si murgh* (thirty birds), are identical with the *Simurgh* (the Divine Bird). Thus, the individual souls find their identity with God. In the *Musibatnama* (Book of Affliction), Attar has exteriorized the experiences of the disciple during the forty days of seclusion until he is directed by the Prophet to enter the "ocean of his own soul," where God is hidden. To find God in the heart that is polished through unceasing meditation and is cleansed from everything that is not Allah is a central problem of Sufism. It is expressed most eloquently in Maulana Jalal al-Din Rumi's (d. 1273) lyrics and his mathnawi. Hailing from present-day Afghanistan, he spent much of his life in Konya. The ecstatic love for the wandering dervish Shams-i Tabrizi transformed the professor Jalal al-Din into Rumi, the mystic who poured out his love, longing, and visions in thousands of lyrical verses that he sang while whirling in ecstatic dance. After Tabrizi disappeared in 1248, Rumi realized the complete union between him and his lost beloved. He turned to a second friend who served, as it were, as his mirror, and then to his disciple Husamuddin Chelebi, at whose request Rumi composed the mathnawi of some twenty-five thousand verses. It has been called "the Qur'an in the Persian tongue." Rumi's talent to see everything created as a sign pointing to a spiritual truth makes his poetry amazingly fresh, and its musical quality remarkable. After Rumi's death, his eldest son and second successor instituted mystical dance; the Mevlevis are still known as the Whirling Dervishes.

Other Persian-writing mystics had expressed their experiences in outwardly simple language in which lover and beloved are each other's mirror and united in the higher unity of love. The most eloquent representative of this love mysticism was the Shirazi master Ruz-bihan Baqli (d. 1209), who sings of chaste love that is the contemplation of a beautiful face, which serves as an educational step toward divine love. These love ideals have inspired the whole range of Persian and Ottoman Turkish poetry. It is the oscillation between metaphorical, i.e., worldly, and real, i.e., divine, love that makes this poetry so fascinating but also almost untranslatable.

Ruzbihan Baqli is not only the author of this book on love but also a commentator on the *shathiyat* (ecstatic utterances) of the Sufis; these are words, paradoxes, at times seemingly areligious sayings, which a Sufi might utter when the experience of union filled him to such an extent that he could no longer control his words.

Expansion: Sufism spread into India around 1200. Before that, the first theoretical work on Sufism in Persian had been composed in Lahore by Hujwiri (d. ca. 1070), whose mausoleum is a place of pilgrimage to this day. Various fraternities grew in the subcontinent and soon a network of convents of the Suhrawardiyya and the music-loving Chishtiyya orders stretched from the southern Punjab to Bengal. Sufism exerted a

Muslim Sufi dervishes (Mevlevis) ecstatically dancing as depicted in a Moghul Indian painting; Himachal Pradesh, Pahari Style, Guler School (ca. 1740), Los Angeles County Museum of Art.

remarkable influence both in cities and rural areas, often, however, with accretions that offended the defenders of pure Islam. Among them was the Naqshbandi order, introduced from Central Asia ca. 1600, whose members tried to fight un-Islamic practices and played an important role in Muslim politics. They were the first to translate into the regional languages religious works in which ecstatic poets sang, in daringly expressive language, of their suffering in love, using indigenous tales and legends.

Ahmad Yesewi (d. 1165) wrote the first Turkish *hikam* (words of wisdom), and Najmuddin Kubra (d. 1221) is important for his visionary accounts and for the foundation of a successful order centered in Iran and Kashmir. Anatolia became the refuge of a number of Sufis who fled from eastern Iran and Central Asia in the wake of the Mongol invasion from 1220 onward. Rumi's presence certainly helped establish Sufism in Anatolia. Along with his refined urban tariqa more rustic fraternities emerged. The Bektashiyya became connected with the Ottoman elite troops, the Janissaries, even though the Bektashis were deeply influenced by Shia doctrines, and, after 1500, Shia Iran was the archenemy of the strictly Sunni Ottomans. The Bektashiyya is the only tariqa that treats women as equals; in other orders they are given merely tertiary status. With the establishment of Istanbul as the Ottoman capital, the great orders and their subgroups came to Turkey, and Sufism influenced Turkish cultural life. The Bektashis were uprooted in 1828 in the first attempt at modernizing the army, but the order continued in the countryside. The final blow came when Ataturk closed the Dervish lodges in 1925. No institutionalized Sufis remain in Turkey, although Sufism still has religious influence.

In Egypt a considerable number of tariqas are active. The same is true for North Africa, where the sober orders such as the Shadhiliyya and its branches (Darqawiyya, Alawiya, etc.) have attracted a number of European and American members. One also finds the beggars' order, the Heddawa. The best expression of North African Sufism is probably the small book of meditation, *Hikam*, by Ibn Ata Allah (d. 1309), which reveals a deep trust in God, in whose hands the human being feels safe and in whose wisdom one discovers even in the smallest movement.

In West Africa, the eighteenth-century renewal of Islam was achieved largely by the orders. The political role of the Tijaniyya or of the Mouridoun in Senegal is worthy of mention in this connection. The same is true for recent Sufi activities in Central Asia and the Caucasus, where Sufi orders, especially the Naqshbandis and the Qadiris, are the backbone of religious resistance against Russification and Marxist theories.

Sufism has often been criticized as backward and dangerous, and even Muslims who appreciated the inner wealth of classical Sufism have complained that it is impossible for Islam to be renewed or reformed as long as Pirism exists, that is, the absolute power of a master over his—often illiterate—followers, which also shows itself in the Pir's engagement in politics. The fact that the seat of the Pir became, in many cases, hereditary (there is no celibacy in the orders) often led to deterioration, as not every son of a Sufi master was spiritually advanced. More recently, Sufism has spread into the Western world. To what extent this is a positive development is not yet clear; it is hoped that the inner treasures of serious Sufism will be preserved by the new disciples.

There are numberless definitions of Sufism, which is like a mighty tree in which sometimes strange birds have built their nests; perhaps Rumi expresses it best:

What is Sufism? To feel joy in the heart at the time of grief.

See also Ghazali, Abu Hamid Muhammad ibn Muhammad al-Tusi; Ibn al-Arabi, Muhyi ad-Din; mysticism; Pir; Rumi, Jalal al-Din; Sufi; tariqa.

sui generis (soo'ee jen'er-is, Lat., "belong to its own kind"), a claim that religion or religious experience is irreducible or unique. Such claims are often made as a defense tactic in the early stages of an academic discipline in order to assert the autonomy of that discipline's subject matter. Thus, Emile Durkheim, the founder of French sociology, claimed that society was *sui generis;* Rudolf Otto, in the *Idea of the Holy* (1917), insisted that religious ("numinous") experience was a "mental state . . . perfectly sui generis and irreducible to any other." *See also* reductionism.

Sukkot (soo-koht'; Heb., "booths"), in Judaism, a seven-day joyous harvest holiday (15–22 Tishrei), during which Jews eat and some even sleep in thatched huts that they construct. The booths evoke the shelters the Israelites built during their trek through the desert. Another observance is taking four species—palm, willow, myrtle, and citron—and waving them in the synagogue while chanting *hallel* psalms (Psalms 113–118) and special poetical prayers called hosannas. *See also* Judaism (festal cycle).

Sumerian religion. *See* Mesopotamian religion.

Sumiyoshi shrine (soo-mee-yoh-shee), a collective group or type of Japanese Shinto shrine dedicated to the Sumiyoshi deity, a protector of seafarers, fishermen, and travelers. *See also* shrine.

Summa Theologiae, the masterwork of the Scholastic theologian Thomas Aquinas (ca. 1225–74) written between 1266 and 1273. The *Summa* is divided into three main parts. Part One, comprising 119 questions, considers God and the procession of all creatures, including humans, from God. Part Two is divided into two main sections. The first discusses, in 114 questions, the supernatural end of the human person, life in heaven with God, and the general principles of the movement to God, the virtues, law, and grace. The second consists of 189 questions concerning the individual virtues that assist the movement to God, the theological virtues (faith, hope, and charity), and the cardinal virtues (prudence, justice, fortitude, and temperance). Part Three was designed to cover Christ, the sacraments, and the end-time. However, Aquinas broke off writing in the midst of the discussion of the sacrament of penance. *See also* Aquinas, Thomas; Scholasticism; Thomism.

Summit Lighthouse. *See* Church Universal and Triumphant.

sumo (soo-moh), a popular form of Japanese wrestling performed with Shinto rituals of purification and protection against evil spirits.

Sun Dance, Sun Dance religion, a widely distributed set of religious rituals found among Plains tribes. The terms *Sun Dance* and *Sun Dance religion,* which were invented by early-twentieth-century interpreters, obscure the rich variety exhibited by these rituals. They also fail to convey the distinct cultural meanings evoked by different tribal symbolic systems. These meanings produce different religious experiences among different cultures, distinguishing groups from one another and giving each group a special sense of origin and identity. The terms capture similarities that may be observed among groups who are interpreted as sharing the dance, but only two groups, the Oglalas and Poncas, actually designate the ritual as a Sun Dance. The Oglala term, *wiwanyag wacipi,* may be translated as "sun-gazing dance." Solar symbolism was widely distributed among the Plains tribes, but the ritual processes described by the popular terms were by no means practiced by all Plains tribes in a dance oriented exclusively toward the sun.

The oldest pattern underlying the variety of expressions is a dance or series of dances oriented around a center pole. With the exception of the Crows, each Plains tribe preserves this motif. Constructed around a forked pole is a circle of upright forked posts. Lodgepoles are laid in the crotch of each of the upright posts. The tapered ends of these poles stretch toward the center, all of them coming to rest in the crotch of the center pole. For the Crows, the ritual enclosure looks more like the frame of a large tepee. In many instances, the ritual enclosure contains an altar that features a painted buffalo skull. The complex of rituals known as the Sun Dance are mainly tribal in character, although many of them are initiated by the vow of an individual. In some instances, a bundle containing special ob-

Representation of a Dakota Sun Dance painted on a buffalo skin by the late-nineteenth-century Sioux Ghost Dance leader Short Bull.

jects is transferred to the individual or family group sponsoring the ceremony. Among groups such as the Blackfeet, Cheyennes, and Arapahoe, the role of women is prominent. Perhaps the most widely shared practice associated with these Plains rituals is the sacrifice that male participants endure; while women often have central roles, they do not participate in physical suffering like the men. In addition to abstention from food, water, and often sexual contact, male participants make spectacular offerings of their bodies to the transcendent powers. A widely used practice involves the piercing of flesh on the chest and back. Skewers are inserted under the skin or muscle and leather thongs are attached to the skewers. The dancers are in some cases suspended from poles by the thongs; in other cases they dance around the center pole, pulling against the skewers until their flesh is torn. Powerful vision experiences often accompany the suffering of the participants. In general, these rituals are performed for the replenishing of the buffalo, the moral renovation of the group, and the wider renewal of the people's world. *See also* dance; North America, traditional religions in; sun worship.

Sunday, the first day of the Christian week. Sunday is a day of worship for most Christians because it became identified as the day on which Christ rose from the dead. *See also* Lord's Day; Sabbath.

Sunna (soon'nuh; Arab., "custom," "tradition"), the exemplary ethical and religious model that Muslims derive from the sayings and deeds of Muhammad. This, for Muslims, supersedes the customary Sunna of the pre-Islamic Arabs. Next to the Qur'an, Sunna is the most important standard for Islamic law. On the practical side, Sunna includes proper ritual actions (prayer, fasting, etc.), personal hygiene, and a host of social, ethical, and family relations. Shiite Muslims regard Sunna as also derived from their *imams*. *See also* hadith; Islamic law.

Sunni (soon'nee; Arab., "custom [of the Prophet Muhammad]"), one of two major branches of Islam, a Sunni majority (approximately 85 percent) and a Shii minority (15 percent). This division occurred over the question of succession: Who was to lead the community after the death of Muhammad? The result was the institutions of the Sunni caliphate and the Shii Imamate. The majority of the community believed that Muhammad died without designating his successor. Thus, upon the Prophet's death, elders selected a successor (*khalifa*, "caliph") as the political leader of the community. The caliph was not a prophet but did assume the mantle of Muhammad as the protector and defender of Islam and the guarantor of a society that was to be guided by God's law (the Sharia, or Islamic law). In contrast, a minority believed that Muhammad had designated his cousin and son-in-law, Ali, the senior male in the Prophet's family, as a religiously inspired leader, or *Imam*. Thus, in a sense, the charisma, though not prophethood, of Muhammad was passed on in these paramount religiopolitical guides or leaders of the community.

By the late eighth century, differences between these two orientations had resulted in the formation of two distinct groups. The majority community came to be called Sunni, those who follow the model example or normative practice (Sunna) of the Prophet. Its more specific self-designation was the people of the Sunna and the community (*ahl al sunna wal jamaa*) of the Prophet. In theory, if not in practice, religious and political authority rested in the community, guided by Islamic law and the consensus of its scholars or leaders (*ulama*). A minority, the followers of Ali, the Shii ("the party of Ali"), believed that religiopolitical authority was vested in its Imams. Community leadership was restricted to the house of the Prophet, specifically a direct descendant of Muhammad and Ali. *See also* Shia.

Sun Ssu-miao (swun soo-myou; fl. ca. 673), a cultured Chinese physician and writer credited with writing numerous Taoist texts associated with alchemy. *See also* alchemy.

Sun Stone, Aztec stone disk, 3.6 meters in diameter, carved by the Mexica Tenochca of Tenochtitlan in the fifteenth or early sixteenth centuries. Discovered beneath the main plaza of Mexico City in 1790, this monument is a complex and sophisticated example of a class of similar disks that represent the sun and the full import of which remains uncertain. It is generally thought that the Sun Stone depicts Mexica-Tenochca expressions of fundamental Mesoamerican cosmological notions about time, space, and sacrifice. Specific calendrical dates, which some believe are significant to Mexica-Tenochca concepts of state history, appear interwoven with the more generally shared glyphic representations of time.

The stone consists of five concentric rings surrounding a center, all of which incorporate religious and mythical themes. In the center of the disk is the head of a deity representing attributes of the sun, the earth, or possibly a combination of both. This figure's toothy mouth displays a tongue that is also a depiction of a sacrificial blade. In the first ring, the first four cosmic ages of mythical time are depicted, encased by the glyph standing for "Four Movement," the name for the fifth age or age of the Aztecs. Mythical sources tell how each of four consecutive cosmic ages or "suns" met with total destruction and how the Aztecs' own sun was also doomed to eventual disappearance by means of famine and earthquake. The twenty day-signs of the Mexica-Tenochca calendar appear in the second ring, and two fire serpents form its outer border. Between their tails is tucked the year date, "Thirteen Reed," which may refer to both the sun and the reign of an important king. Glyphs representing several constellations are carved on the unfinished portions of stone surrounding the disk. *See also* ages of the world; Mesoamerican religion.

sun worship. Solar motifs are prominent in some Plains tribal traditions; these motifs are often accompanied by astral and lunar figures that are related, often by kinship, to the people. The Blackfeet Sun Dance has as one of its central features a bundle known as the Natoas (sun); their tribal traditions include moon and star figures as well. One cannot generalize on the basis of such cases to the entire Plains area. A better approach to the understanding of Plains Indian religions is through the study of particular groups to determine which tribes had solar motifs and which did not. These complex rituals and symbolic expressions, including the ritual known as the Sun Dance, relate to the general welfare of the people and the specific needs of individuals, as well as to hunting, warfare, and other important life processes. *See also* Sun Dance, Sun Dance religion.

Sun Wu-k'ung (suhn woo-kuhng), name for the mischevous monkey character in the Chinese novel *Journey to the West* (sixteenth century); in Buddhism he has the connotation of one who is "aware of emptiness." *See also* Hsi-yu chi.

superhuman beings, beings more than human, possessed of miraculous powers. *See also* religion, definition of.

supernatural religion, a term of contrast with "natural religion," implying a foundation on some sort of divine revelation. *See also* natural religion; typology, classification.

superstition, ignorance, pejorative terms applied to certain religious behaviors and attitudes. Because of a strong conviction on the part of the intellectual elite of Western culture that religion is ultimately irrational, such pejoratives have become a part of its received vocabulary. "Superstition" is a disparaging way of interpreting or explaining religious thought and action that assumes or concludes that either all, or some subset of, religious concepts and the actions they underwrite are inherently irrational. Such explanations are based upon views of the evolution of cultural systems that assume an incremental view of human knowledge and rationality (from "primitive" to "civilized," from "sacred" to "secular," from "traditional" to "modern"). Especially important in such views is the belief that rationality in general, and scientific rationality in particular, steadily increases in coherence, applicability, and reliability, making the need for religious views irrelevant. Religion, in such a view, is regarded as belonging to an earlier, less rational stage, which has gradually been superseded by more adequate forms of interpreting and explaining the world. *See also* origin of religion; typology, classification.

suq. *See* bazaar.

sura (soo'ruh; Arab.), one of 114 literary divisions or chapters of the Qur'an, varying in length from a few to 285 *ayas* (verses). *See also* aya; Islam (authoritative texts and their interpretation).

Suritnal. *See* Korea (festal cycle).

surplice, an outer white garment worn over black robes by clergy and choir in some Christian services.

Surya (soor'yuh; Skt., "sun"), a god of Vedic and later India. He traverses the sky in a chariot drawn by reddish horses and serves as the gods' eye monitoring mortals.

Susano-o (soo-sah-noh-oh), impulsive and occasionally offensive Japanese Shinto deity assigned to rule the underworld. His behavior temporarily drove his sister, the sun goddess Amaterasu, into a cave. *See also* Amaterasu; exorcism; Japanese myth.

Suso, Heinrich (ca. 1295–1366), German Catholic mystic, much influenced by John "Meister" Eckhart, whom he defended in the *Little Book of Truth* (ca. 1327). His classic, *Little Book of Eter-*

nal Wisdom (ca. 1328), is a practical work of religious devotion addressed to lay persons. *See also* Eckhart, John "Meister."

suttee. *See* Sati.

Suzuki, Daisetsu Teitaro (*soo-zoo*-kee dah-ee-set-*soo* tay-tah-roh; 1870–1966), Buddhist scholar and writer, active in Japan and abroad, whose numerous books in both Japanese and English, such as his influential *Essays in Zen Buddhism*, have helped establish the worldwide popularity of Zen Buddhism. *See also* Rinzai.

Suzuki Shosan (*soo-zoo*-kee shoh-sahn; 1579–1655), Japanese samurai who became a Zen Buddhist monk at the age of forty-two. He was the author of a number of works on Buddhism that applied Buddhist morality to everyday life and supported the hierarchical society favored by the government. His work was characterized by a fascination with death as the central religious issue for people. *See also* bushido; seppuku.

svastika (svahs'ti-kuh; Skt.,"that which brings welfare"; Eng. swastika), an ancient symbol of auspicious sacred power. In India, where it adorns temple walls, domestic thresholds, and other boundaries of sacred space, it most likely began as a solar symbol and was originally identified with the god Vishnu. *See also* auspicious, inauspicious (Hinduism); Jainism; Vishnu.

Svedberg, Emmanuel. *See* Swedenborg (Svedberg), Emmanuel.

swami (Skt. *svamin*, "owner," "proprietor," "master," or "lord"), an Indic title of respect for a religious teacher or member of an ascetic (*sannyasi*) order. *See also* guru; sadhu.

sweat, sweat lodge, a saunalike steam bath and structure employed for ritual purification and enjoyment by peoples in all regions of North America except the central and eastern Eskimos, and some tribes in the Great Basin and Southwest. The sweat lodge of the Plains, Eastern Woodlands, and Subarctic is usually covered with canvas, skins, or bark. In preparation for the sweat, heated rocks are placed in the pit at the center of the lodge. Water is ceremoniously poured over the rocks, producing steam. The participants pray and chant.

Among Plains tribes of North America, sweats are used for purification prior to impor-

tant healing, initiation ceremonies, and dances. Use and origin of the sweat varies. For the Pawnee (northern Plains), sweats are personal, without communal ceremony; yet in the Pawnee story traditions the heated stones have healing powers and the Pawnee honor the home of all the animals with communal smoking and teaching in the sweat lodge. The lodge also becomes a place of healing. In Lakota (Plains) tradition the sweat lodge was brought by White Buffalo Calf Woman. According to the Blackfoot (North Central) medicine lodge stories, sweats are necessary to purify oneself after meeting ghosts as well as for healing.

In western Alaska the sweat is held in the men's communal house at the close of the Bladder Festival in addition to being part of other special feasts. Sweats are still part of family enjoyment and cleansing in western Alaska. *See also* Bladder Festival; North America, traditional religions in; purification.

Swedenborg (Svedberg), Emmanuel (swee'den-borg; 1688–1772), Swedish philosopher and mystic whose teachings are perpetuated in the Church of the New Jerusalem (popularly known as the Swedenborgian Church).

Raised a Swedish Lutheran and one of Europe's most distinguished geologists, Swedenborg began to have a series of spiritual experiences (1736–47) that led him to renounce his scientific career. Through dreams, mystic journeys, and communications with spirits, he gained revelations as to the nature of the divine cosmos and the fate of the soul after death.

Swedenborg's fundamental teaching is the "law of correspondences," that there is an exact correlation between the two planes of created existence, the phenomenal and the spiritual. Swedenborg reinterpreted the Christian Trinity, God being manifested in Jesus Christ in three "principles": Father (inexhaustible love), Son (divine wisdom), and Spirit (divine energy, which sanctifies human beings).

The basic elements of Swedenborg's system are most clearly set forth in *Divine Love and Wisdom* (1763). The most complex exposition is in his multivolume commentary on Genesis and Exodus, *Arcana Coelestina* (1749–56).

Within Europe, his teachings became most influential in England. In 1783, the Theosophical Society was formed to study his works and later developed into the Church of the New Jerusalem (1787). Transplanted to America (1792), the General Convention of the New Jerusalem in the United States (1817) is the oldest of the American Swedenborgian churches.

sweet grass, grass used by Native North Americans in a number of religious rituals, as well as by some groups as material for sweet-smelling baskets. Within ritual contexts on the Plains, sweet grass is burned, producing fragrance, believed to be attractive to transcendent beings, and smoke, which is associated with communication with transcendent others and with the ritual purification of humans as they prepare themselves to receive religious power in visions and dreams. *See also* North America, traditional religions in; smoke.

symbol, an object or event designed to stand for or represent something else. Practically anything can serve as a symbol—icons, trees, eruptions, architecture, painting, formulas, invocations, myths, yawning, belching, ordinary language, ritual, and others all may come to stand for or represent something else. This diversity both contributes to the topic's interest and makes for an empirical difficulty in arriving at a satisfactory account or comprehensive theory of symbolism.

Besides this empirical problem, a theory of symbolism must address deep philosophical or conceptual issues. Symbols are by nature relational; they must always be used by creatures capable of self-consciousness, creatures who, if only implicitly, must be able to realize that this stands for that. Thus, the theory of symbolism inevitably raises questions about the nature of thought, and about the place of mind in nature. And there is the complication—held by some to preclude any comprehensive theory of symbolism—that thought itself appears to be symbolic. How can a thinking creature give an account of that which makes possible the very activity of theorizing?

The theory of symbolism is central to an understanding of religion. Many scholars give it precedence over accounts of ritual and belief. The study of symbolism normally includes as a central element of its subject matter the nature of natural language. One is here concerned mainly with nonlinguistic symbols. However, as a means of analyzing the nature of nonlinguistic symbolism, one must be concerned with the difference between nonlinguistic symbolism and the symbolic mechanism at the heart of natural language.

Symbolism and Reference: For many Christians, the cross symbolizes or stands for or represents Jesus' death and resurrection. One may inquire into what the believer means by Jesus' death and resurrection. One may also want to understand the relationship expressed by "symbolizes," "stands for," and "represents." The first inquiry is an empirical, anthropological one; the second is conceptual. A general understanding of the connection between symbol and symbolized, preferably one that analyzes the quoted terms into different, more basic concepts, is required.

According to one theory, influential since Augustine (d. 430), the basic concept is reference. The cross symbolizes Jesus' death and resurrection because it refers to these events. Reference itself can be analyzed in psychological terms: when the believer thinks of the symbol, the believer is caused to think of the thing symbolized. This causality is not blind; the thought process is governed by rules like those essential to linguistic interpretation. Just as competent language users use *cow* only to refer to a cow, so the believer learns the rules necessary to "decode" the symbol of the cross. Of course, the believer learns many such rules—for example, that the priest's blessing refers to Jesus' establishment of the church, that sin refers to the fall from grace, that the manger scene depicted in the stained glass stands for God's act of forgiveness, and so on. In this way, the believer builds an entire symbol system from discrete pieces—actions, concepts, and objects—each of which comes with its own set of interpretive rules.

The building-block theory remains influential in theological circles through the work of Paul Tillich (1886–1965). The German-born Protestant theologian holds that the symbol "participates in the reality for which it stands." According to Tillich, this element of participation makes the relation between symbol and reality nonarbitrary. It is important to note that nothing in the building-block theory requires that the believer explicitly know to what the symbol refers. Thus, in the wider study of religion, the still influential work of the Austrian psychiatrist Sigmund Freud (1865–1939) may be thought of as a variant of this approach. For Freud, religious symbols are individually connected to what they represent; the investigator discovers the correct interpretation of the symbol by tracing its cause (back, according to Freud, to unresolved antisocial or sexual urges). Against the Tillichean view, Freud holds that this relation may change, that the "correct interpretation can only be arrived at on each occasion from the context."

Besides its neutrality to the believer's self-awareness, the building-block approach to symbolism is also neutral to the truth or validity of the symbol in question. While the believer thinks that "God" refers to a supernatural agent, creator of heaven and earth, the outside investigator may, on the basis of the same approach to symbolic materials, come to a different conclusion. Thus, the French sociologist Emile Durkheim (1858–1917) argues that "God" usually refers to society. His interpretive maxim was essentially Freud's: a symbol refers to that which causes it to be employed. The causal connection between symbol and world gives the symbol its discrete, self-contained content. Thus, Tillich, Freud, Durkheim, and the devout believer standing in direct contact with God will likely assign the cross competing referents even as they share a basic approach to symbolism.

Interpreting Symbols: The building-block theory assumes that natural language and other symbolic systems do not differ in kind, that, like words, nonlinguistic symbols have a specifiable content or interpretation. But this is by no means clear. It is not clear that the basic linguistic distinction between literal and nonliteral interpretation carries over into nonlinguistic symbolic materials. If a speaker or writer wants to be understood by an audience, the speaker or writer must use words according to publicly held standards. Competent language users know, explicitly or implicitly, these rules for the correct—that is, the publicly assessable—use of words. Of course, once one has mastered these rules, one is free to innovate to advantage. Indeed, the ability to so innovate may well be a condition of full linguistic competence. One would not normally say that someone has mastered the meaning of an expression such as "Juliet is the sun" if the person thought that the expression could only be used to express a trivial falsehood. It is trivially false, but a competent language user who knows what it (literally) means will also be able to use the sentence toward romantic (and many other) ends. In fact, one can go further: it is because literal meaning is impervious to the context of use that expressions can be put to nonliteral employment.

One way, then, to ask whether nonlinguistic symbols have a determinate content or interpretation is to ask whether, like linguistic materials, they can be put to literal and figurative use. In some communities baptism by immersion is said to symbolize a spiritual cleansing. Does the ritual literally mean spiritual cleansing in the sense that "snow is white" means snow is white? Religious communities do not typically impose on ritual competence interpretive constraints that are as demanding as those that linguistic communities impose on the use of words. Thus, the baptism may call to mind (may "mean") different things to different ritual participants, without putting into question their ritual com-

petence. Indeed, regarding the more abstract symbolism of, for example, the monotheistic traditions, many anthropologists note that only a small percentage of "competent" ritual participants can explicate them in any detail.

Most religious communities impose rigorous constraints on ritual form—on what is said and done. But here the disanalogy with natural language is even clearer. The extensive social constraints on the literal use of words makes possible their nonliteral use; with ritual, that aim has no place, for ritual innovation is generally proscribed. In contrast to semantic or linguistic competence, someone who considered innovation an essential feature of ritual competence would likely be considered ritually *in*competent. The person would likely be said not to have mastered the ritual. This apparently marks a deep difference between semantic and ritual competence.

It is sometimes argued that this distinction is blurred by the ritual participant's ability to imagine novel rituals and make judgments about them. But if the judgment is dismissive then the disanalogy stands, for language users recognize the communicative value of even the deliberate malapropism or the premeditated abuse of grammar. And if the judgment is positive—if the deviation is incorporated into the community's ritual repertoire—then it is not novel after all. By contrast, in no sense do the metaphor and malaprop become true, nor does one often revise one's grammar so as to legitimize the infraction.

In considering whether these disanalogies between linguistic and ritual symbolic systems hold for other forms of nonlinguistic religious systems, the first question is whether the religious community enforces the employment of interpretive rules that yield determinate, literal content. Second, do such rules, if they exist, have as an essential aim the making possible of nonstandard or innovative use of these symbols? The answer seems to be, in each case, no.

Holism: Opposed to the building-block approach to symbolism is the doctrine of symbolic holism. Instead of symbols possessing their content individually, a symbol is said to acquire its meaning through its location in the wider pattern of meaningful symbols. This doctrine has assumed many forms, and has been applied to both linguistic and nonlinguistic systems.

The underlying idea is perhaps clearest when applied to natural language: the use of the word *apple* can symbolize an apple only in the context of talk about color, weight, trees, food, juice, space, and time. Unless a person could speak competently about these things the use of the term apple would be empty. Thus, it is concluded—influentially by, among others, the twentieth-century French linguist Ferdinand de Saussure—that semantic content is diffused throughout a language rather than built up additively out of independently meaningful words. Can the same argument be made for nonlinguistic symbolic systems?

Here one may distinguish a range of holistic approaches. At one end of the spectrum is "extensional holism," so called because it holds that symbols, while given content (meaning) holistically, refer, or at least purport to refer, to real objects, events, or states in the world. This view preserves the notion of reference from the building-block theory, but denies that symbols acquire their meaning through their relation to what they refer to. The ash on the forehead, the rosary, the statue of the virgin, the fish, the cross—for the one who holds them all sacred it will not be possible to separate entirely the content of any of these symbols from that of the others. And presumably such a person would say that each extends to or symbolizes something real. At least in some cases, this thesis has the support of common sense. Yet extensional holism faces a version of the same problem discussed earlier. The reason talk of apples can be holistic (color, weight, trees, food, juice, space, time, etc.) and yet extensional is that most Westerners know what it is to be confronted by one. In order to vindicate an extensional holism as applied to religious, nonlinguistic symbols, one would have to show that the members of a given religious community share determinate concepts (meaning) for the symbols in question.

At the opposite end of the spectrum are holistic approaches to symbolism that entirely discard the notion of extrasymbolic reference. There is, for example, the view that linguistic and nonlinguistic symbols refer to themselves; rather than extending to the external world, they are self-referential or reflexive. In the study of religion, one finds two motives for reflexive holism. First, many theorists doubt whether the very idea of extrasymbolic reference is intelligible. How, it is asked, can a mental (symbolic) entity enter into any specifiable relation with a nonmental entity; a relation of correspondence would seem to require that the two elements share some feature or property—but the mental and physical seem of different orders. If so, symbols can only refer to themselves. Second, scholars of religion have long emphasized the all-encompassing nature of religious symbol systems. There often seems no experience,

event, or object that can escape the purview of some religious symbol. If so, there is no way to stand outside the symbol system to compare it with the world. While both motives are legitimate, the danger inherent in reflexive holism is relativism. If the elements of each symbol system refer only to themselves, then truth must apparently be confined to a given system or framework. But then one cannot defend reflexive holism against other (competing?) views, which presumably are true within their systems.

Occupying a middle position are holistic views generally referred to as structuralist, many of which owe to the work of the twentieth-century French anthropologist Claude Levi-Strauss (b. 1908). Levi-Strauss rejects the thesis that symbols obtain their content in isolation from one another. And, with reflexive holism, he rejects extensionalism in its usual form—that symbols refer, or are at least designed to refer, to the external world. However, he does hold that symbols refer or extend to something outside themselves, namely, to the fundamental categories of the human mind. The aim is nothing less than to document—in full recognition of modern ethnographic knowledge—the ways in which human nature governs cultural, symbolic variation. Levi-Strauss and his followers have argued forcefully that this internal reference is rule-governed and open to systematic investigation, but most anthropologists and linguists have not been persuaded.

Conclusion: While the question is still debated, the arguments are widely held to show that, unlike linguistic symbols (words), nonlinguistic symbols have no semantic content, no determinate meaning. If so, then nonlinguistic symbols must be analyzable primarily on the basis of their context of use; unlike words, nonlinguistic symbols often cannot survive transmission even from person to person. In practice, of course, linguistic and nonlinguistic symbols may well blend into one another. The linguistic symbol whose literal meaning resists all contextual contamination and the nonlinguistic symbol whose interpretation is unconstrained and free—these two can be considered ideal types. However, communication through language would not be possible if literal meaning were not able to remain relatively autonomous against context. This capability is at least not essential to the use of nonlinguistic, including religious, symbols.

Many scholars and perhaps most religious persons would add that religious symbols often gain their richness and depth precisely from their lack of determinate content. Their genius and inexhaustibility lies, it is said, in prompting people to reflect further on their own, and even in refusing to spell out what, in fact, cannot be said. There is a tension here, perhaps unavoidable: to the extent that the richness and depth is supposed to lie in the symbol one must suppose a means of extracting it. But that very means, once discovered, would convert the symbol to a piece of ordinary language. On the other hand, to the extent that the profundity lies somehow either in the symbol user or outside the user and the symbol, the symbol tends toward irrelevance. From a scholarly point of view, it is hard to imagine a general resolution of this tension; from a religious standpoint, it is doubtful that one is wanted. *See also* religion, anthropology of; religion, philosophy of; religious language; semiotics.

Symeon the New Theologian (949–1022), the most influential Greek Orthodox Byzantine mystic. His *Hymns of Divine Loves* emphasizes his central teaching of the gift of an experience of divine light, important in the development of the Hesychast (Gk., "prayer of quiet") movement. *See also* Hesychasm.

synagogue (sin′ah-gog; Gk., "assembly"), the place of Jewish communal worship. In some ancient texts, the Greek term also connotes a congregation of Jews. Since the destruction of the Second Temple in 70, the synagogue has been the principal institutional center of Jewish religious and cultural life. Its primary purposes are worship, education, and assembly.

Unlike the Temple, which was conceived as God's residence and was administered by the priestly caste, the synagogue is a lay institution. From the Middle Ages onward, synagogues have employed a cantor and a sexton, but rabbis became synagogue rather than community employees only in nineteenth-century Western Europe. Most synagogues contain a main sanctuary and classrooms. Large modern ones often have a chapel, school, auditorium, and library as well.

There are no rabbinic rules about synagogue architecture, and synagogues typically conform to the styles of their environment. According to rabbinic practice, synagogues and worshipers should face Jerusalem. The visual center of the sanctuary is the *aron kodesh* (Heb., "holy ark"), which houses the scrolls of the Torah. Covering the ark is a *parokhet* ("curtain"), modeled after the curtain that covered the holy of holies in the Temple. Above the ark usually hangs the *ner tamid* ("eternal light"), which recalls the seven-

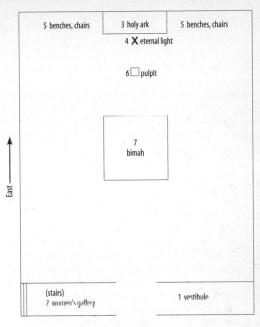

| 5 benches, chairs | 3 holy ark | 5 benches, chairs |

4 **X** eternal light

6 ☐ pulpit

7 bimah

East

(stairs)
2 women's gallery

1 vestibule

synagogue

Jewish houses of worship (synagogues) are not consecrated space and have no required architectural elements. The presence of ten Jewish males over the age of thirteen (*minyan*) and a Torah scroll are sufficient to make any room a synagogue. Nevertheless, a distinctive synagogue architecture developed. The building is usually oriented eastward. One enters through (1) a vestibule, which, in Orthodox and some other synagogues, also has stairs leading to (2) a separate women's gallery. The focal point, raised above the ground on the eastern wall, is a cabinet or niche, capable of being closed from view, containing the Torah scroll(s). This is called (3) the holy ark (Ashkenazic *aron ha-kodesh*; Sephardic *hekhal*). Suspended in front of the ark is (4) an eternal light. Most synagogues provide (5) seats of honor flanking the ark on the eastern wall reserved for synagogue officials, the cantor (*hazzan*), and rabbi. There is also (6) a pulpit or lectern near the ark, which is sometimes portable, sometimes fixed. A second focal point is (7) a raised platform (Ashkenazic *bimah*; Sephardic *tevah*) from which the officiant reads from the Torah scroll and orients the congregation toward Jerusalem for prayers. While commonly in the center, the platform may also be toward the rear (west) wall or integrated into the front, eastern ark area.

branched menorah that burned continuously in the Temple.

The sanctuary also contains the raised *bimah* ("platform"), sometimes called the almemar, from which the *sefer Torah* ("Torah scroll") is read liturgically on every Monday, Thursday, Sabbath (Saturday), and holiday. Although rabbinic rules place the bimah in the center of the sanctuary, facing the ark, in most contemporary Reform and Conservative, and some Orthodox, synagogues it is located in front of the ark, facing the congregation.

Congregations that follow traditional rabbinic practice maintain separate seating for men and women, and women sit either in a balcony or behind a *mehitzah* ("partition"). Reform and Conservative synagogues have mixed seating.

The historic role of the synagogue as the place for the celebration of life-cycle events and for Jewish education, traditionally called "Torah study," persists in modern times. Synagogues typically sponsor weekly religious and Hebrew schools and adult study groups. Other traditional synagogue functions, such as the settlement of disputes, redress of wrongs (for which the worship service may be interrupted), the disbursement of charity, and care of strangers, have been modified or abandoned in many communities.

The origin of the synagogue is obscure. Though it may have emerged in the Babylonian exile as a response to the destruction of the first Temple (587 B.C.), the late (ca. fourth century B.C.) biblical books Ezra and Nehemiah, which allege to describe the Jewish religion practiced by the returnees from Babylonia, do not mention the synagogue. Although first- and second-century texts such as Josephus, Philo, and the New Testament mention synagogues, clear archaeological evidence of synagogues as designated places of worship does not appear until the third century. *See also* ark in Judaism; Falashas; Judaism (art and architecture); Judaism, prayer and liturgy of; Torah scroll.

Synanon, a quasi-religious drug rehabilitation organization established in California in 1958 by Charles Dederich, a former member of Alcoholics Anonymous. Synanon's controversial methods included tightly knit support groups and intense discussion sessions. In these leaderless circles the members may be personally challenged, with the object of attaining eventual honest self-understanding and catharsis. Many members have lived together communally.

In the late 1970s, Synanon received unfavorable publicity from news media reports of alleged child abuse and excessive authoritarianism, and the organization responded with libel suits. A subsequent investigation by the California state attorney general led to numerous indictments. In 1978, charges of attempted murder were made against Dederich and several associates. While none of these cases came to trial, considerable damage was done to the public image of Synanon. Consequently, the organization entered a period of diminished impact in the 1980s and '90s. *See also* Alcoholics Anonymous; North America, new religions in.

syncretism, the process of combining religious elements of diverse origins in a new sect or movement; a term of dubious heritage and limited usefulness, often employed to ascribe insincerity, confusion, or other negative qualities to a nascent religious group. Its usage frequently suggests that while some (non-Western, non-elite, or primitive) religions are formed of a jumble of barely understood components, others (such as Christianity) purportedly exhibit no external influence in their origins and are thus unique and privileged.

The Greek term itself has been traced to a single extant ancient source, *synkretismos*, apparently coined by Plutarch in reference to a Cretan confederation against a common enemy. Its later employment by philosophers and theologians, such as George Calixtus in his seventeenth-century proposal to harmonize Protestant doctrines, and subsequent modern usage indicate conflation with the similar Greek words *synkratizein* ("to combine") or *synkerannumi* ("to mix," "blend").

Following the self-conscious and formal attempts of the fifteenth century to harmonize philosophical points and the later Christian efforts to reconcile increasingly dissimilar sectarian beliefs and practices, the history of modern comparative studies reveals a pattern in the identification of religions as syncretic or syncretistic. Scholars of the turn of the century who struggled unsuccessfully to construct evolutionary patterns of religion seldom included the term *syncretism* in their descriptions of developing cults. But their colleagues, attempting to classify all known religions by "types," resorted to its use to label either transitional phenomena or religions that escaped easy categorization. Thus, for example, one conceived of a primordial phase between polydaemonism and polytheism as a "syncretistic" moment of assimilation and reordering. Other typologists first listed the cult of Marduk in Babylonia and that of Sarapis in Egypt, together with many or all Gnostic sects and Hellenistic religions, as having been the result of efforts to integrate two or more disparate religious traditions; motives ascribed to the followers ranged from attempted monotheism to sincere, if peculiar, universalism to, finally, unavoidable confusion. Interpreters concluded that the intermingling of cultures led naturally to an unconscious assimilation of deities, while conquest allowed a dominant cult to replace the religious system of the conquered.

Underlying this usage were four overlapping assumptions concerning ancient religions, all essentially stemming from a Christian theological bias: first, that Judaism or Christianity alone were revealed traditions and that all others were human inventions, unconnected with divinity or spirituality; second, that the latter, pagan religions evoked no faith or other emotional commitment among their followers and, hence, could be modified without reference to beliefs or needs; third, that the symbol systems of ancient religions were interchangeable and unrelated to their indigenous contexts and thus could be rearranged or introduced into non-indigenous settings without difficulty; and fourth, that ancient priesthoods were, at best, misguided or, at worst, manipulative. The identification of other ancient religious traditions as syncretistic usually presumed the existence of a "pure" tradition precedent to one corrupted by foreign elements or confused with foreign parallels. The treatment of the expansion of the cult of Isis during the Hellenistic period is one example of this, as are Israelite religion in the preexilic era and Mithraism.

Despite its history of intermingled religious doctrines and rituals, Christianity itself has escaped labeling as syncretistic—except in the rare positivistic treatments of the development of Western culture. Only nineteenth- and twentieth-century descriptions of Christianity's encounter with tribal religions in situations of conquest and domination broach the issue, whereupon the new religious movements drawing on both Christian and indigenous elements are labeled "syncretistic." Still, even Christian groups in the Americas and Asia, which have consciously adopted indigenous symbols and interpretations, are only identified as syncretistic when substantial portions of their systems, notably concepts of deity, diverge from assumed standards.

Contemporary usage has, with few exceptions, only added pejorative weight to the term, owing, perhaps, to its unrelenting imprecision. Although commonly used in so-called objective comparative studies to signal the creative interpretive developments in new religions, the term and its contextual connotations—especially in discussions of non-Christian groups—often suggest not only that participants lack a true understanding of the ancestral systems from which they have borrowed symbols, beliefs, and rituals, but also that they have entered a regressive state in religion and in cultural development generally. The newer tenor of the term continues the implication that participants are too loosely bound to their inherited faiths to resist the currents of change in religions. Such perspectives emerge in the analysis of the history of Asian cultures, which, by reducing Buddhist, Tantrist,

or Shinto traditions to doctrines or schools of authority and religious life to exclusivist adherence, neglect the complexity of human experience in a pluralistic society and the interpretive capabilities of spiritual understanding.

Conflicting assessments also confront the changing or "syncretistic" religions of Native Americans—North, Central, and South—who, through that term, are at once pitied for having surrendered their ancient cultures (notwithstanding the tremendous forces against them), censured for efforts to reconstruct or inaugurate separatist religions, and (to a lesser extent) denigrated either for their failure or their success at assimilation. New Age groups are also routinely called "syncretic" as scholars fail to note the historical traditions preceding them, tend to emphasize the transience of individual memberships, and are, indeed, reluctant to include them under the rubric of religion at all. Constructive attempts at systematic clarification of its meaning have, however, regained currency for the term among scholars of Hellenistic religions, especially in Europe.

In view of the fact that no historically known religion has begun in a vacuum but has instead readily drawn on valuable aspects of existent traditions in which its members found meaning, one must conclude that the term at this time has little taxonomic value. *See also* acculturation; typology, classification.

syncretism (Japan). The combining of various religious forms has been a major feature of Japanese religion throughout history. Indeed, persecution when it has occurred has most often been directed toward exclusive devotion to a single tradition. The presence of Buddhism, Shinto, Confucianism, Taoism, folk religion, and more recently Christianity guaranteed not only clashes but also mutual influence and borrowing. Shinto borrowed magic and divination from Taoism, for example, and Buddhism adapted to Japanese folk beliefs concerning the dead and sacred mountains.

One mode of syncretism has been to assign different traditions to different areas of life. For the most part, religious institutions in Japan have been used ad hoc by individuals and groups for the various needs of individual and collective life. The most obvious example is that most Japanese are married in a Shinto wedding and buried with a Buddhist funeral. Similarly, the different social groups an individual may belong to—family, village, occupation, nation, etc.—may entail widely differing religious obligations.

A more deliberate mode of syncretism is to claim an underlying similarity or cosmological connection between two or more traditions. The major example of this has been the theory of essence and manifestation (*honji suijaku*) in which the Shinto *kami* (divinities, divine presences) were said to be the manifestations of various Buddhas and Bodhisattvas, who were their essence. This Buddhist theory predominated until the late nineteenth century, when the government sought to separate Shinto and Buddhism (*shinbutsu bunri*) in order to use the former in constructing a national ideology. *See also* danka system; honji suijaku; Japanese religion; kami; Pure Land; shinbutsu bunri; Shinto; Shugendo; ubasoku.

synod. 1 A meeting of Christian clergy, usually on a regional basis, for the regulation of church life. 2 The permanent governing structure of some Protestant denominations such as the Presbyterians.

Syria, Christianity in. The origins of Christianity in Syria are obscure. Probably by the end of the second century or the beginning of the third, Jewish Christian missionaries had established churches in Edessa, a major commercial center on the eastern fringe of the Roman Empire, and the center of a culture whose primary language was Syriac, an eastern dialect of Aramaic. Edessa was also home to a large Jewish population.

The two major representatives of this early Aramaic Christianity in and around Edessa are Aphrahat (fourth century) and Ephrem Syrus (ca. 306–373). The hymns, or *madrashe,* of Ephrem Syrus are renowned for the way in which they synthesize ancient Mesopotamian, Jewish, Syriac, and Greek Christian traditions. During the fifth and sixth centuries, Syriac-speaking Christians came to be influenced to an ever-greater degree by the theological traditions of Greek Christianity.

The Syriac Christian traditions possess a rich and varied literature ranging from hymnody to translations of Aristotle (d. 322 B.C.), which made possible the introduction of Aristotle to the West via Arabic translations of the Syriac.

The Syriac liturgical traditions developed out of the rites used in the churches in and around the cities of Edessa, Antioch, and Jerusalem. The East Syrian liturgy of the Eucharist (the Liturgy of Addai and Mari) is believed by many to contain remnants of the ancient Aramaic Christianity of Edessa. The ancient Syrian baptismal tradition appears to have placed great emphasis upon an anointing of the baptismal candidate before the baptism, and understood baptism not in terms of death and burial but in terms of the baptism of Christ.

Syriac Christianity can be divided into two major categories: East and West Syrian. The majority of both follow a non-Chalcedonian Christology. East Syrian Christianity, which by the beginning of the fifth century A.D. had existed largely in the Persian Empire, spread through vigorous missionary effort to India and China by the seventh century. This type of Syriac Christianity exists in the Church of the East (erroneously called "Nestorian"), a remnant of which survives in Iraq, Iran, and the United States, in the Malabar Church of southern India, and in the Eastern-rite Catholic Syro-Malabar and Chaldean rites.

West Syrian Christianity continues to exist in small numbers in the Syrian Orthodox church, which is monophysite. There are also small numbers of Eastern-rite Catholic Syrians, and Eastern-rite Catholics of the Syro-Malankara rite in southern India.

Finally, the Maronite Church of Lebanon represents a third type of Syriac Christianity that combined East Syrian and West Syrian liturgical traditions. It entered into communion with the See of Rome in 1204. *See also* Aphrahat; Ephraem Syrus; Maronites; Thomas Christians.

systematic theology. *See* Christian theological systems.j

A B C D E F
G H I J
M N O
R S T U V
W X Y & Z

tabernacle. In the Hebrew Bible, the portable tent that served as a sanctuary during the wilderness wandering (Exodus 25–27, 36–38) and was replaced by the Jerusalem Temple.

Christianity: 1 A receptacle housing the eucharistic elements in Roman Catholic and some Anglican churches. **2** A large building used by evangelical or fundamentalist Protestant congregations for worship and preaching revivals. Occasionally used as a church name (e.g., Mormon Tabernacle in Salt Lake City, Utah).

taboo (ta-*boo'*; Polynesian *tapu,* "forbidden"), objects, persons, and behaviors subject to ritual or religious proscriptions. The term is closely associated with the notion of an innate power or force called *mana,* inherent in all objects, animals, and people, which can cause fortune or misfortune. Taboo prohibits contact with objects that either possess or can invoke harmful mana, the violation of which brings about automatic punishment. The concept of taboo includes things that are avoided as a normal course of action as well as things that are avoided only at specified ceremonial or religious occasions, birth and death rites, and rituals such as the rites of passage between adolescence and adulthood.

Many cultures that observe ceremonial cycles have objects, often food items, that are forbidden for a time prior to and during ceremonial periods. Taboos on behavior include prohibitions of sexual intercourse prior to and during ceremonial periods. Mother-in-law avoidance is practiced by many cultures of the world. The onus of the taboo is upon the son-in-law, who is expected to leave a room or home when the mother-in-law arrives, never to speak directly to her or meet her in public or private. Widespread taboos affect menstruating females. The prohibitions range from relegating the menstruating woman to a place away from the general populace to barring her from food preparation. Other behavioral taboos prohibit a woman from touching her husband's hunting paraphernalia, or a man from seeing his newborn child for a specified time. Penalties for violating taboos range from death to illness to other misfortune, such as divorce, infertility, crop failure, or poor hunting. Most violated taboos can be remedied through ritual ceremony. *See also* Australian and Pacific traditional religions; incest, incest prohibition; mana; origin of religion; purity and impurity.

tabu. *See* taboo.

Ta-chih-tu lun (dah-juhr-doo luhn; Chin., "Treatise on the Great Perfection of Wisdom"), a major treatise on the Buddhist doctrine of emptiness attributed to Nagarjuna. *See also* emptiness; Madhyamaka.

Tachikawa-ryu (tah-chee-kah-wah-ry*oo*), Japanese Buddhist teachings that used sexual intercourse as a means to realize Buddhahood with one's body. It probably arose late in the twelfth century but was denounced by the more mainstream Shingon school and suppressed by the early seventeenth century. *See also* maithuna; sexuality and religion; Shingon-shu; sokushin jobutsu.

T'aebaek, Mt. *See* mountains, sacred.

Taehak. *See* academies (Korea), private and public.

tahara. *See* purity and impurity.

Ta-hsueh (dah-shweh; Chin., "Great Learning"), a classic of later Confucianism. Originally the forty-second chapter of the *Li chi* (Book of Rites), it was first given prominence by Han Yu (768–824). It urges the learner to manifest virtue, cherish people, and rest in perfect goodness. Chu Hsi (1130–1200) significantly edited it, reinterpreting its message to be for all adults seeking to become sages and making it the first of what became orthodox Neo-Confucianism's *Ssu-shu* (Four Books). Later Confucians preferred the older version, arguing that Chu's editing distorted its basic meaning. *See also* Chu Hsi; Confucianism (authoritative texts and their interpretation); Li chi; Ssu-shu.

Ta-hui Tsung-kao (dah-hway dyung-gou; 1089–1163), Chinese Ch'an Buddhist monk who reacted against the literary study of *kung-an* (a paradoxical teaching that transcends logical or conceptual thought) and stressed the role of faith. *See also* Ch'an school; kung-an.

tahur. *See* circumcision.

Tai Chen (d*i* jen; 1723–77), Chinese Confucian polyglot thinker who rejected the abstract methods of Chu Hsi and emphasized inductive and critical investigation of things. *See also* Chu Hsi.

t'ai-chi (t*i*-jee; Chin., "great/supreme," "ultimate/ridgepole"), Chinese philosophical term first found in the *I-ching* (Book of Changes) referring to the Great Ultimate Principle, or ridgepole, supporting the universe. It is the foundation of reality from which duality, the five basic elements, and all things arise and eventually return. *See also* I-ching.

t'ai-chi ch'uan (*ti*-jee chwahn; Chin., "Great Ultimate Boxing"), a Chinese martial arts system based on the philosophical concept of *t'ai-chi* ("Great Ultimate," the foundation of reality). It was synthesized in the early seventeenth century in South China. The original Chen style branched into different styles, becoming more public by emphasizing its numerous health benefits. Today, the Yang style is most popular for this reason. This martial art is a holistic exercise, a dancelike art form and a discipline of moving meditation, offering, at advanced levels, experiential understanding of fundamental Taoist principles. *See also* Chang San-feng; martial arts.

T'ai-chi t'u shou (*ti*-jee *too* shoh; Chin., "Explanation of the Diagram of the Great Ultimate"), a short treatise by Chou Tun-i (1017–73) that became the metaphysical and ethical manifesto of the Sung Neo-Confucian revival. The diagram was highly controversial because of its introduction of the concept of the nonultimate as a cosmological counterpart of the Supreme Ultimate, the highest expression of principle (*li*) and the creative source of the flux of cosmic generation and interaction. *See also* li; Neo-Confucianism; t'ai-chi.

t'ai-hsi (*ti*-shee; Chin., "embryonic breathing"), Taoist physiological procedure and mystical technique of learning to breathe like a fetus in the womb. *See also* physiological techniques (Taoism).

T'ai-hsu (*ti*-shyoo; 1890–1947), a Chinese Buddhist monk and reformer. He worked to educate both monastic and lay Buddhists in doctrine and practice, establish Buddhist study institutes, make Buddhism more intellectually respectable, weed out superstition, and protect the Buddhist establishment from government interference.

T'ai-i (*ti*-yee; Chin., "Grand Unity"). **1** Early Chinese god of the center of the universe. **2** In Taoism, the primordial unity of the cosmos. *See also* cosmology.

T'ai-i chin-hua tsung-chih (*ti*-yee jin-hwah tsoong juhr; Chin., "Comprehensive Instructions on the Golden Flower of the Grand Unity"), a Chinese meditation text attributed to the shadowy ninth-century figure Lu Yen; it was actually composed ca. 1800. It represents the Ch'an-influenced meditative traditions of Chin-tan ("Golden Elixir") Taoism, specifically, a meditative manipulation of internal forces to achieve revitalization and spiritual rebirth. It was translated in 1929 as *The Secret of the Golden Flower* with a commentary by the psychologist Carl Jung. *See also* Chin-tan Taoism.

T'ai-i Taoism (*ti*-yee; Chin., "Supreme One"), the most traditional of the "reformed" Taoist sects. Founded by Hsiao Pao-chen in the twelfth century, it stressed ritual healing and social responsibility instead of the pursuit of immortality. Though popular among emperors (such as Khublai Khan), it was subsumed by Cheng-i Taoism. *See also* Cheng-i Taoism; Taoism.

Tain (tawyn), a short title for *Tain Bo Cuailnge*, "The Cattle-Raid of Cooley," the greatest of the early Irish heroic sagas. This eighth-century tale describes the attempts of the armies of the rest of Ireland, opposed at first only by the warrior Cu Chulainn, to seize a preternatural bull from the province of Ulster. *See also* Celtic religion.

T'ai-p'ing ching (*ti*-ping-jing; Chin., "Scripture of Great Peace"), a Chinese revealed text proclaiming Heaven's will to change the ruling dynasty and outlining the perfect theocratic rule. Twice rejected by Han-dynasty emperors, it inspired the Yellow Turban rebellion in 184, actualizing a messianic ideology frequently rekindled during subsequent revolts. *See also* millenarianism.

T'ai-ping Rebellion (*ti*-ping), a massive antidynastic spiritual, political, and military movement waged against the ruling Ch'ing dynasty (1644–1912) that gained control of south central China from 1849 to 1864. The rebellion was begun by a charismatic Christian convert, Hung Hsiu-chuan, who founded a quasi-Chinese Christian sect, the God Worshiper's Society (Pai Shan-ti Hui), in 1845. Hung declared in his tracts that the Tai-ping T'ien-kuo ("Heavenly Kingdom of the Great Peace") was at hand. Numerous military triumphs brought a dramatic increase in numbers.

This first phase in the history of the movement ended when the rebel armies conquered Nanking and made it the capital of the Heavenly Kingdom. But the decision to attack Peking led to the loss of men and material and the T'ai-ping image of invincibility. Furthermore, conflicts among the movement's ruling elite weakened the rebellion and sapped it of its energy just when it had reached its apex of power and influence. The Ch'ing rulers were supported by a new generation of reformist scholar-officials. Resistance to the Taipings was led by this body of loyal scholarly gentry, who established regional armies inculcated with loyalty and traditional Confucian beliefs. Using these new armies, they were able to crush the T'ai-ping rebellion. An estimated twenty million people were killed over the course of these years. *See also* China, Christianity in; Hung Hsiu-chuan; millenarianism.

T'ai-p'ing Tao (*ti*-ping-dou; Chin., "Way of Great Peace"), a messianic movement founded by Chang Chueh in eastern China whose members were known as the Yellow Turbans. In 184 they instigated a widespread rebellion, accelerating the decline of the Han empire (206 B.C.–A.D. 220). Chang followed Huang-Lao Taoism and was inspired by the *T'ai-p'ing ching* (Scripture of Great Peace), a sacred text with a messianic and utopian ideology that inspired many rebellions. Chang organized his community into thirty-six districts, healed the sick by using confession and charm water, and preached the coming of the "yellow heaven" era. *See also* Chang Chueh; Huang-Lao Taoism; millenarianism; T'ai-p'ing ching.

T'ai Shan (*ti*-shan), China's most sacred mountain and the deity of that mountain. A place of imperial worship, it is today a place of popular pilgrimage. *See also* mountains, sacred.

T'ai-shang kan-ying p'ien (*ti*-shahng gahn-eeng peein; Chin., "Treatise of the Most High on Actions and Retributions"), a morality book from the eleventh century extant in the Taoist canon and numerous reprints. A mixture of Taoist, Buddhist, and folk religious ideas, it purports to be the words of the Taoist sage Lao-tzu teaching the laws of retribution, namely, that good and bad fortune follow naturally from what people do. *See also* Lao-tzu.

Taize, Protestant monastic community founded in France in 1940 and devoted to ecumenism. *See also* monasticism.

tajdif. *See* blasphemy.

Taj Mahal (tahj' ma-hahl'; Persian, corruption of proper name, Mumtaz Mahal, "Chosen One of the Palace"), marble tomb and place of pilgrimage in Agra, India. The shrine was constructed by the Muslim Moghul emperor Shah Jihan (d. 1666) to commemorate his consort, Mumtaz Mahal (d. 1631). It serves principally as a mausoleum, although the shrine complex includes a mosque. The architecture of the shrine fuses Indian and Islamic styles. *See also* Moghul Empire.

Takamagahara (tah-kah-mah-gah-hah-rah; Jap., "high plain of heaven"), the Shinto abode of celestial divinities (*Ama tsu kami*), such as the sun goddess, Amaterasu, in contrast to the underworld of the dead (*Yomi no kuni*) and the middle realm of human habitation (*Ashihara no nakatsu kuni*). *See also* cosmogony; cosmology; Japanese myth; sky.

Talayesva, Don C. (tah-li'-es-vuh; ca. 1890–1987), a member of the Oraibi Village Sun Clan and author of *Sun Chief* (1942), one of four published Hopi (American Southwest) autobiographies, which provides a detailed record of Hopi religious traditions and economic practice. *Sun Chief* is a collaborative work solicited by anthropologist Leo Simmons, who conceived it as an anthropological case study of Hopi culture. It is drawn from oral interviews with Talayesva as well as the autobiographer's own diary entries. As a member of a community notable for its reluctance to document any part of its cultural traditions, Talayesva has been criticized by the Hopis for the graphic and personal nature of his disclosures.

tale type, in folklore, the narrative outline of a tale that has an independent existence. Scholars classify tale types in world folk literature as well as in specific cultures according to the numerical system of A. Aarne and Stith Thompson, *The Types of the Folktale* (2d ed., 1964). It is a general assumption of folklorists that the presence of the same tale type implies a genetic relation. *See also* motif.

talisman. *See* amulet.

Talmud (tahl-mood'; Heb., "study," "knowledge"), in Judaism, a compilation of clarifications and expansions of statements in the Mishnah. There are two Talmuds. One was completed in the Land of Israel ca. 400 to 500 and is called the Talmud of the Land of Israel or, less often, the Palestinian Talmud (in Hebrew, the Yerushalmi, or Talmud of Jerusalem, even though not prepared in Jerusalem). The other concluded in Babylonia, a province at the western frontier of the Iranian Empire corresponding to present-day Iraq, ca. 600 and is called the Talmud of Babylonia (in Hebrew, the Bavli). Both Talmuds are organized as commentaries to the Mishnah. These commentaries to the Mishnah are called *gemara* ("completion," "tradition"), and the Talmuds are often called simply Gemara. The Bavli does not expand upon the earlier one but forms its own discussions in accord with its own program. The Yerushalmi treats thirty-nine of the

Mishnah's sixty-three tractates; the Bavli, thirty-seven of them.

When discussing a rule of the Mishnah, the Talmuds either (1) explain the meaning of the passage, or (2) extend and expand the meaning of the passage. Straightforward explanation of the plain meaning of a law of the Mishnah by far predominates in both Talmuds's readings of the Mishnah. They differ only in their agenda. Both Talmuds contain extensive treatments of the tractates of the Mishnah's second, third, and fourth divisions, which are on appointed times, women, and damages (civil law and government). The Yerushalmi treats most of the Mishnah's first division, on agriculture; the Talmud of Babylonia treats most of the Mishnah's fifth division, on holy things (the sacrificial system of the Temple of Jerusalem and the maintenance of the Temple itself). Neither Talmud addresses the sixth division of the Mishnah, purities, except for the tractate on menstrual uncleanness. The Bavli is the authoritative one and is widely studied as the constitution of Judaism. It received extensive commentaries and supercommentaries, and it has served as the curriculum of Judaism. The Yerushalmi attracted much less attention until very recent times.

The Yerushalmi: The Yerushalmi treats the Mishnah as a composite of discrete and essentially autonomous rules and invariably discusses it in one of four ways: (1) text criticism; (2) exegesis of the meaning of the Mishnah, including glosses and amplifications; (3) addition of scriptural proof texts of the Mishnah's central propositions; and (4) harmonization of one Mishnah passage with another such passage or with a statement of Tosefta. This immensely creative and imaginative approach to the Mishnah vastly expands the range of discourse. But it also obliterates the Mishnah's most striking formal traits and denies the document its own mode of speech and its distinctive and coherent message.

The Bavli: Formed two centuries later, the Bavli treats the Mishnah in the same way. In addition, the Bavli's authorship moves in a direction all its own and systematically comments in large and cogent compositions upon not only the Mishnah but also Scripture, that is, on both the oral and the written Torahs. In the Land of Israel, Mishnah commentary went into the Yerushalmi, and Scripture commentary went into the midrash compilations. But the Bavli's framers included sizable sequences and proportionately substantial compositions—30 to 40 percent—of Scripture units of discourse. These they inserted whole and complete, not in response to the Mishnah's program. The Yerushalmi contains such scriptural commentary in limited volume. This difference between the two Talmuds may account for the greater acceptance of the Bavli.

By extensive resort to units of discourse providing an exegesis of Scripture, the Bavli's framers read their values into the texts of Scripture. In omitting such units, the Yerushalmi's authors lost the opportunity to spell out in a complete way the larger system of Judaism that both Talmuds portray. The key to the Bavli's success lies in the very foundations of its distinctive literary structure, in the redactional-literary decision to lay main beams of its composition upon both the Mishnah and passages of Scripture. The compositors of the Bavli were encyclopedists. Their creation turned out to be the encyclopedia of Judaism, its summa. *See also* Judaism (authoritative texts and their interpretation); Mishnah, the; rabbi.

tama (tah-mah; Jap., "spirit"), in Japanese religion, the animating spirit of *kami* (divinities, divine presences), people, or occasionally a place. Various rituals seek to manipulate it, e.g., to prevent its departure at death and to recall or pacify it after death. *Tama* has two primary forms or modes: *ara-mitama*, active and rough, and *nigi-mitama*, gentle and harmonizing. *See also* kami.

Tambor de Mina. *See* Afro-Brazilian religions.

Tamil, Tamil Nadu. *See* Dravidian.

tan (dahn; Chin., "cinnabar," "mercuric sulfide"), compound used in China to preserve corpses; later it was an element in Taoist elixirs for immortality. *See also* alchemy.

Tan'gun wanggom (tahn-goon wahng-kuhm; Kor., "Royal Khan Sandlewood Prince"), the legendary founder of Choson, the first nation-state on the Korean peninsula. Tan'gun is said to have been born in 2333 B.C., the progeny of the son of the Lord of Heaven and a bear that had been changed into a woman. The Tan'gun calendar dates from the year of his birth. Tan'gun is said to have descended from Mt. Paekdu, established a city at Pyongyang, and called his nation Choson ("Kingdom of the Morning Light"). Later he moved his capital to Mt. T'aebaek and ruled there until King Wu of Chou invested Kija as king of Korea. At this point Tan'gun left and later returned to Mt. T'aebaek where he became a mountain god.

The function of this myth, at the time of its

recording in the thirteenth century, was to present a single myth for all the Korean people at a time when Korea was suffering from repeated invasions from China and Japan. It was meant to replace, or rather preface, all the various clan foundation myths that had been passed on from the Three Kingdoms period (57 B.C.–A.D. 668).

Modern comparative analysis of the myth indicates very strong correspondences with Siberian foundation myths about totem groups among the Tungusic tribes. If there is historical continuity with those myths, then the descent of Tan'gun from Mt. Paekdu, the largest mountain on the Korean northern border, may indicate the migration of the forebears of the Korean people into the peninsula. *See also* Korean foundation myths.

T'an-luan (tahn-lwahn; 476–542 or 554), author of the first systematic treatise on Chinese Pure Land Buddhism and the first great popularizer of Pure Land practices among the laity. He advocated visualization of the Pure Land and invocation of the name of Amitabha Buddha as the Path of Easy Practice, contrasted with the ascetic Path of Difficult Practice. *See also* Pure Land; Pure Land school (China).

Tannisho (tahn-nee-shoh; Jap., "Notes Lamenting Differences"), short Japanese Buddhist text compiled by Shinran's disciple Yuienbo that is one of the most popular guides to Shinran's thought. The first half contains a number of sayings by Shinran and the second half is Yuienbo's critique of several misinterpretations of Shinran's thought. *See also* Shinran.

tan-t'ien (dahn-tyen; Chin., "field of cinnabar"), the Taoist system that divides the human body into three centers. *See also* physiological techniques (Taoism).

Tantra (tuhn'truh; from Skt. root -*tan*, "to extend, span," cognate with Lat. *ten* as in "tension"), also Tantrism and Tantricism, a template term for three overlapping yet distinct themes in Indian and, by diffusion from India, Tibetan, and other Asian esoteric lore.

Indian Tantra: In popular Indian usage, it stands for shamanistic practices of various sorts, as well as for spell-induced witchcraft, some forms of folk divination, and therapy. Second, Tantrism refers to a large set of meditational techniques aimed at liberation (*moksha*) and thought to be a shortcut, albeit a risky one, compared to the orthodox forms of yoga. Third, *Tantrism* is an encompassing term for all ritual that is not Vedic. All women's rites are Tantric by

that definition, and so are village rites other than those performed in the official Sanskrit- and Veda-based ritualistic idiom.

Tantrics, however, see themselves as *yogins* (yoga practitioners) of a special, powerful, and radical kind. Though physical control techniques are shared with *hatha yoga*, there is a strong emphasis on visualization of deities and their mystographic representations (*mandalas*, *yantras*).

Although the eroticized aspects of Tantric praxis and doctrine are vastly exaggerated in both popular Hindu and Indophile Western statements, the "left-handed" (*vamachara*) elements are a central part of Tantrism; vamachara can be seen as the esoteric, "right-handed" (*dakshinachara*) as the exoteric components of Tantrism. In the former, the "five Ms" (*panchamakara*), i.e., the ritual ingestion of meat (*mamsa*), fish (*matsya*), spiced beans thought to be aphrodisiacs (*mudra*), and liquor (*mada*) and sexual intercourse between the male and female adept participants (*maithuna*) in the course of the "circle ritual" (*chakrasadhana*, referring to the circular seating arrangement), are actually performed. "Right-handed" practice replaces these with more conventional substitutes such as milk, coconut, and the meditational visualization of the male and female tutelary deities Shiva and Shakti copulating. To the practicing Tantric, any actual form of sexual congress between males and females of any species is a reflection of the archetypal, divine congress that is seen as replicating itself in myriad forms, thereby generating the universe. Esoterically, however, the reverse flow of the divine energy, visualized as the seminal fluid moving upward during the act, and the retention of semen lead to cosmic involution at the end of each world cycle; in the individual practitioner, it brings about moksha ("salvation"), freedom from rebirth. The panchamakara core ritual, thus, is very contrary to what it seems to the noninitiate. It is not the quest for and the achievement of orgasm but of total control; it is moving away from the senses and the objective world, in diametrical contrast to the ways of the empirical world, the outward-going senses, epitomized in the consummated sexual act. It is easy to see why Tantrics and Tantrism have been and are being looked at with systematic suspicion. The fact that many people—Indian and recently Western as well—often espouse Tantric terminology to camouflage some or all of their sexual activity adds to the negative image Tantrism has on the subcontinent.

The Tantric axiom that the retention of semen in general, but particularly during the panchamakara or *chakra-sadhana*, generates spiritual power as a requisite to the attainment of liberation has extremely ancient roots. The compound *urddhva-retas,* "he whose sperm moves upward," is an epithet of the supreme deity in several Vedic texts that could possibly be viewed as ancestral to Tantric belief and praxis. This assumption seems reinforced by the fact that many of the chants used during "left-handed" Tantric ritual are in fact Vedic chants, sometimes, but not always, modified by purely Tantric accretions.

Buddhist Tantra: Buddhist Tantrism, or Vajrayana, "the vehicle of the thunderbolt," is well preserved and intact in Tibetan Buddhism today, where it is the official teaching of the Tibetan monastic traditions. In no way clandestine like its Hindu counterpart, it follows more complex, but essentially similar practices centering upon the visualization of deities either in the form of *mandalas* or iconically represented, supported in the more advanced phases by sexual contact between the male and female aspirants. In Tibetan religious art, the *than-ka* represents the male and female deities in stylized sexual embrace (*yab yum,* "honorable father honorable mother").

There are some fundamental differences between Hindu and Buddhist Tantric doctrine. The most important is the mirrorlike inversion of the male and the female key properties in the visualization of the deities and in cosmological speculations supporting or deriving from these visualizations. In Hindu Tantric thought, the male deity, Shiva, is totally quiescent, pure knowledge and cognition, and passive; his female consort, Shakti, is what the name implies, power, pure energy. Iconographically, this is represented as the goddess dancing on the chest of the prostrate god. In Vajrayana, by contrast, the male principle of Buddhahood is outgoing energy; his female consort is totally quiescent, pure knowledge, *prajna* ("wisdom"). We do not know the reasons for this inversion of properties, but they are axiomatic in Buddhist and Hindu terms, respectively.

Tantric Texts: The sacred texts of Tantrism form a large corpus. Extant Hindu Tantric texts, often called Shakta texts (i.e., related to *shakti,* the dynamic core concept of Tantric thought), are of relatively recent origin when compared with the Vedic lore. The most authentic and revered Tantras (also referred to as *agamas* and *nigamas* by Tantrics), were compiled between the twelfth and fifteenth centuries. After that time, this literature proliferated, and Tantras are in fact being written even now, since devotees are not concerned about the age of holy writ. The ritualistic

segments contain a large number of Vedic passages, which legitimizes Tantrism as embedded in the Vedic tradition. In Vajrayana, in its extant Tibetan form, Tantric texts (*rgyud*) constitute a sizable portion of the secondary canon, and there are some Tantric texts even in the primary Tibetan canon. The oldest Buddhist texts preserved in Sanskrit (i.e., the *Manjushrimulakalpa* and the *Guhyasamaja Tantra*) probably originated between the sixth and ninth centuries. Just as learned Hindu Tantrics regard Hindu Tantric texts as equal to the Veda, Vajrayana Buddhists regard the Buddhist Tantric corpus as the word of the Buddha.

While the future of Vajrayana is secure, since it is a fully acknowledged integral part of Tibetan Buddhism, Hindu Tantrism has been on a steady decline, mainly due to the generally puritanical attitude of the Hindu religious establishment. The fact that the American counterculture of the 1960s co-opted Tantrism, however superficially, added to a modern Hindu resentment of Tantrism in all forms. Privately, however, middle-class urban Hindus do seek out Tantric help and counsel for all kinds of problems, and there is no shortage of counselors who present themselves as Tantrics, both monastic and lay. *See also* chakras; Goddess (Hinduism); hatha yoga; Kapalika; Kashmir Shaivism; kundalini; liberation; maithuna; mandala; sexuality and religion; Shaktism; Tantrism (Buddhism); yoga.

Tantrism (Buddhism) (Skt. *vajrayana,* "Diamond [or Thunderbolt] Vehicle"), a school of late Indian Buddhism.

Though best known as an exoteric monastic and lay religion, Indian Buddhism has always possessed esoteric traditions. At all periods of its history, certain individuals, in search of perfection, have renounced both "the world" and the monastery and have gone into solitary retreat to practice meditation. Buddhist Tantrism originally emerges as one such esoteric tradition.

Early History: The precise origins of the Vajrayana are obscure, but it is clear that this Buddhist tradition originally took shape in particular Indian religious environments. Several environments of particular importance to Vajrayana include the *stupa* (reliquary mound), with its symbolism and liturgy as reflected in the *mandala,* the cremation/charnal ground with its particular symbolisms and practices, and Indian yogic traditions. Tibetan historians maintain that the Vajrayana goes back to the days of the Buddha, but that, owing to its esoteric nature, it left no historical trace until late in its history.

Later History: Be that as it may, modern scholarship confirms the indisputable existence of Vajrayana in India from the eighth century onward, when it developed an increasingly prominent exoteric and public side. In the eighth century, it began to attain wide popularity in northeastern India, with the Pala dynasty acting as enthusiastic patrons. In the eighth through twelfth centuries, the Vajrayana overtook and passed in popularity other forms of Buddhism, most notably in northeast India. During this period, Vajrayana came to be practiced in all three classical Buddhist contexts, that of the solitary retreat, that of the monastery, and that of lay life. The monastic Vajrayana tended to be scholastic and relatively conventional, while the nonmonastic forms tended to retain the unconventional air of the tradition's earlier days. In the eighth century, Indian masters took Vajrayana to other lands, including China, whence it spread to Japan (Shingon Buddhism), Tibet, and Southeast Asia. After the Muslim conquests culminating in 1200, it continued to survive in certain regions in India (e.g., Orissa), returning once more to a largely esoteric form.

Lacking in its formative period a standardizing environment such as that provided by the monastery, Buddhist Tantrism came to include considerable diversity, partially acknowledged by the (later) scholastic division of Buddhist Tantric traditions into four orders: action Tantra, ritualistic Tantra, Yoga Tantra, and Supreme Yoga Tantra.

Basic Orientation: Buddhist Tantrism is often understood as a branch of the Mahayana, for it shares the same *bodhisattva* (Buddha-to-be) ideal, the same ontology (emptiness), and the same aspiration for the enlightenment of a Buddha. It is to be distinguished from the more conventional (monastic) Mahayana by several features: its primary reliance is upon texts called *tantras* rather than upon the *sutras;* its goal of enlightenment is "in this very lifetime"; it insists upon the necessity of the personal teacher (*guru*) and his role as the source of all wisdom; it emphasizes meditation practice; it uses a characteristic type of liturgical meditation (*sadhana*); and its distinctive enlightened ideal is the *mahasiddha,* an unconventional figure, usually a wandering *yogin* but occasionally a layperson following a worldly occupation.

Tantric Methodology: Tantric method is based on the liturgical visualization of oneself as a Buddha. One becomes qualified to practice Tantric ritual by receiving an initiation from a guru. Having done so, one then begins to practice, often in retreat, one or another type of Tantric meditation ritual, all of which tend to have a similar structure. Having ritually purified the place of practice and one's body, speech,

and mind, the practitioner takes refuge in the Three Jewels (Buddha, Dharma, Sangha) and takes the bodhisattva vow to work for the liberation of all beings. This is followed by a meditation upon emptiness, wherein all concepts of one's historical identity are reduced to nonexistence. In one of the most prevalent types of Tantric practice ("Supreme Yoga Tantra") there then follows the central ritual event: one first creates, step by step, a visualization of oneself as an enlightened deity (a Buddha); this deity is visualized, along with his or her retinue of divine beings, as residing in the center of a mandala; the living reality of the deity is invoked into the visualized form; and one recites the mantra of the deity, through which its full reality is experienced. Following this, one offers praises and presents offerings, and concludes with a dedication of merit. Finally, all is once again dissolved into emptiness.

In more advanced forms, this ritual process may be entirely internalized, with the practitioner's body being visualized as a divine cosmos (mandala), with deities residing at its critical junctures (*chakras*). The process of psycho-physical transformation is here conceived in terms of the movement of the life force (*prana*) through the pathways of experience so that a mode of being (the "central pathway") is found that is awakened and free.

Efficacy of the Tantra: The efficacy of Tantric practice derives from its ability to transform the individual's perspective. Just as self-centered and harmful activity ultimately derives from a mind absorbed in self-serving thoughts, so altruistic actions derive from an enlightened mind. Through a liturgical identification with one or another Buddha, one enacts the dissolution of one's own ego and its replacement with a transcendent awakening and possesses the selfless wisdom, compassion, and activity of an enlightened one.

In the early days of Buddhist studies, it was popular to interpret Vajrayana as a non-Buddhist tradition with a superficial Buddhist veneer. Specialists now reject this view and see Vajrayana as thoroughly Buddhist, and as a classic example of the popularization and monasticization of what was originally an esoteric form of Buddhism. *See also* Amoghavajra; Buddhism (authoritative texts and their interpretation); Esoteric Buddhism in China; Mahayana; mandala; meditation; Nyingma-pa; Shingon-shu; Tantra; Three Jewels; Tibetan religions; Vajrayana.

tanuki (tah-*noo*-kee; Jap., "badger"), an animal with mysterious powers in Japanese folklore. Similar to the fox in its ability to change shape and do harm, it is often a trickster and buffoon. *See also* animals and birds in Japanese religion; Japanese folklore.

Tao (dou; Chin.,"Way"), a principal concept in traditional Chinese thought and religion. As used by Confucians and other ancient schools, it is a generic term for teachings about the conduct of life, but it soon came to be identified with the principles expressed in the writings called the *Lao-tzu* (*Tao-te ching*) and the *Chuang-tzu*. In the *Lao-tzu*, Tao seems to be understood as "the way life operates." It is a concept of a primordial unity from which the phenomenal world evolves and to which all things ultimately return. But the *Lao-tzu* also explains it as a force operating within the phenomenal world, a natural guiding force that leads all things to their fulfillment. Humanity is said to have deviated from the natural course of things ("the Tao"), and much of the *Lao-tzu* is devoted to explaining how to return to it. The Tao is also compared to an archetypal Mother, and its characteristics are identified as feminine qualities such as humility, passivity, and selfless love.

In the *Chuang-tzu*, one finds a different concept of Tao as an indescribable unity transcending all human knowledge and activity. For the *Chuang-tzu*, union with the Tao seems to connote transcending cultural conditioning to experience true reality (a concept that influenced Ch'an/Zen Buddhism). Later religious Taoism revises and extends these understandings of the Tao, conceiving it as a cosmic reality. It is the source of all spiritual power, with which the Taoist connects (and is ultimately united) by means of ritual or meditation. *See also* Chuang-tzu; Taoism; Tao-te ching.

Tao-an (dou-ahn; 312–385), an early Chinese Buddhist monk noted for his literary brilliance and strict discipline. He traveled widely throughout China collecting Buddhist scriptures, compiled the first annotated catalog of Chinese Buddhist texts, and composed many well-received commentaries; he also wrote the first Chinese monastic code for his community. *See also* China, Buddhism in.

Tao-chia, Tao-chiao (dou-jyah, dou-jeou; Chin.,"school of Tao," "sect [or religion] of Tao"), terms used to distinguish between Taoist philosophy (Tao-chia) and Taoist religion (Tao-chiao). Taoist philosophy is a textual tradition that developed out of the writings the *Lao-tzu* and the *Chuang-tzu*. The Taoist religion, while drawing upon these early

texts, developed complex forms of ritual and meditation. *See also* Chuang-tzu; Taoism; Tao-te ching; Tao-tsang.

Tao'chiao. *See* Tao-chia, Tao-chiao.

Tao-ch'o (dou-choh; 562–645), an early master of the Chinese Pure Land School of Buddhism who wrote that the practices of invoking Amitabha mentally and orally with an undivided mind were the best for this decadent age, when humanity's religious capabilities were lower. *See also* Pure Land school (China).

Tao-hsuan (dou-shwuhn; 596–667), Chinese Buddhist monk and scholar who founded the Vinaya school so that monks would have a place to study and receive training in the monastic code. He is also the author of the *Hsu-kao-seng-chuan* (Continued Biographies of Eminent Monks), a valuable source of early Chinese Buddhist biography. *See also* Vinaya school.

T'ao Hung-ching (doo huhng-jing; 456–536), a scholar of the Mao Shan school of Taoism known for his work on their scriptures as well as his alchemical and pharmacological studies. After a succession of prestigious government appointments, T'ao retired to a hermitage at Mao Shan, where he composed *Chen kao* (Declarations of the Perfected), an annotated version of the *Shang-ch'ing ching* (Scriptures of Supreme Purity). In addition to other Taoist works, T'ao wrote a commentary on the ancient *Pharmacopeia of the Sage Shen Nung*. *See also* Chen-kao; Mao Shan; Shang-ch'ing Taoism.

Taoism (dou'iz-uhm), a traditional component of Chinese culture embracing a broad array of moral, social, philosophical, and religious values and activities. The overall concern of Taoism is to liberate people from heedless immersion in mundane activities and reorient them toward the deeper, abiding realities of life. Over the long history of Taoism, people of diverse inclinations understood the fundamental issues differently and developed highly distinct teachings and practices. Nonetheless, from the "Taoist classics" of the *Lao-tzu* (*Tao-te ching*) and the *Chuang-tzu* down through the Taoist religion of modern times, Taoism has been united in an overriding concern with undoing the problems that beset people's individual and social lives. Contrary to certain modern misconceptions, Taoists traditionally concerned themselves not only with individual spiritual transformation but also with society and the world as a whole.

In fact, Taoists traditionally believed themselves—and were often believed by others—to play a unique role as upholders of the moral and spiritual principles that undergird a healthy, well-ordered society. Taoism can properly be styled a holistic value system that emphasizes individual, social, and political reintegration with the beneficent forces inherent in the cosmos, forces generally subsumed under the traditional rubric of "the Tao."

The Debate over "Taoism": To some scholars, "Taoism" is simply a convenient rubric for discussing common concepts in the *Lao-tzu* and the *Chuang-tzu*. Others have argued that Chinese history demonstrates that "Taoism" is a coherent religious tradition that (unlike "folk religion") can be defined in clear social and historical terms. Some scholars maintain that we must differentiate between "Taoism" as an ancient philosophical school and "Taoism" as a later religious tradition, which, they contend, has little or nothing in common with the former. However, most specialists today tend to agree that Taoism actually constituted a single cultural system. This position is especially held by scholars who have done the most intensive study of Taoist history and literature, particularly the diverse array of materials preserved in the Chinese Taoist canon, the *Tao-tsang*, a vast collection of materials pertaining to Taoist history, ritual and meditative communion with the Tao and its hypostases, and the full range of classical Taoist philosophical works and pertinent commentaries. Some scholars insist that we should define the Taoist tradition in terms of the texts preserved in the *Tao-tsang* and those individuals and groups who composed, preserved, and used them. Such a definition results in a fairly amorphous subject for study.

"Mystical" Taoism and "Liturgical" Taoism: From research into the *Tao-tsang* over the last generation, it is clear that the central concern with individual self-perfection first seen in the *Lao-tzu* and the *Chuang-tzu* generally remains a key element of the thought and practice of the later Taoist religion. What is truly distinctive about the later religious tradition is that the "mystical" elements familiar from the philosophical classics are often interwoven with other human concerns. For instance, in the "mystical Taoism" of the *Chuang-tzu* and some meditative traditions within religious Taoism, the individual seems to be conceived as a generalized existential monad—a cog, perhaps, in the cosmos, but not in the community; that is, one's true identity is not seen there as being in any real way tied to one's actual historical context, to one's commu-

nity, or to one's social roles. In the liturgical traditions that developed within the Taoist religion, the opposite is true: the individual is generally understood as a member of the actual human community, of a specific place and time, and involved in a real-life web of interrelationships.

This apparent tension is by no means a polar opposition but rather a broad continuum. Along the "mystical" end of the spectrum, the soteriological models are generally transformative or developmental models of self-cultivation that involve a process of re-perspectivization—a transformative process of self-rediscovery that involves a new mode of perceiving reality. Along the "liturgical" end of the spectrum, the same is sometimes true, but the soteriological media there are primarily moral and ritual. In any event, both "mystical" and "liturgical" Taoism work to focus the individual toward the deeper elements of reality underlying the domain of everyday life and to rectify life through a realignment with those deeper realities. What the liturgical tradition offers is a much more active and interactive mode of effecting that realignment: rather than simply perceiving an underlying harmony with the cosmos (as in the *Chuang-tzu* and Ch'an Buddhism), liturgical Taoism begins with one's localized, contextualized existence. It then carries one to and through a transcendent realm of the sacred and eventually returns to one's everyday life. In this way, the space and time of one's life are newly sacralized (or, at least, their inherent sacrality is newly disclosed). At the same time, the individual is morally and spiritually renewed and, when all goes well, one is newly enabled to undergo a spiritual transformation.

History of the Taoist Religion: The liturgical tradition of religious Taoism is often characterized as representing "popular Taoism" and has long been disparaged by Confucians and modern Westerners as a religion of the superstitious masses. This attitude seems to diminish as one becomes more aware of the complex development of Taoism within Chinese history and culture.

The ground out of which religious Taoism grew was the imperial court of the Han dynasty in the first centuries. Certain thinkers there treasured the sociopolitical ideal of "Grand Tranquillity" (*t'ai-p'ing*), a utopian concept of a world in perfect harmony, as idealized by most of the earlier schools of Chinese thought (including Confucianism). The first Taoist social movements emerged as efforts to actualize that idealized concept, particularly as it was expressed in the *T'ai-p'ing ching*, a text compiled by court intellectuals, building upon many of the central concepts and values of the *Tao-te ching*. During the second century, a man named Chang Tao-ling claimed to have received a covenant from Lord Lao (Lao-chun, a deity identified with the "author" of the *Tao-te ching*) and claimed to be the "Celestial Master" promised in the *T'ai-p'ing ching*. The T'ien-shih (or "Celestial Master") tradition that arose stessed both sociopolitical renewal and individual purification. In the early third century, Chang's grandson allied himself with a northern ruler, forging a lasting tradition of political partnership. For hundreds of years thereafter, Chinese rulers often turned to Taoist leaders for spiritual legitimation of their regime.

In the early fourth century, foreign invasions drove the Celestial Masters into South China, where the indigenous religious traditions centered around efforts to attain health, longevity, and spiritual immortality through the sublimation of biological processes. Those traditions are exemplified in the *Pao-p'u-tzu* of Ko Hung, a maverick Confucian intent to demonstrate that the pursuit of immortality was reasonable and proper for gentlemen of refinement. The encounter between the old southern traditions and Celestial Master Taoism stimulated two new religious traditions. One, known as Shang-ch'ing Taoism, was inspired by revelations from angelic beings known as "Perfected Ones" (*chen-jen*). Guided by those revelations, Shang-ch'ing adherents worked to join the "Perfected Ones" through dedicating themselves to a disciplined process of self-perfection through visualizational meditation (or, for certain advanced adepts, through alchemy). The other new fourth-century tradition, Ling-pao Taoism, was rooted in old southern traditions of talismanic ritual but was reshaped by the stimuli of Mahayana Buddhism and the Shang-ch'ing revelations. The fifth-century Ling-pao master Lu Hsiu-ching developed a new soteriological process focused upon liturgies that soon supplanted the old Celestial Master rites and became the foundation for all later liturgical Taoism. It should be noted, however, that the founders of the Shang-ch'ing and Ling-pao traditions were all well-to-do members of the social and political elite of the day, and liturgical Taoism retained that elite cast for hundreds of years. Throughout T'ang times (i.e., down to the tenth century), great Taoist masters such as Ssu-ma Ch'eng-chen not only developed new meditational practices but also maintained imperial patronage of numerous Taoist abbeys (*kuan*), where male and female priests (*tao-shih*) per-

formed rituals called *chiao* and *chai*, which were designed to integrate society and cosmos. This was Taoism's greatest period, and texts of the period reveal the continuing presence of "classical Taoist" language and values in every aspect of Taoist thought and practice.

The institutional prominence of Taoism was permanently undermined by events of the twelfth and thirteenth centuries, when China was conquered by foreign peoples like the Mongols. Both they and the subsequent rulers of the Ming and Ch'ing dynasties were deeply suspicious of independent religious organizations, and the Taoist liturgical tradition became increasingly marginalized. The early conquest period saw the emergence of several new movements, including some like Ch'uan-chen Taoism, which turned away from the social focus of the medieval liturgical tradition in favor of a more individualized pursuit of self-perfection seen in such meditative processes as "inner alchemy." These beliefs and practices (apparently influenced by Ch'an Buddhism) were swathed in the rhetoric of classical Taoism but actualized in terms of the individualized meditative practices of Shang-ch'ing Taoism and the more Buddhisticized practices of T'ang times.

Here we find a "parting of the way" within what has usually been called "religious Taoism." From the conquest period onward, the "mystical" tradition of Taoism began to grow apart from the liturgical tradition, which had for centuries been the spiritual bulwark of the Chinese empire. From the conquest period on, religiously inclined people began to fall increasingly into two camps: a cultural elite, who practiced a more "mystical," individualized pursuit of spiritual perfection (whether in Taoist or Confucian terms), and a nonelite component, who often cherished Taoist spiritual ideals but faced the practical necessity of making a living. The second group became the main participants in the modern liturgical tradition, particularly in the order known as Cheng-i Taoism. For this second group, the religious life became, by necessity, a profession, and their activities became a public service—a service performed, as always, for the benefit of all, but now underwritten by members of the local community. Under Communist rule, Taoism was outlawed in China, and its prospects for survival have at times seemed quite uncertain. In the Chinese diaspora today, both "liturgical" and "mystical" Taoism endure, though certainly not as in earlier centuries, when Chinese society and culture as a whole were colored and shaped by Taoist values and institutions. *See also* alchemy; Black Head Taoist;

body; Chang Tao-ling; Cheng-i Taoism; chen-jen; chiao; Ch'ing-wei Taoism; Chin-tan Taoism; Ch'uan-chen Taoism; Chuang-tzu; hagiography; Huang-Lao Taoism; Japan, Taoism in; Korea, Taoism in; Lao tzu; Ling-pao Taoism; Lu Hsiu-ching; Lung-men Taoism; Pao-p'u-tzu; physiological techniques (Taoism); Shang-ch'ing Taoism; Shen-hsiao Taoism; Ssu-ma Ch'eng-chen; T'ai-i Taoism; T'ai-p'ing ching; Tao; tao-shih; Tao-te ching; Tao-tsang; Ta-tao Taoism; T'ien-shih Taoism.

Taoism (authoritative texts and their interpretation). *See* Tao-tsang.

Taoism in Japan. *See* Japan, Taoism in.

Tao-sheng (dou-shuhng; ca. 360–434), early Chinese monk who pioneered several concepts that became characteristic of Chinese Buddhism; he was the first to argue against the view that some beings will never attain liberation, to formulate the teaching of sudden enlightenment, and to claim that all sentient beings have the Buddha-nature. *See also* China, Buddhism in.

tao-shih (dou-shuhr; Chin., "Master of the Tao"), a Taoist priest or priestess. Medieval *tao-shih* were often profoundly learned and highly respected among the elite; this was less so later, when they became almost exclusively liturgists. Tao-shih today (generally male) use esoteric knowledge to control spirits and perform public rituals that heal, bless, and protect. *See also* Black Head Taoist.

Tao-te ching (dou-duh jing; Chin., "The Book of the Way and Its Power"), the earliest work of Taoist philosophy, also known as the *Lao-tzu* after its purported author. Probably a mid-fourth-century B.C. creation of intentional vagueness, it is the most widely translated of Chinese classics. *See also* Lao-tzu; Taoism.

t'ao-t'ieh (tou-tyeh; Chin., "glutton"), a term retrospectively applied to an animal-mask motif prominent on Shang (ca. 1766–1122 B.C.) and Chou (ca. 1122–221 B.C.) bronzes. Vertically symmetrical and assembled from disparate parts, usually with horns, prominent eyes, fanged upper jaw, and small clawed arms, the motif is of uncertain symbolism, but it is probably apotropaic and associated with centrality. *See also* Chou religion; Shang religion.

Tao-tsang (dou-dzahng; Chin., "Repository of the Tao," "Taoist canon"), the most comprehensive collection of Taoist texts. The *Tao-tsang* is comparable to

the Buddhist *Tripitaka* as the fundamental collection of religious writings. It contains scriptures based on divine revelation as well as commentaries, historical and geographical treatises, manuals of practice, and literary works relating to the religion. Many of its books are written in an esoteric, priestly language meant to be understood only by the initiated. For this reason, it has been extremely difficult to comprehend or to translate.

Numerous collections of Taoist texts have been compiled over the past fifteen centuries. Only the Ming-dynasty canon, completed by 1444, has survived. The contents of the others can only be known through bibliographical lists, when these survive.

In 471 the first official survey of Taoist texts was ordered by the emperor of the Liu-Sung kingdom. During the T'ang (618–907) and Sung (960–1279) dynasties, three succeeding emperors sent out edicts calling for the submission of all Taoist texts to the capital for copying, compilation, and cataloguing. The first printed *Tao-tsang* (ca. 1120) included nearly fifty-four hundred scrolls. In 1244, a new and much larger collection was assembled by the government of Shansi Province, but that edition, along with the printing blocks and the original texts, was burned by order of Khublai Khan in 1281. During the Ming dynasty, remnants of this collection, along with sections of earlier editions, were again assembled and printed with an added supplement. This is the Taoist canon that survives in the present day and the precursor to the 1926 edition, the first widely available reprint, available in several different photolithographic editions.

The Ming *Tao-tsang* is a prodigious work composed of 1,120 thread-bound volumes and 1,476 titles. It is divided into three primary sections (the "Three Caverns"), each of which is meant to represent a different school of Taoism springing from separate revelatory traditions. The Three Caverns are the Cavern of Realization, containing the scriptures of the Shang-ch'ing ("Highest Clarity") school; the Cavern of Abstruseness, containing the scriptures of the Ling-pao ("Spiritual Treasure") school; and the Cavern of Deities, containing the scriptures of the San-huang ("Three Sovereigns") school. Each of these sections is further subdivided into twelve sections representing various religious genres, such as "basic scriptures," "codes of conduct," etc. There are also four supplements (*Supreme Abstruseness, Supreme Harmony, Supreme Clarity,* and *Upright Unity*), which contain additional texts drawn from scriptural legacies not included in the Three Caverns. *See also* canon; holy books; Ling-pao Taoism; Shang-ch'ing Taoism; Taoism; Yun-chi ch'i-ch'ien.

tao-yin (dou-yin; Chin., "gymnastics"), Taoist physiological technique of stretching and moving like an animal to facilitate the bodily circulation of *ch'i* (vital energy) and attain harmony with the Tao. *See also* physiological techniques (Taoist); Tao.

tapas (tuh'puhs; Skt.), "heat" generated by meditation, ascetic techniques, or ritual performances; it is deployed by gods, demons, ascetics, sages, and heroes and signifies austerity, self-mortification, and internal transformation in Hinduism, Jainism, and some schools of Buddhism. *See also* asceticism; meditation; path of (ritual) action.

Taqlid (tahk-leed'; Arab., lit., "imitation"), a term in medieval Islamic jurisprudence, the convention of limiting legal decisions to repetition of established orthodox rulings, thereby discouraging independent creative interpretation of the law. *See also* Islamic law.

Tara (tahr'uh; Skt., "protectress," "savioress"), Buddhist deity often regarded as goddess of mercy and consort to Avalokiteshvara. A figure of late origin, appearing in India primarily in images and ritual texts of Tantric affiliation (sixth to seventh centuries), she plays an important role in Tantric ritual and meditation and is associated with numerous mantras. Tara is extremely popular in Tibet and an object of both popular devotion and monastic visualizations. Although Tara is most commonly known for her compassion and for the quiet and tender appearance of her iconographic representations, she is also believed to have a fierce form. *See also* Avalokiteshvara; Bodhisattvas; Tantrism (Buddhism).

Targum (tahr-goom'; Aram., "translation"), translation of the Hebrew Bible into Aramaic. Most Targums were written in Palestine or Babylonia between the second and seventh centuries.

tariqa (tah-ree'kuh; Arab., "method," "way"), a brotherhood of Sufi mystics in Islam. Each *tariqa* developed its own characteristic methods of attaining stages and states of mystical union with God. *See* Sufism.

Tarot (tair'oh), a set of cards of uncertain origin used since the Middle Ages for divination and considered a repository of occult wisdom. In addition to four suits—swords, cups, wands, and pentacles—the deck includes twenty-two Greater Trumps of special esoteric significance. The Tarot have been given kabbalistic, theosophical, and Buddhist interpretations, among others. *See also* occult, the.

Tartaros (tahr'tahr-os), in Greek mythology, a gloomy place below Hades, later equivalent to hell. *See also* afterworld; Hades.

Tasawwuf. *See* Sufism.

tasks, heroic, widespread motif in folklore in which the hero must accomplish something difficult or apparently impossible in order to achieve a desired object or goal.

Ta-tao Taoism (dah-dou; Chin., "Great Way"), a populist sect of "reformed" Taoism from the twelfth to the fourteenth centuries. It ignored the pursuit of immortality and stressed the classical Taoist moral values of "yielding," simplicity, humility, and respect for others. Eschewing ritual, it sought healing through prayer. *See also* Taoism.

Tathagata (tuh-tah'guh-tuh; Skt., Pali, "Thus Gone One," "Thus Come One"), in Buddhism an epithet for a Buddha and the title Gautama gave to himself. It suggests that a Buddha has himself traveled the Path he teaches. *See also* Buddhas; Path (Buddhism).

tathata (tuh'tuh-tah; Skt., "Thusness," "Suchness"), a synonym of emptiness used in a wide variety of Mahayana Buddhist literature to refer to the nature of reality; it is explained as meaning that reality ultimately does not change and is therefore "always thus." *See also* emptiness; Mahayana.

Tatian (tay'shun; ca. 120–173), Greek Christian apologist, most active in Syria. He was author of the *Diatessaron* (Gk., "across the four"), an influential harmonized single gospel composed largely of extracts from the four canonical Gospels.

tattooing. *See* mutilation.

Tat tvam asi (tuht tvuhm uh'si; Skt., "you are that"), refrain of a *Chandogya Upanishad* set of eight parables in which a father brings his son to realize, "you are" being (*sat*).

Ta-tung Chen-ching (tah-tuhng jen-jing; Chin., "Scripture of Great Profundity"), an important Shang-ch'ing Taoist scripture revealed to Yang Hsi in the fourth century; it discusses the cultivation of bodily divinities. *See also* Shang-ch'ing Taoism; Yang Hsi.

Tauler, John (tou'ler; 1300–1361), German Catholic Dominican mystic who left no writings except transcripts of his sermons.

tawhid (tou-heed'; Arab., lit., "asserting unity"), the proclamation of the absolute oneness of Allah. It is the primary attestation of faith, expressed in the first half of the Islamic creed: "There is no god but God. . . ." Later theologians and mystics would explore the metaphysical implications of this attestation, but for the majority of Muslims *tawhid* has remained more an act of faith than an expression of dogma. *See also* creed.

taziyah (ta-zee'yah; Arab., "condolences," "consolation," "mourning"). In Iran, *taziyah* came to signify the passion play depicting the sufferings and martyrdom of Husayn ibn Ali (d. 680), his family, and supporters. For Shiis of the Indian subcontinent, taziyah means symbolic representations of the tomb of Husayn and other objects associated with his martyrdom.

Immediately after the death of Husayn, his supporters in Iraq were filled with remorse for having betrayed him. They vowed to keep alive his memory and avenge his blood. Soon these "penitents," as they were called, suffered their master's fate, but their zeal survived and grew into a powerful expression of religious devotion, political protest, and popular art and drama.

Taziyah as a public event began in the tenth century with large processions in Baghdad during Muharram, when the tenth day (Ashura) was observed as a day of public mourning. Large halls (*Husayniyyah*) were built to house these public memorial services.

When the Safavid dynasty in the sixteenth century made Shiism the state religion of Iran, the taziyah passion play evolved, and by the late nineteenth century reached its zenith as a popular art form.

In response to social and political exigencies, the taziyah passion play increasingly is giving way to the memorial services, known in Iran as *rozeh-khaneh*, or as *majalis al-aza* in Arabic-speaking countries. *See also* Husayn ibn Ali.

te (duh; Chin., "virtue," "power"), an integrity of being derived through ritual or military conquest that legitimized a Chinese ruler or saint to have power over other people. People with *te* were natural leaders to whom the people would "attach themselves." For Confucians, te was obtained through ritual acts and moral cultivation.

For Taoists, te was a quality of Tao inherent in all things; one gained it through self-perfection and ego dissolution. By the Han period (206 B.C.–A.D. 220), te was understood as accumulated merit or reward. *See also* kingship, sacred; Tao.

tea ceremony (Jap. *cha no yu*, "hot water tea"; also *chado*, "the way of tea"), the ritual of tea drinking, which originated in China and was cultivated in medieval Japan both as a social pastime and as a ritual in Zen monasteries. In the Momoyama era (1568–1600), tea masters such as Sen Rikyu (1522–91) combined Buddhist discipline with aesthetic creativity to produce the tea ceremony as the focus of an artistic way of life. In the tea ceremony, the tea master creates an aesthetic experience by integrating the small room setting, the season and time of day, utensils, food, charcoal, flowers, scroll, garden, and tea drinking in an intricate ritual. Drawing on religious sentiments and discipline from Zen, Shinto, and Confucianism, the tea ceremony event expresses four basic qualities: *wa*, "harmony" in the integration of host, guests, setting, utensils, and ritual; *kei*, "respect" and sensitivity between host and guests and tea objects; *sei*, "purity," an experience of wholeness and simplicity in the ritual; and *jaku*, "tranquillity," the transformatory experience of lasting inner peace.

tefillin. *See* phylactery.

Teilhard de Chardin, Pierre (tay-yahr' duh shar-dan'; 1881–1955), French Catholic priest, theologian, and distinguished paleontologist. He described the universe in evolutionary terms, with God as a developing part of the process, in which the cosmos becomes increasingly "christified" as a result of the incarnation, all in progress toward a final spiritual unity. As expressed in *The Phenomenon of Man* (1955) and a series of other works, Teilhard proposed the most sweeping modern attempt to reconcile Christian theological tradition with modern science. In 1962, the Vatican issued an official warning against the uncritical acceptance of his ideas.

televangelism, use of modern media for Christian preaching. Through television, many local ministers developed national followings that financed their individual shows, broadcast stations, colleges, and other enterprises. In the 1950s and 1960s, revival meetings were translated to television independently by Billy Graham and Oral Roberts. The Catholic Fulton Sheen had a large television following in the same period. While denominations provided public service programming, major attention was attracted in the 1970s and 1980s by ministers such as Jim Bakker, Jimmy Swaggart, Jerry Falwell, and Pat Robertson, who were only loosely connected to religious bodies beyond those of their own devising. *See also* Worldwide Church of God.

temenos (Gk., "to cut off"), the precinct of an ancient Greek shrine, sometimes defined by a wall or by inscribed markers. *See also* Greek religion; sacred space and sacred time; temple.

Templars, the Poor Knights of Christ and of the Temple of Solomon, a Catholic secret military order founded in the Latin Kingdom of Jerusalem in 1119 and 1120 and condemned as a heresy in 1312. The Templars are of later importance in that they are claimed as ancestors for a number of Western secret societies, including Freemasonry *See also* Crusades; Freemasonry; secret societies.

temple, a building set apart for the presence of a deity and for ritual activities. *See also* architecture and religion; sacred space and sacred time.

Chinese Religion: Chinese temples resemble other traditional Chinese buildings; no sharp distinction exists between secular and sacred forms in China.

The larger temple complexes are walled modular courtyard structures, axially oriented from north to south. The important individual buildings are sited on the axis, often flanked by subsidiary buildings and separated from one another by open courtyards. The most important building is found near the rear (ideally north) end of the ensemble and is the palace of the deity. There the image is enthroned upon an altar facing south toward the entry gate. In the larger temples, this architectural arrangement creates a sense of journey or progression, as the worshiper moves from the secular, ghost-ridden world outside through a series of gates and buildings of ever greater importance until arriving at the image of the chief deity. Temples honoring Confucius, however, substituted a commemorative tablet for an image of the Master.

All important buildings in a temple complex are built on square or rectangular platforms of pounded earth. A temple building is, like all significant buildings in Chinese architecture, essentially a heavy and intricately constructed roof supported by pillars. Walls are unimportant. Thus, the ensemble clearly symbolizes the major elements of Chinese cosmology: heaven is the roof, earth is the platform, and the human realm is in the space between created by the supporting pillars (mountains).

Functionally, the temple is the place where people come to acknowledge the ruling deity, whose help they invoke. They make offerings of food, incense, and paper money; throw divining

Characteristic Hindu temple, showing the gate (foreground), antechamber (low building), and main structure; a temple, in Bhuvaneshvara, Orissa, India.

blocks; and seek oracles. Individuals may come at any time, but on the birthday of the deity, grand celebrations are held. Traditionally temple festivals included operatic performances given to entertain the deity. These were not usually religious in theme but confirmed conventional moral themes of Confucian virtue. The same principle holds today in Taiwan, where the gods and goddesses are often entertained with films and TV.

Local temples functioned as community centers, overseen by a committee of neighborhood or clan leaders. Each had an incense burner where visitors placed their lighted "joss sticks" as offerings to the deity. The smoke rose to the heavens, representing their unity in prayer, and signified the harmony of the community served by the temple. At grand celebrations, images of deities were brought to the main temple to visit the chief god or goddess, creating a kind of network of filial temples and a spiritual bureaucracy.

Temples served as a focus of local pride. The prosperity of a particular locality was indicated by the magnificence of its temple and its good state of repair. When temples were ideally rebuilt or refurbished (preferably every twenty to sixty years), community leaders often called upon Taoist priests to celebrate elaborate festivals of cosmic and community renewal (*chiao*). These were very important events in the life of the community and the history of its temple. *See also* chiao; Chinese religions (art and architecture); ritual.

Japanese Buddhism: Constructed in Japan since the sixth century, Buddhist temples were often seats of not only religious but also cultural, economic, and military power. Their secular power was largely broken in the late sixteenth and early seventeenth centuries. In the Edo period (1615–1868), all Japanese families were required to be associated with a temple. As a result, most of the temples that exist today, but few prominent ones, were founded at that time.

Today, temples are presided over by a married, largely hereditary clergy and a committee of members. Nearly all of them belong to a traditional sect. The main temples of a sect train future clergy and interested laity in traditional monastic and ascetic practices. Local temples perform funerals and ancestral rites for their members and lead them in certain annual rituals of their sect. They may also have kindergartens or other business interests. There are a few nunneries, although women do not perform rites for the laity.

A large portion of Japan's art treasures are to be found in its older temples, which are as important as cultural and tourist centers as they are as religious centers. Most are located in or near the former capitals of Nara and Kyoto. *See also* Japanese religions (art and architecture); ujidera.

A Japanese Shingon Buddhist temple at the sacred Mt. Koya.

Religions of Antiquity: The English word *temple* is derived from the Latin *templum,* which referred to a defined area of sacred space whether or not there was a building within it. Templum could even refer to a particular section of the sky from which augurs derived signs for divination. In many cultures the concept of a sacred space is more significant than that of a sacred building. By "temple" archaeologists and the translators of texts often denote a sacred area with the objects and buildings it contains and sometimes also the social and economic institutions associated with a sacred place.

Temple in Mesopotamia: When a building is erected for the worship of divinity, it is likely to begin as a house similar to that in which the worshipers themselves live. In Near Eastern languages, there is no special word for temple; it is designated by the ordinary word for "house." In ancient Mesopotamia in the third and second millennia B.C. a number of architectural forms were used. The central building, which contained the god's statue and altar, was not distinguished by its size but in time became part of a large complex in an enclosed court. Unlike the practice of the Greeks and Romans, which concentrated on refining and ornamenting the central building, for the Mesopotamians the whole complex of buildings within the sacred area constituted the temple. It had a library of ritual texts (from which much is learned about the use of the temple), storerooms, and quarters for its personnel. It was also a center of economic activity, receiving and exchanging goods. Major temple complexes often included a ziggurat, a platform or mound usually of four or seven levels, surmounted by a shrine. The temples of the chief gods of the various Mesopotamian cities often included shrines of other deities, who might also have their own separate, smaller temples. The temples, conceived of as the home of the gods, were the scene of daily offerings of food as well as of periodic ceremonies on a grander scale.

Temple in Egypt: The temple evolved into a large and elaborate complex in Egypt, where a distinctive national religion flourished for over three thousand years. In the most important temples, impressive gateways (pylons) led into courts with colonnades on three sides beyond which lay colonnaded (hypostyle) halls. The most sacred part of the sanctuary and that to which access was most restricted was dark, farthest from the entrance, and at the highest point in the whole complex. Temples of the sun, however, kept the sacred space open to that deity; mortuary temples contained a burial chamber

that in the course of time came to be built some distance from the rest of the complex and might be cut into a mountainside. Like the major Mesopotamian temples, the Egyptian sanctuaries had quarters for temple personnel and rooms for stores, treasure, and sacred texts. Regular daily attendance of the gods whose residence was in the temple took the form of offerings of food. While the Mesopotamian temples were essentially the residences of local city gods and were built in the cities, the Egyptian gods were those of the whole land and were often at some remove from a town.

Temple in Israel: Although there were other sites, Solomon's temple of Yahweh in Jerusalem (ca. 950 B.C.) came to be ideologically viewed as the Jews' only temple. In origin it shared the characteristics of other Near Eastern temples—it was "The House of the Lord," where the deity received offerings of food as well as animal sacrifice. A vestibule, perhaps in the form of a pylon, formed the entrance of a rectangular building. At the far end was a chamber, the Holy of Holies, which contained the Ark of the Covenant and was accessible only to priests. By some reconstructions, numerous small rooms, reached by stairways in the pylon, were on three floors surrounding the main building. Animals were sacrificed on an altar in front of the temple. Destroyed by the Babylonians in 587 B.C., it was rebuilt several times thereafter, beginning ca. 515 B.C., until the final destruction by the Romans in 70. By that time, the Jews had established many synagogues and houses of prayer that served as their religious buildings.

Temple in Greece: The Minoan civilization on the island of Crete in the Aegean Sea (ca. 3000–1500 B.C.) produced texts that cannot, yet, be translated. Sacred places can only be detected by the objects found in them and, some would argue, by their decoration. There were small shrines in caves and on mountaintops. Certain small, groundfloor chambers in large complexes (referred to as palaces by archaeologists) contained images and ritual vessels. It is also possible that parts of the palaces served as sacred areas, corresponding to Near Eastern temples. The Mycenaean Greeks, who dominated the Aegean ca. 1600 to 1100 B.C., also had chamber shrines. From their deciphered texts it is known that there were numerous places sacred to individual gods, perhaps open-air precincts in addition to chambers, but also possibly separate structures and parts of the "palace" complexes.

The classical Greek temple, a rectangular, stone structure whose gabled roof is supported by columns on all four sides, is likely to be the image evoked by the word temple. The design had a long life in Greece and Rome and was revived in the Renaissance and modern eras for a variety of sacred and secular structures. In the eighth and seventh centuries B.C. the Greeks tried out a number of different types of simple buildings in wood, terra-cotta, and stone, since after a disturbed period there was little continuity with Mycenaean civilization. By the sixth century B.C., the familiar form had become established, though most smaller buildings had columns only at the front. Two orders, or styles, the Doric and Ionic, were distinguished most obviously by the form of the capital at the top of the columns; the Corinthian order was developed later. The larger and richer temples were decorated with terra-cotta and, later, stone sculpture painted in bright colors and representing mythological themes. A few excellent examples of Greek temples, such as the Parthenon in Athens, dedicated to the city's goddess, Athena, have survived in Greece, Asia Minor, Sicily, and Italy.

In terms of cult the temple was not, in fact, indispensable to the Greeks. A sacred space with an altar for sacrifice was more important, and even without a specially demarcated space and a built altar valid sacrifice and prayer were possible. In a sacred precinct containing a temple, animal sacrifice was performed on an eastward-facing altar before the building's main entrance. Access to the interior was not unrestricted, but the priests and officials charged with the care of the building and its contents did not have the power or the duties of their Near Eastern equivalents.

The Greek temple usually, though not always, contained an image of the god and could be spoken of as the god's residence, but this idea was not emphasized. It also contained gifts in the form of images, vessels, arms and armor, furniture, and gold and silver—treasure that might be lent out at interest or donated to the community in an emergency. Within larger precincts might also lie other temples, treasure houses, banquet halls, theaters, and racecourses. The temple was the creation and the responsibility of a community, usually the local city-state. In the Greek world temples more than any other structure embodied civic pride. They begin to appear with the emergence of the city-state and fade in importance with its decline. They were conspicuous evidence of communal piety while also providing a setting for individual piety in the forms of gifts and sacrifices. But their proliferation and elaboration was essentially a political and social phenomenon. They were located both in the towns and the countryside, depending on the character of the cult.

Temple in Italy: The architecture of the Romans and other Italic peoples was much influenced by that of Greek temples, many of which were built by Greeks on Italian soil. But there were also local traditions, seen for instance in the temples of the Etruscans of north-central Italy, which for a long time made greater use of timber and terra-cotta. The developed Roman temples (from ca. 300 B.C. on) were characterized by a high platform on which the temple rested and by the concentration of columns at the front to the neglect of the sides and rear. Compared to the Greek buildings, the Roman temples had an impressive facade but were two-dimensional in effect. Like the Greeks, the Romans performed their animal sacrifices at an altar in front of the building and made only minor offerings, such as incense, on a small altar inside. Even more than the Greek temples, the Roman temples were identified with the authority of the state. Official groups, such as the Senate, used temples as meeting places.

Greek and Roman temples were not designed to accommodate worshipers. Rituals in which laity participated took place outdoors, usually followed by feasting either outdoors or in tents or buildings nearby. *See also* Egyptian religion; Greek religion; Mesopotamian religion; priest/priestess; ritual; Roman religion; sacrifice.

Temple Mount movement, an umbrella term used to encompass diverse, often bitterly divided organizations among Israeli and diaspora Jews and Protestant Christian fundamentalists and evangelicals. The groups seek to constitute, in Jerusalem, Temple worship in a rebuilt Third Temple, which is to be located on the precise site of the Second Temple destroyed by the Romans in the year 70.

The primary motivation for the adherents of these movements is eschatological, a desire to force the end, bringing about in the Jewish view the era of messianic redemption, while for Christians, the goal is to expedite the return of Jesus. That Christian eschatology posits the conversion or destruction of the Jews in this process is tactfully ignored by many of these groups. The primary practical obstacle faced by the Temple Mount movement is the existence on the Haram al-Sharif (Arab., "Noble Sanctuary") of the Dome of the Rock, the third holiest site in Islam and the place from which the Prophet Muhammad is believed to have ascended in his famous Night Journey.

Israel's 1967 capture of the Temple Mount stimulated the Temple Mount movement. The organizations may be divided into those that undertake some form of action in support of the rebuilding of the Temple and those who restrict themselves to an indirect, supporting role. Arguably the best-known Temple Mount group, and the only one to seek to use violent means to achieve its ends, is the Jewish Underground, a group of West Bank settlers primarily affiliated with Gush Emunim's Kiryat Arba settlement in Hebron. The group originally formed around a plot to blow up the Dome of the Rock so as to facilitate the construction of the Temple in the 1970s. The plan was never implemented due to the adherents' inability to get rabbinical authorization for the action, coupled with the preoccupation of the group with acts of vigilante violence throughout the West Bank.

The Temple Mount Faithful headed by Gershon Solomon has been the most visible of the Temple groups. Their attempt to lay a Temple cornerstone on 8 October 1990 resulted in a riot during which Jewish worshipers at the Western Wall were stoned by Arabs worshiping at the Dome of the Rock, while nineteen Muslims were killed and over one hundred wounded by Israeli security forces. Solomon himself never anticipated such a reaction, believing that the Arabs would have no objection to simply moving their mosque elsewhere to make room for the Jewish Temple.

The Jerusalem Temple Foundation (JTF) was most active in the early 1980s. At its peak, the JTF was a primary link between Israeli Jewish activists, American Jewish philanthropists, and American fundamentalist and evangelical Protestants, who contributed both money and scientific expertise. The key Israeli figure in the JTF was Stanley Goldfoot, who collected and disbursed money raised in America for various Temple projects and organizations. The most prominent action carried out by the JTF was a 1983 scientific expedition to the Temple Mount and other religious sites by a team headed by Christian evangelical Lambert Dolphin, and funded by such high-profile members of the American Protestant community as Chuck Smith, Chuck Missler, Terry Risenhoover, and Douglas Krieger. The JTF is still active today, although members have kept a significantly lower profile.

Finally, the Jerusalem Temple Institute, headed by Rabbi Israel Ariel with the assistance of Rabbi Chaim Richman, has concentrated on the reconstruction of Temple implements and assisting in the training, now under way in a variety of Jerusalem *yeshivot* (Heb., "schools"), of young *kohanim* ("priests") for service in the Third Temple. The Temple Institute is closely allied with the B'nai Noah, whose members offer both financial and moral support. Additionally, B'nai Noah leader Vendyl Jones conducts archaeological expeditions, most notably in search of the ashes of the red heifer required by Jewish eschatological tradition to reconsecrate the Temple.

In addition to these activist groups, the Temple Mount movement enjoys the support of a number of groups and individuals who offer assistance ranging from prayers to leading tour groups to the Holy Land to witness Temple activities to fund-raising. The most vociferous of these supporters in Israel are centered at the Christian Embassy in Jerusalem, whose appeals for world support of Temple projects often take the form of a bitter, anti-Muslim polemic. More effective than this approach is the network of Protestant churches in the United States that raises funds for the Temple Mount movement and the religious televangelists who publicize the cause. Perhaps the most notable example of the latter are the appearances by Gershon Solomon on the "700 Club," the television ministry headed by Pat Robertson, Protestant charismatic minister and 1988 candidate for the Republican presidential nomination. *See also* B'nai Noah; Dome of the Rock; Gush Emunim; Jerusalem.

Temple of Heaven, Chinese popular name for the triple-eaved, round building at the north end of the Altar of Heaven complex in Peking, where the Chinese emperor offered New Year's prayers for a successful harvest. *See also* Ming T'ang; Peking; state cult, Chinese.

Templo Mayor (temp-loh' mah-yor'; Span., "great temple"), the largest and most sacred shrine in the fourteenth-century Aztec capital of Tenochtitlan. Called Templo Mayor by the Spaniards, who destroyed it in 1521, it consisted of a huge pyramidal base for two temples dedicated to the great gods Huitzilopochtli (War God) and Tlaloc (God of Agriculture). Called Coatepec (Serpent Mountain) by the Aztecs, it commemorated the myth of Huitzilopochtli's birth and the subsequent dismemberment of his sister Coyolxauhqui, symbolizing the triumph of the sun over the moon and starry sky. It was the supreme place for human sacrifices of captive warriors, coronation ceremonies, and ritual burials of masks, animals, marine animals and shells, and other treasures. Excavations between 1978 and 1982 yielded sculpture, sacrificial victims, masks, and seven superimpositions over the original shrine. *See also* cannibalism; Mesoamerican religion; sacrifice; Tenochtitlan.

Ten Commandments, the word of God spoken to the people of Israel at Mt. Sinai (Exodus 20:1–14 and Deuteronomy 5:6–18). Despite some differences, the two versions are substantially the same in content. God addresses the people in an atmosphere of awesome majesty. This is the God who redeemed the Israelites from their enslavement in Egypt. The people are now consecrated to God's service as "a kingdom of priests and a holy nation."

The tablets on which the commandments are inscribed are the permanent witness to the covenant between God and God's people. The people obligate themselves to live in accordance with the law that God sets down, and God promises to care for the nation of Israel as firstborn son.

As enumerated in Judaism, the first four commandments regulate relations between humanity and God, while the last five regulate relations between human beings. The fifth commandment, the duty to honor one's parents, is a bridge between obligations to God and those to people. Only through parental guidance do children learn their duties. Human parents are thus surrogates for direct divine instruction.

Some Jewish sages taught that the Ten Commandments contain implicitly all the teachings of the Torah. As such, they would understandably have a unique place in Jewish religious practice. At an early time the recital of the Ten Commandments was part of the daily service in the Temple. Opposition developed to efforts to extend this to the synagogue ritual because it would give implied support to those sects who claimed special authority for the Ten Commandments against the rest of the Torah.

The practice in many congregations of standing on the three occasions when the Ten Commandments are publicly read in the synagogue is condemned by some authorities for this reason. *See also* mitzvah; 613 commandments.

Tendai school (tayn-dah-ee), Japanese Buddhist school based on the teachings of the Chinese T'ien-t'ai school. Tendai gave new interpretations to the teachings of its Chinese predecessor and added a number of other doctrinal elements including Tantric Buddhism, Mahayana *Fanwang* precepts, Pure Land, realization of Buddhahood with this very body, and innate enlightenment (*hongaku*). Many Tendai monks performed rituals from several of these traditions. As the most influential Buddhist school in medieval Japan, it produced the founders of the Kamakura traditions of Zen, Pure Land, and Nichiren. *See also* Annen; Enchin; Ennin; Fanwang ching; Hiei, Mt.; hongaku; Ryogen; Saicho; sokushin jobutsu; T'ien-t'ai school.

Tengu (tayn-goo; Jap., "celestial dog"), a Japanese folk demon noted for its long, phallic nose. Of Chinese astrological origin, it haunts lonely, waste places. *See also* demon; Japanese folk religion.

Ten Heavenly Stems and Twelve Earthly Branches, two ancient series of calendrical signs; together the two series generate a sexagenary cycle of sixty unique combinations used in keeping the count of days since the second millennium B.C. *See also* calendar (China); sixty-year cycle.

Ten Kings, in Chinese Buddhist folklore, the deities of ten hells who assign punishments; they were modeled on imperial bureaucrats and later identified with various Bodhisattvas. *See also* afterworld; Bodhisattvas.

Tenno (tayn-noh; Jap., "heavenly sovereign"), title of Chinese origin for the Japanese emperor in use from the seventh century; it is used frequently with the term *heika* ("his majesty"). *See also* kingship, sacred.

Tenochtitlan (te-nohch-teet'lahn; Nahuatl, possibly derived from *nochtli*, "fruit of the prickly pear cactus," and *tetl*, "rock"), political and ritual urban center of the Mexica-Tenochca empire. Founded ca. 1325 to 1371, it fell to Cortes in 1521. The city was located on an island in Lake Texcoco, now buried beneath Mexico City.

The city's name may refer to the story in which an omen appears indicating the site for its main temple. The image of the omen, an eagle grasping a snake in its beak and perching on a prickly pear cactus growing out of a rock, now appears on the Mexican flag.

Tenochtitlan was divided into quadrants aligned with the cardinal directions and four major social divisions. Its ritual district, where sacrifices were regularly offered, was in its exact center and included the primary temple (Templo Mayor) and other religious and educational facilities. *See also* Mesoamerican religion; sacrifice; Templo Mayor.

Tenrikyo (ten-ri-kyor; Jap., "the religion of heavenly truth"), Japanese new religion founded by Nakayama Miki (1798–1887) after she had been possessed by a spirit that eventually identified itself as the creator of humankind. Nakayama's revelations form the basis of Tenrikyo's creed, and her home at Tenri City is seen as the spiritual center of the universe. Followers are taught to live cheerful lives of service to others and to purify themselves of bad thoughts that are seen as spiritual hindrances causing disharmony and misfortune. *See also* Japan, new religions in.

Teresa of Avila (1515–82), Spanish Catholic Carmelite nun and mystic, associated with John of the Cross. A monastic reformer, she addressed a book of spiritual direction, *The Way of Perfection* (posthumously published, 1583), to the nuns of her order. *The Interior Castle* (1588) is her most vivid book of spiritual ascent. Her *Life of the Mother Teresa of Jesus* (1611) remains one of the most powerful Christian autobiographies. *See also* Carmelites; John of the Cross.

term question, debate among nineteenth-century Protestant missionaries to China concerning the best Chinese translation of key biblical terms, especially the word for "God." At issue was whether the terms *Shang-ti* and *T'ien* provided a preexisting theistic vocabulary from ancient China. *See also* Chinese rites controversy; Shang-ti; T'ien.

Tertullian (ter-*tool'*ee-ahn; ca. 160–220), North African Christian theologian, rhetor, and apologist. Best known for his attacks on heretics (especially Marcion), by ca. 210 he had left the Roman church and joined the Montanists. *See also* Montanus.

testimony, in Protestant worship, the public witness of a person's conversion experience and, by extension, the same witness given to an individual to further conversion. *See also* born-again Christian; conversion.

tests, heroic, a widespread motif in folklore, in which the hero (often a figure unlikely to succeed) must be proven by passing a number of perilous trials. *See also* Gilgamesh.

Tetragrammaton (tet'rah-gram'ah-tahn; Gk., "four letters"), the four Hebrew consonants, YHWH, that form the name of God. Because it is forbidden to be pronounced, the word *Adonai* ("Lord") is substituted. A similar practice among devout English-speaking Jews is the use of "G-d" in written texts. The Tetragrammaton has been the subject of much speculation in Jewish and Christian occult thought. *See also* Adonai; G-d; Jehovah; Judaism, God in; YHWH.

thag. *See* thug, thag.

Thammayut (tahm'uh-yut; Skt.; Pali *Dhammayuttika*), a reform movement in the Buddhist monastic community in Thailand begun during the reign of King Rama IV (1851–68), better known as Mongkut, who served as a monk for over twenty-five years before ascending the throne. Convinced that Thai monastic life needed to be reformed by being purged of "superstitious" practices and returned to the model found in the Pali scriptures and commentaries, as king he attempted to put the reforms into practice. During the reign of his son, King Chulalongkorn (1868–1910), Thammayut monks were appointed to extend the program of reform through the Thai monastic community. The Thammayut movement now has the status of official orthodoxy in contemporary Thai Buddhism. *See also* Theravada.

theios aner. *See* divine man.

theism (Gk. *theos*, "god"), belief in the existence of one or more divine beings.

theocracy, theory of politics in which the deity is the supreme ruler of the state; secular government is not acknowledged.

theodicy (Gk. *theos*, "god"; *dike*, "justice"), justification of the goodness and justice of a deity in the face of evil and suffering. The classic question of theodicy is, Why do the innocent (or righteous) suffer? The term *theodicy* was introduced by the philosopher Gottfried Leibniz in the seventeenth century, although the problem of theodicy is central to religion and has been explored in religious texts from ancient to modern times.

The problem of theodicy arises when the suffering of innocent persons is set against two beliefs traditionally associated, in the West, with ethical monotheism. One is the belief that God is absolutely just. The other is the belief that God controls all events in history, being both all-powerful (omnipotent) and all-knowing (omniscient). Taken together, these three ideas—the fact of suffering, God's justice, and God's power—seem contradictory. As the philosopher David Hume (1711–76) suggests in his *Dialogues Concerning Natural Religion* (1779), they appear to form a logical "trilemma." While any two of these ideas can be accepted, adding the third renders the whole logically inconsistent.

Theodicy in its classical Western forms is the effort to resist the conclusion that such a logical trilemma exists. Theodicy aims to show that traditional claims about God's power and goodness are compatible with the fact of suffering. Some students of religion have expanded the term theodicy to apply to religious traditions not involving belief in one just, all-powerful deity. For example, the sociologist Max Weber (1864–1920) uses the term theodicy to refer to any religious effort to explain suffering.

Major Western Theodicies: Western religious traditions have advanced several different theodicies. All of these theodicies try to refine understanding of one or another leg of the "trilemma" to eliminate the apparent contradiction innocent suffering represents.

Sin and the "Free Will" Theodicy: One of the oldest theodicies begins with the observation of suffering but denies that the suffering perceived is innocent. This theodicy is central to the religious viewpoint of the Hebrew prophets, who attributed Israel's misfortunes to the people's ethical and religious trangressions.

The Christian doctrine of original sin gives this theodicy new form. According to this teaching, all human beings participate in or inherit the sin of the first parents, Adam and Eve, whose violation of God's commands (Genesis 3) justly brought death and suffering into the world. With the development of critical philosophy in the West, this emphasis on sin raises many questions. Some thinkers have trouble accepting the idea of inherited sin. Others argue that while sin may explain the suffering created by moral agents (what is sometimes called "moral evil"), it seems less applicable to "natural evils" like earthquakes, floods, or pestilence.

Some also view this theodicy as running counter to traditional claims regarding God's omnipotence and omniscience. If God can foresee and prevent human sinning, why has he not done so? Why did God not create human beings able to avoid sinning, and why does God not step in to prevent moral and religious wrongs?

Responding to this problem, classical theologians such as Augustine (354–430) and Thomas Aquinas (ca. 1225–74) developed what is sometimes called the free will defense of God's justice. They argue that a just being who wishes to bring about the highest degree of goodness in the world would want to create creatures able to respond freely. God has done this and cannot be blamed for the suffering that results from human misuse of freedom.

This approach typifies philosophical theodicies in the West. The seeming logical contradiction between God's goodness, God's power, and the fact of suffering is removed by arguing that certain goods that any all-powerful and perfectly just being would create necessarily entail suffering.

Educative Theodicies: Recognizing the tenuousness of this response in certain cases of innocent suffering, religious thinkers advanced other theodicies. One emphasizes the educative role suffering can play in human life. Paul expressed this view when he affirmed that Christians should "rejoice" in suffering because it produces endurance, character, and hope (Romans 5:3–5).

Sometimes associated with this educative theodicy is the view that sees suffering not as the result of one's own sin but as a penalty vicariously born by the innocent for others' wrongdoing. According to this theodicy, vicarious suffering serves an educative purpose by manifesting the consequences of sin to the world and by helping to purify and uplift the sufferers. This view is foundational to many Christian understandings of Christ's life and death and, by extension, to the vocation of all Christians.

Eschatological Theodicies: Educative theodicies have a shortcoming in that some individuals suffer too much or die too soon to experience the benefits suffering brings. In response to this eschatological solutions were developed to the problem of suffering. These locate fulfillment or reward for innocent suffering in a realm beyond the world. This may be a heavenly domain above, a kingdom of God at the end of time, or some combination of the two.

Theodicy and Mystery: The bitterness of innocent suffering sometimes overwhelms rational efforts at explanation. Because of this, religious thinkers drawing on the Bible sometimes argue that the problem must remain a mystery to human beings because, although God is just, humans lack the knowledge or insight to judge God's ways.

Islam's emphasis on God's absolute sovereignty led it to accentuate this response. The medieval theologian al-Ghazali (d. 1111) affirmed of God that "there is no analogy between His justice and the justice of creatures," and he denied the possibility of human comprehension of God. In the Bible the classical expression of this view appears in the book of Job. Near the end of the book God appears out of a whirlwind. Rebuking Job for his complaints over his suffering and his repeated requests for an explanation, God answers that, as a creature, Job is incapable of understanding or questioning his creator.

Theodicy in Other Religious Traditions: Outside the

sphere of biblically derived monotheism, the theodicy problem exists in Weber's larger sense of how one can religiously understand suffering in the world.

Dualism: Zoroastrian or Parsi religion (along with some later Gnostic traditions such as Manichaeism) offers an essentially dualistic answer to the question of suffering. The world and human life are seen as a realm of cosmic struggle between two deities, one good, one evil. Suffering occurs as human beings are caught in this struggle. A dualistic theodicy spares the good deity from the charge of causing suffering, but it leaves the outcome of the struggle between good and evil in doubt.

Karma and Theodicies: Hinduism and Buddhism share several responses to the problem of suffering. A leading one is the idea of *karma*, a law of moral cause and effect. According to this law, every deed (or volition) eventually reaps its reward either in this life or in a later one when the soul transmigrates and is reincarnated. In a world ruled by karma, innocent suffering does not exist. The child dying in infancy receives the penalty for transgressions committed in some previous life. Because karma applies to all beings in the universe, not even the gods can escape its effects.

The thorough and consistent way karma addresses the problem of suffering leads Max Weber in his *Sociology of Religion* (1922) to characterize it as "the most complete formal solution of the problem of theodicy." Nevertheless, although karma may explain suffering, it provides little comfort to those experiencing it. As a result, Hinduism and Buddhism have each developed further ideas to mitigate or reduce the sense of bondage to suffering. One solution is the Upanishadic teaching linking the individual human soul (Skt. *atman*) with *brahman*, the mystically discerned ground of being. This idea offers spiritually enlightened persons relief from suffering in the knowledge that the immortal soul is "unstained" by deeds or the karmic penalties attached to them.

Buddhism deepens the theodicy problem by defining life itself, the cycle of birth and death, as suffering (*duhkha*). The way out of this cycle is not the idea that the soul or self (*atman*) is immortal, but the recognition that there is no self (*anatman*). Through its doctrine of dependent origination (*pratitya-samutpada*), Buddhism teaches that the seemingly discrete ego is nothing more than a set of complex causal processes that persist because of ignorant craving or thirst (*trisha*). Escape from this painful state of being involves relinquishing the notion of self through a lifelong process of moral and intellectual discipline.

Islam: Questions about God's justice arose early in Islam, but no systematic theodicy emerged until the rise of the Mutazilite school in the eighth century. Affirmation of divine justice formed one of the chief tenets of the Mutazilites, who elaborated a rationalist ethics in which justice represented an objective, intellectually discernible quality with universal application for God as well as humankind. The Mutazilites's critics charged that their theodicy limited God's omnipotence. In reply, Mutazilites developed the view that God could do wrong, but would not. The Mutazilite theodicy, known as the doctrine of "the optimal" (Arab. *al-aslah*), had enormous influence within Islam and was known to such Western thinkers as the seventeenth-century German philosopher Gottfried Leibniz. The rival Asharite school rejected Mutazilite formulations and held that justice is defined solely by God. For Asharites, whatever God does is right. To claim that God acts for the sake of justice is impious. Rather, what God actually does determines justice. Because nothing exists without the will of God, everything that does exist is insuperably right and just; otherwise, it would not exist at all. Such optimistic fatalism became characteristic of Islam. A modified notion of theodicy emerged later in the work of the Asharite theologian and mystic Abu Hamid al-Ghazali (1058–1111), who asserted that "nothing in the realm of possibility is more wonderful than what is." Al-Ghazali's persuasive amalgamation of earlier conflicting notions of theodicy won many adherents but also provoked a long-lasting dispute over theodicy within Islam that endured into the nineteenth century.

theological virtues, the three Christian virtues listed by Paul (1 Corinthians 13:13): faith, hope, and charity. Roman Catholicism understands these virtues as complementary to the cardinal virtues. Protestant thought focuses entirely on the theological virtues. *See also* cardinal virtues.

theology (Gk. *theos*, "god"; *logia*, "sayings"), the discussion of God or the gods. In its classical sense, theology signifies speaking and writing about the Olympic and pre-Olympic gods, as done by Homer and Hesiod. After the rise of Greek philosophy, *theologia* becomes that section of metaphysics that deals abstractly and noncorporeally with the divine being. In Greco-Roman Christianity, in Greek-influenced sectors of Judaism and, later, of Islam, theology is transformed to signify the study of the nature, attributes, and will of the God of revelation. In medieval Christianity, the meaning of theologia expands to include not only God but the entire corpus of doctrine about God's work—creation, redemption, sanctification—in the world. In post-medieval Christianity the normative meaning of the term is the systematic study of Christian dogmas and doctrines or dogmatics. *See also* Christianity (thought and ethics); Christian theological systems; Judaism (thought and ethics); kalam.

Theology of the People (Kor. *Minjung Sinhak*), a twentieth-century Korean Protestant theological movement that seeks to redefine the role of religion vis-a-vis the modern secular state. This movement may be broadly characterized as the Korean equivalent of North and South American liberation theology, in that it draws upon Korean understandings of economic and political power relationships yet seeks to advance both church and state beyond the competitive dichotomies of the past. The greatest impact has been on Protestant church behavior and organization. Some have criticized Protestant churches as organizations rooted in hierarchical rather than democratic models of power holding, contending that this is in direct conflict with the motivations and aspirations of those who seek church membership, i.e., their own self-empowerment. Minjung Sinhak has also criticized the wealth accumulated by Protestant church-capitalism. *See also* Korea, Protestantism in.

theophany, general term for the manifestation of a deity.

theory, an explanatory account of some puzzling or intriguing phenomenon. A theory of religion, then, would see religion as being problematic in some important respect and would represent an attempt to propose a set of principles designed to reduce or eliminate this problematic status. In order to count as a theory, the set of principles would attempt to identify religion's special form, specify its distinctive content, designate its causal origin, and describe its systematic functions. A theory attempts to achieve its explanatory objectives by employing idealizations, that is, by abstracting away from irrelevant details in order to focus upon what was most significant about the phenomenon being accounted for by constructing a model. Such theoretical models are viable and interesting because of their simplicity, coherence, testability, productivity, and suggestive-

ness. *See also* religion, explanation of; religion, the study of.

Types of Theories of Religion: In the history of scholarly inquiry into religion, many theories have been proposed to account for religion's origin, structure, function, and systematic properties. Such theories can be arranged according to type.

Emotivist Theories: Emotivist theories focus on religion's nonintellectual or nonrational features. Such theories consider religious actions and the conceptual schemes that underwrite them to be expressions of emotion: fear, joy, ecstasy, experience of "the numinous," deep unconscious forces, feelings of oneness with the universe. Emotivist theories typically present religion as a nonrational experience, structure, or activity developed over time to fulfill either psychological or social needs.

Emotivist theories of religion assume either positive or negative forms. Positive emotivist theories emphasize the alleged integrative functions that religion is postulated to fulfill in individual and social life. Negative emotivist theories emphasize religion's alleged disintegrative, neurotic, and even pathological features. Under emotivist explanations, whatever conceptual element a religion possesses is said to consist of little more than surface rationalizations that conceal deep and often unconscious individual and social forces. In fact, emotivist theories treat the surface conceptual features of religion as psychological and social expressions that stand in contradiction to the real underlying motivations. Emotivist theories attempt to identify and describe these hidden nonrational features.

Because of their emphasis upon the fulfillment of needs or the expression of hidden motivations, emotivist theories are characteristically functionalist; they attempt to account for the origin or persistence of religious phenomena in terms of the psychological and sociological functions the phenomena serve. Psychological functionalism focuses upon the personal needs that religion is supposed to satisfy. Sociological functionalism is more interested in the requirements and needs that groups evince.

Much criticism both within the philosophy of social science and within the social scientific disciplines themselves has been leveled at the questionable logic and problematic truth claims of functionalist explanations. These explanations continue, nevertheless, to exert a powerful influence on theorizing about sociocultural systems in general and religious systems in particular.

Intellectualist Theories: Unlike emotivist theories,

intellectualist theories focus upon the explanatory interests that human beings in all cultures appear to possess. Intellectualists treat religious conceptual schemes as examples of human theorizing, with the result that religion is treated as simply one form of conceptual cultural activity that human beings with explanatory concerns happen to employ. For example, intellectualist theories of religion consider religious narratives (of which myths are a compelling instance) to be humankind's early, but now outmoded, speculative attempts to explain why the world is the way it appears to be. Myths, according to this view, are theories about puzzling and problematic phenomena presented in narrative form.

Much intellectualist discussion of myth focuses upon the specific medium (metaphor, image, idiom) explanatory thinking employs in its speculations about origins, structures, goals, and elements. Typically intellectualists treat myths as protoscience, or even first science, idiomatically distinct from mature science but conceptually motivated by the same abiding curiosity that is endemic to the human species.

Intellectualist theory has a difficult time explaining why myth as protoscience continues to persist in a culture after a more mature science has emerged in its place. The later, more adequate mode of thought should have replaced such outmoded, earlier explanatory accounts. One intellectualist answer seems to be that where mythic modes of thought successfully maintain themselves even in the presence of mature science they do so as alternative (and subordinate) sociocultural forms.

Intellectualist theories also attempt to account for diverse conceptual schemes among cultures and not only within one culture. When wedded to a progressivistic or evolutionary view of the development of human thought, intellectualism emphasizes the greater precision and verisimilitude of more recent explanations.

When wedded to cultural relativism, and when acknowledging the wide differences among different cultural histories, intellectualism stresses the alternative modes of thought of which human societies are capable. Here the contrast is not between less mature and more mature science but between different forms of science, taking into account differences in idiomatic expression and the different routes that the growth of knowledge has taken in different human societies.

Symbolist Theories: Symbolist theories of religion vary significantly among themselves about the form, content, origin, and function of religion. Except for the view that religious phenomena are symbolic phenomena, that such symbolic phenomena are representations of important features of human experience, and that symbols have a strong aesthetic component, there is little agreement.

Some symbolists argue that the symbolic systems in question represent either psychological or social structures. In the case of the individual, whatever appears in the public expression of the symbol appears first in the (unconscious) experience of the individual and represents, no matter how indirectly, that experience. In the case of social structure, the collective symbols important to the group represent the underlying rationale that acts as the engine of motivation for the group.

Other symbolists are more interested in the evocative role that such symbols play in individual and social life. This approach emphasizes the active role that symbols play in human experience in general, and in religious experience in particular. The issue, here, is what symbols can create, found, or establish rather than how they represent their objects. For example, some symbolists stress the power that symbols have in their capacity to evoke novel experiences such as mystical states. Other symbolists underscore the potential that symbols have for developing new forms of religious discourse. Others point to the formative role of symbols in the development of new worldviews. How all of these creative activities are accomplished, however, is never precisely spelled out. A theory of symbolism that unifies all these modes of creativity still awaits development.

Structuralist Theories: Structuralist theories, like intellectualist theories, see religious forms as instances of the human mind at work. Structuralist theorizing, however, downplays the explanatory interests that human beings are thought to have in favor of the much more prominent concern with categorization and classification that all human societies appear to evince. Structuralists take seriously the idea that human beings require, employ, and move in a world of categories in terms of which all humans beings do their thinking. The style of thinking that results from the employment of these categories is usually binary or oppositional in form. These categories are not constructed abstractly but emerge in the context of narrative development in the growth of cultural forms. For example, while a myth might appear to be an attempt to explain the origins of life, in the structuralist perspective it is more fundamentally a narrative way of circumscribing, defining, and establishing a set of useful cognitive categories in terms of which human beings may interact with the complex environment in which they find themselves. Hence, religious symbols are a subset of a larger group of symbols that give human beings a vantage point on the world around them, especially when that world contains radical differences, puzzling anomalies, or contradictions.

Ideological Theories: Ideological theories of religion are not as concerned with the form or content of religious systems as they are with origins and functions. Ideological theories of religion make a distinction between the actual organization of a human society and the rational (i.e., ideological) system that provides the society with its raison d'etre. What actually goes on in the society, the understanding people have of their society, and the mode of expression that such understanding takes can be miles apart. Hence ideological theories and emotivist theories have much in common, especially when the contradictions between infrastructural and superstructural principles are at stake. Infrastructural principles describe the actual basis for human societies. Superstructural principles emerge from, represent, conceal, and feed back into the infrastructural base.

One of the principal contentions of ideological theories about religion is that religion masks the nature, extent, and causes of the conditions in which oppressed classes find themselves. As such, religion functions as a psychological opiate providing both comfort and illusion to those who have little else to hope for. Here religion is viewed as dulling the senses so that the oppressed not only fail to recognize their condition but are complicit in maintaining it. At the same time the religious ideology is seen as providing social legitimation for the ruling classes. Ideological theories of religion have provided powerful critiques of capitalist societies and have been instrumental in providing an ideology for revolutionary activity in many colonized societies.

Cognitive Theories: Cognitive theories of religion focus their attention on the types of knowledge that human beings are capable of acquiring given the sociocultural systems in which human beings live, and the inherited structures that constrain their formation. Cognitive theorists propose models of the types of competence characteristic of human beings (for example, linguistic competence, symbolic competence, arithmetic competence) and employ formal strategies and techniques available in the cognitive sciences to study them. Of particular interest to cognitivists are those types of human competence that human beings rather easily and rapidly acquire without explicit instruction and that function adequately in social situations without being codified. Scholars of religion operating within a cognitive framework are particularly interested in the type of symbolic competence revealed in the judgments about ritual form that knowledgeable participants in a religious system are capable of making. Some have recently gone so far as to develop formal systems, which are thought to play an important role in religious behavior.

Levels of Analysis in Theories of Religion: Theories of religion cannot only be categorized by types, they also appear at various levels of analysis, specifically the biological, the psychological, and the sociocultural.

Biological theories of religion account for the social and cultural behavior that human beings engage in as particular forms of biological adaptation driven by survival values and providing contexts for reproductive strategies. Such theories employ evolutionary categories to explain the persistence of religion over time as being an evolutionary advantage.

Psychological theories of religion vary according to whether they refer primarily to the unconscious (Freudian and Jungian), to observable behavior (behaviorism), or to the mind (cognitivism). Freudian and Jungian theories concentrate on the affective aspects of religion and the hidden psychological structures that are thought to account for its dynamics. Behavioral theories are concerned primarily with how environmental factors reinforce certain behaviors over time. Cognitive theories are concerned with the complex conceptual forms characteristic of religious systems and devise complex strategies to account for them. Such strategies emphasize either personal or subpersonal features, and employ either statistical or normative judgment techniques. Their main emphasis is upon what a theoretical analysis of the systems of knowledge that human beings possess discloses about sociocultural systems.

Sociocultural theories account for religion either in terms of social relations or in terms of cultural systems. They emphasize the relative autonomy of sociocultural systems from individual control.

Theosophical Society, a Spiritualist organization begun in New York in 1875. Its founding members were Helena Petrovna Blavatsky (1831–91), an aristocratic Russian medium whose writings and psycho-spiritual powers were the real catalysts of the movement; Henry Steel Olcott (1832–1907), an American investigator of Spiritualist phenomena who served as the Society's first president; and William Quan Judge (1851–96), an Irish-born lawyer. Despite its relatively small number of adherents, the Society has been one of the most important conveyors and popularizers of Western occultism and Eastern religious philosophy in the modern world.

The Society embraced a broad program of teaching and activity, subsequently defined under three principal objectives: to form the nucleus for the united human community; to study comparative religion, philosophy, and science; and to investigate the powers latent in humanity. The primary tenets presented in Blavatsky's modern compendiums of Theosophy, especially *Isis Unveiled* (1877) and *The Secret Doctrine* (1888), and in other theosophical writings such as those by Annie Besant and C. W. Leadbeater, include *karma,* reincarnation, the existence of human "subtle bodies," and an elaborate picture of cosmic and terrestrial spiritual evolution.

The Society was established abroad through the travel of its members; branches are in most nations, though it has been most successful in India and the English-speaking world. Since Blavatsky's journey to India in 1879, that country has been a major theosophical center, with the headquarters of the largest worldwide Theosophical Society at Adyar, India. *See also* Blavatsky, Helena Petrovna; North America, new religions in; Olcott, Henry Steel; Theosophy.

Theosophy (the-o'so-fee; Gk., "divine wisdom"), a term used from ancient times through the medieval and modern periods to refer to a particular form of mysticism. Associated with the Hellenistic Gnostics and Neoplatonists; with Meister Eckhart, Nicholas of Cusa, and Jacob Boehme; and with the Jewish Kabbala, the name and tradition of Theosophy has been revived with specific emphases in the Theosophical Society founded by Helena Petrovna Blavatsky (1831–91) and others in 1875.

The theosophical strand of mysticism has generally stressed monism, or seeing the universe in its matter and spirit components as a single unity. At the same time, the theosophical mind characteristically looks with interest "behind the scenes" with a view to detecting the particular processes involving little-known forces or planes of reality that engineer spirit/matter interaction and the interaction of grades of reality up to the meeting of human and divine minds. At this point theosophy presents a program for mystical redemption or enlightenment, typically spelled out with a peculiar juxtaposition of the language of precision and ecstasy.

Fundamental features of traditional theosophical thought include five main tenets. First, adherents believe that a deep spiritual reality exists beneath the surface appearance of the world; particular features of the visible world may have specific relationship to those of the invisible. The heavenly sun, for example, has been said to manifest the place of God or a "Solar Logos." Second, by meditation, intuition, or revelation, often from such higher entities as angels or Masters, humans can establish direct contact with the spiritual realm. Third, the exoteric religions of the world contain veiled esoteric doctrine of the theosophical sort. Some theosophists have worked chiefly within one religion, as did Boehme in Protestant Christianity and ibn Arabi in Islam, while others have emphasized the common mystical core they perceive at the heart of all faiths. Thus, modern theosophists in the lineage of the Theosophical Society have often taken a special interest in Eastern religion, finding Asian thought with its monistic and mystical-experiential bent highly congenial. Fourth, occult powers and psychic phenomena are explored and developed not merely for their own sake or for the this-worldly success their mastery may bring, but also because they are tokens of the reality of hidden nonmaterial forces behind the outer world. And finally, a preeminent role is reserved for those regarded as spiritual masters—either in this world or beyond—and for select, initiatory spiritual circles. Theosophical wisdom, like esotericism generally, is held to be teachable only by one who has fully interiorized it and only to those who are themselves ready. *See also* esoteric movements; Theosophical Society.

Theotokos (thay-oh-tohk'uhs; Gk., "Bearer of God"), an ancient Greek title for Mary, the mother of Jesus Christ, growing from belief that the child she bore is God made flesh. By the logic of the Incarnation she can be called God-bearer or Mother of God. This was affirmed by Council of Ephesus in 431, and the feast day is celebrated January 1. *See also* Mary; Orthodox Church.

Theravada (thai-ruh-vah'duh; Pali, "The Way of the Elders"), the self-chosen name of the relatively diverse Buddhist traditions found in Sri Lanka and Southeast Asia. The name *Theravada* refers to the teachings of ancient monastic elders, which these traditions see themselves as preserving. These teachings are incorporated into a body of commentaries (*atthakathas*) that are uniquely valued by the Theravada; although there is some overlap between the different canons of the various Buddhist traditions, no other school of Buddhism shares the Theravada's commentarial tradition. The Theravada is also notable for its insistence on the historicity of the Buddha and for its use of Pali as a liturgical and scholastic language; for the Theravada, Pali was the language spoken by the Buddha and the Buddhist canon preserved in Pali is the most authentic transmission of his teachings.

The History of the Theravada: The origins of the Theravada are obscure. The Theravada traces its origin to the career of the Buddha himself, but in this self-conception it is like other schools of Buddhism. It was once common for modern scholars to take Theravada's account at face value, at the expense of the claims of other schools; today scholars are increasingly aware that such accounts rather than being historical are to be understood as part of the Theravada's own self-definition.

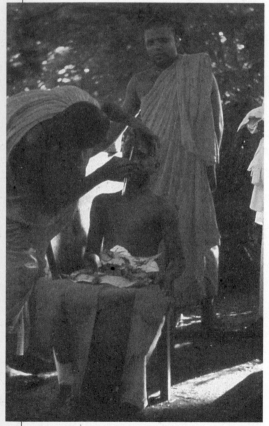

In Colombo, Sri Lanka (1969), a teenage boy takes a first step toward becoming a novice Buddhist monk by having his hair and eyebrows shaved by a monk as a symbol of renunciation. Because his religious status changes by virtue of this initiatory ritual, his cut hair is now sacred and must be caught by cloth on the boy's lap so it does not touch the ground.

The use of Pali is a distinctive trait of the Theravada, but the earliest indications of the use of Pali are found in Burma (Myanmar) and Sri Lanka. One might infer that the Theravada, as we know it, began outside of India. But it is absolutely necessary to posit an Indian background for the Theravada—without such a background it would not be possible to explain the independent emergence of the Theravada in both Burma and Sri Lanka—although there is no easy way to specify exactly what this Indian background might be. It is most likely that the Theravada is a continuation of the school known in ancient India as the Sthaviravada, a Sanskrit cognate with Theravada with the same meaning. The Sthaviravada was one of the eighteen schools of Buddhism that were grouped together pejoratively as the Hinayana (Skt., "Little Vehicle"), by the Mahayana ("Great Vehicle"). Indeed, the Theravada shares the general features attributed to some of those schools, such as a soteriology that gives a central place to the *arhat* ("worthy one," "saint") and the preeminence of monastic life as a context for religious practice. At the same time, however, it is very difficult to find any independent evidence, such as that provided by inscriptions, to prove that the Theravada existed in India before it had emerged in Sri Lanka and Burma.

The contours of the Theravada come into sharper relief in the historical evidence available from Sri Lanka. The Theravada traces its presence in Sri Lanka and Burma to missions sponsored by the great Buddhist emperor Ashoka; this would place the establishment of Buddhism in these areas at about the third century B.C.; some modern scholars argue that this date is too early, especially with respect to Burma. The commentarial tradition so distinctive of the Theravada emerged in the first centuries if not before. It was then preserved in tandem with the Pali canon. These commentaries were originally composed in Sinhala, but they were translated and ordered by Buddhaghosa, the greatest of Theravadin intellectuals, in the fifth century. Buddhaghosa's work in the commentaries and in his doctrinal digest, the *Visuddhimagga*, continues to provide a standard of orthodoxy for most Theravadin thinkers.

Gradually the Theravadin school spread to Southeast Asia from its dual sources in Burma and Sri Lanka, and by the fourteenth century it was the preeminent tradition throughout the region. It thus became incorporated into the daily lives of people in diverse cultures and societies, including the Sinhala people, the Burmese, the Mon, the Shan, the northern Thai, the Lu, the Lao, and the Khmer.

The Theravada, however, also exists as a translocal movement, and some of its appeal historically has been because of its character as a supralocal civilization. There has been constant interchange of ideas, practices, and ordination lineages among elite monks across cultural boundaries throughout history. This gives a considerable degree of homogeneity to the Theravada.

The Religious Thought and Practice of the Theravada: The religious thought and practice of the Theravada may be conveniently summarized with the categories found in what is called a "step-by-step discourse." Discourses of this type are found in the Pali canon, but they continued to be popular in the later Theravada, their basic structure used to order commentarial discussions. A step-by-step discourse includes five parts, ranked in a hierarchy of increasing value: instructions about generosity, morality, meditation, heaven, and the goal of the Buddhist religious life, *nibbana* (Skt. *nirvana*, "liberation"). Almost all of Theravadin religious practice can be interpreted within this rubric. Generosity (*dana*) refers to acts of giving material necessities to monks, nuns, and other worthy subjects. Generosity is a preeminent form of merit making, a major concern of Theravadin practice. One wants to make good merit in order to ensure a satisfactory future by the law of karma, a law of moral cause and effect; the gifting of merit to others is a good action as well. Morality (*sila*) is directly continuous with generosity; it is the development of restraint and positive virtue conducive to a proper religious life. Meditation (*bhavana*) is at the core of the religious life; it is the mechanism for the transformation of the individual, removing obstacles to spiritual advancement as well as generating and cultivating positive traits. Rebirth in heaven is an acceptable goal in Theravadin thought, although it pales in worth and significance when compared with nibbana; thus, it is said that even though heaven is to be striven for, it is also to be renounced. Much of traditional Theravadin thought gave emphasis to elaborate cosmologies with various heavens of differing degrees of pleasure, and particular practices were done in order to gain rebirth in one of these heavens. Nibbana, the ultimate goal of the Theravadin religious life, is the absence of rebirth. It can only be attained by an immediate experience of reality, knowing what really is for oneself. In this experience, one comes to perceive directly that everything in this world is impermanent and without any continuing essence, and with this individual realization there is an end to all suffering. *See also* Buddhism (authoritative texts and their interpretation); Mahayana; Nikaya Buddhism.

Therese of Lisieux (tay-res' leez-yoo'; 1873–97), French Catholic saint, also known as "the Little Flower." Suffering from nervous afflictions, she entered a convent at the age of fifteen and underwent a series of physical and spiritual disturbances. Her espistolary autobiography, *L'histoire d'une ame* (History of a Soul, 1898), was first published with heavy editing and additions; a reliable text has been available since 1956. Therese was canonized in 1925.

theriomorphic (Gk., "in the form of animals"), term applied to deities or representations of deities with animal or animal and human features.

theurgy (thee'uhr-gee; Gk., "sacramental or magical rite"), Greco-Roman magic performed by the aid of spirits, particularly associated with the Neoplatonists, flourishing between the second and fourth centuries. *See also* Neoplatonism.

third eye, in Hinduism, one of the *chakras* ("centers") of psycho-spiritual energy. Located between the eyebrows and sometimes associated with the pineal gland, its activation is said to lead to wisdom and illumination. It is often appealed to in non-Indian occult disciplines. *See also* chakras.

Thirty-nine Articles (1563–71), the only official theological statement within Anglican Christianity. They are not a fixed creed that members are expected to affirm. Today these Articles are primarily a historical testimony to the effects of Protestant thought upon Anglicanism. *See also* Anglicanism.

Thomas a Becket. *See* Becket, Thomas a.

Thomas a Kempis (b. Thomas Hemerken; ca. 1380–1471), German Catholic monk and devotional writer, known for his book *The Imitation of Christ* (1418), one of the two or three most influential works of Christian literature. Primarily aimed at lay piety, it focuses on a Christ-centered life and on moderate austerity.

Thomas Christians, also called Malabar Christians, the general name for those Christians living in the southwest Indian state of Kerala who trace their origin to the missionary activity of the Apostle Thomas. According to the apocryphal third-century *Acts of Thomas*, the apostle brought Christianity to India and was eventually martyred in Mylapore, near Madras. The authenticity of this tradition cannot be established; however, there is evidence that Christians were present in India by the sixth century, probably as a result of missionary activity by the East Syrian Church.

In the fifteenth century, contact between Rome and the Malabar Christians was established by Portuguese missionaries. The Thomas Christians subsequently entered into communion with Rome in 1599, but attempts to Latinize the Malabar liturgy and the imposition of Portuguese bishops resulted in a split in 1653. Following the restoration of the Chaldean hierarchy in 1661, the majority of Malabar Christians (the Syro-Malabar Church) reestablished communion with Rome, while a minority joined the Syrian Orthodox (Jacobite) Church. In addition to these churches there are presently two other major groups of Thomas Christians: an independent (Protestant) Jacobite Church of Mar Thomas that emerged during the nineteenth century, and the Syro-Malankara Church that was reunited with Rome in 1930. *See also* Syria, Christianity in.

Thomism, Roman Catholic theological school based on the work of Thomas Aquinas (ca. 1225–74). *See also* Aquinas, Thomas; Scholasticism; Summa Theologiae.

Thor (thohr), the ancient Norse god of physical strength and thunder. His hammer, Mjollnir, represents the thunderbolt. He travels through the sky in a chariot drawn by two goats and defends the abodes of gods (Asgardr) and humans (Midgardr) by slaying the giants. His name is etymologically preserved in "Thursday." *See also* Nordic religion.

Thoth, an ancient Egyptian god, lord of Hermopolis, scribe of the gods, moon god, and peacemaker among the gods; he is often depicted as a human with an ibis' head. *See also* Egyptian religion.

3HO. *See* Healthy-Happy-Holy Organization.

Three Jewels, also Treasures, the threefold focus of the Buddhist religion: the Buddha; the Dharma, the Truth he rediscovered and taught; and the Sangha, the monastic order he established.

When conceptualized as the Three Jewels, these objects are instances of maximal greatness in the Buddhist scheme of things. Thus, the Buddha of the Three Jewels is not viewed as an ordinary human being or a charismatic religious genius but rather as a Lord (Skt. *Bhagavan*), who is unsurpassed among beings; he is a teacher of gods and humans. His nature is said to be "un-

thinkable," and his good qualities are more than ten million. The Truth he taught is said to be "well-proclaimed by the Lord, thoroughly seen, not subject to time, welcoming all, onward-leading, and to be directly experienced by the wise" (*Visuddhimagga* 7.68), while the "community of the Lord's disciples" is "an incomparable field of merit for the world" (*Visuddhimagga* 7.89).

The Three Jewels are described as the Three Refuges, and a standard part of Buddhist ritual is to affirm verbally, "I go for refuge to the Buddha, I go for refuge to the Dharma, I go for refuge to the Sangha." The Three Jewels are also recipients of worship, with offerings and honor given to images and relics of the Buddha, to texts in which his teachings are written, and to individual monks and nuns as well as the monastic order as a corporate body. The Three Jewels are also important focuses for meditation. *See also* Buddhas; Buddhism; Dharma/dharma; Sangha.

Three Pure Ones. *See* San-ch'ing.

Three Refuges. *See* Three Jewels.

Three Religions/Three Teachings. *See* San-chiao.

Three Stages, Teaching of (Chin. *San-chieh-chiao*), a minor Chinese Buddhist school founded by Hsin-hsing (540–594). Believing that they lived in the last and worst of three periods of progressive deterioration, adherents recommended the reverencing of all beings as potential Buddhas, altruistic activities, and strict discipline. It disappeared during the general suppression of Buddhism in 845. *See also* ages of the world; Degenerate Age of the Dharma.

Three thousand worlds in an instant of thought (Chin. *i-nien san-ch'ien*), a Chinese T'ien-t'ai Buddhist expression for the interpenetration and unity of all existents. *See also* T'ien-t'ai school.

Three Treasures. *See* Three Jewels.

Three Worms. *See* san-ch'ung.

thug, thag (thuhg), in central India during the early nineteenth century, secret associations devoted to Kali, who strangled travelers with a knotted cloth, taking their wealth and offering the dead to the goddess. *See also* Kali.

Tiamat (tee'ah-maht; Babylonian, "sea"), a female, cosmic, chaotic body of water slain by the god

Marduk. *See also* divine combat; Enuma elish; Mesopotamian religion.

tiara, a metal crown of three tiers worn by Christian popes as a sign of their authority. *See also* papacy.

Tibetan Book of the Dead (Tibetan *bar-do-thos-grol*, "liberation through hearing"), a class of Buddhist texts and teachings concerning the *bardo*, an "intermediate state" of extended length between death and rebirth. In the Tibetan texts, a journey through a bardo of forty-nine days is described. The highlights of this journey include unconsciousness at the moment of death (at least for the ordinary person); reawakening in a bodiless condition; and the progressive appearance of the deities, first of a peaceful, later of a wrathful aspect, composing a one-hundred-deity pantheon. According to this teaching, those who see these deities "as they are" attain liberation in the intermediate state, while those who do not will be reborn. By describing the postdeath experience, the texts prepare individuals for death and equip them with knowledge to help them negotiate their way successfully through the bardo. In addition, the "Book" is chanted at the time of death, to assist the deceased in the bardo. Finally, these teachings form the itinerary for the "Black Ati" practice, an important solitary retreat in Nyingma-pa tradition wherein the practitioner is walled up in a cave in total darkness for forty-nine days and by means of various meditative visualizations enters into the bardo experience while still alive. This advanced retreat was considered dangerous but, if successful, particularly efficacious in dismantling the ego. *See also* afterworld; bardo; Tibetan religions.

Tibetan religions. The religion of the peoples who have inhabited the Tibetan plateau shows great diversity. While the dominant tradition for over a thousand years has been Buddhist, Tibetan religion includes a tradition known as Bon (Pon) that is thought by its adherents to be the authentic, pre-Buddhist religion of Tibet. In addition to these two traditions, each of which is diverse in its own right, there is a great variety of popular religious practices having to do with such things as oaths, kingship, and the deities of the land. There also has been a small but significant Muslim minority in Tibet for several centuries.

Tibetan Buddhism: According to Tibetan tradition, Buddhism was first introduced to Tibet in the seventh century, during the reign of the king Songtsen Gampo. A century later, this initial im-

Tibetan pilgrim praying at a cairn beside the Tsang-po River, Tibet (1993). The Tibetan term for pilgrimage, *gnas-kor*, means "circumambulation of sacred places," and pilgrims will often stop and circle a significant place chanting a sacred text.

pulse was reinforced by the royal establishment of a monastery at Samye (bSam-yas). To build the monastery, the Tibetan king called on two Indian Buddhist specialists, a Mahayana scholar-monk from eastern India named Santaraksita and a Tantric saint named Padmasambhava. Tibetan monasticism has inherited the concerns, in one form or another, of all three of these founding figures: a reverence for the secular power of the king, a devotion to monastic discipline and the *bodhisattva* (Buddha-to-be) ideal, and a fascination with the powers and attainments of the independent Tantric adept.

After this introductory phase (known as the "first diffusion of the Dharma [Buddhist teaching]"), Buddhism lost royal support and did not expand aggressively in central Tibet again until the tenth century (in the "later diffusion of the Dharma"). The tenth and eleventh centuries saw the foundation or reformulation of four orders or denominations that have shaped Tibetan Buddhist practice until the present day.

The Kadam-pa order arose from the teaching of an Indian monk-scholar named Atisa (982–1054) and later evolved into the Geluk-pa order that has been associated since the fifteenth century with the lineage of the Dalai Lamas. The Kagyu-pa order was founded by the translator and Tantric master Marpa (1012–92). The Sakya-pa order arose from the work of the translator Drogmi (992–1072). A fourth order, the Nyingma-pa, was formulated in this period and traced its origin to Padmasambhava, the Tantric adept who is said to have played a large role in the first diffusion of the Dharma.

In these early centuries, the focus of attention in Tibetan Buddhism was southward, toward the great monasteries and Tantric lineages of eastern India. When these monasteries were destroyed at the beginning of the thirteenth century, Tibetan Buddhists turned inward for their source of authority and developed many of the texts and practices that give Tibetan Buddhism its distinctive character. The scriptural tradition was organized into an extensive canon, containing the *Kanjur* (the words of the Buddha) and the *Tenjur* (the words of subsequent teachers). The succession of responsibility in the four major orders was increasingly entrusted to *tulkus*, who were understood to be the reincarnations of previous teachers, and the monasteries involved themselves in the struggle for secular power. This process culminated in the seventeenth century, when the fifth Dalai Lama, the leader of the Geluk-pa order, became the secular ruler of Tibet.

In the twentieth century, the isolation of Tibet protected Tibetan Buddhism for a time from the modernist movements that transformed Buddhist traditions elsewhere in Asia. But Chinese domination in the decades after World War II led to the suppression of many Buddhist institutions. Since the 1950s the vitality of Tibetan Buddhism has been maintained, at least in part, by the leadership of the exile community in India, and particularly by the fourteenth Dalai Lama.

The Bon Tradition: The development of the Bon (Pon) tradition in Tibet has closely mirrored the development of Tibetan Buddhism. To its adherents, it is the authentic, pre-Buddhist religion of Tibet. This view of the antiquity of Bon is partially confirmed by documentary evidence. Early sources mention practitioners of Bon who presided over rites for the dead during the period of the ancient Tibetan monarchy (seventh to ninth centuries). But the developed form of Bon that appeared in the fourteenth century contains a complex combination of indigenous and foreign practices. These practices are so similar in form and detail to many of the practices of Tibetan Buddhism that a number of modern scholars have chosen to argue that, while the Bon tradition defines itself in opposition to the Buddhist tradition in Tibet, it is so deeply influenced by the presence of Buddhism that its separate identity is difficult to discern.

The Bon tradition uses the word *bon* as a counterpart of the Buddhist word *chos* (which translates the Indian word *Dharma*). Like Tibetan Buddhists, the practitioners of Bon trace their tradition to a "fully enlightened being" (using the Tibetan word for "Buddha") named Shenrap who came from the land of Tazik, beyond the western boundary of Tibet. Like Tibetan Buddhism, the Bon tradition has a two-part canon, consisting of a Kanjur and Tenjur, and its view of the nature of the world, suffering, and the path to enlightenment is quite similar to the teachings of Tibetan Buddhism. Even the practices of divination and exorcism that are sometimes thought to be distinctive, "indigenous" features of Bon are found in the tradition of the Nyingma-pa school of Tibetan Buddhism.

At the beginning of the twentieth century, the Bon tradition was strongest in eastern Tibet. Since the Chinese invasion in the 1950s Bon monasteries have suffered the same persecution as their Buddhist counterparts, but there continues to be a lively Bon presence in the Tibetan exile community in India and the relaxation of Chinese persecution in the 1980s has made it possible for a number of important Bon institutions to be reestablished in Tibet.

Popular Religion: In addition to the organized traditions of Buddhism and Bon, the Tibetan people have participated in a range of religious practices that some scholars have called the "nameless religion," including beliefs in gods of the sky, earth, mountains, rivers, sun, moon, and stars. Local deities are honored today with a variety of practices such as fixing flags, tree branches, and animal horns or burning juniper branches on high places. An example of a popular festival, in which Buddhist and non-Buddhist elements are liberally intertwined, is the Tibetan New Year. The practice varies from place to place, but frequently involves an atmosphere of carnival and religious competition, in which the forces of chaos are temporarily allowed to run loose and then brought ritually under control. *See also* Avalokiteshvara; bardo; Black Hat; Bon; Buddhism (authoritative texts and their interpretation); Chogyam Trungpa; Dharma Dhatu; dorje; Geluk-pa; Gesar/Geser; Geshe; Kagyu-pa; Kanjur; Karma-pa; lama; Losar; Marpa; Milarepa; Nyingma-

Tibetan pilgrim (1992) holding a small prayer wheel on his way to Mt. Kailas (Tibetan *Ti-se*), the principal sacred mountain in Tibet, venerated as the center of the world, regarded as the home of the tantric god Cakrasamvara, and associated with Milarepa's legendary defeat of a Bon priest.

pa; Padmasambhava; Panchen Lama; prayer flag; prayer wheel; Red Hats; Sakya-pa; Shambhala; Tantrism (Buddhism); Tara; Tibetan Book of the Dead; tulku, Vajrayana.

T'ien (tyen; Chin., "Heaven," "Sky"), name applied to the supreme deity in early Chou-dynasty bronze inscriptions. T'ien is used synonymously with Shang-ti in the *Shu-ching* (Book of History) to assert equivalency with the "Supreme Lord" of the Shang (ca. 1766–1122 B.C.). Heaven in early Chou (ca. 1122–722 B.C.) shared the unpredictable character of Shang-ti but with an admixture of moral intentionality deriving from the Chou doctrine of the Mandate of Heaven (T'ien-ming). Later, as yin-yang and wu-hsing naturalism increased in popularity, Heaven declined in significance outside Confucian circles until a semblance of its former dignity was restored in state worship, beginning in the first century. *See also* Chou religion; cosmology; Shang religion; Shang-ti; Shu-ching; sky; term question; T'ien-ming; wu-hsing; yin and yang.

T'ien-hsin Taoism (tyen-shin; Chin., "Heart of Heaven"), a Chinese tradition of ritual healing founded by a twelfth-century scholar. Its revealed scriptures teach priests how to heal mental illness by drawing down spiritual power from stars. It is still practiced in Thailand. *See also* Taoism.

T'ien-kung. *See* Yu-ti.

T'ien-ming (tyen-ming; Chin., "Mandate of Heaven"), a central tenet of ancient Chinese politico-religious ideology attributed to the Duke of Chou (Chou Kung), who justified the Chou overthrow of the Shang dynasty in mid-twelfth century B.C. by appeal to this doctrine. Its antecedents can be found in Shang attitudes toward the high god Shang-ti and in the perceived correlation of astrological portents with early dynastic transitions. According to the Chou founders, who alluded to the precedent of the Shang usurpation of the preceding Hsia dynasty, Heaven (T'ien) was disposed to bestow the sacred kingship only on a ruler who could be expected to govern the people benevolently and piously. Heaven, the Chou founders insisted, intervened directly in human affairs by signaling the transfer of the "mandate" to rule all under heaven (*ming*, "command," "decree") from an unworthy house to a virtuous one, precipitating the overthrow of tyrants.

Despite a drastic decline in the prestige of the Chou toward the end of the dynasty, the doctrine remained axiomatic in classical Confucianism and in the popular mind. Thinkers such as Confucius were preoccupied with cultivating the moral values of the Shang and Chou dynastic founders in preparation for Heaven's long overdue intervention. Mencius stressed the empowerment of the people, which the doctrine implied. With the establishment of Confucianism as state orthodoxy in the Han dynasty, the concept of Heaven's Mandate became a cornerstone of the imperial ideological edifice, restraining to some degree the absolute power of the emperor. *See also* Chou Kung; Chou religion; kingship, sacred; Shang religion; Shang-ti; T'ien.

T'ien-shih Taoism (tyen-shuhr; Chin., "Celestial Master"), earliest Chinese religious organization, founded in Szechwan by Chang Tao-ling. In 142, Chang claimed to have received a revelation and covenant from the deity Lao-chun. This covenant authorized Chang to establish a new religiopolitical order intended both to supersede existing religious practices and to replace the ineffective Han imperial government. Chang, who took the title of "Celestial Master" (*t'ien-shih*), divided his realm into twenty-four units, in which male or female priests called "libationers" (*chi-chiu*) performed expiatory rituals to heal the sick. All would periodically gather for various communal ceremonies. The laity were instructed in proper morality, sometimes by means of texts such as the *Tao-te ching*. Participants were expected to refrain from worshiping the unapproved deities of "heterodox cults" and to contribute five pecks of "faith-rice" annually (hence the references to the organization in some sources as "The Way of the Five Pecks of Rice," Wu-tou-mi Tao).

In 215, the founder's grandson Chang Lu allied the organization with a warlord and provided legitimation for his new dynasty. Thereafter, many of the most powerful clans participated in the Celestial Master organization. However, it lacked the sophisticated doctrine necessary to interest intellectuals, and it declined sharply after invaders forced its leaders southward in the early fourth century. In the eleventh century, the founder of the Cheng-i sect claimed to be the Celestial Masters' descendant, but there is no evidence of any historical connection. *See also* Chang Tao-ling; Cheng-i Taoism; chi-chiu; Tao-te ching; Wu-tou-mi Tao.

T'ien-t'ai school (tyen t*i*), a school of Chinese Buddhism named after its headquarters on Mt. T'ien-t'ai (Chin., "Heavenly Terrace"). This school taught a complex system of meditation, a way of classifying scriptures, and the threefold truth.

The founder, Chih-i (538–597), was highly regarded as a meditation master and left an encyclopedic work on the subject, *Mo-ho Chih-kuan* (Great Calming and Insight).

He also set criteria by which to classify Buddhist scriptures. Previously, the Chinese were bewildered by the disorganized and mutually contradictory mass of scriptures inherited from India. Working from a paradigm that the Buddha's teachings differed according to the period of his life, the intended audience, and the teaching method used, Chih-i was able to classify the scriptures so as to account for apparent contradictions and place the *Lotus Sutra* as the highest expression of the Buddha's enlightenment.

Finding the Madhyamaka teaching on emptiness too nihilistic, T'ien-t'ai Buddhists affirmed the threefold truth: (1) that things lack absolute existence (the truth of emptiness); (2)

that things have a relative existence based on causes and conditions (the truth of phenomenal existence); and therefore that (3) reality simultaneously affirms and transcends both the first and second premises (the truth of the Middle).

In this way they asserted that all phenomena exist and that they share a common nature and mutually interpenetrate; also all things ultimately depend upon Absolute Mind for their existence. This Mind is undifferentiated in its essence but diverse in its functioning.

The school enjoyed an independent existence until 845, when it perished in the general persecution of Buddhism. *See also* Chih-i; China, Buddhism in; doctrinal classification; Lotus Sutra; Madhyamaka.

T'ien-t'ai Shan (tyen-t*i* shahn; Chin., "Heavenly Terrace"), a mountain in Chekiang Province, China, headquarters of the T'ien-t'ai school of Chinese Buddhism and one of the "four famous mountains" for pilgrimage. *See also* Chiu-hua Shan; mountains, sacred; O-mei Shan; pilgrimage; T'ien-t'ai school; Wu-t'ai Shan.

T'ien-ti. *See* Yu-ti.

T'ien-tsun (tyen-dyuhn; Chin., "Celestial Worthy"), a Taoist title borrowed from early Buddhist translations of the Sanskrit term *bhagavat* ("Lord") and applied to high gods, particularly the anthropomorphized Tao. *See also* Tao.

tilakam (til'uh-kuhm; Skt., "mark on the forehead," "ornament"), forehead mark of special earth, sandalwood, or colored powder (usually red) worn by Hindu men and women sometimes denoting sectarian affiliation. More frequently, it is an adornment when worn by unmarried girls and women whose husbands are alive. *See also* women's rites (Hinduism).

Tilawat al-Qur'an. *See* Qur'an recitation.

Tillich, Paul Johannes (til'ikh; 1886–1965), German-American Protestant theologian who explored the interrelationship of Christianity and culture. Tillich's fundamental work, *Systematic Theology* (1951–63), illustrates his "method of correlation," relating the questions raised by the human existential situation to an interpretation of the symbols of the Christian message. *See also* ultimate concern.

time. *See* sacred space and sacred time.

Tirthankaras. *See* Jainism.

Tiruvaymoli (tihr-*oo*-vay-moh'lee; Tamil, "sacred word of mouth," "word of sacred mouth"), ninth-century Tamil poem of 1,102 verses composed by Nammalvar. After the tenth century, the Shrivaishnava community of South India held this poem to be revelation. It was one of the earliest vernacular Hindu works considered equivalent to the Vedas. The poem portrays Nammalvar's quest for union with Vishnu. Roughly a fourth of the poem speaks from the stance of a girl pining for her beloved. *Tiruvaymoli* has been the focus of ongoing oral and written commentarial tradition since the eleventh century. Selections are recited daily in Shrivaishnava homes and Vishnu temples, and the entire poem is recited during some domestic rituals. *See also* Nammalvar; Shrivaishnavism; Vishnu.

Titans (ti'tuhnz), twelve children of Sky and Earth in Greek myth. They were defeated by Zeus and hurled to Tartaros in Hesiod's *Theogony*. *See also* Hesiod.

tithing, setting aside part of one's income for sacred purposes. The biblical practice of portioning a tenth part of income for the maintenance of worship and the periodic relief of the poor has been taken over in Christianity as a recommended practice, although some groups (e.g., the Mormons) enjoin it as a strict obligation. Less strictly, "tithe" has come to signify any monetary donation made to a religious group. *See also* almsgiving; Zakat.

Ti-tsang (dee-dzuhng), the Chinese name for the Bodhisattva Kshitigarbha. *See also* Kshitigarbha.

t'i-yung (tee-yonq; Chin., "substance and function"), terms coming from Buddhism where *t'i* referred to the "inner body" or "Buddha-body," the essential nature of a person, and *yung* referred to the "outer body," the functioning phenomenal body. The terms are used in nineteenth- and twentieth-century controversies surrounding the influence of Western culture in China when the phrase "Chinese substance and Western function" became popular. *See also* acculturation.

tjuringa (choo-ring'uh; Aranda, "ceremonial object of stone or wood" or "ceremony and its lore"), typically a flat-sided slab or board, ovoid or elongated, ranging from a few inches to several feet in length; used in Australian aboriginal cultures on ceremonial occasions. *Tjuringas* may be plain or have patterns of varying degrees of intricacy incised on their surfaces. In some cases they are painted or rubbed with ochre and fat. They are invariably treated with respect, and often kept secret from all persons who have not attained a suitable degree of initiation. In most aboriginal societies they are never shown to women, even though some tjuringas are said to be owned by women or to originate from mythical ancestresses of the Dreamtime. When not in use they are stored in secret hiding places. Each tjuringa is a tangible reminder of the primordial epoch because it stands for or refers to one of the Dreaming beings who were active on earth at that time; moreover, a tjuringa that is believed to have originated in those days, as many are, is likely to be accepted as containing something of the essence of the being concerned. Other tjuringas are of human manufacture. Tjuringas are retrieved from their hiding places for ceremonial occasions, when they are handled with a care that frequently borders on veneration; their revelation to novices is an essential part of the initiatory process. In addition to their function as objects in which mythic and spiritual significance are condensed, tjuringas have a politico-legal significance as tokens of the rightful claim of a person or group to a place, story, or ceremony, for in aboriginal societies cosmology and power structure are inseparable. *See also* Australian and Pacific traditional religions; Dreaming, the; sacred, profane.

TLV mirror, a Han period (206 B.C.–A.D. 220) Chinese bronze mirror pattern with four L's and inverted V's inside a circle facing four T's sticking out from an inner square; the pattern is a *mandala* (cosmographic diagram) of cosmic harmony found in tombs and also a static imitation of a favorable prognostication on a divining board. *See also* divination; mandala.

tobacco and hallucinogens, substances used by traditional peoples to confer power or ability, often with respect to healing. Illness is perceived as personal, social, or cosmic imbalance, and both diagnosis and cure must address the entire situation out of which imbalance has arisen. Treatment often includes using power or ability to resolve conflicts within the patient, or among the patient and spirit beings or other members of the community, in addition to applying physical remedies. Tobacco and hallucinogens are medicine because they impart to a person the power to communicate and interact with the world of the unseen.

The tobacco plant may be the oldest cultivated in the Americas, and it certainly enjoys the widest ritual use of any plant. Throughout the

Americas tobacco has been smoked by pipe, cigar, and cigarette, blown, snuffed, drunk, imbibed through the nose, chewed, eaten, sucked, licked, and injected rectally. It has been used alone and in conjunction with hallucinogenic plants in shamanic curing, to purify, and to alleviate fatigue, hunger, and thirst.

Tobacco is an important link to the spiritual world. In many traditions tobacco is understood to have been given to human beings by the gods, for whom it is food. Since the gods kept none for themselves, they need human beings to feed them this special plant. This is often accomplished by humans smoking it. Tobacco establishes a relationship of reciprocity between humans and spirits.

For the Venezuelan Warao, tobacco smoke is central to religious life. The Warao employ no other hallucinogen or narcotic but produce ecstatic trance by ingesting massive amounts of tobacco smoke. Warao shamans smoke continually from cane cigars up to two feet long to ensure abundant food for the gods. They travel on spirit journeys over bridges made of smoke, and after death they reside in houses of smoke. These shamans can not only cure, they can launch illness by blowing it through their cane cigars.

Hallucinogens are substances that produce states of altered consciousness. From the perspectives of many religious cultures, hallucinogens allow a person to experience a hidden reality. Practitioners of many religions communicate and interact with the world of unseen powers to gain power, diagnose and cure illness, prophesy, divine the location of stolen objects, and confirm mythic reality.

Many more plant species have hallucinogenic properties than have been used. And although botanically hallucinogens are quite evenly distributed globally, indigenous Americans (particularly Middle and South) have taken greater advantage of these resources than have the inhabitants of the Eastern Hemisphere.

Banisteriopsis caapi, also called "vine of the souls" or *yaje*, is widely used in South America, as are *Virola* and *Anadenanthera*. Use of cactus *Lophophora williamsii* (peyote), *Rivea corymbosa* (morning glory), and a number of hallucinogenic mushrooms (*Psilocybe mexicana* in particular) was severely persecuted by the Spanish Catholics but has endured among several Mexican Indian cultures. Peyote is also widely used in the United States today by the Native American Church. Datura, popularly termed jimsonweed, has been used throughout the Americas, and several Plains Indian tribes have employed the mescal bean (*Sophora secundiflora*) in ritual. The *amanita muscaria*, or flyagaric mushroom, was once used throughout northern Eurasia and is still used in Siberia. Some believe it to be the divine *soma* of the ancient Indo-Europeans. *See also* healing; medium; Native American Church; pipe, sacred; psychoactive plants; Santidade; shamanism; smoke; soma.

Todaiji (toh-dah-ee-jee), one of the seven major Japanese temples of Nara, built by order of Emperor Shomu in 745. The monastery is the site of a great Buddha (Daibutsu), dedicated in 752, and the main ordination platform in Nara-period Japan. It served as an important site for the six Nara schools and headquarters of the Kegon school. From the ninth century onward, Shingon school monks also frequented it. Through patronage and large landholdings, it became a major political force in medieval Japan. Although the temple burned several times, the Daibutsu and its hall were always rebuilt. *See also* Kegon school; Nara schools; Shingon-shu.

T'oegye. *See* Yi Hwang.

tokoyo no kuni (toh-koh-yoh noh *koo*-nee; Jap., "eternal world"), a miraculous Japanese realm of immortality, prosperity, and fertility beyond the sea. According to folk religious belief, divine visitors (*marebito*) travel from there at harvesttime and New Year's to restore vitality to the world. *See also* cosmology; Japanese folk religion; Japanese religions (festal cycle); marebito.

toloache. *See* datura.

Tominaga Nakamoto (toh-mee-nah-gah nah-kah-moh-toh; 1715–46), Japanese Confucian who advanced critical theories about the historical development of Buddhism, Confucianism, and Shinto long before such modern approaches had been introduced from the West. His major writings are *Emerging from Meditation* and *Writings of an Old Man*.

Tonghak. *See* Religion of the Heavenly Way.

Tong'ilgyo. *See* Korea, new religions in.

Tongmaengje. *See* Korea (festal cycle).

T'ongpulgyo. *See* comprehensive Buddhism.

tongues, speaking in. *See* glossolalia.

tonsure, cutting of the hair to signify entrance into Roman Catholic clerical life. Monastic tonsures feature a thin band of hair (the monastic crown) around an otherwise shaven skull.

Tooth Relic, in Buddhism famous relic of the Buddha. Said to have been brought to Sri Lanka in the fourth century, the tooth became a symbol of legitimate sovereignty over the island. It is presently enshrined in the Dalada Maligava in Kandy where it attracts many pilgrims and is the object of a daily cult. *See also* Buddhism (festal cycle); pilgrimage; relics.

The July to August procession (Asala Perahera) of a replica of the Buddha's tooth relic in Kandy, Sri Lanka, 1970. The replica is contained in an elaborate casket atop the largest elephant, "Raja."

Torah (toh'rah; Heb., "instruction"), God's revelation to Moses at Mt. Sinai. The generative symbol of Judaism, Torah stands for God's revelation to Israel, the holy people. "The Torah" refers initially to the Pentateuch, the Five Books of Moses; then, by extension, to the whole of the Hebrew Scriptures or Old Testament; then to the "whole Torah," written and oral. The word for *Judaism* in Judaism therefore is "the Torah." By the end of the fifth and sixth centuries the word *Torah* lost its capital T, becoming *torah,* meaning "that which has the status of The Torah," hence, anything that is authoritative as God's will for Israel. What for nearly a millennium had been a particular scroll or book thus came to serve as a symbol of an entire system. When a rabbi spoke of torah, he meant not only a particular object, a scroll and its contents, but a distinctive and well-defined worldview and way of life. The word torah had come to stand for something one does. Now knowledge of the Torah promised not merely information about what people were supposed to do but ultimate redemption or salvation.

Meanings of Torah: The word Torah bears these six meanings: (1) The Torah can refer to a partic-

ular thing, a scroll containing divinely revealed words. (2) The Torah may further denote revelation, not as an object but as a corpus of doctrine. (3) When one "does Torah," the disciple "studies" or "learns," and the master "teaches," Torah. Hence, while the word Torah never appears as a verb, it does refer to an act. (4) The word also bears a quite separate sense, torah as category, classification, or corpus of rules, e.g., "the torah of driving a car" is a generic usage entirely acceptable to some documents. (5) The word Torah very commonly refers to a status, distinct from and above another status, e.g., "teachings of Torah" as against "teachings of scribes." For the two Talmuds that distinction is absolutely critical to the entire hermeneutic enterprise. (6) Finally, the word refers to a source of salvation, often fully worked out in stories about how the individual and the nation will be saved through Torah. In general, the sense of the word *salvation* is not complicated. It is simply salvation in the way in which Deuteronomy and the Deuteronomic historians understand it: kings who do what God wants win battles; those who do not, lose. So too here, people who study and do Torah are saved from sickness and death, and the way Israel can save itself from its condition of degradation also is through Torah.

Torah as Symbol: In rabbinical literature of late antiquity, the word Torah connotes a broad range of distinct categories of noun and verb, concrete fact and abstract relationship alike, as well as "revealed truth." Accordingly, in Judaism Torah stands for a kind of human being. It connotes a social status and a sort of social group. It refers to a type of social relationship. It further denotes a legal status and differentiates among legal norms. If people wanted to explain how they would be saved, they would use the word Torah. If they wished to sort out their relationships with Gentiles, they would use the word Torah. Torah stood for salvation and accounted for Israel's this-worldly condition and the hope, for both individual and nation alike, of life in the world to come. The Torah symbolized the whole, at once and entire.

The exhaustive expression of the system as a whole in the word Torah explains why the definitive ritual of classical Judaism consisted in studying the Torah. That is why the definitive myth explained that one who studied Torah would become holy, like Moses "our rabbi," and like God, in whose image humanity was made and whose Torah provided the plan and the model for what God wanted of a humanity created in God's image. The framers of the system of Judaism found in the Torah that image of God to which Israel should aspire and to which the sage in fact conformed.

The Development of the Concept: The most important initiative in broadening the meaning of the word Torah occurs in tractate *Abot,* ca. 250, which is attached to the Mishnah as its principal apologetic. There the meaning of "the Torah" as a particular book of revelation is joined by a second sense. In *Abot,* Torah is instrumental. The figure of the sage, his ideals and conduct, forms the goal, focus, and center. The authorship of tractate *Abot* regards study of Torah as what a sage does. The substance of Torah is what a sage says, whether or not the saying relates to scriptural revelation. The sages in tractate *Abot* usually do not quote verses of Scripture and explain them, nor do they speak in God's name. Yet, if a sage says something, it falls into the classification of Torah. *Abot* treats Torah learning as symptomatic, an indicator of the status of the sage, and is the first document of the doctrine that the sage embodies the Torah and is a holy man, like Moses "our rabbi," in the likeness and image of God.

The next major step in the expansion of the meaning of the word Torah is taken by the authorship of the Talmud of the Land of Israel, which treats the Mishnah as equivalent to Scripture. This view is stated by R. Zeira in the name of R. Yohanan: "If a law comes to hand and you do not know its nature, do not discard it for another one, for lo, many laws were stated to Moses at Sinai, and all of them have been embedded in the Mishnah" (Yerushalmi *Hagigah* 1:7.V.B). The Mishnah now is claimed to contain statements made by God to Moses. The passage proceeds to assert that part of the Torah was written down, and part was preserved in memory and transmitted orally. That distinction must encompass the Mishnah, thus explaining its origin as part of the Torah. Hence, a single Torah was revealed and handed down at Mt. Sinai in two forms, part in writing, part orally.

Torah Study as Salvific: The Yerushalmi also holds that because people observed the rules of the Torah, they expected to be saved. If they did not observe, they accepted their punishment. The Torah stands for something more than revelation and life of study, and the sage now appears as a holy, not merely a learned, man because his knowledge of the Torah has transformed him. Accordingly, the word Torah forms the centerpiece of a theory of Israel's history and an account of the teleology of the entire system. Torah ceases to constitute a specific thing or even a category or classification when stories about studying the Torah yield not a judgment

as to status (i.e., praise for the learned man) but promise for supernatural blessing now and salvation in time to come.

To the rabbis the principal salvific deed was to "study Torah," by which they meant memorizing Torah sayings by constant repetition, and, for some sages, profound analytic inquiry into the meaning of those sayings. The innovation is that this act of "study of Torah" imparts supernatural power of a material character. For example, Torah formulas could ward off the angel of death, accomplish other kinds of miracles as well, and serve as incantations. Mastery of Torah transformed the man engaged in Torah learning into a supernatural figure. Through transformation of the Torah from a concrete thing to a symbol, a Torah scroll could be compared to a man of Torah, a rabbi. Once the principle had been established that salvation would come from keeping God's will in general, as Israelite holy men had insisted for so many centuries, it was a small step for rabbis to identify their particular corpus of learning, the Mishnah and associated sayings, with God's will expressed in Scripture, the universally acknowledged medium of revelation. *See also* Judaism (authoritative texts and their interpretation); Mishnah, the; rabbi; revelation; Talmud; Torah study.

Torah scroll, the traditional text of the Pentateuch written on parchment from a ritually clean animal that is the central ritual object of Judaism. Though differences exist between the Ashkenazi (Occidental) and Sephardi (Oriental) customs, in either case the Torah scroll, housed in the ark, is treated with the utmost veneration, and every effort is made to beautify it with different forms of ornamentation. In the case of the Sephardic and other Eastern traditions, the Torah is put into a wooden box decorated with leather or metal. According to Ashkenazi custom, the scroll is covered with a mantle through the top of which protrude the two staves called "trees of life." Upon each of these staves are two finials, and on top of these is the crown. On the day (Simhat Torah) when the cycle reading of the Torah is completed, the scroll is crowned like a bride, recalling the day of revelation at Sinai that itself was likened in the classical rabbinic sources to a wedding celebration. *See also* ark in Judaism; scribe (Judaism); synagogue; Torah.

Torah study (*talmud torah,* Heb., "Torah study"), in Judaism, the study of Torah as an act of worship.

Torah study has been a form of worship in Judaism for nearly two thousand years. Although the practice of Torah study has been changed

Jews in Tel Aviv, Israel, celebrate a newly completed Torah scroll. The scroll is dressed in an embroidered mantle. Projecting through the top of the mantle are the two rods on which the scroll is rolled, covered by two silver finials (*rimmonim*). The poles carried by the men support a wedding canopy (*chuppah*) traditionally held over a new scroll when it is brought into a synagogue for the first time (1970s).

and adapted to fit the circumstances of Jewish life wherever Jews have lived, it has always derived from the rabbinic concept of *talmud torah.*

Definitions: To describe Torah study, one must define the meaning of each term. The meaning of the term *Torah* grows during the rabbinic period. Early on—e.g., in the second-century law code of the Mishnah—Torah has both the specific meaning of the first five books of the Hebrew Bible (Genesis, Exodus, Leviticus, Numbers, Deuteronomy) and the general meaning of the Hebrew Bible as a whole. By the end of the rabbinic period, in the sixth-century Babylonian Talmud, religious authorities had expanded this definition to include the Mishnah itself as well as the interpretation and application of the texts' regulations and principles by learned scholars.

Although the importance of study is mentioned in the Wisdom literature before 70, its identification as worship does not appear until the rabbinic period. Study encompasses several different activities. It focuses primarily on reading and analysis of texts. But it also includes discussing Torah issues with others and mediating on matters of Torah when the mind is otherwise unoccupied—such as during a journey. The central concern is that an individual should focus attention on Torah whenever possible.

Benefits of Torah Study: The benefits of Torah study lie on two levels, individual and national. For the individual, Torah study brings one into the presence of God. And, indeed, frequent study brings one permanently into God's presence through the acquisition of a place in the "world to come." Torah study also has this-worldly benefits. It heals the body's aches and pains and prevents the individual from falling into sin. It furthermore provides the person who becomes adept at it—such as a learned rabbi—with divine protection and sometimes even supernatural power.

The most important benefit of Torah study occurs at the national level, for it brings about the national restoration of Israel. Whereas sacrifice once served to maintain Israel's relationship to God, Torah study now accomplishes that task. Indeed, study is even more important than sacrifice, and for good reason; study is seen in God's eyes as rebuilding the now-destroyed Temple and redeeming the Jews from the nations among which they are scattered. This will happen when the Messiah comes to restructure the world order and raise the people of Israel to their rightful place as God's favored nation. Torah study thus provides the impetus propelling history toward its final goal of saving the people of Israel.

torii (toh-ree-ee; Jap., "bird perch"), symbolic gates marking the sacred boundaries around or in front of a Shinto shrine or other sacred Shinto site. The *torii* has become a primary symbol for Shinto itself. *See also* sacred space and sacred time; Shinto; shrine.

Tosefta (toh-sef-tah'; Heb., "supplements"), a compilation of Supplements to the rabbinic text, the Mishnah. Collected in ca. 200 to 300, the document glosses, expands, or supplies freestanding materials in the language and style of the Mishnah but independent of its content. *See also* Mishnah, the.

totem (toh'tem; Ojibwa *ototeman,* "he is a relative of mine"), nonhuman entity, usually but not always an animal, that symbolizes the spiritual essence, and often the first ancestor, of a group. Totems characteristically inspire strong emotions among those whose groups they represent. Totemic groups—lineages, clans, moieties, etc.—have existed among many peoples around the world, although they are usually associated with tribal societies, as in aboriginal Australia and Native North America. Clan totems such as bear, turtle, and panther seem somewhat typical, although plants and occasionally oddities such as smallpox are also found.

Totems have been central to the development of general theories in both comparative religion and anthropology. The widespread occurrence of totems once inspired speculation that totemism was a universal evolutionary stage in the development of religion. Scholars postulated, for example, an animistic totemic age following belief in demons and preceding ancestor veneration. Later scholars recognized that totemism did not form a unified phenomenon. Theorists had erroneously grouped together diverse, culturally specific systems for relating human and natural worlds. Subsequent explanations for the widespread occurrence of totems have stressed their roles in focusing social solidarity, in defining groups, and in assuring successful environmental adaptation.

More recently, however, anthropologists have argued convincingly that totems are widely distributed because they are intellectually "good to think" rather than pragmatically good to eat. According to these investigators, all totems enter into conceptual systems of differences. Totems stand for opposing social categories of which they are emblems, and group A is to group B as totem A is to totem B. Totemism may tell more about the structure of human cognition than about the universal origins of religion. *See also* Australian and Pacific traditional religions; North America, traditional religions in; origin of religion.

totem pole (toh'tem pohl), a large, half-round cedar pole worked in high relief, usually representing supernatural beings, carved and erected by the Native peoples of the Northwest Coast of North America. These poles, found among Tlingit, Haida, Tsimshian, Bella Coola, Kwakiutl, Nootka, and other nearby peoples, are of several varieties: memorial and mortuary poles, house posts, and poles marking special privileges or commemorating particular people or events. In most cases the sculptures, usually painted, represent intertwined spiritual beings in animal, monster, and human forms, symbolizing kin-group histories and statuses. So-called totem poles—a misnomer, in fact—are frequently compared to European heraldic crests. *See also* North America, traditional religions in; totem.

tradition (Lat. *tradere,* "to hand over"), the transmission of received teaching. In some theological systems, there is a perceived tension between scripture and tradition; in other systems, they are held to be complementary. *See also* bida; exegesis; fundamentalism; hadith; Traditionists.

Judaism: Jewish doctrine holds that at Sinai two Torahs were given and received, one written, i.e., the text of scripture, and one oral, i.e., the large body of detailed elaboration of law and lore. The written Torah could not serve as a system of law without expansion and specification. The Torah prohibits labor on the Sabbath but does not specify which activities constitute prohibited labors. It speaks of marriage and divorce but gives no account of the procedures for consecrating a marriage or ending it. With few exceptions, the law in the written Torah is stated in general terms. Established Jewish doctrine teaches that from the beginning there was an oral tradition that accompanied the written law and gave it specificity.

That oral tradition is held to be the teaching of Moses transmitted through the generations without interruption. The point is expressed in a text that states, "Moses received the Torah at Sinai and handed it over to Joshua; Joshua handed it over to the elders, the elders to the prophets, and the prophets to the men of the Great Assembly" (Mishnah *Abot* 1:1). We have here the key Hebrew terms for receiving the teaching (*kabbalah*) and transmitting the teaching (*massoret*). The messengers of each generation are noted in the official history of the tradition. They are understood to be the conveyors both of the correct text of the written Torah and the elaborated teaching of the oral Torah. In this way God's law is handed down from generation to generation. The oral teaching is recorded in the Talmud and the entire body of associated rabbinic literature. The correct text of scripture and the correct rules of the law are determined only by the received traditions, not by an independent study of the written Torah. *See also* Judaism (authoritative texts and their interpretation); Torah.

Christianity: In Christian faith, tradition is the act of receiving God's revelation in Christ and securing that revelation for subsequent generations. The Greek word for tradition (*paradosis*) is used by Paul to describe his instructions to the church concerning what he had learned from the Lord concerning, e.g., the resurrection (1 Corinthians 15:3) or the celebration of the Eucharist (1 Corinthians 11:23). In subsequent church usage, the word signifies the authentic preservation of the apostolic faith as it is reflected in the preaching of the gospel and its expression in the creeds and usages of the church. The precise relationship between scripture and tradition has been a historically divisive issue between Catholicism and the churches of the Reformation.

A less technical but popular use of the word signifies those practices and usages common to a specific Christian body that distinguish it in some manner. In the Orthodox and Roman Catholic churches, for instance, there is a different tradition concerning married clergy, the manner of choosing bishops, etc., just as the Baptist church has a long tradition of emphasizing the separation of church and state in contrast to the Church of England, which has close church-state ties. *See also* Bible, Christian; Reformation, Protestant; sola scriptura.

traditional religions, Western influence on, the ways in which the Western presence has influenced the process and content of traditional religion. The introduction of written language, especially by missionaries, has profoundly affected the process of tradition, by which beliefs, practices, and attitudes are passed on from generation to generation in a community that assigns authority to the words of the elders. Literacy often shifts authority to the written word and to those who can read, usually the younger generation. The spread of literacy is closely associated with Christianity (and in some cases, Islam); to attend school often means to become a Christian. The children replace the elders as authorities, at least in matters relating to the modern world.

When traditional oral material is put into writing as novels, plays, or poetry, the resulting literature comes to be seen as the property of its composer rather than of the community that preserved and transmitted it. This transition from the communal to the individual may be the most important Western influence on traditional culture, including religion.

The content of the religion of a traditional society is sometimes spoken of in the ethnographic present, as if it had always been what the first missionary or anthropologist reported. The idea of traditional culture and religion as static is largely due to the Western need for unchanging entities to study, govern, or convert. In fact, change in content is normal in traditional religion and culture. Ideas and practices that lose their relevance are forgotten, and others replace them and are included in what is transmitted. This process continues but in a new context. In some areas there has been a process of feedback, by which early written accounts influence the community's self-understanding. If the written account has become the authority, the religion is no longer considered traditional but scriptural. However, often the written account becomes an indirect authority that influences the content of the tradition by being incorporated into the ongoing process.

Some aspects of traditional religion appear to derive from scriptural religion, but the evidence for such incorporation is not definitive. For example, the concept of a supreme God is now accepted as part of the traditional religion in most African societies, but was it part of the tradition before the influence of Islam and Christianity? Although in some cases the new surely has been incorporated into the old, one cannot be sure because no written records are available from before that time.

There has also been a reverse development in which the old is incorporated into the new. An attempt has been made to preserve elements of traditional content in a Westernized context, in which the process of tradition has largely been lost. In Africa the majority of native Christians and Muslims continue to seek the help of traditional healers. Belief in witchcraft is especially prevalent in urban areas, where people of various ethnic groups live side by side. Elements of tradition enter into new religions along with influences from scriptural religions. In churches of Western origin there is often a conscious attempt at indigenization, that is, the use of traditional content in theology and worship. Some educated members consciously seek to revive ancient rituals. The result may be called *neotraditionalism*—a term that designates a situation in which traditional content is preserved without the process of tradition.

The process and the content of traditional religion are closely interrelated. While specific beliefs and rituals may change, tradition is inescapably tied to a sense of communal solidarity. When either one is lost as a result of Western influence, the other goes with it.

It would now be difficult, if not impossible, to find any traditional society where people's understanding of who they are, individually and collectively, and what their tradition involves, has not been influenced at least indirectly by the impact of the West. This does not necessarily mean that traditional religion no longer exists; it still exists wherever the primary authority is in the living word of the elders within the community. *See also* acculturation; mission or missionary movements; modernization; nativistic movements; oral tradition; revitalization movements; traditional peoples, religions of.

Traditionists (Arab. *ahl al-hadith*), Muslims who defer to the authority of Muhammad and his closest companions in matters of religious interpretation and practice over later interpretations, customs, and rational arguments. The Traditionists formed an early, pervasive, and influential movement in Islamic thought and practice that has remained loosely defined. The ninth-century jurist and collector of prophetic sayings (*hadith*), Ahmad ibn Hanbal, became a champion of Traditionist views and an inspiration for Traditionist movements down to the present day. *See also* hadith; Hanbalite; Muslim Brotherhood.

Spirit-mediums link arms to catch a woman in trance during an Afro-Brazilian Umbanda ritual in Rio de Janeiro, Brazil. Having spent the night singing and dancing to drums, the woman has been possessed by the spirit of Pombagira (the Whirling Dove, or Prostitute), the female counterpart of the dangerous trickster Exu.

trance, one of the most common religious altered states of consciousness. It is characterized by extreme disassociation often to the point of appearing unconscious. Trance is a characteristic of ecstatic religions. *See also* altered states of consciousness; ecstasy; medium; shaman.

transcendence, divine attribute, existing above and independently of the material world.

Transcendental Meditation, a neo-Hindu meditative practice of quiet contemplation, taught by Maharishi Mahesh Yogi (b. 1911) through his World Plan Executive Council.

The practice of Transcendental Meditation, also known as the Science of Creative Intelligence or simply TM, is based in classic Hindu religious practice, namely, the attempt to calm the perturbations of the physical body through simple acts of concentration in order to elevate the spiritual self. A special hallmark of TM is the use of a word or short phrase, called the *mantra,* which is repeated quietly or silently as an aid to increased concentration. The meditator who undertakes serious study is promised not only clarity of thought and residual tranquillity from the perception of the world's underlying truth but also increased creativity, productivity in work or study, and overall well-being.

Beginning in the late 1950s, the Maharishi offered this simplified practice of meditation, drawing worldwide attention to his International Meditation Society and his plan to engender a new universal spirituality based in ancient Hindu religious concepts. His popularity burgeoned when members of the Beatles rock music group and other celebrities from the West discovered Transcendental Meditation. The World Plan, announced in 1972, inaugurated the expansion of the teaching organization so as to reach all humanity. Since the late 1970s, however, interest in TM has declined considerably, due, in varying degrees, to declining interest in Asian religions among Western religious seekers, reduced credibility concerning the increasingly fantastic claims of the results of TM, and limits on its access to public institutions in the United States. *See also* Maharishi Mahesh Yogi; North America, new religions in; World Plan Executive Council.

transfiguration of Jesus (Gk. *metamorphosis*), New Testament incident in which Jesus is transformed from human to divine form and displays himself to three disciples on a high mountain (Matthew 17:1–14). *See also* shape shifting.

RELIGIONS OF TRADITIONAL PEOPLES

The religions of traditional peoples comprise the beliefs and practices of people who live in small-scale tribal cultures, particularly in Africa, the Americas, Australia, Oceania, and Indonesia, who until the colonial expansions of the last half-millennium, were largely uninfluenced by the cultures of Europe and Asia.

TERMINOLOGY AND CONCEPTION

Each of the cultures designated as "traditional" has a conception of the world (a cosmology) expressed primarily in terms of a local landscape that extends to celestial, peripheral, and subterranean regions. Each of these cultures distinguishes itself as a people apart from other known peoples. Their worldviews are often rich and complex in detail.

In none of these worldviews is there any concept corresponding to Western connotations of the term *traditional*. None of these peoples would describe their cultures as small in scale or uninfluenced by European or Asian cultures. Nor do any propose a common identity among themselves and all other traditional peoples. The category "traditional" is our conception, not theirs, and realizing this serves to warn us about the limits and character of the knowledge we hold of these peoples.

For much of the twentieth century there has been a growing self-consciousness about what this conglomerate of religious cultures should be called. Terms such as *savage* and *primitive,* once widely used to describe traditional cultures, have been strongly discouraged because they tend categorically either to glorify or denigrate. These terms have persisted, although the bias denoted by the terms is often qualified by placing the terms in quotation marks. *Nonliterate* (or more positively, *exclusively oral*) and *traditional* are more widely used, yet they bear virtually the same prejudices as the other terms.

Behind all of the proposed terms is the conception that there are two categories of culture and religion. One category is tied to the intellectual, cultural, and religious heritage of the West. Though there are great differences among this group, there is a commonness in scale and character among the expansive historical cultures developed in Eurasia that have, particularly during the last five hundred years, greatly expanded throughout the world. The small-scale, usually technologically less advanced, cultures encountered during this expansion were seen as belonging to a different class, type, or kind, usually but not always evaluated as inferior. Even the need for a term by which to call them rests on the presumption that there are two kinds of cultures and religions: Western and "other." Any of the terms chosen, from *savage* to *traditional,* are invariably and unavoidably comparative; they reflect a presupposed contrast between "us" and "them." By calling them primitive we affirm ourselves as civilized. By calling them nonliterate we affirm the importance we attribute to writing. By calling them traditional, meaning a culture uninfluenced by the West, we suggest they are exempt from history and change or that these are of little interest to them. What defines these peoples and their religions for us is something they are thought to lack, but we have.

The issue is one of conception, not terminology. Each of these cultures and their religions might be approached as an integral and complete system on its own terms and in light of its own history. For a few of these cultures such attempts have been made, but the knowledge gained of these cultures is shaped by the expectations of the viewer's conception. The subtle, almost transparent, influence is revealed even by the fact that, as a rule, the religions of traditional peoples have been studied by anthropologists, while the worldwide historical religions have been studied by scholars of religion. A deterrent to considering each of these religions on its own terms is their sheer number: there are thousands of cultures, each with its own language, and few with written histories or religious writings. These conceptions prevent viewers from seeing the cultures clearly.

The position on which all consideration of the religions of traditional peoples must rest is the awareness that virtually everything known about these religions is, to a significant degree, a product of the conceptions that underlie the terms by which we have designated these peoples and their religions. Put differently, what is known of the religions of traditional peoples is influenced by the history of encounter with them. These religious traditions are known almost wholly in terms of how they differ from Western culture, and almost always in terms of something they lack. This lack is not always viewed negatively. Scholars from Jean-Jacques Rousseau to Mircea Eliade have characterized these peoples as pristine, pure, untainted by the messiness of civilization, unburdened by the experience of history. They are noble in their savagery; they are sound ecologists because they live close to nature; they are religious by virtue of their primitiveness. The lack of civilization, the lack of technology, the lack of history may be glorified.

The premises underlying modern anthropology and the study of the religions of traditional peoples are inseparable from the ideas that these peoples represent either what Westerners once were, in the primitive stages of development, or that they hold some pristine knowledge that Westerners, tainted by development and history, have lost and need to regain.

Every bit of information about these peoples is shaped, at least in part, by the viewers and their expectations. One will and must always see the reflections of the viewers in even those reports concerning traditional peoples that appear to be most objectively stated. It is impossible to overcome or avoid the shaping influences of the conceptions underlying all that is known of these religions. Despite the desire to learn about the religions of traditional peoples in their own terms, this endeavor is never free of our own need to define ourselves—our culture and our religion—by comparison to them. The positive and creative approach demands a movement back and forth between both interests; neither one can be denied.

ACTION AND PERFORMANCE

As we approach the religions of traditional peoples, what we see is, in part, what we look for. Even the term *religion* is a case in point. No traditional people is known to distinguish a category that corresponds with the term religion. Further, no matter how we phrase our definition of religion, the term is effectively defined by the kinds of materials we consider religious or reflecting information pertinent to religion. Religion is studied largely by examining written documents—scripture, theological writings, histories, doctrine. In such documents scholars look for distinguishing beliefs, historical events, institutions, and practices. Traditional peoples do not write. Until quite recently, when orthographic systems were introduced making alphabetical rendering of speech possible, the spoken languages of traditional peoples were not written. Thus, traditional peoples produce no scriptures, theological writings, histories, or doctrines. Because they have no written documents, traditional cultures have been assessed as having no worthwhile religions. Their religions might have been overlooked because of the way viewers attempt to look at them.

An alternative perspective is possible. When traditional peoples compare their orality to writing, they stress the immediacy, vitality, control, and sociability of speaking, in contrast to what they understand as the abstraction, stagnation, and depersonalization of writing. This overdraws the contrast, for writing may also be immediate, vital, and enormously creative, and provides a great service in connecting people and events that are historically and spatially distant from one another. It is consistent with the nature of speech that we see it as action and performance, yet writing, though often thought of as a static written or printed page, may also be seen as action and performance. A more fruitful approach to studying the religions of traditional peoples can be achieved by focusing on action and performance, that is, upon the various forms of the enactment of religion. While equally suitable to the religions of all cultures, this approach is especially productive when applied to traditional cultures, because it makes apparent the religions of peoples whose languages are not written.

Anthropologist Colin Turnbull lived for a time with the BaMbuti Pygmy people in the Ituri Forest of Zaire in Africa (*The Forest People: A Study of the Pygmies of the Congo*). While there he participated in a several-month-long ritual. Nightly the men would assemble around a common fire to sing and feast. A voice from the surrounding forest responded to their singing. According to the Pygmies, the forest itself, which not only made the sounds of wild animals, but sang the most beautiful songs, was making the reply to the men's singing. Turnbull learned that the sounds of the forest were made by means of a tubelike trumpet carved from the molimo tree. Turnbull was invited to run with the Pygmies through the forest to the resting place of one of these molimo trumpets. When they reached the trumpet, Turnbull not only saw that it was a piece of metal drainpipe, he also watched as the young Pygmies took turns making rude flatulent noises with the trumpet, prompting uncontrollable laughter among them. Turnbull was shocked and disappointed at the Pygmy actions. However, in time, the Pygmies taught him that what really mattered to them was the sound that the trumpet was capable of producing, and that the trumpet was primarily instrumental to the religious performance. This lesson taught to Turnbull may serve as a metaphor for how anyone may more fully appreciate the religions of traditional peoples.

Two Navajo shamans at work on a sandpainting. This particular design is that of the Moon Painting—to be used in the two-day Sun-Moon curing ceremony. Photographed in Monument Valley, Arizona (ca. 1938).

The sandpaintings of the Navajos and other Native American tribes, quite beautiful in appearance, are more fully appreciated as instruments of healing than as works of art. A person suffering an illness sits in the middle of a Navajo sandpainting, constructed on the floor of a ceremonial lodge. In a ritual act that literally destroys the painting, sands are removed from the figures in the picture and applied to the sufferer. In this act of ritual identification, the sufferer is re-created and given life as represented by the forces of the figures depicted. Sandpaintings are used in ritual processes that are meant to affect the world. It is what they do, not what they express or mean, that is most important.

The vitality commonly attributed by traditional peoples to verbal art forms may be illustrated by the statement attributed to the Eskimo shaman and hunter Orpingalik, "All my being is song and I sing as I draw breath."

Songs are understood to have power when sung, prayers when intoned, names when uttered, stories when told. The content of these verbal forms may be studied, but interpretations are incomplete unless one also comprehends them as enactments and performances.

Rituals are complex composites of song, prayer, story, dance, movement, mask, costume, and other paraphernalia conjoined in a designated space and performed for a specific purpose. Whether a rite of passage, healing ritual, calendrical event, or sustenance rite, the ritual process is the primary enactment and performance of the religious life.

Rather than seeking an articulation of belief and doctrine, one may better understand the religions of traditional peoples by looking at people's actions and what these actions accomplish, even as ways of being and orienting in the world.

TIME AND SPACE

Religion has often been understood in terms of time and space. Religious activities are performed in designated locations (churches, temples, shrines) and times (sabbath, holiday, festival). For no people are space and time simply homogeneous, that is, of equal value. The distinctions any people make within time and space reflect their understanding of the world they live in.

Almost inseparable from the Western intellectual and religious heritage is the assumption that particular temporal and spatial designations are inherently religious. In space, it is the center; in time, the origin. Religion is commonly seen as that which ritually orients a society to their sacred center following a mythic pattern established in the beginning. Based on this perspective, the religions of traditional peoples are often held up as exemplary of the religious. Traditional peoples are recognized as living according to their stories, or myths, which tell of the precedent-setting acts of the gods or ancestors who gave origin to their world and way of life. Rituals are seen as formal actions, performed on the charter of myth, through which human beings continue the sanctioned actions established in the beginning, actions that center, orient, and thereby give meaning to their lives. Myth recounts the paradigmatic creations of the beginning, and ritual (encompassing virtually all of life) replicates these paradigms. Since the religions of traditional peoples are known almost exclusively through their myths and rituals and since the history of traditional peoples is difficult to assess, the almost inevitable implication of this point of view is that they are religious par excellence.

In this view, traditional peoples are distinguished because they live according to models (that is, traditions) established by creators and ancestors; this is the rationale for the term *traditional*. This view denies traditional peoples the experience of history; it denies that they have changed, advanced, or grown over time. It ignores that they have faced adversity and unexpected challenge and managed it successfully. None of these implications is defensible, least of all the implication that nontraditional peoples have no traditions.

Among the most beautiful of all Navajo songs are those that describe the horse:

> Its feet are made of mirage.
> Its gait was a rainbow.
> Its bridle of sun strings.
> Its heart was made of red stone.
> Its intestines were made of water of all kinds.
> Its tail of black rain.
> Its mane was a cloud with a little rain.
> Distant lightning composed its ears.
> A big spreading twinkling star formed its eye and striped its face.
> Its lower legs were white.
> At night beads formed its lips.
> White shell formed its teeth.
> A black flute was put into its mouth for a trumpet.
> Its belly was made of dawn, one side white, one side black.

When sung these songs have the power to heal. Nothing is more representative of the traditional Navajo view of perfection and order than the horse. Yet horses were introduced to North America by the Spanish only four centuries ago. The Navajos, who had migrated from western Canada into the American Southwest only a short time before the Spanish arrived, adapted their way of life to the power of the horse and created themselves and their world in its image. While the horse in Navajo religious conception is cosmic and primordial, historically it is a relatively recent acquisition. So are many of the physical elements strongly identified with the Navajo, who, as a people, are considered among the most traditional in North America: the southwestern desert landscape was occupied a few centuries ago, sheepherding and corn farming came after that, weaving was learned from the neighboring Pueblos, and silver work was introduced by the Spanish. To show that the Navajos' most traditional concepts are relatively recent acquisitions is not to denigrate the Navajo, but to document the extent to which what appears most traditional, that which is least influenced by European cultures, may be that which is creatively adapted from the encounter with European cultures.

The Navajos are no exception and the encounter with Western cultures is not the only stimulus for change. Traditional cultures the world over have almost constantly been in contact with neighboring peoples. In the history of these not always cordial encounters, change, sometimes of major proportion, has occurred. The process of change is often accomplished through the revision of stories that tell of the primordial events, the paradigms established in the creation of the world. Because of the absence of written records, the sequence of changes that would constitute the history of traditional religions is difficult to document. But that does not mean there has been no history.

More obvious examples of the religious adaptations occur in the encounter of traditional peoples with colonists and missionaries. A very well known North American example of a religious response precipitated by the crises of this situation of encounter is the Ghost Dance Movement. As westward expansion across the United States advanced during the nineteenth century, surviving Native American peoples were progressively confined to reservations, with accompanying loss of their way of life and threat to their survival as cultures. Beginning mid-century, waves of prophecy arose, in which visions revealed the impending destruction and restoration of the world. The prophecies included the proposed practice of rituals and transformed ways of life that would assure followers a place in the new world to come.

Throughout Oceania such crisis movements took the form known as cargo cults. With the introduction of money, wage labor, and Western material goods that arrived from an unknown source by ship, these cultures were forced to undergo radical changes in their way of life. The worth of individuals had been unrelated to economic possession. Material goods were limited to food, which was shared equally. The West Ceramese who live on an island west of Papua New Guinea transformed their story of Taro Woman into a story of Coconut Girl, Hainuwele, who could produce by defecation all sorts of foreign goods, from Chinese porcelain to bush knives. The story recounts the occasion of a ritual in which Hainuwele is captured, murdered, dismembered, and buried. From her body parts grew cultivable tubers. By revisioning their story tradition, the West Ceramese incorporate the elements of their crisis situation in such a way that traditional methods of resolution can be used. The story not only acknowledges the situational incongruity of the presence of foreign goods and how they are so mysteriously produced, but also presents a strategy to resolve the incongruity by transforming the disruptive source of these goods into a source of food, tubers, that the Ceramese know how to produce, share, and consume.

Many and varied are the religious responses traditional peoples have made to change. Throughout the twentieth century traditional cultures across the African continent have continually experienced radical change, spawning extensive and often highly creative, though sometimes violent, religious action. While the best-known examples of the changes in the religious histories of traditional peoples are those that have occurred in the encounter with Western colonization, or under the eye of the modern observer, such changes and developments of religion must surely have occurred throughout the history of every traditional culture.

Place distinctions are established in creation stories, in myth. The various Pueblo cultures of the American Southwest tell of the emergence from underworlds onto the present surface of the earth. This emergence place, often identifiable as a specific geographical location, is a point of orientation, though not necessarily a cosmic axis or center. The Hopi identify the emergence place as a particular geological formation in the canyon of the Little Colorado River, some distance to the west of Hopi. The various Hopi clans tell of migrations that eventually led them to their present homes atop the Hopi mesas. An important part of the male initiation process is a journey from Hopi west into this canyon to visit this emergence place. The journey effects a communication with those deities who remain in the lower worlds and a replication of the clan origin and migrations. The place of origin, the *sipapu*, is also replicated as a hole in the floor of the religious lodges (*kivas*) of the Hopi, where it plays a role in some of the Hopi rituals. The Hopi acknowledge as the basic life orientation a facing toward the east. Prayers are made in cornmeal that mark a path from west to east.

The Tjilpa, an Arunta people of Australia, tell stories of their ancestors who, in the time of creation (*Alcheringa*, or the Dreamtime), traveled about their landscape. They camped in one place after another where they met those who lived in that place, conducted initiation rites (invariably involving circumcision and subincision), established some distinctive monument or marker (a rock outcropping, a tree, a stone) that was often the transformed body of one of the ancestors, and, leaving one of the group behind from which a lineage began, traveled on. The Tjilpa can map as an itinerary the events of their Dreamtime onto the landscape around them, a journey during which a sequence of ritual events correspond with known places in their landscape.

Creation, as it is recounted in story, is often a process of making place distinctions and establishing created beings in their appropriate places. Being religious is often considered synonymous with being in the appropriate place. In the religions of traditional peoples there are often figures or characters, ritual and story devices, that introduce dynamics principally by playing against established place designations. These are embodied in what have come to be categorized as tricksters and clowns. A figure common to oral traditions among traditional peoples is one who, on his (and these figures are almost without exception male) own initiative, breaks every rule, violates every space. The figure is characterized as gluttonous, oversexed (often made obvious by having an enormous penis) and without sexual restraint (he sleeps with his daughters, his mother-in-law, and anything animate or inanimate), selfish, overbearing, and wild. Perhaps the most widely known figure of this type to American readers is Coyote, whose stories are told by many Native Americans. The stories of the

A husband and wife have water poured over them at the conclusion of an African healing ritual among the Ndembu, a Bantu-speaking people of northwest Zambia. The Isoma rite cures women who suffer from reproductive problems due to the interference of angry ancestral spirits who have been neglected in some fashion.

trickster figure demonstrate the meaning of created order by the negative consequences to its violation. Yet some of these figures are culture heroes (revealing to human beings how they should live) and even creators (often responsible for such things as death, illness, poverty, and laziness). It has often been a problem for scholars to comprehend the religious value of stories that are explicitly sexual, base, and highly gross in the details of bodily functions, yet wherever these stories are told, traditional peoples almost invariably proclaim the necessity and respect for them and their central character. The rituals of many traditional cultures include performances by clowns, who play the counterpart to tricksters in story traditions.

Place orientations may be discerned in ritual processes as well as in myth. The Isoma ritual of the Ndembu of Zambia is one of a class of women's rituals that deal with temporary barrenness. A woman who has had a number of miscarriages or finds it difficult to become pregnant may attribute the problem to the curse of an ancestor whom she has failed to remember in the appropriate way. Isoma is a complex ritual performed in the bush in a place carefully selected and prepared. Central to the ritual setting is a tunnel that begins at a blocked animal burrow and emerges some distance away. The orientation of the tunnel and the divisions of space, which occur along longitudinal, latitudinal, and altitudinal axes, made by the preparation of the ritual space and in the ritual performance replicate many of the basic divisions in the Ndembu worldview, divisions by which the Ndembu orient themselves. By means of placement and orientation, the ritual actions carefully conducted within this space strongly associate the initiate with the categories and values necessary for her to be a fertile woman. Ritual efficacy is achieved through reorientation within meaningful space.

MOTIVATIONS AND DYNAMICS

There are two broad categories of occasions and situations that motivate religious actions (not exclusive to traditional peoples): transitions and crises in the human life cycle, and occasions related to attaining sustenance.

The life cycle is not a smooth and continuous journey from birth to death. It is a sequence of stages interconnected by ritual passages. The cycle is envisioned differently from one culture to another and the ritual processes, while bearing the common structure of the rite of passage, may reveal much about each religious culture. Common passages for which rituals are performed are conception, birth, puberty, marriage, death, and the initiation into religious societies.

Whatever the occasion or cultural performance, rites of passage have a common, easily identifiable structure. First, the initiates are separated from their position or status in society. This is often effected by physical removal—removal from the village, seclusion in a special enclosure, separation from family. Second, the initiates find themselves in an unidentifiable situation or an unrecognized state of being. This interim phase is called *liminality*, a term that identifies this phase structurally with being on a threshold, being neither here nor there. Symbolically this phase is experienced as death and chaos. Ritually it is commonly effected through antistructure, that is, the reversal and confusion of established structural patterns. Finally, from this liminal phase, the initiate is integrated into the new designated status or position. While the structure of this ritual process may be operative in a variety of passage situations, it is easily adapted to the specific values and concerns of every cultural need.

When the Wiradjuri of eastern Australia deem that it is time to initiate a group of boys into manhood, the boys are forcefully separated from their mothers and their homes. The men enter the village whirling bullroarers and throwing burning brands. The women are covered with branches and blankets, and the initiates are seized and led away into the bush. As the boys are led away they are covered with blankets and forced to look only at the ground where they walk. The boys are told that the spirit Daramulun will come and eat them, then regurgitate them transformed into men. The whirring sound of the bullroarers is identified as the voice of Daramulun. In the extended liminal phase, the boys are often frightened by the sound of Daramulun, whom they fear is coming to eat them. Finally, with bullroarers whirring close by, the men reach under the blanket of each youth and with hammer and chisel knock out an incisor tooth, telling the boys that the spirit is taking their teeth while sparing their lives. Grouped around roaring fires the youths, still covered with blankets, are even more frightened as they hear the voice of Daramulun very close. Suddenly their blankets are pulled from their heads and they are encouraged to look at the men whirling bullroarers, to see for the first time the source of the voice of

Daramulun. They are allowed to experiment with the bullroarers themselves and finally to destroy them. Though they may be disenchanted and fooled, this begins the process of acquiring the stories and knowledge of the tribe. As the youths return to the village, they are transformed and subsequently begin to act as men.

In the liminal phase the symbolic acts of death and transformation are rich and complex. Circumcision, hair cutting, ritual scarring, tattooing, and lip- or ear-piercing are common to the liminal experience and create visible emblems of transformation. Nudity, common dress, and body painting are ways of distinguishing the liminal phase. And while initiates are often forced to undergo ordeals and to subject themselves in humility to every command, they are also often told stories and taught the wisdom of the position into which they are being inducted.

During the life cycle there are many occasions of personal adversity, such as illness, infertility, social conflict, malevolence, and the deaths of friends and family, which are dealt with by religious enactments from praying to the performance of grand ceremonials.

Illness is a very common occasion for religious performances among traditional peoples. In contrast to Western medical practice, which diagnoses illness based on an interpretation of symptoms, traditional religious medicine practices more commonly look for personal, social, or spiritual causes. Subsequently treatment is directed to the rectification of the cause, on the theory that the return of physical or psychological health will follow.

There are many forms of religious healing, from praying and singing to complex ceremonials that engage a large portion of the community and require enormous economic expenditure. Much of the religion of the Navajos of the American Southwest unfolds around concerns for health. There are several dozen major ceremonies whose accompanying story traditions are enormous, and whose ritual processes transpire over a period of nine nights and the intervening eight days, including the intonement of prayers of several hours' duration and the singing in sequence of perhaps five hundred songs. These complex ceremonials often focus first upon removing or rectifying the immediate cause of the illness, followed by a variety of acts that re-create not only the sufferer but the entire surrounding world. Navajo ideas of health correlate with their ideas of the beauty established in the creation of the Navajo world.

Shamanism is another common form of healing that may either be performed as a minimal ritual process or incorporated into complex ceremonials. Shamanism is difficult to define, because it is more effectively thought of as a complex rather than an action with a single definitive characteristic. Perhaps the most prominent shamanic characteristic is the presence of entrancement or ecstasy.

The Pomo of northern California perform shamanic healing. Pomo shamans are commonly women. The simple ritual healing process begins with extensive singing and the use of rattle sticks (long staffs to which are attached shell rattles) shaken and tamped as rhythmic accompaniment. The singing prepares the shaman for entrancement. Kneeling beside the patient, the shaman alternately sings and blows on an eaglebone whistle. In time her body involuntarily begins to shake and convulse. After she has entered a trance, she uses the middle finger of one hand as a diagnostic tool. Time after time she passes it, quivering, slowly over the body of the patient. She returns periodically to some location to which her finger is drawn, finally isolating the point of malevolence. Having found this place, she bends over the patient and sucks the cause of the illness from the body. As the malevolent object enters her body she convulses with its power, but then spits it into a bowl of water that will later be disposed. She may perform this sequence several times until she feels sure she has removed the causal agent.

Traditional peoples generally have remained closely connected with the immediate acquisition of sustenance: they are hunters, gatherers, farmers, fishers. Day-to-day life literally depends upon success in attaining sustenance. Attaining food is, for traditional peoples, as much a religious activity as it is a mechanical one. The profundities and attributes of life are expressed and contemplated in terms related to sustenance.

The religious activities associated with hunting bear are among the oldest and most widely practiced. Bear skulls and leg bones found in caves in the Swiss Alps, and placed in a manner that suggests religious intent, date from the early Paleolithic era, more than half a million years ago. Bear hunting and its accompanying rituals continue to be practiced throughout the circumpolar region by traditional peoples. Though these religious practices differ significantly from culture to culture, there are some common elements. Religious preparations for hunting often involve shamanic encounters with game masters, spiritual beings who control access to game animals. A range of restrictions and required actions characterize the descriptions hunters give of hunting bear, though these are more likely a genre for articulating religious discourse than guidelines for actual hunting. Hunters indicate that they address the bear by ritual names (often kinship terms). They kill the bear only when it is facing a specified direction and after which it has been spoken to in apology for taking its life. The kill is made with certain instruments wielded by the hunter in designated ways. Widely practiced is the ritual treatment of the bear carcass, which may be clothed, fed or given tobacco, and treated with respect. Commonly the muzzle, ears, or head are mounted on a pole as a display of respect for the bear and of success in the hunt. The respectful treatment and disposal of bear bones and any unused remains is widely practiced. Some traditional cultures, such as the Ainu in northern Japan, practice bear sacrifices. In a major ceremonial a two- or three-year-old bear, raised since its capture as a cub, is bound so that its struggles serve only to choke it. In the sacrificial festival, the people taunt and enrage the bear, finally killing it. The bear becomes food for the feast.

The religions of many of the traditional peoples who are agriculturalists are inseparable from the growing cycle. The Pueblo peoples of the American Southwest are continually engaged in a ritual cycle on which all of the mechanical activities of agriculture depend. Rain, pollen, corn, the sun, as well as a whole range of plant, animal, and meteorological phenomena are highly meaningful to these religions, as are the processes of fertilization, growth, maturity, and death.

The Dogon of western Sudan in Africa prepare and cultivate fields in the ar-

West African Dogon tribal village, in the cliffs of Bandiagara, Sanga region, Mali (ca. 1970). The Dogon possess one of the most complex cosmologies and cosmogonies in Africa, an intricate system of sacred signs, and a rich repertoire of ritual and divinatory procedures.

eas around their mountain villages. The layout of the fields and the structure of the granaries replicate the principal cosmic divisions. The Dogon granary is a building of two stories, with four rooms below and four above, each of which is associated with one of the eight kinds of seeds, with one of the organs of the human body, and with one of the organs of the spirit of water. The outer walls of the granary contain the inner organs, and the inner partitions represent the skeleton. The uprights in the four corners represent the arms and legs. The granary was described by one Dogon man, Ogotemmeli, as a woman lying on her back supporting the sky on her outstretched limbs. The granary has exterior stairways in each of the four cardinal directions. Each step is associated with a species of plant, animal, bird, or fish. The common Dogon granary, when idealized, bears the structure of the whole cosmos and of human life as they conceive it.

See also Africa, traditional religions in; agriculture, religious aspects of; Australian and Pacific traditional religions; circumpolar religions; ecological aspects of traditional religions; fishing rites/whaling rites; hunting, religious aspects of; Mesoamerican religion; new religions; nonliteracy; North America, traditional religions in; Orpheus stories in traditional religions; religious themes in the literature of traditional societies; shaman; South American religions, traditional; traditional religions, Western influence on; word (in traditional religions), power of.

transformation. *See* shape shifting.

transformation texts (Chin. *pien-wen*), in Chinese Buddhism, a vernacular retelling of stories from the scriptures or original compositions on Buddhist themes used for evangelizing among the masses. Buddhist scriptures were written in a technical language often on abstract philosophical subjects and were not likely to be of interest to the average Chinese peasant. Therefore, during festivals and other gatherings, popular lecturers and preachers recast scriptural stories and teachings into the local vernacular, often adding poetic and musical settings, in order to present Buddhist teachings in a manner that would be both effective and entertaining. *See also* China, Buddhism in.

translation, to be taken up to the heavens while still alive. *See also* Enoch; occultation.

transmigration of souls. *See* metempsychosis.

transsexuality. *See* gender crossing; gender roles; transvestism, ritual.

transubstantiation, a technical theological term used by Roman Catholics to describe the change of the bread and wine into the body and blood of Christ at Mass. Borrowing from Aristotle's physics, it is held that the substance of the bread and wine changes into the body and blood of Christ while the "accidents" (color, shape, taste, etc.) of the first substance remain. Uniformly rejected by other Christian bodies, this theory has been authoritative in Roman Catholicism since the sixteenth-century Council of Trent, which set forth its position against differing theories of the presence of Christ in the Eucharist proposed by the Reformers. *See also* Eucharist, Christian.

transvestism, ritual, wearing clothing and behaving in a manner characteristic of the opposite sex. It is an element in rituals that express freedom from the norms and social conventions or transcendence of a gendered body. *See also* androgyny; gender crossing; gender roles; rebellion, rituals of; reversal; sexuality and religion.

Treasures, Three. *See* Three Jewels.

trees (Japan), sacred. Trees are venerated as temporary abodes (*yorishiro*) of souls (*tama*) and spirits (*kami*). From ancient times, rites were offered to placate tree spirits before cutting a tree down. Individual trees marked by a sacred rope (*shimenawa*) or groves of trees, especially pine trees and the evergreen sakaki tree, served as the earliest altars for worship and are still commonly found on the grounds of Shinto shrines. Since the Tokugawa period (1600–1868), at New Year's, pine boughs placed over doorways are believed to attract beneficent deities to the house. In popular lore, trees served as places for the descent from the Pure Land of popular Buddhist deities, such as Amida and Kannon. Sacred trees (*reiki*) found floating in the ocean or growing deep in the mountains were often used to carve Buddhist images believed to be filled with numinous power. *See also* Japanese folk religion; kami.

tremendum, a general term for divinity emphasizing the quality of overwhelming external power.

Trent, Council of (1545–63), the nineteenth ecumenical council of the Roman Catholic Church. Held in response to the Protestant Reformation, it clarified Catholic doctrine on most points, such as the issue of transubstantiation, controverted by Protestants and also effected significant Church reform. There were twenty-five sessions over three periods; 1545 to 1547, 1551 to 1552, and 1562 to 1563. The council came too late to restore the unity of the Western Church; its theological canons and decrees made no concessions to Protestant concerns. However, Trent played a major role in reforming and revitalizing the Catholic Church throughout much of Europe. *See also* Counter-Reformation.

Triad Society, a Chinese secret society, so called because of its emphasis on harmony between heaven, earth, and humankind. Also known as the Heaven and Earth Society, it was organized in the 1670s by loyalists who sought to overthrow the Ch'ing dynasty (1644–1912) and restore the Ming (1368–1644). *See also* secret societies.

trickster, a scholarly term used to designate a variety of supernatural figures who appear, in myth, folklore, and ritual, to share in common a capacity to disrupt the ordinary course of natural and social life. Such disruptions are often associated with either creation or with carnival-like periods of reversals. Trickster figures are identified most commonly in Native American and African traditions. It is increasingly doubtful that trickster is a useful generic category. *See also* Coyote.

Tridentine. *See* Trent, Council of.

trimurti (tri-moor'tih; Skt., "having three forms"), an icon concept combining three major Hindu gods—Brahma, Vishnu, and Shiva—sometimes depicted conjoined in a single three-headed figure. The *trimurti* thus simultaneously represents the three universal divine functions of creation, maintenance, and destruction attributed to these deities, respectively. *See also* Brahma; Shiva; Veda, Vedism; Vishnu.

Trinity, the Christian term for the community of God as three divine "Persons" (Father, Son, and Holy Spirit). Although the Trinity, as such, does not occur in the New Testament, the roots of this notion lie in the narratives of Jesus as he is represented as praying to God as his Father and being led by the divine Spirit. Later theological tradition, interpreting these narratives, conceived of God as communal. There are not three gods; the One God is fully present in three different "Persons." How this can be is strictly mysterious. But orthodox Christian theologians have been clear since the Council of Nicaea (325) that everything that the Father is the Son is also, except for fatherhood. Since Constantinople I (381), the Holy Spirit has been understood to be similarly equal to the Father (and Son). The distinctions among the three Persons are therefore relational. None of the three is a person in the modern sense; each is unlimited in being, power, knowledge, and love. *See also* Christology.

tripartition. *See* Indo-European religion.

Tripitaka Koreana (Kor. *Koryo p'alman taejanggyong*), more than eighty-one thousand woodblocks for the printing of over fifteen hundred titles of Buddhist scriptures. A Korean national treasure, this woodblock collection is today housed in the library of Haein Temple on Mt. Kaya near Taegu. The woodblocks were carved in the thirteenth century and constitute one of the oldest versions of the Chinese Buddhist canon.

This thirteenth-century collection is, in part, based on an earlier collection that had been commissioned in the eleventh century by the Koryo king Hyonjong (r. 1009–31) as an act of filial piety for the repose of his parents. This earlier version had taken over forty years to carve and was completed near the end of the reign of King Munjong (r. 1046–83). By the end of the century, a supplementary extension was added to the canon by King Munjong's fourth son, the Buddhist monk Uich'on. It contained the writings of East Asian Buddhists, and its inclusion in the canon marked an elevation of East Asian Buddhist writing to the level of sacred scripture.

Uich'on did not include in his extension any writings by the practitioners of Ch'an Buddhism, a bias that was due to the status of Ch'an Buddhism in Korea, which was considered to be a useless, nonproductive form of Buddhism, and Uich'on's own predilection for T'ien-t'ai Buddhism, which he had helped to establish as a separate sect in Korea. The whole of this first collection with its extension was burned by the Mongols in 1231.

A second carving of the canon was commissioned by King Kojong (r. 1213–59) in the hope that through its merits the Mongol invaders would withdraw. This second canon, carved from 1236 to 1251, differs from the first in that it lacks Uich'on's extension, is based on the Kai-yuan record of Buddhist scriptures, and collates texts from the older Sung-dynasty Shu-pen edition, used for the first carving, with texts of the later Liao-dynasty edition. The blocks of this second canon were first stored at the Kanghwa Palace and later moved to Sonwon Monastery. In 1398 pirate raids forced the collection to be moved to Seoul and a year later it was moved farther inland to its present location at Haein Temple. This second edition, also known as the *Koryo Taejanggyong* (Great Collection of Scriptures of the Koryo), is an important source for all modern editions of the Buddhist canon. *See also* Buddhism (authoritative texts and their interpretation); canon; Haein Temple.

Ts'ai-shen (tsi-shen; Chin., "god of wealth"), deity in Chinese popular religion. Often symbolized by a money tree and casket of jewels, he presides over an array of subordinate deities. *See also* Chinese popular religion.

Ts'ao-tung school (tsou-duhng), a subschool of Chinese Ch'an Buddhism. Unlike the Lin-chi school, the Ts'ao-tung line eschewed the "shock" techniques of beating, shouting, and giving paradoxical responses. Instead, they favored the quieter approach of study, lecture, and silent introspection under the guidance of a meditation master. The point of their practice is to gaze directly upon one's own mind in tranquillity, and they lay no stress on dramatic enlightenment experiences. The school is named after two mountains, Ts'ao and Tung, where the two founders, Pen-chi (840–901) and his teacher Liang-chieh (807–869), lived. *See also* Ch'an school.

Tsou Yen (dzoh yen; ca. 305–240 B.C.), Chinese philosopher associated with the development of the *yin-yang* and *wu-hsing* theories. *See also* wu-hsing; yin and yang.

tso-wang (dzwoh-wahng; Chin., "sit and forget"), important Taoist method of meditation that involves the "forgetting," or obliteration, of ego-identity and the attainment of union with the Tao; it also refers to the condition of the "empty" mind. It is first seen in the *Chuang-tzu*. *See also* Chuang-tzu; meditation; Tao.

tsumi (ts*oo*-mee; Jap., "sin," "pollution"), Shinto term for events requiring religious purification (*harai*). The mythical archetype of many *tsumi* is the disorderly conduct of Susano-o. *See also* exorcism; harai; Susano-o.

Tsung-mi (dzong-mee; 780–841), the fifth and last patriarch of the Hua-yen school of Chinese Buddhism as well as an accomplished Ch'an master. The bitterness of the sudden-gradual controversy led him to write a detailed analysis of sudden and gradual cultivation in order to reconcile the two positions. *See also* Ch'an school; Hua-yen school; sudden-gradual controversy.

Tu-jen ching (doo-ren jinq; Chin., "Scripture of Salvation"), the central text of Ling-pao Taoism. The scripture promises the release of all souls from the purgatories, favorable rebirth, and eventual ascent to the highest heavens through pious recitation in the context of Ling-pao ritual. *See also* Ling-pao Taoism.

Tu Kuang-t'ing (doo gwahng ting; 850–933), a scholar known for works on Taoist liturgy, geography, and biography. Throughout a long career at court, Tu worked to develop a tradition of Taoist scholarship extending back to the second-century Way of the Celestial Masters (T'ien-shih Tao). His major studies include several collections of biographical accounts of Taoist immortals, a work of Taoist geography, and liturgical texts that drew on both fourth-century Spiritual Treasures (Ling-pao) scriptures and second-century practices of the Celestial Masters. His liturgical writings were the basis for later versions of the Taoist *chai* ("fasting") and *chiao* ("communal offerings") rituals. *See also* chai; chiao; Ling-pao Taoism; T'ien-shih Taoism.

tulku (tool'koo; Tibetan), in Tibetan Buddhism a lama who has been recognized as being the incarnation of a previous saint or hierarch. After being recognized, often at a young age, the *tulku* is typically brought to the monastery of his previous incarnation and thoroughly trained first in reading and writing and later in doctrine, dialectics, liturgy, and meditation. Upon maturity, he assumes the official position of his predecessor, usually as abbot of a monastery or group of monasteries, as religiopolitical ruler of a region, or as head of an entire Buddhist sect or subsect. Tulkus of various levels of attainment are known, among the "highest" and best known of which is the Dalai Lama. *See also* Dalai Lama; Karma-pa; Tibetan religions.

Tulsi Das (tool'see dahs'; ca. 1532–1623), a Hindu poet-saint of North India. A devotee of Rama, Tulsi Das celebrated his god in a dozen works in various dialects of Hindi. His epic retelling of the *Ramayana*, the *Ramcaritmanas*, or "Lake of Rama's Deeds," has become a beloved scripture. *See also* Rama; Ramayana.

Tung Chung-shu (duhng juhng-shoo; 179–104 B.C.), an early Han Confucian of the New Text school who successfully advocated the adoption of Confucianism as the official state religion. He established China's first university and wrote the *Ch'un-ch'iu fan-lu*, an exposition in eighty-two chapters (some are later forgeries) on how to apply the production and succession theories of *wu-hsing* and *yin yang* to proper government structure. *See also* Ch'un-ch'iu fan-lu; New Text school; wu-hsing; yin and yang.

Tun-huang (duhn-hwahng), an oasis in northwest China at the edge of the Taklamakan Desert where Buddhist monks hewed rock caves for dwellings and temples beginning in 366. The dry climate has preserved the temple art nearly intact, and researchers have discovered a sealed cave full of manuscripts yielding the earliest known Chinese Buddhist literature. *See also* China, Buddhism in.

turban (Turkish *tülbend*, "muslin" or "gauze"), headgear worn by Sikh men because of their unshorn hair. There is no standard style of tying a turban and turbans are worn in a wide variety of colors. *See also* Five Ks; Sikhism.

turtle/tortoise (China), symbols of oracular wisdom and of longevity. In Shang-dynasty China (ca. 1766–1122 B.C.), tortoises were used for "oracle bone" divination, their lower shells being cracked by heat to obtain answers to questions posed to ancestors. *See also* divination; oracle bones.

Tu-shun (doo-shuhn; 557–640), the first patriarch of the Hua-yen school of Chinese Buddhism. He is an obscure figure, although widely renowned at the imperial court and reputed to be a miracle-worker. No text by him exists, so the content of his teaching is unknown. *See also* China, Buddhism in; Hua-yen school.

tutelary spirit. *See* guardian spirit.

T'u-ti kung (*too*-dee guhng; Chin., "local earth god"), the god of a locality in Chinese popular religion. Subordinate to divinities who protect entire cities or administrative districts, *t'u-ti* are responsible for neighborhoods, streets, buildings, etc. Sometimes deified local heroes, these humble gods maintain registers of all persons in their areas and bless those who worship them. *See also* Chinese popular religion.

Twelver. *See* Ithna Ashari Shia.

twin myth, a theme found in origin stories of tribes in the Americas and Melanesia.

Twins (usually male) are born of a mysterious mother. Their conception is unusual; sometimes they are fathered by the sun. In some stories the mother falls from the sky. The twins may start fighting in the womb before their birth. The mother may die because of the difficult birth of the second twin. One of the twins may be rejected only to take revenge on the mother, killing her. One of the twins may become the culture hero.

In all accounts one of the twins acts positively, the other negatively, in creating the world. In the Seneca (Northeast) story, the struggle of the twins created mountains, streams, disease, and pestilence. The Menominee (Great Lakes) believe that the death of the negative twin brought death to humans, and this twin takes people in death. The Iroquois (Northeast) False Face masks impersonate all the various mistakes and forms of the negative twin's behavior. The Huron (Northeast) tell of Ataentisic (Mother of Humankind), who, in one version of the creation story, slipped through a hole in the sky while chasing a bear. She was pregnant at the time and gave birth to twins. As the twins grew they fought, and the negative twin was killed by his brother. From the drops of his blood flint was produced so that the Huron could make their tools. In the Navajo (American Southwest) story, twins (Monster Slayer and Child Born of Water) are born to Changing Woman (Sun is their father) after First People's emergence. *See also* Changing Woman; North America, traditional religions in.

Tyndale, William (tin'dayl; ca. 1494–1536), English Protestant whose translation of both the New Testament (1525) and the Old Testament (1530–36) of the Bible became the basis for the King James Version, and, hence, for the majority of English translations. As a result of his work, Tyndale was tried as a heretic and burned. *See also* King James Version.

typology, a specifically Christian mode of reading the Old Testament of the Bible as a prefiguration of Jesus by finding narrative parallels between events in Israelite history and events in the life of Jesus. *See also* allegory; exegesis.

typology, classification, a formal arrangement of phenomena according to kinds or categories. The resulting classification is known as a taxonomy. In the study of religion, taxonomies have achieved a high level of popularity. In fact, apart from interpretation, which most scholars regard as essential to the study of religion, the proposal, promulgation, and revision of typologies of religion have been regarded by many scholars as virtually equivalent to the study of religion.

Such taxonomies have ranged from classifying entire sets of religious systems (for example, monotheistic and polytheistic religions, primitive and world religions, tribal, national, and universal religions) to sorting and labeling their components or features (for example, corporate, domestic, and personal rituals, or cosmogonic, anthropogonic, and eschatological myths).

Perhaps the most pervasive and all-inclusive taxonomy involves the distinction between "world" and "primitive" religions (where "world" is further subdivided into categories such as "Western" and "oriental" or "Western" and "Asian"). Many academic programs in the study of religion are built upon such distinctions.

Knowledge of any set of phenomena, whether natural or cultural, comes about not primarily from the application and development of taxonomies but from explanatory theorizing, i.e., from the proposal and testing of principles that are general and systematic, and therefore capable of accounting for the range of phenomena that the explanatory theory aspires to explain. This theoretical approach to religion does not deny the usefulness of taxonomies; it simply insists that any system of classification follow from whatever theories have been adduced to explain religion. Taxonomies are neither substitutes for, alternatives to, nor the generators of theories. They represent intellectual works that have heuristic value once the theoretical work that underwrites them has established its empirical significance and demonstrated its ability to aid in the growth of knowledge. *See also* church/sect; cult; historical religion; nativistic movements; natural religion; popular religion; primitive religion; religion, definition of; revitalization movements; salvation, religions of; sanctification, religions of; supernatural religion; superstition, ignorance; universal and particular; world religions.

tzaddik (Heb., "righteous man"), in Judaism, an individual who is completely righteous in relationship to God and/or to other human beings.

Rabbinic: In the rabbinic writings the term is used in various ways and carries several distinct connotations: those whose behavior goes beyond the strict letter of the law; those endowed with the ability to emulate the creative powers of God, or who are able to annul the decrees of God. Present in rabbinic thought as well is the image of the *tzaddik* as the *axis mundi,* the one who stands at the center of the cosmos and whose actions sustain the world. Related to this is the tradition that a small number of righteous individuals in each generation (variously calculated as thirty, thirty-six, or forty) maintain the world. This was developed as the legend of the thirty-six righteous men (*lamed-vav zaddikim*) and became extremely popular in Jewish mythology and folklore, receiving special emphasis in *kabbalah* and Hasidism.

Kabbalism: The role of the tzaddik became especially prominent in medieval kabbalistic theosophy. Earlier traditions regarding the role of the righteous as the axis mundi were given new significance by the fact that in the kabbalistic system the tzaddik corresponds to the ninth gradation, also called Yesod ("foundation"), which is the bridge that connects the upper masculine emanations and the feminine Presence. The earthly righteous stand in direct relation to that divine grade, strengthening or weakening it in accordance with their deeds: "There is a single pillar that reaches from earth to heaven and its name is righteous (tzaddik). It is named for the righteous (*tzaddikim*). When

there are righteous men in the world, it is strengthened; when there are not, it becomes weak. It sustains the whole world, as it says, 'the righteous is the foundation of the world' (Proverbs 10:25). If it is weakened the world cannot exist. For that reason the world is sustained even by the presence of a single righteous man within it" (*Sefer ha-Bahir,* 102).

Hasidism: The rabbinic and kabbalistic notions of the righteous one standing at the center of the cosmos reached its fullest expression in eastern European Hasidism of the eighteenth and nineteenth centuries. By the second generation of this new social movement, the term tzaddik was used to designate the hasidic master who was the charismatic leader of a particular community. Each tzaddik had his particular court to which his followers would make periodic pilgrimages in order to receive blessings, healings, moral and religious instructions, or practical advice. In addition to his role as preacher and spiritual guide, the tzaddik was reportedly endowed with extraordinary spiritual powers to work miracles and to intercede in behalf of his followers. Utilizing the kabbalistic notion of the tzaddik as a bridge connecting the upper and lower forces, the Hasidic tzaddik was viewed as a ladder connecting heaven and earth, his mystical contemplation elevating heavenward and his leadership role tying him to earth. The tzaddik becomes in Hasidic literature and folklore the intermediary who brings humanity closer to God and God closer to humanity. *See also* Hasidism; holy person; Judaism (mysticism).

tzu-jan (dzuh-rahm; Chin., "spontaneity," "nature," "naturalness"), Taoist belief that patterns of nature are not created but evolve of themselves, that knowledge is innate and not a product of education. *See also* ancestral rites.

ABCDEF
G H I JKL
M N O PQ
RST **U** **V**
WXY&Z

ubasoku (*oo*-bah-soh-koo; Jap., "Buddhist layman"; from Skt. *upasaka*, "one who keeps the Buddhist Five Precepts"), in Japan a term for a variety of Buddhist laymen who combined austerities and recitation of Buddhist phrases with Taoist and folk practices to minister directly to the needs of common people. *See also* Japanese folk religion.

Uchimura Kanzo (*oo*-chee-moo-rah kahn-soh; 1861–1930), Japanese Christian educator and writer; he stressed the ethical imperatives of the Christian faith, organized Bible study groups, and helped to found the *Mu-kyokai* (nonchurch) movement in Japan. *See also* Mu-kyokai.

Udasi (oo-dahs'ee), a North Indian religious sect originating in 1539, when Guru Nanak's son, Srichand, became the first in a lineage of masters that continues today. Most Sikhs now regard it as Hindu, and an early-twentieth-century reform movement removed Sikh *gurdwaras* (houses of worship) from Udasi control. *See also* Sikhism.

Ugarit (u'ga'rit), an ancient city on the north coast of Syria. Excavations at the site, modern Ras Shamra, have been conducted since 1929. Texts written in the local West Semitic script and language, known as Ugaritic, as well as in several other scripts and languages (e.g., Akkadian, Egyptian, Hittite, Hurrian), and dating from the end of the Late Bronze Age (ca. 1400–1190 B.C.), have provided a wealth of cultural information. Myths and legends are in poetic form; letters, administrative documents, and ritual texts are in prose. Most information regarding religion comes from texts in the Ugaritic script and language. The myths and legends provide archaic data presented in high literary form, and the ritual texts give details of everyday practice, but in a prose so laconic as to defy precise interpretation. Proper names, many of which are built on divine names, also provide data on the pantheon of popular belief and veneration. The myths and legends provide the principal points of comparison with the Hebrew Bible in both form and content. They are composed in poetry similar to biblical Hebrew poetry: both are characterized by multilevel parallelism and share rhetorical and stylistic devices as well as particular expressions. In matters of content, these texts provide many of the details of Canaanite religion, to or about which the Hebrew Bible contains reactions or reflections. For example, one can delineate the role of Baal, Athirat, and Anat in Canaanite mythology or, from the details in the depiction of El and Baal, those characteristics that the Hebrew deity Elohim or YHWH shares with each of these Canaanite deities. *See also* Anat; Astarte; Baal; Canaanite religion; Elohim; Israelite religion; YHWH.

Uich'on (uy-chuhn; 1055–1101), an eminent Korean Buddhist monk of the Koryo period (918–1392), Buddhist bibliographer, and the founder of the T'ien-t'ai sect of Buddhism in Korea. Uich'on was the fourth son of King Munjong (r. 1046–83). He lived at Hungwangsa, a royal temple in the capital, where he gathered books from Sung, Liao, and Japan and had texts reprinted and disseminated. Uich'on had studied the Ch'an, T'ien-t'ai, and Hua-yen doctrines in China and in 1086 returned to Korea. With the support of his royal father, he sought to reform Koryo Buddhism and bring about an end to the conflicts between the various meditative and text schools by establishing a new sect that would combine both doctrine and meditation. This he did by establishing the meditative T'ien-t'ai sect, which drew its membership from the Nine Mountain schools of Ch'an and the Hua-yen schools. In Uich'on's view the synthesis of schools was found in the T'ien-t'ai emphasis on concentration or meditation and the exercising of intellect. Pure Land practices of scripture recitation and the invocation of Amitabha's name were considered important steps in the concentration of the mind. *See also* Ch'an school; Hua-yen school; Nine Mountain schools; T'ien-t'ai school; Tripitaka Koreana.

Uisang (uy-sahng; 625–702), one of the three most famous Korean monks of the golden age of Silla Buddhism and the founder of the Hua-yen school of Buddhism in Korea. As a young man of royal lineage, he attempted to travel to China in the company of the Buddhist monk Wonhyo. Though unsuccessful at the time, he was later able to settle at Chungnanshan at Ch'ang-an, where he studied under the Chinese monk Chih-yen (602–668). He also studied alongside and held a lifelong friendship with Chih-yen's most famous disciple and successor, the Serindian monk Fa-tsang (643–712). After a twenty-year stay in China (640–670), Uisang returned to Korea and founded a series of ten temples within the Hua-yen tradition, including the central sect temple of Pusoksa on Mt. T'aebaek, as well as Haeinsa on Mt. Kaya, Pomosa and Hwangboksa on Mt. Chungnan, and Hwaomsa on Mt. Chiri. Uisang insisted on the exclusive use of the *Hua-yen Sutra* as the path of salvation. He and his sect were accorded preeminence by the aristocrats of Unified Silla who may have been drawn to Hua-yen totalism and harmonization of conflicts, as well as the Hua-yen validation of the mundane world as a manifestation of the highest truth. The most famous of his extant works is the 668 *Diagram of the Dharmadhatu According to the One Vehicle of Hua-yen,* a diagram (Skt. *mandala*) of cosmic forces in a wavelike form and autocommentary on Hua-yen doctrines of harmony, nontemporality, and coorigination of all phenomena. *See also* Chih-yen; Fa-tsang; Hua-yen school.

Uiyon (uy-yuhn; fl. sixth century), an eminent Korean Buddhist monk of the Koguryo kingdom and early propagator of Buddhism and Chinese learning beyond the level of the Koguryo royal family and aristocracy. According to the *Lives of Eminent Korean Monks,* Uiyon was fully conversant with the intellectual and religious trends of China at the time, including Confucianism, Dark Learning, and Buddhism, and he taught these traditions throughout the Koguryo kingdom. The *Lives of Eminent Korean Monks* also records that Uiyon traveled to Yeh, the capital of Northern Ch'i (550–577), for discussions with the Chinese monk Fa-Shang on points of Buddhist doctrine and the history of Buddhism in China, and it is from information Uiyon gathered in China that Koreans have traditionally dated their Buddhist history. *See also* National Protection Buddhism.

ujidera (oo-jee-day-rah), Japanese Buddhist clan temples established to pray for both worldly success and the salvation of the clan's ancestors. By the tenth century, clans sometimes supplied many of the high-ranking monks to such temples as well as guaranteed their income. The rise and fall of many monasteries was based on such ties.

ujigami (oo-jee-gah-mee; Jap., "clan deity"), the *kami* (divinity, divine presence) from which Japanese clans (*uji*) were thought to have descended. Many *ujigami* have become guardians of local areas. *See also* Japanese folk religion; kami.

ulama (oo-la-mah; Arab., "learned"), religious authorities of Islam responsible for interpreting divine law and for administrating the Muslim community's familial, educational, legal, and commercial affairs.

Ideally, Muslims should follow the way of life (*Sharia*) ordained by God in the Qur'an and elaborated in the prophetic traditions (*hadith*). After Muhammad's death in 632, pious Muslims knowledgeable in these sources were asked for guidance in matters of faith. By the ninth century, such individuals formed a distinct body widely recognized as the "trustees of the Prophet" or, if Shii, of their *imams* as well.

Theoretically, any sane Muslim can become a member of the *ulama* through diligent study of pertinent Islamic texts under the supervision of qualified teachers. The acceptable branches of religious study have been defined and codified by the ulama to include quranic exegesis, hadith, law and jurisprudence, theology, and mysticism. Although the core curriculum has remained jurisprudence, most scholars have not been exclusively legalists and, until this century, many of the ulama were affiliated with mystical orders.

Besides cultivating and transmitting religious knowledge, the ulama have been essential to its application; they have served as teachers, preachers and prayer-leaders, market-inspectors, arbiters, judges (*qadi*) and jurisconsults (*mufti*), notaries, witnesses, trustees, and heads of mystical orders. The ulama's literacy and learning have also qualified them for important nonreligious state positions such as scribe and private secretary, royal counsel, and vizier. Through these offices, recognition by the state became an additional basis for ulama authority.

The ulama have been necessary for a regime's success, as their cooperation places an Islamic stamp on a government. Scholars sympathetic to the state have frequently issued legal opinions legitimizing a ruler's decisions, and they have accepted government appointments. From the fourteenth until the nineteenth century, the Ottoman ulama were organized and administered as an arm of the state bureaucracy.

Though some religious scholars have acquired wealth and prestige through state appointments, most ulama have not been rich or under direct state control. Thus, the ulama have not formed a class so much as a group, mostly male, originating from all societal levels and tied familially, economically, and ideologically to the communities whose problems and interests they share. Though often serving a regime, the ulama have, nevertheless, represented the Muslim public as advocates and intercessors with the state.

Not surprisingly, many ulama supported twentieth-century independence movements against non-Muslim colonial powers, but subsequent efforts by indigenous regimes to secularize law and education have substantially limited ulama posts and prestige. In addition, those modern Muslim reformers who lack training from a theological academy have also denounced the ulama as moribund, though some ulama, the Ayatollah Khomeini (d. 1989) in Iran, for example, have preached Muslim activism. Yet, the conservative ulama majority remains vital to society, fostering cohesion and stability by continuing to administer the religious needs of the larger Muslim community. *See also* Sharia.

ultimate concern, a theological concept central to the theology of Paul Tillich, a twentieth-century Christian thinker, but partially derived from nineteenth-century religious romanticism, particularly the work of Friedrich Schleiermacher. "Ultimate concern" refers both to the subjective and objective elements putatively present in the relationship between the religious believer and the object or referent of religious commitment. The "concern" attempts to maintain a psychological element or experiential dimension in a description of the religious relationship. The "ultimacy" is meant to emphasize the uniqueness of the religious relationship, thus distinguishing it from all other relationships and regarding it as the presupposition of all other relationships.

Religion as ultimate concern is a popular definition, although inadequate, at the very least, because of its vagueness. *See also* religion, definition of; Tillich, Paul Johannes.

Umayyad (oo-may'yad; Arab.), the Arab dynasty that ruled Islam from 661 to 750. During the reign of the fourth Rightly Guided Caliph of Sunni Islam, Ali (656–661), a dispute broke out as to whether the murder of the third caliph, Uthman (a member of the Umayyad clan), should have been avenged. Arbitration between Ali and the leader of the Umayyad clan (and governor of Syria), Muawiya, went in the favor of Muawiya, who in 661 became caliph. The resulting civil strife among different factions of Muslims was to characterize the Umayyad period and finally lead to the dynasty's collapse in 750. Yet, it was the Umayyads who, for much of the time, were able effectively to administer the newly conquered territories from their capital in Damascus. Under the caliph Abd al-Malik (r. 685–705) Arabic replaced Greek, Pahlevi (old Persian), and other languages used in the chanceries of government. The question raised by Umayyad rule was how to balance the struggle between the newly powerful Arab aristocracy and the non-Arabs incorporated into Islamic society and becoming Muslim in great numbers. The revolution that brought the Abbasids to power in 750 was premised on that conflict. *See also* Abbasid Empire; fitna.

Umbanda (oom-bahn'-dah, derivation uncertain), Brazilian new religion drawing on native Brazilian, African, spiritist, and Christian traditions, led by ritual priestesses and priests under whose guidance mediums accept possession by disembodied spirits in order to enhance personal spiritual development.

Regarded as the most recent and most Brazilian of the Afro-Brazilian groups, the origins of Umbanda are linked with a small group in Niteroi in the 1920s led by Zelio de Moraes that integrated neo-African religion with spiritist cosmology. Guided by the spirit, *O Caboclo das Sete Encruzilhadas* ("The Brazilian-Indian Spirit of the Seven Crossroads"), Moraes and his followers abandoned African-centered doctrines and ritual practices, especially animal sacrifices, and emphasized the charitable spiritual healing rendered by exalted souls in a cosmic hierarchy.

Umbanda communities, now found throughout Brazil after explosive growth in the 1970s and 1980s, continue aspects of all of Brazil's religious past. Brazilindian influence is seen in the prominence of native spirits, use of tobacco and herbal potions, and the mostly stereotypic native symbolism; Roman Catholic theological concepts of salvation, immortality, and hierarchical but benevolent divine-human relationships are central tenets, while saints—construed in terms reminiscent of late medieval traditions—are identified with Indian and African divine powers. The divinities, community structure, and possession rituals were developed from other Neo-African religions and the cosmology from Kardecism.

Each Umbanda center functions independently and, despite two spiritist congresses since the 1940s, significant variations exist among the groups nationwide. Certain general statements may, nonetheless, be made. Umbandist theologians maintain that its universalist teachings emerged with the human race, were influenced by ancient Hindu laws, and continued by the Mayans and by Greek, Egyptian, and Jewish priests; the core of the tradition was preserved in Africa until its revival through the reuniting of three branches of humanity—Indians, Europeans, and Africans—in colonial Brazil. At the pinnacle of the cosmic hierarchy is God the creator, the transcendent source and destination of all spirits. His son Jesus Christ is the *Orixa Maior* (from Yoruban and Portuguese, "great deity"), the highest communicating power; entities below him are other nonincarnate orixas maiores, who make up the Celestial Court, and four categories of formerly incarnate spirits, *orixas menores* ("lesser deities"), who communicate through possessed mediums: *caboclos* or *caboclos*, spirits of dead Brazilindians; *pretos velhos* or *pretas velhas*, souls of dead

An Umbanda altar in Rio de Janeiro, Brazil. Displayed are a variety of orixas (spiritual beings) and saints: St. George (Ogun) on horseback, the Virgin Mary (Iemanja), St. Jerome (Shango), the Old Black, and many others.

African slaves; *criancas*, the spirits of dead children; and *pombagiras* and *exus*, spirits of malicious women and men, especially dead Europeans. Each great deity also heads one of seven quasi-military *linhas* ("lines") of ranked spirits, who assist in spiritual guidance; each line consists of deities, saints, and spirits connected by temperament, natural associations, or mythic identities. According to Umbanda, human beings, composed of body and evolving soul, are bound to the material world through reincarnation and the laws of *karma* and subject to spiritual illnesses resultant from social upheavals, wretched urban surroundings, evil companions, and personal shortcomings. Each human being may, however, improve fate through study, prayer, ritual cleansings, and practice of the highest virtue, charity.

The most important rituals in Umbanda are the *giras* ("dances") conducted by each center's leader, the *pai* or *mai de santo* ("father" or "mother" of the saint/deity") whose guardian spirit protects all participants. The weekly night-time rituals open with songs, which call and welcome the greater deities and dismiss potentially dangerous spirits, and special invocations of one of the categories of the minor powers. The experienced mediums—ritually purified and specially attired—dance to achieve a trance state during which the spirits descend. Bearing positive messages from the higher celestial ranks, the possessing spirits consult with members of the congregation and offer advice on personal problems and cleanse them of evil influences and resultant spiritual sicknesses.

The main ritual room of Umbandist religious centers is halved by a railing separating the congregants from the sacred dance space and from a white-draped altar holding flowers, candles, and sacred symbols such as the statues of the orixas maiores in their familiar forms as Jesus, Mary, and other Catholic saints. While an estimated thirty million participate in Umbanda nationwide, the membership of each center may reach only into the hundreds. Men's and women's participation in Umbanda is remarkably balanced from congregation to leadership, although the mediums are mostly women. With centers principally located in the working-class or new middle-class neighborhoods, Umbanda is still associated with the lower-class or Afro-Brazilian community; despite recently increased prestige and popularity, Euro-Brazilians disclaim knowledge of or participation in its rituals. *See also* Afro-Brazilian religions.

umma (oom′muh; Arab., "community"), generic term for the Muslim community. The model *umma* was the one established by Muhammad in Medina. Membership in the Islamic umma is predicated on bearing witness that there is no God but Allah, and that Muhammad is his messenger. Children, for whom the witness of parents or guardian is sufficient, do so upon attaining the age of reason. The Muslim umma is worldwide and one, not divided by sect, doctrine, or ethnicity, in the Islamic worldview. *See also* Dar al-Islam; Muslim.

umra (oom′ruh; Arab., "visit"), the Islamic visit to the Kaaba shrine in Mecca. Muslim visitors perform circumambulations, run between the hills of Safa and Marwa in commemoration of Hagar's (Arab. *Hajar*) search for water, and observe the state of ritual consecration wherein no hair is cut, no jewelry or scent worn, no sexual activity enjoyed, and no hunting, fighting, or uprooting of vegetation permitted. The *umra* may be performed along with the *Hajj* (pilgrimage), and essentially is identical to its Meccan portion except that this "little hajj" may be performed at any time. Umra is a meritorious observance, whereas the Hajj is (conditionally) obligatory. *See also* Islam (festal cycle); Islam (life cycle); Kaaba; pilgrimage.

Muslims drinking from the well of Zamzam at Mecca, Saudi Arabia, a required stage in the lesser pilgrimage (*umra*) as well as the great pilgrimage (*hajj*).

uncarved block. *See* p'u.

unconditioned. *See* absolute, unconditioned.

unction. *See* anointing.

understanding, the cognitive state that results from having attained a satisfactory explanation of some problematic object, event, or situation. In the study of religion it often is posed not as a cognitive state but as a special strategy (often called *Verstehen* [Ger.]) seen as an alternative to explanation. Many social scientists agree, because they believe that the poverty of generalizations in social science is the consequence of attempting to make social science too much like the physical sciences. So used, "understanding" conveys the idea that a special method of investigation is necessary and available for explicating the concepts of and actions in cultural systems, particularly religion. For a time the term gained wide currency in both the humanities and the social sciences, but its use as a special methodological strategy did not withstand the criticism of philosophers of science. In recent years it has reappeared in theories of hermeneutics, the science of interpretation. *See also* empathy; hermeneutics; religion, explanation of.

underworld. *See* afterworld; Chinvat; cosmology; descent to Hades; descent to the underworld; Hades; heaven and hell; Hel; hell (Christianity); Huang-ch'uan; Orpheus stories in traditional religions; Tartaros; Yama.

Unification Church, or Holy Spirit Association for the Unification of World Christianity, a new religious movement founded in Korea in 1954 by Sun Myung Moon (b. 1920).

Unification theology, based on Moon's interpretation of the Old and New Testaments of the Bible, is to be found in his book *Divine Principle* (1976) and in his speeches circulated within the movement. Jesus was intended to restore the world to its pre-Fall state by marrying, but, murdered before he could complete his mission, he was able to offer only spiritual, not physical, salvation to the world. Moon, believed by his followers to be the Messiah, claims to have laid the foundation for establishing the kingdom of heaven on earth when he married his present wife in 1960. According to Moon, Satan is using communism to try to thwart God's plans.

The most important Unification ritual is the Blessing, when partners whom Moon has matched are married in a mass ceremony. Children born of such marriages are believed to be free of the fallen nature inherited by Adam and Eve's descendants as a result of sexual sin.

Unification-associated organizations own property, run businesses, and sponsor the arts, international conferences, a theological seminary, the Little Angels School, and numerous other ventures. In 1990, the combined North American and European membership was less than five thousand. *See also* Korea, new religions in; Moon, Sun Myung; North America, new religions in.

Unitarianism, a modern liberal religious movement in Europe, Britain, and America denying that God exists as a Trinity. Unitarians trace their origins to free spirits of the sixteenth-century Reformation era such as Faustus Socinus and Michael Servetus (1511–53), and to the liberal movements (1539–1604) that arose in the relative freedom of Poland and Transylvania in the sixteenth and seventeenth centuries. A movement developed in Britain during the seventeenth and eighteenth centuries and was brought to North American shores by John Murray in 1770 and Joseph Priestley in 1794.

Although Unitarianism in New England has continued to remain explicitly Christian though not Trinitarian, the movement in other parts of the United States, especially the Midwest, has at times repudiated a Christian and even a theistic identity. The movement, however, has remained inclusive, eschewing doctrinal tests and consolidating diverse liberal impulses through the merger of the American Unitarian Association with the Universalist Church of America in 1961 to form the Unitarian-Universalist Association (UUA). Universalism was a theologically similar movement that emerged in New England about the same time as Unitarianism.

The UUA embraces a wide latitude of theological or philosophical stances but has consistently allied itself with liberal social and ethical causes. Its headquarters are in Boston, Massachusetts, its polity is congregational, and its membership in the late 1980s stood at about 180,000. *See also* Channing, William Ellery; Protestantism; Servetus, Michael; Socinus, Faustus.

Unitas Fratrum. *See* Hus, Jan.

United House of Prayer for All People. *See* African Americans (North America), new religions among.

universal and particular, a conceptual duality rooted in the human experience of similarities between certain individual entities. This experience is given a formal expression in the theory that puts individuals or specimens into a proximate grouping (species) and then into remoter, wider groupings (genera). *See also* typology, classification.

Universalism. *See* Unitarianism.

universal monarch, mythical "wheel-turning king" (Skt. *cakravartin*), perhaps modeled on the Indian emperor Ashoka, and figuring as a paradigm of kingship in Buddhism. *See also* Ashoka; Dutthagamani; kingship, sacred.

Universal Peace Mission, also Peace Mission movement, founded in 1932 by Father Divine (George Baker, ca. 1880–1965), an advocate of mind power whose followers believe him to be God. *See also* African Americans (North America), new religions among.

unleavened bread, bread baked without yeast, prescribed for Jewish Passover and Christian eucharistic wafers. *See also* host; matzah.

Upanishads (oo-pah'ni-shuhdz; Skt., "sitting nearby"). 1 In a narrow sense, esoteric teachings on the nature of absolute reality given in ancient India by sages to students under their personal tutelage. 2 In a larger sense, a codified collection of Vedic and Hindu canonical texts said to reveal hidden eternal truths regarding the metaphysical connections between the ultimate and the human worlds. The most influential of these were composed between the eighth and fifth centuries B.C. and passed orally through the generations

to qualified seekers of sacred knowledge. The key teachings of the Upanishads revolve around two related notions: the constantly changing world of time, space, and causation experienced by the senses is unreal relative to the unchanging, infinite, and eternal absolute ground of all being and that same ultimate reality is identical to the eternal human soul. Some schools of thought held that this unified, pervasive, and undying world-soul is impersonal, while theistic (often later) interpretations regarded it as a single personal deity, most typically Shiva, Vishnu, or the Goddess. *See also* Hinduism (authoritative texts and their interpretation); karma; liberation; six systems of Indian philosophy; soul.

upaveda (oo-puh-vay'duh; Skt., "secondary knowledge"), a class of Indian sciences including medicine, weaponry and warfare, music, architecture.

Ur (oor; originally Urim, language uncertain), a Sumerian city-state in present-day Iraq, center of the moon god's (Nanna) cult and, in biblical tradition, the first home of Abraham (Genesis 11:31). It achieved political eminence ca. 2100 to 2000 B.C. under the third dynasty of Ur, and became the capital of an empire administered by a vast bureaucracy and reaching into the mountain country to the east and up the Tigris and Euphrates rivers into Syria. From earlier archaeological levels come the famous royal tombs and inscriptions in a very archaic script. *See also* Mesopotamian religon.

Urabon. *See* Obon.

Urantia Book (yoo'ran-shi-yah), the 1955 collection of the American, Spiritualist-influenced teachings of Bill Sadler, redefining Jesus' role in human salvation and cosmic history. *See also* North America, new religions in.

usul al-din (oo-sool' ood-deen'; Arab.), the fundamentals of religion. The *usul al-din* under discussion by theologians (*mutakallimun*) in classical Islam included the being and attributes of God, the justice of God, ethics, divine punishment for sin, and the question of the imamate. In modern Islam, the fundamental beliefs (distinct from the Five Pillars of ritual performance) are in God and his attributes (designated by his ninety-nine beautiful names), his prophets sent to humankind, angels, scriptures, the Day of Judgment, God's omnipotence, and predestination. *See also* creed; Five Pillars; iman; kalam.

usury, collecting interest on a loan. It is forbidden or regulated in many religious traditions, including Judaism, Christianity, and Islam.

Utraquists. *See* Hus, Jan.

vagina dentata (va-ji'nah den-tah'tah; Lat., "vaginal teeth"), motif in stories throughout North and South America, Siberia, Northern Russia, and Greenland.

Women in story traditions may be depicted as having the teeth of a rattlesnake head set in their vaginas. They kill men who would have intercourse with them. As a result, these women may collect the deceased men's hunting equipment, but often these women are able to hunt with their toothed vaginas. A culture hero, sometimes acting the role of a young husband, is often involved in breaking and wearing down the vaginal teeth with a wedge or stone penis, so that intercourse does not end in death.

Vaikhanasa (vi-kah'nuh-suh; Skt., "associated with Vikhanas [name of founder]"), a small Brahman community of hereditary Hindu temple priests in South India. Vaikhanasas conduct devotional services (*puja*) in many Vishnu temples in Tamil Nadu and Andhra Pradesh states, including the famous pilgrimage center at Tirupati. Inscriptions refer to them as early as the eighth century. Their literature, principally in Sanskrit, includes late Vedic ritual material as well as manuals for constructing temples and serving icons within them. Generically called *agama* ("tradition"), these manuals may be compared with texts of the Shaiva and Pancharatra Agamas.

Vaikhanasas insist that they are Vaishnavas "at birth" and that their temple rituals continue Vedic fire sacrifice. This claim to Vedic legitimacy illuminates traditional modes of constructing and expressing continuity in Hindu religious praxis.

Many Vaikhanasas are traditional medical practitioners as well as temple "priests." The community is acutely dependent on a diminishing number of learned elders to preserve its integrity. *See also* Shrivaishnavism; Vishnu.

Vainamoinen (vayn'ah-moy-i-nen; Finnish), an epic hero in oral poetry and the *Kalevala*, a shaman and creator of the cosmos and culture who retreats with the promise to return. *See also* Finnish religion; Kalevala.

Vairochana (vi-roh'chuh-nuh; Skt., "Resplendent One"), a celestial Buddha who holds a central place in Buddhist depictions of the cosmos. He is considered a cosmic Lord, the essence of other Bud-

dhas, and he is an object of worship in some forms of esoteric Buddhism found in Japan. *See also* Bodhisattvas; Buddhas.

Vaishnava Sahajiya (vish'nuh-vuh suh-huh-ji'yah), sixteenth- to nineteenth-century Hindu mystical tradition. Related to the earlier Buddhist Sahajiyas (eighth–thirteenth centuries), Vaishnava Sahajiyas flourished in and around Bengal after the great Vaishnava saint Caitanya (1486–1533). Major teachers such as Mukundadeva (ca. 1650) combined devotional and ascetic practices from Caitanya's Vaishnavism with esoteric psychophysical practices from the Siddha, Nath, and other Tantric traditions involving alchemy, yoga, cosmophysiology, and sexual rituals. Their main goal was to realize within the human body the ultimate state of *sahaja* ("together-born"), in which all dualities are unified and the soul is liberated. Modern groups such as the Bauls continue some of their practices. *See also* Caitanya; Tantra; Vaishnavism.

Vaishnavism (vish'nah-viz-uhm; from Skt. *vaisnava*, "follower of Vishnu"), the extensive complex of Hindu beliefs and practices that honor Vishnu/Krishna as Supreme God; probably the most widely followed kind of Hinduism. Central to this complex is the faith that God loves the person, and that the person should relate to God mainly by *bhakti* ("devotion," "love"), the final reward of which is eternal communion with God. The most famous of this god's many names are Vishnu, Narayana, Hari, Bhagavan, Krishna, and Rama; hence the usage Vishnu/Krishna.

Origins: Vaishnavism's ancient name, Bhagavata ("followers of the Blessed Lord, i.e., Bhagavan"), may clarify its beginnings, for it makes a connection with the movement's two most important literary works: the *Bhagavad Gita* (ca. 150 B.C.) and the *Bhagavata Purana* (*Shrimad Bhagavatam*, ca. 850–900). Though the tradition began earlier, two things became clear by about 200 B.C.: the Bhagavatas related to their god, Krishna, by devotion and accepted the Vedas and Upanishads, the scriptures of Brahmanic Hindu religion. In this process the Brahmanic deities Vishnu and Narayana became identified with Bhagavan Krishna. Thereafter, Krishna has been viewed as an incarnation (*avatara*) of the Supreme God Vishnu (by South Indian Vaishnavas), and Vishnu has been viewed as a subordinate form of the Supreme God Krishna (by North Indian Vaishnavas).

The *Bhagavad Gita* is the earliest full statement of the Bhagavata synthesis. Krishna teaches a path of salvation: desire-free performance of one's born duty should be combined with the meditative wisdom of the Upanishads, suffused by and culminating in loving devotion to Krishna. As Krishna reveals to Arjuna: "I love you well" (18.64).

The Vaishnava Traditions: A new impulse was felt in South India in the sixth to ninth centuries when the twelve Alvars (Tamil, "those deeply immersed") began to express, in Tamil poetry, a much more emotional love for Vishnu and his incarnations. This devotion grew to dominate South and North Indian Vaishnavism and spawned poetry in all the vernaculars. Five classical traditions are recognized, all condemning the impersonalist philosophy of the philosopher Shankara: the Shrivaishnavas and the traditions of Madhva, Nimbarka, Vallabha, and Caitanya.

The Shrivaishnavas, who consider Ramanuja (1017–1137) their greatest theologian, later split into northern and southern schools. The northern, or "monkey," school said Vishnu's grace was like that of a mother monkey saving her baby from danger by swinging through the trees while the baby hangs on (i.e., some human effort is essential). But the southern, "cat," school's figure is a mother cat picking up her kitten by the nape of the neck and carrying it to safety (i.e., Vishnu does everything).

The philosophically acute tradition of Madhva (thirteenth century) teaches a permanent distinction between Vishnu and the soul, and between Vishnu and the world. The appropriate attitude to Vishnu is complete, loving dependence.

The next three traditions, predominantly North Indian, consider Krishna supreme. The tradition of Nimbarka (twelfth–thirteenth centuries), however, worships Krishna and his consort Radha equally. The tradition of Vallabha (1479–1531) emphasizes Krishna's nourishing grace. Krishna chooses and unerringly charms the devotee to salvation, often nullifying both past sin and present ignorance. The tradition of the great ecstatic Caitanya (1486–1533) systematically uses the language of Indian aesthetics to portray the possible relationships between devotee and Krishna. The chief models of the dominant mood, love, are those of servant to Master, friend to Friend, parent to Child, and—uppermost in this tradition—beloved to Lover.

The hero-God Rama is worshiped as supreme by many North Indian Vaishnavas, inspired by Tulsi Das's Hindi version of the epic *Ramayana*.

Other Notable Movements: Vithoba, a local deity identified with Krishna, has a large Vaishnava following in Maharashtra, exemplifying a regional form of a pan-Indian deity. The popular Swami Narayana sect of Gujarat represents a nineteenth-century reform movement directed against the Vallabha tradition. Finally, the International Society for Krishna Consciousness, popularly known as the "Hare Krishnas," was established by a missionary from the Caitanya tradition, A. C. Bhaktivedanta Swami.

Worship: Vaishnava worship, in the home and in the temple, focuses around images believed to be real presences of God. The deity is dressed, symbolically fed, and otherwise served by the devotee in what has been called a kind of "aesthetic yoga." Thus, Vishnu/Krishna brings the devotee actively to final salvation, described as "Entry into the Eternal Game." Vishnu/Krishna has created the world as a game; that is where his chosen join him. *See also* Alvar; avatar; Bhagavad Gita; Bhagavata Purana; Caitanya; Krishna; Madhva; Nimbarka Sampradaya; path of devotion; Rama; Ramanuja; Shrivaishnavism; Tulsi Das; Vallabha Sampradaya; Vishnu.

Vaishya. *See* caste.

vajra (vah'jrah; Skt., "diamond" or "thunderbolt"), important symbol in Tantric Buddhism. Standing alone, the *vajra* indicates enlightenment itself, and particularly its indestructible nature; when used in combination with feminine symbols (the lotus or bell, signifying wisdom), it represents the masculine side of enlightenment (skillful means or compassion). A liturgical scepter used in rituals, it is frequently also an attribute of Tantric deities. Vajra designates the Tantric tradition (Vajrayana, "adamantine vehicle"), the names of deities (Vajradhara, "vajra holder"), the Buddha essence within (vajra nature), the highest meditative states (vajra-upamasamadhi), and songs of realization (vajra songs). *See also* dorje; Tantrism (Buddhism).

Vajrayana (vuhj-ruh-yah'nuh, Skt.), Buddhist term for the vehicle of the diamond or thunderbolt. The term *Vajrayana* is widely used as a designation for the tradition of Buddhist Tantrism. *See also* Esoteric Buddhism in China; Tantrism (Buddhism); vajra.

Vak (vahk; Skt., "speech"), a goddess of Vedic India. Vak especially represents types of sacral speech: "verse," "chant," and "formula." She is often paired with Manas ("Mind") and is later identified with Sarasvati. *See also* Sarasvati; Veda, Vedism.

Valdes, Peter. *See* Waldensians.

Valentine, according to Christian tradition, two third-century martyrs of that name who have been conflated into a single saint honored in the Roman Catholic Church on February 14. The origin of the tradition of honoring love on that day is unknown.

Valentinianism, a Christian Gnostic sect derived from Valentinus, a second-century Christian Gnostic born in Egypt who came to Rome. There, he and his numerous disciples blended into the diversity of Roman Christianity. Valentinus's form of Christianity spread throughout the Roman world and continued until the seventh century. He composed hymns, psalms, poems, and letters, of which only fragments survive. The only known writing of his is a mystical sermon, the *Gospel of Truth,* which describes the search for God and salvation through the Savior who proclaims truth and brings joy and knowledge. Written for initiates, it alludes to but does not discuss fully developed doctrines, leaving it to his many pupils and followers to develop and clarify his original ideas. For instance, responsibility for the tragedy in the divine world that gave rise to material creation is not attached to any one aeon in the writings of Valentinus. The deliberate ambiguity employed when speaking of the cosmic tragedy was eradicated by subsequent writers such as Irenaeus in his accounts of Valentinus's work. Ptolemy identified two Sophias responsible for the tragedy so as to resolve ambiguities in Valentinus's original teaching. The two schools of Valentinianism, Roman and Alexandrian, took different positions regarding Jesus' true nature. The former asserted that Jesus was united to the Holy Spirit at baptism while the latter held that he was conceived and born spiritually.

Valentinians understood themselves to be pneumatics (spiritual ones). The psychics were ordinary Christians who could rise to the pneumatic level or descend to the lowest level of material existence. Valentinians were also known for their allegorical method of explaining Scripture (Ptolemy wrote to Flora to explain the Hebrew Law; Herakleon wrote the earliest commentary on the Fourth Gospel). This respected and ancient mode of textual exposition emerged subsequently in the Christian school of Alexandrian exegesis. In Valentinian understanding, the authority for this method was the apostle Paul, who employed this technique in his letters. *See also* Aion/Aeon; Gnosticism; Ptolemy.

Valhall (val'hol), in Scandinavian mythology Odinn's palace, dwelling place of the band of dead warriors preparing for the last, cosmic battle, Ragnarok. *See also* afterworld; Nordic religion; Ragnarok.

Valkyrja (val'keer-ee-uh; Ger. form, *Valkyrie*), in Scandinavian mythology a female power of death who chooses those who are going to die on the battlefield. *See also* Nordic religion.

Vallabha Sampradaya (vahl'uh-buh suhm-pruh-dah'yuh; Skt.), a Hindu Vaishnava devotional system founded by Vallabha (1479–1531) and his son Vitthala that has about five million followers in northwestern India. The founder's direct male descendants are *gurus* and priests. Holding that the Supreme God Krishna loves and blesses those whom he chooses for his path of grace, followers worship the child Krishna as baby, cowherd boy, and lover of the milkmaids. Philosophically this results in a realistic monism: everything is Krishna and is real. *See also* Krishna; path of devotion; Vaishnavism.

Valmiki (vahl-mee'kee), sage-author of the Hindu epic *Ramayana,* whose legend is part of the *Ramayana.* Sanskrit verse (*shloka*) was born from the sage's sorrowful utterance. Valmiki trained Rama's sons to sing the epic tale. *See also* Hinduism (poetry); Rama; Ramayana.

Vanir (vah'neer), in Scandinavian mythology, a group of fertility gods often consisting of Njordr, Freyr, and Freyja. *See also* Nordic religion.

Varkari Panth (vahr'kuh-ree; Marathi, "pilgrim"), the group of devotees of the Hindu god Vithoba of Pandharpur. Members wear a necklace of tulsi beads, practice vegetarianism, make regular, joint pilgrimages to Pandharpur, and sing devotional songs composed by poet-saints including Jnaneshvar and Namdev (thirteenth century), Eknath (sixteenth century), and Tukaram (seventeenth century).

varnashramadharma (vahrn-ahsh'rah-muh-dahr'muh; Skt.), in Hindu law texts, the particularization of social and religious duty (*dharma*) depending on which of the four social classes (*varnas*) one is born into and what stage of life (*ashrama*) one is in. *See also* ashrama/ashram; caste; dharma.

Varuna (vuh'roo-huh), a god of Vedic and later India. A universal king characteristically paired with Mitra, and associated with the night, Varuna is stern guardian of truth and especially commandments, afflicting deceivers and transgressors with disease. The most impressive ethical force in the *Rig Veda*, he was later demoted to the god of waters. *See also* Mitra; Rig Veda.

Vatican City, an independent state on the Tiber River within the city of Rome, Italy, governed by the pope and containing among other buildings St. Peter's Basilica and the Sistine Chapel. Its territory of 108.7 acres and population of about one thousand make it the smallest country in the world. Established by the Lateran Pacts (1929) between the Kingdom of Italy and the Holy See, it was later ratified by the Republic of Italy in 1948. The pope, whose role as the supreme Pontiff of the Roman Catholic Church is separate from his temporal authority over the state, serves as its absolute monarch. *See also* papacy.

Vatican Council, Second, a council of Roman Catholic Church authorities called by Pope John XXIII, which met intermittently during the years 1962 to 1965.

The pope's notion was that the Church needed to begin a dialogue with the modern world. The bishops assembled developed pastoral (rather than dogmatic) statements about such key issues as how to understand the Church, how the Church ought to operate in the modern world, revelation, ecumenism, and religious liberty. The implementation of the conciliar decrees later became a source of division.

Vayu (vah'yoo; Skt.,"wind"), a god of Vedic and later India. Born from the breath of the First Man, Purusha, he is often identified with breath; his chariot is drawn by ninety-nine or more horses. Companion of Indra, he is best known as the recipient, along with Indra, of the first *soma* drink. *See also* Indra; Purusha; soma.

Veda (vay'duh; Skt.,"knowledge"). 1 The four Vedas of the earliest Sanskrit hymns and verses: *Rig Veda, Sama Veda, Yajur Veda,* and *Atharva Veda.* 2 Equivalent to *shruti,* "revelation," comprising the Vedas, Brahmanas, Aranyakas, and Upanishads as the "eternal" and "unauthored" source of Hinduism. *See also* Hinduism (authoritative texts and their interpretation); Veda, Vedism.

Veda, Vedism. Veda is a collective term for a large corpus of Sanskrit texts dating from the second and first millennia B.C. These texts are the products of the Brahman, or priestly, class among the Indo-European Aryans who invaded and then settled in North India. The term *Veda* is derived from the Sanskrit root *vid-,* "to know," and means "true knowledge." The Vedas are identified with *satya,* "truth," or with *vac,* "speech" or "the word," also in the sense of "truth." Alternatively, the Vedas are equated with the *brahman,* the universal principle that is the ground and end of all knowledge.

The eternal Veda was supposedly revealed to certain semimythical wise men and poets. The Veda is thus categorized by Hindu traditions as *shruti* (lit., "heard," in the sense of an absolutely authoritative revelation that has no human author) as opposed to other and less authoritative texts that are called *smriti* ("remembered," i.e., the handed-down traditional wisdom of human teachers). Adherence to the authority of the Veda (even while largely ignoring its specific contents) provides one of the few yardsticks for orthodoxy within Hinduism.

Preserved only orally until relatively recent times, the Veda was transmitted from teacher to pupil within "schools" (*caranas*) or "branches" (*sakhas*). The Veda is actually divisible into four: the *Rig Veda, Yajur Veda, Sama Veda,* and *Atharva Veda.* Each of these Vedas is comprised of several parts: a *samhita* ("collection" of verses), *brahmana* (explanations and interpretations of the verses), *aranyaka* ("forest texts," or esoteric teachings), and *upanishad* (mystical texts). Finally, each Veda comes in several different recensions, each with its own particular version of the set of texts.

The religion and culture of the ancient Aryans in India is known entirely from what survives among these compositions, which is why it has been dubbed "Vedism." All religions of India can be said to be dependent, in one way or another, on Vedic religion. Hinduism purports to be merely a continuation of the Vedic tradition despite numerous and significant innovations and departures from it. Other religions, e.g., Buddhism and Jainism, originated out of explicit opposition to the doctrines and practices of Vedic religion. These "heterodox" traditions can be said to have been "negatively shaped" by Vedism.

Four principal features of Vedism may be isolated and analyzed: a classificatory bent toward tripartition; a warrior mentality; naturism or the worship of deities who are indistinguishable from natural entities or phenomena; and the cult of fire sacrifice.

Vedic Classifications: The tendency to categorize things and beings into triads was one of the many inheritances Vedism received from its Indo-European roots. Georges Dumezil, the twentieth century's most influential scholar of the Indo-Europeans, has persuasively argued that since the Indo-Europeans belong to a common language family it is probable that they also had certain commonalities in the way they thought. Dumezil has spoken of a shared "ideology" and has found evidence for it by comparing the mythologies, theologies, histories, epics, folk tales, and especially social structures of the various peoples who comprised the Indo-European community. What has emerged from Dumezil's exhaustive and wide-ranging comparisons is the "tripartite ideology," or the Indo-European trait of classifying in triads.

Dumezil's findings for some cultures of the Indo-European world have been received with skepticism. But in the ancient Indian context, at least, Dumezil's hypothesis is borne out. Vedic texts are replete with triads, beginning with the categorization of the social classes of Aryan society into Brahmans (priests), Kshatriyas (rulers and warriors), and Vaishyas (commoners). The cosmos as a whole is also divided into three parts—earth, atmosphere, and sky—and the deities of the Vedic pantheon are assigned to one or another of these three "worlds." Time is organized in this manner as well. The day is analyzed into morning, midday, and afternoon, and the year is divisible into three seasons.

To these Indo-European triads, Vedic classifiers sometimes added a fourth. Thus, to an original complement of three Vedas (the Veda is sometimes referred to as the "threefold wisdom") was later added the *Atharva Veda*, and the "world of heaven" becomes a fourth world in the cosmological scheme. The enlargement of the tripartite classification system into a quadripartite one may very well have been stimulated by an analogous (or causative) historical expansion of Vedic society to include within it the non Aryan indigenous inhabitants of South Asia. These natives the Indo-European invaders originally called *dasas* or *dasyus*, "slaves." Over time, as the invaders themselves became natives and as some of the original inhabitants were assimilated to some degree within Aryan society, the latter came to be known as "Shudras" and took over the bottom rung in the social order: a fourth social class was grafted onto the bottom of a social hierarchy previously consisting of three "twice-born" classes. In any event, the expansion of categorical systems from three to four is a recurring phenomenon in Indian intellectual history. In later Hindu texts, to the three *purusartha*s or "goals of human beings" (pleasure, power, and principle, *kama, artha,* and *dharma*) is added liberation (*moksha*) as a "transcendent fourth." The three *ashrama*s or stages of life—student, householder, and forest dweller —are similarly expanded to include the renunciate's way of life (*sannyasa*).

Veda and Warriors: A second feature of ancient Vedic religion is that it is imbued with the ethos of warriors. The Vedic period in India was one in which the Aryans fought not only with the indigenous peoples of South Asia but also with each other. The social and political order of the time was shaped by competition between numerous small tribes of interrelated people led by "kings" (really more like warlords or gang leaders) who contested with one another for land, power, and wealth (in the form of cattle). The somewhat incestuous nature of Vedic warfare is indicated by the fact that the ancient Sanskrit word for "enemy" is the same term used for "first cousin."

In such a world, the values of the military often prevailed. In the most ancient texts of India, power and dominance were unabashedly embraced and unashamedly displayed. Vedic religion sometimes appears as simply war by other means.

The deities were petitioned for (among other things) victory, the surpassing of others, and the destruction of one's enemies. Among the principal gods worshiped in Vedic religion was Indra, the deified quintessence of the Vedic warrior, known for quaffing huge quantities of the intoxicating soma juice and marauding about fighting the demons. This god stars in an important creation myth of the *Rig Veda*—the universe was created when Indra defeated a cosmic serpent who had coiled around the "waters of life." Indra and similar gods of Vedism are thus the apotheoses of the militarism that characterized the people and times of ancient India.

Naturism: Other gods and goddesses of the pantheon reveal a third feature of Vedism, what might be called Vedic naturism. Many of the Vedic deities are identical to natural phenomena or entities one finds in the cosmological worlds they are assigned to—earth, atmosphere, and sky. In the sky, for example, are gods whose names are also the names for "sun" (Surya, Aditya, Savitar), Candra (the moon), as well as Dyaus, the god of the sky itself. The atmosphere is the cosmic space of the god of wind (Vayu) and the thunder god Indra and his "storm troopers" the Maruts, among others. And this world is the home of the earth goddess (Prithivi). In all cases, the deity and the natural phenomenon or entity are fundamentally indistinguishable: the earth *is* Prithivi, the wind *is* Vayu, the sun *is* Surya, etc. Other deities represent dawn (the goddess Ushas), night (the goddess Ratri), the river (Sarasvati)—and even the forces of chaos or disorder are deified in the figure of Nirriti.

The divine in Vedism is manifest, not transcendent; the sacred is found within nature and not apart from it. This theology is obviously polytheistic, although different deities at different times might be extolled as the highest or even only true god or goddess (and all other deities are then regarded as merely forms of him or her). And, as we shall see, Vedic rituals are usually correlated with the natural rhythms of day and night, new and full moon, the change of seasons, and the solar year.

The deities of the fire sacrifice that played such a central role in Vedic religious life are of special importance. Agni is the god of fire and is therefore among the principal gods of the pantheon. Agni is one of the only deities who is said to live in all three cosmological worlds: he is fire here on earth, lightning in the atmosphere, and his form in the sky is the sun. Furthermore, Agni is the messenger and priest of the gods. Offerings poured into Agni's mouth (i.e., the sacrificial fire) are carried up (via smoke) so that other deities may share in the meal. Agni's role as priest is celebrated in the very first hymn of the *Rig Veda:* "I pray to Agni, the household priest who is the god of the sacrifice, the one who chants and invokes and brings most treasure" (*Rig Veda* 1.1.1).

Vak is the goddess incarnating sacred speech. It is she who represents the power of the *mantra,* or verbal spell that accompanies every ritual action, and it is Vak's power that lies behind the sacrality of the Vedas themselves. In one hymn of self-praise, Vak declares that "I am the one who says, by myself, what gives joy to gods and men. Whom I love I make awesome; I make him a sage, a wise man, a Brahman" (*Rig Veda* 10.125.5).

A third major deity of the sacrifice is Soma, who, like other Vedic divinities, is no different from the part of nature it also names. But what was soma? The texts indicate that it was a plant of some sort that was pressed for its juice, which was offered to the gods in the sacrificial fire as well as consumed by the sacrificer and his priests. But the exact plant that was called by the name "soma" remains a scholarly mystery. What is fairly certain is that the plant's juice had an intoxicating, perhaps even hallucinogenic, effect on the drinker. Witness the following exclamations of bliss that have been preserved in the *Rig Veda:*

> Like impetuous wind, the drinks have lifted me up. Have I not drunk Soma? The drinks have lifted me up, like swift horses bolting with a chariot. Have I not drunk Soma? . . . In my vastness, I surpassed the sky and this vast earth. Have I not drunk Soma? Yes! I will place the earth here, or perhaps

there. Have I not drunk Soma? I am huge, huge! flying to the clouds. Have I not drunk Soma? (10.119)

Vedic Sacrifice: The worship of Agni, Vak, and Soma leads to the fourth characteristic of Vedic religion: the overwhelming importance of the ritual of the fire sacrifice. Most of the Veda is dedicated to the philosophy and practice of the sacrifice, or *yajna.* Utilizing three sacred fires that stood for the three worlds; offering oblations of milk, grain, meat (goats, sheep, cows, and horses were regularly slaughtered), soma, or even human beings (there is some evidence for human sacrifice in Vedic times); and employing anywhere from four to sixteen priests (depending on the complexity of the ritual), the Vedic liturgy is among the most detailed and complicated ever invented.

The power Vedic texts attribute to the sacrifice can hardly be overestimated. It was through the sacrifice that the gods created the world in the beginning, and it is by continual sacrifices even now that the cosmic order, or *rita,* is maintained. It is the responsibility of human beings to see to it that the gods are kept happy and well fed through the offerings of oblations. If the gods are pleased they will reward the sacrificer in various ways, both tangible and spiritual. Over time, the sacrifice took on such efficacy that it was thought to operate automatically. If correctly performed, ritual action would inevitably entail the desired reaction, and pleasing the gods came to take a secondary place to carrying out the details of the sacrifice in the proper manner.

The effects of the sacrifice were threefold. First, the sacrifice was said to have cosmic results. Performed at the junctures of day and night (i.e., dawn and dusk), of the lunar fortnights (i.e., new and full moon), and of the quarters and halves of the year, Vedic rituals were thought to promote the continuity of time itself. Without the daily fire sacrifice, or *agnihotra,* one text claims, the sun would not rise in the morning or set at night. It was the sacrifice that reversed the tendency of nature toward entropy; it was the fire ritual that literally held things together and kept the cosmic order humming along.

The second set of effects of the sacrifice might be called material and sociological. The sacrificer was promised material rewards for offering sacrifices, including such things as good crops, good health, sons (this was an overwhelmingly patriarchal society), wealth, victory over one's enemies, and long life. At another level, the sacrifices one offered were a kind of measuring stick of one's social status. Just as Americans might gauge status by the size of the wedding or celebration one puts on, in Vedic India one's social standing was dependent on the type, size, and frequency of the rituals sponsored. Vedic texts thus speak of the sacrifice's power to create or construct a "self" (*atman*) and a "world" (*loka*) for the sacrificer in this world.

Performance of sacrifice could also result in a "divine self" located in a "world of heaven" for the sacrificer after his death. But like the status ("self") and standing ("world") created by the sacrificer for himself in this life, those of the next life were relative to the sacrificer's ritual resume. The divine self is "born out of the sacrifice," that is, it is the product of the rituals one performs in this life: "The sacrifice becomes the sacrificer's self in yonder world" (*Shatapatha Brahmana* 11.1.8.6), or as another text puts it, the sacrificer "is united in the other world with what he has sacrificed" (*Taittiriya Samhita* 3.3.8.5).

The sacrifice, in sum, was supposed to have a constructive effect—on the cosmos (conjoining the parts of time and providing for temporal continuity), on the human being in this life (creating a social status for the sacrificer), and on the human being after death (for one's destiny in the afterlife was also a product of the rituals one had performed in this life). One is what one does, one's future is the result of one's present actions, and it is here that we can identify the origins of the later Indian law of *karma*.

Already by the sixth or seventh century B.C., new religions with new philosophical assumptions had arisen in India. Vedic religion per se was replaced by Hinduism, Buddhism, Jainism, and other alternatives. Its prestige lives on, however, among the Hindus who revere the Veda as a holy book and who have incorporated some Vedic doctrines and practices into the Hindu tradition. Westerners have recently "discovered" that a handful of Brahmans in India today still perform the Vedic sacrificial rituals, carrying on a tradition that now stretches back some three thousand years. Such Brahmans now enact their archaic rites before the eyes (and cameras and tape recorders) of scholars who are, in their own way, participating in the project to preserve the Vedic tradition. *See also* Aranyakas; Aryans; Atharva Veda; Brahmanas; caste; cosmogony; Hindu domestic ritual; Hinduism; Hinduism (authoritative texts and their interpretation); Indo-European religion; karma; Rig Veda; sacrifice; Sama Veda; Upanishads; Yajur Veda.

Vedanta (vay-dahn'tuh; Skt.), the end or culmina-

tion of the Veda, eternally revealed sacred knowledge; one of six orthodox viewpoints (*darshanas*) of classical Indian thought. Vedanta is the most influential traditional Hindu school of thought to the present day, especially in its nondualistic form. The term *Vedanta* is applied both to the Upanishads (unsystematic sacred texts investigating the ultimate nature of self and cosmos), and a later set of related systems of thought arising from Upanishadic exegesis. Vedanta is sometimes called Uttara (later) Mimamsa (exegesis) to differentiate it from Purva (earlier) Mimamsa, explanation of the ritual-oriented portions of the Veda. The three bases of Vedanta are the Upanishads (especially the oldest ones, such as the *Brihadaranyaka*, *Chandogya*, and *Taittiriya*), the *Brahmasutras* ("aphorisms about *brahman*" summarizing Upanishadic teachings), and the *Bhagavad Gita* ("Song of the Lord").

Vedantan thinkers share certain assumptions, including the authority of the Veda, brahman as cause and substance of phenomenal appearance, the transmigration of the self due to the necessity of experiencing the fruits of one's actions (*karma*), and the possibility of release from the cycle of rebirth.

Several schools developed within Vedanta, holding to quite different views about the nature of ultimate reality (brahman) and its relation with the individual (*jiva*) and real self (*atman*), as well as the nature of liberation from bondage to rebirth. These views, seen most clearly in their respective commentaries on the *Brahmasutras*, include the nondualism of Shankara (ca. eighth century), the qualified (theistic) nondualism of Ramanuja (1017–1137), and the radical dualism of Mudhva (1238–1317). *See also* Bhagavad Gita; Dvaita Vedanta; nondualism, Hindu; six systems of Indian philosophy; Upanishads; Veda, Vedism; Vedanta Sutra.

Vedanta Society, the institutional name for the centers for the teaching of philosophical Hinduism in the United States under the direction of the Ramakrishna Math and Mission headquartered near Calcutta, India. The mission is the work of Swami Vivekananda (1863–1902), a disciple of the modern Hindu saint Ramakrishna. In 1893 Vivekananda attended the World's Parliament of Religions in Chicago, where he attracted considerable attention; within a few years centers staffed by Ramakrishna swamis had been founded in major American cities for the benefit of those who wished to pursue further the Vedanta philosophy and spiritual practice Vivekananda taught.

Vedanta emphasizes that all beings, including all humans, are manifestations of Brahman, the One Reality and human beings' true nature. Although some rituals are performed for those who wish them, public services consist mainly of devotional lectures centering on this theme. There are also monastic communities for monks and nuns. The Vedanta Society has had an influence out of proportion to its relatively small numbers in America, attracting intellectuals such as the novelists Aldous Huxley and Christopher Isherwood. *See also* America, Hinduism in; North America, new religions in; Ramakrishna; Vedanta; Vivekananda.

Vedanta Sutra (vay-dahn'tuh soo'truh; Skt.), one of three central texts, along with the *Bhagavad Gita* and the Upanishads, of the Hindu system called Vedanta, which represents itself as the "end" (*-anta*) or culmination of knowledge (*veda*). Attributed to Badarayana (ca. 400–200 B.C.) and consisting of 555 *sutra*s, which presuppose commentary, the text summarizes, systematizes, and harmonizes the disparate and fragmentary teachings about absolute reality or *brahman* contained in the concluding portions of Vedic literature, namely, the Upanishads (ca. 550 B.C.). Divided into four chapters, the first deals with the nature of absolute reality; the second responds to objections and criticizes opponents; the third details the means to acquire knowledge about the absolute; and the fourth discusses the advantages of such knowledge.

The text apparently favors the view that the absolute is both an impersonal transcendent reality and a personal God identical to and different from creation. Thus, the universe is created through the God's self-transformation even as the God remains entirely unaffected by the process. The text argues against the positions of other Hindu systems, particularly Samkhya and ritualism (*purva mimamsa*), though commentarial traditions have used its ambiguities to sustain arguments in favor of widely varying interpretations. *See also* brahman; Vedanta.

Vedism. *See* Veda, Vedism.

vegetarianism, abstaining from eating flesh (meat, fish), and by some, eggs and dairy products. Religious traditions prescribing vegetarianism include Jains, Pythagoreans, Orphics, and Manichaeans; the medieval Cathari and Bogomils; and sects of Buddhists, post-Vedic Hindus, and Taoists. Historically it is associated with beliefs in reincarnation, the unity of life, bodily purity, sexual abstinence, rejection of sacrificial cults. *See also* Adventists; ahimsa; Bogomils; Catharism; Jainism; Manichaeism; Orphism; Pythagoras; Varkari Panth.

veil, piece of cloth used to conceal. 1 Veiling of women, usually after marriage, is a common practice, especially in Islam. 2 Within Roman Catholicism, nuns wear a veil over their heads and shoulders. "To take the veil" is a popular expression for becoming a nun. 3 Sacred objects are veiled, e.g., the Holy of Holies in the Jerusalem Temple, the Christian eucharistic cup. 4 Persons and objects are veiled as a sign of mourning.

Venus (vee'noos), originally an Italian goddess, later identified with the Greek goddess Aphrodite as patroness of sex, beauty, and generation. She was especially important in legend because, as the mother of Aeneas, she provided a divine origin for the Romans.

Vergil (vuhr'jil; 70–19 B.C.), also Publius Vergilius Maro, Roman poet; author of the *Bucolics*, in which literary pastoral on the peaceful life of shepherds is combined with reference to contemporary disturbances; the *Georgics*, a poetic treatise on farming, which examines the human costs implicit in civilization and progress; and the *Aeneid*, a revival of Homeric epic on the subject of Aeneas, founder of the Roman people, whose journey from the flames of Troy to Italy and subsequent battle for a foothold there provide a powerful image of both the hopes and sufferings implicit in Rome's destiny.

Two features are of special interest in Vergil's engagement with religious themes. First is his interest in deities and cults of the native Italian religion. Though Vergil draws heavily on Greek mythological lore, his care to describe native rites and divinities, often with accounts of their origin, suggests an attempt to preserve and stabilize awareness of traditions that he considers to be of great value: "Fortunate is he who knows the rustic divinities" (*Georgics* 2.493). Second is the importance of fate in the *Aeneid*. Aeneas's journey is a mission of providential destiny, and the prophecies and oracles that Aeneas receives reflect a beneficial cosmic plan both in Aeneas's journey and in the later history of the Roman people—a plan that often appears irreconcilable with the violence and suffering of the human characters in the epic. *See also* Aeneid.

vernacular, the common, living language of a culture; often different from the sacred, archaic language used in religious texts and rituals. *See also* language, sacred.

Verstehen. *See* empathy; hermeneutics; understanding.

Vessantara (ves-ahn'tuh-ruh), legendary prince of the North Indian kingdom of Sivi renowned for his charity, in the Jataka tradition of Pali Buddhism the last *bodhisattva* rebirth prior to Prince Siddhartha. *See also* Buddhas; Buddhism (festal cycle).

Vestals (ve'stuhlz), virgin priestesses of Vesta (the Roman hearth goddess); they were responsible for Vesta's sacred fire in a sanctuary symbolic of the corporate hearth of the Roman people. *See also* priest/priestess; Roman religion.

vestments, Christian liturgical, special clothing used by Christian clergy on ritual occasions. The practice of wearing specifically liturgical garb appears to have arisen in the fifth and sixth centuries. In general, Catholic (Roman- and Eastern-rite) and Orthodox clergy wear liturgical vestments descended from Roman everyday clothing: the alb (a tunic) and the chasuble or cope (a cloak). A wider variation of use exists in the Reformation churches. The twentieth century movements for liturgical reform in a variety of Western churches has to a certain extent brought an ecumenical dimension to the liturgical vestments worn by Western Christian clergy, especially a wider use of the alb.

Via Dolorosa (vi'eh dol'ehro'seh; Lat., "sad road"), traditional route in Jerusalem taken by Jesus from Pilate's judgment hall to the place of crucifixion. *See also* crucifixion; stations of the cross.

vicar (Lat., "substitute"). **1** A salaried Christian priest who administers to a parish but does not receive parish income. **2** In the Anglican Church, a common title for a parish priest.

Vidushaka (vi-doo'shuh-kuh; Skt., "the spoiler"), the buffoon in Sanskrit drama. This grotesque, deformed, ill-educated, Prakrit-speaking Brahman is primarily interested in food, especially sweets. He complements and completes the role of the drama's hero, the *nayaka*, by regularly deflating the latter's lyrical fantasies. *See also* dance; drama and religion.

vihara (vi-hahr'ruh; Skt., and Pali, "residence"), a Bud-

dhist monastery. Although literally a *vihara* is a monk's residence, by extension the term refers to the complexes within which residences are found. Thus, the term is commonly used to refer to Buddhist temples in which a residence is combined with a Buddha image, *stupa* (reliquary mound), and Bodhi Tree. *See also* bhiksu/bhiksuni; Bodhi Tree; monasticism; Sangha; stupa; wat.

The Taktsang, or Tiger's Nest *vihara* (monastery), an important Tibetan Buddhist meditation center and pilgrimage site in western Bhutan. It commemorates the tradition of the arrival of Padmasambhava in Tibet from India in the eighth century, riding on a tiger's back, in order to establish Buddhist Tantrism (Vajrayana).

Viking Brotherhood. *See* Asatru.

Vikings ("those from the bays"), mainly non-Christian Scandinavian seafaring traders, warriors, and adventurers who, from the end of the eighth to the eleventh centuries, raided wide areas of Europe and ranged as far as Persia to the east, Africa to the south, and North America to the west.

Little is known for certain about their religion, which appears to be a warrior-centered Nordic tradition with discernible shamanistic elements. Their most famous ritual is that of shipboard cremation of the dead. *See also* Nordic religion.

village recluses (Korea). Confucian tradition in Korea saw the appearance of two main paths that had also appeared in China, the scholar–civil servant and the scholar-recluse. These two paths point to a fundamental difference in the Neo-Confucian attitude toward scholarship. For some, knowing the truth was knowing how to put the truth into practice in the national government. For others, it was a matter of putting the truth into practice in one's own life and the life of one's community without reference to the government, which was always thought to compromise the truth. This difference had been highlighted in the careers of the twelfth-century Neo-Confucian teachers and was adopted in Korea, where preference and honor were given to those who stayed away from government.

In Korea the ideal of the village recluse (*sarim*) was that of the scholar who exercised pure poverty (*ch'ongbin*). This meant that rather than compromise religious and philosophical principles in government service for the sake of rank and salary, scholars lived in poverty in small villages, studied and wrote commentaries on the classical texts, cultivated empathy with the "good people" (*yang-min*) through the practice of subsistence agriculture, educated their own and village children, and sometimes even established a private academy to teach the sons of other scholars.

The title and mentality of these village recluses, in time, became identified with particular groups of scholars who also served in government. After the various purges of government literati in 1498, 1504, 1519, and 1545, such scholar-bureaucrats as Cho Kwangjo (1482–1519), Yi Hwang (1501–70), and their disciples, who sought to maintain the principles of scholarly self-cultivation, a meditative and ascetic life-style, and uncompromising loyalty to the truth while serving in government became known as *sarim*. They opposed themselves to other scholar-bureaucrats, whom they labeled as *kwanhak*, or "learners for the sake of government office." These sarim, who mostly served in the Office of Remonstrance (Sahonbu), the Office of the Censor-General (Saganwon), and the Office of Special Advisers (Hungmun'gwan), in turn wrote histories of Korean Confucian scholar lineages in which the sarim, their forebears, and descendants were portrayed as the righteous and the oppressed. *See also* Neo-Confucianism; Yi Hwang.

Vimalakirti (vi-muh-luh-keer'tee), protagonist of *The Teaching of Vimalakirti*, an Indian Mahayana Buddhist scripture. As an educated layman, Vimalakirti teaches the ideal of the *bodhisattva* (Buddha-to-be) and the superiority of lay life over the life of a monk. *See also* Mahayana.

Vinaya (vi'nuh-yuh; Skt., Pali, "removal," "rule"), the monastic discipline codified in the *Vinaya* portions of the Buddhist scriptures. Vinaya, as monastic practice itself, is a crucial part of the spiritual development of an individual monk or nun, but it also grounds the communal life of the monastic order. *See also* bhiksu/bhiksuni; Buddhism (authoritative texts and their interpretation); monasticism; Sangha.

Vinaya (Korean Buddhism). The Vinaya is the body of rules that govern the clerical and lay Buddhist community. In Korea these rules were and are derived from Chinese and Korean translations of the Vinaya texts of the Dharmaguptaka sect, which had been brought directly from India in the sixth century, with additions made by various scholastic and meditative lineages.

Koreans have, from the beginnings of Buddhism in the peninsula, been noted for their strict adherence to the Vinaya, especially the rules on celibacy and the separate quartering of monks and nuns. Various governments, including those of Paekche, Silla, and Koryo, have supported Vinaya proscriptions on hunting and the eating of meat. Even in the anti-Buddhist Choson period (1392–1910), Vinaya restrictions on the use of seasonings (garlic, red pepper, onions, and other "hot" spices) and its promotion of vegetarianism affected local and capital cuisines. In the twentieth century, Japanese colonialists introduced Japanese innovations into the Vinaya (clergy marriage and temple inheritance), which caused a split in the Buddhist community, so that there are now two main sects of Buddhism (the Chogye and the T'aeko), distinguished primarily by their interpretations and practice of the Vinaya. *See also* Chogye Buddhism; Vinaya.

Vinaya school (Chin. *Lu-tsung*), a minor school of Chinese Buddhism founded by Tao-hsuan in the seventh century and specializing in the study of the monastic regulations (Vinaya). *See also* Taohsuan; Vinaya.

violence and religion. The relationship of violence and religion clouds the histories of virtually every religious tradition and fascinates some of the keenest theorists of religion. Visions of destruction are ubiquitous in religious symbols, mythology, and rituals, and the histories of most religions leave a trail of blood. Several modern studies set out to show why violence is essential to religious language and images, why violence is justified in religious ethics, and why violence is a natural by-product of political conflicts involving religion in the modern age.

Sacrifice and Symbolic Violence: The savage martyrdom of Husayn in Shiite Islam, the crucifixion of Jesus in Christianity, the sacrifice of Guru Tegh Bahadur in Sikhism, the bloody conquests chronicled in the Hebrew Bible, the battles celebrated in the Hindu epics, and the religious wars described in the Sinhalese Buddhist Chronicles—all these indicate that images of violence are central to virtually every religious tradition. The most familiar emblems of Islam and Sikhism are swords, and the central symbol of Christianity is an execution device, the cross. In Catholic iconography the bleeding, dying savior is often portrayed in graphic detail. In Protestant Christianity the violence is conveyed through words: popular hymns remind the faithful of the "old rugged cross" on which the savior died and urge them to be "washed in the blood of the lamb." The main ritual of Christianity, the Eucharist, involves symbolic cannibalism, the ingestion of the flesh and blood of Jesus. The Catholic doctrine of transubstantiation insists that the eucharistic elements become, in fact, Christ's real body and blood.

The most common forms of violence portrayed in the myths, symbols, and rituals of religion are warfare, sacrifice, and martyrdom. The word *sacrifice* comes from a Latin verb, "to make sacred," and refers to the ritual killing that was especially prevalent in ancient religious traditions, where priests were sacred executioners, and altars were the chopping blocks. The book of Leviticus in the Hebrew Bible provides a detailed guide for sacrificial conduct, and the architecture of ancient Israeli temples reflects the centrality of sacrifice. The most holy figure in Christianity largely eschews the role of priest; instead Christ plays the role of the sacrificed lamb.

The Vedic Agnichayana ritual—some three thousand years old and probably the most ancient ritual still being performed—involves the construction of an elaborate altar for a sacrificial ritual, originally an animal sacrifice. Some speculate that it, and many other ancient rituals, involved human sacrifices. This was certainly true of the ancient Aztec empire, when conquered soldiers were treated royally in preparation for their sacrifice to Huitzilopochtli and other gods; their still-beating hearts would be extracted from their chests and their faces skinned to make ritual masks.

Theories about Symbolic Violence: Most theories about religious violence begin with the concept of sacrifice. In the nineteenth century, E. B. Tylor posits that primitive sacrifice was an attempt to bribe the gods; as religion evolved, sacrifice became internalized in the form of self-renunciation. W. Robertson Smith sees sacrifice as a ritual meal, its destructiveness leading to a covenantal bond. In *The Golden Bough* (1900), James Frazer identifies sacrifice as the key element of religion: the killing of kings and holy men allows the gods to be rejuvenated, and the symbolic sacrifice of modern religion is an extension of this ancient magic. Two sociologists, Henri Hubert and Marcel Mauss, following Emile Durkheim, see the sacrificial victim as mediating between sacred and profane realms. The best-known social theorist of the nineteenth century, Karl Marx, thinks of violence—in the form of class conflict—as fundamental to religion, for he regards religion as both the symptom and instrument of oppression.

In the twentieth century, Sigmund Freud advances a theory of religious violence that by extension accounts for virtually all forms of culture. In *Totem and Taboo* (1913), Freud explains that the destructive instinct in human nature would tear apart a family, a tribe, or a civil society if it were not symbolically displaced and directed toward a sacrificial foe. Freud regards the myth of Oedipus—in which a man kills his father and seduces his mother—as the prototype of all myth. Although many aspects of Freud's theory are discredited, the major theme has survived. Ernst Becker, for instance, accepts that the purpose of violence in religion is to sublimate the violence of real life, and ultimately to deny the reality of death. Weston LaBarre argues that all religion is like the Ghost Dance religion of the Plains Indians: it is an attempt to escape the horrors of cultural conflict and physical destruction, and to appeal for support from immortal forces. In another interesting variant on the Freudian thesis, Rene Girard, in *Violence and the Sacred* (1972), accepts the Freudian point that religion's symbols and rituals of violence evoke, and thereby vent, violent impulses and allow those who embrace them to release their feelings of hostility toward members of their own communities. Parting company with Freud, Girard identifies the basic impulse that needs to be displaced as mimetic desire—the urge to imitate and better one's rival, and to desire what one's rival desires.

A somewhat different explanation of the primacy of violence in religion is offered by Walter Burkert in *Homo Necans* (1972). Burkert concludes that the bloody myths and sacrificial rituals of ancient Greece and other societies allow a group collectively to confront the reality of death, channel the power of violence, increase inner-group solidarity, and give the group a biological advantage for survival.

In addition to these cross-cultural theories, theological explanations account for the violence of a particular religion's symbols and rituals. Images of violence and destruction are often regarded as metaphors for the victory over evil.

Religious Justifications for Violence: Although many of these theories suggest that symbolic violence alleviates the violence of real life, real acts of violence have sometimes been perpetrated or supported by religion. The very words used to characterize fanaticism—a *crusading* spirit, *zealotry*, and acts of *assassins*—are drawn from violent incidents in Christian, Jewish, and Islamic history.

Hindu Violence: In Vedic times, warriors called on the gods to participate in their own struggles, thus merging the two realms. In the later development of Hinduism, the *Bhagavad Gita* gives several reasons why killing in warfare is permissible. Among them is the argument that the soul can never really be killed: "He who slays, slays not; he who is slain, is not slain." Another position given in the *Gita* is based on *dharma* (moral obligation): the duties of a member of the *kshatriya* (warrior) caste involve killing. Mohandas K. Gandhi (1869–1948), like many other modern Hindus who revere the *Gita*, regarded its warfare as allegorical—the conflict between good and evil. Gandhi, who ordinarily ascribed to nonviolence, allowed for an exception to this general rule when a small, strategic act of violence would defuse a greater violence. A more straightforward approach was taken by other Hindu nationalists in this century, including militant Bengali Hindus inspired by Kali, who felt a moral obligation to use force for the cause of Mother India.

Sikh Violence: Although Guru Nanak, the sixteenth-century spiritual master regarded as the Sikhs' founder, is portrayed as a gentle soul, the Sikh movement in time came to be led by members of a militant tribal group, the Jats, and Sikhs have periodically clashed with Moghuls, British, and other Indian rulers. The core of the Sikh community is known as "the army of the faithful" (*dal khalsa*), and their symbol is a double-edged sword. The conquests of the great nineteenth-century ruler, Maharaja Ranjit Singh, and the violent exhortations of the twentieth-century militant, Jarnail Singh Bhindranwale, are both justified by the Sikh doctrine of *miripiri:* the idea that religion is to be victorious in both the spiritual and worldly realms.

Buddhist Violence: The Buddhist ideal of non-injury (*ahimsa*) permits some acts of violence to be justified. Traditional Buddhist teachings require that five conditions be satisfied before anyone is culpable in an act of killing: something must first have been living; the killer must have known that it was alive; the killer must have intended to kill it; there must have been an act of killing; and it must, in fact, have died. It is the absence of the third of these conditions that typically allows for some mitigation of the rule of nonviolence. For instance, many Buddhists will eat meat as long as they have not themselves intended that the animal be slaughtered or been involved in the act of slaughtering. Armed defense—even warfare—has been justified on the grounds that such violence has been in the nature of response, not intent. But to use violence nondefensively—for the purpose of political expansion, for example—is prohibited under Buddhist rule.

Chinese and Japanese Religious Violence: Despite the influence of Buddhism, other religious teachers in Chinese and Japanese traditions have justified violence, often for the sake of maintaining order or expanding the power of the emperor. Beginning in the eleventh century, the Japanese samurai tradition merged Confucian ideals with a warrior ethic to produce something of a religious cult. The ultimate sacrifice was a ritual suicide (*seppuku*) in which the samurai disemboweled himself with his sword and was then decapitated by an assistant. This self-sacrifice was done for reasons of shame, as an atonement for an error, or to protest an act of injustice.

Jewish Violence: As in Hinduism, some of the earliest images of the tradition are the most violent. "The Lord is a warrior," proclaims Exodus 15:3, and the first books of the Hebrew Bible include scenes of utter desolation caused by divine intervention. Rabbinic Judaism, despite several militant clashes with the Romans—including the Maccabean Revolt (166–164 B.C.) and the revolt at Masada (A.D. 73)—is largely nonviolent. At the level of statecraft, the rabbis did sanction warfare, but they distinguished between religious war and optional war. The former they required as a moral or spiritual obligation—to protect the faith or defeat enemies of the Lord. These they contrasted with wars waged primarily for reasons of political expediency.

Christian Violence: The controversy over whether

Christianity sanctions violence has hounded the Christian community from the very beginning. Some argue that Christians are expected to follow Jesus' example of selfless love (*agape*): "Love your enemies and pray for those who persecute you" (Matthew 5:44). Those who take the other side refer to the incident in which Jesus drove the moneychangers from the Temple, and to his enigmatic statement: "Do not think that I have come to bring peace on earth; I have not come to bring peace but a sword" (Matthew 10:34; also Luke 12:51–52). The early church fathers, including Tertullian (d. ca. 220) and Origen (d. ca. 254), asserted that Christians were constrained from taking human life, a principle that prevented Christians from serving in the Roman army. When Christianity was made the state religion by Constantine in the fourth century, it began to reject pacifism and accept the doctrine of just war, an idea first stated by Cicero (d. 43 B.C.) and later developed by Ambrose (d. 397) and Augustine (d. 430). The abuse of the concept in justifying military adventures and violent persecutions of heretical and minority groups led Thomas Aquinas, in the thirteenth century, to reaffirm that war is always sinful, even if it is occasionally waged for a just cause. Some modern Catholic theologians have adapted the theory of just war to liberation theology, arguing that the Church can embrace a just revolution. An American Protestant theologian, Reinhold Niebuhr (1891–1971), argues that Christians ought not be pacifist because they accept the doctrine of original sin, and with it the implication that righteous force is sometimes required to subdue evil in the world. Niebuhr accepts the notion of just war, insisting, however, that when violence is employed to extirpate injustice, it should be as swift and skillful as a "surgeon's knife."

Islamic Violence: Within the Muslim community, violence is justified—even required—as punishment. In Islamic contacts with "the world of conflict" (*dar al harb*) outside the Islamic world, violence is permitted for defensive purposes, and as a tool in subduing an enemy of the faith. Conflict of the latter sort is known as *jihad*, a word that literally means "striving" and is often translated as "holy war." This concept has been used to justify the expansion of Muslim states into non-Islamic areas. But Muslim law does not allow jihad to be used to justify forcible conversion to Islam: the only conversions regarded as valid are those that come about nonviolently, through rational persuasion and change of heart. In recent years Muslim political activists have employed the notion of jihad in justifying militant political acts. According to an influential Egyptian author, Abd Al-Salam Faraj, jihad is

every Muslim's "neglected duty" to defend the faith—violently, if necessary—in the social and political spheres.

The Politics of Religious Terrorism: In the twentieth century, acts of religious violence have been perpetrated by terrorist movements. Images of guerrilla bands of Buddhist monks in Sri Lanka, gun-toting Sikh militants in India, and bomb-wielding Muslim extremists in Lebanon—all these converge to form a picture of militant religious fanaticism that has been global in scope.

These acts of violence have often been committed in a deliberately graphic and extreme way, so as to emphasize their symbolic nature. For that reason they can be analyzed as religious phenomena. Some social scientists see them as political acts as well: David Rapoport views certain forms of religious violence as aspects of political messianism, and Ehud Sprinzak regards them as evidence of a breakdown in democracy. Another approach to the analysis of twentieth-century religious terrorism sees it as part of a larger historical conflict between two views of political order: one characterized by secular nationalism and the other by traditional religious culture. The violent followers of these movements often regard themselves as participating in a cosmic war between the forces of good and evil.

The political analyses of religious violence owe much to Max Weber's insight that the legitimacy of the state is rooted in violence. Since religion is the only entity besides secular nationalism that can give moral sanction to the use of violence, it holds the potential of being fundamentally competitive with it. It should be no surprise, then, that religious violence has erupted in those parts of the world where the legitimacy of the nation-state has been questioned: Ireland, India, Sri Lanka, Israel, Lebanon, and elsewhere in South Asia and the Middle East.

Virashaiva. *See* Lingayat.

Virgin Birth, a cluster of Christian beliefs about Mary's virginity before, during, and after Jesus' birth. She conceived him by the power of the Spirit without sexual intercourse (virginal conception); she delivered him while remaining physically intact (virgin birth); she remained a virgin forever after (perpetual virginity). Virginal conception is briefly attested in the Bible (Matthew, Luke). The other two beliefs developed subsequently, though not without dispute, in tandem with growing church emphasis on the ascetic practice of virginity. *See also* Mary.

Visakha Puja (vis-ahk'ah poo'jah), celebration of the birth, enlightenment, and death of the Buddha. In Buddhist legend each of these three events occurred on the full-moon day of the lunar month of Visakha (April–May). Known as Buddha's Day in the Theravada cultures of Sri Lanka and Southeast Asia, Visakha Puja is the most holy day of the Buddhist calendar. Celebrations focus on the monastery and include circumambulation, sermons on the legendary life of the Buddha, watering Bodhi Trees, bathing Buddha images, and pilgrimages to sacred sites. In Tibet the Buddha's conception or incarnation surpasses in importance the other events in the Buddha's life largely because it was assimilated into the New Year celebration in the first lunar month. In China, Korea, and Japan Buddha images are processed and lustrated in honor of the Buddha's birth. *See also* Buddhism (festal cycle).

Vishnu (vish'noo; Skt.,"he who acts or pervades"), in Hinduism, the pervading protector of the universe. The Vishnu concept appears first in the *Rig Veda*, where Vishnu is already known for his three strides that integrate levels of the cosmos. In Vaishnavism, the Supreme Person is Mahavishnu ("the great Vishnu"), who transforms himself into Brahma to emanate the universe, Vishnu to protect it from within, and Shiva to destroy it. On earth, Vishnu resides in Vaikuntha on White Island in the Milk Ocean to protect and teach, the paradigm for kings. His chief queen, Lakshmi or Shri, is his auspicious wealth and will; his second queen, Bhumi, is his realm of earth and effect; the goddess Durga, his potency for victory, is his third queen or his sister who marries Shiva. Vishnu has no children, but begets many through *avatars* (his assumed forms).

In his temple sanctuaries, Vishnu normally resides in a four-armed human form standing, reclining, or sitting, a right arm holding a discus (symbolizing fire, time, justice) and a left arm a conch shell (water, emancipation from time and justice). Attendants signify other dimensions, e.g., his bird vehicle, Garuda (Veda), his snake couch, Ananta or Adishesha (primordial matter), his attendant, Vishvaksena (Tantra). One or more queens are present as icons or on his body (a mole, a lotus). Royal sovereignty determines relations to Vishnu: the refugee fleeing from sin and evil to Vishnu's feet and living by his grace was taught by Krishna, developed by Ramanuja and other theologians, and extolled by poets like the Alvars and Tulsi Das.

Vishnu is met in the soul through meditation, in the fire through rites, in *mantras* (sacred utterances) through initiation, and in the sun as time—twelve of Vishnu's forms correspond to the months. Common worship includes chanting his one thousand names and singing, telling, and dramatizing stories relating his repeated avatars, notably ten in the four ages: Fish, Tortoise, Boar, and Man-lion in the Krita Yuga; Dwarf, Parashurama, and Rama in the Treta Yuga; Balarama (or Buddha), and Krishna in the Dvapara Yuga; and Kalki in the Kali Yuga. Rama in various *Ramayana*s and Krishna in the *Mahabharata, Bhagavad Gita, Harivamsa, Vishnu Purana,* and *Bhagavata Purana* are most popular. *See also* avatar; Krishna; Shri-Lakshmi; trimurti; Vaishnavism.

vision, the ecstatic experience of seeing a supernatural being.

vision quest, an institutionalized activity characteristic of but not limited to the Plains tribes, by which a special relationship with transcendent powers is sought. For most groups, the vision quest is not, as it is elsewhere in North America, associated with puberty rituals. Among many Plains tribes a general distinction is recognized between dreams and waking visions as means of access to power, although neither of these modes of experience seems necessarily to be more valuable or successful for the vision quest. The general feature informing Plains experience is a deep expectation that visions will occur and that they are necessary for a successful life; persons who have no visions are likely to be marginalized and to understand themselves as spiritually and materially poor. Generally speaking, on the Plains the quest for visions takes a typical form: isolation of the person. For some groups, forms of deprivation, including self-inflicted ordeals, are preparatory to the vision experience; for other groups, preparation excludes ordeals but sometimes includes fasting and other forms of abstinence. The content of the vision experience, while culturally diverse, might include concrete auditory and visual encounters with beings in animal, plant, or other form; some persons have described the experience in terms of disembodied voices or sounds. In many Plains tribes, there is a kind of democratized shamanism, the possibility of the vision experience being open to all, including, in some cases, both men and women. In other groups, like the Pawnees and the Dakotas, powerful vision experiences are associated with a particular class of persons, the shamans; while other persons may have experiences of the inner life, the shamans exercise control over more fundamental and extensive powers. *See also* North America, traditional religions in.

Vivekananda (vi-vay-kah-nahn'dah; b. Narendranath Datta; 1863–1902), a Hindu reformer and Indian culture hero who founded the Vedanta Society (New York, 1895) as well as both the Ramakrishna Mission and the Ramakrishna Order in India (1897). *See also* America, Hinduism in; Ramakrishna; Reform Hinduism; Vedanta Society.

vocation, religious. *See* calling.

Vodou. *See* Voodoo.

Vohu Manah (voh'hoo mah'nah; Avestan, "good mind"), a divinity who proclaimed "the Good Religion," Zoroastrianism's term for itself, to Zoroaster; Vohu Manah's physical symbol is the cow. *See also* Zoroastrianism.

voluntary association, a religious group that one chooses to join as opposed to one into which one has been born or to which one belongs by virtue of citizenship.

Voluspa (voh-luhs-pah'; Icelandic, "Sibyl's Prophecy"), the most famous lay in the Icelandic *Poetic Edda*, probably composed in early eleventh century. It relates the vision of a prophetess who describes the fateful events that lead to Ragnarok, the destruction of the present world order—and the cosmic catastrophe itself. *See also* Edda; Nordic religion.

Voodoo, or Vodou, is the African-Christian new religion born in Haiti, whose followers "serve the divine spirits" in life and rituals and accept possession by those spirits for healing and spiritual guidance. The word *voodoo* derives from the language of the Dahomean Fon communities, in whose traditional religion *vodu* or *vodun* is a "divine spirit." Originally a term used only by outsiders—and then often with a pejorative sense—"Vodou" is now acknowledged as the proper designation for the complex beliefs and practices among the majority of the populace of Haiti.

Voodoo began as the clandestine religion of enslaved African sugar-plantation workers in Haiti in the seventeenth century, but its early history is preserved only in scattered eighteenth-century colonial records and ordinance codes. The reports of covert meetings, dances, funeral practices, and even trance possession

A bloodless Voodoo (or Vodou) offering called *manie sek* ("dry meal") set out on All Souls' Day in Port-au-Prince, Haiti. Various kinds of bread, roasted corn, and coffee are shared by all the participants.

among enslaved and freed Africans indicate that they preserved ancient traditions in the face of enormous obstacles; the development of Voodoo is itself a tribute to the spirit and stamina of those early devotees.

Rooted in the West African Yoruba, Fon, and Angolan communities, as well as in French Roman Catholicism, Voodoo served as the organization and sustenance of the slave revolt leading to Haitian independence and as the symbol for Haitian autonomy and nationalism as the only black republic in the Americas. It has primarily continued African priestly roles, ritual themes, symbolism, and pantheons of named female spirits (especially Ezili) and male ones (Ogou, Damballah-Wedo, Legba). The realities of Haitian life and place have reshaped the details of African mythology connected with each spirit, as well as the concepts of multiple souls and the afterlife. Beyond the importance of African doctrine, symbolism, and fragments of language, a special reverence is maintained for Africa itself as homeland and divine residence as well as symbol for the central virtues of simplicity and directness in rituals and life. Voodoo theology parallels traditional medieval Christianity, for its followers acknowledge a high creator deity, Bondye (Bon dieu), but invoke the intermediary spirits for intercession in human affairs. It is only the intermediaries—identified individually with Christian saints or sacred places—who descend to "mount" their "horses," their followers, during possession rituals. Roman Catholicism provides the ritual framework for the lives of Voodoo members as well, for they not only follow its traditional liturgical calendar for scheduling pilgrimages and lesser ceremonies but also participate in the common rituals of baptism, marriage, and the Mass. Roman Catholic prayers, some still in Latin, form a significant component of some Voodoo rituals, as do other lesser aspects and ritual objects from traditional Catholic festivals.

The divine spirits (*loa* or *lwa*) of Voodoo occupy separate pantheons or nations; two of these, the *Rada*, whose spirits are generous and benevolent, and the *Petro*, whose strong spirits evince terrible powers, dominate worship in urban centers. The higher powers (*lemiste*) are associated with natural dimensions or places, such as sacred springs or cemeteries, and are joined in the spirit world by souls of the dead and ancestral spirits (*lemo*) and sacred twins (*lemarasa*). Individual worshipers, drawn to individual spirits by necessity or similarities in personality or temperament, may choose among them for personal devotion but must not neglect those ancestors and spirits traditionally venerated in the family. Voodoo rituals range from simple devotional acts, such as the lighting of candles with accompanying prayers, to family observances for the family dead to elaborate rituals enhanced by large meals, drumming and singing, and exuberant dance.

The spiritual leaders in the Voodoo community are the male *hungans* and female *mambos;* in their religious roles, they perform divination and healing rituals for individual members, as well as oversee all training and calendrical ceremonies. As elders and teachers, they guide the possession trance dances, which allow the individual divine spirits to be present among their followers, to receive worship, and to offer healing and counsel. In Haiti, rural communities continue Voodoo as a family-centered religion firmly tied to traditional agricultural life, while urban centers have interwoven a wider variety of practices, some structured and formal—including rituals of initiation, funeral rites, pilgrimage to Catholic shrines, and festivals—some less so, including not only divination, but also the making of amulets for luck and protection.

Novels, films, and newspaper reports have sensationalized Voodoo or "hoodoo," falsely identifying it with cannibalism, sorcery, and evil potions. Scholars suggest that the lurid image of Voodoo is the expression of racist hatred of the oppressors for their victims, shaped by their fears of reprisals and revolts. Followers of Voodoo acknowledge that some manipulate its power, and they distinguish between their religion—with its traditional and salutary powers and duties—and the "work of the left hand," malevolent magical practices undertaken for mere personal gain.

The recent history of Voodoo has seen not only several attempts at its suppression by the Roman Catholic Church in Haiti but also recurring efforts there to politicize the religion through co-optation of its leaders, pilgrimage sites, and symbols while unifying its widely varying practices. Haitian Voodoo has spread to several cities in North America, with waves of migration to Miami, New York, and Montreal. Voodoo followers are also a significant presence in New Orleans, where the religion, now commingled with American Christian folk culture, was revitalized by legendary African-American leaders. *See also* Afro-Americans (Caribbean and South America), new religions among.

Votan (voh-tahn'), alternative form of the Norse god Odinn. *See also* Odinn.

votive offering, sacrifice made in fulfillment of a vow. *See also* sacrifice; vow.

vow, a solemn promise that binds one to the performance of a specific religious activity.

Christianity: In Christianity, vows may be private or liturgically celebrated and public (e.g., wedding vows) or promises connected with adoption of a religious form of life (e.g., the monastic vows of poverty, chastity, and obedience).

Vratyas (vrah'tyuhs; Skt.), ancient Indian nomadic band celebrated in the *Atharva Veda;* they were either outside early Vedic communities or perhaps early Vedic warrior-ascetics set apart by special sacrifices, raiding expeditions, and magical practices. *See also* Atharva Veda; Veda, Vedism.

Vulgate, the Latin translation of the Bible by Jerome in the last decades of the fourth century. Jerome translated the Old Testament from the Hebrew rather than the Greek Septuagint as had been common in earlier Latin versions. The Vulgate was confirmed as the official version of the Roman Catholic Church at the Council of Trent (1545–63) and until 1943 all Roman Catholic translations were required to use it. *See also* Bible, translations of the Christian; Jerome.

Vyasa (vi-yah'suh), the Indic seer who diffused the Veda in post-Vedic times. Vyasa divided the Veda into the four known traditions; he then composed a Veda for women and Shudras (the *Mahabharata*), the eighteen Puranas, and the guide to understanding the Upanishads (*Brahmasutras*). *See also* Purana; Upanishads; Veda, Vedism.

A B C D E F
G H I J K L
M N
R S T U V
W X Y & Z

wafer. *See* Eucharist, Christian; host.

wai-tan (*wi*-dahn; Chin.,"external alchemy"), the ritual, chemical, and pharmacological laboratory operations of alchemy in ancient Chinese tradition and in the Taoist religion. *See also* alchemy; nei-tan.

Wakan Tanka (wah'khan tankh'ah; Lakota, "Great Mysterious"), Lakota (Sioux) religious vision of the creative force or power that pervades all things. Though ultimately one force, and shrouded in mystery, Wakan Tanka is manifested in a variety of beings, forces, and material objects. These manifestations are classified into Wakan beings that exhibit creative, but potentially dangerous, energy; and those that exhibit negative, destructive energy. Creative forces are to some extent accessible and manipulatable by shamans, persons who possess special ritual knowledge. Destructive forces are within the purview of negative shamans, who possess ritual knowledge that is in tension with the activities of the former group. The good Wakan beings are known as the "four times four." These sixteen manifestations are subdivided into superior Wakan: Sun, Energy, Earth, and Rock; kindred Wakan: Moon, Wind, White Buffalo Cow Woman, and the Thunder Beings; subordinate Wakan: Buffalo Bull, Bear, Four Winds, and Whirlwind; and Wakan-like entities, which include Spirit, Ghost of Life, the Spirit-like, and Wakan Potency. These beings are related to the people through kinship. Negative Wakan beings include giants, water monsters, dwarflike beings, and Iktomi, the trickster. Some of these beings are interrelated with positive Wakan powers through kinship—for example, Iktomi is the firstborn son of Rock—or inversion—water monsters are inversions of the power of the Thunder Beings. Wakan Tanka, this Manyness that is One, symbolically expresses the mystery and ambiguity of the Lakota religious universe. *See also* mana; North America, traditional religions in.

Waldensians, a Christian group first organized by Peter Waldo (d. 1217), also Valdes, of Lyons. Desiring to live the apostolic life as depicted in the Gospels, the Waldensians renounced their wealth and began to preach in southern France and Italy. Initially orthodox in their beliefs, they failed to win ecclesiastical approval on the grounds that laypeople cannot legitimately preach the gospel. Rebuffed, they became strident in their criticisms of contemporary Catholic life, including the privileges of the clergy and the introduction of a number of practices, including many of the sacraments, not sanctioned by scripture. Subjected to the close scrutiny of Inquisitors, they took refuge in the Piedmont, where they continue to live.

Waldo, Peter. *See* Waldensians.

wali (wa-lee'; Arab., "one who is near"), a "friend of God" or saint in popular and mystical Islam. *See also* baraka; holy person; Sufism.

Wandering Jew, Christian legend of an individual, sometimes named Ahasuerus, who mocked Jesus (or refused him rest) on the way to the crucifixion and was condemned to roam the earth until Jesus' Second Coming.

wang (wahng; Chin., "king"), politico-religious title given to Chinese rulers since the Shang dynasty (ca. 1766–1122 B.C.); under the empire (1644–1912), it referred to a prince.

Wang Che (wahng-jeh; 1112–70), founder of the northern tradition of Taoism known as the Ch'uan-chen, or Total Perfection, school. *See also* Ch'uan-chen Taoism.

Wang Ch'ung (wong chohng; 27–ca. 97), a Chinese Han-dynasty philosopher and proponent of the Huang-Lao and Old Text schools who wrote the *Lung heng,* essays using Taoist naturalism to attack local religious practices. *See also* Huang-Lao Taoism; Old Text school.

Wang Fu-chih (wahng foo-juhr; 1619–92), great critic of the Neo-Confucian schools of Principle and Mind. He rejected the separation of principle (*li*) from vital energy (*ch'i*). *See also* ch'i; Hsin-hsueh; li; Li-hsueh.

Wang Pi (wahng bee; 226–249), a Neo-Taoist Hsuan-hsueh philosopher who found nonbeing to be the ontological basis for all phenomena. Nonbeing, as the "root of beings," is the state of spontaneity wherein everything realizes itself. A sage, embodying nonbeing, has the same emotions as ordinary people, but is fully in accord with moral norms, for moral norms originate in natural human feelings, and the sage can practice them without artificiality. He incorporated Confucian ethics into Taoist philosophy and reanimated the Confucian moral appeal to natural feelings. *See also* Hsuan-hsueh.

Wang Yang-ming (wahng yahng-ming; 1472–1529), most famous philosopher of the Neo-Confucian School of Mind as well as a great teacher, poet, and general. He is best known for his philosophic challenge to Chu Hsi, in which he rejected the notion that principle can be found by means of the external examination of things (*ko-wu*) and for developing the doctrine of the unity of knowledge and action. Wang, through intense personal self-reflection, discovered what he took to be the true Confucian method of insight based on *liang-chih* as the innate knowledge of reality as manifested in the mind. Wang's works continue to be influential on the thought of contemporary Chinese and Japanese religious reformers and philosophers who identify themselves with the Yang-ming school (Jap. *Yomeigaku*). *See also* Hsin-hsueh; ko-wu; liang-chih.

war. *See* violence and religion.

warrior monks (Jap. *sohei*), Japanese Buddhist monks who participated in armed conflict as early as 764. As monasteries became larger and acquired vast landholdings, they began to recruit monks who would bear arms to protect the monastery's interests. Although most conflicts were between monasteries, warrior monks would sometimes march into the capital carrying a palanquin with a *kami* (divinity, divine presence) to press their demands on the government, warning that if officials did not respond, the kami's wrath might be visited upon the city. Warrior monks were particularly powerful during the eleventh and twelfth centuries and were found at leading Buddhist monasteries such as Mt. Hiei and Kofukuji. Their power was effectively destroyed when Oda Nobunaga and Toyotomi Hideyoshi unified Japan in the sixteenth century. *See also* Hiei, Mt.; kami.

wat (waht; Thai, "temple," "monastery"), building complex that is the center of Theravada Buddhist activities in Thailand. Classically a Thai *wat* is divided into two sectors, one where both monks and laity honor and worship the Buddha (*Buddhavasa*), and the other specifically for monastic pursuits (*Sanghavasa*). The former customarily includes a large reliquary tower and one or more adjacent image halls (*vihara*) used for sabbath services and other religious ceremonies. The latter contains monastic living quarters, classrooms, a hall for monastic business, and meditation rooms. The walled wat enclosure often includes a Bodhi Tree, a library for storing palm leaf manuscripts, and guardian lions or serpents protecting the entrances. *See also* monasticism; vihara.

water serpent, a prominent sacred being in many traditional religions. Water serpents (often anacondas in the American tropics) are associated with the undulating forms of rivers, with the Milky Way or Sky River, and with the rainbow that mediates between them. Because the rainbow contains all colors and because of the formlessness of water, water serpents reflect the rotting, fluid union of primordial forms. Throughout the Andean and Amazonian areas, anacondas are believed to be pathonogenic to unprotected persons and may impregnate menstruating adolescents. For mature persons strong enough to absorb their power, anacondas can become spirit helpers. *See also* rainbow snake.

Watts, Isaac (1647–1748), English Protestant hymn writer. *See also* hymnody, Christian.

Way International, The, a biblical research, teaching, and household fellowship ministry (formerly Vesper Chimes) founded in 1942 by Victor Paul Weirville (d. 1985), erstwhile minister of the Evangelical Reformed Church. It became part of the diffuse Jesus movement of the early 1970s and grew through the early 1980s. Its Christology identifies Jesus as the Son of God but not God the Son. The Way has elicited controversy for its alleged anti-Semitism and its weapons training program. The Internal Revenue Service removed The Way's tax exemption for several years. After Weirville's death, schisms weakened the movement. *See also* Jesus movement.

weaving (Japan), a pervasive symbol in Japanese literature and folklore conveying the notion of feminine domesticity, order, and care. Amaterasu (the sun goddess) in Shinto mythology is the cosmic weaver, standing for order against chaos. Influenced by the Chinese Star Festival (Jap. *tanabata*), the "weaver woman" later came to evoke poetically the sadness and desolation of autumn. *See also* Amaterasu; Japanese myth.

Wen-ch'ang (wen-chuhng), the Chinese deity of literature. His cult was most popular among those who sought his help in the civil service examinations.

Wen-tzu (wen-dzuh), a syncretistic Taoist text of uncertain authorship and date containing passages attributed to Lao-tzu and expressing a mystical philosophy.

Wen Wang, Wu Wang (wen wahng, woo wahng; Chin., "Cultured King," "Martial King"; d. 1050; d. 1045), King Wen, who was founder of the Chou dynasty, and King Wu, his son, who completed the task of conquering the Shang dynasty; they are considered sage-kings in the traditional Confucian pantheon.

Wesley, Charles (1707–88), Anglican hymn writer and brother of John Wesley, founder of Methodism. *See also* hymnody, Christian.

Wesley, John (1703–91), ordained Anglican priest, founder (in 1784) of Methodism. *See also* Methodism.

Westminster Abbey, the central church of English Christianity, traditional site for the coronation of British royalty.

An ancient Benedictine abbey, which legend claims was consecrated by Peter in the seventh century, it was restored by Edward the Confessor in 1042. *See also* Anglicanism.

Westminster Confession, the most influential statement among English-speaking Presbyterian Christians. It was produced by the Westminster Assembly called by the Long Parliament in 1643 during the English Civil War. Parliament approved it for the Church of England in 1648 but removed it when the episcopal system was restored in 1660. The Scottish Parliament adopted it in 1649. In form and content it draws on earlier confessions of the Calvinist tradition, especially the Irish Articles of Religion (1615). Scottish Presbyterians were more insistent than the English on subscription to the confession, and this tension has been reflected in American Presbyterianism. *See also* Presbyterianism.

whaling rites. *See* fishing rites/whaling rites.

Wheel of the Dharma, Buddhist symbol. The Buddha's first sermon is entitled "The Setting in Motion of the Wheel of the Dharma," a metaphor for his launching his salvific teaching. Iconographically, the eight-spoked wheel (recalling the noble Eightfold Path) symbolizes the Buddha and his doctrine.

A second Buddhist Wheel of Dharma, that of the wheel-turning universal monarch, serves as one of the seven emblems of the king's sovereignty and is symbolic of his righteous rule. The coexistence of these two wheels expresses the symbiosis in Buddhism of the state and monastic orders. *See also* Buddhas; Dharma/dharma; kingship, sacred.

White, Ellen Gould (1827–1914), foundress of Sev-

enth-Day Adventism in 1844 following the failure of William Miller's advent prophecy. *See also* Adventists; Miller, William; Seventh-Day Adventists.

White Cloud Monastery. *See* Pai-yun Kuan.

White Lotus Society, a syncretistic Chinese sectarian movement originating in the late Sung dynasty (960–1279). Emerging from lay Buddhist associations connected with Pure Land devotionalism, the movement's concern for universal salvation was expressed in a millenarian ideology influenced by Manichaeism, Maitreyan Buddhism, and popular Chinese myths concerning an Eternal Mother who would one day re-create the earth as a paradise for her children. Although lacking central organization, the movement developed its own married clergy, rituals, and temples. Its millenarian message, eventually elaborated in *pao-chuan,* or "precious scrolls," inspired several antigovernment uprisings, including the famous White Lotus Rebellion of 1796 to 1803. *See also* Chinese sectarian religions; millenarianism; secret societies.

white magic, rituals performed for benign purpose, such as healing or fertility. Many North American or European adherents of modern Neo-Paganism or Witchcraft employ the term for their rituals and practices. *See also* Neo-Paganism; witchcraft.

Wholly Other, divine attribute, emphasizing utter transcendence. *See also* transcendence.

Wicca (wik'eh, Old Eng. term for female and male witches), the common term for the many different traditions of Neo-Pagan Witchcraft, also known as "the craft"; a nature religion that celebrates seasonal and life cycles and reveres a Goddess and a God (or a Goddess alone). *See also* Neo-Paganism; witchcraft.

wilderness wandering, in the Hebrew Bible, the period the Israelites spent in the desert between the exodus from Egypt and the entry into Canaan. *See also* Exodus; promised land.

Williams, Roger (ca. 1603–83), founder of the American colony of Rhode Island, which served as a refuge for persecuted Christian dissenting groups. His views on religious freedom are forcefully set forth in *The Bloudy Tenent of Persecution* (1644).

wine. *See* bread and wine.

winter count, calendrical record kept by many Plains tribes. The term itself is descriptive of the Native American practice of reckoning time by means of winters. Typically, winter counts take the form of pictographs painted on the flesh side of the tanned hide of a buffalo or other animal, such as an elk or a deer. Pictographs serve the keeper of the winter count as visual representations of important events; the keeper, or native historian, keeps in memory the text that is associated with each representation on the hide. Typical recorded events include impressive natural occurrences, such as the great meteor shower of 1833, the deaths of persons killed in war or by disease, the successes and failures of raiding parties, the location of tribal camps, descriptions of tribal movements, and the names of significant tribal leaders. *See also* North America, traditional religions in.

Winti. *See* Afro-Surinamese new religions.

Wise, Isaac Mayer (1819–1900), rabbi and pioneer of Reform Judaism in America. Born in Steingrub, Bohemia, he emigrated in 1846 and served as rabbi of Congregations Beth El (1846–50) and Anshe Emeth (1850–54) in Albany, New York. In 1854, he became rabbi-for-life of Congregation Bene Yeshurun in Cincinnati, Ohio.

Wise sought to modernize Judaism and to unite American Jews around a common rite, *Minhag America.* He wrote voluminously, established two newspapers, *The Israelite* (later *American Israelite*) in English and *Die Deborah* in German, and helped create both the Union of American Hebrew Congregations (1873) and the Central Conference of American Rabbis (1889). His major achievement was the founding of an American rabbinical seminary, Hebrew Union College (1875), over which he presided until his death. *See also* Reform Judaism.

Wissenschaft des Judenthums (visen'shahft des yoo'-den-tuhms; Ger., "Science of Judaism"), German Jewish intellectual movement during the first decades of the 1800s. Informed by German university scholarship and Hegelian philosophy, this circle proposed that Judaism and its literature be studied "scientifically"—i.e., comprehensively, objectively, and systematically—so that the historical development and essence of the Jewish religion could be identified.

In the quest for Jewish political emancipation, the Wissenschaft aspired to elevate the dignity of Jews by demonstrating that Judaism was an integral part of Western culture that unfolded in accord with scientific laws. It also aimed to provide the basis for all Jewish religious reform and practice.

Despite a shared historicism and historicist faith that academic study could yield prescriptive lessons for modern Judaism, the Wissenschaft's practitioners drew divergent conclusions about these lessons. A radical Reform wing contended that Judaism had constantly evolved new religious expressions and institutions appropriate to particular times and places. The Wissenschaft thus provided a warrant for their rejection of traditional rabbinic authority and for their own ritual innovations. In contrast, the Historical School, led by Zacharias Frankel (1801–75), head of the Breslau Theological Seminary, held that Judaism was preeminently characterized by a commitment to law and that contemporary observance was mandated.

German Orthodox circles surrounding S. R. Hirsch (1808–88) condemned the Wissenschaft's historical approach as a heresy that undermined the traditional rabbinic belief that the Torah was wholly revealed by God to Moses at Sinai. Nevertheless, the Wissenschaft dominated German Jewish academic and religious circles, even some Orthodox circles, for the remainder of the century. Modern Jewish studies originated in the Wissenschaft, which still influences the curricula of modern liberal rabbinic seminaries. *See also* Conservative Judaism; Reform Judaism.

witch, a word with many different and often contradictory meanings: sorcerer, healer, practitioner of western European forms of shamanism, or member of contemporary nature religion. The word is commonly used to mean a person (usually a woman) with supernatural powers, a spell-caster, an ugly old woman, or a worshiper of the devil. In non-Western cultures, the words translated "witch" usually describe someone who does sorcery for negative purposes. But there is also another tradition in which the word designates either an ancient European practitioner of the healing arts, who uses herbs, divination, and folk magic, or—in modern times—a member of a contemporary earth religion known as Wicca. *See also* Baba Yaga; Goddess religions (contemporary); Skinwalker; witchcraft.

witchcraft (Old Eng. *wicca,* "sorcery"; *wiccian,* "to cast a spell"), human behavior that employs the belief, knowledge, and use of the supernatural to derive results otherwise unattainable.

The lines separating witchcraft from sorcery are not clear from one society to the next or from one observer to the next. Witchcraft and sorcery generally are described as the magical manipulation of the environment by an individual through supernatural forces or powers. Witchcraft and sorcery have destructive impacts on the lives to whom they are addressed, but they provide an overall positive function in that immoral behavior is discouraged. In many societies the powers of witchcraft are thought to be inherited. Sorcery is generally available to those who wish to learn the techniques. While sorcery is apt to cause injury or death through tangible applications such as poisons, witchcraft tends to involve the manipulation of the victim's spiritual components. The concept of persons capable of inflicting pain or injury on others from a remote position dates to Greco-Roman times when three levels of magic were noted: magic of the gods for gods or humans, magic of humans for humans, and magic of humans against humans. The power invoked was neither mortal nor immortal but of a class of spirits called *daimones* (Gk., "demons"). The idea of intermediary spirits has theologically expanded to include the Christian, Jewish, and Islamic angels and saints. Christianity equated angels and saints with good, and in its struggle against Greco-Roman paganism equated demons with the devil or Satan, and thus evil. The stigma that has correlated witchcraft to Satanism exists today.

Witchcraft was formulated in medieval Europe as a Christian heresy. Adherents were believed to have disavowed Christianity and Jesus Christ, made pacts with Satan, participated in orgies and sacrificial infanticide that included their own children, and practiced cannibalism. Missionaries throughout the world encountered other religions and in their zeal lumped all non-Christian practices into one denounced category of witchcraft. Witchcraft was the precursor to and foundation for the witch hunts of early New England. By the early twentieth century, Western witchcraft began to be associated with nature, and in the non-Western world witchcraft continued unabated. In the 1990s witchcraft is found in virtually every corner of the world. With the relative ease of travel and immigration, witchcraft practices are found in most contemporary cities. Shamans, who are generally antidotal to harmful witchcraft, are at times employed by doctors and hospitals to assist in curing a witched person.

Traditional Religion: Witchcraft is frequently active in societies that maintain beliefs in the existence of supernatural, detachable forces or powers that are innate to all things. It focuses in areas of competition for natural and economic resources, where the outward expression of anger is socially unacceptable, and where compensation for the bad is not explainable. The desired end can be success at hunting, success in battle, acquisition of natural resources, or revenge. Competition for affection from potential suitors is frequently cited in witchcraft examples. When one fails to succeed, the blame is invariably placed on improper or incomplete ritual observance or manipulation of the desired outcome by other competing and more powerful witchcraft.

The benefits and detriments of witchcraft to the surrounding society vary. On one hand, witchcraft is used to better one's status in relation to others. On the other hand, witchcraft is used to diminish another's health or status, thereby increasing one's own position relative to the other. Witchcraft can include observations of taboos to bring luck and success to the hunter; in some societies a hunter can gain knowledge of the location of sought-after game (Subarctic); through witchcraft the hunter might induce a game animal to give itself up (Arctic); in other areas hunters use forms of witchcraft to obtain greater physical prowess and cunning over game. In impending battles witchcraft is incorporated in order to vanquish the enemy.

Malevolent or evil witchcraft, frequently called sorcery or black magic, is performed to cause bad luck, ill health, or death to another. The "evil eye" is a concept found in some form on every continent. A person who has the power of the evil eye can, through a gaze, cast an evil spell onto, or malevolent power into, another person. The evil eye can be inflicted upon people, plants, or animals. If it is a milking animal, it will go dry; if it is a plant, it may wither or not produce. A person inflicted with evil eye may become sick and die or go insane. A pregnant woman might abort; a man may not be able to impregnate his wife.

In societies such as the Navajo of the Southwest United States, where harmony and balance with one's environment are paramount, most disruptions of that harmony and balance are frequently believed to be the work of witchcraft. When misfortune strikes a Navajo, that person examines recent behavior to see if anyone might have been offended enough to have used witchcraft. If an incident is discovered where action may be seen as disruptive, even if unintentional, amends will be offered immediately. If no incident is found, the services of a diviner or reader will be sought. The diviner discovers whether the client is being witched, and if so, who the witchcrafter is and what the reason is for the witchcraft. The reasons for Navajo witchcraft are often associated with competition for natural resources such as grazing and water rights, or they are frequently identified with spurned lovers, competition for spouses, and other affairs of the heart. Resolution to witchcraft is offered through making amends, ritual purification, or witching back with more powerful medicine. Witching in retaliation is generally frowned upon because it keeps the universe out of balance and harmony, thereby affecting the whole clan. Often elders will intervene if they suspect revenge is being sought. Among the Yanomamo of the Amazon Basin, *hekwida* spirits can be seen and influenced after the Yanomamo priests and warriors have inhaled a psychedelic drug. The Yanomamo implore the hekwida to go to war and exact revenge for misdeeds performed by neighboring tribes. The havoc the hekwida can create is greatly feared; painful deaths, torture, and infanticide are attributed to them. In this instance witchcraft is used collectively, that is, to the benefit of many; however, if the hekwida are successful, it is possible that the enemies' hekwida will be sent in return as revenge.

Witchcraft serves, in part, as a social control. The fear of witchcraft modifies or defers deviant behavior and encourages amenable relations with family and neighbors. On the other hand, individuals are susceptible to exploitation because of their fear of witchcraft. In any area of the world where there is competition for resources, witchcraft is apt to be present and active.

Contemporary Western Societies: In the United States, Canada, Australia, the United Kingdom, and other parts of Europe, the word *Witchcraft* identifies a contemporary Neo-Pagan nature religion that may have more than a hundred thousand adherents. This religion looks to the pre-Christian nature religions of Europe, worships a Goddess and a God, and is devoted to promoting harmony with the natural world.

Those who call themselves "witches" today fall into several different categories. The majority are those who use magic, divination, herbs, and folk wisdom. A small portion of these are the village healers and cunningmen and -women still found in rural societies. Most, however, are numbered among the countless people who use astrology, spells, charms, and methods of divination either for personal or professional use. Still others belong to Wicca, the burgeoning Neo-Pagan Witchcraft movement that focuses on seasonal celebrations and attunement with the forces of nature. This religious movement has nothing to do with the witchcraft described

in the trial reports of the Inquisition or with Satanism but tends to be confused with them in the popular press. Finally, a small number of families in America and Europe have kept up oral traditions of healing and agricultural magic; in recent years, as a result of the Neo-Pagan Witchcraft revival, they have started calling their practice Witchcraft. There are also a small number of Satanists; occasionally they use the term *witch* to identify themselves.

Neo-Pagan Witchcraft: In 1921, Margaret Murray, an Egyptologist and folklorist, wrote *The Witch-cult in Western Europe*. Murray argued that witchcraft could be traced to pre-Christian times and was the ancient religion of western Europe—a fertility cult centered around a god who in the fashion of James Frazer's *Golden Bough* dies and is reborn. Christianity had co-opted parts of this religion, established churches on its sacred sites, and adopted and transformed its holidays, substituting Christmas, for example, for the old winter solstice celebrations. Later, this ancient religion was forced underground by persecution. Murray's theories were accepted for many years, but few historians now agree with Murray's thesis that an organized pagan religion survived into the times of the persecutions.

Several other writers have proposed that Witchcraft is the survival of ancient European paganism. Among the most interesting and controversial is the American folklorist Charles Godfrey Leland. In 1892 Leland published *Etruscan Roman Remains*, a little-known and fascinating book that traces the names of ancient Etruscan deities as they degenerated into the names of lesser spirit beings who persisted in chants and incantations well into the late nineteenth century. In 1899 Leland published *Aradia or the Gospel of the Witches*, a narrative supposedly based on traditional texts provided by an Italian Witch of his acquaintance. These texts relate the myth of Diana and her daughter Aradia, who comes to earth and teaches Witchcraft to oppressed humanity. Although most contemporary scholars dismiss this account as an invention, Leland's and Murray's writings, along with other books promoting the resurgence of goddess worship, such as *The White Goddess* (1948) by Robert Graves, helped prepare the way for the current revival of Wicca.

In 1939 Gerald B. Gardner, a retired British civil servant was, according to his own claims, initiated into a coven of Witches in the New Forest in England that was practicing an ancient tradition of hereditary Witchcraft. After the last witchcraft act in Britain was repealed in 1951 and replaced by the Fraudulent Mediums Act, Gardner went public. He wrote several books, set up a Witchcraft museum, and founded his own coven. The rituals he created borrowed heavily from folklore, mythology, and Masonic and ceremonial rites (whether or not he was actually initiated into a traditional coven, as he claimed, remains controversial). Gardner's ceremonies were sprinkled with phrases from Ovid, Rudyard Kipling, and Aleister Crowley. In the 1950s Gardner and British writer Doreen Valiente reworked the tradition, and much of the Neo-Pagan Witchcraft revival owes its beginning to their endeavor. In the 1960s, Gardner's variety of Witchcraft found its way to the United States. During the next thirty years, there was a significant growth of Neo-Pagan Witchcraft in the United States and Canada. There are also now groups in Australia, Germany, Holland, Japan, and France.

There are many different traditions in modern-day Wicca, each with its own rituals, names for deities, and organizational structure. A small sampling of the names of some Wiccan traditions includes Alexandrian, Dianic, Gardnerian, Georgian, New Wiccan Church, School of Wicca, Wiccan Shamanism, Welsh Traditionalist, and the Faery Tradition. Many of the traditions honor a particular heritage of western European pre-Christian paganism, such as Celtic, Greek, Norse, or British. In the last ten years, a few Wiccan traditions have incorporated elements of shamanism and Native American religion into their practice.

Many women involved in the revival of goddess religions have also adopted Wicca as their religion. In the United States, there are probably as many feminist Wicca groups—called Dianic Wicca—as there are groups stemming from Gardnerian and other British-based Wiccan traditions. Most (but not all) of these groups focus on the Goddess exclusively; the majority are not open to men.

Overall, Wicca is a very decentralized religion. Within most traditions, worship takes place in covens, a gathering of between three and twenty people who know each other well and have worked and worshiped together. Covens based on the British traditions often require seekers to undergo a year of training and an initiation ceremony before they can join. Covens traditionally meet on the eight seasonal festivals of Wicca (February 1, May 1, August 1, October 31, and the solstices and equinoxes). Covens may also assemble on the new or full moon. In addition, there have been larger gatherings where many covens, or even many differ-

ent traditions, come together to celebrate and to exchange information.

Each tradition and each coven within a tradition is autonomous and plans and designs its own observances. Rituals are held in homes or outside, in a natural setting. There are few established Wiccan temples, although a growing number of Wiccans have bought land on which to hold their rites. Seasonal transitions, rites of passage, initiations, healing ceremonies, and rites for community bonding are commonly celebrated. The use of magic and psychic arts, such as tarot and other forms of divination, play a part in many groups.

The basic tenets of most Wiccan groups are worship of the Goddess in her three aspects, Maiden, Mother, and Crone, and in most non-Dianic groups, worship of her consort, the Horned God; the use of magic within a definite code of ethics, including the Wiccan Rede: "An ye harm none do what ye will"; reverence for nature and ecological principles; belief in pantheism (that the divine is in everything and everything is sacred); belief in polytheism (that there are multiple deities and many different pathways to the divine); and acceptance of reincarnation.

Some critics of modern Wicca see it as an unstable and anarchistic religion, too adverse to hierarchy and structure. Followers of Wicca answer this criticism by insisting that their religion maintains maximum flexibility in order to change and adapt. But in the last ten years, Wicca has begun to institutionalize. In a religion once loosely held together by newsletters and festivals, Wiccan groups have begun to establish legally recognized religious organizations, churches, and seminaries. Representatives of Wicca have also joined in ecumenical activities with other religious groups and have been among the most active of religious groups confronting the environmental crisis. *See also* Europe, new religions in; Goddess religions (contemporary); Neo-Paganism; North America, new religions in; sorcery; Wicca.

witness (Islam). 1 The first pillar of faith and action; embodied by the formal declaration (*shahada*): "There is no god but Allah, and Muhammad is his messenger." This statement concisely acknowledges belief in God's unmatched oneness, eternity, and sovereignty; it also recognizes Muhammad in the foremost rank of prophets. Sincere utterance of the shahada in Arabic confirms membership in the Muslim community and places individuals under its statutory obligations and restrictions.

Repeated by Muslims from cradle to grave, the shahada is an essential component of the call to prayer and of prayer itself. **2** The act of suffering violent death while fighting "in God's path," thus bearing witness to the faith (shahada). Muslims who so perish become martyrs and attain Paradise. Martyrdom has been extended to include those who die in childbirth and on pilgrimage. *See also* Five Pillars; martyr.

Woden (woh'den), also Wodan or Votan, ancient Germanic and Anglo-Saxon name for the Norse god Odinn. *See also* Odinn.

woman-church, a Christian religious community of women and women-identified men. *Woman-church* is a term used to describe both a movement and a concept. As a movement, woman-church refers to a large and loosely affiliated movement of women (although men may be included) who meet for worship together. Many women in the woman-church movement belong to or have come out of the Roman Catholic Church, though Protestant women also belong. Two leading Catholic feminist theologians, Rosemary Radford Ruether and Elisabeth Schussler Fiorenza have written on woman-church.

As a concept, it refers to the possibility or potential of a woman-identified Christian religious community, i.e., Christians gathered in community who hold the existence and experience of women equally valuable with men and who are committed to actively undoing the effects of the prolonged historic exclusion and oppression of women in church and society. *See also* feminism; feminist theology.

women's rites (Hinduism). Hindu rites for women may be performed on a daily, recurring, or occasional schedule. While many of the well-known ones are domestic and performed for the welfare of the family and this-worldly happiness, a few are performed for personal salvation or liberation. Many rituals such as worship at home shrines or temples, pilgrimages, and the singing of devotional songs are similar to patterns of worship practiced by men, but some are unique to married women whose husbands are alive. Underlying many of the rites is the notion that women are carriers of power and rites performed by them have potency. While many rituals conducted by Hindu women share common features in intention and in accessories used, the differences among the many communities, castes, and regions are significant enough to

caution against generalizations. Frequently, though not always, the rituals involve the worship of a goddess.

Early History (ca. 1500–100 b.c.): Sparse evidence from the early Vedas suggests that girls, like boys of the upper classes, underwent a rite of initiation. They were invested with a sacred thread and taught a *mantra* (sacred utterance); this gave them the authority to study the Vedas for salvific knowledge. This study was presumably undertaken in the girl's home or in the house of a teacher. A few women are spoken of as lighting and tending to the sacrificial fire to make ritual offerings to the gods. The epics (ca. 400 b.c.) also speak of women ascetics who probably entered that stage of life after renunciatory rites. By the time the *Laws of Manu* was composed (ca. 100 b.c.–a.d. 100), however, the rite of investing girls with the sacred thread seems to have been abandoned. Marriage is spoken of as the rite of initiation for girls, serving the husband as equivalent to the residence in the house of the teacher, and doing household work as similar to the tending of the sacrificial fire (*Manu Smriti* 2.67). Asceticism and renunciation of family life were not allowed for women.

In southern India, a votive act called *nompu* was undertaken by girls. Bathing themselves ritually in a river or a pond during the Tamil month of Tai (January–February), they prayed to the goddess Parvati. In these rituals some petitioned for a husband and others for a union with a deity. The intentions behind this rite seem to be typical of later women's rites where requests were made either for domestic happiness or otherworldly bliss.

Contemporary Rituals: Daily rituals frequently include lighting of oil lamps and drawing simple or complicated designs (Tamil *kolam;* Hindi *rangoli*) on the threshold of a house and in front of a home shrine. The patterns are drawn with rice powder daily; colored powder is used for important rituals. Personal prayers using Sanskrit or vernacular verses drawn from Hindu texts may be said daily at the home shrine and conclude with ritual bowing before the pictures or images of the deities placed there. While the drawing of the rice patterns may be done both to beautify the house and to keep away evil spirits, the prayers at the home shrine may be for personal spiritual benefit.

Recurring rites are performed on particular days in the lunar cycle during specific months. Many of these rituals are domestic and observed for the welfare of one's husband, the entire extended family, or the community and are considered "auspicious." The generic Sanskrit term

A Hindu woman's ritual drawing (Hindi *rangoli;* Tamil *kolam*) at the threshold of her house in Madras, India (1984). The making of these rice powder protective drawings in front of one's home is a daily women's ritual, most prevalent in South India. A similar drawing will often be made inside the house in front of the domestic shrine.

vrata is used to denote a variety of these votive observances, which may typically involve participation only by unmarried women or married women whose husbands are alive. While Sanskrit manuals describing these rites say that they enable a woman to attain final liberation from the cycle of life and death, most women perform them by praying to a goddess or a family god, petitioning either for marriage or a long life for their husbands. After prayers to the family deity, the women may eat a meal together and distribute emblems of auspiciousness such as betel nuts, betel leaves, bananas, coconuts, turmeric powder, and a red powder called *kumkum,* which is to be placed on one's forehead. These rituals may last from a few minutes to five days, with periods of fasting alternating with communal eating.

In some South Indian variations of these rituals, unmarried and married women tie a yellow thread around their necks on the first day of the Tamil month of Panguni (March–April) in emulation of the heroine Savitri, who through her wisdom protected the life of her husband. In Gujarat, the Gauri Puja is performed by prepubescent girls and involves partial fasting in order to get a good husband. In this rite, girls are also enjoined to sit on the ground for five days, rising as little as possible, so that their bodies are in touch and in harmony with Mother Earth. In many parts of South India, during the month of Adi (July–August) women's rituals are celebrated by many communities and castes. Married women were traditionally enjoined to stay celibate during this month. Brahman women pray to the goddess Lakshmi for domestic happiness. Women of some non-Brahmanic castes carry special pots of water and other ritual items to temples of a local goddess and worship her for the benefit of the entire family. Others cook rice and milk dishes in the temples of the local goddesses and distribute the food. During this month, in the temple of Draupadi Amman, women (along with men) may go into a trance and walk over hot coals in a ceremony called "walking on flowers."

In parts of northern India, during the autumn festival of Navaratri ("Nine Nights") dedicated to the goddesses, women may invite seven prepubescent girls to a home. This is usually done on the eighth day after the new moon, and the girls are venerated as representatives of the goddess Durga. Many women's rites in northern India focus on the welfare of male relatives. During *raksha bandhan* ("tying of the amulet"), which generally occurs around August, girls tie a protective cord around the wrists of their brothers. In the lunar month, which comes between October 15 and November 14, women from the northern states undertake two fasts on the fourth and eighth days of the waning moon. On *karva cauth* women fast all day until they see the moon. This rite is performed for the well-being of the husband. The fast on *hoi ashtami* is undertaken for the health of sons, and women break the fast only after looking at the stars.

Occasional rituals include the *sumangali prarthana* ("worship of married women") practiced in South India and the *mata tedya* ("respectfully inviting the Mother Goddess") in Gujarat. These rituals are done just before a major happy ritual in a family, like a wedding. In the "worship of married women," a family ancestor who died while a woman's husband was still alive is propitiated and her blessings sought for the upcoming events. In the *mata tedya,* women invoke the presence of Durga into a little image or symbol on a plate before them and pray for her blessings.

Life-cycle rituals for upper-caste girls include some of those performed for boys, such as naming the child and the first feeding of solid food. These are required for a woman's wedding sacrament to be valid. Many Hindu communities also celebrate a girl's first menstruation. The girl wears new clothing, fresh flowers in her hair, sits on a specially decorated chair, and is fed special foods. In some regions there are special rituals during pregnancy and the expectant mother is adorned with flowers and protective amulets. These rituals acknowledge the importance of a woman's body and celebrate its life-bearing potential. In many higher castes, however, menstruation and the shedding of blood during childbirth are considered polluting and a ritual bath at the end of a fixed number of days releases the woman from this pollution. *See also* gender roles; Hindu domestic ritual; Hinduism (worship).

Won Buddhism (wuhn; Kor. *Won Pulgyo*), an indigenous Korean Buddhist religion of the twentieth century. Founded in 1924 at Iri City as the Soci-

A Korean Won Buddhist center.

ety for the Research on the Dharma, Won Buddhism is a lay Buddhist religion that syncretistically incorporates ideas and practices not endorsed by the orthodox, monastery-based clerical form of Buddhism. Won Buddhism was deliberately started as a reform of Buddhism outside the traditional clerical institutions by its founder, Sot'aesan Pak Chungbin (1891–1943).

Founder: Pak Chungbin lived and worked in southwest Korea (South Cholla province), an area where Protestantism, Catholicism, and such syncretistic religions as Tonghak and Chungsan'gyo had appeared as part of the lower classes' response to political and economic decay. He was concerned with the state of Buddhism at the end of a long period of Neo-Confucian opposition and neglect. He was also concerned with the increasing spread of Western religious traditions that had little to do with traditional Korean culture and ethical understandings. In his study of the texts of Mahayana Buddhism, Confucianism, and Christianity, he was led to the view that there was a unity to all known religious traditions and that this unity could be experienced through a rigorous disciplined life of lay meditative practice.

Teachings: Won Buddhism teaches that the Buddha is the Buddha Body of Truth (Skt. *Dharmakaya*) and is the ineffable reality behind all things. This Buddha should therefore be worshiped everywhere and not just in Buddha images. The ineffable quality of this Buddha is best represented by a single circle (*won*) and it is the concept of this circle that gives Won Buddhism its name. It also teaches that life is composed of the Four Graces (heaven and earth, parents, fellow human beings, and religious and civil law), which make life possible, and the Four Needs (the lack of self-reliance, the lack of good leaders, the lack of universal education, and the lack of a sense of public service), which are the cause of suffering. The Four Graces are the positive manifestations of the Body of Truth, while the Four Needs are the negative aspects of living in the world.

Members are trained to overcome the Four Needs by disciplining the mind to be free from desires and attachments, to examine the facts of existence to see which lead to happiness or suffering, and to make correct moral choices. This training is supported by the virtues of faith in one's ability to accomplish one's goal, courage of one's conviction, an inquisitive spirit about the nature of things, and sincerity and devotion to one's task. The use of these four virtues to overcome faithlessness, greed, laziness, and foolishness is what Won Buddhism calls "the practice of meditation without reference to time or place."

The organization and worship activities of Won Buddhism closely resemble those of Protestant sects. Won Buddhist temples are located in cities and towns. Worshipers gather at these temples on Sundays and Wednesdays. The main hall of the temples has an altar table with an image of a single circle behind it. Hymns are sung by adherents and sermons are preached by a trained minister. Each temple sponsors service organizations for children, students, teenagers, and adults, with an emphasis on social outreach and public acts of charity. Finally, Won Buddhism accepts the secular culture of today and proposes that wealth, status, and a happy family life come from the congruence of the material and the spiritual worlds and not the exclusion of one or the other. *See also* Korea, new religions in.

Wonhyo (wuhn-hyoh; 617–686), Korean Buddhist monk of the Unified Silla period (seventh–ninth centuries) known as much for his unorthodox life as a monk (he fathered one of Korea's most prominent Confucian teachers, Sol Ch'ong [ca. 661–700]) as for his prolific contributions to Buddhist philosophy and scriptural exegesis.

At a time when most Buddhist monks in Korea were employed by the government as ritualists and preachers of edifying sermons, Wonhyo stands out as a serious philosopher and scholar of Buddhist theory and history. He wrote commentaries on most of the known Mahayana scriptures, summaries of the teachings of the Chinese scriptural schools, explanations of the Vinaya texts, philosophical treatises in Buddhist epistemology and psychology, and assorted synthetic works in which he attempted to consolidate all forms of Buddhism into a single system.

Many scholars see Wonhyo's prolific contributions to Buddhist scholarship as a direct effect of his enlightenment experience. While traveling to China to "obtain the Dharma," he spent one night in a cave. He awoke in the middle of the night to get a drink of water. When he discovered the next morning that the water dipper he had drunk from the night before was a human skull, he was enlightened to the relativity of all things and returned to Silla. Thereafter he refused to be a part of established sectarian Buddhism and devoted the rest of his life to showing that all teachings and practices of Buddhism are part of a single, comprehensive path to enlightenment. He gave up the cloistered life to wander about Silla as a beggar-monk, frequented wine shops, ate meat, and composed and sang songs about Amitabha Buddha for children in the countryside. He later married a Silla princess and fathered a son. *See also* Amitabha; Vinaya (Korean Buddhism).

Wonpulgyo. *See* Korea, new religions in.

word (in traditional religions), power of, the belief that words, especially when spoken, have power or constitute power.

The power of the word is respected in most speech. According to many stories, creation is a speech act. Words are not spoken indiscriminately; their power is inherent in their being spoken or sung. They are powerful forces of creation and destruction. Many medicine people and healers are charged with the responsibility of speaking correctly. Spoken responsibly, words may create beauty and order. In some traditions words are gifts of the culture hero, who steals them from the animals.

Some words, owned and guarded because of their power, may be given to a person during an initiation, a dream, or vision fast. Others are spoken only in secret because of their power. Surrogate words may be used in the language of shamans and other healers.

Stolen or carelessly used, words can create illness and even death. The ability of words to transform demands a constant awareness of how they are learned, used, and remembered. Names are often guarded and carefully used. To know someone's name is to have power over them; therefore, names and naming practices are often very private. *See also* oral tradition.

Word of God. *See* hypostasis; Logos.

worker priests, a group of not more than a hundred French and Belgium Catholic priests who, in the post–World War II period, sought to evangelize the working class by identifying with their trades and living in their midst. The movement sprang from the realization that the working classes were hopelessly alienated from the Roman Catholic Church, and the successful experiences of Catholic priests who had gone to Germany disguised as laborers to aid French workers. Under the inspiration of H. Godin, founder of the *Mission de Paris,* priests began to take jobs as factory laborers, join trade unions, and share in the problems of fellow workers beginning in 1944. Although the movement was seemingly successful, the Vatican intervened to stop the "experiment" in 1953 and 1954, and further restricted the possibility of the clergy working as laborers in 1959. *See also* Christian Socialism.

World Community of Islam , an African-American religious group founded by Wallace Muhammad (Warith Deen Muhammad, b. 1933). An offshoot of the Nation of Islam, it later became known as the American Muslim Mission. *See also* African Americans (North America), new religions among; American Muslim Mission; Muhammad, Wallace D.

World Council of Churches, an international ecumenical organization of Christian churches formally founded in Amsterdam in 1948. The council maintains headquarters in Geneva and is made up of representatives of over three hundred churches—Anglican, Protestant, Eastern Orthodox, and Old Catholic—from more than a hundred nations. Although the Roman Catholic Church is not a member, its relations with the council have become increasingly friendly since Vatican II. The WCC is governed by a General Secretariat, a Central Committee, and a representative Assembly, with three Program Units: "Faith and Witness," "Justice and Service," and "Education and Renewal." *See also* ecumenism.

world parents, a widespread cosmogonic motif in which the present world (and often its inhabitants) is the result of sexual intercourse between two primordial deities, most commonly a Sky Father and an Earth Mother. *See also* Hesiod; Izanagi and Izanami; Japanese myth; Prithivi.

World Plan Executive Council, the organization founded by Maharishi Mahesh Yogi (b. 1911) to coordinate his efforts to teach Transcendental Meditation. *See also* Maharishi Mahesh Yogi; Transcendental Meditation.

world religions, a nineteenth-century taxonomic category designating those religions that transcend national borders, that are inclusive in their mission, and that are centered around notions of salvation. It was developed as a category in opposition to national or ethnic religions.

In older catalogues, only three religions—Christianity, Islam, and Buddhism—met the criteria. More recently, there are seven: Judaism, Christianity, Islam, Hinduism, Buddhism, Confucianism/Taoism, and Shinto. *See also* typology, classification.

World's Parliament of Religions, gathering of representatives of the major religions in Chicago, Illinois, in 1893, at the occasion of the Columbian Exposition. It is most significant for introducing many non-Christian religions to North America. Traditional religions formed no part of the Parliament but were displayed in the Exposition's anthropological museum and the Bazaar of All Nations on the Midway. A second Parliament, celebrating the centennial of the first, was held in Chicago in 1993.

worldview, (Eng. trans. of Ger. *Weltanschauung*), a group's most general, shared ideas concerning life and the world, coupled with the claim that they are somehow grounded in the nature of things. Sometimes suggested as a synonym for "religion." *See also* cosmology.

Worldwide Church of God, a Christian evangelical movement founded in 1933 by Herbert W. Armstrong (1892–1986). Ultimately descended from a splinter group within the Seventh-Day Adventist Church, the Worldwide Church of God pioneered the use of mass media, especially radio (through Armstrong's program, "The Radio Church of God"), television, and periodicals (*The Plain Truth*), to create an independent constituency. From 1945 to 1947, Armstrong added a direct ministry, holding meetings to baptize members of his radio audience. This direct approach was continued with the foundation of Ambassador College (Pasadena, California) in 1947. Between 1974 and 1980 the church was rocked by a series of scandals, which has reduced its membership to one hundred thousand.

While generally accepting Adventist beliefs, the Worldwide Church of God is distinctive in its adherence to British Israelitism, the belief that the Anglo-Saxons of Europe and the United States are the descendants of the Lost Tribes of Israel. *See also* Adventists; British Israelites; Identity Christianity; Seventh-Day Adventists; televangelism.

Wovoka (ca. 1856–1932), Paiute Native American prophet of the 1890s Ghost Dance, also known as Jack Wilson (after a rancher who employed him) and the Messiah (Christ returned to help Native Americans). After 1892, Wovoka corresponded with the help of a local merchant with followers, selling them sacred objects and personal effects, and continued to serve as a shaman. *See also* Ghost Dance; Native Americans (North America), new religions among; prophecy in traditional religions.

wu (*woo;* Chin., "nonbeing," "nothingness," "void"), a Chinese philosophical concept for a primordial state before the differentiation of distinct phenomena. First intimated in the *Lao-tzu* (*Tao-te ching*), the concept was elaborated by third-century *Hsuan-hsueh* thinkers such as Wang Pi, fourth-century Buddhists such as Tao-an, and twelfth-century Neo-Confucians such as Lu Hsiang-shan. *See also* Lu Hsiang-shan; Tao-an; Tao-te ching; Wang Pi.

wu-hsing (*woo-shing;* Chin., "five agents," "five phases"), term for the cosmological principles of wood, metal, fire, water, and earth conceived not as constituent elements of matter but as the efficient action specific to each (e.g., fire burning and rising, water wetting and sinking). First appearing in the *Shu-ching* (Book of History), they were central to Tsou Yen's influential theory that they govern the rise and fall of dynasties. Subsequently, they provided the primary correlative schema for all categories of five employed in the analysis of phenomena: seasons, directions, colors, planets, etc. *See also* cosmology; Tsou Yen.

wu-lun (*woo-luhn;* Chin., "five relationships"), a traditional Confucian theory about human relationships. Basic familial relationships (father-son, husband-wife, elder brother–younger brother), when properly embodied, mature into humane dignity, propriety, and wisdom. Basic societal relationships (ruler-minister, friend-friend) lead to a refined sense of appropriateness and reliability. *See also* Confucianism.

Wu-t'ai Shan (*woo-ti shahn*), mountain in Shansi

Province, China, one of the "four famous mountains" popular as pilgrimage sites for Chinese Buddhist laypeople. *See also* Chiu-hua Shan; mountains, sacred; O-mei Shan; pilgrimage; T'ien-t'ai Shan.

Wu-ti (*woo*-dee; Chin., "five emperors"), mythical Chinese culture heroes. Lists vary; some sources give Fu Hsi (with Nu Kua), Chu Jung (or Shao Hao), Shen Nung, Huang-ti, and Chuan Hsu; others consider the first three of those to be the "three sovereigns" and follow with Huang-ti, Chuan Hsu, Ti Ku (or Shao Hao), Yao, and Shun as the "five emperors." All appear in Han-dynasty (206 B.C.–A.D. 220) and later sources as semidivine ideal rulers of remote antiquity and inventors of various aspects of civilization. *See also* Fu Hsi; Huang-ti; Nu Kua; San-huang; Shen Nung; Yao, Shen, and Yu.

Wu tou-mi Tao (*woo*-doh-mee dou; Chin., "Way of the Five Pecks of Rice"), alternate name for the second-century T'ien-shih ("Celestial Master") organization of Chang Tao-ling; each household in Chang's organization was assessed a tax of five pecks of rice. *See also* Chang Tao-ling; T'ien-shih Taoism.

wu-tsang (*woo*-dsahng; Chin., "five viscera"), medicinal and Taoist term for the key internal organic systems identified as the kidneys, lungs, spleen, liver, and heart. *See also* Chinese medicine.

Wu Wang. *See* Wen Wang, Wu Wang.

wu-wei (*woo*-way; Chin., "nonaction"), the Taoist behavioral ideal of avoiding purposive action intended to effect desired ends. The *Tao-te ching* warns against interfering with the natural course of things ("the Tao"); one should follow one's own natural course and allow all other things to do likewise. Rulers, in particular, are exhorted to *wu-wei* in the *Tao-te ching*, in Confucius's *Analects*, and by later Taoist religious texts such as the *T'ai-p'ing ching*. *See also* Lun Yu; T'ai-p'ing ching; Taoism; Tao-te ching.

Wycliff, John (wik'lif; 1326–84), English Catholic reformer and theologian who inspired one of the early efforts at translating the Bible into English. A professor at Oxford, Wycliff joined controversies on the authority of tradition, on the Eucharist, and on monasticism. The "Wycliff Bible," though supported by him, was in fact authored by his disciples, Nicholas of Hereford (d. ca. 1420) and John Purvey (ca. 1353–1428). His precise relationship to the heretical Lollard movement remains uncertain. *See also* Bible, translations of the Christian; Lollards.

xango. *See* Afro-Brazilian religions.

Yahrzeit (yahr'tsit; Yiddish, "anniversary [of the day of death]"), yearly anniversary of a parent's death determined by the Jewish calendar. Children customarily recite Kaddish, the mourner's prayer of sanctification, in the synagogue, are called to the Torah, and lead the prayers. A memorial candle lit in the home at sundown burns throughout the following day. *See also* Judaism (life cycle).

Yahweh. *See* YHWH.

Yahweh ben Yahweh (b. 1935), founder of the Nation of Yahweh who teaches that African Americans are members of the lost tribe of Judah. *See also* African Americans (North America), new religions among.

Yajur Veda (yuh'joor vay'duh; Skt., "knowledge of sacrificial formulas"), a sacred Vedic Sanskrit text, the manual of the Adhvaryu priest. It is preserved in several recensions and contains collections of prose formulas pronounced during ritual. *See also* Veda, Vedism.

Yaksha (yuhk'shuh; Skt.), an apparition of the deity Brahma in early Vedic and Hindu epic literature, a subtle form that may personify Brahma's creative will as immanent in nature. North Indian Yaksha images from around the beginning of the first century suggest a cult that tapered off, perhaps due to Hindu and Buddhist sectarian developments. *See also* Brahma.

yaksha/yakshi (yuhk'shuh/yuhk'shee; Skt.), male and female deities associated in India with prosperity and fertility in both Hindu and Buddhist traditions.

yakshi. *See* yaksha/yakshi.

Yama (yah'muh), the Hindu god of death and the underworld. He appears in the *Rig Veda* and throughout Indic religious and vernacular literatures. His iconography includes a mace and a noose with which he leads the deceased to join their ancestors. He has a twin sister, Yami, and is often associated with time (*kala*).

Yamaga Soko (yah-mah-gah soh-koh; 1622–85), Japanese scholar of the Ancient Learning (Kogaku) school who developed the way of the samurai (*bushido*) as an ethic of serving the nation. This influenced the Meiji Restoration. *See also* bushido; Kogaku; Meiji Restoration.

Yamato (yah-mah-toh), the ancient name for Nara prefecture, the center of early Japanese culture and polity. It also refers to Japan as a distinctive culture. *See also* Nara.

Yamato-takeru (yah-mah-toh-tah-kay-*roo*), legendary Japanese prince of the second century renowned for courage and ingenuity in the pacification of various *kami* (divinities, divine presences) and rebellious tribes. *See also* Japanese myth; kami.

Yamazaki Ansai (yah-mah-zah-kee ahn-sah-ee; 1619–82), Japanese scholar who created a synthesis of Neo-Confucianism and Shinto called Suiga Shinto. Its emphasis on nationalism and loyalty to the emperor contributed to the Meiji Restoration. *See also* Japan, Confucianism in; Meiji Restoration; Shinto.

Yang Chu (yajng *joo;* ca. fourth century B.C.), ancient Chinese philosopher and opponent of Confucianism who advocated living one's life to completion by not entangling oneself in the world; he is credited with a chapter on hedonism in the *Lieh-tzu. See also* Lieh-tzu.

Yang Hsi (yahng-shee; b. 330), Chinese Taoist who received the Shang-ch'ing revelations between 364 and 370 from the immortal known as Lady Wei Hua-ts'un. *See also* Shang-ch'ing Taoism; Tatung Chen-ching.

yang-hsing (yahng-shing; Chin., "nourish the life principle"), early methods of longevity involving diet, hygiene, and gymnastics associated with the Taoist tradition and traditional Chinese medicine. *See also* Chinese medicine.

Yang Hsiung (yahng shohng; 53 B.C.–A.D. 18), a Chinese Confucian scholar who was criticized for claiming human nature includes a mixture of both good and evil.

yantra (yuhn'truh; Skt., "instrument," "device"), a geometrical diagram used in Tantric ritual and worship and for magical and occult purposes. *Yantras* symbolize the cosmos and its creative dynamism, the Shakti. *See also* Shakti; Tantra.

Yao, Shun, and Yu (you, shuhn, yoo; ca. late third and early second millennia B.C.), mythic culture heroes and "sage-rulers" symbolically reconciling claims of virtue and heredity in Chinese rulership. Yao es-tablished perfect government; he considered his son unworthy and bequeathed the throne to a commoner, Shun. Shun drove the rebellious San Miao tribes from the empire and ceded his throne to Yu, subduer of the great flood. Yu founded the hereditary Hsia dynasty. *See also* Yu (the Great).

yarmulke. *See* skullcap/kippah/yarmulke.

Yashts (yashts'; Avestan, "offering hymns"), Avestan hymns that seem to be reworked pre-Zoroastrian materials; they are not used in Zoroastrian liturgies. *See also* Avesta; Zoroastrianism.

Yasna (yas'nuh; Avestan, "sacrifice"), Zoroastrian daily liturgy of preparation of *haoma* and offerings to fire and water; the term is also the title of the text recited in the ceremony. *See also* Avesta; Zoroastrianism.

Yathrib (yath-reeb'), a pre-Islamic city in Arabia about two hundred miles north of Mecca, renamed al-Madina ("city," short for "City of the Prophet") after the *Hijra* of Muhammad (622). *See also* Medina.

Yazilikaya (yaz-uh-luh-kah'yah), Hittite sanctuary near Boghazkoy (Turkey), where figures of gods, identified by hieroglyphs, and royal mortuary motifs are carved in high relief on rock outcroppings. *See also* Boghazkoy; Hittites.

yeibichai (ya'bi-chay; Navajo *ye'ii,* "holy people" and *bichai,* "its grandfathers"), spirit beings who appear at healing performances in masked form, depicted in sandpaintings and weavings as having elongated humanlike forms. The term's etymology suggests that the *yeibichai* are "the grandfather gods," a rendering supported by the attribute that these figures are essential to health and life and may be called upon as grandfathers. The term refers to the leader of the group, Talking God, who is considered the grandfather of the other ye'ii. Navajos also designate by the term yeibichai the winter healing ceremonial known as Nightway, because it features the public dancing of the yeibichai during the last evenings of the ceremonial. Yeibichai singing has a distinctive falsetto style. *See also* North America, traditional religions in; sandpainting.

Yellow Springs. *See* Huang-ch'uan.

Yellow Turbans. *See* Huang-chin.

yeshiva (yuh-shee'vah), a traditional Jewish academy for talmudic study. The term is also used for a Jewish primary or secondary school that teaches secular as well as religious subjects.

yetzer ha-ra, yetzer ha-tov (yeh'tser hah-rah', hah-tohv'; Heb.), in Judaism, the evil and good impulses that influence human behavior. They tempt to evil and urge the good, but humanity is always free to choose its own way. Sometimes these impulses are personified as independent external powers, the evil impulse as Satan and the good impulse as the angels that oppose Satan.

Yezidis (yez'eh-deez), a small Kurdish-speaking religious group found in Iraq, Iran, and the Caucasus. Deeply influenced by forms of Christianity and Sufism, they claim to be a separate creation from that of Adam. Their worship focuses on the angel Malak Ta'us (peacock angel) who rules the cosmos together with six other angels, the creator deity being remote and uninterested in the world.

Yezidis deny the existence of sin and evil; individuals are purified by successive reincarnations.

The pejorative title *devil worshipers* was applied to them because of their belief that, after Satan repented, he was returned to his original angelic rank.

Yggdrasill (ylg'drah-seel; Old Norse, "Ygg's [Odinn's] horse"), the world tree in Scandinavian mythology, symbolizing the fate and life of the cosmos. *See also* Nordic religion.

YHWH (yah'way), deity's proper name in the Hebrew Bible. In English it is translated "Lord." *See also* Adonai; Jehovah; Judaism, God in; Tetragrammaton.

Yi Chehyon (yi cheh-yon; 1287–1367), a leading Korean poet and essay writer, the disciple of one of the first scholars of Neo-Confucian studies, Paek Ijong (1275–1375). Like many of his contemporaries, Yi Chehyon traveled to China to complete his studies; while there he became acquainted with many Yuan scholars, especially of the North China Han-lin school. He traveled extensively in China, became acquainted with the scholar Chao Meng-fu, and later placed first in the Chinese civil service examination.

Yi Chehyon was more interested in the practical aspects of Confucian policy making and economics than in metaphysical speculation or ritual studies. He was an early Confucian critic of established Buddhism and focused on the economic waste of state-sponsored rituals, temples,

and building projects. He was also concerned with the education of the Koryo monarchs and, after returning from China, wrote a concise history of Korea to serve as a didactic mirror for government. He was later exemplified as the typical loyal Confucian minister upon his death and had the unusual honor of having his spirit tablet placed next to that of King Kongmin (r. 1352–74) in the royal shrine and being worshiped along with his sovereign. *See also* Chu Hsi studies (Korea); Neo-Confucianism.

yidam (yi'dahm; Tibetan, "chosen divinity"), the name given in Buddhist Tantrism to the deity assigned by a master to an initiated disciple for meditation. *See also* Tantrism (Buddhism).

Yiddish, the vernacular of Ashkenazi Jewry in Europe from medieval to modern times. Its vocabulary and structure are derived primarily from German, with elements from Hebrew, Slavic, and romance languages. A fine corpus of Yiddish literature developed in modern times. The majority of the world's native Yiddish speakers died in the Holocaust. *See also* Ashkenazi.

Yi-Gi Debates (yi-gi; Kor. *yigi nonjaeng*), philosophical and religious debates carried out by two factions of sixteenth- and seventeenth-century Korean Confucian scholars. They centered on the question of whether principle (*yi*; Chin. *li*) or material force (*ki*; Chin. *ch'i*) had priority in the genesis of the cosmos. On the surface these debates appear to be arcane philosophical disputes, but because of the role of Neo-Confucian orthodoxy in the Choson period (1392–1910), they were heavily politicized and came to represent the political, philosophical, and regional interests of warring factions within the government.

The debates began with the work of Yi Onjok (1491–1553), who in his commentary on Chou Tun-i's *Muguk taegungnon* (Diagram of the Great Ultimate) and his commentary on the *Taehak changyo poyu* (Great Learning) identified the Great Ultimate as principle, and therefore that which created and was the essence of the universe. Yi Onjok's followers included Yi Hwang (1501–70), who applied this yi monism to a discussion about the nature of the four and seven emotions and demonstrated how the mind, in theory and application, is rooted in the principles that underlie universal processes, and Yi Songnyong (1542–1607), who used the same theory to attack the quietism of Wang Yangming's unity of knowledge and action. These scholars and their disciples formed the Principle

First Faction (Churip'a) and later the Yongnam District Faction (Yongnamp'a).

On the other side of the debate was Ki Tae-sung (1527–72), who inherited traditions of Taoist ki monism from So Kyongdok (1489–1546). Ki's correspondence with Yi Hwang on the four and seven emotions indicated that principle could not exist unless there was a medium in which it could appear. That medium was cosmic material force, which was only later then formed into the universe by the imposition of organizing principles. Ki's disciple Yi Yi (1536–84) continued the debate and noted that the so-called innate emotions were just part of the derived emotions and the principles of things are derived or abstracted from the things themselves. These scholars and their disciples formed the Material Force First Faction (Chugip'a) and later the Kyonggi-Ch'ungch'ong Province school (Kihop'a).

In modern philosophical terminology the difference between these two factions can be characterized as the difference between essentialism (*churi*) and existentialism (*chugi*). The essentialists were conservative and idealistic, emphasizing how the mind must first be perfected so that it adheres to an a priori order of value in all affairs. The existentialists were liberal and pragmatic, emphasizing how the mind creates, develops, and imposes order and values in all affairs. *See also* ch'i; Chu Hsi studies (Korea); li; Neo-Confucianism; Yi Hwang; Yi Yulgok.

Yi Hwang (yi hwahng; 1501–70), one of the most important Korean Confucian scholars of the Choson period (1392–1910). Otherwise known as Yi T'oegye or Master T'oegye, Yi Hwang was born of noble lineage, educated privately by an uncle, and entered the National Academy in 1523. He passed the civil service examination the following year and then worked as a scribe in the central government. After fifteen years of service he retired, but he was later called back into the government to serve as Royal Lecturer. At his second retirement he returned to his hometown and started a private academy on Mt. Tosan near the city of Andong.

T'oegye is famous for his contributions to Korean Neo-Confucian orthodoxy and his defense of Chu Hsi Neo-Confucianism against all other forms. He was the patriarch of the Principle First school and through his disciples in the Yongnam Faction became the most dominant influence in Neo-Confucian circles until the mid-eighteenth century. T'oegye championed the cause of the village recluse (*sarim*) and taught that moral rectitude and self-perfection

must precede social engineering. As a lecturer in the court, T'oegye put all of his efforts into teaching the monarch the basic moral principles of the "Kingly Way." His *Sonhak sipdo* (Ten Diagrams for Sagely Learning) embodies this teaching.

T'oegye's writings on Neo-Confucianism are built upon a strict adherence to the writings of Chu Hsi. T'oegye's commentaries and interpretations of Ch'eng-chu learning became orthodox during the political careers of his disciples and were used in the civil service examination. These teachings were later transmitted to Japan by Kim Songil (1538–93) and played a significant role in the founding of Neo-Confucianism in Tokugawa Japan. In the modern period T'oegye studies have been revived as part of the general recovery of the Korean heritage. *See also* academies (Korea), private and public; Chu Hsi studies (Korea); Neo-Confucianism; village recluses (Korea); Yi-Gi Debates.

yin and yang (yin, yahng; Chin., "shaded," "sunny"), prime correlates of all binary pairs in traditional Chinese cosmology. In their prephilosophical senses, "shade" and "sunshine" were conceived as environmental influences, especially the shady/cool (*yin*) or sunny/warm (*yang*) slopes of hills and valleys; subsequently, they became two polar aspects of primal *ch'i* (vital energy) in cosmological thinking from the third century B.C. The cosmos is seen as evolving by a process of binary division; its manifestation as ch'i generates rarefied and turbid aspects whose universally observable principles are called yin and yang. *See also* ch'i; cosmology.

Yi Saek (yi sak; 1328–96), a Korean Confucian scholar, poet, and literary stylist of the late Koryo period (918–1392), one of the founding fathers of the public study of Neo-Confucianism in Korea. Having spent three years studying Neo-Confucianism in Mongol China (1348–51), Yi Saek returned to Korea and in 1354 placed first and second in the Koryo exam. He was a favorite of King Kongmin (r. 1351–74) and was responsible for the institution of the orthodox Confucian three-year mourning practice. Yi Saek was also the leader of the Koryo-loyalist, pro-Mongol faction, a position that earned him exile at the hands of the new military and scholar elite that appeared in the waning days of the dynasty.

Though a critic of lavish government spending on Buddhist building projects, Yi Saek was an ardent supporter of Ch'an (Son) Buddhism among the laity and at his own expense sponsored lay scripture study societies. He, Chong Mongju (1337–92), and Yi Sungin (1349–92) are generally known as the Three Hermit Scholars because each suffered a forced removal from office as Yi Songgye's military coup d'etat brought the Koryo period to a close. Though Chong Mongju and Yi Sungin were executed by the supporters of Yi Songgye, Yi Saek was not. His age, his standing as dean of the revived Neo-Confucian National Academy, and the fact that those loyal to Yi Songgye were also his students may have kept him from execution. *See also* academies (Korea), private and public; Neo-Confucianism.

Yi Yulgok (yi yool-gohk), pen name of Yi Yi, one of the greatest Korean Neo-Confucian scholars. In his public career Yulgok served as a regional governor, vice-director of the Royal Academy (Seja-won), and First Minister of Personnel, Justice, and Defense.

Unlike Yi Hwang, with whom he is usually paired, Yulgok did not adhere strictly to the Chu Hsi Confucianism, which would become the religious and intellectual orthodoxy of Korea. Yulgok was a student of Hua-yen and Zen Buddhism, studied religious and philosophical Taoism, and took seriously the writings of Wang Yang-ming. Philosophically, he sought to overcome all forms of dualism, theoretical and practical. His work in Confucian ontology (*Treatise on the Way of Heaven*) emphasized the primary and inclusive character of material force (*ki*), since it alone could be manipulated by human effort and will. In this he was the forerunner of the Practical Learning school (Sirhahp'a) of the seventeenth century. He was the chief defender of ki monism in the Yi-Gi Debates and, contrary to most thinkers of the day, proposed that all human emotions are the product of temperament and training of the mind. *See also* Chu Hsi studies (Korea); Neo-Confucianism; Practical Learning school; Yi-Gi Debates.

Yizker (yiz-kuhr'; Yiddish, "May God remember"), Jewish memorial prayer recited primarily on Yom Kippur and derived from medieval German "Memorbuch" tradition, whereby Jews slaughtered by Crusaders were memorialized in a book beginning with a prayer that God might remember (*yizker*) them. *See also* Judaism (festal cycle).

YMCA, YWCA (Young Men's Christian Association, Young Women's Christian Association), parallel but independent lay, nonsectarian organizations for promoting Christianity, health, education, and service among adolescents and adults with international headquarters in Geneva. The YMCA was founded in England in 1844, the YWCA there in 1855. Both organizations began under evangelical aegis and aimed at providing shelter, recreation, and religious life for young adults finding themselves adrift in the industrial cities of Britain and North America. More recently, YMCAs and YWCAs have become ecumenical in outreach and emphasize activities for inner-city young people.

Ymir (ee'meer), a primeval giant of Scandinavian mythology, slain by the younger gods who created the world from his body. *See also* Nordic religion.

yoga (yoh'guh; from Skt. verbal root *yuj*, "to yoke," meaning an "effort," "technique," "joining"), in Indian religions and literature, any strenuous effort in which a committed person employs specific techniques or instruments that contribute to defining a difficult and purposeful activity. Etymologically, yoga suggests a self-disciplined "yoking" to action as well as engagement in processes and things outside oneself. Thus, when warriors in the Indian epic *Mahabharata* (e.g., 5.149.47) prepare for battle by yoking their horses to chariots, they perform a yoga. Yoga also combines with other terms to name various physical and mental disciplines associated with specific persons or systems, such as the formal theology (*darshana*) expounded by Patanjali called Raja Yoga, or Royal Yoga, and the teachings of selfless action (*karma yoga*), devotion to the god (*bhakti yoga*), and knowledge (*jnana yoga*) taught by the incarnate god Krishna in the *Bhagavad Gita*. (ca. first century A.D.). Yoga commonly refers to acts of meditation, concentration, and asceticism, as well as bodily exercises involving the control of breath and other movements; performers of yoga are called either *yogins* (masc.) or *yoginis* (fem.).

Yoga System: Royal Yoga, or Raja Yoga, one of the six systems of Indian philosophy, was first expounded formally in the pithy aphorisms called the *Yoga Sutras* (ca. third century), attributed to the sage Patanjali. Defining yoga as "the cessation of the mental whirlwind" (*Yoga Sutra*,

1.2), Patanjali maintains that through single-pointed concentration (*ekagrata*) one effects isolation (*kaivalya*) of the individual eternal spirit (*purusha*), which is thereby disentangled from matter (*prakriti*) and united with the supreme spirit. Raja Yoga promises to end death and worldly suffering through mastery of techniques and objectives presented in eight hierarchical stages. The first two stages involve purification and preparation for advanced stages. The first, restraint (*yama*), involves physical and ethical prohibitions and injunctions, such as noninjury (*ahimsa*) and truthfulness (*satya*), while the second, discipline (*niyama*), includes virtues such as cleanliness, serenity, and studiousness. The next three stages—posture (*asana*), breath control (*pranayama*), and sensory detachment (*pratyahara*)—are primarily physical disciplines that prepare one for the mental disciplines of concentration (*dharana*), meditation (*dhyana*), absorption (*samadhi*). Mastering these final three disciplines confers superhuman powers (*siddhi*) intended to advance progress toward absorption in the spirit. Raja Yoga's notion of a god (*ishvara*) who may aid yogins toward absorption distinguishes it from the atheistic Samkhya system, with which it shares ideology and vocabulary.

Other Yogas: *Hatha yoga*, traditionally considered a preparation for other religious disciplines, emphasizes mastery of elaborate physical techniques to control the body. Esoteric religious traditions adopt hatha yoga techniques but espouse *kundalini* yoga, a process that awakens the latent spiritual power residing at the base of the spine. Imagined as a goddess in serpent form, Kundalini rises through a series of spiritual centers called *chakras* toward reunion with her consort Shiva in the thousand-petaled lotus (*sahasrara*) at the vault of the skull. *See also* hatha yoga; kundalini; Patanjali; siddhi; six systems of Indian philosophy.

Yogachara (yoh-gah-chah'ruh; Skt., "the practice of yoga"), a major school of Mahayana Buddhist philosophy concerned with the practice of meditation and discipline that leads to the attainment of Buddhahood. Adherents of the school are called Yogacharins ("practitioners of yoga") or Vijnanavadins ("those who hold the doctrine of consciousness").

The school traces its origin to Asanga and Vasubandhu (fourth or fifth century) and, through these two brothers, to the Bodhisattva Maitreya. While many of the fundamental texts of the school are attributed to one or another of these three figures, the question of authorship is highly problematic.

The most distinctive doctrine of the school is the claim that the world consists of nothing but mind. This doctrine has been interpreted as a form of Buddhist idealism in which one denies the reality of the external world but affirms the reality of the mind itself. Yogacharins generally have a more positive attitude toward the nature of ultimate reality than many of their Mahayana opponents. They often compare reality to the ocean, gold, or space and argue that the distinctions of ordinary experience are "adventitious" or temporary defilements of a pure, underlying substance.

Yogachara texts were translated into Chinese as early as the sixth century, and the school achieved considerable popularity in China under the leadership of the great scholar-monk Hsuan-tsang (602–664), who traveled to India, studied with Yogachara masters, and promulgated their teaching in China. The school he founded was eventually eclipsed by other, indigenous Chinese schools, but the Yogachara approach to the fundamental doctrines of the Mahayana continued to have deep influence on Chinese and Japanese speculation about the nature of reality. *See also* Fa-hsiang school; Mahayana; meditation; mind-only.

yombul. *See* Pure Land school (Korea).

Yomi no kuni (yoh-mee noh koo-nee; Jap., "land of darkness"), the dark, defiled, disordered world of the dead in early Shinto cosmology, contrasted with the upper world of superior *kami* (divinities, divine presences; *Takamagahara*) and the middle world of human habitation (*Ashihara no nakatsu kuni*). *See also* afterworld; Ashihara no nakatsu kuni; cosmology; Takamagahara.

Yom Kippur (yohm' kee-poor'; Heb., "day of atonement"), the most solemn day of the Jewish year (10 Tishri), which ends the ten-day period of repentance that Rosh Hashanah begins. Virtually the entire day is spent in the synagogue petitioning God to pardon sins and bestow life for the coming year. No food or drink is consumed from sundown to sundown. *See also* Judaism (festal cycle); Kol Nidre.

yonaoshi (yoh-nah-oh-shee; Jap., "world renewal"), a popular Japanese belief, at the end of the Tokugawa period (1600–1868), that bad times were over and good times of material prosperity and spiritual renewal were at hand; it was strongly influenced by Buddhist messianic ideas of the coming age of Maitreya. *See also* ages of the world; Maitreya; Meiji Restoration.

Yongoje. *See* Korea (festal cycle).

yoni (yoh'nih; Skt., "place of issue," secondarily "womb-chamber"). **1** In Vedic speculation, "the source" of creation, identified with *brahman*. **2** In Hinduism, the emblem of feminine cosmic creativity (Skt. *Shakti*), the highest symbol of Devi, consort of Shiva, corresponding to his *lingam*. Shaiva temples have a circular *yoni*-pedestal for the lingam. In meditational diagrams, especially Tantric, the yoni is a triangle with downward apex. *See* linga; Shiva; Tantra.

Yoshino (yoh-shee-noh), mountainous region south of Kyoto, Japan, associated with *yamabushi* ("mountain ascetics") and recluse poets and famous for its cherry blossoms. *See also* mountains, sacred.

Young Men's Christian Association. *See* YMCA, YWCA.

Young Women's Christian Association. *See* YMCA, YWCA.

Yu. *See* Yao, Shun, and Yu.

Yu (the Great) (yoo; ca. 1900 B.C.), Chinese quasi-mythical culture hero. Magically born from the corpse of his father, the failed flood-tamer Kun, Yu was charged by the sage-ruler Shun with draining a world-engulfing flood. Yu dredged the rivers, leading the floodwaters to the sea, and then surveyed the land, laying out the nine provinces of the Middle Kingdom. Shun then made him emperor; Yu (possibly in this role a historical figure) instituted hereditary rule as Chinese founder of the Hsia dynasty. *See also* cosmogony; myth; Yao, Shen, and Yu.

yuga (yoo'gah; Skt., "conjunction"), an Indic division of time. **1** A system of 5 years containing 62 months of 29$\frac{16}{31}$ days used in conjunction with Vedic ritual. **2** A system of four ages said to represent kalpa, a decline from *dharma*, or law, to *adharma*, lawlessness, and likened to gold, silver, bronze, and iron. Krishna appears "from age to age" to restore the dharma. *See also* ages of the world; cosmogony; Kali Yuga.

Yu-huang Shang-ti. *See* Yu-ti.

Yuiitsu Shinto (yoo-ee-tsoo shin-toh; Jap., "The Only Shinto"), also Urabe Shinto, Yoshida Shinto, a school of Shinto dating from the Heian period (794–1185). Yoshida Kanetomo (1435–1511) was the major systematizer of its highly eclectic doctrines combining Confucian, Taoist, and Shingon Buddhist ideas within a Shinto framework of worship of *kami* (divinities, divine presences). *See also* Shinto.

yukar (yoo-kahr; Ainu, "to imitate"), oral epics and tales of the Ainu, including stories of the gods, culture heros, animals, and people. *See also* Ainu religion.

Yun-chi ch'i-ch'ien (yuhn-jee chee-chen; Chin., "Seven Bamboo Slips from the Cloudy Bookbag"), the most comprehensive general anthology of early Taoist writings in the *Tao-tsang*. Completed by Chang Chun-fang in 1029 for the personal use of the emperor, this selection excludes only ritual texts. *See also* Tao-tsang.

Yun-kang (yuhn-gahng), a set of grottoes near the city of Ta-t'ung, China, that have been carved into Buddhist cave shrines. The project began under the reign of Emperor Hsiao-wen (r. 471–499) and includes monumental figures of the Buddha, the tallest reaching seventy feet in height.

Yu-pu (yoo-boo; Chin., "Step of Yu"), a shamanist dance imitating the limping walk of Yu the Great when he divided water and land. Dancing like a one-legged animal, the shaman beat a drum and fell into a trance to ascend mountains and catch spirits. The term is also seen in Taoist ritual. *See also* shamanism.

Yu-ti (yoo-dee; Chin., "Jade Emperor"), since the T'ang dynasty (618–907), the supreme deity of Taoist and popular pantheons; his birthday is celebrated on the ninth day of the first lunar month. His celestial palace city and government were thought to mirror the earthly imperial capital and its bureaucracy. *See also* Chinese popular religion; Taoism.

Yuzu-nembutsu school (yoo-tsoo nem-boo-tsoo), minor Japanese Buddhist tradition founded by Ryonin (1071–1132) and based on Kegon teachings that an individual's practice permeated that of all humans and that the single practice of the *nembutsu* (recitation of Buddha's name) permeated all other practices. Thus, all could be saved through the nembutsu. *See also* Kegon school; nembutsu.

YWCA. *See* YMCA, YWCA.

Zagreus (zag'ree-uhs), in Greek myth, the son of Zeus and Persephone; he is identified in Orphic myth with Zeus's reborn son, Dionysos-Zagreus. *See also* Dionysos; Orphism.

Zakat (za'kat; Arab., "purity," "alms"), the obligatory alms paid by self-sufficient adult Muslims to aid the Islamic community. Along with belief in one God and his messenger Muhammad, observing daily prayers, fasting during the month of Ramadan, and performing the pilgrimage to Mecca, Zakat is one of the Five Pillars of Islam.

The Qur'an (9:60) designates the ways in which these alms may be used: to aid the poor, the destitute, chronic debtors, and travelers in need, to win converts, ransom slaves, defend the faith, and pay for Zakat collection. But alms help more than those who receive them; Zakat also contributes to purify the giver of selfishness and greed.

Although the Qur'an commands Muslims to give Zakat, it does not stipulate precisely who should pay or how much. These and related matters were addressed by later Muslim jurists who determined a minimum of property exempt from taxation. All wealth above this minimum, including cash, merchandise, minerals, crops, and livestock, was subject to an annual taxation ranging from 2.5 to 20 percent. The Zakat, now clearly a religious tax, was collected and distributed by the state. Over time the collection of alms has been largely abandoned for other more substantial taxes, but giving Zakat remains an individual religious obligation for each capable adult Muslim. *See also* almsgiving; Five Pillars; tithing.

Zamzam Well, one of the stations of ritual performance in Mecca during the Muslim pilgrimage. *See also* pilgrimage.

zandaqa *See* heresy.

Zaydi Shia (zay'di shee'ah; Arab.), or "the Fivers," a subgroup of Shiite Islam. The Zaydi Shia trace their origin to Zayd, one of the great grandsons of the first Shia *Imam* (leader), Ali. Leading a revolt against the ruling dynasty of the time, the Ummayads, he was killed in battle in 740. Those who had supported him developed the view that Zayd, or any such Alid descendant like him, could, through the right combination of religious learning and military capability, lay claim to be an Imam and seek to overthrow an existing illegitimate ruler.

In affirming such a view of the Imam, the followers of Zayd parted company with the majority of the Shia, who held to a doctrine of hereditary but designated succession. The Zaydis's generally militant attitude toward existing rulers forced the group into successive rebellions. During their turbulent history, the Zaydis succeeded in establishing two states, one near the Caspian Sea and the other in Yemen. Here they produced their own legal and theological interpretations of Islam, developing organized Zaydi communities under an Imam. Often in cases where two claimants to leadership appeared simultaneously, the Zaydis argued that in order to present a unified rule, one of the two ought to give up the claim. This often led to divisions within the community. Though most of the early communities have not survived, some being absorbed by other Shia groups, the tradition continues in Yemen, where a Zaydi Imam ruled until the early 1960s. *See also* Shia.

zekhut (zeh-khoot'; Heb.), in Judaism, an untranslatable word that refers to the heritage of virtue and its consequent entitlements. *Zekhut* rests upon the conception that God will do for us what we cannot do for ourselves, when we do for God what God cannot make us do. This heritage of entitlements from Heaven or God therefore derives from a person's action beyond the measure of the law, i.e., an action that God values but cannot command, e.g., uncoerced love. Zekhut results from (1) an action, as distinct from a (mere) attitude, that (2) is precisely the opposite of a sinful one; it is, moreover, an action that (3) may be done by an individual or by the community at large, and one that (4) a leader may provoke the community to do (or not do). Acts of will consisting of submission, on one's own, to the will of Heaven endowed Israel with a lien and entitlement upon Heaven. What one cannot by an act of will impose, one can by free will evoke. What the Israelite cannot accomplish through coercion, he or she can achieve through submission. Zekhut that has been accumulated by the patriarchs may be passed on to Israel, their children. Moses not only attains zekhut but also imparts zekhut to the community of which he is leader, and the same is so for any Israelite. *Zekhut avot,* the heritage of virtue deriving from the patriarchs and matriarchs, stands for the empowerment of a supernatural character to which Israel is entitled by reason of what the patriarchs and matriarchs in particular did long ago. The Israelite possesses a lien upon Heaven by reason of God's love for the patriarchs and matriarchs, God's appreciation for certain things they did, and God's response to those actions not only in favoring them but also in entitling their descendants to do or benefit from otherwise unattainable miracles. No single word in English bears the same meaning. *See also* Judaism (thought and ethics); merit.

Zen (Jap., from Chin. *ch'an,* ultimately from Skt. *dhyana,* "meditation"), the largest school of Buddhism in Japan focusing on methods for the attainment of enlightenment (*satori*). *See also* Ch'an school; Dogen; Eisai; Gozan; Hakuin Ekaku; kung-an; Linchi school; Obaku Zen; Rinzai; Soto school; Ts'aotung school.

Zeus (*zoos*), an ancient Greek god. In origin an Indo-European sky god, he rules from Mt. Olympos as "Father of Gods and Men" after overthrowing his father, Kronos. In myth capricious and violent, he comes to represent justice through his cult role as protector of suppliants, guests, oaths, and the domestic and social orders. *See also* Greek religion; Indo-European religion.

ziggurat (zig'goo-raht; Babylonian, something high and holy), a stepped temple tower, crowned by a shrine, characteristic of ancient Mesopotamia. It served as a meeting place of the gods. *See also* Mesopotamian religion.

Zion, hill in Jerusalem (variously identified). In the Hebrew Bible, it is the place from which God rules the earth.

Zionism, a political program leading to the establishment and development of the Jewish national homeland in the Land of Israel. "Zion" is one of the hills of Jerusalem, the spiritual center of the Jewish homeland.

Before the middle of the nineteenth century, Zionism remained an expectation reflected primarily in the Jews' prayers and dreams of messianic times. The Bible is replete with references to Zion and Jerusalem. Exile in foreign lands and rule by foreigners is balanced with prayers for the return to Zion and the reestablishment of Jerusalem's glory. Though there has been a continuous settlement of Jews in the Land of Israel since biblical days, and though individuals and small groups of Jews migrated there over the centuries, Zionist longings did not enter the realm of debate and action until the nineteenth century.

The Zionist Movement: Zionism is a product of the political development of national states that has occurred during the last one hundred years. Jews organized to solve the problems of Jewish life in the Diaspora and to reestablish an independent Jewish state in the Land of Israel. Beginning with local associations in diverse communities across Europe, especially in the Khovevei Zion ("Lovers of Zion") groups in the Pale of Settlement of the Russian Empire, the movement became institutionalized in 1897 at the first Zionist Congress, in Basel, Switzerland, under the leadership of Theodore Herzl. The Zionists sought to organize the Jewish communities, to purchase land in Palestine, and to engage in international diplomacy in order to establish a Jewish state. At Basel, they announced, "Zionism strives to create for the Jewish people a home in Palestine secured by public law."

Zionism competed with other Jewish political movements. It rejected the liberals' trust that democratic institutions would end discrimination and the revolutionaries' dreams of total transformation of European societies. The Jews were neither a particular group within the working class, to highlight the definition offered by the Bund (the General Union of Jewish Workers in Russia and Poland), nor only a religious community, as defined by the liberals. The Jews, maintained the Zionists, were a nation with the right to a homeland.

Divisions with the Zionist Movement: Diverse themes and factions competed with the Zionist movement. Some sought a haven for the Jewish masses, defining the answer to the Jewish Question as the need to help the poverty-stricken Jews of eastern Europe. Some sought a place where idealistic youth could return to their language while building a new culture and society; they defined the Jewish Question as the decayed condition of Judaism. Others tied these aspirations to the international socialist movement, seeking to combine several dreams by building a model society. Still others saw Zionism as religious return to Zion. Zionists debated strategy as well. Herzl's political Zionists sought international agreements and labor and cultural Zionists encouraged the immigration of idealists who would build the new society. All insisted that only the creation of a national home would solve the Jewish Question.

Factions espousing these positions competed to influence Jews in the Diaspora, to encourage *aliyah* ("immigration"; lit., "ascension," to the Land of Israel), and to gather the resources that would enable them to control the international Zionist movement. Herzl's political Zionism dominated the international movement and the communities in western Europe. Socialist, religious, and general Zionists battled among the Jewish population of eastern Europe.

In the Land of Israel, socialist Zionists established and controlled the institutions of the new community. From its foundation, the Zionist movement has been marked by internal conflict.

Zionism and the Creation of Israel: More than half a century elapsed before the Zionists reached their primary goal. The first major success occurred on November 2, 1917, when the British government issued the Balfour Declaration promising to support the creation of a Jewish national home in Palestine. In 1922, the League of Nations incorporated the declaration into the British mandate over Palestine. For the next twenty-five years, Zionists sought to induce Jews emigrating from Europe, especially the young and able-bodied, to go to Palestine. At the same time, Zionists strove to influence the British to encourage Jewish immigration and to establish self-governing institutions for the Jewish community in Palestine. During the first fifteen years of the British Mandate, 300,000 Jews entered Palestine. By 1935, the 355,000 Jews in Palestine were almost 30 percent of the population. As the number of Jews rose, so did the opposition of Palestinian Arabs to their entry. In 1937, acceding to Arab pressure, which included several bloody pogroms against Jewish settlements in Palestine, the British restricted the immigration of Jews. Between 1937 and 1944, 100,000 Jewish immigrants entered Palestine; from 1945 to mid-1948, 75,000 entered, most of them illegally. The end of World War II witnessed the demise of the British Empire, and on November 29, 1947, the United Nations voted to partition British Palestine, thus permitting the formation of a Jewish state. The State of Israel declared its independence on May 14, 1948. David Ben-Gurion, the leader of Mapai, the Party of Workers of the Land of Israel, was the first prime minister, and Chaim Weizmann, head of the General Zionists, was selected to be the first president. The creation of the State of Israel marks the fundamental victory of the Zionist movement.

Zionism and Contemporary Judaism: With the establishment of the State of Israel, Zionism and Judaism have moved closer. Attacks on Zionism and Israel are interpreted as attacks on Judaism and Jews. Almost all forms of Judaism view Israel as a step in the process of redemption and maintain that Jews have an obligation to support Israel. Relatively few Jews have made *aliyah,* however, choosing instead to invoke prayers and to provide political support and financial resources. At the same time, messianic themes emerged after the 1967 war, when Israel took control of the entire Land of Israel. Zionism continues as well to be at the center of debates over the nature and meaning of the Jewish people, their culture, and religion. *See also* Israel (land, people, state).

Zionist Churches, independent churches in southern Africa influenced by the teachings of John Dowie and his Evangelical Christian Catholic Church (founded in 1896), which was based in Zion City, Illinois. There are more than two thousand such churches in southern Africa, including the Zion Apostolic Church and Isaiah Shembe's amaNazaretha. This term is also used to collectively describe independent churches throughout sub-Saharan Africa that stress direct revelation from God or from angels to African charismatic leaders, a strict abstinence from all forms of African traditional religious practices, and a strong focus on spiritual healing.

Many Zionist churches have millennial expectations in which only those believers who have deep convictions and follow the strict rules of the church community will be able to enter into this new Zion. Both church rules and ritual structures are said to be based on direct revelations to the prophetic founder, but the former often include the dietary regulations found in Leviticus. Zionist churches operated simultaneously as places where southern Africans could freely express their spiritual concerns, experience the relative freedom of African-controlled institutions, and resist the hegemony of oppressive European institutions. *See also* Africa, new religions in.

zodiac. *See* astrology.

Zohar. *See* Judaism (mysticism).

Zoroaster (zohr-oh-as'tuhr; Gk. form of Avestan "Zarathushtra"), founder of the Zoroastrian tradition, author of the *Gathas;* Zoroastrianism flourished in eastern Iran ca. 1000 B.C. *See also* Zoroastrianism.

Zoroastrianism (zohr-oh-as'tree-uhn-iz-uhm), the religion founded by the Iranian-speaking prophet Zarathushtra, Greek Zoroaster. It is known to its followers by the Pahlavi title, *Daena Mazdayasni,* "the Good Religion of the Worshipers of Mazdah." There are presently some 150,000 adherents, the majority living in India in the area of Bombay and in Gujarat. Many of these Zoroastrians, called Parsis, "Persians," moved to India after the Islamization of Iran, their original homeland. Today, many live in other parts of the world, including North America.

Versions of Zoroastrianism were made the official religion of the three major pre-Islamic Near Eastern empires of the Iranians, namely that of the Achaemenids, the Parthians, and the Sassanids; under the last the religion was radically unified. Following the Muslim conquest in the middle of the seventh century, Zoroastrianism was reduced by increasing conversions to Islam. The Turkish and Mongol conquests of Iran saw widespread persecutions, largely reducing the adherents of Zoroastrianism to the desert cities of Kerman and Yazd.

Much has been written about Zoroastrianism because of its probable influence on Judaism, Christianity, and Islam, as these Near Eastern religions developed within the sphere of the Iranian empires.

The high priest in Mozart's opera *The Magic Flute* called Sorastro (a shortened version of Zoroaster/Zarathushtra), Nietzsche's *Also sprach Zarathustra* and his notion of "Uebermensch," and ultimately "Superman" in American cartoon tradition are all evidence of the continuing fascination with Zoroastrianism in the West. In Hellenistic traditions, Zoroaster was considered, along with the Egyptian Hermes Trismegistos, one of the founders of the secret sciences such as alchemy and astrology.

Zarathushtra was a priest and seer who most likely hailed from west-central Asia toward the end of the second millennium B.C. While much of the ritual and conceptual traditions of his religious heritage seem to have been continued in Zoroastrianism, he offered them radically new interpretations in which anthropomorphic thinking (and thus deities) are replaced by a hierarchy of quasi-rationalistic spiritual entities or powers.

Mythology: Zoroastrianism is strictly dualistic, posing the forces of Good against those of Evil. The highest principle, God, uncreated, eternal, and ominiscient, is Ahura Mazda (Ohrmazd), generally translated as "Lord Wisdom," but possibly meaning "Wisdom is the Lord" in Avestan. Ahura Mazda's creative aspect is *Spenta Mainyu,* mostly translated in Christian terms as "Holy Spirit."

In this creative aspect, Ahura Mazda is opposed by an equally uncreated entity called Angra Mainyu, Ahriman, "Evil Spirit," who is always destructive. There is a hierarchy of further emanations of Ahura Mazda, most important of which are six major spiritual principles both abstract and personal. These appear in the three realms of human activities: Vohu Manah, "Good Mind"; Asha, "Truth/Order"; Khshathra, "Realm, Power"; Armaiti, "Proper Mind"; Haurvatat, "Completeness, Health"; and Ameretat, "Immortality." Together with the Holy Spirit, these seven create and guard the seven material creations; the Holy Spirit guards (good) humankind; the others guard animals, fire, sky/metals, earth, water, and plants, respectively. In addition, there are lesser spiritual principles and powers that are opposed by corresponding forces and countercreations of evil.

Space and Time: The physical cosmos is very much geocentric and Ptolemaic, seen as space to attract and confine evil. In various levels of paradise the souls of the good remain until the end of time for a final judgment. In the center of the earth is hell, where the evil are punished. The world is seen as the battleground created by Ahura Mazda for the ultimate elimination of evil.

Perhaps the most fundamental thought of the prophet Zarathustra is the perception of a beginning and an ending of the world. Three saviors will appear at the end of time. Equally important are the ethics of the ending and the recognition of the central role of humankind in salvation. The final outcome of the battle between the forces of good and evil is not predetermined, but depends on choice. Here each individual human plays a vital part, not only to save himself or herself but also to "save the world" using reason and insight. According to Zoroastrianism, the final battle is the first time that humankind is given a central role in the struggle. Later teachings predicted the outcome: eternal life for the good and annihilation for the evil.

Texts: The *Avesta* is the collection of the holy texts of Zoroastrianism, hence the name of the Old Iranian language, Avestan. Most texts are accompanied by *zand,* "interpretation." The main text of Zoroastrianism is the liturgy that accompanies the main ceremony, the *Yasna,* which focuses on seventeen hymns in syllabic meter, the *Gathas,* and a brief central chapter of seven parts, attributed to Zarathushtra. The liturgy is surrounded by the most holy prayers of Zoroastrianism. Later elaboration extended the liturgy to seventy-two chapters. Other main texts include the *Vendidad,* concerned with purity laws. Major compilations of Scripture in Middle Persian include the *Bundahishn* and *Wizidagiha i Zadspram,* which are largely based on interpretations of lost Avestan works.

Worship: The main rite, the *yasna,* is performed daily by a chief priest assisted by another. It is performed in fire temples, which were introduced to Zoroastrianism during Achaemenid times. Fire is the major purifying element in Zoroastrianism, and the yasna constitutes an extremely elaborate cosmic purification rite. The major rite of passage is the initiation into the religion at fifteen when the young receive a sacred shirt and cord. Personal purification rites play a major part in the adherent's life. *See also* Achaemenid; Ahriman; Ahura Mazda; Amesha Spentas; Avesta; Bundahishn; Chinvat; daivas; Denkart; fravashis; Gathas; Haoma; Indo-European religion; Iranian religion; Magi; Mazdak; Mithra; Saosyant; Sassanids; Vohu Manah; Yashts; Yasna; Zoroaster; Zurvan.

zuhd. *See* asceticism.

Zurvan (zoor'vahn; Pahlavi, "Time"), mythic father of twins Ahura Mazda and Ahriman in one Zoroastrian tradition, as reported in Sassanid-period Christian sources. *See also* Ahriman; Ahura Mazda; Zoroastrianism.

Zwingli, Huldrych (tsving'lee; 1484–1531), leader of the Swiss Christian Reformation. He is best known for his dispute (1525) with Martin Luther on the status of the Eucharist. Luther maintained the presence of the body of Christ; Zwingli argued for the Eucharist's symbolic nature. These views are summarized in Zwingli's popular work *On the Lord's Supper* (1526). *See also* Reformed churches.

PHOTOGRAPH CREDITS

In-text photographs:

Akademische Druck- und Verlagsanstalt/Moses Mesoamerican Archive: 706; American Jewish Archives: 104; American Museum of Natural History Library: 1034; S. M. Amin/Aramco World: 613, 993, 1109; Jan Andersson: 303; Aramco World: 711, 712; Arrendadora Internacional/Moses Mesoamerican Archive: 705; Ali S. Asani: 872, 873; John Barker: 107; Berkeley Studio, The United Church of Canada: 239, 255 (left); Edwin Bernbaum: 354, 680, 994, 1060, 1119; Black Star: 627; Barbara Drake Blevens: 116; Jack Breed/FPG International: 1090; Karen McCarthy Brown: 25 (left), 25 (right), 1104, 1125; Jorunn Jacobsen Buckley: 62; John Ross Carter: 98, 156, 1072, 1081; Chapin Mesa Archaeological Museum/ Mesa Verde National Park: 635, 838; Jane Daggett Dillenberger: 236; Jill Dubisch: 821; H. Byron Earhart: 41, 547, 548, 550, 640, 773, 780, 980, 1128, 1138; Diana L. Eck: 2, 6, 43, 44, 68, 73 (left), 80, 105, 375, 402, 421, 451 (left), 650, 772, 842, 1059; Dale Eldred: 175; Rev. Stanley Errett/The United Church of Canada: 102; Foto Marburg/Art Resource, NY: 69; China Galland: 992; Marija Gimbutas: 809, 810; Judith Gleason: 16, 17 (left), 30, 778; Stevan Harrell: 162, 209, 221, 583, John Stratton Hawley: 443, 445, 843, 802, Phoebe Hearst Museum of Anthropology: 92, 300 (left), 704, 752, 802, The Jewish Museum of New York/Art Resource, NY: 575; Christian Jochim: 155, 211; Mark Juergensmeyer: 363, 391, 612, 620, 990, 997, 999 (left), 999 (right); Peter Keen/Aramco World: 66; Wolf Kutnahorsky/Berkeley Studio, The United Church of Canada: 255 (right), 263, 805, 822; Los Angeles Country Museum of Art: 129, 304, 372, 737, 1032; Mary MacDonald: 569, 825; Dorothy McLaughlin/FPG International: 75; Jonathan Meyers/FPG International: 302; National Museum of the American Indian: 800, 958; Nelson-Atkins Museum of Art: 210, 300 (right); John Nunley: 308; Eric Oey: 692, 770; Spencer J. Palmer: 281, 305; James E. Payne: 171, 174, 1098; Jason Pollen: 1, 39; Galen Rowell/Mountain Light Photography: 73 (right), 854, 855, 1027, 1045, 1075, 1077; Scala/Art Resource, NY: 671; Michael Spencer/Aramco World: 299, 713; Gary Sutton: 580 (top), 972; Katrina Thomas/Aramco World: 495, 791; Edith Turner/Victor and Edith Turner Collection: 13, 17 (right), 173, 272, 451 (right), 464, 543, 553, 578, 581 (bottom), 844, 956, 1083, 1086, 1094, 1108; Susan Wadley: 127, 423, 450 (left), 450 (right), 685, 1137; Sabra J. Webber: 364; Robert Weller: 197, 206; Caroline Williams: 327, 334, 474, 496, 497, 520, 527; Mark Woodward: 40, 521 (left), 521 (right).

Insert photographs following page 770:

American Museum of Natural History Library: 39; S. M. Amin/ Aramco World: 29; Arrendadora Internacional/Moses Mesoamerican Archive: 38; John Barker: 21; Zenobia Barlow: 70; O. Baur/from *Longing for Darkness: Tara and the Black Madonna* by China Galland (Viking/Penguin,1991): 16; Berkeley Studio, The United Church of Canada: 17; Edwin Bernbaum: 46, 55, 56; Karen McCarthy Brown: 80; John Ross Carter: 42, 57, 72; Jane Daggett Dillenberger: 15; Jill Dubisch: 27; Diana Eck: 23, 45, 47, 48, 49, 50, 51, 53; Dale Eldred: 31, 58; Werner Forman Archive/Art Resource, NY: 62; Giraudon/Art Resource, NY: 35; Judith Gleason: 40, 76; Louis Goldman/FPG International: 10; Spencer Grant/FPG International: 20; Stevan Harrell: 68, 69; Phoebe Hearst Museum of Anthropology: 2, 36, 43; The Jewish Museum of New York/Art Resource, NY: 14; Christian Jochim: 54, 60; Mark Juergensmeyer: 74; Isaiah Karlinsky/FPG International: 12; Laurel Kendall: 73; Wolf Kutnahorsky/Berkeley Studio, The United Church of Canada: 18; Erich Lessing/Art Resource, NY: 6, 7, 13, 24; Los Angeles County Museum of Art: 52; Ernest Manewal/FPG International: 37; Kenneth W. Morgan: 59; E. Nagele/FPG International: 26; Eric Oey: 44, 65; Spencer J. Palmer: 66, 75; Kimberley C. Patton: 3, 5; James E. Payne: 25; Ken Ross/FPG International: 78; Galen Rowell/ Mountain Light Photography: 63, 64; Gail Shumway/FPG International: 22; Robin Samuel Sierra: 77; Soka Gakkai International-USA: 79; Gary Sutton: 11; Sam Thee/FPG International: 9; Edith Turner/Victor and Edith Turner Collection: 4, 8, 19, 33, 41, 71; Susan Wadley: 28; Robert P. Weller: 67; Nik Wheeler/Aramco World: 30, 32; Caroline Williams: 1; Ian Yeomans/Aramco World: 34; Chun-Fang Yu: 61